ISBN 978-1-334-74323-8
PIBN 10663178

1 MONTH OF
FREE
READING

at
www.ForgottenBooks.com

By purchasing this book you are eligible for one month membership to ForgottenBooks.com, giving you unlimited access to our entire collection of over 700,000 titles via our web site and mobile apps.

To claim your free month visit:
www.forgottenbooks.com/free663178

English
Français
Deutsche
Italiano
Español
Português

www.forgottenbooks.com

Mythology Photography **Fiction**
Fishing Christianity **Art** Cooking
Essays Buddhism Freemasonry
Medicine **Biology** Music **Ancient
Egypt** Evolution Carpentry Physics
Dance Geology **Mathematics** Fitness
Shakespeare **Folklore** Yoga Marketing
Confidence Immortality Biographies
Poetry **Psychology** Witchcraft
Electronics Chemistry History **Law**
Accounting **Philosophy** Anthropology
Alchemy Drama Quantum Mechanics
Atheism Sexual Health **Ancient History**
Entrepreneurship Languages Sport
Paleontology Needlework Islam
Metaphysics Investment Archaeology
Parenting Statistics Criminology
Motivational

BALDHU, an ecclesiastical parish, in the parishes of KENWYN and KEA, union of TRURO, W. division of the hundred of POWDER and of the county of CORNWALL, $3\frac{1}{2}$ miles (S. W. by W.) from Truro. This place derives its name from *Bal-mine-dhu*, or rather *diu*, black; it is about three miles in length and two and a half in breadth, and of hilly and barren surface. The Carnon river forms its boundary on the south, and the Truro and Red-ruth road on the north; the Cornwall railway passes nearly along its boundary on the east. Several mines are wrought, the chief produce of which is black-jack and black tin. The "Old Men's Workings" consist of gigantic excavations in the Elvan rock, open to the sun, in some places more than 150 feet deep, and extending a distance of a mile and upwards: they are probably among the original mines of the county, and are not now wrought. There are also several smelting-houses. The parish was formed in 1847, under the act 6 and 7 Victoria, cap. 37; the living is in the gift of the Crown and the Bishop of Exeter alternately, and has an income of £150. The church was erected in 1847-8, at a cost of £1800, of which sum the Earl of Falmouth, who had the first presentation, contributed £1000; the Incorporated Society, £200; the Diocesan Society, £250; and the Church Commissioners, £260.

BALDOCK (ST. MARY), a market-town and parish, in the union of HITCHIN, hundred of BROADWATER, county of HERTFORD, 18 miles (N. by W.) from Hertford, and 37 (N. by W.) from London; containing 1807 inhabitants. This place, in the reign of Stephen, belonged to the Knights Templars, to whom Gilbert, Earl of Pembroke, had given the site. In a charter of confirmation granted by his descendant William, the place is termed Baudoc, of which the present name is a variation; though some antiquaries derive it from Balbec, supposing the town to have been so called by the Templars, from memory of the city of that name in Syria, from which their order had been expelled by the Saracens. The TOWN is situated near the intersection of the great north road and the Roman Ikeneld-street, between two hills which command an extensive view of a fine open country; and consists principally of one street: the houses are mostly ancient, but interspersed with several of modern erection, and the inhabitants are amply supplied with water. A horticultural society, patronised by the nobility and gentry in the neighbourhood, was established in 1825. The trade is principally in malt, the land in the vicinity being highly favourable to the growth of barley: the fens and marsh land near the town form an extensive grazing district, and cheese of a peculiar quality is made here; there is also a very large brewery. The general market, which was on Saturday, has been discontinued; and a market exclusively for the sale of straw-plat is now held on Friday. The fairs are on the festivals of St. James, St. Andrew, and St. Matthew, each continuing two days; at the last a great quantity of cheese is sold. The county magistrates hold a petty-session here on the first Monday in every month. The parish comprises about 150 acres of land, the soil of which is in general chalky. The living is a discharged rectory, valued in the king's books at £10. 8. 9., and in the patronage of the Crown; net income, £126. The church, erected by the Knights Templars, and nearly all rebuilt in the early part of the fifteenth century, is a spacious structure, partly Norman, and partly in the

133

later English style, with an octagonal steeple built a few years ago; and contains a finely carved oak screen, part of the ancient rood-loft, and a very curious font. There are places of worship for the Society of Friends, Independents, and Wesleyans; and almshouses for twelve aged widows, founded and endowed in 1621, by Mr. John Winne. In cutting through Baldock hill, to form a new turnpike-road, a great number of fossils, consisting of *cornua ammonis*, sharks' teeth, &c. was discovered.

BALDON, MARSH (ST. PETER), a parish, in the union of ABINGDON, hundred of BULLINGTON, county of OXFORD, 6 miles (S. E. by S.) from Oxford; containing 360 inhabitants, and comprising 804 acres. This parish, originally called Meres or Mars and ultimately Marsh-Baldon, derives its distinguishing name from one De la Mare, a descendant of whom was patron of the living in 1381. In 1836, an act was obtained for dividing and allotting lands in the parishes of Marsh-Baldon and Toot-Baldon. The benefice is a rectory, valued in the king's books at £6. 13. 4.; net income, £93; patron, Sir H. P. Willoughby, Bart. The church has a highly picturesque tower, mantled with ivy: over the communion table is a painting of the Salutation, presented by the late Sir Christopher Willoughby. Dr. John Bridges, Bishop of Oxford, who died in 1618, was buried here.

BALDON, TOOT (ST. LAWRENCE), a parish, in the union of ABINGDON, hundred of BULLINGTON, county of OXFORD, $5\frac{1}{4}$ miles (S. E.) from Oxford; containing 269 inhabitants. This place, in Domesday book, is called Baudindon; and was afterwards named Toot Balden or Baldon, probably from one Le Tote, a landed proprietor, to distinguish it from the adjoining parish of Marsh-Baldon. The living is a discharged vicarage, in the gift of Sir H. P. Willoughby: the vicar receives £5. 5. per annum in lieu of tithes, and the interest of £502 raised by private subscription about forty years since.

BALE, or BAITHLEY (ALL SAINTS), a parish, in the union of WALSINGHAM, hundred of HOLT, W. division of NORFOLK, 16 miles (N.) from East Dereham; containing 229 inhabitants. It comprises 1041a. 2r. 38p., of which 824 acres are arable, 100 pasture, and 73 woodland. The living is a discharged rectory, united to that of Gunthorpe, and valued in the king's books at £10. 13. 4.: the tithes have been commuted for £305, and there are 21 acres of glebe. The church is in the decorated and later English styles. Here was anciently a chapel dedicated to St. Botolph.

BALHAM-HILL.—See TOOTING, UPPER.

BALK, a township, in the parish of KIRBY-KNOLE, union of THIRSK, wapentake of BIRDFORTH, N. riding of YORK, $3\frac{3}{4}$ miles (E. S. E.) from Thirsk; containing 89 inhabitants. It comprises about 780 acres, chiefly the property of Viscount Downe.

BALKHOLME, a township, in the parish and union of HOWDEN, wapentake of HOWDENSHIRE, E. riding of YORK, 3 miles (E.) from Howden; comprising by computation 550 acres, and containing 165 inhabitants. It is on the road from Howden to North Cave; and the river Ouse passes not far distant on the south.

BALLAM, a hamlet, in the township of WESTBY with PLUMPTONS, parish of KIRKHAM, union of the FYLDE, hundred of AMOUNDERNESS, N. division of the county of LANCASTER, 3 miles (W. by S.) from Kirkham;

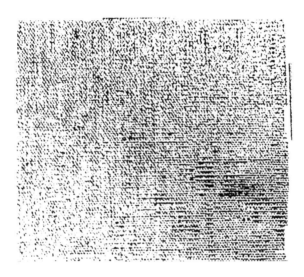

David O. McKay Library

A,

TOPOGRAPHICAL DICTIONARY

OF

ENGLAND,

COMPRISING THE

SEVERAL COUNTIES, CITIES, BOROUGHS, CORPORATE AND MARKET TOWNS,

PARISHES, AND TOWNSHIPS,

AND THE ISLANDS OF GUERNSEY, JERSEY, AND MAN,

WITH

ISTORICAL AND STATISTICAL DESCRIPTIONS:

AND EMBELLISHED WITH

ENGRAVINGS OF THE ARMS OF THE CITIES, BOROUGHS, BISHOPRICS, UNIVERSITIES, AND COLLEGES;

AND OF THE SEALS OF THE VARIOUS MUNICIPAL CORPORATIONS.

BY SAMUEL LEWIS.

Seventh Edition.

IN FOUR VOLUMES.

VOL. I.

FROM ABBAS-COMBE TO CWMYOY.

LONDON:

PUBLISHED BY S. LEWIS AND CO., 13, FINSBURY PLACE, SOUTH.

M.DCCC XLVIII.

TOPOGRAPHICAL DICTIONARY

ENGLAND,

SEVERAL COUNTIES, CITIES, BOROUGHS, CORPORATE AND MARKET TOWNS,

PARISHES, AND TOWNSHIPS,

AND THE ISLANDS OF GUERNSEY, JERSEY, AND MAN,

HISTORICAL AND STATISTICAL DESCRIPTIONS:

AND EMBELLISHED WITH

ENGRAVINGS OF THE ARMS OF THE CITIES, BOROUGHS, BISHOPRICS, UNIVERSITIES, AND COLLEGES;

AND OF THE SEALS OF THE VARIOUS MUNICIPAL CORPORATIONS.

BY SAMUEL LEWIS.

Seventh Edition.

IN FOUR VOLUMES.

VOL. I.

From ABBAS-COMBE to CWMYOY.

LONDON:
PUBLISHED BY S. LEWIS AND CO., 13, FINSBURY PLACE, SOUTH.

M DCCC XLVIII.

LONDON:
GILBERT AND RIVINGTON, PRINTERS,
ST. JOHN'S SQUARE.

PREFACE.

In publishing a SEVENTH EDITION of the TOPOGRAPHICAL DICTIONARY OF ENGLAND, the Proprietors consider it necessary to make a few brief remarks for the information of those Subscribers who may not have seen the more explanatory Preface to the First edition.

With a view to secure a well-condensed and accurate account of every important place possessing either civil or ecclesiastical jurisdiction, several gentlemen of competent talents and industry were originally engaged to make a general survey of the kingdom, and procure, by personal examination, the fullest information upon the different subjects contemplated in the plan of the work; their inquiries being facilitated by printed questions, including every particular to which their attention was to be directed. And the Proprietors beg to return their unfeigned thanks for the courtesy uniformly extended to their agents, during the time they were employed in their pursuit ; and gratefully to acknowledge the prompt assistance received from the resident nobility, gentry, and clergy, and persons holding official situations, many of whom transmitted original manuscripts, containing much highly valuable matter never before published.

It was at first intended that the work should be confined simply to a topographical and statistical account of the various districts ; but considering that a summary of the history of such places as either are, or

A 2

LONDON:
GILBERT AND RIVINGTON, PRINTERS,
ST. JOHN'S SQUARE.

PREFACE.

In publishing a SEVENTH EDITION of the TOPOGRAPHICAL DICTIONARY OF ENGLAND, the Proprietors consider it necessary to make a few brief remarks for the information of those Subscribers who may not have seen the more explanatory Preface to the First edition.

With a view to secure a well-condensed and accurate account of every important place possessing either civil or ecclesiastical jurisdiction, several gentlemen of competent talents and industry were originally engaged to make a general survey of the kingdom, and procure, by personal examination, the fullest information upon the different subjects contemplated in the plan of the work; their inquiries being facilitated by printed questions, including every particular to which their attention was to be directed. And the Proprietors beg to return their unfeigned thanks for the courtesy uniformly extended to their agents, during the time they were employed in their pursuit; and gratefully to acknowledge the prompt assistance received from the resident nobility, gentry, and clergy, and persons holding official situations, many of whom transmitted original manuscripts, containing much highly valuable matter never before published.

It was at first intended that the work should be confined simply to a topographical and statistical account of the various districts; but considering that a summary of the history of such places as either are, or

have been, of importance, would render it more comprehensive and interesting, it was determined to introduce a concise narrative of the principal events which mark their progress from their origin to the present
time.   To effect this, other gentlemen were entrusted with the task of
selecting from general and local histories, authentic records, and manuscripts at the British Museum and other public libraries, notices of the
most remarkable occurrences connected with each spot.

The arrangement of the different places is strictly alphabetical, each
being given under its proper name, and the epithet, if any, by which it
is distinguished from another locality of the same designation, following
after the chief heading.

The ensuing order of subjects, when the topics are noticed in the work,
has been generally adopted :—1. Name of the place, and of the saint to
whom the church is dedicated ; situation ; population, according to the
census of 1841.—2. Origin, and etymology of name ; summary of historical
events, whether national or particular.—3. Local description ; distinguishing features of surface ; soil ; number of acres, &c. ; mines and quarries.
—4. Scientific and literary institutions ; sources of amusement ; commerce, trade, and manufactures ; facilities afforded by rivers, railroads,
canals, &c. ; markets and fairs.—5. Municipal government ; privileges
and immunities ; courts of justice, prisons, &c. ; parliamentary representation.—6. Ecclesiastical and religious establishments ; particulars
respecting livings, tithes, glebe, patronage ; description of churches ; dissenters' places of worship.—7. Scholastic and charitable foundations
and endowments ; benevolent institutions ; hospitals ; almshouses.—8.
Monastic institutions ; antiquities ; mineral springs ; natural phenomena.
—9. Eminent natives and residents ; title which the place confers.

The Maps accompanying the work are corrected up to the present
time, and printed from steel plates.   The Arms and Seals of the
several corporate towns, bishoprics, colleges, &c., have been drawn and
engraved from impressions in wax, furnished by the respective corporate
bodies ; and although they have generally been either enlarged, or reduced, to one size, for the sake of uniformity, yet great care has been

taken to preserve, in each instance, an exact fac-simile of the original. The difficulty of effecting this, from the mutilated state of many of the seals, was kindly removed by Sir George Nayler, and other gentlemen at the Heralds' College, who also furnished the Arms of some of the towns.

Since the publication of the first edition of the Dictionary, the Proprietors have received from the gentry and clergy resident in different parts of the country several thousands of communications, enabling them to embody much additional information, and to correct many statements that had become erroneous in consequence of the lapse of time, or from changes that had otherwise occurred. To the parochial clergy, especially, they are indebted for the contribution, in detail, of those facts with which they are necessarily best acquainted.

In addition to the matter thus obtained, the Proprietors have noticed in the present edition, where needful, the multifarious alterations caused by certain recent legislative enactments. The principal of these enactments are, the Act 2nd and 3rd William IV., c. 45, by which the system of parliamentary representation was remodelled, and new electoral divisions were formed; the Poor-Laws' Act, by which the country was divided into unions; the Act relating to Dioceses and Episcopal Patronage; the Municipal Corporations' Act, which changed the constitution of about one hundred and seventy corporate bodies; and the Tithes' Commutation Act. Diligent use has also been made of the Reports that have been printed under the authority of Parliament, or of Commissions, including the last volumes issued by the Charities' Commissioners, whose labours have been recently completed in 37 folio volumes; and the Report of the Commissioners appointed to inquire into Ecclesiastical Revenues.

Another feature in this new edition is, the introduction of the acreage of nearly every parish, on the authority of resident persons with whom the Proprietors have communicated; which information is the more important, as the returns of government, from the nature of the sources whence they are derived, are for the most part exceedingly inaccurate, and form but an approximation to the fact.

have been, of importance, would render it more comprehensive and interesting, it was determined to introduce a concise narrative of the principal events which mark their progress from their origin to the present time. To effect this, other gentlemen were entrusted with the task of selecting from general and local histories, authentic records, and manuscripts at the British Museum and other public libraries, notices of the most remarkable occurrences connected with each spot.

The arrangement of the different places is strictly alphabetical, each being given under its proper name, and the epithet, if any, by which it is distinguished from another locality of the same designation, following after the chief heading.

The ensuing order of subjects, when the topics are noticed in the work, has been generally adopted :—1. Name of the place, and of the saint to whom the church is dedicated ; situation ; population, according to the census of 1841.—2. Origin, and etymology of name ; summary of historical events, whether national or particular.—3. Local description ; distinguishing features of surface; soil; number of acres, &c.; mines and quarries. —4. Scientific and literary institutions; sources of amusement; commerce, trade, and manufactures; facilities afforded by rivers, railroads, canals, &c.; markets and fairs.—5. Municipal government; privileges and immunities; courts of justice, prisons, &c.; parliamentary representation.— 6. Ecclesiastical and religious establishments; particulars respecting livings, tithes, glebe, patronage ; description of churches ; dissenters' places of worship.—7. Scholastic and charitable foundations and endowments; benevolent institutions; hospitals; almshouses.—8. Monastic institutions; antiquities; mineral springs; natural phenomena. —9. Eminent natives and residents; title which the place confers.

The Maps accompanying the work are corrected up to the present time, and printed from steel plates. The Arms and Seals of the several corporate towns, bishoprics, colleges, &c., have been drawn and engraved from impressions in wax, furnished by the respective corporate bodies; and although they have generally been either enlarged, or reduced, to one size, for the sake of uniformity, yet great care has been

taken to preserve, in each instance, an exact fac-simile of the original.
The difficulty of effecting this, from the mutilated state of many of the
seals, was kindly removed by Sir George Nayler, and other gentlemen at
the Heralds' College, who also furnished the Arms of some of the towns.

Since the publication of the first edition of the Dictionary, the Proprietors have received from the gentry and clergy resident in different
parts of the country several thousands of communications, enabling them
to embody much additional information, and to correct many statements
that had become erroneous in consequence of the lapse of time, or from
changes that had otherwise occurred. To the parochial clergy, especially,
they are indebted for the contribution, in detail, of those facts with
which they are necessarily best acquainted.

In addition to the matter thus obtained, the Proprietors have noticed
in the present edition, where needful, the multifarious alterations caused
by certain recent legislative enactments. The principal of these enactments are, the Act 2nd and 3rd William IV., c. 45, by which the system
of parliamentary representation was remodelled, and new electoral divisions were formed; the Poor-Laws' Act, by which the country was divided
into unions; the Act relating to Dioceses and Episcopal Patronage;
the Municipal Corporations' Act, which changed the constitution of
about one hundred and seventy corporate bodies; and the Tithes'
Commutation Act. Diligent use has also been made of the Reports that
have been printed under the authority of Parliament, or of Commissions,
including the last volumes issued by the Charities' Commissioners,
whose labours have been recently completed in 37 folio volumes; and
the Report of the Commissioners appointed to inquire into Ecclesiastical
Revenues.

Another feature in this new edition is, the introduction of the acreage
of nearly every parish, on the authority of resident persons with whom
the Proprietors have communicated; which information is the more
important, as the returns of government, from the nature of the sources
whence they are derived, are for the most part exceedingly inaccurate,
and form but an approximation to the fact.

The Proprietors cannot entertain the hope that, in a work compiled from such a variety of sources, and containing notices so numerous and diversified, errors have not occurred; indeed, the information, even when collected upon the spot, from the most intelligent persons, has frequently been so contradictory as to require much labour and perseverance to reconcile and verify it. They have, however, regardless of expense, used the most indefatigable exertions to attain correctness, and to render the work as complete as possible; and they, therefore, trust that any occasional inaccuracy will receive the indulgence of the Subscribers.

SUBSCRIBERS.

Abbot, John George, Esq., Cranmer Dykes' House, Gateshead
Abbott, Rev. Christopher, M.A., Kelloe, Durham
Aberdein, Robert Henry, Esq., Honiton
Abney, Rev. Edward Henry, B.A., Vicar of St. Alkmund's, Derby
ABOYNE, The Right Honourable the Earl of
Abraham, John, Esq., Ribblesdale Place, Preston
Abram, Rev. Abraham, Netherton, Liverpool
Acaster, John, Esq., C.E., Liverpool
ACHESON, The Right Honourable Lord Viscount
Ackerley, William, jun., Esq., Solicitor, Wigan
Ackers, James, Esq., M.P.. The Heath, Ludlow
Ackroyd, Robert S., Esq., Field House, Horton, Bradford
Ackroyd, William, Esq., Birkenshaw, Leeds
Ackroyd, William, Esq., Westborn Lodge, Otley
Ackroyd, William, Esq., Horsforth, Leeds
Acland, Sir P. P. F. F., Bart., Fairfield, Bridgwater, Somerset
Acworth, Rev. Jas., M.A., President of Horton College, Bradford
Adair, Alexander, Esq., Heatherton Park, Wellington, Somerset
Adam, James, Esq., Mount Vernon, Liverpool
Adams, Arthur, Esq., J.P., Walsall
Adams, H. C., Esq., Magdalene College, Oxford
Adams, Rev. Richard, Edingthorpe Rectory, near North Walsham
Adams, Rev. Thomas Burrowes, M.A., Aldridge Lodge, Walsall
Adamson, Rev. Edward Hussey, M.A., Windy-Nook, Gateshead
ADELAIDE, The Right Rev. the Lord Bishop of
Adcock, Halford, Esq., Humbaston, Leicester
Addison, George Wilson, Esq., Hall Field, Bowling, Bradford
Addison, Rev. J. Aspinall, B.A., Vicar of Mitton, Yorkshire
Addison, Rev. Thomas, B.A., Vicar of Rillington-cum-Scampston,
Adkins, H., Esq., Edgbaston House, Birmingham   [Malton
Adolphus, J., Esq., Harcourt Buildings, Temple, London
Adshead, Aaron, Esq., Stalybridge
Agar, John, Esq., Brockfield Park, York
Ainger, Rev. T., Hampstead, Middlesex
Airy, Henry Cookson, Esq., Kingthorpe House, Pickering
Aitken, Thomas, Esq., Holmes, Bacup, Rochdale
Aked, Robert, Esq., Shaw-Street, Liverpool
Aked, Thomas, Esq., Shipley Grange, Bradford
Akenhead, Rev. David, B.A., Bishop-Wearmouth
Akroyd and Son, Messrs. James, Halifax
Alanson, Edward, Esq., Walton-on-the-Hill, Liverpool
Alban, Rev. Thomas, M.A., Rector of Snead, Bishop's Castle
Alcock, William N., Esq., Gisburne Park, Skipton
Aldam, William, Esq., M.P., Warmsworth, Doncaster
Alderson, Rev. Christ., M.A., Rector of Kirkheaton, Huddersfield
Alderson, Rev. Jonathan, M.A., Rector of Harthill, Yorkshire
Alderson, Rev. W., M.A., Rector of Aston, Sheffield
Aldred, John, Esq., Wellgate House, Rotherham
Alexander, Vice-Admiral, K.C.B., Fareham, Hants
Allarton, George, Esq., West Bromwich
Allatt and Haxby, Messrs., Solicitors, Ossett, Wakefield
Allbutt, Rev. Thomas, M.A., Vicar of Dewsbury, Craven
Allcroft, Rev. W. R., Whitgift, Goole
Allen, B. F., Esq., Jordan-Street, Preston
Allen, George Charles, Esq., B.C.L., Earl Shilton, Leicestershire
Allen, Rev. George, Incumbent of Great and Little Driffield
Allen, Rev. S., Rector of Wolterton-cum-Wichmere, near Aylsham
Allen, William, Esq., The Lodge, Malton, Yorkshire   [umberland
Allgood, Rev. James, M.A., Vicar of Felton and Framlington, North-
Allhusen, Christian, Esq., Elswick House, Newcastle-upon-Tyne
Allies, Jabez, Esq., F.S.A., Bedford Row, Islington

Allin, W., Esq., Arundel, Sussex
Alston, Rev. Vere, M.A., Rector of Odell, Bedford
Alston, W. C., Esq., J.P., Elmdon Hall, Warwickshire
Ambler, Henry, Esq., Moorside, Ovenden, Halifax
Ames, John, Esq., Green-Street, London, and Pinney House, Devon
Amies, John, Esq., Frettenham, near Coltishall
Amoore, William, Esq., Hastings, Sussex
Anderson, David, Esq., River Head, Driffield
Anderson, Francis, Esq., Fairfield, Liverpool
Anderson, George, Esq., Wingrove House, Newcastle-upon-Tyne
Anderson, George, Esq., Banker, Kirkaldy
Anderson, Henry, Esq., Westoe, South Shields
Anderson, James, Esq., Rose Hill, Wallsend
Anderson, Joseph, Esq., Benwell Tower, Newcastle-upon-Tyne
Anderson, Rev. J. S. M., Brighton
Anderson, Matthew, Esq., Jesmond Cottage, Newcastle-upon-Tyne
Anderson, Robert, Esq., J.P., Westoe, South Shields
Anderson, Rodney, Esq., Solicitor, Ludlow
Anderson, Thomas Darnley, Esq., Everton, Liverpool
Andersson, U. J., Esq., Chapel-Street, Liverpool
Anderton, Francis, Esq., Clayton Villa, Preston
Anderton, George, Esq., Cleckheaton, Leeds
Anderton, James, Esq., Mount Villa, York
Anderton, James Francis, Esq., Haighton House, Preston
Anderton, John, Esq., Wavertree, Liverpool
Anderton, Rev. John, Burscough Hall, Ormskirk
Anderton, W. J., Esq., J.P., Euxton Hall, Chorley
Andrew, Rev. John, B.A., Incumbent of Worsborough, Barnsley
Andrew, Rev. W. W., Vicar of Ketteringham, near Norwich
Andrews, Edward, Esq., Titchfield, Hants
Andrews, Robert, Esq., J.P., Rivington Hall, Bolton-le-Moors
Andrews, William, Esq., Solicitor, Market Harborough
Andrews, William, Esq., Architect, Bradford
Angerstein, John, Esq., Weeting Hall, Norfolk
Angus, Robert, Esq., Liverpool Commercial Bank
Ansdell, John, Esq., Solicitor, Green Bank House, St. Helen's
Ansley, Gilbert, Esq., Houghton Hill, Huntingdon
Anstey, Rev. Charles A., M.A., Assistant Master of Rugby School
Anstis, Bernard, Esq., Liskeard, Cornwall
Anthony, P. L., jun., Esq., Alphington Cottage, Ottery St. Mary
Anyon, Richard, Esq., Chorley, Lancashire
Archbold, James, Esq., J.P., Newcastle-upon-Tyne
Archer, John, Esq., Castle Eaton, Fairford, Gloucestershire
Arkless, Benj., Tantobie, Gateshead
Arkwright, Charles, Esq., Dunstall, Burton-on-Trent
Arkwright, Rev. Joseph, Mark Hall, Harlow, Essex
Armfield, Edward, Esq., Edgbaston, Birmingham
Armitage, James, Esq., Frederic-Street, Birmingham
Armitage, Richard, Esq., Johnson's Buildings, Huddersfield
Armstrong, Rev. Chas. Edw., B.D., Master of Hemsworth Hospital,
Armstrong, Geo., Esq., Abercromby Square, Liverpool [Pontefract
Armstrong, Rev. John, M.A., Wallsend
Armstrong, William, jun., Esq., Wingate Grange, Castle-Eden.
Armstrong, William, Esq., Minories, Jesmond   [Durham
Armstrong, W., Esq., Treasurer to the Corporation of Newcastle
Armytage, Sir George, Bart., Kirklees Park, Dewsbury
Armytage, Lieut.-Col. H., Hyde Park-Street, London
Arnold, J., Esq., Moor Green, Moseley, King's Norton
Arrowsmith, James, Esq., Solicitor, Newport-Pagnell
Arundell, The Honourable Arthur, Springfield, near Horsham
Arundell, W. A., Esq., Lifton Park, Devon .

The Proprietors cannot entertain the hope that, in a work compiled from such a variety of sources, and containing notices so numerous and diversified, errors have not occurred; indeed, the information, even when collected upon the spot, from the most intelligent persons, has frequently been so contradictory as to require much labour and perseverance to reconcile and verify it. They have, however, regardless of expense, used the most indefatigable exertions to attain correctness, and to render the work as complete as possible; and they, therefore, trust that any occasional inaccuracy will receive the indulgence of the Subscribers.

SUBSCRIBERS.

Ashbarry, Josh., Esq., Holme Lacy Cottage, Hereford
Ashburnham, Rev. D., Rector of Catsfield, near Battle
Ashburnham, Rev. J., B.D., Guestling, near Hastings
Ashburnham, Sir William, Bart., Broomham, Hastings
Ashmall, Joseph, Esq., Ediall, Lichfield
Ashton, George, Esq., Seaforth, Liverpool
Ashton, Henry, Esq., Woolton Wood, Liverpool
Ashton, John, Esq., Solicitor, Warrington
Ashton, Thomas, Esq., J.P., Parkfield, Middleton, Lancashire
Ashworth, Edmund, Esq., Egerton, Bolton-le-Moors
Ashworth, Henry, Esq., J.P., The Oaks, Turton, Bolton-le-Moors
Ashworth, John, Esq., Bertinshaw, Turton, Bolton-le-Moors
Ashworth, Messrs. D. and G., Callis Mill, near Halifax
Ashworth, Richard, Esq., Withy Trees, Preston
Askew, Lieut.-Gen. Sir Henry, Pallinsburn, Coldstream, N. B.
Askew, Rich. Croston, Esq., Tynemouth, Northumberland
Aspinall, John, Esq., Smethwick, Birmingham
Astley, Edward, Esq., Roby, Huyton, Liverpool
Astley, Francis L'Estrange, Esq., Burgh Hall, East Dereham, Norfolk
Astley, Sir John Dugdale, Bart., Everleigh House, Wilts
Astley, T. J., Esq., Melton Constable, Dereham, Norfolk
Astley, W. B., Esq., Wellington Lodge, Ryde, Isle of Wight
Aston, Sir Arthur Ingram, G.C.B., Aston Hall, Preston Brook,
Aston, John, Esq., Hereford   [Cheshire
Athy, Robert James, Esq., Ingon Grange, Stratford-on-Avon
Atherley. J., Esq., Arundel, Sussex
Atkin, William, Esq., Little Hulton, Bolton-le-Moors
Atkins, Rev. Henry, Vicar of Arreton, Isle of Wight
Atkins, Henry, Esq., Maddington, Devizes
Atkinson, Adam, Esq., Lorbottle House, Alnwick
Atkinson, Anthony, Esq., Deputy Registrar, Beverley, Yorkshire
Atkinson, Christopher, Esq., Ewart, Wooler
Atkinson, Geo. Clayton, Esq., Tyne Iron Office, Newcastle-upon-
Atkinson, Rev. John Breeks, M.A., West Cowes
Atkinson, John, Esq., Austhorpe Lodge, Leeds
Atkinson, Josh. Robt., Esq., Elmwood House, Leeds [upon-Tyne
Atkinson, Robt. Thos., Esq., Seaton-Delaval Colliery, Newcastle-
Atkinson, Rev. Thos., B.A., Incumbent of Liversedge, Leeds
Atkinson, Rev. William, B.A., Rector of Gateshead-Fell
Atkinson, Wm. Simpson, Esq., Barrowby Hall, Leeds
Atkinson, William, Esq., Ashton Hayes, Tarvin, Cheshire
Atmore, R., Esq., East Harling
Aubrey, H. P. T., Esq., Broom Hall, Oswestry
Austen, Vice-Admiral Sir Francis, K.C.B., Portsdown Lodge
Austin, Joseph, Esq., Headingley, Leeds
AYLESFORD, The Right Honourable the Earl of
Ayre, Rev. Joseph Watson, M.A., Wellingborough
Ayre, Thomas, Esq., Surgeon, Barnsley
Ayton, Henry Isaac, Esq., Seaton-Burn, Colliery, Newcastle-upon.
Ayton, John Featherstone, Esq., Fawcett-Street, Sunderland [Tyne
Ayton, Robinson, Esq., Swathling Cottage, Southampton
Ayton, William, Esq., Sandhill, Newcastle-upon-Tyne
Ayton, Rev. Wm. Alex., B.A., Brompton, Scarborough
Babb, George, Esq., Town Clerk of Great Grimsby
Backhouse, John Church, Esq., Beechwood, Darlington
Bacon, Sir Edmund, Bart., Raveningham Hall, near Beccles
Bacon, George, Esq., Nottingham
Bacon, Rev. Robert, LL.D., Incumbent of Fring, near Rougham
Badcock, Robert, Esq., Wilton, Taunton
Baddeley, Whieldon, Esq., Solicitor, Rocester, Uttoxeter
Badger, Benjamin, Esq., Masbrough Cottage, Rotherham
Badger, Thomas, Esq., Rotherham
Badham, Richard, Esq., Solicitor, Bromyard
Badnall, Rev. Wm., M.A., Wavertree, Liverpool
Bagge, Edward, Esq., Islington, Lynn, Norfolk
Bagge, Richard, Esq.,   do.   do.
Bagge, William, Esq., M.P., Stradsett Hall, near Downham Market
Bagnall, William, Esq., Oakwood, West Bromwich
BAGOT, The Right Honourable Lord
Bailey, Charles, Esq., Kirk-Leatham, Guisborough
Bailey, Joseph, jun., Esq., M.P., Easton Court, Tenbury
Baillie, Rev. J. Farmer, M.A., Great Rissington, Gloucestershire
Bainbridge, Rev. Francis, B.A., Grammar-school, Rothbury
Bainbridge, John, Esq., Moor Park, Harrogate
Bainbrigge, W. H., Esq., Everton, Liverpool
Bainton, John, Esq., Foston Mills, Driffield
Bainton, J. B., Esq., Beverley
Bairstow, John, Esq., J.P., Preston
Bairstow, Messrs. John and James, Hebden-Bridge, Yorkshire
Bairstow, Matthew, Esq., Knott, Keighley
Bairstow, Samuel, Esq., Green Hill, Cross Hills, Skipton
Bairstow, Thomas, Esq., Royd Hill, Sutton, Keighley
Bairstow, Messrs. William and John, Keighley

Baker, Rev. Francis, Wylye, Wilts
Baker, George, Esq., Dringhouses, York
Baker, John, jun., Esq., Cowslip Lodge, Wrington, near Bristol
Baker, Richard, Esq., Midhurst, Sussex
Baker, William, Esq., Fenton, Staffordshire
Baldock, Rev. R., M.A., Langtoft, Driffield
Baldock, William, Esq., Freshfield Cottage, Millbrook, Southampton
Baldrey, Robert, Esq., The Square, Halifax
Baldwin, Henry, Esq., The Square, do.
Baldwin, John, Esq., Carlton Place, do.
Baldwin, William, Esq., J.P., Bilston
Balfour, William, Esq., Bireton Brae, Kirkwall, N.B.
Balguy, Brian Thomas, Esq., Town Clerk of Derby
Balguy, Charles George, Esq., Colwick, Nottinghamshire
Balguy, J., Esq., J.P., Duffield, Derby
Ball, Edwin, Esq., Solicitor, Pershore, Worcestershire
Balshaw, William, Esq., Hill House, Altcar, Ormskirk
Banks, George, Esq., St. Catherine's, Doncaster
Banks, John, Esq., Holt, Norfolk
Banner, Edward, Esq., Grove Park, Liverpool
Bannerman, Alex., Esq., South Cottage, Chorley
Banning, Rev. B., Vicarage, Wellington, Salop
Barber, Edward, Esq., Barston Hall, Warwickshire
Barber, Gilbert, Esq., Winchester
Barber, Rev. John, M.A., Incumbent of Bierley, Bradford
Barber, Joseph, Esq., Solicitor, Brighouse, Halifax
Barber, John, Esq., Derby
Barber, John Sutton, Esq., Blakebrook, Kidderminster
Barber, Rev. Richard, M.A., Incumbent of Heage, Belper
Barclay, Thomas Brockhurst, Esq., Wavertree Lodge, Liverpool
Baring, Rev. Frederick, B.C.L., Itchen Stoke, Alresford
Baring, Sir Thomas, Bart., Stratton Park, Hants
Barker and Cheshire, Messrs., Solicitors, Northwich
Barker, George, Esq., Springfield, Birmingham
Barker, James, Esq., The Hill, Oldham
Barker, James Lamb, Esq., Solicitor, North Shields, Northumber-
Barker, Richard, Esq., Solicitor, Whitefriars, Chester   [land
Barker, Thomas, Esq., Vine Grove, Halifax
Barker, Rev. William, M.A., Vicarage, Broad Clyst, near Exeter
Barkus, William, Esq., Belle Vue, Gateshead
Barkworth, W. H., Esq., Cams Cottage, Hambledon, Hants
Barlow, Edward, Esq., Prestolee, Bolton-le-Moors
Barlow, G. F., Esq., Bryanstone Square, London
Barlow, Rev. Peter, B.A., Cockfield, Darlington
Barlow, William, Esq., Holybourne, Alton, Hants
Barlow, William, Esq., Frances Road, Edgbaston
Barnes, Rev. Joseph, M.A., Vicar of Berwick-upon-Tweed
Barnes, Orlando, Esq., Beeston, Norwich
Barnes, Richard, Esq., Solicitor, Barnard-Castle
Barnes, Thomas, Esq., Whitburn, Sunderland
Barnes, Thomas Addison, Esq., Westoe, South Shields
Barnes, Thomas, Esq., Farnworth, Bolton-le-Moors
Barnett, Horatio, Esq., Solicitor, Walsall
Baron, George, Esq., Drewton, South Cave, Yorkshire
Baron, John, Esq., Belmont, Walton-on-the-Hill, Liverpool
Baron, John Theophilus, Esq., Whitfield House, Roby, Liverpool
Barratt, John, Esq., Harpurhey Hall, Manchester
Barrett, Charles, Esq., Sedgefield, Rusheyford, Durham
Barrow, John Barnes, Esq., Solicitor, St. Helen's
Barrow, Richard Bridgman, Esq., Solicitor, Southwell, Notts
Barrow, William Alexander, Esq., Solicitor, Wigan
Barrow, Wm. Hodgson, Esq., J.P., Southwell, Notts
Barry, James H. Smith, Esq., D.L. and J.P., Marbury Hall, North-
[wich, Cheshire
Barry, Rev. William, M.A., Blisworth, Northampton
Barston, Charles, Esq., Solicitor, Halifax
Bartlelot, George, Esq., Stopham House, near Petworth, Sussex
Bartleman, Alexander, Esq., Tynemouth
Bartlett, Rev. John, Marnwood, near Coalbrook Dale, Salop
Barton, Rev. John Luke, M.A., Hermitage, Hambledon, Hants
Barton, Rev. Miles, Manor House, Little Hoole, Preston
Barton, Nathaniel, Esq., Corsley House, near Frome
Barton, R. B., Esq., Prospect Vale, Fairfield, Liverpool
Barwell, E. H., Esq., Mayor of Northampton in 1843, 1844, 1845
Barwell, N., Esq., Ashfold, near Crawley, Sussex
Barwick, Richard, Esq., Low Hall, Yeadon, Leeds
Bashall, Richard, Esq., Lostock House, near Preston
Bashall, William, Esq., Farington Lodge, Preston
Bass, Isaac, Esq., Brighton
Basset, John, Esq., M.P., Tehidy, Cornwall
Basset, Lady,   do.   do.
Bassett, Rev. H., Glentworth Vicarage, near Spittal, Lincolnshire

SUBSCRIBERS.

Bates, Ely, Esq., West Hill, Halifax
Bates, J. M., Esq., M.D., Newcastle-upon-Tyne
Bates, Jno. Moore, Esq., Mount Pleasant, Heddon-on-the-Wall
Bates, William, Esq., Gambier Terrace, Liverpool
Bath, H. Pyle, Esq., Colestocks, Feniton, Devon
Bathurst, Sir F. H., Bart., Clarendon Park, Wilts
Bathurst, Rev. W. H., M.A., Rector of Barwick-in-Elmet, Leeds
Batson, James, Esq., West Bromwich
Batten, John, Esq., Penzance, Cornwall
Batten, John, Esq., Yeovil, Somerset
Battersby, Rev. W., M.A., Parsonage, Heckmondwike
Battley, Rev. Charles B., M.A., Whitkirk, Leeds
Battye and Firth, Messrs., Solicitors, Birstall
Battye, Wm. Walker, Esq., Thorp Villa, Almondbury, Huddersfield
Bayfield. Rev. B., M.A., Incumbent of Ripponden, Halifax
Bayldon, Rev. J., M.A., Thwing, Bridlington
Bayley, Thomas, Esq., The Black Birches, near Shrewsbury
Bayley, William, Esq., Hastings, Sussex
Baynes, Mrs. General, Woolbrook, Sidmouth, Devon
Bayton, Rev. W. Stevens, Rector of Ford, near Arundel
Beach, William, Esq., Oakley Hall, Basingstoke
Beadon, Edwards, Esq., Highlands, Taunton
Beadon, Rev. F., M.A., Rector of North Stoneham, Hants
Beale, Thomas, Esq., Upton-on-Severn
Beard, Steyning, Esq., Ovingdean, near Brighton
Beasley, John, Esq., Chapel Brampton, Northampton
Beasley, Joseph, Esq., Smethwick, Birmingham
Beatson, William, Esq., Masbrough, Rotherham
Beattie, William, Esq., Warwick-Street, Toxteth Park, Liverpool
Beauchamp, Rev. Thomas, Rector of Buckenham Ferry, Norfolk
Beaumont, Joseph, Esq., Mold Green, Huddersfield
Beaumont, Thomas, Esq., Laura Place, Bradford
Beaumont, Thomas Mills, Esq., Knaresborough
Beaver, Rev. H. N., M.A., Vicar of Gringley-on-the-Hill, Bawtry
Beck, Peter, Esq., Halifax
Beckett, Christopher, Esq., J.P., Meanwood Hall, Leeds
Beckett, John Staniforth, Esq., Barnsley
Beckett, William, Esq., M.P., Kirkstall Grange, Leeds
Beckett, Rev. Wilson, B.A., Vicar of Heighington, Darlington
Beckingsale, William Jeffries, Esq., Newport, Isle of Wight
Beckwith, Rev. Henry, Eaton Constantine, Shrewsbury
Beckwith, Samuel, Esq., Aigburth, Liverpool
Beckwith, Rev. T. F., B.D., Vicarage, East Retford, Notts
Beckwith, William, Esq., Thearne Cottage, Beverley
Beddome, John Reynolds, Esq., M.D., Romsey, Hants
Bedford, John Yeend, Esq., J.P., Pershore Abbey, Worcestershire
Bedinfeld, J. L., Esq., Ditchingham Hall, Bungay
Bedlington, George, Esq., Ovingham, Newcastle-upon-Tyne
Beebee, Rev. Meyrick, M.A., Simonburn Rectory, Hexham
Beeby, Thomas, Esq., Clifton, Biggleswade
Beechey, W. Nelson, Esq., Barge Yard, London
Beed, Rev. J. B., Vicar of Felpham, near Bognor
Beesley, Alfred, Esq., Banbury, Oxon
Beesley, Rev. James, A.M., Vicar of Feckenham, Bromsgrove
Behrens, Sampson Lucas, Esq., Catteral House, Garstang
Belk, Thomas, Esq., Town Clerk of Hartlepool
Bell, Lieut.-Col. C. Hamilton, Auchtertool House, Fifeshire
Bell, G. M., Esq., Claremont Place, Newcastle-upon-Tyne
Bell, Rev. H. Edward, B.A., Vicar of Long-Houghton, Alnwick
Bell, John Thomas Witham, Esq., C.E., Castle-Eden, Durham
Bell, Richard H., Esq., J.P., Lawe, South Shields
Bell, Thomas, Esq., Picton Place, Newcastle-upon-Tyne
Bell, William, Esq., Ford House, Sunderland
Belles, T. W., Esq., Monument Cottage, Edgbaston
Bellhouse, Rev. W. Cocker, B.A., Grammar School, Tadcaster
Bellingham, John, Esq., Rye, Sussex
Bellman, Rev. Edmund, Hainford, near Norwich
Bellwood, Rev. William, Incumbent of Sinnington, Pickering
Benbow, John Henry, Esq., Stone Buildings, Lincoln's Inn, London
Bennett, Joseph, Esq., Surgeon, Wakefield
Bennett, Joseph, B. H., Esq., Tutbury, Burton-on-Trent
Bennett, William, Esq., M.D., Harrogate, Yorkshire
Bennett, Rev. W. C., Vicar of Corsham, Wilts
Benning, Henry, Esq., Barnard-Castle, Durham
Benson, Rev. H. B., M.A., Utterby House, Louth   [Yorkshire
Benson, Rev. Isaac, Incumbent of Acklam and Middlesbrough,
Benson, Rev. John, Norton-sub-Hambden, near Yeovil
Benson, William, Esq., Windsor Terrace, Liverpool
Bentinck, the Hon. and Rev. W. H. E., Rector of Sigglesthorne, Hull
Bentley, Greenwood, Esq., Bradford
Bentley, Henry, Esq., Oulton, Leeds
Bentley, Rev. Robert Henry, Cobridge, Newcastle-under-Lyme

VOL. I.

Beresford, Colonel, Repton Hayes, Burton-on-Trent
Berington, William, Esq., J.P., Little Malvern Court, Worcester
Bernard, Rev. John, B.A., St. Michael's, Toxteth Park
Bernard, Rev. William, Rector of Clatworthy, near Wiveliscombe
BERNERS, The Right Honourable and Rev. Lord
Berry, Grove, Esq., Surgeon, Harrogate
Berry, Rev. Thomas, Christ Church, Bolton-le-Moors
Bertram, Charles, Esq., J.P., Gateshead, Durham
Berwick, Alexander, Esq., J.P., Norton, Ratho, Edinburgh
Best, Rev. Francis, M.A. Rector of South Dalton, Beverley
Best, Rev. Francis, B.A., Flyford Flavell, Worcestershire
Best, Norris, Esq., Bilston
Best, William, Esq., Church Hill Cottage, Wednesbury
Beswicke, Mrs., Pike House, Rochdale
Bethell, Richard, Esq., J. P., Rise, Kingston-upon-Hull
Bethune, Rev. G. M., LL.D., Worth Rectory, near Crawley, Sussex
Betts, Rev. James, Ellingham Rectory, near Bungay
Bevan, Rev. Frederick, Carleton Rode, near Attleburgh
Bevan, John W., Esq., Redruth, Cornwall
Bevan, John, Esq., Clayton Lodge, Aigburth, Liverpool
Bevan, Reece, Esq., J.P., Freckleton House, Wigan
Bevan, Richard Lee, Esq., Flore Fields, Weedon
Bevan, William, Esq., Old Jewry, London
Beverley, William, Esq., Preston Place, Leeds
Bewicke, Mrs. Margaret, Close House, Northumberland
Bewsher, Rev. F. W., M.A., Killingworth, Newcastle-on-Tyne
Bewsher, Rev. James, Lapley, near Wolverhampton
Beynon, William, Esq., Shireland Hill, Smethwick
Bibby, John, Esq., Hart Hill, Allerton, Liverpool
Bickerstaff, John, Esq., Ribblesdale Place, Preston
Bickersteth, Robert, Esq., Liverpool
Bickford, Mr. J. T., Camborne, Cornwall
Biddulph, A. G. Wright, Esq., Burton Park, near Petworth
Bidwill, Joseph G., Felix Hill House, Exeter
Biedermann, Rev. G. A., Rector of Dantsey, Wilts
Bigge, Charles William, Esq., J.P., Linden, Morpeth
Bigge, Rev. H. J., M.A., East Haddon, Northampton
Bigge, Rev. John A., M.A., Incumbent of Ovingham, Newcastle-
Bigland, John, Esq., Bramham, Tadcaster   [upon-Tyne
Bignold, John, Esq., Deane-Street, Edge Lane, Liverpool
Bignold and Mawe, Messrs., Norwich
Bilham, Robert, Esq., Stow Bedon Hall, near Watton
Bill, John, Esq., Trent vale, Newcastle-under-Lyme
Billington, William, Esq., Civil Engineer, Wakefield, Yorkshire
Bills and Mills, Messrs., Darlaston Green Works, Wednesbury
Bilton, Edward, Esq., Newcastle-upon-Tyne
Bingham, Mrs., Harptree Court, Old Down, Somerset
Birch, Rev. Charles, Rector of Sawtrey-All Saints, near Stilton
Birch, Wyrley, Esq., Wretham Hall, near Thetford
Birchall, Thomas, Esq., Ribbleton Hall, Preston
Bird, Lambert, Esq., Kensington, Liverpool
Birkbeck, John, jun., Esq., Settle, Yorkshire
Birkbeck, Thomas, Esq., Stackhouse, Settle
Birket, Charles, Esq., Plungington, Fulwood, Preston
Birkett, Rev. Robert, M.A., Vicar of Kelloe, Durham
Birley, Edmund, Esq., Kirkham
Birley, Thomas, Esq., Milbank, Kirkham
Birley, Thomas Langton, Esq., Kirkham
Birt, John, Esq., Mounton, near Chepstow
Bishop, Rev. Alfred, M.A., Tichborne, Alresford, Hants
Bishop, Henry, Esq., Hastings, Sussex
Bisshopp, Sir Cecil A., Bart., Merton College, Oxford
Bissland, Rev. Thomas, M.A., Rector of Hartley-Maudytt, Alton
Black, William, jun., Esq., Caister, St. Edmund's, near Norwich
Blackburn, Henry Webster, Esq., Prospect House, Bradford
Blackburn, John, Esq., Solicitor, Leeds
Blackburne, Rev. Francis Theophilus, B.A., Cannock, Walsall
Blackburne, John Ireland, Esq., Hale Hall, Warrington
Blackett, Sir Edward, Bart., Matfen, Newcastle-upon-Tyne [Tyne
Blackett, Rev. John Alexander, M.A., Heddon, Newcastle-upon-
Blackwell, Rev. Christopher, M.A., vicarage, Seamer, Scarborough
Blagrave, Anthony, Esq., Harptree Court, Old Down, Somerset
Blair, James, Esq., Solicitor, Uttoxeter
Blair, Stephen, Esq., Mayor of Bolton in 1846
Blake, Rev. E., Bramerton, Norwich
Blake, Silas Wood, Esq., Venne House, Upton, near Wiveliscombe
Blake, William, Esq., Catscy, Trull, near Taunton
Blake, William, Esq., Manor House, Bilston, Skipton
Blakemore, Thomas, Esq., Newport, Salop
Blaker, Anthony, Esq., Southover, Lewes
Blakesley, Charles, Esq., Darlaston Hall, Meriden
Blanchard, James, Esq., J.P., Grimsargh House, Preston
Bland, John, Esq., South Villa, Rotherham, Yorkshire

n

SUBSCRIBERS.

Blane, Rev. Henry, M.A., Bishop-Wearmouth, Durham
Blanshard, W., Esq., M.A., Barrister-at-Law, St. Leonard's Place,
Blayds, John, Esq., Oulton House, Sheffield   [York
Blencowe, Rev. James, Sidmouth, Devon
Blencowe, R. W., Esq., The Hooke, near Chailey, Lewes
Blennerhassett, Rev. John, Rectory, Ryme, Sherborne
Blofeld, Rev. T. Calthorpe, Hoveton House, Norwich
Blommant, Lieut.-Gen., Willett House, near Taunton
Bloome, Matt., Esq., Solicitor, Leeds, Yorkshire
Blount, Sir Edward, Bart., Mawley, Bewdley
Bloxam, Robert, Esq., Newport, Isle of Wight
Bloxham, J. R., Esq., Solicitor, Birmingham
Blundell, R. B. B. H., Esq., J.P., Deysbrook, West Derby
Blundell, Thomas Weld, Esq., J.P., Ince-Blundell Hall
Blundell, William, Esq., J.P., Crosby Hall, Lancashire
Blunt, Edward Walter, Esq., Kempshott Park, Basingstoke
Blunt, Gen. R., K.C.B., Shirley, Southampton
Blyth, Rev. C. Deltick, Rector of Sutton, Bedfordshire
Blyth, Rev. Geo. Blanshard, M.A., Vicar of North Newbald, Mar-
Blyth, H. E., Esq., Sussex Farm, Burnham   [ket-Weighton
Boardman, William, Esq., Farington House, Preston
Bocquet, Francis Samuel, Esq., Laurel Road, Fairfield, Liverpool
Boghurst, P., Esq., Worthing, Sussex
Boissier, Rev. Peter E., M.A., Malvern Wells, Worcestershire
Bold, Nicholas Duckenfield, Esq., South Hill Place, Liverpool
Bolitho, Thomas, Esq., Chyandour, Penzance
Bolshaw, Joshua, Esq., Lunt, Sefton, Liverpool
Bond, Henry Hollier, Esq., Brewood, Wolverhampton
Bond, Rev. John, M.A., Rector of Romansleigh, Devon
Bond, Rev. Robert, The Lawn, Briston, near Holt
Bond, Simon, Esq., Sanderrake, Chipping, Preston
Bonnett, Rev. C. S., Avington, Winchester
Boor, J., Esq., Warminster, Wilts
Booth, James, Esq., Ing House, Liversedge, Leeds
Booth, John, Esq., Crouch Hall, Hornsey
Booth, Joseph Wilkinson, Esq., Solicitor, Wakefield
Booth, Richard, Esq., Basing House, Basingstoke
Booth, Rev. Robert, Rodmell Rectory, near Lewes
Booth, Samuel Lister, Esq., Solicitor, Bramley and Leeds
Booth, Thomas, Esq., Park Iron-Works, near Sheffield
Boothby, Rev. Henry, B.A., Kirby-Misperton, Malton
Borough, Burton, Esq., Chetwynd Park, Newport, Salop
Borrer, W., Esq., Barrow Hill, Henfield, near Steyning
Borthwick, John, Esq., West Newton, Wooler
Bosanquet, Charles, Esq., J.P., Rock, Alnwick
Bosville, A.W., Esq., J.P., Thorpe Hall, Bridlington
Bosworth, John, Esq., St. Ignatius Square, Preston
Botfield, Thomas, Esq., Hopton Court, Cleobury Mortimer
Bottomley, Moses, Esq., Wade House, Shelf, Halifax
Boucher, Rev. James, M.A., Lesbury, Alnwick
Boughey, Sir Thomas, Bart., Aqualate, Staffordshire
Boughey, Rev. John F.F., M.A., Rector of Forton, Newport, Salop
Boughton, Sir W. Edward Rouse, Bart., Downton Hall, Ludlow
Boult, William, Esq., Moulton Hall, near Acle
Boulton, M. P. W., Esq., Tew Park, Oxfordshire
Boulton, Thomas, Esq., Mayor of Stafford 1844   [Honiton
Bourke, Thos., Esq., Worcester Coll. Oxford, and Sidbury Vicarage,
Bourne, The Right Honourable J. Sturges, M.P.
Bourne, James, Esq., J.P., Heathfield House, Wavertree, Liver-
Bourne, R. H., Esq., Solicitor, Staindrop, Durham   [pool
Bousfield, Michael, Esq., Shaw-Street, Liverpool
Boustead, Rev. James, M.A., Stockton-on-Tees
Boutland, Wm., Esq., Bill Quay, Gateshead, Durham
Bouverie, Edward, Esq., J.P., Delapre Abbey, Northampton
Bouverie, Rev. W. Arundell, Rectory, Denton, Harleston
Bowen, Rev. Charles, B.A., Lecturer of Armley, Leeds
Bower, Abraham, Esq., Middlethorpe Hall, York
Bower, Alfred, Esq., Aigburth, Liverpool
Bower, John, Esq., Belle Vue Place, Bradford
Bower, Rev. J. W., B.A., Rector of Barmston, Bridlington
Bower, Robert, Esq., Welham, Malton
Bower, T. B., Esq., Iwerne House, Blandford, Dorset
Bowerman, Richard, Esq., Uffculme, near Wellington, Somerset
Bowers, George, Esq., C.E., Derby Place, Stanley, Liverpool
Bowles, Lieut.-Col. Charles Oldfield, North Aston, Woodstock
Bowles, Rev. C. B., Woking, Surrey
Bowles, H., Esq., Worthing, Sussex
Bowly, Devereux, Esq., Chesterton House, Cirencester
Bowman, James, Esq., Union Bank, Huddersfield   [ford
Bowman, Rev. John, M.A., Incumbent of St. Paul's, Wibsey, Brad-
Bowne, Robert, Esq., Castle House, Winchester
Bowness, Rev. George, M.A., Rector of Rokeby, Barnard-Castle
Bowyer, J., Esq., Petworth, Sussex

Boydell, James, Esq., Oak Farm Iron Works, Dudley
Boyes, James, Esq., Beverley
Boyle, Rev. J., S. C. L., Incumbent of Brighouse, Halifax
Boyles, Rev. C. Gower, M.A., Rector of Buriton
Boys, William, Esq., Bridgwater
Brace, Vice-Adm. Sir Edward, K.C.B., Catisfield Lodge, Fareham
Bracewell, Christopher, Esq., Earby, Skipton
Brackenbury, Bennet, Esq., Solicitor, Gainsborough
Bracknill, Rev. William Samuel, M.A., Grammar School, Nuneaton
Bradburne, Mrs. Mary, Pipe Place, Lichfield
Braddon, William, Esq., Skisdon Lodge, Wadebridge, Cornwall
Bradford, Rev. John, Newton Abbott, Devon
Bradford, Rev. W., Rector of Storrington, Sussex
Bradley, Thomas, Esq., Alnwick, Northumberland
Bradshaw, James, Esq.- Hudcar, Bury, Lancashire
Brady, Henry, Esq., Gateshead
Brameld, Rev. G. W., Louth, Lincolnshire
Bramley, Lawrence, Esq., Halifax
Bramley, Richard, Esq., Campfield House, Leeds
Bramwell, Thomas, Esq., Field House, Gateshead   [pool
Brancker, Rev. P. Whitfield, M.A., Field House, Wavertree, Liver-
Brancker, Thomas, Esq., Pex Hill, Cronton, Prescot
Brandling, C. J., Esq., Dep.-Lieut., Middleton Lodge, Leeds
Brandling, Rev. R.H., M.A. and J.P., Seaton-Burn Hall, Newcastle
Brandling, Robt. W., Esq., J.P., Low-Gosforth, Northumberland
Brandreth, Rev. W. Harper, M.A., Standish, Lancashire
Brawn, George and James, Messrs., Sandhills, Walsall
Bray, Rev. William, M.A., Vicar of Hartley-Wintney, Hants
Brayshaw, Rev. Timothy, M.A., Grammar School, Keighley
Brazier, Henry, Esq., Rye, Sussex
Breckon, Robert, Esq., Solicitor, Whitby
Bree, Rev. W. T., M.A., Rector of Allesley, Coventry
Breed, Richard Foster, Esq., Belmont Road, Liverpool
Breeds, Messrs. Thomas and Co., Hastings
Brereton, Rev. C. D., M.A., Rector of Little Massingham
Brereton, John, Esq., Brinton, East Dereham
Brereton, Rev. Dr. John, Head Master of Grammar School, Bedford ,
Brereton, Joseph, Esq., Speke Hall, Liverpool
Brereton, Robert John, Esq., Blakeney, Norfolk
Brereton, Rev. Shovell, Briningham, Holt, do.
Brereton, Rev. Thomas W., Vicar of Framsden, near Debenham
Bretherton, Peter, Esq., Maghull, Liverpool
Breton, John Frederick, Esq., Lyndhurst, Hants
Breton, Peter, Esq., Southampton
Breton, Thomas, Esq., Bexhill, near St. Leonard's
Brett, Charles, Esq., Exbury House, Fawley, Hants
Brewin, Rev. George, Scrayingham, York
Brewis, Samuel, Esq., Polefield, Prestwich, Manchester
Brewster, Rev. John, M.A., Vicar of Greatham, Stockton-upon-Tees
Brewster, Rev. R. F., M.A., Killingworth, Newcastle-upon-Tyne
Bridge, Richard, Esq., North Curry, near Taunton
Bridge, Sealey, Esq., South Petherton, Somerset
Bridge, S. F., Wellington,   do.
Bridger, Charles, Esq., Winchester
Bridger, H. C., Esq., Buckingham House, near Shoreham
Bridges, Francis S., Horton Hall, Bradford
Bridges, Rev. Nathaniel, Henstridge, near Shaftesbury
Bridgman, Edward, Esq., Coney-Weston Hall, near Thetford
BRIDPORT, The Right Honourable Lord   [Moors
Bridson, Thomas Ridgway, Esq., J.P., Bridge House, Bolton-le-
Brigg, William, Esq., Cross Hills, Skipton, Yorkshire
Briggs, Rev. Fran. B., Vicar of St. Stephen's by Saltash, Cornwall
Briggs, John, Esq., Hemington, Leicestershire
Briggs, Nathaniel, Esq., Ashfield Place, Bradford
Briggs, Rawdon, Esq., South Parade, Wakefield
Briggs, Rawdon, Esq., J.P., Birstwith Hall, Ripley
Brigham, William, Esq., Lair Gate, Beverley, Yorkshire
Brisbane, Lieut.-Gen. Sir T. M., Bart., G.C.B., G.C.H., &c.,
     [Makerstown, Roxburghshire
Briscoe, Musgrave, Esq., Coghurst, near Hastings
Briscoe, Samuel Stone, Esq., D.L. and J.P., Fir-Tree House, Dudley
Briscoe, Mrs., Summerhill, Dudley
Bristow, Robert, Esq., Broxmore Park, Wilts
Bristowe, Samuel Ellis, Esq., Basthorpe Hall, near Newark
Broadbent, James, Esq., Acre House, Lindley, Huddersfield
Broadbent, Samuel, Esq., Bradford, Yorkshire
Broadwood, Rev. John, Bedford House, Worthing
Brock, Thomas Clutton, Esq., Pensax Court, Worcester
Brockett, William Edward, Esq., Bensham Lodge, Gateshead
Brockett, Wm. Henry, Esq., J.P., King James Street, do.
Brockholes, Thomas Fitzherbert, Esq., Claughton Hall
Brockman, Rev. Tatton, Vicar of Rottingdean, near Brighton
Brodie, B. B., Esq., Lincoln's Inn Fields, London

Broke, Sir Arthur de Capel, Bart., Oakley, Kettering
Bromehead, Rev. A. C., M.A., Rectory House, Eckington, Ches-
Bromet, John, Esq., The Grange, Tadcaster, Yorkshire [terfield
Bromfield, Rev. Henry, B.A., Charlecote, Stratford-on-Avon
Bromley, Frederick, Esq., Ashton-under-Lyne
Brook, Charles, Esq., Healey House, Huddersfield
Brook, Mrs. Jonas, West House, Mirfield, Dewsbury
Brook, Joseph, Esq., J.P., Greenhead, Huddersfield
Brook and Freeman, Messrs., Solicitors, do.
Brook, Thomas, Esq., Badsworth, Pontefract
Brook, William Leigh, Esq., Meltham Hall, Huddersfield
Brooke, Charles N., Esq., Walsall
Brooke, John, Esq., Armitage Bridge, Huddersfield
Brooke, John, Esq., Berry Hall, Old Walsingham
Brookfield, Mr. Samuel, Aigburth Vale, Liverpool
Brooks, Wm. Alex., Esq., C.E., Guildhall, Newcastle-upon-Tyne
Brothers, Rev. James, Wissett, near Halesworth
Broughton, William, Esq., Solicitor, Bawtry
Brown, Alexander, Esq., Beilby Grange, Wetherby
Brown, Andrew Cassels, Esq., Duke-Street, Edge Hill, Liverpool
Brown, Rev. Dr., Downside College, Midsomer Norton, Old Down
Brown, Rev. Edward, M.A., Leeds, Yorkshire
Brown, Edward, Esq., Oak Field, Edgbaston
Brown, Francis, Esq., Welbourn, Grantham
Brown, George, Esq., Springfield, Everton, Liverpool
Brown, George, Esq., Rose-Edge Villa, Wavetree, Liverpool
Brown, Isaac, Esq., Cowpen Lodge, Blyth, Northumberland
Brown, James, Esq., J.P., Hare Hills Grove, Leeds
Brown, Rev. James L., B.A., Incumbent of Holbeck, Leeds
Brown, Rev. James Humphrey, M.A., vicar of Dalton-le-Dale,
[Durham
Brown, John, Esq., Clerk to the Justices, Newcastle-upon-Tyne
Brown, John, Esq., Seaton-Delaval, North Shields
Brown, J., Esq., M.D. and J.P., Bishop-Wearmouth, Sunderland
Brown, Rev. John, M.A., and M.R.I.A., Vicar of St. Mary's,
Brown, John, Esq., Lea Castle, Kidderminster [Leicester
Brown, John, Esq., C.E., Dock Yard, Birkenhead, Cheshire
Brown, Rev. William, Great Crosby, Liverpool
Brown, Robert, Esq., Solicitor, Sunderland
Brown, Robert, Esq., Solicitor, Barton-upon-Humber
Brown, Thomas, Esq., Solicitor, Skipton
Brown, Rev. Thomas James, M.A., Portsmouth
Brown, William, Esq., Manor House, Winterborne-Stoke, Devizes
Brown, Rev. William, B.A., Wark, Hexham
Brown, W. Williams, Esq., J.P., Allerton Hall, Chapel-Allerton
Brown, Rev. Wilse, M.A., Egglestone, Barnard-Castle .
Brownbill, William, Esq., Wavertree, Liverpool
Browne, Rev. C. H., Rector of Blo-Norton, near East Harling
Browne, Rev. E. F., St. Werburgh's, Birkenhead
Browne, Rev. J. Geoffrey, A.B., Rector of Kiddington, Woodstock
Browne, J. T. G., Esq., Morley House, near Wymondham
Browne, Rev. Peter, M.A., Blackrod, Bolton-le-Moors
Browne, Thomas, Esq., Thrigby Hall, near Yarmouth
Browne, Thomas, Esq., Amble House, Alnwick
Browne, Thomas Briarley, B.A., Wortley, Leeds
Browne, Rev. Thomas Cooper, M.A., Darnall Hall, Sheffield
Browne, W. J. Utten, Esq., The Lodge, Bramerton, near Norwich
Browne, William W., Esq., Jarrow, South Shields
BROWNLOW, The Right Honourable the Earl
Brownrigg, Rev. Thomas, M.A., Incumbent of Boston, Wetherby
Bruce, Thomas, Esq., Parham Lodge, near Woodbridge
Brumell, H. and G., Messrs., Solicitors, Morpeth, Northumberland
Brunton, John, Esq., C.E., Handsworth
Brunton, Thomas, Esq., Town Clerk, Sunderland
Bruton, Lieut.-Col., Croford, Wiveliscombe, Somerset
Bryans, Rev. Francis, M.A., vicar of Backford, Chester
Buckingham, The Ven. Archd. of, Shanklin Parsonage, Isle of Wight
Buckland, C. E., Esq., Shaftesbury
Buckle, John, Esq., Wyelands, Chepstow, Monmouthshire
Buckle, Joseph, Esq., Lord Mayor of York, 1842-3
Buckley, James, Esq., Quickedge, Mossley
Buckley, John, Esq., J.P., Carr Hill, Ashton-under-Lyne
Buckley, John, Esq., Redgefoot, Todmorden
Bucknell, George, Esq., Crowcombe, near Taunton
Bucknell, Robert, Esq., Hulse, near Milverton, Somerset
Buckner, Rev. C., Perpet. Curate of Mid-Lavant, near Chichester
Buckwell, Rev. William, B.A., Incumbent of Longnor, Stafford-
Bull, Joseph, Esq., Coppice Green, near Shiffnall, Salop [shire
Bull, Rev. Thomas, M.A., Corby, Rockingham
Bulmer, George, Esq., Duncan-Street, Leeds, Yorkshire
Bulwer, Rev. Edward, Sall Rectory, near Reepham
Bulwer, Rev. James, Aylsham, Norfolk
Bulwer, W. E. L., Esq., Heydon Hall, Reepham

Bunkill, Charles, Esq., Wintringham, Brigg, Lincolnshire
Bunney, William, Esq., Solicitor, Kingston-upon-Hull
Bunting, Jabez, jun., Esq., Solicitor, Leeds
Burder, William, Esq., Brineton Villa, Shiffnall
Burdis, Edward Forster, Esq., North of England Bank, Sunderland
Burdon, George, Esq., J.P., Heddon House, Newcastle-upon-Tyne
Burfield, James, Esq., Hastings
Burgh, Henry, Esq., Bittern Lodge, Southampton
Burkitt, John, Esq., Selby, Yorkshire
Burne, T. H., Esq., Loynton Hall, near Newport, Salop
Burnett, Charles M., Esq., Alton, Hants
Burnett, George, jun., Esq., Lead Works, Newcastle-upon-Tyne
Burnett, Thomas Hayton, Esq., Windmill Hill, Gateshead
Burney, Rev. Henry, Wheatley Rectory, near Frome, Somerset
Burningham, Thomas, Esq., Froyle, Hants
Burns, Rev. William, B.D., Farnworth-cum-Kersley, Bolton-le-
Burrell, Bryan, Esq., Bolton, Alnwick [Moors
Burrell, Sir Charles Merrik, Bart., M.P., Knepp Castle, Shipley
Burrell, Henry Peareth, Esq., Little Houghton, Alnwick
Burnell, John, Esq., Iron Founder, Newcastle-upon-Tyne
Burrell, John, Esq., Wakefield, Yorkshire
Burridge, Henry, Esq., Banker, Kirkcaldy, Fife
Burridge, Rev. William, Bradford, Somerset
Burrington, Rev. Gilbert, Rector of Woodleigh, Devon
Burroughes, H. N., Esq., M.P., Burlingham Hall, Norwich
Burroughes, Rev. Jeremiah, Lingwood Lodge, Norwich
Burrow, Thomas Dixon, Esq., Settle, Yorkshire
Burt, Rev. Alexander, Manse of Arngask, Kinross
Burt, Rev. J. T., Perpetual Curate of Seething, Norwich
Burt, Thomas R., Esq., East Grinsted
Burton, Alfred, Esq., St. Leonard's on Sea, Sussex
Burton, Rev. Charles, LL.D., All Saints, Manchester
Burton, Lancelot Archer, Esq., Woodlands, Emsworth, Hants
Burtsal, N., Esq., Bungay, Suffolk
Bury, Charles, Esq., Liphook, Hants
Bury, John, Esq., Coventry
Bury, Robert, Esq., Welches, Bentley, Hants
Busch, Edward, Esq., Austrian Consul, Prince's Park, Liverpool
Busfeild, Rev. Harcourt, M.A., Incumbent of Coley, Halifax
Busfeild, Johnson Atkinson, Esq., Solicitor, Bradford
Busfeild, Rev. J. A., D.D., Rector of St. Michael's, Wood-Street,
[London, and Carlton Vicarage, Skipton
Busfeild, Rev. William, M.A., Rector of Keighley
Busfeild, William, Esq., M.P., Upwood, Bingley, Yorkshire
Bush, Elijah, Esq., Trowbridge, Wilts
Bushell, J., Esq., West Cliffe, Preston
Buston, Roger, Esq., of Buston, Alnwick
Butcher, Rev. James Hornby, Ramsbottom, Bury, Lancashire
Butcher, Robert, Esq., The Grove, Bungay
Buthon, Peter, Esq., Millbrook, Southampton
Butler, Rev. C.R., M.A., Catherington, Hants
Butler, Thomas, Esq., Kirkstall, Leeds, Yorkshire
Butler, William Henry, Esq., Kenilworth
Butler, Rev. William James, B.D., Westbourne, Sussex
Butterfield, Brothers, Messrs., Keighley
Butterton, Rev. George Ash, B.D., Uppingham
Buttery, John, Esq., Nottingham
Buxton, Sir John Jacob, Bart., Schadwell Park, near Thetford
Buxton, Sir T. Fowell, Bart., North Repps, near Aylsham
Byron, James Standish, Esq., J.P., West Ayton, Scarborough
Caffin, Rev. George B., B.A., Brimpton, Berks
Caiger, Capt. Herbert, R.N., Otterbourne, Winchester
Calder, Adam, Esq., Shattor, Kelso, N.B.
Caldwell, H. B., Esq., Hilborow Hall, near Brandon
Caldwell, J. Stamford, Esq., Linley Wood, Newcastle-under-Lyme
Caley, William, Esq., Saltwell House, Gateshead
Callander, John Alexander, Esq., Springfield House, Hyde
Callender, Geo., Esq., Prospect Vale, Liverpool
Callender, S. P., Esq., Bradshaw, Bolton-le-Moors
Calrow, James Richard, Esq., Wood Hill, Bury, Lancashire
Calrow, William, Esq., J.P., Walton Lodge, Preston
CALTHORPE, The Right Honourable Lord
Calthrop, John, Esq., Stanhoe Hall, near Rougham
Calver, Daniel, Esq., Kenninghall, near East Harling
Calvert, William, Esq., Walton-le-Dale, Preston
Cameron, Rev. Charles, M.A., Worsley, Manchester
Cameron, Thomas, Esq., Willow House, Chorley
Camm, Alfred, Esq., Well Holme, Brighouse, York
Campbell, Rev. Charles, Weasenham, near Rougham
Campbell, Rev. Colin, M.A., Sunderland, Durham
Campbell, Rev. Colin, M.A., St. Thomas's, Lancaster
Campbell, Colin, Esq., J.P., Dingle Mount, Liverpool
Campion, Edward, Esq., Hexham, Northumberland

Campion, Francis, Esq., Solicitor, Thorne, Yorkshire
Cane, Rev. T. C., Brackenhurst, Southwell, Notts
Cann, Rev. J. S., Wramplingham Hall, near Wymondham
Cann, W. R., Esq., Casick House, Wymondham
CANTERBURY, His Grace the Lord Archbishop of
CANTILUPE, The Right Honourable Lord
Cantrell, Rev. William, B.A., Alvaston Field, Derby
Capel, Arthur, Esq., Bulland Lodge, near Wiveliscombe, Somerset
Capes, Thomas Hawksley, Esq., Reedness, Goole; and Howden
Cargill, John, Esq., M.D., Eldon Square, Newcastle-upon-Tyne
Cariss, Benjamin, Esq., Osmondthorpe Cottage, Leeds
Carmichael, Alex. G., Esq., Castle Craig, Noblehouse, Peebles
Carne, Edward Clifton, Esq., Falmouth, Cornwall
Carnegie, Rev. J., Seaford, Sussex
Carpenter, George, Esq., Rye, do.
Carr, Rev. Charles, M.A., Rector of Burnby, Pocklington
Carr, Charles, Esq., Seghill, Earsdon, Newcastle-upon-Tyne
Carr, Rev. Cuthbert, B.A., Tynemouth, Northumberland
Carr, C. and W., Messrs., Solicitors, Gomersal, Leeds
Carr, Rev. Henry B., M.A., Alnwick
Carr, John, Esq., Hedgeley House, Whittingham, near Alnwick
Carr, John, Esq., Bondgate Hall, Alnwick
Carr, John, Esq., Solicitor, Skipton, Yorkshire
Carr, John Thomas, Esq., Russian Consul, Newcastle-upon-Tyne
Carr, Rev. John, Alnham Vicarage, Alnwick
Carr, John, Esq., Rosewarth, Newcastle-upon-Tyne
Carr, Ralph, Esq., J.P., Dunston Hill, Gateshead
Carr, Richard, Esq., Stackhouse, Settle
Carr, Richard, Esq., Green House, Balderston, Preston
Carr, Robert, Esq., Solicitor, Masefield
Carr, Rev. W., B.D., Incumbent of Bolton-Abbey, Yorkshire
Carr, William, Esq., Cross House, Wath-upon-Dearne, Rotherham
Carr, William Ridley, Esq., Scotswood, Newcastle-upon-Tyne
Carrick and Lee, Messrs., Solicitors, Brampton, Cumberland
Carrick, Robert, Esq., Croft House, Haltwhistle
Carron Company, Carron, by Joseph Danson, Esq.
Carruthers, W. T., Esq., J.P., Arthington Hall, Otley
Carson, Thomas, Esq., Solicitor, Liverpool
Carter, Charles T., Esq., Newgate-Street, Newcastle-upon-Tyne
Carter, Rev. Edmund, Fleetwood-on-Wyre
Carter, Rev. James, Brewood, Wolverhampton
Carter, Rev. John, D.D., Head Master of Gram. School, Wakefield
Carter, John, Esq., Knottingley, Ferrybridge
Carter, John Thomas, Esq., Hunstanton, near Lynn
Carter, Rev. R. Foster, B.A., Rector of Rowner, Gosport, Hants
Carter, Samuel, Esq., Solicitor, Birmingham
Carter, Rev. T. T., Piddle Hinton, Dorchester, Dorset
Carter, Thomas, Esq., Howden
Carter, Rev. W., B.A., Incumbent of Old and New Malton
Carter, William, Esq., Howden
Carter, William Edward, Esq., Solicitor, Pontefract
Carter, Rev. William, South Bank, Samlesbury, Preston
CARTERET, The Right Honourable Lord
Cartwright, Henry, Esq., Hill Hall, near Eccleshall, Staffordshire
Case, William, Esq., Fareham, Hants
Cash, Newman, Esq., Scarcroft Lodge, Leeds
Cass, William Eden, Esq., Goole
Cassels, Rev. Andrew, M.A., Vicar of Batley, Dewsbury
Cassidi, Rev. Wm., B.A., Vicar of Grindon, Stockton-upon-Tees
Casson, Thomas, Esq., Hatfield Hall, Wakefield
Castell, Rev. William, Vicar of Brooke, near Norwich
Cater, William, Esq., Wraxham Hall, near Stalham
Cator, Rev. Charles, M.A., Rectory, Stokesley
Catt, William, Esq., Bishopstone, near Newhaven
Catterall, Paul, Esq., Winckley Square, Preston
Cautley, Rev. W. G., Earsham Rectory, near Bungay
CAVAN, The Right Honourable the Earl of
Cavendish, The Hon. Richard, Belgrave Square, London
Cazenove, James, Esq., Everton, Liverpool
Chadwick, Charles, Esq., M.D., Park Row, Leeds
Chadwick, J. F., Esq., The Hermitage, Grimsargh, Preston
Chadwick, John, Esq., Broadfield, Rochdale
Chadwick, W., Esq., Chadwick Mount, Everton Valley, Liverpool
Chaffer, Benjamin, Esq., Hope Cottage, Wavertree, Liverpool
Challen, S. H., Esq., Shermanbury Park, Henfield, near Steyning
Chalmers, Rev. Peter, Dunfermline, Fife
Chamberlain, Richard Dineley, Esq., Skipton
Chamberlaine, Rev. George Thomas, Rector of Almsford, Somerset
Chamberlayne, J. Chamberlayne, Esq., Mangersbury House
Chamberlayne, Thomas, Esq., Cranbury Park, Winchester
Chambers, John, Esq., Belle Mont, Chapeltown, Sheffield
Chambers, Thomas W., Esq., Chinton, near Seaford, Sussex
Champney, Thomas Frederick, Esq., Beverley, Yorkshire

Chance, J. T., Esq., Spring Grove, Monument Lane, Birmingham
Chandler, Rev. George, M.A., Treeton, Rotherham, Yorkshire
Chandler, The Very Rev. G., D.D., Dean of Chichester
Chapman, John, Esq., Stakesby, Whitby
Chapman, John Mellar, Esq., Usworth Place, Gateshead
Chapman, John, Esq., J.P. and M.A., Hill End, Mottram-
[in-Longdendale
Chapman, Major-Gen. Sir Stephen, C.B., K.C.B., Fairfield House
Chapman, Robert Stiles, Esq., Little Langford House, Wily
Chapman, Rev. W. S., B.A., Romsey, Hants
Chapman, William Thomas, Esq., Biggleswade
Charleton, John, Esq., Sunderland
Charleton, Robert, Esq., Lee Hall, Hexham
Charleton, Watson, Esq., High Farm, Newcastle-upon-Tyne
Charlton, Anthony, Esq., Solicitor, Morpeth
Charlton, E., Esq., M.D., Eldon Square, Newcastle-upon-Tyne
Charlton, Francis, Esq., Rothwells, Little Hulton, Bolton-le-Moors
Charlton, Philip, Esq., Wytherford Hall, near Shrewsbury
Charlton, St. John C., Esq., Aspley Castle, Wellington, Salop
Charlton, Thomas B., Esq., Chelwell Hall, Nottingham
Charnock, John, Esq., The Avenue, Woodhouse, Leeds
Chaston, James, Esq., Brundish Lodge, Framlingham
Chatfield, Rev. A. W., Vicar of Stotfold, Baldock
Chaytor, M. H., Esq., Union Bank, Sunderland
Cheadle, Rev. James, M.A., Vicar of Bingley, Yorkshire
Cheales, Rev. Henry, M.A., Harbridge, Fordingbridge, Hants
Cheers, W. H., Esq., Papworth Hall, near Caxton, Cambridgeshire
Cheney, E. H. Esq., Badger Hall, Shiffnall, Salop
Chetham, Capt. Sir Edward, K.C.H., C.B., Haslar Hospital
Chevallier, Rev. John, M.D., Aspall Hall, near Debenham
CHICHESTER, The Right Honourable the Earl of
CHICHESTER, The Right Rev. the late Lord Bishop of
Childe, William Lacon, Esq., Kinlet Hall, Salop
Childs, Rev. John, St. Blazey, Cornwall
Chilton, T., Esq., Northumberland Terrace, Everton, Liverpool
Chitty, P. M., Esq., Shaftesbury, Dorset
Cholmley, Col., Howsham, Whitwell, Yorkshire
Chrystie, Captain Thomas, R.N., Hope-Street, Edinburgh
Church, Rev. W. M. H., M.A., Geddington-cum-Newton, Kettering
Clanny, William Reid, Esq., M.D., Sunderland
Clapham, Samuel Blakey, Esq., Aireworth, Keighley
Clapham, Thomas, Esq., Potter-Newton, Leeds
Clapp, Rev. Charles John, Rector of Coulston, near Devizes, Wilts
Clare, Rev. George Boodle, B.A., Incumbent of Shareshill, and
[St. George's, Wolverhampton
Claridge; Henry, Esq., The Mount, York
Clark, Rev. George, M.A., Alton, Hants
Clark, George, Esq., Barnby Moor, East Retford
Clark, Mr. George, Horsham, Sussex
Clark, Rev. John, Incumbent of Hunslet in Leeds, and Domestic
[Chaplain to Lord Howden
Clark, Rev. John Dixon, M.A. and J.P., Belford Hall, Northumber-
Clark, John Graves, Esq., Masboro' Hall, Rotherham   [land
Clark, John, Esq., Architect, Leeds
Clark, John Henry, Esq., Solicitor, Shipston-on-Stour
Clark, Rev. Joseph, M.A., Great Crosby, West Derby
Clark, Lutterell L., Esq., Solicitor, Ludlow
Clark, Rev. Thomas, M.A., Incumbent of Christ Church, Preston
Clark, Thomas, Esq., Incumbent Terrace, Liverpool
Clarke, Abraham, Esq., Holt, near Minehead
Clarke, Rev. Henry, M.A., Incumbent of Guisborough
Clarke, James, Esq., J.P., Swarthdale House, Lancaster
Clarke, Mrs. John, Ashfield House, West Derby
Clarke, Joseph, Esq., Manor House, Kippax, Pontefract
Clarke, Robert C., Esq., Noblethorpe, Barnsley
Clarke, Thomas, Esq., Chard, Somerset
Clarke, Rev. Thomas, M.A., Vicar of Mitcheldever, Hants
Clarke, Thomas, Esq., Alfred Place, Liverpool
Clarke, William, Esq., Aigburth, Liverpool
Clarke, William, Esq., Eton Villa, Wavertree
Clarkson, Henry, Esq., Wakefield, Yorkshire
Clarkson, Rev. Thomas Bayley, M.A., Badsworth, Pontefract
Clavering, John, Esq., Solicitor, Newcastle-upon-Tyne
Claxton, William, Esq., South Hill Grove, Liverpool
Clay, Rev. John, B.D., East Cliff, Preston
Clay, Rev. John, M.A., Vicar of Stanfield, Burton-on-Trent
Clay, John, Esq., Laygate House, South Shields
Clay, Joseph Travis, Esq., Rastrick, Huddersfield
Clay, Patrick, Esq., Mayor of Berwick-upon-Tweed, 1843
Clay, Swift, and Wagstaff, Messrs., Solicitors, Liverpool
Claydon, C. T., Esq., Bawburgh, near Norwich
Clayton, Rev. J. Henry, M.A., Rector of Farnborough, Hants
Clayton, Thos. Greenwood, Esq., J.P., Bierley Hall, Bradford

Clayton, Wm., Esq., J.P., Langcliffe Place, Settle, Yorkshire
Cleather, Rev. G. P., Chirton, Devizes, Wilts
Clegg, Kay, Esq., Solicitor, Oldham
Clements, W. B., Esq., Wadebridge, Cornwall
Clennell, Thos., Esq., J.P., Harbottle Castle, Rothbury
CLEVELAND, His Grace the Duke of
CLIFFORD, The Right Honourable Lord
Clifton, Robert, Esq., Brandon, Suffolk
Clint, Fras. A., Esq., Fairfield, Liverpool ·
Close, Thomas, Esq., Nottingham
Clough, John, Esq., Bootham, Yorkshire
Clough, The Misses, Feltwell, near Brandon
Clubbe, C., Esq., Framlingham
Clutterbuck, Rev. Henry, M.A., vicar of Kempstone, Bedford
Clutterbuck, John, Esq., J.P., Warkworth, Alnwick
Clutton, Messrs. Robert and John, Whitehall Place
Coates, James, Esq., Solicitor, Wetherby
Coates, Peter Eaton, Esq., Stanton Court, Stanton-Drew, Somerset
Cochran, Wm., Esq., Ladge Lane, Liverpool
Cochrane, Rev. James, Cupar, Fife
Cockell, Charles, Esq., Attleburgh
Cockerton, Rev. David, B.A., East Bullington House, Hants
Cockerton, Rev. John, M.A., Dronfield, Sheffield
Cockin, Rev. William, A.M., Head Master of Grammar School of
[Charles 1st, Kidderminster
Cogan, Rev. T. W., Rector of All Saints, Chichester
Coglan, John, Esq., Deane-Street, Liverpool
Colbeck, Harrison, Esq., Leamington House, Newcastle
Colbeck, James, Esq., Whorlton Hall, do.
Colby, Rev. Samuel, Rector of Little Ellingham, near Attleborough
Coldham, H. W., Esq., Anmer Park, near Lynn
Coldham, Rev. J., vicar of Snettisham, do.
Cole, Robert, Esq., Holybourn Lodge, Alton, Hants
Cole, T. Butler, Esq., Kirkland Hall, Garstang
Cole, William, Esq., Newhaven, Sussex
Coleman, Henry John, Esq., Town Clerk of Pontefract
Coleridge, Francis George, Esq., Ottery St. Mary, Devon
Coleridge, Rev. James Duke, LL.D., vicar of Thoverton, do.
Colfox, Wm., Esq., Rax House, Bradpole, near Bridport
Collett, Benjamin, Esq., J.P., Grafton Manor House, Bromsgrove
Collingwood, Edw., Esq., J.P., Dissington Hall, Newcastle-upon-
[Tyne
Collingwood, Edw. John, Esq., High Sheriff, 1844, Lilburn Tower
Collingwood, Fred. John Woodley, Esq., Glanton Pyke, Alnwick
Collins, Rev. Caleb, Rector of Stedham, near Midhurst
Collins, Rev. Oliver Levey, M.A., Parsonage, Ossett, Wakefield
Collinson, Rev. H. King, M.A., Stockton-on-Tees
Collinson, Rev. Rich., B.A., Usworth Parsonage, Gateshead
Collis, Lieut.-Col., Upcott House, Taunton
Collis, Rev. William Blow, M.A., Norton Canes, Walsall
Collison, R. P., Esq., Maghull, Liverpool
Collyer, Rev. J. B., Hackford Hall, near Reepham
Colpoys, Rev. J. A. G., M.A., Rector of Droxford, Alton
Colston, Rev. William, A.M., Broughton Hall, Lechlade
Colt, Capt. W. O., Rownham House, Southampton
Coltart, Wm., Esq., Greenfield House, Liverpool
Commerell, J. W., Esq., Strood Park, Slinfold, near Horsham
Commons, The Library of the House of, by T. Vardon, Esq.
Compton, H. C., Esq., M.P., Manor House, Lyndhurst
Compton, Thomas, Esq., Sompting-Abbots, near Worthing
Comyns, Rev. John, Wood House, Bishops Teignton, Devon
Condell, Wm., Esq., Surgeon to the Duke of Devonshire, Baslow
Constable, Thos., Esq., Manor House, Otley, Yorkshire
Conyers, Edmund Dade, Esq., Coroner, Driffield
Conyngham, Rev. John, Weston Rectory, near Norwich
Coode, Edward, Esq., St. Austell, Cornwall
Cook, Mr. George, Itteringham, near Aylsham
Cook, John, Esq., Solicitor, Scarborough, Yorkshire
Cook, Thos. Linsley, Esq., Wincomblee, Newcastle-upon-Tyne
Cook, William, jun., Esq., Solicitor, Pocklington
Cook, Rev. Dr., St. Andrews, Fife
Cooke, Rev. Alexander, M.A., Loversal, Doncaster
Cooke, Charles H., Esq., Benwell Grove, Newcastle-upon-Tyne
Cooke, Rev. Stephen, Vicar of Oulton, Knapton Hall, Norfolk
Cooke, Thomas, Esq., Newclose, Newport, Isle of Wight
Cooke, Rev. Thomas, Vicarage, Westbury, Wilts
Cookesley, Rev. H. P., Bungay
Cooks, Mrs., Woodhampton, Stourport
Cookson, Daniel, Esq., Solicitor, Newcastle-upon-Tyne
Cookson, Rev. Edward, M.A., Incumbent of St. Mary's, Leeds
Cookson, Rev. Francis Thomas, M.A., St. John's Parsonage, Leeds
Cookson, Isaac Thos., Esq., Newbiggin House, Newcastle-upon-
Cookson, Thomas, Esq., Swinburne Castle, Hexham [Tyne

Cookson, William, Esq., Bill Quay, Gateshead
Coombe, Charles, Esq., Holmes, Broomfield, Somerset
Coombs, Mr. John, Bratton, Westbury, Wilts
Coombs, Rev. William, M.A., Incumbent of St. Catherine's, Wigan
Coope, Rev. W. J., Rector of Falmouth, Summerland, Cornwall
Cooper, Rev. Aug., Syleham Hall, near Harleston
Cooper, Rev. C. B., Morley Rectory, near Wymondham
Cooper, Rev. Douglas, A.B., Hillmorton, Rugby
Cooper, Rev. George Miles, vicar of Wilmington, near Lewes
Cooper, Rev. Henry, Vicar of Rye, Sussex
Cooper, John, Esq., North Cove Hall, near Beccles
Cooper, James Allred, Esq., Solicitor, Bradford, Yorkshire
Cooper, John M., Esq., Solicitor, Sunderland, Durham
Cooper, Joseph, Esq., Oak House, Aigburth, Liverpool
Cooper, Mrs., Lympstone, Devon
Cooper, Samuel, Esq., Solicitor, Sheffield
Cooper, Rev. William, B.D., Rector of West Rasen, Lincolnshire
Cope, Edward, Esq., Solicitor, Birmingham
Cope, William Rogers, Esq., Solicitor, Birmingham
Copeland, William, Esq., Barnard-Castle, Durham
Copeman, Robert, Esq., Hemsley, near Yarmouth
Coppard, Thomas, Esq., Horsham, Sussex
Corbet, E. Goring, Esq., Springfield Cottage, Everton, Liverpool
Corbould, Rev. William, Tacolneston Rectory, Wymondham
Corby, Robert, Esq., Witlingham, near Norwich
Corles, Edward, Esq., Solicitor, Worcester
Corless, Rev. Geo. Jos. Augustine, D.D., Thropton Hall, Rothbury
Cornish, Rev. Sidney W., D.D., Ottery St. Mary, Devon
Corry, George, Esq., Penwortham House, Preston
Cory, Samuel, S., Esq., Allington, Bridport, Dorset
Cosway, Rev. S., M.A., Chute Vicarage, Wilts
Cotes, John, Esq., Woodcote, Shiffnall, Salop
Cottell, Charles, Esq., Everton Road, Liverpool
Cotterell, Sir John B., Bart., Garnons, Hereford
Cotterill, William, Esq., Town Clerk and Coroner, Walsall
Cottle, Rev. H. W., M.A., vicar of Watford, Daventry
Cottle, Rev. James, B.A., Incumbent of St. James, Taunton
Cottom, Rev. George, M.A., Coll. Church, Wolverhampton
Cotton, Benjamin, Esq., Afton House, Freshwater, Yarmouth
Cotton, Rev. Charles Evelyn, LL.B., Rector of Dalbury and Trusley,
Couchman, Rev. John, M.A., Thornby, Northampton [Derby
Coulson, John, Esq., Scagglethorpe, Malton [whistle
Coulson, John Blenkinsopp, Esq., J. P., Blenkinsopp-Hall, Halt-
Coulthard, James Battin, Esq., Hinstead Hill, Bentworth, Alton
Coulthart, John Ross, Esq., Ashton-under-Lyne
Coupe, Thomas, Esq., Oak Vale, Chorley, Lancashire
Courtney, Rev. S., Vicar of Charles the Martyr, Plymouth
Coutts, John, Esq., Wallsend, Newcastle-upon-Tyne
Cove, Rev. Edward, B.A., Rector of Thoresway, near Caistor
Coventry, The Hon. and Rev. Thomas, M.A. and J.P., Severn
[Stoke, Worcestershire
Coventry, The Hon. William, Earl's Croome Court, Worcester
Covey, Rev. Charles, Alderton Rectory, Cheltenham
Cowan, James, Esq., LL.D., Grange, Bishop-Wearmouth
Coward, Chas. Leach, Esq., Solicitor, Masbrough, Rotherham
Cowburn, John, Esq., Solicitor, Settle, Yorkshire
Cowdell, Wm., jun., Esq., Solicitor, Hinckley [Tyne
Cowen, Messrs. Joseph and Co., Blaydon-Burn, Newcastle-upon-
Cowthorpe, Rev. W., Rector of Westmeston cum Chillington, Sussex
Cox, Edward Soresby, Esq., Brailsford House, Derby
Cox, Edward, Esq., Dingle Hill, Liverpool
Cox, George Henry Richardson, Esq., Spondon Hall, Dyke, Derby
Cox, Henry, Esq., Parkfield, Derby
Cox, Rev. James, D.D., Hoxne, near Eye, Suffolk
Cox, Rev. James A., Hatch Beauchamp, Taunton
Cox, Rev. John Edmund, Aldeby, near Beccles
Cox and Co., Messrs., Army Agents, Craig's Court, London
Cox, Rev. Richardson, A.M., Tickenhall, Derby
Cox, William Sands, Esq., F.R.S., Temple Row, Birmingham
Cox, William Thomas, Esq., The Cottage, Spondon, Derby
Cox, William Trevelyan, Esq., Chedington Court, Dorset
Cox, Rev. Rich. Chas., M.A., Vicar of Newcastle-upon-Tyne
Coxon, Rev. Mark, Heswall Rectory, Neston, Cheshire
Coxwell, Geo. S., Esq., James, Newcastle-upon-Tyne
Crabtree, Abraham, Esq., Falkner Square, Liverpool
Craich, John, Esq., Manager of Alloa Colliery Whins, by Alloa
Craig, Rev. Edward, Burton Latimer, Kettering
Crane, Rev. Edwin, B.A., Crowle Vicarage, Worcester
Crane, Henry, Esq., Oakhampton, Stourport
Crankshaw, William, Esq., Prospect House, Samlesbury
CRAVEN, The Right Honourable the Earl of
Craven, John, Esq., Low Mill, Keighley, Yorkshire
Craven, Wm., Esq., Cold Spring House, Cullingworth, Bradford

Craven, William, Esq., Clapton Lodge, Halifax
Crawford, Gibbs, Esq., Paxhill Park, Lindfield, near Cuckfield
Crawhall, Geo., Esq., New House, Stanhope, Durham
Crawhall, Joseph, Esq., St. Ann's House, Newcastle-upon-Tyne
Crawhall, Wm., Esq., Stagshaw Close House, Corbridge
Crea, Henry, Esq., Whittingham, Alnwick
Cresswell, Rev. H., A.B., Vicarage, Creech St. Michael, Taunton
Creswell, John Bowden, Esq., New Court, Topsham, Devon
CREWE, The Right Honourable Lord
Crewe, Rev. Henry Robert, M.A., Rector of Breadsall, Derby
Creyke, Ralph, Esq., J.P., Rawcliffe Hall, Selby
Creyke, Rev. Stephen, M.A., Wigginton Rectory, York
Cripps, J. M., Esq., Novington, near Lewes
Crofts, John, Esq., Solicitor, Bradford
Crompton, Charles Livesay, Esq., Worthington Mills, Wigan
Crompton, John Bell, Esq., J.P., Milford House, Derby
Crompton, Thomas Bonsor, Esq., J.P., Farnworth Mills, Lanca-
Crompton, William Morgan, Esq., Solicitor, Stourbridge [shire
Crook, John Taylor, Esq., Dudlow Lane, Wavertree
Cropper, John, jun., Esq., Dingle Bank, Liverpool
Cropper, Edward, Esq.   do.   do.
Cross, William Assheton, Esq., J.P., Red Scar, Preston
Crosse, Thomas Bright, Esq., J.P., Shaw Hill, Chorley
Crosse, William, Esq., One House Hall, near Stowmarket
Crossland, Thomas P., Esq., Crossland Moor, Huddersfield
Crossley, John, Esq., J.P., Scaitcliffe, Todmorden
Crosthwaite, John, Esq., Woolton Hill, Liverpool
Crow, George, Esq., Ornhams, Boroughbridge
Crowe, Rev. Thomas, Woodside, Thurnham, Lancaster
Crowe, Mr. William, Ashmanhaugh House, near Coltishall
Crowther, George, Esq., Churwell Lane, Leeds
Crowther, Isaac, Esq., Croft House, Morley, do.
Crowther, Rev. James, Monmouth
Crowther, W., Esq., St. John's, Erringden, Halifax
Cruickshank, Robert, Esq., Anglesey Villa, near Alverstoke, Hants
Crump, Rev. John, M.A., Incumbent of Bootle, Liverpool
Cubitt, Capt. Henry, Catton, near Norwich
Cukitt, James T., Esq., of Cukitts, Maghull, Liverpool
Culley, Matthew, Esq., J.P., Fowberry Tower, Wooler [Pagnell
Cumberlege, Rev. Samuel, M.A., Astwood Vicarage, Newport-
Cumming, James, Esq., Upper Parliament-Street, Liverpool
Cummings, James, Esq., Lytham
Cummins, Richard, Esq., Litherland, Liverpool
Cunningham, Rev. Rob., M.A., Polmont House, Falkirk [York
Currer, Rev. Danson Richardson, M.A. and J.P., Clifton House,
Curteis, Rev. Jeremiah, Shelton Rectory, near Long Stratton
Curtis, H. Porter, Esq., Romsey, Hants
Curtis, T.A., Esq., Shaw-Street, Liverpool
Curtis, William, Esq., Alton, Hants
Curzon, Hon. and Rev. Frederic, M.A., Mickleover, Derby
Curzon, The Hon. and Rev. F. E., Mickleover, Derby
Cuthbert, Jas., Esq., Fairfield Cottage, Liverpool
Dadelszen, Edward Von, Esq., Dudlow Lane, Wavertree, Liverpool
Daintry, Rev. John, M.A., Shidfield Parsonage, Fareham
Dale, Daniel, Esq., Montpellier, Liverpool
Dales, Rev. Edward, M.A., Smethwick, Birmingham
Dall, Charles, Esq., Spring Cottage, Samlesbury, Preston
Dall, Joseph, Esq., Mellor Brook, Preston
Dallas, Rev. Alexander R. C., Rector of Wonston, Whitchurch
Dallin, Rev. R., M.A., Vicar of Rudston, Bridlington
Dalton, Rev. William, A.M., The Lloyd, Wolverhampton
Dalziel, William, Esq., Long Horsley, Morpeth
Daman, Stead, and Tylee, Messrs., Romsey, Hants
Danby, Rev. Samuel, M.A., Malton, Yorkshire
Dance, Col. Sir Charles Webb, Barr House, Bishop's Hall, Taunton
Dand, James, jun., Esq., Togston Hall, Alnwick, Northumberland
Dand, Robert, Esq., Field House, Alnwick
Dandy, James, Esq., Oak House, Fulwood, Preston
Daniel, Henry Maddocks, Esq., The Grove, Rainbow Hill, Wor-
Daniel, Knights Francis, Esq., Stockesby Cottage, near Acle [cester
Daniel, Thomas, Esq., Stoodleigh Court, Bampton
Daniell, Edmund John, Esq., Mereden Hall, Coventry
Danks, Samuel, Esq., The Vale, Edgbaston, Birmingham
Dare, Charles Holcomb, Esq., North Curry, Taunton
Darley, Alfred Horatio, Esq., Elvington Hall, York
Darley, Charles, Esq., Thorne, Yorkshire
Darley, Charles Albert, Esq., Burtonfield, York
Darley, Henry Brewster, Esq., J.P., Aldby Park, do.
Darling, George, Esq., Hetton House, Wooler
Darlington, John, Esq., Alison Hall, Chorley
Darlington, Ralph, Esq., Solicitor, Wigan
Darwall, Charles J., Esq., Solicitor, Walsall
Darwin, Edward L., Esq., Solicitor, Chesterfield

Dastim, William, Esq., Beverley
Daubeny, Colonel, K.H., Manse Road Hill, near Frome, Somerset
Daubeny, Rev. Giles, M.A., Rector of Lydiard Tregoz, Swindon
Daubuz, J. B., Esq., Offington House, near Worthing
Davenport, Rev. E. Sharington, Davenport House, Wolverhampton
Davenport, E. D., Esq., Capesthorne, Congleton
Davey, Stephen, Esq., D.L., Redruth, Cornwall
Davey, William, Esq.,   do.   do.
Davids, John, Esq., West Cowes, Isle of Wight
Davidson, H., Esq., Sheriff Clerk of Haddingtonshire, Haddington
Davidson, Robert, Esq., Revelrig, Currie, Edinburgh
Davidson, Robert, Esq., Advocate, York Place, Edinburgh
Davies, Albert, Esq., Rushall Cottage, Pewsey, Wilts
Davies, Rev. Charles Greenall, M.A., Trinity Church, Wakefield
Davies, Rev. David, M.A., Rector of Cliddesdon cum Farleigh
Davies, J. E., Esq., Holt, Bradford, Wilts
Davies, James, Esq., J.P., Elm Lodge, Ludlow
Davies, Rev. Morgan, M.A., late E. I. Co.'s Service, St. Mark's,
Davies, T. W., Esq., Solicitor, Leominster [Northop, Flintshire
Davies, Rev. Thomas, Bayton, near Bewdley
Davis, Rev. John, Ashwick, Old Down, Somerset
Davis, Robert, Esq., Mayor of Gateshead
Davis, William, West Cliffe, Preston
Davison, John, Esq., Brandon White-house, Whittingham
Davison, Robert Aiskell, Esq., Solicitor, Sunderland
Davison, William, Esq., Monk-Seaton, North Shields
Davison, William, Esq., Rothbury
Davy, Capt. John, R.N., Mount Amelia, Ingoldisthorpe, near Lynn
Dawe, Hill, Esq., Ditcheat, near Castle-Cary, Somerset
Dawes, Matthew, Esq., F.G.S., Westbrooke, Bolton-le-Moors
Dawkins, Colonel Henry, Over Norton House, Oxon
Dawson, Christopher, Esq., Brandon, Alnwick
Dawson, C. H., Esq., Royds Hall, Bradford
Dawson, Rev. Henry, Hopdon Rectory, near East Harling
Dawson, Rev. James, Belmont, Bolton-le-Moors
Dawson, Jas., Esq., Windermere, Lancashire
Dawson, Ralph, Esq., Aigburth, Liverpool
Dawson, Robert, Esq., Westoe, South Shields
Dawson, Thomas, Esq., Poundsworth, Driffield
Dawson, William, Esq., Eldon Square, Newcastle-upon-Tyne
Day, Charles, Esq., West Cowes, Isle of Wight
Day, Rev. Edmund, B.D., Incumbent of Norton, Malton
Day, Rev. Henry Thomas, LL.D., Mendlesham Vicarage
Day, Richard, Esq., Bexhill, near St. Leonard's
Day, Rev. Richard, Blyford, Halesworth
Day, Rev. Samuel, St. Austin's, Aigburth, Liverpool
Dayman, Henry, Esq., Millbrook, Southampton
Dayrell, Rev. R. W., Monk-Hopton, Bridgenorth
Deacle, Rev. Hicks, Vicar of Dilham and Honing, near Worstead
Deacon, Rev. George Edward, M.A., Ottery St. Mary, Devonshire
Deacon, Samuel, Esq., Towcester
Dean, John, Esq., Silverwell House, Bolton-le-Moors
Dean, Thomas, Esq., Solicitor, Batley, Yorkshire
Dean, William, Esq., Scausby Hall, Halifax
Deans, Rev. Joseph, M.A., The Vicarage, Melbourne, Derby
Dearden, James, Esq., The Orchard, Rochdale
Dearden, James, Esq., F.A.S. and J.P., The Orchard, Rochdale
Dearden, T. Ferrand, Esq., Solicitor and Coroner, Rochdale
Dees, Robert Richardson, Esq., Solicitor, Newcastle-upon-Tyne
Delafeld, Rev. John, vicar of Tertington, near Arundel
De La Mare, Rev. A., Woolwich Common
Delaunay, L. B., Esq., Hulton House, Blackley, Manchester
Denham, Richard, Esq., Mossley, Sharples, Bolton-le-Moors
Denison, Edmund Beckett, Esq., M.P., Doncaster
Denison, Robert, Esq., J.P., Waplington Manor, Pocklington
Dennett, Thomas P., Esq., Storrington, Sussex
Dennett, William Hugh, Esq., Worthing, do.
Dennis, Rev. Luke, M.A., Beverley
Dent, Ralph, Esq., Streatlam Castle, Barnard-Castle
Dent, Rev. T., Hollin Hall, Billington-Whalley, Blackburn
Denton, John Punshon, Esq., Hartlepool, Durham
Denton, S. B., Esq., M.D., Joy Lodge, Hornsea
Depledge, Joseph Price, Esq., Glass Works, Gateshead
DERBY, The Right Honourable the Earl of
De Ridder, John F. A., Esq., Stanhope Cottage, Windsor. Liverpool
De Sa, Manoel Reviz', St. Alban's House, Ryde, Isle of Wight
De Thoren, Baron, Underdown, Ledbury, Herefordshire
Dew, William, Esq., Swanton Novers, Holt
Dewe, Rev. James Byam, B.A., Ravenfield, Rotherham
Dewes and Sons, Messrs., Solicitors, Coventry
Dewhurst, Isaac, Esq., Skipton-in-Craven
Dewhurst, John, Esq.,   do.
Dewhurst, Thomas, Esq., Clayton Green, Preston

Dewhurst, William, jun., Esq., Ovenden, Halifax
Dewing, R., jun., Esq., Burnham Overy, near Burnham Westgate
Dicker, J. C., Esq., New Hall, Neston, Chester
Dickins, William, Esq., J.P., Cherington, Shipston-on-Stour
Dickins, Charles Scrase, Esq., West Stoke Park, near Chichester
Dickinson, William, Esq., M.D., West Bromwich
Dickon, William, Esq., Beal, Ferrybridge, Yorkshire
Dickson, John M., Esq., Berwick-upon-Tweed
Dickson, J. W., Esq., Camelon House, Falkirk, Stirling
Dickson, W., Esq., Clk. of the Peace for Northumberland, Alnwick
Digby, Rev. William, M.A., Vicar of Coleshill, Warwick
Diggle, Rev. Charles Wadham, Stratfield Turgis, Hartford Bridge
Dighton, Rev. Edward, Cranmore, Shepton Mallet
Dilke, Capt. R.N., Maxstoke Castle, Coleshill
DILLON, The Right Honourable Lord Viscount
Dinmore, Rev. Edward, St. Francis, Goosnargh, Preston
Dinning, Henry, Esq., Elford, Belford, Durham
Dinning, John, Esq., Mavisbush, Lasswade, Edinburgh
Dinsdale, Robert Moses, Esq., J.P., Newsham Park, Staindrop
Ditchfield, Peter, Esq., Mount Pleasant, West Houghton
Dixon, Alexander, Esq., Cleckheaton, Leeds
Dixon, Dixon, Esq., Unthank Hall, Haltwhistle, Northumberland
Dixon, Edward, Esq., Saint Cross, Winchester
Dixon, John, Esq., Alloa
Dixon, Rev. John, B.A., Vicar of Brotherton, Ferrybridge
Dixon, Rev. J., Incumbent of Ingleby-Greenhow and Bilsdale, [Stokesley, Yorkshire
Dixon, Richard, Esq., Holly Cottage, Dilworth, Preston
Dixon, Thomas, Esq., Banker, Chester
Dixon, Rev. W., Incumbent of East Ardsley, Wakefield
Dixon, Rev. W. H., M.A., Vicar of Bishopthorpe, and Chaplain to
Dobb, John, Esq., Wigan [the Archbishop of York
Dobson, Benjamin, Esq., Mere Hall, Bolton-le-Moors
Dobson, John, Esq., Lytham
Dobson, John, Esq., High-Seat House, Newcastle-upon-Tyne
Dobson, Joseph, Esq., Yorkshire District Bank, Selby
Dobson, Richard, Esq., Everton, Liverpool
Dobson, William, Esq., Gouthorpe House, Selby
Docker, William, Esq., Solicitor, Moor Green, Moseley, Birming-
Docker, Rev. Edmund, B.A., Froxfield and Sherard, Hants [ham
Dodd, Rev. Edward, M.A., Northwood, Isle of Wight
Dodd, William John, Esq., Monk-Wearmouth, Durham
Dodds, Isaac, Esq., Hall-Car House, Sheffield
Dodds, Ralph, Esq., Prudhoe-Street, Newcastle-upon-Tyne
Dodman, Martin, Esq., Titchwell, near Burnham Westgate
Dodsley, John, Esq., J.P., Skegby Hall, Mansfield, Notts
Dodson, Rev. Charles, M.A., Rector of Penton-Mewsey, Hants
Dodsworth, George, Esq., Fulford, York
Doherty, John, Esq., Upper Canning-Street, Liverpool
Doig, Rev. Thomas, Torryburn, Fife
Dolben, W. Mackworth, Esq., Finedon Hall, Wellingborough
Dolben, Rev. Charles, B.A., Rector of Ipsley and Spernall, Red- [ditch
Dolby, Miss, Brizes, Brentwood
Dolman, Thomas W. L., Esq., Solicitor, Beverley
Dolphin, Rev. John, South Repps Hall, North Walsham
Donne, W. B., Esq., South Green, Matteshall, near East Dereham
Donnison, Rev. J. W. S., Dove House, Mendham, near Harleston
Donovan, Alexander, Esq., Framfield Park, near Uckfield
Doogood, William, Esq., Solicitor, Bromsgrove
Douglas, Adam Thomson, Esq., Moneylaws, Coldstream
Douglas, Rev. H., M.A., Whickham Rectory, Gateshead
Douglas, The Honourable and Rev. James, Broughton Rectory
Douglas, Rev. Stair, Ashling, near Chichester
Douglas, Wm., Esq., Kirkcaldy, Fife
Douglass, James Ley, Esq., Solicitor, Market Harborough
Dove, Thomas, Esq., Solicitor, Newcastle-upon-Tyne
Dowdeswell, Rev. C., D.D., Stanford Rivers, Romford, Essex
Dowell, Henry, Esq., Solicitor, Sunderland, Durham
Downe, Rev. George E., Rushdon Rectory, Higham Ferrers
Dowsing, Rev. Horatio, North Barsham Rectory, near Walsingham
Dowson, Rev. Henry, M.A., Monk-Frystone, Ferrybridge
Drake, Miss Elizabeth, Castle Thorpe, Stony Stratford
Drake, Sir T. F. E., Bart., Nutwell Court, Woodbury, Devon
Drake, Thomas, Esq., Ashday Hall, Halifax
Dransfield, John, Esq., Solicitor, Penistone, Barnsley
Draper, Thomas, Esq., Wilm Mills, Derby
Drayton, John, Esq., Lyme Regis, Dorset
Dresper, John, Esq., Fairfield Villa, Liverpool
Drewry, James, Esq., The Priory, Burton-on-Trent
Driffield, Charles Edward, Esq., Solicitor, Prescot
Drummond, Henry, Esq., Albury Park, Guildford
Dryden, George, Esq., Bingley, Yorkshire
Dryden, Sir Henry Edward Leigh, Bart., Canons Ashby, Daventry

Dudley, Rev. Samuel George, B.A., Wilcot, Witney, Oxon
Dudley, Walter, Esq., Bloxwich, Walsall
Duesbery, W. D. Thornton, Esq., J.P., Skelton Hall, Yorkshire
Duffield, Francis, Esq., Town Hill House, Bradford
Dugmore, John, jun., Esq., Swaffham
Duke, Rev. Edward, Lake House, near Amesbury, Wilts
Duncan, Alex., Esq., Glenhouse, Denny, Stirling
Duncan, Rev. Joseph R., Manse, Dalkeith, Edinburgh
Duncan, Thos., Esq., C.E., Kensington, Liverpool
Duncan, Rev. W. Wallace, Cleish, Kinross
Dundas, Hon. and Rev. Thos. L., LL.D., Harpole, Northampton
Dunn, Alderman G. T., Esq., J.P., Bath House, Newcastle-upon-
Dunn, Richard, Esq., Heath House, Wakefield [Tyne
Dunn, Thomas, Esq., Mayor of Newcastle-upon-Tyne, 1843
Dunn, Thomas, Esq., Richmond Hill, Sheffield
Dunn, William, Esq., Town Clerk, Lancaster
Duppa, Thomas, Esq., Eardington, Bridgenorth, Salop
Durant, George, Esq., Tong Castle, Salop
Durnford, Mrs., Goodworth Clatford, Andover
Durrant, George, Esq., South Elmham Hall, Harlestone
Durrant, Sir T. H. Estridge, Bart., Scottow Hall, near Norwich
Dusautoy, Rev. William S., M.A., Rector of Exton, Alton, Hants
Dyke, Rev. T. Hart, M.A., Rector of Long Newton, Stockton-on-
Dyson, Jeremiah, Esq., Willow Field, Halifax [Tees
Dyson, Mrs., Elm House, Wavertree, Liverpool
Eadon, Henry, Esq., Snaith, Yorkshire
Eagles, Ezra, Esq., Bedford
Eamonson, Rev. B., M.A., Vicarage, Collingham, Wetherby
Earle, Henry, Esq., Andover, Hants [Yorkshire
Easterby, Rev. Richard D., M.A., Appleton-le-Street, Malton,
Easton, Josiah, Esq., Pawlett, near Bridgwater
Eastwood, John, Esq., Eastwood, Todmorden
Eastwood, William, Esq., Solicitor, Patmos Cottage, do.
Eaton, George, Esq., Spixworth, Norwich
Ebbetts, John, Esq., Cley Old Hall, Cley
Ebsworth, Rev. G. Searl, M.A., Vicar of Ilkeston, near Nottingham
Eccles, William, Esq., Withy Grove, Preston
Ecclesiastical Commissioners, The, Whitehall [Trent
Echalaz, Rev. Theodore, M.A., Lullington Vicarage, Burton-on-
Ecroyd, Benj., Esq., Ashfield Terrace, Bradford
Eddie, Wm. Hesleden, Esq., Barton-upon-Humber
Eddison, John, Esq., Town Clerk of Leeds
Eden, John, Esq., Aigburth Vale, Liverpool
Edge, Charles, Esq., Birmingham
Edgell, Admiral H. H., Standerwick Court, near Beckington
Edinburgh University, The Library of
Edleston and Edleston, Messrs., Solicitors, Nantwich
Edmondson, John, Esq., Mytholmroyd, Halifax
Edmunds, Rev. Edward, B.A., Chester-le-Street, Durham
Edwards, Rev. Edward, A.M., F.A.S., Lynn
Edwards, Rev. Edwin, Perpetual Curate of Ashford cum Thorpe
Edwards, George, Esq., Codsall, Wolverhampton
Edwards, G. N., Esq., Henlow, Biggleswade
Edwards, Isaac, Esq., Aintree, Liverpool
Edwards, Rev. Joseph, B.A., Rector of Croft-with-Yarpole, Leo-
Edwards, Joshua, Esq., Dudley House, Toxteth Park [minster
Edwards, Richard, Esq., J.P., Roby Hall, Prescot
Edwards, Robert, jun., Esq., Liverpool
Edwards, Samuel Bedford, Esq., Arlesey Bury, Biggleswade
Edwards, Somersby, Esq., Solicitor, Long Buckby, Daventry
Edwards, Thomas, Esq., Stoketon, near Saltash, Cornwall
Edwards, T. P., Esq., Millbrook, near Southampton
Edwards, William, Esq., Great Elm, near Frome, Somerset
Edwards, William, Esq., Framlingham
Eedle, Rev. Edward, Vicar of Bersted, near Bognor
Egerton, Francis Thomas, Esq., D.L., Roche Court, Salisbury
Eggington, Alfred, Esq., Town Clerk of Lichfield
Egles, Gabriel, Esq., Southover, Lewes, Sussex
EGREMONT, The Right Honourable the Earl of
Egremont, Rev. Godfrey G., Vicar of Barrow-upon-Humber
Elam, John, Esq., Gildersome, Leeds
ELCHO, The Right Honourable Lord
Eld, Francis, Esq., Seighford Hall, near Stafford
Elkins, Edward, Esq., Newman-Street, London
Ellames, Pattison, Esq., J.P., Allerton Hall, Liverpool
Ellershaw, Rev. Henry, M.A., Conisbrough, Rotherham
Ellerton, Edward, Esq., Gorforth, Leeds
Ellerton, George, Esq., Kippax, Pontefract
ELLESMERE, The Right Honourable the Earl of
Elletson, Josiah Johnson, Esq., Fleetwood-on-Wyre
Elletson, John, Esq., Howden, Yorkshire
Ellins, George, Esq., Droitwich
Elliot, Rev. Wm. Henry, M.A., Curate of Scarborough

Elliott, Rev. E., B.A., Incumbent of New Mill, Huddersfield
Elliott, Rev. George, M.A., Grammar School, Solihull
Elliott, John, Esq., Assistant Clerk of the Peace for Northumber-
Elliott, William Elliott, Esq., Gedling House, Notts   [land
Elliott, William, Esq., The Dales, Edgbaston, Birmingham
Ellis, George, Esq., Tingley House, Dewsbury
Ellis, James, Esq., Green Hill, Bingley
Ellis, John, Esq., High House, Addingham
Ellis, John Luttman, Esq., Petworth, Sussex
Ellis, John, Esq., Dewsbury
Ellis, Joshua, Esq., Highfield House, Dewsbury
Ellis, Rev. John, M.A., Wootton Wawen, Stratford-on-Avon
Ellis, Peter, Esq., Architect, Falkner Square, Liverpool
Ellis, Robert, Esq., Spencer-Street, Everton, Liverpool
Ellis, William, Esq., Yew Tree House, Morley, Leeds
Ellison, Rich., Esq., Solicitor, Tickhill, Yorkshire
Ellison, Rev. Thomas Noel, Rectory, Huntspill, Bridgwater
Elmhirst, Rev. Edward, B.A., Rector of Shawell, Lutterworth
Elmhirst, Rev. George, B.A., Leeds
Elsley, C. H., Esq., Recorder of York
Elswood, A., Esq., Bungay, Suffolk
Elwes, R. C., Esq., Great Billing, Northampton
Embleton, Dennis, Esq., M.D., Newcastle-upon-Tyne
Embleton, Robert, Esq., of Embleton, Alnwick
Emerson, T., Esq., Blaydon Lead-Works, Newcastle-upon-Tyne
Emly, Henry, Esq., New Square, Lincoln's Inn, London
Emmet, John, Esq., Ovendon Grange, Halifax
Empson, Amezia, Esq., Spellow Hill, Boroughbridge
Empson, Jarvis, Esq., Goole Hall, Yorkshire
Enfield, H., Esq., Nottingham
England, George, Esq., Westbury, Wilts
England, Richard, Esq., Binham, near Wells   [Dale
Erskine, The Hon. and Rev. H. D., M.A. and J.P., Kirby-under-
Erskine, Mrs., Dunimaile, Culross, Perth
Esdaile, Edward Jeffries, Esq., Cothelstone House, Bishops-Lydiard
Etty, Rev. S. J., M.A., Wootton Vicarage, Basingstoke
Etwall, Ralph, Esq., M.P., Longstock-Down, Hants
Etwell, William, Esq., Penton Lodge, Andover
Evans, David, Esq., Belper
Evans, George Fabian, Esq., M.D., Birmingham
Evans, Rev. J. H., M.A., Head Master of Grammar School, Sed-
Evans, John, Esq., Chipping, Preston   [bergh
Evans, Rev. Robert Wilson, B.D., Heversham, Milnthorp
Evans, Samuel, Esq., Darley Abbey, Derby
Evans, Samuel Harrison, Esq., Wardwick, Derby
Evans, Thomas, Esq., Hereford
Evans, Thomas, Esq., Lyminster, near Arundel
Evans, Rev. William, B.D. and J.P., Rector of Shipston-on-Stour
Everard, Rev. Daniel, Burnham-Thorpe, near Burnham-Market
Everett, Joseph, Esq., Heytesbury, Wilts
Every, Sir Henry, Bart., Egginton Hall, Burton-on-Trent
Evetts, Rev. Thomas, M.A., Clifton Reynes, Olney, Bucks
Ewbank, Jas., Esq., Redcar House, and Middleham, Yorkshire
Ewbank, William, Esq., Dalby, Whitwell, York
Ewen, J. L., Esq., valewood, near Hazelmere, Surrey
Ewing, George William, Esq., Aigburth, Liverpool
Exall, William, Esq., Amery House, Alton, Hants
EXCISE, Her Majesty's Honourable Commissioners of
Eyre, Rev. A. W., B.A., vicar of Hornsea and Rector of Riston
Eyre, Rev. Charles Wolff, M.A., Hooton-Roberts, Rotherham
Eyre, Charles, Esq., Architect, Birmingham
Eyre, Rev. James, LL.B., North Dalton, Beverley
Eyre, Rev. W., M.A., Rector of Sherfield-upon-Loddon, Hants
Eyston, John, Esq., Welford, Northamptonshire
Eyton, Thomas C., Esq., Donnerville, Wellington, Salop
Fair, James, Esq., Warton Lodge, Lytham
Fairbairn, Peter, Esq., Park Square, Leeds
Falconar, James, Esq., F.S.A., Solicitor, Doncaster
Falkner, Henry, Esq., Southwell, Notts
FALMOUTH, The Right Honourable the Earl of
Fanshawe, Rev. Charles Simon, M.A., Rector of Fawley, Bucks
Fanshawe, Rev. John Faithful, M.A., Incumbent of Lanchester
Farebrother, Rev. Thomas, A.M., Aston, Birmingham
Farley, George, Esq., Crowle Priory, Worcester
Farley, Rev. Thomas, B.D., Rector of Ducklington, Oxon
Farnall, H. Burrard, Esq., Lyme Regis, Dorset
Farrell, Rev. Maurice, Cardington, Bedford
Farrer and Co., Messrs., Lincoln's Inn Fields, London
Farrer, John, Esq., Grove House, Pudsey, Leeds
Farrer, William Frederick, Esq., Brafield House, Olney
Farwell, Rev. William, Rector of St. Martin's, Liskeard
Faulds, Andrew, Esq., Darley Hall, Barnsley
Faulkner, George, Esq., Lime Bank, Crumpsall, Manchester

Faussett, Rev. Bryan, M.A., Cropthorne, Evesham
Fawcett, Rev. Christopher, M.A., Bascombe Rectory, Amesbury
Fawcett, Richard, Esq., Shipley Hall, Bradford
Fawcett, Rev. Robert, B.A., Incumbent of Hilton and vicar of
                                        [Marton, in Cleveland
Fawcett, Rev. Thomas, M.A. and J.P., Rector of Green's Norton,
Fawcus, John, Esq., North Shields   [Towcester
Fawssett, Rev. Richard, M.A., Incumbent of Christchurch, Lei-
                                        [cester
Fayrer, Rev. Robert, Incumbent of Emmanuel Church, Camberwell
Fearenside, John, Esq., Solicitor, Burton, Westmorland
Fearne, Charles, Esq., Leeds
Feilden, Joseph, Esq., Witton Park, Blackburn
Feilden, Sir William, Bart., M.P., Feniscowles, Blackburn
Fellowe, R. G., Esq., Walmer Lodge, Little Hoole, Preston
Fellowes, Rev. Charles. Rector of Shottesham, near Norwich
Fellowes, Captain Sir Thomas, Knt. C.B., R.N., Gosport, Hants
Fendall, Rev. Henry, B.A., vicar of Crambe, Whitwell, York
Fenton, Rev. George, Vicarage, Roystone, Barnsley
Fenton, J. C., Esq., Solicitor, Huddersfield
Fenton, Kirkby, Esq., Leventhorp House, Leeds
Fenton, Robert, Esq., Solicitor, Newcastle-on-Lyme
Fennyhough, Joseph, Esq., Yoxhall, near Burton-on-Trent
Fenwick, Rev. C. Forster, B.C.L., Brook Parsonage, Isle of Wight
Fenwick, H., Esq., Solicitor, Red Barns, Newcastle-upon-Tyne
Fenwick, Henry Wm., Esq., Stand House,   do.
Fenwick, John, Esq., J.P., Preston villa, North Shields
Fenwick, John, Esq., Camp ville,   do.
Fenwick, John Manners, Esq., J.P., Gallow Hill House, Morpeth
Fenwick, John William, Esq., Solicitor, North Shields
Fenwick, T. Wm., Esq., Claremont Place, Newcastle-upon-Tyne
Ferguson, Charles, Esq., Gateshead Low Fell, Durham
Ferguson, Thomas, Esq., Sunderland
Fernandes, José Luis, Belle Vue, Wakefield
Ferrand, W. Busfeild, Esq., M.P., Harden Grange, Bingley
FERRERS, The Right Honourable the Earl
Ferris, Rev. Thomas Boys, M.A., Incumbent of St. Luke's, Leeds
Fessey, Rev. George Frederick, M.A., Rural Dean, Redditch
Festing, Thomas Colson, Esq., Blagdon Court, near Bristol
Fetherstonhaugh, Timothy, Esq., Kirk-Oswald, Penrith
Fetherstone, John, Esq., J.P., Packwood House, Warwickshire
FEVERSHAM, The Right Honourable Lord
Fewtrell, Edwin Alford, Esq., Grammar School, Rotherham
Fidler, Rev. I., B.A., Incumbent of Kelbrook-in-Thornton, Craven
Field, Henry, Esq., Longnor, Staffordshire
Fielden, Rev. U. J., M.A., Rector of Kirk Langley, Derby
Fielden, Brothers, Messrs., Todmorden, Yorkshire
Fielding, H. B., Esq., Church-Street, Lancaster
Fielding, James, Esq., Kerr House, Skircoat, Halifax
Fife, George, Esq., M.D., Sunderland
Fife, Wm. Henry, Esq., Ellison Place, Newcastle-upon-Tyne
Fildes, Jonathan, Esq., Quarry Hill, Rochdale
Fillingham, G., Esq., Syerston, near Newark, Notts
Finch, George, Esq., Solicitor, Worcester   [of Morpeth
Finch, Rev. Thomas, B.A., Chaplain to the County Gaol and Curate
Finney, James, Esq., Elm Vale, Liverpool
Firmstone, George, Esq., Lawnswood, Dudley
Firmstone, Thomas, Esq., Stony Fields, Newcastle-under-Lyme
Firth, Henry Josiah, Esq., Rose Hill, Rotherham
Firth, James, Esq., Upper House, Bowling, Bradford
Firth, Thomas, Esq., Toothill, Huddersfield
Fischer, Charles Anthony, Esq., Walton, Wetherby
Fish, Richard, Esq., Blickling, near Aylsham
Fisher, Edward, Esq., Spring Dale, Huddersfield
Fisher, Frederick, Esq., Solicitor, Doncaster, Yorkshire
Fisher, Henry B., Esq., Conisborough, Doncaster
Fisher, Henry, Esq., Fox Lane Ends, Kirkham   [ton, Liverpool
Fisher, Rev. John Henry, President of St. Edward's College, Ever-
Fisher, Joseph, Esq., Cleeve, Yatton, near Bristol
Fisher, Mr. Robert, Chitterne, Heytesbury, Wilts
Fisher, Rev. Samuel, M.A., Incumbent of Trent Vale, Staffordshire
Fisher, Rev. Thomas, Luccombe, Somerset
Fishlake, Rev. J. R., Little Cheverel, Devizes, Wilts   [Walsall
Fisk, Rev. George, LL.B., Prebendary of Lichfield, and Vicar of
Fitzgerald, Rev. R., B.A., Southington Cottage, Overton, Hants
Fitzpatrick, C. D., Esq., Litherland Park, Liverpool
Fitzroy, Rev. F. T. W. C., Ringstead Rectory, near Lynn
FITZWILLIAM, The Right Honourable the Earl,   2 copies
Flavell, Rev. J. W., Rector of Ridlington, North Walsham
Flavell, Rev. J. W., Rector of Stody with Hanworth, Holt
Fleetwood, George, Esq., Torbuck, Huyton, Liverpool
Fletcher, Rev. Charles, M.A., Southwell, Notts
Fletcher, Rev. Henry Thomas, B.A., St. George's, Chorley

Fletcher, Rev. Horatio S., A.B., Bilston, Staffordshire
Fletcher, James, Esq., North Brook, Leyland, Chorley
Fletcher, Rev. John, M.A., Meaux Abbey, Beverley
Fletcher, Joseph, Esq., Rawcliffe, Goole, Yorkshire
Fletcher, Rev. William, D.D., Collegiate School, Southwell, Notts
Flood, Christopher, Esq., Honiton, Devon
Flood, Samuel, Esq., Leeds
Floud, H. Esq., Upper Tooting, Surrey
Floyd, C. S., Esq., Solicitor, Huddersfield
Flover, Rev. Charles, M.A., Incumbent of Whittington, Lichfield
Foley, J. H. Hodgetts, Esq., M.P., Prestwood, Stourbridge
Foljambe, Thomas, Esq., Holme Field, Thornes, Wakefield
Folkes, Sir W. B., Bart., Hillington Hall, near Lynn
Folliott, George, Esq., Vicar's Cross, Chester
Foote, Ambrose, Esq., Ivy Cottage, West Cowes, Isle of Wight
Forbes, Henry, Esq., Lister Terrace, Bradford
Ford, Abraham Rawlinson, Esq., J.P., Ellel Hall, Lancaster
Ford, Rev. Frederick, M.A., Bramshott, Hants
Ford, Robert L., Esq., Park Place, Leeds
Forde, Matthew, Esq., Bank House, Maghull, Liverpool
Forge, Rev. C., M.A., Incumbent of Mapleton, Hornsea
Formby, Rev. Lonsdale, B.A., Formby
Forrest, The Right Hon. Sir James, Bart., Lord Provost and Lord
 [Lieutenant of the City of Edinburgh
Forster, Rev. John, M.A., Rector of Ryther, Selby
Forster, Rev. John, M.A., Rector of Wickersley, Rotherham
Forster, Rev. Joseph, M.A., Rector of Edmondbyers, Gateshead
Forster, Richard Carnaby, Esq., White House, Gateshead
Forster, Colonel T. W., Halls, Holt, near Melksham
Forster, William, Esq., Solicitor, Alnwick
Forster, William Edward, Esq., Bradford
Forster, William John, Esq., Tynemouth
Forsyth, Thomas, Esq., Wellington Terrace, South Shields
Foster, Rev. A., B.C.L., Kingston, Taunton
Foster, George, Esq., Cliff House, Horbury
Foster, John, Esq., J.P., Banker, Bilston
Foster, John, Esq., Solicitor, Pontefract
Foster, John, Esq., Solicitor, Driffield
Foster, John, Esq., Heptonstall Slack, Hebden-bridge
Foster, John W., Esq., Clapham, Settle, Yorkshire
Foster, Thomas, Esq., Stainforth, Settle
Foster, Mrs. Thomas, The Hill, Woolton, Liverpool
Foster, Rev. Thomas, M.A., Rector of Falstone, Hexham
Foster, William, Esq., Solicitor, Settle
Foster, William Frederick, Esq., South Hill Grove, Toxteth Park
Foster, W. and H., Messrs., Denholme, Bradford
Fothergill, Mark, Esq., Solicitor, Selby, Yorkshire
Foulis, Sir Wm., Bart., Woodhall House, Culloton, Edinburgh
Fountaine, A. Esq., Narford Hall, near Swaffham
Fowler, John, Esq., Berwood Common, Erdington, Birmingham
Fowler, John Coke, Esq., Duffield Bank, Derby
Fowler, Oliver, Esq., Kingsclere, Hants
Fowler, Richard, Esq., Gravelly Hill House, Birmingham
Fowlis, Mark, Esq., J.P., Hesleston House, Malton
Fox, George Colton, Esq., Todwick Grange, Sheffield
Fox, Henderson, and Co., Messrs., London Works, Birmingham
Fox, Rev. Henry, M.A., Churchover, Rugby
Fox, John, Esq., Daisy Lee, Lindley, Huddersfield
Fox, John, Esq., Cleobury Mortimer, Salop
Fox, John, Esq., Woodthorpe, near Nottingham
Fox, Rev. Samuel, M.A., F.S.A., Morley Rectory, Derby
Fox, Rev. Thomas H. Lane, Vicar of Sturminster Newton, Dorset
Fox, William Johnson, Esq., Solicitor, Hatfield, Doncaster
Foyster, Rev. H. S., Hastings
Foyster, Rev. J. G., Rector of All Saints, with St Clements, Hastings
Ffrance, Thomas Robert Wilson, Esq., J.P., Rawcliffe Hall, Gar-
France, Thomas, Esq., Lam Hill, Powick, Worcester [stang
Francis, George Edward, Esq., West End Cottage, Martham
Francis, Thomas, Esq., Mendlesham
Francklin, John, Esq., Gonalston, Southwell, Notts
Franklin, Joseph, Esq., Town Hall, Liverpool
Franklyn, Rev. Thomas Ward, Castle House, Tonbridge Wells
Freeman, Rev. Joseph, B.A., Charwelton, Daventry
Freeman, Thomas, Esq., Ship-Street, Brighton
Freeth, John, Esq., Galton Bridge House, Smethwick, Birmingham
Freke, Colonel Henry, C.B., Hannington Hall, Highworth, Wilts
French, Richard D., St. John, Ilketshall, near Bungay
French, Thomas, Esq., Eye, Suffolk
Friend, William, Esq., Hart Plain House, Catherington, Hants
Frimstone, George, Esq., Lawnswood, Dudley
Frodsham, Samuel, Esq., Ashleigh, Liverpool
Frost, Rev. Joseph Loxdale, M.A., Bingley
Froste, Thomas, Esq., Upper Parliament-Street, Liverpool
Vol. I.

Frowd, Rev. Edward, M.A., Rector of Upper Clatford, Hants
Fry, Edward W., Esq., Thornhill, Handsworth, Birmingham
Fry, Joseph, Esq., Faulkner Terrace, Liverpool
Fry, Rev. Thomas, M.A., Emberton, Newport-Pagnell, Bucks
Fryer, Joseph Harrison, Esq., J.P., Whitley House, North Shields
Fryer, Rev. H. Edmund, M.A., Burley Wood, East Woodhay, Hants
Fulford, Colonel Baldwin, Great Fulford, near Exeter
Fulford, Rev. Francis, Rector of Trowbridge, Wilts
Fuller, John, Esq., Shaw Hill, Halifax, Yorkshire
Fuller, Rev. R. Fitzherbert, Lingfield Lodge, near East Grinstead
Fullerton, John, Esq., J.P., The Manor House, Stretton-on-Duns-
 [more, Coventry
Furbank, Rev. T., M.A., Incumbent of Bramley, Leeds
Furner, William, Esq., Brighton, Sussex [Tyne
Furness, Rev. J. R., M.A., Vicar of Dinnington, Newcastle-upon-
Furness, John, Esq., Preston
Fynney, D. I., Esq., High Park-Street, Liverpool
Gaggs, Thomas, Esq., Howden, Yorkshire
Gale, Edward Morant, Esq., Upham House, Bishop's Waltham
Gale, Rev. J., Rector of Angersleigh, Taunton
Gale, Rev. John Shephard, S.C.L., Hurstbourne Tarrant, Andover
Gale, William, Esq., North Fambridge Hall, Maldon
Galton, J. Howard, Esq., J.P., Hadzor House, Droitwich
Garbert, Jonathan, Esq., Hartlepool
Garbett, Edmund, Esq., Wellington, Salop
Gardiner, George, Esq., Guisley, Leeds, Yorkshire
Gardiner, Rev. R. B., Vicar of Wadhurst, Sussex
Gardiner, Rev. Robert, Uffculm, Devon
Gardiner, Rev. Robert, Wellisford House, Somerset
Gardner, Rev. C., Vicar of East Dean cum Friston, near Eastbourne
Gardner, Rev. Dr., Sansaw, Shrewsbury
Gardner, Edmund Thomas, Esq., Moor Park, Preston
Gardner, John, Esq., Solicitor, Sion Hill, Garstang
Gardner, James, Esq., Hamilton Lodge, Rugeley
Gardner, Richard Cardwell, Esq., Newsham House, Liverpool
Garforth, Thomas, Esq., Elmsley House, Steeton, Keighley
Garland, John, Esq., Netherwood Hall, Wombwell, Barnsley
Garnett, Richard, Esq., Hill Side, Bradford
Garnett, Robert, Esq., Wyerside Hall, Lancaster
Garnett, Rob., jun., Esq., J.P., Moor Hall, Sutton Coldfield
Garnier, The Very Rev. Thomas, Dean of Winchester, Bishop's Stoke
Garrett, J. G., Esq., Portsdown Cottage, Hants
Garrington, Thomas John, Esq., Ribblesdale Place, Preston
Garston, Edgar, Esq., The Mount, Aigburth, Liverpool
Gartside, Henry, Esq., Solicitor, Ashton-under-Lyne
Garvey, Rev. James, M.A., Third Master of Repton School, Derby
Garwood, John, Esq., Solicitor, Hartlepool
Gascoigne, William, Esq., Solicitor, Leeds
Gaskell, Benjamin, Esq., J.P., Thornes House, Wakefield
Gates, William, Esq., Solicitor, Northampton
Gaunt, Matthew, Esq., Solicitor, Leeds
Gaunt, Matthew, Esq., J.P., Highfield House, Leek
Gauntlett, Rev. H., M.A., Cricklade, Wilts
Gay, James, Esq., Thurning Hall, near East Dereham
Geach, Edward, Esq., Liskeard, Cornwall
Geare, John, jun., Esq., Exeter
Gedge, Rev. Joseph, Vicar of Humberston, Grimsby
Geldard, John, Esq., South Benwell House, Newcastle-upon-Tyne
Geldart, Rev. James W., LL.D., R.P.C.L. Cantab., Rector of
 [Deighton, Yorkshire
Geldart, Rev. Richard John, D.D., Rector of Little Billing, North-
Gell, F. Harding, Esq., Lewes, Sussex [ampton
Gem, Rev. Arthur, M.A., Incumbent of Rowington, Warwick
Gem, R. W., jun., Esq., Crescent, Birmingham
Gem, W. H., Esq., The Lozells, Birmingham
George, Rev. W. H., Spaxton Rectory, Bridgwater
German, Thomas, Esq., J.P., Mayor of Preston, 1846
Gibbons, John, Esq., Westbourne Road, Edgbaston, Birmingham
Gibbs, Charles, Esq., Lydiard, Taunton, Somerset
Gibbs, H. C., Esq., Old Broad-Street, London
Gibson, Sir Alex. C. Maitland, Bart., Clifton Hall, Kirkliston, Edin-
Gibson, Rev. Alfred A., Bradley, Basingstoke, Hants [burgh
Gibson, Jasper, Esq., Hexham, Northumberland
Gibson, Rev. John, M.A., Bedlington, Morpeth, Northumberland
Giffard, Rev. James, M.A., Vicar of Wootton, Barrow-upon-Hum-
 [ber, Lincolnshire
Gifford, The Hon. and Rev. John, M.A., Grimley, Worcester
Gilbert, Mrs. Davies, Eastbourne, Sussex
Gilbert, Major Edward, Hartley Lodge, Southampton
Gilbert, Thomas Webb, Esq., Philpot Lane, London
Gilchrist, George, Esq., Berwick-upon-Tweed
Gilderdale, Rev. John, M.A., Lecturer of the Parochial Church,
 [Halifax, Edgerton Lodge, Huddersfield
b

Giles, James, Esq., M.A. and J.P., The Elms, Bare, Lancaster
Gillam and Sons, Messrs., Solicitors, Worcester
Gillett, Joseph Ashby, Esq., Banbury
Gillman, William, Esq., Grassendale, Aigburth, Liverpool
Gills, Robert, Esq., Eldon Square, Newcastle-upon-Tyne
Gilman, S. H. L. N., Esq., Hingham
Gillow, Rev. Richard, Fernyhalgh, Broughton, Preston
Gilpin, Rev. Bernard, Burnham-Market, Norfolk
Girdlestone, Rev. Edward, M.A., Deane, Bolton-le-Moors
Girdlestone, Steed, Esq., Stebbington, near Wansford
Girling, Captain T. A., The Grove, near Holt
Gisborne, Rev. James, M.A., Vicar of Croxall, Lichfield
Gisborne, Matthew, Esq., Walton Hall, Burton-on-Trent
Glassbrook, Rev. Roger, Ribchester, Blackburn
Gleadall, Charles, Esq., Solicitor, Halifax, Yorkshire
Glenton, Frederick, Esq., Bensham Lunatic Hospital, Gateshead
Glover, The Ven. Archdeacon, South Repps, near North Walsham
Glover, Jeremiah, Esq., Field Head, Wakefield
Glover, Robert Mortimer, Esq., M.D., Newcastle-upon-Tyne
Glynne, Sir Stephen, Bart., M.P., Hawarden Castle, Chester
Goddard, Rev. Charles, D.D., Sub-Dean of Lincoln, and Rector of
                                    [Ibstock, Leicestershire
Goddard, Rev. Edward, Vicar of Pagham, near Chichester
Godfrey, T. S., Esq., Balderton Hall, Newark
Godfrey, Rev. W., M.A., Vicar of Rowenstone, Newport-Pagnell
Godson, S. Holmes, Esq., Tenbury, Salop
Godson, William, Esq., Sandall Grove, Doncaster
Goff, Joseph, Esq., Hale House, Salisbury
Goldfrap, Mrs., Clenchwarton Rectory, near Lynn
Goldie, Rev. Thomas Smith, Minister of Coldstream
Golding, Samuel, Esq., Lodge, Walsham-le-Willows, near Ixworth
Goldingham, Herbert George, Esq., Britannia Square, Worcester
Goldney, Gab., Esq., Chippenham, Wilts
Goldsworthy, Major John, Ackworth House, Pontefract
Goldsworthy, John, Esq., Kensington, Liverpool   [Halifax
Gooch, Rev. J. Henry, M.A., Head Master of Grammar School,
Gooch, James, Esq., East Dereham, Norfolk
Gooch, J. W., Esq., Wooton Place, near Bungay
Goodall, Rev. J. J., M.A., Vicar of Bromham and Oakley, Bedford
Goodall, William, Esq., The Heath, Halifax
Goodenough, Rev. R. W., M.A., Vicarage, Whittingham, Alnwick
Goodman, S., Esq., West Chevington, Felton, Northumberland
Goodman, Timothy, Esq., Warminster, Wilts
Goodrich, John, Esq., Hopton, near East Harling
Goodricke, William, Esq., Houghton-le-Spring, Durham
Goodwin, Charles, Esq., Cobland House, Totton, Eling, Hants
Goodwin, Rev. H. J., B.A., Hinchley Wood House, Ashbourn
Goodwin, John, Esq., The Lodge, Stoke-upon-Trent
Goodwin, John Francis, Esq., Aigburth Vale, Liverpool
Gordon, Charles, Esq., Wescombe Park, Honiton, Devon
Gordon, Captain Conway, E.I.C.S., Crescent, Southampton
Gordon, Rev. Hastings, M.A., The Minister of Beverley
Gordon, Captain James, R.N., Whitby, Yorkshire
Gordon, John, Esq., Clerk of the Peace, Bolton-le-Moors
Goring, H. D., Esq., M.P., Highden, near Shoreham
Gorring, H. B., Esq., Seaford, Sussex
Gough, John, Esq., J.P., Perry Hall, Handsworth, Birmingham
Gould, Rev. J. N., B.A., Amberd House, Taunton
Gould, John Scott, Esq., Moredon, North Curry, near Taunton
Gower, Captain Leveson, Bill Hill, near Wokingham
Gowler, Henry, Esq., Rammidge Cottage, Weyhill, Hants
Graburn, William, Esq., Solicitor, Barton-upon-Humber
Grace, Edward N., Esq., Byker-hill, Newcastle-upon-Tyne
Grace, Rev. Henry Thomas, Vicar of Westham, near Eastbourn
Grace, John, Esq., Wallsend, Newcastle-upon-Tyne
Grace, Nathaniel, Esq., Scotswood House, Newcastle-upon-Tyne
Gradwell, Rev. Henry, Claughton, Garstang
Graham, Edward, Esq., The Hall, Worth, near Crawley
Graham, Michael, Esq., Solicitor, Middlesbrough, Yorkshire
Grahamsley, George, Esq., Laverick Hall, Bolldon, Gateshead
Grainge, Middleton, Esq., Sunnyside, Gateshead
Grant, Captain Charles, Glendarrock, Edinburgh
Grant, John, Esq., Nuttall Hall, Bury, Lancashire
Grant, Mr. Jonathan, East Coulston, Devizes, Wilts
Grant, Rev. Robert, Vicar of Bradford-Abbas, Dorset
Grant, William, Esq., Stubbington Lodge, near Portsmouth
Grantham, S., Esq., Stoneham, near Lewes
Grantham, Rev. Thomas, Brambet Rectory, Steyning, Sussex
Gratwick, W. G. K., Esq., Ham, near Arundel
Graves, Rev. Henry, Rector of Middleton St. George, Darlington
Gray, Charles Henry, Esq., Chatham Place, Liverpool
Gray, Edward, Esq., Garesfield House, Gateshead
Gray, John, Esq., East Lilburn, Wooler, Northumberland

Gray, John, Esq., Pagans Hill House, Chew-Stoke, near Bristol
Gray, John, Esq., Wheatfield, Bolton-le-Moors
Gray, Russell, Esq., Barcombe, near Lewes, Sussex
Grazebrook, Thomas W. Smith, Esq., Dallicott House, Claverley
Grazebrook, William, Esq., Summer Hill, Kingswinford, Dudley
Greame, Yarburgh, Esq., J.P., Sewerby House, Bridlington
Greatwood, William, Esq., Solicitor, Birmingham
Greaves, John, Esq., The Grove, Ashbourn, Derbyshire
Greaves, John, Esq., Grove Road, Liverpool
Greaves, Robert D., Esq., Potternewton Lodge, Leeds
Green, A., Esq., Parkgate, Ringmer, near Lewes
Green, Atkinson, and Co., Messrs., Engineers, Wakefield
Green, Edwin, Esq., Havercroft, Wakefield, Yorkshire
Green, Mrs. Elizabeth, Crossland Moor, Huddersfield
Green, Mrs. E. W., Holcombe House, Somersetshire
Green, Henry, Esq., Moreton, near Newport, Salop
Green, Rev. Henry Armel, M.A., Upton Snodsbury, Worcester
Green, James, Esq., Holcombe, near Old Down, Somerset
Green, John, Esq., Darlington
Green, Messrs. John and B., Architects and Engineers, Newcastle-
Green, Rev. John Samuel, M.A., Vicar of Wooler   [upon-Tyne
Green, Thomas, Esq., Ipswich, Suffolk
Green, Thomas Abbott, Esq., Pavenham, Bury, near Bedford
Green, Rev. Valentine, M.A., Rector of Birkin, Ferrybridge
Greenfield, Rev. B. W., M.A., Shirley, Southampton
Greenhalgh, Rev. Henry, Weld-Bank, Chorley
Greenhalgh, James, Esq., Carre Bank, Mansfield
Greenhow, Edward, Esq., M.D., Dockwray-square, North Shields
Greenhow, E. Headlam, Esq., Tynemouth, Northumberland
Greenside, Rev. Ralph, M.A., Rector of Crathorne, Yarm
Greenstreet, Major-General, Brampton, Hants
Greenway, George Cattell, Esq., J.P., East Gate, Warwick
Greenwell, Richard, Esq., Sunderland
Greenwood, Edwin, Esq., J.P., Knowle, Keighley, Yorkshire
Greenwood, James, Esq., Woodlands, Haworth, Keighley
Greenwood, Joseph, Esq., J.P., Spring Head,   do.
Greenwood, Richard, Esq., Solicitor, Gargrave, Skipton
Greenwood, Wm., jun., Esq., Oxenhope Hall, Haworth, Bradford
Greenwood, William Brookwood, Esq., Hinton-Ampner, Hants
Gregory, Rev. H., M.A., Grammar School, Witney
Gregory, William, Esq., Solicitor, Leicester
Gregson, Matthew, Esq., Toxteth Park, Liverpool
Greig, James Robinson, Esq., Chitley, Liphook, Hants
Gretton, John, Esq., Burton-upon-Trent, Staffordshire
Greville, Rev. Joshua, A.M., Duston, Northampton
Grey, G., Esq., Middle Ord, Berwick-upon-Tweed
Grey, George Annett, Esq., Milfield Hill, Wooler
Grey, Thomas Robinson, Esq., J.P., Norton, Stockton-on-Tees
Griesbach, Rev. A. W., B.A., Wollaston, Wellingborough
Griesbach, Rev. W. R., M.A., Vicar of Millington, Givendale, and
                                    [Friday Thorpe, Pocklington, Yorkshire
Griffin, James, Esq., Levins, Edgbaston
Griffith, Rev. John, M.A., Parsonage, Darley Abbey, Derby
Griffith, John, Esq., Alveston, Stratford-on-Avon
Griffith, Rev. Robert C., Corsley Rectory, near Warminster
Griffiths, Henry Moore, Esq., Solicitor, Birmingham
Griffiths, Thomas, Esq., Solicitor, Bishop's Castle
Grigg, Thomas, Esq., Earsham, near Bungay
Grimmer, George, Esq., Manse House, Haddiscoe, near Beccles
Grimston, Henry Estoutreville, Esq., Lingcroft, York
Grooby, Rev. James, Vicar of Swindon, Wilts
Grove, Edward, Esq., LL.D., Shenstone Park, Lichfield
Groves, Captain, Calverleigh, Tiverton, Devon
Grylls, Glynn, Esq., Helston, Cornwall
Gully, John, Esq., Ackworth Park, Pontefract
Gunn, Rev. John, Irstead Rectory, near Norwich
Gunnery, Joseph, Esq., Solicitor, Edge Hill, Liverpool
Gurdon, Rev. Edward, Reymerston, near East Dereham
Gurdon, Rev. Philip, Cranworth, near Shipdham, Norfolk
Gurney, Daniel, Esq., F.A.S., North Runcton Hall, near Lynn
Gurney, Joseph J., Esq., Earlham Hall, near Norwich
Gurney and Birkbeck, Messrs., Norwich
Guy, Joseph, Esq., Solicitor, Gainsborough
Gwyn, John Frauncis, Esq., Ford Abbey, Thorncombe, Devon
Gwyn, W., Esq., Tasburgh Lodge, near Long-Stratton
Hacker, John Heathcote, Esq., Solicitor, Leek, Staffordshire
Hacking, Richard, Esq., Heaton Grove, Bury
Haddington Town Library
Hadlam, Thomas D., Esq., Mayfield, Wavertree
Haggie, Robert Hood, Esq., Willington, Newcastle-upon-Tyne
Hague, John, Esq., J.P., Dewsbury and Drighlington
Haigh, George, Esq., Bradford
Haigh, George, Esq., Waterloo Road, Liverpool

Haigh, Joseph, Esq., Toxteth Park, Liverpool
Haigh, Rev. J., M.A., Incumbent of St. Thomas's, Crooke, Sheffield
Haigh, S. Wood, Esq., Terrace Cottage, Mirfield, Dewsbury
Haigh, Thomas, Esq., Newlaiths Grange, Leeds
Hailstone, Edward, Esq., Horton Hall, Bradford
Hale, Edward, Esq., Hambledon, Hants
Hale, Matthew, Esq., Manor House, Dewsbury
Hale, R. Hale Blagden, Esq., Cottle's House, Melksham
Hale, Rev. Robert, M.A., Settrington House, Malton
Hales, Alfred, Esq., Solicitor, Norton Green Hall, Burslem
Halford, William, Esq., Cintra Cottage, Handsworth
Haliburton, Alexander Fowden, Esq., J.P., Whitley, Wigan
Hall, Rev. E. M., M.A., Incumbent of Idle, Bradford
Hall, G. Blyth, Esq., Stafford
Hall, Gervase Cressy, Esq., Solicitor, Alfreton
Hall, Rev. H. Banks, LL.B., Risley, near Derby   [under-Lyne
Hall, Henry, Esq., Solicitor, and Clerk to the Magistrates, Ashton-
Hall, James, Esq., Scorbrough, Beverley
Hall, Major Jasper, Malshanger, Basingstoke
Hall, John, Esq., Kiveton Park, Sheffield
Hall, Rev. John, Rector of Upper Stondon, and Vicar of Shillington
Hall, Nathaniel, Esq., New Hall, near Henfield, Steyning
Hall, Procter, Esq., Solicitor, Keighley
Hall, Rev. T., Ropsley Rectory, Grantham, Lincolnshire
Hall, Thomas R., Esq., Holly Bush House, Burton-upon-Trent
Hall, Thomas, jun., Esq., J.P., Purston Lodge, Pontefract
Hall, William, Esq., Thorpland Hall, near Fakenham
Hallewell, Benjamin, Esq., Woodhouse, Leeds
Halliday, Andrew, Esq., Preston, Lancashire
Halliday, Rev. Edmund, Trowbridge, Yard House, Taunton
Hallifax, Henry Crawford, Richard's Castle, Ludlow
Halsall, R. J., Esq., A.M., Solicitor, Middleton, Manchester
Haly, Aylmer, Esq., Wadhurst Castle, near Tonbridge
Hambly, Edward, Esq., Wadebridge, Cornwall
Hamerton, James, Esq., M.A., Hellifield Peel, Skipton
Hamilton, F. A., Esq., Bedford-Street South, Liverpool
Hamilton, George E., Esq., Architect, Wolverhampton
Hamilton, Hon. Gustavus F., Burwarton, Ludlow
Hamilton, Rev. James, Rector of Ardingley, near Cuckfield
Hamilton, Rev. Peploe William, M.A., Hoole Lodge, Chester
Hammond, Joshua, Esq., Birmingham
Hammond, Rev. J. Parish, Rector of Minestead-with-Lyndhurst
Hammond, Joseph, Leominster, Herefordshire
Hamond, A., Esq., Westacre High House, near Swaffham
Hamond, Miss, Swaffham
Hamond, Rev. William, M.A., Holdenhurst, Christchurch
Hampshire, H. J., Esq., Upper Parliament-Street, Liverpool
Hampson, Thomas, jun., Esq., Everton, Liverpool
Hampton, Rev. H., Rector of Little Birch, Herefordshire
Hampton, Rev. Henry, M.A., St. James's, Toxteth Park
Hanbury, Edward, Esq., Bloomville Hall, Hacheston
Hanbury, Rev. George, Westacre, near Swaffham
Hanbury, William, Esq., Brown Hills, Lichfield
Hanbury, William, Esq., Moreton House, Colwich, Stafford
Hancocks, William, jun., Esq., Cookley House, Kidderminster
Hand, Rev. John, LL.B., Rector of Handsworth, Sheffield
Hand, Robert William, Esq., Rowley, Stafford
Handforth, Rev. John, B.A., Ashton-under-Lyne
Handley, William Farnworth, Esq., J.P., Banker, Newark
Hankey, James, Esq., Fairfield, Liverpool
Hankinson, Rev. Robert, Walpole St. Andrew, near Lynn
Hanks, James, Esq., Snaith
Hanmer, Rev. George E., M.A., Rector of Loddington and Over-
    [ston, Northamptonshire
Hanmer, Sir John, Bart., Bettisfield Park, near Whitchurch, Salop
Hannay, William, Esq., J.P., Nottingham
Hanson, George, Esq., Wilsden, Bradford
Hanson, Thomas, Esq., Smethwick House, Birmingham
Harbin, George, Esq., Newton House, Yeovil, Somerset
Harbottle, John, Esq., Anick Grange, Hexham
Harcourt, Rev. C. G. V., M.A., Whitton Tower, Rothbury
Harcourt, Henry, Esq., Brampton Bryan, Ludlow
Harcourt, Rev. L. Vernon, West Dean House, near Chichester
Hardcastle, Frederick, Esq., Commercial Bank, Halifax
Hardcastle, Timothy, Esq., Scalby House, Scarborough
Hardcastle, William, Esq., Stainley House, Ripley
Harding, Henry, Esq., Edge Hill Cottage, Lichfield
Harding, Thomas, Esq., Solicitor, Birmingham
Harding, William, Esq., Solicitor and Coroner, Burslem
Hardman, C. F., Esq., Castledown, Hastings
Hardman, John, Esq., Hunter's Lane, Birmingham
Hardy, John, Esq., M.P., Portland Place, London
Hardy, John, Esq., Beaumont-Street, Oxford

Hardy, Thomas, Esq., Birksgate, Huddersfield
Hare, Rev. H. J., Docking Hall, Docking
HAREWOOD, The Right Honourable the late Earl of
Harford, Rev. Alfred, Vicar of Locking, near Cross, Somerset
Hargrave, Joseph, Esq., Monckton Villa, South Shields
Hargrave and Sons, Messrs. James, Kirkstall, Leeds
Hargrave, William, Esq., St. James's Lodge, do.
Hargreaves, George, Esq., Grassendale House, Liverpool
Hargreaves, George, Esq., The Height, Bolton-le-Moors
Hargreaves, William, Esq., Bolton-le-Moors
Harison, W. T., Esq., Folkington, near Eastbourne, Sussex
Harland, William Charles, Esq., M.P., Sutton Hall, York
Harle, William Lockey, Esq., Solicitor, Newcastle-upon-Tyne
Harman, Thomas Leader, Esq., Westwood Park, Southampton
Harneis, Theophilus, Esq., Thorganby Hall, Lincolnshire
Harris, Alfred, Esq., Spring Lodge, Bradford
Harris, Charles, Esq., Fulford Grange, Yorkshire
Harris, Henry, Esq., Heaton Hall, Bradford
Harris, John D., Esq., Leicester
Harris, John, Esq., Civil Engineer, Darlington
Harris, J. D., Esq., Hayne, Launceston, Cornwall
Harris, Rice, Esq., Islington Glass-Works, Birmingham
Harris, W., Esq., J.P., Wootton Hall, Northampton
Harris, William, Esq., Brereton, Rugeley, Staffordshire
Harrison, Alexander, Esq., Solicitor, Birmingham
Harrison, Anthony, Esq., Loygate Cottage, South Shields
Harrison and Brown, Messrs., Solicitors, Wakefield   [Fylde
Harrison, Captain, (late H. E. I. C.,) Maines Hall, Poulton-le-
Harrison, Edward, Esq., Settle, Yorkshire
Harrison, Gilbert Henry, Esq., Hatton House, Ford, Liverpool
Harrison, James, Esq., Architect, Sheffield, Yorkshire
Harrison, James, Esq., Breekfield Road South, Everton, Liverpool
Harrison, James, jun., Esq., Walton-on-the-Hill, Liverpool
Harrison, Rev. John Holden, M.A., Water Orton, Birmingham
Harrison, John, Esq., The Lawn, Belper, Derbyshire
Harrison, Paul, Esq., Bankfield, Poulton-le-Fylde
Harrison, Robert, Esq., Benningholme Hall, Hull
Harrison, Stephen Wright, Esq., Solicitor, Tynemouth
Harrison, Thomas, Esq., Moss Side House, Maghull
Harrison, Washington, Esq., Knowsley Cottage, Driffield
Harrison, Rev. W. B., Rector of Gayton-le-Marsh, Lincolnshire
Harrison, Rev. William Gorst, M.A., Hart, Hartlepool
Harrop, Jonah, Esq., J.P., Bardsley, Ashton-under-Lyne
Hartley, George, Esq., Settle, Craven, Yorkshire
Hartley, Rev. J., B.A., Incumbent of Boroughbridge
Hartley, James, Esq., The Green, Sunderland
Hartley, John, Esq., Summerfield, Wolverhampton
Hartley, John B., Esq., Dock Surveyor, Liverpool
Hartley, S. F., Esq., Shaw Hill, Halifax
Hartley, Rev. William, Balderstone Lodge, Blackburn
Hartopp, Sir Edmund Cradock, Bart., Four Oaks Hall, Sutton
    [Coldfield
Hartopp, William Edward, Esq., J.P., Doe Bank, Sutton Coldfield
Harvey, Charles Whitfield, Esq., Walton-on-the-Hill, Liverpool
Harvey, Richard, Esq., St. Day, Truro, Cornwall
Harvey, Robert R., Esq., Sturminster Newton, Dorset
Harvey, Robert Ellison, Esq., J.P., The Priory, Walton, Liverpool
Harvey, Thomas, Esq., Wavertree Hall, Liverpool
Harvey, William, Esq., St. George's Place, Barnsley
Harward, Rev. John, M.A., Vicar of Wirkworth, Derbyshire
Harward, John, Esq., Solicitor, Stourbridge
Harward, Rev. Thomas, M.A., Winterfold, Kidderminster
Hasker, Rev. William, M.A., Baughurst, Basingstoke, Hants
Hasler, Richard, Esq., Aldingbourne House, near Chichester
Hasluck, Richard, Esq., Handsworth House, Birmingham
Hasted, J. S., Esq., R.N., Tarrington Gurney, Old Down, Somerset
HASTINGS, The Right Honourable Lord
Hatherell, Rev. J. W., Rectory, Charmouth, Dorset
Hattall, H., Esq., Rose House, Stockbridge, Hants
Hawdon, Robert, Esq., Mayor of Morpeth, 1843   [Tyne
Hawdon, William G., Esq., Blaydon-foundry, Newcastle-upon-
HAWKE, The Right Honourable Lord
Hawke, Edward, jun., Esq., Knottingley, Ferrybridge
Hawker, Lieut.-Col., Longparish House, Hants
Hawker, Rear-Adm., K.C.H., Ashford Lodge, Petersfield
Hawkins, John E., Esq., Manor House, Faringdon, Hants
Hawkins, John, Esq., Pontypool, Lancashire
Hawks, George, Esq., J.P., Redheugh, Gateshead
Hawks, Joseph, Esq., Sheriff of Newcastle-upon-Tyne in 1843
Haworth, Benjamin, Esq., M.A., J.P., Hull Bank House, Hull
Hawthorn, William, Esq., C.E., The Cottage, Benwell, Newcastle
Hay, The Hon. and Rev. Somerville, Curate of Bergh-Apton
Hay, William, Esq., Park Square, Leeds

b 2

Haydon, W., Esq., Mill Mead House, Guildford
Hayes, Josiah Anthony, Esq., Canal Office, Wolverhampton
Hayes, William, Esq., Fairfield, Leigh, Manchester
Hayne, Rev. Thomas, M.A., Incumbent of Rastrick, Huddersfield
Haynes, Robert, Esq., Bellavista House, Westbury, Wilts
Haynes, Samuel William, Esq., Solicitor, Warwick
Haythorne, Rev. Joseph, Vicar of Congresbury, Somerset
Hayward, George, Esq., Headingley Hall, Leeds
Hayward, John, Esq., West Chinnock, near Crewkerne
Hayward, Rev. W. Curtis, M.A., Walton Vicarage, Stafford
Haywood, J., Esq., Chad Road, Edgbaston, Birmingham
Haywood, John, Esq., Rotherham
Head, Charles, Esq., Solicitor, Hexham
Head, John, Esq., Everton Village, Liverpool
Head, Rev. Oswald, M.A., Vicar of Lesbury, Alnwick
Headlam, Thomas D., Esq., Mayfield, Wavertree, Liverpool
Heald, George, Esq., The Lodge, Garston, Liverpool
Heald, Rev. W. M., M.A., Vicar of Birstal, Leeds
Heale, Rev. William J., M.A., Penn, Wolverhampton
Healey, Robert, Esq., Great Howarth, Rochdale
Healey, Samuel Robert, Esq., West Bank, Woolton, Liverpool
Heap, Joshua, Esq., Rice House, West Derby
Heath, Rev. Charles, Hanworth, near Aylsham
Heath, Thomas, Esq., Horning, Norwich
Heathcote, J. M., Esq., Connington Castle, Hunts
Heathcote, Richard Edensor, Esq., Apedale Hall, Newcastle-under-
Heathcote, Rev. Thomas Henry, M.A., Vicarage, Leek   [Lyme
Heathcote, William Arthur, Esq., Rolleston, Shrewton, Wilts
Heaton, John, Esq., St. John's Cottage, Little Woodhouse, Leeds
Heaton, William Barnard, Esq., Solicitor, Gainsborough
Hedley, Edward Anthony, Esq., M.D., Link Hall, Alnwick
Hedley, Samuel, Esq., Coxlodge Cottage, Newcastle-upon-Tyne
Hedley, Thomas, Esq., Shieldfield,   do.
Heelis, Thomas, Esq., Skipton Castle
Heffill, Henry, Esq., Diss, Norfolk
Heffill, Rev. W., St. Mark's, Dukinfield, Ashton-under-Lyne
Heginbottom, Samuel, Esq., J.P., Ashton-under-Lyne
Heigham, John Henry, Esq., Hunston Hall, near Ixworth
Hellyer, Thomas, Esq., Ryde, Isle of Wight
Hembrough, John, Esq., Waltham, Grimsby, Lincolnshire
Heming, Rev. H., Lurgashall, near Petworth, Sussex
Hemming, William, Esq., J.P., Fox Lydiate House, Redditch
Hemmingway, Edward, Esq., Oulton Green, Leeds
Henderson, Capt. Geo., R.N., Berkeley Cottage, Bruton, Somerset
Henderson, Lieut.-Col., late Royal Engineers, Southampton
Henderson, William, Esq., Elm, Wolverhampton
Hennah, Rev. W. Veale, B.A., Minister of St. James, East Cowes
Henty, Sam., Esq., Kingston, near Little Hampton, Sussex
Henville, Rev. C. B., M.A., Hamble-le-Rice, Southampton
Henzell, Charles Rutherford, Esq., Newcastle-upon-Tyne
Hepper, James, Esq., Canal Cottage, Shipley, Bradford
Hepworth, Abraham, Esq., Lindley, Huddersfield
Hepworth. Rev. J. W., B.A., Parsonage, Woodkirk, Leeds
Hepworth, Rev. William, Botesdale
Hepworth, Rev. William, vicar of Griston, near Watton
Hepworth, William, Esq., Calder Grove, Wakefield
Herbert, Frederick, Esq., Northleach
Herbert, Miss R., The Hill, near Abergavenny, Monmouthshire
Herbert, Samuel, Esq., Gate Fulford, Yorkshire
Herbert, The Honourable and very Rev. W., Dean of Manchester,
           [and Rector of Spofforth, Wetherby
Herne, Rev. J. Buckworth, Rector of West Hendred, Berks
Heriot, Rev. George, M.A., Incumbent of St. Anne's, Newcastle-
Heseltine, Edward John, Esq., Bank, Rotherham   [upon-Tyne
Hesketh, Sir Thomas George, Bart., Rufford Hall, Ormskirk
Hesketh, Rev. William, M.A., St. Michael's, Toxteth Park, Liver-
Hesleden, Bryan, Esq., Solicitor, Barton-upon-Humber   [pool
Hetherington, Joseph, Esq., Wallsend, Newcastle-upon-Tyne
Hewetson, Joshua, Esq., J.P., Heckley House, Alnwick
Hewett, John Waller, Esq., Fareham, Hants
Hewison, Ions, Esq., Solicitor, Newcastle-upon-Tyne
Hewison, Lawrence, Esq., Benwell Villa, do.
Hewitt, Rev. David, M.A., Horwich, Bolton-le-Moors
Hewitt, Rev. William, M.A., Ancroft, Berwick-upon-Tweed
Hewlett, Rev. Alfred, M.A., Astley, Leigh, Manchester
Hext, Thomas, Esq., Restormill, Lostwithiel, Cornwall
Hey, Rev. Samuel, M.A., Vicar of Ockbrook, Derby
Hey, Rev. Samuel, jun., M.A., Vicar of Sawley, Derby
Heyes, Joseph, Esq., Summerfield, Great Lever, Bolton
Heyes and Pemberton, Messrs., Solicitors, Prescot
Heys, Henry, Esq., Southport, Lancashire
Heys, John, Esq., J.P., Gorse Hall, near Chorley
Heywood, Arthur, Esq., Stanley Hall, Wakefield

Heywood, Robert, Esq., J.P., Newport Terrace, Bolton-le-Moors
Heywood, Thomas, Esq., Charles-Street, Preston
Heyworth, Rev. James, Shirley, near Southampton
Heyworth, Lawrence, Esq., J.P., Yew Tree, West Derby
Hibbert, Joseph, Esq., Solicitor, Clerk to the Magistrates and to
           [the Court of Requests, Hyde, Manchester
Hibbert, R. A., Esq., West Breightmet Hill, Bolton-le-Moors
Hick, Henry, Esq., Solicitor, Stokesley
Hick, John, Esq., Civil Engineer, Highfield, Bolton-le-Moors
Hick, John, Esq., Seafield, Crosby, Liverpool
Hick, Samuel, Esq., Solicitor, Leeds
Hicks, Charles, Esq., Rye, Sussex
Hicks, Thomas, Esq., Hastings, do.
Higginson, Edmund, Esq., Saltmarsh, Bromyard, Herefordshire
Higham, George, Esq., Solicitor, Bone Gate House, Brighouse
Higinbothom, Newburgh, Esq., Holt Lodge, Farnham, Surrey
Hilder, Thomas, Esq., Mays, Selmeston, near Lewes, Sussex
HILL, The Right Honourable the late Lord
HILL, The Right Honourable Lord
Hill, Rev. Benjamin, M.A., Collingtree, Northampton
Hill, Rev. H. T., M.A., Wolverley, Kidderminster
Hill, Rev. John, St. Marie's-on-the-Sands, Southport
Hill, John, Esq., Paulton, near Bath
Hill, Rev. John, The Citadel, Hawkstone, near Shrewsbury
Hill, Rev. J. Oakley, M.A., Dorton and Ashendon, Bucks
Hill, John, Esq., South Cave, Kingston-upon-Hull
Hill, John Hepworth, Esq., M.A., Cantab., Park Square, Leeds
Hill, John, Esq., Balerno Bank, Edinburgh
Hill, Rev. Melsup, B.A., Lye Parsonage, Stourbridge
Hill, Rev. Melsup, Incumbent of St. John's, Kidderminster
Hill, Richard, Esq., J.P., Thornton Dale, Pickering
Hill, Rev. Richard, B.A., Royton, Oldham, Lancashire
Hill, Thomas, Esq., Solicitor, Birmingham
Hill, Captain William, Ryhope, Sunderland
Hill, William Wilkes, Esq., Beeston Hall, Leeds
Hinckley, Rev. John, vicarage, Sheriff-Hales, near Shiffnall
Hincksman, T. C., Esq., Fishergate-Street, Preston
Hinde, Rev. Thomas, M.A., Grammar School, Winwick, Warrington
Hindle, William J., Esq., C.E., Barnsley
Hindmarch, William, Esq., Poulter Close, Gateshead
Hindmarsh, Luke, Esq., Alnbank House, Alnwick
Hipperson, John, Esq., Carleton Rode, near Attleburgh
Hippisley, Lady, Stone-Easton House, Old Down, Somerset
Hird, Henry Wickham, Esq., J.P., Low Moor House, Bradford
Hitchcock, Mr. Harry, Chittern-All Saints, Heytesbury
Hoare, Clement, Esq., Vineyard, Shirley, Southampton
Hobbes, Robert H., Esq., Solicitor, Stratford-on-Avon
Hobson, Richard, Esq., M.D., Park House, Leeds
Hocken, Rev. Wm., Rector of St. Endellion, Camelford, Cornwall
Hodge, Rev. Edward, Woodfield-Badock, Penryn, Cornwall
Hodge, George William, Esq., Solicitor, Newcastle-upon-Tyne
Hodge, W. C., Esq., Pounds, Plymouth
Hodgkinson, Rev. Edmund, M.A., Parsonage, Baildon, Bradford
Hodgkinson, George, Esq., Solicitor, Newark-upon-Trent
Hodgson, Adam, Esq., J.P., Breckfield Lodge, Everton
Hodgson, Alfred, Esq., Snaith, Yorkshire
Hodgson, Dr. D. Stanley, M.A., Grammar School, Bolton-le-
Hodgson, H., Esq., Falkner Square, Liverpool   [Moors
Hodgson, H. B., Esq., Acomb House, York
Hodgson, Rev. John, M.A., M.R.S.L., Hartburn, Morpeth
Hodgson, John, Esq., Bank Side, Hebden Bridge   [Tweed
Hodgson, Thomas, Esq., Morris Hall, Norham, Berwick-upon-
Hodgson, Thomas Bent, Esq., Registrar for W.R., Skelton, York
Hodgson, Thomas Richard Tucker, Esq., Solicitor, Birmingham
Hodgson, William, Esq., Solicitor, Staindrop, Darlington
Hogarth, George, Esq., Banker, Cupar, Fife
Hogge, Rev. Martin, Southacre, near Swaffham
Hoggett, Rev. Thomas A., Biddleston House, Rothbury
Hoghton, Henry, Esq., Hafod, Aberystwith, Cardiganshire
Holden, John, Esq., Woodlands, Gateacre
Holden, Henry, Esq., Solicitor, Chester
Holdich, Rev. T. P., M.A., Oxon, St. John's, Carisbrooke
Holding, William, Esq., Elm Grove, Kingsclere, Hants
Holdsworth, J., Esq., Belle-field, Wakefield
Holford, George C., Esq., New Park, Devizes, Wilts
Holgate, Rev. Thomas Burton, B.A., Vicar of Bishopton, Stock-
Holland, John, jun., Esq., Slead House, Halifax   [ton-upon-Tees
Holland, Rev. S., D.D., Precentor of Cathedral, Chichester
Holland, Rev. T. E. M., Rectory, Stoke Bliss, Tenbury
Holland, Rev. T. A., M.A., Rector of Greatham, Petersfield
Holliday, James, Esq., St. James' Place, Liverpool
Hollier, John, Esq., Thame, Oxon
Hollingberry, T., Esq., Church House, Northiam, near Rye

Hollingsworth, Rev. A. G. H., Vicar of Stow-Market
Hollins, Michael Daintry, Esq., Stoke-upon-Trent, Staffordshire
Hollis, William, Esq., Shire Newton, near Chepstow
Hollond, Robert, Esq., M.P., Allegria, St. Leonard's-on-Sea
Holloway, Horatio, Esq., Marchwood Lodge, Southampton
Holman, Captain Thomas Holloway, R.N., Great Grimsby
Holme, Arthur Hill, Esq., Architect, Liverpool
Holme, Henry, Esq., Solicitor, Leeds
Holme, Rev. James, M.A., Vicar of Kirk-Leatham, Guisborough
Holme, James, Esq., Mount Pleasant, Liverpool
Holme, Samuel, Esq., Holmstead, Mosley Hill
Holmes, Rev. Henry, B.A., Incumbent of Stainforth, Settle
Holmes, James Nathan, Esq., Mosley vale, Aigburth, Liverpool
Holmes, Rev. Joseph, D.D., Head Master of the Grammar School, Holmes, Rev. J., Brooke Hall, near Norwich   [Leeds
Holmes, Rev. J. W., M.A., Stockton-on-the-Forest, York
Holmes, Richard, Esq., Solicitor, Boroughbridge
Holmes, Thomas, Esq., West Grove, Halifax
Holmes, William, Esq., Brookfield, near Arundel, Sussex
Holroyd, John, Esq., White Birks, Ovendon, Halifax
Holroyde, James, jun., Esq., Cheapside,   do.
Holt, Henry, Esq., Mining Engineer, Wakefield   [ventry
Holthouse, Rev. Charles Scrafton, B.A., vicar of Hellidon, Da-
Holy, Thomas Beard, Esq., Norton House, Sheffield
Holyoake, Thomas, Esq., Kinver, near Stourbridge
Hombersley, William, Esq., Peplow Hall, near Hodnet, Salop
Home, R., Esq., Solicitor, Berwick-upon-Tweed
HOME OFFICE, Her Majesty's
Hook, Rev. Walter Farquhar, D.D., The Vicarage, Leeds
Hooke, Benjamin, Esq., Norton Hall, Worcestershire
Hooper, Alfred C., Esq., Ivy Lodge, Worcester
Hooper, Rev. James, M.A., Rector of Kingweston, Somerset
Hope, Thomas Arthur, Esq., Everton Terrace, Liverpool
Hopkenson, John Joseph, Esq., Grimston Hall, York
Hopkins, Rev. Adolphus, M.A., vicar of Clent, Stourbridge
Hopkins, Henry, Esq., Hubborne Lodge, Christchurch, Hants
Hopkins, Peter, Esq., Crown Bank House, Newcastle-under-Lyme
Hopper, Ralph Shipperdson, Esq., M.D., East-Parade, Leeds
Hopper, Thomas, Esq., Sharrow Lodge, Ripon
Hopps, George, Esq., Red House, York
Horley, Edward, Esq., Edge Lane, Liverpool
Hornby, Edmund, Esq., J.P., Dalton Hall, Burton-in-Kendal
Hornby, Hugh, Esq., J.P., Sandown, Wavertree, Liverpool
Hornby, Hugh, Esq., J.P., Ribby Hall, Kirkham
Hornby, Rev. James J., M.A., Winwick, Warrington
Hornby, Rev. William, M.A., St. Michael's-on-Wyre, Garstang
Horncastle, John, jun., Esq., The Yews, Tickhill
Horndon, Rev. D., Bicton Parsonage, Devon
Horne, Rev. William, M.A., Rector of Hotham, Cave, Yorkshire
Hornidge, Samuel Gwinnett, Esq., Bloomsbury Square, London
Horrocks, George, Esq., Fishergate, Preston, Lancashire
Horrocks, Mrs., Lark Hill, Preston
Horsfall, George Henry, Esq., Everton, Liverpool
Horsfall, John Garnett, Esq., Bolton Royde, Bradford
Horsfall, Rev. Richard, M.A., Rectory, Marmanby, Pickering
Horsfall, T. B., Esq., Mayor of Liverpool 1848   [Liverpool
Horsfall, William J., Esq., The Mersey Steel and Iron Company,
Horton, John, Esq., Prior's Lee Hall, near Shiffnall, Salop
Hoste, Derick, Esq., Barwick House, near Docking
Hoste, Rev. James, Rector of Ingoldesthorpe, near Lynn
Hotham, Rev. Charles, M.A., Rector of Roos, Patrington
Hotham, Hon. and Rev. F., Rector of Dennington, Suffolk
Houchen, John, Esq., Wereham Hall, near Stoke Ferry
Houghton, Dugdale, Esq., The Firs, Edgbaston, Birmingham
Houldsworth, William, Esq., Farnsfield House, Notts
Houseman, John, Esq., M.D., M.R.C.S.L., Newcastle-upon-Tyne
Housman, Rev. Thomas, Esq., Christchurch, Catshill, Bromsgrove
How, Rev. G. A., Vicar of Bosham, near Chichester
How, James, Esq., Brook House, Newport, Isle of Wight
Howard, Rev. J. G., M.A., Vicar of St. Michael's, Derby
Howard, Rev. William, Great Witchingham Parsonage, Norfolk
Howard, Hon. and Rev. William, M.A., The Grange, Rotherham
Howard, William, Esq., Hartley House, Plymouth
Howes, Rev. George, Spixworth Parsonage, Norwich
Howey, Thomas, Esq., Lilburn Grange, Wooler
Howitt, Francis T., Esq., Heanor, near Derby
Hoy, James Barlow, Esq., M.P., Thornhill, Southampton
Hoyle, John Theodore, Esq., Solicitor, Newcastle-upon-Tyne
Hoyle, Richard, Esq., Denton Hall,   do.
Hoyle, Robert C., Esq., Aughton Hall, Sheffield
Hoyle, William F., Esq., Solicitor, Rotherham
Hubback, Robert Gumwell, Esq., Stamdrop Hall, Darlington

Hubbersty, Rev. Nathan, M.A., Grammar School, Workworth
Hudson, Rev. G. T., West Harptree, Old Down, Somerset
Hudson, Harrington, Esq., J.P., Bessingby, Bridlington
Hudson, Rev. J., M.A., Chatton, Belford
Hudson, James, Esq., Adwalton, Leeds   [shire
Huet, Rev. William Godfrey, M.A., Rector of Idlicote, Warwick-
Hughes, Rev. D., M.A., Incumbent of Nether-Thong, Huddersfield
Hughes, George Hughes, Esq., J.P., Middleton Hall, Wooler
Hughes, Rev. H. P., Shuttleworth, Bury, Lancashire
Hughes, Rev. Joseph, M.A., Incumbent of Meltham, Huddersfield
Hughes, Thomas, Esq., Hylton Cottage, North Shields
Hughes, William, Esq., Browning's Grove, Framfield, near Uckfield
Hughes, W. Hughes, Esq., F.S.A., &c. &c., Bellevue House, Ryde
Hughes, William, Esq., Fairfield Crescent, Liverpool   [cester
Hughes, William Samuel Price, Esq., Coroner of the County, Wor-
Hughlings, Harry, Esq., Halifax
Huish, John, Esq., Solicitor, Derby
Hull, Rev. Robert P., M.A., Incumbent of Buxton, Derbyshire
Hull, Thomas, Esq., M.D., Beverley
Hulme, John Rhodes, Esq., M.D., Scarborough
Hulse, Sir Charles, Bart., Breamore House, Sarum
Hulton, Rev. Arthur H., B.A., Walmersley, Bury, Lancashire
Humber, John, Esq., Winckley Square, Preston
Humber, William, Esq., Myerscough Hall, Preston
Humberston, Charles, Esq., Brookfield, Walton, Liverpool
Humble, E., Esq., Coldwell Cottage, Chesterfield
Humble, George, Esq., Solicitor, Cleckheaton, Leeds
Humble, Joseph John, Esq., Prudhoe House, Newcastle-upon-Tyne
Hume, Rev. Charles J., M.A., Rector of Meon-Stoke, Alton, Hants
Humfrey, R. B., Esq., J.P., Stoke Albany, Market Harborough
Hunt, Rev. George, Barningham Rectory, near Botesdale
Hunt, John, Esq., Thornington, Coldstream
Hunt, James, Esq., Pittincrieff, by Dunfermline, Fife
Hunter, Adam, Esq., M.D., Park Place, Leeds
Hunter, Rev. Alexander, M.A., Alvechurch, Bromsgrove
Hunter, Charles V., Esq., Kilburne Hall, Derbyshire
Hunter, Cuthbert, Esq., Walker Cottage, Newcastle-upon-Tyne
Hunter, John, Esq., Solicitor, Gateshead
Hunter, Sir Rich., Knt., Dunlany Cottage, Patching, near Arundel
Huntriss, William, Esq., Lord-Street, Halifax, Yorkshire
Huntsman, Francis, Esq., Attercliffe, Sheffield
Hurst, Robert Henry, M.P., Horsham, Sussex
Hurst, William, Esq., Architect, Doncaster
Hustler, John, Esq., Bolton House, Bradford
Hutchinson, Rev. C. E., Can. Res. Chichester
Hutchinson, George, Esq., Ovingham, Newcastle-upon-Tyne
Hutchinson, John, Esq., Caistor, Lincolnshire
Hutchinson, Rev. J., M.A., Bretton Hall, Guisborough
Hutchinson, Timothy, Esq., Egglestone Hall, Barnard-Castle
Hutchinson, William, Esq., C.E., Newcastle-upon-Tyne
Hutchinson, William Johnson, Esq., Grove, Barnard-Castle
Hutchinson, William Parry, Esq., Park Hill Road, Liverpool
Hutt, William, Esq., M.P., Gibside, Gateshead
Hutton, Rev. C. J., Rector of St. John's, Ilketshall, near Bungay
Hutton, Edward, Esq., Solicitor, Milnthorp
Hutton, George, Esq., Carlton, Newark
Hutton, John R., Esq., Solicitor, Sunderland
Hutton, William, Esq., Esplanade, Tynemouth
Hyde, J. B., Esq., St. George's Square, Worcester
Hymers, William, Esq., J.P., Gateshead
Ibbotson, Rev. A., Incumbent of Rawdon, Leeds
Iddins, George Francis, Esq., J.P., The Woodrow, Bromsgrove
Ikin, John Arthur, Esq., Scarcroft Grange,   do.
Ill, Richard, Esq., Mancetter Lodge, Atherstone
Illingworth, Jonathan Akroyd, Esq., Bradford
Imeary, Robert, Esq., Jarrow Lodge, South Shields
Inge, Rev. John Robt., M.A., Incumbent of St. Mary's, Portsmouth
Ingham, Joshua, Esq., M.A. and J.P., Blake Hall, Mirfield, Dews-
Ingham, T. Hastings, Esq., J.P., Marton House, Skipton   [bury
Ingham, William, Esq., Mankinholes, Todmorden
Ingle, John Benjamin, Esq., Bradford
Ingleby, Charles, Esq., Austwick, Settle
Ingleby, Clement, Esq., Cannon Hill, Moseley, Birmingham
Ingledew, John, Esq., Solicitor, Newcastle-upon-Tyne
Ingram, John R., Esq., Haugh End, Halifax
Ingram, J. A., Esq., Solicitor St. Peter, Whits
Ingram, James, Esq., Oak Cottage, Aigburth, Liverpool
Ingram, W. H., Esq., Asles, near Chailey, Lewes
Inman, Thomas, Esq., Hill House, Silverdale, Lancaster
Ireland, Rev. John, Rockfield House, Nunney, near Frome
Iremonger, Rev. F. A., B.A., Shipton-Bellinger Vicarage, Hants
Iremonger, Rev. Thomas L., Vicar of Clatford, Goodworth,   do.

IRISH OFFICE, The, London
Irlam, William, Esq., Solicitor, Liverpool
Irvin, Rev. Thomas, M.A., Vicar of Ormesby, Stockton-upon-Tees
Irvine, Rev. James, M.A., Vicar of Leigh, Manchester
Irving, George, Esq., Chichester, Sussex
Irving, Rev. John W., B.A., Incumbent of Batley-Carr, Dewsbury
Irving, Rev. Lewis H., Abercorn, Linlithgow
Irving, Rev. Thomas, St. Mary's, Osbaldeston, Blackburn
Isaac, John Whitmore, Esq., Doughton House, Worcester
Isaac, Rev. William Lister, M.A., Rector of Pirton and Croome [d'Abitot, Worcestershire
Isham, Sir Justinian, Bart., Lamport Hall, Northampton
Ives, Rev. Cornelius, M.A., Rector of Bradden, Towcester
Iveson, Thomas, Esq., Solicitor, Holmfirth
Jackson, Charles, Esq., Banker, Doncaster
Jackson, Rev. Charles, A.B., Bentley, Farnham
Jackson, Edward, Esq., Beevor Hall, Barnsley
Jackson, Rev. H., B.D., Holt Rectory, Norfolk
Jackson, Rev. H. W., B.A., Incumbent of Coppull, Chorley
Jackson, Hugh William, Esq., Leven, Beverley
Jackson, Rev. John, M.A., Vicar of Dodderhill-with-Elmbridge,
Jackson, John, Esq., Riston Grange, Beverley [Droitwich
Jackson, John, Esq., Beverley
Jackson, Ralph Ward, Esq., Greatham Hall, Stockton-upon-Tees
Jackson, Rev. T. G., M.A., Studley, Warwickshire
Jackson, Thomas, Esq., Great Crosby, Liverpool
Jackson, William, Esq., Knottingley, Ferrybridge
Jackson, William, Esq., Elm House, Old Swan, Liverpool
Jacob, Rev. Philip, M.A., Rector of Crawley, Hants
Jacot, William, Esq., New Hall, Sutton Coldfield
Jacson, John, Esq., Fulwell, Tyldesley, Manchester
Jadis, Rev. John, M.A., Vicar of Humbleton, Hedon, Hull
James, C. F., Esq., Kirknewton House, Wooler
James, Rev. David, F.S.A., St. Mary's, Kirkdale
James, Joseph Green, Esq., Solicitor, Walsall
James, Rev. Moorhouse, M.A., Bedford, Leigh, Manchester
James, Thomas, Esq., Brandon, Alnwick
Jameson, Robert, Esq., Alloa
Jameson, William, Esq., Holly Grove, Roby, Liverpool
Jamieson, Rev. Robert, Currie, Edinburgh
Jardine, Rev. Fergus, Kinghorn, Fife
Jarratt, Rev. Robert, Wellington, Somerset
Jarvis, Sir Raymond, Bart., Fair Oak Park, Bishopstoke, Hants
Jarvis, Messrs. L. W., and Son, Lynn
Jary, W. H., Esq., Blofield Lodge, Norwich
Jee, Richard R., Esq., Mancetter Lodge, Atherstone
Jeffcock, John, Esq., Cowley Manor, Sheffield
Jeffcock, Thomas Dunn, Esq., Brush House, do.
Jeffcock, William, Esq., High Hazles, Sheffield, Yorkshire
Jefferson, Matthew, Esq., Lendings, Startforth, Barnard-Castle
Jefferson, William, Esq., Pontefract
Jefferys, Nath. Newman, Esq., Blightmont, Millbrook, Southampton
Jeffray, Rev. Lockhart William, M.A., Ashton-on-Ribble, Preston
JEFFREY, The Right Honourable Lord
Jeffrey, Rev. John, D.D., Rectory, Otterhampton, near Bridgwater
Jenkins, Rev. David, M.A., Incumbent of Pudsey, Leeds
Jenkins, Rev. William, Vicarage, Sidmouth, Devon
Jenkins, Rev. William, Selham Rectory, near Midhurst, Sussex
Jenkinson, Rev. F., Gnosall, Stafford
Jenkinson, Rev. George, M.A., Lowick, Berwick-upon-Tweed
Jenkinson, Rev. J. S., Hastings
Jennings, Joseph Crew, Esq., Evershot, near Dorchester, Dorset
Jerram, Rev. Charles, M.A., Rector of Witney, Oxon
Jervis, Philip Octavius, Esq., Solicitor, Bishop's Castle, Salop
Jervoise, G. P., Esq., Herriard House, Hants
Jesson, Rev. Cornelius, M.A., Rector of Enville, Stourbridge
Jesson, Thomas, Esq., West Bromwich, Staffordshire
Jesson, Thomas, Esq., Beech House, Bransgore, Christchurch
Jessop, Adam, Esq., Castleford, Pontefract
Jessop, Rev. Thomas, D.D., Bilton Hall, York
Jessop, William, Esq., J.P., Butterly Hall, Alfreton
Jissett, Robert, Esq., Blackdown, Winchester, Hants
Joberns, William Southwell, Esq., Ryde, Isle of Wight
Jobling, Jn. Creswell, Esq., Newton Hall, Newcastle-upon-Tyne
Jobson, William, Esq., Boulmer House, Alnwick
Jodrell, Rev. Henry, B.A., Idsworth, Horndean, Hants
Johnson, Col. C., Douglas, Isle of Man
Johnson, G., Esq., Benwell Colliery, Newcastle-upon-Tyne
Johnson, Captain James, Willow Bank, near Ryde
Johnson, John, Esq., Solicitor, Nottingham
Johnson, John, Esq., Willington, Newcastle-upon-Tyne

Johnson, John, Esq., Brigham, Driffield
Johnson, Rev. R. L., Binderton House, near Chichester
Johnson, Samuel, Esq., Halifax
Johnson, Rev. Samuel, Hinton-Blewett, near Bath
Johnson, Rev. Thomas, M.A., Hinton-Ampner, Alresford
Johnson, Thomas, Esq., Doncaster
Johnston, E., Esq., Abercromby Square, Liverpool
Johnston, William, Esq., Solicitor, Newcastle-upon-Tyne
Johnston, James, Esq., Sands, Kincardine, Perth
Johnstone, Rev. George Henry, B.A., Mainstone Court, Ledbury
Johnstone, James, Esq., Celon by Alloa
Johnstone, R. A., Esq., Alloa House, Stirlingshire
Johnstone, Sir John V. B., Bart., M.P., Hackness, Scarborough
Johnstone, Spearman, Esq., Mount villa, York
Johnstone, Rev. Thomas Bryan, Rector of Clutton, Somerset
Jolliffe, John Twyford, Esq., Ammerdown Park, Kilmersdon, do.
Jones, David, Esq., Hill Top, West Bromwich
Jones, Frederick Robert, Esq., Birk House, Huddersfield
Jones, F. R., jun., Esq., Solicitor, do.
Jones, George Haines, jun., Esq., M.D., Ashling House, Hants
Jones, Rev. Henry, M.A., Vicar of Northop, Flintshire
Jones, Henry Meredith, Esq., Deane-Street, Fairfield, Liverpool
Jones, Rev. John, St. Owen-Street, Hereford
Jones, Rev. John, All Souls, St. Leonard's, Sussex
Jones, Josiah, Esq., Everton Road, Liverpool
Jones, J. A., Esq., Llanarth Court, Abergavenny
Jones, Rev. Robert, M.A., Vicar of Branxton, Coldstream
Jones, Thomas Rock Smith, Esq., Solicitor, Sunderland
Jones, Thomas, Esq., Olive House, near Dudley
Jones, Rev. W., M.A., Rector of Morestead, Winchester
Jones, William, Esq., Falcon House, Oldham
Jope, William, Esq., Tremeddan, Liskeard, Cornwall
Jordan, John, Esq., Whitchurch, Hants
Jowett, Thomas, Esq., Bingley
Jubb, Abraham, Esq., Halifax
Judkins, Capt., Windsor Terrace, Liverpool
Justice, Henry, Esq., Hinstock, near Market-Drayton, Salop
Kay, Duncan James, Esq., South Hill Terrace, Liverpool
Kay, James, Esq., J.P., Turton Tower, Bolton-le-Moors
Kearsley, Edward Tertius, Esq., Shaw-Street, Liverpool
Keck, George Anthony Legh, Esq., J.P., Bank Hall, Ormskirk, [and Stoughton Grange, Leicester
Keeling, Rev. F., M.A., Pockthorpe Hall, Driffield
Keete, Henry W., Esq., M.D., St. Nicholas, Newport, Isle of Wight
Keir, John Mallison, Esq., Solicitor, Barnsley
Kekwick, John, Esq., The Holmes, Rotherham
Kelham, Marmaduke, Esq., Solicitor, Southwell, Notts
Kelham, Robert Kelham, Esq., J.P., Bleasby Hall, Southwell, Notts
Kelk, John, Esq., M.D., Scarborough
Kelsall, James, Esq., Bridge House, Ferrybridge
Kemp, Frederick, Esq., Bispham Lodge, Poulton-le-Fylde
Kemp, F. T., Esq., Swardeston, near Norwich
Kemp, Nathaniel, Esq., Ovingdean House, near Brighton
Kemp, Rev. T. Cooke, B.A., Vicar of East Meon, Hants
Kemp, Rev. Sir W. R., Bart., Gissing, near Diss, Norfolk
Kempson, Rev. Edwin, M.A., Castle Bromwich, Birmingham
Kempson, Rev. W. Brooke, A.M., Rector of Stoke-Lacy, Hereford
Kendal, Rev. Charles Edward, M.A. and J.P., Brindle Rectory
Kendall, James, Esq., Solicitor, Pickering
Kendall, John, Esq., East Ness, Whitwell
Kenmir, George Johnson, Esq., Claremont House, Gateshead
Kennaway, Sir John, Bart., Escot House, Honiton, Devon
Kennaway, Mark, Esq., Exeter, Devon
Kennedy, James, Esq., C.E., Tue Brook, Liverpool
Kennedy, Rev. Lewis Drummond, B.A., Louth
Kennicott, Rev. Richard Dutton, B.A., Horton, Morpeth
Kenrick, Archibald, Esq., West Bromwich
Kenrick, Samuel, Esq., Handsworth Hall, Staffordshire
Kent, Rev. Geo. E., East Winch Hall, near Lynn
Kenyon, Mrs., Swinley, Wigan
Keppel, Hon. Major-Gen. G., Ashley, Lymington, Hants
Keppel, Hon. and Rev. T. R., Warham Rectory, near Wells
KERR, The Right Honourable Lord Robert
Kerrison, M., Esq., Ranworth, near Acle, Norfolk
Kershaw, Rev. J., Esq., Falkner Square, Liverpool
Kershaw, Robert, Esq., Heywood, Lancashire
Kett, George S., Esq., Brooke House, near Norwich
Kidd, Martin, Esq., Solicitor, Holmfirth
Kidd, Rev. Thomas, Croxton Rectory, near St. Neot's
Kilby, Rev. Thomas, M.A., Incumbent of St. John's, Wakefield
Kilner, Rev. William, D.D., Rector of Weyhill, Hants
Killick, Henry, Esq., Walton, Eccleshall, Staffordshire

Kilshaw, William Tyson, Esq., Everton, Liverpool
King, Alfred, Esq., Pembroke Place, Liverpool
King, Alfred, Esq., Solicitor, Warwick, and Queen-Street, Cheap-
King, Rev. Henry, M.A., Middleton, Beverley [side, London
King, Rev. John, M.A., Incumbent of Christ Church, Hull
King, John, Esq., Loxwood House, near Horsham, Sussex
King, J., Esq., Coates, near Petworth
King, Joseph, Esq., Shaw-Street, Liverpool
King, Rev. Joshua, M.A., Woodchurch, Birkenhead
King, R. Meade King, Esq., Walford, near Taunton
King, Thomas, Esq., Kirkleatham, Guisborough
Kinneir, Richard, Esq., M.D., Cirencester
Kinsman, Rev. A.G., M.A., Incumbent of Gildersome, Leeds
Kipling, Thomas, Esq., Barnard-Castle, Durham
Kirlew, George, Esq., The Mount, York
Kirsopp, William, Esq., Solicitor, Hexham
Kittermaster, James, Esq., M.D., Meriden, Coventry
Knapp, Matthew, Esq., J.P., Little Linford House, Newport-Pagnell
Knatchbull, William F., Esq., Babington, Frome
Kneeshaw, Richard, Esq., Upper Parliament-Street, Liverpool
Knight, Sir Arnold James, Knt., M.D.
Knight, Rev. C. Bridges, M.A., Chawton Rectory, Alton, Hants
Knight, Messrs. Charles and John, Cannington, Bridgwater
Knight, Rev. John, Perpetual Curate of Heytesbury, Wilts
Knight, Rev. R. Hervey, M.A., Rector of Weston Favell, North-
Knight, Rev. Thomas, M.A., Rector of Ford, Coldstream [ampton
Knight, Thomas, Esq., Alton, Hants
Knightly, Sir Charles, Bart., Farnley, Daventry
Knighton, Sir William W., Bart., Blendworth Cottage, Horndean
Knipe, Rev. R. R., Rector of Water-Newton, Wansford, Hunts
Knott, Rev. J. M., M.A., Hardwick Priors, Southam
Knott, Samuel, Esq., M.D., Newcastle-upon-Tyne
Knowles and Brown, Messrs., Iron-Works, Rotherham
Knowles, George, Esq., Wood End, Scarborough
Knowles, James, Esq., Eagley Bank, Bolton-le-Moors
Knowles, James, Esq., Solicitor, Bradford Terrace, Bolton-le-Moors
Knowles, Joshua, Esq., J.P., Stormerhill, Tottington, Bury
Knowles, L. and L. H., Messrs., Gomersall, Leeds
Knowlys, John, Esq., Woodsfarm Lodge, near Crawley, Sussex
Kurtz, Charles, Esq., Deane-Street, Edge Hill. Liverpool
Kurtz, A. George, Esq., Kensington, Liverpool
Lacy, Thomas, Esq., Wood Dalling Hall, near Reepham
Ladbroke, James Willis, Esq., Hillyer's, Petworth, Sussex
Laidlay, John, Esq., Fleetwood-on-Wyre
Laidman, John, Esq., Exeter
Laing, George, Esq., Balerno Mill, Currie, Edinburgh
Laing, Philip, Esq., Deptford House, Sunderland
Laird, John, Esq., Birkenhead
Lakeland, Thomas, Esq., Christleton, Chester
Lamb, Sir C. M., Bart., Beauport, near Battle
Lamb, Henry, Esq., The Rookery, Hawley, Kent
Lamb, Henry, Esq., Kettering
Lamb, Henry G., Esq., Solicitor, Kettering
Lamb, John, Esq., Solicitor, Barnard-Castle
Lamb, Thomas, Esq., Solicitor, Lancaster
Lamb, Thomas, Esq., Andover
Lamb, William, Esq., Hay Carr, Lancaster
Lambert, Rev. Burgess, M.A., Misterton, Crewkerne, Somerset
Lambert, Rev. Johnson, M.A., Bowes, Barnard-Castle
Lambert, J., Esq., Solicitor, Alnwick
Lampard, Goodeve, and Bowker, Messrs., Winchester
Lampray, John, Esq., Solicitor, Warwick
Lance, Rev. William, A.M., Rector of Faccombe, Hants
Landon, Rev. James, B.D., Vicar of Aberford, Wetherby
Landon, Rev. George, B.C.L., Richard's Castle, Ludlow
Langham, Herbert, Esq., J.P., Cottesbrooke Park, Northampton
Langham, Sir James Hay, Bart., Glyndbourn, near Lewes, Sussex
Langley, Rev. John, A.M., All Saints, Southampton
Langridge, W. V., Esq., Lewes, Sussex
Langstaff, Owen, Esq., Barnard-Castle
Lardner, J. H., Esq., Rye, Sussex
Larke, H. R., Esq., Brooke, near Norwich
Laslett, William, Esq., Abberton Hall, Worcestershire
Latham, Rev. Henry, Selmeston Vicarage, near Lewes
Latham, John, Esq., Town Clerk of Congleton, Cheshire
Latham, William, Esq., Solicitor, Sandbach, Cheshire
Lauga, Burman, Esq., Waltham, Great Grimsby, Lincolnshire
Lawrell, John, Esq., Waltham, Great Grimsby
Lawrence, Rev. Charles W., M.A., St. Luke's, Liverpool
Lawrence, Captain J. H., East Harptree, Old Down, Somerset
Lawson, William, Esq., Longhirst, Morpeth
Lawton, G. Warner, Esq., Eye, Suffolk
• Layborn, Jonathan, Esq., Wold Cottage, Thwing, Bridlington

Laybourn, Jacob, Esq., Nafferton Lodge, Driffield
Laycock, Thomas, Esq., Fishergate House, York
Layng, Rev. William, M.A., Overstone, Northampton
Lea, Rev. William, Tardebigg, Bromsgrove
Leach, Rev. John, M.A., Tweedmouth, Berwick
Leacroft, William Swymeom, Esq., J.P., Southwell, Notts
Leadbeatter, Thomas, Esq., Solicitor, Mirfield, Dewsbury
Leah, Henry, Esq., J.P., Byerley Hall, Bradford
Leake, James, Esq., Witney, Oxon
Leatham, William, Esq., Beech Lawn, Heath, Wakefield
Leather, James, Esq., Beeston Park, Leeds
Leather, John Towlerton, Esq., C.E., Dam House, Sheffield
Leather, Peter William, Esq., Everton, Liverpool
Leaver, F., Esq., Nottingham [cestershire
Lechmere, Rev. Anthony Berwick, M.A., Hanley Vicarage, Wor-
Ledgard, Francis, Esq., Solicitor, Mirfield, Dewsbury
Ledger, Wilson, Esq., Washington-Street, Everton, Liverpool
Ledsam, Joseph Frederick, Esq., J.P., Chad Hill, Edgbaston
Lee, George, Esq., Threapwood, Hexham
Lee, James, Esq., West Retford House, Notts
Lee, John, Esq., M.D., Daventry, Northamptonshire
Lee, John F., Esq., Kinver, Stourbridge
Lee, R. T., Esq., Grove Hall, Ferrybridge
Lee, Thomas M., Esq., Solicitor, Leeds
Lee, Thomas Eyre, Esq., Camden Lodge, Birmingham
Lee, William, Esq., St. John's, Wakefield
Lee, William, Esq., Huddersfield
Leece, George, Esq., Breck Cottage, Poulton-le-Fylde
Leece, Edward, jun., Esq., Whittle-le-Woods, Chorley
Leech, Rev. W., M.A., Vicar of Shernborne, near Lynn
Leeds, Stephen, Esq., Whitwell, Reepham
Leeke, Rev. H. H., Brockton, Newport, Salop
Leeke, R. M., Esq., Longford Hall, do.
Leeman, George, Esq., Solicitor, York
Leeming, Richard, Esq., Wray, Lancaster
Lees, Henry, Esq., Solicitor, Stalybridge
Lees, John Frederick, Esq., J.P., Werneth, Oldham
Lees, Joseph, Esq., Lower Clarksfield, Oldham
Lefevre, The Right Hon. C. S., Speaker of the House of Commons
Leftwich, Richard, Esq., Aigburth, Liverpool
Legard, George, Esq., J.P., Fangfoss Hall, Pocklington
Legge, Sir Thomas Digby, Bart., Ganton Hall, Yorkshire [ham
Legge, John Robinson, Esq., Solicitor, Houghton-le-Spring, Dur-
Legh, Rev. Peter, M.A., Rector of Newton-in-Makerfield
Le Grice, Rev. Frederick, M.A., Vicar of Great Gransden, Hunts
Le Hunt, P. Bainbridge, Esq., Ashbourn, Derbyshire
LEICESTER, The Right Honourable the late Earl of
Leigh, Frederick, Esq., Collumpton, Devon
Leigh, John Shawe, Esq., Childwall Hall, Liverpool
LEIGH, The Right Honourable Lord
Leigh, Rev. Robert, M.A., Belper, Derby
Leigh, Robert. Esq., Taunton
Leigh, Rev. Wm., M.A., Rector of Pulham-St. Mary, Harleston
Leman, Rev. G. O., Perpetual Curate of Stoven, Brampton Hall
Leman, Rev. Thomas Orgill, Rector of Brampton, near Halesworth
Lemonius, Aug. H., Esq., Bedford-Street South, Liverpool
Lempriere, Captain G. Ourry, R.N., Pelham Lodge, Alton, Hants
Lennon, Rev. Ambrose, St. Alban's, Liscard, Cheshire
LENNOX, The Right Honourable Lord George
Lenthall, Kyffin John W., Esq., Bessels-Leigh, Abingdon, Berks
Leslie, Rev. C. W., St. Leonard's, Sussex
Lethbridge, Rev. Charles, St. Stephen's, Launceston
Lewes, John, Esq., Lewes, Sussex
Lewin, R. Hutchinson, Esq., Bartley Lodge, Southampton
Lewis, Rev. J. H., Episcopal-Episcop. near South Petherton
Lewthwaite, Rev. George, B.D., Rector of Adel, Leeds
Lewty, James Windeyer, Esq., The Firs, Smethwick, Birmingham
Lewty, Thomas Weaver, Esq., Wilden House, Stourport
Lichfield, William, M.A., Nursling Mount, Southampton
Lidbetter, Richard, Esq., Magdalen, near Steyning, Sussex
Lidbetter, Thomas, Esq., Saltworks, Droitwich
Liddell, Christopher, sen., Esq., Shieldfield, Newcastle-upon-Tyne
Liddell, Rev. Henry George, M.A., Rector of Easington, Durham
Light, Rev. H. W. M., B.A., Incumbent of Bramshaw, Hants
Lightoller, Richard A., Esq., Yarrow House, Chorley
Lillingston, Rev. Edward, M.A., Rural Dean, and Incumbent of All
Lind, James, Esq., M.D., Ryde, Isle of Wight [Saints, Derby
Lindley, Charles, Esq., Architect, Mansfield
Lindsay, Robert, Esq., St. Andrews, Fife
Lingwood, Robert M., Esq., Sufton Court, Hereford
Linskill, Rev. John A. P., B.A., Stanhope, Durham
Lipscomb, Rev. Francis, M.A., Rector of Welbury-in-Cleveland
Lister, Francis, Esq., Bank, Goole

Lister, George S. Spofforth, Esq., Ousefleet Grange, Goole
Lister, George Thompson, Esq., Hollin Close, Bolton
Lister, James, Esq., North Everton, Liverpool
Lister, Rev. John, M.A., Incumbent of Stanley, Wakefield
Lister, John, jun., Esq., Gateshead
Lister, John, Esq., Elmfield, Bramley, Leeds
Lister, Rev. J. M., Burwell Park, Louth, Lincoln
Lister, Rev. Joseph Martin, B.A., Muckton-cum-Burwell, Louth
Lister and Son, Messrs. Robert, Scotswood, Newcastle-upon-Tyne
Lister, Samuel Cuncliffe, Esq., Manningham Hall, Bradford
Little, Francis, Esq., Ditton Lodge, Warrington
Little, James, Esq., Deane-Street, Edge Lane, Liverpool
Little, Rev. Robert, B.D.,Yarmouth, Isle of Wight
Littledale, Thomas, Esq., Highfield, West Derby, Liverpool
Littler, Rev. John, Battle, Sussex [end, Glamorgan, South Wales
Llewelyn, Rev. R. Pendrill, M.A., Llangynwyd Vicarage, Bridg-
Lloyd and Summerfield, Messrs., Park Glass-Works, Birmingham
Lloyd, George B., Esq., Bordesley Farm, Birmingham
Lloyd, George, Esq., Stockton Hall, York   [Zouch
Lloyd, Rev. George Wood, D.D., Parsonage, Gresley, Ashby-de-la-
Lloyd, Rev. Henry, M.A., Stockton Hall, York
Lloyd, Sir James M., Bart., Lancing, near Shoreham, Sussex
Lloyd, John Buck, Esq., Aigburth, Liverpool
Lloyd, Rev. Thomas, M.A., Rector of Christeleton, Chester
Lloyd, Thomas, Esq., Chester-Street, Liverpool
Lloyd, Rev. William, Rushall, near Pewsey, Wilts
Lloyd, Rev. W. H. C., Norbury, Rectory, Newport, Staffordshire
Lloyd, Rev. Yarburgh G., M.A., Incumbent of Rawcliffe, Selby
Locke, Wadham, Esq., Codford-St. Mary's, Wiley, Wilts
Lockwood, Rev. Edward Isaac, M.A., St. Mary's, Bedford
Lockwood, Rev. J. W. Knollys, B.A., Incumbent of Ulrome,
                                                   [Bridlington
Lomax, Joseph, Esq., Bradshaw Hall, Bolton-le-Moors
Long, Frederick, Esq., Shabbington, Bucks
Long, Francis Stephen, Esq., Red House, Amesbury, Wilts
Long, Rev. Henry, Newton Rectory, near Long Stratton
Long, R. Kellett, Esq., Dunston Hall, near Norwich
Long, S. M., Esq., Bodney Hall, near Brandon
Long, Walter, Esq., M.P., Rood Ashton House, Trowbridge
Longlands, Rev. T., M.A., vicar of Porchester, Hants
Longridge, William, Esq., Bedlington Iron-Works, Morpeth
Longstaff, Owen, Esq., Barnard-Castle
Longton, James, Esq., Southport, Lancashire
LONSDALE, The Right Honourable the late Earl of
Lonsdale, J. W., Esq., Solicitor, Halifax
Lopes, Sir Ralph, Bart.,Maristow, near Plymouth
Loraine, R. G., Esq., Wallington, Surrey
Lord, James, Esq., Huskisson-Street, Liverpool
Lord, John, Esq., Mayor of Wigan, Standish Hall
Lord, John, Esq., Irwell Terrace, Bacup, Rochdale
Lord, Rev. W. E., Rector of Northiam, near Rye, Sussex
Lovegrove, Joseph, Esq., Horsham, Sussex
Lovett, James, Esq., Priory, Cricklade, Wilts
Lowe, Samuel, Esq., Bradford-Street, Walsall
Lowe, Rev. Thomas, B.A. and J.P., Oldham, Lancashire
Lowes, John, Esq., Allens Green, Haltwhistle
Lowndes, Matthew Dobson, Esq., Edge Lane, Liverpool
Lowndes, R. W. S., Esq., Bletchley, Fenny Stratford
Lowrey, William, Esq., Barmoor, Berwick-upon-Tweed
Lowry, Stephen, Esq., Shieldfield House, Newcastle-upon-Tyne
Loxdale, James, Esq., Barrister at Law, Bilston
Loyd, Edward, Esq., Banker, Manchester
Luard, Peter Francis, Esq., M.D., Warwick and Leamington
Lucas, Henry, Esq., The Green, Newport-Pagnell
Lucas, Rev. St. John W., Rector of East Hatley
Lucy, William, Esq., West Grove, Adgbaston, Birmingham
Lucy, William Charles, Esq., Stratford-on-Avon, Warwickshire
Ludlow, H. G. G., Esq., Heywood House, Westbury, Wilts
Lund, Rev. Thomas, B.D., Rector of Morton, Alfreton
Lund, William, Esq., Key-Street, Liverpool
Lukin, Rev. John, A.M., Rector of Nursling, Hants
Lumb, Henry, Esq., Southgate, Wakefield
Lumb, Rev. Thomas Dawson, M.A., Methley, Leeds
Lundy, Rev. Francis, M.A., Rector of Lockington, Beverley
Lupton, Harry, Esq., Thame, Oxon
Luttrell, Rev. A. Lownes, East Quantoxhead, Bridgwater
Luxmore, Edward, Esq.,Wadebridge, Cornwall
Luxford, Rev. G. C., Bognor, Sussex
Lyddon, Richard, Esq., Wellington, Somerset
Lyddon, Robert, Esq., South Petherton, Somerset
Lyne, Rev. C. P., Rector of West Thorney, near Chichester
Lyne, Edward, Esq., Wadebridge, Cornwall
Lyne, John, Esq., Moorswater Lodge, near Liskeard

Lynn, F. P., Esq., Mindrum Mill, Coldstream
Lyon, Charles Walter, Esq., Silverhill, Barton-under-Needwood
Lyon, David, Esq., Northbrook, Goring, near Worthing
Lyon, James, Esq., Dangstone, near Midhurst
Lyon, Matthew, Esq., Broughton, Manchester
Lyon, Thomas, Esq., Everton, Liverpool
Lyus, George, Esq., Stow-Market
Mabbott, W. C., Esq., The Priory, Southover, near Lewe
Macauley, Francis Edwin, Esq., Solicitor, Halifax
Mac-Carty, Charles E., Esq., Branch Bank of England, Leeds
Macdonald, Rev. Alexander, B.D., Cotterstock, Oundle
Macgregor, Rev. Charles, M.A., St. George's, Wolverhampton
Machell, Rev. Robert, M.A., Etton, Beverley
Mack, Rev. W. B., Rector of Horham, Stradbroke
Mackenzie, Wm., Esq., Grove-Street, Liverpool
MACKENZIE, The Right Honourable Lord
Mackenzie, Alexander, Esq., Doorhay Cottage, Porlock, Somerset
Mackenzie, Rev. William, B.A., Easington, Durham
Mac Gregor, Walter Fergus, Esq., Vauxhall Iron Foundry, Li-
Mac Iver, Charles, Esq., Canning-Street, Liverpool   [verpool
McCormick, William, Esq., Bootle Hall, Liverpool
McGuffog, Messrs. Thomas and William, Preston
McNicoll, John, Esq., Brunswick Steam Saw Mills, Liverpool
Mackreth, Rev. Thomas, M.A. and J.P., Halton, Lancaster
Macpherson, Rev. A., Rothwell vicarage, Kettering
Mactaggart, Peter Lawrie, Esq., Prospect vale, Liverpool
Maddison, George P., Esq., Cramlington, Newcastle-upon-Tyne
Maddison, Rev. John G., A.M., West Monkton, Taunton
Maddock, Edward Dennill, Esq., Everton, Liverpool
Maddock, John Finchett, Esq., Town Clerk of Chester
Maddock, John Dennil, Esq.,J.P., Manor House, Liscard, Cheshire
Maddock, Wm., Esq., Toxteth Park, Liverpool
Maddocks, Rev. John, St. Oswald's, Old Swan, Liverpool
Maddy, William, Esq., Fairfield Mount, Liverpool
Magniac, Hollingworth, Esq., Colworth, Sharnbrook, Bedford
Magor, John P., Esq., Penventon, Redruth, Cornwall
Mahs, Nicholas, Esq., Belmont Road, West Derby, Liverpool
Mainwaring, Rev. James, M.A., Brombro' Hall, Chester
Maister, Rev. H., B.A., Thornaby, Stockton-upon-Tees
Maitland, Rev. Pelham, B.A., Yoxhall, Lichfield
Major, H., Esq., Simonside Hall, Jarrow, Gateshead
Maker, Rev. J. W., Patron and Incumbent of Brede, near Hastings
Makin, Hugh, Esq., Everton, Liverpool   [the-Marsh
Malcolm, Rev. Gilbert, M.A., Rector of Toddenham, Moreton-in-
Malcolm, J., Esq., Lamorbey, Bexley, and Gt. Stanhope-St., London
Maley, Richard, Esq., Bicester
Maling, Rear-Admiral, The Elms, Abberley, Worcester
Maling, Edward Haygorth, Esq., Sunderland
Mallabey, Samuel, Esq., Grendon, Atherstone
Mallows, George, Esq., Wattisfield, near Ixworth
MALMESBURY, The Right Honourable the Earl of
Maltby, Rev. Henry Joseph, M.A., Rector of Eaglescliffe, Yarm
Maltby, Rev. W., M.A., The Terrace, Mansfield
Mammatt, John, Esq., Manor House, Ashby-de-la-Zouch
Mangnall, John, Esq., Sweetloves Hall, Sharples, Bolton-le-Moors
Mann, Rev. Charles, Denver, East Hall, near Downham-Market
Mann, Rev. Joseph, M.A., vicar of Kellington, Ferrybridge
Mann, Joshua, Esq., Mannville, Bradford
Mann, Rev. W. H. G., M.A., vicar of Bowden, Altrincham
Manser, David, Esq., Rye, Sussex
Mant, Arthur, Esq., Storrington, do.
Mant, Thomas, Esq., M.D., Truro Cottage, Hayling, Hants
Manx, Mrs. Martha, Shalden Lodge, Alton,   do.
Marchant, Francis, Esq., M.D., Hemsworth, Pontefract
Margitson, J. T., Esq., Ditchingham House, near Bungay
Marley, John, Esq., High Claremont Place, Newcastle-upon-Tyne
Marriott, John Cary, Esq., Narborough, near Swaffham
Marriott, Mr., Taunton, Somerset
Marris, George, Esq., Solicitor, Caistor
Marrow, William, Esq., Beech Lawn, Garston, Liverpool
Marsden, Rev. A., M.A., Vicar of Gargrave, Skipton
Marsden, John, Esq., Solicitor, Wakefield
Marsh, Henry, Esq., Hatherdon House, Andover
Marsh, R., Esq., Westleigh Hall, Leigh, Manchester
Marsh, Rev. W. H., jun., Esq., Lamas Rectory, near Coltishall
Marshall, George, Esq., Ward End House, Birmingham
Marshall, H. Cowper, Esq., Westwood Hall, Leeds
Marshall, James Garth, Esq., Headingley,   do.
Marshall, John, Esq., Lane Ends, Horsforth, do.
Marshall, John, Esq., Street House, near Bradford
Marshall, Rev. J. W. H., Rector of Ovingdean, near Brighton
Marshall, Michael, Esq., Chew-Magna, near Bristol
Marshall, Richard, Esq., Hornsea House, Yorkshire

Marshall, R., Esq., Higham Place, Newcastle-upon-Tyne
Marshall and Son, Messrs., Spring Mill, Huddersfield
Marshall, William, Esq., Treworgey, near Liskeard, Cornwall
Marshall, Rev. W., Vicar of Naseby, near Welford
Marshall, William, Esq., J.P. and D.L., Penwortham Hall, Preston
Marter, Rev. Richard, A.M., Millbrook, Southampton
Martin, Charles W., Esq., Belvedere, Christchurch, Hants
Martin, James, Esq., Gate-Helmsley
Martin, J. A., Esq., Sidbrook, West Monkton, Taunton
Martin, Peter, Esq., Newport Square, Bolton-le-Moors
Martin, Sir Roger, Bart., Burnham Hall, Burnham-Market
Martin, Thomas, Esq., Havant, Hants
Martin, Thomas, Esq., Edge Hill, Liverpool
Martin, T. J., Esq., Pulborough, near Petworth, Sussex
Martin, William, Esq., Bixley Hall, near Norwich
Martin, William, Esq., Hemingstone Hall, near Needham-Market
Martin, W. Benne, Esq., Worsborough Hall, Barnsley
Martineau, Rev. A., M.A., vicar of Whitkirk, Leeds
Martineau, Rev. James, Park Nook, Princes Park, Liverpool
Martinson, Edward, Esq., High Hedgefield, Newcastle-upon-Tyne
Marton, George, Esq., Capernwray Hall, Lancaster
Martyn, Richard W., Esq., Martock, Somerset
Martyn, Rev. Thomas Waddon, Lifton Rectory, near Launceston
Marwood, William, Esq., Springfield, Everton, Liverpool [hampton
Mason, Rev. H. B., M.A., Grammar School, Brewood, Wolver-
Mason, Captain H. Browne, R.N., Hilfield, Yately, Hants
Mason, Rev. Jacob Montague, M.A., Scarborough
Mason, Mathias, Esq., Solicitor, Barnsley
Mason, Colonel William, Necton Hall, near Swaffham
Massie, Rev. C., Great Finborough, near Stow-Market
Massey, Rev. Thomas, B.A., Hatcliffe Rectory, Great Grimsby
Master, Rev. James Streynsham, M.A., Rector of Chorley, Lanca-
Mather, Edward, Esq., Solicitor, Newcastle-upon-Tyne [shire
Mathew, J. Mee, Esq., F.S.A., Churchyard Court, Temple, London
Matthews, Rev. John Jenkins, Rector of Melbury-Osmond
Matthews, Rev. Thomas, B.A., Rector of Bentworth, Alton, Hants
Matthews, Thomas, Esq., Oak Hill, Maghull
Maton, James, Esq., Manor House, Maddington, Devizes
Matravers, William, Esq., Westbury, Wilts
Maud, Abraham, Esq., Fleets Rilston, Skipton
Maude, Arthur, Esq., Goole
Maude, Francis, Esq., J.P., Alverthorpe Hall, Wakefield
Maude, Rev. Francis, M.A., Incumbent of Hoyland, Barnsley
Maude, John, Esq., Dep.-Lieut. and J. P., Moor House, Stanley,
Maude, Rev. Thomas, M.A., Elvington, Yorkshire [Wakefield
Maugham, Rev. William, Incumbent of Benwell, Newcastle-upon-
Maule, George Frederick, Esq., Huntingdon [Tyne
Maunsell, Thomas P., Esq., M.P., Thorpe Malsor, Kettering
Mawdsley, John, Esq., Hamilton Square, Birkenhead
Mawdsley, John, Esq., Pool Cottage, Seacombe, Cheshire
Maxse, James, Esq., Woolbeding, near Midhurst, Sussex
Maxwell, William Constable, Esq., Everingham Park, Pocklington
May, Thomas, Esq., Basingstoke
Mayall, Messrs. J. and G., Mossley, Ashton-under-Lyne
Mayo, Rev. Charles Erskine, M.A., Dalby Rectory, Stillington
Mayor, Rev. Charles, M.A., Assistant Master of Rugby School
Mc Calmont, Rev. Thomas, B.A., Highfield, Southampton
Mc Carogher, Dr., Chichester
Mc Ghie, Rev. J. Powlett, A.M., Oxon, Vicar of Portsmouth
Mc Kinley, George, Rear-Admiral of the Red, Anglesea villa
Mc Michael, George, Esq., Bridgenorth
Meade, P., Esq., North Curry, near Taunton
Meakin, Mr. John, Brockton, Newport, Salop
Measure, John, Esq., Lincoln's Inn, London
Medhurst, Messrs., Hurstbourne-Tarrant, Andover
Medlycott, Sir William Coles, Bart., Ven House, Milborne Port
Medwin, Rev. T. K., M.A., Head Master of the Grammar School,
[Stratford-on-Avon
Meek, Alderman James, Middlethorpe Lodge, York
Meek, Sturges, Esq., C.E., Liverpool
Meers, Thomas Gay, Esq., Bale, near Holt, Norfolk
Meigh, Job, Esq., J.P., Ash Hall, Hanley, Staffordshire
Meiklam, John, Esq., R.Y.S., Cowes, Isle of Wight
Meldrum, Leslie, Esq., Devon Iron-Works, Alloa
Mellor, Benjamin, Esq., Stainland, Halifax
Melmoth and Son, Messrs., Sherborne, Dorset
Mence, Rev. J. W., B.A., Prestwold, Loughborough
Mence, William Cookes, Esq., Solicitor, Barnsley
Mercer, Rev. William, M.A., Incumbent of St. George's, Sheffield
Mercer, William, Esq., Newton-in-Makerfield, Warrington
Meredith, John, Esq., J.P., Belle Vue, Halesowen
Merest, Rev. J. W. Drage, B.D., Vicar of Staindrop, Durham
Meriman, James, Esq., Ashford House, Cannington, Bridgwater

Merry, John, Esq., J.P., Groveley House, Coston Hacket, Worces-
Meryon, John, Esq., Rye, Sussex [tershire
Messiter, Messrs. G. and H., Wincanton, Somerset
Metcalfe, George, Esq., Northumberland Square, North Shields
Metcalfe, John, Esq., West Bank, Bolton-le-Moors
Metcalfe, Thomas, Esq., West Boldon Hall, Gateshead
Mewburn, Thomas M., Esq., Solicitor, Darlington
Meynell, George, Esq., Barrister at Law, York
Meyer, Philip Herman, Esq., Stondon Place, Ongar
Michell, Rev. H. C., M.A., Minister of Lymington, Hants
Michell, J. C., Esq., East-Street, Brighton
Micklethwait, Rev. John Heaton, B.A., Denton, Otley
Micklethwait, Nathaniel, Esq., Taverham, Norwich
Micklethwaite, Daniel, Esq., South Parade, Wakefield
Micklethwaite, John, Esq., Ardsley House, Barnsley
MIDDLETON, The Right Honourable Lord
Middleton, Edward Chatterton, Esq., Banker, Loughborough
Middleton, Rev. F. G., M.A., Perpetual Curate of Bembridge
Middleton, Rev. Henry, M.A., Incumbent of Codnor-cum-Loscoe,
Middleton, Peter, Esq., Stockeld Park, Wetherby [Derbyshire
Middleton, Sir W. F. F., Bart., Shrubland Park, near Ipswich
Middleton, William, Esq., Hammerwich, Lichfield
Middleton, William, Esq., Solicitor, Leeds
Midgley, Rev. Edward James, B.A., Medomsley, Gateshead
Midgley, James H., Esq., Liverpool
Mildmay, Lady, Dogmersfield Park, Hants
Miller, Miss, Anstey House, Alton, Hants
Miller, Henry, Esq., Winckley Square, Preston
Miller, James, Esq., Newcastle-upon-Tyne
Miller, John, jun., Esq., Brunswick Dock, Liverpool
Millett, Charles, Esq., Hill Place, Droxford, Hants
Milles, W. H., Esq., Filleigh, Chudleigh, Devon
Millett, John N. R., Esq., Penzance
Millett, Richard, Esq., Penzance
Milligan, Robert, Esq., Harden, Bingley
Milligan, Robert, Esq., Acacia, Rawdon, Leeds
Millington, George, Esq., Quarlton Vale, Bolton-le-Moors
Millington, Robert, Esq., Ordsall House, Retford
Mills, John, jun., Esq., Brandeston Hall, near Framlingham
Mills, Stephen, Esq., Elston House, Orcheston St. George, Wilts
Milne, James, Esq., Hay Park, Polmont, Falkirk, N.B. [field
Milne, Rev. John, M.A., vice-Principal of the College, Hudders-
Milne, Rev. Nathaniel, M.A., Rector of Radcliffe, Manchester
Milnthorpe, Thomas, Esq., High Harrogate
Milner, John C., Esq., Thurlstone, Barnsley
Milson, Rev. Thomas, B.A., Woodsome Hall, Huddersfield
Milverton, Miss, Ford Abbey, Thorncombe, Devon
Milward, George, Esq., Manor House, Lechlade, Gloucester
Mitchell, Capt., Fairfield Crescent, Liverpool
Mitchell, Eli, Esq., Solicitor, Ossett, Wakefield
Mitchell, Joseph, Esq., Architect, Sheffield
Mitchell, J., Esq., Wymondham
Mitchell, Rev. Walter, B.A., Attercliffe, Sheffield
Mitchell, W., Esq., Petersfield, Hants
Mitford, Captain Robert, R. N., Hunmanby Hall, Yorkshire
Mitton, Michael and Son, Messrs., Solicitors, Pontefract
Modsley, William, Esq., Laurel Road, Liverpool
Moffat, Andrew Ker, Esq., Beanley, Alnwick
Moffatt, William Lambric, Esq., Architect, Doncaster
Mogg, Rev. H. H., M.A., Stone-Easton, Old Down, Somerset
Mogg, John Geo., Esq., Manor House, Farrington-Gurney, do.
Mogg, William Rees, Esq., Cholwell House, near Bath
Moilliet, James, Esq., Selley Hall, Birmingham
Moilliet. John Lewis, Esq., Abberley Lodge, Worcestershire
Mold, Charles, Esq., Makeny House, Derby
Mole, Francis, Esq., Solicitor, Birmingham
Molesworth, Rev. Hender, Falmouth, Cornwall
Molesworth, Sir Wm., Bart., M.P., Pencarrow, Bodmin, Cornwall
Molyneux, Henry, Esq., Aintree Mill, Liverpool
Molyneux, John Blayds, Esq., Upper Canning-Street, Liverpool
Molyneux, The Misses, Staplands, West Derby, Liverpool
Monck, Charles Atticus, Esq., J.P., Humshaugh House, Hexham
Monks, George, Esq., Arundel, Sussex
Monnington, Rev. George, Bitteswell, Lutterworth
Montgomery, John, Esq., Fir Vale, Wavertree, Liverpool
Montgomery, Rev. Robert, M.A., Rector of Holcott, Northampton
Moon, Rev. Samuel, M.A., Holme, Burton, Westmorland
Moor, Rev. J. H. C., Clifton, near Rugby [Worcester
Moore, Charles Edward, Esq., Upper House, Shelsley Beauchamp,
Moore, Francis George, Esq., M.R.C.S.L., Rotherham
Moore, John, Esq., Mount Vernon Road, Liverpool
Moore, John Bramley, Esq., Carioca Lodge, Aigburth, Liverpool

c

Moore, J. H., Esq., Solicitor, Walsall
Moore, Samuel, Esq., Nottingham
Moore, Thomas, Esq., Architect, Sunderland
Moore, T. S., Esq., Warham All Saints, near Wells
Moore, Thomas Fisher, Esq., La Mancha, Ormskirk
Moore, William, Esq., Wychdon Lodge, Rugeley, Staffordshire
Moorhouse, Thomas, Esq., Solicitor, Halifax
Moorhouse, William, Esq., Marine villa, Knottingley, Ferrybridge
Moorman, Josiah, Esq., Bexhill, near St. Leonard's, Sussex
Moorsom, Constantine Richard, Esq., J.P., Edgbaston, Birmingham
Mordey, William, Esq., Surgeon, Bishop-Wearmouth
More, Rev. Robert H. Gayer, Larden Hall, near Wenlock, Salop
Morecroft, Thomas, Esq., Solicitor, Rock Ferry, Cheshire and [Liverpool
Morehead, Rev. George Jeffery, Easington-cum-Liverton, Gisbo-
Morehouse, Sidney, Esq., Morecroft, Holmfirth [rough
Morewood, Rev. Robert, M.A., Burton, Westmorland
Morewood, W. Palmer, Esq., J.P., Alfreton Hall, Derbyshire, and
Morey, John Egleton, Esq., Doncaster [Ladbroke, Warwickshire
Morfitt, John, Esq., Upper Bank House, Horsforth, Leeds
Morgan, Rev. Frederick, M.A., Rector of Willey, near Lutterworth
Morgan, George, Esq., J.P., Biddlesden Park, Brackley [[Hants
Morgan, Henry Mannington, Esq., Houghton Lodge, Stockbridge,
Morgan, Rev. Nathaniel, M.A., Barston, near Knowle, Warwick- [shire
Morgan, Rev. Thomas, Vicar of Dingestow-with-Tregare, Monmouth
Morgan, William, Esq., Solicitor, Birmingham
Morgan, Wm., Esq., Woodovis, near Tavistock, Devon
Morland, John, Esq., Laburnam House, Milnthorp
Morphew, Rev. T. C., Terrington, near Lynn
Morrice, Rev. William D., B.A., Leeds
Morris, Christopher, Esq., Wigan
Morris, E., Esq., High St. Cliff, Lewes
Morris, Rev. George, M.A., Sarisbury, Southampton
Morris, James, Esq., Solicitor, Coventry
Morris, John Grant, Esq., Grassendale, Aigburth, Liverpool
Morris, Rev. Joseph Ashby, M.A., Vicar of Hampton-in-Arden
Morris, Joseph, Esq., Greenside, Allerton, Bradford
Morris, Rev. L. S., M.A., Rector of Thornton, Skipton
Morris, Rev. Richard, A.M., Vicar of Eatington, Warwickshire
Morris, Thomas, Esq., Elmhurst, Wavertree, Liverpool
Morris, W. E., Esq., Churwell, Leeds
Morrish, Joseph, Esq., Greenside, Allerton, Bradford
Morse, George, Esq., Catton Park, near Norwich
Mortimer, John, Esq., Sen. Surgeon of Haslar Hospital, Gosport
Mortlock, H., Esq., Caxton, Cambridgeshire
Moseley, Rev. Thomas, M.A., Rector of St. Martin's, Birmingham
Mosley, Sir Oswald, Bart., D.C.L., Rolleston Hall, Burton-on- [Trent
Moss, Cottingham, Esq., Aigburth, Liverpool
Moss, John, Esq., Mayor of Derby, 1844
Moss, J. C., Esq., Kempston Lodge, near Swaffham
Mott, Charles, Esq., Haydock Lodge, Ashton-in-Mackerfield
Moultrie, Rev. John, M.A., Rector of Rugby
Mountfield, William, Esq., Laverock Bank, Liverpool
MOUNT SANDFORD, The Right Honourable Lord
Mousley, William Eaton, Esq., Mayor of Derby, 1847
Moxon, Rev. J. B., Rector of Sandringham, near Lynn [shire
Moxon, Rev. William Charles, M.A., Wintringham, Brigg, Lincoln-
Muir, Alexander, Esq., Bradford
Mules, Charles Hawkes, Esq., M.D., Ilminster, Somerset
Mulleneux, James, Esq., Belle Vale, Gateacre
Mundy, Charles J. H., Esq., Mavis-Enderby, Spilsby
Munn, Robert, Esq., Heath Hill, Rochdale
Muntz, G. F., Esq., M.P., Ley Hall, Handsworth, Birmingham
Murgatroyd, William, Esq., Birks House, Bradford
Murrell, Gibbs, Esq., Lesingham House, Surlingham, near Norwich
Murthwaite, Thomas, Esq., Prescot-Street, Liverpool
Murton, George, Esq., Eagley, Bolton-le-Moors
Musgrave, Simeon, Esq., Kirkstall, Leeds
Musgrove, Edgar, Esq., Fern Lodge, Liverpool [verpool
Musker, James, Esq., Rectory Cottage, Walton-on-the-Hill, Li-
Muskett, H., Esq., Clippesby House, near Acle
Muskett, J. S., Esq., Intwood Hall, near Norwich
Musters, Rev. W. M., Colwick Rectory, Nottingham
Myers, William Joseph, Esq., Aigburth, Liverpool
Myres, John James, Esq., Civil Engineer, Preston
Myres, Miles, Esq., Solicitor, Winckley Square, Preston
Mytton, H. G., Esq., Cleobury North, Bridgenorth
Nairn, Philip, Esq., Waren House, Belford
Nanney, Rev. Hugh, B.A., Jarrow Parsonage, Gateshead
Napper, Edward, Esq., Ifold, near Petworth, Sussex
Nash, Frederick, Esq., Ludlow
Naylor, Rev. Martin Joseph, D.D., Rector of Crofton, Wakefield

Naylor, Richard, Esq., Walton Hall, Liverpool
Neill, John, Esq., Manager of the Union Bank, Wakefield
Neilson, Robert, Esq., J.P., Halewood, Liverpool
Nell, David William, Esq., Leeds
Nelson, George Brooke, Esq., do.
Nepean, Rev. Evan, Heydon Rectory, near Reepham
Ness, John, Esq., Helmsley
Netherwood, William, Esq., Skipton
Neumann, Henry, Esq., Edge Lane, Liverpool
Neumann, Rev. John Stubbs, M.A., Hockliffe Rectory, Beds.
Nevill, The Hon. and Rev. C., vicarage, East Grinstead, Sussex
Nevin, Rev. Henry, M.A., Hartlebury, Worcestershire
Nevin, Rev. Thomas, M.A., Battyeford, Mirfield, Dewsbury
Newall, Mrs., Town House, Littleborough, Rochdale [Lyme
Newall, Rev. S., A.M., Incumbent of Tunstall, Newcastle-under-
Newbery, Rev. Thomas, M.A., Incumbent of Shipley-cum-Heaton, [Bradford
Newbould, N., Esq., Golborne House, Newton-in-the-Willows,
Newcastle-upon-Tyne, District Bank of [Warrington
Newington, Charles, Esq., Highlands, Ticehurst, Sussex
Newland, Major R. B., Midhurst
Newlands, James, Esq., Civil Engineer to the Borough of Liverpool
Newlove, Rev. R., M.A., Vicar of Thorner, Leeds
Newman, Edward, Esq., Creech Place, Southwick, Hants
Newman, Edward, Esq., Solicitor, Barnsley
Newman, Edwin, Esq., Yeovil, Somersetshire
Newman, Rev. W. J., B.A., Tankersley, Barnsley
Newman, Rev. W. A., M.A., Curate of St. George's, Wolverhampton
Newnham, Rev. G. W., Chilcompton, Old Down, Somerset
Newsam, Rev. James, M.A., Middlesborough
Newsam, Philip Wm., Esq., Mayor of Warwick, 1844
Newsham, Richard, Esq., J.P., Winckley Square, Preston
Newsham, Rev. Thomas, St. Anthony's, Liverpool
Newton, Henry, Esq., Solicitor, York
Newton, Isaac, Esq., Knaresborough
Newton, Rev. J. Farmer, B.A., Kirby-cum-Broughton, Stokesley
Newton, Samuel, Esq., Croxton Park, Cambridgeshire
Newton, Samuel, Esq., J.P., Green Hall, Atherton, Manchester
Newton, William Leaper, Esq., J.P., Leylands, Derby
Newton, William, Esq., East Retford, Notts
Niblet, J. D. Thomas, Esq., Haresfield, near Gloucester
Nicholetts, John, Esq., South Petherton, Somerset
Nicholls, Samuel, jun., Esq., Bridgenorth, Salop
Nicholls, Thomas, Esq., Axbridge, Somerset
Nicholson, Edward, Esq., Solicitor, Doncaster
Nicholson, George K., Esq., Ravensdowne, Berwick-upon-Tweed
Nicholson, Rev. Henry, Grafton-Underwood, Kettering
Nicholson and Hett, Messrs., Solicitors, Brigg
Nicholson, James, Esq., F.A.S., Thelwall Hall, Warrington
Nicholson, Rev. P. C., M.A., Incumbent of St. James', Hebden- [bridge, Halifax
Nicholson, Captain Ralph, Thornton Park, Berwick-upon-Tweed
Nicholson, Robert, Esq., M.I.C.E., Newcastle upon-Tyne
Nicholson, Robert, Esq., Bradford, Yorkshire
Nicholson, Stephen, Esq., Roundhay Park, Leeds
Nickols, Richard, Esq., Barnsley [field
Nisbett, Marsden, and Co., Messrs., Chapel-town Iron-Works, Shef-
Nixon, Thos., Esq., J.P., Nuthall Temple, Nottingham
Noakes, William, Esq., Ticehurst, Sussex
Noel, Berkeley Plantagenet, Esq., Moxhul Park, Sutton Coldfield
NORFOLK, His Grace the Duke of
Norris, Charles, Esq., St. John's House, Halifax
Norris, Rev. Fred., Rector of Gransden Parva, Caxton
Norris, Rev. George Poole, Roseraddock House, Liskeard
Norris, James Edward, Esq., Savile Hall, Halifax
Norris, Richard, Esq., Lostock Browe, Ulneswalton, Chorley
Norris, Robert, Esq., Everton Valley, Liverpool
Norris, Thomas, Esq., Howick House, Preston
North, Richard Ford, Esq., North Shore Mills, Liverpool
NORTHUMBERLAND, His Grace the Duke of
NORWICH, The Right Honourable the Lord Bishop of
Nottingham Subscription Library
Nowell, James, Esq., Quarry Hill House, Dewsbury
Noyes, H. Crine, Esq., Beaulieu, Hants
Nunns, John, Esq., Windsor Terrace, Liverpool
Oakes, James, Esq., J.P., Riddings House, Alfreton
Oates, Henry, Esq., Spring House, Heckmondwike
Ogel, Rev. J. S., M.A., Preb. Durham, Kirkley Hall, Newcastle
Ogilvy, James, Esq., M.D., Coventry
Ogle, Rev. Edward C., M.A., Vicar of Bedlington, Morpeth
Ogle, Rev. Wm. Reynolds, Meesom Hall, Wellington, Shropshire
Okeover, Haughton Charles, Esq., Okeover Hall, Ashbourn
Oldershaw, The Ven. John, Archdeacon of Norfolk

Oldham, Rev. J. O., M.A., Norland House, Edgbaston
Oldroyd, Thomas, Esq., Solicitor, Dewsbury
Olive, Rev. John, Vicar of Hillingley, near Hailsham
Oliver, George C., Esq., Bramdean Cottage, Alresford
Oliver, Rev. John, B.A., vicar of Warmington, Oundle
Oliver, Royston, Esq., Stansfield, Todmorden
Oliver, Thomas, Esq., Steepleton House, Blandford
Oliver, William, Esq., Walbottle Colliery, Newcastle-upon-Tyne
Olivier, Rev. D. J., Rector of Clifton, Biggleswade
Olliver, William, Esq., Courtlands, near Worthing
Ommanney, Rear-Adm. Sir J. A., K.C.B., Warblington, Havant
ONGLEY, The Right Honourable Lord
Onslow, Hon. Col. Crawley, Upton House, Old Alresford, Hants
Onslow, Rev. Andrew Arthur, B.A., Vicar of Claverdon, Hen-
Openshaw, Henry, Esq., Butcher Lane, Bury   [ley-in-Arden
Ord, Charles O., Esq., Solicitor, Stockton-upon-Tees
Ord, William, Esq., M.P., Whitfield Hall, Northumberland
Orde, Charles W., Esq., Nunnykirk, Morpeth
ORDNANCE, Her Majesty's Honourable Board of
Orford, Thomas, Esq., Toxteth Park, Liverpool
Orger, Rev. William, M.A., Incumbent of Shirley, Southampton
Ormerod, George, Esq., J.P., Fern Hill, Rochdale
Ornsby, Henry W., Esq., Solicitor, Darlington
Orrel, John, Esq., The Beach, Aigburth, Liverpool
Orrell, Robert, Esq., Belmont, Bolton-le-Moors
Orven, Henry, Esq., Solicitor, Worksop, Notts
Osborne, Rev. Edward, M.A., Hook Cottage, Horndean, Hants
Osborne, Rev. George, M.A., Stainby, Colstersworth
Osborne, Joseph, Esq., Spondon, near Derby
Ostler and Sons, Messrs., Grantham
Otter, Rev. W. Bruere, Vicar of Cowfold, near Horsham, Sussex
Overend, Thomas, Esq., Solicitor, Kirkburton, Huddersfield
Overend, Wilson, Esq., J.P., Sheffield
Overman, J. R., Esq., Burnham-Sutton, near Burnham-Westgate
Overton, Rev. C., Cottingham, Kingston-upon-Hull
Overton, Henry, Esq., Solicitor, York
Owen, Henry, Esq., Solicitor, Worksop
Owen, Rev. J. B., M.A., St. Mary's, Bilston
Owen, John, Esq., Tue Brook Villa, West Derby, Liverpool
Owston, Robert, Esq., Solicitor, Brigg, Lincolnshire
Oxley, George, Esq., Park Place, Bradford
Oxley, John, Esq., Moorgate, Rotherham
Oxley, John Fox, Esq., Askerne, Yorkshire
Oxtoby, W. Christopher, Esq., New Road, Driffield
Paddon, John, Esq., Fareham, Hants
Padley, Robert Wilkinson, Esq., Burton Joyce, Nottingham
Padwick, William, Esq., Manor House, Hayling, Hants
Pagan, Rev. Samuel, M.A., Stanningley, Leeds
Page, C. T., Esq., Stiffkey Old Hall, near Wells, Norfolk
Page, Robert, Esq., Charlton-Mackrel, Somerton, Somerset
Page, William, Esq., West Bromwich
Paget, Rev. Edward, M.A., Fair Oak Lodge, Petersfield, Hants
Paige, Rev. Lewis, M.A., Hartlepool, Durham
Pain, Thomas, Esq., Winchester
Paley, Rev. James, Vicar of Lacock, Chippenham, Wilts
Paley, Thomas, Esq., Bowling Hall, Bradford
Palin, Mr. William, Cherrington, near Newport, Salop
Pallet, James, Esq., Solicitor, Birmingham
Palmer, Rev. Dr., Yarcombe, Chard, Somerset   [Tyne
Palmer, Charles M., Esq., St. Mary's Terrace, Newcastle-upon-
Pardow, James, Esq., Studley, Warwickshire
Parfett, W. B., Esq., Eversley, Hants
Pargeter, T. H., Esq., Wollescote, Stourbridge   [Lyme
Paris, Rev. Archibald, M.A., Rectory, Whitmore, Newcastle-under-
Park, Rev. James Allan, M.A., Elwick Hall, Stockton-upon-Tees
Park, Mrs. Waldegrave, Ince Hall, Chester
Parke, John, Esq., Stiffkey Old Hall, near Wells, Norfolk
Parke, Robert, Esq., Withnell Hall, Chorley
Parker, Rev. C. F., Rector of Ringshall, Needham-Market
Parker, George, Esq., Bixley, Norwich
Parker, Rev. Henry, M.A., Rector of Ilderton, Wooler
Parker, Hugh, jun., Esq., Gannow Hill, and of Woodthorpe, Sheffield
Parker, Harrington, Esq., Skelmersdale Hall, Ormskirk
Parker, Rev. John Thomas, M.A., Rector of Bilton, Rugby
Parker, John Clince, Esq., Fair Oak House, Little Bowland, Preston
Parker, John, Esq., M.P., Woodthorpe, Sheffield
Parker, Rev. Pelly, M.A., West Hallum, Derby
Parker, Samuel, Esq., Low Elswick, Newcastle-upon-Tyne
Parker, Thomas H., Esq., Solicitor, Park Hall, Longton
Parker, Capt. W., Clopton Hall, Woolpit, near Stow-Market
Parker, Rev. W. Harris, M.A., Newport, Isle of Wight
Parker, Robert Townley, Esq., J.P., Cuerden Hall, Preston
Parkes, Thos. Wm., Esq., Verulam Buildings, Gray's Inn, London

Parkin, Rev. John, Halton Parsonage, near Hastings
Parkin, Thomas, Esq., Blyth, Nottinghamshire
Parkinson, Rev. A. M., B.A., Cawthorne, Barnsley
Parkyns, G., Esq., Chediston Park, near Halesworth
Parr, Rev. J. Owen, M.A., vicar of Preston
Parr, J. Hamilton, Esq., Upper Parliament-Street, Liverpool
Parrott, John, Esq., Solicitor, Stony Stratford
Parry, Rev. John Peers, M.A., Bothal Park, Morpeth
Parsley, Samuel, Esq., Worle, Somerset
Parsons, Rev. Henry, Rector of Goathurst, Somerset
Partridge, Julius, Esq., Solicitor, Birmingham
Patchett, John T., Esq., Union Bank, Halifax
Pater, Joseph, Esq., Upper Canning-Street, Liverpool
Patrent, Ambrose, Esq., Corton House, Heytesbury, Wilts
Patten, J. Wilson, Esq., M.P., Bank Hall, Warrington
Patten, Edward, Esq., Whitefield House, Everton, Liverpool
Pattinson, Hugh Lee, Esq., Gateshead, Durham
Pattinson, William Watson, Esq., Felling, Gateshead
Patton, William, Esq., Devonshaw House, Dollar
Pattrick, C. George H. S., Esq., Merrimans Hill, Worcester
Paul, G. R., Esq., Portland Lodge, Worthing
PAULET, Right Honourable and Rev. Lord Charles, M.A., Vicar
        [of Wellesbourne, Warwick
Paull, Matthew, Esq., Compton-Pauncefoot, Wincanton
Paver, Christopher, Esq., Peckfield, Selby
Paver, Rev. Richard, Vicar of Brayton, do.   [Farnley, Leeds
Pawson, William, Esq., J.P., Mayor of Leeds, 1842, Lawns House,
Pawson, W., Esq., J.P., Shawdon Hall, Alnwick, Northumberland
Payne, John, Esq., The Cottage, Milverton, Somerset
Payne, Richard Ecroyd, Esq., Roundhay, Leeds   [wich
Payne, Spencer, and Co., Messrs., Phœnix Iron Works, West Brom-
Peachey, Rev. John, Ebernoe, Kirdford, near Petworth, Sussex
Peacock, Anthony, Esq., Rauceby, near Sleaford, Lincolnshire
Peacock, John S., Esq., Solicitor, Darlington
Peacock, John, Esq., Liverpool
Pearce, Francis, Esq., Hadley Lodge, Wellington, Salop
Pearse, Rev. William, Fairlight, near Hastings, Sussex
Pearson, Rev. C. James, B.A., Incumbent of St. John's, Bradford
Pearson, Francis, Esq., Kirkby Lonsdale
Pearson, James, West House, Congleton
Pearson, Rev. John, M.A., Suckley Rectory, Worcester
Pearson, Rev. John, Garencieres, Little Staughton, Bedfordshire
Pearson, Matthew, Esq., Solicitor, Selby
Peason, Thomas, Esq., Croslands, Lockwood, Huddersfield
Pearson, Rev. William, M.A., Norton Parsonage, Sheffield
Pease, Rev. G., M.A., Vicar of Darrington, Pontefract
Peckover, Daniel, Esq., Woodhall, Calverley, Bradford
Pedder, Edward, Esq., Clifton Hall, Kirkham
Peel, The Very Rev. John, M.A., Dean of Worcester
Peel, Lawrence, Esq., Sussex Square, Kemptown, Brighton
Peel, Thomas, Esq., Trenant Park, Looe, Cornwall
Peirson, John, Esq., Thornton Fields, Guisborough
Peirson, John, Esq., Guildhall, Framlingham
Pelham, Hon. and Rev. J. F., Rector of Bergh-Apton, Norwich
Pell, George, jun., Esq., Welford, Northamptonshire
Pellett, Michael, Esq., Arundel, Sussex
Pemberton, Rev. R. N., Millichope Park, Church Sutton
Pemberton, Ralph S., Esq., Usworth House, Gateshead
Pemberton, Richard, Esq., Barnes, Sunderland
Pendarves, Edward W. W., Esq., M.P., Pendarves, Cornwall
Pennington, Richard, Esq., Hindley Lodge, Wigan
Penrice, Rev. Charles, Rector of Little Plumstead, near Norwich
Percival, Samuel, Esq., Abington House, Northampton
Perigal, Rev. Charles, M.A., Vicar of Ellingham, Alnwick
Perkins and Backhouse, Messrs., Architects, Leeds
Perks, John, Esq., Barton-upon-Trent, Staffordshire
Perring, J. P., Esq., Combe-Florey, near Taunton, Somerset
Perry, Rev. Edward, Vicar of Llangattock-Vibon-Abel, Monmouth
Peters, John Weston, Esq., Bridge, South Petherton, Somerset
Pettigrew, Rev. Augustus F., B.A., Bishop-Wearmouth
Peshall, Rev. Samuel D'Oyley, M.A., Oldberrow, Henley-in-Arden
Peyton, Sir John, Bart., Swifts House, Oxon
Phayre, Rev. Richard, West Raynham Rectory, near Rougham
Phear, Rev. John, Earl-Stonham Rectory, Stonham
Philips, Thomas Moss, Esq., Solicitor and Coroner, Wolverhampton
Phillimore, Rev. Robert, M.A., Vicar of Shipton-under-Wychwood
Phillips, George, Esq., Brockton, near Shiffnall, Salop
Phillips, Rev. Herbert, M.A., Rector and Vicar of Folkton, Hun-
Phillips, John Lott, Esq., Staindrop, Darlington   [manby
Phillips, Rev. John M., M.A., Vicar of Skidbrooke, Louth
Phillips, Rev. Samuel J., The Priory, Woolton, Liverpool
Phillips, T. Bentley, Esq., Solicitor, Beverley
Phillips, Thomas John, Esq., Landue, Launceston

c 2

Phillips, Rev. W. J. G., A.M., Vicar of Eling, Hants
Pickcup, Mark, Esq., Solicitor, Bradford
Picton, Rev. Jacob, A.M., Milwich, Staffordshire
Pidcock, Rev. B., M.A., Golden Hill, Newcastle-under-Lyme
Piele, Rev. T. W., Head Master of Repton School, Burton-on-Trent
Pierce, William, Esq., Leominster, Herefordshire
Piercy, John Edwards, Esq., J.P., Warley Hall, Salop
Pierpoint, Matthew, Esq., J.P., Crown-East, Worcester
Pierson, Sir W. H., Knt., Emsworth, near Chichester
Pighills, Joseph, Esq., Apperley Bridge, Bradford
Pigot, Charles, Esq., Solicitor, Wigan
Pigot, Rev. Edward, M.A., Longridge, Preston
Pigott, Francis, Esq., Heckfield, Hants
Pilkington, Captain, R.N., Halnaker Cottage, near Chichester
Pilkington, Messrs. Richard and William, St. Helens, Lancashire
Pillans, Rev. William Huntingdon, M.A., Rector of Hinley, Dudley
Pilling, Albert, Esq., Westfield, Huddersfield
Piuckney, P., Esq., Wilsford House, Wilts
Pinfold, Rev. Charles John, M.A., Rector of Bramshall, Uttoxeter
Piper, Moses, jun., Esq., Wolverley, Kidderminster
Piper, Stephen Edward, Esq., Darlington
Pippet, George, Esq., National Provincial Bank of England, Bar-
Pitman, Harry H., Esq., Exeter   [nard-Castle
Pitman, Rev. Samuel, Oulton Hall, Aylsham
Pix, Thomas, Esq., Woodside, Peasmarsh, near Rye
Platt, Alexander, Esq., Worcester College, Oxford
Platt, George E., Esq., Denne Park, near Horsham
Platts, Rev. George, M.A., Vicar of Sedbergh
Player, G., Esq., Ryde, Isle of Wight
Plowman, Thomas, Esq., North Curry, near Taunton
Plues, Samuel Swire, Esq., Solicitor, Ripon
Plumer, Rev. Charles John, M.A., Norton, Stockton-upon-Tees
Plummer, Matthew, Esq., J.P., Sheriffhill House, Gateshead Fell
Pocock, Rev. G., Vicar of Hailsham, Sussex
Pollard, George Thomas, Esq., Stannary Hall, Halifax
Pollard, John, Esq., Chorley
Pollard, Joshua, Esq., J.P., Crow Trees, Bradford
Pollen, Sir John, Bart., Redenham, Andover, Hants
Pollit, Thomas, jun., Broadgates, Halifax
Pollock, James, Esq., J.P., Gateshead, Durham
Poole, Charles, Esq., Height House, Pudsey, Leeds
Poole, Francis, Esq., Solicitor, Hartlepool
Poole, Rev. Samuel Gower, Glodwick, Oldham
Poole, William Savage, Esq., Solicitor, Kenilworth
Pooley, Rev. David, M.A., Grammar School, Oundle
Pope, Rev. Benjamin, Vicarage, Nether Stowey, Bridgwater
Pope, John, Esq., Symondsbury, Bridport
Popham, C. Wallis, Esq., Trevarno, Helston, Cornwall
Popplewell, William, Esq., Solicitor, South Cave, Hull
Portal, John, Esq., Freefolk-Priors, Overton, Hants
Portal, William, Esq., Laverstoke, Hants
Porteous, James Alison, Esq., Tilgate Lodge, near Crawley, Sussex
Porr, Rev. George, M.A., Monk-Sherborne, Basingstoke
Porter, Charles, Esq., Spital Tongues House, Newcastle-upon-Tyne
Porter, Richard, Esq., Quay Mills, Fareham, Hants
Porter, William Henry, Esq., Dunston, Gateshead
Postlethwaite, Thomas, Esq., Springfield, Everton, Liverpool
Potchett, Rev. Brownlow, Great Ponton Rectory, near Grantham
Potter, Archibald Gilchrist, Esq., Walbottle House, Newcastle-
Potter, Edward, Esq., South Hetton, Durham   [upon-Tyne
Potter, H. G., Esq., Jesmond High Terrace, Newcastle-upon-Tyne
Potter, John, Esq., Solicitor, Walsall
Potter, Samuel, Esq., Birkacre Print Works, Chorley
Potter, William, Esq., J.P., Oxton, Cheshire
Potts, Rev. James, B.A., Whorlton, Barnard-Castle, Durham
Potts, John, Esq., J.P., Benton Park, Newcastle-upon-Tyne
POULETT, The Right Honourable the Earl
Poulton, William, Esq., The College, Huddersfield
Pountney, Rev. H., M.A., St. John's, Wolverhampton
Poutz, Victor, Esq., Edge Hill, Liverpool
Powell, Rev. Henry W., M.A., Laceby, Brigg
Powell, James, Esq., Chichester
Powell, Rev. Richmond, Boxgrove, near Chichester
Powell, William H., Esq., M.D., Fareham, Hants
Power, Rev. Henry, B.A., Farington, Preston
Powley, Rev. J., M.A., Legbourn, Louth
Pownall, James, Esq., J.P., Pennington Hall, Leigh
Pownall, William, Esq., Edge Hill, Liverpool
Powney, Captain John, Orizava, Chudleigh, Devon
Powney, Rev. Henry, M.A., Over Wallop, Hants
Powys, Hon. and Rev. A. Legh, M.A., Titchmarsh, Thrapstone
Poyner, Henry, Esq., Hadley, near Wellington, Salop
Pratt, William Dodd, Esq., Architect, Sunderland

Pratt, Mr. Samuel, Taverham Church Farm, near Norwich
Prescott, Rev. I. Philip, B.A., Romsey, Hants
Prest, John, Esq., York
Preston, Rev. H. Edmund, Tasburgh Rectory, near Long Stratton
Preston, John, Esq., Mearbeck, Settle
Preston, Richard Wheeler, Esq., Beech Hill, Liverpool
Preston, Robert, Esq., Bloxwich Hall, Walsall
Preston, Robert Berthon, Esq., York-Street, Liverpool
Preston, Thomas Baynes, Esq., Solicitor, Skipton
Preston, William, Esq., Rock House, Liverpool
Preston, Rev. William, M.A., Rector of Bulmer, and vicar of
Preston Literary and Philosophical Institution [Whenby, Yorkshire
Pretor, Samuel, Esq., Sherborne House
Price, Charles, Esq., Tenbury, Salop
Price, Rev. William, B.C.L., Brindle, Blackburn
Prickett, Rev. Josiah J., B.A., South Cave, Kingston-upon-Hull
Pridham, George, Esq., Plymouth
Priestley, Peter, Esq., Glead Hill House, Euxton, Chorley
Prime, Richard, Esq., Walberton House, near Arundel
Prior, Rev. Henry, B.A., Saxton, Tadcaster
Pritchard, George, Esq., Broseley, Salop
Pritchard, Henry, Esq., Fairfield, Liverpool
Pritchard, William, Esq., Everton, Liverpool
Pritt, Thomas, Esq., Walnut Bank, Stodday, Lancaster
Procter, Rev. Aislabie, A.B., Alwinton, Rothbury
Procter, Rev. William, B.C.L., Vicar of Bishop Burton, Beverley
Procter, Rev. William, M.A., Doddington, Wooler
Proctor, Rev. George, D.D., Chichester House, Brighton
Proctor, Sir W. B., Bart., Langley Park, Loddon, near Norwich
Protheroe, Rev. T., M.A., Winterslow, Wilts
Prower, Rev. John Merwin, Vicar of Purton, do.
Pryce, S. D., Esq., Redruth, Cornwall
Pullein, Rev. John, M.A., Vicar of Kirkthorpe, Wakefield
Pulley, Rev. William, Hawnes Vicarage, Ampthill, Bedfordshire
Pulleyne, Rev. Benjamin, A.M., Vicar of Sheringham, Holt
Pulteney, John, Esq., Northerwood, Lyndhurst, Hants
Pumfrett, George Betts, Esq., Huntingdon
Pumfrey, Charles, Esq., Solicitor, Droitwich
Purcell, Rev. Jas. G., M.A., Vicar of Worminghall, Thame, Oxon
Purdon, Rev. William C., M.A., Vicar of Loxley, Stratford-on-Avon
Purdy, Robert, Esq., Salthouse, near Cley, Norfolk
Purton, Thomas Pardoe, Esq., Fairtree, Bridgenorth
Putsey, Rev. William, Incumbent of Kirk-Leavington, Yarm
Pye, Rev. William, Saperton, Gloucestershire
Pym, Francis, Esq., The Hasells, Biggleswade
Pym, Rev. Robert, M.A., Rector of Elmley, Wakefield
Pym, Rear-Admiral Sir Samuel, Loosleys, Tamerton, Devon
Quartley, Rev. Henry Reader, M.A., Wolverton, Bucks
Quick, James, Esq., Southampton
Quick, John, Esq., Newton House, Devon
Quinton, William, Esq., Wolverhampton
Raban, William, Esq., Hatch-Beauchamp, near Taunton
Rabett, Rev. Reginald, Bramfield Hall, near Halesworth
Rabone, Edward, Esq., Smethwick Hall, Birmingham
Radcliffe, Alfred, Esq., Everton, Liverpool
Radcliffe, Samuel, Esq., Lower House, Oldham
Radclyffe, Rev. Henry Clifford, B.A., Nun-Monkton, York
Raine, Rev. John, M.A., Vicar of Blyth, Nottinghamshire
Raines, Rev. Charles Alfred, B.A., Jarrow, Gateshead
Ram, Rev. Abel John, M.A., Incumbent of the Minster, Beverley
Ramsay, Rev. E. B., Ainslie Place, Edinburgh
Ramsay, Geo. Heppel, Esq., J.P., Derwent Villa, Newcastle-upon-
Ramsay, Ralph, Esq., Scotswood, Newcastle-upon-Tyne   [Tyne
Ramsay, Sir James, Bart., Banff House, Alyth, Perth
Ramsay, Wm., Esq., Banff House, Alyth, Perth
Ramsbottom, James, Esq., Stand, Manchester
Ramsden, Rev. Edward, M.A., Incumbent of Bradshaw, Halifax
Ramshaw, Rev. Christopher, M.A., Vicar of Fewston, Otley
Ramskill, John, Esq., Solicitor, Pontefract
Rand, John, Esq., J.P., Wheatley Hall, Bradford
Randall, Rev. J., M.A., Incumbent of Hawley, Hants
Randolph, Rev. Charles, M.A., Rector of Kimpton, Andover
Randolph, James, Esq., Milverton, Somerset
Ransom, John, Esq., Holt, Norfolk
Ranson, George Smith, Esq., Solicitor, Sunderland
Rathbone, Richard, Esq., J.P., Eton Lodge, Wavertree
Rathbone, William, Esq., J.P., Green Bank, Liverpool
Raven, John, Esq., Summerfield, near Docking, Norfolk
Ravenshaw, Rev. Edward, Rector of West Kington, Chippenham
RAVENSWORTH, The Right Honourable Lord
Rawlings, Rev. James, M.A., Rector of St. Pinnock, Cornwall
Rawlins, Rev. Christopher, Vicar of Thornton cum Allerthorpe,
Rawlins, George, Esq., Woolverton Park, Hants   [Pocklington

Rawson, Christopher, Esq., Hope House, Halifax
Rawson, Edward, Esq., Ash Grove,   do.
Rawson, George, Esq., Nottingham
Rawson, John, Esq., Solicitor, Bradford
Rawson, Thomas W., Esq., Belvedere, do.
Rawsthorne, Thomas, Esq., Heysham, Lancaster
Rawstorne, Rev. R. Atherton, M.A. and J.P., Hutton Hall
Rawstorne, Walker, Esq., Architect
Ray, Rev. George Henry, M.A., Heanor Hall, Derby
Raymond, Rev. G., Rector of Symondsbury, Bridport [upon-Tees
Raymond, Rev. Jn. Mayne St. Clere, M.A., Norton, near Stockton-
Rayne, Charles, Carville House, Walls End, Newcastle-upon-Tyne
Rayner, J. H., Esq., Seaforth, Liverpool
Rayner, Thomas, Esq., Solicitor, Sheffield
Rayson, Robert, Esq., Stockton-upon-Tees
Rea, James, Esq., North Middleton, Wooler
Rea, Robert Tomkins, Esq., Solicitor, Worcester
Read, Henry, Esq., Worlingham, near Beccles
Read, Mr. James B., Penryn, Cornwall
Read, J. Offley Crewe, Esq., Laverton House, Southampton
Read, John, Esq., Derwent Hall, Sheffield
Read, Rev. Thos. Fr. R., M.A., Rector of Full-Sutton, Pocklington
Read, W. H. Rudston, Esq., M.A., F.L.S., J.P., Hayton,   do.
Reade, Rev. R., B.A., Rector of Romaldkirk, Barnard-Castle
Ready, Rev. H., Rector of Waxham, near Stalham, Norfolk
Reddale, John, Esq., J.P., Dallington Hall, Northampton
Redfern, Thomas, Esq., Daisy Bank, Leek
Redgrave, Mark, Esq., Catton Lodge, Norwich
Redhead, Rev. Thomas F., Rock Ferry, Chester
Redmayne, Thomas, Esq., Taitlands, Stainforth, Settle
Reed, Rev. Christopher, M.A., vicar of Tynemouth
Reed, George, Esq., Manor House, Burnham, Bridgwater
Reed, Henry John, Esq., Solicitor, Newcastle-upon-Tyne
Rees, Rev. Samuel, Vicar of Horsey, North Walsham
Rees, Thomas, Esq., Shaw-Street, Liverpool
Register, the General, Office for Births, Marriages, and Deaths
Reid, James, Esq., Shieldfield, Newcastle-upon-Tyne
Rennoldson, John, Esq., Jesmond Grove, do.
Reynard, Charles, Esq., Hob Green, Ripley
Reynolds, William, Esq., M.D., Allerton Priory
Reynolds, William, Esq., Trevenson, Redruth, Cornwall
Rhoades, Thomas, Esq., Chichester
Rhodes, Rev. James Armitage, M.A., J.P., Horsforth Hall, Leeds
Rice, Rev. Francis W., B.A., vicar of Fairford, Gloucestershire
Rice, Henry, Esq., Newport, Isle of Wight
Rice, Howard, Esq., Stoneham Cottage, Highfield, Southampton
Richards, J. W., Esq., Stapleton, Martock, Somerset
Richards, Rev. S. More, M.A., Incumbent of Thorpe, Rotherham
Richards, Theophilus, Esq., The Cottage, Edgbaston
Richards, Rev. Thos., Vicar of Icklesham, near Winchelsea, Sussex
Richards, Westley, Esq., Ashfield, Edgbaston
Richards, Rev. William, A.M., Reading, Berks
Richardson, Rear-Admiral Sir C., K.C.B., Painsthorpe, Pocklington
Richardson, Col., Life Guards, Blue, Fulford House, York
Richardson, Rev. H., M.A., Bradnop, Leek
Richardson, James Nicholson, Esq., Edge Lane, Liverpool
Richardson, John Cross, Esq., Lily Hill, Pilkington, Manchester
Richardson, Sir John, Bart., Pilfour Castle, Perth
Richardson, John, Esq., Heydon, near Reepham, Norfolk
Richardson, Jonathan, Esq., Shotley Bridge, Newcastle-upon-Tyne
Richardson, Joshua Thomas, Esq., Rochdale
Richardson, Thomas, Esq., Eden Vale, Castle Eden, Durham
Richardson, Rev. William, M.A., Sherburn House,   do.
Richardson, Wormley E., Esq., Riccall Hall, Selby, Yorkshire
Richings, Rev. Frederic Hartshill, B.A., Atherstone, Warwickshire
Richmond, Rev. G., M.A., Grammar School, Haydon Bridge
Ricketts, G. R. G., Esq., Woodside, North Stoneham, Southampton
Rickman, John, Esq., Willingham, near Lewes   [Tyne
Riddell, Edward, Esq., J.P., Cheeseburn Grange, Newcastle-upon-
Ridding, Thomas, Esq., Hawthorn Cottage, Southampton
Ridehalgh, John, Esq., Solicitor, Brigroyd, Halifax
Ridehalgh, Richard, Esq., Solicitor, Bradford
Ridge, William, Esq., Stoneham, near Lewes
Ridley, John, Esq., Solicitor, Newcastle-upon-Tyne
Ridley, John, Esq., Alderman and J.P., do.
Ridley, John, Esq., Park End House, Hexham
Ridley, Sir Mathew White, Bart., Blagdon, Newcastle-upon-Tyne
Ridley, Samuel, Esq., Shieldfield,   do.
Ridley, Thomas, Esq., Solicitor,   do.
Ridley, Thomas Yates, Esq., Morecambe Cottage, Heysham, Lan-
Ridsdale, George, Esq., Old Hall, Wakefield   [caster
Ridsdale, John, Esq., North Grove, Wetherby

Rigby, Rev. J., vicar of Hutton-Cranswick, and P.C. of Beswick.
Riley, John, Esq., Hawksclough, Hebden Bridge   [Driffield
Riley, Richard, Esq., Albyn Bank, Preston
Riley, William T., Esq., Ettingshall Villa, Bilston
Ripley, Edward, Esq., Lodge, Bowling, Bradford
Ripley, George Bates, Esq.,   do.   do.
Ripley, John, Esq., Heath Bank, Wallasey, Cheshire
Rippingall, Rev. S. Frost, Langham, near Holt, Norfolk
Rippon, George, Esq., J.P., Water-ville, North Shields
Rishton, W., Esq., Surveyor to the Corporation of Liverpool
Rising, Robert, Esq., The Shrubbery, Worcester
Rising, William, Esq., Somerton Hall, Yarmouth
Ritso, F. Esq., Cley Hall, near Holt
Ritso, Captain John, South Parade, Doncaster
Robb, Major F. C., E.I.C.S., Woolston Lawn, Southampton
Roberson, Rev. F. Berners, M.A., Ovingham, Newcastle-upon-Tyne
Roberson, Henry, Esq., Healds Hall, Liversedge, Leeds
Robert, Joseph Edward, Esq., Solicitor, Delph, Saddleworth
Roberts, Rev. George, Vicar of Monmouth
Roberts, John, Esq., Oakhill, Prestolee, Bolton-le-Moors
Roberts, Richard, Esq., Solicitor, Birmingham
Robertson, Charles, Esq., Deane-Street, Fairfield, Liverpool
Robertson, Rev. Ebenezer, Rector of Mottiston, Isle of Wight
Robertson, George, Esq., Thornton Dale, Pickering
Robins, Foster, and Co., Messrs., East Cornwall Bank, Liskeard
Robins, Thomas, Esq., Liskeard, Cornwall
Robins, William, Esq., J.P., Hagley House, Worcestershire
Robinson, Benjamin, Esq., M.D., Rotherham
Robinson, Benjamin, Lane, Huddersfield
Robinson, Rev. Christopher, M.A. and J.P., Kirknewton, Wooler
Robinson, Edward, jun., Esq., Newport, Isle of Wight
Robinson, George, Esq., Houghton-le-Spring
Robinson, George, Esq., Solicitor, Rotherham
Robinson, Rev. G. Alington, B.A., Rector of Irby-upon-Humber
Robinson, John, Esq., Craven Bank, Skipton
Robinson, John, Esq., South Shields
Robinson, John E., Esq., Coatham, Guisborough
Robinson, Nicholas, Esq., J.P., Sudley, Aigburth, Liverpool
Robinson, Thomas, Esq., Falkner Square, Liverpool
Robinson, Thomas, Esq., Huddersfield
Robinson, Thomas, Esq., Potternewton and Leeds
Robinson, Thomas, Esq., Darlington
Robinson, Thomas, Esq., Harrogate
Robinson, William, Esq., Everton Crescent, Liverpool
Robinson, William, Esq., Summer Hill, Dudley
Robinson, W. Robinson, Esq., Silksworth Hall, Sunderland
Robinson, Rev. W. B., Rector of Littlington, Lewes
Robinson, Rev. W. Scott, Dirham, Gloucestershire
Robley, Rev. J.. St. Philip's, Salford, Manchester   [Tyne
Robson, Rev. Jas. M.A. and J.P., Ponteland, Newcastle-upon-
Robson, Rev. Jacob, B.D., Tyldesley, Manchester
Robson, John, Esq., Hetton, Durham
Robson, John, Esq., Monk-Wearmouth   [Bridge
Robson, Rev. John Evans, M.A., Incumbent of Hartwith, Pateley
Robson, Joseph, Esq., Gateshead Park, Durham
Robson, Thomas, Esq., The Heath, Halifax
Rodgers, Rev. Charles Ebornl, M.A., vicar of Harworth, Bawtry
Rodgers and Sons, Messrs. Joseph, Cutlers, Sheffield, Yorkshire
Rodick, Thomas, Esq., J.P., Gateacre and Challan Hall
Rodwell, George, Esq., Burnham-Deepdale, Norfolk
Rogers, Arundel, Esq., Helston, Cornwall
Rogers, Edward, Esq., St. Michael's, Toxteth Park
Rogers, Henry, Esq., Thetford
Rogers, John Jenkins, Esq., Huntspill Court, Bridgwater
Rogers, Rev. J., M.A., Canon of Exeter, Penrose, Cornwall
Rogers, Rev. J., M.A., Canon of Exeter, Penrose, Cornwall
Rogers, Joseph, Esq., Cross Flatts House, Beeston, Leeds
Rogers, Rev. R., Rector of Yarlington, Somerset
Rogers, Lieutenant-Colonel W. Cooper, Highfield, Southampton
Rogerson, Edward, Esq., Fazakerley, Liverpool
Rogerson, Thomas, Esq., Grove House, Bramley; and Leeds
Rokeby, Langthorn, Esq., Arthingworth Hall, Northampton [Lynn
Rolfe, Rev. S. C. E. N., Vicar of Heacham, Heacham Hall, near
Rolland, Adam, Esq., Luscar House, by Dunfermline, Fife
Rollason, Abel, Esq., Shepherds Green, Erdington
Rolls, Richard Esq., Solicitor, Banbury
Romney, Rev. John, M.A., Cramlington, Newcastle-upon-Tyne
Ronald, R. W., Esq., Bedford-Street South, Liverpool
Ronalds, Henry, Esq., M.D., Primrose Hill House, Coventry
Rooke, Rev. Willoughby, M.A., Old Alresford, Hants
Rooker, James Gates, Esq., Darlaston, Wednesbury
Roots, Dr. William, Surbiton, Kingston-upon-Thames

Roper, John, Esq., York
Roper, Richard, Esq., Solicitor, Kirkby Lonsdale
Roper, Rev. T. A., Clifton, Nottingham
Roper, Rev. T. R., Wick Hill House, Hove, near Brighton
Rose, Sir George, Bart., M.P., Christchurch, Hants
Rose, Rev. Hyla H., M.A., Erdington, Birmingham
Rose, J. C., Esq., Cransley Hall, near Kettering
Rose, Thomas Bailey, Esq., J.P., Barrister-at-Law, Stoke-upon-
[Trent, Staffordshire
Ross, Col. Malcolm Nugent, K.G.F., Astley Hall
Rosson, John, Esq., J.P., Moor Hall, Ormskirk
Rothwell, Peter, Esq., J.P., Sunning Hill, Bolton-le-Moors
Rothwell, W. M., Esq., Sefton, Lancashire
Rothwell, W. Talbot, Esq., Foxholes, Lancaster [House, Settle
Roughsedge, Hornby, Esq., J.P., Foxghyll, Ambleside; and Bentham
Roughton, Rev. Wentworth, M.A., vicar of Great and Little Har-
[rowden, Wellingborough
Roundell, Richard Henry, Esq., J.P., Gledstone, Skipton
Rous, Rev. George, Rector of Laverton, Somersetshire
Rouse, Joshua, Esq., Barkisland, Halifax
Rowden, Rev. F. Marmaduke, B.A., Highworth, Wilts
Rowden, Mr. John, Heytesbury, Wilts
Rowell, Thomas, Esq., Mayor of Hartlepool in 1843
Rowlandson, Rev. Thomas, B.A., Whittle-le-Woods, Chorley
Rowley, Rev. Thomas, D.D., Bridgenorth, Salop
Rowson, William, Esq., Cliffe Villa, New Brighton
Roxby, James William, Esq., J.P., Ogle Terrace, South Shields
Royden, Thomas, Esq., Frankby Hall, West Kirkby, Cheshire
Royds, Rev. Charles Smith, M.A., Rector of Haughton, Stafford
Royds, Edward, Esq., Everton, Liverpool
Royds, Henry, Esq., Everton Village, Liverpool
Royle, Rev. John, Rector of Compton-Martin, Somersetshire
Royston, Aquila E., Esq., West Parade, Halifax
Rudd, Rev. Edward, D.D., Trebartha Hall, Cornwall
Rudd, J. B., Esq., Guisborough
Rufford, H. F., Esq., J.P., Bellbroughton, Stourbridge
Rumbold, C. E., Esq., M.P., Preston-Candover, Hants
Rushton, Rev. William, B.A., Grammar School, Brewood
Russ, Harry, Esq., Castle-Carey, Somerset
Russell and Sons, Messrs., Wednesbury, Staffordshire
Russell, David, Esq., Solicitor, York
Russell, Rev. H. V., Stottesden Vicarage, near Cleobury-Mortimer,
Russell, John, Esq., Leek [Salop
Russell, Jesse Watts, Esq., J.P., Ilam Hall, Ashbourn
Russell, Samuel, Esq., Blyth, Nottinghamshire
Russell, Messrs. Thomas A. and James, Solicitors, Alnwick
Rutherford, Andr., Esq., M.P., Craigie Hall, Cramond, Edinburgh
Rutland, Mrs. Margaret, Testerton House, near Fakenham
Ryall, John, Esq., LL.D., The Ravenhurst, Harborne, Birmingham
Ryall, William, Esq., Butleigh, Somerset
Ryan, Alex., Esq., Toxteth Park, Liverpool
Ryder, Rev. George Dudley, M.A., Rector of Easton, Winchester
Ryder, John, Esq., Bradford, Manchester
Ryle, Matthew, Esq., Herrington Hill, Houghton-le-Spring
Sabden, Rev. James, M.A., Rector of St. Denis, York
Sadler, John, Esq., Percy Banks, North Shields
Sadler, Joseph, Esq., Winterton, Lincolnshire
Sadler, Richard, Esq., Solicitor, Sutton Coldfield
Sainsbury, Rev. Henry, Rector of Beckington, Somersetshire
Sainsbury, Rev. Langford, M.A., Froyle Parsonage, Alton, Hants
Saint Andrews, University of, Scotland
Salisbury, Edward Dodson, Esq., J.P., Middleton Tower, Lancaster
Salmon, Rev. George, M.A., Shustoke, Coleshill
Salt, Thomas, Esq., Weeping Cross, Stafford
Salt, Titus, Esq., Bradford
Salter, Richard, Esq., Arundel, Sussex
Salter, Thomas, Esq., Attleburgh Hall, Norfolk
Salter, Thomas Bell, Esq., M.D. and F.L.S., Ryde, Isle of Wight
Salter, W. P., Esq., New Hall Farm, Whinburgh, Norfolk
Salwey, John, Esq., Moor Park, Ludlow
Sampson, Rev. T., M.A., Eakring Rectory, Ollerton, Notts
Sanctuary, Thomas, Esq., Worthing, Sussex
Sandbach, Samuel, jun., Esq., Handley, Chester
Sanders, Samuel, Esq., Fernhill Park, Isle of Wight
Sanderson, John, Esq., New Hall, Attercliffe, Sheffield
Sanderson, R., Esq., Gunton Park, and Belgrave Square, London
Sanderson, R. Burdon, jun., Esq., West Jesmond, Newcastle
Sanderson, Rev. T., M.A., Head Master of the Grammar School,
[Wellingborough
Sandford, Charles S. R., Esq., Northfield House, Rotherham
Sandford, Rev. John, M.A., vicar of Dunchurch
Sands, Thomas, Esq., Elm Wood, Mosley Hill, Liverpool

Sandys, Carne, and Vivian, Messrs., Hayle, Penzance
Sant, John, Esq., Spondon, Derby
Satterthwaite, Michael, Esq., Preston
Saunders, Henry, Esq., Solicitor, Kidderminster
Saunders, W. A. F., Esq., Wennington Hall, Lancaster
Savage, Son, and Totley, Messrs., Wolverhampton
Savage, Thomas, Esq., Midsomer-Norton, Somerset
Sawle, Sir J. S. Graves, Bart., Penrice, St. Austell, Cornwall
Say, Rev. Henry, Swaffham, Norfolk
Scarbrough, John, Esq., Wintringham, Brigg
Scatchard, John, Esq., East Keswick, Harewood, Yorkshire
Scatcherd, Thomas, Esq., Boston, Tadcaster
Schobell, Rev. John Samuel, B.A., Vicar of St. Kew, Cornwall
Scholefield, Michael, Esq., Manor House, Temple-Newsom, Leeds
Scholefield, Thomas, Esq., Ivy House, Leeds
Scholefield, William, Esq., Batley House, Baildon, Bradford
Scholes, Joseph Seddon, Esq., Slaithwaite, Huddersfield
Scholes, Thomas Seddon, Esq., Banker, Manchester
Scholfield, E., Esq., M.D., Doncaster
Scholfield, William, Esq., Sand Hall, Howden [Steyning, Sussex
Schomberg, Rev. Alexander William, M.A., Rector of Edburton
Scott, Carteret George, Esq., Malleny, Currie, Edinburgh
Scott, Rev. E., St. John's Parsonage, Wakefield, Yorkshire
Scott, Rev. George Henry, M.A., Ifield, near Crawley; Sussex
Scott, Henry E., Esq., Manchester and Leeds Railway, Wakefield
Scott, John, Esq., J.P., Sunderland
Scott, Joseph, Esq., Badsworth Hall, Yorkshire
Scott, Richard, Esq., Solicitor, Sunderland
Scott, W. L. Fenton, Esq., J.P., Wood Hall, Wetherby
Scott, Rev. Walter, S.T.P., Airedale College, Bradford
Scowcroft, Thomas, Esq., Bradshaw Chapel, Bolton-le-Moors
Scroggs, Lieut.-Col., Standen, Chute, Wilts
Sculthorpe, Rev. Clement Fisher, A.M., vicar of Beoley, Redditch
Scurfield, Robert, jun., Esq., Sunderland
Scutt, Thomas W., Esq., Lewes, Sussex
Seagram, E. F., Esq., Bratton House, Westbury, Wilts
Seagram, W. F., Esq., Warminster
Seagrave, Rev. Samuel Young, M.A., Barton Westcott, Woodstock
Seaton, Rev. John, M.A., Incumbent of Cleckheaton, Leeds
Seckerson, Rev. Edward Barlow, M.A., vicar of High Offley,
Seddon, Rev. David, Vicar of Mottram-in-Longdendale [Stafford
Seddon, John, Esq., Breightmet Fold, Bolton-le-Moors
Sedger, Rev. Thomas, M.A., Chaplain of the County Prison, Stafford
Sedgwick, Abraham, Esq., Larch House, Fulwood, Preston
Sedgwick, Rev. Joseph, M.A., vicar of Scalby, Scarborough
Selby, Prideaux, Esq., Swansfield, Alnwick
Selby, Prideaux J., Esq., Twizell House, Belford, Durham
Semple, George, Esq., Shipley Hall, Bradford
Semple, John, Esq., Canning-Street, Liverpool
Senior, Joseph, Esq., Dalton Lodge, Huddersfield
Senior, Joseph, Esq., Batley, Dewsbury
Seppings, Thomas, Esq., Whitehall, Syderstone, Fakenham
Seppings, William, Esq., Lynn
Sergeantson, Rev. R. J., M.A., vicar of Snaith, Yorkshire
Settle, Joseph, Esq., Oxford-Street, Leeds
Sewell, Messrs., Newport, Isle of Wight
Seymour, George Hicks, Esq., Solicitor, York
Seymour, Capt. Michael, R.N., Cadlington, Horndean, Hants
Seymour, Rev. R., M.A., Rural Dean, Kinwarton Rectory, Alcester
Shackleton, John, Esq., Solicitor, Leeds
Shadwell, W. Lucas, Esq., Hastings, Sussex [Durham
Shafto, Rev. Arthur Duncombe, jun., M.A., Houghton-le-Spring,
Shakespear, Samuel, Esq., Soho Glass Works, Birmingham
Shallcross, John, Esq., Breck Road, Everton, Liverpool
Sharp, David Wilkinson, Esq., Bingley, Yorkshire
Sharp, Rev. John, D.D., Vicar of Doncaster
Sharp, Rev. John, M.A., Incumbent of Horbury, Wakefield
Sharp, John, Esq., Mayor of Lancaster, 1847
Sharp, William, Esq., The Larches, Birmingham
Sharpe, Edmund, Esq., Architect, Lancaster
Sharpe, Rev. F. W., B.A., Tibshelf Vicarage, Alfreton
Sharpe, Samuel, Esq., Docking, Rougham, Norfolk
Sharwood, Rev. John Hodges, M.A., Rowley Regis, Dudley
Shattock, John Esq., Bishop's-Lydeard, Taunton
Shaw, Benjamin L., Esq., Honley, Huddersfield
Shaw, Henry Ossea, Esq., Bury, Lancashire
Shaw, James, Esq., Park Grove, Edgbaston, Birmingham
Shaw, John, Esq., Wolverhampton
Shaw, J. R., Esq., J.P., Arrowe Hall, Birkenhead
Shaw, Messrs. Peter and Son, Micklehurst, Mossley
Shaw, Peter, Esq., Croft Mill, Bottoms, Ashton-under-Lyne
Shaw, Richard, Esq., Seaforth, Liverpool

Shaw, Thomas, Esq., M.A,. Everton, Liverpool
Shaw, William, Esq., Everton Village, Liverpool
Shaw, William, Esq., Miluthorp Cottage, Wakefield
Shaw, William, Esq., Seed Hill, Holmfirth, Yorkshire
Shaw, Mr. W., St. John's Common, Keymer, near Brighton
Shebbear, Joseph Charles, Esq., Basingstoke
Shedden, Captain Lewis, Bittern Manor House, Southampton
Sheehan, John, Esq., Litherland, Liverpool
Sheepshanks, The Rev. and Ven. John, Archdeacon of Cornwall
SHEFFIELD, The Right Honourable the Earl of
Shelley, Rev. John, A.B., Kingsley, Cheadle
Shelley, John Villiers, Esq., Maresfield Park, near Uckfield, Sussex
Shelley, Sir Thomas, Bart., Field Place, near Horsham
Shelton, Charles Jackson, Esq., Bradford
Shephard, John, Esq., Doctors Commons, London
Shepherd, John, jun., Esq., St. Mark's Villa, Woodhouse, Leeds
Shepherd, R., Esq., Solicitor, Driffield
Shepherd, Rev. Robert, M.A., Houghton-le-Spring
Shepherd, Rev. Samuel, B.A., North Somercoates, Louth
Shepherd and Simpson, Messrs., Solicitors, Beverley
Shepherd, Rev. Thomas H., Rector of Clayworth, Bawtry
Shepherd, William, Esq., Solicitor, Barnsley
Sheppard, George, Esq., Fromefield House, near Frome, Somerset
Sheppard, John, Esq., South Hill, Liverpool
Sheppard, Sir Thomas Cotton, Bart., Crakemarsh Hall, Uttoxeter
Sherard, Philip Castel, Esq., Glaton, near Stilton, Hunts
Sherborne, King's School Library
Sherburne, Rev. Thomas, P.P., The Willows, Kirkham
Sheriffe, Rev. T., jun., M.A., Henstead Hall, Wrentham, Suffolk
Sherlock, Rev. Harold H., M.A., Ashton-le-Willows, Warrington
Sherlock, Sidney, Esq., Woodside, Halewood, Liverpool
Sherson, Rev. Robert, M.A., Oxon, Rector of Yaverland
Sherwin, J. Sherwin, Esq., Bramcote Hills, Nottingham
Sherwood, Rev. T. M., Pauntley, Newent, Gloucester
Sherwood, William Stacey, Esq., Architect and Surveyor, Liverpool
Sherwood, Rev. William, B.A., Holybourne, Alton, Hants
Shevill, John Heppell, Esq., Sunderland
Shield, Robert Spencer, Esq., Chester-le-Street
Shields, William, Esq., Gateshead, Durham
Shipley, Joseph, Esq., Wyncote, Allerton
Shipperdson, Rev. Thomas R., M.A., Vicar of Woodhorn, Morpeth
Shirley, Charles, Esq., Midhurst, Sussex
Shirreff, Rev. R. St. John, B.A., Oxon, Blackheath
Shirt, John, Esq., Wales, Sheffield
Shooter, Rev. J., M.A., Vicar of Bishop-Wilton, York
Short, Rev. John Holbeache, M.A., Chaplain of Temple Balsall,
Short, Lieut.-Col. Robert, E.I.C.S., Solihull   [Knowle
Short, Wm., Esq., Toxteth Park, Liverpool
Shorter and Phillips, Messrs., Hastings, Sussex
Shrubb, Rev. Charles, M.A., Vicar of Boldre, Lymington, Hants
Shuckburgh, Sir Francis, Bart., Shuckburgh Park, Warwickshire
Shuckburgh, Mrs., Bourton Hall, Dunchurch
Shutt, Isaac Thomas, Esq., Architect, Low-Harrogate
Siddons, Samuel, Esq., West Bank, Mansfield
Sidebotham, Edward Lowe, Esq., J.P., Aston Hall, Sheffield
Sidebottom, Edward, Esq., Pleadwick Hall, Wakefield
Sidebottom, W., Esq., J.P., Etherow House, Hollingworth, Mottram
Siely, B. C., Esq., Beech Grove, North Walsham
Sigston, William, Esq., Gomersal Hall, Leeds
Sillick, James, Esq., Claremont Place, Newcastle-upon-Tyne
Silver, Rev. Thomas, LL.D., vicar of Charlbury, Oxon
Silvester, Alfred, Esq., Alder House, Atherton, Manchester
Simcoe, Rev. Henry, A., Penheale, Launceston, Cornwall
Simcox, Thomas, Esq., Yew Tree Cottage, Birmingham
Simcox, Rev. Thomas Green, M.A., vicar of North Harborne
Simes, F., Esq., Townend House, Bradford
Simes, Mr. Henry, Vine Hall, near Robertsbridge, Battle
Simpson and Frear, Messrs., Solicitors, Derby
Simpson, Alfred, Esq., Solicitor, Malton
Simpson, Christopher, Esq., East Halton. Skipton
Simpson, Rev. Fred. R., M.A., North Sunderland, Belford
Simpson, Rev. G. F., M.A., Principal of the College, Malton-
                                               [upon-Hull
Simpson, Rev. John, Vicarage, Acklam, Malton
Simpson, Rev. John Pemberton, M.A., Wakefield
Simpson, Joseph Pringle, Esq., Springwell, Bishop-Wearmouth
Simpson, Rev. M., Rector of Mickfield, Stonham, Suffolk
Simpson, Rev. Philip, M.A., Copthorne, Fawley, Hants
Simpson, Robert, Esq., Alnmouth, Alnwick
Simpson, Rev. R. Hutchinson, M.A., Vicar of Monks-Kirby, &c.,
Simpson, Samuel, Esq., The Greaves, Lancaster   [Coventry
Simpson, Rev.Thos., M.A., Perpetual Curate of Cold Kirby, Thirsk
Simpson, Thomas, Esq., M.D., York

Simpson, Rev. William, M.A., Incumbent of Tanfield, Durham
Sinclair, Archibald, Esq., Hill-Side House, Wavertree, Liverpool
Sinclair, Sir John Gordon, Bart., Stevenson House, Haddington
Sinclair, Rev. W., M.A.. Incumbent of St. George's, Leeds
Singleton, John, Esq., Carr House, Rotherham
Siny, Joshua, Esq., Bridgenorth, Salop
Siny, William, Esq., Swancote, Bridgenorth
Sittzer, D., Esq., Rhodes House, Middleton, Manchester
Sitwell, Edward Degge, Esq., Stainsby House, Derby
Sivewright, Charles Kane, Esq., Musbury, Axminster, Devon
Skelley, Thomas, Esq., Freelands, Alnwick
Skelton, Charles Jackson, Esq., Manor-Street, Bradford
Skelton, John, Esq., Field Head, Thorner, Leeds
Skelton, John, Esq., Moor-Allerton House, Leeds
Skelton, Rev. Joseph, M.A., Vicar of Wold-Newton, Hunmanby
Skelton, Rev. Robert, M.A., Rector of Levisham, Pickering
Skey, Robert S., Esq., Newport, Salop
Skidmore, John, Esq., Handsworth, Birmingham
Skirving, W., Esq., Spellow House, Walton-on-the-Hill, Liverpool
Slack, Rev. Sam., M.A., Head Master, Grammar School, Bradford
Slade, Rev. Canon, M.A., Vicarage, Bolton-le-Moors
Slade, Rev. Henry Rapes, D.D., Rector of Kenley, Salop, and Chap-
                        [lain to the Earl of Clarendon
Slade, Mr. Henry, Edington, Westbury, Wilts
Sladen, Thomas, Esq., Mearclough House, Halifax
Slater, Messrs. G. and J., Duncear, Turton, Bolton-le-Moors
Slater, John, Esq., Bleacher, Back o' th' Bank, Bolton-le-Moors
Slater, Joseph, Esq., Duncear, Turton, Bolton-le-Moors
Slater, Rev.Thos. Augustine, R.C.P., Hutton House, Castle Eden
Slatter, Thomas, Esq., Solicitor, Stratford-on-Avon
Slatter, William, Esq., Surgeon, Wakefield
Sleigh, Major-Gen., Shirley House, near Southampton
Slight, Lewis, Esq., Brighton, Sussex
Smalman, John, Esq., Quatford Castle, Bridgenorth
Smart, Daniel, Esq., Emsworth, near Chichester
Smart, John, Esq., Prospect Vale, Liverpool
Smeddle, R., Esq., Bamburgh Castle, Belford
Smetham, J. Esq., Lynn, Norfolk
Smethurst, Richard, Esq., Park Place, Chorley
Smith, Bartholomew, Esq., Timsbury, near Bath
Smith, Bassett, Esq., District Bank, Birmingham
Smith, Charles, Esq., Bearwood House, Erdington, Warwickshire
Smith, Lieut.-Col. Charles, Plainville, York
Smith, Charles Sergison, Esq., Farleigh House, Basingstoke
Smith, Edward, Esq., Armfield Plain. Gateshead
Smith, Rev. Edward Herbert, B.A., Killamarsh, Chesterfield
Smith, George Nicholson, Esq., Surgeon, Goole
Smith, George Pyemont. Esq., M.D., Park Row, Leeds
Smith, Mr. George, Camborne, Cornwall
Smith, George, jun., Esq., Beech Grove, Preston
Smith, Henry, Esq., Snitterfield Wolds, Stratford-on-Avon
Smith, Rev. Hen. Jno., M.A., Incumbent of Birkenshaw, nr. Leeds
Smith, Messrs. Henry and Co., Vulcan Forge, West Bromwich
Smith, James, Esq., Solicitor, Leigh, Manchester
Smith, Rev. J. T. H., M.A., Floore, Northamptonshire
Smith, Rev. Jeremiah, D.D., Brewood and Leamington
Smith, Jeremiah, Esq., Springfield Villa, near Rye, Sussex
Smith, John, Esq., Field House, Horton, Bradford
Smith, John, Esq., Morton, Bingley
Smith, John, Esq.,Weyhill House, Andover, Hants
Smith, John, Esq., St. Anne's, Lewes, Sussex
Smith, Rev. John, Formby, Liverpool
Smith, John, Esq., The Poplars, Birmingham
Smith, John Ashmore. Esq., Solicitor, Hinckley
Smith, John Francis, Esq., Whitbourne Court, Worcester
Smith, John Samuel, Esq., Elm House, Toxteth Park, Liverpool
Smith, Rev. John Tetley, Repton, near Burton-upon-Trent
Smith, John William, Esq., J.P., Oundle, Northamptonshire
Smith, Joseph, Esq., Low Street, Keighley
Smith, Rev. Joseph, Brindle, Preston   [pool
Smith, Joseph, Esq., Warbreck Moor, Walton-on-the-Hill, Liver-
Smith, Lawrence, Esq., Mount Villa, Hurst-Pierepoint, Sussex
Smith, Noel Thomas, Esq., M.D., Newcastle-upon-Tyne
Smith, Richard, Esq., Priory, Dudley
Smith, Rev. Robert, Chaplain at Haggerston Castle, Berwick
Smith, Robert, Esq., Oldcoates, Tickhill
Smith, Rev. Robert, M.A., Kyloe, Belford
Smith, Sampson, Esq., Everton Road, Liverpool
Smith, Samuel, Esq., Darleston, Wednesbury
Smith, Rev. Samuel, M.A., Grindleton, Clitheroe
Smith, Mrs. S, Mackworth, Bersted Lodge, Bognor
Smith, Spencer, Esq., Brooklands, Southampton
Smith, Stephen, Esq., Brown's Place, Robert's Bridge, near Battle

Smith, Tilden, Esq., Vine Hall, near Battle, Sussex
Smith, Thomas, Esq., M.D., Leeds
Smith, Thomas George, Esq., Togston House, Alnwick
Smith, Thompson, Esq., Willington Quay, Newcastle-upon-Tyne
Smith, Walker, Esq., Brotherton, Ferrybridge
Smith, William, Esq., Learmouth, Coldstream
Smith, William, Esq., Benton Lodge, Newcastle-upon-Tyne
Smith, William, Esq., Mayor of Leeds
Smith, Rev. William Henry, M.A., Hinderwell, Guisborough
Smith, William, Esq., Potton, Bedfordshire
Smith, Sir William, Bart., Erdiston House, Worcester
Smith and Summerhill, Messrs., Brockmoor Works, Stourbridge
Smithson, Charles, Esq., Solicitor, Malton
Smithson, Robert, Esq., Holtby Hall, York
Smithson, Samuel, Esq., Heighington, Darlington
Smyth, Rev. C., M.A., Little Houghton, Northamptonshire
Smyth, Rev. George Watson, M.A., Rector of Fyfield, Hants
Smyth, John George, Esq., J.P., Heath Hall, Wakefield
Smyth, Rev. T. Graham, Aldwick Lodge, near Bognor
Smythe, Rev. Patrick Murray, M.A., Tanworth, Henley-in-Arden
Smythe, William Meade, Esq., Deer Park, Honiton, Devon
Snell, Robert, Esq., Wellington Place, Leyland, Chorley
Sneyd, Rev. John, M.A. and J.P., Basford Hall, Leek
Sneyd, William, Esq., Ashcomb, Leek
SODOR AND MAN, The late Right Rev. Lord Bishop of [wick
Somerville, The Hon. and Rev. Wm., M.A., Rector of Barford, War-
Sorby, James, Esq., Gatefield House, Sheffield
Sorsbie, Malin, Esq., Deckham Hall, Gateshead
Southall, Rev. Henry, B.A., Bishampton, Evesham
SOUTHAMPTON, Right Honourable Lord
SOUTHWELL, The Right Hon. Lord Viscount
Southwells and Co., Messrs., Bridgenorth
Sowerby, J. N. P., Esq., Solicitor, Stokesley
Sowerby, Thomas, Esq., Saltwell Vale, Gateshead
Spackman, Charles, Esq., Bradford, Wilts
Sparke, Rev. E. B., Feltwell Rectory, near Brandon
Sparke, Rev. J. H., Gunthorpe, near East Dereham, Norfolk
Sparrow, Charles Frederick, Esq., Solicitor, Wolverhampton
Sparrow, James, Esq., Rye, Sussex
Sparrow, John, Esq., Bramshott Place, Liphook, Hants
Speck, Rev. T., Chichester, Sussex
Speke, Rev. Hugh, M.A., Rector of Dowlish-Wake, Somerset
Spence, Rev. Hugh Maltby, M.A., Rural Dean, and Vicar of West
Spence, Rev. J., M.A., Culworth, Banbury   [Hadden, Daventry
Spence, Rev. John, M.A., Rectory, East Keal, Lincolnshire
SPENCER, The Right Honourable Earl
Spencer, Rev. Charles John, Radwell Rectory, near Baldock, Herts
Spencer, George, Esq., North Gate House, Keighley
Spencer, Rev. Isaac, M.A., The Plantation, York
Spencer, Rev. James, Turton, Bolton-le-Moors   [Tyne
Spencer, John, jun., Esq., Newburn Steel Works, Newcastle-upon-
Spencer, Thomas, Esq., Moat Forge, Tipton
Spencer, William, Esq., South Bank, Edgbaston
Spencer, Rev. William, M.A., Vicar of Dronfield, Sheffield
Spencer, Rev. W. Pakenham, M.A., Rector of Starston, Norfolk
Spilsbury, Rev. Francis Ward, M.A., Willington, Derby
Spode, Mrs., Armitage Park, near Rugeley, Staffordshire
Spooner, The Venerable William, M.A., Archdeacon of Coventry,
                                    [Elmdon, Warwickshire
Sport, Rev. Augustus, M.A., Rural Dean and Vicar, Ravensthorpe,
                                    [Northampton
Spurgeon, Rev. Richard, Rector of Mulbarton, near Norwich
Spurrell, Rev. B., M.A., Deddington, Oxon
Spurrell, D., Esq., Bessingham, near Aylsham, Norfolk
Spurrell, W. D., Esq., Thurgarton,   do.
Spink, George, Esq., Solicitor, Howden
Spink, Henry Hawks, Esq., Tadcaster
Spours, W., Esq., Solicitor, Alnwick
Squires, Richard, Esq., Everton Brow, Liverpool
ST. GERMANS, The Right Honourable the Earl of
St. John, The Hon. Gen., Rough Heath, near Chailey, Lewes
St. John, Rev. H. G., M.A., West Court, Wokingham, Berks
St. Quintin, Thomas, jun., Esq., Hatley Park, Cambridgeshire
St. Quintin, William, Esq., Scampton Hall, Malton
Stables, George, Esq., Solicitor, Horsforth, Leeds
Stables, Henry, Esq., Lockwood House, Huddersfield
Stables, W. W., Esq., Crosland Hall,   do.
Stackhouse, Anthony, Esq., Stainforth, Settle
Staff, J. R., Esq., Norwich
STAFFORD, The Right Honourable Lord
Stafford, W. W., Esq., Hailsham, Sussex
Stagg, Joseph Dickinson, Esq., Middleton, Barnard-Castle
Staincliffe, John, Esq., Over Hall, Mirfield, Dewsbury

Stallard, John, Esq., Worcester
Stamp and Tax Office, Her Majesty's, Edinburgh
Standish, Standish W., Esq., J.P., Duxbury Park, Chorley
Staniford, F., Esq., Eldon Place, Newcastle-upon-Tyne
Staniland, George A., Esq., Brotherton House, Ferrybridge
Staniland, Samuel, Esq., Leeds
Stanley, John, Esq., Newport, Salop
Stanley, Mr. Thomas, Burbage Wharf, near Marlborough, Wilts
Stansfeld, George Micklethwait, Esq., Bradford
Stansfield, James, Esq., Greenbank, Halifax
Stansfield, James, Esq., Solicitor, Ewood, Todmorden
Stanton, Edward D., Esq., Solicitor, Chorley
Starkey, John Jackson, Esq., Canning-Street, Liverpool
Starkey, William, Esq., Wakefield
Starking, Richard, Esq., Heaton Grove, Bury, Lancashire
STATIONERY OFFICE, Her Majesty's
Statter, Robert, Esq., Knowsley, Liverpool
Statter, Thomas, Esq., Stand Hall, Bury, Lancashire
Statter, W., Esq., Wakefield
Staveley, Capt. John, Wales, Sheffield
Stavert, William, Esq., The Hill, Kirkham
Stead, Henry, Esq., Newlaiths, Horsforth, Leeds
Stead, Henry Cox Mason, Esq., Low-Harrogate
Stead, James Fishwick, Esq., Prospect Vale, Liverpool
Stead, Samuel, Esq., Crow Trees, Gomersal, Leeds
Steel, John, Esq., Bradford
Steers, Spencer, Esq., Halewood Green, Liverpool
Stephen, Oscar Leslie, Esq., Trindle House, Dudley
Stephens, Mr. John, Hurcott, near South Petherton, Somerset
Stephens, Rev. Richard, Culvert House, Exeter
Stephens, Thomas, Esq., North Shields
Stephens, Mr. Thomas, White Lackington, Somerset
Stephens, Thomas, Esq., Kensington, Liverpool
Stephenson, Appleton, Esq., Hawsker Hall, Whitby   [Tyne
Stephenson, Robert, and Co., Messrs., Engineers, Newcastle-upon-
Stephenson, William, Esq., Lands House, Holmfirth
Stevens, E., Esq., Watton, Norfolk   [Rollright, Oxon
Stevens, Rev. W. Everett, M.A., Rector of Salford and Little
Stevenson, Mr. Andrew, Kemnay, Kintore, Aberdeenshire
Stevenson, John, Esq., Preston
Steward, Rev. Francis, Rector of Barking, Needham-Market, Suffolk
Stewart, Henry Alexander, Esq., Breeze Hill, Walton-on-the-Hill,
Stewart, John, Esq., Binny House, Uphall, Linlithgow [Liverpool
Stileman, Richard, Esq., The Friars, Winchelsea, Sussex
Stillingfleet, Rev. E. W., B.D., Hotham Cave, Yorkshire
Stitt, James, Esq., Islington, Liverpool
Stockdale, Rev. Henry, B.A., Bawtry
Stockdale, Rev. Walter, B.A., Linwood, Market-Rasen
Stocken, Rev. H., M.A., Incumbent of Arkendale, Knaresborough
Stocker, Rev. W. H. Browell, Incumbent of Horsforth, Leeds ›
Stocks, Joseph, Esq., Upper Shibden Hall, Halifax
Stocks, Robert, Esq., Abden, Kinghorn
Stogdon, Rev. Abraham Horwill, B.A., St. Peter's, Walsall
Stokes, John, Esq., Dunstall Hill, Wolverhampton
Stokes, William, Esq., Willenhall, Walsall
Stone, Charles, Esq., Prebendal House, Thame, Oxon
Stone, Rev. D. S., Walkhampton, near Tavistock
Stone, George, Esq., Taunton, Somerset
Stone, W. T., Esq., Stone Bridge, near Uckfield, Sussex
Storey, Ralph, Esq., Beanley, Alnwick
Storrs, Robert, Esq., Doncaster
Story, Henry, Esq., Solicitor, Newcastle-upon-Tyne
Story, John Bainbridge, Esq., Lockington Hall, Leicestershire
Stott, Henry H., Esq., Newfield, near Haslingden
Stott, Lieut.-Col., E.I.S., Eccleshill Hall, Bradford
Stott, Richard, Esq., South Cottage, Rochdale
Stott, William, Esq., Kersley Mount, Bolton
Stowey, Augustus, Esq., Kenbury, Exminster, Devon
Stracey, John, Esq., Sprowston, near Norwich
Strachan, Ralph, Esq., Kirkliston, Edinburgh
Straker, John, Esq., Point Pleasant, Newcastle-upon-Tyne
Strakers and Love, Messrs., Howdon Dock,   do.
Stratton, John, Esq., Turweston House, Brackley
Stratton, William, Esq., Upavon, Pewsey, Wilts
Streatfeild, R. Shuttleworth, Esq., The Rocks, near Uckfield, Sussex
Strickland, Walter, Esq., Sizergh Castle, Kendal
Stringer, James, Esq., Sand Rock, New Brighton
Stringer, Rev. Thomas, M.A., St. Ann's, Liverpool
Strode, R. C., Esq., Southill House, West Cranmore, Somerset
Strong, P. B., Esq., Trull, Somerset
Strong, Rev. Richard, Horwich, Bolton-le-Moors
Strutt, Jedediah, Esq., J.P., Green Hall, Belper, Derbyshire
Stubbs, John, Esq., Hamstead, Perry Barr, Birmingham

Stubbs, Rev. Jonathan Kirk, M.A., Incumbent of Measham, Ather-
Stubbs, Walter, Esq., Wroxeter and Haye Park, Salop [stone
Sturges, John William, Esq., Beech Field, Doncaster
Sturgis, Rev. Frederick George, Brandsburton, Beverley
Suckling, Rev. Alfred, LL.B., Rectory, Barsham, Beccles, Suffolk
Suckling, John, Esq., Solicitor, Birmingham
Sugden, Joah, Esq., Spring Field House, Huddersfield
Sugden, John Greenwood, Esq., Steeton Hall, Keighley
Sugden, Thomas, Esq., Brighouse, Halifax
Sugden, William, Esq., Eastwood House, Keighley
Sulivan, George James, Esq., Wilbury Park, Amesbury, Wilts
Summerfield, H., Esq., Banker, Warwick
Sumner, Gillyatt, Esq., Woodmansey, Beverley
Sunderland, Rev. S., B.A., Peniston, Barnsley
Sutcliffe, John Crossley, Esq., Lee, Hebden-Bridge
Sutcliffe, John F., Esq., Willow Hall, Halifax
Sutcliffe, Richard, Esq., Lumb Bank, Hebden-Bridge
Sutcliffe, Thomas, Esq., Stoneshay Gate, do.
Sutcliffe, William, Esq., Lower Laith, Todmorden
Sutcliffe, Rev. William, M.A., Weeton, Kirkham
Sutherland, A. J., Esq., Christ-church College, Oxford
Sutherland, A. R., Esq., M.D., F.R.S., F.G.S., 1, Parliament-
Street, London, and Silver Hill, Torquay, Devon
Sutton, H. H., Esq., Fairfield, Liverpool
Sutton, Rev. T. Manners, M.A., Averham Rectory, Newark
Sutton, William Sims, Esq., Solicitor, Birmingham
Swainson, Rev. Charles Litchfield, B.D., Rector of Crich, Daventry
Swainson, Charles, Esq., J.P., Cooper Hill, Walton-le-Dale
Swainson, Charles, jun., Esq., Frenchwood, Preston
Swainson, John, Esq., Aigburth, Liverpool
Swainson, Rev. John, B.A., Old Byland and Kirkdale, Helmsley
Swale, Rev. H. John, M.A., Ingfield, Settle
Swallow, John, jun., Esq., Sterne Mill, Halifax
Swallow, Richard, Esq., Mosborough Hill, Sheffield
Swan, William Robert, Esq., Solicitor, Newcastle-upon-Tyne
Swann, John, Esq., Hutton Hall, York
Swayne, W. C., Esq., Heytesbury, Wilts
Sweet, Rev. Charles B., M.A., Broadleigh, Somerset
Sweetland, William, Esq., Staplake Mount, Starcross, Devon
Syers, Daniel Backhouse, Esq., Walton-on-the-Hill
Sykes, John, Esq., Beech Grove, Leeds
Sykes, Joseph, Esq., Acre Cottage, Lindley, Huddersfield
Sykes, Matthew, Esq., Milas Bridge, Huddersfield
Sykes, Sir Tatton, Bart., Sledmere House, Yorkshire
Sykes, William, Esq., Solicitor, Leeds
Sykes, William, Esq., Mill Bridge, Leeds, Yorkshire
Sykes, Rev. William, vicar of Collumpton, Devon
Symes, Thomas, Esq., Bridgwater, Somerset
Symons, Henry, Esq., Axbridge, Somerset
Sympson, Edmund Walcott, Esq., Winkton, Hants
Syms, Rev. W., West Grinstead, near Horsham, Sussex [School
Tait, Rev. Archibald Campbell, D.C.L., Head Master of Rugby
TALBOT, The Right Honourable the Earl
Talbot, John, Esq., Woodland House, Ashill, near Taunton
Tanner, Henry, Esq., Bishop-Wearmouth
Tanner, Mr. Joseph, Cholderton, Wilts
Tanner, Rev. Thomas, M.A., Incumbent of Bradninch, Devon
Tarleton, Thomas, Esq., Greenwich, Walton, Liverpool
Tate, Captain W. A., E.I.C.S., East Harptree, Somerset
Tate, Rev. William Bunting, M.A., Vicar of Nether Wallop, Hants
Tatham, John, Esq., Canal Bank, Liverpool
Taunton, G. E., Esq., Upper Canning-Street, Liverpool
Taylor, Edward, Esq., Kirkham Abbey, Whitwell, Yorkshire
Taylor, George, Esq., Solicitor, Stalybridge
Taylor, Rev. Harrison, M.A., Treeton, Rotherham
Taylor, Herbert, Esq., M.D., Uttoxeter House, Staffordshire
Taylor, James, Esq., D.L., Moseley Hall, Birmingham
Taylor, James, Esq., J.P., The Hall, Todmorden
Taylor, John, Esq., Castle Eden, Durham
Taylor, John, Esq., Silverwell House, Bolton
Taylor, Rev. Mascie Domville, Lymme Hall, Warrington
Taylor, Rev. Robert, M.A., Incumbent of Hartlepool
Taylor, Robert, Esq., Treeton, Rotherham
Taylor, Rev. Robert, M.A., Rector of Clifton-Campville, Tamworth
Taylor, Robert, Esq., Warbreck Moor, Walton-on-the-Hill, Liver-
Taylor, Thomas, Esq., J.P., Wigan [pool
Taylor, Thomas, Esq., Dudworth, Barnsley
Taylor, Thomas, Esq., St. John's, Wakefield
Taylor, Thomas, Esq., Long Benton, Newcastle-upon-Tyne
Taylor, Thomas, Esq., Cricklade, Wilts
Taylor, Thos. Lambe, Esq., Starston Place, near Harlestone, Norfolk
Taylor, Rev. W. R., Holt, Norfolk

Taylor, William, Esq., J.P., Moss Cottage, Preston
Taylor, Rev. W. Addington, B.A., Rector of Litchborough, Tow-
Taylor, William, Esq., Pembroke Place, Liverpool [cester
Taylor, William Bewley, Esq., Brooms, near Stone
Tayton, William, Esq., Pattesley House, near Rougham
Teal, Henry, Esq., Stourton Lodge, Rothwell, Leeds
Teale, Edward J., Esq., Solicitor, Leeds
Teale, William, Esq., do. do.
Tee, Charles, Esq., Pindar Oaks, Barnsley
Teed, Rev. Frederick, B.A., Rector of St.Michael's, Lewes, Sussex
Teesdale, Christopher, Esq., Sudley Cottage, near Bognor, Sussex
Teesdale, Symes, and Weston, Messrs., Fenchurch-Street, London
Tempest, Col. J. Plumbe, Tong Hall, Leeds
Temple, William, Esq., Bishopstrow House, near Warminster
Templer, James, Esq., Bridport, Dorset
Templer, Rev. G. H., M.A., Shapwick, Glastonbury, Somerset
Tench, Rev. John, B.D., Rector of Great Rollright, Oxon
Tennant, Charles A., Esq., Solicitor, Dewsbury
Tennant, John C., Esq., Roby, Liverpool
Tennant, Rev. Ottiwell, Rector of Upton, Hunts
TENTERDEN, The Right Honourable Lord
Terrell, William, Esq., Stoke-under-Hamdon, Yeovil, Somerset
Terry, Stephen, Esq., Dummer House, Basingstoke
Tetley, Richard, Esq., Fremont, West Derby, Liverpool
Tetley, Thomas William, Esq., Everton, Liverpool
Tewart, John, Esq., Glanton, Alnwick
Thacker, William, Esq., Muchall Hall, Penn, Staffordshire
Thew, Edward, jun., Esq., Lesbury House, Alnwick
Thistlethwaite, Rev. George, M.A., Ribby, Kirkham
Thoburn, James, Esq., Paradise Row, Blyth
Thomas, Edwin, Esq., Worcester
Thomas, Francis Henry, Esq., Hereford
Thomas Inigo, Esq., Ratton, near Eastbourne
Thomas, Joshua, Esq., Town Clerk, Tewkesbury
Thomas, William, Esq., M.D., Wakefield
Thomas, Rev. W. P., LL.B., Drake's Place, Wellington, Somerset
Thompson, Arthur, Esq., Oxford-Street, Liverpool
Thompson, Benjamin Blaydes, Esq., Solicitor, Tadcaster
Thompson, Benjamin, Esq., Park Gate, Guiseley, Leeds
Thompson, Charles F., Esq., Green Mount Hall, Manchester
Thompson, Corden, Esq., M.D., Sheffield
Thompson, Edward, Esq., Salters' Hall, London
Thompson, Rev. F., LL.B., Carham, Coldstream
Thompson, Rev. F. B., B.A., Eaglescliffe, Yarm
Thompson, George, Esq., Sunderland
Thompson, Rev. Sir Hen., Bart., M.A., Holy Trinity, Fareham, Hants
Thompson, H. Stafford, Esq., Fairfield, York
Thompson, James, Esq., Wakefield
Thompson, John, Esq., Solicitor, Sheffield
Thompson, Rev. Joseph, M.A., Satley, Wolsingham
Thompson, Joseph, Esq., Bradford, Yorkshire [upon-Hull
Thompson, Rev. Joseph, M.A., Incumbent of Marfleet, Kingston-
Thompson, Robert, Esq., Clerk to the Union, Thistleton in Kirk-
Thompson, Rev. William, B.A., Rector of Addingham, Skipton [ham
Thompson, William, Esq., Lewes, Sussex
Thomsett, William, Esq., Halford, Warwickshire
Thomson, Rev. George Selby, M.A., Rothbury
Thornborrow, William, Esq., Bridge Cottage, Roughton, Paxton
Thornely, John, Esq., J.P., Dodworth Green, Barnsley
Thornewill, John, Esq., Solicitor, and Clerk to the Magistrates,
[Burton-on-Trent
Thornhill, Thomas, Esq., Woodleys, Woodstock, Oxon [pool
Thornhill, Wilkinson, Esq., St. Clement's Terrace, Windsor, Liver-
Thorns, Joseph, Esq., Green House, Ossett, Wakefield
Thornton, Henry, Esq., Montpelier Terrace, Liverpool
Thornton, Stephen, Esq., Moggerhanger House, St. Neot's
Thornton, Mrs., The Elms, West Derby
Thorold, Sir John C., Bart., Syston Park, Grantham
Thorold, Richard, Esq., J.P., Weelsby, Great Grimsby
Thorold, W. M., Esq., Wigthorpe, Worksop, Notts
Thorp, Rev. Charles, M.A., Sandford, near Enstone, Oxon
Thorp, Rev. Henry, M.A., Perpetual Curate of Topsham, Devon
Thorp, Richard, Esq., Monk Bretton, Barnsley
Thorpe, William, Esq., Solicitor, Thorne
Threlfall, Richard, Esq., Ribblesdale Place, Preston
Thring, Rev. W. D., D.D., Rector of Sutton-Veny, Warminster
Thruston, John, Esq., Weston Hall, Harling, Norfolk
Thursfield, Rev. R. P., Heckbury, Shiffnall, Salop
Thurston and Liddle, Messrs., Newport, Salop
Thwaite, Samuel, Esq., Woodlands, Halifax
Thwaites, J. B., Esq., Paradise House, Burnham, Bridgwater
Tibbits, James, Esq., Town Clerk of Warwick .1

Wheatley, William, Esq., Royds House, Hopton, Mirfield, Dews-
Wheeler, Rev. Daniel, Blagdon, Somerset   [bury
Wheeler, Henry, Esq., Middleton, Manchester
Wheldon, Thomas, Esq., Solicitor, Barnard-Castle
Wheler, Rev. H. Trevor, M.A., Berkley Rectory, Frome, Somerset
Whichcote, Sir T., Bart., Aswarby Park, Falkingham, Lincolnshire
Whitacre, John, Esq., Wood House, Huddersfield
Whitaker, Alfred, Esq., Frome, Somersetshire
Whitaker, Frederick, Esq., Bampton, Oxon
Whitaker, Rev. G. H., M.A., Vicar of Garforth, Leeds
Whitaker, James, Esq., Bramham, Tadcaster
Whitaker, James, Esq., J.P., Broadclough, Rochdale
Whitaker, Rev. John Fielding, St. Joseph's, Liverpool
Whitaker, Jonas, Esq., J.P., Greenholme, Otley
Whitaker, Joshua, Esq., Ossett, Wakefield
Whitaker, Rev. Thos. W., M.A., The Rectory, Stainton-by-Bridge,
Whitby, William, Esq., Prospect Vale, Liverpool   [Derby
White, David B., Esq., M.D., Newcastle-upon-Tyne
White, Capt. Frederick, Saxby Hall, Barton-upon-Humber
White, Rev. James, B.A., Wood Lynch, Bonchurch, Isle of Wight
White, James, Esq., Wooldringfold, Horsham, Sussex
White, Rev. J. Neville, B.D., Rector of Tivetshall, Norfolk
White, John, Esq., Upper Wood House, Rawdon, Leeds
White, John, Esq., Warden of Whixley Hospital, York
White, Joseph, Esq., Anfield House, Romsey, Hants
White, Robert, Esq., Woodhouse Grove, Leeds
White, Thomas W., Esq., Nursling, Southampton
White, Rev. William, M.A., Vicar of Stradbroke, Suffolk
White, William Lambert, Esq., Yeovil, Somerset
Whitehead, Rev. James, Broomfield, Ainsworth, Bolton-le-Moors
Whitehead, John, Esq., Harlem Hey, Elton, Bury
Whitehead, John, Esq., Cambridge
Whitehead, Matthias, Esq., J.P., The Crescent, Selby   [worth
Whitehead, Ralph Radcliffe, Esq., Royal George Mills, Saddle-
Whitehead, Major-General Sir Thomas, K.C.B., Uplands, Preston
Whitehead, Thomas, Esq., Meanleys, Tyldesley, Manchester
Whiteley, John Denton, Esq., Stainland, Halifax
Whiteley and Sons, Messrs. John, Calder Side, Hebden-Bridge
Whitfield, Edward, Esq., Elswick Villa, Newcastle-upon-Tyne
Whitfield, William, Esq., Solicitor, Rotherham
Whitham, Joseph, Esq., Kirkstall, Leeds
Whitley, Edward, Esq., West Coker, Yeovil, Somerset
Whitley, George, Esq., Solicitor, Liverpool
Whitley, John, Esq., Solicitor,   do.
Whitmore, Rev. Ainslie H., Leasingham Rectory, Sleaford
Whitmore, Thomas, Esq., Apley Park, Bridgenorth, Salop
Whittaker, John, Esq., Hurst, Ashton-under-Lyne
Whitten, James Sibley, Esq., Mayor of Coventry, 1844
Whittington, Rev. Thomas J., M.A., Winwick, Warrington
Whyatt, Messrs. George, and Son, Openshaw, Manchester
Wickham, James, Esq., Sutton-Scotney House, Whitchurch
Wickham, Rev. Robert, M.A., Twyford, Winchester
Wickham, William, Esq., Bullington House, Whitchurch
Wickham, William, Esq., Winchester
Wicksted, Charles, Esq., Shakenhurst, Cleobury-Mortimer
Wignall, Rev. William, St. Saviour's, Bamber Bridge
Wilberforce, William, Esq., Oriel College, Oxford
Wilby, John, Esq., Solicitor, Wakefield, Yorkshire   [terfield
Wilcocks, Rev. W. Wright, M.A., Incumbent of Ridgeway, Ches-
Wild, Richard, Esq., Bank House, Shuttleworth, Rochdale
Wild, Rev. William Taylor, B.D., Vicar of Westow, Whitwell
Wilde, Rev. Spencer D., Fletching, near Uckfield, Sussex
Wilding, Rev. James Henry, M.A., Rector of St. Helen and St.
Wilding, William, Esq., Netherton, Liverpool   [Alban, Worcester
Wilkins, Rev. Edw., M.A., Rector of Hempstead, Stalham, Norfolk
Wilkinson, Rev. C., M.A., Vicar of Bardsey, Wetherby
Wilkinson, Rev. Edmund, Vicar of Chipping, near Preston
Wilkinson, Rev. H. T., Weston Rectory, Harling, Norfolk
Wilkinson, Henry, Esq., New House, Thornley, Preston
Wilkinson, John Etridge, Esq., Dunston Lodge, Gateshead
Wilkinson, Rev. J. A., St. Mary's, Liverpool
Wilkinson, Rev. Marmaduke, M.A., Redgrave Rectory, Botesdale
Wilkinson, Rev. Wm. Hutton, M.A., Incumb. of All Saints, Portsea
Wilkinson, William, Esq., Brow Bridge, Elland, Halifax
Wilkinson, Rev. W. G., Bubwith Vicarage, Howden
Wilks, John, Esq., Solicitor, Dewsbury
Willan, Robert, jun., Esq., Solicitor, Barnsley
Willan, Whaley, Esq., Solicitor, Bentham, Lancaster
Willders, J. W., Esq., Chesterton House, Stilton
Willebois, H., Esq., Marham House, near Downham-Market
Willett, Henry Goodrich, Esq., J.P., The Lightwoods House, Staf-
                                                            [fordshire
Williams, Rev. E., B.A., Perpetual Curate of Linfield and Ascot

Williams, Rev. H. J., vicar of Buckland-Denham, Somerset
Williams, Rev. James P., Sidlesham, near Chichester, Sussex
Williams, John, Esq., Burncooso, Truro, Cornwall
Williams, John, Esq., Retley Hill, Wellington, Salop
Williams, John, Esq., J.P., Pitmaston, Worcester
Williams, John, Esq., M.D., Beverley   [Hull
Williams, Rev. Preston J., M.A., Sigglesthorne, Kingston-upon-
Williams, Rev. Stephen, Magor, Newport, Monmouth
Williams, William, Esq., Hallatrow, near Bath, Somerset
Williams, Rev. William, B.A., Rector of Aston, Ludlow
Williams, Rev. W., B.D., vicar of Stokesay, Ludlow
Williams, William, Esq., Summerfield House, West Bromwich
Williamson, Captain, Crawley, Hants
Williamson, Rev. R. H., M.A., Incumbent of Holy Trinity, Dar-
Willington, John S., Esq., Newport, Isle of Wight   [lington
Willis, Rev. Arthur, M.A., Master of the Grammar School, Ludlow
Willis, Capt. Edward, Polygon, Cheetham Hill, Manchester
Willis, George, Esq., Sopley Park, Ringwood, Hants
Willis, Richard, Esq., Halstead, Prescot
Willmore, John, Esq., Oldford, Handsworth, Birmingham
Willmot, George, Esq., Erdington, Birmingham
Willoby, W. and E., Messrs., Solicitors, Berwick-upon-Tweed
Willoughby, Edward Croxall, Esq., Solicitor, Sutton Coldfield
Willoughby, Henry, Esq., Birdsall Hall, Malton
Willson, John, Esq., Quarry House, Northowram, Halifax
Wilson, Mrs., Elm Farm, Liverpool
Wilson, Benjamin, Esq., Bank House, Mirfield, Dewsbury
Wilson, Charles, Esq., Wellington Road, Wavertree, Liverpool
Wilson, Charles Thomas, Esq., Oundle
Wilson, Frederick W., Esq., Solicitor, Sheffield
Wilson, George, Esq., M.D., Alnwick
Wilson, George St. V., Esq., Redgrave Hall, near Botesdale
Wilson, Henry, Esq., Solicitor, Alford
Wilson, Henry, Esq., Stowlangtoft Hall, near Ixworth, Suffolk
Wilson, Sir Isaac, Knt. and M.D., Fareham, Hants
Wilson, J., Esq., Solicitor, Goole
Wilson, James William, Esq., Solicitor, Louth
Wilson, John, Esq., Union Bank, Huddersfield
Wilson, John, Esq., Pershore, Worcestershire
Wilson, J. W. R., Esq., Broughton Hall, near Preston
Wilson, Joseph, Esq., Clifford, Sheffield
Wilson, Joseph Radcliffe, Esq., Solicitor, Stockton-upon-Tees
Wilson, Knowlton, Esq., M.D., Sheffield
Wilson, R., jun., Esq., Solicitor, Hartlepool
Wilson, Rev. Samuel, M.A., vicar of Warter, Pocklington
Wilson, Samuel, Esq., Willow Bank, Derby Breck, Liverpool
Wilson, Thomas, Esq., Woolton, Liverpool
Wilson, Rev. Thomas, M.A., Incumbent of Walton, Wetherby
Wilson, Thomas, Esq., Merchant, Kingston-on-Hull
Wilson, Thomas, Esq., Hornsea, Yorkshire
Wilson, Thomas, Esq., Shotley Hall, Newcastle-upon-Tyne
Wilson, John, Esq., Fell House, Gateshead Low Fell
Wilson, Thomas, Esq., Birkby House, Huddersfield
Wilson, Major Thomas, Titchfield, Hants
Wilson, Rev. T. D. Holt, Rector of Hinderclay, near Botesdale
Wilson, Rev. William, M.A., Incumbent of Ryhope, Sunderland
Wilson, W. Murray, Esq., Horsforth, Leeds
Wilson, Rev. William, Palgrave Rectory, near Diss, Norfolk
Wilson, Rev. William, D.D., vicar of Holy-Rood
Wilson, William, Esq., Beech Lane, Aigburth, Liverpool
Wilson, William Henry Bowen Jordan, Esq., Olton Hall, Solihull
Wimble, Nehemiah, Esq., Lewes, Sussex
Winch, Henry, Esq., J.P., Seacombe, Cheshire
Windham, W. H., Esq., Felbrigg Hall, Norfolk
Winearls, R. G., Esq., Marham, near Downham-Market
Winfield, John Fawkener, Esq., The Hawthorns, Edgbaston
Wing, Rev. Wm. M.A., Rector of Stibbington, Wansford, Hunts
Winn, Charles, Esq., J.P., Nostal Priory, Wakefield
Winn, Joseph, Esq., Newlay House, Leeds
Winn, William Henry, Esq., Springfield, Everton, Liverpool
Winnington, Rev. Francis, Rectory House, near Bromyard
Winpenny, Rev. J., Incumbent of Yarm
Winslow, Rev. Richard, Wilton, Taunton, Somerset
Winslow, John, Esq., Lashlake, Thame
Winstanley, John, Esq., Fishergate, Preston
Winstanley, Rev. J. Robinson, D.D., vicar of Bampton, Oxon
Winstanley, William, Esq., Chaigeley Manor, Clitheroe
Winterbottom, Thomas M., Esq., M.D., Westoe, South Shields
WINTERTON, The Right Honourable the Earl of
Wise, Rev. John Henry, Stradbrooke, Suffolk
Wiseman, William Wood, Esq., Ossett, Wakefield
Witham, H. T. M., Esq., J.P., Lartington Hall, Barnard-Castle
Wither, Rev. Harris Jervois Bigg, M.A., Worting Rectory, Hants

Wither, Rev. Lovelace Bigg, M.A., Tangier Park, Hants
Wither, Rev. William Bigg, B.C.L., Otterbourne, do.
Withers, William, Esq., Church House, Holt, Norfolk
WODEHOUSE, The Right Honourable Lord
Wodehouse, Edmund, Esq., M.P., Bracondale, near Norwich
Wollaston, Rev. W. C., Rector of East Dereham, Norfolk .
Wollen, Rev. J., Bridgwater, Somerset
Wallocombe, Rev. John, M.A., Rector of Stowford, Cornwall
Wonham, Mr. W. K., Bognor, Sussex
Wood, Charles Thorold, Esq., Campsall Park, Doncaster
Wood, Christopher, Esq., Oaken Terrace, Wolverhampton
Wood, George, Esq., Morston Hall, Blakeney, Norfolk
Wood, Rev. Hugh, B.A., Rector of Blore, Ashbourn
Wood, Rev. John Ryle, M.A., Chaplain to the Queen and the Queen
    [Dowager, College, Worcester
Wood, Rev. John A., M.A., Beadnell, Belford
Wood, John, Esq., Thedden Grange, Alton, Hants
Wood, John, Esq., Woodlands, Darlington
Wood, Joseph, Esq., Woolley Moor, Wakefield
Wood, Joseph, Esq., Sandal,   do.
Wood, Rev. Leonard Charles, B.A., Singleton, Poulton-le-Fylde
Wood, Rev. Peter, Rector of Broadwater, near Worthing, Sussex
Wood, Thomas, Esq., Arthingworth, Northamptonshire
Wood, William, Esq., Mayor of Pontefract in 1841
Wood, William Cole, Esq., Martock, Somerset
Woodcock, Rev. George, M.A., Barbourne House, Worcester
Woodcock, Part, and Scott, Messrs., Solicitors, Wigan
Woodall, Henry, Esq., North Dalton, Beverley
Woodall, John, Esq., J.P., The Crescent, Scarborough
Woodall, William Edward, Esq., Solicitor,   do.
Woodd, Basil T., Esq., J.P., Aldborough Lodge, Boroughbridge
Woodhams, William R., Esq., Hammond's House, Udimore, Rye
Woodhead, William Wright, Esq., Solicitor, Sheffield
Woodhouse, John, Esq., Solicitor, Bolton-le-Moors
Woodhouse, Samuel, Esq., Norley Hall, Northwich
Woodman, William, Esq., Town Clerk of Morpeth
Woodroffe, Skynner George, Esq., Farthinghoe Lodge, Brackley
Woodroffe, Rev. T., M.A., Oxon, Rector of Calbourne, Isle of Wight
Woods, Edward, Esq., C.E., Edge Hill, Liverpool
Woods, George, Esq., Walton-on-the-Hill, Liverpool
Woods, Henry, Esq., Wigan
Woods, James, Stow-Market, Suffolk
Woods, Miss, Shopwyke, near Chichester, Sussex
Woods, Samuel, jun., Esq., Woolton Grove, Liverpool
Woods, William, Esq., Newcastle-upon-Tyne
Woodward, Rev. Thos., M.A., Hopton-Wafers, Cleobury-Mortimer
Woodyatt, T. M., Esq., Kinver Screw Manufactory, Stourbridge
Wooldridge and Son, Messrs., Winchester, Hants   [Birmingham
Woolley, Rev. Henry Rushworth, M.A., Rector of Handsworth,
Woolley, Rev. John, D.C.L., Rossall College, Fleetwood
WORCESTER, The Right Rev. the Lord Bishop of
Wordsworth, Rev. William, B.A., Monk Bretton, Barnsley
Workman, Rev. William, A.M., Rector of Eastrop, Basingstoke
Wormald, Frank, Esq., Field Head, Mirfield, Dewsbury
Wormald, Henry, Esq., South Parade, Wakefield
Wormald, Percival, Esq., Moor Lane, Gomersal, Leeds
Wormald, Smith, Esq., Tickton Grange, Beverley
Wormald, William, Esq., Solicitor, Leeds
Worrall, John, Esq., Knotty Ash House, Liverpool
Worsley, Charles C. Seymour, Esq., Newport, Isle of Wight
Worsley, Rev. Charles, M.A., Oxon, do.   do.
Worsley, Rev. Henry, D.D., Oxon, Rector of Gatcombe, do.
Worsley, Rev. Perryman, M.A., Rector of Little Ponton, Grantham
Worsley, Thomas, Esq., Cubley, Penistone, Barnsley

Worsley, Sir William, Bart., Hovingham Hall, Whitwell
Worsop, John Arthur, Esq., Landford House, Wilts
Worthington, George, Esq., Solicitor to the Docks, Liverpool
Worthington, H. B., Esq., C.E., Lancaster
Wrench, Rev. J. G., D.C.L., Salehurst Vicarage, Sussex
Wright, Adam, Esq., Kirkham
Wright, Rev. Charles, J.P., Hill Top, Bolton-le-Moors
Wright, Rev. Charles, B.A., Vicar of St. Peter's, Derby
Wright, Chas., Esq., Mattishall Burgh Cottage, near East Dereham
Wright, Mrs. E., Feniton, near Honiton, Devon
Wright, Francis Bowcher, Esq., Hinton-Blewett, near Bath
Wright, Francis, Esq., Revell Grange, Stannington, Sheffield
Wright, Ichabod, Esq., Mapperley, Nottinghamshire
Wright, James, Esq., Ravenhill, near Rugeley, Staffordshire
Wright, James, Esq., Blyth, Northumberland
Wright, Rev. John Marsden, M.A., Tatham, Lancaster
Wright, John Francis, Esq., Kelvedon Hall, Ongar, Essex
Wright, Joshua Collett, Esq., Beckwith House, Harrogate
Wright, R., Esq., Dep.-Lieut., Sands House, Rushyford, Durham
Wright, Rev. R. J. W., M.A., Winchester, Hants
Wright, Robert, Esq., Stand House, Wavertree
Wright, Thomas G., Esq., M.D., South Parade, Wakefield
Wright, William, Esq., Silsden, Keighley
Wright, Rev. W., B.A., Principal of the College, Huddersfield
Wrigley, Thomas, Esq., Waterloo Villa, Halifax
Wyatt, Rev. Arthur M., M.A., Perry Bar, Birmingham
Wyatt, Hugh P., Esq., Cissbury, near Worthing
Wyatt, Rev. Thomas, North Lodge, Worthing
Wylam, William, Esq., Prospect Cottage, Gateshead
Wyld, Rev. Thomas, Rector of North Wraxall, Chippenham
Wylde, William, Esq., Banker, Southwell, Notts
Wylie, Robert, Esq., J.P., Beverley
Wymer, Rev. Edward, Rector of Westwick, Norfolk
Wynch, Rev. Henry, Rector of Pett, near Winchelsea, Sussex
Wyndham, Col. George, Petworth Park, Petworth,   do.
Wynn, Jeremiah, Esq., Wolverhampton
Wythe, Thomas, Esq., Manor House, Middleton, near Lynn
Yaldwyn, Mrs. M., Blackdown House, near Petworth, Sussex
YARBOROUGH, The Right Honourable the Earl of
Yard, Thomas, Esq., Bucklands, Ryde, Isle of Wight
Yarker, Rev. Luke, M.A. and J.P., Vicar of Chillingham, Belford
Yate, Rev. Charles, B.D., Vicar of Holme-on-Spalding-Moor,
Yates, Charles, Esq., Birmingham   [Market-Weighton
Yates, Henry, Esq., Halsnead, Prescot
Yates, Henry, Esq., Salisbury House, West Derby, Liverpool
Yates, Rev. H. S., Henlow, Biggleswade, Bedfordshire
Yates, Miss J., Hoole Hall, Chester
Yates, James, Esq., Barbot Hall, Rotherham
Yates, John, Esq., Everton, Liverpool
Yates, Rev. William, M.A., Eccleston, Chorley
Yeates, John, Esq., J.P., Park Head, Kendal
Yeatman, Rev. H. F., Stock House, Dorset
Yerbury, Francis, Esq., Belcomb House, Bradford, Wilts
Yewdall, William, Esq., Buxton House, Rawdon, Leeds
YORK, His Grace the Lord Archbishop of
York, E., Esq., J.P., Wighill Park, Tadcaster   [London
Yorke, The Hon. Eliot Thomas, M.P., Norfolk-Street, Park Lane,
Yorke, The Hon. and Rev. Grantham, M.A., Edinburgh
Young, James, Esq., West Docks, South Shields   [Spring
Young, Rev. J. D., Master of the Kepier School, Houghton-le-
Young, Thomas, Esq., Northumberland Square, North Shields
ZETLAND, The Right Honourable the Earl of
Zwilchenbart, Emmanuel, Esq., Roselands, Aigburth, Liverpool

A

TOPOGRAPHICAL DICTIONARY

OF

ENGLAND.

ABBAS-COMBE, or TEMPLE-COMBE (ST. MARY), a parish, in the union of WINCANTON, hundred of HORE-THORNE, E. division of SOMERSET, 4½ miles (S. by W.) from Wincanton, on the road to Blandford; containing 461 inhabitants. It derived the name of Temple-Combe from the military order of Knights Templars, who had an establishment here, which at the Dissolution possessed a revenue of £128. 7. 9. Some remains of the chapel attached to the old priory-house are still to be seen. The parish comprises by measurement 1884 acres of land; and contains good building-stone of the granite species, and limestone, both of which are quarried. The living is a rectory, valued in the king's books at £9. 9. 4½., and in the gift of the Rev. Thomas Fox: the tithes have been commuted for £370, and the glebe consists of 38 acres. The church has a tower on the south side of the nave. There is a place of worship for Independents.

ABBERBURY, county SALOP.—See ALBERBURY.

ABBERLEY (ST. MICHAEL), a parish, in the union of MARTLEY, Lower division of the hundred of DOD-DINGTREE, Hundred-House and W. divisions of the county of WORCESTER, 12 miles (N. W. by N.) from Worcester; containing 559 inhabitants. This place, formerly *Abbotsley*, comprises 2564 acres of land, of which the arable and pasture are in equal portions, with about 70 acres of wood; the surface is well watered, and the soil rather above the average in fertility. The village is situated to the right of the road leading from Worcester to Ludlow, in a valley surrounded by hills whose summits afford delightful prospects: from one eminence eleven counties may be seen. Coal of good quality is wrought, and there are large quarries of excellent stone for building, and of stone for repairing roads. Abberley Hall, a beautiful Italian edifice, was purchased in 1844, with its surrounding demesne, from the Misses Bromley by the late J. L. Moilliet, Esq., by whom considerable improvements and alterations were made, in the purest taste; the whole of the interior was destroyed by fire on the

VOL. I.—1

25th December 1845; but the exterior remains quite perfect, and the mansion is now undergoing complete repair.

The living is a rectory, valued in the king's books at £11. 10. 2½., and in the gift of Mrs. Moilliet; incumbent, the Rev. Francis Severne, whose tithes have been commuted for £333. 8., with two acres of glebe and a house. Certain impropriate tithes have been commuted for £100. The church is a neat ancient edifice, picturesquely situated on the east side of the village, and has a wood-shingle spire 99 feet high, with four bells; the architecture is of various styles, one of the windows presenting an excellent specimen of the Saxon arch. A school was founded under gifts made by Elizabeth and Victoria Walsh, in 1717; it has an income of £15 per annum, in addition to a house and garden: the school-house was rebuilt by Robert Bromley, Esq., in 1791. On Abberley hill, in the midst of a thickly-planted wood, stands an oak, said to have been a sapling from the oak-tree under which St. Augustine in the 6th century invited the Welsh bishops to a conference, as recorded by Milner in his Church History: the parent tree was afterwards consumed by fire. William Walsh, the poet, and a correspondent of Pope's and Addison's, was born in the parish in 1663: at the close of Pope's *Essay on Criticism*, are some touching lines to his memory.

ABBERTOFT, a hamlet, in the parish of WIL-LOUGHBY, union of SPILSBY, Wold division of the hundred of CALCEWORTH, parts of LINDSEY, county of LINCOLN, 7 miles (S. E.) from Alford; containing 23 inhabitants. This place, called also Habertoft, lies in the south-eastern portion of the parish, and is one of several hamlets within its limits. The Orby drain passes in an eastern direction here.

ABBERTON (ST. ANDREW), a parish, in the union of WINSTREE, hundred of WINSTREE, N. division of ESSEX, 4½ miles (S.) from Colchester; containing 248 inhabitants. It is situated about a mile

B

and a half to the east of the river Colne, and comprises by measurement 1067 acres. There are some gravel-pits, which afford good materials for repairing the roads; and chalk can be obtained at a distance of three miles, being brought by vessels into the Strode of Mersea island. The living is a rectory, valued in the king's books at £14. 7. 8½., and in the patronage of the Crown : the tithes have been commuted for £300, and there are 50 acres of glebe. The church is a small neat building, on an elevated site, with a square tower of brick. There is a place of worship for Wesleyans.

ABBERTON, a parish in the union, and Upper division of the hundred, of PERSHORE, Pershore and E. divisions of the county of WORCESTER, 10 miles (E.) from Worcester, on the road to Alcester ; containing 81 inhabitants. Henry VIII. granted the whole of the manor or lordship to Thomas and Francis Sheldon, whose family continued to be owners of the parish, until it passed into the possession of the present proprietor, William Laslett, Esq. The parish comprises 971a. 1r. 35p., one-half of which is fine pasture land, much esteemed for its dairy and feeding produce ; the soil is sand and clay : there are quarries of sandstone and limestone, and coal exists. Abberton Hall, the manor-house, the seat of Mr. Laslett, is in the centre of the estate, on an eminence overlooking a park of nearly 500 acres of pasture ; it stands on a level with the Malvern hills, and commands a mos beautiful panoramic view of the Malvern and Bredon hills, the Lench woods, and vale of Evesham. The living is a rectory, valued in the king's books at £5. 8. 1½., in the patronage of Mr. Laslett, and incumbency of the Rev. Francis Best : the tithes have been commuted for £173. 10., and there is a glebe of 2½ acres. The church is an ancient stone edifice, situated near the manor-house : two acres of land in the parish of Flyford-Flavel, near Huntings farm, belong to Abberton, and the rent is applied to the repair of the building. There are mineral springs, whose waters, bitter and cathartic, are supposed to be little inferior in virtue to those of Epsom and Cheltenham.

ABBERWICK, a township, in the parish of EDLINGHAM, union of ALNWICK, N. division of COQUETDALE ward and of NORTHUMBERLAND, 4 miles (W.) from Alnwick ; containing 170 inhabitants. It includes the north-eastern part of the parish, adjoining Alnwick moor ; and near it runs the river Aln, which is here joined by the Lemmington brook. The great tithes have been commuted for £136, and the vicarial for £77.

ABBEY, a tything, in the parish, union, and hundred of AXMINSTER, Honiton and S. divisions of DEVON; containing 76 inhabitants.

ABBEY-LANDS, a township, in the parish and union of ALNWICK, E. division of COQUETDALE ward, N. division of NORTHUMBERLAND ; containing 295 inhabitants.

ABBOT'S-ANN (ST. MARY), a parish, in the union of ANDOVER, partly in the hundred of WHERWELL, but chiefly in that of ANDOVER, Andover and N. divisions of HANTS, 2¼ miles (S. W. by W.) from Andover ; containing 619 inhabitants. This place anciently belonged to Hyde Abbey, Winchester, in the earliest rolls of which it is noticed as the manor of Anna, and in later ones as Abbottes-Anne. In a field about a mile south-east of the church, were discovered a few years since the remains of what is believed to have been a Roman villa. Some,

2.

however, have imagined them to be the ruins of a monastery, as the field is still called Monaster Field, and the opinion is favoured by the names of this and the neighbouring village of Monkston. At the beginning of the eighteenth century, the property passed by purchase into the Pitt family, by one of whom, Governor Pitt (who brought the Pitt diamond into Europe), the church was rebuilt. The parish comprises about 3000 acres, and is intersected by the Andover and Salisbury road ; a canal from Andover to Southampton passes within a mile. The living is a rectory, valued in the king's books at £42. 17. 6., and in the patronage of Miss Burrough : the tithes have been commuted for £790, and there are about 50 acres of glebe, and a good glebe-house. The church is a substantial brick edifice relieved with stone, with a handsome tower. There is a place of worship for Independents.

ABBOT'S-ASTLEY.—See ASTLEY, ABBOT'S.—And other places having a similar distinguishing prefix will be found under the proper name.

ABBOTSBURY (ST. NICHOLAS), a parish, and formerly a market-town, in the union of WEYMOUTH, hundred of UGGSCOMBE, Dorchester division of DORSET, 8¼ miles (W. S. W.) from Dorchester, and 129 (S. W. by W.) from London ; containing, with the hamlets of Rodden and Elworth, 1005 inhabitants. The name of this place is evidently derived from its ancient possessors, the abbots of the monastery of St. Peter here, which is supposed to have been founded in 1044, by Orcus, or Orking, steward of the household of Canute the Great, and Tola his wife, for monks of the Benedictine order. According to the register of the abbey, it appears that a church was erected at a very early period, by Bertulphus, a priest. This having afterwards become a place of retreat for the West Saxon kings, and the territory having passed into the possession of Canute, lands to a considerable extent were given by him to Orcus, by whom, dying without issue, they were granted to the church, built a long time previously, and then forsaken and in decay, on account of its having been frequently infested by pirates. Orcus erected the monastery, which occupied a large extent of ground, and, in progress of time, was endowed with rich grants and divers immunities, and was frequently rebuilt : the remains consist of a gateway and portions of the walls. Its revenue, at the Dissolution, was estimated at £485. 3. 5. : it was granted to Sir Giles Strangeways, and on its site was erected a mansion, which, having been garrisoned for the king, in 1644, was attacked by Sir Anthony Ashley Cooper, and burnt to the ground. The church was also occupied by a party of royalists, who surrendered before it sustained any damage.

The TOWN, situated in a valley surrounded by lofty hills, near the sea-shore, consists of three streets, partially paved, and is well supplied with water : the western part of it was consumed by fire in 1706. Fishing is the chief occupation of the inhabitants, great quantities of mackerel being taken on the coast. The weaving of cotton was introduced about fifty years since, but has of late much declined. The market, which was on Thursday, has fallen into disuse ; it was granted, together with two fairs, to Sir John Strangeways in the 8th of James I., a former market, granted to one of the abbots, and held on Friday, having been long discontinued. One of the fairs has also been lost ; the other, which is for sheep and toys, is held on the 10th of July. The LIVING is a discharged vicarage, valued in the king's books at £10 ; net income, £140 ; patron and impropriator, the Earl of Ilchester, whose tithes have been commuted for £127. 10. The church is a large handsome structure in the later style of English architecture, with a square embattled tower ; and is thought to contain the remains of the founder of the abbey and his wife, which were removed hither from the conventual church at the Dissolution. A school, originally founded for twenty boys, was further endowed in 1754, by Mrs. Horner, with £21 per annum, for instructing ten additional boys. St. Catherine's chapel, supposed to have been erected in the reign of Edward IV., stands on an eminence south-west of the town, and serves only as a land-mark : it is built wholly of freestone dug out of the hill on which it is situated ; the roof is finely groined, and on each side of the edifice is a handsome porch. About a mile and a half to the west of Abbotsbury is an ancient intrenchment, occupy- ing an area of nearly 20 acres ; and near the town is a cromlech.

ABBOTSHAM (ST. HELEN), a parish, in the union of BIDEFORD, hundred of SHEBBEAR, Great Torrington and N. divisions of DEVON, 2 miles (W.) from Bideford, containing, with the hamlets of Shepperton and Little- ham, 414 inhabitants. This parish, which is situated on the shore of Barnstaple bay, is distinguished for a memorable victory over the Danes, who besieged the fortress called Kenwith or Kenwic Castle, towards the close of the ninth century : their main western army was routed ; 1200 of them, including their leader, were slain, and their consecrated standard was captured. The living is a discharged vicarage, valued in the king's books at £16. 4. 7. ; it is in the patronage of the Crown, and the owners and occupiers of land are the impropriators. The great tithes have been commuted for £32. 10., and the vicarial for £120 ; there are nearly 34 acres of glebe.

ABBOT-SIDE, HIGH, a township, in the parish of AYSGARTH, wapentake of HANG-WEST, N. riding of YORK, 1¼ mile (N. W. by W.) from Hawes ; containing, with the chapelries of Hardraw and Helbeck-Lunds, and the hamlets of Cotterdale, Fosdale, Litherskew, Sedbusk, Shaw, and Simonstone, 574 inhabitants. The two townships of Abbot-Side received their names from the monks of Jervaulx Abbey, who had considerable pro- perty in the district. This township, which comprises by computation 13,000 acres, is altogether wild and mountainous, and consists of moors, dales, and ravines ; it is rich in springs, waterfalls, rocks, and caves, and a variety of interesting natural curiosities. The magnifi- cent cataract *Hardraw Scarr*, 102 feet in height, with its stupendous rocks and romantic caverns, and the eleva- tion of *Shunner Fell*, 2329 feet above the level of the sea, and commanding views of several counties, are both situated in the township. The river Ure, on which are several beautiful waterfalls, rises at the head of the valley. A rent-charge of £163 has been awarded to Trinity Col- lege, Cambridge, in lieu of the impropriate tithes.

ABBOT-SIDE, LOW, a township, in the parish of AYSGARTH, wapentake of HANG-WEST, N. riding of YORK; containing, with the hamlets of Grange, Bow- bridge, Helme, and Shawcote, 166 inhabitants. This place is on the north side of the river Ure, and com- prises by computation about 5000 acres of land : Whit- field Gill, in which is the picturesque waterfall called

3

Whitfield Force, separates the township from that of Askrigg. Here the monks of Jervaulx abbey were first seated, and afterwards maintained a cell. The impro- prlate tithes have been commuted for £42, payable to Trinity College, Cambridge.

ABBOTSLEY (ST. MARGARET), a parish, in the union of ST. NEOT'S, hundred of TOSELAND, county of HUNTINGDON, 4½ miles (S. E.) from St. Neot's ; contain- ing 443 inhabitants. It comprises about 1700 acres, and is bounded by a brook formed by the draining of the adjacent lands, and which, passing onward for three or four miles, discharges itself into the river Ouse at St. Neot's. The pillow-lace manufacture affords em- ployment to the female population. The living is a dis- charged vicarage, valued in the king's books at £8. 17. ; net income, £85 ; patrons and impropriators, the Master and Fellows of Balliol College, Oxford. The glebe con- sists of 185 acres, of which 125 were allotted to the vicar in lieu of the small tithes, on the inclosure of the waste lands in 1837 ; the glebe-house has been rebuilt. The church consists of a nave, chancel, two aisles, and a tower, with a north and south porch, a west entrance through the tower, and a chancel door ; it is supposed to have been erected between the accessions of William Rufus and Edward III., and was thoroughly repaired in 1837. A Roman road once passed along the western boundary of the parish, and in its tract coins of the Roman emperors are occasionally found. Dr. Abbott, father of Charles Abbott, speaker of the house of com- mons, subsequently created Lord Colchester, was vicar here in the reign of George II.

ABBOTSTON (ST. PETER), a parish, in the union of ALRESFORD, hundred of BOUNTISBOROUGH, Winches- ter and N. divisions of HANTS, 2¾ miles (N. W.) from New Alresford. The living is a rectory, united to the vicarage of Itchin-Stoke, and valued in the king's books at £13. 6. 8. : the church is in ruins. Here are the re- mains of some religious house, of which there is no authentic account.

ABDASTON, STAFFORD.—See ADBASTON.

ABDON (ST. MARGARET), a parish, in the union of LUDLOW, hundred of MUNSLOW, S. division of SALOP, 12 miles (S. W. by W.) from Bridgnorth ; containing 155 inhabitants. It comprises upwards of 1100 acres, of which about 190 are arable, 664 meadow and pasture, and 260 waste land ; the surface is very irregular, and the soil a strong red clay in the higher grounds, with a sheep-walk, having much gorse and fern ; the lower grounds are more favourable to agriculture. A few pits on the hills yield an inferior coal, much of which is used in lime-works; formerly there were several iron-forges in the neighbourhood. The living is a discharged rec- tory, valued in the king's books at £3. 6. 8. ; patron, the Hon. S. Herbert ; net income, £147, arising from tithes and a small estate, with 49 acres of glebe, of which 22 are in the parish of Stoke St. Milborough. The church is a rude structure, with walls of great thickness ; much of it appears to have been rebuilt about 150 or 200 years ago : in the chancel is a window in the decorated style. Abdon Burf, on the summit of Brown Clee hill, is a re- markable oval inclosure of basalt stones, evidently British ; the area measures from north to south 1317 feet, and at its widest point from east to west is 660 feet ; huge blocks of stone are scattered within it, several of them arranged in circles. B 2

ABERFORD (*St. Richard*), a parish, and formerly a market-town, in the Lower division of the wapentake of Skyrack, W. riding of York, 7 miles (S. by E.) from Wetherby, and 186¾ (N. N. W.) from London, on the road to Carlisle ; comprising the townships of Aberford, Parlington, and Sturton-Grange, and containing 1071 inhabitants, of whom 782 are in the township of Aberford. The town, which is in the parishes of Aberford and Sherburn, is built on the gentle acclivity of a rock of limestone, near the small river Cock, a stream abounding with trout and eels, over which is an excellent stone bridge. It consists principally of one long street : the houses are in general of stone, and many of them are handsome ; the air is pure and salubrious, and the environs are thickly studded with elegant villas. The parish comprises 3820 acres of fertile land ; there are extensive strata of limestone, and a productive coal-mine, from which a railway has been laid down to a depôt in the town, and an extensive trade is carried on in coal. The Leeds and Selby railway passes within three miles. The market, which was on Wednesday, has been discontinued ; but a customary market is held on Friday, and fairs take place on the last Monday in April and May, the first Monday in October, the first Monday after the 18th of that month, and the first Monday after the 2nd of November. The magistrates hold a petty-session for the division every Thursday, and the town is a polling-place for the West Riding. The living is a discharged vicarage, valued in the king's books at £6. 1. 8., and in the patronage of Oriel College, Oxford, to which establishment, and the Misses Gascoigne, the impropriation belongs ; net income of the vicar, £305. The church is an ancient structure, in the early, decorated, and later styles of English architecture. There is a place of worship for Wesleyans. At the distance of a mile north of Aberford are vestiges of Castle-Cary, an ancient Norman fortification ; and the scene of the battle of Towton, which decided the long continued war between the houses of York and Lancaster, is within two miles of the town. The Roman road is the parish boundary south of the bridge, and cuts off a small district on the north, called Greystone Field. The Rev. Mr. Waters, a former incumbent, died at the advanced age of 114 years.

ABERGAVENNY (*St. Mary*), a market-town and parish, and the head of a union, in the division and hundred of Abergavenny, county of Monmouth, 16 miles (W. by N.) from Monmouth, and 145 (W. by N.) from London, on the road to Brecon ; comprising the hamlets of Hardwick and Llwyndû, and containing 4953 inhabitants, of whom 2720 are in the town. This was the *Gobannium* of Antoninus, a Roman station so called from the river *Gobannius*, now Gavenny, from which, also, the present name of the town is formed, by prefixing the Welsh word *Aber*, denoting its situation near the mouth of the river. Soon after the Conquest, a castle was erected here, on an eminence overlooking the Usk, by Hameline de Balun or Baladun, one of William's followers ; and it was besieged and taken in 1215, by Llewelyn, Prince of Wales : the only remains are the exterior walls, which appear to have been erected in the time of Henry II., and within which a neat modern house has been built. De Balun also founded a priory for Benedictine monks, in honour of the Blessed Virgin, the revenue of which, at the Dissolution, was £59. 4. ; it stood in Monk-street.

The town, which is lighted with gas and well supplied with water, is beautifully situated at the extremity of a pass, where the mountains abruptly terminate ; and is watered by the rivers Usk, Gavenny, and Kibby, over the first of which is an ancient bridge of fifteen arches, including several dry arches on each side. The streets are narrow, and the houses irregularly built ; but considerable improvements have been made by the enlargement of the market-place, and the removal of numerous projections in front of the buildings ; and the salubrity of the air, and the picturesque beauty of the scenery, attract many visiters during the summer months. Assemblies are occasionally held. The trade is principally in wool, a considerable quantity of which is sold on the market-days during the months of June and July : the mountains in the neighbourhood abound with coal and iron-stone, and in the surrounding districts numerous iron-works have been established. The Monmouthshire and Brecon canal, which passes within a mile of the town, affords great facility in distributing to every part of the kingdom the produce of the mines : there is also a tram-road to Hereford ; and an act was passed in 1846, for a railway from Pontypool, by Abergavenny, to Hereford. The market-days are Tuesday and Saturday, the former chiefly for corn : the fairs are held on the third Tuesday in March, May 14th (which is the principal), June 24th, the Tuesday before July 20th (at which two a great quantity of wool is sold), Sept. 25th, and Nov. 19th. The charter of incorporation, by which the government of the town was vested in a bailiff, recorder, and twenty-seven burgesses, was forfeited in the reign of William III., and the town is now within the jurisdiction of the county magistrates, who hold a petty-session every Wednesday. The powers of the county debt-court of Abergavenny, established in 1847, extend over the greater part of the registration-district of Abergavenny.

The living is a discharged vicarage, valued in the king's books at £10. 0. 7½. ; net income, £451 ; patron, C. Bailey, Esq. ; impropriator, Mrs. Bagot. The church is a spacious structure, the body and aisles of which were taken down in 1828, and rebuilt, and galleries erected ; there are several very ancient monuments, principally of the Herberts, some of whom were killed at the battle of Agincourt. A neat building in the Tudor style, forming an oblong square, with a handsome church dedicated to the Holy Trinity in the centre, was erected in 1840, at the sole expense of Miss Rachel Herbert, of The Hill, near the town ; the south side of the square consists of a residence for the minister and four cottages, the north side having the same number of cottages, and a schoolroom for fifty girls, with apartments for the mistress. Miss Herbert, who has endowed the cottages, for aged women, is patroness for life, and the bishop of the diocese will afterwards appoint to the living, which is endowed with £3000. There are two places of worship for Baptists, and one each for Independents, English and Welsh Wesleyans, and Roman Catholics. The free grammar school, founded by Henry VIII. in 1543, and formerly under the management of the corporation, was, on the forfeiture of their charter, placed under the control of the Master and Fellows of Jesus College, Oxford, who appoint the master, with preference to a fellow of that college ; a writing-master, also, is appointed. The school-house was the parochial church of St. John, which was converted to this purpose at the

4

Dissolution : about the middle of the last century it was rebuilt; but still, having an embattled tower, it presents the appearance of an ecclesiastical structure. William Prichard, in 1623, founded a scholarship in Jesus College, to which boys educated here are eligible. The poor law union of Abergavenny comprises 26 parishes or places in the county of Monmouth, and 2 in the county of Hereford, and contains a population of 50,834. A variety of Roman coins, some bricks inscribed " Leg. II. Aug.," and a sudatory, have been discovered in the town ; and within half a mile of it are the remains of a Roman camp, near which was a chapel of ease, now converted into a farmhouse. Abergavenny confers the title of Earl on the family of Neville ; the earldom, like the earldoms of Arundel and Berkeley, is a local dignity, attached to the possession of the castle, and is the only one now subsisting of those baronies with which the Norman warriors, who assisted in the subjugation of Wales, were rewarded.

ABERYSTWITH (St. Peter), a parish in the union, division, and hundred of Abergavenny, county of Monmouth, 9 miles (S. W. by W.) from Abergavenny ; containing 11,272 inhabitants. This parish, which is sometimes called Blaenau, comprises 11,788 acres, whereof 4640 are common or waste. It abounds with valuable mines of iron, worked on a very extensive scale ; and is intersected by numerous tram-roads, communicating with the Brecon and Monmouth canals, leading to Newport, where the produce of the various works is shipped. A quarry of stone used for roofing and paving, is partially worked. There are villages in the parish, connected with the iron-works at Ebbwvale, Nant-y-Glo, Coalbrook-vale, Blaina, and Cwmelyn. The living is a perpetual curacy, endowed with nearly the whole of the rectorial tithes, and in the gift of the Earl of Abergavenny : the impropriate tithes have been commuted for £5. 10., and those of the incumbent for £300. The church is a plain structure, erected in 1827. A church district named Nant-y-Glo was formed in 1844, and one named Beaufort in 1846, by the Ecclesiastical Commission ; both livings are in the gift of the Crown and the Bishop of Llandaff, alternately. There are places of worship for Baptists, Wesleyans, Calvinists, and Ranters.

Arms.

ABINGDON, a borough and market-town having exclusive jurisdiction, and the head of a union, locally in the hundred of Hormer, county of Berks, of which it is the county town, 6 miles (S.) from Oxford, 26 (N. N. by N.) from Reading, and 56 (W. N. W.) from London ; containing, exclusively of that part of the parish of St. Helen which is without the borough, and actually in the hundred of Hormer, 5585 inhabitants ; of whom 4947 are in the parish of St. Helen, and 638 in that of St. Nicholas. This place, according to a manuscript in the Cottonian library quoted by Dugdale, was, in the time of the Britons, a city of considerable importance, and distinguished as a royal residence, to which the people resorted to assist at the great councils of the nation. By the Saxons it was called *Scovechesham*, or *Sewsham ;* but it acquired the name of Abbendon, " the town of the abbey," on the removal hither, in 680, of a monastic institution previously founded at Bagley Wood, now an extra-parochial liberty in the vicinity, by Cissa, viceroy of Centwine, ninth king of Wessex ; on which institution Ceadwalla, the king's son and successor, bestowed the town and its appendages. After the establishment of the monastery, Offa, King of Mercia, on a visit to Abingdon, was so much pleased with the situation that he erected a palace here, in which he and his immediate successors, Egferth and Cenwulf, occasionally resided. The monastery continued to flourish till 871, when it was destroyed by the Danes ; in consequence, Edred, grandson of Alfred, in 955 laid the first stone of a new monastery, which was completed after his death by the abbot of Ethelwold and his successor Ordgar, and which, from the extent of its endowments and privileges, subsequently augmented by Edgar and Canute the Great, was raised to the dignity of a mitred abbey. William the Conqueror in 1084 celebrated the festival of Easter at Abingdon, where he was sumptuously entertained by Robert D'Oilly, one of the most powerful barons of the time, under whose care the king left his son Henry to be educated in this convent, where the prince imbibed those acquirements which afterwards procured for him the surname of Beauclerc. At the Dissolution, the revenue of the abbey was £1876. 10. 9. A nunnery was also founded here by Cilla, niece of Cissa, who presided over it till her death, when it was removed to Witham : the site was afterwards given, by Edward VI., to Christ's hospital in this town. The Guild of the Holy Cross was instituted in St. Helen's church prior to the reign of Richard II., and appears to have been refounded in that of Henry V., when the brethren erected bridges at Burford and Culhamford, where the ferry across the river Thames was so dangerous that passengers and cattle had been frequently lost. It was dissolved in 1547, at which period its revenue amounted to £85. 15. 6.

In the early part of the civil war of the seventeenth century, Charles I. garrisoned Abingdon, where he established the head-quarters of his cavalry ; but on the retreat of the royal forces to Oxford, in 1644, the Earl of Essex took possession of it, and garrisoned it for the parliament ; and a few days afterwards, Waller's army, which had been stationed near Wantage, entered the town, and among other excesses destroyed the cross in the market-place, at which, in 1641, the accommodation with the Scots had been celebrated by 2000 choristers. This cross is particularly noticed by Camden for its beauty, and was the model of one afterwards erected at Coventry. Sir Stephen Hawkins in 1645, and Prince Rupert in the following year, attacked the garrison unsuccessfully : on these occasions the defenders put every Irish prisoner to death, without trial ; whence the expression " Abingdon law."

The town, which is pleasantly situated at the influx of the small river Ock into the Thames, is handsomely built, and consists of several spacious streets diverging from the market-place ; it is well paved and lighted, under a local act of the 6th of George IV., and is amply supplied with water. The several bridges near the town have been widened and improved by voluntary contributions, and the causeway connected with Culham bridge forms a pleasant promenade. An act for inclosing lands was passed in 1841. Races take place in September, at which time, also, assemblies are held in the council-chamber. The manufacture of woollen goods was formerly carried on to a great extent, but has quite declined; and during the late war, Abingdon had a good trade in sail-cloth, sacking, and coarse manufactures of a similar description; but, owing to the competition of the establishments in the north of England and in Scotland, this source of employment has also declined. The trade now consists in corn and in malt, which are sold to a considerable extent. Several wharfs and ware-houses have been constructed, where the Wilts and Berks canal joins the Thames, near its confluence with the Ock; and the Oxford branch of the Great Western railway has a station three miles south-east of the town, in the county of Oxford. The market-days are Monday, chiefly for corn, and Friday, for provisions only: fairs for horses and horned-cattle are held on the first Monday in Lent, May 6th, June 20th, Aug. 5th, Sept. 19th, the Monday before Old Michaelmas-day (a statute fair), Monday after Oct. 12th (a great market), and Dec. 11th; and there is also a fair for wool.

The BOROUGH was incorporated by Philip and Mary in 1555-6, and other charters were granted by Elizabeth, James I., and George III., chiefly confirmatory of the original, by which the corporation was styled the "Mayor, Bailiffs, and Burgesses of the borough of Abing-don." Under the Municipal act of 1836 the corpora-tion is now styled the "Mayor, Aldermen, and Bur-gesses," which has been adopted as the motto of a new seal; and consists of a mayor, 4 aldermen, and 12 councillors: the burgesses are about 300 in number, and the mayor, late mayor, and recorder, with four others, are justices for the borough, of which the municipal and parliamentary boundaries are the same. There is a court of sessions quarterly, with jurisdiction over felonies and misdemeanors; the magistrates hold a petty-session every Tuesday; and courts leet and view of frankpledge are held by the mayor within a month after Easter and Michaelmas. The county debt-court of Abingdon, esta-blished in 1847, has jurisdiction over the greater part of the registration-district of Abingdon. The old borough gaol has been converted into a police station-house and other uses, and the borough justices have the privilege of committing prisoners to the county bridewell; the prisoners, however, being supported out of the borough rate. The town returns a member to parliament; the mayor is returning officer. The members for the county are elected at Abingdon; and the county magistrates hold a petty-session on alternate Mondays for the Abingdon division. The market-house is a spacious and elegant building of freestone, erected by the corporation in 1678, having a commodious hall in which the Nisi Prius court at the assizes is held, and public business connected with the borough or county is transacted. The county bridewell, a handsome stone edifice, erected in 1811, at an expense of £26,000, comprises a court-house, in which the crown court at the summer assizes, and the July county sessions, are held; the October ses-sions take place here and at Reading alternately.

Abingdon comprises the parishes of ST. HELEN and ST. NICHOLAS; the former including, in the out-parish, part of the townships of Shippon and Northcourt, and the whole of Sandford, Barton, and Pumney; and the latter, the remainder of Shippon and Northcourt, with

some lands in Sunningwell and Bayworth, which are all without the limits of the borough. The living of St. Helen's is a vicarage, with the rectory of St. Nicholas and the chapelry of Drayton annexed, valued in the king's books at £29. 11. 3., and having a net income of £255; it is in the patronage of the Crown. The church is a handsome structure in the early English style, with a square embattled tower surmounted by a lofty spire. The church of St. Nicholas, built about the close of the thirteenth, or commencement of the fourteenth, century, has some remains of Norman architecture. Mr. Wrig-glesworth left lands and tenements, in Abingdon, for the support of a lecture in St. Helen's church, to be de-livered every Saturday evening from Michaelmas to Lady-day, and at the church at Marcham (a village two miles and a half distant) on every Sunday morning from Lady-day till Michaelmas. There are places of wor-ship for Baptists, the Society of Friends, Independents, and Wesleyans. The Free Grammar school, for the education of "Threescore and thirteen" boys, was founded in 1563, by John Royse, and endowed with two mes-suages in Birchin-lane, London, now occupied by part of the premises belonging to the London Assurance Company. In 1608, William Bennett, of " Marlborowe," left land in "Brodeblunsdon" for the maintenance of six poor scholars in Royse's school; these are elected by the master and governors of Christ's hospital in this town, and, from the increase of the funds, are clothed, and instructed also in writing and arithmetic. In 1609, Thomas Tesdale gave certain lands in the county of Warwick, to maintain an usher, whose salary is £120 per annum. The school is entitled to six scholarships at Pembroke College, Oxford, established by Thomas Tesdale, two to be filled by the founder's kin, and the others from the school at large; and to four more scholarships at the same college, instituted by Richard Wightwick, two for the founder's kin.

Christ's Hospital, on the west side of St. Helen's church, erected in 1446, originally belonged to the fra-ternity of the Holy Cross, on the dissolution of which establishment, in 1547, the inhabitants applied through Sir John Mason, to Edward VI., for the restoration of their lost estates, and the foundation of an hospital for the relief of the poor of the town. In compliance with this application the monarch, by letters-patent in 1553, founded the hospital under its present name, and incor-porated twelve persons for its government, called "The Master and Governors of the Hospital of Christ." It consists of almshouses for six poor men, six women, and a nurse, with cloisters, and a handsome hall, where prayers are read morning and evening to the inmates. An almshouse was built in 1718, for eighteen men or women; and there is another, near the river Thames, for six men or women, to which Mr. Beasley, in 1826, bequeathed £600 stock, the interest to be paid weekly, and Thomas Knight, Esq., in 1836, left £600 three and a half per cents. St. John's hospital, in the Vineyard, was endowed before the Reformation, for six poor men, and rebuilt by the corporation in 1801; B. Bedwell, Esq., was a liberal contributor to it, and Mr. Beasley added £600 stock to the endowment. An almshouse near St. Helen's church was erected in 1707, by Charles Twitty, for the maintenance of three men and three wo-men; bequests of £200 each, by John Bedwell in 1799, and Samuel Cripps in 1819, and of £600 three per cent.

6

stock by Mr. Beasley in 1826, have been added to the original endowment. There are also houses for four men and four women, endowed in 1733, by Benjamin Tomkins. The union of Abingdon comprises 27 parishes or places, in the county of Berks, and 11 in that of Oxford, and contains a population of 18,789. The remains of the abbey consist chiefly of the gateway entrance, which, though greatly mutilated, displays some beautiful details of the later style of English architecture. St. Edmund, Archbishop of Canterbury; Sir John Mason, British ambassador at the court of France, and chancellor of the University of Oxford; and the late Lord Colchester, were natives of this place; which confers the title of Earl on the family of Bertie.

ABINGER (St. James), a parish, in the union of Dorking, First division of the hundred of Wotton, W. division of Surrey, 4½ miles (S. W. by W.) from Dorking; containing 920 inhabitants. This parish is noticed in the Domesday survey, under the appellation of Abinebourne; it comprises 5547 acres, of which 374 are common or waste, and includes a small hamlet called Hammer, from an iron-hammer mill formerly here. Abinger Hall is the pleasant seat of Lord Abinger. The living is a rectory, valued in the king's books at £12. 8. 1½., and in the gift of the Evelyn family: the tithes have been commuted for £584, and there are 85 acres of glebe. The church, which occupies an elevated site, is an ancient edifice, with a low wooden tower and pyramidal spire. Sir James Scarlett was raised to the peerage by the title of Baron Abinger in 1835, having previously been appointed chief baron of the exchequer; he died in 1844.

ABINGHALL (St. Michael), a parish, in the union of Westbury, hundred of St. Briavells, W. division of the county of Gloucester, 4 miles (N. by W.) from Newnham; containing 239 inhabitants. This place, formerly called Abbenhall, derived its name from being the residence of the abbots of Flaxley. It contains 691 acres, of which 306 are arable, 238 pasture, and 121 woodland; the surface is hilly, and the soil in general sandy, but towards the east rich and fertile. There are mines of coal and iron-ore, and stone is quarried; facilities of conveyance are afforded by tram-roads and by the Severn. The manufacture of paper is carried on to a considerable extent at Gun's mills, formerly an iron-furnace; the machinery is worked by a stream issuing from St. Anthony's well, the water of which is reputed to be efficacious in cutaneous diseases. The living is a discharged rectory, valued in the king's books at £6. 6. 8., and in the gift of the Dean of Llandaff: the tithes have been commuted for £136. 17., and there are 26 acres of glebe. The church is an old edifice, in the early English style.

ABINGTON (St. Peter and St. Paul), a parish, in the hundred of Spelhoe, union, and S. division of the county, of Northampton, 1½ mile (E. N. E.) from Northampton; containing 143 inhabitants. This was the residence and burial-place of Elizabeth Hall, grand-daughter of the immortal Shakspeare, and widow of Thomas Nash; she married Sir John Bernard, lord of the manor of Abington, and resided here till her death. The parish comprises 1140 acres; it is bounded on the south and south-east by the river Nene, and the roads to Kettering and Wellingborough pass through it. The living is a rectory, valued in the king's books at £20;

net income, £200; patron, John Loyd, Esq. The church was rebuilt in 1825, with the exception of the tower, which is ancient and of square form, with pinnacles.

AB$_{IN}$G$_{TON}$, GREAT (St. Mary), a parish, in the union of Linton, hundred of Chilford, county of Cambridge, 2¼ miles (N. W.) from Linton; containing 358 inhabitants. This place was formerly in the possession of the Veres, earls of Oxford, to one of whom a market on Friday, to be held here, was granted about 1256, with a fair on the festival of St. Lawrence, both of which have been long discontinued. The living is a vicarage, valued in the king's books at £7. 16. 3.; net income, £62: patron and impropriator, T. Mortlock, Esq. The tithes, with some exceptions, were commuted for land under an inclosure act passed in 1801.

ABINGTON-IN-THE-CLAY, or Abington-Pigots (St. Michael), a parish, in the union of Royston, hundred of Armingford, county of Cambridge, 4½ miles (W. N. W.) from Royston; containing 232 inhabitants. It had formerly the privilege of holding a market on Friday, granted about the year 1335 to the Bassingbourns. The parish comprises 1239a. Sp., of which 885 acres are arable, 268 meadow, 64 wood, and 19 occupied by cottages. The living is a rectory, valued in the king's books at £16. 2. 3½., and in the gift of M. G. F. Pigott, Esq.: the tithes have been commuted for £354, and there are 28 acres of glebe.

ABINGTON, LITTLE (St. Mary), a parish, in the union of Linton, hundred of Chilford, county of Cambridge, 2¾ miles (N. W. by N.) from Linton; containing 277 inhabitants. This place appears to be of some antiquity, its church having been given by Stephen, Earl of Brittany, to the monastery of St. Neots in York; subsequently to which, the prior of Pentney, in Norfolk, possessed it. The living is a discharged vicarage, valued in the king's books at £7. 6. 5½.; patron, T. Mortlock, Esq. The tithes were commuted for land and a money payment by an inclosure act in 1801.

AB-KETTLEBY (St. James), a parish, in the union of Melton-Mowbray, hundred of Framland, N. division of the county of Leicester, 3 miles (N. W. by N.) from Melton-Mowbray, on the road to Nottingham; containing, with the hamlet of Holwell, 380 inhabitants. This parish is situated near the border of Nottinghamshire, and comprises 2127 acres, of which 660 are arable, and 1467 pasture. The living is a vicarage, valued in the king's books at £15. 10. 5., and in the patronage of the Rev. Thomas Bingham: the tithes for the waste grounds inclosed in the parish were commuted for land by an inclosure act in 1761. At Holwell is a chapel of case.

ABLINGTON, a tything, in the parish of Bibury, union of Northleach, hundred of Brightwell's-Barrow, E. division of the county of Gloucester, 5½ miles (N. W. by N.) from Fairford; containing 96 inhabitants. The vicarial tithes have been commuted for £364.

ABLINGTON, a hamlet, in the parish of Fighel-dean, union and hundred of Amesbury, Everley and Pewsey, and S. divisions of Wilts; containing 137 inhabitants.

ABNEY, a hamlet, in the parish of Hope, union of Bakewell, hundred of High Peak, N. division of the county of DERBY, 4¾ miles (N. E.) from Tideswell; containing, with Abney-Grange, 102 inhabitants.

ABRAM, a township, in the parish and union of WIGAN, hundred of WEST DERBY, S. division of the county of LANCASTER, 3 miles (S. S. E.) from Wigan; containing 901 inhabitants. This township was originally called Adburgham, and afterwards Abraham, and gave name to an ancient family of landowners, of whom Gilbert de Abram and John Abraham are mentioned in the reigns of Henry IV. and Henry V. It comprises 1769 acres, of which 442 are arable, and 1327 pasture; the soil is chiefly clay. Several coal-mines are in operation; and the Duke of Bridgewater's canal skirts the township. There are some ancient seats, among which is Abram Hall, a moated brick mansion existing since the time of Henry VI. A district church dedicated to St. John has been built, towards defraying the expense of which the Incorporated Society granted £200: the living is a perpetual curacy, in the gift of the Rector, with a net income of £146. A school-house was erected in 1824, at the cost of Mrs. Bevan, of Lowton House. The tithes have been commuted for £242.

ABRIDGE, a hamlet, in the parish of LAMBOURN, union and hundred of ONGAR, S. division of ESSEX, 6½ miles (N. N. W.) from Romford. This place, which is on the high road to Chipping-Ongar, and is bounded on the north by the river Roding, was formerly called Affebruge, or Affebridge; it has within the last few years rapidly increased, and contains several handsome houses. A chapel of ease was erected in 1833; and there is a place of worship for Wesleyans.

ABSON.—See WICK and ABSON.

ABTHORPE (ST. JOHN THE BAPTIST), a parish, in the union and hundred of TOWCESTER, S. division of the county of NORTHAMPTON, 3 miles (W. S. W.) from Towcester; containing, with the hamlets of Charlock and Foscot, 449 inhabitants. This parish was formerly a chapelry dependent upon the vicarage of Towcester, from which it was separated by act of parliament in 1737. It is situated on the right bank of the river Tow, which bounds it on the north-west; and consists of 1895a. 3r. 17p., whereof two-thirds are arable and the remainder pasture. Limestone is quarried. The female population is employed in the manufacture of lace. The living is a vicarage not in charge; net income, £184, with a house; patrons, alternately, the Bishop of Lichfield (to whom the impropriation belongs) and the trustees of Mrs. Jane Leeson's charity estate. The tithes were partially commuted for land under an inclosure act in 1822, and those of the Bishop have been recently commuted for £220; there are about 50 acres of impropriate glebe. Mrs. Leeson, by will dated in 1646, bequeathed certain property to the poor in this and other villages, and also for the instruction of children in a school-house here, previously erected at her expense: the estate at Abthorpe comprises a dwelling-house and about 60 acres of land, together with an allotment of nearly 57 acres under the act of inclosure.

ABY (ALL SAINTS), a parish, in the union of LOUTH, Marsh division of the hundred of CALCEWORTH, parts of LINDSEY, county of LINCOLN, 3 miles (N. W. by W.) from Alford; containing, with the hamlet of Greenfield, 312 inhabitants. The living is a discharged vicarage, united, in 1732, to the rectory of Belleau, and valued in the king's books at £6. 3. 6.
8

ACASTER-MALBIS (HOLY TRINITY), a parish, in the union of YORK, partly in the AINSTY wapentake, W. riding, but chiefly in the wapentake of OUSE and DERWENT, E. riding, of YORK, 4½ miles (S. by W.) from York; containing 748 inhabitants, of whom 322 are in the township of Acaster-Malbis. This place partly derives its name from the family of Malby, who flourished here for some centuries after the Conquest, until at length a daughter and heiress was married to Fairfax of Walton, created Viscount Emley. It comprises by computation 1839 acres, and is intersected by the navigable river Ouse. The living is a perpetual curacy; net income, £56; patron and impropriator, Sir F. Lawley, Bart. A school is endowed with land given by John Knowles in 1603.

ACASTER-SELBY, a township, in the parish of STILLINGFLEET, E. division of AINSTY wapentake, W. riding of YORK, 7¼ miles (S. by W.) from York; containing 188 inhabitants. This place, which anciently belonged to the abbot of Selby, is pleasantly situated on the banks of the navigable river Ouse. A college for a provost and two or three fellows, one of whom was to instruct children, was founded here by Robert Stillington; the revenue, at the Dissolution, was £33. 10. 4.

ACCONBURY, or ACORNBURY (ST. JOHN THE BAPTIST), a parish, in the Upper division of the hundred of WORMELOW, union and county of HEREFORD, 4 miles (S.) from Hereford; containing 158 inhabitants. This parish comprises 1590 acres by computation, and is intersected by the old road from Ross to Hereford, and on its western side by that between Hereford and Monmouth. A nunnery of the order of St. Augustine was founded here, in the reign of John, by Margery, wife of Walter de Lacy, to the honour of the Holy Cross; the revenue, at the Dissolution, was £75. 7. 5¼. The remains have been converted into a farmhouse, but some stone coffins are still preserved. The living is a perpetual curacy; net income, £53; patrons, the Governors of Guy's Hospital, London. The vaults of the church contain the ashes of many illustrious persons, among whom are the first duke of Chandos, and an earl of Carnarvon. On the summit of Acconbury hill, celebrated for its fine plantations and its drives, are traces of a large Roman encampment, the rampart of which, on the east side, is plainly discernible.

ACCRINGTON, a post-town, in the parish of WHALLEY, union of HASLINGDEN, Higher division of the hundred of BLACKBURN, N. division of LANCASHIRE, 5½ miles (E. by S.) from Blackburn; comprising the chapelry of Old, and the township of New, Accrington; and containing 8719 inhabitants, of whom 1811 are in Old, and 6908 in New, Accrington. This place was possessed by the Lacys, by one of whom, Robert, it was given to the monks of Kirkstall; it was subsequently restored by the monks, and, like other lands of the Lacys, came to the crown. Henry VIII. granted lands here to different persons, and among others, probably to the Kenyons : in 1650 Roger Kenyon is described as "the able and orthodox minister of Accrington." Within the last few years the place has acquired considerable importance, from its situation in the calico-printing district; and some large establishments for spinning cotton-thread, and weaving and printing calico, have been formed. An act for lighting the township with gas, and supplying the inhabitants with water, was passed in 1841. Here is a station of the East Lancashire railway : the line runs hence, to Blackburn westward, to Burnley north-east-ward, and to Haslingden southward; three branches here uniting. Old Accrington contains about 739 acres, and New Accrington 2450. The living is a perpetual curacy; net income, £180; patrons, the Hulme Trustees; appropriator, the Archbishop of Canterbury. The chapel was taken down and rebuilt upon a larger scale in 1826, and improved in 1838 : it is a plain structure, with a tower in which are six musical bells ; is elegant within; and has a handsome organ. An additional church was erected in 1840, in the form of a cross, at an expense of above £7000, defrayed by Messrs. Hargreaves and Co., and other inhabitants; it is dedicated to Christ, and the living is a perpetual curacy, in the gift of Trustees. There are places of worship for Baptists, Wesleyans, and Swedenborgians; also a national school, erected by subscription in 1816, and towards the support of which Jonathan Peel, Esq., in 1824, gave £1000.

ACHURCH.—See THORPE-ACHURCH.

ACKLAM (St. John the Baptist), a parish, in the union of MALTON, wapentake of BUCKROSE, E. riding of YORK; containing the townships of Acklam-with-Barthorpe, and Leavening ; and having 845 inhabitants, of whom 411 are in Acklam-with-Barthorpe, 7¼ miles (S.) from Malton. The parish comprises about 4000 acres : the surface is elevated, including a portion of the wolds, from which a most extensive view of the surrounding country is obtained ; and the scenery is in many parts beautifully romantic. The soil in the valley is a strong clay, in other parts of lighter quality; and stone of a good kind for building is largely quarried. The living is a discharged vicarage, valued in the king's books at £5; net income, £108; patron, the Chancellor of the Cathedral of York. The church, rebuilt in 1790, is a neat structure with a square tower, and contains 250 sittings. There are places of worship for Primitive Methodists and Wesleyans.

ACKLAM-IN-CLEVELAND, a parish, in the union of STOCKTON-UPON-TEES, W. division of the liberty of LANGBAURGH, N. riding of YORK, 3 miles (S. E. by E.) from Stockton ; containing 97 inhabitants. This parish, which is on the road from Stokesley to Stockton, and bounded on the west by the river Tees, includes parts of the townships of Linthorpe and Ayresome, and comprises an area of about 1050 acres ; the surface is varied, but generally flat. The soil in the eastern portion is clay, and in the western sandy ; the lands are nearly all arable, and in good cultivation. The Stockton and Middlesborough railway passes through the parish. Acklam Hall has been lately re-fronted, and is a spacious and handsome mansion of brick, pleasantly situated in grounds well laid out, and ornamented with plantations. The village is on the road side. The living is a perpetual curacy, in the patronage of the Archbishop of York, the appropriator, and has a net income of £44 : the church, which had become dilapidated, was rebuilt in 1772, and is a neat structure, covered with Westmorland blue slates.

ACKLINGTON, a township, in the parish of WARKWORTH, union of ALNWICK, E. division of COQUETDALE ward, N. division of NORTHUMBERLAND, 10½ miles (S. S. E.) from Alnwick; containing 301 inhabitants. The manor formed a part of the barony of Warkworth,

and at a very early period belonged to the Percys, earls of Northumberland, in whose family it still remains. The village, which is pretty large, is situated a little to the south of the river Coquet, and about midway be-tween the sea and the road from Alnwick to Morpeth. The tithes have been commuted for £232. 18. payable to the Bishop of Carlisle, and £50. 9. to the vicar. Coal is obtained in the township.

ACKLINGTON-PARK, a township, in the parish of WARKWORTH, union of ALNWICK, E. division of COQUETDALE ward, N. division of NORTHUMBERLAND, 9 miles (S. S. E.) from Alnwick; containing 133 inhabitants. This place lies on the south side of the river Coquet, not very far distant from the sea, and in a fine secluded situation : it belongs to the Duke of Northumberland. There is a coarse woollen manufactory. The tithes have been commuted for £55. 11. payable to the Bishop of Carlisle, and £1. 3. to the vicar.

ACKTON, a township, in the parish of FEATHERSTONE, Lower division of the wapentake of AGBRIGG, W. riding of YORK, 3½ miles (W.) from Pontefract; containing 76 inhabitants. This place, called also Aikton, a probable corruption of Oak Town, from the number of oak-trees growing in its vicinity, comprises by computation 1090 acres of land. Aikton Hall belonged to Langdale Sunderland, Esq., of Halifax, who raised a troop of horse for Charles's service, and was at the battle of Marston Moor : Cromwell fined him £878.

ACKWORTH (St. Cuthbert), a parish, in the Upper division of the wapentake of OSGOLDCROSS, W. riding of YORK, 3¼ miles (S. S. W.) from Pontefract ; containing 1828 inhabitants. This parish, which ocenpies an elevated situation, comprises 2537a. 3r. 27p. of profitable land, and 36 acres of roads and waste ; the soil is fertile ; the surface is boldly undulated, and richly embellished with wood. Freestone of excellent quality is abundant, and there are some extensive quarries of it at Moor Top, in the parish. The village, which is divided into High and Low Ackworth, is situated on rising ground near the source of the river Went, and contains numerous neat and well-built houses, with several pleasant villas in the immediate neighbourhood. Ackworth Park is a beautiful seat. Handloom weaving is carried on to a limited extent. The living is a rectory, valued in the king's books at £22. 1. 0½., and in the patronage of the Crown, in right of the duchy of Lancaster ; net income, £403. The tithes were commuted for land and a money payment, under an act of inclosure, in 1774 ; the glebe comprises 152 acres. The church, an ancient structure situated in Upper Ackworth, has at various times undergone much alteration and repair. There is a place of worship for Wesleyans.

The school here belonging to the SOCIETY OF FRIENDS was originally and for some years an appendage to the Foundling Hospital of London, for which purpose it was originally built, at an expense of £13,000, defrayed by subscription, aided by a grant from parliament. Upon its separation from that institution, the house, with 84 acres of land attached to it, was purchased in 1777 by Dr. Fothergill and two or three other gentlemen of the Society of Friends for £7000; and it was afterwards appropriated as a school for the education of the children of the less wealthy members of that community. The buildings are situated between High and Low Ackworth; and now comprise arrangements for the recep-

C

tion of 180 boys and 120 girls; the land has been extended to 274 acres. The hospital and school at High Ackworth were built by Mrs. Mary Lowther, who in 1741 endowed them with 17 acres of land, now producing £30 per annum, and with £700 invested at 5 per cent interest.

ACLE (St. Edmund), a parish, in the union of Blofield, hundred of Walsham, E. division of Norfolk, 11 miles (E.) from Norwich; containing 864 inhabitants. This place, at the time of the Norman Conquest, became a fief of the crown, and was granted by William to Roger Bigod, who obtained for it the privilege of a market and a fair; and in the reign of Richard II. the inhabitants were exempted from all tolls and suits of shire and hundred, and invested with several valuable immunities. The parish comprises 3164a. 2r. 8p., a large portion of which is grazing land reclaimed from marshy ground; the uplands consist of a fine loamy soil, and are exceedingly fertile. The village is situated on the road from Norwich to Yarmouth, and on a gentle eminence rising from the banks of the navigable river Bure, over which is a stone bridge of three arches, and of great elevation. The living is a rectory, valued in the king's books at £20, and in the gift of Lord Calthorpe: the tithes have been commuted for £720, and there are about twenty acres of glebe, and a good rectory-house. The church, which is chiefly in the decorated style, consists of a nave and chancel, with a circular tower the upper part of which is octagon; and the edifice was thoroughly repaired and beautified in 1834. At Weybridge, a small priory for Augustine canons was founded in the reign of Edward I., by Roger Bigod, Earl of Norfolk; the revenue at the Dissolution was £7. 13. 4.

ACOMB (St. Stephen), a parish, in the Ainsty wapentake, W. riding of York; containing 880 inhabitants, of whom 774 are in the township of Acomb, 2½ miles (W.) from York, on the road to Leeds via Wetherby. This parish, anciently Ascham, comprises by measurement 1920 acres, and is bounded on the north by the river Ouse, on which is a small wharf for coal, lime, &c., adjacent to the Darlington railway; the soil is of a sandy and gravelly nature, and the air remarkably salubrious. Several mansions and villas here are ocenpied by families of the first respectability. The village has a neat appearance; the York and North-Midland railway passes near it, at Hob Moor. Part of Knapton, and also part of Dringhouses, are in the parish, and churchwardens are elected for these places along with those for Acomb. The living is a discharged vicarage, valued in the king's books at £3. 9. 2.; net income, £109; patron and incumbent, the Rev. Isaac Spencer. The peculiar of Acomb formerly belonged to the Treasurer in the Cathedral of York, but was surrendered, with the rectory, to the Crown in 1547; and in 1609 was granted by James I. to Thomas Newark and his heir. The tithes of the townships of Acomb and Holgate were commuted for land and a money payment, by an inclosure act in 1774. The church, rebuilt in 1831-2 by subscription, is an elegant structure with a graceful spire, and, standing on the highest ground in the vicinity of York, has a very picturesque appearance; it contains 609 sittings, of which 212 are free. There are places of worship for Wesleyans and Primitive Methodists. Half a mile from the village is a hill, supposed to be the tumulus of Septimius Severus, who died at York.

10

ACOMB, EAST, a township, in the parish of Bywell St. Peter, union of Hexham, E. division of Tindale ward, S. division of Northumberland, 8 miles (E.) from Hexham; containing 37 inhabitants. It is situated about a mile north from Bywell, and consists of two farms; Peepee, a pleasant hamlet, lies at a little distance westward. This, and many other parts of the Bywell estate, are covered with trees of a remarkably fine growth, which impart to the landscape a rich and luxuriant aspect.

ACOMB, WEST, a township, in the parish of St. John Lee, union of Hexham, S. division of Tindale ward and of Northumberland, 1¾ mile (N.) from Hexham; containing 571 inhabitants. This place, anciently Hameshaly, belonged to the prior of Hexham, and is supposed to have been the favourite retreat of St. John of Beverley: on the dissolution of the priory it came to the crown; in 1724 it was the property of the Coatsworth family, and subsequently of the Jurins and Hunters. The township is bounded on the south by the river Tyne: coal is obtained within its limits; and the Newcastle and Carlisle railway passes through it. The great tithes have been commuted for £65.

ACORNBURY.—See Acconbury.

ACRISE (St. Martin), a parish, in the union of Elham, partly in the hundred of Folkestone, but chiefly in that of Loningborough, lathe of Shepway, E. division of Kent, 5 miles (N.N.W.) from Folkestone, near the road to Canterbury; containing 207 inhabitants. The parish comprises 1033 acres, of which 55 are common or waste land, and 126 in wood. The living is a rectory, valued in the king's books at £7, and in the patronage of the Crown: the tithes have been commuted for £217, and there are nearly 44 acres of glebe.

ACTON, a township, in the parish of Weaverham, union of Northwich, Second division of the hundred of Eddisbury, S. division of Cheshire, 4½ miles (W. N. W.) from Northwich; containing 382 inhabitants. This place, sometimes called Acton-in-Delamere, was part of the ancient inheritance of the Duttons, from whom it passed by marriage to the Geralds and Fleetwoods: it subsequently came by purchase to the Ashton family. The township comprises 1102 acres of land, of a clayey and sandy soil: the Liverpool and Birmingham railway and the Grand Trunk canal pass through it, and on the former a station has been fixed here.

ACTON (St. Mary), a parish, in the union and hundred of Nantwich, S. division of Cheshire; comprising the townships of Acton, Aston-juxta-Mondrum, Austerson, Baddington, Brindley, Burland, Cholmondstone, Cool-Pilate, Edleston, Faddiley, Henhull, Hurleston, Poole, Stoke, Worleston, and part of Soond; and containing 4134 inhabitants, of whom 328 are in the township of Acton, 1¼ mile (N. W. by W.) from Nantwich. This place was the scene of some hostilities during the parliamentary war. In October 1643, the church and Dorford Hall were occupied by the royalists, on whose retreat both were garrisoned by the parliament. They were afterwards captured by the king's troops under Lord Byron; but, on the raising of the siege of Nantwich, Sir Thomas Fairfax compelled the garrisons to surrender, and among the prisoners were sixty officers, including Col. Monk, afterwards Duke of Albemarle. In the township of Acton are 674 acres; the soil is half clay and half sand. The Chester and Crewe railway crosses the Middlewich and Wardle canal at the Chol-mondstone lock in this parish. The living is a vicarage, valued in the king's books at £19. 9. 7.; net income, £324; patron and impropriator, John Tollemache, Esq., of Tilston Lodge : the great tithes of Acton township have been commuted for £41. 6., and the vicarial tithes for £26. 14. The church exhibits some curiously orna-mented windows; the tower is partly in the early style of English architecture. At Burley-Dam is a second church, the living of which is a perpetual curacy, in the gift of Viscount Combermere; net income, £100. A grammar school is endowed with £16 per annum, and a house; and there is a school in connexion with the National Society. Sir Roger Wilbraham founded and endowed two almshouses in 1613.

ACTON (St. Mary), a parish, in the union of Brent-ford, Kensington division of the hundred of Ossul-stone, county of Middlesex, 5 miles (W.) from London; containing, with the hamlets of East Acton and Steyne, 2665 inhabitants. The name is supposed to be derived from the Saxon word Ac, signifying oak, and tun, a town; the neighbourhood having, in former times, abounded with timber of that description, and some land in the parish, from time immemorial, having been called Old Oak common. Previously to the battle of Brentford, in 1642, the Earls of Essex and Warwick had their head-quarters here; and on Cromwell's return to London, after the battle of Worcester, the lord presi-dent and council of state, the members of the house of commons, and the lord mayor, aldermen, and citizens of London, met him at this place, when the recorder delivered a congratulatory address, after which they at-tended him to the metropolis, forming altogether a train of more than three hundred carriages. The parish com-prises 2251 acres, of which 85 are common or waste : the village consists chiefly of one long street, and is plentifully supplied with water; the Paddington canal and the Great Western railway run through. A pleasure-fair is held on Holy-Thursday. The living is a rectory, valued in the king's books at £14; net income, £968; patron, the Bishop of London. The church, which ex-hibits portions in the later style of English architecture, with modern insertions, was enlarged and repaired, at the expense of the inhabitants, in 1825. There is a place of worship for Independents, and the detached buildings of a private mansion have been fitted up as a Roman Catholic chapel. At East Acton are handsome almshouses, built and endowed by the Goldsmiths' Com-pany, for twelve men and twelve women. In a garden on Old Oak common is a mineral spring, formerly held in general repute, but now disused.

ACTON, with Old Felton, a township, in the parish of Felton, union of Alnwick. E. division of Coquetdale ward, N. division of Northumberland, 7½ miles (S.) from Alnwick, on the road to Morpeth; containing 111 inhabitants. This place extends between one and two miles north of the village of Felton. Acton House is a handsome mansion; and North Acton Hall is also a fine structure, beautifully situated : the adjoin-ing lands are fertile and picturesque. The impropriate tithes have been commuted for £40.

ACTON (All Saints), a parish, in the union of Sudbury, hundred of Babergh, W. division of Suf-folk, 3 miles (N. E. by N.) from Sudbury; containing 555 inhabitants. It comprises 2811a. 21p., whereof 69

acres are common or waste. There are several small hamlets, that which is called "The Village" being the principal. The living is a vicarage, valued in the king's books at £9. 6. 8.; patron and impropriator, Earl Howe : the great and small tithes have been each commuted for £375. The church is neat, and contains some ancient and very handsome brasses.

ACTON-BEAUCHAMP (St. Giles), a parish, in the union of Bromyard, Upper division of the hundred of Doddingtree, Worcester and W. divisions of the county of Worcester, 4 miles (S. E.) from Bromyard; containing 217 inhabitants. The area is 1524 acres, of which 717 are arable, 570 pasture, 150 woodland, and 82 hop-ground, &c.; the surface is very hilly, and the soil mostly a strong clay, but in some parts sandy; the scenery is beautiful, and embraces extensive views. The parish is intersected by the roads from Worcester to Hereford, and from Bromyard to Malvern; and is sur-rounded on all sides except the east by the county of Hereford. There are quarries of stone for building. The living is a discharged rectory, valued in the king's books at £4, and in the patronage of Mrs. Cowpland : the tithes have been commuted for £270, and the glebe consists of 42 acres, with a house. A school is supported by the rector. Here are some mineral springs.

ACTON-BURNELL (St. Mary), a parish, in the unions of Atcham and Church-Stretton, hundred of Condover, S. division of Salop, 7 miles (S.) from Shrewsbury; containing, with Ruckley and Langley, 394 inhabitants. This place, which is of considerable anti-quity, is on a branch of the Roman Watling-street. It takes the adjunct to its name from the family of Burnell, of whom Robert, Bishop of Bath and Wells, and Lord High Chancellor in the reign of Edward I., had a castle in the parish, of which there are still some remains. In 1283, a council or parliament was held here, at which was enacted the law of "Statute merchant;" the king and his court were accommodated in the castle, the lords assembled in a great hall erected for them in the park, and the commons met in a very large barn belonging to Shrewsbury Abbey, whose gable ends have been pre-served to the present time. Besides the Watling-street, a causeway passes through the parish; and there are a Roman bridge, and an early specimen of Saxon antiquity called the Moat. The parish comprises by computation 2400 acres. The living is a rectory, with the chapelry of Langley, valued in the king's books at £6. 10., and in the gift of Sir E. J. Smythe, Bart. : it has a net in-come of £350; the glebe consists of about 70 acres, with a good house. The church, which is cruciform, was built in 1264, and is a splendid specimen of architecture : its internal decorations are of a highly ornamental cha-racter. There is a Roman Catholic chapel. Nicholas Burnell, a distinguished warrior in the reign of Edward III., was born and buried here.

ACTON-GRANGE, a township, in the parochial chapelry of Daresbury, parish and union of Runcorn, hundred of Bucklow, N. division of the county of Chester, 2¾ miles (S. W. by S.) from Warrington; containing 175 inhabitants. The manor was the pro-perty of the convent of Norton, and in the reign of Henry VIII., 1545, was purchased by the crown, with other estates of that monastery, by the ancestor of the present proprietor, Sir Richard Brooke, Bart. The township comprises 855 acres; it is separated from

Lancashire by the river Mersey, and is intersected by the Liverpool and Birmingham railway, and the Bridgewater canal.

ACTON, IRON.—See IRON-ACTON.

ACTON-PIGOT, a hamlet, in the parish of ACTON-BURNELL, union of CHURCH-STRETTON, hundred of CONDOVER, S. division of SALOP, 6¾ miles (W. N. W.) from Much-Wenlock ; comprising 391 acres, and containing 40 persons. There was formerly a chapel, the remains of which still exist.

ACTON-REYNALD, a township, in the parish of SHAWBURY, union of WEM, liberty of the borough of SHREWSBURY, N. division of SALOP, 7½ miles (N. N. E.) from Shrewsbury ; containing 159 inhabitants.

ACTON-ROUND, a parish, in the union of BRIDG-NORTH, hundred of STOTTESDEN, S. division of SALOP, 3¾ miles (S. S. E.) from Much-Wenlock, and 6 (W. N. W.) from Bridgnorth ; containing 180 inhabitants. This parish, which is intersected by the road from Much-Wenlock to Bridgnorth, comprises by computation 2126a. 2r. ; the soil is a red clay ; the prospect embraces the Clee hills, the highest in the county. The living is a perpetual curacy ; net income, £85 ; patron and impropriator, Sir John Acton, Bart. Certain tithes were commuted for land under an inclosure act in 1773 : there are about 25 acres of glebe, of which 14 are near Bromsgrove, in Worcestershire, and 11 in the parish of Stottesden. The church is a neat edifice, the walls of which are ornamented with monuments to the memory of the Actons, by one of whom, Sir Richard, the chancel was built in 1761.

ACTON-SCOTT (ST. MARGARET), a parish, in the union of CHURCH-STRETTON, hundred of MUNSLOW, S. division of SALOP, 3 miles (S. by E.) from Church-Stretton ; containing 204 inhabitants. It is situated on the new road from Wenlock to Bishop's Castle, and contains by measurement 1600 acres of land, all cultivated, excepting about 200 under plantation and coppice. The surface is hilly, abounding in bold, and in some parts romantic, scenery ; the soil comprises several varieties ; and stone is quarried for building and the repair of roads. The living is a discharged rectory, valued in the king's books at £5. 10., and in the gift of E. W. W. Pendarves, Esq. : the tithes have been commuted for £230, and there are 61 acres of glebe.

ACTON-TRUSSELL, a parochial chapelry, in the parish of BASWICK, union of PENKRIDGE, E. division of the hundred of CUTTLESTONE, S. division of the county of STAFFORD, 3½ miles (N. N. E.) from Penkridge ; containing, with Bednall, 574 inhabitants. The township of Acton and Bednall comprises 2551 acres, of which 1400 are arable, and the remainder grass, with a few acres of plantation ; the soil is a good gravelly loam. Acton lies west of Bednall, adjoining the river Penk and the Staffordshire and Worcestershire canal. The living is a perpetual curacy, with that of Bednall united ; net income, £234 ; patrons, the Trustees of William Hulme. The glebe-house was built in 1842 by the Rev. Matthew Davies, the incumbent ; it commands extensive and beautiful views : the glebe consists of 32 acres. The chapel of Acton, dedicated to St. James, is an ancient edifice in the early English style, with a square tower : Bednall chapel, dedicated to All Saints, was rebuilt in 1844, and consecrated in July 1846 ; it is a neat structure with a bell-turret. There is a national school.

12

ACTON-TURVILLE (ST. MARY), a parish, in the union of CHIPPING-SODBURY, Lower division of the hundred of GRUMBALD'S ASH, W. division of the county of GLOUCESTER, 5¾ miles (E.) from Chipping-Sodbury ; containing 311 inhabitants. This place, which lies on the border of Wiltshire, is exceedingly well situated with respect to means of communication, roads branching off from the village to the towns of Malmesbury, Chippenham, Bath, and Chipping-Sodbury, respectively. The living is a vicarage not in charge, united to the rectory of Tormarton in 1344.

ADBASTON (ST. MARGARET), a parish, in the union and of the county of STAFFORD, 4 miles (W. by S.) from Eccleshall ; comprising the townships of Adbaston, Bishop's Offlow, Flashbrook, and Tunstall, and the hamlet of Knighton ; and containing 610 inhabitants, of whom 39 are in the township of Adbaston. The parish consists of about 4000 acres, divided into nearly equal portions of arable and pasture, with a small quantity of woodland. The soil belongs to a number of proprietors, several of whom reside upon their estates here. In Adbaston are only a few scattered houses. The living is a perpetual curacy, in the patronage of the Dean of Lichfield ; net income, £100 : the tithes have been commuted for £562. 10. per annum, and the incumbent receives a rent-charge of £2. 10. The church stands near the Hall and the parsonage, and is an ancient structure.

ADBOLTON, formerly a parish, now a hamlet in the parish of HOLME-PIERREPOINT, union of BING-HAM, S. division of the wapentake of BINGHAM and of the county of NOTTINGHAM, 3 miles (E. S. E.) from Nottingham ; containing 25 inhabitants. The living, a discharged rectory, valued in the king's books at £2. 13. 9., was in 1707 consolidated with the rectory of Holme-Pierrepoint : the church is in ruins.

ADDERBURY, EAST (ST. MARY), a parish, in the union of BANBURY, hundred of BLOXHAM, county of OXFORD, 3 miles (N. by E.) from Deddington ; containing, with the township of West Adderbury, the hamlets of Barford St. John, Bodicot, and Milton, 2525 inhabitants. This place, in Domesday book called *Edburberie*, probably derived that name from St. Edburgh, to whom many religious establishments in this part of the country were dedicated. In the court rolls of New College, Oxford, to which the lordship belongs, the name is written " Ebberbury ;" and Henry de Knyghton relates that, by a council of bishops held at Oxford, a blasphemous impostor, condemned for assuming the office and pretending to the wounds of Christ, was crucified at " Abberbury," now Adderbury. The PARISH comprises about 5900 acres, of which 1120 are in West Adderbury, 1240 in Bodicot, 800 in Milton, and 700 in Barford St. John. In the eastern part of the village stood a magnificent ancient mansion, belonging to the Duke of Argyll, afterwards the residence of the Earl of Rochester, and the remains of which are now incorporated with a modern seat.

The living is a vicarage, valued in the king's books at £21. 4. 9½. ; net income, £818 ; patrons and appropriators, the Warden and Fellows of New College. The church, situated on elevated ground, is a handsome cruciform structure in the early and decorated English styles, with a massive square tower strengthened by angular buttresses, and crowned with a pierced parapet, from within which rises an octagonal spire, having at the base four octagonal pyramids surmounted with vanes. Between the north transept and the east end of the chancel is an octagonal turret, crowned with battlements. The chancel, of beautiful proportions, and built by William of Wykeham, is lighted by windows of elegant design, lately restored : part of the ancient rood-loft, of exquisite workmanship, is remaining; also some fine tracery; and the whole of the interior is replete with rich details, interspersed with grotesque ornaments. In the hamlets of Bodicot and Barford St. John are other churches, both ancient structures, supposed to have been erected in the fourteenth century; and the old parsonage, now a farmhouse, retains much of its original character. There is a place of worship for Wesleyans.

ADDERBURY, WEST, a township, in the parish of EAST ADDERBURY, union of BANBURY, hundred of BLOXHAM, county of OXFORD, 2 miles (N.) from Deddington ; containing 442 inhabitants.

ADDERLEY (ST. PETER), a parish, in the union of DRAYTON, Drayton division of the hundred of NORTH BRADFORD, N. division of SALOP, 4 miles (N. by W.) from Drayton ; containing 404 inhabitants. It is situated on the Liverpool and Shrewsbury road, and the Chester and Ellesmere canal ; and comprises 3750a. 1r. 23p., of which 962½ acres are arable, 2493½ pasture and meadow, and 294 woodland. The living is a rectory, valued in the king's books at £11. 6. 0½., and in the patronage of the Rev. H. C. Cotton, for the next turn; afterwards, of Richard Corbett, Esq., of Adderley Hall. The tithes have been commuted for £666. 16. ; and there are about 19 acres of glebe, with a glebe-house, rebuilt in 1800. The parish has sundry donations for doles of bread to widows each Sunday, and for a distribution of money on St. Thomas's day ; also an alternate turn with Muckleston, of money to place six poor boys at school, and two as apprentices.

ADDERSTONE, a township, in the parish of BAM-BROUGH, union of BELFORD, N. division of BAMBROUGH ward and of NORTHUMBERLAND, 3 miles (S. E. by S.) from Belford ; containing 302 inhabitants. The manor was possessed by the ancient family of Forster, from whom it came, in 1763, to John William Bacon, Esq., by whom the present handsome mansion, which stands near the site of the old hall, on the west bank of the Warn, was erected, and whose successor sold the estate to J. Pratt, Esq.

ADDINGHAM (ST. MICHAEL), a parish, in the union of PENRITH, LEATH ward, E. division of CUMBERLAND, 1½ mile (S. E.) from Kirk-Oswald ; containing, with the townships of Gamblesby, Glassonby, Hunsonby and Winskel, and Little Salkeld, 735 inhabitants. It is bounded on the west by the river Eden, and the Roman road called Maiden-way may be traced here in many parts of its course : there are some quarries of red freestone. The living is a vicarage, valued in the king's books at £9. 4. 7.; net income, £253 ; patrons and appropriators, the Dean and Chapter of Carlisle. The church is situated in the township of Glassonby : at Gamblesby are places of worship for Independents and Wesleyans; also one for the latter at Hunsonby ; and there are well-endowed free schools at Hunsonby and Maughamby. At Little Salkeld is a remarkable monument supposed to be Druidical, commonly called ' Long Meg and her Daughters," consisting of 67 stones

13

varying in shape and height, which form a circle about 350 feet in diameter; and in the same township was anciently a chapel, the site of which, according to tra. dition, was at a village called Addingham, on the eastern bank of the Eden, where human bones, crosses, and other remains, have been dug up. Dr. Paley, the cele. brated theological writer, held the living.

ADDINGHAM (ST. PETER), a parish, in the union of SKIPTON, partly in the E. division of the wapentake of STAINCLIFFE and EWCROSS, and partly in the Upper division of the wapentake of CLARO, W. riding of YORK, 6 miles (E. by S.) from Skipton ; containing 1753 inha. bitants, of whom 1527 are in the township of Adding. ham. It is situated on the western side of the river Wharfe, and within the liberty of Clifford's Fee, and comprises about 4000 acres, of which 900 are open common : the soil is fertile, and the surface varied and pleasing ; freestone of good quality is abundant, and ex. tensively quarried. Farfield Hall, in the parish, is a handsome mansion in the Italian style, originally built by the Earl of Burlington, and is finely situated, commanding beautiful views of the river and of the pictu. resque valley through which it flows. The village, which consists of irregularly detached houses, extends nearly a mile in length : a portion of the inhabitants are employed in cotton and worsted mills, and in hand-loom weaving. The living is a discharged rectory, valued in the king's books at £9. 7. 8½.; income about £400, with a glebe-house beautifully situated ; patron, the Rev. William Thompson. The tithes of the township have been commuted for £197, and the glebe consists of 20 acres. The church, which was rebuilt in 1757, is a neat structure with a square tower, and is seated on an eminence overlooking the river ; it contains 450 sittings. There are places of worship for the Society of Friends, Primitive Methodists, and Wesleyans. On Counter Hill, about a mile from the village, are the remains of a Roman encampment, and some traces of a Roman road. A massive and antique ring of gold was found in the churchyard some years since.

ADDINGTON (ST. MARY), a parish, in the union, hundred, and county of BUCKINGHAM, 1¾ mile (W.N.W.) from Winslow ; containing 84 inhabitants. It comprises about 1500 acres ; the surface is in general level, and the soil good pasture. The living is a rectory, valued in the king's books at £9. 9. 7.; net income, £200 ; patron, John Poulett, Esq. : the glebe consists of 100 acres. On the border of the parish is a place called " Gallows Gap," where, in the reign of Edward III., a gallows was erected by the family of Molines, who, as lords of the barony, possessed the power of trying and executing capital offenders.

ADDINGTON (ST. MARGARET), a parish, in the union of MALLING, hundred of LARKFIELD, lathe of AYLESFORD, W. division of KENT, 8 miles (N. W. by W.) from Maidstone ; containing 208 inhabitants. The parish comprises 942 acres, whereof 70 are under wood. Here is one of those land springs very common in the eastern part of Kent, called the Ailbourn, which breaks out with great impetuosity once in seven or eight years, directing its course into a trench dug for its reception, till it arrives at the Leybourn rivulet, the trout in which, at other times white, it turns to a red colour. The living is a rectory, valued in the king's books at £6. 6. 8. ; net income, £160 ; patron, the Hon. J. W. Stratford :

the glebe consists of 26 acres. The church is pleasantly situated in the midst of foliage on rising ground within a valley, near which are remains, supposed to be Druidical.

ADDINGTON (St. Mary), a parish, in the union of Croydon, First division of the hundred of Wallington, E. division of Surrey, 3½ miles (E. S. E.) from Croydon; containing 580 inhabitants. The manor is held by the singular tenure of making and presenting to the king, at his coronation, a mess of pottage called *mewpergynon*; subject to the performance of which, a carucate of land here was granted to Tezelin, cook to William the Conqueror. The parish comprises by admeasurement 3635 acres, 500 of which are under wood or uncultivated. The village is situated at the foot of a range of hills to which it gives its name; and adjacent to these hills also is Addington Place, which, in 1807, was purchased by Dr. Sutton, Archbishop of Canterbury, with the funds arising from the sale of the archiepiscopal palace at Croydon. The mansion was originally erected by Alderman Trecothick, on the site of an ancient edifice said to have been a hunting seat of Henry VIII.; it was improved by Dr. Sutton, and has been rebuilt with the addition of wings, and the grounds much extended, by Dr. Howley. The living is a discharged vicarage, valued in the king's books at £4. 16. 5½.; patron, the Archbishop; impropriators, the landowners. The great and small tithes have been commuted, the former for £559. 18. 6., and the latter for £208. 4.; and there is a small glebe. The church, consisting of a nave, chancel, and south aisle, with a low, square, embattled tower, was thoroughly repaired in 1843: in the chancel lie the remains of Archbishop Sutton. Near the church is an eminence called Castle hill, on which it is said a castle anciently stood; and on the brow of the hill adjoining Addington common, and now in the park, are several low tumuli, in which urns have been found.

ADDINGTON, GREAT (All Saints), a parish, in the union of Thrapston, hundred of Huxloe, N. division of the county of Northampton, 4½ miles (S. W.) from Thrapston; containing 266 inhabitants. It is situated on the left bank of the navigable river Nene, and comprises 1233a. 3r. 31p.; the surface is pleasantly diversified with hill and dale, and the soil runs through many varieties. The living is a rectory, valued in the king's books at £10. 12. 8½.; net income, £315; patron and incumbent, the Rev. James Tyley. The tithes were commuted for 327 acres of land and a money payment, under an inclosure act, in 1803.

ADDINGTON, LITTLE (St. Mary), a parish, in the union of Thrapston, hundred of Huxloe, N. division of the county of Northampton, 3¾ miles (N.) from Higham-Ferrers; containing 299 inhabitants. The parish is bounded by the river Nene, and consists of 1104a. 3r. 29p. of a moderately productive soil. On the opposite side of the Nene runs a branch of the London and Birmingham railway, from Northampton to Peterborough, with a station at a convenient distance from this place. The living is a discharged vicarage, endowed with the great tithes, and valued in the king's books at £7. 12.; net income, £245; patron, G. Capron, Esq. The tithes of the parish were commuted for land and a money payment, under an inclosure act, passed in the year 1830.

14

ADDLE, or Adel (St. John the Baptist), a parish, in the Upper division of the wapentake of Skyrack, W. riding of York; containing 1121 inhabitants, of whom 785 are in the township of Addle-cum-Eccup, 5¾ miles (N. N. W.) from Leeds. This place, anciently called Adhill, from the Ada of the Saxons, and in some documents Adel, was the site of the Roman station *Burgodunum*, of which some traces, with many inscribed stones, fragments of urns, and the remains of an aqueduct, were discovered in 1702 on an adjacent moor. Near this moor are still the vestiges of a camp 120 yards in length, and 90 yards in breadth, in which Roman altars, numerous coins, and various other relics, have been found. The parish is bounded on the north by the river Wharfe, and comprises by computation 8000 acres; the surface is varied, and the scenery generally of pleasing character. The hamlet of Eccup, which is near the site of the camp, abounds with springs of excellent water, from which the Leeds new water-works are supplied. The living is a rectory, valued in the king's books at £16. 3. 4.; net income, £623; patron, W. T. Carruthers, Esq.: the glebe comprises 164 acres, with a good house. The church is a venerable structure of Norman design, and one of the most perfect specimens of that style in the kingdom; the south doorway is highly enriched, and many of its details are of great elegance. Thos. Kirk, Esq., in 1701, bequeathed to the poor the sum of £800, which has been laid out in the purchase of two houses and 82 acres of land.

ADDLESTONE, an ecclesiastical district, in the parish and union of Chertsey, Second division of the hundred of Godley, W. division of Surrey; containing about 2000 inhabitants. The lands were inclosed in 1808, and include a considerable extent of meadow; the dwellings are much scattered, and interspersed with several seats and villas. A church in the early English style, dedicated to St. Paul, and affording accommodation for 800 persons, has been erected at an expense of about £3000, raised by subscription; it has been endowed with £2000 by Miss Wightwick, whose family has long resided in the parish, and the patronage is vested in the Bishop of Winchester. The consecration took place in Jan. 1838; and the benefice was augmented in 1841 by the Ecclesiastical Commissioners to £150 per annum. Near the west end of the church is a parsonage-house, built by subscription at a cost of £970. An ancient and venerable tree here, called the Crouch oak, is stated by tradition to have in former ages marked the boundary of Windsor Forest, in this direction; and Queen Elizabeth is said to have dined beneath its shadow : the girth, at two feet from the ground, is 24 feet.

ADDLETHORPE (St. Nicholas), a parish, in the union of Spilsby, Marsh division of the wapentake of Candleshoe, parts of Lindsey, county of Lincoln, 9½ miles (E. S. E.) from Alford; containing 238 inhabitants. This parish is about 2000 acres of land, on the coast, and is subject to encroachments of the sea, against which it is necessary to maintain an embankment at a considerable expense. The living is a discharged rectory, valued in the king's books at £9. 10. 2½., and in the gift of the Crown: the tithes have been commuted for £140, and the glebe consists of about 7 acres. The church is a fine specimen of the perpendicular style, and consists of a nave, north and south aisles, and a tower. There is a place of worship for Methodists.

ADFORTON, with STANWAY, PAYTON, and GRANGE, a township, in the parish of LEINTWARDINE, union of KNIGHTON, hundred of WIGMORE, county of HEREFORD, 8½ miles (W. S. W.) from Ludlow; containing 288 inhabitants, and comprising 1565 acres. The surface is boldly undulated, and the southern portion well wooded. On an eminence at the northern extremity are the remains of a Roman encampment called Brandon camp. The road from Leintwardine to Wigmore passes through the village of Adforton.

ADGARLEY, a township, in the parish of URSWICK, union of ULVERSTON, hundred of LONSDALE north of the Sands, N. division of the county of LANCASTER, 2 miles (S. E. by E.) from Dalton; containing 45 inhabitants.

ADISHAM (HOLY INNOCENTS), a parish, in the union of BRIDGE, hundred of DOWNHAMFORD, lathe of ST. AUGUSTINE, E. division of KENT, 2¾ miles (S. W. by S.) from Wingham; containing 372 inhabitants. It lies a little to the east of the high road from Canterbury to Dover, and comprises 1815 acres, of which 189 are in wood. The living is a rectory, with the perpetual curacy of Staple annexed, valued in the king's books at £28. 3. 1½., and in the gift of the Archbishop of Canterbury: the tithes have been commuted for £747, and there are about 13 acres of glebe, with a house. The church is a large cruciform edifice with a low tower, in the early style of English architecture, except the large window of the transept, which is in the decorated style; the altar-piece is embellished with curious paintings on wood of the Four Evangelists.

ADLESTROP (ST. MARY MAGDALENE), a parish, in the union of STOW-ON-THE-WOLD, Upper division of the hundred of SLAUGHTER, E. division of the county of GLOUCESTER, 3¾ miles (E. by N.) from Stow; containing 200 inhabitants. It is bounded on the south-east by the road from Stow to Chipping-Norton, and on the south-west by the river Evenlode; and is situated on the borders of Oxfordshire, not far distant from the southern extremity of the county of Warwick. The living is a rectory not in charge, annexed to that of Broadwell: the tithes were partially commuted for land, under an inclosure act, in 1775. The church, with the exception of the tower, was rebuilt in 1764.

ADLINGFLEET (ALL SAINTS), a parish, in the union of GOOLE, Lower division of the wapentake of OSGOLDCROSS, W. riding of YORK; comprising the townships of Eastoft, Fockerby, and Haldenby; and containing 448 inhabitants, of whom 199 are in the township of Adlingfleet, 9½ miles (S. E.) from Howden. This parish is situated on the borders of Lincolnshire, between the rivers Ouse and Trent, and contains 4580 acres, forming a continuation of the great level of Hatfield Chase; the soil is chiefly clay, and, though the surface is flat, the scenery is pleasing. The living is a vicarage, valued in the king's books at £9. 12. 11., and has a net income of £280; it is in the patronage of the Crown, and the impropriation belongs to Catherine Hall, Cambridge. The tithes for the townships of Adlingfleet, Fockerby, and Haldenby, were commuted for land and a money payment, under an inclosure act, in 1767. The church, which is a small edifice, was repaired in 1828 at an expense of £500. There are two places of worship for Methodists; and at Fockerby is a free grammar school.

15

ADLINGTON, a township, in the parish of PRESTBURY, union and hundred of MACCLESFIELD, N. division of the county of CHESTER, 5 miles (N. by W.) from Macclesfield; containing 1159 inhabitants. Adlington Hall, a very ancient and curious structure with a garden of cut yew hedges, which has long been the residence of the family of Legh, was garrisoned for Charles I. in the civil war, and taken by the parliamentarian forces on the 14th of Feb. 1645, after a fortnight's siege: in the south-east angle is a small domestic chapel, handsomely fitted up, licensed by the Bishop of Lichfield and Coventry in the 25th of Henry VI. The township comprises 4019 acres; the soil is clayey, and there are some valuable mines of coal, and quarries of flagstone. A manorial court is held in May and December, at which debts under 40s. are recoverable.

ADLINGTON, a township, in the parish of STANDISH, union of CHORLEY, hundred of LEYLAND, N. division of the county of LANCASTER, 4 miles (N.) from Wigan; containing 1130 inhabitants. The Adlington family held lands here in the reign of Edward II., and for many subsequent generations: the Aughtons, also, resided here for several centuries; and, latterly, the knightly family of Clayton were lords of the manor. The village is about midway between the Preston and Wigan and the Preston and Bolton railways; and the road from Wigan to Chorley, and the Leeds and Liverpool canal, also afford means of communication. The townships of Adlington, Anderton, Duxbury, and Heath-Charnock, in the parish, form a district chapelry; and a church, a neat structure in the Norman style, has been erected by Her Majesty's Commissioners, containing 629 sittings, of which 331 are free: the living is a perpetual curacy, with a net income of £150, in the gift of the Rector. The tithes have been commuted for £120. 14.

ADMARSH, LANCASTER.—See BLEASDALE.

ADMASTON, a hamlet, in the parish of BLITHFIELD, union of UTTOXETER, hundred of SOUTH PIREHILL, N. division of STAFFORDSHIRE, 7½ miles (S. S. W.) from Uttoxeter; containing 59 inhabitants. It lies about a quarter of a mile east of the church; and contains a few houses, and the free school, founded by the Bagot family in 1729.

ADMINGTON, a hamlet, in the parish of QUINTON, union of SHIPSTON, Upper division of the hundred of KIFTSGATE, E. division of the county of GLOUCESTER, 6¼ miles (N. E. by N.) from Chipping-Campden; containing 197 inhabitants.

ADMISTON, or ATHELHAMPTON, a parish, in the union of DORCHESTER, hundred of PIDDLETOWN, Dorchester division of DORSET, 6 miles (E. N. E.) from Dorchester; containing 74 inhabitants. This place is said to have been the principal residence of the Saxon kings of Wessex, but there is no satisfactory evidence of the truth of that opinion. The living is a rectory, with that of Burleston annexed, valued in the king's books at £2; net income, £200; patron, the Earl of Mornington. The church is a small edifice, repaired by Sir Robert Long in 1740, before which it contained an apartment supposed to have been anciently inhabited by a rector or custos.

ADSTOCK (ST. CECILIA), a parish, in the union, hundred, and county of BUCKINGHAM, 3 miles (N. W.) from Winslow, on the road to the town of Buckingham; containing 419 inhabitants. This parish consists of 1128 acres of cultivated arable and pasture land, inclosed under an act of parliament passed in 1797, when an allotment was awarded to the incumbent in lieu of tithes. The living is a rectory, valued in the king's books at £13. 16. 3.; patron, the Bishop of Lincoln; net income £235, arising from 300 acres of land. In the time of the plague, in 1665, the contagion having extended to Buckingham and Winslow, a market was held at this place.

ADSTONE, a chapelry, in the parish of CANONS-ASHBY, union of TOWCESTER, hundred of GREENS-NORTON, S. division of the county of NORTHAMPTON, 6¾ miles (W. N. W.) from Towcester; containing 196 inhabitants. Mention occurs of the monks of Canons-Ashby as owners of land here, in the reign of Henry III.: in the time of Edward II. the king granted them the liberty of free warren in all their demesne lands in Adstone, and from this period the monastery seems to have held the manor until the Dissolution. The chapelry comprises by computation 1400 acres of land, about equally divided in arable and pasture; it is partially undulated, and watered by a stream which falls into the river Tow. Good sandstone is quarried for building. The living is a donative; patrons, the Corporation of the Sons of the Clergy, who have estates here, and who, with Worcester College, have given a small endowment to secure permanent duty. The chapel, dedicated to All Saints, is remarkable for the simplicity and dignity of its architecture, and is supposed to have been dependent on Canons-Ashby, at which place the inhabitants still continue to bury. In 1813 the corporation repaired the chapel, and in 1843-4 restored the dilapidated parts of the building, adding a chancel.

ADVENT, or ST. ADVEN, a parish, in the union of CAMELFORD, hundred of LESNEWTH, E. division of CORNWALL, 1¾ mile (S.) from Camelford; containing 291 inhabitants. It comprises 4222 acres, of which 2400 are common or waste; the surface is hilly, and the soil slaty, and interspersed with large granite stones: the river Camel flows on the northern boundary. The living is a rectory, not in charge, annexed to that of Lanteglos cum Camelford.

ADWALTON.—See DRIGHLINGTON.

ADWELL (ST. MARY), a parish, in the union of THAME, hundred of LEWKNOR, county of OXFORD, 1¾ mile (S. by E.) from Tetsworth; containing 46 inhabitants. It comprises about 500 acres of land, bounded on the north-east by the road between Oxford and High Wycombe. The living is a discharged rectory, valued in the king's books at £4. 13. 9., and in the patronage of Mrs. F. Webb: the incumbent's tithes have been commuted for £111, and £9 are payable to the Dean and Canons of Windsor; there are about 15 acres of glebe. Here is an ancient intrenchment called Adwell Cop, supposed by Dr. Plott to have been constructed by the Danes, about the year 1010.

ADWICK-LE-STREET (ST. LAWRENCE), a parish, in the union of DONCASTER, N. division of the wapentake of STRAFFORTH and TICKHILL, W. riding of YORK; containing 554 inhabitants, of whom 120 are in the township of Hampole, and 434 in that of Adwick-le-Street, 4 miles (N. W. by N.) from Doncaster. This place, which is said to derive the adjunct to its name from its situation on a Roman road, is intersected by the

16

great northern road, and contains 1543a. 3r. 22p.; 595 acres are grass, 924 arable, and 24 wood and plantation. The village is pleasantly situated on a declivity, and watered by a stream that flows eastward to the Don. The living is a rectory, valued in the king's books at £4. 13. 4.; net income, £364; patron, John Fullerton, Esq.: the glebe consists of 8 acres. The church is a neat structure, with a nave, chancel, north aisle, and tower, and has several ancient altar tombs, richly carved, erected in memory of the Fitzwilliam, Washington, and other families. A spring of pure water, in the parish, is in some repute for healing weak eyes.

ADWICK-UPON-DEARNE, a parish, in the union of DONCASTER, N. division of the wapentake of STRAFFORTH and TICKHILL, W. riding of YORK, 7 miles (W. by S.) from Doncaster; containing 108 inhabitants. The parish comprises 1105a. 1r. 22p., of which 704 acres are arable, 385 meadow and pasture, 8 acres homesteads and orchards, and 6 canal; the surface is varied, and the surrounding scenery richly diversified. The village is beautifully situated on the southern acclivity of the picturesque vale of Dearne, and near it run the Midland railway and the Dearne and Dove canal. The living is a perpetual curacy, annexed to the vicarage of Wath-upon-Dearne. There was a church at an early period, which in the former part of the reign of Henry I. was given to the monastery of St. Oswald of Nostell, then newly founded: this edifice, which is the present parochial church, retains its primitive simplicity, and is the purest specimen remaining in the deanery of Doncaster of the original village churches; it has a nave and chancel, with a little shed in which two bells are hung. A powerful chalybeate spring was discovered on the glebe land in 1820.

AFF PIDDLE or PUDDLE, a parish, in the union of WAREHAM and PURBECK, hundred of HUNDRED'S BARROW; Wareham division of DORSET, 9 miles (E. by N.) from Dorchester; containing, with Bryant's-Puddle tything, and the hamlet of Pallington, 507 inhabitants. The parish comprises 3541 acres, whereof 1130 are common or waste. The living is a discharged vicarage, valued in the king's books at £8. 14. 9.; patron and impropriator, J. Frampton, Esq. The great tithes have been commuted for £354, and the vicarial for £46. 10.; the glebe consists of 1½ acre. The pulpit in the church bears date 1540, and is beautifully ornamented with carvings.

AGDEN, a township, in the parish of MALPAS, union of WREXHAM, Higher division of the hundred of BROXTON, S. division of the county of CHESTER, 2¼ miles (S. E.) from Malpas; containing 97 inhabitants. It comprises 508 acres of land, the soil of which is clay. The tithes have been commuted for £63.

AGDEN, a township, partly in the parish of Rostherne, but chiefly in that of BOWDON, union of ALTRINGHAM, hundred of BUCKLOW, N. division of the county of CHESTER, 5½ miles (N. N. W.) from Nether Knutsford; containing 95 inhabitants. The manor was held by a family of the same name: a moiety of it passed by female heirs to the families of Daniel and Venables; the other moiety, by purchase, to the Savages, who sold it to the family of Venables in 1619. William Venables married the heiress of the Daniels; and in 1727 the heiress of George Venables was married to Sir T. P. Chetwode, Bart., in whose family the property continues.

The township comprises 500 acres; the soil is chiefly loam. The Duke of Bridgewater's canal passes through. The tithes of that part in the parish of Bowdon have been commuted for £16. 13., payable to the Bishop of Chester, and £16 to the vicar.

AGELTHORPE, or AGGLETHORPE, a township, in the parish of COVERHAM, union of LEYBURN, wapentake of HANG-WEST, N. riding of YORK, 3¼ miles (W. S. W.) from Middleham; containing 195 inhabitants. It comprises by computation 1090 acres, and includes within its limits the places called Ashgill, Tupgill, Brackengill, Giles Alley, Scotescue Park, Bird Ridding, and Coverham. The Cover river, which has its source near the great Whernside mountain, here passes on the south, and flows north-eastward to the Ure. The monks of Coverham had land here, valued at £1. 6. 8. per annum; and the village, which is situated on the northern acclivity of the romantic Coverdale, is remarkable for its ancient Hall, now a farmhouse, which once belonged to the Topham family, and afterwards to the Chaytors.

AGLIONBY, a township, in the parish of WARWICK, union of CARLISLE, CUMBERLAND ward, E. division of CUMBERLAND, 3¾ miles (E.) from Carlisle; containing 137 inhabitants

AGNES (ST.), a market-town and parish, in the union of TRURO, W. division of the hundred of PYDER, and of CORNWALL, 8½ miles (N. W. by W.) from Truro, and 263 (W.) from London; containing 7757 inhabitants. This place, formerly called *Breanic*, or *Bryanic*, is situated in an extensive mining district, on the northern coast of the county, and is hilly and barren, the town consisting principally of cottages inhabited by miners. The rocks on this part of the coast are precipitous, and the character of the scenery for the greater part boldly picturesque. On a pyramidical rocky eminence, 664 feet above the level of the sea, is St. Agnes' beacon, formed out of an ancient cairn or tumulus, and which, during the late war with France, was kept constantly in readiness to communicate intelligence in the event of any invasion: it has since that time been greatly diminished by the removal of the stone for repairing the fences in the neighbourhood. At the base of the hill are vestiges of a strong vallum, supposed to have been constructed by the Romans, and which anciently extended for nearly two miles in a circular direction. The district was formerly worked only for tin, of which the principal mine, called " Seale Hole," after having produced an immense quantity of ore, was discontinued some years since. Copper-mines were subsequently opened, and have been worked with very great success. The PORT, which is a member of that of St. Ives, carries on a trade principally with Ireland and Wales, in the exportation of copper-ore and fire-clay, and the importation of coal, iron, machinery, limestone, and grain. After many fruitless attempts, a pier of moorstone, here called "Trevannance," was constructed by a company in 1794; and the harbour has been improved within the last few years: it affords safe anchorage to about eight or ten vessels of one hundred tons' burthen, but can only be entered at high water. A pilchard fishery was established in 1802, which gives employment to about forty men. The market is on Thursday; a fair takes place on the 30th of April, and courts for the duchy are held here in October, at which constables and other officers are appointed.

The parish comprises 8294 acres, of which 3633 are common or waste. The living is a vicarage not in charge, united to that of Perranzabuloe: the vicarial tithes have been commuted for £265, and the appropriate, belonging to the Dean and Chapter of Exeter, for £250. The church is an ancient structure, built chiefly of granite, with a small spire of the same material. A church district named Mount Hawke was formed in 1846, by the Ecclesiastical Commission, out of the parishes of St. Agnes and Illogan; and another, named Mithian, was formed out of St. Agnes' and three other parishes: the living of each is in the gift of the Crown and the Bishop alternately. There are places of worship for Bryanites, Independents, and Wesleyans. The free school, founded by the Rev. St. John Elliott in 1760, has a small endowment, arising from funds bequeathed by him for charitable uses; and another school is endowed with £5 per annum. Near the site of an ancient chapel, in a dingle called Chapelcomb, was the famous well of St. Agnes, of which many miraculous stories are recorded. Opie, the celebrated painter, was born in the parish in 1761; he died in the year 1807.

AIGBURTH, or AIGBURGH, a district chapelry, in the township of GARSTON, parish of CHILDWALL, union and hundred of WEST DERBY, S. division of LANCASHIRE, 4 miles (S. E.) from Liverpool; containing 1031 inhabitants. In the reigns of Elizabeth and James the family of Brettargh possessed this place; in that of Charles I. it was held by the Tarletons. It afterwards passed to various hands, among others to the Tarletons again, and more recently, by purchase, to the family of Alderman Porter, of Liverpool. Aigburth is a wealthy and fashionable district extending along the banks of the Mersey, and studded with the noble mansions and splendid villas of the Liverpool bankers and merchants, the salubrity of the air and the delightful scenery inviting their residence here. The land is beautifully undulated, and there are fine views of the river, the Welsh mountains, the county of Chester, and the ocean. The living is a perpetual curacy, in the patronage of certain Trustees; net income, £200. The chapel, dedicated to St. Anne, was erected in 1837, at a cost of £4000, and is a good edifice in the Norman style, with a highly decorated interior; the east window is of stained glass, representing Christ healing the Leper: the tower is 65 feet high, with a richly ornamented battlement. A Roman Catholic chapel, dedicated to St. Augustine, was built in 1837, at an expense of £1800; it is in the early English style, with a neat interior, and adjoining are a school, and a house for the priest, the Rev. Samuel Day. A school for boys and girls in connexion with the Established Church, is supported by subscription. There is a curious mausoleum erected by the well-known Dr. Solomon, who had a residence in the chapelry.

AIGHTON, with BAILEY and CHAIGLEY, a township, in the parish of MITTON, union of CLITHEROE, Lower division of the hundred of BLACKBURN, N. division of the county of LANCASTER, 5 miles (W. by S.) from Clitheroe; containing 1795 inhabitants. Aighton, under the name of *Haighton*, was granted by Ilbert de Lacy, prior to 1102, with other lands, to a family who is supposed to have taken the surname of Mitton. The hospitallers of St. John of Jerusalem had lands in *Aiton* in the 20th of Edward I. The three hamlets of Aighton, Bailey, and Chaigley, meet on the north and south

AILE

AINS

summit of the eastern side of the crescent of Longridge Fell. Aighton occupies the east-south-east brow, whence it gradually recedes by a gentle decline into a finely wooded country, watered by the Hodder and the Ribble. It is remarkable as the seat of the Roman Catholic COLLEGE of STONYHURST. The heads of the college having been driven from their establishment at Liege by the proscriptions of the French revolution, were induced, in consequence of the mitigation of the penal enactments in this country against Roman Catholic seminaries, to seek an asylum here. In 1794 a long lease was obtained of the mansion of Stonyhurst, the ancient seat of the Sherburne family, and of the farm, on moderate terms, from the late Thomas Weld, Esq.; and at great expense, a large and handsome new building was added to the house. The whole now comprises, a hall of study, seven class-rooms, a library, museum, room for philosophical apparatus, exhibition-room, music-room, drawing-room, recreation-hall, chambers for the president and directors, apartments for the professors and teachers, and, in the upper stories, dormitories for the students, &c.: the public rooms in the new building, which is 300 feet in length, as well as those in the old mansion, are on a noble scale. The area of the college, the play-grounds, and the gardens, occupy upwards of ten acres; and the stately pile, with its towers and park-like grounds, forms a magnificent object to the whole of the surrounding country. On the south angle of the front of the college, is a handsome chapel dedicated to St. Peter, of which the first stone was laid in 1832.

AIKE, a township, partly in the parish of ST. JOHN, borough of BEVERLEY, but chiefly in that of LOCKINGTON, union of BEVERLEY, Bainton-Beacon division of the wapentake of HARTHILL, E. riding of YORK, 7 miles (N. by E.) from the town of Beverley; containing 98 inhabitants. This place comprises about 630 acres, of which upwards of 200 are in the parish of St. John : it was formerly an island, but by means of draining has been connected with the surrounding country, although it is still low and swampy. The tithes were commuted for land and a money payment, under an inclosure act passed in 1771.

AIKTON (ST. ANDREW), a parish, in the union of WIGTON, CUMBERLAND ward, E. division of CUMBERLAND, 4 miles (N. N. E.) from Wigton; comprising the townships of Aikton, Biglands with Gamblesby, Wampool, and Wiggonby; and containing 802 inhabitants, of whom 318 are in the township of Aikton. The parish comprises 5491 acres, of which 160 are common or waste. The living is a rectory, valued in the king's books at £14. 13. 1½.; net income, £546; patron, the Earl of Lonsdale. A school has been endowed by Margaret Hodgson, with houses and land valued at £150 per annum, and is free to the poor of Aikton, Burgh-upon-Sands, and Beaumont, and to all persons of the founder's name.

AIKTON, county of YORK.—See ACKTON.

AILBY, a hamlet, in the parish of RIGSBY, Wold division of the hundred of CALCEWORTH, parts of LINDSEY, county of LINCOLN; containing 53 inhabitants.

AILESWORTH, a hamlet, in the parish of CASTOR, union and soke of PETERBOROUGH, N. division of the county of NORTHAMPTON, 2¾ miles (E. by S.) from Wansford; containing 363 inhabitants. It is situated on the road from Wansford to Peterborough.

18

AINDERBY-MYERS, with HOLTBY, a township, in the parish of HORNBY, union of BEDALE, wapentake of HANG-EAST, N. riding of YORK, 3¼ miles (S. by E.) from Thirsk; containing 82 inhabitants. It is situated in the vale of a rivulet, and comprises about 879 acres of land. Holtby Hall is a handsome mansion, seated in a pleasant park, on the west side of Leeming-Lane.

AINDERBY-QUERNHOW, a township, in the parish of PICKHILL, union of THIRSK, wapentake of HALLIKELD, N. riding of YORK, 5¼ miles (W. S. W.) from Thirsk; containing 92 inhabitants. This place derives the adjunct to its name from the querns, or millstones, obtained from the how or hill in the parish : it comprises an area of 527a. 18p. The impropriate tithes have been commuted for £150, payable to Trinity College, Cambridge.

AINDERBY-STEEPLE (ST. HELEN), a parish, in the union of NORTHALLERTON, wapentake of GILLING-EAST, N. riding of YORK; containing 760 inhabitants, of whom 262 are in the township of Ainderby-Steeple, 3 miles (W. S. W.) from Northallerton. The parish comprises the townships of Ainderby-Steeple, Morton, Thrintoft, and Warlaby, and consists by measurement of 4599 acres; Ainderby-Steeple extends over 1129 acres. The living is a discharged vicarage, valued in the king's books at £13. 6. 8., and has a net income of £200; the patronage and impropriation are vested in the Crown. The church is a handsome structure, on a bold eminence, and from its lofty tower, which may be seen at the distance of 30 miles, the place derives the affix of Steeple.

AINSTABLE, with RUCKROFT (ST. MICHAEL), a parish, in the union of PENRITH, LEATH ward, E. division of CUMBERLAND, 4½ miles (N. N. W.) from Kirk-Oswald, and 10 miles (N. by E.) from Penrith; comprising 4177a. 18p., and containing 501 inhabitants. This parish, which is bounded on the west by the river Eden, and on the east and south by the Croglin, abounds with beautiful scenery, particularly in the vale of Croglin, and in the vicinity of Nunnery, the seat of Major Aglionby, who has erected a spacious and elegant mansion on the site of a Benedictine convent founded here by William II., the revenue of which at the Dissolution was £18. 18. 8. The living is a discharged vicarage, valued in the king's books at £8. 8. 2.; net income, £225; patron and impropriator, Major Aglionby. The vicarial tithes and all moduses were commuted for land under an inclosure act in 1818. The nave of the church was rebuilt in 1816, and the chancel soon afterwards. Near the parsonage-house is a chalybeate spring. John Leake, M.D., founder of the Westminster Lying-in Hospital, and author of some esteemed medical works, was born here, in 1729.

AINSWORTH, or COCKEY-MOOR, a parochial chapelry, in the parish of MIDDLETON, union of BURY, hundred of SALFORD, S. division of the county of LANCASTER, 3 miles (E. by N.) from Bolton, on the road to Bury; containing 1598 inhabitants. The family of Aynesworth, located here, was of considerable antiquity, and is mentioned in the reigns of Edward III. and Richard II., at which latter time John de Aynesworth was of Pleasington, in Blackburn parish. The lordship passed to the Asshetons of Middleton, at what period does not appear; but by the marriage of the younger coheiress of that family, it became the property of the Earl of Wilton, in whose grandson, the present earl, it is now vested. The township comprises by measurement about 1200 acres: the population is chiefly employed in two large cotton-mills and some bleach-works, in calico-printing, and in collieries and extensive stonequarries. The village is called Cockey-Moor, and this name is better known than the name of the township. There is a station of the Bury and Bolton railway. Ainsworth Hall has been modernised, and now possesses few traces of antiquity. The LIVING is a perpetual curacy, in the gift of the Rector of Middleton. The rectorial tithes have been commuted for £48; the glebe belonging to the perpetual curate consists of 55 acres, with a house. The church was formerly surrounded by a moat, and stood in the centre of a common; it was rebuilt in 1832, in the early English style, has a square tower, and, standing on an eminence, is seen at a great distance. There is a neat place of worship for English Presbyterians, built in 1715, enlarged in 1773, and altered in 1845; it has a considerable endowment, with a residence for the minister or curator: the present curator is the Rev. James Whitehead, who succeeded his father-in-law, the Rev. Joseph Bealey. Near the church are excellent national schools. The late Sir Ralph Assheton, Bart., gave a piece of ground and a house, now valued at about £15 a year, for the maintenance of a schoolmaster. Roman coins have been found.

AINTREE, a township, in the parish of SEFTON, union and hundred of WEST DERBY, S. division of the county of LANCASTER, 6 miles (N. N. E.) from Liverpool; containing, in 1846, about 430 inhabitants. William of Aintree, in the reign of Henry III., left a daughter and heiress, Alice, who married into the Maghull family; and an heiress of the latter, Joanna, married into the family of Molyneux, who thus became proprietors of this place. The township lies on the road from Liverpool to Ormskirk, and the Liverpool race-course is within its limits. The tithes have been commuted for £135.

AIRTON, a township, in the parish of KIRBY-IN-MALHAM-DALE, union of SETTLE, W. division of the wapentake of STAINCLIFFE and EWCROSS, W. riding of YORK, 6½ miles (S. E. by E.) from Settle; containing 217 inhabitants. This place, which comprises by computation 2790 acres of rich grazing land, derives its name from the river Aire, on which it is situated, and which takes its rise in Malham Tarn, a few miles above the village. The population is chiefly agricultural, but some of the inhabitants find employment in a cotton-mill. The land is divided among several owners: among former proprietors were the monks of Bolton, Fountains, and Nostell Priory. There are places of worship for Methodists and Quakers, the latter built in 1700. Alice Ellis, in 1709, left a house and 29 acres of land for apprenticing children.

AISBY, a hamlet, in the parish of HAYDOR, union of GRANTHAM, wapentake of ASWARDHURN, parts of KESTEVEN, county of LINCOLN; containing 190 inhabitants.

AISBY, a hamlet, in the parish and wapentake of CORRINGHAM, union of GAINSBOROUGH, parts of LINDSEY, county of LINCOLN; containing 63 inhabitants.

AISHOLT, or ASHOLT (ALL SAINTS), a parish, in the union of BRIDGWATER, hundred of CANNINGTON, W.

19

division of SOMERSET, 7¼ miles (W. by S.) from Bridgwater; containing 201 inhabitants, and comprising 1252 acres, of which 240 are common or waste. Limestone is quarried, and used for agricultural purposes. The living is a rectory, valued in the king's books at £7. 12. 3½.; net income, £280; patrons, the family of West: the glebe consists of 60 acres, and there is a good glebe-house.

AISKEW, a township, in the parish and union of BEDALE, wapentake of HANG-EAST, N. riding of YORK, ½ mile (N. E.) from Bedale; containing 658 inhabitants. This place, which is pleasantly situated on the north side of the Bedale beck, comprises by computation 1950a. 2r. 9p. There are two places of worship for Anabaptists, and one for Roman Catholics. Near Leases Hall, a neat mansion, with pleasant grounds, is Cloven hill, the supposed site of a battle, and where human bones have often been found.

AISLABY, a township, in the parish of EAGLES-CLIFFE, union of STOCKTON, S. W. division of STOCKTON ward, S. division of the county of DURHAM, 1½ mile (W. by N.) from Yarm; containing 128 inhabitants. There was anciently a chapel dedicated to St. Thomas the Martyr, which was founded by William de Aslakby (now Aislaby) and Agnes his wife, in 1313; and the place was ·for several generations the residence of the family of Pemberton, whose mansion has been converted into an inn and several other tenements. The township is pleasantly situated on the northern bank of the Tees, by which it is separated from Yorkshire.

AISLABY, or AYSLEYBY, a chapelry, in the parish and union of WHITBY, E. division of the liberty of LANGBAURGH, N. riding of YORK, 3 miles (S. W. by W.) from Whitby; containing 346 inhabitants. The township comprises about 1080 acres, abounding in the most picturesque scenery, interspersed with several neat mansions: in the neighbourhood are numerous quarries of excellent stone, wrought for various purposes, and shipped from Whitby. The living is a perpetual curacy, in the patronage of Mrs. R. Boulby, with a net income of £87: the chapel is dedicated to St. Margaret. About a mile from the village is a fine spring called St. Kilda's well, which runs directly into the river Esk, two miles from its source.

AISLABY, a township, in the parish of MIDDLETON, union, and W. division of the lythe, of PICKERING, N. riding of YORK, 1½ mile (W. N. W.) from Pickering; containing 128 inhabitants. This place is on the road from Pickering to Helmsley; the surface is undulated, and the scenery pleasingly varied; there are quarries of sandstone for building, and limestone. Aislaby Hall is finely situated.

AISMUNDERBY, with BONDGATE, a township, in the parish and liberty of RIPON, W. riding of YORK; containing 614 inhabitants. It adjoins Ripon on the south, is partly within that borough, and comprises 1055 acres, whereof 25 are common or waste: in the immediate vicinity are several handsome villas, and a little to the south lies the hamlet of Quarry Moor, noted for its lime-works. The tithes have been commuted for £24 payable to impropriators, and £38 to the Dean and Chapter of Ripon.—See BONDGATE.

AISTHORPE (ST. PETER), a parish, in the wapentake of LAWRESS, parts of LINDSEY, union and county of LINCOLN, 6 miles (W. N. W.) from the city of Lincoln;

D 2

containing 82 inhabitants. It comprises by measurement 807 acres, and is intersected by the road from Lincoln to Barton. Stone is quarried for building purposes, and for making roads. The living is a discharged rectory, with the vicarage of West Thorpe annexed, valued in the king's books at £4. 10.; net income, £289; patrons, the Milnes family : the glebe consists of an acre and a half, with a cottage. The church is a plain edifice, erected about 45 years since, and consists of a nave, chancel, and tower.

AKEBAR, a township, in the parish of FINGALL, union of LEYBURN, wapentake of HANG-WEST, N. riding of YORK, 5 miles (N. E. by E.) from Middleham; containing 30 inhabitants. It is on an acclivity opposite to Fingall, and comprises an area of 760 acres.

AKELD, a township, in the parish of KIRK-NEWTON, union of GLENDALE, W. division of GLENDALE ward, N. division of NORTHUMBERLAND, 3 miles (N. W. by W.) from Wooler; containing 182 inhabitants. It comprises 2362 acres, of which 1300 are arable, 100 plantation, and the remainder pasture. The surface is mountainous in the southern portion, but level on the north-east; the soil is various, and the scenery pleasing : whinstone is obtained in abundance. The village is situated near the river Glen, which runs through the township; and on the road from Wooler to Kirk-Newton. The vicarial tithes have been commuted for £56, and the impropriate for £1. 13. Vestiges of a burial-place are discernible, but there are no traces of any place of worship. On a hill, which ranges three miles in length, is a Roman camp, two inner walls of which are very perfect : a Roman brass bowl was found at Milfield Place, in the township, in 1842.

AKELY (ST. JAMES), a parish, in the union, hundred, and county of BUCKINGHAM, 2¾ miles (N. by E.) from the town of Buckingham; containing 362 inhabitants. This parish, according to a survey made in 1794, when the common was inclosed, comprises 1232a. 1r. 26p.; the soil is a stiff clay, with the exception of some light land in that part which formed the common. The living is a rectory, valued in the king's books at £6. 2. 4.; net income, £245; patrons, the Warden and Fellows of New College, Oxford. There was formerly a chapel of ease at Stockholt, in the parish.

AKENHAM (ST. MARY), a parish, in the union and hundred of BOSMERE and CLAYDON, E. division of SUFFOLK, 4½ miles (N. by W.) from Ipswich; containing 117 inhabitants. The living is a discharged rectory united to that of Claydon, valued in the king's books at £9. 11. 5½.: the tithes of the parish have been commuted for £260, and there are 20 acres of glebe.

Seal and Arms.

ALBAN'S (ST.) a borough and market-town having separate jurisdiction, and the head of a union, locally in the hundred of CASHIO, or liberty of ST. ALBAN'S, county of HERTFORD, 12½ miles (W. by S.) from Hertford, and 20 (N. W. by N.) from London; containing, with those portions of the parishes of St. Michael and St. Peter which extend beyond the limits of the borough, 8604 inhabitants. This place, which is

separated from the site of the Roman *Verulamium* by the small river *Ver*, derived its name and origin from the magnificent monastery established here by Offa, King of Mercia, in commemoration of St. Albanus, the proto-martyr of Britain. Verulam, according to the Roman historians, was founded by the Britons, at an earlier period than London : it was the chief station of Cassivellaunus, at the time of the invasion of Cæsar, who describes it as a place of great military strength, well defended by woods and marshes; and appears to have consisted of rude dwellings constructed of wood, and to have been surrounded by a rampart and fosse. In the reign of Nero it was accounted a *Municipium*, or free city; in that of Claudius it was surprised by Boadicea, Queen of the Iceni, who slaughtered the chief part of the Roman and British inhabitants. After its restoration, it continued to be a primary station of the Romans until their final departure from Britain. During their occupation of it, Albanus, an eminent citizen, who had been converted to Christianity by Amphibalus, in 293, boldly refusing to abjure his new religion, was beheaded on the hill called Holmhurst; on which spot the monastery was erected at the close of the eighth century (in 793) for 100 Benedictine monks. About the middle of the fifth century, Verulam was occupied by the Saxons, and received the name of *Watlingceaster*, from the Roman highway called Watling-street, on which it stood.

According to Matthew Paris, the present town owes its origin to Ulsinus, or Ulsig, the sixth abbot, who, about the year 950, built a church on each of the three principal roads leading from the monastery, dedicated respectively to St. Stephen, St. Michael, and St. Peter, and encouraged the neighbouring inhabitants to erect houses, by supplying them with money and materials. Fritheric, or Frederic, the thirteenth abbot, opposed the march of the Norman conqueror, by causing the trees on the road side, near Berkhampstead, to be cut down and laid across the way; he was also principally instrumental in exacting from that sovereign an oath to observe the ancient laws of the realm. William subsequently deprived this church of a great portion of its lands, and would have destroyed the monastery, but for the interposition of Archbishop Lanfranc. The monks and the inhabitants had frequent quarrels; and, in the reign of Richard II., the insurgents in Wat Tyler's rebellion were aided by the latter in besieging the monastery. On their dispersion, the king repaired hither, attended by Judge Tresilian and 1000 soldiers, to try the delinquents, and many of the townsmen were executed. The king remained eight days, on one of which the commons of the county assembled by his command, and, in the great court of the abbey, swore to be thenceforward faithful subjects. A sanguinary battle was fought here on the 22nd of May, 1455, between Henry VI. and the Duke of York, in which the Lancastrians were defeated, their leader, the Duke of Somerset, killed, and the king himself made prisoner. On the 17th of February, 1461, another engagement took place on Bernard heath, north of the town, when Queen Margaret compelled the Earl of Warwick to retreat with considerable loss : after this action, the town was plundered and much damaged. On the introduction of printing into England, about 1471, a press was put up in the abbey, from which issued some of those early specimens that are now so eagerly sought for by collectors: the first translation of the Bible was also made here. During the civil war between Charles I. and the parliament, a party of soldiers, under the Earl of Essex, garrisoned the town, and destroyed the beautiful cross, which was one of those erected by Edward I. in memory of his queen.

The TOWN is situated chiefly on the summit and northern declivity of a considerable eminence, and consists principally of three streets, the abbey church standing on the hill near the point where they meet. That part of it which forms the old line of the great north road is narrow, and contains many ancient houses; but the other parts are spacious and neatly built. It is well paved, and lighted with gas, under a local act obtained in 1803, and is supplied with water from wells in the upper part of the town. By a diversion of the main road, about three hundred yards to the south, the former circuitous and dangerous route through the town is avoided; and on this new line of road, which is about two miles in length, some handsome villas, and one of the most commodious inns in the county, called the Verulam Arms, have been erected. The manufacture of straw-plat, in which about eight hundred persons are employed, is the chief occupation of the lower class of inhabitants: a silk-mill, occupying the site of the abbey-mill, affords employment to three hundred young persons; and in a mill for spinning cotton-wicks for candles, formerly applied to the cutting and polishing of diamonds, about sixty persons are engaged. Coal is conveyed for the supply of the town, from the Grand Junction canal at Boxmoor, about six miles distant. The market is on Saturday, for corn, straw-plat, and provisions: there is a fair on March 25th and 26th, for cattle and horses; and a statute-fair is held on Oct. 11th, and the two following days.

St. Alban's is styled a BOROUGH in the record of Domesday, in which it is stated to have contained forty-six burgesses, who were the demesne men of the abbot; and the town continued under his jurisdiction (with the exception of a brief interval in the reigns of Edward II. and III.) until the Dissolution, when the possessions of the monastery were surrendered to the crown. The inhabitants were incorporated in the 7th of Edward VI., by a charter which was modified in subsequent reigns, and confirmed in the 16th of Charles II. By the act of the 5th and 6th of William IV., cap. 76, the corporation bears the title of the "Mayor, Aldermen, and Burgesses," and consists of a mayor, four aldermen, and twelve councillors, together forming the council of the borough; the municipal and parliamentary boundaries are now the same. The town first received the elective franchise in the 35th of Edward I.: the privilege was suspended from the 5th of Edward III. till the first of Edward VI., since which time the town has continued to return two members to parliament. The right of election was formerly vested in the freemen, whether resident or not, and in those householders who had been six months resident in the borough, paying scot and lot; but by the act of the 2nd of William IV. it was confined to the resident burgesses and the £10 householders, the latter 709 in number: the mayor is returning officer. The limits of the parliamentary borough were extended by the act of the 2nd and 3rd of William IV., cap. 64; they formerly comprised, by computation, 308 acres, and are now estimated to contain 425. The mayor, the late mayor, and

21

the recorder, are justices of the peace, and hold courts of quarter-session: the mayor presides at a court of aldermen, on the first Wednesday in every month, for the transaction of public business; and petty-sessions are held every Saturday. The magistrates for the liberty, also, hold quarter-sessions here. The liberty surrounds, and is entirely distinct from, the borough, the magistrates of the one having no jurisdiction in the other; it comprises the divisions of Barnet, Watford, and St. Alban's, and extends into twenty-two parishes. The powers of the county debt-court of St. Alban's, established in 1847, extend over the registration-district of St. Alban's, and the greater part of the districts of Hatfield and Welwyn, and Hemel-Hempstead. The former town, hall was originally the charnel-house of the monastery; a handsome and commodious edifice was erected in 1830. The ancient prison of the monastery is now appropriated to the confinement of criminals committed for the borough and liberty.

The venerable ABBEY, rich in lordships and immunities, continued to flourish under a succession of forty abbots, who enjoyed both spiritual and temporal autho. rity, having a palatine jurisdiction similar to that exercised by the Bishops of Durham and Ely; they had also a precedence from Pope Adrian IV. over all other abbots, with an exclusive exemption from the payment of Peter's pence, which, according to Camden, they possessed the power of collecting throughout the county, and applying to their own use. Henry VIII. granted the abbey, which at the Dissolution had a revenue, according to Dugdale, of £2102. 7. 1., to Sir Richard Lee; but re. tained the church, since made parochial, which Edward VI., in 1553, granted for a pecuniary consideration to the mayor and burgesses. The church is a cruciform structure, six hundred feet in length, and consists of a nave, two aisles, a choir, presbytery, lady chapel, and two transepts, with a large square tower rising from the intersection. The choir is separated from the nave by St. Cuthbert's screen, which, with the elaborately carved screen over the altar, the ceiling (partly groined, and partly enriched with Mosaic paintings), and the tombs of Humphrey, Duke of Gloucester, and Abbot Ramryge, presents a rich and imposing appearance. The tower, supported on four arches, the two transepts, and a great part of the choir, were built of Roman tiles from the ancient city of Verulam, about the year 1077, and exhibit the Norman style of architecture; the remainder, erected about the reign of Henry III., is in the early English style, with sharply pointed arches. Many fine brasses, in memory of the abbots, were taken by Cromwell's soldiers, and the church was much damaged by the prisoners who were confined in it during the parliamentary war.

The town comprises the parish of St. Alban, or the Abbey parish, and parts of the parishes of St. Michael and St. Peter. The living of St. Alban's is a rectory, valued in the king's books at £10; net income, £111; patron and incumbent, Dr. Nicholson, who purchased the advowson from the corporation. A lectureship was founded in the church in 1640, by Francis Combe, who endowed it with £10 per annum. The living of St. Peter's is a vicarage, valued in the king's books at £9. 0. 10.; net income, £308; patron, the Bishop of Ely. The church, erected by Abbot Ulsinus, in 948, has been rebuilt within the last fifty years. The living of St.

Michael's is a vicarage, valued in the king's books at £10. 1. 8.; net income, £300; patron and impropriator, the Earl of Verulam. The church is a small edifice, erected by the same abbot, and contains, in a niche on the northern side of the chancel, a finely-sculptured alabaster statue of Lord Bacon, who was interred here. *St. Mark's* church, at Colney Heath, was consecrated in December, 1845; it is in the Norman style, and cost £1300: the materials externally are Cowley white brick, and Bath stone. The living is a perpetual curacy, in the gift of Trustees. There are places of worship for Particular Baptists, the Society of Friends, Independents, Wesleyans, and Unitarians. The *Free Grammar school* was erected in or about the year 1569, by the mayor and burgesses, under their charter of incorporation bestowed by Edward VI.; and was endowed by letters-patent of Elizabeth and James I., granting power to the mayor and burgesses to license dealers in wine in the borough. The schoolroom, adjoining the Abbey church, was the beautiful chapel of the Virgin. Dr. Aubrey Spencer, Bishop of Jamaica, and Dr. George Spencer, Bishop of Madras, were educated here. The almshouses called *Marlborough Buildings*, containing apartments for thirty-six persons of both sexes, were built and endowed by Sarah, Duchess Dowager of Marlborough, in 1736: they occupy three sides of a quadrangle, on the site of the old manor-house of Newland-Squillers; and the income, arising from property in the counties of Warwick and Surrey, now amounts to £757 per annum. The church lands, appropriated to the repairs of the abbey, together with several benefactions for the same purpose, produce a revenue of £220. The poor law union of St. Alban's comprises eight parishes or places, and contains a population of 17,051.

In the town is a high square brick tower with a house attached, called the *Clock House*, built by one of the abbots in the reign of Henry VIII., and conveyed to the corporation in the 29th of Elizabeth; the house and lower part of the tower are used as a shop, and in the upper part is a public clock. At the distance of half a mile to the south-east, are some fine remains of the nunnery of *Sopwell*, founded in 1140 by Abbot Geoffrey de Gorham, and of which the Lady Juliana Berners was at one time prioress: like the monastery, it was built of Roman tiles and bricks, and partly of flints. Of two hospitals founded by the abbots, and dedicated respectively to St. Julian and St. Mary de Pratis, there is not a single vestige. On the left of the road leading to Dunstable, a few fragments of the ancient walls of Verulam are still discernible; and in a field adjoining the town, called New England, are some hills supposed to have been the site of the camp of Ostorius, and thence vulgarly styled Oyster hills. There is a mineral spring in a garden near St. Michael's bridge. Matthew Paris, one of the most eminent of the old English historians, was a monk in the abbey; and among the most distinguished natives of the town may be enumerated Alexander Necham, a poet and scholastic divine; Sir John Mandeville, the celebrated traveller; and Sir John King, and Sir Francis Pemberton, two eminent lawyers. Breakspear's farmhouse, in the vicinity, was the birthplace of Nicholas Breakspear, the only Englishman that ever sat in the papal chair; on his elevation he assumed the name of Adrian IV.: he was a great benefactor to the abbey. St. Alban's gives the title of Duke to the family

22

of Beauclerc; and the representative of the family of Grimstone enjoys the title of Earl of Verulam.

ALBERBURY, or ABBERBURY (ST. MICHAEL), a parish, in the union of ATCHAM, partly in the hundreds of CAWRSE and DEYTHUR, county of MONTGOMERY, NORTH WALES, but chiefly in the hundred of FORD, S. division of SALOP, 8¼ miles (W.) from Shrewsbury; containing, in the English portion, which includes the township of Alberbury and the chapelry of Wollaston, 1065 inhabitants, of whom 638 are in the township of Alberbury. This parish, the Welsh name of which is Llanvihangel-yn-Ghentyn, is partly bounded by the river Severn, and is intersected by the Roman Watling-street. There are some remains of a castle, built in the reign of Henry II., by Fulk Fitz-Warine, who founded an abbey for Black monks of the order of Grandmont, vestiges of which may also still be traced about a mile from the castle: on the suppression of alien priories, Henry VI. gave the abbey site to the college of All Souls, Oxford, to which it still belongs. The parish comprises 1000 acres: coal is abundant, but none is at present worked. The living is a discharged vicarage, valued in the king's books at £5. 10.; net income, £187; patrons and impropriators, the Warden and Fellows of All Souls' College. The tithes of a part of the parish have been commuted for £498 payable to the college, and £47 payable to the vicar. The glebe consists of 20 acres. There are also incumbencies at Wollaston and Criggion, the former, in the gift of the Vicar of Alberbury, and the latter in that of V. Vickers, Esq.

ALBOURNE (ST. BARTHOLOMEW), a parish, in the union of CUCKFIELD, hundred of TIPNOAK, rape of BRAMBER, W. division of SUSSEX, 2¼ miles (W. N. W.) from Hurst-Pierrepoint; comprising about 1400 acres. The living is a rectory, valued in the king's books at £7. 14. 2., and in the gift of John Goring, Esq.: the tithes have been commuted for £310, and the glebe consists of 10 acres. The church is an ancient structure; the nave is separated from the chancel by a fine Norman arch, and there is a north transept, added a few years since by C. Goring, Esq. Albourne Place is said to have been built by Bishop Juxon, who retired hither after the death of Charles I, and resided here till the Restoration.

ALBRIGHTON (ST. MARY), a parish, and formerly a market-town, in the union of SHIFFNALL, Shiffnall division of the hundred of BRIMSTREE, S. division of SALOP, 7½ miles (N. W.) from Wolverhampton; containing 1058 inhabitants, and comprising 3424a. 1r. 33p. Pepperhill, an ancient mansion here of the Talbot family, is now converted into a farmhouse. The living is a vicarage, endowed with nearly the whole of the rectorial tithes, and valued in the king's books at £5. 10.; net income, £651; patrons, alternately, the Haberdashers' Company, and the Governors of Christ's Hospital, London: the glebe consists of 27 acres. The church, which has partly been rebuilt, has a Norman tower, with a small Saxon arch outside; the chancel is also ancient, and has a fine window; in the north-east angle, on a monument dated 1504, are effigies of a knight of the Talbot family, and of his lady, one of the Gifford family. The Duke of Shrewsbury lies buried here. A free school is principally supported from the tolls of the fairs, which are held on March 5th, May 23rd, July 18th, and Nov. 9th, for horned-cattle, sheep, and hogs.

ALBRIGHTON (St. John), a parish, in the union of Atcham, hundred of Pimhill, N. division of Salop, 4 miles (N.) from Shrewsbury; containing 85 inhabitants. It is on the road from Shrewsbury to Whitchurch and to Ellesmere. The living is a perpetual curacy, in the gift of the Spurrier family; net income, £52.

ALBURGH (All Saints), a parish, in the union of Depwade, hundred of Earsham, E. division of Norfolk, 3¼ miles (N. E. by N.) from Harleston; containing 589 inhabitants, and comprising by measurement 1512 acres. The living is a rectory, valued in the king's books at £12; net income, £395; patron, the Earl of Effingham, who must present a member of St. John's College, Cambridge: the glebe comprises about 7 acres. The church consists of a nave and chancel, with a lofty embattled tower; the nave is separated from the chancel by the remains of a beautiful carved screen, formerly highly gilt. Some town lands, left by Richard Wright before the reign of Henry VIII., are let for about £70, applied in aid of the poor-rate.

ALBURY (St. Mary), a parish, in the union of Bishop-Stortford, hundred of Edwinstree, county of Hertford, 4½ miles (N. W.) from Bishop-Stortford; containing 641 inhabitants. It is near the borders of Essex. The living is a vicarage, valued in the king's books at £7. 9. 7.; net income, £264; patron, the Treasurer of St. Paul's Cathedral. A pleasure-fair is held in July.

ALBURY (St. Helen), a parish, in the union of Thame, hundred of Bullington, county of Oxford, 3¼ miles (W. by S.) from Thame; containing, with the hamlet of Tiddington, 244 inhabitants. The parish is on the borders of Buckinghamshire, and is watered by the Thame. The living is a rectory, valued in the king's books at £9. 2. 8½.; net income, £276; patron, the Earl of Abingdon. The church has been lately rebuilt, principally through the munificence of the earl, and is fitted up throughout with open sittings of handsome old oak.

ALBURY (St. Peter and St. Paul), a parish, in the union of Guildford, Second division of the hundred of Blackheath, W. division of Surrey, 4 miles (E. S. E.) from Guildford; containing 1079 inhabitants. It comprises 4503 acres, of which 612 are common or waste, and includes the hamlets of Brooke and Little London; the sub-soil in general is chalk and sand. The living is a rectory, valued in the king's books at £17. 12. 8½., and in the gift of Henry Drummond, Esq.: the tithes have been commuted for £482. 10., and there are 78 acres of glebe. The old church is in the early English style, occupying a picturesque situation in Albury Park; it contains two singular octagonal pillars, resting upon circular bases of Sussex marble, supposed to have been removed from a Roman temple which stood on Blackheath. A new church has been erected by Mr. Drummond, a cruciform edifice in the later English style; and there is an Irvingite chapel, erected under the same auspices. Dr. Horsley, Bishop of St. Asaph, was for some time rector of Albury.

ALBY (St. Ethelbert), a parish, in the union of Aylsham, hundred of South Erpingham, E. division of Norfolk, 4¾ miles (N. by E.) from Aylsham; containing 299 inhabitants. This place, which was anciently called Oslby, is intersected by the road from Aylsham to Cromer, and includes the hamlets of Alby

23

Common and Alby Hill; it comprises about 840 acres, whereof 634 are computed to be arable, 80 pasture, and 100 common or heath inclosed in 1840. The living is a discharged rectory, valued in the king's books at £7. 11. 8½., and in the gift of the Earl of Orford : the tithes have been commuted for £196, and there are 13 acres of glebe, with a small house. The church is in the early and decorated English styles.

ALCESTER, a liberty, in the parish of St. James, borough of Shaftesbury, locally in the hundred of Monckton-up-Wimborne, county of Dorset; containing 334 inhabitants.

Seal and Arms.

ALCESTER (St. Nicholas), a market-town and parish, and the head of a union, in the Alcester division of the hundred of Barlichway, S. division of the county of Warwick, 15 miles (W. S. W.) from Warwick, and 103 (N. W.) by W.) from London; containing 2399 inhabitants. The name of this place is a contraction of Alnceastre, denoting its situation on the river Alne. Its position on the line of the Ikeneld-street (which may still be traced within a mile to the north-west), and the discovery of numerous relics of antiquity, afford evidence of its having been a Roman station; which by most antiquaries has been identified with the Alauna of the Itineraries. In the time of the Saxons it was a place of great importance, and a royal residence; the inhabitants being described by Capgrave as given to luxury and viciousness, from an abundance of worldly wealth. Egwin, third bishop of Huicca, who first preached Christianity here, founded the abbey of Evesham; and at a general synod held at this place, at which were present Bertwald, Archbishop of Canterbury, and Wilfred, Archbishop of York, the endowments of that house were confirmed. Alcester is said to have been formerly of much greater extent than at present, and to have contained three parochial churches; which opinion is corroborated by the discovery of human skeletons, and numerous foundations of ancient buildings, in that part of the parish called the Blacklands, now an extensive meadow, lying between the present town and the bridge over the Alne, to which, in all probability, it formerly extended; and also by the site of a monastery founded in 1140, by Ralph de Boteler, for Benedictine monks, afterwards made a cell to the abbey of Evesham, and valued at the Dissolution at £101. 14. per annum. The remains have been converted into a farmhouse, and are situated about half a mile to the north-east of the town, in the centre of which, according to Leland, they originally stood.

In the reign of Henry I. the place was a free borough, and in that of Henry II. it was rated, among the other boroughs in the county, at four marks as a yearly aid. In the 21st of Edward I., Sir Walter de Beauchamp, lord of a moiety of the manor, obtained the grant of an annual fair for eight days, to begin on the eve of St. Giles; which time being found inconvenient, the eve of St. Faith was appointed by another charter in the 30th of that monarch's reign. In the 28th of the same reign

Beauchamp also received a grant of free warren in all his demesne lands here and elsewhere. His son Walter, in the 13th of Edward II., obtained a charter for another fair, to be held annually for eight days, beginning on the eve of St. Barnabas the Apostle; and his brother and successor, Giles, procured in the 14th of Edward III., a charter to fortify and embattle his manor-house here. His great-grandson, Sir John Beauchamp, purchased the other moiety of the manor from the family of Bortreaux, and, having thus become lord of the whole, obtained, in the 25th of Henry VI., a charter confirming the privilege of a court leet with waifs and estrays, a market, and all other privileges enjoyed by his predecessors.

The TOWN is pleasantly situated on the river Arrow, at its confluence with the Alne, in a fertile and richly-cultivated vale, surrounded with finely-wooded eminences; and consists of one principal street, from which, near the market-place, others diverge in the direction of the roads to Birmingham, Stratford-upon-Avon, and Evesham. The houses are in many instances well built, and of handsome appearance, occasionally interspersed with ancient buildings having projecting upper stories, and many modern brick-built cottages. The principal manufacture is that of needles and fish-hooks, in which from 500 to 600 persons are employed. The market, which is well supplied with corn, is on Tuesday; the fairs, principally for cattle, horses, and sheep, are on Jan. 26th, March 23rd, May 18th, July 27th, Oct. 18th, and Dec. 7th. The town is within the jurisdiction of the county magistrates, and a court leet is held annually in November, when bailiffs and constables are appointed by the steward of the manor. The powers of the county debt-court of Alcester, established in 1847, extend over the whole of the registration-district of Alcester, except the parish of Ipsley. The town-hall, situated in the centre of the market-place, is a plain building, of which the lower part, appropriated to the use of the market, is of stone, supported on circular arches and round Tuscan columns.

The parish comprises by measurement 1200 acres of good fertile land, and extends to the Ridge Way, which separates a portion of the county from that of Worcester. The LIVING is a discharged rectory, valued in the king's books at £14. 18. 10., and in the gift of the Marquess of Hertford: the income arises from land granted in lieu of tithes, comprising 90 acres, and valued at £215 per annum. The church, formerly dedicated to St. Andrew, was built in the beginning of the thirteenth century; but of the original structure only the tower remains, the battlements of which, together with the body of the church, were rebuilt in 1732, when the edifice was dedicated to St. Nicholas; it has been lately rendered more commodious by extensive galleries erected at the expense of the rector. The exterior preserves a characteristic appearance, harmonizing with the tower, to which the interior, with a flat ceiling supported on round Tuscan pillars separating the aisles from the nave, forms a striking contrast. Near the altar is a tomb with recumbent effigies of Sir Fulke Greville and his lady, finely sculptured and coloured; also an elegant monument to the second marquess of Hertford, in which his effigy, in a sitting posture, is beautifully represented in white marble. Two chantries were formerly existing in the church; one in a chapel of "Our Lady," founded by one of the Botelers of Oversley; and the other by

John, son of Giles de Beauchamp, in the 36th of Edward III. There are places of worship for Baptists, the Society of Friends, Independents, Wesleyans, and Unitarians. The free school, which is open to all the boys of the parish, was instituted in 1592, by Walter Newport, of Goldney, in the county of Northampton, who endowed it with £400, producing £20 per annum, which is paid to the master, who has also a house and garden rent-free: there are but few boys on the foundation. The poor law union of Alcester comprises 18 parishes and places in the county of Warwick, and 4 in that of Worcester; and contains a population of 16,833. Beauchamp's Court, the ancient manor-house, now a farm, about a mile and a half distant, gives the title of Baron to the Earl of Warwick.

ALCISTON, a parish, in the union of WEST FIRLE, hundred of ALCISTON, rape of PEVENSEY, E. division of SUSSEX, 7¼ miles (E. S. E.) from Lewes; containing 275 inhabitants. This manor was given, with others, to Battle Abbey by the Conqueror, whose grant was confirmed by Henry I.: on the surrender of the abbey, in 1539, the king became seised of the lordship, and gave it to Sir John Gage and Philippa his wife, to hold *in capite* by knight's service. Alciston Place was occupied by an ancestor of the present Lord Gage in 1585. The parish comprises about 2100 acres of land, a portion of which consists of chalky downs. The living is a discharged vicarage, united by act of council in 1840 to the vicarage of Selmeston, and valued in the king's books at £6. The church has some remains of Norman architecture, with an admixture of the early English style.

ALCOMBE, a hamlet, in the parish of DUNSTER, union of WILLITON, hundred of CARHAMPTON, W. division of DORSET; containing 259 inhabitants.

ALCONBURY (ST. PETER AND ST. PAUL), a parish, in the hundred of LEIGHTONSTONE, union and county of HUNTINGDON, 4½ miles (N. W.) from Huntingdon; containing 823 inhabitants, and comprising about 4000 acres. A fair is held on Midsummer-day. The living is a discharged vicarage, with the living of Alconbury-Weston annexed, valued in the king's books at £8. 6. 1.; net income, £162; patrons and appropriators, the Dean and Chapter of Westminster. The glebe comprises 186 acres. There is a place of worship for Wesleyans.

ALCONBURY-WESTON, a parish, in the hundred of LEIGHTONSTONE, union and county of HUNTINGDON, 6 miles (N. W.) from Huntingdon; containing 491 inhabitants. The living is annexed to the vicarage of Alconbury.

ALCUMLOW, with MORETON.—See MORETON.

ALDBOROUGH (ST. MARY), a parish, in the union of ERPINGHAM, hundred of NORTH ERPINGHAM, E. division of NORFOLK, 6 miles (N.) from Aylsham; containing 293 inhabitants. It comprises 788a. 9p., of which 434 acres are arable, 287 pasture and meadow, and 20 woodland. A stock and pleasure fair is held on June 22nd. The living is a discharged rectory, valued in the king's books at £8, and in the gift of Lord Suffield: the tithes have been commuted for £199. 10., and the glebe consists of 26 acres, with a good house. The church, chiefly in the decorated style, contains several neat memorials to the family of Gay, and some sepulchral brasses to the Herewards, from whom the Gays were descended.

24

ALDBOROUGH, or AL-
DEBURGH (St. Peter and
St. Paul), a sea-port and
parish, ·and formerly a representative borough and a
market-town, in the union,
and locally in the hundred,
of Plomesgate, S. division
of Suffolk, 25 miles (N.
E. by E.) from Ipswich, and
94 (N. E.) from London;
containing 1557 inhabitants.

Seal and Arms.

This place takes its name
from its situation on the river Alde; it was formerly of
very considerable extent and importance, possessing many
valuable privileges. Owing to the inroads of the sea
(which, within the last century, has destroyed the market-
place, with an entire street and a great number of houses),
it has been reduced to an inconsiderable town; but from
the salubrity of the air and the convenience of the shore
for sea-bathing, it has lately become a place of fashionable
resort during the summer; baths for the accommodation of visiters have been erected, and machines are kept
on the beach. The town is situated in a pleasant vale,
rather below the level of high-water mark, having the
river Alde on the north, and on the south the navigable
river Ore, which flows from Orford to this place; it is
sheltered by a steep hill, the extended summit of which
forms a magnificent terrace, affording a delightful promenade, and a beautifully diversified prospect embracing
the North Sea. The strand, the descent to which from
the town is gradual, consists of firm sand, favourable
for bathing and walking. At the southern extremity of
the main street, which is nearly a mile in length, are a
battery, on which, during the late war, two eighteen-
pounders were mounted, another of five guns, and a
martello tower, for the protection of the coast. The old
houses are in general ill-constructed, but those erected
by families residing here during the season, or for the
accommodation of visiters, are well built and respectable;
among them is an elegant marine villa, in the Italian
style, built by the late Leveson Vernon, Esq. There is
a public subscription library, situated on the Head; a
neat and commodious theatre is open for a few weeks
during the season; and assemblies are held occasionally
at the principal inns.

The trade consists chiefly in the exportation of corn,
and the importation of coal and timber; in which forty-
six vessels, averaging fifty-two tons' burthen, are employed. The custom-house is a neat and convenient
building near the quay; the harbour is safe and commodious, and attracts a number of seafaring people and
fishermen, by whom the town is principally inhabited.
Many of these are Trinity-house pilots, who form themselves into small associations, and purchase swift-sailing
cutters, in which they traverse the North Sea, frequently
approaching the coast of Norway, in search of vessels
requiring assistance. The chief employment of the other
inhabitants consists in the taking and drying of herrings
and sprats, the latter of which are found here in profusion, and exported to Holland; soles and lobsters of
superior flavour arc taken also in abundance. The
market, on Wednesday and Saturday, has been discon-
tinned; the fairs are held on March 1st and May 3rd.
Aldborough claims to be a borough by prescription:

the earliest charter extant was granted by Henry VIII.
in 1529, after which it received several others, the last
and governing charter being granted by Charles I. in
1637. The officers of the corporation are two bailiffs,
ten capital and twenty-four inferior burgesses, a recorder,
town-clerk, two chamberlains, two serjeants-at-mace, and
others; and the bailiffs, late bailiffs, and recorder, are
exclusively justices of the peace for the borough, which
is co-extensive with the parish. The revenue arises
principally from the proceeds of the town marshes,
comprising 188 acres of land used for depasturing cattle,
which were purchased in 1610, and are vested in trustees. The town-hall is an ancient building of timber,
under which is the common gaol, consisting of a single
cell, for the confinement of disorderly persons; the magistrates generally commit to the county gaol. The
borough first exercised the elective franchise in the
13th of Elizabeth, from which time, until its disfranchisement by the Reform act, in the 2nd of William IV.,
it returned two members to parliament. The parish
comprises by measurement 1150 acres: it contains a
small portion of good arable land, but chiefly consists of
heath, and of land laid out in sheep-walks. The living
is a discharged vicarage, valued in the king's books at
£33. 6. 8., with a net income of £220; it is in the patronage of F. J. V. Wentworth, Esq., and there is a
manor of 13 acres attached to it: it is an
ancient structure of flint and freestone, standing on the
summit of a hill at the northern extremity of the town,
with a square embattled tower surmounted by a turret,
affording an excellent landmark for mariners. There
are places of worship for Particular Baptists, Independents, and Wesleyans. This was the birth-place of the
poet Crabbe.

ALDBOROUGH (St. Andrew), a parish, partly in
the wapentake of Hallikeld, N. riding, but chiefly in
the Lower division of the wapentake of Claro, W. riding,
of York; comprising the ancient borough towns of
Aldborough and Boroughbridge, and the townships of
Minskip, Rocliff, and Upper and Lower Dunsforth, in
the W. riding, with part of that of Humberton with
Milby, and the whole of Ellenthorpe, in the N. riding;
and containing 2473 inhabitants, of whom 615 are in
the township of Aldborough, 16½ miles (N. w. by W.)
from York, and 205½ (N. N. W.) from London. The
town, which is situated upon the southern bank of the
river Ure, and upon the line of the northern Watling-
street, was the celebrated and important Roman station
called *Isurium Brigantium*, and received from the Saxons
the name of *Eald-burgh*, denoting its antiquity even in
their time. Its destruction is attributed to the Danes,
by whom it was sacked and burnt to the ground, about
the year 870. The elective franchise was granted by
Philip and Mary, in 1558; but by the Reform act the
borough was deprived of the privilege of returning members: the right of election was vested in the inhabitants
paying scot and lot, in number about sixty; and the
bailiff, who was appointed by the electors, was the returning officer. The town is now only a rural village,
beautifully situated. The parish comprises 4600 acres;
the scenery is varied, and in some points picturesque.
The living is a discharged vicarage, valued in the
king's books at £9. 19. 5.; net income, £368; patrons
and appropriators, the Dean and Chapter of Ripon.
The tithes of the township of Aldborough were com-
E

muted for land and a money payment, by an inclosure act, in 1808. The church, supposed to have been built out of the ruins of *Isurium*, has several antique monuments, and on the outside a figure of Mercury, 2½ feet in length. At Boroughbridge, Dunsforth, and Rocliff, are other incumbencies. There is a 'place of worship for Independents. The foundations of the walls of the ancient city, which included a quadrilateral area of 2500 yards, may still be traced. Near the centre are vestiges of a mount called the Borough Hill, removed in 1783, and believed, from the remains then discovered, to have been the site of a Roman temple ; and about a hundred paces from the south wall is a semicircular outwork, named Studforth, 200 feet long, with a slope of 30 feet, forming a lofty terrace, on the south side of the town. Many Roman remains, consisting of tessellated pavements, military weapons, coins, &c., have at various times been discovered, and are preserved in the pleasuregrounds of Aldborough Lodge, where are remains of a Roman encampment. In the village is a beautiful tessellated pavement, under a wood covering.

ALDBOURN (*St. Michael*), a parish, and formerly a market-town, in the union of Hungerford, hundred of Selkley, Marlborough and Ramsbury, and N. divisions of Wilts, 6 miles (N. E.) from Marlborough ; containing 1556 inhabitants. The name is compounded of the Saxon terms *Ald*, old, and *bourne*, a brook. Aldbourn anciently gave name to a royal chase, granted by Henry VIII. to Edward Seymour, Duke of Somerset, and which for a long period served only as a rabbit-warren, but is now inclosed and cultivated. Previously to the battle of Newbury, in the reign of Charles I., a sharp skirmish took place here between the parliamentarian forces and the royalists. In 1760, a fire consumed seventy-two houses ; and in 1817, twenty were destroyed by a similar calamity. The parish comprises 8495*a*. 3*r*. 19*p*., of which 5037 acres are arable, 839 meadow and pasture, and 226 woodland ; the surface generally is undulated, and the quality of the soil is various, presenting a sand-gritty substance together with red clayey gravel and black turfy mould, and in some places chalk and flint. The town is situated in a fertile valley ; it has a willow-factory for bonnet frames, in which about 100 females are employed. The living is a vicarage, valued in the king's books at £26. 6. 3.; patron, the Bishop of Salisbury ; appropriators, the Dean and Chapter of Winchester. The great tithes have been commuted for £1475, and the small tithes for £210 : the rectorial glebe comprises about 120 acres ; the vicarial consists chiefly of allotments made under an act of parliament, and is valued at £262 per annum. The church, an ancient structure exhibiting portions in the Norman style, has a tower erected at the cost of John of Gaunt, Duke of Lancaster ; and the southern part of the vicarage-house is supposed to be the remains of a hunting seat which belonged to him. There is a place of worship for Wesleyans. Near a farmhouse called Pierce's Lodge, are vestiges of a British encampment; and in the neighbourhood may be seen various artificial mounds of earth.

ALDBROUGH (*St. Bartholomew*), a parish, in the union of Skirlaugh, Middle division of the wapentake of Holderness, E. riding of York ; comprising the townships of Aldbrough, Newton-East, and Newton-West, with part of Great and Little Cowden ; and con-
26

taining 1119 inhabitants, of whom 845 are in the township of Aldbrough, 11½ miles (N. E. by E.) from Hull. The township of Aldbrough comprises upwards of 4000 acres, of which two-thirds are arable, and one-third is pasture : the soil, generally, is strong and tenacious ; and bricks and tiles are manufactured. The village, which is large and convenient, is pleasantly situated on an eminence about a mile from the sea, and includes some good houses and shops, and a large hotel, lately built, for the accommodation of visiters who resort hither for sea-bathing. The living is a discharged vicarage, valued in the king's books at £13. 15., and in the patronage of the Crown, with a net income of £350 : the rectorial tithes for the lordship of Aldbrough were commuted for land, under an inclosure act, in 1764. The church, the oldest in Holderness, is a large edifice, and contains a circular stone bearing this Saxon inscription : " Ulf commanded this church to be built for the soul of Hanum and Gunthral." Ulf was lord of the place, and had a castle here, every vestige of which, except the moat, has been destroyed. The chantry on the north side of the chancel contains a very splendid monument of Sir John de Melsa and his lady : the knight was governor of the city of York from 1292 to 1296, and a great warrior ; his massive helmet is preserved. There is a place of worship for Wesleyans. Slight traces of a Roman road are discernible in the vicinity.

ALDBROUGH, a township, in the parish of Stanwick St. John, union of Richmond, wapentake of Gilling-West, N. riding of York, 7 miles (W. S. W.) from Darlington ; containing 544 inhabitants. It is a large and pleasant village, situated on a small rivulet, and the lands in the vicinity are fertile and productive. Carlton Hall, a mile to the north, was formerly the seat of S. B. M. Barrett, Esq., who built a school here. There is a place of worship for Wesleyans.

ALDBURY (*St. John the Baptist*), a parish, in the union of Berkhampstead, hundred of Dacorum, county of Hertford, 3 miles (E. by N.) from Tring; containing 790 inhabitants, and comprising 2102 acres, of which 280 are common or waste. The village is pleasantly situated at the foot of the Chiltern hills, whose summits are crowned with thick plantations ; the Tring station of the London and Birmingham railway is only about a mile distant from the church. The living is a rectory, valued in the king's books at £20. 8. 6½., and in the gift of the Earl of Bridgewater's trustees : the tithes have been commuted for £374, and the glebe comprises 32 acres. The church is in the early style of English architecture, and contains an altar-tomb of an armed knight in a recumbent posture, and his lady ; also another, with brasses, to a knight and his lady, and their nine sons and three daughters ; both executed in the richest style of ancient sculpture. There are two places of worship for Baptists.

ALDCLIFFE, a township, in the parish of Lancaster, hundred of Lonsdale south of the Sands, N. division of the county of Lancaster, 1 mile (S. W.) from Lancaster ; containing 111 inhabitants. This place is mentioned in Domesday book. Roger de Poictou granted lands here to the priory of Lancaster, and a lease of the manor was confirmed to the prior by Duke Henry of Lancaster. In the reign of Elizabeth, Aldcliffe belonged to the Daltons of Thurnham ; and about 1731 the principal part of the estate came by purchase to the family of Dawson, of whom was Edward Dawson, Esq., of Aldcliffe Hall, a spirited agriculturist, who improved the property, and inclosed the chief part of Aldcliffe Marsh. The township comprises 600 acres of very fertile land, whereof 390 are in grass, and 210 arable: the surface is undulated; and from the higher grounds are fine views of the river Lune, which flows on the west, and beyond which extend the waters of Morecambe bay. The Lancaster canal passes on the east. Besides the inclosed lands, the proprietor, who is lord of the manor, claims 367 acres adjoining the Lune. A very fine freestone is found within the township. £25 per annum are paid as a commutation for the small tithes.

ALDEBURGH.—See ALDBOROUGH.

ALDEBY (ST. MARY), a parish, in the union of LODDON and CLAVERING, hundred of CLAVERING, E. division of NORFOLK, 3 miles (N. E.) from Beccles; containing 496 inhabitants. It is bounded on the south by the navigable river Waveney, which separates it from the county of Suffolk; and comprises 3043 acres by admeasurement. The living is a perpetual curacy; net income, £120; patrons and appropriators, the Dean and Chapter of Norwich. The church, a cruciform structure with a south chapel, is partly in the early English style; the entrance to the west is through a rich Norman doorway; the tower rises between the nave and chancel. £40, the rental of land, are annually distributed among the poor. Here was a small priory, a cell to the Benedietine abbey of Norwich.

ALDENHAM (ST. JOHN THE BAPTIST), a parish, in the union of WATFORD, hundred of CASHIO, or liberty of ST. ALBAN's, county of HERTFORD, 2¼ miles (N. E. by E.) from Watford; containing, with the hamlet of Theobald-Street, 1662 inhabitants. The living is a vicarage, valued in the king's books at £24, and in the gift of the Trustees of P. Thellusson, Esq.: the impropriate tithes have been commuted for £778, and the vicarial for £110. The church is in the early English style, and contains some highly ornamented screen-work, the effigies of two females in stone, and an enriched font. A free grammar school was founded and endowed in 1599, by Richard Platt, citizen of London, for sixty children, to be chosen from among the poor of Aldenham and the families of freemen of the Brewers' Company, London. In consequence of a great improvement in the value of the property, the master and wardens of the company, who were constituted the governors, decided upon extending its benefits; and the present buildings, called the "Upper and Lower Schools," were erected in 1825, the latter school being designed for the sons of farmers and labourers of Aldenham, on the national system. The same munificent benefactor endowed six almshouses.

ALDERBURY (ST. MARY), a parish, and the head of a union, in the hundred of ALDERBURY, Salisbury and Amesbury, and S. divisions of WILTS, 3 miles (S. E. by E.) from Salisbury; containing, with Farley and Pitton chapelries, 1440 inhabitants. The living is a discharged vicarage, in the patronage of the Bishop of Salisbury, with a net income of £162: the great tithes were commuted for land and an annual money payment, under an inclosure act, in 1803. At Farley and Pitton are chapels of ease. There is a place of worship for Wesleyans; also a small endowed free school. The poor law union of Alderbury comprises 22 parishes or places.

27

and contains a population of 14,171. A monastery formerly existed at Ivy Church, in the parish, the site of which is now occupied by a modern residence.

ALDERFORD (ST. JOHN THE BAPTIST), a parish, in the union of ST. FAITH's, hundred of EYNSFORD, E. division of NORFOLK, 3¼ miles (S. E. by S.) from Reepham; containing 44 inhabitants. This parish is bounded on the south by the river Wensum, and intersected by the road from Norwich to Reepham; it comprises 431a. 16p., chiefly arable. The living is a discharged rectory, with the vicarage of Attlebridge consolidated, valued in the king's books at £4. 6. 8.; patrons, the Dean and Chapter of Norwich. The tithes of the parish have been commuted for £137, and the glebe consists of 7 acres, with a small cottage. The church is in the early, decorated, and later English styles, and consists of a nave and chancel, with a square tower; the font is curiously and elaborately sculptured.

ALDERHOLT, a tything, in the parish and hundred of CRANBORNE, union of WIMBORNE and CRANBORNE, Wimborne division of DORSET; containing 404 inhabitants.

ALDERLEY (ST. MARY), a parish, in the union and hundred of MACCLESFIELD, N. division of the county of CHESTER, 6 miles (W. N. W.) from Macclesfield, containing 1538 inhabitants, of whom 455 are in the township of Upper Alderley, 679 in that of Lower Alderley, and 404 in that of Great Warford. This parish comprises by computation 6009 acres of fertile land, whereof 1971 are in Upper, and 2353 in Lower Alderley; the prevailing soils are clay and sand. The surface is greatly diversified, and towards the north-east rises gradually, forming an elevation called Alderley Edge, which terminates abruptly, and commands an extensive view. Alderley Park, the seat of Lord Stanley, forms an interesting feature in the landscape; in the grounds is a sheet of water called Radnor Mere, a wood near which contains some of the finest beech-trees in England. A few of the inhabitants are engaged in weaving for the manufacturers of the neighbouring towns. The Manchester and Birmingham railway passes through the parish. The living is a rectory, valued in the king's books at £14. 10. 10.; net income, £514; patron, Lord Stanley. Besides the church, there is a chapel at Birtles, the incumbency of which is in the gift of T. Hibbert, Esq. The parish contains also places of worship for Wesleyans, and one for Baptists at Great Warford. An ancient school-house in the churchyard, some time after its erection, was endowed with the sum of £250, which has been placed at interest in the hands of Lord Stanley, who pays the master £10 per annum; another school is principally supported by his lordship. On Alderley Edge is a fine spring, called the Holy Well.

ALDERLEY (ST. KENELME), a parish, in the union of CHIPPING-SODBURY, Upper division of the hundred of GRUMBALD's-ASH, W. division of the county of GLOUCESTER, 2 miles (S. S. E.) from Wotton-under-Edge; containing 174 inhabitants. The village is pleasantly situated on an eminence between two streams which unite and fall into the river Severn at Berkeley; and commands an extensive and interesting view to the south and south-west. There is a manufactory of cloth, affording employment to between one and two hundred persons. Cornua ammonis and other fossils are found. The living is a discharged rectory, valued in the king's

E 2

books at £11. 4. 7., and in the gift of R. H. B. Hale, Esq.: the tithes have been commuted for £155. 5. 8., and there are about 25 acres of glebe. The Rev. Potter Cole was in 1730 presented to this benefice, which he held till the year 1800. Sir Matthew Hale, lord chief justice in the reign of Charles II., was born here, Nov. 1st, 1609, and lies interred in the churchyard.

ALDERMASTON, or ALDMERSTON (ST. MARY), a parish, and formerly a market-town, in the union of BRADFIELD, hundred of THEALE, county of BERKS, 10 miles (S. W. by W.) from Reading; containing 662 inhabitants. This place was distinguished by various military operations in the civil war. The royal army under the command of Col. Gage, on its way from Oxford to Basing House in 1643, halted at the village: on its return, finding the enemy in possession of the place, the troops were ordered to march by a different route. The Earl of Essex was here with his army in the same year, and proceeded hence by Padworth and Bucklebury heath to Newbury, immediately before the second battle fought near that town. The parish comprises 3689a. 6p., and is intersected by the river Kennet. Fairs are held on May 6th, July 7th, and Oct. 11th. The living is in the gift of the lord of the manor, and valued in the king's books at £12. 12. 8½. The tithes were formerly appropriated to the priory of Sherborne, subject to the payment of a small quit-rent to Queen's College, Oxford; but since the reign of Elizabeth they have belonged to the lord of the manor; they have been commuted for £535. The church is an ancient structure, and contains several fine monuments of the families of Orchard, De la Mere, and Foster.

ALDERMINSTER (ST. MARY), a parish, partly in the Upper division of the hundred of OSWALDSLOW, but chiefly in the Upper division of the hundred of PERSHORE, union of STRATFORD-UPON-AVON, Blockley and E. divisions of the county of WORCESTER, of which it is a detached portion, surrounded by Warwickshire, 5 miles (S. S. E.) from Stratford; containing 508 inhabitants. The parish comprises 3073a. 3r. 26p.; it is bounded on the south-west by the river Stour, and has a great variety of soil. There are three manors, viz.: Aldermaston, Apthrop, and Goldecote, the last containing the handsome seat of Gustavus Smith, Esq. The village is situated on the London and Birmingham road. The living is a discharged vicarage, valued in the king's books at £7; the patronage and impropriation belong to the Crown. The great tithes have been commuted for £188. 4., and those of the incumbent for £160. 19.; the glebe comprises 20 acres in this parish, and 3½ acres in that of Bengworth, near Evesham. The church is a curious cruciform edifice, with a low tower; the nave is in the Norman style: a new gallery was added in 1839.

ALDERNEY, an island, dependent on, and under the jurisdiction of, the states of Guernsey; situated 6 leagues (N. E.) from that island, and 7 miles (W.) from Cape La Hogue, in Normandy (from which it is separated by a strait, called by the French Raz Blanchard, and by the English the Race of Alderney); and containing 1030 inhabitants. This island, named in old English records Aurney, Aureney, and Aurigny, by which last name it is still designated by the French geographers, is supposed to have been the Riduna of Antoninus; but little of its history is known prior to the time of Henry

28

III., in the fourth year of whose reign an act of parliament was passed, by which it appears that one moiety of the island belonged to that monarch, and the other moiety to the Bishop of Coutances. From an extent of the crown, made in the fourth year of the reign of James I., the whole of the island seems to have been the property of the king, who was entitled to the amends, or fines, and the perquisites of the court; to the treizièmes, or thirteenths, upon the sale of lands; and to the wrecks, and other princely rights and royalties; but it was subsequently granted in fee-farm to successive tenants. George III., by letters-patent under the great seal, bearing date Dec. 14th, 1763, in consideration of the surrender of the former lease or patent, and for other considerations therein specified, granted the island to John Le Mesurier, Esq., for 99 years, with a proviso for resuming the lease at any time, upon payment to the lessee of such amount of money as should have been disbursed in improving the mansion called the Governor's house, and the other premises. In this grant was included the advowson of the church and chapel, with power to levy duties upon all vessels coming into the port of the island, in the same proportion as they are levied in the harbour of St. Peter's Port, in Guernsey. The rights and property of the island were, however, purchased by government from J. Le Mesurier, Esq., of Poole, who was the last governor.

The approach to the island, particularly in stormy weather, is dangerous, from the rapidity and diversity of the currents, which at spring tides rush in contrary directions, with a velocity of six miles an hour; and from the numerous rocks by which it is surrounded. These rocks were fatal to Prince Henry, son of Henry I., who was wrecked on his return from Normandy, in 1119; and, in 1744, to the Victory man-of-war, which was lost with the whole crew, consisting of 1100 men: the French fleet, notwithstanding, escaped through the passage here after its defeat at La Hogue, in 1692. About seven miles to the west are the Caskets, a cluster of rocks rising to a height of twenty-five or thirty fathoms from the water, and about one mile in circumference. On the south-west side of the cluster is a naturally-formed harbour, in which a frigate may shelter as in a dock; steps are cut in the rock, and conveniences are provided for hauling up boats: there is a smaller and less compact harbour on the north-east side. On these rocks three light-houses have been erected, furnished with revolving reflectors.

The ISLAND, which is four miles in length, one mile and a half in breadth, and nearly ten miles in circumference, shelves considerably to the north-east, and is intersected by deep valleys. The whole of the southern and eastern parts, from La Pendante to La Clanque, is bounded by cliffs varying in elevation from 100 to 200 feet, and presenting picturesque and striking scenery; the northern and eastern sides have lower cliffs, alternating with small bays and flat shores. The bay of Bray is remarkably fine, affording good anchorage to vessels, and at low water the sands are very extensive: Longy bay is also commodious; and Craby harbour, in which at spring tides the water rises to the height of twenty-five feet, affords every facility for a wet-dock. A harbour of refuge was commenced in the early part of the year 1847. The east side of the island consists chiefly of reddish sandstone, and the west side principally of porphyry, neither of which rocks is found in large masses in any of the other islands of the group. About one-half of the land is in cultivation; the remainder consists of common and furze land, affording good pasturage for sheep, but insufficient for cattle. The soil, though light and sandy, is in general productive, and the system of agriculture similar to that of Guernsey; but the general appearance of the land is bare, as few trees and no thorn hedges are to be seen, the inclosures being formed by walls of loose stones, and furze banks. Of the Alderney breed of cows, which has taken its name from this island, Jersey and Guernsey furnish by far the greater number for exportation, this island but very few. The town is situated nearly in the centre of the isle, and, with the exception of the Governor's house, contains few buildings worthy of notice; it is partially paved, and well supplied with water: there is a good road to Bray harbour, and another to Longy bay, where was an ancient nunnery, subsequently used as barracks during the war, and, since the peace, converted into an hospital, and a depôt for military stores. The pier, near which are several houses, is of rude construction, with but one projecting arm, and affording shelter to vessels only from the north-east.

The CIVIL JURISDICTION is exercised by a judge and six jurats, the former of whom is nominated by the governor, and the latter elected by the commonalty; they hold their several appointments for life, unless removed for misbehaviour, or malversation in office. The judge and jurats, with the queen's officers, viz., the procureur, or attorney-general; the comptroller, or solicitor-general; and the greffier, or registrar, who is also nominated by the governor, compose the court, the decision of which, however, is not necessarily definitive, being subject to an appeal to the royal court at Guernsey, and from that to the queen in council. In all criminal cases the court of Alderney has only the power of receiving evidence, which is transmitted to the superior court of Guernsey, where judgment is pronounced, and the sentence of the law executed. The entire jurisprudence is similar to that of Guernsey, as appears by the order of the royal commissioners sent to the island by Queen Elizabeth, in 1585. The judge and jurats, together with the douzainiers, the latter being twelve men chosen by the commonalty for their representatives, compose the assembly of the states of the island, wherein all ordinances for its government are proposed. But the douzainiers have only a deliberate voice, and no vote, the judge and jurats alone deciding upon the expediency of any proposed measure. The governor, or his lieutenant, must be present at each assembly, but has no vote in it. The public acts were first registered at Alderney in 1617, and the first contract was enrolled in the year 1666. The privileges of the charter are inherited by birth, or obtained by servitude.

It is not known at what time the CHURCH was built: it is an ancient edifice, not entitled to architectural notice; the tower was added to it in 1767, and a chapel near it was erected in 1763. The net income of the incumbent is £120. From the year 1591 to 1607 Alderney was without an officiating minister; baptisms and marriages were solemnized at Guernsey, and registered in the parish of St. Saviour. There is a place of worship for Wesleyans. A school for boys, and another for girls, were founded by J. Le Mesurier, Esq., the last
29

governor; the building was erected in 1790. A general hospital was erected in 1789, and is supported by subscription. There still exists part of a castle begun by the Earl of Essex, in the reign of Queen Elizabeth, but never finished; the ruinous foundations yet bear that favourite's name. The islet of Burhou, lying to the westward, is used as a rabbit-warren.

ALDERSEY, a township, in the parish of CODDINGTON, union of GREAT BOUGHTON, Higher division of the hundred of BROXTON, S. division of the county of CHESTER, 8¾ miles (S. E. by S.) from Chester; containing 138 inhabitants. The soil is clayey. Salt-works were carried on here in the middle of the sixteenth century; and there is still a brine spring in the neighbourhood, but it is not worked, owing to the distance from which coal must be brought for that purpose.

ALDERSHOTT (ST. MICHAEL), a parish, in the hundred of CRONDALL, Odiham and N. divisions of the county of SOUTHAMPTON, 3 miles (N. E. by N.) from Farnham; containing 685 inhabitants. It is situated on the road between Farnham and Guildford; and comprises 4130 acres, of which 731 are arable, 550 pasture, 130 woodland, 20 acres sites and gardens, 19 hops, and 2700 common. The Basingstoke canal passes within a mile and a half of the village. The living is a perpetual curacy; net income, £64; patrons, J. Eggar, S. Andrews, J. Alden, and W. Tice, Esqrs.; impropriators, the Master and Brethren of the Hospital of St. Cross, Winchester. The church contains a curious monument to the Titchbourne family, whose ancient seat has been converted into a farmhouse. There are some remains of an extensive Roman camp on Brixbury Hill.

ALDERTON (ST. MARGARET), a parish, in the union of WINCHCOMB, Upper division of the hundred of TEWKESBURY, E. division of the county of GLOUCESTER, 4¼ miles (N. N. W.) from Winchcomb; containing, with the hamlet of Dixton, 411 inhabitants. It comprises by admeasurement 1750 acres; the surrounding country is beautiful, and extensive views are commanded from the hills. Near Alderton Hill stood the fine old mansion, recently taken down, where one of the ancestors of the family of Tracy (Lord Sudely) was born; and at Dixton is a large manor-house, where the Higfords, who have been great benefactors to the parish, resided for several centuries. The living is a rectory, valued in the king's books at £22. 1. 10½.; net income, £337; patron and incumbent, the Rev. C. Covey. The glebe consists of 230 acres, allotted in lieu of tithe, and the tithes for the hamlet of Dixton have been commuted for a rent-charge of £150: a handsome and commodious parsonage-house has been built by the present rector, on an eminence. The church, which is an ancient structure, is distinguished for the elegance of its arches. Numerous fossils are found in the stone-quarries in the parish.

ALDERTON (ST. MARGARET), a parish, in the union of POTTERSPURY, hundred of CLELEY, S. division of the county of NORTHAMPTON, 3¾ miles (E. S. E.) from Towcester; containing 166 inhabitants. On the north the parish is bounded by the river Tow, and on the east partly by the road leading from Northampton to Stony Stratford. It consists of 869a. 20p.; the surface is boldly undulated, and the village stands on the western declivity of an eminence. The living is a rectory, annexed to that of Grafton-Regis, and valued in the king's books at £12.

ALDERTON (St. Andrew), a parish, in the union of Woodbridge, hundred of Wilford, E. division of Suffolk, 7 miles (S. E. by S.) from Woodbridge ; containing 620 inhabitants. It comprises 2377 acres, of which 368 are common or waste. The living is a rectory, valued in the king's books at £14. 18. 4., and in the patronage by turns of the lords of the four manors in the parish, of whom the Bishop of Norwich, as lord of Alderton Hall, is one. The tithes have been commuted for £630, and there are about 22 acres of glebe.

ALDERTON (St. Giles), a parish, in the union of Malmesbury, forming a detached portion of the hundred of Chippenham, and N. divisions of Wilts, 9 miles (N. W. by N.) from Chippenham ; containing 183 inhabitants. It comprises 1584 acres, of which a considerable portion is waste land. Stone is quarried suitable for building and the repair of roads. The living is a perpetual curacy, in the gift of J. Neeld, Esq. : the tithes have been commuted for £145, and the glebe consists of 47 acres. The present church has been lately built, with much taste, and has a square tower surmounted by a spire : the former church was a very ancient structure.

ALDERWASLEY, a chapelry, in the parish of Wirksworth, union of Belper, hundred of Appletree, S. division of the county of Derby, 2¼ miles (E. by S.) from Wirksworth ; containing 398 inhabitants. The manor anciently belonged to the Ferrars family, and was afterwards annexed to the earldom and duchy of Lancaster. The Le Foune or Fawne family held lands here in the reign of Henry III., and their heiress intermarried with the Lowes, who obtained a grant of the manor from Henry VIII. : the Hurt family afterwards became possessed of the manor, through an heiress of the Lowes. The township comprises 3054 acres, of which 32 are common or waste. There are iron-works and furnaces for smelting lead-ore in the neighbourhood. The chapel belongs to F. Hurt, Esq., who appoints the chaplain.

ALDFIELD, a chapelry, in the parish of Ripon, Lower division of the wapentake of Claro, W. riding of York, 3½ miles (W. by S.) from Ripon ; containing 132 inhabitants. This village, which is beautifully situated in the woody vale near Fountain's Abbey, is resorted to on account of its mineral springs, discovered about 1698, and whose sulphureous quality is said to be stronger than that of the Harrogate water. The surrounding scenery comprises all the variety of Matlock, in Derbyshire. The living is a perpetual curacy, in the patronage of Earl De Grey ; net income, £72. Rent-charges amounting to £59. 12. have been awarded as a commutation for the tithes ; £38 are payable to the trustees of Smith's charity, and £21. 12. to the Dean and Chapter of Ripon.

ALDFORD (St. John the Baptist), a parish, in the union of Great Boughton ; comprising the townships of Aldford and Churton in the Higher, and those of Buerton and Edgerley in the Lower, division of the hundred of Broxton, S. division of the county of Chester ; and containing 835 inhabitants, of whom, 488 are in the township of Aldford, 5 miles (S. by E.)

from Chester, on the road to Farndon and Holt. This place, which had formerly a market and a fair, derives its name from an ancient ford on the river Dee ; the stream divides it on the west from the county of Denbigh, North Wales, and a good bridge has been erected. In the reign of Henry II. a castle was built, of which at present only the earth-works, nearly adjoining the church, are remaining ; and in the reign of Charles I. a garrison was placed here by Sir William Brereton, during the siege of Chester. The parish contains by measurement 2764 acres, whereof 1194 are in the township of Aldford ; of the latter the soil is loam, gravel, and clay : there are two quarries of red sandstone. The living is a rectory, valued in the king's books at £16. 17. 8½., and in the gift of the Marquess of Westminster : the tithes of the township have been commuted for £315, and the glebe comprises 21 acres, with a large and commodious house. The church stands on the verge of the castle moat, and has been repaired in various styles ; in the churchyard is the recumbent effigy of a female, sculptured in red stone. Schools are supported ; and there are six almshouses for aged widows, endowed with £22 per annum. Vestiges of a Roman road connecting the northern and southern branches of the Watling-street, are discernible in the parish.

ALDHAM, a parish, in the union of Lexden and Winstree, Witham division of the hundred of Lexden, N. division of Essex, 6 miles (E. N. E.) from Great Coggeshall ; containing 382 inhabitants. This place is situated on the river Colne, by which it is bounded on the north ; and comprises an area of 1512 acres, whereof 27 are common or waste. Fairs are held at the hamlet of Ford-street on Easter-Tuesday and Nov. 1st. The living is a rectory, valued in the king's books at £12 ; net income, £327 ; patron, the Bishop of London. The church is a rude edifice, with a small wooden turret. A national school is supported ; and £22 per annum, bequeathed by an unknown benefactor, are divided among 16 married persons who have not received parochial relief during the preceding twelve months. The Rev. Philip Morant, author of the History of Essex, was rector of the parish ; he died Nov. 26th, 1770, aged 70 years, and was interred in the chancel of the church, where a monument has been erected to his memory. The learned Sir John Marsham, one of the six-clerks in chancery, and author of several valuable works, was proprietor of Bourchiers Hall (now a farmhouse), in the reign of Charles I., to whose fortunes he was a firm adherent.

ALDHAM (St. Mary), a parish, in the union and hundred of Cosford, W. division of Suffolk, 2 miles (N. N. E.) from Hadleigh ; containing 293 inhabitants. It comprises 1742a. 1r. 33p., and has, for the most part, a hilly surface ; the land consists of arable, pasture, and wood, the last of which is tithe-free ; the soil is a stiff clay, and produces good corn. The living is a rectory, valued in the king's books at £10. 13. 4. ; net income, £290 ; patron, Thomas Barret Lennard, Esq. : the glebe consists of 45 acres. The church is situated on a hill, and is built of flint and stone, with a round tower : the advowson formerly belonged to the earls of Oxford, whose arms are carved on the oak benches fitted up in the church in 1537. Dr. Rowland Taylor suffered martyrdom on the common of the parish, in 1555.

ALDINGBOURNE (*St. Mary*), a parish, in the union of WEST HAMPNETT, hundred of BOX and STOCK-BRIDGE, rape of CHICHESTER, W. division of SUSSEX, 4¼ miles (E. by N.) from Chichester; containing, with the hamlets of Lydsey and Westergate, 772 inhabitants. This was formerly the residence of the bishops of Chichester, whose palace here was destroyed in the parliamentary war by Sir William Waller on his march to Arundel; a castellated building near the palace, situated on a mound surrounded with a moat, was demolished at the same time. The road from Chichester to Arundel, and the Portsmouth and Arun canal, both pass through the parish. The living is a vicarage, valued in the king's books at £5. 10. 5.; net income, £212; patron, the Dean of Chichester. The church is a cruciform structure in the Norman style, with a square embattled tower which terminates the north transept: the south transept is an ancient chapel, having an entrance by a fine Norman doorway. At Lydsey was a chapel founded prior to the year 1282, of which there are now no remains.

ALDINGHAM (*St. Cuthbert*), a parish, in the union of ULVERSTON, hundred of LONSDALE north of the Sands, N. division of the county of LANCASTER, 5¾ miles (S.) from Ulverston; containing 907 inhabitants. Immediately after the Conquest, Aldingham was granted to Michael Flandrensis or le Fleming, sometimes called de Furness, who is supposed to have accompanied William I. to England. The parish is situated on the western shore of Morecambe bay, which has encroached so much upon the lands that the church, said to have been formerly in the centre of the parish, is now within the reach of a high tide. The soil is a friable loam and marl, constantly melting down; and the sea threatens greater ravages: the present area is about 7500 acres, whereof two-thirds are arable. The population is principally engaged in the cultivation of the land, and several neat farm-houses have recently been erected by the Earl of Burlington. Limestone is quarried, and there are numerous limekilns. The Tarn beck flows from Urswick beck, southward, to Gleaston, in the parish, where it receives the name of the Gleaston beck; it falls into the bay near the small hamlet of Roosebeck.

The living is a rectory, valued in the king's books at £39. 19. 2., and in the patronage of the Crown; net income, £1093. The church is supposed to have been founded by Michael le Fleming: the present edifice is a low, long, and narrow structure, with whitened walls, and chipstones of red stone; the tower, supported by buttresses and surmounted by pinnacles, is strong and bulky. The churchyard is protected from the sea by an artificial rampart of stone, which appears to be of some antiquity. In the village of Gleaston are the mouldering ruins of a castle which, according to tradition, was built by the lords of Aldingham immediately after the sea had swept away the lower part of the parish; the date is uncertain. The ruins consist of two towers, nearly perfect, on the west side, and there are traces of towers on the east; the interior is now a browsy pasture, of uneven surface, covered in many places with masses of fallen stone. From a promontory on the coast, which was once surrounded by a moat, and is supposed to have been an exploratory station during the incursions of the Picts and Scots, is an extensive prospect over the counties of Westmorland and York.

ALDINGTON (*St. Martin*), a parish, in the union of EAST ASHFORD, partly in the liberty of ROMNEY-MARSH, but chiefly in the franchise and barony of BIRCHOLT, lathe of SHEPWAY, E. division of KENT, 5½ miles (W. by N.) from Hythe; containing 733 inhabitants. It is crossed by the South-Eastern railway; and comprises 3576 acres, of which 320 are in wood. The living is a rectory, with the chapel of Smeeth annexed, valued in the king's books at £38. 6. 8.; net income, £1014; patron, the Archbishop of Canterbury. The church displays the early English style in its general structure; the tower presents a specimen of very good masonry. Erasmus, the celebrated divine, was rector of the parish.

ALDINGTON, a hamlet, in the parish of BADSEY, union of EVESHAM, Upper division of the hundred of BLACKENHURST, Pershore and E. divisions of the county of WORCESTER, 2 miles (E.) from Evesham; containing 102 inhabitants. At the time of the Domesday survey, this was a *berewic*, or corn-farm, annexed to the manor of Offenham, and held by the abbey of Evesham: in the reign of Henry III. the abbot built a grange here. The hamlet comprises 642 acres, forming the northern part of the parish; on the west it is bounded by the Avon, and on the north by a stream which falls into that river. The soil is of the most fertile quality. There is a small, but very respectable village; and the manor-house is well designed, and pleasantly situated.

ALDRIDGE (*St. Mary*), a parish, in the union of WALSALL, S. division of the hundred of OFFLOW and of the county of STAFFORD, 4 miles (N. E. by E.) from Walsall; containing, with the chapelry of Great Barr, 2083 inhabitants, of whom 1005 are in the township of Aldridge. This parish, anciently *Alrewich*, comprises 7752 acres, whereof 480 are common or waste land : in the township of Aldridge are about 2500 acres, all arable, with the exception of 100 of grass and 20 woodland. The soil is principally sandy and gravelly, producing good crops if well manured; much of the surface is elevated, the celebrated Barr Beacon being the highest hill in the inland counties. The neighbourhood affords a kind of red clay, well adapted for the finer sort of flower-pots, tiles, &c.; it is thirty feet deep, and makes, also, superior blue bricks for building, The Blue-tile works of Messrs. G. and J. Brawn were established here in 1825; the excellence of the tiles consists in their lightness, durability, and colour, being similar to slate : about 100 hands are employed in this species of manufacture. The trade is greatly facilitated by the Wyrley and Essington Extension canal, now incorporated with the Birmingham canal, and which passes a short distance west of the village. There is not a running stream in the parish; the Bourne rivulet separates it from Shenstone, and the old London and Chester road passes at the east end. The village is pretty, and contains some good houses : about a mile southward of it is Aldridge Lodge, occupying elevated ground, surrounded with 200 acres, and commanding a panoramic view of the circumjacent country; it is the property of the Rev. Thomas Burrowes Adams, M.A. Druids' Heath and Mill Green, two hamlets in the manor of Aldridge, are also within a mile of the village. The LIVING is a rectory, with the perpetual curacy of Great Barr annexed, valued in the king's books at £8. 1. 3.; patron, Sir E. D. Scott, Bart.: the tithes have been commuted for

£1300 per annum; and there are 70 acres of glebe, with a good glebe-house situated near the church, near which, also, is the residence of Edward Tongue, Esq. The church was partly rebuilt in 1842, at a cost of £728; it has a monument of a Knight Templar, and its square tower is very ancient. There are two free schools, one of them with an endowment of £126 per annum, founded in 1718 by the Rev. John Jordan; and the other for girls, of whom six are instructed in consideration of an endowment of £12 per annum arising from land left by Mrs. Wheeley. A national and Sunday school is supported by subscription. At the back of the church is a small tumulus.

ALDRINGHAM (ST. ANDREW), a parish, in the union and hundred of BLYTHING, E. division of SUFFOLK, 2½ miles (N. by W.) from Aldborough; containing, with the hamlet of Thorpe, 401 inhabitants. The parish derives its name from the river Alde (by some improperly called the Hundred brook), which separates it from Aldborough; it comprises 1736 acres, whereof 323 are common or waste. A market was formerly held, which has fallen into disuse: there is a small fair on St. Andrew's day, called Cold Fair. The living is a perpetual curacy; net income, £59; patron and impropriator, Lord Huntingfield, whose tithes have been commuted for £205. There is a place of worship for Particular Baptists.

ALDRINGTON, EAST, a parish, in the union of STEYNING, hundred of FISHERGATE, rape of LEWES, E. division of SUSSEX, 3 miles (W. by N.) from Brighton; containing about 650 acres. This place is by Camden, Stillingfleet, and others, identified with the Portus Adriani of the Romans; and urns, skeletons, pottery, and other relics of Roman antiquity have been frequently discovered in this and the adjoining parishes; which appear to have been the first points of attack when the Saxons began to infest the coasts. It is bounded on the south by the English Channel, which has made such encroachments on the land as to have completely destroyed the village; and the parish is now without any population, except one individual returned in the last census. The road and railway from Brighton to Shoreham both pass through it. The living is a discharged rectory, valued in the king's books at £7. 10. 2½.; net income, £294; patrons, the Masters and Fellows of Magdalene College, Cambridge. The church is in ruins.

ALDSTONE.—See ALSTON.

ALDSWORTH (ST. PETER), a parish, in the union of NORTHLEACH, hundred of BRIGHTWELL'S BARROW, E. division of the county of GLOUCESTER, 3½ miles (S. E.) from Northleach; containing 365 inhabitants. The living is a perpetual curacy, in the gift of the Vicar of Turkdean; net income, £66. The tithes were commuted for land and an annual money payment, by an inclosure act, in 1793. The peculiar of Aldsworth is regularly inhibited during the bishop's visitation, although his right has been and still continues to be resisted by the patron and ordinary of the peculiar, notwithstanding an award of the Dean of Arches, in 1741, in the bishop's favour.

ALDSWORTH, a tything, in the parish and union of WEST BOURNE, hundred of WEST BOURNE and SINGLETON, rape of CHICHESTER, W. division of SUSSEX; containing 118 inhabitants. It is situated in the northern extremity of the parish.
32

ALDWARK, a township, in the parish of ALNE, union of EASINGWOULD, wapentake of BULMER, N. riding of YORK, 6½ miles (E. S. E.) from Boroughbridge; containing 224 inhabitants. This place comprises 2217 acres, of which 57 are common or waste. The village is seated in the vale of the Ouse, and nearly a mile to the south is Aldwark bridge, a substantial wooden structure, which crosses the river and its banks by twenty-seven arches and culverts. The vicarial tithes have been commuted for £75, and the impropriate for £3. 11.

ALDWARK, a township, in the parish of ECCLESFIELD, union of WORTLEY, N. division of the wapentake of STRAFFORTH and TICKHILL, W. riding of YORK, 2½ miles (N. E.) from Rotherham. Aldwark, or "the old work," the ancient seat of the Clarelles, Fitzwilliams, and Foljambes, lies remote from the rest of the parish, and has consequently never been considered a part of Hallamshire: its long line of resident proprietors presents a fine subject for the genealogist and antiquary. A few years since, the extensive corn and oil mills on the opposite side of the river Don were burnt down.

ALDWARK, a township, in the parish of BRADBORNE, union of BAKEWELL, hundred of WIRKSWORTH, S. division of the county of DERBY, 5¾ miles (N. W. by W.) from Wirksworth; containing 82 inhabitants. The manor was given to the monks of Darley by Sewall, ancestor to the Shirley family: Queen Elizabeth granted it to the Hardwickes, whose heiress brought it to Sir William Cavendish, ancestor of the Duke of Devonshire.

ALDWICK, a tything, in the parish of PAGHAM, union of WEST HAMPNETT, hundred of ALDWICK, rape of CHICHESTER, W. division of SUSSEX; containing 203 inhabitants.

ALDWINKLE (ALL SAINTS), a parish, in the union of THRAPSTON, hundred of HUXLOE, N. division of the county of NORTHAMPTON, 4 miles (N.) from Thrapston; containing 272 inhabitants. It is situated on the navigable river Nene, and contains about 1000 acres. The living is a rectory, valued in the king's books at £12. 4. 2.; net income, £311; patron, the Rev. R. Roberts, D.D. The tithes were commuted for land and a moneypayment, by an inclosure act, in 1792; the land comprises 205 acres. The church is remarkable for its beautiful tower; there are some windows in the decorated English style, and a small ornamented chapel adjoining the southern side of the chancel. The sum of £30 per annum, the rental of a plantation of twelve acres, is divided between the poor of the two parishes of Aldwinkle All Saints and St. Peter. There is a chalybeate spring. The poet Dryden was born in the parsonage-house, in 1631.

ALDWINKLE (ST. PETER), a parish, in the union of THRAPSTON, hundred of HUXLOE, N. division of the county of NORTHAMPTON, 3¾ miles (N. by E.) from Thrapston; containing 183 inhabitants. The river Nene, which is navigable to the North Sea, and communicates with the Northampton canal, flows through the parish. Here are the remains of a singular cruciform building, called Liveden, erected by the Tresham family, and richly decorated with sculpture, especially round the cornice, which exhibits a Roman Catholic legend and a variety of religious symbols. The living is a rectory, valued in the king's books at £11. 6. 3.; net income, £230; patron, Lord Lilford: the glebe consists of 183 acres. There is a place of worship for Particular Baptists. Fuller, author of *The Worthies of England* and other learned works, was born in the parish.

ALDWORTH (St. Mary), a parish, in the union of Wantage, hundred of Compton, county of Berks, 4½ miles (E. by S.) from East Ilsley; containing 314 inhabitants. This place, which is supposed by Hearne to have been a Roman station, comprises 1785a. 3r. 32p., and nearly the whole is cultivated land; the village is situated on an eminence commanding extensive and interesting views. The living is a vicarage, valued in the king's books at £8. 16. 0½.; patrons and impropriators, the Master and Fellows of St. John's College, Cambridge. The great tithes have been commuted for £400, and the vicarial for £100; the impropriate glebe consists of 27, and the vicarial of 16, acres. The church is an ancient structure of simple character, containing eight altar-tombs, on which are nine recumbent figures, under highly enriched arches, elegantly sculptured, supposed to represent different members of the De la Beche family, and to have been executed in the fourteenth century.

ALEMOUTH.—See Alnmouth.

ALETHORPE, an extra-parochial liberty, locally in the parish of Fakenham, union of Walsingham, hundred of Gallow, W. division of Norfolk, 2 miles (N. E. by E.) from Fakenham; containing 8 inhabitants. It comprises 237 acres of land.

ALEXTON (St. Peter), a parish, in the union of Billesdon, hundred of East Goscote, N. division of the county of Leicester, 3½ miles (W. by N.) from Uppingham; containing 81 inhabitants. This parish, which is separated from Rutland by the river Eye, and is situated near the road from Leicester to Cambridge, comprises 997a. 28p., nearly the whole of it good grazing land, and, with the exception of 200 acres, tithe-free; the soil is a stiff clay, and the surface undulated and pleasingly wooded. The ancient Hall, built in the reign of Elizabeth, is adorned with avenues of Scotch and Balm of Gilead firs, which are considered the finest in this part of the country. The living is a rectory, valued in the king's books at £6. 18. 4.; net income, £140; patron, Lord Berners. Attached are 24 acres of glebe within the parish, and two in Belton Field. The church was built in 1594, by Edward Andrewes.

ALFOLD (St. Nicholas), a parish, in the union of Hambledon, First division of the hundred of Blackheath, W. division of Surrey, 8½ miles (S. E. by S.) from Godalming; containing 519 inhabitants. The parish comprises 2726a. 1r. 33p., whereof 72 acres are common or waste, and abounds with oak, ash, and elm: in parts there is a bed of stone, which is used for repairing roads, but is not hard enough for building. The Arun and Wey Junction canal passes through. The living is a rectory, valued in the king's books at £6. 11. 2., and in the gift of the Sparkes family: the tithes have been commuted for £355, and the glebe comprises 14 acres. The church consists of a nave, chancel, and south aisle, with a tower surmounted by a small spire: the parsonage-house is situated on the south side of the churchyard.

ALFORD (St. Wilfred), a market-town and parish, in the union of Spilsby, Wold division of the hundred of Calceworth, parts of Lindsey, county of

Vol. I.—33

Lincoln, 34 miles (E.) from Lincoln, and 137 (N. by E.) from London; containing 1945 inhabitants. This place, which derives its name from an old ford over a stream that twice runs through it, is a small, though ancient, town; and is described by Leland as consisting of one street of mean buildings, covered with thatch. Since that writer's time, however, it has been considerably improved, particularly during the last 20 years: it is pleasantly situated, and is one of the polling-stations for the parts of Lindsey. The market is held on Tuesday, and fairs occur on Whit-Tuesday and the 8th of November: a court leet takes place annually, and petty-sessions once in every three weeks. The parish comprises about 1000 acres of land. The living is a discharged vicarage, with the living of Rigsby annexed, valued in the king's books at £10, and in the patronage of the Bishop of Lincoln; the appropriator, with a net income of £122: the church is a large structure of stone, repaired with brick, and is embellished by a tower commanding very extensive views of the adjacent districts; it has many ancient monuments. There are places of worship for Primitive Methodists, Baptists, Independents, and Wesleyans.

The free grammar school was founded and endowed by Francis Spanning, in 1565; and its revenue has been considerably augmented by subsequent benefactions of land at Farlesthorpe,Thoresthorpe,Woodthorpe, Strubby, and Cumberworth, containing in the whole 260 acres, and yielding an annual rent of £268. 18.; together with the living of Saleby, the patronage being vested in the governors. By a charter obtained in 1576, it was made a royal foundation, to be called "The Free Grammar School of Queen Elizabeth," and the management vested in eleven governors, who are a body corporate, and have a common seal. It has two quinquennial fellowships at Magdalene College, Cambridge; and there is a scholarship of £6. 8. 6. per annum at Jesus' College, Cambridge, for students from Alford, Caistor, or Louth schools. The premises consist of a substantial brick house for the master, with two commodious rooms adjoining, and a large garden in the town. Another school, in which 130 children of both sexes are instructed, was founded by John Spendluffe, who endowed it with an estate now producing £70 per annum. Almshouses for six poor people were erected and endowed by Sir Robert Christopher, Knt., in 1668; the endowment was subsequently augmented by Lord Harborough, in 1716. A salt spring, efficacious in scurvy, jaundice, &c., was discovered in 1670. Alford confers the title of Viscount on the family of Brownlow.

ALFORD (All Saints), a parish, in the union of Wincanton, hundred of Catsash, E. division of Somerset, 1¾ mile (W. by N.) from Castle-Cary; containing 90 inhabitants. The living is a rectory, consolidated with that of Hornblotton by act of parliament in 1836, and valued in the king's books at £9. 9. 9.; patron and incumbent, the Rev. J. G. D. Thring. The tithes have been commuted for £140, and there are 40 acres of glebe. At a farmhouse, called Alford Well, about three-quarters of a mile from the church, is a saline chalybeate spring, now disused.

ALFRETON (St. Mary), a market-town and parish, in the union of Belper, hundred of Scarsdale, N. division of the county of Derby, 14 miles (N. N. E.) from Derby, and 140 (N. N. W.) from London; com-

F

prising the township of Alfreton, the manor of Riddings (in which is Ironville), and the townships or hamlets of Swanwick, Greenhill-Lane, Newlands, Summercotes, and Birchwood ; and containing 7577 inhabitants, of whom 1774 are in Alfreton township. This place, called in King Ethelred's charter to Burton Abbey " Alfredingtune," and in Domesday book " Elfretune," is supposed to have derived its name from Alfred the Great. At the time of the Norman survey it was the property of Roger de Busli, and in the Pipe-Rolls of the reign of Henry II. it is recorded that Randulph was then enfeoffed of the barony of Alfreton ; he served the office of sheriff of the counties of Derby and Nottingham, in the 9th year of that reign. Fitz-Randulph, his son, the founder of Beauchief Abbey, in this county, and said to have been one of the murderers of Thomas à Becket, was also sheriff of the same counties, in the 12th and subsequent years of the same king ; and the like honour descended to his son William, whose heir, Robert, in the 13th of John, was certified to hold half a knight's fee in the adjoining manor of " Ryddinges," and in " Watnow" in Nottinghamshire. On the death of Thomas Fitz-Randulph the manor of Alfreton was transferred, in moieties, to William de Chaworth and Robert de Latham, who married his sisters, co-heiresses. The first charter for a market here was granted to Thomas de Chaworth, son of William, and to Robert de Latham, in the 36th of Henry III., and was renewed to one of their successors in the 5th of Edward VI. Thomas de Chaworth had free warren granted him in the 41st of Henry III. ; and in the 4th of Edward III. he claimed a park at Alfreton, with the privilege of having a gallows, tumbrell, and pillory, for the use of the manor. He purchased Robert de Latham's moiety. The last of the race was William de Chaworth, whose only daughter married John Ormond in the time of Henry VII. ; and by the heiress of the latter, the manor passed to Sir Anthony Babington, of Dethick, in this county, by whose grandson it was sold, about 1565, to John Zouch, of Codnor. After a sale by a son of Zouch, in 1618, to Robert Sutton, it finally passed, by purchase in 1629, to Anthony Morewood and his son Rowland, in whose descendants it still continues, the present possessor being William Palmer Morewood, Esq.

The parish comprises 4550 acres of land. The town is pleasantly situated on the brow of a hill, sloping towards the south, and consists of four streets in the form of a cross, with a market-place at the point of intersection ; the houses are irregularly built, but some of them are good specimens of the ancient style of domestic architecture. The manufacture of stockings is carried on to a considerable extent in the parish ; and there are large iron-works at Riddings and extensive collieries there, as well as in Alfreton, Greenhill-Lane, and the other townships. The produce is conveyed by the Cromford canal, a branch of which passes through Riddings and Summercotes : the Midland railway runs within about a mile and a half of the town ; and roads to Chesterfield, Mansfield, Nottingham, Derby, and Matlock pass through it. An act was passed in 1845 for making a railway from the parish of Alfreton to Sawley, on the Midland railway ; the line is called the Erewash Valley railway, and communicates with the Mansfield and Pinxton line. The market-day is Friday ; and fairs are held on January 26th, Easter-Tuesday, Whit-Tuesday,

34

July 31st, October 7th, and November 24th, the last being the day for the annual hiring of servants in husbandry. The town is a polling-place for the Northern division of the county ; and petty-sessions are held here : the powers of the county debt-court of Alfreton, established in 1847, extend over part of the registration-districts of Belper, Chesterfield, Mansfield, and Basford. The living is a discharged vicarage, valued in the king's books at £7. 18. 9. ; net income, £150 ; patron, Mr. Morewood : the great tithes have been purchased by the Landowners. The church is an ancient structure, with an embattled tower crowned by pinnacles. At Riddings is a second church. There are places of worship within the township of Alfreton for Wesleyans, General Baptists, and Independents.

ALFRICK, a hamlet, in the parish of SUCKLEY, union of MARTLEY, Upper division of the hundred of DODDINGTREE, Worcester and W. divisions of the county of WORCESTER, 7 miles (W. by S.) from Worcester ; containing 434 inhabitants. This place is bounded on the north by the river Teme, and comprises 1542a. 1r. 17p., whereof 83 acres are common or waste ; the surface is undulated, the land in good cultivation, and the scenery, enriched with wood, is generally of pleasing character, and in some parts picturesque. The heights of Old Storage command fine views. The inhabitants are chiefly employed in agricultural pursuits, and many of the females in making gloves for the manufacturers in Worcester. The road from Bromyard to Worcester passes through the hamlet. The tithes have been commuted for £240. 10. : the glebe land here consists of about four acres and a half. There is a chapel of ease, dedicated to St. Mary, in which marriages, baptisms, and burials are solemnized. A school for the instruction of ten poor children has an endowment of £8 per annum, arising from a bequest of £100 left by Richard Lloyd, Esq., in 1729, and which has been vested in the schoolhouse and land.

ALFRISTON (ST. ANDREW), a parish, in the union of EASTBOURNE, hundred of ALCESTON, rape of PEVENSEY, E. division of SUSSEX, 9 miles (S. E.) from Lewes ; containing 668 inhabitants. It is bounded on the east by the Cuchmere river, and comprises about 2000 acres, of which 600 are common or waste ; the soil is rich and fertile, and the produce of the orchards and gardens is remarkable for quality and exuberance. The village, beautifully situated in a valley near the river, was formerly of much greater extent than at present, and in the centre is an ancient cross, where probably a market was held. The living is a discharged vicarage, valued in the king's books at £11. 16. 0½., and in the patronage of the Crown ; net income, £135 ; impropriators, the Trustees of " Smith's Charity." The church is an ancient cruciform structure, in the decorated and later English styles, with a central tower surmounted by a spire. There is a place of worship for Independents. On the neighbouring downs are several barrows, in some of which urns, spear-heads, and other relics of antiquity have been found.

ALGARKIRK (ST. PETER AND ST. PAUL), a parish, in the union of BOSTON, wapentake of KIRTON, parts of HOLLAND, county of LINCOLN, 6 miles (S.) from Boston ; containing 754 inhabitants. This place derives its name from the Saxon Earl Algar, who in 870, aided by his seneschals Wibert and Leofric, obtained a victory over the Danes in this neighbourhood, but was defeated and slain on the day following : a statue of stone in the churchyard is said to have been erected to his memory. The parish comprises by admeasurement 5041 acres. The living is a rectory, with the living of Fosdyke annexed, valued in the king's books at £50. 18. 1½.; patron and incumbent, the Rev. Basil Beridge. The tithes have been commuted for £990, and the glebe, including that of Fosdyke, comprises 500 acres. The church, which is partly in the Norman and partly in the early English style, is rich in its details, and contains monuments to the Beridge family since the time of James I. The parsonage-house has a very picturesque appearance. About £38 per annum, the amount of various bequests, are distributed among the poor, who are also eligible to the benefit of Sir Thomas Middlecott's hospital at Fosdyke.

ALHAMPTON, a tything, in the parish of DITCHEAT, hundred of WHITSTONE, E. division of SOMERSET, 2¾ miles (N. W. by N.) from Castle-Cary ; containing 386 inhabitants. There was formerly a chapel.

ALKERTON, a tything, in the parish of EASTINGTON, union of WHEATENHURST, Lower division of the hundred of WHITSTONE, E. division of the county of GLOUCESTER, 3 miles (W.) from Stroud; containing 1108 inhabitants.

ALKERTON (ST. MICHAEL), a parish, in the union of BANBURY, hundred of BLOXHAM, county of OXFORD, 6 miles (W. N. W.) from Banbury; comprising 691a. 24p., and containing 190 inhabitants. The living is a rectory, valued in the king's books at £6. 3. 9.; net income, £153; patron, J. Dent, Esq. The tithes were commuted for land and a money payment, by an inclosure act, in 1776. The church is beautifully situated on elevated ground ; the tower rises from between the nave and the chancel, and the building has some sculpture in the mouldings of the outer walls. Thomas Lydiat, the learned mathematician and chronologer, was born at Alkerton in the year 1572; he became its rector, and was interred here.

ALKHAM (ST. ANTHONY), a parish, in the union of DOVOR, hundred of FOLKESTONE, lathe of SHEPWAY, E. division of KENT, 5 miles (W. by N.) from Dovor; containing 595 inhabitants. It comprises 3145a. 2r. 28p., including 300 acres of woodland, and 100 of common ; the surface is hilly, and the soil chalky, except at the tops of the hills, where it is a stiff clay. The living is a vicarage, with the living of Capel-le-Ferne annexed, valued in the king's books at £11 ; patron and appropriator, the Archbishop of Canterbury : the appropriate tithes have been commuted for £500, and the vicarial for £213. 10.; there are 9½ acres of appropriate glebe, and about 3 of vicarial. The church is partly Norman, and partly early English : the interior, which has been much improved of late years, has a venerable and interesting aspect, and there are some ancient monumental stones. According to Domesday book, a church existed here in the time of Edward the Confessor.

ALKINGTON, a tything, in the parish, and Upper division of the hundred, of BERKELEY, union of THORNBURY, W. division of the county of GLOUCESTER, 1¼ mile (S. E.) from Berkeley ; containing 1175 inhabitants. The village of Newport, on the great road from Gloucester to Bristol, is situated in this tything, and is the central posting-place between those cities ; it con-
35

tains several inns. There is a place of worship for Independents.

ALKINGTON, a township, in the parish of WHITCHURCH, Whitchurch division of the hundred of NORTH BRADFORD, N. division of SALOP, 2 miles (S. by W.) from Whitchurch.

ALKMONTON, a township, in the parish of LONGFORD, hundred of APPLETREE, S. division of the county of DERBY, 5¾ miles (S. by E.) from Ashbourn ; containing 102 inhabitants. There was anciently an hospital dedicated to St. Leonard, between this place and Hungry-Bentley, in the same parish, to which Walter Blount, Lord Mountjoy, was a benefactor, in 1474. The hospital shared the fate of most other similar establishments, whose constitutions were mingled with religious observances, at the time of the Reformation, and was abolished in 1547. The manor of Alkmonton afterwards belonged successively to the Barnesley, Browne, Stanhope, and Evans families. A chapel of ease has recently been erected, containing 120 sittings. The tithes have been commuted for £28. 15. payable to the rector, and £26 to the vicar, of Longford.

ALKRINGTON, a township, in the parish of PRESTWICH-CUM-OLDHAM, union of OLDHAM, hundred of SALFORD, S. division of the county of LANCASTER, 4½ miles (N. N. E.) from Manchester ; containing 338 inhabitants. The Levers were seated here from the middle of the seventeenth century ; and in Alkrington Hall was collected by Sir Ashton Lever the celebrated Leverian museum of rare productions of nature and art, for the sale of which, by lottery, Sir Ashton obtained an act of parliament, in 1785. The holder of the successful ticket was Mr. Parkinson, who exhibited the museum in London for some time, but eventually sold it by auction, and it was thus dispersed. Alkrington comprises 788 acres, of which 74 are common or waste land : the population is chiefly agricultural. The Messrs. Lees are the proprietors of nearly the whole township. It is included in the ecclesiastical district of Tongue, which see. The tithes have been commuted for £40.

ALLCANNINGS (ST. ANNE), a parish, in the union of DEVIZES, hundred of SWANBOROUGH, Devizes and N. divisions of WILTS, 5¾ miles (E.) from Devizes ; comprising the chapelry of Etchilhampton and the tythings of Allington and Fullaway, and containing 851 inhabitants. On the downs is St. Anne's hill, on which a large fair for sheep and horses is held on the 6th of August. The Kennet and Avon canal affords facility for the conveyance of goods. The living is a rectory, valued in the king's books at £31. 16. 10½., and in the gift of Lord Ashburton : the tithes, including those of Etchilhampton, have been commuted for £1204. 5., and the glebe comprises 36 acres. The church is an ancient structure in the Norman style. There is a chapel of ease at Etchilhampton. Miss Anne Lavington, in 1828, bequeathed £500, the interest to be distributed among the poor at Christmas.

ALLEN, ST. (ST. ALLEN), a parish, in the union of TRURO, W. division of the hundred of POWDER and of CORNWALL, 4 miles (N. by W.) from Truro; containing 652 inhabitants. It comprises 3061 acres, of which 216 are common or waste. The living is a vicarage, valued in the king's books at £8. 13. 4.; patron, the Bishop of Exeter; impropriator, the Earl of Falmouth. The great tithes have been commuted for £265, and the vicarial
F 2

for £147; there are 95 acres of glebe. The parish contains a Danish encampment.

ALLENDALE, a market-town and parish, in the union of HEXHAM, S. division of TINDALE ward and of NORTHUMBERLAND, 7 miles (S.) from Haydon-Bridge, 9¾ miles (S. W. by W.) from Hexham, and 286 (N. N. W.) from London; comprising the grieveships of Allendale town, Broadside, Catton, High and Low Forest, Keenly Park and West Allen High and Low; and containing 5729 inhabitants. The TOWN, which includes 1217 persons, is irregularly built on an acclivity gradually rising from the eastern bank of the river Allen, over which a bridge was erected in 1825. The market is on Friday: fairs are held on the Friday before the 11th of May, on the 22nd of August, and the first Friday after the festival of St. Luke, for horses, cattle, and sheep; and a cattle show, which has been established within the last few years, is annually held. In the market-place are the ruins of a cross. The PARISH derives its name from the river Allen, a small but rapid stream which rises in the hamlet of Allenheads, in East Allen, and Coalcleugh, in West Allen, and falls into the river Tyne about three miles to the west of Haydon-Bridge, where is a station of the Newcastle and Carlisle railway. The inhabitants are chiefly employed in the lead-mines, which are on a large scale, producing upwards of 3500 tons of lead annually. There are several works for grinding and washing the ore, and two extensive smelting-houses, one having an horizontal chimney 2½ miles long, with a terminus upwards of 780 feet above the ground-floor of the mill, and the other a chimney 1½ mile in length, and 700 feet above the ground-floor; in one of these smelting-houses twenty-one tons pass through the furnace weekly, and a considerable quantity of silver is separated. Limestone is extensively quarried, and there are also numerous quarries of stone of good quality for building.

The LIVING is a perpetual curacy; net income, £130; patron, T. W. Beaumont, Esq. The church is of stone, rebuilt in 1807. Within the parish also are four chapels, in the gift of the incumbent of Allendale, viz. St. Peter's, rebuilt in 1825, a perpetual curacy, of which the net income is £120; the chapel at Nine-Banks, partially rebuilt about 1816, a perpetual curacy, with an income of £124; the chapel at the Carr Shield, or West Allen High chapel, built in 1822, also a perpetual curacy, of which the income is £109; and that of Allenheads, described under its proper head. There are places of worship for the Society of Friends and Wesleyans. A free school for the children of parishioners is endowed with two tenements, bequeathed by William Hutchinson in 1692, producing a rental of £24; and with other premises and thirty-two acres of land, in Broadside, purchased with a legacy of Christopher Wilkinson in 1700, and yielding £38 per annum. Various other schools are connected with the different places of worship in the parish; and some small sums, the principal of which is an annuity of £10 from Shield's charity, are distributed annually among the poor. There are several chalybeate springs; and at a place called Old Town, about three miles to the north-west, are vestiges of an ancient intrenchment, of a square form, supposed to be Roman.

ALLENHEADS, a hamlet (formerly a distinct parish) in the parish of ALLENDALE, S. division of TINDALE ward and of NORTHUMBERLAND, 17 miles (S. S. W.)

from Hexham. The chapel here was built by Col. Beaumont, in 1826, on the site of one erected in 1701 by Sir William Blackett, for the religious duties of the miners, who at that time attended prayers every morning at six o'clock; it is now considered a domestic chapel, and near it is a good house for the minister, occupied by the incumbent of St. Peter's, described in the preceding article, who officiates in both chapels. There are several veins of lead-ore in the neighbourhood, which are worked to a considerable extent.

ALLENSFORD, a hamlet, in the parish of SHOTLEY, union of HEXHAM, E. division of TINDALE ward, S. division of NORTHUMBERLAND, 13 miles (S. E.) from Hexham. This place is on the north side of the river Derwent, over which is a stone bridge.

ALLENSMORE (ST. ANDREW), a parish, in the hundred of WEBTREE, union and county of HEREFORD, 4 miles (S. W.) from Hereford; containing 668 inhabitants. The parish is intersected by the road from Hereford to Monmouth, and consists of 1820 acres, the surface being generally level, with an ample proportion of timber. The living is a discharged vicarage, rated in the king's books at £5. 12. 6., and endowed with £400 royal bounty; patron, the Dean of Hereford. The appropriate tithes have been commuted for two rent-charges, each of £125, one payable to the Dean, and the other to the Dean and Chapter; the vicarial tithes have been commuted for £175, and a rent-charge of £7. 6. is paid to impropriators. There are 30 acres of glebe.

ALLENTON, or ALLWINTON (ST. MICHAEL), a parish, in the union of ROTHBURY, W. division of COQUETDALE ward, N. division of NORTHUMBERLAND; comprising the townships of Allenton, Biddleston, Borrowdon, Clennell, Fairhaugh, Farnham, Linbriggs, Netherton, North and South Sides, Peals, and Sharperton; and containing 1255 inhabitants, of whom 78 are in the township of Allenton, 19 miles (W. by S.) from Alnwick. The parish is of great extent, stretching from the parish of Rothbury to Scotland, and 20 miles from east to west; and consists almost entirely of porphyritic mountains, presenting very abrupt elevations, covered with short thick grass, valuable for rearing sheep. The river Coquet rises within its limits, and here pursues a winding course through a very narrow valley, the mountains rising in many parts almost perpendicularly from its bed; it is joined by the Alwine, which gives name to the parish. The living is a vicarage not in charge, with the curacy of Hallystone annexed; net income, £130, with a glebe-house lately built; patron, the Duke of Northumberland; impropriators, Thomas Clennell, Esq., and others. The church is an ancient edifice, greatly disfigured by repairs. Here was formerly an hospital belonging to the Templars, and on the south side of the Coquet are vestiges of an old structure, called Barrow Peel, to the west of which is Ridlee-Cairn Hill, supposed to have been a burial-place of the ancient Britons. Throughout the district are numerous other remains of the Britons, consisting of encampments, cromlechs, &c.; and at Chew green, near the Scottish border, are the remains of a very extensive Roman station, the next to the north from Bremenium, High Rochester.

ALLER, a hamlet, in the parish of HILTON, union of BLANDFORD, hundred of WHITEWAY, Blandford division of DORSET; containing 91 inhabitants.

ALLER (St. *Andrew*), a parish, in the union of Langford, hundred of Somerton, W. division of Somerset; 6¼ miles (W.) from Somerton; containing 559 inhabitants. Guthrum, the Danish chief, received baptism at this place, under the sponsorship of Alfred the Great, after the victory obtained by that monarch over the Danes at *Ethandune*. Aller Moor was the scene of a battle between the royalists and the parliamentarians in 1644. The living is a rectory, valued in the king's books at £36. 15., and in the gift of Emanuel College, Cambridge; the tithes have been commuted for £590, and the glebe comprises 66 acres. Dr. Ralph Cudworth, author of *The Intellectual System of the Universe*, was born here in 1617.

ALLERBY, or Alwardby.—See Oughterside.

ALLERFORD, a tything, in the parish of Selworthy, union of Williton, hundred of Carhampton, W. division of Somerset; containing 181 inhabitants.

ALLERSTON (St. *Mary*), a parish, in the union and lythe of Pickering, N. riding of the county of York, 5 miles (E. by S.) from Pickering; containing 414 inhabitants. The parish comprises by measurement 9110 acres, of which about 4800 are arable and pasture, 240 wood and plantations, and the remainder large tracts of moor abounding with peat and turf : the surface is varied, in some parts mountainous, and the lands on the south side, which are low, are frequently overflowed by the Derwent. Coal is supposed to exist, but has not been wrought. The village is situated at the foot of the moors of Pickering forest, and on the northern verge of the fertile marshes of the vale of Derwent. The living has been united to the vicarage of Ebberston since 1242 : the church is an ancient edifice, with a lofty square tower.

ALLERTHORPE, a parish, in the union of Pocklington, Wilton-Beacon division of the wapentake of Harthill, E. riding of York; containing, with the townships of Allerthorpe and Waplington, 199 inhabitants, of whom 154 are in the township of Allerthorpe, 1½ mile (S. W. by W.) from Pocklington. The general surface of the parish is flat and well wooded. It consists of 1543a. 1r. 33p., of which about 670 acres are arable, 420 meadow or pasture, and 450 common land tithe-free; the soil is of a light and various quality, but chiefly sandy. On the east the parish is bounded by the Pocklington canal, and it is also contiguous to the road between York and Market-Weighton. The living is annexed to the vicarage of Thornton : the appropriate tithes have been commuted for £246. 2. 6., and the vicarial for £73. 12.; there are a glebe-house and 3 acres of glebe. In the church is a very fine font.

ALLERTHORPE, with Swainby, N. riding of York.—See Swainby.

ALLERTON, a township, in the parish of Childwall, union and hundred of West Derby, S. division of the county of Lancaster, 5¼ miles (S. E.) from Liverpool; containing in 1846 about 800 inhabitants. At the time of the Domesday survey, three thanes held "Alretune;" which was in the possession of Geoffrey de Chetham in the reign of Henry III., and of the Lathoms in that of Henry VIII. It was sold in 1670 to the Percivals, who in 1732 sold it to the Hardmans; and from them it was purchased by Messrs. Clegg and Roscoe. The township comprises 1531 acres, and con-

sists partly of a luxuriant vale, and partly of gently-rising hills, which command fine views of the river Mersey at its widest part, with portions of Cheshire and North Wales. The air is salubrious, and the scenery adorned with wood; the soil is of various quality, in some parts sandy, and in others a stiff clay. Allerton Hall was until 1816 the residence of William Roscoe, the elegant historian of Leo X., and is now the seat of Pattison Ellames, Esq. : the apartments contain numerous valuable paintings, and a beautiful marble statue of Sappho, by John Gibson, of Rome. Wyncote is the residence of Joseph Shipley, Esq. ; and Allerton Priory, of Theodore Woolman Rathbone, Esq. Here is a large Druidical monument called Calder Stones, in digging round which, more than sixty years ago, urns of coarse clay were found, containing human bones : the stones were surrounded with a neat iron palisade in 1845 ; and not far distant is the residence of Joseph N. Walker, Esq., named, after them, Calderstones. There is a quarry of red sandstone. The tithes have been commuted for £228 payable to the lessee of the Bishop of Chester, and £43 payable to the vicar of the parish. A church was erected in 1848, at a cost of £5000, by James Holme, Esq. ; it is in the early English style, with a tower and spire, and, standing on rising ground, is a picturesque and commanding object. The living is a perpetual curacy, in the gift of Mr. Holme.

ALLERTON, a township, in the ecclesiastical district of Wilsden, parish and union of Bradford, wapentake of Morley, W. riding of York, 4 miles (W. N. W.) from Bradford; containing 1914 inhabitants. This township is part of the ancient manor of Allerton-cum-Wilsden, and comprises by measurement 1872 acres. A very considerable portion of waste has, under the provisions of an act of parliament, obtained in 1840, by Mrs. Ferrand, the owner of the manor, in concurrence with the principal freeholders, been inclosed, and is rapidly coming into profitable cultivation. Of the whole land, about 1100 acres are meadow and pasture, 550 arable, and 40 wood and plantation ; the soil is not unfertile, and the substratum is chiefly coal and freestone of good quality ; the surface is varied. There are several ancient mansions, formerly the seats of distinguished families, of which Crossley, Shuttleworth, and Allerton Halls, are still remaining ; Dean House, the asylum of the celebrated Oliver Heywood, during the times of the Tudors and Stuarts, is now divided into tenements. The township consists chiefly of scattered houses, and the inhabitants are principally employed in the worsted manufacture, and in coal-mines and quarries. There are places of worship for General Baptists, Independents, and Wesleyans.

ALLERTON-BYWATER, a township, in the parish of Kippax, Lower division of the wapentake of Skyrack, W. riding of York, 4¼ miles (N. W.) from Pontefract ; containing 490 inhabitants. This place comprises about 870 acres, and is situated at the confluence of the rivers Aire and Calder, where extensive wharfs and stations have been constructed by the Aire and Calder Company : part of the houses near the bridge form a suburb of Castleford. Large glass-works have been established. The tithes are commuted for land and a money payment, by an inclosure act, in 1803.

ALLERTON, CHAPEL, a parish, in the union of Axbridge, hundred of Bempstone, E. division of

SOMERSET, 3 miles (S.) from Cross; containing 331 inhabitants. The living is a discharged rectory, valued in the king's books at £10. 8. 4.; net income, £223; patrons, the Dean and Chapter of Wells. There are 15 acres of glebe. The church is a small edifice, formerly a chapel to Wedmore.

ALLERTON, CHAPEL, W. riding of the county of YORK.—See CHAPEL-ALLERTON.

ALLERTON-MAULEVERER (ST. MARTIN), a parish, in the Upper division of the wapentake of CLARO, W. riding of YORK, 4½ miles (E.) from Knaresborough; containing 277 inhabitants, of whom 258 are in the township of Allerton-Mauleverer with Hopperton. This place obtained its distinguishing name from the family of Mauleverer, one of whom, named Richard, in the reign of Henry II. founded here an alien priory of Benedictine monks, the revenue of which was given by Henry VI. to King's College, Cambridge. The parish is wholly the property of Lord Stourton; and comprises 2170 acres, of which 1180 are arable, 820 meadow and pasture, and 170 woodland and plantations. The mansion here, which, with the estate, was purchased by his lordship's grandfather for £163,800, is a handsome structure in the Grecian style; and attached to it is a neat Roman Catholic chapel. The village is pleasantly situated about half a mile from the great road between London and Edinburgh. The living is a perpetual curacy; net income, £65; patron, Lord Stourton. The church is an ancient cruciform structure. The late Duke of York resided here in 1786, 1787, and 1789.

ALLERTON, NORTH.—See NORTHALLERTON.

ALLESLEY, or AWESLEY (ALL SAINTS), a parish, in the union of MERIDEN, Kirkby division of the hundred of KNIGHTLOW, N. division of the county of WARWICK, 2 miles (N. W. by W.) from Coventry, on the road to Birmingham; containing 963 inhabitants. It comprises by measurement 4155a. 3r. 30p., of which 1213 acres are arable, 2453 pasture, and 171 woodland; the land is in good cultivation, the surrounding scenery is pleasingly varied, and the village neatly built. Sandstone is quarried for rough building purposes. The Rev. Edward Neale is lord of the manor. Fairs are held for cattle on February 5th, March 4th, June 17th, August 7th, September 4th, October 7th, and December 11th. The LIVING is a rectory, valued in the king's books at £17. 18. 9.; patron and incumbent, the Rev. W. T. Bree: the tithes have been commuted for £786, and the glebe comprises nearly 40 acres. The church is an ancient structure in the early and later Norman styles, with modern additions in bad taste: a gallery was erected in 1838. £43 per annum, derived from land and houses in Meriden and Allesley, have been bequeathed for beautifying the church. There is a free school for boys, towards which Mrs. Flint, in 1705, gave land producing £42. 9. per annum, and a house for the master; a girls' school is supported by subscription. The sum of £16 yearly, left by an unknown benefactor, is distributed among the poor; and there are various other small benefactions. The moat and mound of an ancient castle are visible at the rear of the Hall. Fossil wood of a siliceous kind is dug up from the gravel.

ALLESTREE (ST. ANDREW), a parish, in the union of BELPER, hundred of MORLESTON and LITCHURCH, S. division of the county of DERBY, 2 miles (N.) from Derby; containing 507 inhabitants. The family of
38

Alestrey or Alastre, so called from this place, are mentioned in deeds of the thirteenth century; they resided in the village, and were at that time retainers to the Lords Audley. At the period of the visitation of 1634, the elder branch had been settled at Turnditch; but it probably was extinct before the visitation of 1662, when the younger branch only, settled at Alvaston, is named. The parish lies on the road from Derby to Matlock, and comprises 1030 acres, whereof 900 are pasture, 80 arable, and 50 woodland; the soil is loam and marl; the land is elevated, and the undulations of the surface are beautiful. The river Derwent flows on the east. The living is a perpetual curacy, united to the vicarage of Mackworth: the church is an ancient structure, with a square tower, and contains several monuments of the Mundys; the sittings are 300 in number. There is a place of worship for Wesleyans. Some schools, for which buildings were erected by William Evans, Esq., of Allestree Hall, are supported by that gentleman.

ALLEXTON.—See ALEXTON.

ALLHALLOWS, a parish, in the union of WIGTON, ALLERDALE ward below Derwent, W. division of CUMBERLAND, 6¾ miles (S. W. by S.) from Wigton; comprising by admeasurement 1860 acres, and containing 235 inhabitants. This place, which was anciently a chapelry in the parish of Aspatria, is bounded on the south by the river Ellen; and contains some quarries of freestone and limestone, and a vein of coal of inferior quality. The living is a perpetual curacy; net income, £80; patron and appropriator, the Bishop of Carlisle. The tithes were partially commuted for land, under an inclosure act, in 1817. A little southward of Whitehall is an intrenchment twenty-eight yards square, surrounded by a ditch.

ALLHALLOWS, a parish, in the union and hundred of Hoo, lathe of AYLESFORD, W. division of KENT, 9 miles (N. E.) from Rochester; containing 268 inhabitants. It is bounded on the north by the Thames, and comprises 2460 acres, of which 300 are marsh, and 23 wood. The living is a discharged vicarage, valued in the king's books at £8. 7. 11., and in the patronage of the Dean and Chapter of Rochester: the appropriate tithes, belonging to the Dean and Chapter, have been commuted for £620, with a glebe of 11 acres, and those of the incumbent for £185, with a glebe of 39 acres.

ALLINGTON (ST. SWITHIN), a parish, in the union of BRIDPORT, hundred of GODDERTHORNE, Bridport division of DORSET, ¾ of a mile (N. W.) from Bridport; containing 1545 inhabitants. This parish, formerly a chapelry in that of Bridport, comprises 582a. 3r. 5p., of which 281 acres are arable, 249 pasture, and 51 homesteads. The river Brid, or Birt, runs through the locality, which may be considered as a continuation of the town of Bridport, and is within the limits of the borough. Great quantities of hemp and flax are raised in the vicinity, and a manufacture of home and sail cloth is carried on, affording employment to a considerable number of persons. A fair for cheese and pedlery is held on the first Wednesday in August. The living is a perpetual curacy, in the gift of the Rev. Henry Fox: the tithes have been commuted for £190. The church is in the Grecian style; it was erected in 1827, and contains 800 sittings, of which 400 are free. An hospital for lepers, dedicated to St. Mary Magdalene, existed here, which, at the Dissolution in 1553, was valued at

£7. 8. 4. An ancestor of the celebrated John Wesley was ejected from the ministry of Allington as a non-juror.

ALLINGTON (St. LAWRENCE), a parish, in the union of MALLING, hundred of LARKFIELD, lathe of AYLESFORD, W. division of KENT, 1¾ mile (N. N. W.) from Maidstone; containing 49 inhabitants. It is situated on the western side of the Medway, nearly opposite Aylesford; and comprises 706 acres, of which 245 are woodland. The living is a discharged rectory, valued in the king's books at £6. 16. 8.; net income, £145, with a glebe-house, lately built; patron, the Earl of Romney. Sir Thomas Wyatt, a distinguished poet in the reign of Henry VIII., was born at Allington Castle, the remains of which have been converted into a farmhouse.

ALLINGTON, a tything, in the parish and union of SOUTH STONEHAM, hundred of MANSBRIDGE, Southampton and S. divisions of the county of SOUTHAMPTON; containing 536 inhabitants.

ALLINGTON, a parish, in the union and hundred of AMESBURY, Salisbury and Amesbury, and S. divisions of WILTS, 3½ miles (E. S. E.) from Amesbury; containing 94 inhabitants. The living is a rectory, valued in the king's books at £14. 13. 4.; net income, £236; patron, the Earl of Craven.

ALLINGTON, a tything, in the parish of ALLCANNINGS, union of DEVIZES, hundred of SWANBOROUGH, Devizes and N. divisions of WILTS, 4 miles (E. N. E.) from Devizes; containing 188 inhabitants. The tithes belong to the Dean and Canons of Westminster. There is a place of worship for Particular Baptists.

ALLINGTON, EAST (St. ANDREW), a parish, in the union of KINGSBRIDGE, hundred of STANBOROUGH, Stanborough and Coleridge, and S. divisions of DEVON, 3½ miles (N. E. by N.) from Kingsbridge; containing 729 inhabitants, and comprising 2348 acres. The living is a rectory, valued in the king's books at £32. 2. 1., and in the patronage of Mrs. Fortescue: the tithes have been commuted for £485, and the glebe consists of 80 acres. In the church is a wooden screen, which, like the pulpit, is much enriched with carved work.

ALLINGTON, EAST (St. JAMES), a parish, in the union of NEWARK, wapentake of WINNIBRIGGS and THREO, parts of KESTEVEN, county of LINCOLN, 5 miles (N. W.) from Grantham; containing 276 inhabitants. The living is consolidated with a mediety of the rectory of Sedgebrook, to the incumbent of which an allotment of land was given as a commutation for the tithes of the manor, by an inclosure act, in 1793.

ALLINGTON, WEST, in the county of DEVON.— See ALVINGTON, WEST.

ALLINGTON, WEST (HOLY TRINITY), a parish, in the union of NEWARK, wapentake of LOVEDEN, parts of KESTEVEN, county of LINCOLN, 5½ miles (N. W. by W.) from Grantham; containing 120 inhabitants. In this parish is the seat of T. Earle Welby, Esq., a handsome edifice, partly in the Elizabethan style, and commanding a distant view of Foston and the city of Lincoln. The living is a rectory, valued in the king's books at £3. 13. 11½., and in the patronage of the Crown; net income, £262.

ALLITHWAITE, LOWER, a township, in the parish of CARTMEL, union of ULVERSTONE, hundred of LONSDALE north of the Sands, N. division of the county

39

of LANCASTER, 2 miles (S.) from Cartmel; containing 807 inhabitants. This township has sometimes been named Cartmel Church Town. To the north, not far from the shore, are some remains of Wraysholme Tower, which was a fortified house, of strong masonry, in the 14th century: Abbot Hall, in the hamlet of Kents, is supposed to have been a residence of the priors of Cartmel. In some fields called Chapel Fields, human skeletons have been exhumed. The church and part of the town of Cartmel (which see) are in the township.

ALLITHWAITE, UPPER, a township, in the parish of CARTMEL, union of ULVERSTON, hundred of LONSDALE north of the Sands, N. division of the county of LANCASTER, 3¼ miles (N. E.) from Cartmel; containing 740 inhabitants. A conical rock in this township, called Castlehead, is supposed, from some imperial coins found on the spot, to have once had Roman inhabitants. It had the appearance of a rough neglected wood, till the late J. Wilkinson, Esq., the great iron-master, improved and adorned all around, by cutting paths, and planting trees and shrubs wherever the soil invited the hand of cultivation. In effecting these improvements, many relics of antiquity were found, rings, Roman money, fibulæ, ornaments, and fossils, and the bones of animals that no longer inhabit this country. At the foot of the rock is a house built by Mr. Wilkinson, and afterwards occupied by Mr. Legh, who married his daughter; it is now in the possession of Robert Wright, Esq. At a short distance from it is a pyramidical mausoleum of iron, twenty tons in weight, which, until 1828, pressed the mortal remains of its founder: in that year, however, the remains of Mr. Wilkinson were removed to the churchyard of Lindale.

ALLONBY, a chapelry, in the parish of BROMFIELD, union of WIGTON, ALLERDALE ward below Derwent, W. division of CUMBERLAND, 9 miles (N. N. W.) from Cockermouth; containing 811 inhabitants. The village, comprising about 200 houses, is situated on the coast of Allonby bay, which opens to the Solway Firth and the Irish Sea; and is much frequented as a bathing-place, the sands being extremely smooth and firm. It was noted for a herring-fishery, but this has greatly declined, owing to the herrings having almost totally deserted the neighbouring sea; a few of the inhabitants are, however, still occupied in fishing. The living is a perpetual curacy; net income, £94; patron, the Vicar of Bromfield. The chapel, dedicated to Christ, was built at the expense of Dr. Thomlinson and some relatives, in 1744; and a school was endowed in 1755, by Mrs. Thomlinson, his relict, with £100, since laid out in land producing £8 per annum. There is a place of worship for the Society of Friends. Captain Joseph Huddart, F.R.S., an eminent naval engineer and hydrographer, was born here in 1741, and in the chapel is a handsome monument erected to his memory, at a cost of £500.

ALLOSTOCK, a township, in the parish of GREAT BUDWORTH, union and hundred of NORTHWICH. S. division of the county of CHESTER, 5 miles (S. by W.) from Nether Knutsford; containing 427 inhabitants. In the reign of Edward I. the manor was conveyed by John de Lostock to the Grosvenors, who had their chief residence here; it afterwards fell to the Leicesters and Shakerleys. The township comprises 2155 acres; the soil is sand and clay. There is a place of worship for Unitarians.

ALLOWENSHAY, a hamlet, in the parish of KINGS-TON, union of CHARD, hundred of TINTINHULL, W. division of SOMERSET; containing 212 inhabitants.

ALLSTONEFIELD.—See ALSTONFIELD.

ALLTON, with IDRIDGEHAY.—See IDRIDGEHAY.

ALLWINTON, county of NORTHUMBERLAND.—See ALLENTON.

ALMELEY (ST. MARY), a parish, partly in the hundred of WOLPHY, but chiefly in that of STRETFORD, union of WEOBLEY, county of HEREFORD, 4½ miles (S. E.) from Kington, near the road to Hereford; containing 642 inhabitants. It comprises 3352 acres, of which 1500 are meadow and pasture, 1300 arable, and 552 woodland; the surface is undulated and extensively wooded, and the soil, for the most part, is a sandy loam, having a wet sub-soil of marl and clay. A tram railway for the conveyance of coal from Brecon to Kington, passes through the parish. The living is a vicarage, valued in the king's books at £6. 17. 11.; patron and appropriator, the Bishop of Hereford. The great tithes have been commuted for £300, and the vicarial for £207. 10.; the appropriate glebe contains 19, and the vicarial 55, acres. The church is partly Norman, and partly in the English style. About three-quarters of a mile north-west of it, was probably once a castle; part of the ditch, &c., being traceable, and the farm there called Old Castle. Sir John Oldcastle, Lord Cobham, executed in 1417 for his attachment to the Lollards, was a native of the parish.

ALMER (ST. MARY), a parish, in the union of BLANDFORD, hundred of LOOSEBARROW, Wimborne division of DORSET, 5¾ miles (S. S. E.) from Blandford-Forum; containing, with the hamlet of Mapperton, 189 inhabitants. It comprises 1129 acres of land, presenting a flat appearance; the soil is light, with a chalk and gravel bottom. The living is a rectory, valued in the king's books at £13. 5. 8., and in the patronage of the family of Drax: the tithes have been commuted for £265, and the glebe consists of 35 acres. The church is a small edifice, built by General Erle.

ALMHOLME, a hamlet, in the parish of ARKSEY, union of DONCASTER, N. division of the wapentake of STRAFFORTH and TICKHILL, W. riding of YORK, 3 miles (N. by E.) from Doncaster; containing 69 inhabitants. The term holme or holmes is a generic name for low and level pasture lands near water; which is descriptive of the neighbourhood of this place. The hamlet is situated in the north-eastern extremity of the parish; the river Don runs a little on the east, and on the north flows a tributary of that river.

ALMINGTON, a township, in the parish and union of DRAYTON-IN-HALES, N. division of the hundred of PIREHILL and of the county of STAFFORD, 1½ mile (E. by N.) from Drayton; containing 189 inhabitants.

ALMODINGTON, a hamlet (formerly a parish) in the parish of EARNLEY, union of WEST HAMPNETT, hundred of MANHOOD, rape of CHICHESTER, W. division of SUSSEX, 6 miles (S. W. by S.) from Chichester. The living, a rectory, was consolidated in 1524 with that of Earnley; and the church has fallen into ruins.

ALMONDBURY (ALL SAINTS), a parish, in the union of HUDDERSFIELD, Upper division of the wapentake of AGBRIGG, W. riding of YORK, 1¾ mile (S. E.) from Huddersfield, on the old road to Sheffield; comprising the townships of Almondbury, Austonley, North
40

and South Crossland, Farnley-Tyas, Holme, Honley, Lingards, Linthwaite, Lockwood, Marsden, Meltham, Nether Thong, and Upper Thong; and the hamlets of Berrybrow, Crossland Moor, Deanhouse, Meltham-Mills, Longley, Lowerhouses, Netherton, and Rashcliffe; and containing 37,315 inhabitants, of whom 8828 are in the township of Almondbury. According to Camden, this was the Cambodunum of Antoninus, the site of which he places on the summit of a neighbouring hill, where are vestiges of a rampart and the remains of a fortification; but some later writers are of opinion that these are Saxon remains, as no Roman relics have ever been found, and there are no ancient roads leading to the place. The same author states that in the early Saxon times a royal vill existed here, with a church, built by Paulinus, and dedicated to St. Alban, from which circumstance arose the name Albanbury, since softened into Almondbury. This church is supposed to have been afterwards burnt in the war between Penda, King of Mercia, and Edwin of Northumbria, the latter of whom had a palace here; and it appears that no church from that period was known till after the year 1090, when the manor came into the possession of the Lacy family, of whom Alice de Lacy and her son Henry presented to the rectory in 1187, prior to which time a church had been erected most probably by Gilbert de Lacy, the first lord.

The inhabitants of this populous and extensive district are principally engaged in the manufacture of fancy goods and woollen cloth, for which there are numerous establishments. The parish comprises 26,055a. 3r. 37p.; there are several coal-mines, and some stone-quarries, the produce of which is chiefly applied to building purposes. In the 39th of George III. an act was passed for inclosing the waste lands in the townships of North Crossland and Honley; in the 9th of George IV., one for reclaiming those in Austonley and Upper Thong; and in 1830 similar acts were passed for Meltham and Nether Thong: in 1837 an act was procured for making certain reservoirs in the parish. Fairs are held on Easter and Whit Mondays, and on Nov. 23rd for swine and cattle.

The LIVING is a vicarage, valued in the king's books at £20. 7. 11.; net income, £250; patrons and impropriators, the Governors of Clitheroe school, to whom the rectory, &c., were given by the crown at the Dissolution, previously to which they had belonged to the College of Jesus, at Rotherham. There are 16 acres of glebe, with a good vicarage-house rebuilt about 1774. The church, an ancient and venerable structure, erected on the site of the original church, in 1552, and which had fallen into a state of general dilapidation, was in 1840, through the spirited efforts of a few of the inhabitants, thoroughly restored, with the most scrupulous regard to the preservation of its pristine character, and is now one of the most beautiful churches in the West riding. At the end of the north aisle is a chapel belonging to the Earl of Dartmouth, and at the extremity of the south aisle one belonging to the Beaumont family: there are two oak chests of great antiquity, richly carved; and round the upper part of the walls, close to the ceiling, are some verses in Saxon characters. There are also churches at Holme-Bridge, Crossland, Farnley-Tyas, Linthwaite, Meltham, Meltham-Mills, Lockwood, Marsden, Nether Thong, Upper Thong, Milns-Bridge, Armitage-Bridge, and Honley; and within the township of Almondbury are two places of worship for Wesleyan Methodists, and one for the New Connexion. A free grammar school was founded by letters-patent of James I.; the annual income amounts to £91, arising from lands and rent-charges demised by Robert Nettleton and other bene-factors.

ALMONDSBURY (ST. MARY THE VIRGIN), a parish, in the union of THORNBURY, comprising the tything of Almondsbury in the Lower division of the hundred of BERKELEY, the tythings of Gaunts-Earthcote and Lea in the Lower division of that of THORNBURY, and the tythings of Hempton and Patchway, Over, and Lower Tockington, in the Lower division of the hundred of LANGLEY and SWINEHEAD, W. division of the county of GLOUCESTER; and containing 1584 inhabitants, of whom 603 are in Almondsbury tything, 7 miles (N. by E.) from Bristol. This parish is situated near the river Severn, and comprises 6927 acres of land, which, with the exception of 137 acres of common or waste, is rich pasture in good cultivation: sandstone is quarried, chiefly for rough building purposes. The village is situated at the foot of a ridge of limestone rocks, in which lead-ore has been found in small quantities, and of which the old roof of Berkeley Castle was partly composed; and the views from the heights, along which passes the road from Gloucester to Bristol, are beautiful and extensive, embracing the whole estuary of the Severn, and the opposite coast of Wales. The living is a discharged vicarage, in the gift of the Bishop of Gloucester and Bristol, and valued in the king's books at £20: the tithes have been commuted for £1150. 13. 4., and there are two acres of glebe. The church, situated in that part of the parish which is in the hundred of Berkeley, is a very handsome cruciform structure, in the early English style, with a tower and spire at the intersection; it has been extensively repaired and altered within the last few years. There is a place of worship for Wesleyans; also a school endowed with £30 per annum from lands left by an unknown benefactor for the use of the church, producing £210 per annum.

ALMSFORD (ST. ANDREW), a parish, in the union of WINCANTON, hundred of CATSASH, E. division of SOMERSET, ¾ of a mile (N.) from Castle-Cary; containing 293 inhabitants, and comprising 844a. 1r. 18p. The living is a rectory, valued in the king's books at £7. 12. 1., and in the gift of F. Woodford, Esq.: the tithes have been commuted for £215, and the glebe consists of 60 acres, with a glebe-house. The church is a small neat structure.

ALNE (ST. MARY), a parish, in the union of EASING-WOULD, wapentake of BULMER, N. riding of YORK; comprising the townships of Aldwark, Alne, Flawith, Tholthorp, Tollerton, and Youlton; and containing 1703 inhabitants, of whom 494 are in the township of Alne, 4¼ miles (S. S. W.) from Easingwould. The parish contains by computation 10,900 acres, of which 1900 are in the township of Alne; the surface is level, and comprises every variety of soil. A fair for cattle and sheep is held on the Tuesday next after the 8th of October. The York and Newcastle railway passes through the parish. The living is a discharged vicarage, valued in the king's books at £10; net income, £370; patron and impropriator, Sir C. B. Codrington: a small glebe-house was obtained by exchange with the patron, in 1842. The church, an

VOL. I.—41

ancient edifice with a square tower, was repewed about thirty years since. There are places of worship for Wesleyans at Alne and Tollerton. Remains exist of a religious house subordinate to St. Mary's at York.

ALNE, GREAT (ST. MARY MAGDALENE), a parish, in the union of ALCESTER, Alcester division of the hundred of BARLICHWAY, S. division of the county of WAR-WICK, 2¼ miles (N. E. by E.) from Alcester; containing 404 inhabitants. It comprises by computation 1800 acres, and is bounded on the south, and partly on the east, by the river Alne. The living is a rectory, annexed, with the perpetual curacy of Weethley, to the rectory of Kinwarton: the church has been enlarged within the last few years. Part of the glebe belonging to Kinwar-ton rectory is situated in this parish. There is a national school.

ALNESBORNE, an extra-parochial district, locally in the parish of NACTON, hundred of COLNEIS, E. division of SUFFOLK, 2¼ miles (S. E.) from Ipswich; adjoining the river Orwell; and containing 39 inhabitants. Here was a small priory of Austin canons, dedicated to the Virgin Mary, and suppressed about the year 1466: there are still the remains of a chapel.

ALNEY, a small island in the river Severn, partly in the parish of MAISEMORE, E. division of the county of GLOUCESTER, and partly in the parishes of ST. MARY-DE-LODE and ST. NICHOLAS, city of GLOUCESTER. This island, which is formed by a division of the river into two streams, and comprehends several acres of rich pasture land, was by the Saxons called Oleneag, and is memorable for the interview which took place here in 1016, between Edmund, King of the Saxons, and Canute, leader of the Danes, whose armies had been drawn up at Deerhurst in battle array for some time, without either giving the signal for the attack. Edmund at length challenged Canute to single combat, which the latter refused on the plea of inequality, proposing, instead, a reference to the principal officers of both armies; this was accepted by Edmund, and, after a short conference on the island, peace was concluded between them by a partition of the kingdom.

ALNHAM (ST. MICHAEL), a parish, in the union of ROTHBURY, N. division of COQUETDALE ward and of NORTHUMBERLAND; consisting of the townships of Alnham, Prendwick, Screnwood, and Unthank; and containing 256 inhabitants, of whom 141 are in the township of Alnham, 6 miles (W. by S.) from Whittingham, and 14 (W. by S.) from Alnwick. The parish forms part of the Cheviot range of mountains, and occupies about 12,000 acres, almost entirely occupied as sheep-walks: excellent building-stone is obtained. The living is a discharged vicarage, endowed with part of the great tithes, and valued in the king's books at £3. 17. 1.; net income, £74; patron, the Duke of Northumber-land; impropriator of the remainder of the great tithes, J. C. Tarleton, Esq. There are about ten acres of glebe. The church has a plain Norman arch between the nave and chancel. Near it are the ruins of an ancient tower, which the late duke fitted up for a parsonage; and on Castle Hill is a semicircular encampment, defended by a high double rampart and deep trench, within which is a range of uncemented stones.

ALNMOUTH, or ALEMOUTH, a small sea-port, and a township, in the parish of LESBURY, union of ALNWICK, S. division of BAMBROUGH ward, N. division of NORTH-

G

UMBERLAND, 5¼ miles (E. S. E.) from Alnwick; containing 480 inhabitants. This township, which takes its name from its situation on a tongue of land projecting into the sea, near the mouth of the river Alne, comprises 180 acres of land of a light soil, in equal portions of arable and pasture; the surface is undulated, and there are good land and sea views: stone for building is procured from the rocks on the shore. Formerly a considerable trade was carried on in the export of corn, flour, eggs, and pork, to London, and of wool to the manufacturing districts of Yorkshire; but the trade is now limited: the imports are timber, iron, bark, &c., from foreign ports, and groceries, seeds, bones, hardware, and other merchandise, coastwise. The business of ship-building, which prevailed here, has entirely declined. The village is resorted to for bathing, and the sands, being very firm, form a fine promenade; hot baths are always in readiness at the Schooner inn. By an encroachment of the sea, and a change in the course of the river, a small island has been formed, on which, until 1807, were the remains of an old chapel dedicated to St. John the Baptist, the site of which was originally on the main land: the hill, called the Church Hill, whereon it stood, is rapidly yielding to the combined action of the sea and atmosphere. The tithes have been commuted for £30. 1. 6., of which £26. 15. 10. are payable to the vicar, who has a glebe of about three-quarters of an acre. There is a place of worship for Wesleyans.

Corporation Seal.

ALNWICK (ST. MARY AND ST. MICHAEL), a market-town and parish, and the head of a union, in the E. division of COQUETDALE ward, N. division of NORTH-UMBERLAND, of which it is the county town, 33 miles (N. by W.) from Newcastle, and 306 (N. by W.) from London; comprising the townships of Alnwick, South-side, Shieldykes, Abbey-Lands, Canongate, Denwick, and Hulne Park; and containing 6626 inhabitants. This place, which is of great antiquity, was occupied at a very early period by the Danes or Saxons, who called it *Ealnwic*, from its situation near the river Alne, and built a strong CASTLE for its defence on a site supposed to have been previously occupied by a Roman fortress. The castle thus erected, after the Norman Conquest, became the baronial residence of Ivo de Vesey, lord of Alnwick, to whom the barony had been given by the Conqueror. In 1093, it was besieged by Malcolm III., King of Scotland, and bravely defended by Mowbray, Earl of Northumberland; upon which occasion, Malcolm and his son Edward were both killed; the former, according to the Chronicle of Alnwick Abbey, by one of the garrison, under pretence of presenting to him, in token of submission, the keys of the fortress at the point of a lance; and the latter in his eagerness to revenge the death of his father, in an unguarded assault of the enemy, from whom he received a mortal wound. The remembrance of this siege is preserved by a cross erected about a mile north of the town, on the spot where the Scottish monarch is supposed to have fallen; it was rebuilt in 1774 by the Duchess of Northumberland, a lineal descendant of the king.

42

In 1135, the town was taken by David, King of Scotland; in 1174 it was besieged by William, at the head of 80,000 Scottish forces, but was successfully defended by William de Vesey, Robert de Stuteville, Ranulph de Glanville, and others, who took the monarch prisoner, and sent him to London, where he was kept in confinement till released by his subjects, who paid £100,000 for his ransom. In 1215, Alnwick was nearly reduced to ashes by King John; but it appears to have been speedily rebuilt, for, within five years from that date, Gualo, the pope's legate, summoned a general council of the Scottish bishops to be held here, for the regulation of some ecclesiastical abuses. In 1328, it was again besieged by the Scots, under Robert Bruce, but without success; and in 1411, the castle was embattled, and the town surrounded with a strong wall, to protect them from the predatory incursions of the Scots. Notwithstanding these fortifications, the town was again assailed by the Scots, who in 1448 set fire to it in retaliation for the burning of Dumfries by the English. After the battle of Hexham in 1463, the castle, which was in the interest of the house of Lancaster, was summoned by the Earl of Warwick; but the garrison, though unable to sustain a protracted siege, retained possession till they were relieved by Sir George Douglas, who, arriving at the head of a considerable force, afforded them an opportunity of retiring unmolested.

The TOWN is pleasantly situated on the irregular declivity of an eminence rising from the bank of the river Alne, over which, at the northern extremities, are two neat stone bridges. The streets are spacious, well paved, and lighted with gas; the houses, built of stone, are chiefly of modern erection; and the inhabitants are amply supplied with water from cisterns and reservoirs, and by pumps in various parts, erected at the expense of the corporation. Near the south entrance of the town is a fine column, eighty-three feet in height, upon an eminence at the side of the road: it is called the Percy Tenantry Column, having been raised by the agricultural tenantry of the second duke of North-umberland, in 1816, in grateful commemoration of his Grace's liberality at various periods, when the distress of the times had rendered the payment of rent in many cases difficult, and in some altogether impracticable. There is also an elegant column, erected in 1814, on Camp Hill near the town, in commemoration of the various victories obtained by the British during the war, and of the restoration of peace. A subscription library was established in 1783; but this was dissolved in 1833, and an improved institution was formed in 1834, which now contains nearly 2000 volumes. In 1824, a mechanics' institute was founded, for which a handsome building was erected in 1831, containing a lecture-room, library, and other accommodations. The trade and manufactures of the place are not of much importance; yet there are some extensive breweries and tanneries, and the parish abounds with coal, limestone, freestone, and whinstone. The Newcastle and Berwick railway passes between the town and the sea-coast. The market, abundantly supplied with corn and provisions, is held on Saturday: fairs for cattle and horses are held on May 12th, the last Monday in July, and the first Tuesday in October; and there are other fairs, on the first Saturday in March and in November, for hiring servants. A fish-market was opened in 1830.

Alnwick is a BOROUGH by prescription, having no royal charter of incorporation; though, from the capricious mode of choosing the freemen, which is ascribed to King John, it would appear that its prescriptive right was at least tacitly acknowledged by that sovereign: an established corporation is also recognised by an inoperative charter of Henry III., as well as by several ancient existing grants of the De Vesey family. The present corporation consists of twenty-four common-councilmen, who, at a meeting held on the 29th of September, nominate eight out of their number, and return the names to the steward of the manor, by whom, at the next court leet, four are appointed to act as chamberlains for the ensuing year. The common-councilmen are chosen from among the resident freemen of the several incorporated companies or fraternities, ten in number, viz., the Cordwainers, Skinners and Glovers, Merchants, Tanners, Weavers, Blacksmiths, Butchers, Joiners, Tailors, and Coopers. A chamberlain's clerk and other officers are appointed by the common-councilmen. The freedom is inherited by the sons of freemen, provided they have first been made free of one of the trading companies; it may also be acquired by a servitude of seven years to a freeman residing in the borough. Each candidate, on taking up his freedom, is subjected to the ludicrous ceremony of passing through a miry pool, thence called the "Freemen's well." A bailiff is appointed by the Duke of Northumberland for the manor. The corporation possess no magisterial authority, the town being wholly within the jurisdiction of the county magistrates, who hold petty-sessions on the first and third Saturday in every month. Courts leet and baron are held at Easter and at Michaelmas, under the Duke of Northumberland, as lord of the manor; and a manorial court is held also for the township of Canongate. The quarter-sessions for the county take place here at Michaelmas, in rotation with Hexham, Morpeth, and Newcastle. The county court is held here monthly; the powers of the county debt-court of Alnwick, established in 1847, extend over the registration-district of Alnwick. The election of parliamentary representatives for the northern division of the county, and also the election of coroners for the county, take place here. The town-hall, erected in 1731, is a handsome stone building surmounted by a square tower, and stands on the west side of the market-place, an extensive area in the centre of the town, on the south side of which is a large building erected by the late Duke of Northumberland, containing in the upper part a spacious assembly-room and a news-room, and affording underneath a covered area for the sale of butchers' meat and poultry. The house of correction, near the Green Bat, was erected in 1807.

The LIVING is a perpetual curacy; net income, £175; patron and impropriator, the Duke of Northumberland. The impropriate tithes of Southside township have been commuted for £183. 15. 6. The church is a spacious and venerable structure, in the later style of English architecture, with a neat tower, and consists of a nave, north and south aisles, and a chancel. The roof of the chancel is richly groined and ornamented; on the sides are some ancient stalls carved in tabernacle work, and at the east end are three altar-tombs, on which are recumbent figures of stone, finely sculptured, but without date or inscription. The chancel was repaired and

43

beautified in 1781, by the first duke of Northumberland; and in 1818, the church was repewed and repaired, the late duke contributing £300 towards the expense. On repairing the north aisle, two statues of stone, one representing a king and the other supposed to be the figure of a martyr, were found about two feet below the surface of the ground; they are now placed beneath the tower, at the western extremity of the church. St. Paul's church, erected by the Percy family, was consecrated in October, 1846: the living is in the gift of his Grace. There are places of worship for Independents, a United Secession Relief congregation, Presbyterians, Wesleyans, New Connexion of Methodists, and Unitarians; and a Roman Catholic chapel rebuilt in 1836. The poor law union of Alnwick comprises 62 parishes or places, and contains a population of 18,768.

The ancient CASTLE, now the magnificent residence of the Duke of Northumberland, is a noble and stately structure comprising two wards, the whole put into a state of thorough repair by the grandfather of the present owner, with a due regard to the preservation of its original style, and its ancient character as one of the most splendid baronial residences in the kingdom. The extensive park and demesnes abound with beautifully varied walks, commanding a rich diversity of scenery, and a fine assemblage of strikingly interesting objects, among which the venerable ruins of Alnwick and Hulne Abbeys are conspicuous. *Alnwick Abbey* was founded in 1147, by Eustace Fitz-John, who endowed it for Præmonstratensian canons, and dedicated it to St. James and the Blessed Virgin: the abbot was summoned to parliament in the reigns of Edward I. and II. It continued to flourish till the Dissolution, when its revenue was estimated at £194. 7.; the remains consist of a gateway, which has been fitted up as a lodge to the parks (which are stocked with deer and a very fine breed of buffaloes), and, with the abbey grounds, forms a highly interesting feature. *Hulne Abbey*, about three miles from the town, but within the limits of the park, is beautifully situated on the slope of an eminence. It was founded about the year 1240, according to some authorities by William de Vesey, and according to others by Ralph Fresborn after returning from the crusades, for Carmelite friars, and is said to have been the first house of that order established in England; it was amply endowed by William de Vesey and his successors, and Fresborn became the first abbot. The site was granted in the reign of Elizabeth to Thomas Reeve and others, and was afterwards purchased by the Percy family. The remains, which are beautifully mantled with ivy, are very considerable; part of the buildings has been fitted up as a residence for a gamekeeper. Bale, the eminent biographer, was one of the brethren of this ancient monastery. Opposite to the remains of the abbey, a road, winding round a lofty eminence, leads to *Brislee Hill*, on the summit of which is a noble column, ninety feet high, with a spiral staircase leading to the balcony, which commands an extensive and delightful prospect, embracing the hills of Cheviot and Teviotdale; the hill of Flodden; the castles of Bamborough, Dunstanburgh, and Warkworth; the isle of Coquet, the port of Alnmouth, and various other interesting objects. At Alnwick, also, was an ancient hospital, founded by Eustace de Vescy, and dedicated

G 2

to St. Leonard; likewise a chapel dedicated to St. Thomas: and in Walkergate-street is an old house, the doorway and windows of which prove its ecclesiastical origin. There are some remains of the town walls, which were defended by four square massive gateway towers, of which Bondgate, now the only one entire, was built by the son of the renowned Hotspur; on the site of Pottergate tower a handsome tower gateway has been erected, in the later style of English architecture. At Sheep-layers-on-the-Moor, and at Rugley-Moorhouse farm, are encampments supposed to be of Danish origin, but nothing is recorded of their history. Alnwick gives the title of Baron Louvaine of Alnwick to the Earl of Beverley.

ALPERTON, a hamlet, in the parish of HARROW-ON-THE-HILL, union of HENDON, hundred of GORE, county of MIDDLESEX; containing 242 inhabitants.

ALPHAMSTONE, a parish, in the union of SUD-BURY, hundred of HINCKFORD, N. division of ESSEX, 5 miles (N. E.) from Halstead; containing 314 inhabitants. This parish, which includes the hamlet of Bures, and contains 1557a. 2r. 37p., was anciently parcel of the possessions of the abbey of Bury St. Edmund's, except a portion that belonged to Richard Fitz-Gilbert, which, after the Conquest, was divided among several proprietors. The soil is rich, and constitutes fine corn-land; the scenery is picturesque. A pleasure-fair is held on the first Thursday in June. The living is a rectory, valued in the king's books at £11, and in the gift of the Crown: the tithes have been commuted for £440, and the glebe consists of 28 acres. The church, an ancient building of flint, consisting of a nave with a south aisle and chancel, lighted by small lancet-shaped windows, is finely situated on an eminence, commanding an extensive and richly varied prospect: the tower, with the bells, fell down about fifty years since.

ALPHETON, a parish, in the union of SUDBURY, hundred of BABERGH, W. division of SUFFOLK, 3 miles (N. N. E.) from Long Melford; containing 321 inhabitants, and comprising 1200 acres by admeasurement. The living is a rectory, valued in the king's books at £10. 1. 8.; patron and incumbent, the Rev. T. G. Dickenson. The tithes have been commuted for £286; and there are 40 acres of glebe, with a good parsonage-house pleasantly situated near the turnpike-road. The church contains a mural monument to Lieut. Sheppard, who received a wound in the head at the attack on Boulogne in 1805, which caused his death ten years after; the old painted glass has been lately collected, and, with the addition of new, formed into two neat windows.

ALPHINGTON (ST. MICHAEL), a parish, in the union of ST. THOMAS, hundred of WONFORD and S. divisions of DEVON, 1½ mile (S.) from Exeter; containing 1286 inhabitants. This place, an ancient manor whose lords had the power of inflicting capital punishment, is skirted by the Exe, and intersected by the Exeter canal. It comprises 2223 acres by computation; granite is found in some parts, and at the Porkham quarry good building-stone is obtained. Fairs for cattle are held on the first Wednesday after the 20th of June, and in the beginning of October. The living is a rectory, valued in the king's books at £34. 6. 8., and has a net income of £852; the glebe consists of 27 acres, with an excellent parsonage-house built by the

44

late Rev. William Ellicombe, whose son, the Rev. Richard Ellicombe, is the present patron and incumbent. The church contains a circular Norman font, with intersecting arches and scroll ornaments. There is a place of worship for Wesleyans.

ALPINGTON, a parish, in the union of LODDON and CLAVERING, hundred of LODDON, E. division of NORFOLK, 1½ mile (N.) from Brooke, and 6 miles (S. E.) from Norwich, on the road from Norwich to Bungay; containing 197 inhabitants, and comprising 530a. 3r. 12p. The living, a rectory, is united to Yelverton, and there are no remains of the church. About 9½ acres of land were allotted to the poor for fuel, at the time of the inclosure.

ALPRAHAM, a township, in the parish of BUNBURY, union of NANTWICH, First division of the hundred of EDDISBURY, S. division of the county of CHESTER, 3½ miles (S. E. by E.) from Tarporley; containing 520 inhabitants. The township comprises 1596 acres, of which 10 are common or waste; the soil is sand and clay. The impropriate tithes have been commuted for £106, payable to the Haberdashers' Company, London. There is a place of worship for Wesleyans.

ALRESFORD (ST. PETER), a parish, in the union and hundred of TENDRING, N. division of ESSEX, 6½ miles (S. E. by E.) from Colchester; containing 289 inhabitants. The parish is bounded on the west by the river Colne, and takes its name, which is supposed to be a modification of Aldersford, from an ancient ford across that river: the lands are elevated, and the soil generally of a light sandy quality. The living is a discharged rectory, valued in the king's books at £8, and in the gift of Brasenose College, Oxford: the tithes have been commuted for £348, and there is a glebe of 30 acres. The church, a small edifice, with a spire of shingles, was, according to an inscription in the chancel, written in Norman French, erected by Anfrid or Anfrey de Staunton.

ALRESFORD, NEW, a market-town and parish, and the head of a union, in the liberty of ALRESFORD, Alton and N. divisions of the county of SOUTHAMPTON, 6 miles (N. E. by E.) from Winchester, and 57 (S. W. by W.) from London, on the high road to Winchester; containing 1578 inhabitants. This place, which derives its name from its situation near a ford on the river Arle, was given to the church of Winchester by Cenwalh, King of the West Saxons, after his baptism by Bishop Birinus; and about 1220, Godfrey de Lucy, Bishop of Winchester, restored the market, then fallen into disuse. On May-day, 1690, the town was destroyed by fire, previously to which it was so prosperous that there was not an individual requiring parochial relief; and in 1710 a similar calamity occurred. The PARISH comprises by computation 730 acres; the surface is flat in some parts, and in others hilly; the soil, which is light and chalky, is in general good. Alresford pond is a fine piece of water, through which runs the river Itchen. The northern embankment is formed by a causeway nearly 500 yards in length, which, previously to the construction of the present road through Bishop's-Sutton, in 1753, constituted part of the main road to London. It was accomplished by Bishop de Lucy, under a grant from King John, with a view to the improvement of the prelate's grounds, and to increase the depth of the river Itchen, which was formerly navigable to Alresford, though of late it has ceased to be so higher than Winchester; and as a recompense for this arduous undertaking, the bishop obtained, for himself and his successors, the entire royalty of the river from the reservoir to the sea. Among the seats in the neighbourhood are those of Lord Rodney (formerly the residence of his ancestor, the gallant admiral), the family of Tichbourne, and Lord Ashburton, which last, called the Grange, is a beautiful copy of the Parthenon at Athens. The market is on Thursday; and fairs are held on Holy-Thursday, the last Thursdays in July and Nov., and the Thursday next after Old Michaelmas-day, almost exclusively for sheep.

Alresford was incorporated at a very early period, and returned one representative to parliament in the 23rd of Edward I. The corporation consists of a bailiff, appointed by the Bishop of Winchester (as lord of the manor), and eight burgesses, who, by virtue of a lease from the bishop, receive the tolls of the market, but exercise no magisterial authority. A court leet is held at Michaelmas, when the bailiff is chosen; and the county magistrates hold a petty-session weekly, for the division of Alton. The living is a rectory, annexed, with that of Medsted, to the rectory of Old Alresford: the glebe comprises 18 acres. There are places of worship for Independents and Roman Catholics. H. Perrin, in 1698, founded a school for nineteen boys, sons of poor tradesmen in the town, and in the neighbouring villages of Old Alresford, Sutton, and Tichbourne; it is endowed with a good house for the master, and fifty-two acres of land, now let for £100 per annum. The poor law union of which this town is the head comprises 13 parishes and places, and contains a population of 7092. At Bramdean, about three miles distant, a tessellated pavement was discovered some years ago, one part of which represents the wrestling match between Hercules and Antæus.

ALRESFORD, OLD (ST. MARY), a parish, in the union of ALRESFORD, hundred of FAWLEY, Winchester and N. divisions of the county of SOUTHAMPTON, ¾ of a mile (N.) from New Alresford; containing 502 inhabitants. This parish, which is divided from that of New Alresford by the river Itchen, comprises 3265 acres, whereof 40 are common or waste; the surface is hilly, and the soil light and chalky, but tolerably good. The hamlet of Hamsworth is included in the measurement of this parish, but is rated with that of Medsted. The living is a rectory, with the rectories of New Alresford and Medsted annexed, valued in the king's books at £49. 12. 8½., and in the gift of the Bishop of Winchester; the glebe comprises 40 acres.

ALREWAS (ALL SAINTS), a parish, in the union of LICHFIELD, N. division of the hundred of OFFLOW and of the county of STAFFORD, 5½ miles (N. E. by N.) from Lichfield; containing, with the hamlets of Fradley and Orgreave, 1658 inhabitants, of whom 1173 are in the township of Alrewas. This parish is bounded by the Trent on the north, and the Tame on the east, and contains 4329a. 31p.; it is intersected by the Trent and Mersey, and the Coventry canals, and there is a station of the Birmingham and Derby railroad 1½ mile from the village. A manufactory of tape employs about ninety hands. Courts leet and baron for the manor are held twice a year: the custom of Borough English prevails. The living is a discharged vicarage, valued in the king's

45

books at £5. 6. 8.; patron, the Prebendary of Alrewas and Weeford in the Cathedral of Lichfield. The great tithes have been commuted for £439. 15., and the vicarial for £250: there is glebe-land, together with land allotted in lieu of tithes upon the common; the impropriator has 102a. 25p., and the vicar 37a. 2r. 10p., with a glebe-house. The church is chiefly in the Norman style, and contains monuments to the family of Turton, a member of which was chief justice of the king's bench in the time of William III. There are places of worship for Wesleyans and Ranters. Viscount Anson was baron of Orgreave, where he had an estate, which still remains in the possession of the family. The Roman Ikeneld-street intersects the parish.

ALREWAS-HAYES, an extra-parochial liberty, locally in the parish of ALREWAS, N. division of the hundred of OFFLOW and of the county of STAFFORD, 5½ miles (N. N. E.) from Lichfield; containing 92 inhabitants, and comprising 1200 acres. This place was formerly an open forest or chase; and at the time of the Conquest, perhaps formed the extensive wood at Alrewas mentioned in Domesday book: it was not wholly inclosed until 1826. The Fazeley and the Trent and Mersey canals unite here.

ALSAGER, a chapelry, in the parish of BARTHOMLEY, union of CONGLETON, hundred of NORTHWICH, S. division of the county of CHESTER, 4 miles (W.) from Church-Lawton; containing 445 inhabitants. The manor was at an early period in the possession of the Vernon family, and subsequently in that of the family of Minshull: about the reign of Henry III. it was held by the Alsagers, who became extinct in the male line in 1768, by the death of John Alsager, Esq., when the property devolved to his three sisters. The chapelry is situated on the road from Barthomley to Lawton, and comprises 2076 acres; the soil is chiefly sand, clay, and fox-bench. On the heath is a mere, which, though small, is picturesque. The living is a donative, in the patronage of the owner of the manor; the income is £105, arising from 63 acres of land. A rent-charge of £240 has been awarded as a commutation in lieu of the tithes. The chapel is a handsome edifice, consecrated in 1790, and contains a monument to the memory of Col. Tryon, who was engaged in the Peninsular war. There is a place of worship for Wesleyans; also a small school founded and endowed, in 1789, by Mary, Judith, and Margaret Alsager, owners of the manor, who likewise built and endowed the chapel.

ALSOP-LE-DALE, with EATON, a chapelry, in the parish of ASHBOURN, hundred of WIRKSWORTH, S. division of the county of DERBY, 5½ miles (N. by W.) from Ashbourn; containing 67 inhabitants. Alsop is the Elleshope of the Domesday survey. The manor was given by the crown to William de Ferrars, Earl of Derby, from whom it passed in succession to various families. Eaton was an appendage to the manor of Parwich, and was granted by King John to the family of Ferrars; about 1518 it appears to have belonged to the Vernons, of Haddon. The road from Ashbourn to Buxton lies in the vicinity of both places. The living is a perpetual curacy, in the patronage of the inhabitant freeholders; net income, £49. The chapel, dedicated to St. Michael, is of Norman architecture, with many modern alterations. A large half-timbered building here is in good preservation.

ALSTON, or ALSTON-MOOR (ST. AUGUSTINE), a market-town and parish, forming a union of itself, in LEATH ward, E. division of CUMBERLAND, 29 miles (E. S. E.) from Carlisle, and 287 (N. N. W.) from London; comprising the township of Alston, and the chapelry of Garrigill, the former containing 4588, and the latter 1474, inhabitants. Mining in this district is of some antiquity, several charters having been granted to the miners of "Alderston" in the 13th century. In 1282 the manor was granted by Edward I. to Nicholas de Veteripont, and in 1333 Edward III. confirmed to his son, Robert de Veteripont, and to the *monetarii*, or coiners, many important privileges. In the reign of Henry V. the manor and mines were let to William Stapleton; and, subsequently, Alston became the property of the Hyltons of Hylton Castle, in the county of Durham, and lastly of the Radcliffe family, with whom it continued until the attainder of the last earl of Derwentwater, in 1716, when it was granted by the crown to the Governors of Greenwich Hospital.

The parish comprises by computation about 40,000 acres, and includes two considerable villages, Garrigill and Nent Head, the latter on the eastern border of the parish, each 4 miles from Alston, and each containing about 500 persons. The TOWN of Alston, consisting of about 1650 inhabitants, is situated on the declivity and base of Middlefell hill, in a narrow valley, near the confluence of the rivers Nent and South Tyne, over each of which is a neat stone bridge. The houses, which are irregularly and rather meanly built, are chiefly of stone, roofed with slate, and the streets are inconveniently steep; the inhabitants are supplied with water conveyed by pipes from an excellent spring, about half a mile distant, into four punts or cisterns, conveniently placed in different parts of the town. A subscription library was established in 1821, to commemorate the coronation of George IV.; races are held on Easter Monday and Tuesday. A new line of road has been made, under the superintendence of M'Adam, from Hexham to Penrith, through Alston, which is shorter by several miles than the old road by way of Carlisle. Several of the contiguous eminences command beautiful views of the surrounding country, particularly Hartside, which embraces the counties of Cumberland and Westmorland, including Ullswater, and the mountains of the lake district, Solway Firth, and the adjacent Scottish shore.

The immediate vicinity, which is inclosed on the west by the mountains Cross Fell and Hartside, and on all sides by high lands, is equally remarkable for the sterility of the soil and the abundance of its MINERAL wealth. The lead-mines, in which the inhabitants are chiefly employed, and of which there are no fewer than thirty-eight in the parish, are very productive: the ore contains a proportion of silver, averaging from eight to ten ounces per ton; and one of the mines opened at Yadmoss in 1828, has produced ore containing ninety-six ounces of silver in each ton. Copper has also been found in the same vein with the lead, and in many instances the same mine has been worked for copper-ore of excellent quality, and lead-ore rich in silver. The grand aqueduct level, called "Nent Force," was cut by the trustees of Greenwich Hospital: this subterraneous canal is five miles in length, from its mouth, near the town, to the shaft of the mine, and boats and guides were once kept in readiness to conduct those who might wish to explore
46

it. In the mines are several extensive caverns, splendidly decorated with fluor-spar, shot into crystals of every form and hue; and, where the yellow copper-ore and pyrites are intermingled, nothing can exceed the brilliancy with which the prismatic colours are reflected. Of these caverns, Tutman's Hole has been explored to the distance of a mile from the entrance; in that at Dun Fell, on the side of Alston-Moor, the chambers and windings are so intricate, that visiters have been glad to avail themselves of some clue to their return. The other minerals found here are pyrites of iron containing small particles of gold, tessellated ore, zinc, phosphate and sulphate of lead, cobalt, &c. The Crow coal, found on the moor, at a small depth below the surface, contains pyrites in large proportion; it burns with little flame, but emits an intense heat, and, mixed with clay, is made into balls for fuel. There are two large smelting-furnaces; and several machines, worked by water, for crushing and washing the ore. The principal manufacture is that of woollen yarn, which is carried on in an extensive mill recently built; there is also a public brewery on a large scale. The market is on Saturday; fairs take place on the last Thursday in May, Friday before the last day of September, and the first Thursday in November. At Nent Head, a customary market is held every Thursday. Two of the county magistrates hold a petty-session at the Swan inn, on the first Friday in every month; and courts leet and baron occur in the months next after Easter and Michaelmas. The powers of the county debt-court of Alston, established in 1847, extend over the registration district of Alston, and the parishes of Kirkhaugh and Knaresdale.

The LIVING is a discharged vicarage, valued in the king's books at £7. 13.; net income, £180; patrons and impropriators, the Governors of Greenwich Hospital. The tithes, with certain exceptions, were commuted for an allotment of land, under an inclosure act, in 1803. The church, rebuilt in 1770, is a neat edifice with a tower. A chapel of ease, a plain and unadorned building erected by subscription about 1780, is maintained at Garrigill; and at Nent Head is a distinct incumbency, in the gift of the Vicar. There are places of worship for the Society of Friends, Independents, and Primitive and Wesleyan Methodists. The grammar school was rebuilt by subscription, in 1828, and is endowed with £29. 8. per annum: no scholars are gratuitously instructed, but the master, in consideration of the endowment, is limited to a certain scale of charges. The Roman road called the Maiden-way crosses the western part of the parish, where it may be distinctly traced; and on Hall hill, a little below the bridge over the Tyne, are the foundations of an ancient fortress, surrounded by a moat. On Gildersdale Fell is a stagnant pool, covered with mud several inches thick, which is used by the neighbouring people as paint: it produces colours resembling yellow ochre and Spanish brown, but has not been analyzed.

ALSTON, a chapelry, in the parish of ASHBURTON, union of NEWTON-ABBOT, hundred of TEIGNBRIDGE, Teignbridge and S. divisions of DEVON, 2½ miles (N. E. by E.) from Ashburton. It comprises 1010 acres by computation; the surface is hilly, and the sub-soil consists of limestone, clay, and sharp gravel. The chief produce arises from corn land and orchards, the cultivators of which are in general independent freeholders.

ALSTON, a township, in the chapelry of LONGRIDGE, parish of RIBCHESTER, union of PRESTON, hundred of AMOUNDERNESS, N. division of the county of LANCASTER, 6 miles (N. E.) from Preston; containing 807 inhabitants. The township comprises 1989a. 1r. 12p. of land; and within its limits is part of the village of Longridge, a large, thriving, stone-built place, situated near the summit of Longridge Fell, and of which the other portion is in the township of Dilworth. Among the principal owners of the soil are the Earl of Derby and Sir Henry Hoghton, Bart. The line of the Preston and Clitheroe railway passes through the lower part of the township. Alston Hall is now a farmhouse. The tithes have been commuted for £150, payable to the Bishop of Chester, and £20 to the vicar. There are some small charities.

ALSTONE, a hamlet, in the parish and hundred of CHELTENHAM, union of WINCHCOMB, E. division of the county of GLOUCESTER, ¾ of a mile (N. W. by W.) from Cheltenham. This place is situated on the river Chelt, over which is a viaduct for the Bristol and Birmingham railway, which proceeds hence to the parish of Swinton. A church was consecrated in 1840, a handsome and spacious structure containing 2085 sittings. Here is a chalybeate saline spa, for an account of which see CHELTENHAM.

ALSTONE, a chapelry, in the parish of OVERBURY, Middle division of the hundred of OSWALDSLOW, Pershore and E. divisions of the hundred of WORCESTER, 6½ miles (E. by S.) from Tewkesbury; containing 89 inhabitants. It comprises 575 acres, and forms part of a detached portion of the parish, surrounded on all sides, except the north-west, by the county of Gloucester. The village lies a short distance south of the road from Tewkesbury to Stow-on-the-Wold. The chapel is dedicated to St. Margaret, is a very ancient building with a square tower, and contains about 90 sittings.

ALSTONFIELD (ST. PETER), a parish, in the union of LEEK, hundred of NORTH TOTMONSLOW, N. division of the county of STAFFORD, 7 miles (N. N. W.) from Ashbourn; comprising the chapelries of Elkstone, Warslow, Longnor, and Quarnford, and the townships of Alstonfield, Fairfieldhead, Heathy-Lee, and Hollinsclough; and containing 4701 inhabitants, of whom 654 are in the township of Alstonfield. This parish, which is fifteen miles in length, is situated at the northern extremity of the county, and is bounded on the west by Cheshire, and on the east by Derbyshire, from which it is separated by the river Dove: the township comprises 2862 acres. The living is a discharged vicarage, valued in the king's books at £8. 11. 4.; net income, £112; patron and impropriator, Sir John Crewe, Bart. The church is in the early English style, with an embattled tower crowned with pinnacles; the nave is separated from the aisles by finely pointed arches; the pulpit and reading-desk were the gift of the poet Cotton, who resided at Beresford Hall. There are six chapels exclusively of the parish church, those in Heathy-Lee and Hollinsclough having been lately built, principally at the expense of Sir G. Crewe.

ALTCAR (ST. MICHAEL), a parish, in the union of ORMSKIRK, hundred of WEST DERBY, S. division of the county of LANCASTER, 6 miles (W. by S.) from Ormskirk; containing 490 inhabitants. This place seems to be the *Acrer* of the Domesday survey, at which period it
47

was held by Uctred; it was afterwards held by the abbots of Merivale, and continued with them till the Dissolution, soon after which it was possessed by the family of Molyneux. The parish takes its name from the river *Alt*, and the word *car*, meaning low land; and comprises 3582 acres, mostly in meadow and pasture: the surface is level, and the soil partly alluvial and partly a sandy loam containing a mixture of marl. The Alt bounds the parish on the south, having various channels by which the marshes here are drained, and the lower lands thus present the appearance of a Dutch farm with drains and embankments. The grounds are subject to floods, which are carried off by a steam-engine, erected in 1842, the water being thrown into the Alt, which merges into the Irish Sea at Formby Point. A large quantity of hay is produced in the parish; and there is a good stone-quarry, the material of which is used for building purposes. A court baron is held annually in May, and an adjourned court in October. The principal village, called Great Altcar, is a straggling place, consisting chiefly of farmhouses, extending on a slight eminence towards the church, which stands in the western extremity of the parish. Little Altcar is a hamlet adjacent to Formby; and Altcar Hall is an ordinary farmhouse, over the door of which were formerly the arms of the noble family of Molyneux. The living is a perpetual curacy; net income, £108; patron and impropriator, the Earl of Sefton. The church is a neat structure with a campanile tower, erected in 1746, and repaired in 1841. A school, built in 1840, is supported by subscription, aided by £8 per annum from the noble patron; and the interest of a few small bequests is appropriated to the poor. On the coast, near the mouth of the Alt, oak, ash, and fir trees are dug up, after ages of immersion in a subterranean forest at that place.

ALTERNON (ST. NUNN), a parish, in the union of LAUNCESTON, hundred of LESNEWTH, E. division of CORNWALL, 7¾ miles (W. S. W.) from Launceston; containing 1334 inhabitants. The parish comprises 12,039 acres, of which 4174 are common or waste. Fairs are held at Five-Lanes, in the parish, on the Monday after June 24th, and the first Tuesday in November. The living is a vicarage, valued in the king's books at £18. 5.; net income, £320; patrons and appropriators, the Dean and Chapter of Exeter. There is a place of worship for Wesleyans.

ALTHAM, a township and parochial chapelry, in the parish of WHALLEY, union of BURNLEY, Higher division of the hundred of BLACKBURN, N. division of the county of LANCASTER, 5 miles (W.) from Burnley; the township containing 349 inhabitants. Under the name of *Elvetham*, the manor was granted by the first Henry de Lacy to Hugo, a Saxon: John de Alvetham, Hngo's descendant, left an heiress who married into the Banastre family, and thus sprang the Banastres of Altham, who occupied the manor-house for five centuries. The parochial chapelry comprises the townships of Altham (in which are 868 acres), Clayton-le-Moors, and New and Old Accrington. The river Calder forms the northern boundary of Altham township: on the east it is increased by a nameless brook from Huncoat; and the Hyndburne, after flowing as the western boundary of the chapelry, forms its confluence with the Calder at the north-west extremity of Clayton-le-Moors. Coal is obtained in the vicinity. The living is a perpetual curacy; net income, £117; patron, R. T. W. Walton, Esq. The chapel is dedicated to St. James. The Wesleyans have a place of worship; and there is a Roman Catholic chapel, erected in 1825.

ALTHORNE (St. *Andrew*), a parish, in the union of Maldon, hundred of Dengie, S. division of Essex, 4 miles (N. W.) from Burnham; containing 418 inhabitants. It is situated on the estuary of the river Crouch, from the overflowing of which the lands are protected by very strong embankments, nine feet high, constructed by labourers from Holland, whose descendants are still resident here. The living is a vicarage, united to the rectory of Creeksea in 1811, and valued in the king's books at £14; impropriator, Thomas Wilson, Esq. The great tithes have been commuted for £454. 5. 6., the small tithes for £155. 15.; and there are more than six acres of glebe. The church is a small edifice, containing, in the aisles, two brass plates with inscriptions in the old English character, one to the memory of Margaret Hycklot, the other to William Hycklot, "who paid for the workmanship of the walls of this church," and died in 1508.

· ALTHORP (St. *Oswald*), a parish, in the union of Thorne, W. division of the wapentake of Manley, parts of Lindsey, county of Lincoln, 11 miles (W. by N.) from Glandford-Brigg; containing, with the townships of Amcotts and Keadby, 1184 inhabitants. The living is a rectory, valued in the king's books at £25, and in the patronage of the Crown; net income, £400. The tithes of the township of Althorp have been commuted for corn-rents under an act obtained in 1794. There is a chapel of ease at Amcotts.

ALTHORPE, an extra-parochial liberty, in the hundred of Newbottle-Grove, county of Northampton; containing 55 inhabitants. It comprises 790 acres of land.—See Brington.

ALTOFTS, a township, in the parish of Normanton, Lower division of the wapentake of Agbrigg, W. riding of York, 3¼ miles (N. E. by E.) from Wakefield; containing 704 inhabitants. This place is situated on the south side of the river Calder, across which is a horse-ferry, and near the Midland railway. There is an aqueduct of elegant design for the Aire and Calder canal. The ancient hall of Altofts is said to have been the residence of Admiral Frobisher. Stone of good quality is quarried, and many fossils are found. The impropriate tithes have been commuted for £344, payable to Trinity College, Cambridge, and the vicarial for £69. 10. Here is a school, endowed by Mrs. Susannah Dodsworth, with £20 per annum, for which 15 girls are clothed and instructed.

ALTON (St. *Lawrence*), a market-town and parish, and the head of a union, in the hundred of Alton, Alton and N. divisions of the county of Southampton, 17 miles (E. N. E.) from Winchester, and 47 (S. W. by W.) from London; containing 3139 inhabitants. The name of this town, which is a slight modification of *Auleton* or *Aultone*, is descriptive of its great antiquity. It was a royal demesne in the time of Alfred the Great; and is noticed in the Saxon Chronicle as the scene of a sanguinary battle which was fought between the Saxons and the piratical Danes, who, having landed on this part of the coast in 1001,—plundered and laid waste the country till they reached this place, at that time called "Aethelinga-dene." Here the men of Hampshire had assembled
48

in order to oppose their further progress; but notwithstanding that great numbers of the invaders were slain, the latter remained in possession of the field of battle, whence they afterwards marched northward. At the time of the Norman survey, the town belonged to the abbot of St. Peter's, Winchester; and in the reign of Edward I. it returned one member to parliament. During the civil war of the seventeenth century, the place was occupied by a detachment of the royal army, under the command of Sir Ralph Hopton; but, in 1643, it was taken by the parliamentarian forces under Sir William Waller, after an engagement in which Col. Bowles was killed at the church-door, and his regiment taken prisoners.

The town is situated at the source of the river Wey, and consists of three principal streets, which are lighted under an act obtained for that purpose; the houses are in general neatly built, and of pleasing and cheerful appearance. A public library, on a plan calculated to meet the wants of the working mechanics, was established in 1837; it is in a state of prosperous advancement, and lectures are occasionally given to the members. The environs are beautifully picturesque, and the adjacent district richly fertile; the lands are watered by a fine stream, which crosses the town under the streets and houses, and in the surrounding scenery the church forms a conspicuous and interesting feature. The parish comprises by measurement 3896 acres; the surface is generally hilly, and the soil consists principally of chalk and gravel. The manufacture of bombazines was formerly carried on to a very considerable extent, but is now totally discontinued; a great quantity of hop bagging is made, and a paper manufactory is set in motion by the Wey, at no great distance from its source. There are also two large breweries in the town, and in the vicinity are about 200 acres of ground laid out in the cultivation of hops, the malt and the ale of Alton being in high repute. An act was passed in 1846 for the construction of a railway to Farnham and Guildford, 19 miles in length. The market, formerly held on Saturday, but since 1840 altered to Tuesday in every alternate week, is chiefly for cattle and sheep, and, from the great agricultural resources of the neighbourhood, is rapidly increasing: fairs for horses and cattle take place annually on the last Saturday in April, and Sept. 29th, the former for the manor of Alton Westbrook, and the latter for that of Alton Eastbrook. The county magistrates hold petty-sessions here for the division; and a court leet is held once a month by the steward of the manor, at which debts under 40s. are recoverable. The powers of the county debt-court of Alton, established in 1847, extend over the registration district of Alton. The town-hall, situated in the market-place, was rebuilt by subscription in 1812.

The living is a vicarage, with the livings of Binstead, Holybourne, and Kingsley annexed, valued in the king's books at £15; patrons and appropriators, the Dean and Chapter of Winchester. The great tithes have been commuted for £770, and the vicarial for £496. The church is a spacious structure, in the later style of English architecture, with some portions of earlier date; it has a square embattled tower surmounted by a spire, and has been enlarged by the addition of a north aisle; on its northern wall is a curious painting of our Saviour's life. There are places of worship for the Society of

Friends, and Independents. The free grammar school at Anstey, in the parish, was founded in the reign of Charles I., by John Eggar, and has an endowment of £74. 10. per annum. The poor law union of Alton comprises 19 parishes or places, and contains a population of 11,299. Roman urns, coins, and other antiquities have been found in the neighbourhood; and in cleaning the church, in 1839, portraits of Henry VI. and several bishops were discovered. William de Alton, a Dominican friar, who lived in the time of Edward II., and wrote a treatise on the universality of the pollution of mankind by original sin; John Pitts, an eminent biographer, author of a work entitled "De Illustribus Angliæ Scriptoribus;" and William Curtis, an eminent botanist, author of the "Flora Londinensis," editor of the Botanical Magazine, and founder of a botanical garden near the Magdalene Hospital, and afterwards of a more extensive establishment at Brompton; were natives of the town.

ALTON, county of STÁFFORD.—See ALVETON.

ALTON BARNES or BERNERS (ST. MARY), a parish, in the union of DEVIZES, hundred of SWANBOROUGH, Devizes and N. divisions of WILTS, 7 miles (E.) from Devizes; containing 167 inhabitants. The Kennet and Avon canal flows a little south of the village. The living is a rectory, valued in the king's books at £6. 18. 11½., and in the gift of New College, Oxford: the tithes have been commuted for £449, and the glebe consists of about 50 acres.

ALTON-PANCRAS (ST. PANCRATIUS), a parish and liberty, in the union of CERNE, Cerne division of DORSET, 8¼ miles (N.) from Dorchester; containing 248 inhabitants. The two manors, or parcels of demesne land, called Alton Borealis and Alton Australis, till lately constituted the endowment of two prebends in the cathedral of Salisbury. The living is a discharged vicarage, valued in the king's books at £9; net income, £120; patrons, the Dean and Chapter of Salisbury, who are also appropriators. The church is dedicated to St. Pancratius, a nobleman of Phrygia, who suffered martyrdom under Diocletian at Rome in the third century.

ALTON-PRIORS, a chapelry, in the parish of OVERTON, union of PEWSEY, hundred of ELSTUB and EVERLEY, Everley and Pewsey, and S. divisions of WILTS, 7 miles (E. by N.) from Devizes; containing, with the tything of Stowell, 251 inhabitants. The chapelry is separated on the north from the principal portion of the parish by a range of hills that stretches across the country in this part; and the Kennet and Avon canal passes at a short distance on the south. The chapel is dedicated to All Saints.

ALTRINCHAM, a market-town and chapelry, and the head of a union, in the parish of BOWDON, hundred of BUCKLOW, N. division of the county of CHESTER, 7 miles (N. by E.) from Knutsford, and 180 (N. W. by N.) from London; containing 3399 inhabitants. The town is situated near Bowdon Downs, and, though small, contains several respectable dwelling-houses, the salubrity of the air

Arms.

rendering it a place of general resort for invalids from Manchester; it is watched and lighted under the general act of the 11th of George IV., and is characterised throughout by cleanliness and neatness. The trade principally consists in the spinning of yarn, the making and weaving of cotton by hand-looms, and by machinery driven by steam, for the manufacturers at Manchester and other adjacent towns. The Duke of Bridgewater's canal from Manchester to Runcorn passes within three-quarters of a mile of the town, affording a facility for conveyance for coal; and in 1845 and 1846 acts were passed, the first for a railway to Manchester, since completed, and the second for a railway from Birkenhead, by Altrincham, to Stockport. Early potatoes are cultivated here to a great extent for the Manchester market. The market-days are Tuesday and Saturday, the latter for butchers' meat; the fairs, chiefly for the sale of live stock, are held on April 29th, August 5th, and November 22nd.

Altrincham was made a free borough in the reign of Edward I., by charter of Hamon de Massey, lord of the barony of Dunham-Massey, and the burgesses were empowered to have a guild-merchant, and to choose a *præpositus*, or bailiff; but the only privilege they now possess is that of electing a mayor at a court leet held in autumn, when a jury of burgesses present three of their own body to the steward, who appoints one to the office, which however is merely nominal, the duty extending only to the opening of the fairs. A steward is chosen by the lord of the barony of Dunham-Massey, and this officer appoints a bailiff; there are also two constables, who are chosen by the leet jury. The powers of the county debt-court of Altrincham, established in 1847, extend over part of the registration-district of Altrincham. The township comprises 657 acres, of which 38 are common or waste: the soil is loam. The living is a perpetual curacy; patron, the Vicar of Bowdon; net income, £150. The tithes have been commuted for £48. 14., payable to the Bishop of Chester, and £43 to the vicar. The chapel, dedicated to St. George, is a plain brick building, erected by subscription in 1799. There are two places of worship for Methodists, and one for Unitarians. The poor law union of Altrincham comprises 39 parishes or places, and contains a population of 31,019.

ALVANLEY, a chapelry, in the parish of FRODSHAM, union of RUNCORN, Second division of the hundred of EDDISBURY, S. division of the county of CHESTER, 3 miles (S. S. W.) from Frodsham; containing 314 inhabitants, and comprising 1532 acres of land, whereof the soil is clay and sand. The manor was held under the earls of Arundel at an early period by Richard de Pierpoint and Robert de Alvanley, who sold it to Sir Philip de Orreby; and it came by marriage, in the reign of Henry III., to the Arden family. When Sir Richard Pepper Arden, master of the rolls, was created a peer, in 1801, he took the title of Lord Alvanley from this place; and it is now held by his son and successor, the present lord. The living is a donative; net income, £47; patron, Lord Alvanley. The chapel is dedicated to St. Mary. A Sunday school has been established.

ALVASTON, a township, in the parish, union, and hundred of NANTWICH, S. division of the county of CHESTER, 2½ miles (N. E.) from Nantwich; containing

40 inhabitants. The ancient manor of Alvaston was possessed by the Bromley family, but no manor now exists : in 1788 the principal estate came by purchase to the Fosters. In the township is the common of Croach or Beam-heath, which in 1285 was given by Richard Alvaston to the whole community of the town of Wich-Malbank, now Nantwich ; but it being deemed more for the benefit of the persons interested, the common was inclosed by act of parliament, in 1803. The township comprises 610 acres, of which 450 are in Beam-heath ; the soil is partly sand and partly clay. Races are held annually. The tithes have been commuted for £82. 7. 6.

ALVASTON, a chapelry, in the parish of St. Michael, Derby, union of Shardlow, hundred of Morleston and Litchurch, S. division of the county of Derby, 3½ miles (S. E. by E.) from Derby ; containing 493 inhabitants. The manor, then called Alewoldestune, was held by Tochi at the time of the Domesday survey ; and belonged afterwards to Ralph Fitz-Germund, founder of Dale Abbey, whose descendant Matilda gave Alvaston to that monastery. In 1547 it was granted to the Needham family, from whom it passed to various hands. It was esteemed a chapelry in the 12th century. The area is 1355 acres ; the chapelry is pleasantly situated near the river Derwent, on the London road, and the Derby canal runs through. The living is a perpetual curacy, in the gift of the parishioners, with a net income of £116 : the tithes were commuted for land, under an inclosure act, in 1802 ; the glebe here consists of about 67 acres, and portions of land have been purchased in Leicestershire and Derbyshire by an allowance from Queen Anne's Bounty. There is a place of worship for Wesleyans ; and schools are aided by the trustees of Gilbert's charity, which provides also for the repair of the chapel.

ALVECHURCH (St. Lawrence), a parish, in the union of Bromsgrove, forming a detached portion of the Middle division of the hundred of Oswaldslow, locally in the Upper division of the hundred of Half-shire, Northfield and E. divisions of the county of Worcester, 4½ miles (E. N. E.) from Bromsgrove ; containing 1633 inhabitants. This was the occasional residence of the bishops of Worcester, who had a palace here in the reign of Henry II., which after the sale of the manor by the parliament, in 1648, was suffered to fall to decay, and has now entirely disappeared. The parish comprises 6599 acres, and the Birmingham and Worcester canal runs through it. Needles are made here in the rough state, and taken to Redditch to be finished. A sandstone-quarry is in operation. Fairs for cattle and sheep are held on the 22nd of April and 10th of August. The living is a rectory, valued in the king's books at £24. 16. 8., and in the gift of the Bishop of Worcester : the tithes have been commuted for £1100, with 96 acres of glebe, and a house. The church has Norman pillars, but the chancel displays the early English style, and the tower is more modern ; in the interior is a monument dated 1315, of Sir Thomas Blanchfont, represented as a cross-legged knight. There are places of worship for Wesleyans and Baptists. £36 per annum are appropriated to the instruction of children ; the original benefactor is not known, but Dr. Warth left £100 in augmentation. A school-house was built in 1839 ; the school is on the national plan, for 50

boys and 30 girls, and is well supported by subscription. There is also an excellent Sunday school. An hospital for a master, six brethren, and two sisters, was incorporated by Queen Elizabeth ; it is endowed with £33. 6. 8., exclusively of keeping the tenements in repair. The Roman Ikeneld-street passes through the parish, in its course from Alcester towards Lichfield. The learned Dr. Hickes, author of the *Thesaurus Septentrionalium Linguarum*, was incumbent here.

ALVELEY (St. Mary), a parish, partly within the liberty of the borough of Bridgnorth, but chiefly in the hundred of Stottesden, union of Bridgnorth, S. division of Salop, 6½ miles (S. S. E.) from Bridgnorth ; containing, with Nordley-Regis township, and Romsley liberty in the borough of Bridgnorth, 1062 inhabitants. It comprises 6435 acres, including Romsley, which contributes one-third towards the church-rate, but is independent of the parish in other respects : the road from Shrewsbury to Cheltenham passes through it, and the river Severn is its boundary on one side. There are some works for the manufacture of iron, and several quarries, the stone of which is used for building, and made into wheels for mills and manufactures. Alveley was one of the five prebends in the royal free chapel of the castle of Bridgnorth, valued in the reign of Henry III., at sixty marks, and is still reputed and rated as such in the Office of the First Fruits. The living is a perpetual curacy, recently endowed with £300, the donations of various persons, which were placed in the hands of the Ecclesiastical Commissioners by whom, in consideration thereof, the net income, previously £90, was augmented £17 ; patron and impropriator, Col. Gatacre. The church is a fine edifice, a mixture of Norman and early English architecture, with a curious old painted window in the clerestory, supposed to have been built in the time of the Tudors. In the south wall of the chancel, three fine early English sedilia and a piscina were recently discovered, in a mutilated state, by the incumbent ; they were concealed by plaster : the patron has had them restored. There is a private chapel attached to Coton Hall, in the parish. A free school was endowed in 1616, by John Grove, to whom is a monument of brass on the floor of the chancel of the church, bearing the date 1616 ; the master resides in a house rent-free, and receives £20 per annum. Five "decayed labourers" receive £6 each, annually, from property bequeathed by the same individual. Thomas Grove, his son, also conveyed some land to trustees, for "the poorest of the poor people," the proceeds to be distributed yearly.

ALVERDISCOT (All Saints), a parish, in the union of Torrington, hundred of Hartland, Braunton and N. divisions of Devon, 4½ miles (N. E.) from Torrington ; containing 332 inhabitants. This parish, which is situated on the old road from Torrington to Barnstaple, comprises by computation 2000 acres. The living is a rectory, valued in the king's books at £13. 3. 11¼., and in the gift of William Lee, Esq. : the tithes have been commuted for £156. 8., and the glebe comprises 36 acres. The church contains some elegant marble monuments to the families of Hoody and Welch, former proprietors of the manor : it has been recently repewed and beautified, and a small vestry-room has been added. There is a place of worship for a congregation of Wesleyans.

ALVERSTOKE (St. Mary), a parish, comprising the sea-port town of Gosport, the watering-place called Anglesey, and the chapelry of Forton, in the liberty of ALVERSTOKE and GOSPORT, Fareham and S. divisions of the county of SOUTHAMPTON; and containing 13,510 inhabitants. This place is situated on the shore of Alverstoke bay. According to an ancient chronicle, Henry de Blois, Bishop of Winchester, and brother of King Stephen, on his return from Normandy, being overtaken by a storm in the bay, between the Isle of Wight and Alverstoke, made a solemn vow to build a church on the spot where he should first land in safety; and, having landed at this place, is said to have erected the parish church, in fulfilment of his vow, about the year 1130. The parish comprises 3031 acres, whereof 142 are common or waste: the scenery is varied, and in the western part of the parish are several small rural villages which have a pleasing aspect, and contrast finely with the more stately edifices in other parts of it. The village of Alverstoke is pleasantly situated about half a mile from the bay, and within a quarter of a mile from the elegant new buildings of Anglesey.

The living is a rectory, valued in the king's books at £21. 6. 0½., and in the gift of the Bishop of Winchester: the tithes have been commuted for £1250, and the glebe consists of 45 acres. The church, which occupies a site in the village beautifully secluded by trees, has undergone many changes since its foundation, and is now in a state of renovation, which has been effected with a judicious regard to its original character: a tablet was erected in 1844, to the memory of the officers and soldiers of the 44th regiment, who fell in the Affghan war. There are several churches and chapels in the parish; one at Gosport, consecrated in 1696, and dedicated to the Holy Trinity; a small chapel closely adjoining the liberty of Gosport; another at Elson, on the northern side of the parish; one, lately erected, very near to the parish church, among the new buildings at Anglesey; and one at Forton. The church at Elson is dedicated to St. Thomas, and was consecrated in Aug. 1845: the living is a perpetual curacy, in the patronage of the Rector. The dissenters, also, have several places of worship.

ALVERTHORPE, a township, comprising the ecclesiastical districts of Alverthorpe and Thornes, in the parish and union of WAKEFIELD, Lower division of the wapentake of AGBRIGG, W. riding of YORK, 1½ mile (W. N. W.) from Wakefield; containing 5930 inhabitants. This township, including Westgate Common, a suburb of the borough of Wakefield, comprises by computation 3000 acres. The land is rich and fertile, and in profitable cultivation; the surface is varied; the substratum abounds with coal of good quality, and several mines are in operation. The village of Alverthorpe is pleasantly situated, and the township includes also the village of Thornes, and the hamlets of Fanshaw, Kirkham Gate, and Silcoates. The population is chiefly employed in the spinning of woollen and worsted yarn, and in the manufacture of woollen cloth and worsted stuffs, for which there are several mills and large factories; the manufacture of rope and twine is also carried on to a considerable extent. Alverthorpe church, dedicated to St. Paul, was erected in 1826, at an expense of £8000, chiefly by grant of the Parliamentary Commissioners: it is a handsome structure in the early English style,

51

with a square embattled tower crowned with pinnacles, and contains 1600 sittings, of which 800 are free. The living is a perpetual curacy, in the gift of the Vicar of Wakefield; the income, previously £72, was augmented in 1841 with £78 per annum by the Ecclesiastical Commissioners, and a neat residence for the minister was built in 1842. The small tithes were commuted for land and a money payment, under an act of inclosure, in 1793. There is a place of worship for Wesleyans. The Northern Congregational School at Silcoates House was instituted in 1830, for the board and education of the sons of ministers of the Independent denomination.

ALVERTON, a hamlet, in the parish of KILVINGTON, union of NEWARK, S. division of the wapentake of NEWARK and of the county of NOTTINGHAM, 7½ miles (S. by W.) from Newark; containing 26 inhabitants.

ALVESCOTT, a parish, in the union of WITNEY, hundred of BAMPTON, county of OXFORD, 6 miles (S. S. E.) from Burford; comprising 2021a. 29p., and containing 357 inhabitants. The living is a rectory, valued in the king's books at £8. 16. 8.; net income, £371; patrons, the family of Neate. All the tithes were commuted for land and corn-rents, under an inclosure act, in 1796. The church is an ancient structure, consisting of a nave with semi-transepts, a massive western tower, and a chancel, which has been rebuilt, and contains some mural monuments. Goddard Carter, Esq., in 1723, left a rent-charge of £10, directing one-half to be applied in educating poor children, and the remainder in apprenticing them.

ALVESDISTON (St. Mary), a parish, in the union of TISBURY, hundred of CHALK, Hindon and S. divisions of WILTS, 7½ miles (E. by N.) from Shaftesbury; containing 263 inhabitants. This parish takes its name from Aileva, who held lands here at the time of the Norman survey: it contains about 2733 acres. The living is a discharged vicarage, united to the rectory of Broad-Chalk and the vicarage of Bower-Chalk; impropriators, the Provost and Fellows of King's College, Cambridge. The church has a font of great antiquity, and in one of the aisles are four handsome mural monuments of marble to the memory of the Wyndham family.

ALVESTON (St. Helen), a parish, in the union of THORNBURY, partly in the Lower, but chiefly in the Upper, division of the hundred of LANGLEY and SWINEHEAD, W. division of the county of GLOUCESTER, 1 mile (S. by E.) from Thornbury; containing 841 inhabitants. This parish lies on the road from Bristol to Birmingham, and comprises by computation 2600 acres, including some waste lands, for the inclosure of which an act was passed in 1836: the land is almost entirely pasture, and is thickly clothed with elm, beech, and oak. The scenery is grand, and the parish being situated on a high ridge, commands extensive views of the Severn and the surrounding country. The living is a vicarage, annexed to that of Olveston: the tithes have been commuted for £319, and the glebe comprises 25 acres. The church, situated at some distance from the village, is a small edifice in the later English style, with a low square embattled tower. There is a place of worship for a congregation of Wesleyans. Some remains of a Roman encampment are to be seen in a part of the parish called the Abbey.

II 2

ALVESTON (St. James), a parish, in the union of Stratford-on-Avon, Snitterfield division of the hundred of Barlichway, W. division of the county of Warwick, 2 miles (E. N. E.) from Stratford; containing 793 inhabitants. It is situated on the river Avon, and comprises by measurement 2700 acres, whereof four-fifths are arable land; the remainder is pasture by the river side, with 150 acres of wood. The road from Stratford to Wellesbourn-Hastings passes through the parish. The living is a vicarage, valued in the king's books at £6; net income, £220; patron, the Rector of Hampton-Lucy; impropriator, George Lucy, Esq.: the glebe consists of 90 acres. The church, rebuilt in 1839, at an expense of about £2500, chiefly raised by sub-scription, is in the early English style, with a square tower: the east window, presented by the patron, con-tains a full length figure of St. James, and the arms of the Lucy family; the interior of the edifice is very neatly and conveniently fitted up. A school is supported by subscription.

ALVETON, or Alton (St. Peter), a parish, in the union of Cheadle, S. division of the hundred of Tot-monslow, N. division of the county of Stafford, 4½ miles (E. by S.) from Cheadle; comprising the town-ships of Alton, Cotton, Denston, and Farley; and con-taining 2390 inhabitants, of whom 1168 are in Alton township. The extensive manor of Alton became the property of John Talbot, first earl of Shrewsbury, by his marriage with the heiress of the Furnival family, and has remained with his descendants to the present time. The living, before the Reformation, was connected with the abbey of Croxden, to which the benefice was attached by Bertram de Verdun of Alton Castle, in 1176, after he had founded the abbey. The ruins of the castle still remain, on the summit of a rock 300 feet above the bed of the Churnet: on the opposite bank of the river are the magnificent mansion and park of the Earl of Shrews-bury.

The parish contains between 7000 and 8000 acres, whereof 2251 are in Alton township: there are lime-stone-quarries in the township of Cotton, and some copper-mines at Ribden; and a paper-mill is in opera-tion. The Uttoxeter branch of the Trent and Mersey canal runs through the parish, its course being for some miles parallel with that of the Churnet, over which it is carried by means of an aqueduct. The village is ro-mantically situated on the banks of the river, which here flows through a fertile vale; on the summit of an adja-cent eminence is a lofty tower, commanding extensive and varied prospects. The living is a discharged vicar-age, valued in the king's books at £5. 16. 5½., and in the gift of the Earl of Shrewsbury: the tithes have been commuted for £433 payable to his lordship and others, and £250 payable to the vicar; the glebe comprises 5 acres, with a house. The church, which displays a mixture of the Norman and English styles, was repaired and enlarged in 1831. There is a chapel at Cotton. The Calvinistic, Wesleyan, and Primitive Methodists have places of worship; and a Roman Catholic chapel has been erected at Alton-Towers by the earl. At Bun-bury, in the parish, are the remains of a very extensive fortress, of an irregular form, ascribed to Ceolred, King of Mercia about 715; it is defended on three sides by a double vallum, and on the fourth by a steep declivity.

52

ALVINGHAM (St. Adelwold), a parish, in the union of Louth, Marsh division of the hundred of Louth-Eske, parts of Lindsey, county of Lincoln, 4 miles (N. E.) from Louth; containing 313 inhabitants. It comprises by computation 1600 acres, and is inter-sected by the Louth navigation. The living is a perpetual curacy, with that of Cockerington St. Mary annexed, in the patronage of the Bishop of Lincoln, who, as appro-priator, owns about 400 acres of land, allotted in lieu of tithes at the inclosure in 1819, and from the produce of which the incumbent's stipend is paid. The church was rebuilt in 1826, and is a neat and commodious building, situated in the same churchyard as that of Cockerington. A priory of Gilbertine nuns and canons, dedicated to the Virgin Mary and St. Adelwold, was founded here in the reign of Henry II., which, at the Dissolution, was valued at £141. 15. per annum.

ALVINGTON, a parish, in the hundred of Bledis-loe, W. division of the county of Gloucester, 5½ miles (N. E.) from Chepstow; containing 340 inhabit-ants, and comprising by estimation 1550 acres. The abbot of Llantony, previously to the Reformation, ex-ercised capital jurisdiction in this manor, which subse-quently passed through various hands to the Highfords, of Dixton, from whose coheir it was purchased by the father-in-law of the present proprietor, who resides at Clanna House, in the parish. The road from Gloucester to Chepstow runs through Alvington, and the river Severn flows on the east. The living is consolidated with the rectory of Wollaston.

ALVINGTON, a hamlet, in the parish of Brimpton, union of Yeovil, hundred of Stone, W. division of Somerset; containing 65 inhabitants.

ALVINGTON, WEST (All Saints), a parish, in the union of Kingsbridge, hundred of Stanborough, Stanborough and Coleridge, and S. divisions of Devon, 1 mile (W. S. W.) from Kingsbridge; containing 998 inhabitants. It comprises 3676 acres; the surface is very hilly, the soil chiefly arable, and a large quantity of peculiarly fine cider is made. The living is a vicarage, with the perpetual curacies of South Huish, Malborough, and South Milton annexed, valued in the king's books at £62. 16. 10½.; net income, £685; patrons and ap-propriators, the Dean and Chapter of Salisbury. The glebe comprises 2 acres here, and 1½ in each of the parishes of Malborough and South Milton. The church contains some good screen-work in carved oak, and a beautiful monument to a member of the Bastard family, whose ancient seat has been converted into a farm-house.

ALWALTON (St. Andrew), a parish, in the union of Peterborough, hundred of Normancross, county of Huntingdon, 5 miles (N. N. W.) from Stilton; con-taining 329 inhabitants. The parish is situated on the river Nene, which here separates the counties of Hunt-ingdon and Northampton, and on the great north road, near its intersection with the road from Lynn to North-ampton; it comprises 910a. 3r. 38p., of which the soil is fertile, and the surface beautifully varied. On the banks of the Nene are found great blocks of grey fossil stone, susceptible of a very high polish. The living is a rectory, valued in the king's books at £3. 5. 10., and in the gift of the Dean and Chapter of Peterborough: the tithes were commuted for 197 acres of land and a money payment, under an inclosure act, in 1805. The church exhibits in the body of the building a singular combination of Norman and early English architecture : it has been new roofed in appropriate style, and the chancel restored to its pristine elegance by the rector, who has also built a handsome parsonage-house. There is a place of worship for Wesleyans. Dr. Timothy Neve, archdeacon of Huntingdon, was buried here in 1757.

ALWINGTON (*St. Andrew*), a parish, in the union of Bideford, hundred of Shebbear, Great Torrington and N. divisions of Devon, 4 miles (S. W. by W.) from Bideford ; containing, with the hamlets of Fairy Cross, Ford, and Woodtown, 392 inhabitants ; and comprising by measurement 2603 acres. The living is a rectory, valued in the king's books at £17. 4. 9½., and in the gift of the Rev. I. T. Pine Coffin : the tithes have been commuted for £241, and there are 60 acres of glebe. In the church, over the door of the chancel, is a curious ancient monument to a member of the Coffin family. In Yeo Vale, so called from the river Yeo, which runs through it, are the remains of a chapel. There is a parochial school ; also a place of worship for Wesleyans ; and almshouses for three poor persons.

ALWOODLEY, a township, in the parish of Harewood, Upper division of the wapentake of Skyrack, W. riding of York, 5½ miles (N.) from Leeds ; containing 281 inhabitants. It comprises by computation 1250 acres, chiefly the property of G. L. Fox, Esq. ; the ancient Hall, the seat of Sir Gervase Clifton, who died in 1666, is now a farmhouse. The soil is fertile, and the lands are generally in good cultivation ; the surface is undulated.

AMBERLEY, county of Gloucester.—See Hampton, Minchin.

AMBERLEY, a chapelry, in the parish of Marden, hundred of Broxash, union and county of Hereford, 5¾ miles (N. N. E.) from Hereford ; containing 32 inhabitants, and comprising 378 acres.

AMBERLEY, a parish, in the hundred of West Easwrith, rape of Arundel, W. division of Sussex, 5 miles (N. N. E.) from Arundel ; containing, with Rackham hamlet, 722 inhabitants. The bishops of Chichester had a residence here, erected at the close of the fourteenth century by Bishop Rede, and which is said to have been plundered and dismantled in the parliamentary war by the army under Waller : the gateway is perfect, and, with other remains, has a bold and striking appearance in the views of the surrounding district. The parish comprises by measurement 2878 acres, and is bounded on the west by the river Arun : the village occupies an elevated situation on a sandstone rock ; and towards the south rises a range of steep downs, above which is a large knoll called Amberley Mount. The living is a vicarage, with that of Houghton united, valued in the king's books at £7. 5. 7½. ; net income, £166 ; patron and appropriator, the Bishop. The tithes have been commuted in 1813 for 117 acres of land in this parish, and 16 in that of Angmering. The church has a nave of Norman, and a chancel of early English, architecture, separated by a Norman arch much enriched.

AMBERSHAM, NORTH, a tything, in the parish of Steep, union of Midhurst, hundred of Easebourne, rape of Chichester, county of Sussex, 2½ miles (E. N. E.) from Midhurst ; containing 189 inhabitants.

AMBERSHAM, SOUTH, a tything, in the parish of Steep, union of Midhurst, hundred of Easebourne,

rape of Chichester, county of Sussex, 2½ miles (E. by N.) from Midhurst ; containing 189 inhabitants.

AMBLE, a township, in the parish of Warkworth, union of Alnwick, E. division of Coquetdale ward, N. division of Northumberland, 9 miles (S. E.) from Alnwick ; containing 724 inhabitants. The village is pleasantly situated on an eminence near the mouth of the river Coquet, where a harbour has been formed under an act obtained in 1838, by which the value both of the soil and the minerals here has been greatly enhanced. The place was anciently of much greater importance, as is evident from the discovery of circular foundations of houses, of unhewn and uncemented stones of British origin, and of Roman coins : a paved causeway also was discovered a few years since, extending in a direction towards the old bed of the Coquet. There are valuable and extensive mines of coal in the township, the produce of which is exported to France and other parts. The tithes have been commuted for £170. 19. 6. payable to the Bishop of Carlisle, and £46. 8. 10. to the vicar of the parish.—See Warkworth.

AMBLECOAT, a hamlet, in the parish of Old Swinford, union of Stourbridge, S. division of the hundred of Seisdon and of the county of Stafford, ½ a mile (N.) from Stourbridge ; containing 1623 inhabitants. It is situated on the north side of the small river Stour, and comprises about 600 acres, whereof the surface is undulated. There are fire-clay pits, clayworks, glass-houses, and iron-works, of which last those of James Foster, Esq., of Stourton Castle, are among the largest in the kingdom. The Wolverhampton and Stourbridge road passes through the hamlet. The tithes have been commuted for £220. A district church, erected at a cost of £4300, chiefly raised by subscription, was opened for divine service on 7th August 1842 ; it is built of fire-brick : the living has been endowed by the Earl of Stamford, and is in his gift. There are places of worship for Wesleyans, and Methodists of the New Connexion ; also a national school on the Madras system, with about 350 children ; a Church Sunday school, of 300 children more ; and two small dissenting schools.

AMBLESIDE, a market-town and parochial chapelry, partly in the parish of Windermere, but chiefly in that of Grasmere, Kendal ward and union, county of Westmorland, 25 miles (W. S. W.) from Appleby, and 274 (N. W. by N.) from London ; containing 1281 inhabitants. The name, anciently written *Hamelside*, probably derived from the Saxon *Hamol*, signifying a sheltered habitation. The town is situated near the site of a Roman station of considerable extent, supposed by Horsley to have been the *Dictis* of the *Notitia* ; the earth-works of the fortress remain, and various Roman relics and foundations of buildings have been discovered. It stands on the acclivity of a steep eminence, near the northern extremity of the lake Windermere, in a district pre-eminently distinguished for the beauty of its scenery ; and consists chiefly of one street, lighted with naphtha, but not paved : the houses, though detached and irregular, are well built. Tourists frequently make this their head-quarters, as many delightful excursions may be taken hence, to view the sublimely romantic and richly varied scenery of the lake district. The river Rothay flows in the vicinity, and at the upper extremity of the town is a beautiful waterfall called Stockgill

Force. There were until lately a few manufactories for linsey-woolsey, but they have been relinquished; a bobbin-mill only, is at present carried on. Stone and slate are quarried; and a peculiar kind of marble, of a dusky green colour, veined with white, is found. The market, granted in 1650 to the celebrated Countess of Pembroke, is on Wednesday and Saturday; and fairs are held on Whit-Wednesday and the 13th and 29th of October, to which a court of pie-poudre is attached : the market-house was built about the year 1796, on the site of the former.

The inhabitants received a charter in the reign of James II., under the authority of which they elect a mayor annually on Christmas-eve; but he does not possess magisterial authority, the town being entirely within the jurisdiction of the county justices, who hold a petty-session every fortnight. The powers of the county debt-court of Ambleside, established in 1847, extend over the sub-registration-districts of Ambleside and Hawkshead. The township comprises 1583 acres, whereof about 800 are common or waste; the soil is of a sandy quality. The living is a perpetual curacy, with a net income of £80; it is in the patronage of Lady Fleming, and the impropriation belongs to Sir R. Fleming, Bart. A rent-charge of £27, of which £14 are payable by Ambleside below Stock, and £13 by Ambleside above Stock, has been awarded to the rector of Windermere, as a commutation in lieu of tithes. The chapel, situated in that part of the town which is in the parish of Grasmere, was made parochial by the Bishop of Chester in 1675, and was rebuilt in 1812 ; it is a plain edifice. The Independents have a place of worship. The free grammar school was founded and endowed by John Kelsick, in 1721 ; the annual income exceeds £150. Bernard Gilpin, surnamed "The Northern Apostle," was born at Kentmere, and Judge Wilson at Troutbeck, near the town. The residence of Dove's Nest, on the road to Bowness, was for some time occupied by Mrs. Hemans; and Fox-How, to the west of the town, was the residence of the late Dr. Arnold.

AMBROSDEN (St. Mary), a parish, in the union of Bicester, hundred of Bullington, county of Oxford, 2½ miles (S. E. by S.) from Bicester; comprising the chapelries of Arncott and Blackthorn, and containing 892 inhabitants, of whom 181 are in the hamlet of Ambrosden. This place is supposed by Bishop Kennet, who was formerly incumbent of the parish, to have derived its name from Ambrosius Aurelius, the celebrated British chief, who encamped here during the siege of Alchester by the Saxons. The living is a discharged vicarage, valued in the king's books at £11. 17.; net income, £228 ; patron, Sir G. O. P. Turner, Bart. ; appropriator, the Bishop of Oxford. The tithes were commuted for land, under an inclosure act, in 1814. The church is stated to have been built in the latter part of the reign of Edward I., on the site of the original Saxon, or Norman, edifice, whose northern entrance still remains ; it is in the early English style, with an embattled tower, on the east and west fronts of which are some curious devices in plaster, and among the rest one of the paschal lamb.

AMCOTTS, a chapelry, in the parish of Althorp, union of Thorne, W. division of the wapentake of Manley, parts of Lindsey, county of Lincoln, 11¼ miles (E. S. E.) from Glandford-Brigg; containing 417

54

inhabitants. The chapel is dedicated to St. Thomas à Becket. The tithes were partially commuted for land, under an inclosure act, in 1779; and the impropriate tithes have been recently commuted for £5. There is a place of worship for Wesleyans.

AMERSHAM, or Agmondesham (St. Mary), a market-town and parish, and the head of a union, in the hundred of Burnham, county of Buckingham, 33 miles (S. E. by S.) from Buckingham, and 25¾ (W. N. W.) from London ; containing 3645 inhabitants. The town is situated in a pleasant valley, through which flows the Misburne, a stream falling into the Colne near Uxbridge ; it is surrounded by wood-crowned hills, and consists principally of one street, well paved : there is a plentiful supply of water. In the reign of Henry V. several of the inhabitants were burnt at the stake for professing the tenets of the Lollards ; and in that of Mary, many of them suffered a similar fate : a spot of ground, occupying a circle of about 24 feet, is pointed out on the east side of the town as the place on which they suffered, and on which, it was supposed, no vegetation could be matured ; but, in 1842, the ground was opened by means of a subscription fund, and found to contain nothing but flints, which served as a sort of drainage, and impeded culture. A manufactory for silk crape has been some time established, and many females are employed in the making of lace and straw-plat; wooden chairs are also made for exportation. The market is on Tuesday ; and fairs are held on Whit-Monday and Sept. 19th. The town was a borough by prescription, and sent burgesses to parliament from the 28th of Edward I. to the 2nd of Edward II., but made no subsequent return until the 21st of James I., from which time it continued to send two members till it was disfranchised by the act of the 2nd of William IV. cap. 45. A constable and other officers are appointed at the court leet of the lord of the manor. The town-hall, situated in the centre of the town, is a handsome brick edifice resting on piazzas, erected by Sir Wm. Drake : the lower part is appropriated to the market ; the upper, which is surmounted by a lantern turret, is used for transacting public business.

The parish contains by measurement 7855 acres of land, in general hilly, and resting upon a sub-soil of chalk, flint, and clay : the hamlet of Coleshill is included in it. The Living is a rectory, valued in the king's books at £48. 16. 1½., and in the gift of Thos. Tyrwhitt Drake, Esq. : the tithes have been commuted for £1500, and there are about 123 acres of glebe. The church is a spacious edifice of brick coated with stucco ; the chancel and an adjoining mausoleum contain several interesting monuments, exhibiting some beautiful specimens of sculpture, by the hand of Bacon. There are two places of worship for Baptists, and one for the Society of Friends. A free grammar school was instituted by Dr. Robert Chaloner, canon of Windsor, who, by his will dated June 20th, 1620, endowed it with £20 per annum, since augmented to more than £80 ; and in an apartment adjoining the grammar schoolroom is a writing-school, established in 1699, by Lord Cheyne, and endowed with a rent-charge of £20. An almshouse for six aged widows was founded by Sir Wm. Drake, Bart., and endowed by him in 1667 : the income, arising from land and property in the funds, was augmented with a bequest of £300 by Wm. Drake, jun., in

1796, and now amounts to about £150. A fund of £87 per annum, arising from land and the three per cents., is applied, under the will of William Tothill, of Shardeloes, in apprenticing children. The union of Amersham comprises 10 parishes or places, and contains a population of 18,207 : the workhouse is a good building in the Elizabethan style of architecture, erected at, a cost of nearly £7000 ; it stands on the road to Wycombe, and will accommodate 350 paupers.

AMERTON, a township, in the parish and union of STOWE, S. division of the hundred of PIREHILL, N. division of STAFFORDSHIRE, ¾ of a mile (N. W.) from Stowe; containing 120 inhabitants. It lies on the road from Stafford to Uttoxeter, and has a small village or hamlet, chiefly inhabited by persons engaged in agriculture.

AMESBURY (ST. MARY AND ST. MELORIUS), a town and parish, and the head of a union, in the hundred of AMESBURY, S. division of WILTS, 7 miles (N.) from Salisbury, and 78 (W. S. W.) from London ; containing 1171 inhabitants. This place was anciently called Ambresbury, and that name is probably derived, not from Aurelius Ambrosius, as hitherto generally supposed, but from the combined appellations of Stonehenge and an ancient camp, both situate in the parish and near the town ; viz. Ambres, holy or anointed stones, and burg, or bury, a camp ; " the holy stones near the camp." A monastery for 300 monks is stated to have been founded here by Ambruis, a British monk, or, more probably, by Ambrosius ; it was destroyed by Gurthurm, or Gurmundus, a Saxon chief. After the conversion of the Saxons to Christianity, a synod was held at Amesbury, in the reign of King Edgar, to adjust the differences that existed between the regular and the secular clergy, which had been previously discussed in an assembly held at Calne. About 980, Elfrida, widow of the same king, founded here a nunnery of the Benedietine order, which she dedicated to St. Mary and to St. Melorius, a Cornish saint, in expiation, it is supposed, of the murder of Edward, her step-son, at Corfe Castle. In 1177, the abbess and nuns were expelled, on the ground of incontinence ; and Henry II. made it a cell to the foreign abbey of Fontevrault. Queen Eleanor, widow of Henry III., assumed the veil in this convent, where she died in 1291. It was at length made denizen ; and at the Dissolution its revenue was £558. 10. 2.

The manor and principal estates of Amesbury originally appertained to the abbey, and at the Reformation were granted to the Lord Protector Somerset, from whose family they were carried by the marriage of a female descendant into the family of Bruce, subsequently earls of Amesbury. They afterwards passed by sale to Lord Carlton, who left them by will to the Duke of Queensberry, husband to the celebrated duchess; and on the death of the last duke, they descended by entail to Lord Douglas of Bothwell Castle, by whom they were sold to Sir Edmund Antrobus, at whose decease they passed to his nephew, the present baronet. A mansion was built by the Somerset family nearly on the site of the ancient abbey ; it has been taken down by Sir Edmund Antrobus, who is replacing it by an extensive and elegant edifice, judiciously preserving the magnificent saloon of the former building. The town is situated in a valley on the banks of the Avon, and consists of two streets ; it is neither paved nor lighted, but is well supplied with water. The market, which was on Friday, has been discontinued : fairs are held on May 17th, June 21st, and December 21st.

The parish comprises 5600 acres ; the surface is undulated, and the soil a gravelly loam upon a chalky subsoil. The LIVING is a perpetual curacy, in the gift of the Dean and Canons of Windsor, with a net income of £141 : about 5 acres of land in the parish of Hungerford, purchased by Queen Anne's Bounty, belong to it. The church, originally of Norman architecture, has recently undergone a thorough repair ; it is warmed by two very handsome stoves, which cost £189, and were presented by Sir Edmund Antrobus. There is a place of worship for Wesleyans. In 1677, John Rose bequeathed property for the establishment of a superior and a secondary school, the former for boys, and the latter for boys and girls : the endowment consists of a farm in the parish of Ditchett, county of Somerset, comprising 52½ acres, and of a messuage and garden at Amesbury in the rent-free occupation of the master. Here is also a school founded under the will of Mr. Henry Spratt, in 1708, and endowed with land now let for £50 per annum; other schools are supported by subscription. The poor law union of Amesbury comprises 23 parishes or places, and contains a population of 7698. To the west of the river is an ancient encampment with a vallum and deep fosse, occupying an area of forty acres, commonly attributed to Vespasian, but undoubtedly of British origin : the road from Amesbury to Warminster is cut through its rampart. The poet Gay passed much of his time at Amesbury, under the roof of his generous patrons, the Duke and Duchess of Queensberry.

AMINGTON, with STONY-DELPH, a township, in the parish and union of TAMWORTH, Tamworth division of the hundred of HEMLINGFORD, N. division of the county of WARWICK, 2¾ miles (E.) from Tamworth ; containing 276 inhabitants, and comprising 2191 acres. This place is intersected by the river Anker, the Coventry canal, and the road from Tamworth to Ashby-de-la-Zouch. It was the property of the late C. E. Repington, Esq., for the benefit of whose widow it is now vested in the hands of trustees ; on her death it will devolve to Captain E. H. A'Court, R.N.

AMOTHERBY, a chapelry, in the parish of APPLETON-LE-STREET, union of MALTON, wapentake of RYEDALE, N. riding of YORK, 3 miles (N. W. by W.) from Malton ; containing 239 inhabitants. This chapelry, which is bounded on the north by the river Rye. is situated on the road from Malton to Kirkby-Moorside. The surface is undulated, and the scenery highly picturesque ; the soil in the upland parts is rich, and in the valleys inferior ; limestone of fine quality is extensively quarried. The tithes were commuted for land and a money payment, in 1776. There is a chapel of ease, and a school is endowed with 20 acres of land.

AMPHIELD, a hamlet, in the parish and union of HURSLEY, hundred of BUDDLESGATE, Fawley and N. divisions of the county of SOUTHAMPTON, 4 miles (S. S. W.) from Romsey. This pleasant village is situated on the high road to Winchester, and is inhabited by a considerable rural population. A district church has been erected, chiefly at the expense of William Heathcote, Esq.; it is dedicated to St. Mark, and the incumbency is in the gift of the Vicar.

AMPLEFORTH (St. Hilda), a parish, in the union of Helmsley, partly in the wapentake of Birdforth, and partly in that of Ryedale, N. riding of York; containing 446 inhabitants, of whom 207 are in the township of Ampleforth, 4½ miles (S. W. by S.) from Helmsley. This parish, anciently Ampleford, comprises by measurement 2270 acres. The village, which is long, and pleasantly situated, extends into the three hamlets of Ampleforth St. Peter, Ampleforth-Birdforth, and Oswaldkirk-Quarter; it lies at the base of the hill which runs up to Hamilton, and on the south commands a beautiful view of the valley of De Mobray, embracing on the south-east Gilling Castle, and on the south-west Newborough Park, which give to the vicinity a rich and diversified appearance. The living is a discharged vicarage, valued in the king's books at £4. 6. 5½.; net income, £261; patron, the Archbishop of York. By an inclosure act in 1806, 199 acres were allotted in lieu of the vicarial tithes of the parish, and óf all tithes for the township of Ampleforth. The church is an ancient structure, with a Norman doorway beautifully carved and flowered. There is a place of worship for Wesleyans. At Oswaldkirk-Quarter is Ampleforth College, a Roman Catholic establishment, founded in 1802 by the members of the College of Dieulouard, near Pont à Mousson, in Lorraine, whose property was confiscated in the French revolution; the students, about fifty in number, are instructed in the ancient and modern languages, mathematics, &c. The establishment has been several times enlarged; it is situated in the midst of extensive pleasure-grounds, and commands some beautiful views of the surrounding country. Half a mile north of the village are the remains of a Roman camp; near which was discovered in March 1808, by the Rev. Robert Nixon, a barrow formed by a large circle of stones about ten feet in diameter, in which an urn and several ancient coins were found.

AMPNEY, or Ashbrook (St. Mary the Virgin), a parish, in the union of Cirencester, hundred of Crowthorne and Minety, E. division of the county of Gloucester, 3½ miles (E.) from Cirencester; containing 121 inhabitants. It is situated on the southern side of the road from Fairford to Cirencester; and has good quarries of limestone for building. The living is a perpetual curacy: net income, £72, derived from 57 acres of land; patron and impropriator, Col. Beach. The church stands at a distance from the village, and is a small structure.

AMPNEY, or Easington (St. Peter), a parish, in the union of Cirencester, hundred of Crowthorne and Minety, E. division of the county of Gloucester, 4¼ miles (E. by S.) from Cirencester; containing 196 inhabitants. This parish, which is situated on the London road, is of small extent, comprising by measurement only 533 acres: quarries of stone are slightly worked for mending the roads, and for fences; and some tiles are made here. The living is a perpetual curacy; net income, £90; patron, the Bishop of Gloucester and Bristol; appropriators, the Dean and Chapter of Gloucester. On Rambury farm are the remains of a Roman camp, called Rambury Ring.

AMPNEY-CRUCIS (The Holy Rood), a parish, in the union of Cirencester, hundred of Crowthorne and Minety, E. division of the county of Gloucester, 3½ miles (E.) from Cirencester; containing, with the

hamlet of Hilcot-End, 591 inhabitants. It comprises by measurement 3088 acres. The soil is various, in some parts of very inferior quality, and in others tolerably fertile; stone suitable for repairing the roads is quarried. The living is a discharged vicarage, valued in the king's books at £6. 9. 0½., and in the patronage of the Crown; net income, £84; impropriator, G. G. Blackwell, Esq. The church has an embattled tower, and some portions of ancient architecture, among which is a handsome Norman arch dividing the nave from the chancel. Here is a charity school, endowed in 1719, by Robert Pleydell, Esq., with a rent-charge of £80.

AMPNEY, DOWN (All Saints), a parish, in the union of Cirencester, chiefly in the hundred of Crowthorne and Minety, E. division of the county of Gloucester, 4 miles (S. W. by W.) from Fairford; containing 425 inhabitants. A portion of this parish lies in the northern division of the adjoining county of Wilts, and in the hundred of Highworth. The manor-house, a very interesting specimen of ancient architecture, was formerly one of the many seats of the Hungerford family, and is situated precisely on the border line of the two shires. The living is a discharged vicarage, valued in the king's books at £10. 5. 8.; net income, £116; patrons and appropriators, the Dean and Canons of Christ-Church, Oxford. The church was built about the year 1260, by the Knights Templars, to whom Edward I. had granted the living; it is chiefly in the early English style, with a tower surmounted by a spire.

AMPORT (St. Mary), a parish, in the union of Ludgershall, hundred of Andover, Andover and N. divisions of the county of Southampton, 4¼ miles (W. by S.) from Andover; containing, with the tythings of East Cholderton and Sarson, 771 inhabitants, and comprising 3594 acres. The living is a vicarage endowed with the rectorial tithes, with the living of Appleshaw annexed, and valued in the king's books at £25. 7. 11.; patrons, the Dean and Chapter of Chichester. The tithes of Amport have been commuted for £830, and there are 70 acres of glebe. Pursuant to the will of the Rev. Thomas Sheppard, D.D., dated in 1812, a school, and an almhouse consisting of six tenements, were built here by his widow, who vested in trustees the sum of £9000 for the maintenance of six widows, for a schoolmistress's salary, medical attendance, and the repair of the buildings.

AMPTHILL (St. Andrew), a market-town and parish, and the head of a union, in the hundred of Redbornestoke, county of Bedford, 7 miles (S. by W.) from Bedford, and 45 (N. W. by N.) from London; comprising by computation 1882 acres, and containing 201 inhabitants. In the reign of Henry VI., Sir John Cornwall, created Lord Fanhope, built a castle on the manor of Ampthill, which, about the year 1530, came into the possession of the crown, and was made the head of an honour by act of parliament. Catherine of Arragon, while the business of her divorce was pending, resided here, where she received the summons to attend the commissioners at Dunstable, which she refused to obey; and in memory of this, the Earl of Ossory, in 1770, erected on the site of the castle a handsome column, with an appropriate inscription by Horace Walpole, Earl of Orford. The modern seat of Ampthill is chiefly remarkable for the number of very ancient oaks which ornament the park. The TOWN, pleasantly situated between two hills, is irregularly built, paved with pebbles, and amply supplied with water; it has been of late considerably improved by the removal of old buildings, and the erection of a good market-house. The Bedford branch of the London and Birmingham railway passes on the north-west. The market is on Thursday; fairs take place on the 4th of May and 30th of November, for cattle. The county magistrates hold petty-sessions for the hundred at this town; and a court for the honour is held in the moot-house, an ancient building, under the lord high steward, by whom constables and other officers are appointed. The county debt-court of Ampthill, established in 1847, has jurisdiction over the registration-district of Ampthill.

The LIVING is a discharged rectory, valued in the king's books at £10. 6. 8., and in the gift of the Crown, with a net income of £330: the tithes were commuted for land and corn-rents, under an inclosure act, in 1806. The church is a handsome cruciform structure, in the decorated and later English styles, with a square embattled tower rising from the centre. There are places of worship for Independents, the Society of Friends, and Wesleyans. A school was endowed by Mrs. Sarah Emery, in 1691, with lands producing £30 per annum, half of which is given to the parish of Meppershall. There is also a feoffee charity of about £100 per annum, derived from land and houses, for the benefit of the necessitous and industrious poor; and about a quarter of a mile from the town an hospital, founded by John Cross, in 1690, which affords a comfortable asylum for nine men and four women, who each receive about £20 per year, with bedding, coal, &c. The union of Ampthill comprises 19 parishes or places, and contains a population of 15,681.

AMPTON (ST. PETER), a parish, in the union of THINGOE, hundred of THEDWESTRY, W. division of SUFFOLK, 5¼ miles (N. by E.) from Bury St. Edmund's; containing 147 inhabitants. In this parish, which comprises 736a. 3r. 4p., is the seat of Lord Calthorpe, scarcely surpassed for beauty of situation by any mansion or grounds in Suffolk. The living is a discharged rectory, valued in the king's books at £5. 2. 1., and in the gift of his lordship: the tithes have been commuted for £120, and the glebe consists of 20 acres. Calthorpe's school, adjoining the churchyard, was founded and endowed in 1705, by James Calthorpe, Esq., and has property in land consisting of about 430 acres, and yielding a rental of £384; in addition to which, Henry Edwards in 1715 bequeathed £100, with which, and other accumulations, £1017 three per cent. consols were purchased, paying a dividend of £30. On Ampton green is an almshouse for four unmarried women, founded under the will of Mrs. Dorothy Calthorpe dated 1693, and endowed with £700 Old South Sea Annuities.

AMWELL, GREAT (ST. JOHN THE BAPTIST), a parish, in the union of WARE, hundred and county of HERTFORD, 1¼ mile (S. E. by S.) from Ware; containing 1545 inhabitants. The parish contains 2443a. 1r. 12p., of which 268 acres are common or waste. It is situated between the river Lea and the road from Cambridge to London; and is supposed to take its name from "Emma's Well," which is now absorbed by the New River. The village of Amwell, particularly that part of it adjacent to the church, is one of the most

beautiful in the county; and within the limits of the parish is situated the East India College, founded in 1806, for the education of youths intended for the civil service of the company, and which contains accommodation for 105 students. A pleasure fair is held on Whit-Monday. The living is a discharged vicarage, valued in the king's books at £6; patrons, the Rev. Mordaunt Barnard and others; impropriator, E. F. Whittingstall. Esq. The great tithes have been commuted for £418. 11. 6., and the vicarial for £232; the glebe consists of 35 acres, with a house in a fine situation, built in 1840. The chancel of the church is separated from the nave by three very ancient arches, supposed to be Saxon. Hoddesdon chapel, a handsome brick edifice, is in the parish; and among the schools is a national school for girls, endowed about 1820 by Mrs. E. Jones with £40 per annum. The remains of a Roman encampment are visible between the church and the vicarage-house. Amwell has been the residence of some celebrated literary characters, among whom may be named Izaak Walton, the noted angler; Mr. Scott, author of several poems and tracts; and Hoole, the distinguished translator of Tasso, and biographer of Mr. Scott. The remains of Warner, the historian, were interred in the churchyard.

AMWELL, LITTLE, a liberty, in the parish of ALL SAINTS, HERTFORD, union, hundred, and county of HERTFORD, 1¼ mile (S. E. by S.) from Ware; containing 461 inhabitants. Here is a chapel of ease to the vicarage of All Saints. The New River, which supplies the metropolis with water, has its source in a spring that rises in this liberty, called Emma's Well.

ANCASTER (ST. MARTIN), a parish, in the union of GRANTHAM, wapentake of LOVEDEN, parts of KESTEVEN, county of LINCOLN, 6¾ miles (N. E.) from Grantham, on the road to Sleaford; containing, with the hamlets of West Willoughby and Sudbrook, 530 inhabitants. This place occupies the site of a Roman station, which Horsley conjectures to have been Causennæ, but the name of which has not been satisfactorily ascertained: it was formerly of much greater extent than it is at present, and various coins, foundations of buildings, vaults, and other relics of the Romans, have been discovered. During the civil war of the seventeenth century, the parliamentarian forces were defeated here by the royalists, under the command of Col. Cavendish. The parish comprises about 3000 acres, of which 2780 are arable, 200 pasture, and 14 woodland; the soil is light, and the surface well wooded. The celebrated "Ancaster" quarries (which are really in the adjoining parish of Wilsford) yield beautiful building-stone. The living is a discharged vicarage, valued in the king's books at £6. 13. 4., and in the patronage and incumbency of the Rev. Mr. Warren; net income, £151, arising from 120 acres of glebe. The church is an ancient and handsome building, with a tower surmounted by a tall slender spire; the arches on the north side of the nave are Norman, and those on the south of early English architecture; the font is singularly elegant. There is a place of worship for Wesleyan Methodists. Ancaster formerly gave the title of Duke to the family of Bertie.

ANCROFT, a parochial chapelry, in the union of BERWICK-UPON-TWEED, ISLANDSHIRE, N. division of NORTHUMBERLAND, 6 miles (S.) of Berwick; containing 1670 inhabitants, of whom 491 are in the township.

I

It includes the villages of Ancroft, Cheswick, Haggerston, Scremerston, and Greenses, the first of which appears, from the numerous foundations of houses that have been discovered in the adjoining fields, to have been formerly of much greater extent than it is at present. The chapelry comprises 9622 acres, mostly arable, and is rich in mineral produce. Limestone is very abundant, and is quarried to a great extent for the supply of the neighbouring districts; freestone and coal are likewise wrought in considerable quantities. The great road from London to Edinburgh passes through. The scenery is finely diversified, and enlivened with some handsome seats, among which is Ladythorn, in the village of Cheswick, occupying an elevated situation, and commanding a view of Holy Island, the Farn Islands, the coast from Bambrough Castle to Berwick, and the Cheviot hills in the distance. The living is a perpetual curacy; net income, £131; patrons and appropriators, the Dean and Chapter of Durham. The church, a Norman structure, originally a chapel of ease to Holy Island, but now parochial, was enlarged in 1836, at an expense of £550, raised. by subscription: the tower was so constructed that it served as a place of residence for the curate, and afforded him a protection from the Scottish marauders; it was until lately roofless, and an ash-tree, which had its root in the vaulted floor of the first story, spread over its battlements. There is a second incumbency at Scremerston.—See SCREMERSTON and HAGGERSTON.

ANDERBY (St. Andrew), a parish, in the union of SPILSBY, Marsh division of the hundred of CALCEWORTH, parts of LINDSEY, county of LINCOLN, 4½ miles (E. by S.) from Alford; containing 243 inhabitants. The parish comprises 1200 acres by computation, and extends to the coast of the North Sea, which bounds it on the east; the village is scattered, and is in the manor of Bilsby, a neighbouring parish. The living is a discharged rectory, with that of Cumberworth united, valued in the king's books at £13. 10. 2½.; net income, £548; patrons, the President and Fellows of Magdalene College, Cambridge. On the inclosure of the parish, a fixed money payment of £65. 7., and 8 acres of land, were assigned to the rector, in lieu of tithes for the portion inclosed. The church is a plain edifice. There is a place of worship for Wesleyan Methodists.

ANDERSTON, or ANDERSON (St. Michael), a parish, in the union of BLANDFORD, hundred of COOMBSDITCH, Blandford division of DORSET, 6 miles (S.) from the town of Blandford; containing 43 inhabitants. This parish, which is situated on the river Winterbourne (here a comparatively insignificant stream), comprises by measurement 566 acres, of which 414 are arable, and 152 meadow and pasture. The living is a rectory, valued in the king's books at £6. 19. 1., and in the gift of S. B. Tregonwell, Esq.: the tithes have been commuted for £120, and there are four acres of glebe. The church is an ancient edifice, and the place of sepulture of the Tregonwells, whose former manor-house, a spacious building in the Elizabethan style, and in which is a chamber hung with decayed tapestry, is now the union workhouse.

ANDERTON, a township, in the parish of GREAT BUDWORTH, union of NORTHWICH, hundred of BUCKLOW, N. division of the county of CHESTER, 1¾ mile (N. W. by N.) from Northwich; containing 331 inhabitants. The manor was held at an early period by the

58

family of Lostock, from whom Urian de St. Pierre, who died seised of it in 1286, had obtained it by gift. It afterwards passed to the Cokeseys, Grevilles, and Suttons, and in 1600 was purchased of the last-named family by Sir Peter Warburton, whose daughter and heiress brought it in marriage to the Stanleys, of Alderley. The township comprises 495 acres; the soil is partly clay and partly sand. It is intersected by the river Weaver, on the northern bank of which there is an almost uninterrupted line of salt-works: the Grand Trunk canal also passes through.

ANDERTON, a township, in the district chapelry of ADLINGTON, parish of STANDISH, union of CHORLEY, hundred of LEYLAND, N. division of the county of LANCASTER, 4¾ miles (S. E. by S.) from Chorley, on the road from that town to Bolton; containing 339 inhabitants. This place gave name to a family which was seated here at an early period; it comprises about 800 acres, and has coal-mines, and good stone-quarries. The tithes have been commuted for £157.

Seal and Arms.

ANDOVER (St. Mary), a borough, market-town, and parish, having exclusive jurisdiction, and the head of a union, locally in the hundred of ANDOVER, Andover and N. divisions of the county of SOUTHAMPTON, 26 miles (N. by W.) from Southampton, and 64 (W. S. W.) from London; comprising the hamlets of Charlton, Hatherden, King's Enham, Little London, Smannell, Wildhern, and Woodhouse, and the chapelry of Foxcote; and containing 5013 inhabitants. Andover, or, according to the charter, seal, and official documents, Andever, is a corruption of the Saxon Andeafara, which signifies the passage of the Ande, denoting the proximity of the town to the small river Ande or Anton. In the church at this place, Anlaf, King of Norway, in 994 received the sacrament of confirmation, under the sponsorship of King Ethelred, promising that he would never. more come in a hostile manner to England, which engagement he religiously observed.

The TOWN, which is situated on the border of the Wiltshire downs, and near the edge of an extensive woodland tract forming the north-west portion of the county, is neat, airy, and well built; it consists principally of three long streets, is well paved under an act obtained in 1815, lighted with gas supplied by a company lately formed among the inhabitants, and plentifully supplied with water. The manufacture of silk has, of late, entirely superseded that of shalloons, which was formerly carried on to a great extent; and the construction of a canal from the town, through Stockbridge, to Southampton Water, has materially improved its trade, particularly in corn, malt, and timber, of which last a vast quantity is forwarded from Harewood Forest, for the supply of Portsmouth dockyard. In 1846 an act was passed for the construction of a railway from Basingstoke, by Andover, to Salisbury. The principal market is on Saturday, and there is a smaller one on Wednesday: the fairs are on Mid-Lent Saturday and Old May-day, for horses, cattle, cheese, and leather; on the 16th of November for sheep; and on the following day for horses, hops, cheese, &c. Three miles west of Andover, and within the out-hundred belonging to the town, is Weyhill, where an annual fair is held, which, originating in a revel anciently kept on the Sunday before Michaelmas-day, has gradually become the largest and best attended fair in England. It takes place on October 10th and six following days, by charter of Queen Elizabeth, confirmed by Charles II. The first day is noted for the sale of sheep, of which the number sold has frequently exceeded 170,000; on the second day farmers hire their servants; after which, hops, cheese, horses (particularly cart colts), cloth, &c., are exposed for sale. An additional fair, principally for sheep, was instituted in 1829, and is held on the 1st of August.

The inhabitants appear to have received charters of INCORPORATION from Henry II. and Richard I., but the oldest now in their possession is one bestowed in the 6th of King John's reign : several others were subsequently granted, and that under which the borough was until recently governed, is dated in the 41st of Elizabeth. By the act of the 5th and 6th of Wm. IV. c. 76, the government is now vested in a mayor, four aldermen, and twelve councillors, assisted by a recorder, town-clerk, and other officers : the municipal boundaries are co-extensive with those of the parish, which is about twenty-two miles in circumference, and include the parish of Knights-Enham, locally in Andover parish. The borough sent representatives to all the parliaments of Edward I., but made no return after the first of Edward II. till the 27th of Elizabeth, since which period it has continued to send two members : the right of election was formerly vested in the bailiff and corporation, in number about twenty-four, but was extended by the act of the 2nd of William IV., cap. 45, to the £10 householders; the mayor is the returning officer. Courts of session are held quarterly; courts leet occur at Easter and Michaelmas; and the county magistrates hold a petty-session every Monday for the neighbouring district. The powers of the county debt-court of Andover extend over the registration-districts of Andover and Whitchurch. The town-hall was erected in 1825, at an expense of £7000, towards defraying which each of the then members for the borough, Sir J. W. Pollen, Bart., and T. A. Smith, Esq., presented £1000 : it is a handsome and spacious building of stone, surmounted by a cupola; on the ground-floor is the market-house, over which are a council-room for transacting the business of the corporation, and a hall for holding the quarter-sessions.

The LIVING is a vicarage, valued in the king's books at £17. 4. 3½.; net income, £350; patrons and impropriators, the Warden and Fellows of Winchester College. The late church was an ancient building with a Norman doorway at the west end : it having become dilapidated, a new edifice was erected by the late Dr. Goddard, presenting a splendid example of the early English style; the interior is finished in a most chaste and beautiful manner, and the windows of the chancel are filled with coloured glass. There are places of worship for Baptists, the Society of Friends, Independents, and Wesleyans. A grammar school was founded and endowed in 1569, by John Hanson, whose benefaction was subsequently increased by Richard Kemys. In 1719, John Pollen, Esq., one of the representatives of the borough,

erected a school-house, and endowed it with £10 per annum, for twenty children; in 1725, James Sambourne bequeathed £1000 for the instruction of twenty-four children of Hatherden. An hospital for eight poor men was founded by John Pollen, Esq.; and six unendowed almshouses for women were built with funds bequeathed by Catherine Hanson, who also gave an acre of ground planted with trees, to be appropriated as a walk for the recreation of the inhabitants. The union of Andover comprises 28 parishes or places in the county of Hants, and 4 in that of Wilts, and contains a population of 16,990. The Roman road from Winchester to Cirencester passed near Andover, and is yet visible in Harewood coppice; and, besides two or three small encampments near the town, there is a large one, about a mile to the south-west, on. the summit of Bury hill. Some beautiful specimens of Roman pavement have recently been discovered in the neighbourhood. Andover gives the inferior title of Viscount to the Earl of Suffolk.

ANDWELL, an extra-parochial district, in the union and hundred of BASINGSTOKE, Basingstoke and N. divisions of the county of SOUTHAMPTON, 4½ miles (E.) from Basingstoke; containing 26 inhabitants. It comprises about 130 acres of land.

ANGERSLEIGH (ST. MICHAEL), a parish, in the union of TAUNTON, hundred of TAUNTON and TAUNTON-DEAN, W. division of SOMERSET, 4 miles (S. S. W.) from Taunton; containing 42 inhabitants. It comprises by measurement 411 acres, of which the arable and pasture are in nearly equal portions. The living is a discharged rectory, valued in the king's books at £4. 19. 4½., and in the gift of the Rev. Henry Tippets Tucker : the tithes have been commuted for £98, and there are 18 acres of glebe.

ANGERTON, HIGH, a township, in the parish of HARTBURN, union of MORPETH, W. division of MORPETH ward, N. division of NORTHUMBERLAND, 7 miles (W.) from Morpeth; containing 75 inhabitants. This place is noticed in the year 1262 as the residence of the Baroness Theophania, widow of Hugh de Bolbeck, who was sheriff of Northumberland, governor of several castles, and held other offices of importance : from the Bolbecks, both High and Low Angerton went in regular descent to the Howards, with whom they continued until within the last few years. The township extends to the village of Hartburn, and comprises 1197 acres of rich loamy soil, whereof 550 are arable, 571 pasture, and the remainder woodland. The vicar receives £125. 9. for the tithes of this place.

ANGERTON, LOW, a township, in the parish of HARTBURN, union of MORPETH, W. division of MORPETH ward, N. division of NORTHUMBERLAND, 7½ miles (W. by S.) from Morpeth; containing 64 inhabitants. A branch of the Greys, of Howick, resided here in the 17th century, as tenants under the Earl of Carlisle. It comprises 1075 acres, of which 383 are arable, 646 pasture, and 45½ wood : the river Wansbeck runs through, and is bordered by rich pastures. The village stands on a dry ridge of gravelly alluvium, with the Wansbeck on the north, and flat marshy gullies nearly round the other three sides. The tithes have been commuted for £106, payable to the vicar.

ANGLESEY, a newly-erected watering-place, in the parish of ALVERSTOKE, liberty of ALVERSTOKE and GOSPORT, Fareham and S. divisions of the county of

SOUTHAMPTON, 2 miles (W. S. W.) from Gosport. This interesting place occupies an elevated site at a small distance from Stoke's Bay, and nearly opposite to the town of Ryde in the Isle of Wight. The mild temperature of the climate, the beauty and variety of the surrounding scenery, the facilities for sea-bathing, and the goodness of the roads in its vicinity, have united to render it eligible as a watering-place, and it has already obtained a considerable degree of patronage, which is rapidly increasing. The first building erected was Uxbridge House, the seat of Robert Cruickshank, Esq., the founder of the town; the first stone of which was laid in 1826, by the Earl of Uxbridge, for his father, the Marquess of Anglesey, from whom the place derives its name. The buildings consist of a noble terrace and crescent, and are situated within a spacious area inclosed with iron-railing, and tastefully laid out and ornamented with shrubs and flowers : within the inclosure is a fine elevated terrace-walk, commanding a view of the Isle of Wight, Stoke's Bay, the Mother Bank, and St. Helen's, with the shipping passing between Spithead and Portsmouth harbour. A commodious hotel was built in 1830, and being found too small for the accommodation of the increasing number of visiters, a house in the adjoining crescent was subsequently added to it: there are also reading-rooms and public baths, and a chapel of ease. The bay affords good anchorage for vessels; and a communication is kept up with Portsmouth harbour, the dockyard, and the other naval arsenals in the vicinity, by Haslar lake, a branch of the harbour.

ANGLEZARKE, a township, in the chapelry of RIVINGTON, parish of BOLTON, union of CHORLEY, hundred of SALFORD, S. division of the county of LANCASTER, 3 miles (E. S. E.) from Chorley; containing 164 inhabitants. The township comprises 1857 acres; it is mostly mountainous, abounding with game, and is chiefly the property of William Standish Standish, Esq., of Duxbury, who is lord of the manor. At White Coppice is a cotton-mill: several quarries in the township produce a fine hard gritstone, of whitish appearance, in great request for the paving of roads and streets; and grey slate is sometimes obtained in small quantities. The lead-mines here were wrought more than 130 years ago: after being discontinued for some time, they were again opened by Sir Thomas Standish; and about 70 years since, they were wrought a third time, by his son, Sir Francis Standish, who relinquished the works about 1790. In 1823 the Messrs. Thompson, of Wigan, commenced operations anew, but they were unsuccessful, and the works were in consequence abandoned. These mines contain immense quantities of the carbonate of barytes, a mineral whose value was unknown until about the year 1782, when the visit of two Frenchmen to the mines led to the knowledge of its nature and properties: Dr. Withering and Dr. Crawford subsequently drew the attention of all Europe to the newly discovered mineral. The carbonate of barytes found here consists of 22 parts of carbonic acid, and 78 parts of barytes. At Brookhouse Farm, where are powerful springs, was commenced on 7th April, 1847, the construction of works and reservoirs for supplying water to Chorley; and it is proposed to supply the town of Liverpool also with water from this place : the distance to Liverpool is twenty miles, but the great elevation at Anglezarke renders the position chosen most favourable for the purpose.

ANGMERING, EAST and WEST (ST. PETER), a parish, in the union of PRESTON (under Gilbert's act), hundred of POLING, rape of ARUNDEL, W. division of SUSSEX, 5 miles (S. E. by E.) from Arundel; containing 1002 inhabitants. It comprises East and West Angmering and Bargeham, formerly all distinct parishes, which were consolidated in 1573, and now form one parish, containing 4229 acres; 1933 acres are arable, 1895 pasture, and the rest wood. East Angmering had anciently a weekly market, and an annual fair on the 31st of July; but the former has been long discontinued, and the latter has degenerated into a mere pleasure-fair. The living comprises the rectory of West Angmering, with the vicarage of East Angmering consolidated, valued jointly in the king's books at £21. 9. 8.; patrons, the family of Reeks; impropriator of the vicarage, the Rev. J. Usborne. The impropriate tithes have been commuted for £26, the rectorial for £290, and the vicarial for £8. 5. The church is a handsome structure in the later English style, with a square embattled tower, and contains several monumental tablets to the Gratericke family. A school was founded by William Older, who in 1679 endowed it with a cottage and garden, and 30 acres of land at East Angmering, now producing £90 per annum. On the lands of the church farm on the western borders of the parish, a Roman bath was discovered in 1819.

ANGRAM, a township, in the parish of LONG MARSTON, W. division of AINSTY wapentake, W. riding of YORK, 5 miles (N. E. by N.) from Tadcaster; containing 78 inhabitants. The road from York to Wetherby passes at a short distance on the north.

ANGRAM-GRANGE, a township, in the parish of COXWOLD, union of EASINGWOULD, wapentake of BIRDFORTH, N. riding of YORK, 4¾ miles (N.) from Easingwould; comprising 438a. 3r. 24p., and containing 24 inhabitants. The impropriate tithes have been commuted for £106, payable to Trinity College, Cambridge.

ANICK, a township, in the parish of ST. JOHN LEE, union of HEXHAM, S. division of TINDALE ward and of NORTHUMBERLAND, 1¾ mile (N. E. by E.) from Hexham; containing 146 inhabitants. It comprises 360 acres, of which 270 are arable, and 90 meadow and pasture. About 9 acres are on the south side of the Tyne, and the remainder, including an island of 13 acres of grass land, are on its northern bank, gradually and beautifully sloping to the river, which sometimes overflows the grounds in its vicinity; the soil is various, but rendered productive by manure. The Newcastle and Carlisle railway skirts the township on the south. At Hexham Bridge End is a large brewery. The tithes have been commuted for £75. 13. 4. payable to the impropriators, and £28. 6. 8. to the perpetual curate.

ANICK-GRANGE, a township, in the parish of ST. JOHN LEE, union of HEXHAM, S. division of TINDALE ward and of NORTHUMBERLAND, 1½ mile (E. N. E.) from Hexham; containing 40 inhabitants. It formerly belonged to the monastery of Hexham.

ANLABY, a township, partly in the parish of HESSLE, but chiefly in that of KIRK-ELLA, county of the town of HULL, union of SCULCOATES, E. riding of YORK, 3¼ miles (W.) from Hull; containing 423 inhabitants. This place was anciently a possession of a family of the same name, and in 1100 a great part of the estate passed, by intermarriage with its heiress, into the family of Legard.

The township comprises about 2020 acres, including the adjacent hamlets of Wolfreton and Tranby, the former of which, consisting of 355 acres, is partly in the township of Kirk-Ella. There is a place of worship for Wesleyans.

ANMER (St. Mary), a parish, in the union of Docking, hundred of Freebridge-Lynn, W. division of Norfolk, 11 miles (N. E.) from Lynn; containing 175 inhabitants. The parish comprises 1359 acres, of which 184 are common or waste. The living is a discharged rectory, valued in the king's books at £9. 0. 1., and in the gift of H. Coldham, Esq.: the tithes have been commuted for £194, and the glebe consists of 70 acres. The church, which is picturesquely situated in the grounds of the Hall, is chiefly in the decorated and later styles, and consists of a nave and chancel, with a chapel on the south side, and an embattled tower. On opening a tumulus a few years ago in the park, a fine Roman urn, containing bones and ashes, was discovered.

ANN, ABBOT'S.—See Abbot's-Ann.

ANNE (St.), or Briers.—See Owram, South.

ANNESLEY (All Saints), a parish, in the union of Basford, N. division of the wapentake of Broxtow and of the county of Nottingham, 10 miles (N. N. W.) from Nottingham; containing, with the hamlets of Annesley-Woodhouse and Wandesley, and the extraparochial district of Felly, 315 inhabitants. This parish comprises 3030 acres by measurement; it is intersected by the road from Nottingham to Kirkby-Sutton, and is irregular in its surface, which in many parts rises into mountainous ridges. The soil rests on red sandstone, of which there are some quarries supplying an inferior material used chiefly for walls and small houses. The village is picturesquely situated; several of its inhabitants are engaged in the manufacture of stockings. The living is a perpetual curacy; net income, £52; patron and impropriator, J. Musters, Esq. The church is ancient, and has a tower with two bells.

ANNFIELD-PLAIN, a colliery village, in the township of Kyo, parish and union of Lanchester, W. division of Chester ward, N. division of the county of Durham, 11 miles (S. S. W.) from Gateshead. This place has risen into some importance, and its population has increased to 500, in consequence of the opening of a coal-pit, whose produce is conveyed to the shipping by the Pontop and South Shields railway. There is a place of worship for Primitive Methodists.

ANSLEY (St. Lawrence), a parish, in the union of Atherstone, Atherstone division of the hundred of Hemlingford, N. division of the county of Warwick, 3 miles (S. by W.) from Atherstone; containing 701 inhabitants. It lies on the road from Nuneaton to Coleshill, and comprises by measurement about 2700 acres of land in equal portions of arable and pasture, with about 37 acres of woodland; the soil is stiff, and very fertile, the surface low and undulated, and the scenery in parts picturesque. Coal exists, but is not worked. The population is partly engaged in the weaving of ribbons. The living is a discharged vicarage, valued in the king's books at £6. 6. 8., and in the patronage of the Crown; net income, £116; impropriator, W. S. Dugdale, Esq. The church, which is very ancient, has a fine square tower, and a Norman arch divides the nave from the chancel. A school is sup-

ported by subscription. There are some remains of an old castle.

ANSLOW, or Annesley, a township, in the parish of Rolleston, union of Burton-upon-Trent, N. division of the hundred of Offlow and of the county of Stafford, 3¾ miles (N. W. by W.) from Burton; containing 278 inhabitants. The manor is now held by the family of Williams. The late Sir John Williams, Knt., one of the judges of the realm, who died in 1846, came into possession in right of his wife, daughter of Davies Davenport, Esq., of Capesthorne, in the county of Chester, whose ancestor purchased it in 1739 from the Mainwarings, of Whitmore, in Staffordshire, to whom it had descended by marriage from the ancient family of Boghay. The township includes the hamlets of Callingwood and Stockdale-Ridding. There was a chapel here before the Reformation; there is now a place of worship for Wesleyans.

ANSTEY, a hamlet, in the parish of Hilton, union of Blandford, hundred of Whiteway, Blandford division of Dorset; containing 200 inhabitants.

ANSTEY, a parish, in the union of Buntingford, hundred of Edwinstree, county of Hertford, 4 miles (N. E.) from Buntingford; containing 497 inhabitants. It is situated on the road to Cambridge through Barkway, and comprises 2051a. 3r. 11p. A fair is held on July 15th. The living is a rectory, valued in the king's books at £21. 13. 4.; net income, £504; patrons, the Master and Fellows of Christ's College, Cambridge. Corn-rents were assigned to the rector under a private act in 1826, as a commutation in lieu of tithes. The church is a cruciform edifice, with a central tower surmounted by a short spire supported by Saxon arches, and is said to have been built from the ruins of a castle erected by Eustace, Earl of Boulogne, soon after the Conquest, traces of which are still visible.

ANSTEY (St. Mary), a parish, in the union of Barrow-upon-Soar, hundred of West Goscote, N. division of the county of Leicester, 3¼ miles (N. W.) from Leicester; containing 838 inhabitants. This place, formerly called Hanstigie or Anstige, is situated between the forests of Charnwood and Leicester; and at the dissolution of religious houses belonged to the priory of Ulverscroft, with a reserved rent of 3s. 4d., and a pound of pepper, due to the Lord of Groby. The living is consolidated with the rectory of Thurcaston: the church was rebuilt by the incumbent in 1844, and is now a beautiful edifice, with the old tower; the cost was £4000. There is a place of worship for Wesleyans. In 1376, certain lands, described as "lying in the fields of Anstey in Wolfdale," were granted by John Lenerych, of Leicester; and in 1490 the "Brereyard" was devised by Thomas Martyn and William Haket, and vested in trustees for the repair of the church, bridges, and causeways of this place.

ANSTEY (St. James), a parish, in the union of Foleshill, hundred of Knightlow, N. division of the county of Warwick, 5½ miles (N. E.) from Coventry; containing 224 inhabitants. This place is situated on the road from Coventry to Wolvey heath, and thence to Leicester; it was originally called Heanstige, from the Saxon heun, high, and stige, a path-way. The parish comprises by computation 1000 acres, and, with the exception of about 300 acres, is the property of the Dean and Canons of Windsor; the Oxford canal passes

61

through the village. Anstey Hall, erected 150 years ago, is a noble mansion of brick and stone, the seat of Lieut.-Col. H. W. Adams, C.B. The living is a vicarage, not in charge, with a net income of £63 ; it is in the patronage of the Crown, and the Dean and Canons are appropriators. The church is said to have been founded in the time of Henry I.

ANSTEY (St. James), a parish, in the union of Tisbury, hundred of Dunworth, Hindon and S. divisions of Wilts, 5¼ miles (S. E. by S.) from Hindon ; containing 329 inhabitants. It comprises 1000 acres ; the surface is hilly in some parts, and the soil chalky and sandy. The living is a perpetual curacy, in the patronage of Lord Arundel ; net income, £22. Here was a commandery of the Knights Hospitallers, founded by Walter de Tuberville in the reign of John, and the revenue of which at the Dissolution was £81. 8. 5. ; its remains have been coverted into a farmhouse. Dr. Richard Zouch, an eminent civilian, and judge of the court of admiralty, in the reign of Charles I., was a native of the place.

ANSTEY, EAST (St. Michael), a parish, in the union and hundred of South Molton, South Molton and N. divisions of Devon, 4 miles (W. S. W.) from Dulverton ; containing 240 inhabitants. This parish, which is situated on the road to Barnstaple, comprises 2392 acres, whereof 805 are common or waste : there are some quarries of stone, worked for building and other purposes. The living is a rectory, valued in the king's books at £11 ; net income, £180 ; patron, T. S. Jessopp, Esq. The church is a plain neat edifice, with a tower ; the churchyard commands an extensive view.

ANSTEY-PASTURES, an extra-parochial liberty, in the union of Barrow-upon-Soar, hundred of West Goscote, N. division of the county of Leicester, 3¾ miles (N. W.) from Leicester ; containing 15 inhabitants. This place, which was formerly parcel of the " Ffrith of Leicestre," and of the ancient duchy of Lancaster, was granted in the 27th of Elizabeth to Thomas Martyn and others, on a lease of 31 years, and after the expiration of that term was purchased, in the 4th of James I., from Robert, Earl of Salisbury, lord treasurer of England, by Robert Martyn, of Anstey, whose descendants have a seat here. The liberty comprises 250 acres of land. The sum of £40 per annum, arising from lands allotted under an inclosure act, is applied to the repair of the highways and bridges ; and £10, and a further sum from Lord Stamford, are annually distributed in bread and linen among the poor.

ANSTEY, WEST (St. Petrock), a parish, in the union and hundred of South Molton, South Molton and N. divisions of Devon, 3½ miles (W.) from Dulverton ; containing 279 inhabitants, and comprising 3008 acres, of which 1036 are common or waste. Here are some quarries of stone for building. The living is a vicarage, valued in the king's books at £10. 16. 8. ; patrons and appropriators, the Dean and Chapter of Exeter. The great tithes have been commuted for £76. 17., and the vicarial for £112 ; the glebe consists of 37½ acres. The church is a substantial edifice with a tower, and is in good repair.

ANSTON, NORTH and SOUTH (St. James), a parish, in the union of Worksop, S. division of the wapentake of Strafforth and Tickhill, W. riding of York, 6½ miles (W. N. W.) from Worksop ; containing,

with the township of Woodsetts, 1102 inhabitants. The parish is on the road from Sheffield to Worksop, and comprises about 4000 acres, of which the surface is varied, and the scenery picturesque. Freestone of good quality and of a beautiful colour is extensively wrought, and from the quarries has been raised stone for the new houses of parliament. The manufacture of malt, starch, and nails, is carried on to a moderate extent. The villages, once called Church Anstan and Chapel Anstan respectively, are pleasantly situated on opposite eminences, between which flows one of the little streams that unite and form the Ryton ; they are exceedingly neat and clean, and the rivulet, after leaving their immediate vicinity, passes into a glen, where stands Woodmill. The Chesterfield canal bounds the parish on the north. The living is a perpetual curacy, in the patronage of the Prebendary of Laughton-en-le-Morthen in York Cathedral, with a net income of £84 : the tithes for the manor of North Anston were commuted, in 1767, for an allotment of land and a money payment. The church is a neat structure in the later English style, and consists of a nave, aisles, and chancel, with a square tower surmounted by a small spire ; it contains some monuments to the Lizour, Beauchamp, and D'Arcy families, with a finely sculptured figure of a lady bearing an infant in her arms. There are places of worship for Independents and Wesleyans. Between the villages is situated an endowed school.—See Woodsetts.

ANTHONY (St.) in Meneage, a parish, in the union of Helston, W. division of the hundred of Kerrier and of the county of Cornwall, 7 miles (S. by W.) from Falmouth ; containing 313 inhabitants. During the civil war of the seventeenth century, a small intrenchment here, called Little Dinas, was occupied by the royalists, for the defence of Helford harbour, but was captured by the parliamentarian forces under Sir Thomas Fairfax, in 1646. The parish is situated on the estuary of the river Helford, and divided by a creek that runs into it from the Nase Point to Gillan. It comprises by measurement 1510 acres ; the high grounds command fine views. The living is a discharged vicarage, valued in the king's books at £4. 15. 10., and in the patronage of the Crown ; impropriators, the family of Gregor : the tithes have been commuted for £210 for the impropriate, and £140 for the vicarial ; and the glebe comprises 62½ acres. The church, situated at the foot of the promontory of Little Dinas, within fifty yards of the sea, is an ancient and elegant structure, with a tower built of a very fine granite said to have been brought from Normandy. There is a place of worship for Bryanites. At Conderra, in 1735, was found a very large number of Roman brass coins, chiefly of the Emperor Constantine and his family. The parish had a cell to the priory of Tywardreth.

ANTHONY (St.) in Roseland, a parish, in the union of Truro, W. division of the hundred of Powder . and of the county of Cornwall, 9¼ miles (S. W. by S.) from Tregony ; containing 144 inhabitants. It lies at the extreme point of Roseland, a verdant and bold promontory, connected on the north by a narrow isthmus with the parish of Gerrans. The living is a donative, in the patronage of the family of Spry : the tithes have been commuted for £118. The church, beautifully situated on the border of a navigable lake, separating this parish from St. Mawes, contains some handsome monuments to the Spry family, of which one, by Westmacott, is to the memory of Sir Richard Spry, Rear-Admiral of the White. An Augustine priory, subordinate to that of Plympton in the county of Devon, existed here till the general Dissolution; its remains have been converted into a private residence called Place House.

ANTHONY, WEST (St. Anthony and St. John the Baptist), a parish, in the union of St. Germans, S. division of the hundred of East, E. division] of Cornwall, 5½ miles (S. E.) from St. Germans; containing, with the chapelry of Torpoint, 2894 inhabitants. The living is a discharged vicarage, valued in the king's books at £12. 17. 8½., and in the gift of the family of Carew, the impropriators: the incumbent's tithes have been commuted for £307. 3. 6., with a glebe of 6 acres, and the great tithes for £284. 13. The incumbency of Torpoint is in the gift of the Vicar. There is a place of worship for Wesleyans. A small endowed school was founded in 1766, by Sir Coventry Carew, Bart.

ANTHORN, a township, in the parish of Bowness, union of Wigton, Cumberland ward, and E. division of Cumberland, 8 miles (N. W. by N.) from Wigton; containing 207 inhabitants. Here is a school with a small endowment.

ANTINGHAM, a parish, in the union of Erpingham, hundred of North Erpingham, E. division of Norfolk, 2½ miles (N. W.) from North Walsham; containing 271 inhabitants. It is intersected by the road from North Walsham to Cromer, and comprises 1509a. 3r. 36p., of which 1356 acres are arable, 33 pasture and meadow, 56 woodland, and 13 water, consisting of two lakes forming the principal source of the river Ant, which was made navigable to the eastern boundary of the parish in 1806. The living of Antingham St. Mary is a discharged rectory, valued in the king's books at £6. 3. 1½.; patron, Lord Suffield. Antingham St. Margaret's is also a discharged rectory, consolidated with the living of North Walsham, and valued at £5. 6. 8. The tithes of St. Mary's have been commuted for £340, with nearly 16 acres of glebe; and those of St. Margaret's for £28. 10. The church of St. Mary is chiefly in the decorated style, with an embattled tower: in the churchyard are the remains of the church of St. Margaret, consisting of its tower and some of its side walls. Neat schoolrooms were erected by the late Lord Suffield, at a cost exceeding £2000.

ANTROBUS, a township, in the parish of Great Budworth, union of Runcorn, hundred of Bucklow, N. division of the county of Chester, 5 miles (N. N. W.) from Northwich; containing 489 inhabitants. Antrobus Hall and demesne belonged to the family of Antrobus from an early period till the reign of Henry IV., when it was sold to the Venables family, who resided here for many generations. The estate was purchased in 1808 of Edward Townshend, Esq., of Chester, by Edmond Antrobus, Esq., a descendant of the former proprietors, and is now the property of Sir Edmund W. Antrobus, Bart. The township comprises 1947 acres, of which 308 are common or waste land; the soil is clay and moss.

ANWICK (St. Edith), a parish, in the union of Sleaford, wapentake of Flaxwell, parts of Kesteven, county of Lincoln, 4¾ miles (N. E.) from Sleaford; containing 314 inhabitants. The living is a discharged vicarage, united, with the rectory of Dunsby, to the

rectory of Brauncewell, and valued in the king's books at £5. 3. 11½.; impropriator, S. Hazelwood, Esq. The tithes were commuted for land and corn-rents, under an inclosure act, in 1791.

APESTHORPE.—See Applesthorpe.

APETHORPE (St. Leonard), a parish, in the union of Oundle, hundred of Willybrook, N. division of the county of Northampton, 4¼ miles (S. W. by W.) from Wansford; containing 269 inhabitants. The parish is situated on the road from King's Cliff to Oundle, and on the Willybrook, at the border of Rockingham forest; and comprises 1669a. 15p., a portion of which is occupied by Apethorpe Hall, the seat of the Earl of Westmoreland. The living is a perpetual curacy; net income, £80; patron, the Bishop of Peterborough. The church contains a sumptuous monument to the memory of Sir Anthony Mildmay, Bart., and his lady; and another with the recumbent figure of an infant, the eldest son of Lord Burghersh, beautifully sculptured by a Florentine artist. The Earl of Westmoreland, by indenture in 1684, charged a farm with the payment of £36 annually in lieu of certain rent-charges assigned by his ancestors, for apprenticing boys and girls of Apethorpe, Wood-Newton, Nassington, and Yarwell.

APETON, a township, in the parishes of Bradley and Gnosall, union of Newport, W. division of the hundred of Cuttlestone, S. division of the county of Stafford. It lies about two miles west-by-north from the village of Bradley, and two and a half south-east from that of Gnosall. A tributary to the Penk flows in the vicinity.

APLEY (St. Andrew), a parish, in the W. division of the wapentake of Wraggoe, parts of Lindsey, and county of Lincoln, 3 miles (S. W.) from Wragby; containing 162 inhabitants. It comprises 1660 acres, of which 250 are woodland; the surface is flat, and the soil a cold clay, subject to inundation from a stream that divides Apley from the parish of Stainfield. The living is a perpetual curacy, valued in the king's books at £6; net income, £20; patron and impropriator, T. Tyrwhitt Drake, Esq. Formerly a church existed; but at present there is only a small building erected on its site, in which the minister reads the funeral service, and the parishioners hold their vestries.

APPERLEY, a township, in the parish of Bywell St. Peter, union of Hexham, E. division of Tindale ward, S. division of Northumberland, 2½ miles (S. by E.) from Bywell; containing 34 inhabitants. It is situated at a short distance from the border of the county of Durham, and comprises 316 acres of land. The Roman Watling-street passes on the south-west; and a stream, tributary to the Tyne, flows in nearly the same direction.

APPERLY, with Whitefield, a hamlet, in the parish of Deerhurst, Lower division of the hundred of Westminster, union of Tewkesbury, E. division of the county of Gloucester, 4½ miles (S. W. by S.) from Tewkesbury; containing 420 inhabitants. There is a place of worship for Wesleyans.

APPLEBY (St. Michael), a parish, in the union of Ashby-de-la-Zouch, partly in the hundred of Repton and Gresley, S. division of the county of Derby, but chiefly in the hundred of Sparkenhoe, S. division of Leicester, 5¼ miles (S. W. by S.) from Ashby; comprising 2803a. 3r., and containing 1075 inhabitants.

The living is a rectory, valued in the king's books at £20. 9. 4½.; net income, £750, with a house; patron, George Moore, Esq. The tithes were commuted for land and a money payment, under an inclosure act, in 1771. The church, which is in Leicestershire, was repaired and repewed in 1830, when some windows of painted glass were added by private donation; it contains a curious monument to Sir Stephen and Lady Appleby. A free grammar school was founded in 1699 by Sir John Moore, Knt., lord mayor of London in 1682, who endowed it with an estate at Upton, consisting of 298 acres of land, producing about £315 per annum; the buildings, forming a spacious structure, were erected by Sir Christopher Wren.

APPLEBY (St. Bartholomew), a parish, in the union of Glandford-Brigg, N. division of the wapentake of Manley, parts of Lindsey, county of Lincoln, 7 miles (N. W. by N.) from Glandford-Brigg; containing, with the hamlet of Raventhorpe, 505 inhabitants. The living is a discharged vicarage, valued in the king's books at £10. 4.; net income, £150; patron, C. Winn, Esq.

Seal and Arms.

Obverse.   *Reverse.*

APPLEBY, an incorporated market-town, having separate jurisdiction, and formerly a representative borough, locally in East ward, union of East ward, county of Westmorland, of which it is the chief town, 274 miles (N. N. W.) from London; containing 1075 inhabitants. This place is thought, but on uncertain grounds, to have been a Roman station: Camden, from a similarity of name, erroneously calls it *Aballaba*; while Horsley considers it to have been the Roman *Galacum*. A Roman road passed near it from Langton, on the east, to Redland's Bank on the north-west; and some antiquities of the Romans have been discovered in the vicinity. It has long been the head of a barony, sometimes called the barony of Westmorland; the rest of the county, which forms the barony of Kendal, having been anciently included in Lancashire and Yorkshire. The barony was granted by the Conqueror to Ranulph de Meschines, whose son Ranulph, having in his mother's right succeeded to the earldom of Chester, gave it to his sister, the wife of Robert d'Estrivers. It afterwards came into the possession of the Engains and Morvilles, and was seized by the crown, in consequence of the participation of a member of the latter family in the murder of Thomas à Becket. King John bestowed it, together with the "Sheriffwick and rent of the county of Westmorland," upon Robert de Veteripont, Lord of Curvaville, in Normandy, whose grandson, Robert, joining the confederated barons, in the reign of Henry III., it escheated to the crown; it was restored, however, to the two

64

younger daughters of Robert, and subsequently, by marriage, came into the possession of the illustrious family of Clifford, whose descendants, the Tuftons, earls of Thanet, have ever since enjoyed it, with all its rights and dignities.

Appleby was anciently of much greater magnitude than it is at present, as is evident from the situation of a township called *Burrals* (Borough Walls), a mile distant, and from the discovery of old foundations at the distance of more than two miles, to which the suburbs formerly extended. An ancient record, about the period of the reign of Edward I., makes mention of a sheriff of Applebyshire; from which it appears that the town gave name to one of those districts into which Edward the Confessor divided the earldom of Northumberland. It retained its importance from the time of the Romans until the year 1176, when William, King of Scotland, surprised the castle, and destroyed the town; from which calamity, however, it had so far recovered in the reign of Henry III., that a court of exchequer was established here. A Carmelite monastery was founded at Battleborough, in the parish of St. Michael, in 1281, by the Lords Vesey, Clifford, and Percy; the site of which is now occupied by a neat modern mansion, called the Friary. In the year 1388 the town was again totally laid waste by the Scots, from the effects of which it never afterwards recovered; so that, in the reign of Philip and Mary, it was found necessary to reduce the ancient fee-farm rent, due to the crown, from twenty marks to two. In 1598 it was nearly depopulated by the plague, and its market was consequently removed to Gilshaughlin, a village five miles distant. At the commencement of the parliamentary war, the castle was garrisoned for the king by the Lady Anne Clifford, Countess of Pembroke and Montgomery, and it continued in his interest until after the battle of Marston-Moor, when all the northern fortresses fell into the possession of the parliament.

The town is pleasantly situated on the river Eden, by which it is almost surrounded. It is well paved, and amply supplied with water, and consists of one spacious street, intersected at right angles by three smaller streets, and terminated at one extremity by the castle, and at the other by the church of St. Lawrence; at each end also is a handsome stone obelisk, or cross. An ancient stone bridge of two arches, over the Eden, connects the suburb of Bongate with the borough. The castle stands on a steep and richly-wooded eminence rising from the river. It suffered much in the wars with Scotland, especially in the reigns of Richard II. and Henry IV.; and of the original structure, said to be of Roman foundation, only a detached portion called Cæsar's tower, and a small part of the south-east end, remain: the greater part was rebuilt by Lord Clifford, in the reign of Henry VI., and again by Thomas, Earl of Thanet, in 1686. The castle is of square form, and contains several apartments of noble dimensions, adorned with a large and valuable collection of ancient family portraits; the magnificent suit of gold and steel armour worn by George Clifford in the tilt-yard, when he acted as champion to his royal mistress Queen Elizabeth, is also preserved here, as too is the famous genealogical picture of the Veteriponts, Cliffords, and Tuftons. The shrievalty of the county of Westmorland is hereditary, and has descended lineally through the male and female line from the year 1066 to the present time. The castle has been from time immemorial the temporary residence of the judges travelling the northern circuit, who are entertained here at the expense of the Earl of Thanet. In the vicinity of the town are lead-mines worked by the London Mining Company; also quarries of red freestone used for building; and at Coupland-Beck is a carding and spinning mill, where yarn is spun for coarse woollen cloth, stockings, and carpets. The market is on Saturday: fairs are held on the Saturday before Whit-Sunday, for cattle; on Whit-Monday for linen-cloth, and the hiring of servants; and the second Wednesday in June (commonly called Brampton Fair), and the 21st of August, for horses, cattle, sheep, woollen cloth, cheese, and other articles. The market-house, or the Cloisters, is a handsome structure near the church, rebuilt by the corporation in 1811, in the early style of English architecture, after a design by Mr. Smirke.

This is a BOROUGH by prescription, and received a charter of incorporation from Henry I., with privileges equal to those of York, which were confirmed by Henry II., King John, Henry III., Edward I., and Edward III.; the last monarch's charter reciting that the borough had been seized by Edward II. for an arrear of rent, and was then in the possession of the crown; and granting the town again to the burgesses, on the same terms as before. The present officers of the corporation are a mayor, deputy-mayor, twelve aldermen, and sixteen common-councilmen, assisted by a recorder, town-clerk, two coroners, two chamberlains, a sword-bearer, mace-bearer, two serjeants-at-mace, and two bailiffs; the mayor is a justice of the peace, but exercises only a limited jurisdiction. Petty-sessions are held here by the county magistrates every Saturday; the assizes for the county also take place here, and the general quarter-sessions are held alternately at Appleby and Kendal, the Easter and Michaelmas at the former, and the Epiphany and Midsummer at the latter. The powers of the county debt-court of Appleby, established in 1847, extend over the registration-district of East Ward. The town-hall is a large ancient edifice in the principal street. The county gaol and house of correction has been adapted to the radiating plan: adjoining it is the shire-hall, built in 1771. The borough sent members to parliament from the 23rd of Edward I., but was disfranchised by the act of the 2nd of William IV. cap. 45: the right of election was vested in the holders of burgage tenements, in number about 200; and the mayor was the returning officer. It is the place of election of knights of the shire, for which also it has been constituted a polling-place.

The town is situated in the parishes of St. Lawrence and St. Michael, that portion of it which is in the latter being named Bongate: St. Lawrence's contains a population of 1354, and St. Michael's one of 1165. The LIVINGS of both are vicarages. That of St. Lawrence is valued in the king's books at £9. 5. 2½., and has a net income of £306; it is in the patronage of the Dean and Chapter of Carlisle, and attached to it are 51 acres of ancient glebe, and 252 allotted in lieu of tithes. That of St. Michael is valued at £20. 13. 9.; net income, £175; patron, the Bishop of Carlisle. The tithes of the manor of Appleby were commuted for land, under an inclosure act, in 1772: the Dean and Chapter are appropriators of both parishes. The church of St. Lawrence

is partly in the decorated, and partly in the later, style of English architecture; it contains the remains of Anne, the celebrated Countess of Pembroke, Dorset, and Montgomery, who died in 1675, and of her mother, the Countess of Cumberland, to the memory of each of whom there is a splendid marble monument. The church of St. Michael is situated about three-quarters of a mile south-east of the town; and about three miles and a half from it, between the villages of Hilton and Murton, is a place of worship for Wesleyans.

The free grammar school, founded by the burghers, existed long before the dissolution of religious houses, but was established on its present foundation in the 16th of Elizabeth, when the management was vested in ten governors, who are a corporate body: the endowment, arising from different sources, is about £200 per annum. It has five exhibitions, of £8 per annum each, to Queen's College, Oxford, founded by Thomas, Earl of Thanet, in 1720, and is entitled to send candidates for one of Lady Elizabeth Hastings' exhibitions to the same college. Dr. Bedel, Bishop of Kilmore; Dr. Barlow, Bishop of Lincoln; Drs. Smith and Waugh, Bishops of Carlisle; and Dr. Langhorne, the translator of Plutarch, were educated in the school. St. Ann's hospital, for 13 aged widows, was founded and endowed in 1653, by the Countess of Pembroke; the revenue arising from land is about £490, and it has a considerable funded property. The building, which is quadrangular, comprises 13 distinct habitations and a neat chapel; the chaplain and sisters are appointed by the Earl of Thanet, as heir of the countess, who left also various lands at Temple-Sowerby for repairing the church of St. Lawrence, the school-house, town-hall, and bridge. In the neighbourhood were two ancient hospitals for lepers, dedicated respectively to St. Leonard and Nicholas; the estate of the latter was applied by the countess towards the endowment of her almshouse. There was also a chapel at the western end of the stone bridge of St. Lawrence; and the ruins of another have been found at Chapel hill. About a mile north of the village of Crackenthorpe, on the ancient Roman way, was a Roman encampment; and a little further to the north was discovered, on sinking the foundation of a new bridge, in 1838, between the parish of St. Michael and Kirkby-Thore, a variety of Roman coins and other antiquities. At Machill bank, near the Roman way, urns have been found in circular pits of clay, apparently dug for their reception. Thomas de Appleby, Bishop of Carlisle, and Roger de Appleby, Bishop of Ossory, were natives of the town.

APPLEDORE, a small sea-port town, in the parish of NORTHAM, union of BIDEFORD, hundred of SHEB-BEAR, Great Torrington and N. divisions of DEVON, 3 miles (N.) from Bideford; containing 2174 inhabitants. This spot is celebrated in history for the many battles between the Saxons and the Danes which took place in the immediate vicinity, more especially for the decisive and important victory obtained by Earl Odun and the men of Devon, over a large army of Danes under the command of Hubba, who, in the reign of Alfred, landed here with thirty-three ships. The invaders were repulsed with great slaughter and the loss of their leader, who, being taken prisoner, was beheaded on a hill in the neighbourhood, on which a stone has been erected to mark the spot, and which still retains the name of

K

Hubberstone hill. The TOWN is pleasantly situated on the shore of Barnstaple bay, and, from its facilities for sea-bathing, the mildness of its climate, and the romantic beauty and variety of the surrounding scenery, has been gradually growing into importance as a favourite watering-place. The beach, which is from two to three miles in length, is a firm level sand, affording an excellent promenade ; and there are other agreeable walks and rides in the vicinity. The streets are for the greater part narrow and inconvenient, but leading down to the beach, they are ventilated by a current of pure air ; and the atmosphere, impregnated with saline particles from the sea, and softened by the adjacent hills, is considered very favourable for invalids. There is a market well supplied with fish, and with every other kind of provisions. The Burrows, a fine tract of land, on which every inhabitant householder has the right of common, is defended from the sea by an embankment called Pebbleridge, which is nearly two miles in length, 150 feet broad at the base, and considerably higher than high-water mark. The parish church at Northam being about a mile and a half distant, a district church has been lately erected here by subscription, containing 550 sittings, of which 275 are free : the living is a perpetual curacy in the gift of the Vicar, with a net income of £150. There is a place of worship for Independents.

APPLEDORE (ST. PETER AND ST. PAUL), a parish, in the union of TENTERDEN, partly in the liberties of ROMNEY MARSH, but chiefly in the hundred of BLACKBOURNE, lathe of SCRAY, W. division of KENT, 6 miles (S. E. by S.) from Tenterden ; containing 561 inhabitants. The parish comprises 2963 acres, of which 63 are common or waste, and 60 in wood. Some trade is carried on in coal, timber, and other merchandise, by means of the Royal Military canal, which passes close to the village. The living is a vicarage, with the living of Ebony annexed, valued in the king's books at £21 ; net income, £185 ; patron and appropriator, the Archbishop of Canterbury. The church is a spacious edifice in various styles, with a Norman tower which appears to have formed part of the ancient castle on whose site the church is built. There is a place of worship for Wesleyans.

APPLEDRAM (ST. MARY), a parish, in the union of WEST HAMPNETT, hundred of Box and STOCKBRIDGE, rape of CHICHESTER, W. division of SUSSEX, 1¾ mile (S. W.) from Chichester ; containing 156 inhabitants. It is bounded on the west by the harbour of Chichester, and is of very small extent. Considerable business is done in the timber and coal trade at Dell Quay. The manor-house, crowned with turrets, and surrounded by a moat, is a good specimen of the style of domestic architecture of the reign of Henry VIII. : near it are the remains of another ancient house, now occupied by a farmer. The living is a perpetual curacy, valued in the king's books at £14 ; net income, £34 ; patrons and appropriators, the Dean and Chapter of Chichester. The church is in the early English style.

APPLEFORD, a chapelry, in the parish of SUTTON-COURTNEY, union of ABINGDON, hundred of OCK, county of BERKS, 3½ miles (S. E.) from Abingdon ; containing 187 inhabitants, and comprising 843 acres, of which 77 are common or waste. Here is a station of the Oxford branch of the Great Western railway. The chapel is dedicated to St. Peter and St. Paul. The

tithes have been commuted for £344. 10., payable to the Dean and Canons of Windsor. A free school was founded and endowed by Edmund Bradstock, for the education of twenty poor children, seven from the chapelry of Appleford, and the remainder from the rest of the parish of Sutton.

APPLESHAW, a parish, in the union and hundred of ANDOVER, Andover and N. divisions of the county of SOUTHAMPTON, 5 miles (N. W. by W.) from Andover ; containing 372 inhabitants. Fairs for the sale of sheep are held on May 23rd, Oct. 9th, and Nov. 4th and 5th. The living is annexed to the vicarage of Amport : the church, erected in 1832 at an expense of £1300, is a neat edifice, containing 270 sittings, of which 86 are free. There is a school with a small endowment.

APPLESTHORPE, or APESTHORPE (ST. PETER), a parish, in the union of EAST RETFORD, North-Clay division of the wapentake of BASSETLAW, N. division of the county of NOTTINGHAM, 5 miles (N. by E.) from East Retford ; containing 109 inhabitants. It comprises 783a. 3r. 27p., and is bounded on the east by the river Trent ; the surface is flat, and the soil a stiffish clay ; the land near the Trent is rich meadow. The living is a perpetual curacy ; net income, £81 ; patron, the Bishop of Lincoln. The tithes were commuted for land, under an inclosure act, in 1795. The church has been more than a century in ruins, and the inhabitants attend that at North Leverton : there is, however, a burial-ground, which was inclosed in 1833.

APPLETHWAITE, a township, in the parish of WINDERMERE, union and ward of KENDAL, county of WESTMORLAND, 5¼ miles (S. E.) from Ambleside ; containing 436 inhabitants. In the township are several beautiful villas, among which is Calgarth Park, commenced in 1789 by Dr. Watson, Bishop of Llandaff, who occupied it till his death in 1816 : his remains were interred at Bowness. The residence of Elleray, then the property of Professor Wilson, of Edinburgh, was visited in 1825 by Sir Walter Scott and George Canning, Mr. Wordsworth being also present at the meeting ; and during the visit, a most splendid regatta took place on Windermere lake under the direction of Professor Wilson. Rayrigg, on the road to Bowness, was a residence of Mr. Wilberforce's. Two bobbin-mills afford employment to a portion of the population. The tithes have been commuted for £27.

APPLETON (ST. LAWRENCE), a parish, in the union of ABINGDON, hundred of OCK, county of BERKS, 5½ miles (N. W.) from Abingdon ; comprising 1981a. 2p., and containing, with the township of Eaton, 496 inhabitants. It is bounded on the north-west by the river Thames, which separates it from the county of Oxford, and on the south-east by a small stream called the Ouse. The surface undulates gently from the banks of the Thames, and the scenery is pleasingly diversified ; the soil near the river is of a clayey quality, and in the more elevated lands a rich and fertile loam. The living is a rectory, valued in the king's books at £13. 5., and in the gift of Magdalene College, Oxford : the tithes have been commuted for £455, and the glebe comprises 32 acres. The church contains a few monuments to the Fettiplace family. There are some remains of two ancient manor-houses, each surrounded by a moat. Dr. Edmund Dickinson, author of a work entitled Delph.

Phœnicizantes, tracing to the Bible the origin of the heathen mythology, was born here in 1624.

APPLETON, with HULL, an ecclesiastical district, in the parish of GREAT-BUDWORTH, union of RUNCORN, E. division of the hundred of BUCKLOW, N. division of the county of CHESTER, 2 miles (S. S. E.) from Warrington, on the road to Northwich; containing 1753 inhabitants. The manor, with its hamlets of Hull and Stockton, belonged in the reign of Henry III. to Geffrey Dutton, and subsequently passed, with Budworth, to Sir Peter Warburton, Bart. Bradley, another manor, was given by Geffrey, son of Adam de Dutton, to the ancestor of Thomas Daniers or Daniel, whose daughter and heiress, in the reign of Edward III., brought it by marriage to the Savage family; in 1622 it was the seat of the Greggs, and at a later period was held by the Egertons, of Oulton, of whom it was purchased in 1800 by Richard Wilson, Esq. The township was inclosed by an act passed in 1764, and comprises 3048 acres; the soil is clay and sand, with rock, but the first prevails : the Bridgewater canal passes through. A court baron is held by R. E. E. Warburton, Esq. Appleton Hall is the seat of Thomas Lyne, Esq. The living is a perpetual curacy, with a net income of £150, and a residence; patrons, Thomas and Gilbert Greenall, Esqrs.: the church is a plain structure, erected at a cost of £1000. At Stockton Heath is a chapel dedicated to St. Thomas, the incumbent of which has an income of £124. There is also a place of worship for Wesleyans; and a school for infants, boys and girls, is supported by subscription.

APPLETON, LANCASHIRE.—See WIDNESS.

APPLETON (ST. MARY), a parish, in the union and hundred of FREEBRIDGE-LYNN, W. division of NOR-FOLK, 8 miles (N. E. by E.) from Lynn; comprising 876a. 1r. 7p., of which 508 acres are arable; and containing 25 inhabitants. The living is a discharged vicarage, valued in the king's books at £8, and in the gift of the Hon. C. S. Cowper: the impropriate tithes have been commuted for £10, and the vicarial for £8. The church has fallen into ruins.

APPLETON, a township, in the parish of CATTE-RICK, union of RICHMOND, wapentake of HANG-EAST, N. riding of YORK, 2 miles (S. by W.) from Catterick; containing 91 inhabitants. It comprises about 1480 acres of land, and includes the hamlets of East and West Appleton.

APPLETON-LE-MOORS, a township, in the parish of LASTINGHAM, union of PICKERING, wapentake of RYEDALE, N. riding of YORK, 3¼ miles (E. N. E.) from Kirkby-Moorside; containing 322 inhabitants. It comprises about 2570 acres, of which nearly 1300 are open moorland : the river Seven passes on the east, and the road from Kirkby-Moorside to Pickering on the south. There is a place of worship for Wesleyans. John Stockton, in 1839, left £10 a year for the instruction of children.

APPLETON-LE-STREET (ALL SAINTS), a parish, in the union of MALTON, wapentake of RYEDALE, N. riding of YORK; comprising the townships of Amotherby, Appleton, Broughton, Hildenley, and Swinton; and containing 944 inhabitants, of whom 185 are in the township of Appleton, 3¾ miles (W. N. W.) from Malton. This parish, which is bounded on the north by the river Rye, is situated on the road to Thirsk; the surface is

67

undulated, and the scenery richly diversified. Limestone of excellent quality is abundant, and extensively quarried. The living is a vicarage, with the chapel of Amotherby, valued in the king's books at £7. 8. 6½.; net income, £515 ; patron and incumbent, the Rev. J. J. Peach ; impropriators, the Earl of Carlisle, F. Cresswell, Esq., and others. The church is in the Norman style, with a square tower.

APPLETON-ROEBUCK and NUN-APPLETON, a township, in the parish of BOLTON-PERCY, W. division of AINSTY wapentake, W. riding of YORK, 7½ miles (S. S. W.) from York ; containing 564 inhabitants. This place comprises by computation 2800 acres, chiefly the property of the Milner family, whose splendid mansion, Nun-Appleton Hall, stands in an extensive and finely wooded park, near the confluence of the rivers Ouse and Wharfe : the house was built by Thomas, Lord Fairfax, on the site of a Cistercian priory for nuns, founded by Alice de St. Quintin at the commencement of the thirteenth century. The village is situated in the vale of a rivulet. There is a place of worship for Wesleyans.

APPLETON-UPON-WISK, a parish, in the union of NORTHALLERTON, W. division of the liberty of LANG-BAURGH, N. riding of YORK, 7¼ miles (S. S. W.) from Yarm ; containing 600 inhabitants. The manor, at the time of the Domesday survey, was in the hands of the Conqueror, and was then styled *Apeltune :* it was afterwards granted by the monarch to Robert de Brus, lord of Skelton, who gave it to the abbey of St. Mary at York ; and with that institution it continued till the Dissolution, when it was bestowed by Henry VIII. upon Sir Charles Brandon, Knt. The parish is bounded on the south by the river Wisk, and is about two miles in length from east to west, and a mile and a half broad. It comprises 1827a. 2r. 25p., of which 1101 acres are arable, 666 grass land, 27 wood, and 32 acres cottages, gardens, roads, and waste : the soil is a strong clay ; and the fields, which adjoining the river are low, rise from it by a gradual and easy ascent towards the north. The manufacture of linen affords employment to about 100 of the inhabitants. The village is situated at the southern extremity of the parish, in the most westerly part of Cleveland, and is intersected by the roads between Richmond and Stokesley, and Northallerton and Yarm. The living is annexed to the rectory of Great Smeaton ; impropriator, the Rev. J. Hewgill. The church is a small ancient building. There are places of worship for Independents, Primitive Methodists, and Wesleyans.

APPLETREE, a hamlet, in the parish of ASTON-LE-WALLS, union of BANBURY, hundred of CHIPPING-WARDEN, S. division of the county of NORTHAMPTON, 7 miles (N. N.Æ.) from Banbury ; containing 92 inhabitants, and comprising 526a. 30p. It is situated on the borders of Oxfordshire, which bounds it on the south-west.

APPLETREE-WICK, a township, in the parish of BURNSALL, union of SKIPTON, E. division of the wapentake of STAINCLIFFE and EWCROSS, W. riding of YORK, 9 miles (N. E. by N.) from Skipton ; containing 467 inhabitants. This township, which forms the eastern side of Wharfdale, and includes the hamlets of Gateup and Skireholm, comprises by computation 7740 acres, chiefly forming a high moorland district affording tolerable pasture. The village is pleasantly situated ; a fair for

K 2

horses and cattle is held in it annually on the 25th of October, under a charter granted in the reign of Edward III. Christ-church in Skireholm was erected in 1837 by subscription, at a cost of £240, as a chapel of ease to the mother church ; it is a neat small edifice. William Craven, lord mayor of London in 1611, and whose son was created Baron Craven in the 2nd, and Earl of Craven in the 16th, of Charles II., was a native of this place.

ARBORFIELD (ST. BARTHOLOMEW), a parish, in the union of WOKINGHAM, hundred of SONNING, county of BERKS, 5 miles (S. E. by S.) from Reading; comprising 1468a. 2r. 25p., and containing 300 inhabitants. The living is a rectory, valued in the king's books at £8, and in the gift of Lord Braybrooke : the tithes have been commuted for £398. The village of Arborfield Cross, about a mile from the church, is partly in this parish, and partly in that of Hurst.

ARBURY, with HOUGHTON and MIDDLETON.—See HOUGHTON.

ARCLEBY, a hamlet, in the parish of PLUMBLAND, union of COCKERMOUTH, ALLERDALE ward below Derwent, W. division of CUMBERLAND, 7 miles (N. N. E.) from the town of Cockermouth. There are some coalworks in the vicinity.

ARCLID, a township, in the parish of SANDBACH, union of CONGLETON, hundred of NORTHWICH, S. division of the county of CHESTER, 2 miles (E. N. E.) from Sandbach ; containing 121 inhabitants. It comprises 530 acres ; the prevailing soil is sand. The impropriate tithes have been commuted for £29, and the vicarial for £39.

ARDEN, with ARDENSIDE, a township, in the parish of HAWNBY, union of HELMSLEY, wapentake of BIRDFORTH, N. riding of YORK, 8 miles (N. W. by W.) from Helmsley ; containing 137 inhabitants. A small Benedietine nunnery in connexion with Rivaulx Abbey, about four miles distant, was founded here about 1150, the revenue of which, at the Dissolution, was £12 : Arden Hall is built upon its site. In 1757, John Smales and Gregory Elsley bequeathed £120. 5., directing the produce to be applied to the instruction of six boys.

ARDINGLEY, or ERTHINGLEY, a parish, in the union of CUCKFIELD, hundred of BUTTINGHILL, rape of LEWES, E. division of SUSSEX, 6 miles (N. E. by N.) from Cuckfield ; containing 742 inhabitants. It is situated on the road to Brighton through Lindfield, and is intersected by the London and Brighton railway. In the hamlet of Hepsted Green a pleasure-fair is held on the 30th of May. The living is a rectory, valued in the king's books at £19. 5. 10.; net income, £498 ; patron, J. W. Peyton, Esq. The church is a handsome structure, in the decorated English style, and contains several ancient monuments to the Culpepper family.

ARDINGTON (THE HOLY TRINITY), a parish, in the union and hundred of WANTAGE, county of BERKS, 2¾ miles (E.) from Wantage; containing 405 inhabitants. It comprises by computation 2190 acres, and is intersected by the Wilts and Berks canal. The surface is flat, except at the northern extremity, which contains a portion of the chalk hills extending through this county and Wiltshire. The northern part has some good meadow lands, and the middle is a rich loam well adapted for corn. The living is a discharged vicarage, valued in the king's books at £8. 7. 9., and in the

68

patronage of the Dean and Canons of Christ-Church, Oxford.: the church has a narrow south aisle divided from the nave by pointed arches, and at the east end a small transept. The Roman Ikeneld-street passed through the parish.

ARDLEIGH (ST. MARY), a parish, in the union and hundred of TENDRING, N. division of ESSEX, 4¾ miles (N. E.) from Colchester; containing 1605 inhabitants. This parish, which comprises 4953 acres, is situated on the road from Colchester to Harwich, and has a station of the Colchester and Ipswich railway, midway between the stations of Colchester and Manningtree. A fair is held on September 29th. The living is a discharged vicarage, valued in the king's books at £11. 0. 10., and in the patronage of the Crown ; net income, £258. The church is an ancient structure partly rebuilt of brick, with the original square embattled tower of stone. There is a place of worship for Wesleyans. In 1571 William Littlebury bequeathed a farm called Wrabnass, now let for £250 per annum, for the instruction of boys of Ardleigh, Dedham, and other places adjacent.

ARDLEY (ST. MARY), a parish, in the union of BICESTER, hundred of PLOUGHLEY, county of OXFORD, 4 miles (N. W. by N.) from Bicester ; containing 168 inhabitants. It contains by measurement 1469 acres, and is situated on the road from Oxford to Northampton. Lace is manufactured here. The living is a rectory, valued in the king's books at £5. 12. 8½., and in the gift of the Duke of Marlborough : the tithes have been commuted for £283, and the glebe comprises 60 acres. The main body of the church was rebuilt in a plain style about 50 years since. In Ardley wood are the foundations of an ancient castle built by the Normans, in the reign of Stephen, on the site of a fortification which had been raised by Offa, King of Mercia : they are nearly circular, and comprise an area about sixty yards in diameter, surrounded by a moat.

ARDSLEY, a township and chapelry, in the parish of DARFIELD, wapentake of STAINCROSS, W. riding of YORK, 2 miles (E. by S.) from Barnsley ; containing 1226 inhabitants. Hand-loom weaving of linen, and the manufacture of fancy drills, are carried on here : a coal-pit is in operation, and there is a valuable stonequarry from which grindstones of a very superior quality are supplied to the Sheffield and Birmingham manufacturers. The Dearne and Dove canal runs through the township. The chapel, dedicated to Christ, a cruciform structure in the Norman style, was erected in 1841, on a site given by Sir George Wombwell, Bart., at an expense of £1200, of which £400 were contributed by the lord of the manor, £200 by the Incorporated Society, £120 by the vicar of Darfield, and the rest by private individuals : it contains 500 sittings, one-third of which are free. The living is a perpetual curacy in the gift of the Vicar of Darfield, with a net income of £120, and a parsonage-house. The tithes have been commuted for £203, half payable to Trinity College, Cambridge, and half to the rector. There is a place of worship for Wesleyans.

ARDSLEY, EAST, a parish, in the union of WAKEFIELD, Lower division of the wapentake of AGBRIGG, W. riding of YORK, 3½ miles (N. W. by N.) from Wakefield ; containing 900 inhabitants. This parish, which is in the honour of Pontefract, comprises about 1600 acres of fertile land : the village is situated on the road to Bradford, and the surrounding scenery is pleasing. There are extensive coal-mines. The living is a perpetual curacy; net income, £369; patron and impropriator, the Earl of Cardigan. The tithes of East and West Ardsley were commuted for land, under an inclosure act, in 1826. The church has a square tower. There is a place of worship for Wesleyans.

ARDSLEY, WEST (*St. Mary*), a parish, in the union of Wakefield, Lower division of the wapentake of Agbrigg, W. riding of York, 5¼ miles (S. S. W.) from Leeds; containing 1420 inhabitants. This place, in some documents called Woodkirk, from its ancient church of wood, formerly belonged to Nostall Priory, subordinate to which a cell of Black canons was founded here, and endowed with land by one of the family of Soothill, in expiation of the murder of a child: its revenue at the Dissolution amounted to £17, and the foundations of the building may still be traced. The parish comprises by measurement 2300 acres of fertile land: the substratum abounds with coal of excellent quality, of which there are some extensive mines in operation. Fairs for horses, &c., are held on August 24th and September 17th. The living is a perpetual curacy; net income, £265, derived from land; patron and impropriator, the Earl of Cardigan, who is lord of the manor. The church, an ancient structure in the early English style, having fallen into dilapidation, was partly rebuilt in 1832, and the chancel in 1834; the ancient stalls and monuments have been preserved in the present structure, and among the latter is a monument to Sir John Topcliffe, chief justice and master of the mint in the reigns of Henry VII. and VIII., who resided at Topcliffe Hall, now a farmhouse. The Wesleyans have a place of worship.

ARDWICK, a township, forming two ecclesiastical districts, in the parish and borough of Manchester, union of Chorlton, hundred of Salford, S. division of the county of Lancaster, 1 mile (S. E. by E.) from Manchester; containing 9906 inhabitants. This is a wealthy suburb of Manchester, comprising 496 acres, and chiefly inhabited by merchants of that town. For ecclesiastical purposes the township is divided into two districts, the Manchester and Birmingham railway being the line of separation : this railway is here joined by the Manchester and Sheffield line. The railway called the Ardwick Junction is a third line connected with the township, measuring 1¾ mile in length, and reaching from Ardwick to the Ashton branch of the Manchester and Leeds railway. The living of St. Thomas' is a perpetual curacy; net income, £294; patrons, the Dean and Canons of Manchester. The church has been twice enlarged during the present incumbency, viz. in 1831 and 1836, at a cost in both instances of £2000, the building being lengthened at each end, and a tower erected in a campanile form : the interior is neat, and the altar ornamented by an original picture, by Bassano, of the Presentation in the Temple, the gift of William Townend, Esq., late of Ardwick. The living of St. Silas' is also a perpetual curacy, in the patronage of Five Trustees. The church was built in 1841, at a cost of £4564; it is in the Norman style, with a tower and spire. The Wesleyans and Independents have places of worship; and there is a public cemetery of eight acres, opened in 1838, at a cost of £18,000. In both districts are excellent schools.

69

ARELEY, KING'S, or Lower Areley (*St. Bartholomew*), a parish, in the union of Martley, Upper division of the hundred of Doddingtree, the Hundred-House and W. divisions of the county of Worcester, ½ a mile (S. W. by W.) from Stourport; containing 423 inhabitants. The parish comprises 1449 acres, whereof two-thirds are arable and the remainder pasture, with the exception of sixty acres of common or waste. It is separated from Stourport by the river Severn, and fully partakes of the beauty of the surrounding district; the general surface is irregular, and the higher grounds are clothed with wood. Across the western boundary of the parish, nearly from north to south, a range of hills or high grounds extends from Stagberry, in the parish of Ribbesford, towards the Abberley hills : from the base of these hills the land generally slopes to the Severn. The living is a rectory, valued in the king's books at £9, and in the patronage of the Rector of Martley: the tithes have been commuted for £358, and there is a glebe of 41 acres, with a house. The church is situated on a considerable eminence commanding a fine prospect and nearly overhanging the river, which flows through a rich valley at the base. In the burial-ground is a singular sepulchral monument, of the date of about 1690, supposed to commemorate Sir Harry Coningsby, of Hampton Court, who lived in seclusion in this parish, in consequence of the loss of his only child.

ARELEY, UPPER (*St. Peter*), a parish, in the union of Kidderminster, S. division of the hundred of Seisdon and of the county of Stafford, 4 miles (N. by W.) from Bewdley; containing 667 inhabitants. The parish comprises 3803a. 3r. 12p., whereof 58 acres are common or waste; the surface is undulated, the soil generally good, and the scenery very fine. A thin stratum of coal is worked; and there are quarries of red freestone, of which large blocks are raised for building, and which is also used for grindstones and millstones. Areley Castle, the seat of the late Earl of Mountnorris, who, when Viscount Valentia, published his interesting travels in the east, is now the residence of his nephew, A. L. Annesley, Esq., who succeeded to his English and Irish estates. The village occupies a romantic situation near the margin of the river Severn. The living is a perpetual curacy; patron and impropriator, Mr. Annesley; incumbent, the Rev. John Allen. The great tithes have been commuted for £391. 7., and those of the incumbent for £305 : the impropriate glebe consists of 199 acres; the glebe belonging to the incumbent contains about half an acre, with a good house. The church, which is situated on an eminence commanding a fine prospect, was first built by Henry de Port, in the reign of Henry I., and was rebuilt in the time of Edward I. : the interior was renovated and beautified at the expense of the late Earl of Mountnorris, who also built a handsome school-house, with a residence for the master, and endowed the school with £21 per annum. In Areley wood are the remains of a Roman camp; at Hawkbatch a Roman town and bridge are said to have existed, and many Roman coins have been found in that part of the parish. There are mineral springs, which are said to be something like the Harrogate waters, and have been used for medicinal purposes.

ARGAM, or Ergam (*St. John the Baptist*), a parish, in the union of Bridlington, wapentake of

DICKERING, E. riding of YORK, 5½ miles (N. W.) from Bridlington; containing 30 inhabitants. The parish is situated near the road leading from Bridlington to Malton, and comprises by computation 510 acres of land. The living is a discharged rectory, valued in the king's books at £4, and in the patronage of C. Grimston, Esq., with a net income of £21. The church was one of the chapels of Hunmanby, until it was appropriated to the abbey of Bardensey; few traces of it now remain.

ARKENDALE, a chapelry, in the parish of KNARESBOROUGH, Lower division of the wapentake of CLARO, W. riding of YORK, 4 miles (N. E.) from Knaresborough; containing 261 inhabitants. This place comprises 1516a. 2r. 35p., of which more than two-thirds are arable, and the remainder meadow and pasture, with 4½ acres of wood. The soil is partly sand, but mostly clay, producing good crops of wheat, barley, oats, and turnips; the surface is hilly, and picturesque, the higher grounds commanding extensive views. The village is situated at the distance of a mile from the Boroughbridge and Wetherby, and the Boroughbridge and Knaresborough, roads. The living is a perpetual curacy, in the patronage of the Vicar of Knaresborough, with a net income of £90: the tithes of the manor were commuted for land, under an inclosure act, in 1773, and a rent-charge of £107 has been lately awarded as a commutation for tithes. The chapel, dedicated to St. Bartholomew, was rebuilt in 1836, at a cost of about £750, raised by subscription, aided by a grant of £100 from the Incorporated Society; it is a handsome edifice of white brick and stone, in the early English style, with a square embattled tower, and contains 210 sittings, of which 144 are free. A parsonage-house, pleasantly situated on an eminence, was built in 1841. There is a place of worship for Wesleyans.

ARKENGARTH-DALE, otherwise ARKENDALE (ST. MARY), a parish, in the union of RICHMOND, wapentake of GILLING-WEST, N. riding of YORK, 12 miles (W. by N.) from Richmond; containing 1243 inhabitants. This is a large moorland parish, the most interesting part of which is its picturesque dale, about eight miles long, and beautifully studded with rural hamlets, whereof the principal are Arkle, Booze, Eskeylith, Langthwaite, Whaw, Seal-houses, and Dale-head. It comprises by computation 14,256 acres; 3200 are pasture and meadow, 5 arable, 51 wood, 50 public road, and 10,950 common land. The district abounds in lead-ore, lying principally in high and bleak moors, in the vicinity of the Arkle rivulet, on whose south side the mountain called *Water Crag* rises 2186 feet above the level of the sea: the lead-mines are of great antiquity, some of them having been worked in the reign of King John, and they are still very productive. There are also extensive smelting-works, where more than 1000 tons of lead are made into ingots yearly; and two excellent slate-quarries are in operation. The road leading from Reeth, in Swaledale, to Kirkby-Stephen and Brough, in Westmorland, passes through the whole length of the parish. The living is a perpetual curacy, in the patronage of Sir John Lowther, Bart., the impropriator, with a net income of £123, and a house. The present church, built in 1818, stands about half a mile from the site of the old edifice, and is a neat stone structure capable of accommodating from 500 to 600 persons; the cost of its erection, between £2000 and

£3000, was defrayed, partly by money bequeathed by the late George Brown, Esq., and partly by the Rev. John Gilpin. At Langthwaite are places of worship for Primitive Methodists and Wesleyans.

ARKESDEN (ST. MARY), a parish, in the union of SAFFRON-WALDEN, hundred of UTTLESFORD, N. division of ESSEX, 3 miles (E.) from Newport, and 9 miles (N.) from Bishop-Stortford; containing 498 inhabitants. It comprises 2297a. 2r. 28p.; the surface is undulated, the soil a heavy and tenacious clay. The living is a discharged vicarage, valued in the king's books at £13. 6. 8.; net income, £181; patron and impropriator, R. B. Wolfe, Esq. It was formerly endowed with a portion of the great tithes, which were commuted for land and a corn-rent, under an inclosure act, in 1814. The church, a spacious and handsome structure with a square embattled tower, in the later English style, is finely situated on the slope of a hill; the north aisle was built by Thomas Alderton, of London, who founded a chantry here in the reign of Hen. VII.

ARKHOLME, with CAWOOD, a chapelry, in the parish of MELLING, hundred of LONSDALE south of the Sands, N. division of the county of LANCASTER, 10 miles (N. E.) from Lancaster, on the road to Kirkby-Lonsdale; containing 407 inhabitants. This place is mentioned in the Domesday survey. Roger de Monte Begon gave to the Cluniac priory of Thetford the wood called "Cainueda;" and in the reign of Edward I. Geoffrey de Nevill obtained the grant of a market and fair to be held in the township. It comprises 2756 acres, whereof 2466 are meadow and pasture, 160 arable, and 130 waste, forest, &c.; the surface is generally level, being part of the vale of the Lune, which river flows beautifully in this vicinity. Stone for building is quarried, and the population are employed in agriculture and the manufacture of baskets and other articles of osier-work, several osier-beds being found along the river. The living is a perpetual curacy, with a net income of £65, and a house; patron, the Vicar of Melling. The church is an ancient plain structure, with a bell-tower. A school is supported by subscription. Behind the church is a tumulus.

ARKLESIDE, a hamlet, in the township of CARLTON-HIGHDALE, parish of COVERHAM, union of LEYBURN, wapentake of HANG-WEST, N. riding of YORK, 8 miles (S. W.) from Middleham. The tithes belong to the incumbent of Coverham, the monks of which place had lands here, producing £6. 13. 4. per annum.

ARKSEY (ALL SAINTS), a parish, in the union of DONCASTER, N. division of the wapentake of STRAFFORTH and TICKHILL, W. riding of YORK, 3 miles (N. by E.) from Doncaster; containing 1056 inhabitants, of whom 266 are in the hamlet of Arksey, and 697 in that of Bentley. The parish comprises the hamlets of Stockbridge, Almholm, Shaftholme, Bodles, Doncaster Bridge-End, and Scawthorpe; and consists of about 5220 acres of fertile land in a champaign district of rich loam: it is bounded on the east by the river Don, and watered by two of its tributary streams. The living is a vicarage, valued in the king's books at £12. 17. 6., in the patronage of Sir William Bryan Cooke, Bart., the impropriator, with a net income of £113: the tithes were commuted for land and a money payment, under an inclosure act, in the 7th and 8th of George IV. The church consists of a nave, chancel, aisles, transepts, and

70

a tower with a low spire rising from the centre; the interior is rich in heraldic insignia, and the windows have much stained glass in good preservation. The free grammar school here was built in pursuance of the will of Sir George Cooke, and has an endowment of £40 per annum, left by Sir Bryan Cooke in 1660. An alms-house for 12 poor inhabitants is endowed with £120 per annum.—See BENTLEY.

ARLECDON (ST. MICHAEL), a parish, in the union of WHITEHAVEN, ALLERDALE ward above Derwent, W. division of CUMBERLAND, 5¼ miles (E. N. E.) from Whitehaven; consisting of the townships of Arlecdon, Frizington, and Whillymoor; and containing 558 inhabitants, of whom 211 are in Arlecdon township. It comprises 5311a. 3r. 15p.; and possesses coal, iron-ore, limestone, and freestone. Fairs for cattle are held on April 24th, the first Friday in June, and Sept. 17th. The living is a perpetual curacy, in the patronage of the Bishop of Chester; net income, £100. The tithes for the township of Arlecdon were commuted for land, under an inclosure act, in 1819. The present church was consecrated Aug. 25th, 1829; divine service is also performed in a Sunday school, lately erected, and licensed by the bishop. On an estate called Cringle-gill is a chalybeate spring, the water of which is stated to possess similar properties to that of Harrogate.

ARLESCOTE, a township, in the parish of WAR-MINGTON, union of BANBURY, Burton-Dasset division of the hundred of KINGTON, S. division of the county of WARWICK, 5½ miles (E. S. E.) from Kington; containing 43 inhabitants. This place was given soon after the Conquest to the Earl of Mellent, who bestowed a portion of it on the monks of Preaux. The manor, after the Dissolution, passed from the crown to the Andrews family.

ARLESTON, with SYNFIN, a liberty, in the parish of BARROW, union of SHARDLOW, hundred of APPLE-TREE (though locally in the hundred of REPTON and GRESLEY), S. division of the county of DERBY, 4½ miles (S. by W.) from Derby; containing 85 inhabitants. The manor of Arleston was conveyed, in 1426, to the Bothes, whose descendant died seised of it in 1519; it afterwards came to the Blounts, and from them to Sir John Harpur, ancestor of the Crewes. Synfin belonged in the reign of Edward I. to the family of Toke, who were succeeded by the Bothes; and this estate came also, in the reign of Charles I., to the ancestor of Sir John Crewe, Bart. Synfin moor, a large common, on which the Derby races were held, was inclosed about 1804.

ARLESTON, a hamlet, in the parish and union of WELLINGTON, hundred of SOUTH BRADFORD, N. division of SALOP; containing 181 inhabitants.

ARLEY (ST. WILFRID), a parish, in the union of NUNEATON, Kirby division of the hundred of KNIGHT-LOW, N. division of the county of WARWICK, 8 miles (N. N. W.) from Coventry; containing 265 inhabitants. The parish is traversed by the road from Coventry to Tamworth, and comprises 1929a. 29p. of land, the greater portion of which is pasture and meadow; 140 acres are wood, and 20 common or waste. The soil is variable, some parts good, and some stiff clay; the sur-face is undulated, and the scenery picturesque. Lime in considerable quantities, and stone for the roads, are obtained here. The chief proprietor is Alfred Ashley Vaughton, Esq., of Fillongley Lodge. The living is a

rectory, valued in the king's books at £9. 0. 7½.; patron and incumbent, the Rev. R. R. Vaughton: the tithes have been commuted for £336. 8., and the glebe con-sists of 74 acres. The church is an ancient edifice, with a square tower. £20 yearly out of lands producing up-wards of £200 per annum, left by William Avery, and a donation of the interest of £600 in the new three-and-a-half per cents., by John and Francis Holmes, go to-wards the support of a free school. A Sunday school is supported by the rector.

ARLEY, UPPER, STAFFORD.—See ARELEY, UPPER.

ARLINGHAM (ST. MARY THE VIRGIN), a parish, in the union of WHEATENHURST, Upper division of the hundred of BERKELEY, W. division of the county of GLOUCESTER, 1½ mile (S. E. by E.) from Newnham; containing 793 inhabitants. The parish is situated on a nook of land formed by a curvature of the Severn, by which river it is bounded on three sides, and across which is a ferry to Newnham: from an eminence called Barrow hill is a very extensive and pleasing view. The living is a vicarage, valued in the king's books at £19. 7. 3½., and in the patronage of Mrs. Hodges, to whom also the impropriation belongs; net income, £193. The tithes were commuted for land and corn-rents, by an inclosure act, in 1801. There is a place of worship for Wesleyans. Mrs. Mary Yate, in 1765, endowed a school for boys and girls with a rent-charge of £40; she also gave an additional rent-charge of £40 for the benefit of the poor.

ARLINGTON (ST. JAMES), a parish, in the union of BARNSTAPLE, hundred of SHERWILL, Braunton and N. divisions of DEVON, 6¼ miles (N. E. by N.) from Barnstaple; containing 206 inhabitants. The parish comprises 4000 acres, and is intersected by the river Yeo. Arlington Court, a spacious and handsome man-sion in the Grecian-Doric style, is situated here. The living is a rectory, valued in the king's books at £13. 18. 1½.; net income, £272; patron, J. P. Chichester, Esq. The church, which has lately been rebuilt by the patron, contains a beautiful monument in marble to one of the Carey family, and the figure of a female crowned.

ARLINGTON, a tything, in the parish of BIBURY, union of NORTHLEACH, hundred of BRIGHTWELL'S-BAR-ROW, E. division of the county of GLOUCESTER, 4¾ miles (N. W.) from Fairford; containing 371 inhabitants.

ARLINGTON (ST. PANCRAS), a parish, in the union of HAILSHAM, hundred of LONGBRIDGE, rape of PEVEN-SEY, E. division of SUSSEX, 3 miles (W. S. W.) from Hailsham; containing 686 inhabitants. A priory of Black canons was founded at Michelham, in this parish, in honour of the Holy Trinity, by Gilbert de Aquila, in the reign of Henry III.; it continued to flourish till the Dissolution, when its revenue was estimated at £191. 19. 3.: the remains have been converted into a farmhouse, on the north side of which are various pillars and arches, still in tolerable preservation. The parish comprises 5100 acres by admeasurement. The living is a discharged vicarage, valued in the king's books at £10. 6. 11.; net income, £156; patron, the Prebendary of Woodhorne in the Cathedral of Chichester; impro-priator, Mrs. Attree. The church is an ancient structure in the decorated English style. At Upper Dicker Com-mon, in the parish, is a church dedicated to the Holy Trinity, to which a chapelry district was assigned in 1843, comprising parts of the parishes of Arlington, Chiddingly, and Hellingly: the patronage belongs to the Bishop. There is a place of worship for Wesleyans. In the hamlet of Milton is the site of Barlow Castle, over-looking the river Cuckmere.

ARLSEY (St. Peter), a parish, in the union and hundred of Biggleswade, county of Bedford, 6 miles (S.) from Biggleswade; containing 820 inhabitants. This place is in the Domesday survey noticed as a market-town, and in 1270 Stephen Edworth, then lord of the manor, obtained a confirmation of the grant for its market, and a grant of a fair on the festival of St. Peter and St. Paul, both of which have been long discontinued. The parish is bounded on the north by the river Ivel, and on the west by the Hiz, both of which unite in the north-west extremity. It is intersected by the road from Baldock to Bedford, and comprises by measure-ment 2303 acres, of which about 1600 are arable, 500 pasture, 20 wood, and 50 common; the sub-soil is gravel and clay. The women and children are employed in the straw-plat manufacture. The living is a discharged vicarage, with the rectory of Astwick annexed, and valued in the king's books at £8 per annum; it is in the patronage of Mrs. Roger Smith. At the inclosure of the parish, 255 acres were allotted in lieu of tithes, and there are 15 acres of grass land round the glebe-house. The church is a neat edifice. There is a place of worship for Wesleyans. At Etonbury, near the road to Baldock, are the remains of a Roman encampment; and a spot still called the Hermitage, was the site of an ancient religious house.

ARMATHWAITE, a chapelry, in the parish of Hes-ket-in-the-Forest, union of Penrith, Leath ward, E. division of Cumberland, 5 miles (N. W.) from Kirk-Oswald. The village is beautifully situated on the western bank of the Eden, over which is a good stone bridge of four arches. Armathwaite Castle, a handsome modern edifice, built on the site of an ancient fortress, occupies a rocky elevation, at the foot of which flows the Eden; in the reign of Henry VIII. it was, with the estate, the property of John Skelton, the poet-laureat. The living is a perpetual curacy; net income, £50; patrons, the Trustees of Mr. Milbourne, in whom also the impropriation is vested. The chapel was rebuilt by Richard Skelton in 1668, having for some time previously been used as a shed for cattle.

ARMIN, a chapelry, in the parish of Snaith, union of Goole, Lower division of the wapentake of Osgold-cross, W. riding of York, 2 miles (N. N, W.) from Goole; containing 593 inhabitants. This chapelry, the name of which signifies the "mouth of the Aire," is bounded on the north-west by that river, and is situated on the road from Doncaster to Hull. The living is a perpetual curacy; net income, £71; patrons, the Earl of Beverley, and N. E. Yarburgh, Esq.; impropriator, the earl. The chapel is dedicated to St. David.

ARMINGHALL (St. Mary), a parish, in the union and hundred of Henstead, E. division of Norfolk, 3 miles (S. E. by S.) from Norwich; comprising by com-putation 650 acres, and containing 79 inhabitants. The living is a perpetual curacy; net income, £66; patrons and appropriators, the Dean and Chapter of Norwich, whose tithes have been commuted for £229. 10. The church is chiefly in the early English style, and consists of a nave and chancel, with a square tower. An old house near it has a very rich and curious porch, on the

72

door of which is written, in ancient characters, "Pray for the soul of Master William Ely, who caused this to be made an hospital in the year 1487."

ARMITAGE (St. John), with Handsacre, a parish, in the union of Lichfield, S. division of the hundred of Offlow and of the county of Stafford, 3 miles (E. S. E.) from Rugeley; containing 967 inhabitants. This place was formerly called Hermitage, from a tradi-tion that a hermit anciently resided in a sequestered spot between the church and the river Trent. The parish is intersected by the Grand Trunk canal, is skirted by the Trent, and lies on the main road from Lichfield to Uttoxeter, in a beautiful and fertile part of the county exceedingly well wooded; it comprises 1921a. 2r. 24p., whereof 821 acres are arable, 829 pasture, 100 wood, and 70 acres gardens. Bricks and tiles are made to some extent. The living is a perpetual curacy, in the patronage of the Bishop of Lichfield; net income, £100, with a small glebe. The tithes formerly belonged to a canonry in Lichfield cathedral, which being suppressed, they have fallen to the Ecclesiastical Commissioners; they have been commuted for £336. The body of the church was rebuilt, and a south aisle added, in the Nor-man style, in 1845, at a cost of £1500; the old porch, also, was restored: the font is curious, and very ancient. There is a place of worship for Independents; and a national school for boys and girls, established in 1839.— See Handsacre.

ARMLEY, a chapelry, in the parish of St. Peter, liberty of the borough of Leeds, W. riding of York, 2½ miles (W. by N.) from Leeds; containing 5676 in-habitants. This chapelry comprises 939a. 1r. 18p.; the soil is tolerably fertile, and excellent building-stone abounds; the surface is boldly undulated, and from the east side, looking towards Headingley, the scenery is picturesque. Armley House is a noble mansion of the Ionic order, situated in an extensive and richly-wooded park. The old Hall, anciently the residence of the Hop-tons, lords of the manor, is now a farmhouse. The village is situated on the west side of the river Aire, and extends for a considerable distance along the acclivities of the vale: the Leeds and Liverpool canal passes in a direction nearly parallel with the river, and also the new road from Stanningley to Leeds, completed in 1836. The inhabitants are employed in extensive woollen-mills. The chapel, dedicated to St. Bartholomew, and originally erected in the reign of Charles I., was rebuilt in 1835, at an expense of £1000, of which £300 were granted by the Incorporated Society, and the remainder raised by sub-scription; it contains 930 sittings. The living is a perpetual curacy, in the patronage of the Vicar of Leeds, with a net income of £204, and a glebe-house. A Sun-day evening lecture was established in 1841, and is sup-ported at the sole expense of Mr. Gott; the lecturer has a liberal income, and a commodious house. The Dean and Chapter of Oxford receive a tithe rent-charge of £30. There are places of worship for Wesleyans, Primitive Methodists, and Methodists of the New Con-nexion. Almshouses for 12 poor widows, and a national schoolroom for 500 children, were erected near the chapel in 1832, by the late Benjamin Gott, Esq.; they form a handsome range of buildings in the Elizabethan style. Above the village is a lofty eminence named Giant's hill, on which are the remains of some works supposed to have been a Danish fort; there were some others on two eminences called the Red and White War hills, but they were destroyed in the formation of the canal.

ARMSCOTT, a hamlet, in the parish of NEWBOLD, union of SHIPSTON-UPON-STOUR, Upper division of the hundred of OSWALDSLOW, Blockley and E. divisions of the county of WORCESTER, 3 miles (N. by W.) from Shipston; containing 139 inhabitants, and comprising 714 acres. It is in the southern part of the parish, a short distance westward of the river Stour, and on the road from Chipping-Campden to Warwick.

ARMSTON, a hamlet, in the parish and hundred of POLEBROOK, union of OUNDLE, N. division of the county of NORTHAMPTON, 2¼ miles (E. S. E.) from Oundle; containing 26 inhabitants, and comprising 784 acres. It is situated near the right ·bank of the river Nene, and in the south-western part of the parish.

ARMTHORPE (ST. MARY), a parish, in the union of DONCASTER, S. division of the wapentake of STRAFFORTH and TICKHILL, W. riding of YORK, 4 miles (E. N. E.) from Doncaster; containing, with the hamlet of Nutwell, 449 inhabitants. This place, in Domesday book called Ernulfestorp, was the property of the monks of the abbey of Roche, who had a grange here, at which the official resided who managed this part of the estates of the establishment, and who was sometimes a brother of the house: they had also an officer called their forester. The parish comprises 3810 acres, and includes the farms of Holm-Wood and Waterton, the latter of which was long the seat of the ancient family of its own name, one of whom several served the office of high sheriff, and one was master of the horse to Henry V. The village consists of scattered houses, and is situated on a declivity. The living is a rectory, valued in the king's books at £8. 18. 9., and in the patronage of the Crown, with a net income of £366: the tithes were commuted for land and a money payment, by an inclosure act, in 1775. The church is a small building, with an octagonal turret, and exhibits a good specimen of the original country churches for small parishes. The Primitive Methodists have a place of worship.

ARNCLIFFE (ST. OSWALD), a parish, partly in the union of SKIPTON, and E. division of the wapentake of STAINCLIFFE and EWCROSS, but chiefly in the union of SETTLE, and W. division of that wapentake, W. riding of YORK, 4 miles (N. by W.) from Kettlewell; comprising the townships of Buckden, Hawkeswick, and Litton, and the chapelry of Halton-Gill; and containing 834 inhabitants, of whom 182 are in the township of Arncliffe. This parish consists by estimation of 35,860 acres, nearly all in grass, including 5800 in Arncliffe township; and is bounded on the west by Pennygent, a mountain 2270 feet high, and on the north by Camm Fell, 2245 feet high. The district consists of two valleys, separated by an almost impassable mountain: one of these, called Langstrothdale, is watered by the Wharfe, which has its rise here; and the other, called Littondale, by the Skirfare, which forms a junction with the Wharfe at the bottom of the valley. The air is for the greater part of the year piercing, owing to, the vicinity of the high hills just mentioned, which being often capped with snow, render the winds cold and sharp. There is a cotton-mill in the village, but grazing forms the chief occupation of the inhabitants. The living is a discharged vicarage, valued in the king's books at £13. 6. 8.; net

income, £50, with an excellent glebe-house; patrons and appropriators, the Master and Fellows of University College, Oxford: the tithes have been commuted for £483. 7. The church, with the exception of the tower, was taken down and rebuilt in 1805: the chancel has just been again rebuilt by subscription, and in the same style as the tower; and several windows of that charac. ter have been inserted in the body of the edifice. At Halton-Gill and Hubberholme are chapels, the livings of which are in the patronage of the Vicar of Arncliffe.

ARNCLIFFE, INGLEBY (ST. ANDREW), a parish, in the union of STOKESLEY, W. division of the liberty of LANGBAURGH, N. riding of YORK, 7 miles (S. W. by W.) from Stokesley; containing 329 inhabitants. There appears, from Domesday book, to have been anciently two manors in the parish, Ingleby and Arncliffe, which after the Conquest were held by King William, when they were styled Engelebi and Erneclive; the estates were subsequently granted to Robert de Brus, as parcel of the barony of Skelton, to be held of the king in capite; and among the families which have at different periods owned property here, occur those of Bruce, Fauconberge, Ingelram, Colville, and Mauleverer. The parish is in the district called Cleveland, and comprises 1850 acres, of which about 1200 are arable, 300 woodland and plantations, and the remainder meadow and pasture. The lands are chiefly the property of William Mauleverer, Esq., the descendant of the Norman baron who came over with the Conqueror from Normandy, and whose family have continued here since that period. The surface is undulated, and the high grounds command fine views of the vale of Cleveland, the distant hills of Richmond, and the sea; the hills are richly wooded, and the scenery in many parts is beautifully picturesque; the soil is a strong clay. Freestone of good quality is plentiful; but as there is little demand, it is not wrought to any great extent. The village of Ingleby, the only one in the parish, is neatly built, and occupies a retired situation on the summit of a gentle ridge, at a short distance from the road between Stokesley and Thirsk. The living is a perpetual curacy, in the patronage of Bryan Abbs, Esq., the impropriator, with a net income of £49: the tithes have been commuted for £125. The church is a neat plain structure with a campanile turret, erected in 1822, at an expense of £500, raised by subscription.

ARNCOTT, a chapelry, in the parish of AMBROSDEN, union of BICESTER, hundred of BULLINGTON, though locally in the hundred of PLOUGHLEY, county of OXFORD, 2¼ miles (S. E. by S.) from Bicester; containing 331 inhabitants.

ARNE, a parochial chapelry, in the union of WAREHAM and PURBECK, hundred of HASILOR, Wareham division of DORSET, 4 miles (E. by N.) from Wareham; containing 168 inhabitants; and comprising 1068a. 2r. 21p., exclusive of 1754 acres of common or waste. The village is situated on the shore of Poole harbour, between Wareham and Brownsey Island. On the summit of an eminence connected with a bank of gravel or pebbles, extending north-eastward into the harbour, is a large barrow, which was formerly used as a beacon. The living is a perpetual curacy, in the patronage of the Rector of Warcham. The chapel, dedicated to St. Nicholas, is a plain structure of ancient date.

ARNESBY (ST. PETER), a parish, in the union of LUTTERWORTH, hundred of GUTHLAXTON, S. division

L

of the county of LEICESTER, 8½ miles (S. by E.) from Leicester; containing 505 inhabitants. It is situated on the road from Leicester to Welford, and comprises about 1250 acres of land, nearly all pasture; the soil is chiefly a clay of a strong quality. The population is principally employed in the stocking manufacture. The living is a discharged vicarage, valued in the king's books at £5. 16. 8.; patron, John Sherwin, Esq.: the tithes have been commuted for £60, and the glebe comprises 25 acres. The church is a substantial edifice in good repair, containing about 400 sittings. There is a place of worship for Baptists. Two allotments of land, comprising together 16½ acres, and producing £50. 13. per annum, are appropriated to the benefit of the poor. Robert Hall, the distinguished theological writer, was born here in 1764; the building in which he preached his first sermon is now a barn.

ARNFORD-CUM-NEWTON, a hamlet, in the township of HELLIFIELD, parish of LONG PRESTON, union of SETTLE, W. division of the wapentake of STAINCLIFFE and EWCROSS, W. riding of YORK. This place, of which mention is made in one of the oldest Craven charters, belonged to the monks of Fountains, with whom it continued till the Dissolution, when it became the property of the Greshams.

ARNOLD (ST. MARY), a parish, in the union of BASFORD, N. division of the wapentake of BROXTOW and of the county of NOTTINGHAM, 4 miles (N. by E.) from Nottingham; containing, with part of the hamlet of Daybrook, 4509 inhabitants. It comprises by admeasurement 4349 acres, of which 2610 are arable, 1330 meadow and pasture, 294 wood and plantation, and the remainder roads, waste, &c.; the soil in the eastern part is clay, but elsewhere of a sandy nature. The village, which is remarkably healthy, and well supplied with water, is about three-quarters of a mile long, and a quarter broad, situated in the midst of the ancient forest of Sherwood, and surrounded by a beautifully undulated country. The inhabitants are principally employed in the manufacture of cotton hose, gloves, &c.; and the cotton stockings made here are as fine as those produced at any other place in England. A small fair is held on the first Wednesday after Sept. 19th. The living is a discharged vicarage, valued in the king's books at £7. 17. 8,. and in the patronage of the Duke of Devonshire; impropriator, T. Holdsworth, Esq. The small tithes have been commuted for £210, and there are 90 acres of glebe. The church is a large handsome edifice in the later English style, with a tower; a tablet in the interior records various charitable bequests amounting to about £150 per annum. There are places of worship for Wesleyans, Wesleyans of the New Connexion, Baptists, and Independents; and a Chartist meeting-house. On Cockliff hill, the highest ground in the county, are the remains of a Roman encampment.

ARNOLD, a township, partly in the parish of LONG RISTON, and partly in that of SWINE, union of SKIRLAUGH, N. division of the wapentake of HOLDERNESS, E. riding of YORK, 6 miles (E. N. E.) from Beverley; containing 154 inhabitants. This place, in the 13th century, belonged to the family of de Roos; the Hildyards afterwards held the lands for a considerable period, and among other proprietors occurs the abbot of Meaux. The township belongs, in nearly equal parts, to the two parishes, and comprises by computation 2000 acres: the village,
74

which is long and scattered, is situated to the north of the Lamwith stream. There are places of worship for Independents and Primitive Methodists.

ARNSIDE, a hamlet, in the township and parish of BEETHAM, union and ward of KENDAL, county of WESTMORLAND, 4 miles (S. W.) from Milnthorpe. It is situated in the southern part of the parish, near the border of Lancashire, and at the point where the river Kent expands into the bay of Morecambe. The scenery is beautiful: the house of Woodclose, here, surrounded by 50 acres of land, is the residence of Robert Preston Rodick, Esq.; and Morecambe Cottage, that of his brother, Thomas Rodick, Jun., Esq. A curious cave was discovered in 1844; it has a narrow entrance, but contains several large chambers. Here, also, are the ruins of the Tower of Arnside, which is supposed to have been erected to command the bay.

ARNWOOD, a tything, in the parish of HORDLE, union of LYMINGTON, hundred of CHRISTCHURCH, Lymington and S. divisions of HAMPSHIRE; containing 543 inhabitants. It stands in the northern part of the parish, on the borders of the New Forest.

ARRAM, a township, in the parish of LECKONFIELD, union of BEVERLEY, Hunsley-Beacon division of the wapentake of HARTHILL, E. riding of YORK, 3 miles (N. by E.) from Beverley; containing 117 inhabitants. This is a long scattered village, situated to the east of Leckonfield, and near the right bank of the river Hull.

ARRAM, a district, in the parish of ATWICK, union of SKIRLAUGH, N. division of the wapentake of HOLDERNESS, E. riding of YORK, 11½ miles (N. E.) from Beverley; containing 50 inhabitants. This place, in Domesday book styled Argun, and in other records Ergham, came at an early period into the possession of Meaux Abbey, to which institution Sir Steven Ergham gave some land here about 1190: the canons of Bridlington also had some interest in the property. The manor comprises about 500 acres: the manor-house, a neat residence, was built about the time of James I., but has been much modernised.

ARRAS, a hamlet, in the parish of MARKET-WEIGHTON, union of POCKLINGTON, Holme-Beacon division of the wapentake of HARTHILL, E. riding of YORK, 3 miles (E.) from Market-Weighton. The hamlet is situated on the Wolds, and on the road from Market-Weighton to Beverley. It is supposed there was a village here during the conflicts of the Saxons and Danes, if not at the time of the Romans, as the foundations of buildings have been discovered in a field, as have also fragments of chariot wheels, and the heads of arrows.

ARRETON (ST. GEORGE), a parish, in the liberty of EAST MEDINA, Isle of Wight and S. divisions of the county of SOUTHAMPTON, 3 miles (S. E.) from Newport; comprising by computation 9000 acres, and containing 1964 inhabitants. It abounds with limestone, which is extensively quarried for building purposes, and for burning into lime. The living is a discharged vicarage, valued in the king's books at £21; net income, £220; patron and impropriator, J. Fleming, Esq.: the small tithes have been commuted for £245, and there are 20 acres of glebe. The church, an ancient building with a heavy embattled tower, contains a brass effigy of a Knight Templar.

ARRINGTON (*St. Nicholas*), a parish, in the union of Caxton and Arrington, hundred of Wetherley, county of Cambridge, 5¾ miles (S. S. E.) from Caxton; containing 317 inhabitants, and comprising about 1300 acres. The living is a vicarage, valued in the king's books at £7. 6. 3.; net income, £69; patrons and impropriators, the Master and Fellows of Trinity College, Cambridge, who have commuted the tithes for £390. There are 22 acres of glebe.

. ARROW (*Holy Trinity*), a parish, in the union of Alcester, partly in the Alcester, and partly in the Stratford, division of the hundred of Barlichway, S. division of the county of Warwick, 1 mile (S. W.) from Alcester; containing, with Ragley and the hamlet of Oversley, 543 inhabitants. The parish is situated in the western part of the county, on the border of Worcestershire; and consists of 3983 acres, a considerable portion of which is attached to the beautiful demesne and interesting grounds of Ragley Park. The surface is agreeable, the river Arrow flowing through from north to south, with other streams in different directions, and the whole is thickly interspersed with wood, the rateable annual value of which in the parish is returned at £600. The roads from Alcester to Stratford and Evesham intersect the parish. The living is a rectory, valued in the king's books at £10. 10. 7½.; net income, £248; patron, the Marquess of Hertford. The church is an ancient structure, the tower of which was rebuilt in 1760.

ARROWE, or Arrow, a township, in the parish of Woodchurch, union, and Lower division of the hundred, of Wirrall, S. division of the county of Chester, 4½ miles (W. S. W.) from Birkenhead; containing 122 inhabitants. It lies on the Claughton and Hinderton road, and comprises 752 acres, whereof 97 are in wood, 17 roads, 266 park, and the rest arable and pasture; the soil is a stiff clay, and the surface elevated, commanding very extensive views. A moiety of the manor was in the Thornton family in the reign of Edward II., and passed by successive female heirs to the Duttons and Gerards; the other moiety was in the family of Tildesley in the reign of Henry VII. The manor has of late years been frequently alienated: one-half of it was left in 1527 to the free grammar school at Warrington, and was purchased in 1840 by John Ralph Shaw, Esq., who now owns the whole township, and who in 1835 built the Hall, a mansion of stone, in the Elizabethan style. From the tower of Arrowe Hall can be seen Black Comb, in the county of Cumberland, and the Snowdon range of hills in North Wales.

ARROWTHORNE, a township, partly in the parish of Hornby, but chiefly in that of Brompton-Patrick, union of Leyburn, wapentake of Hang-East, N. riding of York, 5 miles (S. by S.) from Catterick; containing 81 inhabitants. It is situated to the west of the demesne of Hornby Castle, and comprises about 850 acres of land.

ARTHINGTON, a township, in the parish of Addle, Upper division of the wapentake of Skyrack, W. riding of York, 4½ miles (E.) from Otley; containing 336 inhabitants. This place is situated in Wharfdale, and abounds with interesting scenery; Arthington Hall is in the township. A convent of Cluniac nuns founded here in the twelfth century, by Piers de Ardington, was valued at the Dissolution at £19: the site is occupied by a farmhouse called the "Nunnery."

75

ARTHINGWORTH (*St. Andrew*), a parish, in the union of Market-Harborough, hundred of Roth-well, N. division of the county of Northampton, 4½ miles (S. by E.) from Harborough; containing 242 inhabitants. It comprises 1593 acres, of which 1293 are pasture, 245 arable, and 55 woodland; the soil is of various qualities, a great part being a strong clay; the grazing grounds are very fine. The living is a rectory, valued in the king's books at £12. 2. 8½.; net income, £323; patron, the Rev. Henry Ralph Rokeby. The tithes were commuted for land, under an inclosure act, in 1767; the glebe consists of 215 acres of land, and a house. The church is an ancient structure, with a handsome well-proportioned square tower of later date. A school is endowed with about 24 acres of land at Ashley, producing £40 per annum.

ARTHURET (*St. Michael*), a parish, in the union of Longtown, Eskdale ward, E. division of Cumberland, ¾ of a mile (S.) from Longtown; comprising the townships of Breconhill, Lyneside, Longtown, and Netherby, and containing 2859 inhabitants. This parish is situated on the border of Scotland, where in 1337 a Scottish army crossed, which, marching eastward, destroyed about twenty villages; and at the chapel of Solom, a small oratory which anciently stood near the spot called the Chapel Flosh, commissioners from England and Scotland met in 1343, to settle the boundaries of the respective countries. On Solom Moss, in 1542, the Scots, 10,000 in number, but discontented with their commander, Oliver Sinclair, a favourite of the Scottish monarch, allowed themselves to be defeated by a small body of about 500 English troops, under the command of Dacres and Musgrave, and it is said that 1000 of them were made prisoners, amongst whom were 200 noblemen, esquires, and gentlemen. The parish comprises about 11,000 acres, and there are quarries of white and red freestone within its limits. The living is a rectory, valued in the king's books at £3. 2. 1.; net income, £687; patron, Sir J. R. G. Graham, Bart. The church was rebuilt in 1609, with the exception of the tower, which was not erected till 1690: in the churchyard is a rude cross with a pierced capital, near which were interred the remains of Archibald Armstrong, court jester to James I. and Charles I., and a native of the parish. An artificial tumulus, in the form of a prostrate human figure, near the church, is said to have been raised over the body of a chieftain slain in the above-mentioned battle.

ARTILLERY-GROUND, OLD, a liberty, in the union of Whitechapel, locally in the Finsbury division of the hundred of Ossulstone, county of Middlesex; containing 1558 inhabitants. It forms one of five divisions of the liberty of the Tower, and is detached.

ARTINGTON, a tything, in the parish of St. Nicholas, Guildford, union of Guildford, First division of the hundred of Godalming, W. division of Surrey, 1 mile (S. by W.) from Guildford; containing 687 inhabitants. Artington lies on the west side of the river Wey, and, according to tradition, was once the principal part of the town of Guildford. Some lands here were given in the reign of Henry III. to the nuns of Wherwell, in Hampshire, who continued in the possession of them until the dissolution of their nunnery in the time of Henry VIII. The rents of "Ertindon

L 2

belonging to the establishment then amounted to £1. 1. 2. per annum.

Arms.

ARUNDEL (*HOLY TRINITY*), a borough, market-town, and parish, having exclusive jurisdiction, locally in the hundred and rape of ARUNDEL, W. division of SUSSEX, 10 miles (E. by N.) from Chichester, and 55 (S. by W.) from London; containing 2624 inhabitants. This place, which derives its name from its situation in a dale watered by the river Arun, is first noticed in the will of Alfred, who bequeathed the castle and a few adjacent residences to his nephew Athelm. The castle, which was rebuilt by Roger de Montgomery at the time of the Conquest, was, in the reign of Henry I., besieged and taken from Montgomery's son, Robert de Belesme, who had rebelled against his sovereign, and settled by that monarch on his second wife Adeliza, who by a subsequent marriage conveyed it to William D'Albini, Lord of Buckenham, in the county of Norfolk. Matilda, daughter of Henry I., asserting her claim to the throne in opposition to Stephen, landed at Littlehampton in 1139, and was received and protected for several days in this castle against the forces of her opponent; in recompense for which service, her son Henry II., on his accession, granted the castle and honour of Arundel to William D'Albini and his heirs for ever. William, the fourth earl, dying without heirs male, the property was divided among his four sisters, and the castle and manor of Arundel descended to John Fitzalan, son of the second sister, in whose family they continued till 1580, when they passed to Philip Howard, Earl of Surrey, descendant of another of the sisters, who had married Thomas, Duke of Norfolk. On the earl's attainder in 1589, the castle and manor of Arundel reverted to the crown; and they continued to form part of the royal possessions till the death of Queen Elizabeth. The property was restored by James I. to Thomas, son of Philip, from whom, in uninterrupted succession, it has descended to the present proprietor, Henry Charles, Earl of Arundel and Duke of Norfolk. During the civil wars the castle was garrisoned for the parliament, but in 1643 was taken by the royalists under the command of Lord Hopton, who placed in it a garrison of 200 men, and appointed Col. Ford, high sheriff of the county, governor. Being, however, afterwards besieged by Sir William Waller, it finally surrendered after a defence of seventeen days, was dismantled as a place of defence, and so far destroyed as to unfit it for a baronial residence. The CASTLE is situated on the summit of a high hill, and defended on two sides by the precipitous acclivity of the ground, and on the other by deep fosses. The walls originally inclosed an area 950 feet in length, and 250 feet in width, in the centre of which was the keep, a circular tower of great strength 100 feet in height, built on an artificial mound, and evidently of Norman origin. After remaining in a ruinous state till 1720, Thomas, Duke of Norfolk, restored part of the buildings, and erected others of modern style, making Arundel his occasional residence. Charles, the 11th duke, in 1791

made considerable additions; the north-west front was built in 1795, and the wing that contains the library and other apartments was completed in 1801. The entrance, which is by a deeply recessed Norman arched doorway, leads to the grand staircase and gallery, the latter of which, 195 feet in length, opens into the Barons' hall, erected in commemoration of the triumph of the barons in obtaining *Magna Charta*. The library is a strikingly magnificent apartment, 117 feet in length and 35 feet wide, panelled throughout with mahogany and cedar exquisitely carved, with a richly ornamented roof. The chapel is an elegant structure in the decorated English style, the walls of which are strengthened with slender enriched buttresses, terminating in crocketed pinnacles; the interior is lighted by windows of excellent design. The banqueting-room, formerly the ancient chapel, the saloon, and all the other state apartments of this magnificent structure, are of corresponding splendour. The entire range of building occupies three sides of a quadrangle, and the expense of restoration and the erection of new portions has already amounted to £400,000. The pleasure-grounds and gardens are tastefully laid out, and the park, which abounds with stately timber, comprises 1200 acres; the surrounding country presents richly varied scenery, and from the higher grounds within the park, and especially from the towers of the castle, are obtained extensive prospects. The castle is the head of the honour of Arundel, and confers on its possessor the title of Earl without creation, a feudal right which was adjudged by parliament, in the 11th of Henry VI., to an ancestor of the present Duke of Norfolk.

The TOWN is pleasantly situated on rising ground within four miles of the sea, and chiefly on the north bank of the river Arun, over which is a neat stone bridge of three arches. The houses are in general well built, and many of them modern and of handsome appearance; the streets, which are lighted with gas, are paved under an act of the 25th of George III., and the inhabitants plentifully supplied with excellent water. A considerable coasting-trade is carried on. The imports are chiefly butter, bacon, pork, lard, grain, and starch, from Ireland; grain and cheese from Holland; grain, oilcake, wine, fruit, and eggs, from France; timber, mostly from the Baltic; and coal from Newcastle and Scotland. The exports are principally oak-timber, corn, flour, and bark, to the west of England and Liverpool, and to Ireland. The port has a custom-house with the usual officers, and also affords a facility of intercourse between London and the Mediterranean, enabling the fruit ships from the latter to perform two voyages in the season: ships drawing sixteen feet of water can enter. The Brighton and Portsmouth railway passes to the south of the town, and has a station near Leominster, where the Arun is crossed by a bridge of peculiar construction. A canal also, connecting the Arun with the Thames and with Portsmouth, affords a medium of conveyance to various parts. There are two breweries on a large scale for the supply of the neighbourhood. The market is on Tuesday, chiefly for corn, the sale of which is considerable; and on every alternate Tuesday there is a large cattle-market : a few years since, a building was erected by subscription on the quay, for the purpose of a corn-market. The fairs are held on May 14th, Sept. 25th, and Dec. 17th, chiefly for cattle and pedlery; but, since the cattle-markets were established, they have been but little attended. Arundel is a BOROUGH by prescription, and has had a corporation from the time of the Conquest: the government is vested in a mayor, three aldermen, and twelve councillors, and the mayor and late mayor are justices of the peace; the municipal and parliamentary boundaries of the borough are the same, and are co-extensive with those of the parish. Petty-sessions are held by the county magistrates every alternate Tuesday, in an elegant town-hall erected by the late Duke of Norfolk, at an expense of £4000. The powers of the county debt-court of Arundel, established in 1847, extend over part of the registration-district of Worthing. The borough returned two members to parliament from the time of Edward I. to the 2nd of William IV., when it was destined thenceforward to send only one: the mayor is the returning officer.

The parish comprises 1834 acres, of which 30 are common or waste land. The LIVING is a discharged vicarage, valued in the king's books at £5. 0. 10.; net income, £199; patron, the Earl of Albemarle. The church, situated at the upper end of the town, was greatly damaged by the forces of Sir William Waller, who occupied it during the siege of the castle; but the whole was restored by the late duke. It is a large and ancient cruciform structure, with a low well-built central tower, surmounted by an obtuse leaden spire painted white; the style is chiefly later English, and the interior is very neatly fitted up. At the east end is the Norfolk chapel, consisting of a nave and north aisle divided by three fine arches, and lighted by windows of elegant design: this is the burial-place of the noble family of Howard, and it contains some interesting monuments. There is a place of worship for Independents. The Benedictine monastery of St. Nicholas, to which William D'Albini, the second earl, annexed the then vacant rectory of Arundel, was founded by Robert de Montgomery; the establishment flourished for two centuries, but was so greatly impoverished by Edward III., that it was neglected till the reign of Richard II., when the Earl of Arundel dissolved it, and founded in its place the College of the Holy Trinity, for a master, twelve chaplains, two deacons, two sub-deacons, and four choristers. This college continued to flourish till the Dissolution, when its revenues were estimated at £168. 0. 7.: part of the original building was converted by Charles, Duke of Norfolk, into a Roman Catholic chapel and a residence for his chaplain. The earl founded also the hospital of the Holy Trinity for a master and poor brethren, the revenue of which at the Dissolution was valued at £93. 18. 6¾.: on the rebuilding of the bridge over the Arun, in 1724, a considerable portion of the edifice was removed to furnish materials for that structure. The learned Chillingworth, who had joined the royal army, was taken prisoner during the siege of the castle by the parliamentarians, and confined in the episcopal palace of Chichester, where he died.

ARVANS (ST.), a parish, in the union and division of CHEPSTOW, partly in the hundred of RAGLAN, but chiefly in the Upper division of the hundred of CALDICOT, county of MONMOUTH, 2¼ miles (N. W. by N.) from Chepstow; containing, with the hamlet of Portcasseg, 354 inhabitants. This parish, which is washed on the north-east by the river Wye, and situated on the 77

road from Monmouth to Chepstow, comprises by computation 2840 acres, and abounds in romantic scenery, which, in many situations, is of great diversity. From Piercefield Park, a splendid seat, the views are remarkably magnificent, and embrace numerous reaches of the Wye, the Severn, and a great range of the surrounding country. The mansion, situated on an eminence, in the midst of fine plantations, is a superb elevation of freestone, consisting of a centre and two wings, and much admired for its tasteful architecture: on the spacious staircase are four beautiful pieces of Gobelin tapestry which belonged to Louis XVI., representing subjects in the natural history of Africa. The living is a perpetual curacy; net income, £53; patron and impropriator, the Duke of Beaufort: about 50 acres of land of indifferent quality, contained in two small farms in other parishes, belong to the curacy. The church is in the early English style, with a square tower. Remains exist of two ancient chapels, dedicated respectively to St. Kingsmark and St. Lawrence: in the park, where is a chalybeate spring, are the remains of an encampment; and there is a small intrenchment in the hamlet of Portcasseg.

ARYHOLME, with HOWTHORPE, a township, in the parish of HOVINGHAM, union of MALTON, wapentake of RYEDALE, N. riding of YORK, 7¼ miles (W.) from Malton; containing 36 inhabitants.

ASBY, GREAT (ST. PETER), a parish, in the union and division of EAST ward, county of WESTMORLAND, 4½ miles (S. by W.) from Appleby; containing, with the townships of Asby-Windewath, Asby-Coatsforth, and Little Asby, 407 inhabitants, of whom 222 are in the first, with the hamlet of Garthern; 129 in the second; and 56 in the third, with the hamlet of Asby-Overgrange. It comprises by computation 6500 acres, and is bounded on the south by the parish of Crosby-Garret and by Orton Fells; the surface is diversified with hills and valleys, and watered by numerous rivulets, near the margin of one of which, in the hollow called Asby Gill, is Plate hole, a remarkable cavern, intersected by a small stream, and which has been explored to an extent of more than 500 yards. The substratum is principally limestone, and on the common belonging to the manor has been lately discovered a very valuable fossil marble. The living is a rectory, valued in the king's books at £23. 13. 4.; patron, Sir F. F. Vane; net income, £205. The church is a very ancient structure with lofty gables, and strengthened by massive buttresses: the parsonage-house occupies the site of a nunnery, the chapel and prison of which are still partly remaining, the latter being used as a cellar. There was formerly a chapel at Little Asby, dedicated to St. Leonard. A school-house was built in 1688, by George Smith, citizen and merchant-tailor of London, to which Dr. Thomas Smith, Bishop of Carlisle (who was born at Whitewall, near the village), gave £100. Near the church is St. Helen's well.

ASCOT, BERKS.—See WINKFIELD.

ASCOTE, CHAPEL, an extra-parochial liberty, in the S. division of the hundred of KNIGHTLOW, S. division of the county of WARWICK, 9 miles (N. W. by N.) from Southam; containing 10 inhabitants, and comprising 600 acres.

ASCOTT, a hamlet, in the parish of WING, union of LEIGHTON-BUZZARD, hundred of COTTESLOE, county of BUCKINGHAM; containing 98 inhabitants.

ASCOTT, a hamlet, in the parish of GREAT MILTON, union and hundred of THAME, county of OXFORD, 4½ miles (N.) from Bensington; containing 29 inhabitants.

ASCOTT-UNDER-WYCHWOOD (HOLY TRINITY), a parish, in the union of CHIPPING-NORTON, hundred of CHADLINGTON, county of OXFORD, 5¾ miles (N. E. by N.) from Burford; containing 463 inhabitants. The parish is divided into two portions, Earl's-Ascott and Ascott-Regis; the village is pleasantly situated in a valley on the bank of the river Evenlode, near the border of Wych-wood Forest. The living is a perpetual curacy; net income, £100; patron, the Vicar of Shipton. The church is a neat ancient building. There is a place of worship for Particular Baptists.

ASENBY, a township, in the parish of TOPCLIFFE, wapentake of HALLIKELD, N. riding of YORK, 5¾ miles (N.) from Boroughbridge; containing 261 inhabitants. It is situated on the south-western acclivities of Swaledale, and comprises by computation 1131 acres, mostly occupied in farms. A bed of gravel affords excellent material for repairing roads; and a bed of coal-shale shows itself on the eminences of the dale. The tithes have been commuted for £250 payable to the impropriator, £64. 10. to the vicar of Topcliffe, and £20 to the Dean and Chapter of York.

ASGARBY (ST. ANDREW), a parish, in the union of SLEAFORD, wapentake of ASWARDHURN, parts of KESTEVEN, county of LINCOLN, 2¾ miles (E.) from Sleaford; containing, with the hamlet of Boughton, 77 inhabitants. The living is a vicarage, united in 1737 to the rectory of Kirby-le-Thorpe, and valued in the king's books at £10. 14. 4½. The church is in the later English style, with a lofty tower surmounted by a fine crocketed spire.

ASGARBY (ST. SWITHIN), a parish, in the union of HORNCASTLE, W. division of the soke of BOLINGBROKE, parts of LINDSEY, county of LINCOLN, 2 miles (N. by W.) from Bolingbroke; containing 131 inhabitants. It comprises by computation 1950 acres, two-thirds of which are pasture, and one-third arable; the soil is a sandy loam. The living is a perpetual curacy, in the patronage of the Bishop of Lincoln; net income, £55, with three acres of glebe. The church is a small plain edifice, built about forty years ago. There are some vestiges of an encampment, probably formed during the civil wars, and near which human skeletons are frequently dug up.

ASH, a hamlet, in the parish of SUTTON-ON-THE-HILL, union of BURTON-UPON-TRENT, hundred of APPLETREE, S. division of the county of DERBY, 8 miles (W. S. W.) from Derby; containing 51 inhabitants. It contains 692 acres of strong land; and a neat small village, a mile east from Sutton. The place was the property of the Sleigh family, from whom it came to the Chethams, and subsequently to the Cottons. The vicarial tithes have been commuted for £83.

ASH, a hamlet, in the parish of THROWLEY, union of OAKHAMPTON, hundred of WONFORD, Crockernwell and S. divisions of DEVON, 7¼ miles (E. S. E.) from Oakhampton. John Churchill, Duke of Marlborough, the celebrated general, was born here in 1650.

ASH, county of DURHAM.—See ESH.

ASH (ST. PETER AND ST. PAUL), a parish, in the union of DARTFORD, hundred of AXTON, DARTFORD, and WILMINGTON, lathe of SUTTON-AT-HONE, W. division of KENT, 9 miles (N. E.) from Seven-Oaks; containing 663 inhabitants. It comprises 3022 acres, of which 1780 are arable, 180 meadow, 624 woodland, 244 cinque-foil, 169 hop-ground, and 21 furze and waste; the surface is hilly and well wooded, and the soil in some parts chalky, but chiefly a stiff loam. The living is a rectory, valued in the king's books at £9. 18. 4., and in the gift of the family of Lambard; the tithes have been commuted for £675, and there are 20 acres of glebe. A school is endowed with £20 per annum.

ASH, a hamlet, in the parish and hundred of MARTOCK, union of YEOVIL, W. division of SOMERSET; containing 322 inhabitants. Here is a district church dedicated to the Trinity: the living is in the gift of the Vicar.

ASH (ST. PETER), a parish, under Gilbert's act, partly in the First division of the hundred of GODLEY, and partly in the First division of the hundred of WOKING, W. division of SURREY, 4½ miles (N. E. by E.) from Farnham; containing, with Frimley chapelry and Normandy tything, 2236 inhabitants. The parish is intersected by the Basingstoke canal and the South-Western railway, and comprises, with Normandy, about 4000 acres, of which 2041 are common or waste; and including Frimley, about 10,015 acres. A species of sandstone, dug out of the common, is used for building; and pebbles are found, susceptible of a bright polish, which are commonly called Bagshot diamonds. The village is long and scattered, and situated in a dreary part of the country: south-eastward of it is Henley Park, which, being on an eminence, forms a beautiful contrast with the wild heath around. The living is a rectory, valued in the king's books at £15. 18. 11½.; net income, £473; patrons, the Warden and Fellows of Winchester College. The church, previously to the dissolution of monasteries, was attached to the abbey of Chertsey. There is a chapel at Frimley. Dr. Young is said to have written a portion of the Night Thoughts at the rectory-house, then the residence of Dr. Harris, who married a sister of the poet, and was incumbent from 1718 to 1759.

ASH-BOCKING (ALL SAINTS), a parish, in the union and hundred of BOSMERE and CLAYDON, E. division of SUFFOLK, 6 miles (E. by S.) from Needham-Market; comprising by measurement 1398 acres, and containing 321 inhabitants. The living is a discharged vicarage, endowed with the rectorial tithes, and valued in the king's books at £9. 18. 6½.; it is in the patronage of the Crown. The incumbent's tithes have been commuted for £375, and £3 per annum are paid to the rector of Hemingstone; the glebe consists of about 11 acres.

ASH, CAMPSEY (ST. JOHN THE BAPTIST), a parish, in the union of PLOMESGATE, hundred of LOES, E. division of SUFFOLK, 2 miles (E.) from Wickham-Market; containing 374 inhabitants. In the reign of Richard I., Theobald de Valoins gave his estate here to his two sisters, that they might build a nunnery in honour of the Virgin Mary; it was of the order of St. Clare, or the Minoresses, and at the Dissolution had a revenue of £182. 9. 5.: a portion of the building still remains. A collegiate chapel, in honour of the Annunciation, was also founded here; by Maud, Countess of Ulster, for a warden and four secular priests, in 1347, seven years after which the establishment was removed to Bruisyard. The parish comprises by measurement 1813 acres. The living is a rectory, valued in the king's books at £14. 5., and in the gift of Thellusson's Trustees : the tithes have been commuted for £430, and there are 9½ acres of glebe.

ASH-GILL, a hamlet, in the township and parish of COVERHAM, union of LEYBURN, wapentake of HANG-WEST, N. riding of YORK, 1¾ mile (W.) from Middleham. Here is a noted training-ground for horses, the property of the Lister family.

ASH, GREAT, a township, in the parish of WHITCHURCH, Whitchurch division of the hundred of NORTH BRADFORD, N. division of SALOP, 2¼ miles (S. E. by E.) from Whitchurch ; containing 204 inhabitants.

ASH, LITTLE, a township, in the parish of WHITCHURCH, Whitchurch division of the hundred of NORTH BRADFORD, N. division of SALOP, 2¾ miles (S. E. by E.) from Whitchurch ; containing 208 inhabitants. A church, erected by subscription, was consecrated Aug. 31st, 1837 : the living is a perpetual curacy, in the gift of the Rector.

ASH-NEAR-SANDWICH (ST. NICHOLAS), a parish, in the union of EASTRY, hundred of WINGHAM, lathe of ST. AUGUSTINE, E. division of KENT, 3 miles (E.) from Wingham ; containing 2077 inhabitants. This place is by most antiquaries identified with the *Rutupium*, or *Urbs Rutupiæ*, of the Romans, one of the earliest stations, if not the first, in the island, and supposed by Camden to have been established by that people for the protection of their haven called *Portus Rutupensis*, the landing-place of their fleets, and the usual passage into Britain. According to Bede, the station was called by the Saxons *Reptaceastre*, and subsequently, by Alfred of Beverley, *Richeberg*, from which its present name Richborough is derived. Of the ancient city every vestige has disappeared, and the site is now covered with cornfields : part of the citadel alone remains, consisting of portions of the walls, about 200 feet in length, varying from ten to thirty feet in height, and about twelve feet thick, forming one of the most interesting relics of Roman antiquity in the kingdom. The parish is intersected by the road from London to Deal, and bounded on the north by the river Stour, over which are two ferries. It comprises 6872a. 1r. 36p., of which 3128 acres are arable, 3258 meadow, 331 orchard and garden, 100 hop ground, 49 wood, and 6 rectorial glebe ; the soil is rich and fertile. Pleasure-fairs are held on April 5th, and Oct. 11th. The living is a perpetual curacy ; net income, £147 ; patron and appropriator, the Archbishop of Canterbury. The church is a handsome building in the early and later English styles. A chapel of ease dedicated to the Trinity was erected in 1841, in the early English style, partly by subscription and partly by aid of a grant from the Church Building Society. There are two small places of worship for Wesleyans ; and a free school, founded, and endowed with £75 per annum, in 1714, by the Cartwright family.

ASH-PRIORS (HOLY TRINITY), a parish, in the union of TAUNTON, W. division of the hundred of KINGSBURY and of the county of SOMERSET, 6 miles (N. W. by W.) from Taunton ; comprising by computation 600 acres, and containing 226 inhabitants. The name of this place is a corruption of *Esse Prioris*, "the property of the prior," which related to a house here, anciently used for a country residence by the prior of Taunton.

79

The church and principal parts of the village are beautifully situated on rising ground, commanding a fine view of Taunton-Dean. There are some quarries of red sandstone, which is of good quality for building, and is also burnt for manure. The living is a perpetual curacy, in the gift of Sir Thomas Buckler Lethbridge, Bart., with a net income of £70 : the tithes have been commuted for £110. The church, a neat structure in the later English style, has been enlarged by the addition of a new aisle, and beautified, at the expense of Sir T. B. Lethbridge. Priory House, of which a small portion yet remains, was the residence of the celebrated Admiral Blake.

ASHAMPSTEAD (ST. CLEMENT), a parish, in the union of BRADFIELD, hundred of MORETON, county of BERKS, 10 miles (N. W. by W.) from Reading ; containing 404 inhabitants. It comprises 1666a. 1r. 32p., of which 1350 acres are in cultivation ; there are 70 acres of beech-wood, 250 of coppice, and 100 common. The living is annexed to the vicarage of Basildon ; impropriator, R. Hopkins, Esq.

ASHAMPSTEAD, a chapelry, in the parish of LEWKNOR, union of WYCOMBE, hundred of DESBOROUGH, county of BUCKINGHAM, 3¼ miles (N. W.) from Great Marlow. The chapel is dedicated to St. Mary de More.

ASHBOURN (ST. OSWALD), a market-town and parish, comprising the townships of Hulland, Hulland-Ward, Hulland-Intacks, Sturston, and Yeldersley, in the hundred of APPLETREE ; the township of Clifton and Compton, in the hundred of MORLESTON and LITCHURCH ; and the chapelry of Alsop-le-dale and Eaton, the hamlet of Newton-Grange, and the liberty of Offcote-Underwood, in the hundred of WIRKSWORTH ; S. division of the county of DERBY ; the whole containing 4884 inhabitants, of whom 2246 are in the town, 13½ miles (N. W. by W.) from Derby, and 140 (N. W. by N.) from London. This place, which at the time of the Conquest was held in royal demesne, is in Domesday book called *Esseburn*. No event of importance occurred until the 17th century, when, in 1644, a battle was fought here between the royalists and the parliamentarians, the former of whom were defeated with considerable loss. Charles I. was at Ashbourn during the battle, and again in 1645, on his march to Doncaster, at the head of 3000 horse, when a skirmish took place, in which the royalists defeated Sir John Gell, the leader of the parliamentarian forces in this part of the country : during his stay the king attended divine service at the church. Charles Edward Stuart, accompanied by the Dukes of Athol and Perth, on their return from Derby in 1745, remained for one night in the town, taking forcible possession of the manor-house, from which they expelled Sir Brooke Boothby and his family. On Sir Brooke's return, he found the names of the officers written in chalk upon the doors of the apartments they had severally occupied :

of these inscriptions, which were overlaid with white paint, some are preserved, and the bedroom where the Pretender slept is still shown.

The TOWN is beautifully situated in a deep vale, near the eastern bank of the river Dove, over which there is a bridge of stone: the houses are principally built of red brick, and roofed with slate; the streets are partly paved, and the inhabitants are well supplied with water and with gas. The entrance from London is highly picturesque, commanding a fine view of the beautiful vale on the left, and of Ashbourn Hall, the seat of Sir William Boothby, Bart., on the right: the vicinity abounds with pleasing and richly varied scenery. The reading and news rooms, the libraries, are respectably supported. The manufacture of cotton and tambour lace is carried on to a considerable extent, and a great quantity of cheese and malt is sent to the metropolis and other towns; but the principal support of the town is derived from its market and numerous fairs. The market is on Saturday: the fairs are held on the first Tuesday in Jan. and on Feb. 13th, for horses and cattle; the second Monday in March, for horses, cattle, and cheese; April 3rd, May 21st, and July 5th, for horses, cattle, and wool; August 16th and Sept. 20th, for horses and cattle; the third Monday in Sept., for horses, cattle, and cheese; and Nov. 29th, for horses. The powers of the county debt-court of Ashbourn, established in 1847, extend over the greater part of the registration-district of Ashbourn; and courts leet and baron are held annually under the lord of the manor, at which constables and other officers for the town are appointed. A prison was built in 1844.

The parish comprises 7043 acres. The LIVING is a discharged vicarage, with the rectory of Mappleton united, valued in the king's books at £5. 4. 7.; net income, £134; patron, the Bishop of Lichfield. The church, erected in 1240 by Hugh de Patishull, Bishop of Coventry, is a spacious cruciform structure, in the early style of English architecture, with a central tower surmounted by a lofty and richly ornamented octagonal spire: the interior has lately undergone extensive repairs and embellishments. The northern part of the chancel, appropriated as a sepulchral chapel to the Boothby family, contains, among others, an exquisitely sculptured monument by Banks, to the memory of Penelope, only child of Sir Brooke Boothby, who died at the age of five years: this is said to have suggested to Chantrey the design of his celebrated monument in Lichfield cathedral. At Alsop, Clifton, and Parlich are additional churches. There are places of worship for Wesleyans, Independents, and others. The free grammar school was founded in 1585, under a charter of Queen Elizabeth, and endowed with estates purchased by the inhabitants, from the proceeds of which, £131. 10. per annum, with a house and garden, are given to the master, and £65. 15., with a house, to the usher. An English school was founded in 1710, and endowed with £10 per annum, by Nicholas Spalden, for the instruction of thirty boys, till they should be fit to enter the grammar school; he also endowed a school for thirty girls under twelve years of age, the mistress of which has £10 per annum. In addition to these, a national school is carried on; a savings' bank was erected in 1843, and there are several almshouses, founded at various periods, and some of them endowed

with considerable funds. The poor-law union of Ashbourn comprises 61 parishes and townships, of which 17 are in Staffordshire. In the neighbourhood formerly stood a chapel dedicated to St. Mary, which previously to its being taken down some years ago, was used as a malt-house.

ASHBRITTLE (St. John the Baptist), a parish, in the union of Wellington, hundred of Milverton, W. division of Somerset, 6¾ miles (W.) from Wellington; containing 540 inhabitants, and comprising 2489a. 2r. 10p., of which 95 acres are common or waste. The parish is situated on the borders of the county of Devon, and includes the tything of Greenham. Fairs are held in Feb. and Oct. The living is a rectory, valued in the king's books at £19. 3. 11½., and in the gift of J. Quick, Esq.: the tithes have been commuted for £400, and the glebe consists of 80 acres.

ASHBURNHAM (St. James), a parish, in the union of Battle, hundred of Foxearle, rape of Hastings, E. division of Sussex, 4½ miles (W. by S.) from Battle; containing 790 inhabitants. The manor, with the exception only of a few years, has been from a time anterior to the Conquest in the continued possession of the noble family of Ashburnham, whose mansion-house here is beautifully situated, and surrounded by a fine park. The parish comprises about 3600 acres; and was once noted for the smelting of iron-ore. The living is a vicarage, with the rectory of Penhurst annexed, valued in the king's books at £8. 13. 4.; patron and impropriator, the Earl of Ashburnham. The great tithes of the parish have been commuted for £260, and the vicarial for £239; the glebe consists of 6 acres. A lectureship was founded in 1631 by R. Bateman, Esq., and others, with an endowment of £40 per annum for two sermons every week; it is in the gift of the coheiresses of the late Sir Hugh Bateman, the last surviving trustee. The church, situated behind Ashburnham House, is a neat cruciform edifice in the decorated English style, with a tower; the south transept contains a gallery for the family, and in the north are handsome monuments to William and John Ashburnham, and their wives: in a glass case lined with red velvet, are preserved the watch of Charles I., and portions of the dress which he wore when he was beheaded. There are several mineral springs in the parish.

Seal and Arms.

ASHBURTON (St. Andrew,) a borough, market-town, and parish, in the union of Newton-Abbott, hundred of Teignbridge, Teignbridge and S. divisions of Devon, 19 miles (S. W.) from Exeter, and 192 (W. by S.) from London, on the road to Plymouth; containing 3841 inhabitants. This town, anciently called Aisbertone, in the time of Edward the Confessor belonged to Brietric, and at the Conquest to Judael de Totnais. It seems by Domesday book to have then been part of the demesne of the crown, being therein described as "Terra Regis." The place was subsequently annexed to the see of Exeter: in 1310, Bishop Stapylton obtained for it a grant of a market and four fairs; and in 1672, another market,

chiefly for wool and yarn spun in Cornwall, was procured by Mr. John Ford, which has long been discon-
tinned. It was made a stannary town by charter of
Edward III., in 1328, being then noted for the mines of
tin and copper which abounded in the neighbourhood.
Henry IV., in the third year of his reign, granted a
charter, declaring that " the men of the manor of Aisbertone, which is ancient demesne of our Crown," should be
free from paying toll throughout the kingdom. It also
appears that Ashburton belonged to the crown in the
time of Charles I., as that king bestowed the manor
upon his son Charles, when he created him Prince of
Wales. How it was alienated by the crown is unknown ;
but in the reign of Charles II. it was the property of
Sir Robert Parkhurst, and Lord Sondes, Earl of Feversham, the former of whom sold his moiety to Sir John
Stawell, of Parke, in South Bovey, by whose executors
it was sold to Roger Tuckfield, Esq., from whom Lord
Clinton, the present proprietor of one moiety of the
borough, claims. The other moiety was, about the
same time, purchased by Richard Duke, Esq., and
is now vested in Sir L. V. Palk, Bart. In the parliamentary war, Ashburton, having been previously occupied by the royal troops under Lord Wentworth, was
taken by Sir Thomas Fairfax, on his march westward,
in January 1646.

The TOWN is situated about a mile and a half from
the river Dart, and consists principally of one street of
considerable length : the houses are built of stone, and
roofed with slate, which is obtained from quarries in the
vicinity. The inhabitants are well supplied with water;
the river Yeo, a rapid stream, runs through the town
and turns several mills. There is a book society; and
card and dancing assemblies, and music meetings, are
frequently held in a handsome suite of rooms at the
Golden Lion inn. The environs abound with objects of
interest, and the scenery on the banks of the river is
celebrated for its picturesque and romantic beauty. The
manufacture of serge and other woollen goods for the
East India Company is carried on to a very great
extent in the town and neighbourhood ; there are some
mills for fulling cloth and for the spinning of yarn, and
in addition to the slate-quarries, mines of tin and copper
are still worked. An act was passed in 1846, for constructing a railway from the South-Devon railway at
Newton-Abbott to Ashburton, 10½ miles long. The
market is on Saturday ; and fairs are held on the first
Thursdays in March and June, the first Thursday after
the 10th of Aug., and on the 11th of Nov., which last is
a great sheep fair. Ashburton is a borough by prescription : a portreeve, bailiff, constables, and subordinate officers are appointed annually at a court leet held
by the steward of the borough ; but they have no magisterial authority. A stannary court is held occasionally.
The borough made two returns to parliament, in the
26th of Edward I. and the 8th of Henry IV., but not
subsequently until 1640, when the franchise was restored
by the last parliament of Charles I. ; and until the
passing of the Reform act it continued to return two
members. It now returns only one, the elective franchise being in the resident freeholders and the £10
householders of the entire parish ; the portreeve is the
returning officer.

The parish comprises 5074 acres, of which 584 are
common or waste. The LIVING is a vicarage, with the

livings of Bickington and Buckland-in-the-Moor annexed, valued in the king's books at £38. 8. 11½. ;
patrons and appropria'tors, the Dean and Chapter of
Exeter. The great tithes have been commuted for
£390, and the vicarial for £528; the glebe consists
of 60 acres. The church, which was formerly collegiate,
is a venerable and spacious cruciform structure in the
later English style, with a square embattled tower.
There are places of worship for Particular Baptists, Independents, and Wesleyans. The free grammar school
was founded in the 3rd of James I. by William Werring,
and endowed with lands, a portion of which had belonged
to the dissolved chantry of St. Lawrence, a fine ancient
building with a tower and small spire, now appropriated
to the use of the school, and for public meetings : the
original endowment was augmented by subsequent benefactions ; and two scholarships, each of £30 per annum,
in Exeter College, Oxford, were founded in favour of
boys educated at the school, by the late Mr. Gifford.
The free school, in which 180 children are educated, was
endowed in 1754, by Lord Middleton, and John Harris,
Esq., then representatives of the borough, in gratitude
for the liberality of their constituents; and in 1831 an
excellent school-house was built, at the expense of £500.
Inconsiderable vestiges of a chapel, which belonged to
the abbot of Buckfastleigh, are still discernible in the
walls of a house occupied by Mr. Parham. John Dun-
ning, Baron Ashburton, the eminent lawyer, was born
here, Oct. 18th, 1731 ; he died ·Aug. 18th, 1783, and
was interred in the church. Dr. Ireland, Dean of
Westminster, and Mr. Gifford, editor of the Quarterly
Review, were also natives of the place. The title of
Baron Ashburton was revived in 1835, in the person of
Alexander Baring, Esq., nephew, by marriage of his
father's sister, of the celebrated lawyer above noticed.

ASHBURY (St. Mary), a parish, in the union of
Farringdon, hundred of Shrivenham, county of
Berks, 6¼ miles (N. W. by W.) from Lambourn ; containing, with the tythings of Idstone and Odstone, and
the hamlet of Kingstone-Winslow, 819 inhabitants. It
comprises 5600 acres, a large portion of which is appropriated to dairy-farms. The living is a vicarage, valued
in the king's books at £11. 8. 1½. ; net income, £375 ;
patron, the Bishop of Bath and Wells, who presents one
of three candidates nominated by Magdalene College,
Oxford. The rectory is a sinecure, valued at £30. 12. 6.,
and now in the hands of the Ecclesiastical Commissioners; net income, £567. The tithes were commuted
for land, valued at about £500 per annum, and a money
payment, by an inclosure act in 1770; the glebe consists of 25 acres. The Roman road called the Ikeneld-
way passes near the village; and in the parish is an
intrenchment named Alfred's Camp, near which are two
barrows. Here are also a tumulus and cromlech,
popularly designated " Wayland Smith," with which is
connected a tradition, introduced by Sir Walter Scott in
his romance of Kenilworth.

ASHBURY (St. Mary), a parish, in the union of
Oakhampton, hundred of Black Torrington, Black
Torrington and Shebbear, and N. divisions of Devon,
5¼ miles (S. W. by W.) from Hatherleigh ; containing
65 inhabitants. It contains about 1450 acres, in general
of a clayey soil. The living is a discharged rectory, valued in the king's books at £5. 13. 4., and in the gift of
the Crown ; income, £96. There are 120 acres of glebe. .
M

ASHBY (St. Peter), a parish, in the union of Caistor, wapentake of Bradley-Haverstoe, parts of Lindsey, county of Lincoln, 6¼ miles (S. by W.) from Grimsby; containing, with the hamlet of Fenby, 211 inhabitants. This parish, which is situated on the old road from Grimsby to Louth, and on the borders of the Wolds, comprises, with Fenby, 1637 acres by admeasurement; the soil is fertile, and the sub-soil generally chalk; the surface is undulated. The living is a rectory, valued in the king's books at £14. 10. 10., and in the gift of the Crown: the tithes have been commuted for £252, and the glebe comprises 45 acres. The church, a very ancient structure in the early English style, with a square tower, contains an oak pulpit richly carved, and an elegant octagonal font, supported on a clustered pedestal, and panelled in quatrefoil: there are also two handsome monuments, one of which is to the memory of Sir William and Lady Frances Wray. There is a chapel of ease at Fenby; also a place of worship in the parish for Wesleyans. In 1641 six almshouses were built by Dame Wray, and endowed by her son Sir Christopher with a rent-charge of £30.

ASHBY (St. Helen), a parish, in the union of Spilsby, Wold division of the wapentake of Candleshoe, parts of Lindsey, county of Lincoln, 2¼ miles (E. by N.) from Spilsby; containing 160 inhabitants. It comprises 906 acres by measurement. The living is a discharged rectory, valued in the king's books at £7. 10. 2½.; net income, £157, arising from 185 acres of land allotted in 1811 in lieu of tithes by an inclosure act; patrons, the Representatives of the late Dr. Fowler, Bishop of Ossory. The church was rebuilt in 1841.

ASHBY, a township, in the parish of Bottesford, union of Glandford-Brigg, E. division of the wapentake of Manley, parts of Lindsey, county of Lincoln, 6½ miles (W. by S.) from Glandford-Brigg; containing 429 inhabitants. The village is large and pleasant, and the township comprises about 2100 acres, extending over the western ridge of the Wolds to the river Trent, near which is a tract of moory land that has just undergone the process of warping. There is a decoy, perhaps in wild-duck and other aquatic birds; in the immediate vicinity of which, a handsome mansion was built in 1841, by H. Healey, Esq. Forty acres of land were awarded to the vicar of the parish at the inclosure. There are places of worship for Wesleyans and Primitive Methodists.

ASHBY (St. Mary), a parish, in the East and West Flegg incorporation, hundred of West Flegg, E. division of Norfolk, 4 miles (N.) from Acle. This parish, which was consolidated with those of Thirne˜and Oby in 1604, now comprises about 1900 acres, whereof 800 are marsh and meadow land. The three places form one rectory, valued in the king's books at £10, and in the gift of the Bishop of Norwich: the tithes have been commuted for £690. Ashby consists of only one farm; it had formerly a church, of which there are very slight remains. The parsonage-house, a respectable residence, is in Oby, and has a glebe of about 23 acres.

ASHBY (St. Mary), a parish, in the union of Loddon and Clavering, hundred of Loddon, E. division of Norfolk, 7½ miles (S. E.) from Norwich; containing 263 inhabitants. The waste lands were inclosed under an act passed in 1837. The living is a rectory, united to that of Carleton, and valued in the king's books at £6.

82

The church consists of a nave and chancel, with a square tower; the entrance on the south is through a rich Norman doorway.

ASHBY (St. Mary), a parish, in the union and hundred of Mutford and Lothingland, E. division of Suffolk, 6 miles (N. W.) from Lowestoft; containing 53 inhabitants, and comprising 1003 acres. The living is a discharged rectory, valued in the king's books at £6, and in the gift of the family of Anguish: the tithes have been commuted for £205, and the glebe consists of about 22 acres. The church is a small thatched building, having a tower circular at the base, and octangular above.

ASHBY, CANONS (St. Mary), parish, in the union of Daventry, hundred of Greens-Norton, S. division of the county of Northampton, 8 miles (W. by N.) from Towcester; containing 252 inhabitants. This place is remarkable as the residence of the family of the poet Dryden, who obtained their property here chiefly by marriage with Elizabeth, daughter of Sir John Cope, in the reign of Mary: Erasmus Dryden, of Canons-Ashby, was made high sheriff of the county in the 40th of Elizabeth, and advanced to the dignity of a baronet in 1619. The parish consists of 3070a. 29p., of which 1715a. 29p. are exclusive of the chapelry of Adstone; a portion is occupied by a well-wooded park. Here was a priory of Black canons, founded about the time of John, and the revenue of which at the Dissolution was £127. 19.: in the alienation no endowment was reserved for the service of the church, and consequently there is now no incumbency.

ASHBY, CASTLE (St. Mary Magdalene), a parish, in the union of Hardingstone, hundred˜of Wymmersley, S. division of the county of Northampton, 8 miles (E. by S.) from Northampton; containing 172 inhabitants. It appears to derive the prefix to its name from an ancient castle which is thought to have stood near the site of the present magnificent mansion of the Marquess of Northampton, where the foundation stones of a large building have been discovered. The parish comprises 1889a. 2r. of land, the greater part arable; the soil is a strong clay, the sub-soil mostly limestone, in some parts gravel. The living is a rectory, valued in the king's books at £17. 9. 7., and in the gift of the marquess: the tithes have been commuted for £237. 18. 2., and the glebe consists of 120 acres. The church forms a picturesque object in his lordship's grounds, and is principally in the decorated style of English architecture; the north entrance is through a beautiful Norman arch in good preservation. Some skeletons and warlike weapons of an early date have been dug up in the neighbourhood.

ASHBY, COLD (St. Denis), a parish, in the union of Brixworth, hundred of Guilsborough, S. division of the county of Northampton, 11½ miles (N. W. by N.) from Northampton; containing 443 inhabitants. This parish, which comprises by computation 2077 acres, forms a verdant tract of elevated ground, and is traversed on the north-east by the road from Northampton to Leicester. From the bold declivity terminating the lofty ridge upon which the village stands, extensive and beautiful prospects are obtained of the surrounding country. The living is a vicarage, valued in the king's books at £6. 0. 5.; net income, £230; patron and incumbent, the Rev. W. Mousley; impropriators, the family of Buxton: the glebe consists of about 120 acres of good arable land. The church was repaired and re-pewed in 1840, at which time the incumbent presented a new organ and two stained-glass windows. Here is a school endowed with £18 per annum, and with £6 arising from land. Richard Knowles, the historian of the Turkish Empire, was born here in 1540.

ASHBY-DE-LA-LAUNDE (St. Hybald), a parish, in the union of Sleaford, wapentake of Flaxwell, parts of Kesteven, county of Lincoln, 6¼ miles (N. by W.) from Sleaford; containing 157 inhabitants. It comprises 2580a. 3r., of which 2296 acres are arable, 222 grass, and 62 woodland, &c. The living is a dis-charged vicarage, valued in the king's books at £6. 8. 4.; net income, £299; patron and impropriator, the Rev. John King.

ASHBY-DE-LA-ZOUCH (St. Helen), a market-town, parish, and the head of a union, in the hundred of West Goscote, N. division of the county of Leicester, 18 miles (N. W. by W.) from Leicester, and 115 (N. W. by N.) from London; containing, with part of the ecclesias-tical district of Woodville and part of the chapelry of Blackfordby, 5652 inhabitants. The name appears to be derived from the Saxon *Asc*, an ash, and *bye*, a habitation: it received the adjunct by which it is dis-tinguished from other towns of the same name, from the family of La Zouch, in whose possession it continued from the latter part of the twelfth to the close of the fourteenth century. Sir William Hastings, created Baron Hastings by Edward IV., and who was beheaded by Richard III., built a strong castle here in the reign of the former monarch, in which Mary, Queen of Scots, while in the custody of the Earl of Huntingdon, was for some time kept in confinement; and in this castle also Anne, consort of James I., and her son Prince Henry, were magnificently entertained by 'the fourth earl of Huntingdon, on their journey from York to London in 1603. At the commencement of the parliamentary war, the fifth earl was one of the first that appeared in arms for the king in Leicestershire, and Ashby Castle was garrisoned for his majesty by the earl's second son, Col. Henry Hastings, who was made general of the king's forces in the midland counties, and, for his services to the royal cause, was in 1643 created Baron Lough-borough. The king was here, on his march to and from Leicester, in May and June 1645. After sus-taining a siege of several months from the army under Fairfax, Lord Loughborough surrendered the castle to Col. Needham, in February 1646, on honourable terms, the garrison being allowed to march out with all the honours of war. The castle was one of the fortresses demolished by order of a committee of the house of commons, about the end of the year 1649: the re-maining portions form an extensive and interesting mass of ruins, consisting of the great tower, the chapel, the kitchen tower, and a part evidently of much earlier date than the tower, as some portion of it was standing in the time of Richard I. The late Marquess of Hastings expended a considerable sum in repairing parts of these ruins, and arresting the progress of decay; and on the site of a building which stood to the north of the castle, and at right angles with it, erected for the accommoda-tion of the suite of James I. when visiting the Earl of Huntingdon, he raised a handsome structure in the later English style, designated the Manor-house.

The town, a great part of which was destroyed by fire in 1753, is pleasantly situated on the banks of the small river Gilwisthaw, at the north-western extremity of the county; and consists principally of one very spacious street, with two smaller streets extending in a parallel di-rection, and containing several substantial and well-built houses. It is lighted with gas, and measures have been lately taken for supplying it with water. South of the town stand the Ivanhoe Baths, a handsome structure of the Doric order, erected in 1826. The building consists of a centre, containing a spacious pump-room, sur-mounted by a lofty dome with rich architectural decora-tions; and of two wings, in each of which are six baths provided with every accommodation. The water is furnished from an adjacent mine, and contains, accord-ing to a recent analysis by Dr. Ure, larger proportions of the salts of chlorine combined with bromine than any other mineral water in the kingdom; it is employed both internally and externally, as a remedial agent in many chronic diseases, with great advantage. Com-modious pleasure-grounds are attached to the baths; and the town contains lodging-houses, a handsome hotel, a theatre, and other sources of attraction requisite in a place of fashionable resort.

Ashby is situated in an extensive carboniferous dis-triet; the principal collieries are at Moira, and are the property of the Marquess of Hastings. The coal is worked at a thousand feet from the surface, and is of a superior quality; large quantities are transported to the southern and western counties, and it has been recently introduced in London with great success. The neighbour-ing wolds, which are now inclosed and populous, abound with minerals, particularly ironstone; there is also found an excellent clay, used for making yellow ware, extensive manufactories of which are carried on at Woodville and Gresley. A canal passes within three miles south-westward of the town, with which it is con-nected by a railroad; and after continuing a course of more than thirty miles, unimpeded by a single lock, it forms a junction with the Coventry canal. The market is on Saturday; and fairs are held on Shrove-Monday, Easter-Tuesday, Whit-Tuesday, the last Monday in Sept., and the 10th of Nov., for horses and cattle: this is stated to be the best market for strong horses in England. A constable and two headboroughs are ap-pointed at the court leet of the lord of the manor. The powers of the county debt-court of Ashby, established in 1847, extend over the registration-district of Ashby.

The parish comprises about 7000 acres. The living is a discharged vicarage, valued in the king's books at £14. 10. 4.; net income, £417; patron and impropri-ator, the Marquess of Hastings. 150 acres of land belong to the living in this parish, and 33 in that of Whitwick. The church is a spacious structure in the decorated English style, and contains, in an adjoining sepulchral chapel, several monuments of the Hunting-don family, among which is one to the memory of Francis, Earl of Huntingdon, and his countess, de-serving particular notice. A church dedicated to the Holy Trinity was erected at an expense of £3000, on a site given by the late marquess, and was consecrated on the 13th of August 1840; it is a handsome structure, and contains 900 sittings, of which 600 are free. The cost of the building was defrayed by subscription, aided by the Incorporated Society, the Church Commissioners.

M 2

83

and the Board at Leicester. The living is a perpetual curacy, in the gift of the Vicar of Ashby : towards the endowment the Additional Curates' Society granted £500, and the fund for the purpose now amounts to £1950, the interest of which and the pew-rents constitute the income of the minister. At Woodville is a district church : in the township of Blackfordby is a chapel of ease ; and there are places of worship in the parish for Baptists, the Connexion of the Countess of Huntingdon, Independents, and Wesleyans.

The free grammar school was founded in 1567, by Henry, Earl of Huntingdon, and others, and endowed with 120 houses and 75 acres of land. It provides instruction to upwards of 100 boys ; and has three exhibitions of £40 a year to either of the two universities, and ten exhibitions of £10 per annum to Emmanuel College, Cambridge, founded by Francis Ash, merchant, of London, together with a lectureship of £20 a year from the same foundation. A Blue-coat school was instituted in 1669, and endowed with £25' per annum, by Isaac Dawson ; and a Green-coat school was established and endowed by Alderman Newton, of Leicester : they are now united, and contain about 50 boys. The Rev. Simeon Ash, a native of Ashby, gave £50 per annum, directing that £10 should be appropriated to the apprenticing of two boys yearly in some corporate town, and that the remainder should be distributed among the poor. The union of which Ashby is the head comprises seventeen parishes or places in the county of Leicester, and eleven in the county of Derby, and contains a population of 14,234. A great number of Roman coins has been found here. Bishop Hall, an eminent divine and satirist, and Dr. John Bainbridge, a celebrated astronomer and mathematician, were born in the town, the former in 1574, and the latter in 1582.

ASHBY-FOLVILLE (ST. MARY), a parish, in the union of MELTON-MOWBRAY, hundred of EAST GOSCOTE, N. division of the county of LEICESTER, 6 miles (S. W. by S.) from Melton-Mowbray ; containing, with the chapelry of Bardsby, 437 inhabitants. It comprises 2829a. 1r. 13p. of which 2298 acres are pasture, 461 arable, and 70 woodland. The living is a discharged vicarage, valued in the king's books at £9 ; net income, £170 ; patron, Mr. Black ; impropriators, the family of Johnston. Lord Carrington, in 1673, founded and endowed an almshouse for seven poor men or women, the endowment of which produces £135 per annum.

ASHBY MAGNA (ST. MARY), a parish, in the union of LUTTERWORTH; hundred of GUTHLAXTON, S. division of the county of LEICESTER, 4 miles (N. by E.) from Lutterworth ; containing 337 inhabitants, and comprising by measurement 2000 acres. The living is a vicarage, valued in the king's books at £7. 18. 11½. ; net income, £120 ; patron and impropriator, the Earl of Aylesford. The glebe consists of 49 acres.

ASHBY, MEARS (ALL SAINTS), a parish, in the union of WELLINGBOROUGH, hundred of HAMFORDSHOE, N. division of the county of NORTHAMPTON, 4 miles (W. by S.) from Wellingborough ; containing 496 inhabitants. It comprises 1500 acres, of which more than two-thirds are arable land ; and is beautifully situated about a mile from the road between Wellingborough and Northampton, and two miles distant from the navigable river Nene. There is an extensive quarry of excellent freestone, from which many mansions have been

84

built. The living is a discharged vicarage, valued in the king's books at £4. 13. 9., and in the gift of Mrs. Maria Newby ; net income, £235 : the glebe consists of about 20 acres, with a house in good repair. The south side of the church has been rebuilt ; the tower is very ancient. A free school is endowed with land assigned, on the inclosure of waste grounds, in lieu of property purchased with a bequest of £200 by Sarah Kinloch, in 1720 ; the rental is about £60. Land also, producing about £30 per annum, is appropriated to the repair of highways and bridges.

ASHBY PARVA (ST. PETER), a parish, in the union of LUTTERWORTH, hundred of GUTHLAXTON, S. division of the county of LEICESTER, 3 miles (N. N. W.) from Lutterworth ; containing 179 inhabitants. It comprises about 750 acres, of which three-fourths are pasture land ; the soil is clay and gravel. Within a mile and a half is a station on the Midland railway. The living is a rectory, valued in the king's books at £5. 7. 6., and in the patronage of the Crown ; net income, £98 : the glebe consists of 34 acres. Mrs. Goodacre, in 1830, bequeathed the whole of her property, amounting to £6574, after payment of all debts and legacies, to her niece Mrs. Bowyer ; who, in pursuance of the testator's will, expended a part of the money in erecting almshouses for eight widows, and two schoolrooms with dwelling-houses ; and laid out the residue in the purchase of estates producing £150 a year for their endowment. On the inclosure of the parish in 1665, fourteen acres of land, yielding £28 per annum, were allotted towards the reduction of the poor-rates, and three acres, producing £7 per annum, to the repair of the church.

ASHBY-PUERORUM (ST. ANDREW), a parish, in the union of HORNCASTLE, hundred of HILL, parts of LINDSEY, county of LINCOLN, 4¼ miles (E. N. E.) from Horncastle ; containing, with the hamlet of Stainsby, and Holbeck extra-parochial, 111 inhabitants. Ashby Puerorum, which comprises 1500 acres, chiefly arable, derives its affix from its connexion with the singing boys of Lincoln Cathedral, for whose benefit the great tithes are received. The living is a discharged vicarage, valued in the king's books at £6. 13. 2. ; net income, £118 ; patrons, the Dean and Chapter.

ASHBY ST. LEDGER'S (ST. MARY AND ST. LEODGARE), a parish, in the union of DAVENTRY, hundred of FAWSLEY, S. division of the county of NORTHAMPTON, 3½ miles (N.) from Daventry ; containing 257 inhabitants. This parish, which comprises 1902a. 2r. 4p., is bounded on the east by the Roman Watling-street, and situated near the London and Birmingham railway and the Union canal. The living is a discharged vicarage, valued in the king's books at £6. 13. 4., and in the patronage of the Senhouse family ; net income, £130, which arises from 66 acres of glebe. The church is in the later English style ; it contains a richly ornamented screen and rood-loft, and in the windows are some remains of ancient painted glass. Sir William Catesby, favourite of Richard III., and owner of the manor, was buried within the altar-rails, under a marble slab with a rich brass in fine preservation ; and Robert Catesby, the conspirator, of the time of James I., resided here, where he had property.

ASHBY, WEST (ALL SAINTS), a parish, in the union and soke of HORNCASTLE, parts of LINDSEY, county of LINCOLN, 1¾ mile (N.) from Horncastle; containing, with the hamlets of Farthorpe and Middlethorpe, 534 inhabitants. It is pleasantly situated at the foot of the Wolds, on the road from Horncastle to Louth, and is intersected in the western part by the river Bane, and in the eastern by the river Waring. The whole extent by measurement is 2900 acres, of which two-thirds are arable, and one-third meadow and pasture; the soil is extremely fertile. The village is one of the most pleasing in the county, and remarkable for the neatness of its buildings, the excellence of the roads leading to it, and the beauty of the surrounding scenery. The living is a perpetual curacy; net income, £54; patron and appropriator, the Bishop of Carlisle. The church is a handsome edifice in the later English style, with a square embattled tower, and partly mantled with ivy.

ASHCHURCH (ST. NICHOLAS), a parish, in the union, and Lower division of the hundred, of TEWKESBURY, E. division of the county of GLOUCESTER, 2¼ miles (E. N. E.) from Tewkesbury; containing, with the tythings of Aston-upon-Carron, Fiddington with Natton, Northway with Newton, and Pamington, 743 inhabitants. This parish, the name of which was originally Eastchurch, from its relative situation to the church of Tewkesbury, is on the road from Tewkesbury to Stow, and comprises by computation 3150 acres. A station on the Birmingham and Gloucester railway is situated close to the village. The living is a perpetual curacy; net income, £48; patron and incumbent, the Rev. John Askew. The tithes were partially commuted for land, under an inclosure act, in 1811; the glebe consists of about 25 acres. The church is a handsome edifice, chiefly in the English style, with a square embattled tower crowned with pinnacles; the south entrance is by a Norman porch of elegant design. Mrs. Smithsend bequeathed £400, appropriating £7. 7. per annum to the Sunday school, and the remainder to the purchasing of blankets for distribution annually among the poor. A spring resembling the Cheltenham waters was discovered a few years since.

ASHCOMBE, a parish, in the union of ST. THOMAS, hundred of EXMINSTER, Wonford and S. divisions of DEVON, 2½ miles (E.) from Chudleigh; containing 297 inhabitants. This parish is situated near the sea-coast, and comprises 2000 acres, of which 500 acres of common and waste have recently been planted; the remainder is arable, pasture, and orchard: the soil is a red loam. The living is a rectory, valued in the king's books at £18, and in the patronage of the Crown: the tithes have been commuted for £242, and the glebe comprises 30 acres. The church, a cruciform structure in the early and decorated English styles, was dedicated 22nd Nov. 1259; it contains many ancient stalls of carved oak. During some recent repairs, part of an old breviary was found between the ceiling and the roof, written in the reign of Richard II.; it is now in the British Museum.

ASHCOTT (ALL SAINTS), a parish, in the union of BRIDGWATER, hundred of WHITLEY, W. division of SOMERSET, 5 miles (W. S. W.) from Glastonbury; containing, with the hamlet of Pedwell, 843 inhabitants. This parish, which is bounded on the south by the Polden hills, and intersected by the road from Glastonbury to Bridgwater, formerly belonged to the abbey of

85

Glastonbury. A fair for cattle is held on January 9th. The living is a perpetual curacy, annexed to the vicarage of Shapwick: the impropriate tithes have been commuted for £158. 16., the vicarial for £155, and £9. 10. are paid to the rector of Walton-cum-Street; the glebe consists of 45 acres. There is a place of worship for Wesleyans. In 1737 Richard Miles bequeathed a sum of money, since vested in land, now producing £70 per annum, which is distributed among the poor.

ASHDON (ALL SAINTS), a parish, in the union of SAFFRON-WALDEN, hundred of FRESHWELL, N. division of ESSEX, 3¾ miles (N. E. by E.) from Saffron-Walden; comprising by computation 3681 acres, and containing, with the hamlet of Little Bartlow, 1164 inhabitants. The living is a rectory, valued in the king's books at £28. 3. 4.; net income, £691; patrons, the Master and Fellows of Caius College, Cambridge. The church, situated on an eminence, is a spacious and ancient structure, with a low square tower surmounted by a small spire covered with lead: the parsonage-house, a handsome residence, about a quarter of a mile to the north, stands pleasantly on rising ground.

ASHE, a tything, in the parish of STOURPAIN, union of BLANDFORD, hundred of PIMPERNE, Blandford division of DORSET; containing 64 inhabitants.

ASHE (HOLY TRINITY), a parish, in the union of WHITCHURCH, hundred of OVERTON, Kingsclere and N. divisions of the county of SOUTHAMPTON, 5¼ miles (E. N. E.) from Whitchurch; comprising by computation 1667 acres, and containing 160 inhabitants. The living is a rectory, valued in the king's books at £9. 11. 5½.; net income, £350; patron, W. H. Beach, Esq.: the glebe consists of about 32 acres.

ASHELDHAM (ST. LAWRENCE), a parish, in the union of MALDON, hundred of DENGIE, S. division of ESSEX, 2 miles (N. E.) from Southminster; containing 219 inhabitants. This parish, which is situated on the sea-shore, comprises an area of about 3 square miles. The living is a discharged vicarage, valued in the king's books at £16. 13. 4.; patron, the Bishop of London; appropriators, the Dean and Chapter of St. Paul's. The tithes have been commuted for £408. 10., and there are 40 acres of glebe. The church is a plain building, consisting of a nave and chancel, with a low square tower.

ASHELWORTH (ST. ANDREW, or ST. BARTHOLOMEW), a parish, in the union of GLOUCESTER, Upper division of the hundred of BERKELEY, though locally in the hundred of DUDSTONE and KING'S BARTON, W. division of the county of GLOUCESTER, 5½ miles (N. by W.) from Gloucester; containing 594 inhabitants. It is skirted on the south-east by the navigable river Severn, and comprises about 1600 acres, of which two-thirds are pasture, and one-third arable. Several parts of the manor-house display considerable antiquity; and the parsonage, now a farmhouse, affords a peculiarly fine specimen of wood-work. The living is a discharged vicarage, valued in the king's books at £10. 2. 11.; net income, £187; patron, the Bishop of Gloucester and Bristol. The tithes were commuted for land and an annual money-payment, under an inclosure act, in 1797. The church consists of a nave, south aisle, and two chancels, with a tower and spire.

ASHEN, a parish, in the union of RISBRIDGE, hundred of HINCKFORD, N. division of ESSEX, 2½ miles (S. W. by S.) from Clare; comprising by measurement

1574 acres, and containing 321 inhabitants. The village is pleasantly situated on elevated ground, commanding fine prospects; and the parish is richly wooded. John Elwes, celebrated for his great wealth and penurious habits, was proprietor of the manor of Ashen, to which he succeeded on the decease of his uncle, Sir Harvey Elwes. The living is a rectory, valued in the king's books at £8, and in the patronage of the duchy of Lancaster: the tithes have been commuted for £390, and there are 16 acres of glebe. The church is an edifice of small dimensions, chiefly of stone, with a square embattled tower, and contains several monuments of great antiquity. According to Bishop Tanner, here was a priory of Augustine friars in the seventeenth of Edward II.

ASHENDON (St. Mary), a parish, in the union of Aylesbury, hundred of Ashendon, county of Buckingham, 6½ miles (N.) from Thame; containing, with the hamlet of Pollicot, 312 inhabitants. The living is a perpetual curacy, with that of Dorton annexed; net income, £106; patrons, the Dean and Canons of Christ-Church, Oxford. The church formerly contained several lofty and elegant marble monuments to the ancient family of Falconer, of Ashendon: in a large recess of the south wall, under an ornamented arch, to the left of the communion-table, is the recumbent effigy of a crusader with chain mail.

ASHERIDGE, a hamlet, in the parish of Chesham, union of Amersham, hundred of Burnham, county of Buckingham; containing 129 inhabitants.

ASHFIELD, with Ruthall, a township, in the parish of Prior's-Ditton, union of Bridgnorth, hundred of Munslow, S. division of Salop, 8¾ miles (W. S. W.) from Bridgnorth; containing 55 inhabitants.

ASHFIELD (St. Mary), a parish, in the union of Bosmere and Claydon, hundred of Thredling, E. division of Suffolk, 2½ miles (E.) from Debenham; comprising 1565a. 2r. 19p., and containing, with the hamlet of Thorpe, 343 inhabitants. The living is a perpetual curacy; net income, £53; patron and impropriator, Lord Henniker, who has commuted the tithes for £465. The glebe comprises three acres, with a small cottage. The church has long been dilapidated, though parts of the walls and of the steeple remain: the cemetery, however, is still used for interment. There is a chapel of ease at Thorpe, dedicated to St. Peter: it is in the English style, with a round tower, which is very old and must have belonged to a more ancient edifice; the chapel was repaired by George Pitt, Esq., in 1739. There is also a burial-ground at Thorpe.

ASHFIELD, GREAT (All Saints), a parish, in the union of Stow, hundred of Blackburn, W. division of Suffolk, 5 miles (E. S. E.) from Ixworth; containing 396 inhabitants. The living is a perpetual curacy; net income, £54; patron and impropriator, Lord Thurlow, whose ancestor, the lord chancellor, was born here in 1732. The church is in the early and decorated styles, and consists of a nave, chancel, and north aisle, with a square tower surmounted by a small spire. Nicholas Firmage, by his will dated in 1620, gave some land for a minister to preach a sermon every Sunday forenoon; four-fifths of the rent are now paid to a lecturer.

ASHFORD, a chapelry, in the parish and union of Bakewell, hundred of High Peak, N. division of the county of Derby, 2 miles (N. W. by W.) from Bakewell; containing 950 inhabitants, and comprising 2562a. 1r.

13p. The village is pleasantly situated in a vale watered by the river Wye, over which are three stone bridges. Mills for sawing and polishing marble, being the first established for that purpose in England, were erected on its banks in 1786, and are supplied from the celebrated quarries of black marble in the vicinity. The living is a perpetual curacy; net income, £102; patron, the Vicar of Bakewell; appropriators, the Dean and Chapter of Lichfield. The chapel, dedicated to the Holy Trinity, is in various styles, part being early English; the first erection was a chantry, established here by Godfrey, son of Wenun Wyn, in 1257. There is a place of worship for General Baptists; another, originally founded by the nonconformist divine, William Bagshaw, styled "the Apostle of the Peak," has been subsequently used by different sects. A school endowed with £8. 13. 4. per annum, is further supported by a donation of £20 from the Duke of Devonshire. Edward Plantagenet, Earl of Kent, resided in a mansion near the church, of which there are no vestiges except the moat that surrounded it.

ASHFORD (St. Peter), a parish, in the union of Barnstaple, hundred of Braunton, Braunton and N. divisions of Devon, 2 miles (N. W.) from Barnstaple; containing 174 inhabitants. This parish is situated on the navigable river Taw, by which it is bounded on the south; and comprises by measurement 339 acres, two-thirds of which are arable, and the remainder grazing, meadow, and orchard, with 38 acres of common. The living is a discharged vicarage, endowed with the rectorial tithes, and valued in the king's books at £8. 13. 9.; it is in the patronage of the Crown, and the tithes have been commuted for £85, with a glebe of 7 acres.

ASHFORD (St. Mary), a market-town, parish, and the head of the union of West Ashford, in the hundred of Chart and Longbridge, lathe of Shepway, E. division of Kent, 20 miles (S. E. by E.) from Maidstone, and 54 (E. S. E.) from London; containing 3082 inhabitants. This place, originally Asscheford, rose from the ruins of Great Chart, an ancient market-town, which gave name to the hundred, and was destroyed during the Danish wars. The town is a liberty of itself: it is situated on an eminence rising from the northern bank of the small river Stour, over which is a bridge of one arch; the houses are modern and well built, and the principal street, which is nearly half a mile long, is lighted. A suite of assembly-rooms has been erected on the site of the ancient manor and market-house, and assemblies occasionally take place; there are two subscription libraries, and races are held annually for one day. The only branch of manufacture is that of linen, which is carried on to a small extent. The market is on Tuesday and Saturday; there is a cattle-market on the first and third Tuesday in every month; and fairs are held on May 17th, Sept. 9th, and Oct. 24th, for general merchandise, and in the first week in Aug. for wool. A new turnpike-road, in a more direct line than the old road, has lately been completed between the town and Canterbury; and the South-Eastern railway passes near it: an act was obtained in 1845 for a railway to Hastings, 29 miles long; a railway was opened to Canterbury in Feb. 1846, and extended to Ramsgate, April, same year. Great works have just been formed for the construction of steam-engines and the manufacture of carriages, for the South-Eastern Company's use;

some of the piles of building are of extraordinary dimensions. A court leet is held annually, at which a constable, borough-holder, and other officers are appointed. The powers of the county debt-court of Ashford, established in 1847, extend over the registration-districts of East and West Ashford.

The parish comprises 2800a. 3r. 17p., of which about 290 acres are woodland, and 92 acres roads, waste land, and the town. The LIVING is a vicarage, valued in the king's books at £18. 4. 2.; net income, £460; patrons and appropriators, the Dean and Chapter of Rochester: the glebe comprises about 14 acres. The church, formerly collegiate, is a spacious and handsome cruciform structure in the later English style, with a lofty and elegant tower rising from the centre, and at the southern entrance a fine Norman arch: it was rebuilt in the reign of Edward IV., by Sir John Fogge, Knt., who erected the beautiful tower, and founded the college for a master, two chaplains, and two secular clerks. In a small chapel adjoining the south-western transept are three sumptuous monuments of variegated marble, to the memory of the Smyths of Westenhanger, and one to the Duchess of Athol. There are places of worship for Particular Baptists, the Society of Friends, the Connexion of the Countess of Huntingdon, and Wesleyans. The free grammar school was founded in 1636, by Sir Norton Knatchbull, who endowed it with £30 per annum, and vested the appointment of a master in his own family; national schools are supported by subscription, and by a bequest in land, producing £35 a year, from Dr. Turner, in 1702. The poor-law union of West Ashford comprises 12 parishes and places, and contains a population of 11,329. A mineral spring was discovered a few years ago, in a field called Sparrows gardens. Robert Glover, an industrious antiquary of the sixteenth century; his nephew, Thomas Miller, eminent as a herald and genealogist; and Dr. John Wallis, the celebrated mathematician, were natives of the place. It confers the inferior title of Baron on the family of Keppel, earls of Albemarle.

ASHFORD (ST. MICHAEL), a parish, in the union of STAINES, hundred of SPELTHORNE, county of MIDDLESEX, 4 miles (N. by N.) from Chertsey; containing 524 inhabitants. It comprises 1378a. 3r. 14p., of which the greater portion is arable, and about 100 acres meadow and pasture; the surface is generally flat, and the soil a gravel resting on blue clay. The surrounding scenery is pleasing, and enlivened by several handsome residences. The living is annexed to the vicarage of Staines; impropriator, J. Irving, Esq. The great tithes were commuted in 1809 for land and a money payment, under an inclosure act; and the vicarial tithes have since been commuted for £100: there is a glebe of 26½ acres. The church is a small edifice, built in 1796, at the expense of the principal inhabitants. A Sunday school is endowed with the interest of £438, three and a half per cent. consols.

, ASHFORD, a hamlet, in the parish of ILTON, union of CHARD, hundred of ABDICK and BULSTONE, W. division of SOMERSET; containing 13 inhabitants.

ASHFORD-BOWDLER (ST. ANDREW), a parish, in the union of LUDLOW, hundred of MUNSLOW, S. division of SALOP, 2 miles (S. by E.) from Ludlow; containing 96 inhabitants. This parish lies on the road to Worcester, and comprises 630 acres in equal portions of

arable and pasture; the views are picturesque and beautiful, and bounded by the Clee hills on the east, and the High Vinealls on the west. On the east flows the Teme, dividing the parish from Ashford-Carbonell: a bridge connects the two places. The living is a perpetual curacy; net income, £55; patron, Charles Walker, Esq., of Ashford Court. The church is ancient, with a steeple.

ASHFORD-CARBONELL (ST. MARY), a parish, in the union of LUDLOW, partly in the hundred of MUNSLOW, but chiefly in that of STOTTESDEN, S. division of SALOP, 3¼ miles (S. S. E.) from Ludlow; containing 266 inhabitants. It is situated on the river Teme, and comprises about 1500 acres. There are stone-quarries. The road leading from Ashford-Bowdler north-eastward to Cainham intersects the parish; and the Leominster canal runs very near its southern extremity. On the bank of the Teme is the residence of Ashford Court. The living is a rectory, annexed to that of Little Hereford: the tithes have been commuted for £325. The church stands a little to the north of Ashford Court.

ASHFORDBY, or ASFORDBY (ALL SAINTS), a parish, in the union of MELTON-MOWBRAY, hundred of EAST GOSCOTE, N. division of the county of LEICESTER, 3 miles (W.) from Melton-Mowbray; containing 482 inhabitants. It comprises by measurement 1800 acres, which two-thirds are grazing, and one-third arable land; and is situated on the river Wreak, which communicates with the Leicester and Melton-Mowbray navigation, and over which is a bridge. The living is a rectory, valued in the king's books at £15. 11. 8., and in the patronage of the Rev. A. Burnaby, the present incumbent, and his two sisters, with a net income of £455: the tithes were commuted for land in 1761, under an inclosure act.

ASH-HOLM, a township, in the parish of LAMBLEY, union of HALTWHISTLE, W. division of TINDALE ward, S. division of NORTHUMBERLAND, 19½ miles (W. by S.) from Hexham. This place, which is snugly seated under banks clothed with luxuriant woods, and where the course of the Tyne is suddenly intercepted by a high promontory called the Shaftbill, was the seat of the ancient family of Wallace, whose honourable career and success in life have enabled them to extend their property in the county far beyond the limits of this their patrimonial estate. James Wallace was attorney-general in 1780, and his son Thomas also filled offices of state, for which he was in 1828 created Baron Wallace, of Knaresdale. The Romans had a signal station here, the area of which is rectangular, 35 yards by 24; it is defended on three sides by steep escarpments, and on the east, and partly on the south, is cut off from the main land by a ditch 60 feet wide and 25 deep. There is a good millstone quarry.

ASHILL (ST. NICHOLAS), a parish, in the union of SWAFFHAM, hundred of WAYLAND, W. division of NORFOLK, 3 miles (N. W.) from Watton; containing 637 inhabitants. It comprises by computation 2991 acres, of which 2367 are arable, and 584 meadow and pasture; the soil is in some parts light and gravelly, and in others strong and clayey. The living is a rectory, valued in the king's books at £19. 13. 6½.; patron and incumbent, the Rev. B. Edwards. The incumbent's tithes have been commuted for £979; a rent-charge of £21 is paid to the rector of Great Cressingham; and there are 30 acres of glebe, with a good house. The church is chiefly in the later style of English architecture. There is a place of worship for Wesleyans. At the time of the inclosure, 73 acres of land were allotted to the poor.

ASHILL, a parish, in the union of CHARD, hundred of ADDICK and BULSTONE, W. division of SOMERSET, 4 miles (N. W.) from Ilminster ; containing 438 inhabitants. This place, which is situated on the road from Bridport to Taunton and Tiverton, belonged in the reign of Edward II. to Thomas de Multon, who obtained for the inhabitants the grant of a weekly market on Wednesday, and of fairs on the festivals of the Virgin Mary, St. Simon and St. Jude. A portion of ground which for many years has been contested by the parishes of Ashill and Broadway, was in 1685 the scene of a conflict between Monmouth, on his retreat from Sedgemoor, and a party of the king's forces. The parish comprises by admeasurement 1790 acres of profitable land, under good cultivation ; the scenery is pleasantly diversified, and in some parts enriched with wood. A fair is still held in the village on the Wednesday in Easter-week. The living is a discharged vicarage, valued in the king's books at £6. 0. 10. ; patron, the Prebendary of Ashill in the Cathedral of Wells. The great tithes have been commuted for £204. 10. 8., with a glebe of 60 acres ; the vicarial tithes have been commuted for £118. 13. 4., and there are 24 acres of land attached, at Bewley Down, Dorset. Some remains exist of an ancient seat belonging to Nicholas Wadham, founder of Wadham College, Oxford. A chalybeate spring is carefully preserved.

ASHINGDON (ST. ANDREW), a parish, in the union and hundred of ROCHFORD, S. division of ESSEX, 2½ miles (N. by W.) from Rochford ; containing 119 inhabitants. This place is thought by the best writers to have been the scene of the battle of Assandune, in which Canute the Dane, after a sanguinary contest, vanquished the Saxons under Edmund Ironside. The parish comprises 1165a. 1r. 11p. The living is a discharged rectory, valued in the king's books at £8. 13. 4., and in the gift of the Nottidge family : the tithes have been commuted for £285, and there are 20 acres of glebe.

ASHINGTON, with SHEEPWASH, a township, in the parish of BOTHAL, union of MORPETH, E. division of MORPETH ward, N. division of NORTHUMBERLAND, 4½ miles (E. by N.) from Morpeth ; containing 76 inhabitants. The persons who are first named in the records as connected with the property here, are the Morwicks, Lumleys, and Fitzhughs ; the family of Essendon (the modern Ashington) are mentioned as lords of the manor at the close of the 13th century, and the most important landowners since that period have been the families of Coventre and Fenwick, from whom the place has descended to the Duke of Portland. The township comprises 583 acres of land, of which 444 are tillage, 112 grass, and 27 wood ; the grounds are very beautiful in some places by the side of the river Wansbeck, which is navigable for keels and small boats as far as Sheepwash, where it is crossed by a bridge. The tithes have been commuted for £109. 6.—See SHEEPWASH.

ASHINGTON (ST. VINCENT), a parish, in the union of YEOVIL, hundred of STONE, W. division of SOMERSET, 3 miles (E. S. E.) from Ilchester ; comprising by computation 560 acres, and containing 71 inhabitants. The parish is finely wooded and fertile, the land rising gently from the river Yeo, which bounds it on the east

and north ; and looking over a rich and extensive vale, the view is terminated at unequal distances by a bold range of hills from the south-east to the north-west. The living is a discharged rectory, valued in the king's books at £6. 3. 4., and in the patronage of the family of Williams : the tithes have been commuted for £125, and there are 32 acres of glebe, with a house. The church is a small neat structure, having a turret with two bells ; at the eastern end, on the outside, is a small niche with three human figures, which admit a conjecture that they refer to the history of St. Vincent, who was burnt alive at Valentia, in Spain, in the year 304.

ASHINGTON cum BUNCTON (ST. PETER AND ST. PAUL), a parish, in the union of THAKEHAM, hundred of WEST GRINSTEAD, rape of BRAMBER, W. division of SUSSEX, 5 miles (N. W.) from Steyning, and on the road from London to Worthing ; containing 282 inhabitants. The living is a rectory, valued in the king's books at £8. 5. ; net income, £189 ; patron, G. Wyndham, Esq. The church is in the later English style, and has some fragments of stained glass in its windows. At Buncton is a chapel of ease, with remains of Norman arches on the outside of the chancel.

ASHLEY cum SILVERLEY (ST. MARY), a parish, in the union of NEWMARKET, hundred of CHEVELEY, county of CAMBRIDGE, 3¼ miles (E. by S.) from Newmarket ; containing 417 inhabitants. These two places, which are now consolidated, comprise 2143a. 3r. 25p. At Silverley are only a farmhouse and two cottages, with the tower of the ruined church ; at Ashley are the ruins of an old church situated in the burial-ground. The living is a rectory, with the vicarage of Silverley annexed, valued in the king's books at £8 ; patron, the Marquess of Bute ; net income, £150, arising out of 272 acres of land allotted in lieu of tithes on the inclosure. The church is a small plain edifice.

ASHLEY, a township, in the parish of BOWDON, union of ALTRINCHAM, hundred of BUCKLOW, N. division of CHESHIRE, 5 miles (N. N. E.) from Knutsford ; containing 377 inhabitants. It comprises 2072 acres, of a clayey and sandy soil. Ashley Hall, the ancient manorial mansion, which is approached by a fine avenue of stately walnut-trees, is remarkable for containing eleven original portraits of gentlemen of this county, ancestors of the Grosvenors, Cholmondeleys, and other families, who formed a club during the progress of the Pretender through the north, in 1715, when the expediency of joining his standard was debated, and the casting vote against the measure was given by Thomas Asheton, the owner of the mansion. Arden House, with 140 acres of land adjacent, is the property of John Orrell, Esq. The tithes have been commuted for £197 payable to the Bishop of Chester, and £8 to the vicar.

ASHLEY (ST. MARY), a parish, in the union of MARKET-HARBOROUGH, hundred of CORBY, N. division of the county of NORTHAMPTON, 5 miles (W. by S.) from Rockingham ; containing 323 inhabitants. On the north the parish is bounded by the river Welland, which separates it from Leicestershire ; it consists of 1182a. 2r. 20p. of a rich and fertile soil. The living is a rectory, valued in the king's books at £17 ; net income, £320 ; patron and incumbent, the Rev. Richard Farrer. The tithes were commuted for land and a money payment, under an inclosure act, in 1806.

ASHLEY (St. Mary), a parish, in the union of Stockbridge, hundred of King's Sombourn, Winchester and N. divisions of the county of Southampton, 3½ miles (S. S. E.) from Stockbridge; containing 102 inhabitants. It comprises by measurement 1857 acres, of which 1270 are arable, 400 wood, and 187 pasture, waste, &c.; the soil rests chiefly on chalk. The living is a rectory, valued in the king's books at £7. 16. 3.; patron and incumbent, the Rev. James Hannay: the tithes have been commuted for £350, and the glebe comprises about 40 acres. The church is an ancient and curious structure, in the early English style. There are vestiges of several Roman camps, and a circular intrenchment of considerable dimensions, supposed to be British, or Danish.

ASHLEY, a tything, in the parish of Milton, union of Lymington, hundred of Christchurch, Lymington and S. divisions of Hants; containing 552 inhabitants. It is situated to the east of the village of Milton, and on the road from Lymington to Christchurch.

ASHLEY (St. John the Baptist), a parish, in the union of Market-Drayton, N. division of the hundred of Pirehill and of the county of Stafford, 6 miles (N. N. E.) from Market-Drayton; containing 853 inhabitants. It comprises 2800a. 3r. 32p. of fertile land. The living is a rectory, valued in the king's books at £10. 2. 8½., and in the patronage of Thomas Kinnersley and H. C. Meynell, Esqs.: the tithes have been commuted for £370, and the glebe comprises 40 acres. The church is a handsome structure in the early English style, and contains splendid monuments and effigies of the six Lords Gerard, the last of whom died in 1807; also an elegant monument by Chantrey to Thomas Kinnersley, Esq., father of the present patron. There are places of worship for Wesleyans and Roman Catholics.

ASHLEY (St. James), a parish, in the union of Tetbury, hundred of Malmesbury, Malmesbury and Kingswood, and N. divisions of Wilts, 5 miles (N. by W.) from Malmesbury; containing 96 inhabitants. The living is a discharged rectory, valued in the king's books at £9. 16. 5½., and in the patronage of the Duchy of Lancaster: the tithes have been commuted for £210, and there are 34 acres of glebe.

ASHLEY-GREEN, a hamlet, in the parish of Chesham, union of Amersham, hundred of Burnham, county of Buckingham; containing 536 inhabitants.

ASHLEY-HAY, a township, in the union of Belper, parish of Wirksworth, hundred of Appletree, S. division of the county of Derby, 1¾ mile (S.) from Wirksworth; containing 272 inhabitants. The road from Wirksworth to Derby passes here.

ASHLEY LODGE.—See Godshill-Wood.

ASHLEY, NORTH, a tything, in the parish, union, and hundred of Ringwood, Ringwood and S. divisions of Hants; containing 237 inhabitants.

ASHLING, EAST and WEST, tythings, in the parish of Funtington, union of Westbourne, hundred of Bosham, rape of Chichester, W. division of Sussex; containing, respectively, 310 and 455 inhabitants.

ASHMANHAUGH (St. Swithin), a parish, in the union of Tunstead and Happing, hundred of Tunstead, E. division of Norfolk, 2 miles (E. by N.) from Coltishall; containing 180 inhabitants. It comprises

665a. 2r. 23p., of which 571 acres are arable, 29 pasture and meadow, and 37 woodland. The living is a perpetual curacy, in the patronage of the family of Preston; net income, £42; appropriator, the Bishop of Norwich, whose tithes have been commuted for £145, and who has a glebe of 5½ acres. The church, which is chiefly in the early style, was thoroughly repaired and new-pewed, and the tower rebuilt in 1840.

ASHMANSWORTH (St. James), a parish, in the union of Kingsclere, hundred of Evingar, Kingsclere and N. divisions of the county of Southampton, 7 miles (S. S. W.) from Newbury; comprising 1798 acres by measurement, and containing 220 inhabitants. The soil is strong clay mixed with flint stones, and rests on chalk, the district being a portion of the high range of chalk hills which form the northern boundary of the South Downs. The living is annexed to the rectory of East Woodhay: the tithes have been commuted for £371, and the glebe comprises 26 acres.

ASHMORE (St. Nicholas), a parish, in the union of Shaftesbury, hundred of Cranborne, Shaston division of Dorset, 5 miles (S. E.) from Shaftesbury; containing 242 inhabitants. It comprises 2342 acres, of which 643 are common or waste; the soil is heavy and flinty, and the ground elevated, rising 720 feet above the level of the sea. The living, which formerly belonged to the abbey of Tewkesbury, is a rectory, valued in the king's books at £7. 19. 9½.; net income, £389; patron, the Rev. C. Chisholme. The glebe consists of about 30 acres. The church, erected in 1433, is a plain edifice of stone and flint.

ASHOLT, county of Somerset.—See Aisholt.

ASHORN, a township, in the parish of Newbold-Pacey, union of Stratford-on-Avon, Warwick division of the hundred of Kington, S. division of the county of Warwick, 6½ miles (N. N. W.) from Kington; containing 274 inhabitants.

ASHOVER (All Saints), a parish, in the union of Chesterfield, partly in the hundred of Wirksworth, but chiefly in that of Scarsdale, N. division of the county of Derby, 7 miles (S. S. W.) from Chesterfield; containing, with the chapelry of Dethwick-Lea, and the hamlet of Holloway, 3482 inhabitants. This place, which was formerly a market-town, and, according to Domesday book, had a church at the time of the Conquest, occupies a pleasant site near the rivers Amber and Milntown, and within three miles of the Midland railway. The parish comprises 9700a. 2r. 37p., of which 62 acres are waste; the soil is various, and the lands are in good cultivation. Coal, ironstone, millstone, gritstone, and lead-ore are found; and the Gregory lead-mine here, 300 yards deep, is said to have once been the richest in the kingdom, though its present produce is inconsiderable. The manufacture of stockings is carried on to a small extent, and the working of tambour lace affords employment to the greater part of the female population. Fairs for cattle and sheep are held on the 25th of April and the 15th of October. Ashover is in the honour of Tutbury, duchy of Lancaster: constables and other officers are appointed at the court leet of the lord of the manor. The living is a rectory, valued in the king's books at £24. 3. 1½.; net income, £481; patron, the Rev. Joseph Nodder. The tithes were commuted for land, under an inclosure act, in 1776; the glebe comprises 150 acres. The church is a spacious edifice,

N

built in 1419, with a very handsome spire, and contains a Norman font of curious design, and several monuments to the family of Babington. The chapel at Dethwick-Lea forms a distinct incumbency. There are places of worship for Primitive and Wesleyan Methodists; and a school endowed with £23 per annum.

ASHOW (St. Mary), a parish, in the Kenilworth division of the hundred of KNIGHTLOW, union, and S. division of the county, of WARWICK, 2½ miles (S. E. by E.) from Kenilworth; containing 172 inhabitants. The parish contains by measurement 1000 acres, of which about 800 are arable and pasture, and 200 woodland; the soil is chiefly red sand and clay. The lands are intersected by the river Avon. The living is a rectory, valued in the king's books at £6. 2. 1., and in the patronage of Lord Leigh: the tithes have been commuted for £216. 17., and the glebe consists of about 12 acres.

ASHPERTON (St. Bartholomew), a parish, in the union of LEDBURY, hundred of RADLOW, county of HEREFORD, 5¼ miles (N. W. by W.) from Ledbury; containing 604 inhabitants. It comprises by measurement 1741 acres; and is intersected by the road from Leominster to Ledbury, and the new canal from Ledbury to Hereford. The living is annexed to the vicarage of Stretton-Grandsome: the tithes have been commuted for £350. 15.; and there is a quarter of an acre of glebe, on which a school-house for boys has been built. The parliamentary army was stationed at a place in the parish, still called Cromwell's Walls.

ASHPRINGTON (St. David), a parish, in the union of TOTNES, hundred of COLERIDGE, Stanborough and Coleridge, and S. divisions of DEVON, 3 miles (S. E.) from Totnes; containing 588 inhabitants. This parish, which comprises about 2380 acres, is intersected by the old road to Dartmouth, and washed by the Hareburne and the Dart, which latter river brings up colliers and coasters. Ochre and iron are frequently met with; and slate, dunstone, and limestone abound. The living is a rectory, valued in the king's books at £29. 1. 8.; net income, £520; patron, the Rev. G. T. Carwithen. The glebe consists of 25 acres.

ASHREIGNEY, or RING'S ASH (St. James), a parish, in the union of TORRINGTON, hundred of NORTH TAWTON, South Molton and N. divisions of DEVON, 4 miles (W. by S.) from Chulmleigh; containing 1088 inhabitants. The parish comprises 4800 acres, of which 410 are common or waste. The living is a rectory, valued in the king's books at £24, and in the patronage of the Rev. J. T. Johnson: the tithes have been commuted for £450, and there are 70 acres of glebe. A national school is endowed with £10 per annum.

ASHTEAD (St. Giles), a parish, in the union of EPSOM, Second division of the hundred of COPTHORNE, W. division of SURREY, 2 miles (S. W. by S.) from Epsom; containing 618 inhabitants. It comprises 2516a. 25p., of which 511 acres are common or waste; and is pleasantly situated on the road from London, by Dorking, to Bognor and Worthing. A small fair is held on the 4th of May. Ashtead Park is a fine structure of white brick, and is said to have cost nearly £100,000; it is surrounded by a demesne of 140 acres: here is preserved a very valuable collection of pictures. The living is a rectory, valued in the king's books at £13. 15. 5., and in the patronage of the Hon. Fulk Greville Howard

and Hon. Mrs. Howard: the tithes have been commuted for £549. 12. 6., and there are 12½ acres of glebe. The church is a neat building, beautifully situated in Ashtead Park. An hospital for six poor widows was founded by Lady Diana Fielding, and endowed with property producing £32. 7. per annum. Here is a mineral spring, the water of which is similar to that of the Epsom wells. A Roman encampment may be traced round what is now the churchyard and part of Ashtead Park; and the great Roman road by Noviomagus (now Woodcote Park) passes along the south side of the parish. Sir Robert Howard, the poet, resided here in the time of Charles II., by whom, it is said, he was often visited.

ASHTED, a district, in the parish and union of ASTON, Birmingham division of the hundred of HEMLINGFORD, N. division of the county of WARWICK. This place, which adjoins the town of Birmingham on the north-east, and now forms a portion of that borough, consists of good streets of well-built houses, and some pleasant detached cottages and villas. About forty years ago it contained but a few hundred residents; the present population is very little, if at all, short of 25,000. At the extremity of Great Brooke-street are the Vauxhall gardens, which have lately been laid out very tastefully, and where concerts and displays of fireworks take place during the summer; in the same street are the barracks erected soon after the Birmingham riots in 1791, a handsome range of building, with a riding-school, hospital, and magazine, also a spacious area for the exercise of cavalry, and a smaller for parade. From its proximity to Birmingham, the hamlet participates in the trade and manufactures of that town; there are a large glasshouse, flour-mills, and various other works, with several wharfs on the line of the Birmingham canal. From Ashted verge four lines of railway, the London, the Gloucester and Bristol, the Grand Junction, and the Derby, of all of which, as they proceed from Birmingham, the Vauxhall gardens command a full view. Adjoining the barracks is an episcopal chapel dedicated to St. James, formerly the dwelling-house of Dr. Ash, from whom the hamlet takes its name: it was purchased for about £2700, and consecrated Sept. 7th, 1810; in 1810 it was repaired at an expense of £848, and in 1836 enlarged at a cost of £1300. The living is a perpetual curacy; net income, £210; patrons, the Hon. Frederic Gough and the Ven. Archdeacons Spooner and Hodson, as trustees. Here is a national school.

ASHTON, a township, in the parish of TARVIN, union of GREAT BOUGHTON, Second division of the hundred of EDDISBURY, S. division of the county of CHESTER, 7½ miles (E. N. E.) from Chester; containing 401 inhabitants. The manor was held in the reign of Edward I. by the Mainwaring family, from whom it descended by female heirs to the Veres and Trussells: about 1580 it was sold by Edward Vere, Earl of Oxford, to Sir Christopher Hatton, from whom it passed by successive sales to various owners. The property of Ashton-Hayes was purchased in 1843 from Booth Grey, Esq., by William Atkinson, Esq., of Manchester, who has much improved the mansion and grounds, and introduced the latest system of agriculture. The township comprises 1222 acres; the soil is of a sandy quality. The tithes have been commuted for £109 payable to the Dean and Chapter of Lichfield, and £81. 10. to the vicar of the parish.

ASHTON (St. John the Baptist), a parish, in the union of St. Thomas, hundred of Exminster, Teignbridge and S. divisions of Devon, 4 miles (N. by W.) from Chudleigh ; containing 319 inhabitants. It comprises 1726a. 3r. 5p., of which about 200 acres are furze and fir plantations. The sudden inundations of the river Teign, which bounds the parish on the east, frequently occasion much damage. Several mines of manganese are worked by contractors from Cornwall, who pay to the lord of the manor a duty on the tonnage; and large quantities of the mineral are supplied to the Manchester and other manufacturers, for bleaching their goods. The living is a rectory, valued in the king's books at £11. 10. 2½.; patron and incumbent, the Rev. George Ware, whose tithes have been commuted for £256, and who has a glebe of 50 acres. The church contains a very finely carved wooden screen and rood-loft.

ASHTON, with Eye-Moreton, a township, in the parish of Eye, union of Leominster, hundred of Wolphy, county of Hereford, 3¾ miles (N. N. E.) from Leominster ; containing 294 inhabitants. The tithes have been commuted for £40 payable to the Bishop of Hereford, and £311 payable to the vicar of the parish, besides which the latter receives 5s. per acre on all hopgrounds.

ASHTON, or ASHTON-UPON-RIBBLE, with Lea, Cottam, and Ingol, a township, in the parish and union of Preston, hundred of Amounderness, N. division of the county of Lancaster, 2 miles (W. by N.) from Preston, and on the Fylde road, containing 710 inhabitants. Tulketh, in the township, was originally inhabited by a body of monks from the monastery of Savigny, in Normandy, under the immediate direction of Evanus, and who, on seating themselves here, chose him to be their first abbot ; they afterwards removed to Furness. The township is washed by the river Ribble on the southern boundary, and comprises 3347 acres, whereof 801 are in Ashton, 1668 in Lea, and 878 in Cottam and Ingol; the surface is generally flat, and the soil clay and marl. The Lancaster canal and the Preston and Wyre railway pass through. Sir Henry Bold Hoghton, Bart., is lord of the manor of Ashton and Lea. The township has been formed into an ecclesiastical district, the living of which is a perpetual curacy, in the patronage of the Vicar of Preston ; income, £100, with a house. The church, dedicated to St. Andrew, was built in 1836, and is a neat structure of stone, in the Norman style, with a tower and spire. The great tithes have been commuted for £235, and the vicarial for £13. There is a Roman Catholic chapel at Lea, built in 1800 ; the priest has a house and six acres of land. Excellent schools, built by subscription in 1846, with a residence for the master and mistress, are near the church ; and Tulketh Hall, now a large school, stands on a hill overlooking the Preston marshes and the river Ribble. At Lea is a school endowed in 1784 by S. Neeld ; the property consists of a farmhouse and 25 acres of land, producing £82 per annum.

ASHTON, with Stodday, a township, in the parish and union of Lancaster, hundred of Lonsdale south of the Sands, N. division of the county of Lancaster, 3¼ miles (S. S. E.) from Lancaster ; containing 185 inhabitants. Ashton is remarkable as the ancient seat of the De Courcys, out of which family it passed by mar-

riage to John de Coupland, the hero of Neville's Cross. It was possessed in 1454 by the Lawrences, and came subsequently by marriage to the Butlers, Radcliffes, and Gerards ; an heiress of the last named married James, Earl of Arran, created fourth duke of Hamilton in 1679. The township comprises 1350 acres of land ; the surface is undulated, in some parts of high elevation, and the views of Lancaster Castle and town and of the surrounding country are beautiful. Ashton Hall, once the seat of the knightly family of Leyburne, and now the property of the Duke of Hamilton, is a quadrangular edifice, with a projecting wing to the east, and a square tower with angular turrets on the west ; it was probably erected in the fourteenth century, but the numerous alterations and additions which it has undergone, have left little of the ancient baronial mansion. Stodday Lodge is the residence of William Assheton Cross, Esq.; in the gardens are some Roman antiquities. Walnut Bank is the picturesque residence of Thomas Pritt, Esq. The impropriate tithes have been commuted for £22. A free school has an income of nearly £50 per annum.

ASHTON (St. Michael), a parish, in the union of Potterspury, hundred of Cleley, S. division of the county of Northampton, 7 miles (S. by E.) from Northampton ; containing 417 inhabitants. This parish, which is bounded on the south by the river Tow, comprises by measurement 1100 acres of highly fertile land, chiefly arable ; and is situated near the Grand Junction canal, and intersected by the London and Birmingham railway. The living is a rectory, valued in the king's books at £10, and in the patronage of the Crown ; net income, £275, arising from 235 acres of land allotted in lieu of tithes on the inclosure of the parish. The church is a very ancient structure, with a square tower, and contains a Norman font, several good brasses, and a figure of a Knight Templar. There is a place of worship for Baptists.

ASHTON, a hamlet, in the parish of Ufford, union of Stamford, soke of Peterborough, N. division of the county of Northampton, 4½ miles (S. E.) from Stamford ; containing 101 inhabitants. The tithes were commuted for corn-rents, under an inclosure act, in 1796.

ASHTON, a chapelry, in the parish and union of Oundle, hundred of Polebrook, N. division of the county of Northampton, 1¼ mile (E. by N.) from Oundle ; containing 172 inhabitants, and comprising 1308a. 3r. 20p. It is situated on the right bank of the river Nene, and is intersected by the road from Oundle to Peterborough. A school was erected in 1708, by Elizabeth Creed, under the will of her daughter Jemima, who endowed it with land producing £44 per annum; it has also a fund of £200 in the three per cent. consols.

ASHTON-BLANK.—See Aston-Blank.

ASHTON, a tything, in the parish and hundred of Bishop's-Waltham, union of Droxford, Droxford and N. divisions of the county of Southampton ; containing 310 inhabitants.

ASHTON, COLD (Holy Trinity), a parish, in the union of Chipping, hundred of Puckle-Church, W. division of the county of Gloucester, 5½ miles (N.) from Bath ; containing 414 inhabitants. In the memorable battle of Lansdown, the parliamentarians, who had marched from Bath to attack the royalist forces intrenched on Furze hill, were defeated, after a severe conflict, and driven up the valley of Ashton Lodge, where

N 2

in the hour of victory, the gallant Sir Beville Granville, who commanded the royalists, received a mortal wound, of which he expired in the rectory-house of this place. The parish is situated on the road from Bath to Gloucester, and contains by measurement 2400 acres. The living is a rectory, valued in the king's books at £17. 1. 8.; net income, £492; patrons, the family of Batchellor. The glebe consists of 88 acres. The church was erected in 1406, by Thomas Key; and to perpetuate the memory of the founder, keys of a durable material are carved over every window and door, and on many parts of the interior of the building. The venerable Bishop Latimer was incumbent of the parish prior to his advancement to the episcopal dignity, and in the church is an ancient stone pulpit, in which he preached. The descendants of Sir Richard Whittington, lord mayor of London in the years 1397, 1406, and 1419, reside here, in an old mansion bearing date 1664.

ASHTON-GIFFORD, a township, in the parish of CODFORD ST. PETER, union of WARMINSTER, hundred of HEYTESBURY, Warminster and S. divisions of WILTS, 3 miles (S. E. by E.) from Heytesbury; containing 141 inhabitants.

ASHTON - IN - MAKERFIELD, or ASHTON-LE-WILLOWS, a township, in the union of WIGAN, hundred of WEST DERBY, S. division of the county of LANCASTER, 5 miles (S.) from Wigan, and 7 miles (N. N. W.) from Warrington. The township was until lately, with Haydock, a chapelry in the parish of Winwick; and consists of three parts, viz.: the Town-End, the Brynn-End, and the Garswood-End, comprising together 6057 acres, and containing 5915 inhabitants. By an act of parliament for the division of Winwick, passed in 1845, the Brynn-End and the Garswood-End were made a separate parish, called the rectory of Ashton; the Town-End was annexed to the adjoining township of Haydock, and the two places formed into another and distinct parish, called the vicarage of St. Thomas (the Apostle) in Ashton. The district forms part of the great coal-field of Lancashire; it is dry and healthy, the surface level, and the soil a heavy clay. One of the great lines of road from London to Edinburgh runs through the town of Ashton, and other facilities of communication are furnished by the Sankey canal, the Leeds and Liverpool canal, and the Liverpool and Manchester railway; the last being two miles distant, at Newton. The place has long been famous for the manufacture of locks and hinges; and employment is also afforded to the inhabitants in several cotton and other manufactories, and in the working of the contiguous extensive and valuable coal-mines. The lord of the manor, Sir John Gerard, Bart., holds a court leet every September. A fair is held on the 21st and 22nd of the same month.

The rectory of Ashton is endowed with the tithes of the whole township, which have been commuted for £600; patron, the Earl of Derby: the next presentation, however, will be exercised by the present rector of Winwick, should a vacancy occur during his incumbency. The church, dedicated to the Trinity, is situated near Downall-Green, in Garswood-End; it was built in 1838, principally at the expense of the rector of Winwick, and is a cruciform edifice in the early English style: the cost was £2600. The rectory-house adjoins the church, as also does a handsome and commodious school-house: twelve acres of land surrounding the rectory have been
92

purchased for glebe. The vicarage of St. Thomas is in the patronage of the Rector of Ashton; net income, £300, arising partly from 24 acres of glebe and the tithes of the township of Haydock: there is a glebe-house. The church stands in almost the centre of the town : it was rebuilt in 1715, was enlarged in 1784, and again in 1815, and has a campanile turret with a clock. A free grammar school, at Seneley Green, was founded in 1588 by Robert Byrchall, and is endowed with £50 per annum. The Independents, Quakers, Unitarians, and Roman Catholics have places of worship. Many curious fossils are found in the coal-mines.

ASHTON-KEYNES (HOLY CROSS), a parish, in the union of CRICKLADE and WOOTTON-BASSET, hundred of HIGHWORTH, CRICKLADE, and STAPLE, Cricklade and N. divisions of WILTS, 4½ miles (W.) from Cricklade; containing, with the chapelry of Leigh, 1332 inhabitants. The living is a vicarage, valued in the king's books at £16; income, £325; patron and impropriator, J. Pitt, Esq. There is a chapel of ease at Leigh.

ASHTON, LONG (ALL SAINTS), a parish, in the union of BEDMINSTER, hundred of HARTCLIFFE with BEDMINSTER, E. division of SOMERSET, 3 miles (S. W. by W.) from Bristol; containing, with the hamlets of Kingcot, Providence, Yanleigh, Bower-Ashton, and Rounham, 1926 inhabitants. It comprises by computation 4112 acres, of which 1132 are arable, 2328 pasture, and 428 woodland, waste, &c. The living is a discharged vicarage, valued in the king's books at £10. 17. 11.; net income, £117; patrons and impropriators, Sir J. Smyth, Bart., and the family of Langton. There were formerly a chapel and a hermitage at Rounham Ferry, in the parish. In 1661, Francis Derrick gave a piece of land producing about £8 per annum; in 1760, Anne Smyth left a rent-charge of £10; and, in 1822, John Stanton gave £100; which funds are applied towards the support of a school further maintained by subscription. On the eastern point of Ashton hill are two intrenchments called Burwalls and Stokeleigh, now overgrown with wood, which appear to have been Roman camps; and recently, in forming the line of the Bristol and Exeter railway, the foundation of the wall of an ancient village was discovered, with numerous coins of Constantine and Severus, and domestic utensils.

ASHTON, STEEPLE (ST. MARY), a parish, partly in the union of WESTBURY and WHORWELSDOWN, and partly in that of MELKSHAM, hundred of WHORWELSDOWN, Whorwelsdown and N. divisions of WILTS; containing, with the chapelry of Semington, and the tythings of West Ashton, Hinton, and Littleton, 1941 inhabitants, of whom 848 are in the village of Steeple-Ashton, 4 miles (E. by S.) from Trowbridge. This place derived the adjunct by which it is distinguished from other localities of the same name, from the lofty spire of its church, which was first injured, and then struck down by lightning in 1670. It was formerly of some importance, and had the grant of a market in the reign of Edward III., which was confirmed in that of Richard II., with the addition of an annual fair. In the time of Henry VIII. Leland states that the clothing trade was carried on here to a very considerable extent, but it has ceased to exist; the market also has been for many years discontinued, but the fair, though now ill attended, is still held on the 19th of September. Steeple-Ashton contains by estimation 5400 acres, of which

2120 are arable, 2660 pasture, and 540 woodland; Semington consists of 1195a. 1r. 24p., of which 213 acres are arable, and 923 pasture. The living is a vicarage, valued in the king's books at £17. 2. 6.; net income, £852; patron, the Master of Magdalene College, Cambridge, who is restricted in his presentation to one of three senior foundation fellows. The tithes, exclusively of the tythings, have been commuted for £362. 10., payable to the College, £285 payable to the vicar, £18. 2. to the rector of Trowbridge, and £10 to the impropriator. The church is a spacious structure in the later English style, built between the years 1480 and 1500, and has a lofty square embattled tower at the west end, crowned with pinnacles, and a north and south porch of elegant design. There is a chapel of ease at Semington, which probably was in early times a parish; it is in the later English style. At West Ashton also is a church, forming a distinct incumbency. John Hicks bequeathed £5 per annum for teaching children, and John Togwell a further sum for the same purpose; which have been laid out in the purchase of £519. 10. 7., three per cent. consols. The parish is remarkable for fossils of the coral-rag formation.

ASHTON-UNDER-HILL (St. Barbara), a parish, in the union of Evesham, partly in the Upper division of the hundred of Tewkesbury, but chiefly in the hundred of Tibaldstone, E. division of the county of Gloucester, 8 miles (E. N. E.) from Tewkesbury; containing 342 inhabitants, and comprising about 1300 acres. The living is annexed to the vicarage of Beckford, and the impropriation belongs to W. Wakeman and J. Blackburne, Esqs.: the tithes were commuted for land and a money payment, under an inclosure act, in 1773.

Arms.

ASHTON-UNDER-LYNE (St. Michael), a market-town, parish, parliamentary borough, and the head of a union, in the hundred of Salford, S. division of the county of Lancaster, 6 miles (E.) from Manchester, 58 (S. E.) from Lancaster, and 197 (N. W. by N.) from London; comprising the parochial divisions of Ashton-town, Audenshaw, Hartshead, and Knott-Lanes; and containing 46,296 inhabitants. The primary part of the name of this place is derived from the Saxon words *æyc,* an ash, and *tun,* an inclosed place or town; the adjunct *under-Lyne* is of obscure etymology, and various hypotheses have been ventured in elucidation of its origin. The most probable seems to be that of Mr. John Ross Coulthart, of Croft House, Ashton, who ascribes the term to the situation of the town near to or *under* the *line* or chain of hills which separates Yorkshire from Lancashire, popularly denominated "the back-bone of England." The original proprietors, the Asshetons, a family distinguished in the early period of English history, exercised the power of life and death; and a field on the west side of the Old Hall, through which now passes the Ashton branch of the Manchester and Sheffield railway, was the place of execution, and is still known by the name of the Gallows' Meadow. In the reign of Henry VI., when the feudal

93

system was generally relaxed, Sir Ralph Assheton, still inheriting extraordinary privileges, exercised them with great rigour and exactitude; and in order that no fines or forfeits might be lost for the want of strict supervision, it was customary for him, clad in black armour and mounted on a charger, with a numerous retinue of dependents, to perambulate the manor in person at uncertain intervals, taking cognizance of every infraction of his rights as a baron, levying from his tenants, by force if necessary, all fines for heriots, weifs, strays, &c., and rigidly punishing with the stocks, imprisonment, or death, all offences committed within his jurisdiction. To commemorate the abhorrence in which Sir Ralph's conduct was held, the ceremony of "riding the black lad" was instituted, and is still observed on every Easter-Monday. The effigy of a man of colossal dimensions, clad in black, is placed on a horse, and, followed by a rabble, is led in procession through the principal streets of the borough, while the promoters of the cavalcade beg small sums from door to door; at night, the effigy is dismounted at the old market-place, and after being torn to pieces, the fragments are usually burned amid the execrations of the populace.

The town is situated on a gentle declivity, on the northern bank of the river Tame, above which it is elevated from 30 to 40 feet; the old streets are narrow and irregular, but those recently formed. are remarkably spacious, and consist of substantial and handsome houses. It is well paved, lighted with gas, cheaply and abundantly supplied with water, and is rapidly improving under the management of local commissioners of police. A mechanics' institution was founded in 1825; the present commodious premises are situated at the top of Church-street, immediately adjoining the western gates of the parish church. The reading-room of the institution is well supplied with periodicals, and the library contains upwards of 1200 volumes of standard works : the number of subscribers is 164. In 1846, a Floral and Horticultural Society was formed for the purpose of promoting, by means of prizes to exhibitors, the general cultivation of tulips, herbaceous plants, fruits, &c. The Barracks, which are capable of accommodating a small battalion of infantry and a troop of cavalry, are eligibly situated on the road to Mossley, at a distance of about a mile from the town; they were erected in 1843, at a cost of £42,500, and are fitted up with baths and every convenience for both officers and men. The site, occupying six acres, was given by the lord of the manor.

The principal trade is in spinning, power-loom weaving, and other branches of the cotton manufacture; and there are few instances on record of a town making such rapid progress as this in wealth and population. In 1775, the population of the town was only 2859; in 1801, 6500; in 1811, 7800; in 1821, 9222; in 1831, 14,671; and in 1841, 22,689. In 1750, the inhabitants were humbly engaged in spinning and weaving cotton by hand, in their cottages: in 1785, Arkwright's machines gave an impetus to the trade; but even so late as 1794, there were only eleven spinning-rooms or small factories. At present there are in active operation within the borough, 77 large factories; and within a radius of two miles from the parish church are 160, of 5199 horse-power, consuming weekly upwards of 2,000,000 lb. of raw cotton, employing on the average nearly 23,000 workpeople, representing a capital of not less than £4,000,000, and sending out of the district yarn and power-loom cloth of not less value than £4,500,000 annually. Formerly, ginghams, muslins, and shawls were manufactured to a considerable extent; but the profit arising from spinning and manufacturing cotton being greater, those branches have fallen into decay. Wool and beaver hats, also, were a few years ago extensively manufactured in the neighbourhood; but the preference recently given by the public to silk hats, has nearly ruined the trade, and produced great distress among the workmen engaged in it. The whole district abounds in excellent coal, which, after supplying the home consumption, is conveyed in large quantities to Manchester and other parts by means of a branch of the Manchester, Sheffield, and Lincolnshire railway, by a branch of the Manchester and Leeds railway, and the Ashton, Huddersfield, and Peak-Forest canals; which all touch here.

The MARKET, which, previously to the establishment of the cotton trade, had been discontinued, was restored in 1828 by act of parliament, and a commodious market-place was formed, the Earl of Stamford and Warrington giving 14,000 square yards of land for a site. This spacious area was opened July 2nd, 1830; and near its eastern extremity is a large quadrangular edifice consisting of 26 butchers' shops, let at rents varying from £10 to £13 per annum. Four and a half per cent. of the gross produce of the tolls is claimed by the lord of the manor, and the remainder, which is very considerable, goes to the Commissioners of Police, and enables that body to carry out many improvements. The principal market-day is Saturday; and in 1846 a weekly cattle-market, on Tuesday, was established: markets are also held on Monday and Wednesday. By royal grant, dated 1284, two fairs were conferred; and in a confirmation of the grant to Sir John de Assheton in 1413, it was directed that they should be held, one on the eve, feast, and morrow of St. Swithen (July 14th, 15th, and 16th), and the other on the eve, feast, and morrow of St. Martin (Nov. 9th, 10th, and 11th). The present fairs, however, are held on March 23rd, April 29th, July 25th, Nov. 21st; and, for the sale of horned-cattle, sheep, pigs, &c., on the second Thursday in every month. Business is facilitated by the Ashton, Stalybridge, Hyde, and Glossop Bank, founded in 1836; and by branches of the Manchester and Liverpool District Bank, and Saddleworth Bank. There is also a savings' bank.

The town was incorporated in the reign of Henry VI., but is now under the jurisdiction of the county magistrates acting for the division, who hold petty-sessions every Monday, Wednesday, and Saturday in the Town-hall, a handsome stone structure of the Corinthian order, built in 1840, at an expense of £7500. The building contains a court-room, news-room, prison, police-office, a residence for the principal police-officer, sundry committee-rooms, and a spacious public hall 83 feet by 40, where balls, concerts, lectures, and large public meetings take place. The internal regulation of the town is vested, by an act passed in 1827, in all owners or occupiers of premises within the borough, of the clear yearly value of £35 and upwards, called *Police Commissioners*, who levy police rates, appoint deputy and other salaried constables, and keep the town properly lighted, cleansed, and watched. Besides the officers appointed by the Commissioners, the Earl of Stamford and Warrington's leet steward annually swears into office at the Michaelmas court, for the service of the manor, a mayor (who acts as returning officer at parliamentary elections), three constables, four assistant constables, from 12 to 24 jurymen, 12 bye-law men, two bailiffs, two pounders, three afferors, an inspector of weights and measures, two market-lookers, three ale-tasters, and two bellmen. A charter of incorporation, however, has just been granted by the crown, under which many changes will take place. Though courts leet have generally fallen into desuetude, the one held here is singularly useful in recovering fines under 40s., and abating nuisances within the manor, which otherwise could only be recovered and abated by tedious and expensive processes at law: the court has been held from time immemorial, every six months, in the ancient manor court-house, a curiously formed structure, erected in 1636, near the old market-cross. The county debt-court of Ashton, established in 1847, has jurisdiction over part of the registration-district of Ashton and Oldham. The inhabitants are empowered by the Reform act to return one member to parliament, the right of election being vested in the £10 householders: the borough is co-extensive with the Ashton-town parochial division, and contains 1319 acres, and 671 registered electors; the entire parish containing 9300 acres. The poor are under the management of the guardians of the Ashton union, which comprises Ashton-town, Audenshaw and Droylsden, Knott-Lanes, Hartshead, Denton and Haughton, Dukinfield, Newton and Godley, Stayley, and Mottram-in-Longdendale, with an aggregate population of 101,598.

The LIVING is a rectory, valued in the king's books at £26. 13. 4., and at £1409 in the parliamentary return of 1833. The Grelles, as lords of Manchester, were the earliest owners of the advowson; but in 1304, William de Merchia, parson of Manchester, usurped the patronage, which he retained until the De la Warres, by right of relationship to the Grelles, recovered it in 1339. In 1427, Thomas De la Warre, baron and rector of Manchester, conveyed the advowson to Sir John de Assheton, whose descendants possessed it for upwards of a century; at length, through the Booths of Dunham-Massey, it became heritably vested in the earls of Stamford. The church, which is a handsome structure in the later English style, standing on elevated ground near the south-eastern extremity of the town, was at one time a chapel of ease to the church of Manchester; the date of its foundation is not known, but it clearly appears by the Taxation of Pope Nicholas IV., 1291, that the living was then one of considerable importance. During the lifetime of Sir Thomas Assheton, who died in 1516, the church was extensively repaired, and was enlarged; but for several generations afterwards, the fabric underwent few changes: in January, 1791, however, it was so severely damaged by a thunder storm, that in the following year it was wholly repewed at the cost of the seat-holders, and the belfry and roof repaired at the expense of the parishioners. The present lofty square tower (which contains a clock, and an excellent peal of ten bells), and the whole of the north side of the church, were built in 1820-21: while these improvements were in progress, a fire broke out which destroyed the principal timbers of the west end, and consumed a noble-toned organ, with many curiously-carved antique embellishments. From 1821 to 1840, the edifice was in a very dilapidated condition, and no steps were taken during that period to rebuild the ruined south wall and renovate the interior : on the 18th of May, 1840, however, the foundation stone of a new south wall was laid, and in the course of four years from that time, the whole fabric underwent such complete restoration that, for correct architectural design, harmonious distribution of ornament, and elaborate carving in oak, there are few churches of the same size in the north of England comparable with it. The expense of the renovation, which amounted to £6849, was defrayed proportionately by the patron, the rector, and the seatholders ; by general voluntary contributions ; and the proceeds of a bazaar. The east window is of beautiful design, and the walls within the communion rails, to the height of eight feet above the encaustic pavement, are lined with rich tabernacle stone-work ; the gilded recessed compartments being interspersed with sacred mottoes and emblematical representations. At the west end is an exceedingly fine organ, built in 1845, at a cost of £1155, and which was presented by Mr. Edward Brown, of The Firs. A short distance to the south of the church, is a school, rebuilt in 1827 at a cost of £800, which is occupied on Sundays by upwards of 1400 children, and on other days of the week as a school in connexion with the National Society.

At the western extremity of the town is St. Peter's Church, a rich specimen of the decorated style, erected in 1821 at a cost of £14,000, of which sum £12,688 were given by the Parliamentary Commissioners, and the remainder by the inhabitants. It is internally 142 feet long by 65 wide, and is capable of seating 1821 persons ; the galleries, which have 800 sittings, being entirely appropriated to the poor : the western gallery contains a fine-toned organ, erected in 1831 at an expense of £600. The eastern elevation has a spacious circular window; the western is characterized by a remarkably fine tower, 128 feet in height, ornamented with buttresses at the angles, and surmounted with a perforated parapet and crocketed pinnacles. The living is a perpetual curacy in the gift of the Rector, returned in 1833 as being worth £137 per annum : by an order in council, in 1840, an ecclesiastical district was annexed to it, in pursuance of the 59th of George III., cap. 134. To the east of the church is a school, a spacious building, erected in 1836 at a cost of £1400, partly defrayed by public grants and partly by subscription ; the number of Sunday-school children in attendance exceeds 1350, and the number of infants and other week-day scholars, in connexion with the National Society, is about 500. Attached to this school is a library of 360 volumes. The district of Christ Church was constituted in March, 1846, and became an ecclesiastical parish in 1847, under the act 6 and 7 Victoria, cap. 37 ; it comprises about 1000 acres of level land. The church, situated in the Charlestown suburb, was built in 1847, at a cost of about £3000, and is a cruciform structure in the early English style, containing 852 sittings, mostly free : connected with it is an excellent school for boys, girls, and infants, with a house for the master. The living is a perpetual curacy ; net income, £150 ; patrons, alternately, the Crown and the Bishop of Chester. Other churches are described under the head of Audenshaw, Hurst, Mossley, &c. There are

places of worship, and, generally, schools also, belonging to the Independents, Wesleyans, Independent Methodists, Primitive Methodists, Methodists of the New Connexion, Baptists, Stephenites, Latter-day Saints, and Israelites : the last-named sect, who are understood to hold the doctrines promulgated by Joanna Southcott, have a chapel or sanctuary in Church-street, built in 1825, at a cost of £9500, entirely defrayed by Mr. John Stanley. The British school, near Ryecroft, built in 1846-7, cost nearly £3000, and will accommodate 1000 children. There are several charitable institutions ; and the working classes maintain 20 sick and burial societies, having in the aggregate 14,500 members. Mr. Coulthart states in his report on Ashton, published by Her Majesty's Commissioners for inquiring into the state of large towns, that the operatives have also three boards of health or self-supporting medical associations ; that the aggregate number of members belonging to them is 5600 ; and that the average annual number of cases treated is 6650.

Among the ANTIQUITIES is the ˙Old Manor-House, situated on a promontory near the parish church, grimly overlooking the adjacent country, and the numerous factories on the banks of the Ashton canal and the river Tame. It is a large irregularly-constructed pile, having underground cells, spacious galleries, massive doorways, and round towers at the corners, which last peculiarity is considered to be indicative of a very remote origin ; the moats, court-yards, and drawbridges, however, have all disappeared, and scarcely any thing remains to attest that it was at one time the fortified baronial residence of the Asshetons. The date of its erection is unknown, but title-deeds satisfactorily prove that it existed in a style of feudal grandeur in 1380 ; it is now used by the agents of the Earl of Stamford and Warrington as a place of business when collecting rents, and is also occasionally occupied by his lordship when visiting the town or shooting in the neighbourhood. The Manorial Corn-mills, on the north bank of the Tame, at a distance of about 400 yards from the Old Hall, are very ancient, though the date of their erection, and the changes they have undergone, are not recorded ; it appears, however, by the rent-roll of the manor, dated 1422, that the mills were in existence at that time, that the milner was " John of the Edge," and his annual rent, 16s. 4d., the mills being kept in repair by the lord. The dates discoverable in the buildings are comparatively modern. One of the mills has recently been appropriated to cotton-spinning, and the other is in full operation as a soak-mill, the tenants of the manor being still obliged to grind their corn here, though the ancient custom of taking the sixteenth measure as toll, has been discontinued, and in lieu a scale of charges in money has been substituted. The parish Workhouse and Almshouses, which are situated on the east side of the market-place, occupy a site of 1562 square yards : the date of these buildings must be very remote, but that of 1684, on the lintel of a door, is the only one now visible. Druidical basins, hollowed out of the solid rock, and used by the Druids in rites of purification, exist in the bottom of the Medlock, in Rocher Vale ; but a weir having been thrown across the river a few yards above the basins, they are covered with a stratum of debris many feet in thickness. At Park Bridge, also, are a very ancient hand-millstone, and a curiously sculptured block of granite, dated 1496, which were found in 1845 at the bottom of an old draw-well belonging to Mr. Samuel Lees. There are chalybeate springs near Water-houses, and at Lees; lime-springs at Bardsley brewery, and at Lime Hurst; and in 1845 a strong chalybeate spring was discovered when sinking a pump at Mr. Richmond's residence, in Bardsley Vale. None of the springs in the neighbourhood indicate the presence of sulphur, but so strongly impregnated with iron is the water last referred to, that it is wholly unfit for any but medicinal purposes. Vegetable fossil remains are found in great abundance and variety in the coal-pits and stone-quarries of the parish; and occasionally, specimens of the animal kingdom are met with.

ASHTON-upon-Mersey (St. Martin), a parish, in the union of Altrincham, hundred of Bucklow, N. division of the county of Chester, 1¾ mile (N.) from Altrincham; comprising the township of Sale, and part of the township of Ashton, the former containing 1309 inhabitants, and the latter, together with the remaining part of the township, in the parish of Bowdon, 1105. A moiety of the manor was held for many generations by the Carringtons, and passed by a female heir of that family to the Booths, from whom it descended to the earls of Stamford and Warrington. The other moiety was possessed by the Hondfords, from whom it came to the Breretons; it afterwards became the property of Viscount Allen, who sold it in 1749 to George, Earl of Warrington, grandfather of the present Earl of Stamford and Warrington, now lord of the whole manor. The township of Ashton is situated, as the name of the parish implies, on the banks of the Mersey; and comprises 1479 acres: the soil is of a sandy and light quality, and large quantities of potatoes and other early produce are grown for the supply of Manchester. The road from Altrincham to Manchester, and the Duke of Bridgewater's canal, intersect the parish. A court leet is held. The living is a rectory, valued in the king's books at £13. 4. 7.; net income, £608; patron and incumbent, the Rev. C. B. Sowerby. Besides the church, there are places of worship for Calvinists, Wesleyan and Primitive Methodists, and Unitarians; and in the township of Sale is a school endowed with land and tenements producing £25. 15. per annum. John Okell, Esq., left £80; Thomas Ashton, Esq., £40; and Mrs. Safe, £23; the proceeds whereof are distributed among the poor.

ASHTON-upon-Ribble, parish of Preston, Lancashire.—See Ashton.

ASHTON, WEST, a tything, in the parish of Steeple-Ashton, union of Westbury and Whorwelsdown, hundred of Whorwelsdown, Whorwelsdown and N. divisions of Wilts; containing 307 inhabitants. A church was consecrated in Oct. 1846; it was built and endowed by Walter Long, Esq., who is patron, and is a simple yet elegant structure, conspicuous in every direction. The tithes have been commuted for £410 payable to the vicar of the parish, and £3. 15. to the rector of Trowbridge.

ASHURST, a parish, in the union of Tonbridge, hundred of Washlingstone, lathe of Aylesford, W. division of Kent, 4¾ miles (W.) from Tonbridge-Wells; containing 224 inhabitants. It is bounded by the river Medway, and intersected by the road from East Grinstead to Tonbridge-Wells; and contains 891 acres, of

17th century under the will of Henry Colborn or Cole-bron, who bequeathed £1000 in trust to the Merchant Tailors' Company, by whom the master is appointed. On Harborough Hill, in the parish, are the remains of a quadrangular encampment, probably an exploratory station of the Romans. The Rev. Ralph Cudworth, D.D., Master of Christ's College, Cambridge, and author of the *Intellectual System*, was vicar of the parish, and died here in 1688.

ASHWELL (ST. MARY), a parish, in the union of OAKHAM, hundred of ALSTOE, county of RUTLAND, 3 miles (N. by W.) from Oakham ; containing 223 inhabitants. It comprises 1800 acres by measurement; the soil is fertile, and a coarse kind of stone is quarried for inferior buildings, and for the roads. The Melton-Mowbray and Oakham canal passes within a mile of the parish. The living is a rectory, valued in the king's books at £20. 16. 3., and in the gift of Viscount Downe : the tithes have been commuted for £412, and the glebe comprises 130 acres. The church is a neat substantial structure, in the later English style.

ASHWELTHORPE (ALL SAINTS), a parish, in the union and hundred of DEPWADE, E. division of NOR-FOLK, 3½ miles (S. E. by S.) from Wymondham ; con-taining 469 inhabitants. The road from New Buckenham to Norwich runs through the parish. The living is a discharged rectory, with that of Wreningham *cum* Nay-land annexed, valued in the king's books at £6. 13. 4. ; net income, £648; patron, Lord Berners. The incum-bent resides in the Hall, an ancient residence of the Knyvett family, moated on three sides. The church, which is chiefly in the decorated style, consists of a nave and chancel, with a chapel on the north side, and a square embattled tower ; in the chancel is an altar-tomb, on which are the effigies of Sir Edward and Lady de Thorpe.

ASHWICK (ST. JAMES), a parish, in the union of SHEPTON-MALLET, hundred of KILMERSDON, E. divi-sion of SOMERSET, 3¾ miles (N. by E.) from Shepton-Mallet ; comprising 1527a. 2r. 34p., and containing 945 inhabitants. There are many quarries, supplying a material for building and for making lime. At the vil-lage of Oakhill, which stands partly in this parish and partly in Stoke-Lane and Shepton-Mallet, are some good residences, and a public brewery ; and the road from Bath to Exeter, and another from Bristol to Weymouth, run through the parish. The living is a perpetual curacy; net income, £113; patron, the Vicar of Kilmersdon ; impropriator, J. Twyford Jolliffe, Esq. The great tithes have been commuted for £28. 10., and those of the in-cumbent for £59. 15. ; the glebe consists of 2½ acres. The curacy was separated from the vicarage of Kilmers-don in 1826, at which time also the church was rebuilt, with the exception of the tower; it is a neat structure, accommodating about 550 persons. There are places of worship for Independents, Unitarians, and Methodists. On the south-western side of the parish, near the Fosse-way, is a Roman camp, with a double intrenchment, called Mashury Castle.

ASHWICKEN (ALL SAINTS), a parish, in the union and hundred of FREEBRIDGE-LYNN, W. division of NORFOLK, 5 miles (E. by S.) from Lynn ; containing 78 inhabitants. It comprises 1178a. 2r., of which 638 acres are arable, 378 pasture and meadow, 150 heath, and 12 woodland ; the surface is a good deal undulated. The

living is a rectory, with that of Leziate annexed, valued in the king's books at £6. 13. 4. ; patron and incumbent, the Rev. John Freeman. The tithes have been com-muted for £238, and the glebe comprises 10 acres. The church is chiefly in the later English style, with a square tower.

ASHWORTH, a parochial chapelry, in the parish of MIDDLETON, union of BURY, hundred of SALFORD, S. division of the county of LANCASTER, 3¼ miles (W.) from Rochdale ; containing 325 inhabitants. A family named Ashworth was seated here as early as the 13th century, and appears to have been succeeded by the Holts : Richard Holt, an active supporter of the royal cause in the civil war, had his estate sequestrated in 1643 ; but it was afterwards restored. The manor came subsequently into the possession of the Wilbraham family. Ashworth comprises by measurement 1025 acres ; the soil is fertile, the scenery romantic, and the lower part of the township is thickly studded with large oak-trees. The substratum abounds in coal, of which a mine is in operation ; and stone of good quality for building is also obtained in great quantity : a fulling-mill affords employment to some hands. The living is a perpetual curacy, in the patronage of Wilbraham Egerton, Esq. ; net income, £119. The rectorial tithes have been commuted for £15, and the glebe consists of 62 acres. The chapel, a plain stone fabric, dedicated to St. James, stands on the summit of a hill to the north of Ashworth Hall ; it was for the most part rebuilt in 1789, and in 1837 the chancel, which was part of a former edifice, was taken down, and the east end of the chapel considerably enlarged. The burial-ground commands an extensive view of the adjacent hills and vales. A daily school, founded by Mr. Egerton in 1828, is partly supported by that gentleman, by whom, also, premises for a Sunday school were built in 1838.

ASKE, a township, in the parish of EASBY, union of RICHMOND, wapentake of GILLING-WEST, N. riding of the county of YORK, 1¾ mile (N.) from Richmond ; containing 92 inhabitants. The township comprises 1610 acres of well-cultivated land ; the soil is productive, and the scenery embraces fine prospects of the surround-ing country. Aske Hall, one of the seats of the Earl of Zetland, is a spacious and elegant castellated mansion, situated on rising ground in a large and beautiful park, and embosomed in noble woods of fine old timber, and pleasure-grounds of varied surface : many of the views from the residence are of striking beauty. The noble earl's inferior title is Baron Dundas of the manor of Aske, conferred in 1794.

ASKERNE, a township, in the parish of CAMPSALL, union of DONCASTER, Upper division of the wapentake of OSGOLDCROSS, W. riding of YORK, 7¼ miles (N.) from Doncaster ; containing 468 inhabitants. Askerne, during the present century, has risen from an inconsiderable village into an elegant and fashionable watering-place. It is pleasantly situated near the road, on a rocky accli-vity ascending gently from the foot of an extensive plain ; and its hotels and bathing establishments, surrounded by gardens, orchards, and plantations, all agreeably harmonising together, give it an interesting and commanding appearance. Here is a sheet of water called Askerne pool, covering seven acres, a few yards from which rises a sulphureous spring, highly celebrated for more than a century as a powerful remedy in scrofu-

O

lous, rheumatic, and gouty complaints : it is also reputed for its virtue in dyspepsia, palsy, and pulmonary consumption. Boarding-houses have been erected for the accommodation of visiters. The tithes were commuted for land in 1814.

ASKERSWELL (ST. MICHAEL), a parish, in the union of BRIDPORT, hundred of EGGERTON, Bridport division of DORSET, 4 miles (E.) from Bridport; containing 233 inhabitants. It contains about 1200 acres; the soil is chalky, and the surface hilly. The living is a rectory, valued in the king's books at £9. 2. 6.; net income, £160; patron, the Rev. James Cox. The glebe contains 23 acres, with a house.

ASKERTON, a township, in the parish of LANERCOST, union of BRAMPTON, ESKDALE ward, E. division of CUMBERLAND, 6¼ miles (N. N. E.) from Brampton; containing 496 inhabitants. The castle here, a small building with lofty turrets, situated on a rocky knoll on the southern bank of the rivulet Cambeck, and commanding a most extensive view of the adjacent country, is partly ruinous and used as stables; but much of it has been recently modernised in the interior, and the building is now inhabited by a farmer. It was in ruins in Camden's time, but was repaired by the Dacres in the 16th century, and over a mantel-piece in what was once the dining-hall is an inscription, "Tho. Carleton, Jun., 1575," the date of the repair. Askerton comprises the ancient parish of Kirk Cambeck, the church of which was destroyed by the Scots in the reign of Edward II.; the tithes are held on lease from the Dean and Chapter of Carlisle.

ASKHAM, a parish, in the union of EAST RETFORD, South-Clay division of the wapentake of BASSETLAW, N. division of the county of NOTTINGHAM, 2¾ miles (N.) from Tuxford; containing, with Rockley hamlet, 288 inhabitants. The parish contains about 1440 acres: the surface is undulated, and the soil clayey; the village is skirted on the north by the stream called North Beck, which is subject to inundations after heavy rains. The living is a perpetual curacy, annexed, with that of Stokeham, to the vicarage of East Drayton : two acres of land, and the tithes of hops, form the principal value of the curacy. There are almshouses for six widows.

ASKHAM (ST. PETER), a parish, in WEST ward and union, county of WESTMORLAND, 4¾ miles (S.) from Penrith; containing 635 inhabitants. It comprises 4264 acres, of which 2049 are tithable, 2150 wood and common, and 65 tithe-free; the surface is partly undulated and partly hilly, and the soil rests principally on limestone and peat. The river Lowther bounds the parish on the east, and the Dale beck on the south. The living is a discharged vicarage, endowed with a portion of the rectorial tithes, and valued in the king's books at £6; net income, £156; patron, and impropriator of the remainder of the great tithes, the Earl of Lonsdale. The tithes have been commuted for £238. 17., of which £114. 5. are payable to the impropriator, and £124. 12. to the vicar: the glebe comprises 56 acres. A school was endowed in 1813, with subscriptions amounting to £420, part of which has been vested in the purchase of land.

ASKHAM-BRYAN, or GREAT ASKHAM (ST. NICHOLAS), a parish, in the AINSTY wapentake, W. riding of YORK, 4 miles (W. S. W.) from York; containing 342 inhabitants. This place derives its name partly from

98

Bryan Fitz-Alain, who held it of the honour of Richmond, paying 5s. per annum to the warden of the castle of that town : the families of Mowbray, Stapleton, and Grey have also owned the estate. The parish comprises by measurement 1808 acres, three-fourths of which are arable, and the rest meadow, with some few plantations; the surface is flat, and the soil composed chiefly of gravel and clay. Contiguous to the church passes the York and North-Midland railway. The living is a perpetual curacy; net income, £120; patron, Colonel Croft, of Stillington Park. The tithes were commuted for land, by an inclosure act, in 1811. There is a place of worship for Wesleyans.

ASKHAM-RICHARD, or LITTLE ASKHAM (ST. MARY), a parish, in the AINSTY wapentake, union and W. riding of YORK, 3½ miles (N. E.) from Tadcaster; containing 232 inhabitants. In the 9th of Edward II. the priory of Burlington held this manor; the patronage of the church was exercised by the nuns of Monkton till the Dissolution, when the privilege was granted to the Vavasour family. The parish comprises by measurement 929 acres, of which about three-fourths are arable, and the remainder meadow or pasture; the surface is generally level, and the soil of a gravelly and clayey quality. The road from Leeds to York, and the York and North-Midland railway, cross each other near this place; where also is Askham Hall. The living is a discharged vicarage, valued in the king's books at £4. 13. 4.; net income, £200 : patron, Col. Croft. The tithes were commuted for land in 1813. There is a place of worship for Wesleyans.

ASKRIGG, a market-town and chapelry, in the parish of AYSGARTH, wapentake of HANG-WEST, N. riding of YORK, 57 miles (W. N. W.) from York, and 247 (N. W. by N.) from London; containing 726 inhabitants. The town is situated on an eminence rising from the northern bank of the river Ure, and upon the road from Richmond to Lancaster; the lands near it are almost entirely occupied as pasture and the surrounding country exhibits some fine waterfalls and picturesque scenery. It was formerly a place of considerable note, but has fallen into decay; there is a woolcarding mill, and in the neighbourhood are lead-mines, but they are not very productive. The market is on Thursday : fairs are held on May 11th, July 11th and 12th, and Oct. 28th; and there is also a fair for general traffic and recreation on the first Thursday in June. By the act of the 2nd and 3rd of William IV. cap. 64, Askrigg was made a polling-place for the North riding. The township comprises 4741 acres, of which 1948 are common or waste. The living is a perpetual curacy; net income, £100; patron, the Vicar of Aysgarth. The tithes have been commuted for £84, payable to Trinity College, Cambridge. The chapel is an ancient structure, dedicated to St. Oswald. There is a place of worship for Wesleyans. The Yorebridge free grammar school, in the chapelry, was founded for the sons of inhabitants, in 1601, by Anthony Besson, who endowed it with an inn named the Black Swan, in York, and a plot of about two acres and a half of ground called the Intack, producing upwards of £200 per annum, which is paid to the master, who has also a house and garden rent-free. Almshouses were founded, and endowed with £2000 three per cent. consols., in 1807, by Christopher Alderson, for six poor widows of the townships of Askrigg and Low Abbotside, each of whom has £10 per annum. —See AYSGARTH, BAINBRIDGE, &c.

ASKWITH, or ASQUITH, a township, in the parish of WESTON, Upper division of the wapentake of CLARO, W. riding of YORK, 3 miles (N. W.) from Otley; containing, with Askwith-Moorside, 398 inhabitants. It comprises by computation 3180 acres, and includes the hamlets of Upper and Lower Snowden: the village, which is scattered, is pleasantly situated on the northern acclivities of Wharfdale, and the river Wharfe winds its devious course on the south and west. The tithes were commuted for land, in 1779. There are places of worship for Primitive Methodists and Wesleyans.

ASLACKBY (St. JAMES), a parish, in the union of BOURNE, wapentake of AVELAND, parts of KESTEVEN, county of LINCOLN, 2¼ miles (S. S. E.) from Folkingham; containing, with the hamlets of Graby and Milthorpe, 507 inhabitants. It is situated on the road from London to Hull, and comprises by measurement 3420 acres; the soil is various, and the surface pleasingly diversified with hill and dale, and richly embellished with wood. The river Forty-foot, which is navigable from Bourne to Boston, skirts the eastern extremity of the parish. The living is a vicarage, valued in the king's books at £12. 10. 7½.; net income, £453; patron and impropriator, R. F. Barstow, Esq. The tithes are compounded for the above sum, and the glebe comprises 39 acres. The church is a handsome edifice in the decorated and later English styles, with an embattled tower crowned with pinnacles. Here was a preceptory of Knight Templars, which, on the abolition of their order, became a commandery of the Hospitallers.

ASLACTON (St. MICHAEL), a parish, in the union and hundred of DEPWADE, E. division of NORFOLK, 3½ miles (W. by S.) from Long Stratton; containing 404 inhabitants, and comprising about 1130 acres. The living is a perpetual curacy; net income, £58; patron and impropriator, John Cooper, Esq., whose tithes have been commuted for £340. The church, which is chiefly in the perpendicular style, consists of a nave, chancel, and south aisle, with a circular tower.

ASLACTON, a township, in the parish of WHATTON, union of BINGHAM, N. division of the wapentake of BINGHAM, S. division of the county of NOTTINGHAM, 2¾ miles (E. by N.) from Bingham; containing 424 inhabitants. The tithes were commuted for land and a money payment, in 1780. This was the birth-place of Cranmer.

ASPALL, a parish, in the union and hundred of HARTISMERE, W. division of the county of SUFFOLK, 1 mile (N. by W.) from Debenham; containing 132 inhabitants. The river Deben rises in this parish, which comprises 834a. 3r. 26p. The living is a perpetual curacy; net income, £149; patron, impropriator, and incumbent, the Rev. John Chevallier, M.D., whose residence is the ancient moated mansion of Aspall Hall.

ASPATRIA (St. KENTIGERN), a market-town and parish, in the union of WIGTON, ALLERDALE ward below Derwent, W. division of CUMBERLAND; comprising the townships of Aspatria with Brayton, Hayton with Medlo, and Oughterside with Allerby; and containing 1921 inhabitants, of whom 988 are in the township of Aspatria with Brayton, 9 miles (N. by E.) from Cockermouth. This village, which derives its name from Gospatrick, father of the first lord of Allerdale, 99

extends for a considerable distance along the side of a hill, and has recently assumed somewhat the character of a town, by the erection of several good and substantial dwelling-houses. A pitched market for corn is held on Thursday. The parish comprises by measurement 7064 acres, and is bounded on the west by the Solway Frith, and on the south-east and south by the river Ellen. It contains a vein of red freestone at Hayton, and coal at Oughterside. The Maryport and Carlisle railway passes through, and has a station here. The living is a vicarage, valued in the king's books at £10. 4. 2.; net income, £249; patron and appropriator, the Bishop of Carlisle. The tithes were partially commuted in 1817 for land. The church was originally in the Norman style, but there are no remains of its ancient character except two arches. A place of worship for Independents was built in 1827. In 1790 a barrow was opened in the vicinity, when the skeleton of a man, with the corroded remains of some military weapons, &c., was discovered.

ASPEDEN (St. MARY), a parish, in the union of BUNTINGFORD, hundred of EDWINSTREE, county of HERTFORD, ¾ of a mile (S.) from Buntingford; containing 529 inhabitants. It comprises about 1340 acres of land, the soil of which is clayey; the rivulet Rib runs through the district, and falls into the Lea near Hertford. The living is a rectory, valued in the king's books at £15. 5. 2½.; patron, Lady Mexborough. The tithes have been commuted for £400, and the glebe consists of nearly 23 acres. W. and R. Freeman in 1668, and Mrs. Cater in 1704, gave land for the education of children, now producing £17. 5. per annum; and R. Freeman assigned an additional plot for clothing them. In 1684, Dr. Seth Ward, Bishop of Sarum, founded an almshouse for two men and two women, and endowed it with £41. 12. a year.

ASPLEY, a township, in the parish of ECCLESHALL, union of STONE, N. division of the hundred of PIREHILL and of the county of STAFFORD, 3 miles (N. by W.) from Eccleshall; containing 34 inhabitants. It is situated on a lofty summit; and is the property of various persons. The tithes have been commuted for £86. 18. 6., payable to the Dean and Chapter of Lichfield.

ASPLEY, with FORDHALL, a hamlet, in the parish of WOOTTON-WAWEN, union of STRATFORD, Henley division of the hundred of BARLICHWAY, S. division of WARWICKSHIRE; containing 126 inhabitants.

ASPLEY-GUISE (St. BOTOLPH), a parish, in the union of WOBURN, hundred of MANSHEAD, county of BEDFORD, 2½ miles (N. by W.) from Woburn; containing 1139 inhabitants. It comprises by measurement 2033 acres, of which 1953 are arable, and the remainder woodland, plantations, and heath; the prevailing timber is elm, and the plantations chiefly fir. The inhabitants obtained in 1207 the grant of a market to be held on Friday, and a fair on June 17th; but both have been long discontinued. The living is a rectory, valued in the king's books at £15. 16. 10½.; net income, £215; patron, the Duke of Bedford. The tithes were commuted for 85 acres of land, and an annual payment of £60, in 1760. The church contains several ancient and interesting monuments, among which are an altar-tomb with the effigy of Sir Edward Sadlier in chain armour, and another with an effigy in brass of one of the family of Guise. There is a place of worship for Wesleyans, O 2

ASPULL, a township, in the ecclesiastical district of HAIGH, parish and union of WIGAN, hundred of SALFORD, S. division of the county of LANCASTER, 3 miles (N. E. by E.) from Wigan; containing 2772 inhabitants. The families of de Lathom, Ince, and Gerrard had lands here, and the last named anciently held a manorial court. The manor was transferred by sale to the Earl of Balcarres by William Gerrard, Esq.; it now appertains to the manor of Haigh. The township comprises 1879 acres, of which 1145 are pasture, 377 arable, 40 woodland, and 100 common or waste; and abounds with Cannel coal and other seams of various quality, worked by the Earl of Balcarres and others. There is a cotton-mill of 80-horse power. Hindley Hall, in this township, is on the border of the township of Hindley, *which see.* There is a school with an endowment of £11 per annum. The tithes have been commuted for a rent-charge of £214.

ASSELBY, a township, in the parish and union of HOWDEN, wapentake of HOWDENSHIRE, E. riding of YORK, 2 miles (W. by S.) from Howden; containing 293 inhabitants. This place, in Domesday-book *Aschilebi,* was held at the Conquest chiefly by the Bishop of Durham and Earl Morton; the Aislabys subsequently had property here, and are supposed to have taken their name from that of the township. It comprises by computation 1200 acres; the land is very rich and prolific, and the gardens supply large quantities of fruit for the markets in the West riding. Asselby Island, containing about 10 acres, is seated in the river Ouse, which flows at a short distance on the south of the village; it belongs to the parish of Drax. There is a place of worship for Wesleyans.

ASSERBY, a hamlet, in the parish of BILSBY, union of SPILSBY, Wold division of the hundred of CALCEWORTH, parts of LINDSEY, county of LINCOLN; containing 54 inhabitants.

ASSINGDON, county of Essex.—See ASHINGDON.

ASSINGTON (ST. EDMUND), a parish, in the union of SUDBURY, hundred of BABERGH, W. division of SUFFOLK, 5 miles (E. S. E.) from Sudbury; containing 778 inhabitants. Assington Hall was purchased by Robert Gurdon, in the reign of Henry VIII., from Sir Piers Corbet, and has ever since been the residence of that family. A double stratum of cement stone has been found in the parish, and is now regularly manufactured. The living is a discharged vicarage, endowed with part of the rectorial tithes, and valued in the king's books at £10; patron, and impropriator of the remainder of the great tithes, John Gurdon, Esq. The impropriator's tithes have been commuted for £361. 15. 3., and the vicarial tithes for £444. 7. 10.; the glebe comprises about 14 acres.

ASTBURY (ST. MARY), a parish, chiefly in the union of CONGLETON, consisting of the townships of Eaton and Somerford-Booths in the hundred of MACCLESFIELD, and the market-town of Congleton, and the townships of Astbury-Newbold, Buglawton, Davenport, Hulme-Walfield, Moreton with Alcumlow, Odd Rode, Radnor, Smallwood, and Somerford, in the hundred of NORTHWICH, county of CHESTER; and containing 14,890 inhabitants, of whom 641 are in Astbury-Newbold. This parish comprises by computation 20,000 acres, and contains a bed of limestone, from twenty-five to thirty yards in thickness, of which considerable quantities are procured
100

and burnt; it is based on a species of gritstone, excellent for building. The Macclesfield canal passes at a short distance to the east of the village. The living is a rectory, valued in the king's books at £68, and in the patronage of the Trustees of Lord Crewe; net income, upwards of £1500. The church is a spacious and beautiful structure, in every style of architecture from the early English to the later English, but chiefly the latter: the interior contains several stalls, a rood-loft, and some fine screen-work; the roofs are of oak, richly carved; the east window is highly enriched, and there are some fine specimens of stained glass. The tower, which stands at the north-west angle of the church, and is surmounted by an elegant spire, appears to have belonged to a former edifice. There are also churches or chapels at Congleton, Buglawton, Mossley, Rode, Smallwood, and Somerford; together with several places of worship for dissenters, in the parish. The sum of £50 per annum, the bequest of John Holford in 1714, is partly distributed among the poor, and partly applied in apprenticing children. The parish contains some petrifying springs.

ASTERBY (ST. PETER), a parish, in the union of HORNCASTLE, N. division of the wapentake of GARTREE, parts of LINDSEY, county of LINCOLN, 7 miles (N.) from Horncastle; containing 256 inhabitants. The living is a discharged rectory, valued in the king's books at £8. 0. 10.; net income, £210; patron, T. Southwell, Esq. A national school, for the parishes of Asterby and Goulsby, is endowed with a rent-charge of £10 per annum.

ASTHALL (ST. NICHOLAS), a parish, in the union of BAMPTON, county of OXFORD, 3 miles (E. by S.) from Burford; containing, with the hamlet of Asthall-Leigh, 389 inhabitants. This place was formerly the residence of Sir Richard Jones, one of the judges of the court of common pleas in the reign of Charles I.; and there are still some remains of the ancient manor-house near the church, which are now converted into a farmhouse. The living is a discharged vicarage, valued in the king's books at £7. 9. 4½.; net income, £100; patrons and impropriators, the Provost and Fellows of Eton College. The tithes were commuted for a money payment and an allotment of land, in 1812. The church contains some interesting monuments, among which is a recumbent effigy on a stone coffin, under an enriched arched canopy, said to be the tomb of Alice Corbett, mistress of Henry I., and mother of Reginald, Earl of Cornwall. In the parish is a barrow of considerable height, supposed to be a sepulchral monument, and near which the Roman Akeman-street passes.

ASTHORPE, a hamlet, in the parish of WILLOUGHBY, union of SPILSBY, Wold division of the hundred of CALCEWORTH, parts of LINDSEY, county of LINCOLN; containing 16 inhabitants.

ASTLEY, a district chapelry, in the parish and union of LEIGH, hundred of WEST DERBY, S. division of LANCASHIRE, 3 miles (E.) from the town of Leigh; containing 2011 inhabitants. This township comprises about 2620 acres; 900 are uncultivated moss, and of the remainder about one-fifth is in tillage. The land lies low, and the principal drainage is from north to south to the brook running east and west from the adjoining township of Worsley; the soil of about 1500 acres is or has been a peat moss, and that of the remainder is chiefly a clayey loam. A colliery producing excellent engine-coal was lately established, on an extensive scale; Messrs. Arrowsmith, cotton-spinners, have a mill here, and there is a considerable number of silk-weavers by hand. The Liverpool and Manchester railway runs over part of Chat Moss in the southern district of the township; the Duke of Bridgewater's canal passes through the centre of the township, and the road from Manchester to Leigh through the northern part. Astley Hall, or Damhouse, situated in the township of Tyldesley, but on the borders of that of Astley, was built in 1650 by Adam Mort, from whom it has passed to his descendant and present representative, Mrs. Ross, lady of Col. Malcolm Nugent Ross, who has greatly enlarged the mansion. Of Morley Hall, the seat of a branch of the Tyldesleys, but little is now remaining, it having been converted into a farmhouse and rebuilt. The living is a perpetual curacy, in the gift of the Vicar of Leigh; incumbent, the Rev. Alfred Hewlett; net income, £250, with a house erected about 1703 by Thomas Mort, whose ancestors had founded the chapel and school of Astley in the preceding century. The chapel was rebuilt in 1760; a tower was added in 1842, and a new north aisle in 1847. There is a place of worship for Wesleyans. Besides the school founded by the Mort family, and which is free for 24 children, national schools have been established for boys and girls; also an infants' school in connexion with the Church, and a school belonging to the Wesleyans.

ASTLEY, a chapelry, in the parish of St. MARY, union of ATCHAM, liberties of SHREWSBURY, N. division of SALOP, 5 miles (N. N. E.) from Shrewsbury; containing 264 inhabitants. The living is a perpetual curacy with a net income of £56, in the patronage of five Trustees, by order of the court of chancery: the impropriation is vested in the Trustees of Shrewsbury grammar school, whose tithes have been commuted for £211. Mrs. Elizabeth Jones, in 1733, agreeably to the request of her deceased husband, bequeathed a farm here, let for £60 per annum, of which about £40 are appropriated for the benefit of the poor of Atcham, £10 to the poor of Astley, and £6 to the minister: it is also charged with the payment of £5 to the organist of St. Mary's.

ASTLEY (St. MARY), a parish, in the union of NUNEATON, Kirby division of the hundred of KNIGHT-LOW, N. division of the county of WARWICK, 4½ miles (W. S. W.) from Nuneaton; comprising 2555 acres, and containing 371 inhabitants. A short distance to the north of the church is a mansion, erected in the sixteenth century, on the site of a more ancient baronial castle: in the interior are a chair and table, which, according to an inscription, were those used by Henry, Marquess Grey and Duke of Suffolk, father of Lady Jane Grey, when concealed in a hollow tree in the vicinity. The living is a perpetual curacy; net income, £60; patrons and impropriators, the family of Newdegate. The church was made collegiate, and rebuilt in the form of a cross, with a lofty spire, in the reign of Edward III., by Lord Thomas de Astley, many of whose family were interred here; the ancient choir, now forming the body of the church, is the only portion of the building remaining. The revenue of the college, at its dissolution, was £46. 8.

101

ASTLEY (St. PETER), a parish, in the union of Martley, Lower division of the hundred of DODDING-TREE, Hundred-House and W. divisions of the county of WORCESTER, 3 miles (S. W. by S.) from Stourport; containing 834 inhabitants. An alien priory of Benedietine monks was founded here by Ralph de Todeni, in the reign of William I.; it was annexed to the college of Westbury, in that of Edward IV., and given, at the Dissolution, to Sir Ralph Sadleir. The parish is bounded on the east by the river Severn, and comprises 2960a. 3r. 10p., whereof about 450 acres are woodland: the surface is very unequal, and rather hilly; the soil is a sandy loam, and highly productive; and the scenery picturesque. There are quarries of red sandstone. Woodhampton House, the seat of Mrs. Cookes, is a commodious mansion at the foot of a well-wooded hill; and among other handsome residences are Oakhampton and Hill House. The LIVING is a rectory, valued in the king's books at £15. 13. 4.; patrons, I. Russell Cookes, Esq., and the Trustees of the late Rev. D. J. J. Cookes. The tithes have been commuted for £750, and the glebe consists of 20 acres of land, of a very mixed quality; the rectory-house adjoins the church. The church, pleasantly situated on a hill, is an ancient building chiefly of Norman architecture, and supposed to have been erected about the year 1090, and the Gothic tower about 1500; in 1839 a north aisle was added, and the edifice entirely restored: there are altar-tombs with recumbent effigies of members of the family of Blount. A free school is endowed with about £20 per annum, left by Mrs. Mercy Pope in 1717. Cottages have been built at Redstone Ferry, the site of an ancient hermitage excavated in a lofty cliff by the side of the river.

ASTLEY, ABBOTS, a parish, in the union of BRIDGNORTH, hundred of STOTTESDEN, S. division of SALOP, 2 miles (N.) from Bridgnorth; containing 657 inhabitants. This parish, which comprises about 3200 acres, is intersected by the road from Bridgnorth to Broseley, and by the river Severn. The living is a perpetual curacy, in the patronage of the family of Whitmore: the tithes have been commuted for £255. 15., and there are 51½ acres of rectorial glebe. The church, which is in the later English style, was built in 1638; the chancel is of modern date. A parochial school was endowed by Mrs. C. Phillips, in 1805, with £300 in the three per cent. consols.

ASTLEY-BRIDGE, an ecclesiastical parish, in the parish and union of BOLTON, hundred of SALFORD, S. division of the county of LANCASTER, 1½ mile (N.) from Bolton, on the roads to Blackburn and Belmont; containing 2325 inhabitants. This parish was formed in 1844, out of the townships of Little Bolton and Sharples, under the act of the 6th and 7th of Victoria, cap. 37. It comprises 1468 acres, and the rivers Astle and Eagle forming its southern and eastern boundary. The population is chiefly employed in bleach-works and cotton-mills. The living is a perpetual curacy, in the patronage of the Crown and the Bishop of Chester, alternately; net income, £150. The church, dedicated to St. Paul, was erected in 1847, at a cost of £3000, raised by subscription aided by public grants: the body of the edifice is in the Norman style; and the tower, surmounted by a spire, is early English. The Wesleyans have a place of worship; and there are some national schools.

ASTON, a hamlet, in the parish of IVINGHOE, union of LEIGHTON-BUZZARD, hundred of COTTESLOE, county of BUCKINGHAM, 1¾ mile (N. N. E.) from Ivinghoe: containing 446 inhabitants.

ASTON, a hamlet, in the parish of HOPE, union of CHAPEL-EN-LE-FRITH, hundred of HIGH PEAK, N. division of the county of DERBY, 6½ miles (N. N. E.) from Tideswell; containing 111 inhabitants.

ASTON, a hamlet, in the parish of AVENING, union of STROUD, hundred of LONGTREE, E. division of the county of GLOUCESTER; containing 221 inhabitants.

ASTON, or PIPE-ASTON (ST. GILES), a parish, in the union of LUDLOW, hundred of WIGMORE, county of HEREFORD, 4 miles (S. W. by W.) from Ludlow; containing 52 inhabitants; and comprising 733 acres. The surface is undulated and well-wooded; the soil is of an inferior quality. The parish runs up to the High Vinealls, and to the boundary of Richard's-Castle parish; from the height is a complete panoramic view, including the Brecon, Radnor, Cardigan, and Montgomery hills. The road from Ludlow to Wigmore also Presteign passes through. The living is a discharged rectory, valued in the king's books at £2. 13. 4.; net income, £84; patron, Sir Wm. E. Rouse Boughton, Bart. The church, an ancient structure, was restored and repewed, and an eastern window added, in 1844: the arch over the entrance door has a curious stone engraving, representing the Lamb bearing the Cross. Near the road, opposite a farmhouse, is a tumulus.

ASTON (ST. MARY), a parish, in the hundred of BROADWATER, union and county of HERTFORD, 3¼ miles (S. E.) from Stevenage; containing 556 inhabitants. The living is a rectory, valued in the king's books at £26. 11. 8.; patron and incumbent, the Rev. James Ellice. The tithes have been commuted for £460, and the glebe consists of 42½ acres.

ASTON, with COTE, a hamlet, in the parish and hundred of BAMPTON, union of WITNEY, county of OXFORD, 4 miles (S. S. W.) from Witney; containing 729 inhabitants, and comprising 2017 acres, of which 630 are common or waste. A handsome chapel was built in 1839, chiefly by the three portionists of Bampton, who perform divine service. The tithes have been commuted for £556, of which £550 are payable to the portionists, and £6 to the Dean and Chapter of Exeter.

ASTON, a township, in the parish and union of WEM, Whitchurch division of the hundred of NORTH BRADFORD, N. division of SALOP; containing 212 inhabitants. There is a place of worship for Wesleyans.

ASTON, a township, in the parish and union of WELLINGTON, hundred of SOUTH BRADFORD, N. division of SALOP; containing 84 inhabitants.

ASTON, with BURSTON and STOKE, a township, in the parish and union of STONE, S. division of the hundred of PIREHILL, N. division of the county of STAFFORD, 2 miles (S. S. E.) from Stone; containing 773 inhabitants. This township is situated in the southeastern part of the parish. Aston lies on the southwest side of the Trent, opposite to Stoke, which is a long straggling village on the Lichfield road, near the Trent and Mersey canal; Burston is a small hamlet on the Trent, containing several good houses. Aston Hall is the property of Lord St. Vincent. In the summer of 1846, a church (St. Saviour's) was erected and endowed by Lord and Lady St. Vincent; the living is a perpetual

curacy, in the patronage of his Lordship. The tithes have been commuted for £396. One of the sons of Wulphere, King of Mercia, is said to have suffered martyrdom at Burston.

ASTON, a township, in the parish of MUCKLESTON, union of MARKET-DRAYTON, N. division of the hundred of PIREHILL and of the county of STAFFORD, 8 miles (W. S. W.) from Newcastle-under-Lyme; containing 283 inhabitants. It lies in the northern part of the parish, and on the western border of the county.

ASTON, a hamlet, in the parish of SEIGHFORD, S. division of the hundred of PIREHILL, union, and N. division of the county, of STAFFORD, 2½ miles (W.) from Stafford. The manor-house here was formerly the residence of the Count de L'Age, who married into the Palmer family, through whom the property came to that noble. The house subsequently belonged to Lord Ashburton, from whom it was lately purchased, together with the estate and manor adjoining, by the Rev. Charles Smith Royds, rector of Haughton, the present possessor. The land is of a rich loamy quality; and the Presford brook, famous for its trout and cray-fish, passes by the hamlet, at a short distance in front of the house, to the north of which it falls into the river Sow. The manor-house, called Aston Hall, is beautifully situated on a sloping bank, north of the ancient castle of Stafford, and is a gable-ended mansion, built probably in the sixteenth or seventeenth century. A few fields distant from it, and close to the village of Derrington, is a handsome church, lately erected at the expense of the Rev. Mr. Royds, who gave the site and a spacious piece of ground for a churchyard: the building is of stone, is in the decorated style, and has a bell-turret at the west end containing two bells, and a campanile over the vestry with one bell. The chancel is laid in Mosaic and encaustic tiles, and there are eight stone stalls ornamented with hoods, and worked into bosses, crockets, and finials; the pulpit and font are also of stone, and very handsome. This church is upwards of two miles from the parish church; and has been endowed by Mr. Royds, to whom the patronage belongs. In the time of the Reformation, there existed a chapel at Derrington dedicated to St. Edmund, a Saxon prince, in a field now called the Chapel field; it was then destroyed. The Presford brook was a favourite resort of Izaak Walton.

ASTON (ST. PETER AND ST. PAUL), a parish, and the head of a union, in the Birmingham division of the hundred of HEMLINGFORD, N. division of the county of WARWICK; adjoining the town of Birmingham, part of which is within its limits; and comprising the hamlets of Ashted, Castle and Little Bromwich, Erdington, Saltley with Washwood, Ward-End, Water-Orton, Witton, Deritend with Bordesley, and Duddeston with Nechells; containing together 45,718 inhabitants, of whom 2896 are in Aston manor. This extensive parish, the name of which was originally Eston (East town), includes several manors anciently belonging to the earls of Mercia, under whom that of Aston, at the time of the Conquest, was held by Godmund the Saxon. The manor, with other extensive possessions, was afterwards granted by William the Norman to Fitz Ausculf, one of his followers, who fixed his baronial residence at the Castle of Dudley in the county of Stafford, of which barony this place formed a part. Fitz Ausculf was succeeded by Gervase Paganell, whose nephew, Ralph Somery, about the commencement of the reign of John, granted the manor to Thomas de Erdington ; and in the early part of the reign of Edward I. it became the property of Thomas de Maidenhach, who obtained from that monarch extensive privileges, with exemption from the jurisdiction of the county and hundred courts, and a charter of free warren throughout the whole of his demesnes here. The manor was purchased in 1366 from the heiress of de Maidenhach by John atte HOLT, of Birmingham, and remained for many generations in the possession of his lineal descendants, of whom several were distinguished for their talents and for the important stations they occupied in society. Edward Holt, sheriff of the county in 1574, resided in the adjoining manor of Duddeston, there being at that time in Aston only an ancient house, probably of timber, situated on the bank of the river Tame near the church, and the site of which, now overgrown with trees, is discoverable only by part of the moat by which it was surrounded.

On the demise of Edward Holt in 1593, the estate descended to his son Thomas, the most distinguished member of the family, who is represented by Dugdale as eminent for his literary acquirements. He was sheriff in 1600 : on the arrival of James VI. of Scotland to assume the crown of England, he attended that monarch in his route from Yorkshire, where he received the honour of knighthood ; and in 1612 he was created one of the order of baronets, then recently instituted. Sir Thomas Holt inclosed the park, and erected the present stately Hall of Aston, unrivalled in these parts for beauty and magnificence, which he commenced in 1618, and completed in 1635. On the breaking out of the civil war in the reign of Charles I., he zealously embraced the royal cause, and to the utmost of his fortune assisted the king, who spent two nights at the Hall a few days previously to the battle of Edgehill. He was nominated ambassador to the court of Spain, but was excused on account of his extreme age and infirmity, which also prevented him from following the camp ; his son Edward, however, accompanied the monarch to Oxford, where he was during the siege. Sir Thomas was imprisoned for his attachment to his sovereign ; and during his absence, the Hall was assaulted, and, after a resolute defence by his servants, plundered by a party of soldiers of the parliamentarian army, who battered it with cannon, the marks of which are still visible on the south wall of the building, and on the massive oak staircase, where the balls that penetrated the mansion are still preserved. The estate was decimated, and subjected to contributions ; the damages it sustained being estimated at £20,000.

Sir Thomas died in 1654, aged 83 ; and the property passed through successive baronets, his descendants, to Sir Lister Holt, who dying without issue in 1770, left it to his widow Sarah for her life, and afterwards to his brother Charles and his heirs male, with succession to his friend Heneage Legge, Esq., the Rt. Rev. Lewis Bagot, Bishop of St. Asaph, and Wriothesley Digby, Esq. After the death of Lady Sarah, and of Sir Charles Holt and the bishop without issue male, the estate passed to Mr. Legge and Mr. Digby, the former of whom occupied the Hall and park ; and in 1817, both being widowers and childless, these gentlemen entered into an agreement with the heirs of Sir Lister Holt, Mary Elizabeth, 103

daughter of Sir Charles, her husband Abraham Bracebridge, and their creditors, for the sale of the estate, which was confirmed by act of parliament in 1818. The property, in pursuance of this arrangement, was in part divided, and the remainder sold in lots to pay off the incumbrances. The HALL and park were purchased by Messrs. Whitehead and Greenway of Warwick, bankers, by whom the mansion and the contiguous portion of the park were granted on lease to James Watt, Esq., of Soho, son of the celebrated philosopher and improver of the steam-engine ; who in 1823 purchased the manor from the trustees, and in 1828 served the office of sheriff for the county. Since it became the residence of Mr. Watt, this venerable mansion, which is beautifully situated in a park embellished with ancient wood, and with thriving plantations of modern growth, has undergone very little alteration : it has simply been repaired from the injuries of time ; a west porch has been added, and several of the offices have been rebuilt. The Hall is a spacious and elegant structure in the Elizabethan style, containing a noble hall in which was formerly a portrait of Sir Thomas Holt from Vandyke, and numerous stately apartments, with a picture gallery, library, and chapel ; and, as seen from the public road and from various other points of view, displays a splendid monument of the correct taste and munificence of its founder.

The parish comprises 12,534 acres of land, of which a considerable portion is in a high state of cultivation ; and contains numerous populous and thriving villages. The LIVING is a vicarage, valued in the king's books at £21. 4. 9½. ; net income, £2075 ; patrons, the Executors of the late vicar, the Rev. George Peake, who obtained it by purchase from the trustees of the Holt family. The church, which was built at various periods, is an ancient structure, partly in the early and partly in the later English style, with a handsome tower surmounted by a graceful spire, which, seen in combination with the foliage of the park and the lofty gables of the Hall, forms a picturesque feature in the landscape. The interior was modernised in 1790, and much of its original character has been lost : a ceiling of plaister has been substituted in place of the old groined roof ; and the chantry chapel at the east end of the south aisle, erected by Thomas de Erdington, and the piscina and sedilia, have been removed. In the windows are some fine specimens of painted glass by Eginton. Of the ancient monuments several still remain, among which are, an altar-tomb with recumbent figures, to the memory of William Holt and his wife ; two with recumbent figures in alabaster, to members of the Erdington family ; and one of similar character, to Walter de Arden and Eleonora his wife, erected in the early part of the 15th century, and of exquisite design. There are additional churches at Castle-Bromwich, Water-Orton, Ward-End in Little Bromwich, Bordesley, Deritend, Erdington, Ashted, and Duddeston. A school is endowed with a house and garden, valued at £25 per annum ; and there are several national and Lancasterian schools, and a school of industry, in the parish. A school-house was erected in 1843, in Villa-street, in the district of Lozells, which part of the parish is under the superintendence of the Rev. D. N. Walton, curate of Aston : this establishment is called the Aston Church District Institution ; it will contain upwards of 250 persons, and divine service is regularly performed in it every Sunday evening. The district comprises the neighbourhoods of the Lozells, Round-Hills, and Park, and includes a population of about 3000. There is also a society of young men, called the Lozells Society for mental cultivation, who meet at stated times for the reading and discussion of essays. Almshouses for five men and five women were founded in 1656, by Sir Thomas Holt, who endowed them with a rent-charge of £88 on his manor of Erdington. The poor law union of Aston comprises five parishes and places, containing a population, according to the last census, of 50,928.—See BIRMINGHAM, and the articles on the hamlets.

ASTON (*ALL SAINTS*), a parish, in the union of ROTHERHAM, S. division of the wapentake of STRAFFORTH and TICKHILL, W. riding of YORK, 8¼ miles (E. by S.) from Sheffield; containing, with the hamlet of Aughton and part of Ulley, 763 inhabitants. This place is noticed in Domesday book, in which a church is mentioned as existing here. The parish is bounded on the western side by the river Rother, is on the road from Worksop to Sheffield, and is intersected by that from Rotherham to Mansfield; it comprises about 3000 acres, chiefly arable land, with not more than about 30 acres of wood. The surface is bold and elevated, and the views extend over the hills of North Derbyshire and the Yorkshire moors; the soil is mostly light, very fertile, and rests on a stratum of coarse dark sandstone, beneath which coal of good quality is found. The Midland railway passes on the west for a distance of two miles. The LIVING is a rectory, valued in the king's books at £12. 15. 2½., and in the patronage of the Duke of Leeds: the tithes have been commuted for £740, and there are about 34 acres of glebe. The church is a neat stone building, with a tower at the west end: the chancel, which has recently been renovated by the incumbent, the Rev. W. Alderson, contains kneeling marble effigies of the "good Lord D'Arcy," who died in 1628, and three of his wives, a fourth having survived him; the east window is of stained glass, and occupied chiefly with the arms and impalements of the D'Arcy family. In the hamlet of Aughton are places of worship for Calvinists and Wesleyans. The parish is remarkable for having been for many years the residence of the Rev. William Mason, the poet, its then rector, who here composed some of his most beautiful works, and who reduced to practice his rules for English gardening, in the garden which pertained to the rectorial manse: he died in 1797, and was buried in the church, where is a tablet to his memory.

ASTON, ABBOT'S (*ST. JAMES*), a parish, in the union of AYLESBURY, hundred of COTTESLOE, county of BUCKINGHAM, 5½ miles (N. N. E.) from Aylesbury; containing 356 inhabitants. The parish comprises by measurement 2131 acres; the village is beautifully situated on a hill overlooking the vale of Aylesbury, within half a mile of the road from Oxford to Cambridge. A large supply of excellent butter is sent to the London market. The women and children are employed in the manufacture of lace and straw-platting. The living is a vicarage, valued in the king's books at £6. 7. 11.; net income, £143; patron, the Earl of Chesterfield. About 90 acres of land in the parish, with the tithes of the hamlet of Burston, belong to the benefice.

104

ASTON-BLANK (*ST. ANDREW*), a parish, in the union of NORTHLEACH, hundred of BRADLEY, E. division of the county of GLOUCESTER, 4½ miles (N. by E.) from Northleach; containing 302 inhabitants. This parish, which comprises 2200 acres, is situated about half a mile from the Stow road, and is bounded on the north and north-east by the river Windrush. The neighbourhood has been much improved by the inclosure of waste lands, and by the plantations made by the lord of the manor. The living is a discharged vicarage, valued in the king's books at £6. 12. 4.; net income, £151; patron, the Crown. The tithes were commuted for land and annual money payments, in 1795; the glebe consists of 3 acres.

ASTON-BOTTERELL (*ST. MICHAEL*), a parish, in the union of CLEOBURY-MORTIMER, hundred of STOTTESDEN, S. division of SALOP, 9 miles (S. W. by W.) from Bridgnorth; containing, with the chapelry of Bold, 173 inhabitants. This place derives the adjunct to its name from the family of Botterell, by whom the manor was held under the earls of Arundel in the reign of Henry III. It is situated on the road from Bridgnorth to Ludlow, and comprises 2238a. 22p.: limestone is obtained for manure, but in very small quantity, and basaltic stone for the repair of the roads. There was formerly a blast-furnace here, in which the iron was smelted with charcoal, the cinder hill from which also forms materials for the roads. By a charter of Henry III. a market was held on Tuesday, and a fair at Michaelmas; but both have been long discontinued. The living is a rectory, valued in the king's books at £7. 1. 0½., and in the gift of the Duke of Cleveland: the tithes have been commuted for £345, and there are 70 acres of glebe. In the church is an altar-tomb, on which are recumbent figures, supposed to be of the Botterell family. During some late repairs, on the whitewash being removed from the interior walls, were exposed various texts from Scripture in old English characters; and, on the left of the porch, a figure of death.

ASTON-BY-BUDWORTH, a township, in the parish of GREAT BUDWORTH, union of ALTRINCHAM, hundred of BUCKLOW, N. division of the county of CHESTER, 3 miles (N. N. E.) from Northwich; containing 405 inhabitants. Arley, in this township, has been the seat of the Warburton family ever since the reign of Henry VII. The Hall was lately rebuilt in a very handsome style; and a chapel, attached to the mansion, has been erected by the present representative of the family, A. E. E. Warburton, Esq. The township comprises 2860 acres; the soil is chiefly clay. The village is situated at the distance of about a mile from the main road between London and Liverpool, and the same distance from the Trent and Mersey canal. In the centre of the township are the remains of an ancient moated mansion, with an old bridge. A petrifying spring rises on the Gore farm.

ASTON-BY-SUTTON, a parochial chapelry, in the parish and union of RUNCORN, hundred of BUCKLOW, N. division of the county of CHESTER, 1 mile (S. by W.) from Preston-Brook; containing 508 inhabitants, of whom 206 are in the township of Aston. The manor belonged as early as the reign of Wm. I. to the family of Aston, of whom Thomas Aston was created a baronet by Charles I. in 1628; he was an officer in the king's service, and was actively engaged in the civil war, as was also Sir Arthur Aston, who was a personal friend of Charles. The title became extinct in the commencement of the eighteenth century. The chapelry comprises 2974a. 30p., whereof about 535 acres are arable, 1950 meadow and pasture, 410 woodland, and the remainder homesteads and gardens. Of the whole acreage, 1001 are in Aston township, which is chiefly of a clayey and sandy soil; the land is cultivated in a judicious manner, and is well wooded. The township lies on the river Weaver, which is navigable here and flows through the hamlet of Sutton into the Mersey. The Chester and Warrington road runs on the north of the township, and the Liverpool and Birmingham railway passes through it. Aston Hall, a handsome mansion, built about the close of the 17th century, and surrounded by an extensive park, is the seat of Sir Arthur Ingram Aston, G.C.B.; it stands on elevated ground, and commands fine views of the estuary of the Weaver, and of the Lancashire shore on the north-west. The living is a curacy, in the patronage of Sir Arthur; net income, £88: There was formerly a chapel at Middleton-Grange; and after it fell into decay, about the year 1450, another was erected on the present site, at Aston, which was made a parochial chapel by grant of Dr. John Bridgeman, Bishop of Chester, in 1635. It was rebuilt on an enlarged scale in 1737, is of red sandstone, and consists of a nave and chancel, with a belfry turret at the west end; there are several memorials of the Aston family.

ASTON-CANTLOW (St. John the Baptist), a parish, in the union of ALCESTER, Stratford division of the hundred of BARLICHWAY, S. division of the county of WARWICK, 4 miles (N. E. by E.) from Alcester; containing, with part of the hamlet of Wilncote, 1089 inhabitants. This place appears to have derived the adjunct to its name from the family of Cantelu, or Cantelupe, of whom William de Cantelupe received from Henry III. a confirmation of the lordship, together with a market and fair. John de Hastings, into whose possession it had come, claimed by prescription, in the 13th of Edward I., a court leet, with assize of bread and beer, weifs, gallows, and free warren, all which were allowed. The parish comprises 4758 acres, and is intersected by the river Alne, on the left bank of which the village is situated. The Stratford canal also passes through. The living is a discharged vicarage, valued in the king's books at £9. 9. 7.; net income, £93; patron, the Rev. R. S. Carles; impropriator, the Earl of Abergavenny. The chapel of St. Andrew, Wilncote, was built in the year 1841.

ASTON-CHETWYND, a township, in the parish of EDGMOND, union of NEWPORT, Newport division of the hundred of SOUTH BRADFORD, N. division of Salop, 1½ mile (S. S. E.) from Newport; containing 385 inhabitants.

ASTON, CHURCH, a chapelry, in the parish of EDGMOND, union of NEWPORT, Newport division of the hundred of SOUTH BRADFORD, N. division of Salop, 1 mile (S.) from Newport; containing 512 inhabitants. The chapel is dedicated to St. Andrew.

ASTON-CLINTON (St. Michael), a parish, in the union and hundred of AYLESBURY, county of BUCKINGHAM, 2¾ miles (W. by N.) from Tring, on the London road; containing, with the hamlet of St. Leonard, 1025 inhabitants, of whom 847 are in the township of Aston-

Clinton. The Grand Junction canal passes through the parish. The cottagers manufacture straw-plat and lace. The living is a rectory, valued in the king's books at £23. 6. 10¼.; net income, £506; patrons, the Principal and Fellows of Jesus' College, Oxford. The tithes, with the exception of those for woodland, were commuted for land and a money payment, in 1814. At St. Leonard's is an incumbency in the gift of Trustees. There is a place of worship for Baptists.

ASTON, EAST, a tything, in the parish of LONG-PARISH, union of ANDOVER, hundred of WHERWELL, Andover and N. divisions of HANTS; containing 109 inhabitants.

ASTON-EYRE, a chapelry, in the parish of MORVILL, union of BRIDGNORTH, hundred of STOTTESDEN, S. division of SALOP, 4¼ miles (W. by N.) from Bridgnorth; containing 130 inhabitants. The living is a perpetual curacy, annexed to that of Morvill: the tithes have been commuted for £218. The chapel is a small structure in the Norman style, of the 12th century, and consists of a nave and chancel, the latter and a great part of the former having been lately rebuilt. Over the south doorway of the nave is a perfect and beautifully carved tympanum, lately exposed, representing the Entry of Our Lord into Jerusalem, with the people strewing palm-branches in his path. Nearly adjoining the chapel are the remains of a religious house now a farmhouse, supposed to have been a priory under the abbey of Wenlock.

ASTON-FLAMVILLE (St. Peter), a parish, in the union of HINCKLEY, hundred of SPARKENHOE, S. division of the county of LEICESTER, 2 miles (E. S. E.) from Hinckley; containing, with the chapelry of Burbage, 1909 inhabitants. This parish comprises 4097 acres, of which 3057 are in Burbage; the portion of arable is computed to be 1450 acres, of woodland 149 acres, and the rest is pasture. It is chiefly the property of Sir E. C. Hartopp, Bart., who is lord of the manor. The place is famous for its cheese. The living is a rectory, valued in the king's books at £33. 12. 8½.; net income, £878; patron, Earl de Grey. The tithes of Burbage have been commuted for a rent-charge of £677; the tithe at Aston is about £31. 18., and is a modus. The glebe consists of about 120 acres. The church is very ancient.—See BURBAGE.

ASTON-GRANGE, a township, in the parochial chapelry of ASTON, parish and union of RUNCORN, hundred of BUCKLOW, N. division of the county of CHESTER, 3¼ miles (E.) from Frodsham; containing 27 inhabitants. The manor of Aston-Grange, anciently Maurice-Aston, was given to the monks of Stanlow (who afterwards removed to Whalley) by John Lacy, constable of Chester; in the 37th of Henry VIII., 1545, it was purchased of the crown by the Brooke family, of Norton, and it was held by them until a few years since. The township is now the property of Sir Arthur Aston, and comprises 442 acres of land, the soil of which is chiefly clay and sand. The Liverpool and Birmingham railway passes a little to the east.

ASTON-INGHAM, a parish, in the union of NEWENT, hundred of GREYTREE, county of HEREFORD, 3 miles (S. W. by W.) from Newent; containing 621 inhabitants. This parish comprises 1944 acres, of which about 100 are common or waste; it is bounded on the east and south by a portion of the county of Gloucester, and is intersected by the road from Newent to Mitchel-Dean. The surface exhibits considerable undulations, and numerous patches of woodland ; the soil is of average productiveness. There are some quarries of limestone, and also of stone for building. The living is a rectory, valued in the king's books at £7. 7. 1.; patron, the Rev. Henry Lawson Whatley, the present incumbent. The tithes have been commuted for £350, and there are about 100 acres of glebe, and a good house.

ASTON-JUXTA-MONDRUM, a township, in the parish of ACTON, union and hundred of NANTWICH, S. division of the county of CHESTER, 4 miles (N.) from Nantwich ; containing 164 inhabitants. It comprises 1193 acres, of a clayey soil. The Chester and Crewe railway passes close to the place, near which it is conducted over the Weaver by a bridge of 8 arches, 60 feet above the level of the river. The impropriate tithes have been commuted for £71. 5., and the vicarial for £26. 7.

ASTON-LE-WALLS (ST. LEONARD), a parish, in the union of BANBURY, hundred of CHIPPING-WARDEN, S. division of the county of NORTHAMPTON, 8½ miles (N. N. E.) from Banbury ; containing, with the hamlet of Appletree, 252 inhabitants. This parish, which is intersected in its north-eastern extremity by the road from Banbury to Daventry, comprises 1528 acres, of a highly productive soil ; the substratum is rock, and stone is quarried for repairing the roads and for rough building. The living is a rectory, valued in the king's books at £9. 9. 7.; net income, £343 ; patrons, the President and Fellows of St. John's College, Oxford. The glebe comprises 140 acres. The church is an ancient structure in the early English style, with a low Norman tower. There is a Roman Catholic chapel.

ASTON MAGNA, a hamlet, in the parish of BLOCKLEY, union of SHIPSTON-ON-STOUR, Upper division of the hundred of OSWALDSLOW, Blockley and E. divisions of the county of WORCESTER, 2¾ miles (N.) from Moreton-in-the-Marsh ; containing 223 inhabitants. Here is a district church, dedicated to St. John ; the living of which is a perpetual curacy in the gift of Lord Redesdale, with a net income of £105. The vicarial tithes have been commuted for £95.

ASTON, MIDDLE, a township, in the parish of STEEPLE-ASTON, union of WOODSTOCK, hundred of WOOTTON, county of OXFORD, 3 miles (S. by E.) from Deddington ; containing 111 inhabitants, and comprising 842a. 3r. 20p.

ASTON-MORRIS, a tything, partly in the parish of BURNHAM, union of AXBRIDGE, hundred of BEMPSTONE, E. division, and partly in the parish of HUNTSPILL, union of BRIDGWATER, hundred of HUNTSPILL and PURITON, W. division, of SOMERSET ; containing 239 inhabitants.

ASTON, NORTH (ST. MARY), a parish, in the union of WOODSTOCK, hundred of WOOTTON, county of OXFORD, 2 miles (S. S. E.) from Deddington, and 8 (N. E.) from Woodstock ; comprising by measurement 1260 acres, and containing 289 inhabitants. The Oxford canal forms a boundary of the parish on the east. The views from the grounds of the mansion here are very extensive, and of the most pleasing description. On the village green, which is one of the prettiest in the county, are some fine elms, and other full-grown trees. The living is a discharged vicarage, valued in the king's books at
106

£6. 10.; net income, £133 ; patron, J. Wills, Esq. The church consists of a nave, aisles, and chancel, of unequal height, with a tower picturesquely covered with ivy ; in a chantry on the south side of the chancel is an elegant tomb, with recumbent effigies of a male and female, supposed to be those of Sir John Anne and Alicia his wife.

ASTON-PIGOT, a township, in the parish of WORTHEN, hundred of CHIRBURY, S. division of SALOP, 11 miles (N. E.) from Montgomery ; containing 78 inhabitants.

ASTON-ROGERS, a township, in the parish of WORTHEN, hundred of CHIRBURY, S. division of SALOP, 2½ miles (N. E.) from Worthen ; containing 174 inhabitants. The village is situated on the road between Shrewsbury and Montgomery.

ASTON-ROWANT (ST. PETER AND ST. PAUL), a parish, in the union of THAME, hundred of LEWKNOR, county of OXFORD, 3½ miles (S. E.) from Tetsworth ; containing, with the townships of Chalford and Kingston-Blount, 885 inhabitants. The parish comprises 2800 acres by computation ; the surface is in general flat, and the soil composed of chalk, sand, and deep clay. Many of the females are employed in lace-making. The living is a vicarage partly endowed with the great tithes, with the living of Stokenchurch annexed, and valued in the king's books at £16. 18. 11. ; net income, £176 ; patron, the Crown. The remainder of the great tithes have been commuted for land under an act of inclosure. The church is partly in the early and partly in the later style of English architecture, and contains some ancient brasses. There is a place of worship for Independents at Kingston. Near the close of the seventeenth century, a large Roman vessel, containing five smaller ones, was discovered in Kingston field, within the parish, at the distance of about a furlong from the Ikeneld-street.

ASTON-SANDFORD (ST. MICHAEL), a parish, in the union of AYLESBURY, hundred of ASHENDON, county of BUCKINGHAM, 3 miles (E. N. E.) from Thame ; containing 86 inhabitants. It comprises 669a. 2r. 14p., of which 473 acres are tithable. The living is a rectory, valued in the king's books at £12. 16. 0½., and in the patronage of Mrs. Susannah Barber : the tithes have been commuted for £107, and the glebe consists of 53½ acres. The church is in the later English style, and has a wooden tower with three bells. The remains of the Rev. Thomas Scott, a learned and pious commentator on the Scriptures, and for some time rector, were interred in the chancel.

ASTON-SOMERVILLE (ST. MARY), a parish, in the union of EVESHAM, Lower division of the hundred of KIFTSGATE, E. division of the county of GLOUCESTER, 3½ miles (S. S. E.) from Evesham ; containing 89 inhabitants. It is situated on the river Isperne, and comprises by measurement 1000 acres, of which three-fourths are arable, and the rest pasture land ; the soil is a deep strong clay. The living is a rectory, valued in the king's books at £9. 3. 4., and in the patronage of Lord Somerville : the tithes have been commuted for £230, and there are about 40 acres of glebe. The church, a plain edifice, contains a monument to the late Lord Somerville, author of some tracts and essays on Agriculture and Rural Economy ; he was a native of this place, and was interred here in 1819.

ASTON, STEEPLE (St. Peter), a parish, in the union of Woodstock, hundred of Wootton, county of Oxford, 6 miles (N. N. E.) from Woodstock; containing 580 inhabitants. This place is thought to have been occupied by the Romans, as a tessellated pavement was discovered in the vicinity in the 16th century. The parish includes the villages of Steeple-Aston and Middle Aston, and comprises 1875a. 2r. 37p.: it is skirted by the river Cherwell and the Oxford canal; and the Oxford and Rugby railway intersects a part of it. Limestone is quarried for building. The apricot-tree is cultivated extensively by the cottagers, and there are about twenty apple-orchards. The living is a rectory, valued in the king's books at £16. 2. 8½.; net income, £582; patrons, the Principal and Fellows of Brasenose College, Oxford. The church is an ancient edifice, partly rebuilt in 1842: the north aisle, chancel, and tower are early English, and other portions in the decorated style. In a chapel on the north side of the chancel are recumbent effigies of Sir Francis Page and his lady, to whom the manor of Middle Aston formerly belonged: Sir Francis destroyed some monuments of the Dinham family to make room for his own, which was erected in his life-time. In the parish chest is preserved part of the hangings of the altar of the church, of the 14th century, richly embroidered; in the churchyard are the steps and base of a perpendicular cross. A school is endowed with £20 per annum, and a house and garden, from a bequest in 1640, by Dr. Samuel Radcliffe, principal of Brasenose College, who founded two scholarships in that college, to be supplied, if possible, from the school; he also founded an almshouse here for poor women. An account of the history and antiquities of the parish was published at Deddington, in the county, in 1845. Near the village, a strong chalybeate spring was discovered in 1833.

ASTON-SUB-EDGE (St. Andrew), a parish, in the union of Evesham, Upper division of the county of Gloucester, 1¼ mile (N. N. W.) from Chipping-Campden; containing 134 inhabitants. This parish comprises by measurement 850 acres. Norton-Burnt House, so called from the greater portion of it having been destroyed by fire while the seat of Sir William Knight, Bart., is the property of the Earl of Harrowby, who, with Lord and Lady Sandon, occasionally resides here. The living is a rectory, valued in the king's books at £10. 2. 3½.; net income, £204; patron, the Earl. An allotment of 100 acres of land has been given in lieu of tithes. The church is a plain, neat edifice, erected in 1795, on the site of the old structure.

ASTON-TIRROLD (St. Michael), a parish, in the union of Wallingford, hundred of Moreton, county of Berks, 3½ miles (S. W. by W.) from Wallingford; containing 343 inhabitants. Bishop Gibson supposes this to be the place called in the Saxon Chronicle Aescesdune, where Ethelred I. and his brother Alfred defeated the Danes, in 871; but Gough, with greater probability, considers the battle to have been fought at Ashdown Park, near East Ilsley. The parish comprises 1650 acres by survey, and is situated near the Great Western railway. The living is a rectory, valued in the king's books at £10. 12. 11., and in the patronage of Magdalene College, Oxford: the tithes have been commuted for £278, and the glebe consists of 36 acres.

ASTON-UPON-CARRON, a tything, in the parish of Ashchurch, union of Tewkesbury, Lower division of the hundred of Tewkesbury, E. division of the county of Gloucester, 4¼ miles (E. N. E.) from Tewkesbury; containing 179 inhabitants.

ASTON-UPON-TRENT (All Saints), a parish, in the union of Shardlow, hundred of Morleston and Litchurch, S. division of the county of Derby, 6½ miles (S. E.) from Derby; comprising the townships of Aston, Shardlow, and Great Wilne; and containing 1952 inhabitants, of whom 646 are in Aston township. The manor was granted after the Reformation to Sir William Paget, and subsequently passed to the Ropers, from whom it was purchased in 1649 by the Holden family. A grant of a market and fair was obtained in 1256, but both have been long discontinued. The township of Aston contains 1770 acres of arable and pasture land, the soil of which is in some parts gravel and in others clay; the surface is generally level. It lies on the road from London to Manchester; and the Great Trunk navigation joins the river Trent below Shardlow, at which place are extensive wharfs. The parish contains some plaster pits. The living is a rectory, valued in the king's books at £29. 15.; net income, £1030; patron, E. A. Holden, Esq. The tithes were commuted for land in 1762; there is a glebe-house, with glebe now comprising 383 acres. A chapel of ease has been erected at Shardlow; and the Wesleyans have a place of worship. In the village are some subscription schools; and six almshouses for widows, the rector having the nomination of the inmates.

ASTON-UPTHORP, a chapelry, in the parish of Blewberry, union of Wallingford, hundred of Moreton, county of Berks, 3¼ miles (W. S. W.) from Wallingford; containing 159 inhabitants. It forms a part of the parliamentary borough of Wallingford, and comprises 1270a. 1r. 2p. The chapel is said to be one of the most ancient in England.

ASTON, WEST, a tything, in the parish of Long-Parish, union of Andover, hundred of Wherwell, Andover and N. divisions of Hants; containing 170 inhabitants.

ASTON, WHITE LADIES (St. John the Baptist), a parish, in the union of Pershore, Lower division of the hundred of Oswaldslow, Worcester and W. divisions of the county of Worcester, 5 miles (E. by S.) from Worcester; containing 367 inhabitants. The ancient manor-house of this place, pulled down a few years since, was the abode of Oliver Cromwell, the night before the celebrated battle of Worcester. On the road to Evesham is a high hill called Lowe hill, which is bishop's land, and is supposed to be the Oswalds Lawe, or Mount, that gives name to the hundred. The parish comprises 1224a. 2r. 24p., in about equal portions of arable and pasture, with 10 acres of wood; the surface is undulated, the soil of mixed quality, and from Lowe hill are beautiful views of the Malvern hills and the surrounding country. The roads from Worcester to Alcester and Evesham pass through the parish, and the Spetchley station of the Gloucester and Birmingham railway is only about a mile and a half distant. The living is a vicarage, valued in the king's books at £6. 17. 3½., and endowed with the great tithes; patron, R. Berkeley, Esq. The tithes have been commuted for £250. 5. 9., and there are about two acres of glebe, and a glebe-house. The church is an ancient building, with a white wooden spire, and contains a curious old font. Springs of water appear very near the surface of the soil, in this parish.

ASTROP, a hamlet, in the parishes of KING's SUTTON and NEWBOTTLE, hundred of KING's SUTTON, union of BRACKLEY, S. division of the county of NORTHAMPTON, 5¼ miles (W.) from Brackley; containing 224 inhabitants. Here is a mineral spring called St. Rumbald's well, which, in the latter part of the seventeenth century, was much frequented.

ASTWELL, a hamlet, partly in the parish of SYRESHAM, but chiefly in the parish of WAPENHAM, union of BRACKLEY, hundred of KING's SUTTON, S. division of the county of NORTHAMPTON, 5½ miles (N. N. E.) from Brackley; containing 46 inhabitants, and comprising, with the hamlet of Falcutt, 1790a. 3r. 36p.

ASTWICK (ST. GUTHLAKE), a parish, in the union and hundred of BIGGLESWADE, county of BEDFORD, 3¾ miles (N. W. by N.) from Baldock; containing 84 inhabitants. This parish is situated on the road from Baldock to Biggleswade, a little to the north of that between Baldock and Shefford, and lies on the border of Hertfordshire. It is bounded by the river Ivel, which separates it from the parish of Stotfold; and comprises by measurement 640 acres of arable land : the soil is heavy, and the sub-soil clay. The living is a rectory, united in 1764 to the vicarage of Arlsey, and valued in the king's books at £6. 13. 4.

ASTWOOD (ST. PETER), a parish, in the union of NEWPORT-PAGNELL, hundred of NEWPORT, county of BUCKINGHAM, 6 miles (E. N. E.) from Newport-Pagnell, on the road to Bedford; containing 243 inhabitants. This place was at the Conquest surveyed as part of the adjoining parish of Hardmead, and belonged to William Fitzanculph, from whom it descended by marriage to Fulk Paganell, the founder of Newport-Pagnell. The parish comprises 1259a. 1r. 7p., and is high table-land, which recedes on each side; the soil is "galt," a kind of clay mixed with lime and chalk. The female population are employed in the manufacture of lace. The living is a vicarage, valued in the king's books at £6. 6. 8., endowed with the great tithes, and in the patronage of the Lord Chancellor : the tithes have been commuted for £230. 11. 6., of which £29. 10. have been resigned for land; the glebe consists of 14 acres, with a house built in 1843. The church is an ancient structure, with a square tower; it contains a rather handsome Norman font, and a brass monument of three figures, representing a man and his two wives. There is a place of worship for Independents.

ASWARBY (ST. DENIS), a parish, in the union of SLEAFORD, wapentake of ASWARDHURN, parts of KESTEVEN, county of LINCOLN, 4 miles (N. by W.) from Folkingham; containing 119 inhabitants. It comprises about 1500 acres, and is situated on the road from London to Lincoln. The living is a rectory, valued in the king's books at £12. 4. 7., and in the gift of Sir T. Whichcote, Bart. : the tithes have been commuted for £327. 12., and there are 47 acres of glebe, and a good house. The church, a handsome building in the pointed style, was extensively repaired, and its chancel rebuilt, in 1840, at the expense of the patron and incumbent. There is a chalybeate spring. Aswarby Hall is a large mansion, situated in a well-wooded park.

ATHERSTONE, a market-town, chapelry, and the head of a union, in the parish of MANCETTER, Atherstone division of the hundred of HEMLINGFORD, N. division of the county of WARWICK, 20 miles (N. by E.) from Warwick, and 105 (N. W. by N.) from London, on the road to Chester; containing 3743 inhabitants. The name of this place, in Domesday book written *Aderestone*, is by Dugdale derived from its Saxon possessor *Edred* or *Aldred*, and thence called *Edredestone* or *Aldredestone*; by others its name is deduced from its situation near Mancester, or Mancetter, the *Manduessedum* of the Romans, reckoning from which station here was the nearest milliarium on the line of the Watling-street, and hence called Hither-stone or Atherstone. In 1485, the Earl of Richmond, previously to the battle of Bosworth Field, entered the town on the 20th of August, encamped his forces in a meadow north of the church, still called the Royal meadow, and took up his own quarters at an ancient inn, now the Three Tuns, where he passed the night. Here he had an interview with the Stanleys, and concerted those measures which secured him the victory in the celebrated battle that took place on the 22nd, and which terminated the war between the houses of York and Lancaster.

The TOWN has one principal street, containing many ancient and several modern houses, and from which another street branches to the market-place; it is paved, well lighted, and amply supplied with water. There is a circulating library; and assemblies are held occasionally in the town-hall, a neat brick building on the piazzas. Stone is quarried for road-making and for walls; and the manufacture of hats and caps, chiefly of a coarse kind, for soldiers and the West India trade, was formerly carried on to a considerable extent; but since the termination of the war, and the abolition of the slave trade, it has declined, there being little demand for soldiers' caps and none for negroes' hats. The Trent Valley railway, completed in 1847, runs by the town; and the Coventry and Fazeley canal passes at its northwestern extremity, where extensive coal and lime wharfs have been constructed. The market, granted in the 31st of Henry III., is on Tuesday; and fairs are held on April 7th and July 18th, for cattle; Sept. 19th, 20th, and 21st, for cattle, cheese, and pedlery, on the Tuesday after which is a statute-fair; and on Dec. 4th, which is a great show-fair for cattle, &c. The county magistrates hold a petty-session weekly: the hundred court is held here in rotation with other towns; and a court leet annually, at which constables and other officers are appointed. The powers of the county debt-court of Atherstone, established in 1847, extend over nearly the whole of the registration-district of Atherstone.

The township comprises 842 acres, chiefly pasture land. The LIVING is a perpetual curacy; net income, £150; patron, the Vicar of Mancetter. The chapel is dedicated to St. Mary; it formerly belonged to the monks of Bec, in Normandy. There are places of worship for Independents and Methodists; also a convent of the Dominican order, the foundation stone of which was laid in Sept. 1837, and a chapel attached to which, dedicated to Our Blessed Lady of the Rosary, was opened Oct. 6th, 1841. A grammar school was founded in the 5th of Elizabeth, 1573, by Sir William Devereux of Merevale, Thomas Fulner, and Amyas Hyll, and a charter of incorporation was obtained: in 1749 the school-
109

room was divided, and the grammar school is now conducted in one part, and an endowed English school in the other. The endowment amounts to £302 per annum, of which the master has £150 and the English master £50, and £60 are appropriated for repairs, contingent expenses, and a building fund; the residue being paid in augmentation of the head master's salary. Upwards of forty scholars are at present on the foundation. The poor law union of Atherstone comprises nine parishes and places in the county of Warwick, and five in the county of Leicester, and contains a population of 10,866. Drayton, the poet, and one of the earliest topographical writers, was, according to Dugdale, born here.

ATHERSTONE-UPON-STOUR, a parish, in the union of STRATFORD-UPON-AVON, Kington division of the hundred of KINGTON, S. division of the county of WARWICK, 3 miles (S.) from Stratford; containing the village of Ailston, 93 inhabitants. The parish is nearly surrounded by the county of Gloucester; it consists of 1030 acres, and is intersected by the river Stour and the road from Stratford to Shipston. The living is a rectory, valued in the king's books at £13. 1. 8.; patron and incumbent, the Rev. Thomas Cox, D.D. The tithes have been commuted for £253.

ATHERTON, a chapelry, in the parish and union of LEIGH, hundred of WEST DERBY, S. division of the county of LANCASTER, 12 miles (W. by N.) from Manchester, and on the road from Leigh to Bolton; containing, with the village of Chowbent, 4475 inhabitants. This place was held of the barons of Warrington by Robert de Atherton, in the reign of John; and in this knightly family the manor descended through many generations, successively allied to the Byrons, Warrens, Ashtons, Butlers, Catterals, Conyers, Irelands, and Bolds: by the marriage of the late Lord Lilford with the heiress of Atherton, the manor came to his lordship's family. The chapelry comprises 2323a. 3r. 35p., and abounds with valuable stone and extensive coalmines. Two-thirds of the population are employed in the cotton and silk manufactures, in the working of the collieries, and in making nails; and the remaining third in agricultural pursuits. A cattle-fair is held in January, and holiday fairs on the 29th of June and 24th of August. Atherton Hall, a superb edifice, built by the Atherton family in the early part of the 18th century, at an expense of about £63,000, was taken down in 1825; Alder Ilouse, an ancient mansion of stone, of peculiar architecture, is the residence of Alfred Silvester, Esq. The village of Atherton includes that of Chowbent, the name of the latter being now in disuse. Petty-sessions are held every alternate Monday. The living, endowed about 1720 by Sir Richard Atherton, is a perpetual curacy, in the patronage of Lord Lilford, with a net income of £100: the tithes have been commuted for £118 per annum. The present chapel is dedicated to St. John the Baptist, and is a plain structure, built in 1810: the former edifice originally belonged to dissenters, and was consecrated in 1723, for the service of the Church, by Dr. Wilson, Bishop of Sodor and Man. There are places of worship for Unitarians and Baptists; and infants' and day schools, in connexion with the chapel, built in 1840.

ATLOW, a parish, in the hundred of APPLETREE, S. division of the county of DERBY, 5 miles (E. N. E.) from Ashbourn; containing 156 inhabitants. This is the *Etelaw* of Domesday book. The manor once belonged to Henry de Ferrars, and was held under him or his immediate heirs by the ancestor of the ancient family of Okeover. It lies north of the road from Ashbourn to Belper. The living is a perpetual curacy, in the gift of Mr. Okeover: the impropriate tithes have been commuted for £110. The church is a dilapidated structure, situated in the middle of a field. Near the village is a high hill, called "Magger's Bush," which affords an extensive prospect.

ATTENBOROUGH (ST. MARY), a parish, in the union of SHARDLOW, S. division of the wapentake of BROXTOW, N. division of the county of NOTTINGHAM, 6 miles (S. W.) from Nottingham; containing, with the township of Toton and the hamlet of Chilwell, 1036 inhabitants, of whom 124 are in the village of Attenborough. This parish, the surface of which is diversified with boldly swelling undulations, comprises about 2580 acres, whereof 1480 are in Chilwell and 1100 in Toton: the river Erewash passes through. The village has now the appèarance of a lonely and deserted place, but is said to have been formerly considerable; in a field near it is the stump of the town cross, called " St. Mary's Cross," the numerous dwellings around which have long since disappeared. It is supposed that the liability to floods from the Trent, caused the inhabitants to fix themselves in the drier locality of Chilwell. The living is a discharged vicarage, with the perpetual curacy of Bramcote annexed, valued in the king's books at £4. 15.; net income, £250; patròn and impropriator, George Saville Foljambe, Esq. The tithes of Attenborough have been commuted for £280, half payable to the trustees of the late Chesterfield school, and half to the vicar: the glebe consists of about 40 acres. The church is situated at Toton, and is a large edifice, with a nave, aisles, and chancel, and a tower (with five bells) surmounted by a handsome spire; the pillars of the nave and aisles are those of a former and probably yet larger structure. In 1688, Thomas Charlton, of Chilwell, bequeathed one pound yearly to the minister, on the condition of his preaching a sermon on the 5th of November, in relation to the events which took place on that day; and several small sums were left by different members of his family, and others, which are distributed annually to the poor. Attenborough is the birthplace of Henry Ireton, son-in-law of Cromwell, and lord deputy of Ireland in the time of the Commonwealth.

ATTERBY, a township, in the parish of BISHOP'S NORTON, union of CAISTOR, E. division of the wapentake of ASLACOE, parts of LINDSEY, county of LINCOLN, 10¼ miles (W. N. W.) from Market-Rasen; containing 142 inhabitants. The tithes were commuted for land in 1769.

ATTERCLIFFE, a chapelry, in the parish and union of SHEFFIELD, S. division of the wapentake of STAFFORTH and TICKHILL, W. riding of YORK, 1½ mile (N.E.) from Sheffield; containing 4156 inhabitants. This place is situated on the road from Sheffield to Worksop and Rotherham, and, together with the hamlet of Darnall, occupies a triangular area at the south-eastern extremity of the parish, bounded on the north by the river Don, and on the east by the small river Carbrook. The village is well built, and contains several handsome houses. The manufacture of steel is carried on extensively, and many of the inhabitants are employed in making anvils

110

and agricultural implements: at Royds Mills is a gold and silver refinery. The old chapel, at the eastern extremity of the village, was erected in 1629 by Stephen Bright and William Spencer, Esqs., and others of the principal inhabitants, who endowed it with £10 per annum; it is now only used for the performance of the funeral service. Christ church, the first stone of which was laid by the Duke of Norfolk, assisted by Earl Fitzwilliam, in 1822, was completed at an expense of £14,000, of which £11,700 were granted by the Parliamentary Commissioners, and consecrated in 1826; it is a handsome structure in the later English style, with a square embattled tower crowned with pinnacles. The living is a perpetual curacy, in the patronage of the Vicar of Sheffield. There are places of worship for Independents and Wesleyans.

ATTERTON, a hamlet, in the parish of WITHERLEY, union of ATHERSTONE, hundred of SPARKENHOE, S. division of the county of LEICESTER, 3¼ miles (E. by N.) from Atherstone; containing 84 inhabitants.

ATTINGTON, an extra-parochial liberty, in the hundred of THAME, county of OXFORD, 1 mile (E. by N.) from Tetsworth; containing 8 inhabitants. It comprises 434 acres of land.

ATTLEBOROUGH, a hamlet, in the parish and union of NUNEATON, Atherstone division of the hundred of HEMLINGFORD, N. division of WARWICKSHIRE, 1 mile (S. S. E.) from Nuneaton; containing 1095 inhabitants. This being part of the lordship of Nuneaton, was entirely possessed by the nuns of the convent of that name. The hamlet lies on the road from Nuneaton to Wolvey. A neat church in the later English style, with a tower and spire, has been lately completed, containing 511 sittings, of which 347 are free: it is dedicated to the Trinity; and the living is a perpetual curacy in the gift of the Vicar, with a net income of £120.

ATTLEBRIDGE (ST. ANDREW), a parish, in the union of ST. FAITH, hundred of TAVERHAM, E. division of NORFOLK, 8 miles (N. W.) from Norwich; containing 94 inhabitants. This parish, which is situated on the road from Norwich to Fakenham, comprises 1237a. 2r. 34p. The living is a discharged vicarage, united to the rectory of Alderford, and valued in the king's books at £4. 6. 10½.: the vicarial tithes have been commuted for £70, and there are 10 acres of glebe; the impropriate tithes have been commuted for £162. 18. The church is a handsome structure in the decorated English style, with a square embattled tower.

ATTLEBURGH, or ATTLEBOROUGH (ST. MARY), a market-town and parish, in the union of WAYLAND, hundred of SHROPHAM, W. division of NORFOLK, 15 miles (S. W. by W.) from Norwich, and 94 (N. E. by N.) from London; containing 1959 inhabitants. This place derives its name from *Atheling*, or Attlinge, a Saxon chieftain, by whom it is supposed to have been originally founded; and from a *burgh* or fortress, by which it was defended against the frequent incursions of the Danes. It was anciently the capital of Norfolk, and the residence of Offa and Edmund, kings of East Anglia; and was subsequently the seat of the Mortimer family, the site of whose baronial hall is still encompassed by a moat. In the reign of Richard II., Robert de Mortimer founded a collegiate establishment, in the church of the Holy Cross, for a warden and four secular priests; the revenue was estimated at £21. 16. 3., and, with the site, was granted to the Earl of Essex. The TOWN, of which a considerable portion was destroyed by fire in 1559, is at present of very inconsiderable extent, consisting principally of one long street ; it lies on the road from Norwich to Thetford, and has a station on the Norwich and Thetford railway, being about midway between those places. The market is chiefly for corn, and is on Thursday ; fairs are held on the Thursday before Easter and Whitsuntide, and on the 15th August. The powers of the county debt-court of Attleburgh, established in 1847, extend over the registration-districts of Guiltcross and Wayland. The former town comprised the two parishes of Attleburgh Major and Minor; the first a rectory, valued in the king's books at £19. 8. 9. ; and the second a vicarage, valued at £8. 2. 6.: they are now united, and the present parish comprises 5251a. 1r. 25p., of which 3955 acres are arable, and 1244 meadow and pasture. The livings constitute one rectory, in the patronage of the Rev. Sir E. B. Smyth, Bart. : the tithes have been commuted for £1500, and the glebe comprises 17 acres, with a handsome house. The church is a venerable cruciform structure in the decorated English style, with a square embattled tower rising from the centre, and a porch of elegant design ; it was repaired and beautified in 1844, at a cost of £1200. There are places of worship for Baptists and Wesleyans. The patron has allotted 24 acres of land to the poor, in small lots, for garden-ground ; 57a. 2r. were also assigned to them at the time of the inclosure, and 20 acres for the repairs of the church. A house called the College-house occupies the site of the ancient college. There are two springs in the parish, slightly chalybeate.

ATWICK (St. LAWRENCE), a parish, in the union of SKIRLAUGH, N. division of the wapentake of HOLDERNESS, E. riding of YORK, 2¼ miles (N. N. W.) from Hornsea ; containing 300 inhabitants. The parish is bounded on the east by the German Ocean, and comprises, with the manors of Arram and Skirlington, about 2186 acres, the soil of which is a stiff, but very fertile, clay. The surface begins to rise here in gentle undulations, and prepares the traveller for the hill and dale of the Wolds ; the view towards Bridlington-Quay and Flamborough Head is beautiful. The village is situated near the sea, from whose encroachments it has occasionally sustained considerable damage ; and it appears from measurements repeated for a series of years, that the sea gains from the land an average of three yards annually. The LIVING is a discharged vicarage, valued in the king's books at £4. 7. 11., and in the patronage of the Lord Chancellor, with a net income of £149 ; impropriator, B. O. Mitford, Esq. The tithes for the township of Atwick were commuted for 26a. 3r. of land and a money payment of £15, under an act in 1769; and under the recent act, the remaining tithes have been commuted for a rent-charge of £210. 11., of which £107 for the hamlet of Arram are not payable when the land is in the hands of the owner, it having been the property of the dissolved abbey of Meaux. The church formerly belonged to the priory of St. Mary, Bridlington, to which it was granted by the family of de Roos in the 12th century ; it is situated at the extreme end of the village, upon rather elevated ground, and consists of a nave and chancel, with a small square embattled tower of brick, which last was built in 1829. A school has an endowment of £35 per annum. In the centre of the village

stands a rude stone cross of great antiquity, with a Latin inscription upon its base, now nearly defaced ; and near the church is ground bearing evidence of having been the site of a religious house ; also a series of fish-ponds, and a "holy well," the water of which is inexhaustible, and of the greatest purity.

ATWORTH, a tything and chapelry, in the parish of GREAT BRADFORD, union and hundred of BRADFORD, Westbury and N. divisions and Trowbridge and Bradford sub-divisions of WILTS, 4 miles (N. E. by N.) from Bradford ; the tything containing 824 inhabitants. The chapel, with the exception of the tower, was rebuilt a few years since : there is a second chapel at South Wraxall. The living is a perpetual curacy ; income, £195 ; patrons, the Dean and Chapter of Bristol.

AUBORN (St. PETER), a parish, in the Lower division of the wapentake of BOOTHBY-GRAFFO, parts of KESTEVEN, union and county of LINCOLN, 6¼ miles (S. W. by S.) from Lincoln ; containing, with a part of the township of Haddington, 436 inhabitants. The living is a discharged vicarage, valued in the king's books at £7. 13. 10.; net income, £54 ; patron, the Rev. H. Neville. There is a place of worship for Wesleyans.

AUBURN, county of YORK.—See FRAISTHORPE.

AUCKLAND, BISHOP, a market-town and chapelry, in the parish of St. ANDREW, union of AUCKLAND, N. W. division of DARLINGTON ward, S. division of the county of DURHAM, 10½ miles (S. W.) from Durham, and 252 (N. by W.) from London ; containing 3776 inhabitants. This place, in common with others in the immediate vicinity, derives its name from the great number of oak-trees that formerly grew in the neighbourhood ; and its prefix from a palace, in which the bishops of the diocese, who are lords of the manor, occasionally reside. The town, which is in the centre of the parish, is pleasantly situated on a considerable eminence, near the confluence of the rivers Gaunless and Wear, in a fertile district abounding with coal and limestone, and remarkable for the salubrity of the air. The streets are badly payed ; the houses are well built, and the inhabitants are plentifully supplied with water. The palace, originally erected in the reign of Edward I. by Bishop Anthony Beck, and subsequently enlarged, was much injured by Sir Arthur Haslerigg, to whom it was sold by the Parliamentary Commissioners ; but after the Restoration it was repaired by Bishop Cosin : it stands in a beautiful park to the north-east of the town, and is a spacious structure, surrounded with plantations and pleasure-grounds watered by the Gaunless. The chapel attached to the palace is a fine edifice in the early and decorated styles, built originally by Bishop Beck, and repaired about 1660 by Bishop Cosin, whose remains are deposited in it. The market is on Thursday ; the fairs are in March and October, but on no fixed day. The Bishop-Auckland and Weardale railway, constructed chiefly for the conveyance of coal, and a few passengers, branches off from the Stockton and Darlington railway at Shildon, and passes near the town ; it takes a course of eight miles, and terminates by a short branch in the township of Crook. It passes over numerous embankments and bridges in its progress, and through several tunnels, and various roads are carried over it : the embankment at Holdforth alone cost £11,000, and the line was completed at an expense of £96,000, of which £72,000 were raised in original shares, and the remainder by loan. In 1846 an act was passed for a line to the Lancaster and Carlisle railway in Westmorland. The county magistrates hold petty-sessions monthly; and courts leet and baron are held annually, at the former of which a bailiff and other officers are appointed. The powers of the county debt-court of Bishop-Auckland, established in 1847, extend over the registration-district of Auckland.

The chapel, dedicated to St. Anne, is small, and very inadequate to the purposes for which it was designed. There are places of worship for the Society of Friends, Independents, and Wesleyans. The free grammar school was founded by James I., and is endowed with land, a house and garden for the master, and a rent-charge, producing an income of about £60 per annum ; the management is vested in twelve governors, who are a body corporate, and have a common seal : the school-room, over which is St. Anne's chapel, was rebuilt in 1783. A school for twenty boys was founded by Mr. Walton, in 1772. A central school on Dr. Bell's system, for 200 children, was established in 1810, by Bishop Barrington, who also founded a school of industry for girls, in 1815. Almshouses for two men and two women were founded and endowed by Bishop Cosin, in the reign of Charles II.; the inmates are clothed every third year, and receive an allowance of about £15 per annum each.

AUCKLAND, ST. ANDREW, a parish, in the union of AUCKLAND, partly in the S. E., but chiefly in the N. W., division of DARLINGTON ward, S. division of the county of DURHAM. In the S. E. division are the townships of Byers-Green, Coundon-Grange, Eldon, Middlestone,Midridge, Midridge-Grange, Old-Park,West-erton, and Windleston ; while the N. W. division includes the market-town of Bishop-Auckland, the cha-pelries of St. Helen Auckland and Hamsterley, and the townships of St. Andrew, West Auckland, North and South Bedburn, Barony, Binchester, Coundon, Even-wood, Hunwick with Helmington, Lynesack with Softley, Newfield, Newton-Cap, Pollard's Lands, Shildon, and East Thickley ; the whole containing 19,100 inhabitants, of whom 1367 are in the township of St. Andrew, 1 mile (S.) from Bishop-Auckland. This extensive parish com-prises by computation 11,195 acres, and contains six considerable villages ; it abounds with coal and limestone, and its surface is highly varied. The Stockton and Darlington railroad passes through it ; and in 1837 an act was obtained for constructing the Bishop-Auckland and Weardale railway, which branches from the Stockton and Darlington at Shildon, and passes within a quarter of a mile of Bishop-Auckland, which see.

The LIVING is a perpetual curacy, with the chapelry of St. Anne ; net income, about £550, nearly half of which arises from a bequest by Bishop Barrington; patron, the Bishop of Durham ; impropriators, the Land-owners of the parish. The tithes attached to the living have been commuted for £46. 10.; and there is a glebe valued at £117 per annum. The church, a spacious cruciform structure, was made collegiate for the secular canons ejected by Bishop Carileph from his cathedral of Durham, in 1082 ; and in 1292 was endowed by Bishop Beck for a dean and nine prebendaries: three or four additional prebends were founded by Bishop Langley, in 1428. At the Dissolution, the deanery was valued at £100. 7. 2., and the prebends at £79. 16. 8.:
112

the dean's house and some of the prebendal houses have been converted into residences for farmers. There are distinct incumbencies at Byers-Green, Coundon, Escomb, Etherley, Hamsterley, St. Helen's, and Shildon ; also places of worship for Independents, Ranters, the Society of Friends, and others. The union comprises 33 parishes and places, and contains a population of 21,979.

AUCKLAND, ST. HELEN, a chapelry, in the parish of ST. ANDREW, union of AUCKLAND, N. W. division of DARLINGTON ward, S. division of the county of DURHAM, 3 miles (S. S. W.) from Bishop-Auckland ; containing in the township of St. Helen (which constitutes only a small portion of the chapelry) 720 inhabitants. At the St. Helen's colliery, numerous ovens are employed in the manufacture of coke for the use of the engines on the Stockton and Darlington railway. Large quantities of coal are sent from the mines in the neighbourhood to be shipped at Stockton and Middlesborough on the Tees. The living is a perpetual curacy, valued in the king's books at £13. 9. 4., and in the gift of the Bishop of Durham ; net income, £120. The impropriate tithes, belonging to the landowners, have been commuted for £119. 1. 6., and those of the perpetual curate for £6.7.; there is a glebe of 23 acres.

AUCKLAND, WEST, a township, in the parish of ST. ANDREW, union of AUCKLAND, N. W. division of DARLINGTON ward, S. division of the county of DURHAM, 3½ miles (S. W. by S.) from Bishop-Auckland ; contain-ing 2310 inhabitants. This place is situated at the junc-tion of the high road from Durham to Barnard-Castle with that from Darlington to Wolsingham ; the river Gaunless winds in a devious course through the town-ship. There is a place of worship for Wesleyans ; and a free school, founded by Mrs. Margaret Hubback in 1798, is endowed with about £30 per annum, and con-ducted on the national plan. The place gives the title of Baron to the family of Eden, who formerly resided here : the estates now belong to Sir R. J. Eden, Bart.

AUDENSHAW, a division, in the union and parish of ASHTON-UNDER-LYNE, hundred of SALFORD, S. divi-sion of the county of LANCASTER, 5 miles (E. by S.) from Manchester ; comprising the villages of Auden-shaw, Hooleyhill, Littlemoss, North-street, Walkmill, Waterhouses, and Woodhouses ; and containing 5374 inhabitants. The name of this place, in ancient docu-ments written Aldwinshagh, is said to be derived from the Saxon Aldwin, an elder or chieftain, and Shagh, a wood. It is supposed to have belonged prior to the Conquest to some Saxon thane, whose residence was on or near the site of the present village, which exhibits appearances of earlier cultivation than the surrounding district, the latter consisting mostly of woods and mo-rasses. A small hamlet in the division derives its name of Danehead from its situation at the head of an extensive valley called "the Danes," probably from some battle which took place there between that people and the Saxons ; it is traversed by a stream which falls into the river Mersey.

The inhabitants are chiefly employed in the various branches of the hat manufacture, in silk and cotton weaving and spinning, and calico-printing. The Ashton and Oldham canals, and the Manchester and Sheffield railway, pass through the division ; and a large reservoir has been constructed here for supplying the town of Manchester with water. The village of Audenshaw is

AUDLEY (St. James), a parish, in the union of NEWCASTLE-UNDER-LYME, N. division of the hundred of PIREHILL, and of the county of STAFFORD, 5 miles (N. W.) from Newcastle, on the road to Nantwich; containing 4474 inhabitants, and consisting of the townships of Audley, Bignall-End, Eardley-End, Halmer-End, Knowl-End, Park-End, and Talk-o'-th'-Hill. This place was originally given by Hervey de Stafford to the barons of Aldeleigh, or Audley, who erected the baronial residence of Heyley Castle, commanding an extensive range of the surrounding country. The parish, which comprises about 11,000 acres, and is almost entirely appropriated to dairy-farming, abounds with excellent iron-stone and coal, the latter of which is sent in large quantities by the Trent and Mersey canal to Cheshire, and to other parts. The living is a discharged vicarage, valued in the king's books at £6. 13. 4.; patron, the Rev. Edward Gilbert: the vicarial tithes have been commuted for £430, and the impropriate, belonging to George Tollet, Esq., for £664. The church is in the early style of English architecture, with a decorated chancel, and an embattled tower crowned with pinnacles. At Talk-o'-th'-Hill is another church; and there are numerous places of worship for dissenters in the parish. The free grammar school, founded in 1622 by Edward Vernon, has an endowment in land producing £125. 18. per annum. Near the village are vestiges of an intrenchment; and on the western boundary of the parish are situated, on a lofty rock, the remains of the ancient and strong castle of Heyley, the ascent to which, on the south side, is more than 100 yards in height. About a mile from the church is a pellucid spring of water, always flowing. Audley gives the title of Baron to the family of Touchet.

AUGHTON, a chapelry, in the parish of HALTON, hundred of LONSDALE south of the Sands, N. division of the county of LANCASTER, 7 miles (N. E.) from Lancaster; containing 134 inhabitants. The lord of Halton exercises the manorial rights of Aughton. The Oliverian survey, made in June, 1650, recommends that Aughton should be added to Gressingham, owing to its distance from the parish church; but Robert Burton, in 1697, obviated this inconvenience by erecting and endowing a chapel and school here; and Mr. Lawson subsequently enlarged the endowment by the bequest of Lower Highfield. The chapelry is beautifully situated on the banks of the river Lune, which bounds it on the north; the scenery is mountainous, and the views extensive. There is stone for building purposes. The living is a perpetual curacy; net income, £110, with a house; patron, the Rector of Halton. The chapel, dedicated to St. George, is situated on a hill.

AUGHTON (St. Michael), a parish, in the union of ORMSKIRK, hundred of WEST DERBY, S. division of the county of LANCASTER, 2 miles (S. W.) from Ormskirk, on the road to Liverpool; containing 1560 inhabitants. "Achetun" was held before the Conquest by Uctred, the Saxon proprietor of Dalton and Skelmersdale; the manor, or parts of it, subsequently came to the families of Acton or Aughton, Bradshagh, and Scarisbrick, and more recently to the families of Hesketh, Molyneux, and Plumbe, which last assumed in 1824, in addition to their own, the arms and name of Tempest. The PARISH comprises 3943a. 14p. of titheable land, whereof 1534 acres are arable, 900 meadow, 1492 pas-

Q

ture, 9 wood, and 8 glebe: Aughton Moss, which contains several hundred acres, not titheable, was inclosed in 1814. From the elevated situation of the parish, principally upon an extended eminence declining from Ormskirk to the south of Aughton church, it commands an extensive view of the country around. The *Sudell*, a tributary of the Alt, has its source here, dividing Aughton and Lydiate, and joining the Alt below the latter; a rivulet named *Meer*'brook, also, separates the parish from the town of Ormskirk. The Liverpool, Ormskirk, and Preston railway passes through. The estate of *Moor Hall*, the property of John Rosson, Esq., was in the possession of the Stanleys, of Hooton, at a very remote period : in 1566, Peter Stanley, a younger branch of that family, rebuilt the hall in its present form, as stated in an inscription in old English raised letters over the porch. *Aughton Old Hall*, the ancient residence of the Aughtons, is now a farmhouse : *New Hall*, built in the 17th century, became the property of the Plumbe family. The LIVING is a rectory, valued in the king's books at £14. 15. 5.; net income, £800, with a house : patron, John Plumbe Tempest, Esq. A portion of the tithes was commuted under the inclosure act for 85 acres of land, which, with the glebe, are of the annual value of £105. The church is an ancient structure, with a steeple in the centre. The Roman Catholic chapel here, built in 1767, and enlarged in 1823, is dedicated to the Blessed Virgin, and has a small endowment. There were formerly distinct traces of an intrenchment on Aughton Common, raised during the time of the Commonwealth; but the inclosure and the plough have combined to obliterate this vestige of intestine war.

AUGHTON (*ALL SOULS*), a parish, partly in the union of HOWDEN, and partly in that of POCKLINGTON, Holme-Beacon division of the wapentake of HARTHILL, E. riding of YORK; containing, with the chapelry of East Cottingwith and the township of Laytham, 634 inhabitants, of whom 217 are in the township of Aughton, 8½ miles (N. N. W.) from Howden. The parish is situated on the left bank of the navigable river Derwent, and presents a tolerably level surface. The living is a discharged vicarage, valued in the king's books at £4; net income, £90, with a glebe-house erected in 1839 by the Rev. John Earle, incumbent; patron, James Fletcher, Esq. The church, the chancel of which was rebuilt in 1839, has a low embattled tower, built by Christopher, son of the unfortunate Robert Aske who was beheaded at York in the reign of Henry VIII., 1537, as a principal in the insurrection called the "Pilgrimage of Grace," occasioned by the suppression of the monasteries. On the chancel floor is a fine brass slab, on which are graven the effigies of Richard Aske and his lady, who died in the fifteenth century. Near the east bank of the river Derwent the moats and trenches of an ancient castle are still visible; and in the vicinity of the church is a large mound of earth, the site of the castellated mansion of the Aske family.

AUGHTON, a township, in the parish of ASTON, union of ROTHERHAM, S. division of the wapentake of STRAFFORTH and TICKHILL, W. riding of YORK, 8 miles (E.) from Sheffield; containing 108 inhabitants. This place, called in Domesday book Actone, Hactone, and Hacstone, was formerly the residence of the family of West, of whom was Sir William West, a soldier in the army of Henry VIII., and who had, in reward for his

114

services, beneficial grants of abbey lands: the family resided here till the latter end of the reign of Elizabeth. The township is situated on the Rotherham and Mansfield road, and separated from the county of Derby by the river Rother; the surface is varied : coal is found, and there is a mine at present in operation. The Midland railway passes through the township. There are places of worship for Independents and Wesleyans.

AUKBOROUGH (*ST. JOHN THE BAPTIST*), a parish, in the union of GLANDFORD-BRIGG, N. division of the wapentake of MANLEY, parts of LINDSEY, county of LINCOLN, 10½ miles (W.) from Barton-upon-Humber; containing, with the hamlet of Walcot, 528 inhabitants. The living is a discharged vicarage, valued in the king's books at £10; net income, £209; patrons, the Bishop of Lincoln, and the family of Constable. The vicarial tithes of Aukborough have been commuted for £12, and the incumbent has a glebe of 53 acres. There is a place of worship for Wesleyans; also a free school endowed with £16. 13. per annum. The place is thought by Dr. Stukeley to have been the *Arquis* of the geographer of Ravennas.

AUKLEY, a township, in the parish of FINNINGLEY, union of DONCASTER, partly in the Hatfield division of the wapentake of BASSETLAW, N. division of the county of NOTTINGHAM, and partly in the soke of DONCASTER, W. riding of the county of YORK, 5¼ miles (N.) from Bawtry; containing 418 inhabitants. This township comprises about 2391 acres, of which 827 are in the Nottinghamshire portion. In 1838, a chapel of ease was erected at a cost of £700, containing 250 sittings; and there is a place of worship for Wesleyans.

AULT-HUCKNALL, a parish, in the union of MANSFIELD, hundred of SCARSDALE, N. division of the county of DERBY, 5½ miles (N. W. by W.) from Mansfield; containing, with the hamlets of Rowthorne and Stainsby, 678 inhabitants. It comprises by measurement 4285 acres, the soil of which is two-thirds sandstone, and one-third magnesian limestone; and forms a fine agricultural district. The manor of HARDWICKE, lies on the south side of the parish, and on the border of Nottinghamshire, from which it is separated by the river Meden or Mayden. It was granted by King John, in 1203, to Andrew de Beauchamp; the Hardwickes possessed it for six generations; and Elizabeth, daughter of John Hardwicke, Esq., brought it to Sir William Cavendish, from whom it descended to its now noble possessor, the Duke of Devonshire.

The present HALL of Hardwicke was built by the Countess of Shrewsbury in the reign of Elizabeth; its situation is exceedingly picturesque and beautiful, standing in a fine park containing 621 acres of land, embellished with venerable oaks of most gigantic size. It is of stone, with a parapet of open work at the top, and at each extremity a lofty tower. The state apartments are very magnificent; several of the rooms are hung with tapestry of exquisite workmanship, particularly the audience hall, where is represented the story of Ulysses. The gallery is about 170 feet long and 26 wide, extending the whole length of the eastern side of the house, and hung with tapestry, on a part of which is the date 1478 : it is probable that this, as well as many articles of the furniture, celebrated for its antique character, was removed from the old Hall, or from Chatsworth when that splendid mansion was being rebuilt. Among other excellent pictures, are portraits of Elizabeth, Lady Jane Grey, Sir Thomas More, Cardinal Pole, Bishop Gardiner, the first earl of Devonshire, and Thomas Hobbes. The ancient Hall, standing near the mansion, appears to have been a very fine structure, and, from its style of architecture, could not have been built any great length of time before the present edifice. The LIVING of the parish is a discharged vicarage, valued in the king's books at £6. 0. 5.; patron and impropriator, the Duke of Devonshire. The vicarial tithes have been commuted for £105, and there are more than 27 acres of glebe; the impropriate tithes have been commuted for £34. At Hardwicke is a school, towards the support of which Thomas Whitehead, in 1729, bequeathed a house and land producing £23. 15. per annum; it is also endowed with property in the parish of Edensor.

AULTON, county of DERBY.—See ALLTON.

AUNSBY (ST. THOMAS à BECKET), a parish, in the union of SLEAFORD, wapentake of ASHWARDHURN, parts of KESTEVEN, county of LINCOLN, 5 miles (N. W. by W.) from Falkingham; containing 117 inhabitants. It is situated on the road from Lincoln to London, and comprises 1089 acres. The living is a rectory, valued in the king's books at £6. 0. 7½., and in the patronage of J. A. Houblon, Esq.: the tithes have been commuted for £249, and there are about 11 acres of glebe, and a glebe-house. The church, which is in the early English style, is a small edifice, having in the windows some remains of beautifully stained glass: the font also has some remarkable ornaments.

AUST, a chapelry, in the parish of HENBURY, union of THORNBURY, Upper division of the hundred of HENBURY, W. division of the county of GLOUCESTER, 4¼ miles (W. S. W.) from Thornbury; containing 191 inhabitants. This place derived its name, anciently Austre Clive, signifying "the southern cliffs," from its situation on the south bank of the Severn, among bold and lofty cliffs projecting into the river, which is here two miles in breadth. About half a mile below the village, which is surrounded by salt marshes, and immediately opposite to the estuary formed by the junction of the Severn and the Wye, is the ferry called the Old Passage, supposed to have been the Vectis of the Romans. Alabaster is procured in great quantities; and those rare minerals, the sulphate and carbonate of strontian, are found in the cliffs which line the banks of the Severn. The chapel is in the ancient English style. The place is distinguished as having been the residence of Wycliffe.

AUSTELL, ST. (THE HOLY TRINITY), a market-town, parish, and the head of a union, in the E. division of the hundred of POWDER, and of the county of CORNWALL, 34 miles (S. W.) from Launceston, and 252 (W. S. W.) from London; containing 10,320 inhabitants. This place was in the reign of Henry VIII. an obscure village, and first rose into importance from its vicinity to Polgooth and other considerable mines. In the civil war, part of the army under the Earl of Essex was quartered here; and the town was taken by Charles I. a short time prior to the capitulation of the parliamentarians near Lostwithiel, in 1644. In 1760 the great road from Plymouth to the Land's End was brought through the place, which is now a considerable thoroughfare. The TOWN is pleasantly situated in a
115.

well-cultivated district, on the south side of a hill sloping gradually to a small stream; the streets are paved, and lighted with gas, and the inhabitants are well supplied with water. The trade principally consists of the produce of the numerous mines of tin and copper, and in china-stone and clay of a very superior quality, which are found here in great abundance; the manufacture of coarse woollen cloth is also carried on to a small extent. The mines in the vicinity are exceedingly productive, and, from the improved manner of working them, promise continued prosperity to the town, the population of which has been trebled within the last twenty years. The parish comprises 8678 acres, of which 3121 are common or waste: freestone of excellent quality abounds; and near the harbour of Pentewan is a very extensive quarry, from which have been raised materials for the erection of many churches and mansions in the county. Several harbours have been formed in different parts. Many vessels are engaged in the importation of coal from Wales, for the use of the mines, and in the exportation of copper-ore for smelting, and of china-stone and clay to the different potteries and for the use of linen-bleachers. The principal part of the grain tin produced in Cornwall is obtained here, and blowing-houses for melting it have been erected near the town. A considerable pilchard fishery is also carried on, in which many boats, fitted out from the different harbours, are employed. The market, which is considerable for corn and provisions, is on Friday; and there are fairs on the Thursday next after Palm-Sunday, the Thursday after Whit-Sunday, the nearest Friday to July 23rd, and on Nov. 30th. In 1842 an act was obtained for providing a new market-place, and regulating the fairs. The town is within the jurisdiction of the county magistrates, by whom constables and other officers are appointed; and the Blackmore, the most considerable of the stannary courts, is held here. The powers of the county debt-court of St. Austell, established in 1847, extend over the whole of the registration-district of St. Austell.

The LIVING is a vicarage, valued in the king's books at £21, and in the patronage of the Crown; impropriators, Miss Rashleigh, and J. B. Tremayne, Esq. The tithes produce £537. 16., and the glebe comprises about an acre, with a large garden. The church combines various styles of English architecture, and has a very handsome tower richly ornamented with sculpture. Two church districts, named respectively Charlestown and Treverbyn, were endowed in 1846 by the Ecclesiastical Commission: each of the livings is in the alternate gift of the Crown and the Bishop of Exeter. There are places of worship for Baptists, Bryanites, Calvinists, the Society of Friends, Primitive and Wesleyan Methodists, Warrenites, and Plymouth Brethren. The poor law union of St. Austell comprises fifteen parishes and places, and contains a population of 31,417. At Menacuddle and Towan, in the parish, are baptismal wells, over which are ancient buildings in the early English style, covered with arched roofs of granite. In one of the celebrated tin stream-works of Pentewan, the bones of men, of oxen of enormous size, of a whale, and of animals now unknown, have been found.

AUSTERFIELD, a chapelry, in the parish of BLYTHE, union of DONCASTER, N. division of the wapentake of STRAFFORTH and TICKHILL, W. riding of YORK, 1¼
Q 2

mile (N. N. E.) from Bawtry; containing 314 inhabitants. This place is in Domesday book called Oustrefield, and derives its name probably from some old form of the cardinal point of the compass, east; though the name is said by some·to be derived from the Roman general Ostorius, who was defeated here by the Britons. It was formerly the property, in succession, of the families of Busli, Vipont, De Spenser, and Neville, from whom it passed to the crown; and has since descended, with Bawtry, to the present owner. The township comprises 2710 acres, including the hamlet of Brancroft and Finningley Park. The small tithes of the common were commuted for land in 1765.

AUSTERSON, a township, in the parish of ACTON, union and hundred of NANTWICH, S. division of the county of CHESTER; containing 55 inhabitants. It comprises 699 acres, of a clayey soil. The vicarial tithes have been commuted for £20. 3. 5., and the impropriate £91. 12.

AUSTHORPE, a township, in the parishes of WHITKIRK and GARFORTH, Lower division of the wapentake of SKYRACK, W. riding of YORK, 3½ miles (E.) from Leeds; containing 173 inhabitants. It is situated near the railway and turnpike-road from Leeds to Selby. The impropriate tithes have been commuted for £150. 6., payable to Trinity College, Cambridge, and the vicarial for £6. 19.; there is a glebe of about 2½ acres. John Smeaton, distinguished as a civil engineer, and who rebuilt the Eddystone lighthouse, was born here in the year 1724.

AUSTHWAITE, with BIRKER.—See BIRKER.

AUSTONLEY, a township, in the ecclesiastical district of HOLME-BRIDGE, parish of ALMONDBURY, union of HUDDERSFIELD, Upper division of the wapentake of AGBRIGG, W. riding of YORK, 7 miles (S. S. W.) from Huddersfield; containing 1940 inhabitants, mostly engaged in the manufacture of woollen cloth, for which there are numerous mills. The township comprises about 1760 acres, and consists of a deep valley, and large tracts of mountain and moor.

AUSTREY (ST. NICHOLAS), a parish, in the union of TAMWORTH, Tamworth division of the hundred of HEMLINGFORD, N. division of the county of WARWICK, 6½ miles (N.) from Atherstone; containing 479 inhabitants. The parish is situated in the northern part of the county, on the border of Leicestershire, which bounds it on the east; and consists of 2080 acres. The living is a vicarage, valued in the king's books at £8, and in the patronage of the Crown; net income, £162. The church was thoroughly repaired and the chancel rebuilt in 1845, at a cost of £2000. A school is endowed with the interest of £150, bequeathed by Miss Toon, and is also supported partly by the trustees of a charity for apprenticing boys and other purposes, and partly by subscription.

AUSTWICK, a township, in the parish of CLAPHAM, union of SETTLE, W. division of the wapentake of STAINCLIFFE and EWCROSS, W. riding of YORK, 4 miles (N. W.) from Settle; containing 599 inhabitants.· This place, in the Domesday survey "Oustewic," includes the hamlet of Wharfe, and part of that of Feizor. It is situated beneath the shelter of a rocky and precipitous projection of the Ingleborough mountain; and comprises by computation 5400 acres, a considerable portion of which is freehold, and leasehold on long leases; the
116

lands are chiefly in pasture. The population is partly employed in the weaving of cotton. The village is neatly built; a fair for cattle is held in it on the Thursday before Whitsuntide, and is generally well attended. A chapel was erected in 1840, at the expense of Charles Ingleby, Esq., and his sister, the late Miss E. A. Ingleby; the living is held with the vicarage of Clapham.

AUTHORPE (ST. MARGARET), a parish, in the union of LOUTH, Wold division of the hundred of LOUTH-ESKE, parts of LINDSEY, county of LINCOLN, 6¼ miles (N. W.) from Alford; containing 117 inhabitants. It comprises 921a. 1r. 13p.; the substratum is a chalk rock of good quality, which is burnt into lime. The living is a discharged rectory, valued in the king's books at £5. 13. 4., and in the patronage of Robert Vyner, Esq.: the tithes have been commuted for £158, and there are 29 acres of glebe. The church is an ancient structure. There is a place of worship for Wesleyans.

AVEBURY (ST. JAMES), a parish, in the union of MARLBOROUGH, hundred of SELKLEY, Marlborough and Ramsbury, and N. divisions of WILTS, 6¼ miles (W. by S.) from Marlborough; containing, with the tythings of Beckhampton and Kennet, 751 inhabitants. This parish, in which the river Kennet has its source, comprises about 4641 acres; the soil is a light earth resting on chalk, and the surface is undulated. The village is built on a portion of the area anciently occupied by a stupendous monument called Abury, supposed to have been constructed by the Britons, for the purposes of religious worship or national assemblies. It consisted of an extensive ditch and rampart, including double circles of large unhewn stones, many of which have been broken, and used as materials for building the houses in the village, and for other purposes. In the vicinity are several barrows, and among them the very large and remarkable one, close to the turnpike-road, called Silbury hill, which covers an area of five acres and thirty-four perches, and exceeds in dimensions every similar work in Great Britain, being 2027 feet in circumference at the base, and 120 at the summit; its sloping height is 316 feet, and its perpendicular height 170 feet. Within a short distance of this are remarkable stones termed the Grey Wethers, and about a mile north of the village is a cromlech. The living is a discharged vicarage, to which that of Winterbourne-Monkton was united in 1747, valued in the king's books at £9; net income, £178; patron, the Crown; impropriators, the family of Hopkins. The glebe consists of 16 acres. The church is of Norman architecture. An alien priory, dependent on the Benedictine abbey of Bocherville in Normandy, was founded here in the reign of Henry I. Robert of Avebury, who wrote a history of Edward III., is supposed to have been a native of the place.

AVELEY (ST. MICHAEL), a parish, and formerly a market-town, in the union of ORSETT, hundred of CHAFFORD, S. division of ESSEX, 1¾ mile (N. E.) from Purfleet, and 7 miles (S. S. E.) from Romford; containing 849 inhabitants. This parish, which comprises by computation 2615 acres, is separated from that of West Thurrock by the creek Marditch. The village, though now small, was once of some importance. The living is a discharged vicarage, valued in the king's books at £14. 10. 5.; patron, the Bishop of London; appropriators, the Dean and Chapter of St. Paul's. The great tithes have been commuted for £453. 15., and the vicarial for £327 ; the appropriate glebe consists of 30 acres, and there is one acre of vicarial glebe. The church is an ancient edifice, with a square tower of flint and stone, formerly surmounted by a lofty spire, which was blown down in 1703.

AVENBURY (St. Mary), a parish, in the union of BROMYARD, hundred of BROXASH, county of HEREFORD, 1½ mile (S. E.) from Bromyard ; containing 382 inhabitants. The parish is intersected by the river Frome, and also by the road from Bromyard to Ledbury, and comprises 3178 acres, including about 200 acres of hop grounds ; a small portion of limestone is found within its limits. The living is a vicarage, valued in the king's books at £7. 8. 9.; net income, £80 ; patron, the Crown ; impropriator, E. Higginson, Esq., whose tithes have been commuted for £422. 15., and who has a glebe of 60½ acres. The church and its large endowments were anciently attached to the abbey of Dore.

AVENING (St. Mary), a parish, in the union of STROUD, hundred of LONGTREE, E. division of the county of GLOUCESTER, 3 miles (N.) from Tetbury ; containing 2227 inhabitants. It is a polling-place for the eastern division of the county. The living is a rectory, valued in the king's books at £24, and in the patronage of the Heirs of the late Dr. Brooke: the tithes have been commuted for £760, and the glebe comprises 104 acres. The church is supposed to have been built by the abbess of Caen, in Normandy, to whom the manor belonged till the suppression of alien priories in the reign of Henry V. At Nailsworth is an incumbeney in the gift of Trustees. There is a place of worship for Particular Baptists ; also an endowed school in which six boys are clothed and educated.

AVERHAM (St. Michael), a parish, in the union of SOUTHWELL, N. division of the wapentake of THURGARTON, S. division of the county of NOTTINGHAM, 3¼ miles (W. by N.) from Newark ; containing, with the township of Staythorpe, 264 inhabitants. This place suffered from the hostilities of the contending parties during the reign of Charles I. At the time of the siege of Newark, many skirmishes occurred here ; and in 1644, the ancient manor-house, then belonging to Robert Sutton, Lord Lexington and Baron of Averham, and which had been the residence of the family from 1250, was destroyed. The parish comprises by measurement 2011 acres of fertile land; it is situated on the river Trent, and is intersected by the road from Newark to Southwell and Mansfield. The scenery is pleasing; and the village, with the church, which is on the margin of the river, forms a beautiful object in the landscape. The living is a rectory, with that of Kelham annexed in 1775, valued in the king's books at £20 ; patron, John Henry Manners Sutton, Esq. The tithes of Averham have been commuted for £787, and the glebe comprises nearly 58 acres. The church is a very ancient structure, in the early English style, with a square embattled tower. There are some remains of a Roman camp and a watch-tower on Michael Barrow hill.

AVETON-GIFFORD (St. Andrew), a parish, in the union of KINGSBRIDGE, hundred of ERMINGTON, Ermington and Plympton, and S. divisions of DEVON, 3¼ miles (S. E.) from Modbury ; containing 1057 inhabitants. It is situated on the river Avon, which is navigable to the English Channel, and over which is a

bridge, on the road leading to South Enford. The lords of the manor had formerly the power of inflicting capital punishment. The living is a rectory, valued in the king's books at £38. 1. 8.; net income, £586 ; patron, James Pitman, Esq. The church is an ancient structure, in the early style of English architecture, with later additions.

AVILLE, a hamlet, in the parish of DUNSTER, union of WILLITON, hundred of CARHAMPTON, W. division of SOMERSET; containing 17 inhabitants.

AVINGTON, a parish, in the union of HUNGERFORD, hundred of KINTBURY-EAGLE, county of BERKS, 2 miles (E. by S.) from Hungerford ; containing 93 inhabitants, and comprising 1143a. 1r. 3p. The living is a rectory, valued in the king's books at £8, and in the patronage of Sir Robert Burdett, Bart.; the tithes have been commuted for £299. 10., and the glebe consists of 6 acres. The church exhibits a curious specimen of Norman architecture, having an arch separating the chancel from the nave, with an obtuse depending point in the centre : the font, which is also of Norman design, is adorned with sculptured figures under arches.

AVINGTON (St. Mary), a parish, in the hundred of FAWLEY, Winchester and N. divisions of the county of SOUTHAMPTON, 4¼ miles (N. E. by E.) from Winchester ; containing 204 inhabitants. Avington House, a mansion of the Duke of Buckingham's, is situated near the bank of the river Itchen, in a demesne tastefully laid out : near the house are some fine old trees, and the sloping grounds behind it are embellished with thriving plantations. Charles II. while engaged in his projected palace at Winchester, spent much of his time here. The living is a rectory, valued in the king's books at £11. 11. 10½., and in the patronage of the Bishop of Winchester: the tithes have been commuted for £264. 13. 6., and the glebe comprises about 25 acres.

AVON, a tything, in the parish of SOPLEY, union and hundred of CHRISTCHURCH, Ringwood and S. divisions of HANTS ; containing 207 inhabitants. It is situated to the north of the village of Sopley, and near the east bank of the river Avon.

AVON, a hamlet, in the parish of STRATFORD-UNDER-THE-CASTLE, union of ALDERBURY, hundred of UNDERDITCH, Salisbury and Amesbury, and S. divisions of WILTS ; containing 23 inhabitants.

AVON, a tything, in the parish of CHRISTIAN-MALFORD, union and hundred of CHIPPENHAM, Chippenham and Calne, and N. divisions of WILTS, 3 miles (N. E.) from Chippenham ; containing 76 inhabitants. It lies south of the village of Christian-Malford, and near the Great Western railway and the river Avon, which latter flows hence to Chippenham.

AVON-DASSET.—See DASSET, AVON.

AWBRIDGE, a hamlet, in the parish of MITCHELMERSH, union of ROMSEY, hundred of BUDDLESGATE, Romsey and S. divisions of the county of SOUTHAMPTON ; containing 345 inhabitants.

AWLISCOMBE (St. Michael), a parish, in the union of HONITON, hundred of HEMYOCK, Honiton and N. divisions of DEVON, 2 miles (W. by N.) from Honiton ; containing 590 inhabitants. It comprises 2127 acres, of which 183 are common or waste, and is bounded by the river Otter on the south ; the surface is hilly, and the soil in general a rich productive marl, chiefly laid out in pasture. The living, which before the Dissolution was attached to the abbey at Tavistock, is a discharged vicarage, valued in the king's books at £12. 10. 10.; patron, the Duke of Bedford. The vicarial tithes have been commuted for £200, and £170 are paid to the trustees of Kelland's charity; the glebe consists of thirty acres, with a house. The church was erected about the time of Henry VI., and has a handsome stone screen, and a magnificent window finely ornamented: it is in excellent order, having been repaired in 1838, at an expense of nearly £500. The remains of a large encampment supposed to be Roman, and called Hembury fort, are in the parish.

AWNBY, with HOLYWELL.—See HOLYWELL.

AWRE (ST. *ANDREW*), a parish, in the union of WESTBURY, hundred of BLEDISLOE, W. division of the county of GLOUCESTER; containing, with Blakeney, a post-town in the parish, and the tythings of Awre, Bledisloe, Hagloe, and Etloe, 1277 inhabitants. This parish, which is intersected by the road from Gloucester to Chepstow, forms a promontory of the river Severn, and comprises 4082 acres by admeasurement; the port of Gatcomb, and a town named Pomerton'once included within it, do not now exist. The living is a vicarage, valued in the king's books at £10. 5., and in the patronage of the Haberdashers' Company, London : the impropriate tithes have been commuted for £400, and the vicarial for £450. 7.; the glebe consists of nearly 9 acres, and there is a glebe-house, recently built. Besides the parochial church, there is a chapel at Blakeney, where are also a Baptist chapel and a national school. In the register, it is recorded that Thomas Sternhold and John Hopkins, who collected the metrical version of the Psalms, resided in the parish.

AWSWORTH, a chapelry, in the parish of NUTHALL, S. division of the wapentake of BROXTOW, N. division of the county of NOTTINGHAM, 7½ miles (N. W. by W.) from Nottingham; containing 294 inhabitants. This place borders upon Derbyshire, and has a small village on the Nottingham canal. The living is a perpetual curacy; net income, £101; patron, the Rector : the incumbent resides in a neat house, built in 1843. The chapel was consecrated about 1760. A poor person from this chapelry is eligible to Ilkeston almshouse.

AXBRIDGE (ST. JOHN THE *BAPTIST*), a market-town and parish, having separate jurisdiction, and the head of a union, locally in the hundred of WINTERSTOKE, E. division of SOMERSET, 18 miles (S. by W.) from Bristol, and 130 (W. by S.) from London; containing 1045 inhabitants. This place, which derives its name from a bridge over the river Axe, was formerly the residence of some of the West Saxon monarchs, by whom it was invested with many privileges. The TOWN is of mean appearance, and indifferently paved, but amply supplied with water. The chief occupation of the poorer ·class of inhabitants was the knitting of stockings, but that trade was destroyed by the introduction of machinery, and the prosperity of the town declined until a fresh impulse was given to it by the drainage of the adjacent levels,

Corporation Seal.

in which Sir Richard Cholmondeley, who commanded the former, was slain. The TOWN, which is irregularly built, is pleasantly situated on the declivity of a hill, near the confluence of the rivers Axe and Yarty, over the first of which three bridges have been erected; it is paved, partially lighted, and amply supplied with water from several good springs. Races are held in August at Shute hill, three miles distant; and there are assemblies occasionally at the George hotel. The manufacture of carpets, which had been established for nearly a century, has been recently transferred to Wilton, and the only manufacture now carried on is that of tape. The parish produces stone of good quality for building, and for burning into lime. The market is on Saturday; and fairs are held on the first Tuesday after April 25th, the first Wednesday after June 24th, and the first Wednesday after Oct. 10th. Courts leet and baron are held annually by the lord of the manor, at the former of which constables and other officers are appointed. The powers of the county debt-court of Axminster, established in 1847, extend over the registration-district of Axminster, and two adjacent parishes.

The LIVING is a vicarage, with the livings of Kilmington and Membury annexed, valued in the king's books at £44. 6. 8.; net income, £975; patron, the Bishop of Exeter. The tithes have been commuted for £608 payable to the impropriators, and £608 payable to the vicar. The church is an ancient structure, of various styles; the entrance is under a fine Norman arch richly moulded; the interior is of the early English style, with later insertions: the pulpit and reading-desk are curiously carved. There are places of worship for Independents, Wesleyans, and Roman Catholics. The poor law union of Axminster comprises 11 parishes and places in the county of Devon, and 6 in that of Dorset; and contains a population of 20,585. About a mile south of the town, on the bank of the river Axe, are the remains of Newenham Abbey, consisting of the chapel, kitchen, and other parts; and at the distance of three miles, is an intrenchment called Musbury Castle.

AXMOUTH, a parish, in the union and hundred of AXMINSTER, Honiton and S. divisions of DEVON, 2¾ miles (S. by E.) from Colyton; containing, with the extra-parochial liberty of Horsedown, 645 inhabitants. This place, from the numerous traces of Roman occupation on the eastern bank of the river Axe, which intersects the parish, is supposed to have been the *Moridunum* of the Romans. The manor formerly belonged to the abbey of Sion, in Middlesex, and was given at the Dissolution by Henry VIII. to his queen Catharine Parr, as part of her dower; it reverted at her death to the crown, and was granted by Edward VI., in 1552, to Walter Erle. In the year 1839, a very remarkable and extensive subsidence of the surface took place about a mile and a half from the village, on the farms of Dowlands and Bindon, near the coast. The parish contains 3788a. 3r. 9p., the surface of which is beautifully diversified with hill and dale; the soil on the hills is chalky, well adapted for corn and the pasturage of sheep, while that in the valleys is a strong clay and marl, and is excellent dairy-land. Limestone and good building-stone are abundant. The village is situated near the mouth of the river Axe, which here falls into the English Channel; near its influx a commodious harbour has been constructed by Richard Hallet, Esq., which is accessible to
119

coasting-vessels of 200 tons' burthen. The living is a vicarage, endowed with one-third of the rectorial and vicarial tithes, and valued in the king's books at £22. 19. 2.; net income, £230; patron, J. H. Hallet, Esq., who, with others, is impropriator of the remainder of the tithes. The glebe comprises 30 acres. The church is a very ancient Norman structure, having two Saxon arches, and a fine specimen of the zig-zag arch in the north porch, now converted into a vestry-room. On an extra-parochial estate of about 200 acres called Roosdown, in the centre of the parish, is a chapel endowed with certain lands from Queen Anne's Bounty, but no duty has been performed in it within the memory of man. On Hawksdown hill is a large encampment supposed to be of Roman or Danish origin.

AYCLIFFE (ST. *Acca*), a parish, partly in the union of DARLINGTON, and partly in that of SEDGEFIELD, S. E. division of DARLINGTON ward, S. division of the county of DURHAM, 5 miles (N.) from Darlington; containing 1372 inhabitants, of whom 823 are in the township of Great Aycliffe. This place is supposed by Spelman to be the ancient "Aclea," where synods were held in 782 and 789; and two old Saxon crosses lately discovered in the churchyard, apparently warrant that conjecture. The parish is situated in the southern portion of the county, and comprises 10,716 acres of arable and pasture land in nearly equal portions, of which 2134 are within the township of Great Aycliffe; the soil generally is tolerably fertile, and the pastures are rich. Magnesian limestone of very pure quality is extensively quarried. The village is pleasantly situated on the road from Darlington to Durham, and on the west bank of the river Skerne, on which are a spinning-mill, and a mill for the manufacture of brown paper, but not now in use. The Clarence railway intersects the parish, and joins the Stockton and Darlington railway within a distance of three-quarters of a mile; the railway from York to Newcastle also skirts the village. The living is a vicarage, valued in the king's books at £20, and in the gift of the Dean and Chapter of Durham: the tithes have been commuted for £386. 1. 8. payable to the vicar, £165. 3. 8. to the Dean and Chapter, and £238. 7. 2. to other impropriators. The church is a very ancient structure, partly Norman, and partly in the early English style, and contains 500 sittings, of which 70 are free; the old porch has been restored, several new windows have been inserted, and the structure has been generally repaired.

AYCLIFFE, SCHOOL, a township, in the parish of HEIGHINGTON, union of DARLINGTON, S. E. division of DARLINGTON ward, S. division of the county of DURHAM, 7¼ miles (N. by W.) from Darlington; containing 25 inhabitants. This place, anciently called *Scholacley*, gave name to a resident family, of whom John de Scholacley died in 1350; it was a manor belonging to the Nevills, and was granted in 1411 by Lord Nevill to Robert De Binchester, to be held of the bishop by military service, suit at the head courts of the county, and a payment yearly at the Durham exchequer. The vicarial tithes have been commuted for £7 4. 16.

AYDON, a township, in the parish of CORBRIDGE, union of HEXHAM, E. division of TINDALE ward, S. division of NORTHUMBERLAND, 5½ miles (E. by N.) from Hexham; containing 83 inhabitants. The Reed family once occupied a good house and a small estate here; at present several families have land in the township. Lead-ore and coal exist, but in very small quantities. Several Roman relics have been found, including two urns, the effigy of a human being, &c.

AYDON-CASTLE, a township, in the parish of CORBRIDGE, union of HEXHAM, E. division of TINDALE ward, S. division of NORTHUMBERLAND, 6½ miles (E. by N.) from Hexham; containing 25 inhabitants. The castle which gives name to the township stands on the west side of a deep precipice, at whose foot runs a small rivulet; it appears to have been of great extent and strength, and was encompassed by an outer wall, in which the loop-holes still remain. The fortress was destroyed by the Scots during their inroad into England, which ended in their defeat at the battle of Nevill's Cross, in 1346.

AYLBURTON, a chapelry, in the parish of LIDNEY, union of CHEPSTOW, hundred of BLEDISLOE, W. division of the county of GLOUCESTER, 4½ miles (S. W. by W.) from Blakeney; containing 468 inhabitants. The chapel is dedicated to St. Mary.

AYLESBEAR (ST. CHRISTOPHER), a parish, in the union of ST. THOMAS, hundred of EAST BUDLEIGH, Woodbury and S. divisions of DEVON, 8 miles (E.) from Exeter; containing, with the tything of Newton-Poppleford, 982 inhabitants. It comprises by computation 2701 acres, of which 1033 are arable, 823 meadow and pasture, 92 orchard, 53 coppice, and 700 common or waste land; and is bounded on the east by the river Otter: the surface is hilly, and the soil divided between a stiff cold clay and light sand. There is a silk and ribbon manufactory. The living is a discharged vicarage, valued in the king's books at £16. 2. 4.; net income, £123; patron and incumbent, the Rev. H. W. Marker, to whom, and the rector of Huxham, the impropriation belongs. The glebe contains about 44 acres. There is a chapel of ease at Newton-Poppleford.

AYLESBURY (ST. MARY), a borough, market-town, parish, and the head of a union, in the hundred of AYLESBURY, county of BUCKINGHAM, of which it is the county town, 16½ miles (S. E. by S.) from Buckingham, and 38 (N. W. by W.) from London by way of Watford; containing, with the hamlet of Walton, 5429 inhabitants. This place appears to have been one of the strongholds of the ancient Britons, from whom it was taken in the year 571 by Cutwulph, brother of Ceawlin, King of the West Saxons; and to have had a castle of some importance, from which circumstance probably it derives its Saxon appellation *Aeglesburge*, of which its present name is only a slight modification. In the reign of the Conqueror it was a royal manor; and some lands here were granted by that monarch, upon the extraordinary tenure that the owners should provide straw for the monarch's bed, sweet herbs for his chamber, and two green geese and three eels for his table, whenever he should visit Aylesbury. In the civil war of the seventeenth century, the town was garrisoned for the parliament; but it does not appear to have had any further connexion with the transactions of that period.

The TOWN is pleasantly situated on a gentle eminence, in a fertile vale extending from Thame, in Oxfordshire, to Leighton in Bedfordshire; and is lighted with gas, and paved under the direction of a body called "the Incorporated Surveyors," who derive their funds from land and houses devised by John Bedford: the inha-

120

bitants are amply supplied with water. The houses are principally of brick, and the town has been greatly improved by the erection of some handsome private residences at the entrances into it from London and Buckingham. The only manufacture is that of bone lace, which is carried on upon a very limited scale. Ducklings and tame rabbits are bred in great numbers, for the supply of the London market. The market, which is amply supplied, is on Saturday; and fairs are held on the Friday after the 18th of Jan., the Saturday before Palm-Sunday, May 8th, June 14th, Sept. 25th, Oct. 12th: those in Jan., May, and Oct. not being chartered, are free from toll, and those in Sept. and Oct. are also for hiring servants. The river Thame, which separates the town from Walton, is not navigable; but a canal, beginning at the hamlet, communicates with the Grand Junction canal at Marsworth. The branch railway from this town, to the London and Birmingham line, was opened in June 1839, and is one continued level throughout, seven miles in length. There is a florists' and horticultural society, which from its foundation has been liberally supported, and has produced some fine shows of flowers and fruit.

The inhabitants received their first CHARTER from Queen Mary, in the year 1554, but the corporation soon lost their privileges, by neglecting to fill up vacancies: the town is now within the jurisdiction of the county magistrates, who hold petty-sessions daily; and constables and other officers are appointed at the court leet of the lord of the manor. The elective franchise was conferred also in 1554, and notwithstanding the loss of its charter, the borough has continued, since that time, to return two members to parliament. The right of election was originally vested in the corporation alone; and in the reign of Queen Anne, a disputed return for this place, in the cause of Ashby *v.* White, occasioned so serious a contest between the two houses, respecting the power of electors to bring actions against returning officers; for refusing to receive their votes, that the queen was obliged to prorogue the parliament, leaving the case undecided. After the loss of the charter, the two members were elected by the pot-wallopers; and in 1804, in a case of notorious bribery, an act was passed, extending the right of voting to the freeholders of the three hundreds of Aylesbury. The constables are the returning officers. The Lent assizes, and the quarter-sessions for the county, are held, and the knights of the shire elected, here: the powers of the county debt-court of Aylesbury, established in 1847, extend over the greater part of the registration-district of Aylesbury, and twelve adjacent parishes. The county hall, the magistrates' chamber, and offices of the clerk of the peace, form one range of brick building, of modern erection, with the county gaol and house of correction, which is well adapted to the classification of prisoners.

The LIVING is a discharged vicarage, valued in the king's books at £24. 18. 1.; net income, about £300; patron, the Bishop of Lincoln. The great tithes have been commuted for land: the vicar has a house and garden, with two plots of land in lieu of tithes. An afternoon lecture, long supported by subscription, was endowed by the Marquess of Buckingham, about the close of the last century, with a rent-charge of £18, in consideration of which the vicar has for many years given a third service. The church is an ancient cruciform structure in the decorated English style, with some earlier portions, and a low central tower; the western entrance is very rich: on the north side of the chancel is a chantry chapel, now used as a vestry-room, in which are still remaining some traces of Norman character; and on the south side is another chantry chapel, now belonging to the grammar school. From the number of Roman tiles still found in several parts of the building, it is probable that a tessellated pavement originally constituted the floor of the whole. At Walton is a church, the living of which is a perpetual curacy, in the gift of the Church-Patronage Society. There are places of worship for the Society of Friends, Independents, and Wesleyans, and one for Particular Baptists in the hamlet of Walton.

The *Free Grammar School* was founded by Sir Henry Lee, Knt., about the year 1611, and endowed with about £8 per annum, which was greatly augmented by Henry Phillips, Esq., who, by will in 1714, left £5000 in trust to be invested in land: the property consists of a manor and estate at Broughton-Abbots, in the parish of Bierton, and upwards of £1800 in the three per cent. consols, producing together an income of about £540. Thomas Hickman, in 1695, bequeathed land and houses (five of which are occupied as almshouses) now let for £73 per annum, which, after defraying the expenses of repairs and other small charges, is distributed among decayed tradesmen and tradesmen's widows not receiving parochial relief. William Harding, of Walton, by his will proved in 1719, devised certain lands and tenements now let for £289 per annum, by means of which about fourteen children are apprenticed annually, with premiums of £20 each; and there are also several charities for different purposes under the management of the churchwardens. A county infirmary, erected at the northern end of the town, chiefly through the exertions of John Lee, Esq., of Hartwell House, was opened for the reception of patients on the 23rd of October, 1833 ; it is a spacious building, consisting of a centre and two wings, the former of stone, and the latter of brick stuccoed in imitation of stone. The poor law union of Aylesbury comprises 40 parishes and places, and contains a population of 22,134. A monastery was founded here about the year 600, and dedicated to St. Osyth; and there were also two hospitals for lepers, dedicated respectively to St. John and St. Leonard, which had fallen into decay prior to the year 1360. A convent for Grey friars, the only one in the county, was established in 1387, by James, Earl of Ormond: its site was subsequently occupied by a mansion belonging to Sir John Baldwin, Knt., lord chief justice of the common pleas; but during the civil war the house sustained so much damage, that it has never since been inhabited as a seat. John Wilkes resided at Aylesbury for a long time, and for some years represented the borough in parliament. The place gives the titles of Earl and Marquess to the ancient family of Bruce.

AYLESBY (St. Lawrence), a parish, in the union of Caistor, wapentake of Bradley-Haverstoe, parts of Lindsey, county of Lincoln, 5 miles (W. by S.) from Great Grimsby; containing 201 inhabitants. This parish, which is intersected by the road from Grimsby to Brigg, comprises by computation 2000 acres ; there are several plantations, but the greater portion of the land is arable. The living is a perpetual curacy; net

income, £73; patron and incumbent, the Rev. T. T. Drake. The tithes have been commuted for £537. 6. 8., and there are 36 acres of impropriate glebe. The church is an ancient structure, with a tower, on the outside of which, near the summit, are two large elder-trees which bear fruit and are flourishing.

AYLESFORD (St. Peter), a town and parish, in the union of Malling, hundred of Larkfield, lathe of Aylesford, W. division of Kent, 3½ miles (N. N. W.) from Maidstone; containing 1344 inhabitants. This place was called *Saissenaighobail* by the Britons, in commemoration of their having here defeated the Saxons; and by the latter, after their settlement in the country, *Eaglesford*, of which the present name is a corruption. In the battle above mentioned, which took place in 455, Horsa, the brother of Hengist, on the side of the Saxons, and Catigern, the son of Vortigern, on the side of the Britons, were slain. In 893, Alfred defeated the Danes at Fenham, in the parish; and in 1016, Edmund Ironside, in a fierce encounter with those invaders, pursued them to this place with great slaughter, and drove them hence to Sheppy. In 1240, Ralph Frisburn, on his return from the Holy Land, founded a Carmelite monastery, under the patronage of Richard, Lord Grey, of Codnor : many parts of the building are entire, though the greater portion of the site is occupied by a mansion erected by Sir William Sedley, and now the residence of the Earl of Aylesford. The parish contains 4260a. 2r. 29p., of which 1721 acres are arable, 628 meadow and pasture, 1428 woodland, 152 hop plantation, 53 orchard, and about 196 common and waste: the surface is marked by numerous chalk hills. In the northern part the soil is various ; the southern part, which is often overflowed by the Medway, has a soil of loam and gravel: the substratum abounds with stone, which is quarried for building sea-walls and for the roads. The town is pleasantly situated on the north-east bank of the river, over which is an ancient stone bridge of six arches ; and has one principal street, on whose north side the ground rises abruptly to an elevation of 100 feet. A paper-mill, by the side of a small stream, is the only manufactory. A pleasure-fair is held on the 29th of June.

The living is a vicarage, valued in the king's books at £10 ; patrons and appropriators, the Dean and Chapter of Rochester. The rectorial tithes have been commuted for £630. 15., and the vicarial for £597. 11. ; the glebe contains 14 acres, with a house. The church is an ancient structure, and contains monuments to the memory of Sir Paul Rycaut, Sir John Colepepper, and Sir Caleb Banks. There is a place of worship for Wesleyans. An hospital, dedicated to the Holy Trinity, was founded in 1617, for a warden and six aged persons, by Sir William Sedley, partly in performance of the will of his brother John, dated in 1605, and partly of his own free gift; it is endowed with two farms in the parish of Frittenden, let for £135 per annum. Fragments of military weapons are frequently discovered here. At Horsted is a monument of upright stones, erected, as is supposed, to the memory of Horsa ; and three miles distant is another, called Kit's Cotty House, to the memory of Catigern. Sir Charles Sedley, a celebrated wit and poet in the reign of Charles II., was born at the Stoars, in the parish. Aylesford confers the title of Earl on the family of Finch.

R

AYLESTONE (ST. ANDREW), a parish, in the union of BLABY, partly in the hundred of GUTHLAXTON, and partly in that of SPARKENHOE, S. division of the county of LEICESTER, 2½ miles (S. by W.) from Leicester; containing, with the township of Glen Parva and the chapelry of Lubbesthorpe, 757 inhabitants. It is situated on the road to Lutterworth, and contains about 2700 acres; the Duke of Rutland is lord of the manor. The Union canal passes through the parish, and soon after joins the river Soar. The living is a rectory, valued in the king's books at £31. 8. 11½.; net income, £845; patron, the Duke of Rutland. The tithes were commuted for 350 acres of land, in 1767.

AYLMERTON (ST. JOHN THE BAPTIST), a parish, in the union of ERPINGHAM, hundred of NORTH ERPINGHAM, E. division of NORFOLK, 2¾ miles (W. S. W.) from Cromer; containing 289 inhabitants. It is intersected by the road from Cromer to Holt, and comprises 1581a. 8p., of which 916 acres are arable, 190 pasture and meadow, and 470 woodland and water; the views of the ocean from the high grounds are exceedingly fine. The living is a discharged rectory in medieties, with the livings of Felbrigg, Melton, and Runton united, valued together in the king's books at £6. 11.; net income, £370; patron, W. H. Windham, Esq. The tithes of Aylmerton have been commuted for £220, and the glebe consists of 41½ acres. The church is in the decorated and later English styles, with an embattled tower; in the interior is a handsome carved screen, and on the south side of the chancel a piscina and two stone stalls.

AYLSHAM (ST. MICHAEL), a market-town and parish, and the head of a union, in the hundred of SOUTH ERPINGHAM, E. division of NORFOLK, 12¼ miles (N. by W.) from Norwich, and 121 (N. E. by N.) from London; containing 2448 inhabitants. This place, which is situated on the high road from Norwich to Cromer, was during the reigns of Edward II. and III. the chief seat in the county for the manufacture of linens, then distinguished by the appellation of "Aylsham Webs." This branch of manufacture was subsequently superseded by that of woollen cloths; and in the time of James I. the inhabitants were principally employed in the knitting of worsted hose, and in the manufacture of stocking-pieces for breeches, and waistcoat-pieces, which was carried on here till the introduction of machinery. The TOWN is pleasantly situated on a gentle acclivity rising from the south bank of the river Bure, and is well built, containing many handsome houses. The trade consists for the most part in corn, coal, and timber, for which its situation is extremely favourable; the river is navigable to Yarmouth for barges of 40 tons' burthen, and a spacious basin and commodious wharfs have been constructed here for the greater facility of trade. The market, formerly on Saturday, is now on Tuesday, and is amply supplied with corn and provisions of all kinds: fairs, which are well attended, are held on March 23rd, and the last Tuesdays in Sept. and Oct., the last one being a statute-fair. The town was formerly governed by a bailiff, and had several privileges, of which exemption from serving on juries at the assizes and sessions still remains. The powers of the county debt-court of Aylsham, established in 1847, extend over the registration-district of Aylsham.

The parish comprises 4311a. 2r. 4p., of which 350

the Crown : the vicarial tithes have been commuted for £341. 19. There is a chapel, a very ancient structure, at Leinthall-Earls, the living of which is in the gift of the Vicar. In the parish are two schools; one at Aymestrey, endowed by William Onneslo, in 1515; and the other at Leinthall-Earls, endowed by William Hewes, in 1634. Several small charities belong to the poor. On the north side of the village, above the inn, is the supposed site of a small Roman camp, recently used as a bowling-green ; and in the township of Yatton are the sites of British and Roman camps, the former occupying the high ground called Croft Ambrey, and the latter the Pyon Grove : the embankments of both are well worth the visit of the antiquary.

AYNHO (St. Michael), a parish, and formerly a market-town, in the union of Brackley, hundred of King's Sutton, S. division of the county of North-ampton, 2¾ miles (E. by N.) from Deddington ; contain-ing 662 inhabitants. The parish occupies the south-western extremity of the county, on the borders of Oxfordshire, which bounds it on the west and south ; it comprises 2219a. 1r. of rich and highly productive land. The road from Buckingham to Deddington, as well as the Oxford canal, intersects it. The village, which is of considerable extent, is situated on a rocky eminence, from whose base issues a copious spring called the " Town Well." A charter was obtained in the 17th of Edward II., for a weekly market and a fair annually at Michaelmas ; but both have long since been discon-tinned. The living is a rectory, valued in the king's books at £25. 5. 5.; net income, £500; patron, W. R. Cartwright, Esq. The church has a fine tower of the 14th century : the body of the building was taken down in 1723, and rebuilt in the tasteless manner of the period. A free school was founded by Mrs. Mary Cart-wright, in 1671, and endowed with a rent-charge of £20. Here was anciently an hospital dedicated to St. John and St. James, founded about the time of Henry II., and in 1484 united to Magdalene College, Oxford, by gift of the patron, William Fitz-Alan. The Roman Portway, a vicinal road, ran through the parish, and is visible at the eastern end of the village. Shakerley Marmion, a dramatic writer, was born at the manor-house in 1602 ; and Robert Wild, a Presbyterian minister, and a poet and satirist, held the living during the Common-wealth.

AYOTT (St. Lawrence), a parish, in the union of Welwyn, hundred of Broadwater, county of Hert-ford, 3¼ miles (W. by N.) from Welwyn ; containing 134 inhabitants. This parish, during the heptarchy, formed part of the possessions of the last of the Saxon monarchs ; and a spot in the immediate vicinity, still called Dane End, commemorates a signal defeat of the Danes by King Ethelwulph. The parish comprises by computation 900 acres. The living is a rectory, valued in the king's books at £8. 13. 4.; net income, £180 ; patron, Lionel Lyde, Esq. The glebe consists of 20 acres. The church is a neat brick edifice, with a hand-some portico of stone, of the Dorie order, the whole erected in 1787, at an expense of £6000, by Sir Lionel Lyde, from a design by Revett, the celebrated Italian architect : the ruins of the old church, a quarter of a mile distant, are considerable, and under the belfry of its embattled tower is an altar-tomb, with recumbent figures of a knight and his lady.

AYOTT (St. Peter), a parish, in the union of Welwyn, hundred of Broadwater, county of Hert-ford, 1¼ mile (W. by S.) from Welwyn ; containing 240 inhabitants. It comprises about 1200 acres of land ; the surface is in general elevated, and the soil a mixture of gravel and clay. The river Marran divides it from the parishes of Welwyn and Codicote : the village is pleasantly situated on the side of the great north road, and is skirted by Brocket Hall Park, the property of Lord Melbourne, a small part of which stands in the parish. The living is a rectory, valued in the king's books at £7. 8. 6½., and in the gift of Lady Mexborough : the tithes have been commuted for £245. 12. 6., and there are 49 acres of glebe. The church, a neat octa-gonal building, was erected about a century since by a former rector, Dr. Freeman, who built also the steeple, on the opposite side of the churchyard.

AYSGARTH (St. Andrew), a parish, in the wapen-take of Hang-West, N. riding of York ; comprising the townships of High and Low Abbotside, Askrigg, Aysgarth, Bainbridge, Bishopdale, West Burton, Car-perby cum Thoresby, Hawes, Newbiggin, Thoralby, and Thornton-Rust ; and containing 5725 inhabitants, of whom 269 are in the township of Aysgarth, 8½ miles (W.) from Middleham. This parish, which is about 22 miles long, and from 4 to 8 or 9 wide, contains 96,000 acres. It comprehends the upper part of the splendid valley called Wensley dale, and the surface is strikingly diversified with high moorlands and fertile vales, famed for grouse and other game ; the grounds are principally in pasture, and the district is noted for its superior dairy productions, butter and new-milk cheeses. The village is pleasantly situated near the river Ure, which rises in the parish, and in its progress forms cataracts at Ays-garth, Askrigg, Hardraw, and West Burton. There is a sheet of water, named Semer water, covering about 500 acres, and abounding with fish of several varieties ; the Ure, also, abounds with trout of a rich flavour, as well as with the greyling, and affords to the angler at certain seasons sport not generally to be met with. At a short distance above Aysgarth Force, is Yore bridge, built in 1539, a curious and interesting structure, which rises in one elliptical arch of 32 feet, with a span of 70 feet, exhibiting numerous petrifactions in its concave, and having its battlements festooned with verdant ivy : this bridge commands a fine view of the falls made by the river in its course through rocks in some parts craggy and abrupt, and in others beautifully intermingled with foliage. There are some veins of lead, and strata of coal. A coarse description of knitted hosiery is manufactured by the females and children of the lower classes, for the use of sailors, and for exportation. The living is a discharged vicarage, valued in the king's books at £19. 6. 8.; net income, £137 ; patrons and appropriators, the Master and Fellows of Trinity College, Cambridge. The church is in the early English style, with a square embattled tower, which was height-ened in the reign of Henry VIII., when the whole build-ing was renovated : the chancel is separated from the nave by an elegant and highly enriched screen and rood-loft, said to have been removed from the abbey of Jervaulx. There are other churches at Askrigg, Hawes, Hardraw, Lunds, and Stalling-Busk. The Society of Friends have places of worship at Aysgarth, Bainbridge, Hawes, and Counterside ; and the Wesleyans at Ays-

123

R 2

garth, Burton, Thoralby, Carperby, Askrigg, Bainbridge, and Gayle: at Thornton-Rust the Calvinists have a meeting-house; and at Hawes the Independents and Sandemanians one each. Mary, Queen of Scots, was imprisoned for a short time at Nappa Hall, an ancient mansion in the parish.—See ASKRIGG, &c.

AYSLEBY, N. riding of YORK.—See AISLABY.

AYSTON (ST. MARY), a parish, in the union of UPPINGHAM, hundred of MARTINSLEY, county of RUTLAND, 1 mile (N. W. by N.) from Uppingham; containing 88 inhabitants. It comprises by measurement 870 acres, of which about one-quarter is arable, and the remainder pasture; the surface is undulated, and the soil partly a red loam, and partly a white clay. The village is situated a quarter of a mile from the road between Oakham and Uppingham. The living is a rectory, valued in the king's books at £8. 7. 8½.; net income, £183; patron, George Fludyer, Esq. The tithes are commuted for a modus of 14d. per acre, and there are 70 acres of glebe, and a glebe-house. The church is a plain neat structure, in the pointed style, except the three arches that divide the north aisle from the body of the church, which are round.

AYTHORPE-ROOTHING.—See ROOTHING.

AYTON-BANKS.—See EIGHTON-BANKS.

AYTON, EAST, a chapelry, in the parish of SEAMER, union of SCARBOROUGH, PICKERING lythe, N. riding of YORK, 5 miles (S. W. by W.) from Scarborough; containing 362 inhabitants. The village is situated in a valley remarkable for the beauty of its scenery, through which flows the river Derwent. The chapel, dedicated to St. John the Baptist, is an ancient structure, with a square tower. The tithes were commuted in 1768, for land and a money payment. There is a place of worship for Primitive Methodists.

AYTON, GREAT (ALL SAINTS), a parish, in the union of STOKESLEY, W. division of the liberty of LANGBAURGH, N. riding of YORK; containing 1216 inhabitants, of whom 1014 are in the township of Great Ayton, 3 miles (N. E. by E.) from Stokesley. This parish, which is on the road from Stokesley to Guisborough, consists of the townships of Great Ayton, Little Ayton, and Nunthorpe, and comprises about 5640 acres; the lands are chiefly arable and pasture in nearly equal portions; the surface is diversified, and much of the scenery is very beautiful. A large seam of whinstone runs across the whole district, passes through the parish, and is wrought in several quarries; the stone is a hard blue, of excellent quality, and much used in making roads. Iron-ore is also found, and a mine was opened at Cliffrigg-Woods, but the works have been for some time discontinued. There are two oil-mills and three tanneries; and the manufacture of linen, once a flourishing trade here, still affords employment to a few of the inhabitants. The living is a perpetual curacy, in the patronage of the family of Marwood, the impropriators, with a net income of £82. The church is a neat unadorned edifice of considerable antiquity, with a square tower; the chancel is separated from the nave by an enriched Norman arch. There is a second church at Nunthorpe, forming a separate incumbency. The Independents, Primitive Methodists, Wesleyans, and Society of Friends have places of worship. A school founded in 1704 by Michael Postgate, and rebuilt in 1785, has an endowment of about £10 per annum: at

this school the celebrated navigator, Captain Cook, received a portion of his education, at the expense of Thomas Scottowe, Esq., whom his father served as manager of a farm. There is also a large agricultural school connected with the Society of Friends; and in the middle of the village are three almshouses, built by subscription.

AYTON, LITTLE, a township, in the parish of GREAT AYTON, union of STOKESLEY, W. division of the liberty of LANGBAURGH, N. riding of YORK, 3¼ miles (E. N. E.) from Stokesley; containing 65 inhabitants. At the time of the Conquest this was an ancient demesne of the crown; the manor was soon afterwards granted to the family of Malbisse, and subsequently passed to the Lords Eure, of Easby. There was once a chapel here, built by Sir William Malbisse, Knt., about 1215; but no remains are now visible. The township comprises about 1170 acres; its small and scattered hamlet is on a branch of the river Leven, and near the road from Stokesley to Guisborough.

AYTON, WEST, a township, in the parish of HUTTON-BUSCEL, union of SCARBOROUGH, PICKERING lythe, N. riding of YORK, 5¼ miles (S. W. by S.) from Scarborough; containing 305 inhabitants. This township is bounded on the east and south by the river Derwent, which separates it from East Ayton; and comprises about 2000 acres, of which one-third is woodland and moor, and the remainder arable and pasture. The surface is finely varied, and the scenery picturesque; the hills are richly wooded to their summits, and the low grounds are watered by the Derwent, over which is a handsome bridge of four arches. Stone of excellent quality for building and for burning into lime is quarried. The village is situated on the road from York to Scarborough, and above it are the remains of Ayton Tower: of this once spacious baronial residence, one wing only is remaining, but the extensive lines of foundations on every side still indicate its former importance. There is a place of worship for Wesleyans. The tithes were commuted for land and a money payment, under an act, in 1792.

AZERLEY, a township, in the parish of KIRKBY-MALZEARD, Lower division of the wapentake of CLARO, W. riding of YORK, 4 miles (N. W.) from Ripon; containing 836 inhabitants. It comprises 4470 acres, of which 57 are common or waste; and includes the villages of Galpha and Mickley. The tithes have been commuted for £220. 16. payable to Trinity College, Cambridge, £45 to the vicar of the parish, and £5 to the Dean and Chapter of Ripon. There is a chapel at Mickley, erected by the family of the late Col. Dalton, of Sleningford Park; also a place of worship for Wesleyans in the township.

B

BABCARY (HOLY CROSS), a parish, in the union of LANGPORT, hundred of CATSASH, E. division of SOMERSET, 4¾ miles (E.) from Somerton; containing 465 inhabitants, and comprising by computation 2500 acres. The living is a rectory, valued in the king's books at £13. 10. 5., and in the gift and incumbency of the Rev. W. H. Twemlow. The rector's tithes have been commuted for £400, besides which a sum of £8. 15. is payable to an impropriator; the glebe comprises 45 acres. The Wesleyans have a place of worship.

BABINGLEY (St. Felix), a parish, in the union and hundred of Freebridge-Lynn, W. division of Norfolk, 8½ miles (N. N. E.) from Lynn; containing 54 inhabitants. It is intersected by the road from Lynn to Wells, and comprises 849a. 3r. 25p., of which 214 acres are arable, 390 pasture and meadow, 98 woodland, and 139 heath; the surface is low and flat, and the soil in some parts light and gravelly, and in others good meadow earth. The living is a discharged rectory, annexed to that of Sanderingham, and valued in the king's books at £4. 13. 4.: the tithes have been commuted for £102. The church is supposed to be the oldest in the county, and is said to have been originally erected by Felix, the apostle of the East Angles, to whom it was afterwards dedicated.

BABINGTON (St. Margaret), a parish, in the union of Frome, hundred of Kilmersdon, E. division of Somerset, 5½ miles (W. N. W.) from Frome; containing 163 inhabitants. It comprises 800 acres; and contains abundance of limestone, and some coal, of which a mine is in full operation. The living is a discharged rectory, valued in the king's books at £10, and in the gift of Col. Jolliffe: the tithes have been commuted for £116, and the glebe consists of about 7 acres. There is a place of worship for Wesleyans; also a school endowed with £20 per annum, bequeathed in 1758 by Elizabeth Long.

BABRAHAM (St. Peter), a parish, in the union of Linton, hundred of Chilford, county of Cambridge, 4½ miles (N. W.) from Linton; containing 217 inhabitants. It comprises by computation 2500 acres; and is intersected by the Cambridge and Colchester road, and bounded on the south-west by the road from London to Newmarket. A splendid mansion in the Elizabethan style has lately been erected, which, with the park, gardens, and pleasure-grounds, contributes greatly to the ornamental scenery of the locality. The living is a discharged vicarage, valued in the king's books at £6. 5. 10.; patron and impropriator, R. J. Adeane, Esq. The great tithes have been commuted for £28, and the small for £125; the glebe consists of 4 acres. The church is an ancient building in the decorated style, situated in the pleasure-grounds of the patron, to the memory of several branches of whose family it contains some handsome monuments. There is a free school, supported from bequests by Levinus and James Bush, Esqrs., and Judith Bennett, who also left an endowment for an almshouse for six women, and £25 per annum for apprenticing poor boys; the income is now £134.

BABUR, county of Norfolk.—See Bawburgh.

BABWORTH (All Saints), a parish, in the union of East Retford, Hatfield division of the wapentake of Bassetlaw, N. division of the county of Nottingham, 1¼ mile (W.) from East Retford; containing 577 inhabitants. It comprises 5882a. 3r. 38p., of which about 5028 acres are arable, 370 meadow and pasture, and 479 woodland; the surface is undulated, and the scenery enriched with wood. The Chesterfield canal bounds the parish on the north. The living is a rectory, valued in the king's books at £14. 19. 2., and in the gift of the Hon. J. B. Simpson: the tithes have been commuted for £815, and the glebe consists of 20 acres. The church is a small
125

neat edifice in the later English style, with a square embattled tower crowned with pinnacles, and has been recently repewed and beautified. Lindley Simpson, Esq., in 1781, bequeathed the profits of a share in the Chesterfield canal for the support of a school, to which also the gentry of the neighbourhood contribute. A schoolroom was built in 1836, at the expense of J. Rogers, Esq., and has been licensed for the celebration of divine service.

BACHE, a township, in the parish of St. Oswald, Chester union of Great Boughton, Lower division of the hundred of Broxton, S. division of the county of Chester; containing 18 inhabitants. It comprises 93 acres, of a loamy soil. Bache Hall was garrisoned for the parliament in the early part of the civil war, and destroyed during the siege of Chester, in 1645.

BACKFORD (St. Oswald), a parish, in the union of Great Boughton, partly in the Higher division of the hundred of Wirrall, and partly in the Lower division of the hundred of Broxton, S. division of the county of Chester; comprising the townships of Backford, Caughall, Chorlton, Lea, and Mollington-Tarrant; and containing 556 inhabitants, of whom about 200 are in the township of Backford, 4 miles (N.) from Chester, on the road to Birkenhead. During a great part of the 13th and 14th centuries, the manor was held by the Masseys, of Timperley; about the year 1580 it was sold to Thomas Aldersey, by whom it was soon afterwards alienated to the Birkenheads, who resided at Backford Hall until the family became extinct in the male line in 1724. The parish comprises 3006 acres, whereof 687 are in Backford township, and of a sandy and clayey soil. The Ellesmere canal skirts the parish on the south; and at Mollington is a station of the Chester and Birkenhead railway. The vicinity of the place to the city of Chester renders it cheerful and desirable for residence. The living is a discharged vicarage, valued in the king's books at £5. 0. 5.; net income, £230; patron and appropriator, the Bishop of Chester: the tithes of Backford township have been commuted for £64 and £46. 3., payable respectively to the bishop and the vicar. The church was rebuilt in the reign of Anne, with the exception of the tower and chancel, built in that of Henry VI. A school is partly supported by subscription; and an excellent school-house was erected in 1844, under the auspices of the vicar, the Rev. Francis Bryans, at a cost of £345, raised by subscription, aided by public grants.

BACKSHAW, a hamlet, in the parish of Holwell, union of Sherborne, hundred of Brownshall, county of Dorset; containing 16 inhabitants.

BACKWELL (St. Andrew), a parish, and formerly a market-town, in the union of Bedminster, hundred of Hartcliffe with Bedminster, E. division of Somerset, 7¼ miles (S. W. by W.) from Bristol; containing, with the hamlets of Churchtown, Downside, Farley, Moorside, and West-town, 1161 inhabitants. It includes some extensive collieries, and some quarries producing a kind of calcareous stone of a reddish colour, variegated with blue and white veins, and which is susceptible of a very high polish. The weekly market, granted by Edward II. has been long discontinued; but a fair for cattle and pedlery is held on the 21st of September. The living consists of a sinecure rectory and a discharged vicarage; the rectory valued in the king's books at £11. 16. 3., with a net income of £253; the vicarage valued at £6. 19. 9½., with a net income of £144; patron of both, the Marquess of Bath.

BACKWORTH, a township, in the parish of EARS-DON, union of TYNEMOUTH, E. division of CASTLE ward, S. division of NORTHUMBERLAND, 7 miles (N. E. by N.) from Newcastle-upon-Tyne; containing 413 inhabitants. This place formerly belonged to Tynemouth priory, and afterwards to the Grey family, by whom it was sold to the late Duke of Northumberland, for £95,000. The soil is fertile, and favourable to the growth of wheat; the district abounds in coal, and an extensive colliery is in operation, the produce of which is of a superior quality, and known as "Northumberland Wallsend." The great tithes have been commuted for £107. Sir Charles Grey, Knt., the governor of Barbadoes, was born at Backworth House.

BACONSTHORPE (ST. MARY), a parish, in the union of ERPINGHAM, hundred of SOUTH ERPINGHAM, E. division of NORFOLK, 3½ miles (E. S. E.) from Holt; containing 326 inhabitants, and comprising 1332a. 3r. 38p. The manor was long held by the Bacons, one of whom was the learned John Bacon, who died in 1346. The living is a rectory, valued in the king's books at £9, and in the gift of John Thurston Mott, Esq.: the tithes have been commuted for £340, and there are 33 acres of glebe, with a handsome house. The church was partly destroyed by the fall of the steeple in 1729, but was thoroughly repaired, chiefly at the expense of the Rev. Mr. Hewitt, in 1779.

BACTON, a parish, in the union of DORE, hundred of WEBTREE, county of HEREFORD, 11½ miles (S. W. by W.) from Hereford; containing 140 inhabitants. The parish comprises 1177 acres, and is bounded on the east by the river Dore: the land is fertile in corn and apples, and a considerable quantity of cider is made; there is a large supply of excellent limestone. The living is a discharged rectory, valued in the king's books at £3. 13. 4., and in the patronage of Francis Hamp, Esq.: the tithes have been commuted for £122. 9. The church contains, in the north side of the chancel, a monument of the Corinthian order, with a curious inscription, to the memory of Mrs. Blanche Parry, of Newcourt, in the parish, and for many years maid of honour to Queen Elizabeth. Mrs. Blanche Parry, in 1589, bequeathed as much land as would produce 140 bushels of wheat and rye, to be divided among the poor of Bacton and the hamlet of Newton; and there are other bequests to the poor, recorded on a stone slab in the church. Some chalybeate springs have been discovered within the last few years.

BACTON (ST. ANDREW), a parish, in the TUNSTEAD and HAPPING incorporation, hundred of TUNSTEAD, E. division of NORFOLK, 4½ miles (N. E. by E.) from North Walsham; containing 513 inhabitants. The parish comprises 1629a. 14p., of which 1327 acres are arable, and 275 pasture and meadow. Bacton-green is a fishing-village on the coast, having three curing-houses; six large and several small boats employed in the herring, crab, and lobster fishery; and many vessels engaged in the coal-trade. A fair is held on the first Monday in August. The living is a discharged vicarage, endowed with a portion of the rectorial tithes, and valued in the king's books at £5. 3. 1½., net income, £263; patrons, and impropriators of the remainder of the great tithes, 126

the family of Wodehouse. The glebe consists of 28 acres, with a house. The church, situated on an eminence, is chiefly in the decorated style, and contains a handsome and elaborately sculptured font. There is a place of worship for Particular Baptists. At Bromeholme are the remains of a priory for Cluniac monks, founded by W. De Glanvill in 1113.—See BROMEHOLME.

BACTON (ST. MARY), a parish, in the union and hundred of HARTISMERE, W. division of SUFFOLK, 6½ miles (N.) from Stow-Market; containing 800 inhabitants. The parish comprises 2226 acres, of which 91 are common or waste. The living is a rectory, valued in the king's books at £19. 12. 3½.; and in the patronage of H. D. Hemsworth, Esq.: the tithes have been commuted for £736, and there are nearly 52 acres of glebe. The church is chiefly in the decorated style, and consists of a nave, chancel, and aisles, with an embattled tower surmounted by a shingled spire.

BACUP, a consolidated chapelry, in the townships of NEWCHURCH and SPOTLAND, parishes of WHALLEY and ROCHDALE, union of HASLINGDEN, Higher division of the hundred of BLACKBURN, N. division of LANCASHIRE, 7 miles (N. by W.) from Rochdale; containing 7279 inhabitants. The village or town is situated in a beautiful valley, from which the ground ascends on both sides to high moorland, abounding in game. The soil is alluvial, inclined to clay; and coal, and excellent stone for building, are in great plenty: at Dulesgate is a bed of hard coal similar to that of Halifax. The river Erewell or Irwell, which takes its rise at Cliviger, two miles and a half to the north, runs through the village, where a tributary stream joins it; and the roads from Rochdale to Burnley, and from Todmorden to Haslingden, cross each other in the middle of the village. The population is chiefly employed in cotton factories. A cattle-fair is held on the first Tuesday in every month; and fairs are also held on the Tuesday and Wednesday before Good-Friday, the first Friday and Saturday in June, and the 25th and 26th of October. An act was passed in 1846, for constructing a branch line connecting Bacup with the Leeds and Manchester railway; and another act has been obtained, for a branch in connexion with the East Lancashire railway. Fern Hill, a mansion situated on an eminence overlooking the valley, is the seat of George Ormerod, Esq.; and at Broadclough, about half a mile up the vale, is the seat of James Whitaker, Esq.

The consolidated chapelry was allotted in 1843. The living is a perpetual curacy, in the patronage of the Hulme Trustees, with a net income of £150, and a house; the chapel, dedicated to St. John, was consecrated in 1788. There are two places of worship for Particular Baptists, and two for Wesleyans. A mechanics' institution and a British school stand on the site of the original Baptist meeting-house, which was erected in 1692, and was for a considerable number of years the only place of worship in the village. A national school is supported in connexion with St. John's chapel. At Broadclough are the remains of an intrenchment, called the "Dykes," respecting the antiquity of which no tradition exists. It is cut out from the gentle slope of an eminence, and in one direction is nearly parallel to the horizon for more than 600 yards: a part of the line, for about 100 yards, appears to have been levelled; and more than 400 yards present a trench 54 feet in breadth at the bottom, and of proportionate depth. So gigantic and singular a work could only have been intended for some military purpose: it was probably one side of a vast British camp, designed to have been carried round the eminence, but left unfinished. Bacup is included in the forest of Rossendale, of which the first portion inclosed was Brandwood, in this district, granted about the year 1200, by Roger de Lacy, to an ecclesiastical establishment; the remainder was disforested in the reign of Henry VII.

BADBURY, a tything, in the parish of CHISLEDON, union of HIGHWORTH and SWINDON, hundred of KINGSBRIDGE, Swindon and N. divisions of WILTS; containing 395 inhabitants.

BADBY (ST. MARY), a parish, in the union of DAVENTRY, hundred of FAWSLEY, S. division of the county of NORTHAMPTON, 2¼ miles (S. S. W.) from Daventry; containing 624 inhabitants. It is intersected by the road from Daventry to Banbury, and consists of 2147a. 30p., in equal portions of arable and pasture. The village is situated on the declivity of a hill. There are quarries of hard blue ragstone in the neighbourhood. The living is a discharged vicarage, with the living of Newnham annexed, valued in the king's books at £14; net income, £306; patrons and appropriators, the Dean and Canons of Christ-Church, Oxford. A Sunday school is endowed with the interest of £191. 17. three per cent. annuities. On a lofty eminence called Arbury hill, is an intrenchment, supposed to be Roman.

BADDESLEY-CLINTON (ST. MICHAEL), a parish, in the union of SOLIHULL, Solihull division of the hundred of HEMLINGFORD, N. division of the county of WARWICK, 7 miles (N. W.) from Warwick; containing 115 inhabitants. The parish is intersected by the Warwick and Birmingham canal, and skirted by the road between those two places: it comprises 1310 acres. The living is a donative, valued in the king's books at £4. 6. 8., and is in the patronage of the family of Ferrers, to whom also the impropriation belongs; net income, £27. There is a Roman Catholic chapel.

BADDESLEY-ENSOR (ST. MICHAEL), a parish, in the union of ATHERSTONE, Atherstone division of the hundred of HEMLINGFORD, N. division of the county of WARWICK, 3 miles (W. N. W.) from Atherstone; containing 579 inhabitants. The parish is situated on the road from the Watling-street to the Bentley turnpike-road; and comprises by computation 1125 acres, in about equal portions of arable and pasture, with small interspersions of wood. The land is very elevated, commanding a panoramic view of the surrounding country, including Bromsgrove-Lickey, Barr-Beacon hill, and, beyond, Lichfield, Cannock Chase, &c.; the prevailing soil is a stiff clay. A coal-mine is in operation. The living is a perpetual curacy, in the patronage of the Inhabitants, with the approval of the vicar of Polesworth; net income, £66, with a parsonage of picturesque appearance. The present church, erected by W. S. Dugdale, Esq., in the style of the 13th century, was consecrated in September 1846. There is a Sunday school; and at Bentley is a day school supported by Mr. Dugdale, to which the children of this parish go.

BADDESLEY, NORTH, a parish, in the union of HURSLEY, hundred of MANSBRIDGE, Romsey and S. divisions of the county of SOUTHAMPTON, 3 miles (E.

by S.) from Romsey; containing 302 inhabitants. It comprises about 2000 acres, of which 1500 are under cultivation, and a considerable quantity common. Here was anciently a preceptory of Knights Templars. The living is a donative; net income, £100; patron and impropriator, T. Chamberlayne, Esq. The glebe-house is a cottage residence, with 2 acres of land attached. The church is very ancient.

BADDESLEY, SOUTH, a chapelry, in the parish of BOLDRE, union of LYMINGTON, partly in the E. division of the NEW FOREST, and partly in the hundred of CHRISTCHURCH, Lymington and S. divisions of the county of SOUTHAMPTON, 2 miles (E. N. E.) from Lymington; containing 1238 inhabitants. The living is a donative, endowed with £12 per annum rent-charge on the estate of Pylewell, the proprietor of which is patron. The chapel is a neat edifice, capable of accommodating 200 persons.

BADDILEY (ST. MICHAEL), a parish, in the union and hundred of NANTWICH, S. division of the county of CHESTER, 3 miles (W. S. W.) from Nantwich; containing 275 inhabitants. The manor belonged, as early as the time of William I., to the family of Praers; and in the reign of Edward III. passed, by marriage with the co-heiresses of William Praers, to the Bromleys, Hondfords, and Mainwarings, in which last family it ultimately became solely vested. The parish comprises 2300 acres of land, the soil of which is clay and sand: the Ellesmere canal passes through. Baddiley Hall, once the noble residence of the Mainwarings, is now a farmhouse. The living is a discharged rectory, valued in the king's books at £24. 3. 6., and in the gift of John Tollemache, Esq.: the tithes have been commuted for £195; the glebe consists of nine acres, and a house built in 1844. The church is of oak, and of great antiquity; the upright timbers, being much decayed, were cased with brick in 1811, but the roof and ceiling are still in fine preservation. About £50, obtained from 39 acres of land, are yearly distributed among the poor.

BADDINGTON, a township, in the parish of ACTON, union and hundred of NANTWICH, S. division of the county of CHESTER, 1½ mile (S. S. W) from Nantwich: containing 137 inhabitants. It comprises 1102 acres of land, whereof clay is the prevailing soil. The Liverpool and Birmingham Junction canal passes near. A rent-charge of £134 has been awarded as a commutation for the impropriate tithes, and one of £28. 18. for the vicarial.

BADDOW, GREAT (ST. MARY), a parish, in the union and hundred of CHELMSFORD; S. division of ESSEX, 1 mile (S. E.) from Chelmsford; containing 2022 inhabitants. It comprises 3620a. 1r. 27p., of which 150 acres are common or waste: the village is very pleasantly situated, and inhabited by several highly respectable families. A large brewery was established about seventy years since. The living is a vicarage, valued in the king's books at £18. 6. 8., and in the patronage of Mrs. Bullen; impropriator, J. A. Houblon, Esq. The great tithes have been commuted for £636, and the vicarial for one of £495. 15.: the glebe belonging to the impropriator comprises about 22 acres, and the vicar's glebe one acre. The church contains some ancient monuments, one of which, in the south aisle, is very beautiful, representing the figure of a child, in a mournful attitude supporting the bust of a female. A free school was founded in 1731, by Jasper Jefferey, of London, and endowed with property invested in the purchase of estates now producing an annual income of about £168.

BADDOW, LITTLE (St. Mary), a parish, in the union and hundred of Chelmsford, S. division of Essex, 5 miles (E. N. E.) from Chelmsford ; containing, with the hamlet of Middle Mead, 592 inhabitants. It is bounded on the north by the navigable river Chelmer, on which are two large flour-mills with convenient quays. The living is a discharged vicarage, valued in the king's books at £8. 2. 2. ; patron and impropriator, Col. Strutt, who is also patron of the rectory, which is a sinecure valued at £7. 13. 4. The impropriate tithes have been commuted for £358, the vicarial for £197. 5. 6., and the rectorial for £126. 17. : the rectorial glebe comprises 40,'and the vicarial 5, acres. The church is an ancient edifice, with a tower at the west end, and consists of a nave and chancel, in which latter is a stately monument of marble to Henry Mildmay, of Graces. Here is a place of worship for Independents. In 1717, Edmund Butler bequeathed 160 'acres of land and 36 acres of woodland, for the clothing and education of children of this parish and that of Boreham ; the whole is now let for £130 per annum ; and to this income are added £11, the rent of two cottages, and £15. 1., annual dividends on three and a half per cent. stock.

BADGER, or Bagsore (St. Giles), a parish, within the liberties of the borough of Wenlock, union of Shiffnall, locally in the hundred of Brimstree, S. division of Salop, 5 miles (S.) from Shiffnall ; containing 137 inhabitants. The parish comprises by measurement 920 acres : red sandstone of good quality is obtained, and from the quarries was raised the stone for the erection of the church. The neighbourhood also abounds with stately timber, and from one oak alone was procured wood for the pulpit, pews, and all the other interior fitting-up of the church. Here is a narrow rocky dingle, richly wooded, through which flows a small river ; walks have been tastefully formed, and the spot is much resorted to in the summer. · The living is a discharged rectory, valued in the king's books at £4. 13. 4., and in the gift of R. H. Cheney, Esq. : the tithes have been commuted for £254. 10. 6., and the glebe comprises 25 acres. The church was erected about 1835, at the expense of the patron, and is in the later English style, and embellished with stained glass.

BADGEWORTH (St. Mary), a parish, in the union of Cheltenham, Upper division of the hundred of Dudstone and King's Barton, E. division of the county of Gloucester, 4 miles (S. W. by W.) from Cheltenham ; containing, with the hamlets of Bentham, Little Shurdington, and Little Witcombe, 903 inhabitants, of whom 210 are in the hamlet of Badgeworth. The living is a vicarage, with the living of Great Shurdington annexed, valued in the king's books at £20. 11. 3.; net income, £295 ; patron, Joseph Ellis Viner, Esq.; impropriators, the Principal and Fellows of Jesus College, Oxford, in whom the great tithes are vested for the support of a school at Abergavenny, subject to a deduction of £16 per annum paid to Christ-Church College, Cambridge. The church is in the early English style, with some later portions, and has a very handsome
128

tower. On an estate called Cold Pool is a ·mineral spring, the water of which is similar to that of Cheltenham.

BADGINGTON, or Bagendon (St. Margaret), a parish, in the union of Cirencester, hundred of Crowthorne and Minety, E. division of the county of Gloucester, 3¼ miles (N.) from Cirencester ; containing 172 inhabitants. It comprises by measurement 1100 acres of land in good cultivation : stone of inferior quality is raised for road-making and rough building. The living is a discharged rectory, valued in the king's books at £8. 4. 4½., and in the gift of Jesus College, Oxford : the tithes have been commuted for £200, and the glebe consists of about 78 acres.

BADGWORTH (St. Congar), a parish, in the union of Axbridge, hundred of Winterstoke, E. division of Somerset, 2½ miles (S. W. by W.) from Axbridge : containing 321 inhabitants. The living is a rectory, valued in the king's books at £25. 15., and in the gift of Sir J. Mordaunt, Bart.: the tithes have been commuted for £432. 9., and the glebe comprises 85½ acres.

BADIALTON.—See Bathealton.

BADINGHAM (St. John the Baptist), a parish,.in the union and hundred of Hoxne, E. division of Suffolk, 14 miles (N. by E.) from Woodbridge ; containing 864 inhabitants, and comprising 3172a. 26p. The living is a rectory, valued in the king's books at £22. 16. 8., and in the gift of the Gorton family : the tithes have been commuted for £875, and there are 25 acres of glebe. The church has a nave and chancel, and an embattled tower.

BADLESMERE (St. Leonard), a parish, in the union and hundred of Faversham, Upper division of the lathe of Scray, E. division of Kent, 4¼ miles (S.) from Faversham ; containing 122 inhabitants. It comprises 1150 acres, of which 118 are in wood ; the surface is hilly, and the soil clay and chalk. A fair is held on Nov. 5th. The living is a discharged rectory, with that of Leaveland united, valued in the king's books at £5. 2., and in the patronage of Lord Sondes : the tithes have been commuted for £400, and the glebe consists of 13 acres. A parsonage-house was built in 1836.

BADLEY (St. Mary), a parish, in the union and hundred of Bosmere and Claydon, E. division of Suffolk, 2 miles (W. N. W.) from Needham ; containing 83 inhabitants. This parish comprises about 1200 acres. It is situated on the navigable river Gipping, by which it is bounded on the north-east ; and is traversed by the road from Ipswich to Bury-St. Edmund's. The living is a perpetual curacy ; net income, £40 ; patron and impropriator, the Earl of Ashburnham. The church is an ancient structure, containing many memorials of the Poleys.

BADMINTON, GREAT (St. Michael), a parish, in the union of Chipping, Upper division of the hundred of Grumbald's-Ash, W. division of the county of Gloucester, 6½ miles (E. by N.) from Chipping-Sodbury ; containing 552 inhabitants. This parish, together with Little Badminton, is nearly all included within the boundary wall of Badminton Park, the seat of the Duke of Beaufort, whose ancestor, the first duke, built a princely mansion in the reign of Charles II., on the site of an ancient house belonging to the Boteler family. The roads from Cheltenham and Cirencester to Bath unite here. The living is a discharged vicarage, valued in the king's books at £5. 5. 7½.; net income, £7; patron, the Duke of Beaufort, by whose family the church was rebuilt in 1785. Mary, Duchess Dowager, in 1705 gave a rent-charge of £94 for the endowment of an almshouse for three men and three women, and a school for poor children.

BADMINTON, LITTLE, a tything, in the parish of Hawkesbury, union of Chipping-Sodbury, Upper division of the hundred of Grumbald's-Ash, W. division of the county of Gloucester; containing 127 inhabitants. Here was a chapel to the vicarage of Great Badminton, now in ruins.

BADSEY (St. James), a parish, in the union of Evesham, Upper division of the hundred of Blackenhurst, Pershore and E. divisions of the county of Worcester, 2¾ miles (E. by S.) from Evesham; containing, with the hamlet of Aldington, 497 inhabitants. This place belonged to the abbey of Evesham, even before the Conquest; and in the reign of Edward III. the abbot provided a garden and buildings here, for the retirement of sick and convalescent monks from the establishment. The parish comprises 1795 acres, and is bordered on the west by the navigable river Avon, which here receives a small brook, which in its course turns several mills, including a silk-mill. It is crossed from west to east by the road from Evesham to Chipping-Campden. The village consists of an airy street, with some substantial dwellings. The living is a perpetual curacy, valued in the king's books at £5. 6. 8.; net income, £150; patrons and appropriators, the Dean and Canons of Christ-Church, Oxford. The church stands in an open burial-ground rising gently from the street, whence its remarkably pretty tower and ancient yew-tree are seen with good effect.

BADSHOT, a tything, in the parish and hundred of Farnham, W. division of Surrey, 2 miles (N. E. by E.) from Farnham; containing, with the tything of Runfold, 1410 inhabitants.

BADSWORTH (St. Mary), a parish, in the Upper division of the wapentake of Osgoldcross, W. riding of York; containing 750 inhabitants, of whom 200 are in the township of Badsworth, 5 miles (S.) from Pontefract. This parish, which is on the road from Wakefield to Doncaster, comprises the townships of Badsworth, Thorp-Audlin, and Upton, and consists of about 4320 acres of productive land, of which 1750 are in the first-named township, the property of the Earl Fitzwilliam, and the centre of a sporting district called the Badsworth Hunt. The place was the residence of Col. Bright, an eminent officer in the parliamentarian army, who was created a baronet soon after the restoration, and was buried in the church. The living is a rectory, valued in the king's books at £32. 5. 10., and in the patronage of the Earl: the tithes have been commuted for £500, and the glebe comprises 168 acres. The church is an ancient structure in the decorated English style, with later insertions, and was thoroughly repaired in 1826, at an expense of £500. There is a place of worship for Wesleyans.

BADWELL-ASH (St. Mary), a parish, in the union of Stow, hundred of Blackbourn, W. division of Suffolk, 5 miles (E.) from Ixworth; containing 458 inhabitants. The living is a perpetual curacy, with a net income of £69, and is in the patronage of Miss R.

VOL. I.—129

Clough, to whom the impropriation belongs, and whose tithes have been commuted for £357. The church is in the decorated style, and consists of a nave, chancel, and south aisle, with an embattled tower.

BAGBOROUGH, WEST (Holy Trinity), a parish, in the union of Taunton, hundred of Taunton and Taunton-Dean, W. division of Somerset, 8 miles (N. W. by W.) from Taunton; containing 449 inhabitants. The parish is situated in a fertile district, watered by numerous streams from the hills in the vicinity, and abounds with pleasingly diversified scenery; it comprises by measurement 1972 acres, of which 762 are arable, 742 meadow, 150 woodland, and 120 common. The living is a rectory, valued in the king's books at £18. 10. 10.; patron and incumbent, the Rev. J. B. B. Clarke, whose tithes have been commuted for £295. 4., and who has a glebe of 63 acres.

BAGBURY, a hamlet, in the parish of Evercreech, union of Shepton-Mallet, hundred of Wells-Forum, E. division of Somerset; containing 23 inhabitants.

BAGBY, a township, in the parish of Kirby-Knowle, union of Thirsk, wapentake of Birdforth, N. riding of York, 2¼ miles (E. S. E.) from Thirsk; containing, with the hamlet of Islebeck, 317 inhabitants. This township is separated from the main part of the parish by intervening portions of other parishes, and is situated near Thirkleby, about 4 miles distant from the parochial church. It is intersected by the York and Newcastle railway. There is a chapel of ease here; also a place of worship for Wesleyans.

BAGGRAVE, a liberty, in that part of the parish of Hungerton which is in the hundred of Gartree, union of Billesdon, N. division of the county of Leicester, 8½ miles (E. N. E.) from Leicester, containing 27 inhabitants.

BAGINGTON (St. John the Baptist), a parish, in the union of Warwick, Kenilworth division of the hundred of Knightlow, S. division of the county of Warwick, 3½ miles (S. by E.) from Coventry; containing 245 inhabitants. It is situated between the rivers Avon and Sow, the former bounding it on the east, and the latter on the west; and consists of 1650 acres, of which a considerable portion is attached to Bagington Hall. The Duke of Hereford, afterwards Henry IV., previously to the day appointed for the combat between him and the Duke of Norfolk at Coventry, in the reign of Richard II., took up his residence in an ancient castle in the parish, of which there are now no remains. The hall was built in 1706 (the old manor-house having in that year been destroyed by fire) by William Bromley, Esq., speaker of the house of commons, and subsequently one of the principal secretaries of state. The London and Birmingham railway passes in the vicinity, and here is a station on the line. The living is a rectory, valued in the king's books at £8. 1. 8., and in the patronage of the Rev. W. D. Bromley: the tithes have been commuted for £355, and there is a glebe of 19 acres. A school conducted on the national plan is supported by an endowment.

BAGLEY-WOOD, an extra-parochial liberty, in the hundred of Hormer, county of Berks, 3½ miles (N. by E.) from Abingdon; containing 21 inhabitants. and comprising 390 acres. A monastery was founded here by Cissa, viceroy of Centwine, ninth king of Wessex;

S

which was removed to Abingdon in 680, that town and its appendages having been assigned to it by Ceadwalla.

BAGNALL, a township, in the parish of BUCKNALL, union of STOKE-UPON-TRENT, N. division of the hundred of PIREHILL and of the county of STAFFORD, 3¾ miles (N. E.) from Hanley; containing 347 inhabitants. This is an agricultural township, formerly included in the extensive parish of Stoke, from which it was separated in 1807. Here is a chapel, rebuilt in 1834, at a cost of £520.

BAGNOR, a tything, in the parish of SPEEN, union of NEWBURY, hundred of FAIRCROSS, county of BERKS, 2 miles (N. W.) from Speenhamland; containing 165 inhabitants.

BAGSHOT, a chapelry, in the parish of WINDLESHAM, union of CHERTSEY, First division of the hundred of WOKING, W. division of SURREY, 12 miles (N. N. W.) from Guildford, and 26 (W. S. W.) from London, on the great western road; containing 1071 inhabitants. This place, formerly called Holy Hall, gives name to a tract of heath land, which was anciently more extensive, a great part having been inclosed and cultivated. It was once a residence of the kings of England, who had a mansion here, and a park, which was laid open after the civil war in the reign of Charles I.: the house was occupied by the late Duke of Gloucester. On the borders of Bagshot Heath are some handsome villas. The chapel was built in 1819 by subscription, aided by a grant of £200 from the Incorporated Society, in consideration of which 225 sittings are free. There are places of worship for Independents, Wesleyans, and Baptists; and an almshouse for six men and women, built in 1761, by James Butler, Esq.

BAGSHOT, a hamlet, in the parish of SHALBOURN, union of HUNGERFORD, hundred of KINWARDSTONE, Marlborough and Ramsbury, and S. divisions of WILTS; containing 194 inhabitants.

BAGTHORPE (ST. MARY), a parish, in the union of DOCKING, hundred of GALLOW, W. division of NORFOLK, 2 miles (E.) from Great Bircham; containing 78 inhabitants. It comprises 750a. 2r. 26p., of which about 600 acres are arable, 72 pasture and meadow, and 70 woodland. The living is a discharged rectory, valued in the king's books at £5. 10., and in the gift of the Chad family: the tithes have been commuted for £140, and there are eight acres of glebe. The church is in the early English style.

BAGTHORPE, a hamlet, in the parish of SELSTON, union of BASFORD, N. division of the wapentake of BROXTOW and of the county of NOTTINGHAM, 3 miles (S. E.) from Selston; containing 566 inhabitants. It is the central division of the parish, and lies on the road from Greasley to Selston. Here is Wansley Hall, anciently the seat of Sir Ranulph de Wandesley; near which, in 1830, an urn full of silver coins was found.

BAGULEY, a township, in the parish of BOWDON, union of ALTRINCHAM, hundred of BUCKLOW, N. division of the county of CHESTER, 6¼ miles (W. by S.) from Stockport; containing 505 inhabitants. This was at an early period the property of the Baguleys, whose heiress brought it to the Leghs; the latter sold it, and in 1722 it belonged to Viscount Allen, of whom it was purchased by the Jacksons, of Rostherne. The township comprises 1769 acres, of which 114 are common

taining 431 inhabitants. The scenery is of a romantic description, and there is a long range of lofty crags, which extends to the point where the kingdom of Scotland and the counties of Cumberland and Northumberland meet.

BAINBRIDGE, a township, in the parish of Aysgarth, wapentake of Hang-West, N. riding of York, 1½ mile (S. W.) from Askrigg; containing 786 inhabitants. This township comprises by computation 14,210 acres, and takes its name from its situation on the river Bain, which is here crossed by a good stone bridge on the Aysgarth road, and is a considerable stream tributary to the neighbouring Ure, over which is also a bridge on the Askrigg road, about half a mile from the former. The Bain is supplied from the lake Seamer-Water, which is of considerable extent and has its source among the mountains of Raydale-side, a secluded valley within the township; the lake has two beautiful cataracts on its north-western side, and is a favourite resort of several kinds of waterfowl. Overlooking the mouth of the lake stands the beautiful rural hamlet of Counter-side, opposite the Roman station on Addlebrough mountain. The station, with the camp beneath, commanded an important and extensive district, now comprised, with its various ramifications, under the name of Wensley dale, and varying from the wildest mountain to the richest vale scenery in England, though but imperfectly known to tourists. Near the camp have been found divers Roman relics, including a statue of the Emperor Commodus. At Stalling-Busk, in Raydale-side, is a church, the living of which is in the gift of the Vicar of Aysgarth: at Bainbridge the Wesleyans and Society of Friends have places of worship; and the Friends have also a meeting-house at Counter-side. The celebrated Dr. John Fothergill was born at Carr-End, in the district.

BAINTON (St. Mary), a parish, in the union of Stamford, soke of Peterborough, N. division of the county of Northampton, 4½ miles (S. E.) from Stamford; containing 161 inhabitants. The parish is situated on the road from London to Stamford, and near the river Welland, which is navigable to Boston; it comprises 993a. 1r. 31p. of fertile land, and contains some quarries of stone chiefly used for rough building and road-making. The living is united to the rectory of Ufford; the tithes were commuted for corn-rents in 1796. The church exhibits some interesting specimens of early English architecture. On the east of the parish are remains of the Roman road to Lincoln.

BAINTON, a hamlet, in the parish of Stoke-Lyne, union of Bicester, hundred of Ploughley, county of Oxford, 3 miles (N.) from Bicester. The great tithes have been commuted for £233, and the vicarial for £57.

BAINTON (St. Andrew), a parish, in the union of Driffield, Bainton-Beacon division of the wapentake of Harthill, E. riding of York, 5¾ miles (S. W.) from Great Driffield; containing 452 inhabitants. This place, in which a beacon was anciently erected on an eminence near the village, to warn of approaching danger, gives the name to this division of the wapentake. The parish comprises 3280 acres, which include Neswick, and of which two-thirds are arable, and the remainder meadow and pasture with a small portion of woodland. The living is a rectory, valued in the king's books at

131

£35. 14. 9½.; net income, £757; patrons, the President and Fellows of St. John's College, Oxford. The land attached comprises about 602 acres, the tithes of Bainton having been commuted for land in 1774. The church is an ancient structure, the tower of which exhibits a part only of its octagonal spire, the other part having fallen down about the middle of the last century: the interior, which was repaired in 1842, contains several interesting antiquities. There are places of worship for Primitive Methodists and Wesleyans. The petty-sessions for the Bainton-Beacon division are held here once a month.

BAITHLEY, county of Norfolk.—See Bale.

BAKEWELL (All Saints), a market-town and parish, and the head of a union (exclusively of a portion which is in the union of Chapel-en-le-Frith), in the hundred of High Peak, N. division of the county of Derby; comprising the townships of Ashford, Baslow with Bubnell, Beeley, Blackwell, Brushfield, Buxton, Calver, Chelmorton, Curbar, Flagg, Froggatt, Harthill, Hassop, Great Longstone with Holme, Little Longstone, Monyash, Over and Nether Haddon, Rowland, Great Rowsley, Sheldon, Taddington with Priestcliffe, and part of Wardlow; and containing 10,363 inhabitants, of whom 1976 are in the town, 26 miles (N. W.) from Derby, and 152 (N. W. by N.) from London. The Saxon name of this place, Baderanwylla, or Badde cum Well, of which its present appellation is a contraction, is derived from a chalybeate spring, which was in great repute prior to the year 924, when Edward the Elder is said to have built a castle, or fort, in the vicinity. The town is in an improving state: it is situated on the river Wye, in a beautiful and picturesque vale, about four miles from the confluence of the Wye and Derwent, and at nearly an equal distance from Buxton and Matlock, between which places is an excellent road, leading by Bakewell through a district replete with pleasingly diversified scenery. Two miles south of the town is Haddon Hall, the property of the Duke of Rutland, one of the largest and most perfect baronial mansions in the kingdom : about three miles towards the north-east is Chatsworth House, the princely seat of the Duke of Devonshire; and two miles and a half to the north is Hassop Hall, the seat of the Earl of Newburgh. The chalybeate baths have been lately re-established by the Duke of Rutland; the principal bath is 33 feet long, 16 wide, and of proportionate depth, and is constantly supplied with fresh water, which, on its influx, emits a considerable quantity of carbonic acid gas, and possesses a temperature of 60° of Fahrenheit. There are also shower-baths and a private warm-bath, with suitable accommodations; and a news-room has been added to the establishment. An agricultural society has been formed, the members of which hold their meetings in Bakewell and Chesterfield alternately, generally in October.

Near the entrance into the town from Ashford stands a cotton-mill, erected by the late Sir Richard Arkwright, in which about 300 persons are employed; and in the immediate vicinity are extensive lead-mines, and quarries of black and grey marble, and of chertz, which last is used in the Staffordshire potteries, in manufacturing earthenware. The market is on Friday : on every alternate Monday there is a cattle-market, which is now extremely well supplied with store and fat cattle

S 2

and sheep; and fairs are held on Easter-Monday, Whit-Monday, Aug. 26th, the Monday next after Oct. 10th, and the Monday after Nov. 11th, for horses and horned-cattle. One of the quarter-sessions for the county was formerly, and a petty-session for the hundred of High Peak on the first and third Friday in every month, is still, held here. A mineral court is also held for the manor, according to the local articles and customs of the lead-mines within it, which have prevailed from time immemorial. The powers of the county debt-court of Bakewell, established in 1847, extend over the greater part of the registration-district of Bakewell.

The parish comprises about 70,000 acres, chiefly hilly ground affording excellent pasture for sheep and cattle, and of which the Dukes of Rutland and Devonshire are the principal proprietors. The LIVING is a discharged vicarage, valued in the king's books at £40; net income, £350; patrons and appropriators, the Dean and Chapter of Lichfield. The tithes for the townships of Bakewell and Over Haddon were commuted, with some exceptions, for land and a money payment, in 1806. The church is a spacious cruciform structure, partly Norman, and partly in the early English style: the central tower, which was surmounted by a lofty spire, becoming dangerous from the failure of the pillars that supported it, has been taken down. Within are several magnificent altar-tombs of alabaster, with recumbent figures, and a stone font of great antiquity; in the churchyard is a cross, decorated with rude sculpture. At Baslow, Beeley, and Buxton, are churches, the livings of which are in the gift of the Duke of Devonshire; and at Ashford, Chelmorton, Great Longstone, Monyash, Sheldon, and Taddington, are others the livings of which are in the gift of the Vicar. There are places of worship for Independents, Wesleyans, and others. A free school was founded by Lady Grace Manners in 1636, and endowed with £15 per annum, which has been augmented with £35 per annum by the Duke of Rutland. St. John's hospital, for six aged men, was founded and endowed in 1602, by Sir John Manners Sutton and his brother; the income amounts to £40. A dispensary and a lying-in institution have been established. The poor law union of Bakewell comprises above 50 parishes and places, and contains a population of 31,319. Dr. Thomas Denman, an eminent physician, and father of Lord Denman, chief justice of the queen's bench, was born here in 1733.

BALBY, with HEXTHORP, a township and ecclesiastical parish, in the parish, union, and soke of DONCASTER, W. riding of YORK, 1½ mile (S. S. W.) from Doncaster; containing 486 inhabitants. It lies on the east side of the river Don, on the roads from Doncaster to Rotherham and Worksop; and comprises 1420 acres, whereof 640 are the property of the corporation of Doncaster, who are lords of the manor. There are a brewery and some tanneries. The parish was formed in August, 1846, under the act 6 and 7 Victoria, cap. 37. The church, the site for which, and for some schools, was given by the corporation, was built by subscription, in 1847; and the living has been endowed with £150 per annum by Miss Elizabeth Goodman Banks, of St. Catherine's, in whom the patronage is vested. The first meetings of the Society of Friends, under their founder George Fox, were held at Balby and the neighbouring village of Warms-worth.

132

BALCOMB (ST. MARY), a parish, in the union of CUCKFIELD, partly in the hundred of STREET, but chiefly in the hundred of BUTTINGHILL, rape of LEWES, E. division of SUSSEX, 4 miles (N.) from Cuckfield; containing 1542 inhabitants. It comprises about 4170 acres; and is intersected by the London and Brighton railway, which here passes through its principal tunnel, the construction of which was attended with much difficulty on account of the extraordinary swelling of the earth when exposed to the air. Midway between Balcomb and Cuckfield, the line is carried over the river Ouse by a viaduct 462 yards in length and 60 yards high, which rests on 37 arches. The living is a rectory, valued in the king's books at £15. 18. 6½., and in the gift of the family of Bethune: the tithes have been commuted for £450, and the glebe comprises 70 acres. About a quarter of a mile from the church is a spring, the water of which is similar in its properties to the Tonbridge waters.

BALDERSBY, a township, in the parish of TOP-CLIFFE, wapentake of HALLIKELD, N. riding of YORK, 5¾ miles (N. N. E.) from Ripon; containing 296 inhabitants. This place is on the road from Thirsk to Ripon, and comprises by computation 1600 acres; the river Swale passes on the east, and on the west is the great Roman road now called Leeming-Lane.

BALDERSTON, a chapelry, in the parish, union, and Lower division of the hundred, of BLACKBURN, N. division of the county of LANCASTER, 4½ miles (N. W.) from Blackburn, on the road between Whalley and Preston; containing 585 inhabitants. The manor was possessed by the Balderstons, by two coheiresses of whom it was brought, in moieties, to the Harringtons and Talbots. A portion subsequently passed to the Dudley family; and after the execution of the celebrated Sir Edmund Dudley for high treason, an inquisition was taken, 1st Henry VIII., when it was found that the manor was an escheat to the crown. The property was afterwards possessed by Mr. Cross, who, some years since, sold it to Joseph Feilden, Esq. The township comprises 1704a. 1r. 3p., of which 141 acres are woodland and plantation, and the remainder arable and pasture; the soil is a stiff clay, and the scenery beautiful, with extensive views. The river Ribble forms the northern boundary for more than a mile and a half. Part of the ecclesiastical district of Mellor-Brook is within the chapelry. The living of Balderston is a perpetual curacy in the gift of the Vicar of Blackburn, with an income of £118: the chapel is dedicated to St. Leonard. There is a national school for the poor.

BALDERTON (ST. GILES), a parish, in the union of NEWARK, S. division of the wapentake of NEWARK and of the county of NOTTINGHAM, 2 miles (S. E.) from Newark; containing 899 inhabitants. The parish comprises 3600 acres of land, with a clayey and sandy soil, and of which the Duke of Newcastle is one of the chief proprietors: the village consists of several well-built and substantial houses, and the surrounding scenery is agreeably diversified. The living is a vicarage, annexed to that of Farndon: the glebe comprises about 33 acres. The church is a very handsome edifice, principally in the later English style, with a lofty spire, and has a richly-ornamented Norman porch of exceeding beauty and in good preservation. A school has been endowed by William Alvey, with a rent-charge of £18.

BALDHU, an ecclesiastical parish, in the parishes of KENWYN and KEA, union of TRURO, W. division of the hundred of POWDER and of the county of CORNWALL, 3½ miles (S. W. by W.) from Truro. This place derives its name from *Bal-mine-dhu*, or rather *diu*, black; it is about three miles in length and two and a half in breadth, and of hilly and barren surface. The Carnon river forms its boundary on the south, and the Truro and Redruth road on the north; the Cornwall railway passes nearly along its boundary on the east. Several mines are wrought, the chief produce of which is black-jack and black tin. The " Old Men's Workings" consist of gigantic excavations in the Elvan rock, open to the sun, in some places more than 150 feet deep, and extending a distance of a mile and upwards: they are probably among the original mines of the county, and are not now wrought. There are also several smelting-houses. The parish was formed in 1847, under the act 6 and 7 Victoria, cap. 37; the living is in the gift of the Crown and the Bishop of Exeter alternately, and has an income of £150. The church was erected in 1847-8, at a cost of £1800, of which sum the Earl of Falmouth, who had the first presentation, contributed £1000; the Incorporated Society, £200; the Diocesan Society, £250; and the Church Commissioners, £260.

BALDOCK (ST. MARY); a market-town and parish, in the union of HITCHIN, hundred of BROADWATER, county of HERTFORD, 18 miles (N. by W.) from Hertford, and 37 (N. by W.) from London; containing 1807 inhabitants. This place, in the reign of Stephen, belonged to the Knights Templars, to whom Gilbert, Earl of Pembroke, had given the site. In a charter of confirmation granted by his descendant William, the place is termed Bandoc, of which the present name is a variation; though some antiquaries derive it from Balbec, supposing the town to have been so called by the Templars, in memory of the city of that name in Syria, from which their order had been expelled by the Saracens. The TOWN is situated near the intersection of the great north road and the Roman Ikeneld-street, between two hills which command an extensive view of a fine open country; consists principally of one street: the houses are mostly ancient, but interspersed with several of modern erection, and the inhabitants are amply supplied with water. A horticultural society, patronised by the nobility and gentry in the neighbourhood, was established in 1825. The trade is principally in malt, the land in the vicinity being highly favourable to the growth of barley: the fens and marsh land near the town form an extensive grazing district, and cheese of a peculiar quality is made here; there is also a very large brewery. The general market, which was on Saturday, has been discontinued; and a market exclusively for the sale of straw-plat is now held on Friday. The fairs are on the festivals of St. James, St. Andrew, and St. Matthew, each continuing two days; at the last a great quantity of cheese is sold. The county magistrates hold a petty-session here on the first Monday in every month. The parish comprises about 150 acres of land, the soil of which is in general chalky. The living is a discharged rectory, valued in the king's books at £10. 8. 9., and in the patronage of the Crown; net income, £126. The church, erected by the Knights Templars, and nearly all rebuilt in the early part of the fifteenth century, is a spacious structure, partly Norman, and partly in the

later English style, with an octagonal steeple built a few years ago; and contains a finely carved oak screen, part of the ancient rood-loft, and a very curious font. There are places of worship for the Society of Friends, Independents, and Wesleyans; and almshouses for twelve aged widows, founded and endowed in 1621, by Mr. John Winne. In cutting through Baldock hill, to form a new turnpike-road, a great number of fossils, consisting of *cornua ammonis*, sharks' teeth, &c. was discovered.

BALDON, MARSH (ST. PETER), a parish, in the union of ABINGDON, hundred of BULLINGTON, county of OXFORD, 6 miles (S. E. by S.) from Oxford; containing 360 inhabitants, and comprising 804 acres. This parish, originally called Meres or Mars and ultimately Marsh-Baldon, derives its distinguishing name from one De la Mare, a descendant of whom was patron of the living in 1381. In 1836, an act was obtained for dividing and allotting lands in the parishes of Marsh-Baldon and Toot-Baldon. The benefice is a rectory, valued in the king's books at £6. 13. 4.; net income, £93; patron, Sir H. P. Willoughby, Bart. The church has a highly picturesque tower, mantled with ivy: over the communion table is a painting of the Salutation, presented by the late Sir Christopher Willoughby. Dr. John Bridges, Bishop of Oxford, who died in 1618, was buried here.

BALDON, TOOT (ST. LAWRENCE), a parish, in the union of ABINGDON, hundred of BULLINGTON, county of OXFORD, 5¼ miles (S. E.) from Oxford; containing 269 inhabitants. This place, in Domesday book, is called Baudindon; and was afterwards named Toot Balden or Baldon, probably from one Le Tote, a landed proprietor, to distinguish it from the adjoining parish of Marsh-Baldon. The living is a discharged vicarage, in the gift of Sir H. P. Willoughby: the vicar receives £5. 5. per annum in lieu of tithes, and the interest of £502 raised by private subscription about forty years since.

BALE, or BAITHLEY (ALL SAINTS), a parish, in the union of WALSINGHAM, hundred of HOLT, W. division of NORFOLK, 16 miles (N.) from East Dereham; containing 229 inhabitants. It comprises 1041a. 2r. 38p., of which 824 acres are arable, 100 pasture, and 73 woodland. The living is a discharged rectory, united to that of Gunthorpe, and valued in the king's books at £10. 13. 4.: the tithes have been commuted for £305, and there are 21 acres of glebe. The church is in the decorated and later English styles. Here was anciently a chapel dedicated to St. Botolph.

BALHAM-HILL.—See TOOTING, UPPER.

BALK, a township, in the parish of KIRBY-KNOLE, union of THIRSK, wapentake of BIRDFORTH, N. riding of YORK, 3¼ miles (E. S. E.) from Thirsk; containing 89 inhabitants. It comprises about 780 acres, chiefly the property of Viscount Downe.

BALKHOLME, a township, in the parish and union of HOWDEN, wapentake of HOWDENSHIRE, E. riding of YORK, 3 miles (E.) from Howden; comprising by computation 550 acres, and containing 165 inhabitants. It is on the road from Howden to North Cave; and the river Ouse passes not far distant on the south.

BALLAM, a hamlet, in the township of WESTBY with PLUMPTONS, parish of KIRKHAM, union of FYLDE, hundred of AMOUNDERNESS, N. division of the county of LANCASTER, 3 miles (W. by S.) from Kirkham;

containing 60 inhabitants. It lies on the road from Westby to Lytham, and is divided into Higher and Lower Ballam.

BALLIDON, a chapelry, in the parish of BRAD-BORNE, hundred of WIRKSWORTH, S. division of the county of DERBY, 5¾ miles (N. N. E.) from Ashbourn; containing 92 inhabitants. At the time of the Domesday survey the manor belonged to Ralph Fitzhubert, and for some generations afterwards was held by the family of Herthill, whose heiress brought it to the Cokaines in the 15th century. In the reign of Elizabeth it was sold to Sir Anthony Ashley, and subsequently came to other families, among whom were the Boothbys, and the Murrays, earls of Mansfield. The chapel is very ancient, and contains a curious font.

BALLINGDON, a parish, in the union of SUDBURY, hundred of HINCKFORD, N. division of ESSEX, ½ a mile (S. W. by W.) from Sudbury; containing 843 inhabitants. After the decay of the parochial church, the village of Ballingdon, which had been previously only a chapelry in the parish of Brundon, became the head of the parish. The soil in some parts is a stiffish clay, retaining moisture, and in others a sandy loam, forming some of the best arable land in the district. The living is a rectory, valued in the king's books at £6. 13. 4., and in the patronage of the family of Windham. The inhabitants resort to the church of All Saints, Sudbury, and contribute towards the church-rate of that parish.

BALLINGHAM (ST. DUBRITIUS), a parish, in the union of Ross, Upper division of the hundred of WORMELOW, county of HEREFORD, 7 miles (N. by W.) from Ross; containing 149 inhabitants. The parish is situated on the right bank of the Wye, that river surrounding it on all sides except the west: it comprises 840 acres. The living is a perpetual curacy; net income, £165; patron and impropriator, Sir E. F. S. Stanhope, Bart. The tithes have been commuted for £177. 10.

BALLS-POND, an ecclesiastical district, in the parish of ISLINGTON, Finsbury division of the hundred of OSSULSTONE, county of MIDDLESEX, 2 miles (N.) from London. This populous suburb of the metropolis is of modern origin, and consists principally of uniform ranges of houses. A very large open area, surrounded by a wall and cattle-shed, with a handsome entrance, was formed for a market-place, intended to supersede the celebrated market in Smithfield; and an act for opening it as a general cattle-market was procured by its enterprising proprietor, Mr. Perkins; but it was soon after closed from want of business, and no cattle have been sold there for some years. A church dedicated to St. Paul was erected in 1827, at an expense of £10,947; it is a handsome structure in the later English style, with a low square tower embattled and crowned with pinnacles. The living is a perpetual curacy; net income, £335; patron, the Vicar of Islington. The Independents have a place of worship, and there are almshouses belonging to the London Benefit Societies, the Tilers' and Brick-layers' Company, the Cutlers' Company, and the Dyers' Company. Samuel Rogers, the eminent poet, was born in that part of Newington green which is within the district.

BALNE, a township, in the parish of SNAITH, Lower division of the wapentake of OSGOLDCROSS, W. riding of YORK, 5¼ miles (S. W. by W.) from Snaith; containing 341 inhabitants. It comprises by computation 2750
134

acres, of which about 115 are woodland; the soil is chiefly of a sandy nature. The village, which is scattered, lies to the south of the Knottingley and Goole canal. The Wesleyans and Primitive Methodists have each a place of worship.

BALSALL, a chapelry, in the parish of HAMPTON-IN-ARDEN, union of SOLIHULL, Solihull division of the hundred of HEMLINGFORD, N. division of the county of WARWICK, 4½ miles (S. E. by E.) from Solihull; containing 1160 inhabitants. It comprises 4824 acres; and is partly bounded on the west by the river Blythe, and skirted on the east by the road between Kenilworth and Coleshill. The chapel, dedicated to St. Mary, was originally the church of a preceptory founded here by the Knights Templars, to whom Roger de Mowbray had given the lordship: it was repaired in 1823, at a cost of £979. The living is a perpetual curacy; patrons, the Governors of Balsall Hospital, in whom the impropriation is also vested. Lady Katherine Leveson, in 1670, devised the manor for the erection and endowment of an hospital for twenty women. The hospital was incorporated in the first year of the reign of Queen Anne, and eleven trustees were appointed, with power to enlarge the buildings and increase the number of inmates, which now amounts to thirty; exclusively of whom, the establishment comprises a master, under-master, apothecary, matron, and nurse. The annual receipts are about £1500, of which the master, in addition to his stipend, receives £50 as perpetual curate of Balsall; a sum of £50 is also paid to the vicar of Long Itchington.

BALSCOT, a chapelry, in the parish of WROXTON, union of BANBURY, hundred of BLOXHAM, county of OXFORD, 5 miles (W. N. W.) from Banbury; containing 199 inhabitants. The village contains some interesting remains of ancient domestic architecture. The chapel is a small but neat edifice in the decorated English style, with a tower of remarkably graceful proportions on the south side of the building: the font is Norman. Until 1821, the dead were interred at Wroxton; but on the 28th of August in that year the chapelyard here was consecrated.

BALSHAM (HOLY TRINITY), a parish, in the union of LINTON, hundred of RADFIELD, county of CAMBRIDGE, 3 miles (N. E. by N.) from Linton; containing 1271 inhabitants. It comprises about 4500 acres, the soil consisting principally of clay and chalk. The living is a rectory, valued in the king's books at £39. 16. 8.; net income, £1104; patrons, the Governors of the Charter house, London. The tithes were commuted for land and a money payment in 1801. A little westward from the village are Gogmagog hills, on the summit of which are remains of a circular camp with a double rampart, supposed to be British. The ancient trench called Fleam-Dyke commences in the vicinity. Hugh de Balsham, founder of Peter-house College, Cambridge, was born and is interred here; and Thomas Sutton, founder of the Charter house, resided at the place.

BALTERLEY, a township, in the parish of BAR-THOMLEY, union of NEWCASTLE-UNDER-LYME, N. division of the hundred of PIREHILL and of the county of STAFFORD, 6½ miles (N. W. by W.) from Newcastle; containing 316 inhabitants. This is the only part of the parish lying in Staffordshire, the remainder being in the county of Chester. The township comprises 800 acres, and the tithes have been commuted for £134.

BALTONSBOROUGH (St. Dunstan), a parish, in the union of Wells, hundred of Glaston-Twelve-Hides, E. division of Somerset, 5 miles (S. E.) from Glastonbury; containing 718 inhabitants. It is annexed to the vicarage of Butleigh.

BAMBER-BRIDGE, an ecclesiastical district, in the chapelry of Walton-le-Dale, parish, and Lower division of the hundred, of Blackburn, union of Preston, N. division of the county of Lancaster, 3½ miles (S. S. E.) from Preston, on the road to Chorley; containing about 3000 inhabitants. The soil of the district is a stiff clay; the surface is undulated, and the scenery picturesque. The village, which is very pleasant, is the spot where the Claytons established print-works as early as 1760. A cotton-mill, belonging to William Eccles, Esq., employs 500 hands; another, the property of Richard Bashall, Esq., employs a like number; and a third, the property of Richard Ashworth, Esq., employs 250. Among the seats in the vicinity are, Lostock Hall, the residence of William Clayton, Esq.; Withy Grove, the residence of Mr. Eccles; and Lostock House, the residence of Mr. Bashall. Bamber-Bridge House, the original seat of the Clayton family, is now divided into several dwellings. The Blackburn and Preston railway has a station at this place. The living is a perpetual curacy, in the patronage of the Vicar of Blackburn, with a net income of £150, and a residence. The church, dedicated to Our Saviour, is a very neat structure in the Romanesque style, with a graceful spire; it was built in 1837, at a cost of £2200. Robert Townley Parker, Esq., of Cuerden Hall, has erected a vault under the chancel, as the future burial-place of his family. There is a national and Sunday school, in which more than 400 children receive instruction.

BAMBROUGH (St. Aidan), a parish, in the union of Belford, N. division of Bambrough ward and of Northumberland; comprising the chapelries of Beadnell, Lucker, and North Sunderland, and the townships of Adderstone, Bambrough, Bambrough-Castle, Bradford, Budle, Burton, Elford, Fleetham, Glororum, Hoppen, Mouson, Newham, Newstead, Outchester, Ratchwood, Shorestone, Spindlestone, Swinhoe, Tughall, Warenford, and Warenton; and containing 4231 inhabitants, of whom 375 are in the township of Bambrough, 4¾ miles (E. by N.) from Belford. Bambrough, originally called Bebbanburg, was prior to the Conquest a royal burgh, and the residence of several of the kings of Northumbria. It sent two members to parliament in the 23rd of Edward I., and in the reign of Edward III. furnished one ship for the expedition against Calais; it had also a market, which has long been discontinued. The surrounding district, formerly called Bambroughshire, was a separate franchise, in the possession of various privileges, now become obsolete. The village occupies an airy and pleasant situation near the sea and Budle bay. The living is a perpetual curacy; net income, £121; patron, the Trustees of Lord Crewe, who, with other proprietors, are the impropriators. The church, with another long since in ruins, was given by Henry I. to the priory of Nostel in Yorkshire, whereupon a small convent of Augustine canons was founded here, in 1137, as a cell to that priory, the revenue of which at the Dissolution was £124. 15. 7. There were also a college, an hospital dedicated to St. Mary Magdalene, and a house of Preaching Friars. At Beadnell,

Lucker, and North Sunderland are separate incumbencies. The church estate, which is situated at Fowberry, in Bambrough township, consists of a farmhouse, outbuildings, and about 63 acres of land, let for £100 per annum.

BAMBROUGH-CASTLE, a township, in the parish, and N. division of the ward, of Bambrough, union of Belford, N. division of Northumberland, 5 miles (E. by N.) from Belford; containing 59 inhabitants. This township is principally distinguished for its castle, built about the middle of the sixth century, by Ida, the first Anglo-Saxon king of Northumbria. In 642 it was besieged by Penda, King of Mercia, who, after an unsuccessful attempt to set it on fire, was compelled to retreat. In the beginning of the eighth century, Berthfrid, guardian of Osred, the young Northumbrian king, defended it against the usurper Eadulph, who was taken prisoner and put to death. It was plundered and almost demolished by the Danes in 993, but was soon restored. After the Norman Conquest it was held by Robert de Mowbray, on whose insurrection against William Rufus it was besieged, and, after an obstinate defence, surrendered to that monarch, who threatened, unless it were given up, to put out the eyes of Mowbray, who had been taken prisoner. During the war between Stephen and the Empress Matilda, and the protracted struggle between the houses of York and Lancaster, the castle sustained repeated sieges: it was taken in 1463 by Margaret of Anjou, queen of Henry VI., on her route to Hexham, after landing at Berwick, on her return from France, and at length became dilapidated in the reign of Henry VII. The castle and manor were granted in the reign of James II. to John Forster, one of whose descendants having joined the Pretender, they were confiscated to the crown, and were purchased by Lord Crewe, Bishop of Durham, who, in 1720, devised to trustees his manors of Bambrough and Blanchland, then producing £1312 and now £8126 per annum, for charitable purposes. The income is appropriated to the erection and repair of churches, the support of exhibitions and fellowships, the relief of the poor, the foundation and endowment of schools, the maintenance of the establishment at Bambrough Castle, the improvement of Sunderland harbour (for which £5000 have been paid out of the funds), and various improvements along the coast. Under the direction of Dr. Sharp, Archdeacon of Durham, the castle was repaired in 1757, the keep being set apart for the occasional residence of the trustees; and the whole is maintained in repair, with its furniture, by an estate left by Dr. Sharp for the purpose.

The castle is situated on the summit of a steep rock, which projects into the sea and rises perpendicularly to the height of 150 feet above low-water mark, being accessible only on the south-east side, where is the ancient gateway flanked with a circular tower on each side, and formerly defended by a trench cut through a narrow isthmus communicating with the main land. Within a short distance of this is a more modern gateway, with a portcullis; and a little further on is a round tower. The keep, which is of Norman architecture, and the most ancient part of the building, is a lofty square structure. In 1773, the ruins of a church or chapel, erected in the castle during the Norman period, were discovered; and the font, richly carved, is preserved, among other curiosities, in the keep. In the castle-yard are granaries, in which corn is stored to be sold to the poor at proper times; and a market is opened every Tuesday and Friday, when the industrious poor are supplied with meal and grocery at the cost price. In another part of the castle-yard is a dispensary, at which a surgeon attends twice every week; and from the surplus revenue the trustees have established two national schools, for which schoolrooms have been appropriated in the castle, and which are free to all poor children who may come. Thirty girls, between the ages of nine and sixteen, are admitted to board and lodge, and are likewise provided with clothes and washing. In 1778, the trustees founded a library, to which Dr. Sharp generously bequeathed the whole of his valuable books, including the greater part of the library of Dr. Sharp, Archbishop of York; and this collection, including nearly 6000 volumes, is open to persons residing in the neighbourhood, under certain regulations. A principal object of the establishment is also to afford assistance to shipwrecked mariners.

BAMBURGH.—See BAUMBER.

BAMFORD, a hamlet, in the parish of HATHERSAGE, union of CHAPEL-EN-LE-FRITH, hundred of HIGH PEAK, N. division of the county of DERBY, 6¼ miles (N. by W.) from Stoney-Middleton; containing 297 inhabitants, and comprising 1456 acres, of which 700 are common or waste. The impropriate tithes have been commuted for £33. 9., and the vicarial for £4; there is a glebe of 33 acres.

BAMFORD, LANCASHIRE.—See BIRTLE.

BAMPTON (ST. MICHAEL), a market-town and parish, in the union of TIVERTON, hundred of BAMPTON, Collumpton and N. divisions of DEVON, 21 miles (N. by E.) from Exeter, and 162 (W. by S.) from London; containing 2049 inhabitants. Bampton is supposed by Bishop Gibson to have been the Beamdune of the Saxon Chronicle, where, in 614, the Britons were defeated with great slaughter by Cynegils, King of the West Saxons. Other antiquaries, referring this event to Bindon in Dorset, derive its ancient names Bathermtown and Bathrumpton from the river Batherm, which flows into the Exe, about one mile and a quarter below the town; and thence, by contraction, deduce the present name. The parish contains between 7000 and 8000 acres: the surface is marked by numerous hills formed of limestone; the soil runs through several varieties, and is liable, especially in the valleys, to inundations from the rivers Exe and Batherm. The town is pleasantly situated in a vale; the houses are irregularly built of stone, and amply supplied with water. The principal branch of manufacture is that of serge: limestone is obtained in large quantities, and of excellent quality. The market is on Wednesday: fairs are held on Whit-Tuesday and the last Thursday in October; and on the Wednesday before Lady-day and the last Thursday in November are two large markets, both of which are well attended. At the fairs and great markets a large number of sheep are sold, which, from the excellence of the pastures, are remarkable for size and flavour. A portreeve, two constables, and other officers, are appointed annually by the lord of the manor. The living is a discharged vicarage, valued in the king's books at £20; net income, £118; patron, E. Rendell, Esq.; impropriator, Charles Chichester, Esq., whose tithes have been commuted for

136

£720: the vicar has a glebe of two acres. The church is a spacious structure in the early English style, containing several monuments to the earls of Bath. At Petton, four miles distant from the church, is a chapel, in which divine service is performed every Sunday; at Shillingford are the ruins of an old chapel. There is a place of worship for Particular Baptists. In the town is a spring strongly impregnated with iron. The site of an ancient castle erected in 1336, by a member of the family of Cogan, is still discernible on a mount. John de Bampton, a Carmelite monk, and the first who read Aristotle publicly at Cambridge, was a native of the town.

BAMPTON (ST. MARY), a town and parish, in the union of WITNEY, hundred of BAMPTON, county of OXFORD, 16 miles (W. by S.) from Oxford, and 70 (W. N. W.) from London; comprising the hamlets of Aston, Brighthampton, Chimney, Lew, and Weald, the chapelry of Shifford, and the township of Bampton; and containing 2734 inhabitants, of whom 778 are in the township. This place, called by the Saxons Bemtune, was a town of some importance during the heptarchy, and for a considerable period afterwards: in the reign of Edward the Confessor it was annexed to the diocese of Exeter, by Leofric, chaplain to that monarch, and first bishop of the see. It is bounded on the south by the river Isis, on which are some convenient wharfs: the houses are neatly built, and the inhabitants are plentifully supplied with water, which springs through a gravelly soil. There are a subscription library and a newsroom. A considerable trade was formerly carried on in leather, but it has greatly declined. A fair is held on the 26th and 27th of August, the former day being for the sale of horses. Bampton has two divisions for the transaction of its civil affairs, the one called the eastern and the other the western; the justices in petty-sessions for the former division meet at Witney, and for the latter at Burford, and courts leet of the joint proprietors of the manor are held, at which constables and other officers are appointed. A town-hall has been erected in the market-place by subscription.

The LIVING is a vicarage, in three portions, each valued in the king's books at £10. 0. 10., and in the patronage of the Dean and Chapter of Exeter: net income of the first portion, £544; of the second, £492; and of the third, £510. The tithes, with certain exceptions, were commuted in 1812, for land and corn-rents. The church is a spacious cruciform structure, partly Norman, and partly in the early English style, with a massive square embattled tower surmounted by an octagonal spire; the Norman doorway leading into the south transept, and the semi-porch and western entrance, in the early English style, are fine specimens, and the interior of the belfry, which is in its original state and perfectly entire, is a beautiful specimen of Norman decoration. There are chapels of ease at Shifford, Lew, and Aston. The free school was founded in 1635, by Robert Vesey, of Chimney, who endowed it with £200, which, with subsequent benefactions, was laid out in the purchase of eight acres of land, now let for £28 per annum: in 1784, £400 stock was given for the instruction of ten additional scholars. There are slight remains of a castle supposed to have been erected in the reign of John, and of a quadrangular form, with towers at the angles, and bastions at the entrance on the east and west sides. A field called Kinsey is supposed to have been originally the "King's Way." Phillips, the author of the "Splendid Shilling," a poem on Cider, &c., was born here in 1676.

BAMPTON (St. Patrick), a parish, in West ward and union, county of Westmorland, 9 miles (S.) from Penrith ; containing, with part of Mardale chapelry, 579 inhabitants. This parish comprises by measurement 3720 acres, and is intersected by the river Lowther. Here is a beautiful lake, called Hawsewater, about three miles long, and half a mile broad, its head being environed by an assemblage of lofty mountains, its eastern side sheltered by well-planted rocky eminences, and its western bordered by cultivated fields. The living is a discharged vicarage, valued in the king's books at £7. 5., and in the patronage of the Crown ; net income, £101. The impropriate tithes belong to the Earl of Lonsdale and the trustees of the free grammar school, of whom the former has £164, and the latter £54. 8. ; the vicarial tithes have been commuted for £19. 16. The church was rebuilt on the site of the former, in 1726 : the vicarage-house was rebuilt also, about the same period, by Dr. Gibson, Bishop of London. The free school was founded in 1627, by Thomas Sutton, D.D., who vested in trustees the sum of £500, collected in the parish of St. Saviour, Southwark, and other places, with which a portion of the rectorial tithes of Bampton was purchased. A school at Roughill was established by Edmund Noble, and endowed with £9. 15. 10. per annum ; and in 1723 Richard Wright founded a school at Measand, which he endowed with property producing £50 per annum. Here are also three parochial libraries, established respectively in 1710, 1750, and 1757, and comprising in the aggregate upwards of 800 volumes. Thomas Gibson, M.D., (who married the daughter of Richard Cromwell, son of the Protector,) physician-general to the army, and author of a *System of Anatomy*, was a native of High Knipe, in the parish ; where also was born, in 1669, his nephew, Edmund Gibson, D.D., Bishop of London, and editor of two improved editions of Camden's *Britannia*, and other learned works.

BAMPTON, KIRK (St. Peter), a parish, in Cumberland ward, E. division of Cumberland, 6½ miles (W.) from Carlisle ; comprising the townships of Kirk-Bampton, Little Bampton, and Oughterby ; and containing 536 inhabitants, of whom 193 are in the township of Kirk-Bampton. This parish is of oblong form, much greater in extent from east to west than from north to south. In the east is the village of Kirk-Bampton, a little to the south-west of which lies Oughterby, and in the west is Little Bampton township. The living is a discharged rectory, valued in the king's books at £14. 17. 10. ; net income, £100 ; patrons, alternately, the Earl of Lonsdale and Sir Wastell Brisco, Bart. There are two chalybeate springs, one of them discovered in 1826, near Fingland Rigg ; the other, called Toddel Well, has been long known.

BAMPTON, LITTLE, a township, in the parish of Kirk-Bampton, Cumberland ward, E. division of Cumberland, 5 miles (N. by E.) from Wigton ; containing 212 inhabitants. The tithes have been commuted for £58. 6. 6. payable to the Dean and Chapter of Carlisle, and £66. 13. 6. to the rector. The river Wampool flows at a short distance from the western boundary of the township.

BANBURY (St. Mary), a borough, market-town, and parish, and the head of a union, chiefly in the hundred of Banbury, county of Oxford, but partly in that of King's-Sutton, S. division of the county of Northampton, 22 miles (N.) from Oxford, and 69 (N. W.) from London ; containing, with the township of Neithrop and the hamlets of Grimsbury and Nethercote, 7366 inhabitants. This place, called by the Saxons *Banesbyrig*, is supposed to have been occupied by the Romans, which opinion is corroborated by the discovery of Roman coins and an altar, the latter relic having been preserved under an archway in front of an inn, until about the year 1775 : there is also, in a field near the south entrance to the town, a sort of amphitheatre, now called "the Bear Garden," presenting two rows of seats cut in the side of a hill, and of very ancient date. About the year 1135, a castle was built here by Alexander, Bishop of Lincoln, who, when taken prisoner by King Stephen, was compelled to resign this, with Newark and other fortresses which he had erected. It was afterwards restored to the see, and long continued to be one of the residences of the bishops, but in the first of Edward VI. was re-signed to the crown : it is described by Leland, in the reign of Henry VIII., as "a castle having two wards, and each ward a ditch ; in the outer is a terrible prison for convict men ; in the north part of the inner ward is a fair piece of new building of stone." During the war between the houses of York and Lancaster, the neighbourhood was the scene of a sanguinary conflict, in 1469, between a vast body of insurgents from the north (said to have been privately encouraged by the Earl of Warwick) and the army of Edward IV., commanded by the Earl of Pembroke, who had been joined by Lord Stafford with about 5000 men. The armies met on a plain called Danesmoor, near Edgcot, five miles from Banbury ; and a conflict ensued, somewhat advantageous to the insurgents. In the evening, the king's forces having retired to Banbury, a quarrel took place between Pembroke and Stafford respecting quarters at the inn ; in consequence of which, Lord Stafford quitted the town with his followers, and left Pembroke alone to meet the enemy (who had encamped on a hill near the town) on the following day. In the battle which ensued the royal army was defeated, with the loss of 4000 men ; and the gallant Pembroke and his brother, Sir Richard Herbert, being taken prisoners, were on the next day beheaded at this place, together with ten other gentlemen of the king's party.

At the commencement of the civil war of the seventeenth century, the inhabitants espoused the cause of the parliament with so much zeal as to give occasion to the mirth and raillery of some writers of that and subsequent periods. The castle was at first garrisoned for the parliament, but was surrendered to the king in the week following the battle of Edge Hill, Oct. 1642 ; it withstood a slight siege from the parliamentarians in 1643, and a very severe one in 1644. After the affair at Cropredy-Bridge, three miles to the north, on the

Seal and Arms.

29th of June in that year, the siege was pressed with the utmost vigour; Col. John Fiennes, a son of Lord Saye, having brought to the assistance of the besieging party all the disposable forces from Northamptonshire and Warwickshire. A breach being effected, an assault was made on Sept. 23rd, but without success. At length, on Oct. 25th, the Earl of Northampton, having defeated the parliamentary cavalry on the south side of the town, was enabled to relieve the garrison, after the siege had continued thirteen weeks, and when the defenders had eaten all their horses except two : the defence was conducted by Sir William Compton. In 1646 the castle was again besieged, by Col. Whalley, who encamped before it ten weeks ; and the king having now joined the Scottish army, and further resistance being useless, the garrison capitulated on honourable terms. Of this once massive fortress the only vestige is a part of one of the walls, on which a cottage has been erected, and the site is now occupied by fruitful gardens.

The TOWN is pleasantly situated in a fertile valley, on the banks of the small river Cherwell, which separates this county from Northamptonshire ; it formerly consisted of old streets irregularly built, but has been greatly improved under an act passed in the 6th of George IV. for paving, lighting, and watching the borough. The shops are excellent, the streets for the most part wide and airy, and the footpaths well paved : the carriage ways are macadamized with a durable kind of ironstone brought from the border of Leicestershire ; the streets are lighted with gas, and the supply of water is generally abundant. A subscription library and mechanics' institute have been established. The manufacture of plush, shag, and girth-webbing was formerly carried on to a considerable extent, but has of late somewhat declined. Banbury was noted for a peculiar kind of cheese, but has long since lost this distinction ; its *cakes*, however, still enjoy great and deserved celebrity. The Oxford canal passes close to the town, communicating with all parts of the kingdom, and affording facility for every kind of trade ; and the Oxford and Rugby railway, commenced in 1846, runs close to Banbury, on the east side. The market is on Thursday, and, from the situation of the town in a fertile and populous agricultural district, is much frequented. Fairs are held on the first Thursday after Old Twelfth-day and the three preceding days (which fair is celebrated for the trade in horses), the third Thursdays in Feb., March, and April, Holy-Thursday, the third Thursdays in June, July (for cattle and wool), August, and Sept., the Thursday after Old Michaelmas (which is also a statute-fair for the hiring of servants), the third Thursday after Old Michaelmas, the third Thursday in Nov., and the second Thursday before Christmas.

The inhabitants were originally incorporated in 1554, by Queen Mary, who granted them a CHARTER, in consideration of services rendered in the suppression of the Duke of Northumberland's rebellion upon her accession to the throne. A second was bestowed by James I. in 1609; and in 1718, George I. conferred the charter by which, until the passing of the Municipal Reform act, the borough was governed. The corporation, since the passing of the act, has consisted of a mayor, 4 aldermen, and 12 councillors, and the number of burgesses is about 350 : a commission of the peace has been issued

138

lage is situated on a gentle eminence. The living is a rectory, valued in the king's books at £9. 3. 6½., and in the patronage of the Crown, with a net income of £800 : the glebe comprises 34 acres. The church, a large handsome building with a square tower surmounted by a wooden spire, was founded by Sir Hugh Bardolp, Knt., whose effigy is in a chapel belonging to the church, and some trifling remains of whose family seat are still visible in the parish. There are places of worship for Primitive and Wesleyan Methodists. About 150 acres of fen land were awarded for the benefit of the poor, at the inclosure.

BANK NEWTON, a township, in the parish of GARGRAVE, union of SKIPTON, E. division of the wapentake of STAINCLIFFE and EWCROSS, W. riding of YORK, 6 miles (W.) from Skipton ; containing 129 inhabitants. This township, which is situated in the western portion of the parish, comprises by computation 2280 acres, all in meadow and pasture ; some of the inclosures are among the largest in the district of Craven.

BANKS, LANCASHIRE.—See CROSSENS.

BANKS-FEE, or SOUTH-FIELD, a hamlet, in the parish of LONGBOROUGH, union of STOW-ON-THE-WOLD, Upper division of the hundred of KIFTSGATE, E. division of the county of GLOUCESTER, 1½ mile (N. by W.) from Stow. The small tithes have been commuted for £125.

BANNINGHAM (ST. BOTOLPH), a parish, in the union of AYLSHAM, hundred of SOUTH ERPINGHAM, E. division of NORFOLK, 2 miles (N. E.) from Aylsham ; containing 329 inhabitants. The parish comprises about 1000 acres of land, of which the surface is flat, and the soil a strong loam on brick earth. The living is a rectory, valued in the king's books at £10. 15. 10., and in the gift of S. Bignold, Esq. : the tithes have been commuted for £375, and the glebe consists of 18 acres. The church is in the decorated and later English styles, with a lofty embattled tower. There is a place of worship for Primitive Methodists.

BANNISTER-HALL, a hamlet, in the chapelry of WALTON-LE-DALE, parish, and Lower division of the hundred of BLACKBURN, union of PRESTON, N. division of the county of LANCASTER, 4 miles (S. E.) from Preston. It is situated on the river Darwen. The soil is various, but very good, the surface level, and the scenery picturesque and beautiful. Here are the extensive print-works of Messrs. Charles Swainson and Co., remarkable for producing the finest chintz work, wrought by blocks ; this establishment was commenced about 1770, and employs 300 hands. Iron, salt, and magnesia are obtained in the hamlet. Frenchwood, near Preston, close to which is the confluence of the Darwen and the Ribble, is the residence of Mr. Swainson. There is a mineral spring.

BANSTEAD (ALL SAINTS), a parish, in the union of EPSOM, First division of the hundred of COPTHORNE, W. division of SURREY, 3½ miles (E. S. E.) from Epsom ; containing 1168 inhabitants. It is situated on high ground, on the chalk hill which stretches into Kent ; and comprises 5463 acres, chiefly in pasture : 1375 acres are common or waste. Banstead Downs are remarkable for their verdure ; and the fine pasturage they afford to numerous flocks of sheep has long rendered the excellence of Banstead mutton proverbial : a considerable portion of them has, however, been brought under tillage of late years. The living is a perpetual curacy, valued in the king's books at £13. 8. 7½.; patron and incumbent, the

139

Rev. W. L. Buckle. The great tithes, belonging to the Rev. Mr. Buckle and R. Hudson, Esq., have been commuted for £393, the vicarial for £300, and a rent-charge of £201. 5. 9. is payable to the trustees of Newport grammar school ; the glebe consists of 6½ acres. The church is built of flints, and consists of a nave, aisles, and chancel, with a tower surmounted by a lofty spire. There is a place of worship for dissenters in the hamlet of Tadworth.

BANWELL (ST. ANDREW), a parish, in the union of AXBRIDGE, hundred of WINTERSTOKE, E. division of SOMERSET, 5 miles (N. N. W.) from Axbridge ; containing 1819 inhabitants. The manor has been in the possession of the bishops of Bath and Wells since the time of Edward the Confessor, with the exception of the short reign of Edward VI. ; one of them built an episcopal palace here, the remains of which, in the early part of the last century, were converted into a private residence, called Banwell Court. The park was subsequently divided into inclosures, which were assigned on lease for lives. Some of the leases, however, were lately bought up, and the ground disposed in a tasteful manner, by forming plantations, with drives conducting to pleasing and richly variegated prospects. The late Bishop Law, also, in 1827, erected a cottage ornée for his own accommodation, and that of the numerous visiters which the discovery of two caverns in the rock, one denominated the Bone, and the other the Stalactite cavern, has attracted hither. The PARISH comprises by measurement 5000 acres of land, of which the soil is fertile, and the substrata abound in mineral varieties ; limestone and blue lias are quarried, and lead, iron, and copper ore were formerly worked to a very great extent. The manufacture of paper is carried on, affording employment to about 80 persons. The village is pleasantly situated under the Mendip Hills, in a vale watered by a copious stream issuing from a spring formerly in repute for medicinal properties,·and from which the place is supposed to have taken its name. A fair for fat-cattle is held on the 18th of January. The Bristol and Exeter railway passes through the parish, in which a station has been established. The LIVING is a vicarage, valued in the king's books at £26. 0½.; patrons and appropriators, the Dean and Chapter of Bristol : their tithes have been commuted for £225, and the vicarial for £702. The church is a fine specimen of the later English style, and contains a richly carved screen and rood-loft, a finely sculptured stone pulpit, and windows of stained glass. There is a place of worship for Wesleyans. A monastery was founded at Banwell by one of the early Saxon kings, to the abbacy of which Alfred the Great appointed Asser, his subsequent biographer : it was entirely demolished in the Danish irruptions ; and although restored, it never recovered its former splendour, and fell to decay several years before the suppression of religious houses. The summit of a neighbouring eminence is crowned by a British earthwork, inclosing within its irregular rampart an area of about twenty acres ; and about a quarter of a mile from this is an intrenchment nearly square, in the centre of which the ground is elevated in the form of a cross.

BAPCHILD (ST. LAWRENCE), a parish, in the union and hundred of MILTON, Upper division of the lathe of SCRAY, E. division of KENT, 1¼ mile (E. S. E.) from Sittingbourne ; containing 338 inhabitants. Ecclesi-

T 2

astical councils were held here during the heptarchy, in commemoration of one of which, convened under Archbishop Brightwald in 794, an oratory or chapel was erected, of which there are still some remains. The parish comprises 1058 acres, whereof 94 are in wood. The living is a discharged vicarage, valued in the king's books at £8; patrons and appropriators, the Dean and Chapter of Chichester. The great tithes have been commuted for £435. 5., and the vicarial for £165. 5. 6.; the appropriate glebe consists of 5 acres, and the vicarial of 1½ acre. The church is principally in the early English style, with modern insertions, and has a shingled tower.

BAPTON, a tything, in the parish of FISHERTON-DE-LA-MERE, union of WILTON, hundred of WARMINSTER, though locally in the hundred of DUNWORTH, Warminster and S. divisions of WILTS, 6 miles (N. by E.) from Hindon; containing 143 inhabitants.

BARBON, a chapelry, in the parish of KIRKBY-LONSDALE, union of KENDAL, LONSDALE ward, county of WESTMORLAND, 4 miles (N. N. E.) from Kirkby-Lonsdale; containing 315 inhabitants. The township comprises 4204 acres, of which 1960 are common or waste; the soil is light and gravelly, and its surface undulated, rising to the summit of Barbon Fell. Peat is in abundance, and there is a small vein of coal. The North-Western railway runs through the chapelry. The living is a perpetual curacy; net income, £90; patron, the Vicar of Kirkby-Lonsdale. The chapel, and a schoolroom adjoining it, were built by subscription, in 1815; the school has a small endowment, bequeathed by John Garnett, in the year 1721.

BARBY (ST. MARY), a parish, in the union of RUGBY, hundred of FAWSLEY, S. division of the county of NORTHAMPTON, 6 miles (N. N. W.) from Daventry; containing, with Onely, 640 inhabitants. This parish, which is bounded by Warwickshire on the north-west and partly on the south, comprises by measurement 3353 acres, nearly all pasture; it is intersected by the Oxford canal, and situated near the London and Birmingham railway. The living is a rectory, valued in the king's books at £30. 2. 11.; net income, £894; patrons, the Trustees of the Rev. C. Williams. "Barby Town Lands" consist of property left for charitable uses, and vested in feoffees; part of it comprises eight cottages and an acre and a half of garden-ground, valued together at £37 per annum, which is applied in aid of a school.

BARCHESTON (ST. MARTIN), a parish, in the union of SHIPSTON-ON-STOUR, Brails division of the hundred of KINGTON, S. division of the county of WARWICK, ½ a mile (E. S. E.) from Shipston; containing, with the hamlet of Willington, 193 inhabitants. The living is a discharged rectory, valued in the king's books at £13. 6. 8.; net income, £193; patron and incumbent, the Rev. G. D. Wheeler.

BARCOMBE (ST. MARY), a parish, in the union of CHAILEY, hundred of BARCOMBE, rape of LEWES, E. division of SUSSEX, 4 miles (N. by E.) from Lewes; containing 1028 inhabitants. It comprises 3106 acres, whereof 305 are common or waste; and is bounded on the east by the river Ouse, on which is a flour-mill that has existed since the Conquest, and has been for more than a century in the possession of the family of Mr. Russell Gray, who has also established an extensive oil-

nard : the tithes have been commuted for £465, and there are 63 acres of glebe, with a handsome parsonage-house. The church is a small ancient edifice, with a low tower, and contains some monuments to the Walford family. A school, now conducted on the national plan, was endowed in 1774, with £18 per annum, by Sarah Barnard, who also endowed an almshouse for five widows.

BARDFIELD-SALING (St. *Margaret*), a parish, in the union of Dunmow, hundred of Freshwell, N. division of Essex, 5¾ miles (N. E.) from Dunmow; containing 381 inhabitants, and comprising about 1100 acres. The living is a donative ; net income, £75 ; patron, W. Sandel, Esq. ; impropriator, J. M. Raikes, Esq. It was returned in the reign of Henry VIII. as a chantry, and granted to Henry Needham, by whom it was conveyed to George Maxey, but it was recovered by suit in chancery, on condition of his being allowed to appoint the chaplain.

BARDNEY (St. *Lawrence*), a parish, in the W. division of the wapentake of Wraggoe, parts of Lindsey, union and county of Lincoln, 10 miles (W.) from Horncastle ; containing, with the hamlet of Southrow, 1192 inhabitants. It comprises by measurement 5019 acres, of which 1711 are arable, 2500 pasture, and 808 woodland. The living is a discharged vicarage, valued in the king's books at £7 ; net income, £60 ; patron and appropriator, the Bishop of Lincoln, whose tithes have been commuted for £280, exclusively of Southrow. There is a place of worship for Wesleyans. A free grammar school was founded in 1711 by Thomas Kitchen, who endowed it for the benefit of the children of Bardney, Bucknall, and Tupholm, with a salary of £35 per annum for the master, together with a house and garden. There is also an almshouse for fourteen widowers and widows. A monastery here, in which Ethelred, King of Mercia, became a monk in 704, was destroyed by the Danes in 870 ; and, about the period of the Conquest, was restored for a society of Bene-dietine monks, by Gilbert de Gaunt, Earl of Lincoln : the revenue, at the Dissolution, amounted to £429. 7.

BARDON-PARK, an extra-parochial liberty, in the union of Market-Bosworth, hundred of Sparkenhoe, S. division of the county of Leicester, 9½ miles (N. W. by W.) from Leicester ; containing 63 inhabitants. This place comprises about 1200 acres of land. Bardon hill is the highest and most conspicuous elevation in the county, and is 853 feet above the level of the sea : a greater extent of surface is visible from its summit than from any equal altitude in the kingdom, chiefly owing to its central situation and the absence of any contiguous hills by which the range of view might be obstructed. Upwards of 5000 square miles, or 3,000,000 of acres, may be seen, it is said, from this summit.

BARDSEA, a township, in the parish of Urswick, union of Ulverston, hundred of Lonsdale north of the Sands, N. division of the county of Lancaster, 3 miles (S. by E.) from Ulverston ; containing 263 inhabitants. Here are several malt-kilns, and in the neighbourhood is a copper-mine. A school is endowed with a rent-charge of £8.

BARDSEY (*All Saints*), a parish, in the Lower division of the wapentake of Skyrack, W. riding of York ; containing, with the townships of Bardsey-with-Rigton, Wothersome, and part of Wike, 469 inhabitants,
141

of whom 364 are in the township of Bardsey-with-Rigton, 5 miles (S. W. by S.) from Wetherby, on the road to Leeds. This parish, which comprises 2600 acres, contains some quarries of excellent stone for building, in which are found many fossils ; and abounds with pleasing scenery. The village is situated in the picturesque vale of a small rivulet, near the Wetherby road ; Rigton lies on the opposite side of the valley. The living is a discharged vicarage, valued in the king's books at £4. 1. 8. ; net income, £270 ; patron and impropriator, George Lane Fox, Esq. The church is an ancient structure in the Norman style, of which it is an elegant specimen : near it is a mound called Castle Hill, the supposed site of a Roman fortress. A school was endowed by Lord Bingley, in 1726, with 27 acres of land, which produce £20 per annum. Congreve, the dramatist, thought to have been born at Bardsey-Grange, was baptized here, in 1669.

BARDSLEY, an ecclesiastical district, in the parish and union of Ashton-under-Lyne, hundred of Salford, S. division of the county of Lancaster, on the road to Oldham ; containing about 2500 inhabitants. This district is in the Knott-Lanes division of the parish ; and the river Medlock, and the Manchester and Oldham canal, both run through it. The surface is elevated, and undulating ; the soil tolerably good ; and the scenery picturesque. The population is mostly employed in coal-mines, which are wrought to a great extent, the coal being of excellent quality ; and stone is also abundant in the neighbourhood. There are a cotton-mill, and a large brewery. Bardsley House, overlooking the glen of the Medlock, is the seat of John Jonah Harrop, Esq. Many generations of the Bardsley family held the estate, under the lords of Ashton, by the feudal payment of a rose and one penny, annually : the property subsequently came, by marriage, to the Tetlows ; and after having been out of the family for some time, was again purchased in 1681 by Jonah Harrop. In the glen is the house of Riversvale. The living is a perpetual curacy, with an income of £150, and a residence ; patrons, the Trustees of Hulme's Charity. The church, dedicated to the Holy Trinity, was built in 1844, at a cost of £2000 ; it stands on an eminence, and is a cruciform structure in the Norman style, with a square tower. The Primitive Methodists have a place of worship ; and excellent national schools have been built, at a cost of £1400. Sixty gold coins of the reigns of James and Charles I. were found in an old stable here, in 1822.

BARDWELL (St. *Peter and St. Paul*), a parish, in the union of Thingoe, hundred of Blackbourn, W. division of Suffolk, 2¼ miles (N. by E.) from Ixworth ; containing 826 inhabitants. The living is a rectory, valued in the king's books at £7. 17. 1., and in the gift of St. John's College, Oxford : the tithes have been commuted for £780, and there are 33 acres of glebe. The church is in the decorated style, and consists of a nave and chancel, with a lofty embattled tower ; in the windows are several beautiful specimens of ancient stained glass. There is a place of worship for Particular Baptists. The Town estate, left by William Beetson and others, [consists of a building termed the Guildhall, occupied by the poor, six cottages, and several pieces of land containing 68 acres ; yielding in the whole £87 per annum.

BARE, a hamlet, in the township of POULTON, BARE, and TORRISHOLME, parish of LANCASTER, hundred of LONSDALE south of the Sands, N. division of the county of LANCASTER, 3¼ miles (N. W. by N.) from Lancaster; containing 120 inhabitants. Bare was a part of the Saxon manor of "Haltune," and one of those places whose tithes were granted by Roger de Poictou to the priory of Lancaster. The hamlet comprises 230a. 1r. 18p., and is beautifully situated on the shore of Morecambe bay, commanding fine views of the opposite shore of Furness, Piel Castle, the Lake mountains, Ingleborough, and the valley of the Lune. The soil on the hills is light, and very favourable for early potatoes; in the lower grounds it is rich clay and moss. The population is employed in fishing and agriculture. The Elms is the beautiful seat of James Giles, Esq., M.A., mayor of Lancaster in 1845-6. The air here is very salubrious and bracing.

BARFORD (ST. BOTOLPH), a parish, in the corporation and hundred of FOREHOE, E. division of NORFOLK, 3½ miles (N.) from Wymondham; containing 417 inhabitants. The parish comprises 1052a. 3r. 15p., of which 852 acres are arable, 192 meadow and pasture, and 8 woodland and plantations. The living is a discharged rectory, valued in the king's books at £4. 8. 4.; patron and incumbent, the Rev. H. Francklin. The tithes have been commuted for £350, one-half of which is paid to the Dean and Chapter of Norwich, and the other to the rector; the glebe comprises 31 acres, equally divided between the Dean and Chapter and the rector. The church is a small edifice, in the early and later English styles, with a square tower. There is a place of worship for Wesleyans.

BARFORD, an extra-parochial liberty, adjoining the parish of RUSHTON, in the union of KETTERING, hundred of BOTHWELL, N. division of the county of NORTHAMPTON, 3 miles (N. by W.) from Kettering; containing 9 inhabitants. It comprises 360 acres, of a rich and highly productive soil, and is intersected by the north branch of the river Nene, and bounded by the road from Kettering to Rockingham on the east.

BARFORD (ST. JOHN), a chapelry, in the parish of EAST ADDERBURY, union of BANBURY, hundred of BLOXHAM, county of OXFORD, 2¾ miles (N. W. by W.) from Deddington; containing 126 inhabitants, and comprising by computation 700 acres. The church is a small edifice, with a tower within the square of the nave, at the south-west corner, open to the church; the doorway is of plain Norman design.

BARFORD (ST. PETER), a parish, in the Warwick division of the hundred of KINGTON, union and county of WARWICK, 3 miles (S. by W.) from Warwick; containing 849 inhabitants. Barford was for three centuries the residence of the ancestors of Charles Thomas Warde, Esq., now of Clopton, in the county. Of this family was Rowley Warde, an eminent lawyer in the reigns of James and Charles I., commonly called Old Serjeant Warde, and in the parish register styled the Right Worshipful Rowley Warde; who died at the age of 96, about the year 1650. His son, Thomas Warde, barrister at law, served as an officer in the army of Charles at the battle of Edge Hill, and kept the royal flag flying on the top of the church tower here, facing his own house; which caused Cromwell's army after the battle, on its march to Kenilworth Castle, eight
142

miles distant, to fire shots at the tower, the marks of which still remain. The mill on the river Avon at Barford, now belonging to the Earl of Warwick, was either granted or sold by Charles II. to this Thomas Warde, he having been instrumental in obtaining for the king and his royal father several sums of money to assist them in their distress, in the rebellion. The PARISH is pleasantly situated on the left bank of the Avon, which flows through a finely varied tract of country from the grounds of Warwick Castle; it comprises 1594 acres of land, and the higher parts present very fine views. The village contains several handsome houses. The living is a rectory, valued in the king's books at £11. 11. 0½.; net income, £869; patron, John Mills, Esq.: the tithes were commuted for land and a money payment in 1760. Thomas Warde, Esq., an eminent antiquary, sold the advowson for £500, in 1740, to the Rev. John Mills. The old church was built in the reign of Henry VI.; the late church in that of Henry VII.; and the present edifice, which incorporates the ancient tower, in 1844: it contains 604 sittings, and cost about £2500. The windows are of painted glass: the eastern one is in five compartments, embellished with figures of the Four Evangelists and the patron saint; the colours are peculiarly rich, and the effect of the whole window striking and beautiful; it was executed at the cost of the neighbouring families, to the memory of Jane, widow of the late Charles Mills, Esq., and daughter of the Hon. Wriothesley Digby. Under the chancel is a vault for the family of Mills, to members of whom are five urns on pedestals in the chancel wall. Formerly there was a tomb to the memory of a rector of Wellesbourn, who died about the year 1200; the tomb was long since destroyed, but the inscription, on stone, has been built into the wall of the church. Among other relics is a curious tablet of freestone, part of a monument, which the rector, the Rev. William Somerville, has had placed in the wall of the vestry, with this inscription: "Here lyeth the body of Thomas Warde, Gentleman, parson of Barford, 2d son of Thomas and Martha Warde; he died in 1532." A school here is endowed with about £48 per annum, arising from benefactions of John Beale in 1672, and the Rev. Thomas Dugard in 1677.

BARFORD (ST. MARTIN), a parish, in the union of WILTON, hundred of CAWDEN and CADWORTH, Salisbury and Amesbury, and S. divisions of WILTS, 2½ miles (W.) from Wilton; containing, with Grovely Wood, extra-parochial, 599 inhabitants. It is situated on the Shaftesbury road, and comprises 2246a. 3r. 2p. The living is a rectory, valued in the king's books at £24. 2. 8½., and in the patronage of All Souls' College, Oxford: the tithes have been commuted for £627. 5., a portion of which belongs to the church of Salisbury, and a small part to the adjoining rectory of Baverstock; the glebe consists of 92 acres.

BARFORD, GREAT (ALL SOULS), a parish, in the hundred of BARFORD, union and county of BEDFORD, 6 miles (E. N. E.) from Bedford; containing 814 inhabitants. It is situated on the navigable river Ouse, which forms its south-eastern boundary, and over which is a neat bridge. The living is a discharged vicarage, united to that of Roxton, and valued in the king's books at £9: the tithes were commuted for land and a money payment, in 1820. There is a place of worship for Wesleyans.

BARFORD, GREAT (St. Michael), a parish, in the union of Banbury, hundred of Wootton, county of Oxford, 2½ miles (W. N. W.) from Deddington; containing 370 inhabitants. The living is a perpetual curacy, valued in the king's books at £6. 5.; net income, £67; patron and impropriator, John Hall, Esq. The tithes were commuted for land and a money payment, in 1807. The church is rather peculiar in its character, and striking in its appearance; it stands on a high bank: the tower is placed at the east end of the south aisle, and there is a very fine Norman doorway: the edifice has no north aisle. A school, conducted on the national system, was founded by the late William Wilson, Esq., of Worton.

BARFORD, LITTLE (St. Mary), a parish, in the union of St. Neot's, hundred of Biggleswade, county of Bedford, 2½ miles (S. by W.) from St. Neot's; containing 190 inhabitants. This parish, which comprises by computation 1240 acres, is situated on the river Ouse, by which it is bounded on the west, and close to the road from Biggleswade to St. Neot's; the soil is in some places, and especially near the river, is exceedingly rich and productive. The living is a rectory, valued in the king's books at £13. 16. 3., and in the patronage and incumbency of the Rev. John Alington: the tithes have been commuted for £250, and the glebe consists of 45 acres. The church is an ancient building, with a Norman arch over the south door, and a curious wooden screen between the nave and the chancel. Nicholas Rowe, the dramatic writer, and poet-laureate to George I., was a native of the place.

BARFORTH, a township, in the parish of Forcett, union of Teesdale, wapentake of Gilling-West, N. riding of York, 6 miles (E.) from Barnard Castle; containing 114 inhabitants. It is on the south bank of the Tees, and comprises by computation 1750 acres: a ferry crosses the river to the county of Durham. Within the township are the inconsiderable remains of a village called Old Richmond, formerly a Roman station; and also the ruins of an ancient chapel.

BARFREYSTON (St. Mary), a parish, in the union and hundred of Eastry, lathe of St. Augustine, E. division of Kent, 5 miles (S. by E.) from Wingham; containing 125 inhabitants. It comprises 500 acres, chiefly arable. The living is a discharged rectory, valued in the king's books at £7. 14.; net income, £160; patrons, the President and Fellows of St. John's College, Oxford. The church, which is supposed to be of the date of the twelfth century, presents a fine specimen of Norman architecture, especially in the southern porch, which is richly ornamented with varied mouldings. There are numerous tumuli in this and the adjoining parishes.

BARHAM (St. Giles), a parish, in the hundred of Leightonstone, union and county of Huntingdon, 6 miles (N. N. E.) from Kimbolton; containing 107 inhabitants. The living is a perpetual curacy, in the patronage of the Bishop of Ely; net income, £58.

BARHAM (St. John the Baptist), a parish, in the union of Bridge, hundred of Kinghamford, lathe of St. Augustine, E. division of Kent, 6½ miles (S. E. by S.) from Canterbury; containing 1151 inhabitants. It comprises by measurement 4470 acres, of which 2147 are arable, 1301 pasture, 998 woodland, and 24 acres hops; and is celebrated for its pleasant and spacious
143

downs, on which the Canterbury races are held in August. The living was till lately annexed to the rectory of Bishopsbourne. Barham gives the title of Baron to the family of Noel.

BARHAM (St. Mary), a parish, in the union and hundred of Bosmere and Claydon, E. division of Suffolk, 4 miles (N. N. W.) from Ipswich; containing, with the inmates of the union workhouse, 576 inhabitants. The parish comprises about 1500 acres, and is bounded on the west by the navigable river Gipping. Shrubland Hall, formerly the seat of a branch of the Bacon family, descended from the Lord Keeper Bacon, and now of Sir William F. F. Middleton, Bart., has been greatly improved by the present proprietor, and is a splendid residence. The living is a rectory, valued in the king's books at £12. 10. 5.; net income, £342; patrons, the family of Longe. The church is a handsome edifice, chiefly in the decorated style, consisting of a nave and chancel with a square tower on the south side, and the chancel contains many monuments to the Bacons and Southwells. In a field called Chapel Field, the floor of an ancient chapel was lately turned up by the plough. A Roman road passed through Shrubland Park; and in the year 1840 a Roman apartment six feet square, and a bath five feet four inches long, two feet nine inches deep, and three feet wide, were discovered. The late Duke of Gloucester resided at Shrubland when in command of the district.

BARHOLME (St. Martin), a parish, in the union of Stamford, wapentake of Ness, parts of Kesteven, county of Lincoln, 3¾ miles (W. by N.) from Market-Deeping; containing 165 inhabitants. This parish, including the hamlet of Stowe, comprises by measurement 1500 acres, of which 400 are in Stowe, and of the remainder, 1000 are arable and 100 pasture: the soil is for the most part gravelly, and in some parts fen. The living is a discharged vicarage, to which that of Stowe was united in 1772, valued in the king's books at £5. 11. 8.; net income, £147; arising from 70 acres of land allotted on the inclosure in lieu of tithe; patrons and impropriators, the Governors of Oakham and Uppingham schools. The church is an ancient structure, partly in the Norman and early English styles, with a tower which, from an inscription in verse, appears to have been erected in 1648.

BARKBY (St. Mary), a parish, in the union of Barrow-upon-Soar, hundred of East Goscote, N. division of the county of Leicester, 5 miles (N. E.) from Leicester; containing, with the chapelries of Barkby-Thorp and North Thurmaston, 849 inhabitants, of whom 70 are in Barkby-Thorp. The living is a vicarage, valued in the king's books at £10; net income, £250; patron and impropriator, W. A. Pochin, Esq. The tithes, with some exceptions, were commuted for land in 1762. The church has been repewed.

BARKESTONE (St. Peter and St. Paul), a parish, in the union of Bingham, hundred of Framland, N. division of the county of Leicester, 4 miles (W. N. W.) from Belvoir Castle; containing 403 inhabitants. It comprises about 2000 acres, and is intersected by the Grantham and Nottingham canal: the soil is a dark-coloured tenacious clay, and the surface a gentle acclivity. The living is a discharged vicarage, valued in the king's books at £7. 5. 5.; net income, £114; patron and impropriator, the Duke of Rutland. The church was partly rebuilt and enlarged, and entirely refitted, in 1840. Daniel Smith endowed a school for the instruction of sixteen boys and ten girls of the parishes of Barkestone and Plungar, to which has been added a national school; and another for 26 girls is supported by the lady of the manor: a Sunday school is endowed with £20 per annum.

BARKHAM (ST JAMES), a parish, in the union of WOKINGHAM, hundred of CHARLTON, county of BERKS, 2 miles (S. W. by W.) from Wokingham; containing 248 inhabitants. It comprises 1362a. 1r. 5p., of which 743 acres are arable, 212 meadow and pasture, and 290 waste, common, and roads. The living is a rectory, valued in the king's books at £5. 15. 7½., and in the patronage of C. Leveson Gower, Esq. : the tithes have been commuted for £368, and there are 22 acres of glebe. The church, a neat building, has been lately repaired, and contains a small organ.

BARKING (ST. MARGARET), a parish, and formerly a market-town, in the union of ROMFORD, hundred of BECONTREE, S. division of ESSEX, 23 miles (S. W.) from Chelmsford, and 7 (N. E.) from London; containing 8718 inhabitants, of whom 3751 are in the town of Barking, exclusively of 987 men and boys engaged in the fishery, who were at sea at the time of the enumeration. The name of this place, formerly written *Berking*, is by some deduced from the Saxon words *Beorce*, a birch-tree, and *Ing*, a meadow; by others from *Berg-Ing*, signifying a fortification in the meadows, probably from an ancient intrenchment about a quarter of a mile on the road to Ilford, of which there are still considerable vestiges. The town derived its early importance from a very extensive and distinguished abbey, founded in 670, by Erkenwald, Bishop of London, for nuns of the Benedictine order, and dedicated to the Virgin Mary, which was governed by a long succession of abbesses, of whom many were of noble, and some of royal, descent. In 870, Barking was burnt by the Danes, the abbey destroyed, and many of the nuns were massacred, and the rest dispersed; but the abbey was afterwards rebuilt, about the year 970, by Edgar, whose queen, Elfrida, presided over it after his decease; and at the Dissolution its revenue amounted to £1084. 6. 2¾. Soon after the Conquest, William retired to the town, till the completion of the Tower of London, which he was then building to keep the citizens in subjection; and here he was visited, during the preparations for his coronation, by Edwin, Earl of Mercia, and Morcar, Earl of Northumberland, with many of the English nobles, who swore fealty to him on the restoration of their estates.

The TOWN is situated on the small river Roding, which, after flowing in two branches, unites with the Thames about two miles below: it is lighted with gas, by a company recently formed. The inhabitants are principally occupied in the fishery; a number of vessels sail to the Dutch and Scottish coasts, and, on their return, the fish is forwarded to Billingsgate in smaller vessels. There is a convenient wharf at Barking creek, which is navigable to Ilford for vessels of eighty tons' burthen, by which the neighbourhood is supplied with coal and timber; and near it is a large flour-mill, formerly belonging to the abbey. A fair is held on Oct. 22nd. The upper part of the building which was formerly the market-house, is appropriated to the purpose of a town-hall: attached to it is a small prison.

the south ; and the township comprises part of the village of Ripponden, and numerous scattered hamlets. The inhabitants are partly employed in wool-combing, and in the manufacture of the coarser kinds of woollen cloth, which is carried on to a small extent. The grammar school here, an ancient structure, was endowed in 1657 with £200 by Mrs. Sarah Gledhill : a house for the master was erected in 1780, with a good garden attached to it ; and the endowment now produces £40 per annum, which is paid to the master for teaching twelve children.

BARKSTON, a township, in the parish of SHER-BURN, Upper division of the wapentake of BARKSTONE-ASH, W. riding of YORK, 5 miles (S. by E.) from Tadcaster ; containing 323 inhabitants. It comprises about 1130 acres, chiefly arable, and generally fertile land : the road from Tadcaster to Pontefract intersects the township ; and the York and North-Midland railway passes on the east, and the Leeds and Selby railway on the south. The tithes were commuted for land and money payments in 1772. There is a place of worship for Wesleyans. The hundred court was formerly held, probably under a large ash-tree, in this village, and hence the name of the wapentake of Barkstone-Ash.

BARKSTONE-IN-THE-WILLOWS (ST. NICHO-LAS), a parish, in the union of NEWARK, wapentake of LOVEDEN, parts of KESTEVEN, county of LINCOLN, 4 miles (N. N. E.) from Grantham ; containing 413 inhabitants. It comprises by estimation 2083 acres, of which 1331 are arable, 549 pasture or meadow, and 44 woodland ; besides which, there are 65 acres, chiefly arable, on which a small tithe-modus is payable : the soil is light, varying from clay to sand. The river Witham, which is scarcely navigable, passes through the parish.. A pleasure-fair is held in October. The living is a rectory, in the patronage of the Prebendary of North Grantham in the Cathedral of Salisbury, valued in the king's books at £13. 7. 6.; the tithes have been commuted for £610, and there are about 19 acres of glebe. The church is supposed to have been built in the reign of John. The Wesleyans have a place of worship. There is a small endowment for a school; and an alms-house for six people is endowed with £43 per annum.

BARKWAY (ST. MARY MAGDALENE), a town and parish, in the union of ROYSTON, hundred of EDWINS-TREE, county of HERTFORD, 4 miles (S. S. E.) from Royston, 13¾ miles (N. N. E.) from Hertford, and 35 (N.) from London, on the road to Cambridge ; containing, with the hamlets of Newsells and Nuthampstead, 1291 inhabitants. In the reign of Henry III. a grant of a market now disused, and of a fair which is still held on July 20th, was obtained for this place. Nearly the whole town was destroyed by fire in the reign of Elizabeth, and again in 1748. It is pleasantly situated on rising ground, and consists principally of one street : the houses in general are modern and neatly built, and the inhabitants ·are well supplied with water. The parish comprises chiefly arable land, with a large extent of wood, and a small portion of pasture. The living is a vicarage, consolidated in 1800 with the rectory of Reed, and valued in the king's books at £14 ; the im-propriation belongs to Mrs. Vernon Harcourt : the tithes were commuted for land in 1801. The church is a spacious structure combining various styles, with a square embattled tower. There is a place of worship

for Independents ; and a charity school for boys has an endowment of £10 per annum.

BARKWITH, EAST (ST. MARY), a parish, in the union of HORNCASTLE, E. division of the wapentake of WRAGGOE, parts of LINDSEY, county of LINCOLN, 3 miles (N. E.) from Wragby ; containing 255 inhabitants. It is situated on the road from Lincoln to Louth ; the soil is fertile, and abounds with a fine chalk marl, which is used as manure. The living is a discharged rectory, valued in the king's books at £11. 10. 10.; net income, £195 ; patron, G. F. Heneage, Esq., who is lord of the manor. The church is in the later style of English architecture, with an embattled tower, and has a font of very ancient date, highly ornamented ; in a niche over the porch is a figure of the Virgin and Child. There is a place of worship for Wesleyans.

BARKWITH, WEST (ALL SAINTS), a parish, in the union of HORNCASTLE, E. division of the wapentake of WRAGGOE, parts of LINDSEY, county of LINCOLN, 2½ miles (N. E.) from Wragby ; containing 130 inhabitants. It contains by computation 700 acres ; and is situated on the road between Lincoln and Louth, the church stand-ing at the thirteenth milestone from each of those towns. The living is a discharged rectory, valued in the king's books at £5. 5.; net income, £160, derived from 114 acres of land in lieu of tithes ; patron, C. D. Holland, Esq. There is a glebe-house in good repair, with a handsome garden. The church is a plain build-ing with an old tower.

BARLASTON (ST. JOHN THE BAPTIST), a parish, in the union of STONE, S. division of the hundred of PIRE-HILL, N. division of the county of STAFFORD, 4½ miles (N. by W.) from Stone ; containing 591 inhabitants. The parish comprises 2087a. 2r. 23p. of inclosed land, with about 60 acres of waste : the Grand Trunk canal passes through. The village, which is well built, is delightfully situated near the summit of a lofty acclivity on the east side of the vale of the Trent, commanding extensive and beautiful views : Parkfield is a hamlet of pleasant houses on a terrace above the Trent. Barlaston Hall, a handsome mansion, stands near the north end of the village. The living is a perpetual curacy ; net income, £150 ; patron, the Duke of Sutherland. The church is a modern building of brick, with an ancient stone tower ; it was enlarged in 1830, when a new gallery was erected. There is a school for 28 children, to which Thomas Mills, in 1800, bequeathed £12 per annum ; it is also endowed with a cottage and garden.

BARLAVINGTON, a parish, in the union of SUT-TON (under Gilbert's act), hundred of ROTHERBRIDGE, rape of ARUNDEL, W. division of SUSSEX, 4½ miles (S.) from Petworth ; containing 132 inhabitants. The living is a discharged rectory, valued in the king's books at £5. 13. 4.; patrons, the family of Biddulph. The tithes have been commuted for £100, and there are 8 acres of glebe.

BARLBOROUGH (ST. JAMES), a parish, in the union of WORKSOP, hundred of SCARSDALE, N. divi-sion of the county of DERBY, 8 miles (N. E. by E.) from Chesterfield ; containing 804 inhabitants. It comprises by estimation 3305 acres, of which 2000 are arable, and 1150 pasture and meadow land ; and is intersected by the roads from Chesterfield to Worksop, and from Rotherham to Mansfield, which cross here at right angles. There are some collieries in operation, and two

                                                           U

quarries of limestone. Barlborough Hall is a spacious and interesting edifice of the Elizabethan style. The living is a rectory, valued in the king's books at £10. 1. 5½., and in the patronage of the Rev. C. H. R. Rodes; the tithes have been commuted for £600, and there are 73 acres of glebe. The church is a handsome structure, with a square tower. In 1752, Margaret and Mary Pole founded an almshouse for six poor persons, and endowed it with an estate now producing £75 per annum.

BARLBY, a chapelry, in the parish of HEMING-BROUGH, union of SELBY, wapentake of OUSE and DERWENT, E. riding of YORK, 1½ mile (N. E. by E.) from Selby; containing 387 inhabitants. This township, which has a long village, comprises 1411 a. 3r. 15p.; about 900 acres are rich arable land, and the remainder pasture and common. The living is a perpetual curacy; net income, £65; patron, the Vicar of Hemingbrough: the great tithes produce £369 per annum. The chapel is a neat brick edifice with an octagonal turret, built about 1777.

BARLESTON, a chapelry, in the parish and union of MARKET-BOSWORTH, hundred of SPARKENHOE, S. division of the county of LEICESTER, 3' miles (N. E.) from Market-Bosworth; containing 580 inhabitants, a portion of whom are employed in the weaving of stockings. The chapel is dedicated to St. Giles.

BARLEY (ST. MARGARET), a parish, in the union of ROYSTON, hundred of EDWINSTREE, county of HERTFORD, 2¼ miles (N. E. by N.) from Barkway; containing 792 inhabitants. It contains by computation 2500 acres, and the road from Barkway to Cambridge runs through the village. The living is a rectory, valued in the king's books at £26. 13. 4., and in the patronage of the Bishop of Ely: the tithes have been commuted for £581, and the glebe consists of 32 acres. A school is endowed with £10 per annum.

BARLEY, with WHITLEY-BOOTHS, a township, in the parish of WHALLEY, union of BURNLEY, Higher division of the hundred of BLACKBURN, N. division of the county of LANCASTER, 5 miles (W. by N.) from Colne; containing 686 inhabitants. These are two adjoining villages at the foot of Pendle hill; Whitley-Booths is north of Barley, and distant from it about half a mile. The area of the township is 1564 acres. In this part the general *patois* of the county becomes almost peculiar, being more rugged. An annual wake is held on Midsummer-day.

BARLEYTHORPE, a chapelry, in the parish, union, and soke of OAKHAM, county of RUTLAND, 1 mile (N. W. by W.) from Oakham; containing 200 inhabitants. The chapel is dedicated to St. Peter.

BARLING (ALL SAINTS), a parish, in the union and hundred of ROCHFORD, S. division of ESSEX, 4½ miles (E. S. E.) from Rochford; containing 326 inhabitants. The parish comprises 1258a. 3r. 10p., and is skirted by a creek which flows into the river Thames from Rochford: it comprises the manors of Barling and Mucking, the former of which is the property of the Dean and Chapter of St. Paul's, London, by gift from Edward the Confessor. Here are several good oyster-beds. The living is a vicarage, valued in the king's books at £18; patrons and appropriators, the Dean and Chapter. The great tithes have been commuted for £342, and the vicarial for £171; the glebe comprises about 27 acres.

the chapel, staiths, jetties, &c.; and John Blanchard endowed a lectureship, the appointment to which is vested in the inhabitants. Here are two mineral springs called St. Peter's and St. Helen's wells, one chalybeate, the other sulphureous.

BARMBY-ON-THE-MOOR (ST. CATHERINE), a parish, in the union of POCKLINGTON, Wilton-Beacon division of the wapentake of HARTHILL, E. riding of YORK, 1¾ mile (W.) from Pocklington; containing 475 inhabitants. It comprises 2471a. 1r. 26p., of which about two-thirds are arable, and the remainder pasture, and moorland abounding with game; the surface is for the most part level, with a soil generally sandy. The village, which is of considerable length, stands on the Hull and York road, and was anciently a market-town, and of much greater importance than at present, having received a grant of various immunities, such as freedom from toll, &c., which the inhabitants still enjoy, subject to the payment of a small sum annually to the Dean and Chapter of York. The ancient manor-house is surrounded by a moat. The living is a discharged vicarage, valued in the king's books at £5. 6. 8.; net income, £50; patron, the Dean of York. The tithes were commuted for land and a money payment, in 1777. The church is an ancient structure in the Norman style, with later additions: the original square tower has been surmounted with a neat and well-proportioned spire of later English character, and a handsome window inserted. There are places of worship for Wesleyans and Primitive Methodists.

BARMER, a parish, in the union of DOCKING, hundred of GALLOW, W. division of NORFOLK, 8 miles (W. N. W.) from Fakenham; containing 61 inhabitants. It comprises 1294a. 3r. 31p., nearly all arable; there are 100 acres of plantation. The living is a perpetual curacy; net income, £5; patron and impropriator, Thomas Kerslake, Esq. The church, which had been long in ruins, was converted by the father of the present patron into a mausoleum.

BARMING (ST. MARGARET), a parish, in the union and hundred of MAIDSTONE, lathe of AYLESFORD, W. division of KENT, 2½ miles (W. by S.) from Maidstone; containing 540 inhabitants. This parish, which comprises 745a. 3r. 4p., is intersected by the road from Maidstone to Tonbridge, and by the river Medway, which is crossed by a stone bridge leading to East Farleigh, and by another of wood, called St. Helen's bridge, on the road to West Farleigh. The soil is rich, and peculiarly adapted to the cultivation of hops and fruit, of which latter a large quantity is sent to the London market. There are 66 acres of common, The living is a rectory, valued in the king's books at £12. 17. 1., in the patronage of the Crown: the tithes have been commuted for a rent-charge of £400, subject to increase or decrease according to the increase or decrease of hops and fruit; and there are 70 acres of glebe. Here was a Roman villa, the foundations of which were taken up a few years ago, when coins of the Lower Empire, and of Edward I. and later English monarchs, were found. The abbess of St. Helen's, London, had a summer retreat here; but there are no remains of the house. The poet Smart resided upon his paternal estate in the parish; and the Rev. John Harris, D.D., author of a *History of Kent*, a *Dictionary of Arts and Sciences*, &c., formerly held the living.

147

BARMING, WEST, a hamlet (formerly a parish), locally in the parish of NETTLESTEAD, union of MAIDSTONE, hundred of TWYFORD, lathe of AYLESFORD, W. division of KENT, 3 miles (S. W.) from Maidstone; containing 44 inhabitants. It comprises 323 acres of land; and the river Medway, over which is a modern bridge, flows along the southern border of the hamlet. The living, which was a rectory, has been consolidated with that of Nettlestead, and the church is in ruins. The place is now deemed extra-parochial.

BARMOOR, a township, in the parish of LOWICK, union and E. division of GLENDALE ward, N. division of NORTHUMBERLAND, 7 miles (N. by E.) from Wooler. In 1417, the lords marchers assembled here, at the head of a force amounting to 100,000 men, against the Scots, who, on hearing of their approach, retreated within their own territory. The English army also encamped in the vicinity prior to the battle of Flodden, on the night after which the English general slept at Barmoor wood. A fair was formerly held at Cross Hills, between this place and Lowick. The tithes have been commuted for £298. 16. 3. payable to the Dean and Chapter of Durham, and £10. 11. 8. to the impropriators.

BARMPTON, a township, in the parish of HAUGHTON-LE-SKERNE, union of DARLINGTON, S. E. division of DARLINGTON ward, S. division of the county of DURHAM, 2½ miles (N. E. by N.) from Darlington; containing 124 inhabitants. The township comprises by computation 1502 acres, of which 887 are arable, and 615 grass land: the soil is a productive clay, with a small part gravel; and the scenery pleasing and picturesque. The principal farm was occupied some years since by the brothers Collings, who contributed so much to improve and bring into public notice the breed of shorthorned cattle: at their sale in 1812, Comet, one of their bulls, was disposed of for the enormous sum of 1000 guineas, and Lily, a cow, for 400 guineas. The tithes have been commuted for £255.

BARMSTON, a township, in the parish of WASHINGTON, union of CHESTER-LE-STREET, E. division of CHESTER ward, N. division of the county of DURHAM, 4¾ miles (W.) from Sunderland; containing 81 inhabitants. This place was once the property of the very ancient family of Hilton, of whom Sir Robert, in 1322, granted to his chaplain all the wax and honey of his wild bees in Barmston Park; it afterwards came to the Lilburnes and the Tempests. On the banks of the river Wear is an iron-foundry, and within the limits of the township is also a mineral spring. The tithes have been commuted for £128.

BARMSTON (ALL SAINTS), a parish, in the union of BRIDLINGTON, N. division of the wapentake of HOLDERNESS, E. riding of YORK, 6 miles (S. by W.) from Bridlington; containing 254 inhabitants. This is a remarkably fine agricultural parish, comprising by measurement 2290 acres, chiefly arable, of a loamy soil excellent for the growth of all sorts of grain: on the east is the sea, which every year washes away a small portion of the land; and the coast abounds with gravel, large quantities of which are used for repairing the roads. The village is pleasantly situated at the northern extremity of Holderness, on the road from Hull to Bridlington and Scarborough. The living is a rectory, valued in the king's books at £13. 11. 10½., and in the patron-

U 2

age of Sir H. Boynton, Bart.: the rent-charge in lieu of tithes is about £680, and there are 38 acres of glebe in the parish, and 67 in the township of Ulrome, which is partly in the parish of Skipsea. The church is in the decorated English style, and has a nave, chancel, and south aisle, with an embattled tower at the south-west angle. In the chancel is a table-monument of white alabaster, highly ornamented, and having a recumbent effigy of a knight in plate armour, supposed to represent Sir Martin de la See, who so signally assisted Edward IV. after that monarch had landed at Ravenspurn, in 1471. There is a church at Ulrome; and a place of worship for Wesleyan Methodists has been erected in the parish.

BARNACK (St. John the Baptist), a parish, in the union of Stamford, soke of Peterborough, N. division of the county of Northampton, 3½ miles (S. E.) from Stamford; containing, with the hamlets of Pilsgate and Southorpe, 860 inhabitants. The living is a rectory, valued in the king's books at £28. 10.; net income, £1025; patron, the Bishop of Peterborough. The tithes were commuted for corn-rents, under an inclosure act, in the 39th and 40th of George III. The church is an interesting and very ancient structure,' in the early Norman and English styles, with a tower, the lower part of which, from the character of the arch opening from it into the nave, is evidently of more ancient date than the earliest of the Norman details, and probably one of the very few specimens of Saxon architecture remaining in the kingdom. A school is supported by subscription, and by a donation from the funds of the poor's estate, which consists of fifty-one acres and five tenements, producing a rental of £72. An act for inclosing lands was passed in 1841.

BARNACLE, a hamlet, in the parish of Bulkington, union of Nuneaton, Kirby division of the hundred of Knightlow, N. division of the county of Warwick, 6 miles (N. E.) from Coventry; containing 263 inhabitants. It is mentioned in the Conqueror's survey, and is supposed to have anciently belonged to the family of Fitzwith. In the time of Elizabeth the manor was granted to Michael Fielding, from whom it descended to Basil Fielding, Earl of Denbigh.

BARNACRE, with Bonds, a township, in the parish and union of Garstang, hundred of Amounderness, N. division of the county of Lancaster, 2¼ miles (N. E.) from Garstang; containing 628 inhabitants. The township comprises 4478a. 2r. 2p., in about equal portions of arable and pasture, and nearly all the property of the Duke of Hamilton: the surface is undulated, and the soil various, and rich towards the Wyre, which river divides the township from Garstang. The Lancaster and Preston railway passes through for about two miles. Excellent stone is obtained from a quarry here; and there are two cotton-mills. Woodacre Hall was a residence of a former Duchess of Hamilton. The impropriate tithes have been commuted for £148. 1. 9., payable to W. Standish, Esq. At Bonds are the relics of Greenhalgh Castle, which was held for the king by the Earl of Derby, in 1643, during the parliamentary war, and subsequently destroyed by Cromwell: it was erected by Thomas Stanley, Earl of Derby, in the reign of Henry VII., for the protection of his newly acquired estates; and is mentioned by Camden, as being situated near " the swift stream of the Wyr."

from the southern bank of the Tees, the bridge over which at this place was repaired in 1771, after the injury it had sustained in that year by the memorable flood that swept away most of the bridges on the Tees and Tyne. It has undergone considerable improvement of late years, by the formation of new streets, and the removal of unsightly objects. The houses are built of white freestone, and have a very handsome appearance: the streets are well paved; they were lighted with gas in 1834, and the inhabitants are amply supplied with water from springs in the neighbourhood. The environs are remarkably pleasant, and the Vale of Tees abounds with romantic scenery. There are two book societies, one in conjunction with Staindrop; also a mechanics' institution founded in 1852, under the auspices of H. T. M. Witham, Esq., of Lartington Hall. On the banks of the river are the extensive flax, tow, and spinning mills of Messrs. Ullathorne and Longstaff, established in 1798, and whose manufacture of shoe-makers' thread gives employment to between 400 and 500 hands: there are also four carpet manufactories, employing a large number of persons; and two iron-foundries. The market is on Wednesday: there is a cattle-market every fortnight; and fairs are held on the Wednesday in Easter and Whitsun weeks. A fair on St. Mary Magdalene's day has nearly fallen into disuse. The magistrates hold a petty-session once in every month; and a baronial court for the recovery of debts under 40s. is held quarterly: the powers of the county debt-court of Barnard-Castle extend over the registration-district of Teesdale. The town-hall, situated in the market-place, is an octagonal structure, erected in 1747, by Thomas Breaks, a native of the place; the upper part is used for the transaction of business, and the lower for the market.

The township comprises 3860a. 32p., exclusively of waste, water, and the site of the town: the land is generally good, and is divided in equal portions of arable, and meadow and pasture; the moorlands abound in game. The LIVING is a perpetual curacy, in the patronage of the Vicar of Gainford, with a net income of £224; impropriator, as lessee under Trinity College, Cambridge, John Bowes, Esq.: the great tithes have been commuted for £211. 8. 10., and those of the vicar for £292. 14. 10. The chapel, dedicated to St. Mary, is an ancient and spacious cruciform structure, in the decorated and later English styles, with a square embattled tower at the south-west angle: the bells were recast about twenty-five years since, by subscription. There are places of worship for Independents, Primitive Methodists, and Wesleyans. An hospital, for the residence and maintenance of three aged widows, was founded by John Balliol, about the 14th of Henry III., and dedicated to St. John the Baptist; the income is nearly £200 per annum. About two miles north-west of the town is a chalybeate spring, which is approached by walks through highly varied scenery of the most pleasing description. A Roman coin of the Emperor Trajan was dug up in the churchyard, in the year 1824. Sir John Hullock, one of the late barons of the exchequer; William Hutchinson, Esq., author of the *History and Antiquities of the County of Durham*, and who resided at the Grove, and died in the year 1814; and George Edwards, Esq., M.D., a political writer of distinction, were natives of the chapelry. It gives the titles of Viscount and Baron Barnard to the Duke of Cleveland.

149

BARNARDISTON (*ALL SAINTS*), a parish, in the union and hundred of RISBRIDGE, W. division of SUF-FOLK, 3 miles (N. E.) from Haverhill; containing, with the extra-parochial liberty of Monks' Risbridge, 217 inhabitants. This parish, which comprises by computation 1500 acres, was originally the seat of, and gave name to, the family of Barnardiston, long resident in the adjoining parish of Kedington. The living is a discharged rectory, valued in the king's books at £7. 10. 5.; net income, £191; patron and incumbent, the Rev. Valentine Ellis.

BARNBROUGH, or BARMBROUGH (*ST. PETER*), a parish, in the union of DONCASTER, N. division of the wapentake of STRAFFORTH and TICKHILL, W. riding of YORK, 6¼ miles (W.) from Doncaster; containing, with Harlington, 508 inhabitants. This place has long been in the possession of the family of More; John More, only son and heir of Sir Thomas, the celebrated chancellor of England, having obtained it by marriage with Ann Cresacre, whose family had settled here in the reign of Edward I. The parish is on the north side of the river Dearne, and comprises about 1947 acres, of which 273 acres are common or waste; the soil is mostly a strong fertile clay, resting on a substratum of excellent lime and freestone. Barmbrough Hall, the former seat of the Cresacres and Mores, is in a retired situation near the church; and the Grange, which once belonged to the religious house of Nostel, and has, since the Dissolution, been in succession the residence of various families, stands in the meadows near the Dearne, not far from the hamlet of Harlington. The village is situated in the vale. The living is a rectory, valued in the king's books at £23, and in the patronage of the Chapter of the Collegiate Church of Southwell: the tithes have been commuted for £534, and there are 100 acres of glebe. The church, built in the fourteenth century, is a neat structure with a tower, and contains a highly-wrought tomb to a member of the Cresacre family. There is a place of worship for Wesleyans.

BARNBY (*ST. JOHN THE BAPTIST*), a parish, in the incorporation and hundred of MUTFORD and LOTHING-LAND, E. division of SUFFOLK, 4 miles (E. by S.) from Beccles; containing 296 inhabitants. It comprises by measurement 1010 acres; and is situated on the road from Lowestoft to Beccles, and bounded on the north by the navigable river Waveney, which separates it from the county of Norfolk. The living is a discharged rectory, annexed to the vicarage of Mutford, and to the rectory of Wheatacre, All Saints, in Norfolk; it is rated in the king's books at £6: the tithes have been commuted for £170, and there are nearly 4 acres of glebe.

BARNBY, a township, consisting of the villages of EAST and WEST BARNBY, in the parish of LYTHE, union of WHITBY, E. division of the liberty of LANGBAURGH, N. riding of YORK, 5¼ miles (W. by N.) from Whitby; containing 262 inhabitants. These two villages lie about a couple of miles to the south-west of that of Lythe, not far from the road between Whitby and Guisborough. The township anciently belonged to a family of the same name; mention occurring of Robert de Barneby, who held the lands under Peter de Manley, lord of Mulgrave.

BARNBY-IN-THE-WILLOWS (*ALL SAINTS*), a parish, in the union of NEWARK, S. division of the wapentake of NEWARK and of the county of NOTTING-

HAM, 4¾ miles (E. by S.) from Newark; containing 266 inhabitants, and comprising by measurement 1400 acres. The living is a discharged vicarage, valued in the king's books at £5. 9. 9½., and in the patronage of the Chapter of the Collegiate Church of Southwell : the incumbent's tithes have been commuted for £219. 10., with a glebe of 29 acres, and those of the impropriators for £140, with a glebe of 42 acres. There is a place of worship for Wesleyans. Flawford, a farm of 250 acres, anciently belonged to the Knights Templars.

BARNBY-MOOR, with BILBY, a township, in the parish of BLYTH, union of EAST RETFORD, Hatfield division of the wapentake of BASSETLAW, N. division of the county of NOTTINGHAM, 3½ miles (N. W.) from East Retford; containing 221 inhabitants. It comprises by measurement 1918 acres, chiefly arable : the soil is of a sandy nature, and the chief crops are wheat, barley, and oats. The scenery is pleasingly diversified, and in some parts picturesque. The great north road, and the Trent and Chesterfield canal, pass through the township. The tithes were commuted for land in 1807.

BARNBY-UPON-DON (ST. PETER), a parish, in the union of DONCASTER, S. division of the wapentake of STRAFFORTH and TICKHILL, W. riding of YORK; containing 629 inhabitants, of whom 510 are in the township of Barnby, 5¾ miles (N. E. by N.) from Doncaster. The parish comprises the townships of Barnby and Thorp-in-Balne. The village of Barnby, the "residence of Beorn," is pleasantly situated close to the river Don, on the road between Doncaster and Thorne, and consists of somewhat picturesque houses, among gardens and orchards, in a flat country; the rest of the township is for the most part inclosed and cultivated land, with scarcely a house erected upon it. The LIVING is a discharged vicarage, valued in the king's books at £9. 12. 6., with a net income of £105; the patronage and impropriation belong to Thomas Gresham, Esq., who is chief landowner : the tithes were commuted for land and annual money payments in 1803. The church is a well-built structure of very ancient date, with a chancel the property of the Gresham family, which contains some handsome monuments to their ancestors and others. There are places of worship for Primitive and Wesleyan Methodists.

BARNES (ST. MARY), a parish, in the union of RICHMOND, W. division of the hundred of BRIXTON, E. division of SURREY, 5 miles (W. S. W.) from London; containing 1461 inhabitants. This parish comprises 936 acres of land, of which 176 are common or waste; the soil is for the most part gravelly, and the surface flat. The village is pleasantly situated on the southern bank of the river Thames, and contains several well-built houses, particularly on the terrace facing the river, which commands an extensive view of the opposite bank, and forms a peculiarly interesting promenade, from the constant traffic on the Thames, and the continned succession of pleasure-boats passing between London and Richmond, and in other aquatic excursions. The Barnes station of the Richmond railway is 5½ miles distant from Nine Elms, London. At Barn-Elms, in the vicinity, so called from a row of stately elm-trees, is an ancient mansion called Queen Elizabeth's Dairy, which was the residence of Jacob Tonson, the eminent bookseller, who built a room for the meetings of the members of the "Kit-Kat Club," portraits

150

of some of whom adorn the walls; these have been engraved and published, and among them are several of the most distinguished English literati of the early part of the last century. Elizabeth granted the manor-house to Sir Francis Walsingham, who, in 1589, enter-wards that sovereign and her court here : it was after-wards the residence of the Earl of Essex, who had espoused the daughter of Sir Francis, the widow of Sir Philip Sidney; and is now that of the Rt. Hon. Sir Launcelot Shadwell, Vice-Chancellor. A court leet is held at Putney, by the lord of the manor, at which constables and other officers are appointed for Barnes.

The LIVING is a rectory, valued in the king's books at £9. 3. 4., and in the patronage of the Dean and Chapter of St. Paul's, London : the tithes have been commuted for £315, and there are 8 acres of glebe. The church is an ancient edifice in the early English style, built of flint and freestone, with a square tower of brick, having an octagonal turret at one angle, which appears to have been added in 1500 : it was enlarged in 1838, by subscription, on the north side of the chancel. Mrs. Mary Wright, in 1804, bequeathed £500, which were invested in the purchase of £824. 11. three per cent. consols.; and Mr. John Biggs, in 1837, left £500 : the interest of both sums is applied in keeping their tombs in repair, and for the benefit of the poor. Robert Beale, who was employed by Elizabeth to communicate to Mary, Queen of Scots, the sentence which had been passed upon her, and who was afterwards sent to Fotheringay Castle to see it carried into effect, died here in 1601. Cowley, the poet, resided here for some time.

BARNESLEY, county of YORK.—See BARNSLEY.

BARNET-BY-THE-WOLD (ST. MARY), a parish, in the union of GLANDFORD-BRIGG, S. division of the wapentake of YARBOROUGH, parts of LINDSEY, county of LINCOLN, 5 miles (E. N. E.) from Glandford-Brigg; containing 679 inhabitants. This parish, which is on the road from Brigg to Caistor, comprises by survey 2600 acres : the soil, partly chalk and sand, is rich and fertile, and the chief produce barley and turnips; a considerable portion of the land is in pasture. The living is a discharged vicarage, valued in the king's books at £6. 4. 2.; net income, £305; patron and appropriator, the Bishop of Lincoln. The tithes were commuted for land in 1766. There are places of worship for Independents, Primitive Methodists, and Wesleyans.

BARNET, CHIPPING (ST. JOHN THE BAPTIST), a parish, town, and the head of a union, in the hundred of CASHIO, or liberty of ST. ALBAN'S, county of HERTFORD, 14 miles (S. W. by S.) from Hertford, and 11 (N.) from London, on the great north road; containing 2485 inhabitants. This place, called also High Barnet, from its situation on the summit of a hill, derives its distinguishing name from the privilege granted to the monks of St. Alban's, of holding a market here. On April 5th, 1471, the decisive battle which terminated in the defeat and death of the Earl of Warwick, and established Edward IV. on the throne, took place on Gladmore Heath, a mile north-west of the town; in commemoration of which, an obelisk was erected by Sir Jeremy Sambrook, at the junction of the roads from Hatfield and St. Alban's, near Hadley Common. The TOWN, which is pleasantly situated, consists principally of one street, more than a mile in length; the houses, though interspersed occasionally with a few of more respectable appearance, are in general mean, and the inhabitants scantily supplied with water. A new road, entering from London, was made in 1826, by means of an embankment across the valley, at an expense of £15,000. The great railway from London to York will pass near. The races, held on Barnet Common, and for some time discontinued, have lately been revived; and a hall has recently been erected, by shareholders, for public meetings, concerts, lectures, &c. The market was on Monday, and was chiefly noted for the sale of pigs, but has been discontinued. A fair is held on April 8th and 9th, for cattle and horses, and on the 10th there is a pleasure-fair; another, considered the largest in England for horned-cattle, commences on Sept. 4th, and continues the three following days, on the last of which the races are held. The magistrates for the liberty hold a meeting here on the first Thursday in every month; and two constables and two headboroughs are appointed at the court leet of the lord of the manor, held at Easter. The powers of the county debt-court of Barnet, established in 1847, extend over the registration-district of Barnet and the parish of Hendon.

The LIVING is united to the rectory of East Barnet: the church was built by one of the abbots of St. Alban's, in the fifteenth century, and is a venerable structure in the style of that period, but has undergone several alterations. There is a place of worship for Independents. A free school was established in 1573 by Queen Elizabeth, and was further endowed, in 1676, by Alderman Owen, and in 1734 by the Rev. Humphrey Hall; the income amounts to about £35. There is also a national school, supported partly by a bequest from Mrs. Allen in 1725, since invested in land let for £57 per annum. Jesus' hospital, for six elderly women, was founded in 1679, by James Ravenscroft, and was further endowed with the residue of the produce of £500 left by Mrs. Barcock, in 1731, after distributing £10 annually to the poor; and with a moiety of the dividends of £800 reduced Bank annuities, bequeathed by Ann Mills, in 1784: the income is £273. In 1728, Mr. John Garret founded six almshouses for aged widows, the income of which has been augmented by bequests, and now amounts to £50; and six others, for married couples, were erected a few years ago, at an expense of £1022, by the trustees of a charity founded by Eleanor Palmer, and producing £153 per annum, two-thirds for the parish of Chipping-Barnet, and the remainder for that of St. Pancras. The Leather-sellers' Company likewise erected almshouses, the first stone of which was laid in July, 1837, by the master of the company, Mr. R. Thornton, who presented the amount of the contract, £1208. There are other charities for the relief of the poor, the principal of which are, Valentine Poole's, producing £51 per annum; an inclosure of Barnet Common, amounting to 135 acres, let for £167; and the dividends on £898 three per cent. reduced annuities, under the will of Keene Fitzgerald, Esq., in 1829. A rental of £41, arising from a plot of ground in the parish of Stepney, assigned by deed of James Ravenscroft, Esq., in 1679, is applied to repairing the church. On Barnet Common has been built the workhouse for the poor law union of Barnet, which comprises nine parishes and places, under the care of fourteen guardians. On this common is a mineral

151

spring, the water of which contains a considerable portion of calcareous glauber, with a small portion of sea-salt.

BARNET, EAST (THE VIRGIN MARY), a parish, in the union of BARNET, hundred of CASHIO, county of HERTFORD, 10¼ miles (N.) from London; containing 598 inhabitants. It comprises 1702a. 20p., and the village is pleasantly situated near the town of Chipping-Barnet; the houses are neatly built, and the general appearance of the place is pleasingly picturesque. The air is salubrious, but the supply of water is scanty, and the quality not very good. The living is a rectory, with the living of Chipping-Barnet annexed, valued in the king's books at £22. 2. 8½., and in the patronage of the Crown: the tithes, with those of Chipping-Barnet, have been commuted for £860. 5. 9., and there are 31½ acres of glebe, with an allotment. The church formerly belonged to the monastery of St. Alban's: in the churchyard is a handsome monument to the memory of Sir Simon Houghton Clarke, Bart. A building was erected on Barnet Common in 1839, by Enos Durant, Esq., of High Canons, which has been licensed by the bishop for the performance of service. On a hill opposite to the church, called Monk's Frith Garden, the abbots of St. Alban's anciently had a villa. In the neighbourhood are several mineral springs.

BARNET, FRYERN (ST. JAMES), a parish, in the union of BARNET, Finsbury division of the hundred of OSSULSTONE, county of MIDDLESEX, 8¼ miles (N. by W.) from London; containing, with the hamlet of Colney-Hatch and a portion of that of Whetstone, 849 inhabitants. It is supposed that an abbey anciently existed here from which the place obtained the prefix to its name, and that the old manor-house, now taken down, was the summer residence of the abbots. The land is tithe-free, if cultivated by resident proprietors, but if let to tenants the exemption ceases. Courts leet and baron are held on the Friday in Whitsun-week. The living is a rectory not in charge, in the patronage of the Dean and Chapter of St. Paul's, London; net income, £255. The church is a small and very ancient structure, in the Norman style; the chancel was rebuilt some years since. Almshouses for twelve aged persons were founded, and endowed with £10 a year, in 1612, by Lawrence Kemp, Esq., of London. John Walker, author of the "English Pronouncing Dictionary," was born here in 1732.

BARNEY (ST. MARY), a parish, in the union of WALSINGHAM, hundred of NORTH GREENHOE, W. division of NORFOLK, 5 miles (E. N. E.) from Fakenham; containing 276 inhabitants. It comprises 1389a. 3r. 31p., of which the greater portion is arable land. The living is a discharged vicarage, valued in the king's books at £6. 13. 4.; patron and impropriator, Lord Hastings. The great tithes have been commuted for £168, and the vicarial for £104; there is a glebe of 38½ acres. The church is in the early and later English styles, and consists of a nave, chancel, and south chapel, with a square embattled tower. The Wesleyans and Baptists have places of worship.

BARNHAM (ST. GREGORY AND ST. MARTIN), a consolidated parish, in the union of THETFORD, hundred of BLACKBOURN, W. division of SUFFOLK, 3 miles (S.) from Thetford; containing 412 inhabitants, and comprising 5184a. 3r. 32p. The living of St. Gregory's,

valued in the king's books at £7. 11. 10½., and that of
St. Martin's, at £8. 5. 5., now form one rectory, united
to that of Euston: the tithes have been commuted for
£423. 2., and there are about 95 acres of glebe. The
church of St. Gregory is the parochial church; St.
Martin's is in ruins, but the steeple is standing.

BARNHAM (St. Mary), a parish, in the union of
West Hampnett, hundred of Avisford, rape of
Arundel, W. division of Sussex, 6 miles (S. W. by W.)
from Arundel; containing 125 inhabitants. It comprises about 700 acres, and is intersected by the Arundel and Portsmouth canal. The living is a discharged
vicarage, valued in the king's books at £7. 15.; net
income, £67; patron, the Bishop of Chichester; impropriators, the family of Postlethwayte. The church is in
the early English style; the north isle was a chantry,
founded by John Le Taverner in 1409, and was taken
down at the Dissolution.

BARNHAM-BROOM (St. Peter and St. Paul), a
parish, in the incorporation and hundred of Forehoe,
E. division of Norfolk, 4¾ miles (N. N. W.) from
Wymondham; containing 494 inhabitants. This parish
comprises by measurement 1760 acres: at the western
boundary is a small stream, on which is a flour-mill:
the common was inclosed in 1811, when 19 acres were
allotted to the poor for fuel. The living is a rectory,
with that of Bixton and the vicarage of Kimberly
united, valued in the king's books at £12. 8. 1½.;
net income, £524, with 19 acres of glebe, and a house;
patron, Lord Wodehouse. The church is a handsome
structure in the later English style, with a square embattled tower. There was formerly a church dedicated
to St. Michael in the same churchyard.

BARNHILL, a hamlet, in the parish of Malpas,
Higher division of the hundred of Broxton, S. division
of the county of Chester, 10 miles (S. E. by S.) from
Chester. The petty-sessions for the hundred are held
here.

BARNINGHAM (St. Andrew), a parish, in the
union of Thetford, hundred of Blackbourn, W.
division of Suffolk, 4 miles (N. N. E.) from Ixworth;
comprising by measurement 1556 acres, and containing
508 inhabitants. The living is a discharged rectory,
with that of Coney-Weston annexed, valued in the king's
books at £13. 9. 2.; net income, £770; patron, R.
Hunt, Esq. The glebe consists of about 25 acres. The
church is in the decorated style, with an embattled
tower. There is a place of worship for Wesleyans.
Land and tenements called the Town estate are let for
about £35 per annum, applied to the repairs of the
church and general parochial purposes; and the sum
of £21, the rental of an allotment of 20 acres, is laid
out in coal for poor families.

BARNINGHAM (St. Michael), a parish, in the
union of Teesdale, wapentake of Gilling-West, N.
riding of York; containing 600 inhabitants, of whom
337 are in the township of Barningham, 2 miles
(S. S. W.) from Greta-Bridge. The parish includes the
townships of Barningham, Hope, Scargill, and part of
Newsham, and comprises 10,771 acres, of which 3255
are common or waste: in the township of Barningham
are 3620 acres. On the west are high moors and fells,
but on the east is a fine and fertile champaign country,
in the most open part of the dale of Greta: in his poem
of Rokeby, Sir Walter Scott alludes in eulogistic terms

habitants, of whom 1849 are in the township of Bar-noldswick. This place was the original seat of the monks of Kirkstall, who were settled here from 1147 until 1153, and of whose abode there are still some re-mains. The parish includes the townships of Brogden, Coates, and Salterforth, and comprises 6073a. 2r. 8½p. ; the surface is boldly diversified, rising into hills of lofty elevation, and in some parts intersected with deep and narrow glens. In the vicinity are extensive and valuable limestone-quarries. The Leeds and Liverpool canal passes through the parish in a direction nearly north and south. The village, which is spacious, is situated in a secluded part of a valley, and sheltered by lofty hills ; the inhabitants are chiefly employed in the cotton manufacture, for which there are three mills, and many are engaged in hand-loom weaving. The LIVING is a perpetual curacy, in the patronage of Richard Hodgson, Esq., with a net income of £162 ; impropriators, the landowners. The original church was built probably as early as 1080, and the existing structure bears marks of a date not long subsequent to the removal of the monks, who built it after having levelled the first edifice to the ground in consequence of the opposition made by the rector and inhabitants to their intrusive entry among them ; it is seated on the brink of a deep glen, from which it obtained the name of Gill church. A chapel of ease, dedicated to St. James, was erected in the centre of the village in 1837, at an expense of £1700, raised by subscription, aided by a grant of £200 from the Ripon Diocesan Society, and the same sum from the Incorporated Society ; it is a neat structure in the early English style. There are places of worship for Baptists and Wesleyans.

BARNSHAW, with GOOSTREY.—See GOOSTREY.

Arms.

BARNSLEY, a market-town and chapelry, in the parish of SILKSTONE, wapen-take of STAINCROSS, W. riding of YORK, 14 miles (N.) from Sheffield, 38 (S. by W.) from York, and 177 (N. W. by N.) from London ; containing 12,310 inhabit-ants. This place, in the Domesday survey "Bernes-leye," and called also Bleak Barnsley from the exposed situation of the original town, now a hamlet in the chapelry, was anciently celebrated for the manufacture of steel wire, which is still carried on to a moderate ex-tent. The favourable situation of the present town in the heart of a district abounding in coal, iron, and stone, amply supplied with water, and intersected with canals in almost every direction, affording facilities of commu-nication with many of the principal towns in the king-dom, rendered it peculiarly eligible for the purposes of trade ; and the introduction of the linen manufacture, towards the close of the last century, appears to have laid the foundation of its subsequent increase, and its present prosperity. Since the introduction of that branch of manufacture the place has been steadily ad-vancing in importance, and so rapid has been its pro-gress, that within the last thirty years its population has been nearly quintupled. The chief articles manufactured -here for many years were the coarser kinds of linen

goods, principally towelling, sheeting, dowlas, and duck ; but about the year 1810, the manufacture of hucka-backs, diapers, damasks, broad sheeting, and the finer sorts of linen, was attempted and carried on with com-plete success ; and since that period, the improvement made in this branch of manufacture has been such as to rival in fineness of texture and beauty of pattern, the most costly productions of Scotland and Ireland.

The TOWN is pleasantly situated on the acclivity of a hill rising from the bank of the river Dearne, and con-sists of several streets, of which the more ancient are narrow and irregularly formed, but those of more modern date spacious, and uniformly built. Con-siderable improvements have been made by the erection of good houses on the sites of many that have been removed ; by the widening of some streets ; and the building of others : and the houses being generally of stone, procured in the neighbourhood, the town has a handsome and imposing aspect. The streets are lighted with gas by a company of shareholders established under an act of parliament in 1821, with a capital of £6000, raised in shares of £10 each ; and the inhabitants are supplied with water by another company established under a more recent act, and having a capital of £9000. The water, which is of excellent quality, is obtained from the Dearne, about a mile from the town. The public rooms were erected in 1837, at an expense of £1500, by a proprietary of £25 shareholders ; the principal front is of the Ionic order, and the building contains a sub-scription library and news-room communicating with each other, so as to form one room occasionally for the delivery of lectures. The news-room is embellished with an original full-length portrait of the Duke of Wellington, painted by H. P. Briggs, Esq., R.A., and a likeness of Archdeacon Corbett, by the same artist. The mechanics' institution for the promotion of science by mutual instruction and stipendiary lectures, was esta-blished in 1837, and has a good library. The theatre, a neat plain building, was erected in 1814, at a cost of £1400, and is opened at intervals. The hall for the so-ciety of Odd Fellows, forming a branch of the Man-chester union, is a handsome structure of the Grecian-Ionic order, erected in 1836 at an expense of £1100, in shares of £1 each ; the great room in which the lodges are held is elegantly decorated, and of ample dimensions. The environs of the town present a pleasing diversity of scenery, and the land is richly cultivated : among the numerous seats are the mansions of Earl Fitzwil-liam, Lord Wharncliffe, Sir W. Pilkington, Bart., and F. T. W. V. Wentworth, Esq.

The inhabitants are chiefly employed in the linen manufacture, and, at present, the demand for drills has become so extensive as to form the principal branch of TRADE ; not less than 4000 hand-looms are constantly employed in weaving these articles in an endless variety of patterns, producing annually more than 220,000 pieces of drill, each fifty yards in length. So great, indeed, is the number of hands engaged in this depart-ment, that the manufacturers of the other articles have been obliged to introduce power-looms, which are well adapted to the heavier kinds of linen, and in the super-intendence of which the weavers obtain higher wages than they previously earned by hand-loom weaving. The total amount of the linens manufactured averages about £1,000,000 per annum : the Barnsley ducks, so

X

BARN

generally in demand for smock-frocks, have been for some time superseded by a fabric of thicker and warmer texture, called "drabbets." In the town and its vicinity are extensive works for bleaching, some dye-houses, and two large calendering establishments; there are also flax-mills for spinning yarn, but the greater portion of the yarn used in the factories here is brought from Leeds, and still more distant places. There are several iron-foundries, and two manufactories for steel-wire, the produce of which is used by the needle-makers. Coal of excellent quality is obtained in the immediate vicinity; one seam, called the Barnsley thick bed, averages about ten feet in thickness, and there are other extensive mines in operation, the produce of which, with the iron and freestone with which the district abounds, forms a considerable source of trade. Great facilities of conveyance are afforded by the Barnsley canal, which was constructed in 1794, and extends from the river Calder, near Wakefield, to the Dearne and Dove canal at this place; the Midland railway, also, passes within two miles and a half of the town. The market, which is toll-free for all kinds of grain, is on Wednesday, and there is also a market for provisions on Saturday; fairs for cattle and horses are held on May 13th and Oct. 11th, a great market for live-stock on the last Wednesday in February, and another for swine on the Wednesday before Old Michaelmas-day. The town is within the liberty of the honour of Pontefract, and its management is vested in commissioners chosen at the court of quarter-sessions, under an act, 3rd George IV., cap. 25, for lighting, paving, watching, and improving the place. A court baron for the manor of Barnsley and Dodworth is held annually by the steward, and a court of petty-sessions every Wednesday by the magistrates of Staincross wapentake. The powers of the county debt-court of Barnsley, established in 1847, extend over the registration-district of Ecclesfield, and part of that of Wortley. The court-house is a neat substantial building, erected in 1833 at an expense of £1300, of which £500 were raised by rate, and the remainder by subscription: it contains the various rooms for holding the courts, and for the transaction of business relative to the town; and the hall contains a full-length portrait of the late Lord Wharncliffe, lord-lieutenant of the county, by Briggs.

The chapelry comprises by measurement 2116 acres. The chapel, dedicated to *St. Mary*, with the exception of the tower, has been rebuilt of freestone found in the neighbourhood, at a cost of £12,000, raised by rate on the inhabitants: the present structure is in the later English style, and contains 1050 sittings; the east window is embellished with paintings of Our Saviour, the Virgin Mary, and the Four Evangelists, in stained glass. The living is a perpetual curacy; net income, £225; patron, the Archbishop of York. The church dedicated to *St. George*, to which a district has been assigned, was erected in 1823 by the Parliamentary Commissioners, at an expense of £6500: it is a handsome structure in the later English style, with some details of more ancient character, and has turrets at the angles, and embattled parapets; it contains 1174 sittings. The living, which is endowed with £1500 three-and-a-half per cent. stock, has a net income of £150; patron, the Archbishop. A church district named *St. John's* was formed in 1844, and endowed by the Ecclesiastical Com-

154

dated the town, and did much damage to the property of the inhabitants. During the civil war of the seventeenth century, it was distinguished for its adherence to the cause of the parliament, and was the scene of frequent conflicts between the two parties, being alternately in the possession of each.

The TOWN is pleasantly situated in a fertile vale sheltered by a semicircular range of hills, on the east bank of the river Taw, near its confluence with the Yeo; and consists of several spacious and well-paved streets, containing many well-built houses. The barracks, formerly appropriated to the reception of cavalry, were purchased from government in 1818, by H. Hole, Esq., and converted into a handsome range of dwelling-houses with gardens and coach-houses attached, called Ebberly-place, and forming an interesting feature in the appearance of the town; there is a similar range of building, named Trafalgar-place, at Newport, close to the town. The inhabitants are amply supplied with excellent water, conveyed by pipes from the distance of half a mile; and the town is lighted with gas. The air is salubrious, and the surrounding scenery agreeably and richly diversified. Several charming walks upon the winding banks of the Taw (over which is a stately stone bridge of eighteen arches, within a few years considerably widened, and improved by iron railings) extend for nearly a mile; and one of them, called the North walk, is shaded by lofty elm-trees, and commands a fine view of the junction of the rivers Taw and Yeo, which here expand into a beautiful bay. On the quay is a handsome piazza of the Doric order, called Queen Anne's walk, surmounted by a statue of that sovereign, and formerly used as an exchange by the merchants for the transaction of their business. A light and elegant theatre has been erected in one of the chief streets; and there are assembly, reading, and billiard rooms, which are well attended.

The TRADE consists principally in the importation of deals from North America and the Baltic; wines, spirits, and fruits direct from the places of their growth; coal and culm from South Wales; and shop goods, chiefly groceries, from London and Bristol; and in the exportation of corn and other agricultural produce, oak-timber and bark, leather, wool, tiles, earthenware, &c. The quay, on which is the custom-house, is extensive and commodious; but, from the accumulation of sand, the part which the navigation of the river is obstructed, it is not accessible to vessels of more than 100 tons' burthen. A few years since, the port obtained the privilege of bonding wines, spirits, and other articles of colonial produce; and by warrant of the lords of the treasury, lately issued, Ilfracombe has been deprived of the character of a separate port, and is now united as a creek to the port of Barnstaple. The Taw Vale railway and dock have been constructed here under the provisions of an act of parliament obtained for that purpose: the line extends from Penhill, in the parish of Fremington, to this place, is two miles and a half in length, and in its course passes under a tunnel 418 yards long; it was completed at an expense of £20,000. In 1846 an act was passed for the extension of this railway, 31 miles, to the Exeter and Crediton line at Crediton. The manufacture of serge and inferior broad-cloths has long been established; and in the town and neighbourhood are three factories for patent lace, or bobbin-net, employing more than

155

1000 persons. There are also six tan-yards and two paper-mills; an iron-foundry was established in 1822; and great quantities of bricks, tiles, and coarse earthenware are manufactured. Limestone of good quality is found within four miles of the town, and lead-ore has been discovered in the vicinity, but at such a depth from the surface as to afford little encouragement for the opening of mines. The market is on Friday; and there are great markets on the Fridays before March 16th, April 21st, and July 27th, and on the second Friday in December. A great market for cattle, for which this place is celebrated, is also held monthly; and a fair for horses, cattle, and sheep, on Sept. 19th, which is continued for three days.

Corporation Seal.

The inhabitants have received various charters of INCORPORATION, of which that of James I., in the 8th year of his reign, was the governing charter, until the passing of the act 5th and 6th William IV., c. 76, when the borough was divided into two wards, and the control vested in a mayor, six aldermen, and 18 councillors. The elective franchise was granted in the reign of Edward I., since which time the borough has regularly returned two members to parliament. The right of election was once vested in the corporation and free burgesses, in number about 700; but, by the act of the 2nd of William IV., cap. 45, it was confined to the resident burgesses only, and extended to the £10 householders of the borough, the limits of which, both for parliamentary and municipal purposes, include by computation 980 acres: the mayor is the returning officer. Courts of quarter-session are held for the borough, for determining on all offences not capital; and a court of record, having jurisdiction over the four neighbouring hundreds, is held on alternate Mondays, for the recovery of debts to any amount, and for other business relative to the police of the borough. The powers of the county debt-court of Barnstaple, established in 1847, extend over the greater part of the registration-district of Barnstaple. The guildhall, in which the courts are held, is a spacious building, erected by the corporation in 1826; and contiguous to it is a handsome market-place for butchers' meat, with convenient shops. A substantial and convenient prison, containing 20 cells, was erected some years since, at the joint expense of the inhabitants and the corporation.

The LIVING is a discharged vicarage, valued in the king's books at £15. 8. 9.; net income, £324; patron, Lord Wharncliffe; impropriator, R. N. Incledon, Esq. The church is a spacious and ancient structure, with a spire. A church district, named *St. Mary Magdalene's*, was formed in 1845, under the 6th and 7th of Victoria, cap. 37, and endowed by the Ecclesiastical Commissioners: the living is a perpetual curacy with an income of £150, in the patronage of the Crown and the Bishop of Exeter alternately. The church, commenced in Oct. 1844, and consecrated in Nov. 1846, is a simple and elegant structure of beautiful proportions, in the early English style, from a design of Mr. B. Ferrey's. The cost, about £3500, exclusive of £500 for the site, was

X 2

raised by subscription, aided by a grant from the Church Building Society; the tower and spire were the gift of the first appointed incumbent. Another church, that of the *Holy Trinity*, a very handsome cruciform building in the later English style, has been erected at an expense of nearly £10,000, defrayed almost wholly by the Rev. John James Scott; the site was presented by Mr. Charles Roberts. This edifice was consecrated in June, 1845; and the living is a perpetual curacy, in the gift of the Rev. J. J. Scott. There are places of worship for Baptists, the Society of Friends, Independents, and Wesleyans. The free grammar school, of uncertain foundation, was endowed in 1649 by R. Ferris, and a small annuity was added in 1760 by the Rev. John Wright: the school-house, an ancient building in the churchyard, formerly belonged to the Cluniac monastery established here by Judael de Totnais. Jewell, the celebrated Bishop of Salisbury; Thomas Harding, Jesuit professor at Louvain; and Gay, the poet, who was born in the neighbourhood, received the rudiments of their education in the school. The charity school, for clothing and educating 50 boys and 24 girls, was founded in 1710, and is maintained by the rent of land purchased with several benefactions, and by subscription.

Litchdon almshouse, an ancient building, consisting of a centre and two wings, in one of which is a chapel, was founded in 1624, and endowed with a considerable estate by John Penrose, Esq., for 40 aged persons of either sex. Horwood's almshouses, for sixteen people, established in 1658, and Paige's almshouses, established in 1553, and enlarged in 1656, were both endowed by the respective founders whose names they bear. The late Mr. Roberts, in 1830, gave £500 four per cent. annuities, the interest to be distributed among the poor of the various almshouses, in number 70 persons; and an elegant building, comprising three sides of a square, and containing twelve almshouses, has lately been erected near Litchdon almshouse, at the expense of Mr. Charles Roberts, son of the above-named gentleman, for 24 decayed housekeepers. A noble hospital, or infirmary, for the reception of the afflicted poor of the north of Devon, was erected by subscription in 1826; it is a lofty and handsome structure, situated on the south-east of the town. An extensive establishment, called the North Devon Dispensary, was also founded in 1830. The union of Barnstaple comprises 39 parishes and places, and contains a population of 37,452. On the quay is an ancient building, now used as a warehouse, said to have been a chantry chapel dedicated to St. Anne. A priory was founded by Judael de Totnais, soon after the Conquest, and dedicated to St. Mary Magdalene, for monks of the Cluniac order; it was at first a cell to the abbey of St. Martin de Campis, at Paris, but was afterwards made denizen, and flourished till the Dissolution, when its revenue was estimated at £123. 6. 9. Some notice also occurs of a house of Augustine friars, and of an hospital dedicated to the Holy Trinity, founded here; but no particulars are recorded.

BARNSTON, a township, in the parish of WOOD-CHURCH, union, and Lower division of the hundred, of WIRRALL, S. division of the county of CHESTER, 4½ miles (N. by W.) from Great Neston; containing 206 inhabitants. A moiety of the manor belonged to a family of the same name, and afterwards to a branch of the Bennets of Wollaston; the other moiety passed by

living is a rectory, to which that of Barnwell All Saints was united in 1821, valued in the king's books at £17. 2. 1.; net income, £298; patron, Lady Montagu. The tithes of the two parishes were commuted for land and corn-rents in 1830; there are 26 acres of glebe, and an excellent parsonage-house. The church is a fine specimen of the early and decorated English styles, with a tower and spire. There is a free school, founded in the 2nd of James I. by the Rev. Nicholas Latham, who also established an almshouse for 14 infirm men and women, bequeathing estates for these purposes, and for the relief of persons in distress. The income was augmented in 1824, by a bequest from Mr. William Bigley, of London, who also left an endowment for building a school-house, and educating and clothing 15 girls of Barnwell St. Andrew and Oundle. In the reign of Henry I. a baronial castle was erected here by Reginald le Moine, of which there are considerable remains, including the principal gateway.

BARNWOOD (St. Lawrence), a parish, in the Upper division of the hundred of Dudstone and King's Barton, union, and E. division of the county, of Glou-cester, 1½ mile (E. S. E.) from Gloucester; containing 383 inhabitants. The road from Gloucester to Cirencester, and the Bristol and Birmingham railway, pass through the parish, which is also intersected by the Roman Fosse-way. The living is a vicarage, not in charge; patrons and appropriators, the Dean and Chapter of Gloucester. The great tithes have been commuted for £350, and the vicarial for £176; the glebe comprises nearly half an acre.

BARONY, with Evenwood, a township, in the parish of St. Andrew Auckland, union of Auckland, N. W. division of Darlington ward, S. division of the county of Durham; containing 1729 inhabitants. This place is situated on the north side of the river Gaun-less, over which is a bridge leading to Evenwood; and contains the hamlets of Morley, Ramshaw, and Tofthill. The Bishop of Durham, as lord of the manor, holds courts leet and baron in March and October, at which debts to the amount of 40s. are recoverable.

BARR, GREAT, a parochial chapelry, in the parish of Aldridge, union of Walsall, S. division of the hundred of Offlow and of the county of Stafford, 5½ miles (N.) from Birmingham; containing 1078 inhabit-ants. This place lies on the road between Birmingham and Walsall, and comprises about 5000 acres: the sur-face is elevated; the soil varies from a light to a heavy quality, and the scenery is beautiful, presenting from the celebrated Barr beacon a very extensive view. Excel-lent limestone is obtained, of a peculiar degree of hard-ness suitable for under-water work, as it sets quickly and firmly. At Newton is a station of the Liverpool and Birmingham railway. The Hall, which has long been the seat of the Scott family, stands in a romantic vale, having an extensive lawn and deer-park, with a fine sheet of water in front; the grounds are abundantly planted, and the sylvan beauties of the place owe much to the taste of the poet Shenstone. The living is a perpetual curacy, annexed to the rectory of Aldridge. The chapel, dedicated to St. Margaret, stands on an eminence shaded by a number of lofty elms; it was re-built in the latter part of the last century by Joseph Scott, Esq., afterwards Sir Joseph Scott, Bart., and is in the Grecian style, with a handsome spire. There are

157

seven painted windows, copied from designs by Sir Joshua Reynolds at New College, Oxford; the eastern window is elaborately painted by Eginton, of Birming-ham. The chapel lands consist of about 66 acres of land on Barr common, obtained at the inclosure in 1799 from Sir Joseph Scott, in exchange for the Chapel Hills, which had been held from time immemorial. John Addyes, in 1722, bequeathed property for the erection and endowment of a free school for thirteen boys, which number by subsequent benefactions has been augmented to twenty; the endowment consists of a house and land, the latter let for nearly £50 per annum.

BARRASFORD, a township, in the parish of Chol-lerton, union of Hexham, N. E. division of Tindale ward, S. division of Northumberland, 7 miles (N. by W.) from Hexham; containing 209 inhabitants. At this place, which, with the exception of a small free-hold, is the property of the Duke of Northumberland, Robert de Umfraville in 1303 obtained license from Edward I. to hold a market on Wednesdays, and a fair on November 11th, both of which have been discon-tinned. The tithes have been commuted for £126. 6. payable to the Mercers' Company, of London, and £54. 2. 11. to the vicar of the parish.

BARRAWAY, a chapelry, in the parish of Soham, union of Newmarket, hundred of Staploe, county of Cambridge, 2¼ miles (S. S. E.) from Ely; contain-ing 71 inhabitants. The chapel is dedicated to St. Ni-cholas.

BARRINGTON (All Saints), a parish, in the union of Royston, hundred of Wetherley, county of Cam-bridge, 6¾ miles (S. W. by S.) from Cambridge; con-taining 533 inhabitants. The living is a discharged vicarage, valued in the king's books at £7. 14. 4.; net income, £107; patrons, the Master and Fellows of Trinity College, Cambridge, to whom also the impro-priation belongs. The tithes were commuted for corn-rents in 1796. The church has been repaired within a few years.

BARRINGTON (St. Mary), a parish, in the union of Langport, hundred of South Petherton, W. divi-sion of Somerset, 3¾ miles (N. E.) from Ilminster; con-taining, with the hamlet of Barrington-hill, 531 inhabit-ants, and comprising by computation 900 acres. Hemp and flax are extensively cultivated. About a mile from the village is the terminus of the canal recently cut by the Parret Navigation Company, by means of which, in conjunction with the rivers Isle and Parret, a commu-nication is obtained with the town of Bridgwater. The living is a perpetual curacy; net income, £84; patron John Lee Lee, Esq., as lessee of the advowson under the Dean and Chapter of Bristol. The tithes have been commuted for £396.

BARRINGTON, GREAT (St. Mary), a parish, in the union of Stow-on-the-Wold, Lower division of the hundred of Slaughter, E. division of the county of Gloucester, 3¼ miles (N. W.) from Burford; con-taining 553 inhabitants. It comprises about 1700 acres; the soil is partly stiff clay and partly light earth, and the parish abounds with freestone of excellent quality, which was obtained stone for the erection of Blenheim House, and the repairs of Westminster Abbey. The Windrush, a branch of the Thames, runs through the parish. The living is a discharged vicarage, valued in the king's books at £7. 6. 8., and in the gift of Lord Dynevor, whose seat of Barrington Park is situated in the parish : the great tithes, payable to his lordship, have been commuted for £213. 15., and those of the incumbent for £195. 16., with a glebe of 42 acres. The church is a handsome edjfice, in the later English style, with an embattled tower.

BARRINGTON, LITTLE (St. Peter), a parish, in the union of Northleach, Lower division of the hundred of Slaughter, E. division of the county of Gloucester, 3 miles (W. N. W.) from Burford; containing 208 inhabitants, and comprising about 1000 acres. The living is a discharged vicarage, valued in the king's books at £4. 19. 2., with a net income of £100; the patronage and impropriation belong to the Crown. Under an inclosure act in 1759, land and money payments were given in lieu of all tithes for the manor, the money payments being for the small tithes of the old inclosures. Schools are partly supported by the surplus revenue of an estate left for repairing the church.

BARRON'S-PARK, a hamlet, in the parish of Desford, union of Market-Bosworth, hundred of Sparkenhoe, S. division of the county of Leicester, 5 miles (W.) from Leicester; containing 18 inhabitants.

BARROW (St. Bartholomew), a parish, in the union of Great Boughton, Second division of the hundred of Eddisbury, S. division of the county of Chester, 4½ miles (E. N. E.) from Chester; containing 668 inhabitants. This place consists of Great and Little Barrow. It was given by Ranulph, Earl of Chester, to his nephew William de Albini, Earl of Arundel. By Edward III. to Sir Roger de Swinerton, an heiress whose family brought them, in marriage, to Sir John Savage, who was knighted by Henry V. at the battle of Agincourt. They afterwards came to the noble family of Cholmondeley. The parish comprises 2774 acres, the soil of which is sand and clay, the ground is elevated, and there is a fine view of the city of Chester, with the Welsh hills in the distance. The road from Chester to Northwich passes on the south. The living is a rectory, valued in the king's books at £19. 16. 2½., and in the gift of Lord H. Cholmondeley : the tithes have been commuted for £460, with a house. A school is endowed with about £6 per annum. Here was a commandery of the Knights Hospitallers, founded in the reign of Henry II., and valued at the Dissolution at £107. 3. 8.

BARROW (St. Wilfrid), a parish, in the union of Shardlow, partly in the hundred of Appletree, and partly in that of Morleston and Litchurch, S. division of the county of Derby, 5¾ miles (S.) from Derby; containing 641 inhabitants. The manor, at the time of the Domesday survey, was held by Godwin under Henry de Ferrars. An estate here, which had been parcel of the manor of Melbourne, was annexed to the see of Carlisle before 1273, and was held on lease, under the bishops, by the family of Coke. This estate was enfranchised by act of parliament in 1704, and became the property of Daniel Dalrymple, Esq., by purchase from Lord Melbourne, about the year 1800. The parish includes the chapelry of Twyford with Stenson, and the liberty of Sinfin with Arleston; and comprises about

1140 acres, whereof two-thirds are arable, and the rest pasture, with small plantations : the soil is chiefly a light loam, and the scenery picturesque. The river Trent bounds the parish on the south, and the Trent and Mersey canal passes through. The living is a discharged vicarage, valued in the king's books at £5. 6. 5½.; net income, £105.; patron, the Rev. John Latham. The tithes have been commuted for £245; and the glebe consists of about 40 acres. In addition to the parochial church, there is a chapel of ease at Twyford. The Wesleyans and Independents have places of worship; and a school is endowed with £8 per annum, the gift of Elizabeth Sale in 1702. A preceptory of Knights Templars formerly existed here.

BARROW, a village and sea-port, in the township of Hawcoat, parish of Dalton, union of Ulverston, hundred of Lonsdale north of the Sands, N. division of the county of Lancaster, 5 miles (S. W. by S.) from Dalton, and 9 (S. W.) from Ulverston, the post-town. This place is situated at the south-western extremity of the district of Furness, opposite to the isle of Walney and Old Barrow island. The trade consists chiefly in the export of malt, slate, and iron-ore, of which two last articles vast quantities are brought from the mines and quarries in the vicinity by the Furness railway : an excellent pier of wood was built by the railway company in 1846. The land near the village is mostly arable, the surface rather uneven, and the soil a stiff clay. About a mile on the road to Dalton is a chapel in connexion with the Establishment, built by subscription in 1845.

BARROW, a township, in the parish of Hallystone, union of Rothbury, W. division of Coquetdale ward, N. division of Northumberland, 9½ miles (W. N.W.) from Rothbury; containing 22 inhabitants. It is situated on the south side of the Coquet river, near the confluence of the Barrow burn.

BARROW, a chapelry, in the parish of Cottesmore, union of Oakham, hundred of Alstoe, county of Rutland, 5 miles (N. by E.) from Oakham; containing 142 inhabitants. The tithes were commuted for land and a money payment, under an inclosure act of the 39th and 40th of George III.

BARROW (St. Giles), a parish, in the union of Madeley, liberties of the borough of Wenlock, S. division of Salop, 3½ miles (E. by S.) from Much Wenlock; containing 383 inhabitants. The living is a perpetual curacy, annexed to the rectory of Willey : the tithes payable to the impropriator have been commuted for £283. 2., and those to the perpetual curate for £3. 15. Here is a small free school, to which £10 per annum were bequeathed in 1631 by John Slaney, who also founded an almshouse for six persons.

BARROW, a tything, in the parish of Kingsbury-Episcopi, union of Langport, E. division of the hundred of Kingsbury, W. division of Somerset, 5 miles (N. N. E.) from Ilminster; containing 242 inhabitants. The impropriate tithes have been commuted for £245. A conical hill, in a great degree the work of art, was raised here to Ina, King of the West Saxons, who is said to have been buried at this place; near it is a mansion of considerable antiquity.

BARROW (All Saints), a parish, in the union and hundred of Thingoe, W. division of Suffolk, 6¾ miles (W.) from Bury; containing 995 inhabitants, and comprising 2665*a*. 2*r*. 33*p*., of which 156 acres are common or waste. The living is a rectory, valued in the king's books at £23. 9. 9½., and in the patronage of St. John's College, Cambridge: the tithes have been commuted for £810, and there are 62 acres of glebe. The church is a spacious building of the time of Henry III. or Edward I. There is an endowment of about £21 per annum for the education of children. A rental of £36 (subject to a deduction of £3. 12. 4.) arising from land and tenements assigned by deed of the Rev. John Crosier, in the 12th of Elizabeth, is applied to the purposes of a church-rate; and about £20 are distributed among the poor. The Rev. Philip Francis, the translator of Horace, was rector of this parish.

BARROW-GURNEY (HOLY TRINITY), a parish, in the union of BEDMINSTER, hundred of HARTCLIFFE with BEDMINSTER, E. division of SOMERSET, 5 miles (S. W.) from Bristol; containing 303 inhabitants. It comprises 2026 acres, of which 339 are arable, 1448 pasture, 97 wood, and 16 common. The living is a donative; net income, £71; patron, Montague Gore, Esq. A Benedictine nunnery was founded here about 1200, the revenue of which, at the Dissolution, was valued at £29. 6. 8.: the site is occupied by a fine old mansion in the Elizabethan style.

BARROW, NORTH (ST. NICHOLAS), a parish, in the union of WINCANTON, hundred of CATSASH, E. division of SOMERSET, 2¼ miles (S. W.) from Castle-Cary; containing 140 inhabitants. The living is a discharged rectory, valued in the king's books at £7. 17. 8½., and in the patronage of Lord Portman: the tithes have been commuted for £115, and there are about 41 acres of glebe.

BARROW, SOUTH (ST. PETER), a parish, in the union of WINCANTON, hundred of CATSASH, E. division of SOMERSET, 3¾ miles (S. W. by S.) from Castle-Cary; containing 140 inhabitants. The living is a perpetual curacy, with a net income of £80, and in the patronage of Mrs. Toogood, to whom also belong the tithes, which have been commuted for £245.

BARROW-UPON-HUMBER (HOLY TRINITY), a parish, in the union of GLANDFORD-BRIGG, N. division of the wapentake of YARBOROUGH, parish of LINDSEY, county of LINCOLN, 2¼ miles (E.) from Barton-upon-Humber; containing 1662 inhabitants. Henry VIII. landed at this place on his route to Thornton Abbey. The parish is situated on the river Humber, and on the road from London through Peterborough and Lincoln ▸to Hull; it comprises 4720 acres, of which 3000 are arable, and the remainder meadow and pasture, with one or two small plantations. The soil of the arable land is a strong rich loam, and there is also some fine turnip land; in that part of the parish near the Humber, the soil is a kind of clay warp, apparently embanked from the river at some early period. The village, which is large and well built, comprises a spacious street, at the south end of which is an area called the market-place, with an ancient cross; the view of Hull and neighbouring parts of Yorkshire is very fine. A manufactory of glue is carried on, affording employment to about 20 persons. A market for cattle, held once a fortnight, was commenced in 1832, but afterwards discontinued; and in the same year was established a ferry for passengers and cattle, from a place called New Holland, in this parish, to Hull, a
159

distance of 2¾ miles. The LIVING is a discharged vicarage, valued in the king's books at £9. 16.; net income, £348: the patronage and impropriation belong to the Crown. The tithes were commuted for corn-rents and a money payment in 1797. The church is an ancient Norman structure, with a handsome tower of later English architecture, and exhibits appearances of having been repaired at different times and in various styles. There are places of worship for Wesleyans, Primitive Methodists, and Independents. About a mile north-westward from the village is an intrenchment called the Castle, supposed to have been a British camp; and near it are several barrows. A monastery was founded about the middle of the seventh century, by Wulphere, King of Mercia; and in digging on the site, a little north of the village, some years since, a coffin, a valuable gold ring, and other remains were found. Harrison, the inventor of the chronometer for discovering the longitude at sea, and who, in 1763, received a premium of £20,000 from the Board of Longitude, was a native of the place.

BARROW-UPON-SOAR (HOLY TRINITY), a parish, and the head of a union, partly in the hundred of EAST, but chiefly in that of WEST, GOSCOTE, N. division of the county of LEICESTER; containing 5913 inhabitants, of whom 1837 are in Barrow proper, 3 miles (E. S. E.) from Loughborough. The parish consists of Barrow proper, a part of the market-town of Mountsorrel; the chapelries of Quorndon and Woodhouse, and the consolidated chapelry or district of St. Paul's, Woodhouse-Eaves; the manor of Beaumanor; and the hamlets of Mapplewell, Charley, and Alderman-Haw. It comprises 9100 acres of land, the soil of which is of various kinds, from the finest meadow and richest loam to cold clayey and sterile mountain. The district has for many centuries been noted for its excellent lime, which is made from a hard blue-lias stone, and is extensively used in works where great hardness is necessary: the pier at Ramsgate was built with it, after all other kinds of lime had failed; and from its property of hardening under water, it has been used in Holland. Near Mountsorrel and Quorndon are very extensive and valuable quarries of granite; the midland counties are hence supplied with material for the repair of roads, and the stone is also used for architectural purposes. In Charnwood forest are quarries of primitive slate, which for centuries has been used for covering buildings, and is in much request for tombstones, and many domestic purposes. Barrow proper, and Mountsorrel and Quorndon, are situated on the river Soar, which is navigable through the parish; and here is an intermediate station of the Midland railway, whose course is continued over the Soar by a viaduct of five arches, each spanning 30 feet.

The living is a vicarage, valued in the king's books at £15. 2. 8½., and in the patronage of St. John's College, Cambridge: the tithes have been commuted for 180 acres of land. There are three other incumbencies, in the three chapelries; and places of worship for Wesleyans, Baptists, Primitive Methodists, and Roman Catholics. The free grammar school is endowed with land producing £110 per annum, bequeathed by the Rev. Humphrey Perkins in 1717. An almshouse for six widowers or "ancient bachelors" was founded in 1686 by the Rev. Humphrey Babington, who endowed it with an estate now producing about £500 per annum : the number of inmates has been increased to eleven aged men and a nurse, and six aged widows. The whole of the property belonging to the parish, applied to charitable purposes, amounts to about £1400 per annum. The poor law union of which Barrow is the head, comprises 30 parishes and places, and contains a population of 19,695. William Beveridge, the learned Bishop of St. Asaph, was born here in 1638, in a house which is still standing.

BARROWBY (*All Saints*), a parish, in the union of Grantham, wapentake of Loveden, parts of Kesteven, county of Lincoln, 2 miles (W.) from Grantham ; containing, with the hamlets of Breather-Hills, Casthorpe, and Stenwith, 799 inhabitants. The parish comprises 4330*a*. 1*r*. 21*p*. of fertile land, intersected by the Grantham canal. The Duke of Devonshire, who is proprietor of about one-half of the soil, is lord of the manor : the ancient Hall is now a farmhouse. The living is a rectory, valued in the king's books at £31. 1. 5½. ; net income, £1084 ; patron, the Duke. The church is a neat edifice in the pointed style, with a tower and spire. There are places of worship for Independents and Wesleyans. At Nenbo, in the parish, Richard de Malebisse in 1198 founded an abbey of Præmonstratensian canons in honour of the Blessed Virgin, which at the Dissolution had a revenue of £115. 11. 8.

BARROWDEN (*St. Peter*), a parish, in the union of Uppingham, hundred of Wrandike, county of Rutland, 7 miles (S. W.) from Stamford ; containing 658 inhabitants. It comprises 1997 acres, whereof 388 are common or waste ; and is bounded on the south by the river Welland, which separates the counties of Rutland and Northampton. Excellent rugs are manufactured from sheep-skins ; also parchment, glue, leather for the binding of books, hat-linings, &c. The living is a rectory, valued in the king's books at £14. 13. 1½., and in the gift of the Marquess of Exeter : the glebe consists of 26 acres, and a glebe-house has recently been erected ; the rector's tithes have been commuted for £588. 13., and £30. 3. are also paid to the incumbent of South Luffenham. There is a place of worship for Baptists.

BARROWFORD, a township, in the parochial chapelry of Colne, parish of Whalley, union of Burnley, Higher division of the hundred of Blackburn, N. division of the county of Lancaster, 2½ miles (W.) from Colne ; containing 2630 inhabitants. This place in the reign of Henry VII. constituted two vaccaries, called Over and Nether Barrowford. It is a large township at the junction of several streams flowing into the Colne water ; and comprises 1342 acres. The spinning and manufacture of cotton prevail extensively. Carr Hall was the property of Richard Towneley in 1760, and afterwards of Col. Clayton ; Park Hill was long the seat of the Banisters. A district church has been erected, dedicated to St. Thomas ; the living is a perpetual curacy, in the gift of Hulme's Trustees, and the incumbent has a net income of £150. There is a place of worship for Wesleyans.

BARSBY, a chapelry, in the parish of Ashby-Folville, union of Melton-Mowbray, hundred of East Goscote, N. division of the county of Leicester, 6 miles (S. W. by S.) from Melton-Mowbray ; containing 291 inhabitants. It comprises 914 acres, of which 774 are pasture, and 140 arable.

Dissolution (4th of Elizabeth) to John Fisher and others. The parish is almost surrounded by the small river Blythe, and comprises by computation 1844 acres ; the adjacent country abounds with good scenery, and with objects of interest, and the village is pleasantly situated on an eminence commanding a fine prospect. The Birmingham and Warwick canal approaches within a mile, and the London and Birmingham railway within a mile and a half, of the village. Edward Barber, Esq., who is a large proprietor, has a mansion here. The living is a rectory, annexed to that of Berkeswell : the tithes have been commuted for £180. The church is a plain edifice of brick, erected about the commencement of the last century, upon the site of the ancient structure. A school, in connexion with the church, has just been built.

BARTESTREE, a chapelry, in the parish of Dor-MINGTON, hundred of GREYTREE, union and county of HEREFORD, 4½ miles (E.) from Hereford ; containing 44 inhabitants. The chapelry is situated near the right bank of the river Froome, and is crossed by the road from Hereford to Ledbury ; it comprises 410 acres. The living is a perpetual curacy, united to the vicarage of Dormington. A rent-charge of £90 has been awarded as a commutation for the vicarial tithes. The chapel is dedicated to St. James.

BARTHERTON, a township, in the parish of WYBUNBURY, union and hundred of NANTWICH, S. division of the county of CHESTER, 2¼ miles (S. S. E.) from Nantwich ; containing 32 inhabitants. It comprises 406a. 3r. 12p., of a clayey soil. The Grand Trunk canal passes in the vicinity. The tithes have been commuted for £32 payable to the Bishop of Lichfield, and £5. 19. 6. to the vicar.

BARTHOLOMEW HOSPITAL (ST.), an extra-parochial liberty, in the hundred of EASTRY, lathe of ST. AUGUSTINE, E. division of KENT, ¾ of a mile (S.) from Sandwich ; containing 54 inhabitants, and comprising about 20 acres.—See SANDWICH.

BARTHOLOMEW (ST.), HYDE-STREET, county of SOUTHAMPTON.—See WINCHESTER.

BARTHOMLEY (ST. BERTOLINE), a parish, partly in the union of NEWCASTLE, N. division of the hundred of PIREHILL and of the county of STAFFORD, but chiefly in the hundred of NANTWICH, unions of CONGLE-TON and NANTWICH, S. division of the county of CHESTER ; containing 2725 inhabitants, of whom 422 are in the township of Barthomley, 6½ miles (S. by E.) from Sandbach. In the civil war, a troop of Lord Byron's passing through this place, on the 22nd of December, 1643, made an attack upon the church, into which some of the inhabitants had gone for safety. The troop soon gained possession of it, and having set fire to the forms and matting, made such a smoke as caused fifteen men to retreat to the steeple, where they called for quarter ; their assailants, however, having gotten them into their power, are said to have stripped them all naked, and murdered twelve in cold blood, three only being suffered to escape. The parish includes the townships of Alsager, Balterley, Crewe, and Haslington, and comprises by computation 11,000 acres, whereof 1981 are in the Barthomley township : the surface is flat, and the soil light and sandy ; there are several excellent beds of marl. The living is a rectory, valued in the king's books at £25. 7. 1., and in the gift of the Trustees of Lord

VOL. I.—161

Crewe : the tithes have been commuted for £429 pay. able to impropriators, and £729 belonging to the in. cumbent, who has also a glebe of 90 acres. The church exhibits various styles, and has a Norman porch on the northern side ot the chancel. There are separate in. cumbencies at Alsager and Haslington ; and a school endowed with about £10 per annum.

BARTHORPE, a hamlet, in the parish of ACKLAM, union of MALTON, wapentake of BUCKROSE, E. riding of YORK, 9½ miles (S. by W.) from Malton ; containing 51 inhabitants. This place, also called Barthorpe-Bottoms, is picturesquely situated on the west side of the Wolds : the river Derwent passes on the west at a distance of about three miles.

BARTINGTON, a township, in the parish of GREAT BUDWORTH, union of RUNCORN, hundred of BUCKLOW, N. division of the county of CHESTER, 3¾ miles (N. W.) from Northwich ; containing 89 inhabitants. It comprises 300 acres, of a sandy soil. The tithes have been commuted for £30. 14., of which £29 are payable to the Dean and Chapter of Christ-Church, Oxford.

BARTLEY REGIS, a tything, in the parish of ELING, union of NEW FOREST, hundred of REDBRIDGE, Romsey and S. divisions of the county of SOUTHAMP. TON ; containing 288 inhabitants.

BARTLOW (ST. MARY), a parish, in the union of LINTON, hundred of CHILFORD, county of CAMBRIDGE, 2 miles (E. S. E.) from Linton ; containing 89 inhabit. ants. This place was supposed to have been the scene of the conflict between Canute the Great and Edmund Ironside, which took place in 1016, and in commemora. tion of which four artificial mounds on the lands near Bartlow farm were thought to have been erected ; but on the exploration of these mounds between 1832 and 1840, all the remains discovered were evidently of Roman origin. The parish comprises by computation 360 acres : a fair is held on the 12th of June. The living is a rectory, valued in the king's books at £19. 16. 8. ; net income, £259 ; patron, the Rev. John Bullen. The church has a circular tower, of Norman architecture, said to have been built in the eleventh century ; the body of the building is of the fifteenth century. On the south wall of the nave is a curious painting of St. Christopher, discovered in 1817, on the erection of a monument to Sir William Blackett. There is a place of worship for Wesleyans in the hamlet of Bartlow.

BARTLOW, LITTLE, or STEVENTON-END, a ham. let, in the parish of ASHDON, union of LINTON, hundred of FRESHWELL, N. division of ESSEX, 2¼ miles (S. E.) from Linton ; containing 216 inhabitants. This place, supposed to have been formerly a distinct parish, is civilly included in Ashdon, but ecclesiastically, and as connected with the militia, is considered to be in Bart-low, county of Cambridge.

BARTON (ST. PETER), a parish, in the union of CHESTERTON, hundred of WETHERLEY, county of CAM-BRIDGE, 3½ miles (W. S. W.) from Cambridge ; contain-ing 319 inhabitants. It comprises by measurement 1772 acres, of which about 1622 are arable, and 150 pasture. The living is a vicarage, valued in the king's books at £8. 11. 3., and in the gift of the Bishop of Ely : the great tithes, belonging to King's College, Cambridge, have been commuted for £400, and those of the incum-bent for £135, with a glebe of 36½ acres. In 1839, an act was obtained for inclosing lands.

BARTON, a township, in the parish of FARNDON, union of GREAT BOUGHTON, Higher division of the hundred of BROXTON, S. division of the county of CHESTER, 9½ miles (S. S. E.) from Chester; containing 169 inhabitants. The manor was anciently held under the barony of Malpas by the family of Barton, some monuments of whom, with their effigies, were formerly to be seen in Farndon church; it was afterwards long held by the noble family of Cholmondeley. The township comprises 470 acres; the soil is clay and sand. The impropriate tithes have been commuted for £105.

BARTON, with BRADNOR and RUSHOCK, a township in the parish and union of KINGTON, hundred of HUNTINGTON, county of HEREFORD, ¾ of a mile (N. E.) from Kington; containing 426 inhabitants.

BARTON, a township, in the parish and union of PRESTON, hundred of AMOUNDERNESS, N. division of the county of LANCASTER, 4½ miles (N. N. W.) from Preston; containing 413 inhabitants. It lies on the road, railway, and canal from Preston to Lancaster, and comprises 2400 acres; about 600 are arable, 500 meadow, 90 wood, and the remainder pasture. The surface is undulated, being at the foot of the Bleasdale fells, the peculiar swell of which is continued in a lower degree throughout the township; and the distant fells, and the winding, rural, and wooded lanes, render the scenery varied and pleasing. From the upper grounds are obtained extensive views over the level Fylde, with the sea beyond, embracing the Cumberland and Welsh hills when the atmosphere is clear. The soil is deep and productive, but retentive of moisture, as is the subsoil, which for the most part is a reddish clay, with occasionally marl, sand, peat, and limestone. There are indications of coal in the higher parts; and a quarry of limestone is wrought, more valuable for building purposes than for burning. The township constitutes part of the chapelry of Broughton, and there is a private chapel on the Barton estate for the convenience of the tenantry, the surplus seats being let to the inhabitants of the adjoining township of Myerscough. This chapel, which was in existence before the Reformation, is in the Italian-Gothic style, with a handsome doorway, and has a stained window enriched with the arms of the families now and formerly connected with the estate: the building was enlarged in 1845, by the late George Jacson, Esq., at a considerable expense. Barton Cross, a conspicuous and venerable ruin, which stood where three lanes meet, was mischievously pulled down by some idle persons in 1845.

BARTON (ST. GEORGE), a parish, in the union of BASFORD, N. division of the wapentake of RUSHCLIFFE, S. division of the county of NOTTINGHAM, 6¾ miles (S. W. by S.) from Nottingham; containing 382 inhabitants. It is bounded by the river Trent, which is here navigable. The living is a rectory, valued in the king's books at £19. 3. 9.; net income, £360; patron, the Archbishop of York. The tithes were commuted for land and a money payment, in 1759. The church has several monuments of the Sacheverel family. On the lofty eminence of Brent's hill, south of the village, are the remains of a Roman camp; and in the vicarage farmyard is a Roman pavement.

BARTON (ST. DAVID), a parish, in the union of LANGPORT, hundred of CATSASH, E. division of SOMERSET, 5 miles (N. E. by N.) from Somerton; contain-

perpetual curacies, the latter in the patronage of the
Vicar of St. John's, Stanwick, and the former in that
of the Vicar of Gilling. In 1840, the churches being
in a dilapidated condition, the two curacies were consolidated into one benefice, and a new church was
erected by subscription. The parish is on the road
from Richmond to Darlington, and comprises about
2900 acres, of which 2335 are in the township of Barton; about two-thirds of the land are arable and in profitable cultivation, and the remainder meadow and pasture, with a small portion of woodland. The village is
pleasantly situated on the banks of a small rivulet, and
has an ancient cross in the centre. The living is a perpetual curacy, in the alternate patronage of the Vicars
of Stanwick and Gilling, with a net income of £120;
impropriators, John Allan, Esq., of Blackwell, and others.
The great tithes have been commuted for £125, and
those of the incumbent of Gilling for about £75; 23¾
acres of glebe here are attached to the benefice of Easby,
and 37¼ belong to that of Gilling. There is a place of
worship for Wesleyans.

BARTON-BENDISH, a parish, in the union of
DOWNHAM, hundred of CLACKCLOSE, W. division of
NORFOLK, 4 miles (N. by E.) from Stoke-Ferry; containing 455 inhabitants. This place derives the affix to
its name from a dyke called Bendish, constructed here
by the Saxons as a boundary line to the hundred; it
formerly consisted of the three parishes of St. Andrew,
St. Mary, and All Saints, the two latter of which have
been consolidated. The whole comprises 4126a. 24p.,
whereof 3316 acres are arable, 450 meadow and pasture, and the remainder fen and waste. The living of
St. Andrew's is a rectory, valued in the king's books at
£14, with a net income of £260, and in the patronage
of the Crown: the tithes were commuted in 1777 for
308 acres of land, and the glebe comprises 26 acres.
The church is a handsome structure in the early
and later English styles, with a square embattled tower,
and a south porch in the Norman style. The livings of
St. Mary's and All Saints' form a rectory, valued at
£11, with a net income of £300, and in the gift of Sir
H. Berney, Bart.: the tithes were commuted for 320
acres of land, and the glebe comprises 10 acres, with a
house. The church of St. Mary is chiefly in the early
English style, with a small belfry, the tower having
fallen in the reign of Anne: of the church of All Saints
there are no remains. In the hamlet of Eastmore was
anciently a chapel, dedicated to St. John the Baptist.
There is a place of worship for Wesleyans.

BARTON-BLOUNT, a parish, in the union of BUR-
TON-UPON-TRENT, hundred of APPLETREE, S. division
of the county of DERBY, 11 miles (W.) from Derby;
containing 68 inhabitants. The manor was held in
1296 by the de Bakepuze family, from whom the place
acquired the name of Barton-Bakepuze; and after it
had passed into the possession of their successors, the
Blounts, it obtained its present affix. The families of
Merry, Simpson, Curzon, and Bradshaw subsequently
possessed the manor. The manor-house was garrisoned
in October 1644, by Col. Gell, on behalf of the parliamentarians. The living is a discharged rectory, valued
in the king's books at £4. 19. 1.; net income, £69;
patron, F. Bradshaw, Esq.

BARTON, EARL'S (ALL SAINTS), a parish, in the
union of WELLINGBOROUGH, hundred of HAMFORD-
163

SHOE, N. division of the county of NORTHAMPTON, 3¾
miles (S. W.) from Wellingborough; containing 1079
inhabitants. This place is situated a mile northward
from the navigable river Nene, and about the same distance from the Northampton and Peterborough railway,
which has a station here; it comprises 2330 acres of a
fertile soil. The greater part of the inhabitants are employed in shoe and mat making. The living is a discharged vicarage, valued in the king's books at £10, and
in the patronage of the Crown; net income, £183,
chiefly arising from 88 acres of land allotted on the
inclosure in lieu of tithes; impropriator, T. R. Thornton, Esq., holding 280 acres. The church is a curious
edifice, presenting specimens of various styles of architecture, and having a massive tower of rude Saxon construction. There are places of worship for Baptists and
Wesleyans; also a national school erected in 1844, a
neat building in the Elizabethan style. Almshouses for
three poor people were founded by Mrs. Mary Whitworth in 1823. To the north of the church is a large
tumulus or barrow, of Roman origin.

BARTON-END, a hamlet, in the parish of HORSLEY,
union of STROUD, hundred of LONGTREE, E. division
of the county of GLOUCESTER; containing 268 inhabitants.

BARTON, GREAT, or BRAMBLE (HOLY INNOCENTS),
a parish, in the union of THINGOE, hundred of THED-
WASTRY, W. division of SUFFOLK, 2¼ miles (N. E. by
E.) from Bury; containing 774 inhabitants. The living
is a discharged vicarage, valued in the king's books at
£10. 15. 7½., and in the patronage of Sir H. E. Bunbury,
Bart., whose seat is here: the tithes, with certain exceptions, were commuted for land and a money payment
in 1802. The produce of about 100 acres of land is
applied to the purchase of fuel for the poor, and to parochial purposes.

BARTON-HARTSHORN (ST. JAMES), a parish, in
the union, hundred, and county of BUCKINGHAM, 4¼
miles (W. S. W.) from Buckingham; containing 165
inhabitants. The living is a perpetual curacy, with
that of Chetwood annexed; net income, £80; patrons
and impropriators, the families of Bracebridge and
Viger.

BARTON-IN-FABIS, NOTTS.—See BARTON.

BARTON-IN-THE-BEANS, a township, partly in
the parishes of SHACKERSTONE and NAILSTONE, but
chiefly in that of MARKET-BOSWORTH, union of MAR-
KET-BOSWORTH, hundred of SPARKENHOE, S. division
of the county of LEICESTER, 2¼ miles (N. by W.) from
Market-Bosworth; containing 161 inhabitants. Here
was formerly a chapel.

BARTON-IN-THE-CLAY (ST. NICHOLAS), a parish,
in the union of LUTON, hundred of FLITT, county of
BEDFORD, 3¼ miles (S.) from Silsoe; containing 855
inhabitants. This place, which derives its distinguishing affix from its position at the commencement of the
clayey soil under Barton Hill, is situated on the road
from Luton to Bedford, and on the border of Hertfordshire: the manor formerly belonged to the monks of
Ramsey, since whose possession it has been in the
hands of many different families. The living is a
rectory, valued in the king's books at £26. 9. 7.; net
income, £317; patron, the Crown. The tithes were
commuted for land and a money payment in 1809.
There is a place of worship for Particular Baptists; and
Y 2

a school is endowed with property producing about £50 per annum, the bequest of Edward Willes in 1807.

BARTON-LE-STREET (St. Michael), a parish, in the union of Malton, partly in the wapentake of Bulmer, but chiefly in that of Ryedale, N. riding of York; containing 419 inhabitants, of whom 185 are in the township of Barton, 6 miles (N.) from Whitwell. This parish is bounded on the north by the river Ryle; and, including the townships of Coneysthorpe and Butterwick, comprises by computation 3200 acres, of which about 1500 are in the township of Barton. The surface is undulated, and the scenery beautifully varied; the soil is of moderate quality, and limestone for building and for burning into lime is extensively quarried. The living is a rectory, valued in the king's books at £14. 8. 6½.; net income, £450; patron, Hugh M. Ingram, Esq. The church, an ancient structure with a campanile turret, is said to have been erected with materials from the ruins of St. Mary's Abbey, York; it contains some curious specimens of sculpture. A chapel was erected at Coneysthorpe in 1837, at the expense of the Earl of Carlisle, sole proprietor of that township.

BARTON-LE-WILLOWS, a township, in the parish of Crambe, union of Malton, wapentake of Bulmer, N. riding of York, 10½ miles (N. E.) from York; containing 207 inhabitants. There is a place of worship for Wesleyans.

BARTON, ST. MARY, a hamlet, in the parish of St. Mary-de-Lode, Gloucester, union of Gloucester, Middle division of the hundred of Dudstone and King's Barton, E. division of the county of Gloucester; containing 1674 inhabitants.

BARTON, ST. MICHAEL, a hamlet, in the parish of St. Michael, Gloucester, union of Gloucester, Middle division of the hundred of Dudstone and King's Barton, E. division of the county of Gloucester; containing 1116 inhabitants. A church has been built and endowed by subscription, the living of which is in the gift of the Bishop of the diocese.

BARTON-MILLS, Little Barton, or Barton Two-grind (St. Mary), a parish, in the union of Mildenhall, hundred of Lackford, W. division of Suffolk, 1 mile (S. E.) from Mildenhall; containing 640 inhabitants, and comprising by measurement 2000 acres. The living is a rectory, valued in the king's books at £14. 15. 10.; net income, £550; patron, the Crown. The tithes were commuted for land and a money payment in 1796. There is a place of worship for Particular Baptists. The sum of about £13 per annum, the rental of fourteen acres of fen land, devised by the Rev. James Davies in 1692, is distributed amongst the poor.

BARTON-ON-THE-HEATH (St. Lawrence), a parish, in the union of Chipping-Norton, Brails division of the hundred of Kington, S. division of the county of Warwick, 3½ miles (E.) from Moreton-in-Marsh; containing 212 inhabitants. The parish is situated at the southern extremity of the county, and comprises 1145a. 3r. 34p., of which about one-third is arable, and 85 acres woodland; at its south-western point is a pillar, called the "Four-Shire stone," where the counties of Gloucester, Worcester, Warwick, and Oxford meet. The living is a rectory, valued in the king's books at £12. 17. 11.; net income, £364; patrons, the President and Fellows of Trinity College, Oxford.

pasture and meadow, 35 woodland, and 167 water; and is situated on the navigable river Ant, which opens out into a large lake or broad on the east side of the parish. The living is a discharged vicarage, with the rectory of Irstead united, valued in the king's books at £3. 13. 4.; patron and appropriator, the Bishop of Norwich. The great tithes of Barton-Turf have been commuted for £290, and the vicarial for £168, per annum; there is half an acre of glebe belonging to the bishop, and the vicar's glebe comprises 27½ acres, besides 7½ in Neatshead parish. The church contains handsome monuments to the Norris family. Under the inclosure act, about thirty acres of land were allotted to the poor for fuel.

BARTON-UNDER-NEEDWOOD, a parochial chapelry, in the parish of TATENHILL, union of BURTON-UPON-TRENT, N. division of the hundred of OFFLOW and of the county of STAFFORD, 6 miles (S. W. by W.) from Burton; containing 1459 inhabitants. This place, in Domesday book called Bertune, gave name to one of the five wards into which the ancient royal forest of Needwood was divided. Edward the Confessor granted it to Henry de Ferrers, from whom it passed to the Somervilles, and afterwards to the earls of Derby, one of whom forfeited the property by rebellion in 1263, when Henry III. gave it to his youngest son, Edmund, Earl of Lancaster. It subsequently reverted to the crown as a part of the duchy of Lancaster, and was sold by Charles I. in 1629 to the citizens of London, of whom it was purchased by Sir Edward Bromfield. The TOWNSHIP comprises 3798a. 24p., in about equal portions of arable and pasture; the surface is elevated and undulating, and the scenery picturesque. About a mile east of the village, is the hamlet of Barton-Turning; and further eastward is a handsome bridge, of stone and iron, lately erected across the Trent to Walton, at a cost of £7000. The Grand Trunk canal passes through the chapelry; and there is a station on the Birmingham and Derby railway. Courts leet and baron are held annually in October; and fairs on May 3rd and November 28th. Among the seats are, Barton Hall, Yewtree House, Newbold Manor, and Silverhill; the last, which is the seat of C. W. Lyon, Esq., is built in the Elizabethan style, and the views from it are extensive and beautiful. The LIVING is a perpetual curacy, with a net income of £135; patron, the Dean of Lichfield. The chapel, dedicated to St. James, is a handsome building in the later style, with a square tower and pinnacles; it was erected in the reign of Henry VIII. by the Rev. John Taylor, D.D., a native of the place. The free grammar school was founded in 1593 by Thomas Russell, who, by will, left money for its erection, and endowed it with an annuity of £21. 10., to be paid out of property in the parish of Shoreditch, London, held in trust by the Drapers' Company, who have increased the annuity; besides which, the master has a house and three acres of land: the boys are instructed on Dr. Bell's system. A school for girls is partly supported by an endowment of £20 per annum by the late Thomas Webb, Esq.; and numerous small sums are appropriated to the relief of the poor. There are several saline springs.

BARTON-UPON-HUMBER (ST. PETER), a market-town and parish, in the union of GLANDFORD-BRIGG, N. division of the wapentake of YARBOROUGH, parts of LINDSEY, county of LINCOLN, 34 miles (N.) from Lincoln, and 167 (N.) from London; containing 3495 in-
165

habitants. This place, called in the Norman survey Berton super Humber, is of great antiquity, and is thought to have been a Roman station; which opinion is in some degree confirmed by the direction of the streets, which intersect each other at right angles. During the Saxon and Danish contests it was of considerable importance, and is said to have been surrounded by a rampart and fosse, some remains of which, called the Castle Dykes, are still perceptible. On the invasion of Anlaff and his confederates in the reign of Athelstan, he is supposed to have landed part of his forces and posted them here to act in concert with the main body of his army, which was stationed at Barrow, previous to the great battle of Brunnam, which took place in the adjoining township, now Burnham. At the time of the Conquest, Barton was noted for its commerce, and was one of the manors bestowed by William the Conqueror on his nephew, Gilbert de Gaunt, who had a castle here. It continued to flourish as a commercial town till Edward I. gave to Wyke-upon-Hull the appellation of "King's town upon Hull," and made it a free borough, at which time the trade of Barton began to decline.

The TOWN is pleasantly situated on the south bank of the river Humber, at the foot of the northern termination of the range of chalk hills called the Lincolnshire Wolds; and is of considerable extent, consisting of several streets, in which are numerous good dwelling-houses with gardens and orchards attached, and combining with the advantages of a market-town the pleasing appearance of a rural village. The trade is principally in corn, flour, malt, coal, and bones for manure. There are a large ropery and sacking manufactory; two tanneries, in one of which the larch bark is used for the finer kinds of leather; an extensive foundry for church bells, carried on by Mr. James Harrison, whose grandfather obtained a premium for the best time-piece for finding the longitude at sea; and large manufactories for starch and malt. In the vicinity is a chalkstone-quarry, producing great quantities of stone, the larger pieces of which are used for repairing the banks of the Humber and other rivers, and for the construction and repair of jetties, and the smaller for mending roads; the finest quality is sold for making plaster of Paris, and shipped for foreign markets. The market, under an ancient grant, is on Monday, and is well supplied with corn and with provisions of every kind; a market is also held every alternate Monday for fat-cattle, and a fair, chiefly for toys, on Trinity-Thursday and the following day. The ancient ferry to Hessle, across the Humber, which is here about a mile broad, is appurtenant to the manor, which is vested in the crown: it has been for a long time granted to different lessees, and is now combined with the Hull ferry, under lease to the corporation of that town, who have established a steam-packet. There is a station on the Hull and Selby railway at Hessle, just mentioned; and an act was passed in 1846 for extending the New Holland branch of the Gainsborough and Grimsby railway, to Barton: the extension is four miles long. The town is under the jurisdiction of the county magistrates, who hold a petty-session every fortnight; and constables and other officers are appointed at the court leet of the manor, which is held annually under the crown. The powers of the county debt-court of Barton, established 1847, extend over the Barton sub-registration-district.

The parish comprises 6240 acres, of which about 700 are arable, and 100 plantation; the land adjoining the Humber is of a clayey quality, but the greater part is a fine soil resting upon chalk. The LIVING is a vicarage, valued in the king's books at £19. 4. 8.; net income, £261; patrons and impropriators, the Uppleby family. The great tithes were granted by Gilbert de Gaunt to the abbey of Bardney; and, at the inclosure of the waste lands, the tithe allotment and glebe of the rectory amounted to more than 1000 acres. The church is a spacious structure, principally in the decorated English style, with a tower, of which the upper part is evidently early Norman, and the lower of a much more remote date, being probably one of the very few specimens of Saxon architecture remaining in the kingdom. There is also a church dedicated to St. Mary, formerly called the chapel of All Saints, which, having no endowment, is supposed to have been built as a chapel of ease to St. Peter's, and which, according to tradition, was rebuilt by the merchants of Barton; it is partly Norman, but chiefly in the early English style, of which the tower is a very elegant specimen. There are places of worship for Wesleyans, Independents, and Primitive Methodists, and a Roman Catholic chapel lately erected. In the south part of the parish is a small encampment, supposed to have been an outpost to the larger station at Burnham, and which has long been planted with trees, and is now styled Beaumont Cote. In November, 1828, a Roman urn of unburnt clay, and of excellent workmanship, was dug up in the West Field of Barton, near the line of the ancient road to Ferriby: it contained human bones unconsumed; and near the spot where it had been deposited was a human skeleton, the bones of which mouldered into dust on exposure to the air.

BARTON-UPON-IRWELL, a township, in the parish of Eccles, hundred of Salford, S. division of the county of Lancaster, 5½ miles (W. by S.) from Manchester; containing 10,865 inhabitants. The township lies on both banks of the Irwell from Trafford Park to Davyhulme, where the river becomes the boundary line till it falls into the Mersey: the Mersey and the Glazebrook also form boundaries. The manufacture of calico and nankeen goods is carried on. The Duke of Bridgewater's canal crosses the Irwell here, by means of a stone aqueduct of three arches, which was the first constructed in England over a navigable river; and the Liverpool and Manchester railway also passes through the township. Barton Old Hall, a brick edifice, now a farmhouse, was the seat successively of the Barton, Booth, and Leigh families. A church dedicated to St. Catherine, a neat stone building with an elegant octagonal spire rising to a height of about 100 feet from the ground, was consecrated on the 25th of October, 1843; the site is elevated, and commands extensive prospects. The living is a perpetual curacy, in the patronage of the Bishop of Chester, Vicar of Eccles, and others. There are places of worship for Wesleyans, Independents, Independent Methodists, the New Connexion, Unitarians, and Roman Catholics. The Eccles parochial school, in the township, is endowed with pew-rents, amounting to £8 per annum; and in another school, twenty children are partly paid for by the trustees under the will of Mr. James Bradshaw. There is also a national school capable of accommodating 240 children, with a residence for the master.—See PATRICROFT.

BARWICK, a hamlet, in the parish of ABBOT'S ROOTHING, hundred of ONGAR, N. division of ESSEX; containing 126 inhabitants.

BARWICK (ST. MARY), a parish, in the union of DOCKING, hundred of SMITHDON, W. division of NORFOLK, 11 miles (N.) from Rougham; containing 32 inhabitants. It comprises 1233a. 3r. 19p., and contains Barwick House, a neat brick mansion. The living is a discharged vicarage, valued in the king's books at £6; patron and impropriator, Mr. Hoste: the great tithes have been commuted for £132, and the vicarial for one of £100; there are 45 acres of glebe.

BARWICK (ST. MARY MAGDALENE), a parish, in the union of YEOVIL, hundred of HOUNDSBOROUGH, BERWICK, and COKER, W. division of SOMERSET, 1¾ mile (S. by E.) from Yeovil; containing, with the hamlet of Stoford, 446 inhabitants. It is situated near the road between Yeovil and Dorchester, and comprises by measurement 784 acres. Flax-spinning is carried on to some extent; and sheep and cattle fairs are held on June 11th and Sept. 28th. The living is a discharged rectory, valued in the king's books at £7. 14. 7., and in the gift of John Newman, Esq.: the tithes have been commuted for £245, and there are 46 acres of glebe.

BARWICK-IN-ELMET (ALL SAINTS), a parish, in the Lower division of the wapentake of SKYRACK, W. riding of YORK, 7 miles (N. E. by E.) from Leeds; containing 2275 inhabitants, of whom 1836 are in Barwick township. This place was the seat of Edwin, King of Northumbria, and had its name from a castle of great magnitude and strength, founded by that monarch on an eminence called Hall-Tower Hill, and the walls of which inclosed an area of upwards of thirteen acres. On the banks of Grimsdike rivulet, which flows on the west, was fought in 655 the great battle between the Northumbrians and Mercians, when Penda and many of his vassal princes were slain. The parish comprises by measurement 8325 acres, whereof 1440 are in the township of Roundhay, and the remainder in Barwick township, which includes Barnbow, Kiddal-with-Potterton, and Morwick-with-Scholes: the substratum consists for a great part of coal and limestone. The Leeds and Selby railway passes through. The living is a rectory, valued in the king's books at £33. 12. 6., and in the patronage of the Duchy of Lancaster, with a net income of £1200: the church is a handsome structure, in the later English style. At Roundhay is a district church. There is a place of worship for Wesleyans. A school, endowed with £14 per annum, is conducted at Barwick; and at Stanks is a school supported by the rector, the schoolroom of which, built in 1839, is licensed for public worship.

BASCHURCH (ALL SAINTS), a parish, in the union of ELLESMERE, hundred of PIMHILL, N. division of SALOP, 8 miles (N. W. by N.) from Shrewsbury; containing 1491 inhabitants. It is intersected by the Ellesmere canal; and comprises 8213a. 1r. 10p., exclusively of the chapelry of Little Ness, which by computation contains 1300 acres: red sandstone for building is quarried. The living is a discharged vicarage, valued in the king's books at £10. 16., and in the patronage of the Crown; net income, £203; impropriators, certain Landowners in the parish: the glebe comprises 40 acres. At Little Ness is a chapel of ease. Vestiges of a Roman camp may be traced in the neighbourhood.

167

BASFORD, a township, in the parish of WYBUN-BURY, union and hundred of NANTWICH, S. division of the county of CHESTER, 4¾ miles (E.) from Nantwich; containing 85 inhabitants. It comprises 642a. 3r. 29p., of a clayey, loamy, and sandy soil. The Liverpool and Birmingham railway passes through the township, and has a station on Basford Heath. The tithes have been commuted for £58 payable to the Bishop of Lichfield, and £6. 6. to the vicar of Wybunbury.

BASFORD (ST. LEODGARIUS), a parish, and the head of a union, in the N. division of the wapentake of BROXTOW and of the county of NOTTINGHAM, 2½ miles (N. W. by N.) from Nottingham; containing 8688 inhabitants. This parish, which is pleasantly situated in the vale of the river Leen, has a rich sandy soil, and is ornamented around the extensive village of Old Basford with well-wooded scenery, thickly studded with modern mansions. Newly-rising and populous villages, the houses of which are chiefly built of brick and covered with blue slate, have lately sprung up in several parts, the principal of them being New Basford, Carrington on the Mansfield road, Mapperley-place, and Sherwood. New Basford is situated at the southern extremity of the old village, and consists of several good streets which cross each other at right angles, and the principal occupants of which are persons employed in the manufacture of bobbin-net. The parish abounds with numerous springs of soft water; it has been selected as a place well adapted for the bleaching of cotton-hose and lace, and several large factories have been established for the manufacture of those articles. The living is a vicarage, valued in the king's books at £8. 17. 7., and in the patronage of the Crown; net income, £260; impropriator, the Duke of Newcastle: the tithes were commuted for land in 1792. The church, which is situated at the southern extremity of the village, was repaired in 1819, when it received an addition of 212 free sittings. A church district named New Basford was formed in 1847 by the Ecclesiastical Commissioners; patrons, the Crown and the Bishop alternately. At Carrington is a church dedicated to St. John. There are places of worship for Wesleyans, Methodists of the New Connexion, and Baptists. The poor law union of Basford comprises 43 parishes, of which 38 are in the county of Nottingham, and 5 in the county of Derby, and contains a population of 59,634; the workhouse was formerly the house of industry for 32 parishes in the county, and is a modern stone building.

BASFORD, a township, in the parish of CHEDDLE-TON, union of CHEADLE, N. division of the hundred of TOTMONSLOW and of the county of STAFFORD, 3 miles (S. by E.) from Leek; containing 349 inhabitants. The river Churnet and the Uttoxeter canal pass on the west.

BASHALL-EAVES, a township, in the parish of MITTON, union of CLITHEROE, W. division of the wapentake of STAINCLIFFE and EWCROSS, W. riding of YORK, 3 miles (W. by N.) from Clitheroe; containing 279 inhabitants. This place, long distinguished as the residence of the Talbots, has been variously designated Beckshalgh, Batsalve, Bakesholf, and Bashall; the first orthography is the true one, viz., Beckshalgh, or "the hill by the brooks," which agrees precisely with its situation: in Domesday book it is styled Baschelf. The township comprises about 3640 acres, and includes the small hamlets of Exa and Pagefold: the river Ribble passes on the east. John Taylor, Esq., of Moreton, is lord of the manor. There is a place of worship for Wesleyans.

BASILDON (St. Bartholomew), a parish, in the union of Bradfield, hundred of Moreton, county of Berks, 8 miles (N. W. by W.) from Reading; containing 812 inhabitants. This place appears to have been anciently a place of much greater importance than it is at present, being noticed in Domesday book as having two churches; and in the reign of Edward II. the inhabitants obtained the grant of a weekly market, and a fair on St. Barnabas' day. The parish comprises 3083a. 6p., of which 52 acres are roads and waste; the soil varies, but is principally flinty; the ground is hilly, and the vicinity abounds with picturesque scenery. The river Thames here separates the counties of Oxford and Berks, and is crossed by a viaduct of four arches on the line of the Great Western railway, erected at a cost of £25,000. The living is a discharged vicarage, with the living of Ashampstead annexed, valued in the king's books at £7. 14. 4½.; patrons, alternately, the family of Sykes and the Trustees of the late Rev. C. Simeon. The great tithes have been commuted for £770, and the vicarial for £215 per annum; the glebe comprises 19 acres. The church contains some hatchments of the family of Fane, formerly proprietors of the estate; also some chaste monuments belonging to the family of Sir Francis Sykes, Bart. In excavating for the railway, a beautiful tessellated pavement was discovered a few inches below the surface of an elevated spot, not far from the Thames; and coins of Vespasian in a high state of preservation, domestic utensils, and several skeletons, with a Roman sword lying near them, were also found in the immediate neighbourhood.

BASILDON, a chapelry, in the parish of Laindon, union of Billericay, hundred of Barstable, S. division of Essex, 4½ miles (S. E. by S.) from Billericay; containing 157 inhabitants. This is a place of considerable antiquity, and contains three manors. The mansion of the manor of Barstable was about half a mile from the chapel of Basildon, and is said to have been surrounded by a town that gave name to the hundred; which is rendered probable by the fact, that foundations of houses have been ploughed up in the vicinity, as well as considerable quantities of human bones. The record of Domesday informs us that the estate of Barstable had been taken from a Saxon freeman, and given to Odo, Bishop of Bayeux; in the reign of Edward III., it was generally holden, with the hundred, of the king. The chapel, dedicated to the Holy Cross, is a neat and substantial edifice, consisting of a nave and chancel, with an embattled tower surmounted by a spire. The tithes have been commuted for £280, and there is a glebe of 23 acres.

BASING (St. Mary), a parish, in the union and hundred of Basingstoke, Basingstoke and N. divisions of the county of Southampton, 2 miles (E. N. E.) from Basingstoke; containing 1172 inhabitants. This place is remarkable for having been the scene of the defeat of King Ethelred I. by the Danes, in 871. At the period of the Norman survey, Hugh de Port held fifty-five lordships in the county, of which Basing was the head. The castle was rebuilt, in a sumptuous manner, by Sir William Paulet, Knt., a lineal descendant from Hugh de 168

Port, created Marquess of Winchester by Edward VI., and one of the most polite noblemen of the age : here, in 1560, he entertained Queen Elizabeth, who honoured his great-grandson William, the fourth marquess, with a visit, in 1601. John, the fifth marquess, distinguished himself for his gallant defence of his house at Basing, in the cause of Charles I., through a series of sieges that lasted for two years, at the end of which, in Oct. 1645, it was stormed and taken by Cromwell, who ordered it to be burned to the ground. The fortress and its outworks occupied an area of about fourteen acres and a half, through which the Basingstoke canal now passes; the remains consist principally of the north gateway and part of the outer wall. The river Loddon and the London and Southampton railway run through the parish, which comprises about 4000 acres; the surface is undulated, and the soil chalk, clay, and gravel. The living is annexed to the vicarage of Basingstoke: the great tithes, payable to Magdalen College, Oxford, have been commuted for £705, with a glebe of 19 acres, and those of the incumbent for £475. The church is a large ancient structure, with a central tower, and contains the family vault of the Paulets, in which all the dukes of Bolton of that family have been interred.

BASINGSTOKE (St. Michael), a municipal borough, a market-town, and the head of a union, in the hundred of Basingstoke, Basingstoke and N. divisions of the county of Southampton, 18 miles (N. E.) from Winchester, and 45 (W. S. W.) from London, on the great western road; containing 4066 inhabitants. In the early part of the Saxon dynasty, Basingstoke was inferior to Old Basing; but at the time of the Conquest it had obtained the superiority, since, in the record of Domesday, it is described as a royal demesne, and as having a market. In 1261, Henry III., at the request of Walter de Merton, founded an hospital here for six poor priests, with preference to those from Merton College, Oxford. In the reign of Henry VIII., Sir William (afterwards Lord) Sandys, in conjunction with Fox, Bishop of Winchester, instituted a guild and erected a beautiful chapel, which he dedicated to the Holy Ghost. This fraternity was dissolved in the time of Edward VI., and the revenue was vested in the crown; but in the reign of Mary it was re-established, and the income appropriated to the maintenance of a priest, for the celebration of divine service, and the instruction of young men and boys belonging to the town. During the civil war, it was suppressed by Cromwell, and the estates were seized by the parliament; but through the intercession of Dr. Morley, Bishop of Winchester, they were restored in 1670, and appropriated to their former use. Of the chapel, and the buildings connected with it, there are some remains on an eminence at the south-western side of the town, consisting of the south and east walls, and an hexagonal tower at the north-west angle.

The town is pleasantly situated in a fertile and well-cultivated district, near the source of the small river Loddon, and consists of several streets, containing neat

Corporation Seal.

and well-built houses; it is paved under an act of parliament granted in 1815, is amply supplied with water, and lighted with gas. Races formerly took place in Sept., but they have been discontinued; a spacious reading-room has lately been erected. The trade is principally in corn and malt; it is extensive, and is greatly facilitated by the situation of the town at the junction of five principal roads, and by the Basingstoke canal, which communicates with the river Wey near its confluence with the Thames. The London and Southampton railway, also, has a station here. The Great Western railway company have a line to Reading, 15 miles long, under an act passed in 1845; and an act was passed in 1846 for a railway from near Basingstoke to Andover and Salisbury, 32 miles long. The chief market is on Wednesday, and has lately been made a pitched market for corn; there is a minor market on Saturday. Fairs take place on Easter-Tuesday, the Wednesday next after Whitsuntide, and Oct. 11th, which last is also a statute-fair: the one formerly held on Basingstoke downs, for cheese and cattle, is now held near the cattle-market, and is entirely a cattle-fair.

The GOVERNMENT, by charter of incorporation granted by James I. and confirmed by Charles II., was vested in a mayor, seven aldermen, and seven burgesses, assisted by the usual officers; who were superseded in 1836 by a mayor, four aldermen, and 12 councillors, appointed under the Municipal Corporations' act. Four justices, besides the mayor, act for the town, the county magistrates having concurrent jurisdiction. The latter hold a petty-session here for the division, on the first and third Wednesdays in every month; and a court leet is held under the lord of the manor, the jurisdiction of which comprises nineteen tythings. The powers of the county debt-court of Basingstoke, established in 1847, extend over the registration-districts of Basingstoke and Hartley-Wintney. The town sent members to parliament from the 23rd of Edward I. to the 4th of Edward II., when, it is supposed, the privilege ceased at the solicitation of the inhabitants. The old town-hall has been taken down, and a new and very handsome edifice erected in its stead, containing, besides a good basement, a spacious market for corn, a justice-room of ample dimensions, and a waiting-room on the ground floor. The ball-room is of an elegant and chaste character and of good proportions, being 60 feet long and 30 wide, with a convenient orchestra, council-room, ante-room, &c. The expense of this structure, which was erected from a design by Mr. Lewis Wyatt, was defrayed partly from the funds of the corporation, and partly by subscription. Behind it is a market-place for meat, fish, and vegetables.

The parish of Basingstoke is co-extensive with the borough, and contains 4036 acres, of which 107 are common or waste; the surface consists of hill and dale, and the soil is good light earth, suited to the production of barley. The LIVING is a discharged vicarage, with the livings of Basing and Upper Nately annexed, valued in the king's books at £30. 16. 5½.; patrons and appropriators, the President and Fellows of Magdalen College, Oxford. The great tithes of Basingstoke have been commuted for £783. 7., and the vicarial for £494. 13.; there are 17 acres of glebe belonging to the college, and 1¼ acre of vicarial glebe. The church is a spacious and handsome structure in the later English style, with a
VOL. I.—169

low embattled tower, and contains a small parochial library, the gift of Sir George Wheler. There are places of worship for the Society of Friends, the Connexion of the Countess of Huntingdon, and Independents. The free grammar school, called "the Holy Ghost Chapel School," and originally founded in the reign of Henry VIII. in connexion with the guild of the Holy Ghost, was re-established, after the dissolution of the fraternity in the time of Edward VI., by Queen Mary, and has now a revenue exceeding £200, arising from 105 acres of land. Dr. Joseph Warton, a poet and refined critic, and his brother Thomas, the poet-laureate, received the early part of their education here, under their father, Thomas Warton, B.D., some time professor of poetry in the University of Oxford, and subsequently master of the school. The Blue-coat school, in which ten boys are clothed, maintained, and educated, was founded and endowed in 1646, by Richard Aldworth. Almshouses for eight aged men or women, each of whom receives £6. 18. per annum, were founded and endowed by Sir James Deane, Knt., in 1607. The poor law union of Basingstoke comprises 37 parishes and places, of which 36 are in the county of Southampton, and one in the county of Berks; and contains a population of 16,636. On an eminence in the vicinity is an ancient encampment of an elliptical form, 1100 yards in circumference, called Aubrey Camp. John de Basingstoke, a learned Greek scholar, and the intimate friend of Matthew Paris; Sir James Lancaster, an eminent navigator, who, in the reign of Elizabeth, explored the Arctic Sea, and who was a great benefactor of the town; and Thomas Warton, above-mentioned, were natives of the place.

BASINGTHORPE (THOMAS à BECKET), in the union of GRANTHAM, wapentake of BELTISLOE, parts of KESTEVEN, county of LINCOLN, 3¾ miles (N. W.) from Corby; containing, with the hamlet of Westby, 137 inhabitants. It comprises 1790 acres, the property of the Earl of Dysart. The living is a vicarage, valued in the king's books at £8. 17. 6., and in the patronage of the Earl: the vicarial tithes have been commuted for £190, and the impropriate for one of £230; there are 4 acres of glebe.

BASLOW, a chapelry, in the parish and union of BAKEWELL, hundred of HIGH PEAK, N. division of the county of DERBY, 4 miles (N. E.) from Bakewell; containing 962 inhabitants. This place is situated on the river Derwent, and on the road from Bakewell to Chesterfield. The inhabitants are partly employed in the cotton manufacture, and there are some quarries of ordinary building-stone. The living is a perpetual curacy; net income, £115; patron, the Duke of Devonshire; impropriator, the Duke of Rutland : the tithes (those on wool and lamb excepted) were commuted for land in 1822. The chapel, which is chiefly in the later English style, has a tower and low spire at the western end of the north aisle. There are two places of worship for Wesleyans; and about half a mile from the village is Stanton-Ford school, endowed with about £15 per annum.

BASSALEG (ST. BASIL), a parish, in the union and division of NEWPORT, hundred of WENTLLOOG, county of MONMOUTH, 2¾ miles (W.) from Newport; containing, with the hamlets of Duffryn, Graig, and Rogerstone, 1731 inhabitants. The parish is partly bounded by the river Severn, and comprises about 6500 acres, of which
Z

2633 are arable, 3146 meadow and pasture, and 722 woodland; it is intersected by the river Ebn and the Monmouthshire canal, and the Rumney railway joins the Sirhowey railway here, at a place called Pye Corner. The living is a discharged vicarage, valued in the king's books at £14. 13. 6½., and in the gift of the Bishop of Llandaff : the glebe consists of about one acre ; and the tithes have been commuted for £864. 18., of which £509. 19. belong to the bishop. There is a place of worship for Particular Baptists ; and a free school, endowed with £20 per annum, is conducted on the national plan. On the brow of a hill a mile from the village, is a circular intrenchment called *Craeg-y-Saesson*, supposed to have been a Saxon camp; a mile from which is one named *Pen-y-Park Newydd*, probably a fortress of the Britons. A priory was founded in 1101, which became a cell to the abbey of Glastonbury.

BASSENTHWAITE (*St. Bridget*), a parish, in the union of Cockermouth, Allerdale ward below Derwent, W. division of Cumberland, 5 miles (N. W. by N.) from Keswick ; containing 536 inhabitants. The parish comprises about 7000 acres, much of which is wet heavy land ; it includes a portion of the lofty mountain Skiddaw, situated at its south-eastern extremity, and is intersected by the river Derwent. The beautiful lake of Bassenthwaite, or Broadwater, covers about 1500 acres, and the parish is enriched throughout with scenery of a sublime character. There is a mine of antimony in the neighbourhood, and lead-ore has also been found. The living is a perpetual curacy ; net income, £123; patrons and appropriators, the Dean and Chapter of Carlisle : the tithes were commuted for land in 1770. In addition to the parochial church, there is a chapel of ease.

BASSET-HOUSE, an extra-parochial liberty, in the union of Market-Bosworth, hundred of Sparkenhoe, S. division of the county of Leicester, 6 miles (N. E.) from Hinckley ; containing 30 inhabitants. The liberty is situated near the road from Leicester to Hinckley, about midway between the two towns; and comprises 191 acres of land. It belonged to the Basset family, and passed from them to the Harringtons, Greys, and more recently to the Arkwrights.

BASSINGBOURNE (*St. Peter*), a parish, in the union of Royston, hundred of Armingford, county of Cambridge, 3¼ miles (N. W. by N.) from Royston ; containing, with the hamlet of Kneesworth, 1774 inhabitants. A fair is held on the festival of St. Peter and St. Paul. The living is a vicarage, valued in the king's books at £7. 0. 10. ; net income, £224; patrons and appropriators the Dean and Chapter of Westminster : the tithes were commuted for land and a money payment, in 1801. A room adjoining the north aisle has been appropriated to the reception of a parochial library, founded in 1717, by Edward Nightingale.

BASSINGHAM (*St. Michael*), a parish, in the union of Newark, Lower division of the wapentake of Boothby-Graffo, parts of Kesteven, county of Lincoln, 8 miles (E. N. E.) from Newark, and 9 miles (S. W. by S.) from Lincoln ; containing 792 inhabitants. It is situated on the river Witham, and comprises 3015a. 28p., of which 1430 acres are arable, about 1494 meadow and pasture, and the remainder roads and waste; the soil is partly clay and partly gravel, and the surface uniformly flat. The living is a

170

rectory, valued in the king's books at £26. 16. 8. ; net income, £483; patrons, the President and Fellows of Corpus Christi College, Oxford : the glebe comprises 157 acres. The church is a handsome structure, the tower of which has been rebuilt within the last fifty years. There are two places of worship for Wesleyans, and one for Primitive Methodists.

BASSINGTON, a township, in the parish of Eglingham, union of Alnwick, N. division of Coquetdale ward and of Northumberland, 3½ miles (N. W. by W.) from Alnwick ; containing 11 inhabitants. This place, which is situated on the north side of the Aln, near its junction with the Eglingham burn, derives its name from *bassin*, an old word signifying rushy, and *ton*, a place of abode ; and the surrounding fields, notwithstanding the progress of cultivation, still very much abound with the common rush. The impropriate tithes have been commuted for £16.

BASTON (*St. John the Baptist*), a parish, in the union of Bourne, wapentake of Ness, parts of Kesteven, county of Lincoln, 3¼ miles (N. N. W.) from Market-Deeping ; containing, with Thetford, 765 inhabitants. The living is a discharged vicarage, valued in the king's books at £6. 1. 3., with a net income of £231 ; it is in the patronage of the Crown, and the impropriation belongs to Brown's Hospital at Stamford. The tithes were commuted for an allotment of land, in the year 1801.

BASWICH, or Berkswich (*Holy Trinity*), a parish, partly in the union of Stafford, and partly in that of Penkridge, E. division of the hundred of Cuttlestone, S. division of the county of Stafford, 2 miles (E. S. E.) from Stafford ; consisting of the chapelry of Acton-Trussell with Bednall, and the townships of Baswich and Brompton ; and containing 1438 inhabitants, of whom 626 are in the township of Baswich. This parish, which lies on the road from Stafford to Lichfield, comprises by measurement 4951 acres, whereof 1644 are in Baswich township : the soil is gravelly, productive, and suitable to the growth of turnips and barley. The surface is undulated, and the scenery picturesque, and the land entirely agricultural : the rivers Penk and Sow skirt the parish ; the Staffordshire and Worcestershire canal passes through it, and the Liverpool and Birmingham railway within two miles. Part of Cannock chase is within the parish. In Baswich township are the hamlets of Milford, Radford, Walton, and Weeping-Cross. The living is a vicarage not in charge ; net income, £238 ; patrons, John Newton Lane, Esq., and the Rev. William Inge. The church is an ancient structure with a square tower. A chapel of ease has been erected at Walton, on a site presented by the Earl of Lichfield : it is in the early English style, with open sittings ; the chancel has a window of triple lancet shape, embellished with stained glass, and a smaller window is also painted. The chapels of Acton and Bednall form a separate incumbency. A national and Sunday school is supported by subscription ; at Milford is a day school maintained by Mrs. Levett ; and a school at Brockton, in the parish, is endowed with 7a. 1r. of land, supposed to have been given by Mrs. Dorothy Bridgman, and for the proceeds of which nine children are taught.

BATCOMBE (*St. Mary*), a parish, in the union of Cerne, hundred of Yetminster, Cerne division of

DORSET, 3 miles (N. W. by W.) from Cerne-Abbas; containing 171 inhabitants. It comprises by computation 1149 acres, of which 172 are arable, 539 pasture, 28 orchard, 27 woodland, and 383 common : the soil is a deep black mould. The living is a discharged rectory, united in 1772 to that of Froome-Vauchurch, and valued in the king's books at £9. 9. 9½. : the tithes have been commuted for £130, and there are 45 acres of glebe. The church is a handsome structure in the early English style, with a finely carved roof of oak, and a square tower ; on the north side is a private aisle for sepulture, anciently belonging to the family of Minterne.

BATCOMBE (*St. Mary*), a parish, in the union of SHEPTON-MALLET, hundred of WHITESTONE, E. division of SOMERSET, 3 miles (N. by E.) from Bruton ; containing 780 inhabitants. It comprises by measurement 3170 acres, of which 670 are arable. The living is a rectory, with the perpetual curacy of Upton-Noble annexed, valued in the king's books at £26. 14. 4½.; net income, £690 ; patron and incumbent, the Rev. J. Browne. There is a place of worship for Wesleyans.

BATCOMBE, a tything, in the ancient parish of NYLAND, union of AXBRIDGE, hundred of GLASTON-TWELVE-HIDES, E. division of SOMERSET; containing 11 inhabitants.

Arms.

BATH, a city, having separate jurisdiction, and the head of a union, locally in the hundred of BATH-FORUM, E. division of SOMERSET, 12 miles (E. by S.) from Bristol, 19 (N. N. E.) from Wells, and 107 (W.) from London, on the direct road to Bristol ; containing, with the whole of the parish of Walcot, 38,314 inhabitants, and with those of Bathwick, and Widcombe and Lyncombe, 53,206. The name of this city is obviously derived from its medicinal springs, the efficacy of which has been celebrated from remote antiquity. It is stated to have been a British town prior to the Roman invasion, and to have been named *Caer Badon*, or "the place of baths," from an accidental discovery of the medicinal properties of its waters by Bladud, son of Lud Hudibras, King of Britain ; who, according to the fabulous histories of those times, having been banished from court on account of leprosy, came to this place, and being cured of the disease by using the waters, built a palace here after his accession to the throne, and encouraged the resort of persons affected with cutaneous disorders. So favourably was this account received even till the eighteenth century, that a statue of Bladud was erected in the King's bath, with an inscription to that effect, in 1699. The researches of modern historians, however, have induced them to reject the tradition as entirely destitute of support, and to ascribe the foundation of the city to the ROMANS, who, in the reign of Claudius, having ascertained the healing quality of its waters, constructed, on a skilful and extensive plan, their *balnea*, consisting of *frigidaria, tepidaria, olothesia, sudatoria*, &c., for the better enjoyment of the luxury of the bath, and gave to the station the name *Aquæ Solis*. They erected a temple to Minerva,

171

with many votive altars, and numerous other buildings, the remains of which, discovered at various periods, strikingly indicate their splendour and magnificence. They also surrounded the city with walls twenty feet in height, and of prodigious thickness, including an area in the form of an irregular pentagon, of which the larger diameter was 1200 feet, and the smaller 1140. In the centre were the *prætorium*, the baths, and the temple; and in the walls were four gates terminating the principal streets, from which they constructed roads leading to the neighbouring stations, *Verlucio, Ischalis, Abona,* &c. After the departure of the Romans from Britain, Bath, then called *Caer Palladwr*, "the city of the waters of Pallas," remained in the possession of the Britons for more than a century, being disturbed only by one or two unsuccessful attacks of the Saxon chieftains, Ælla and Cerdic, who were bravely repulsed by the renowned King Arthur.

In the year 577 the Saxons, having nearly overrun the kingdom, fell with irresistible fury on the western part of England ; and having gained the memorable battle of Deorham, about eight miles distant, Bath fell a prey to their ravages, and was abandoned to indiscriminate plunder. Its temple was destroyed, its altars were overthrown, and its baths and other splendid monuments of Roman grandeur reduced to a heap of ruins. How long it continued in this desolate state is uncertain, but probably the Saxons, after having retained uninterrupted possession of it for a time, took means to effect its restoration : they rebuilt the walls and other fortifications upon the original foundations, with the old materials, cementing them with a liquid substance, which time has rendered harder than stone ; and it is likely that they also directed their attention to the baths, which they soon restored ; for the Saxon names of the city were *Hat Bathur*, "hot baths," and *Ace mannes ceaster*, "city of invalids." After their conversion to Christianity, a nunnery was erected here, in 676, which was destroyed during the wars of the heptarchy ; on its site a college of Secular canons was founded, in 775, by Offa, King of Mercia, who had taken Bath from the King of Wessex, and annexed it to his own dominions. He also rebuilt the conventual church of St. Peter, in which Edgar was crowned king of England, by Dunstan, Archbishop of Canterbury, in 973 ; and the anniversary of this coronation continued to be celebrated in the time of Camden, in commemoration of the numerous privileges which had been granted to the citizens on that occasion. Edgar converted the college into a Benedictine monastery, which, with the church, was demolished by the Danes.

At the time of the NORMAN survey, Bath contained 178 burgesses, of whom 64 held under the king, 90 under different feudatories of the crown, and 24 under the abbot of St. Peter's. In the first year of the reign of William Rufus, Geoffrey, Bishop of Coutances, and Robert de Mowbray, who had risen in support of the claim of Robert, Duke of Normandy, to the throne of England, obtained possession of the city by assault, and reduced the greater part of it to ashes. From this calamity, however, it soon recovered, under the favour of John de Villula, who, on his promotion to the see of Wells, about the year 1090, purchased the city from Henry I. for 500 marks, and built a new and spacious church for that see, removing the episcopal chair

Z 2

to this place, where, during the festival of Easter in 1107, he had the honour of entertaining Henry I. In the turbulent reign of Stephen, Bath suffered greatly from its proximity to Bristol, then the head-quarters of the Empress Matilda, and was alternately occupied by the adherents of both parties. It continued in the possession of its bishops until 1193, when Bishop Savaric transferred it to Richard I. in exchange for the abbey of Glastonbury; this monarch made it a free borough, and invested it with many privileges, in consequence of which it began to participate in the commerce of the country, and to increase in wealth and importance. The manufacture of woollen cloth, which was commenced in England in the year 1330, was established here under the auspices of the monks, on which account the shuttle was introduced into the arms of the monastery.

During the civil war in the reign of CHARLES I., Bath was fortified for the king; but the Marquess of Hertford, who commanded the royal forces, having retired into Wales, it fell into the hands of the parliamentarians, and became the head-quarters of the army raised by Waller in this part of the country to retrieve the loss which his party had sustained in the battle of Stratton. In 1643, the battle of Lansdown, in the immediate neighbourhood, took place, when the royalists, notwithstanding many local disadvantages, drove the parliamentary forces from the field, and compelled them to retire into the city; in commemoration of which, a monument was erected on the spot in 1720. After this battle the royalists regained possession of the city, which they held till it was finally surrendered to the parliament in 1645. On the restoration of Charles II., the citizens presented a congratulatory address through the celebrated William Prynne, then one of their representatives; and in the autumn of 1663, the king paid a visit to Bath, on which occasion his chief physician having recommended the internal use of the waters, the adoption of this practice became general. After the suppression of Monmouth's rebellion, four persons, who had been condemned by Judge Jeffreys, were executed here.

The CITY continued within the limits prescribed to it by the Romans till the year 1720, and its suburbs consisted merely of a few scattered houses : celebrated only for the medicinal properties of its hot springs, it was for several years visited merely by invalids. The perseverance of Mr. John Wood, an enterprising architect, who was encouraged by the proprietors of land in the vicinity, about the year 1728, first led to its improvement; and the excellent quarries of freestone in the neighbourhood facilitated the execution of an enterprise which has embellished it with splendid edifices, and raised it to the highest rank as a place of fashionable resort. The town is pleasantly situated on the banks of the river Avon, along which its buildings extend more than two miles, decorating the acclivities, and crowning the summits, of the fine range of hills by which it is environed. Over that part of the Avon which skirts the eastern side of the town, are two stone bridges, one of ancient, the other of modern, erection : a handsome iron bridge has been constructed, connecting Walcot with Bathwick, and affording a direct entrance from the London road into that improving part of the town ; and more recently, a similar structure, called the North Parade bridge, has

172

been erected, connecting the parades with Bathwick and Widcombe. Three smaller bridges on the suspension principle, one near Grosvenor-buildings, the other two on the Tiverton side of the city, add to the public convenience.

Among the earliest of the modern improvements is Queen's-square, the houses in which are decorated with columns and pilasters of the Corinthian order ; in the centre is an obelisk 70 feet high, erected in 1738 by Beau Nash, to commemorate the visit of the then Prince and Princess of Wales, who occupied a house in the square. The Circus is a noble range of uniform edifices, and the Royal Crescent, also, is characterised by a simple grandeur of elevation, and has, in front, an extensive lawn, which slopes gradually until bounded by a noble avenue leading to and forming part of the Royal Victoria Park, which comprises walks of the most attractive character, and a spacious carriage drive. Above the Crescent are St. James's-square, Cavendish-place and crescent, Somerset-place, and Lansdown-crescent, rising successively above each other, and forming so many stations from which may be seen the central parts of this elegant city, encircled as in an amphitheatre of gracefully swelling hills. In the lower part of the town considerable improvements are in progress ; the houses which formerly obscured the abbey have been removed, and that ancient and noble edifice has undergone a thorough repair, under the care and from the funds of the old corporation. Through Orange-grove, in the centre of which is an obelisk commemorating the restoration of the Prince of Orange to health by drinking the waters, a carriage-road has been formed ; and other alterations are in progress, contributing much to the convenience of the public. In the new town, on the eastern bank of the Avon, is Laura-place, a neat range in the form of a lozenge, from which proceeds Great Pulteney-street, an extended series of mansions, at the extremity of which are Sydney gardens, occupying a spacious area surrounded by buildings forming Sydney-place, not inferior in beauty and elegance to the most splendid part of the city. Bath has been lighted with gas since 1819. The hills which surround it abound with springs, within 50 feet of their summits, and no forcing apparatus is required for supplying any part of the town : an act for a better supply of water, was passed in 1846.

All the BATHS belong to the corporation, except some small ones, formerly the property of the Duke of Kingston. In 1811, fears being entertained of the escape of the hot springs, considerable sums were laid out in puddling the ground through which they rise; and more recently, an individual, in boring for a well, reached one of the hot springs, and the aperture was not closed without much expense. No inconvenience, however, is at present felt from a deficiency of water in any of the baths. In the 29th of George III. a statute, called the Bath Improvement act, was obtained, principally for the improvement of the baths and pump-room, under which commissioners were appointed, with power to levy tolls and raise money on mortgage of them ; and the corporation, in addition to the payment of an annual sum towards the reduction of the debt thus incurred, disbursed £7163, and gave up buildings and other property valued at £9000, towards the improvements. These improvements consisted principally in rebuilding the pump-room, and in the removal of houses, for the purpose of securing the springs, and rendering the approaches to the baths and pump-room more commodious: the property improved under the act was finally vested in the corporation. The grand pump-room, the centre of attraction during the fashionable season, was erected in 1797, and is a handsome building, eighty-five feet in length, forty-eight in width, and thirty-four in height. The interior is lighted by a double range of windows, and decorated with pillars of the Corinthian order, supporting a rich entablature and a lofty covered ceiling: at the west end is an orchestra, and at the eastern a well-executed marble statue of the celebrated Beau Nash, under whose superintendence as master of the ceremonies, the elegant amusements of the place were for many years regulated. The principal entrance is through a portico of four lofty columns of the Corinthian order, supporting a triangular pediment, under the tympanum of which is inscribed, "ΑΡΙΣΤΟΝ ΜΕΝ ΥΔΩΡ." The King's bath contains 364 tons of water, and is conveniently fitted up with seats and recesses, having also a handsome colonnade of the Doric order, with the statue of Bladud, the traditionary patron of the waters. The Queen's bath, adjoining it, has likewise suitable apartments. The Cross bath, so called from a cross erected in the centre of it, and the Hot bath, so named from its superior degree of heat, the mean temperature being 117° of Fahrenheit, have the convenience of dry and vapour baths; and a small pump-room has been erected. The waters contain carbonic-acid and nitrogen gases, sulphate and muriate of soda, sulphate and carbonate of lime, and silicious earth, with a minute portion of oxyde of iron; and are efficacious in gout, rheumatism, palsy, biliary obstruction, and cutaneous disorders. The corporation, with great liberality and taste, have also erected several private baths for the accommodation of invalids and others; besides a swimming-bath of very large dimensions, probably unrivalled for beauty and commodiousness.

A Literary and Philosophical Institution was established in 1820: the buildings, occupying the site of the lower assembly-rooms, which were burnt down in 1820, are of the Doric order. The Mechanics' Institution in Queen's-square, erected in 1839, is an appropriate structure in the Grecian style. The Bath and West of England Society for the encouragement of Agriculture, the Arts, Manufactures, and Commerce, for the distribution of premiums and medals, was instituted here in 1777, at the suggestion of Mr. Edmund Rack; and there are many excellent circulating libraries, the terms of which are reasonable. A handsome building for the Savings' bank has been erected in Charlotte-street, at an expense of £2500. Among the chief SOURCES OF AMUSEMENT are the subscription assemblies and concerts, which are held during the season, under the superintendence of a master of the ceremonies, whose office, being equally honourable and lucrative, has been warmly contested by the successive candidates. The rooms are superbly elegant; the ball-room is 105 feet long, 43 wide, and 22 high, and the card-rooms, library, and rooms for refreshment, are furnished in a style of great splendour. The city assemblies, for those who are not eligible as subscribers to the upper rooms are held, by permission of the corporation, in the banquet-room of the guildhall. The Theatre, a well-adapted edifice, in the centre of the city, among the buildings of which it
173

is distinguished by the loftiness of its elevation, is handsomely fitted up and decorated; the ceiling is divided into compartments embellished with exquisite paintings by Cassali, removed from Fonthill Abbey. The building was completed in 1805, and is regularly open during the season; it has been long and deservedly eulogized for the excellence of the performances, and many actors who have attained the highest degree of eminence on the London stage have made their debût here. Sydney gardens afford an agreeable promenade at all times, and during the summer attract numerous assemblages to public entertainments and exhibitions of fireworks, upon which occasions they are brilliantly illuminated. The Subscription Club-house, in York-buildings, containing a spacious suite of rooms, is established upon the plan of most of the superior club-houses in London; the annual subscription is six guineas and a half. There are subscription billiard-rooms in Milsom-street, to which those are admissible who are eligible to the assembly-rooms; also two extensive riding-schools, in one of which is a spacious covered ride for invalids in unfavourable weather. Lansdown and Claverton down afford delightful equestrian excursions, displaying much variety, and abounding in interesting scenery. The races take place on Lansdown, the week after Ascot races; there is also a spring meeting in April. On this down, the late Mr. Beckford erected a tower of considerable height and beauty, commanding a most extensive prospect of the surrounding country.

The town is favourably situated for TRADE: the river is navigable to Bristol, and the Kennet and Avon canal maintains an inland communication with London and the intermediate places. The Great Western railway, from London to Bath and Bristol, was opened throughout on the 30th of June, 1841; most of the heaviest works of the line occur in the neighbourhood of this city. The Bath viaduct extends 800 feet in length, and 30 in breadth, and rests on 65 segmental arches, of about 20 feet span, constructed of Bath stone, and presenting a uniformity of design with the other buildings of the city; connected with this work is an oblique wooden bridge, formed at an angle of 28°, supported on stone piers, and crossing the river Avon, with openings of 99 feet span, by which the railway is carried 36 feet above the level of the river. The Bath station, which covers a space of 13,500 square feet, is elevated 30 feet above the contiguous ground, and is approached by an ascending carriage-way from Pierrepoint-street. An act was passed in 1846 for making a branch of 7½ miles, from Bath, to the Wilts, Somerset, and Weymouth railway. The only branches of manufacture carried on are those of woollen cloth, Bath coating, and kerseymere, which are made in the vicinity. The markets are held on Wednesday and Saturday, in an area behind the guildhall, the wings of which form the principal entrances: the market-house is extensive and commodious. The corn and cattle markets are in Walcot-street, and were built about 30 years since, by the corporation, at an expense of £6000; the coal-market is in the Saw-close. The fairs are on Feb. 14th and July 10th.

The city enjoyed, under Edgar and other Saxon monarchs, many valuable MUNICIPAL privileges, which were afterwards confirmed by Richard I. and other monarchs, subsequently recognised and enlarged by a

Corporation Seal.

charter of Queen Elizabeth, and finally by George III., who made such modifications in the charter as the increasing importance of the place required. By the act 5th and 6th of William IV. cap. 76, the corporation consists of a mayor, fourteen aldermen, and forty-two councillors, constituting the council of the borough, which is divided into seven wards; the magistrates are twelve in number, and the police force comprises a principal, two superintendents, twelve inspectors, and 132 constables. Since the passing of the above act, quarter-sessions, having been applied for by the council, and granted, are regularly held before the recorder; and as lords of the manor, the corporation hold a court leet, at which the town-clerk presides. The powers of the county debt-court of Bath, established in 1847, extend over the registration-district of Bath, and part of that of Keynsham. The corporation possess a large revenue applicable to civic purposes, and also hold some property called the Bath Common estate, lying to the west of the city, in trust for all the resident citizens, who participate equally in its profits; it comprises about 100 acres, let as a grazing-farm, and is a parcel of the ancient manor or grange of Barton Regis. The elective franchise was conferred in the reign of Edward I., since which time the city has continued to return two members to parliament; the borough consists of 3534 acres; the mayor is returning officer. The *Guildhall* is an elegant structure of freestone : the front is decorated with a portico of four lofty Corinthian columns, rising from a rustic basement, and supporting a triangular pediment with a rich entablature and cornice, in the tympanum of which are the city arms, and on the apex a finely sculptured figure of Justice; above the cornice is a handsome balustrade, with urns. The building comprises on the ground floor a vestibule, sessions-hall, offices for the courts of record and requests, and for the chamberlain and town-clerk; and in the upper story, a magnificent suite of apartments formerly devoted to civic entertainments. In the mayor's room is a beautiful head of Minerva, or Apollo, of gilt brass, which was discovered in 1727, sixteen feet below the surface of the ground, in Stall-street, and is thought to be part of a mutilated statue, the remainder of which is buried near the same spot. The prison is a spacious building, occupying an area of 60 feet in front and 80 feet in depth, with a large court-yard, and cells in which delinquents are confined previously to their committal to the county gaol.

Jointly with Wells, Bath is the head of a diocese comprising very nearly the whole of the county of Somerset; the income of the bishop is £5000. The parish of St. Peter and St. Paul, or the Abbey parish, and the parish of St. James, form a rectory, with the vicarage of Lyncombe and Widcombe (*which see*) annexed : the living is valued in the king's books at £20. 17. 11.; net income, £750; patrons, the Trustees of the Rev. Charles Simeon. The Abbey church is a venerable and finely-proportioned cruciform structure, in the later English

Arms of the Bishopric.

style, of which it forms one of the purest specimens : from the intersection an irregularly quadrilateral tower rises to the height of 162 feet. It occupies the site, and is built partly with the materials, of the conventual church of the monastery founded by Osric in 676, which had subsisted, under different forms of government, for more than 800 years. This church having become dilapidated, Bishop Oliver King (as it is said, admonished in a dream, of which a memorial is sculptured on the west front,) began to rebuild it in 1495; but dying before it was completed, and the citizens refusing to purchase it from the commissioners of Henry VIII,. the walls were left roofless, till Dr. James Montague, bishop of the diocese, aided by a liberal contribution from the nobility and gentry resident in the county, completed it, in the year 1606. The revenue of the monastery, at the Dissolution, was £695. 6. 1¼. The edifice has now, as before noticed, undergone a thorough repair and embellishment at the expense of the corporation; but not in accordance with the simplicity of its original style of architecture. St. James's church, rebuilt in 1768, is an elegant structure in the later English style. The *Octagon* chapel, in Milsom street, was erected in 1767, and is much admired : the living is in the patronage of the Rev. G. G. Gardiner. The living of the parish of St. Michael was until recently annexed to the Abbey rectory; but is now a distinct rectory, with a net income of £182 : the church, rebuilt in 1835, is of early English character, with a lofty and well-proportioned spire of great beauty.

The parochial church of St. Swithin, Walcot, a spacious edifice within the liberty of the city, was rebuilt in 1780 : the living is a discharged rectory, valued in the king's books at £6. 19. 9½.; net income, £600; patron, the Rev. S. H. Widdrington. *Christ church* was erected by subscription, in 1798, for the especial accommodation of the poor, and is a handsome building in the later English style. *All Saints'*, Lansdown-place, erected in 1794, is a good specimen of the decorated style, and has twelve fine windows in which the heads of the Apostles are painted, and an east window with a painting of the Last Supper. These two churches, with that of *St. Stephen*, Lansdown, are presented to by the rector of Walcot. Portland chapel until lately belonged to the Roman Catholics, but is now in connexion with the Church of England : *Margaret* chapel, in Margaret-buildings, is a spacious and handsome structure of early English architecture. These two chapels, with that of *St. Thomas*, are presented to by the Rev. S. H. Widdrington. Trinity church, in St. James's street, is of recent erection : the living is a district rectory; net Mary's chapel, Queen-square, was built by subscription in 1735, and is a handsome Grecian edifice; the exterior of the Doric, and the interior of the Ionic, order. There is also a chapel in Avon-street, the incumbency of which is in the gift of the Rector of Trinity. At Lambridge is the church of St. Saviour, Walcot : the living is a district rectory, in the gift of the Rev. Dr.

teeth, and amber beads, discovered in the burial-places of the Britons ; also a small silver coin, having on the obverse a rude head in profile, and on the reverse a star, or wheel. Among the *Roman* were found, in 1753, a pedestal with a Latin inscription ; in 1755, parts of the Roman baths, and several of the large tubulated bricks, which conveyed the heat to the *sudatoria* ; and in 1790 a votive altar, fragments of fluted Corinthian columns, basso-relievos, and other relics of the temple of Minerva, besides numerous coins of the emperors Nero, Trajan, Adrian, Antonine, Gallienus, Claudius Gothicus, Maxentius, and Constantine, with some of Carausius, who assumed the Roman purple in Britain. On digging the foundation of the new bridge over the Avon to Walcot, the remains of an old ford were observable, and a leaden vessel was found, containing some hundreds of *denarii*, and several small brass coins from the time of the Emperor Valens to that of Eugenius : for the reception of these a room was appropriated by the corporation, in which they are deposited, with a due regard to classification. The *Saxon* remains, exclusively of coffins, &c., consist of what is still visible in the city walls erected by the Saxons on the Roman foundation, in which are inserted fragments of the ruined temple, pieces of sculpture, and parts of triumphal arches, intermixed with the original materials. In a stone coffin has been discovered a small copper box, in the form of a rouleau, divided into two parts ; the upper part being covered by a slide, probably intended for perfume, and the lower part filled with small silver coins resembling the early Saxon *scattæ*. *John Hales,* called the "ever memorable," was a native of the city, and received the rudiments of his education in the grammar school. *Benjamin Robins,* a celebrated mathematician, and the writer of the account of Commodore Anson's voyage round the world, was also born here, in 1707. And closely connected with Bath for several years, though not a native, was *Ralph Allen, Esq.,* of Prior Park, an elegant mansion one mile south of the city, which was in his time the resort of several of the wits and literati of the age : this gentleman, supposed to be the original of Fielding's *Allworthy* in his novel of *Tom Jones,* died in 1764, and was interred at Claverton, where is a handsome monument to his memory. Bath gives the title of Marquess to the family of Thynne, of Longleat House.

BATHAMPTON (St. Nicholas), a parish, in the union of Bath, hundred or liberty of Hampton and Claverton, though locally in the hundred of Bath-Forum, E. division of Somerset, 1¾ mile (N. E. by E.) from Bath ; containing 355 inhabitants. The living is a discharged vicarage, consolidated with that of Bath-Ford, and valued in the king's books at £7. 17. 1. ; impropriator of Bathampton, Robert Fisher, Esq. The great tithes have been commuted for £120, and the vicarial for £130.

BATHEALTON, or Badialton (St. Bartholomew), a parish, in the union of Wellington, hundred of Milverton, W. division of Somerset, 3 miles (S.) from Wiveliscombe ; containing 135 inhabitants. It comprises by computation 860 acres, the soil of which is fertile, and in fine cultivation ; stone of good quality for building is quarried to a considerable extent. The living is a rectory, valued in the king's books at £7. 2. 6., and in the patronage of the Rev. Edward Webber : the tithes have been commuted for £195, and the glebe comprises 45 acres, with a house. The church was erected in 1572. A mile westward is a circular intrench-ment called Castles, within the area of which some Roman coins have been discovered.

BATH-EASTON (St. John the Baptist), a parish, in the union of Bath, hundred of Bath-Forum, E. division of Somerset, 3 miles (N. E.) from Bath; contain-ing, with a portion of the liberty of Easton and Amrill, 2191 inhabitants. The parish comprises 1605 acres, of which 83 are common or waste. The village, divided into Upper and Lower, is situated near the Great Western railway, and on the London road, in a pleasant valley bounded by lofty hills on the west, north, and east, and by the Lower Avon on the south. On the western side is Salisbury hill, on the summit of which are vestiges of an intrenchment, nearly circular, supposed to have been constructed by the Saxons when they besieged Bath, in 577 : some antiquaries are of opinion that this hill was anciently crowned by a temple, erected by Bladud in honour of Apollo. The living is a discharged vicarage, with the perpetual curacy of St. Catherine annexed, valued in the king's books at £9. 6. 5., and in the gift of the Dean and Canons of Christ-Church, Oxford : the tithes have been commuted for £210 payable to the Dean and Canons, and £300 to the incumbent, who has also a glebe of 3 acres. The church is in the later English style, with a square tower 100 feet high; it was enlarged in 1834 by the addition of an aisle. There is a place of worship for Wesleyans. In 1818 a national school was built by the late learned and estimable vicar, the Rev. J. J. Conybeare. At a villa here, resided Sir John Miller, whose lady established a literary festival for the recitation of prize poems, which were pub-lished under the title of "Poetical Amusements :" she died in 1781.

BATH-FORD (St. Swithin), a parish, in the union of Bath, hundred of Bath-Forum, E. division of So-merset, 3½ miles (E. N. E.) from Bath; containing 1099 inhabitants. The village is situated in a picturesque neighbourhood, on the banks of the Avon, which was anciently crossed by a ford; and the Great Western railway passes through the parish. The manufacture of paper affords employment to more than forty persons. The living is a discharged vicarage, with that of Bath-ampton consolidated, valued in the king's books at £8. 18.; patrons, the Dean and Chapter of Bristol; im-propriator of Bath-Ford, John Wiltshire, Esq. The great tithes of the parish have been commuted for £114, and the vicarial for £160; there are 12 acres of glebe. Here are vestiges of a Roman camp, and a tumulus : in 1691, a Roman hypocaust with a Mosaic pavement, an altar, urns containing coins, and other ancient relics, were discovered.

BATHLEY, a township, in the parish of North Muskham, union of Southwell, N. division of the wapentake of Thurgarton, S. division of the county of Nottingham, 4 miles (N. N. W.) from Newark; con-taining 252 inhabitants. It comprises 1193 acres of land. The village is small and scattered. A place of worship for Methodists was erected in 1844.

BATHWICK, a parish, in the union of Bath, hun-dred of Bath-Forum, E. division of Somerset; con-taining 4973 inhabitants. This elegant suburb to the city of Bath, from which it is separated by the river Avon, at the beginning of the last century consisted only

176

of a few scattered houses unpleasantly situated on an extensive marsh frequently inundated by the river. From the discovery here of a large portion of those in-teresting relics which are deposited in the museum at Bath, this place appears to have formed, at a remote period of antiquity, no inconsiderable part of that city, and to have retained its importance during the succes-sive occupation of Bath by the Britons, Romans, and Saxons. Within the last twenty years, it has greatly in-creased in extent and population, and it now contains some of the most elegant ranges of building which adorn that city : it is connected with Bath by handsome bridges over the Avon. The Kennet and Avon canal, in its course through Sydney-gardens, has been made available to the introduction of a pleasing variety into the grounds; and two elegant iron bridges, which have been erected over it, form an interesting feature in the scenery of the place. There is a manufactory for broad cloth in the parish; and, in addition to the Kennet and Avon canal, the Somersetshire coal canal passes through it. The living comprises a consolidated rectory and vicarage, with the rectory of Wolley annexed; the rectory of Bath-wick valued in the king's books at £3. 6. 8., and the vicarage, at £8. 3. 4.: patron, Lord W. Pawlett. The tithes of the parish have been commuted for £105, and there are 5 acres of glebe. The church, which was erected in 1820, is a handsome and spacious structure in the decorated English style, with a beautiful altar-piece painted and presented by Mr. B. Barker. In Henrietta-street is Laura chapel, erected in 1796 : the living is in the gift of the Rev. E. Tottenham.

BATLEY (All Saints), a parish, in the union of Dewsbury, partly in the Lower division of the wapen-take of Agbrigg, and partly in the wapentake of Mor-ley, W. riding of York; containing 14,278 inhabit-ants, of whom 7076 are in the township of Batley, 2 miles (N.) from Dewsbury. This place is of great antiquity, its name signifying in Saxon "the Field of Batt or Batta;" it is noticed in the Domesday survey as having a church, which was granted in the reign of Henry I. to the canons of St. Oswald in Nostal Priory. The manor was for eighteen generations held by the Copley family. The parish comprises 6390 acres, of which 2140 are in the township of Batley, 2590 in that of Morley, 1120 in that of Gildersome, and 540 in that of Churwell; the two former are in the Agbrigg divi-sion, and the two latter in that of Morley. The soil is fertile, and the substratum abounds with coal and free-stone of good quality; the population is partly agricul-tural, but mostly employed in the manufacture of wool-len-cloths, blankets, pilot-cloth, carpets, coverlets, and flushings. The village is pleasantly situated on the Dewsbury and Gomersal road, in a valley watered by a small rivulet; and is very extensive. The living is a discharged vicarage, valued in the king's books at £16. 11. 8.; net income, £200; patrons, alternately, the Earls of Cardigan and Wilton. The tithes for the town-ship of Batley were commuted for land in 1803. The church, which was rebuilt in the reign of Henry VI., is a handsome structure in the later English style, with a square machicolated tower : on the north of the chancel is the chapel belonging to Howley Hall, the seat of Lord Saville in the reigns of James I. and Charles I., to whom he was councillor of state. At Gildersome and Morley are district churches. There are places of worship for

Baptists, Independents,' Methodists of the New Connexion, and Wesleyans. A free grammar school was founded by the Rev. William Lee, who, in 1612, endowed it with a house and garden for the master, and with lands now producing an income of £133.

BATLEY-CARR, an ecclesiastical district, in the parish and union of DEWSBURY, wapentake of MORLEY, W. riding of YORK, 1 mile (N.) from Dewsbury; containing 2144 inhabitants. This place, which is situated in a pleasant valley on the Bradford road, forms a suburb of Dewsbury, part of which township is included within its district; and is inhabited chiefly by persons employed in the manufacture of woollen-cloths, pilot-coatings, and druggets. The church, dedicated to the Holy Trinity, was erected at an expense of £2000, raised by subscription, aided by Joshua Ellis, Esq., of Highfield; Mr. Ellis also subscribed £500 towards its endowment, and Mrs. Ellis presented a rich and massive service of communion plate. It was consecrated on the 5th of October, 1841, and is a handsome structure in the later English style, with a square embattled tower crowned with pinnacles. The living is a perpetual curacy; net income, £150; patron, the Vicar of Dewsbury.

BATSFORD (ST. MARY), a parish, in the union of SHIPSTON-ON-STOUR, Upper division of the hundred of KIFTSGATE, E. division of the county of GLOUCESTER, 2 miles (N. W.) from Moreton-in-the-Marsh; containing 79 inhabitants, and comprising 922a. 1r. 27p. The railroad from Stratford-on-Avon to Moreton terminates here. The living is a rectory, valued in the king's books at £13. 3. 9., and in the patronage of the Dean and Canons of Christ-Church, Oxford: the tithes have been commuted for £255, and the glebe consists of 96 acres. The church was rebuilt in 1822, at the expense of Lord Redesdale, who has a handsome seat here, and whose relative, Lord Chancellor Freeman, was buried in the church in 1710.

BATTERSBY, a township, in the parish of INGLEBY-GREENHOW, W. division of the liberty of LANGBAURGH, N. riding of YORK, 5¼ miles (E. by S.) from Stokesley; containing 93 inhabitants. This was an ancient demesne of the crown, and according to the Domesday survey was called Badresbi; it was afterwards the property of the Balliols, and at an early period came to the Percys, with whom it continued till the time of Elizabeth, after which the estate passed to the Eures and the family of Foulis. The township lies near the road between Whitby and Stokesley, through Kildale; and forms part of the district named Cleveland.

BATTERSEA (ST. MARY), a parish, in the union of WANDSWORTH and CLAPHAM, partly in the E., but chiefly in the W., division of the hundred of BRIXTON, E. division of SURREY, 3 miles (S.) from London; containing, with the hamlet of Penge (which see), 6887 inhabitants. This place, in Domesday book called Patricesey or Peters-ey, was so named from having anciently belonged to the abbey of St. Peter at Westminster: it was formerly of much greater extent than it is at present. The family of St. John had a venerable mansion here, which was the favourite resort of Pope, who, when visiting his friend Lord Bolingbroke, usually selected as his study, in which he is said to have composed some of his celebrated works, a parlour wainscoted with cedar, overlooking the Thames. The parish comprises 2108a. 2r.

39p., whereof 390 acres are common or waste; and the village is pleasantly situated on the southern bank of the river, over which is a wooden bridge, connecting it with Chelsea. The neighbourhood has long been celebrated for the production of vegetables for the London market, especially asparagus, which was first cultivated here. There are several manufactures, including chymical-works, large cement-works, a brewery, malt-house, lime and whitening manufactories, a silk factory, a pottery for crucibles, and Brunel's machinery for sawing veneers; and along the banks of the Thames are some coal-wharfs: the manufacture of kid gloves is also carried on very extensively. The London and Southampton railway, for the present, has its commencement at Nine-Elms, in the parish, the offices at which station, fronting the road, exhibit a neat elevation and arcade, and contain all the necessary apartments. Immediately behind is the passengers' shed, extending nearly 300 feet, with four lines of way, and resting on two lines of iron columns twelve feet high; other lines of way lead to the carriage, horse, and locomotive departments, which were unfortunately injured by an accidental fire recently, to the extent of £40,000. The county magistrates hold a meeting at Wandsworth, an adjoining parish, where also the lord of the manor holds a court leet, at which a headborough and constables for Battersea are appointed.

The LIVING is a vicarage, valued in the king's books at £13. 15. 2½.; net income, £982; patron and impropriator, Earl Spencer. The church, which was handsomely rebuilt of brick, in 1777, has a tower surmounted by a small spire, and, standing on the margin of the river, forms an interesting object viewed from the water. The window over the altar is decorated with portraits of Henry VII., his grandmother Margaret Beauchamp, and Queen Elizabeth, in stained glass; and there are some interesting sepulchral monuments, among which are, one by Roubilliac to the memory of Viscount Bolingbroke and his lady, and one to the memory of Edward Winter, an officer in the service of the East India Company, on which is recorded an account of his having, singly and unarmed, killed a tiger, and on foot defeated sixty Moors on horseback. Collins, author of the Peerage and Baronetage of England; his grandson, David Collins, Lieutenant-Governor of New South Wales, and author of a History of the English Settlement there; and William Curtis, a distinguished botanical writer, were buried here. St. George's chapel, in Battersea Fields, a neat building in the later style of English architecture, was erected in 1829, partly by a subscription of £2277 among the parishioners, partly by a rate amounting to £1327, and partly by a grant from the Parliamentary Commissioners; the minister is appointed by the vicar, and derives his stipend from a subscription fund of £1450, and from the pew-rents. In the hamlet of Penge is a small chapel capable of accommodating about 200 persons, built by subscription, in 1838. Christ Church, Battersea Fields, was commenced in May, 1847, the foundation-stone being laid by the Hon. Mr. Eden, late incumbent of the parish, recently appointed to the bishopric of Sodor and Man: the cost of the church is estimated at £7000. There are places of worship for Baptists and Wesleyans. A school for the instruction of twenty boys, to which a national school has been united, was founded and endowed by Sir Walter St. John, in 1700, and has an endowment of £85 per annum. Sir Walter and Lady St. John left £300, directing the interest to be applied in apprenticing boys or girls; and there are several other charitable bequests, the principal of which is one by John Parvin, who left £2000 four per cent. bank annuities. Here is a very important training college for masters of national schools. The workhouse for the union, pleasantly situated on St. John's Hill, in the parish, was built in 1838, at an expense of about £16,000.

BATTISFORD (ST. MARY), a parish, in the union and hundred of BOSMERE and CLAYDON, E. division of SUFFOLK, 3 miles (W. S. W.) from Needham-Market; containing 520 inhabitants, and comprising 1544a. 3r. 2p. The framework of the late Royal Exchange, London, erected by Sir Thomas Gresham, was made here; Sir Thomas residing in the adjoining parish of Kingshall, and having considerable property in this. The living is a discharged vicarage, endowed with the rectorial tithes, and valued in the king's books at £8. 0. 7½.; patron and incumbent, the Rev. Edward Paske, whose tithes have been commuted for £400. The church is chiefly in the decorated English style, and consists of a nave and chancel; the interior was thoroughly repaired in 1841. Here was a commandery of the Knights Hospitallers, the revenue of which, at the Dissolution, was £53. 10.

BATTLE, or BATTEL (ST. MARY), a market-town, parish, and the head of a union, in the hundred of BATTLE, rape of HASTINGS, E. division of SUSSEX, 7 miles (N. W.) from Hastings, 63 (E. by N.) from Chichester, and 56 (S. E.) from London; containing 2999 inhabitants. This place, previously called Epiton, derives its present name from the memorable battle fought here, October 14th, 1066, between Harold, King of England, and William, Duke of Normandy. Though generally called the battle of Hastings, it took place at this town, where, in fulfilment of a vow, the Conqueror founded a magnificent abbey for monks of the Benedictine order, in which were preserved, until its suppression, the sword and royal robe worn by him on the day of his coronation, and the celebrated roll on which the names of the warriors who accompanied him to England were inscribed. He conferred on it the privilege of sanctuary, raised it to the dignity of a mitred abbey, and invested its abbots with the power of saving a criminal from execution, if accidentally passing at the time: at the Dissolution, its revenue was £987. 0. 10½.

The parish is situated in a beautiful valley, bounded on the west, south, and south-east by wood-crowned eminences. The town, which is built on rising ground, consists chiefly of one irregular line of houses forming three several streets, well lighted with gas, and amply supplied with water. The manufacture of fine gunpowder, established at a very early period, and for which the town has attained the highest celebrity, is carried on to a very great extent; and there is a large tannery. The market, granted by Henry I. on Thursday, has fallen into disuse, but a corn market is held on the second Tuesday in every month. The fairs are on Whit-Monday, and Nov. 22nd and two following days; and a large sheep-fair is held on the 6th of September: a great number of horned-cattle are sent from this part of the country to the London market. The town is within the jurisdiction of the county magistrates, who hold petty-sessions here for the district on the second Tuesday in

178

the month; but this being a franchise, the inhabitants are exempt from serving on juries at the assizes and sessions for the county. A coroner and other officers are appointed at the court leet of the lord of the manor. Here is a house of correction, appropriated for the reception of persons apprehended in the Battle district of the county, and of others summarily convicted by the magistrates, whose terms of imprisonment do not exceed one month.

The LIVING is a vicarage, valued in the king's books at £24. 13. 4.; net income, £396; patron and impropriator, Sir Godfrey V. Webster, Bart. The church is a spacious structure, partly Norman, and partly in the early and later English styles, with a square embattled tower; and contains some ancient brasses, and a fine altar-tomb to Sir Henry Browne. There are places of worship for Baptists, Wesleyans, and Unitarians. In 1791, Mrs. Elizabeth Langton bequeathed £1500 for the instruction of fifteen boys and fifteen girls, and £200 for purchasing books, from the interest on which sums a master and mistress are allowed £60 per annum. The poor law union of Battle comprises fourteen parishes and places, under the care of eighteen guardians, and contains a population of 12,034 inhabitants. Of the ancient abbey there are still considerable remains; the gateway, a beautiful specimen of the decorated English style, is in entire preservation, and many parts of the conventual buildings have been retained in the present magnificent mansion of Battle Abbey. Southward of the grounds is a place called Tellman Hill, where William is reported to have mustered his army the evening before the battle; and to the north is another, named Callback Hill, from which it is said he recalled his troops from pursuing the vanquished enemy. The Rev. Edmond Cartwright, D.D., a celebrated writer, but better known as the inventor of the power-loom, was buried here.

BATTLEBURN, a hamlet, in the parish of KIRKBURN, union of DRIFFIELD, Bainton-Beacon division of the wapentake of HARTHILL, E. riding of YORK, 3½ miles (W. S. W.) from Great Driffield; containing 14 inhabitants. It comprises, with Eastburn, one farm.

BATTLEFIELD (ST. MARY MAGDALENE), a parish, in the union of ATCHAM, liberties of SHREWSBURY, N. division of SALOP, 3 miles (N. N. E.) from Shrewsbury; containing 64 inhabitants. This place derives its name from a sanguinary battle fought here on the 22nd of July, 1403, between Henry IV. and the rebels under Percy, Earl of Northumberland; in which nearly 2300 gentlemen (among whom was Lord Henry Percy, the valiant Hotspur), and about 600 private soldiers, were slain. The king, in grateful commemoration of his victory, immediately founded on the spot a college for Secular clerks, the revenue of which, at the Dissolution, was £54. 10. 4. The parish comprises by computation 700 acres, and is situated on the road from Shrewsbury to Whitchurch and Drayton. A fair for horned-cattle and sheep is held on the 2nd of August. The living is a perpetual curacy, with a net income of £240, derived from land; it is in the patronage of Mrs. Corbet, to whom also the impropriation belongs. The church, built upon the spot on which the battle of Shrewsbury was fought, suffered much in the time of the commonwealth, but would, if restored, be a beautiful specimen of the perpendicular style.

BATTLESDEN (St. Peter), a parish, in the union of Woburn, hundred of Manshead, county of Bedford, 3 miles (S. S. E.) from Woburn, on the road from Dunstable to Fenny-Stratford; containing 179 inhabitants. The manor was in 1706 purchased by Allen Bathurst, Esq., a distinguished political character during the reigns of Anne and George I., the former of whom created him a baron, of Battlesden, which was for some years his country seat, and the resort of the most celebrated wits of the time, until it passed to another family. The living is a rectory, with that of Potsgrove annexed, valued in the king's books at £12. 9. 7.; net income, £306; patron, Sir G. P. Turner, Bart.

BATTRAMSLEY, a tything, in the parish of Boldre, union of Lymington, E. division of the hundred of New Forest, Lymington and S. divisions of the county of Southampton; containing 302 inhabitants.

BATTYEFORD, a hamlet, in the parish of Mirfield, union of Dewsbury, Lower division of the wapentake of Agbrigg, W. riding of York. This place is situated on the river Calder, near the western extremity of the parish, and on the road between Dewsbury and Elland; the surface is undulated, the soil good, producing earlier crops than the neighbouring districts, and the scenery rich and beautiful. There are several coal-mines, which afford employment to a portion of the population, but the inhabitants are chiefly engaged in the woollen manufacture, and in making cards for the machinery in the cotton and woollen mills, which latter branch of industry is carried on to a considerable extent. The Calder and Hebble navigation, and the Manchester and Leeds railway, pass in the vicinity. A district church was erected in 1840, on a site given by Benjamin Wilson, Esq., at an expense of £1778, of which £700 were granted by the Incorporated Society, and the remainder subscribed by the landowners and parishioners: it is dedicated to Christ. The living, a perpetual curacy in the patronage of the Vicar, was augmented in 1841 to £150 a year by the Ecclesiastical Commissioners.

BAUGHURST, a parish, in the union of Kingsclere, forming a detached portion of the hundred of Evingar, Kingsclere and N. divisions of the county of Southampton, 7 miles (N. W. by N.) from Basingstoke; containing 528 inhabitants. It comprises 1675a. 15p.; and is intersected by a turnpike-road from Basingstoke to Aldermaston, Newbury, &c. The living is a rectory, valued in the king's books at £7. 12. 1., and in the gift of the Bishop of Winchester: the tithes have been commuted for £339. 8., and there are 2 acres of glebe.

BAULDOXFEE, a tything, in the parish of Eling, union of New Forest, hundred of Redbridge, Romsey and S. divisions of the county of Southampton; containing 931 inhabitants.

BAULKING, a chapelry, in the parish of Uffington, union of Shrivenham, county of Berks, 3½ miles (S. E. by S.) from Great Farringdon; containing 193 inhabitants, and comprising 1442a. 1r. 13p. The chapel is dedicated to St. Nicholas; the vicarial tithes have been commuted for £165, and the impropriate for £150.

BAUMBER, or Bamburgh (St. Swithin), a parish, in the union of Horncastle, N. division of the wapentake of Gartree, parts of Lindsey, county of Lincoln, 4 miles (N. W.) from Horncastle; containing 371
179

inhabitants. This place, in Domesday book called Bade. burgh, is supposed to have taken its name from the river Bane, on which it is situated; it stands on the road between Horncastle and Lincoln, and contains by computation nearly 4000 acres. The manor and parish formerly belonged to the earls of Lincoln, who became dukes of Newcastle, and the remains of whose ancient mansion may still be seen. The living is a perpetual curacy; net income, £37; patron, the Duke of Newcastle.

BAUNTON (St. Christopher), a parish, in the union of Cirencester, hundred of Crowthorne and Minety, E. division of the county of Gloucester, 1¾ mile (N. by E) from Cirencester; containing 187 inhabitants. The living is a perpetual curacy, in the patronage of Miss Masters, to whom also the impropriation belongs; net income, £67. The Roman Fosse-way passes along the eastern border of the parish.

BAVANT, NORTON.—See Norton-Bavant.

BAVERSTOCK (St. Edith), a parish, in the union of Wilton, hundred of Cawden and Cadworth, Hindon and S. divisions of Wilts, 8 miles (W.) from Salisbury; containing, with the hamlet of Hurdcott, 194 inhabitants. This parish, which is situated near the road from Salisbury to Hindon, and on the river Nadder, comprises 1168 acres by measurement; the soil is fertile, and chalk, clay, and green sandstone are found in abundance, the last containing numerous fossils. The living is a rectory, valued in the king's books at £11. 10. 2½., and in the gift of Exeter College, Oxford: the tithes have been commuted for £295, and the glebe consists of 52 acres. The church was repewed a few years since, and otherwise underwent considerable repair; and on the occasion of re-opening it, in July 1834, the foundation-stone of a parochial school, adjoining it, was laid by the Bishop of Bath and Wells. There is a spring called Merrywell, the water of which is efficacious in curing diseases of the eye.

BAVINGTON, GREAT, a township, in the parish of Kirk-Whelpington, union of Bellingham, N. E. division of Tindale ward, S. division of Northumberland, 14 miles (N. N. E.) from Hexham; containing 69 inhabitants. This place has been possessed by various families, including the Umfravilles, Strothers, Swinburnes, Shaftos, Ogles, and Harles; and is now the property of several persons. The lofty hills of basalt which form a marked and peculiar feature of this township, are part of a vast bed which may be traced from Cumberland, by Glenwhelt and the Roman wall, to Little Swinburn, where it divides into two branches. The western sides of the hills are very precipitous; and the soil, except of that portion called the Plashetts, is for the principal part dry, rich, and mostly in grass; on the whinstone hills it is thin, and apt to burn in droughty summers. A lead-mine was opened here some years since, but the speculation failed. The impropriate tithes have been commuted for £25. 19. 7., and the vicarial for £35. 10. 7. There is a place of worship for Scottish Presbyterians.

BAVINGTON, LITTLE, a township, in the parish of Thockrington, union of Bellingham, N. E. division of Tindale ward, S. division of Northumberland, 12 miles (N. N. E.) from Hexham; containing 91 inhabitants. This place is on the road from Alnwick to Hexham, and has been the seat of the Shaftos since the
2 A 2

BAWD

reign of Edward I. Bavington Hall, the residence of
the present representative of that family, is a handsome
mansion surrounded with fine plantations. The Erring
burn has its source in the township.

BAWBURGH, or BABUR (ST. MARY AND ST. WAL-
STAN), a parish, in the union and hundred of FOREHOE,
E. division of NORFOLK, 5 miles (N. W.) from Norwich;
containing 404 inhabitants. This place is distinguished as the birthplace of St. Walstan; he lived at
Taverham, where he died in 1016, and his remains
were removed hither, and enshrined in a chapel in the
parish church. The resort of pilgrims to visit his
shrine greatly enriched the vicar and officiating priests,
who, in 1309, rebuilt the church; but the chapel in
which the remains of the saint were deposited was demolished in the reign of Henry VIII., though the walls
are still a little above the surface of the ground. The
road from Norwich to Walton, and the river Yare, run
through the parish. The living is a vicarage, valued in
the king's books at £13. 17. 6.; net income, £100;
patrons and appropriators, the Dean and Chapter of
Norwich. The great tithes have been, commuted for
£227, and there are 93 acres of appropriate glebe. The
church is in the early English and later styles; the
nave is separated from the chancel by the remains of a
beautifully carved screen. There is a place of worship
for Wesleyans.

BAWDESWELL (ALL SAINTS), a parish, in the
union of MITFORD and LAUNDITCH, hundred of EYNS-
FORD, E. division of NORFOLK, 4 miles (W. by S.) from
Reepham; containing 582 inhabitants. The road from
Norwich to Fakenham runs through the village. The
living is a discharged rectory, valued in the king's
books at £7; net income, £208; patron, E. Lombe,
Esq. The church is in the later English style, with a
square brick tower built at the west end of the chancel
in 1740. There is a place of worship for Wesleyans.
John Leeds, in 1730, bequeathed a house and 16 acres
of land, now let for about £20 per annum, to provide
instruction for 12 boys of Bawdeswell, and 8 of Foxley;
and at the inclosure in 1808, two acres of land were
allotted as gravel, and 35 acres for fuel to the poor.

BAWDRIP (ST. MICHAEL), a parish, in the union of
BRIDGWATER, hundred of NORTH PETHERTON, W.
division of SOMERSET, 3¼ miles (N. E. by E.) from
Bridgwater; containing 425 inhabitants. The living is
a rectory, valued in the king's books at £15. 19. 7., and
in the gift of Edward Page, Esq.: the tithes have been
commuted for a rent-charge of £340, and the glebe consists of 38½ acres.

BAWDSEY (ST. MARY), a parish, in the union of
WOODBRIDGE, hundred of WILFORD, E. division of
SUFFOLK, 8½ miles (S. E. by S.) from Woodbridge;
containing 468 inhabitants. The parish is situated on
the coast of the North Sea; and at the mouth of the
river Deben is a haven, which affords convenient anchorage for small vessels. In the 11th of Edward I. permission was obtained for a market to be held on Friday,
but it has long been discontinued; there is, however, a
fair on September 8th. The living is a discharged
vicarage, valued in the king's books at £6. 13. 4., and
in the patronage of the Crown: the tithes have been
commuted for £193 payable to the vicar, and £305
payable to the executors of the late John Wilson Shephard, Esq. The old church, which had a large and
180

interred in the chancel of the chapel; the remains have been converted into a farmhouse.

BAXBY, York.—See Thornton.

BAXTERLEY, a parish, in the union of Ather- stone, Atherstone division of the hundred of Hemling- ford, N. division of the county of Warwick, 4 miles (W. by S.) from Atherstone; containing 228 inhabit- ants. This parish lies in a sequestered part of the county; is three miles from the Kingsbury station on the Birmingham and Derby railway; and comprises 804 acres of fertile land, and 70 acres of common and wood. It stands high; the views are beautiful, and include the Barr-Beacon, Bromsgrove-Lickey, &c. The whole parish is the property of W. S. Dugdale, Esq. Limestone is found, but is not wrought. The living is a discharged rectory, valued in the king's books at £5, and in the alternate patronage of the Crown and Mr. Dugdale : the tithes have been commuted for £182, and the glebe consists of 46 acres, let for £94 per annum. The church is in the Norman style, having been built in the reign of William the Conqueror: the tower was rebuilt in 1607, by Hugo Glover, brother of Mrs. Lewis who was burnt at Coventry for her adherence to the Protestant faith, during the Popish persecution in the reign of Mary, and whose remains were interred in the church. A day and Sunday school was built by sub- scription in 1839.

BAYDON (St. Nicholas), a parish, in the union of Hungerford, hundred of Ramsbury, Marlborough and Ramsbury, and N. divisions of Wilts, 1¾ mile (N. E.) from Aldbourn; containing 335 inhabitants. This parish, which is situated on the road from Ciren- cester to Newbury, comprises by measurement 2350 acres of fertile land; the village stands on an eminence, on the high road, commanding extensive and finely varied prospects over the surrounding country. The living is a perpetual curacy; net income, £110; patrons and impropriators, the family of Meyrick: at the in- closure, in 1779, land was apportioned in lieu of tithes. The church is an ancient and very handsome edifice, containing some Norman details. There are places of worship for Wesleyans and Baptists. The celebrated Sir Isaac Newton had a residence, with a small estate, in the parish.

BAYFIELD (St. Margaret), a parish, in the union of Erpingham, hundred of Holt, W. division of Norfolk, 2¾ miles (N. W.) from Holt; containing 21 inhabitants. It is pleasantly situated in the deep and well-wooded vale of the Glaven, and comprises 780a. 1r. 26p., of which 682 acres are arable, 76 pasture and meadow, and 41 woodland; the surface is undulated, and the views from the higher grounds are very fine. The living is a discharged sinecure rectory, valued in the king's books at £4, and in the patronage of Mrs. J. E. Best: the tithes produce £168. The church, which is mantled with ivy, has long been in ruins.

BAYFORD (St. Mary), a parish, in the union, hundred, and county of Hertford, 3 miles (S. S. W.) from Hertford; containing 357 inhabitants. It com- prises by admeasurement 1612 acres of land; the soil is clay. The living is annexed to the rectory of Essen- don : the tithes have been commuted for £282. The church is a neat brick edifice, built by subscription in 1804, and containing an ancient octangular font orna- mented with quatrefoils and roses.

BAYFORD, a hamlet, in the parish of Stoke- Trister, union of Wincanton, hundred of Norton- Ferris, E. division of Somerset, 1¼ mile (E. N. E.) from Wincanton; containing 222 inhabitants.

BAYHAM, a hamlet.—See Frant.

BAYLHAM (St. Peter), a parish, in the union and hundred of Bosmere and Claydon, E. division of Suffolk, 3 miles (S. by E.) from Needham-Market; containing 275 inhabitants. The river Orwell and the Stow-Market and Ipswich canal bound this parish, which comprises 1332a. 3r. 19p., and is intersected by the road from Colchester to Stow-Market. The living is a rectory, valued in the king's books at £12. 4. 9½., and in the gift of the Rev. J. C. Aldrich: the tithes have been commuted for £300, and the glebe consists of 39 acres.

BAYNTON, a tything, in the parish of Edington, hundred of Whorwelsdown, Whorwelsdown and N. divisions of Wilts; containing 33 inhabitants.

BAYSWATER, a hamlet, in the parish of Pad- dington, Holborn division of the hundred of Ossul- stone, county of Middlesex, 1 mile from Cumber- land-gate, London, on the Uxbridge road. Bayswater, which may now be considered as a suburb to the metropolis, consists of several ranges of neat houses, and of some handsome detached residences; it has been much increased by ranges of new buildings branching off from the main street towards the north, and is de- sirable as a place of residence from its vicinity to Ken- sington gardens, which are situated on the south. The district is lighted with gas, and the inhabitants are sup- plied with water from a reservoir originally constructed for the use of Kensington Palace, and subsequently granted to the proprietors of Chelsea water-works, on the condition that the supply of the palace should be regularly continued. Sir John Hill, M.D., a voluminous writer, resided here many years, and cultivated the plants from which he prepared his medicines, on the spot now occupied by the proprietor of the Bayswater tea-gardens. An episcopal chapel was built by Mr. Edward Orme, in 1818.

BAYTON (St. Bartholomew), a parish, in the union of Cleobury-Mortimer, Lower division of the hundred of Doddingtree, Hundred-House and W. divisions of the county of Worcester, 1¾ mile (S. E. by S.) from Cleobury-Mortimer; containing 468 in- habitants. This parish is bounded on the north and west by a portion of Shropshire, from which it is partly divided by the river Rea; it comprises 1748a. 1r. 11p., and is intersected by the road from Worcester to Cleo- bury-Mortimer. The surface is hilly, but the land is well cultivated; and coal is obtained to some extent. Shakenhurst is a handsome seat on the margin of the county. The living is a discharged vicarage, united to that of Mamble, and valued in the king's books at £5. 0. 2½.: the tithes were some years since commuted for 140 acres of land. The church, a plain edifice, has been recently enlarged, and the old spire replaced by a square tower. A free school is supported by sub- scription.

BAYWORTH, a hamlet, in the parish of Sunning- well, hundred of Hormer, county of Berks; con- taining 75 inhabitants. Here was formerly a chapel of ease to the rectory of Sunningwell, but it has gone to decay.

BEACHAMPTON, or BEAUCHAMPTON (St. Mary), a parish, in the union, hundred, and county of BUCK-INGHAM, 2½ miles (S. by W.) from Stony-Stratford, and 4½ (S. W.) from Wolverton station; containing 248 in-habitants. It comprises about 1500 acres of land, in general clayey and stoney; and is intersected by the river Ouse, and situated near the Grand Junction canal, from which there is a branch canal to Buckingham. Lace-making is carried on. The living is a rectory, valued in the king's books at £14. 16. 5½., and in the gift of Caius College, Cambridge: the tithes have been commuted for £345, and the glebe comprises 31 acres. The church has some remains of the decorated style. William Elmer founded a free grammar school in 1652, and endowed it with freehold lands now producing £70 per annum; he also bequeathed £5 per annum for apprenticing a poor boy, and there are other charities amounting to about £110. The remains of the fine old mansion of Lord Latimer, whose widow was married to Henry VIII., are still to be seen, with the royal arms in different parts.

BEACHAMWELL.—See BEECHAMWELL.

BEACHFIELD, a township, in the parish of WOR-THEN, hundred of CHIRBURY, S. division of SALOP; containing 35 inhabitants.

BEACHLEY, a chapelry, in the parish of TIDEN-HAM, hundred of WESTBURY, W. division of the county of GLOUCESTER, 3 miles (S. S. E.) from Chepstow; containing 224 inhabitants. This place is situated on a small peninsula at the mouth of the Wye, formed by the junction of that river with the Severn, over which latter is the Old Passage ferry, lately improved by the erection of stone piers and an establishment of steam-packets; it is remarkable for its early vegetation, the salubrity of its air, and the beauty of its surround-ing scenery. The living is a perpetual curacy; net in-come, £16; patron, the Vicar of Tidenham; impropri-ator, C. S. Stokes, Esq. The chapel, which is in the early English style, was consecrated on Sept. 10th, 1833, and is dedicated to St. John; it was made a district church in 1842.

BEACONSFIELD (ALL SAINTS), a market-town and parish, in the union of AMERSHAM, hundred of BURN-HAM, county of BUCKINGHAM, 36 miles (S. E. by S.) from Buckingham, and 23¼ (W. by N.) from London; containing 1732 inhabitants. This parish comprises 4548a. 11p., of which 3568 acres are arable and meadow land, 778 woodland, and 172 road and waste. The town, which occupies 29 acres, is situated on a hill, and is supposed to have derived its name from a beacon for-merly erected there; it consists of four streets, which meet in a convenient market-place in the centre, and the houses are in general well built, of handsome ap-pearance, and amply supplied with water. The en-virons, in which there are some handsome seats, abound with beautiful scenery, and the air is remarkably salu-brious. The market is on Thursday; the fairs, chiefly for horses, horned-cattle, and sheep, are held on Feb. 13th and Holy-Thursday. The living is a rectory, va-lued in the king's books at £26. 2. 8½.; net income, £545; patrons, the President and Fellows of Magdalene College, Oxford. The church is an ancient building of stone and flint, with a tower, and contains a mural tablet to the memory of Edmund Burke, who died at his seat called Gregories, in the parish, and was interred here:

a local jurisdiction, a mayor, and a prison; but it is now united with Canterbury, the archbishops of which once had a palace here, long since converted into a private dwelling-house. The parish comprises by measurement 1139 acres, of which 64 are in wood. The living is a vicarage, valued in the king's books at £6; net income, arising from tithes, £170, with a permanent addition of £50 annually from the Archbishop, who is patron and appropriator.

BEAL, with Lowlin, a township, in the parish of Kyloe, union of Berwick-upon-Tweed, in Island-shire, N. division of Northumberland; adjoining Berwick, and containing 180 inhabitants.

BEALINGS, GREAT (St. Mary), a parish, in the union of Woodbridge, hundred of Carlford, E. division of Suffolk, 2 miles (W.) from Woodbridge; containing 377 inhabitants. It comprises 965 acres of land; the surface is hilly, and the soil light, and subject to inundation from a confluence of small streams, which run into the river Deben at Woodbridge, and thence into the sea. The living is a discharged rectory, valued in the king's books at £10. 4. 7., and in the gift of Edward Moor, Esq.: the impropriate tithes have been commuted for £8. 10., and the rectorial for £297. 5.; there are 11 acres of glebe.

BEALINGS, LITTLE (All Saints), a parish, in the union of Woodbridge, hundred of Carlford, E. division of Suffolk, 2¾ miles (W. by S.) from Woodbridge; comprising by admeasurement 712 acres, and containing 322 inhabitants. The living is a rectory, valued in the king's books at £6. 7. 3½.; net income, £140; patron, F. Smythies, Esq.

BEAMINSTER, a market-town and parish, in the union and hundred of Beaminster, Bridport division of Dorset, 17½ miles (W. N. W.) from Dorchester, and 137¼ (W. S. W.) from London; containing, with the tything of Langdon, 3270 inhabitants. During the civil war in the reign of Charles I., Prince Maurice, commanding a party of royalists engaged in besieging Lyme, took up his quarters in this town, which, a few days after, was nearly reduced to ashes by fire, stated by some historians to have been occasioned by accident, and by others to have been the result of a quarrel between the French and the Cornish men in the service of the king, who set fire to it in five different places. It was rebuilt by means of a parliamentary grant of £2000, but was again nearly destroyed by a fire which occurred in 1684: in 1781, it experienced a similar calamity, but the greater part of the buildings having been insured, it soon recovered its former prosperity. The town is pleasantly situated on the river Birt, which is formed by the union of several small springs that rise in the immediate vicinity; the houses are in general modern and well built, and the inhabitants are amply supplied with water. The manufacture of woollen-cloth, which formerly flourished here, is at present on the decline, and that of sail-cloth is now the principal source of employment; there is also a pottery for the coarser kinds of earthenware. The market, granted to William Ewel, prebendary of Sarum, in the 12th of Edward I., is on Thursday; and a fair is held on Sept. 19th, for cattle. Constables and other officers are appointed at the court leet of the lord of the hundred. The quarter-sessions for the county, now held at Dorchester, were formerly held here; and in 1638, an order of session was issued

183

for building a house of correction at the expense of the division. The town-hall is a neat and commodious edifice, in which the public business is transacted.

The parish contains the manors of Beaminster Prima and Secunda, both till lately forming prebends in the Cathedral of Salisbury; the former valued in the king's books at £20. 2. 6., and the latter at £22. 5. 7½. The living is a vicarage, annexed to that of Netherbury: the great tithes have been commuted for £220, and those of the incumbent for £300. The church, founded in honour of the Nativity of the Blessed Virgin, is a stately edifice in the later style of English architecture, with a fine tower 100 feet high, richly ornamented with sculptured designs of the Crucifixion, the Resurrection, the Ascension, and other subjects of scriptural history. There is a place of worship for Independents. The free school was founded in 1684, by Mrs. Frances Tucker, who endowed it with £20 per annum for the master, leaving also £30 per annum for apprenticing boys: the endowment now produces about £140, and the number of scholars is 100. The Rev. Samuel Hood, father of Lords Hood and Bridport, was master of the school early in the eighteenth century. An almshouse for eight aged persons was founded in 1630, by Sir John Strode, of Parnham, Knt., the income of which amounts to £20. Gilbert Adams, Esq., in 1626, gave £200 to the poor; and the Rev. William Hillary, in 1712, bequeathed the reversion, after ninety-nine years, of land in the parish of Carscombe, worth £35 per annum, for the benefit of twelve distressed families. The Knowle estate, in the parish, has been in the possession of the Daniels since the reign of Henry VIII., and there is a burial-ground for the family upon it. Dr. Thomas Sprat, Bishop of Rochester; and the Rev. Thomas Russel, Fellow of New College, Oxford, who distinguished himself by his defence of Warton's *History of English Poetry*, were natives of the town.

BEAMISH, a township, in the chapelry of Tanfield, parish of Chester-le-Street, union of Lanchester, Middle division of Chester ward, N. division of the county of Durham, 7½ miles (S. S. W.) from Gateshead; containing, with the township of Lintz-Green, 2671 inhabitants. It stands in the wooded vale of Team, which expands itself near the house of Beamish into a fine strath, bordered on all sides by rising grounds of irregular form, richly clothed with luxuriant forest-trees. The mansion, which contains some curious old portraits, is one of the best family residences in the county, having been much improved, and is remarkable for the handsome evergreens that ornament its pleasure-grounds: the old park of Beamish occupies an upland site to the south of the Team. There is a great quantity of coal in the township, worked from what is called the Tanfield colliery, near Beamish.

BEAMSLEY, a township, in the union of Skipton, Upper division of the wapentake of Claro, W. riding of York, 6½ miles (E. by N.) from Skipton; containing 235 inhabitants. This township, which includes Great Beamsley in the parish of Skipton, and Little Beamsley in that of Addingham, is on the eastern side of the river Wharfe, and comprises by computation 1820 acres of fertile land; Beamsley Hall is a handsome mansion pleasantly situated. A tithe rent-charge of £20 is payable to the rector of Addingham. There is a place of worship for Wesleyans. An hospital was founded and

BEAR

BEAU

endowed in 1593 by Margaret, Countess of Cumberland, for 13 poor women, 7 of them from Skipton, 5 from Silsden, and one from Stirton with Thorlby; and an estate at Harewood was left to the charity by her daughter, Anne, Countess of Pembroke. In 1809, timber was felled on the lands to the amount of £1176, of which part was invested in the Navy 5 per cents. The inmates have each separate apartments, and the buildings contain a chapel, in which prayers are read daily by a chaplain, who has £20 per annum; the Earl of Thanet, as representative of the founder, is trustee, and the annual income is £332.

BEANACRE, a tything, in the parish, union, and hundred of MELKSHAM, Melksham and N. divisions of WILTS; containing 257 inhabitants.

BEANLEY, a township, in the parish of EGLINGHAM, union of ALNWICK, N. division of COQUETDALE ward and of NORTHUMBERLAND, 9¼ miles (W. N. W.) from Alnwick; containing 176 inhabitants. This was formerly the head of a barony, the lord of which had the power of inflicting capital punishment; Gallow-Law, on the north side of the Breamish, being the place of execution. It comprises about 2000 acres, of which 1000 are pasture and moorland, and 1000 arable; the soil, generally, is a light gravel, the surface mountainous, and the views very extensive. On an elevated spot called Beanley Plantation are vestiges of an encampment, having a double fosse and rampart; the road which led to it is plainly discernible. Another encampment existed on Beanley Moor. Percy's Cross, erected in memory of Sir Ralph Percy, an officer attached to the Lancasterian party, who fell in battle against the Yorkists, in 1464, stands on Hedgeley Moor, a short distance from Gallow-Law. The impropriate tithes produce £125. 18., and the vicarial £55. 18.

BEARD, a hamlet, in the parish of GLOSSOP, union of HAYFIELD, hundred of HIGH PEAK, N. division of the county of DERBY, 4¼ miles (N. W. by N.) from Chapel-en-le-Frith; containing 290 inhabitants.—See NEW-MILLS.

BEARL, a township, in the parish of BYWELL ST. ANDREW, union of HEXHAM, E. division of TINDALE ward, S. division of NORTHUMBERLAND, 4 miles (E.) from Corbridge; containing 36 inhabitants. This is a large farm, standing nearly two miles north from Bywell, and was some years since the property of Mr. Anthony Wailes and Mrs. Charlton, of whom it was purchased by T. W. Beaumont, Esq., for £22,000. The road from Corbridge to Heddon passes at a short distance north of the village.

BEARLEY (ST. MARY), a parish, in the union of STRATFORD-UPON-AVON, Snitterfield division of the hundred of BARLICHWAY, S. division of the county of WARWICK, 4¼ miles (N. N. W.) from Stratford; containing 231 inhabitants, and comprising 939 acres. In Domesday book it is written Burlei, a name afterwards assumed by a family who possessed it, and resided here. Some of the lands were anciently given to the monks of Bordesley, and, on the dissolution of that monastery, were granted by the crown to the Throckmortons, from whom they passed to other families. The living is a perpetual curacy; net income, £62; patrons, the Provost and Fellows of King's College, Cambridge. There is a school in which the greater portion of the children are paid for by the wealthier landowners.

184

BEARSTEAD (HOLY CROSS), a parish, in the union of MAIDSTONE, hundred of EYHORNE, lathe of AYLESFORD, W. division of KENT, 2½ miles (E.) from Maidstone; containing 605 inhabitants. It is intersected by the lower Dover road, and comprises 1090 acres, of which about 400 are arable, and the rest pasture, including 100 common or waste; the surface is undulated, the soil sandy, and the chief produce hops and corn. A fair is held on the third Tuesday in July; and there are petty-sessions on the first Monday in every month. The living is a discharged vicarage, valued in the king's books at £6. 7. 4½.; net income, £191; patrons and appropriators, the Dean and Chapter of Rochester: there are about two acres of glebe. The church is an ancient edifice, in the early English style, with a square tower.

BEARSTON, a township, in the parish of MUCKLESTON, union of DRAYTON, Drayton division of the hundred of NORTH BRADFORD, N. division of SALOP, 4¾ miles (N. E. by N.) from Drayton; containing 101 inhabitants.

BEARWARD-COTE, a township, in the parish of ETWALL, union of BURTON-UPON-TRENT, hundred of APPLETREE, S. division of the county of DERBY, 5 miles (W. S. W.) from Derby; containing 36 inhabitants. The manor is mentioned in the Domesday book as being held under Henry de Ferrars, and in 1297 was held under the Earl of Lancaster. The Bonningtons possessed it in the reign of Henry IV., and sold it to the Turners in 1672: the manor afterwards passed, among other families, to the Cottons.

BEAUCHAMP-ROOTHING.—See ROOTHING.

BEAUCHAMP-STOKE.—See BEECHING-STOKE.

BEAUCHIEF-ABBEY, an extra-parochial liberty, formerly part of the parish of NORTON, in the union of ECCLESALL-BIERLOW, hundred of SCARSDALE, N. division of the county of DERBY, 3½ miles (N. W. by N.) from Dronfield; containing 74 inhabitants. The living of this place is a donative; patron, P. Pegge Burnell, Esq. The chapel is a small edifice, erected about 1660, with the exception of the tower, which formed part of a monastery of Præmonstratensian canons founded here in 1183 by Robert Fitz-Ranulph, and dedicated to St. Thomas à Becket, the revenue of which at the Dissolution was £157. 10. 2. The liberty, comprising about 1000 acres, was exempted from assessment for taxes, by a deed executed at a court held at Richmond, March 14th, 1601.

BEAUDESERT (ST. NICHOLAS), a parish, in the union of STRATFORD-UPON-AVON, Henley division of the hundred of BARLICHWAY, S. division of the county of WARWICK, ½ a mile (E.) from Henley; containing 205 inhabitants. This place derives its name from a strong castle erected here soon after the Conquest by Thurstane de Montfort, which, from the beauty of its situation, was called Beldesert, and continued the chief seat of his descendants for several ages, but was probably either demolished or suffered to go to ruin about the time of the war between the houses of York and Lancaster, that the contending parties might not take advantage of it in their military operations. The parish comprises 1242a. 2r. 19p., of which 586 acres are arable; it is almost entirely surrounded by a range of hills, and is intersected by the Birmingham road: the soil is tolerably good, and consists principally of clay and marl. The living is a rectory, valued in the king's books at £7. 16. 0½., and in the gift of the Crown : the tithes have been commuted for £170, and the glebe consists of 141 acres, with a glebe-house. The church is partly Norman, and partly in the early English style, with a richly ornamented Norman arch between the nave and the chancel. The Rev. Richard Jago, a poet of some note, was born here in 1715, during the incumbency of his father.

BEAULIEU, a liberty, in the union of NEW FOREST, Southampton and S. divisions of the county of SOUTHAMPTON, 6¼ miles (N. E.) from Lymington, on the road to Hythe; containing, with an extra-parochial district within its limits, 1339 inhabitants. This place is situated on a river of the same name, which rises in the New Forest, at the foot of a hill about a mile and a half to the north-east of Lyndhurst, and is navigable for vessels of fifty tons' burthen to the Isle of Wight channel, which bounds the parish on the south. On reaching the village, the river spreads into a wide surface covering several acres, on the eastern side of which stood Beaulieu Abbey, founded in 1204, by King John, for thirty monks of the reformed Benedictine order, and dedicated to the Blessed Virgin Mary : its revenue, at the Dissolution in 1540, was £428. 6. 8. It had the privilege of sanctuary, and afforded an asylum to Margaret of Anjou, wife of Henry VI., after the battle of Barnet, and to Perkin Warbeck, in the reign of Henry VII. Beaulieu has long been noted for the manufacture of coarse sacking : near the village of Sowley, within the liberty, were formerly two large mills belonging to some iron-works; and at Buckler's Hard, another populous village in the liberty, situated on the Beaulieu river, and inhabited principally by workmen employed in ship-building, many vessels of war have been built. At Sowley is a fine sheet of water, abounding with pike, some of which are of very large size, weighing nearly 28lbs. Fairs for horses and horned-cattle are held on April 15th and September 4th.

The LIVING is a donative; net income, £85; patron and impropriator, Lady Montagu. The chapel, dedicated to St. Bartholomew, was the refectory of the abbey, the church of which, situated to the south-east, has been entirely destroyed ; it is a plain building of stone, with strong buttresses, and has a beautiful stone pulpit, the only one similar to which in the kingdom, is that at Magdalene College, Oxford : the edifice was enlarged in 1840. There is a place of worship for Particular Baptists. The ruins of the abbey are situated in a beautiful valley, nearly circular in form, bounded by well-wooded hills ; and are surrounded by a stone wall, nearly entire in many places, and mantled with ivy. Near the abbey was a building, called an hospital, occupied by the Knights of St. John of Jerusalem, where travellers and persons in distress were relieved, and the revenue of which, at its dissolution, was £100; it was founded a little previously to the abbey, and, from the beauty of its situation, gave the name of *Beaulieu* to the place. About two miles distant, and very near the sea-shore, is Park Farm, anciently one of the granges attached to the abbey, and which, like others appertaining to that establishment, possessed the privilege of having divine service celebrated in it, under a bull of Pope Alexander I. The chapel is remaining, though much dilapidated, and adjoins the farmhouse, a massive stone building of equal antiquity : its length is 42 feet, and breadth about 14; the interior is divided into two com-

partments by a stone screen, which reaches to the roof. At a short distance from this, on the road to Beaulieu, are the ruins of the extensive barn and the chapel of St. Leonard, the former measuring in length 226 feet, in breadth 77, and in height 60 : here was the principal grange belonging to the abbey.

BEAU-MANOR, an extra-parochial liberty, in the hundred of WEST GOSCOTE, N. division of the county of LEICESTER, 3 miles (S. W.) from Loughborough; containing 87 inhabitants. This place was anciently the residence of the Beaumont family, who, in 1389 and 1390, had the honour of entertaining Richard II. and his queen at their mansion called Beau-Manor Park. It afterwards became the residence of Frances, Duchess of Suffolk, niece of Henry VIII., and mother of Lady Jane Grey; and subsequently of Sir William Hericke, one of the tellers of the exchequer in the reign of James I. In 1725 a new manor-house was built; the park and scenery around are remarkably picturesque and beautiful, and some very large timber-trees form a prominent feature in the landscape.

BEAUMONT (ST. MARY), a parish, in the union of CARLISLE, CUMBERLAND ward, and E. division of the county of CUMBERLAND, 4 miles (N. W. by W.) from Carlisle; containing 288 inhabitants. About the year 1323, Robert Bruce, King of Scotland, encamped with his army for five days at the village, and hence sent detachments to ravage the circumjacent country. The parish comprises by measurement 1497 acres of land; the soil of which is a rich black loam, alternated with sand; the village is pleasantly situated on the river Eden, and the Carlisle canal passes through the parish. At the hamlet of Sandsfield, on the western bank of the Eden, vessels of sixty tons' burthen, belonging to the port of Carlisle, receive and discharge their cargoes. There is an extensive salmon-fishery in the river, the property of the Earl of Lonsdale. The living is a discharged rectory, united to that of Kirk-Andrews-upon-Eden in 1692, and valued in the king's books at £8. 1. 8. : the glebe consists of about 12 acres. The church stands upon a considerable elevation. The celebrated wall of Severus crossed the parish.

BEAUMONT *cum* MOZE (ST. LEONARD), a parish, in the union and hundred of TENDRING, N. division of ESSEX, 7¼ miles (S. E. by S.) from Manningtree, and 13 (E.) from Colchester; containing 451 inhabitants. It comprises 3046 acres, whereof 692 are common or waste ; and lies near the extremity of an inlet of the North Sea between the Naze and Harwich. The tide comes up to Beaumont wharf, which is connected with a short canal, for conveying coal, corn, and manure, to and from London. The living is a rectory, to which that of Moze was united in 1678, valued in the king's books at £18, and in the gift of the Governors of Guy's Hospital: the tithes have been commuted for £775, and there are 46 acres of glebe. The church is a plain edifice, having a piscina in the chancel : the church at Moze has been demolished. There is a small place of worship for Wesleyans. Some silver coins were dug up in 1806.

BEAUMONT-CHASE, an extra-parochial district, in the union of UPPINGHAM, partly in the hundred of WRANGDIKE, and partly in that of MARTINSLEY, county of RUTLAND, 1½ mile (W. by S.) from Uppingham ; containing 22 inhabitants. It lies on the border of the county, next to Leicestershire, and comprises 696 acres.

BEAUMONT-LEYS, an extra-parochial liberty, in the hundred of WEST GOSCOTE, N. division of the county of LEICESTER, 2 miles (N. N. W.) from Leicester; containing 29 inhabitants. In 1276 Dalby hospital had lands here by gift of Simon Montfort, and at the suppression of the Knights Templars they were given to the Hospitallers, who, in 1482, exchanged them with the king for the advowson of Boston church, in Lincolnshire. Leicester Abbey had also property in " Beaumund." The liberty comprises 1047 acres of land.

BEAUSALL, a chapelry, in the parish of HATTON, union of WARWICK, Snitterfield division of the hundred of BARLICHWAY, S. division of the county of WARWICK, 4½ miles (N. N. W.) from Warwick; containing 292 inhabitants. This place comprises 1600a. 1r. 25p., whereof 968 acres are arable, 599 meadow and pasture, 9 woodland, and 24 acres homesteads and gardens. Beausall common is in the township.

BEAWORTH, a tything, in the parish of CHERITON, union of ALRESFORD, hundred of FAWLEY, Winchester and N. divisions of the county of SOUTHAMPTON, 4¾ miles (S. by W.) from Alresford; containing 153 inhabitants. Many hundreds of coins, supposed to be of William the Conqueror and William Rufus, were discovered in June 1833; an account of which appeared in the 26th volume of the *Archæologia*.

BEAWORTHY (ST. ALBAN), a parish, in the union of OAKHAMPTON, hundred of BLACK TORRINGTON, Black Torrington and Shebbear, and N. divisions of DEVON, 10 miles (N. N. W.) from Oakhampton; containing 405 inhabitants. The parish comprises 1931 acres, of which 1243 are common or waste, and is intersected by the road from Oakhampton to Holsworthy; the land is of a clayey quality. The living is a discharged rectory, valued in the king's books at £6. 6.; net income, £143; patron, Sir William Molesworth, Bart. There is a place of worship for Wesleyans.

BEBINGTON (ST. ANDREW), a parish, in the union, and Lower division of the hundred, of WIRRALL, S. division of the county of CHESTER; consisting of the ecclesiastical district of Tranmere, and the townships of Higher and Lower Bebington, Poulton *cum* Spittle, and Storeton; and containing 5008 inhabitants, of whom 844 are in Higher Bebington, and 1187 in Lower Bebington, 5 miles (S.) from Birkenhead. The manor of *Higher Bebington* was held for several generations by the family of Bebington, the elder branch of which became extinct in the reign of Richard II.: a younger branch settled at Nantwich. Richard Bebington, of this family, had six sons and a brother slain at the battle of Flodden Field. The manor passed with the heiress of the elder branch to the Minshulls, whose heiress, in the 17th century, brought it to the Cholmondeleys: it was sold in 1736, under an act of parliament, to several persons, among whom was the Orred family. The Lancelyns appear to have possessed lands in *Lower Bebington* as early as the Conquest; their heiress brought the manor in the reign of Elizabeth to the Greens, and it continued in the male line of that family till 1711. It was subsequently possessed by Mrs. Parnell, who died in 1792, bequeathing the estate to her relative, Joseph Kent, Esq., who, conformably with her will, assumed the name of Green. The PARISH is situated on the banks of the river Mersey, and is intersected by the road from Neston to Birkenhead, and the railway from Chester to Birken-

north and west. It consists of several spacious streets, diverging from the market-place, well paved, and lighted with gas; the houses in general are well built, and the inhabitants are amply supplied with water. The corn-exchange and assembly-rooms form two handsome ornamental buildings. The environs, which abound with pleasing scenery, afford agreeable walks; and races are held annually on a fine course near the town, on which are two commodious stands. The trade is principally in corn, malt, and coal, and is considerable: the market is on Saturday, and fairs are held on Whit-Monday for cattle, and Oct. 2nd for horses and pedlery; there are also statute-fairs.

Adjoining the town is a tract of fen land, originally about 1400 acres in extent, which was granted by Henry VIII. in 1540 (after the dissolution of the abbey of Bury St. Edmund's, to which the manor belonged,) to William Rede and his heirs, in trust, for the benefit of himself and other inhabitants of the town; there are now remaining about 940 acres, and upwards of 200 more are held for charitable purposes. In 1543 the inhabitants were incorporated by letters-patent of Henry VIII., but, in consequence of protracted disputes between them and the family of Rede, concerning the grant of the fen lands, the charter was surrendered to Queen Elizabeth, and a new one granted in 1584, which was confirmed in 1588, and by James I. in 1605. The government is now vested in four aldermen, and twelve councillors, from whom a mayor is chosen; the borough is co-extensive with the parish. A court of quarter-sessions is held for the county; petty-sessions are held for the district every Saturday, and manor courts occasionally. The county debt-court of Beccles, established in 1847, has jurisdiction over part of the two registration-districts of Wangford, and Loddon and Clavering.

The parish contains 1893a. 2r. 14p., of which 950 acres are common; the soil on the high grounds is wet and clayey, and in the lower parts sandy. The LIVING is a rectory, consolidated with the vicarage of St. Mary Ingate; the rectory valued in the king's books at £21. 12. 3½., and the vicarage at £7. 6. 8.: the tithes have been commuted for £350. The church is a spacious and elegant structure, in the later style of English architecture, and consists of a nave, chancel, and aisles; the porch is of beautiful design and elaborate execution, and the interior is appropriately ornamented. A collection of books, formerly kept in a room over the porch, has been removed to the subscription library established in 1836. A chapel for reading the burial service, and a burial-ground, were consecrated in 1823; and a cemetery, with a chapel for all denominations, was established in 1840. There are places of worship for Baptists, Independents, and Methodists. A grammar school was endowed under the will, dated in 1714, of the Rev. Dr. Fauconberge, a native of the town, with an estate of 132 acres in the parish of Corton, producing about £183 per annum. Dr. Routh, the learned president of Magdalene College, Oxford, received the rudiments of his education here. The free school in Ballygate-street was founded and endowed in 1631, by Sir John Leman, Knt., alderman of London, who devised several parcels of land for its support, containing altogether 112 acres, and yielding a rent of £196. An ancient hospital for lepers, of uncertain foundation, with a chapel dedicated to St. Mary Magdalene, was granted in 1676, to the

corporation of Beccles, for the benefit of the poor. Here were also several guilds; and an ancient church, dedicated to St. Peter, distinct from the present church.

BECCONSALL, with HESKETH.—See HESKETH.

BECHTON, a township, in the parish of SANDBACH, union of CONGLETON, hundred of NORTHWICH, S. division of the county of CHESTER, 2¼ miles (S. E.) from Sandbach; containing 809 inhabitants. The manor was held by the Bechtons in the reign of Edward II.; it came afterwards in moieties to the Davenports and Fittons, and later to the Wilbrahams and Egertons. The township lies on the road from Sandbach to Church-Lawton; and comprises 3800 acres, of which sand is the prevailing soil. The Grand Trunk canal passes close to the salt-works here. The impropriate tithes have been commuted for £192. 11. 10., and the vicarial for £192. 18. 9.

BECKBURY (ST. MILBURGH), a parish, in the union of SHIFFNALL, liberties of the borough of WENLOCK, S. division of SALOP, 4 miles (S.) from Shiffnall; containing 312 inhabitants. It is situated about two miles south of the great Holyhead road, and comprises by measurement 1321 acres: red rockstone is found, suitable for building. The living is a discharged rectory, valued in the king's books at £5. 3. 4., and in the gift of the Lord Chancellor: the tithes have been commuted for £333, and there are 31 acres of glebe, with a house. In the church is a table-monument of alabaster to the memory of Richard Houghton and his lady. In the Windmill field is a tumulus, which was opened in 1840, and which, about four feet beneath the surface, contained human bones.

BECKENHAM (ST. GEORGE), a parish, in the union of BROMLEY, hundred of BROMLEY and BECKENHAM, lathe of SUTTON-AT-HONE, W. division of KENT, 1¼ mile (W.) from Bromley, and 10 (S. S. E.) from London; containing 1608 inhabitants. The name of this place, compounded of the Saxon terms Bec, a brook, and Ham, a dwelling, is derived from a small stream which passes through the parish, and falls into the river Ravensbourne. In the reign of Henry VIII., Charles Brandon, Duke of Suffolk, entertained that monarch when on his journey to visit Anne of Cleves, with great pomp, at the manor-house. The parish comprises 3575 acres, of which 307 are woodland, and 102 common or waste. The village is pleasantly situated, and contains some neat dwelling-houses: in the neighbourhood are many handsome villas. The Croydon railway passes along the north-western angle of the parish. A fair, chiefly for toys, is held on the Monday before St. Bartholomew's day. The living is a rectory, valued in the king's books at £16. 18. 9., and in the gift of J. Cator, Esq.: the tithes have been commuted for £893. 10., and there are 27 acres of glebe. The church is a neat structure erected about the beginning of the seventeenth century, with a lofty spire which, having been destroyed by lightning in 1790, was lately rebuilt. Mrs. Mary Watson, in 1790, bequeathed property for the instruction of children, which was vested in the purchase of £1401 New South Sea annuities, producing an annual dividend of £42, to which subsequent benefactions have been added; a school-house was erected in 1818. Dr. Asheton, the projector of a plan for providing for widows by survivorship, was rector of the parish towards the close of the 17th century.

BECK

BECKERMET (St. Bridget), a parish, in the union of Whitehaven, Allerdale ward above Derwent, W. division of Cumberland; containing 630 inhabitants. The village of Great Beckermet lies partly in this parish, and partly in that of Beckermet St. John, 3 miles south from Egremont. The parish is situated on the north bank of the Calder, adjoining the ocean, and contains the sequestered ruins of Calder Abbey, described under Calder-Bridge. Freestone is obtained. The living is a perpetual curacy; net income, £87; patron and impropriator, H. Gaitskell, Esq. The parochial church stands about half a mile south-west of the village; and a church in the early English style has just been erected at Calder-Bridge, at the expense of Capt. Irwin.

BECKERMET (St. John), a parish, in the union of Whitehaven, Allerdale ward above Derwent, W. division of Cumberland; containing 468 inhabitants. The living is a perpetual curacy; net income, £57; patron and impropriator, H. Gaitskell, Esq. The church is a small ancient edifice. A portion of the town of Egremont is included within this parish; in which also stands a private residence called Woto-Bank, with whose etymology is connected an interesting fabulous tale, chosen by Mrs. Cowley for the subject of a romantic poem entitled *Edwina*, published in 1794.

BECKETT, a tything, in the parish and hundred of Shrivenham, county of Berks, 4¾ miles (S. W. by S.) from Farringdon; comprising 792a. 2r. 25p., and containing 42 inhabitants. The manor, soon after the Conquest, became the property of the crown, and the manor-house was occasionally a royal residence. Dr. Shute Barrington, Bishop of Durham, was born here in 1734.

BECKFORD (St. John the Baptist), a parish, in the union of Winchcomb, partly in the hundred of Tibaldstone, and partly in the Upper division of the hundred of Tewkesbury, E. division of the county of Gloucester, 6 miles (E. N. E.) from Tewkesbury; containing, with the hamlets of Grafton, Bangrove, and Didcote, 461 inhabitants. This parish, which comprises about 1800 acres, is situated on the road from Tewkesbury to Evesham; and abounds with freestone of good quality. The living is a vicarage, with the living of Ashton-under-Hill annexed, valued in the king's books at £16. 16. 10½.; net income, £317; patron, the Rev. John Timbrill, D. D.; impropriator, W. Wakeman, Esq.: the tithes were commuted for land and a money payment in 1773. The church is a very ancient structure. Here is a Roman Catholic chapel. An alien priory of Augustine canons, a cell to the abbey of St. Martin and St. Barbara, in Normandy, formerly existed here: upon its suppression, the revenues amounted to £53. 6. 8. per annum.

BECKHAM, EAST (St. Helen), a parish, in the union of Erpingham, hundred of North Erpingham, E. division of Norfolk, 4½ miles (W. by S.) from Cromer; containing 56 inhabitants. The parish comprises about 800 acres, nearly all arable land. The living is annexed to the rectory of Aylmerton, and the church has long been a ruin.

BECKHAM, WEST (All Saints), a parish, in the union of Erpingham, hundred of South Erpingham, E. division of Norfolk, 3 miles (E.) from Holt; containing 179 inhabitants. It comprises by measurement 835 acres, of which 767 are arable, 18 pasture, and 50

BECKLEY (*St. Mary*), a parish, in the union of HEADINGTON, hundred of BULLINGTON, county of OXFORD, 4 miles (N. N. W.) from Wheatly; containing, with the hamlets of Studley and Horton, 763 inhabitants. The manor was part of the private property of Alfred the Great : in the thirteenth century it belonged to Richard, Earl of Cornwall, who had a castellated mansion here, formerly the residence of the barons of St. Walery, and a portion of the site of which is now occupied by a dovecote, supposed to be a relic of the fortress. The living is a vicarage, valued in the king's books at £8; net income, £112 : it is in the patronage of the family of the incumbent, the Rev. T. L. Cooke, to whom, and the Earl of Abingdon and Sir Alexander Croke, the impropriate tithes belong. The church is in the early and decorated English styles, with an embattled tower between the nave and chancel, and contains some monuments to the Crokes, of Studley. The Roman road from Alchester to Wallingford passed through the parish, and fragments of Roman pottery have been found in the vicinity.

BECKLEY (*All Saints*), a parish, in the union of RYE, hundred of GOLDSPUR, rape of HASTINGS, county of SUSSEX, 7 miles (W. N. W.) from Rye; containing 1412 inhabitants. The parish is bounded on the north by the river Rother, which separates the counties of Kent and Sussex : it comprises by measurement 4800 acres, of which about 1500 are in woods and plantations, and the remainder arable and pasture land in good cultivation ; about 360 acres are planted with hops. Iron-ore and sandstone are found, and formerly there was an extensive furnace for smelting iron-ore. The village is pleasantly situated on the road from Rye to London; the surrounding scenery is rich in sylvan beauty, and from many parts extensive and finely varied prospects are obtained. The living is a rectory, valued in the king's books at £11. 6. 8., and in the gift of University College, Oxford : the tithes have been commuted for £1000, and the glebe comprises 25 acres, with a house built in 1840 by the patrons. The church is a handsome edifice in the decorated English style. The Wesleyans have a place of worship. There are several chalybeate springs.

BECK-ROW, a hamlet, in the parish and union of MILDENHALL, hundred of LACKFORD, W. division of SUFFOLK; containing 744 inhabitants. It is situated to the north-west of the village of Mildenhall.

BECKSWELL.—See BEXWELL.

BEDALE (*St. Gregory*), a market-town, parish, and the head of a union, chiefly in the wapentake of HANG-EAST, but partly in that of HALLIKELD, N. riding of YORK ; containing 2803 inhabitants, of whom 1250 are in the town, 33½ miles (N. W) from York, and 223 (N. N. W.) from London. The parish comprises 8702*a*. 1r. 24*p*., and contains the townships of Aiskew, Bedale, Burrell with Cowling, Crakehall, Firby, and Langthorne, and the hamlet of Rands-Grange. The town, which has been considerably improved of late, is of prepossessing appearance ; it is pleasantly situated on the banks of a stream flowing into the river Swale, near Scruton, and consists principally of one street, which is lighted with gas from works erected in 1836. The houses are in general of brick, and irregularly built ; the air is pure, and the neighbourhood, which is well cultivated, affords many pleasant walks and much pic-

189

turesque scenery. Among the more recent buildings is a handsome structure erected in 1840, containing apartments for the savings' bank, a suite of assembly-rooms, and apartments for holding petty-sessions. Several extensive wool-staplers carry on business here, and give employment to numerous wool-combers. An act was passed in 1846, enabling the York and Newcastle Railway Company to make a branch line to Bedale, 7 miles in length. The market is on Tuesday ; and on the same day in alternate weeks is a large fair for fat-cattle and sheep, established in 1837. Other fairs are held on Easter-Tuesday, Whit-Tuesday, and July 5th and 6th, for horses, horned-cattle, and sheep ; and Oct. 10th and 11th, and the last Monday but one before Christmas-day, for cattle, sheep, hogs, and leather, the supply of the last article being the most considerable of any in the north of England. The horses are generally of superior value, the surrounding country being famed for its breed of hunters and race-horses.

The LIVING is a rectory, valued in the king's books at £89. 4. 9½., and in the alternate patronage of Miss Pierse, and Myles Stapylton, Esq. : the tithes have been commuted for £1713. 16. 3., and there are 176 acres of glebe. The church is in the early English style, and has a square embattled tower crowned by pinnacles, and of remarkable strength, having been used as a place of security from the incursions of the Scots : it contains several interesting monuments, one of which is to the memory of Sir Brian Fitz-Alan, lord-lieutenant of Scotland in the reign of Edward I., who resided in a castle near the church, of which there are no remains. A district church was erected in 1840 at Crakehall. There are places of worship for Methodists, Particular Baptists, and Roman Catholics. A school for boys, formerly in the churchyard, was removed in 1816 to a more convenient room erected by Henry Pierse, Esq., in the market-place ; it is supposed to have existed prior to the dissolution of religious houses, and was endowed by Queen Elizabeth with £7. 11. 4. per annum, and afterwards by the Countess of Warwick with £13. 6. 8. per annum. The latter sum, together with a gratuity of £50 from the rector, and £10 from the Hazleflatt estate, is paid to the master ; the first sum of £7. 11. 4. being appropriated to the instruction of scholars in the old building in the churchyard, which was re-opened as a grammar school a few years ago. Samwaies hospital, a neat stone building, containing apartments for six men, was founded by P. Samwaies, D.D., in 1698 ; the Widows' hospital was founded by Robert Younge about 1666, for the residence of three widows. There are numerous bequests for the poor. The union of Bedale, comprising 23 parishes and places, contains a population of 8596. Sir Christopher Wray, lord chief justice of the court of queen's bench in the reign of Elizabeth, was a native of the place.

BEDBURN, NORTH, a township, in the parish of ST. ANDREW AUCKLAND, union of AUCKLAND, N. W. division of DARLINGTON ward, S. division of the county of DURHAM, 5¾ miles (N. W.) from Bishop-Auckland ; containing 457 inhabitants. This place, which was anciently a possession of the Eure family, comprises the hamlets of Green-Head and Fir-Tree, and lies on the north side of Witton-le-Wear : the river Wear passes on the west. Smelting-works are said to have been carried on at a place now called Smelt-house.

BEDBURN, SOUTH, a township, in the chapelry of HAMSTERLEY, parish of ST. ANDREW AUCKLAND, union of AUCKLAND, N. W. division of DARLINGTON ward, S. division of the county of DURHAM, 8 miles (N. W. by W.) from Bishop-Auckland; containing 350 inhabitants. This township, which is situated between the river Wear and the Bedburn rivulet, comprises 8068 acres, whereof 5000 are arable, meadow, and pasture, 1068 wood and plantations, and the remainder waste; the soil is light and sandy, but not unfertile. The surface is diversified with hills and glens, and the neighbourhood abounds with picturesque and romantic scenery. At the north-western extremity of the township is an earthwork of remote antiquity, called "The Castles," of oblong form, surrounded by a lofty rampart of loose pebble-stones, with an outer ditch, supposed to have been a British fortress. At Bedburn Forge is a manufactory for edge-tools, spades, &c., which, prior to the year 1820, was used for bleaching linen cloth and yarn by a chemical process.

BEDDINGHAM (ST. ANDREW), a parish, in the union of WEST FIRLE, hundred of TOTNORE, rape of PEVENSEY, E. division of SUSSEX, 2 miles (S. E.) from Lewes; containing 268 inhabitants. The parish comprises 2283a. 3r. 1p., and includes part of the South Downs; it is bounded on the west by the river Ouse, and is intersected by the road from Lewes to Eastbourne. The living is a discharged vicarage, with that of West Firle united, valued in the king's books at £9. 10. 10.; net income, £345; patrons, alternately, the Bishop, and the Dean and Chapter, of Chichester. The impropriation of Beddingham belongs to the Dean and Chapter, and that of West Firle to Viscount Gage. The church is a handsome structure, and has evidently been of larger dimensions than at present. Several relics of antiquity, consisting of swords, bracelets, and Roman coins, with some skeletons, were dug up in a field in 1800.

BEDDINGTON (ST. MARY), a parish, in the union of CROYDON, Second division of the hundred of WALLINGTON, E. division of SURREY, 1½ mile (W.) from Croydon; containing, with the hamlet of Wallington, 1453 inhabitants. This parish comprises 3909 acres, whereof 98 are common or waste, and is intersected by the river Wandle; the soil is light and gravelly, and towards the north the surface is flat. The living is a rectory, valued in the king's books at £13. 16. 8., and in the patronage of Capt. Carew: the tithes, with those of Wallington, have been commuted for £1200, and there are 49 acres of glebe. The church, beautifully situated in Beddington Park, close to the ancient mansion, is a handsome edifice with a fine tower, chiefly in the later English style; it was built in the reign of Richard II., and contains some monuments to the memory of the Carew family. Several schools are supported by subscription; and there are bequests to the poor, the principal of which is one of £1000 by Mrs. A. P. Gee, in 1825. The first orange-trees introduced into England are said to have been planted in Beddington Park. Roman urns and other relics have been discovered.

BEDFIELD (ST. NICHOLAS), a parish, in the union and hundred of HOXNE, E. division of SUFFOLK, 4¾ miles (W. N. W.) from Framlingham; containing 358 inhabitants. The parish comprises 1268 acres, of which

for a residence to William de Beauchamp, to whom Henry restored the barony which he had forfeited in the preceding reign. Of this fortress, only a part of the intrenchments, and the site of the keep, now converted into a bowling-green, remain. The ancient barons of Bedford were lord almoners at the coronation of the kings of England; and as an inheritor of part of the barony, the Marquess of Exeter officiated at that of George IV., receiving the usual perquisite of a silver alms-basin, and the cloth upon which the sovereign walked from Westminster Hall to the Abbey. During the civil war in the reign of Charles I., this town, which had been garrisoned for the parliament, surrendered to Prince Rupert, in 1643; the parliamentary troops, under Col. Montague, afterwards entered it by stratagem, and carried off some money and horses, which had been brought thither for the use of the royalists.

The TOWN is pleasantly situated in a fertile vale watered by the river Ouse, which is here navigable for barges, and over which is a handsome stone bridge of five arches, erected in 1813 at an expense of £15,137, and replacing a former bridge of great antiquity. It consists of one spacious street, nearly a mile in length, intersected at right angles by several smaller streets; and is rapidly increasing, from the advantages of gratuitous education at the excellent and richly endowed free schools, adapted to every class of the community, operating as an inducement to families to settle here. The town is well paved, lighted with gas, and amply supplied with water. Races are held in the spring and autumn, a king's plate having been run for, the first time, at the autumnal meeting of 1832; assemblies take place during the winter, and a small theatre is opened occasionally. There is a public library, with an extensive and well-assorted collection of valuable books, and a museum; and several book-clubs have been established.

The principal branches of manufacture are those of lace and straw-plat, in which many women and children are employed; a good deal of iron is manufactured into agricultural implements, and a considerable trade in corn and coal, by means of the Ouse, is carried on with Lynn and the intermediate places. A railway from Bedford to the Bletchley station of the London and North-Western line, was opened in November, 1846; it is about 16½ miles long, almost a dead level, and cost between £16,000 and £17,000 per mile. In 1846, an act was passed for making a branch of nearly eight miles from the great London and York railway, to Bedford. The market-days are Monday, for pigs only; and Saturday, for corn and provisions: the former market is held in the southern, and the latter in the northern, division of the town. The fairs are on the first Tuesday in Lent, April 21st, July 6th, Aug. 21st, Oct. 12th, and Dec. 19th, for cattle; and there is a wool-fair also on the 6th of July. The GOVERNMENT, until 1836, was in accordance with a charter of incorporation granted by Charles II., confirming the prescriptive privileges of the borough and the charters previously granted; but by the act of the 5th and 6th of William IV., cap. 76, the corporation now consists of a mayor, 6 aldermen, and 17 councillors, exclusively of the mayor, who belongs to the last-named class; and the borough is now divided into two wards, the municipal and parliamentary boundaries being the same. The mayor is a justice of the peace by virtue of

191

his office, and four other gentlemen have been appointed justices, concurrently with the county magistrates. The borough first sent representatives to parliament in the 23rd of Edward I., since which time it has returned two members; the mayor is returning officer. The county debt-court of Bedford, established in 1847, has jurisdiction over the registration-district of Bedford. The assizes and quarter-sessions for the county are held in the town, where also the election of the knights of the shire takes place; the sessions-house, rebuilt in 1753, is a neat stone edifice, in St. Paul's square. The county gaol, rebuilt in 1801, is a handsome structure surrounded by a high brick wall, at the north-western entrance into the town, and contains seven wards or divisions for the classification of prisoners, with airing-yards, in one of which is a tread-mill. The county penitentiary, or new house of correction, a large brick building on the road to Kettering, was erected in 1819.

The borough comprises the PARISHES of St. Cuthbert, St. John, St. Mary, St. Paul, and St. Peter Martin. The parish of *St. Cuthbert* comprises about 250 acres by measurement. The living is a discharged rectory, valued in the king's books at £5. 9. 4½., and in the patronage of the Crown, with a net income of £129: the tithes were commuted for land and annual money payments in 1795. The church, rebuilt in 1846 in the Anglo-Saxon style, is a neat edifice, and cost £1600. The parish of *St. John* contains by computation 18 acres. The living is a rectory not in charge, with the mastership of St. John's hospital, in the town, annexed; net income, about £380: the advowson till lately belonged to the corporation. The church is a neat structure in the later English style, with a handsome tower, but it has been much modernised. The parish of *St. Mary* contains 490 acres, of which 275 acres are plough land, and 215 pasture; the soil is gravel. The living is a rectory, valued in the king's books at £11. 4. 9½.; net income, £273; patron, the Bishop of Lincoln: the tithes were commuted for land and a money payment in 1797. The church, which is of early date, shows few marks of its antiquity, except in the tower, in which are good specimens of the Norman arch, recently discovered: great improvements have of late been made in the interior of the edifice, by removing the wall which divided the nave from the north aisle, and substituting stone arches and columns of light and handsome structure; the chancel, also, has been fitted up with stalls, in oak, with sculptured finials, and the nave and aisle with open sittings. In the immediate neighbourhood of this church stood, until the reign of Edward VI., another church, dedicated to St. Peter Dunstable: from its materials the aisle of the surviving church was built; and in the late alterations, a doorway was discovered in the outer wall of this aisle, in one of the spandrils of which are the clear marks of St. Peter's emblem, the cross keys.

The parish of *St. Paul* contains 771a. 1r. 34p., the greater part of which is arable, the pasture being chiefly on the banks of the Ouse; the surface is level, rising gradually on the north towards Clapham hill. The living is a vicarage, valued in the king's books at £10, and in the patronage of Lord Carteret, with a net income of £230; the glebe consists of about 63 acres. The church, a portion of which was built in the 12th century, is a spacious and venerable structure, partly in the early and partly in the decorated English style, with a handsome tower surmounted by an octagonal spire, and a north and south porch in the later style. An additional church, dedicated to the *Holy Trinity*, was erected in the pointed style, in 1839-40, by subscription, aided by £500 from the Incorporated Society; it contains 1000 sittings, of which 500 are free, and Lord Carteret has contributed £2700 towards its endowment. The living is a perpetual curacy, in the gift of the Vicar of St. Paul's. The parish of *St. Peter Martin* comprises 547a. 3r. 18p. The living is a rectory, valued in the king's books at £11. 13. 1½., and in the patronage of the Crown; net income, £204: the tithes were commuted for land and annual money payments in 1795. The church is an ancient edifice, with a tower, the upper part of which has been recently restored, and having at the southern entrance a beautiful Norman arch: the first stone of an enlargement of the building, was laid in October, 1845. There are places of worship for Baptists, Independents, Wesleyans, and Moravians; and a chapel lately erected, denominated the Primitive Episcopal or Reformed Church of England, the minister of which styles himself Bishop.

The *Free Grammar school* of the Bedford charity was founded in 1556, and endowed with property, consisting of houses and land, by Sir William Harpur, a native of the town, and lord mayor of London in 1561, whose statue, in white marble, is placed in a niche over the entrance. It has eight exhibitions of £80 per annum each, tenable for four years, in any one of the Universities of Oxford, Cambridge, or Dublin, six of which are restricted to boys whose parents are inhabitants of the town, and the remaining two are open to all scholars educated in the school, whether or not children of inhabitants. Under the same endowment there are an English commercial school, confined to the children of the settled inhabitants of the town; a national school for boys and girls; and an hospital for the maintenance and education of fifty children of both sexes: the entire amount given annually in apprentice fees is £1500. Handsome school premises in connexion with the charity were lately erected, to which an extensive addition in a corresponding style of architecture has been since made. From the same fund were founded and endowed twenty almshouses, each containing four apartments, for ten aged men and ten aged women, decayed housekeepers; and forty-six additional houses have since been erected, on the northern side of Dame Alice-street, so called in honour of the founder's lady. The sum of £800 is annually given, in marriage portions of £20 each, to maidens of good character in the town, being daughters of resident householders belonging to any of the parishes; £500 for the relief of decayed housekeepers; and other pecuniary donations to the poor; all arising from the same endowment, which, owing to the increased rental of the estate, yields an annual income of more than £13,000. A school was founded in 1727, and endowed with lands producing £46. 10. per annum, by Mr. Alexander Leith; and a Green-coat school, now united to the national school, was established in 1760, and endowed with £33. 15. per annum, by Alderman Newton, of Leicester, for twenty-five boys, for clothing whom the endowment is now appropriated. The house of industry, erected by act of parliament, in 1796, at a cost of £5000, is now the workhouse of the Bedford union, which comprises forty-four parishes and places, and contains a
192

population of 31,767. The county lunatic asylum, a handsome brick building on the road to Ampthill, was erected in 1812, at an expense, including the furniture, of £17,975; and a wing being added in 1842, it will now accommodate sixty-five patients. The county infirmary, on the same road, is a substantial edifice with a stone front, towards the erection and endowment of which the late Samuel Whitbread, Esq., gave £10,000, and Lord Hampden £1000; it contains a small museum, and a medical library consisting of nearly 2000 volumes. The Marquess of Tavistock, at the election for the county in 1826, presented £2000 to the institution, in lieu of entertaining the freeholders; and the Duke of Bedford contributes £100 per annum. Eight almshouses, for unmarried persons of either sex, were founded and endowed in 1679, by Mr. Thomas Christie. An hospital, dedicated to St. John the Baptist, is supposed to have been established and partly endowed by Robert de Parys; its revenue, at the dissolution of religious houses, was £21. 0. 8.; the charity was then confirmed, and the mastership is now annexed to the rectory of St. John's.

A monastery of uncertain foundation existed here at a very early period, in the chapel of which, Offa, King of Mercia, who had been a great benefactor to it, was buried; the chapel being afterwards undermined by the Ouse, sank with the tomb of that monarch into the river. About three-quarters of a mile west of the town, on the bank of the river, are some remains of the conventual buildings of Caldwell Priory, which was instituted in the reign of John, by Robert, son of William de Houghton, for brethren of the order of the Holy Cross, and the revenue of which, at the Dissolution, was £148. 15. 10. At Newenham, a mile east of the town, are considerable vestiges of a priory of Black canons, which, in the reign of Henry II., was removed thither from Bedford, where it had been originally founded by Simeon Beauchamp; and at Elstow church, formerly *Helenstowe*, two miles distant, on the road to Clophill, are the interesting ruins of a nunnery established by Judith, niece of William the Conqueror, and dedicated to the Holy Trinity, and to St. Helen, mother of Constantine the Great; the revenue, at the Dissolution, was £325. 2. 1. John Bunyan, author of the *Pilgrim's Progress*, was confined for twelve years and a half in the county gaol, from which he was ultimately released on the intercession of the Bishop of Lincoln. Bedford confers the title of Duke on the noble family of Russell.

BEDFORD, a district chapelry, in the parish and union of LEIGH, hundred of WEST DERBY, S. division of the county of LANCASTER, ½ a mile (E. S. E.) from Leigh; containing 4187 inhabitants. It lies on the road from Leigh to Warrington, and is of level surface; the soil is of various qualities. The Messrs. Bickham and Pownall have a very large silk power-loom mill on the banks of the Bridgewater canal, established in 1844, and in connexion with which they employ, in and out of doors, more than 1000 persons. There are four cotton-mills, an iron-wire and machine mill, and a brewery: four collieries, also, are in operation. The church, dedicated to St. Thomas, was erected in 1840, at an expense of £3000, and is a neat structure of brick, with a tower. The living is a perpetual curacy, with a net income of £150; patron, the Vicar of Leigh. There are places of worship for Wesleyans and Roman Catholics.

BEDFORD-CIRCUS, a precinct and chapelry, in the county of the city of EXETER, S. division of DEVON; containing 190 inhabitants.

BEDFORDSHIRE, an inland county, bounded on the north and north-east by Huntingdonshire, on the east by the county of Cambridge, on the south-east and south by that of Hertford, on the south-west and west by that of Buckingham, and on the north-west by that of Northampton. It lies between the parallels of 51° 50′ and 52° 22′ (N. Lat.), and between the meridians of 9′ and 42′ (W. Lon.); and includes 463 square miles, or 296,320 statute acres. There are 21,235 inhabited houses, 519 uninhabited, and 210 in progress of erection; and the population amounts to 107,936, of whom 52,190 are males, and 55,746 females. At the time of the Roman conquest of Britain, this territory formed part of the possessions of the *Cassii*; and on the consolidation of the Roman dominion, it was included in the division of Southern Britain, called *Flavia Cæsariensis*. During the heptarchy, the northern part appears to have been occupied by the South Mercians, and the southern by the East Saxons. Bedfordshire, by the act founded on the recommendation of the Ecclesiastical Commissioners, is now within the diocese of Ely, and province of Canterbury: it forms an archdeaconry, in which are included the deaneries of Bedford, Clapham, Dunstable, Eaton, Fleet, and Shefford; and contains 123 parishes. For purposes of civil jurisdiction it is divided into nine hundreds, namely, Barford, Biggleswade, Clifton, Flitt, Manshead, Redbornestoke, Stodden, Willey, and Wixamtree. It contains the borough, market, and county town of Bedford; the corporate and market-town of Dunstable; and the market-towns of Ampthill, Biggleswade, Harrold, Leighton-Buzzard, Lnton, Potton, and Woburn. Two knights are returned to parliament for the shire, and two burgesses for the borough of Bedford. The county is included in the Norfolk circuit, and the assizes and sessions are held in the shire-hall at Bedford, at which town are the county gaol and old house of correction, and the penitentiary or new house of correction.

The form of the county is a very irregular parallelogram, the sides of which are deeply indented by projecting, and in some instances nearly isolated, portions of the adjoining shires. The SOIL comprises every species commonly seen in upland districts, from the strongest clay to the lightest sand; although the various kinds are frequently found in remarkably small patches, and so intermixed that no accurate delineation of them can be given. The agricultural improvements that have taken place in modern times, but which have not been very extensively introduced, are mainly owing to the exertions of the fifth duke of Bedford. The county has long been noted for its abundant produce of wheat and barley, the Vale of Bedford being one of the finest corn districts in the country; rye and oats are cultivated only to a limited extent, as beans are thought more profitable, and on the clay soils are less exhausting than oats. The natural meadows on the banks of the rivers are distinguished for their richness, but the quantity of pasture land is not very considerable; in the southern part of the county, however, and in the neighbourhoods of Ampthill and Woburn more especially, are many large dairy-farms, the produce of which, being chiefly butter, is sent to the London market. The breeding and fat-

tening of calves are carried on in the vicinity of Biggles. wade. The woods occupy about 7000 acres, and are nearly all situated on the slopes of the hills, which consist of cold wet woodland clays; various extensive plantations have been made by the principal proprietors. The high chalky downs, which constitute a large portion of the southernmost part of the county, comprise about 4000 acres of bleak and barren land, in many parts consisting only of a mass of hard chalk, called hurlock, or clunch, with a slight covering of loamy soil, barely sufficient to nourish a scanty crop of indifferent herbage. The northern acclivities of the Chiltern hills are, in many places, the steepest in the county, and are totally inaccessible to the plough; but, with the exception of this tract, the waste lands occupy only a very small proportion of its surface.

The *Manufactures* are almost entirely confined to the platting of straw and the making of thread-lace, the latter being pursued in every part of the county, excepting only in the southern districts, where it has been superseded by the straw manufacture. Straw-platting was formerly confined to the chalk district, at the southernmost extremity of the county, but was so much encouraged about the commencement of the present century, as to spread rapidly over the whole southern part of it, as far as Woburn, Ampthill, and Shefford. Here many of the male, and nearly the whole female, population are employed in this manufacture; as those of the middle and northern parts are in making thread-lace. A considerable quantity of mats is made in the vicinity of the Ouse, to the north-west of Bedford. The principal rivers are the Ouse and the Ivel; the former becomes navigable at Bedford, and the latter at Biggleswade, and they unite at Tempsford. The Grand Junction canal crosses a small south-western portion of the county, in the valley of the Ouzel, near Leighton-Buzzard; and the Bedford branch of the London and Birmingham railway, passing by the towns of Ampthill and Woburn, is almost wholly within the county.

Bedfordshire contained the Roman station called by Antonine *Durocobrivæ*, and by Richard of Cirencester *Forum Dianæ*, at Dunstable; and that designated by Ptolemy Σαληναι, and by the geographer of Ravennas *Salinæ*, near the village of Sandy. It was intersected by the great Roman roads lkeneld-street and Watling-street, by a military way running for a considerable distance within its south-eastern border, and by several vicinal ways. The most remarkable military intrenchment is that called Totternhoe Castle, on the brow of a high hill about two miles to the north-west of Dunstable, consisting of a lofty circular mount surrounded by a ditch and ramparts: a little south-eastward of this is a camp in the form of a parallelogram, about 500 feet long, and 250 broad. About a mile from Dunstable is the large circular encampment of Maiden Bower, about 2500 feet in circumference, and formed by a single ditch and rampart. There is another extensive fortification of the same kind, and nearly of a circular shape, near Leighton-Buzzard: a third circular intrenchment, 112 feet in diameter, is situated about four miles from Bedford, on the road to Eaton-Socon; and on a hill overlooking the site of the ancient *Salinæ*, is a large Roman camp of an irregular oblong form. At the period of the Reformation, there were fourteen religious houses, besides a commandery of the Knights Hospitallers, six hospitals and one college of priests : the most considerable remains are those of Elstow Abbey and Dunstable Priory, and there are smaller vestiges of Warden Abbey, of the Grey friars' Monastery at Bedford, and of the priories of Bushmead, Harrold, Newenham, and Caldwell. Of ancient castles there are few remains, except the strong earthworks which yet mark their sites, and of which the most remarkable are situated at Arlsey, Bedford, Bletsoe, Cainhoe, Mappershall, Puddington, Ridgmont, Risinghoe, Sutton, Thurleigh, Toddington, and Yielding. Among the mansions of the landed proprietors, those most worthy of particular notice are Woburn Abbey, and Ampthill, Luton-Hoo, Wrest, Brogborough, Bletsoe, and Melchbourn Parks. There are mineral springs at Barton, Bedford, Bletsoe, Blunham, Bromham, Bushmead, Clapham, Cranfield, Holcutt, Milton-Ernest, Odell, Pertenhall, Risley, Silsoe, and Turvey; they possess different properties, some being saline, and others chalybeate, but none of them are much frequented.

BEDHAMPTON, a parish, in the union of HAVANT, hundred of PORTSDOWN, Fareham and S. divisions of the county of SOUTHAMPTON, ¾ of a mile (W.) from Havant; containing 533 inhabitants. It comprises by measurement 2415 acres, about one-half of which is under tillage, and the other divided in nearly equal portions between woodland and pasture; the soil in the lower part is a rich black loam, and in the upper part a strong clay. There are some chalk-pits, and two extensive flour-mills. The village is delightfully situated on the shore of Langston harbour, and commands splendid views: there are some fine springs of water, to one of which considerable medicinal qualities are attributed. The living is a rectory, valued in the king's books at £10. 3. 9.; patron, the Rev. St. John Alder: the tithes have been commuted for £320. 10., and the glebe consists of 26 acres. The church is a very neat structure.

BEDINGFIELD, or BEDINGFELD (ST. MARY), a parish, in the union and hundred of HOXNE, E. division of SUFFOLK, 5 miles (S. S. E.) from Eye; containing 336 inhabitants, and comprising 1753a. 1r. 7p., of which 21 acres are common or waste. The living is a discharged rectory, valued in the king's books at £8, and in the gift of J. J. Bedingfield, Esq., whose family received their name from the parish: the tithes have been commuted for £400, and the glebe consists of 3 acres, with a good parsonage-house. The church is in the early English style, and has a nave and chancel, with an embattled tower. The produce of land, to the amount of about £35 per annum, is partly applied to the repairing of the church, and partly to general purposes; and £15 per annum, from land left by B. Bedingfield and S. Pakes, are distributed among the poor. There are several ancient moated houses; a few years ago some silver coins were found of Edward I., and a curious leaden seal of Pope Innocent VI. has been dug up in the glebe.

BEDINGHAM (ST. ANDREW), a parish, in the union of LODDON and CLAVERING, hundred of LODDON, E. division of NORFOLK, 4¼ miles (N. W. by W.) from Bungay; containing 316 inhabitants. It comprises 1340 acres, of which 70 are common or waste. The living is a discharged vicarage, valued in the king's books at £5; patron and impropriator, J. W. Gooch, Esq.: the great tithes have been commuted for £280. 10., and the vicarial for £141. 3.; the glebe comprises about

194

11 acres. The church consists of a nave, chancel, and aisles, with a chapel at the east end of each aisle, and a circular tower the upper part of which is octagonal; the font is curiously sculptured, and in the chancel are some handsome monuments to the Stow family. Another church, dedicated to St. Mary, formerly stood in the churchyard; and the living consisted of medieties, which have long been united.

BEDLINGTON (ST. CUTHBERT), a parish and division, in the union of MORPETH, N. division of the county of NORTHUMBERLAND, 5½ miles (S. E. by S.) from Morpeth; containing 3155 inhabitants, of whom 2023 are in the township of Bedlington. This district was purchased about the beginning of the tenth century by Cutheard, second bishop of Chester, who gave it to the see, by which means it was annexed in jurisdiction to the body of the county palatine of Durham lying between the Tyne and the Tees; it anciently had courts and officers of justice within its own limits, appointed under commission from the Bishop of Durham. The TOWN or village stands on high ground, in a pleasant situation, and consists principally of one long street of considerable width, forming a kind of sloping avenue to the river Blyth, which glides past, between steep banks. The parish, commonly called Bedlingtonshire, and including the townships of North Blyth, Cambois, Choppington, Netherton, and East and West Sleekburn, is on the coast of the North Sea, and is bounded on the north by the Wansbeck, and on the south by the Blyth, which is navigable for small craft, and affords facility of conveyance for the produce of the Bedlington iron-works. At these works, which are among the oldest and most extensive in the kingdom, are manufactured chain-cables, bolts, bar and sheet iron, and all the heavier articles in wrought iron, which are conveyed to the port of Blyth, where they are shipped for London : the buildings occupy an exceedingly romantic site, the banks on each side of the river rising to a considerable height, while the impatient waters hasten rapidly along, and, in passing over a dam, form a very beautiful cataract. There are also some extensive collieries, and several quarries producing grindstones, scythe-stones, and whetstones of superior quality. Petty-sessions are held occasionally. The LIVING, of which the net income is £454, is a vicarage, valued in the king's books at £13. 6. 8., and in the gift of the Dean and Chapter of Durham, who are also appropriators. The great tithes of the township have been commuted for £361. 10., and the vicarial for £40. 8. 4.; there are 234 acres of vicarial glebe. The church is dedicated to St. Cuthbert, whose remains are said to have rested here, on the flight of the monks from Durham upon the approach of the Conqueror, in 1069; it was enlarged and repaired in 1818. At the eastern extremity of the village is a petrifying spring, called Spinner's Well.

BEDMINSTER (ST. JOHN THE BAPTIST), a parish, and the head of a union, partly in the county of the city of BRISTOL, and partly in the hundred of HARTCLIFFE with BEDMINSTER, E. division of SOMERSET, 1½ mile (S. by W.) from Bristol; containing, with the tythings of Bishport and Knowle, 17,862 inhabitants. This large and populous place anciently consisted only of a few cottages; but, from its proximity to Bristol, from which it is separated only by the new cut formed for the conversion of the natural channel of the river Avon into a floating-harbour, and also from its situation on the main road from the western counties, it has become a considerable suburb to that city. Here are tanneries and rope-walks, and many of the inhabitants are employed in collieries. The parish comprises about 5000 acres, chiefly pasture land, and in the environs are several gardens, with the produce of which the occupiers supply the city of Bristol. The living is a discharged vicarage, with the perpetual curacies of St. Mary's and St. Thomas' Redcliffe and Abbot's-Leigh annexed, valued in the king's books at £10. 3. 4., and in the gift of the Prebendary of Bedminster and Redcliffe : the appropriate tithes have been commuted for £69, and the vicarial for £400. The church displays various portions of ancient architecture, with modern insertions : a spire on the tower was thrown down in 1563. St. Paul's district church, in the later English style, with a tower, was erected in 1831, by grant of the Parliamentary Commissioners, at an expense of £8673 : the living is a vicarage not in charge; net income, £180; patron, the Vicar of Bedminster. At Bishport is a district church dedicated to St. Peter. There are places of worship for Baptists, Independents, and Methodists, of which that belonging to the Independents is one of the most handsome and spacious buildings of the kind in the kingdom; the principal entrance is adorned with Grecian columns, and the exterior coated with freestone. Schools are maintained by voluntary contributions; and an hospital, including also a dispensary, has been lately instituted. About the close of the twelfth century, Robert de Berkeley founded an hospital, dedicated to St. Catherine, for a master and several poor brethren; it stood on the western side of a street near the extremity of Brightlow bridge, and was subsequently used as a glass-manufactory, but has since been converted into small tenements. Another hospital was founded by a member of the same family, but every vestige of it has disappeared. The poor law union of Bedminster comprises twenty-three parishes and places, and contains a population of 36,268.

BEDNALL.—See ACTON-TRUSSELL.

BEDSTONE (ST. MARY), a parish, in the union of KNIGHTON, hundred of PURSLOW, S. division of SALOP, 4½ miles (N. E.) from Knighton; containing 139 inhabitants. It comprises 908 acres, of which 99 are common or waste; the surface is diversified with hill and dale, and the soil in general a sharp gravelly earth. The living is a discharged rectory, valued in the king's books at £4. 13. 4.; net income, £230; patron, E. Rogers, Esq. The tithes have been commuted for £110.

BEDWARDINE (ST. JOHN), a parish, in the union of WORCESTER, Lower division of the hundred of Os-WALDSLOW, Worcester and W. divisions of the county of WORCESTER, ¼ of a mile (S. W. by W.) from Worcester; containing 2663 inhabitants. This parish, which is bounded on the east by the Teme and the Severn, comprises about 250 acres of land. The village is pleasantly situated on an eminence rising from the western bank of the latter river, by which it is separated from the city of Worcester. The chief employment of the females here is glove-making. The allotment system has been introduced by the vicar. Among the seats are Pitmaston, Broughton House, and Crow's Nest, with grounds, well planted, attached to each; and

in the village are many handsome and substantial houses and shops. A fair is held on the Friday before Palm-Sunday, on which day (by ancient usage, originating in a grant of certain privileges by the prior of Worcester, in the reign of Edward IV.) the mayor and corporation of the city walk in procession through the village.

The living is a discharged vicarage, valued in the king's books at £13. 6. 8.; net income, £635; patrons and appropriators, the Dean and Chapter of Worcester. The church is an ancient edifice, partly Norman, but chiefly in the early English style, with a square tower; and stands at the junction of the Bromyard and Bransford roads. It is said to have been a chapel of ease to the mother church, originally at Wick, and to have been made the parish church in 1371 : an organ was presented in 1841 by John Williams, Esq., of Pitmaston, who also gave about £300 towards the repair and enlargement of the edifice. The Wesleyans have a place of worship. Charity schools for twelve boys and twelve girls, afterwards united, were respectively founded and endowed by Milbarrow Doelittle in 1719, and Mercy Herbert in 1722, each granting land for the purpose. An infants' school, in which 120 children are instructed, was built in 1843. A rent-charge of £25 was bequeathed by Timothy Nourse, in 1698, for apprenticing children and clothing aged persons; and among other charities are, several bequests for the benefit of the poor, four almshouses for aged widows, a district-visiting clothing club, a Sunday-school clothing club, an infants'-school clothing club, and a coal club; the clothing clubs being under the auspices of the clergy. There is also a parochial lending library.

BEDWARDINE, ST. MICHAEL, county of WORCESTER.—See MICHAEL (ST.), BEDWARDINE.

BEDWAS (ST. BARROG), a parish, in the union of NEWPORT, partly in the hundred of CAERPHILLY, county of GLAMORGAN (South Wales), but chiefly in the Lower division of the hundred of WENTLLOOG, county of MONMOUTH ; containing 800 inhabitants, of whom 458 are in the hamlet of Upper Bedwas, and 284 in that of Lower Bedwas, 9 miles (W. by N.) from Newport. This parish, which is intersected by the river Rumney, comprises 4207 acres, whereof 339 are common or waste ; it abounds with coal, and some mines are in full operation. The living is a rectory, with the living of Ruddry annexed, valued in the king's books at £10. 14. 9½., and in the patronage of the Crown : the great tithes of Bedwas, belonging to the Bishop of Llandaff, have been commuted for £187. 12. 6., and the bishop has also 100 acres of glebe. A school is endowed with £23 per annum, derived from land.

BEDWELTY (ST. SANNAN), a parish, in the union of ABERGAVENNY, division of BEDWELTY, hundred of WENTLLOOG, county of MONMOUTH, 16 miles (N. W.) from Newport ; containing, with the hamlets of Ish-lawrcocd, Ushlawrcoed, and Mambole, 22,413 inhabitants. The parish comprises 14,516 acres, of which 3931 are common or waste : it contains extensive veins of ironstone, and is intersected in every direction by numerous tramroads; the Rumney railway, also, commences here, and joins the Sirhowey railway in the parish of Bassaleg. There are several foundries on a very large scale, for an account of which *see* Tredegar. The Rock inn is a polling-place for the election of knights of the shire. The living is a perpetual curacy;

2 C 3

BEDW

net income, £150; patron, the Bishop of Llandaff. The
church is of early English architecture: the churchyard,
which commands extensive and variegated prospects, is
surrounded with some trifling remains of an intrenchment. A district church was lately erected at Tredegar,
by aid of grants from the Parliamentary Commissioners
and the Incorporated Society; and in 1839, an act was
passed to empower the Rumney Iron Company to erect
and endow another church, the living of which is in the
gift of the Bishop. There are places of worship for Baptists, Independents, and Wesleyan and Calvinistic Methodists.

Arms.

BEDWIN, GREAT
(St. Mary), an incorporated
market-town and a parish, in
the union of Hungerford,
hundred of Kinwardstone,
Marlborough and Ramsbury,
and S. divisions of Wilts,
5½ miles (S. W. by W.) from
Hungerford, 23 (N.) from
Salisbury, and 70½ (W. by
S.) from London; including
the tythings of Crofton with
Wolfhall, East and West

Grafton, Martin, Wexcombe, and Wilton; and containing 2178 inhabitants. This place, supposed by Dr.
Stukeley to be the *Leucomagus* of Ravennas, derives its
name from the Saxon *Beeguyn*, or *Bedgwyn*, expressive
of its situation on an eminence in a chalky soil. It was
anciently a city of great extent, and the metropolis of
Cissa, one of the three sons of Ælla, the Saxon chieftain,
who invaded Britain in 477; and Cissa, when viceroy
of Wiltshire and part of Berkshire, is said to have enlarged and strengthened Chisbury Castle, now a noble
relic of Saxon earthwork, about a mile to the north-east
of the town, in the parish of Little Bedwin. In 674, a
battle was fought here between Wulfhere, King of
Mercia, and Æscuin, a nobleman in the service of Sax-
burga, Queen of Wessex; in which, after a desperate
struggle, the latter was victorious. The PARISH comprises by measurement 9353 acres of land, chiefly arable,
with a good quantity of wood and some pasture and
down; the soil consists principally of mellow earth,
resting on chalk. The surface presents numerous softly-
rounded eminences, crowned with luxuriant plantations
overhanging the picturesque valleys; and to the south
the hills rise higher, and stretch towards Salisbury
Plain. The Kennet and Avon canal passes through the
parish, and affords a medium for the conveyance of
excellent coal. The market is on Tuesday; and fairs
are held on April 23rd and July 26th: the market-
house is an ancient building situated in the principal
street.

A portreeve, who is customarily called mayor, a
bailiff, and other officers, are annually chosen at the
court leet of the lord of the manor. The borough sent
representatives to all the parliaments of Edward I.,
from the close of whose reign to the 9th of Henry V.,
there were frequent intermissions; but since then
it constantly returned two members, until its disfranchisement by the act of the 2nd of William IV., cap.
45. The LIVING is a vicarage, valued in the king's books
at £8. 10. 10.; net income, £212; patron and impropriator, the Marquess of Ailesbury. The church, the

196

from Coventry to Nuneaton. Fairs for cattle are held, but they are not much frequented. The living is a rectory, valued in the king's books at £10. 3. 11½., and in the gift of the Earl of Aylesford : the tithes have been commuted for £270, and the glebe comprises 200 acres. The church, in the year 1827, underwent a thorough repair, and was considerably enlarged; an organ was erected in 1844. There are places of worship for Baptists, Independents, and Wesleyans. The Rev. Nicholas Chamberlain, a former rector, left by will dated June 24th, 1715, property now producing about £1000 per annum, to be applied to the erection and support of schools and almshouses : upwards of 500 children are taught on the national plan, under the will ; and a number of aged men and women, with a nurse to attend them, are lodged in the houses.

BEEBY (*All Saints*), a parish, in the union of BARROW-UPON-SOAR, hundred of EAST GOSCOTE, N. division of the county of LEICESTER, 6 miles (N. E. by E.) from Leicester ; containing 115 inhabitants. It comprises by measurement 1418 acres, of which 219 are arable, and the remainder pasture. The living is a rectory, valued in the king's books at £15. 2. 6., and in the gift of the Earl of Shaftesbury : the tithes have been commuted for £300, and the glebe consists of 34 acres, with an excellent residence. The church is a handsome structure in the decorated English style, with a square embattled tower, surmounted by about 10 feet of a spire, which was commenced, but not completed.

BEECH, a village, in the parishes of STONE and SWINNERTON, union of STONE, N. and S. divisions of the hundred of PIREHILL, N. division of the county of STAFFORD ; containing 120 inhabitants. The village stands on a lofty eminence. Beech quarter, in which it is partly included, is in Stone parish, and contains also the villages of Darlaston, Tittensor, and Walton.

BEECHAMWELL, a district comprising the parish of *All Saints* and the united parishes of *St. John* and *St. Mary*, in the union of SWAFFHAM, hundred of CLACK-CLOSE, W. division of NORFOLK, 5 miles (W. S. W.) from Swaffham ; containing 246 inhabitants. The district consists of 3813 acres, of which about 2000 are rabbit-warren : the whole was the property of the late J. Mot-teux, Esq., lord of the manor, who left his Norfolk estates to the Hon. C. S. Cowper. The living of All Saints' is a discharged rectory, with that of Shingham annexed, valued in the king's books at £6. 13. 4., and in the patronage of the Crown ; the tithes of All Saints' have been commuted for £98, and the glebe contains 3 acres : the church is a ruin. St. John's and St. Mary's are discharged rectories consolidated, valued jointly at £9. 13. 4.; net income, £191; patron, the Hon. Mr. Cowper. The church of St. John's was taken down many years since ; that of St. Mary's is an ancient structure, thoroughly repaired in 1835.

BEECH-HILL, a tything, in the parish of STRAT-FIELD-SAYE, union of BASINGSTOKE, hundred of READ-ING, county of BERKS, 6 miles (S. by W.) from Read-ing ; containing 261 inhabitants, and comprising 811a. 18p. There is a place of worship for Particular Bap-tists.

BEEDING or BEAUCHAMP STOKE (*St. Ste-phen*), a parish, in the union of DEVIZES, hundred of SWANBOROUGH, Devizes and N. divisions of WILTS, 5¼ miles (E. by S.) from Devizes ; containing 187 inhabit-

197

ants. It is situated between the Marlborough downs and Salisbury Plain, and comprises about 800 acres of well-cultivated land, the soil of which consists of clay, sandy loam, and a dark rich mould. The living is a rectory, valued in the king's books at £7. 2. 11., and in the gift of George Wylde Heneage, Esq. : the tithes have been commuted for £285, and there are 30 acres of glebe. On recently opening a tumulus, a quantity of stags' horns and human bones was discovered.

BEEDING (*St. Peter*), a parish, partly in the union of STEYNING, and partly in that of HORSHAM, hundred of BURBEACH, rape of BRAMBER, W. division of SUSSEX ; comprising Upper and Lower Beeding, and containing 1389 inhabitants, of whom 614 are in the former, 1 mile (E.) from Steyning. The living is a discharged vicarage, valued in the king's books at £8; net income, £112; patrons and impropriators, the President and Fellows of Magdalen College, Oxford, who receive a tithe rent-charge of £650, and have 84 acres of glebe. The church consists of a nave and chancel separated by a screen, with a low embattled tower at the west end, and seems to have had formerly a south aisle, as there are two arches remaining in the south wall. At Lower Beeding is a district church. An alien priory of Benedictine monks was founded about 1075, the revenue of which, amounting to £26. 9. 9., was given to Magdalen College in 1459 : it stood on the brow of a high bank on the north side of the church, but every vestige of the build-ing was removed about fifty years since, when the rec-tory-house was built upon its site. A large tumulus was opened on Beeding Hill in 1800, in which more than 100 Roman urns were found.

BEEDING, LOWER, an ecclesiastical district, in the parish of BEEDING, union of HORSHAM, hundred of BURBEACH, W. division of SUSSEX, 4 miles (E. S. E.) from Horsham ; containing 775 inhabitants. This place, which comprises the forest of St. Leonard and the estate called New Park, is intersected by a branch of the river Arun which has its source within the forest near Ash-fold. Ironstone is found ; and building-stone of excel-lent quality is plentiful, and extensively quarried. In 1840 a church was erected for Lower Beeding at Plum-mer's plain, on the road from Handscross to Horsham, by subscription, aided by a grant from the Incorporated Society ; it is a neat edifice, and contains about 200 sittings, of which one-half are free. The living is en-dowed with a rent-charge on land of £135, and is in the gift of the President and Fellows of Magdalen College, Oxford, who have built a handsome parsonage-house, attached to which are 20 acres of land. A chapel, dedi-cated to St. John, was erected on the Coolhurst estate in 1839, at the expense of Charles Scrase Dickins, Esq., who also gave the site, which includes an extensive ceme-tery. The celebrated Lord Erskine resided for many years at Holmebush, in the parish.

BEEDON (*St. Nicholas*), a parish, in the union of WANTAGE, hundred of FAIRCROSS, county of BERKS, 2 miles (S. W. by W.) from East Ilsley ; containing, with the tything of Stanmore, 334 inhabitants ; and comprising 2026a. 1r., of which 119 acres are common or waste. The living is a discharged vicarage, valued in the king's books at £6. 10. 10. : the tithes have been commuted for £171 per annum, of which £27 are payable to Sir J. Reade, Bart., the patron, and £144 to the incumbent, who has also 28½ acres of glebe.

BEEFORD (St. Leonard), a parish, chiefly in the union of Driffield, but partly in the unions of Bridlington and Skirlaugh, N. division of the wapentake of Holderness, E. riding of York; comprising the townships of Beeford and Dunnington, and the chapelry of Lissett; and containing 977 inhabitants, of whom 766 are in the township of Beeford, 8 miles (E. S. E.) from Driffield. This place is of considerable antiquity, it being recorded in Domesday book that there was a church here at the time of that survey; which church was given, within a century after the Conquest, to the priory of Bridlington, by Ernald de Montbegun. The parish is on the road from Hull, through Beverley, to Bridlington and Scarborough, and comprises about 4000 acres; 897 are pasture, 120 woodland, and the remainder arable. The village is long and straggling; and on the road towards Upton are many small garths or inclosures, where houses seem formerly to have existed. The living is a rectory, valued in the king's books at £22, and in the patronage of the Archbishop of York, with a net income of £779: the tithes of Beeford township were commuted for land and a money payment in 1766. The church, which stands nearly in the centre of the village, is a spacious edifice, in a rich style of architecture, and consists of a nave, south aisle, and chancel, with a tower, which is of handsome appearance, and presents a good specimen of the later English. At Lissett is a chapel of ease, dedicated to St. James. There are places of worship for Independents and Wesleyans. An experiment has been made here of the allotment system, with about 20 acres of land divided into 68 gardens, and the advantages derived have been very great.

BEELEY, a chapelry, in the parish and union of Bakewell, hundred of High Peak, N. division of the county of Derby, 4 miles (E. by S.) from Bakewell; containing 406 inhabitants. The living is a perpetual curacy; net income, £98; patron, the Duke of Devonshire; impropriator, the Duke of Rutland: land and a money payment were assigned in lieu of all tithes in 1811. The chapel is dedicated to St. Anne. There is a place of worship for Wesleyans.

BEELSBY (St. Andrew), a parish, in the union of Caistor, wapentake of Bradley-Haverstoe, parts of Lindsey, county of Lincoln, 7 miles (S. W.) from Grimsby; containing 181 inhabitants. It comprises by computation 2200 acres; and contains some chalk-quarries, supplying a material for the roads and for making lime. The land is the property of R. J. Adeane, Esq., of Babraham Hall, Cambridgeshire, and is let in two farms, the occupiers of which have carried the cultivation to a height almost unequalled in any other part of the wapentake. The living is a rectory, valued in the king's books at £8. 17. 6., and in the patronage of the Chapter of the Collegiate Church of Southwell; net income, £500: the glebe consists of about a quarter of an acre. The church stands on a lofty hill; it is a small building, and includes a portion of an ancient structure.

BEENHAM-VALLENCE (St. Mary), a parish, in the union of Bradfield, hundred of Reading, county of Berks, 8 miles (W. S. W.) from Reading; containing 421 inhabitants. It comprises 1732a. 1r. 14p., and is bordered on the south by the Kennet and Avon canal. The living is a discharged vicarage, valued in the king's books at £7. 17.; net income, £211; patrons, the family

BEER-HACKET (*St. Michael*), a parish, in the union and hundred of Sherborne, Sherborne division of Dorset, 5 miles (S. W. by S.) from Sherborne; containing 103 inhabitants, and comprising 907 acres, of which 53 are common or waste. The living is a discharged rectory, valued in the king's books at £6. 2. 8½., and in the gift of the family of Munden, and W. Helyer, Esq., the latter of whom has every fourth presentation: the tithes have been commuted for £164, and the glebe consists of 38 acres.

· BEER REGIS (*St. John the Baptist*), a town and parish, in the union of Wareham and Purbeck, hundred of Beer Regis, Wareham division of Dorset, 7 miles (N. W.) from Wareham, and 113 (S. W.) from London; comprising the tythings of Milbourn-Styleham and Shitterton; and containing 1684 inhabitants. This place, which is supposed by Dr. Stukeley to have been the *Ibernium* of Ravennas, derives its name from the Saxon *Byrig*, and the adjunct *Regis* from its having been held in royal demesne. Elfrida, after the murder of her step-son, is said to have retired hither to avoid suspicion; and King John, who occasionally made this his residence, granted the inhabitants the privilege of a market, in the seventeenth year of his reign. Edward I. made it a free borough, but it does not appear to have ever returned any members to parliament. A great part of the town was destroyed by fire in 1634: it experienced a similar calamity in 1788, and in 1817 another destructive fire occurred, in which the parish registers were burnt. The parish comprises 7898 acres, whereof 1825 are common or waste; the cultivated land is arable, lying on chalk, and the surface is in general hilly. The town is pleasantly situated on the small river Beer; the houses, in general, are modern and well built, and the inhabitants are amply supplied with water. The market was on Wednesday, but has fallen into disuse: a fair is held on September 18th and the four following days, on Woodbury Hill, for horses, horned-cattle, sheep, cloth, and cheese. The living, which, in conjunction with that of Charmouth, formerly constituted the golden prebend in the cathedral of Salisbury, is a vicarage, with the vicarage of Winterbourne-Kingston annexed, valued in the king's books at £25. 5., and in the gift of Balliol College, Oxford; net income, £330. The great tithes of Beer Regis have been commuted for £820. 7. 6., and the vicarial for £305. 2. 6. The church is a spacious ancient structure, with a square embattled tower crowned with pinnacles. There are places of worship for Independents and Wesleyans. A charity school was founded and endowed by Thomas Williams, Esq., in 1719; the annual income is about £20. On Woodbury Hill, about half a mile from the town, is a circular camp comprehending an area of ten acres; and to the west of it are the site of the ancient chapel of Sancta Anchoretta, and a well called Anchoret's well. Dr. John Moreton, Archbishop of Canterbury, and a cardinal; and Dr. Tuberville, Bishop of Exeter, were natives of the place.

BEERHALL, a tything, in the parish and union of Axminster, county of Dorset. It was until recently included within the county of Devon.

BEES, ST. (*St. Bega*), a parish, in the union of Whitehaven, Allerdale ward above Derwent, W. division of Cumberland; comprising the town of Whitehaven, and the townships of St. Bees, Ennerdale, 199

Eskdale, Wasdale-Head, Hensingham, Kinneyside, Lowside Quarter, Nether Wasdale, Preston Quarter, Rottington, Sandwith, and Weddiker; and containing 19,687 inhabitants, of whom 557 are in the township of St. Bees, 2¾ miles (W. by N.) from Egremont. The parish extends for about ten miles along the coast, which in some parts is rocky and precipitous; and contains coal, limestone, and freestone: lead-ore is obtained at Kinneyside, where there are smelting-furnaces; and iron-ore was formerly got in Eskdale. A lighthouse erected in 1717, and subsequently destroyed by fire, was rebuilt in 1822, on a promontory called St. Bees' Head; it is furnished with nine reflectors, affording a strong light, which, from its elevated position, is seen at a great distance. The living is a perpetual curacy; net income, £103; patron and impropriator, the Earl of Lonsdale, whose tithes in the township of St. Bees have been commuted for £166. There are four separate incumbencies at Whitehaven, and one each at Ennerdale, Eskdale, Hensingham, Lowswater, Wasdale-Head, and Nether Wasdale; nearly the whole of them in the gift of the Earl. The parish church was formerly the conventual church of a monastery founded about 650, by Bega, or Begogh, an Irish female, who subsequently received the honour of canonization. The monastery was destroyed by the Danes, but was restored in the reign of Henry I., by William de Meschines, lord of Copeland, as a cell to the abbey of St. Mary at York; and in 1219 was pillaged by the Scots. Its revenue, at the Dissolution, was estimated at £149. 19. 6. The church is cruciform, and has a strong tower of early Norman architecture, but the rest of the edifice is in the decorated English style: the nave is used for the celebration of divine service. The chancel, which had long lain in a ruinous state, was repaired in 1819, and fitted up as a school of divinity, in connexion with a clerical institution founded by Dr. Law, Bishop of Chester, for the benefit of young men intended for holy orders, who do not complete their studies at Oxford or Cambridge, but receive ordination after having studied for a certain period at this place; they can, however, only enter upon their ministry within the province of York.

In addition to this, there is a celebrated *Free Grammar school*, founded by letters-patent dated April 24th, 1583, obtained by Edmund Grindall, Archbishop of Canterbury, whereby its management is intrusted to a corporation of seven governors, of whom the provost of Queen's College, Oxford, and the rector of Egremont, are always two, the former enjoying the privilege of nominating the master, who chooses an usher. The annual income, arising from land, is £125; and the school enjoys the advantage of a fellowship and two scholarships at Queen's College, Oxford, with the privilege of sending a candidate to be examined for one of five exhibitions, founded at the same college by Lady Elizabeth Hastings; a fellowship and three scholarships at Pembroke College, Cambridge; a scholarship of £4 a year at Magdalen College, Cambridge; and, in failure of scholars from the school at Carlisle, eligibility to two exhibitions founded by Bishop Thomas, at Queen's College, Oxford.

BEESBY, formerly a distinct parish, now united to Hawerby, in the union of Caistor, wapentake of Bradley Haverstoe, parts of Lindsey, county of Lincoln, 8¼ miles (N. W. by N.) from Louth; contain-

ing 43 inhabitants. The living is a rectory, consolidated
with that of Hawerby : the tithes of Beesby have been
commuted for £221. 17. 7., and there are nearly 44
acres of glebe.

BEESBY-in-the-Marsh (St. Andrew), a parish,
in the union of Louth, Wold division of the hundred of Calceworth, parts of Lindsey, county of
Lincoln, 3¼ miles (N. by E.) from Alford; containing
157 inhabitants. It comprises 1169a. 2r. 20p., of which
627 acres are arable, 518 meadow and pasture, and 26
woodland and plantations : the surface is slightly varied, and the scenery of pleasing character; the soil is
a silty clay. The living is a rectory, valued in the
king's books at £13. 10. 2½., and in the patronage of
the Crown : the tithes have been commuted for £212. 17.,
and the glebe comprises 42 acres. The church was
nearly rebuilt in 1840, at an expense of £300, chiefly by
subscription, aided by a parochial rate.

BEESTON, a hamlet, partly in the parish of
Northill, and partly in that of Sandy, union of Biggleswade, hundred of Wixamtree, county of Bedford, 3 miles (N. N. W.) from Biggleswade; containing
406 inhabitants.

BEESTON, a township, in the parish of Bunbury,
union of Nantwich, First division of the hundred of
Eddisbury, S. division of the county of Chester, 3¾
miles (S. S. W.) from Tarporley; containing 428 inhabitants. This place takes its name from a castle
founded by Ranulph de Blundeville, about 1220, and
which was made a royal garrison in the war between
Henry III. and the confederate barons. In 1643, the
castle was held by a detachment of the parliamentarian
forces, but was subsequently taken by the royalists, who,
after sustaining a protracted siege in 1645, were compelled, from want of provisions, to surrender it to the
parliamentarians, by whom it was demolished early in
the following year. The remains occupy an eminence
overlooking the Vale Royal, and include part of a tower
which guarded the principal entrance to the inner court,
flanked by semicircular bastions, and surrounded by a
moat excavated in the solid rock : the outer walls were
defended by eight round towers irregularly placed, and
now covered with ivy. The township comprises 1921
acres, the soil of which is light and clayey; it is the
property of J. Tollemache, Esq. The Beeston station
of the Chester and Crewe railway is exactly midway
between the two termini, being 10½ miles from each.
Of the ancient mansion of the Beeston family, who long
resided here, there are but small remains.

BEESTON (St. Andrew), a parish, in the union
of St. Faith's, hundred of Taverham, E. division of
Norfolk, 4 miles (N. N. E.) from Norwich; containing
46 inhabitants. It comprises by measurement 622
acres, of which 404 are arable, 137 pasture, and 81
woodland; and is intersected by the road from Norwich to North Walsham. The living is a discharged
rectory, valued in the king's books at £3. 6. 8.; net
income, £217; patron, F. R. Reynolds, Esq. There are
some slight remains of the church, which was destroyed
two or three centuries since. Beeston Old Hall, built
in 1610, is a fine specimen of ancient domestic architecture.

BEESTON (St. Lawrence), a parish, in the Tunstead and Happing incorporation, hundred of Tunstead, E. division of Norfolk, 10 miles (E. N. E.) from

varied, rising into eminences of considerable elevation, and the scenery is pleasingly diversified; the substratum abounds with coal of good quality, which has been wrought for more than two centuries, and of which several mines are still in operation. The village is on an eminence commanding a view of the town of Leeds, and the surrounding country; the air is remarkably salubrious, and several of the houses are neatly built. The inhabitants are chiefly employed in the collieries and in the woollen manufacture. The living is a perpetual curacy, in the patronage of the Vicar of Leeds, with a net income of £189, and a glebe-house. The chapel, dedicated to St. Mary, is an ancient structure in the early English style, of which, notwithstanding numerous alterations and repairs, it still retains some well-executed details; in the east window are some remains of stained glass. A pewter flagon and a plate of the same material have been used in the celebration of the communion ever since the reign of Richard I.; the cup is of silver, very ancient in form, but without a date. There is a place of worship for Wesleyans; and some small bequests are distributed among the poor.

BEESTON REGIS (*All Saints*), a parish, in the union of ERPINGHAM, hundred of NORTH ERPINGHAM, E. division of NORFOLK, 3 miles (W. N. W.) from Cromer; containing 265 inhabitants. The parish comprises 822*a*. 1*r*. 17*p*., of which 526 acres are arable, 54 meadow, 21 woodland, and the remainder heath and common; the surface is undulated, and the soil clayey and sandy. The living is a discharged rectory, valued in the king's books at £16, and in the patronage of the Duchy of Lancaster: the tithes have been commuted for £135; the glebe originally consisted of 21 acres, all of which have been washed away by the sea, excepting 4½ acres. The church is chiefly in the decorated English style, with a square embattled tower: on the south side of the chancel are two sedilia of stone, and a piscina; and in the north aisle is an altar-tomb with effigies in brass. A school was erected in 1836. Here are some remains, consisting chiefly of the west end of the church, with a small tower, and part of the chapter-house, of a priory of Augustine canons, founded in the reign of John by Lady Isabel de Cressey, and the revenue of which, at the Dissolution, was £50. 6. 4.

BEETHAM (*St. Michael*), a parish, in the union and ward of KENDAL, county of WESTMORLAND; containing, with the townships of Farleton, Haverbrack, Methop with Ulpha, and Witherslack, 1656 inhabitants, of whom 845 are in the township of Beetham, 1¼ mile (S.) from Milnthorpe. The parish comprises by computation 12,000 acres, and is situated at the south-western extremity of the county, on both sides of the estuary of the river Kent, which is navigable for small craft as far as the hamlet of Storth, and on the shore of which are two wharfs, where slate and other articles are shipped for various ports on the western coast. The Kendal and Lancaster canal, the river Belo, and some smaller streams, also intersect the parish, through which a new road was formed between Lancaster and Ulverston, about 1820. The scenery is very beautiful, of great variety, and in some parts of romantic character. The sands are well adapted for bathing, though the place is not much resorted to for that purpose. There is a manufactory for paper and pasteboard at the village, and limestone abounds within the parish. The LIVING is a

discharged vicarage, valued in the king's books at £13. 7. 4., and in the patronage of the Duchy of Lancaster; net income, £159; impropriator, G. Wilson, Esq.: there is a glebe-house. The church is an ancient structure, of a mixed style of architecture. There is a second church at Witherslack, forming a separate incumbency. A grammar school, built about 1663, and rebuilt in 1827, has an endowment of £40 per annum, arising from land. Near the school-house stood an ancient chapel, dedicated to St. John, where human bones have frequently been dug up: the site has been converted into a garden. Beetham Hall, formerly a fortified mansion situated within a spacious park, is now in ruins; and at a short distance to the south are the ruins of Helslack and Arnside towers, which were probably erected to guard the bay of Morecambe, there being remains of similar towers on the opposite shore. In digging a grave near one of the pillars in the nave of the Church, in Aug. 1834, upwards of 100 silver coins, chiefly of the reigns of William the Conqueror and his son William Rufus, with a few of Edward the Confessor and Canute the Dane, were discovered.

BEETLEY (*St. Mary*), a parish, in the union of MITFORD and LAUNDITCH, hundred of LAUNDITCH, W. division of NORFOLK, 3 miles (N. by W.) from East Dereham; containing 394 inhabitants. This parish, into which a portion of the ancient parish of Bittering has merged, comprises about 2200 acres. The living is a discharged rectory, annexed to that of East Bilney, and valued in the king's books at £9. 7. 11. The church is chiefly in the decorated English style, with a square tower; on the south side of the chancel is a piscina of good design.

BEGBROOK (*St. Michael*), a parish, in the union of WOODSTOCK, hundred of WOOTTON, county of OXFORD, 2½ miles (S. E. by S.) from Woodstock; containing 110 inhabitants, and comprising 609*a*. 2*r*. 39*p*. The living is a rectory not in charge, in the patronage of Brasenose College, Oxford: the tithes have been commuted for £145, and there are 37 acres of glebe. The church is in the Norman style, of which it contains some good details. A little westward from the church is an ancient military work, called Round Castle.

BEIGHTON (*St. Mary*), a parish, in the union of ROTHERHAM, hundred of SCARSDALE, N. division of the county of DERBY, 6 miles (E. S. E.) from Sheffield; containing 1121 inhabitants. This parish, which is situated on the banks of the river Rother, comprises by measurement 3009 acres, and contains several coalmines; stone is quarried for building and for mending roads; and the manufacture of scythes is carried on in the hamlet of Hackenthorpe. The Midland railway passes through the parish, and has a small station here. The living is a discharged vicarage, endowed with some rectorial tithes of Hackenthorpe, and valued in the king's books at £6. 11. 10½.; net income, £250; patron, Earl Manvers: the tithes were commuted for land and corn-rents in 1796, and the glebe consists of about 36 acres, with a parsonage-house. The church was re-pewed in 1816; on a beam of the roof is a date, supposed to be 1100. There is a place of worship for Wesleyans at Hackenthorpe. Some ancient earthworks on the east bank of the Rother, about half a mile from Beighton, are thought to have formed part of a Roman station.—See HACKENTHORPE.

BEIGHTON (*ALL SAINTS*), a parish, in the union of BLOFIELD, hundred of WALSHAM, E. division of NOR-FOLK, 2 miles (S. W. by S.) from Acle ; comprising 1016*a*, 37*p*., and containing 288 inhabitants. The living is a discharged rectory, valued in the king's books at £13, and in the gift of R. Fellowes, Esq.: the tithes have been commuted for £420, and there are ten acres of glebe. The church, chiefly in the decorated style, consists of a nave, chancel, and south aisle, with a low square tower, and contains remains of a carved screen.

BEIGHTON, county of SUFFOLK.—See BEYTON.

BELAUGH (*ST. PETER*), a parish, in the union of AYLSHAM, hundred of SOUTH ERPINGHAM, E. division of NORFOLK, 1¾ mile (S. E.) from Coltishall ; containing 161 inhabitants. It comprises 854*a*. 3*r*. 18*p*., of which 647 acres are arable, 182 pasture and meadow, and 21 water. The village is picturesquely situated on the summit and side of an abrupt acclivity, which rises within a semicircular curve of the river Bure. The living is a discharged rectory, with the vicarage of Scottow consolidated, valued in the king's books at £6; patron, the Bishop of Norwich. The tithes of the parish have been commuted for £222, and there are two acres of glebe, with a small house; a rent-charge of £12. 5. is also payable to the rector out of the parish of Hoveton, St. John. The church was repaired in 1831.

BELBANK, a township, in the parish of BEW-CASTLE, union of LONGTOWN, ESKDALE ward, E. division of CUMBERLAND ; containing 445 inhabitants. There are collieries and lime-works at Oakshaw, in the township.

BELBANK, a township, in the parish of STAPLE-TON, union of LONGTOWN, ESKDALE ward, E. division of CUMBERLAND, 9 miles (N.) from Brampton; containing 124 inhabitants.

BELBROUGHTON (*HOLY TRINITY*), a parish, in the union of BROMSGROVE, Lower division of the hundred of HALFSHIRE, Stourbridge and E. divisions of the county of WORCESTER, 5 miles (N. W. by N.) from Bromsgrove, on the road to Stourbridge; containing 1765 inhabitants. The parish is divided into the manors of Belbroughton, Brian's Bell, Fairfield, and Broomhill. It comprises 4733 acres, of which a considerable portion is pasture land ; the soil is fertile, producing wheat, barley, turnips, &c.; the surface is rather hilly. The manufacture of hay-knives and scythes is carried on extensively; and fairs take place on the last Monday in April, and the Monday before St. Luke's day. Mr. Rufford, banker, has a mansion here. The living is a rectory, valued in the king's books at £19; net income, £1244; patron, the President and Fellows of St. John's College, Oxford. The church is a handsome structure, with a tower and spire; it stands on the south-west side of the village, on the eastern bank of a good stream of water, which turns several mills. There is an endowment of about £10 per annum for the instruction of children. In 1833, a Roman jar, containing more than a hundred coins of the early emperors, was found on the Fern estate, near Fairfield.

BELBY, a township, in the parish and union of HOWDEN, wapentake of HOWDENSHIRE, E. riding of YORK, 1½ mile (E. by N.) from Howden ; containing 58 inhabitants. It is situated on the road between Howden and Balkholme, and comprises by computation 440 acres of land, laid out in two farms.

BELCHAMP-OTTON (*ST. ETHELBERT AND ALL SAINTS*), a parish, in the union of SUDBURY, hundred of HINCKFORD, N. division of ESSEX, 5¼ miles (N. by E.) from Castle-Hedingham ; containing 389 inhabitants. This place derives the adjunct to its name from an ancient possessor called Otton, or Otho, who held it in the reign of Henry II., and whose descendant, Otho Fitz-William, was sheriff of Essex and Hertfordshire for several successive years. The parish contains some of the highest land in the county, and comprises about 1600 acres, the soil of which is of a clayey quality. The living is a rectory, valued in the king's books at £12, and in the gift of the Rev. E. H. Dawson : the appropriate tithes belonging to the rector of Ovington have been commuted for £76. 15., and the incumbent's for £443. 5.; there are 31 acres of glebe, of which 30 are annexed to Ovington. The church, a small edifice, was repaired in 1800, when a handsome tower was erected on the site of part of a more ancient structure of Norman character.

BELCHAMP ST. PAUL'S (*ST. ANDREW*), a parish, in the union of SUDBURY, hundred of HINCKFORD, N. division of ESSEX, 3 miles (S. E. by E.) from Clare ; containing 731 inhabitants. This parish comprises by measurement 2557 acres, and, like the parishes of Belchamp-Otton and Belchamp-Walter, obtained its Norman appellation in consequence of its fertility and the beauty of its situation. It was granted by Athelstan to the cathedral of St. Paul, London, by the Dean and Chapter of which it is still possessed. The village consists of a few houses round Cole Green, on which a fair for cattle is held on the 11th of December. The living is a vicarage, valued in the king's books at £14 ; patrons and appropriators, the Dean and Chapter : the great tithes have been commuted for £288. 14., and the vicarial for £200 ; there are 79 acres of glebe. The church is a handsome edifice in the later English style, and consists of a nave, north aisle, chancel, and square tower ; in the chancel is a large window of elegant design, embellished with stained glass.

BELCHAMP-WALTER (*ST. MARY*), a parish, in the union of SUDBURY, hundred of HINCKFORD, N. division of ESSEX, 4 miles (W.) from Sudbury ; containing, with North-Wood and North-End, extra-parochial, 698 inhabitants. It is skirted on the south-east by a small brook, which separates it from the parish of Bulmer, and falls into the river Stour. The Hall, situated near the church, is a spacious mansion of modern erection, and contains many stately apartments, and a splendid collection of paintings by the first masters. The living is a discharged vicarage, consolidated with that of Bulmer, and valued in the king's books at £6. The church is a handsome edifice, partly of stone and partly of brick, and consists of a nave and chancel, with a tower; the chancel contains a marble monument to the Raymond family, and there are also some remains of a very ancient monument to one of the earls of Essex.

BELFORD (*ST. MARY*), a parish, and the head of a union, partly in ISLANDSHIRE, but chiefly in the N. division of BAMBROUGH ward, N. division of NORTHUM-BERLAND ; comprising the townships of Delchant, Easington, Easington-Grange, Elwick, Middleton, and Ross ; and containing 1789 inhabitants, of whom 1157 are in the market-town of Belford, 48 miles (N. by W.)

from Newcastle-upon-Tyne, and 318 (N. by W.) from London. The parish comprises about 7500 acres. The town is situated on a gentle eminence within two miles of the sea, of which, and of Holy Island, the Farne Islands, and Bambrough Castle, there is a fine view from the high ground on the north : the foundations of an ancient chapel may still be traced on Belford crag. It has a very pleasing appearance, and consists principally of two spacious streets, intersected by a few narrow lanes; the houses are irregularly built : the inhabitants are amply supplied with water. The neighbourhood abounds with diversified scenery and agreeable walks. Belford is mainly indebted for its rise to the spirited exertions of Mr. Dixon, a former proprietor of the manor, who built several houses on a larger and more convenient scale, cleared away unsightly objects, and established a woollen-manufactory, a tannery, &c. : his father had previously procured the privilege of holding a market and fairs. The parish abounds with coal, limestone, and freestone ; and considerable quantities of cockles, called Budle cockles, are got upon the coast. The market is on Tuesday, and is noted for corn, much of which is sold for exportation ; the fairs are on the Tuesday before Whitsuntide, and Aug. 23rd. The powers of the county debt-court of Belford, established in 1847, extend over the registration-district of Belford. The Newcastle and Berwick railway passes between the town and the sea-coast. The living is a perpetual curacy, endowed with 191 acres of land in two distant parishes ; net income, £147 ; patron and impropriator, the Rev. J. D. Clark. The church is at the north-western extremity of the town, and has been lately rebuilt in the early English style. There are places of worship for the United Secession and Presbyterians. The poor law union of Belford comprises 34 townships, of which 33 are in the county of Northumberland, and one in the county of Durham ; and contains a population of 6421. About a mile to the south-west of the town is a quadrilateral intrenchment, having an entrance on the north-east, and defended by a wide ditch and a double rampart : it is by some supposed to have been a stronghold, or place of security from the incursions of the Scots, during the border wars; by others it is thought to be of Danish origin. There are a few mineral springs.

BELGRAVE (St. Peter), a parish, in the union of Barrow-upon-Soar, partly in the hundred of West Goscote, but chiefly in that of East Goscote, N. division of the county of Leicester, 1¾ mile (N.N.E.) from Leicester ; containing, with the chapelries of Birstal and South Thurmaston, 2609 inhabitants. During the civil wars, Belgrave was the scene of many skirmishes between the royalist and parliamentarian forces ; and a field adjoining the village is called " Camp close," from part of the army under Prince Rupert having been there encamped, in 1645, at the siege of Leicester. The parish is situated on the road to Manchester, and intersected by the Leicester canal, the navigable river Soar, and the Midland railway. It comprises 1396 acres of arable and pasture land ; the soil is in general light, and the substrata are chiefly gravel, sand, marl, and clay. The inhabitants are principally employed by the hosiers of Leicester in the manufacture of stockings and socks, particularly the latter. The living is a vicarage, valued in the king's books at £13. 6. 8.; net income, £146 ;

203

patron, the Bishop of Lichfield, to whom, in right of his see, belongs the rectory, worth about £1150 per annum. The glebe of the vicarage is 25 acres, with a house erected in 1825. The church, a handsome and spacious structure, is chiefly in the decorated style of English architecture, with a square embattled tower, and a fine Norman doorway at the south entrance. At South Thurmaston is a separate incumbency. There are places of worship for Baptists, Ranters, and Wesleyans. On the inclosure of the parish, a common containing 47 acres was set apart for the town cottagers not having a right of common ; and 23 acres, with several cottages and a house, were vested in trustees for the repair of the church. Here are traces of the Roman fosse-road leading to Newark and Lincoln.

BELLASIS, a township, in the parish of Stannington, union and W. division of Castle ward, S. division of Northumberland, 6 miles (S. by E.) from Morpeth. The name, which has been variously written Beleasise, Belessys, Belasyse, &c., signifies " a handsome place," but the spot does not now, whatever its past appearance may have been, bear out the title; it is in a low situation, sheltered with rising ground to the north, and has the Blyth before it, the winding waters of which are made deep and slow by the wears of Stannington mill.

BELLASIZE, a township, in the parish of East-rington, union of Howden, wapentake of Howden-shire, E. riding of York, 5¼ miles (E. by S.) from Howden; containing, with the hamlet of Bennetland, 306 inhabitants. This place comprises by computation 1400 acres ; and includes, besides Bennetland, the farm of Green Oak, one of the three Newland farms. The village is small and scattered, and situated south of the road leading from Howden to North Cave. The impropriate tithes have been commuted for £82. 17. 6., and the vicarial for £4. 2. 1.

BELLCHALWELL, a parish, in the union of Sturminster, hundred of Cranborne, Sturminster division of Dorset, 8 miles (W. N. W.) from Blandford-Forum; containing 225 inhabitants, and comprising 1308 acres, of which 222 are common or waste. The living is a discharged rectory, united in 1776 to the rectory of Fifehead-Neville, and valued in the king's books at £7. 15. The tithes have been commuted for £260, and there are 3 acres of glebe.

BELLEAU (St. John the Baptist), a parish, in the union of Louth, Marsh division of the hundred of Calceworth, parts of Lindsey, county of Lincoln, 5 miles (N. W. by N.) from Alford ; containing, with the chapelry of Claythorpe, 193 inhabitants. The name (Belle eau) is derived from a fine stream of water, which issues from a chalk hill with considerable force. The living is a discharged rectory, to which the vicarage of Aby was united in 1732, valued in the king's books at £13. 3. 9.; net income, £300 ; patron, Lord Willoughby de Eresby.

BELLERBY, a chapelry, in the parish of Spennithorn, union of Leyburn, wapentake of Hang-West, N. riding of York, 13 miles (N. N. W.) from Bedale; containing 350 inhabitants. It is situated on the road from Richmond to Leyburn, and comprises 2917a. 2r. 28p. The living is a perpetual curacy ; net income, £70; patron and impropriator, Mr. Chaytor : the tithes were commuted for land in 1770. The chapel is a small edifice. There is a place of worship for Wesleyans.

2 D 2

BELL

BELLESTER, a township, in the parish and union of HALTWHISTLE, W. division of TINDALE ward, S. division of NORTHUMBERLAND, 16 miles (W. by S.) from Hexham; containing 116 inhabitants. The manor has, in common with other possessions in the neighbourhood, been the property of various families of consideration, and its history commences at an early period, it being conjectured that the family of Roos, of Hamlake, obtained it in marriage with Isabella, daughter of William the Lion, King of Scotland. Here are the ruins of a castle which once belonged to the Blenkinsopps, consisting of a grey pile of towers, with modern additions made in good taste by the present owner; rich, flat, alluvial ground surrounds the building on every side, and on the east and south its demesne lands are walled in with woody banks formed by the South Tyne river. The township includes the hamlet of Park, and comprises 988 acres, of which 211 are common or waste. There is a place of worship for Wesleyans.

BELLINGDON, a hamlet, in the parish of CHESHAM, union of AMERSHAM, hundred of BURNHAM, county of BUCKINGHAM; containing 173 inhabitants.

BELLINGHAM (ST. CUTHBERT), a parish, and the head of a union, in the N. W. division of TINDALE ward, S. division of NORTHUMBERLAND; comprising the townships of Charlton East and West Quarters, Leemailing, The Nook, and Tarretburn Quarter; and containing 1730 inhabitants, of whom 672 are in the market-town of Bellingham, 30 miles (W. N. W.) from Newcastle, and 298 (N. N. W.) from London. This place, from the remains of several camps apparently of Roman origin, is supposed to have been occupied by that people; but little of its early history is recorded. The Lords de Bellingham are said to have had a castle, or baronial seat, here, erected on an eminence still called Hall Field, and of which there are some slight remains. In the reigns of Richard II. and Henry IV. the manor and castle were in the possession of Richard de Bellingham; the estate afterwards became the property of the Earl of Derwentwater, upon whose attainder it was given to the governors of Greenwich Hospital. The TOWN is pleasantly situated on the northern bank of the North Tyne, between that river and a stream called Hareshaw burn, over which, near the eastern extremity of the town, a good stone bridge was erected in 1826. The rocks on each side of the burn rise precipitously to the height of 100 feet, and the water at Hareshaw-linn has a perpendicular fall of thirty feet. The smelting of iron-ore has been recently introduced by the Hareshaw Company, who have erected furnaces for the purpose, and the works already afford employment to 250 persons: many are also employed in the iron and coal mines, which are extensively worked; and sandstone of good quality for building is quarried. Fairs for cattle are held on the first Saturday after the 15th of September, and on the 12th of November. The powers of the county debt-court of Bellingham, established in 1847, extend over the registration-district of Bellingham.

This was formerly part of the extensive parish of Simonburn, which was divided into six distinct parishes by act of parliament in 1811; it comprises by measurement 20,124 acres, of which from 7000 to 8000 are moorland, abounding with grouse and other game. The LIVING is a rectory not in charge, in the patronage of the Governors of Greenwich Hospital: the tithes have

204

of several streets, is partially paved, lighted with gas, and amply supplied with water. There are five mills for the spinning of cotton, &c., belonging to Messrs. Strutt, who make their own machinery on the spot; two of these, 'and a bleaching-mill and dyehouse, are about a mile and a half lower down the river, over which the proprietors have built a neat stone bridge of two arches. Here are also two of the largest manufactories in the kingdom for silk and cotton hose, established in 1790 by Messrs. Ward, Brettle, and Ward, and now carried on by Messrs. Ward, Sturt, Sharpe, and Ward, and by George Brettle and Company, who employ more than 6000 persons, principally in the surrounding villages. The nails made here, especially those for the shoeing of horses, are much in demand. The Midland railway has a station at Belper. The market is on Saturday, and fairs are held on May 12th and Oct. 31st, for horned-cattle, sheep, and horses. The county magistrates hold a petty-session for the district every Wednesday; and courts for the manor are held when occasion requires, under the steward: the powers of the county debt-court of Belper, established in 1847, extend over part of the registration-districts of Belper and Basford.

The parish comprises 2852 acres, whereof two-thirds are pasture, and the remainder arable, with a little woodland and some ornamental planting. The LIVING is a perpetual curacy; net income, £158; patron, the Vicar of Duffield; impropriator, Lord Beauchamp. The present chapel, dedicated to St. John the Baptist, was erected in 1824, at an expense of upwards of £12,000, which was partly defrayed by a parliamentary grant; it is a handsome structure, in the decorated English style, with a lofty pinnacled tower. The old chapel, built by John of Gaunt, and the burial-ground of which is still used, is now a district church. Divine service is also performed in Bridge-Hill. There are places of worship for Baptists, Independents, Wesleyans, Primitive Methodists, and Unitarians; and a Lancasterian school, in which 500 children are taught, is supported by the proprietors of the cotton-works. Henry Smith, Esq., endowed two almshouses, and bequeathed an estate producing £30 per annum, directing the rental to be divided equally between the minister and the poor of Belper; two other almshouses were endowed by James Sims, with £12 per annum. The union of Belper comprises 35 parishes and places, and contains a population of 46,235. In a field in the neighbourhood may still be traced the massive foundations of the mansion in which John of Gaunt resided.

BELSAY, a township, in the parish of BOLAM, union of CASTLE ward, N. E. division of TINDALE ward, S. division of NORTHUMBERLAND, 13 miles (N. W.) from Newcastle-upon-Tyne; containing 312 inhabitants. The township comprises 2516 acres: the soil is of great variety, and, with the exception of some fine grass-land within the park, mostly arable, and of medium or inferior quality; there are considerable .quarries of lime and freestone. Belsay Hall, a splendid edifice of Grecian character, built by Sir Charles Monck, stands on a dry knoll, and partly occupies the site of the late chapel of Belsay; the structure is of the Doric order, and forms a square of upwards of a hundred feet. The ancient castle, supposed, from its style, to have been built in the reign of King John, stands not far from the Hall, at the head of a vale, backed by a woody 205

hill; and is reckoned one of the most perfect specimens, and certainly one of the most imposing, of Norman castellated architecture in the county. The vicarial tithes have been commuted for £10. 12. 6. On the top of the how, or hill, west of the castle, is an old Roman camp, the fosses of which are still very perfect; and below it along the back of the hill, the old village of Belshow, or Belsay, originally stood. The hill was sacred to the British god Bel, whence its name.

BELSHFORD (ST. PETER AND ST. PAUL), a parish, in the union of HORNCASTLE, N. division of the wapen-take of GARTREE, parts of LINDSEY, county of LINCOLN, 5 miles (N. E. by N.) from Horncastle; containing 554 inhabitants. It comprises about 2600 acres, of which the soil is various, and the surface very uneven; excellent limestone is found in the north-east portion of the parish. The living is a rectory, valued in the king's books at £18. 6. 8., and in the gift of the Crown, with a net income of £425: the tithes were commuted for land in 1804. There are places of worship for Primitive and Wesleyan Methodists.

BELSTEAD (ST. MARY), a parish, in the incorporation and hundred of STAMFORD, E. division of SUFFOLK, 3¾ miles (S. W.) from Ipswich; containing 261 inhabitants. It comprises about 1000 acres of land, of which the surface is hilly, and the soil light. The living is a discharged rectory, valued in the king's books at £7. 6. 0½, and in the gift of the Rev. Isaac Lockwood: the tithes have been commuted for £290, and there is a glebe of 55 acres. The church contains a tablet to the memory of Admiral Sir Robert Harland.

BELSTONE (ST. MARY), a parish, in the union of OAKHAMPTON, hundred of BLACK TORRINGTON, Black Torrington and Shebbear, and N. divisions of DEVON, 3 miles (E. S. E.) from Oakhampton; containing 208 inhabitants. This place, the name of which in the Saxon language signifies " the town of Belus, or the Sun," is situated on the great Falmouth road, by which it is divided from the parish of Sampford-Courtney; it is bounded on the east by the river Taw, which separates it from South Tawton, and on the west by the river Okemont, which separates it from the parish of Oak-hampton. According to computation it comprises about 1500 acres, of which 800 are inclosed, and with the exception of a small portion of woodland, are arable, and in good cultivation. Copper-ore is found among the mineral strata, and was formerly wrought: granite is raised in great quantities. The manufacture of blan-kets is carried on to a considerable extent, affording employment to the poor of several adjoining parishes. The living is a discharged rectory, valued in the king's books at £9. 0. 1.: net income, £154; patron, the Rev. John Hole: the glebe comprises 76 acres, with a substantial house erected in 1836. The church is an ancient structure in the Norman style. There are some remains of a Druidical circle.

BELTINGHAM, a hamlet, in the township of RID-LEY, parish and union of HALTWHISTLE, W. division of TINDALE ward, S. division of NORTHUMBERLAND, 5½ miles (E. by S.) from Haltwhistle. This place is beautifully situated upon a gentle eminence on the south side of the Tyne, and is said to have been anciently a market-town, but now consists only of four dwellings: the Newcastle and Carlisle railway passes in the vicinity. Here is a chapel supposed to have been formerly a domestic chapel to the castle of Williamswyke, but at present appropriated to public worship; it is an ancient and handsome edifice of the period of Henry VII., with elegant windows, so large and numerous, as to have led Mr. Hodgson the historian of Northumberland, to call it "a cage of light." The living is a perpetual curacy, in the patronage of the Vicar of Haltwhistle, with a net income of £75.

BELTON (*St. John the Baptist*), a parish, in the union of Loughborough, hundred of West Goscote, N. division of the county of Leicester, 5 miles (S. W. by S.) from Kegworth; containing, with the extra-parochial liberty of Grace-Dieu, 718 inhabitants. The parish comprises by measurement 1179 acres, and the liberty of Grace-Dieu 1029 acres: the soil is generally a good loam, and the surface level: limestone, porphyries, and greywacke slate are found. Many of the inhabitants are employed in framework knitting. A considerable fair for horses and cattle is held on the Monday next after Trinity week. The living is a discharged vicarage, valued in the king's books at £8. 18. 4.; net income, £204; patron, the Marquess of Hastings: the glebe consists of 117 acres. There are places of worship for Baptists and Methodists. A convent for fourteen nuns of the order of St. Augustine was founded at Grace-Dieu, in the reign of Henry III., 1240, by Roesia de Verdun, or Jocosa Varadon. In this nunnery, prior to its dissolution, great irregularities were discovered as to the lives and conduct of its inmates; and though it was licensed to continue for some time after the general suppression in 1536, it was finally surrendered in 1539, when its revenue was £101. 8. 2¼.: the remains are still to be seen. Sir John Beaumont, author of a poem entitled *Bosworth Field*, and brother of Francis Beaumont, the celebrated dramatist, was born at Grace-Dieu in 1582.

BELTON (*St. Peter and St. Paul*), a parish, in the union of Grantham, wapentake of Loveden, parts of Kesteven, county of Lincoln, 2½ miles (N. N. E.) from Grantham; containing 176 inhabitants. The living is a rectory, valued in the king's books at £12. 3. 6½., and in the gift of the Earl Brownlow :· the tithes have been commuted for £465, and the glebe comprises about 30 acres. Belton gives the title of Baron to Earl Brownlow.

BELTON (*All Saints*), a parish, in the union of Thorne, W. Division of the wapentake of Manley, parts of Lindsey, county of Lincoln, 1¾ mile (N.) from Epworth; containing, with the hamlets of Beltoft, Carr-house, Mosswood, Sandtoft, Westgate, and Woodhouse, 1706 inhabitants. At the hamlet of Sandtoft, a church was built for the Dutch and French Protestants brought over by Cornelius Vermuyden, in the reign of Charles II., to assist in draining the marshes. In opposition to this undertaking, serious riots occurred : the church was materially injured, and soon fell into decay. The females of the hamlet who intermarried with the strangers retained their maiden names after marriage, not choosing to adopt those of their foreign husbands. The living is a perpetual curacy, formerly in the gift of the Corporation of Lincoln, who, by the Municipal act, were directed to dispose of it. There is a place of worship for Wesleyans.

BELTON (*St. Peter*), a parish, in the union of Uppingham, soke of Oakham, county of Rutland, 4 miles (W. N. W.) from Uppingham; containing, with

206

Gunthorpe Lodge, 402 inhabitants. It is separated from Leicestershire by the small river Eye, and comprises 970a. 1r. 4p. of arable and pasture land in nearly equal portions; the soil is chiefly clay and gravel. The living is a vicarage, annexed to the rectory of Wardley; impropriators, the family of Bishop, and J. Eagleton, Esq. An allotment of land and a money payment were assigned, in lieu of tithes, in 1794; the glebe comprises 66 acres, with a parsonage-house, recently rebuilt by the incumbent. The church is an ancient structure, chiefly in the Norman style, and contains 400 sittings. A school is endowed with £15. 15. per annum.

BELTON (*All Saints*), a parish, in the incorporation and hundred of Mutford and Lothingland, E. division of Suffolk, 4½ miles (S. W.) from Great Yarmouth; containing 465 inhabitants. This parish, which includes the hamlet of Browston, is situated on the navigable river Waveney, and comprises 2012 acres. The living is a discharged rectory, valued in the king's books at £17. 15., and in the patronage of the Bishop of Norwich : the tithes have been commuted for £440, and there are 19 acres of glebe.

BELVOIR, an extra-parochial liberty, in the union of Grantham, partly in the soke of Grantham, parts of Kesteven, county of Lincoln, but chiefly in the hundred of Framland, N. division of the county of Leicester, 7 miles (W. by S.) from Grantham; containing 109 inhabitants. At the Conquest, the manor of Belvoir was held by Robert de Todenei, standard-bearer to William I., and whose son took the name of Albini from his marriage into a family of that name in Bretagne. King Stephen granted it to Ranulf Gernon, Earl of Chester; but in the reign of Henry II. the Albinis regained possession of it, and their heiress brought it in marriage to the family of De Ros, barons of Hamlake. In 1461, Thomas, Lord Ros, was attainted of high treason, and the honour, castle, and lordship of Belvoir were granted to William, Lord Hastings; but in 1483 his property was restored to him : subsequently, Eleanor, the sister and co-heir of Edmund, Lord Ros, married Sir Robert Manners, and the estates became vested in that family, which was afterwards ennobled. The liberty is the sole property of the Duke of Rutland, and comprises 678 acres of land.

His Grace's seat, Belvoir Castle, is one of the most magnificent mansions in the kingdom; it stands upon a lofty eminence, the sides of which are formed into terraces, at various heights, diversified with shrubs, while the base is covered with large trees, forming a complete woodland. The original foundation of the castle is involved in considerable doubt, but it is ascribed to Robert de Todenei, of whose fortress there still remains the tower, which forms the centre of the present edifice. The mansion has been at various times rebuilt or enlarged : it was completely restored in 1668, by the then Earl of Rutland,; and the present possessor had expended more than £200,000 upon alterations and improvements, when on the 26th of October, 1816, during the progress of the works, a calamitous fire consumed a great part of the building, with furniture, works of art, and upwards of one hundred pictures by the ancient and other great masters, involving a loss the amount of which was never estimated. The whole of the superb structure has been reconstructed or repaired since the fire : it is of vast extent, built of freestone, with a north-west and south-west wing, and ornamented with turrets. On the summit of Black-berry hill is a mausoleum, in which repose the two last dukes, the celebrated Marquess of Granby, and the late duchess; it contains a statue of her grace in the act of ascending to the skies, executed in Parian marble by Matthew Wyatt. The priory of Belvoir, dedicated to St. Mary, was founded near the castle, by Robert de Todenei, about 1076, for four Black monks of the order of St. Benedict, as a cell to St. Alban's: at the Dissolution, when the revenue was £135, it was granted to the Manners and Terwhit families.

BEMBRIDGE, a district chapelry, in the parish of BRADING, liberty of EAST MEDINA, Isle of Wight division of the county of SOUTHAMPTON, 4½ miles (S. E.) from Ryde by the ferry across the mouth of Brading harbour. This village, which formerly consisted only of fishermen's huts, has within the last few years become a highly interesting watering-place; and though of small extent, is the favourite resort of persons who wish to combine with the benefit of sea-bathing the enjoyment of pleasing retirement. It is situated in a beautifully secluded spot at the eastern extremity of the island of which it forms one of the most picturesque portions, and has a safe and commodious harbour for pilots and fishermen: the rides in the vicinity abound with good scenery, and the neighbourhood affords walks commanding fine views of the country adjacent. The living is a perpetual curacy, in the patronage of the Vicar of Brading, with a net income of £100: the church, dedicated to the Holy Trinity, a neat edifice in the later English style, containing 475 sittings, was erected in 1827.

. BEMERSLEY, a township, in the parish of NOR-TON-ON-THE-MOORS, union of LEEK, N. division of the hundred of PIREHILL and of the county of STAFFORD, 6¼ miles (N. N. E.) from Newcastle-under-Lyme; containing 211 inhabitants. This township includes a part of the hamlet of Whitfield, one mile north of Norton; also a small village; and a pleasant mansion called Greenway Bank.

BEMERTON (ST. ANDREW), a parish, in the union of WILTON, hundred of BRANCH and DOLE, Salisbury and Amesbury, and S. divisions of WILTS, 2 miles (W. by N.) from Salisbury; containing 109 inhabitants. The living is a rectory, united to that of Fugglestone. The place is remarkable for the celebrity of three of its rectors,—George Herbert, commonly called "the Divine," who died in 1635; John Norris, a metaphysical writer, who died in 1711; and Archdeacon Coxe, the traveller and historian, who died in 1828. The first greatly repaired the church, and rebuilt the parsonage-house at his own expense.

BEMPTON (ST. MICHAEL), a parish, in the union of BRIDLINGTON, wapentake of DICKERING, E. riding of YORK, 3¼ miles (N. N. E.) from Bridlington; containing 313 inhabitants. The parish is bounded by the North Sea, and comprises about 1600 acres, partly arable and partly grass, the latter being some of the richest grazing and feeding pastures in the East riding. The village is pleasantly situated near Flamborough Head, on the road to Scarborough. The living is a perpetual curacy, in the patronage of H. Broadley, Esq., the impropriator, and has a net income of £51: the tithes were commuted for land and a money payment in 207

1765. The church, rebuilt at the expense of the patron in 1829, is a small neat structure, with a tower at the west end. There is a place of worship for Wesleyans. Bempton was separated from the priory of Bridlington in 1474.

BENACRE (ST. MICHAEL) a parish, in the union and hundred of BLYTHING, E. division of SUFFOLK, 5 miles (N. E.) from Wangford; containing 194 inhabitants. It comprises 259a. 1r. 37p., and is situated on the sea-coast: about half a mile from the shore is a sheet of fresh water, called Benacre Broad, comprising 100 acres, and abounding with pike and other fish. Benacre Hall, a large mansion, is the seat of Sir T. S. Gooch, Bart. The living is a rectory, with that of Easton-Bavent and the vicarage of North-Ales consolidated, valued in the king's books at £18, and in the gift of Sir T. S. Gooch; the tithes have been commuted for £354, and there are 24 acres of glebe. The church consists of a nave and chancel, with a square tower. An urn containing coins of Vespasian, Trajan, Adrian, Antoninus Pius, and Marcus Aurelius, was discovered here more than sixty years since, in forming a road from Yarmouth to London.

BENAGER.—See BINEGAR.

BENEFIELD (ST. MARY), a parish, in the union of OUNDLE, hundred of POLEBROOK, N. division of the county; of NORTHAMPTON, 3½ miles (W.) from Oundle; containing 533 inhabitants. This parish, including the lordship of Liveden, comprises 4468 acres, of which above 300 are woodland, and the remainder chiefly pasture; the soil is a strong tenacious clay, with an upper surface of dark loam, and the ground is varied with some gentle undulations, though generally level. There are two villages about a mile apart, distinguished as Upper and Lower Benefield, the road from Oundle to Great Weldon proceeding through both. The living is a rectory, valued in the king's books at £35. 9. 7.; net income, £622; patron, Jesse Watts Russell, Esq., lord of the manor, and proprietor of the parish, with the exception of Liveden. The tithes were commuted for land in 1820: the old glebe, with a house and garden, is valued at £30 per annum; the entire glebe now consists of 470 acres. The church comprises a nave, north and south aisles, and a deep chancel with a chapel at the north side, and has a tower and spire; the style of the body of the edifice is the transition Norman, and of the chancel, the decorated. The whole has been just restored, and part rebuilt, and the chancel richly illuminated throughout with painting, as practised in medieval times; the windows are of stained glass, and the oak carving highly finished. About a furlong to the west of the village are nine of those cavities in the earth commonly called "Swallows," into which the waters of the land-floods flow and disappear.

BENENDEN (ST. GEORGE), a parish, in the union of CRANBROOKE, hundred of ROLVENDEN, Lower division of the lathe of SCRAY, W. division of KENT, 3¼ miles (S. E.) from Cranbrooke; containing 1594 inhabitants. The parish comprises 6507 acres, of which 104 are common or waste, and 750 in wood. It lies to the south of the London and Dover railway. Fairs for horses and horned-cattle are held on May 15th and Aug. 4th. The living is a discharged vicarage, valued in the king's books at £17. 12. 6.; patron and impropriator, T. L. Hodges, Esq.: the great tithes have been commuted for £500, and the vicarial for one of £151. The church was built in 1672, the former edifice having been damaged by lightning. Edward Gibbon, in 1602, founded a school, which was subsequently endowed with property producing £114 per annum.

BENFIELDSIDE, a township, in the chapelry of MEDOMSLEY, parish and union of LANCHESTER, W. division of CHESTER ward, N. division of the county of DURHAM, 14 miles (N. W. by N.) from Durham; containing 1074 inhabitants. The bishops of Durham formerly appointed foresters or keepers of their woods of Benfieldside, and elsewhere, within the parish. The township is on the river Derwent, which here separates the county from Northumberland; and is intersected by the Derwent and Shotley-Bridge, and the Newcastle and Stanhope, roads. It comprises 1828a. 1r. 25p., of which 1019 acres are arable, 410 pasture, 318 wood, and 80 acres highways, buildings, waste, &c.; the soil is generally clay upon a substratum of freestone rock, and the surface hilly, some of the highest hills being 700 or 800 feet above the level of the sea. There are mines of coal and ironstone, quarries of freestone in great variety, and some fine clay; the manufacture of paper is extensively carried on, and there are an iron-foundry, a saw-mill, a flour-mill, &c. A branch to Medomsley of the Pontop and South Shields railway terminates about 1½ mile from Shotley-Bridge. The lands are chiefly tithe-free. One of the first meeting-houses for the Society of Friends in the north of England was established in the township; there are also places of worship for Primitive Methodists and Wesleyans.—See SHOTLEY-BRIDGE.

BENFLEET, NORTH (ALL SAINTS), a parish, in the union of BILLERICAY, hundred of BARSTABLE, S. division of ESSEX, 2½ miles (S. S.E.) from Wickford; containing 364 inhabitants. This district, previously to its subdivision into the North and South parishes at present recognized, was the usual landing-place of the Danish pirates during their incursions into this part of the country in the 9th century; and towards the close of that century, Hesting, one of their chiefs, erected a strong castle here, in which was deposited the plunder he obtained from the inhabitants, and which was, in 894, demolished by Alfred the Great, who took Hesting's wife and two of her sons prisoners, with all their booty, to London. The parish of North Benfleet comprises about 2200 acres of flat land, of which about 700 form a portion of the isle of Canvey. The living is a rectory, valued in the king's books at £16; present net income, £600; patron and incumbent, the Rev. C. R. Rowlatt. The church has a small wooden tower with two bells, and a spire.

BENFLEET, SOUTH (ST. MARY), a parish, in the union of BILLERICAY, hundred of BARSTABLE, S. division of ESSEX, 4 miles (S. W. by S.) from Rayleigh; containing 707 inhabitants, and comprising 3056a. 1r. 32p. The village is pleasantly situated on the border of a creek which separates it from Canvey Island; and several other creeks enter the parish from the river Thames, which are noted for producing good oysters. A fair is held on the 24th of August. The living is a discharged vicarage, valued in the king's books at £16. 5. 5.; net income, £242; patrons, the Dean and Chapter of Westminster; impropriator, J. Perry, Esq. The church is a handsome edifice with a tower of stone, surmounted by a lofty spire of wood.

BENNINGHOLME, with BENNINGHOLME-GRANGE, a township, in the parish of SWINE, union of SKIR-LAUGH, Middle division of the wapentake of HOLDER-NESS, E. riding of YORK, 9 miles (N. by E.) from Hull ; containing 108 inhabitants. This place is in Domesday book called *Benincol.* In the reign of John, permission was given by the proprietors to certain ecclesiastics to fish in and render navigable the stream of Lamwith here. Among the chief owners of land in former times were the Constables, who had possessions in the township so early as the time of Henry III. : several of the farm-houses contain ancient remains. The township comprises about 1200 acres, of which 800 are arable and in cultivation, and the remainder meadow and pasture, interspersed with plantations ; the surface is level, and the scenery of pleasing character.

BENNINGTON (ST. PETER), a parish, in the hundred of BROADWATER, union and- county of HERT-FORD, 5½ miles (E. S. E.) from Stevenage ; containing 605 inhabitants. This place, which is of great antiquity, is said to have been the residence of the kings of ·Mercia, who had a palace here ; and on an intrenched eminence to the west of the church was a castle, of which little more than the site remains. The parish is intersected by the river Bene, and comprises 2900a. 1r. 6p., the soil of which rests principally on chalk ; the cottagers are chiefly employed in the making of straw-plat. The living is a rectory, valued in the king's books at £19, and in the gift of the family of Proctor : the tithes have been commuted for £635, and there are 90 acres of glebe. There is a place of worship for Wesleyans.

BENNINGTON (ALL SAINTS), a parish, and formerly a market-town, in the union of BOSTON, wapentake of SKIRBECK, parts of HOLLAND, county of LINCOLN, 5 miles (E. N. E.) from Boston ; containing 539 inhabitants. This place belonged to the family of Bay, of whom William Bay was summoned to the grand council at Westminster in 1353, as member for Boston : the ancient family mansion, Bay Hall, is still entire. The parish is situated on the sea-coast, and intersected by the road from Boston to Wainfleet : it comprises by measurement 2814a. 1r. 12p., of which two-thirds are pasture, and the remainder arable ; the soil is rich, and the substratum principally clay. The living is a rectory, valued in the king's books at £33. 8. 11½., and in the gift of the Earl of Ripon. On the inclosure of the fens and marsh lands in 1818, land was allotted in lieu of tithes ; the land comprises 426 acres, valued at £895 per annum. The church is a handsome structure in the decorated and later English styles, and contains a curious font ; on the floor of the chancel is a marble slab, from which the brasses inlaid in it were removed during the parliamentary war, under which are the remains of Bishop Wainfleet. There is a place of worship for Primitive Methodists ; also a well-endowed school. A chantry once existed here, and near the glebe-house is a piece of ground called the Chantry Pasture.

BENNINGTON, LONG (ALL SAINTS), a parish, in the union of NEWARK, wapentake of LOVEDEN, parts of KESTEVEN, county of LINCOLN, 7 miles (N. W.) from Grantham ; containing, with Bennington-Grange, extra-parochial, 1007 inhabitants. This parish, which is situated on the great north road, and bounded on

the north-east by the river Witham, comprises 4000 acres of land of a clayey soil, and has some good stone.quarries. The living is a discharged vicarage, with the living of Foston annexed ; it is valued in the king's books at £20. 1. 10., and has a net income of £463 ; the patronage and impropriation belong to the Duchy of Lancaster. The tithes were commuted for a corn-rent and an allotment of land in 1784 ; the glebe consists of about 30 acres. There is a place of worship for Wes-leyans. An alien priory of Cistercian monks was founded here about 1175, the revenue of which, in the reign of Richard II., was £50 per annum. There is a mineral spring strongly impregnated with iron.

BENNIWORTH (ST. JULIAN), a parish, in the union of HORNCASTLE, E. division of the wapentake of WRAGGOE, parts of LINDSEY, county of LINCOLN, 6½ miles (E. N. E.) from Wragby ; comprising by computation 2700 acres, and containing 488 inhabitants. The living is a rectory, valued in the king's books at £23. 8. 6¼. ; net income, £506 ; patron, G. F. Heneage, Esq.: the tithes were commuted for an allotment of land in 1770.

BENRIDGE, with KIRKLEY and CARTER-MOOR, a township, in the parish of PONTELAND, union, and W. division of CASTLE ward, S. division of NORTHUMBER-LAND, 9½ miles (N. W. by N.) from Newcastle-upon-Tyne ; containing 168 inhabitants. This place comprises 1085 acres, of which 27 are common or waste ; it is situated to the south of the river Blyth, and east of the road from Newcastle to Rothbury.

BENRIDGE, a township, in the parish of MIT-FORD, union of MORPETH, W. division of MORPETH ward, N. division of NORTHUMBERLAND, 2 miles (W. N. W.) from Morpeth ; containing 70 inhabitants. This place, formerly Benrigge, or the "high ridge," derives its name from its situation on the slope of a lofty ridge of land that runs through the township from east to west. Possessions have been held here by the families of Bertram, Eure (of which was Sir Ralph Eure, a man of consideration in the county), Bolbeek, Herle, Greystock, and Dacre ; the present owners of the estate are the Howards, represented by the Earl of Carlisle. The township comprises 1085 acres of open ground, and about 20 of wood ; and consists of several farms, three of which form a straggling hamlet, on the south side of the highway between Stanton and Morpeth, and probably occupy the site of the ancient vill. The impropriate tithes have been commuted for £84.

BENSINGTON, or BENSON (ST. HELEN), a parish, in the parliamentary borough and the union of WAL-LINGFORD, partly in the hundred of DORCHESTER, but chiefly in that of EWELME, county of OXFORD, 1½ mile (N. N. E.) from Wallingford ; containing, with the hamlets of Fifield, Preston-Crownmarsh, and Roke, 1234 inhabitants. In this parish was a strong fortress of the Britons, from whom it was taken on their defeat at Bedford, in 571, or, according to some authorities, in 560, by Cealwyn, third king of the West Saxons. It subsequently fell into the power of the Mercians, from whom it was seized by Cuthred, King of the West Saxons, who, revolting from Ethelbald, King of Mercia, defeated him at Burford in 752 ; but it was finally surrendered by the West Saxons to Offa, King of Mercia, who, enraged at the obstinate resistance of the garrison, dismantled the fortifications. The Roman way leading from Alchester to Wallingford crossed the Thames here ; and there was anciently a royal palace in the vicinity. The parish contains 2880a. 2r. 13p., of which 2119 acres are arable, 344 meadow, 92 woodland, and 200 pasture. The living is a perpetual curacy; net income, £180 ; patrons and appropriators, the Dean and Canons of Christ-Church, Oxford. The great tithes have been commuted for £1046, with a glebe of 17½ acres, and those of the incumbent for £157. 10., with a glebe of 3½ acres.

BENTFIELD, a hamlet, in the parish of STANSTED-MOUNTFITCHET, union of BISHOP-STORTFORD, hundred of CLAVERING, N. division of ESSEX, 1¾ mile (N. W. by N.) from Stansted-Mountfitchet ; containing 496 inhabitants. It is situated near the river Stort.

BENTHALL (ST. BARTHOLOMEW), a parish, in the union of MADELEY, liberties of the borough of WENLOCK, S. division of SALOP, 2½ miles (N. E. by N.) from Wenlock ; containing 587 inhabitants, who are principally employed in potteries. The navigable river Severn flows past the place. The living is a perpetual curacy ; net income, £93 ; patron, the Vicar of Wenlock ; impropriator, Thomas Harries, Esq.

BENTHAM, a hamlet, in the parish of BADGE-WORTH, Upper division of the hundred of DUDSTONE and KING'S BARTON, E. division of the county of GLOUCESTER, 4 miles (S. W. by S.) from Cheltenham; containing 236 inhabitants.

BENTHAM (ST. JOHN THE BAPTIST), a parish, in the union of SETTLE, W. division of the wapentake of STAINCLIFFE and EWCROSS, W. riding of YORK ; containing 3535 inhabitants, of whom 2180 are in the township of Bentham, 10 miles (W. N. W.) from Settle. This parish is situated on the confines of the county of Lancaster, and comprises 25,811a. 13p., of which 7972a. 27p. are in the township of Bentham ; of the latter portion about 2000 acres are common or waste: the soil is poor, resting on a substratum of gritstone. The surface is varied, and the lands are watered by the rivers Greta and Wenning ; the former has its source in the higher parts of the parish, and the latter in the adjoining parish of Clapham, and both after flowing through the parish fall into the river Lune. The township contains the villages of Upper and Lower Bentham. The inhabitants are chiefly employed in the spinning of flax and the weaving of linen, for which extensive mills have been erected by Messrs. Hornby and Roughsedge ; and there are some potteries for various kinds of earthenware. A market is held on Monday at Upper Bentham; and fairs take place on the 5th of February, Easter-Tuesday, the 22nd of June, and the 25th of October.

The LIVING is a rectory, valued in the king's books at £35. 7. 8½., and in the patronage of James William Farrer, Esq. : the tithes have been commuted for £675, and there is a good glebe-house. The church, situated at Lower Bentham, is a handsome structure in the later English style, with a square embattled tower ; the nave was rebuilt and enlarged in 1832. An additional church, in the later English style, with a square embattled tower crowned by pinnacles, has been erected at Upper Bentham, by Hornby Roughsedge, Esq., at an expense of £1800 ; the east window is embellished with stained-glass, and contains a painting of the Last Supper. There is a chapel at Ingleton, in the parish, a very ancient edifice : also one at Ingleton-Fell. The free school was

county of WARWICK, 3 miles (S. W.) from Atherstone; containing 266 inhabitants. It lies on the road from Atherstone to Coleshill, and comprises 1835 acres. The chapel, which was dedicated to the Holy Trinity, has long been in ruins.

BENTLEY, a village, in the parish of ROWLEY, wapentake of HARTHILL, Hunsley-Beacon division, E. riding of YORK, 2½ miles (S.) from Beverley; containing 62 inhabitants. This place is situated in the northern part of the parish, and on the road from Beverley to Hessle. In a hedge, east of the village, stands part of one of the ancient crosses that marked the limits of the sanctuary of Beverley minster.

BENTLEY, a township, in the parish of ARKSEY, union of DONCASTER, N. division of the wapentake of STRAFFORTH and TICKHILL, W. riding of YORK, 2 miles (N. W. by N.) from Doncaster; containing 790 inhabitants. This village is about a mile from that of Arksey, and has grown up round an ancient manor-house, now known only by its site, but which was formerly the seat of some very eminent persons, and the head of one of the most considerable tenancies of the castle and honour of Tickhill. The tithes were commuted for land and a money payment under an act passed in the 7th and 8th of George IV. There is a place of worship for Wesleyans.

BENTLEY, FENNY (ST. MARY MAGDALENE), a parish, in the hundred of WIRKSWORTH, S. division of the county of DERBY, 2½ miles (N. by W.) from Ashbourn; containing 343 inhabitants. The manor belonged to a branch of the Beresfords of Staffordshire, who settled at this place in the reign of Henry VI. The elder branch of the Beresfords of Bentley, soon became extinct in the male line, and the manor came, by marriage with their heiress, to the Beresfords of Staffordshire, from whom it passed into various hands. Of the manor-house, a castellated mansion, there are still some remains. The parish is situated on the road from Ashbourn to Tissington, and comprises about 1000 acres, mostly good pasture land : there is a limestone-quarry. The living is a discharged rectory, valued in the king's books at £6. 12. 10., and in the gift of the Bishop of Lichfield : the tithes have been commuted for £60, and the glebe consists of 35 acres, with a house. The church is a small structure with a square tower, and has a curious richly-carved screen : it contains a monument, with figures of his sixteen sons and five daughters, to one of the Beresford family, who distinguished himself in the wars with France, and died in 1473.

BENTLEY, GREAT (ST. MARY), a parish, in the union and hundred of TENDRING, N. division of ESSEX, 8 miles (E. S. E.) from Colchester; containing 1005 inhabitants. This parish, which on the west is bounded by a small creek flowing into the river Colne, is about eleven miles in circumference; the surface is diversified with hill and valleys, and the general scenery is cheerful. Fairs are held on the Monday after Trinity-Monday, for cattle; the last Friday in Sept., for sheep; and the Monday after St. Swithin's-day. The living is a discharged vicarage, valued in the king's books at £7, and in the patronage of the Bishop of London : the impropriate tithes, belonging to the landowners, have been commuted for £674, and the vicarial for £250; the glebe consists of 13 acres. A rent-charge of £59 is also paid to Gonville and Caius College, Cambridge. The

church, beautifully situated near a pleasant green, is a spacious and venerable structure, in the Norman style. There is a place of worship for Wesleyans; and a school is endowed with about £15 per annum.

BENTLEY, HUNGRY, a liberty, in the parish of LONGFORD, hundred of APPLETREE, S. division of the county of DERBY, 5¾ miles (S.) from Ashbourn; containing 83 inhabitants. The manor belonged to Henry de Ferrars when the Domesday survey was taken; afterwards to the Blounts, lords Mountjoy; and more recently to the Browne and Wilmot families. The small village is about two miles west of the village of Longford. The vicarial tithes have been commuted for £67. 10. Here was a chapel, long since demolished.

BENTLEY, LITTLE (ST. MARY), a parish, in the union and hundred of TENDRING, N. division of ESSEX, 5 miles (E.) from Colchester; containing 472 inhabitants. It comprises 2000a. 2r. 14p., of which 1660 acres are arable, 135 pasture, and 162 woodland. The living is a rectory, valued in the king's books at £13, and in the patronage of Emmanuel College, Cambridge : the tithes have been commuted for £650, and there are 58 acres of glebe. The church is an ancient building, consisting of a nave, north aisle, and chancel, with a tower of stone. A chantry was founded by Sir John Le Gros. There is a place of worship for Wesleyans; and a school is partly supported by the rector.

BENTLEY-PAUNCEFOOT, a township, in the parish of TARDEBIGG, union of BROMSGROVE, Upper division of the hundred of HALFSHIRE, DROITWICH and E. divisions of the county of WORCESTER, 3 miles (W. by S.) from Redditch; containing 238 inhabitants. It comprises 1587 acres, whereof two-thirds are arable, 70 acres woodland, and the rest pasture. The soil is partly light and partly a strong marl, and of full average fertility : the surface is elevated, moderately undulated, and well watered; and the scenery pleasing. The principal proprietor, and lord of the manors of Upper and Lower Bentley, is William Hemming, Esq., of Foxlydiate House, a handsome seat in the vicinity. Bentley Lodge is an elegant mansion, surrounded by fertile lawns, pleasant walks, and extensive drives. The township seems to have been formerly a distinct chapelry : in consequence of a dispute which arose between the parishioners, searches were made, and the ruins of the old chapel found. It was dedicated to St. Stephen.

BENTON, LITTLE, a township, in the parish of LONG BENTON, union of TYNEMOUTH, E. division of CASTLE ward, S. division of NORTHUMBERLAND, 2½ miles (N. E.) from Newcastle; comprising an area of 573a. 3r. 10p., whereof 24 acres are common or waste. A part of the population is employed in Bigge's-main colliery. Benton Park mansion, originally built a century ago, and enlarged in 1769, came by purchase, in 1838, with 90 acres of demesne, into the possession of Mr. Potts, who has entirely re-beautified the interior. The vicarial tithes have been commuted for £9. 7., and those of corn and hay for £135. 17. In the park grounds is an old font, with the date 1069.

BENTON, LONG (ST. BARTHOLOMEW), a parish, in the union of TYNEMOUTH, E. division of CASTLE ward, S. division of NORTHUMBERLAND, 3½ miles (N. E. by N.) from Newcastle-upon-Tyne; containing 8711 inhabitants, of whom 2451 are in the township of Long Benton. This parish is bounded on the south by the river Tyne.

and intersected from east to west by the North Shields and Newcastle railway, and turnpike-road; it extends eight miles and a half from north to south, and at the widest point is about three in breadth. The whole comprises, with the townships of Weetsleet, Killingworth, Little Benton, and Walker, 8869a. 2r. 7p. The township of Long Benton, occupying about the middle of the parish, consists of 3301a. 35p., of which 85 acres are common or waste. On the banks of the river are various large manufactories, and staiths for shipping coal; and the district contains many extensive collieries, which are now nearly exhausted as respects coal for domestic purposes, though much remains applicable to steam-furnaces: in Weetsleet and Walker townships are some freestone-quarries. The village of Long Benton, consisting for the most part of one long street, is built upon a rock, in a pleasant and healthy situation. The LIVING, a discharged vicarage valued in the king's books at £3. 1. 3., is in the gift of Balliol College, Oxford, in whose favour an impropriation was made, on the grant of Sir Philip Somervyle, in 1342. The corn and hay tithes have been commuted for about £1500, of which £687. 11. are derived from the township of Long Benton, and the vicarial tithes for £120, of which £52 are for the township; the glebe consists of about 80 acres. The church, which stands in a spacious burial-ground, a short distance north of the village, was rebuilt, with the exception of the chancel, in 1791. At Walker is a separate incumbency. There are several places of worship for dissenters. The Roman wall of Severus passed through the parish before its immediate termination at Wallsend: on the line of this wall was an ancient chapel, and another chapel is traditionally spoken of as having stood near Low Weetsleet; both have long since disappeared. Among the eminent persons connected with the place, may be named the celebrated Dr. Charles Hutton, and George Stephenson, the railway engineer, the former of whom, when a boy, worked in the pits at Long Benton colliery, and the latter was a brakesman at Killingworth colliery.

BENTWORTH (St. Mary), a parish, in the union of Alton, hundred of Odiham, Basingstoke and N. divisions of the county of Southampton, 4 miles (W.) from Alton; containing 609 inhabitants. On the loss of Normandy, Peter, Archbishop of Rouen, obtained license, in the 9th of Edward III., to alienate his manor of "Binterworth," which he held in free socage, to William de Melton, Archbishop of York. The living is a rectory, valued in the king's books at £14. 10. 5., and in the gift of the Rev. Thomas Matthews: the tithes have been commuted for £907. 10., and the glebe comprises 90 acres with a house. George Withers, the poet, was born here in 1588.

BENWELL, a district chapelry comprising the township of Benwell and part of that of Elswick, in the parish of St. John, Newcastle, union of Newcastle, W. division of Castle ward, S. division of Northumberland; containing 2415 inhabitants, of whom 1433 are in the township of Benwell, 2½ miles (W.) from Newcastle. This place, anciently Benwall, or By-the-Wall, the Roman wall having passed this way, is supposed to occupy the site of the Condercum of the Notitia. The township comprises by measurement 1074 acres, chiefly elevated land, rising gradually and beautifully from the Tyne; the soil is generally good, and

BEPTON, or BEBTON, a parish, in the union of MIDHURST, hundred of EASEBOURNE, rape of CHICHESTER, W. division of SUSSEX, 2¾ miles (S. W.) from Midhurst; containing 207 inhabitants. The parish comprises a portion of the South Downs, and part of it is comprehended within the borough of Midhurst. It contains by estimation 1098 acres, of which 312 are arable, 434 meadow and pasture, 100 woodland, and 252 common and down land. The living is a rectory, valued in the king's books at £8, and in the gift of the family of Poyntz : the tithes have been commuted for £140, and the glebe comprises 20 acres. The church consists of a nave and chancel, and is in the early English style.

BERDON (ST. NICHOLAS), a parish, in the union of BISHOP-STORTFORD, hundred of CLAVERING, N. division of Essex, 5 miles (S. W.) from Newport; containing 391 inhabitants. It is on the east borders of the county of Hertford, and comprises 1771a. 3r. 37p.; the soil, which is chiefly strong and heavy, is in some parts light, but generally fertile. An act for inclosing lands was obtained in 1838, at which time 13 acres were appropriated for the recreation of the inhabitants. The living is a perpetual curacy, till lately annexed to the vicarage of Ugley : the tithes are impropriate in the patrons, the Governors of Christ's Hospital, and have been commuted for £360. The church is an ancient edifice. A priory of Augustine canons was founded in the reign of Henry III., the revenue of which at the Dissolution amounted to £35. 5. 1¼. The Rev. Joseph Mede, a learned commentator on the Book of Revelation, was born here in 1586.

BERE-CHURCH (ST. MICHAEL), a parish, in the union, and within the liberties of the borough, of COLCHESTER, N. division of Essex, 2¼ miles (S. by W.) from Colchester; containing 146 inhabitants. The living is a perpetual curacy ; net income, £100 ; patron and impropriator, Sir G. H. Smyth, Bart., of Bere-Church Hall, to whose family, and to Lord Audley, there are monuments in the church.

BERGH-APTON (ST. PETER AND ST. PAUL), a parish, in the union of LODDON and CLAVERING, hundred of CLAVERING, E. division of NORFOLK, 7½ miles (S. E.) from Norwich; containing 564 inhabitants. It comprises 1938a. 3r. 21p.; and was formerly two parishes, Bergh and Apton. The living is a rectory, to which a mediety of the rectory of Holveston is annexed, valued in the king's books at £13. 6. 8., and in the gift of the Earl of Abergavenny : the tithes have been commuted for £585, and the glebe comprises 48 acres, with a handsome house attached. The church, situated on an eminence, is a neat cruciform structure, enlarged in 1838. There is a town estate, consisting of 60 acres, which lets for £80, applied to general purposes ; also a poor's estate, comprising 23 acres, which lets for £26 per annum. A church existed at Apton, dedicated to St. Martin, but there are no remains of it.

BERGHOLT, EAST (ST. MARY), a parish, in the incorporation and hundred of SAMFORD, E. division of SUFFOLK, 3½ miles (N. W.) from Manningtree; containing 1461 inhabitants. This place, the name of which implies " Wooded Hill," comprises 3063a. 2r. 34p. It is pleasantly situated in the most cultivated part of the county, on a spot overlooking the fertile valley of the Stour; and the vicinity is remarkable for the beauty of its gentle declivities, luxuriant meadows, well-tilled up-213

lands, and woods and streams : the river Stour forms the southern boundary of the parish. The Knights Templars had a manor here. The living is a rectory, consolidated with that of Brantham : the tithes have been commuted for £820, and there are 20½ acres of glebe. The church is a large and handsome edifice, of which the steeple was never finished. There is a place of worship for Independents. Lettice Dykes, in 1589, gave property, now producing about £40 per annum, to endow a free school, which was built by subscription on land given by Edward Lamb. John Constable, the distinguished painter, was born here in 1776; and of the scenery of the neighbourhood he used often to speak, as having made him an artist.

BERGHOLT, WEST (ST. MARY), a parish, in the union of LEXDEN and WINSTREE, Colchester division of the hundred of LEXDEN, N. division of Essex, 3½ miles (N. W.) from Colchester ; containing 822 inhabitants. It comprises 2274a. 18p., of which 1733 acres are arable, 119 pasture, 108 wood, and 312 common or waste. The living is a rectory, valued in the king's books at £10 ; net income, £454 ; patron, William Fisher, Esq. The church is an ancient edifice, consisting of a nave and south aisle separated by massive pillars, and a chancel, with a wooden turret surmounted by a shingled spire. A chantry was founded here in 1331, by J. De Bures, for a priest to officiate at the altar of the Virgin Mary. There is a place of worship for Wesleyans.

BERKELEY (ST. MARY), a market-town and parish, in the union of THORNBURY, Upper division of the hundred of BERKELEY, W. division of the county of GLOUCESTER, 17 miles (S. W.) from Gloucester, 19 (N. E.) from Bristol, and 114 (W. by N.) from London ; comprising the tythings of Alkington, Breadstone, Ham, Hamfallow, and Hinton, and the chapelry of Stone ; and containing 4405 inhabitants. This place, according to Sir Robert Atkyns, the historian of Gloucestershire, derives its name from the Saxon Beorc, a birch-tree, and Leas, a pasture ; whence it has been inferred that the parish was formerly remarkable for the growth of birch-trees. From the fertility of the soil, and its contiguity to the river Severn, it was always a place of considerable importance ; and at a very early period it gave name to the great manor of Berkeley, which during the heptarchy was held of the crown, at £500. 17. 2. per annum, by ROGER de BERKELEY, a near relative of Edward the Confessor, and lord of Dursley, from whom the earliest authentic pedigree of the Berkeley family is deduced. Berkeley, notwithstanding the residence of the oldest branches of the family in their castle at Dursley, was a market-town ; and had a nunnery endowed with the large manor. The time of the foundation of this establishment, and the name of the founder, are not known ; but its suppression, prior to the Conquest, was effected by the perfidious avarice of Earl Godwin, who, in order to obtain its ample revenues, introduced his nephew into the convent for the purpose of seducing the sisterhood, and, on the accomplishment of the design, artfully reporting to his sovereign the state of the establishment, procured its dissolution, and was rewarded for his treachery with a grant of its lands. A few years afterwards, William the Conqueror, professing high regard for all the relatives of Edward the Confessor, granted the manor of Berkeley to Roger Berkeley, of Dursley, by whose descendants it was held till the reign of Henry II., when, refusing to pay the fee-farm rent, and also taking part with Stephen, they were dispossessed by the former monarch, who bestowed the manor upon Robert Fitzhardinge, the descendant of a younger son of the king of Denmark, and at that time mayor of Bristol, who, being a man of great wealth, materially assisted Henry in his contest with Stephen. Fitz-Hardinge, however, was so greatly annoyed in his new possession by the Berkeleys of Dursley, that Henry II. interfered to make peace, which he ultimately effected by arranging a marriage between Maurice, son of Robert Fitz-Hardinge, and the daughter of Roger de Berkeley, upon which the former assumed the name of Berkeley. From this union descended the present family of Berkeley; the male issue of the Berkeleys of Dursley became extinct in 1382.

The CASTLE, erected during this reign, at the south-east end of the town, out of the ruins of the ancient nunnery, was considerably enlarged by successive proprietors in the reigns of Edward II. and III., and became one of the principal baronial seats in the kingdom. It has been connected with many transactions of intense political interest, and in the reign of John was one of the places of rendezvous for the confederate barons, who extorted from that monarch the grant of Magna Charta. Edward II. after his deposition was detained a prisoner in the castle under the alternate custody of Lords Berkeley, Montravers, and Gournay; and, during the illness of the first, by whom he had always been treated with kindness and humanity, was barbarously murdered by the two latter: the room and bed in which the murder was perpetrated are still shown to persons visiting the castle. During the reigns of Henry VI. and Edward IV. the town suffered materially from the attacks of the Earl of Warwick, who, in right of his wife, laid claim to the castle, of which he endeavoured to obtain possession by force; and in the civil war of the 17th century, being garrisoned for the king, it was besieged by the parliamentarians, to whom, after a vigorous resistance of nine days, it was compelled to surrender. The castle and estates are now the property of Earl Fitz-Hardinge, to whom they were devised by his father, the late Earl of Berkeley. The castle occupies a site nearly circular in form. The entrance from the outer into the inner court is through a massive arched portal, on the left of which is the keep, a fine specimen of Norman military architecture, containing the dungeon chamber, without either window or chimney, in which Edward II. was confined; in the floor is an opening to the dungeon, which is twenty-eight feet deep. The great hall was built in the reign of Edward III.

The TOWN is situated on a gentle eminence in the beautiful vale of Berkeley, at the distance of two miles from the river Severn, the tides of which, flowing up the Berkeley Avon, render it navigable to the town for vessels of forty or fifty tons' burthen. At present, the place consists only of two streets irregularly built, the principal of which is well paved and contains a few good houses: the surrounding scenery is pleasing; and the ancient castle, which has been partly modernised as the residence of Earl Fitz-Hardinge, forms an interesting feature in the landscape. The trade is principally in coal, which is brought from the Forest of Dean, by the rivers Severn and Avon, for the supply of the neighbourhood. The Berkeley and Gloucester ship canal joins the Severn

and tower are later English : under the chancel is a handsome crypt. Certain lands in the parish are charged, by a recent order of the Lord Chancellor, with the payment of £50 per annum for a schoolmaster ; and there are considerable funds for the benefit of the poor, of which the churchwarden and rector are trustees.

BERKHAMPSTEAD, or NORTH-CHURCH (ST. MARY), a parish, in the union of BERKHAMPSTEAD, hundred of DACORUM, county of HERTFORD, 1½ mile (N. W. by W.) from Great Berkhampstead ; containing 1265 inhabitants. It comprises 3885a. 2r., of which about 1600 acres are arable, and 206 wood ; and surrounds Great Berkhampstead : the village is situated in a valley. The living is a rectory, valued in the king's books at £21. 1. 3., and in the patronage of the Duchy of Cornwall : the tithes have been commuted for £900, and there are nearly 11 acres of glebe. On the top of the western hill are the small but interesting ruins of Marlin chapel, which is supposed to have been demolished by Oliver Cromwell ; the walls are chiefly supported by ivy of strong and luxuriant growth, and in the area are large timber-trees.

Arms.

BERKHAMPSTEAD, GREAT (ST. PETER), a market-town and parish, and the head of a union, in the hundred of DACORUM, county of HERTFORD, 25½ miles (W. by S.) from Hertford, and 26 (N. W. by W.) from London ; containing 2979 inhabitants. The Saxon name of this place, *Berghamstede*, is derived from its situation, either on a hill or near a fortress, which latter, from the site of the present town, appears to be the more probable. It is a town of considerable antiquity, the kings of Mercia having had a castle here, to which circumstance may be attributed its early growth and subsequent importance. According to Spelman, Wightred, King of Kent, assisted at the council held here in 697. At the time of the Conquest, William, on his arrival at the place, was met by Stigand, Archbishop of Canterbury, who tendered his submission ; but on leaving Berkhampstead, the king's march was greatly obstucted by the opposition of Frederick, abbot of St. Alban's, who caused the roads to be blocked up, by cutting down the trees, and, on William's arrival at St. Alban's, exacted an oath from him that he would observe the ancient laws of the realm, particularly those of Edward the Confessor. Robert, Earl of Moreton, to whom the Conqueror gave the town, built a castle, which was subsequently taken from his son William, who had rebelled against Henry I., and by that monarch's order razed to the ground. Henry II. held his court here for some time, and conferred many privileges on the town. The castle was rebuilt in the reign of John, and soon after besieged by Louis, Dauphin of France, who had come over to assist the barons that were in arms against the king. In the 11th of Edward III., Berkhampstead sent two representatives to the great council at Westminster ; and James I., who selected the place as a nursery for his children, granted the inhabitants a charter of incorporation ; but they were so impoverished during the civil war in the reign
215

of his son Charles I., that they were unable to maintain their privileges, and the charter became forfeited.

The TOWN is pleasantly situated in a deep valley, on the south-western bank of the river Bulbourne, and consists of two streets intersecting at right angles, the principal of which, nearly a mile in length, contains several handsome houses ; the air is highly salubrious, and the inhabitants are amply supplied with water. Assemblies are held regularly during the season. The manufacture of wooden bowls, spoons, and other articles of a like kind, formerly prevailed, but it is on the decline ; and the making of lace, which was also carried on extensively, has given place to the platting of straw, in which the female part of the population are chiefly employed. The Grand Junction canal, which passes by the town, affords an extensive line of inland navigation ; and the railroad from London to Birmingham runs close to the canal, and has a station at this point. The market is on Saturday ; the market-house is an ancient building in the centre of the town. Fairs are held on Shrove-Tuesday and Whit-Monday, and there is also a statute-fair at Michaelmas. The county magistrates hold a petty-session on the first and third Tuesdays in every month ; and a court leet for the honour of Berkhampstead, which is part of the duchy of Cornwall, is held at Michaelmas. The prison is used as a house of correction, and for the confinement of malefactors previously to their committal to the county gaol.

The parish comprises 4341 acres, of which 1197 are common or waste. The LIVING is a rectory, valued in the king's books at £20, and in the patronage of the Duchy of Cornwall : the tithes have been commuted for £434, and there are two acres of glebe. The church is a spacious cruciform structure, exhibiting some fine portions of the several styles of English architecture ; the tower, rising from the intersection, and highly enriched with sculpture, was built by Richard Torrington, in the reign of Henry VIII. Within the church are two chapels at the eastern end, one dedicated to St. John, the other to St. Catharine ; and some interesting monuments. There are places of worship for Baptists, the Society of Friends, and Independents. The free grammar school was instituted in the time of Henry VIII., and endowed with lands belonging to the dissolved guild of St. John the Baptist : in the succeeding reign it was made a royal foundation ; the master, usher, and chaplain, were incorporated by act of parliament ; and the warden of All Saints' College, Oxford, was appointed visiter. A charity school called the Blue-coat school, for twenty boys and ten girls, was founded in 1727, by Thomas Bourne, who endowed it with £8000 ; the property now consists of £9300 in the New South Sea annuities. Almshouses for six aged widows were founded in 1681, and endowed with £1000, by Mr. John Sayer ; whose endowment was augmented with £300 by his widow, in 1712 ; with £26. 5. per annum by Mrs. Martha Deere, in 1784 ; and with £400 by the Rev. Geo. Nugent and Mrs. Elizabeth Nugent, in 1822. King James I. gave £100, and Charles I. £200, for providing employment and fuel for the poor, and there are several other bequests for charitable uses. The union of which the town is the head comprises ten parishes and places, of which seven are in the county of Hertford, and three in that of Bucks ; and contains a population of 11,512. There are slight vestiges of the ancient residence of the Mercian kings, on the north side of the town; and at the north-east end of Castle-street are the remains of the castle, consisting principally of walls of an elliptical form, defended on the north-west side by a double, and on the other sides by a triple, moat: the entrance was at the south-east angle, where there are two wide piers, between which probably was the drawbridge. An hospital, dedicated to St. James, formerly existed; but there are no vestiges of it. At the end of the High-street is a spring of clear water, called St. James's well, to which medicinal properties are attributed. The poet Cowper was born in the town in 1731.

BERKHAMPSTEAD, LITTLE (ST. ANDREW), a parish, in the union, hundred, and county of HERTFORD, 4¾ miles (S. W. by S.) from Hertford; containing 555 inhabitants. The surface is hilly, and the soil consists of clay and gravel. The living is a rectory, valued in the king's books at £7. 8. 6½., and in the gift of the Marquess of Salisbury: the tithes have been commuted for £250. 18. 4., and there are nearly 39 acres of glebe. At How Green is a place of worship for Wesleyans. On an elevated situation near an old manor-house, a circular tower of brick 100 feet in height, termed the Observatory, has been erected, which commands an extensive prospect.

BERKLEY (ST. MARY), a parish, in the union and hundred of FROME, E. division of SOMERSET, 2¾ miles (E. N. E.) from Frome, and on the road from Bath to Salisbury; containing 496 inhabitants. This place appears to have formed part of the possessions of the Newborough family, who were relatives to, and came over to England with, William the Conqueror, and one of whose descendants, Thomas Newborough, was interred in the church in 1531. The parish comprises about 1800 acres, is richly wooded, and abounds with pleasing scenery; freestone resembling that of Bath, but of harder quality, is extensively quarried for building, and limestone abounds. The living is a rectory, valued in the king's books at £7. 9. 7., and in the gift of Sir John Mordaunt: the tithes have been commuted for £354, and the glebe comprises 55¼ acres. The church was erected in 1751. Sir John Colborne, afterwards Lord Seaton, resided in the rectory-house for some time.

BERKSHIRE, an inland county, bounded on the north by Oxfordshire and the southern part of Buckinghamshire, on the east by the counties of Buckingham and Surrey, on the south by that of Southampton, on the west by that of Wilts, and at its north-western extremity, for a very short distance, by that of Gloucester. It extends from 51° 21′ to 51° 48′ (N. Lat.), and from 34′ 30″ to 1° 43′ (W. Lon.); and contains nearly 726 square miles, or about 464,500 statute acres. There are 31,653 houses inhabited, 1590 uninhabited, and 201 in the course of erection; and the population amounts to 161,147, of whom 80,231 are males, and 80,916 females. At the period of the conquest of Britain by the Romans, the south-eastern part of the county was inhabited by the Bibroci, a small portion of it, on the south side, by the Segontiaci; and the remaining more extensive tract by the Attrebatii, or Attrebates. Under the Roman dominion it was included in the great division called Britannia Prima; and in the time of the heptarchy it formed part of the powerful kingdom of the West
216

Saxons, or Wessex. Berkshire is in the diocese of Oxford, province of Canterbury, and forms an archdeaconry, in which are comprised the deaneries of Abingdon, Newbury, Reading, and Wallingford, containing 148 parishes. For purposes of civil government it is divided into the hundreds of Beynhurst, Bray, Charlton, Compton, Cookham, Faircross, Farringdon, Ganfield, Hormer, Kintbury-Eagle, Lambourn, Morton, Ock, Reading, Riplesmere, Shrivenham, Sunning, Theale, Wantage, and Wargrave. It contains the borough and market towns of Abingdon, Reading, Wallingford, and Windsor: the incorporated market-towns of Maidenhead, Newbury, and Wokingham; and the other market-towns of Farringdon, Hungerford, East Ilsley, Lambourn, and Wantage. Under the act of the 2nd of William IV. cap. 45, the county sends to parliament three knights of the shire: Reading and Windsor continue to return two representatives each; the number for Wallingford has been restricted by the statute to one; and Abingdon still sends one, as heretofore. It is included in the Oxford circuit: the Lent assizes and the Epiphany sessions are held at Reading; the summer assizes and midsummer sessions at Abingdon; the Michaelmas sessions at either of these towns, at the option of the magistrates; and the Easter sessions at Newbury. The county gaol and house of correction is at Reading, and the county house of correction at Abingdon.

The SURFACE of Berkshire comprises four grand natural divisions: the first is the great Vale of White Horse, which is bounded on the south by the White Horse hills (a continuation of the Chiltern range), on the east and north by the Thames, and on the west by Wiltshire, constituting the whole north-western part of the county. Here, along the banks of the Thames, is a fertile but narrow range of meadows, seldom exceeding half a mile in breadth, from which the land rises in most parts gradually, forming moderately elevated ridges, or distinct eminences. Between these hills and the chalk range, with a gentle inclination towards the south, lies the Vale, properly so called, remarkably productive of every kind of grain and pulse. The next grand division comprises the chalk hills, which form so prominent a feature in the western part of the county, presenting towards the Vale a steep declivity, mostly bare of wood, but clothed with a fine sward. The third great natural division consists of the Vale of the Kennet, containing a variety of richly diversified scenery. The fourth is the Forest district, which comprises the remaining eastern part of the county, being the whole of that lying eastward of the Loddon, except a detached range of chalk hills included between the Thames and an imaginary line drawn from Maidenhead to Wargrave, and which may be considered as forming a collateral part of the second division, or chalk district. The surface of the Forest district is agreeably varied, particularly in Windsor Forest, and the views from Windsor Terrace are of unrivalled beauty; but it contains the greatest quantity of waste land of any in the county, the most extensive tracts of waste being situated on the south side of it, and one of them, called Maidenhead Thicket, on the north.

The SOILS are various, but those of a chalky or gravelly nature predominate. Owing to the great extent of barren heaths in the south and east parts of the county, and of sheep-walks on the chalk hills, the quantity of land in cultivation does not exceed the general average of the kingdom. The total amount of arable land is computed at 255,000 acres; the rotations of crops are of infinite variety, but wheat and barley are the principal. The natural grass lands, bordering on the rivers, and in the dairy district occupying the western part of the Vale of White Horse, together with other dry pastures, parks, &c. but exclusively of the sheep downs of the chalk districts, are computed to comprise about 97,000 acres, of which 72,000 are included in the Vale. The dairy district includes the greater part of the hundreds of Shrivenham and Farringdon, and smaller portions of those of Ganfield and Wantage; the cheese made in it is for the most part of the kind known by the name of "Single Gloucester," and a large quantity is annually sent down the Thames to the metropolis. The native breed of hogs is the most esteemed of any in Great Britain.

The WOODLANDS occupy about 30,000 acres, much of which consists of coppices, of which those in the Vale of the Kennet supply large quantities of hoops and brooms to the London market. The best wooded tracts are in Windsor Forest, on the south side of the Kennet, and in several parishes to the north of that river; and Bagley wood, near Oxford, is one of the largest. A considerable extent of boggy land in the vicinity of Newbury is planted with alder-trees, the wood of which, at eight or nine years' growth, is made into rakes, prongs, shafts for mops and besoms, &c. Along the banks of the Thames and on its islands are numerous osier-beds; and in every other suitable situation osier plantations are objects of considerable attention, more especially along the courses of the rivers Kennet and Loddon: the greater part of the produce, after being prepared for the basket-makers, is conveyed by the Thames to London. The celebrated Royal forest of Windsor was formerly of much greater extent than it is at present, having comprised large portions of the counties of Surrey and Bucks, and the whole south-eastern part of Berkshire, as far as Hungerford, on the border of Wiltshire: the Vale of the Kennet was disafforested by charter in 1226, and the circuit of the forest is now reduced to about 56 miles. The greater part is under tillage; and Windsor Great Park was reduced by George III. from 3800 to 1800 acres, 2000 acres having been brought into cultivation. The forest is computed to comprehend 69,600 acres, of which about 5500 are inclosed lands belonging to the crown; 29,000, other private property; 600, encroachments upon the wastes; and the remaining 24,500 acres, open forest land, including heaths and water.

Berkshire was formerly one of the principal seats of the clothing-trade, which, about the middle of the 17th century, was carried on to a very considerable extent, particularly at Abingdon, Reading, and Newbury, and in their vicinities. Sacking and sail-cloth were also made at Abingdon and Wantage; and silk is yet manufactured on a small scale at Wokingham. There are some large breweries, especially at Windsor, which is celebrated for its ale; several paper-mills on the banks of the Kennet; and numerous corn-mills. The principal rivers are the Thames, the Kennet, the Loddon, the Ock, and the Lambourn. The Thames forms the entire northern boundary of Berkshire, in a circuitous course

of nearly 105 miles, in the whole of which it is navigable; and is augmented by the influx of all the others before it quits the county. The Kennet is navigable, partly by means of artificial collateral cuts, to its junction with the Thames a little below Reading. The Kennet and Avon canal, constructed under an act obtained in 1794, connects the navigable channel of the former river at Newbury with that of the latter at Hackson bridge, near Shrivenham, traverses the Vale of White Horse, to the Thames at Abingdon. The north-western part of the shire also derives some advantage from the Oxford and the Thames and Severn canals; and the south-eastern, from the Basingstoke canal. The Great Western railway enters the county a little to the east of Maidenhead, and passes on the south side of that town, to Reading, after which it skirts the border of the county as far as to the north of Basildon Park; it then crosses the Thames into Oxfordshire, and runs for a short distance along the boundary of that county, recrossing the Thames a little above South Stoke, and again entering Berkshire, whence it proceeds, by Dudcote and Wantage, into Wilts. At Dudcote branches off a line in a northern direction, by Abingdon, to Oxford.

The REMAINS of ANTIQUITY are various and interesting. The Roman stations were, Spinæ, at the present village of Speen; that called Bibractè, the exact site of which is yet undecided; and an important station, the name of which has not been transmitted to modern times, at Wallingford. Several Roman roads crossed the county; but it is difficult to reconcile their courses to any general theory, or to fix with precision the exact places to which they tended. The principal were, one from Glevum, now Gloucester, to London; and the Ikeneld-street, which enters from Oxfordshire at Streatley, where it divides into two branches, one of which, under the name of the Ridgway, runs along the entire northern verge of the chalk hills, and may be regarded as the main line, and the other, under the name of the Westridge, passes by Hampstead Hermitage, the Long Lane, and the vicinity of Newbury, to Old Sarum, in Wilts. Another very ancient, and perhaps a Roman, road enters from Wiltshire, on the north-western confines of the county, under the name of the Port-way, and appears to have taken a direction towards some spot south of Wallingford. There are also numerous remains of camps, of which it is thought that Letcombe Castle and Uffington Castle, both occupying commanding situations on the downs, were constructed by the Britons and subsequently used by the Romans. In a field about half a mile from Little Coxwell is a space of fourteen acres, styled Cole's Pits, in which are 273 pits, for the most part circular, and excavated in the sand to the depth of from seven to twenty-two feet: they are supposed to mark the sites of ancient British habitations. Near Uffington Castle is the rude figure of a horse, giving name to the hills and vale of White Horse; it is formed by cutting away the turf on the steep brow of the chalk hill above Uffington, and occupies about an acre of ground. At a little distance from this is a mount called Dragon hill, supposed to mark the place of interment of some British chieftain;

and many tumuli are dispersed over the downs, especially in the way from Uffington to Lambourn, where a group of them has acquired the name of the " *Seven Barrows.*"

Within the limits of the county were anciently twelve religious houses, including an alien priory, and two commanderies of the Knights Hospitallers ; also three colleges, of which that of the royal chapel of St. George, at Windsor, still remains ; and ten hospitals, five of which yet exist, namely, two at Abingdon, and one each at Donnington, Lambourn, and Newbury. Of the magnificent abbey built by Henry I. at Reading, little more than rude heaps of stones can now be seen ; but there are considerable remains of the church of the Grey friars there, converted into a bridewell. There are likewise some vestiges of the monasteries of Abingdon, Hurley, and Bisham, and of the collegiate church of Wallingford. The fragment of a wall, and extensive ditches and earthworks, indicate the site of the important castle of Wallingford ; and there yet exist ruins of the gateway of that of Donnington. The most remarkable mansion, in point of antiquity, is the manor-house at Appleton, which appears to be of as remote a date as the reign of Henry II. Berkshire has for a series of centuries derived some degree of celebrity from containing, at its easternmost extremity, one of the chief residences of the kings of England,—the vast and magnificent pile of Windsor Castle ; and there are also many seats of the nobility and gentry, distinguished for their architectural beauties. The mineral waters are unimportant, the following only possessing any note, *viz.*, a mild cathartic at Cumner ; a weak chalybeate at Sunninghill ; a strong chalybeate in the parish of Wokingham, called Gorrick Well ; and some springs near Windsor, of the quality of the Epsom waters. The county gives the title of Earl to the family of Howard, Earls of Suffolk and Berkshire.

BERKSWICH.—See BASWICH.

BERMONDSEY (St. MARY MAGDALENE), a parish and union, in the borough of SOUTHWARK, E. division of the hundred of BRIXTON and of SURREY, 1½ mile (S. S. E.) from London ;—containing 34,947 inhabitants. This place, in Domesday-book, is described as a royal demesne, and, in other ancient records, as having been occasionally the residence of William the Conqueror, and his successor, William Rufus, who had a palace here. In 1089, a priory for Cluniac monks was founded by Aldwin Child, a citizen of London, as a cell to the abbey of La Charité in France, from which establishment brethren of that order are said to have been sent hither through the influence of Lanfranc, Archbishop of Canterbury. To this monastery William Rufus and some of his successors were great benefactors. Henry I. gave the palace to the monks, for the enlargement of their cloister, reserving part of it as a residence for himself, in which King John having subsequently resided, it obtained the appellation of King John's Palace, and has been by some antiquaries considered rather the original site than, as it was in reality, only an appendage to the monastery. This establishment increased so much in wealth and importance that it was found necessary to enlarge the buildings ; and an hospital was erected adjoining it in 1213, for the reception of their converts and the education of children of indigent parents, which was dedicated to St. Thomas

218

the Martyr. In the 45th of Edward III. it was sequestrated, with other alien priories, to the use of the crown, but was re-established. Richard II. elevated it into an abbey, and it retained its grandeur and importance till the Dissolution, when its revenue was estimated at £548. 2. 5¾. The site appears to have been very extensive, comprising the present churchyard, and an adjoining area, still called King John's Court ; and vestiges of the place and conventual buildings may be traced in the gardens of the houses which have been erected on the site : a gateway, which was standing in 1807, has been taken down, in order to form Abbeystreet. Bermondsey owes its origin to the monastery, in the vicinity of which a gradual accumulation of buildings had formed a village in the reign of Edward III. when a church was founded by the prior, for the use of the inhabitants. Catherine of France, widow of Henry V., lived in retirement in the monastery, where she died in 1436 ; here also, in 1486, Elizabeth, queen of Edward IV. who had been sentenced by the council to forfeiture of lands, ended her life in confinement.

Bermondsey is situated on the southern bank of the river Thames. The houses are in general ancient and irregularly built, but there are several modern and handsome structures ; the streets are paved, and lighted with gas, and the inhabitants are supplied with water from the South London and the Southwark water-works. An act for more effectually paving, lighting, and otherwise improving the parish, was passed in 1845. A great alteration has lately taken place by the formation of the London and Greenwich railway, which commences near the foot of London bridge, and crosses the parish by means of a magnificent viaduct of lofty arches, for the construction of which numbers of houses were purchased by the directors and pulled down along the line. The Bricklayers' Arms branch of the Croydon railway is almost exclusively within the parish ; it was opened in May 1844, and is about 1¾ mile long : the cost was defrayed jointly by the Croydon and South-Eastern Railway Companies. The tanning of leather is carried on to a very great extent ; there are numerous woolstaplers, fellmongers, curriers, and manufacturers of vellum and parchment, besides an extensive hat-factory, some vinegar-works, a distillery, and brewery. The situation is also favourable to other trades ; there are a small dock and several yards for boat-builders, and within the parish are likewise rope-makers, anchorsmiths, and stave-merchants, and an establishment for the printing and dyeing of calico. About 200 acres of land are cultivated for the production of vegetables.

The LIVING is a rectory, valued in the king's books at £15. 8. 11½., and in the patronage of the family of Knapp ; net income, £514. The parish church, of which the west front and tower were repaired and embellished in 1830, is in the later English style. A district church, dedicated to St. James, was completed in 1828, partly by a grant from the Parliamentary Commissioners, at an expense of £21,412 ; it is a handsome edifice in the Grecian style, with a tower, and a portico of four pillars of the Ionic order : an altar-painting, of the Ascension, which cost £500, the bequest of Mr. J. Harcourt, was put up in 1845. The living is a perpetual curacy ; net income, £300 ; patron, the Rector of Bermondsey. A church district named Christchurch was endowed by the Ecclesiastical Commission in 1845, and one named

St. Paul's in 1846: a church has just been consecrated in the former district, which has consequently become an ecclesiastical parish; the edifice is in the Romanesque style, built at a cost of about £4600, exclusive of the site, and situated at an angle formed by a road crossing the road to Lower Deptford. There are places of worship for Independents and Wesleyans; and a handsome and spacious Roman Catholic chapel erected in 1834, at a cost of about £6000. Close to it is a convent of the Sisters of Mercy, erected in 1839, for about forty inmates, with a private chapel and a schoolroom for 300 female children; it cost about £4000. " The Bermondsey Free School," for sixty boys, who are instructed in reading, writing, and arithmetic, was founded in 1709, by Josiah Bacon, who left £700 for building the premises, and £150 per annum for its endowment; the schoolroom, which was erected in 1718, in the Grange road, is a neat brick building, having a bust of the founder in a niche over the entrance. The united " Charity Schools," established in 1712, are supported partly by an endowment of £109 per annum. In 1770, a chalybeate spring was discovered, and a spa established which, for many years, was a celebrated place of entertainment. Israel Mauduit, an ingenious writer on politics and commerce, was born in Bermondsey in 1708.

BERNERS-ROOTHING.—See ROOTHING.

BERRICK-PRIOR, a liberty, in the parish of NEWINGTON, union of WALLINGFORD, hundred of EWELME, county of OXFORD, 4¼ miles (N. N. E.) from Wallingford; containing 181 inhabitants.

BERRICK-SALOME, a chapelry, in the parish of CHAGROVE, union of WALLINGFORD, hundred of EWELME, county of OXFORD, 2½ miles (N.) from Bensington; containing 164 inhabitants. The chapel is dedicated to St. Helen. Here is a school with a small endowment.

BERRIER, a township, in the parish of GREYSTOCK union of PENRITH, LEATH ward, E. division of CUMBERLAND, 8 miles (W. by S.) from Penrith; containing, with the township of Murrah, 127 inhabitants, of whom 65 are in Berrier. Mary Jackson, in 1799, left £230 in reversion, to found and endow a school for girls, which was built by subscription in 1828.

BERRINGTON, a township, in the parish of KYLOE, union of BERWICK-UPON-TWEED, in ISLANDSHIRE, N. division of NORTHUMBERLAND; adjoining Berwick, and containing 316 inhabitants.

BERRINGTON, a hamlet, in the parish of CHIPPING-CAMPDEN, union of SHIPSTON-ON-STOUR, Upper division of the hundred of KIFTSGATE, E. division of the county of GLOUCESTER; containing 158 inhabitants.

BERRINGTON (ALL SAINTS), a parish, in the union of ATCHAM, hundred of CONDOVER, S. division of SALOP, 5½ miles (S. E. by S.) from Shrewsbury; containing 651 inhabitants. The navigable river Severn passes through the parish. The living is a rectory, valued in the king's books at £10. 12. 1., and in the gift of Lord Berwick: the tithes have been commuted for £520 payable to the rector, and £74 payable to impropriators; the glebe consists of 31 acres.

BERRINGTON, a hamlet, in the parish and union of TENBURY, Upper division of the hundred of DODDINGTREE, Hundred House and W. divisions of the county of WORCESTER, 2 miles (W. by S.) from Tenbury; containing 207 inhabitants. The hamlet comprises 1274a. 2r. 9p., and forms the most eastern district of the county, being bounded on the north by the river Teme, and surrounded on the west and south by a portion of the county of Hereford.

BERROW (ST. MARY), a parish, in the union of AXBRIDGE, hundred of BRENT with WRINGTON, E. division of SOMERSET, 9½ miles (W. by S.) from Axbridge; containing 578 inhabitants. The parish is situated on a small inlet from the Bristol Channel, to which it gives the name of Berrow bay, and by which it is bounded on the west. It comprises 1650 acres of land; the range of sand-hills that bound the coast contain many botanical and entomological rarities. The living is a discharged vicarage, valued in the king's books at £13. 11. 10½.; patron, the Archdeacon of Wells. The great tithes have been commuted for £102, and the impropriator has 18 acres of glebe: the vicarial tithes have been commuted for £218. 13., and there is an acre of vicarial glebe. The church is likely to be buried in the sands, which have accumulated to such an extent, that the wall of the churchyard is twenty feet below the surface of the ground. There is a place of worship for Wesleyans.

BERROW (ST. FAITH), a parish, in the union of UPTON-ON-SEVERN, and in a detached part of the Lower division of the hundred of OSWALDSLOW, locally in the Lower division of the hundred of PERSHORE, Upton and W. divisions of the county of WORCESTER, 7 miles (W.) from Tewkesbury; containing 480 inhabitants. This beautiful parish, about a mile in breadth, extends in an eastern direction three miles from the summit of Raggedstone hill or the Gloucester beacon, and from the Keysand hill, which latter forms the southern limit of the Malvern range. There is a sudden descent for a quarter of a mile to the foot of the hill, whence the country is undulated, with here and there deep narrow ravines alternating with low flat ridges or terraces of considerable extent; the entire surface, dotted with fruit and forest trees, presenting to the eye a varied landscape. At the western extremity of the parish, where it touches the parishes of Eastnor and Bromsberrow, the three counties of Worcester, Hereford, and Gloucester unite. The area is about 2100 acres, whereof four-tenths are arable, five-tenths pasture, and one-tenth woodland with 72 acres of common or waste: the soil is a rich loam, but the system of cultivation might be much improved, and a better mode of drainage adopted. Quarries of limestone and roadstone are wrought in the parish. The road between Tewkesbury and Ledbury passes near its northern border. The LIVING is a perpetual curacy, valued in the king's books at £7. 18. 4.; patrons and appropriators, the Dean and Chapter of Worcester. The tithes have been commuted for £350, of which £40 are paid to the incumbent, whose total income is £100 : there are 44 acres of glebe land; and a cottage named the Vicarage, with a rood of garden ground attached. The church is a small building in the decorated and later English styles, and consists of a chancel, nave, and south aisle, with a western tower, and north porch; the chancel, which is of good proportions, has been built since the erection of the nave: the edifice will afford accommodation to about 250 persons. A national school, taught by a mistress, has just been established.

BERRY-POMEROY (St. Mary), a parish, in the union of Totnes, hundred of Haytor, Paignton and S. divisions of Devon, 1½ mile (E. N. E.) from Totnes; containing with the township of Bridgetown, 1149 inhabitants. This place derives its distinguishing appellation from a family of that name, one of whom, Ralph de Pomeroy, soon after the Conquest founded a castle here, of which there are still some remains. The parish comprises by measurement 4335 acres, whereof 2629 are arable, 1204 pasture, 237 woodland, 167 orchard, and 62 common or waste, and is intersected by the navigable river Dart; the low lands are rich and fertile, abounding in irrigated meadows and fruitful orchards, and on the high grounds are produced excellent crops of corn. The living is a vicarage, valued in the king's books at £18. 19. 7.; patron and impropriator, the Duke of Somerset: the great tithes have been commuted for £400, and the vicarial for £420, with a glebe of 3 acres. The church contains a finely-carved screen and rood-loft. A chapel in the pointed style was erected at Bridgetown, at the expense of the patron, in 1832.

BERRYN-ARBOR (St. Peter), a parish, in the union of Barnstaple, hundred of Braunton, Braunton and N. divisions of Devon, 2¾ miles (E. by S.) from Ilfracombe : containing 899 inhabitants. It comprises by computation 5000 acres of fertile land : limestone of fine quality is quarried to a considerable extent. The living is a rectory, valued in the king's books at £34. 15. 10. ; patrons, in turn, the Bishop of Exeter, the Fursdon family, the Rev. E. W. Richards, and J. D. Basset, Esq. : the tithes have been commuted for £545, and the glebe comprises 130 acres, with a house. The church is a neat edifice, with a handsome tower. There is a place of worship for Independents. Bishop Jewell, celebrated for his support of the Protestant faith, was born here in 1522.

BERSTED, SOUTH (St. Mary Magdalene), a parish, in the hundred of Aldwick, rape of Chichester, W. division of Sussex, 6 miles (S. E.) from Chichester; containing, with the town of Bognor, and the tythings of North and of South Bersted, and Shripney, 2490 inhabitants, of whom 194 are in North Bersted. It comprises 2455 acres, of which about 1575 acres are arable, 774 pasture, and 6 woodland ; the surface is pleasingly varied, and the soil in general a rich loam resting upon a reddish clay or brick earth, and in some parts sand and gravel. The village, which formerly consisted only of a few fishermen's cottages, has been greatly improved. The living is a vicarage, valued in the king's books at £7. 18. 9.; patron, the Archbishop of Canterbury; appropriators, the Dean and Chapter : the great tithes have been commuted for £810, and those of the vicar for £400. The church, erected in 1400, is a plain edifice, with a tower surmounted by a low spire of shingles ; in the churchyard is the tomb of Sir Richard Hotham, Knt., founder of the town of Bognor. A chapel dedicated to St. John was erected at Bognor, and consecrated in 1822. Stephen de "Berghestede," who was elevated to the see of Chichester in 1262, was a native of the place; and Dr. Lloyd, Bishop of Oxford, was vicar.

BERWICK, a parish, in the union of West Firle, hundred of Longbridge, rape of Pevensey, E. division of Sussex, 3 miles (E. S. E.) from Lewes ; containing 199 inhabitants. It is bounded on the east by the Cuckmere river, and intersected by the road from Lewes to 220.

Eastbourne, and comprises 1060 acres, of which 330 are common or waste; the soil is chiefly chalk, clay, and rich loam. The Berwick station of the Brighton and Hastings railway is equidistant from the station at Lewes and that at Pevensey. The living is a rectory, valued in the king's books at £13. 6. 8., and in the gift of John Ellman, Esq. : the tithes have been commuted for £387. 10., and the glebe consists of 21 acres. The church is a handsome structure in the later English style, with a tower formerly surmounted by a spire, which was destroyed by lightning in 1774. Wood fossils are found in a sand-pit.

BERWICK (St. James), a parish, in the union of Wilton, hundred of Branch and Dole, Salisbury and Amesbury, and S. divisions of Wilts, 8 miles (N. W.) from Salisbury; containing 247 inhabitants. This parish is situated on the road from Salisbury to Devizes, and comprises by computation 2300 acres of arable and pasture land, of which the soil is fertile, and the substratum chiefly chalk; many sheep are fed on the Downs. A fair is held on the 4th of October. The living is a discharged vicarage, valued in the king's books at £8. 10. ; net income, £54 ; patron, Lord Ashburton. The great tithes have been commuted for £133, and the vicarial for £30 : there is an acre of glebe. The church is a very substantial building, having in the north transept a curious stone pulpit, which has been much noticed by antiquaries, and until within these few years was used by the officiating minister.

BERWICK (St. John), a parish, in the union of Tisbury, hundred of Chalk, Hindon and S. divisions of Wilts, 5½ miles (E. by S.) from Shaftesbury; containing 419 inhabitants. It comprises about 1700 acres; the surface is hilly, and the soil consists of all the varieties of clay, chalk, and sand. The living is a rectory, valued in the king's books at £26. 13. 4., and in the gift of New-College, Oxford : the tithes have been commuted for £500, and there are 53½ acres of glebe. The church is a handsome edifice in the later English style. There is a place of worship for Baptists. About a mile southward from the village is an intrenchment called Winkelbury Camp, supposed to have been constructed by the Romans.

BERWICK (St. Leonard), a parish, in the union of Tisbury, hundred of Dunworth, Hindon and S. divisions of Wilts, 1 mile (E.) from Hindon ; containing 41 inhabitants. This parish, which is situated on the road from London to Exeter, comprises by measurement 1200 acres of fertile land. A fair for sheep is held on St. Leonard's day; it is numerously attended. The manor-house, now in ruins, was for many years the residence of the Howe family, of whom Sir George Howe had the honour to entertain the Prince of Orange in 1688. The living is a rectory, with the perpetual curacy of Sedghill annexed, valued in the king's books at £8. 6. 8.; net income, £374 ; patron, J. Bennet, Esq.

BERWICK-BASSETT (St. Nicholas), a parish, in the union of Marlborough, hundred of Calne, Marlborough and Ramsbury, and N. divisions of Wilts, 8 miles (N. W. by W.) from Marlborough; containing 175 inhabitants. It comprises by measurement 1388 acres of fertile land, of which about one-third is pasture : there are about 8 acres of wood. The ancient manor-house, many ages since the residence of the Goddard family, is still remaining. The living is a perpetual curacy, united to the vicarage of Calne. The church is a neat plain edifice, and contains a carved screen and font. Henry Webb, in 1775, endowed a school with £14 per annum.

BERWICK-HILL, a township, in the parish of PONTELAND, union and W. division of CASTLE ward, S. division of NORTHUMBERLAND, 9¼ miles (N. N. W.) from Newcastle-upon-Tyne; containing 112 inhabitants. The township comprises 1594a. 27p., of which two-thirds are arable, and the remainder grass land and waste; the soil is of a strong quality, producing good crops, particularly of grain. The surface is elevated, and commands fine and extensive views; on the south is Prestwick Carr; and the river Pont flows on the west and north. The tithes have been commuted for £244. 11. 4. payable to Ralph Carr, Esq., and £22. 14. 2. to the vicar of Ponteland.

BERWICK-IN-ELMETT.—See BARWICK.

BERWICK, LITTLE, a chapelry, in the parish of ST. MARY, SHREWSBURY, N. division of SALOP; containing 271 inhabitants. The living is a perpetual curacy; net income, £54; patrons, the Earl of Tankerville and others. Near the chapel is an almshouse consisting of sixteen tenements, erected under the will of Sir Samuel Jones dated in 1672, and endowed by him with £80 per annum; he also bequeathed £40 per annum as a stipend for the minister, and £20 per annum towards repairing the chapel and almshouses, all charged on the Berwick estate. The property of the charity, with funds derived from other sources, yields an income of £183.

Arms.

BERWICK - UPON - TWEED (*HOLY TRINITY*), a port, borough, market-town, parish, and county of itself, and the head of a union, 64 miles (N. by W.) from Newcastle-upon-Tyne, and 334 (N. by W.) from London; containing 8484 inhabitants. The name of this town, which Leland supposes to have been originally Aberwick, from the British terms, *Aber*, the mouth of a river, and *Wic*, a town, is by Camden and other antiquaries considered to be expressive merely of a hamlet, or granary, annexed to a place of greater importance. Such appendages are usually in ancient records styled *berewics*, and the town is thought to have obtained its name from having been the *grange* or *berewic* of the priory of Coldingham, ten miles distant. The earliest authentic notice of Berwick occurs in the reign of Alexander I. of Scotland, and in that of Henry II. of England, to the latter of which monarchs it was given up, with four other towns, by William the Lion, in 1176, as a pledge for the performance of the treaty of Falaise, by which, in order to obtain his release from captivity after the battle of Alnwick, in 1174, he had engaged to do homage to the English monarch as lord paramount for all his Scottish dominions. Richard I., to obtain a supply of money for his expedition to the Holy Land, sold the vassalage of Scotland for 10,000 marks, and restored this and the other towns to William, content with receiving homage for the territories only which that prince held in England. King

John, upon retiring from an unsuccessful invasion of Scotland, burnt the town, which the Scots almost immediately rebuilt.

In 1291, the commissioners appointed to examine and report on the validity of the title of the respective claimants to the crown of Scotland, met at Berwick, and pursued the investigation which led to the decision in favour of John Balliol. Edward I. having compelled Balliol to resign his crown, took the town by storm in 1296, when a dreadful carnage ensued; here he received the homage of the Scottish nobility in the presence of a council of the whole nation, and established a court of exchequer for the receipt of the revenue of the kingdom of Scotland. Wallace, in the following year, having laid siege to the town, took and for a short time retained possession of it, but was unsuccessful in his attempt upon the castle, which was relieved by the arrival of a numerous army. Edward II., in prosecuting the war against Scotland, assembled his army here repeatedly, and hence made inroads into the enemy's territory. Robert Bruce obtained it in 1318, and, having raised the walls and strengthened them with towers, kept it, notwithstanding attacks from Edward II. and III., until it surrendered to the latter after the celebrated battle of Hallidown Hill, within the borough, which took place on the 19th of July, 1333. From Edward IV. and his successors it received several charters and privileges in confirmation and enlargement of the charter granted by Edward I., in which the enjoyment of the Scottish laws as they existed in the time of Alexander III. had been confirmed. After having been exposed during the subsequent reigns to the continued aggressions of the Scots and the English, Elizabeth repaired and strengthened the fortifications, and new walled part of the town : the garrison which had for some time been placed in it, was continued till the accession of James to the English throne, when its importance as a frontier town ceased. During the civil war in the reign of Charles I., it was garrisoned by the parliament.

The TOWN is pleasantly situated on the northern bank, and near the mouth, of the river Tweed, over which is a handsome stone bridge of fifteen arches, built in the reigns of James I. and Charles I., and connecting it with Tweedmouth on the south. The streets, with the exception of St. Mary gate, usually called the High-street, Castlegate, Ravensdowne, the Parade, and Hide-hill, are narrow, but neatly paved, and the houses are, in general, well built : the town is lighted with gas, and an abundant supply of water is obtained by pipes laid down to the houses from the public reservoirs, which are the property of the corporation. Fuel is also plentiful, there being several collieries on the south, and one on the north, side of the river, within from two to four miles of the town. A public library was established in 1812, and a reading-room in 1842; the theatre, a small neat building, is opened at intervals, and there are assembly-rooms. The new fortifications, which are exceedingly strong, have displaced those of more ancient date, of which only a few ruins now remain ; they afford an agreeable promenade, much frequented by the inhabitants. The present works consist of a rampart of earth, faced with stone : there are no outworks, with the exception of the old castle, which overlooks the Tweed, and is now completely in ruins, and an earthen battery at the landing-place below the Magdalen fields. The line of works below the river is almost straight, but to the north and east are five bastions, to two of which there are powder magazines : the harbour is defended by a four and a six gun battery near the governor's house; and a saluting battery, of twenty-two guns, commands the English side of the Tweed. There are five gates belonging to the circumvallation, by which entrance is obtained. The barracks, which were built in 1719, form a small quadrangle, neatly built of stone, and afford good accommodation for 600 or 700 infantry. To these was recently attached the governor's house, for officers' barracks; but that building and the ground adjoining, formerly the site of the palace of the kings of Scotland, have been sold by the crown to a timber-merchant, and are now occupied for the purposes of his trade. The PORT was celebrated in the time of Alexander III. for the extent of its traffic in wool, hides, salmon, &c., which was carried on both by native merchants, and by a company of Flemings settled here; the latter of whom, however, perished in the conflagration of their principal establishment, called the Red Hall, which was set on fire at the capture of the town and castle by Edward I. At present, there is a considerable coasting-trade, though it has somewhat declined since the termination of the continental war: the exports are corn, wool, salmon, cod, haddock, herrings, and coal; and the imports, timber-deals, staves, iron, hemp, tallow, and bones for manure. About 800 men are employed in the fishery: the salmon and trout, of which large quantities are caught, are packed in boxes with ice, and sent chiefly to the London market; great quantities of lobsters, crabs, cod, haddock, and herrings are also taken, and a large portion forwarded, similarly packed, to the metropolis. The principal articles of manufacture, exclusively of such as are connected with the shipping, are, damask, diaper, sacking, cotton-hosiery, carpets, hats, boots, and shoes; and about 200 hands are employed in three iron-foundries, established within the present century. Steam-engines, and almost every other article, such as the gas-light apparatus for Berwick, Perth, and several other places, was manufactured here, and iron-works have lately been erected at Galashiels and at Jedburgh by the same proprietors. The HARBOUR is naturally inconvenient, the greater part of it being left dry at ebb-tide; it has, however, been recently deepened by several feet, and vessels of large tonnage come to the quay. The river is navigable only to the bridge, though the tide flows for seven miles beyond it: on account of the entrance being narrowed by sand-banks, great impediments were occasioned to the navigation till the erection, in 1808, of a stone pier on the projecting rocks at the north entrance of the Tweed; it is about half a mile in length, and has a light-house at the extremity. This, together with the clearing and deepening of the harbour, has materially improved the facilities of navigation, and been of great importance to the shipping interest of the place. On the Tweedmouth shore, for a short space, near the Carr Rock, ships of 400 or 500 tons' burthen may ride in safety. The smacks and small brigs, formerly carrying on the whole traffic of the place, are now superseded by large and well-fitted steam-vessels, schooners, and clipper-ships. There are numerous and extensive quays and warehouses, with a patent-slip for the repair of vessels; and the town has 222

the advantage of a railway to Edinburgh, in continuation of the railway along the east coast hence to Newcastle-upon-Tyne: the great railway bridge over the Tweed here, was commenced in the spring of 1847. The market, which is well supplied with grain, is on Saturday, and there is a fair on the last Friday in May, for black-cattle and horses; statute-fairs are held on the first Saturday in March, May, August, and November.

By charter of INCORPORATION granted in the second year of James I., the government was vested in a mayor, bailiffs, and burgesses; and there were, besides, an alderman for the year, a recorder, town-clerk, town-treasurer, four sergeants-at-mace, and other officers; but the control now resides in a mayor, six aldermen, and eighteen councillors, together composing the council, by whom a sheriff and other officers are appointed. The borough is distributed into three wards, and its municipal and parliamentary boundaries are the same; the mayor and late mayor are justices of the peace, and twelve other gentlemen have been appointed to act under a separate commission. Berwick was one of the royal burghs which, in ancient times, sent representatives to the court of the four royal burghs in Scotland; and on being annexed to the kingdom of England, its prescriptive usages were confirmed by royal charter. It sent representatives to parliament in the reign of Henry VIII., since which time it has continued to return two members. The right of election was formerly vested in the freemen at large, in number about 1140; the resident freemen and certain householders are now the electors, and the sheriff is returning officer. The limits of the borough include the townships of Tweedmouth and Spittal, on the south side of the river. The corporation hold courts of quarter-session for the borough, and a court of pleas every alternate Tuesday for the recovery of debts to any amount; a court leet, also, is held under the charter, at which six petty constables are appointed. The powers of the county debt-court of Berwick, established in 1847, extend over the registration-district of Berwick. The town-hall is a spacious and handsome building, with a portico of four massive columns of the Tuscan order: a portion of the lower part, called the Exchange, is appropriated to the use of the poultry and butter market; the first story contains two spacious halls and other apartments, in which the courts are held and the public business of the corporation transacted, and the upper part is used as a gaol. The whole forms a stately pile of fine hewn stone, and is surmounted with a lofty spire, containing a peal of eight bells, which on Sunday summon the inhabitants to the parish church.

The LIVING is a vicarage, valued in the king's books at £20; net income, £289; patrons and appropriators, the Dean and Chapter of Durham. The church is a handsome structure in the decorated English style, built during the usurpation of Cromwell, and is without a steeple. One of the Fishbourn lectureships is established here. There are places of worship for members of the Scottish Kirk, the Associate Synod, the Scottish Relief, Particular Baptists, Wesleyans, and Roman Catholics. A school for the instruction of the sons of burgesses in English and the mathematics was founded and endowed by the corporation, in 1798; to each department there is a separate master, paid by the corporation, and the average number of pupils is about 300.

The burgesses have also the patronage of a free grammar school, endowed in the middle of the seventeenth century by Sir William Selby, of the Moat, and other charitable persons. The Blue-coat charity-school was founded in 1758 by Captain Bolton, and endowed with £800, since augmented with several benefactions, especially with one of £1000 by Richard Cowle, who died at Dantzic in 1819; the whole income is £155, which is applied to educating about 150 boys, of whom 40 are also clothed. The school of industry for girls, established in 1819, affords instruction to 106 girls; and there are several infant, Sunday, and other schools. A pauper lunatic house was erected in 1813, and a dispensary established in 1814. A considerable part of the corporation land is allotted into "meadows" and " stints," and given rent-free to the resident freemen and freemen's widows, according to seniority, for their respective lives. Among the most important bequests for the benefit of the poor, are, £1000 by Richard Cowle, £1000 by John Browne in 1758, and £28 per annum by Sarah Foreman in 1803. The poor law union of which the town is the head comprises seventeen parishes and places, sixteen of them being in the county of Durham; and contains a population of 20,938. Some remains are still visible of the ancient castle of Berwick, and of a pentagonal tower near it; also of a square fort in Magdalen fields, and some entrenchments on Hallidown Hill. All vestiges of the ancient churches and chapels of the town, the Benedictine nunnery said to have been founded by David, King of Scotland, the monasteries of Black, Grey, White, and Trinitarian friars, and three or four hospitals, have entirely disappeared. The Magdalen fields, already mentioned, belonged to the Hospital of St. Mary Magdalen. During the reigns of William the Lion, and of Edward I., II., III., and other Scottish and English monarchs, Berwick was a place of mintage, and several of its coins are still preserved. There is a mineral spring close to the town, which is occasionally resorted to by invalids.

BESFORD, a township, in the parish of SHAWBURY, union of WEM, hundred of PIMHILL, N. division of SALOP, 3¾ miles (S. E. by E.) from Wem; containing 167 inhabitants.

BESFORD (ST. ANDREW), a parish, in the union, and Upper division of the hundred, of PERSHORE, Pershore and E. divisions of the county of WORCESTER, 3 miles (W. by S.) from Pershore; containing 179 inhabitants. The parish comprises 1320 acres of arable and pasture land in nearly equal portions; and is intersected by the Birmingham and Gloucester railway. The living is annexed to the vicarage of St. Andrew's, Pershore, and valued in the king's books at £3: the church stands in the village, and is an ancient structure of unknown date, containing about 100 sittings.

BESKABY, an extra-parochial place, connected with the parish of CROXTON-KEYRIAL, in the hundred of FRAMLAND, N. division of the county of LEICESTER, 7 miles (N. E.) from Melton-Mowbray; containing 7 inhabitants. The manor of "Bescoldeby" was held in 1363 by Andrew Luttrell, for Croxton Abbey; the Furnivals subsequently held lands here. The area is 843 acres. The chapel is in ruins.

BESSELSLEIGH (ST. LAWRENCE), a parish, in the union of ABINGDON, hundred of HORMER, county of BERKS, 4 miles (N. W.) from Abingdon; containing 106
223

inhabitants. It takes its name from the ancient family of Bessels, an heiress of which conveyed the estate by marriage to the Fettyplaces; and Sir Edmund Fettyplace sold it, about 1620, to Wm. Lenthall, master of the rolls, and speaker of the house of commons in the Long parliament, from whom it has descended to Kyffin J. W. Lenthall, Esq. The old manor-house was pulled down about fifty years since: Cromwell, who was a frequent visiter, usually concealed himself in a room to which the only access was by a chair let down and drawn up with pulleys. The parish comprises 872a. 1r. 21p. The living is a discharged rectory, valued in the king's books at £4. 17. 3½., and in the gift of Mr. Lenthall: the tithes have been commuted for £230, and the glebe consists of 26 acres. Sir John Lenthall, son and heir of the speaker, and governor of Windsor Castle, was buried in the chancel of the church in 1681.

BESSINGBY (ST. MAGNUS), a parish, in the union of BRIDLINGTON, wapentake of DICKERING, E. riding of YORK, 1½ mile (S. W.) from Bridlington; containing 66 inhabitants. The parish is on the road from Bridlington to Driffield, and a short distance from Bridlington bay, which stretches on the east; it comprises about 1230 acres of land, the property of Harrington Hudson, Esq., who is lord of the manor, and resides at Bessingby Hall. The living is a perpetual curacy, in the patronage of Mr. Hudson, with a net income of £59: the tithes were commuted for land and a money payment in 1766. The church, rebuilt in 1766, contains several handsome monuments to the Hudson family, one of them a fine basso-relievo of a female .e$^{x}p_{iring}$ in the arms of her attendants.

BESSINGHAM (ST. MARY), a parish, in the union of ERPINGHAM, hundred of NORTH ERPINGHAM, E. division of NORFOLK, 8 miles (N.) from Aylsham; containing 139 inhabitants. It comprises about 510 acres, of which 307 are arable, and 197 pasture; the soil is various, but chiefly strong, with brick earth, and the surface generally undulated, but in some parts flat. The living is a discharged rectory, valued in the king's books at £4. 6. 8., and in the gift of the Arden family: the tithes have been commuted for £125, and there are 25 acres of glebe. The church is chiefly in the perpendicular style, with a circular tower.

BESTHORPE (ALL SAINTS), a parish, in the union of WAYLAND, hundred of SHROPHAM, W. division of NORFOLK, 1 mile (E. by S.) from Attleburgh; containing 536 inhabitants. It comprises 2132a. 1r. 21p., of which 1471 acres are arable, and 610 meadow and pasture; the soil in general is wet and heavy. The road from London to Norwich, by way of Thetford, passes through the parish. The living is a discharged vicarage, valued in the king's books at £5. 6. 10½.; net income, £250; patron and impropriator, the Earl of Winterton, lord of the manor: the glebe comprises 35 acres. The church is a handsome cruciform structure, in the early and decorated English styles, with a square embattled tower at the west end; it was thoroughly repaired in 1840.

BESTHORPE, a chapelry, in the parish of SOUTH SCARLE, union, and N. division of the wapentake of NEWARK, S. division of the county of NOTTINGHAM, 8 miles (N. N. E.) from Newark; containing 327 inhabitants. This place comprises 1168 acres of land; and has a good village near the Fleet river, and two miles west-north-west from the village of Scarle. The tithes have been commuted for £269. 5. 8., of which £44 are payable to the vicar of South Scarle. The chapel was rebuilt in 1844, at a cost of £400, raised by subscription. There is a place of worship for Wesleyans; and a school is endowed with £8. 12. per annum. Some remains exist of an ancient mansion in the style of the period of James I., with a tower and pointed gable roof.

BESWICK, an extra-parochial district, in the hundred of SALFORD, S. division of the county of LANCASTER, 1½ mile (E.) from Manchester; containing 345 inhabitants. This place, which comprises 95 acres, and which at the beginning of the present century had only one solitary house, is indebted for its present extent and increase in population, to its contiguity to the town of Manchester.

BESWICK, a chapelry, in the parish of KILNWICK, union of BEVERLEY, Bainton-Beacon division of the wapentake of HARTHILL, E. riding of YORK, 6½ miles (N. by W.) from Beverley; containing 211 inhabitants. It is situated on the road from Driffield to Beverley; and comprises upwards of 2000 acres, chiefly arable, and very flat, having been once a marsh. The living is a perpetual curacy, with a net income of £65 : the chapel is a plain thatched building, with a wooden steeple.

BETCHCOTT, a township, in the parish of SMETHCOTT, union of CHURCH-STRETTON, hundred of CONDOVER, S. division of SALOP; containing 32 inhabitants. It is south-west of Smethcott village.

BETCHTON.—See BECHTON.

BETCHWORTH (ST. MICHAEL), a parish, in the union, and First division of the hundred, of REIGATE, E. division of SURREY, 3¼ miles (W. by S.) from Reigate; containing 1140 inhabitants. This place is noticed in Domesday book as Becesworde, and the manor was anciently held by the earls of Warren and Surrey, one of whom in the 12th century gave the advowson to the convent of St. Mary Overy, Southwark. The parish comprises 3067 acres, whereof about 500 are common or waste land; it contains some good seats, and several respectable cottage residences. The living is a discharged vicarage, valued in the king's books at £7. 8. 11½.; patrons, the Dean and Canons of Windsor; impropriators, the Rt. Hon. Henry Goulburn, and Sir Benjamin Brodie, Bart.: the great tithes have been commuted for £295. 15. 4., and the vicarial for £200. The church was renovated in 1838. At Brockham Green is a church lately built by subscription. A school is endowed with £20 per annum, and there are several charities for the benefit of the poor. Brockham Lodge was the summer retreat of Capt. Morris, the well-known lyric poet, who died in 1838, at the age of 93.

BETHERSDEN (ST. BEATRICE), a parish, in the union of WEST ASHFORD, hundred of CHART and LONG-BRIDGE, lathe of SHEPWAY, E. division of KENT, 6 miles (W. S. W.) from Ashford; containing 1011 inhabitants. It comprises 6345 acres, of which 798 are woodland, and 300 common. A considerable quantity of a species of grey marble, used for columns and the internal ornaments of various neighbouring churches, is obtained from quarries in the northern part of the parish. A fair is held on the 1st of July. The living is a vicarage, valued in the king's books at £12; net income, £165; patron, the Archbishop of Canterbury; impropriator, Earl Cornwallis: the great tithes have been commuted

for £481, and there are 78 acres of glebe. Here is a place of worship for Particular Baptists.

BETHNAL-GREEN (ST. MATTHEW), a parish, and a union of itself, in the borough of the TOWER HAMLETS, Tower division of the hundred of OSSULSTONE, county of MIDDLESEX, 2½ miles (N. E. by E.) from St. Paul's; containing 74,088 inhabitants. This very extensive parish was separated by act of parliament, in 1743, from the parish of Stepney, to which it was formerly a hamlet; and is divided into four districts called Church, Green, Hackney-road, and Town divisions. It is supposed to have derived its name from Bathon Hall, the residence of a family of that name, who had considerable possessions here in the reign of Edward I., and from a spacious green, to the east of which is the site of an episcopal palace called Bishop's Hall, said to have been the residence of Bonner, Bishop of London. The popular legendary ballad of the "Blind Beggar of Bethnal-Green," the hero of which is said to have been Henry de Montfort, the son of the Earl of Leicester, has reference to an ancient castellated mansion, built in the reign of Elizabeth by John Kirby, a citizen of London, and now converted into a private lunatic asylum.

The houses in general are meanly built of brick, and consist of large ranges of dwellings, inhabited chiefly by journeymen silk-weavers, who work at home for the master-weavers in Spitalfields; but considerable improvements have been made, and some handsome ranges have been erected on the line of the Hackney-road, in the district of St. John's, and at Cambridge-heath, and more recently in that part of the parish once called Bonner's Fields, but now Victoria Park. This park, designed as a place of healthful resort and recreation for the population of the east end of London, already attracts an immense number of visiters; great progress has been made in the plantations, and building speculation is very active in its vicinity. The parish is lighted with gas; the streets are partially paved, and the inhabitants are supplied with water by the East London Company's works: an act making further provision for paving, lighting, and cleansing the public ways, was passed in 1843. There are a very extensive cotton-factory; a large manufactory for waterproof hose, made of flax, without seam, and of any length and diameter, chiefly for the use of brewers and for firemen; a mill for the manufacture of all kinds of printing-paper; some white-lead and colour works; two extensive establishments for the manufacture of worsted lace and gimp; and a brewery. A great quantity of land is in the occupation of market-gardeners. The Regent's canal passes through the parish, which is also crossed by the Eastern-Counties railway.

The LIVING is a rectory not in charge; net income, £614; patron, the Bishop of London. The church, erected in 1746, is a neat brick building, ornamented with stone. St. John's district church was built in 1828, by grant from the Parliamentary Commissioners, at an expense of £17,638, and is a handsome edifice of brick faced with stone, in the Grecian style, with a tower surmounted by a cupola : the living is a perpetual curacy, with a net income of £190, in the gift of the Bishop. Ten additional districts or ecclesiastical parishes have been formed; and the expense of erecting a church in each of them has been estimated at more than £75,000, raised by subscription, aided by a grant of £10,000

room has been taken down for the line of the Eastern Counties railway, and rebuilt on a new site. Another, called "Friar's Mount school," contains seventy boys, and is partly supported by subscription. The alms-houses founded by Captain Fisher in 1711, and those belonging to the companies of Drapers and Dyers, are situated in the parish. Trinity Hospital at Mile-End, was erected in 1695, on land given by Captain Henry Mudd, an elder brother of the Trinity House, and endowed, in 1701, by Captain Robert Sandes, for twenty-eight masters of ships, or their widows. The union workhouse, recently erected, is near Victoria Park. The Roman road from the western counties of England to the ferry over the river Lea, at Old Ford, passes through the northern part of the parish. Sir Richard Gresham, father of Sir Thomas Gresham who built the Royal Exchange; Sir Thomas Grey, Knt.; and Sir Balthazar Gerbier, a celebrated painter and architect, who designed the triumphal arch for the entrance of Charles II. into London on his restoration; were residents at the place. Ainsworth, the compiler of the Latin Dictionary, kept an academy here for some years; and Caslon, who established the celebrated type-foundry in Chiswell-street, lived here in retirement till his decease in 1766.

BETLEY (St. Margaret), a parish, in the union of Newcastle-under-Lyme, N. division of the hundred of Pirehill and of the county of Stafford, 7½ miles (W. by N.) from Newcastle; containing 884 inhabitants. It is situated on the road from Newcastle to Nantwich, and near the confines of Cheshire, the boundary line between the two counties extending here through the middle of a fine lake of 80 acres, called Betley Mere. The parish comprises by measurement 1381 acres of fertile land: red sandstone of fine quality for building is wrought; and facility for the conveyance of produce is afforded by the Liverpool and Birmingham railway, which passes near the village. The village is uncommonly neat, and is greatly ornamented by two very handsome seats in its immediate vicinity, Betley Hall and Betley Court. A fair for cattle takes place on the 31st of July: a market, on Friday, has long been of such trivial consequence, that it may be said to be obsolete. Within a mile to the south of Betley is Wrine-Hill, a scattered village on an eminence, partly in this parish and partly in that of Wybunbury in Cheshire. The living is a perpetual curacy; net income, £150; patron and impropriator, G. Tollet, Esq.: the glebe comprises 60 acres; and a good parsonage-house has been built by the present incumbent. The tithes have been commuted for £270. The church is an ancient half-timbered edifice, of which the chancel was rebuilt in 1610, and the tower in 1713; it affords a specimen of the earliest attempts at Gothic architecture, on which account, though inferior to many churches in the neighbourhood, it deserves notice: the building was restored in 1842. There is a place of worship for Wesleyans; also a national school for boys and girls, with a small endowment.

BETSOME, a hamlet, in the parish of Southfleet, union of Dartford, hundred of Axton, Dartford, and Wilmington, lathe of Sutton-at-Hone, W. division of Kent; containing 188 inhabitants.

BETTERTON, a tithing, in the parish of Lockinge, hundred of Wantage, county of Berks, 2¼ miles (E. S. E.) from Wantage; containing 17 inhabitants.

2 G

BETTESHANGER (St. Mary), a parish, in the union and hundred of Eastry, lathe of St. Augustine, E. division of Kent, 4 miles (S. S. W.) from Sandwich; containing 18 inhabitants. It comprises 397 acres, whereof 38 are wood. The living is a discharged rectory, valued in the king's books at £6. 4. 4.; net income, £166; patron F. E. Morrice, Esq. The church was repewed in 1835; the north and south entrances are under Norman arches, ornamented with zigzag mouldings, and beneath the arch over the latter is a figure of Christ: there are several monuments, one of which, to the memory of Vice-Admiral Morrice, is very handsome.

BETTISCOMBE, a parish, in the union of Beaminster, liberty of Frampton, Bridport division of Dorset, 6 miles (w. by S.) from Beaminster; containing 53 inhabitants, and comprising 667a. 2r. 16p. The living is a rectory, valued in the king's books at £8. 2. 3½., and in the gift of the family of Sheridan: the tithes have been commuted for £1401, and the glebe consists of 54½ acres.

BETTON, a township, in the parish and union of Drayton-in-Hales, Drayton division of the hundred of North Bradford, N. division of Salop; 2 miles (N. N. E.) from Drayton; containing 254 inhabitants. This place lies on the road from Drayton to Norton, and the river Tern here separates the county from Staffordshire. The tithes have been commuted for £123, payable to the free grammar school of Shrewsbury.

BETTUS (St. Mary), a parish, in the union of Knighton, hundred of Purslow, S. division of Salop, 6 miles (N. W.) from Knighton; containing, with the townships of Rugantine and Trebodier, and part of Kevencalonog, 452 inhabitants. The living is a perpetual curacy; net income, £57; patron and impropriator, the Earl of Powis.

BETTWS (St. David), a parish, in the union and division of Newport, hundred of Wentlloog, county of Monmouth, 1½ mile (N. W. by W.) from Newport; containing 90 inhabitants, and comprising by measurement 1132 acres. The living is annexed to the vicarage of St. Woollos: the incumbent's tithes have been commuted for £42, and the great tithes, belonging to the Bishop of Gloucester, for £82. 10.

BETTWS-NEWYDD, a parish, in the union of Abergavenny, division and hundred of Raglan, county of Monmouth, 4 miles (N. by E.) from Usk; containing 106 inhabitants. The parish comprises about 1200 acres, of which three-sixths are arable, two-sixths pasture, and one-sixth woodland. It is situated nearly in the centre of the county, is bounded on the west by the river Usk, and intersected by the road from Usk to Abergavenny; the surface is undulated, and from the elevated grounds some good views are obtained. The living is a perpetual curacy, annexed to the vicarage of Llanarth: the vicarial tithes have been commuted for £51. 6., and there is a glebe of about 3 acres. The church is an ancient structure, remarkable for a very curiously carved rood-loft; and in the churchyard are some fine yew-trees.

BEVERCOATS (St. Giles), a parish, in the union of East Retford, South-Clay division of the wapentake of Bassetlaw, N. division of the county of Nottingham, 2½ miles (W. N. W.) from Tuxford; containing 44
.226

inhabitants, and comprising 800 acres. The living is a vicarage, united to that of West Markham : the church is in ruins.

BEVERIDGE.—See Boveridge.

Seal and Arms.

BEVERLEY, a borough, market-town, and the head of a union, in the E. riding of York, 9 miles (N. W.) from Hull, 29 (E. S. E.) from York, and 183 (N.) from London; comprising the parishes of St. John, St. Martin, St. Mary, and St. Nicholas, the first of which includes the townships of Aike, Eske, Molescroft, Storkhill with Sandholme, Thearne, Tickton with Hull-Bridge, Weel, and Woodmansey with Beverley-Park; and containing 8759 inhabitants. This place, from the woods with which it was formerly covered, was called Deirwalde, implying the forest of the Deiri, the ancient inhabitants of this part of the country. By the Saxons, probably from the number of beavers with which the river Hull in this part abounded, it.was called Beverlega, and subsequently Beverlac, from which its present name is deduced. About the year 700, John, the fifth archbishop of York, rebuilt the church, and founded in the choir a monastery of Black monks, dedicated to St. John the Baptist; in the nave a college of seven presbyters or secular canons, with seven clerks, dedicated to St. John the Evangelist; and in the chapel of St. Martin, adjoining the church, a society of nuns. This collegiate and monastic establishment was richly endowed by the founder and successive benefactors, and became the retreat of the archbishop, who, after having filled the see of York for 33 years, with a reputation for extreme sanctity, spent the remainder of his life in retirement and devotion; and, dying in 721, was canonized by the title of St. John of Beverley. The foundation of the monastery naturally led to the erection of buildings in the immediate neighbourhood, and appears to have been the origin of the town, which gradually grew up around it. In the year 867, it was nearly destroyed by the Danes in one of their incursions under Inguar and Ubba, who murdered many of the monks, canons, and nuns; but after remaining for three years in a state of desolation, it was partly restored by the monks, who again established themselves at the place.

In the early part of the tenth century, Athelstan, marching against the confederated Britons, Scots, and Danes, caused the standard of St. John of Beverley to be carried before his army, and, having returned victorious, bestowed many privileges upon the town and monastery. He founded a college for secular canons, which, at the Dissolution, had an establishment consisting of a provost, eight prebendaries, a chancellor, precentor, seven rectors, and nine vicars choral, and a revenue of £597. 19. 6. He also conferred on the church the privilege of sanctuary, the limits of which, extending for a mile around the town, were marked out by four crosses (the remains of three of which are still standing), erected at the four principal entrances: an account of the culprits who took refuge within its walls during the 15th and 16th centuries has been

ported on eight pillars, each of one entire stone. There was formerly a market on Wednesdays, the market-place for which has a neat cross, but is of smaller area than the former : there is also a market-place for the sale of fish, built in an octagonal form. Fairs are held on the Thursday before Old Valentine's-day, on Holy-Thursday, July 5th, and November 6th, chiefly for horses, horned-cattle, and sheep ; and on every alternate Wednesday is a great market for sheep and horned-cattle. The fairs and cattle-markets are held at Norwood, where is a spacious opening.

The prescriptive privileges of the BOROUGH have been confirmed and extended by several charters, especially in 1572 by Queen Elizabeth, who, also, in 1579 assigned certain chantry lands and tenements for the repairing of the minster, and four years subsequently gave other lands for the support of the minster and St. Mary's church. By the dissolution of the monastic institutions, the town had suffered so much, that a few years afterwards it was unable to pay its portion of taxes (£321) due to the crown; and in consequence of a petition to the queen, she remitted them during royal pleasure. The corporation now consists of a mayor, six aldermen, and eighteen councillors ; the borough is divided into two wards, and, as at present constituted, comprises only the parishes of St. Martin, St. Mary, and St. Nicholas. The liberties, comprehending certain townships in the parish of St. John (which extends into the northern division of the wapentake of Holderness), were severed from the borough by the act of the 5th and 6th of William IV., c. 76, except as regards the election of members to serve in parliament, and were united to the East riding. The mayor and late mayor are justices of the peace, and there are eight other justices appointed under a commission from the crown : petty-sessions are held weekly. Among the privileges which the freedom of the borough confers is the right of pasturing cattle, under certain restrictions, on four pastures, containing about 1200 acres, and managed under an act obtained in 1836. The elective franchise was conferred in the time of Edward I., but was not exercised from the end of that reign till the 5th of Elizabeth, since which the borough has continued to return two members to parliament. The right of election was formerly vested in the freemen generally, whether resident or not; but, by the act of the 2nd of William IV., cap. 45, the non-resident electors, except within seven miles of the borough, were disfranchised, and the privilege was extended to the £10 householders of the borough and liberty, over which latter the limits were extended. The mayor is returning officer. The general quarter-sessions for the East riding are held here; and for that division also, Beverley is a polling-place in the election of parliamentary representatives. The powers of the county debt-court of Beverley, established in 1847, extend over the registration-district of Beverley, and part of that of Skirlaugh. The guildhall has been repaired and beautified, and is a neat building : adjoining it stands the gaol, lately erected, but now used only for debtors, and for securing prisoners previously to examination. The house of correction for the riding is a spacious building, erected at an expense of £16,000, at the extremity of the town, on the road to Driffield and Scarborough; the principal front has a portico of four Ionic columns, with a handsome pediment.

2 G 2

The MINSTER, formerly the church belonging to the monastery of St. John, is now the parochial church of the united parishes of *St. John* and *St. Martin:* the living is a perpetual curacy, of which the net income (with the value of the parsonage-house) is about £195; patrons, the Trustees of the Rev. Charles Simeon. The impropriators of St. John are, the representatives of Sir M. Warton; the impropriation of St. Martin's belongs to the crown. Two curates are appointed, who perform divine service twice every day; each having a stipend of about £132, paid out of the minster estates and funds, appropriated by act of parliament to that purpose. The Minster, as already observed, was almost entirely rebuilt in 1060, by Kinsius, Archbishop of York. In 1664, some workmen, whilst opening a grave in the chancel, discovered a sheet of lead, enveloping some relics, with an inscription in Latin, purporting that, the ancient church having been destroyed by fire in 1188, search was made for the relics of St. John of Beverley, which, the next being found, were again deposited near the altar. It is not known at what precise period the present church was built, though probably in the early part of the reign of Henry III. It is a venerable and spacious cruciform structure, in the early, decorated, and later styles of English architecture, with two lofty towers at the west end; and though combining these several styles, it exhibits in each of them such purity of composition and correctness of detail, as to raise it to an architectural equality with the finest of the cathedral churches, to which it is inferior only in magnitude. The west front is the most beautiful and perfect specimen we have of the later English style, the whole front is pannelled, and the buttresses, which have a very bold projection, are ornamented with various tiers of niche-work, of excellent composition, and most delicate execution. The nave and transepts are early English, of which the fronts of the north and south transepts are pure specimens. The choir is partly in the decorated style, with an exquisitely beautiful altar-screen and rood-loft, which, though unequalled in elegance of design and richness of detail, were long concealed by a screen of inferior composition, put up within the last century. The east window is embellished with stained glass, collected from the other windows, and skilfully arranged. Near the altar is the Frydd-stool, formed of one entire stone, with a Latin inscription offering an asylum to all criminals who should flee to this sanctuary; and on an ancient tablet are the portraits of St. John of Beverley and King Athelstan, with a legend recording the monarch's grant of freedom to the town. In the choir is a superb and finely-executed monument, the celebrated Percy shrine, erected in the reign of Edward III., to the memory of one of the Percy family; and in the north transept is a fine altar-tomb : both are in the decorated style. Behind the minster is the ancient manor-house belonging to Beverley Park.

The living of *St. Mary's* is a vicarage, with the rectory of *St. Nicholas'* united, valued in the king's books at £14. 2. 8., and in the patronage of the Crown; net income, £289. St. Mary's, now the parochial church for the united parishes, is a highly interesting structure, and contains portions in the various styles from the Norman to the later English; the towers at the western end are finely pierced, and the octagonal turrets flanking
28

the nave are strikingly elegant. The roof of the chancel, which is in the decorated style, is richly groined, and the piers and arches are well proportioned; there are some interesting monuments, and a font in the later style. The churches of St. Martin and St. Nicholas have long since gone to decay. The *Minster chapel of ease*, in the parish of St. Martin, was erected at a cost of £3300 : the first stone was laid by Mr. Atkinson, then mayor, on the 20th May, 1839, and the chapel was consecrated on the 8th of October, 1841. There are places of worship in the town for Baptists, the Society of Friends, Independents, and Primitive and Wesleyan Methodists.

The *Grammar school* is of uncertain origin, though it appears to have existed at a remote period. The fixed endowment is £10 per annum, which was bequeathed in 1652, by Dr. Metcalf, and is augmented with £90 per annum by the corporation, who have the appointment of the master; this grant, however, will be discontinued on the next avoidance. There are several yearly exhibitions at Cambridge University for natives of Beverley educated at the school. The Blue-coat charity school was established by subscription in 1709, for the maintenance, clothing, and education of poor children; the annual income, arising from subsequent benefactions, is at present about £126. There is also an endowed school for 80 girls; and a school in which are about 70 boys and 85 girls, is supported by the interest of £2000 stock, bequeathed in 1804 by the Rev. James Graves, incumbent of the minster. Beverley contains seven sets of almshouses, or charities, in which more than 90 poor people are gratuitously lodged, pensioned, and clothed, viz.: Fox's hospital, Routh's hospital, the Corporation almshouses, Warton's hospital and charities, Sir Michael Warton's hospital, and Tymperon's hospital. Several hundreds of pounds are produced from a number of miscellaneous benefactions. Sir Michael Warton, Knt., in 1724 bequeathed £4000 (laid out in the purchase of an estate near Spilsby, in Lincolnshire, of which the annual rent is now £900), as a perpetual fund for keeping the minster in repair; and Mr. Robert Stephenson, in 1711, left an estate now producing from £70 to £100 per annum, for the maintenance of "Nonconformist preaching ministers." The poor law union of Beverley comprises 36 parishes and places, and contains a population of 18,957. Alfred of Beverley, a monkish historian of the twelfth century, is supposed to have been born here; and Dr. John Alcock, Bishop of Ely, and founder of Jesus' College, Cambridge; Dr. Fisher, Bishop of Rochester, a martyr to his religious tenets in the reign of Henry VIII.; and Dr. Green, Bishop of Lincoln, an elegant scholar, and one of the writers of the *Athenian Letters*, published by Lord Hardwicke; were also natives of the town. It gives the title of Earl to the family of Percy.

BEVERSTONE (ST. MARY), a parish, in the union of Tetbury, Upper division of the hundred of BERKELEY, W. division of the county of GLOUCESTER, 2 miles (N. W.) from Tetbury; containing 178 inhabitants. This place is of very remote antiquity, and there are still some remains of a castle in which a meeting was held, in 1048, by Earl Godwin and his son, for the alleged purpose of aiding Edward the Confessor to repress the incursions of the Welsh. The castle in the reign of Edward III. was enlarged and repaired by

Seal and Arms.

BEWDLEY, a borough, market-town, and chapelry, having separate jurisdiction, in the parish of RIBBESFORD and union of KIDDERMINSTER, locally in the Lower division of the hundred of DODDINGTREE, and in the Hundred-House and W. divisions of the county of WORCESTER, 14 miles (N. W.) from Worcester, and 126 (N. W.) from London; containing 3400 inhabitants. This place, in Camden's "Britannia" called *Bellus Locus* from the pleasantness of its situation and the beauty of the surrounding scenery, anciently obtained also the appellation of *Beaulieu*, of which its present name is a corruption. In the 13th of Henry IV., a petition was presented to parliament from the "men of Bristowe" and Gloucester, praying that they might navigate the river Severn without being subject to new taxes levied by the men of *Beaudley*. At this time Bewdley appears to have enjoyed many privileges, among which was that of sanctuary for persons who had shed blood: it was extra-parochial, but, by letters-patent granted by Henry VI., was annexed to the parish of Ribbesford. Edward IV. gave the inhabitants a charter of incorporation in the twelfth year of his reign; and Henry VII. erected a palace here for his son Arthur, who was married in it by proxy to Catharine of Arragon: the prince dying soon after at Ludlow, his corpse was removed to this town, where it lay in state previously to interment in the cathedral of Worcester. Bewdley was formerly included in the marches of Wales, but by an act of parliament, passed in the reign of Henry VIII., was added to the county of Worcester. During the civil war in the time of Charles I., that monarch, who had been driven from Oxford by the parliamentary forces, retired with the remnant of his army to this town, where he encamped, in order to keep the river Severn between himself and the enemy. Whilst staying here, he was attacked by a party of Scottish cavalry, when several of his officers, and seventy men, were made prisoners; and in these attacks the palace was greatly damaged: the site is now occupied by a dwelling-house, and not a single vestige of the original edifice can, with certainty, be traced. The more ancient part of the town was built at a greater distance from the river, and the portion now called Load-street is supposed to have been merely the place where the inhabitants loaded their boats: there were four gates, two of which were standing in 1811, but have since been entirely demolished.

The TOWN is beautifully situated on the western bank of the river Severn, over which a light and elegant stone bridge was erected in 1797: the street leading from the bridge diverges right and left, but extends farther in the latter direction; it is paved, and lighted with gas. The houses in this street are in general well built, and of respectable appearance, and there are some handsome residences in the vicinity, among the most distinguished of which are Winterdyne, Ticknell, Spring Grove, and Ribbesford House; the inhabitants are amply supplied with water, the air is salubrious, and the surrounding scenery richly and pleasingly diversified.

Some years since, Bewdley was a place of considerable trade, having two markets and four fairs, and for a long period was the mart from which the neighbouring towns were supplied with grocery and other articles of consumption; but in consequence of the recent construction of canals, that portion of its trade has been diverted to other towns. The manufacture of woollen caps, known by the name of Dutch caps, was introduced here in consequence of the plague prevailing at Monmouth, where it had previously been carried on, and being encouraged by legislative enactments in the reign of Elizabeth, it continued for some time to flourish, but has now declined, and the present trade is principally in malt, the tanning of leather, and the making of combs. The market is on Saturday; and fairs are held on April 23rd, July 26th, and December 10th and 11th. The inhabitants were first incorporated in the 12th of Edward IV.: they received additional privileges from Henry VII., which were confirmed by Henry VIII.; and James I. granted a new charter. The corporation now consists of a mayor, four aldermen, and twelve councillors; the mayor and late mayor are justices of the peace, and two permanent magistrates have also been appointed. Bewdley sent members to parliament so early as the reign of Edward I., after which there was a long intermission. The elective franchise was again conferred by James I., since which time it has returned one member to parliament : the borough embraces the town of Stourport, three miles distant, also the Forest of Wire : the mayor is the returning officer. The town-hall is a neat building of stone, erected in 1808, with a front decorated with six square pilasters supporting a pediment, in which are the arms of the family of Lyttelton; under the hall is the entrance into the market-place, which has an arcade on each side for stalls, and an open area in the centre; at the extremity are two small prisons, one for malefactors, the other for debtors.

The township comprises 2840 acres. The LIVING is a perpetual curacy, endowed with £8 per annum, paid out of the exchequer, the revenue of a dissolved chantry which formerly existed here; net income, £220; patron, the Rector of Ribbesford. The chapel, a neat stone edifice, at the upper end of the street leading from the bridge, was erected in 1748, by the old corporation, aided by a subscription among the inhabitants and a brief, and has recently undergone considerable alteration by the expenditure of more than £800, contributed by the corporation and the inhabitants. There are places of worship for Baptists, the Society of Friends, Wesleyans, and Unitarians. The free grammar school, founded and endowed in 1591, by William Monnox or Monnoye, and further endowed in 1599 by Humphrey Hill, was made a royal foundation by charter' of James I.; the endowment, augmented by subsequent benefactions, produces an income of £46. The Blue-coat school, for thirty boys and thirty girls, has been enlarged, and united to the National School Society, two good rooms having been built for 160 children. Almshouses for six aged men, founded by Mr. Sayer, of Nettlestead, in the county of Suffolk, and endowed with £30 per annum, were rebuilt in 1763, by Sir Edward Winnington, bart., member for the borough. Burlton's almshouses, for fourteen aged women, were founded and endowed in 1645; and eight other houses were erected, and endowed with £6 per annum, in 1693, by Thomas Cook. John

Tombes, a celebrated biblical critic of the seventeenth century; and Richard Willis, Bishop of Winchester, and principal founder of the Society for Promoting Christian Knowledge, were natives of the town.

BEWERLEY, a township, in the chapelry and union of PATELEY-BRIDGE, parish of RIPON, Lower division of the wapentake of CLARO, W. riding of YORK, 11¼ miles (W. S. W.) from Ripon; containing 1329 inhabitants. This extensive moorland township includes the village of Greenhow-Hill, and comprises 5872 acres, whereof 2983 are common or waste : the vicinity formerly abounded with valuable lead-mines, which were worked to a considerable extent. The tithes have been commuted for £52, payable to the Dean and Chapter of Ripon. At Greenhow are places of worship for Primitive Methodists and Wesleyans; and a school endowed with a house and land, producing about £20 per annum. There are remains of an ancient chapel.

BEWHOLME, a township, in the parish of NUNKEELING, union of SKIRLAUGH, N. division of the wapentake of HOLDERNESS, E. riding of YORK, 3½ miles (N. W.) from Hornsea; containing 199 inhabitants. The principal landowners have been the families of Fauconberg, St. Quintin, and De la Pole; the monastery of Swine also held possessions here, which were afterwards, in the reign of Mary, granted, under the designation of "the Grange of Bewhall," to John Constable, to be held in capite by military service. The village, which is pleasant and well built, and on a commanding eminence, extends over a considerable space.

BEWICK, NEW, a township, in the parish of EGLINGHAM, union of GLENDALE, N. division of COQUETDALE ward and of NORTHUMBERLAND, 9½ miles (N. W. by W.) from Alnwick; containing 121 inhabitants. It comprises about 1200 acres of arable land : the river Breamish and the great north road to Edinburgh form portions of the boundary line. The impropriate tithes have been commuted for £140. 14,. and the vicarial for £57. 15.

BEWICK, OLD, a township, in the parish of EGLINGHAM, union of GLENDALE, N. division of COQUETDALE ward and of NORTHUMBERLAND, 10 miles (N. W. by W.) from Alnwick, on the road to Wooler; containing 176 inhabitants. It is bounded on the west by the river Breamish, and comprises about 5000 acres, of which 1000 are arable, 50 woodland, and the remainder pasture and moorland. The village, which is well built, commands an extensive and delightful prospect. The impropriate tithes have been commuted for £176. 2. 6., and the vicarial for £110. 5. There was anciently a chapel dedicated to the Holy Trinity, the ruins of which are situated a little to the north-west of the village; it was destroyed by the Puritans, was restored in 1695, but again fell into decay. On Bewick Hill is a British encampment of a semicircular form, with a double rampart; and at Harehope burn, half a mile eastward, is another, supposed to have been an outwork.

BEXHILL (ST. PETER), a parish, in the union of BATTLE, hundred of BEXHILL, rape of HASTINGS, E. division of SUSSEX, 8 miles (S.) from Battle; containing 1916 inhabitants. It is bounded on the south by the English Channel, and comprises 6000 acres by computation; the surface is pleasingly varied, and in the northern parts richly embellished with wood; about 70 acres are planted with hops. The village, which is situated on an eminence, commands extensive prospects; and the coast road from Dovor, by way of Hastings and St. Leonard's, to Brighton, passes through it. Here also is a station of the Hastings and Brighton railway. The living is a vicarage, endowed with the rectorial tithes, and valued in the king's books at £24. 10. 2½.; net income, £977 : patron, the Bishop of Chichester. The church is an ancient cruciform structure, partly in the early and partly in the later English style, with a low embattled tower. A chapel of ease has been erected on Little Common, and there is a place of worship for Wesleyans. Sir Richard de la Wyche, 13th bishop of Chichester, died here. There are several chalybeate springs.

BEXLEY (St. Mary), a parish, in the union of Dartford, partly in the hundred of Lessness, but chiefly in the hundred of Ruxley, lathe of Sutton-at-Hone, W. division of Kent, 3 miles (W.) from Dartford; containing, with the hamlets of Blendon, Bridgend, and Upton, 3955 inhabitants. The manor was purchased from the crown in the reign of James I., by the celebrated antiquary William Camden, who conveyed it to the University of Oxford, in trust, to found a professorship of ancient history. The parish comprises 5025 acres, of which 1093 are woodland. The living is a vicarage, rated in the king's books at £13. 4. 7.; patron, Viscount Sidney; impropriators, the coheiresses of Thomas Latham, Esq.: the rectorial tithes have been commuted for £1046, and the vicarial for £700. 10. A chapel of ease was erected on Bexley Heath in 1836, by subscription, aided by a grant from the Church Building Society; and a district chapel was built in 1840 at Halfway-street, at the expense of John Malcolm, Esq., in whom the patronage is vested. The Right Hon. Nicholas Vansittart, on retiring from the chancellorship of the exchequer, was created Baron Bexley, March 1st, 1823.

BEXTON, a township, in the parish of Knutsford, union of Altrincham, hundred of Bucklow, N. division of the county of Chester, 1 mile (S. S. E.) from Knutsford; containing 96 inhabitants. The manor was for many centuries in moieties, one of which passed from the Bextons to the Tableys, and from them to the Daniels, who, in 1699, purchased the other moiety of Lord Cholmondeley: the whole came by purchase, in 1775, to the Leicester family. The township comprises 520 acres, the soil of which is clay and sand; about one-fourth is arable, and the remainder pasture: the surface of the land is level.

BEXWELL (St. Mary), a parish, in the union of Downham, hundred of Clackclose, W. division of Norfolk, 1 mile (E.) from Downham; containing 70 inhabitants, and comprising 1177a. 3r. 17p. The manor anciently belonged to William de Bexwell, to whom Henry III. granted permission to hold a market on Thursday, and a fair on Whit-Monday. The living is a discharged rectory, valued in the king's books at £7. 11. 8., and in the patronage of the Bishop of Ely: the tithes have been commuted for £330, and the glebe consists of 41 acres. The church is built of ragstone obtained in the vicinity.

BEYTON, or Beighton (All Saints), a parish, in the union of Stow, hundred of Thedwastry, W. division of Suffolk, 5 miles (E. by S.) from Bury; containing 384 inhabitants, and consisting by measurement

231

of 1625 acres. The living is a discharged rectory, valued in the king's books at £4. 3. 9., and in the patronage of the Crown : the tithes have been commuted for £210, and the glebe comprises 10 acres. The church has a round tower with buttresses.

BIBURY (St. Mary), a parish, in the union of Northleach, partly in the hundred of Bradley, and partly in that of Brightwell's-Barrow, E. division of the county of Gloucester, 5 miles (N. W.) from Fairford; comprising the chapelry of Winson, and the tythings of Ablington and Arlington, and containing 1077 inhabitants. It comprises by measurement upwards of 4000 acres, chiefly arable land. The living is a vicarage, valued in the king's books at £13. 1. 5½.; net income, £1023; patron, W. Strahan, Esq. There is a chapel of ease at Winson, two miles distant from the parochial church. Thomas Tryon, author of a curious work entitled The Way to Health, Long Life, and Happiness, published in 1691, was a native of the place.

BICESTER (St. Eadburg), a market-town and parish, and the head of a union, in the hundred of Ploughley, county of Oxford, 12½ miles (N. E. by N.) from Oxford, and 55 (N. W. by W.) from London; comprising the townships of Market-End and King's-End, and containing 3022 inhabitants. This place, by the Saxons called Burenceaster and Burnacester, both implying a fortified place, is supposed to derive its name either from its founder, Birinus, a canonized Saxon prelate; from Bernwood, a forest in Buckinghamshire, not far from which it is situated; or from the small stream of the Bure, on which it stands. A priory for a prior and eleven canons of the Augustine order was founded in 1182, and dedicated to St. Eadburg, by Gilbert Basset, Baron of Haddington, and his wife, Egiline de Courteney: the revenue, at the Dissolution, was £167. 2. 10. In 1355, a royal license was granted to Nicholas Jurdan, warden of the chapel of St. John the Baptist, for the establishment of an hospital for poor and infirm people; but the design does not appear to have been carried into execution. During the civil war in the reign of Charles I., the inhabitants suffered by repeated exactions levied on them by both parties; and, in 1643, a skirmish took place, in which the royalists were defeated and driven through the town.

Bicester is situated in a valley, on the banks of a stream which falls into the river Ray, which joins the Cherwell, near Islip; it is neatly built, and amply supplied with water. The female inhabitants are employed in making pillow-lace; and the town is noted for excellent malt-liquor. The market is on Friday; and fairs are held on the Friday in Easter-week, the first Friday in June, August 5th, and the third Friday in December; there are also statute-fairs on the first three Fridays after Michaelmas. The county magistrates hold petty-sessions for the district every Friday: the powers of the county debt-court of Bicester, established in 1847, extend over the registration-district of Bicester. The LIVING is a discharged vicarage, valued in the king's books at £16; net income, £250; patron and impropriator, Lady Page Turner: the tithes for King's-End were commuted for land and annual money payments in 1793. There is an excellent parsonage-house, with a large and productive garden; the premises have been greatly improved by the incumbent, the Rev. J. W. Watts. The church, which is supposed to have been built about the year 1400, on the site of a former edifice, is a spacious and handsome structure with a lofty square tower, and contains many interesting monuments and some antique sculptures. There are places of worship for Independents and Wesleyans. A school is supported partly by endowment; and lands producing about £200 per annum, and a few minor charitable bequests, are appropriated to the relief of the poor. The union of Bicester comprises 38 parishes and places, of which 36 are in the county of Oxford, and two in that of Bucks, and contains a population of 15,201; the union house is situated near the town. In the vicinity, on the London-road, is Graven-hill Wood, on the north side of which ran the Akeman-street; and not far from the town, on the west side, is St. Eadburg's well, famous before the Reformation for miraculous cures, and which proved very useful in supplying water to the town during the dry summer of 1666. In making some excavations in 1819, the foundations of the priory, a vast mass of sculptured fragments, pieces of painted glass, and other relics, were discovered.

BICKENHALL, a parish, in the union of TAUNTON, hundred of ABDICK and BULSTONE, W. division of SOMERSET, 5½ miles (S. E. by E.) from Taunton; containing 264 inhabitants. The living is annexed to the rectory of Staple-Fitzpaine: the tithes have been commuted for a rent-charge of £200, and there are about 8½ acres of glebe.

BICKENHILL, CHURCH (ST. PETER), a parish, in the union of MERIDEN, Solihull division of the hundred of HEMLINGFORD, N. division of the county of WARWICK, 8½ miles (E. by S.) from Birmingham; containing, with Church, Middle, Lyndon, and Marston Quarters, 774 inhabitants. This place is of considerable antiquity, and included Kington, or Kingsford, now partly in this parish and partly in that of Solihull, the church of which was given to the nuns of Mergate, now Market-street, in the 5th of Henry III. by Henry le Notte, owner of the Marston-Hall estate. The parish comprises 3771a. 3r. 17p., of which the soil is in some parts a stiff clay, and in others of a lighter quality. It is situated near the London and Birmingham and the Stratford and Warwick canals, and is intersected by the London and Holyhead road, and the London and Birmingham and the Derby railways, the rateable value of the railway property in the parish being £2652. Many improvements have lately taken place. The living is a discharged vicarage, valued in the king's books at £7. 17. 3.; patron, the Earl of Aylesford: the incumbent's tithes have been commuted for £325, and the glebe consists of 19 acres, with a vicarage-house. The church, on whose site, according to Dugdale, a beacon existed in very early times, is an ancient structure chiefly in the Norman style, with a tower, but has received some subsequent additions of inferior character. A national school is supported by subscription.

BICKER (ST. SWITHIN), a parish, in the union of BOSTON, wapentake of KIRTON, parts of HOLLAND, county of LINCOLN, 1½ mile (N. E. by N.) from Donnington; containing, with the extra-parochial liberties of Copping-Sike and Ferry-Corner, 925 inhabitants. The parish is situated on the road from Donnington to Boston, and bounded on the west by the navigable river Forty-foot, which falls into the Witham at Boston. 232

It comprises by measurement 3579 acres, of which one-half is arable, and the other half pasture and meadow; the soil is chiefly sand and clay; the surface is flat, and, being subject in part to inundation, has been much improved by draining. The living is a discharged vicarage, valued in the king's books at £15; net income, £560, arising from 270 acres of land given in lieu of tithes on the inclosure; patrons and appropriators, the Dean and Chapter of Lincoln. The church is an ancient structure, with a central tower. There is a place of worship for Wesleyans.

BICKERING, a hamlet, in the parish of HOLTON, union of LINCOLN, W. division of the wapentake of WRAGGOE, parts of LINDSEY, union and county of LINCOLN, 2 miles (N. by W.) from Wragby.

BICKERSTAFFE, a township and ecclesiastical district, in the parish and union of ORMSKIRK, hundred of WEST DERBY, S. division of the county of LANCASTER, 3½ miles (S. E.) from Ormskirk; containing 1579 inhabitants. This was very early the seat of a family of the same name, from whom it passed to the Athertons and the Stanleys: the Earl of Derby is now proprietor of the entire township. It comprises 6291 acres, whereof 3550 are arable, 2250 pasture, 41 wood, and 450 common or waste. The soil is a sandy loam, part inclining to moor, and part to clay, with a red sandstone formation, beneath which is abundance of coal; the surface is elevated, presenting distant views of the Welsh hills and the sea. There is a quarry of a hard blueish stone; and two excellent collieries are in operation. The living is a perpetual curacy, in the patronage of the Earl of Derby; income, £150, with a house: the impropriate tithes have been commuted for £750. The church, dedicated to the Holy Trinity, and erected in 1843 at an expense of £2500, is in the early English style, with an apse at the east end, and a square tower surmounted by a graceful spire of great height, forming a conspicuous object in the surrounding scenery. The cost of the church, the endowment, and parsonage-house, with most of the cost of the schools, was defrayed by the noble patron. Bickerstaffe Hall, now a farmhouse, was the seat of the Stanley family. The present earl, in the lifetime of his father, the late earl, in 1832, was created a peer by the title of Lord Stanley, of Bickerstaffe; and his son, the present Lord Stanley, was, under the same circumstances, summoned to the upper house, in 1844, as Baron Stanley, also of this place.

BICKERSTON.—See BIXTON.

BICKERTON, a township, in the parish of MALPAS, union of NANTWICH, Higher division of the hundred of BROXTON, S. division of the county of CHESTER, 4¾ miles (N. N. E.) from Malpas; containing 401 inhabitants. The township comprises 1755 acres, of which 600 are common or waste; the soil is light. A church has been built, in aid of which the Incorporated Society contributed £120; 222 of the sittings are free: the living is a perpetual curacy in the gift of the Rector, with a net income of £120. The tithes have been commuted for a rent-charge of £110. On the summit of a hill is an intrenchment called Maiden Castle.

BICKERTON, a township, in the parish and union of ROTHBURY, W. division of COQUETDALE ward, N. division of NORTHUMBERLAND, 4¾ miles (W. by S.) from Rothbury; containing 18 inhabitants. It stands upon a pleasant level, the moorlands forming a semi-

Carew, "king of the beggars," was born in the par.
sonage-house, his father being .the rector, and was
buried here.

BICKLEIGH, a parish, in the union of PLYMPTON
ST. MARY, hundred of ROBOROUGH, Midland-Roborough and S. divisions of DEVON, 7 miles (N. N. E.)
from Plymouth; containing 469 inhabitants. The
Dartmoor and Plymouth railway passes along the
parish. The living is a vicarage endowed with the great
tithes, with the living of Sheepstor annexed, valued in
the king's books at £11. 4. 7., and in the gift of Sir
Ralph Lopes, Bart. : the tithes of Bickleigh have been
commuted for £172. 10., and there are 33 acres of glebe.
The patron lately rebuilt the church, and the new edifice
was consecrated in August 1839.

BICKLEY, a township, in the parish of MALPAS,
union of NANTWICH, Higher division of the hundred of
BROXTON, S. division of the county of CHESTER, 3½
miles (E. N. E.) from Malpas ; containing 489 inhabitants. It comprises 2092 acres ; the soil is clay, gravel,
and peat. On the 18th of July, 1657, about a quarter
of an acre of elevated ground, covered with full-grown
trees, sank suddenly, with a noise resembling thunder,
to such a depth below the surface of the surrounding
ground, that even the summits of the trees were not
visible, from their total immersion in water ; the water
has long been dried up, and the chasm, called the
Barrell-Fall, from being situated on the Barrell farm,
is now quite dry. There is a place of worship for Wesleyans.

BICKMERSH, a hamlet, in the parish of WELFORD,
union of STRATFORD-ON-AVON, Stratford division of the
hundred of BARLICHWAY, S. division of the county of
WARWICK, 5¾ miles (S. by E.) from Alcester ; containing, with Little Dorsington, 130 inhabitants. The
hamlet is situated on the borders of Gloucester and
Worcester, being surrounded, except on the north, by
those counties ; it comprises 1240 acres. A chapel was
founded in the reign of Henry II. by William Foliot,
then lord of the manor.

BICKNACRE, a hamlet, partly in the parish of
DANBURY, and partly in that of WOODHAM-FERRIS,
union and hundred of CHELMSFORD, S. division of
ESSEX; containing 304 inhabitants.

BICKNELL.—See BICKENHALL.

BICKNOLLER, a parish, in the union of WILLITON,
hundred of WILLITON and FREEMANNERS, W. division
of SOMERSET, 13 miles (N. W.) from Taunton ; containing 345 inhabitants. It comprises 1320 acres, of which
560 are arable, 250 meadow and pasture, 81 plantation,
wood, and orchard, and 340 common. The living is a
vicarage not in charge ; patrons and appropriators, the
Dean and Chapter of Wells : the rectorial tithes have
been commuted for £139, and the vicarial for £77. 10. ;
there are 2½ acres of glebe. Two fortifications, named
Trendle Castle and Turk's Castle, together with the
ruins of a beacon, occupy the summit of an eminence
near the village ; and a variety of Roman coins has been
found in the vicinity.

BICKNOR, or CHURCH-BICKNOR (ST. JAMES), a
parish, in the union of HOLLINGBOURNE, hundred of
EYHORNE, lathe of AYLESFORD, W. division of KENT,
4½ miles (S. S. W.) from Sittingbourne; containing 46
inhabitants. It comprises 631 acres, of which 467 are
arable and pasture, principally the former, and the

remainder is wood; the surface slopes to the north-east, and the soil is clay mixed with flint. The living is a discharged rectory, valued in the king's books at £5. 10.; net income, £115; patron, the Lord Chancellor: there are about 20 acres of glebe. Here are the remains of a Danish intrenchment, and vestiges of an old British town burnt by the Danes when ravaging this part of the country.

BICKNOR, ENGLISH (St. Mary), a parish, in the union of Monmouth, hundred of St. Briavells, W. division of the county of Gloucester, 3 miles (N.) from Coleford; containing 576 inhabitants. It comprises 2411a. 1r. 4p., and lies within the Forest of Dean, on the eastern bank of the Wye, opposite to Welsh-Bick-nor. The manor exceeds the parish in extent by 728 acres. There are mines of coal and iron, the former of which are worked; and stone is quarried for building and road-making. The living is a rectory, valued in the king's books at £13. 6. 8., and in the gift of Queen's College, Oxford: the tithes have been commuted for £390, and the glebe comprises 9 acres, with a house. The church has some portions in the Norman style, and stands within the area of an ancient fortification, the fosse belonging to which may still be traced.

BICKNOR, WELSH (St. Margaret), a parish, in the union of Monmouth, hundred of Wormelow, county of Hereford, 7 miles (S. by W.) from Ross; containing 74 inhabitants. This parish comprises 850a. 23p., of which 348 are arable, 226 meadow and pasture, 149 wood, and 54 common and roads. It is almost surrounded by the river Wye, the banks of which are rich in picturesque scenery. The soil is various, partaking of sand and gravel, generally light, a rich mould in some parts, and in others clay; the surface is hilly, and in a few places consists of rock. At Court-field, a private mansion about half a mile off, is a Roman Catholic chapel; and tradition relates that Henry V. was nursed there, under the care of the Countess of Salisbury, who, according to the same authority, is represented by a recumbent stone figure in the church. The living is a discharged rectory, valued in the king's books at £4. 6. 8., and in the gift of the Lord Chancellor: the tithes have been commuted for £152. 10., and there are about 18 acres of glebe. The church, which is in the early English style, contains an antique chalice, said to have been brought into Europe with the Saracens; the lid is of beaten silver, and it bears other evidences of high antiquity.

BICKTON, a chapelry, in the parish of St. Chad, liberty of the borough of Shrewsbury, N. division of Salop, 3½ miles (N. W. by W.) from Shrewsbury; containing, with the hamlet of Calcott, 560 inhabitants. The navigable river Severn runs through the chapelry, which is also intersected by the Roman Watling-street. The living is a perpetual curacy; net income, £60; patron, the Vicar of St. Chad's.

BICKTON, a tything, in the parish and union of Fordingbridge, Ringwood and S. divisions of the county of Southampton; containing 273 inhabitants.

BICTON (Holy Trinity), a parish, in the union of St. Thomas, hundred of East Budleigh, Woodbury and S. divisions of Devon, 3¾ miles (W. S. W.) from Sidmouth; containing, with the hamlet of Yettington, 198 inhabitants. It comprises 684 acres of inclosed land, and there are supposed to be 500 acres of common;

the soil is in general sandy, and the surface hilly: the river Otter borders the parish. The possessor of the manor was formerly obliged to "find a county gaol," but was discharged from that obligation by an act of parliament, within the last fifty years. The living is a rectory, valued in the king's books at £12. 13. 4., and in the gift of the family of Rolle: the tithes have been commuted for £160. 17., and there are 50 acres of glebe.

BIDBOROUGH (St. Lawrence), a parish, in the union of Tonbridge, hundred of Washlingstone, lathe of Aylesford, W. division of Kent, 3 [miles (S. W.) from Tonbridge; containing 260 inhabitants. It comprises by measurement 1300 acres, of which about 360 are arable, 390 pasture and meadow, 43 acres hops, and 507 common. The soil is a mixture of iron-sand, sandstone, and clay, and is not very productive; the surface is hilly and irregular. The living is a discharged rectory, valued in the king's books at £5. 4. 4½., and in the patronage of the Trustees of W. Gay, Esq.: the tithes have been commuted for £179. 4., and there are 79 acres of glebe. The church is an ancient structure, with a Norman doorway in the earliest period of that style. There are some chalybeate springs.

BIDDENDEN (All Saints), a parish, in the union of Tenterden, hundred of Barclay, Lower division of the lathe of Scray, W. division of Kent, 5 miles (E. by N.) from Cranbrook; containing 1486 inhabitants. It comprises 7207a. 2r. 20p., of which 1100 acres are in wood, and is situated on the Maidstone and Tenterden road, and near the South-Eastern railway; the soil is clayey, and the surface in some parts rather hilly. The place was once famous for its clothing-trade, which has entirely decayed. Fairs, chiefly for horses and Welsh cattle, are held on Old Lady-day and November 8th. The living is a rectory, valued in the king's books at £35, and in the patronage of the Archbishop of Canterbury: the tithes have been commuted for £687, and the glebe consists of about 18 acres of land of good quality, with a commodious residence. The church is a fine structure in the later English style, with an embattled tower, and is capable of accommodating 1000 persons. There is a meeting-house for dissenters. John Mayne, in 1566, bequeathed a sum for the erection of a school-house, and endowed it with a rent-charge of £20. 3. 4. A distribution of bread and cheese to the poor takes place on Easter-Sunday, the expense of which is defrayed from the rental of about 20 acres of land, the reputed bequests of the Biddenden Maids, two sisters of the name of Chulkhurst, who, according to tradition, were born joined together by the hips and shoulders, in the year 1100, and, having lived in that state to the age of thirty-four, died within six hours of each other.

BIDDENHAM (St. James), a parish, in the hundred of Willey, union and county of Bedford, 2½ miles (W. by N.) from Bedford; containing 345 inhabitants. The family of the Botelers, of whom was Sir William Boteler, lord mayor of London in 1515, were settled here for ten generations. The property afterwards passed into the family of Lord Trevor, subsequently created Viscount Hampden; and on the decease of John, the last viscount, in 1823, it was bequeathed to the Hon. George Rice, eldest son of Lord Dynevor, who assumed the name of Trevor. The parish is bounded on the south, west, and north by the river

234

Ouse, and on the east by the borough of Bedford; and is intersected by the road from that town to Newport-Pagnell, a little to the south of which thoroughfare the village is situated. The soil is good, though gravelly; and the scenery picturesque. The living is a discharged vicarage, valued in the king's books at £8; net income, £100; patron and impropriator, the Hon. Mr. Trevor: the glebe consists of 43 acres, with a good house. The church contains a handsome font, and several memorials to the Botelers. A national school here has an endowment.

BIDDESHAM, a parish, in the union of AXBRIDGE, hundred of BEMPSTONE, E. division of SOMERSET, 3 miles (W. by S.) from Axbridge; containing 145 inhabitants. It is recorded that the Danes were defeated here by the Saxons in the reign of Alfred. The parish is bounded by the river Axe on the north, and the road from Bridgwater to Cross on the south; and comprises by measurement 574 acres. The living is in the patronage of the Bishop of Bath and Wells: the tithes have been commuted for £137, and the glebe consists of 14 acres, with a house. The church contains a singing-gallery, lately erected at the expense of the incumbent and parishioners.

BIDDESTONE (ST. NICHOLAS AND ST. PETER), a parish, in the union and hundred of CHIPPENHAM, Chippenham and Calne, and N. divisions of WILTS, 4¼ miles (W.) from Chippenham; containing 452 inhabitants, of whom 428 are in the division of St. Nicholas, and 24 in that of St. Peter. The living is a discharged rectory, with the perpetual curacy of Slaughterford annexed, valued in the king's books at £2. 18. 4., and in the gift of Winchester College: the tithes have been commuted for £33. 10., and the glebe consists of 6 acres. The church contains a monument to the memory of Edmund Smith, A.M., a poet of some repute, who died in the neighbourhood, in 1709.

BIDDLESDON (ST. MARGARET), a parish, in the union of BRACKLEY, hundred and county of BUCKINGHAM, 3½ miles (N. E. by E.) from Brackley; containing 169 inhabitants. An abbey of Cistercian monks was founded here in 1147, the revenue of which, at the Dissolution, was £142. 1. 3. The manor was afterwards given to Thomas, Lord Wriothesley, and passed by purchase to the Peckhams, from whom the estate was seized by Queen Elizabeth, in satisfaction of a debt due to the crown, and given to Arthur, Lord Grey. On the attainder of this nobleman's son, in 1603, it was conferred on Sir George Villiers, afterwards Duke of Buckingham: it was sold in 1681 to Mr. Sayer; was purchased of his family by Earl Verney; and in 1791, from a descendant of the earl's, by George Morgan, Esq. The parish lies on the borders of Northamptonshire. In 1315, Edward II. granted to the convent a market on Monday, and a fair on St. Margaret's day. The living is a perpetual curacy; net income, £69; patron, G. Morgan, Esq.

BIDDLESTON, a township, in the parish of ALLENTON, union of ROTHBURY, W. division of Co-QUETDALE ward, N. division of NORTHUMBERLAND, 7¾ miles (N. W. by W.) from Rothbury; containing 140 inhabitants. The manor was granted, in 1272, to Sir Walter Selby, Knt., and has ever since continued in the possession of his descendants. The township is on the road from Clennel to Netherton, and south of
235

the Netherton burn, which flows at a short distance from the village. The manor-house, a commodious stone building of modern erection, occupies the summit of a gentle declivity, commanding, on the south, a fine prospect of the vale of Coquet. There is a place of worship for Roman Catholics.

BIDDULPH (ST. LAWRENCE), a parish, in the union of CONGLETON, N. division of the hundred of PIREHILL and of the county of STAFFORD, 3¾ miles (S. E. by. S.) from Congleton; containing 2314 inhabitants. It comprises 5200 acres, of which 310 are open common; the surface is elevated, and the soil is in excellent cultivation: the river Trent has its source in the northern part, under a high rocky ridge called Mole Cop. The parish is divided into the four hamlets of Over Biddulph or Overton, Middle and Nether Biddulph, and Knypersley; it abounds in coal, has several quarries of hard and durable stone, and contains manufactories for cotton and earthenware, and iron-works. In 1837 an act was obtained for making a new road hence to Congleton. Biddulph Hall, at the north end of the parish, was anciently the residence of the Biddulph family: Knypersley Hall was the seat of a family of that name, and afterwards of the Gresleys, and is now the property and residence of J. Bateman, Esq. The living is a discharged vicarage, valued in the king's books at £4. 9. 8.; patron and impropriator, Mr. Bateman. The great tithes have been commuted for £180. 8., and the vicarial for £90; the glebe consists of 34 acres. The church was an ancient edifice, but has lately been rebuilt, with the exception of the tower, at an expense of £2000. There is a place of worship for Wesleyans on Biddulph Moor; and a school is endowed with about £14 per annum. Here are the ruins of a Druidical temple, and near them the remains of three curious caves excavated in the solid rock.

Corporation Seal.

BIDEFORD (ST. MARY), a sea-port, incorporated market-town, and parish, having separate jurisdiction, and the head of a union, locally in the hundred of SHEBBEAR, Great Torrington and N. divisions of DEVON, 39 miles (N. W. by W.) from Exeter, and 201 (W. by S.) from London; containing 5211 inhabitants, of whom 4830 are in the town. This place, called also Bytheford, of which its modern appellative is a variation, derives its name from being situated near an ancient ford on the river Torridge. It was a town of some importance in the time of the Saxons : in early records it is styled a borough, and in the reigns of Edward I. and II. returned members to parliament; but the burgesses having pleaded inability to supply the usual pecuniary allowance to their representatives, this distinction was withdrawn. In 1271, Richard de Grenville, to whose ancestor Bideford had been granted in the reign of William Rufus, obtained for it a market and a fair; and, in 1573, Queen Elizabeth incorporated the inhabitants, and made the town a free borough. From that time it rapidly increased as a place of trade, and the expeditions of Sir Walter Raleigh to Virginia and of Sir Richard Grenville to Carolina, established the basis of its foreign commerce. During the civil war in the reign of Charles I., two small forts were erected on the banks of the river, and a third at Appledore, which was garrisoned for the parliament; they were taken for the king by Col. Digby, after the battle of Torrington, Sept. 2nd, 1643. Between this period and the beginning of the eighteenth century, Bideford was in its highest prosperity. The weaving of silk was introduced in 1650, and after the revocation of the edict of Nantes, in 1685, many French Protestants settled in the town, and established the manufacture of silk and cotton; a great quantity of wool was imported from Spain, and in 1699 its trade with Newfoundland was inferior only to that of London and Exeter. From 1700 to 1755, the imports of tobacco exceeded those of every port except London.

The TOWN is situated on the river Torridge, which in spring tides rises to the height of twenty-two feet above the level of low-water mark. The greater part is built on the acclivity of the western bank of the river, and is connected with that on the eastern side by a noble stone bridge of twenty-four arches, of which some are of sufficient span to allow free passage for vessels of sixty tons' burthen. The bridge was erected in the early part of the fourteenth century, by a subscription raised in the counties of Devon and Cornwall, under the auspices of Grandison, Bishop of Exeter, who being influenced by a dream of Gornard, the parish priest, granted indulgences to all who should contribute to the work: a considerable estate in houses and lands, for keeping it in repair, is vested in trustees. The town consists of several streets, some of which are well paved and lighted; the houses are in general of respectable appearance, and the town is amply supplied with water. There are assembly and reading rooms on the quay; and from the salubrity of the air, the picturesque beauties of the surrounding scenery, and the improved facility of communication with Barnstaple and Torrington, owing to the new roads that have been made, Bideford has become a place of considerable resort.

The PORT, including within its jurisdiction Appledore and the harbours of Clovelly and Hartland, also a convenient station for wind-bound vessels, carries on a considerable colonial and coasting trade. The principal exports are sails, cordage, British manufactured goods, and articles of general supply, to the fisheries of Newfoundland and the British colonies in North America, oak-bark to Ireland, apples to Scotland, earthenware to Wales, and corn and flour to Bristol; the imports are timber from America and the Baltic, and limestone, coal, and culm, from Bristol and Wales. The river, in spring tides, is navigable for vessels of 300 tons' burthen, as far as the bridge, two miles and a half above which it is connected, by means of a sea-lock, with the Torrington canal. The quay, 1200 feet in length, and of proportionate breadth, has been greatly improved. Ship-building is extensively carried on: during the late war, several frigates were launched at this port, and there are eight or ten dockyards, in which smaller vessels are built. The principal articles of manufacture are cordage, sails, and common earthenware; there are also several tan-yards, and a small lace-manufactory. Culm and black mineral paint are found in the vicinity, and on the rectorial glebe; some old culm-mines have been lately re-opened, with every prospect of advantage. The

market days are Tuesday and Saturday, and fairs are held on Feb. 14th, July 18th, and Nov. 13th. The inhabitants were originally incorporated by charter of the 16th of Elizabeth, confirmed and extended by another granted by James I.; the government is now vested in a mayor, four aldermen, and twelve councillors, of whom the mayor and late mayor are justices, and there are four other permanent magistrates appointed by the crown: the borough and parish are co-extensive. The recorder holds a court of quarter-sessions; petty-sessions are held monthly, and there is a court of record for the recovery of debts to any amount. The powers of the county debt-court of Bideford, established in 1847, extend over the registration-district of Bideford, and part of Barnstaple district. The town-hall, erected in 1698, is a neat and commodious building, having two prisons underneath, one for malefactors, the other for debtors; and a gaol and bridewell have been lately built on the eastern side of the river. A handsome hall called the Bridge Hall was erected in 1758, by the trustees of the Bridge estate, with a schoolroom adjoining.

The parish comprises 2758 acres, of which 287 are common or waste. The LIVING is a rectory, valued in the king's books at £27. 7. 6., and in the patronage of Lewis William Buck, Esq.; the tithes have been commuted for £590, and the glebe consists of 48 acres. The church is a spacious cruciform structure in the early English style, containing a handsome stone screen, and some interesting monuments. There are places of worship for Baptists, Independents, and Wesleyans. The free grammar school, of remote foundation, was rebuilt in 1657, and in 1689 was endowed by Mrs. Susannah Stuckley with an estate of £200 value; a good house was purchased for the master with money arising from the sale of timber on the estate, which now lets for £56 per annum. A charity school is supported by the trustees of the Bridge estate, and by subscription; a building has likewise been erected for a national school. Almshouses in Maiden-street, for seven families, were erected in 1646, by John Strange, alderman of Bideford; and an hospital in the Old Town, for twelve families, was built pursuant to the will of Henry Amory, who died in 1663. The poor law union of Bideford comprises 18 parishes and places, and contains a population of 19,568. Sir Richard Grenville, who distinguished himself in 1591, in an action fought near the island of Flores, with a Spanish fleet; Thomas Stuckley, an eccentric character, the supposed original of Sterne's *Captain Shandy*; Dr. John Shebbeare, a noted political writer, born in 1709; and the Rev. Zachary Mudge, a learned divine, and master of the grammar school, were natives of Bideford. The Rev. James Hervey, author of the *Meditations* and other popular works, was curate of the place from 1738 till 1742.

BIDFORD (ST. LAWRENCE), a parish, in the union of ALCESTER, Stratford division of the hundred of BARLICHWAY, S. division of the county of WARWICK, 4 miles (S. by E.) from Alcester; containing, with the hamlets of Barton, Broom, and Marcliff, 1567 inhabitants. This place is situated on the northern bank of the navigable river Avon, and the river Arrow skirts the parish on the west. It was an ancient demesne of the crown, having been in the possession of Edward the Confessor, and was principally held by the monarchs

and Everton; and northward, the Channel, bounding the horizon. These objects are also viewed from the top of the lighthouse. A school is endowed with £15 per annum, and a house and garden for the master.

BIELBY, a chapelry, in the parish of Hayton, union of POCKLINGTON, Holme-Beacon division of the wapentake of HARTHILL, E. riding of YORK, 3½ miles (S. by W.) from Pocklington; containing 273 inhabitants. It comprises about 1220 acres of land, of which a great part, together with the manor, belongs to Merton College, Oxford: the village, which is of neat appearance, is in the vicinity of the Pocklington canal. The tithes were commuted in 1814 for an allotment of land: the chapel is an ancient building, dedicated to St. Giles, and is served by the vicar. There is a place of worship for Wesleyans.

BIERLEY, NORTH, a township, in the parish and union of BRADFORD, wapentake of MORLEY, W. riding of YORK, 2 miles (S.) from Bradford; containing 9512 inhabitants. This township comprises by computation 3264 acres, of which 2250 are pasture, 276 arable, 238 woodland, and about 500 waste. The old Hall has been rebuilt in a handsome modern style; it is beautifully situated in grounds tastefully embellished, and in front of the house is a noble cedar of Lebanon, presented when a seedling to Dr. Richardson of Bierley by Sir Hans Sloane, more than a century since, and which has attained a stately and majestic growth. Royds Hall, which has been for many years the residence of the Dawson family, was originally built by the Rookes, who held the manor from the time of Henry VIII., till the close of the last century; it is in the ancient English style. The manor of Royds Hall, together with the minerals underneath the estate, was purchased from the last proprietor in 1788, by the ancestors of Messrs. Hird, Dawson, and Hardy, who originally established the celebrated *Low Moor* iron-works, now the most important in the north of England, both for extent, and for the superior quality of their produce. The works comprise furnaces, forges, tilts, and mills, on a very extensive scale, both for the manufacture of pig and bar iron, and for rolling and slitting it into sheets, bars, and rods, with foundries for the casting of cannon and ordnance of all kinds. Boilers for steam-engines, sugar-pans for the East and West Indies, water-pipes of large calibre, and a great variety of other articles, are manufactured here. The *Bierley* iron-works were commenced in 1810 by Henry Leah and James Marshall, Esqrs., and their partners, who hold on lease from Miss Currer all the minerals under the east end of Bierley, together with those under her estates in the townships of Bowling and Okenshaw. These works are confined to the manufacture of pig-iron, which, being the produce of ore from the same mine, is equal in quality with that of the Low Moor and Bowling works; they are conducted on an extensive scale. A worsted-mill has been built near the Low Moor. Bierley chapel was erected in 1766, in the township of Bowling, though immediately bordering on the north-east of North Bierley, by Richard Richardson, Esq., son of Dr. Richardson, but was not consecrated till 1824; it was enlarged by Miss Currer in 1828, and 1831, principally for the accommodation of the poor, and is a beautiful structure in the Grecian style. The living is a perpetual curacy, with a good house, and is in the patronage of Miss Currer, whose liberal addition of £40 per annum augments the income to £200.—See WIBSEY.

BIERTON (ST. JAMES), a parish, in the union and hundred of AYLESBURY, county of BUCKINGHAM, 1½ mile (N. E. by E.) from Aylesbury; containing, with the hamlet of Broughton, 605 inhabitants. The living is a vicarage, with the livings of Bùckland, Quarrendon, and Stoke-Mandeville annexed, valued in the king's books at £20. 10.; net income, £272; patrons and appropriators, the Dean and Chapter of Lincoln. A Sunday school on the national plan is endowed with £10 per annum. Mr. Hill, in 1723, gave property, directing the proceeds to be applied in clothing poor men, and in educating and apprenticing children.

BIGBURY (ST. LAWRENCE), a parish, in the union of KINGSBRIDGE, hundred of ERMINGTON, Ermington and Plympton, and S. divisions of DEVON, 4 miles (S.) from Modbury; containing 652 inhabitants. The parish comprises by computation 2500 acres, whereof 2100 are arable, 150 meadow, 200 wood and brake, and 50 garden and orchard. It is bounded on the east by the river Avon, which falls into Bigbury bay, an inlet of the English Channel, the navigation of which is somewhat dangerous. The living is a rectory, valued in the king's books at £28. 7. 11., and in the patronage of the Livingston family; net income, £658.

BIGBY (ALL SAINTS), a parish, in the union of CAISTOR, S. division of the wapentake of YARBOROUGH, parts of LINDSEY, county of LINCOLN, 4½ miles (E.) from Glandford-Brigg; containing, with the hamlets of Kettleby and Kettleby-Thorp, 245 inhabitants. It comprises 2784 acres, of which 1484 are meadow and pasture, and 1300 arable land. The village was formerly of considerable celebrity, from containing Kettleby Hall, the residence of the Roman Catholic family of Tyrwhitt, from whom the De Ros family claim their title; but of this once splendid mansion there are now no remains. The living is a rectory, valued in the king's books at £31. 10. 10., and in the gift of Robert C. Elwes, Esq.: the tithes have been commuted for £726, and there are 28 acres of glebe. The church contains monuments of great beauty and considerable antiquity.

BIGGE'S QUARTER, a township, in the parish 'of LONG HORSLEY, union of MORPETH, W. division of MORPETH ward, N. division of NORTHUMBERLAND, 8 miles (N. N. W.) from Morpeth; containing 252 inhabitants. The lands of this place, which was once called Linden Quarter, and Carlisle's Quarter, continued in fee in the family of Merlay and their descendants, from the time of Henry I. till the last century, when the Earl of Carlisle sold them. The township is situated on the river Coquet, and on the road to Edinburgh through Wooler; and comprises 2666 acres of pasture and meadow, and 193 of wood. The soil is for the most part clay; much of the land lying on each side of the road between the village of Long Horsley and Linden, is of excellent quality, and the whole is more or less fertile: improvements have been made during the present century by draining and planting. Quarries of coarse free-stone are worked for building purposes.

BIGGIN, a township, in the parish of WIRKSWORTH, hundred of APPLETREE, S. division of the county of DERBY, 5½ miles (E. by N.) from Ashbourn; containing 149 inhabitants. Here was formerly a church or chapel, not even the site of which is now known. The township

was once considered to be in the parish of Kniveton, but it has been deemed for nearly four centuries part of Wirksworth.

BIGGIN, with NEWTON.—See NEWTON.

BIGGIN, a township, in the parish of KIRK-FENTON, Upper division of the wapentake of BARKSTONE-ASH, W. riding of YORK, 6¾ miles (W. N. W.) from Selby; containing 126 inhabitants. It comprises by computation, including the area of Little Fenton, 2250 acres: the village, which is small, is situated north of the road from Sherburn to Cawood. Allotments of land and money payments were assigned in lieu of all tithes and moduses for the township, under an inclosure act, in 1770. The plant teasel (Dipsacus Fullonum), used in dressing woollen-cloth, is said to have been first cultivated here on its introduction into England.

BIGGINS, HIGHER and LOWER, hamlets, in the township and parish of KIRKBY-LONSDALE, union of KENDAL, LONSDALE ward, county of WESTMORLAND, the former ¾, the latter ¼, of a mile (S. W.) from Kirkby-Lonsdale; containing 150 inhabitants. These hamlets lie on the borders of Lancashire. There is a limestone-quarry.

BIGGLESWADE (ST. ANDREW), a market-town and parish, and the head of a union, in the hundred of BIGGLESWADE, county of BEDFORD, 10½ miles (E. S. E.) from Bedford, and 45 (N. N. W.) from London, on the road to York; containing, with the hamlets of Holme and Stratton, 3807 inhabitants, and comprising 4200 acres, of which 200 are common or waste. The town is pleasantly situated on the river Ivel, which is crossed by two stone bridges, and which, by act of parliament, has been made navigable to its junction with the Ouse, whereby the neighbourhood is supplied with coal, timber, and various articles of merchandise. A large portion of the town was destroyed by fire in 1785, to which circumstance its handsome appearance may partly be attributed. It is lighted with gas, and has been lately much improved by the erection of new buildings; the houses are uniformly of brick, the air is pure and salubrious, and the inhabitants are supplied with excellent water from numerous springs. The environs, abounding with elegant villas and picturesque scenery, present a pleasing appearance. The making of white thread-lace and edging, and straw-plat, affords employment to a considerable part of the female population; much 'of the traffic of the town arises from its situation on the great north road, and the railway from London to York will' pass by. The market, which is on Wednesday, is much resorted to for grain, and fairs are held on Feb. 13th, the Saturday in Easter-week, Whit-Monday, and Nov. 8th, for horses and live stock of every kind; a fair on August 2nd has been discontinued. The county magistrates hold a petty-session for the hundreds of Biggleswade, Clifton, and Wixamtree: the powers of the county debt-court of Biggleswade, established in 1847, extend over the registration-district of Biggleswade.

The LIVING is a discharged vicarage, valued in the king's books at £10; patron, the Prebendary of Biggleswade: the rectorial tithes have been commuted for £937. 10., and the vicarial for £312. 10.; the glebe consists of a small piece of land. The church, formerly collegiate, is a venerable structure in the early English style: the chancel was rebuilt in 1467, by John Reeding, Archdeacon of Bedford, whose arms are carved on some

intendence of Samuel Lysons, Esq., the antiquary and topographer; near it a Roman road was very distinctly marked, leading from Chichester, by Pulborough, to Dorking. Charlotte Smith, the novelist, wrote many of her works at this place, where her father, N. Turner, Esq., was resident.

BILBOROUGH (St. Martin), a parish, in the union of Basford, S. division of the wapentake of Broxtow, N. division of the county of Nottingham, 4 miles (W. N. W.) from Nottingham; containing 267 inhabitants. The hamlet of Broxtow, in the parish, was once a place of considerable importance, and gave name to the wapentake. There are some coal-works. The living is a discharged rectory, valued in the king's books at, £3. 12. 6.; net income, £273; patron, T. Webb Edge, Esq.: land was assigned to the rector in 1808, in lieu of tithes. Some interesting remains exist of an ancient manor-house.

BILBROUGH, a parish, in the Ainsty wapentake, W. riding of York, 4¼ miles (N. E.) from Tadcaster; containing 216 inhabitants. It is situated on the road between Tadcaster and York, and comprises by computation 1410 acres of generally fertile land: the village, which is small but pleasant, is seated on an eminence at a short distance from the road. A chantry was founded here in 1492, by John Norton, lord of the place, who ordained that £4. 6. 8., in land and inclosure, should be paid to Sir William Dryver, priest, and his successors, to pray for the souls of the founder, his wife, and children. The living is a perpetual curacy, in the gift of T. L. Fairfax, Esq.: the tithes have been commuted for £270. There is a place of worship for Wesleyans. Thomas, Lord Fairfax, the celebrated parliamentary general, who died in 1671, was interred in the church.

BILBY, with Barnby-Moor.—See Barnby-Moor.

BILDESTON, or Bilson (St. Mary), a parish, and formerly a market-town, in the union and hundred of Cosford, county of Suffolk, 5 miles (N. N. W.) from Hadleigh, 14½ miles (W. N. W.) from Ipswich, and 66 (N. E. by N.) from London; containing 857 inhabitants. It comprises 1289a. 2r. 28p. of land, the soil of which is a strong productive clay. The manufacture of blankets and woollen-cloth was formerly carried on, and subsequently the chief employment of the inhabitants consisted in spinning yarn; but this also has much declined. The market was held on Wednesday; there are fairs on Ash-Wednesday and Holy-Thursday. The living is a rectory, valued in the king's books at £12. 16. 10½.; patron and incumbent, the Rev. Charles Johnson : the tithes have been commuted for £412. 4. 6., and there are 50 acres of glebe. The church is a handsome spacious structure. There is a place of worship for Baptists. A chapel existed here, dedicated to St. Leonard, in which divine service was performed long after the Reformation.

BILHAM, a township, in the parish of Hooton-Pagnell, union of Doncaster, N. division of the wapentake of Strafforth and Tickhill, W. riding of York, 7 miles (W. N. W.) from Doncaster; containing 75 inhabitants. It comprises about 600 acres, and contains strata of coal and limestone; excellent sandstone, also, used in the foundries at Rotherham and Sheffield, is procured. Bilham House is a handsome mansion, built, or greatly improved, in the last century by Thomas Selwood, Esq., who made it his principal seat. Subsequently a beautiful prospect-house was erected on the highest adjacent ground, by the late Mr. Hewet, at a cost of £1500; it consists of three stories, and from the summit may be seen in clear weather the cathedrals of York, Lincoln, and Southwell, together with a hundred churches.

BILLERICAY, a market-town and chapelry district, and the head of a union, in the parish of GREAT BUR-STEAD, hundred of BARSTABLE, S. division of ESSEX, 9½ miles (S. S. W.) from Chelmsford, and 24 (E. N. E.) from London; containing 1284 inhabitants. The name, anciently written *Beleuca*, is of uncertain derivation, and of the history of the town few particulars of importance are recorded: by some it has been called *Villa Ericæ*, the "Village of Heath." From the discovery of Roman urns containing bones, glass vessels, and other relics, and from the traces of a Roman vallum and ditch formerly visible at Blunt's Walls, nearly a mile distant, the place appears to have been known to the Romans, who probably had a station here, though the exact site has not been ascertained. The TOWN is pleasantly situated on the road from London to Southend, on an eminence overlooking an extensive and richly cultivated vale, and commanding a fine prospect of the surround-ing country, which abounds with beautiful scenery, and a distant view of the shipping on the Thames: it has of late been much improved by the erection of several large and well-built houses. The only branches of manufacture are those of silk braid, laces, and wire ribbon, which are at present declining. The Eastern Counties railway passes a few miles to the north-west. Here were barracks, which have been converted into the workhouse for the union, which comprises 26 parishes and places, and contains a population of 14,934. The market is on Tuesday; and fairs, granted in 1476 by Edward IV,. are held on Aug. 2nd and Oct. 7th; the former chiefly a pleasure-fair, and the latter a cattle-fair. Courts leet and baron are held on the Thursday in Whitsun-week, when constables and other officers for the internal regulation of the town are appointed. The living is a perpetual curacy, in the patronage of the Bishop of London; net income, £120. The chapel, dedicated to St. Mary Magdalene, is a brick building in the centre of the town, erected probably in the 14th century. There are places of worship for Baptists, the Society of Friends, and Independents. The Rev. Mr. Bayley, rector of Benfleet, in 1654 bequeathed an estate at Laindon, producing £45 per annum, for the education of 15 children; and 5 more are taught in one school, and 10 in another, from the interest of an endowment of £500 consols.

BILLESDON (ST. JOHN THE BAPTIST), a parish, and the head of a union, in the hundred of GARTREE, S. division of the county of LEICESTER, 9 miles (E. by S.) from Leicester, on the road to Uppingham; containing, with the chapelries of Goadby and Rolleston, 878 inhabitants. An annual fair, chiefly for pleasure, is held in April, but is not much attended: there are a few stocking-frames employed in the parish. The living is a vicarage, valued in the king's books at £14. 10.; net income, £279, arising from 156 acres of land; patron, H. Greene, Esq.; impropriators, R. Linney, Esq., and others. The church has been lately repewed. There are chapels of ease at Goadby and Rolleston; and a place of worship for Baptists. A school built in 1650, by William Sharp, has since been endowed with property producing

ing is a rectory, valued in the king's books at £10. 2. 11., and in the patronage of Earl Brownlow : the tithes have been commuted for £349, and there are 8 acres of glebe, with a house. In the church is a curious Norman font.

BILLINGBOROUGH (ST. ANDREW), a parish, in the union of BOURNE, wapentake of AVELAND, parts of KESTEVEN, county of LINCOLN, 3 miles (E.) from Folkingham ; containing 999 inhabitants. This parish, which is situated on the borders of the Fens, comprises 2239a. 6p. of land in nearly equal portions of arable and pasture ; stone of inferior quality is quarried for repairing the roads. A fair, chiefly for wooden-ware, is held on the 2nd and 3rd of July at Stow Green, about a mile and a half distant ; and also a horse-fair. The living is a discharged vicarage, valued in the king's books at £6. 1. 8. ; net income, £237, arising from 137a. 3r. of land ; patron and impropriator, Earl Fortescue. The church has a fine tower and spire, and displays chiefly the decorated style of English architecture. There are places of worship for Calvinists and Wesleyans. Mary Toller, in 1671, gave land producing about £34 per annum, for the endowment of a free school, which is conducted on the national plan. The Roman Cor Dyke passes within a mile to the east of the village. There are some chalybeate springs.

BILLINGE, CHAPEL-END, a township and chapelry, in the parish and union of WIGAN, hundred of WEST DERBY, S. division of the county of LANCASTER, 5½ miles (S. W.) from Wigan, on the road to St. Helen's ; containing 1550 inhabitants. Billinge anciently gave name to a family the chief line of which terminated about the reign of Edward I., in a female heir, who married into the Heyton family. The estate was afterwards possessed by the Bisphams, Owens, and Leighs. The whole district comprehended in the name was formerly one township divided into two hamlets, which are now separate townships called respectively Billinge Chapel-End and Billinge Higher-End ; the affix to this, the southern portion, being given to it because it contained the chapel. The township of Chapel-End comprises 1044 acres, of which 830 are arable, 174 pasture, 27 wood, and 13 common. The population are engaged in agriculture, hand-loom weaving, in quarrying stone, and in collieries, of which last the produce is abundant and of excellent quality. The living is a perpetual curacy, in the patronage of the Rector of Wigan ; net income, £156 : the tithes have been commuted for £189. 7. 6. The chapel was built in 1650, and rebuilt in 1718, and is in the early English style, with a campanile tower. At Birchley is a Roman Catholic chapel. A school is endowed with £40 per annum.

BILLINGE, HIGHER-END, a township, in the chapelry of UP HOLLAND, parish and union of WIGAN, hundred of WEST DERBY, S. division of the county of LANCASTER, 5 miles (W. S. W.) from Wigan ; containing 712 inhabitants. It comprises 1302 acres, whereof 492 are arable, 682 pasture, 40 wood, and 88 common : the surface is elevated, presenting very extensive prospects from Billinge Beacon ; the soil is of various quality. A coal-mine and three stone-quarries are in operation. The tithes have been commuted for a yearly rent-charge of £216. 13. The Wesleyan Methodists have a place of worship ; and a school is endowed with £20 per annum.

BILLINGFORD (ST. LEONARD), a parish, in the union of DEPWADE, hundred of EARSHAM, E. division of NORFOLK, 1½ mile (E.) from Scole ; containing 219 inhabitants. This parish, anciently called Pryleston, is intersected by the road from Bury to Yarmouth, and bounded on the south by the river Waveney, which separates it from Suffolk. It comprises 1037 acres, whereof 20 are common or waste. The living is a discharged rectory, with that of Little Thorpe annexed, valued in the king's books at £9 ; net income, £264 ; patron, G. St. Vincent Wilson, Esq. : there are about 20 acres of glebe. The church consists of a nave and chancel, separated by the remains of a carved screen, and has a low square tower.

BILLINGFORD, a parish, in the union of MITFORD and LAUNDITCH, hundred of EYNSFORD, E. division of NORFOLK, 6 miles (N. N. E.) from East Dereham ; containing 353 inhabitants. This parish is bounded on the south and west by the river Wensum, and comprises by computation 1800 acres, of which 1470 are arable, 320 pasture, and 10 woodland. The living is a discharged rectory, valued in the king's books at £7. 10., and in the patronage of the Rt. Hon. E. Ellice : the tithes have been commuted for £360, and there are 27 acres of glebe. The church is an ancient structure in the early English style, with an octangular tower ; the font is of Norman character, and on the south side of the chancel is a piscina. There is a place of worship for Primitive Methodists. At Beck Hall, in the parish, the birthplace of Chancellor Bacon, and the ancient seat of the Coke family, an hospital, with a chapel dedicated to St. Thomas à Becket, was founded in the beginning of the reign of Henry III.

BILLINGHAM (ST. CUTHBERT), a parish, in the union of STOCKTON-UPON-TEES, N.E. division of STOCKTON ward, S. division of the county of DURHAM ; comprising the townships of Cowpen-Bewley and Newton-Bewley, and the chapelry of Wolviston ; and containing 1653 inhabitants, of whom 782 are in the township of Billingham, 2½ miles (N. N. E.) from Stockton. This place is distinguished as the scene of a battle fought in the time of Eardulph, King of Northumbria. It was given to the convent of Durham by William the Conqueror, upon a scrap of parchment which is preserved among the muniments there, and which is not so large as the space occupied by this notice. The parish comprises 5409a. 2r. 25p. : it is bounded on the south and east by the river Tees ; and the road from Stockton to Sunderland passes through the village. The Clarence railway commences at Port Clarence, about three miles distant eastward, near Haverton Hill, north of the river Tees, in the parish, where shipping staiths have been erected ; and pursues a course nearly east till it joins the Stockton and Darlington railway at Sim Pasture, in the parish of Heighington. The Stockton and Hartlepool railway quits the Clarence railway here by a gentle curve, and proceeds in a north-eastern direction. The LIVING is a vicarage, valued in the king's books at £11. 3. 1½. ; patrons, the Dean and Chapter of Durham. The great tithes have been commuted for £810. 18., and the vicarial tithes for £132. 11. ; there are also about 110 acres of glebe appurtenant to the vicarage. The original church, of which little remains, is supposed to have been built by Egbrid, Bishop of Lindisfarn, about the year 830, and to have been given by him to the church of St.

Cuthbert, Durham; the present edifice is very ancient, with pointed arches, and a lofty Norman tower. The chapel of Wolviston forms a separate incumbency. There is a place of worship for Methodists.

BILLINGHAY (St. Michael), a parish, in the union of Sleaford, First division of the wapentake of Langoe, parts of Kesteven, county of Lincoln, 9½ miles (N. E.) from Sleaford; containing, with the townships of Dogdyke and Walcott, 2095 inhabitants. The parish comprises 7827a. 2r. 22p., and is situated on the road from Sleaford to Horncastle : a stream called Billinghay Skirth is navigable for small coal-vessels, and runs into the river Witham about 3½ miles from the village. An act was passed in 1840 for the more effectual drainage of land. The living is a discharged vicarage, valued in the king's books at £13. 4.; net income, £450; patron, Earl Fitzwilliam. The vicarial glebe consists of about 230 acres, with a house. There are places of worship for dissenters.

BILLINGLEY, a township, in the parish of Darfield, N. division of the wapentake of Strafforth and Tickhill, W. riding of York, 6½ miles (E. by S.) from Barnsley; containing 220 inhabitants. This place, which is the property of Earl Fitzwilliam, is in the heart of a rich agricultural district : a coal-pit was opened some years since, but it has been abandoned. The village is pleasantly situated on the declivity of an eminence. The tithes have been commuted for £190, equally divided between the rector of the parish, and Trinity College, Cambridge. There is a place of worship for Wesleyans.

BILLINGSHURST (St. Mary), a parish, in the union of Petworth, hundred of West Easwrith, rape of Arundel, W. division of Sussex, 7½ miles (S. W. by W.) from Horsham; containing in East and West Billingshurst 1439 inhabitants. It comprises 5903 acres, of which 20 are common or waste : the soil is generally clay, upon a substratum of sandstone or beds of Sussex marble. The river Arun, and the Arun and Wey Junction canal, pass through the parish; and the village is situated on the road from London to Arundel and Bognor. It is a post-town, with a corn-market on alternate Tuesdays; and at the hamlet of Adversam fairs are held for horses, cattle, and pigs. The living is a vicarage, valued in the king's books at £9. 6. 0½.: the incumbent's tithes have been commuted for £200, with a glebe of 12 acres; and the impropriate tithes, belonging to Sir C. F. Goring, Bart., the patron, for £916, with a glebe of 3 acres. The church consists of a nave, chancel, and aisles, with a tower surmounted by a lofty shingled spire. There are places of worship for Independents and Unitarians.

BILLINGSIDE, a township, in the parish and union of Lanchester, W. division of Chester ward, N. division of the county of Durham, 13 miles (N. W.) from Durham; containing 13 inhabitants. It comprises about 340 acres, and is situated north of the road between Shotley-Bridge and Lanchester : the river Derwent passes about three miles distant on the west.

BILLINGSLEY (St. Mary), a parish, in the union of Bridgnorth, hundred of Stottesden, S. division of Salop, 6 miles (S. by W.) from Bridgnorth; comprising about 1300 acres, and containing 149 inhabitants. Under the name Billigesleage, historians mention this place as the scene of a congress held between King Harold, and

242

Griffin, Prince of Wales, at which they engaged to observe mutual peace and amity. The living is a discharged rectory, valued in the king's books at £4. 13. 4., and in the patronage of the Duke of Cleveland; the tithes have been commuted for £186, and there are twelve acres of glebe. Dr. Thomas Hyde, professor of oriental literature at Oxford, was born here in 1636.

BILLINGTON, a chapelry, in the parish and union of Leighton-Buzzard, hundred of Manshead, county of Bedford, 2 miles (S. E.) from Leighton; containing 323 inhabitants. It is situated on the road from Leighton to London through Hemel-Hempstead, and comprises by computation 1050 acres : the Grand Junction canal, and London and Birmingham railway, pass within two miles of the church. The living is a perpetual curacy, in the patronage of the Inhabitants; net income, £45. The church is supposed to have been erected about 300 years ago.

BILLINGTON-LANGHO, a township and district chapelry, in the parish, union, and Lower division of the hundred, of Blackburn, N. division of the county of Lancaster, 5½ miles (N. N. E.) from Blackburn; containing 988 inhabitants. In the reign of Stephen the manor was held by a family of the same name. A moiety of it was subsequently possessed by the abbey of Whalley, the other moiety being held by the Hodlestons; and in the reign of Philip and Mary, Sir Thomas Holcroft, the great dealer in abbey lands, died seised of the manor, which afterwards became the property of the Ashtons. Langho is supposed to have been the scene of a battle that occurred between Wada, a Saxon duke, one of the murderers of Ethelred, and Ardulph, King of Northumbria, in the year 798, when the former was defeated, and his army put to flight. The chapelry is bounded on the north and east by the river Calder, and in other parts by the Ribble; and comprises about 1800 acres. The surface is hilly, and the scenery very interesting : the soil is cold and wet, and in some places are pits of marl, sunk to a great depth; also quarries of stone, principally used in draining. The inhabitants are partly employed in hand-loom weaving. The Blackburn and Clitheroe railway passes through. The living is a perpetual curacy, in the patronage of the Vicar of Blackburn; net income, £120. The chapel is seated in the hamlet of Langho, and is called Langho chapel; it is an ancient structure : in the south wall of the chancel is a piscina of elegant design; and inserted in the east wall is a font of a single stone, beautifully enriched with tracery. There is a Roman Catholic chapel. An asylum for insane patients was for some time conducted by the late Dr. Chew, and is now conducted by Dr. Hindle with every attention to the comfort and benefit of the inmates. A school for the instruction of the poor is supported by an endowment, and two schoolrooms have been built.

BILLISBORROW, or Billsborough, a township, in the parish and union of Garstang, hundred of Amounderness, N. division of the county of Lancaster, 4½ miles (S. S. E.) from Garstang, on the road to Preston; containing 157 inhabitants. The family of Billisburgh was early seated here, and in the reign of Edward II. the Banasters are mentioned as holding lands in "Billesworth." The township comprises 784 acres; the surface is undulated, the soil various and fertile, and the scenery picturesque. The river Brock passes through; and there is a station, called the Brock station, on the Lancaster and Preston railway. In the township is a paper-mill. The impropriate tithes have been commuted for £104. 3. There is a place of worship for Wesleyans. John Cross, in 1718, bequeathed property producing about £70 per annum, with a house, for the endowment of a free school for the townships of Billisborrow and Myerscough.

BILLOCKBY (*All Saints*), a parish, in the East and West Flegg incorporation, hundred of West Flegg, E. division of Norfolk, 2½ miles (N. E.) from Acle; containing 71 inhabitants. The road from Norwich to Yarmouth intersects the parish. The living is a discharged rectory, valued in the king's books at £2. 8. 9.; patron and incumbent, the Rev. William Lucas : the tithes have been commuted for £147, and the glebe comprises about 2 acres. The church forms a picturesque ruin, the chancel only being fitted up for divine worship.

BILL-QUAY, a village, in the chapelry of Nether Heworth, parish of Jarrow, E. division of Chester ward, N. division of the county of Durham, 3 miles (E.) from Gateshead. This place, which has its name from being situated opposite to Bill Point, is a manufacturing district, running along the south margin of the river Tyne. The Arkendale and Derwent Mining Company have works here, where lead-ore is occasionally smelted, and where is a large mill for rolling sheet-lead, and making the various oxides of that metal, called "litharge" and "red lead :" the extraction of silver is performed by a patent process. Some extensive greenglass, bottle works have been established for nearly a century and a half. There are thirteen cinder ovens in operation; a tar, naphtha, and turpentine distillery; and an establishment for distilling oil from bones, the calx of which, after having been reduced to ashes, is used in making ivory-black, &c. Among other manufactories is one for preparing colours, and making mustard; and Mr. Boutland has a large ship-building yard and floating-dock. In a deep dene called Catdene, now overgrown with forest-trees and thorns, are extensive quarries, from which it is said the stone was obtained for building the walls of Newcastle.

BILLY-ROW, with Crook.—See Crook.

BILNEY, EAST (St. Mary), a parish, in the union of Mitford and Launditch, hundred of Launditch, W. division of Norfolk, 5 miles (N. N. W.) from East Dereham; containing 218 inhabitants. It comprises 541a. 28p., of which 338 acres are arable, 140 meadow and pasture, and 46 woodland and plantations. The living is a discharged rectory, with that of Beetley, and valued in the king's books at £5. 14. 2.; patron, John Collison, Esq. : the tithes of the parish have been commuted for £112, and there are 26 acres of glebe, with a handsome parsonage in the Elizabethan style. The church is an ancient structure with a low tower. William Pearse, Esq., in 1840 built almshouses for 3 aged couples, and endowed them with land producing £63 per annum. Thomas Bilney, a learned divine, who was burnt at Norwich, in the year 1531, for preaching against popery, is said to have been born here.

BILNEY, WEST (St. Cecilia), a parish, in the union and hundred of Freebridge-Lynn, W. division of Norfolk, 6¼ miles (S. E. by E.) from Lynn; containing 298 inhabitants. The parish is intersected by

the road and railway from Lynn to Norwich, and comprises by measurement 2414 acres, of which about 1500 are arable, 770 meadow, pasture, and heath, and 130 woodland. The railway has a station here. The living is a perpetual curacy; net income, £60; patron and impropriator, John Dalton, Esq. The church is chiefly in the early English style.

BILSBY (*Holy Trinity*), a parish, in the union of Spilsby, Wold division of the hundred of Calceworth, parts of Lindsey, county of Lincoln, ¾ of a mile (E. by N.) from Alford; containing, with the hamlets of Asserby and Thurlby, 584 inhabitants. It comprises by computation 2800 acres, of which about 1000 are arable, and 1800 pasture and meadow. The living is a vicarage, valued in the king's books at £13. 3. 4.; patron, James Mason, Esq.; impropriators, the Trustees of Caistor grammar school : the vicarial tithes have been commuted for £150, and the glebe consists of 15 acres. The church, a very ancient edifice, has recently undergone great alterations and repairs, having been previously in a very dilapidated state. There is a place of worship for Wesleyans; and a school has a small endowment of £5 per annum.

BILSDALE, WEST SIDE, a township, in the parish of Hawnby, union of Helmsley, wapentake of Birdforth, N. riding of York, 8 miles (N. W. by N.) from Helmsley; containing 168 inhabitants. This is a moorland township, extending in length between seven and twelve miles, and rising in lofty fells at Ryedale Head; it comprises by computation 6090 acres. The river Seth flows on the east in a direction nearly from north to south. In 1757, John Smales and Gregory Elsley bequeathed £120. 5., directing the proceeds to be applied to teaching six poor boys.

BILSDALE-MIDCABLE, a chapelry, in the parish and union of Helmsley, wapentake of Ryedale, N. riding of York, 7 miles (N. N. W.) from Helmsley; containing, with Bilsdale-Kirkham, 738 inhabitants. This place is on the east side of Ryedale, and includes the hamlets of Crosett and Chapel-Yate; it comprises by computation 8380 acres, of which a large portion is high moorland. The chapel, built about 20 years since, and dedicated to St. Hilda, is a neat structure with a square tower : the living is a perpetual curacy, in the patronage of the Vicar of Helmsley, and has a net income of £91. There is a place of worship for the Society of Friends. Upon Studfast hill, in this district, the site of a Druids' temple was discovered in 1824.

BILSINGTON (St. Peter and St. Paul), a parish, in the union of East Ashford, partly in the liberty of Romney Marsh, but chiefly in the hundred of Newchurch, lathe of Shepway, E. division of Kent, 8 miles (S. S. E.) from Ashford; containing 385 inhabitants. The parish consists of 2843 acres, of which about 557 are in wood. It comprises the manors of Bilsington Superior, or the Priory, and Bilsington Inferior, or the Moat; and the proprietor for the time being is cupbearer to the king at his coronation, on which occasion he presents three maple cups to his majesty, and, on performing that office in person, receives the honour of knighthood. The upper part of the parish is thickly wooded, and in that portion lying in Romney Marsh are some luxuriant pastures : the soil is clay, alternated with sand; the chief crops are wheat, oats, beans, peas, and hops. Over the Royal Military canal, which passes

                    2 I 2

BILS

through the parish, is a neat bridge, and adjoining it a coal and timber wharf. A fair for toys is held on the 5th of July. The living is a perpetual curacy; net income, £49; patrons and impropriators, the family of Cosway, whose tithes have been commuted for £615. A priory for Black canons was founded here, before the year 1253, by John Mansell, provost of Beverley, who dedicated it to the Blessed Virgin; its revenue was valued at the Dissolution at £81. 1. 6., and was granted in exchange for other lands to the Archbishop of Canterbury.

BILSON, county of SUFFOLK.—See BILDESTON.

BILSTHORPE (ST. MARGARET), a parish, in the union of SOUTHWELL, South-Clay division of the wapentake of BASSETLAW, N. division of the county of NOTTINGHAM, 5 miles (S.) from Ollerton; containing 244 inhabitants, and comprising 1420 acres. The living is a discharged rectory, valued in the king's books at £5. 1. 8.; patron, the Earl of Scarborough: the tithes have been commuted for £372, and there are 75 acres of glebe. The church stands on an eminence above the village; the tower, which has two bells, appears to have been built in 1663.

BILSTON, a market-town and chapelry, in the parish, borough, and union of WOLVERHAMPTON, N. division of the hundred of SEISDON, S. division of the county of STAFFORD, 3 miles (S. E.) from Wolverhampton, 19 (S. by E.) from Stafford, and 120 (N. W.) from London; containing 20,181 inhabitants. This place, which formerly belonged to the portionists or prebendaries of Wolverhampton, and in their charter is called " Bilsreton," was a royal demesne at the time of the Conquest, and in the reign of Edward III. was, under the appellation of " Billestune," certified to be exempt from toll. It comprises part of the manor of Stowheath, and the whole of the manor of Bradley, separated from each other by a brook which, rising at Sedgley, about two miles distant, forms one of the tributaries of the river Tame, and flows through the township. Previously to the introduction of the ironworks, Bilston merely contained a few private houses; and its population in 1695, according to the census then taken, was only 1004; but from the abundance and rich quality of its coal and ironstone, and the consequent establishment of the iron-trade, it rapidly increased in extent and population, and has become one of the largest manufacturing places in the county.

The TOWN is situated on rising ground in the centre of a district abounding with foundries, forges, furnaces, steam-engines, and other works necessary for the various processes of the iron manufacture, of which the smoke by day and the fires by night present a scene singularly impressive. It extends nearly two miles in length, is irregularly built, and lighted with gas; the principal streets contain several substantial and handsome houses, and throughout the neighbourhood are scattered, in every direction, the numerous habitations of persons employed in the different works. The manufacture of tin, japanned and enamelled wares of every kind, iron-wire, nails, screws, iron gates and palisades, machinery, steam-engines, and all the heavier articles in the iron-trade, is carried on to a very considerable extent; there are some mills for forming pig-iron into bars, and many iron and brass foundries. Clay, of which the coarser kind of pottery-ware is made, and a particularly fine

244

BINBROOKE, a district (formerly a market-
town) comprising the parishes of *St. Gabriel* and *St.
Mary*, in the union of WALSHCROFT, S. division of the
wapentake of WALSHCROFT, parts of LINDSEY, county
of LINCOLN, 8 miles (E. N. E.) from Market-Rasen.
There are extensive rabbit-warrens in the neighbourhood, and considerable business is done in the dressing of skins for furriers. A fair is held on Easter-
Tuesday, on which day are also horse-races. St.
Gabriel's, containing, with the extra-parochial liberty
of Orforth, 708 inhabitants, is a discharged vicarage,
valued in the king's books at £8; present income, £75;
patron, the Bishop of Lincoln. The church is in ruins.
St. Mary's, containing 501 inhabitants, is a discharged
rectory, valued in the king's books at £10. 4. 2., and
in the patronage of the Crown; net income, £291.
The church is a small plain edifice. The Wesleyans
have a place of worship.

BINCHESTER, a township, in the parish of ST.
ANDREW AUCKLAND, union of AUCKLAND, N. W. division of DARLINGTON ward, S. division of the county of
DURHAM, 2 miles (N. by E.) from Bishop-Auckland;
containing 43 inhabitants. Binchester appears to have
been a Roman station, called *Vinovia* by Antoninus,
and *Binovium* by Ptolemy, and situated on the Fosse-way.
Mr. Cade considers it to have been sacred to Bacchus,
and to have derived its name, *Vinovium*, from the festivals held here in honour of that deity. The fortress
occupied an elevated site rising from the bank of the
river Wear, and the whole station comprised about
twenty-nine acres of ground, within which, and in the
vicinity, the remains of a hypocaust, some altars, urns,
and other relics, were found at different times. These
remains were preserved in the court-yard of the mansion-house till the year 1828, when they were destroyed
by the owner of the estate, to assist in forming the
walls of a coal-pit; one altar only was saved, which has
been deposited in the library of the Dean and Chapter
of Durham.

BINCOMBE (*HOLY TRINITY*), a parish, in the union
of WEYMOUTH, liberty of FRAMPTON, Dorchester division of DORSET, 5 miles (S. by W.) from Dorchester;
containing 170 inhabitants. It comprises by measurement 1000 acres, of which the soil is strong, the surface
hilly, and the pasture land in general excellent. There
are some quarries of a very fine durable stone, easily
worked, a great quantity of which has been used in the
public buildings at Dorchester. The living is a rectory,
with that of Broadway annexed, valued in the king's
books at £9. 1. 5½.; patrons, the Master and Fellows
of Caius College, Cambridge. The tithes of Bincombe
have been commuted for £180, and those of Broadway
for £290. 10. 6.; the glebe in Bincombe comprises
about 30 acres, and in Broadway 20. The church is a
small structure with a square tower. Numerous barrows are visible on the neighbouring downs.

BINDERTON, a parish, in the union of WEST
HAMPNETT, hundred of WESTBOURN and SINGLETON,
rape of CHICHESTER, W. division of SUSSEX, 4 miles
(N.) from Chichester; containing 75 inhabitants. It
comprises by measurement 1345 acres of land, of which
the soil is chalky, and the surface hilly. The living is
endowed with a portion of the tithes, and is annexed to
the living of West Dean and Singleton. The old church
was taken down, and the present one erected a short dis-

tance from it about the year 1680, by Thomas Smyth, Esq.; it has not been consecrated, and is private property.

BINEGAR (*Holy Trinity*), a parish, in the union of Shepton-Mallet, hundred of Wells-Forum, E. division of Somerset, 4 miles (N.) from Shepton-Mallet; containing 338 inhabitants. It comprises 1100 acres; and lies on the great road from Bristol to Exeter, through Shepton-Mallet. A large fair noted for the sale of horses, formerly held at Wells, was removed hither in the seventeenth century, in consequence of the plague, and is held during the whole of Whitsun-week. The living is a rectory, valued in the king's books at £13. 12. 8½., and in the patronage of the Prebendary of Whitchurch in the Cathedral of Wells: the tithes have been commuted for £250; and the glebe consists of 44 acres, with a good residence. The church contains a monument to the Rev. Mr. Tuson, a former rector, and his wife, Lady Frances Tuson, one of the Somerset family. There is a place of worship for Wesleyans at Gurney Slade.

BINFIELD (*All Saints*), a parish, in the union of Easthampstead, hundred of Cookham, county of Berks, 3 miles (N. W.) from Bracknell; containing 1242 inhabitants. The parish comprises 3218a. 30p., of which 1660 acres are arable, 1275 meadow, and 282 woodland; and is situated in the midst of the tract called the Royal Hunt, in Windsor Forest. It is distinguished as the residence of Pope, who lived with his father in the village, where, at the age of sixteen, he composed his earliest poems; and in a retired part of the forest, consisting entirely of beech-trees, on the edge of a common within half a mile of the house, is a large tree on the trunk of which, about twelve feet from the ground, was inscribed by George, Lord Lyttelton, in capital letters, " here pope svng,"—which inscription is annually renewed. The living is a rectory, valued in the king's books at £18. 17. 1., and in the patronage of the Crown: the tithes have been commuted for £800, and there are 20 acres of glebe. The church has portions in different styles: the north entrance is Norman; a few windows are early English, but most of them, with the tower and south doorway, are of the decorated English style; one large window is of a later character. Mrs. Macaulay, the historian, is buried here. There is a place of worship for Wesleyans; and a national school has an endowment of £37. 15. per annum, arising from land. On the summit of a hill, near Binfield Place, are the remains of a very large encampment defended by a double ditch, named " Cæsar's Camp," and supposed to have been occupied by Julius Cæsar in his invasion of Britain. About half a mile to the south of this camp is a raised road ninety feet wide, with a trench on each side, pointing in a direction from east to west, and called the " Devil's Highway."

BINGFIELD, a chapelry, in the parish of St. John Lee, union of Hexham, S. division of Tindale ward and of Northumberland, 6½ miles (N. N. E.) from Hexham; containing 111 inhabitants. It occupies an eminence above five miles north-north-east from St. John Lee, and the road from Corbridge to Cowden passes on the west. The chapel is dedicated to St. Mary. The tithes have been commuted for £150. 10. payable to the Mercers' Company, London, and £27. 14. 6. to an impropriator. A school is endowed with £10 per annum. Near the Ering burn, a little northward from the
246

village, is a mineral spring, the water of which is so powerful that neither fish nor any kind of insect can live in it, and which was said by the celebrated Dr. Werge to be in no respect inferior to Gisland spa.

BINGHAM (*All Saints*), a market-town and parish, and the head of a union, in the N. division of the wapentake of Bingham, S. division of the county of Nottingham, 10 miles (E.) from Nottingham, and 123 (N. W. by N.) from London; containing, with part of the township of Newton, 1998 inhabitants. This place was possessed previously to the Conquest by two Saxon chieftains, and appears to have been anciently more extensive than at present: it had a college, or guild, in honour of St. Mary. The parish, which comprises by computation 2985a. 1r. 37p., is bounded on the east by the river Smite or Snite, and intersected by the road from Nottingham to Grantham; the road from Nottingham to Newark passes within a mile of the town, the canal from Nottingham to Grantham within three miles, and the Trent within three and a half. The soil is various, but generally very good, and the surface level, except to the north and south, where it is more elevated. The town is pleasantly situated in the vale of Belvoir, and consists chiefly of two parallel streets, one of which leads directly into a spacious market-place; some smaller streets have been formed within the last thirty years. The houses, though irregularly built, are neat, and several of them of handsome appearance; the town is well paved and amply supplied with water. The market is on Thursday; and fairs are held on Feb. 9th, 10th, 11th, and 12th, the first Thursday in May, Whit-Thursday, May 31st, and Nov. 8th and 9th, for horses principally, and also cattle, sheep, hogs, &c. The powers of the county debt-court of Bingham, established in 1847, extend over the greater part of the registration-district of Bingham.

The living is a rectory, valued in the king's books at £44. 7. 11., and in the patronage of the Earl of Chesterfield: the tithes have been commuted for £1400, and there are about 34 acres of glebe, with a good residence. The church is an ancient and spacious cruciform structure, partaking of the early and decorated English styles, with a square embattled and highly enriched tower, crowned with the remains of statues, which have been substituted for pinnacles, and surmounted by a lofty spire, which, with the upper stage of the tower, is of later erection: within the church are some beautiful specimens of foliage and sculpture, of elegant design and elaborate execution. There are places of worship for Primitive and Wesleyan Methodists. The poor law union comprises 40 parishes and places, of which 38 are in the county of Nottingham, and two in the county of Leicester; and contains a population of 16,196. The Roman Fosse-way, in its course through the parish, passes by a large mound called Castle Hill, the site of an ancient fortress. Mr. Robert White the astronomer, and editor of the Ephemeris which bears his name, was a native of Bingham, and is interred here; a mural tablet in the church is inscribed to his memory. Abbot, Archbishop of Canterbury; Wren, Bishop of Ely; and Hanmer, Bishop of Bangor, were successively rectors of the parish, from which they were promoted to their respective sees, in the seventeenth century.

BINGLEY (*All Saints*), a parish and market-town, in the union of Keighley, Upper division of the wapentake of SKYRACK, W. riding of YORK; containing 11,850 inhabitants, of whom 10,157 are in the town (including Micklethwaite), 37 miles (W. S. W.) from York, and 202 (N. N. W.) from London. This place is one of the thirty-two lordships granted by the Conqueror to Erneis de Berun, from whose descendants it was conveyed to the Paganells and the Gants, and afterwards to the Cantilupe family, from whom it was purchased by Robert Benson, Baron Bingley, and ambassador to the court of Vienna, in the reign of Anne. The manor subsequently passed, by marriage with the heiress of Baron Bingley, to George Fox, Esq., who assumed the surname of Lane, and was created Baron Bingley in 1762; and on the death of the second baron in 1773, it came to the ancestor of George Lane Fox, Esq., the present lord. The town is situated on the sides and summit of a gentle eminence: it is bounded on the west by the river Aire, and on the east by the Leeds and Liverpool canal; and consists chiefly of one long street, on the road from Keighley to Bradford, in the manufactures of which latter place it largely participates. The houses are built of stone, with which the neighbourhood abounds; the streets are lighted with gas, from works erected in 1837, and the inhabitants are amply supplied with water. The air is salubrious; and the environs, which are richly wooded, abound with pleasingly varied scenery. The worsted and cotton manufactures, for which there are several large establishments, are carried on in the town, which has been gradually increasing for the last twenty years in population and extent: the manufacture of paper is carried on at Morton, where are also a cotton-mill and four worsted-mills; and there is likewise a considerable trade in malt. The Leeds and Bradford Extension railway passes under part of the town by a tunnel of masonry, about 150 yards long. The market, originally granted to the Gant family in the reign of John, is on Tuesday; and fairs for horned-cattle are held on the 25th of January and of August, and for horses on the two following days in August. Petty-sessions are held every month.

The parish, including the townships of East and West Morton, comprises 13,000 acres, of which number nearly 10,000 are in Bingley with Micklethwaite; the soil is generally fertile, and in good cultivation. A considerable portion of the township of Bingley belongs to the Ferrand family, whose ancestor came over to England with William the Conqueror, and whose descendants have ever since continued at this place. The LIVING is a discharged vicarage, valued in the king's books at £7. 6. 8., and in the patronage of the Crown; impropriator, the Rev. W. Penny: the great tithes have been commuted for £410, and the small for £300. The church is a spacious and venerable structure with a square embattled tower, in the later English style, and, having suffered much dilapidation, was restored in the reign of Henry VIII.; it contains several monuments to the Ferrand and Busfield families. Two church districts, named respectively Morton and Cullingworth, have been endowed by the Ecclesiastical Commissioners: each of the livings is in the gift of the Crown and the Bishop of Ripon, alternately. There are places of worship for Baptists, Independents, Primitive Methodists, and Wesleyans. The free grammar school was founded in the reign of Henry VIII., and endowed with land and tenements producing at present £260 per annum, subject to
247

certain payments to the poor: the premises comprise a large schoolroom, and a house and garden for the master. Mrs. Sarah Rhodes, in 1784, gave five cottages, which she endowed as almshouses for five aged widows, who receive £3 per annum each. Thomas Busfeild, Esq., in 1767, bequeathed the interest on £800; and there are also several bequests for distribution in bread and clothes among the poor, and for other charitable uses. John Nicholson, the Airedale poet, was buried here in May, 1843.

BING-WESTON, a quarter, in the parish of WORTHEN, hundred of CHIRBURY, S. division of SALOP; containing 91 inhabitants.

BINHAM (HOLY CROSS), a parish, in the union of WALSINGHAM, hundred of NORTH GREENHOE, W. division of NORFOLK, 5 miles (S. W.) from Wells; containing 502 inhabitants. This place was the site of a Benedictine priory, founded in the reign of Henry I. by Peter de Valoines, nephew of William the Conqueror, as a cell to the abbey of St. Alban's, and which flourished till the Dissolution, when its revenue was returned at £140. 5. 4. The parish comprises 2241a. 1r. 3p., of which 1825 acres are arable, and 386 pasture and meadow. In the village is the shaft of an ancient market-cross; a fair is still held there on the 26th of July and three following days, chiefly for cattle and for pleasure. The living is a discharged vicarage, valued in the king's books at £6. 13. 4.; patron and impropriator, T. T. Clarke, Esq.: the great tithes have been commuted for £200, and the vicarial for £100; the glebe comprises about an acre. The church is the nave of the priory church, of which there are other remains, consisting of portions of the transepts; and is chiefly in the Norman style, with some later details. The poor have some lands and a house called the Guildhall, producing £41. 5. per annum.

BINLEY, a tything, in the parish of BOURNE, union of WHITCHURCH, hundred of EVINGAR, Kingsclere and N. divisions of the county of SOUTHAMPTON; containing 138 inhabitants.

BINLEY (ST. BARTHOLOMEW), a parish, in the union of FOLESHILL, Kirby division of the hundred of KNIGHTLOW, N. division of the county of WARWICK, 3 miles (E. by S.) from Coventry; containing, with the liberty of Earnsford, 233 inhabitants. This parish, consisting of 1469 acres, is situated on the road from Coventry to Lutterworth, and intersected by the London and Birmingham railway, the portion of which passing through the parish is of the rateable annual value of £270. The living is a donative curacy; net income, £52; patron and impropriator, Earl Craven. The present church was built by the sixth lord Craven, and consecrated in 1772. The Rev. Thomas Wagstaffe, who wrote a defence of Charles I., was born here; he died at Rouen in 1770.

BINNINGTON, a township, in the parish of WILLERBY, wapentake of DICKERING, E. riding of YORK, 7 miles (W. by N.) from Hunmanby; containing 61 inhabitants. It is situated on the road from Hunmanby to Sherburn, and comprises by computation 910 acres of land. The river Hartford flows at a short distance north of the village. The great tithes were commuted for land and corn-rents under an inclosure act obtained in 1801, and the vicarial by a similar act passed in 1803.

BINSEY (*St. Margaret*), a parish, in the union of ABINGDON, and liberty of the city of OXFORD, locally in the hundred of WOOTTON, county of OXFORD, 2 miles (N. W.) from Oxford; containing 61 inhabitants. The soil is good meadow and grazing land, but the surface is in general low, and subject to inundation from the river Isis, on the banks of which the parish is mostly situated. The living is a perpetual curacy; net income, £90; patrons, the Dean and Chapter of Christ-Church, Oxford. The church is of great antiquity, having belonged to the monastery of St. Friedeswide at Osney.

BINSTEAD (*Holy Cross*), a parish, in the ISLE of WIGHT incorporation, liberty of EAST MEDINA, Isle of Wight and S. divisions of the county of SOUTHAMPTON, 1 mile (W.) from Ryde; containing 278 inhabitants. In the vicinity are the ancient quarries from which was taken part of the stone for the erection of Winchester cathedral. The soil is a rich marl, and the lands are in profitable cultivation. The living is a discharged rectory, valued in the king's books at £1. 7. 1.; net income, £80; patron, the Bishop of Winchester. The church is said to have been built by one of the early bishops of Winchester. At Quarr are the remains of an abbey of Cistercian monks, which was founded in 1132, by Baldwin de Redveriis, then lord of the island; its revenue at the Dissolution was estimated at £184. 1. 10.

BINSTED (*St. Nicholas*), a parish, in the union and hundred of ALTON, Alton and N. divisions of the county of SOUTHAMPTON, 3¾ miles (E. by N.) from Alton; containing 1055 inhabitants. It is extremely fertile, and the surrounding country is pleasantly varied; about 120 acres are planted with hops. The parish includes the forest of Alice-Holt, comprising 1800 acres, inclosed by act of parliament in 1816. The living is a vicarage not in charge, annexed, with the livings of Holybourne and Kingsley, to that of Alton.

BINSTED (*St. Mary*), a parish, in the union of WEST HAMPNETT, hundred of AVISFORD, rape of ARUNDEL, W. division of SUSSEX, 2 miles (E. by S.) from Arundel; containing 111 inhabitants. It comprises 1086 acres, of which 424 are arable, 244 pasture, and 418 woodland; and is crossed by the road from Arundel to Bognor. The living is a vicarage, endowed with the great tithes, valued in the king's books at £5. 17. 8½., and in the patronage of the Dowager Countess of Newburgh: the tithes have been commuted for £175. The church is a small plain building.

BINTON (*St. Peter*), a parish, in the union of STRATFORD-UPON-AVON, Stratford division of the hundred of BARLICHWAY, S. division of the county of WARWICK, 3¾ miles (W. by S.) from Stratford; containing 269 inhabitants. This place is written *Benintone* in Domesday book, and a family of the same name were lords of the manor during several reigns. The manor afterwards came to the Wyncotes, Throckmortons, and Walters; from which last it was purchased by the family of the Marquess of Hertford. The parish is bounded on the south by the river Avon, over which is a bridge continuing the road leading to Chipping-Campden: it comprises 1228 acres. There are quarries of excellent limestone, producing also marble. The living is a rectory, valued in the king's books at £8. 10.; net income, £140; patron, the Marquess. An allotment of land, and a money payment, were assigned in lieu of moduses

248

and certain tithes for this parish and Old Stratford, in 1779.

BINTREE (*St. Swithin*), a parish, in the union of MITFORD and LAUNDITCH, hundred of EYNSFORD, E. division of NORFOLK, 2 miles (S. E. by S.) from Guist; containing 409 inhabitants. This parish, which is bounded on the west by the river Wensum, and situated on the road from Norwich to Fakenham, comprises 1443*a*. 3*r*. 11*p*., of which 1117 acres are arable, 247 pasture, and 26 plantation: some of it is good wheat land, and other parts good turnip and barley soil. The living is a rectory, with that of Themelthorpe annexed, valued in the king's books at £10; net income, £462; patron, Lord Hastings. The church is a handsome structure in the early and later English styles, with a square embattled tower, and a south transept, and contains a richly carved screen, and some other interesting details. The poor have twenty-five acres allotted on the inclosure of the parish in 1796, and now producing £50 per annum; and the half of £30, rent of land bequeathed by an unknown benefactor.

BIRBECK-FELLS, a township, partly in the parish of ORTON, EAST ward and union, and partly in the parish of CROSBY-RAVENSWORTH, WEST ward and union, county of WESTMORLAND, 4 miles (W. S. W.) from Orton; containing 200 inhabitants, and comprising 1250 acres, of which 770 are common or waste. The Birbeck embankment, on the line of the Lancaster and Carlisle railway, contains 200,000 cubic yards of earthwork, and the viaduct here is 45 feet in height, the arches being similar to those of Borrow viaduct. The vicarial tithes have been commuted for £18. 9. A free school at Greenholme, for the education of the children of Birbeck-Fells, Bretherdale, Rounthwaite, and Low Scales, is endowed with land producing about £40 per annum, purchased with a bequest of £400 by George Gibson, in 1733.

BIRCH, a district chapelry, in the parish of MANCHESTER, union of CHORLTON, hundred of SALFORD, S. division of the county of LANCASTER, 3 miles (S.) from Manchester, on the road to Congleton. The living is a perpetual curacy, in the patronage of J. Dickinson, Esq.; net income, £160. The chapel, dedicated to St. James, is supposed to have been originally built by a member of the family of Birch, and was rebuilt in 1846; it is one of the best specimens of ecclesiastical architecture in this neighbourhood, and consists of a nave, chancel, and aisles, with a tower and spire placed at the north-west corner, within the square of the plan. Adjoining is a neat school. Birch Hall, a seat of the Haverseges, passed from them to the Birches; and it is conjectured that the plans laid by James, Earl of Derby, for seizing Manchester for Charles I., were disconcerted by the councils of Col. Birch and his compeers, held here.

BIRCH, a village, in the parish of MIDDLETON, union of OLDHAM, hundred of SALFORD, S. division of the county of LANCASTER, 2½ miles (W. N. W.) from Middleton. This place is half-way between Rochdale and Manchester: the road from Manchester to Heywood runs through the village; and the Rochdale canal, and Manchester and Leeds railway, pass along the eastern side of the district chapelry of Birch. The spinning of cotton, and the manufacture of gingham, are carried on to a limited extent. The living is a perpetual curacy, in the patronage of the Rector of Middleton, with a net in-

discharged rectory, with that of Bircham-Tofts annexed, valued in the king's books at £7. 13. 4.; patron, the Marquess of Cholmondeley. The tithes of this parish have been commuted for £218, and those of Bircham-Tofts for a like sum; in Bircham-Newton are 48, and in Bircham-Tofts 32 acres of glebe.

BIRCHAM-TOFTS (St. *Andrew*), a parish, in the union of Docking, hundred of Smithdon, W. division of Norfolk, 7¼ miles (S. S. W.) from Burnham-Westgate; containing 142 inhabitants. The living is a discharged rectory, annexed to that of Bircham-Newton, and valued in the king's books at £6. 13. 4.

BIRCHANGER (St. *Mary*), a parish, in the union of Bishop-Stortford, hundred of Uttlesford, N. division of Essex, 2 miles (N. E.) from Bishop-Stortford; containing 386 inhabitants. It was given by Richard II. to William of Wykeham, for the endowment of New College, Oxford, the Warden and Fellows of which are the present proprietors. The parish comprises 1051a. 23p., of which 730 acres are arable, 185 meadow, and 97 woodland. The living is a rectory, valued in the king's books at £9. 13. 4., and in the gift of the college: the impropriate tithes have been commuted for £50, and the rectorial for £310; there are 24 acres of glebe, with a handsome house. The church, pleasantly situated on the summit of a hill, near the London road, is a small ancient edifice with a round tower, and contains a fine Norman arch. Richard de Newport founded here, in the reign of John, an hospital dedicated to St. Mary and St. Leonard, for a master and two chaplains; the revenue, in the 26th of Henry VIII., was £31. 13. 11.

BIRCHER, a township, in the parish of Yarpole, union of Leominster, hundred of Wolphy, county of Hereford, 5½ miles (N. by W.) from Leominster; containing 257 inhabitants. It lies on the road from Leominster to Ludlow. The village is a short distance north-east of that of Yarpole; and on the north-west is an extensive common, called Bircher or Highwood common.

BIRCHES, a township, in the parish of Great Budworth, union and hundred of Northwich, S. division of the county of Chester, 3¼ miles (E. S. E.) from Northwich; containing 8 inhabitants. In the reign of Edward II. the manor passed with the heiress of Nicholas de Birches, by marriage, to the Winningtons, in whose family it continued for many generations. It came to the Starkeys in Charles I.'s reign; and in 1695 was the property of Mrs. Elizabeth Dobson, who bequeathed it to the Cholmondeley family, in trust, for the education of two boys, one to be the son of a counsellor, and the other the son of a divine of the Church of England. The township comprises 138 acres: the soil is clay. The road from Northwich to Twemlow passes on the south.

BIRCHFIELD, a hamlet, in the parish of Handsworth, union of West Bromwich, S. division of the hundred of Offlow and of the county of Stafford, 2 miles (N.) from Birmingham, on the road to Walsall. This place lies in the eastern part of the parish, and close to the borders of the county of Warwick. It contains a few handsome residences, the principal of which are those of William Haughton, Esq., and George Bragg, Esq.; the former a large mansion with about 76 acres of land, and the latter having about

2 K

40 acres. The other residences situated in the hamlet are small.

BIRCHINGTON (*ALL SAINTS*), a parish, within the cinque-port liberty of DOVOR (of which it is a member, though locally in the hundred of RINGSLOW, or ISLE of THANET), union of THANET, lathe of ST. AUGUSTINE, E. division of KENT, 3½ miles (W. by S.) from Margate; containing 874 inhabitants, and comprising by admeasurement 1283 acres of arable, and 290 acres of pasture land. It is said to have been anciently called Birchington in Gorend, from a place called Gorend on the seashore, where tradition reports the church to have stood until it was destroyed by the falling of the cliff. The village is on the road from Margate to Canterbury, and a pleasure-fair is held in it on the Monday and Tuesday at Whitsuntide. At Quex Park, a fine old seat, is preserved a curious gilt chair, which was used by William III. when he occupied Quex, whilst waiting for favourable winds to convey him to Holland, and was borrowed by Sir William Curtis for the use of George IV., when he embarked at Ramsgate for his Hanoverian dominions, in 1821. The living is united, with that of Acole, to the vicarage of Monkton. On the north side of the church is Quex chapel, belonging to the manor of Quex, where are interred several of the family of Crispe, to whom there are some very interesting monuments and brasses. A place of worship for dissenters was erected a few years since; and there is a school, founded under the will, dated Feb. 13th, 1707, of Mrs. Anna Gertrude Crispe, who bequeathed 47 acres of land in Birchington and Monkton for charitable purposes.

BIRCHOLT (*ST. MARGARET*), a parish, in the union of EAST ASHFORD, franchise and barony of BIRCHOLT, lathe of SHEPWAY, E. division of KENT, 4 miles (E. by S.) from Ashford; containing 37 inhabitants. It comprises 299 acres. The living is a rectory, valued in the king's books at £2. 10. 10.; net income, £50; patron, Sir E. Knatchbull, Bart. The church is in ruins.

BIRCHOVER, a chapelry, in the parish of YOULGRAVE, union of BAKEWELL, hundred of HIGH PEAK, N. division of the county of DERBY, 1 mile (N. by W.) from Winster; containing, with the hamlet of Gratton, 112 inhabitants.

BIRCHWOOD, a hamlet, in the district of RIDDINGS, parish of ALFRETON, union of BELPER, hundred of SCARSDALE, N. division of the county of DERBY, about 3 miles (S. S. E.) from the town of Alfreton. The neighbourhood abounds in coal and iron.

BIRDALL, with RAISTHORPE.—See RAISTHORPE.

BIRDBROOK (*ST. AUGUSTINE*), a parish, in the union of RISBRIDGE, hundred of HINCKFORD, N. division of ESSEX, 7 miles (N. W.) from Castle Hedingham; containing 557 inhabitants. This parish, which is separated from the county of Suffolk by the river Stour, comprises an area of about 2240 acres, and is beautifully situated on a hill descending to the north and south, and commanding a richly diversified prospect. The soil is a deep sandy loam, extremely favourable to the growth of forest timber, especially oak, of which there are many noble and stately trees. The living is a rectory, valued in the king's books at £19, and in the patronage of Clare Hall, Cambridge: the tithes have been commuted for £600, and there are 99 acres of glebe. The church has some fine details in the early English style. The Roman road from Colchester to Cambridge passed

sion of the county of LANCASTER, 2 miles (S. W.) from the town of Chorley. This place is situated on the river Yarrow, and is about half a mile distant from the Coppull station on the North-Union railway. The vale here is very beautiful; there are large lodges, or reservoirs, of fine spring water, resembling what are seen in Westmorland and Cumberland. Here is an excellent coalmine. Formerly an iron-forge was in operation; but in the year 1784 it was converted into print-works, which are still carried on, employing about 300 hands. The present proprietors of the works are Messrs. Mc Naughton, Potter, and Company.

BIRKBY, a township, in the parish of CROSS-CAN-NONBY, union of COCKERMOUTH, ALLERDALE ward below Derwent, W. division of CUMBERLAND, 1¾ mile (E. N. E.) from Maryport; containing 89 inhabitants.

BIRKBY, a township, in the parish of MUNCASTER, union of BOOTLE, ALLERDALE ward above Derwent, W. division of CUMBERLAND, 2¼ miles (E. by S.) from Ravenglass; containing 119 inhabitants. Extensive ruins of a British or Danish city, called Barnscar, are visible on Birkby Fell.

BIRKBY (ST. PETER), a parish, in the union of NORTHALLERTON, wapentake of ALLERTONSHIRE, N. riding of YORK; consisting of the townships of Birkby and Little Smeaton, and the chapelry of Hutton-Bonville; and containing 256 inhabitants, of whom 74 are in the township of Birkby, 6 miles (N. N. W.) from Northallerton. This parish comprises about 3000 acres of land, of which two-thirds are arable, and one-third pasture with a little wood; the soil is a productive clay, and the surface, though not hilly, gently undulated: some parts are subject to inundation from the Wiske river. The York and Newcastle railway, passing to the east of Hutton-Bonville Hall, and slightly curving to the west of Birkby, crosses the Wiske. The living is a discharged rectory, valued in the king's books at £6. 13. 4., and in the patronage of the Bishop of Ripon: the tithes have been commuted for £205, and there are 4 acres of glebe, and an excellent parsonage-house lately built. The church, erected in the year 1776, is a plain brick building. At Hutton-Bonville is a chapel dedicated to St. Lawrence.

BIRKDALE, a township, in the parish of NORTH MEOLS, union of ORMSKIRK, hundred of WEST DERBY, S. division of the county of LANCASTER, 7½ miles (N. W.) from Ormskirk; containing 557 inhabitants. The manor, in the reign of Henry IV., was held by the Hallalls; and the Gerards of Bromley became possessed of the estate by purchase, in the 17th century: from the latter it passed to the Mordaunts, and from them to the Blundell family. The township comprises 2235a. 2r. 32p., and lies on the coast; the shore here is remarkable for its flatness and number of sandbanks, highly dangerous to shipping in strong westerly winds. Some years ago, a farm in the township was overwhelmed in the sand. There is a good schoolroom, where divine service is performed once every Sunday by one of the clergymen attached to the parish church. A court-leet appertains to this place.

: BIRKENHEAD, a rising sea-port, market-town, and township, in the union, and Lower division of the hundred, of WIRRALL, S. division of CHESHIRE; situated less than a mile, by ferry, (W.) from Liverpool, 16 miles N. by W.) from Chester, 32 (W. by S.) from Manchester, and 202 (N. W.) from London; containing about 25,000 inhabitants, and comprising the ancient extraparochial district or chapelry of Birkenhead, the former township of Claughton, in Bidstone, and part of that of Oxton, in Woodchurch. Though of recent origin as a town and port, this place is of considerable antiquity. A PRIORY for sixteen Benedictine monks was founded here about 1150, in honour of St. Mary and St. James, by Hamon de Massey, third baron of Dunham-Massey: according to Leland, it was subordinate to the abbey of St. Werburgh, at Chester; but from the power exercised by the monks, Bishop Tanner considers it to have been independent. The priors sat in the parliaments of the earls of Chester, and enjoyed all the dignities and privileges of palatinate barons, seldom riding out unless attended by their chamberlains and marshals; while the office of their seneschal was a prize worthy of the emulation of the most knightly houses in the county. The priory had considerable endowments: the adjacent rectories of Backford and Bidstone, with most of the lands in those parishes, were among its possessions, and it had also property in various parts of Lancashire. The right of ferryage across the Mersey was given to the prior in 1282, and confirmed by subsequent grants; and in a charter dated the 20th February 1318 (11th of Edward II.), he obtained license to build houses for lodging all such persons using the ferry as should be detained on account of contrary weather and the frequent storms. Up to that time there had not been any accommodation for sojourners here, and the priory had in consequence been burthened, and the passengers "much wearied and very greatly grieved." Subsequently the priors obtained a house, situated in the present Water-street, where such produce as remained unsold on the market-days was deposited till the next market. The revenues of the establishment were, according to Dugdale, valued at the Dissolution at £90. 13., and, according to Speed, at £102. 16. 10. Of the buildings, the last use of which was as a girls' school, for all the country for many miles round, nothing remains but a small portion of a Gothic window covered with ivy. The Priory House, which was garrisoned by the royalists, and captured by the parliamentarians in 1644, stands at the back of the church of St. Mary.

The greater portion of the priory estates in Cheshire was granted to Ralph Worsley, a junior member of the family of that name settled at Worsley, in Lancashire; and after his death, without male issue, the lands became the property of his grandson, Thomas Powell, of Birkenhead, whose eldest son was created a baronet in 1628. The manor continued in this family until 1703 or 1704, when it was sold to John Cleveland, Esq., of Liverpool, during the year of his mayoralty. This gentleman, and his second son (the eldest having died young),'were successively members for the borough of Liverpool for many years; they resided in Cleveland-square, several of the streets near which are called after parties connected with them. Alice, the only daughter and heiress of the former, married Francis Price, of Bryn-y-pys, in the county of Flint, and had issue Richard Price, Esq., who assumed the name of Parry, became a privy councillor for Ireland, and was buried in the old chapel at Birkenhead, yet occasionally used, in 1782. He was twice married, first to Dorothy, daughter of Sir John Byrne, and sister of Sir Peter Byrne Leycester, Bart., of Tabley;

and had issue Francis Parry Price, of Bryn-y-pys. The last-named married Francisca, daughter of Henry Offley Wright, Esq., of Mottram, in Cheshire ; and his son is Francis Richard Price, Esq., late lord of the manor of Birkenhead, which now belongs to William Jackson, Esq., of Claughton Hall.

Few places have, in the same short space of time, made such rapid progress as the township of Birkenhead. For centuries an inconsiderable place, it has suddenly become a large and important town ; and what was once regarded as an outskirt of the great port of Liverpool, is now going hand in hand with that mart of commerce, in extending the facilities for the trade of the country, and in increasing the prosperity of those residing on the shores of the noble estuary of the Mersey. The first steam-boats were introduced on the Mersey in 1815, at which time Birkenhead contained but a few insignificant and isolated cottages. In 1833 an act was passed for the improvement of the place ; in 1840 a railway was opened hence to Chester. The first stone of the docks was laid on the 23rd of October, 1844, by Sir Philip de Malpas Grey Egerton, Bart., M.P. for the southern division of the county ; and on the 5th of April, 1847, a portion of the docks, a number of dock warehouses, the extension of the Chester railway to the quays, and the park, were all formally opened by Lord Morpeth. The increase in the population has been commensurate with the great and rapid improvement of the town and the establishment of its various public works. In 1818 there were only three houses besides the priory and a few straggling cottages, and Woodside ferry-house ; and the population did not exceed 50 : in 1821 it was only 200 ; it had risen in 1831 to 2569, and in 1841 was 8227. The number of inhabitants in 1844 was about 14,000, and there were then at least 2315 houses in the township, exclusively of 503 houses in the course of erection. An actual survey and valuation were made in August 1823, by the late Mr. William Lawton, land-surveyor, of all the property in the township, when it was found that there were only 61 houses, cottages, fields, or other property that could be assessed ; and that their annual value was £3101. 4. 6. In 1837 the property was assessed at £25,781 per annum ; in 1840, at £42,778 ; and in 1844, at £64,481.

The TOWN is admirably situated on the Mersey, which separates it from Liverpool, on the east ; while on the north it is bounded by Wallasey Pool, soon to be converted into the great Float and the low-water basin. The direction of the chief streets is from north-west to south-east ; they include Conway-street, Laird-street, Beck-with-street, Price-street, and Cleveland-street, and are crossed at right angles by shorter streets, among which are Hamilton, Argyll, Lord, Camden, Park, Exmouth, Cathcart, and Victoria streets. Hamilton-square ocenpies 6½ acres of ground, surrounded on every side by elegant stone-fronted houses, four stories high, rusticated to the first story course, and built in the Doric style of architecture ; the wing houses having four bold columns in front, supporting handsome friezes and parapets. The garden and walks of the square are inclosed by a parapet and iron-railings, and are tastefully laid out for the special use of the neighbouring occupants. The town is well drained : in 1833 an act was obtained for paving and improving it, for regulating the police, and establishing a market ; this act was amended by another

252

passed in 1838, and in 1841 an act was obtained for lighting the township with gas, and supplying the inhabitants with water. The Water-works are situated in Oxton, and are the property of a private company. Their level is 104 feet above the sea : the borings and sinkings are 294 feet in depth, through an uninterrupted stratum of red sandstone formation ; and from the elevation of the works, a supply of water is provided even above the tops of the houses in Hamilton-square. The Market was opened in July 1845, and is very centrally situated ; its general form is somewhat similar to that of St. John's market at Liverpool, being a quadrangular building, 430 feet long, and 131 wide. The hall is covered with wrought-iron roofs of a light and elegant construction, which are divided into three bays, the centre one supported upon two rows of columns, connected by arched cast-iron girders ; an arrangement that divides the hall into three arcades. Of these, the middle arcade is of thirty feet span, and the two exterior arcades have each a span of fifty feet. The whole building, which is fire-proof, is surrounded by an open area, protected by a low parapet wall with a handsome cast-iron railing ; this area affords a free communication with the vaults, which form the basement story, and promotes the thorough ventilation of the stores, so necessary for preserving all articles of food in a fresh and wholesome condition. The cost of the market, including the outside footpaths and curbing, was nearly £35,000. The Slaughter-houses are situated in Jackson-street ; they are built of freestone, and have walls of a massive character. The principal entrance is through a large gateway, over which is a lodge for the keeper, and on the right and left are sheds or pens for cattle, each butcher having stalls set apart for his own beasts, and for forage ; the slaughter-rooms have all the necessary mechanical aids for the purpose, with abundance of hot and cold water, and thorough and efficient drainage. The ground purchased for these houses, and which will eventually be occupied by new erections when required by the increasing wants of the township, is 1000 yards.

The project of turning the capabilities of WALLASEY POOL to advantage was first conceived by the late Mr. William Laird, who purchased from Mr. Price, in May 1824, fifty acres of land on the margin of the pool, adjoining the site of the present Dock Company's warehouses, for an establishment for iron ship-building. Having bought other, additional, land, and with a view of bringing the matter prominently before the public, Mr. Laird and Sir John Tobin caused a survey to be made by Mr. Thomas Telford, Mr. Robert Stephenson, and Mr. Alexander Nimmo, civil engineers ; and their report was so favourable, that a private company was formed, and every preparation made for proceeding to parliament, in 1828, for power to construct docks, warehouses, and wharfs. The corporation of Liverpool, on hearing of the project, made overtures for the purchase of the land on the margin of the pool from Mr. Laird and Sir John Tobin, the holders of it : after some negotiation the purchase was concluded, the amount paid being £84,657 ; and purchases were afterwards made from other frontagers on both sides of the pool by the corporation, to the extent of £100,000 more. The pool continued in the possession of the corporation until 1843, when that body, requiring funds to carry on various works they had then in hand, disposed of some land to Mr. John Laird for 10s. per yard; a large portion of the land thus transferred being that sold by Mr. Laird's father to the corporation in 1828, and for which only 3s. a yard had been paid. The conditions upon which Mr. Laird made the purchase were, that he should have the right of constructing docks or wharfs for the use of shipping, on a lease of seventy-five years; and no sooner had that agreement been effected, than other parties bought large portions of the land, in eligible situations along the pool, with the view of building docks and warehouses.

The commissioners of Birkenhead being then fully convinced of the practicability of the scheme going forward, and of the important influence it would exercise as to the future prospects of the town, appointed J. M. Rendel, Esq., as their civil engineer, and gave notice of their intention to apply to parliament for the requisite powers to construct extensive works, embracing a sea-wall from Woodside to Seacombe, docks at Bridge-End, and a tidal basin of thirty-seven acres, accessible at all times of the tide by vessels of not more than twelve feet draft; a basin, for the use of coasters, of sixteen acres; and a dam to pen up the waters of Wallasey Pool, and make that portion lying between Bridge-End and the Wallasey bridge into an immense float, similar to that at Bristol, convenient gates and locks being formed for the access of vessels to it from the tidal basin. The determination to proceed to parliament was formed on the 19th of July, 1843, at the house of Mr. Laird; and by 'a somewhat remarkable coincidence, the bill giving full powers to carry out the project passed the third reading in the house of lords on the 19th of July, 1844. In less, therefore, than four years from the original determination to proceed to parliament; in less than three years from the obtaining of the bill; and in less than two years and a half from the laying of the foundation stone, the public were called upon to celebrate, under Lord Morpeth's auspices, the completion of the first portion of the undertaking. |

The DOCKS bound, or will bound, the town on the north and north-east, and partly on the east; ranging from the pier of Woodside ferry to the Wallasey bridge. The Pool, which was originally an inlet or creek of the Mersey, will form the great Float of 150 acres; it divides Birkenhead from Poolton with Seacombe, in the parish of Wallasey, and will communicate on the east with a low-water basin of thirty-seven acres, and on the south-east with a three-acre dock, called Bridge-End. This last will be connected on the north with the low-water basin, and on the south-east its connexion with the Woodside dock, which communicates, also on the south-east, with a tidal basin of sixteen acres for coasters and other vessels: the entrance to the Woodside dock is fifty feet wide. Thus a total accommodation will be afforded equal to more than 200 acres. The great sea-wall on the east will be broken only by an entrance 300 feet in width to the low-water basin of thirty-seven acres: this basin is excavated to the depth of twelve feet below low-water spring tides, will be walled with convenient wharfs, and in every respect made suitable as a place of refuge for the numerous vessels visiting the port. At the southern extremity of the sea-wall is the basin of sixteen acres: this is bounded on the south by the Woodside ferry-pier, and has two entrances, north and south, formed by the construction of an oblong

253

island between the basin and the river. It is thus seen, that the two great basins last described are the only portions of the docks of Birkenhead that immediately adjoin the Mersey.

The *Dock Warehouses* belong to a joint-stock company, called the Birkenhead Dock Warehouse Company, the bill for legalizing which was successfully carried through parliament in 1845. This company purchased a large extent of frontage on the south side of the Pool, and laid it out, with a view to the accommodation and increase of trade generally: the first portion of their warehouses, containing an amount of space sufficient for the stowage of 80,000 tons of goods, was opened in April, 1847. Adjoining their property is the new goods' station of the Chester and Birkenhead Railway Company, whose line is now carried round the whole of the Dock Company's property, by which all cartage is avoided, and the goods delivered direct from the vessel's side or the warehouse to all parts of the country, with safety, speed, and cheapness. The warehouses come under the denomination of what the insurance offices call fire-proof: each set is detached; water is laid on, and the whole are surrounded by a wall twelve feet high, with convenient entrance-gates and yards. In order to provide accommodation for the various workmen connected with the warehouses, the company have built a number of airy, well-lighted, and well-ventilated dwellings at the junction of Ilchester-road and Stuart-street. They are sixty in number, and have an abundant supply of pure water, with all the modern and most approved conveniences (some of them being perfectly unique) for sanitary purposes: they are built on the Scotch principle of having *flats* of four or five stories, one over another; and a good kitchen and two small bed-rooms are allotted to each family. The custom-house department is under that of Liverpool, and the entries passed on the Liverpool side answer for Birkenhead. A large establishment has been some time formed, belonging to Mr. Laird, for the construction of iron vessels, and at which many have been already built; there are also copper-mills, a varnish-manufactory, an iron-foundry, gun-works, a patent-slip for repairing ships, a boiler-yard, and other establishments.

There are three FERRIES, with an hotel at each; namely, the Woodside ferry, the Monks', and the Birkenhead. The right of ferry across the river has, for nearly five centuries, been a fruitful source of litigation: under the 27th of Edward III. pleadings were instituted against the prior; and it was the subject of two actions in the years 1838 and 1839, when it may be presumed to have been at length finally settled, as the jury returned in both cases that " Mr. Price had an ancient right of ferry from Birkenhead to Liverpool." These two actions were brought by the Woodside Ferry Company against the trustees of the Monks' ferry, who, soon after the verdict was delivered, sold their ferry, and their splendid building, the Monks' hotel, to the railway company, by whom it has been re-sold to the commissioners of the township. The commissioners have also purchased Mr. Price's ancient right of ferry, extending over all the township, except the Birkenhead hotel premises. The slips at *Woodside* are excellent: a fine pier runs down between them, which is twenty feet wide; a row of lamps illuminates each slip at night, and the pier forms a delightful promenade, where contractors with the ferry have the privilege of walking : at the extremity is a small lighthouse. The *Monks' ferry* hotel is the largest hotel in Birkenhead, and is advantageously situated on the verge of the river, from which it presents a very fine appearance. The *Birkenhead* ferry, the property of the corporation of Liverpool, by whom it was purchased a few years ago, is the most southern of the ferries, and has a fine commodious slip, but shorter than the slips at the other ferries, owing to the greater depth of water close to the shore. The hotel, which is very spacious, stands on a delightful and almost isolated site, close to the point forming the northern boundary of the indenture of Tranmere Pool. From the house and pleasure-grounds the most charming views are obtained of the river and shipping, the Lancashire shore from Bootle·bay to Runcorn, with Liverpool on the east, and the whole basin of the Mersey on the south ; also of the Cheshire shore, the Rockferry, &c. A new pier has recently been built from the top of the slip, running northward, parallel with the river ; and this is found to be extremely convenient for passengers landing or embarking during the height of spring tides.

The *Birkenhead and Chester railway*, sixteen miles in length, connects the town with the midland counties and the metropolis ; and in 1846 an act was passed for a railway from Hooton, about midway between Birkenhead and Chester, to Warrington, Altrincham, and Stockport, thus completing a direct railway communication between the town and Manchester, Lancashire generally, and Yorkshire. The Birkenhead and Chester line originally commenced at Grange-lane ; but in 1844 an extension under the town was formed, which brings the line almost to the water's edge, at the Monks' ferry. The tunnel is about 500 yards long, and has excavated and embanked approaches ; the inclinations fall towards the river, and the line curves a little to the right in going down : there is one shaft near the middle for ventilation. About 242 yards of the tunnel were driven through sand and clay, and 255 through indurated sandstone. The arch is semicircular, and two feet in extreme thickness : it is partly constructed of stone and partly of brick, as the emergencies required ; and the crown of it is lined throughout with brickwork, and pointed with cement. The area of the station or yard at the ferry is very large ; from the mouth of the tunnel to the quay, about 250 feet long, and about 120 in width between the high retaining rails. Another act was passed in 1845, for making a line from Grange-lane to Bridge-End and the docks : this second extension is about a mile long, and has two new stations, one for passengers between Canning-street and Bridge-street, and the other for goods, adjoining the dock warehouses.

The COMMISSIONERS of the town were originally constituted under an act of parliament, 3rd William IV., which received the royal assent on the 10th of June, 1833. The mayor and bailiffs of Liverpool for the time being, and the four junior aldermen, together with sixty other persons named in the act, were appointed the commissioners ; the rate-payers having the privilege of supplying vacancies in the sixty, from whatever cause they might occur. The act of the 1st Victoria, which received the royal assent on the 11th June, 1838, repealed the clauses in the former act relating to the com-
254

missioners, their number, and mode of election ; and enacted that there should be twenty-four commissioners, three of them appointed by the town-council of Liverpool, and the remainder elected by the rate-payers. In 1846 an act was passed for the exclusion of the three Liverpool members. The qualification for a commissioner is a rating to the poor to the value of £35, or the possession of property to the value of £1500 : one-third of the commissioners retire annually, but they are eligible for re-election. For the convenience of public business, the following committees have been appointed by the board ; Watching and Lighting, Improvement, Finance, Market, Road, Ferry, and Health : the chairman and vice-chairman are *ex officio* members of all committees. Birkenhead is not subject to church rates or any other claims of an ecclesiastical character ; and it may be added that, as the general sewerage of the place is effected by the land proprietors, no rate is levied on the inhabitants for the purpose. The commissioners have only authority to levy dock dues on the shipping using their docks ; on goods no duties are levied. The powers of the county debt-court of Birkenhead, established in 1847, extend over the registration-district of Wirrall. The town-hall contains the bridewell, and various offices for parochial purposes, and is situated in Hamilton-street ; the front is of stone from the Storeton-hill quarries, and presents to the eye a neat elevation in the Grecian style. But the whole of the buildings have been found unsuited to the necessities of the township, and will be cleared away when the new buildings now in contemplation shall have been completed.

The township comprises an area, including Claughton and part of Oxton, of about 1388 acres, or two square miles : Claughton contains 575 acres, a large portion of which is converted into a public park and villa grounds ; and it has, together with a small part of Oxton, been incorporated by a recent act of parliament with the township of Birkenhead. The project of a PUBLIC PARK originated with Mr. I. Holmes, one of the commissioners, and a committee was appointed to take the subject into consideration : some time afterwards, the project was revived by Mr. Jackson ; and the commissioners, having agreed to purchase the land, obtained an act of parliament, the royal assent to which was given on the 1st Sept. 1843. The area consists of 180 acres, laid out in admirable taste by Mr. Paxton, with every variety of landscape-gardening, including plantations of shrubs, flower-beds, verdant vales, picturesque lakes, ornamental bridges, and serpentine walks, with extensive drives, cricket and archery grounds, &c. A margin of 350,000 yards of land is available for sale to erect villas, and 114 acres are dedicated to the public for their free use and enjoyment for ever. It is expected that the sales of the marginal land will reimburse the township for the cost of the whole : from 70,000 to 80,000 yards have been already sold, at an average price of about 6s. 6d. per yard. The park entrance is through a handsome archway for carriages, and two minor archways for foot passengers ; on each side are uniform lodges, two stories in height, and built of the purest freestone : the noble architectural appearance of the whole, presenting a fine specimen of the Ionic style, is deservedly admired. *Claughton Hall*, the residence of William Jackson, Esq., the lord of the manor, and late chairman of the commissioners, is a very elegant and commodious building, of fine white veined freestone from Storeton, erected with great taste, and having four fronts, one to each cardinal point; the principal entrance is on the west. The house stands on an elevated site sloping gradually eastward, and commands, as do the lawn and pleasure-grounds in front, an extensive and uninterrupted view of the public park below, the pool, the Wirrall peninsula northward, the river and shipping, and the whole of Birkenhead and Liverpool, which, save where the water intervenes, appear to be blended into one huge metropolis. *Oxton Hill* lies to the south of Claughton. Comparatively but a few years ago, it was a barren heath; it is now, to a great extent, covered with fine houses and villas, with gardens, fields, woods, and pleasure-grounds, and is, in fact, a village of itself. The air in this elevated locality is extremely salubrious, and the prospect from almost any point uninterrupted and delightful, embracing a vast extent of land, and town and marine scenery. *Clifton Park* is well worthy of being named among the beauties of Birkenhead; the entrance lodge is in Grange-lane: after a turn on the road there is a slight ascent, and on each side a number of elegant mansions have been erected, rising one above another on the slope of the hill. Other places within a short distance are also very attractive, especially to visiters from the counties inland; among these may be mentioned New Brighton, Leasowe, West Kirby, and, particularly, Hoylake, on the west point of the peninsula.

St. Mary's church is an elegant and well-built structure of stone, in the pointed style, erected by F. R. Price, Esq., then lord of the manor. In 1817 a considerable purchase of land was made by Messrs. Grindrod, Hetherington, and Addison, who, in their contract with Mr. Price, stipulated, among other things, that a new church should be built, which was accordingly commenced in July, 1819, the foundation stone being laid by Lord Kenyon, and the direction confided to the eminent architect, Mr. Rickman. The living is in the patronage of William Jackson, Esq. The churchyard includes the ancient burial-ground of the abbey, in which are a number of tombs of very old date. The church of the *Holy Trinity*, situated in Price-street, is somewhat remarkable, as regards design and architectural ornament; it is in the Norman style, but considerably modified, is built of stone, is 102 feet in extreme length, 56 feet in breadth, and will accommodate 1000 persons. The principal entrance is by a deep, recessed, ornamented doorway, having two windows above supported on small arches, grotesque heads being introduced at the various points of contact; the tower rises to the height of 88 feet, and is highly embellished with mouldings and pierced work. The living is in the patronage of H. Williams, Esq. *St. John's* church is of new red sandstone, and was built at the expense of J. S. Jackson, Esq., Joseph Mallaby, Esq., and others; it stands in Grange-lane road, and presents one of the most perfect specimens of the early English style in the neighbourhood, is of very imposing appearance, and of large dimensions. In the chancel are stained-glass windows representing St. John, St. Paul, and St. Peter, and in the north and south aisles are others, with various arms. The living is in the patronage of Trustees. *St. James's* church, of yellow sandstone, and in the early English style, was built at the united cost of W. Potter, Esq., W. Jackson, Esq., and the

255

Messrs. Laird, for the use of the labouring classes resident in the dock cottages. A church dedicated to *St. Anne*, and situated in Beckwith-street, has just been completed from designs furnished by William Cole, Esq., architect, at the expense of Mr. Potter; it is of red sandstone, and in the pointed style of architecture. The last-named gentleman has erected another church at *Claughton Firs*, in a similar style. There are places of worship for Calvinists, Independents, Quakers, Welsh Methodists, Wesleyans, and Roman Catholics, one in connexion with the Scottish Kirk, and one for Seceders. The Scottish church is situated in Conway-street, and is one of the principal edifices in the locality, combining neatness of form with internal convenience and fitness: there is a small portion of land attached, used as a burial-ground.

A Theological College, under the patronage of the Bishop of Chester, prepares young men as clergymen for foreign missions, and others as pastors to foreigners in the port of Liverpool and Birkenhead: the course of study includes the ordinary University course, with a greater proportion of theology and biblical literature. The Birkenhead Mechanics' Institution was established in 1840, and has been perseveringly carried on under very fluctuating circumstances. Numerous schools have been founded for the poor. A house is at present used as an infirmary, but the erection of a spacious building has been determined on; the commissioners have agreed to give an acre of land for the purpose, and a sum amounting to several thousand pounds has already been subscribed. A lying-in hospital has been established in a house at the entrance of Clifton Park, through the exertions of several charitable ladies and those of Dr. C. E. H. Orpen; and there is a dispensary, yet but an infant institution. Flaybrick hill, where extensive stone-quarries are formed for the town purposes, especially for the construction of the docks, is intended ultimately to be the public cemetery. From the bowels of this hill fine stone has been for many years extracted; but the excavation made has been filled up with the rubbish thrown out, and in such a manner as to leave a hill of pyramidal form, the high side of which will be appropriated to catacombs and tombs, ornamented with shrubs and flowers.

BIRKENSHAW, an ecclesiastical district, in the parish of BIRSTAL, wapentake of MORLEY, W. riding of YORK, 6½ miles (E.) from Leeds; containing 3000 inhabitants, of whom 1803 are in the hamlet. This place, which is situated at the junction of the Leeds and Halifax, and Dewsbury and Bradford turnpike-roads, in the heart of a district abounding with coal, iron-ore, and building-stone, has been rapidly increasing in importance, and is now an extensive, populous, and thriving village. The inhabitants are chiefly employed in the coal-mines, and in the extensive worsted factories of the Messrs. Ackroyd and others; in the combing of wool; and in the weaving of stuffs and woollen-cloths, the former for the Bradford, and the latter for the Leeds market. The church, dedicated to St. Paul, was erected in 1829, at an expense of £2929, by the Parliamentary Commissioners, on a site given by the late Emanuel Emmet, Esq.: it is in the early English style, with a square embattled tower crowned with pinnacles and surmounted by a spire, and contains 702 sittings. The living is a perpetual curacy, in the gift of the Vicar of

Birstal, with a net income of £150, and a handsome residence built in 1835 at an expense, including the purchase of nearly five acres of land, of £2000.

BIRKER, with AUSTHWAITE, a township, in the parish of MILLOM, union of BOOTLE, ALLERDALE ward above Derwent, W. division of CUMBERLAND, 7½ miles (E. by N.) from Ravenglass; containing 105 inhabitants. It is within the limits of the chapelry of Eskdale, in the adjoining parish of St. Bees, and the inhabitants marry and bury there. The neighbourhood abounds with picturesque scenery, heightened and diversified by the lake Devock-water, and the water-falls of Birker Force and Stanley Gill.

BIRKIN (ST. MARY), a parish, in the Lower division of the wapentake of BARKSTONE-ASH, W. riding of YORK; comprising the townships of Birkin, West Haddlesey, Chapel Haddlesey, Temple-Hurst, and Hurst-Courtney; and containing 921 inhabitants, of whom 169 are in the township of Birkin, 4 miles (N. E. by E.) from Ferry-Bridge. The parish is intersected by the Selby canal, and bounded on the south by the river Aire. It is nine miles long, and comprises 5890 acres, of which about 3355 are arable, 2000, pasture, and 45 woodland; the soil varies in quality, part being light, and adapted to the growth of barley and turnips, and part being of a stronger nature, and well suited for wheat and beans. The surface is varied, the scenery pleasingly diversified, and the air salubrious. The living is a rectory, valued in the king's books at £36; net income, £1008; patron, the Rev. Thomas Hill. The church, erected in the 12th century, is a very curious and perfect specimen of Norman architecture, and contains a chancel particularly worthy of notice: there is an inscription by Whitehead, the poet laureate, commemorating Elizabeth Wright, wife of a former rector. A chapel of ease was erected, in 1836, at Chapel Haddlesey, upon the site of one which, being very dilapidated and insufficient for the accommodation of the parishioners there, was pulled down. The Wesleyan Methodists have small places of worship at Chapel Haddlesey and Temple-Hurst.

BIRKSCEUGH, CUMBERLAND.—See BRISCO.

BIRLEY (ST. PETER), a parish, in the union of WEOBLEY, hundred of STRETFORD, county of HEREFORD, 4 miles (E. by N.) from Weobley; containing 172 inhabitants. The parish comprises by measurement 934 acres, of which 48 are common or waste; the surface is rather flat, and the soil principally clay, but in some places inclining to gravel. On the west, Birley is bounded by the road from Hereford to Pembridge. The living is a discharged vicarage, consolidated with that of King's Pion, and valued in the king's books at £5. 9. 7. BIRLING (ALL SAINTS), a parish, in the union of MALLING, hundred of LARKFIELD, lathe of AYLESFORD, W. division of KENT, 3 miles (N.) from Town Malling; containing 511 inhabitants, and comprising 1883a. 2r. 35p., of which 178 acres are woodland. The living is a vicarage, valued in the king's books at £6. 9. 4½.; patron and impropriator, the Earl of Abergavenny. The great tithes have been commuted for £118. 9. 11., and the vicarial for £170; there are 8 acres of glebe. Foundations of buildings have been discovered in a field near the church.

BIRLING, a township, in the parish of WARKWORTH, union of ALNWICK, E. division of COQUETDALE

ward, N. division of NORTHUMBERLAND, 6¼ miles (S. E.) from Alnwick; containing 80 inhabitants. It is situated on the road from Warkworth to Lesbury, and is the property of the Duke of Northumberland: the river Coquet flows on the south. The tithes have been commuted for £95. 8., payable to the Bishop of Carlisle, and £32. 7. to the vicar of the parish.

BIRLINGHAM (ST. JAMES), a parish, in the union, and Upper division of the hundred, of PERSHORE, Pershore and E. divisions of the county of WORCESTER, 3 miles (S. S. W.) from Pershore; containing 390 inhabitants. The parish is surrounded on all sides, except the west and a portion of the north, by a bend of the navigable river Avon; and comprises 1274a. 2r. 22p., of which 700 acres are pasture, 470 arable, and 13 woodland: the surface is moderately undulated, and the soil highly fertile. The village contains several respectable houses. The living is a rectory, valued in the king's books at £9. 17. 11.; net income, £205; patron and incumbent, the Rev. Robert Eyres Landor. The church is a neat stone structure with a tower: in the chancel are two windows with ancient stained glass.

BIRMINGHAM, a celebrated manufacturing town and a borough, locally in the Birmingham division of the hundred of HEMLINGFORD, N. division of the county of WARWICK, 18 miles (N. W. by W.) from Coventry, 20 (N. W.) from Warwick, and 109 (N. W.) from London; containing in the parish 138,215, and, with the parish of Edgbaston, and the hamlets of Bordesley, Deritend, and Duddeston with Nechels (which, though in the parish of Aston, form parts of the town, and are included within the borough), 182,922 inhabitants. The name of this town has been traced by its local antiquary, the late Mr. Hamper, through no less than 140 variations, and its etymology is involved in great uncertainty. Dugdale, from its Saxon termination, deduces it from the first Saxon lord; while others assign to it an origin of much higher antiquity, inferring that, with more probability, the first Saxon proprietor took his name from that of the town, which they suppose to have been originally "Bromwych," from the quantity of broom formerly growing in the neighbourhood; from which circumstance also are derived the names of two villages in the immediate vicinity, called respectively Castle Bromwich and West Bromwich. In proof of the high antiquity of the place, and also of its having been distinguished for the manufacture of arms and warlike instruments prior to the Roman invasion, may be adduced the great number of exhausted coal-mines on a common of large extent, called Wednesbury Old Field, within a short distance of the town, and the prodigious accumulation of scoria produced by the smelting of iron, at Aston furnace, on the border of the parish. Both of these it is concluded must have been the work of many centuries; as in the latter, though continually receiving additions, no perceptible increase has been observed within the memory of the oldest inhabitant. From its situation near the Ikeneld-street, the town is

Arms.

supposed to have been the *Bremenium* of the Romans. During the time of the Saxons, it appears to have been governed by two constables, and to have obtained the grant of a weekly market on Thursday.

In the Conqueror's survey the place is noticed under the name "Bermengeham;" and from the reign of Henry I. till that of Henry VIII., the manor and lordship were held by a distinguished family from whom, according to Camden, "the noble and warlike family of the Bremichams, earls of Louth, in Ireland," who were instrumental in assisting Strongbow, Earl of Pembroke, in the conquest of that country, "had both their original and name." Of this family were William de Bermingham, who attended Edward I. into Gascony, where he was made prisoner at the siege of Bellegarde in 1297, and his descendant William, who was summoned to parliament by the title of William, Lord Birmingham, in the 1st of Edward III. The lordship continued in the possession of that family till the 37th of Henry VIII., when by the artifices of John Dudley, afterwards Duke of Northumberland, who at that time held the castle of Dudley, and was ambitious of adding to it the manor of Birmingham, which he had no hope of purchasing, it was wrested from Edward de Birmingham, whom that unprincipled nobleman had by a fictitious charge of felony, supported by perjured hirelings, reduced to the necessity of ransoming his life by the sacrifice of his estate. On the attainder and execution of the duke, in the reign of Mary, the manor escheated to the crown; and, in 1643, a descendant of the Bermingham family through the female line, named Humble Ward, was raised to the peerage as Baron Ward of Birmingham, which title was subsequently absorbed in the superior dignities of Viscount Dudley and Ward, and Earl of Dudley. Of the ancient manor-house, a memorial is preserved in the name of the site, at present occupied by the Smithfield market, and which for many years has retained the appellation of "the Moat," from the intrenchment by which the mansion was surrounded. In St. Martin's church are the recumbent effigies of a crusader and an ecclesiastic, both members of the Bermingham family.

Few events of importance occur in the history of the place prior to the commencement of the civil war of the 17th century, when the inhabitants, with those of Coventry and Warwick, embraced the cause of the parliament, and in 1642, after the king had passed through the town on his route from Shrewsbury, immediately before the battle of Edge-Hill, seized the royal carriages and plate, which they sent to Warwick Castle. In the following year, Prince Rupert, whom the king had despatched with a detachment of 2000 of the royal army, to open a communication between Oxford and York, was, on his arrival at Birmingham, intercepted in his progress by a company of foot belonging to the parliamentarians. This company, reinforced by a troop of horse from Lichfield, and assisted by the inhabitants, having thrown up some works on the summit of Bordesley, since called Camp-hill, on the line of approach from the Oxford road, and having blocked up all the smaller avenues, fired upon the prince's army, and obstinately opposed its entrance into the town. A sharp conflict ensued, which was of longer duration than could have been expected from the great disparity of the numbers; the parliamentarians were driven from their

station, and the prince, after much difficulty, obtained an entrance by another avenue. A second attempt to obstruct his progress was made by the inhabitants, who were animated in their resistance by a clergyman who acted as governor, and who, being taken prisoner during the action, and refusing to accept quarter, was, after the battle, put to death at the Red Lion inn. At length, exasperated by the determined resistance of the inhabitants and the death of the Earl of Denbigh, who had been shot by an officer in the service of the parliament, the prince set fire to the town; which, however, after several houses had been burnt, was saved from further devastation by the payment of a heavy fine. In 1791 occurred the memorable riots, which originated in the meeting of about eighty persons on Thursday, the 14th of July, to celebrate the anniversary of the French revolution by a dinner, at the Royal Hotel; and on the 15th of July, 1839, another riot took place, occasioned by the Chartists, who committed numerous and serious outrages.

The most prominent and interesting features in the history of Birmingham are, the extraordinary increase of the town, the progressive improvements of its manufactures, and the wide extension of its trade and commerce. For these advantages it is indebted to the rich mines of ironstone and coal with which the northern and western districts of the neighbourhood abound, and to the numerous canals and railways by which it is connected with all parts of England; carrying on through these channels not only an immense trade with every town of importance in the kingdom, but also exporting its manufactures and its merchandise to every quarter of the civilized world, and receiving, in return, the produce of every country. In the reign of Henry VIII., Leland describes Birmingham as inhabited "by smithes that use to make knives and all manner of cutting tooles, and lorimers that make bittes, and a great many nailours." In the reign of Elizabeth, it is described by Camden as "swarming with inhabitants, and echoing with the noise of anvils; but the upper part rising with abundance of handsome buildings;" and his continuator, Bishop Gibson, in the reign of Anne, mentions "its artificers in iron and steel, whose performances in that way are greatly admired both at home and abroad." Prior to the restoration of Charles II., the town had for centuries consisted merely of one long street, extending from the hamlet of Deritend to the present Bull-street; and its population, till that period, probably did not amount to 5000. In 1711, its public edifices were only the parish church of St. Martin, the chapel of St. John in Deritend, the Old and New meeting-houses, and the free grammar school of King Edward VI. In 1731, it had received the addition of St. Philip's church and the Blue-coat charity school, and at that time its population had increased to 8254. In Westley's Plan of Birmingham, which was published in that year, and which accurately delineates the state of the town, not a house appears northward of St. Philip's church, with the single exception of an ancient mansion called New Hall, of which a memorial is preserved in the name of New Hall street, now leading to its site. From 1731 to 1778, the chapels of St. Bartholomew and St. Mary were the sole additions to the public buildings of the town, which at the latter period contained 42,550 inhabitants. From 1778 to 1801, St.

Paul's chapel, the general hospital, the dispensary, the Old and New Libraries, the barracks, and the theatre, were added to its public edifices; and, during the same interval, its population, including the hamlets, increased to 69,384. Since this period, so rapid has been the increase of the buildings in the suburbs, that upwards of 100,000 inhabitants have been added to its population.

The TOWN is advantageously situated on an eminence at the north-western extremity of the county, bordering closely on the counties of Stafford and Worcester, from the former of which it is separated only by a small brook. On every side, except the north-west, it is approached by an ascent; and the streets, which are in general spacious, are well paved and flagged, lighted with gas, and, being commonly on a declivity, always clean. The houses, most of which are modern and well built, and of which several of more recent erection are large and handsome, are chiefly of brick; but, since the introduction of Roman cement, many have been new-fronted, and nearly throughout the town and its environs (the latter of which are thickly studded with the pleasant villas and private houses of merchants, manufacturers, and tradesmen) are presented spécimens of elegance in almost every style of architecture. The inhabitants are amply supplied with water from pumps attached to their houses, and with soft water of excellent quality from two fine wells at Digbeth, in the lower part of the town. On entering from London, either through Coventry or through Oxford, the road, by a stone bridge over the river Rea at Deritend, leads up an ascent into an area called the Bull-ring, formerly used as the market-place, in the centre of which is a statue in bronze of Admiral Viscount Nelson, finely executed by Westmacott, at an expense of £3000, raised by subscription.

The *Old Library*, in Union-street, originally established in 1779, is a stone building, comprising a spacious depository for the books, of which there are more than 30,000 volumes: the *New Library*, instituted in 1796, and for which the present building in Temple-row West was erected about twenty years since, though upon a smaller scale than the Old library, is similarly conducted. The *News-room*, on Bennet's-hill, erected in 1825, is a neat edifice: the interior comprises one large reading-room, opening through folding-doors at one end into two smaller apartments, and there is also a suite of rooms, in which copies of the public records and books of reference are deposited. The press of this town attained considerable eminence when Baskerville printed that series of works which in typographical beauty have never since been equalled. After his decease in 1775, his exquisite types could obtain no purchaser in Britain, and were therefore sold to a literary society at Paris, and subsequently taken to Kehl by Beaumarchais, to print his edition of the works of Voltaire. The *Philosophical Society*, in Cannon-street, was formed in 1800, and in 1810 the members extended their plan, and added to their rooms a commodious theatre for the delivery of lectures. A *Mechanics' Institute* was founded in 1825, and there are several other literary and scientific institutions. One of these, an institution called the *Polytechnic*, for the instruction of the working classes and others at a cheap rate, and advancing their moral and intellectual character, was established in 1843; in con-

nexion with it are a news-room, library, and baths. The *Botanical and Horticultural Society* was instituted in 1828, when a spaciods plot of ground in a delightful situation at Edgbaston, granted on lease by Lord Calthorpe, was converted into gardens, in which have been erected a conservatory and other requisite buildings. The *Society of Arts*, in New-street, was formed in 1821; the building is a chaste and elegant specimen of the Corinthian order, comprising an exhibition-room (a circle 52 feet in diameter, lighted from the roof), and several smaller apartments for casts from the antique sculptures, and other departments of the art, with a well-assorted library. The Institution for Promoting the Fine Arts was established in 1828, for the encouragement of artists resident within 30 miles of Birmingham: it is now incorporated with the Society of Arts; and a handsome building of the Grecian-Doric order, with fluted columns supporting a rich entablature and cornice, which had been erected for its use on the south side of St. Philip's churchyard, is now used for various literary and scientific purposes.

The *Theatre*, in New-street, is a spacious and well-arranged building, consisting of a pit, two tiers of boxes, and a gallery, together capable of accommodating 2500 persons. It was originally built in 1774: the interior was destroyed by fire in 1792, and again, with the exception of the present front, in January, 1820; but it was rebuilt during the same year, at an expense of £14,000, subscribed in shares. *Assemblies* are held periodically during the winter, at the Royal Hotel; the room, which is spacious and elegantly embellished, is also appropriated to the subscription concerts, which are supported by more than 300 members, and conducted on a scale combining the first-rate talent of the metropolis with the professional skill of the town. The triennial musical festivals, for which Birmingham has become so pre-eminently distinguished, originated in aid of the funds of the General hospital, for which purpose the committee, on its being opened in 1779, had recourse to a performance of sacred music under the direction of a London professor: the receipts are now very large. The *Town-hall*, intended for the transaction of public business and the holding of large meetings, and more especially with a view to the efficient performance of the music at the triennial festivals, was erected under the provisions of the Street Commissioners' act obtained in 1828, and was opened in 1834, at an expense of £18,000, defrayed by a rate on the inhabitants. It is a stately and magnificent structure of colossal dimensions, substantially built of brick, and cased with Anglesey marble presented to the town by Sir R. Bulkeley, Bart., proprietor of the Penmon quarries: the design was modelled by Mr. Harris from the temple of Jupiter Stator at Rome, and the edifice was built by Messrs. Hanson and Welsh, architects, of Liverpool. The interior of the hall is 140 feet in length, 65 feet in breadth, and 65 feet in height from the floor to the ceiling; and the result of the performances proves it to be the finest room in Britain for musical effect. The organ was built by Hill of London, at an expense of £6000, and in its dimensions is unequalled even by those of Haarlem and Rotterdam.

It is not easy to trace with accuracy the origin of the numerous branches of TRADE and MANUFACTURE which, in addition to those described by Leland, have been introduced into the town, and which, from their taste and variety, as well as for the high degree of perfection to which they have attained, procured for the place, from Mr. Burke, the designation of the "Toy-shop of Europe." The toy trade appears to have been adopted in the reign of Charles II., brass-founding in that of William III., and the buckle trade about the same period; the last, after exercising the ingenuity of the manufacturer in every variety of form, pattern, and material, declined about the year 1812, and is now nearly extinct. The leather trade, which was carried on at a remote period, has also experienced a very great diminution. It is un-certain at what time the button trade was first intro-duced, but it has continued to flourish from a distant period, and, though much lessened, is still a source of employment to thousands. The manufacture of fire-arms was commenced towards the close of the seven-teenth century, and during the last war the government contracts for muskets alone averaged 30,000 per month. In 1813, the gun-makers of the town obtained an act of parliament for the erection of a proof-house, in which, under a heavy penalty, all barrels of fire-arms are sub-jected to a severe test; and though the manufacture of fire-arms has necessarily diminished since the peace, it is still carried on to a very great extent, and since the erection of the proof-house the manufacture of fowling-pieces and pistols has increased. Among the almost in-numerable branches of trade are, light and heavy steel goods (here called toys), brass and iron founding, sad-dlery, military accoutrements, fire-arms, swords, and cutlery of various kinds; jewellery; gold, silver, plated, and japanned goods; buttons; medals; gilt, silver, ivory, bone, and other toys; glass; wood-turnery; metal-rolling; tools and implements of all kinds; mills; ma-chinery of all sorts; and steam-engines on every known principle. Casting, modelling, die-sinking, engraving, and other processes connected with the various manu-factures, have likewise been brought to the greatest perfection; also the cutting of glass, of which there are brilliant specimens in the show-rooms of the town.

With the manufactures is intimately connected the celebrated establishment at Soho, about a mile to the north of the town, and within the parish of Hands-worth, under which head it is described. Collis and Co.'s manufactory, in Church-street, has a splendid suite of show-rooms attached to it, replete with costly and elaborate specimens of workmanship in gold, silver, plated-ware, or-molu, cut-glass, medals, bronzes, and the crystallized bases of metals and semi-metals: among the more massive productions is a statue in bronze of George IV.; and in a suitable room built for the purpose is a metallic vase of vast dimensions, a fac-simile in size, form, and embellishment, of the Grecian vase of Lysip-pus in the gardens of Warwick Castle. The show-rooms of Messrs. Elkington, manufacturers of plated goods, also contain articles of exquisite design. The pin-factories are very interesting, and give employment to numbers of children; the manufactories for japanned-ware and papier-maché are considered the most beautiful objects for tasteful inspection in the town, and improve-ments are continually being introduced by Messrs. Jen-nens and Bettridge, Mr. Lane, Messrs. M'Callum and Hodgson, Mr. Farmer, and Mr. Sutcliffe, all manufac-turers of papier-maché. There are several extensive brass and iron foundries; rolling and slitting mills of

great power; and three manufactories of metallic hot-houses and conservatories, in one of which a hot-house and conservatory were made for the Duke of Northum-berland, at an expense of £50,000. The Cambridge-street works, established in 1820 by Mr. R. W. Winfield, and at which between 300 and 400 persons are employed in the production of every variety of ornamental and rough brass-founding, gas-fittings, metallic bedsteads, and other useful articles, are justly celebrated. Beau-tiful bronze castings are produced by the Messrs. Mes-senger, and fine brass-work for lamps, &c., by the Messrs. Ratcliff. The manufacture of glass has greatly increased within the last twenty years, during which period five or six glass-houses have been erected; also numerous mills for cutting and polishing it. The Islington glass-works, erected in 1814, are capable of employing nearly 500 hands in the various departments, and are conducted by Mr. Rice Harris, whose attention has been directed for several years to the pressing or stamping of glass, and who has so far succeeded in his attempts at improvement in this respect, that it is diffi-cult to distinguish the articles thus produced from the richest cut articles. The Park works, first erected about 1785, were then the only glass-works in the neighbourhood, and have been carried on ever since for the manufacture of flint-glass; they now belong to Messrs. Lloyd and Summerfield, and the Soho works, erected in 1803, to Mr. Samuel Shakespear. Companies have been established for supplying materials for the different works, among which are the Birmingham Copper Company, the Birmingham Mining Company, the Brass Company, and the Brades' Iron and Steel Com-pany. There are chemical laboratories on a large scale, for the production of articles necessary in the processes of manufacture; a distillery; and several breweries, of which the Wharstone, Deritend, and New breweries are the chief.

The trade of the town is greatly promoted by nume-rous Canals, of which Birmingham may be regarded as the common centre; namely, the Birmingham, con-structed in 1768, and for the supply of which a reservoir of 19 acres was excavated to the depth of 20 feet, near the town; the Birmingham and Fazeley, constructed in 1783; the Worcester and Birmingham, in 1791; the Warwick and Birmingham, in 1793; and the Bir-mingham and Liverpool Junction, in 1826. The town is also a grand centre of RAILWAY communication. A railway was opened to *London* Sept. 17th, 1838: the present station here, which is 250 feet above the level of the London terminus, is at the north-eastern extre-mity of Birmingham, adjoining the station of the Liver-pool line. The *Liverpool* line is carried over Lawley-street by a viaduct 1000 feet in length, supported on 28 segmental arches of 30 feet span: the principal depôt is at Duddeston, about half a mile from the terminus. These two important lines now belong to a joint com-pany called the London and North-Western; and the Birmingham and *Derby* railway, opened Aug. 5th, 1839, and the Birmingham and *Bristol* railway, completed in 1844, both belong to the Midland company. An act was passed in 1845, giving power to the London and North-Western company to make a railway from their London line to the centre of Birmingham, nearly one mile long; and in 1847 the works were commenced: the extension runs from the present station, across the adjacent canal, by St. Bartholomew's churchyard, then through Park-street, and under High-street, to the rear of the grammar school, where a new station will be erected, upon an "end" of ground extending from Worcester-street to Navigation-street. The Midland company, also, received power in 1846 to improve their line at Birmingham, by making an extension a mile and a quarter long, and forming a new junction with the London railway. Other acts were passed in the same year, for the construction of a railway to *Lichfield*; a railway to the *Oxford and Rugby* line near Fenny-Compton; another, called the *Birmingham, Wolverhampton, and Dudley,* joining the Oxford and Wolverhampton line after a course of 11 miles, and having a branch to Dudley 3½ miles long; and a fourth, called the *Birmingham, Wolverhampton, and Stour Valley,* which runs to Wolverhampton, and to the Liverpool railway in Bushbury parish, with a branch of 3½ miles to Dudley.

The principal MARKET is on Thursday, for corn, horses, cattle, sheep, and pigs. There are also markets on Monday and Saturday for provisions, and on Tuesday for hay and straw; and two fairs, for three days each, are annually held, one commencing on the Thursday in Whitsun-week, and the other on the last Thursday in September, which is also a great fair for onions. The market was for many years held in the open air, in the wide area fronting St. Martin's church, till the year 1834, when the present market-place was erected by act of parliament, at an expense of £20,000, on a more commodious site obtained by taking down the houses on one side of the area: it is a handsome building, fronted with Bath stone, and forms a conspicuous object on ascending the hill from Digbeth. The market for cattle and horses, and also that for hay and straw, are held in Smithfield, a spacious area. Birmingham is supplied with bread, at, perhaps, a cheaper rate than any other town in England. From the great scarcity of wheat in 1795, and the difficulty to the small capitalist of obtaining a foreign supply, bread became so dear as to induce a number of gentlemen to form a flour and bread company, which soon became very flourishing. Their example was followed by the millers, who became bakers also, and the competition was so great that the ordinary bakers could not sell at the same price as the mills; which have continued since that time to possess nearly the whole of the trade, the bakers existing principally by making fancy bread. It is customary, also, for many of the inhabitants to buy the flour, to make it up at their own homes, and have it baked by hire.

The town was formerly governed by a high and a deputy constable, but has been incorporated by CHARTER under the 5th and 6th of William IV., cap. 76. The borough comprises the parishes of Birmingham and Edgbaston, and the hamlets of Deritend with Bordesley, and Duddeston *cum* Nechels; and is divided into thirteen wards, *viz.,* Lady-wood, containing 8787 inhabitants; All Saints, 13,719; Hampton, 11,037; St. George's, 19,648; St. Mary's, 14,685; St. Paul's, 8973; Market-hall, 13,014; St. Peter's,

Corporation Seal.

16,773; St. Martin's, 13,325; St. Thomas's, 18,254; Edgbaston, 6609, Deritend and Bordesley, 18,019; and Duddeston *cum* Nechels, 20,079. Each ward returns three members to the town-council, with the exception of Duddeston *cum* Nechels, Deritend and Bordesley, and St. Peter's, each of which sends six councillors. Thus, the total number of councillors is forty-eight; and there are sixteen aldermen, out of whom, or the councillors, a mayor is chosen. The manorial officers consist of a high bailiff (who is also clerk of the market), a low bailiff, two constables for Birmingham, a constable for Deritend, a headborough, two ale-conners, two flesh-conners, two affeerers, and two leather-sealers; who are chosen annually at the court leet of the lord of the manor, at Michaelmas. By the act of the 2nd of William IV., cap. 45, Birmingham was constituted a parliamentary borough, with the privilege of sending two members; the mayor is the returning officer. The powers of the county debt-court of Birmingham, established in 1847, extend over the registration-districts of Aston and Birmingham, and part of those of King's Norton, Meriden, and West Bromwich. The court of bankruptcy, established in 1842, and held daily in Waterloo-street, embraces several counties. The public office, in Moor-street, is a commodious building with a handsome stone front, and comprises a well-arranged court-room, in which the magistrates hold their sittings, with apartments for the street commissioners and other officers for the internal regulation of the town: behind is a prison for the confinement of offenders previously to their committal to the county gaol at Warwick. A new borough gaol was commenced in 1846. The superintendence of the police is entrusted to the council; the paving and lighting of the streets, and the general improvement of the town, are under the direction of 100 commissioners, and the management of the poor is vested in overseers and guardians. Large baths for the working classes were established in 1846; and in the same year an act was passed for a public cemetery.

Prior to the year 1715, Birmingham comprised only one parish, and for all civil purposes it is still so considered; but in its ECCLESIASTICAL arrangements it at present comprises the five parishes of St. Martin, St. Philip, St. George, St. Thomas, and All Saints. The living of St. MARTIN's is a rectory, valued in the king's books at £19. 3. 6½., and in the gift of Trustees; net income, £1048. The parochial church is an ancient structure in the decorated English style, with a square tower having pinnacles at the angles, and surmounted by a lofty and finely-proportioned spire, with the exception of which the whole building, originally of stone, was cased with red brick in 1690; the interior contains several monumental effigies, of some of which the details are finely executed. *St. Mary's* church, in the parish of St. Martin, erected by subscription in 1774, on a site given by Miss Weaman, is an octagonal brick building with a small steeple of stone: the living is a perpetual curacy, in the gift of Trustees, with a net income of £350. *St. Paul's* church, in the same parish, built by subscription in 1779, on a site given by C. Colmore, Esq., is a handsome edifice in the Grecian style, with a steeple, which was added to it in 1820, and is much admired for the beauty and lightness of its character; the interior is elegantly arranged, and the altar-piece ornamented with a painting, in glass, of the Conversion of St. Paul. The living is a perpetual curacy; net income, £170; patron, E. Latimer, Esq. *St. Bartholomew's*, built in the year 1749, is a plain brick edifice with a cupola, and has been recently enlarged; the interior is a good specimen of the Tuscan order, and the altar-piece is richly carved. The living of ST. PHILIP's is a rectory not in charge; patron, the Bishop of Worcester. The church, erected in 1725, unfortunately of a perishable kind of stone, is a handsome building combining the Corinthian and Doric orders, with a tower supporting a dome surmounted by a cupola; the churchyard, which is very spacious, is surrounded with elegant buildings of modern date. *Christ-church*, in the parish of St. Philip, erected by subscription at a cost of about £26,000, and usually called the "Free church," was consecrated July 6, 1813, and is a neat structure of stone, with a portico of the Tuscan order and a spire: the living is a perpetual curacy, with a net income of £200; patron, the Bishop. *St. Peter's*, Dale-end, also in the parish of St. Philip, erected by grant of the Parliamentary Commissioners, at a cost, including the site, of about £19,000, and consecrated Aug. 10th, 1827, is a building of stone, with a handsome portico of the Doric order, and a small lantern tower surmounted by a dome. It was partially destroyed by fire in 1830, but in 1837 was re-opened for divine service, having been restored by subscription, at the cost of nearly £5000. The building will accommodate 2170 persons, and is much admired for its chaste simplicity, beautifully decorated roof, noble organ, and handsome stained-glass window at the east end, representing the Ascension. The living is in the gift of the Rector of St. Philip's. The living of ST. GEORGE's is a rectory not in charge, in the patronage of Trustees; net income, £550. The church, erected in 1822, by grant of the commissioners and subscription of the inhabitants, at an expense of £12,735, is a fine specimen of the early and decorated English styles, with a square embattled tower. The living of ST. THOMAS' is a rectory not in charge, in the patronage of Trustees; net income, £150. The church, erected in 1829, by subscription, aided by the commissioners, is a chaste and elegant structure of the Ionic order, with a tower and cupola surmounted by a double cross, and having the tower connected, in the lower stages, with the sides of the building by elegant Ionic quadrants; the interior is neatly arranged, with galleries supported on plain Doric columns. The expense of its erection was £14,222. The living of ALL SAINTS' is a rectory not in charge, in the patronage of Trustees: the church, built in 1833, at a cost of £3817, by subscription, aided by the commissioners, is a neat brick edifice of later English architecture, with facings of stone.

Bishop Ryder's church, built in commemoration of the late prelate of that name, was consecrated Dec. 18th, 1838; it contains 1574 sittings, of which 813 are free, and the expense of erection was £4300. The living is in the gift of Trustees. The want of adequate accommodation for the increasing population, lately induced an appeal to the wealthier inhabitants for the erection of ten additional churches, for which purpose a meeting was held in the town-hall, at which the Bishop of Worcester presided, when it was resolved to open a subscription, and within three months the sum of £20,000 was subscribed. Five of the churches have been consecrated: the first completed was that of St. Matthew,

261

Duddeston, in the parish of Aston. *St. Mark's* church, the second, cost £4405, including an endowment of £1000, and was consecrated July 29th, 1841; it is a neat building with lancet windows, contains 1000 sittings, and has schoolrooms in connexion with it, erected at an expense of £1250. The living is in the gift of Trustees. *St. Luke's* church, which cost about £3700, was consecrated Sept. 28th, 1842, and is situated on the Bristol-road; it is in the Norman style, has 1100 sittings, and some schools were built in connexion with it in 1843, at a cost of £1140. The interior is well fitted up, partly by means of special gifts made by several gentlemen; there are a handsome organ, a pulpit and desk of oak, a painted window, and other fittings up of appropriate design. The living is in the gift of Trustees. *St. Stephen's* church, in the parish of St. George, situated in Newtown-row, cost £3200, and was consecrated July 24th, 1844: the living is in the gift of the Crown and Bishop alternately. The fifth church is that of St. Andrew, Bordesley, consecrated Sept. 30th, 1846. A church district called *St. Jude's* was formed out of the parishes of St. Martin and St. Philip, and a benefice endowed, in 1846, by the Ecclesiastical Commissioners, under the act 6 and 7 Victoria, cap. 37: the incumbent is appointed by the Crown and the Bishop alternately; and at present, divine service is performed in the national school, Pinfold-street. In the spring of the year 1847, the foundation-stone was laid of a new church at the Church of England cemetery, Birmingham. Other churches are described in the articles on Edgbaston, Deritend, Bordesley, Duddeston, and other places adjacent. There are places of worship for Baptists, the Society of Friends, Independents, Primitive and Wesleyan Methodists, Swedenborgians, and Unitarians; a Scottish church, and two Roman Catholic chapels. Of these, Zion chapel, the Baptist and the Carr's Lane meeting-houses, Ebenezer chapel, and one or two of the Methodist meeting-houses, are spacious and handsome structures.

The QUEEN's COLLEGE, established in 1828 by the indefatigable exertions of William Sands Cox, Esq., F.R.S., and incorporated by royal charter in 1843, and again in 1847, already takes a high rank among similar foundations in this country. It is, pre-eminently, a college of medicine and surgery, but combines a thorough course of classical

College Seal.

education. The institution is under the direction and management of a council, and professors in surgery and medicine; and, in the classical department, of distinguished teachers in the various branches of learning, and the arts and sciences. Clinical lectures are delivered in the theatre every week; other lectures are given on regulated days, and examinations take place weekly: the lectures qualify for examinations for the medical diplomas of the University of London, the Royal College of Surgeons, and the Society of Apothecaries; and the council grant certificates also for the degrees of B.A., M.A., B.C.L., and D.C.L., to be conferred by the University of London upon the students. The interest of £1000 is applied to the purchase of two prizes, called the Warneford Gold Medals, either in equal or unequal amount; the compositions for them to be of a religious as well as scientific nature. The Jephson prize, of twenty guineas, is awarded to the student who passes the best public examination in all the branches of medicine and surgery; and besides various other prizes, and medals in gold and silver, are certificates of honour, to induce emulation in proficiency and good conduct. Four resident scholarships, also, have been founded by the Rev. Dr. Warneford, of £10 each, to be held for two years, and are conferred upon students who have resided in the college at least twelve months, and have distinguished themselves for diligence, and for regular attendance on divine worship, and the religious instruction of the warden. Dr. Warneford's gifts altogether amount to £5000. Connected with the college are a museum of human and comparative anatomy, containing upwards of 2000 preparations; and an extensive museum illustrative of zoology, geology, and other departments of natural history. The library contains upwards of 2500 volumes, and receives the quarterly, monthly, and weekly periodicals of medicine, surgery, and general science. The foundation stone of a new building for the institution was laid on the 18th August, 1843 : St. James's chapel, attached to the college, was consecrated in November, 1844.

The FREE GRAMMAR SCHOOL, in New-street, was founded in 1552, by Edward VI., who endowed it by charter with the revenues of the dissolved guild of the Holy Cross, which occupied the site of the present buildings; and vested the management in twenty inhabitants of the manor. The annual value of the property was then £21; but the whole of the estates being in Birmingham, the increase of houses has led to a vast increase in the income, which is now about £7000 per annum, and in a few years will be doubled. The buildings having become dilapidated, and the enhanced resources demanding enlarged usefulness, an act was passed in 1831 authorising the governors to take the school down and erect new premises, and, after fully providing for the greater efficiency of classical learning, to establish an additional school " for modern languages and the arts and sciences," and elementary schools for the poorer children of the town of both sexes. This act was amended by another, obtained in 1837, when more extensive powers were given; and an edifice has been completed, which, for magnificence and extent, is almost unequalled, and may fitly be named a college. It is a beautiful structure in the later English style, erected under the superintendence of Mr. Barry, and presents one of the finest specimens of modern collegiate architecture in the kingdom. The extremities, from north to south, consist of the houses of the head and second masters; the intermediate space is occupied with the schoolrooms, library, corridors, &c. The entrance, from New-street, leading into a corridor, has the library on the left hand, in which has been erected a chimney-piece, an interesting relic of the former school, of marble, finely sculptured, and surmounted by an exquisite bust of Edward VI.: the corresponding room, on the right, is appropriated to lectures. A noble stone staircase, under a lofty pointed arch, leads into a corridor of great beauty, with stained windows, and forming a communication between the two schoolrooms. The grammar

262

school on the south is a spacious apartment of striking appearance, eighty-six feet in length, and of proportionate width and height; the wainscot fittings are of massive oak, and the lofty roof, of stained wood, much conduces to its effect. The room for the commercial school, on the north, is of similar length and height, but narrower, and is embellished with the arms of Edward VI. and William IV., carved in stone. The establishment consists of a head master, whose salary is about £1000 per annum, independent of the privilege of taking eighteen boarders; a second master with a salary of £400, and the power of taking twelve boarders; three classical assistants, a mathematical master, a chief and two assistant masters of English literature, and masters in modern languages, drawing, writing, &c. There are ten exhibitions of £50 per annum, tenable for seven years at either University, and for which the sons of inhabitants of the town and manor have a preference; the other benefits of the school are open to boys of Birmingham and the vicinity, and to the boarders of the head and second masters. The number of boys exceeds 450. The governors have erected five elementary schools, for the instruction of the poorer classes, in different parts of the town, where about 750 children are educated, under the superintendence of the head master, the Rev. J. Prince Lee.

The *Blue-coat school* was founded in 1722, upon land belonging to the rectory of St. Philip's, and conveyed, by the bishop and the trustees for erecting that church, for the purpose of maintaining children of poor members of the Church of England, and instructing them in her principles : by the accumulation of benefactions it is now possessed of property to the amount of £1000 per annum. The buildings, which were enlarged in 1794, and are well arranged, have an extensive stone front in St. Philip's churchyard. The *Asylum* for deaf and dumb children was founded in 1812, and a commodious building in the antique style was erected on a site of ground in Calthorpe-street, Edgbaston, granted on liberal terms by Lord Calthorpe. There are also numerous national, Lancasterian, infants', and other schools, supported by subscription. The *Magdalen Asylum*, of which the bishop of the diocese is patron, is a noble institution; the chapel attached to it was opened April 28th, 1839, having cost about £1400, raised by subscription. The *General Hospital*, first established in 1779, has since been much enlarged, and the buildings, consisting of a centre and two wings, handsomely erected of brick, now comprise 19 wards, capable of admitting 200 patients. The foundation stone of the *Queen's Hospital*, Edgbaston, was laid on the 18th of June, 1840 : this institution is in union with Queen's College; the building occupies an elevated site, and consists of a centre and two wings called respectively the Victoria and Adelaide wards, the whole containing 150 beds. The *Dispensary*, in Union-street, was established by subscription in 1794, and affords medical relief to about 4000 patients annually; the building consists of a centre and two wings of stone, with four lofty pilasters supporting a triangular pediment, in the tympanum of which is a basso-relievo of the "Good Samaritan." The Self-supporting Dispensary, on the plan of Mr. Smith, of Southam, is maintained by small annual subscriptions of the poor, aided by those of honorary members. The Infirmary for the cure of Bodily Deformity, established under the patronage of the Earl of Dartmouth in 1817, and the Infirmary for Diseases of the Eye and Ear, established by Mr. Hodgson, surgeon, in 1823, are liberally supported. Another important institution is the Asylum for Infant Poor, forming an excellent school of industry, in which 300 children are maintained, clothed, and employed in platting straw and heading pins, and other kinds of work suited to their age. The Licensed Victuallers' Asylum, commenced in the spring of 1847, is designed in the Elizabethan style, to accommodate ten families, and is situated in the Bristol road. There are several charitable endowments, which lapse of time has greatly enhanced in value, and of which the chief is Lench's trust, bequeathed in the reign of Henry VIII., by the trustees of which many almshouses for aged females have been erected.

About a mile from the town is a chalybeate spring, which, though known to possess highly medicinal properties, is not much noticed. Three miles to the west, and within a few hundred yards of the Ikeneld-street, are the remains of a large quadrangular encampment surrounded by a triple fosse, which, from the extent of the area (more than thirty acres), is supposed to be of Danish origin : pieces of armour, broken swords, and battle-axes, have been ploughed up in the vicinity. Some inconsiderable vestiges of an ancient priory are still visible in the cellars of some houses in the square which now occupy its site ; and great numbers of human bones, and skulls with teeth having the enamel perfect, have been found in the immediate neighbourhood, parts of which still bear the names of the Upper and Lower Priory. At the western extremity of the town was an hospital dedicated to St. Thomas the Apostle, the revenue of which, in the 26th of Henry VIII., was £8. 5. 3.

BIRSTAL, a chapelry, in the parish of BELGRAVE, union of BARROW-UPON-SOAR, hundred of WEST GOSCOTE, N. division of the county of LEICESTER, 3 miles (N. by E.) from Leicester ; containing 438 inhabitants. This chapelry is bounded on the east by the river Soar, and comprises 1128 acres of arable and pasture land, of which the soil is generally light, and the substrata are sand, marl, and blue clay. The inhabitants are chiefly employed in the manufacture of hosiery, connected with the trade of Leicester. At the time when the inclosure of waste lands, 165 acres were allotted to the impropriate rectory in lieu of tithes, from which, with the exception of about 100 acres, the whole of the chapelry is exempt. The chapel, dedicated to St. James, was in 1823 severely damaged by lightning, which injured the steeple and part of the nave ; and by consent of the ordinary and the archdeacon the steeple was not restored, on condition of enlarging the north side of the chapel, which was done, and the whole of the nave rebuilt, at an expense of £600.

BIRSTAL (ST. PETER), a parish, partly in the union of BRADFORD, and partly in that of DEWSBURY, wapentake of MORLEY, W. riding of YORK, 7 miles (S. W.) from Leeds, on the road to Huddersfield ; containing 29,723 inhabitants. This parish comprises by computation about 13,000 acres, and includes the chapelries of Cleckheaton, Drighlington, Liversedge, and Tong, and the townships of Gomersal, Heckmondwike, Hunsworth, and Wyke ; the soil is various, but generally fertile, and the lands in the agricultural districts are in a good state of cultivation, producing fine crops of grain.

The surface is beautifully diversified with hills and valleys, watered by numerous rivulets, and the scenery is in many parts picturesque ; the substratum abounds with excellent coal and freestone, and at Hunsworth with iron-ore. The village of Birstal is situated in the township of Gomersal, at the base and on the acclivity of an eminence commanding a fine view of the adjacent district. The inhabitants are chiefly employed in the woollen and worsted manufactures, which are carried on extensively in the various townships, and in the making of cards for machinery ; the chief articles are woollen-cloths, blankets, and worsted stuffs. A savings' bank has been for some years in active operation. The LIVING is a discharged vicarage, valued in the king's books at £23. 19. 2.; net income, £289, with a good house ; patron, the Bishop of Ripon ; impropriators, the Master and Fellows of Trinity College, Cambridge. The church is a handsome structure in the later English style, with a lofty square embattled tower, and contains numerous monuments. There are ten other churches and incumbencies, which are described under their respective townships ; and also places of worship for Wesleyans, Independents, Moravians, and Methodists of the New Connexion. A free school, now merged in a national school, was endowed by the Rev. William Armitstead, in 1556, with a rent-charge of £5, for which, with a bequest of £100 from Mrs. Murgatroyd, the master instructs several children gratuitously. The school is a spacious building, erected in 1819, at an expense of £1200, principally defrayed by William Charlesworth, Esq., of Brier Hall, a native. Dr. Priestley, equally distinguished for his discoveries in chemistry and his controversial writings, was born at Fieldhead, in the parish, in 1733.

BIRSTWITH, a township, in the parish of HAMPSTHWAITE, Lower division of the wapentake of CLARO, W. riding of YORK, 5 miles (N. W. by W.) from Harrogate ; containing 676 inhabitants.

BIRTHORPE, a chapelry, in the parish of SEMPERINGHAM, union of BOURNE, wapentake of AVELAND, parts of KESTEVEN, county of LINCOLN, 2½ miles (E.) from Folkingham ; containing 52 inhabitants. Allotments of land were assigned in lieu of tithes in 1768.

BIRTLE, with BAMFORD, a township, in the parish of MIDDLETON, union of BURY, hundred of SALFORD, S. division of the county of LANCASTER, 2½ miles (E. N. E.) from Bury ; containing 1753 inhabitants. The name was formerly written Birkle and Berkle, and denotes a ley or field of birch. The township extends over 1480 acres, whereof 100 are arable, 1000 pasture, 135 woodland, 40 water, and the remainder moor. The surface is hilly, and diversified with glens : the soil of the higher part is poor ; but in the lower grounds, near the river Roche (which separates the township from Heap, for a mile and a half), it is richer land. The population is chiefly employed in the cotton and woollen mills in the neighbourhood ; several collieries are in operation, and quarries of good stone are wrought. Birtle is westward of Bamford, and is the larger hamlet of the two; both lie near the road from Bury to Rochdale. In the township are also the small village of Kenyon Fold ; a place called Hagg Lee ; and Nat Bank, a romantic spot where the Roche sweeps along a deep narrow vale, lined by meadows and wood. A church was built in 1846, at a cost of £1100 ; it is a neat structure with a campanile tower : the living is a perpetual curacy, in the patronage of the Rector of Middleton, who has given the tithes of the township, £33 per annum, to the incumbent. The Wesleyans and Primitive Methodists have places of worship ; and there is a Sunday school, established in 1833. An eminence denominated Castle Hill was probably the place where a small watch-tower stood in the ages of feudalism.

BIRTLES, a township, in the parish of PRESTBURY, union and hundred of MACCLESFIELD, N. division of the county of CHESTER, 3 miles (N. W.) from Macclesfield ; containing 60 inhabitants. The township comprises 566 acres, of a black, light, soil : its general surface is undulated, rising in some parts into eminences richly clothed with wood. Birtles Hall and demesne belonged for many generations to the Birtles family. There are various tumuli in the neighbourhood ; and fragments of urns have been discovered.

BIRTLEY, a township, in the parish and union of CHESTER-LE-STREET, Middle division of CHESTER ward, N. division of the county of DURHAM, 3 miles (N.) from Chester-le-Street ; containing 1759 inhabitants. In Bishop Hatfield's time this place belonged to a family of its own name, and subsequently formed part of the forfeitures of the Earl of Westmorland, on the attainder of that nobleman. The township comprises 1344 acres, of which two-thirds are arable land ; the surface is undulated, the soil chiefly clay, and the views, which are very extensive, embrace Lumley and Lambton Castles, and Ravensworth vale. Coal is abundant throughout the township ; and freestone is quarried for building purposes, and for grindstones. Salt-works were in operation here at a very early period : Sir William Lambton, in his petition to parliament, particularly enumerates, among other losses inflicted by the Scottish army, the total destruction of his "salt-works" at Birtley. In the latter part of the last century a strong brine-spring was discovered, which now produces about 1200 tons of salt per annum : the brine is conveyed from the spot whence it issues, to the bottom of a coal-pit, from which it is raised in pumps by the colliery steam-engine. Large iron-works were established in 1829, in which pig and bar iron, castings and engines are made, employing nearly 200 hands. There are several railways for conveying the coal ; at Ouston colliery is a railway passing to the Tyne, distant six miles : the road from Durham to Newcastle, also, intersects the township. A full church service is performed in a licensed chapel every alternate Sunday. There is a place of worship for Wesleyans ; also a Roman Catholic chapel.

BIRTLEY, a parochial chapelry, in the union of BELLINGHAM, N. E. division of TINDALE ward, S. division of NORTHUMBERLAND, 5 miles (S. E. by S.) from Bellingham ; containing, with the township of Broomhope with Buteland, 472 inhabitants. It is situated on the east of the North Tyne : the land in the northern part is mountainous and sterile, but near the bank of the river it is of better quality. Coal and limestone are found in the vicinity. The place was separated from the parish of Chollerton, and formed into a chapelry, in 1765. The living is a perpetual curacy ; net income, £84 ; patron, the Duke of Northumberland. The chapel is a small ancient edifice. The great tithes of the High and Low divisions of Birtley have been commuted for £70, and the vicarial tithes for £129.

264

BIRTS-MORTON (St. Peter and St. Paul), a parish, in the union of UPTON-UPON-SEVERN, Lower division of the hundred of PERSHORE, Upton and W. divisions of the county of WORCESTER, 5½ miles (E. S. E.) from Ledbury ; containing 313 inhabitants. It comprises 1198a. 2r. 29p., of which 46 acres are common or waste ; the surface is varied, and the scenery richly diversified. The manor-house is an ancient edifice, surrounded by a moat. The living is a rectory, valued in the king's books at £7. 8. 1½. ; patron and incumbent, the Rev. S. Thackwell : the tithes have been commuted for £320. 10. 6., and there are 27 acres of glebe. The church is an ancient cruciform edifice, with a window of stained glass. A school was endowed with six acres of land, now let for £14 per annum, by the Rev. Samuel Juice in 1703.

BISBROOKE, or PISBROOKE (St. John the Baptist), a parish, in the union of UPPINGHAM, hundred of WRANDIKE, county of RUTLAND, 1¾ mile (E.) from Uppingham ; containing 211 inhabitants. It comprises about 2000 acres of land, of which the soil is invariably red, light, and very fertile, and the situation rather hilly ; a considerable quantity of vegetables and fruit of excellent quality is grown. The manor is one of the most ancient possessions of the Duke of Rutland. The living is a discharged vicarage, valued in the king's books at £6. 0. 4. ; net income, £252 ; patron and impropriator, the Duke of Rutland. His Grace holds an allotment of land in lieu of the rectorial tithes ; and there are about 100 acres of glebe, chiefly at Bisbrooke, but partly at Uppingham.

BISCATHORPE (St. Helen), a parish, in the union of LOUTH, E. division of the wapentake of WRAGGOE, parts of LINDSEY, county of LINCOLN, 8 miles (N. E. by E.) from Wragby ; containing 63 inhabitants. The living is a discharged rectory, valued in the king's books at £5. 11. 4., and in the patronage of the Crown ; present net income, £180.

BISCOTT, BEDFORDSHIRE.—See LIMBURY.

BISHAM (All Saints), a parish, in the union of COOKHAM, hundred of BEYNHURST, county of BERKS, 4½ miles (N. W.) from Maidenhead ; containing 659 inhabitants. The parish comprises 2341a. 3r. 35p., of which 1662 acres are arable, 231 meadow and pasture, and 385 woodland and coppice ; the soil is gravelly, with a small portion of chalk, and the surface in general hilly. On the north flows the river Thames, the banks of which are adorned with interesting scenery and many pleasing seats. The rolling of copper into sheets, and the making of copper-bolts for the navy, and of pans and other vessels in copper, are carried on to a considerable extent. Temple mills, esteemed among the most complete and powerful of the kind in the kingdom, received their name from having been in the possession of the Knights Templars, who established a preceptory here on receiving a grant of the manor from Robert de Ferrariis, in the reign of Stephen. This institution, on the dissolution of the society, was succeeded by an Augustine priory, founded in 1338 by William de Montacute, Earl of Salisbury, and the revenue of which, in the 26th of Henry VIII., amounted to £327. 4. 6. It was surrendered in 1536, was re-founded by the king for a mitred abbot and thirteen Benedictine monks, and was finally dissolved on the 10th of June, 1538. The abbey was frequently visited by Henry VIII., and also by Elizabeth, who resided here some time, a large state apartment being still called the Queen's council-chamber: a very small portion only of the conventual building can be traced in the mansion which now occupies its site. The living is a discharged vicarage, valued in the king's books at £7. 13. 1.; net income, £156; patron and impropriator, George Henry Vansittart, Esq. The church contains some costly monuments of the Hoby family, who resided in the abbey from the time of Elizabeth till about the year 1780: one of them, in beautiful preservation, was brought in the sixteenth century from Paris, where Sir Thomas Hoby died ambassador to that court.

BISHAMPTON (St. Peter), a parish, in the union of Pershore, Middle division of the hundred of Oswaldslow, Pershore and E. divisions of the county of Worcester, 4 miles (N. E. by N.) from Pershore; containing 410 inhabitants. The parish comprises 1828a. 1r. 1p., mostly arable land, the remainder pasture, and is situated near the Avon : stone is quarried for the repair of roads. The living is a discharged vicarage, valued in the king's books at £7. 9. 9½.; patron, the Bishop of Worcester; impropriator, the Earl of Harrowby. The glebe consists of 80 acres of land, given in lieu of tithes, and valued at £100 per annum; with a glebe-house in good repair. The church, which is partly in the pointed style, was erected in the sixteenth century, and has a noble square tower with six bells, and an organ presented by the vicar, for the period of his incumbency, in 1839. A school is partly supported by the Earl of Harrowby.

BISHOP-AUCKLAND.—See Auckland, Bishop. *And all places having a similar distinguishing prefix will be found under the proper name.*

BISHOP'S-BOURNE (St. Mary), a parish, in the union of Bridge, hundred of Kinghamford, lathe of St. Augustine, E. division of Kent, 4 miles (S. E. by S.) from Canterbury; containing 334 inhabitants. It comprises 2002 acres, of which 437 are in wood. The living is a rectory, valued in the king's books at £39. 19. 2.; net income, £1240; patron, the Archbishop of Canterbury. The tithes of the parish have been commuted for £500; and the glebe, which consists of 1a. 20p., with premises, is valued at £60 per annum. Richard Hooker, author of the *Ecclesiastical Polity*, was incumbent.

Corporation Seal.

BISHOP'S-CASTLE (St. John the Baptist), an incorporated market-town, and a parish, having separate jurisdiction, in the union of Clun, locally in the hundred of Purslow, S. division of Salop, 19 miles (N. W. by N.) from Ludlow, 20¼ (S. W. by S.) from Shrewsbury, and 157 (N. W. by W.) from London ;· containing 1781 inhabitants, of whom 1510 are within the borough. This place derives its name from a castle belonging to the bishops of Hereford, that stood here, but of which the site alone, now a bowling-green attached to the Castle inn, and some small portions of the inclosing walls, can be traced. A subterraneous passage is said to have led from this castle to another at some distance; the arched entrance to the passage is shown in the garden of an adjoining house ; but it is scarcely distinguishable from the heaps of stones found in various parts of the hill on which the castle stood.

The town is partly situated on the summit, but chiefly on the steep declivity, of a hill : the houses in general are meanly built of unhewn stone, with thatched roofs; though, in detached situations, there are several good edifices of modern erection. The market is on Friday, and is well supplied with grain, which is sold by sample : the market-house, built by the late Earl of Powis, is a handsome structure of stone, supported on piazzas; the area is used as a corn-market, and the upper part as a schoolroom. The fairs are on the Friday before the 13th of Feb., for cattle and sheep; on the Friday preceding the 25th of March, which is a very large fair for horned-cattle; on the first Friday after May-day, a pleasure and statute fair ; July 5th, formerly a great wool-fair; and Sept. 9th and Nov. 13th, for horned-cattle, sheep, and horses. The government, by charter granted in the 15th year of the reign of Elizabeth, and confirmed and extended by James I., is vested in a bailiff, recorder, and fifteen capital burgesses, assisted by a town-clerk, chamberlain, two serjeants-at-mace, and subordinate officers : the bailiff, late bailiff, and recorder, are justices of the peace. The elective franchise was conferred in the 26th of Elizabeth, from which time, until its disfranchisement in the 2nd of William IV., the borough returned two members to parliament. The corporation hold a court of session quarterly for the borough, on the next Wednesday after the general quarter-sessions for the county ; the bailiff, the late bailiff or justice, and the recorder, preside. The powers of the county debt-court of Bishop's-Castle, established in 1847, extend over the registration-district of Clun, the parish of Churchstoke, and the township of Aston. The town-hall is a plain brick edifice on pillars and arches, built by the subscription of the burgesses, in 1750, with a prison on the basement story for criminals, and above it one for debtors.

The township of Bishop's-Castle comprises 1717 acres, of which 96 are common or waste. The living is a vicarage, valued in the king's books at £9. 12. 1.; net income, £350; patron and impropriator, the Earl of Powis. The great tithes of the borough have been commuted for £125, and the vicarial for £230, with a glebe of 12 acres, and a house. The church is a fine old structure, partly in the Norman style, with a square embattled tower crowned with pinnacles : it was burnt in the parliamentary war, by Cromwell, and has been repaired without a due regard to the original architecture. There are places of worship for Independents and Primitive Methodists. The free school was founded in 1785, by Mrs. Mary Morris, in memory of her first husband, Mr. John Wright, of Wimbledon, in Surrey, merchant, a native of Bishop's-Castle, and was endowed with £1000 in the three per cents., since increased to £1598. Jeremy Stephens, author of various doctrinal works, and the learned coadjutor of Sir Henry Spelman in the compilation of the *English Councils*, was a native of the place.

BISHOP'S-DALE, a township, in the parish of Aysgarth, wapentake of Hang-West, N. riding of York, 12 miles (S. W. by W.) from Middleham ; containing *107 inhabitants. This place comprises 4805 acres of land, adjoining the mountainous part of the West riding; 915 acres are common or waste. The neighbourhood contains several waterfalls, and abounds with picturesque scenery: small quantities of lead-ore are found. The tithes have been commuted for £76. 15., payable to Trinity College, Cambridge.

BISHOP'S-FEE, a liberty, in the parish of ST. MARGARET, union and borough of LEICESTER, though locally in the hundred of GARTREE, S. division of the county of LEICESTER. The magistrates for the borough and county exercise concurrent jurisdiction throughout the liberty, the inhabitants of which pay church and poor rates to the parish of St. Margaret, but are assessed for the king's taxes with the hundred of Gartree, the petty-sessions for which are occasionally held here.

BISHOPSIDE, HIGH and LOW, a township, in the chapelry and union of PATELEY-BRIDGE, parish and liberty of RIPON, W. riding of YORK, 10¼ miles (W. S. W.) from Ripon; containing 1937 inhabitants. The township includes the market-town of Pateley-Bridge, and the hamlets of Fell-Beck, Raikes, Smelt-house, Wath, Whitehouses, and Wilsill; and comprises 5813 acres of land, on the northern acclivities of Nidderdale: about 4000 acres are high uncultivated moor, abounding in grouse and other game. The tithes have been commuted for £55, payable to the Dean and Chapter of Ripon. At Raikes is a school endowed under the will of Miss Alice Sheppard, in 1806, with £1000 navy five per cents., for clothing and educating twenty-two boys and four girls; and for a similar purpose Dr. William Craven left £800 of the same stock, in 1812. John Lupton, in 1720, bequeathed a house and 12 acres of land, latterly let for £36 a year, for four widows; and there are a few smaller charities.

BISHOPSTON, a chapelry, in the parish of OLD STRATFORD, Stratford division of the hundred of BARLICHWAY, S. division of the county of WARWICK, 2¾ miles (N. N. W.) from Stratford; containing 51 inhabitants. This place was originally called Bishopsdone, and owed the former part of its name to the bishops of Worcester, to whom Stratford belonged, and the latter to its situation at the foot of a hill. For many generations the hamlet was the property of a family who took their name from it. It was at length conveyed by a female heir to the family of Sir William Catesby, after which it had several possessors. The living is a perpetual curacy; net income, £25; patron, the Vicar of Stratford. A new chapel was consecrated in 1843; it is in the early English style, contains 192 sittings, and cost £1000.

BISHOPSTON (ST. JOHN THE BAPTIST), a parish, in the union of WILTON, hundred of DOWNTON, though locally in the hundred of CHALK, Salisbury and Amesbury, and S. divisions of WILTS, 3½ miles (S. by W.) from Wilton; containing 569 inhabitants, and comprising by estimation 4265 acres. The living consists of a vicarage and a sinecure rectory united, the former valued in the king's books at £12. 1. 3., and the latter at £19. 14. 2.; patron, the Earl of Pembroke. The tithes have been commuted for £960, and there are 30½ acres of glebe. The church is a handsome cruciform edifice, in the decorated English style of architecture; and in it are preserved two stone coffins, said to have contained the relics of two bishops, from which circum-
266

stance the parish is traditionally reported to have derived its name.

BISHOPSTON (ST. MARY), a parish, in the union of HIGHWORTH and SWINDON, hundred of RAMSBURY, Swindon and N. divisions of WILTS, 6½ miles (E.) from Swindon; containing 704 inhabitants. It comprises by computation 4000 acres, and is situated near the Wilts and Berks canal, and the Great Western railway. The living is a vicarage, valued in the king's books at £6. 6. 8., and in the gift of the Bishop of Salisbury: about 150 acres of land, valued at £200 per annum, were allotted at the time of the inclosure in lieu of tithes; and there is a vicarage-house. The Primitive Methodists have a place of worship; and a parochial school is supported by bequests, amounting to about £40 per annum.

BISHOPSTONE, a hamlet, in the parish of STONE, union and hundred of AYLESBURY, county of BUCKINGHAM; containing 274 inhabitants.

BISHOPSTONE (ST. LAWRENCE), a parish, in the union of WEOBLEY, hundred of GRIMSWORTH, county of HEREFORD, 7 miles (W. N. W.) from Hereford; containing 304 inhabitants. It comprises by measurement 672 acres, of which 307 are arable, 328 meadow, and 38 woodland; the surface is hilly, and on Bishopstone hill is a quarry of good freestone. The living is a discharged rectory, with the vicarage of Yazor annexed, valued in the king's books at £7. 7. 6.; net income, £429; patron, Sir R. Price, Bart.: the glebe comprises 60 acres. The church is an ancient structure in the early English style, containing some monuments to the Berrington family, and has been recently repaired and decorated.

BISHOPSTONE, MONMOUTH.—See BISHTON.

BISHOPSTONE, a tything, in the parish of MONTACUTE, union of YEOVIL, hundred of TINTINHULL, W. division of SOMERSET; containing 257 inhabitants.

BISHOPSTONE, a parish, in the union of NEWHAVEN, hundred of BISHOPSTONE, rape of PEVENSEY, E. division of SUSSEX, 1¼ mile (N. W. by N.) from Seaford; containing 288 inhabitants. The parish comprises 1810a. 10p., of which 1040 acres are arable, and 770 down and pasture land; it is bounded on the west by the river Ouse, and on the south by the English Channel, which within the last twenty years has made considerable encroachment on the land. The road from Newhaven to Seaford passes through. The living is a discharged vicarage, valued in the king's books at £8. 13. 4.; patron, the Bishop of Chichester; net income, £88. The church is an ancient structure in the early Norman style, with a tower. The Rev. James Hurdis, D.D., professor of poetry in the University of Oxford, and author of the *Village Curate* and other interesting poems, was born in the hamlet of Norton, in the parish, in 1763, and was buried in the church. On the Downs are several barrows.

BISHOPSTROW (ST. ADELME), a parish, in the union and hundred of WARMINSTER, Warminster and S. divisions of WILTS, 1½ mile (E. S. E.) from Warminster; containing 296 inhabitants. It is situated on the river Wily, and bounded on the north by the Downs; and comprises 1030 acres. The living is a rectory, valued in the king's books at £11. 10., and in the gift of Sir Dugdale Astley, Bart.: the tithes have been commuted for £225, and there are about 11 acres of glebe.

n the parish is an estate called the Berries, supposed to have been a Roman station, where in 1791 two earthen vessels were found, containing several thousand small brass coins of the Lower Empire; there is also a meadow called Pitmead, where, in 1786, a discovery was made of the remains of some extensive Roman villas, and of several tessellated pavements within them.

BISHOP'S-WOOD, a liberty, in the township and parish of BREWOOD, union of PENKRIDGE, E. division of the hundred of CUTTLESTONE, S. division of the county of STAFFORD, 2¼ miles (W. by N.) from Brewood. This place is an open common, in the vicinity of Kiddernore Green.

BISHOPTHORPE (ST. ANDREW), a parish, in the union of YORK, AINSTY wapentake, W. riding of YORK, 3 miles (S. by W.) from York; containing 404 inhabitants. This place was called originally St. Andrew's Thorpe, from the dedication of its church, which formerly belonged to the priory of St. Andrew's at York; and obtained its present appellation in the reign of Henry III., when Walter de Grey, Archbishop of York, purchased the manor, and erected a house here, which, since the destruction of Cawood Castle in the parliamentary war, has been the residence of his successors in the see. The palace is now a large and magnificent building, having been improved by several subsequent possessors, and especially by Archbishop Drummond, by whom it was greatly enlarged in 1766. Walter de Grey also built here a chapel, in the early English style, in which he founded a chantry for the souls of King John and himself, and of all faithful deceased; this is now the private chapel of the archbishop, and the most ancient part of the palace. The parish comprises by computation 760 acres, of which 464 are arable, and 164 pasture. The living is a discharged vicarage, valued in the king's books at £4; net income, £134; patron, the Archbishop: the vicarage-house was considerably enlarged in 1825. The church was rebuilt in 1768, by Archbishop Drummond, and ornamented by him with a handsome window, removed from Cawood Castle; and the edifice again requiring very extensive repairs, it was restored and embellished in 1842, by the present archbishop, at an expense of about £1500. The notorious Guy Fawkes is said to have been a native of this place, and it is certain that he was a schoolfellow of Thomas Morton, Bishop of Durham, at the free grammar school at York.

BISHOPTON (ST. PETER), a parish, in the union of SEDGEFIELD, S. W. division of STOCKTON ward, S. division of the county of DURHAM; containing, with the townships of Newbiggin and Little Stainton, 473 inhabitants, of whom 362 are in Bishopton township, 6 miles (W. by N.) from Stockton. The parish comprises 4016a. 1r. 10p., of which 2102 acres are in the township, and of these latter 1273 are arable, 790 pasture, 12 woodland, and 20 waste: the soil is various; gravel of good quality is obtained in abundance for the highways. The Clarence railway, and the Stockton and Darlington railway, run in a direction nearly parallel on each side of the village, which is pleasantly situated on an eminence, about a mile and a half from the former, and 4 miles from the latter. The living is a discharged vicarage, valued in the king's books at £4. 5. 10., and in the patronage of the Master of Sherburn Hospital: the tithes of the parish, belonging to the vicar, the master

of the hospital, and the lessee of the corn tithes, have been commuted for £639. 1.; and there is a glebe of 67 acres. The church was partly rebuilt in 1790. In a field at the eastern extremity of the village is a large mound, with vestiges of an intrenchment, which is supposed to have been part of the fortifications that guarded the mansion of the faithful Roger de Conyers, from whom William de St. Barbara, elect Bishop of Durham, received powerful assistance in his struggle against Comyn, the usurper of the see, about the middle of the twelfth century.

BISHOPTON, a township, in the parish and liberty of RIPON, W. riding of YORK, 2¼ miles (N. by W.) from Ripon; containing 108 inhabitants. It is situated on the north bank of the Skell, forming a western suburb of Ripon; and comprises 118 acres of land. The tithes have been commuted for £58. 18. 7. payable to the impropriators, and £20. 10. to the Dean and Chapter of Ripon.

BISHPORT, a tything, in the parish and union of BEDMINSTER, hundred of HARTCLIFFE with BEDMINSTER, E. division of SOMERSET; containing 270 inhabitants. This place was formerly called Bishopsworth, and had a chapel standing in the time of Edward VI. A district church, St. Peter's, was consecrated in April, 1843; it is a beautiful specimen of Norman architecture. The living is in the gift of the Vicar of Bedminster.

BISHTON, a hamlet, in the parish of TIDENHAM, hundred of WESTBURY, W. division of the county of GLOUCESTER; containing 425 inhabitants.

BISHTON (ST. CADWALLADER), a parish, in the union of NEWPORT, Christchurch division of the hundred of CALDICOT, county of MONMOUTH, 6 miles (S. E.) from Newport; containing 187 inhabitants. It comprises about 1200 acres; the surface, though level, is elevated, and commands a fine view of the Severn and the country on the opposite bank. The living is a perpetual curacy, in the patronage of the Archdeacon of Llandaff: the church is in the early English style of architecture. There are some remains of an ancient castle.

BISHTON, a township, in the parish of COLWICH, S. division of the hundred of PIREHILL, union, and N. division of the county, of STAFFORD, 1 mile (S. E.) from Colwich; containing 173 inhabitants. It is situated on the eastern side of the Trent, on the road from Colwich to Colton; and contains a handsome seat, called Bishton Hall.

BISLEY (ALL SAINTS), a parish, in the union of STROUD, hundred of BISLEY, E. division of the county of GLOUCESTER, 4 miles (E. N. E.) from Stroud, and 7 (S. E.) from Gloucester; containing 5339 inhabitants. The parish, according to survey in 1841, comprises 7912 acres, whereof 864 are common. The town or village, to which the privilege of a market was granted by James I., is situated partly on the acclivity of a hill, and partly in the vale beneath it, which is watered by a small stream; the streets are irregularly formed, and contain some houses of respectable appearance. In Lypiatt Park, amidst beautiful scenery, is situated the manor-house of Bisley and Stroud, noted as the place where Guy Fawkes and the other conspirators met and consulted, prior to carrying their evil designs into effect: the apartment which they used is still shown. The inhabitants of the parish are chiefly employed in the manufacture of broad-cloth, which is carried on to a considerable extent; silk is also manufactured, and stone is quarried for building and for pavements. The market has been discontinued; but fairs are held on May 4th and Nov. 12th, chiefly for sheep.

The LIVING is a vicarage, valued in the king's books at £19. 10. 5., and in the patronage of the Lord Chancellor: the great tithes, belonging to T. M. Goodlake, Esq., have been commuted for £1204, and those of the incumbent for £748. 15., with a glebe of 17 acres, and a vicarage-house. The church is a spacious and handsome structure, partly in the decorated and partly in the later English style, with a tower surmounted by a spire 130 feet high, which forms a conspicuous landmark: in the churchyard is an octagonal cross. At Chalford is a district church; and a chapel of ease has been built at Oakridge, containing 380 sittings. At Bussege is a beautiful little church, erected at a cost of £2000 by twenty students of different colleges of Oxford; it is in the decorated style, is dedicated to St. Michael and All Angels, and was consecrated in Oct. 1846. There are places of worship for Independents, Baptists, and Wesleyans. The free school is supported by a portion of the produce of lands left for the repair of the church, the payment of the clerk, and the salary of a schoolmaster; with it has been incorporated a Blue-coat school. The common is reported to have been given to the poor by Roger Mortimer, Earl of March, in the reign of Edward III.; it then comprised 1200 acres, but a considerable part of it has been inclosed. At Lilly-house, a hamlet south of the town, a vaulted chamber has been discovered, with several adjoining apartments, having tessellated pavements, and niches in the walls. Some other relics of antiquity, supposed to be Roman, were found at Custom-Scrubs, another hamlet, in 1802; and in Oct. 1841, near Lillygate, was discovered an extensive range of Roman chambers, whose communications with each other were distinctly marked, and of which a part exhibited the supports and bases of tessellated floors. Many fragments of glazed pottery, antique glass, implements, stags' bones, sacrificial knives, &c., were found, as were also 1223 coins of various emperors, some in a state of cohesion.—See CHALFORD.

BISLEY (ST. JOHN THE BAPTIST), a parish, in the union of CHERTSEY, First division of the hundred of GODLEY, W. division of SURREY, 4 miles (S. E.) from Bagshot; containing 321 inhabitants. It comprises by computation 700 acres: the soil is rather light, but yields good corn; the surface is moderately undulated. The lands belonged to the convent of Chertsey for several centuries, the whole being then included within the manor of Byfleet. The living is a rectory, valued in the king's books at £7. 16. 8.; net income, £188; patron, John Thornton, Esq.: 28 acres of land in this parish, and 9 in that of Purbright, belong to the rectory. The church, part of which is built with timber and brick, covered with plaster, is said to be six centuries old; near it is a chalybeate spring, called St. John the Baptist's well.

BISPHAM, a parish, in the union of the FYLDE, hundred of AMOUNDERNESS, N. division of the county of LANCASTER; comprising the townships of Bispham with Norbreck, and Layton with Warbreck; and containing 2339 inhabitants, of whom 371 are in Bispham

the county of SOUTHAMPTON, 3 miles (S.) from the town of RINGWOOD; containing, with the tything of Bistern with Crow, 562 inhabitants. This place is situated on the road to Christchurch, and on the river Avon, which abounds with excellent trout, grayling, and other fish. The old chapel formerly attached to the House here was taken down many years since, and a church has been erected at an expense of £1000, on a site given by J. Miles, Esq.: the living is a curacy, in the patronage of the vicar of Ringwood. There are several barrows, and some remains of a Roman encampment.

BITCHFIELD (ST. MARY MAGDALENE), a parish, in the union of GRANTHAM, wapentake of BELTISLOE, parts of KESTEVEN, county of LINCOLN, 3¼ miles (N. by W.) from Corby, and 8 (S. E. by S.) from Grantham; comprising about 1360 acres, and containing 160 inhabitants. The living is a discharged vicarage, valued in the king's books at £5. 11. 5½.; net income, £134; patron and appropriator, the Bishop of Lincoln; there are about 5 acres of glebe. The church was consecrated and endowed by Hugh de Wells, who presided over the diocese from the year 1209 to 1234. There are some remains of a Roman encampment.

BITCHFIELD, a township, in the parish of STAMFORDHAM, union of CASTLE ward, N. E. division of TINDALE ward, S. division of NORTHUMBERLAND, 13 miles (N. W.) from Newcastle-upon-Tyne; containing 36 inhabitants. The township comprises 717a. 9p. The tithes have been commuted for £18. 14. 4., of which £18. 4. 3. are payable to the vicar. The remains of an old castle formerly belonging to the Fenwicks are now used as a farmhouse.

BITTADON (ST. PETER), a parish, in the union of BARNSTAPLE, hundred of BRAUNTON, Braunton and N. divisions of DEVON, 6¼ miles (N. by W.) from Barnstaple; containing 78 inhabitants. It comprises about 1000 acres, and is situated on the road from Barnstaple to Ilfracombe; the soil is light, and the principal part of the land being high and exposed, it is much used for summer pasture. The living is a discharged rectory, valued in the king's books at £5. 2. 8½., and in the patronage of W. A. Yeo, Esq.: the tithes have been commuted for £73, and there are 23 acres of glebe. The church is very small, with a low turret.

BITTERING, LITTLE (ST. PETER), a parish, in the union of MITFORD and LAUNDITCH, hundred of LAUNDITCH, W. division of NORFOLK, 5 miles (N. W.) from East Dereham; containing 18 inhabitants. It comprises 398a. 2r., of which 289 acres are arable, 96 pasture, and 17 plantation and heath. The living is a discharged rectory, valued in the king's books at £2. 13. 6½., and in the patronage of the Dover family: the tithes have been commuted for £70, and there are nearly 45 acres of glebe. The church is in the early English style; the font is Norman.

BITTERLEY (ST. MARY), a parish, in the union of LUDLOW, partly in the hundred of MUNSLOW, but chiefly in the hundred of OVERS, S. division of SALOP, 4½ miles (E. N. E.) from Ludlow; containing, with the townships of Cleeton, Henley, Hill-upon-Cot, Middleton, and Snitton, 1098 inhabitants, of whom 204 are in Bitterley township. The parish comprises 6587a. 3r., of which 256 acres are common or waste, and is situated on the road from Ludlow to Birmingham: there are quarries of stone for rough building, and extensive coal-mines; and

269

ironstone is found. The living is a rectory, with the chapelry of Middleton, valued in the king's books at £18. 6. 3., and in the patronage of the Rev. C. Walcot: the tithes have been commuted for £740, and there are 57 acres of glebe, with a residence. The parochial church is an ancient edifice. There is a place of worship for dissenters. John Newborough, in 1712, gave £400, with which land was purchased now producing £36 per annum, towards the support of a free school.

BITTERN, an ecclesiastical district, in the parish of SOUTH STONEHAM, hundred of MANSBRIDGE, Southampton and S. divisions of the county of SOUTHAMPTON, 2 miles (N. E.) from Southampton; containing 881 inhabitants. This place is identified by most antiquaries with the Roman station Clausentum, and various relics of Roman times have been found on the spot. A church was erected in 1838, at an expense of £2000, raised by subscription, aided by a grant of £300 from the Incorporated Society; it is a handsome edifice in the later English style, situated on an eminence.

BITTERSCOTE, a liberty, in the township of FAZELEY, parish and union of TAMWORTH, S. division of the hundred of OFFLOW and of the county of STAFFORD, 1 mile (S. S. W.) from Tamworth; containing 44 inhabitants. This liberty comprises about 350 acres of land.

BITTESBY, a liberty, in the parish of CLAYBROOKE, union of LUTTERWORTH, hundred of GUTHLAXTON, S. division of the county of LEICESTER, 3 miles (W. by N.) from Lutterworth; containing 28 inhabitants.

BITTESWELL (ST. MARY), a parish, in the union of LUTTERWORTH, hundred of GUTHLAXTON, S. division of the county of LEICESTER, 1 mile (N. by W.) from Lutterworth; containing 495 inhabitants. This parish is situated on the road from Hinckley to Lutterworth, and near the Midland railway; it comprises by measurement 1729 acres, of which the soil is strong, the surface flat, and the land chiefly pasture. The living is a vicarage, valued in the king's books at £4. 3. 0½.; net income, £428, arising from 306 acres of land apportioned in lieu of tithes; patrons, alternately, the Haberdashers' Company, and the Governors of Christ's Hospital, London, to whom also the impropriation belongs. The church is a handsome structure, in the decorated English style. The Roman Watling-street passes along the verge of the parish. There is a mineral spring.

BITTON (ST. MARY), a parish, in the union of KEYNSHAM, Upper division of the hundred of LANGLEY and SWINEHEAD, W. division of the county of GLOUCESTER; containing, with the chapelries of Hanham and Oldland, and the district of Kingswood, 9338 inhabitants, of whom 2413 are in the hamlet of Bitton, 6¼ miles (E. S. E.) from Bristol. This parish is bounded on the south by the river Avon, and comprises by admeasurement 7602 acres; the surface is varied. The substratum abounds with coal, which is worked to a considerable extent; large quantities of iron-ore are found, and copper is rolled at Swineford: the manufacture of hats, pins, and paper, is also carried on. A railway runs through the hamlet for the conveyance of coal to the Avon; the Via Julia also passes through it. The living is a discharged vicarage, valued in the king's books at £18. 15.; patron, the Prebendary of Bitton in the Cathedral of Salisbury. The tithes of the hamlet of Bitton have been commuted for £310 and £265, payable respectively to the impropriator and the vicar : the glebe consists of 7 acres, with a residence. The church is a large and handsome edifice, partly Norman and partly in the later English style, with a finely ornamented tower. There are separate incumbencies at Hanham and Kingswood ; a chapel of ease at Oldland ; and places of worship for Independents, Moravians, and Wesleyans. At Field Grove is a mineral spring.

BIX-BRAND (St. James), a parish, in the union of Henley-upon-Thames, hundred of Binfield, county of Oxford, 4 miles (N. W. by N.) from Henley ; containing 427 inhabitants. This parish, with that of Bix-Gibwen St. Michael united, and now usually called Bix, comprises altogether about 3000 acres, of which 2000 are chiefly arable, 750 woodland, chiefly beech, and 250 waste land. The soil is principally chalk, with gravel and clay in some places ; the surface is hilly, and the valleys run into the Chiltern range of hills. The living is a rectory, valued in the king's books at £9. 15. ; net income, £487 ; patron, the Earl of Macclesfield : the glebe consists of about 50 acres, with a house. The church of Bix-Gibwen is in ruins.

BIXLEY (St. Wandegisilus), a parish, in the union and hundred of Henstead, E. division of Norfolk, 3 miles (S. E. by S.) from Norwich ; comprising 640 acres of arable and pasture, and containing 110 inhabitants. The road from Norwich to Bury passes through the parish. The living is a discharged rectory, with that of Earl-Framingham united, valued in the king's books at £5 ; net income, £608 ; patrons, the family of Brereton. The church is an ancient edifice, built by William de Dunwich, in 1272, and was formerly the resort of numerous pilgrims to the shrine of its tutelar saint.

BIXTON, or Bickerston (St. Andrew), a parish, in the incorporation and hundred of Forehoe, E. division of Norfolk, 5½ miles (N. by W.) from Wymondham. The living is a rectory, united, with the vicarage of Kimberly, to the rectory of Barnham-Broom, and valued in the king's books at £2. 6. 8. : the church is in ruins.

BLABY (All Saints), a parish, and the head of a union, in the hundred of Guthlaxton, S. division of the county of Leicester, 5 miles (S. W.) from Leicester ; containing, with the chapelry of Countessthorp, 1896 inhabitants. It is intersected by the Union canal, and comprises 1250 acres, exclusively of the chapelry, which consists of 1200 acres ; the soil is various, and the surface generally level. The worsted manufacture is carried on to a considerable extent. The living is a rectory, valued in the king's books at £15. 5., and in the patronage of the Crown; net income, £350. On the inclosure of waste in 1776, an allotment of 400 acres was assigned in lieu of tithes. The parish contains places of worship for Baptists and Wesleyans. The poor law union of Blaby comprises 22 parishes and places, and contains a population of 13,699.

BLACKAUTON (St. Michael), a parish, in the union of Kingsbridge, hundred of Coleridge, Stanborough and Coleridge, and S. divisions of Devon, 5 miles (W. by N.) from Dartmouth ; containing, with the chapelry of Street, 1449 inhabitants, of whom 420 are in the village of Blackauton. It comprises 5217

270

acres, of which 105 are common or waste ; the soil is in general good, the surface hilly. The living is a discharged vicarage, valued in the king's books at £15. 8. 9.; net income, £122; patron, Sir H. P. Seale, Bart. ; impropriator, A. Welland, Esq. : the glebe consists of 9 acres, with a residence. The church contains a Norman font, and a wooden screen richly carved. An additional church has been built at Street, containing 400 sittings, of which 200 are free, the Incorporated Society having granted £250 towards the expense : the Vicar is patron. There is a place of worship for a congregation of Wesleyans.

BLACKBOROUGH (All Saints), a parish, in the union of Tiverton, hundred of Hayridge, Cullompton and N. divisions of Devon, 4 miles (E. S. E.) from Cullompton ; containing 112 inhabitants. The living is a rectory, valued in the king's books at £4, and in the patronage of the Wyndham family : the tithes have been commuted for £80, and the glebe consists of 74 acres. The church having become dilapidated, a new one of elegant design was erected at the expense of the third earl of Egremont, of agate, of which an almost inexhaustible quarry has been discovered in the Black Down hills, a portion of which range is included within the limits of the parish. Whetstones for sharpening scythes ; and the Sun Dew (Drosera rotundifolia), a plant confined to particular localities ; are found in great abundance.

BLACKBROOK, or Blakebrook, a hamlet, in that part of the parish of Kidderminster which is called the Foreign, union of Kidderminster, Lower division of the hundred of Halfshire, Kidderminster and W. divisions of the county of Worcester, ½ a mile (W.) from Kidderminster. Several new houses have been erected in this agreeable part of the environs of Kidderminster.

BLACKBURN (St. Mary), a parish, and the head of a union, in the Lower division of the hundred of Blackburn, N. division of the county of Lancaster ; comprising the market-town and newly-enfranchised borough of Blackburn, the chapelries of Balderston, Billington-Langho, Over Darwen, Salesbury, Samlesbury, and Tockholes, and the townships of Clayton-le-Dale, Cuerdale, Lower Darwen, Dinkley, Eccleshill, Great and Little Harwood, Livesey, Mellor, Osbaldeston, Pleasington, Ramsgrave, Rishton, Walton-le-Dale, Wilpshire, and Witton; and containing 71,711 inhabitants, of whom 36,629 are in the town, 31 miles (S. E. by S.) from Lancaster, and 210 (N. N. W.) from London. This place takes its name from a small rivulet near the town, which, from the turbid state of the water, was anciently called Blakeburn, or "the yellow bourne." A castle is said to have been built here, probably by the Romans, which, after their departure from the island, was occupied successively by the Britons and the Saxons ; but there are no vestiges of it, nor can even its site be distinctly ascertained. Blackburn was formerly the capital of a district called Blackburnshire, which for many ages was a dreary and uncultivated waste. In the reign of Elizabeth, it was distinguished as a good market-town, and in the middle of the following century was celebrated for its supplies of corn, cattle, and provisions. The town is pleasantly situated at the distance of about half a mile from the river Derwent, in a valley sheltered by a ridge of hills, extending from the north-east to the north-west, and consists of several streets, irregularly formed, but containing some well-built and many respectable houses: it is only indifferently paved, is lighted with gas, and amply supplied with water under an act passed in 1845. There are assembly-rooms, a subscription library, a scientific institution, and a theatre, which was erected in 1818.

The manufacture of Blackburn checks, and subsequently that of Blackburn greys, a mixture of linen and cotton, which formerly flourished here to a considerable extent, have been superseded by the manufacture of calico, muslin, and cotton goods: nearly 50,000 pieces of the last are on an average made weekly, about 10,000 persons being employed; and the value of these goods, exclusively of dyeing and printing, is estimated at more than £2,000,000 sterling per annum. There are large factories for the spinning of cotton; and throughout the entire parish are printing, dyeing, bleaching, and other establishments connected with the manufacture. Some of the earliest and most important improvements in the spinning and manufacture of cotton originated with James Hargreave, a carpenter in this town, who was the inventor and patentee of the spinning-jenny, since so generally adopted. The introduction of machinery excited a powerful sensation among the workmen of the neighbourhood, and created such tumultuous proceedings on the part of the populace, who destroyed several of the factories in which it was used, that the inventor was driven from the town; while many individuals who had invested large capitals in the establishment of cotton-factories, were so intimidated, that they embraced the earliest opportunity of withdrawing their investments, and of removing to places where they might employ them with security. There are at present about 100,000 spindles in operation in the town and neighbourhood, which produce about 35,000lb. of yarn weekly.

The Leeds and Liverpool canal passes the town, and affords communication with the Mersey, the Dee, the Ouse, the Trent, the Humber, the Severn, and the Thames, forming a most extensive line of inland navigation. The Blackburn and Preston railway, running hence to the Farington station of the North-Union line, three miles south of Preston, was opened in June, 1846; and the distance by railway between the two towns has been since diminished, by avoiding the angle at Farington. The Blackburn, Darwen, and Bolton railway, 14½ miles in length, was opened in May 1847. The station here is on a large scale, the length of the building being 252 feet and its mean breadth about 40 feet: the platform is 330 feet long, and the four lines of rails in front of it are covered with an iron roof in one span: the station is lighted by a plate-glass Louvre light, 16 feet wide at the top of the roof, and extending along its whole length. There is a railway to Accrington, Burnley, &c.; also a line to Clitheroe, &c. The market-days are Wednesday and Saturday: the fairs are held on Easter-Monday (which continues during the whole week), May 12th and the two following days, and October 17th; a cattle-fair is also held every second Wednesday throughout the year. An act was passed in 1841, for improving the streets, and for the erection of a town-hall and market-places. A spacious covered market was erected in 1847, in King William-street; it is a reetangular building in the Italian style, 60 feet long and 36

wide, with an iron roof supported by two rows of iron pillars dividing the market into three parallel walks, with distinct entrances at both ends to each. Over the middle entrance of the front elevation rises a lofty campanile tower, containing a public clock; and excellent light and ventilation are afforded by a series of windows at each side, where are also entrances. The fish-market is held in Fleming's-square. One side of this square is occupied by a spacious cloth-hall, built for the exhibition and sale of Yorkshire woollen-cloths, a great quantity of which is brought hither; but it is now seldom used for that purpose, the stalls for the sale of these cloths being erected in the streets. Blackburn is within the jurisdiction of the magistrates acting for the hundred to which it gives name, and which is co-extensive with the ancient Blackburnshire; and two high constables are appointed, one for the upper, and one for the lower, division, for which latter, together with Whalley, a court of petty-session is held here: its local concerns are under the superintendence of commissioners. An act was passed in 1841, vesting in the overseers of the poor the town moor for sale or other disposal. The powers of the county debt-court of Blackburn, established in 1847, extend over the registration-district of Blackburn. By the 2nd of William IV., cap. 45, the place was constituted a borough, with the privilege of sending two members to parliament, to be elected by the £10 householders of the township, including about 4160 acres: the returning officer is appointed annually by the sheriff.

This extensive parish, which is fourteen miles in length, and ten in breadth, was formerly part of Whalley, on being separated from which it was, on account of its sterility, endowed with a fourth part of the tithes of that parish, in addition to its own. The LIVING is a vicarage, valued in the king's books at £8. 1. 8.; net income, £893; patron and appropriator, the Archbishop of Canterbury. The church, formerly the conventual church of the monastery of Whalley, was rebuilt in the reign of Edward III., and again in that of Henry VIII.; but in 1819 it was taken down, with the exception of the tower and the Dunken chapel, and a new building was completed in 1826, on the site of the old grammar school, at an expense of upwards of £30,000, raised by a rate. The Dunken chapel was used for the performance of parochial duties during the interval, but has been since taken down, so that the tower is the only part of the old church now remaining. The present spacious and elegant edifice is in the later English style, with a lofty square tower, highly enriched, and crowned with a pierced parapet and crocketed pinnacles; the roof of the nave was burned down in January, 1831. The district church of St. Paul remained unconsecrated from the time of its erection until a few years since, when it was united to the Establishment: the living is a perpetual curacy, in the patronage of the Vicar of Blackburn, with a net income of £150. The district churches of St. John and St. Peter are both neat modern edifices: the livings are perpetual curacies; net income of St. John's, £150, and of St. Peter's, £153. They are in the patronage of the Vicar, in whom is also vested the presentation of the perpetual curacies of St. Michael and Trinity, both formed in 1839, and of All Saints; net income of St. Michael's, £150, and of All Saints', £100. A chapel dedicated to St. Clement has been erected; and the Vicar likewise presents to the incumbencies of Balderstone, Bamber-Bridge, Billington-Langho, Lower and Over Darwen, Feniscowles, Great Harwood, Mellor, Mellor-Brook, Salesbury, Samlesbury, Tockholes, Walton, and Witton. In the town are places of worship for Baptists, the Society of Friends, Independents, Wesleyans, Primitive Methodists, and Warrenites, also a Scottish kirk and a Roman Catholic chapel; and in the rural parts of the parish are various other meeting-houses for different denominations.

The free grammar school was founded in the reign of Elizabeth, who placed it under the superintendence of fifty governors resident in the town, who are a corporate body, and appoint a master: it is endowed with land in the neighbourhood, producing £120 per annum; and there are 30 boys on the foundation. The Rev. Robert Bolton, an eminent divine, and one of the compilers of the Liturgy, was a native of the town, and received the rudiments of his education in this school. In 1764, Mr. John Leyland bequeathed £250 for the instruction of girls, which sum has been augmented by subsequent benefactions, and at present 90 girls are taught and clothed. Several national schools have been erected; a dispensary was established in the year 1823; and there are a ladies' society for the relief of poor women during child-birth at their own houses, a strangers' friend society, and several other charitable institutions. The union of Blackburn comprises the entire parish, with the exception of the townships of Cuerdale, Samlesbury, and Walton, which are in the union of Preston; together with four townships of the parish of Whalley: it contains a population of 75,091.

BLACK-BURTON.—See BURTON, BLACK.

BLACK-CARTS, forming with RYEHILL an extra-parochial liberty, in the union of HEXHAM, N. W. division of TINDALE ward, S. division of NORTHUMBERLAND, and containing 17 inhabitants. It comprises 447 acres of land.

BLACK-CHAPEL, a chapelry, in the parish of GREAT WALTHAM, union and hundred of CHELMSFORD, S. division of ESSEX, 9 miles (N. by W.) from Chelmsford. The living is a perpetual curacy, in the patronage of certain Trustees; net income, £20.

BLACKDEN, a township, in the parish of SANDBACH, union of CONGLETON, hundred of NORTHWICH, S. division of the county of CHESTER, 6½ miles (S. S. E.) from Knutsford; containing 266 inhabitants. The township comprises 581 acres; the prevailing soil is sand. The impropriate tithes have been commuted for £70, and the vicarial for £52. 18.

BLACKFORD, a chapelry, in the parish of WEDMORE, union of AXBRIDGE, hundred of BEMPSTONE, E. division of SOMERSET, 5¼ miles (S. by W.) from Axbridge. It comprises by measurement 1600 acres; stone of good quality for building is quarried. The living is a perpetual curacy, in the patronage of the Vicar of Wedmore, with a net income of £105 : the impropriate tithes have been commuted for £150, and the impropriate glebe comprises 20 acres. The chapel is a modern building, towards defraying the expense of which the Incorporated Society gave £200. The manor was given as part of the endowment of Bruton Hospital, by Hugh Saxey, Esq., the founder; and two boys are annually sent from this place to be educated at that institution. Here is a mineral spring.

272

BLACKFORD (ST. MICHAEL), a parish, in the union of WINCANTON, hundred of WHITLEY, though locally in the hundred of HORETHORNE, E. division of SOMERSET, 4½ miles (W. S. W.) from Wincanton; containing 178 inhabitants. It is situated in a fertile vale on the road from London to Exeter, and comprises by measurement 566 acres of profitable land; the scenery is generally pleasing. There are quarries of stone for building and other purposes. The living is a discharged rectory, valued in the king's books at £6. 11. 0½.; and in the patronage of the Trustees of the late J. H. Hunt, Esq.: the tithes have been commuted for £160, and there are nearly 25 acres of glebe, with a residence. The church is in the early English style, with a Norman arch over the entrance. The Wesleyans have a place of worship.

BLACKFORDBY, a chapelry, in the parishes of ASHBY-DE-LA-ZOUCH and SEAL, union of ASHBY, hundred of WEST GOSCOTE, N. division of the county of LEICESTER, 2¾ miles (W. N. W.) from Ashby; containing 478 inhabitants. It comprises 530 acres, principally pasture land. The Ashby canal crosses the Wolds south of this place. The chapel is dedicated to St. Margaret. There is a place of worship for Wesleyans; and a school is supported by subscription.

BLACKHEATH, a village, in the parishes of GREENWICH, LEWISHAM, and LEE, hundred of BLACK-HEATH, lathe of SUTTON-AT-HONE, W. division of KENT, 5 miles (S. E.) from London, on the road to Dovor. This place, which takes its name either from the colour of the soil, or from the bleakness of its situation, was, prior to the erection of the numerous villas with which it now abounds, the scene of many important political transactions. In 1011, the Danes, having landed at Greenwich, encamped on the heath, and, among other barbarities, put to death Alphege, Archbishop of Canterbury, who had refused to sanction their extortions, and who was afterwards canonized. In the reign of Richard II., the insurgents under Wat Tyler, amounting to 100,000 men, took up their station here, whence they marched to London. In 1400, Henry IV. held an interview at the place with the Emperor of Constantinople, who came to solicit aid against Bajazet, Emperor of the Turks; and in 1415, the lord mayor and aldermen of London, in their robes of state, attended by 400 of the principal citizens, clothed in scarlet, came hither in procession to meet Henry V., on his triumphant return after the battle of Agincourt. In 1451, Henry VI. met many of the followers of Jack Cade, who submitted to his authority, and on their knees implored and obtained his pardon; and here, the following year, that monarch assembled his forces to oppose Richard, Duke of York, who aspired to the throne. In 1497, the Cornish rebels, headed by Lord Audley, who had advanced into Kent, encamped near Eltham, and awaited the approach of Henry VII., on whose arrival a battle ensued, on the 22nd of July, in which the insurgents were defeated, and their leader, together with two of his associates, taken and executed. In 1519, Campejo, the pope's legate, was received here in great state by the Duke of Norfolk, with a numerous retinue of bishops, knights, and gentlemen, who conducted him to a magnificent tent of cloth of gold, whence, after having arrayed himself in his cardinal's robes, he proceeded to London; and at this place, in 1540, Henry VIII. appointed an interview with Ann of Cleves, previously to their marriage, which was celebrated with great pomp at Greenwich.

Blackheath is pleasantly situated on elevated ground, commanding diversified and extensive views of the surrounding country, which is richly cultivated, and abounds with fine scenery, in which Greenwich hospital and park, and the river Thames, are prominent objects. There are many elegant villas, among which the Paragon, a handsome range of building, is eminently conspicuous : on the west, and within the park, is the residence occupied by the late Princess Sophia of Gloucester. Wricklemarsh House, once the noblest ornament of the heath, erected early in the last century by Sir Gregory Page, was razed to the ground in 1787, by the different purchasers to whom it had been sold in lots by public auction ; its site, now called Blackheath Park, is occupied by handsome villas. There are two episcopal chapels on that part of the heath in the parish of Lewisham. Another at Kidbrooke, an extra-parochial district on the north side of the heath, was built by the late Dr. Greenlaw ; and on the declivity of the hill opposite Kentplace, is the church of the Holy Trinity, in the early English style, with two towers surmounted by spires at its east end. St. Peter's church, Blackheath Park, is an elegant structure of stone, of decorated and later English architecture, with a slender pinnacled tower, above which rises a beautiful spire ; it forms a conspicuous and interesting object in the surrounding landscape, and was erected in 1829 by John Cator, Esq., at an expense of £15,000.

The Blackheath proprietary school, in connexion with King's College, London, is a neat building, situated on the rise of the hill near Blackheath Park. In Lee Park, also, is a handsome building after the model of the Propylæum at Athens, erected as a proprietary school for classical and general literature. Morden College, a noble institution for the support of decayed merchants, was founded in 1695, by Sir John Morden, Bart., an opulent Turkey merchant, who endowed it with the manor of Old Court : the establishment consists of 40 brethren (each of whom receives £60 per annum, with attendance), a chaplain, and a treasurer ; and the management is vested in seven trustees, who must be either Turkey merchants, or directors of the East India Company. The premises, which occupy a spacious quadrangle, are handsomely built of brick, with quoins and cornices of stone, and are surrounded with a piazza : over the entrance are statues of the founder and his lady, whose portraits are in the hall ; and in the chapel are the arms of Sir John, who was interred here in 1708. The Watling-street, or Roman road from London to Dover, which passed over the heath, may still be traced : in 1710, several Roman urns were dug up, two of which were of fine red clay, one of a spherical, and the other of a cylindrical, form ; and in 1803, several urns were discovered in the gardens of the Earl of Dartmouth, about a foot below the surface of the ground, which were presented by his lordship to the British Museum.—See LEWISHAM.

BLACKLAND (St. PETER), a parish, in the union, parliamentary borough, and hundred of CALNE, Chippenham and Calne, and N. divisions of WILTS, 1¾ mile (S. E.) from Calne ; containing 81 inhabitants. The living is a discharged rectory, valued in the king's books at £3. 10. 10. ; net income, £160 ; patron, the

Rev. James Mayo. Allotments of land were assigned in 1813 in lieu of certain tithes.

BLACKLEY, a chapelry, in the parish and union of MANCHESTER, hundred of SALFORD, S. division of the county of LANCASTER, 3½ miles (N. N. E.) from Manchester, on the road to Middleton and Rochdale ; containing 3202 inhabitants. It comprises about 1000 acres ; the surface is undulated, and the scenery picturesque and beautiful. The population is employed in weaving, bleaching, and dyeing cotton and silk ; the silk-dye works of Messrs. Louis and Michael Delannay are among the establishments that are carried on here. The living is a perpetual curacy ; net income, £150, with a house built in 1838 ; patrons, the Dean and Canons of the Cathedral of Manchester, to whom a rent-charge of £203. 11. 4. per annum has been lately assigned in lieu of tithes. The chapel, dedicated to St. Peter, was previously to the Reformation a domestic chapel belonging to Blackley Hall, and, after a period of disuse, was purchased by the inhabitants, in 1610 ; it was rebuilt in 1844, at a cost of £3300, raised by subscription and public grants, and is in the early English style, with a square tower. There are places of worship for Wesleyans and Unitarians. A school has an endowment of £5 per annum : in 1838, Miss Alsop, of Litchford Hall, founded another, and endowed it with £60 per annum ; and a national school was built at Crab Lane in 1842.

BLACKMANSTONE, a parish, in the union and liberty of ROMNEY-MARSH, though locally in the hundred of WORTH, lathe of SHEPWAY, E. division of KENT, 3 miles (N. by E.) from Romney ; containing 10 inhabitants. It comprises 276 acres of pasture, and 12 of arable land, the latter being the glebe. The living is a rectory, valued in the king's books at £4 ; net income, £36 ; patron, the Archbishop of Canterbury. The church is in ruins.

BLACKMORE (St. LAWRENCE), a parish, in the union of ONGAR, hundred of CHELMSFORD, S. division of ESSEX, 3½ miles (N. W. by W.) from Ingatestone ; containing 709 inhabitants. The parish comprises by computation 2400 acres, of which about 100 are woodland, 800 pasture, and the rest arable ; and derives its name from the dark colour of the soil, which is generally a rich wet loam. The living is a perpetual curacy, valued in the king's books at £6. 13. 4. ; net income, £83 ; patrons and impropriators, the Representatives of the late C. A. Crickett, Esq. The church belonged to a priory of Black canons, founded here by Adam and Jordan de Samford, and which was dissolved in the 17th of Henry VIII. ; the revenue, amounting to £85. 9. 7., was applied by Cardinal Wolsey towards the endowment of his two colleges at Oxford and Ipswich, and on his attainder, in 1529, was appropriated to the crown. Blackmore was the frequent residence of Henry VIII., whose natural son, Henry Fitzroy, Duke of Somerset, was born here.

BLACKMORE, a tything, in the parish, union, and hundred of MELKSHAM, Melksham and N. divisions of WILTS ; containing 279 inhabitants.

BLACKPOOL, a chapelry and bathing-place, in the township of LAYTON with WARBRICK, parish of BISP-HAM, union of the FYLDE, hundred of AMOUNDERNESS, N. division of the county of LANCASTER, 4 miles (S. W. by W.) from Poulton, 19 (W. by N.) from Preston, and 25 (S. W. by W.) from Lancaster ; containing 1304 inhabitants. This place perhaps acquired its name from a boggy pool at the southern end of the village: until within the last 90 years it was an inconsiderable hamlet; but owing to its eligibility for sea-bathing, it has become a very favourite locality. No bathing-place can be better situated; it opens out to the sea, is refreshed by a pure and bracing air, presents a fine smooth sand, new modelled by every tide, but always firm, safe, and elastic, and is furnished with excellent accommodations. The village at the height of the season commonly numbers a thousand visiters; many of them of rank and fashion, mixed with good company from the manufacturing districts. The houses of public reception, and the villas, are scattered along the coast, and in the rear are the habitations of the villagers; when viewed from the sea, the place has a large and imposing appearance. The parade forms an agreeable promenade, from which there is an extensive view of the fells in Westmorland and Cumberland, and the mountains in North Wales. Assemblies occasionally take place at the principal hotels; a news-room has been established; and much is otherwise done to conduce to the pleasure and comfort of the increasing number of families who sojourn here. The sea has receded towards the south, but appears to have encroached considerably on the shore towards the north; a large rock called Penny-stone, lying on the sands about half a mile from the shore, is stated by tradition to mark the site on which a public-house formerly stood. An act was passed in 1845 for making a branch to this village of the Preston and Wyre railway; the branch, 3¾ miles long, has been completed, and the communication between Blackpool and the important town of Preston is thus easy and rapid. Fox Hall, once a sequestered residence of the gallant family of Tildesley, is now a farmhouse. The living is a perpetual curacy in the patronage of certain Trustees; net income, £150, with a house. The chapel was built in 1821, at a cost of £1150, and has been twice enlarged. There is a place of worship for Wesleyans; and a free school, established in 1817, is conducted on Dr. Bell's plan. In the peat bog here, numerous antediluvian trees are found.— See SOUTH-SHORE.

BLACKROD, a chapelry, in the parish of BOLTON, union of WIGAN, hundred of SALFORD, S. division of the county of LANCASTER, 4½ miles (S. S. E.) from Chorley; containing 2615 inhabitants. This is the site of a Roman station, named *Coccium* by Antonine and *Rigodunum* by Ptolemy, which was situated on the Watling-street; and from its central position, and its commanding every object between Rivington Pike and the sea, it was most suitable for a military station. In the reign of John, Hugh le Norries had possessions here; and subsequently Hugh de *Blakerode* held a carucate of land, of the fee of William Peverel. The manor came at a later period to the Bradshaws and the Stanleys; and in the 10th of Elizabeth was found in the possession of Sir William Norreys' family, on his death: it afterwards passed to the Lindsays, and Lord Balcarres is the present lord. The township is situated on the river Douglas, and on the road from Bolton to Chorley: it comprises 2344a. 2r. 22p., of which the surface is hilly, and the soil good; 207 acres are common or waste land. Coal is obtained: the spinning of cotton and the printing of calico are carried on; and the trade is facilitated by a branch of the Lancaster canal, and the Manchester,

Bolton, and Preston railway, which pass through. A fair for toys and pedlery is held on the first Thursday after the 12th of July. The living is a perpetual curacy; net income, £100, with a house; patron, the Vicar of Bolton. The tithes of the Bishop of Chester have been commuted for £98. The chapel, dedicated to St. Catherine, was principally built in the reign of Elizabeth, and has a tower with a peal of bells: it stands on elevated ground, and forms a most conspicuous object for four miles in the line of road from Chorley. There is a place of worship for Wesleyans. A free grammar school, under the superintendence of trustees, is endowed with about £140 per annum, being the produce of various benefactions. John Holmes, in the year 1568, founded an exhibition at Pembroke College, Cambridge, for a scholar on this foundation: the funds having accumulated, three exhibitioners are now appointed, receiving respectively £60, £70, and £80 per annum, for four years. In 1845, a handsome national school-house, with a master's residence attached, was built at an expense of £1000, for the accommodation of 500 children. In 1829, John Popplewell, Esq., M.D., a native of Bolton, among other munificent bequests to the parish, left by will sums altogether amounting to £3500 to this township, to be applied as follows: the interest of £1000 to augment the incumbent's salary; the interest of £1900 to be given annually, after certain deductions, in bread and clothing to the poor; of £400, for clothing boys or girls of the free grammar school; and of £200, for twelve pairs of blankets to old women. Anne and Rebecca, the sisters of this benefactor, left £2150 (part of a sum of £12,600, in the three per cents., bequeathed by them to the whole parish) to this township, for similar benevolent uses. Here stood an ancient castle, the entrance to which, the fosse, &c., were discernible within the memory of persons now living; and many relics have been found in a field which is still called the "Castle field."

BLACKTHORN, a chapelry, in the parish of AMBROSDEN, union of BICESTER, hundred of BULLINGTON, county of OXFORD, 3 miles (S. E. by E.) from Bicester; containing 380 inhabitants. The chapel is in ruins. Roman Akeman-street enters the county here, and proceeds over Blackthorn Hill, in its course through the parish. The custom of running at the quintal or quintain, the origin of which is attributed to the Romans, was anciently observed on the occasion of a wedding in the chapelry.

BLACKTOFT, a parish, in the union of HOWDEN, wapentake of HOWDENSHIRE, E. riding of YORK; comprising the townships of Blacktoft and Scalby, in which latter is the extra-parochial place of Cheapsides; and containing 552 inhabitants, of whom 333 are in the township of Blacktoft, 8 miles (E. S. E.) from Howden. The parish consists by computation of 2241 acres: the surface is level; the soil has been latterly much improved by warping, and is now well drained. The views are very fine, and include the adjacent hills of Yorkshire and Lincolnshire. The village is situated on the northern bank of the Ouse, one mile above its confluence with the Trent, and occasionally vessels ride opposite to it, its roads affording the best anchorage between Hull and Selby; the steam-packets of those places pass daily. The river is very broad in this part, and leaves at low water an extensive bed of sand, which

BLAC   BLAC

s used for the ballasting of small craft. The Hull
and Selby railway crosses the parish near Scalby. The
living is a perpetual curacy, in the gift of the Dean and
Chapter of Durham, and has a net income of £198, by
augmentation from the patrons, with a new and convenient parsonage-house. The tithes of the township of
Blacktoft have been commuted for £568, payable to the
Dean and Chapter. The church is a neat substantial
edifice, built in 1841.

BLACK TORRINGTON.—See TORRINGTON, BLACK.

BLACKWALL, a hamlet, in the parish of STEPNEY,
borough of TOWER HAMLETS, union of POPLAR, Tower
division of the hundred of OSSULSTONE, county of
MIDDLESEX, 4 miles (E.) from Cornhill, London. This
place, which is situated near the influx of the river Lea
into the Thames, consists chiefly of a few irregularly-
formed streets, which are paved, and lighted with gas:
the houses, many of which are of wood, and of mean
appearance, are inhabited chiefly by shipwrights, and
persons employed in the docks; they are supplied with
water by the East London Company. It has long been
noted for a very large private yard for ship-building,
and a wet-dock, once belonging to Mr. Perry: the former was purchased by Sir Robert Wigram, Bart., and
is still applied to the same use; and the latter by the
East India Dock Company, for the formation of their
locks, which were commenced in 1804, and completed
in 1806. These docks, situated at the eastern extremity of the hamlet, and surrounded by a lofty wall, consist of an outer and an inner dock, communicating by
locks and flood-gates; the entrance from the river is by
a basin, nearly three acres in extent, from which vessels
sail directly into the docks. At Blackwall reach, adjoining the hamlet, are the West India docks, similarly constructed, but upon a more extensive scale. In 1836, an
act was obtained for making a railway from Fenchurch-
street, London, to Blackwall, with branches to the East
and West India docks; and this work, which was begun
with a capital of £600,000, afterwards augmented, was
opened to the public 4th July, 1840: the station is on
an extensive scale, and the offices fronting the Brunswick
wharf have a very imposing effect from the river. An
act was passed in 1846, empowering the Eastern
Counties Railway Company to make a line from the
Pepper warehouses at the East India docks to the Thames
Junction railway in Essex: the line is about three furlongs in length.—See LONDON.

BLACKWATER, a large village, in the parish of
YATELY, hundred of CRONDALL, Odiham and N. divisions of the county of SOUTHAMPTON, 15 miles (E. N. E.)
from Basingstoke. It occupies a low situation on the
great western road, at the point of junction of the three
counties of Southampton, Surrey, and Berks, and on the
western bank of the river Blackwater, which is here
crossed by a bridge: on the northern side of the road is
a range of handsome buildings, appropriated as resi-
lences for the masters of the adjoining college of Sandhurst. A fair for cattle and sheep is held on Sept. 8th.
There are places of worship for Particular Baptists.

BLACKWELL, or BLACKHALL, HIGH, a town-
ship, in the parish of St. CUTHBERT, CARLISLE, union
of CARLISLE, CUMBERLAND ward, E. division of CUM-
BERLAND, 2½ miles (S.) from Carlisle; containing 315
inhabitants. The manor was given by Margaret de
Wigton, heiress of Sir John de Wigton, to Sir Robert
275

Parvinge, serjeant-at-law, and afterwards lord high-
chancellor, in the reign of Edward III., for successfully
conducting her cause against Sir Robert de Bridekirk,
who had impugned her title to the barony of Wigton.

BLACKWELL, or BLACKHALL, LOW, a town-
ship, in the parish of St. CUTHBERT, CARLISLE, CUM-
BERLAND ward, union of CARLISLE, E. division of the
county of CUMBERLAND, 2 miles (S.) from the city of
Carlisle; containing 181 inhabitants.

BLACKWELL, a township, in the parish and union
of BAKEWELL, hundred of HIGH PEAK, N. division of
the county of DERBY, 3¼ miles (S. W.) from Tideswell;
containing 68 inhabitants.

BLACKWELL (St. WERBURGH), a parish, in the
union of MANSFIELD, hundred of SCARSDALE, N. division of the county of DERBY, 3¼ miles (N. E. by E.) from
Alfreton; containing 477 inhabitants. It comprises by
measurement 1675 acres, and abounds in coal, which is
close to the surface; two mines are at present worked,
affording employment to a part of the population, and
about 50 persons are engaged in the stocking manufacture. Stone is quarried for road-making. The living
is a discharged vicarage, valued in the king's books at
£5. 4. 2.; patron and impropriator, the Duke of Devonshire: the great tithes have been commuted for £170
and the vicarial for £101; the glebe consists of an acre
and a half. The church was rebuilt in 1824; its site is
a bed of coal, which, a short distance from it, has a
peculiar appearance, jutting out four or five yards above
the turnpike-road: the churchyard contains one of the
oldest yew-trees in England. There is a place of worship
for dissenters.

BLACKWELL, a township, in the parish and union
of DARLINGTON, S. E. division of DARLINGTON ward,
S. division of the county of DURHAM, 1¼ mile (S. W.
by S.) from Darlington; containing 299 inhabitants. A
stone bridge of three arches has been erected over the
river Tees, which is navigable here; and a railway from
Darlington to York passes in the vicinity. There is a
place of worship for Wesleyans. The Grange, in the
township, was the property and residence of George
Allan, Esq., the ingenious antiquary.

BLACKWELL, a hamlet, in the parish of TREDING-
TON, union of TEWKESBURY, Upper division of the
hundred of OSWALDSLOW, Blockley and E. divisions of
the county of WORCESTER, 2½ miles (N. N. W.) from
Shipton-upon-Stour; containing 204 inhabitants, and
comprising 669 acres. The village lies one mile west of
the village of Tredington.

BLACKWOOD, with CROBOROUGH, a township, in
the parish of HORTON, union of LEEK, N. division
of the hundred of TOTMONSLOW and of the county of
STAFFORD, 4 miles (W.) from Leek; containing 526
inhabitants. The soil belongs to a number of freeholders.

BLACON, with CRAB-WALL, a township, in the parish
of HOLY TRINITY, CHESTER, union of GREAT BOUGH-
TON, Higher division of the hundred of WIRRALL, S.
division of the county of CHESTER, 2 miles (W. N. W.)
from Chester, on the road to Parkgate; containing 61
inhabitants. The manor appears to have been in the
Mainwaring family at the time of the Domesday survey,
and to have passed by successive female heirs to the
Trussels, and the Veres, earls of Oxford; it was sold by
the latter to Sir Christopher Hatton, and subsequently
2 N 2

passed to the noble family of Crewe. The township comprises 1112 acres, whereof two-thirds are arable and one-third grass land: the soil is a strong clay. The Ellesmere canal passes through the township. Crabwall Hall, is a handsome mansion, lately built by Samuel Farmer, Esq.

BLADON (St. Martin), a parish, in the union of Woodstock, hundred of Wootton, county of Oxford, 2 miles (S.) from Woodstock; containing, with the hamlet of Hensington, 687 inhabitants. The living is a rectory, with the chapelry of Woodstock annexed, valued in the king's books at £16. 0. 5.; net income, £329; patron, the Duke of Marlborough. The church was built at the expense of the third duke, in 1804, when the former, a fine ancient edifice, was taken down. A fortification, supposed to be of Saxon origin, existed here; and some records of a battle fought at this place are extant.

BLAENAU, Monmouth.—See Aberystwyth.

BLAENAVON, a parochial chapelry, chiefly in the parish of Llanover, division and hundred of Abergavenny, county of Monmouth, 5 miles, (S. W.) from Abergavenny. The village, which has of late assumed the appearance of a thriving town, is situated in a mountainous district, near the source of the Avon Lloyd, whence it derives its name; many of the houses are excavated in the solid rock. The neighbourhood abounds with iron-ore, coal, and limestone. Iron-works on an extensive scale, belonging to the Blaenavon Company, were completed in 1789, since which they have been progressively increasing: the greater portion of the pig-iron is conveyed by means of a canal and a tram-road to Newport, whence it is exported; and another portion, together with iron, coal, and limestone, is sent to Llanfoist, for supplying Abergavenny, Hereford, &c., on the same conveyance, round the Blorange mountain and down its declivities, by means of an inclined plane. A customary market is held on Saturday. The living is a perpetual curacy; net income, £114; patrons, the Blaenavon Company. There are two places of worship for Baptists; and for Presbyterians, and Calvinistic, Primitive, and Wesleyan, Methodists, one each. Near the iron-works stands a spacious free school, on the national plan, endowed in 1816 by Mrs. Hopkins.

BLAGDON, a tything, in the parish of Cranborne, union of Wimborne and Cranborne, hundred of Monckton-up-Wimborne, Wimborne division of Dorset; containing 36 inhabitants.

BLAGDON, a township, in the parish of Stannington, union and W. division of Castle ward, S. division of Northumberland, 6¾ miles (S.) from Morpeth. This place, which lies on the south side of the Blyth, was formerly called Blakedene, and was part of the ancient barony of Morpeth: the family of Fenwick flourished on the spot for three centuries, the 15th, 16th, and 17th; it is now the property of Sir M. White Ridley, Bart., who resides at Blagdon Hall. The present mansion owes its origin to M. White, Esq., who died in 1749, since which time valuable additions and improvements have been made; it is a very extensive pile, and the main front, facing the south, has a sumptuous suite of rooms on the ground-floor, consisting of a saloon, dining and drawing rooms, and library, in all 135 feet long. The Blakedene, bordered by forest-trees, runs behind the house, on the north.

276

BLAGDON (St. Andrew), a parish, in the union of Axbridge, hundred of Winterstoke, E. division of Somerset, 8 miles (N. E. by E.) from Axbridge; containing 1178 inhabitants. This is said to have been anciently a royal residence; and some ruins at Reg-hill-bury are traditionally asserted to be the remains of the palace. The parish comprises an area of about 4000 acres, in good cultivation, and the scenery is pleasingly diversified. The substrata are chiefly limestone, which is burnt for manure, and sandstone of good quality for building; lapis calaminaris is also found. The living is a rectory, valued in the king's books at £29. 13. 9.; net income, £430; patron, James George, Esq. The church, with the exception of the tower, which is of elegant design, has been rebuilt within the last few years, by subscription, aided by a grant of £500 from the Incorporated Society. There is a place of worship for Wesleyans. Thomas Baynard, in 1687, gave land now producing an income of £17. 10., for the instruction of children: John Leman gave land for apprenticing children, which now yields £13 per annum; and there are other bequests for the benefit of the poor. Dr. John Langhorne, the poet and miscellaneous writer, and for some time rector of the parish, is interred in the churchyard; the celebrated Toplady was for two years curate.

BLAGRAVE, with Hadley, a tything, in the parish and hundred of Lambourn, union of Hungerford, county of Berks; containing 446 inhabitants, of whom 204 are in Blagrave. It comprises 3065a. 20r. 14p.

BLAISDON (St. Michael), a parish, in the union and hundred of Westbury, W. division of the county of Gloucester, 9 miles (W.) from Gloucester; containing 264 inhabitants. The village was considerably reduced by fire in 1699, which event is recorded on a tablet in the church, stating that the damage was estimated at £4210. 18. 9. The living is a discharged rectory, valued in the king's books at £5. 7. 3½., and in the patronage of the family of Gordon.

BLAKEMERE (St. Leonard), a parish, in the union of Weobley, hundred of Webtree, county of Hereford, 10½ miles (W. by N.) from Hereford; containing 183 inhabitants, and consisting of 898 acres. On the south-west the parish is bounded by very elevated ground. The living is a discharged vicarage, united to that of Preston-upon-Wye, and valued in the king's books at £3.

BLAKENEY, a chapelry, in the parish of Awre, union of Westbury, hundred of Bledisloe, W. division of the county of Gloucester, 15 miles (S. W. by W.) from Gloucester. The village is pleasantly situated near the river Severn, which is here navigable. Fairs are held on the 12th of May and of November. The living is a perpetual curacy; net income, £232; patrons, the Haberdashers' Company, London. The chapel is dedicated to All Saints. There is a place of worship for Baptists.

BLAKENEY (St. Nicholas, St. Mary, and St. Thomas the Apostle), a small sea-port, post-town, and parish, in the union of Walsingham, hundred of Holt, W. division of Norfolk, 26 miles (N. N. W.) from Norwich, and 134 (N. E.) from London; containing 1021 inhabitants. This place was called Snitterley in the time of Henry III., who granted it a market: it assumed its present name in the reign of Edward III., in the 31st of which a statute was passed for the regulation of the fish trade, which was then carried on to a large extent, and attracted a great number of German merchants, several of whom fixed their residence in the town. It is chiefly noted for its excellent harbour, which is well situated for sheltering vessels, and has been improved under an act obtained .in 1817 : the trade consists principally in coal, timber, and deals, hemp, iron, tar, tallow, oil-cakes, &c., of which the importation is considerable ; the exports are chiefly corn and flour. There is an ancient guildhall, relative to which some old deeds are yet extant. The parish comprises 1061a. 10p.; the soil is chiefly of a sandy nature, but beds of chalk are found in various parts, and between the towns of Blakeney and Clay runs the river Glaven, which, emptying itself into the sea, assists in forming the harbour. The LIVING is a rectory, united to the livings of Little Langham, Glandford, and Cockthorpe, and valued in the king's books at £26. 13. 4. The tithes of Blakeney have been commuted for a rent-charge of £170, and an allotment of land ; the glebe consists of 16 acres. The church, which stands on an elevation a little south of the town, is a handsome and spacious structure, partly in the early and partly in the later English style, with a lofty embattled tower which serves as a landmark to mariners. The Wesleyans have a place of worship. There are some remains, consisting principally of several fine arches, of an ancient monastery for Carmelites or White friars, of which Sir William de Roos, Knt., and the Lady Maud his wife, were among the chief founders ; it was established in 1295, and was dedicated " to the honour of God, and the Virgin Mary." In this monastery John de Baconthorpe, a learned divine and acute metaphysician, became a friar; he was born here, and died in London in 1346.

BLAKENHALL, a township, in the parish of WYBUNBURY, union and hundred of NANTWICH, S. division of the county of CHESTER, 5½ miles (S. E. by E.) from Nantwich ; containing 257 inhabitants. The township comprises 1547a. 2r. 36p. The tithes have been commuted for £198. 10., of which £168 are paid to an impropriator. The trustees of the charity estate of Sir Thomas Delves, who died in 1727, pay £10 annually to a schoolmistress for the instruction of girls of the township.

BLAKENHAM, GREAT, or BLAKENHAM SUPER AQUAS (ST. MARY), a parish, in the union and hundred of BOSMERE and CLAYDON, E. division of SUFFOLK, 5 miles (N. N. W.) from Ipswich ; containing 180 inhabitants. Walter Gifford, Earl of Buckingham, appropriated the manor, in the time of William II., to the monks of Bec in Normandy, who established a cell here, which being suppressed with other alien priories, the manor was given by Henry VI. to Eton College. The Stow-Market and Ipswich canal passes along the south-eastern side of the parish, which comprises 869a. 1r. 8p. The living is a discharged rectory, valued in the king's books at £6. 16. 0½., and in the gift of the College : the tithes have been commuted for £195, and there are upwards of eight acres of glebe.

BLAKENHAM, LITTLE, or BLAKENHAM SUPER MONTEM (ST. MARY), a parish, in the union and hundred of BOSMERE and CLAYDON, E. division of SUFFOLK, 5 miles (N. W.) from Ipswich ; containing 119 inhabit-

ants, and comprising 1046a. 1r. 9p. The living is a rectory, valued in the king's books at £10. 3. 4., and in the gift of the Jackson family : the tithes have been commuted for £244, and the glebe consists of 33 acres.

BLAKESLEY (ST. MARY), a parish, in the union of TOWCESTER, hundred of GREENS-NORTON, S. division of the county of NORTHAMPTON, 4 miles (W. N. W.) from Towcester ; containing 830 inhabitants. The parish comprises 3834a. 1r. 3p., of which 2175a. 1r. 3p. are in the portion exclusively of the hamlet of Woodend : the soil varies from poor cold clay to warm red gravel and loam ; the surface is gently undulated, and since the inclosure, about eighty years ago, nearly two-thirds of the land have been laid out in pasture. A branch of the Tow, which rises at Preston, runs through the parish for about two miles. Quarries of red sandstone are worked for building, and limestone for mending roads. A statute-fair is held on the first Friday after the 22nd of September. The living is a discharged vicarage, valued in the king's books at £9. 17.; net income, £176; patron, John Wight Wight, Esq. In 1760 land was assigned in lieu of tithes, and by the late act a rent-charge of £43. 7. is paid to the impropriator, and one of £41. 6. to the vicar ; there are ten acres of glebe. A free school was founded by William Foxley, in 1669, and endowed with property now producing about £85 per annum ; a Sunday school is endowed with a bequest of £200 by Sir John Knightley, Bart. There are also other charities. Blakesley Hall was anciently a religious house, occupied by a fraternity of the order of St. John of Jerusalem ; and among a number of productive farms, is one of 200 acres, once the property of Dryden.

BLANCHLAND, otherwise SHOTLEY HIGH-QUARTER, a chapelry, in the parish of SHOTLEY, union of HEXHAM, E. division of TINDALE ward, S. division of NORTHUMBERLAND, 10 miles (S. by E.) from Hexham ; containing 476 inhabitants. It is situated on the north side of the river Derwent, and is celebrated for its lead-mines, which have been extensively worked for a long period, and from which large quantities of ore are still raised : the proprietors have a smelting-furnace at Jeffries'-Rake, in the county of Durham. The village is in a narrow deep green vale, inclosed by heathy hills and morasses; the population is chiefly employed in the mines. The living is a perpetual curacy; net income, £198 ; patrons and impropriators, Lord Crewe's Trustees. The chapel was formed in 1752, by the Trustees, out of the tower and aisles of an abbey of Præmonstratensian canons founded by Walter de Bolbec, in 1175, in honour of the Blessed Virgin, and the abbot of which was elevated to the house of peers in the 23rd of Edward I. : the establishment, at the time of the Dissolution, consisted of an abbot and fourteen canons, and the revenue amounted to £44. 9. 1. After having passed through various hands, the estate was purchased by Bishop Crewe, who bequeathed it and other property for charitable purposes. Besides that part converted into a chapel, the principal gateway and other portions of the conventual buildings are still visible.

BLANDFORD (ST. MARY), a parish, in the union of BLANDFORD, hundred of COOMBS-DITCH, Blandford division of DORSET, ¾ of a mile (S.) from Blandford-Forum ; containing 407 inhabitants. This parish, situated near the river Stour, and on the road to Dorchester, comprises 1557 acres of arable and pasture land in nearly equal portions; the soil is generally chalk. The living is a rectory, valued in the king's books at £15. 17. 8½., and in the patronage of Miss Burrough: the tithes have been commuted for £300, and there are 40 acres of glebe. The church, with the exception of the tower, was rebuilt in 1711, by Governor Pitt, ancestor of the Earl of Chatham and of Lord Camelford; it is in the Grecian style, and contains the remains of many of the Pitt family. Browne Willis, the antiquary, was born here, Sept. 14th, 1682. In 1833, six skeletons were discovered about a quarter of a mile from Blandford Bridge; a single skeleton was also found a short distance from the others, and a variety of Roman coins, a Greek coin, a bronze figure of Our Saviour, and a glass vessel two inches in length, evidently formed in a mould, and impressed with two grotesque heads.

Corporation Seal.

BLANDFORD-FORUM (St. Peter and St. Paul), a parish, in the union of Blandford,comprising the borough and market-town of Blandford-Forum and the township of Pimperne, in the hundred of Pimperne, Blandford division of Dorset, 16 miles (N. E.) from Dorchester, and 104 (S. W.) from London; containing 3349 inhabitants. This place derived its name from its situation near an ancient ford on the river Stour, called by the Romans *Trajectus Balaniensis*. It was nearly destroyed by an accidental fire in 1579, but was soon afterwards rebuilt. During the civil war in the reign of Charles I., it suffered severely for its loyalty to that monarch; in 1644 it was plundered by the parliamentarian forces under Major Sydenham, and, not being fortified, became an easy prey to the contending parties, by whom it was frequently assailed and alternately possessed. In 1677, and in 1713, it again suffered greatly from fire, and in 1731 was, with the exception of forty houses only, consumed by a conflagration, which destroyed also the hamlets of Blandford St. Mary and Bryanston, in which only three dwellings were left. After the last calamity, which is recorded on a marble tablet over a pump near the church, it was rebuilt by act of parliament, in 1732.

The town is pleasantly situated on the road from London to Exeter, within a curve of the river Stour, over which is a bridge; the streets are regularly formed and well paved, the houses modern and uniformly built of brick, and the inhabitants amply supplied with water. A theatre, a neat and commodious building, is opened occasionally; and races, which have been established for more than a century, are annually held in August, near the town, the course being one of the best in the kingdom. The manufacture of lace of a very fine quality, equal, if not superior, to that made in Flanders, and valued at £30 per yard, formerly flourished here: the making of shirt-buttons, for which Blandford has long been noted, and which formerly afforded employment to a very considerable number of females in the town and the adjacent villages, is now almost discontinued. The market is on Saturday; the fairs, chiefly for horses, horned-cattle, sheep, and cheese, are held on March 7th,

278

July 10th, and Nov. 8th, and to each a court of piepoudre is attached. Blandford is a borough by prescription, and is parcel of the duchy of Lancaster, the arms of which are borne on the corporation seal; it has also a charter, granted by King James I., who, by separate letters-patent, gave the manor and vill to the bailiff and burgesses. By the act of the 5th and 6th of William IV., cap. 76, the corporation now consists of a mayor, four aldermen, and twelve councillors; the mayor and late mayor are justices of the peace. A court leet is held; and the county magistrates hold petty-sessions here for the division: the powers of the county debt-court of Blandford, established in 1847, extend over the greater part of the registration-district of Blandford. The town-hall is a neat edifice of Portland stone, supported on pillars, with an entablature. The burgesses exercised the elective franchise from the 23rd of Edward I. till the 22nd of Edward III., when it was discontinued.

The living is a vicarage, valued in the king's books at £12. 8. 1½.; patrons and appropriators, the Dean and Chapter of Winchester. The great tithes have been commuted for £152. 10., and the vicarial for £112. 10.; there are nearly 13 acres of glebe belonging to the appropriators. The church is a handsome modern edifice in the Grecian style, with a tower surmounted by a cupola and ornamented with a balustrade and urns. There are places of worship for Independents and Wesleyans. The free school, to the north-west of the church, is of uncertain foundation: it has a small endowment. The Blue-coat school, for the clothing and instruction of twelve boys, and for apprenticing three of them, was founded by Archbishop Wake, who in 1728 bequeathed £1000 for these purposes: this sum was expended in purchasing New South Sea annuities, and, by repeated additions, the total amount now standing to the account of the trust is £1716, yielding a dividend of £51. 9. There is also a small sum for the instruction of four boys, arising from a benefaction of William Williams, who in 1621 left £3000, laid out in land now producing £465 per annum, for instruction and other charitable purposes. In 1685, almshouses for ten aged persons were founded by George Ryves; the income is about £260. In the churchyard are others supported by property bequeathed by Sir Edward Uvedale, and occupied by five poor women. The union of Blandford comprises thirty-three parishes or places, and contains a population of 13,856. On a hill to the north of the town was formerly an intrenchment, inclosing an area 300 paces in length and 200 in breadth, which has long been under cultivation; the only relic now visible is an adjoining barrow. Sir Thomas Ryves, LL.D., a learned antiquary and civilian; the Rev. Bruno Ryves, D.D., publisher of the *Mercurius Rusticus* (an early newspaper in the time of the parliamentary war) and one of the writers of the Polyglot Bible, who was born in 1596; the Rev. Thomas Creech, M.A., translator of *Lucretius*, born in 1659; William Wake, Archbishop of Canterbury, born in 1657; Edward Wake, uncle to that prelate, and founder of the institution for the Sons of the Clergy; Dr. Lindsey, Archbishop of Armagh; Dr. Samuel Lisle, Bishop of Norwich; and the Rev. Christopher Pitt, translator of Virgil's *Æneid*, who died in 1748, and was buried in the church; were natives of the parish. Blandford gives the title of Marquess to the Duke of Marlborough.

BLANKNEY, or BLACKNEY (ST. OSWALD), a parish, in the union of SLEAFORD, Second division of the wapentake of LANGOE, parts of KESTEVEN, county of LINCOLN, 10 miles (N.) from Sleaford; containing, with the hamlet of Linwood, 640 inhabitants. It comprises by computation 5000 acres, chiefly arable land. The living is a rectory, valued in the king's books at £16. 10. 7½.; net income, £752; patron, C. Chaplin, Esq. On Blankney heath are the remains of a British camp about eighty yards in diameter, with a fosse; the site has been recently planted by Mr. Chaplin.

BLASTON (ST. MICHAEL), a chapelry, in the parish of HALLATON, union of UPPINGHAM, hundred of GARTREE, S. division of the county of LEICESTER, 7 miles N. E.) from Market-Harborough; containing, with Blaston St. Giles, 102 inhabitants. The chapel is a small plain building. Another chapel, called the Nether chapel, dedicated to St. Giles, was founded by Richard I., to whom the manor belonged, and rebuilt about 1710: it is a donative belonging to the lord of the manor; patron, the Rev. G. O. Fenwick. The tithes of Blaston St. Michael's, payable to the minister of Hallaton, have been commuted for £74, and there is a glebe of 7 acres: the incumbent of Blaston St. Giles' receives £169, and has a glebe of 44 acres.

BLATCHINGTON, or BLETCHINGTON, EAST (ST. PETER), a parish, in the union of NEWHAVEN, hundred of FLEXBOROUGH, rape of PEVENSEY, E. division of SUSSEX, ¼ of a mile (N.) from Seaford; containing 163 inhabitants. It comprises by measurement 700 acres, of which 405 are arable, and 295 pasture; and is bounded on the south by the English Channel, and intersected by the road from Newhaven to Seaford. The living is a discharged rectory, valued in the king's books at £14; net income, £88; patron, the Rev. R. N. Dennis. The church is a neat edifice in the early English style of architecture.

BLATCHINGTON, WEST (ST. PETER), a parish, in the union of STEYNING, hundred of WHALESBONE, rape of LEWES, E. division of SUSSEX, 1½ mile (N. W. by W.) from Brighton; containing 64 inhabitants. The living is a discharged rectory, consolidated with the vicarage of Brighton, and valued in the king's books at £6. 4. 4½.: the tithes have been commuted for £200. The church is in ruins. On an elevated spot commanding an extensive range of the coast, were discovered in 1818 the site and some vestiges of a Roman villa.

BLATCHINWORTH, with CALDERBROOK, a township, in the parish and union of ROCHDALE, hundred of SALFORD, S. division of the county of LANCASTER, 5 miles (N. E.) from Rochdale; containing 4456 inhabitants.—See LITTLEBOROUGH.

BLATHERWYCKE (HOLY TRINITY), a parish, in the union of OUNDLE, hundred of CORBY, N. division of the county of NORTHAMPTON, 8 miles (W. S. W.) from Wansford, and 8 (E. N. E.) from Rockingham; containing 236 inhabitants, with a portion of Rockingham forest, said to be extra-parochial. This parish, which is intersected by the road from Kettering to Stamford, comprises 2105a. 2r. 39p. The living is a rectory, valued in the king's books at £14. 13. 3.; net income, £394; patron, Augustus Stafford, Esq.: the glebe consists of about 400 acres, with a house. Blatherwycke anciently included two parishes, united in 1448, since which one of the churches, dedicated to St. Mary

Magdalene, has been demolished; the existing structure is a mixture of the Norman and early English styles. There are a chalybeate and a sulphureous spring in Blatherwycke Park.

BLAWITH, a chapelry, in the parish and union of ULVERSTON, hundred of LONSDALE north of the Sands, N. division of the county of LANCASTER, 7 miles (N.) from Ulverston; containing 186 inhabitants. Portions of the manors of Ulverston, Egton with Newland, Torver, and Conishead, constitute this township. The living is a perpetual curacy; net income, £59; patron and impropriator, T. R. G. Braddyll, Esq. The chapel existed in 1715. In 1772 Margaret Lancaster bequeathed £50, and in 1777 William Lancaster gave £110, for the support of a school.

BLAXHALL (ST. PETER), a parish, in the union and hundred of PLOMESGATE, E. division of SUFFOLK, 3¾ miles (E. by N.) from Wickham-Market, and 7 (N. E.) from Woodbridge; containing 173 inhabitants. It comprises 1975 acres, of which 115 are common or waste. The living is a rectory, valued in the king's books at £20, and in the gift of Andrew Arcedeckne, Esq.: the tithes have been commuted for a yearly rent-charge of £510, and there are 80 acres of glebe.

BLAXTON, a township, in the parish of FINNINGLEY, union and soke of DONCASTER, W. riding of the county of YORK, 4¾ miles (N. by E.) from Bawtry; containing 183 inhabitants.

BLAYDON, a village, in the parish of WINLATON, union of GATESHEAD, E. division of CHESTER ward, N. division of the county of DURHAM, 4 miles (W.) from Newcastle-upon-Tyne; containing 1114 inhabitants. This place is situated on the south of the Tyne; the soil is generally light, but produces good wheat, turnips, and potatoes, and the scenery is varied with hill and dale, wood and water. The river affords great facility for the conveyance of coal, of which immense quantities are sent in keels from the Townley-main, Blaydon-main, and Cowen's collieries, to the shipping at Shields. There is an extensive manufactory and depôt for lead; the lead is brought from the Allendale and Weardale mines, where it is smelted, to the works here, where it is manufactured, and shipped for the London market. At this place are also some white-lead and sulphuric-acid works, established in 1839; an iron manufactory for chains, nails, &c.; a cast-iron foundry for ovens, stoves, engines, and other articles; a coke and lamp-black factory; a steel and iron forge; and a fire-brick manufactory. A good road from Newcastle crosses the Tyne by an elegant suspension-bridge at Scotswood, and forms a junction with the Gateshead and Hexham turnpike here; the Newcastle and Carlisle railway, also, has a station at which the trains meet from Newcastle and Gateshead. A church, for which a site was given by Mr. Beaumont, was consecrated in August, 1845; it is called St. Cuthbert's. There are places of worship for Wesleyans, Primitive Methodists, and Methodists of the New Connexion.

BLAYDON-BURN, a hamlet, in the parish of WINLATON, union of GATESHEAD, W. division of CHESTER ward, N. division of the county of DURHAM, 6 miles (W. S. W.) from Newcastle-upon-Tyne. It is picturesquely situated on the Tyne, at the confluence of a small rivulet or burn; and has an extensive establishment where fire-bricks fire-clay retorts for gas-works, flint for potteries, and almost every article of which fire-clay is susceptible, are manufactured : the first fire-clay made into bricks in this part of the country, was produced at these works about 80 years ago. A colliery is in full operation, employing from 200 to 300 hands ; and there is a private railway winding through the romantic dell of Blaydon-Burn, opened in 1841, and extending to the Tyne, whence goods are conveyed by wherries to Newcastle and Shields, and there shipped.

BLAZEY (ST.), a parish, in the union of St. Austell, E. division of the hundred of Powder and of the county of Cornwall, 4 miles (E. N. E.) from St. Austell ; containing 3284 inhabitants. The parish comprises 1480 acres, of which 71 are common or waste ; the surface is hilly, and in the lower grounds is subject to inundation. The substratum is rich in mineral produce, and mines of copper and tin are extensively wrought. The living is a vicarage, in the gift of Col. Carlyon : the impropriate tithes have been commuted for £120, and the vicarial for the same amount. A church district named Par was formed in 1846 out of the parishes of St. Blazey and Tywardreth, by the Ecclesiastical Commission. There are places of worship for Wesleyans.

BLEADON (St. Peter), a parish, in the union of Axbridge, hundred of Winterstoke, E. division of Somerset, 5¾ miles (W. N. W.) from Axbridge ; containing, with the hamlets of Oldmixton and Shipslade, 778 inhabitants. It comprises 2745 acres, whereof 854 are common or waste. The navigable river Axe passes through the parish, and a considerable trade in coal is carried on. The living is a rectory, valued in the king's books at £27. 7. 8½.; net income, £469, patron, the Bishop of Winchester. Meric Casaubon, D.D., an eminent critic and divine, and son of the celebrated Isaac Casaubon, was collated to the benefice about 1624. Here are vestiges of a British settlement, but the Roman road on which it stood can scarcely be traced ; and there are several barrows on an eminence in the vicinity.

BLEANE.—See Cosmus (St.) and Damian.

BLEASBY, a hamlet, in the parish of Legsby, union of Caistor, W. division of the wapentake of Wraggoe, parts of Lindsey, county of Lincoln ; containing 123 inhabitants.

BLEASBY (St. Mary), a parish, in the union of Southwell, Southwell division of the wapentake of Thurgarton, S. division of the county of Nottingham, 4 miles (S. S. E.) from Southwell ; containing 353 inhabitants. It comprises 1468a. 1r. 5p., of which 760 acres are arable, and the remainder meadow and pasture : the surface presents hill and vale ; the soil is clay and sand. The village occupies a secluded situation on the western side of the river Trent, over which is a ferry ; it is a pleasant, straggling place. Within the limits of the parish are the hamlets of Notown, Goverton, and Gibsmere, and Heaselford ferry, near which the Trent forms two channels, and encompasses an island of twenty acres, called the "Knabs." The living is a discharged vicarage, in the patronage of the Chapter of the Collegiate Church of Southwell, valued in the king's books at £4 ; it is held with the perpetual curacy of Morton, and has a net income of £115. The tithes were commuted for land in 1777 ; the vicarial portion consists of 58 acres, and there is a vicarage-house, built in 1843. The church is an ancient edifice, in the early English style, with modern alterations, and is in good repair.

BLEASDALE, a chapelry, in the parish of Lancaster, union of Garstang, hundred of Amounderness, N. division of the county of Lancaster, 7 miles (E. by N.) from Garstang ; containing 249 inhabitants. The forest of Bleasdale, which is held of the crown, in right of the duchy of Lancaster, comprises about 8490 acres, and is co-extensive with the township ; it is wild and mountainous, and the upper ridge of hills joins the county of York : the soil is of a clayey quality. There is a good stone-quarry ; also a paper-mill. Six thousand acres belong to William Garnett, Esq., whose house here, called Bleasdale Tower, is the residence of his son, W. J. Garnett, Esq. The living is a perpetual curacy, in the patronage of the Vicar of Lancaster ; net income, £73, with a house : there are about 22 acres of glebe. The chapel, called Admarsh Chapel, is a neat edifice with a square tower, rebuilt in 1835 ; it has a beautiful east window of stained glass, executed by Ward of London, the gift in 1840 of Mr. Sergeant Bellasis. A school here has an endowment of £22 per annum.

BLEATARN, a hamlet, in the parish of Warcop, East ward and union, county of Westmorland, 4¾ miles (W. by S.) from Brough. John Tailbois, in the reign of Henry II., gave the manor to the abbot of Byland, in Yorkshire, who founded a cell in the vicinity, the ruins of which indicate the conventual buildings to have been somewhat extensive. The Sawbridge estate, and others within the manor, are tithe-free if occupied by their respective owners, but subject to the claim if held by a tenant. Limestone abounds.

BLECHINGDON (St. Giles), a parish, in the union of Bicester, hundred of Ploughley, county of Oxford, 5 miles (E. by N.) from Woodstock ; containing 638 inhabitants. It is bordered on the south-west by the Oxford canal ; and contains quarries of stone well adapted for building and paving. The living is a rectory, valued in the king's books at £12. 9. 4½., and in the gift of Queen's College, Oxford : the tithes have been commuted for £272. 18., and the glebe consists of 209½ acres. Leonard Power, by will in 1620, endowed an almshouse for four poor persons ; it was rebuilt about the end of the last century, and £33 per annum are assigned for the support of the inmates. Dr. Mills, Principal of St. Edmund's Hall, Oxford, and author of the Prolegomena, was rector of the parish ; he was interred in the church, and a handsome monument has been erected to his memory.

BLEDINGTON (St. Leonard), a parish, in the union of Stow-on-the-Wold, Upper division of the hundred of Slaughter, E. division of the county of Gloucester, 4 miles (S. E. by E.) from Stow ; containing 354 inhabitants. It comprises by computation 1400 acres, and is divided from Oxfordshire by the Evenlode stream, by which the flat grounds are sometimes flooded ; the soil is gravelly, with some clay, and the surface level. The living is a discharged vicarage, valued in the king's books at £6. 13. 4. ; net income, £88 ; patrons and appropriators, the Dean and Canons of Christ-Church, Oxford, to whom land and a money payment were assigned in lieu of tithes in 1769.

BLEDLOW (Holy Trinity), a parish, in the union of Wycombe, hundred of Aylesbury, county of Buckingham, 5½ miles (E. S. E.) from Thame ; containing 1205 inhabitants. It comprises 4112a. 1r. 1p., of which about 500 acres are woodland, 100 pasture, and one-third of the rest meadow and two-thirds arable. There are two paper-mills, and females find employment by making cotton and blond lace by hand on pillows. The living is a discharged vicarage, valued in the king's books at £16. 9. 7.; net income, £250; patron, Lord Carrington : land and money payments were assigned in 1809, in lieu of all tithes, woodlands excepted. The church was erected about the year 1200. At Bledlow Ridge, three miles from the church, is a chapel, which was rebuilt by subscription in 1835, and is vested in three trustees; the vicar, who is also chaplain, being one. There is also a Wesleyan meeting-house at Bledlow Ridge; and several endowments, amounting to about £30 per annum, have been left to the poor.

BLENCARN, with KIRKLAND.—See KIRKLAND.

BLENCOGO, a township, in the parish of BROM-FIELD, union of WIGTON, CUMBERLAND ward, E. division of CUMBERLAND, 4½ miles (W. by S.) from Wigton; containing 211 inhabitants. The Rev. Jonathan Boucher, who published a *Supplement to Dr. Johnson's Dictionary*, was born here in 1738.

BLENCOW, GREAT, a township, in the parish of DACRE, union of PENRITH, LEATH ward, E. division of CUMBERLAND, 5 miles (W. N. W.) from Penrith ; containing 64 inhabitants. In 1772 land and a money payment were assigned to the impropriator in lieu of tithes. A grammar school, of high repute, was founded in 1576 by Thomas Burbank, who endowed it with property now producing about £200 per annum : a new schoolroom, and a house for the master, were built in 1793. The late Lord Ellenborough received a part of his early education at this school, which has also produced several distinguished clergymen.

BLENCOW, LITTLE, a township, in the parish of GREYSTOCK, union of PENRITH, LEATH ward, E. division of CUMBERLAND, 4¾ miles (W. N. W.) from Penrith; containing 69 inhabitants. Near an ancient house, once the residence of the Blencows, are some dispersed ruins of buildings, particularly those of a chapel, with a burial-ground adjoining; and near the road is an inclosed cemetery, in which stands a stone cross, with the arms of the family engraved on it.

BLENDON, a hamlet, in the parish of BEXLEY, union of DARTFORD, hundred of LESSNESS, lathe of SUTTON-AT-HONE, W. division of KENT; containing 122 inhabitants.

BLENDWORTH (ST. GILES), a parish, in the union of CATHERINGTON, hundred of FINCH-DEAN, Petersfield and N. divisions of the county of SOUTHAMPTON, ¾ of a mile from Horndean; containing 280 inhabitants. It comprises 1421a. 1r. 23p., of which 611 acres are arable, 146 meadow, 386 downs, and 253 woodland : the soil is chalky, and the surface level and dry. The living is a rectory, valued in the king's books at £6. 7. 8½., and in the gift of the Rev. Edward Langton Ward : the tithes have been commuted for two rent-charges, £130 payable to the incumbent of Chalton, and £243 to the rector of Blendworth, who has also a glebe of 6 [acres. William Appleford, in 1695, gave £200 in trust, to be invested in land, and the proceeds applied to education.

BLENHEIM-PARK, an extra-parochial district, in the liberty of OXFORD (though locally in the hundred of WOOTTON), union of WOODSTOCK, county of OXFORD ; containing 109 inhabitants. This district was granted in

1704, by Queen Anne, to John Churchill, Duke of Marl-borough, in reward of the splendid victory obtained by him over the French and Bavarians, on the 2nd of August, near the village of Blenheim; and the grant was confirmed by parliament in the following year, when the house of commons voted the sum of £500,000 for the erection of a palace. The structure was completed in 1715, after a design by Sir John Vanbrugh, and is a magnificent pile 850 feet in extreme length, generally considered to be the only public work of magnitude sufficient for the full development of the genius of that architect, and consequently regarded as his *chef d'œuvre*. In the centre of the principal front is a projecting portico of the Corinthian order supporting a triangular pediment, crowned on the apex by a statue of Minerva, and displaying in the tympanum the armorial bearings of the duke; at each extremity of the front is a lofty massive tower. The demesne, which comprises 2940 acres, and is inclosed by a wall twelve miles in circuit, is intersected by the river Glyme, which passes in its several windings under bridges of elegant design, and expands into a noble and beautifully picturesque lake, 250 acres in extent. On a fine lawn is a column 130 feet in height, surmounted by a colossal statue of the duke, holding in one hand his baton of command, and in the other a figure of Victory. In different parts of the grounds are temples, grottoes, and statues of beautiful design; and the numerous lodges at the various entrances into the widely-extended demesne, form interesting features in the scenery of the contiguous villages : the principal approach is from Woodstock, under a triumphal arch. The Roman Akeman-street passes through the northern portion of the park, and may be distinctly traced near the lodge.

BLENKINSOPP, a township, in the parish and union of HALTWHISTLE, W. division of TINDALE ward, S. division of NORTHUMBERLAND, 1½ mile (W.) from Haltwhistle; containing 845 inhabitants. This has long been the property of the Blenkinsopp family. In 1399 "Thomas de Blencansopp" had a license to fortify his mansion : it occurs in the list of border castles about 1416 ; and in 1488 its proprietor committed the custody of it to Henry Percy, Earl of Northumberland, at that time warden of the west and middle marshes, when it is supposed that the Blenkinsopps abandoned it finally as a residence. The township comprises 4725 acres, whereof 3844 are common or waste; and is situated on the road from Newcastle to Carlisle, and near the site of the Roman station *Magna*, now called Caer Voran, which latter name it must have received from the ancient Britons, probably from having been placed under the tutelage of the virgin goddess Minerva, *Caer l'orwen* or *Morwen* signifying Maiden's fort. The foundations of buildings and traces of streets are still evident to the view ; the Roman wall is strongest near this station, and at the distance of a quarter of a mile is more than twelve feet high and nine broad. The geological features of the district are generally interesting, and the township abounds in mineral wealth : coal of good quality is very extensively wrought by a company, and near the collieries are quarries of grey slate and limestone. The Newcastle and Carlisle railway passes through the township, and attains its summit level a mile and a half to the north-west of the village of Greenhead (*which see*), where four locomotive engines are usually stationed. Blenkinsopp

Castle, the seat of the ancient family of that name, and now in the possession of their descendant, John Blenkinsopp Coulson, Esq., is a venerable pile of grey massive walls, with a farmhouse attached, used as the residence of the agent of the colliery.

BLENNERHASSET, with KIRKLAND, a township, in the parish of TORPENHOW, union of WIGTON, ALLERDALE ward below Derwent, W. division of CUMBERLAND, 8¼ miles (S. W.) from Wigton; containing 224 inhabitants. A meeting-house here for Independents was rebuilt in 1828.

BLETCHINGLEY (ST. MARY), a parish, and formerly a borough and market-town, in the union of GODSTONE, First division of the hundred of TANBRIDGE, E. division of SURREY, 21 miles (S.) from London; comprising 5370 acres, whereof 220 are common or waste; and containing 3546 inhabitants. This town, which is pleasantly situated on the road from Godstone to Reigate, is of considerable antiquity; a castle was erected here soon after the Conquest, by Gilbert, Earl of Clare, which was demolished by Prince Edward, after the battle of Lewes, in 1264, and the foundations alone are now remaining. Fairs are held on May 10th and Nov. 2nd, for horses, hogs and lean-cattle. Shortly after quitting the London and Brighton railway near Reigate, the South-Eastern railway at this place enters a tunnel 1080 yards in length. A bailiff and other officers are appointed at the court leet of the lord of the manor. The borough received the elective franchise in the 23rd of Edward I., from which time it continued to return two members to parliament, until its disfranchisement by the act of the 2nd of William IV., cap. 45.

The LIVING is a rectory, valued in the king's books at £19. 19. 4½., and in the gift of H. Chawner, Esq.: the tithes have been commuted for £1185, and there are 90 acres of glebe. The church is a spacious and venerable structure, in the early English style of architecture, with a low tower: the south chancel is entirely occupied by a magnificent monument to the memory of the first Sir Robert Clayton, Knt., and his lady, whose effigies in white marble stand on a projecting base; the knight is represented in his robes, as lord mayor of London. There are several other monuments, of which the principal is that of Sir William Bensley, Bart., R.N., by Bacon. John Thomas, Bishop of Rochester, and Sir Thomas Cavendish, master of the revels to Henry VIII., were also interred here; the former was at one time incumbent, as was also Archbishop Herring. There is a place of worship for Independents. Thomas Evans, in 1633, founded a free school for 20 boys, and endowed it with land now producing £20 per annum. The town is near a Roman road; and at Pendhill, in the parish, some workmen in 1813 discovered part of the foundations of a Roman bath, the different apartments in which were paved, and some of the walls lined with tiles. The union workhouse is a spacious building near the town, erected in 1839.

BLETCHLEY (ST. MARY), a parish, in the union of NEWPORT-PAGNELL, hundred of NEWPORT, county of BUCKINGHAM; containing, with part of the chapelry of Fenny-Stratford, and the township of Water-Eaton, 1415 inhabitants. Walter Gifford, Earl of Buckingham, possessed by grant from William Rufus the whole landed property of this parish, which was inherited by Richard

282

de Clare, Earl of Hertford, who had married his granddaughter, Roesia; from the latter family it passed to the Greys, who continued to hold the manor for upwards of 400 years, until the attainder of Thomas, Lord Grey, in 1603. It was given by James I. to George Villiers, Duke of Buckingham, whose descendant sold it, in 1674, to the eminent physician, Dr. Thomas Willis, grandfather of Browne Willis, the celebrated antiquary. The parish is intersected by the London and Birmingham railway, of which the Bletchley and Fenny-Stratford station is situated here: a branch line was opened to Bedford in November, 1846; and an act was passed in the same year, for a railway to Oxford. The living is a rectory, valued in the king's books at £29. 13. 1½.; net income, £456; patron, J. Fleming, Esq.: in 1810, land and a money payment were assigned in lieu of tithes. The church was repaired at the expense of Browne Willis, by whom a large sum was expended upon the internal decorations. William Cole, the Cambridge antiquary, was rector of the parish from 1753 to 1767.

BLETSOE (ST. MARY), a parish, in the hundred of WILLEY, union and county of BEDFORD, 6½ miles (N. N. W.) from Bedford; containing 420 inhabitants. It comprises about 2000 acres: the soil is gravel and clay; the surface is in some parts rather hilly, and the meadows are occasionally flooded by the river Ouse, which runs through the parish. Here are the remains of an ancient castle formerly belonging to Lord Bolingbroke, and part of which has been destroyed for the materials. The living is a rectory, valued in the king's books at £17, and in the patronage of Lord St. John: the tithes have been commuted for £333. 18. 9., and there are 34 acres of glebe. A bequest of £8 per annum is applied to the support of a Sunday school. There is a mineral spring, issuing from a bed of chalk, runs through the village; it turns several mills within three miles, and falls into the river Thames at Wallingford. The living is a discharged vicarage, valued in the king's books at £16. 6. 10½., and in the patronage of the Bishop of Salisbury: the great tithes have been commuted for £1100, and the vicarial tithes for £232. 13.; there are 217½ acres of impropriate glebe, and 1a. 3r. belonging to the vicar. In addition to the parochial church, there are chapels of ease at Aston-Upthorp and Upton. William Malthus, by will dated Nov. 16th, 1700, after specifying certain bequests, directed the residue of his estate to be sold, and the money to be invested in land: the net income is about £916; the trustees allow £161 for the support of ten boys at Reading, and other sums for the instruction, clothing, and apprenticing of children in Blewberry. An almshouse for one poor man was founded, and endowed with £271. 13. 4., by Mr. Bacon, in 1732; the lands are let for £38 per annum.

BLEWBERRY (ST. MICHAEL), a parish, in the union of WANTAGE, partly in the hundred of MORETON, but chiefly in that of READING, county of BERKS, 4½ miles (N. E. by N.) from East Ilsley; containing, with the chapelries of Aston-Upthorp and Upton, and the liberty of Nottingham-Fee, 1096 inhabitants. The parish comprises upwards of 4000 acres, of which about 2500 are arable, and the rest pasture and meadow: the soil is partly of a cold, chalky nature, but round the village it is a strong clay loam, and in other parts gravel and peat. A large stream, issuing from a bed of chalk, runs through the village; it turns several mills within three miles, and falls into the river Thames at Wallingford. The living is a discharged vicarage, valued in the king's books at £16. 6. 10½., and in the patronage of the Bishop of Salisbury: the great tithes have been commuted for £1100, and the vicarial tithes for £232. 13.; there are 217½ acres of impropriate glebe, and 1a. 3r. belonging to the vicar. In addition to the parochial church, there are chapels of ease at Aston-Upthorp and Upton. William Malthus, by will dated Nov. 16th, 1700, after specifying certain bequests, directed the residue of his estate to be sold, and the money to be invested in land: the net income is about £916; the trustees allow £161 for the support of ten boys at Reading, and other sums for the instruction, clothing, and apprenticing of children in Blewberry. An almshouse for one poor man was founded, and endowed with £271. 13. 4., by Mr. Bacon, in 1732; the lands are let for £38 per annum.

large edifice called the Charter-house, supposed to have. een used as a place of worship previously to the Re- irmation, was taken down a few years since. A field etween Blewberry and Aston is thought to have been ie scene of a severe conflict between the Saxons under thelred and his brother Alfred, and the Danes, the itter of whom were defeated with great slaughter; and i forming a new turnpike-road, in 1804, many human keletons and military weapons were found near the pot. The parish is intersected by a Roman and a British bad, termed respectively Ickleton and Grimsditch. here is an encampment of considerable extent on a hill alled Blewberton; and Loughborough Hill, the loftiest minence in the county, has also been crowned by an ncient work, apparently constructed for purposes of arfare.

BLICKLING (ST. ANDREW), a parish, in the union of AYLSHAM, hundred of SOUTH ERPINGHAM, E. division of NORFOLK, 1¼ mile (N. W. by N.) from Aylsham; containing 356 inhabitants. Before the Conquest the manor was in the possession of Harold, afterwards king of England: William I. settled the whole on the see: and after the foundation of Norwich cathedral, the bishops held the demesne in their own hands, and had a palace here. Charles II., with his queen, visited the Hall, in their progress through the county, in 1671. The edifice is of brick, in the Elizabethan style; it is environed with large old trees, and situated in a beautiful park of about 700 acres. The road from Aylsham to Holt passes through the parish, which is bounded on the north-east by a branch of the river Bure: the area is 2114a. 2r. 12p., of which 924 acres are arable, 755 meadow and pasture, 401 woodland and plantations, and the remainder common or waste. The living is a rectory, with that of Erpingham annexed, valued in the king's books at £10. 13. 4., and in the patronage of the Dowager Lady Suffield: the tithes of the parish have been commuted for £400, and the glebe comprises 17 acres. The church, which is picturesquely situated near the Hall, is in the decorated and later styles, and consists of a nave, chancel, and aisles, with a low square tower.

BLIDWORTH (ST. MARY), a parish, in the union of MANSFIELD, Southwell division of the wapentake of THURGARTON, S. division of the county of NOTTING-HAM, 5 miles (S. S. E.) from Mansfield; containing, with the hamlets of Lower Blidworth, Bottoms, Fishpool, and Rainworth, and the extra-parochial places of Lindhurst and Haywood-Oaks, 1154 inhabitants. At the time of the Norman survey this formed a berewic to Oxton, and in the 3rd of Henry V. was given by that monarch to the college of Southwell. The parish comprises 5302a. 3r. 10p. The village is nearly in the centre of the ancient forest of Sherwood, in all the perambulations of which, from the reign of Henry I. to that of Charles II., it is mentioned as a forest town: it is pleasantly situated upon an eminence, surrounded by some of the finest scenery of the forest. The "Queen's Bower" and "Langton Arbour" are still pointed out as the sites of hunting-seats of King John; and "Fountain Dale" and "Rainworth" are both celebrated in the annals and ballads of Robin Hood. Rainworth gives name to the forest rivulet that rises near Robin Hood's hills. A portion of the population is employed as frame-work knitters of stockings, and in glove-making and running

283

lace. A fair for sheep is held on Old Michaelmas-day. The living is a discharged vicarage, valued in the king's books at £4, and was till lately in the alternate gift of the two prebendaries of Oxton, on the decease of one of whom, his right of patronage devolved to the Bishop of Ripon; net income, £188. The tithes were commuted for land and a money payment in 1769 and 1806; the glebe comprises 140 acres. The original church becoming dilapidated, the present edifice was erected in 1740, and re-roofed and enlarged in 1839 at an expense of above £1000. There is a place of worship for Wesleyans. In a field near the village is a rocky formation of sand and gravel, commonly called plum-pudding stone; it is fourteen feet high and eighty-four in circumference, and is supposed to have been a Druidical idol. At the inclosure in 1806, upwards of 1000 acres were planted, which are now in a very flourishing condition.

BLINDBOTHEL, a township, in the parish of BRIGHAM, union of COCKERMOUTH, ALLERDALE ward above Derwent, W. division of CUMBERLAND, 2½ miles (S.) from Cockermouth; containing 100 inhabitants. As a commutation in lieu of tithes, land was assigned to the impropriator in 1812.

BLINDCRAKE, with ISELL.—See ISELL.

BLISLAND (ST. PRATT), a parish, in the union of BODMIN, hundred of TRIGG, E. division of CORNWALL, 4½ miles (N. N. E.) from Bodmin; containing 688 inhabitants. It comprises 5643 acres, of which 2460 are common or waste. A cattle-fair is held on the Monday next after September 22nd. The living is a rectory, valued in the king's books at £13. 10.; net income, £571; patron and incumbent, the Rev. F. W. Pye. There is a place of worship for Wesleyans.

BLISWORTH (ST. JOHN THE BAPTIST), a parish, in the union of TOWCESTER, hundred of WYMMERSLEY, S. division of the county of NORTHAMPTON, 4½ miles (S. S. W.) from Northampton; containing 882 inhabitants. It is intersected by the road from Northampton to Towcester, and comprises 1914 acres, including 50 acres occupied by the London and Birmingham railway, the annual value of which property in the parish is returned at £2357. About two-thirds of the land are arable, and 68 acres in wood; the surface is undulated, the scenery pleasing, and the soil various. The whole, with the exception of the rectory and church lands, belongs to the Duke of Grafton, who is lord of the manor. The Grand Junction canal, entering the parish by means of a tunnel from the parish of Stoke-Bruerne, continues its course northward towards Braunston; and the Northampton canal branches out of it, at the extremity of the parish. Much good stone for lime and building is sent by canal to the neighbouring counties. Here also is a station on the line of the railway, which passes a short distance from the village, and has a cutting through blue limestone rock, about two miles long, with an average depth of fifty feet: the quantity of rock removed was estimated at 1,200,000 cubic yards, and the expense of the cutting at £200,000. The Peterborough railway commences at Blisworth; it passes close to the town of Northampton, and through the heart of the county, by Wellingborough, Higham-Ferrers, and Thrapstone. The living is a rectory, valued in the king's books at £20. 3. 9.; net income, £435; patron and incumbent, the Rev. William Barry. The glebe-house, built in 1841, is in the Elizabethan style. As a

2 O 2

commutation in lieu of tithes, with the exception of the tithe of underwood, land and a money-payment were assigned in 1808 : the tithe of underwood was commuted in 1845. The church is an ancient edifice with a square tower, and contains a tomb to an ancestor of the Wake family of Courteenhall. The Baptists have a place of worship. A free school is endowed with £10. 4. 7. per annum, paid by the crown.

BLITHBURY, a hamlet, in the parish of MAVESYN-RIDWARE, union of LICHFIELD, N. division of the hundred of OFFLOW and of the county of STAFFORD, 8 miles (N. by E.) from Lichfield ; containing 144 inhabitants. It lies on the north side of the parish, in the vale of the Blithe. Here Hugo Mavesyn settled in the reign of Henry I., and founded a church and priory. The priory was dedicated to St. Giles, and occupied by Benedictine monks ; but no traces of it now remain.

BLITHFIELD (ST. LEONARD), a parish, in the union of UTTOXETER, hundred of SOUTH PIREHILL, N. division of the county of STAFFORD, 4¼ miles (N.) from Rugeley ; containing, with Newton liberty and Admaston hamlet, 390 inhabitants. The Bagot family, of great eminence and antiquity, possessed this and the adjoining estate of Bagot's-Bromley, at the time of the Domesday survey. In 1195 Hervey Bagot married the heiress of Baron Stafford ; his son assumed the surname and title of Stafford, and became progenitor to the succeeding barons and earls of Stafford, and dukes of Buckingham. Of that branch of the family resident at Blithfield and Bromley, was Sir John Bagot, Knt., ancestor of Hervey Bagot, who was created a baronet in 1627 : William Bagot was made a baron in 1780. Blithfield Hall, the family seat, is an ancient mansion with embattled towers and walls ; it stands in the vale of the Blithe or Blythe, on a beautiful lawn, and contains a large and valuable collection of paintings, among which are portraits of many distinguished persons. Bagot's Park, which forms part of Lord Bagot's pleasure-grounds, is distant a mile and a half to the north-east, in the parish of Abbot's-Bromley ; and is well wooded with ancient oaks, and stocked with deer. The living is a rectory, valued in the king's books at £10. 19. 2., and in the patronage of the noble baron ; net income, £388. The church stands a quarter of a mile west of Admaston. Elizabeth Bagot and Jane Jones, in 1729, gave land now producing about £35 per annum, which is applied to the support of a school on the national system ; and there are some benefactions for distribution among the poor, one of which, of £10 per annum, was left in 1702 by Sir Walter Bagot.

BLOCKHOUSE, an extra-parochial liberty, in the city, union, and county of WORCESTER; containing 1280 inhabitants. A district church, dedicated to St. Paul, was consecrated in 1845 ; it is a handsome brick structure with a small square tower, erected at a cost of £2200, raised by subscription and a grant from the Church Building Society. The living is a perpetual curacy in the patronage of the Bishop, with a net income of £150. On each side of the entrance to the church stands a Sunday school.

BLOCKLEY (ST. PETER AND ST. PAUL), a parish, in the union of SHIPSTON, Upper division of the hundred of OSWALDSLOW, Blockley and E. divisions of the county of WORCESTER, 3¼ miles (N.·W. by W.) from Moreton ; surrounded by Gloucestershire and a small
284

portion of Warwickshire; comprising the townships of Blockley, and the hamlets of Aston Magna, Dorne, Ditchford, Draycot, and Paxford ; and containing 2136 inhabitants, of whom 1412 are in the township of Blockley. It consists of 7571 acres, of which 3190 are arable, 4035 meadow and pasture, and 341 wood; the soil is rich and fertile. The surface is irregular and undulated, and the scenery produced by its shady groves, fruitful vales, and sloping hills, is very pleasing : the land is in good cultivation. There are several silk-mills, worked by small streams which rise in Dovedale, a short distance hence. Fairs are held on the Tuesday next after Easter-week, for cattle, and Oct. 10th, for hiring servants ; a manorial court is occasionally held under the Bishop of Worcester, who is lord of the manor, and the petty-sessions for the division are held here. The living is a vicarage, valued in the king's books at £54 ; net income, £762 ; patron and appropriator, the Bishop: the tithes were commuted for land in 1772. The church is partly Norman, and partly in the early English style; the interior is spacious, and consists of a nave, chancel, and north aisle, with a small gallery at the west end, and is appropriately decorated : the tower was rebuilt in 1725, at the expense of the inhabitants. At Aston is a separate incumbency. There is a place of worship for Baptists. Premises for a school upon the national plan, were built some years since by Lord Northwick ; the endowment, arising from various sums bequeathed by the ancestors of his lordship, amounts to £12. 14. per annum. In a charter of King Burhred, dated 855, mention is made of a monastery which then existed, and which was subsequently annexed to the bishopric of Worcester: the bishops had a palace here. The Roman Fosse-way passed between this village and Moreton, and urns and other Roman remains have been found on Moor Hill. There are several chalybeate springs.

BLODWELL.—See LLAN-Y-BLODWELL.

BLOFIELD (ST. ANDREW), a parish, and the head of a union, in the hundred of BLOFIELD, E. division of NORFOLK, 7 miles (E.) from Norwich; containing 1112 inhabitants. It comprises about 2252 acres; and the road from Norwich to Yarmouth runs through the village, in which is a branch post-office. Petty-sessions are held at the Globe inn every alternate Monday. The living is a rectory, valued in the king's books at £23. 6. 8.; net income, £896 ; patrons, the Master and Fellows of Gonville and Caius College, Cambridge: the glebe consists of about 62 acres, with a handsome house erected in 1806. The church is in the later style, with a lofty square embattled tower surmounted at each angle by a figure of one of the Evangelists. The Independents have a place of worship. The rent of about 37 acres of land awarded at the inclosure, is distributed in coal among the poor. The union of Blofield comprises 32 parishes or places, and contains a population of 10,555.

BLO-NORTON (ST. ANDREW), a parish, in the union and hundred of GUILT-CROSS, W. division of NORFOLK, 5 miles (S. by E.) from East Harling ; containing 435 inhabitants. It comprises 1133a. 2r. 22p., of which 841 acres are arable, 227 pasture, and the remainder, wood and waste land, and roads. The living is a discharged rectory, valued in the king's books at £5. 6. 3. ; patron and incumbent, the Rev. Charles Howman Browne, whose tithes have been commuted for £330, and who has

(N. by W.) from Sleaford; containing 67 inhabitants. This parish is situated near the road from Sleaford to Lincoln, and comprises about 1200 acres, of which 700 are arable, 250 pasture and meadow, and the remainder waste; stone is quarried, and made into lime. Bloxham Hall is a fine old mansion, enlarged in 1825, and surrounded by extensive pleasure-grounds. The living is a rectory, to which the vicarage of Digby was united in 1717, valued in the king's books at £9. 9. 4½., and in the patronage of R. A. Christopher, Esq.: the tithes of the parish have been commuted for £209. 5. 2., and the glebe comprises 18 acres, with a house. The church is a neat edifice; in the chancel are deposited the remains of many members of the Manners family, late the possessors of the lordship.

BLOXHAM (St. Mary), a parish, in the union of BANBURY, hundred of BLOXHAM, county of OXFORD, 3 miles (S. W. by S.) from Banbury; containing, with the chapelry of Milcombe, 1543 inhabitants. A petty-session is held once every month. The living is a discharged vicarage, valued in the king's books at £17. 9. 4., and in the gift of Eton College, with a net income of £262 : land and annual money payments were assigned in lieu of tithes in the 39th and 40th of George III. The church, which is justly admired for loftiness of elevation and beauty of design, was greatly damaged during the war between the houses of York and Lancaster, but was repaired in the reign of Henry VIII., and beautified by Cardinal Wolsey. It is principally in the early and decorated English styles, with some Norman remains, and has a highly enriched tower of four stages, strengthened by angular buttresses ornamented with canopied niches rising to the third stage; the fourth stage, of smaller dimensions, gradually becomes octagonal, corresponding with the lofty crocketed spire by which it is surmounted. At Milcombe is a chapel of ease; and there is a place of worship in the parish for Baptists; also a free school established in 1831, which was endowed by the will of Mr. Job Faulkner with the interest of £666. 13. 4. three per cent. consols.

BLOXWICH, a chapelry district, in the parish and union of WALSALL, S. division of the hundred of OFFLOW and of the county of STAFFORD, 2 miles (N. N. W.) from Walsall, on the road to Stafford; containing 3801 inhabitants. In Domesday book this place is described as being held by the king, and having a wood three furlongs in length and one in breadth. From its vicinity to Walsall, it participates in a considerable degree in the manufactures and trade of that town ; and advantage is derived from the Essington and Wyrley canal, which passes through the district. The land is of level surface, and the soil gravelly and sandy. Extensive coal and iron mines are in operation : the colliery opened by Messrs. Walter Dudley and Company in 1840, employs 350 hands. Bridle-bits and awl-blades are made in great quantities; and at Goscote is a foundry. The LIVING is a perpetual curacy; net income, £150, with a house. The church, dedicated to St. Thomas, is a neat edifice with a square tower ; it was rebuilt in 1790 and enlarged in 1833, and is in good repair. By an order of council, in August 1842, a district was assigned, comprehending the village of Bloxwich, and the hamlets of Little Bloxwich, Goscote, Blakenall, Coalpool, Harden, and part of the Birchills.

There are places of worship for Wesleyans and Primitive Methodists ; and, at Harden, a Roman Catholic chapel. A national school is supported by subscription; at Blakenall is an infants' school.

BLOXWORTH (St. *Andrew*), a parish, in the union of WAREHAM and PURBECK, hundred of COOMBS-DITCH, Wareham division of DORSET, 8 miles (S.) from Blandford ; containing 306 inhabitants. It comprises about 3000 acres, of which 900 are arable, 400 pasture, 200 meadow, 80 woodland (chiefly coppice), and the remainder heath; the soil is various, in some parts clay, in others chalk alternated with sand. The living is a rectory, valued in the king's books at £15. 7. 1., and in the gift of the family of Pickard : the tithes have been commuted for £279, and the glebe consists of 35 acres. The church is an ancient structure in the later English style, with a square embattled tower. On a hill called Woolsbarrow, situated on the heath, about a mile towards the east, are vestiges of a small fortification supposed to be of Danish origin, the ramparts and trenches of which may be traced : near it are several tumuli.

BLUBBER-HOUSES, a township, in the parish of FEWSTON, Lower division of the wapentake of CLARO, W. riding of YORK, 8 miles (N. by W.) from Otley ; containing 99 inhabitants. It comprises about 3600 acres, chiefly moorland and pasture, with a small proportion of arable land ; the surface is strikingly varied. At Brandith Craggs, a range of lofty rocks, situated in the neighbourhood, is a rocking-stone easily moved with one hand, though its weight cannot be less than 20 tons.

BLUNDESTON (St. *Mary*), a parish, in the incorporation and hundred of MUTFORD and LOTHINGLAND, E. division of SUFFOLK, 3¼ miles (N. W.) from Lowestoft ; containing 592 inhabitants. It is situated on the navigable river Waveney, which forms its boundary on the south-west. The living is a discharged rectory, with that of Flixton united, valued in the king's books at £13. 6. 8., and in the gift of the family of Anguish : the tithes have been commuted for £610, and there are nearly 13 acres of glebe. Here is a place of worship for Wesleyans. The Rev. Gregory Clarke, in 1726, gave land for the instruction of children, of the annual value of about £11.

BLUNHAM (St. *Edmund*), a parish, in the union of BIGGLESWADE, hundred of WIXAMTREE, county of BEDFORD, 5¼ miles (N. N. W.) from Biggleswade, and on the great north road; containing, with the hamlet of Muggerhanger, 1050 inhabitants. The parish is situated at the junction of the Ivel with the Ouse, which is navigable to Bedford. It comprises 2589 acres, whereof 1785 are arable, 424 meadow, 250 pasture, and 130 plantation ; the soil is light and convertible, the surface level, and the meadow lands subject to floods. A large portion of the females are employed in the manufacture of pillow-lace, and in preparing straw-bonnet plat. In the reign of Edward II., the inhabitants obtained the grant of a weekly market on Wednesday, and of an annual fair on the festival of St. James, both which have long been discontinued. The living is a rectory, valued in the king's books at £46. 2. 11., and in the patronage of Earl de Grey; net income, £731, derived from about 600 acres of land. The church is a commodious, plain structure ; the interior and the tower appear of different

habitants. This parish comprises 2353a. 2r. 29p., and is situated on the road from Lincoln to Barton-on-Humber, by which it is bounded on the east; the soil is various, but chiefly consists of loam, clay, and sand, and the surface is rather level. Limestone is quarried for building, and the repair of roads. The living is a rectory, valued in the king's books at £19, and in the patronage of the Crown : the tithes have been commuted for £557, and there are nearly two acres of glebe, with a residence. A tessellated pavement was discovered a few years since in a field, a few inches below the surface, in a perfect state. There are mineral springs.

. BLYMHILL (St. Mary), a parish, in the union of Shiffnall, W. division of the hundred of Cuttlestone, S. division of the county of Stafford, 6 miles (W. N. W.) from Brewood ; containing 632 inhabitants. It comprises by measurement 2433 acres, mostly of a strong loamy soil : the commons, called the Heath and the Lawn, were inclosed about 35 years ago. High Hall, now occupied by a farmer, is seated on a charming eminence, and is supposed to have been the residence of William Bagot, who was lord of Blymhill in the reign of Henry II. The hamlet of Brineton is in this parish. The living is a rectory, valued in the king's books at £13. 10. 7½., and in the gift of the Earl of Bradford : the tithes have been commuted for £560, and there are 76½ acres of glebe. The church was rebuilt, with the exception of the tower and chancel, in 1719. Schoolrooms have been erected, chiefly at the expense of the rector. The late incumbent, the Rev. Samuel Dickenson, was a learned and ingenious naturalist.

BLYTH (St. Martin), a parish, in the unions of Doncaster, East Retford, and Worksop ; partly in the N. and partly in the S. division of the wapentake of Strafforth and Tickhill, W. riding of York ; and partly in the Hatfield division of the wapentake of Bassetlaw, N. division of the county of Nottingham ; 31¼ miles (N. by E.) from Nottingham, and 151½ (N. N. W.) from London, on the old road to York ; containing 3488 inhabitants, of whom 811 are in the village of Blyth. This place, anciently called Blia and Blida, was chiefly noted in former times for its religious and charitable establishments. In 1088, a priory was founded in honour of the Blessed Virgin, by Roger de Builly and his wife Muriel, for monks of the Benedictine order ; which, though considered as an alien priory, being in some respects subordinate to the abbey of the Holy Trinity, near Rouen, in Normandy, was yet spared at the suppression of alien priories, and subsisted till the general dissolution, when its revenue was estimated at £126. 8. 2. An hospital for lepers, dedicated to St. John the Evangelist, was founded by Hugh de Cressy, lord of Hodsock, in the reign of John, for a warden, three chaplains, and brethren, whose revenue at the Dissolution was £8. 14. Of these buildings, as well as of a strong castle which is known to have been anciently erected here, there are scarcely any remains, nearly the whole having been demolished by wanton hands, or decayed by time ; the monastic institution occupied the site and grounds of the present Hall, a handsome mansion of considerable magnitude which stands near the church,-in a situation surrounded by beautiful scenery. The lord of the honour of Tickhill had a castle at Blyth, where he exercised the usual feudal rights of a lord paramount ; in the immediate neighbourhood was one of

287

the five places which alone were licensed for holding tournaments, and several records are preserved of royal and noble blood having been shed in these dangerous sports.

The parish is nearly 11 miles in extreme length, and contains the chapelries of Bawtry and Austerfield, and the townships of Barnby-Moor, Blyth, Hodsock, Ranskill, Torworth, and part of Styrrup ; it comprises 15,477a. 11p. of fertile land, of which 1257 acres are in the township, and is intersected by the river Idle. The town or village, which is four miles from Bawtry, is pleasantly situated on the east bank of the Ryton, on a gentle ascent; and is clean and well built, and amply supplied with water. The market, which was formerly held on Wednesday, has been discontinued ; the fairs are on Holy-Thursday and October 20th. The living is a discharged vicarage, valued in the king's books at £14. 9. 4½.; gross income, £751 ; patrons and impropriators, the Master and Fellows of Trinity College, Cambridge. The great tithes of the township of Blyth have been commuted for £295, and those of the vicar for £170. 8.: there are in the township nearly three acres of vicarial glebe. The church is a lofty structure partly in the Norman style, and formed the ante-choir of the splendid cruciform church of the priory ; it has a handsome tower in the later style of English architecture, with crocketed pinnacles. At Austerfield and Bawtry are chapels of ease. There are places of worship for the Society of Friends and Wesleyans ; and a school endowed with land producing £12 per annum. Some almshouses for six aged people, supposed to have been originally an appendage to the hospital founded by Hugh de Cressy, have been lately rebuilt ; and there are also almshouses for two aged women, endowed with £10 per annum, under the management of the Society of Friends ; besides other charitable bequests for the relief of the poor.

BLYTH, NORTH, a township, in the parish and division of Bedlington, union of Morpeth, N. division of Northumberland, 8½ miles (E. S. E.) from Morpeth ; containing 123 inhabitants. The village is situated on a peninsula upon the northern side of the river Blyth, opposite to the port and town of South Blyth, and is chiefly inhabited by fishermen and pilots. The manufacture of salt and of earthenware was formerly carried on to a considerable extent, but has been wholly discontinued. There are several store-houses for corn, and a quay. A little to the north-east of the village is a large cluster of rocks, called the Row-cars, which appear at low-water mark, though there are five fathoms of water close to the ledge.

BLYTH, SOUTH, or BLYTH NOOK, a sea-port and chapelry, partly in the parish of Horton, chiefly in that of Earsdon, union of Tynemouth, E. division of Castle ward, S. division of Northumberland, 9½ miles (E. S. E.) from Morpeth, 16 (N. N. E.) from Newcastle, and 283 (N. N. W.) from London ; containing, with the lordship of Newsham, and exclusively of that part of the

Seal.

town which is in the parish of Horton, 1921 inhabitants. The river and port were of much importance to the bishops of Durham in ancient times, and are named in the records with the Tyne, Wear, and Tees, as subject to their jurisdiction, with all the royal rights appertaining to their possession. The place was the property of a younger branch of the Cramlingtons in the reign of Elizabeth, and in the time of Charles I. was possessed by Robert Cramlington; but his estate being sequestrated by the parliament, it was purchased by a wealthy London merchant, by whom it was sold to Col. Thomas Ratcliff; and is now in the possession of Sir M. White Ridley, Bart., a descendant of the family to which the martyred Bishop Ridley belonged. In August, 1795, the Duke of York, accompanied by Prince William of Gloucester, reviewed the troops encamped on the coast of Northumberland, upon Blyth sands, the whole force consisting of 13 regiments, who performed their various evolutions in the presence of nearly 60,000 persons.

The TOWN, which is advantageously situated on the north side of the Blyth, at its influx into the North Sea, is remarkably pleasant and well built; and though at the commencement of the present century it was of slight importance, and its streets narrow and few, it is now extensively engaged in commerce, and ranks among the most bustling small sea-ports of the kingdom. The trade consists principally in the export of coal from the Cowpen and other collieries, and the importation of various articles of local consumption. The produce of the Bedlington iron-works, which are about three miles distant, is brought down the Blyth to this port for shipment; it includes a great number of locomotive engines and vast quantities of machinery, justly noted for their excellence, and which are sent to all parts of the world. In a recent year, 8 foreign and 120 coasting vessels, with cargoes, entered inwards, and 223 foreign and 826 coasting vessels cleared outwards; 190,000 tons of coal were exported, and the amount of duties received was £1641: the number of ships registered as belonging to the port and to Seaton-Sluice, is 100. The river near its mouth abounds with sea-fish, and the higher parts of the stream are frequented by fresh-water fish of extremely fine quality. The harbour, the entrance to which is at all times free from obstruction, is quite secure, even during the most tempestuous weather, but is accessible only to vessels of moderate burthen; the tide flowed over an extensive waste on the western side of it, but, with a view to counteract this, a quay has been formed on the margin of the river. A circular stone lighthouse was built in 1788, and there is also a beacon-light, called the Basket-Rock light: a dry-dock was constructed in 1811. The custom-house here had formerly the control of the coast as far south as Cullercoats, where large quantities of coal were shipped, and the vessels had to pay their dues and clear out at Blyth; but since the Tyne has risen into such importance, the whole is now under the Newcastle customs. Ship building and repairing (for which latter there is a patent-slip), and likewise sail-making, are carried on: there are some roperies, a large brewery, and extensive timber, iron, and slate yards; also two steam, and three wind flour-mills. A branch of the Newcastle and Berwick railway extends to this place. There are excellent and commodious inns; and vapour, shower, and warm baths. A bench of magistrates hold a monthly court.

288

The chapel was erected by the then Sir M. W. Ridley, in 1751: the living is a donative curacy, in the patronage of the present baronet, with a net income of £93. The tithes have been commuted for £227. 6. There are places of worship for Presbyterians, Scottish Seceders, Wesleyans, and Methodists of the New Connexion. George Marshall, author of a miscellaneous volume of poems, and *Letters from an Elder to a Younger Brother*, was born at the place.

BLYTHBURGH (*Holy Trinity*), a parish, and formerly a market-town, in the union and hundred of BLYTHING, E. division of SUFFOLK, 4 miles (S. S. W.) from Wangford; containing, with the hamlets of Hinton and Bulcamp, 837 inhabitants. Among the relics of antiquity that have been found are some Roman urns, dug up about 1768; which circumstance, together with the termination of the name of the parish, affords evidence of its having been a Roman station. In 654, a battle was fought at Bulcamp, between Anna, King of the East Angles, and Penda, King of Mercia, of whom the latter was victorious, and the former was slain, together with his son Ferminus, and interred in the church, whence their remains were afterwards removed to Bury St. Edmund's. A priory of Black canons, of uncertain foundation, was given by Henry I. to the abbey of St. Osyth, in the county of Essex, to which it remained subordinate till the Dissolution, when its revenue was valued at £48. 8. 10. The parish comprises 3711 acres, and is situated on the river Blyth; the quality of the land varies from a mixed soil to a sandy loam. The living is a perpetual curacy; net income, £45; patron, Sir Charles Blois, Bart.: the tithes have been commuted for £505. The church, a spacious and handsome building, but much dilapidated, consists of a nave, chancel, and aisles, with a lofty embattled tower; it was formerly profusely ornamented with paintings, sculpture, monumental brasses, and stained glass, but the three first were destroyed in the time of Cromwell, and of the last only a few fragments remain. The house of industry for the union of Blything is situated at Bulcamp; the union comprises 49 parishes or places, and contains a population of 27,319. A portion of the ruins of the priory may still be discerned, and there are some slight remains of an ancient chapel, called Holy Rood chapel.

BLYTHFORD (*All Saints*), a parish, in the union and hundred of BLYTHING, E. division of SUFFOLK, 2¾ miles (E. by S.) from Halesworth; containing 223 inhabitants. The parish is bounded on the south by the river Blyth, and comprises 953 acres. The living is a private donative, of which the stipend is optional, in the patronage of the Rev. Jeremy Day: the impropriate tithes have been commuted for £72. The church consists of a nave and chancel, with an embattled tower; the entrances on the north and south are through decorated Norman doorways.

BLYTH-NORNEY, a hamlet, partly in the parish of BLYTH, and partly in that of HARWORTH, union of WORKSOP, Hatfield division of the wapentake of BASSETLAW, N. division of the county of NOTTINGHAM, 2 miles (N.) from Blyth; containing 75 inhabitants. It is situated on the north bank of the river Idle, and opposite to the village of Blyth.

BLYTON (*St. Martin*), a parish, in the union of GAINSBOROUGH, wapentake of CORRINGHAM, parts of

LINDSEY, county of LINCOLN, 4 miles (N. E.) from Gainsborough; containing, with the township of Wharton, 647 inhabitants, and comprising 4002a. 3r. The living is a vicarage, valued in the king's books at £12; net income, £399; patron and impropriator, the Earl of Scarborough. The tithes were commuted for land in the 36th of George III.; the vicarial portion consists of 260 acres. There is a place of worship for Wesleyans; and a school is endowed with £20 per annum.

BOARDLEY, with HETTON, a township, in the parish of BURNSALL, union of SKIPTON, E. division of the wapentake of STAINCLIFFE and EWCROSS, W. riding of YORK, 8 miles (N. N. W.) from Skipton; containing 191 inhabitants. It comprises about 4980 acres, stretching in a northern direction on both sides of a rivulet to its source; a great portion of the soil is open moorland. At the time of the inclosure, 15a. 2r. 3p. were allotted to the poor in lieu of right of commonage.

BOARHUNT, a parish, in the union of FAREHAM, hundred of PORTSDOWN, Fareham and S. divisions of the county of SOUTHAMPTON, 2 miles (N. E.) from Fareham; containing 232 inhabitants. It comprises about 8000 acres of land; the surface is marked by gentle undulations, and the soil consists of chalk, sand, and clay. From the top of Portsdown bill, which skirts the parish, is one of the finest views in England. Beneath is the harbour of Portsmouth, studded with shipping; in the distance is the famous anchorage of Spithead, while the hills of the Isle of Wight close the landscape to the sea: on the other side is a richly wooded country, chiefly planted with oak, and forming a far-extended valley which terminates at the foot of a range of hills. Portsdown fair is of fashionable resort. The living is a donative, annexed to that of Southwick: the tithes have been commuted for £47. 2. The church is in the early English style; it was formerly the chapel of a Cistercian monastery, of which there are still traces. Five chantries were founded here by William of Wykeham. There is a place of worship for Wesleyans. On that part of Portsdown within the parish, a monument has been erected in memory of Lord Nelson, which also serves as a beacon. Several Roman urns have been found in the park of Mr. Thistlethwayte.

BOARSTALL (ST. JAMES), a parish, in the union of BICESTER, hundred of ASHENDON, county of BUCKINGHAM, 7½ miles (S. S. E.) from Bicester; containing 252 inhabitants. This place formed part of the ancient demesnes of the Anglo-Saxon kings, who had a palace here, which was frequently the residence of Edward the Confessor, when enjoying the pleasure of the chase in Bernwood forest. According to tradition, corroborated by the records of the manor, the forest was at that time infested by a wild boar, which, after committing great depredation, was killed by a hunter named Nigel, to whom the king granted some lands here to be held by the tenure of cornage, or the service of a horn. Nigel erected a spacious manor-house on these lands, which continued in the possession of his descendants till the beginning of the fourteenth century, when the estate was conveyed by marriage to Richard de Handlo, who, in 1322, obtained permission of the king to fortify his mansion at Boarstall, and convert it into a castle. In the early part of the civil war, Boarstall Castle was garrisoned for the king, but was evacuated in 1644, and immediately seized by the parliamentarian forces sta-

tioned at Aylesbury: it was retaken by Col. Gage, and again garrisoned for the king; but, after holding out for some time, it was ultimately surrendered to General Fairfax, in 1646. The old mansion was demolished by the late Sir John Aubrey, and the only part remaining is the gateway tower, which is quadrangular and defended by embattled turrets at the angles, with portions of the moat by which it was surrounded, and over which is a bridge of two arches. The parish comprises by measurement 2550 acres, of which 100 are woodland, and the rest is divided between arable and pasture. It was formerly a chapelry in the parish of Oakley, from which it was separated in 1418. The living is a perpetual curacy, annexed to that of Brill; impropriator, Sir T. D. Aubrey, Bart. The church erected in 1818 by Sir John Aubrey on the site of the former edifice, is a neat building.

BOBBING (ST. BARTHOLOMEW), a parish, in the union and hundred of MILTON, Upper division of the lathe of SCRAY, E. division of KENT, 1¼ mile (W. by N.) from Milton; containing 404 inhabitants, and comprising by measurement 1070 acres, of which 157 are in wood. A fair is held on September 4th. The living is a vicarage not in charge, in the gift of the Rev. G. Simpson, who is also impropriator of one-third of the parish; the remainder is impropriate in R. Hinde, Esq. The great tithes have been commuted for £194. 12., and the vicarial for £140; there are 35 acres of glebe. The church is composed of two aisles, two chancels, and a western tower. A benefaction of £50 from Ann Gibbon has been invested in land, now producing £6. 6. per annum, for which seven girls are instructed. At Keystreet, a small hamlet in the parish, corruptly so called from Caius'-street (Caii Stratum), a Roman highway, is a gravel-pit of unusual size and depth, from which the Romans perhaps obtained part of the materials for making the road.

BOBBINGTON (ST. MARY), a parish, in the union of SEISDON, partly in the hundred of BRIMSTREE, S. division of SALOP, but chiefly in the S. division of the hundred of SEISDON and of the county of STAFFORD, 8 miles (W. N. W.) from Stourbridge; containing 418 inhabitants. It comprises 2676a. 3r. 9p., strong land, mostly arable; the surface is undulated, and the scenery highly picturesque. The living is a perpetual curacy; net income, £97; patron, T. Whitmore, Esq., of Apley Park, Salop: the tithes have been commuted for £543. The church is a neat structure, with a square tower; it was repewed in 1828. There is a place of worship for Wesleyans; also a free school built in 1792 by Hannah Cobbett, who endowed it with four acres of land and £1400 three per cents.

BOBBINGWORTH (ST. GERMAN), a parish, in the union and hundred of ONGAR, S. division of ESSEX, 2¼ miles (N. W.) from Ongar; containing 357 inhabitants. This parish, which comprises 1400 acres, is of very uneven surface, rising into hills of moderate elevation, and commanding in some parts pleasing and in others highly enriched scenery; the village is built round a pleasant green, and has a cheerful aspect. The living is a rectory, valued in the king's books at £13. 6. 8., and in the patronage of Capel Cure, Esq.: the tithes have been commuted for £446. 5., and there are 35 acres of glebe. The church, which is at some distance from the village, appears to have been erected at different periods; the chancel is the most ancient part, and has a handsome east window of the decorated English style.

BOCKENFIELD, a township, in the parish of FELTON, union of MORPETH, E. division of MORPETH ward, N. division of NORTHUMBERLAND, 8½ miles (N. by W.) from Morpeth; containing 127 inhabitants. Near this place, which lies west from Eshott and comprises 1970 acres, is an eminence called Helm-on-the-Hill, over which the road from Morpeth to Alnwick was once carried, but which is now avoided by a new branch, formed some years since, on its west side. Here was formerly a chapel.

BOCKHAMPTON, a tything, in the parish and hundred of LAMBOURN, union of HUNGERFORD, county of BERKS, ¾ of a mile (S. E. by E.) from Lambourn; containing 78 inhabitants. It comprises, by survey in 1806, 1098a. 1r. 15p.

BOCKING (ST. MARY), a parish, in the union of BRAINTREE, hundred of HINCKFORD, N. division of ESSEX, 1 mile (N.) from Braintree; containing 3437 inhabitants. The parish comprises 4490a. 1r. 12p., of which 3460 acres are arable, 617 meadow and pasture, 262 woodland, and 30 acres hop-grounds; and is intersected by the river Blackwater, which puts in motion the machinery of several corn-mills and silk-factories. The lands rest on a substratum of clay partially mixed with chalk; that portion under tillage produces fair average crops. The village, one of the most extensive in the county, has one principal street reaching to the town of Braintree, and containing several well-built houses. The living is a rectory, valued in the king's books at £35. 10., and in the gift of the Archbishop of Canterbury: the tithes have been commuted for £1360, and there are nearly 114 acres of glebe. The church, built partly of flints and stone, is a spacious and handsome structure in the early English style, with a square embattled tower, and contains many interesting monuments. John Gauden, Bishop of Worcester, established a school for boys, and endowed it with land now producing £50 per annum. An almshouse, endowed with about £8 per annum, was built by license of Henry VI., as a *Maison Dieu*, or " God's House," by John Doreward, who gave to it, and the chaplain of his chantry in the parish church, his manor of Tendring and a rentcharge on all his lands in the county; but this revenue, it is supposed, was lost at the Dissolution.

BOCKLETON (ST. MICHAEL), a parish, in the union of TENBURY, chiefly in the Upper division of the hundred of DODDINGTREE, Tenbury and W. divisions of the county of WORCESTER, but partly in the hundred of BROXASH, county of HEREFORD, 5 miles (S.) from Tenbury; containing, with the hamlet of Hampton-Charles in the latter county, 358 inhabitants. The parish comprises 2440 acres, of which 1026 are pasture, 936 arable, and 88 woodland; there are also some cider orchards and hop-grounds. The soil is in general a reddish clay, on a substratum of coarse limestone or freestone; and the surface is gently undulated. The living is a perpetual curacy; net income, £127; patrons, the Salwey family: the glebe consists of rather more than 100 acres. The church, a substantial edifice of stone, has a chancel at the east end, a tower, and two Norman doorways on the north and south; it has lately undergone considerable repair. There is a national school.

290

BOCONNOC, a parish, in the union of LISKEARD, hundred of WEST, E. division of CORNWALL, 3¾ miles (E. N. E.) from Lostwithiel; containing 312 inhabitants. In 1644, during the parliamentary war, Charles I. resided for a short time at Boconnoc House, where he had a narrow escape from assassination, having been fired at by a rebel while walking in the grounds. In the park are vestiges of lead-mines, one of which was wrought in the seventeenth century, and again about the middle of the eighteenth. The living is a discharged rectory, with which that of Broadoak was consolidated in 1742, valued in the king's books at £9. 17. 8., in the family of Grenville. The tithes of Boconnoc have been commuted for £185, and of Broadoak for £195; in the latter parish is a glebe of 83½ acres. The church contains a font of considerable beauty.

BODDINGTON (ST. MARY MAGDALENE), a parish, in the union of TEWKESBURY, partly in the Lower division of the hundred of WESTMINSTER, and partly in that of the hundred of TEWKESBURY, E. division of the county of GLOUCESTER, 3¾ miles (N. W. by W.) from Cheltenham; containing 414 inhabitants. This place is distinguished as the scene of the last great battle fought (in 893) between Alfred the Great and the Danes, who, having intrenched themselves, were surrounded by the king with the whole force of his dominions, with the view of reducing them by famine. After having been compelled to eat their horses, many perished from hunger, and the remainder made a desperate sally upon the English; a great number fell in the action, but a considerable body effected their escape. The living is annexed to the vicarage of Staverton.

BODDINGTON, LOWER and UPPER (ST. JOHN THE BAPTIST), a parish, in the union of BANBURY, hundred of CHIPPING-WARDEN, S. division of the county of NORTHAMPTON, 9¾ miles (S. W. by S.) from Daventry; containing 675 inhabitants, of whom 324 are in the lower, and 351 in the upper, division. The parish is situated on the confines of Oxfordshire and Warwickshire, the three-shire-stone which marks the bounds of the respective counties being at its western extremity. It comprises 3020a. 3r. 31p., of which 1721a. 34p. are in Upper, and 1299a. 2r. 37p. in Lower Boddington; of the former number 1286 acres are pasture, and the remainder arable, and of the latter 1088 are pasture, and the remainder arable. The surface is diversified by several elevations, and the soil is in general clayey. The living is a rectory, valued in the king's books at £20, and in the gift of Emmanuel College, Cambridge; net income, £850, derived from 470 acres of land: there is a glebe-house. The church is a very ancient edifice, with a square tower. The Wesleyans have a place of worship. The family of Lupworth, in 1600, gave 18 acres of land to the poor of Upper Boddington, who now occupy it in garden plots; the annual rent is £38, with which coal is purchased, and distributed to the poor on St. Thomas's day. Richard Lamprey, in 1758, gave a tenement for a school-house; and the interest of £300, being the amount of different benefactions, is paid to a master for instructing poor children.

BODENHAM (ST. MICHAEL), a parish, and anciently a market-town, in the union of LEOMINSTER, hundred of BROXASH, county of HEREFORD, 8½ miles (N. N. E.) from Hereford; comprising the townships of Bodenham,

Bowley, Bryan-Maund, Whitechurch-Maund, and the Moor; and containing 1017 inhabitants, of whom 341 are in the township of Bodenham. The parish is intersected by the river Lug, and comprises 4974a. 3r. 3p., of which the surface is hilly, and the soil a stiff clay. Walter Devereux, in 1379, obtained permission to hold a market on Tuesday, and a fair on the eve, day, and morrow of the Assumption of Our Lady; but they have been long discontinued. The living is a vicarage, valued in the king's books at £12. 1. 5½.; net income, £686; patrons, the family of Arkwright : the tithes were commuted for land and corn-rents in 1802; the glebe consists of 469 acres. There is a place of worship for Wesleyans; also a small endowed school. Thomas Mason, Esq., in 1773, bequeathed nine acres of land, for the benefit of poor housekeepers.

BODENHAM, WILTS.—See NUNTON.

BODHAM (ALL SAINTS), a parish, in the union of ERPINGHAM, hundred of HOLT, W. division of NORFOLK, 3¼ miles (E.) from Holt; containing 292 inhabitants. This parish comprises about 1400 acres, and has a pleasant village on an acclivity near the source of the river Glaven : the heath was inclosed in 1808, and much of it has been planted. The living is a discharged rectory, valued in the king's books at £9, and in the patronage of Thomas J. Mott, Esq. : the tithes have been commuted for £375. The church, which is in the later English style, consists of a nave and chancel, with a square embattled tower.

BODIAM (ST. GILES), a parish, in the union of TICEHURST, hundred of STAPLE, rape of HASTINGS, E. division of SUSSEX, 2 miles (S. W.) from Sandhurst, and 12 (S. S. E.) from Lamberhurst; comprising 1594 acres, and containing 377 inhabitants. A castle was erected here in 1386 by Sir Edward Dalyngrudge, which, during the civil war in the reign of Charles I., was dismantled by the parliamentarian troops; the remains are in some parts tolerably entire, and the whole, though in a dilapidated state, still forms a stately and magnificent pile. The parish is bounded on the south by the river Rother, which is here navigable; and on the north and north-east by the county of Kent. The living is a vicarage endowed with the rectorial tithes, valued in the king's books at £6. 18. 6½.; patron, the Rev. J. Image. The tithes have been enumerated for £320, and the glebe comprises 10 acres. The church is a neat edifice in the later English style, with a low square embattled tower.

BODICOT, a chapelry, in the parish of EAST ADDERBURY, union of BANBURY, hundred of BLOXHAM, county of OXFORD, 1¾ mile (S. by E.) from Banbury; containing 729 inhabitants. It comprises about 1240 acres; the surface is gently undulated, and the scenery generally of pleasing character. On the north-eastern boundary flows the river Cherwell, which here separates the county from Northamptonshire; the chapelry is intersected by the Oxford canal, which runs near to and almost parallel with the river, and the road leading from Banbury southward to East Adderbury runs through the village. The chapel, dedicated to St. John the Baptist, was nearly wholly rebuilt, and reconsecrated in April, 1844; the cost amounted to £1575 : the tower is on the north side. There is a place of worship for Particular Baptists. Bodicot Cross was standing in the middle of the village, until the early part of the present century.

Corporation Seal.

BODMIN (ST. PETROCK); a parish, and the head of a union, in the hundred of TRIGG, E. division of CORNWALL; containing, with the municipal borough of Bodmin, 4643 inhabitants, of whom 4025 are in the borough, 20½ miles (S. W. by W.) from Launceston, and 234½ (W. S. W.) from London, on the western road. This place, in the Cornish language called *Bosvenna*, "the houses on the hill," and in ancient charters *Bos-mana* and *Bod-minian*, "the abode of the monks," owes its origin to a MONASTERY founded by King Athelstan, in 936, on the site of a cell for four brethren established by St. Petrock about 518, and which had been previously a solitary hermitage, originally occupied by St. Guron. Historians are widely at variance concerning the claims which Bodmin possesses to the distinction of having been the primary seat of the bishopric of Cornwall. Dr. Borlase, whose opinion has been entertained by others, states that Edward the Elder in 905 conferred upon it this honour, which it retained till 981, when, the town, church, and monastery having been burnt by the Danes, the episcopal chair was removed to St. Germans. But this has been strenuously combated by Mr. Whitaker, in his work entitled *The Ancient Cathedral of Cornwall Historically Surveyed*, in which he shows that the see was founded in 614, and that St. Germans was made the original seat of it; asserting, on the authority of a grant by King Ethelred, that the monastery of Bodmin was annexed by that monarch, in 994, to the episcopate of St. Germans, and that both places combined to furnish a title to the future prelates until the annexation of the bishopric of Cornwall to that of Crediton, in the county of Devon, in 1031, about twenty years after which Exeter was made the head of the diocese. He refers the Danish conflagration to the monastery of St. Petrock at Padstow, and in this conclusion he is borne out by the flourishing state of the church at Bodmin, as described in Domesday book, where its possessions are enumerated, including 68 houses, with the privilege of a market. This religious house, under different renewals of the establishment, the last of which was by one Algar, in 1125, appears to have been successively inhabited by Benedictine monks, nuns, secular priests, monks again, and canons regular of the order of St. Augustine, whose prior, from the circumstance of his possessing a gallows and a pillory, had evidently the power of inflicting capital punishment. Its revenue at the Dissolution amounted to £289. 11. 11.: the site and demesne were granted to Thomas Sternhold, one of the first translators of the Psalms into English metre. St. Petrock was buried here; for, says Leland, "the shrine and tumbe of St. Petrok yet stondith in thest part of the chirche."

The town appears to have increased rapidly after the Conquest. Leland describes the market as being "lyke a fair for the confluence of people," and enumerates, in addition to the parochial church and the cantuary chapel near it, two other chapels; a house and church of Grey friars, begun by John of London, a merchant, about

1239, augmented by Edward, Earl of Cornwall, and in the time of Elizabeth converted into a house of correction for the county; and two hospitals, dedicated respectively to St. Anthony and St. George; besides the hospital of St. Lawrence, a mile off. Norden, also, says, "It hath been of larger recite than now it is,.as appeareth by the ruynes of sundrye buyldings decayde." William of Worcester, citing the register in the church belonging to the Grey friars, states that 1500 of the inhabitants died of the plague, about the middle of the fourteenth century. It was one of those decayed towns in the county to repair which an act was passed in the 32nd of Henry VIII.

In 1496, Perkin Warbeck, the pretended duke of York, on landing in Cornwall, assembled here a force of 3000 men, with which he marched to attack the city of Exeter; and in 1498, an insurrection of the Cornish men was organized, under the influence of Thomas Flammoc, a lawyer, and Michael Joseph, a farrier, in this town, who, being chosen leaders, conducted the insurgents to Wells, where they were joined by Lord Audley, who placed himself at their head. The rebels continued their march into Kent, and encamped at Eltham, where, in the battle of Blackheath, they were surrounded by the king's troops, made prisoners, and dismissed without further punishment; but Lord Audley, Flammoc, and Joseph, were executed as ringleaders. During the depression of trade and agriculture, in the reign of Edward VI., the Cornish men, attributing their distresses to the Reformation, assembled at Bodmin to the number of 10,000, under the command of Humphrey Arundel, governor of St. Michael's Mount, and, being countenanced by the inhabitants, encamped at Castle Canyke, near the town. The insurgents marched thence to besiege Exeter, demanding the re-establishment of the mass and the restoration of the abbey lands; but, after having reduced the inhabitants of that city to extreme privation, they were defeated by Lord Russell, who had been sent with a reinforcement to the relief of the citizens. Subsequently to their dispersion, Sir Anthony Kingston, provost-marshal, who had been sent to Bodmin to punish the insurgents, is said to have hanged the mayor at his own door, after having been hospitably entertained in his house. During the civil war in the reign of Charles I., the town, which had no permanent garrison, was alternately occupied by each party, till, in 1646, General Fairfax finally took possession of it for the parliament. After the Restoration, Charles II. visited the place on his journey to Scilly, and humorously declared it to be the most polite town through which he had passed, "one-half of the houses being prostrate, and the remainder uncovered."

The TOWN is situated on a gentle elevation rising out of a vale, between two hills, almost in the centre of the county: it consists of several streets, the principal of which is a mile in length; it is well paved, and the inhabitants are amply supplied with water. The races, which formerly took place annually after the summer assizes, have been discontinued for several years; the course, which is one of the best in England, is about a mile and a half distant. In July an annual procession of the populace, on horseback and on foot, carrying garlands of flowers, was till lately made to a place in the vicinity, called Halgaver Moor: this ceremony, the memorial of some ancient festival, was called "Bodmin

Riding." The manufacture of bone lace, which formerly flourished, has given place to that of shoes, a great quantity of which is exposed for sale in the neighbouring markets and fairs; there are also a large tan-yard and a brewery. A railway has been constructed to Wadebridge. The market is on Saturday: fairs are held on Jan. 25th, the Saturday preceding Palm-Sunday, the Tuesday and Wednesday before Whitsuntide, July 6th, and Dec. 6th, for horses and horned-cattle; large cattle-fairs are also held in the hamlet of St. Lawrence on Aug. 21st, and Oct. 29th and 30th. The inhabitants were incorporated in the 12th century, by Richard, Earl of Cornwall; and charters were subsequently granted by Edward III., Richard II., Elizabeth, and George III. By the act of the 5th and 6th of William IV., c. 76, the corporation now consists of a mayor, four aldermen, and twelve councillors, of whom the mayor and late mayor are justices of the peace, and hold petty-sessions weekly for the borough. The shire-hall is a substantial building of granite, 104 feet long and 56 broad, erected by the county, at an expense of £8000, upon a portion of the site of the ancient convent of Grey friars; it was first opened at the Midsummer sessions of 1838. Nearly adjoining, elegant and commodious lodgings for the accommodation of the judges of assize were erected by the town-council, at an expense of nearly £4000; and in consequence of these improvements, both the assizes were, by order of the privy council, July 6th, 1838, appointed to be holden at Bodmin, the summer assize only having been previously held here. The quarter-sessions for the county are also held at the place. The powers of the county debt-court of Bodmin, established in 1847, extend over the registration-district of Bodmin. The elective franchise was conferred in the 23rd of Edward I., since which time the borough has continued to return two members: the limits of the borough were extended for parliamentary purposes, in 1832, to 13,651 acres; the mayor is returning officer. The county gaol and house of correction, built in 1780 on Mr. Howard's plan, and since greatly enlarged for the proper classification of prisoners, is a neat and compact building.

The parish comprises 4586 acres, whereof 330 are common or waste. The LIVING is a discharged vicarage, valued in the king's books at £13. 6. 8., and in the gift of Lady Basset; net income, £283. The church, formerly the conventual church of the monastery, was rebuilt in 1472, and is a spacious structure chiefly in the later style of English architecture, with a venerable tower on the north side, formerly surmounted by a lofty spire, which was destroyed by lightning in 1699; the interior contains some exquisitely carved oak, a large Norman font curiously sculptured, and several interesting monuments. Near the altar was a small chapel, taken down in 1776, in which the shrine of St. Petrock was preserved till the Reformation; and at the north side of the chancel is a fine altar-tomb of grey marble, resembling that of Henry VII. in Westminster Abbey, and on which is a recumbent effigy of Prior Vivian, removed from the ancient priory. In the churchyard is a building supposed to have been a chantry chapel, dedicated to St. Thomas, with a crypt underneath; it was used, until a few years since, for the free grammar school, and is at present occupied as a national school for girls. There are places of worship for Bryanites, the Connexion of the Countess of Huntingdon, and Wesleyans. The grammar school was founded by Queen Elizabeth, who endowed it with £4. 13. 8. per annum, payable out of the exchequer : no appointment has been made since the death of the late master. The poor law union of Bodmin comprises 21 parishes or places, and contains a population of 20,800. The county lunatic asylum was built here in 1820, at an expense of £15,177, including the furniture; it is of an octagonal form, consisting of six ranges, each containing two galleries.

About a mile to the west of the town are some remains of the hospital of St. Lawrence, originally endowed for nineteen lepers, two sound men and women, and a priest, who were incorporated by Queen Elizabeth in 1582, from whom they received the grant of a market, now discontinued, and two fairs, still held. There are three intrenchments in the parish, namely, Castle Canyke, the Beacon (near the town), and one in Dunmere wood; and above the ford at Nantallon a Roman camp has lately been discovered, in which coins of Vespasian and Trajan, and some pottery were found. On the north side of the town is a ruined tower, called Berry Tower, 418 feet above the level of the sea; it belonged to the chapel of the Holy Rood, and was built in the reign of Henry VII.

BODNEY (St. Mary), a parish, in the union of Swaffham, hundred of South Greenhoe, W. division of the county of Norfolk, 9 miles (N. N. E.) from Brandon ; containing 98 inhabitants. This parish comprises 2605a. 18p., of which 1384 acres are arable, 1177 meadow and pasture, and 43 woodland and plantations ; much ground is also rabbit-warren. The ancient Hall was for some time the retreat of the nuns of Montargis, of whom Eloise Adelaide de Bourbon, daughter of the Prince-de Condé, assumed the veil here in 1805, and is interred at this place. The house has been rebuilt in a handsome style. The living is a discharged rectory, united to that of Great Cressingham, valued in the king's books at £6. 7. 3½. : the tithes have been commuted for £195. The church is a plain thatched building, with an ornamented window, and a wooden belfry.

BOGNOR, a market and post town, chapelry, and bathing-place, in the parish of South Bersted, hundred of Aldwick, rape of Chichester, W. division of Sussex, 7 miles (S. E.) from Chichester, and 67 (S. W. by S.) from London ; containing 576 inhabitants. This place, anciently called *Bogenor*, implying, in the Saxon language, " a rocky shore," was prior to 1790 an insignificant village, inhabited only by a few labourers and fishermen; but in that year, Sir Richard Hotham, Knt., perceiving the natural advantages which it possessed, erected a handsome villa for his own residence, and several lodging-houses, which he furnished at considerable expense for the accommodation of visiters. The town is chiefly resorted to by persons suffering from pulmonary complaints, and such as dislike the tumult and expense of more populous watering-places ; it has also been visited by numerous members of the royal family. The whole is divided into Upper and Lower ; the former consisting of several beautiful marine villas, standing in grounds tastefully laid out ; the latter comprising the town, pleasantly situated near the peninsula of Selsey, on a plain at the foot of the South Down

293

hills, which shelter it from the north and east winds. The parade and drive along the coast have of late years been greatly improved, and extend about two miles, forming a delightful promenade, and commanding most extensive sea and land views.

The town is paved, macadamized, and supplied with water from pumps; and its internal regulation, under a general act of improvement passed in 1835, is vested in a body of commissioners. On the Steine are warm and cold baths, conveniently arranged ; and for those who prefer the open sea there are numerous bathing-machines on the beach. Here are two subscription libraries ; and a handsome assembly-room, with refreshment and other apartments, erected in 1837. Races occasionally take place on the sands. Bognor is celebrated for prawns and the silver-mullet, great quantities of which are sent to London and Brighton ; and off the coast are extensive oyster-beds. A large brewery here is noted for its ale ; and there is a small manufactory for Roman cement, made from the Kidney rock which abounds in the sands. The Brighton and Portsmouth railway passes a few miles to the north of the town. The markets, established within a few years, and for which a market-place has been erected, are on Thursday and Saturday ; and a fair is held on the 5th and 6th of July. The living is a perpetual curacy ; patron, the Archbishop of Canterbury ; net income, £107, with a good residence. The chapel, dedicated to St. John, is a neat building, with an embattled tower at the east end ; it was consecrated in 1822. There are places of worship for Independents and Wesleyans. In opening the rocks, various fossils have been discovered ; beautiful agates and pebbles, and, after storms and high tides, pyrites, are found in profusion on the beach.

BOLAM, a township, in the parish of Gainford, union of Auckland, S. W. division of Darlington ward, S. division of the county of Durham, 5 miles (S. by W.) from Bishop-Auckland ; containing 119 inhabitants. It is situated on a lofty ridge of limestone, commanding an extensive prospect to the south and west ; and comprises 950 acres, of which 500 are arable, 438 grass land, and 12 wood : the soil, with a trifling exception of cold clay, is productive. The township is remarkable for a whinstone dyke, which proves itself to be of later formation than the coal-field through which it runs, as the coal is, on both sides of the stone where they have come into contact, converted into cinders : this dyke, the vein of which in some parts is twelve yards wide, extends from Cockfield to the east, in a direction nearly west, as far as has yet been ascertained, and is much used. This dyke may be traced in a line through nearly the whole of the northern counties. Ironstone is found here in abundance ; and the whinstone dyke before mentioned crosses the township. The quarries are worked, supplying a material for the repair of roads. The rectorial tithes have been commuted for £62. 10., payable to Trinity College, Cambridge, and the vicarial for £46. 10. A chapel has been recently erected. William Garth, father of the celebrated Sir Samuel, physician and poet, was a landowner in the place ; and the name of the family occurs twice in the parochial register of Gainford in the year 1747.

BOLAM (St. Andrew), a parish, in the union, and partly in the W. division, of Castle ward, but chiefly in the W. division of Morpeth ward and N. E. division of Tindale ward, N. and S. divisions of Northumberland ; comprising the townships of Trewick, Bolam, Bolam-Vicarage, Gallow-Hill, Belsay, Bradford, Harnham, and Shortflatt ; and containing 603 inhabitants, of whom 66 are in the township of Bolam, and 17 in that of Bolam-Vicarage, 9½ miles (W. S. W.) from Morpeth. It derives its name from being situated on a *bol*,

.or high swell of land. The old town of Bolam had its
grant of a market and fair from Edward I., and consisted of a castle, a church, and two rows of houses
running from east to west : the tower of the castle was
standing some years since ; and on the commanding
hill near Bolam House, the seat of Lord Decies, where
it stood, are intrenchments of a period anterior to the
Conquest. The parish comprises upwards of 7000
acres, of which 1116 are in the township of Bolam. A
large portion of the soil is a dark earth resting on clay,
and there are fine portions of a sandy loam with a substratum of freestone, and also coal and limestone ; in
the township of Bolam a great part is rich grass land,
interspersed with many thriving plantations, and a small
but picturesque lake has been formed by the noble
owner. The living is a vicarage, valued in the king's
books at £6. 13. 4., and in the patronage of the Crown :
the great tithes have been commuted for £247. 3. 8.,
and the vicarial for £72. 10. 6. ; the glebe consists of
about 130 acres. The township of Bolam-Vicarage
comprises only the glebe land, lying on the eastern side
of the church, which is of the Norman style. A branch
of the Watling-street, called the "Devil's Causeway,"
may be distinctly traced about a mile westward ; and
near it are two large barrows, and a stone pillar of rude
form, with a tumulus which, on being opened, was found
to contain a coffin. On an intrenched rock, on the
north-east side of Bolam moor, is a British camp.

BOLAS, GREAT (St. John the Baptist), a parish,
in the union of Wellington, Newport division of the
hundred of South Bradford, N. division of Salop,
7 miles (N.) from Wellington ; containing 288 inhabitants. This parish, which is situated on the road from
Wellington to Drayton, comprises by measurement 1845
acres ; the surface is pleasingly varied, and watered by
the rivers Mees and Terne, which add greatly to the
fertility of the soil and beauty of the scenery. There are
two quarries of red sandstone, used for building. The
living is a rectory, valued in the king's books at £7. 9. 4½.,
and in the patronage of Lord Hill : the tithes have been
commuted for £330, and there are about 49 acres of
glebe. The church is a plain neat edifice, of comparatively modern erection, and in good repair.

BOLD, a township, in the parish and union of
Prescot, hundred of West Derby, S. division of the
county of Lancaster, 4½ miles (E. S. E.) from Prescot ;
containing 712 inhabitants. The family of Bold resided
here even previously to the Conquest, and preserved an
uninterrupted succession of male heirs down to the time
of Peter Bold, Esq., parliamentary representative for the
county, who died in 1761. The whole estate passed, in
1803, from his daughter Anna Maria to the husband of
her sister, Thomas Patten, Esq., who assumed the name
of Bold ; and by an heiress of the latter family, it became vested in the Hoghtons, of Hoghton Tower. The
present elegant mansion of Bold Hall was built after a
design by Leoni : the old Hall, a curious edifice, is now
the farming-house belonging to it. The township comprises 4261 acres of land. The impropriate tithes have
been commuted for £335. 17., payable to Trinity College, Cambridge, and the vicarial for £117. 19. 5. The
Rev. Richard Barnes, promoted to the see of Carlisle
in 1570, and to that of Durham in 1577 ; and his
brother, John Barnes, the chancellor, were natives of the
place.

the year 1724, and reckoned among his ancestors the amiable reformer, Bernard Gilpin; he died here, April 5th, 1804.

BOLDRON, a township, in the parish of BOWES, union of TEESDALE, wapentake of GILLING-WEST, N. riding of YORK, 2 miles (S. W. by S.) from Barnard-Castle; containing 169 inhabitants. It lies in the manor of Bowes, and comprises by computation 1340 acres. The road from Brough to Barnard-Castle passes north of the village. The impropriate tithes have been commuted for £80.

BOLE (*ST. MARTIN*), a parish, in the union of GAINSBOROUGH, North-Clay division of the wapentake of BASSETLAW, N. division of the county of NOTTING-HAM, 3½ miles (S. W. by S.) from Gainsborough; containing 191 inhabitants. It comprises about 1460 acres of land, of which the soil is a strong clay producing excellent red wheat, and the surface flat and liable to inundations from the river Trent, which divides the parish from the county of Lincoln. The Bole ferry is now a mile distant from the village; the river, about twenty years ago, having formed a new course. The living is a discharged vicarage, valued in the king's books at £4. 13. 4.; net income, £84; patron, the Bishop of Lincoln: there are 20 acres of glebe. The church is a small ancient structure, and has a handsome pinnacled tower with three bells.

BOLEHALL, with GLASCOTE, a township, in the parish and union of TAMWORTH, Tamworth division of the hundred of HEMLINGFORD, N. division of the county of WARWICK, 1 mile (S. S. E.) from Tamworth; containing 495 inhabitants, and comprising 1193 acres. The road from Atherstone to Tamworth crosses the township, which is also intersected by the Coventry canal and the Birmingham and Derby railway.

BOLINGBROKE (*ST. PETER AND ST. PAUL*), a parish, in the union of SPILSBY, W. division of the soke of BOLINGBROKE, parts of LINDSEY, county of LINCOLN, 30 miles (E. S. E.) from Lincoln, and 129 (N.) from London; containing 919 inhabitants. A castle was built by William de Romara, Earl of Lincoln, of which his descendant, Alicia de Lacey, was dispossessed by Edward II. Henry IV. was born in this fortress, and from it took the name of Henry of Bolingbroke: it was nearly demolished in the civil wars, the south-west tower being all that remains. At this period also the church suffered so considerably, that it was almost reduced to a ruin; one aisle of it only has been rebuilt, at the corner of which is a low tower. Bolingbroke is situated in a wide and pleasant valley, near the source of a small river which runs into the Witham: the public road passing through the town to Spilsby, has been superseded by a new line about two miles distant, which ascends Keal Hill. There is a manufactory for earthenware. The market formerly held on Tuesday has been discontinued, but a fair is still held on St. Peter's day. The living is a discharged rectory, to which that of Hareby was united in 1739, valued in the king's books at £9. 19. 2., and in the gift of the family of Bosanquet: the glebe consists of 345 acres, the income of which amounts to £456; and an excellent parsonage-house has lately been built, at a cost of £2000. There is a place of worship for Wesleyans; also a free school, with a trifling endowment in land. The village and district of New Bolingbroke have lately risen up on lands in the

295

fen belonging to Bolingbroke; a curate has been appointed by the rector.

BOLLIN-FEE, a township, in the parish of WILMS-LOW, union of ALTRINCHAM, hundred of MACCLESFIELD, N. division of the county of CHESTER, 6 miles (S. W.) from Stockport; containing 2212 inhabitants. The township comprises 2484 acres, of which 89 are common or waste; the soil is principally clay. The tithes have been commuted for £378, and there is a glebe of 71 acres.

BOLLINGTON, a township, partly in the parish of ROSTHERN, but chiefly in that of BOWDON, union of ALTRINCHAM, hundred of BUCKLOW, N. division of the county of CHESTER, 5½ miles (N. by W.) from Nether Knutsford; containing 316 inhabitants. The manor was anciently parcel of the barony of Dunham-Massey. Hamo, one of the barons, gave a moiety of it with his daughter to Geffery Dutton, from whose descendants the portion passed by a female heir to the Radcliffes, earls of Sussex, and by sale to the Carringtons, from whom it came, through the Booths, to the earls of Stamford and Warrington, afterwards possessors of the whole estate. The township consists of 585 acres. The tithes of that part in the parish of Bowdon have been commuted for £30 payable to the Bishop of Chester, and £15 to the vicar of Bowdon. At a place called Pump hill is a tumulus, in which human bones have been found.

BOLLINGTON, a township, in the parish of PREST-BURY, union and hundred of MACCLESFIELD, N. division of the county of CHESTER, 2½ miles (N. by E.) from Macclesfield; containing 4350 inhabitants. In this township are 1120 acres, of a sandy and a clayey soil. The village lies on the banks of a small stream called the Bolling, from which its name is derived. For more than twenty years it has been exceedingly prosperous: there are cotton and silk factories, and collieries; and at Kerridge Hill, which is partly in this township and partly in that of Rainow, are quarries of freestone and slate, worked to a considerable extent, the produce being chiefly sent to the neighbouring towns. The Macclesfield canal passes through the township. A district church dedicated to St. John, erected by grant from the Parliamentary Commissioners, was consecrated July 7th, 1834: the living is a perpetual curacy, in the gift of the Vicar, with a net income of £174. The Wesleyans have a meeting-house.

BOLLOM, a hamlet, in the parish of CLARE-BOROUGH, union of RETFORD, North-Clay division of the wapentake of BASSETLAW, N. division of the county of NOTTINGHAM, 1 mile (N.) from Retford; containing 103 inhabitants. This is a romantic place, on the east side of the river Idle; and comprises 223 acres of land. Half a mile eastward are some cottages called Bollom-lane Houses. There was anciently a chapel, the site of which is still called Chapel yard.

BOLNEY (*ST. MARY MAGDALENE*), a parish, in the union of CUCKFIELD, partly in the hundred of BUTTING-HILL, but chiefly in the half-hundred of WYNDHAM, rape of LEWES, E. division of SUSSEX, 3½ miles (W. S. W.) from Cuckfield; containing 713 inhabitants. It comprises 3482 acres, of which 42 are common or waste. The London and Brighton road by way of Hixted passes through the parish, within half a mile of the village. The land is chiefly arable and pasture, with a tract of wood forming part of the forest of St. Leonard; it is generally poor, being a thin soil over sandstone, but in some places there is a good stiff clay. Sandstone abounds, and iron-ore is found. The living is a discharged vicarage, valued in the king's books at £5. 5. 2½.; patron, the Prebendary of Hove in the Cathedral of Chichester; impropriators, W. and C. Marshall, Esqrs.; net income, £162.

BOLNHURST (ST. DUNSTAN), a parish, in the hundred of STODDEN, union and county of BEDFORD, 7 miles (N. by E.) from Bedford, on the road to Kimbolton; containing 344 inhabitants. It comprises 2166a. 3r. 13p., of which the surface is undulated, and the soil a stiff cold clay. The living is a rectory, endowed with only one-third of the tithes, and valued in the king's books at £9; net income, £159; patron, the Rev. H. W. Gery; impropriators of the remaining two-thirds of the tithes, Capt. Duberly and others.

BOLSOVER (ST. MARY), a parish, and formerly a market-town, in the union of CHESTERFIELD, hundred of SCARSDALE, N. division of the county of DERBY, 6 miles (E. by S.) from Chesterfield, 28½ (N. N. E.) from Derby, and 145½ (N. by W.) from London; containing, with the hamlets of Glapwell, Ockley, Whaley, Oxcroft, Stanfree, Shuttlewood, Woodside, and Woodhouse, 1512 inhabitants. This place, called Belesoure prior to the Conquest, was noted for a CASTLE erected immediately after by William Peveril, who had obtained the grant of several manors in England. The castle, which was remarkably strong, on the extinction of the Peveril family became a royal fortress, and sustained a siege in the war of the barons, by whom, together with the Castle of the Peak, it was garrisoned against King John. In 1215, William, Earl of Ferrers, retook both these castles from the barons, and was made governor of them, as a reward for his fidelity. In the reign of Henry VII. the castle became the property of the Earl of Shrewsbury, and in that of Elizabeth was given to his step-son, Sir Charles Cavendish, who rebuilt the greater portion of it, and erected a magnificent suite of state apartments on the site of the original Norman structure, which had become ruinous. His eldest son, William, afterwards Duke of Newcastle, erected the spacious riding-house, and the long range of buildings, now in ruins, which crown the beautiful terrace. In these stately and splendid halls he thrice entertained Charles I. and his court, and upon one occasion, when the queen was present, expended £15,000. During the civil war, while the duke was abroad, the castle sustained a siege, and, after being defended for some time by the Marquess of Newcastle, surrendered to the parliamentarians, from whom it was purchased by Sir Charles, the duke's younger brother. The Duke of Portland, who is proprietor of the castle, and lord of the manor of Bolsover, inherits from the Cavendish family. The keep is in an excellent state of preservation, and is at present the residence of the Rev. J. H. Gray, vicar of Bolsover; it occupies a lofty eminence commanding an extensive prospect.

The TOWN is large and well built, and is pleasantly situated on rising ground, environed on every side, except where the ground forms a natural rampart, with a deep intrenchment. The chief pursuit of the inhabitants is agriculture; at present no manufacture is carried on, but formerly the place was celebrated for buckles

and tobacco-pipes. Facility of conveyance is afforded by the Midland railway, which has a station at Chesterfield; and to the east of the town is the road from Mansfield to Rotherham. It is within the jurisdiction of the court for the honour of Peveril, held at Lenton, near Nottingham: a court leet belonging to the lord of the manor is held every third week, for the recovery of debts under 40s.; and there is a fair on Midsummer-day. The PARISH comprises 4590 acres of land, whereof 82 are wood. South-west of the town the surface declines to a fine open valley, and on the east approaches to a level undulating country; the scenery of the valley is exceedingly beautiful, and in the distance is seen hill rising over hill for more than twenty miles. The soil is calcareous, and the substratum consists of thick beds of limestone of two or three varieties. The quarries here supply excellent building-stone, which is extensively used in the town and neighbourhood, and has been raised for the erection of parts of the new houses of parliament; the material is of a durable nature, but more suitable for exterior than inner work. Coal-mines, also, are wrought, on a limited scale. The chief proprietor of land, after the Duke of Portland, is the Duke of Devonshire; and there are a great number of other owners, the farms being generally small.

The LIVING is a discharged vicarage, valued in the king's books at £5. 19. 4.; net income, about £110; patron and impropriator, the Duke of Portland, who receives about £800 per annum as tithe rent: the glebe consists of 28 acres of arable land. The church, situated in the town, is a spacious structure, and consists of a nave, chancel, and south aisle: it is said to be partly Norman, but is probably of later construction; with the exception of an arch, the general style is early English, of which the spire is a good specimen. In the chancel is a mutilated piece of sculpture, of very ancient workmanship, representing the Virgin and the Infant Jesus, and, perhaps, the Magi; with camels looking over the manger. The Cavendish family have a sepulchral chapel, terminating the aisle; it was built in 1618, and contains some very splendid monuments: in one corner of the chancel, also, is a flat stone, with an inscription round it in square letters, and a number of figures in outline, evidently of great age. The Wesleyans and Independents have places of worship; that belonging to the latter was formerly a Presbyterian chapel, in which Archbishop Secker officiated for some time. An endowed school was built in 1755 by the Countess of Oxford and Mortimer: it had dwindled into insignificance, and become almost useless; but in 1844 was placed under the National Society, and opened on an improved system. Mrs. Isabella Smithson, in 1761, bequeathed £2000 to the poor of Bolsover; the payment being resisted by her executors, a suit was instituted, and in 1770 the full amount, with £956 interest, was recovered. The annual proceeds are chiefly paid as marriage portions, of £25 each, to five young women of the parish; and in default of that number of young women in any year, the portions unclaimed, and the residue, are appropriated in sums not exceeding three guineas annually, to poor persons upwards of 55 years of age. The Duke of Portland lately set apart some land as allotments for the poor, and about 135 families have already been assigned plots of ground. In the parish is a ferruginous spring; and partly inclosing the

conferred upon matters affecting their respective interests; and on the 5th of Sept., in the 5th of Henry VIII., a short time previously to the battle of Branxton, a congress was held here, at which several noblemen and other distinguished persons, with a train of about 26,000 troops, were present. An hospital for a master, three chaplains, thirteen lepers, and other lay brethren, was founded and endowed prior to 1225, by Robert de Roos, Baron of Wark, in honour of St. Thomas the Martyr, or the Holy Trinity, and made subordinate to the abbey of Rivaulx, and the priory of Kirkham, in Yorkshire. Several stone chests, and urns containing ashes, charcoal, and fragments of human bones, together with a celt, have been discovered at a short distance from the place. The tithes here of the Dean and Chapter of Durham have been commuted for £196.

BOLTON, a chapelry, in the parish of MORLAND, WEST ward and union, county of WESTMORLAND, 4 miles (N. W. by W.) from Appleby; containing 383 inhabitants. About a mile north of the village, an iron bridge, thirty yards in length, was constructed across the Eden, at the expense of the landowners on both sides of the river, in 1816. The living is a perpetual curacy; net income, £80; patron, the Vicar of Morland : the tithes were commuted for land in 1808. The chapel is dedicated to All Saints. A meeting-house for Methodists was built in 1818; and there is a free school endowed with £13 per annum.

BOLTON, a township, in the parish of BISHOP-WILTON, union of POCKLINGTON, Wilton-Beacon division of the wapentake of HARTHILL, E. riding of YORK, 2¾ miles (N. W.) from Pocklington; containing 98 inhabitants. It comprises 960 acres by computation; and has a neat and pleasant village seated on a gentle acclivity. The vicarial tithes have been commuted for £41. 4. 6., and the impropriate for £6. 2. There is a place of worship for Wesleyans.

BOLTON, a township, in the parish of CALVERLEY, union of BRADFORD, wapentake of MORLEY, W. riding of YORK, 1½ mile (N. N. E.) from Bradford; containing 683 inhabitants. This township, including the hamlets of Hodgsonfold, Lowfold, and Outlanes, with part of the hamlet of Undercliffe, comprises by measurement 699 acres; the surface is varied, and the scenery of pleasing character. There are quarries of slate and flagstone in full operation; and the Bradford canal passes through the township. The Wesleyans have a place of worship.

BOLTON-ABBEY, a chapelry and township, in the parish and union of SKIPTON, E. division of the wapentake of STAINCLIFFE and EWCROSS, W. riding of YORK, 6 miles (E. N. E.) from Skipton; the township containing 127 inhabitants. This place derives its name from its magnificent abbey of canons regular of the order of St. Augustine, founded originally at Embsay, and dedicated to the Virgin Mary and St. Cuthbert, by William de Meschines and Cecilia his wife, in 1121, and removed to this place, about the year 1151, by their daughter and heiress Adeliza, who had married William Fitz-Duncan, nephew of the King of Scotland. The establishment continued to flourish till the Dissolution, when its revenues were estimated at £302. 9. 3. Of this once stately and magnificent structure the nave is perfect, and appropriated as a parochial chapel; the north and south transepts and the choir are in ruins. The choir, which is the most ancient part of the church, is in the Norman style of architecture, with later insertions; the windows, apparently altered from the original openings, are in the decorated English style. The township comprises by computation 3000 acres, situated in the vale of the river Wharfe, which pursues its varied course through a district abounding with scenery of romantic character, combining features of intense interest, among which the venerable remains of the abbey are conspicuous. The acclivities that inclose the vale are in some parts richly wooded; and in others, masses of rugged rock rise precipitously from the margin of the river, which flows almost under the east window of the abbey. Towards the north of the ruins is a verdant expanse of level lawn, studded at intervals with clusters of elm and ash of stately growth, and skirted by a thick wood of oak, interspersed with protruding rocks of barren aspect. In the distance are the venerable groves of Bolton Park, beyond which are seen the craggy heights of Simonseat and Bardon Fell, finely contrasting with the softer beauties of the luxuriant vale, which, gradually contracting its limits, scarcely affords a passage for the Wharfe between the densely wooded banks which overhang its stream. In this part of the vale is a beautifully picturesque cascade, formed by a tributary of the Wharfe descending from a rocky glen into the river, near its disappearance in the deep cleft of a rock which obstructs its course. The road leading from Skipton to Harrogate passes at the distance of about half a mile from the abbey. The living is a perpetual curacy; net income, £111; patron, the Duke of Devonshire. A free grammar school was founded in 1697, by the Hon. Robert Boyle. who endowed it with a rent-charge of £20, and other property, making in the aggregate an income of £100; the master has a good house and garden.

BOLTON-BY-BOWLAND (St. Peter), a parish, in the union of Clitheroe, wapentake of Staincliffe and Ewcross, W. riding of York, 3½ miles (W.) from Gisburn, and 15 (W. by S.) from Skipton; containing 993 inhabitants. This place was anciently owned by the Pudsey family of Bolton Hall, of whom Sir Ralph Pudsey afforded to Henry VI. an asylum in his mansion after the battle of Hexham. The parish comprises by computation 4940 acres; the lands are mostly in good cultivation, and the prevailing scenery is pleasingly diversified. Bolton Hall is an ancient mansion, beautifully situated in an extensive and tastefully embellished demesne; in one of the apartments, a pair of boots, a pair of gloves, and a spoon, left here by Henry VI., are carefully preserved. The village stands on one of the streams flowing into the river Ribble; a large fair, chiefly for cattle, is held in it on the 28th of June and two following days. The living is a rectory, valued in the king's books at £11. 13. 4., and in the patronage of Mrs. Littledale: the tithes have been commuted for £335, and the glebe comprises 100 acres, with a good house. The church is a venerable structure, in the later English style, having a square embattled tower, and contains a monument to Sir Ralph Pudsey, with a slab of grey Craven limestone, on which are sculptured in bold relief the effigies of himself, his three wives, and twenty-five children. The Independents have a place of worship. There is a spring at Fooden, strongly impregnated with sulphur; and at Holden is a picturesque cascade.

BOLTON-CASTLE, a chapelry, in the parish of Wensley, union of Leyburn, wapentake of Hang-

WEST, N. riding of York, 7¼ miles (N. W. by W.) from Middleham; containing 230 inhabitants. On the brow of a hill are the ruins of a castle built by Richard, Lord Scrope, chancellor of England in the reign of Richard II., and endowed with £106. 15. 4. per annum, for a chantry of six chaplains. Mary, Queen of Scots, was kept a prisoner here for about two years, and was removed hence to Tutbury in 1569; she inscribed her name on a pane of glass, which was removed to Bolton Hall a few years since. During the parliamentary war, the castle was defended for the king by Colonel Scrope and a party of the Richmondshire militia, and sustained a pressing siege, which terminated in its surrender to the insurgents in 1645. The north-eastern tower fell down in 1761, and the eastern and northern sides are entirely in ruins; the west front is in good repair. The living is a perpetual curacy, with that of Redmire annexed; net income, £115; patron, the Rector of Wensley. The chapel is dedicated to St. Oswald.

BOLTON-LE-MOORS (St. Peter), a parish, and the head of a union, in the hundred of Salford, S. division of the county of Lancaster; comprising the borough and market-town of Bolton, the chapelries of Blackrod, Bradshaw, Harwood, Little Lever, and Turton, and the townships of Anglezarke, Breightmet, Edgeworth, Entwistle, Darcy-Lever, Longworth, Lostock, Quarlton, Rivington, Sharples, and Tonge with Haulgh; and containing 73,905 inhabitants, of whom 33,610 are in Great, and 16,153 in Little, Bolton, 43 miles (S. S. E.) from Lancaster, and 197 (N. W. by N.) from London. This place, which derives the adjunct to its name from its situation on the moors, was of little importance prior to 1337, when the emigrant Flemings, who fixed their residence here, introduced the manufacture of woollen-cloth, and laid the foundation of its future increase as a manufacturing town. After the revocation of the edict of Nantz, also, many of the French refugees, attracted by the means of employment which its trade at that time afforded, took up their abode in the town. At the commencement of the civil war in the reign of Charles I., the inhabitants espoused the cause of the parliament, by whom the town was garrisoned, and in whose possession it remained till 1644, when Prince Rupert, advancing with 10,000 men to the relief of Lathom House, which was besieged by a body of 2000 parliamentary troops, compelled them to raise the siege and retire into this town. Being joined by the Earl of Derby from the Isle of Man, the prince assembled his forces on the moor to the south-west of the town, and there held a council of war, at which it was resolved to carry the place by storm. Pursuant to this, an assault was made with great spirit and bravery, which, however was met by equal intrepidity from the garrison, now consisting of 3000 men; and the assailants, after performing numerous acts of valour, were compelled to retreat, with the loss of 200 of their force. A second council of war was then convened, and a second attack determined upon, which, at his earnest request, was entrusted to the Earl of Derby: this loyal noble-

Borough Seal.

man, placing himself at the head of a gallant band of only 200 Lancashire men, principally his own tenantry and their sons, led on the van, by marching directly to the walls, where the conflict was for some time carried on with desperate valour on both sides; but the earl, bearing down all opposition, entered the town, and put the whole garrison into the utmost consternation. The royalists pursued the enemy in every direction, killing all whom they encountered; and at last plundered the town, which remained for some time in their possession, but was ultimately given up to the parliament. After the disastrous battle of Worcester, the gallant earl, who had come from the Isle of Man to the assistance of Charles II., being taken prisoner, was condemned by a military tribunal at Chester, and sent under an escort to this place, where he was beheaded.

The manor of Bolton, which is of considerable antiquity, was alienated by Roger de Maresey, with his other lands between the rivers Ribble and Mersey, to Ranulph de Blundeville, Earl of Chester, for 240 marks of silver, and a pair of white gloves, to be presented annually at Easter. It afterwards passed through the families of Ferrers and Pilkington, and was confiscated to the crown on the attainder of Sir Thomas Pilkington, in the 1st of Henry VII., for his adherence to the cause of Richard III. at the battle of Bosworth-Field. Henry granted it to his relation, Thomas, Lord Stanley, then created Earl of Derby; but a considerable portion of the property having been confiscated by parliament, during the period of the Commonwealth, the manor of Bolton is at present held, in unequal proportions, by five lords.

The TOWN, comprising the townships of Great and Little Bolton, which are separated by the rivulet Croal, was greatly enlarged under an act of parliament obtained in 1792,.for inclosing Bolton Moor, of which more than 250 acres were divided into allotments, now partly occupied with buildings. The powers of the commissioners appointed under that act were extended by an act in 1817, since which time three spacious squares, several ranges of buildings, and a few public edifices, have been erected; 428 houses in Great Bolton, and 196 in Little Bolton, were built during one year, and considerable improvement has been made in the roads leading to the town. It is lighted with gas by a company incorporated in 1820, whose powers were extended by an act passed in 1843; and the inhabitants are supplied with excellent water, brought from the high lands in Sharples, five miles north of Bolton, by pipes, and conveyed by an iron main of eighteen inches diameter to the various parts of the town. This undertaking was first established at an expense of £40,000, subscribed in shares of £50 each, by a company formed in 1824, for whose use a handsome stone building was erected, in front of which a an emblematical tablet representing a Naiad seated by a fountain, pouring water from a ewer to a thirsty child. The company obtained a new act in 1843, extending its powers to the adjacent townships; and in 1847 an act was passed, enabling the municipal corporation to purchase or take a lease of the water-works, and to improve the town generally. The theatre is regularly open during the season; a town-hall was erected a few years since, in which concerts occasionally take place, and here are three public libraries. Splendid baths, with public rooms for assemblies, concerts, and lectures, were
299

erected in 1846, at a cost exceeding £4000. The Exchange Buildings, erected in 1825, form a neat edifice of stone, with two Ionic columns at the entrance: the lower room, which is of ample dimensions, is appropriated to the transaction of general business, and fitted up as a news-room; the upper part contains a library and reading-rooms. A mechanics' institute was established in 1825. Temporary barracks have been provided for the accommodation of two companies of infantry.

The principal branch of MANUFACTURE, and to the introduction of which Bolton owes its present extent and importance, is that of cotton, in the improvement of which many ingenious and valuable discoveries originated in this town. Sir Richard Arkwright, a resident here, after he had established his works at Derby and Nottingham, brought the spinning-jenny and the water-frame machines to perfection; and Samuel Crompton, who was also an inhabitant of Bolton, invented a machine called the mule, combining the properties of both, for which, after receiving two several donations of £105 and £400, subscribed as acknowledgments of his merit, he was ultimately remunerated by parliament with a grant of £5000. Previously to the introduction of the cotton-trade, some weavers who arrived in this country from the palatinate of the Rhine, had added to the manufacture of woollen-cloth that of a fabric, partly composed of linen-yarn chiefly imported from Germany, and partly of cotton. The chief articles were fustian, jean, and thickset: velvet, entirely of cotton, was first made here in 1756, and muslin, quilting, and dimity succeeded. After the introduction of the improved machinery, several factories were established, but, being chiefly worked by water, they were on a small scale; the subsequent employment of steam enabled the proprietors to enlarge their works, and the adoption of power-looms contributed greatly to improve and extend the trade.

There are at present in Bolton sixty-one cotton-factories. At fifty-six of these are engines of the aggregate power of 1685 horses, and 793,800 throstle spindles; the number of power-looms is 2131, and the weight of raw cotton annually used 13,705,636 lb.: in fifty-five of the factories are consumed 69,278 tons of common coal and 888 tons of cannel coal. The bleaching-grounds are also very extensive, and more than 10,000,000 pieces of cloth are annually bleached. Among them are three large establishments, in each of which from 130,000 to 150,000 pieces are, on the average, finished every month, in two of them is used engine-power equal to 120 horses, and in one alone are annually consumed 16,000 tons of coal. There are twenty-one iron-founders and machine-makers, of whom thirteen have engines of the aggregate power of 433 horses, and employ 2793 hands; use 18,390 tons of metal, and consume 28,150 tons of coal and 3231 tons of coke: machinery of all kinds, and mills of every description, are made. A paper-mill manufactures annually 470 tons of paper, and consumes 3640 tons of coal. The neighbourhood abounds with coal; and veins of lead-ore and of calamine have been worked at Rivington, but they have not been found productive. The total amount of horse-power in the various works carried on in the borough, in 1846, was 3816; of this aggregate, steam-engines supplied the power of 3654 horses, and
2 Q 2

water-wheels of 162. The Bolton and Leigh and the Kenyon and Leigh Junction railways connect the town with the Liverpool and Manchester railway at Kenyon; the whole line is nine miles and three-quarters in length. A direct railway to Manchester, 10 miles long, was opened in May 1838; a railway to Euxton, a few miles south of Preston, in June 1843; and a railway to Darwen and Blackburn, 14½ miles long, in 1847. An act, also, was passed in 1845 for the construction of a railway from Liverpool, by Wigan and Bolton, to Bury, there to join a branch of the Manchester and Leeds line. The canal to Manchester was constructed in 1791; a branch to Bury diverges from it at Little Lever, in this parish. The market-days are Monday and Saturday: there are fairs on July 30th and 31st, and Oct. 13th and 14th, for horned-cattle, horses, pigs, and pedlery; and a fair for lean-cattle every alternate Wednesday, from Jan. 5th to May 12th. The market is held in the area of the new square, in the centre of which is a handsome cast-iron column, 30 feet high, rising from a pedestal in the form of a vase, and supporting a lantern which is lighted with gas.

The town was formerly within the jurisdiction of the county magistrates, and its internal GOVERNMENT was under the regulation of officers appointed at the court leet of the lord of the manor; but on the 11th Oct. 1838, a charter of incorporation was granted under the Municipal act, and it is now governed by a mayor, 12 aldermen, and 36 councillors. On May 9th, 1839, the queen decreed that a court of quarter-sessions should be held here. The number of magistrates is 17. It was made a parliamentary borough by the act of the 2nd of William IV., cap. 45, with the privilege of returning two members to parliament, the right of election being vested in the £10 householders; the limits of the borough comprise 1748 acres. The county debt-court of Bolton, established in 1847, has jurisdiction over the registration-district of Bolton. The town-hall, already mentioned, at Little Bolton, was built at an expense of £2000; and it is in contemplation to erect a similar structure in Great Bolton, more suited to the importance of the town than the present rooms in which the business is transacted.

The parish comprises by computation 31,000 acres. The LIVING is a discharged vicarage, valued in the king's books at £10. 3. 1½.; net income, £464; patron and appropriator, the Bishop of Chester. The church is a spacious structure, of the style of architecture termed Perpendicular or later English: it has a splendid east window by Wailes, of Newcastle, one of his best productions, and forming an obituary window, erected by the vicar, the Rev. James Slade, M.A. and his relatives, at the cost of £300; a beautiful font of Caen stone was recently erected by Matthew Dawes, Esq., F.G.S., in memory of his parents, and among some interesting monuments is one by Chantrey in the Chetham chapel to John Taylor, Esq., and his family. A district church dedicated to the *Holy Trinity* was erected in 1825, at an expense of £13,412, defrayed by a grant from the Parliamentary Commissioners; it is a handsome edifice in the later English style, with a tower. The living is a perpetual curacy, in the gift of the Vicar of Bolton, on whose voidance the district will become a separate parish in the gift of the Bishop: the net income, previously £120, was augmented in 1842 with
300

£30 per annum by the Ecclesiastical Commissioners. The district church dedicated to *St. George*, in Little Bolton, was erected by subscription in 1796: the living is a perpetual curacy, in the patronage of the Vicar; net income, £168. *Emmanuel* church, built in 1838, at a cost of £2200, originated in a desire on the part of the parishioners to present a service of plate to the vicar, who requested the fund might be applied rather to the building of a church in the most destitute part of the town; it is a handsome structure in the early English style, with a tower and spire. The living is a perpetual curacy, augmented in 1841 by the Ecclesiastical Commissioners to £150, and in the presentation of the Vicar. *Christ church*, built as a meeting-house in 1818, for Methodists of the New Connexion, was purchased from the trustees in 1841, and licensed for divine worship according to the rites of the Church of England, the minister and greater part of the congregation having conformed thereto: it was consecrated as the church of one of the new parishes under the 6th and 7th Victoria, cap. 37, in 1844; and is of brick, with a handsome Norman porch, and windows of the same style of *terra cotta*. The living is a perpetual curacy, with an endowment of £150 per annum from the Ecclesiastical Commissioners; patrons, the Crown and the Bishop alternately. A church district, called *St. John's*, was formed in Little Bolton, in May, 1846, under the same act, and the erection of a church was commenced in 1847; the edifice is in the decorated style, will seat 1000 persons, and was built at a cost of £3500. The district became an ecclesiastical parish on the consecration of the church: the living is a perpetual curacy; net income, £150; patrons, the Crown and Bishop alternately. A chapel dedicated to *All Saints*, also in Little Bolton, has been restored, and made a district church: the living is a perpetual curacy; net income, £128; patron, T. Tipping, Esq. A Scottish church, in the early English style, was erected by subscription, in 1846. There are also places of worship for Baptists, Independents, Unitarians, the Society of Friends, Swedenborgians, Methodists, and Roman Catholics; and, besides these, ten churches in chapelries and rural townships within the parish. Connected with the parish church is a lectureship, endowed by the Rev. James Gosnell in 1622, and considerably augmented by a grant of land from the Earl of Derby.

The free grammar school, containing 60 boys, was founded by Robert Lever, citizen of London, who, in 1641, bequeathed estates now producing about £350 per annum, with which the revenue of a school previously existing has been united, amounting in the whole to £485: there is a small exhibition to either of the Universities. Robert Ainsworth, compiler of the *Latin Dictionary*, and Dr. Lempriere, compiler of the *Classical Dictionary*, were masters of the school; and the former had been educated here. A charity school was founded and endowed in 1693, by Nathaniel Hulton, for the instruction of 30 boys and 30 girls; the income is £277. The "Churchgate Charity School" was founded in 1714, by Thomas Marsden, who endowed it with a house, &c., now producing £14. 10. per annum; in addition, £10 per annum are allowed to the master from Brooks' charity, accruing from pews in the parish church. Other schools are supported by subscription; and there are various Sunday schools, of which that in connexion with the parish church, is a large and handsome building of freestone, in the later English style, erected in 1819 at an expense of £1800. A dispensary was established in 1814: a clothing society is supported chiefly by ladies; and there is a society for the relief of poor women during child-birth, formed in 1798. In 1829, John Popplewell, Esq., a gentleman of the medical profession, and a native of the parish, bequeathed £4500, the interest to be applied in providing clothing and bread for the poor of Great and Little Bolton, and the township of Turton; the interest of £2000, to found scholarships for the grammar school; of £400, to repair All Saints' chapel; and of £3500, to the township· of Blackrod, for various uses. The bequests of this benefactor altogether amounted to £15,099, vested in the three per cent. consols.; to which his sisters, Anne and Rebecca, added in 1831 the interest of £12,600 in the same stock, for similar benevolent purposes. Elizabeth Lum, in 1840, built six almshouses at the Tealds, in Little Bolton, for twelve widows or spinsters above sixty years of age, who each receive a weekly allowance. The union of Bolton comprises the entire parish with the exception of Anglezarke, Blackrod, and Rivington, and, in addition, eleven other chapelries and townships; and contains a population of 97,519. There are several strong chalybeate springs in the parish. John Bradshaw, president of the court which sentenced Charles I. to the scaffold, is said to have been born near the town.

. BOLTON-LE-SANDS (ST. MICHAEL), a parish, in the hundred of LONSDALE south of the Sands, N. division of the county of LANCASTER; containing 1774 inhabitants, of whom 671 are in the township of Bolton, 4 miles (N.) from Lancaster, on the road to Kendal. On the foundation of the priory at Lancaster, Roger de Poictou gave to it the church of "Boelton," with the tithes of the lordship, and half a carucate of land; and in the Testa de Nevill, several transactions are mentioned of a family of the local name, as occurring in the registry of the priory. The manor of Bolton, on the suppression of religious communities, seems to have passed to the crown. The parish comprises the townships of Bolton, Slyne with Hest, and Nether Kellet, and the chapelry of Over Kellet. Bolton township comprises 1574a. 3r., chiefly arable land; the surface is undulated, and the soil principally loam, with a gravelly subsoil. It is beautifully situated on Morecambe bay, having views of the Lake mountains and the opposite shore of Furness. · The living is a discharged vicarage, valued in the king's books at £4. 15., and in the patronage of the ·Bishop of Chester, who is appropriator. The church has a noble square tower: the body was rebuilt in 1816; as was the chancel in 1846, in the early English style, at a cost of £600, by John Holden, Esq., of Woodlands, Gateacre, near Liverpool, as a memorial of his late wife, the daughter of John Walmsley, Esq., of Richmond House, Lancaster. The windows of the chancel are of stained glass, by Wailes, of Newcastle; the eastern window depicts the Crucifixion and Ascension, and the rest contain family arms. The chapel at Over Kellet forms a distinct incumbency. The free school was founded in 1619, by Thomas Assheton, and has an income of £27, arising from the original endowment and subsequent benefactions. The interest of £250, left in 1838 by Richard Sparling Berry, Esq.,

is given in rewards to parents who educate their children without parochial relief, in the township of Bolton. The arm of a Saxon stone cross, and the remains of the cross from the churchyard, are preserved.

BOLTON-PERCY (ALL SAINTS), a parish, in the AINSTY wapentake, W. riding of YORK; containing 1040 inhabitants, of whom 241 are in the township of Bolton-Percy, 4 miles (E. by S.) from Tadcaster. This parish, which is bounded on the south-west by the river Wharfe, comprises the four townships of Bolton-Percy, Appleton-Roebuck, Colton, and Steeton; and contains about 7320 acres. The soil is generally a strong clay, with portions of a lighter kind; the surface is level, and interspersed with small plantations and woods. Bricks and tiles are manufactured. The York and North-Midland railway passes through the parish, in which is a station. The living is a rectory, valued in the king's books at £39. 15. 2½.; net income, £1540; patron, the Archbishop of York. The church, built in 1423, by Thomas Parker, rector, is a neat structure with a square tower; it is decorated with a quantity of stained glass, and contains several monuments to the Fairfax family.

BOLTON-DEARNE (ST. ANDREW), a parish, in the union of DONCASTER, N. division of the wapentake of STRAFFORTH and. TICKHILL, W. riding of YORK, 7¾ miles (N. by E.) from Rotherham, and upon the road from Doncaster to Barnsley; containing 671 inhabitants. At the time of the Conquest here was a church, with its attendant priest; also a mill; and the country appears to have been in a higher state of cultivation than the lands around. The place became the residence of several families of some consideration, and seems to have been from early times a rich and flourishing spot. It lies on the line of road traced by those who consider that a Roman road existed from Templeborough to Castleford; and it is certain there was a bridge over the Dearne here at a remote period, the pontage of which was early a subject of dispute, as is recorded in the Hundred rolls. The PARISH comprises by measurement 2400 acres, of which about one-third is grass, and the remainder arable: the soil is various, in some parts a strong clay, in others a light sand; and the substratum abounds with excellent sandstone, which is extensively quarried. The village is beautifully situated on the northern acclivities of the vale of Dearne, having a good bridge over the river, said to occupy the site of a Roman ford; and about a mile northward is the pleasant hamlet of Goldthorpe. A statute-fair for hiring servants is held on the second Thursday in November. The living is a perpetual curacy, valued in the king's books at £6. 15. 5.; net income, £88; patrons, the Executors of the late W. H. Marsden, Esq., in whom are vested the impropriate tithes, which have been commuted for £580. The church is an ancient edifice, chiefly in the Norman style, with a tower at the west end. There is a place of worship for Wesleyans.

BOLTON-UPON-SWALE, a chapelry, in the parish of CATTERICK, union of RICHMOND, wapentake of GILLING-EAST, N. riding of YORK, 1¾ mile (N. E.) from Catterick; containing 960 inhabitants, of whom 96 are in Bolton township. It comprises the townships of Bolton, Whitwell, Kiplin, Ellerton, Scorton, and Uckerby; and is separated from that of Catterick by the river Swale. The living is a perpetual curacy, in the gift of the Vicar of Catterick, with a net income of £100; the chapel, dedicated to St. Mary, is ornamented with a lofty tower, and its burial-ground contains a neat pyramidal monument, erected by subscription, in 1743, over the grave of Henry Jenkins, a native of this place, who died in the year 1670, at the age of 169, and is the oldest Englishman on record. A free school was founded in the beginning of the last century by Leonard Robinson; and there is a large nunnery, with a ladies' boarding school attached.

BONBY (St. Andrew), a parish, in the union of Glandford-Brigg, N. division of the wapentake of Yarborough, parts of Lindsey, county of Lincoln, 5½ miles (S. S. W.) from Barton-on-Humber; containing 386 inhabitants. This parish, in ancient records called Bondeby, is on the road from Barton to' London, and comprises by survey 2427 acres, equally divided between arable and pasture: the eastern half is high land, part of the Wolds, and the western half part of the Ancholme level; the soil is a peat moor, upon a stratum of clay. There are some quarries of chalkstone, which is raised for manure. The Ancholme river and Ancholme canal pass through the parish. The living is a discharged vicarage, valued in the king's books at £6. 4. 4.; net income, £233; patron and impropriator, Lord Yarborough. The church is an ancient edifice, with a square tower. There are places of worship for Primitive Methodists and Wesleyans. In the reign of John, a priory was established here.

BONCHURCH (St. Boniface), a parish, in the liberty of East Medina, Isle of Wight division of the county of Southampton, ½ a mile (N. E.) from Ventnor; containing 302 inhabitants. This place, lying on the south coast of the island, is of remote antiquity; its church, which is one of the oldest in the neighbourhood, appears to have been originally founded by some monks of the abbey of Lyra, in Normandy, who were sent over to convert the fishermen on this coast to Christianity. The parish comprises 540 acres, whereof 77 are common or waste. The living is a discharged rectory, with that of Shanklin annexed, valued in the king's books at £6. 15. 5.; net income, £134; patrons, Charles Popham Hill, Esq., and the Trustees of the late J. Popham, Esq. The tithes of the parish of Bonchurch have been commuted for a yearly rent-charge of £51. 10., and the glebe consists of 4¾ acres. Admiral Hobson was a native of the parish.

BONDGATE, with Aismunderby, a township, in the parish and liberty of Ripon, W. riding of York, ½ a mile (S.) from Ripon; containing 614 inhabitants, of whom 541 are in Bondgate. The township adjoins Ripon, of which Bondgate forms the southern suburb. An hospital for two poor women was founded here by one of the archbishops of York, about the time of King John.

BONDINGTON, a hamlet, in the parish of Dunster, union of Williton, hundred of Carhampton, W. division of Somerset; containing 16 inhabitants.

BONDS, with Barnacre.—See Barnacre.

BONEHILL, a liberty, in the chapelry of Fazeley, parish and union of Tamworth, S. division of the hundred of Offlow and of the county of Stafford, 1½ mile (S. W. by W.) from Tamworth; containing 323 inhabitants. It lies on the north side of Drayton manor. The Fazeley canal passes through it.

302

hundred of CALCEWORTH, parts of LINDSEY, county of LINCOLN, 3 miles (S. S. E.) from the town of Alford; containing 14 inhabitants.

. BONWICK, a township, in the parish of SKIPSEA, union of SKIRLAUGH, N. division of the wapentake of HOLDERNESS, E. riding of YORK, 11½ miles (E. S. E.) from Driffield; containing 29 inhabitants. Bonwick, or Bovingwick, is not named in the Domesday book, being probably included, with Skipsea and other parts of the parish, in the "adjacent lands" of the manor of Cleton. The place consists of two farms, respectively designated High and Low Bonwick. A rent-charge of £25. 5. 3. has been awarded as a commutation for the tithes, payable to the Archbishop of York.

BOOKHAM, GREAT (ST. NICHOLAS), a parish, in the union of EPSOM, hundred of EFFINGHAM, W. division of SURREY, 2½ miles (W. S. W.) from Leatherhead; containing 963 inhabitants. It comprises by measurement 3242 acres, of which 1446 are arable, 629 meadow and pasture, 264 woodland, 105 acres gardens and buildings, 23 public road, and 775 common. Within the parish is the estate of Polesden, which was the property of Sheridan, soon after whose decease it was purchased by Joseph Bonsor, Esq., whose son, of the same name, is the present possessor. The living is a discharged vicarage, endowed with a moiety of the rectorial tithes, and valued in the king's books at £9. 17. 3½.; patron, the Rev. W. Heberden. The rectorial tithe rent-charge is £442, and the vicarial £165; there are 12 acres of glebe. The church is an ancient structure in the early English style, and contains numerous handsome monuments. Sir George Shiers, Bart., in 1690 bequeathed a rent-charge of £36. 3. for apprenticing children, and other charitable purposes.

· BOOKHAM, LITTLE, a parish, in the union of EPSOM, hundred of EFFINGHAM, W. division of SURREY, 3½ miles (W. S. W.) from Leatherhead; containing 237 inhabitants. This parish, which is on the road from London to Guildford, and bounded by the river Mole, contains 945 acres, of which 112 are woodland, and 129 common or waste; the soil comprises clay, gravel, and chalk. The living is a discharged rectory, valued in the king's books at £6. 15. 7.; patron and incumbent, the Rev. G. P. Boileau Pollen. The tithes have been commuted for £154, and £10 are paid to the Vicar of Effingham; there are 41 acres of glebe. The church has some memorials to the Pollen and Boileau families. Certain tenements in London, producing about £65 per annum, were assigned by Sir Benjamin Maddox, a moiety to the clergyman, and the other moiety for the benefit of the poor and the parish clerk, and for repairing the church and the highways.

BOOLEY, a township, in the parish of STANTON-UPON-HINE-HEATH, union of WEM, Whitchurch division of the hundred of NORTH BRADFORD, N. division of SALOP; containing 178 inhabitants.

BOOTH, a hamlet, in the township of KNEDLINGTON, parish of HOWDEN, wapentake of HOWDENSHIRE, E. riding of YORK, 2 miles (S. W.) from Howden; containing 36 inhabitants. The village lies on the northern bank of the river Ouse, across which is a ferry.

BOOTH, NEW LAUND, with FILLEY-CLOSE and REEDLEY-HALLOWS, a township, in the parish of WHALLEY, union of BURNLEY, Higher division of the hundred of BLACKBURN, N. division of the county of

303

LANCASTER, 2 miles (N.) from Burnley; containing 412 inhabitants. These three places are ancient vaccaries of Pendle; they comprise 815 acres. The river Calder divides Filley-Close and New Laund from Reedley-Hallows; and the Leeds and Liverpool canal also passes through the township.

BOOTH, OLD LAUND, a township, in the chapelry of NEWCHURCH-in-PENDLE, parish of WHALLEY, union of BURNLEY, Higher division of the hundred of BLACKBURN, N. division of the county of LANCASTER, 3 miles (N.) from Burnley; containing 481 inhabitants. It lies on the north-east side of Pendle forest, and consists of 246 acres, with scattered houses amidst tolerably wooded pastures. Old Laund Hall is a very ancient strongly-built fabric; it was some time since purchased by Mr. Greenwood, of Palace House, from the lords of Clitheroe. A church dedicated to St. Anne was built at Fence, in Old Laund, in 1837, and endowed by the late Mrs. Holden, of Palace House : the living is a perpetual curacy, in the patronage of the Holden family. There is a national school.

BOOTHBY (ST. ANDREW), a parish, in the Higher division of the wapentake of BOOTHBY-GRAFFO, parts of KESTEVEN, union and county of LINCOLN, 10 miles (N. W. by N.) from Sleaford; containing 214 inhabitants. The living is a rectory, valued in the king's books at £11. 12. 3½.; net income, £638; patron, J. Fullerton, Esq. The tithes were commuted for land in 1771.

BOOTHBY-PAGNELL (ST. ANDREW), a parish, in the union of GRANTHAM, wapentake of WINNIBRIGS and THREO, parts of KESTEVEN, county of LINCOLN, 5¼ miles (N. N. W.) from Corby; containing 132 inhabitants. The living is a rectory, valued in the king's books at £11. 10. 5., and in the patronage of J. Litchford, Esq.: the tithes have been commuted for £312. 14., and there are upwards of 121 acres of glebe.

BOOTHEN, a township, in the parish and union of STOKE-UPON-TRENT, N. division of the hundred of PIREHILL and of the county of STAFFORD, 1 mile (S.) from Stoke; containing 144 inhabitants. The river Trent and the Grand Trunk canal pass in the vicinity of this place.

BOOTHS, HIGHER, a township, in the parish of WHALLEY, union of HASLINGDEN, Higher division of the hundred of BLACKBURN, N. division of the county of LANCASTER, 2 miles (N.) from Rawtenstall, and 2½ (N. N. E.) from Haslingden; containing 3652 inhabitants. This township comprises 2606 acres of land; it is on the road from Manchester to Burnley, and includes the villages of Goodshaw-Booth, Goodshaw-Fold, Crawshaw-Booth, Low-Clough, and Sunny-Side, all of them within the district of Rossendale. The tenures are copyhold, of the honour of Clitheroe. Coal and stone are wrought; there are two extensive calico-printing establishments, and many cotton-mills. Among the more remarkable residences in the township are, Crawshaw-Booth Hall, an ancient stone building; Rake; and Low-Clough; and near the print-works at Sunny-Side, are the elegant mansions of their owners. Goodshaw has a chapel, to which a district has been assigned, co-extensive with the township : the living is a perpetual curacy, with a net income of £150; patrons, the Hulme Trustees. The chapel stands on Morrell Height; it was erected in the reign of Henry VIII., and rebuilt in 1829.

The Wesleyans, Baptists, Primitive Methodists, and Society of Friends have places of worship; and there are several schools, one of which, situated at Crawshaw-Booth, and in connexion with the Church, was built in 1835-6.

BOOTHS, LOWER, a township, in the parish of WHALLEY, union of HASLINGDEN, Higher division of the hundred of BLACKBURN, N. division of the county of LANCASTER; containing 2464 inhabitants. It comprises 948 acres, extends to the banks of the Irwell, and includes part of the thriving village of Rawtenstall: the farms, which are small, are chiefly copyhold. The inhabitants are principally employed in the cotton and woollen mills in the neighbourhood. The Unitarians have a place of worship, originally built for an Independent congregation. Lower Booths, like the preceding township, is in the district of Rossendale.

BOOTLE (ST. MICHAEL), a market-town and parish, and the head of a union, in ALLERDALE ward above Derwent, W. division of CUMBERLAND, 5½ miles (S. S. E.) from Ravenglass, and 282 (N. W. by N.) from London; containing 696 inhabitants. The name of this place, formerly written "Bothill," is supposed to be derived from the booths erected on a hill above the town, for the watchmen whose duty it was to light the beacon on its summit, upon the discovery of any ships in the Irish Channel which might appear to threaten a descent upon the coast. A Benedictine nunnery was founded at Seton, in the parish, by Gunild, daughter of Henry de Boyvill, fourth lord of Millorn; to which Henry IV. annexed the hospital of St. Leonard, in Lancaster. Its revenue, at the Dissolution, was £13. 17. 4.: there are still some remains. The TOWN is pleasantly situated within two miles of the sea; the houses are neatly built, and the inhabitants well supplied with water. The land in the neighbourhood is in a high state of cultivation, and the environs abound with pleasing scenery: the Corney and Bootle Fells, eminences in the adjoining forest of Copeland, afford extensive views; and from Black Coombe, which is nearly 2000 feet high, may be seen the coast of Scotland, the Isle of Man, and the mountains of North Wales. The trade is principally in corn, pork, and bacon, which are sent to Liverpool: the market is on Saturday; and fairs are held on April 5th and Sept. 24th, for the sale of corn, and for hiring servants; and April 26th and August 3rd, for horses, horned-cattle, and sheep.

The parish comprises 5800 acres, of which 900 are common or waste. The LIVING is a rectory, valued in the king's books at £19. 17. 3½., and in the patronage of the Earl of Lonsdale: the tithes have been commuted for £436, and there are 14 acres of glebe. The church is a very ancient edifice, much modernised by successive repairs; the interior contains some interesting monuments, among which is an effigy on a brass plate of Sir Hugh Askew, and has been lately enlarged. A place of worship for Independents was built in 1780. A free school was founded in 1713, by Henry Singleton, who endowed it with £200, which sum, with subsequent benefactions, produces about £20 per annum. The poor law union of Bootle comprises 12 parishes or places, and contains a population of 5516. At Selker bay, a small inlet of the sea, are sometimes seen the remains of vessels, which are traditionally said to have been Roman galleys, sunk there at the time of an invasion by that

304

people; and at Esk-Meols are vestiges of an encampment, where Roman coins and fragments of altars have been frequently discovered.

BOOTLE, with LINACRE, a township and chapelry, in the parish of WALTON-ON-THE-HILL, union and hundred of WEST DERBY, S. division of the county of LANCASTER, 4 miles (N.) from Liverpool; containing in 1846 about 4090 inhabitants. Four thanes at the time of the Domesday survey held "Boltelai" as four manors. Afterwards the district belonged to Warin Bussel, whose daughter married Roger Fitz-Richard; and the son of the latter, Richard Fitz-Roger, founder of Lytham, left four coheiresses, through whom the lands passed into as many families. The manor subsequently was held by the Mores, and from them was purchased by the Stanleys. At this place are some works for supplying the town of Liverpool with water, from a spring which formerly discharged itself at Bootle bay, on the coast, after turning a mill within half a mile of its source. The project of bringing the water to Liverpool was suggested so early as the 8th year of Queen Anne, when Sir Cleave More, the second baronet, obtained a private act of parliament for the purpose. Anciently there were paper-works and flour-mills at Bootle; the latter were destroyed by fire some years ago.

The township is beautifully situated on the shores of the Mersey, at its mouth; and comprises 837 acres of land, the property of the Earl of Derby. The soil is light and good, resting on a substratum of red sandstone, which is used for building; the beach is firm, of great extent, and much resorted to for bathing, and horse exercise. The village is well built; there are numerous elegant villas, and ranges of houses inhabited by the merchants of Liverpool, and some excellent hotels and lodging-houses with every accommodation for visiters. The expansive views of the sea, the Cheshire coast, and mountains of Wales, &c., are highly attractive in this quarter. Bootle Hall is the seat of William MᶜCormick, Esq. The living is a perpetual curacy, in the patronage of W. S. Miller, Esq.; net income, £250. Rent-charges amounting to £235 have been awarded as commutations for the tithes. The chapel, dedicated to St. Mary, was built in 1820, and was enlarged and a tower added in 1847; it is a cruciform structure, with a neat interior. There are places of worship for Wesleyans and Baptists; and a Roman Catholic chapel, dedicated to St. James, has been just built at a cost of £3500: it is in the early English style, with a square tower and a spire; and schools and a house for the priest are attached.

BOOTON (ST. MICHAEL), a parish, in the union of ST. FAITH'S, hundred of SOUTH ERPINGHAM, E. division of NORFOLK, 1 mile (E. S. E.) from Reepham; containing 241 inhabitants. It is intersected by the road from Norwich to Reepham, and comprises 1040 acres. The living is a discharged rectory, valued in the king's books at £7. 12. 6., and in the gift of H. Elwin, Esq.: the tithes have been commuted for £294, and there are about 23 acres of glebe. The church is chiefly in the decorated style, with a square embattled tower. At the inclosure, in 1811, twenty acres were allotted to the poor.

BORASTON, SALOP.—See BURASTON.

BORDEAN, a tything, in the parish and hundred of EAST MEON, union of PETERSFIELD, Petersfield and N.

BORE

A church dedicated to the Holy Trinity was built in 1822, at an expense of £14,235, raised by subscription of the inhabitants, aided by a grant from the Parliamentary Commissioners; it is in the later English style, combining a rich variety of architectural details. The living is a perpetual curacy; patron, the Vicar of Aston. In 1846, a district, or ecclesiastical parish, was formed of part of the hamlet, under the act 6 and 7 Victoria, cap. 37, by the name of St. Andrew's, Bordesley; and a church was consecrated the same year. The edifice is in the decorated style, and is neat and substantial, consisting of a nave, chancel, and aisle, with an engaged tower surmounted by a spire; the cost was about £4000, and was defrayed by a Church Building Society. The patronage of the benefice is in the Bishop of Worcester and five Trustees, alternately; the income, £150, is a grant by the Ecclesiastical Commissioners. In the hamlet are twelve almshouses for aged persons, built by Mr. Dowell, whose widow appoints the inmates: one of the houses is appropriated as a chapel.

BORDESLEY, a hamlet, in the parish of TARDE-BIGG, union of BROMSGROVE, Upper division of the hundred of HALFSHIRE, Droitwich and E. divisions of the county of WORCESTER, 5½ miles (E. S. E.) from Bromsgrove. A Cistercian abbey, in honour of the Blessed Virgin Mary, was built in 1138, by the Empress Matilda; and its revenue, a short time previously to the Dissolution, was estimated at £392. 8. 6.: the chapel, dedicated to St. Stephen, subsisted for some time afterwards. Bordesley Hall, surrounded by an extensive and well wooded park, is in this vicinity, but in the parish of Alvechurch, and about a mile and a half south-east of Alvechurch village: the mansion stands on rising ground, and is handsomely built.

BOREHAM (ST. ANDREW), a parish, in the union and hundred of CHELMSFORD, S. division of ESSEX, 4 miles (N. E. by E.) from Chelmsford; containing 1034 inhabitants. This parish derives its name from the Saxon Bore, "a market," and Ham, "a village;" and is supposed to have been anciently a place of considerable importance. The land is generally elevated; the soil is fertile though varying in quality, and the general appearance is greatly enriched with wood, which seems to have been formerly more abundant than at present. New Hall, in the parish, is part of a much larger mansion greatly adorned by Henry VIII., who having obtained the manor in exchange for other property, raised it into an honour: his daughter, the Princess Mary, also resided here for several years. It is now occupied by a society of English nuns, who were driven from Liege by the fury of the French republicans, and who now superintend the education of about eighty young ladies. The village is pleasantly situated on the road to Colchester; and the Chelmer navigation bounds the parish on the south. The living is a vicarage, valued in the king's books at £10. 3. 9., and in the patronage of the Bishop of London: the impropriate tithes have been commuted for £680, and the vicarial for £440; there are 21 acres of glebe belonging to the impropriator, and 18 to the vicar. The church is a handsome edifice, consisting of a nave, with north and south aisles, and a chancel, between which and the nave rises a lofty square embattled tower; the south aisle was added by Sir Thomas Radcliffe, and contains an elegant monument with statues of Robert, first Earl of Sussex, his son, and grandson.

2 R

BORESFORD, with PEDWARDINE, a township, in the parish of BRAMPTON-BRYAN, union of KNIGHTON, hundred of WIGMORE, county of HEREFORD, 3 miles (S. E.) from Knighton; containing 102 inhabitants. The hamlet of Boresford is situated in the northern part of the county, near the borders of Radnorshire; and both hamlets lie a short distance south of the village of Brampton-Bryan, and of Brampton-Bryan Park. The earls of Kinnoul enjoy a seat in the house of lords, as barons Hay, of Pedwardine: here was formerly a castle belonging to the family.

BORLEY, a parish, in the union of SUDBURY, hundred of HINCKFORD, N. division of ESSEX, 2¼ miles (N. W. by W.) from Sudbury; containing 188 inhabitants. This parish, which comprises 776a. 3r. 9p., and is bounded on the east by the river Stour, derives its name from the Saxon words signifying "Boar's Pasture." The manor, at the time of the Norman survey, belonged to Adeliza, Countess of Albemarle, half sister to William I.; and descended to many illustrious families closely allied to the crown: it afterwards passed to the Waldegrave family, whose descendants are the present proprietors. The living is a rectory, valued in the king's books at £9, and in the gift of Earl Waldegrave: the tithes have been commuted at £276. 10., and there are 10½ acres of glebe. The church, which stands on an eminence commanding an extensive prospect, is a small ancient edifice, containing an elegant monument to the Waldegraves.

BORLEY, a village, in the parish of OMBERSLEY, union of DROITWICH, Lower division of the hundred of OSWALDSLOW, Worcester and W. divisions of the county of WORCESTER, 8 miles (N. by W.) from Worcester. It lies on the east side of the Severn, and about a mile and a half north-west from the village of Ombersley.

BOROUGHBRIDGE, a hamlet, in the parishes of LING, OTHERY, and WESTON-ZOYLAND, partly in the hundred of ANDERSFIELD, and partly in that of WHITLEY, union of BRIDGWATER, W. division of SOMERSET; containing 93 inhabitants. Collinson, the county historian, states the name to be derived from "a large borough or mount, very high and steep," and a stone bridge of three lofty arches, which here crosses the navigable river Parret: this mount is situated within an inclosure, on the eastern side of the river, and has generally been considered as formed by nature; but the same author supposes it to be a work of art, raised for a tumulus. It is crowned with the ruins of an ancient cruciform chapel, which was dedicated to St. Michael, and dependent on the abbey of Athelney. Though previously in a dilapidated state, it was greatly damaged during the parliamentary war, when it was occupied as a military post by a small party of royalists, who, after having successfully resisted various assaults, were compelled to surrender to a body of parliamentarians, detached against them by General Fairfax.

BOROUGHBRIDGE, a market-town and chapelry, in the parish of ALDBOROUGH, Lower division of the wapentake of CLARO, W. riding of YORK, 17½ miles (N. W. by W.) from York, and 206 (N. N. W.) from London; containing 1024 inhabitants. This place, which has risen into importance since the decline of Aldborough, within half a mile of which it is situated, derives its name from a bridge erected here over the river Ure, soon after the Conquest, when the road was diverted

from Aldborough, and brought through this town. In 1318, it was burnt by Earl Douglas, at the head of a band of Scots, who ravaged the northern parts of England. In 1322, a battle was fought near the bridge, between the forces of Edward II. and those of the celebrated Earl of Lancaster; the latter were defeated, and the earl, having taken refuge in the town, which was assaulted on the following day, was made prisoner and conveyed to Pontefract, where he was soon afterwards beheaded. Of this battle, a memorial was exhibited in the number of human bones, swords, fragments of armour, and other military relics, which, in raising the bank of the Ure in 1792, were found near the spot. The TOWN has been greatly improved, and is pleasantly situated on the southern bank of the river, over which is a handsome stone bridge on the site of a former one of wood: the streets are partially paved, and the inhabitants are amply supplied with water from springs and from the river. A court-house was built in 1836. The trade of the town is principally derived from its situation on the high road to Edinburgh. In 1846 an act was passed, enabling the York and Newcastle Railway Company to make a branch to Boroughbridge, 5¾ miles long. The market is on Saturday; and large fairs are held on April 27th, June 22nd, Aug. 16th, Oct. 23rd, and Dec. 13th, each for two days: the fair in June, which continues for a week, is chiefly celebrated for horses and hardware, and the others are for cattle and sheep. In the market-place, which is in the centre of the town, is a handsome fluted column of the Doric order, twelve feet high. The constables and other officers are chosen annually at the court leet of the lord of the manor. The elective franchise was conferred in the reign of Mary, from which time the borough returned two members to parliament, until disfranchised by the 2nd and 3rd of William IV., cap. 45.

The LIVING is a perpetual curacy; net income, £83; patron, the Vicar of Aldborough. Besides the chapel, there are places of worship for Particular Baptists and Wesleyans. To the west of the town are three large pyramidal stones, ranged in a straight line, in a direction from north to south; the central one, which is the largest, is 30½ feet in height: they are vulgarly called the Devil's Arrows, and were originally four in number. The purpose of their erection is involved in obscurity: some suppose them to have been raised in memory of a reconciliation effected between Caracalla and Geta, sons of the Emperor Severus who died at York. Camden considers them to have been Roman trophies; but though they may probably have been used by that people as metæ in the celebration of their chariot races, their origin appears to be more remote. Stukeley refers them to the earliest times of the Britons, and is of opinion that here was the great Panegyre of the Druids, where the inhabitants of the neighbouring district assembled to offer the sacrifices. From its proximity to Aldborough, a celebrated Roman station, the town hàs become the depository of numerous relics, consisting of tessellated pavements and coins, several of which have been found here; and in the immediate vicinity, the remains of a Roman wall are still discernible.

BOROUGH-FEN, an extra-parochial district, in the soke of PETERBOROUGH, N. division of the county of NORTHAMPTON, 5 miles (N. E. by N.) from Peterborough; containing 192 inhabitants.

ı BORROWASH, a hamlet, partly in the parish of OCKBROOK, hundred of MORLESTON and LITCHURCH, and partly in the parish of SPONDON, hundred of APPLE-TREE, union of SHARDLOW, S. division of the county of DERBY, 4½ miles (E. by S.) from Derby; containing about 650 inhabitants. This hamlet lies on the high road from Derby to Nottingham; and is watered by the river Derwent, on which are the mills of Messrs. Towle, where the manufacture of lace-thread is carried on, giving employment to about 250 hands. The Derby canal runs near the place; and it has a station on the Midland railway. The Wesleyans have a place of worship; there are also a day, and an infants', school.

· BORROWBY, a township, in the parish of LEAKE, union of NORTHALLERTON, wapentake of ALLERTON-SHIRE, N. riding of YORK, 5 miles (N.) from Thirsk; containing 401 inhabitants. It is situated on the road between Thirsk and Stokesley, and comprises by computation 1280 acres, including Gueldable, in which are 500 acres. The Bishop of Ripon is lord of the manor of Borrowby. There is a place of worship for Wesleyans.

BORROWBY, a township, in the parish of LYTHE, union of THIRSK, E. division of the liberty of LANG-BAURGH, N. riding of YORK, 11¼ miles (W. N. W.) from Whitby; containing 81 inhabitants. This place was formerly styled Bergebi, as it appears written in Domesday survey; and was the property of the Manleys, of Mulgrave, with which barony the estate has descended to the present lord: at the time of the Conqueror's survey it had been laid waste. The township comprises about 650 acres, in the western part of the parish. The village is on the acclivities of a narrow dale, and north of the road between Whitby and Guisborough.

BORROWDALE, a chapelry, in the parish of CROSTHWAITE, union of COCKERMOUTH, ALLERDALE ward above Derwent, W. division of CUMBERLAND, 6 miles (S. by W.) from Keswick; containing 369 inhabitants. The romantic scenery of this district has elicited deserved eulogy from numerous tourists. The Bowder stone, situated in the vale, is esteemed the largest detached piece of rock, entitled to the denomination of a single stone, in England; it is 62 feet in length, and 84 in circumference, and contains about 23,090 feet of solid stone, weighing upwards of 1771 tons: the upper part projects considerably over the small base on which it rests, and it is not unusual for parties of pleasure to regale under it. The celebrated black-lead, or wad, mine of Borrowdale, is about nine miles from Keswick, near the head of the valley, in the steep side of a mountain facing the south-east. The lead is found in lumps or nodules, varying in weight from 1oz. to 50lb., imbedded in the matrix; and the finer sort is packed in barrels, sent to London, and deposited in the warehouse belonging to the proprietors of the mine, where it is exposed for sale to the pencil-makers on the first Monday in every month: that of an inferior description is chiefly used in the composition of crucibles, in giving a black polish to articles of cast-iron, and in various anti-attrition compositions. Black-lead is found in various parts of the world, but in none to so great an extent, and of the same degree of purity, as here: an inferior kind has been discovered in the shires of Ayr and Inverness, in Scotland, but it is unfit for pencils. Here are also several quarries of blue slate:

a copper-mine was formerly worked; and lead-ore exists to a limited extent in the mountain. A soft paleish substance, commonly called Borrowdale soap, is found, which, having undergone a chymical process, similar to that by which the black-lead is hardened, is used for slate pencils. A fair for sheep is held on the first Wednesday in September. The living is a perpetual curacy; net income, £80; patron, the Vicar of Crosthwaite. The chapel was rebuilt a few years since. On the summit of Castle Crag, a conical hill covered with wood, are vestiges of a military work. Near a lake at the lower extremity of the dale is a salt-spring, the water of which is of a quality somewhat similar to that of Cheltenham.

BORROWDON, a township, in the parish of AL-LENTON, union of ROTHBURY, W. division of COQUET-DALE ward, N. division of NORTHUMBERLAND; containing 165 inhabitants. It is situated about a mile south-west from Netherton, from which it is separated by a small stream; and belongs to various proprietors. About a mile and a half to the south-west stands Charity Hall, which was left to the poor of Rothbury parish, and from that circumstance derives its name. Several British axe-heads of flint have been found.

BORWICK, or BEREWIC, a township, and formerly a chapelry, in the parish of WALTON, hundred of LONS-DALE south of the Sands, N. division of the county of LANCASTER, 2½ miles (S.) from Burton-in-Kendal; containing 214 inhabitants. The Whyttyngtons and Brearleys were early possessed of Berewic, the name of which denotes a subordinate manor; it afterwards passed, by marriage, to the Standishes and Townleys, and more recently to the family of Strickland, a branch of which took the name of Standish. One of the bedrooms of the Hall was the ancient domestic chapel; and adjoining was the priests' closet, beneath which still remains a secret place, into which the persecuted ecclesiastics, on pressing part of the floor, suddenly descended, eluding for the time all search. When Charles II. was here in August, 1651, "he was little aware," says Dr. Whittaker, "in how few days he was to be indebted for his crown and life to a similar contrivance:" the king lodged for one night at the Hall, on his way to Worcester, and his army encamped a short distance from it.

The township is separated from Capernwray and Carnforth by the river Keer, and comprises 836 acres, whereof two-thirds are arable, and the remainder pasture, with about ten acres of woodland. The surface is undulated; the soil good, a little light and gravelly upon a limestone substratum in parts, and in other parts grit: the scenery is picturesque, with a view of Warton Cragg and Morecambe bay. There is good limestone; it carries a fine polish, and also produces excellent lime for manure. The Lancaster and Kendal canal runs through the township. The Hall is now the property of Walter Strickland, Esq.; Linden Hall is the seat of William Sharp, Esq., and is picturesquely situated. The great tithes have been commuted for £111. The chapel of the township has fallen into neglect.

BOSBURY (HOLY TRINITY), a parish, in the union of LEDBURY, hundred of RADLOW, county of HERE-FORD, 4 miles (N. by W.) from Ledbury; containing 1137 inhabitants. The parish is intersected by the Ledbury and Worcester road, and comprises by computation 4500 acres, of which the soil is a stiff red clay saturated with moisture, and the surface varied hill and dale. The Gloucester and Ledbury canal wharf is a mile distant. The living is a discharged vicarage, endowed with one-fourth of the rectorial tithes, and valued in the king's books at £10. 3. 8.; patron, the Bishop of Hereford: the impropriate tithes have been commuted for £420, and the vicarial for £399. 18. The church, which is in various styles, is an ancient edifice, containing some interesting monuments. There is a place of worship for Wesleyans; and a grammar school, endowed by Sir Rowland Morton, has an income of about £135. The bishops of Hereford had a palace here, the remains of which have been converted into farm-offices.

BOSCASTLE, a small sea-port, and formerly a market-town, in the parishes of FORRABURY and MINSTER, hundred of LESNEWTH, E. division of CORN-WALL, 5 miles (N. N. W.) from Camelford, and 230 (W. by S.) from London; containing 807 inhabitants. This place takes its name from a castle erected by some of the family of Bottereaux, who settled here in the reign of Henry II.; only the site remains. The town is romantically situated on the northern coast of the county, and contains several respectable houses. A pilchard-fishery, established a few years since, but soon afterwards relinquished, contributed greatly to the improvement of the quay, which is accessible to ships of 300 tons' burthen. The port is a member of the port of Padstow; and a considerable trade is carried on in corn, Delabole slate, and manganese, of which last there is a mine in the neighbourhood. The fairs are on August 5th, for lambs, and November 22nd, for ewes and cattle. There is a place of worship for Wesleyans; and some remains of an ancient chapel dedicated to St. John, are visible.

BOSCOBEL, an extra-parochial district, in the union of SHIFFNALL, hundred of BRIMSTREE, S. division of SALOP, 7½ miles (E.) from Shiffnall; containing 18 inhabitants. It comprises 549 acres of land. Boscobel House is celebrated in history as the place where Charles II. concealed himself, in Sept. 1651, after the disastrous battle of Worcester, secure in the incorruptible integrity of five brothers, in humble life, named Penderell. The house has been considerably modernised; but the place of concealment, called the Sacred Hole, is carefully preserved, and in front of the house is a Latin inscription, traced with white pebbles in the pavement, recording the circumstance. The Royal Oak, thought to have sprung from an acorn of the tree to which the unfortunate monarch retired for greater security when his pursuers were searching the house and out-buildings, stands near the middle of a large field, adjoining the garden; it is surrounded by an iron-railing, and has an inscribed brass plate affixed to it.

BOSCOMB (ST. ANDREW), a parish, in the union and hundred of AMESBURY, Salisbury and Amesbury, and S. divisions of WILTS, 3¾ miles (S. E. by E.) from Amesbury, and on the road between Salisbury and Marlborough; containing 156 inhabitants. The living is a rectory, valued in the king's books at £13. 17. 1.; net income, £330; patron, the Bishop of Salisbury. Four almshouses were endowed with a rent-charge of £24, by John Kent, Esq., by will proved in 1710. This was once the residence of the celebrated Richard Hooker, 308

who held the living, and here wrote some part of his Ecclesiastical Polity.

BOSDEN, county of CHESTER.—See HANDFORTH.

BOSHAM (HOLY TRINITY), a parish, in the union of WEST BOURNE, hundred of BOSHAM, rape of CHICHESTER, W. division of SUSSEX, 4 miles (W. by S.) from Chichester; containing, with the tythings of Broadbridge, Creed, Fishbourne, Gosport, and Walton, 1091 inhabitants. This place, called by the Saxons Bosenham, probably from the woods by which it was surrounded, was anciently of great importance, and, in the reign of Edward the Confessor, was the occasional residence of Earl Godwin, whose son Harold, afterwards King of England, sailing from Bosham on an excursion of pleasure, in 1056, was driven by a storm on the Norman coast, and made prisoner by Count Ponthieu. In the time of Henry II. the place was constituted the head of a hundred and manor, and endowed with various immunities, which were fully confirmed by James I., and of which several are still recognised. The parish is bounded on the east and south by the harbour of Chichester, and comprises 3194 acres, whereof 94 are common or waste. The inhabitants are chiefly employed in the oyster-fishery: the village is pleasantly situated at the upper extremity of the creek to which it gives name, and is neatly built. The living is a discharged vicarage, valued in the king's books at £6. 11. 3.; net income, £120; patrons and appropriators, the Dean and Chapter of Chichester, whose tithes have been commuted for £1318. 13., and who possess a glebe of 88 acres. The church, built about the year 1120, by William Warlewast, Bishop of Exeter, was made collegiate for a dean and five secular canons or prebendaries, and was a royal free chapel, exempt from ecclesiastical jurisdiction, till the Dissolution, when it was made parochial. It is a stately edifice, chiefly early English, with some Norman details, and later additions: the south aisle was restored, and other improvements effected, in 1845. There is a place of worship for Independents. A small monastery for five or six brethren was founded in 681, by Adelwach, and placed under the superintendence of Dicul, an Irish monk. Herbert, secretary to Thomas à Becket, and afterwards made cardinal by Pope Alexander III., was a native of the place.

BOSLEY, a chapelry, in the parish of PRESTBURY, union and hundred of MACCLESFIELD, N. division of the county of CHESTER, 4¾ miles (E. N. E.) from Congleton; containing 552 inhabitants. The manor passed in 1327 to Isabel, mother of Edward III., and from Henry VI. came by grant to the Stanleys in 1454: it was afterwards held by Lord Monteagle, the hero of Flodden; passed to the Fittons about 1540; and is now vested in their successor, the Earl of Harrington. The chapelry is situated on the road from Manchester to Derby, and comprises about 2500 acres; it is skirted by the river Daine, and intersected by the Macclesfield canal. There are a silk-spinning factory and a cotton-mill, in which upwards of 100 people are employed. The living is a perpetual curacy; net income, £82; patron, the Vicar of Prestbury: the glebe comprises about 30 acres.

BOSSALL (ST. BOTOLPH), a parish, partly in the wapentake of BIRDFORTH, but chiefly in that of BULMER, N. riding of YORK; consisting of the chapelries of

Butter-Crambe, Claxton, and Sand-Hutton, and the townships of Bossall, Harton, and part of Flaxton-on-the-Moor; and containing 1184 inhabitants, of whom 77 are in the township of Bossall, 4 miles (S.) from Whitwell. The parish comprises 9820 acres; and is bounded by the river Derwent on the south and east, and intersected by the road from York to Scarborough. The village was formerly large, but at present consists of only three or four houses: foundations of buildings have been discovered in an adjoining field, thence called "Old Bossall." Courts leet are held for the several manors in the parish. The living is a vicarage, valued in the king's books at £12; net income, £445; patrons and appropriators, the Dean and Chapter of Durham. The church is a handsome cruciform structure, with a steeple rising from the centre. There are chapels at Sand-Hutton, Claxton, and Butter-Crambe.

Seal and Arms.

BOSSINEY with TREVENA, in the parish of TINTAGELL, union of CAMELFORD, hundred of LESNEWTH, E. division of CORNWALL, 4½ miles (N. W.) from Camelford; containing 296 inhabitants, of whom 219 are in Trevena. Bossiney and Trevena are two villages, about a quarter of a mile distant from each other, situated on a bleak and rugged part of the northern coast. A fair is held at the latter on the first Monday after Oct. 19th. Bossiney was made a free borough in the reign of Henry III., by Richard Earl of Cornwall, brother to that monarch; and a mayor, whose office is merely nominal, is chosen annually by a jury of burgesses empannelled by his predecessor, at the court leet held in October, when constables and other inferior officers are likewise appointed. The elective franchise was conferred in the 7th of Edward VI., from which time the borough returned two members to parliament, until it was disfranchised by the act of the 2nd of William IV., cap. 45. The town-hall, a small building, is appropriated also to the use of a charity school, which is chiefly supported by the mayor and burgesses, who appoint the master, and allow him a salary of £20 per annum. There are some remains of King Arthur's Castle, on the top of a stupendous rock, formerly part of the main land, but now connected with it only by a narrow isthmus: the summit comprises an area of thirty acres of pasture; but the acclivities are so steep that it is almost inaccessible to the sheep that graze on it.

ᵗ BOSSINGTON, a tything, in the parish of PORLOCK, union of WILLITON, hundred of CARHAMPTON, W. division of SOMERSET; containing 133 inhabitants.

BOSSINGTON (ST. JAMES), a parish, in the union of STOCKBRIDGE, hundred of THORNGATE, Romsey and S. divisions of the county of SOUTHAMPTON, 3½ miles (S. W. by S.) from Stockbridge; containing 60 inhabitants. The Roman road from Salisbury to Winchester passes through. The living is annexed to that of Broughton: the church was built in 1840, by Mr. Elwes.

, BOSTOCK, a township, in the parish of DAVENHAM, union and hundred of NORTHWICH, S. division of
309

the county of CHESTER, 2¾ miles (N. W. by W.) from Middlewich; containing 190 inhabitants. This place gave name to a family descended from Osmerus, lord of Bostock in the reign of William the Conqueror: the heiress of the elder branch brought the manor in the latter part of the 15th century to the Savages. In 1755 it was sold by Sir Thomas Whitmore to the Tomkinsons. The township comprises 1523 acres; the soil is sand and clay. The Liverpool and Birmingham railway passes about a mile to the west of the village. The tithes have been commuted for £75. 11.

BOSTON (ST. BOTOLPH), a borough, port, market-town, and parish, and the head of a union, in the wapentake of SKIRBECK, parts of HOLLAND, county of LINCOLN, 34 miles (S. E.) from Lincoln, and 116 (N.) from London; containing 12,942, and, with certain extra-parochial grounds, 13,507 inhabitants. This place derived its name from St. Botolph, a Saxon, who founded a monastery here about the year 650; from which circumstance it was called Botolph's Town, since contracted to Boston. The monastery, which was erected on the north side of the present church, was destroyed by the Danes in 870, and its remains have been converted into a dwelling-house, styled Botolph's Priory. From the discovery of the foundations of several buildings, urns, and other relics of antiquity, in 1716, the place is supposed to have been of Roman origin; and according to Dr. Stukeley, the Romans built a fort at the entrance of the river Witham, over which they had a ferry, at a short distance to the south of the town. In the reign of Edward I., Robert Chamberlayne, having assembled some associates disguised as ecclesiastics, secretly set fire to the town, and, while the inhabitants were endeavouring to extinguish the flames, plundered the booths of the rich merchandise exposed for sale at the fair, and burnt such goods as they were not able to carry away. So rich is the town represented to have been at the time of this fire, that veins of melted gold and silver are said to have run in one common current, down the streets. In 1285, Boston suffered greatly from an inundation of the river; and the mercantile ardour of the inhabitants having been checked by the plunder of the fair and the conflagration of the town, its prosperity began to decline. In the early part of the reign of Edward II., however, it was made a staple port for wool, leather, tin, lead, and other commodities, which soon gave a new impulse to the spirit of commercial enterprise; and the settlement in England of the Hanseatic merchants, who established a guild here, tended so powerfully to revive the former prosperity of the town, that, in the reign of Edward III., it sent deputies to three grand councils held at Westminster, and contributed 17 ships and 261 men towards the armament for the invasion of Brittany.

Arms.

The TOWN is situated on the banks of the river Witham, which divides it into two wards, east and west, connected by a handsome iron bridge of one arch, erected by the corporation in 1807, at an expense of £22,000, under the superintendence of Mr. Rennie.

The streets are well paved, and lighted with gas, under acts passed in the 16th and 46th of George III. for the general improvement of the town ; and many handsome buildings have been erected. The inhabitants were till recently scantily supplied with water, which the more opulent collected from rain, in cisterns attached to their houses, and the poorer brought from the river, or from pits in the neighbourhood. Frequent attempts to procure a better supply, by boring, failed ; and in Feb. 1829, after expending £1800, the last undertaking was relinquished. An act, however, was passed in 1846, by which this inconvenience has been remedied. There are two subscription libraries ; a handsome suite of assembly rooms, built by the corporation in 1820 ; a commodious theatre, erected in 1806 ; and a theatre of arts, exhibiting views of various cities, with appropriate moving figures, which is open every Wednesday evening. About half a mile from the town are Vauxhall Gardens, which, during the season, are brilliantly illuminated, and numerously attended ; they were designed by Mr. Charles Cave in 1813, and comprise about two acres of ground : in the centre is an elegant saloon sixty-two feet wide.

Seal of the ancient Admiralty Jurisdiction, now abolished.

The TRADE of the port, from an accumulation of silt in the river, which impeded its navigation, had begun to decline about the middle of the last century, but was revived by forming a canal, deepening the river, and enlarging the harbour. The exports consist chiefly of the agricultural produce of the county ; the imports include timber, hemp, tar, and iron from the Baltic : a considerable coasting-trade is carried on, which of late years has rapidly increased. Since the fens adjoining the town have been drained and cultivated, a tract of rich land, of nearly 70,000 acres, has been obtained, which, besides producing grain, feeds a number of sheep and oxen, remarkable for their size and fatness : oats in great quantity are shipped to various parts of the coast, and wool to the manufacturing districts in Yorkshire, whence coal and other articles are brought in return. The quay, which is conveniently adapted to the loading of vessels, is accessible to ships of 100 tons' burthen. The custom-house, a commodious building, was erected at the public expense : the pilot-office was built in 1811 ; the establishment consists of a master, twelve pilots, and a few supernumeraries. The Witham is navigable to Lincoln, from which place, by means of canals communicating with the Trent, there is an inland navigation to almost every part of the kingdom. A loop or diverging line of the London and York railway will pass by the town : an act was passed in 1846 for a railway to Grantham, Nottingham, and Ambergate ; and another act, also passed in 1846, authorises the formation of a railway to Louth and Grimsby. About 40 boats are employed in the fishery, and shrimps of superior quality, soles, smelts, and herrings are taken in profusion : in 1772, the corporation erected a fish-market, which was taken down, and a new one upon a larger scale erected, in 1816. The market is on Wednesday and Saturday,

by an octagonal lantern turret, in the later English style; the tower, which is 300 feet high, and was formerly illuminated during the night, forms a conspicuous landmark for mariners traversing the North Sea. An additional church was erected some years since, by subscription: the living is a perpetual curacy, endowed with £100 per annum by the Corporation, who are the patrons. There are places of worship for General and Particular Baptists, the Society of Friends, Independents, Methodists, Unitarians, and Roman Catholics. The free grammar school, founded and endowed in 1554, under the above grant of Philip and Mary, is subject to the control of the trustees for charitable purposes appointed under the act of the 5th and 6th of William IV.: the schoolroom was built in 1567, and a convenient house for the master in 1826. A school was founded in 1707, by Mr. Laughton, who endowed it with lands in Skirbeck, producing about £50 per annum, since augmented by other benefactors; and a Blue-coat school, founded in 1713, for clothing and instructing boys and girls, and two national and Lancasterian schools, established in 1815, are supported by subscription. A general dispensary was instituted in 1795. The poor law union of Boston comprises 27 parishes or places, and contains a population of 34,680. Of the numerous monastic establishments which formerly existed in the town and its vicinity, there remain only some slight vestiges of the Black or Dominican friary, established in the year 1288. The ancient church of St. John, formerly the parish church, has been totally removed, but the cemetery is still used as a burying-ground. Fox, the martyrologist, was a native of the town. Boston confers the title of Viscount on the Irby family.

BOSTON, a village, forming with CLIFFORD a township, in the parish of BRAMHAM, Upper division of the wapentake of BARKSTONE-ASH, W. riding of YORK, 3 miles (S. S. E.) from Wetherby; containing 1566 inhabitants, of whom 1014 are in Boston. This large and commanding village is of recent growth. It arose in consequence of the discovery, in 1744, of a mineral spring here, which was called Thorp-Arch Spa on account of Thorp-Arch, in the vicinity, affording the nearest accommodation for visiters, before the building of the village of Boston, where the first house was erected in 1753. The water is of a saline taste, of a slightly sulphureous smell, and possessed of purgative and diuretic qualities: it is taken in larger quantities than the Harrogate water, and is efficacious in cases of general relaxation, bilious and dyspeptic complaints, and glandular obstructions. For the accommodation of the visiters to this place of fashionable resort, there is a pump-room, with hot and cold baths, the conveniences of which, together with the salubrity of the air, and the situation of the spot, in a valley, on the southern side of the river Wharfe (the village communicating with Thorp Arch by a good stone bridge), contribute greatly to increase the sanative effect of the spa water. The powers of the county debt-court of Boston, established in 1847, extend over the registration-district of Tadcaster, and the townships of Linton and Wetherby. A chapel, a neat plain building, erected on land given by Mr. Samuel Tate, was consecrated in 1815: the living is a perpetual curacy; net income, £146; patron, the Vicar of Bramham. There is a place of worship for Wesleyans.—See CLIFFORD.

311

BOSWORTH, HUSBAND'S (*ALL SAINTS*), a parish, in the union of MARKET-HARBOROUGH, hundred of GARTREE, S. division of the county of LEICESTER, 6 miles (W. S. W.) from Harborough; containing 953 inhabitants. The river Welland bounds the parish on the south and south-east, and the Avon on the north-west; the Grand Union canal crosses the western part of it, being conducted through a tunnel, 1170 yards in length, to the northern side of the village. The living is a rectory, valued in the king's books at £24. 15. 7½.; net income, £929; patron, the Rev. J. T. Mayne. The church had its spire greatly damaged through a storm of thunder and lightning, in July, 1755. There are places of worship for Particular Baptists, Wesleyans, and Roman Catholics. A school for boys is partly supported by a bequest of £15 per annum; and a school for boys and girls, partly by Miss Turvile.

BOSWORTH, MARKET (*ST. PETER*), a parish, and the head of a union, in the hundred of SPARKENHOE, S. division of the county of LEICESTER; comprising the chapelries of Barleston, Carlton, Shenton, and Sutton-Cheney, and part of the townships of Barton-in-the-Beans and Osbaston; and containing 2539 inhabitants, of whom 1135 are in the town of Market-Bosworth, 7 miles (N. by W.) from Hinckley, and 13 (W. by S.) from Leicester. This place, in Domesday book called *Bosworde*, takes the prefix to its name from a market granted to the inhabitants in the reign of Edward I. The neighbourhood is celebrated as the scene of a decisive battle fought on the 22nd of Aug. 1485, between Richard III. and the Earl of Richmond, afterwards Henry VII. This battle, the last of the sanguinary conflicts between the houses of York and Lancaster, took place on Redmoor Plain, in the lordship of Sutton-Cheney, a long tract of uneven ground extending in the direction of Atherstone from about a mile below Bosworth, now inclosed, and since that event better known as Bosworth-Field. On a hill about two miles south-west of the town, is a small spring, inclosed with rough stones in the form of a pyramid or obelisk, and which bears the name of "King Richard's Well:" according to tradition, the king quenched his thirst here during the action; and this circumstance has been commemorated by Dr. Parr, who visited the spot in 1813, in a short Latin inscription placed immediately above the spring. Numerous swords, shields, spurs, and other military relics, have been dug up in the neighbourhood.

The TOWN, which is pleasantly situated on an eminence, contains some respectable houses, and is well supplied with water. The manufacture of worsted-stockings is carried on here, and in the adjacent villages, to a considerable extent; and great facility has been given to trade by the Ashby and Coventry canal, which, passing within a mile of the town, affords a medium for supplying it with coal and other articles. The soil is good, but often clayey; it rests on gravel, with a substratum of sand, and is remarkable that the best land is on the hills. There is a market on Wednesday; and fairs are held on May 8th, for horses, horned-cattle, and sheep, and July 10th, which is called the Cherry fair: there are also statute-fairs on Oct. 2nd and about a fortnight before Martinmas. The powers of the county debt-court of Market-Bosworth, established in 1847, extend over the registration-district of Market-Bosworth.

The LIVING is a rectory, valued in the king's books at £55. 18. 4.; net income, £903; patron, Sir W. W. Dixie, Bart., of Bosworth Hall: the tithes were commuted for land and money payments in 1794. The church is a spacious ancient structure, with a beautiful spire, and contains many interesting monuments, among the finest of which is one to some members of the Dixie family. There are chapels of ease at Barleston, Carlton, Shenton, and Sutton-Cheney; also places of worship in the parish for Baptists and Independents. The free grammar school, which is open to all boys of the parishes of Bosworth and Cadeby, was founded in 1593, by Sir Wolstan Dixie, Knt., who endowed it with lands, and with two fellowships of £30 and four scholarships of £10 per annum each, at Emmanuel College, Cambridge. In consequence of some abuses, the affairs were in chancery for nearly 50 years, during the greater part of which time the establishment was discontinued; but in 1827 new premises were begun, whích were opened on the 1st of Feb. 1830, and form a very handsome pile. The Rev. Anthony Blackwall, an eminent classical scholar, was master, and the celebrated Dr. Johnson, for a short time, usher; Richard Dawes, the learned critic, was educated here under the former. The poor law union of Bosworth comprises 28 parishes or places, and contains a population of 13,600. This is the birthplace of Thomas Simpson, the eminent mathematician, who died here in 1761, and was interred at Sutton-Cheney, where a tablet has lately been erected to his memory.

BOTCHERBY, a township, in the parish of St. Cuthbert, Carlisle, Cumberland ward, union of Carlisle, E. division of Cumberland; containing 125 inhabitants. It lies east of Carlisle.

BOTCHERGATE, a township, in the parish of St. Cuthbert, Carlisle, Cumberland ward, union of Carlisle, E. division of Cumberland; containing 5460 inhabitants.—See Carlisle.

BOTCHESTON, a hamlet, in the parish of Ratby, union of Market-Bosworth, hundred of Sparkenhoe, S. division of the county of Leicester, 6 miles (E. N. E.) from Market-Bosworth; containing 37 inhabitants.

BOTESDALE, a chapelry and post-town, and formerly a market-town, in the parish of Redgrave, union and hundred of Hartismere, W. division of Suffolk, 25 miles (N. N. W.) from Ipswich, and 86 (N. E. by N.) from London, on the road to Norwich; containing 633 inhabitants. The name, a contraction of *Botolph's Dale*, is derived from Botolph, the tutelar saint of the chapel, and from the dale in which the place is situated. The town consists principally of one long street, which extends into the parishes of Rickinghall Superior and Inferior; the houses are indifferently built: the inhabitants are amply supplied with water from wells. A small fair for cattle and pedlery is held on Holy-Thursday; and there are courts leet and baron held at Whitsuntide; at the former of which constables and other officers are appointed. The chapel is a small and rather mean building, of some antiquity. A free grammar school for six boys was founded and endowed in 1561, by Sir Nicholas Bacon.

BOTHAL (St. Andrew), a parish, in the union of Morpeth, E. division of Morpeth ward, N. division of Northumberland; containing the townships of Ashington with Sheepwash, Bothal-Demesne, Longhirst,

moor, some portions of which, however, have been lately improved by draining, and by warpage from the Trent. The living is a discharged vicarage, united in 1727 to the vicarage of Messingham, and valued in the king's books at £10: the tithes of Ashby, Bottesford, and Yaddlethorpe, were commuted for land and corn-rents, under an inclosure act, in 1794; and those of Burringham, Holme, and East Butterwick, have been commuted for a rent-charge. The church is an ancient structure of a mixed character of architecture, with a square tower, and Norman porch. There are places of worship at Ashby and Burringham for Wesleyans, and one at Yaddlethorpe for Primitive Methodists.

BOTTESLAW, a township, in the parish and union of STOKE-UPON-TRENT, N. division of the hundred of PIREHILL and of the county of STAFFORD; containing 65 inhabitants. This is a township of scattered farms, lying north of the town of Stoke; it belongs to several proprietors.

BOTTISHAM (*HOLY TRINITY*), a parish, in the union of NEWMARKET, hundred of STAINE, county of CAMBRIDGE, 6 miles (W. S. W.) from Newmarket; containing 1484 inhabitants. The parish comprises about 5000 acres, of which 400 are pasture, and the rest arable, with the exception of a few acres of woodland. A considerable part of the village was destroyed by fire in 1712. The petty-sessions are held here. The living is a discharged vicarage, valued in the king's books at £16; net income, £258; patrons and impropriators, the Master and Fellows of Trinity College, Cambridge. The tithes were commuted for land and a money payment in 1801. The church contains the tomb of Elias de Beckingham, justiciary of England in the reign of Edward I. At Bottisham Lode is a place of worship for Particular Baptists. Sir Roger Jenyns, Knt., founded a school in 1730, and endowed it with £20 per annum. The poor also derive benefit from a bequest of £118 per annum by the Rev. W. Pugh, late vicar, who died in 1825; one of £25 per annum, by Henry Sheppard; and £5 per annum, by another benefactor. A small priory of Augustine canons, dedicated to the Blessed Virgin and St. Nicholas, was founded at Anglesey, in the parish, by Henry I.; the revenue, in the 26th of Henry VIII., was £149. 18. 6.: the site is now occupied by a farmhouse, in the walls of which a portion of the conventual buildings is visible. Soame Jenyns, author of the *Evidences of Christianity* and a volume of poems, was a native of the parish.

BOTTOMS, a hamlet, in the parish of BLIDWORTH, union of MANSFIELD, Southwell division of the wapentake of THURGARTON, S. division of the county of NOTTINGHAM; containing 250 inhabitants.

BOTUS-FLEMING, a parish, in the union of ST. GERMANS, S. division of the hundred of EAST, E. division of CORNWALL, 3 miles (N. W.) from Saltash; containing 250 inhabitants. The parish comprises 937 acres, of which 21 are common or waste. The living is a rectory, valued in the king's books at £16. 15. 7½.; net income, £190; patrons, the family of Spry. In the centre of a field, on the northern side of the village, stands a pyramidal monument erected to the memory of Dr. William Martin, of Plymouth, who died in 1762.

BOTWELL, a hamlet, in the parish of HAYES, union of UXBRIDGE, hundred of ELTHORNE, county of MIDDLESEX; containing 373 inhabitants. It lies to the south of the village of Hayes, and near the Grand Junction canal.

BOUGHTON (*ALL SAINTS*), a parish, in the union of DOWNHAM, hundred of CLACKCLOSE, W. division of NORFOLK, 1¼ mile (N.) from Stoke-Ferry; containing 209 inhabitants. The parish comprises 1323*a*. 1*r*. 27*p*., of which 721 acres are arable, 519 meadow and pasture, 24 woodland and plantations, and 43 common allotted to the poor at the inclosure. The living is a discharged rectory, valued in the king's books at £10; patron, Sir W. J. H. B. Folkes, Bart.: the tithes have been commuted for £410, and the glebe comprises 30 acres, with a small house. The church is an ancient structure in the early English style, with a square embattled tower.

BOUGHTON, a hamlet, in the parish of WEEKLEY, county of NORTHAMPTON.—See WEEKLEY.

BOUGHTON (*ST. JOHN THE BAPTIST*), a parish, in the union of BRIXWORTH, hundred of SPELHOE, S. division of the county of NORTHAMPTON, 3¾ miles (N.) from Northampton; containing 389 inhabitants. This parish, formerly called Buckton, is bounded on the west and north by the river Nene, and intersected by the road from Northampton to Leicester; and comprises by computation about 1400 acres: limestone is quarried, principally for the roads. A chartered fair for cattle and for manufactured wares is held on the 24th of June, and two following days. The living is a rectory, valued in the king's books at £20. 9. 7.; net income, £368; patron, Col. R. W. H. Howard Vyse: the tithes have been commuted for 184 acres of land; and a house has been lately built by Col. Vyse, in which the rector, now Rev. G. S. Howard Vyse, resides. The church, having been enlarged, was reconsecrated in March 1847. There is a place of worship for Wesleyans. Humphrey's charity, consisting of about 49 acres of land and three tenements, in Pitsford, the rent of which is £160 per annum, is applied by the feoffees, according to the will of the benefactor, in providing coal for the poor, apprenticing children, mending the highways, and repairing the church. Some slight remains still exist of an ancient family mansion, the residence of Lord Strafford.

BOUGHTON, a parish, in the union of SOUTHWELL, Hatfield division of the wapentake of BASSETLAW, N. division of the county of NOTTINGHAM, 1¾ mile (N. E. by E.) from Ollerton; containing 309 inhabitants, and comprising 1750 acres. About 135 acres are common, and 50 wood. The parish is intersected by the river Maun, over which a bridge was erected by subscription in 1812, the ford that previously existed being often dangerous. On the bank of the river is a deep cavity, in the rock of red sandstone, called Robin Hood's Cave, near which is New England, a district of about 50 acres, inclosed from the forest land many years ago. The village is small and scattered, and is situated at the foot of Cockin Hill, a steep acclivity which forms the east side of the parish, and the boundary of the South Clay division. The living is a perpetual curacy, annexed to the vicarage of Kneesall: the church is a plain building, with a belfry turret. The Baptists have a place of worship.

BOUGHTON-ALUPH (*ALL SAINTS*), a parish, in the union of EAST ASHFORD, hundred of WYE, lathe of SHEPWAY, E. division of KENT, 4 miles (N. N. E.) from Ashford; containing 524 inhabitants. It is bounded on the east by the river Stour, and comprises 2418 acres,

314

of which 400 are in wood; the soil is to a great extent chalky. The living is a vicarage, valued in the king's books at £6. 5.; patrons, the Trustees of Dr. Breton; impropriator, the Rev. J. Billington: the tithes have been commuted for £600, and there are 28 acres of glebe. The church is a spacious cruciform structure, built of flint and ashlar-stone, with a low central tower.

BOUGHTON, GREAT, a township, and the head of a union, in the parish of ST. OSWALD, CHESTER, Lower division of the hundred of BROXTON, S. division of the county of CHESTER; containing 949 inhabitants. This place was given by Hugh Lupus to the convent of St. Werburgh; it came, in the reign of Edward VI., to Sir Richard Cotton, who parcelled it out among several fee farmers. The principal mansion, with its demesne, was for some generations vested in a younger branch of the Davenport family, from whom it passed by female heirs to the family of Currie. The township comprises 731 acres. It is intersected by two turnpike-roads to Chester, one from Whitchurch, and the other from Nantwich; and near their junction has been formed a considerable village, which unites with one of the streets of Chester. The Chester and Nantwich canal, and the Chester and Crewe railway, also pass through it; and the river Dee adjoins on the west. Across the middle of the township stretches a belt of deep rich loam, which, from its proximity to Chester, lets at a high rate for garden-ground; the rest is a clayey soil, held by milkmen, butchers, &c. The poor law union of Great Boughton comprises 99 parishes or places, of which 96 are in Cheshire, and 3 in the county of Flint, North Wales; and contains a population of 49,085.

BOUGHTON-MALHERB (*ST. NICHOLAS*), a parish, in the union of HOLLINGBOURN, hundred of EYHORNE, lathe of AYLESFORD, W. division of KENT, 1½ mile (S. W. by S.) from Lenham; containing 512 inhabitants, and comprising 2699 acres. This parish is divided by a ridge of hills into two districts, Boughton Upland and Boughton Weald, the latter so called from its situation within the Weald of Kent. The family of Wotton resided here for a considerable period, and this is the birthplace of its most accomplished member, Sir Henry Wotton, who was employed by James I. in several foreign embassies, and whose biography is written by Izaak Walton. The remains of the mansion, on a panel in which is inscribed the date 1579, have been converted into a farmhouse. The living is a rectory, valued in the king's books at £13. 15., and in the patronage of Earl Cornwallis: the tithes have been commuted for £300, and the glebe comprises six acres. The church is situated on the summit of the ridge of hills, and is a handsome edifice with a square tower at the west end; it contains several interesting monuments to members of the family of Wotton, and a mural tablet to Dr. Sharpe, chaplain to Queen Elizabeth, James I., and Prince Henry.

BOUGHTON-MONCHELSEA (*ST. PETER*), a parish, in the union of MAIDSTONE, hundred of EYHORNE, and extending into the hundred of MAIDSTONE, lathe of AYLESFORD, W. division of KENT, 4 miles (S. by E.) from Maidstone; containing 1106 inhabitants. It comprises 2296 acres, and is intersected by a ridge of hills, the summit of which forms the northern boundary of the Weald of Kent, and on the southern declivity of which are several stone-quarries. The living is a vicarage, valued in the king's books at £7. 13. 4.; net income, £395; patrons and appropriators, the Dean and Chapter of Rochester. The church, a small edifice with a handsome tower, has been partly rebuilt, the body of it having been destroyed by fire in 1832; there are some remarkable monuments, especially one to the memory of Sir Christopher Powell.

BOUGHTON, SPITTLE, an extra-parochial liberty, in the union of GREAT BOUGHTON, and county of the city of CHESTER; containing 191 inhabitants.

BOUGHTON-UNDER-BLEAN (ST. PETER AND ST. PAUL), a parish, in the union of FAVERSHAM, hundred of BOUGHTON-UNDER-BLEAN, lathe of SCRAY, E. division of KENT, 3 miles (S. E. by E.) from Faversham; containing 1373 inhabitants. This place derives its distinguishing epithet from the adjacent forest of Blean, which was anciently the haunt of wild boars, wolves, and other beasts of chace; but the description applies more particularly to the situation of that part of the parish which is now called South-street. The parish comprises 2349a. 3r. 27p.; 1220 acres are arable, 274 meadow, 161 pasture, 109 wood, 262 in hops, 209 in orchards, 18 occupied by homesteads, and 45 in gardens. Boughton-street is on elevated ground, and was not built till after the formation of the present high road to Canterbury, through the king's forest of Blean, before which time the old Watling-street crossed the river Stour at Shalmsford bridge, and entered Canterbury near the castle. A fair for toys and pedlery is held on the Monday after St. Peter's day. The living is a vicarage, valued in the king's books at £9. 4. 9½.; net income, £300; patron, the Archbishop of Canterbury; appropriators, the Dean and Chapter. The church contains several ancient monuments, and its internal architecture is of a pleasing character; the spire fell down about the close of the sixteenth century. There is a place of worship for Wesleyans. About 28 acres of land, and other considerable charities, have been bequeathed for the benefit of the poor. In 1716, a human skeleton, by the side of which lay a sword and a brass coin struck in the reign of Antoninus Pius, was dug up.

BOULBY.—See EASINGTON-in-CLEVELAND.

BOULDON, a township, in the parish of HOLDGATE, union of LUDLOW, hundred of MUNSLOW, S. division of SALOP; containing 61 inhabitants.

BOULGE (ST. MICHAEL), a parish, in the union of WOODBRIDGE, hundred of WILFORD, E. division of SUFFOLK, 3 miles (N. N. W.) from Woodbridge; containing 45 inhabitants, and comprising 545 acres by measurement. The living is a discharged rectory, with that of Debach annexed, valued in the king's books at £3. 12. 1.; patron and incumbent, the Rev. O. S. Reynolds. The tithes of the parish have been commuted or £133, and there are nearly 4 acres of glebe. The church is very small.

BOULMER, with SEATON-HOUSE, a township, in the parish of LONG HOUGHTON, union of ALNWICK, S. division of BAMBROUGH ward, N. division of NORTHUMBERLAND, 5 miles (E. by N.) from Alnwick; containing 153 inhabitants. The township comprises 63a. 1p., all arable land, with the exception of about 30 acres of grass. The village is situated on the sea-shore, and is chiefly inhabited by fishermen, whose boats are moored in Boulmer bay, a natural basin (environed by rocks) 800 yards long and 400 broad, and the entrance

315

to which is 12 feet deep at low water. Here is a coastguard station. The vicarial tithes have been commuted for £78. 19. 6., and the impropriate for £27. 12.

BOULSDON, with KILLCOT, a tything, in the parish and union of NEWENT, hundred of BOTLOE, W. division of the county of GLOUCESTER, 1¼ mile (S. by W.) from Newent; containing 417 inhabitants.

BOULSTON.—See BOLSTONE.

BOULTHAM (ST. HELEN), a parish, in the Lower division of the wapentake of BOOTHBY-GRAFFO, parts of KESTEVEN, union and county of LINCOLN, 3 miles (S. W. by S.) from Lincoln; containing 72 inhabitants. The living is a discharged rectory, valued in the king's books at £7. 15. 2., and in the patronage of the Trustees of the late R. Ellison, Esq.; net income, £126. The tithes were commuted for land and corn-rents in 1803.

BOULTON, a chapelry, in the parish of ST. PETER, DERBY, union of SHARDLOW, hundred of MORLESTON and LITCHURCH, S. division of the county of DERBY, 3½ miles (S. E. by E.) from Derby; containing 171 inhabitants. It comprises 791a. 3r. 4p., and is intersected by the Derby canal: the village has several neat houses. The living is a perpetual curacy, in the patronage of the Proprietors of land in the chapelry; net income, £120. The tithes were commuted for land and a money payment in 1802; the incumbent then received 29 acres, besides which he has 37 acres in other places. The chapel was enlarged and repaired in 1840, at a cost of £480.

BOURN (ST. MARY), a parish, in the union of CAXTON and ARRINGTON, hundred of LONGSTOW, county of CAMBRIDGE, 1¼ mile (S. E. by E.) from Caxton; containing 909 inhabitants. Here was a castle, which was destroyed during the war with the barons in the reign of Henry III. The living is a discharged vicarage, valued in the king's books at £9. 15. 10., and in the gift of Christ's College, Cambridge: the great tithes, belonging to the college, have been commuted for £593, with a glebe of 219 acres, and the incumbent's tithes for £188. 13., with a glebe of 4 acres. A school, established in 1819, is endowed by the Countess De la Warr with £20 per annum. A mineral spring here was formerly in high repute.

BOURN, SURREY.—See WRECKLESHAM.

BOURN-MOOR, a township, in the parish of HOUGHTON-LE-SPRING, union of CHESTER-LE-STREET, N. division of EASINGTON ward and of the county of DURHAM; containing 891 inhabitants. This township, which is bounded by Bidick on the north, was separated from that district about eighty years since, probably on account of the population attached to the collieries: the name appears to have been derived from the stream called Moors-burn, which falls into the river Wear in Lumley Park. It comprises 500 acres, of which 375 are arable, 100 grass land, and 25 waste. At New Lambton, in the township, is a brine well 97 fathoms deep, where salt-works were established in 1815. There is a place of worship for Wesleyans.

BOURNE (ST. PETER AND ST. PAUL), a parish, and the head of a union, in the wapentake of AVELAND, parts of KESTEVEN, county of LINCOLN, 36 miles (S.) from LINCOLN, and 97 (N.) from London; containing, with the hamlets of Cawthorpe and Dyke, 3361 inhabitants. This place takes its name from a stream of remarkably pure water, issuing from a copious spring

2 S 2

contiguous to the town, near the Castle Hill, and called the Bourn-Eau; *bourn* being the Saxon term for brook or torrent. Though little of its early history is known, the town is supposed, from the discovery of Roman coins and tessellated pavements, to have been anciently of some importance. When the Danes invaded England in the ninth century, Marcot, the Saxon lord of Bourne, with a few of his own vassals and a detachment from Croyland Abbey, after an obstinate engagement, defeated a party of them who had made an inroad into this part of Lincolnshire. Prior to the time of Edward the Confessor a castle was erected here, of which the trenches and mounds are still discernible : it appears to have included an area of more than eight acres. In 1138, Baldwin, a descendant of Walter Fitz-Gilbert, to whom the town was given by William Rufus, founded a priory for canons of the order of St. Augustine, the site alone of which, now called the Trenches, is visible : the revenue, at the Dissolution, was £197. 17. 5. In the seventeenth century, Bourne was twice nearly destroyed by fire.

The parish comprises about 10,000 acres. The town is intersected by the Hull, Lincoln, and London road, and consists principally of one very long street, the houses in which are in general modern and well built. A considerable trade in leather was formerly carried on, and several extensive tan-yards were at work ; but this branch of industry has altogether declined. A canal has been constructed to Spalding and Boston, by which means the town is supplied with coal, timber, and other commodities. The market is on Saturday; the fairs are on April 7th, May 7th, and October 29th. The county magistrates hold a meeting every Saturday ; and courts of session for the parts of Kesteven are held quarterly : the powers of the county debt-court of Bourne, established in 1847, extend over the registration-district of Bourne. The town-hall, erected at an expense of £2500, on the site of a former one built by William Cecil, lord treasurer in the reign of Elizabeth, is a spacious handsome edifice, under which is the market-place.

The LIVING is a discharged vicarage, valued in the king's books at £8; patron, the Rev. J. Dodsworth. An allotment of 232 acres of land made to the vicar in lieu of tithes, in 1768, is let on lease, producing £320 per annum. The church, though spacious, appears to be only part of a larger structure ; it is very ancient, and principally Norman, but contains several portions in the early and later styles of English architecture, and has two towers of mixed character, of which the southern is considerably higher than the other, and is crowned with pinnacles. There were formerly two towers at the west front, one of which was taken down about 140 years since. The interior, which has lately been repewed, and greatly beautified and repaired, consists of a nave, and north and south aisles, and chancel ; on each side of the nave are some massive round pillars and arches. The western entrance is a fine specimen of the later style, and over it is a large window of good composition. Within are some interesting monuments, a finely enriched font of the later style, and a stoup under a crocketed canopy ; also a slab to the memory of the Rev. W. Dodd, vicar, and Elizabeth his wife, parents of the Rev. Dr. Dodd, who was born here in 1729, and was executed at Tyburn for forgery, in June, 1777.
316

There are places of worship for Presbyterians and Wesleyans. A grammar school for 30 children was founded in 1653, and endowed with £30 per annum and a school-house by William Trollope, Esq., who also endowed an hospital for six aged men ; and William Fisher, by will, in 1627, endowed with land then let at £30 per annum, an almshouse for the same number of women : a national school, established in 1830, is endowed with £42 per annum. The poor law union of Bourne comprises 37 parishes or places, and contains a population of 19,832. There is a mineral spring in the town, formerly of great repute. William Cecil, created Baron Burleigh by Queen Elizabeth, was born here in 1521.

BOURNE (ST. MARY), a parish, in the union of WHITCHURCH, hundred of EVINGAR, Kingsclere and N. divisions of the county of SOUTHAMPTON, 3 miles (N. W. by W.) from Whitchurch ; containing, with the tythings of Binley, Egbury, Stoke, Swampton, and Week, 1152 inhabitants, of whom 384 are in Bourne tything. The parish comprises 6727 acres, whereof 21 are common or waste. The living is annexed to the vicarage of Hurstbourn-Priors : the tithes have been commuted for £110, and the glebe comprises 63 acres. The estate of the Earl of Portsmouth is charged with the annual payment of £16. 16. to a mistress for teaching 18 children ; the school-building has been lately enlarged, and 130 children are taught by a master and mistress, to the former of whom his lordship allows £21, the remainder of the expenses being raised by subscription.

BOURNE, EAST.—See EASTBOURNE.

BOURNE, WEST (ST. JOHN THE BAPTIST), a parish, and the head of a union, in the hundred of WESTBOURNE and SINGLETON, rape of CHICHESTER, W. division of SUSSEX, 7¾ miles (W. N. W.) from Chichester; containing, with the tythings of Aldsworth, Hermitage, Nutbourne, Prinsted, and Woodmancot, 2093 inhabitants. It comprises 3714 acres, whereof 220 are common or waste. The village, which was formerly a trading town of some importance, is pleasantly situated on a small stream, which is crossed by a bridge uniting Hermitage (through which passes the road from Chichester to Portsmouth) with the small brisk sea-port of Emsworth, in the county of Southampton. On the south is Thorney Channel, passable at low water for carriages to and from Thorney Island. The living is a discharged vicarage, valued in the king's books at £10. 10. 5., and in the gift of the Rector, with a net income of £280 : the rectory is a sinecure, valued at £24. 13. 4. ; net income, £870 ; patrons, the family of Newland. The church is a neat commodious structure in the later English style, with a well-proportioned spire of oak : the principal entrance is approached by an avenue of eight yew-trees, remarkable for their size ; and on the arch of the doorway are carved the heraldic bearings of Lord Maltravers, with an inscription almost illegible, of about the time of Edward IV. Henry Smith bequeathed land in 1642, now producing £60 per annum, for the apprenticing of children, and for the poor. The union of West Bourne comprises 12 parishes, and contains a population of 6668.

BOURNEMOUTH, a village, in the parish, union, and hundred of CHRISTCHURCH, Ringwood and S. divisions of the county of SOUTHAMPTON, about 6 miles

(W. by S.) from Christchurch. This village, which is situated on the sea-shore, has become a place of fashionable resort for bathing, and, from a secluded and unfrequented spot, has been tastefully laid out in a series of villas of pleasing character, in various styles of architecture. A spacious hotel, commanding an extensive view of the sea, with the Isles of Wight and Purbeck, was built by the late Sir G. Jervis, the proprietor of the lands, for the reception of visiters; and a range of commodious baths has been erected on the beach; forming together a handsome suite of buildings, from the centre of which rises a tower of picturesque character, into which the fines of the various chimneys are conveyed. A church has been very recently built by the Jervis family.

BOURTON, a tything, in the parish and hundred of Shrivenham, union of Farringdon, county of Berks, 7 miles (S. W. by S.) from Farringdon; containing 396 inhabitants; and, according to a survey in 1838, comprising 1182 acres.

BOURTON, a hamlet, in the parish, union, hundred, and county of Buckingham, 1½ mile (E.) from Buckingham; containing 48 inhabitants.

BOURTON, a chapelry, in the parish and liberty of Gillingham, union of Mere, Shaston division of Dorset, 2½ miles (S. W. by W.) from Mere; containing 901 inhabitants. The living is a perpetual curacy, in the patronage of the Vicar and Inhabitants; net income, £50. The chapel has been enlarged within the last few years. There is a place of worship for Wesleyans.

BOURTON, with Easton, a tything, in the parish of Bishop's Cannings, union of Devizes, hundred of Potterne and Cannings, Devizes and N. divisions of Wilts; containing 216 inhabitants.

BOURTON, BLACK (St. Mary), a parish, in the union of Witney, hundred of Bampton, county of Oxford, 4 miles (S. W.) from Witney; containing 331 inhabitants, and comprising about 2250 acres. The living is a discharged vicarage; net income, £151; patrons and appropriators, the Dean and Canons of Christ-Church, Oxford: the tithes have been commuted for £95. The church is in the early English style: in the chancel are the remains of Sir Arthur Hopton, ambassador to the court of Spain in the reign of Charles I., and at the east end of the north aisle are several monuments to the Hungerford family; the pulpit is of stone, exquisitely sculptured in the decorated English style.

BOURTON, FLAX, a parish, in the union of Bedminster, hundred of Portbury, E. division of Somerset, 5½ miles (W. by S.) from Bristol; containing 232 inhabitants. This place derives the adjunct by which it is distinguished from other places of the same name, from the manor having anciently belonged to the abbot of Flaxley, in the county of Gloucester. The parish is situated at the base of a chain of hills forming the commencement of the Mendip range, and, from the higher grounds, commands a fine view of the Bristol Channel, with the distant sea; it comprises an area of 621a. 2r. 3p. of fertile land. The village is pleasantly situated on the road to Weston-super-Mare, at the extremity of the parish; and the Bristol and Exeter railroad passes in the immediate vicinity. The living is a perpetual curacy, in the patronage of the Rector of Nailsea: the tithes have been commuted for £95. The

317

church is a small edifice, chiefly in the Norman style, with a low embattled tower; the entrance is under a beautiful arch of Norman character: in the churchyard are the remains of a very ancient cross.

BOURTON, GREAT and LITTLE, a township, in the parish of Cropredy, union and hundred of Banbury, county of Oxford, 3 miles (N.) from Banbury; containing 593 inhabitants. The tithes were commuted for land and money payments in 1777. In Great Bourton is an interesting chapel, in the early English style, now used as a school and house for the master: the school was endowed by Mr. Thomas Gill, with rent-charges on lands now belonging to Sir Egerton Leigh and others, producing a net income of £18 per annum.

BOURTONHOLD, a hamlet, in the parish, union, hundred, and county of Buckingham; containing 614 inhabitants.

BOURTON-ON-THE-HILL (St. Lawrence), a parish, in the union of Shipston, partly in the Upper division of the hundred of Tewkesbury, and partly in the Upper division of that of Westminster, E. division of the county of Gloucester, 2 miles (W. by N.) from Moreton; containing 542 inhabitants. The living is a rectory, with the living of Moreton annexed, valued in the king's books at £14; net income, £675; patron and incumbent, the Rev. S. W. Warneford: the tithes were commuted for land and corn-rents in 1821. Sir Thomas Overbury, an ingenious writer in the reign of James I., who was poisoned while a prisoner in the Tower, was born here in 1581.

BOURTON-ON-THE-WATER (St. Lawrence), a parish, in the union of Stow-on-the-Wold, Lower division of the hundred of Slaughter, E. division of the county of Gloucester, 4 miles (S. S. W.) from Stow; containing 943 inhabitants. The living is a rectory, with the living of Lower Slaughter annexed, valued in the king's books at £27. 2. 8½., and in the patronage of Wadham College, Oxford; net income, £475. The church is a modern edifice, having a tower at the western end, rising from a rustic basement, with Ionic pilasters at the angles, and surmounted by a balustrade, urns, and cupola; within is a colonnade of the Ionic order. There is a place of worship for Particular Baptists; and a school is endowed with £12 per annum, accruing from property bequeathed by Anthony Collett, in 1719. The Roman Fosse-way passes through the parish; and about a quarter of a mile from the village is a square intrenchment, where coins, and other relics of the Romans, have been discovered: a paved aqueduct was formerly visible on one side of it. John Foster, author of the *Essays*, resided for some time in the village.

BOURTON-UPON-DUNSMOOR (St. Mary), a parish, in the union of Rugby, Rugby division of the hundred of Knightlow, N. division of the county of Warwick, 4 miles (W. by S.) from Dunchurch; containing, with the tything of Draycot, 390 inhabitants. The manor was held by the Verdons, lords of Brandon. In the time of Henry III. it came to the Garshales, in which family it continued in the male line for several generations; it afterwards passed by marriage to the Burdets and Staffords, and from the latter was purchased by the Shuckburghs, of Birdingbury. The parish comprises about 2000 acres, divided into arable and pasture; the surface is undulated, the scenery pic-

BOVE

turesque: limestone abounds. The living is a rectory, valued in the king's books at £19. 17. 3½., and in the patronage of Mrs. Shuckburgh; net income, £450. The tithes were commuted for land in 1765. The church is an ancient edifice. The Baptists have a place of worship; and there is a small school.

BOUSTEAD-HILL, a township, in the parish of Burgh-upon-the-Sands, union of Carlisle, Cumberland ward, and E. division of Cumberland, 7½ miles (W. N. W.) from Carlisle; containing 74 inhabitants.

BOVENEY, LOWER, a chapelry, in the parish and hundred of Burnham, union of Eton, county of Buckingham, 2 miles (W.) from Eton; containing, with the liberty of Upper Boveney, 362 inhabitants, and comprising 407 acres, of which 70 are common or waste. The chapel, in which divine service is performed once a month, is dedicated to St. Mary Magdalene. The great tithes have been commuted for £97, and the vicarial for £25.

BOVERIDGE, a tything, in the parish of Cranborne, union of Wimborne and Cranborne, hundred of Monckton-up-Wimborne, Wimborne division of Dorset; containing 174 inhabitants. Here is a chapel of ease, lately rebuilt.

BOVEY, NORTH (St. John the Baptist), a parish, in the union of Newton-Abbot, hundred of Teignbridge, Crockernwell and S. divisions of Devon, 1¾ mile (S. W. by S.) from Moreton-Hampstead; containing 660 inhabitants, and comprising 4299 acres, of which 2780 are common or waste. The lords of this manor formerly exercised the power of inflicting punishment for capital crimes. The vicinity is noted for mines of tin, which are worked to a considerable extent. A fair for cattle is held on the Monday next after Midsummerday. The living is a rectory, valued in the king's books at £22. 10. 5., and in the patronage of the Earl of Devon: the tithes have been commuted for £325, and there are 26 acres of glebe.

BOVEY-TRACEY (St. Thomas à Becket), a parish, in the union of Newton-Abbot, hundred of Teignbridge, Teignbridge and S. divisions of Devon, 4 miles (W. by S.) from Chudleigh; containing 1823 inhabitants. This place derives the affix to its name from the family of Tracey, barons of Barnstaple, to whom the manor anciently belonged, and who were descendants of William de Tracey, the chief agent in the assassination of St. Thomas à Becket of Canterbury, in 1170. An encounter took place between the royalist and parliamentarian forces on Bovey-Heathfield. The parish is pleasantly situated near the road from Exeter to Plymouth, and comprises 7186a. 22p., all fertile land with the exception of about 900 acres, which are common or waste: the substrata are chiefly coal of inferior quality, granite, and stone. A manufactory for earthenware is established on Bovey-Heathfield, for which purpose the remains of an ancient building, formerly the priory of Indiho, and subsequently a private mansion, were appropriated in 1772. A canal from Teignmouth to Ventiford bridge, about four miles from the village, and a railroad from the Haytor Rocks to the same place, have been constructed by George Templar, Esq., for the conveyance of wrought granite; they also afford facility for bringing coal, sea-sand, and lime, and sending away Bovey coal, and pipe and potter's clay, which are found here in great plenty. The place is under the government

318

which the central arch was considerably larger than the rest; and from the inconvenient narrowness of the bridge, a wooden platform was constructed on the outside of one of the parapets, for the accommodation of foot passengers. An act for rebuilding it was obtained in 1834, and a new bridge was opened with much ceremony on the 14th of Feb. 1839, consisting of one flat elliptical arch, 66 feet in span, rising to the height of 13 feet from the water level, and defended with solid parapets. The village is pleasantly situated; the streets are paved, and lighted with gas, and the inhabitants are supplied with water by the East London Company's works. The manufacture of porcelain, formerly carried on to a considerable extent, has been discontinued; and the fair held at Whitsuntide has, within the last few years, been entirely suppressed. A little to the north of the town, runs the Eastern Counties railway. The powers of the county debt-court of Bow, established in 1847, extend over the parishes of Bow and Bromley, and the registration-district of West Ham. Three head-boroughs and a constable are annually appointed at the court leet of the lord of the manor.

It was formerly a chapelry in the parish of Stepney, from which it was separated in 1730. The LIVING is a rectory; net income, £319; patrons, the Principal and Fellows of Brasenose College, Oxford, by whom an addition was made, a few years since, to the stipend of the rector. The church, founded in 1613, by Sir John Jolles, who endowed it for thirty-four boys of this parish and that of Bromley. Another school for fifty boys was founded in 1701, by Mrs. Prisca Coburne, who endowed it with houses and lands at that time producing £40 per annum; and from the increased value of the property, the income, on the expiration of the present leases, will amount to £500: a schoolroom has been built for 100 children of each sex, the school being under the inspection of the rectors of Bow, and four adjoining parishes. Sir John Jolles also founded and endowed almshouses for eight people; and there are other charitable bequests for the relief of the poor, including one of £1400 in the funds under the will of Mrs. Margaretta Browne, dated in 1826, out of the dividends of which the sum of £20 is paid to the rector.

BOWCOMBE, a hamlet, in the parish of CARIS-BROOKE, liberty of WEST MEDINA, ISLE of WIGHT division of HANTS; containing 93 inhabitants.

BOWDEN, GREAT (St. PETER), a parish, in the union of MARKET-HARBOROUGH, hundred of GARTREE, S. division of the county of LEICESTER; containing, with the town of Harborough, 3698 inhabitants. The parish comprises upwards of 3000 acres, principally rich grazing-land; the river Welland bounds it on the south, and a branch of the Union canal passes near the village. The living is a perpetual curacy; net income, £86; patrons, the Dean and Canons of Christ-Church, Oxford. There is a separate incumbency in the town.

BOWDEN, LITTLE (St. NICHOLAS), a parish, in the union of MARKET-HARBOROUGH, hundred of ROTH-WELL, N. division of the county of NORTHAMPTON, ½ a mile (E. S. E.) from Harborough; containing, with the hamlet of Little Oxendon, 439 inhabitants. The parish is situated on the border of Leicestershire, from which it is separated by the river Welland; and comprises by computation 2366a. 2r. 10p., of which three-fourths are pasture, and one-fourth arable, the surface being moderately undulated, and the soil of the most productive quality. It is closely connected with Harborough by means of two bridges over the Welland, and the roads from that town to Northampton and Kettering intersect the parish. The living is a rectory, valued in the king's books at £15. 4. 2.; net income, £293; patron and incumbent, the Rev. John Barlow. The tithes were commuted for land and money payments in 1779.

BOWDEN'S-EDGE, a township, in the parish and union of CHAPEL-EN-LE-FRITH, hundred of HIGH PEAK, N. division of the county of DERBY, 1½ mile (N. E.) from Chapel-en-le-Frith; containing 1021 inhabitants.

BOWDON, or BOWDEN (St. NICHOLAS), a parish, in the union of ALTRINCHAM, hundred of BUCKLOW, N. division of the county of CHESTER; comprising the chapelries of Altrincham and Carrington, the townships of Ashley, Baguley, Bowdon, Dunham-Massey, Hale, Partington, and Timperley, and part of the townships of Agden, Ashton-upon-Mersey, and Bollington; the whole containing 9373 inhabitants, of whom 549 are in the township of Bowdon, 1 mile (S. W. by S.) from Altrincham. The manor was anciently parcel of the barony of Dunham-Massey; a moiety of it was given, about 1278, to the priory of Birkenhead by Hamon de Massey, the fifth of that name, and the other moiety passed to a younger branch of the Massey family. The Bowdens, Booths, Holcrofts, and Breretons afterwards possessed the lands; and more recently the whole manor became the property of the Earl of Stamford and Warrington. The parish comprises by admeasurement 16,918 acres, whereof 770 are in the township of Bowdon; the soil of the latter is a sandy loam. The living is a vicarage, valued in the king's books at £24, and in the gift of the Bishop of Chester: the tithes have been commuted for rent-charges amounting altogether, for the bishop, to £1671. 6., and for the vicar, to £364; the vicar's glebe comprises 37½ acres. The rectorial tithes are leased by the bishop to the Earl of Stamford and Warrington, who, as lord of the barony of Dunham-Massey, appoints four churchwardens for the parish. The church is an ancient structure, commanding an extensive and pleasing panoramic view of the surrounding country: it was annexed to the see of Chester by Henry VIII., on the dissolution of Birkenhead priory. There are three chapels, forming separate incumbencies; viz., Altrincham, built in 1799; Carrington, built about 1760, at the cost of the Countess of Stamford; and Ringway, the date of which is uncertain. Edward Vawdrey, about the year 1600, gave £4 per annum towards the endowment of a grammar school: the schoolroom was rebuilt at the expense of the parishioners, about 1670, and again in 1806. A national school is supported by subscription; and there are also a school for boys at Seamons Moss, and one for boys and girls at Littleheath, the latter founded and endowed by the late Mr. Thomas Walton. The Earl of Warrington in 1754 gave £5000, now amounting to £5610 three per cent. reduced bank annuities, for educating or apprenticing children of the parish, and for the relief of the poor of this and the parish of Barnwell All Saints. A Roman road passed through the parish.

BOWER-CHALK (*Holy Trinity*), a parish, in the union of WILTON, hundred of CHALK, Salisbury and Amesbury, and S. divisions of WILTS, 7½ miles (S. W.) from Wilton; containing 447 inhabitants. The living is a discharged vicarage, united to the consolidated rectory of Broad Chalk and vicarage of Alvediston.

BOWER-HINTON, with HURST, a hamlet, in the parish and hundred of MARTOCK, union of YEOVIL, W. division of SOMERSET; containing 688 inhabitants.

BOWERS-GIFFORD (*St. Margaret*), a parish, in the union of BILLERICAY, hundred of BARSTABLE, S. division of ESSEX, 4½ miles (S. W. by W.) from Rayleigh; containing 249 inhabitants. It comprises about 2400 acres; and is bounded on the south by Holly and East havens, which afford a navigable communication with the Thames. The living is a rectory, valued in the king's books at £25, and in the patronage of Mrs. Curtis; net income, £564. The church is a small ancient edifice, with a tower surmounted by a shingled spire, and consists of a nave and chancel.

BOWES (*St. Giles*), a parish, in the union of TEESDALE, wapentake of GILLING-WEST, N. riding of YORK, 6 miles (W. by N.) from Greta-Bridge; containing 850 inhabitants, of whom 763 are in the township of Bowes, and 87 in that of Gillmonby. This place, from its situation on one of the Roman military roads, and from the discovery of numerous relics of antiquity (among which was a votive inscription to the Emperor Adrian, on a stone slab used in the time of Camden as the communion-table in the church), appears to have been the site of a Roman station. Most antiquaries have identified it with the *Lavatræ* of Antonine, where the first Thracian cohort was stationed, in the reign of Severus, and where also, towards the decline of the Roman empire, were fixed the head-quarters of the " *Numerus Exploratorum*," and their prefect, under the " *Dux Britanniæ*." At the time of the Conquest, there were still vestiges of a town, which had been destroyed by fire, from which circumstance Camden supposes the present name of the place to be derived; and within the vallum of the Roman fortress, and with part of the materials, a castle was soon afterwards built by Alan, Earl of Richmond, of which there are considerable remains, occupying the summit of an eminence declining on the south towards the river Greta.

The village consists principally of one street, nearly three-quarters of a mile in length; and has long been noted for its boarding-schools, to which numerous pupils are sent from London, on grounds of economy. It is situated near the verge of Stanemore, and on the banks of the Greta, over which, at the distance of two miles, is a natural bridge of picturesque character, called " God's bridge," formed by a rude arch of limestone rock, sixteen feet in the span, and twenty feet in breadth, affording a passage for carriages. Lead-ore, ironstone, and some coal are found in the neighbourhood. A market which was held on Friday, and a fair on Oct. 1st, have both fallen into disuse. The LIVING is a perpetual curacy; net income, £90; patron and impropriator, T. Harrison, Esq. There is a place of worship for Wes-

leyans. A free grammar school was founded in 1693, by William Hutchinson, who gave an estate now producing £258 per annum, for the instruction of children and for supplying the poor with coal. This place is interesting as the scene of Mallet's pathetic ballad of *Edwin and Emma*, which has reference to Roger Wrightson and Martha Railton, both of whom, according to the parish register, were interred here in the same grave, March 15th, 1714.

BOWESDEN, a hamlet, in the parish of LOWICK, union of GLENDALE, E. division of GLENDALE ward, N. division of NORTHUMBERLAND, 9¼ miles (N.) from Wooler. The ancient family of Carr sold their paternal estate here to the late Sir Francis Blake, Bart. The village is long and scattered. A sepulchral urn was turned up by the plough, several years since, at Bowesden-Hollins; and in the year 1800, some workmen, in levelling a barrow in the neighbourhood, discovered two inverted urns, containing calcined human bones.

BOWLAND-FOREST, HIGHER DIVISION, a township, in the parish of SLAIDBURN, union of CLITHEROE, W. division of the wapentake of STAINCLIFFE and EwCROSS, W. riding of YORK; containing 181 inhabitants. In the time of our Saxon ancestors, as at a much later period, the forest here was distinguished for archery; and hence the name of Bow-land. The township, which lies north-west of Slaidburn, and is high moorland, with scattered houses, includes the hamlets of Dunslop, Batterax, and Burnend; and comprises, with the Lower division of Bowland-Forest (the two forming the district called Bolland Liberty), 17,800 acres. The forest was granted by Charles II. to General Monk, from whom it descended to the dukes of Buccleuch; and is now the property of P. E. Towneley, Esq. The herds of wild deer in it were destroyed about forty years ago. The tithes have been commuted for £180.

BOWLAND-FOREST, LOWER DIVISION, a township, in the chapelry of WHITEWELL, parish of WHALLEY, union of CLITHEROE, wapentake of STAINCLIFFE and EwCROSS, W. riding of YORK; containing 330 inhabitants. It lies west and south-west of Slaidburn, includes the hamlets of Browsholme and Harrop (*which see*), and comprises 5170a. 2r. 39p., whereof 600 acres are wood, 200 moorland, 50 arable, and the rest pasture. The surface is undulated, the soil various; and from the elevation of the township, it commands most extensive views. There is abundance of limestone, and some calamine. The Roman Watling-street enters at Dawford bridge, and, taking a northern course, passes into Newton township. The chapel of Whitewell stands in this division; and the widows residing here are first presented to Waddington hospital. There is a chalybeate spring.—See WADDINGTON and WHITEWELL.

BOWLAND, LITTLE, with LEAGRAM, a township, in the parish of WHALLEY, union of CLITHEROE, Lower division of the hundred of BLACKBURN, N. division of LANCASHIRE, 15 miles (N. N. E.) from Preston; containing 273 inhabitants, of whom 133 are in Little Bowland. This district is three miles in length from north to south, and two miles and a half in breadth from east to west. In Little Bowland are 1768a. 3r. 4p., and in Leagram 1424a. 1r. 39p., mostly grazing-land; the surface is very undulated. On the limestone here, is a brown soil; in other places the soil is peaty: there is an excellent limestone-quarry, in which fossils are found.

The river Hodder divides the counties of York and Lancaster in this part. Fair-Oak House, a very ancient mansion in which is much carved oak, is, with 483 acres of land, the property of John Clince Parker, Esq.: the lordship of Leagram, long a possession of the Sherburnes, became latterly the property of the Weld family, of Leagram House. There are some remains of a Roman camp. A strong petrifying spring adjoins the Hodder.

BOWLD, a hamlet, in the parish of IBBURY, union of CHIPPING-NORTON, hundred of CHADLINGTON, county of OXFORD; containing 59 inhabitants.

BOWLEY, a township, in the parish of BODENHAM, union of LEOMINSTER, hundred of BROXASH, county of HEREFORD; containing 206 inhabitants.

BOWLING, a chapelry, in the parish and union of BRADFORD, wapentake of MORLEY, W. riding of YORK, 1 mile (S. E.) from Bradford; containing 8918 inhabitants. The township is situated on the slope of a hill on the east side of Low Moor, and comprises by computation 1438 acres, of which by far the greater portion is pasture; the surface is varied, and the surrounding scenery in some parts enlivened with plantations. Bolling or Bowling Hall is a stately and spacious mansion of venerable aspect. The substratum abounds with coal and iron-ore, which have been wrought for more than half a century by the Bowling Iron Company, whose works here are among the most extensive in England: the accumulated heaps of refuse from the mines, forming huge mounds surrounding the excavations, have been planted with trees. The village consists chiefly of one long street, rising by a gradual ascent from the town of Bradford to Dudley Hill, on the Wakefield road; the houses are of stone and well built, and there are numerous clusters of modern cottages inhabited chiefly by persons employed in the iron-works. The chapel, dedicated to St. John, and consecrated in Feb. 1842, was erected at the sole expense of the Iron Company, at a cost of £4000; it is a handsome structure in the later English style, with a square embattled tower and well-proportioned spire, and contains 1000 sittings, of which 300 are free. The living is a perpetual curacy; net income, £150; patron, the Vicar of Bradford. There are places of worship for Primitive Methodists and Wesleyans.

BOWNESS (ST. MICHAEL), a parish, in the union of WIGTON, CUMBERLAND ward, and E. division of the county of CUMBERLAND; comprising the townships of Anthorn, Bowness, Drumburgh, and Finland; and containing 1488 inhabitants, of whom 624 are in the township of Bowness, 14 miles (W. N. W.) from Carlisle. The parish comprises by measurement 9294 acres, of which 4953 are arable, 1088 meadow, 3152 common, moss land, or peat, and 42 wood. The village stands on a rocky promontory, commanding a fine view of the Solway Firth, on the coast of which it is situated; and occupies the site of the Roman station *Tunnocellum*, where, according to the Notitia, a marine cohort (*cohors prima Ælia Classica*) was placed. At the distance of about a mile was the western extremity of the Picts' wall, vestiges of which are conspicuous in various parts of the parish, as well as vestiges of *Gabrosentum*, another Roman station. Coins and other relics of the Romans, among which was an image of the god *Terminus*, have been discovered; and from the foundations of houses

and streets, which cultivation has exposed to view, this place has evidently been of greater extent than it is at present. The ship-canal from Carlisle terminates near the village. The living is a rectory, valued in the king's books at £21. 13. 11½.; net income, £393; patron, the Earl of Lonsdale: there are 57 acres of good glebe, and 272 acres of common land, the latter only partly cultivated, and very inferior.

BOWNESS, a post-town, in the parish of WINDERMERE, KENDAL ward and union, county of WESTMORLAND, 9 miles (W. N. W.) from Kendal. This town or village, which contains the parish church, is beautifully situated on the eastern shore of Windermere Lake; and, from the many objects of deep interest in its immediate vicinity, has been steadily advancing in extent and importance, as a place of favourite resort for visiters, who, in their excursions to the lakes, take up their abode here during the summer months. Two excellent hotels, the Royal (so called in commemoration of Her Majesty Queen Adelaide's visit in 1840) and the Crown, and some lodging-houses, have been built in the village for their accommodation; and in the neighbourhood are several handsome villas erected by persons whom the beauty of the situation has induced to fix their permanent residence here. Pleasure-boats, with fishing-tackle, for parties visiting the lake, are always to be had, and also conveyances for excursions in the environs, which afford a rich display of romantic scenery, and in many points command extensive views of highly varied and strikingly impressive beauty. Two steamers ply during the summer up and down the lake, touching at Ambleside, Waterhead, Low Wood, Bowness, the Ferry inn, and Newby-Bridge; and the Kendal and Windermere railway, opened in 1847, brings the traveller from the south to a point (Orrest head) where a spacious hotel has been built, about a mile and a half distant from Bowness. The char of the lake is in high repute, and is potted in great quantities, and sent to all parts of the country. A free grammar school established in 1600 has an endowment of about £60 per annum; a new school-house was lately erected, at an expense of £1500, by Mr. Bolton, of Storr's Hall, in the parish. The building is situated on a hill overlooking the village, and contains two large schoolrooms; the first stone was laid by William Wordsworth, the eminent poet, in 1836.—See WINDERMERE.

BOWOOD, a tything, in the parish of NETHERBURY, union and hundred of BEAMINSTER, Bridport division of DORSET, 2¾ miles (W. S. W.) from Beaminster. A chapel of ease, capable of accommodating upwards of 500 persons, was erected by subscription a few years since.

BOWOOD, an extra-parochial liberty, in the union and hundred of CALNE, Chippenham and Calne, and N. divisions of WILTS, 3½ miles (S. E. by E.) from Chippenham; containing 68 inhabitants. It comprises 1320 acres of land. Here is the magnificent seat of the Marquess of Lansdowne, occupying elevated ground, and consisting of three distinct parts, erected at different periods, and consequently exhibiting various styles of architecture: the main front is adorned with a portico of the Doric order, and commands a splendid view of the park and pleasure-grounds, the natural beauties of which have been heightened by the skilful and judicious application of art. The apartments are fitted up in the most sumptuous style, and are embellished with many valuable pictures.

BOWSCALE, a township, in the parish of GREY-STOCK, union of PENRITH, LEITH ward, county of CUMBERLAND, 10 miles (W. N. W.) from Penrith; containing 31 inhabitants.

BOWTHORP, with MENTHORP.—See MENTHORP.

BOWTHORPE (ST. MICHAEL), a parish, in the incorporation and hundred of FOREHOE, E. division of NORFOLK, 3½ miles (W. by N.) from Norwich; containing 34 inhabitants. It comprises 750 acres, in one farm. The church was used, at the beginning of the seventeenth century, as a storehouse for grain, but, by a decree in chancery obtained in 1635, was restored to its original purpose; in 1792 it was unroofed, and only a portion of the walls now remains. The living was formerly a rectory, in the patronage of the Dean and Canons of the College of St. Mary-in-the-Fields, at Norwich, who, in 1522, petitioned the bishop for its reduction to a curacy: since 1635 the living has been a donative.

BOX (ST. THOMAS à BECKET), a parish, in the union and hundred of CHIPPENHAM, Chippenham and Calne, and N. divisions of WILTS, 7 miles (S. W. by W.) from Chippenham; containing 2274 inhabitants. The parish comprises 4135 acres, of which 217 are common or waste. An extensive bed of freestone of a peculiar quality exists here, called Bath stone, from the circumstance of the greater part of that city having been built with it: it forms a considerable article of exportation to almost every part of the empire. At a short distance north-west of the village, which is beautifully situated in a rich valley, and on the road from London to Bath, is a mineral spring, containing a very large proportion of sulphur and carbonic acid. The Great Western railway, which passes through the parish, here enters a tunnel, 1¾ mile in length, 30 feet wide, 25 feet high above the rails, and having 11 shafts for affording air and light, each 25 feet in diameter, and some of them nearly 300 feet in depth from the surface of the ground. The living is a vicarage, valued in the king's books at £15. 8. 9.; patron and incumbent, the Rev. H. D. C. S. Horlock; impropriator, W. Northey, Esq. The great tithes have been commuted for £490. 6. 4., and the vicarial for £408. 3. 8.; there is an acre of glebe. A charity school has an income of nearly £30 a year, arising from lands. On Cheney-Court farm, north of the spa, and about five miles from Bath, a variety of coins was dug up in 1813, indicating that a large Roman villa once existed on the spot; and several Roman pavements are in the premises near the church.

BOXDEN, with HANDFORTH.—See HANDFORTH.

BOXFORD (ST. ANDREW), a parish, in the union of NEWBURY, hundred of FAIRCROSS, county of BERKS, 4½ miles (N. W. by N.) from Newbury; containing, with the tything of Westbrook, 612 inhabitants; and comprising 2769a. 2r. 23p., according to a survey in 1839. The living is a rectory, valued in the king's books at £20; patron and incumbent, the Rev. G. Wells, whose tithes have been commuted for £880, and who has a glebe of 10½ acres. In the church is a monument to James Anderton. There is a place of worship for Wesleyans.

BOXFORD (ST. MARY), a parish, in the union, and partly in the hundred, of COSFORD, but chiefly in that

Thomas Wyatt, the poet. The abbey contained a celebrated rood, which, together with the image of St. Rumbald, was taken away, and publicly destroyed at St. Paul's Cross, in 1538 : there are still some remains of the buildings. The parish comprises 5745 acres, of which 1100 are in wood. It is noted for the manufacture of paper of a superior quality. The living is a vicarage, valued in the king's books at £12. 19. 2.; net income, £834 ; patrons and appropriators, the Dean and Chapter of Rochester. The church is a neat small edifice, with a handsome square tower. An extensive rabbit-warren, part of the possessions of the abbey, lies beneath the chalk hill here ; and there was another near Penenden Heath (about half of which is in this parish), but it has been brought into cultivation. A small stream that rises just below the church, and runs through the village, is said to petrify wood with an incrustation resembling brown unpolished marble.

BOXMOOR.—See HEMEL-HEMPSTEAD.

BOXTED (ST. MARY), a parish, in the union of LEXDEN and WINSTREE, Colchester division of the hundred of LEXDEN, N. division of ESSEX, 5 miles (N.) from Colchester ; containing 856 inhabitants. It comprises 3082 acres, of which 2432 are arable, 576 meadow, and 74 woodland ; and is bordered on the north by the navigable river Stour. The living is a discharged vicarage, valued in the king's books at £7. 13. 9.; patron, the Bishop of London ; impropriator, J. Josselyn, Esq. The great tithes have been commuted for £520, and the vicarial for £220 : the glebe belonging to the impropriator comprises more than 61 acres ; the vicar's, not quite four. The church is an ancient edifice with a tower, and has been repewed within the last few years ; it contains an elegant monument to Sir Richard Blackmore, physician to William III., and author of several medical and other works.

BOXTED, a parish, in the union of SUDBURY, hundred of BABERGH, W. division of SUFFOLK, 5¾ miles (N. E.) from Clare ; containing 200 inhabitants. This place has long been the residence of the Poley family ; the mansion is a spacious and ancient edifice. The living is a rectory not in charge, consolidated with that of Hartest : the tithes have been commuted for £375. 10. The church is a small edifice, adjoining the chancel of which is a family vault of the Poleys, containing some monuments of very delicate sculpture in marble.

BOXWELL (ST. ANDREW), a parish, in the union of TETBURY, Upper division of the hundred of GRUMBALD'S ASH, W. division of the county of GLOUCESTER, 5 miles (E. by S.) from Wotton-under-Edge, and 6 (W.) from Tetbury ; containing 334 inhabitants. This place derives its name from a plantation of box-trees, one of the most considerable in the kingdom, and from a copious spring of water that issues from it. A nunnery was established at a very early period, which is said to have been destroyed by the Danes, and of which the possessions were subsequently annexed to the abbey of Gloucester. Charles II. rested at the ancient manorhouse on his route from Boscobel to Bristol; and Prince Rupert, when governor of that city, made it a place of frequent resort. The parish comprises 2243 acres, of which 30 are box-wood, 100 woodland, about 300 pasture, and the remainder arable ; it is situated on the road from Cheltenham to Bath. The soil is fertile, and

323

there are some good quarries of oolite freestone. The living is a rectory, valued in the king's books at £23. 4. 9½.; patron and incumbent, the Rev. R. W. Huntley : the tithes have been commuted for £375, and there are 68 acres of glebe. The church is a very ancient structure, with a tower. At Leighterton is a chapel of ease. In a field at the same place is a large barrow.

BOXWORTH (ST. PETER), a parish, in the union of ST. IVES, hundred of PAPWORTH, county of CAMBRIDGE, 6½ miles (N. E. by N.) from Caxton ; containing 326 inhabitants. The living is a rectory, valued in the king's books at £18. 12. 3½., and in the patronage of George Thornhill, Esq. : the tithes have been commuted for £490, and the glebe comprises 126 acres. The church contains a monumental bust of Dr. Saunderson, F.R.S., the blind professor of mathematics at the University of Cambridge ; he died and was buried here, in 1759.

BOYATT, a tything, in the parish of OTTERBOURNE, union of HURSLEY, hundred of BUDDLESGATE, Winchester and N. divisions of the county of SOUTHAMPTON ; containing 160 inhabitants.

BOYCUTT, a hamlet, in the parish of STOWE, union, hundred, and county of BUCKINGHAM, 3 miles (N. W. by W.) from Buckingham ; containing 35 inhabitants.

BOYLESTONE (ST. JOHN THE BAPTIST), a parish, in the union of UTTOXETER, hundred of APPLETREE, S. division of the county of DERBY, 6 miles (E. by N.) from Uttoxeter ; containing 343 inhabitants. The manor is described in the Domesday survey as one of the possessions of Henry de Ferrars. It was afterwards held in moieties, which became for a time separate manors ; the Cotton family possessed it for many generations, and it subsequently came to the Fitzherberts, Venables, Grosvenors, and others. The parish comprises 1700 acres, mostly pasture and dairy-farms ; the surface is undulated, and the soil marl. The living is a discharged rectory, valued in the king's books at £6. 0. 2.; net income, £260 ; patron, the Rev. W. Hurst: an allotment of land, and money payments, were assigned in 1783 in lieu of tithes. The church is a neat structure in the early English style, with a square Flemish tower, and stands very picturesquely ; it was restored in 1843-4, at a cost of £550. The Wesleyans and Primitive Methodists have places of worship. An excellent school-house, with a residence for the master and mistress attached, was built in 1844, at a cost of £570 ; the site was purchased and presented by John Broadhurst, Esq., of Acton : the schools are on the national plan.

BOYNTON (ST. ANDREW), a parish, in the union of BRIDLINGTON, wapentake of DICKERING, E. riding of YORK, 2 miles (W. by N.) from Bridlington ; containing 100 inhabitants. It is on the road from Bridlington to Malton, and comprises by computation 2100 acres, the property of Sir George Strickland, Bart. ; the family were anciently seated at Strickland, in the county of Westmorland, but the principal branch has been settled here more than two centuries. Boynton Hall, the residence of the baronet, is a lofty and handsome mansion, beautifully situated upon an eminence in a richly wooded park ; the acclivities present some fine plantations, and a large sheet of water ornaments the grounds. On an elevated ridge, south of the Hall, is a pavilion erected by the late Sir George, from which is obtained an extensive prospect both of sea and land, particularly of Bridlington bay and the eastern heights of the Wolds. The village is in the vale of a rivulet flowing in an eastern direction to the coast. The living is a discharged perpetual curacy, valued in the king's books at £7.14.2., and in the patronage of Sir George Strickland, the impropriator, with a net income of £141 : land and a money payment were assigned in 1777, in lieu of tithes. The church, which was rebuilt in the early part of the last century, consists of a nave and chancel, with a handsome tower; in the chancel are several monuments to the Strickland family.

BOYTON, a parish, in the union of LAUNCESTON, partly in the hundred of BLACK TORRINGTON, N. division of the county of DEVON, but chiefly in that of STRATTON, E. division of CORNWALL, 5 miles (N. by W.) from Launceston; containing, with the hamlet of Northcott, in Devon, 600 inhabitants. It comprises between 4000 and 5000 acres : the soil is clay, and in general very shallow, the surface rather hilly; there is a' considerable quantity of coppice. The Bude and Launceston, or Tamar, canal intersects the parish. A fair is held on August 5th. The living is a perpetual curacy, net income, £123; patron, the Rev. G. Prideaux; impropriator, H. Thompson, Esq. Between this place and North Tamerton is an ancient thatched building, called Hornacott Chapel, now occupied by a labourer.

BOYTON (ST. ANDREW), a parish, in the union of WOODBRIDGE, hundred of WILFORD, E. division of SUFFOLK, 8 miles (E. by S.) from Woodbridge; containing 239 inhabitants. The parish comprises 1650 acres; the soil is for the most part light and heathy, with some few acres of marsh, and the surface level. The living is a rectory, valued in the king's books at £5. 12. 1., and in the gift of the Trustees of Mrs. Mary Warner : the tithes have been commuted for £388, and the glebe consists of 23 acres. An almshouse was built in 1743, and liberally endowed by Mrs. Warner.

BOYTON (ST. MARY), a parish, in the union of WARMINSTER, hundred of HEYTESBURY, Warminster and S. divisions of WILTS, 1 mile (W. by S.) from Codford; containing, with the township of Corton, 360 inhabitants. This parish, which is situated near the road from Bath to Salisbury, and intersected by the river Willey, comprises by measurement 3720 acres. The mansion-house of the Lamberts, adjoining the church, is an ancient edifice in the Elizabethan style, the grounds of which retain their original character; the terrace, walks, and hedges of yew-trees still remain as they probably appeared in 1660. The living is a rectory, valued in the king's books at £27. 17. 3½., and in the patronage of Magdalene College, Oxford : the tithes have been commuted for £560, and the glebe comprises 20 acres. The church is an ancient and picturesque structure, in the early and decorated English styles, with a porch of elegant design ; the interior is embellished with a beautiful circular window, and in the south aisle is a sepulchral chapel, now belonging to the Lambert family, but originally built by the Giffards. Giffard, the friend of the younger Long Espée, was interred here. There is a place of worship for Baptists. Aylmer Bourke Lambert, the celebrated botanist, was born in the parish.

BOZEAT (ST. MARY), a parish, in the union of WELLINGBOROUGH, hundred of HIGHAM-FERRERS, N.
324

division of the county of NORTHAMPTON, 5¾ miles (N.) from Olney; containing 845 inhabitants. This parish is situated on the border of Bedfordshire, and comprises 2537a. 3r. 8p., of which above 120 acres are woodland; the surface is in some parts hilly, especially at the north end, and in others level ; the soil is a cold clay. Limestone is quarried. The road from Wellingborough to Olney passes through the village. The living is a discharged vicarage, with the rectory of Strixton consolidated, valued in the king's books at £8 ; net income, £183 ; patron, Earl Spencer; impropriators, the representatives of the late Dr. Laurence, Archbishop of Cashel: the glebe comprises 120 acres. Land and annual money payments were assigned in 1798, in lieu of tithes. There is a place of worship for Wesleyans.

BRABOURNE (ST. MARY), a parish, in the union of EAST ASHFORD, franchise and barony of BIRCHOLT, lathe of SHEPWAY, E. division of KENT, 7 miles (E. by S.) from Ashford; containing 889 inhabitants. It comprises by measurement 3504 acres, and is crossed by the railway from London to Dovor : there are 227 acres of wood. Extensive cavalry and infantry barracks were erected a few years since. A fair for toys and pedlery is held on the last day in May. The living is a vicarage, with the rectory of Monk's-Horton consolidated, valued in the king's books at £11. 12. 6., and in the gift of the Archbishop of Canterbury. The great tithes of Brabourne, belonging to his Grace, have been commuted for £613, with a glebe of 82 acres; and those of the incumbent for £270, with a glebe of one acre, and a residence. The church is very ancient, and contains numerous interesting monuments. There is a chapel for Calvinistic Baptists.

BRACEBOROUGH, or BRACEBURGH (ST. MARGARET), a parish, in the union of STAMFORD, wapentake of NESS, parts of KESTEVEN, county of LINCOLN, 7 miles (N. E.) from Stamford ; containing, with the hamlet of Shillingthorpe, 231 inhabitants. The living is a rectory, valued in the king's books at £9. 10., and in the patronage of the Crown, with a net income of £195 : corn-rents were assigned in the 39th and 40th of George III. in lieu of tithes. There is a fine spring called the Spa, with convenience for bathing ; its waters are beneficial in cases of scurvy.

BRACEBRIDGE (ALL SAINTS), a parish, in the wapentake of BOOTHBY-GRAFFO, parts of KESTEVEN, union and county of LINCOLN, 2¼ miles (S. by W.) from Lincoln ; containing 127 inhabitants. The living is a vicarage, valued in the king's books at £3. 9. 9½., and in the patronage of the family of Bromehead ; net income, £203 ; impropriators, Edward Gibbeson, Esq., of Red Hall, and William Colegrave, Esq. The church is ancient, and consists of a nave, chancel, and south aisle, with a tower.

BRACEY (ST. MARGARET), a parish, in the union of GRANTHAM, wapentake of WINNIBRIGGS and THREO, parts of KESTEVEN, county of LINCOLN, 4½ miles (W. by N.) from Falkingham, and 7 (E.) from Grantham ; containing 155 inhabitants. The living is a vicarage, united to that of South Grantham : the impropriate tithes have been commuted for £132. 17. 6., and the vicarial for £55. The church is a small structure, without a tower ; the exterior cornice is curiously wrought with the heads of men, foxes, roses, &c.

BRACE-MEOLE (*ALL SAINTS*), a parish, in the union, and partly within the borough, of SHREWSBURY, N. division of SALOP, 1½ mile (S.) from Shrewsbury; containing 1195 inhabitants. It comprises 2487*a*. 3*r*. 3*p*., of which 1079 acres are arable, 1382 meadow, pasture, and homesteads, and 25 woodland. The living is a discharged vicarage, valued in the king's books at £5; patron, the Ven. Edward Bather, Archdeacon of Salop; impropriators, the landowners. The great tithes have been commuted for £119, and the vicarial for £391 : there are 11 acres of glebe. The Shrewsbury house of industry, a noble building, stands in the parish.

BRACEWELL (*ST. MICHAEL*), a parish, in the union of SKIPTON, E. division of the wapentake of STAINCLIFFE and EWCROSS, W. riding of YORK, 9 miles (W. by S.) from Skipton; containing 153 inhabitants. This place is called in ancient documents *Breis-well* and *Brais-well*, signifying " the well on the bray " or " brow." The parish comprises by computation 1920 acres : the surface is beautifully undulated, and the hills are covered with luxuriant verdure; the lands are chiefly in pasture. The ancient manor-house, now a ruin, consisted of a centre with two boldly projecting wings, built of brick in the reign of Henry VIII.; and to the north of it are the remains of a former house of stone, in which an apartment called " King Henry's parlour " was the retreat of Henry VI. There are some quarries of excellent limestone, which is used both for building and for burning into lime. The village is pleasantly situated and neatly built : on the north the parish adjoins the turnpike-road between Gisburn and Skipton; and the Leeds and Liverpool canal passes about two miles east of the church. The living is a discharged vicarage, valued in the king's books at £2. 2. 9½., net income, £123; patron and impropriator, Earl de Grey. The church, nearly adjoining the manor-house, and probably founded by the Tempest family, is an ancient structure chiefly in the Norman style, enlarged by the addition of a north aisle in the reign of Henry VII. : it has a plain Norman doorway on the south, and a similar arch divides the chancel from the nave; it contains the family-vault of the Tempests, whose armorial bearings embellish several of the windows. On the summit of two hills, called Howber and Gildersber, are remains of military works, said to have been thrown up by the army of Prince Rupert, on its march through Craven, in 1664.

· BRACKEN, a township, in the chapelry of KILN-WICK, union of DRIFFIELD, Bainton-Beacon division of the wapentake of HARTHILL, E. riding of YORK, 6¾ miles (S. W. by S.) from Driffield; containing 33 inhabitants. It is on the road from Beverley to·Malton, and comprises about 600 acres. The village was formerly populous; and contained a chapel, the cemetery belonging to which remains undisturbed.

BRACKENBOROUGH, a chapelry, in the parish of LITTLE GRIMSBY, union of LOUTH, wapentake of LUD-BOROUGH, parts of LINDSEY, county of LINCOLN, 2½ miles (N.) from Louth; containing 63 inhabitants.

· BRACKENFIELD, an ecclesiastical district, in the parish of MORTON, union of CHESTERFIELD, hundred of SCARSDALE, N. division of the coun y of DERBY, 4 miles (N. W.) from Alfreton; containing 459 inhabitants. The family of Heriz possessed Brackenfield, then called Brackenthwayte, in the reign of King John; it after-

325

wards became the property of the Willoughbys, and in later times of the Turbutt family. The district comprises 1557*a*. 24*p*., whereof 452 acres are arable, 905 pasture, and 63 wood : it is skirted by the Midland railway. Framework knitting is carried on. The living is a perpetual curacy, in the patronage of the Rector of Morton; net income, £32, derived from the interest of £1000, Queen Anne's Bounty. A rent-charge of £176. 15. has been awarded as a commutation of the tithes. The chapel, dedicated to the Holy Trinity, was rebuilt in 1846. There is a place of worship for Primitive Methodists; and a national school, for which a house was built in 1844, is supported by subscription.

BRACKENHILL, a township, in the parish of ARTHURET, union of LONGTOWN, ESKDALE ward, E. division of CUMBERLAND, 4¼ miles (E. by N.) from Longtown; containing 373 inhabitants. In this township is the small hamlet of Easton, which anciently gave name to a parish, long since included within the parishes of Arthuret and Kirk-Andrews-upon-Esk.

BRACKENHOLME, with WOODHALL, a township, in the parish of HEMINGBROUGH, union of HOWDEN, wapentake of OUSE and DERWENT, E. riding of YORK, 3½ miles (N. N. W.) from Howden; containing 77 inhabitants. It is situated in the vale of the Derwent, and comprises about 1200 acres : the village is on the road from Howden to Hemingbrough.

BRACKENTHWAITE, a township, in the parish of LORTON, union of COCKERMOUTH, ALLERDALE ward above Derwent, W. division of CUMBERLAND, 8½ miles (W. by S.) from Keswick; containing 116 inhabitants. The neighbourhood abounds with beautiful and picturesque scenery.

BRACKLEY, an incorporated market-town, a parish,and the head of a union, in the hundred of KING's-SUTTON, S. division of the county of NORTHAMPTON, 20 miles (S. W. by S.) from Northampton, and 64 .(N. W. by W.) from London; containing 2121 inhabitants, of whom 887 are in the parish of St. James, and 1234 in that of St. Peter, which includes the hamlet of Halse. This place derives its name from the Anglo-Saxon *Bracken*, signifying fern, with which the neighbourhood formerly abounded : it was a Saxon burgh of considerable importance, but was greatly injured by the Danes. In the reign of John, Saher de Quincy, Earl of Winchester, joined the confederate barons at Stamford, and marched with them to Brackley, whence they sent a remonstrance setting forth their grievances to the king, who was then at Oxford. In the reign of Henry III. two splendid tournaments were held on a plain called Bayard's Green, near the town. Edward II., who conferred many privileges upon Brackley, made it a staple town for wool; and in the reign of Edward III., having become famous for its trade, it sent three representatives, as " Merchant Staplers," to a grand council held at Westminster. In the time of Henry VIII., the plague raging violently at Oxford, the fellows and scholars of Magdalen College removed to this town, and resided in an hospital founded

Seal and Arms.

by Robert le Bossu, Earl of Leicester, about the middle of the twelfth century, and of which there are considerable remains; the chapel, with a broad low tower on the north-west side, being still entire.

The TOWN, which was formerly of much greater extent, is on the border of Buckinghamshire, and is situated on the declivity of a hill, near a branch of the river Ouse, whose source is in the immediate vicinity: it is divided into two portions, New and Old; the latter, which is the smaller, is without the limits of the borough. The principal street, nearly a mile in length, extends from the bridge up the acclivity of the hill, and contains many good houses, mostly built of stone; there is an abundant supply of water. The inhabitants are chiefly occupied in the making of bobbin-lace, and boots and shoes. The market is on Wednesday; the fairs are principally for horses, horned-cattle, and sheep, and are on the Wednesday after Feb. 25th, the second Wednesday in April, the Wednesday after June 22nd, the Wednesday after Oct. 11th (a statute-fair), and Dec. 11th, which is a great fair for cattle and wearing-apparel. The inhabitants are supposed to have received their first charter of incorporation in the reign of Edward II., and subsequent charters were granted in the 2nd and 4th of James II., by which the government is vested in a mayor, six aldermen, and twenty-six burgesses. The elective franchise was conferred in the 1st of Edward VI., the borough from that time returned two members to parliament, but was disfranchised by the 2nd of William IV., cap. 45. The powers of the county debt-court of Brackley, established in 1847, extend over the registration-district of Brackley. The town-hall, a handsome building in the centre of the town, supported on arches, under which the market is held, was erected in 1706, by Scroop, Duke of Bridgewater, at a cost of £2000.

Brackley comprises the parishes of St. Peter and St. James, which, though ecclesiastically united, are distinct as regards civil affairs; the former consists of 3716 acres, and the latter of 430a. 3r. 36p. The LIVING is a consolidated vicarage, valued in the king's books at £19. 1. 6.; net income, £359; patron, the Earl of Ellesmere. Under an inclosure act, in 1829, land and a money payment were assigned in lieu of tithes; and under the recent act, impropriate tithes have been commuted for a rent-charge of £167. 10., and vicarial for one of £238. 6. 10. The church of St. Peter is an ancient building, with a low embattled tower, and contains a Norman font of curious design: St. James', formerly a parochial church, is now a chapel of ease. There is a place of worship for Wesleyans. The free grammar school was founded about the year 1447, by William of Wainfleet, who endowed it for ten boys, with £13. 6. 8. per annum, which sum is paid by the society of Magdalen College, Oxford, to whom the site of the ancient hospital was granted at the time of its dissolution. A national school is supported by subscription; and a school-house, of Bath stone, for an infants' school, has been built by the Earl of Ellesmere, at a cost of £400. Almshouses for six aged widows were founded by Sir Thomas Crewe, in 1633, and endowed with a rent-charge of £24, which was increased, in 1721, by his descendant, Lord Crewe, Bishop of Durham, to £36. The poor law union of Brackley comprises 30 parishes or places, of which 25 are in the county of Northampton, 3 in that of Buckingham, and 2 in that of Oxford; and
326

contains a population of 13,508. The site of a castle built by one of the Norman barons, is still called the Castle Hill. Samuel Clarke, an eminent orientalist, and one of the coadjutors of Walton in publishing the Polyglot Bible, was born here, in 1623; and Dr. Bathurst, Bishop of Norwich, who died in 1837, was also a native. Brackley gives the title of Viscount to the Earl of Ellesmere.

BRACKNELL, a large posting-village, in the parish of WARFIELD, union of EASTHAMPSTEAD, hundred of COOKHAM, county of BERKS; 4 miles (E.) from Wokingham, on the road to Windsor. Fairs are held on April 25th, August 22nd, and October 1st.

BRACON-ASH (ST. NICHOLAS), a parish, in the union of HENSTEAD, hundred of HUMBLEYARD, E. division of NORFOLK, 6 miles (S. W.) from Norwich; containing 293 inhabitants. The road from Buckenham to Norwich intersects the parish. The living is a rectory, valued in the king's books at £10, and in the patronage of the family of Berney; net income, £245. The church is partly in the early and partly in the decorated style, and consists of a nave, chancel, and south aisle, with a mausoleum on the north side belonging to the Berney family. Lord Thurlow was born at the old Hall in 1730.

BRADBORNE (ALL SAINTS), a parish, partly in the hundred of APPLETREE, but chiefly in that of WIRKSWORTH, S. division of the county of DERBY, 5 miles (N. N. E.) from Ashbourn; comprising the township of Aldwark, the chapelries of Atlow, Ballidon, and Brassington, and the hamlet of Lea-Hall; and containing 1303 inhabitants, of whom 187 are in Bradborne township. The manor was one of those belonging to Henry de Ferrers at the time of the Domesday survey; in the reign of John it was conveyed to the Bradborne family, of whom Henry de Bradborne was executed at Pomfret, in 1322, for his adhesion to Thomas, Earl of Lancaster. In Elizabeth's reign the manor came to Sir Humphrey Ferrers; and subsequently to the noble family of Townshend, and the family of Gell of Hopton Hall. The parish abounds with limestone. The living is a discharged vicarage, valued in the king's books at £8. 3. 4.; net income, £119; patron and impropriator, the Duke of Devonshire. The tithes of the township of Bradborne have been commuted for £144. 15., whereof £37. 10. are payable to the impropriator, and £107. 5. to the vicar: there are two acres of glebe, with a glebe-house. At Brassington and Atlow are separate incumbencies, and at Ballidon a chapel of ease. A school is partly supported by subscription: a school-house was built by W. Evans, Esq., in 1844.

BRADBURY, a township, in the parish and union of SEDGEFIELD, N. E. division of STOCKTON ward, S. division of the county of DURHAM, 2½ miles (E.) from Rushyford, and 10½ (S. by E.) from Durham; containing 167 inhabitants. Mr. Cade, the antiquary, considered the name of this place to be a corruption of Brimesbury, where King Athelstan encamped in 937, when he gained a decisive victory over the Danes; but it is more probable that the battle was fought at Bramby, in Lincolnshire. The township is bounded on the south-east by the river Skerne, which separates it from the parish of Great Aycliffe; and comprises 2043 acres, in equal portions of arable and pasture: the surface is rather level, pretty well wooded, and presents almost every variety of soil. £3000 have recently been expended in effectually draining the marshes, which promise to become good grazing-land. The York and Newcastle railway runs through the township for two miles. Here was a chapel of ease dedicated to St. Nicholas, of which there are no vestiges; the curate's house is still standing. The tithes have been commuted for £233; and there is a glebe of 63 acres.

BRADBY, a chapelry, in the parish of REPTON, union of BURTON-UPON-TRENT, hundred of REPTON and GRESLEY, S. division of the county of DERBY, 3 miles (E.) from Burton; containing 298 inhabitants. Near the chapel is the site of a baronial mansion, which was fortified by royal licence in the year 1300. The materials are supposed to have been used by the first earl of Chesterfield in the erection of a residence which he garrisoned for the king in 1642, and which, after a short defence, was captured by a strong detachment sent by Col. Gell; it was taken down in 1780. The living is a donative; net income, £80; patron, the Earl of Chesterfield. The inhabitants marry and bury at Repton.

BRADDEN (ST. MICHAEL), a parish, in the union of TOWCESTER, hundred of GREEN'S NORTON, S. division of the county of NORTHAMPTON, 3¼ miles (W.) from Towcester; containing 171 inhabitants. This parish is bounded on the south-east by the river Tow, and comprises by measurement 1011 acres, whereof about two-thirds are in permanent pasture. The soil is generally strong, inclining to clay; the surface rather undulated, with gentle inclinations and slopes; and the meadows subject to occasional floods. Stone is quarried for road-making. The living is a rectory, valued in the king's books at £14. 6. 8.; net income, £227, arising from 192 acres of land, allotted at the inclosure of the parish in lieu of tithes; patron and incumbent, the Rev. C. Ives: there is a glebe-house. The church is of an indistinct style of architecture; the date of its erection is unknown, but it appears to have been restored about the beginning of the 18th century. A school is supported by the clergyman and the parishioners. There existed a curious old manor-house, supposed to have been built by the Hospitallers of St. John of Jerusalem; but it became necessary, from its ruinous state, to take it down in 1818.

BRADENHAM (ST. BOTOLPH), a parish, in the union of WYCOMBE, hundred of DESBOROUGH, county of BUCKINGHAM, 4¼ miles (N. W.) from Wycombe; containing 226 inhabitants. The living is a discharged rectory, valued in the king's books at £5. 3. 9., and in the patronage of Mrs. A. Hearle; net income, £190. Catherine Pye, by deed dated in 1713, gave land for the instruction of children.

BRADENHAM, EAST (ST. MARY), a parish, in the union of SWAFFHAM, hundred of SOUTH GREENHOE, W. division of Norfolk, 2 miles (N. W.) from Shipdham; containing 368 inhabitants. It comprises 2340a. 3p., of which 1013 acres pay a modus of £34. 8. in lieu of tithes. The living is a rectory, valued in the king's books at £12. 2. 8½., and in the patronage of Thomas Adlington, Esq.: the remainder of the tithes have been commuted for a rent-charge of £352. 9., and the glebe comprises a little more than three acres, with a house. The church is a spacious structure in the later English style, with a square embattled tower; it was

327

thoroughly repaired in 1833, and contains some handsome monuments. There is a place of worship for Independents.

BRADENHAM, WEST (ST. ANDREW), a parish, in the union of SWAFFHAM, hundred of SOUTH GREENHOE, W. division of NORFOLK, 3 miles (N. W.) from Shipdham; containing 364 inhabitants. It comprises by computation 1682a. 3r. 30p., of which 972 acres are arable, 615 pasture and waste, and 95 wood and plantation. The living is a discharged vicarage, valued in the king's books at £7. 1. 10½.; patron and appropriator, the Bishop of Ely: the appropriate tithes have been commuted for £210, and the vicarial for £160; there are nearly eight acres of glebe belonging to the bishop, and nearly 58 to the vicar. The church, situated on an eminence, is an ancient structure in the later English style, with a square embattled tower at the west end of the south aisle: in the chancel are three sedilia of stone, and a piscina of elegant design.

BRADESTON.—See BRAYDESTON.

BRADFIELD (ST. ANDREW), a parish, and the head of a union, in the hundred of THEALE, county of BERKS, 8 miles (W.) from Reading; containing 1042 inhabitants. The parish comprises 4057a. 3r. 19p., according to a survey made in 1838. The living is a rectory, valued in the king's books at £19. 7. 8½., net income, £788; patron and incumbent, the Rev. T. Stevens. A parochial school, or school of industry, was established by the parish officers for the purpose of giving employment and instruction to poor children; the arrangements are superintended by the family of the rector, who chiefly support another school. The union of Bradfield comprises 29 parishes or places, of which 25 are in Berks, 3 in the county of Oxford, and one in the county of Southampton; and contains a population of 15,557. A monastery was founded here by King Ina, before 699.

BRADFIELD (ST. LAWRENCE), a parish, in the union and hundred of TENDRING, N. division of ESSEX, 3 miles (E. S. E.) from Manningtree; containing 995 inhabitants. It is bounded on the north by the river Stour, and comprises by computation 2270 acres: the greater portion of the land rises to a considerable elevation above the marshes; and the soil, chiefly a fine impalpable loam, is uncommonly fertile. A fair is held on the last Monday in July. The living is a discharged vicarage, united, with the living of Manningtree, to the rectory of Mistley, and valued in the king's books at £12. 13. 4.: the great tithes, belonging to the trustees of the late Col. Rigby, have been commuted for £422, with a glebe of 32 acres; and those of the incumbent for £193, with a glebe of 11 acres. The church is an ancient edifice, partly in the later English style, and partly of a much earlier date. There is a place of worship for Wesleyans. Sir Harbottle Grimston, master of the rolls under Charles II., and an eminent writer on the law, was born here.

BRADFIELD (ST. GILES), a parish, in the TUNSTEAD and HAPPING incorporation, hundred of TUNSTEAD, E. division of NORFOLK, 2½ miles (N. N. W.) from North Walsham; containing 195 inhabitants. One mediety of the living is a discharged rectory, valued in the king's books at £3. 15. 7½., and in the patronage of Lord Suffield; the other is a donative, annexed to the vicarage of Thorpe-Market. The tithes

of the rectory have been commuted for £160, and those
belonging to the vicar of Thorpe for £55 ; there are 2½
acres of glebe. The church is chiefly in the early style,
and consists of a nave and chancel, with a square tower ;
the font is handsomely sculptured.

BRADFIELD, a parochial chapelry, in the parish of
ECCLESFIELD, union of WORTLEY, N. division of the
wapentake of STRAFFORTH and TICKHILL, W. riding of
YORK, 6¾ miles (N. W. by W.) from Sheffield ; containing 6318 inhabitants. It comprises about 33,700 acres,
in a mountainous part of the county, and lying between
the river Don and the borders of Derbyshire ; the Loxley, the Ewden, and several smaller streams wind
through it in various directions. The district abounds
with slate, flag, and fire and building stone. Game
abounds on the moors, and is strictly preserved. Fairs
are held on June 17th and December 9th. The living is
a perpetual curacy, with a net income of £186, and in
the patronage of the Vicar of Ecclesfield, who, with the
curate of Bradfield and others, has the impropriation.
The chapel was repewed about 1800, by the feoffees of
sundry parcels of land consisting of about 250 acres,
appropriated by a decree of the Commissioners of
Charitable Uses, 13th James I., for the repairs of the
chapel and defraying the expenses attending the celebration of divine service, being such as are usually
discharged by a church-rate : the income is about £170
per annum. There are district churches at Oughti-
bridge, Stainington, and Wadsley, and chapels at
Bolsterstone and Midhope ; also several places of
worship for dissenters. Near the chapel is a Saxon
camp in a very perfect state, and on the moors are
several Druidical remains : many Roman coins have
also been found.

BRADFIELD-COMBUST, or BRADFIELD-MANGER
(ALL SAINTS), a parish, in the union of THINGOE, hundred of THEDWASTRY, W. division of SUFFOLK, 5½
miles (S. S. E.) from Bury St. Edmund's ; containing
192 inhabitants, and comprising 836 acres. It is situated on the road from Bury to Sudbury. The living is
a discharged rectory, valued in the king's books at
£4. 19. 7., and in the patronage of the Rev. H. J.
Hasted : the tithes have been commuted for £230, and
the glebe comprises five acres. This was the birthplace
and the residence of Arthur Young, the celebrated
writer on agriculture, and author of various miscellaneous works.

BRADFIELD ST. CLARE, a parish, in the union
of THINGOE, hundred of THEDWASTRY, W. division of
SUFFOLK, 6 miles (S. E. by S.) from Bury St. Edmund's ;
containing 240 inhabitants. The living is a rectory,
valued in the king's books at £7. 4. 7.; patron, the
Rev. Robert Davers : the tithes have been commuted
for £272. 15., and there are 29 acres of glebe.

BRADFIELD ST. GEORGE, or MONKS-BRAD-
FIELD, a parish, in the union of THINGOE, hundred of
THEDWASTRY, W. division of SUFFOLK, 4½ miles (S. E.)
from Bury St. Edmund's ; containing 479 inhabitants.
An inconsiderable fair is held at Whitsuntide. The
living is a rectory, with that of Rushbrook, and valued
in the king's books at £11. 17. 3½.; net income, £550;
patron, the Marquess of Bristol. The church stands
upon the highest ground in this part of the county, and
has a very lofty square tower, from the summit of which
sixty parish churches may be seen ; in one of the upper

Arms.

BRADFORD (St. Peter), a borough, market-town, and parish, and the head of a union, in the wapentake of Morley,W. riding of York, 10 miles (W. by S.) from Leeds, 34 (S. W.) from York, and 196 (N. N. W.) from London; comprising the townships of Allerton, North Bierley, Bowling, Bradford, Clayton, Eccleshill, Heaton, Manningham, Shipley, and Wilsden, and the chapelries of Haworth, Horton, and Thornton; the whole containing 105,257 inhabitants, of whom 34,560 are in the town. This place during the heptarchy formed part of the extensive parish of Dewsbury, from which it appears to have been separated soon after the Conquest. The manor of Bradford, which in the Domesday survey is described as a barren waste, was given to Ilbert de Lacy, who attended the Conqueror from Normandy, and fought under his standard at the battle of Hastings. Ilbert had 150 other manors in the county, which he formed into a seigniory, called the Honour of Pontefract; and in the same family was vested the barony of Clitheroe, in the shire of Lancaster. The frequent intercourse between the proprietors of these two baronies, which were separated by a wide tract of dreary, rugged, and uninhabited country, rendered some intermediate station requisite either for refreshment or security, in a journey of such difficulty and danger, at a time when feudatory wars were raging between the various chieftains among whom the lands were divided; and the comparatively fertile and pleasant vale in which the town of Bradford is situated, appears to have been selected for that purpose. There is evidence of a castle existing here in the time of the Lacys, which, as a baronial seat, would naturally assume that character; and the inhabitants in its immediate neighbourhood, whom even the temporary residence of a chieftain and his retinue would attract, are styled burgesses in an inquisition taken after the death of Henry de Lacy, the last earl of Lincoln. In this inquisition, which is dated 1316, notice also occurs of a fulling-mill, a soke corn-mill, a market on Sunday, and other particulars; from which it would appear that the town, originating in the residence of the Lacy family, had already attained no inconsiderable degree of importance. In the time of Henry III., Bradford paid more tallage to the king than Leeds, though smaller in extent. During the wars between the houses of York and Lancaster, it suffered much from the hostilities of the contending parties; and in compensation the inhabitants, though firm adherents of the house of Lancaster, received from Edward IV. exemption from toll, and a grant of two annual fairs of three days each. From this time the town continued to prosper without interruption; in the reign of Henry VIII., it had become equal to Leeds in extent and population, and far exceeded it in manufacturing importance.

During the civil war in the reign of Charles I., the town was garrisoned for the parliament, whose cause the inhabitants zealously supported. In 1642, it was attacked by a detachment of the royalist forces from Leeds, that took post at Undercliffe, in the immediate vicinity; but after one or two assaults, in which they were repulsed, the assailants retreated to Leeds, from which a stronger detachment was sent with no better success. Sir Thomas Fairfax soon afterwards took the command of the garrison in person, and marched out to meet the Earl of Newcastle, who had fixed his head-quarters at Wakefield, and who now obtained a signal victory over Fairfax: the parliamentarians, after their defeat, retreated to Bradford, and the earl, who took up his head-quarters at Bolling Hall, and brought his artillery to bear on the town, commenced a regular siege. Fairfax, seeing the dangerous position in which he was placed, endeavoured to make his escape by a desperate sally, in which Lady Fairfax, who accompanied him, was made prisoner, but generously sent back with an escort by the earl in his own carriage. The town now surrendered, and was garrisoned by the royalists, from whom, after the Earl of Newcastle had marched against the Scots, it was taken by Col. Lambert for the parliamentarians, in whose possession, after one or two attempts to retake it, it ultimately continued.

The prosperity of Bradford received a severe check during this struggle; its trade was so much impeded, that nearly half a century elapsed before it recovered its former importance, and Leeds, which had been inferior to it as well in population as in extent, now became greatly its superior in both. The woollen manufacture, for which it had from a very remote period been celebrated, and for which it is noticed by Leland in the reign of Henry VIII., was at its height in the reign of Charles I.; but after the breaking out of the parliamentary war, the town lost its consequence as the principal seat of that manufacture, and languished till the middle of the last century. It then began to revive; on the subsequent introduction of the worsted manufacture, it fully recovered its previous importance, and since that time it has been rapidly advancing in prosperity.

The TOWN is pleasantly situated at the junction of three fertile valleys, and is supposed to have derived its name from a ford over a stream which, rising in the western hills, flows through it into the river Aire. It is built partly in the bottom, but principally on the acclivities of the valley, at various elevations; and though some of the streets in the more ancient part are narrow and irregularly formed, most of those of modern date are spacious and handsome. The houses are chiefly of stone, and roofed with slate: many of them are large and substantially built; and in the suburbs are numerous excellent houses and pleasant villas, inhabited by merchants and the proprietors of the various factories in Bradford and its vicinity. The streets are well paved, and lighted with gas from works erected at an expense of £15,000, by a proprietary of 600 £25 shareholders, under an act obtained in the 3rd of George IV., subject in its provisions to an act of the 43rd of George III. for paving, lighting, watching, and improving the town and neighbourhood. The inhabitants were until lately very inadequately supplied with water from works established by a company, incorporated by act of parliament in 1790. The water was conveyed by pipes from a spring at Brown Royd Hill into a reservoir at Westgate, capable of bolding only 15,000 gallons; some of the larger houses, which were not supplied from this source, had wells attached to them, and the remainder were supplied by water-carriers from wells belonging to various proprietors, most of which were sunk to a depth of more than 100 yards. Great efforts have, however, been made, for some years, to obtain a more ample supply from Many-wells, a copious spring of pure water, about eight miles from the town ; a company of shareholders recently subscribed a capital of £45,000, and an act for their incorporation was passed in 1842. The air, though sharp, is healthy; and the environs abound with pleasing scenery.

. A subscription library, containing a well assorted collection of nearly 8000 volumes, supported by 140 shareholders and annual subscribers of a guinea each ; and a public newsroom, supported by 200 subscribers, were opened in 1828, in the *Exchange Buildings*, a handsome structure of freestone in the Grecian style, erected at an expense of £7000, by a proprietary of £25 shareholders. It comprises various apartments, of which those on the ground-floor are appropriated to the library and newsroom, while on the first-floor is a spacious and elegant assembly-room for concerts, balls, exhibitions, and public meetings : the late Miss Jowett bequeathed £1000 towards liquidating the outstanding claims for the erection of the edifice. A mechanics' institution was formed in 1825, but after a short time discontinued; and in 1832 another was established, for which an appropriate building was erected in 1839, at an expense of £3300. It is situated at the junction of Well-street with the new road to Leeds ; and contains a theatre for the delivery of lectures, a library of 3000 volumes, and a museum in which is a good collection of specimens in natural history, antiquities, various models, and machinery : an exhibition, including also a collection of paintings, was opened to the public for fifteen weeks in 1840, and the receipts for admission amounted to £2345.

The staple TRADE is the worsted manufacture; the woollen manufacture is carried on to a considerable extent in several parts of the parish, and that of cotton on a smaller scale. For the spinning of worsted-yarn, and the weaving of worsted goods, there are not less than 112 large mills in the parish, of which 38 are situated in the town : in these are 88 steam-engines of the aggregate power of 2059 horses, and 20 water-wheels of 87-horse power ; and the number of persons engaged is 10,896. In the woollen manufacture are six extensive mills, chiefly in the adjoining townships ; the machinery is propelled by 5 steam-engines of 150-horse power, and one water-wheel of 12-horse power, and the number of persons employed is 681. For the cotton manufacture there are two mills, worked by a steam-engine of 14-horse power, and 3 water-wheels of 22-horse power ; affording occupation to 98 persons. A very considerable number of persons are also engaged in hand-loom weaving. The *Piece Hall*, in Kirkgate, was erected by the merchants and manufacturers, in 1773, for the exhibition and sale of worsted stuffs; and is a neat building, 144 feet in length, and 36 in breadth, containing an upper and lower chamber. The larger manufacturers display and sell their goods in the spacious warehouses attached to their factories ; yet on market days, the hall is crowded with numerous manufacturers from neighbouring places, and by multitudes of dealers who resort to the town as the principal mart of the worsted manufacture. It is open every Thursday from ten till twelve in the morning, and from two till four in the afternoon. Much business is transacted on Monday in the woollen-trade ; and of

330

late years, a considerable trade in English and foreign wool has sprung up, large quantities of wool being transmitted hence to the various parts of the clothing district. The quantity consumed in the manufactures of the parish in a recent year, was 17,135,704 pounds ; nearly equal to the aggregate quantities of Keighley, Bingley, Halifax, and Wakefield. The *Bradford Canal*, which communicates with the Leeds and Liverpool canal at Shipley, affords facility of conveyance for the manufactures of the town, and also for the rich mineral produce of the surrounding district, which abounds with coal, limestone, and freestone of excellent quality ; it is three miles in length, and has a fall of 87 feet in its whole extent, with 12 locks. A railway was opened to Leeds in July, 1846 ; and an extension, from Shipley to Colne in Lancashire, has since been completed. The market, which is amply supplied with corn, cattle, and provisions of all kinds, is on Thursday ; and fairs for horses, cattle, sheep, and various articles of merchandise, are held on March 3rd, June 17th, and Dec. 9th ; the two last continuing for three days each. The market-place, built by the lord of the manor in 1824, comprises a spacious area, round which are ranged shops for butchers, poulterers, greengrocers, and dealers in other necessaries ; and above, on three sides of the area, are ranges of stalls and shops for the sale of fancy articles. The market for cattle is held in an inclosed area in Duke-street ; swine, of which great numbers are brought to the town, are exposed for sale in the streets.

By the act of the 2nd and 3rd of William IV., Bradford was invested with the elective franchise, and constituted a BOROUGH, with the privilege of returning two members to parliament. The right of election is in the resident £10 householders, and the returning officer is appointed by the sheriff of the county ; the borough comprises the townships of Bradford, Manningham, Bowling, and Horton. The town is within the jurisdiction of the magistrates for the West riding, and the adjourned Midsummer quarter-sessions are held here : the powers of the county-debt court of Bradford, established in 1847, extend over the registration-district of Bradford. The court-house is a handsome building of freestone, in the Grecian style ; in front is a rustic basement projecting boldly from the centre, above which is a portico of four Ionic columns, supporting an entablature and cornice surmounted with a triangular pediment. The watch-house, with a depôt for fire-engines, was built in 1837, at a cost of £1400.

The PARISH comprises by computation 33,323 acres, of which 1198 are in the township of Bradford. A very considerable portion is hilly moor, affording but indifferent pasture; and the land under cultivation being divided into small farms, occupied chiefly by persons who are also employed in the domestic woollen and stuff manufactures, or in the factories, the system of agriculture pursued is susceptible of much improvement. The soil near the town, and generally in the lower parts of the parish, is a loam on a substratum of clay, and the lands in the bottoms of the valleys produce abundant crops. The substratum is rich in mineral produce, abounding with coal, ironstone, freestone, and mill-stone-grit, all of which are extensively wrought: of the last the town is mostly built ; it is raised in large blocks, and, together with great quantities of flagstone, is sent to London, and some of the principal towns in

,the kingdom. The millstone-grit is abruptly cut off to ,the east and south of the town by the coal-measures, which form the northern boundary of the large York-shire-coal-field; and in these strata are found the rich iron-ores so extensively used in the Low Moor, Bowling, and Bierley iron-works. The coal is of two kinds, distinguished as the black bed and the better bed; the former found at various distances from the surface, with a roof of argillaceous ironstone; and the latter about forty yards below the former, varying in thickness, and extending to the magnesian limestone formation in the south. To these valuable mines and quarries, and to the numerous rivulets that intersect the parish, may be in a great degree attributed the importance of the town, as the principal seat of a wide and prosperous manufacturing district.

The LIVING is a vicarage, valued in the king's books at £20; net income, £437, with a good house; patrons, the Trustees of the late Rev. C. Simeon. An afternoon lectureship was founded in the seventeenth century, by Peter Sunderland, who also presented part of the communion-plate. The parish church is a spacious and venerable structure, with a massive square embattled tower strengthened by double buttresses at the angles, and crowned with angular and central pinnacles, rising from a perforated parapet. The western entrance is through a handsome arch, above which is a large window, in the later English style; the south porch is modern: the walls of the aisles are strengthened with buttresses of several stages, and those of the nave are embattled. The nave is separated from the aisles by a series of finely clustered columns, and lighted by a range of clerestory windows; the east window, which is of modern insertion, is large, enriched with tracery, and embellished with some portions of ancient stained glass. *Christ Church*, erected on a site presented by Benjamin Rawson, Esq., was completed in 1815, at an expense of £5400, raised by subscription, towards which a lady unknown contributed £800, through the Rev. Dr. Gaskin, of London; it was enlarged in 1826 by the assistance of the Incorporated Society, and in 1836 was new roofed and repaired at an expense of £1000. The incumbency is a perpetual curacy; net income, £160; patron, the Vicar. The churches dedicated to *St. James* and *St. John* are described under the article Horton, in which township they are situated; as also *St. Jude's* church under the article on the township of Manningham. Other churches have been erected at Bierley, Bowling, Buttershaw, Clayton, Daisy-Hill, Denholme-Gate, Eccleshill, Haworth, Horton, New Leeds, Manningham, Oxenhope, Shipley, Stanbury, Thornton, Wibsey, and Wilsden: the greater part of the livings are in the Vicar's gift. There are places of worship for Baptists, the Society of Friends, Independents, Primitive Methodists, Wesleyans, Unitarians, and Roman Catholics; the gateway of the Unitarian meeting-house is an ancient massive piece of masonry, removed from Howley Hall on its demolition.

The *Free Grammar School*, which is of very early date, was refounded and richly endowed by Edward VI.; and, by charter of Charles II. in 1662, was placed under the direction of thirteen governors, of whom the vicar of Bradford is one *ex officio*. The school-house was rebuilt on a more eligible site, under an act of parliament, in 1818, and comprises a neat dwelling-house for the

331

master, and a library. The endowment exceeds £500 per annum, and the number of scholars on the foundation is by the statutes limited to fifty; the scholars are eligible to exhibitions founded in Queen's College, Oxford, by Lady Elizabeth Hastings. At Undercliffe, about a mile to the north-east of the town, is the *Airedale Independent College*, a handsome edifice of freestone, with a stately portico, and occupying a considerable eminence; it affords accommodation for twenty students, each of whom has a private study and separate bedroom, and contains a library, lecture-room, and dining-room, with apartments for the tutors, one of whom is always resident. At Horton is a *Baptist College*, founded in 1804. The *Infirmary*, in Westgate, erected in 1842 at a cost of £5000, contains wards for 60 patients, and is gratuitously attended by two physicians, two surgeons, and two apothecaries: this institution now unites the business of a dispensary; the buildings in Darley-street, where a separate establishment existed, having been vacated in 1843. The union of Bradford comprehends the whole of the parish except the township of Haworth, and eight townships in the parishes of Birstal and Calverley; including in the whole twenty-two townships, and containing a population of 132,164. The learned and eloquent John Sharp, Archbishop of York in the reign of William III., was a native of the place.

BRADFORD-ABBAS (*St. Mary*), a parish, in the union and hundred of SHERBORNE, Sherborne division of DORSET, 4 miles (W. S. W.) from Sherborne; containing 652 inhabitants. It comprises 1139a. 1r. 30p., of which 774 acres are arable, 336 pasture, and 29 woodland: the soil is partly of a sandy and partly of a stony nature; the surface is generally hilly, and where flat subject to inundation. The river Ivel passes through. The living is a vicarage, with which the rectory of Clifton-Mabank was united in 1824, valued in the king's books at £7. 17. 11., and in the gift of the Warden and Fellows of Winchester College, who exchanged the living of Milbourne-Port for this in 1824. The Marquess of Anglesey has commuted his share of the great tithes for £193. 17. 11.; the Warden and Fellows receive £45, and the vicarial tithes of the parish have been commuted for £156: the glebe belonging to the impropriator comprises nearly nine acres, and that of the vicar nearly 9½. The church is an elegant structure in the later English style, with a lofty square embattled tower of graceful elevation. The Rev. William Preston, in 1738, gave an estate now worth £24 per annum; and in 1781, Mark West and William Read gave property producing £12. 5. per annum; for which sums children are educated on the national system.

BRADFORD, GREAT (*Holy Trinity*), a market-town and parish, and the head of a union, in the hundred of BRADFORD, N. and Westbury divisions, and Trowbridge and Bradford subdivisions, of WILTS, 8 miles (S. E.) from Bath, 31½ (N. W.) from Salisbury, and 102 (W. by S.) from London; comprising 11,272 acres, and including the ancient chapelries of Atworth, Holt, Limpley-Stoke, Winsley, and South Wraxall, and the tythings of Leigh with Woolley, and Trowle; the whole containing 10,563 inhabitants, of whom 3836 are in the town. This place, from a ford over the river Avon, was called by the Saxons *Bradenford*, of which its present name is a contraction. During the heptarchy, a battle took place here between Cenwalh, King of the West

2 U 2

Saxons, and a formidable party of his own subjects,'who had rebelled against him, under the command of his kinsman Cutbred ; when the latter were defeated with great slaughter. In 706, Aldhelm, bishop of Sherborne, founded an abbey at the place, which he dedicated to St. Lawrence, and which, after its destruction by the Danes, was rebuilt and converted into a nunnery by Ethelred, who annexed it to a larger establishment of the same kind at Shaftesbury, in 1001.

The TOWN is beautifully situated on the acclivity of a steep hill forming part of a line of eminences on the northern side of the river Avon, over which here are an ancient bridge of four, and a modern bridge of nine, arches, both affording agreeable prospects. The view of the town, which consists of three regular streets ranged above each other at different elevations on the side of the hill, is strikingly picturesque : the houses, built of stone, are in general handsome, and many of them elegant; and the inhabitants are amply supplied with water from springs. Various designs have been carried into effect for the improvement of the town : in 1839 an act was passed for paving, lighting, watching, and otherwise improving it; some of the streets have been widened, and considerable alterations made for the furtherance of business. A book society and a news-room have been established. The principal branch of manufacture is that of woollen-cloth (said by Leland to have flourished in the reign of Henry VIII.), partien-larly of the cloth composed of the finer kind of Spanish and Saxony wool, for the dyeing of which the water of the river is highly favourable. There are numerous fac-tories, affording employment to many men, women, and children, in the town and neighbourhood. Ladies' cloth, kerseymere, and fancy pieces, are also manufactured to a considerable extent. The Kennet and Avon canal, which provides an increased facility of conveyance to various parts of the kingdom, passes close to the town, and a commodious wharf has been formed on its bank. The act also for constructing the Wilts, Somerset, and Weymouth railway, passed in 1845, sanctions the forma-tion of a branch to Bradford, 1¾ mile in length. The market is on Saturday: the fairs are on Trinity-Mon-day, and the day after St. Bartholomew's day ; the latter held at Bradford-Leigh, a hamlet in the parish.

Bradford sent members to parliament in the 23rd of Edward I., but since that time it has made no return. Petty-sessions are held here alternately with Trow-bridge : the powers of the county debt-court of Brad-ford, established in 1847, extend over nearly the whole of the registration-district of Bradford. A small ora-tory, on the south-western side of the bridge, formerly belonging to the monastery of St. Lawrence, has been converted into a place of confinement for offenders pre-viously to their committal to the county gaol. The LIVING is a discharged vicarage, with the living of West-wood annexed, valued in the king's books at £10. 1. 3.; patrons and appropriators, the Dean and Chapter of Bristol. The great tithes of Bradford have been com-muted for £1485, and the small for £1000; the appro-priate glebe consists of 260 acres, and the vicarial of 3. The church, a spacious handsome structure, suffered greatly from fire in 1742, and has undergone extensive repair; the windows contain some modern stained glass, the altar is embellished with a good painting of ‚the Last Supper, and there are several stately monu-

332

ments of marble. A district church dedicated to Christ has been erected, the incumbent of which, appointed by the Vicar, has a net income of £150 ; and there are five chapels attached to the three per-petual curacies of Holt, Atworth with South Wraxall, and Winsley with Limpley-Stoke. There are also places of worship for Baptists, Independents, the Society of Friends, the Connexion of the Countess of Huntingdon, Wesleyans, and Unitarians. A free school is endowed with land producing £40 per annum. Two almshouses here, one founded by Mr. John Hall for aged men, the other for aged women, are supposed to have been an appendage to the monastery, of which, and of other re-ligious establishments formerly existing, there are still some slight remains. The poor law union of Bradford comprises eight parishes or places, seven of them in Wilts, and one in Somerset ; and contains a population of 13,379. Many curious fossils have been found in the quarries adjoining the town.

BRADFORD-PEVERELL (ST. MARY), a parish, in the union of DORCHESTER, hundred of GEORGE, Dorches-ter division of DORSET, 3¼ miles (N. W. by W.) from Dorchester; containing, with the hamlet of Muckleford, 355 inhabitants. This parish, which comprises by mea-surement 2180 acres, is situated on the river Frome, and bounded on the north by the main road from Dor-chester to Yeovil, and on the south by the road to Bridport. There is an old Roman way in a straight line from the village to Dorchester ; and in the vicinity are several tumuli, some of which, on being opened, were found to contain urns, burnt bones, coins, and various other relics of the Romans. The living is a rectory, valued in the king's books at £11. 2. 11.; net income, £229; patrons, the Warden and Fellows of Winchester College : corn-rents were assigned in lieu of tithes in 1798, and there are about 50 acres of glebe, with an excellent house. The church is a plain edifice : a good arch divides off the chancel ; and on stained glass in one of the windows is the coat of arms of William of Wykeham.

BRADFORD, WEST, a township, in the parish of MITTON, union of CLITHEROE, W. division of the wapentake of STAINCLIFFE and EWCROSS, W. riding of YORK, 2 miles (N.) from Clitheroe; containing 366 inhabitants. The township comprises by computation 1700 acres, chiefly in pasture; it is intersected by the road from Grindleton to Waddington, and the river Ribble passes on the south-east, at a very short dis-tance from the village.

BRADGATE.—See BROADGATE.

BRADING (ST. MARY), a market-town and parish, in the liberty of EAST ME-DINA, Isle of Wight division of the county of SOUTH-AMPTON, 4 miles (S.) from Ryde, and 95 (S. W.) from London ; containing 2701 in-habitants. The parish com-prises 9555 acres, of which 8156 are arable, pasture, and ground occupied by cottages and gardens ; the remainder being the cliff, the harbour of Brading, and roads and waste. The town, which was formerly of

Corporation Seal.

considerable importance, as appears from its being styled "the King's Town of Brading" in the legend of its common seal, is situated to the south of the harbour, and may be approached by vessels of small burthen. Repeated attempts have been made to exclude the sea by an embankment; the last was by Sir Hugh Myddelton, the projector of the New River, who had effected this, when, during a wet season, the whole of the works, which had been raised at an expense of £7000, were destroyed by a spring tide. In the parish is Sandown fort, a quadrangular fortification, flanked by four bastions, and encompassed by a ditch; it was constructed in the reign of Henry VIII., on a level with the beach, and, having been greatly neglected after the rise of the English navy, was repaired during the late war, and made the most considerable fortress in the island.

· The town consists principally of one long street, the houses in which are irregularly built; the inhabitants are plentifully supplied with water from public wells. The market, which is amply supplied with corn, is on Monday; and fairs are held on the 12th of May and 2nd of October. The government, by charter of incorporation granted prior to the reign of Edward VI., is vested in a senior and junior bailiff, two justices (who are the bailiffs of the preceding year), two constables, a steward, and other officers; the bailiffs are appointed at the court leet of the town. The town-hall is now partly used as a schoolroom; the lower portion contains a prison, and is also used for the market. The living is a discharged vicarage, valued in the king's books at £20, and in the gift of Trinity College, Cambridge: the tithes have been commuted for £1645, of which £1285 are payable to the college, £330 to the incumbent, and £30 to an impropriator; the glebe attached to the living consists of 3½ acres, and that belonging to the college of 16½ acres. The church is said to have been built in 704 by Wilfred, Bishop of Chichester, who here baptized his first converts to Christianity; it is a spacious structure with a tower, and some probable remains of Saxon architecture are preserved in the nave, though the building has undergone many alterations in other parts. A church was built at Bembridge in 1827; and in 1846 an additional church was erected, which occupies a lofty and conspicuous position, at Sandown. There is a place of worship for Wesleyans.—See BEMBRIDGE.

BRADLE, a tything, in the parish of CHURCH-KNOWLE, union of WAREHAM and PURBECK, hundred of HASILOR, Wareham division of the county of DORSET; containing 97 inhabitants.

BRADLEY, a tything, in the parish of CUMNER, union of ABINGDON, hundred of HORMER, county of BERKS, 5 miles (N. N. W.) from Abingdon; containing 7 inhabitants.

BRADLEY, a township, in the parish of MALPAS, union of WREXHAM, Higher division of the hundred of BROXTON, S. division of the county of CHESTER, 2 miles (S. E. by E.) from Malpas; containing 99 inhabitants. In this township are 820 acres, of a clayey soil. The tithes have been commuted for £72.

BRADLEY (ALL SAINTS), a parish, in the hundred of APPLETREE, union of BURTON-UPON-TRENT, S. division of the county of DERBY, 3 miles (E. by S.) from Ashbourn; containing 271 inhabitants. At the time of the Domesday survey, the manor belonged to Henry de

333   ·

Ferrers; and at a very early period it became the property and seat of the ancient family of Kniveton: Sir Andrew Kniveton, in 1655, sold the estate to the Meynells. Bradley comprises 2374a. 3r. 23p., the soil of which is, in nearly equal portions, strong and light. The living is a rectory, valued in the king's books at £5. 19. 9½., and in the patronage of the Bishop of Lichfield: the tithes have been commuted for £262, and the glebe comprises 55 acres. The church is a small ancient structure. There is a chalybeate spring, but not much used.

BRADLEY, with SINWELL.—See SINWELL.

BRADLEY (ST. GEORGE), a parish, in the union of CAISTOR, wapentake of BRADLEY HAVERSTOE, parts of LINDSEY, county of LINCOLN, 3 miles (S. W.) from Grimsby; containing 106 inhabitants. The living is a discharged rectory, valued in the king's books at £5. 10. 10., and in the patronage of Sir John Nelthorpe, Bart.: the tithes have been commuted for £245, and there are nearly 7 acres of glebe.

BRADLEY (ALL SAINTS), a parish, in the union of BASINGSTOKE, hundred of OVERTON, Basingstoke and N. divisions of the county of SOUTHAMPTON, 8¼ miles (S.) from Basingstoke; containing 125 inhabitants. It comprises about 1100 acres, of which 850 are arable, 23 meadow, and 220 woodland. The living is a rectory, valued in the king's books at £8. 13. 4., and in the patronage of C. E. Rumbold, Esq.: the tithes have been commuted for £185, and there are 21 acres of glebe. The church is a small plain edifice, with 80 sittings.

BRADLEY, a chapelry, in the parish of FLADBURY, union of DROITWICH, Middle division of the hundred of OSWALDSLOW, Droitwich and E. divisions of the county of WORCESTER, 6¼ miles (E. S. E.) from Droitwich; containing, with the hamlet of Stock, 251 inhabitants, of whom 160 are in Bradley. It comprises 1096 acres of land, of rather level surface, and lies on the road from Droitwich to Stratford. The chapel has lately been put into excellent repair, at the joint expense of the congregation and the rector.

BRADLEY, BOTH, a township, in the parish of KILDWICK, union of SKIPTON, E. division of the wapentake of STAINCLIFFE and EWCROSS, W. riding of YORK, 2½ miles (S. S. E.) from Skipton; containing 557 inhabitants. This township, which consists of the two hamlets of Upper and Lower Bradley, comprises 1576 acres, whereof 209 are common or waste, the whole the property of the Earl of Burlington; the soil is fertile, and stone is quarried. The tithes have been commuted for £43. 15. payable to the Dean and Chapter of Christ-Church, Oxford, and £23 to the vicar of the parish. There are places of worship for Primitive Methodists and Wesleyans, and a burial-place belonging to the Society of Friends.

BRADLEY, GREAT (ST. MARY), a parish, in the union and hundred of RISBRIDGE, W. division of SUFFOLK, 6½ miles (N. by E.) from Haverhill; containing 544 inhabitants, and comprising by computation 2306 acres. The living is a rectory, valued in the king's books at £17. 1. 5½., and in the patronage of the Trustees of the Rev. W. S. Parr Wilder, the present incumbent: the tithes produce £650 per annum, and the glebe comprises about 50 acres. The church is an ancient structure.

BRADLEY-IN-THE-MOORS (*ALL SAINTS*), a parish, in the union of CHEADLE, S. division of the hundred of TOTMONSLOW, N. division of the county of STAFFORD, 4 miles (E. S. E.) from Cheadle; containing 72 inhabitants. It lies near the road from Cheadle to Rocester, and comprises about 650 acres of land: the Earl of Shrewsbury is lord of the manor and principal owner of the soil. The living is a perpetual curacy; net income, £58; patron and impropriator, the Earl of Shrewsbury, whose rectory is valued in the king's books at £17. 11. 8. The church is a small edifice.

BRADLEY-JUXTA-STAFFORD (*ALL SAINTS*), a parish, in the W. division of the hundred of CUTTLESTONE, union, and S. division of the county, of STAFFORD, 3¾ miles (N. W.) from Penkridge; containing, with the liberties of Billington and Woollaston, 649 inhabitants. The parish comprises by measurement nearly 6000 acres of fertile land, the greater part arable, the rest pasture and meadow; and is situated near the Liverpool and Birmingham railway, and the Grand 'Trunk canal. The living is a perpetual curacy; net income, £75; patron, the Duke of Sutherland; impropriators, the Earl of Lichfield, Lord Willoughby de Broke, and other landowners. The church is a neat and substantial structure, lately new-pewed and thoroughly repaired. There is a place of worship for Wesleyans. The free grammar school is of early and obscure foundation; the endowment arises from land producing about £130 per annum. At Billington are traces of an old encampment, said to have been a British station and afterwards possessed by the Saxons.

BRADLEY, LITTLE (*ALL SAINTS*), a parish, in the union and hundred of RISBRIDGE, W. division of SUFFOLK, 6 miles (N. by E.) from Haverhill; containing 33 inhabitants, and comprising by measurement 976 acres. The living is a discharged rectory, valued in the king's books at £5. 0. 10., and in the patronage of W. and C. Lamprell, Esqrs.: the tithes have been commuted for £250. The church, though small, is of very considerable antiquity, with a round tower; in it lies buried John Day, the celebrated printer, and it contains also some ancient and curious monuments.

BRADLEY, MAIDEN (*ALL SAINTS*), a parish, in the union of MERE, partly in the hundred of NORTON-FERRIS, E. division of the county of SOMERSET, but chiefly in the hundred of MERE, Warminster and S. divisions of WILTS, 5¾ miles (N. by W.) from Mere; containing, with the tything of Yarnfield, 700 inhabitants. The parish is the property of the Duke of Somerset, who has a seat here; and comprises 4208 acres, of which 1400 are arable, 1860 pasture, 506 down, and 362 wood: the soil is various, and for the most part good rich land. The district abounds with romantic and interesting scenery; there are two singular knolls of chalk, separated from each other by the turnpike-road leading to Wincanton. Fairs, formerly of importance, are held on April 25th and September 21st. About three-quarters of a mile to the north-east of the village, and now forming part of the buildings of a farm called Priory Farm, are the remains of an hospital founded by Manasser Biset, about the close of the reign of Stephen or the beginning of that of Henry II., and dedicated to the Blessed Virgin. It was for leprous women, under the care of some secular brethren, who were afterwards changed by Herbert, Bishop of Sarum, into a prior and

canons of the Augustine order; and at the Dissolution, the revenue was £197. 18. 8. The living is a perpetual curacy; net income, £111; patrons and appropriators, the Dean and Canons of Christ-Church, Oxford. The church contains a monument, finely executed, to the memory of Sir Edward Seymour, Bart., of political celebrity in the reigns of Charles II., William and Mary, and Anne.

BRADLEY, NORTH (*ST. NICHOLAS*), a parish, in the union of WESTBURY and WHORWELSDOWN, hundred of WHORWELSDOWN, Whorwelsdown and N. divisions of WILTS, 2 miles (S.) from Trowbridge; containing, with the chapelry of Southwick, 2427 inhabitants, of whom 1043 are in North Bradley tything. The parish is bounded on the west by the river Frome, and comprises by measurement 3978 acres, of which 2764 are pasture, 927 arable, and 287 woodland; the soil is for the most part a strong clay, and the surface hilly, except to the north, where a small portion is level. Bradley stream enters from the south, and, pursuing a northern course, empties itself into the Trow. The living is a discharged vicarage, valued in the king's books at £11; net income, £398; patrons and impropriators, the Warden and Fellows of Winchester College. In the tything of Southwick, at the extremity of the parish, is an additional church, called Christ Church, erected under the auspices of the late Dr. Daubeny, Archdeacon of Sarum, and incumbent of the parish. At a short distance from the parish church is a neat edifice of Bath freestone, erected and endowed in 1808, by the archdeacon, as an asylum for aged persons of respectable character, reduced to poverty; and attached to the asylum is a school. The endowment consists of property invested in the funds, producing about £120 per annum. A building called the Vicar's poor-house was erected by the same munificent benefactor, for the reception of twelve poor persons. There is one place of worship for Wesleyans, and two for Particular Baptists.

BRADLEY, WEST, a parish, in the union of WELLS, hundred of GLASTON-TWELVE-HIDES, E. division of SOMERSET, 4¾ miles (E. S. E.) from Glastonbury; containing 116 inhabitants. The living is annexed to the vicarage of East Pennard: the appropriate tithes, payable to the Bishop of Bath and Wells, have been commuted for £30, and those belonging to the incumbent for £50; there is a glebe of 12½ acres.

BRADMORE, a parish, in the union of BASFORD, N. division of the wapentake of RUSHCLIFFE, S. division of the county of NOTTINGHAM, 6¼ miles (S.) from Nottingham; containing, with the hamlet of Parbrook, 416 inhabitants. The parish is on the Nottingham and London road, through Loughborough; and comprises by computation 1560 acres. It is of oblong form, extending from east to west; and is bounded on the north by the parish of Ruddington, on the north-east by the parish of Plumtree, on the south-east by that of Keyworth, on the south by Bunny parish, and on the west by Gotham. The village stands on an eminence, close to the high road, and about a mile distant from the village of Bunny. The living is a vicarage, annexed to that of Bunny: the church, with the exception of the steeple, was destroyed by fire, and has not been rebuilt. A place of worship for a congregation of Wesleyans was erected in 1830.

Corporation Seal.

BRADNINCH (St. Dí-
sen), a town and parish,
having separate jurisdiction,
in the union of TIVERTON,
locally in the hundred of
HAYRIDGE, N. division of
DEVON, 8 miles (N. E.) from
Exeter, and 170 (W.) from
London; containing 1714
inhabitants. This place, anciently called *Braineis*, was
of some importance in the
time of the Saxons: in the
reign of John it received many privileges, which were
increased by Henry III.; and in the reign of Edward
III. it was annexed to the duchy of Cornwall. In this
and in the preceding reign it sent representatives in
parliament, from which, on account of its poverty, it
was excused in the time of Henry VII., on the payment
of a fine of five marks. During the civil war the town
suffered considerably, from its proximity to Exeter, and
was alternately in the possession of the royalists and the
parliamentarians; in the year 1665 it was almost destroyed by fire. The parish comprises 4351a. 27p., of
which 4184 acres are arable, meadow, pasture, and
orchard. The town is pleasantly situated on an
eminence, environed by hills on all sides except the
south and south-west, and consists principally of neatly
thatched and white-washed cottages. The woollen-
trade was formerly carried on, but little now remains;
the chief branch of manufacture at present is that of
paper, for which there are three mills, affording employment to sixty or seventy of the inhabitants. Iron-
ore has been found in the neighbourhood, but works
have not been established. The Bristol and Exeter
railway passes by the town. The market has been discontinued; fairs are held on May 6th and Oct. 2nd.
The first charter of incorporation was granted by
Reginald, Earl of Cornwall, and others were bestowed
by King John and James I.; the latter of these, as enlarged in 1667, is the governing charter, under which the
corporate body consists of a mayor, twelve masters, and
an indefinite number of free burgesses, with a recorder,
town-clerk, two serjeants-at-mace, and constables. The
mayor, late mayor, and recorder, are justices of the
peace for the borough. The corporation holds a court
of session quarterly: a mayor's court for the recovery
of debts under 40s. is held monthly; and petty-sessions
are also held monthly, and frequently every Monday.
The guildhall is a small building. The living is a perpetual curacy; net income, £102; patrons and appropriators, the Dean and Canons of Windsor, whose tithes
have been commuted for £584, and who have 120 acres
of glebe. The church is an ancient structure, with a
tower and other portions of later date; the chancel is
separated from the nave by a richly carved oak-screen:
the whole was repaired in 1842, and with such skill and
success that the original character of the venerable
structure has been preserved in all its pristine beauty.
There is a place of worship for Particular Baptists.
Bradninch gives the title of Baron to the dukes of
Cornwall, who are styled barons of Braines.

BRADNINCH, a precinct, in the county of the city
of EXETER, S. division of DEVON; containing 55 inhabitants.

335

BRADNOP, a township, in the parish and union
of LEEK, N. division of the hundred of TOTMONSLOW
and of the county of STAFFORD, 2 miles (E. S. E.) from
Leek; containing 442 inhabitants, many of whom are
employed in copper-mines. This place lies on the road
from Leek to Ashbourn, and belongs to a number of
owners.

BRADON, NORTH and SOUTH (St. Mary Magdalene), a parish, in the union of LANGPORT, hundred
of ABDICK and BULSTONE, W. division of SOMERSET,
3¾ miles (N. by E.) from Ilminster; containing 41
inhabitants. The living is a sinecure rectory, valued
in the king's books at £5. 4. 4½., and in the patronage of the Wyndham family: the impropriate tithes
have been commuted for £55, and the vicarial for £50.
The church is in ruins. Adjoining this parish was one
called Gouze-Bradon, now depopulated, and the church
and other buildings entirely destroyed.

BRADPOLE (Holy Trinity), a parish, in the union
of BRIDPORT, hundred of BEAMINSTER-FORUM and
REDHONE, Bridport division of DORSET, 1 mile (N. N. E.)
from Bridport; containing 1357 inhabitants. It comprises 998a. 2r. 16p., of which 566 acres are arable, 182
meadow, 100 pasture, and 18 woodland. The living is
a discharged vicarage, valued in the king's books at
£8. 13. 1½., and in the patronage of the Crown; net
income, £199. A new church was consecrated in
August 1846, containing 400 sittings, mostly free. The
inhabitants formerly interred their dead at Bridport;
but by a composition made in 1527, they were allowed
to inter in their own churchyard, on paying annually a
small acknowledgment to the rector of Bridport.

BRADSHAW, a chapelry, in the parish and union
of BOLTON, hundred of SALFORD, S. division of the
county of LANCASTER, 2 miles (N. E.) from Bolton;
containing 827 inhabitants. The family of Bradshaw·
were seated here in the 16th century, and of this family
was John Bradshaw, who presided at the trial of
Charles I., and was subsequently chancellor of the duchy
of Lancaster. The township is situated on the east
bank of the Bradshaw brook, which separates it from
Turton and Harwood; and on the road from Bolton to
Burnley. It comprises 1380 acres; the surface is undulated, and the scenery picturesque, and enriched with
several good plantations: the land is chiefly in pasture.
A colliery and a stone-quarry are in operation. The
bleach and print works of Messrs. Callender, Bickham,
and Company, employ 500 hands; and there are also
two cotton-mills at work. Bradshaw Hall, an irregular
building embosomed in trees, affords a beautiful specimen of the style of architecture that prevailed in the
early part of the seventeenth century; and the arms of
the Bradshaws are still to be seen, both in the stained
glass of the window, and cut on stone over the hall-door.
The living is a perpetual curacy; net income, £150;
patron, the Vicar of Bolton. The chapel was rebuilt in
1847. There is a small Baptist place of worship; and
a school-house is let rent-free to a master. President
Bradshaw was the son of Henry Bradshaw, and of
Catherine, daughter and coheiress of Ralph Winnington, of Offerton. He was baptized at Stockport, December 10th, 1602; married Mary, the daughter of Thomas
Marbury, of Marbury, in the county of Chester; and
died (without issue) December 16th, 1659, just before
the Restoration, thus escaping the fate of other mem-

bers of the "High Court of Justice" which condemned the unfortunate Charles to the scaffold.

BRADSHAW, an ecclesiastical district, in the parish and union of HALIFAX, wapentake of MORLEY, W. riding of YORK, 3½ miles (W.) from Halifax; containing 3499 inhabitants. This district was formed subsequently to the erection of a church here in 1838; the scenery is strikingly diversified, and from the summit of Soil-hill is a very extensive view, embracing the cathedral and city of York, with the adjacent country for 40 miles around. The inhabitants are chiefly employed in the various worsted-mills, in wool-combing and hand-loom weaving, and in collieries and quarries. The church, dedicated to St. John, was erected at an expense of £1200, of which £800 were given by the late Mrs. Elizabeth Wadsworth, and the remainder by the Parliamentary Commissioners; it is a neat structure in the early English style, with a square tower, and contains 350 sittings, of which 125 are free. The living is a perpetual curacy, in the patronage of the Vicar of Halifax, with a net income of £150. There are places of worship for Wesleyans, Primitive Methodists, and Methodists of the New Connexion. A national school was erected by Mrs. Wadsworth, who endowed it with £20 per annum; and that lady also bequeathed funds for the erection and endowment of six almshouses for aged females; the buildings were completed in 1841, and form a neat range in the Elizabethan style.

BRADSHAW-EDGE, a township, in the parish and union of CHAPEL-EN-LE-FRITH, hundred of HIGH PEAK, N. division of the county of DERBY; containing 1850 inhabitants. It includes a principal part of the town of Chapel-en-le-Frith. The Hall, which is now a farm-house, was the seat of the ancient family of Bradshaw.

BRADSTONE (ST. NUN), a parish, in the union of TAVISTOCK, hundred of LIFTON, Lifton and S. divisions of DEVON, 4¼ miles (S. E. by E.) from Launceston; containing 166 inhabitants. The living is a discharged rectory, valued in the king's books at £6. 7. 2., and in the patronage of the Bishop of Exeter: the tithes have been commuted for £210, and there are 50 acres of glebe.

BRADWALL, a township, in the parish of SANDBACH, union of CONGLETON, hundred of NORTHWICH, S. division of the county of CHESTER, 2 miles (N. by W.) from Sandbach; containing 344 inhabitants. In this township are 2037 acres, of a clayey and sandy soil. The tithes have been commuted for £159. 7. 7. payable to the impropriator, £158. 11. 8. to the vicar of the parish, and £5. 1. to the rector of Brereton.

BRADWELL (ST. LAWRENCE), a parish, in the union of NEWPORT-PAGNELL, hundred of NEWPORT, county of BUCKINGHAM, 3½ miles (E. by S.) from Stoney-Stratford; containing 381 inhabitants. It is situated near the Wolverton station of the London and Birmingham railway, and comprises 1671a. 2r. 27p., of which 161 acres are woodland. The living is a vicarage, endowed with the great tithes, valued in the king's books at £5. 11. 0½., and in the patronage of the Crown: the tithes have been commuted for £250, and there are six acres of glebe. The sum of £13. 13. is applied annually in relieving the poor, and towards instructing children.

BRADWELL, a township, in the parish of HOPE, union of BAKEWELL, hundred of HIGH PEAK, N. divi-
336

sion of the county of DERBY, 4½ miles (N. N. E.) from Tideswell; containing 1273 inhabitants. The population are chiefly engaged in the lead and calamine works in the vicinity, the manufacture of these articles being carried on to a considerable extent. About the year 1807, a huge natural excavation, called the Crystallized Cavern, was discovered: it is approached by a narrow entrance, leading to a spacious area, the sides of which are lined with crystallizations of singular beauty; and its separate parts are recognised by different names, such as the Grotto of Paradise, the Grotto of Calypso, Music Chamber, &c. The tithes have been commuted for £84 payable to the Dean and Chapter of Lichfield, £12 payable to the impropriator, and £7 to the vicar. There are meeting-houses for Wesleyans and Unitarians.

BRADWELL (ST. NICHOLAS), a parish, in the incorporation and hundred of MUTFORD and LOTHINGLAND, E. division of SUFFOLK, 3 miles (S. W.) from Yarmouth; containing 270 inhabitants. Breydon Water bounds the parish on the north. The living is a rectory, valued in the king's books at £28, and in the patronage of Lord G. Osborne: the tithes have been commuted for £630. The church contains a monument to the ancient family of Vesey, and an octagonal font on an ascent of two steps.

BRADWELL-ABBEY, an extra-parochial liberty, in the union of NEWPORT-PAGNELL, hundred of NEWPORT, county of BUCKINGHAM, 3¼ miles (E. S. E.) from Stoney-Stratford; containing 21 inhabitants. It comprises 425 acres of land. A priory of Black monks, dedicated to St. Mary, was founded about the time of Stephen, by Meinfelin, Baron of Wolverton, originally as a cell to the monastery at Luffield; the revenue, in the 23rd of Henry VIII., was £53. 11. 2. The site is now occupied by a farmhouse.

BRADWELL-JUXTA-COGGESHALL (HOLY TRINITY), a parish, in the union of BRAINTREE, hundred of WITHAM, N. division of ESSEX, 2 miles (W. by S.) from Coggeshall; containing 293 inhabitants. It derives its name, originally Broadwell, from a copious spring to the north of the Hall: the river Pant, or Black-water, flows through a small hamlet in the parish, to which it gives its name. The living is a rectory, valued in the king's books at £12, and in the gift of M. P. C. Brunwin, Esq.: the tithes have been commuted for £345, and the glebe consists of 31 acres. The church is a small edifice with a tower, and contains several ancient and handsome alabaster monuments.

BRADWELL-NEAR-THE-SEA (ST. THOMAS THE APOSTLE), a parish, in the union of MALDON, hundred of DENGIE, S. division of ESSEX, 12 miles (E.) from Maldon; containing 1034 inhabitants. The parish is situated at the mouth of the river Black-water, and is bounded on the east by the North Sea; it comprises 4733a. 3r. 18p., of which 3156 acres are arable, 972 pasture, 60 wood, and 134 common or waste. Camden places the Saxon city of Æthancestre at or near this place, which he also identifies with the Roman station Othona, where the Numerus Fortensium was posted under a commander styled Count of the Saxon Shore, at the decline of the Roman empire in Britain. A fair is held on the 24th of June. The living is a rectory, valued in the king's books at £48, and in the gift of the Rev. T. Schreiber: the tithes have been commuted for £1300, and there are nearly 254 acres of glebe, with a house built by Sir H. Bate Dudley between 1781 and 1786. The church, rebuilt in 1706, is a handsome edifice, with a stone tower surmounted by a lofty spire, and is situated on elevated ground commanding fine prospects. An ancient chapel, called Capella-de-la-Val, of uncertain foundation, has long been in ruins. There is an endowed school in the parish.

BRADWOOD-WIDGER, a parish, in the union of HOLSWORTHY, hundred of LIFTON, Lifton and S. divisions of DEVON, 6 miles (N. E.) from Launceston; containing 923 inhabitants. The parish comprises by computation 5000 acres, of which 1500 are common or waste; the soil is chiefly clay, and the surface hilly. It is bounded by the river Bradwood on the south and north, and the river Carey on the west. The place belonged to the Priory of Frithelstock, and, on the dissolution of monasteries, was conferred by Henry VIII. on the Dean and Chapter of Bristol. A fair is held on the Tuesday next after Midsummer-day. The living is a perpetual curacy, with that of German's-Week annexed, valued in the king's books at £8. 3. 4.; net income, £148; patrons and appropriators, the Dean and Chapter. About 70 acres of glebe are attached to the curacy. There is a place of worship for Wesleyans.

BRADWORTHY (ST. JOHN THE BAPTIST), a parish, in the union of BIDEFORD, hundred of BLACK TORRINGTON, Holsworthy and N. divisions of DEVON, 7 miles (N. by W.) from Holsworthy; containing 1081 inhabitants. It comprises 7800 acres, of which 100 are common or waste. The reservoir of the Bude canal, occupying an extent of 75 acres, is chiefly in the parish. The living is a vicarage, with the perpetual curacy of Pancrasweek annexed, valued in the king's books at £25. 5. 5., and in the patronage of the Crown; net income, £243; impropriators, Mrs. E. Langdon and the Rev. R. Kingdon. There is a place of worship for Wesleyans.

· BRAFFERTON, a township, in the parish of AYCLIFFE, union of DARLINGTON, S. E. division of DARLINGTON ward, S. division of the county of DURHAM, 4½ miles (N. by E.) from Darlington; containing 211 inhabitants. This township, which is situated on the line of the York and Newcastle railway, contains 2312 acres; and comprises the ancient manor of Ketton, which was granted by Bishop Carilepho to the convent of Durham, and is now the property of the Rev. Sir Charles Hardinge, Bart. While Ketton was in the occupation of the late Charles Colling, who died in 1830, it was celebrated for its fine breed of short-horned cattle. The tithes have been commuted for £144. 10. payable to the vicar, and £73 to the Dean and Chapter of Durham.

BRAFFERTON (ST. PETER), a parish, in the union of EASINGWOULD, wapentakes of HALLIKELD and BULMER, N. riding of YORK; containing 873 inhabitants, of whom 179 are in the township of Brafferton, 4½ miles (N. E.) from Boroughbridge. The parish includes the townships of Helperby and Thornton-Bridge, and comprises 4565 acres: the village adjoins Helperby on the east side of the river Swale. The York and Newcastle railway intersects Pill-Moor. The living is a discharged vicarage, valued in the king's books at £9. 15. 6., and in the patronage of the Crown, with a net income of £307; appropriator, the Archbishop of York. The

church was rebuilt in 1832, at the expense of £1300, raised by subscription. Brafferton Spring, north-east of the village, is a noted fox-cover.

BRAFIELD-ON-THE-GREEN (ST. LAWRENCE), a parish, in the union of HARDINGSTONE, hundred of WYMMERSLEY, S. division of NORTHAMPTONSHIRE, 5 miles (E. by S.) from Northampton; containing 428 inhabitants. It comprises about 1300 acres, including between fifty and sixty acres of woodland, and is mostly arable; the surface is undulated, and the soil principally clay, and generally fertile. Gravel and stone are obtained, but only fit for the repair of roads. Shoes are made by the greater portion of the male population, and pillow-lace by nearly all the females. The village lies on the Northampton and Bedford road, and within a mile of the Peterborough railway, which passes through about two acres of land belonging to the Rev. Christopher Smyth. The living is a discharged vicarage, annexed to that of Little Houghton, and valued in the king's books at £6. 13. 6¼. The church was in the early English style; but the character of the body of it was completely destroyed about fifty years ago, when the edifice underwent a thorough repair : the tower remains in its original state, but its beauty is much spoiled by unsightly buttresses. The Baptists have a small place of worship; and there is a handsome school-house, lately built by the vicar, the Rev. C. Smyth, who also supports an infant school. Coal and clothing clubs have been established.

BRAILES (ST. GEORGE), a parish, in the union of SHIPSTON-UPON-STOUR, Brailes division of the hundred of KINGTON, S. division of the county of WARWICK, 4 miles (E. by S.) from Shipston; containing, with the hamlets of Chelmscote and Winderton, 1284 inhabitants. Prior to the Conquest, this lordship was in the possession of Edwin, Earl of Mercia; and subsequently, including Chelmscote and Winderton, it yielded to the Conqueror "no less than £55 yearly, with 20 horseloads of salt." Henry III., in 1248, granted a charter for a market here on Monday, which has been long discontinued; also a fair, which is held on Easter-Tuesday. In the 13th of Edward I., William de Beauchamp, Earl of Warwick, then owner of the manor, claimed by prescription, and was allowed certain privileges; viz., a gallows, with assize of bread and beer. The parish contains 5407 acres of land, whereof about 2000 are arable and 3000 pasture; the village is situated on the turnpike-road from Shipston to Banbury, and is of considerable extent. There is a manufactory for livery shag, plush, &c., in which nearly 100 persons are employed. The LIVING is a vicarage, valued in the king's books at £25; net income, £344; patron, John Thornton, Esq. Under an inclosure act passed in 1784, land and annual money payments were assigned in lieu of all tithes and moduses, for Lower Brailes. The church was probably erected in the time of the Conqueror, and was given in the reign of his son, Henry I., to the canons of Kenilworth. It is a large and handsome edifice, combining the early, decorated, and later English styles, with a lofty tower (supported by tall buttresses and crowned with battlements and pinnacles) containing six bells, the largest of which weighs more than two and a half tons; the interior was modernised in 1824. A guild consisting of a warden, brethren, and sisters, was founded in the church by Richard Nevill, Earl of War-

wick; the revenue, in the 37th of Henry VIII., was
£18. 13. 2., out of which a grammar school was then
supported. There was anciently a chapel at Chelmscote,
in which a chantry for four priests was founded by
Thomas de Pakinton, of Brailes, in 1322. The Society
of Friends and the Roman Catholics have places of
worship; and a free school, probably founded about
the end of the reign of Henry VIII., is endowed with
an improved income of £70. In Upper Brailes, at the
distance of 1¼ mile from the church, is a chalybeate
spring, the water of which has been used with considerable advantage in cases of scrofula.

BRAILSFORD (ALL SAINTS), a parish, in the hundred of APPLETREE, S. division of the county of DERBY,
7 miles (N. W. by W.) from Derby; containing, with
the township of Ednaston, 756 inhabitants, of whom
539 are in that portion exclusive of the township. The
manor, which in the reign of the Confessor had belonged
to Earl Wallef, was one of those given, by William the
Conqueror to Henry de Ferrers, under whom it was
held by Elsin, ancestor of the ancient family of Brailsford. From the Brailsfords the property passed by
marriage to the Bassetts, and from them in the same
way to the Shirleys: the manor now belongs to the
Evans family. The parish comprises 4296a. 33p.,
whereof two-thirds are pasture, and the remainder
arable and woodland; it is situated on the road from
Derby to Ashbourn. Brailsford House and Culland
Hall are the property of the family of Cox. The
living is a rectory, with that of Osmaston annexed,
valued in the king's books at £9. 19. 2., and in the
patronage of Earl Ferrers. The tithes of the parish
have been commuted for £500, and the glebe consists of
about 72 acres, valued at £100 per annum, with a residence. The church, which stands on an eminence, is a
handsome edifice with a tower; some portions of it are
in the Norman style, but its architecture is chiefly of the
early part of the 15th century. On the floor are several
alabaster slabs: two of them have effigies, in scroll
lines, of knights in armour; and on a third is the representation of a priest in his vestments. The Wesleyans
and Primitive Methodists have places of worship; and
schools built in 1831, by William Evans, Esq., are supported by subscription. The Venerable Archdeacon
Shirley, rector of Brailsford, was raised to the bishopric
of Sodor and Man, in 1846, but only held the prelacy a
few months, his death occurring in April 1847.

BRAINTFIELD (ST. ANDREW), a parish, in the
union of HERTFORD, hundred of CASHIO, or liberty of
ST. ALBAN'S, though locally in the hundred of HERT-
FORD, county of HERTFORD, 3½ miles (N. W.) from
Hertford; containing 201 inhabitants. The living is a
rectory, valued in the king's books at £11. 6. 8., and
in the patronage of Abel Smith, Esq.: the tithes have
been commuted for £326, and there are about 35 acres
of glebe. According to Matthew Paris, this was the
first preferment held by Thomas à Becket; and a
small pond near the parsonage-house still bears his
name.

BRAINTREE (ST. MICHAEL), a market-town and
parish, and the head of a union, in the hundred of
HINCKFORD, N. division of ESSEX, 11 miles (N. by E.)
from Chelmsford, and 40 (N. E.) from London; containing 3670 inhabitants. This place is described in
Domesday book under the head of " Raines," including

Methodists. An ancient grammar school, in which the eminent naturalist, John Ray, received his education, is supported partly by an endowment of land now let for £18 a year, bequeathed by J. Coker, Esq., partly by an annuity of £45 left by the Rev. James Burgess, and partly by voluntary contributions. In the reign of Charles I., Henry Smith, alderman of London, who, from the habit of wandering like a beggar, accompanied by his dog, obtained the appellation of " Dog Smith," bequeathed £2800 to the poor of this and 13 other parishes; and there are many other charities in the town, yielding altogether nearly £200 per annum. The union of Braintree comprises 14 parishes or places, and contains a population of 15,097 : the workhouse, calculated for the reception of 300 inmates, cost £6342. About half a mile distant there were, till lately, the ruins of a church founded before the Conquest, and formerly the parish church : the site of a Roman camp, now called the Cherry Orchard, is pointed out; and many sepulchral urns, fragments of Roman pottery, and Roman coins, have been found, besides three British gold coins, supposed to be of Boadicea. This was the scene of one of the earlier martyrdoms, that of Richard Pygott, in the reign of Mary. Samuel Dale, M.D., editor of the *History and Antiquities of Harwich*, resided here, and assisted Ray in collecting the more rare plants in Essex ; and the Rev. Mr. Challis, professor of astronomy at Cambridge, is a native of the place.

BRAISEWORTH, a parish, in the union and hundred of HARTISMERE, W. division of SUFFOLK, 1¾ mile (S. S. W.) from Eye; containing 151 inhabitants. It is within the parliamentary borough of Eye. The living is a discharged rectory, valued in the king's books at £4. 8. 1½., and in the gift of Major-General Sir E. Kerrison, Bart. : the tithes have been commuted for £195, and there are 20 acres of glebe. The church is in the early style, and consists of a nave and chancel; the entrances on the north and south sides are by Norman doorways, that on the north being exceedingly rich in workmanship.

BRAITHWAITE, a township, in the parish of CROSTHWAITE, ALLERDALE ward above Derwent, W. division of CUMBERLAND, 2¾ miles (W. by N.) from Keswick ; containing 318 inhabitants. The village lies at the foot of Winlatter Fell, the summit of which, gained by a steep ascent of two miles and a quarter, embraces prospects of a most sublime character. A woollen manufactory is carried on; and lead-mines have been worked.

BRAITHWAITE, LEATH ward, CUMBERLAND.—See MIDDLESCEUGH.

BRAITHWAITE, a hamlet, in the parish of KIRK-BRAMWITH, union of DONCASTER, Upper division of wapentake of OSGOLDCROSS, W. riding of YORK, 3½ miles (W. by S.) from Thorne ; containing 107 inhabitants. It is on the north bank of the river Don, and nearly a mile from the village of Kirk-Bramwith.

BRAITHWELL (ST. JAMES), a parish, partly in the union of DONCASTER, and partly in that of ROTHER-HAM, S. division of the wapentake of STRAFFORTH and TICKHILL, W. riding of YORK ; containing, with the chapelry of Bramley, 800 inhabitants, of whom 447 are in the township of Braithwell, 6½ miles (E. by N.) from Rotherham. In acknowledgment of a subscription raised here towards the ransom of Richard I., when

made captive in Germany, a charter for a market and fair was granted to this place on his return from the Holy Land : the former is disused, but the latter is held on the first Wednesday in May; and a cross still remains in the centre of the village, with an inscription in Norman French, dated 1191, commemorating the event. The parish comprises 2930 acres, of which 69 are waste, and the soil is partly limestone and partly clay ; in the township are 1368 acres of arable land, 502 meadow, and 7 wood. The country is high, and slightly inclines to the south-east : a great part of the township is uninclosed, and cultivated in very long slips of ground belonging to various proprietors, which gives the surface a bleak appearance in that neighbourhood; but in other portions there is a considerable quantity of wood. The inhabitants manufacture stockings of excellent quality; red-ochre is made, and lime burnt. The LIVING is a discharged vicarage, valued in the king's books at £7. 7. 6., and in the patronage of the Crown : all the tithes of Bramley belong to the vicar, and the impropriator of the rest of the parish is the Earl of Scarborough ; the incumbent's tithes have been commuted for £351, and those of the earl for £368. The church is an ancient edifice, with a square tower ; an arch, of very early style, separates the chancel from the nave. At Bramley is a chapel of ease ; also a place of worship for Wesleyans. Of the several powerful springs in the parish, the chief are the Town well and Holy well.

BRAKES, a township, in the parish of LEINTWARDINE, union of LUDLOW, hundred of WIGMORE, county of HEREFORD ; containing 156 inhabitants.

BRAMBER (ST. NICHOLAS), a parish, in the union and hundred of STEYNING, rape of BRAMBER, W. division of SUSSEX, 1 mile (E. S. E.) from Steyning, and 50 miles (S. by W.) from London; containing 138 inhabitants. This place was noted for a castle built by the descendants of William de Braiose, upon whom the lands had been bestowed by the Conqueror. In the reign of Edward III., the castle was garrisoned by John de Mowbray, Duke of Norfolk, for the protection of the town and shore from the expected attack of the French, who were hovering off the coast. It was also garrisoned by the parliamentarian forces during the civil war. The village is situated on the river Adur, which is navigable for small vessels ; and, though once of considerable extent and importance, consists at present only of a few cottages. It was a borough by prescription, and returned members to parliament in the 23rd of Edward I. : after that time it frequently omitted, and was occasionally represented in conjunction with Steyning, till the 7th of Edward IV., from which period it regularly continued to return two representatives, until its disfranchisement in the 2nd of William IV. The parish comprises by computation 850 acres, of which 280 are arable, 425 down, and 145 other pasture. The LIVING is a discharged rectory endowed with only one-third of the tithes, with the vicarage of Buttolphs united, and valued in the king's books at £10. 6. 8.; it is in the patronage of the President and Fellows of Magdalene College, Oxford, who are impropriators of the remaining two-thirds of the tithes of Bramber, and of all the rectorial tithes of Buttolphs. The tithes of Bramber have been commuted ; the impropriate for £113. 6.; and the incumbent's for £56. 13. The church, formerly cruciform, is a small ancient edifice, now consisting only of a nave and chancel, but containing some fine portions in the Norman style, with a low square tower. The ancient and once formidable castle, occupied a quadrilateral area, 560 feet in length, and 280 in breadth, surrounded by a wide and deep moat; the remains consist principally of part of a square Norman tower, of great solidity, some detached portions of the walls to the north-west, and the mount whereon stood the keep. On altering a road near the river, an old bridge of excellent workmanship was discovered, upon which had stood a chapel; at Beddington was an hospital dedicated to St. Mary Magdalene, the founder of which is unknown.

BRAMCOTE, a parish, in the union of SHARDLOW, S. division of the wapentake of BROXTOW, N. division of the county of NOTTINGHAM, 5 miles (W. by S.) from Nottingham; containing 732 inhabitants. The parish comprises about 1000 acres of rich sandy land; it occupies several lofty hills, and the scenery, interspersed with some large and handsome mansions, is highly picturesque. From the village, which is situated on a considerable eminence, and is one of the prettiest in the county, is a fine view of the town of Nottingham, and of the country for many miles round. Coal is obtained, and excellent bricks are made to a great extent; a number of persons are also employed in the lace and stocking manufacture. The Nottingham canal passes through the parish. The living is a perpetual curacy, annexed to the vicarage of Attenborough: on the inclosure of land in 1771, 4½ acres were allotted to the vicar; and a parsonage was built here in 1843, at a cost of £1500. The church stands on an abrupt eminence. A square rock here is a natural curiosity.

BRAMCOTT, a hamlet, in the parish of BULKINGTON, union of NUNEATON, Kirby division of the hundred of KNIGHTLOW, N. division of the county of WARWICK, 4 miles (S. E.) from Nuneaton; containing 73 inhabitants.

BRAMDEAN (ST. SIMON AND ST. JUDE), a parish, in the union of ALRESFORD, hundred of BISHOP'S SUTTON, Droxford and N. divisions of the county of SOUTHAMPTON, 4 miles (S. by E.) from Alresford; containing 225 inhabitants. The parish comprises 1204 acres, whereof 159 are common or waste. It is pleasantly situated, and in the village, which is irregularly built and of rural appearance, are several handsome detached residences: the surrounding scenery is picturesque; and the view of the vale of Bramdean, from the church, which is on the brow of a hill, is very beautiful. The living is a rectory, valued in the king's books at £8. 14. 9½., and in the patronage of the Bishop of Winchester: the tithes have been commuted for £224, and there are 10½ acres of glebe. The church has recently been repaired and decorated in an appropriate style, and, from its beautiful situation, partly embowered among trees, forms an interesting feature. Near the manor-house of Woodcote is a tessellated pavement in tolerable preservation.

BRAMERTON (ST. PETER), a parish, in the union and hundred of HENSTEAD, E. division of NORFOLK, 4¼ miles (S. E. by E.) from Norwich; containing 229 inhabitants. It comprises 728a. 3r. 34p., whereof 106 acres are common or waste; and is bounded on the north by the navigable river Yare, from which rises an extensive and beautiful common, in the hills of which are found a great variety of fossils. The living is a dis-

340

session of the county was secured to Henry IV. The extensive village of Bramham is pleasantly situated in the vale of a small rivulet, on the great north road; the neighbourhood is undulated, and abounds with rich and beautiful scenery. There are good stone-quarries for building and other purposes. The living is a discharged vicarage, valued in the king's books at £6. 7. 6.; net income, £159; patrons and appropriators, the Dean and Canons of Christ-Church, Oxford. The church is an ancient and elegant structure, in the decorated English style. There are chapels, forming separate incumbencies, at Boston and Clifford; and places of worship in the parish for Wesleyans and Ranters. Visible remains of the Watling-street exist on Bramham Moor, a mile north of the village: from the middle of this moor is an extensive prospect of a well-cultivated district, which abounds with freestone, limestone, and coal.

BRAMHOPE, a chapelry, in the parish of OTLEY, Upper division of the wapentake of SKYRACK, W. riding of YORK, 3 miles (E. S. E.) from Otley; containing 350 inhabitants. This chapelry, which is situated on high ground overlooking the valley of Wharfdale, comprises 1290 acres of fertile land. The village is irregularly built, and the surrounding scenery is varied. The living is a perpetual curacy, in the patronage of six Trustees, appointed by the founder, and has a net income of £50: land was assigned in lieu of tithes, in 1805.

BRAMLEY (ALL SAINTS), a parish, in the union and hundred of BASINGSTOKE, Basingstoke and N. divisions of the county of SOUTHAMPTON, 4¼ miles (N. by E.) from Basingstoke; containing 428 inhabitants. The living is a discharged vicarage, valued in the king's books at £7. 3. 6½.; patrons and impropriators, the Provost and Fellows of Queen's College, Oxford. The great tithes have been commuted for £510, and the vicarial for £150; there are about 21¼ acres of glebe belonging to the impropriators, and nearly five to the vicar.

BRAMLEY, a parish, in the union of HAMBLEDON, First division of the hundred of BLACKHEATH, W. division of SURREY, 3 miles (S. by E.) from Guildford; containing 970 inhabitants. This parish, which is described in the Norman survey under the name of Bronlegh, comprises about 4420 acres, and, in the southern part, abounds with natural beauties, particularly where it adjoins Hascomb and Dunsfold: the Arun and Wey Junction canal crosses it. In its ecclesiastical concerns it is annexed to the parish of Shalford: the great tithes have been commuted for £126, and the vicarial for £160. The church, dedicated to the Holy Trinity, is built in the form of a cross, with a small chapel on the south side, and is of the character of the 15th century; it contains several neat monuments.

BRAMLEY, a chapelry, in the parish of ST. PETER, liberty of the borough of LEEDS, W. riding of YORK, 4 miles (W. N. W.) from Leeds; containing 8875 inhabitants. It is on the Leeds and Halifax road, and comprises by computation 2387 acres. The substratum abounds with slate of good quality, and with freestone of great firmness of texture, in high repute for building, and of which large quantities are sent to most of the principal towns in the kingdom, by the Leeds and Liverpool canal, which passes through the township, and connects the two great ports of Liverpool and Hull. The village is pleasantly situated near the new Stanningley road, on a boldly undulated and richly wooded eminence, over-

341

looking Airedale; it is nearly a mile in length, built chiefly of stone, and, viewed in connexion with the scenery of the vale beneath, has a very imposing aspect. The inhabitants are chiefly employed in the manufacture of woollen-cloth, for which there are not less than twenty large mills in full operation in the village and adjacent hamlets, Stanningley, Rodley, Newlay, and White Cote; many are also engaged in the freestone quarries of Bramley Fall, on the south side of the river Aire. The chapel, supposed to have been originally founded by the monks of Kirkstall Abbey, has undergone so many alterations, that little of its ancient character remains; it was enlarged in 1833, when a spire was added to it, at an expense of £700, raised by subscription. The living is a perpetual curacy, in the patronage of the Vicar of Leeds, with a net income of £289. A church, dedicated to St. Thomas, has been erected at Stanningley, which see. The great tithes of the chapelry have been commuted for £100, and the small for £15. There are places of worship for Baptists, Primitive Methodists, and Wesleyans.

BRAMLEY, a chapelry, in the parish of BRAITHWELL, union of ROTHERHAM, S. division of the wapentake of STRAFFORTH and TICKHILL, W. riding of YORK, 4¼ miles (E.) from Rotherham; containing 353 inhabitants. This place belonged to the abbey of Roche, the abbot of which had a grange here, that became, after the Dissolution, a seat of the Spencers. The family of Eyre lived in a house called the Hall, in the village, for several generations. The township comprises about 977 acres of land. The chapel is a small ancient fabric. There is a place of worship for Wesleyans.

BRAMPFORD-SPEKE (ST. PETER), a parish, in the union of ST. THOMAS, hundred of WONFORD, Wonford and S. divisions of DEVON, 4¼ miles (N. by E.) from Exeter; containing 393 inhabitants. The parish is pleasantly situated on the river Exe, by which it is bounded on the east; the scenery is richly varied, and derives great beauty and interest from the proximity of the river. The number of acres is about 1500; the soil is rich and fertile. A fair, chiefly for pleasure, is held at Michaelmas. The living is a vicarage, valued in the king's books at £10, and in the patronage of the Crown; net income, £216; impropriators, the family of May: the glebe comprises 39 acres of moderately good land. The church is an ancient cruciform structure, with a handsome embattled tower.

BRAMPTON (ST. MARTIN), a market-town and parish, and the head of a union, in ESKDALE ward, E. division of CUMBERLAND; containing, with the townships of Easby and Naworth, 3304 inhabitants, of whom 2754 are in the town, 9½ miles (N. E. by E.) from Carlisle, and 305 (N. by W.) from London. According to Camden, this was the site of the Roman station Bremetenracum, which some modern writers, with more probability, have fixed at Old Penrith. The town sustained extensive damage during the wars of Edward II.; of which, as well as of its earlier importance, it still exhibits evident marks. In Nov. 1715, a large force under the command of Mr. Forster, who had received a general's commission from James Stuart, entered the town, where they proclaimed the Pretender; and hence marched to Penrith. During the rebellion of 1745, the young Pretender led his troops hither, to observe the motions of Gen. Wade, who was mistakenly reported to be marching from Newcastle to the relief of Carlisle; and after remaining here several days, he proceeded to Carlisle, which had surrendered to his arms.

The TOWN is situated between the small rivers Irthing and Gelt, tributaries to the Eden, about one mile south of the former, and two and a half from the point where they unite; and lies about two miles south of the Picts' wall. It occupies a deep narrow vale embosomed in hills, and consists principally of two streets irregularly built, and a spacious market-place; the houses have been mostly rebuilt, and are of handsome appearance: the inhabitants are well supplied with water. The manufacture of gingham employs nearly 700 persons: there are two breweries. The railway between Newcastle and Carlisle passes a mile and a half to the south, and is connected with the town by a good road, and also by means of the Earl of Carlisle's railway, which reaches to the extensive coal and lime works at Tindal Fell, and by which coal and lime are brought hither in abundance. The market is on Wednesday, and is well supplied with corn, admitted toll-free; fairs are held on April 20th, the second Wednesday after Whitsuntide, the second Wednesday in Sept., and the 23rd of Oct., for horned-cattle, horses, and pigs. The county magistrates hold a petty-session every alternate Wednesday; and courts leet and baron for the barony of Gilsland are held at Easter and Michaelmas, in the town-hall, a neat octagonal edifice with a cupola, erected by the Earl of Carlisle in 1817, on the site of the former hall, in the market-place, the lower part being formed into a piazza, under which butter, eggs, poultry, &c., are sold on the market-day.

The LIVING is a vicarage, valued in the king's books at £8; net income, £466; patron and impropriator, the Earl of Carlisle: in 1777, land was assigned in lieu of tithes. The present church was built in 1788, out of the chapel and tenements of an almshouse, and with the materials of the old church, the chancel of which is still remaining on the southern bank of the river Irthing, about a mile west of the town, being used for the performance of the funeral service for those who are interred in the cemetery. The church was greatly enlarged in 1827 at an expense of £1800: on which occasion the Rev. Mr. Ramshay presented five bells and an organ. There are places of worship for Independents, Primitive and Wesleyan Methodists, and Presbyterians. The poor law union comprises 14 parishes or places, and contains a population, according to the last census, of 10,525.

Two miles east of Brampton, and about a mile south of the Irthing, commanding a fine view of the vale of St. Mary, through which that river flows, is *Naworth Castle*, the ancient baronial seat of the lords of Gilsland, the earliest notice of which occurs in the 18th of Richard II. The walls, including two large square towers in the front, besides others at the angles, inclose a quadrangular area, each side of which measures 40 paces: the hall, 70 or 80 feet in length, and of proportionate width and height, displays all the magnificence of feudal grandeur; and the chapel, to which there is a descent of several steps, is decorated with a profusion of armour. The dungeons of the castle, which were the prison for the barony, are in their original state; they consist of three cells underground, and one above, and the strong iron rings to which the prisoners were chained are yet remaining. A great portion of this splendid

BRAM

BRAM

were, until lately, vestiges of a burying-place called Cor-Lowe, considered to be of greater antiquity than the period of the Roman occupation of Britain. In various parts of the high grounds of the parish are found oysters, muscles, and other shell-fish, in a fossil state; and the cactus and other tropical plants are also met with imbedded in the stone. The living was for some time held by Dr. Edmund Cartwright, inventor of the power-loom and carding-machine.

BRAMPTON (St. Mary), a parish, in the hundred of Leightonstone, union and county of Huntingdon, 1¾ mile (W. by S.) from Huntingdon; containing 1164 inhabitants. This parish, which is seated on the navigable river Ouse, and on the road from London to Cambridge, comprises 3110 acres; about three-fourth parts are arable, and the soil is generally sandy but fertile. The living is a discharged vicarage, valued in the king's books at £8. 1. 4.; net income, £160; patron, the Prebendary of Brampton in the Cathedral of Lincoln. The great tithes have been commuted for £93. 10. The church is partly in the decorated and partly in the later English style, with a fine south porch enriched with elegant tracery; it was rebuilt in 1635, and repewed in 1835. Samuel Pepys, secretary to the admiralty in the reigns of Charles II. and James II., and elected president of the Royal Society in 1684, was born here.

BRAMPTON, a chapelry, in the parish of Torksey, union of Gainsborough, wapentake of Well, parts of Lindsey, county of Lincoln, 7½ miles (S. S. E.) from Gainsborough; containing 130 inhabitants.

BRAMPTON (St. Peter), a parish, in the union of Aylsham, hundred of South Erpingham, E. division of Norfolk, 2¾ miles (S. E.) from Aylsham; containing 263 inhabitants. It comprises by computation 441 acres, and is bounded on the east by the navigable river Bure: the soil is various, the arable land being principally loam; and the surface is somewhat uneven. The living is a discharged rectory, valued in the king's books at £5, and in the patronage of R. Marsham, Esq.: the tithes have been commuted for £148. 19. 4., and there are about 14 acres of glebe. The church is chiefly in the early English style, and consists of a nave, chancel, and south aisle, with a tower circular at the base and octangular above. From several urns containing calcined bones, this is conjectured to have been the place of interment connected with the Roman station at Burgh, on the opposite side of the river.

BRAMPTON (St. Mary), a parish, in the union of Market-Harborough, hundred of Corby, N. division of the county of Northampton, 4 miles (E. by. N.) from Harborough, on the road to Rockingham; containing 104 inhabitants. The parish comprises by measurement 2387 acres; there are good quarries of stone for building. The living is a rectory, valued in the king's books at £21. 6. 8.; net income, £346; patron, Earl Spencer: there are 132 acres of glebe, with a residence. The church is a fine specimen of the early English style, with a lofty spire, and contains some sepulchral brasses rather mutilated, and an ancient mural monument with two figures kneeling in the costume of the time, belonging to the Norwich family, formerly lords of the manor. A house in the parish, once an inn known as the "Hermitage," appears to have been a religious house, surrounded by a moat. Richard Cumberland, afterwards Bishop of Peterborough, was some time rector.

343

BRAMPTON (St. Peter), a parish, in the union and hundred of Blything, E. division of Suffolk, 3 miles (N. W.) from Wangford; containing 322 inhabitants. It comprises 2002a. 1r. 5p., and is situated on the road from Halesworth to Beccles. The living is a discharged rectory, valued in the king's books at £20, and in the patronage of the Rev. G. O. Leman: the tithes have been commuted for £433. 5. 6., and there is a commodious rectory-house, with a glebe of about 12 acres. The church consists of a nave and chancel with an embattled tower. A Sunday school is endowed with £9. 6. per annum; and the rents of an estate are applied to the repairs of the church, the relief of the poor, and other purposes.

BRAMPTON, a township, in the parish of Long Martin, East ward and union, county of Westmorland, 2½ miles (N.) from Appleby; containing 304 inhabitants. The tithes have been commuted for £165, and there is a glebe of nearly 40 acres.

BRAMPTON-ABBOTS (St. Michael), a parish, in the union of Ross, hundred of Greytree, county of Hereford, 1 mile (N.) from Ross; containing 197 inhabitants. This parish, which comprises by computation 1500 acres, is situated on the left bank of the river Wye, and in the heart of a rich and fertile district, abounding with picturesque and romantic scenery; it is intersected in the eastern part by the road from Ledbury to Ross. The living is a rectory, valued in the king's books at £12, and in the patronage of the Bishop of Hereford: the tithes have been commuted for £321. 2. 6., and the glebe comprises 8 acres.

BRAMPTON-BIERLOW, a township, in the parish of Wath-upon-Dearne, union of Rotherham, N. division of the wapentake of Strafforth and Tickhill, W. riding of York, 6 miles (S. E.) from Barnsley; containing 1704 inhabitants. This township, which is situated on the Dearne and Dove canal, in a district abounding with coal, comprises 3168a. 2r. 14p., of which 1633 acres are arable, 1203 grass land, 245 wood, 76 acres homesteads, orchards, &c., and 9 canal. Extensive iron-works have been established, and several mines of coal are in full operation; affording employment to the principal part of the population of the township.

BRAMPTON-BRYAN (St. Barnabas), a parish, in the union of Knighton, partly in the hundred of Knighton, county of Radnor, South Wales, but chiefly in the hundred of Wigmore, county of Hereford, 10 miles (W. by S.) from Ludlow; containing, in the English portion, with the township of Boresford with Pedwardine, 250 inhabitants. The parish comprises about 3000 acres, of which 1200 are arable, 1470 pasture, and 330 woodland; and is bounded on the north by the river Teme, and intersected by the road from Ludlow to Knighton. The village was nearly destroyed in the parliamentary war; the castle, also, was burnt by the royalists in 1643, and is now a ruin, consisting chiefly of an arched gateway flanked by two circular towers, and fragments of the outer walls. Sir Robert de Harley obtained this castle and estate in the reign of Edward II., by marriage with the coheiress of Sir Bryan de Brampton; and it has since continued in that noble family. A great fair for horned-cattle, horses, and sheep, is held on June 22nd. The living is a rectory, valued in the king's books at £5. 11. 0½., and in the

gift of the Earl of Oxford : the tithes have been commuted for £345, and there are 16 acres of glebe. The
church, which was destroyed in 1643, was rebuilt in
1650, and is a plain edifice, containing 350 sittings, of
which 150 are free : the Earl of Oxford, lord treasurer,
was buried here. About a mile from the church is Cox-
wall Knoll, on the summit of which are vestiges of a
camp anciently occupied by the brave Caractacus, and
now overgrown with oak-trees : a brass celt, either
British or Roman, was found at Litton in 1843. A
school is endowed with property given by the second
Earl of Oxford in 1720, amounting to £18 per annum.

BRAMPTON, CHAPEL, a parish, in the union of
BRIXWORTH, hundred of NEWBOTTLE-GROVE, S. division of the county of NORTHAMPTON, 4 miles (N. N. W.)
from Northampton; containing 229 inhabitants. It is
situated on the river Nene, and the Northampton and
Welford road ; and comprises 1250 acres of rich land, in
equal portions of arable and pasture, with about 16
acres of wood : the soil is a red-sand loam, and red
sandstone is obtained. Earl Spencer is the sole owner.
The female population is employed in making pillow-
lace. In ecclesiastical matters, Chapel-Brampton is annexed to Church-Brampton ; and its church has been
long demolished. There is a small dissenting place of
worship for all 'denominations ; a boys' school is supported by John Beasley, Esq., and a girls' school by his
lady. One of the fine springs here is particularly good
for weak eyes.

BRAMPTON, CHURCH (ST. BOTOLPH), a parish,
in the union of BRIXWORTH, hundred of NEWBOTTLE-
GROVE, S. division of the county of NORTHAMPTON,
4 miles (N. W. by N.) from Northampton ; containing
169 inhabitants. This parish, which is situated on the
road from Northampton to Welford, and bounded by
the river Nene on the east, comprises by computation
1125 acres of rich land in equal portions of arable and
pasture, interspersed with fox-covers and plantations,
and mostly the property of Earl Spencer. Good stone
is obtained for building. The living is a rectory, valued
in the king's books at £25. 19. 7., and in the patronage
of Corpus Christi College, Oxford ; net income, £400,
arising from 332 acres of land allotted long since in lieu
of tithes : there is a glebe-house. The church is partly
in the decorated, and partly in the later, style of English
architecture, and contains a large circular font ; the
stairs of the rood-loft and some ancient benches remain :
the chancel was repaired in 1844. There are parochial
and Sunday schools, supported by Mr. and Mrs.
Beasley.

BRAMPTON-EN-LE-MORTHEN, a township, in
the parish of TREETON, union of ROTHERHAM, S. division of the wapentake of STRAFFORTH and TICKHILL,
W. riding of YORK, 5¼ miles (S. E. by E.) from Rotherham ; containing 139 inhabitants. Two centuries since,
this place was the residence of several families of property and consequence; and in the church of Treeton
is a choir called Brampton choir, which is paved with
monumental stones placed over the remains of the
families of Vesey, Bradshaw, and Lord, who had mansions in the village, which have long been deserted by
their owners. The freeholders of Brampton acknowledge no mesne manor over them. The township comprises 1090 acres : the road from Rotherham to Tickhill
passes about two miles north of the village.
344

BRAMPTON, LITTLE, with ROD.—See ROD.

BRAMSHALL (ST. LAWRENCE), a parish, in the
union of UTTOXETER, S. division of the hundred of
TOTMONSLOW, N. division of the county of STAFFORD,
2 miles (W. by S.) from Uttoxeter ; containing 170 inhabitants. This place, formerly called Broomshelf from
the surface once abounding in broom, was a lordship of
the Staffords, and passed subsequently to the family of
Erdeswicke. It is situated on the road from Uttoxeter
to Stafford, and comprises 1276a. 1r. 38p. of fertile
land, of which the greater portion is pasture ; the soil is
gravelly, the surface undulated, and the scenery beautifully picturesque. Here are several dairy-farms. The
living is a discharged rectory, valued in the king's books
at £4. 3. 9., and in the patronage of Lord Willoughby
de Broke : the tithes have been commuted for £145, and
there are nearly 43 acres of glebe, and a glebe-house.
The church, a plain edifice, was erected at the expense of
Lord Willoughby de Broke.

BRAMSHAW (ST. PETER), a parish, in the union
of NEW FOREST, partly in the hundred of CAWDEN and
CADWORTH, Salisbury and Amesbury, and S. divisions
of WILTS, but chiefly in the N. division of the hundred
of NEW FOREST, Romsey and S. divisions of the county
of SOUTHAMPTON, 3 miles (N.) from Stony Cross ; containing, with the hamlets of Furzley and Brook, and the
extra-parochial places of Eyeworth-Lodge and Amber-
wood-Cottage, 793 inhabitants, of whom 474 are in the
county of Southampton. The parish comprises by measurement 3560 acres, and is intersected by the road from
Southampton to Salisbury. In that portion of the New
Forest which lies on its borders to the south-east,
William Rufus was killed by an arrow, shot by Walter
Tyrrell at a stag, but which, glancing by the animal,
struck the royal breast, and occasioned the monarch's
death : a stone, erected on the spot where the oak-tree
stood whence the arrow was shot, commemorates the
event. The living is a vicarage, described in the king's
books as not in charge ; patrons and appropriators, the
Dean and Chapter of Salisbury. The rectorial tithes
have been commuted for £149, and the vicarial for £60 ;
there are about 20 acres of glebe, a portion of which is
in Lyndhurst. The vicarage-house was erected in 1841,
in lieu of a former one supposed to be more than 300
years old. Of the ancient church, which stands upon
an eminence, and overlooks a considerable portion of the
New Forest, the nave alone is standing ; the east end,
and north and south aisles, being entirely new : in the
building of these latter portions, in 1829, some very
grotesque heads were found inclosed in the old walls.
There are places of worship for Calvinists and Wesleyans.

BRAMSHILL, GREAT, a tything, in the parish of
EVERSLEY, union of HARTLEY-WINTNEY, hundred of
HOLDSHOTT, Odiham and N. divisions of HAMPSHIRE,
1¾ mile (N. W. by N.) from Hartford-Bridge ; containing 175 inhabitants.

BRAMSHILL, LITTLE, a tything, in the parish of
EVERSLEY, union of HARTLEY-WINTNEY, hundred of
HOLDSHOTT, Odiham and N. divisions of HAMPSHIRE ;
containing 10 inhabitants.

BRAMSHOTT (ST. MARY), a parish, in the hundred
of ALTON, Petersfield and N. divisions of HAMPSHIRE,
4½ miles (W. by N.) from Haslemere ; containing, with
the hamlet of Liphook, 1313 inhabitants. This parish,

acres, with a handsome parsonage-house. The church, which is in the early and decorated English styles, consists of a nave, chancel, and aisles, with a square embattled tower; it was thoroughly repaired in 1832. A free school and almshouses were built by Robert Smith, about the close of the sixteenth century, and endowed with 72 acres of land by his sister; the endowment produces about £70 per annum.

BRANCEPETH (St. Brandon), a parish, in the unions of Durham, Auckland, and Lanchester, N. W. division of Darlington ward, S. division of the county of Durham, comprising the townships of Brandon with Byshottles, Crook with Billy-Row, Hedley-Hope, Hemlington-Row, Stockley, and Wellington; and containing 2151 inhabitants, of whom 352 are in the township of Brancepeth, 4¼ miles (S. W.) from Durham. The name is supposed to be a corruption of *Brawn's path*, in allusion to the number of wild boars that formerly infested the district, and for the purpose of hunting which the Duke of Gloucester, afterwards Richard III., frequently resorted to this place, where his maternal ancestors, the Nevills, had a fortress. This fortress was almost entirely taken down by the late Matthew Russel, Esq., who erected on its site the present Brancepeth Castle. Coal is found, and there are some quarries of stone. The living is a rectory, valued in the king's books at £60. 10. 5., and in the patronage of R. E. D. Shafto, Esq.: the tithes have been commuted for £985. 12. The church is a fine cruciform edifice, highly decorated within; the chancel is stalled and wainscoted with oak carved in tabernacle work, and has an ornamented ceiling. At Crook is a living in the Rector's gift. There are some medicinal springs of a vitriolic and sulphureous kind.

BRANDESTON (All Saints), a parish, in the union of Plomesgate, hundred of Loes, E. division of Suffolk, 4 miles (S. W.) from Framlingham; containing 555 inhabitants. The Hall was for many generations the seat of the Revet family. The living is a discharged vicarage, valued in the king's books at £8. 13. 4., and in the patronage of the Rev. John Smythe; net income, £100: there is a glebe of about 16 acres, with a good residence. The church consists of a nave and chancel, with an embattled tower.

BRANDISTONE *cum* Guton (St. Nicholas), a parish, in the union of St. Faith's, hundred of Eynsford, E. division of Norfolk, 3 miles (E. S. E.) from Reepham; containing 137 inhabitants. The parish is chiefly the property of Magdalen College, Oxford; and comprises 757a. 2r. 24p., of which 634 acres are arable, 103 meadow and pasture, and 20 common. The living is a discharged rectory, valued in the king's books at £7. 12. 8¼., and in the gift of the College: the tithes have been commuted for £240, and the glebe comprises 11½ acres. The church consists of a nave, chancel, and north aisle; with a circular tower, the upper part octagonal, at the west end of the aisle: the font is Norman. There was formerly another church, dedicated to St. Swithin.

BRANDON, with Byshottles, a township, in the parish of Brancepeth, union of Durham, N. W. division of Darlington ward, S. division of the county of Durham, 3 miles (W. S. W.) from Durham; containing 467 inhabitants. It comprises by computation 3460 acres. The village is occasionally called East Brandon,

2 Y

to distinguish it from a farm-hold within the township, bearing the name of West Brandon. Here is a paper manufactory. Burn Hall, a handsome mansion here, was built about twenty years since, near the site of an ancient residence. The tithes have been commuted for £311. 15. 10. On the summit of Brandon Hill is an oblong mount, or tumulus, supposed to have been either the site of a beacon, or the burial-place of some departed hero.

BRANDON, a township, in the parish of Egling-ham, union of Glendale, N. division of Coquetdale ward and of Northumberland, 4 miles (N. N. W.) from Whittingham ; containing 147 inhabitants. It comprises 1020 acres, mostly arable land, with about 20 of wood ; the surface is undulated, and the soil light and gravelly, and good for barley and turnips. Brandon White House, to the east of the village, was the seat of the Collingwood family, who possessed the estate for a long period of years. A chancel wall and numerous tombs indicate the site of an ancient church.

BRANDON (St. Peter), a market-town and parish, in the union of Thetford, partly in the hundred of Grimshoe, W. division of Norfolk, but chiefly in the hundred of Lackford, W. division of Suffolk, 40 miles (N. W.) from Ipswich, and 78 (N. N. E.) from London ; containing 2002 inhabitants. The parish comprises 6759a. 10p., of which the soil is generally a sandy loam, and the substratum chalk ; the meadow-land is flat, and subject to floods. The town consists of two portions, designated Town-street and Ferry-street, a mile distant from each other ; the latter, which is the chief portion, stands upon the road from London to Lynn, and on the southern bank of the Little Ouse, or Brandon river. The stream forms the northern boundary of Suffolk, and is here crossed by a neat stone bridge ; it is navigable to Thetford and to Lynn. A line of railway between Brandon and Norwich was opened in July, 1845 ; and there is railway communication with Ely, and towns beyond, in a western direction. Imbedded in a stratum of chalk a mile westward from the town, lie continuous strata of the finest flint, of which gun-flints are made in abundance, and conveyed to various parts of the world, employing about 200 hands in the manufacture. In addition, the town has a considerable traffic in corn, seeds, malt, coal, timber, iron, bricks, tiles, &c. ; and there are some extensive rabbit-warrens in the neighbourhood, from which 150,000 rabbits are sent annually to the London markets. About 160 females are employed in preparing and cutting rabbit and hare skins for making hats, and felts for the clothiers in Yorkshire. A brewery has also been established. The market is on Thursday, for corn and seeds; there are fairs on Feb. 14th, June 11th, and Nov. 11th; and a fair at Broomhall, about half a mile distant, on July 7th, for stock.

The Living is a rectory, with that of Wangford annexed, valued in the king's books at £20. 18. 1½., and in the patronage of Thomas Everard Cartwright, Esq. : the tithes have been commuted for a gross rent-charge of £560, and there are 102 acres of glebe. The church, which is situated midway between the two streets, is in the later style, and consists of a nave, chancel, and south aisles, with a lofty embattled tower at the west end. There are places of worship for Primitive and Wesleyan Methodists. A free school was founded in
346

1646, by Robert Wright, who endowed it with a rent-charge of £40 ; it was further endowed with 8 acres of land under the Bedford Level act, and with 3 under the Brandon Inclosure act, producing £11. 18. per annum. Joanna, widow of John Wright, in 1664 bequeathed £13 per annum for keeping the school-house in repair, and for the relief of the poor : an almshouse was founded in Ferry-street for seven widows, by Humphrey Hall, in 1698 ; and some almshouses founded by a person named Curteis, for three parishioners, were rebuilt near the church in 1840. Various other bequests have been made for the benefit of the poor, amounting in the aggregate to about £100 per annum. Brandon Camp, a square earthwork guarded by a single trench and a rampart, is supposed to have been the Bravinium of the Romans, and to have been occupied by Ostorius Scapula previously to his decisive victory over the brave Caractacus. The Duke of Hamilton and Brandon takes his English title from the place.

BRANDON, a hamlet, in the parish of Wolstan, union of Rugby, Kirby division of the hundred of Knightlow, N. division of the county of Warwick, 6 miles (E. S. E.) from Coventry ; containing 252 inhabitants, and consisting of 1946 acres. Here was a castle, built soon after the Conquest, either by Geffrey de Clinton, or his son-in-law, Norman de Verdune, and which was garrisoned in the 7th of Richard I., and destroyed by the barons in the reign of Henry III. It is supposed to have been rebuilt by Theobald, a descendant of Norman, who appears to have enjoyed the privilege of free warren in all his demesne lands here, together with a court leet, gallows, and assize of bread and beer : there are no remains. A station of the London and Birmingham railway is situated in the hamlet, and the rateable annual value of railway property here is returned at £1400.

BRANDON PARVA (All Saints), a parish, in the incorporation and hundred of Forehoe, E. division of Norfolk, 5 miles (N. N. W.) from Wymondham ; containing 222 inhabitants. It comprises about 1000 acres. The living is a discharged rectory, valued in the king's books at £8. 3. 9., and in the patronage of F. R. Reynolds, Esq. : the tithes have been commuted for £315, and the glebe comprises 17 acres, with a small house. The church is in the later English style, with a square embattled tower.

BRANDSBURTON (St. Mary), a parish, in the union of Skirlaugh, N. division of the wapentake of Holderness, E. riding of York ; containing 718 inhabitants, of whom 34 are in the township of Moortown, and 684 in that of Brandsburton, 8½ miles (N. E.) from Beverley. The church of St. John de Beverley had property here so early as the time of Athelstan, and a grant of lands was made to that establishment ; and among the families who held possessions in the place at an early date, occurs that of St. Quintin. The township of Brandsburton comprises 4484 acres, whereof 506 are common or waste. The village, which is large, well built, and in a very flourishing condition, is situated on the lower road from Hull to Bridlington and Scarborough. Here is a large show for horses on the 11th of April ; and a fair is held on May 14th. The market-cross stands in the centre of the village. The living is a rectory, valued in the king's books at £24. 13. 4.; net income, £895 ; patrons, the Master and Fellows of

St. John's College, Cambridge. The church, which is principally in the later style of English architecture, is situated on a slight eminence, and when seen from the south-west is highly picturesque, the old trees about it adding greatly to the effect; it is of considerable size, and consists of a nave, aisles, and chancel, with a low embattled tower. There is a place of worship for Wesleyans, and another used alternately by the Independents and Primitive Methodists.

BRANDSBY (*All Saints*), a parish, in the union of Easingwould, wapentake of Bulmer, N. riding of York, 14 miles (N. by W.) from York; containing with Stearsby, 304 inhabitants. The parish is situated on the road from York to Helmsley, and comprises 3048a. 20p., of which 1425 acres are arable, 1169 pasture, 219 woodland, and 165 moor: the soil varies in different situations, being rich in the vale, and light on the hills; the surface is undulated, and the scenery picturesque. Good limestone is quarried for building and other purposes. The living is a rectory, valued in the king's books at £9. 8. 11½., and in the patronage of F. Cholmeley, Esq.: the tithes have been commuted for £588, and there are 68 acres of glebe. The church, which is surmounted by a handsome cupola, was erected in the year 1770. There is a Roman Catholic chapel at Brandsby Hall.

BRANDY-STREET, a hamlet, in the parish of Selworthy, union of Williton, hundred of Carhampton, West division of the county of Somerset; containing 29 inhabitants.

BRANSBY, a township, in the parish of Stow, union of Gainsborough, wapentake of Well, parts of Lindsey, county of Lincoln, 8 miles (N. W.) from Lincoln; containing 107 inhabitants.

BRANSCOMBE (*St. Winifred*), a parish, in the union of Honiton, hundred of Colyton, Honiton and S. divisions of Devon, 4¾ miles (E.) from Sidmouth; containing 956 inhabitants. The parish is bounded on the south and east by the British Channel, and comprises 2987 acres, of which 462 are common or waste; in some parts its scenery is beautiful and romantic. The living is a vicarage, valued in the king's books at £18. 15. 10., and in the gift of the Dean and Chapter of Exeter, the appropriators: the great tithes have been commuted for £268; and those of the incumbent for £225, with a glebe of 3 acres. The founder of Wadham College, Oxford, was buried here.

BRANSDALE, EAST SIDE, a hamlet, in the parish of Kirkby-Moorside, union of Helmsley, wapentake of Ryedale, N. riding of York, 11 miles (N. W.) from Pickering; containing 134 inhabitants. This place, and Bransdale, West Side, form one township, and comprise about 3000 acres of land: they are separated by a stream running in a direction from north-north-west to south-south-east. There is a chapel of ease in the hamlet of Cockan, in the township.

BRANSDALE, WEST SIDE, a hamlet, in the parish of Kirkdale, union of Helmsley, wapentake of Ryedale, N. riding of York, 11 miles (N. by W.) from Helmsley; containing 80 inhabitants.

BRANSFORD, a chapelry, in the parish of Leigh, union of Martley, Lower division of the hundred of Pershore, Worcester and W. divisions of the county of Worcester, 3¾ miles (W. S. W.) from Worcester; containing 277 inhabitants. The parish comprises 1034

347

acres of rich land, whereof two-thirds are arable, and the remainder pasture. It is situated on the south of the river Teme, in the eastern part of the parish, and is crossed from north to south by the road from Worcester to Hereford. The chapel, dedicated to St. John the Baptist, is an ancient structure, containing about 100 sittings.

BRANSGORE, a chapelry, in the parish and hundred of Christchurch, Ringwood and S. divisions of the county of Southampton, 5 miles (N. E. by N.) from Christchurch. The living is a perpetual curacy; net income, £73; patron, the Vicar of Christchurch. The chapel was built in 1822, at an expense of £2800, defrayed by the Parliamentary Commissioners; and is a neat edifice in the later English style, with a tower and spire. National schoolrooms were built by subscription, in the year 1839.

BRANSTON, or Braunston (*St. Guthlake*), a parish, in the union of Melton-Mowbray, hundred of Framland, N. division of the county of Leicester, 9 miles (S. W. by W.) from Grantham, containing 333 inhabitants, and comprising about 2200 acres. The living is a rectory, valued in the king's books at £15. 10. 5.; net income, £350, derived from land; patron, the Duke of Rutland: there is a good rectory-house. The church has been recently embellished with a handsome east window, and refitted with open seats; the pulpit is of stone, after the model of that of St. Peter's, Oxford.

BRANSTON (*All Saints*), a parish, in the wapentake of Langoe, parts of Kesteven, union and county of Lincoln, 4½ miles (S. E.) from Lincoln; containing 1122 inhabitants. The living is a rectory, valued in the king's books at £18. 17. 11.; net income, £677; patron and incumbent, the Rev. P. Curtois: land was assigned in 1801, in lieu of tithes. There is a place of worship for Wesleyans.

BRANSTONE, a township, in the parish and union of Burton-upon-Trent, N. division of the hundred of Offlow, and county of Stafford, 2 miles (S. W. by W.) from Burton; containing 441 inhabitants. The village is seated on the north bank of the river Trent, and the road from Burton to Lichfield passes through it. Sinai Park, which occupies a fine eminence, was the summer retreat of the abbots of Burton. On the top of the hill are the lines of an encampment.

BRANTHAM (*St. Michael*), a parish, in the incorporation and hundred of Samford, S. division of Suffolk, 1 mile (N. by E.) from Manningtree; containing 404 inhabitants. It comprises 1922a. 2r. 20p., of which 1860 acres are in cultivation; the river Stour, which here divides into two branches, is navigable on the southern side of the parish. The living is a rectory, with that of East Bergholt consolidated, valued in the king's books at £25. 10., and in the patronage of Emmanuel College, Cambridge: the tithes of the two parishes have been commuted for £1320, and there are 42¾ acres of glebe. There was formerly a chapel in the hamlet of Catawade.

BRANTHWAITE, a township, in the parish of Dean, union of Cockermouth, Allerdale ward above Derwent, W. division of Cumberland, 6 miles (S. W.) from Cockermouth; containing 300 inhabitants. Several years since, a considerable quantity of a ferruginous kind of limestone, called catscalp, was obtained here, and sent to the iron-works at Clifton and Seaton; but this branch of trade has ceased. There are quarries of white freestone, a woollen manufactory, a paper-mill, and two corn-mills. The Methodists have a place of worship.

BRANTINGHAM (*All Saints*), a parish, in the union of Beverley, partly in the Hunsley-Beacon division of the wapentake of Harthill, and partly in the wapentake of Howdenshire, E. riding of York; comprising the townships of Thorpe-Brantingham and Ellerker, and containing 635 inhabitants, of whom 112 are in Thorpe-Brantingham, 2 miles (S. E. by E.) from South Cave. It comprises 3370 acres, chiefly arable and pasture land, besides some thriving plantations, which contribute much to the beauty of the scenery. The living is a discharged vicarage, valued in the king's books at £12. 9. 2.; net income, £176; patrons and appropriators, the Dean and Chapter of Durham. The great tithes have been commuted for £25, and the vicarial for £7; there is an appropriate glebe of 3 acres, and a vicarial glebe of 2. The church is in the perpendicular style, with some traces of Norman architecture in the porch. There is a chapel of ease at Ellerker.

BRANTON, a township, in the parish of Eglingham, union of Glendale, N. division of Coquetdale ward and of Northumberland, 9¼ miles (S. S. E.) from Wooler; containing 119 inhabitants. Some antiquaries have supposed that this is the Roman station *Bremenium*. The township comprises 1143 acres, whereof two-thirds are arable, and the remainder pasture, including 16 acres of plantation. There is a fine freestone quarry, out of which Lilburne tower was built. The village is situated on the south side of the Breamish, and at a short distance west of the road from Morpeth to Wooler. The vicarial tithes have been commuted for £60. 10. There is a place of worship for Presbyterians.

BRANTON, or Brampton, a hamlet, in the parish of Cantley, union of Doncaster, S. division of Strafforth and Tickhill wapentake, W. riding of York, 4 miles (S. E.) from Doncaster; containing 286 inhabitants. The river Torne passes at a short distance east of the village. A national school was opened in 1835, which is also used as a chapel of ease on Sunday evenings.

BRANTON-GREEN.—See Dunsforth, Upper.

BRANXTON, a parish, in the union of Glendale, W. division of Glendale ward, N. division of Northumberland, 4¾ miles (E. S. E.) from Coldstream, and 9¼ (N. W.) from Wooler; containing 261 inhabitants. This parish comprises by measurement 1535 acres, and is situated about half a mile to the south of the road from Wooler to Coldstream. The battle of Flodden, in 1513, was principally fought here: the Earl of Surrey drew up his men, after crossing the Till, on the flat ground immediately under Kingchair or Kingshire Hill, the foot of which bounds the parish. The battle was hotly contested from the south to the north of Branxton, especially about the church and village, and thence to the north of the Wooler road. In Westfield, about 150 yards from the turnpike-road, on Sir Henry Askew's property, is an unhewn pillar of basalt, about five feet high, and more than three feet in diameter, commemorative of the battle; it is called the King's stone, and is said to point out the place where King

348

BRAUGHIN (*St. Mary*), a parish, in the union of
Bishop-Stortford, hundred of Braughin, county of
Hertford, 10 miles (N. E.) from Hertford, and 28 (N.)
from London ; containing, with part of the hamlet of
Puckeridge, 1358 inhabitants. This place, in the Norman survey called *Brachinges*, and by the Saxons *Brook-
ing*, from the streams and meadows in its vicinity, was
anciently a market-town of considerable importance,
and a demesne of the Saxon kings : by some historians
it is supposed to have been a Roman station, and the
remains of a camp may still be distinguished. The town
or village is pleasantly situated on the small river Quin,
near its confluence with the Rib, and even now exhibits
traces of its former greatness. The market, which was
granted in the reign of Stephen, has been discontinued ;
but a fair is held on Whit-Monday and the following
day. The living is a vicarage, valued in the king's books
at £19. 13. 4.; net income, £192 ; patron, the Rev. W.
Tower : in 1812, land and corn-rents were assigned in
lieu of all tithes. The church is a handsome and spacious edifice, with a square embattled tower surmounted
by a spire. There is a place of worship for Independents. On a lofty eminence to the south of the village,
are the remains of an encampment, of which part of the
vallum and fortifications may be traced : the form is
quadrilateral, and the area contains nearly 40 acres ;
the south-western angle is rounded, and on the north is
a triple rampart.

BRAUNCEWELL (*All Saints*), a parish, in the
union of Sleaford, wapentake of Flaxwell, parts of
Kesteven, county of Lincoln, 4¾ miles (N. N. W.)
from Sleaford ; containing 125 inhabitants.. The parish
is situated on the road from London to Lincoln ; and,
including the hamlet of Dunsby, comprises 2430 acres
by measurement. Since the improvements of the last
century, and the introduction of extraneous manures,
the soil, formerly poor, has been much enriched ; and
the village, which had fallen into decay, has been rebuilt : freestone of the upper oolite formation is quarried. The living is a discharged rectory, with the vicarage of Anwick and the rectory of Dunsby united, valued
in the king's books at £9. 8. 11½.; net income, £580 ;
patron, the Marquess of Bristol. The church, a very
substantial structure, was rebuilt in 1814. Some traces
of the foundations of the church of Dunsby may still
be seen, on a spot called Old Dunsby.

BRAUNSTON, anciently Brandeston (*All Saints*),
a parish, in the union of Daventry, hundred of Fawsley, S. division of the county of Northampton, 2¾
miles (N. W.) from Daventry ; containing 1469 inhabitants. The parish comprises by computation 2962 acres,
and the small brook Leam separates it from Warwickshire : the road from Daventry to Coventry, forming
part of the Holyhead road, passes through it ; and the
Oxford and Grand Junction canals unite here. The
village, which once consisted of two detached portions, called Great and Little Braunston, commands,
from the brow of a steep declivity, an extensive opening
into Warwickshire. The living is a rectory, valued in the
king's books at £31. 2. 11.; net income, £837 ; patrons,
the Principal and Fellows of Jesus College, Oxford.
About 390 acres of land were assigned in lieu of tithes,
in 1766 ; and there is an excellent glebe-house, lately
erected. The church is in the decorated English style,
consisting of a nave, north and south aisles, and chan-

cel, with a handsome square embattled tower, crowned
with pinnacles at the angles, and surmounted by a
crocketed octangular spire, rising to the height of 150
feet : standing on a bank, the edifice forms a fine feature
in the country, visible for many miles round.   There
are places of worship for Calvinistic Baptists and Wesleyans ; and a national school is supported partly by an
endowment of £29 per annum, arising from land bequeathed by Mr. William Makepeace in 1733.   A pit on
the side of the old road to Daventry has produced a
large number and variety of organic remains, and an
almost complete series of rocky stratifications ; and
some very scarce plants have been found in the parish.
Dr. Edward Reynolds, Bishop of Norwich, and an able
political writer, was incumbent here.

BRAUNSTON, or BRANSTON (ALL SAINTS), a
parish, in the union and soke of OAKHAM, county of
RUTLAND, 2 miles (S. W.) from Oakham ; containing
443 inhabitants.   It comprises between,1500 and 2000
acres, of which the greater portion is arable ; the soil is
various, but chiefly clay of inferior quality.   An act of
parliament was passed in 1801, for inclosing the waste
lands. The living is annexed to the vicarage of Hambleton : the church is a small neat edifice.

BRAUNSTONE, a chapelry, in the parish of GLEN-
FIELD, union of BLABY, hundred of SPARKENHOE, S.
division of the county of LEICESTER, 2¾ miles (S. W.
by W.) from Leicester ; containing 195 inhabitants.
This place, which is separated from the parish of Aylestone by the river Soar, comprises about 1700 acres ;
the soil is partly clay and partly of lighter quality,
forming good arable and pasture land, and the surface
is pleasingly diversified with hill and dale.   The chapel
is dedicated to St. John the Baptist.

BRAUNSTONE-FRITH, an extra-parochial district,
in the union of BLABY, hundred of SPARKENHOE, S. division of the county of LEICESTER, 2 miles (W. S. W.)
from Leicester ; containing 7 inhabitants.

BRAUNTON (ST. BRANNOCK), a parish, in the union
of BARNSTAPLE, hundred of BRAUNTON, Braunton and
N. divisions of DEVON, 5 miles (W. N. W.) from Barnstaple ; containing 2274 inhabitants. The parish is supposed to derive its name from that of its patron saint. It
comprises 9150 acres, of which 3723 are common or
waste ; on the west it is bounded by the Bristol Channel,
and on the south by the navigable river Taw, at the
mouth of which is a lighthouse.   A tract of land, comprising about 900 acres, and formerly overflowed by the
sea, is considered the richest in the county.   There is a
mine of manganese. The living is a vicarage, valued in
the king's books at £16. 3. 6½. ; net income, £450 ;
patron, the Dean of Exeter. There is a place of worship
for Independents. A free school was founded by the Rev.
William Chaloner, in 1667 ; the endowment was augmented by Arthur Acland, Esq., in 1690, and the income
is now £75. The remains of some ancient chapels exist.

BRAWBY, a township, in the parish of SALTON,
union of MALTON, wapentake of RYEDALE, N. riding
of YORK, 6½ miles (N. W.) from Malton ; containing
218 inhabitants. This place is situated at the confluence
of the Seven and Dove rivers with the Rye, and comprises
by computation 1080 acres of fertile land. The vicarial
tithes have been commuted for £13.   There is a place
of worship for Wesleyans.

BRAWITH, with KNAYTON.—See KNAYTON.

Cherry, Esq., who endowed it with £500, to which Townley Ward, Esq., added £100 three per cents. ; and there is a national school for girls at Bray Wick, endowed with £16 per annum by the late Whitshed Keene, Esq., of Hawthorn Hill. Jesus' Hospital was founded in 1627, by William Goddard, for forty poor persons, six of them to be free of the Fishmongers' Company, under whose management it is placed : attached is a chapel.

BRAY-EATON.—See EATON, BRAY.

BRAY, HIGH (ALL SAINTS), a parish, in the union of BARNSTAPLE, hundred of SHERWILL, Braunton and N. divisions of DEVON, 7 miles (N. by W.) from South Molton ; containing 314 inhabitants. It comprises 3790a. 2r. 25p., of which 1447 acres are arable, 533 meadow and pasture, 311 wood, and 1400 common land. The living is a rectory, valued in the king's books at £14. 6. 8., and in the patronage of T. P. Acland, Esq. : the tithes have been commuted for £360, and there are 89½ acres of glebe.

BRAYBROOK (ALL SAINTS), a parish, in the union of MARKET-HARBOROUGH, hundred of ROTHWELL, N. division of the county of NORTHAMPTON, 2½ miles (S. E.) from Harborough ; containing 420 inhabitants. The parish is on the road between Harborough and Kettering, which bounds it on the north ; and comprises by computation 2778a. 2a. 39p., whereof 2543 acres are pasture, 215 arable, and 20 plantation. The soil is of first-rate quality, and watered by numerous streams ; the village is very healthy. The living is a rectory, valued in the king's books at £23. 6. 10½.; net income, £600 ; patron and incumbent, the Rev. J. Field : there are 313 acres of glebe, together with tithes of the old inclosure, now commuted into a rent-charge ; also a spacious glebe-house. The church is a very handsome edifice in the decorated English style, consisting of a nave, north and south chancel, and two aisles ; in the south chancel is an elaborately wrought monument to Sir Nicholas Griffin. There is a place of worship for Baptists. Braybrook gives the title of Baron to the family of Neville-Griffin.

BRAYDESTON (ST. MICHAEL), a parish, in the union and hundred of BLOFIELD, E. division of NORFOLK, ½ a mile (S.) from Blofield ; containing 126 inhabitants. It comprises about 700 acres, of which 378 are arable, and 139 marsh land ; and is bounded on the south by the navigable river Yare, from the valleys of which the land rises in gentle acclivities : the soil varies from a fine (in some places stiff) brick earth to a light sand. The prospects from the high land over the vale of the Yare are much admired. The Norwich and Yarmouth railway passes through the parish. The living is a discharged rectory, united to that of Strumpshaw, and valued in the king's books at £5. 6. 8. The church consists of a nave and chancel, with a square tower : the ruins of another church, dedicated to St. Clement, were pulled down about 30 years ago. Three Roman urns, containing calcined bones, were found in digging a sand-pit near the site of the demolished church.

BRAYDON, a hamlet, in the parish of PURTON, union of CRICKLADE and WOOTTON-BASSET, hundred of HIGHWORTH, CRICKLADE, and STAPLE, Cricklade and N. divisions of WILTS, 4½ miles (S. S. W.) from Cricklade ; containing 60 inhabitants. The impropriate tithes have been commuted for a rent-charge of £55, and the vicarial for one of £50.

351

BRAYFIELD, COLD (ST. MARY), a parish, in the union of NEWPORT-PAGNELL, hundred of NEWPORT, county of BUCKINGHAM, 2¾ miles (E. by N.) from Olney ; containing 83 inhabitants. The manor anciently belonged to the Blossomvilles, and afterwards to the Staffords ; in Elizabeth's reign it was held by the Mordaunts. In 1669 it came by purchase to the Boddingtons, from whom it passed by marriage to the Dymocks ; and about 1714 the estate was sold to the Farrer family. The parish lies on the borders of Bedfordshire, and is bounded on the south and east by the river Ouse : the village is on the road from Olney to Bedford. The living is annexed to the vicarage of Lavendon. As a commutation in lieu of tithes, land and a money payment were assigned in 1801, when the parish was inclosed by act of parliament.

BRAYTOFT (ST. PETER AND ST. PAUL), a parish, in the union of SPILSBY, Wold division of the wapentake of CANDLESHOE, parts of LINDSEY, county of LINCOLN, 5 miles (E. by S.) from Spilsby ; containing 235 inhabitants. It comprises 1815a. 2r. 26p., and is situated on the road from Spilsby to Burgh and Skegness : by a drainage navigation which approaches within three miles, corn may be forwarded to the market at Boston. The living is a discharged rectory, valued in the king's books at £18. 3. 6., and in the patronage of the Lord Chancellor : the tithes have been commuted for £322. 18. payable to the incumbent, and £18. 7. belonging to an impropriator : the glebe consists of 31½ acres. The church is built chiefly of brick. The nave is supported by five pointed arches, springing from octangular pillars, and surmounted by a row of clerestory windows ; and above the arch which opens into the chancel is a painting of the Spanish Armada : the font is ancient, and adorned with escutcheons emblazoned with devices representing the Saviour's passion : the east end of each aisle is taken off by screen-work for a chapel. The porch was rebuilt in 1715, and the tower in 1747. The family of Braytoft resided here in 1281 ; their ancient residence was taken down in 1698. Braytoft was the birthplace of the Rev. T. Scott, author of a very copious Biblical Commentary, and various other publications of considerable merit.

BRAYTON, with ASPATRIA.—See ASPATRIA.

BRAYTON (ST. WILFRID), a parish, in the union of SELBY, Lower division of the wapentake of BARKSTONE-ASH, W. riding of YORK ; comprising the townships of Barlow, Brayton, Burn, Gateforth, Hambleton, and Thorpe-Willoughby ; and containing 1974 inhabitants, of whom 307 are in the township of Brayton, 1 mile (S. W.) from Selby. The parish comprises by measurement 10,690 acres, of which 660 are woodland ; it is partly skirted by the river Ouse, and intersected by a canal which connects that river with the Aire. The soil is principally of a sandy nature, but its quality varies, and in some parts it is of a reddish cast ; the surface is generally level. Brayton Barf and Hambleton Haugh, two noted hills, covered with trees, are conspicuous objects in this flat district, and are seen at a great distance. The Leeds and Selby railway passes through the parish, one of its stations being at Hambleton. The living is a discharged vicarage, valued in the king's books at £7. 14. 4½.; net income, £268 ; patrons, the Hon. E. R. Petre and the Prebendary of Wistow, the former of whom is impropriator : the glebe comprises

140 acres, with a good residence. The church exhibits various styles of architecture : the tower is Norman, and is surmounted by an octagonal lantern, from which rises a lofty spire in the later English style ; the south doorway, and the arch leading into the chancel, are Norman, highly enriched ; the chancel is in the decorated, and the nave in the later, English style. At Barlow, three miles from the parish church, is a small chapel, a plain brick building, rather ancient ; there is also a chapel at Gateforth.

BREADSALL (*All Saints*), a parish, in the union of Shardlow, hundred of Appletree, though locally in that of Morleston and Litchurch, S. division of the county of Derby, 3 miles (N. E. by N.) from Derby ; containing 620 inhabitants. This place was for several centuries the property of the ancient family of the Harpurs, ancestors of the Crewes, of whose mansion there are still some picturesque remains near the church. A house of friars Eremites, afterwards converted into a priory of Augustine monks, was established at an early period, as is supposed by some member of the Dethic family ; its revenue at the Dissolution amounted to £18. 0. 8. The site, with the adjoining lands, was granted by Edward VI., in 1552, to Henry Duke of Suffolk, and came soon afterwards to other hands. The parish is situated on the Midland railway, the Derby and Eaton canal, and the road to Chesterfield ; and comprises by measurement 2219 acres of fertile land, mostly pasture. There are quarries of coarse gritstone. The village, which is ancient and well built, is situated in the vale of the Derwent, and at the foot of a hill which shelters it from the north and north-east winds. The living is a rectory, valued in the king's books at £28. 2. 8½. ; net income, £580, arising from land allotted in lieu of tithes in 1815 ; patron, Sir John Harpur Crewe, Bart. There is an excellent rectory-house. The church is a large handsome structure with a lofty spire, in the early and decorated English styles, and having a fine Norman arch at the principal entrance ; it contains some rich specimens of carved oak, and an ancient stone font : on the south side of the chancel is a monument to the memory of Erasmus Darwin, the poet, who died here in 1802. The Methodists have a place of worship. A school is endowed with £10. 8. per annum, arising from a bequest of £200 by the Rev. John Clayton, in 1745 ; excellent schools and a house for the master were built a few years ago, the former by Sir George Crewe, and the latter by the incumbent. There are remains of a Roman encampment ; and in a field belonging to the glebe is a very perfect tumulus, crowned by a venerable oak. John Hieron, a non-conformist divine of some celebrity, was incumbent from 1644 till 1662.

BREADSTONE, a tything, in the parish of Berkeley, union of Thornbury, Upper division of the hundred of Berkeley, W. division of the county of Gloucester, 2 miles (E. N. E.) from Berkeley ; containing 140 inhabitants.

BREAGE (*St. Breage*), a parish, in the union of Helston, W. division of the hundred of Kerrier and of the county of Cornwall, 3 miles (W. by N.) from Helston ; containing 6166 inhabitants. The parish is situated on the road from Falmouth to Penzance, and bounded on the south by the sea for nearly seven miles ; it abounds in mineral ores, chiefly copper and tin, with

BREASTON, a chapelry, in the parish of SAWLEY, union of SHARDLOW, hundred of MORLESTON and LITCHURCH, S. division of the county of DERBY, 7¾ miles (E. S. E.) from Derby; containing 712 inhabitants. The manor of Breaston, when the Domesday survey was taken, was held with Risley, by Roger de Busli. The chapelry comprises 1250 acres, whereof two-thirds are pasture, and the rest arable, with some woodland. Here is a station on the Midland railway; and the Nottingham and Derby canal passes through. The living is a perpetual curacy, annexed to that of Risley. A rent-charge of £361, formerly belonging to the prebend of Sawley (a suppressed dignity), has been awarded as a commutation of the tithes; and there is a glebe of nearly 24 acres. The chapel, dedicated to St. Michael, is a neat edifice, with a square tower surmounted by a curious spire. The Wesleyan Methodists have a place of worship.

BRECCLES, LITTLE, NORFOLK.—See SHROPHAM.

BRECKENBROUGH, with NEWSHAM, county of YORK.—See NEWSHAM.

BRECKLES (ST. MARGARET), a parish, in the union of WALSINGHAM, hundred of WAYLAND, W. division of NORFOLK, 5 miles (S. E. by S.) from Watton; containing 160 inhabitants. The parish comprises 1600 acres, the property of Sir E. Kerrison, Bart. There was formerly a lake of 100 acres, which was drained about 40 years since, and now affords rich pasturage. The Hall is an ancient mansion of brick, in the Elizabethan style. The living is a discharged vicarage, valued in the king's books at £7. 17. 11.; net income, £41, arising from Queen Anne's Bounty; patron and impropriator, Sir E. Kerrison. The church is an ancient structure in the early and later English styles, with a circular tower, and contains a large Norman font, which is elaborately sculptured.

BREDBURY, a township, in the parish and union of STOCKPORT, hundred of MACCLESFIELD, N. division of the county of CHESTER, 2¼ miles (N. E. by E.) from Stockport; containing 3301 inhabitants. The manor was held under the Stockports, by the family of Bredbury, whose heiress brought a moiety of it to the Ardens; the other moiety was for several generations in the Davenports of Henbury, from whom it passed by a female heir to Sir Fulke Lucy: the whole now belongs to the Arden family. The township comprises 2236 acres, the soil of which is clay, gravel, and sand; the surface is undulated or hilly. Coal-mines are wrought; and there is a cotton-mill. The road from Stockport to Hyde, and the Peak Forest canal, pass through the township; and the rivers Goit and Tame bound it on the south and north, respectively. There are three old Halls, of which Arden Hall is a place of great antiquity. A church district, called St. Mark's, was constituted by the Ecclesiastical Commissioners in 1846: the living is in the gift of the Crown and the Bishop of Chester, alternately. Hatherlow Independent chapel, here, was built at the cost of O. Heyworth, Esq., of Oakwood Hall; the Primitive Methodists, also, have a place of worship. The tithes have been commuted for £156.

BREDE (ST. GEORGE), a parish, in the union of RYE, partly in the hundred of STAPLE, but chiefly in that of GOSTROW, rape of HASTINGS, E. division of SUSSEX, 4 miles (S. by W.) from Northiam; containing 1151 inhabitants. This parish, distinguished by the

divisions of Broad Oak and Brede High, is bounded on the south by the Brede channel, which is navigable for barges, and over which is a bridge; and is intersected in the eastern portion by the road from London to Rye. It comprises 4834a. 3r. 8p., whereof 1960 acres are arable, 1091 pasture, and 1316 woodland; the soil is favourable for the growth of hops, which are successfully cultivated. The village is pleasantly situated on a hill commanding extensive and finely varied prospects. The living is a rectory, valued in the king's books at £12. 10. 5.; net income, £702; patron and incumbent, the Rev. J. W. Maher. The church consists of a nave, aisles, and chancel, with a square embattled tower surmounted by a low spire, the whole thoroughly repaired in 1840. There is a place of worship for Wesleyans at Broad Oak; and the union workhouse is in the parish. Dr. Horne, Bishop of Norwich, in 1790, was a native of Brede.

BREDENBURY, a parish, in the union of BROMYARD, hundred of BROXASH, county of HEREFORD, 3 miles (W. N. W.) from Bromyard; containing 46 inhabitants. The parish comprises by measurement 540 acres, of which the soil is of a clayey nature, and the surface for the most part hilly; it is intersected by the road from Leominster to Bromyard. The living is a discharged rectory, valued in the king's books at £2. 1. 10½., and in the patronage of Charles Dutton, Esq.: the tithes have been commuted for a yearly rent-charge of £53. 9., and the glebe consists of 50 acres, of which 30 are in the parish of Bockleton. The church is a neat small edifice.

BREDFIELD (ST. ANDREW), a parish, in the union of WOODBRIDGE, hundred of WILFORD, E. division of SUFFOLK, 2½ miles (N.) from Woodbridge; containing 468 inhabitants, and comprising by measurement 1067 acres. The living is a discharged vicarage endowed with the rectorial tithes, with the livings of Lowdham and Petistree consolidated in 1827; it is valued in the king's books at £4. 4. 2., and is in the patronage of the Crown. The tithes of the parish have been commuted for £318, and the glebe comprises 27 acres. There is a small place of worship for Baptists.

BREDGAR (ST. JOHN THE BAPTIST), a parish, in the union and hundred of MILTON, lathe of SCRAY, E. division of KENT, 4 miles (S. W. by S.) from Sittingbourne; containing 540 inhabitants. The parish comprises by measurement 1727 acres, of which 1072 are arable, 400 pasture, 180 woodland, and 21 acres hops: the soil is in many parts a good marl, and the substratum chalk; the surface is undulated, and the higher grounds crowned with woods. A fair is held on the first Monday after the 29th of June. The living is a discharged vicarage, valued in the king's books at £9; patron and impropriator, Sir E. C. Dering, Bart.: the great tithes have been commuted for £375, and the vicarial for £210; there are about 2 acres of glebe, with a house and garden. The church, which is partly of Norman architecture, was built about five centuries ago, and, prior to the Dissolution, had a small college attached to it: it is endowed with land for repairs. A Methodist meeting-house was erected about 1800.

BREDHURST (ST. PETER), a parish, in the union of HOLLINGBOURN, hundred of EYHORNE, lathe of AYLESFORD, W. division of KENT, 5 miles (S. S. E.) from Chatham; containing 131 inhabitants. It comprises 600 acres, of which 274 are in wood. The ancient village is said to have stood at a short distance, near a wood, where several wells are still visible. The living is a perpetual curacy, in the patronage of the Rector of Hollingbourn, and endowed with the tithes, which have been commuted for £130 : there are 9 acres of glebe. The church is a small edifice, consisting only of one aisle and a chancel, with a tower surmounted by a low spire: adjoining it is a small ruinous chapel in the early English style, formerly the burial-place of the family of Kemsley. There is a small dissenters' place of worship.

BREDICOT (ST. JAMES), a parish, in the union of PERSHORE, Lower division of the hundred of OSWALD-SLOW, Worcester and W. divisions of the county of WOR-CESTER, 3¾ miles (E.) from Worcester; containing 53 inhabitants. It is a small parish, comprising only 337 acres, whereof two-thirds are arable, and the remainder pasture; the surface is undulated, the soil a good rich marl, and the scenery picturesque. The Birmingham and Gloucester railway intersects the parish from north to south, nearly on a level with the surface. The living is a discharged rectory, valued in the king's books at £3. 18. 1½.; net income, £120, derived from land : patrons, the Dean and Chapter of Worcester. The church, an ancient structure, was thoroughly repaired, re-pewed, and beautified, in 1843, at a cost of £300, defrayed principally by the rector, the Rev. William Godfery. In 1839, some workmen excavating for the railway, found a small Roman urn of red clay, containing about 140 copper coins; it was met with at the depth of two feet in the earth, under the boughs of an old pollard elm, just by Bredicot Court.

BREDON (ST. GILES), a parish, in the union of TEWKESBURY, chiefly in the Middle, but partly in the Upper, division of the hundred of OSWALDSLOW, Pershore and E. divisions of the county of WORCESTER, 3¾ miles (N. E. by N.) from Tewkesbury; containing, with the chapelries of Norton and Cutsdean, and the hamlets of Bredon, Hardwick with Mitton, Kinsham, and Westmancote, 1567 inhabitants. This place was given by Ethelbald, King of Mercia, before the year 716, to his kinsman, Eanulph, who founded a monastery here in honour of St. Peter, which, previously to the Conquest, was annexed to the bishopric of Worcester. The parish comprises by computation between 5000 and 6000 acres, of which 963 are in the hamlet of Bredon, and is situated on the road between Tewkesbury and Pershore; the river Avon separates it from Gloucestershire. The soil is in general strong, producing good wheat and beans. The Birmingham and Gloucester railway passes through the village, where there is a station. From Bredon Hill (on which are quarries of stone suitable for building) is a pleasing view of the vales of Evesham and Cotswold, including the winding course of the Severn : the hill is crowned by a Roman encampment with a double trench. The living is a rectory, valued in the king's books at £72. 11. 0½.; net income, £1498, arising from 1100 acres of land, assigned in lieu of tithes, under inclosure acts, in 1775 and 1808 ; patron, Jacob Jones, Esq. : there is a glebe-house. The church has been recently restored by the incumbent and parishioners, and is a fine edifice with a tower and spire. The porch and principal doorways are excellent examples of the Norman style : the tower, which stands be-

354

ıf Worthington with Newbold liberty. A cell for Black :anons was founded soon after 1144, by the prior and nonks of St. Oswald, Nosthall, to whom the church and ome lands here had been given by Robert Ferrers, Earl ıf Nottingham ; its revenue, at the Dissolution, amounted o the sum of £25. 8. 1. The church which belonged to t is now the parochial church. The parish comprises ıy computation between 2000 and 2500 acres : the soil n general is very strong, and chiefly calculated for ɣrowing wheat ; the surface is hilly. The village is ituated at the foot of an elevated limestone rock, the ummit of which stands the church : there are considerble lime-works. The living is a discharged vicarage, alued in the king's books at £6. 2. 8. ; net income, ¦205 ; patron and impropriator, the Earl of Stamford nd Warrington : in 1759, land and money payments ʋere assigned in lieu of all tithes for the manor. At Vorthington is a separate incumbency. There is a place f worship for Wesleyans. By deed in 1736, Francis Jommins gave £300 towards the support of a school or boys, and Eliza Commins £583 for a girls' school ; n which endowments a national school has been estaılished.

BREEM, a chapelry, in the parish of NEWLAND, nion of MONMOUTH, hundred of ST. BRIAVELL'S, V. division of the county of GLOUCESTER, 5½ miles W. by S.) from Blakeney ; containing 441 inhabitants. The living is a perpetual curacy ; net income, £52 ; atron, the Vicar of Newland. The chapel is dedicated o St. James.

BREIGHTMET, or BRIGHTMEAD, a township, in the arish and union of BOLTON, hundred of SALFORD, S. division of the county of LANCASTER, 2 miles (E. by N.) rom Bolton, on the road to Bury ; containing 1309 inabitants. The manor of this place, forming part of the ossessions of Henry, Duke of Lancaster, in the reign of Edward III., seems to have been comprehended within he manor of Manchester. In the 1st of Richard III. t was one of the forfeited estates of "our rebell" Sir Thomas St. Leger, and was by that king conferred pon Lord Stanley. The ill-fated Sir Thomas, although e had married the Duchess of Exeter, sister of Richard, ost, not only his estates by attainder, but his life by he hands of the public executioner. The TOWNSHIP omprises 825 acres of land, mostly pasture ; the soil is ed and gravelly, on a substratum of red rock, and the cenery viewed from the hills is very extensive. Several ollieries are at work, in one of which the vein of coal three yards thick ; and there is a stone-quarry. Two otton-mills are in operation, and a few of the inhabitnts are employed in weaving quilts and counterpanes y hand : at Breightmet-Fold are the extensive bleachorks, established seventy years ago, of John Seddon, Esq. The river Irwell separates this township from onge. Among the chief residences here, are, Breightnet Hall, a substantial stone building, long possessed y the Parker family, who, and the Earl of Derby, are he principal owners of the soil; Oaken Bottom, formerly he residence of the Cromptons ; and Crompton-Ford, n elegant mansion. R. A. Hibbert, Esq., has a cottage esidence at West Breightmet, with good views. In 729, William Hulton gave land for the erection of a chool, which was built in 1750, and is endowed with ¦30 per annum. About sixty years ago, twelve Roman rns of earthenware were found in the township, a little

below the surface, containing ashes of the dead ; but on being exposed to the air they mouldered into dust : the vessels were of cylindrical form, and within the top of each was a small bone. Camden supposed that the *Coccium* of Antoninus was near this place.

BREIGHTON, a township, in the parish of BUB-WITH, union of HOWDEN, Holme-Beacon division of the wapentake of HARTHILL, E. riding of YORK, 5¼ miles (N. W. by N.) from Howden ; containing 204 inhabitants. The village lies on the eastern bank of the river Derwent, opposite to Menthorpe. The farm of Gunby, in the township, was given by the Conqueror to his standard-bearer, Gilbert Tison, whose posterity took the name of *De Guneby*, and resided in the old mansionhouse for many generations.

BREINTON (ST. MICHAEL), a parish, in the hundred of GRIMSWORTH, union and county of HEREFORD, 2 miles (W.) from Hereford ; containing 362 inhabitants. It comprises 1539a. 28p., of which about two-thirds are arable ; on the south it is bounded by the river Wye. The living is a perpetual curacy, valued in the king's books at £1. 10., and in the patronage of the Dean of Hereford ; appropriators, the Dean and Chapter. The great tithes have been commuted for £210, and those of the incumbent for £135.

BREMHILL (ST. MARTIN), a parish, chiefly in the union of CALNE, but partly in that of CHIPPENHAM, hundred of CHIPPENHAM, Chippenham and Calne, and N. divisions of WILTS, 4¼ miles (E.) from Chippenham ; containing 1550 inhabitants. This parish comprises by computation 6000 acres : the soil is chiefly a sandy loam ; the surface is partly hilly, and partly a fine vale. Facilities of communication are afforded by the Wilts and Berks canal. The Roman Watling-street passed through the parish, and in the vicinity is the course of the ancient rampart Wansdyke. At the hamlet of Studley was a Roman station, thought to have been an outpost to the more important station of *Verlucio*, the site of which was ascertained by Sir Richard Colt Hoare to be near Wanshouse, about four miles distant : numerous coins, chiefly of Constantine, and some British earthenware, have been dug up. Avebury, a celebrated temple of the Britons, supposed to have been raised in honour of Teutates, their chief Celtic deity ; and Tan hill and Silbury, two lofty eminences appropriated to the performance of their pagan rites, are situated within a short distance : on Tan hill a fair is held on Aug. 6th. The living is a vicarage, endowed with the rectorial tithes, with the living of Highway annexed, valued in the king's books at £15. 15. ; net income, £406 ; patron, the Bishop of Salisbury. Under an inclosure act in 1775, land and a money payment were assigned to the impropriator in lieu of tithes on certain lands in the parish : there are about 230 acres of glebe, with a residence. The church is a venerable and interesting edifice, with a massive square tower adorned with battlements and pinnacles ; between the aisle and chancel is a handsome rood-loft, beautifully carved : the chancel contains several monuments, and in the churchyard are numerous epitaphs written by the late vicar, the Rev. Mr. Bowles, the poet, who in 1827 published a description of the parish. Near the church are the ivy-mantled remains of a portion of the tenements belonging to the grange of the abbot of Malmesbury. At Foxham is a chapel of ease, dedicated to St. John the Baptist.

BREMILHAM, or Cowich, a parish, in the union and hundred of Malmesbury, Malmesbury and Kingswood, and N. divisions of Wilts, 2 miles (W. by S.) from Malmesbury; containing 47 inhabitants. The living is a discharged rectory, valued in the king's books at £4. 1. 8., and in the patronage of the Hon. and Rev. R. Bowles: the tithes have been commuted for £106.

BRENCHLEY (All Saints), a parish, in the union of Tonbridge, hundred of Brenchley and Horsemonden, lathe of Aylesford, W. division of Kent, 4½ miles (N.) from Lamberhurst; containing 2472 inhabitants. The parish comprises 7698 acres, of which 1693 are common or waste, and 1010 in wood. It abounds with iron-ore; and there are some mineral springs, similar in their properties to those of Tonbridge. A cattle-fair is held annually at the hamlet of Matfield Green. The South-Eastern railway passes through the parish. The living is a vicarage, valued in the king's books at £12. 18. 9.; net income, £749; patron and impropriator, G. Courthorpe, Esq. The church is an ancient cruciform structure, built chiefly of sandstone, with a lofty tower. There is a place of worship for Particular Baptists.

BRENDON (St. Brendon), a parish, in the union of Barnstaple, hundred of Sherwill, Braunton and N. divisions of Devon, 15½ miles (E.) from Ilfracombe; containing 271 inhabitants. The parish comprises 4497 acres, of which 3000 are common or waste. The living is a discharged rectory, valued in the king's books at £9. 4., and in the patronage of John Knight, Esq.: the tithes have been commuted for £167, and there are 50 acres of glebe.

BRENKLEY, a township, in the parish of Dinnington, union and W. division of Castle ward, S. division of Northumberland, 7½ miles (N. by W.) from Newcastle-upon-Tyne; containing 56 inhabitants. It lies above three miles north-east from Ponteland, and nearly a mile west from the great post road. The tithes have been commuted for £141, payable to Merton College, Oxford, and £9 to the vicar.

BRENT, EAST (St. Mary), a parish, in the union of Axbridge, hundred of Brent with Wrington, E. division of Somerset, 4¾ miles (W. S. W.) from Axbridge; containing, with the hamlets of Edingworth and Rooksbridge, 849 inhabitants. This place appears to have been the scene of various military transactions at an early period; and on the summit of a lofty conical hill termed Brent Knoll, are vestiges of a large double intrenchment, within which, and at the base of the hill, numerous Roman relics have been found. The West Saxons are also supposed to have occupied this position, in their contests with the Mercians; and it is related that Alfred defended himself here against the Danes. A plot of ground to the south retains the name Battleborough, probably from some battle having been fought upon it. The parish is situated on the road from Bridgwater to Bristol, and near the Bristol and Exeter railway; and comprises by computation 3000 acres. The living is a vicarage, valued in the king's books at £30. 11. 3.; patron and appropriator, the Bishop of Bath and Wells: the great tithes have been commuted for £90, and the vicarial for £690; the glebe comprises about 70 acres. The church is a very ancient structure, with a tower and spire together 130 feet

in the time of the civil war. There is a place of worship for Bryanites.

BRENTFORD, a market-town, and the head of a union; comprising Old Brentford, in the parish of EALING, Kensington division of the hundred of OSSULSTONE, and New Brentford, in the parish of HANWELL, hundred of ELTHORNE, county of MIDDLESEX, of which it is the county town; 7 miles (W. by S.) from Hyde-park Corner, and on the great western road; New Brentford containing 2174 inhabitants, and Old Brentford 5058. This place, formerly called *Brainforde*, takes its name from an ancient ford on the small river Brent. In 1016 Edmund Ironside, having compelled the Danes to raise the siege of London, pursued them to this place, where they were routed with great slaughter. A chapter of the order of the Garter was held here in 1445; and, in the 25th of Henry VI., an hospital for a master and several brethren, of the Nine Orders of Angels, was founded in a chapel beyond the bridge, at the western end of the town, once known as West Brentford : the revenue appears to have been £40, and the site was granted to Edward, Duke of Somerset, in the 1st of Edward VI. In 1558, six Protestants were burnt here at the stake. In the great civil war the place was the scene of a battle, in which the royalists, though victorious, were obliged to retire from the field, by the sudden arrival of a strong reinforcement to the enemy from London. For his services in this battle, which occurred on the 12th of November, 1642, Patrick Ruthen, Earl of Forth in Scotland, was created an English peer by the title of Earl of Brentford, which title was subsequently conferred by William III. upon Mareschal Schomberg, who had accompanied him to England at the Revolution. Several skirmishes also took place in 1647, between the royal guards stationed here and the parliamentary troops quartered at Hounslow.

The TOWN consists of one street, more than a mile in length, paved, and lighted with gas, under an act of parliament obtained in 1825 and amended in 1842. The river Thames runs parallel with the street; and over it, at the eastern extremity of the town, is a handsome stone bridge leading to Kew : the Brent, uniting the Grand Junction canal with the Thames, crosses Brentford on the west; and over this is a neat stone bridge erected by the county in 1825, replacing a bridge of great antiquity, at one time supported by a toll levied upon Jewish passengers exclusively. There are a large malt-distillery, an extensive brewery, and a soap-manufactory; but the chief trade of the town is derived from its situation on the great western road (now much diminished, however, by the construction of the Great Western railway), and from the union of the canal with the Thames. The market is on Tuesday; and fairs are held on May 17th, 18th, and 19th, for cattle, and September 24th, 13th, and 14th, for toys and pedlery. The town is within the jurisdiction of the county magistrates, who hold a petty-session for the division every alternate week : the powers of the county debt-court of Brentford, established in 1847, extend over the registration-district of Brentford. The parliamentary elections for the county take place at New Brentford.

The LIVING of New Brentford is a perpetual curacy; net income, £283; patron, the Rector of Hanwell. The rectorial tithes have been commuted for £60, and the vicarial for £85. The chapel, dedicated to St. Law-

rence, with the exception of the tower was rebuilt of brick in 1762 : annexed to it is the residence of the minister. The chapel of Old Brentford, dedicated to St. George, was rebuilt in 1770, by subscription : the living was augmented in 1842 to £168 per annum by the Ecclesiastical Commissioners, and is a perpetual curacy in the gift of the Vicar of Ealing. There are places of worship for Particular Baptists, Primitive Methodists, and Wesleyans. A charity school for boys, established by subscription in 1703, was endowed by Lady Capel, in 1719, with the twelfth part of an estate, yielding at present £37. 10. per annum : the endowment, enlarged by subsequent benefactions, produces an annual income of £143. There is a national school, partly supported by an endowment. The poor law union of Brentford comprises 10 parishes or places, and contains a population of 37,054. Human skeletons have at various times been dug up in the neighbourhood.

BRENTINGBY, a chapelry, in the parish of WYFORDBY, union of MELTON-MOWBRAY, hundred of FRAMLAND, N. division of the county of LEICESTER, 2½ miles (E. by S.) from Melton-Mowbray; containing 54 inhabitants. The chapelry comprises about 600 acres : the soil is partly a cold clay, and partly of much richer quality; the pastures are luxuriant, and Stilton cheese is made here and in the neighbourhood. There is a curious old manor-house, repaired in 1846. The Melton-Mowbray and Oakham canal passes through the district. The chapel is an ancient structure.

BRENT-TOR (ST. MICHAEL), a parish, in the union and hundred of TAVISTOCK, Tavistock and S. divisions of DEVON, 4 miles (N.) from Tavistock ; containing 169 inhabitants. This place partly derives its name from its situation on a lofty eminence or tor, which, differing materially in its strata from all other tors in Dartmoor Forest, is by geologists supposed to have been originally a volcanic eruption. It comprises 887 acres, whereof 100 are common or waste. The small river Lid runs through the parish; in which are also a fine sheet of water called Stowford Lake, and some mines of manganese. The village is built on the acclivity of the eminence; and the church, occupying its summit, forms a conspicuous landmark to vessels entering Plymouth harbour. The living is a perpetual curacy; net income, £60; patron and impropriator, the Duke of Bedford.

BRENTWOOD, a district chapelry and market-town, in the parish of SOUTH WEALD, union of BILLERICAY, hundred of CHAFFORD, S. division of ESSEX, 11 miles (S. W.) from Chelmsford, and 18 (E. N. E.) from London, on the road to Norwich; containing 2362 inhabitants. The name, which is of Saxon origin, signifies a burnt wood; the woods that once occupied the site having been burnt down. The hamlet comprises by computation 395 acres. The town is pleasantly situated on a commanding eminence, and consists principally of one street; the houses are in general ancient, and irregularly built : the inhabitants are supplied with excellent water from wells. Races take place occasionally on a common near the town. There are cavalry barracks at Warley, about a mile and a half distant. A large ale and porter brewery and malting establishment was established about 30 years since; the produce is chiefly for home consumption, and about 5000 quarters of malt are annually sent to London. The Eastern Counties railway runs near the town ; the station here is of red brick, and in the Elizabethan style. The market, lately revived, is on Saturday ; the fairs are on July 18th and Oct. 15th, and are for horses and cattle. Courts leet and baron are held by the lord of the manor of South Weald : petty-sessions for the division take place every Thursday ; and the assizes were formerly held here. The powers of the county debt-court of Brentwood, established in 1847, extend over the registration-district of Ongar, and part of that of Billericay. A portion of the old town-hall has been converted into shops.

The LIVING is a perpetual curacy ; net income, £124, with a residence ; patron, Christopher T. Tower, Esq. The old chapel, dedicated to St. Thomas à Becket, was originally founded early in the thirteenth century, by David, Abbot of St. Osyth, and is now used for a national school, a new chapel having been erected by a grant from the Incorporated Society, and by subscription ; it is a plain edifice, with lancet windows. There is a meeting-house for Independents, and the Roman Catholics have chapels at Pilgrim Hatch and Thorndon Hall. The free grammar school was founded and endowed in 1537, by Sir Anthony Browne, Knt., and is open to all boys residing within three miles of Brentwood ; the income arising from the endowment is £1452, which is paid to the master, subject to an allowance of £10 per annum each to five alms-persons, and to the expense of keeping the school premises and almshouses in repair. An exhibition of £6 per annum to Caius College, Cambridge, was founded by Dr. Plume, with preference to Chelmsford, Brentwood, and Maldon. The Roman station *Durositum* is supposed to have been situated in the vicinity.

BRENZETT (ST. EANSWITH), a parish, in the union of ROMNEY-MARSH, partly in the hundred of ALOES-BRIDGE, but chiefly in the liberty of ROMNEY-MARSH, lathe of SHEPWAY, E. division of KENT, 4½ miles (N. W. by W.) from Romney ; containing 228 inhabitants. It comprises by computation 1768a. 2r. of marshy land, subject to flood. The living is a vicarage, valued in the king's books at £7. 18. 11½. ; net income, £73 ; patron and impropriator, the Rev. W. Brockman, as lessee of the Archbishop of Canterbury. The church is an ancient edifice, with a tower surmounted by a spire. There is a place of worship for Wesleyans.

BREOCK, ST. (ST. BREOKE), a parish, in the union of ST. COLUMB MAJOR, hundred of PYDER, E. division of CORNWALL, 1 mile (W. S. W.) from Wadebridge ; containing 1733 inhabitants. The parish comprises 6846 acres, of which the soil is generally shelfy, and the surface hilly, with some large coppice woods in the valleys ; 1719 acres are common or waste. It is situated on the road between Launceston and Falmouth, and on the river Camel, by which it is bounded on the north and east, and over which is a handsome bridge of 16 arches. The river is navigable for two miles above Wadebridge ; and a railway has been completed to Bodmin and Simonward, with branches to Ruthyn Bridge and Wynford Bridge. There are iron-mines at Pawton, and an iron-foundry : copper has been found, but not now of such quality as to pay the expense of raising it ; slate is obtained for building purposes. Fairs are held on March 2nd, May 12th, June 22nd, and October 10th. The living is a rectory, valued in the king's books at £41. 10. 10., and in the patronage of Sir W. Moles-
358

worth, Bart. : the tithes have been commuted for £966. 4. 11., and the glebe consists of about 83 acres, with a residence. In the church are some old monuments of the Tredenick and Vyal families, now extinct. There are a chapel of ease at Wadebridge ; and places of worship in the parish for Independents, Wesleyans, and Bryanites. Dr. Hall, Bishop of Exeter in the reign of Charles I., held the living here *in commendam*. On the summit of an eminence which commands an extensive view of the coast, are the remains of an ancient cromlech.

BRERETON, with SMETHWICK (ST. OSWALD), a parish, in the union of CONGLETON, hundred of NORTH-WICH, S. division of the county of CHESTER, 3 miles (N. E. by N.) from Sandbach ; containing 666 inhabitants. The parish comprises by measurement 4200 acres, of which the soil is clay and sand ; and is situated on the road from London to Liverpool, and on the Manchester and Birmingham railway. The ancient residence of the lords Brereton, from whom the place derived its name, is a fine old mansion in good preservation, lately purchased by its present occupier, John Howard, Esq. The living is a rectory, valued in the king's books at £7. 0. 5., and in the patronage of the family of Royds ; net income, £681 : the glebe consists of about 20 acres. The church, a stately structure in the later style of English architecture, with a roof of carved oak, was formerly a chapel of ease to the church at Astbury, but was made parochial, and endowed with the tithes of Brereton *cum* Smethwick, in the reign of Henry VIII. ; it contains monuments of Lord Brereton and the Smethwick family. There is a place of worship for Independents ; and a school has an endowment of £4 per annum.

BRERETON, a chapelry district, in the parish of RUGELEY, union of LICHFIELD, E. division of the hundred of CUTTLESTONE, S. division of the county of STAF-FORD, 1¼ mile (S. E.) from Rugeley ; containing about 1160 inhabitants. This district is the south-eastern portion of the parish. The river Trent forms its boundary on the north-east, and the Grand Trunk canal passes through it, communicating by two railroads with collieries of considerable extent belonging to Earl Talbot and the Marquess of Anglesey. The scenery is extremely beautiful, presenting the varieties of woodland, moorland, well-cultivated fields, and hill and dale : a large portion of Cannock Chase is included in the district ; the remainder is partly pasture, and partly arable land. The village lies on the road from Lichfield to Stafford, and is distant seven miles from the former, and nine from the latter place ; it contains several well-built houses.

The living is a perpetual curacy, in the patronage of the Vicar of Rugeley, endowed partly by private benefaction, and partly by grants from Queen Anne's Bounty and the Ecclesiastical Commissioners ; net income, £120, with a parsonage-house, and nine acres of glebe. The church, named St. Michael's, stands on the brow of a hill by the side of the road ; it was built in 1837, at the cost of nearly £1800, and is a cruciform structure with lancet windows, containing 422 sittings, of which 222 are free. Its situation has been happily chosen to set it off to advantage, and it is much admired. A national school for boys was established in 1843, and is supported by subscription ; there is also a national school for girls, founded by Miss Sneyd. A boys' day school, established by Miss Birch, was endowed by her with £70 per annum ;

and the same lady founded almshouses for six poor people, to each of whom she left a perpetual allowance of 4s. per week. This last school and the almshouses are in connexion with the Wesleyan Methodists, who have here a place of worship.

BRESSINGHAM (St. John the Baptist), a parish, in the union of Guiltcross, hundred of Diss, E. division of Norfolk, 2½ miles (W.) from Diss; containing 647 inhabitants. The parish comprises 2364 acres, of which 1569 are arable, 634 pasture, and 76 woodland; and is situated on the road from Thetford to Diss, and bounded on the south by the river Waveney, which separates it from Suffolk. The living is a rectory, valued in the king's books at £15, and in the patronage of C. Bidwell, Esq.: the tithes have been commuted for £604. 16.; there are 37 acres of glebe. The church was rebuilt, with the exception of the chancel, in 1527, having been commenced some time previously by Sir Roger Pilkington, Knt., lord of the manor; it is in the decorated style, and consists of a nave, chancel, and aisles, with an embattled tower. Conduit Meadow, in the parish, is so called from a spacious conduit, now in a ruinous state, constructed by Sir Richard de Boyland, to supply some baths and an extensive moat which encompassed his grounds.

BRETBY, county of Derby.—See Bradby.

BRETFORTON (St. Leonard), a parish, in the union of Evesham, Upper division of the hundred of Blackenhurst, Pershore and E. divisions of the county of Worcester, 3¾ miles (E.) from Evesham; containing 511 inhabitants. The lands belonged to the abbey of Evesham even before the Conquest. The parish is situated on the border of Gloucestershire, which bounds it on the east and south: it is intersected by the road from Evesham to Campden, and comprises 1632 acres. The soil is various, but the greater part is stiff clay; and the surface is flat. The village is of neat and respectable appearance. The living is a discharged vicarage, valued in the king's books at £6. 5.; net income, £82; patron, Admiral Morris; impropriators, the landowners. Land and a money payment were assigned to the vicar, in lieu of all tithes, in 1765; the glebe consists of 90 acres. The church is spacious and airy, with a well-built tower at the west end; a chapel juts out on the north and south, and the building is thus rendered cruciform.

BRETHERDALE, a township, in the parish of Orton, East ward and union, county of Westmorland, 8 miles (S. W.) from Orton; containing 82 inhabitants. The manor belonged to Byland Abbey, Yorkshire, but at the Dissolution was purchased by the family of Wharton, and is now the property of the Earl of Lonsdale. A rent-charge of £22. 9. 10. has been awarded as a commutation for the vicarial tithes; the rectorial were purchased by the landowners in 1618.

BRETHERTON, a township and ecclesiastical district, in the parish of Croston, union of Chorley, hundred of Leyland, N. division of the county of Lancaster, 10 miles (N. N. E.) from Ormskirk; containing 33 inhabitants. This place was the manorial residence of the Banastres or Banisters, previously to the reign of 'dward III.; and a Thomas Banastre, who is conjectured to have been of this family, was beheaded in the reign of Edward II. by Thomas, Earl of Lancaster, for his active opposition to that powerful and factious baron. The township comprises 2292 statute acres, of which

359

816 are arable land, 618 meadow, 732 pasture, 13 woodland, and 113 acres gardens, &c.; the surface is rather flat, and the soil a stiff clay, marsh, loam, and hazel. The river Lostock bounds the township; the rivers Douglas and Yarrow meet here, and run into the Ribble about a mile distant: here is also a branch of the Leeds and Liverpool canal, and the Liverpool and Preston turnpike-road runs across the township from Bank bridge to Cara-House bridge. Bank Hall, the seat of George Anthony Legh Keck, Esq., was built in 1608, and restored in the Elizabethan style, in 1832. The living is a perpetual curacy, in the patronage of the Rector of Croston; net income, £150, with a house erected in 1847. The tithes have been commuted for £325, payable to the rector of Chorley, and £45 to the rector of Croston. The church, dedicated to St. John the Baptist, was consecrated on the 26th of June, 1840; it is in the early English style, and cost £1260. There are places of worship for Wesleyans and Independents. A free school was built in 1654, at the expense of James Fletcher, who endowed it with £230, to which various donations have been added.

BRETSFORD, a hamlet, in the parish of Wolstan, union of Rugby, Kirby division of the hundred of Knightlow, N. division of the county of Warwick, 6½ miles (E. by S.) from Coventry; containing 148 inhabitants. The name is a corruption of Bradforde, and is derived from the breadth of a ford here. In the 11th of Henry III., Nicholas de Verdon, lord of the manor, obtained a special charter for a weekly market on Tuesday; and his descendant, Theobald, had the power of life and death both at this place and Brandon, with other privileges. Here was anciently a chapel dedicated to St. Edmund, supposed by Sir William Dugdale to have been founded by one of the Turviles.

BRETTENHAM (St. Mary), a parish, in the union of Thetford, hundred of Shropham, W. division of Norfolk, 4 miles (E. by S.) from Thetford; containing 62 inhabitants. It comprises 2001 acres, of which 573 are common and heath. The living is a discharged rectory, valued in the king's books at £5. 12. 6., and in the patronage of the Bishop of Ely: the tithes have been commuted for £200, and the glebe comprises 18 acres. The church is in the decorated style, and consists of a nave only; the chancel, with the parsonage-house, having been burnt down in 1693: the entrance on the south is by a Norman doorway. Roman coins of Vespasian and other emperors, and urns, have been dug up.

BRETTENHAM (St. Mary), a parish, in the union and hundred of Cosford, W. division of Suffolk, 4 miles (N. N. W.) from Bildeston; containing 367 inhabitants. This place is supposed by some to have been the site of the Roman station Combretonium, which others have endeavoured to fix at Brettenham in Norfolk; but the distances in the Itineraries justify neither of these suppositions. The station was most probably Burgh, near Woodbridge, where are evident remains of a Roman post. The parish comprises by computation 1300 acres. The living is a rectory, valued in the king's books at £11. 3. 11½., and in the patronage of the Crown; net income, £377.

BRETTON, MONK, a township and district chapelry, in the parish of Royston, wapentake of Staincross, W. riding of the county of York, 1½ mile (N. E.) from

Barnsley; the township containing 1719 inhabitants. The chapelry includes Upper and Lower Cudworth, and comprises 3809 acres, of which 2129 are in Monk-Bretton township and tithe-free. It is intersected by the Barnsley canal and the Midland railway: the population has rapidly increased within the last ten years, and many persons are employed in linen weaving and bleaching. A district church dedicated to St. Paul, containing 700 sittings, was built at a cost of £1200, defrayed principally by subscription, and was consecrated 9th June, 1840; it is in the Anglo-Norman style, built of stone supplied from quarries here, and occupies a site given by Sir George Wombwell, Bart., lord of the manor. The living is in the patronage of the Vicar of Royston, with a net income of £150. A priory of the Cluniac order was founded in the reign of Henry II., the remains of which may still be seen: at the Dissolution, its revenues amounted to £323. 8. 2. An almshouse, comprising six tenements, is supposed to have been founded by Dame Mary Talbot, in 1654; Sir G. Wombwell allows 50s. annually to each, and repairs the buildings.

BRETTON, WEST, a chapelry, partly in the parish of SANDALL MAGNA, Lower division of the wapentake of AGBRIGG, and partly in the parish of SILKSTONE, wapentake of STAINCROSS, union of WAKEFIELD, W. riding of YORK, 6 miles (S. S. W.) from Wakefield; containing 564 inhabitants. This place, which is on the Denby-Dale road to Manchester, is the property and residence of Thomas Wentworth Beaumont, Esq., lord of the manor; and contains by computation 1992 acres, tithe-free, of which 760 are within the limits of the demesne of Bretton Hall. The present Hall was erected by Sir William Wentworth, Bart., in 1730, when the original mansion of the family, with the adjacent chapel, was taken down; considerable additions were made by the late Col. Beaumont and his lady, after designs of Sir Jeffrey Wyatville, and many improvements have been completed by the present proprietor. Henry VIII. and suite slept three nights in the old mansion; and the panels, chairs (the latter of oak, curiously carved), and draperies of his bedroom were removed to the new Hall. The park abounds with sylvan scenery, enlivened by the windings of the river Dearne, which flows through a picturesque valley, and in the southern part of the grounds expands into two beautiful lakes; the upper lake is called Virginia Water, and is surrounded by bold rocky banks, with drives and walks enriched by grottos and Virginian plants. The chapel is a handsome edifice in the Grecian style, built in 1737, by Sir William Wentworth; it is the private property of Mr. Beaumont, who pays the chaplain, but it is open to the public.

BREWARD, ST., or SIMONWARD (ST. BRUARD), a parish, in the union of CAMELFORD, hundred of TRIGG, E. division of CORNWALL, 6¾ miles (N. by E.) from Bodmin; containing 724 inhabitants. It comprises 9230 acres, of which 2780 are common or waste. The surface is boldly undulated; and the lofty hills of Rough Tor (contracted from Rowtor) and Brown Willy are both within the limits of the parish. From the latter, which is 1368 feet above the level of the sea, a most extensive view is obtained over the English and Bristol Channels; and on the summit of the former are the remains of an ancient building supposed to have been a chapel, and a Logan stone. The living is a discharged vicarage, valued in the king's books at £8, and in the patronage of the 360

Dean and Chapter of Exeter: the tithes have been commuted for £150 payable to the Dean and Chapter, and £290 payable to the vicar, who has also 70 acres of glebe. The church is an ancient structure, partly Norman, and partly in the later style of English architecture. There are some circles of stones in the vicinity of the parish.

BREWERS, ISLE.—See ISLE-BREWERS.

BREWHAM-LODGE, an extra-parochial liberty, in the hundred of NORTON-FERRIS, E. division of SOMERSET, 5 miles (E. by N.) from Bruton; containing 8 inhabitants. This place consists of one estate, comprising nearly 800 acres; and acquired its extra-parochial privileges from having been one of King John's hunting-seats: a wood in the vicinity retains the name of King's Wood. Alfred's Tower, here, was erected by Henry Hoare, Esq., in commemoration of a victory obtained in the vicinity by that prince over the Danes: it is a triangular brick building, 155 feet in height, surmounted at each angle by a turret; and over the entrance is an inscription, recording the good qualities and noble exploits of Alfred. About half a mile towards the north-east is a small oval encampment, called Jack's Castle, which is thought to be of Danish construction; and human bones, spears' heads, and urns containing the ashes of burnt bones, have been dug up in the neighbourhood, which was the scene of various conflicts between the Saxons and the Danes.

BREWHAM, NORTH and SOUTH (ST. JOHN THE BAPTIST), in the union of WINCANTON, hundred of BRUTON, E. division of SOMERSET; containing 905 inhabitants, of whom 392 are in North Brewham, 3½ miles (E. N. E.) from Bruton. This parish takes its name from the river Brew, and is divided into two distinct parishes having one church: North Brewham comprises 2023a. 2r. 10p., of which about 100 acres are woodland and 139 common or waste; and South Brewham, 2661a. 2r. 30p., of which 1845 acres are pasture, 379 arable, and 437 wood. The soil is mostly clay, and stony in some places, and in some parts tolerably good mould; the surface is much diversified with hill and dale, and thickly wooded. The living is a perpetual curacy; net income, £102; patron and impropriator, Sir H. R. Hoare, Bart.: the tithes of North Brewham have been commuted for £169, and those of South Brewham for £180. The church is a neat edifice, lately repaired at a great expense; in the churchyard are the shaft of an old cross, and two fine yew-trees. A chapel formerly stood at North Brewham, the remains of which have been converted into a barn.

BREWHOUSE-YARD, an extra-parochial liberty, in the union of RADFORD, S. division of the wapentake of BROXTOW, N. division of the county of NOTTINGHAM; containing 110 inhabitants. This district adjoins the town of Nottingham, lying south-east of the Castle rock, and on the north bank of the Leen. It was formerly under the jurisdiction of the castle, and had a malt-kiln and brewhouse for the use of the garrison; but in 1621 James I. constituted it a distinct constabulary. A society, called the "Philadelphians," or the "Family of Love," from the love they professed to bear all men, even the most wicked, used to meet here; their founder was one David George, an Anabaptist, of Holland, who first propagated his doctrines in Switzerland, where he died in 1556.

for a weekly market, which has long been disused; and Edward III. exempted the burgesses from the payment of toll throughout the kingdom : this exemption is not now claimed, but the inhabitants still enjoy the right of cutting wood in the Forest of Dean, which they form into hoops and other articles, and send to Bristol. The parish comprises by computation 3312 acres, of which 1477 are meadow and pasture, 1307 arable, 508 woodland, and 20 waste. There are several coal-works in the vicinity; and until lately a court was held for regulating matters in dispute among the miners, but an act was passed in 1842 for abolishing this court. The living is annexed to the vicarage of Lidney : the appropriate tithes, belonging to the Dean and Chapter of Hereford, have been commuted for £215, the vicarial tithes for £229, and the impropriate for £8. The church is a small cruciform edifice, principally in the Norman and early English styles.

BRICETT, GREAT (St. Mary and St. Lawrence), a parish, in the union and hundred of Bosmere and Claydon, E. division of Suffolk, 3½ miles (E. N. E.) from Bildeston; containing 214 inhabitants, and comprising 912a. 3r. 21p. The living is a perpetual curacy; net income, £100; patrons and impropriators, the Provost and Fellows of King's College, Cambridge. A priory of Augustine canons was founded about 1110, by Ralph Fitz-Brien, in honour of St. Leonard; the possessions of which, on the suppression of alien priories, were given by Henry VI. to the Provost and Fellows.

BRICETT, LITTLE, in the union and hundred of Bosmere and Claydon, E. division of Suffolk, 4½ miles (S. S. W.) from Needham-Market; containing 25 inhabitants. It was formerly a separate parish, but is now a hamlet to Offton : the living, a discharged rectory, was consolidated with the vicarage of Offton, when the church fell into decay, about the year 1503.

BRICKENDON, a liberty, in the parish of All Saints, Hertford, union, hundred, and county of Hertford, 3 miles (S. by W.) from Hertford; containing 757 inhabitants.

BRICKHILL, BOW (All Saints), a parish, in the union of Newport-Pagnell, hundred of Newport, county of Buckingham, 2 miles (E.) from Fenny-Stratford; containing 566 inhabitants. The parish is intersected by the Roman Watling-street; and comprises by computation 1550 acres, the soil of which is various, being sandy on the hills, and heavy clay in other parts : a very hard species of ironstone is quarried for building. Many females and children are employed in making lace and platting straw. The living is a rectory, valued in the king's books at £15. 0. 2½., and in the patronage of Queen's College, Cambridge; net income, £370. Land and annual money payments were assigned under an inclosure act, in 1790, in lieu of tithes; the land consists of 250 acres. The church was enlarged a few years since. Charles Porrett, in 1633, left several bequests for charitable purposes. There is a national school, and the poor have 198 acres of heath land. The remains of the Roman station *Magiorintum* are still visible here, and coins are frequently turned up by the plough.

BRICKHILL, GREAT (St. Mary), a parish, in the union of Newport-Pagnell, hundred of Newport, county of Buckingham, 2¾ miles (S. E. by S.) from Fenny-Stratford; containing 721 inhabitants. The manor was anciently possessed by the Beauchamps, from whom it passed by female heirs to the Bassets and Greys. Richard Grey, Earl of Kent, sold it in 1514 to the Somersets, and the Somersets, in 1549, to the Duncombes; from this last family it passed to the Bartons and Pauncefots. The parish is bounded on the west by the Levet river, and on the east by the road from Fenny-Stratford to Dunstable: the London and Birmingham railway passes within about a mile and a half of the church. The living is a rectory, valued in the king's books at £18. 2. 11.; net income, £425; patron, P. P. Duncombe, Esq.: land was assigned in 1771, in lieu of tithes, and other tithes have been recently commuted for a rent-charge of £80. In the church are monuments to several of the early families connected with the parish. There are places of worship for Baptists and Wesleyans; and a sum of £5 is annually contributed by Mrs. Duncombe for instructing a few children.

BRICKHILL, LITTLE (ST. MARY); a parish, in the union of NEWPORT-PAGNELL, hundred of NEWPORT, county of BUCKINGHAM, 2 miles (E. S. E.) from Fenny-Stratford; containing 563 inhabitants. This place, which is situated on the great road to Holyhead, was at an early period of considerable importance, and received the grant of a market by charter dated in 1228: a fair was at the same time bestowed, to be held on the festival of St. Mary Magdalene; and by subsequent charter, another, on May 12th. The latter fair is still held, and there is also one on the 18th October; but both are insignificant. The assizes were formerly held here, and for the last time in 1638; the gallows stood upon a heath about a mile distant, and between the years 1561 and 1620 the names of forty-two executed criminal offenders appear among the burials in the parochial register. The parish comprises by computation 1254 acres; the quality of the soil is various, a strong clay being found on the level ground, and on the hills a light sand. The manufacture of plat and lace affords employment to about 200 persons. Prior to the inclosure in 1796, the living was a discharged vicarage, which it is still considered to be, or will be after the next presentation, although at present designated a perpetual curacy: it is in the patronage of the Archbishop of Canterbury, as impropriator of the rectory, which is valued in the king's books at £9; net income of the minister, £119. Under the inclosure act, land and annual money payments were assigned in lieu of tithes; the glebe consists of 58 acres. The church is an ancient structure of English architecture. There is a place of worship for Wesleyans; and an endowment of £5 per annum is applied in teaching poor boys. Fine specimens of sulphate of lime have been found.

BRICKLEHAMPTON, a chapelry, in the parish of ST. ANDREW, PERSHORE, union, and Upper division of the hundred, of PERSHORE, Pershore and E. divisions of the county of WORCESTER, 3¼ miles (S. E.) from Pershore; containing 173 inhabitants. The parish is bounded by the river Avon, and intersected by the road between Evesham and Pershore; it contains 859 acres. The living, which is valued in the king's books at £2. 14. 2., is annexed to the vicarage of Pershore: the chapel, dedicated to St. Michael, is a neat stone edifice with a brick tower.

BRICKLETON, a tything, in the parish of HURST-BOURN-TARRANT, union of ANDOVER, hundred of PAS-

TROW, Kingsclere and N. divisions of the county of SOUTHAMPTON; containing 145 inhabitants.

BRIDEKIRK (ST. BRIDGET), a parish, in the union of COCKERMOUTH, ALLERDALE ward below Derwent, W. division of CUMBERLAND; comprising the townships of Bridekirk, Great and Little Broughton, Dovenby, Papcastle, Ribton, and Tallentire; and containing 2112 inhabitants, of whom 121 are in the township of Bridekirk, 2 miles (N. by W.) from Cockermouth. This parish, which takes its name from its patron saint, contains some quarries of limestone and white freestone, and extends about five miles along the northern bank of the river Derwent, near which the land is fertile; a wet soil, incumbent on clay or limestone, prevails on its northern side. The living is a discharged vicarage, valued in the king's books at £10. 13. 4., and in the patronage of Mrs. Dykes; net income, £137; impropriators, Mrs. Dykes, the Earl of Lonsdale, William Brown and J. S. Fisher, Esqrs., and Captain Senhouse. The church is an ancient edifice, principally in the Norman style, but modernised a few years since, by the erection of a new tower, and the enlargement of several windows: it contains a singular font, which, according to Camden, was brought from the Roman station at Papcastle, exhibiting, in rude relief, various designs symbolical of the serpent and the forbidden fruit, the expulsion of Adam and Eve from Paradise, the baptism of Christ, &c., likewise a Runic inscription. Sir Joseph Williamson, secretary of state in the reign of Charles II.; and Thomas Tickell, the poet and essayist, born in 1686, were natives of this place, each during the incumbency of his father.

BRIDE (ST.) WENTLLOOG, a parish, in the union and division of NEWPORT, Upper division of the hundred of WENTLLOOG, county of MONMOUTH, 5¼ miles (S.) from Newport; containing 247 inhabitants. It comprises by computation 1300 acres, chiefly rich moorland, and generally level; the river Usk is to the east, and the Bristol Channel to the south. The living is vicarage, with the living of Coedkernew united, value in the king's books at £4. 18. 1½.; patron, the Bishop of Llandaff. The tithes have been commuted for £62. 4 payable to the bishop, and £41. 19. to the incumbent the glebe consists of one acre.

BRIDE'S (ST.) NETHERWENT, a parish, in the union of CHEPSTOW, hundred of CALDICOT, county o MONMOUTH, 8 miles (E. by N.) from Newport; containing 179 inhabitants, of whom 128 are in the town ship of St. Bride's. This parish, with the hamlet o Llandevenny, comprises by admeasurement about 100 acres; the soil of Llandevenny is principally pasture The living is a discharged rectory, valued in the king' books at £6. 16. 3., and in the patronage of the famil of Perry: the tithes have been commuted for £14! and the glebe consists of 52 acres. The church is a ancient structure.

BRIDEFORD (ST. THOMAS à BECKET), a parish, i the union of ST. THOMAS, hundred of WONFORI Crockernwell and S. divisions of DEVON, 4 mile (E. by N.) from Moreton-Hampstead; containing 56 inhabitants. The rectory-house of Brideford was occu pied by a detachment of parliamentarian forces, pre viously to their encounter with the royalists at Bovey Heathfield, in the vicinity. The parish is bounded o the north and east by the river Teign, and intersecte in the northern part by the main road from Exeter to Moreton ; the number of acres is 4100, by computation. The soil is various, though generally fertile, and the substratum is interspersed with mineral produce : some shafts have been sunk for lead and for manganese, with every reasonable prospect of success; and there are quarries of good granite, which is wrought for various purposes. The living is a rectory, valued in the king's books at £13. 15., and in the patronage of Sir Lawrence Vaughan Palk, Bart.: the tithes have been commuted for £375, and the glebe consists of 238 acres, with a house. The church, a handsome edifice in the decorated and later English styles, was greatly enlarged and embellished in the reign of Henry VIII., and has an elegant rood-loft, a fine screen, and a richly carved pulpit; the chancel is of much earlier date. In the granite rocks, to the north-west of the parish, are some singular caverns ; and various celts and ancient coins have been found.

BRIDESTOWE (St. Bridget), a parish, in the union of Oakhampton, hundred of Lifton, Lifton and S. divisions of Devon, 6½ miles (S. W.) from Oakhampton; containing 1128 inhabitants. It comprises 3682 acres, of which 2337 are meadow and pasture, 1049 common and moor, and 296 woodland ; the soil is on a clay bottom, and the surface hilly, and intersected with some fruitful valleys : the tract of common was originally part of Dartmoor. The village is pleasantly situated on the road to Falmouth, and the surrounding scenery is enlivened by several seats. Fairs for cattle take place on the first Wednesday in June, and July 29th. The living is a rectory, with that of Sourton annexed, valued in the king's books at £32. 17. 11.; net income, £424; patron, the Bishop of Exeter : the glebe consists of 60 acres, with a corps land annexed comprising several estates, part of which has been disposed of to redeem the land-tax. The church exhibits some Norman details, and is approached by a stately avenue of lime-trees ; the tower was rebuilt in 1830, at an expense of £590, and is a handsome embattled structure. On the recent destruction of a very old church which had been converted into a poor-house, a perfect Roman arch was rescued from the ruins, and placed at the entrance of the churchyard. In ploughing a field at Millaton, in the parish, a sepulchral urn of stone, with a human skull, and some silver coins of Richard II., were discovered.

BRIDGE (St. Peter), a parish, and the head of a union, in the hundred of Bridge and Petham, lathe of St. Augustine, E. division of Kent, 3 miles (S. E. by S.) from Canterbury; containing 817 inhabitants. It comprises 1161 acres, of which 204 are in wood ; the surface is varied, and the soil in some parts chalk, alternated with a rich and fertile loam. The village is situated on the road to Dovor, at the base of two considerable hills ; and, from the salubrity of the air, has much increased within the last few years, and become the residence of many respectable families. The river Stour passes through the parish. The living is a vicarage, annexed to that of Patrixbourne : the church is principally in the Norman style, with a spire. There is a place of worship for Wesleyans. The poor law union of Bridge comprises 22 parishes or places, and contains a population of 10,981 ; the workhouse is a plain brick building.

BRIDGE-END, a hamlet, in the parish of Horbling, union of Bourne, wapentake of Aveland, parts of Kesteven, county of Lincoln, 3¾ miles (W.) from Donington ; containing 46 inhabitants. It lies on the road from Donington to Grantham, and about a mile and a half north-east of the village of Horbling.

BRIDGEFORD, GREAT and LITTLE, hamlets, in the parish of Seighford, S. division of the hundred of Pirehill, union, and N. division of the county, of Stafford, about 3½ miles (N. W.) from Stafford ; the one containing 83, and the other 154, inhabitants. These hamlets are seated on opposite banks of the river Sow, by which they are separated ; and the road from Stafford to Eccleshall passes through both. The village of Seighford is distant, southward, about a mile. The land is fertile, and highly cultivated, like the other portions of the parish.

BRIDGEHAM (St. Mary), a parish, in the union of Guiltcross, hundred of Shropham, W. division of Norfolk, 2 miles (W. by S.) from East Harling ; containing 328 inhabitants. It comprises 2702a. 28p., of which 1248 acres are arable, 426 meadow, 846 heath and furze, 75 sheep-walk, and 35 plantation. The living is a rectory, valued in the king's books at £11. 1. 0½., and in the patronage of the Crown: the tithes have been commuted for £371, and the glebe comprises a little more than 15 acres. The church is chiefly in the decorated style, and consists of a nave and chancel, separated by a carved screen ; the font is large, and curiously sculptured. There is a place of worship for Wesleyans.

BRIDGE-HILL, an ecclesiastical district, in the townships of Duffield and Belper, parish and union of Duffield, hundred of Appletree, S. division of the county of Derby. It embraces all that part of the town of Belper which lies west of the Midland railway ; and is about two miles in length, and a mile and a half in its greatest breadth. A part of the district is very steep, hilly, and rugged ; the lands are watered by the fine stream of the Derwent, and the road from Derby to Matlock passes through. The cotton and nail manufactures are carried on by a portion of the population. The district was formed in August 1845, under the act 6th and 7th of Victoria, cap. 37 ; and until the proposed erection of a church, divine service is performed in a licensed room belonging to an inn : the estimated cost of the church is £2000. Within the district are places of worship for Baptists, Wesleyan Methodists, Methodists of the New Connexion, and Plymouth Brethren. A stone, having the arms of John of Gaunt, is still preserved in the gable of a house on Mount Pleasant.

BRIDGEMERE, a township, in the parish of Wybunbury, union and hundred of Nantwich, S. division of the county of Chester, 7 miles (S. E.) from Nantwich ; containing 219 inhabitants. It comprises 1075a. 1r. 11p. The impropriate tithes have been commuted for £105, and the vicarial for £15.

BRIDGEND, a hamlet, in the parish of Bexley, union of Dartford, hundred of Lessness, lathe of Sutton-at-Hone, W. division of Kent ; containing 138 inhabitants.

BRIDGE-RULE, a parish, in the union of Holsworthy, partly in the hundred of Black Torrington, Holsworthy and N. divisions of Devon, and partly in the hundred of Stratton, E. division of Cornwall,

4 miles (W.) from Holsworthy; containing 497 inhabitants, of whom 276 are in the western or Cornwall portion. This parish, which comprises by computation 3600 acres, and is situated on the Tamar, derives its name from a bridge over that river, and from Ruald or Reginald, lord of the manor soon after the Conquest. The part in Cornwall is intersected by the Bude canal, cut chiefly for the conveyance of sand to Launceston, the road from which place to Stratton also passes through the parish. The soil is various, about one-half being good arable and pasture land, and the remainder moor and marsh; the substratum is chiefly clay, with a deep mould above, where the soil is good: the surface, in general, is hilly. Stone is quarried for road-making and building purposes. A fair is held on the 21st of June. The living is a discharged vicarage, endowed with a portion of the rectorial tithes, and valued in the king's books at £14; net income, £150; patron, the Rev. T. H. Kingdon; impropriators of the remainder of the great tithes, the Landowners. The land appertaining to the vicarage consists of about 160 acres, and an excellent glebe-house has been built. The church, which stands in Devonshire, has a tower cased with granite. There are places of worship for Primitive and Wesleyan Methodists.

BRIDGE-SOLLERS (St. Andrew), a parish, in the union of Weobley, hundred of Grimsworth, county of Hereford, 6½ miles (W. N. W.) from Hereford; containing 65 inhabitants. It comprises 725a. 9p., of which 360 acres are pasture, 355 arable, and 10 woodland. The parish is intersected by the river Wye, and partly bounded on the west by a portion of Offa's Dyke, which here abuts upon the left bank of that stream; it is crossed from east to west by the road from Hereford to Kington. The living is a discharged vicarage, endowed with a portion of the rectorial tithes, and valued in the king's books at £8. 10.: the whole tithes have been commuted for £178. 4., of which £45 belong to Sir J. G. Cotterell, Bart., the patron, £23 to the Dean and Chapter of Hereford, and £110. 4. to the incumbent, who has also an acre of glebe.

BRIDGETOWN, a township, in the parish of Berry-Pomeroy, union of Totnes, hundred of Haytor, S. division of Devon; containing 644 inhabitants.

BRIDGFORD, EAST (St. Mary), a parish, in the union of Bingham, N. division of the wapentake of Bingham, S. division of the county of Nottingham, 3 miles (N. by W.) from Bingham; containing 1110 inhabitants. Here, says Horsley, was the Margidunum of the Romans, numerous relics of whom have been discovered in the vicinity, particularly gold, silver, and brass coins of various emperors. Stukeley describes the place as lying within a mile of the station Ad Pontem: he adds, that "the Romans had a bridge across the Trent, with great buildings, cellars, and a quay for vessels to unload at;" and near a place called the Old-Wark Spring, have been found, according to the same authority, "Roman foundations of walls, and floors of houses, composed of stones set edgeways into clay, and liquid mortar run upon them." The parish comprises by computation 1777 acres, and is bounded on the north by the Trent, and on the south by the Fosse road, leading from Newark to the Nottingham and Grantham road: the soil is loamy, with some good tillage and pas-

Alfred the Great: it was afterwards enlarged by Robert de Belesme, Earl of Shrewsbury, who erected, or probably rebuilt, the castle, and fortified the town with walls and six strong gates, some portions of which are still remaining. On the earl's rebellion against his sovereign, Henry I., in 1102, the town and castle were besieged, and, after an obstinate defence, were surrendered to the victorious monarch, who gave them to Hugh de Mortimer. This grant was confirmed by Stephen; but it appears to have been little more than nominal, since "*Præpositi*," or provosts, were appointed to collect the revenue for the crown. Mortimer having risen in rebellion against Henry II., that monarch laid siege to the castle, which he nearly demolished, and in this state it lay until the reign of John; he afterwards confirmed to the inhabitants all the privileges and franchises which they had enjoyed under Henry I. In 1216, King John passed a day in the town, on his march to Worcester, where he was soon afterwards interred; in 1263, the place was taken by Simon de Montfort, Earl of Leicester.

During the civil war in the reign of Charles I., Bridgnorth, being a royal garrison, was in 1646 attacked by the parliamentarians, who gained an entrance through the churchyard, and, the royalists retiring into the castle, set fire to the town, which was nearly consumed. The parliamentarians having made the church of St. Leonard their magazine, the royalists planted cannon on the round tower of the castle, and set fire to the church; the flames spread to an adjoining college, and entirely destroyed it. The castle was now closely invested, but being strongly fortified both by nature and art, it sustained a siege of three weeks without receiving any material injury. The besiegers, despairing of success, had begun to undermine the rock on which it was built, when the garrison, having exhausted all their ammunition, capitulated on honourable terms, and retired to Worcester.

The TOWN is most romantically situated on the banks of the river Severn, which divides it into two parts, called Upper and Lower. The Upper Town is built on the summit and steep acclivities of a rock rising abruptly to the height of 180 feet from the western bank of the river, and presents an appearance singularly picturesque. Crowning the summit of the rock, at the southern extremity, are the small ruins of the square tower of the castle, declining considerably from the perpendicular line, and the modern church of St. Mary Magdalene; while at the northern extremity is the venerable church of St. Leonard, with its lofty square embattled tower, crowned with pinnacles. Upon the castle-hill walk, and forming a conspicuous object, is the reservoir, a capacious flat square tank, supported on lofty pillars of brick, assuming at a distance the appearance of a handsome portico. On the side of the rock rising from the river are several successive tiers of detached houses, intermixed with caverns and rude dwellings, and interspersed with gardens, shrubberies, and lofty trees. The walk round the castle-hill is defended by a palisade of iron, and commands a most extensive view of the surrounding country, which abounds with picturesque scenery, being richly diversified by cultivated fields, well-watered meadows, wood-crowned eminences, and barren rocks. Two streets, containing well-built houses, lead from St. Mary's church into the High-street, and

there are others of a similar character. Over the river is a stone bridge of six arches, leading into the Lower Town, the streets in which contain some modern and several ancient houses; among the latter is Cann Hall, a very antique structure in the Elizabethan style, where Prince Rupert resided in 1642, when he addressed a letter to the jury empanelled for the choice of town officers, entreating them "to select such men for their bailiffs as were well affected to his Majesty's service." The town is partially paved, and the inhabitants are supplied with soft water from the river, and with spring water from Oldbury, at the western extremity of Bridgnorth. The public library in St. Leonard's churchyard, a handsome octagonal brick building lighted by a dome, was founded by the Rev. Hugh Stackhouse, to whose memory a marble tablet has been erected over the fireplace: it was extended, by subscription, from a theological to a general library, and contained more than 4000 volumes; but is now chiefly restricted to theological works; and a new general library has been recently erected on the castle-hill. A theatre, a neat and commodious edifice of stone, was erected in 1824, on part of the site of the ancient moat of the castle, accidentally discovered; it has been since sold, and converted into shops. Races are held in July, on a race-course about a mile from the town.

The TRADE principally arises from the navigation of the river, which affords every facility for the conveyance of goods; but it has declined in consequence of the more certain transit by canals: some vessels are built; and a great quantity of malt of very superior quality, and of grain, is sent to various parts of the country. The iron-trade has greatly declined; but there is a foundry where a good deal of casting is done, and nails are made to a small extent: two carpet-manufactories were established about 1810, and increased at subsequent periods; and there is a considerable manufactory for tobacco-pipes. The market, held on Saturday, is abundantly supplied with wheat, barley, and beans, to the growth of which the land in the neighbourhood is particularly favourable. The fairs are on the third Tuesday in February; third Tuesday in March, for horned-cattle and sheep; May 1st, a pleasure and statute fair; third Tuesday in June, for wool and cattle; first Tuesday in August, for lamb's-wool and cattle; third Tuesday in September, for cattle, sheep, and cheese; October 29th, a large fair for salt butter, cheese, hops, and nuts; and on the first Tuesday after the Shrewsbury December fair, which is a great fair for cattle and general merchandise.

Seal now disused.   *Present Seal.*

The town is a BOROUGH by prescription: the first charter respecting which there is any certainty was granted by King John, in the 16th of his reign, and subsequent charters were bestowed by Henry III. and VI. By the act of the 5th and 6th of William IV., cap. 76, the corporation now consists of a mayor, four aldermen, and twelve councillors; the mayor is a justice of the peace, and there are thirteen other magistrates, appointed by a separate commission. A court of record, for the recovery of debts to any amount, was formerly held, but is now disused; general sessions of the peace are holden quarterly before the recorder, and petty-sessions by the mayor and borough justices once a fortnight. The powers of the county debt-court of Bridgnorth, established in 1847, extend over the registration-district of Bridgnorth. The municipal limits of the borough comprehend the parishes of St. Mary, St. Leonard, part of Quatford, and the liberty of Quatt-Jarvis; and comprise 3006 acres of pasture and meadow land, 70 of arable, and 5 of wood. The borough received the elective franchise in the 23rd of Edward I., and from that time has continued to return two members to parliament: the right of election was formerly vested in all the burgesses, whether resident or not; but is now, by the act of the 2nd of William IV., cap. 45, confined to the resident burgesses within seven miles, and extended to the £10 householders. The mayor is returning officer. The borough for parliamentary purposes embraces 10,731 acres, of which 5137 are arable, 5539 meadow and pasture, and 55 wood. The town-hall, erected about the year 1646, is a spacious building of timber framework and plaster, supported on pillars and arches of brick forming a covered area for the use of the market: above, is a large room where the public business of the corporation is transacted, besides a smaller apartment in which meetings of the council are held.

Bridgnorth town comprises the parishes of *St. Mary Magdalene* and *St. Leonard*, containing, respectively, 2773 and 2997 inhabitants; and gives name to a royal peculiar, of which the late Thomas Whitmore, Esq., was lay dean. The living of St. Mary Magdalene's is a perpetual curacy; net income, £258; patron, the Representative of the late Mr. Whitmore. The church, formerly the chapel belonging to the castle, and exempted by King John from all ecclesiastical jurisdiction, was made parochial in the 4th of Edward III., and rebuilt of freestone, in 1792, at the cost of about £8000; it is a handsome edifice in the Grecian style, with a lofty tower surmounted by a cupola. The interior is supported by a line of plain stone pillars of the Ionic order, and of large dimensions, extending from the entrance along each side of the body of the church. The living of St. Leonard's is also a perpetual curacy; net income, £288; patron, the Representative of Mr. Whitmore. The church, once collegiate, was erected in 1448, on the site of a structure raised in the reign of Richard I.; and was originally a magnificent edifice, comprising seven different chapels, the arches leading into which from the present nave, and now walled up, are still discernible. It suffered greatly while in the possession of the parliamentarians, during the civil war, and was consequently rebuilt, with the exception of the tower, in 1646. In each of the parishes is a parsonage-house, purchased partly from Queen Anne's Bounty, and partly by the impropriator; and about 20 acres of excellent land are attached to the livings, being a devise of Francis Wheeler in 1682: the rent, with some deductions leav-

ing about £90 per annum, is divided between the incumbents. There are places of worship for Baptists, Wesleyans, Presbyterians, and Irvingites. The free grammar school was established in 1503, and has three exhibitions to Christ-Church College, Oxford, founded by Mr. Careswell in 1689; the property, which is chiefly in land near the town, produces an annual income of about £80. The Blue-coat charity-school, kept in an old castellated brick building, over one of the ancient gates, was instituted in 1720, and is supported partly by a small endowment arising from benefactions vested in the funds; the entire income is about £100 a year. There is also a national school, maintained by subscription. The hospital in St. Leonard's churchyard, for ten aged widows, was founded in 1687, by the Rev. Francis Palmer, rector of Sandby, in Bedfordshire; the income is about £120. The almshouses in Church-lane, endowed with estates producing £130 per annum, under the direction of the trustees of charities within the borough, are for twelve widows or single daughters of burgesses. The poor law union of Bridgnorth comprises 29 parishes or places, and contains a population of 16,118.

At the southern extremity of the High-street is part of an arch which formed the entrance to the castle ward; also some portions of the walls, which inclosed an area of fourteen acres. At the northern extremity of the town, on the west bank of the river, are the remains of a convent of Grey friars, which have been converted into a malt-house: the great hall, or refectory, is still nearly in its pristine state; and the panelled oak ceiling, the stone fireplace, and many of the windows, though the lights are stopped with plaster, are in entire preservation. About a quarter of a mile south of the Lower Town was an hospital for lazars, converted in the reign of Edward IV. into a priory, and now a private mansion. In making the shrubberies to the north of the house, in 1823, thirty-seven bodies were discovered lying in rows, within eighteen inches from the surface, having evidently been buried in winding sheets and without coffins; they were in good preservation, the teeth still retaining their enamel. Some slight vestiges of the church may be traced in the walls of the out-buildings. There are also remains of several fortifications in the neighbourhood, it having been the scene of frequent battles between the Saxons and the Danes. About a mile south of the town, on the eastern bank of the river, is a large mount, with a trench on all sides except the west, on which it is defended by a rocky precipice overhanging the Severn; Robert de Montgomery had here a strongly-fortified palace. Half a mile eastward lay the forest of Morfe, which, in Leland's time, was a "hilly ground, well wooded; a forest, or chace, having deer," and for which a forester and steward were appointed from the time of Edward I. to that of Elizabeth. The brother of King Athelstan is stated to have passed the life of a hermit here; and a cave in a rock, still called the Hermitage, is supposed to have been his solitary abode. On a portion of the tract are five tumuli in quincunx, under some of which the remains of human skeletons have been discovered. The sylvan features of the forest long since disappeared, and the whole, comprising between 5000 and 6000 acres, was inclosed in 1815. Dr. Thomas Percy, Bishop of Dromore in Ireland, and compiler of *Reliques of Ancient English*

Poetry, was a native of Bridgnorth; and the house in which he is said to have been born, in 1728, is still remaining.

BRIDGWATER (St. Mary), a port, borough, market-town, and parish, having separate jurisdiction, and the head of a union, locally in the hundred of NORTH PETHERTON, W. division of SOMERSET, 35 miles (S. W.) from Bristol, and 137 (W. by S.) from London; containing 10,449 inhabitants. This place was given to Walter de Douay, one of William's followers, at the time of the Conquest, and was thence called "Burg.. Walter" and "Brugge Walter," by which names, both signifying Walter's burgh or borough, it is designated in various ancient records. William de Briwere, to whom it was granted in the reign of Henry II., built a castle in the following reign, combining the strength of a fortress with the splendour of a baronial residence; and obtained from King John the grant of a market and a fair. He founded the hospital of St. John, for a master, brethren, and thirteen poor persons of the order of St. Augustine, whose revenue at the Dissolution was £120. 19. 1¼.; he also constructed the haven, and began to erect a stone bridge of three arches over the river Parret, which was completed by Sir Thomas Trivet in the reign of Edward I. His son William founded a monastery for Grey friars, about 1230, and dedicated it to St. Francis. The barons, during their revolt against Henry III., took possession of the town in 1260.

In the civil war of the 17th century, the inhabitants embraced the royal cause; and the castle being strongly fortified, the people of the surrounding district deposited therein their money, plate, &c. The parliamentarians under Fairfax invested the town, and laid close siege to the castle: both were resolutely defended; but the town being fired on both sides of the bridge, the garrison capitulated on terms of personal indemnity, and surrendered the fortress, with all the treasure in it, and 1000 prisoners, into the hands of the enemy. The castle, having sustained considerable damage during the siege, was demolished in 1645, and the sally-port and some detached portions of the walls are all that now remain. In the reign of James II. the inhabitants favoured the pretensions of the Duke of Monmouth, who, on his arrival from Taunton, was received with great ceremony by the corporation, and proclaimed king. He remained for some time in the town; and having, from the tower of the church, reconnoitred the royal army encamped on Sedgemoor, he rashly resolved to hazard the battle that terminated so fatally to his ambition. His adherents in the town suffered greatly for their attachment to his cause, under the legal severity of Jeffreys, and the military executions of Kirke.

The TOWN is pleasantly situated in a well-wooded and nearly level part of the county, the view being bounded on the north-east by the Mendip hills, and on the west by the Quantock hills: the river Parret divides it into two parts, connected by a handsome iron bridge of one arch. The streets are spacious and well paved, and the

Arms.

town is lighted with gas, under an act obtained in 1834: the houses, chiefly of brick, are uniform and well built; and there is an ample supply of excellent water from springs. The western part is particularly clean. In the eastern part, termed Eastover, very great improvement has been effected. There is a foreign trade, consisting in the importation of wine, hemp, tallow, and timber; but the trade of the port is principally coastwise. Coal is brought free of duty from Monmouthshire and Wales, and is conveyed into the interior of the country by a canal to Taunton, Tiverton, Ilminster, and Chard, and by the river to Langport and Ilchester: in 1837, an act was obtained to enable the company of proprietors to continue the line of the canal below the town. That portion of the Bristol and Exeter railway, extending from Bristol to Bridgwater, was opened June 14th, 1841; and the remaining portion of the line, between Bridgwater and Exeter, was completed in May, 1844. In 1845 an act was passed for improving the navigation of the river, extending the quays, and making a short railway between the quays and the Bristol and Exeter railway; and another act, passed in 1846, authorises a railway from Bridgwater to Stoford, on the coast, where a harbour has been projected. The quay is accessible to ships of 200 tons' burthen, and furnished with every appendage requisite for the convenience of commerce. A principal source of employment is the making of bricks for general use, and scouring-bricks; the latter composed of a mixture of clay and sand deposited by the river: they are usually called Bath or Flanders' brick, and this is the only place in the kingdom where they are made. The market-days are Tuesday, Thursday, and Saturday; Thursday's market is for cheese, corn, and cattle, and is much frequented. The market-house, lately erected, is a handsome building, surmounted with a dome and lantern, and having a semicircular portico of the Ionic order. The fairs are on the first Monday in Lent, July 24th, October 2nd (which continues for three days), and December 27th.

The first charter of INCORPORATION was bestowed in the reign of John, and others were subsequently granted by Edward II. and III., Henry IV., VII., and VIII., Mary, Elizabeth, James I., and Charles I. and II. Under the act of the 5th and 6th of William IV., c. 76, the corporation now consists of a mayor, 6 aldermen, and 18 councillors; the number of magistrates is 13. The borough first sent representatives to parliament in the 23rd of Edward I., since which time it has continued to return two members. The right of election was formerly vested in the householders resident within the borough (which comprised 158 acres), paying scot and lot; but it was extended, by the act of the 2nd of William IV., cap. 45, to the £10 householders of an enlarged district containing 742 acres, which, both for parliamentary and municipal purposes, forms the present borough: the mayor is the returning officer. The corporation hold quarterly courts of session for the trial of all offenders, except those accused of capital crimes; and a court of record for the recovery of

Corporation Seal.

debts to any amount. The powers of the county debt-court of Bridgwater, established in 1847, extend over the registration-district of Bridgwater. The summer assizes, alternately with Wells, and the summer-sessions for the county, are held here. The judges' mansion is a handsome modern edifice, containing apartments for the judges, the borough court-rooms, and a room for the grand jury. The borough prison contains distinct de-partments for debtors and criminals, the latter of whom are only confined here previously to trial, or to their committal to the county gaol.

The LIVING is a vicarage, with the rectory of Chilton Trinity united, valued in the king's books at £11. 7. 6., and in the patronage of the Crown, with a net income of £342 : the impropriation belongs to the corporation. The parish church is an ancient and handsome struc-ture, with a square embattled tower and a lofty spire : it has a rich porch in the decorated style of English architecture, and the altar is embellished with a fine painting of the Descent from the Cross, found on board a captured French privateer, and presented by the Hon. A. Poulett. An additional church, dedicated to the *Holy Trinity*, was erected in 1840, at an expense of £4000, and was consecrated on the 16th of June, in that year ; it is a substantial structure in the later English style, and contains 1100 sittings : a good altar-piece was presented by Mr. Baker, an artist. The living is a perpetual curacy, in the Vicar's gift ; net income, £150. The church of *St. John the Baptist*, Eastover, completed in April 1845, and consecrated in August 1846, was built by the Rev. John Moore Capes, at a cost of nearly £10,000, and is a very handsome structure in the early English style, with stained-glass windows; it has an organ which cost £600, presented by another member of the Capes family. An ecclesiastical parish is annexed to it under the 6th and 7th Vict., cap. 37, and the living is a perpetual curacy in the gift of the Bishop of Bath and Wells ; net income, £150. There are places of worship for Baptists, the Society of Friends, Independents, Wes-leyans, Roman Catholics, Unitarians, and others. The free grammar school was founded in 1561, and endowed by Queen Elizabeth with £6. 13. 4. per annum, charged on the tithes, to which two donations of £100 each were added : it is under the control of the corporation, who appoint the master, and under the inspection of the bishop of the diocese. A school, now conducted on Dr. Bell's system, was established by Dr. John Morgan, in 1723, and endowed with 97 acres of land ; the management is exercised by charity trustees appointed by the lord chancellor, under the Municipal act. A school was also instituted in 1781, by Mr. Edward Fackerell, who endowed it with the dividends on £3000 in the three per cent. consols., and rents, producing to-gether an annual income of £174, for educating the children of his relatives. The infirmary, a commodious building, was established in 1813, and is supported by subscription. The union of Bridgwater comprises 40 parishes or places, with a population of 31,778. Ad-miral Blake was born here in 1599, and received the rudiments of his education in the grammar school.

BRIDLINGTON, or BURLINGTON (ST. MARY), a parish, and the head of a union, in the wapentake of DICKERING, E. riding of YORK ; comprising the town-ships of Bridlington, Buckton, Hilderthorpe with Wils-thorpe, and Sewerby with Marton, the hamlet of Easton,

BRIDPORT (St. Mary), a sea-port, borough, market-town, and parish, having separate jurisdiction, and the head of a union, in the Bridport division of Dorset, 14¾ miles (W.) from Dorchester, and 134 (W. S. W.) from London, on the high road to Exeter; containing 4787 inhabitants. This was a town of some importance in the time of Edward the

Seal of the New Corporation.

Confessor, and is mentioned in Domesday book as having a mint and an ecclesiastical establishment. During the civil war in the reign of Charles I. it was garrisoned by the parliament; but, not being a place of much strength, was alternately in the possession of each party. In 1685 it was surprised by some troops in the interest of the Duke of Monmouth, under Lord Grey; these were defeated by the king's forces, and twelve of the principal insurgents were afterwards executed. The TOWN is situated in a fertile vale surrounded by hills, having on the west the river Bride or Brit, from which it takes its name, and on the east the Asher, over which are several bridges : these rivers unite a little below the town, and fall into the sea at the harbour, about a mile and a half to the south. It is chiefly formed by three spacious streets, containing many handsome modern houses; and is partially paved, amply supplied with water, and well lighted with gas. A mechanics' institution, containing a reading-room, and lecture and class rooms, has been built at the expense of H. Warburton, Esq., a late member for the borough.

The TRADE of the port consists principally in the importation of hemp, flax, and timber, from Russia and the Baltic, and timber from America and Norway: there is also a considerable coasting-trade, by which the adjacent towns are supplied with coal from the north of England, with culm from Wales, and with other articles of general consumption. Many coasting-vessels, particularly smacks, for the trading companies of Scotland, are built at this port; they are considered remarkable for strength, beauty, and fast sailing. The harbour is situated at the bottom of the bay formed by Portland Point, on the east, and the headlands near Torbay on the west. An act for restoring and rebuilding it was obtained in the 8th of George I., the preamble to which recites that, by reason of a great sickness that had swept away the greater part of the wealthy inhabitants, and other accidents, the haven was choked with sand, and the piers had fallen into ruins: the work was begun in 1742, and, by the expenditure of large sums, great improvement was made. Another act was obtained in 1823, since which more than £20,000, raised on the security of the rates and duties, have been expended, so that the harbour is now perfectly safe and commodious. This is a bonding port for wines, spirits, hemp, iron in bars, timber, tallow, hides, and other articles; the amount of import duties is somewhat more than £6200 per annum. An act was passed in 1845, for the construction of the Wilts, Somerset, and Weymouth railway, with a branch of 11¼ miles to this town. The principal articles of manufacture are nets, lines, small twine, shoe-thread, girth-

3 D

webbing, cordage, and sail-cloth, for the use of the home and colonial fisheries, particularly those of Newfoundland and Nova Scotia: 10,000 persons are generally thus employed in the town and neighbourhood. In the reign of Henry VIII., the cordage for the whole of the English navy was ordered to be made at Bridport, or within five miles of it, exclusively. The markets are on Wednesday and Saturday; fairs are held on April 6th and Oct. 11th, for horses, horned-cattle, and cheese, and there is a smaller fair on Holy-Thursday.

Old Corporation Seal.

The GOVERNMENT, until recently, was regulated by charter of incorporation, originally granted by Henry III., confirmed by Richard II., Henry VII., Edward VI., and Elizabeth, and renewed and extended by James I. and Charles II. By the act of the 5th and 6th of William IV., cap. 76, the corporation now consists of a mayor, six aldermen, and eighteen councillors; and the borough has been divided into the north and south wards, the municipal and parliamentary boundaries being the same: the number of magistrates is eight. The elective franchise was conferred in the 23rd of Edward I., since which time the borough has regularly returned two members to parliament. The right of election was formerly vested in the inhabitants of the borough (which comprised 92 acres), paying scot and lot, in number about 250; but the act of the 2nd of William IV., cap. 45, extended it to the £10 householders of an enlarged district, containing by computation 388 acres. The mayor is returning officer. The powers of the county debt-court of Bridport, established in 1847, extend over the greater part of the registration-districts of Bridport and Beaminster. The town-hall is a handsome building of brick and Portland stone, containing, in the upper story, a large room for judicial and other purposes, a council chamber, town-clerk's offices, &c.: it was erected in 1786 on the site of the ancient chapel of St. Andrew, in the centre of the town, by an act of parliament. There is also a lock-up house for the confinement of prisoners before committal.

The LIVING is a discharged rectory, valued in the king's books at £10. 12. 3½.; net income, £166; patron, the Earl of Ilchester. The church, which appears to have been erected in the reign of Henry VII., about 1485, is a handsome and spacious cruciform structure, chiefly in the later English style, with a square embattled tower seventy-two feet high, rising from the centre, and crowned with pinnacles: it contains many interesting monuments; among them is an altar-tomb of William, son of Sir Eustace Dabrigecourt, of Hainault, related to Queen Philippa. There are places of worship for the Society of Friends, Independents, Wesleyans, and Unitarians. A free school was founded and endowed in 1708, by Daniel Taylor, one of the Society of Friends; and there are almshouses and other charities, under the management of trustees appointed in 1837, by the court of chancery. A handsome stone building for the poor law union of Bridport, and a register and other offices, have been lately erected;

miles (N. N. E.) from Newcastle-upon-Tyne; containing 97 inhabitants. It comprises an area of 515 acres, and contains quarries of excellent freestone, and an extensive colliery opened some years ago by Lord Ravensworth and partners : the whole township belongs to the Ogle family, of Causey Park, near Morpeth. Here are the ruins of an ancient castle, of great interest to antiquaries, and very similar in appearance to Loch Leven Castle in Scotland, where Queen Mary was confined.

BRIERLEY, a township, in the parish and union of LEOMINSTER, hundred of WOLPHY, county of HEREFORD ; containing 89 inhabitants.

BRIERLEY, a township, in the parish of FELKIRK, wapentake of STAINCROSS, W. riding of YORK, 6½ miles N. E. by E.) from Barnsley ; containing 491 inhabitants. This township, which includes the hamlet of Brimethorpe, is situated on the road from Barnsley to Pontefract, and comprises about 2490 acres : a coal-pit s in operation. Grimethorpe Hall, an ancient mansion, had formerly a small Roman Catholic chapel, and extensive pleasure-grounds. The tithes of this place, with those of South Hiendly and Shafton, have been commuted for £716.19. payable to the Archbishop of York, and £114. 8. to the vicar of the parish ; there is a glebe of 1¼ acre. The Wesleyans have a place of worship. On the lofty hill of Ringstead is a venerable oak measuring thirteen yards in circumference, the hollow of which is sufficient to admit of six men sitting round a able.

BRIERLEY-HILL, a district chapelry, in the parish of KING'S SWINFORD, union of STOURBRIDGE, N. division of the hundred of SEISDON, S. division of the county of STAFFORD, 2¼ miles (N. N. E.) from Stourbridge. This is a populous village and chapelry, consisting of several streets, and having in its vicinity numerous collieries, and iron-works on a large scale ; team-boilers and various other heavy articles in iron being manufactured here. There are also glass-works, and some potteries. It appears by an old deed, that coal and ironstone were obtained at this place as early as the 16th of Edward III. The living is a perpetual curacy, with a net income of £210 ; patron, the Rector of King's Swinford ; impropriator, Lord Ward. The chapel was erected in 1767, was enlarged in 1823 and again in 1837, and will now accommodate nearly 2000 persons : a magnificent organ has lately been erected at an expense of 400 guineas. In 1834, a national school was built for 500 children, at a cost of £700, whereof £270 were given by the Lords of the Treasury ; and in 1846, a handsome infant school was added, the expense of which was £400. The first minister here, was the Rev. Thomas Moss, author of the elegant little poem called The Beggar's Petition ; he afterwards removed to Trentham, as domestic chaplain to the Marquess of Stafford.

BRIERS, county of YORK.—See OWRAM, SOUTH.

BRIERTON, a township, in the parish of STRANTON, union of STOCKTON-UPON-TEES, N. E. division of STOCKTON ward, S. division of the county of DURHAM, 3¼ miles (E. N. E.) from Stockton ; containing 27 inhabitants. The manor belonged from the earliest date of the records to the family of Graystock. It afterwards passed to the Dacres; and Lord William Howard, who married Elizabeth, younger sister and coheiress of

George, Lord Dacre, seems to have had the Durham estates on partition with his brother, the Earl of Arundel, husband of Anne, the elder sister. The place was subsequently the property of the Blacketts.

BRIERY-COTTAGES and GRETA-MILLS, an extra-parochial district, connected with the chapelry of ST. JOHN CASTLERIGG, parish of CROSTHWAITE, union of COCKERMOUTH, ALLERDALE ward below Derwent, W. division of the county of CUMBERLAND ; containing 100 inhabitants.

BRIERYHURST, or BREREHURST, a hamlet, in the parish of WOLSTANTON, union of WOLSTANTON and BURSLEM, N. division of the hundred of PIREHILL and of the county of STAFFORD, 5½ miles (N.) from Newcastle ; containing 1518 inhabitants. It comprises an area of 922 acres, and includes the eastern portion of Merocop, a rugged and lofty hill dividing the counties of Stafford and Chester : the district is rich in mineral produce, and the hamlet contains mines of coal and ironstone, which are extensively worked at Kidsgrove and in the immediate vicinity. Several blast furnaces for smelting iron-ore have been erected by Thomas Kinnersly, Esq. A handsome church has been built and endowed by Mr. Kinnersly, capable of accommodating 400 persons : it has a tower, in which are six bells and a clock ; and nearly adjoining are a parsonage and school-house, erected by the same gentleman. They are all situated in a secluded spot, embosomed in woods, and have a very picturesque appearance. There is a place of worship for Wesleyans.

BRIGG.—See GLANDFORD-BRIGG.

BRIGHAM (ST. BRIDGET), a parish, comprising the borough and market-town of Cockermouth, and the townships of Blindbothel, Brigham, Buttermere, Eaglesfield, Embleton, Gray-Southan, Mosser, Setmurthy, and Whinfell, in the union of COCKERMOUTH, ALLERDALE ward above Derwent, W. division of CUMBERLAND ; the whole containing 7397 inhabitants, of whom 490 are in the township of Brigham, 2 miles (W.) from Cockermouth. This parish is situated among the lakes Bassenthwaite, Buttermere, Crummock, and Loweswater, which, with the rivers Derwent and Maron, form its boundaries ; and is intersected by the Cocker, which falls into the Derwent at Cockermouth. The surface is hilly, but since the inclosure of the waste land, the high grounds have been chiefly brought into cultivation : there are quarries of limestone, freestone, and blue slate, and a mine of coal has been opened. The village, which contains some respectable dwelling-houses, is built upon an eminence on the south bank of the Derwent, commanding a richly diversified prospect. The living is a discharged vicarage, valued in the king's books at £20. 16. 0½ ; net income, £190 ; patrons and impropriators, the family of Lowther, to whom, in 1813, land was assigned in lieu of all tithes for the township of Brigham. The church, situated at the distance of half a mile from the village, has a handsome window of five lights in the decorated style, at the east end of the south aisle ; a curious circular window of the same date ; and a monumental arch richly canopied. A chapel of ease was erected by the Rev. Dr. Thomas, in 1840 ; and there are separate incumbencies at Buttermere, Cockermouth, Embleton, Lorton, Mosser, Setmurthy, and Wythrop. The dissenters have several places of worship.

BRIG BRIG

BRIGHAM, a township, in the parish of Foston-upon-Wolds, union of Driffield, wapentake of Dickering, E. riding of York, about 5½ miles (S. E.) from Driffield; containing 147 inhabitants. It is situated on the navigable river Hull, near Frodingham Bridge, and comprises by computation 1470 acres. Land and money payments were assigned in lieu of tithes, in 1766. There is a place of worship for Wesleyans.

BRIGHOUSE, an ecclesiastical district, in the township of Hipperholme-cum-Brighouse, parish and union of Halifax, Upper division of the wapentake of Morley, W. riding of York, 4 miles (E. by N.) from Halifax; containing 3200 inhabitants. This flourishing and rapidly increasing place, which has grown into some importance within a comparatively recent period, is beautifully situated on the road from Bradford to Huddersfield, and in the fertile valley of the Calder; the village is spacious and well built, and contains many handsome houses. An act for lighting and otherwise improving the place, was passed in 1843. In the immediate vicinity are pleasing villas and detached ranges of building, forming a considerable appendage to the village, and adding much to the appearance of the surrounding scenery. The manufacture of worsted and cotton goods is carried on, several large mills being in full operation; the manufacture of cards used in the woollen, flax, and cotton trades, is also carried on to a great extent, and there are some flour-mills, and tanneries. In the neighbourhood are the valuable quarries called Cromwell Bottom, from which large quantities of building and flag stone are sent to various parts of the kingdom, by the Calder and Hebble navigation. The river Calder forms the southern boundary of the township, and at the village is a station on the old Leeds and Manchester railway, with a spacious depôt for merchandise. A fair for cattle and pigs is held on the day after the festival of St. Martin. The church, dedicated to St. Martin, was erected at an expense of £3200, principally a grant from Her Majesty's Commissioners, and was consecrated in 1830; it is a good edifice in the later English style, with a square embattled tower crowned by pinnacles, and contains 1150 sittings, of which 500 are free. The living is a perpetual curacy, at present in the patronage of the Vicar of Halifax, with an income of £150, and a handsome parsonage-house erected at a cost of £1600.—See Hipperholme.

BRIGHTHAMPTON, a hamlet, in the parish of Bampton, union of Witney, hundred of Bampton, county of Oxford, 4¾ miles (S. E. by S.) from Witney; containing 120 inhabitants.

BRIGHTLING (St. Thomas à Becket), a parish, in the union of Battle, partly in the hundred of Henhurst, but chiefly in that of Netherfield, rape of Hastings, E. division of Sussex, 4 miles (N. W.) from Battle; containing 692 inhabitants. This parish comprises about 4000 acres, of which 1020 are arable, 850 meadow and pasture, 120 common, 120 acres hop-grounds, and 1630 wood. It is diversified with gentle undulations, rising in some places to a considerable eminence; the highest parts of Rose Hill have an elevation of more than 600 feet above the level of the sea. Limestone and sandstone are found in abundance, and great quantities of the latter are quarried for building; ironstone was formerly wrought, and there were furnaces for the smelting of iron-ore. The living is a rec-

372

tory, valued in the king's books at £11; patron and incumbent, the Rev. J. B. Hayley, whose tithes have been commuted for £642. The church is a handsome edifice, chiefly in the later English style, with a low embattled tower, and contains several neat monuments, among which is one to John Fuller, Esq., whose bust is finely sculptured by Chantrey. The Rev. William Hayley, who collected ample materials for a History of Sussex, and whose manuscripts are in the British Museum, was rector of the parish, and was interred here. At Rose Hill is a chalybeate spring.

BRIGHTLINGSEA (All Saints), a parish, in the union of Lexden and Winstree, hundred of Tendring, N. division of Essex, 9 miles (S. E.) from Colchester; containing 2005 inhabitants. It constitutes a peninsula, formed by the estuary of the river Colne on the west, and that of a smaller river on the east; and comprises 3090 acres, of which 128 are common or waste. The living is a discharged vicarage, valued in the king's books at £17. 0. 5.; patron, the Bishop of London; impropriator, M. D. Magens, Esq.: the great tithes have been commuted for £240, and the vicarial for £150. The church is situated about a mile and a half from the village. There is a place of worship for Wesleyans.

BRIGHTON (St. Nicholas), a sea-port, borough, market-town, and parish, in the hundred of Whalesbone, rape of Lewes, E. division of Sussex, 30 miles (E.) from Chichester, and 52 (S.) from London; containing 46,661 inhabitants. This place, in the Saxon Brighthelmstun, in Domesday book Bristlemeston, and now, by contraction, generally Brighton, is supposed to have taken its name from the Saxon bishop, Brighthelme, who resided in the vicinity. It was anciently a fortified town of considerable importance, and by some antiquaries is thought to have been the place where Cæsar landed on his invasion of Britain; an opinion probably suggested by the quantity of Roman coins found in the town, the vast number of human bones, of extraordinary size, which have been discovered for nearly a mile along the coast westward, and the traces of lines and intrenchments in the immediate vicinity, bearing strong marks of Roman construction. From a fortified town, it was, by successive encroachments of the sea, reduced to a comparatively inconsiderable village; and soon after the Conquest the place was inhabited principally by fishermen. It was frequently assaulted by the French, by whom, in the reign of Henry VIII., it was plundered and burnt; and as a protection against their future attacks, fortifications were erected, which were repaired and enlarged by Queen Elizabeth, who built a wall, with four lofty gates of freestone, for its better defence. After the fatal battle of Worcester, Charles II. arrived here on the 13th of October, 1651, and on the following morning embarked for France, in a small vessel belonging to the port, which landed him safely at Feschamp in Normandy, and which, after the Restoration, was taken into the royal navy as a fifth-rate, and named the "Royal Escape." In the years 1665 and 1669, an ir-

Town Seal.

-uption of the sea destroyed a considerable part of the own, and inundated a large tract of land adjoining; nd in 1703, 1705, and 1706, the fortifications were ndermined, and many houses destroyed by tremen- lous storms and inundations that threatened its anni- hilation.

In the reign of George II., Brighton began to rise nto consideration as a bathing-place, from the writings f Dr. Russell, a resident physician, who recommended he sea-water here, as containing a greater proportion of alt than that of other places, and being therefore more fficacious in the cure of scrofulous and glandular com- plaints. Its progress was accelerated in 1760 by the discovery of a chalybeate spring, the water of which being successfully administered as a tonic, in cases of nfirm or debilitated constitutions, the town became the resort of invalids from all parts of the country; and it ultimately obtained the very high rank which it now enjoys as a fashionable watering-place, under the auspices of George IV., who, in 1784, when Prince of Wales, commenced the erection of a palace here.

The TOWN is pleasantly situated on elevated ground rising gently on the east and west from a level called the Steyne, supposed to have been the line of the ancient Stayne-street, or Roman road from Arundel to Dorking. It adjoins a bay of the English Channel, formed by the promontories of Beachy Head and Worthing Point; ex- tends nearly three miles from east to west; and is sheltered by a range of hills on the north and north-east, and by the South Downs. Its form, including the more recent additions, is quadrangular; and the streets, which are spacious, and intersect each other at right angles, are well paved, and lighted with gas : an act was obtained in 1834, for more plentifully supplying the town with water; in 1839 and 1843 acts were procured for the better lighting of the town, and in 1839 one for the establish- ment of a general cemetery. The houses in the older part are irregularly built, but the more modern part con- sists of handsome ranges of uniform buildings, many of which are strikingly elegant, and situated on the cliffs. Kemp Town, in the extreme east, contains some splendid mansions : there are also fine ranges of building, with a square, in the extreme west, towards Hove; and in other parts are agreeable squares. The Pavilion, begun in 1784, and completed in 1827, by George IV., is in the oriental style of architecture, on the. model of the Kremlin at Moscow. It has a handsome stone front, 200 feet in length, with a circular building in the centre, surrounded by an arcade of elliptic form, with interco- lumniations carried up to the parapet, and crowned with a splendid oriental dome, terminating in a slender and richly-embellished finial, and encircled with four mina- rets of.nearly equal elevation. The central range is connected, by corridors of circular buildings, crowned with domes of similar character, but of smaller dimen- sions, with two quadrangular and boldly-projecting wings, round which are carried arcades similar to that of the centre, with lofty pagoda roofs, and minarets rising from the angles. The interior contains a splendid vestibule and grand hall, a Chinese gallery of costly magnificence, a music-room, banqueting-room, rotunda, and numerous stately apartments, all decorated in the most sumptuous style of oriental splendour. Connected with the palace on the west, is the private royal chapel, consecrated in 1822; and behind it are the royal stables,

373

a circular structure, appropriately designed in the Arabian style, and surmounted by a dome of glass : on the east side of the quadrangle in which they are situated, is a racquet-court, and on the west a riding- house.

Hot and cold sea-water, vapour, and shower baths have been constructed in the town, with every regard to the convenience of the invalid : those at the New Steyne hotel are supplied with water raised from the sea, to the height of 600 feet, by an engine, and conveyed through a tunnel excavated in the rock. The chalybeate spring, about half a mile west of the old church, is inclosed within a neat building; and the water, which deposits an ochreous sediment, has been found very beneficial as a restorative, and is in high repute : the German spa, also, near the Park, affords every variety of mineral water, artificially prepared. There are several public libraries : assemblies are held at the Ship hotel, in which are spacious rooms superbly fitted up; and a concert and ball room, in Cannon-place, lately erected, is said to be one of the best adapted to its purpose in the kingdom. The theatre, erected in 1807, is externally an unadorned building, with a plain portico, but is elegantly fitted up within. The races, which continue for three days, are held on the Downs, in the first week in August. The Royal Gardens, to the north of the town, including a spacious cricket-ground, are appropriated to various amusements; and the Downs afford pleasant and extensive rides. The Old Steyne is adorned with a bronze statue of George IV. by Chantrey, erected in 1828, at an expense of £3000, raised by subscription; and comprises the North and South Parades, and several other agreeable walks : the inclosures have been much improved of late, and are ornamented with a fountain, which was completed in 1846. The splendid suspension chain pier, constructed in 1821, at an expense of £30,000, under the superintendence of Capt. Sir S. Brown, R.N., forms a favourite promenade, 1130 feet in length : during a violent storm on the 15th of October, 1833, it sustained considerable injury, but it was effectually re- paired by subscription, under the direction of Capt. Brown. The Esplanade, 1200 feet long and 40 feet wide, connects the pier with the Steyne. Among the more recent improvements is the construction of a sea-wall, on the beach in front of the town, extending from Mid- dle-street to Kemp Town, a distance of a mile and a half; it forms one compact and solid mass, presenting a formidable barrier to further encroachments of the sea : a beautiful carriage drive was formed, and the total ex- pense of the undertaking exceeded £100,000. There are barracks for infantry in the town, and for cavalry at the distance of a mile, on the road to Lewes. The artillery barracks on the western cliff, where there is a battery of heavy ordnance for the defence of the beach, are now used as dwelling-houses.

Steam-vessels sail from this place or Shoreham to Dieppe and Havre; but few vessels discharge their cargoes on the beach, the great quantity of articles for the supply of the town being landed at Shoreham har- bour, and thence conveyed hither by land carriage or railway. The principal branch of trade is the fishery, in which about 100 boats are employed : the mackerel season commences in April, and the herring season in October; and soles, turbot, skate, and other flat fish, are also taken in great quantities, and sent to the

London market. The making of nets and tackle for the fishermen, the materials of which are brought from Bridport, affords employment to a portion of the inhabitants. The London and Brighton railway was constructed by a company, incorporated by act of parliament passed in July 1837, by which they were empowered to raise a joint-stock capital of £1,800,000, and by loan £600,000. The line was opened Sept. 21st, 1841. It diverges from the London and Croydon railway, about 9¼ miles from London, and reaches its termination at Church-street, Brighton, whence there is a branch of 5½ miles to Shoreham, opened in May, 1840 : the Shoreham branch has been since extended to Worthing, Arundel, Chichester, and Portsmouth ; and a line has been completed from Brighton to Lewes and Hastings. The Brighton station is an elegant structure in the Grecian style, surrounded by a colonnade, above which is a handsome balustrade. The market was established by act of parliament, in 1773 : the principal day is Thursday, but there are daily markets for the supply of the inhabitants. The fairs are on Holy-Thursday and Sept. 4th. A new and commodious market-house was built on the site of the old workhouse, in 1829. By the act of the 2nd of William IV., cap. 45, the town was constituted a borough, consisting of the parishes of Brighton and Hove, with the privilege of sending two members to parliament ; the returning officer is annually appointed by the sheriff of the county. The town is within the jurisdiction of the county magistrates, who hold meetings every Monday and Thursday. A constable, eight headboroughs, and other officers are chosen annually at the court leet for the hundred ; and the direction of police and parochial affairs is entrusted, under an act of parliament, to a corporate body of 112 commissioners elected by the inhabitants, who appoint a town-clerk, surveyor, collectors of tolls and duties, police officers, &c. The powers of the county debt-court of Brighton, established in 1847, extend over the registration-district of Brighton, and part of that of Steyning. A new town-hall has been erected on the site of the old market-house, near the centre of the town, at an expense of £30,000 ; it is a very large edifice, ornamented with three stately porticoes, and contains offices for the magistrates, commissioners, directors of the poor, &c., the lower part being used as a market-place.

The LIVING is a vicarage, with the rectory of West Blatchington consolidated, valued in the king's books at £20. 2. 1½.; net income, £1041 ; patron, the Bishop of Chichester ; impropriator, T. R. Kemp, Esq. The parish church is a spacious ancient structure, partly in the decorated, and partly in the later, English style, with a square embattled tower, which, from the situation of the church on the summit of a hill, 150 feet above the level of the sea, serves as a landmark to mariners. It contains a fine screen of richly carved oak, and an antique font, said to have been brought from Normandy in the reign of William the Conqueror, which is embellished with sculptured representations of the Last Supper, and of the miracles of our Saviour. St. Peter's church is an elegant structure at the north end of the town, in the later English style, with a square embattled tower crowned with pinnacles, erected in 1827, at an expense of £18,000, partly by the Parliamentary Commissioners, and containing 1840 sittings, of which 940 are free. The living is a perpetual curacy ; net income, £350 ;
374

patron, the Vicar. The *Chapel Royal*, in Prince's-place, erected in 1793, is a neat plain edifice, containing 900 sittings, of which 200 are free : the living is a perpetual curacy ; net income, £180 ; patron, the Vicar. The church of *St. James*, in St. James's street, contains 1000 sittings, of which 300 are free : the living is a perpetual curacy ; net income, £181 ; patrons, the Trustees of the late N. Kemp, Esq. The church of *St. Mary*, in the same street, is a handsome structure in the Grecian style, with a portico of the Doric order, and contains 1100 sittings, of which 240 are free : the living is a perpetual curacy ; net income, £100 ; patron and incumbent, the Rev. H. V. Elliott. The church of *St. George*, in Kemp Town, is a well-built edifice in the Grecian style, containing 1450 sittings, of which 390 are free : the living is a perpetual curacy ; net income, £150 ; patrons, L. Peel, Esq., and the Rev. J. S. M. Anderson, the incumbent. The church of the *Holy Trinity*, Ship-street, contains 900 sittings, of which 200 are free : the living is a perpetual curacy ; net income, £150 ; patron and incumbent, the Rev. C. E. Kennaway. *St. Margaret's*, Cannon-place, was built in 1827, is in the Grecian style, and contains 1000 sittings, of which 200 are free : the living is a perpetual curacy, in the gift and incumbency of the Rev. F. Reade, with a net income of £150. The church of *All Souls*, Upper Edward-street, erected in 1833, contains 1100 sittings, nearly all free : the living is a perpetual curacy ; net income, £100 ; patron, the Vicar. *Christ-Church*, in the Montpelier-road, was consecrated April, 1838, and contains 1076 sittings, of which 624 are free : the living is a perpetual curacy, in the gift of the Vicar ; net income, £420. The church of *St. John the Evangelist*, Carlton-Hill, contains 1225 sittings, of which 625 are free : the living is a perpetual curacy, in the patronage of the Vicar ; net income, £90. The foundation-stone of *All Saints'* church, West-street, was laid in April, 1846 ; the building is in the early decorated style, and was erected partly by the Church Commissioners, partly by the Wagner family, and partly by general subscription. A neat church, with a spire, has also been just completed at Kemp Town ; and besides these is *St. Andrew's*, Waterloo-street, in Hove parish. There are places of worship for Baptists, Independents, the Society of Friends, the Connexion of the Countess of Huntingdon, Huntingtonians, Scottish Seceders, Wesleyans, and others ; also Bethel chapel, belonging to the Mariners' Friend Society ; a Roman Catholic chapel, and a synagogue.

Brighton College, opened January 26th, 1847, provides for the sons of noblemen and gentlemen a course of education of the highest order, in conformity with Church principles. It was established by a proprietary, who appoint a patron, four vice-patrons, and a council consisting of a president, four vice-presidents, and twelve other members : there are a principal, a vice-principal and theological tutor, a head-master, and seven assistant-masters. The pupils are divided into two departments, the senior and the junior ; and those in the former wear an academical dress : three scholarships of £30 a year each have been founded. The building occupies an elevated site at Kemp Town, near the new church, and is in the Elizabethan style ; it is of compact form, and the grounds around it are inclosed by a substantial wall, in some parts very lofty. Of the numerous *Free Schools* the principal are, the school in Gardener-

several excellent hotels and boarding-houses have been built; and the accommodation which the place affords, the salubrity of its air, and the convenience of bathing, have made it the residence of eminent merchants, and the resort of visiters generally of the wealthy classes. The sandy beach is very smooth, dry, and firm; and the water on the shore, beautifully pellucid. From the higher grounds are extensive views of the Welsh mountains, the opposite port of Liverpool, and the shipping on the Mersey. A reservoir has been constructed for supplying the inhabitants with water, and on the shore is a spring of fine fresh water, which, though covered over by the tide, is perfectly pure when the sea retires. Upon the Black rock, where the Mersey enters the Irish Channel, is a very strong fort, mounting fifteen large guns, and approached from the main land by a drawbridge; and further off the shore is a small light-house, on the plan of the Eddystone, built of Anglesey marble at a cost of £34,500, defrayed by the corporation of Liverpool: it rises ninety feet, and is completely surrounded at high tides, like the fort, by the water. Steamers run to and from Liverpool every hour. A site and £500 have been offered for building a church, and plans are in progress for its erection. The masses of sandstone near the Black rock, called the Red and Yellow Noses, well merit the attention of the naturalist, being worn by the action of the sea into a variety of caverns of the most romantic forms; a tunnel has been cut through one of them from the beach, forming a private entrance up to Cliffe Villa.

BRIGHTSIDE-BIERLOW, a township, in the parish and union of SHEFFIELD, N. division of the wapentake of STRAFFORTH and TICKHILL, W. riding of YORK, 3 miles (N. E.) from Sheffield; containing 10,089 inhabitants. This populous and very extensive township, parts of which form suburbs to the borough of Sheffield, partakes in the manufactures of the surrounding district. Several large steel-works, foundries, and iron-forges have been established; and the manufacture of table-knives and cutlery of various kinds, and of scythes and agricultural implements, is carried on to a great extent: there are also quarries of excellent building-stone. The village of Brightside is situated on the river Don, and in the immediate vicinity are several pleasing villas, and some richly varied scenery; Wincobank hill is about 300 feet above the river, and commands a prospect unusually fine and extensive. Here is a station on the Sheffield and Rotherham railway; and a new road to Barnsley has been constructed, leading through the romantic dell of Burngreave to Pitsmoor, and avoiding the precipitous hill of Pye Bank. Three ecclesiastical districts, called Brightside, Pitsmoor, and Wicker, respectively, were constituted in August, 1845, under the act 6th and 7th of Victoria, cap. 37: each living is in the gift of the Crown and the Archbishop of York alternately. The district of Brightside extends from the east-north-east suburbs of Sheffield, in the direction of Rotherham, its middle and greatest breadth being about a mile; Wicker is an immediate suburb of Sheffield, and more to the north lies Pitsmoor. There are several places of worship for dissenters. At Wincobank are remains of Roman fortifications and embankments.

BRIGHT-WALTHAM.—See WALTHAM, BRIGHT.

BRIGHTWELL (ST. AGATHA), a parish, in the union and parliamentary borough of WALLINGFORD, hundred of MÓRETON, county of BERKS, 2½ miles (W. N. W.) from Wallingford; containing 611 inhabit. ants. The parish comprises 1958a. 1r. 15p., and is bounded on the north by the river Thames, and on the south by the Tadsey: the soil is a rich loam, partly mixed with gravel; the surface is high on the northern boundary, but in other parts level. The castle here was given up by Stephen to Henry II., then Duke of Normandy, after the treaty of peace concluded between him and Matilda at Wallingford, and was probably soon afterwards demolished, for its site is not even known, though conjectured to have been within the moat where the manor farmhouse now stands. The living is a rectory, valued in the king's books at £44. 17. 11., and in the patronage of the Bishop of Winchester: the tithes have been commuted for £855, and there are 51 acres of glebe. The church contains a monument to the memory of Thomas Godwyn, D.D., author of a treatise on Jewish and Roman antiquities, and who died rector in 1642. There is a meeting-house for dissenters.

BRIGHTWELL (ST. JOHN THE BAPTIST), a parish, in the union of WOODBRIDGE, hundred of CARLFORD, E. division of SUFFOLK, 5½ miles (E. by S.) from Ipswich; containing 81 inhabitants, and comprising about 800 acres. The Hall, a fine old building belonging to the Barnardiston family, was pulled down about 1730. The living is a rectory, with the perpetual curacy of Foxhall annexed; net income, £54; patron, Sir J. K. Shaw, Bart.

BRIGHTWELL-BALDWIN (ST. BARTHOLOMEW), a parish, in the union of HENLEY, hundred of EWELME, county of OXFORD, 5 miles (S. W. by S.) from Tetsworth; containing, with the tything of Cadwell, 312 inhabitants. This parish, which takes its name from its crystal springs, comprises 1569a. 4p.; about 356 acres are pasture, and 40 woodland. The old mansion of the Stone family was burnt down in 1786, and the present was erected in 1790. The living is a rectory, valued in the king's books at £18. 16.; net income, £494; patron, W. F. L. Stone, Esq. Under an inclosure act in 1802, land and corn-rents were assigned in lieu of tithes. The church is a picturesque edifice in the decorated English style, with a tower, the front of which is elaborately enriched with canopied niches; in the chancel are some flemish brasses, and on the floor some ancient tiles with figures. To the north of the church is the sepulchral chapel of the families of Carleton, Stone, and Lowe, whose mansions are in the parish. At Bushy-Leas, between this place and Chagrove, a curious glass vessel, surrounded by twelve Roman sepulchral urns, has been dug up. Herbert Westphaling, afterwards Bishop of Hereford, and Dr. William Paul, Bishop of Oxford, held the living.

BRIGMERSTON, a hamlet, in the parish of MILSTON, union and hundred of AMESBURY, Everley and Pewsey, and S. divisions of WILTS; containing 33 inhabitants.

BRIGNALL (ST. MARY), a parish, in the union of TEESDALE, wapentake of GILLING-WEST, N. riding of YORK, 1 mile (S. W. by W.) from Greta-Bridge; containing 190 inhabitants. This place for many years formed one of the numerous manors possessed by the Scrope family, and some remains of an old Hall adjoining the village were removed in the present century. From the Scropes the property came into the hands of

Lord Barrymore, and from him descended to the Edens, of Windleston, in the county of Durham; it was purchased by the late John Bacon Sawrey Morritt, Esq., of Rokeby Park, from Sir R. J. Eden, Bart., for £66,000, and thus became an appendage to the beautiful demesne of Rokeby. The parish is bounded on the south and east by the picturesque river Greta, and comprises by computation 2000 acres, of which nearly three-fourth parts are pasture, one-fourth arable, and 100 acres woodland; the surface is undulated, the soil generally a loamy clay. There are some quarries of fine grey slate. The living is a vicarage, endowed with the rectorial tithes, and valued in the king's books at £8. 2. 6.; it is in the patronage of the Crown: the tithes have been commuted for £271, and there are about 63 acres of glebe. The church was rebuilt in 1834. The remains of a large Roman camp which commanded the ford on the river, are visible at Greta-Bridge; it was surrounded by a triple fosse, and relics of antiquity and Roman coins have frequently been dug up in its precincts.

BRIGSLEY (ST. HELEN), a parish, in the union of CAISTOR, wapentake of BRADLEY-HAVERSTOE, parts of LINDSEY, county of LINCOLN, 5 miles (S. by W.) from Great Grimsby; containing 125 inhabitants. It comprises by measurement upwards of 800 acres, half arable, and half meadow. The living is a discharged rectory, valued in the king's books at £7. 4. 4., and in the patronage of the Chapter of the Collegiate Church of Southwell; net income, £55.

BRIGSTOCK (ST. ANDREW), a parish, in the union of THRAPSTON, hundred of CORBY, N. division of the county of NORTHAMPTON, 22 miles (N. E.) from Northampton; containing 1262 inhabitants. It embraces 6013a. 3r. 21p., a large portion of which is occupied by parks and plantations; the village is of some extent, and situated about the middle of the parish. The lands formerly belonged to the dukes of Montague, whose ancient manor-house is still remaining. James I. granted a weekly market to be held on Thursday, and fairs on the festivals of St. Mark the Evangelist, St. Bartholomew the Apostle, and St. Martin: the market has long since fallen into disuse, but the fairs are still held. By a custom that prevails in the manor, if any man die seized of copyhold lands or tenements which descended to him in fee, his youngest son inherits; but if they were purchased by him, they fall to the eldest son. The living is a vicarage, with the living of Stanion annexed, valued in the king's books at £11. 17. 3¾.; net income, £236; patron, the Duke of Cleveland. The church has some Norman remains, amidst various alterations of later date; the tower is of very rude workmanship, and plastered.

BRILL (ALL SAINTS), a parish, in the union of THAME, hundred of ASHENDON, county of BUCKINGHAM, 7 miles (N. W. by N.) from Thame; containing 1449 inhabitants. Here was a palace belonging to the kings of Mercia, which was subsequently a favourite residence of Edward the Confessor, who frequently came hither during the hunting season, to enjoy the pleasures of the chase in Bernwood Forest. After the Conquest, Henry II., attended by his chancellor Thomas à Becket, kept his court here, in 1160 and 1162; and Henry III., in 1224: King John also appears to have resorted to the place, as there are some remains of a building called after him. In 1642, a garrison stationed here for the

376

king was attacked by a detachment of the parliamentary forces under the patriotic Hampden, but the latter were repulsed with considerable loss. The PARISH comprises 3100 acres of fertile land, of which 2395 are meadow and pasture, 310 arable, and 240 wood. Lace-making is carried on; and there is a small manufactory for earthenware. Brill and Ashendon Hills abound with interesting geological features, and numerous specimens of fossil remains; and the former also with excellent yellow ochre, of which considerable quantities have been conveyed to distant parts. There are likewise some quarries of stone used for roads, and for burning into lime; building-stone is occasionally found, and there is an excellent quarry of iron sandstone. From its elevated situation, the place commands a most extensive and richly varied prospect, comprehending a panoramic view of nine counties; and the salubrity of the air, and the nearness of Dorton spa, have made it the frequent resort of invalids, for whose accommodation several well-built lodging-houses have been erected. A fair granted to Sir John Molins, in 1346, has been revived within the last few years, and is held on the Wednesday next after Old Michaelmas-day.

The LIVING is a perpetual curacy, with that of Boarstall annexed; net income, £101; patron and impropriator, Sir T. D. Aubrey, Bart. The church is a small edifice of considerable antiquity, partly in the Norman style, with a low tower and spire; the entrance is through a rude porch in the south wall, over which is the date 1654, probably the period when the church was repaired after the parliamentary war. There are places of worship for Wesleyans and Independents. A national school was established in 1815, and united with a school founded by Samuel Turner, Esq.; it is endowed with £60 per annum, arising from £2000 three per cent. consols., bequeathed by Sir John Aubrey in 1825. On the disafforestment of Bernwood Forest, under a commission appointed in the 21st of James I., an allotment was set apart for the benefit of the poor, consisting of a farmhouse and buildings, with 181 acres of land, let at a clear rent of £120. On the north side of Muswell Hill, partly in this parish and partly in that of Piddington, stood the hermitage of St. Werburgh, a cell to the priory of Chetwood.

BRILLEY (ST. MARY), a parish, in the union of KINGTON, hundred of HUNTINGDON, county of HEREFORD, 6¼ miles (N. E. by N.) from Hay; containing 587 inhabitants. The parish is situated on the border of Wales, which bounds it on the north and west; and is partly encircled on the south by the river Wye. It consists of 3771 acres, and exhibits much rural and interesting scenery, the surface being in a great degree diversified by bold hills and deep dales, remarkably well wooded, and watered by numerous streams. The road from Kington to Hay crosses from north to south. The living is united to the vicarage of Kington, and the Bishop of Hereford is appropriator.

BRIMFIELD, a parish, in the union of TENBURY, hundred of WOLPHY, county of HEREFORD, 4 miles (S. by E.) from Ludlow; containing 591 inhabitants. This parish is situated on the borders of Shropshire, and comprises 1807 acres, of which nearly 700 are arable, and the rest pasture, with the exception of 76 acres of common or waste and about 50 acres of hop-ground; the surface is moderately undulated, with a large portion

of wood, and the soil above the average fertility. The roads from Ludlow to Tenbury and to Leominster branch off at the village, which is of some extent; the parish is intersected by the Leominster canal, and bounded by the river Teame. The proposed Hereford and Shrewsbury railway is intended to pass through the confines of Brimfield. The living is a perpetual curacy; patron and appropriator, the Bishop of Hereford: the great tithes have been commuted for £155, and those of the incumbent for £125; two acres of glebe appertain to the bishop. The nave and chancel of the church were rebuilt, in a plain style, in 1834; but the tower is of some antiquity.

BRIMINGTON (ST. MICHAEL), a parish, in the union of CHESTERFIELD, hundred of SCARSDALE, N. division of the county of DERBY, 2 miles (N. E.) from Chesterfield; containing 780 inhabitants. This place was severely afflicted by the plague in 1603. The manor of Brimington, formerly an appendage of Newbold, was successively in the families of Breton, Loudham, and Foljambe, the last of whom sold it about 1800: the family of Brimington was extinct in the time of Edward III. The parish, which was separated from that of Chesterfield in 1844, comprises 1252a. 25p., and is situated on the road from Chesterfield to Worksop, on the Chesterfield canal, and near the Midland railway. Stone is quarried for building purposes. An act was passed in 1841, for inclosing the waste lands. The living is a perpetual curacy; net income, £102; patron, the Vicar of Chesterfield: there are 9 acres of glebe, with a house. The church was rebuilt by subscription, in 1847. There are places of worship for Primitive Methodists and Wesleyans; and a national school, built in 1840, is supported by subscription.

BRIMPSFIELD (ST. MICHAEL), a parish, in the union of CIRENCESTER, hundred of RAPSGATE, E. division of the county of GLOUCESTER, 8 miles (E. N. E.) from Cirencester; containing 417 inhabitants. It comprises by measurement 2612 acres, of which nearly equal portions are arable and pasture, with 250 acres of wood; the soil varies considerably, but is generally a light loam. A part of the land lies high, being on the Cotswold hills, but it is interspersed with some fertile and well-wooded valleys, possessing much beauty: the river Stroudwater has its source within the parish. Good building-stone is found. The living is a discharged rectory, with that of Cranham consolidated, valued in the king's books at £9. 12. 1., and in the patronage of William Goodrich, Esq.: the tithes of Brimpsfield have been commuted for £303, and of Cranham for £162; the glebe contains 32 acres. The church is a small ancient structure. The Roman Ermin-street passes along the northern side of the parish. An alien priory of Benedictine monks, subordinate to the abbey of St. Stephen, at Fontenay, in Normandy, anciently existed here; also a castle, destroyed by Edward II. on his march from Cirencester to Worcester.

BRIMPTON (ST. PETER), a parish, in the union of NEWBURY, hundred of FAIRCROSS, county of BERKS, 6 miles (E. by S.) from Newbury; containing 412 inhabitants. It comprises 1689a. 2r., of which about 80 acres are common and roads. The living is a vicarage, valued in the king's books at £7, and in the patronage of the Rev. G. B. Caffin: the tithes have been commuted for £320, and the glebe comprises 15 acres. At the period of the Norman survey there were two churches in the parish; and the remains of an ancient ecclesiastical edifice are visible at a farmhouse, about half a mile from the present church. The Knights Hospitallers appear to have had an establishment here, in the time of Henry III.

BRIMPTON (St. Andrew), a parish, in the union of Yeovil, hundred of Stone, W. division of Somerset, 2¼ miles (W. S. W.) from Yeovil; containing, with the hamlets of Alvington and Houndstone, 123 inhabitants. The living is a discharged rectory, valued in the king's books at £7. 7., and in the patronage of the family of Williams : the tithes have been commuted for £130,' and there are about 30 acres of glebe.

BRIMSCOMB-PORT, an ecclesiastical parish, in the parish of Minchin-Hampton, union of Stroud, hundred of Bisley, E. division of the county of Gloucester, 2 miles (S. S. E.) from Stroud; comprising the hamlets of Chalford, Hyde, Burley, Brimscomb, and Cowcombe. This place obtained its name from a basin of the Thames and Severn canal within the hamlet, a large sheet of water, on the margin of which are the spacious wharfs and warehouses of the canal company. In the village, which is chiefly inhabited by persons employed in the clothing-trade, are two extensive mills for the manufacture of superfine broad-cloths and kersey-meres, affording employment to 500 persons. Here is a station of the railway from Swindon to Gloucester; it is 2¼ miles from the Stroud station. The living is a rectory, in the gift of D. Ricardo, Esq. There is a place of worship for Wesleyans.

BRIMSLADE.—See Savernake-Forest.

BRIMSTAGE, a township, in the parish of Brom-borrow, union, and Lower division of the hundred of Wirrall, S. division of the county of Chester, 3¾ miles (N. by E.) from Great Neston; containing 161 inhabitants. The manor was held by the family of Dom-ville, as early as the reign of Edward I., and passed by a succession of female heirs to the families of Hulse, Troutbeck, and Talbot. The township comprises 1012 acres, of which 42 are waste : the soil is clay. The impropriate tithes have been commuted for £103.

BRIND, with Newsholme or Newsham, a town-ship, in the parish of Wressel, union of Howden, Holme-Beacon division of the wapentake of Harthill, E. riding of York, 2¼ miles (N. by W.) from Howden; containing 231 inhabitants. The Hull and Selby railway passes by the place.

BRINDLE (St. James), a parish, in the union of Chorley, hundred of Leyland, N. division of the county of Lancaster, 4¾ miles (N. by E.) from Chor-ley; containing 1401 inhabitants. This place appears to have been granted, by the superior tenant of the crown, soon after the Conquest, to a family who were designated from their possessions. The manor passed by the marriage of the heiress of " Sir Peter de Bryn, of Brynhill," to the Gerards, with whom it continued till the reign of Henry VIII., when Sir William Cavendish is found patron of the living, though the manor did not come into the possession of the Cavendish family until the middle of last century. The parish is elevated land, and comprises 2900 acres, of which the soil is clay and sand; about one-third is arable, and the rest pasture, garden-ground, and waste : the river Lostock passes at the south-western extremity, where it receives

a nameless brook, whose slender stream flows near the village. There are two valuable stone-quarries in the parish; one at Duxon Hill, producing large millstones, which are frequently exported to Ireland; and the other at Denham Hill, where good ashlar is obtained in abundance. Chemical works, established in 1830, by Mr. Thomas Coupe, employ 30 hands; and here are also some print-works. The Blackburn and Preston railway runs through, and the Leeds and Liverpool canal skirts, the parish.

The living is a discharged rectory, valued in the king's books at £12. 8. 4., and in the patronage of the Duke of Devonshire : the tithes have been commuted for £500; and there are more than 11 acres of glebe, with a glebe-house and other buildings. The church is in the early English style, with a square tower; the body of the edifice was rebuilt in 1817 : in the churchyard is a stone coffin, and in the parsonage, an ancient font. The Roman Catholic chapel here, is dedicated to St. Joseph, and is the property of the Benedictines; it was built in 1786, and is a neat structure, situated in a vale. A free school, supposed to have been founded by Peter Burs-cough, has funds consisting of about £335, lent on in-terest, producing £16. 16. per annum; and near the Roman Catholic chapel is a school which was erected by Mr. Joseph Knight, of Chelsea, a native of the parish, with a house for the master and mistress, who receive £25 per annum.

BRINDLEY, a township, in the parish of Acton, union and hundred of Nantwich, S. division of the county of Chester, 4½ miles (W. N. W.) from Nant-wich; containing 184 inhabitants. It comprises 1071 acres, of which the soil is clay and a strong loam. The impropriate tithes have been commuted for £66. 5., and the vicarial for £26. 11.

BRINDLEYS, an extra-parochial liberty, in the union of Howden, Holme-Beacon division of the wapen-take of Harthill, E. riding of York, 3½ miles (N. by W.) from Howden; containing 8 inhabitants. It com-prises about 173 acres of farm land.

BRINGHURST (St. Nicholas), a parish, in the union of Uppingham, hundred of Gartree, S. division of the county of Leicester; containing, with the town-ship of Drayton and the chapelry of Great Easton, 840 inhabitants, of whom 92 are in the township of Bring-hurst, 2¼ miles (W. by N.) from Rockingham. The living is a vicarage, valued in the king's books at £11. 15.; net income, £241; patrons and appropria-tors, the Dean and Chapter of Peterborough. Land and a money payment were assigned in 1804, in lieu of tithes for the townships of Bringhurst and Drayton. There is a chapel of ease at Great Easton.

BRINGTON (All Saints), a parish, in the union of Thrapston, hundred of Leightonstone, county of Huntingdon, 5½ miles (N. by W.) from Kimbolton; containing 129 inhabitants. This parish, which is situ-ated within half a mile of the road from Huntingdon to Northampton, comprises by measurement 1014 acres. The living is a rectory, with the livings of Bythorn and Old Weston united, valued in the king's books at £34. 3. 6½.; net income, £492; patrons, the Master and Fellows of Clare Hall, Cambridge. Land and a money payment were assigned in lieu of tithes, in 1804.

BRINGTON (St. Mary), a parish, in the union of Brixworth, hundred of Newbottle-Grove, S. divi-

three miles along the north side of the river Coquet, and is crossed by the high road from Weedon Bridge: the soil is a strong clay. Here are extensive strata of limestone, and a mine of coal. A priory for Augustine canons was founded in the time of Henry I., by Osbertus Colatarius, in honour of St. Peter: the establishment, at the time of the Dissolution, consisted of ten religious, and the revenue was rated at £77. It was beautifully situated within a curvature of the Coquet, which flows close to the walls; and now forms an interesting ruin, exhibiting specimens of Norman architecture. On the hill above the priory are traces of a Roman town, in connexion with a military way; and the foundations of the piers of a Roman bridge are discernible when the water is low.

BRINKBURN, LOW WARD, a township, in the parochial chapelry of LONG FRAMLINGTON, union of ROTHBURY, E. division of COQUETDALE ward, N. division of NORTHUMBERLAND; containing 57 inhabitants, and comprising 579 acres.

BRINKBURN, SOUTH SIDE, a township, in the parish of FELTON, union of ROTHBURY, W. division of MORPETH ward, N. division of NORTHUMBERLAND, 9 miles (N. N. W.) from Morpeth; containing 55 inhabitants.

BRINKHILL (ST. PHILIP), a parish, in the union of SPILSBY, hundred of HILL, parts of LINDSEY, county of LINCOLN, 6½ miles (N. N. W.) from Spilsby; containing 168 inhabitants. It comprises about 1000 acres, of which the soil is a red marl, and the surface hilly. The living is a discharged rectory, valued in the king's books at £8; net income, £137; patron, R. Cracroft, Esq.: land was assigned in lieu of tithes, in 1773. There is a place of worship for Wesleyans. In a stratum of blue clay in the village, are found veins of barren marcasite.

BRINKLEY (ST. MARY), a parish, in the union of NEWMARKET, hundred of RADFIELD, county of CAMBRIDGE, 5½ miles (S. by W.) from Newmarket; containing 366 inhabitants. The living is a rectory, valued in the king's books at £13. 6. 8.; net income, £241; patrons, the Master and Fellows of St. John's College, Cambridge: land and a money payment were assigned in 1811, in lieu of tithes. The parish is entitled to the fifth part of an estate at Oakington, producing in the whole £100 per annum, given by Mrs. Elizabeth March, in 1729; it is paid to a master for the instruction of children.

BRINKLOW (ST. JOHN THE BAPTIST), a parish, in the Kirby division of the hundred of KNIGHTLOW, N. division of the county of WARWICK, 6½ miles (E.) from Coventry, on the road to Market-Harborough; containing 793 inhabitants. This place derives its name from a large tumulus, on which stood the keep or watch-tower of a very ancient castle of uncertain erection, of which there are no remains. In the reign of John, Nicholas de Stuteville, lord of the manor, received the grant of a market to be held on Monday, and a fair on the festival of St. Margaret. The parish comprises 1393*a*. 3*r*. 22*p*.: about 150 acres are wood, and of the remainder, one-third is arable, and two-thirds pasture; the surface is level, and the soil a good strong loam. The labourers who work at Combe Field reside here, and the number of cottages is therefore considerable. The Oxford canal passes within a quarter of a mile of the parish; and the Roman fosse-way, on the line of which are some traces of an encampment, bounds it on the east. The living is a rectory, valued in the king's books at £17. 10., and in the patronage of the Crown; net income, £228. The church is built in the style which prevailed in the reign of Henry VII. There is a place of worship for Independents. The interest on £60 given by the Rev. W. Fairfax, in 1761, is applied to instruction; as is also the interest of £800 left in 1789 by William Edwards, after deducting £13. 19. for bread distributed to the poor.

BRINKWORTH (St. Michael), a parish, in the union and hundred of Malmesbury, Malmesbury and Kingswood, and N. divisions of Wilts, 4 miles (W. N. W.) from Wotton-Basset; containing, with the tything of Grittenham, 1694 inhabitants. It is intersected by the Great Western railway; and comprises 5450 acres, of which 4759 are pasture, 472 arable, and 219 woodland. The living is a rectory, valued in the king's books at £23. 9. 2., and in the gift of Pembroke College, Oxford: the tithes have been commuted for £735, and the glebe comprises 150 acres.

BRINNINGTON, a township, in the parish and union of Stockport, hundred of Macclesfield, N. division of the county of Chester, 2 miles (N. E. by N.) from Stockport; containing 5331 inhabitants, most of whom are employed in the cotton manufacture. The manor was the property of the De Masseys, and subsequently of the Stockports, who were succeeded by the Dukenfields, by whom the lands were held as early as 1327; it continued theirs until about the year 1770, when it passed to the Astley family, of whom it was purchased by James Harrison, Esq. The township comprises 750 acres, of a clayey soil; and contains Portwood, *which see*. The tithes have been commuted for £30.

BRINSLEY, or Brunsley, a hamlet, in the parish of Greasley, union of Basford, S. division of the wapentake of Broxtow, N. division of the county of Nottingham, 2 miles (N. N. W.) from Greasley; containing 1139 inhabitants. It comprises 888 acres of land, mostly the property of the Duke of Newcastle and the Earl of Mexborough. In this vicinity are extensive collieries, and near the village is a large coal-wharf on the Nottingham and Cromford canal. A neat chapel of ease was built in 1838, at a cost of about £1200, raised by subscription, aided by £200 from the Church Building Society; the Duke of Portland gave £100, and the land, and stone. There is a place of worship for Wesleyans.

BRINSOP (St. George), a parish, in the union of Weobley, hundred of Grimsworth, county of Hereford, 5½ miles (N. W.) from Hereford; containing 116 inhabitants. It comprises by computation 1334 acres. The living is a discharged vicarage, valued in the king's books at £4; patron and appropriator, the Bishop of Hereford: the great tithes have been commuted at £170, and the small at £104; the glebe comprises 190 acres, and a vicarage-house has recently been built. The church is partly of Norman architecture; it has a window of painted glass of great antiquity.

BRINSWORTH, a township, in the parish and union of Rotherham, S. division of the wapentake of Strafforth and Tickhill, W. riding of York, 2¼ miles (S. S. W.) from Rotherham; containing 241 in-

governor, Scroop, Earl of Wiltshire, Sir Henry Green, and Sir John Bushy, to be beheaded; in the same year, parliament exempted the place, by "land and water," from the jurisdiction of the lord high admiral.

In 1471, the Duke of Somerset, Earl of Devonshire, and other nobles in the interest of the house of Lancaster, entering into a confederacy against Edward IV., assembled their forces here, and were greatly assisted by the inhabitants (who were attached to the Lancastrian cause), in their attempts to replace Henry VI. upon the throne. Henry VII. visited Bristol in 1485, on which occasion the citizens, to evince the greater respect, appeared in their best apparel; but the king, thinking their wives too richly dressed for their station, imposed a fine of twenty shillings upon every citizen who was worth £20. During the civil war in the reign of Charles I. the city was garrisoned by the parliamentarians, who appointed Nathaniel Fiennes governor. The king, sensible of the importance of the place, endeavoured to gain possession of it by means of his partisans within the town; but their proceedings having been discovered, Alderman Yeomans and Mr. Bourchier were hanged as traitors, by order of the governor. In 1643, Prince Rupert closely invested the city, which surrendered on the third day; and the king, arriving soon after, remained for a short time, and attended divine service in the cathedral on the following Sunday. Bristol continued in the possession of the royalists for nearly two years; but, after sustaining a vigorous assault with incredible valour, the garrison capitulated to Fairfax, and Cromwell soon afterwards ordered the castle and the fortifications to be demolished. The city was the scene of a serious riot, in the autumn of 1831, during the progress of the Reform bill in parliament. It commenced by an attack upon the recorder, who was opposed to that measure, on his entrance into the city, prior to holding the quarter-sessions, on Saturday the 29th of October, and, owing to the want of energy on the part of the civil and military authorities, continued until the Monday following, during which period the gaols were broken open and burnt. The episcopal palace, mansion-house, and custom-house, were destroyed; and many private dwellings, particularly in Queen-square, were set on fire.

The CITY is pleasantly situated in a valley, near the confluence of the rivers Avon and Frome; the old town, which forms the nucleus of the present, consists of four principal streets, diverging at right angles from the centre, and intersected by smaller streets. The houses in the interior of the town are mostly ancient, being built of timber and plaster, with the upper stories projecting; but in the outer parts are spacious streets and squares, containing good houses, uniformly built of stone and brick. The town is well paved, lighted with gas, and supplied with excellent water from springs, and from public conduits, originally laid down by the monks, in convenient situations: an act for its better supply with water was passed in 1846. A handsome stone bridge of three wide arches over the Avon, which flows through the town, was completed in 1768, on the site of a former one, connecting the northern with the southern part; and over the river Frome is a swing bridge, admitting of the passage of ships. The theatre, said to have been admired by Garrick for its just proportions and arrangement, was built by Mr. Powell, in 1766; it is opened during the winter season, and has been the nursery of some of the best performers on the London stage. The City Library, in King-street, a handsome stone edifice beautifully ornamented with sculpture and literary emblems, contains a large collection of books and numerous manuscripts. The Philosophical Institution in Park-street, a neat building with a Grecian portico, contains reading-rooms, a theatre in which lectures are delivered, a laboratory, a philosophical apparatus, an extensive museum, and a room for the exhibition of paintings. The Statistical Society was instituted in Nov. 1836, soon after the meeting of the British Association; and the Academy of the Fine Arts, more recently. The Exchange, in Corn-street, erected about the year 1760, by the corporation, at an expense of more than £50,000, is a spacious and elegant structure, 110 feet in length, with a rustic basement; in the centre are handsome columns of the Corinthian order, forming the principal entrance, and supporting a pediment, in the tympanum of which are the king's arms: the edifice is principally used as a corn-market. The Commercial Rooms, erected in 1811, and having a portico of four pillars of the Ionic order, contain apartments for the despatch of business, and a reading-room; the principal hall is 60 feet in length, 40 feet wide, and 25 feet high. The Post-office is a neat building of freestone, to the west of the Exchange. A handsome structure called the Victoria Rooms, intended for public assemblies, was lately erected from the designs of Mr. Charles Dyer; it is situated near the top of Park-street, and is built entirely of Bath stone. The south front, which is the principal, has a noble octo-style Corinthian portico, recessed within the building as well as advanced forward; the grand hall is a noble apartment, 117 feet by 55, and 48 in height.

Bristol is represented by Malmsbury as having been, so early as the reign of Henry II., a "wealthy city, full of ships from Ireland, Norway, and every part of Europe, which brought to it great commerce." It carries on an extensive TRADE with the West Indies, North and South America, and the countries bordering on the Baltic and Mediterranean seas: the principal articles of importation are sugar, rum, coffee, tobacco, wine, corn, timber, tar, turpentine, &c.; those exported consist chiefly of the produce of the manufactories within the town and neighbourhood. It has also a great coasting-trade, and considerable intercourse with Ireland. Of late, a new and important feature in the commerce of the place was introduced, by the establishment of steam communication with North America: the large steam ship, the "Great Western," which sailed from the port on the 2nd June, 1838, was the first steamer which crossed the Atlantic by the power of steam only. In 1842, 336 British ships of the aggregate burthen of 63,227 tons, and 49 foreign ships of 9671 tons, entered the port. The total tonnage in that year was 403,627; and in 1845, 492,720.

A few years since, a considerable reduction was made by the corporation in the local dues; and the port was materially enlarged and improved, in 1803, by changing the course of the Avon, and damming up its old channel, to form an extensive floating-dock, communicating by means of reservoirs with the river and the quay; to which vessels have access at any time, and from which they may sail directly into the Bristol Channel. Over this new course of the Avon two handsome iron bridges were erected, and the entire work was completed, in

Corporation Seal.

Obverse.   Reverse.

granted, the principal of which were by Henry III., Edward III., Henry VII., Elizabeth, Charles II., and Queen Anne. By the act of the 5th and 6th of William IV., cap. 76, the corporation now consists of a mayor, sixteen aldermen, and forty-eight councillors, and the city is divided into ten wards; a sheriff, recorder, and other officers required by the act, are also appointed, and the total number of magistrates is twenty-five. The elective franchise has been exercised since the 23rd of Edward I., two members being returned. The right of election was formerly vested in the freeholders and free-men at large, in number about five thousand; but, by the act of the 2nd of William IV., cap. 45, the non-resident freemen, except within seven miles of the city, were disfranchised, and the privilege was extended to the £10 householders of an enlarged district : the ancient boundary comprised about 784 acres, but the present embraces by estimation 4674. The sheriff is return-ing officer. A court of general sessions of the peace is held quarterly before the recorder, who is sole judge; prisoners charged with offences not cognizable at the sessions are removed for trial at the assizes for the county of Gloucester. A court of assize and nisi prius is held annually at the close of the summer assizes for the western circuit, at which the senior judge on that circuit presides. A court called the Tolzey court (from having been anciently held at the place where the king's tolls, or dues, were collected), is held by prescription every Monday under the sheriff, in his character of bailiff of the hundred, aided by a steward, who must be a barrister of three years' standing; its jurisdiction extends over the whole of the county of the city, and on the river down to the Flat and Steep Holmes, below Kingsroad, twenty miles from the city. It takes cogni-zance of all actions for debt, and other civil actions, to an unlimited amount, arising within the city; it also holds pleas of ejectment, and issues processes of attach-ment on the goods of foreigners sued for debt. A branch of this, similar in all its proceedings and juris-diction, is the court of pie-poudre, held for fourteen days in the open air, in the Old market, commencing on the 30th of September; and during this period the proceed-ings in the Tolzey court are suspended. The powers of the county debt-court of Bristol, established in 1847, extend over Bristol, Clifton, Bedminster, and part of Keynsham. The court of bankruptcy, established in 1842, and held daily, embraces several counties. The guildhall lately pulled down to make way for a new edifice, was a very ancient building, decorated with the arms of Edward VI., those of George IV., and a statue of

Charles II.; and contained, in the north wing, a small chapel dedicated to St. George, founded in the reign of Richard II., by William Spicer, mayor. The new guild-hall is similar in style to the new Palace of Westminster, and was erected in 1845; the front is elaborately en-riched, and ornamented in the centre by a handsome tower. The Council-house, for the transaction of civic affairs, is an elegant edifice of freestone, of the Ionic order, with a handsome portico and balustrade, and or-namented with a figure of Justice over the pediment. Merchants' Hall, Coopers' Hall, and others formerly be-longing to trading companies, and many of them good buildings, are now appropriated to private uses. The common gaol comprises ten wards, with day-rooms and airing-yards, for the classification of prisoners. The house of correction was destroyed by fire, by the rioters, in 1831, except a few of the cells, which have been re-paired. Lawford's Gate prison, without the city, is ap-propriated to that part of the suburbs lying in the county of Gloucester.

Bristol was separated from the diocese of Salisbury in 1542, and raised into a SEE, the jurisdiction of which extended over the county of the city, the county of Dor-set, and a few parishes in the shire of Gloucester. By the act of the 6th and 7th of William IV., cap. 77, the sees of Gloucester and Bristol have been united, and new limits assigned :

Arms of the Bishopric.

Dorsetshire has been transferred to Salisbury. The establishment of Bristol consists of a dean, six (to be reduced to four) canons or prebendaries, four honorary canons, an archdeacon, a chancellor, four minor canons, a deacon, sub-deacon, and other officers : the Dean and Chapter possess the patronage of the minor canonries, and of thirty-three benefices. The Cathedral, dedicated to the Holy Trinity, was the collegiate church of a priory of Black canons, founded by Robert Fitzharding in 1148, and raised into an abbey in the reign of Henry II., the revenue being at the Dissolution £767. 15. 3. It is a venerable and highly-finished cruciform structure, with a lofty square embattled tower rising from the centre, strengthened with buttresses and crowned with pin-nacles; it contains portions in the early, decorated, and later English styles, in all of them exhibiting specimens of the purest design and most elaborate execution. The nave was destroyed during the parliamentary war : the roofs of the choir and transepts, all of equal height and finely groined, are supported on clustered columns, richly moulded; and the remaining parts, from the striking beauty of their details, afford evidence of the grandeur of the interior when entire. At the entrance into the choir is an empannelled screen, ornamented with carvings of the minor prophets; and in several small chapels of exquisite beauty are many interesting monuments, among which may be noticed those of Robert Fitz-harding and several of the abbots and bishops; of Mrs. Draper, the eulogized Eliza of Sterne; Lady Hesketh, celebrated by Cowper; and the wife of the Rev. William Mason, with a beautiful epitaph written by that poet : there is also a bust of Southey. The chapter-house, a spacious edifice, highly enriched, in the latest style of Norman architecture, and part of the cloisters in the later English style, are still remaining ; the entrance gateway, in the lower part Norman, and in the upper part later English, is in excellent preservation.

The city comprised within its ancient limits, the PARISHES of All Saints, St. Augustine, Christ-Church, St. Ewin or Owen, St. John the Baptist, St. Leonard, St. Mary-le-Port, St. Mary Redcliffe, St. Michael, St. Nicholas, St. Peter, St. Stephen, St. Thomas, and St. Werburgh, besides Temple parish or Holy Cross ; part of the parishes of St. James, St. Paul, and St. Philip and St. Jacob ; and the extra-parochial ward of Castle Precincts, which has no church, and is exempted from all ecclesiastical assessments. By the Municipal act the parish of Clifton, part of Westbury-upon-Trym, and those portions of the parish of St. Philip and St. Jacob, and of the united parishes of St. James and St. Paul, which were in the county of Gloucester, with part of the parish of Bedminster, in Somerset, have been comprehended within the county of the city of Bristol. The living of *All Saints'* is a discharged vicarage, valued in the king's books at £4. 3. 4. ; net income, £160 ; patrons and appropriators, the Dean and Chapter of Bristol. The church, to which a tower was added in 1716, is a very ancient structure ; the interior is a fine specimen of the early English style, and contains a magnificent monument, by Rysbrack, to the memory of Edward Colston, an eminent philanthropist, and a great benefactor to the city. The living of *St. Augustine's* is a discharged vicarage, valued at £6 ; net income, £320 ; patrons and appropriators, the Dean and Chapter. The church, which was built about the year 1480, combines various portions in the early, with several in the later, English style. The living of *Christ-Church* parish is a discharged rectory, with that of *St. Ewin's* united, valued in the king's books at £11. 10. ; net income, £390 ; patron, the Rev. J. Strickland. The church is a handsome modern edifice in the Grecian style, with a lofty tower of two stages, decorated with light columns and pilasters, and surmounted by an octangular turret and spire. The living of *St. John the Baptist's* is a discharged rectory, with which that of *St. Lawrence's* was consolidated in 1578, valued at £7. 4. 7. ; net income, £150. The church is a handsome edifice, chiefly in the later English style ; a gallery was erected in 1833 with 120 sittings. The living of *St. Leonard's* is a discharged vicarage, with that of St. Nicholas' united, valued at £12 ; net income, £253 ; patrons and appropriators, the Dean and Chapter. The living of the parish of *St. Mary-le-Port* is a discharged rectory, valued at £7 ; net income, £150 ; patron, the Duke of Buckingham. The church is a very ancient structure, of early English architecture, with a square embattled tower crowned by pinnacles.

The living of *St. Mary's Redcliffe* is a perpetual curacy, with that of St. Thomas' united, and, with the living of Abbot's-Leigh, is annexed to the vicarage of Bedminster ; it is valued in the king's books at £12. 6. 3. The church was founded in 1376, by Simon de Burton, mayor, and after the damage it sustained from a violent storm, in 1445, that blew down two-thirds of the spire, was extensively repaired by William Cannyngs. It is a spacious and magnificent cruciform structure, with a lofty and finely-proportioned tower at the west end, surmounted

ception of the tower, which was added to it in 1385, rebuilt in 1761, is in the later style of English architecture; it is highly ornamented within, and contains a monument to the memory of Robert Thorne, founder of the grammar school. In this church, the Litany was first celebrated in English, in 1543.

The living of *St. James'* is a perpetual curacy; patrons, Trustees; net income, £551. The church, anciently collegiate, was made parochial in 1347, when the tower was added; the interior contains some fine portions in the Norman style, particularly a curious circular window: the edifice was restored in 1846. Robert, Earl of Gloucester, founder of the priory of St. James, to which the church belonged; and Eleonora, niece of King John, who is said to have been forty years confined in Bristol Castle; are supposed to lie interred in the church. The living of *St. Paul's* is a perpetual curacy; net income, £513. The living of the parish of *St. Philip and St. Jacob* is a discharged vicarage, valued in the king's books at £15, and in the gift of Trustees; net income, £440; impropriator, R. C. Blathwayte, Esq. The church, founded in the twelfth century, is a spacious and handsome structure in the early English style, with a lofty square embattled tower : 700 additional sittings have been lately provided.

St. Mark's, commonly called the mayor's chapel, in College-green, formerly collegiate, is a small edifice containing elegant specimens of the early, decorated, and later styles of English architecture, with a beautiful tower. The altar-piece, a few years since restored, contains some handsome niches in the later style, and fine tabernacle work ; and to the east of the tower is a small chapel, now used for a vestry-room, with a ceiling of fan tracery of exquisite workmanship. There are several episcopal chapels, the principal of which are, *Foster's*, in Steep-street, and *Colston's*, on St. Michael's Hill. *Trinity* chapel, a neat building in the later English style, was erected at an expense of £8800, of which £6000 were granted by the Commissioners for Building New Churches : the living is a perpetual curacy, with a net income of £140, in the patronage of the Vicar of the parish of St. Philip and St. Jacob. *St. George's* church, in Great George-street, is a handsome structure, with a portico of the Dorie order : the living is a vicarage, not in charge; net income, £285; patrons and appropriators, the Dean and Chapter. The church of *St. Barnabas*, near Ashley-place, in St. Paul's parish, was consecrated Sept. 1843, and is a plain edifice with a tower and spire, the whole erected at a cost of £2200 : the living is a perpetual curacy in the gift of the Incumbent of St. Paul's, with a net income of £150. *St. Luke's* church, in the parish of St. Philip and St. Jacob, cost £2700, and was consecrated a few days after that of St. Barnabas : the living is a perpetual curacy in the gift of the Vicar. The same parish contains the churches of *St. Simon* and *St. Jude*, each of them a perpetual curacy, in the alternate patronage of the Crown and the Bishop, and each having a net income of £150. Part of St. Paul's parish, and part of that of Horfield, now form the district of *St. Andrew Montpelier*, for which a church was consecrated January 1845 ; the building is cruciform, of correct though plain design, and in the style which prevailed at the end of the 13th century : the living is a perpetual curacy; net income, £150; patron, the Bishop. A district named *The Weir* was formed in

1846, out of the parishes of St. Paul, St. Peter, and St. Philip and St. Jacob, and endowed by the Ecclesiastical Commissioners. There are places of worship for Baptists, the Society of Friends, the Connexion of the Countess of Huntingdon, Independents, Primitive and Wesleyan Methodists, Moravians, Scotch Seceders, Swedenborgians, Unitarians, and Roman Catholics, besides two synagogues. An act for establishing a general cemetery was obtained in 1837.

The free grammar school was founded in 1532, by Robert Thorne, who bequeathed £1000 for the purpose. This sum, together with houses and land belonging to the dissolved hospital of St. Bartholomew, was appropriated to its erection and endowment, and various benefactions having since been made, the school now possesses 590 acres of land and some houses; it has several exhibitions, and two small fellowships at St. John's College, Oxford. The grammar school in College-green is attached to the cathedral, and endowed with £40 per annum, for the instruction of the choristers by one of the minor canons. The free grammar and writing school in the parish of Redcliffe, was established by letters-patent granted in the 13th of Elizabeth, and endowed by Alderman Whitson and others, with annuities amounting to £21. Queen Elizabeth's hospital, founded in 1586 by John Carr, an opulent citizen, whose endowment of it, increased by subsequent benefactions, produces about £2400 per annum, is under the management of charity trustees : a new building for this hospital was erected in 1845, the front of which is 400 feet long ; it stands on the side of Brandon hill, between Bristol and Clifton. The free school in St. Augustine's parish, called Colston's Hospital, was instituted in 1708, by Edward Colston, who endowed it for 100 boys : Chatterton was maintained for seven years in this school, and within that period is thought to have composed several of his poems. The free school in Temple parish was endowed with £80 per annum by Mr. Colston. The Merchants' Hall school, in St. Stephen's parish, was established in 1738, by Susannah Holworthy, and endowed by her and other benefactors ; the Merchants' Society, in part of whose hall the school is held, pay a master £80 per annum. The school in Pile-street, for boys of the parishes of Redcliffe and St. Thomas, is supported partly by an endowment of £20 per annum, by Mr. Colston ; the income is about £170. The Red Maids' school was founded in 1627, and endowed by Alderman Whitson, for girls : a building in the more eligible collegiate style, has been erected for it on a more eligible site, from the designs of Mr. C. Dyer. There are also, a school in Temple parish, endowed with a permanent fund for girls ; the Diocesan school, containing 240 boys and 120 girls ; the Clergy Daughters' school, established in 1833 ; Ellbridge's school for girls, supported by endowment ; and national and other schools opened in various parts of the city.

Trinity hospital, or almshouse, for ten aged men and thirty-six poor women, is of very ancient date ; the endowment, increased by benefactions, produces £790 per annum, and the premises consist of two separate ranges of buildings, on opposite sides of Old Market-street, to one of which is attached a neat chapel. *Foster's* almshouses, in Steep-street, were founded and endowed, in 1492, by John Foster, merchant, for fourteen aged persons, whose revenue is at present about

£330 ; they are built of stone, and have a small chapel annexed. *Temple* hospital was founded and endowed in 1613, by the Rev. Dr. White ; its revenue amounts to upwards of £600, and the number of the inmates has been increased to 24 : the premises consist of two parallel ranges of buildings, connected at one end by a wall, the area forming a garden. Two almshouses of stone, one in Temple-street, containing twelve tenements, and the other in the old market-place, containing sixteen, were founded in 1679, by *Alderman Stevens;* the endowment, consisting of 354 acres of land, produces £750 per annum. The *Merchants'* almshouses, in King-street, were founded by John Welch and other mariners, in the 4th of Elizabeth ; they are endowed with £1000, the bequest of Richard Jones, Esq., of Stowey, and comprise 31 tenements, occupied by nineteen seamen and twelve women. *Colston's* almshouses, on St. Michael's Hill, were founded and endowed in 1696, by Edward Colston, for twelve aged men and twelve aged women ; the income is about £300. *Mrs. Sarah Ridley,* in 1716, founded an almshouse, which she endowed with £2200, for five bachelors and five maids; the endowment was augmented by Mr. John Jocham with £1000, and, with subsequent benefactions, produces £155 per annum. The almshouses in Milk-street were founded in 1722, by *Mrs. Elizabeth Blanchard,* who endowed them for five aged persons ; the income is £95. The revenue arising from the various charitable endowments amounts to nearly £17,000 per annum. The *Infirmary,* the great medical and surgical school for the western counties, is conducted on a plan of truly beneficent liberality, and embraces every possible case of calamity or disease ; it was opened for the reception of patients in 1786, and is nobly supported by donations and voluntary subscriptions. The building to which a new wing was added a few years since, at an expense of £10,000, is spacious and well arranged, and in an open and healthy situation. A new hospital and dispensary have been instituted in the populous parish of Bedminster, on the Somersetshire side of the city ; and numerous other charitable and benevolent institutions are extensively patronized.

Of the ancient fortifications,—the tower gateway, a plain arch at the end of John-street, and St. John's gate, under the tower of St. John's church, decorated with statues and much ornamented, are all that now exist. There are partial remains of some of the numerous RELIGIOUS HOUSES which once flourished in the city and its immediate vicinity, comprised in the buildings of the schools and charitable institutions established by the corporation and by individuals. Of these houses the principal were, a priory of Benedictine monks, to the north-east of the city, founded by Robert, Earl of Gloucester, in the latter part of the reign of Henry I., or the beginning of that of Stephen ; a nunnery, to the north of the city, established in the time of Henry II., by Eva, widow of Robert Fitzharding, of which she was prioress, and the revenue of which, at the Dissolution, was £21. 11. 3. ; St. John's hospital, on the road to Bath, instituted in the reign of King John, the revenue of which was £51. 10. 4.; St. Catherine's hospital, founded in the reign of Henry III., by Robert de Berkeley, and the revenue of which was £21. 15. 8.; St. Lawrence's hospital for lepers, established in the time of Henry III.; an hospital dedicated to the Blessed Virgin and St. Mark, instituted in 1229, by Maurice de.

386

Gaunt, and the revenue of which was £140 ; a house of Black friars, by the same founder, who also erected a college of calendaries; a house of Grey friars, established in 1234 ; a house of White friars, instituted in 1267 by Edward I., when Prince of Wales ; an establishment for Augustine friars, founded in the reign of Henry II., by Simon and William Montacute; and Trinity hospital, near Lawford's Gate, established by John Barstable in the time of Henry V. In excavating for the Great Western railway, about the beginning of June, 1839, a remarkably fine tusk of the mammoth was discovered, lying on a bed of new red sandstone, about seven feet below the surface, between the Bristol cotton-works and St. Philip's bridge; some very fine specimens of iron and lead ores were also found near the same spot.

The city is distinguished as the birthplace of many *Eminent Characters,* among whom may be noticed Sebastian Cabot, who first discovered the continent of North America, in 1498; Hugh Elliot, who discovered Newfoundland, in 1527 ; William Grocyn, Greek professor at Oxford in the beginning of the sixteenth century ; Tobias Matthew, Archbishop of York ; the Rev. Mr. Catcott, author of a treatise on the Deluge ; Sir William Draper, who distinguished himself by his epistolary replies to the strictures of Junius ; Admiral Sir William Penn ; the Rev. John Lewis, author of the Life of Wycliffe, History of the Translations of the Bible, &c.; the poet Chatterton ; Mrs. Mary Robinson, from the sweetness of her poetry called the British Sappho; Edward Colston, merchant, who died in 1721, and Richard Reynolds, one of the Society of Friends, and a proprietor of the iron-works at Colebrook-dale, both distinguished for their munificent charities; Thomas Edward Bowditch, the African traveller ; Robert Southey ; and Sir Thomas Lawrence, Bird, and several other artists of eminence. Bristol gives the titles of Earl and Marquess to the family of Hervey.

BRISTON (*ALL SAINTS*), a parish, in the union of ERPINGHAM, hundred of HOLT, W. division of NORFOLK, 4 miles (S. S. W.) from Holt; containing 963 inhabitants. It comprises 2824*a.* 1*r.* 5*p.*, of which about 2181 acres are arable, 242 meadow, pasture, and woodland, and 400 waste and common ; the village, which is considerable, is situated near the springhead of the river Bure. A swine and sheep market is held every Tuesday, a cattle-fair on the 26th of May, and a wake on the day after Old Michaelmas-day. The living is a discharged vicarage, valued in the king's books at £4. 9. 9½., and in the gift of the Rev. Robert Bond : the impropriation belongs to Winton charity; the glebe contains 39½ acres. The church, which is in the decorated and later English styles, and consists of a nave and chancel, formerly had a north aisle, the arches, though pulled up, being still visible; the tower fell down in 1724. There are places of worship for Independents, Wesleyans, and Primitive Methodists.

BRITFORD, or BURFORD (*ST. PETER*), a parish, in the union of. ALDERBURY, hundred of CAWDEN and CADWORTH, Salisbury and Amesbury, and S. divisions of WILTS, 1½ mile (S. E. by S.) from Salisbury ; containing, with the hamlets of East Harnham and Longford, 878 inhabitants. A stream in the parish was cut for a canal in the reign of Charles II., to form a line of communication with Christchurch, in the county of Southampton; but owing to the shifting of the sand, it was never

ompleted. The manufacture of horse-hair is carried
n to a limited extent; and a large fair for sheep is
eld on Aug. 12th. The living is a vicarage, valued in
he king's books at £13; net income, £281; patrons
nd appropriators, the Dean and Chapter of Salisbury.
he great tithes have been commuted for £700, and the
lebe comprises 39 acres; the vicarial have been com-
uted for £350, and the glebe comprises one acre. The
iurch, a spacious cruciform structure, with a central
,wer, contains a tomb considered by some to be that
: the Duke of Buckingham, who was beheaded by
ichard III.

BRITTENTON, a hamlet, in the parish of STAND-
AKE, union of WITNEY, hundred of BAMPTON, county
f OXFORD; containing 162 inhabitants.

BRITWELL, a liberty, in the parish and hundred of
URNHAM, county of BUCKINGHAM, 4 miles (N. N. W.)
'om Eton; containing 94 inhabitants.

BRITWELL-PRIOR, a chapelry, in the parish of
EWINGTON, union of HENLEY, hundred of EWELME,
ıunty of OXFORD, 6¼ miles (S. S. W.) from Tetsworth;
ıntaining 52 inhabitants. The mansion-house was
rmerly a nunnery, and subsequently belonged to the
eld family.

BRITWELL-SALOME (ST. NICHOLAS), a parish, in
the union of HENLEY, hundred of LEWKNOR, county of
OXFORD, 5½ miles (S. by W.) from Tetsworth; containing 233 inhabitants. It comprises 726a. 3r. 26p., exclusively of ground occupied by a beech wood on the
west side of Britwell Hill. An act for inclosing lands
was passed in 1842. The living is a rectory, valued in
the king's books at £6. 19. 2.; net income, including
glebe, £200; patron, the Earl of Carrington. The lower
Ikeneld-street passes under the hill.

• BRIXHAM (VIRGIN MARY), a sea-port, market-
town, and parish, in the union of TOTNES, hundred
of HAYTOR, Paignton and S. divisions of DEVON, 27¾
miles (S.) from Exeter, and 198 (W. S. W.) from London;
containing 5684 inhabitants. This town, at which William, Prince of Orange, landed on the 5th of November,
1688, is pleasantly situated near the southern extremity
of Torbay, on the west side; and is irregularly built,
though containing many good houses, several of which
are on the cliffs above the harbour: a handsome column
of granite has been erected on the spot where the prince
landed. The inhabitants are amply supplied with water;
the air is salubrious, the environs pleasant, and its vicinity to Torquay renders it desirable as a place of residence. During the late war, it was of some importance
as a garrison town, the barracks, at Bury Head, being
sufficiently spacious to accommodate several regiments;
they are inclosed in two regular fortresses, which, with
the ditches and drawbridges, remain in complete repair,
though the barracks have been dismantled. The PORT
is a member of that of Dartmouth, and carries on a
considerable coasting-trade, in which 120 vessels, of
from 60 to 150 tons' burthen, are employed; they are
also engaged in the foreign fruit-trade during the season.
The harbour, consisting of two basins, communicating
with each other, is safe and commodious; the outer
basin was formed by the erection of a second pier, which
was begun in 1803, and completed in 1809, by subscription, under an act authorizing the lords of the
manor to raise £6000 on security of the tolls. On the
liquidation of the debt now due, it is in contemplation
387

to erect another pier, on the eastern side of the harbour,
towards Bury Head; in furtherance of which object, an
act for improving the pier, harbour, and market, and
for the formation of a breakwater, was obtained in
1837: vessels will then be enabled to ride in perfect
safety during easterly winds, and Brixham will be a
safe harbour for both homeward and outward bound
ships. During spring-tides the water rises to the height
of 24 feet at the pier-head. There are 105 vessels of
from 20 to 45 tons' burthen, and 64 smaller boats, engaged in the fishing-trade, which is carried on to a considerable extent; the fish caught are chiefly turbot and
soles, for the supply of the London, Bath, and Exeter
markets. The trade of the town was derived some increase from being the rendezvous of ships of war, which
here lay in their supply of water. There are some extensive quarries of marble in the vicinity. The market-
days are Tuesday and Saturday; a fair is held on Whit-
Tuesday and two following days.

The parish is divided into Higher and Lower Brixham, and comprises 5213a. 3r. 12p., of which 777 acres
are common or waste. The LIVING is a discharged
vicarage, with the perpetual curacy of Churston-Ferrers
annexed, valued in the king's books at £52. 15., and in
the patronage of the Crown; impropriator, Miss Knollis;
net income, £494, with a house. The church, situated
in Higher Brixham, is an ancient structure, containing
some interesting monuments, among which is the cenotaph of the late Judge Buller; it was enlarged in 1825.
The church at Lower Brixham was erected about the
year 1822, by the vicar, aided by a large subscription,
and by a grant of £1200 from the Parliamentary Commissioners, and was made a district church by act of
the 58th of George III.; it is a neat building in the
English style, and contains 300 free sittings. The living
is a perpetual curacy, in the gift of the Crown; net income, £150. There are places of worship for Baptists
and Wesleyans. At Higher Brixham is Lay Well, the
water of which ebbs and flows about nine times in an
hour; the variation is about an inch and a quarter.
Bury Head is said to have been the site of a Roman
fortress: several ancient coins, in excellent preservation, were found in the vicinity in 1830.

BRIXTON, a parish, in the union of PLYMPTON
ST. MARY, hundred of PLYMPTON, Ermington and
Plympton, and S. divisions of DEVON, 5 miles (E.) from
Plymouth; containing 823 inhabitants. This parish
comprises 2838a. 33p.; and the road from Plymouth
to Exeter, through Totnes, and that from Plymouth to
Dartmouth, through Modbury and Kingsbridge, intersect the village. Quarries of slate and marble are
wrought, the marble being used for building, for the
making of lime, and for mending roads; coal and culm
are imported, and agricultural produce and slate are exported, by means of the river Yealm, which forms the
southern boundary of the parish. The living is a perpetual curacy; net income, £124; patrons, the Dean
and Canons of Windsor; impropriator, T. Splatt, Esq.,
whose tithes have been commuted for £642. The church
is a remarkably neat structure, in the later English style,
and is supposed to have been built about the close of the
fifteenth century, with the exception of the chancel,
which is part of a former chapel. Lewis Fortescue, a
baron of the exchequer in the reign of Henry VIII., was
born at Spriddleston; and Elizæus Heale, of the Inner
3 D 2

Temple, in the reign of Elizabeth, who was called
" Pious uses Heale," from his bequeathing £1500 per
annum for charitable purposes, was born at Wollaton;
both which places are in Brixtone parish.

BRIXTON, or BRIGHSTONE (*St. MARY*), a parish,
in the liberty of WEST MEDINA, Isle of Wight incorporation and division of the county of SOUTHAMPTON,
7 miles (S. W. by W.) from Newport; containing 710
inhabitants. The village is pleasantly situated, commanding an extensive view of the British Channel; and
in the neighbourhood are several of those chasms which
form so distinguishing a feature in this part of the coast.
The living is a rectory, valued in the king's books at
£30. 3. 4., and in the patronage of the Bishop of Winchester : the tithes have been commuted for £670. The
church is of very primitive character, with a massive
tower surmounted by a low spire of lead; the interior
is neatly fitted up. The rectory-house is a pleasant
residence, and the glebe comprises 5 acres. The Rev.
Noel Digby, rector, conveyed in 1814 an estate in trust
for the establishment of a school. The celebrated
Bishop Ken was rector of the parish, as was also the
present Bishop Wilberforce.

BRIXTON, an ecclesiastical district, in the parish
and union of LAMBETH, E. division of the hundred of
BRIXTON and of the county of SURREY, 4½ miles (S.
S. W.) from London; containing 10,175 inhabitants.
This is one of the most agreeable suburbs of the metropolis, and is divided into two parts, North Brixton and
Brixton Hill. It consists principally of a line of road
leading from Kennington to Streatham, upwards of two
miles in length, on each side of which are ranges of neat
and well-built houses, with others in detached situations
surrounded by small shrubberies. Within its limits,
also, is Tulse Hill, a gradual ascent from the church,
declining a little towards the east, and returning near
its greatest acclivity into the main road at Brixton Hill.
On both sides are elegant villas and handsome cottages,
the country residences of respectable families, commanding a fine view of the metropolis, and rich prospects
over the adjacent country. Works on a very extensive
scale have been formed for supplying the neighbourhood
with water. On Brixton Hill stands the house of correction for the county, containing ten wards and ten
day-rooms for the classification of prisoners ; the tread-
mill, completed in 1821, was the first established.

The church, dedicated to St. Matthew, and consecrated in June, 1824, was erected pursuant to an act of
parliament for dividing the extensive and populous
parish of Lambeth into five districts, Brixton being one.
It is in the Grecian style, with a handsome portico supported by four fluted columns of the Doric order at the
west, and contains 1926 sittings, of which 1022 are free ;
the expense of its erection amounted to £15,192, and
was defrayed by Her Majesty's Commissioners. The
tower was struck down by lightning, April 24th, 1842.
The living is a district incumbency ; net income, £650 ;
patron, the Archbishop of Canterbury. At Denmark
Hill, in the district, is a chapel dedicated to St. Matthew.
Holland Chapel, North Brixton, is a neat edifice, with a
bell-turret ; it was built in 1823, for Independents, but
has for some years been an episcopal proprietary chapel.
There are three places of worship for Independents, and
one each for Wesleyans and Unitarians. The St. Ann's
Society, for the maintenance, clothing, and education of

bitants. The living is a rectory, annexed to that of Cottered, and valued in the king's books at £10 : the church is in ruins.

BROADFIELD, a tything, in the parish of WRING-TON, union of AXBRIDGE, hundred of BRENT with WRINGTON, E. division of SOMERSET; containing 575 inhabitants.

BROADGATE, or BRADGATE, an extra-parochial liberty, in the hundred of WEST GOSCOTE, N. division of the county of LEICESTER, 5 miles (N. W.) from Leicester; containing 7 inhabitants. Here are the ruins of a mansion once the property of the noble family of Grey of Groby, of which was the accomplished and unfortunate Lady Jane Grey, who was born here in 1537. The ruins are small, chiefly composed of brick, and exhibit no signs of architectural grandeur, the house having been a large but low building in the form of a square, and turreted at each corner; it was built in the early part of the 16th century, by Thomas, Lord Grey, second Marquess of Dorset. Situated on the verge of Charnwood forest, it combined the variety of rocky and mountainous scenery on one side, and a rich and fertilized plain on the other. The grounds of which the park is formed, are about six miles in circumference, and surrounded and intersected by walls; they are well stocked with deer, and an extensive rabbit-warren supplies the neighbouring town of Leicester. A small stream, abounding in trout, enters the park near the church of Newtown-Linford, and, working its way amidst the rock and wood with which this part of the demesne is overspread, adds materially to the romantic beauty of the scenery. The Earl of Stamford and Warrington is the proprietor of Broadgate, which consists of about 1200 acres.

BROADGREEN, a hamlet, in the parish of BROAD-WAS, union of MARTLEY, Lower division of the hundred of OSWALDSLOW, Worcester and W. divisions of the county of WORCESTER; containing 113 inhabitants. It lies a short distance north of the road from Worcester to Bromyard, and half a mile north-east of the village of Broadwas.

BROADHEATH, a hamlet, in the parish of HALLOW, union of MARTLEY, Lower division of the hundred of OSWALDSLOW, Worcester and W. divisions of the county of WORCESTER, 3 miles (N. W.) from Worcester; containing 482 inhabitants. In this hamlet is a chapel of ease, dedicated to Christ, and built by subscription in 1836. A meeting-house was erected by Lady Huntingdon's Connexion, in 1825; and there is also a national school.

BROADHEMBURY (ST. ANDREW), a parish, and formerly a market-town, in the union of HONITON, hundred of HAYRIDGE, Cullompton and N. divisions of DEVON, 5 miles (N. W.) from Honiton; containing 851 inhabitants. The parish, according to a recent survey, comprises 4704 acres, of which 2513 are arable, 1101 meadow and pasture, 243 woodland and plantations, 139 orchard ground, and the remainder common and waste: there are some quarries of whetstone. The manor formerly belonged to the Abbot of Dunkeswell, who obtained for it the grant of a market and fair; the former has long been discontinued, but the latter is still held, for cattle, on the 11th of December. The living is a discharged vicarage, valued in the king's books at £16. 17.; net income, £227; patrons and appropriators, the Dean and Chapter of Exeter. The church is an ancient structure with a handsome tower, and contains 450 sittings. There is a place of worship for dissenters. In the village of Carswell was a small monastery, subordinate to the priory of Montacute; and Hembury Fort comprises the remains of an encampment. The Rev. A. Montague Toplady, the celebrated defender of Calvinistic principles, was vicar of the parish.

BROADHOLME, a hamlet, in the parish of THORNEY, union, and N. division of the wapentake, of NEWARK, S. division of the county of NOTTINGHAM, 1 mile (E. by N.) from Tuxford; containing 90 inhabitants. A small Præmonstratensian nunnery was founded here, in the latter part of the reign of Stephen, by Agnes de Camvile, in honour of the Blessed Virgin Mary; the revenue, in the 26th of Henry VIII., was estimated at £16. 15. 2.

BROADMAYNE (St. MARTIN), a parish, in the union of DORCHESTER, hundred of GEORGE, but locally in that of CULLIFORD-TREE, Dorchester division of DORSET, 4 miles (S. E. by S.) from Dorchester; containing 490 inhabitants. It is situated on the road from Dorchester to Wareham, and comprises by admeasurement 1500 acres, chiefly arable land; the soil is chalky, and the produce consists principally of wheat, barley, oats, and turnips. Bricks, of excellent quality, are made to a considerable extent. The living is a rectory, annexed to that of West Knighton, and valued in the king's books at £15. 4. 2.: land and a money payment were assigned in 1805, in lieu of tithes. The church is in the Norman style. Many tumuli of great antiquity may be seen in the neighbourhood.

BROADOAK (St. MARY), a parish, in the union of LISKEARD, hundred of WEST, E. division of CORNWALL, 6¾ miles (W. S. W.) from Liskeard; containing 303 inhabitants. The living is a discharged rectory, consolidated, in 1742, with the rectory of Boconnoc (which see), and valued in the king's books at £8. 13. 4. The church contains a handsome font.

BROADSIDE, a grieveship, in the parish of ALLENDALE, union of HEXHAM, S. division of TINDALE ward and of NORTHUMBERLAND; containing 123 inhabitants.

BROADSTAIRS, a small sea-port and hamlet, in the parish of St. PETER, union of THANET, hundred of RINGSLOW, or ISLE of THANET, lathe of St. AUGUSTINE, E. division of KENT, 2 miles (N. E. by N.) from Ramsgate, 4 (S. E. by S.) from Margate, and 75 (E.) from London; containing 1459 persons. This place, anciently called Bradstow, exhibits many vestiges of its former importance; and though subsequently reduced to an inconsiderable village, inhabited only by a few fishermen, it has lately risen into celebrity as a place of fashionable resort for sea-bathing, and is visited in the season by many respectable families, for whose accommodation several new buildings, and warm baths with every requisite appendage, have been erected. There are two public libraries, an assembly-room, and an excellent hotel. Her present Majesty, when Princess Victoria, often resided here with the Duchess of Kent during the summer months, at Pierremont House. Leading down to the shore is a stone arch, or portal, with walls built of flint, in which were gates and a portcullis, with a drawbridge attached to it, erected to protect the

outh by the British Channel. The number of acres is stimated at 2650, of which about 150 are detached. he soil is rich and fertile, especially along the sea-shore, onsisting of a deep rich loam, bearing luxuriant crops f wheat; the climate is mild and genial, being defended rom the north and north-east winds by the range of he South Down hills, and myrtles and evergreens of ll kinds flourish in perfection. The LIVING is a rectory, alued in the king's books at £36; net income, £602; atron and incumbent, the Rev. Peter Wood. The hurch is a spacious and venerable cruciform structure, artly in the Norman and early English styles, with a ow central tower, and a turret at the south-west angle; he interior is 139 feet in length, and 90 feet in breadth long the transepts. The chancel is richly groined, and he arch leading into it from the nave is in the richest tyle of the later Norman; it is lighted by a handsome ast window, and contains several canopied stalls finely culptured, and, in a recess on the south side, a bench urmounted by a Norman arch. In the chancel is a uperb monument to the memory of Thomas Lord De Warre, who died in 1526; and on the east side of ie south transept is a monument to Thomas, Lord De Warre, who died in 1554, and was buried in the hurch. The whole of the interior has been recently estored, at an expense of £1200. There are two hurches at Worthing, forming separate incumbencies. n the north of the parish is an eminence called Ciss-ury Hill, containing 20 acres, surrounded by a vallum, nd supposed to have been originally a British encamp-ent, subsequently adopted by the Romans, and lastly y the Saxons, from one of whose kings, Cissa, it is hought to derive its name.

BROADWAY (St. NICHOLAS), a parish, in the union of WEYMOUTH, hundred of CULLIFORD-TREE, Dor-hester division of DORSET, 5 miles (S. S. W.) from Dorchester; containing 498 inhabitants. This parish, which is situated on the Weymouth and Dorchester oad, and intersected by the river Wey, comprises by dmeasurement 11,000 acres, about one-third being rable. There are some fine quarries from which stone s obtained for lime and for building. At the hamlet f Nottingham is a mineral spring, used for medicinal urposes. The living is a rectory, annexed to that of 3incombe, and valued in the king's books at £7. 15. 2½.: he glebe contains about 100 acres. The southern en-rance of the church is distinguished by a beautiful Vorman arch of very early date. There is a place of vorship for Wesleyans.

BROADWAY (St. ALDELME), a parish, in the union f CHARD, hundred of ABDICK and BULSTONE, W. division of SOMERSET, 2½ miles (W. by N.) from Ilmin-ter; containing, with the tythings of Capland, Broad-vay, and Rapps, 570 inhabitants. The name of this dlace was given as descriptive of the situation of the ew scattered huts which were constructed at an early veriod, along each side of a broad path leading through vhat was then the forest of Roche, or Neroche, so de-iominated from a Roman encampment called Roche or lachiche Castle, on the edge of Blackdown Hill. The arish comprises 2012a. 3r. 32p., of which 1043 acres re arable, 850 meadow and pasture, 99 acres orchards nd gardens, and 19 wood. The living is a perpetual uracy; net income, £167; patron and impropriator, he Rev. William Palmer, D.D. The church belonged,

until the Reformation, to the abbey of Bisham in Berks, and is a fine cruciform structure, with an ancient tower at the west end, and windows in the later English style : in the churchyard is a beautiful cross on a pedestal, ornamented with figures of saints.

BROADWAY (St. EADBURGH), a parish, in the union of EVESHAM, Upper division of the hundred of PERSHORE, Pershore and E. divisions of the county of WORCESTER, 6 miles (S. E.) from Evesham; containing 1687 inhabitants. The parish comprehends by admea-surement 4692 acres, of which two-thirds are pasture, and the rest arable; it forms the south-eastern extre-mity of the county, is surrounded on all sides except the north by that of Gloucester, and intersected by the road from Worcester to London. The population is principally engaged in agriculture. There are some quarries of good freestone. The village is pleasantly situated on a plain, and is about three-fourths of a mile in length; the houses are principally of stone, and many of them ancient, forming a very wide street. In the time of Henry III. this place had a market on Friday, and a fair on the eve of St. John; but both have been long extinct. A post-office has been established. The living is a discharged vicarage, valued in the king's books at £10. 17., and in the patronage of certain Trustees; net income, £212 : land and an annual money payment were assigned in lieu of the tithes of the manor, in 1771. A new church was erected in 1840, on the site of a chapel of ease, an ancient and small building; it is in the early English style, with a handsome tower at the west end, and is capable of containing 1000 per-sons. There are places of worship for Independents, Wesleyans, and Roman Catholics. Thomas Hodges, in 1686, gave land for the instruction of 20 poor boys, which was exchanged for an allotment of 62 acres under an inclosure act, now producing £74 per annum.

BROADWELL (St. PAUL), a parish, in the union of STOW-ON-THE-WOLD, Upper division of the hundred of SLAUGHTER, E. division of the county of GLOUCESTER, 1½ mile (N. N. E.) from Stow; containing 345 inhabit-ants. It derives its name from a spring which rises within its limits. The living is a rectory, with that of Adlestrop annexed, valued in the king's books at £23. 11. 10½.; net income, £643; patron, Lord Leigh. The tithes of Broadway were commuted for land and an annual payment in money, in 1792.

BROADWELL (St. PETER AND St. PAUL), a pa-rish, in the union of WITNEY, hundred of BAMPTON, county of OXFORD, 5¼ miles (S.) from Burford; contain-ing, with the hamlet of Filkins, and the chapelries of Holwell and Kelmscott, 1051 inhabitants. The living is a discharged vicarage, valued in the king's books at £8. 14. 4½.; net income, £270; patron, the Rev. T. W. Goodlake; impropriators, the Master and Fellows of Trinity College, Oxford, who lease the impropriation to W. Hervey, Esq. The tithes were commuted in 1775, for land and annual money payments. The church is a spacious cruciform structure, with a massive western tower surmounted by a spire; in the chancel are some mural monuments to the Colston family. Near the churchyard are the remains of a cross. At Holwell and Kelmscott are chapels of case. On the estate of Broad-well Grove may be traced the line of the Roman Akeman-street, which continues its course towards *Akeman-ceastre* (Bath).

BROADWELL, a hamlet, in the parish of LEAMING-TON-HASTINGS, union of RUGBY, S. division of the hundred of KNIGHTLOW, S. division of the county of WARWICK, 2 miles (S. S. E.) from Leamington-Hastings; containing 220 inhabitants. It is said to have taken its name from a broad well or spring here. The road from Rugby to Southam passes on the west.

BROADWINSOR (ST. JOHN THE BAPTIST), a parish and liberty, in the union of BEAMINSTER, Bridport division of DORSET, 3 miles (W. by N.) from Beaminster; containing, with Little Winsor, which is in Redhone hundred, 1661 inhabitants. It comprises by admeasurement 6215 acres, of which 1222 are arable, 4579 meadow and pasture, and 292 wood and orchards. The living is a vicarage, valued in the king's books at £15. 8. 9., and in the patronage of the Bishop of Salisbury: the tithes have been commuted for £1282. 10., of which £750 are paid to the vicar, who has a glebe-house, and 9 acres of land; the impropriators have a glebe of 85 acres. A chapel of ease was erected at Blackdown in 1840, in the early English style, and dedicated to the Holy Trinity; it is a neat and substantial building, and will accommodate 300 persons.

BROADWOOD-KELLY, a parish, in the union of OAKHAMPTON, hundred of BLACK TORRINGTON, Black Torrington and Shebbear, and N. divisions of DEVON, 5½ miles (E. N. E.) from Hatherleigh; containing 471 inhabitants. The parish comprises 2400 acres, of which 557 are common or waste. The living is a rectory, valued in the king's books at £19. 7. 6.; net income, £238; patron, the Rev. John Hole.

BROADWOOD-WIDGER, county of DEVON.—See BRADWOOD-WIDGER.

BROBURY (ST. MARY), a parish, in the union of WEOBLEY, hundred of GRIMSWORTH, county of HEREFORD, 8¾ miles (E.) from Hay; containing 71 inhabitants. It is bounded on all sides, except the north-east, by a bend of the river Wye, and comprises 487 acres, the soil being of the full average productiveness, and the surface moderately wooded. The river is here crossed by a bridge leading to Bredwardine. The living is a discharged rectory, valued in the king's books at £4; net income, £180; patron and incumbent, the Rev. N. D. H. Newton.

BROCKDEN, or BROGDEN, a township, in the parish of BARNOLDSWICK, union of SKIPTON, E. division of the wapentake of STAINCLIFFE and EWCROSS, W. riding of YORK, 9¼ miles (W. S. W.) from Skipton; containing 219 inhabitants. The township comprises by computation 1670 acres, including Admergill, which adjoins Lancashire, and is ecclesiastically connected with the chapelry of Colne, in the parish of Whalley, in that county.

BROCKDISH (ST. PETER AND ST. PAUL), a parish, in the union of DEPWADE, hundred of EARSHAM, E. division of NORFOLK, 3¼ miles (S. W. by W.) from Harleston; containing 466 inhabitants. The road from Bury St. Edmund's to Yarmouth passes through the parish, and the river Waveney separates it from the county of Suffolk. The living is a rectory, valued in the king's books at £10, and in the gift of the France family: the tithes have been commuted for £340, and there are 24 acres of glebe. The church, which is chiefly in the later English style, consists of a nave, chancel, and south aisle, with an embattled tower; the

nave and chancel are divided by the remains of a carved screen. There is a place of worship for Wesleyans.

BROCKENHURST, a parish, in the union of LYMINGTON, E. division of the hundred of NEW FOREST, Lymington and S. divisions of the county of SOUTHAMPTON, 4¼ miles (N. by W.) from Lymington; containing 928 inhabitants. The village is of Saxon origin, and is mentioned in Domesday book under the name *Broceste*. It is beautifully situated on an eminence, on the road from Lyndhurst to Lymington, and commands a finely varied prospect over a considerable portion of the New Forest. The parish comprises 2880 acres, of which 547 are common or waste; the soil is in some places a strong clay loam. The Boldre or Lymington river flows past the northern extremity of the village. The living is united to that of Boldre. The church stands on an artificial mound, and, though somewhat disguised by modern alterations, exhibits various portions of early Norman architecture; it was enlarged in 1834. There is a place of worship for Baptists. Watcombe House, in Brockenhurst Park, was for three years the residence of John Howard, the philanthropist.

BROCKFORD, a hamlet, in the parish of WETHER-INGSETT, union and hundred of HARTISMERE, W. division of SUFFOLK, 1¼ mile (E. S. E.) from Mendlesham, and on the road from London to Norwich; containing 277 inhabitants.

BROCKHALL (ST. PETER AND ST. PAUL), a parish, in the union of DAVENTRY, hundred of NEWBOTTLE-GROVE, S. division of the county of NORTHAMPTON, 2 miles (N. by E.) from Weedon; containing 59 inhabitants. The parish comprises about 850 acres, consisting chiefly of pasture and plantations; it is intersected in its western portion by the Grand Junction canal, and the London and Birmingham railway, which has a station at Weedon, also runs through it. On that part of the Watling-street which passes by the gate of Mr. Thornton's premises, is found the uncommon plant called field eryngo. The living is a rectory, valued in the king's books at £13, and in the gift of the family of Thornton: the tithes have been commuted for £160. 6., and there is a good glebe-house, with upwards of 8 acres of glebe, exclusively of 30 acres in the adjoining parish of Floore. The church is a small ancient structure, adjoining Mr. Thornton's mansion, partly Norman, and partly in the early English style. Chalybeate springs are found in this and the neighbouring parishes, all deriving their mineral qualities from the inferior oolite, the escarpment of which forms the hills of the district, ranging north-east and south-west.

BROCKHAMPTON, with KNOWLE, a tything, in the parish and hundred of BUCKLAND-NEWTON, union of CERNE, Cerne division of DORSET, 12 miles (N. by E.) from Dorchester; containing 188 inhabitants.

BROCKHAMPTON, GLOUCESTER.—See SOUTHAM.

BROCKHAMPTON, a chapelry, in the parish and union of BROMYARD, hundred of BROXASH, county of HEREFORD, 3¼ miles (E. N. E.) from Bromyard; containing 88 inhabitants; and comprising, with the township of Norton, 2879 acres, exclusively of 133 in the extra-parochial place of Lower Brockhampton. It is a rich and fertile district. A free chapel was built some years ago, the right of presentation to which belongs to John Barneby, Esq.

BROCKHAMPTON (*Holy Trinity*), a parish, in the union of Ross, hundred of Greytree, county of Hereford, 6 miles (N.) from Ross; containing 132 inhabitants. The parish is beautifully situated on the left bank of the river Wye, and abounds with picturesque scenery. It comprises by admeasurement 785 acres, about 150 of which are pasture, and the rest arable, with the exception of about 60 acres of woodland, consisting chiefly of oak and elm. The soil is fertile, and is formed principally of the detritus of the old red sandstone; there are some quarries of good building-stone, and also stone for the roads. The village is pleasantly seated near the bank of the river, which is here navigable for barges of 40 tons' burthen. The living is a perpetual curacy; net income, £74; patrons and appropriators, the Dean and Chapter of Hereford. The great tithes have been commuted for £125, and the incumbent's for £63. 10. The church, a neat edifice in the later English style, has a tower and two bells, and a piscina for holy-water at the entrance door; in the churchyard is an ancient cross. A little to the north of the village are the remains of a Roman encampment with a double trench.

BROCKHAMPTON, a tything, in the parish of Newington, union of Wallingford, hundred of Ewelme, county of Oxford, 6½ miles (N.) from Wallingford; containing 113 inhabitants.

BROCKHAMPTON, a tything, in the parish, union, and liberty of Havant, Fareham and S. divisions of the county of Southampton; containing 109 inhabitants.

BROCKHOLES.—See Grimsargh.

BROCKLEBANK, with Stoneraise, a township, in the parish of Westward, union of Wigton, Allerdale ward below Derwent, W. division of Cumberland, 5½ miles (S. E.) from Wigton; containing 617 inhabitants.

BROCKLESBY (*All Saints*), a parish, in the union of Caistor, E. division of the wapentake of Yarborough, parts of Lindsey, county of Lincoln, 10 miles (S. E.) from Brigg; containing, with Newsham extraparochial, and the hamlet of Limber Parva, 243 inhabitants. It comprises by computation 2454 acres, of which 1614 are pasture, 380 arable, and 460 woodland. The living is a discharged rectory, valued in the king's books at £9. 10. 10.; net income, £287; patron, the Earl of Yarborough: the tithes were commuted in 1812, for land and corn-rents. A monastery of the Præmonstratensian order, in honour of St. Mary and St. Martial, was founded at Newsham, by Peter de Gousla, in 1143 : at the Dissolution it had a revenue of £114. 1. 4.

BROCKLEY (*St. Nicholas*), a parish, in the union of Bedminster, hundred of Chewton, E. division of Somerset, 9 miles (S. W.) from Bristol; containing 171 inhabitants. This parish, which is beautifully situated on the road from Bristol to Weston-super-Mare, comprises by computation 700 acres. There are some quarries of limestone of excellent quality. Lead-ore exists in the eastern part of the parish, and there are numerous basaltic columns, similar to those forming the Giant's Causeway in Ireland. About a quarter of a mile to the south-east of the church, is a strikingly romantic glen called Brockley-Coombe, nearly a mile in length, inclosed on each side by steep banks of rugged rocks, rising to the height of nearly 300 feet, and thickly interspersed with trees of luxuriant growth. The Bristol and

Exeter railway skirts the parish, about a mile to the north of the church. The living is a discharged rectory, valued in the king's books at £9. 18. 4.; net income, £128; patrons, the Trustees of the late Rev. Wadham Pigott. The church is an ancient structure, with a square embattled tower, and a south porch; the interior displays much elegance.

BROCKLEY (*St. Andrew*), a parish, in the union and hundred of Thingoe, W. division of Suffolk, 6¾ miles (S. S. W.) from Bury St. Edmund's; containing 380 inhabitants, and comprising by computation nearly 1500 acres. The living is a rectory, valued in the king's books at £10. 4. 2.; net income, £330; patron and incumbent, the Rev. William Sprigge. The rectory-house was consumed on the night of the 6th of April, 1841, by an accidental fire which destroyed property to the amount of £2000. The church is an ancient structure.

BROCKMOOR, an ecclesiastical parish, in the parish of King's Swinford, union of Stourbridge, N. division of the hundred of Seisdon, S. division of the county of Stafford, 2½ miles (S. W.) from Dudley; containing about 3500 inhabitants. It is nearly a mile and a half in length, and three-quarters of a mile in breadth in the broadest part, tapering to a point at one extremity : the surface is varied. The Stourbridge Extension canal bounds the parish on the west side; the road from Dudley to Stourbridge, by Brierley Hill, passes on the east; and the Oxford, Worcester, and Wolverhampton railway passes through. The inhabitants are employed in coal-mines, iron-manufactories, and a brick-factory. Brockmoor was formed into a separate ecclesiastical district in September, 1844, under the act 6th and 7th Victoria, cap. 37; and, conformably with its provisions, became a new parish on the consecration of a church, in December, 1845. The edifice is in the Norman style; is of handsome appearance, with stained-glass windows in the chancel; and was built at a cost of about £3000, provided by church building societies, aided by subscription. A parsonage-house, which stands in an acre of ground, was erected at an expense of £900, whereof £500 were contributed by Lord Ward, and the same nobleman presented two acres for a churchyard. There is a place of worship for Wesleyans; also a commodious school-house, recently built, with rooms for boys, girls, and infants, and apartments for the master and mistress : the cost of its erection, about £1000, was provided by the National Society, the Privy Council, and subscription.

BROCKSFIELD, a township, in the parish of Embleton, union of Alnwick, S. division of Bambrough ward, N. division of Northumberland, 2¾ miles (N. N. E.) from Alnwick; containing 24 inhabitants. It comprises 312 acres; the soil is of an inferior nature, but several young healthy plantations are scattered over the township.

BROCKTHROP (*St. Swithin*), a parish, in the union of Wheatenhurst, Middle division of the hundred of Dudstone and King's Barton, E. division of the county of Gloucester, 4 miles (S. E.) from Gloucester; containing 169 inhabitants. This place is situated on the road between Gloucester and Stroud, near the head of a small stream which falls into the Severn. The living is a discharged vicarage, endowed with a portion of the rectorial tithes, and valued in the king's books at £7. 17. 6.; it has the perpetual curacy of Whaddon annexed, and is in the patronage of the

Dean and Chapter of Gloucester for two turns, and J. Pitt, Esq., for one : net income, £186.

BROCKTON, a township, in the parish of WORTHEN, hundred of CHIRBURY, S. division of SALOP, 7½ miles (N. E.) from Montgomery ; containing 303 inhabitants.

BROCKTON, a township, in the parish of BASWICH, E. division of the hundred of CUTTLESTONE, union, and S. division of the county, of STAFFORD, 4 miles (S. E. by E.) from Stafford ; containing 238 inhabitants. The township comprises about 800 acres. There is an excellent freestone-quarry ; and from a fine stratum of clay large quantities of bricks are made. Brockton Hall is an ancient mansion situated in a pleasant park : near it is Brockton Lodge.

BROCKWEAR COMMON, an extra-parochial district, adjoining the parish of HEWELSFIELD, in the union of CHEPSTOW, hundred of ST. BRIAVELL'S, W. division of the county of GLOUCESTER, 5½ miles (N. N. E.) from Chepstow ; containing 212 inhabitants.

BROCKWORTH (ST. GEORGE), a parish, in the Upper division of the hundred of DUDSTONE and KING'S BARTON, union, and E. division of the county, of GLOUCESTER, 4 miles (E. S. E.) from Gloucester ; containing 409 inhabitants. This parish, which is situated on the old road from Gloucester to Cirencester, comprises by measurement 1840 acres : stone for the roads is found. The living is a discharged vicarage, valued in the king's books at £6. 3. 4. ; patron and impropriator, J. Watts, Esq. : the tithes have been commuted for £151, and the glebe comprises 26 acres. The church is a very ancient structure, with a low central tower ; in the chancel is a handsome marble monument to Sir Christopher Guise. The parish is crossed by the Ermin-street.

BRODSWORTH (ST. MICHAEL), a parish, in the union of DONCASTER, N. division of the wapentake of STRAFFORTH and TICKHILL, W. riding of YORK, 5½ miles (N. W. by W.) from Doncaster ; containing, with the township of Brodsworth and the hamlets of Pigburn and Scawsby, 467 inhabitants. It abounds with limestone of superior quality, which is extensively quarried. The living is a discharged vicarage, valued in the king's books at £6. 6. 10¼. ; net income, £367 ; patron, the Archbishop of York. An allotment of land was given in lieu of tithes, in 1815. The Brodsworth estate belonged to Peter Thellusson, Esq., and is now vested in trustees, according to the singular will of that gentleman, who directed that the greater part of his immense property should be allowed to accumulate, and at a future fixed period, in default of a male heir, be applied towards discharging the national debt.

BROKENBOROUGH (ST. JOHN THE BAPTIST), a parish, in the union and hundred of MALMESBURY, Malmesbury and Kingswood, and N. divisions of WILTS, 1¾ mile (N. W. by N.) from Malmesbury ; containing 429 inhabitants. It comprises about 3000 acres of land, nearly the whole of which is the property of the Earl of Suffolk, who is lord of the manor : the river Avon runs through the parish. The living is annexed, with that of Charlton, to the vicarage of Westport St. Mary. In excavating the ground in the parish, near the mouth of the Kennet, for the Great Western railway, a sword, several human skulls, and some horse-shoes were found near the surface ; probably the spot was the scene of a battle in the wars of Charles I.

BROKENHAUGH, EAST and WEST, a township, in the parochial chapelry of HAYDON, union of HEXHAM, N. W. division of TINDALE ward, S. division of NORTHUMBERLAND, 6 miles (W. by N.) from Hexham ; containing 250 inhabitants. It is situated on the west of the South Tyne river, and is divided into farms.

BROMBLOW, or BROMLOW, a quarter, in the parish of WORTHEN, hundred of CHIRBURY, S. division of SALOP ; containing 468 inhabitants.

BROMBORROW (ST. BARNABAS), a parish, in the union of WIRRALL, partly in the Lower, but chiefly in the Upper, division of the hundred of WIRRALL, S. division of the county of CHESTER, 11 miles (N. N. W.) from Chester, on the road to Birkenhead ; containing, with the township of Brimstage, 450 inhabitants. This parish is enumerated, by the learned editor of the Saxon Chronicle, among the places which, from the similarity of name, may claim to be the scene of the decisive action fought at Brunanburh, between the Saxons under Athelstan, and the Danes under Anlaf and Constantine, the latter of whom were defeated : other writers, however, disallow the claim. A monastery was founded at this place, then called Brimesburgh, by Ethelfleda, the celebrated Countess of Mercia, about 912 ; but it was demolished previously to the Conquest, subsequently to which period the manor was given by Ranulph de Gernons, Earl of Chester, to the monks of the abbey of St. Werburgh. Prince Edward, when Earl of Chester, granted a licence in 1277 for a market here on Monday, and a fair on the eve, festival, and morrow of St. Barnabas ; both these have long been discontinued. The PARISH is bounded on the east by the river Mersey, and comprises 1525 acres, whereof 630 are arable, 813 meadow, 69 wood, and the remainder waste. The surface is level, the soil partly sandy loam and partly marl and clay, and the scenery rich and varied : there are good stone-quarries. The Rev. J. Mainwaring is the chief owner of the land, and resides at Bromborrow Hall. The living is a perpetual curacy ; net income, £92 ; patrons, the Dean and Chapter of Chester. The church has been rebuilt, and is of plain pointed architecture ; the chancel window is of stained glass, with representations of Our Saviour and the sacramental emblems. A school is supported by the incumbent. Petrifying powers are attributed to a spring here.

BROMBY, a township, in the parish of FRODINGHAM, union of GLANDFORD-BRIGG, E. division of the wapentake of MANLEY, parts of LINDSEY, county of LINCOLN, 7½ miles (W. N. W.) from Glandford-Brigg ; containing 160 inhabitants. It comprises 2995 acres, of which 819 are common or waste land, and is chiefly in the vale of the Trent. The village is situated about a mile south of Frodingham. There are places of worship for Wesleyans and Primitive Methodists.

BROME, or BROOME (ST. MICHAEL), a parish, in the union of LODDON and CLAVERING, hundred of LODDON, E. division of NORFOLK, 2½ miles (N. N. E.) from Bungay ; containing 610 inhabitants. The parish is bounded on the south by the navigable river Waveney, which separates it from the county of Suffolk ; it comprises 1442 acres, whereof 24 are common or waste. The living is a discharged rectory, valued in the king's books at £6. 13. 4., and in the patronage of Sir W. F. F. Middleton, Bart. : the tithes have been commuted for £286, and there is a good glebe-house, with about 28 acres of land.

valued in the king's books at £4. 15. 7½., and in the gift of the Marquess of Bristol : the tithes have been commuted for £270, and the glebe consists of an acre and a half. The church is a neat edifice.

BROMFIELD (*St. Kentigern*), a parish, in the union of Wigton, partly in Cumberland ward, E. division, but chiefly in Allerdale ward below Derwent, W. division, of Cumberland ; comprising the chapelry of Allonby, and the townships of Blencogo, Dundraw with Kelsick, Langrigg with Mealrigg, and West Newton ; and containing 2312 inhabitants, of whom 364 are in the township of Bromfield with Crookdake and Scales, 6 miles (W. by S.) from Wigton. It is situated on the shore of the Solway Firth. The living is a vicarage, endowed with part of the rectorial tithes, and valued in the king's books at £22 ; net income, £270 ; patron, the Bishop of Carlisle ; impropriator of the remainder of the great tithes, Sir Henry Fletcher, Bart. The tithes were commuted for land in 1817. There is a separate incumbency at Allonby. A free school, in the churchyard, was founded by Richard Osmotherly in 1612, and endowed with £10 a year : this was subsequently augmented by a donation of £100 from the family of Tomlinson ; and in 1805, Mr. Tomlinson bequeathed £1400, one-fourth of which was assigned to the school. In a field belonging to the vicar, the site of Mungo Castle is visible.

BROMFIELD (*St. Mary*), a parish, in the union of Ludlow, hundred of Munslow, S. division of Salop, 3 miles (N. W. by W.) from Ludlow, on the road to Shrewsbury ; containing 531 inhabitants. The surface is undulated, the soil various, and the scenery beautiful. Of 6110*a*. 3*r*. 37*p*., the area of the parish, nearly equal portions are arable and pasture, the latter preponderating ; and there is much fine wood, particularly around Oakley Park, the seat of the Hon. R. H. Clive, which is charmingly situated on the banks of the river Teme. Good stone is obtained for building. The living is a vicarage, valued in the king's books at £6 ; net income, £334, with a house built in 1845 ; patron and impropriator, Mr. Clive. The church, which has a square tower, was repaired in 1842. It is part of a larger church that belonged to a Benedictine priory established as a cell to the abbey of St. Peter at Gloucester, about 1155, on the site of a college of prebendaries, or Secular canons, of earlier foundation : the revenue, at the Dissolution, was £78. 19. 4.

BROMFLEET, a township, in the parish of South Cave, union of Howden, Hunsley-Beacon division of the wapentake of Harthill, E. riding of York, 4¼ miles (S. W.) from South Cave ; containing 206 inhabitants. The township is situated on the north side of the Humber, and comprises about 1220 acres, forming a level district of rich marshes, including part of Walling fen, inclosed in 1780. There is a place of worship for Wesleyans. The line of the Hull and Selby railway passes in the vicinity.

BROMHALL, a township, in the parish of Wrenbury, union and hundred of Nantwich, S. division of the county of Chester, 3¾ miles (S. S. W.) from Nantwich ; containing 157 inhabitants. It comprises about 1200 acres, of a clayey and sandy soil. The impropriate tithes have been commuted for £124, and the vicarial for £33. 11. 5., the latter sum payable to the incumbent of Acton.

3 E 2

BROMHAM (St. Owen), a parish, in the hundred
of Willey, union and county of Bedford, 3 miles
(W. N. W.) from Bedford; containing 314 inhabitants.
This place is situated on the banks of the Ouse, over
which is a neat bridge of 25 arches (including 22 across
the meadows) on the line of road from Bedford to Newport-Pagnell. It is recorded that, in the years 1399 and
1648, the waters of the river had so far deserted their
channel, that persons walked in its bed for nearly three
miles in this part of its course. The parish comprises
1798 acres, the soil of which, in the northern part, is a
heavy clay, and in the other parts a light sand, resting
on a deep gravel; an excellent coarse building-stone is
quarried, beneath which is a thin stratum of a softer
stone, suitable for sculpture, and which hardens upon
exposure to the air. The females are employed in making pillow-lace. The living is a vicarage, with that of
Oakley annexed, valued in the king's books at £8; net
income, £336; patrons, the Provost and Fellows of
Eton College: there is a good glebe-house, built in
1831, with 18 acres of glebe. The church is pleasantly
situated in the centre of the Park, the village standing
partly round it, in the form of a crescent; it was built
in the reign of Edward IV., and the interior was neatly
restored in 1844, at a cost of £100. In 1825 the tower
was struck by lightning, which forced out two of the
southern windows. This edifice contains some handsome monuments to the families of Trevor and Dyve, of
which latter was Sir Lewis Dyve, commander for
Charles I. of the Newport-Pagnell district in the civil
war. When about to be executed after the king's death,
Sir Lewis threw himself from a great height into the
Thames, and escaped by his skill in swimming. He
was the great antagonist of Sir Samuel Luke, of Cople
Hall, now a farmhouse, where Dr. Butler wrote *Hudibras*.
There is a day and Sunday school; also a library of
three hundred volumes, presented by Lord Trevor to the
vicar and parishioners.

BROMHAM (St. Nicholas), a parish, in the union
of Devizes, hundred of Potterne and Cannings, Devizes and N. divisions of Wilts, 4 miles (N. W.) from
Devizes; containing 1558 inhabitants. This place,
which is situated near the Roman road from Marlborough to Bath, appears to have been a villa of the
Romans. In 1763, a tessellated pavement and other
remains of Roman baths were discovered, which were
more fully explored in 1840, when four others were
cleared from the earth in which they had lain so many
centuries imbedded. The lordship, previously to the
Conquest, belonged to Harold, Earl of the West Saxons,
and subsequently king of England. Spye Park, about
two miles north of the village, in the reign of Charles II.
was the property and occasional residence of the Earl of
Rochester. The manufacture of fine broad-cloth, and
of kerseymeres, is carried on to a moderate extent. The
living is a rectory, valued in the king's books at
£12. 16. 0½., and in the gift of the family of Starkey:
the tithes have been commuted for £780, and there are
79 acres of glebe. The church contains a mural tablet
to the memory of Henry Season, M.D., the projector of
a well-known almanack; and in an ancient chapel, at
the east end, are several monuments to the family of
Baynton, formerly lords of the manor. There are places
of worship for Baptists and Wesleyans. Dr. George
Webb, consecrated Bishop of Limerick in 1634, and the

vided. It contains an ancient Norman font, and various interesting monuments, among which are those of several of the bishops of Rochester; of Dr. Hawkesworth, author of the *Adventurer*, who was a native of the place; and of Elizabeth, wife of Dr. Johnson, who was buried here. A district church, dedicated to the Trinity, has been erected on the common, in the later English style: the living is a perpetual curacy; patron, the Bishop; net income of the incumbent, £120. There are places of worship for Independents and Methodists. A national school is partly supported by subscription: fifteen boys and as many girls are clothed by means of the dividends on £1400 stock, purchased with donations, the chief of which were by the Rev. George Wilson in 1718, and Launcelot Tolson in 1726. *Bromley College*, at the north-eastern extremity of the town, was founded in 1666, by John Warner, Bishop of Rochester, who endowed it with £450 per annum, for the residence and support of 20 widows of loyal and orthodox clergymen, to each of whom he assigned £20 per annum, and to a chaplain £50. This endowment has been augmented by many subsequent benefactions. In 1767, the Rev. William Hetherington bequeathed £2000 Old South Sea annuities; in 1774, Dr. Zachary Pearce, Bishop of Rochester, gave £5000 in the same stock; in 1782, William Pearce, the bishop's brother, bequeathed £12,000; in 1823, Walter King, Bishop of Rochester, gave £3000 three per cents.; and in 1824, Mrs. Rose bequeathed £8000. There are at present 40 widows resident in the college, who have £38 per annum each, with occasional diocesan grants; two additional widows, who occupy the treasurer's wing, and receive £20 a year each; and three out-pensioners, each of whom has £30 a year from the gift of Bishop King. The chaplain's salary has been advanced to £150. The college is a handsome appropriate pile of building of red brick, faced with stone, surrounding two quadrangular areas; it is encircled by about four acres of land, tastefully laid out. The poor law union of Bromley comprises 16 parishes or places, and contains a population of 16,079.

BROMLEY, ABBOTS (ST. *NICHOLAS*), a parish, in the union of UTTOXETER, S. division of the hundred of PIREHILL, N. division of the county of STAFFORD, 12½ miles (E.) from Stafford, and 130 (N. W. by N.) from London; containing 1508 inhabitants. This place is bounded on the south-west by the river Blythe, and derives its distinguishing name from a Benedictine monastery founded at Blythebury, in the neighbourhood, in the latter part of the reign of Henry I., or the beginning of that of Stephen, by Hugh Mavesyn, and dedicated to St. Giles. The parish comprises 9392a. 17p., and contains the manor of Abbots or Paget's Bromley, the property of the Marquess of Anglesey; the manor of Bagots-Bromley, the ancient possession of the Bagot family, of Blithfield Hall, to whom it belonged prior to the Conquest; the manor of Bromley-Park, consisting of upwards of 900 acres, belonging to the Earl of Dartmouth; and the liberty of Bromley-Hurst. The trade is principally in malt, which is sold to some extent. The market here has been discontinued for many years: the market-house is an ancient building covered with shingles. The fairs are on March 11th, May 22nd, and September 4th, and are chiefly for cattle. The turnpike-road from Uttoxeter to Lichfield passes through the

397

village, which is six miles distant from the former, and twelve from the latter place.

The living is a discharged vicarage, valued in the king's books at £5. 1. 8.; net income, about £155; patron and impropriator, the Marquess of Anglesey. The church is an ancient structure, partly in the decorated and partly in the later English style, with a Norman entrance; it has undergone considerable repairs, and been much modernised. There is a place of worship for Independents. A free school was founded in 1606, by Richard Clarke, who left £300 to purchase land for its endowment; the annual income is £20. An hospital was founded in 1702, by Lambard Bagot, Esq., who bequeathed £800 for its erection and endowment, for six aged men, three of this parish, and one from each of the parishes of Yoxhall, Hanbury, and Tatenhill; the income was augmented by Charles Bagot, Esq., and a matron has been added, who, as well as each of the inmates, receives a stipend of £10 per annum.

BROMLEY, GERRARD'S, a township, in the parish of ECCLESHALL, union of STONE, N. division of the hundred of PIREHILL and of the county of STAFFORD, 6 miles (N. W.) from Eccleshall; containing 33 inhabitants. This place is included in Broughton quarter. The tithes have been commuted for £83 payable to the Dean and Chapter of Durham, and 18s. to the vicar of the parish.

BROMLEY, GREAT (ST. *GEORGE*), a parish, in the union and hundred of TENDRING, N. division of Essex, 4½ miles (S. S. W.) from Manningtree; containing 738 inhabitants. This parish, which includes an area ten miles in circumference, belonged, at the time of the Norman survey, to Geoffrey de Magnaville. An act for inclosing lands was passed in 1843. The living is a rectory, valued in the king's books at £16. 16. 0½.; net income, £698; patrons, the family of Graham. The church is a handsome and spacious structure, with a lofty tower of elegant design, and consists of a nave, aisles, and chancel, the roofs of which are lofty and beautifully enriched. There is a place of worship for Wesleyans.

BROMLEY, KING'S (ALL *SAINTS*), a parish, in the union of LICHFIELD, N. division of the hundred of OFFLOW and of the county of STAFFORD, 5 miles (N. by E.) from Lichfield; containing 718 inhabitants. The manor was anciently called *Brom Legge*, and derived its present name from having been the property of the crown for nearly two centuries after the Norman Conquest, previously to which time it had been distinguished as the residence of the earls of Mercia. Leofric, the husband of the famous Lady Godiva, died here in 1057; and she was herself buried here. The road from Lichfield to Ashbourn in Derbyshire runs through the parish, and the river Trent passes by the village, about a mile from which is a wharf communicating with the Grand Trunk canal. The parish comprises 3463a. 3r. 16p., of which upwards of 1700 acres are arable, 1300 pasture and meadow, and nearly 200 in plantations. Bromley Hall is a handsome mansion surrounded by an extensive park. The living is a perpetual curacy, in the patronage of the Prebendary of Alrewas and Weeford in the Cathedral of Lichfield; net income, £72. The great tithes have been commuted for £320, and the small for £105; the glebe consists of 10 acres. The church is partly in the early English style, and is adorned with large and beautiful windows; it contains monuments to the families of Agard, Newton, and Lane. There is a place of worship for Wesleyans. A school was founded in 1699, by the Rev. Richard Crosse, who endowed it with property now producing £110 per annum; almshouses for 7 widows were also founded, and partly endowed, by him.

BROMLEY ST. LEONARD'S (St. Mary), a parish, in the union of Poplar, Tower division of the hundred of Ossulstone, county of Middlesex, ½ a mile (S.) from Bow, and 3½ miles (E.) from Cornhill, London; containing 6154 inhabitants. The name appears to have been derived from *Brom*, broom, and *Ley*, a field, indicating that a great quantity of broom anciently grew in the vicinity. The village is lighted with gas, and supplied with water by the works of the East London Water Company: there is a distillery on a large scale, near the western entrance into it. A communication with the Regent's canal has been formed by a cut from the river Lea, made by Sir Charles Duckett. Two headboroughs and a constable are annually appointed at the manorial court; and the parochial affairs are under the superintendence of a select vestry. The living is a donative; net income, £190; patron, John Walter, Esq.; impropriators, the Mann family. The church, a small plain structure comprising only a nave and chancel, is surrounded by a high wall, and exhibits some remains of Norman architecture, containing also, in the southern wall of the chancel, some stone seats. It is part of a larger edifice, the conventual church of a Benedictine nunnery founded soon after the Conquest, by William, Bishop of London, and dedicated to St. Leonard: the society consisted of a prioress and nine nuns, whose revenue, in the 26th of Henry VIII., was rated at £121. 16. At New Town is a second church, the living of which is a perpetual curacy; net income, £100; patron, the Incumbent of Bromley. The Bow Wesleyan meeting-house stands in the parish. National and infants' schools are supported by subscription, and a Sunday school is endowed with £1400 three per cents., from the interest of which the minister is paid £20 per annum, to catechise the children once a month, and for an annual examination. Seventeen children of the parish are entitled to receive education at Sir John Jolles's school at Stratford: Sir John also founded eight almshouses for the poor at Stratford and Bromley, opposite to which are almshouses established for the benefit of decayed sail-makers, by John Edmonson; at the upper extremity, between the two rows of almshouses, is a neat chapel.

BROMLEY, LITTLE (St. Mary), a parish, in the union and hundred of Tendring, N. division of Essex, 3½ miles (S. S. W.) from Manningtree; containing 426 inhabitants. It comprises by measurement 1841 acres, of which 1500 are arable, 80 pasture, 38 woodland, and about 220 acres roads and waste. The living is a rectory, valued in the king's books at £8, and in the patronage of Wadham College, Oxford: the tithes have been commuted for £560, and there is a good glebe-house, with 11 acres of land. The church is a plain edifice, with a stone tower.

BROMPTON, a hamlet, in the parishes of Chatham and Gillingham, parliamentary borough of Chatham, union of Medway, hundred of Chatham and Gillingham, lathe of Aylesford, W. division of Kent; con-

which is in the parish, 1534 inhabitants, of whom 609 are in the township of Brompton, 8 miles (S. W. by W.) from Scarborough. This is said to have been the residence of the kings of Northumberland; and on an eminence called Castle Hill, are the foundations of an ancient castle, about half a mile from which is Gallows' Hill, the place of execution for criminals within the barony. The Cayley family, of whom Sir William Cayley was distinguished for his services to King Charles I. and II., have been located here for more than two centuries. The parish comprises by measurement 10,180 acres, of which about 6000 are arable; the pasture, meadow, and heath cover 4000 acres, and about 180 are wood: the soil varies in quality in different situations, and the scenery in many parts is picturesque and beautiful. Limestone, in which some fossils are found, is quarried for building, for agricultural purposes, and the repair of roads; and a kind of slate is also obtained, used for roofing houses: a factory for bricks, coarse pots, &c., employs about fifteen persons. A fair is annually held for the sale of pigs, from which the name of Swine Brompton is sometimes given to the parish. The living is a discharged vicarage, valued in the king's books at £12; net income, £103; patron, Sir George Cayley, Bart., to whom the impropriation also belongs: the tithes were commuted in 1768, for land and a money payment. The church, which is one of the most spacious and elegant in the county, is in the decorated style, with a square tower surmounted by a graceful spire. At Snainton is a chapel of ease. There are three places of worship for Wesleyans, and one for Primitive Methodists, John of Brompton, a monkish historian, who compiled a laborious work on the early annals of England, including the period between the years 558 and 1198, is supposed to have been born here: he lived twenty years in the Benedictine abbey of Whitby, during the abbacy of John of Skelton, which commenced in 1413.

BROMPTON-PATRICK (St. Patrick), a parish, in the union of Leyburn; comprising the townships of Brompton-Patrick and Newton-le-Willows, and part of those of Arrowthorne and Scotton, in the wapentake of Hang-East, and part of the chapelry of Hunton in the wapentake of Hang-West, N. riding of York; and containing, with the whole of Arrowthorne, Hunton, and Scotton, 1130 inhabitants, of whom 181 are in the township of Brompton-Patrick, 3¾ miles (N. W. by W.) from Bedale. The living is a perpetual curacy; net income, £100; patron, the Bishop of Chester: C. H. Elsley, Esq., is impropriator of the lay rectory, which is valued in the king's books at £34. 13. 1½. Mr. Elsley's tithes in the township of Brompton-Patrick have been commuted for £81, and his glebe consists of 91 acres. The church is an ancient edifice in the decorated English style, and the chancel is particularly admired, but the tower is considered a deformity: tradition relates that the original one having been blown down in a storm, the present was erected, in 1572.

BROMPTON-RALPH (St. Mary), a parish, in the union of Williton, hundred of Williton and Free-Manners, W. division of Somerset, 3½ miles (N.) from Wiveliscombe; containing 492 inhabitants. It comprises by admeasurement 2700 acres, of which 1460 are arable, 760 pasture and meadow, and 120 wood. An act for the inclosure of lands was passed in 1842. The

living is a rectory, valued in the king's books at £17. 10. 5., and in the patronage of Gen. Blommant and the Rev. T. Sweet Escott: the tithes have been commuted for £400. The greater part of the church was rebuilt in 1738. Between Combe and Holcombe, in the parish, are vestiges of an encampment supposed to have been constructed by the Romans.

BROMPTON REGIS (St. Mary), a parish, in the union of Dulverton, hundred of Williton and Free-Manners, W. division of Somerset, 5 miles (N. E.) from Dulverton; containing 875 inhabitants. This place anciently constituted a hundred; and in the reign of Henry II. a priory was endowed by William de Say, for Black canons, and dedicated to St. Nicholas: it was an appendage of Glastonbury Abbey, and continued till the Dissolution, when its revenue was £98. 14. 9½. About two miles to the south of the church are some remains of this establishment, called Barlynch Priory; and in the burial-ground have been discovered several stone coffins, containing skeletons. The parish is bounded on the south-west by the river Exe, which receives many mountain-streams, all stocked with trout. It comprises about 8000 acres, of which a considerable portion is un-inclosed moorland, abounding with black game; and in the woods are great numbers of the wild red-deer peculiar to this country, for the hunting of which a subscription pack of hounds was formerly kept. The surface is diversified with hills and valleys, richly wooded with coppices of oak and hedge-rows of beech, and abounding in romantic scenery; the vales are watered by the river Had Yeo. There are quarries of good building-stone. A weekly market and two annual fairs were granted to the lord of the manor, Sir Thomas de Bessilles, Knt.; the market has long since fallen into disuse; but the fairs are still held, in May and Oct., for cattle and sheep. The living is a discharged vicarage, valued in the king's books at £12. 5. 7½.; patrons, the Master and Fellows of Emmanuel College, Cambridge; impropriators, Trustees of various parishes. The rectorial tithes have been commuted for £176, and the vicarial for £421. 15.; and there is a good glebe-house, with about 30 acres of land; also an estate in another parish, belonging to the vicarage. The church has a curiously carved screen, separating the nave from the chancel. Three Roman tumuli are visible on an adjacent eminence; and at a mount called Hadborough, near the western extremity of Haddon Hill, Roman coins have been found.

BROMPTON-UPON-SWALE, a township, in the parish of Easby, union of Richmond, wapentake of Gilling-East, N. riding of York, 1¾ mile (N. W.) from Catterick; containing 399 inhabitants. It is situated on the north side of the river Swale, and on the road from Catterick to Richmond; and comprises by computation 1710 acres of land.

BROMSBERROW (St. Mary), a parish, in the union of Newent, hundred of Botloe, W. division of the county of Gloucester, 4 miles (S. E.) from Led-bury; containing 283 inhabitants. This parish, which anciently formed part of Malvern Chase, was for many years the property of the Yate family, from whom it was purchased by the late David Ricardo, Esq.; it comprises 1803 acres, of which about 1000 are arable, 381 meadow and pasture, 119 wood, and 76 common or waste. The soil is rather of a sandy nature; the surface is strikingly varied, and the scenery, which is greatly enriched with wood, is highly picturesque. Keysend Hill, the last of the Malvern range, is within the parish. The hill of Conygree, which is partly artificial, is near the church, and is of oval form, about 50 feet high and 700 yards round the base : it is thought to have been a hill-altar where the Druids held an annual assembly for judicial and other purposes. The living is a rectory, valued in the king's books at £7. 15.; patron, Earl Beauchamp : the tithes have been commuted for £350, and there is a good glebe-house, with a glebe of 55 acres. The church is an ancient edifice, with a low tower ; adjoining the chancel is the mausoleum of the Yate family, built about a century since.

BROMSGROVE (St. John the Baptist), a market-town and parish, the head of a union, and formerly a borough, in the Upper division of the hundred of Half-shire, Droitwich and E. divisions of the county of Worcester, 13 miles (N. E. by N.) from Worcester, 13 (S. W.) from Birmingham, and 116 (N. W.) from London; containing 9671 inhabitants. This place, anciently Bremesgrave, was a royal demesne at the time of the Conquest, and continued to be so till the reign of Henry III.: it returned members to parliament in the 23rd of Edward I. During the civil war it was the head-quarters of a party of royalists employed in the siege of Hawkesley House, about three miles distant, which, in 1645, was fortified and garrisoned by the parliament. The town is pleasantly situated on the western bank of the river Salwarp, and consists principally of one street, extending for a considerable distance along the Birmingham and Worcester turnpike-road ; the houses are in general substantial and well built ; and the inhabitants amply supplied with water. In 1846 an act was passed for paving and otherwise improving the place. The principal articles of manufacture are nails and silk buttons : potatoes, for the Bristol and other markets, are extensively cultivated in the neighbourhood. The Birmingham and Worcester canal passes within three miles to the east; and the Birmingham and Gloucester railway has one of its principal stations a mile and a quarter distant. The market is on Tuesday ; the fairs are on June 24th and October 1st. The town is within the jurisdiction of the county magistrates : a bailiff and other officers are appointed at the court leet of the lord of the manor, held at Michaelmas ; and a court is held every third week, for the recovery of debts under 40s. The town-hall is a neat and commodious building, in the centre of the town.

The parish comprises 10,968 acres : the soil is in some parts fertile, in others of inferior quality. To the north of the town is Bromsgrove Lickey, a range of lofty hills, commanding an extensive and diversified prospect of the surrounding country ; a considerable part, comprising a tract of 2000 acres, has been inclosed, and produces good crops of clover, turnips, and potatoes. A spring rising among these hills divides into two streams, one of which, flowing northward, joins the river Rea, and, uniting with the Trent, falls into the North Sea ; the other, running into the Stour, joins the Severn, and empties itself into the Irish Sea. The living is a vicarage, valued in the king's books at £41. 8. 1½. ; patrons and appropriators, the Dean and Chapter of Worcester, whose tithes have been commuted for £1200, and whose glebe consists of 75a. 3r. 22p. :

the vicarial tithes have been commuted for £1100, and the glebe consists of 1a. 2r., with a house. The church is a very ancient structure, combining portions in the Norman style and the decorated and later English styles, of which last the tower and spire are fine specimens ; the interior contains many interesting monuments. A district church was built at Catshill in 1837. There are places of worship for Baptists, Primitive Methodists, Independents, and Wesleyans ; and a Roman Catholic chapel at Grafton, an extra-parochial liberty adjoining. A free grammar school was instituted, with an endowment of £7 per annum, by charter of Edward VI., confirmed by Queen Mary ; and the original endowment was augmented with £50 per annum by Sir Thomas Cookes, Bart., of Bentley, who in 1714 founded six scholarships, of £50 per annum each, in Worcester College, Oxford, for this school and four others in the county ; and six fellowships, of £150 per annum each, in the same college, to which, as vacancies occur, those who hold the scholarships succeed. Thomas Hawkes, in 1809, left £1000 four per cent. bank annuities for the benefit of the poor ; and there are several other endowments. The union of Bromsgrove comprises 15 parishes or places, of which 11 are in the county of Worcester, 2 in that of Salop, and one in each of the counties of Stafford and Warwick ; and contains a population of 22,357. At Dadford, two miles from the town, are the remains of a small priory of Præmonstratensian canons founded by Henry I., now part of a farmhouse. At Shepley are some traces of the Roman Ikeneld-street ; near Gannow is a petrifying spring.

BROMWICH, CASTLE, a chapelry, in the parish and union of Aston, Birmingham division of the hundred of Hemlingford, N. division of the county of Warwick, 5½ miles (E.) from Birmingham ; containing 779 inhabitants. It comprises 2587a. 3r. 21p., of which about two-thirds are arable land of good quality, with a pretty fair proportion of wood and plantations ; the surface is undulated, and the scenery highly picturesque. The northern boundary of the chapelry is formed by the river Tame, by which a flour-mill, beautifully situated, is propelled : the Birmingham and Derby railway has a station here. Castle-Bromwich Hall, the property of the Earl of Bradford, who is lord of the manor, is an ancient and interesting mansion. The hamlet is seated on a gentle acclivity, and contains several well-built houses. The living is a donative, in the patronage of the Earl, with a net income of £315 per annum. The chapel, dedicated to St. Mary and St. Margaret, is a neat brick structure, with a square tower, and has a handsome interior ; it was erected in 1729, by Sir John Bridgman, Bart., ancestor of the Earl of Bradford, and the circumstance is recorded on a tablet in the building. There is a boys' school, endowed with land in the hamlet producing about £35 per annum, in the hands of trustees, with a house and garden for the master ; it is further aided by subscription : there is also a girls' school. In the Castle field is a mound, artificially constructed, and supposed to be of Roman origin.

BROMWICH, LITTLE, a hamlet, in the parish and union of Aston, Birmingham division of the hundred of Hemlingford, N. division of the county of Warwick, 3 miles (N. E.) from Birmingham ; containing 262 inhabitants. The hamlet is bounded by the river Tame on the north, and the river Cole on the south ;

BROM

BROM

ınd is intersected by the road between Birmingham and Coleshill, and the London and Birmingham railway : the surface is flat and well-wooded, and the soil a sandy loam. Ward-End Hall, an old farmhouse near the church of Ward-End (*which see*), with about 100 acres if land, comprising the 30 acres mentioned in Dugdale's *Warwickshire* as the Park, is the property of Thos. Hutton, Esq., and is occupied by a member of his family. The manor-house at Allum Rock is the property of W. Webb Essington, Esq., and the residence of Isaac Marshall, Esq.; Ward-End House is the property and residence if George Marshall, Esq.

BROMWICH, WEST (*ALL SAINTS*), a town and parish, and the head of a union, in the hundred of OFFLOW SOUTH, S. division of the county of STAFFORD, situated about 6 miles (N. W.) from Birmingham, 5 miles (E.) from Dudley, and 4 (S.) from Walsall ; adjoining the town of Wednesbury; and containing, in 1841, 26,121 inhabitants. The name has been variously written at different periods as Bromwic, Bromwych, Bromich, Bromwhiche, and Bromwidge. It is derived from the *room* supposed to have once grown plentifully in the neighbourhood, and *wic*, a Saxon word signifying village : *West* appears to have been added to distinguish the place rom Castle-Bromwich, Little Bromwich, and Bromvycham, as Birmingham was once called. The parish is not mentioned in the Domesday survey ; but it appears rom other records to have belonged to the barony of Dudley, and in the time of Henry III. Walter de Everons, and his two coparceners, held the town of Bromwich if Roger de Somery. In the 21st of Edward I. one Richard Bassett was lord of the manor, which the amily of Freebody afterwards appear to have held ; and Cecily, daughter and heiress of William Freebody, narrying John Stanley, conveyed it to him : she died in 1553. The manor remained in the Stanleys for about a century, when Sir Edward Stanley sold it to his cousin, Sir Richard Shelton, Knt., from whose family it passed about 1700 to Sir Samuel Clarke, whose descendants now sold some of the property; though the greater part was sold by Mr. Clarke Jervoise in 1822, when the manor and several of the estates were purchased by the Earl of Dartmouth.

The PARISH comprises nearly 6000 acres ; about two-thirds of the cultivated land are arable, and the remainder pasture : a considerable portion of land is occupied with buildings, collieries, and brick-yards. On the east lies the parish of Handsworth, on the south lie Smethwick parish and Oldbury township, on the west the parishes of Rowley-Regis and Tipton, on the north Wednesbury, and on the north-east Barr. The river Tame, which is but a small stream here, bounds the parish for nearly nine miles : the whole circumference is about thirteen miles. The surface presents no striking feature; it is gently undulated, and from Sandwell Park up the valley of the Tame the country is picturesque and well wooded. The soil for the most part is light and sandy on the higher grounds, and a sandy loam in other parts, with, generally, a substratum of sand and gravel ; clay abounds in numerous places, and is extensively used in the manufacture of bricks. The water, in many of the wells, is strongly impregnated with iron ; and there are some springs at Wigmore that are considered medicinal, but they have never been properly analysed, and have only a local reputation. A large tract nearly in the centre of

VOL. I.—401

the parish, and surrounding Christ Church, was formerly a common and rabbit-warren ; it was inclosed about 1805, together with all the other waste lands, and now forms some of the most valuable land in the district. *Sandwell Hall*, situated on the site of a Benedictine priory, was the residence of the ancient and wealthy family of Whorwood, which continued to reside here till the close of the 17th century, when it became by purchase the property of the earls of Dartmouth, whose principal seat it now is, and who, as already mentioned, purchased the manor in 1822. Several of the Whorwoods received the honour of knighthood : in 1572 Thomas Whorwood was a member for the county ; and in 1573, 1596, 1604, 1632, and 1654 the family served the office of high sheriff. The present mansion is a large, square, stuccoed building, with a portico of stone pillars ; it has every accommodation for a noble family, and contains a handsome library, a neat chapel, and a large collection of valuable paintings, including some fine specimens of the old masters. The park covers a space of about 700 acres, fenced round for the greater part with a high wall, and contains some fine timber. The old manor-house, called *Bromwich Hall*, stands about a mile to the north-west of the church, and forms a pile of irregular buildings, half timber, surrounded with numerous out-houses, and by lofty walls : it is now divided into several dwellings. The *Oak House*, one of the oldest buildings in the parish, was the residence of the Turtons, who are said to have dwelt upon the spot upwards of 600 years : the last of the name died here in 1768. It is a fine specimen of the half-timbered mansions of the Elizabethan age, and is in tolerably good repair.

This place, which is situated in an extensive manufacturing and mining district, has, within a few years, risen with amazing rapidity from a state of comparative insignificance, to a degree of importance, for the variety and extent of its manufactures and trade, that is almost unparalleled. In 1750, the population appears to have been 1825 souls : in 1801, it was 5687 : in 1831 it had increased to 15,337 ; and by the last census, in 1841, it had reached to upwards of 26,000. The greater part of the parish presents the appearance of a large straggling town, the buildings being scattered about without much order, but dense enough in some parts to form streets, especially along the Holyhead road, where, in the High street, are shops of every description, a convenient market-place, and a good hotel. A literary institution was established in 1836. One great cause of the rapid increase of the place, is its mines of COAL and IRONSTONE, which occupy, as far as they are at present ascertained, rather more than half the parish : the principal bed of coal is the Thick or Ten-yard coal, but there are also all the other measures of coal and ironstone which usually accompany it, forming the well-known basin of South Staffordshire. Some peculiar features in the coal measures of the parish are worthy of notice. To the north, the Thick coal, which there lies from 100 to 140 yards deep, is suddenly terminated by a range or fault running nearly east and west, and passing from Holloway Bank to the front of Bromwich Hall ; on the north side of this fault, thin measures of coal and ironstone are met with near the surface, that usually lie at a considerable depth below the Thick coal. It was formerly supposed that no coal existed under the New Red-sandstone formation, and that a line of fault running nearly north and south

3 F

from a point a little to the west of the old church, in a direct line to Oldbury, terminated the coal-field; but within the last few years five pairs of pits have been sunk over this fault, and after passing through about 150 yards of the red-sandstone measures, the coal measures have been found, and the Thick coal obtained, at the depth of about 300 yards. It is still uncertain, however, how much further the coal extends in this direction; for another dislocation of the measures occurs to the west of Sandwell Park wall, running nearly in the direction of Spon Lane, beyond which no borings that have hitherto taken place, satisfactorily prove the existence of coal. There are at the present time altogether about thirty pairs of pits in the Thick coal, capable of raising at a fair average about 12,000 tons per week; but the quantity procured is subject to great variation from the state of trade and other causes. After the Thick coal has been obtained, the lower mines both of coal and ironstone are worked, and about fifteen pairs of pits are now thus employed.

The MANUFACTURE of IRON has become a most important branch of business. That it was carried on here at a very early period, we have evidence in the fact of an old smelting-furnace having stood in a meadow near Bromwich Old-Forge; the smelting-works, however, went to decay, and no pig-iron was made in the parish till Messrs. John Bagnall and Sons commenced their three furnaces at Golds Green, in 1820. Since then, three others have been erected at the Union by Messrs. Philip Williams and Sons, and three at Crookhay by Mr. Thomas Davies; each of these is capable of making from ninety to one hundred tons of pig-iron per week. Before the introduction of the steam-engine, the only power available for manufactures was the water-wheel; accordingly, along the stream of the Tame are to be found the sites of many old corn-mills and iron-works. Of the latter were Golds Hill, originally a small slitting-mill; Bustleholm, a rod-mill; and Bromwich Old-Forge. This last is probably the oldest iron-work in the parish; it is mentioned by Dr. Wilkes in his *View of Staffordshire*, in 1735, and was subsequently carried on by Messrs. Jesson and Wright, who in 1774 obtained a patent for making malleable iron from the pig, with raw coal and coke without charcoal. They afterwards erected the Bromford works near Oldbury. Among the iron-works now in operation, are the Golds Hill and Golds Green works, where, in conjunction with their works at Toll-End, and the Imperial works in the adjoining parishes of Tipton and Wednesbury, Messrs. Bagnall and Sons are capable of furnishing upwards of 750 tons of iron per week, and where a considerable portion of the rails of the railroads of this country and also of the continent has been manufactured. The other principal iron-works are, the Albion works, belonging to Mr. Walter Williams; those of Bromford, belonging to John Dawes and Sons; Roway, to E. Page and Sons; Great Bridge, to Mr. James Batson; Church Lane, to Underhill, Whitehouse, and Company; the works of the Phœnix Patent Galvanized-Iron Company; Vulcan Forge, for hammered-iron, belonging to Henry Smith and Company; Crookhay, to Mr. Thomas Davies; &c. The cast-iron founding business is also carried on to a great extent; and in the hollow-ware branch, consisting of pots, kettles, &c., the firms of Messrs. Izons and Company, W. Bullock and Company, and A. Kenrick and Sons,

Church district church is a handsome stone structure with tower in the florid English style, built principally at he charge of the Church Commissioners, at a cost of bout £19,000; it was consecrated in 1829, and contains 200 sittings. The living is a perpetual curacy; net income, £330; patrons, the Earl of Dartmouth and Trustees. *St. James'* district church was erected in 1841, by voluntary contributions (of which the earl ubscribed £1300), aided by grants from the Incorporated Society and the Lichfield Diocesan Society; it is a neat building with 1009 sittings. The living is a perpetual uracy, in the gift of the Incumbent of West Bromwich. *Holy Trinity* district church was erected at a cost of £3400, raised by subscription, aided by a grant of £500 rom the Lichfield Diocesan Society; it is an elegant building of brick, with a square tower and pinnacles, and contains 930 sittings, whereof 430 are free : this church was consecrated in August 1841. The living is in the gift of five Trustees, and has been endowed with £1000 by Thomas Hood and Edwin Bullock, Esqrs.: a parsonage, the site of which, and that for the church, were given by George Silvester, Esq., of the Elms, was built in 1843. There are many places of worship for Dissenters of different denominations. The Wesleyans have five meeting-houses, of which the largest, Wesley Chapel, is capable of holding 2000 persons : the Independents have four meeting-houses, the Baptists two, the Roman Catholics one; and the Primitive Methodists, Ranters, and others, have four or five small places of meeting. Nearly all the churches and meeting-houses have large schools attached to them; but there is no endowed school. Of the benefactions left to the parish, the principal is that of Walter Stanley, lord of the manor, who by deed of trust dated March 12, 1613, gave a house and certain lands in Aston, and Sutton-Coldfield, in the county of Warwick, for the maintenance of a preacher in the church of West Bromwich. Upon the erection of Christ Church an act was obtained, by which one-half of the rents arising from the property was appropriated to the incumbent of the parish, and the other half to the minister of Christ Church; a second act was obtained in 1840, enabling the trustees to grant building-leases, and a great part of the estate has been leased out. The annual income now derived from it is about £300. The union of West Bromwich comprises six parishes or places, and contains a population of 52,596.

Some of the foundations of *Sandwell Priory* are still traceable in the back part and offices of the present mansion, where may be seen a stone coffin, which was dug up there. On the lawn in front of the house, the "Sanctus Fons," or Holy Well, from which the priory derived its name, is still remaining. The priory was founded in the latter part of the reign of Henry II. or the beginning of that of Richard I., by William, son of Guy de Ophene or Offney: it was dedicated to St. Mary Magdalen, and was one of those houses which were given in the 17th of Henry VIII. to Cardinal Wolsey; its spiritualities were at that time of the yearly value of £12, and its temporalities amounted to £26. 8. 7. Eventually, it was granted to the Whorwoods, of Compton and Stourton Castle. At *Friars' Park* is said to have been an establishment of Mendicant friars in connexion with the priory at Sandwell; but not a trace of it now exists, nor any record that is authentic. A tes-

sellated pavement was discovered in 1841. William Parsons, the gigantic porter of James I., was a native of the parish.

BROMYARD (St. Peter), a market-town and parish, and the head of a union, in the hundred of Broxash, county of Hereford, 14 miles (N. E.) from Hereford, and 126 (N. W. by W.) from London; containing 2927 inhabitants. The town is pleasantly situated on the road from Worcester to Hereford, near the river Frome, in a rich and fertile district abounding with orchards and hop-plantations; and consists of several well-paved streets. The ancient market-hall and butter-cross, an unsightly structure, has been taken down, leaving the space open; and on the site of some old buildings adjoining, a commodious market-house has been erected, with fixed stalls and benches. Races are held annually on the Downs, an extensive common adjoining the town, and are generally well attended. The market, chiefly for live-stock, butter, cheese, and poultry, is on Monday; and fairs are held on the last Monday in Jan., the Thursday before the 25th of March, on May 3rd, the Thursday before St. James's day, and the Thursday before the 29th of October. Petty-sessions for the district are held on Monday, at Dumbleton Hall, an ancient mansion purchased by subscription and appropriated as a town-hall, containing a spacious court-room for the sessions, and accommodation for the weekly meetings of the savings'-bank trustees, and monthly meetings of the turnpike commissioners. Courts leet and baron are also held twice in the year under the Bishop of Hereford, who is lord of the manor. The powers of the county debt-court of Bromyard, established in 1847, extend over the registration-district of Bromyard. A new police station house, with a residence for the constable, was built in 1843.

The parish, including the townships of Winslow, Norton, and Linton, comprises 7921 acres, of which 202 are in the town of Bromyard : the land is in a high state of cultivation, producing hops of excellent quality, of which there are nearly 700 acres under cultivation. The surface is varied with hills, and the lower grounds are watered by a brook that flows through the parish into the river Frome. The LIVING consists of a sinecure rectory and a vicarage : the rectory, of which the net income is £612, is divided into three portions, in the gift of the Bishop of Hereford; and the vicarage, of which the net income is £600, is in the patronage of the Portionists. The church is an ancient and spacious structure in the Norman style, and contains a curious font; the accommodation has been increased by the erection of a gallery at the west end, containing a hundred sittings all free. Brockhampton chapel, in the township of Norton, recently built by the Barneby family, is a handsome edifice in the later English style. There are places of worship for the Society of Friends, Independents, and Primitive Methodists. The free grammar school was founded by Queen Elizabeth, and endowed with £16. 14. 11¾. per annum, augmented with £20 per annum by John Perrin, alderman and goldsmith of London, in 1656. John Perrin also endowed a weekly divinity lecture by six beneficed clergymen, to be elected by the churchwardens and 12 of the principal inhabitants of this, his native parish, with several other benefactions, for which the Goldsmiths' Company are trustees. A national school, in which are 100 girls, is supported by endowment. An

almshouse was founded in the reign of Charles II., by
Phineas Jackson, forty years vicar of the parish, who
also founded various others, in which seven aged widows
are comfortably provided for. The poor law union of
Bromyard comprises 33 parishes or places, of which 30
are in the county of Hereford, and 3 in that of Worcester; and contains a population of 11,494.

BRON-Y-GARTH, a township, in the parish of St.
Martin, hundred of Oswestry, N. division of Salop,
5 miles (N.) from the town of Oswestry; containing
324 inhabitants.

BROOK (St. Mary), a parish, in the union of East
Ashford, partly in the hundred of Wye, but chiefly in
that of Chart and Longbridge, lathe of Shepway,
E. division of Kent, 4½ miles (E. by N.) from Ashford;
containing 158 inhabitants. It comprises by admeasurement 582 acres: about half is arable, and the remainder
pasture, with 55 acres of wood, part of which consists of
oak; the soil is wet and heavy. The South-Eastern
railway runs within 2½ miles. The living is a discharged rectory, valued in the king's books at £7. 7. 3.,
and in the patronage of the Dean and Chapter of Canterbury: the tithes have been commuted for £145, and the
glebe comprises 10 acres. The church is in the Grecian
style of architecture.

BROOK, or Gasper, a tything, in the parish of
Stourton, union of Mere, hundred of Norton-Ferris,
E. division of Somerset, 5 miles (N. E.) from Wincan-
ton; containing 288 inhabitants.

BROOK (St. Mary), a parish, in the liberty of West
Medina, Isle of Wight division of the county of
Southampton, 5 miles (S. E.) from Yarmouth; containing 150 inhabitants. It is bounded on the south by the
sea, and comprises 712 acres, of which 490 are arable,
and 222 pasture: the village is seated in a sheltered
valley formed by two lofty hills. The living is a discharged rectory, valued in the king's books at £1. 18. 9.;
net income, £250; patron and incumbent, the Rev. Collingwood Fenwick. The church, a small edifice partly
overspread with ivy, is situated on rising ground, and
consists of a nave and chancel, with a low tower. On
Brook Down are several tumuli, each of which is encompassed with a fosse. Vestiges of a Roman encampment, and the remains of an amphitheatre, are discernible
in the parish; and several human skeletons and daggers
have been found.

BROOK, a hamlet, in the parish of Bramshaw,
union of New Forest, N. division of the hundred of
New Forest, Romsey and S. divisions of the county
of Southampton; containing 347 inhabitants.

BROOK, a tything, in the parish and hundred of
King's-Sombourn, union of Stockbridge, Romsey
and S. divisions of the county of Southampton; containing 86 inhabitants.

BROOK, NORTH and SOUTH, two tythings, in
the parish and hundred of Mitcheldever, union of
Winchester, Winchester and N. divisions of the county
of Southampton; containing respectively 224 and 602
inhabitants.

BROOKE (St. Peter), a parish, in the union of
Loddon and Clavering, hundred of Clavering, E.
division of Norfolk, 7 miles (S. E. by E.) from Norwich; containing 756 inhabitants. It is situated between the rivers Yare and Waveney, and comprises
2119a. 2r. 11p., of which about 1387 acres are arable,

BROOMFIELD (St. Mary), a parish, in the union and hundred of Chelmsford, S. division of Essex, 2½ miles (N.) from Chelmsford; containing 820 inhabitants. This parish is supposed to have derived its name from the profusion of broom growing in the immediate vicinity. It is on the road to Braintree, and comprises by computation 2000 acres of fertile land, of which about four-fifths are arable, and the remainder, with the exception of a few acres of wood, meadow and pasture. The living is a discharged vicarage, valued in the king's books at £7. 13. 4.; net income, £161; patron, the Bishop of London; impropriator, H. Finch, Esq. The church, a very ancient edifice with a circular tower, has many interesting details in the Norman style: the vicarage-house is a handsome residence. The learned Patrick Young died at the vicarage-house, in 1652; he was keeper of the king's library, and superintended the printing of the *Septuagint* from the Alexandrian MSS. The Rev. Thomas Cox, who translated from the French Dupin's *Life of Christ*, and also his *Ecclesiastical History*, and compiled part of a *History of England*, and of the *Magna Britannia*, was vicar of the parish.

BROOMFIELD (St. Margaret), a parish, in the union of Hollingbourn, hundred of Eyhorne, lathe of Aylesford, W. division of Kent, 6 miles (E. S. E.) from Maidstone; containing 146 inhabitants, and comprising 1420 acres. The living is a perpetual curacy, united to that of Leeds. On the southern side of the parish extends a tract of woodland, called King's Wood, and within its limits is a rabbit-warren; the total extent of woodland is 266 acres.

BROOMFIELD (St. Mary and All Saints), a parish, in the union of Bridgwater, hundred of Andersfield, W. division of Somerset, 4¾ miles (N.) from Taunton; containing 497 inhabitants. The living is a perpetual curacy; net income, £78; patron and impropriator, Col. Hamilton, whose tithes have been commuted for £375: the glebe comprises nearly 30 acres. In the churchyard is a stone cross, somewhat mutilated.

BROOMHAUGH, a township, in the parish of Bywell St. Andrew, union of Hexham, E. division of Tindale ward, S. division of Northumberland, 7¾ miles (E. S. E.) from Hexham; containing 100 inhabitants. This place is situated about three miles southeast of Corbridge, on the road from Newcastle to Hexham, and is bounded on the north by the river Tyne: the scenery is picturesque. There is a small land-sale colliery, and good building-stone is obtained. The village is inhabited by labourers in husbandry; and the Newcastle and Carlisle railway enters it through a tunnel 135 yards in length. A national school has been established, in which church service is performed. There is a place of worship for Baptists.

BROOMHILL, in the union of Rye, partly in the hundred of Goldspur, liberty of Winchelsea, rape of Hastings, county of Sussex, but chiefly in the hundred of Langport, liberty of Romney-Marsh, lathe of Shepway, E. division of Kent, 3½ miles (E. by S.) from Rye; containing 123 inhabitants. This place, which was anciently a parish, is a member of the port, and forms part of the town, of Romney. The church, which stood within the limits of Kent, was destroyed, with the village, in the reign of Edward I., by an inundation of the sea.

BROOMHOPE, with BUTELAND.—See BUTELAND.

BROOMLEY, a township, in the parish of BYWELL ST. PETER, union of HEXHAM, E. division of TINDALE ward, S. division of NORTHUMBERLAND, 7¾ miles (E. S. E.) from Hexham ; containing 314 inhabitants. This place is situated on the Hexham road, to the south of the river Tyne, about one mile south-by-west from Bywell. Old Ridley lies a short distance to the south-east, and a little further in the same direction is New Ridley, a small village surrounded by several farms.

BROOM-PARK, a township, in the parish of ED-LINGHAM, union of ALNWICK, N. division of COQUET-DALE ward and of NORTHUMBERLAND, 5½ miles (W.) from Alnwick ; containing 63 inhabitants. The township is finely situated between the Aln river and the Lemmington burn : it contains a noble mansion, the seat of the Burrell family, the pleasure-grounds around which are well laid out ; and the neighbouring country affords a variety of pleasing views. Many tumuli, supposed to be places of sepulture of the ancient Britons, are found here, and in the vicinity. A tithe rent-charge of £34 is paid to the Dean and Chapter of Durham.

BROOMRIDGE, a hamlet, in the parish of FORD, union of GLENDALE, W. division of GLENDALE ward, N. division of NORTHUMBERLAND, 5¾ miles (N. by W.) from Wooler. Camden considers this to have been the place, called *Brunanburh*, where King Athelstan defeated Constantine, King of Scotland, Anlaf the Dane, and Eugenius, a petty prince of Cumberland. About half a mile to the south is Haltwell Sweire, the scene of an encounter, in 1558, between the English under Sir Henry Percy and the Scots under Earl Bothwell, the former of whom sustained a defeat.

BROOMSTHORPE, a parish, in the union of DOCK-ING, hundred of GALLOW, W. division of NORFOLK, 5½ miles (N. N. E.) from Rougham ; containing 10 inhabitants. It comprises 430 acres, forming one farm, belonging to Lord Henry Cholmondeley. The church was destroyed before the reign of Elizabeth, and the benefice abolished. Here was a guild, in honour of St. John, to whom it is supposed the church was dedicated.

BROSELEY (ST. LEONARD), a market-town and parish, in the union of MADELEY, franchise of WEN-LOCK, S. division of SALOP, 2 miles (S.) from Iron-bridge, 14 (S. E.) from Shrewsbury, and 144 (N. W.) from London, on the road from Worcester to Shrewsbury ; containing 4829 inhabitants. This place, in ancient records called *Burwardesley*, derived its importance from the numerous mines of coal and ironstone in the neighbourhood, which made it the resort of miners ; and in proportion as the works proceeded, it increased in population and magnitude. The town is irregularly built, on an eminence rising abruptly from the western bank of the river Severn, to which its eastern extremity extends, and from which its western extremity is nearly two miles distant. It consists principally of one long street, from which a few smaller streets branch towards the different collieries and other works : the houses, in general of brick and of mean appearance, are occasionally intermixed with some of more respectable character ; and in detached situations are several handsome and spacious edifices. The trade consists partly in ironstone-mining operations ; but, from the exhausted state of the mines, this branch of trade, as well as that in coal, has

declined. There are still, however, numerous coal-pits, iron-foundries, and furnaces ; and fine earthenware, tobacco-pipes, bricks, and tiles, are made to a great extent : the fire-bricks for building furnaces are in high repute, and, by means of the Severn, are sent to various parts of the kingdom. A considerable portion of the population are employed in the china manufacture, at Coal-port, in the adjoining parish of Madeley. The market is on Wednesday ; the fairs are on the last Tuesday in April, and Oct. 28th, and are chiefly for pleasure, though a considerable number of pigs are sold. The town is within the jurisdiction of the borough of Wenlock ; courts leet for the manor are held in the town-hall in April and October, and at the latter four constables are appointed. The town-hall is a handsome brick building, in the centre of the town, supported on pillars and arches, the basement forming a spacious market-place : the first story contains a room where the petty-sessions and public meetings are held (used also as an assembly-room), and two smaller apartments. There is a small prison attached to the building, for the confinement of debtors, and for criminals previous to their committal by the borough magistrates.

The parish comprises 1912a. 2r. 14p. ; the soil is fertile. The LIVING is a rectory, with that of Linley united, valued in the king's books at £7. 18. 6½., and in the gift of Lord Forester : the tithes have been commuted for £453, and the glebe comprises 11½ acres. The church, with the exception of the ancient tower, which is of stone, has been rebuilt of brick ; but something of its original character is preserved in the interior, in the octangular pillars and pointed arches that support the roof. A chapel, dedicated to St. Mary, was built in 1759, by Mr. Francis Turner Blythe, in a part of the parish called Jackfield, at a considerable distance from the church ; it is a neat brick building, with a square embattled tower crowned by pinnacles. The living is a perpetual curacy, in the patronage of Francis Blythe Harris, Esq. There are places of worship for Baptists, Wesleyans, Primitive Methodists, and Independents ; and national schools are supported by subscription. In 1750, John Barret, Esq., a native of the place, bequeathed £110, which sum, augmented with a legacy of £100 by Mr. Richard Edwards, and several smaller sums, amounting in the whole to £380, was invested in the purchase of land, upon which the town-hall and other houses have been erected : the rents are distributed among the poor.

BROTHERTOFT, a chapelry, in the parish and wapentake of KIRTON, union of BOSTON, parts of HOL-LAND, county of LINCOLN, 4 miles (W. N. W.) from Boston ; containing 122 inhabitants.

BROTHERTON (ST. EDWARD THE CONFESSOR), a parish, in the Lower division of the wapentake of BARK-STONE-ASH, W. riding of YORK ; containing 1744 inhabitants, of whom 1613 are in the township of Brotherton, 1 mile (N. N. W.) from Ferry-Bridge. The village of Brotherton, anciently called *Broyerton*, is memorable as the birthplace of Prince Thomas (Thomas de Brotherton), of whom Margaret, second wife of Edward I., was suddenly delivered in June 1300, after taking the amusement of hunting in the neighbourhood. The young prince was created earl of Norfolk, and earl marshal of England ; and from him, in the female line, descended the Mowbrays, dukes of Norfolk. The parish s bounded on the south and west by the river Aire, and comprises by computation rather more than 2000 acres, of which 607 are in the township of Brotherton, 850 in that of Byrome with Pool, and 750 in the township of Sutton. The soil is generally fertile, and the surface pleasingly undulated, in some parts rising to considerable elevations ; limestone of very superior quality is quarried for the supply of the neighbouring district, and there are many kilns for burning it into lime. Extensive works were established in 1840, by James Kelsall and Company, for the manufacture of glass-bottles of every description. Facility of conveyance is afforded by the river Aire, which is navigable here, and by the York and North-Midland railway, which passes through the parish. The living is a discharged vicarage, valued in the king's books at £5. 6. 8.; net income, £192 ; patrons and ap-proprietors, the Dean and Chapter of York. The church, erected in 1300, was almost entirely rebuilt in 1843, at a cost of £3250, of which £2000 were given by the Ramsden family, to whose ancestors there are some good monuments. In the chancel is a monument to Stephen Owen, vicar, who was deprived of his benefice by the usurper Cromwell ; also one to the Rev. Charles Daubuz, a French refugee, and author of a *Commentary on the Revelations*, who was vicar of the parish, and died in 1717. There are places of worship for Independents and Wesleyans.

BROTTON, a parochial chapelry, in the union of Guisborough, E. division of the liberty of Lang-baurgh, N. riding of York ; containing 468 inhabit-ants, of whom 319 are in the township, 6 miles (N. E. by E.) from Guisborough. This place is styled in the Domesday survey *Broctune.* The chapelry includes the ownships of Brotton, Skinningrove, and Kilton ; is situated on the shore of the North Sea, and on the road etween Guisborough and Whitby ; and comprises by easurement 3742 acres, of which a great portion is rable land. The surface is mountainous on the sea-oast, and in other parts generally diversified with hills : he soil is a hard clay, occasionally of a good quality, nd the scenery in many places interspersed with wood nd plantations. The living is a perpetual curacy, nnexed to that of Skelton : the tithes of the township elong to the Archbishop of York, and have been com-uted for £340. The church, erected in 1777, at the xpense of the parishioners, is a plain edifice, standing n the summit of an elevated ridge which is washed by he sea. There is a place of worship for Wesleyans. ossils, agates, snake-stones, and other petrifactions have een found.

BROTHERWICK, a township, in the parish of Arkworth, union of Alnwick, E. division of Co-uetdale ward, N. division of Northumberland, miles (W.) from Warkworth ; containing 10 inhabit-ats. It is situated on the west side of the river oquet, which is navigable to within a quarter of a mile f Warkworth. The tithes have been commuted for 24. 12. payable to the Bishop of Carlisle, and £4. 18.) the vicar of the parish.

BROUGH, with Shatton, a hamlet, in the parish of Iope, union of Chapel-en-le-Frith, hundred of High 'eak, N. division of the county of Derby, 5 miles N. N. E.) from Tideswell ; containing 80 inhabitants. place called the Castle, near the junction of two small treams, the Noe and the Bradwell Water, was evidently

407

the site of a Roman station, probably *Crococolana*; and numerous Roman relics have been discovered, also coins (among which is a gold one of Vespasian), and rude busts, one being of Apollo. The Dean and Chapter of Lichfield receive a tithe rent-charge of £68.

BROUGH, or BURG, under Stainmoor (St. Michael), a parish, in East ward and union, county of Westmorland ; comprising the townships of Brough, Brough-Sowerby, and Hilbeck, and the chapelry of Stainmoor or Stainmore ; and containing 1694 inhabit-ants, of whom 899 are in the market-town of Brough, 8 miles (S. E. by E.) from Appleby, and 262 (N. N. W.) from London, on the high road to Glasgow. This town occupies the site of the ancient *Vertera* or *Veteris*, where, towards the decline of the Roman empire in Britain, a prefect, with a band of *directores*, was stationed. It was partly built with the ruins of that fort, from which circumstance it probably derived its appellation ; and is distinguished from other places of the same name by the affix of Stainmoor, from its vicinity to an exten-sive ridge of rocky mountains that separates this county from Yorkshire. It flourished as a place of consider-able importance prior to the Conquest, soon after which a conspiracy was formed here, by the northern English, against the government of William. At what time the castle was erected is not precisely known ; but in 1174 it was nearly demolished by William, King of Scotland, who laid waste the town : the building was subsequently restored, and, in 1521, was nearly destroyed by a fire that broke out after the celebration of a Christmas festival by Lord Clifford ; it remained in a ruinous state till 1660, when it was repaired by Lady Ann Clifford, Countess Dowager of Pembroke. The fortress was si-tuated upon an eminence, abruptly steep towards the north and west ; and on the south and east, where the acclivity is more gentle, was defended by a ditch and a strong rampart. The remains consist of some massive towers, of which the keep, a large square tower with turrets at the angles, called Cæsar's Tower, was almost perfect in 1792, when the lower portion of one of the angles fell down, leaving the upper adhering by the cement only to the main building. Great part of it has within the last few years been removed, and the re-mainder is in a state of progressive dilapidation.

The town, divided into Market-Brough and Church-Brough, is pleasantly situated, and crossed by the Swin-dale beck, a tributary of the river Eden : it consists principally of one long street, the houses in which are rather commodious than handsome ; the inhabitants are well supplied with water. Several of the females are employed in knitting white-yarn stockings. The market, granted in 1331, by Edward III., to Robert, Lord Clifford, is on Thursday, but is of little note ; corn is admitted toll-free. Fairs are held on the Thursday before Whit-Sunday and September 30th, the latter of which, called Brough-Hill fair, is held on a common, two miles from the town, and is celebrated for the sale of linen and woollen cloth, wearing-apparel, articles of hardware, and live-stock ; cattle-fairs are also held in the town, on the second Thursday in March and April. The parish comprises by computation 20,000 acres, of which about one-half is inclosed and cultivated, and the remainder waste ; .the soil of the higher parts of the inclosed land, with the exception of a few portions of extremely fine quality, is sterile, and that of the lower portions rich and fertile, and equally adapted either for arable or pasture. The surface is varied with hills, and the lower grounds are watered by two small rivulets, of which one divides this parish from that of Kirkby-Stephen, and the other flows through the town, as already observed, into the river Eden. Coal is abundant; several mines are in operation for the supply of the neighbouring district, and there are quarries of freestone, limestone, and slate.

The parish was formerly a chapelry in Kirkby-Stephen. The living is a vicarage, valued in the king's books at £8. 8. 9.; net income, £492; patrons, the Provost and Fellows of Queen's College, Oxford, to whom the rectory and advowson were given at the request of Robert Egglesfield, founder of that college, and for several years rector of Brough. The church is a large handsome structure of great antiquity, to which a square embattled tower was added in 1513: the windows are ornamented with richly stained glass, which, from an inscription on one of them appears to be of the time of Henry VIII.; the pulpit is formed of one entire stone, and within the church are several interesting monuments. There is a chapel at Stainmoor, forming a separate incumbency. The Independents, Primitive Methodists, and Wesleyans have places of worship. The free school is endowed with £6. 18. 11., a portion of the revenue of a dissolved chantry and hospital founded in 1506 by John Brunskill, the former for two chaplains, one of whom was to instruct the children of the parish in grammar; the present building was erected by Lord Thanet. Many Roman coins and other antiquities have been found at various times near the castle, and, within the last thirty years, an earthen vessel full of silver *quinarii*, many of which are in good preservation. Cuthbert Buckle, lord mayor of London in 1593, was born at Brough.

BROUGH, a township, in the parish of CATTERICK, union of RICHMOND, wapentake of HANG-EAST, N. riding of YORK, 1½ mile (W.) from Catterick; containing 88 inhabitants. It comprises about 1050 acres of fertile land, the property of Sir W. Lawson, Bart., lord of the manor, who resides at Brough Hall, a handsome mansion, much improved by Sir John Lawson in the seventeenth century. An elegant Roman Catholic chapel was commenced in 1834, and finished in 1837, at a cost of £12,000, defrayed by Sir W. Lawson; it is a splendid structure in the early English style, with an east window of beautifully stained glass, executed by Willement.

BROUGH, with DRINGHOE and UPTON, a township, in the parish of SKIPSEA, union of BRIDLINGTON, N. division of the wapentake of HOLDERNESS, E. riding of YORK, 9 miles (S. by W.) from Bridlington; containing 190 inhabitants, of whom 90 are in Brough. The hamlet derives its name from a castle erected here by Drogo de Bevere, who came over with the Conqueror, and was lord of the seigniory of Holderness. The only remains now existing of this fortress, are the outworks, and the high artificial mound on which stood the keep: the outer rampart of the outworks is at least half a mile in circumference; and the outer bank of the keep, which commands a very extensive prospect, is 500 yards round. A market and two fairs were granted to the inhabitants of the place by Edward III., the former to be held weekly, and the latter annually.

BROU

pense of the Rev. Anthony Lund, V.G., who also built a house for the priest, and endowed the chapel with five acres of land. A school in the chapelry, which was rebuilt in 1845, has an endowment of £120 per annum; and adjacent to the Roman Catholic chapel is a school built by the Rev. Richard Gillow. There are some small charities.

BROUGHTON-cum-Kersal, a township, and ecclesiastical district, in the parish of Manchester, union and hundred of Salford, S. division of the county of Lancaster, 2 miles (N. N. W.) from Manchester, on the new road to Bury; containing 3794 inhabitants. This is a wealthy suburb of Manchester, abounding in villas, good streets, and elegant ranges of houses, chiefly the residences of the merchants of that town, and nearly all built within the last fifteen years. The surface of the township is undulated, the soil gravel, sand, and clay, and the scenery picturesque: the river Irwell passes through. The Manchester races take place here. Kersal Hall and Kersal Cell are old mansions, the latter belonging to Miss Atherton. The living is a perpetual curacy, in the patronage of the Rev. John Clowes, of Broughton Hall, and others; net income, £400, with a house. The great tithes have been commuted for £100. The church, dedicated to St. John the Evangelist, and in the debased perpendicular style, was completed in 1839, at an expense of about £7000: a chancel, in the decorated style, with painted windows by Hardman of Birmingham, was added by the present incumbent in 1846. There is a place of worship for Wesleyans. A day school near the church was built in 1845.

BROUGHTON, or Barrow-Town (St. Mary), a parish, in the union of Glandford-Brigg, E. division of the wapentake of Manley, parts of Lindsey, county of Lincoln, 4 miles (N. W.) from Glandford-Brigg; containing, with the township of Castlethorpe, 913 inhabitants. This place derives its name from a large barrow or tumulus near the western extremity of the village. It is situated on the Roman road from Lincoln to the Humber at Winteringham, and was a Roman station, which, in the time of the emperors Honorius and Arcadius, was occupied by the prefect of the Dalmatian horse, auxiliary to the 6th Legion, and which Horsley supposes to have been the station called *Prætorium.* Numerous relics of the Romans have at various times been found. The manor for several ages belonged to the family of Radford, till, in 1455, Sir Henry Radford engaging in the rebellion of the Earl of Rutland and others against Henry VI., it became forfeited upon his attainder of high treason: subsequently it came into the possession of the Andersons, of which family was Sir Edmund Anderson, chief justice in the reign of Elizabeth, who presided at the trial of Mary, Queen of Scots, in Fotheringay Castle. The parish is situated on the river Ancholme, which falls into the Humber at Brigg; it is bounded on the south-east by the road to Barton, and comprises 6912 acres, of which 1200 are wood, and 863 common land. A fair is held at Midsummer. The living is a rectory, valued in the king's books at £21; net income, £824; patron, Ellys Anderson Stephens, Esq.: the glebe comprises 80 acres. The church, which was extensively repaired in 1826, is an ancient edifice, with a tower surmounted at one angle by a circular turret; it contains some interesting monuments. Gokewell, a Cistercian nunnery, founded by William de Alta

3 G

Ripa prior to 1185, stood in the north-west part of the parish; the only remains are a doorway in a farmhouse which has been erected on the site.

BROUGHTON (St. ANDREW), a parish, in the union of KETTERING, hundred of ORLINGBURY, N. division of the county of NORTHAMPTON, 2¾ miles (S. W.) from Kettering; containing 593 inhabitants. This parish, which is on the road from Kettering to Northampton, comprises 1675a. 1r. 20p. There are some quarries of stone applicable to rough building. The living is a rectory, valued in the king's books at £21. 9. 7., and in the patronage of the Duke of Buccleuch: the tithes were commuted at the inclosure of the parish, for 320 acres of land, valued at about £440 per annum. The church is a handsome structure, in the later English style. There is a place of worship for Wesleyans. On the inclosure 61 acres, now producing £95 per annum, were allotted in exchange for land bequeathed by Edward Hunt, in 1674, for poor widows and other aged persons of Broughton, Kettering, and Rothwell.

BROUGHTON (St. MARY), a parish, in the union of BANBURY, hundred of BLOXHAM, county of OXFORD, 2 miles (W. S. W.) from Banbury; containing, with the hamlet of North Newington, 629 inhabitants. The parish is pleasantly situated on the road from Banbury to Shipston-upon-Stour. Broughton Castle was erected by the De Broughton family about the reign of Edward I.: many interesting portions of the original building remain, but the greater part of the present mansion was erected by the Fenys or Fiennes family, about the reign of James I. The castle was a place of sufficient strength to oppose some resistance to the royalist troops after the battle of Edge-Hill. The whole of the buildings have a venerable and interesting appearance, and are surrounded by a deep moat, 80 feet broad, over which is a bridge forming the only entrance, through a square embattled gateway tower. The interior contains several magnificent apartments, adorned with paintings, and displaying some beautiful specimens of ancient architecture. The living is a rectory, valued in the king's books at £18. 16. 0½.; net income, £539; patron and incumbent, the Rev. Charles F. Wyatt. The church, situated near the bridge leading to the castle, is an interesting structure, chiefly of the thirteenth century, but partly in the decorated and partly in the later style of English architecture, and contains some splendid monuments.

BROUGHTON (St. MARY), a parish, in the union of WEM, liberties of the borough of SHREWSBURY, N. division of SALOP, 3½ miles (S. by W.) from Wem; containing 188 inhabitants. It comprises about 800 acres, of which 500 are arable, and the rest pasture: roadstone is quarried. The living is a perpetual curacy; net income, £67; patron and impropriator, Lord Hill: the glebe comprises about 30 acres.

BROUGHTON, a hamlet, in the parish of STOKE, union of TAUNTON, hundred of TAUNTON and TAUNTON-DEAN, W. division of SOMERSET; containing 26 inhabitants.

BROUGHTON (St. MARY), a parish, in the union of STOCKBRIDGE, hundred of THORNGATE, Romsey and S. divisions of the county of SOUTHAMPTON, 3 miles (W. S. W.) from Stockbridge; containing, with the chapelry of Pittleworth and tything of French-Moor, 1009 inhabitants. This place is by Camden identified with the Roman station Brige, which Salmon refers to a hill

repair of roads. The living is a rectory, valued in the king's books at £35. 13. 4., and in the gift of Sir R. Sutton, Bart. : the tithes have been commuted for £691. 1., and there is a good glebe-house, with a glebe of about 5 acres. The church has a handsome spire which rises to an elevation of 50 yards. There are places of worship for Wesleyans and the Society of Friends. Bishop Warburton was rector of the parish, and is supposed, during his residence here of 20 years, to have endowed by will dated July 18th, 1735, the former with £8, and the latter with £20. 10., per annum.

BROUGHTON, CHURCH (St. Michael), a parish, in the union of Burton-upon-Trent, hundred of Appletree, S. division of the county of Derby, 8½ miles (E.) from Uttoxeter; containing, with the hamlet of Sapperton, 652 inhabitants. It comprises by computation, 2224 acres. The manor was granted by Edward VI., in 1552, to Sir William Cavendish; the Duke of Devonshire is now lord, and principal owner. The living is of pleasing appearance. The living is a discharged vicarage, valued in the king's books at £6. 13. 4.; net income, £228; patron, John Broadhurst, Esq. : the tithes of the manor were commuted for land and a money payment in 1773. The church is a venerable edifice with an embattled tower; the north side has been rebuilt, and the whole was repaired and new-pewed in 1845: in the chancel are three stone stalls. There is a place of worship for Primitive Methodists. A school was founded about 1745, by subscription, to which the Duke of Devonshire was the principal contributor; and the sum raised was invested in land, the rental of which is about £30 per annum.

BROUGHTON, EAST, a chapelry, in the parish of Cartmel, union of Ulverston, hundred of Lonsdale north of the Sands, N. division of the county of Lancaster, 2 miles (N. by E.) from Cartmel; containing 458 inhabitants. The families of Marshall and Machell had long a seat here : the Thornboroughs were also a long time resident, and subsequently to 1621 held one of two manors, which afterwards descended to the Rawlinsons. The township having often been confounded with Broughton in Furness, the names of East Broughton and Broughton-in-Cartmel have been adopted. The living is a perpetual curacy; net income, £67; patron, the Earl of Burlington. The chapel, which was consecrated in 1745, is dedicated to St. Peter. A national school for girls was commenced in the year 1830.

. BROUGHTON-GIFFORD (St. Mary), a parish, in the union and hundred of Bradford, Westbury and N. divisions, and Trowbridge and Bradford subdivisions, of Wilts, 2 miles (W.) from Melksham; containing 741 inhabitants. This parish, which is situated on the road from Melksham to Bradford, and bounded on the southeast by the Lower Avon, comprises 1677 acres, of which 39 are common or waste; the soil is good, and great quantities of gravel are dug. The population is partly employed by the manufacturers of Trowbridge, Melksham, and Staverton, in the weaving of cloth, in which about 300 persons, and many of their children, are engaged. The living is a rectory, valued in the king's books at £19. 3. 11½., and in the patronage of the Crown : the tithes have been commuted for £450, and the glebe comprises nearly 33 acres. The church is a spacious and ancient structure, with a massive square embattled tower. There are places of worship for Baptists and Wesleyans.

411

BROUGHTON, GREAT, a township, in the parish of Bridekirk, union of Cockermouth, Allerdale ward below Derwent, W. division of Cumberland, 4½ miles (W.) from Cockermouth; containing 562 inhabitants. The village lies on the southern slope of an eminence rising from the river Derwent. The tithes were commuted for land in 1819. Joseph Ashley built an almshouse for four women, and a schoolroom, which he endowed by will dated July 18th, 1735, the former with £8, and the latter with £20. 10., per annum.

BROUGHTON, GREAT and LITTLE, a township, in the parish of Kirkby-in-Cleveland, union of Stokesley, W. division of the liberty of Langbaurgh, N. riding of York, 2 miles (S. E.) from Stokesley; containing 511 inhabitants. The village of Great Broughton is regularly built, upon a spacious common or green, and the houses which run in a direction nearly north and south, are neat, and in good repair. A portion of the population is engaged in the linen manufacture. There is a meeting-house for Wesleyans. On the top of a mountain near this place, is a rude monument consisting of a large collection of stones, some of an immense size, called the Wain stones, which, it has been conjectured, were raised over the remains of a Danish warrior.

BROUGHTON-HACKET (St. Leonard), a parish, in the union, and Upper division of the hundred, of Pershore, Worcester and W. divisions of the county of Worcester, 5 miles (E.) from Worcester; containing 154 inhabitants. This parish which is nearly encircled by the river Bow, so called from the direction of its course, comprises 365 acres, whereof two-thirds are arable and the remainder pasture; the soil is rich, and the surface has a gentle declivity from the village, which is situated on an elevated ridge. The road from Alcester to Worcester crosses the parish from east to west, and the Spetchley station on the Birmingham and Gloucester railway is only a mile and a half distant. There are some stone-pits, producing specimens (in which marine shells are imbedded) susceptible of a polish that renders them in appearance not inferior to the Derbyshire marble; a valuable blueish limestone, also, which supplies the city of Worcester and places adjacent with lime for building and manure, abounds. The living is a discharged rectory, valued in the king's books at £8. 1. 0½., and in the patronage of the Crown; net income, £73, with a house built in 1845 : the tithes were commuted for land and a money payment in 1807. The church is an ancient structure partly early English, and was repewed and thoroughly repaired in 1843, at a cost of nearly £200.

BROUGHTON-IN-AIREDALE (All Saints), a parish, in the union of Skipton, E. division of the wapentake of Staincliffe and Ewcross, W. riding of York, 3½ miles (W. by S.) from Skipton; containing 407 inhabitants. The Saxon name of this place, implying a fortified town, bears testimony to its antiquity; vestiges of works may still be traced, and various relics, either of British or Roman origin, have been discovered. From its situation between the town of Skipton, which was garrisoned by the royalists, and that of Thornton, which was occupied by the parliamentarians, the place suffered much during the civil war. The parish is bounded on the west by the river Aire, and comprises by computation 3950 acres; there is a considerable portion of high land

3 G 2

affording pasture. The living is a discharged vicarage, valued in the king's books at £5. 16. 0½.; net income, £190, with a good house; patrons and appropriators, the Dean and Chapter of Christ-Church, Oxford. The church is an ancient structure, with a square tower. There is a chalybeate spring.

BROUGHTON-IN-FURNESS, a market-town and chapelry, in the parish of KIRBY-IRELETH, union of ULVERSTON, hundred of LONSDALE north of the Sands, N. division of the county of LANCASTER, 29 miles (N.W.) from Lancaster, and 270 (N. W. by N.) from London; containing 1250 inhabitants. The town is situated on the southern declivity of a gentle eminence, and is in the form of a square; the houses are built of stone, and roofed with blue slate. In the centre of it is a spacious square area, the ground for forming which was given by John Gilpin, Esq., and in which his widow erected a handsome lofty obelisk. Previously to the introduction of machinery, the spinning of woollen-yarn prevailed to a considerable extent in private houses: the making of brush-stocks and hoops at present furnishes employment to many of the inhabitants, particularly the latter, from the number and extent of the coppices on Furness Fells. There was formerly a very extensive tract of uncultivated land called Broughton Common, nearly all of which is now inclosed. The surrounding country is very mountainous, abounding with mines of iron and copper ore, and with slate-quarries; a great quantity of slate is shipped at Dudden Sands, for conveyance coastwise. Iron, grain, malt, oak-bark, and hoops, are also sent from the same spot, in vessels averaging about 60 tons' burthen; and from a place about half a mile below Dudden Bridge, in vessels of 25 tons' burthen, for which the estuary is navigable at the flow of the tide. An act was passed in 1846 for extending the Furness railway to this place. The market is on Wednesday: fairs are held on April 27th and August 1st, for horned-cattle, and on the 6th of October, for horned-cattle and sheep; those in April and October, are likewise statute-fairs for the hiring of servants, and all are much frequented by the clothiers from Yorkshire. The living is a perpetual curacy; net income, £108; patron, J. Sawrey, Esq.; appropriators, the Dean and Chapter of York, whose tithes were commuted for land in 1828. The chapel is dedicated to St. Mary Magdalene. Edward Taylor, by will dated in 1784, bequeathed £100, on condition that £60 should be raised by subscription, for the benefit of a grammar school.

BROUGHTON, LITTLE, a township, in the parish of BRIDEKIRK, union of COCKERMOUTH, ALLERDALE ward below Derwent, W. division of CUMBERLAND, 4½ miles (W. by N.) from Cockermouth; containing 344 inhabitants. A meeting-house was built by the Society of Friends, in 1656; and one by the Baptists, in 1672. Here is a manufactory for tobacco-pipes and coarse earthenware. Abraham Fletcher, a self-taught mathematician of no inconsiderable eminence, author of the *Universal Measurer*, was born here in 1714; he was the son of a tobacco-pipe maker, and in early life laboured at that occupation.

BROUGHTON, NETHER (ST. MARY), a parish, in the union of MELTON-MOWBRAY, hundred of FRAMLAND, N. division of the county of LEICESTER, 5¾ miles (N. W.) from Melton-Mowbray; containing 412 inhabitants. It comprises 2225 acres. The soil is a stiff

dward IV., Thomas Bellers released all his lands in his manor to Richard Boughton, with whose descendants it continued for several generations. It afterwards assed with a female heir to Sir Egerton Leigh. The hapelry is situated on an eminence near the confluence f the Avon and Swift rivers, and on the road from ugby to Lutterworth; and comprises by measurement 53 acres. The chapel is dedicated to St. Michael. The reat tithes belong to Rugby grammar school, founded by Lawrence Sheriff, who was born here.

BROWSHOLME, a hamlet, in the township of Bowland-Forest Lower division, chapelry of White-well, parish of Whalley, union of Clitheroe, wapen-take of Staincliffe and Ewcross, W. riding of York, 5½ miles (N. W.) from Clitheroe; containing 150 inhabitants. This hamlet, which has lately been disforested, comprises 1720 acres, whereof about 350 are woodland: t is the property of Thomas Goulburne Parker, Esq. Browsholme Hall, the seat of the Parker family for more than three centuries, is a large mansion of red stone, with a centre, two wings, and a small façade in front, of the time of Elizabeth and of James I.: it contains many oak rooms, with oak furniture; and a good library, having a valuable collection of MSS., paintings, some coins, and armour. The Roman Watling-street passes through the hamlet.

BROWSTON, a hamlet, in the parish of Belton, hundred of Mutford and Lothingland, E. division of Suffolk; containing 64 inhabitants.

BROXA, a township, in the parish of Hackness, union of Scarborough, liberty of Whitby-Strand, N. riding of York, 7¾ miles (W. N. W.) from Scarborough; containing 65 inhabitants. It comprises 1858 acres, of which 509 are arable, 619 pasture, 445 wood, and 285 waste or moor.

BROXBOURN (St. Augustine), a parish, in the union of Ware, hundred and county of Hertford; containing, with the chapelry of Hoddesdon, part of which is in the parish of Great Amwell, 2386 inhabitants. In the time of William the Conqueror, the manor belonged to Adeling, wife of Hugh de Grentemaisnill; it afterwards came to the Knights Templars, and lastly to the prior and brethren of the hospital of St. John of Jerusalem, who occupied the more ancient part of the present mansion of Broxbournbury. James I., on his way from Scotland, was entertained at the manor-house, where he was met by many of the nobility and the officers of state. The parish is situated on the north road, and bounded on the east by the river Lea, which separates it from the county of Essex; the New River, also, flows through it. The scenery is pleasingly diversified, and the views from many parts are extensive, embracing some mansions of great interest and beauty. The sweeps of woodland in different places are strikingly picturesque; and in Broxbournbury Park are some fine specimens of oak, elm, and Spanish chesnut. The parish comprises by admeasurement 4379 acres, whereof 2582 are in the hamlet of Hoddesdon: the soil, which is fertile, lies upon a bed of gravel of very fine quality. The Lea has a wharf about 200 yards from the church: a station of the Eastern Counties railway has been built here, of red brick and quadrangular form, in the Elizabethan style; and a little beyond it, in the valley of the Lea, the line is continued for about two miles on an embankment twelve feet high. The living is a dis-
413

charged vicarage, valued in the king's books at £12. 6. 5½.; patron and appropriator, the Bishop of London. The great tithes have been commuted for £197. 8., and the vicarial for £147. 8.; the appropriate glebe consists of 62½ acres. The church is a large handsome edifice, in the later English style, with a square tower supporting an octagonal spire, and a north and south chapel, the former rich in detail: there are an ancient font and several very fine monuments, of which those to Lady Elizabeth Say, Sir John Say, and Sir Henry Cock, are the most remarkable. A chapel was built in Hoddesdon about 1730; and the Independents and Quakers have each a place of worship. By deed in 1727, the Hon. Letitia Monson gave £1000, since laid out in Bank annuities, for endowing an almshouse for six widows.

BROXHOLME (All Saints), a parish, in the wapentake of Lawress, parts of Lindsey, union and county of Lincoln, 6¼ miles (N. W.) from Lincoln; containing 145 inhabitants. The parish comprises 1304 acres of land, and is bounded on the west by the river Till. The property was purchased by Lord Monson, a few years ago, by Frederick Robinson, Esq., now lord of the manor. The living is a rectory, valued in the king's books at £9. 10., and in the gift of Mr. Robinson: the tithes have been commuted for £250, and there is a good glebe-house, with 68a. 33p. of glebe.

BROXTED (St. Mary), a parish, in the union and hundred of Dunmow, N. division of Essex, 3 miles (S. W.) from Thaxted; containing 737 inhabitants. This place, anciently called Chawreth, is supposed to have derived its present name from a brook or rivulet which has its source here, and flows into the river Chelmer at Tiltey. The parish comprises 3098a. 3r. 1p., of which 2195 acres are arable, 503 pasture, 138 woodland, and the remainder gardens and waste. The soil is richly fertile, and the surface rises in some parts into considerable elevations, commanding fine views of the surrounding country. The living is a discharged vicarage, valued in the king's books at £7; patron and impropriator, R. de Beauvoir, Esq. The great tithes have been commuted for £660, and the vicarial for £200; there is a good glebe-house. The church, pleasantly situated on the brow of a hill, is an ancient edifice with a wooden turret.

BROXTON, a township, in the parish of Malpas, union of Great Boughton, Higher division of the hundred of Broxton, S. division of the county of Chester, 5 miles (N.) from Malpas; containing 464 inhabitants, and comprising 1638 acres, the soil of which is sand and clay. It has given name to a hundred, which, at the time of the Norman survey, was called Dudestan. The tithes have been commuted for £170.

BRUEN-STAPLEFORD, county of Chester.—See Stapleford, Bruen.

BRUERA.—See Churton-Heath.

BRUERN, an extra-parochial liberty, in the union of Chipping-Norton, hundred of Chadlington, county of Oxford, 3¼ miles (N. by E.) from Burford; containing 46 inhabitants, and comprising 3510 acres of land. An abbey for Cistercian monks, dedicated to the Blessed Virgin Mary, was founded by Nicholas Basset, in 1147; the revenue of which, at the Dissolution, amounted to £124. 10. 10.: the site was granted in the reign of James I., to Sir Anthony Cope, whose family built a mansion here, which was accidentally destroyed by fire.

BRUISYARD (ST. PETER), a parish, in the union
and hundred of PLOMESGATE, E. division of SUFFOLK,
4½ miles (N. W.) from Saxmundham; containing 296
inhabitants. It comprises by admeasurement 1126 acres:
the soil is a fertile clay, the surface is undulated, and
the lower grounds are watered by a small river. The
living is a perpetual curacy; net income, £62; patron
and impropriator, the Earl of Stradbroke, whose tithes
have been commuted for £92. The church is an ancient
structure, chiefly in the later English style, with a circular tower at the west end, and consists of a nave and
chancel, with a chapel on the south side, in which is a
slab, bearing the effigies, in brass, of Michael Hare and
his lady. A collegiate chapel, in honour of the Annunciation, was founded at Campsey, for a warden and
four Secular priests, by Maud, Countess of Ulster, in
1347, seven years after which the establishment was
removed to Bruisyard: the site and possessions, in
1366, were surrendered to an abbess and nuns of the
order of St. Clare, who continued here until the general
suppression, when their annual revenue was estimated at
£56. 2. 1. It was granted by Henry VIII. to Sir
Nicholas Hare, and came by marriage to the family of
Rous.

BRUMSTEAD (ST. PETER), a parish, in the TUN-
STEAD and HAPPING incorporation, hundred of HAPPING,
E. division of NORFOLK, 1 mile (N.) from Stalham;
containing 116 inhabitants. It comprises by measurement 788 acres, of which 652 are arable, 22 wood, and
the remainder marsh; the soil of the arable land is
fertile. The living is a discharged rectory, valued in
the king's books at £6. 5. 7½., and in the gift of the
Earl of Abergavenny: the tithes have been commuted
for £240, and there is a glebe of 23 acres, with a parsonage-house erected in 1841. The church is chiefly in
the decorated style, and has a lofty embattled tower.
At the inclosure in the year 1805, 12 acres were allotted
to the poor.

BRUNDALL (ST. LAWRENCE), a parish, in the
union and hundred of BLOFIELD, E. division of NOR-
FOLK, 6½ miles (E. by S.) from Norwich; containing
52 inhabitants. It is bounded on the south by the navigable river Yare; and comprises about 559 acres, the
whole arable, excepting about 133 acres of common.
The Brundall estate, consisting of a mansion and 143
acres of land, was sold to Mr. Tuck, in 1845, for £12,500.
The Norwich and Yarmouth railway passes through the
parish. The living is a discharged rectory, consolidated
with the livings of Witton and Little Plumstead, and
valued in the king's books at £4. 10.: the tithes have
been commuted for £145, and the glebe comprises
nearly 14 acres. The church is a plain structure, chiefly
in the early English style. In the 38th of Henry III.,
William de St. Omer received a grant of a fair to be
held here.

BRUNDISH (ST. LAWRENCE,) a parish, in the
union and hundred of HOXNE, E. division of SUFFOLK,
4½ miles (N. by W.) from Framlingham; containing 525
inhabitants. The living is a perpetual curacy, united to
the vicarage of Tannington: the tithes have been commuted for £572, of which £467 are payable to the Bishop
of Rochester, and £105 to the incumbent, who has also
10½ acres of glebe. The church is a handsome structure, chiefly in the later English style, with a square
embattled tower: under an arched canopy in the north

on the north bank of the river Taw, and near the road from Bideford to Exeter, comprises by computation 1300 acres. A few women are occasionally employed in weaving serges by hand-loom. Adjoining the church-yard is a green of about 3 acres, on which are marks of the foundations of houses, supposed to have been the ancient village, which, according to tradition, was destroyed by fire, and of which only one house is remaining. The living is a perpetual curacy; patron and impropriator, G. Luxton, Esq. The church, a small ancient edifice in the early English style, is situated on a hill overlooking the river; the chancel is divided from the nave by a carved oak screen, and contains a good painting of Queen Anne. Abbotsham, a farmhouse in the parish, is thought to have been the occasional residence of the abbot of Hartland, to which abbey this parish was annexed.

BRUSHFORD (ST. MARY MAGDALENE), a parish, in the union of DULVERTON, hundred of WILLITON and FREEMANNERS, W. division of SOMERSET, 1¾ mile (S. by E.) from Dulverton; containing 340 inhabitants. This parish, which is situated on the river Exe, and on the road from Minehead to Exeter, comprises by computation 2067 acres: there are some good stone-quarries, and a very fine gravel for garden-walks is found in abundance. A fair for cattle and sheep is held on the 2nd of August, at Langridge farm, in the parish. The living is a rectory, valued in the king's books at £15. 1. 5½., and in the alternate patronage of the Earl of Carnarvon and the Sydenham family; the tithes have been commuted for £305, and the glebe comprises 40 acres. The church is a plain neat edifice.

BRUTON (ST. MARY), a market-town and parish, in the union of WINCANTON, hundred of BRUTON, E. division of SOMERSET, 12 miles (S. E.) from Wells, and 110 (W. by S.) from London; comprising, with the chapelry of Wyke-Champflower, the tything of Redlynch, and part of Discove, 2074 inhabitants, of whom 1885 are in the town. This place takes its name from the river Bri or Bru, which rises in the adjoining forest of Selwood. Prior to the Conquest it was distinguished for an abbey founded by Algar, Earl of Cornwall, in 1005, for monks of the Benedictine order; upon the ruins of which, William de Bohun in the time of Stephen erected a priory for Black canons, which was raised into an abbey in the beginning of the reign of Henry VIII., by William Gilbert, the prior, by whom it was almost rebuilt: it was dedicated to the Blessed Virgin, and its revenue, at the Dissolution, was £480.17.2. The abbey, after its suppression, became the residence of the lords Fitzharding and Berkeley, who sold the manor to the Hoare family, in 1777; the remains have been converted into a parsonage-house, and the other vestiges consist of the altars, the tomb of the last abbot, and an ancient well. The TOWN is pleasantly situated at the base of a steep hill, and along the side of a romantic combe, watered by the Bru, over which is a stone bridge: it consists principally of one well-paved street; the houses are in general neatly built. The manufactures were once considerable, but are now confined chiefly to stockings and machinery; about 250 persons are employed in silk-throwing. The market is on Saturday; the fairs are on April 23rd, and Sept. 17th. The town-hall, a spacious building, of which the lower part was used for the market, and the upper contained a large
415

court-room where the petty-sessions were held, is now converted into tenements.

The parish is situated on the road from Bath to Weymouth, and comprises by measurement 3713 acres; stone of good quality for building is quarried to a considerable extent. The LIVING is a perpetual curacy; net income, £138; patron and impropriator, Sir H. R. Hoare, Bart., whose tithes have been commuted for £130. 8. The glebe comprises 20 acres. The church is a spacious and handsome structure chiefly in the later English style, with a square embattled tower crowned by pinnacles and elaborately decorated, and two porches, having over the entrance the arms of some of the abbots. The roof is of open timber frame-work, richly carved and of elegant design; the chancel is of modern erection, and in the Grecian style: the tomb of Prior Gilbert is preserved. There is a chapel at Wyke-Champflower, and another at Redlynch; and the Independents have a place of worship. The free grammar school was founded by deed dated Sept. 24th, 1519, by Richard Fitzjames, Bishop of London, Sir John Fitzjames, chief justice of England, and Dr. John Edmonds, who endowed it with estates now producing altogether £280 per annum: it has four exhibitions, of £50 per annum each, to either of the universities. An hospital for fourteen aged men, the same number of women, and sixteen boys who are also educated and apprenticed, was founded about 1618, by Hugh Saxey, auditor of the household to Queen Elizabeth and James I., who endowed it with estates at present worth £1381. 11. per annum. The buildings, which were completed about 1636, form a spacious quadrangle near the west end of the town, and are in the Elizabethan style: in one of the wings is a neat chapel, with a schoolroom below it; and over the entrance to the hall is the bust of the founder: the eastern side of the quadrangle was rebuilt some years since. Many marine shells and fossils have been dug up at Creech Hill, where was an encampment, and on which also a beacon formerly stood: human skeletons and skulls have been found at Lawyat; and at Discove, the remains of a tessellated pavement were discovered in 1711. The benevolent founder of the hospital, the two Fitzjames's, the Earl of Falmouth, who was killed in a naval engagement in 1665, and Dampier, the celebrated navigator, were born here.

BRYAN-MAUND, a township, in the parish of BODENHAM, union of LEOMINSTER, hundred of BROX-ASH, county of HEREFORD; containing 153 inhabitants.

BRYANSTON (ST. MARTIN), a parish, in the union of BLANDFORD, hundred of PIMPERNE, Blandford division of DORSET, 1½ mile (N. W. by W.) from Blandford-Forum; containing 144 inhabitants. It is situated on the river Stour, which forms its northern boundary; and comprises 1691 acres. The soil is generally chalky, but fertile; the surface is varied, and the lower grounds are subject to occasional inundation from the river, on whose banks are some tracts of fine meadow-land. The living is a rectory, united to that of Durweston, and valued in the king's books at £8. 11. 5½.: the tithes have been commuted for £177.

BRYANTS-PIDDLE, a tything, in the parish of AFF-PIDDLE, union of WAREHAM, hundred of HUN-DRED'S-BARROW, Wareham division of DORSET, 9¼ miles (E. by N.) from Dorchester; containing 64 inhabitants.

BRYNGWYN (St. Peter), a parish, in the union
of Abergavenny, division and hundred of Raglan,
county of Monmouth, 1½ mile (N. W.) from Raglan;
containing 306 inhabitants. The parish is situated near
the left bank of the river Usk, and intersected by the old
and new roads from Monmouth to Abergavenny. It
contains by estimation about 1250 acres, of which 513
are arable, 688 pasture and meadow, 10 woodland, and
the remainder roads, waste, &c.; the surface is boldly
undulated, and from some elevated portions, especially
from a place called Camp Hill, very beautiful views are
obtained: the soil consists of different combinations of
clay and gravel. Petty-sessions for the division of
Raglan are held on the third Monday in each month, at
Cross Buchan, in the parish. The living is a discharged
rectory, valued in the king's books at £4. 8. 9., and in
the gift of the Earl of Abergavenny: the incumbent's
tithes have been commuted for £164, and the glebe consists of about 39 acres, with a good parsonage-house,
enlarged and considerably improved by the rector, the
Rev. W. Crawley. A. Jones, Esq., is impropriator of the
tithes of five farms, which have been commuted for £66.
The church is an ancient structure.

BRYNING, with Kellamergh, a township, in the
ecclesiastical parish of Warton, parish of Kirkham,
union of the Fylde, hundred of Amounderness, N. division of the county of Lancaster, 2¾ miles (S. W. by W.)
from Kirkham; containing 152 inhabitants. So early
as the reign of Edward I., these two places appear
to have been considered as one township; and in
Edward IV.'s reign the Bethun family held lands in
both. Kellamergh gave name to a family when it was
usual to pass lands without dating the deeds of conveyance, or before the 18th of Edward I.: that manor was
subsequently held by a grant from the crown, by the
Middletons, who also held " Brenninge." The township
comprises 1043a. 1r. in equal portions of arable and
pasture; the surface is rather level, and the soil principally a strong clay. The tithes have been commuted
for £164 payable to the Dean and Chapter of Christ-
Church, Oxford, and £35. 19. to the vicar.

BUBBENHALL, or Bobenhall (St. Giles), a
parish, in the Kenilworth division of the hundred of
Knightlow, union, and S. division of the county, of
Warwick, 5½ miles (S. S. E.) from Coventry; containing 262 inhabitants. In the time of Edward I., John
Fitzwith was lord of the manor, which came afterwards
by marriage to John Beauchamp, who was the first person created a baron, in England, by a patent, temp.
Richard II. 1387; he was attainted of treason the same
year, and was hanged, drawn, and quartered. From the
29th of Elizabeth the manor was possessed by the family
of Wootton, with whom it continued during several
reigns. The parish comprises 1114 acres, of which 78
are woodland, and the rest chiefly arable; it is partly
bounded by the river Avon on the north. The living is
a perpetual curacy; net income, £70; patron, the
Bishop of Worcester.

BUBNELL, a township, in the parish and union of
Bakewell, hundred of High Peak, N. division of the
county of Derby, 2¾ miles (S. E.) from Stoney-Middleton; containing 128 inhabitants. The great tithes of
the township have been commuted for £169 payable to
the impropriators, and £7 payable to the Dean and
Chapter of Lichfield.

containing 716 inhabitants. This place owes its origin to William D'Albini, Earl of Chichester, who, disliking the situation of a castle which had been built at Old Buckenham about the time of the Conquest, demolished that structure, and erected another here, in the reign of Henry II. The new castle was pleasantly situated on an eminence to the east of the former, and consisted of a keep, two round towers, a grand entrance tower, and a barbican, inclosed with embattled walls surrounded by a fosse. Its owner, who had view of frankpledge, and the power of life and death, obtained from Henry many privileges for his new burgh, among which were 'those of holding a mercate court, the assize of bread and ale, and a market; and the lord of the manor still claims the right of officiating as butler at the coronation of the kings of England. The TOWN is pleasantly situated; the houses are neatly built, and there is an ample supply of water. The market (on Saturday) has fallen into disuse; the fairs for horses, cattle, &c., are on the last Saturday in May, and Nov. 22nd and 23rd, and a statute-fair for hiring servants is held a fortnight before Old Michaelmas-day. A high bailiff is chosen annually at the " Portman" court, and a court baron and court leet are held by the proprietor of the manor. The parish comprises about 330 acres, 80 of which are uninclosed common, and the rest chiefly arable. The LIVING is a perpetual curacy, and has a net income of £115 : it is in the patronage of the Inhabitants, who pay a yearly modus of $3\frac{1}{2}d.$ in the pound on the rental in lieu of tithes. The church is an ancient and handsome structure, containing portions of several orders of architecture, and has a square tower with six bells : the north aisle was rebuilt in 1749, by the aid of several distinguished families ; the chancel is separated from the north aisle by a richly carved screen, and contains some interesting monuments. There are places of worship for Methodists.

BUCKENHAM, OLD (*All Saints*), a parish, in the union of GUILTCROSS, hundred of SHROPHAM, W. division of NORFOLK, 3 miles (S. S. E.) from Attleburgh ; containing 1255 inhabitants. This was anciently a place of considerable importance, and is supposed to derive its name either from *Boccen*, a beech-tree, and *Ham*, a dwelling-place ; or from an allusion to the bucks, or deer, that thronged the adjacent forests. It was given by the Conqueror to William D'Albini, whose son of the same name married the widow of Henry I., became Earl of Chichester, and founded a priory for Augustine canons, in honour of St. James the Apostle, about the middle of the twelfth century. At the Dissolution, the establishment consisted of a prior and eight canons, whose revenue was estimated at £131. 11. Here were three guilds, dedicated respectively to St. Margaret, St. Peter, and St. Thomas the Martyr. The parish comprises 4820a. 1r. 7p., of which 3703 acres are arable, 1050 pasture, 49 wood, and 18 water : the common was inclosed in 1790. The living is a perpetual curacy, in the patronage of the Inhabitants, with a net income of £102 : the tithes have been commuted for £1527. 18. The church has a thatched roof, and an octagonal tower with five bells. There are places of worship for Baptists, Sandemanians, and Primitive Methodists.

BUCKENHAM PARVA or TOFTS (*St. Andrew*), a parish, in the union of SWAFFHAM, hundred of GRIMSHOE, W. division of NORFOLK, 6 miles (N. E.) from Brandon ; containing 77 inhabitants. It comprises by

3 H

admeasurement 650 acres, of which about one-fifth is wood and plantation, and the remainder arable and pasture land in equal portions. The estate belongs chiefly to the Hall, a large handsome mansion in a spacious park, built in the reign of Charles II. : the road from London to Watton passes through the park. The living is a discharged rectory, valued in the king's books at £3, and in the patronage of the Rev. T. Newman. The church has long been demolished, together with the village of Buckenham.

BUCKENHILL, a township, in the parish of WOOL-HOPÉ, union of LEDBURY, hundred of GREYTREE, county of HEREFORD, 8½ miles (N. by E.) from Ross; containing 137 inhabitants.

BUCKERELL, or BOKERELL (ST. MARY), a parish, in the union of HONITON, hundred of HEMYOCK, Honiton and N. divisions of DEVON, 3 miles (W.) from Honiton; containing 360 inhabitants. This place was anciently the property of the Pomeroys, of Bury, and was given, in the reign of John, by Sir Henry Pomeroy to his second son Sir Geoffrey, from whom, by marriage of his descendant in the female line, it was conveyed to the Fulfords and Gwynnes, of Ford Abbey. A hamlet in the parish, now called Weston, but anciently Weringstone, was a manor belonging to Dunkeswell Abbey, and, after the Dissolution, was granted by Henry VIII. to John Drake, merchant. The surface of the parish is intersected by a semicircular ridge of hills; and near Godford Cross is a rill of water, which has its rise under Wulphere Church, so designated from the Saxon chieftain of that name, whose stronghold was Hembury Fort. Hembury-Fort House, originally built by Admiral Graves, was once called Cockenhayes, and a Roman road leading to it is still known as Cockenhay-street; it is situated directly under the ancient fort, and forms an interesting feature in the landscape. Deer Park, which occupies the site of an old lodge and chace, after the Conquest was held by Matthew de Buckington, from whose crest (a buck) and the rill previously noticed, the parish is supposed to have derived its name. The village is pleasantly situated near the banks of the Otter; a pleasure-fair is held there on the first Monday in September. The living is a discharged vicarage, valued in the king's books at £10. 0. 2½.; patrons, the Dean and Chapter of Exeter; impropriator, J. Northcote, Esq. The vicarial tithes have been commuted for £135. The church is an elegant structure in the later English style, and contains a richly carved oak screen separating the nave from the chancel, some monuments to the family of Admiral Graves, and the Gwynnes of Ford Abbey, and an elegant tablet to the memory of Elizabeth, late wife of the Rev. E. E. Coleridge, the present incumbent, by whom the church, to which an aisle was added in 1839, has been restored and beautified. A vicarage-house was built in 1829. Andrew Buckerell, mayor of London in 1232 and for five successive years, was a native of the parish.

BUCKFASTLEIGH (HOLY TRINITY), a market-town and parish, in the union of TOTNES, hundred of STANBOROUGH, Stanborough and Coleridge, and S. divisions of DEVON, 2¾ miles (S. W. by W.) from Ashburton; containing 2576 inhabitants. This place, which was formerly of considerable importance, derived its origin and name from a Cistercian abbey, founded about the year 1137, and the abbot of which had the power of

BUCKHOW-BANK, a township, in the parish of DALSTON, union of CARLISLE, ward, and E. division of the county, of CUMBERLAND, 5½ miles (S. S. W.) from Carlisle; containing 636 inhabitants. The village lies on the eastern bank of the river Caldew, and there are several cotton-mills within the township, in connexion with the manufacturers at Carlisle. The soil is very favourable to the growth of wheat.

BUCKINGHAM (ST. PETER AND ST. PAUL), a parish, and the head of a union, in the hundred and county of BUCKINGHAM, 17 miles (N. W.) from Aylesbury, and 57 (N. W. by W.) from London; comprising the borough and market-town of Buckingham (which has a separate jurisdiction), the chapelry of Gawcott,

Seal and Arms.

the hamlets of Bourton, Bourtonhold, and Lenborough, and the precinct of Pre-bend-End; and containing 4054 inhabitants, of whom 1816 are in the township, or principal district, of Buckingham. This place is of great antiquity, and is supposed to have derived its name from the Saxon *Bucca*, a "stag" or "buck," *ing*, a "meadow," and *ham*, a "village;" being surrounded with extensive forests well stocked with deer. In 915, Edward the Elder fortified both sides of the river, where the town is situated, with high ramparts of earth, to protect the inhabitants from the incursions of the Danes; the remains are still visible. In 941, the Danes perpetrated dreadful outrages in the neighbourhood, and in 1010 took possession of the town as a place of safety. In the reign of Edward III., Buckingham sent three representatives to a council of trade held at Westminster, at which time it was a considerable staple for wool; but upon the removal of that mart to Calais, its prosperity declined, and it finally became one of those decayed towns for which relief was granted by parliament, in 1535. About this period the assizes, formerly held here, were removed to Aylesbury; but in 1758, Lord Cobham obtained an act for holding the summer assizes at Buckingham. In 1644, Charles I. fixed his head-quarters at the place; and Sir William Waller, after the battle of Cropredy-Bridge, and Fairfax, after his defeat at Boarstall House, in this county, took up their stations here. In 1724, the inhabitants suffered severely from an accidental fire, which destroyed several entire streets, and many of the houses have not yet been rebuilt. Her Majesty and Prince Albert visited the town in January, 1845.

· BUCKINGHAM is pleasantly situated on a peninsula formed by the river Ouse, which nearly encompasses the town and is crossed by three stone bridges, two of them of great antiquity: that on the London road is a neat structure of three arches, erected about the year 1805, by the Marquess of Buckingham. It is divided into three districts, *viz.*, the Borough, Bourton-Hold, and the Prebend-End, the first of which contains the principal streets: the houses in general are built of brick; the streets are paved but not flagged, and are lighted with gas. The trade chiefly consists in the sorting of wool, the tanning of leather, and the manufacture of lace; and before the introduction of that manufacture into Not-

419

tingham, where machinery is used, lace-making afforded employment to a large portion of the female inhabitants. In the vicinity are several limestone-quarries, and a quarry of marble of a darkish brown colour and exceedingly hard, but which, as it can neither endure the weather nor retain a polish, is not now worked. The river affords facility of conveyance; and there is a canal, which joins the Grand Junction at Cosgrove: an act was passed in 1846 for the formation of a railway from Brackley, by Buckingham, to the Oxford and Bletchley line. The market is on Saturday, and there is also a very good market, exclusively for calves, every Monday. Fairs, chiefly for the sale of cattle, sheep, and horses, are held on Old New-Year's day, the last Monday in January, March 7th, the second Monday in April, May 6th, Whit-Thursday, July 10th (a wool-fair), September 4th, October 2nd, the Saturday after Old Michaelmas-day (which is also a statute-fair for the hiring of servants), November 8th, and December 13th.

The town was first incorporated by Queen Mary, in 1554, and another charter was granted by Charles II.; but it having been surrendered, the charter of Mary continued to be the governing one, until the passing of the Municipal act, by which the government is vested in a mayor, four aldermen, and twelve councillors, assisted by a recorder, town-clerk, and other officers. The jurisdiction extends over the town and parish, and the total number of magistrates is nine. The borough has constantly returned two representatives to parliament since the 36th of Henry VIII.: the right of election, prior to the act of the 2nd of William IV., cap. 45, was vested exclusively in the bailiff and twelve principal burgesses, but, by that act, was extended to the £10 householders of an enlarged district of 18,265 acres. The mayor is returning officer. A court of quarter-sessions was granted in 1836. There was also, until lately, a court wherein any action might be brought, provided the amount sought to be recovered did not exceed £20; but this court has been superseded by the county debt-court of Buckingham, established in 1847, which has jurisdiction over the registration-districts of Buckingham and Winslow. The town-hall is a spacious and convenient brick building, nearly in the centre of the town. The old borough gaol, a square stone edifice, was built by Lord Cobham, in 1758; it has been lately enlarged, and, by internal improvement, adapted to the system of classification.

The parish comprises by computation 4680 acres: the soil is a good loam, alternated with gravel; the surface is rather hilly, and the surrounding scenery pleasingly varied. The LIVING is a discharged vicarage, valued in the king's books at £22; patron, the Duke of Buckingham; impropriators, the landowners: the present net income, £200, is about to be considerably increased by means of the Tithe Commutation act, under which certain ancient payments in lieu of tithes have been found invalid. The old church, having been for many years in a very dilapidated condition, fell down on March 26th, 1776, and the present edifice was erected in 1781, at a cost, it is said, of £7000, in addition to the old materials. It does not occupy the site of the former church, but that of an ancient castle, supposed to have been built by one of the earls of Buckingham subsequently to the Conquest, and the foundations of which

3 H 2

are occasionally discovered. The structure has a square embattled tower surmounted by a well-proportioned spire. The interior is handsomely fitted up in the Grecian style : the altar is ornamented with a good copy of Raphael's Transfiguration, over which is a beautifully painted window, presented by the late Duke of Buckingham, on his elevation to the dukedom, and said to have cost £1300 ; and at the west end is the finest-toned organ in the county. At Gawcott is a separate incumbency. There are places of worship for Independents, the Society of Friends, and Wesleyans. The free grammar school was instituted by Edward VI., who endowed it with the revenue of a dissolved chantry in the town ; the master is appointed by the corporation. The schoolroom was the chapel of a chantry founded in 1268, by Matthew Stratton, Archdeacon of Buckingham, and dedicated to St. John the Baptist and Thomas à Becket : the original entrance, a Norman arched doorway, is still remaining ; and there are in the chapel some remains of seats put up in the old church in the reign of Edward VI., very curiously carved. The union comprises 29 parishes or places, of which 28 are in the county of Buckingham, and one in the county of Oxford ; and contains a population of 14,239. Buckingham gives the titles of Duke and Marquess to the family of Temple, whose magnificent seat is at Stowe, about two miles to the west.

BUCKINGHAMSHIRE, an inland county, bounded on the south and south-west by Berkshire, on the west by the county of Oxford, on the north-west and north by that of Northampton, on the north-east by that of Bedford, on the east by those of Bedford and Hertford, and on the south-east by Middlesex. It extends from 51° 26′ to 52° 12′ (N. Lat.), and from 28′ to 1° 8′ (W. Lon.) ; and comprises an area of about 740 square miles, or 473,600 statute acres. The county contains 31,087 inhabited houses, 1159 uninhabited, and 206 in course of erection ; and the population amounts to 155,983, of whom 76,482 are males, and 79,501 females.

The territory composing the present county of Buckingham is thought by Camden to have been anciently inhabited by the *Cassii* or *Cattieuchlani.* Mr. Whitaker, the learned historian of Manchester, was of opinion, that only that part of the county bordering on Bedfordshire was originally occupied by the *Cassii,* and that they afterwards seized upon the territories of the *Dobuni,* who had previously obtained possession of the rest by conquest from the *Ancalites.* Under the Roman dominion it was included in the great division called *Flavia Cæsariensis ;* and on the complete establishment of the heptarchy, it became part of the powerful kingdom of Mercia. Buckinghamshire is in the diocese of Oxford and province of Canterbury, and, with the exception of a few parishes, constitutes an archdeaconry, in which are the deaneries of Buckingham; Burnham, Mursley, Newport, Wadsden, Wendover, and Wycombe ; the number of parishes is 202. For civil purposes it is divided into the hundreds of Ashendon, Aylesbury, Buckingham, Burnham, Cottesloe, Desborough, Newport, and Stoke. It contains the borough and market-towns of Aylesbury, Buckingham, Great Marlow, and High Wycombe ; and the market-towns of Amersham, Beaconsfield, Chesham, Ivinghoe, Newport-Pagnell, Olney, Prince's-Risborough, Fenny-Stratford, Stony-

osgrove, on the Northamptonshire border; and the ʃendover navigation joins it at Bulborne, on the confines of Hertfordshire. The *Great Western railway* enters the county at Iver, in its progress from Middlesex, and quits it at Taplow, where it enters the county of Berks. The *London and Birmingham* railway enters the county ſ Ivinghoe, and, after a course of 25 miles, quits it at Hanslope, for Northamptonshire. The *Aylesbury* railway proceeds from that town through a portion of the county of Herts, near Tring, and joins the London and irmingham line, of which it is a branch; the line is even miles in length. A small part of the *Bedford* ʃranch of the London and Birmingham railway, is also ithin the county.

Buckinghamshire contained the Roman station *Maʃovintum*, the remains of which are visible on a small elevation in the "Auld Fields," about a quarter of a ʃile from Fenny-Stratford, where an abundance of coins ʃnd foundations of buildings have been dug up. It was ʃrossed by the Ikeneld-street, Watling-street, and Akeman-street, and by several vicinal ways, of which there ʃre traces in different parts. Camden is of opinion that ʃhere was a Roman town at Burg-hill, now contracted ʃto Brill, in the western part of the county: numerous ʃelics of Roman occupation, such as coins, pavements, ʃc., have been found at Wycombe and in its vicinity; ʃnd coins have also been found near Prince's-Risborough ʃnd Ellesborough. Above the village of Medmenham ʃre the remains of a large camp, nearly square, formed ʃy a single ditch and vallum, and inclosing an area of ʃbout seven acres; and in a wood near Burnham is an ʃblong intrenchment of the same kind, vulgarly called 'Harlequin's Moat." Near Ellesborough are some ʃtrong earthworks on the side of the Chiltern Hills, at ʃne corner of which is a high mount styled the Castle ʃill, or Kimble Castle, and commonly supposed to have ʃeen the site of the residence of the British king Cunoʃeline. On the top of the hill at West Wycombe are ʃhe remains of a circular encampment; and those of ʃnother are discernible near High Wycombe, at a place ʃamed Old, or All, Hollands. At Danesfield, on the ʃanks of the Thames, is a nearly circular intrenchment, ʃlesignated Danes' Ditch; at Cholsbury is a nearly cirʃular camp, formed by a double ditch; and the manorʃouse of the adjacent village of Hawridge is built within ʃn ancient circular intrenchment. There are also some ʃarge intrenchments at Hedgerby-Dean, and a remarkʃble ditch runs thence to East Burnham. Near the ʃower Ikeneld way, in the parish of Ellesborough, is a ʃnoated area of an irregular form, in most places about ʃifty paces in breadth. A considerable rampart of earth, ʃnder the common name of Grimesdike, runs nearly east ʃnd west through a part of the county, upon the Chiltern ʃills, where it may be traced for some miles; and on ʃhe side of the chalk hills near Risborough is cut a great ʃross called White Leaf Cross, of unknown antiquity, ʃvhich has been considered the memorial of some victory ʃ̧ained by the Anglo-Saxons over the Danes.

Prior to the Reformation there were twenty-one *Religious Houses;* including four alien priories, one commandery of the Knights Hospitallers, and a college of ʃhe society of *Bonhommes* at Ashridge, near the confines ʃf Hertfordshire, the only house of that order in England, excepting that at Edingdon in Wiltshire. The ʃounty contained, besides, ten hospitals, one of which,

at Newport-Pagnell, refounded by Queen Anne, consort of James I., still exists; also the well-known royal·college of Eton, founded by Henry VI. There are very considerable remains of Nutley Abbey, converted into a farmhouse and offices; and some vestiges of those of Burnham, Medmenham, and Great Missenden, and of the college of *Bonhommes:* part of St. Margaret's nunnery, in the parish of Ivinghoe, is yet standing, and is occupied as a dwelling-house. No mural remains exist of any fortress, but some earthworks point out the sites of those which stood at Castlethorpe, Lavendon, and Whitchurch, the first was called Hanslope Castle. The most remarkable ancient mansions are, Gayhurst, built in the reign of Elizabeth, and Liscombe House; and among the seats of the landed proprietors, those most distinguished for their architectural beauties are, the magnificent mansion of Stowe, Wycombe Abbey, Ashridge Park (partly in Herts), and the modern mansion at Tyringham. Buckinghamshire gives the title of Earl to the family of Hobart-Hampden.

BUCKLAND, *cum* CARSWELL (ST. MARY), a parish, in the union of FARRINGDON, hundred of GANFIELD, county of BERKS, 3¾ miles (E. N. E.) from Farringdon; containing 946 inhabitants. It is situated on the road from Oxford to Bath, and bounded on the north by the navigable river Isis, on the banks of which a wharf has been constructed. Some quarries of good buildingstone are extensively wrought; and a pleasure-fair is held in August. Buckland House, the seat of Sir J. Throckmorton, Bart., was erected in 1757, and is pleasantly situated. The living is a discharged vicarage, valued in the king's books at £18. 4. 7.; patron and appropriator, the Bishop of Gloucester and Bristol: the great tithes have been commuted for £863. 10., and the vicarial for £275. 8.; the glebe comprises 30 acres. The church, a neat edifice, contains a monument to a Duke of Somerset, who was interred here. There is a place of worship for Baptists, and a Roman Catholic chapel is attached to Buckland House.

BUCKLAND (ALL SAINTS), a parish, in the union and hundred of AYLESBURY, county of BUCKINGHAM, 3 miles (W. N. E.) from Tring; containing 537 inhabitants, and comprising 1497 acres. An act was passed in 1842 for inclosing lands in the parish. The living is annexed, with the livings of Quarrendon and Stoke-Mandeville, to the vicarage of Bierton. There is a place of worship for Wesleyans.

BUCKLAND (ST. MICHAEL), a parish, in the union of WINCHCOMB, Lower division of the hundred of KIFTSGATE, E. division of the county of GLOUCESTER, 6 miles (W. S. W.) from Chipping-Campden; containing, with the hamlet of Laverton, 377 inhabitants. The living is a rectory, valued in the king's books at £29. 6. 8.; net income, £222; patron, Sir T. Phillips, Bart.: the tithes were commuted in 1779, for land and a money payment. The church is a fine structure, in the later English style; some of the windows contain specimens of ancient stained glass. James Thynne, by deed in 1707, gave land now producing upwards of £100 per annum, for teaching poor children, and other charitable purposes.

BUCKLAND (ST. ANDREW), a parish, in the union of BUNTINGFORD, hundred of EDWINSTREE, county of HERTFORD, 3 miles (N.) from Buntingford; containing 435 inhabitants. It comprises by computation 2000 acres, of which 500 are woodland, 50 pasture, and the remainder good arable land; the soil is fertile, and the surface varied. The living is a rectory, valued in the king's books at £20, and in the patronage of King's College, Cambridge: the tithes have been commuted for £330, and the glebe comprises 38 acres. The church is in the later English style.

BUCKLAND (ST. NICHOLAS), a parish, in the union and hundred of FAVERSHAM, Upper division of the lathe of SCRAY, E. division of KENT, 3 miles (N. W. by W.) from Faversham; containing 19 inhabitants. It consists of 978 acres, of which 35 are in wood. The living is a discharged sinecure rectory, valued in the king's books at £5. 6. 8.; net income, £167; patron, Sir John Tyssen Tyrrell, Bart. The church has long been in ruins.

BUCKLAND (ST. MARY), a parish, in the union of CHARD, partly in the S. division of the hundred of PETHERTON, and partly in the hundred of MARTOCK, but chiefly in that of ABDICK and BULSTONE, W. division of SOMERSET, 6 miles (W. by S.) from Ilminster; containing 696 inhabitants. This parish was the scene of some sanguinary conflicts between the Saxons and the Danes, and various relics of warlike implements have been found in the neighbourhood. It comprises 3494 acres, of which 210 are common or waste. A fair for cattle and toys is held on the Wednesday and Thursday next after September 20th. The living is a rectory, valued in the king's books at £12. 19. 9½., and in the patronage of Lieut.-Gen. Popham: the tithes have been commuted for £350, and the glebe consists of 37½ acres. The churchyard contains a mutilated stone cross. On the edge of Blackdown Hill are the remains of a Roman fortification, called Neroche Castle; and on the summit of the same ridge, a little further on, by the side of the road leading to Chard, is a huge collection of flint stones, lying in heaps upwards of 60 yards in circumference, styled Robin Hood's Butts, and supposed to be the rude sepulchral memorials of warriors who fell in battle.

BUCKLAND (ST. PETER), a parish, in the union, and First division of the hundred, of REIGATE, E. division of SURREY, 2¼ miles (W.) from Reigate; containing 364 inhabitants. This parish, which is situated on the road from Dorking to Reigate, and bounded on the south by the river Mole, comprises by computation 1800 acres. The soil is partly chalk, forming a portion of the great ridge extending through Surrey, and partly a blue clay, alternated with sand; the surface is hilly, and the surrounding scenery very pleasing. The living is a rectory, valued in the king's books at £11. 12. 11., and in the patronage of All Souls' College, Oxford; net income, £337. The church consists of a nave and chancel; .in some of the windows are the remains of stained glass.

BUCKLAND-BREWER (ST. MARY AND ST. BENEDICT), a parish, and formerly a market-town, in the union of BIDEFORD, hundred of SHEBBEAR, Great Torrington and N. divisions of DEVON, 5 miles (S. by W.) from Bideford; containing 1103 inhabitants, of whom 312 are in the village. This place derives its distinguishing appellation from its ancient proprietor, Lord Brewer, whose seat, Orleigh Court, is still remaining: he gave a portion of the manor to the abbot of Dunkeswell, who obtained the privilege of a weekly market and an annual

BUCKLAND-MONACHORUM (*HOLY TRINITY*), a parish, and formerly a market-town, in the union of TAVISTOCK, hundred of ROBOROUGH, Midland-Roborough and S. divisions of DEVON, 4 miles (S. by E.) from Tavistock; containing 1411 inhabitants. This place acquired the adjunct to its name from an abbey founded in 1278, by Amicia, Countess Dowager of Devonshire, in honour of the Virgin Mary and St. Benedict; to which she removed a society of Cistercian monks from the Isle of Wight. In 1337, the abbot obtained permission to castellate his monastery; and during the parliamentary war it was garrisoned by Sir Richard Grenville. The revenue of the society, in the 26th of Henry VIII., was estimated at £241. 17. 9. The estate came by purchase into the possession of the renowned Sir Francis Drake; and a modern mansion, beautifully situated on the banks of the Tavy, has been erected, called Buckland Abbey, now the property of Sir T. T. F. E. Drake, Bart.; but there are still some interesting remains of the abbey. The parish comprises 6386 acres, of which 1889 are common or waste. The village, which contains some curious old houses,. a mutilated stone cross, and a few ancient inscriptions, is mean in appearance, but picturesquely situated. A fair is held on Trinity-Monday. The Plymouth and Dartmoor railway crosses the parish on the east. The living is a vicarage, valued in the king's books at £19. 8. 9., and in the gift of the family of Nichols: the great tithes, belonging to Sir T. Drake, have been commuted for £175. 8.; and those of the incumbent for £291. 10., with a glebe of 52 acres. The church consists of a nave, two aisles, and two small transepts, with a fine tower supporting four octagonal turrets, embattled, and surmounted by pinnacles; it contains, among several others, a finely executed monument by Bacon, to the memory of Baron Heathfield, the brave defender of Gibraltar.

BUCKLAND-NEWTON (*HOLY ROOD*), a parish, in the union of CERNE, hundred of BUCKLAND-NEWTON, Cerne division of the county of DORSET, 4 miles (N. E. by N.) from Cerne; comprising the tythings of Brockhampton, Buckland, Duntish, Knowle, Mintern Parva, and Plush; and containing 914 inhabitants, of whom 310 are in the tything of Buckland. The parish is on the great road from Weymouth to Bath, and comprises by measurement 6018 acres, of which about 1241 are arable, 4085 meadow and pasture, 237 woodland, and 308 common. The substratum is chalk, in which are imbedded some few flints; and a little sandstone is found on the western confines. The living is a vicarage, valued in the king's books at £16. 19. 9½.; patrons, the Dean and Chapter of Wells; impropriators, the representatives of Leonard Pount, Esq., who have commuted their tithes for £745: the vicarial tithes have been commuted for £550; 104 acres of glebe belong to the impropriators, and 19½ to the vicar. The church is in the early and later English styles; the chancel has lancet windows: a gallery, containing 120 sittings, was built in 1821. At Plush is a chapel of ease, more ancient than the church. The Independents have a place of worship. There are some remains of a Roman camp.

BUCKLAND-RIPERS, a parish, in the union of WEYMOUTH, hundred of CULLIFORD-TREE, Dorchester division of DORSET, 3½ miles (N. W. by N.) from Melcombe-Regis; containing 118 inhabitants. It comprises 1205 acres by computation: the soil is a strong clay, producing good crops of grain; the surface is hilly, and the surrounding scenery pleasing. The living is a discharged rectory, valued in the king's books at £5. 9. 2., and in the patronage of Q. H. Stroud, Esq.: the tithes have been commuted for £200, and the glebe comprises nine acres.

BUCKLAND-TOUTSAINTS, a chapelry, in the parish of LODDISWELL, union of KINGSBRIDGE, hundred of COLERIDGE, Stanborough and Coleridge, and S. divisions of DEVON, 2½ miles (N. E.) from Kingsbridge; containing 56 inhabitants.

BUCKLAND, WEST (ST. PETER), a parish, in the union of SOUTH MOLTON, hundred of BRAUNTON, South Molton and N. divisions of DEVON, 6 miles (N. W.) from South Molton; containing 275 inhabitants. It comprises 1339 acres, of which 259 are common or waste: stone for the roads is quarried in several parts. The living is a rectory, valued in the king's books at £13. 13. 4., and in the gift of the Baroness Bassett: the tithes have been commuted for £190; there is a good glebe-house, and the glebe comprises 32 acres. The church has a carved wooden screen, highly enriched, separating the nave from the chancel. There is a place of worship for Wesleyans.

BUCKLAND, WEST (ST. MARY), a parish, in the union of WELLINGTON, W. division of the hundred of KINGSBURY, locally in that of TAUNTON and TAUNTON-DEAN, W. division of SOMERSET, 2¾ miles (E.) from Wellington; containing 887 inhabitants. The living is annexed to the vicarage of Wellington: the church is partly in the Norman style, with later additions. There is a place of worship for Wesleyans.

BUCKLEBURY, anciently BURGHULBURY (ST. MARY), a parish, in the union of BRADFIELD, partly in the hundred of READING, and partly in that of FAIRCROSS, county of BERKS, 7 miles (E. N. E.) from Newbury; containing, with the tythings of Bucklebury, Hawkridge, and Marlston, 1277 inhabitants, of whom 1065 are in Bucklebury tything. The parish comprises 6025a. 7p., of which 3443 acres are arable, 1000 copse-wood, 726 meadow, and 854 common land. The living is a vicarage, valued in the king's books at £17; patron and impropriator, W. H. H. Hartley, Esq., lord of the manor: the great tithes have been commuted for £75. 10., and the vicarial for £340; the glebe consists of nearly 31 acres, with a glebe-house. The church contains a monument to the memory of Viscountess Bolingbroke, and others to the ancient family of Winchcombe; a good organ was presented by the late incumbent, the Rev. W. Hartley. Not far from the church stood the old manor-house, which, from decay, was taken down in 1833, when some very ancient arches of carved oak, with several pieces of coin and tessellated pavement, were discovered: there are still some remains of a subterraneous passage, through which the celebrated Lord Bolingbroke is reported to have escaped.

BUCKLESHAM (ST. MARY), a parish, in the union of WOODBRIDGE, hundred of COLNEIS, E. division of SUFFOLK, 5 miles (E. S. E.) from Ipswich; containing 255 inhabitants. The parish comprises 1799 acres, of which 41 are common or waste. The soil is of a mixed quality, the greater portion light; and till within the last few years, a considerable portion was uninclosed heath: the surface is boldly undulated, and the lower grounds are watered by a stream which flows through

the Napton canals meet in the parish. The living is a discharged vicarage, valued in the king's books at £8, and in the patronage of the Rev. H. White: the tithes have been commuted for £427. 5. The church, a neat edifice in good repair, has been beautified, and several of the windows embellished with stained glass. There is a Roman Catholic chapel at Hampton Hill, the seat of Lord Dormer. A parochial school is endowed with £22. 11. per annum, a portion of the rental of land bequeathed in 1701 by Job Marston.

BUDBY, a township, in the parish of EDWINSTOW, union of SOUTHWELL, Hatfield division of the wapentake of BASSETLAW, N. division of the county of NOTTINGHAM, 3 miles (N. W. by W.) from Ollerton; containing 127 inhabitants, and comprising 1312 acres. In Domesday book it is called "Buteby," and described as *soc* of the king's great manor of Mansfield, of which it is now held in fee by Earl Manvers. The village consists of Gothic cottages, and is seated at the south-west corner of Thoresby Park, under a thickly-wooded acclivity, and on the south side of the Medin, which is here crossed by a neat bridge. North and South Budby forests are uninclosed, but form excellent sheep-walks. A school for girls, established in 1791, is under the patronage of the Countess Manvers.

BUDDLE-HILL, a hamlet, in the parish of SELWORTHY, union of WILLITON, hundred of CARHAMPTON, W. division of SOMERSET; containing 28 inhabitants.

BUDE, a village and small sea-port, on the coast of the Bristol Channel, in the parish, union, and hundred of STRATTON, E. division of CORNWALL, 2 miles (N. W.) from Stratton; containing 189 inhabitants. This village has of late years become a place of resort for bathing, and the trade has received a stimulus from the construction of the Bude canal: the imports are coal and limestone from Wales, and grocery, &c., from Bristol; and timber, bark, and grain, are sent away. The harbour is inaccessible to ships of large burthen, on account of the sands; those connected with it do not average more than 50 tons each, though vessels of 120 tons' burthen have often entered. Lime is burnt in considerable quantities, and a great deal of sand conveyed inland for manuring the soil. A chapel has been erected at the expense of Sir T. D. Acland, Bart., in whom the patronage is vested; and there is a place of worship for Wesleyans. On Chapel rock, near the breakwater, formerly stood a chapel.

BUDEAUX, or BUDOCK, ST., a parish, in the union of PLYMPTON ST. MARY, hundred of ROBOROUGH, Roborough and S. divisions of DEVON, 4½ miles (N. W. by N.) from Plymouth; containing 790 inhabitants. This place, which is beautifully situated on an eminence rising from the river Tamar, from which it is distant about three-quarters of a mile, was, during the parliamentary war, the scene of a conflict between the royalists under Sir Richard Grenville, and the forces of the garrison of Plymouth, then in the possession of the parliamentarians. The royalists, who had strongly fortified the church of St. Budock, as their chief station while besieging the garrison, were driven into it by a sally of the besieged, under Colonel Martin, the governor; and Major Stuckley, with several officers and about 100 men were made prisoners. The parish comprises by computation 2500 acres, of which 120 are in the county of

Cornwall : there are some quarries of slate, and of stone of inferior quality. The river is navigable for vessels of small burthen from Saltash-ferry, about a mile distant, to the Weirhead, at certain times of the tide. A fair is held on the 29th of May. The living is a perpetual curacy, in the patronage of the Vicar of St. Andrew's, Plymouth : the tithes have been commuted for £350; the income of the curacy is about £113. The church, which was re-built in 1563, is a neat structure in the later English style. There are places of worship for Wesleyans ; and a school has an endowment of about £86 per annum, arising from land.

BUDLE, a township, in the parish of BAMBROUGH, union of BELFORD, N. division of BAMBROUGH ward and of NORTHUMBERLAND, 3¾ miles (E. by N.) from Belford ; containing 102 inhabitants. The township is on the coast, and comprises 600 acres, of which 450 are arable, and 150 pasture including about 20 acres of plantation ; the views embrace a large extent of the sea-shore, with Bambrough Castle and Holy Island. Whin-stone is quarried, and very extensive flour-mills are in operation. The village lies on the southern shore of a fine bay, and on the east side of the Warn rivulet ; the adjacent coast abounds with cockles of a superior fla-vour. Vessels of ten feet draught come up to the harbour one mile from the mills. The tithes have been commuted for £24. 5. payable to the impropriator, and 14s. to the perpetual curate of Bambrough.

BUDLEIGH, EAST (ALL SAINTS), a parish, and formerly a market-town, in the union of ST. THOMAS, hundred of EAST BUDLEIGH, Woodbury and S. divisions of DEVON, 4½ miles (W. S. W.) from Sidmouth ; con-taining 2319 inhabitants. The antiquity of this place is evinced by its having given name to the hundred. It is pleasantly situated on the shore of the English Channel, to which it is open on the south ; and is sheltered on other sides by hills of moderate elevation. From the excellent accommodations which have been provided for sea-bathing at Budleigh-Salterton, within the parish, where hot and cold baths have been constructed, and preparations made for the reception of visiters, that hamlet is rising into repute as a watering-place. The market was anciently held on Sunday, and afterwards on Monday; a pleasure-fair is still held on Easter-Tues-day. The parish comprises 2622 acres, of which 338 are waste ; the surface is hilly, and the lower lands are watered by the river Otter. The living is a discharged vicarage, with the perpetual curacy of Withycombe-Rawleigh annexed, valued in the king's books at £30 ; net income, £318; patrons, the family of Rolle ; impro-priators, the landowners. In addition to the parochial church, there is a chapel of ease in the later English style, erected in 1813 at the expense of Lord Rolle. The Wesleyans have a place of worship. At Poer Hayes is an ancient mansion, celebrated as the birthplace of Sir Walter Raleigh ; and some remains exist of an old chapel dedicated to St. James.

BUDOCK (ST. BUDOKE), a parish, in the union of FALMOUTH, E. division of the hundred of KERRIER, W. division of CORNWALL, 1½ mile (W. by S.) from Fal-mouth ; containing 1979 inhabitants. This parish, which is bounded on the east by Falmouth bay and the English Channel, and crossed in one part by the road from Fal-mouth to Penryn, was distinguished for a collegiate church erected on Glaseney Moor in 1720, in honour of the

Blessed Virgin and St. Thomas of Canterbury, by Wal-ter Bronescombe, Bishop of Exeter. It continued till the Dissolution, at which time its revenue amounted to £205. 10. 6.; the buildings are said to have occupied a site of three acres, to have been inclosed with an em-battled wall, and to have had a subterraneous commu-nication with the church of Gluvias. Within the parish are Pendennis Castle, and Dunstanville and Green-Bank terraces, forming the principal part of the Barton of Penwarris, and adjoining the town of Falmouth. The parish comprises 3899 acres, of which 236 are common or waste ; the surface is diversified with hill and dale, and generally well cultivated; and the views from the higher parts, both of sea and land, are extensive and commanding. Granite is largely quarried for exporta-tion to London, at a place called the Budock Rocks, and near Swan Pool, a lake about a quarter of a mile in cir-cumference, and separated from the sea by a bar of sand : there is also a copper-mine. The living is a vicarage, united to that of St. Gluvias : the tithes of Budock have been commuted for £800, of which £420 are payable to the vicar. The church is pleasantly situated on a hill ; and contains portions in the later English style, and some interesting monuments to the family of Killegrew, of whom Sir John Killegrew was governor of Pendennis Castle in the reign of Henry VIII. Penwarris chapel was built in 1828, at a cost of about £1800, on Dunstan-ville-terrace ; it contains 594 sittings, 307 of which are free, and is in the gift of the Vicar. There are two places of worship for Wesleyans.

BUDVILLE, LANGFORD, county of SOMERSET.— See LANGFORD-BUDVILLE.

BUDWORTH, GREAT (ST. MARY AND ALL SAINTS), a parish, in the unions of RUNCORN, ALTRINCHAM, and NORTHWICH, county of CHESTER ; containing 17,103 inhabitants, of whom 677 are in the township of Great Budworth, 3 miles (N. by E.) from Northwich. The manor was possessed, in the beginning of Henry III.'s reign, by Geoffrey de Dutton, who from his residence at this place was sometimes called de Budworth ; Peter, his grandson, removed to Warburton, assumed that name, and was the immediate ancestor of the Warburton family, in whom the property became vested. Geoffrey gave a third part of Budworth to the prior and convent of Norton, whose estate here, after the Dissolution, was granted by Henry VIII. to the Grimsditches ; it was afterwards divided and sold in severalties. This is the largest parish in Cheshire, next to Prestbury, being fifteen miles in length and ten in breadth, and compris-ing 26,676 acres, whereof 789 are in Budworth town-ship. It contains the townships of Anderton, Antrobus; Appleton, Aston by Budworth, Barnton, Bartington, Budworth, Cogshall, Comberbach, Crowley, Dutton, Little Leigh, Marbury, Marston, Peover-Inferior, Pick-mere, Plumbley, Seven-Oaks, Stretton, Tabley-Inferior, Whitley Inferior and Superior, and Wincham, in the hundred of BUCKLOW ; the chapelry of Hartford, and the townships of Castle-Northwich and Winnington, in the hundred of EDDISBURY ; and the townships of Allostock, Birches, Hulse, Lack-Dennis, Lostock-Gralam, North-wich, and Nether Peover, part of Rudheath lordship, and the parochial chapelry of Witton, in the hundred of NORTHWICH. The village of Budworth is pleasantly situated on a gentle acclivity, near two sheets of water called Budworth-mere, or Marbury, and Pickmere ; and

shire: the income from the property is now about £130. Horse-races were formerly held on a four-mile course in the parish.

BUERTON, a township, in the parish of ALDFORD, union of GREAT BOUGHTON, Higher division of the hundred of BROXTON, S. division of the county of CHESTER, 5 miles (S. S. E.) from Chester ; containing 81 inhabitants. The manor was held of the Aldfords in the reign of Edward I. by the family of Pulford, by service either of repairing a certain portion of Aldford Castle, or of assisting in the ward of it. From the Pulfords the manor passed successively by female heirs to the Grosvenors, of Hulme, and the Stanleys, of Hooton. The township lies east of the river Dee, and comprises 600 acres of land, the soil of which is clay.

BUERTON, a township, in the parish of AUDLEM, union and hundred of NANTWICH, S. division of the county of CHESTER, 2 miles (E.) from Audlem ; containing 512 inhabitants. This manor was anciently in a family of the same name, and afterwards, for several generations, in the Pooles, of Poole, in Wirrall : it was sold in 1725 by Francis Poole to the Dicken family of Woollerton, in Shropshire, of whom it was purchased by Sir Thomas Broughton, Bart. Another estate here, was, as early as the reign of Edward IV., the property of the Gamuls, of whom the brave and loyal Sir Francis Gamul was created a baronet by Charles I. : on his death in 1654, the estate devolved to his two daughters, one of whom married into the Brerewood family, who sold it to the Warburtons. The township comprises 2602 acres, of which the prevailing soil is clay. The village lies near the southern border of the county, and on the road from Audlem to Eccleshall. In 1779, James Holbrook bequeathed £400 to trustees, to provide bread for the poor during the winter months.

BUGBROOKE (ST. MICHAEL), a parish, in the hundred of NEWBOTTLE-GROVE, union, and S. division of the county, of NORTHAMPTON, 6 miles (W. S. W.) from Northampton ; containing 953 inhabitants. The London and Birmingham railway and the Grand Junction canal pass through the parish, which is bounded on the north by the river Nene, and on the west by the Roman Watling-street. It comprises by admeasurement 2188 acres, nearly equally divided between arable and pasture. The railway occupies 49 acres, and the rateable annual value of such property, in the parish, is returned at £3600 : the Weedon station is distant four miles. The living is a rectory, valued in the king's books at £34 ; net income, £800, with a good glebe-house ; patron and incumbent, the Rev. J. H. Harrison. The church exhibits various styles of English architecture ; it has a square tower surmounted by a spire, and contains a fine wooden screen, and an octagonal font highly enriched : the interior was repaired in 1828 ; and the churchyard enlarged in 1845. There are places of worship for Particular Baptists and the Society of Friends.

BUGLAWTON, an ecclesiastical district, in the parish of ASTBURY, union of CONGLETON, hundred of NORTHWICH, S. division of the county of CHESTER, 1 mile (N. E. by E.) from Congleton, on the road to Buxton ; containing 1864 inhabitants. This was a seat of the Touchet family, from nearly the time of the Conquest. Sir John Touchet, who distinguished himself in the wars with France, and was slain in an engagement with the Spanish fleet before Rochelle, married the sister and co-

heir of Nicholas, Lord Audley, in consequence of which
union his posterity enjoyed the title of Lord Audley.
In 1565 the manor belonged to the Bagnall family, from
whom it passed to the Mainwarings, and subsequently to
the Staffords and Egertons. The township comprises 4048
acres, of which the surface is undulated, and the soil clay
and loam, with rock : there is a good stone-quarry. The
rivers Dane and Davenshaw propel five silk-mills, three
cotton-mills, and a corn-mill, which afford employment to
the population. The living is a perpetual curacy; net
income, £150, with a house; patron, the Rector of
Astbury. The tithes have been commuted for £240.
The church, dedicated to St. John, was erected in 1840,
and is in the Norman style, with a tower. There is a
place of worship for Wesleyans; and adjacent to the
church is an excellent school. A mineral spring, the
water of which contains sulphur, a small quantity of
Epsom salts, and calcareous earth, has proved serviceable in scorbutic diseases.

BUGTHORPE (ST. ANDREW), a parish, in the union
of POCKLINGTON, wapentake of BUCKROSE, E. riding of
YORK, 7 miles (N. N. W.) from Pocklington; containing 296 inhabitants. The parish comprises about 1990
acres; the soil is a strong clay, and the surface level
with rising ground to the north, east, and south. The
living is a discharged vicarage, valued in the king's
books at £20; net income, £111; patron, the Archbishop of York. Land was given under an inclosure act,
in 1777, in lieu of the great tithes. The church is an
ancient structure with a square tower.

BUILDWAS (HOLY TRINITY), a parish, in the union
of MADELEY, Wellington division of the hundred of
SOUTH BRADFORD, N. division of SALOP, 3 miles
(W. N. W.) from Iron-Bridge; containing 273 inhabitants. This place is celebrated for the stately and venerable remains of its ancient Cistercian abbey, founded in
honour of St. Mary and St. Chad, by Roger, Bishop of
Chester, in 1135; the establishment continued to flourish
till the Dissolution, when its revenue was returned at
£129. 6. 10. The ruins are romantically situated on
the south bank of the river Severn, which here flows
through a deep and secluded vale, and consist principally of the roofless nave, transept, and lower portions
of the central tower of this once beautiful structure.
The parish comprises by measurement 2034 acres of
rich arable and pasture land ; the substratum is chiefly
limestone, which is quarried to a great extent, for agricultural and building purposes, and also for the works
in the adjoining district of Coalbrook-Dale. The Severn
affords every facility of conveyance, and near the abbey
is a handsome cast-iron bridge constructed by Telford,
in 1796, on the site of a former stone bridge, which had
been destroyed by a flood in the preceding year; it consists of one arch, 130 feet in span, and 24 feet above
the surface of the river. The road over it leads through
a romantic dingle to the town of Much Wenlock;
communication is also maintained by the road from
the adjoining town of Iron-Bridge to Shrewsbury. The
living is a donative, in the gift of Walter Moseley, Esq.,
proprietor of the parish : the church, rebuilt in 1720, is
a neat edifice. On the 27th of May, 1773, a remarkable
land-slip occurred here, when more than 18 acres were,
by a sudden disruption, carried forward with such
impetuous velocity as to stop the current of the Severn,
and take possession of its ancient bed.

man style, with a low spire, and consists only of a nave, at the east end of which is a beautiful Norman arch, that led into the chancel, now destroyed; there is a similar arch at the south entrance.

BULLINGHAM, a parish, in the hundred of WEB-TREE, union and county of HEREFORD, 2 miles (S.) from Hereford; containing 412 inhabitants, of whom 129 are in Upper, and 283 in Lower, Bullingham. This parish comprises 1679 acres, of which 705 are in Upper Bullingham; it is bounded on the north by the river Wye, and is intersected by the road from Hereford to Ross. The living is a perpetual curacy; net income, £109; patron, the Bishop of Hereford; appropriators, the Dean and Chapter. The church was enlarged some years since.

BULLINGTON, a chapelry, in the parish of GOL-THO, W. division of the wapentake of WRAGGOE, parts of LINDSEY, union and county of LINCOLN, 2¾ miles (W.) from Wragby; containing 52 inhabitants. The parish is situated on the road from Lincoln to Louth, and comprises by computation 780 acres; it formerly belonged to the knightly family of Metham, which is now extinct. Here are inconsiderable remains of a religious house founded by Simon Fitz-William, or De Kyme, in honour of the Blessed Virgin Mary, as a priory and convent for both sexes, under the rule of St. Gilbert of Sempringham: the revenue, at the time of the Dissolution, was £187. 7. 9.

BULLINGTON (ST. MICHAEL), a parish, in the union of ANDOVER, hundred of WHERWELL, Andover and N. divisions of the county of SOUTHAMPTON, 5 miles (S. by W.) from Whitchurch; containing 187 inhabitants. It comprises 1623 acres, of which 23 are common or waste; the soil is of a mixed quality, but generally fertile. The surface is varied, rising in some parts into hills of moderate elevation; and the lower grounds are watered by a branch of the river Test, which flows through the parish. The living is annexed, with that of Tufton, to the vicarage of Wherwell: the tithes of Bullington have been commuted for £361. 13., of which £272. 6. are payable to the impropriator, who has a glebe of 15 acres, and £89. 7. to the incumbent. At a place called Titbury Hill is an intrenched area of about ten acres, in which square stones, Roman coins, and the remains of some wells have been discovered.

BULLOCK'S-HALL, a township, in the parish of WARKWORTH, union of MORPETH, E. division of MOR-PETH ward, N. division of NORTHUMBERLAND, 10½ miles (N. N. E.) from Morpeth; containing 19 inhabitants. It formed part of the ancient chapelry of Chivington, and the chapel for the district was situated near its limits. The tithes have been commuted for £24 payable to the Bishop of Carlisle, and £4. 12. to the vicar of the parish.

BULMER (ST. ANDREW), a parish, in the union of SUDBURY, hundred of HINCKFORD, N. division of ESSEX, 2 miles (W. S. W.) from Sudbury; containing 775 inhabitants. The parish comprises by measurement 2759 acres, of which 83 are common or waste: the soil is generally productive, and in some parts exuberantly fertile, producing abundant crops of grain; several acres are planted with hops, which thrive well. The surface is elevated, and the higher grounds command extensive and finely varied prospects. The living is a discharged vicarage, with that of Belchamp-Walter consolidated, endowed with a portion of the great tithes, and valued in the king's books at £8; net income, £445; patron, Samuel Milbank Raymond, Esq.; impropriator, excepting where the land is tithe-free, Charles Hammersley, Esq. The church is a plain edifice of stone, with a square tower, and contains an ancient font of considerable beauty. Here was a chantry endowed with lands, which, on the suppression, were annexed to the manor of Butlers.

BULMER (St. Martin), a parish, in the union of Malton, wapentake of Bulmer, N. riding of York, 3 miles (N. W.) from Whitwell; containing 983 inhabitants, of whom 324 are in the township of Bulmer. This parish, which gives name to the wapentake, is bounded on the east by the river Derwent, and comprises the townships of Bulmer and Welburn, the latter in the eastern part. In the township of Bulmer are 1622 acres, of which 929 are arable, 511 meadow and pasture, and 177 woodland: the soil is generally a fine bright loam; the surface is diversified with hills, commanding extensive views, and the scenery is picturesque. Limestone is quarried for building and agricultural purposes. The living is a rectory, valued in the king's books at £11, and in the patronage of the Earl Fitzwilliam, with a net income of £395: the tithes were commuted for land under an inclosure act, in 1777; the glebe now consists of 210 acres. The church is an ancient edifice with a square tower at the west end, and contains a monument of a Knight Templar. There is a place of worship for Wesleyans.

BULPHAN (St. Mary), a parish, in the union of Orsett, hundred of Barstable, S. division of Essex, 10 miles (E. S. E.) from Romford; containing 254 inhabitants. This parish, which anciently belonged to the nunnery of Barking, is bounded on the west by the brook of Dunton, and comprises 1667a. 15p., including 222 acres of common. The living is a rectory, valued in the king's books at £23, and in the patronage of the family of Hand: the tithes have been commuted for £405. 12., and the glebe comprises 15 acres. The church is a small edifice, with a belfry of wood surmounted by a spire; on the south side of the chancel are some remains of an ancient chapel.

BULVERHYTHE (St. Mary), an ancient parish, and a member of the town and port of Hastings, in the union and rape of Hastings, hundred of Bexhill, E. division of Sussex, 1½ mile (E.) from Bexhill; containing 37 inhabitants. This place, formerly a haven called Bollifridé, is said to derive its name from the circumstance of William the Conqueror, who is supposed to have landed here, having granted to an ancestor of the Pelham family as much land as he could cover with a bull's hide, which was made extensive by the expedient of cutting it into slips. The parish is bounded on the south by the English Channel, which has considerably encroached on the land; and is intersected by the road from Dovor to Brighton, by way of Hastings: along the coast are several martello towers, and there are some remains of an ancient church or chapel.

BULWELL (St. Mary), a parish, in the union of Basford, N. division of the wapentake of Broxtow and of the county of Nottingham, 3¾ miles (N. W. by N.) from Nottingham; containing 1577 inhabitants. This place derives its name from a copious spring called "Bull-well," to which the cattle from the adjoining
430

forest of Sherwood, previously to its inclosure, were accustomed to resort. The parish includes the ancient soc of Hemshill. It is situated on the river Leen, and comprises by measurement 1631 acres, mostly arable and meadow land in nearly equal portions, and lying on both bank of the river; 177 acres are common or waste. Th substratum is chiefly limestone, which produces lime of excellent quality, and coal abounds, and is extensivel wrought. The population is partly employed in the manufacture of lace and the weaving of stockings: there are three corn-mills, and one for the spinning of cotton, all propelled by water, and several bleaching-grounds and printing-establishments connected with the cotton manufacture, in which about 300 persons are employed. The village is pleasantly situated near the river, and contains many substantial and well-built houses of stone. Courts leet and baron are held by the lord of the manor, who has the power to prove wills and grant administrations, and to hold a court of copyhold for the manor, in which the custom of Borough-English prevails. The living is a discharged rectory, valued in the king's books at £5. 5. 10., and in the patronage of the Rev. Alfred Padley, who is lord of the manor: the tithes have been commuted for £273. 10., and the glebe comprises 60 acres. The church is a small neat edifice, situated to the east of the village, on the highest ground in the parish; it was enlarged about the year 1775. There are places of worship for Baptists, Wesleyans, Primitive Methodists, and another sect; and a free school endowed with four acres of land, producing £20 per annum.

BULWICK (St. Nicholas), a parish, in the union of Oundle, hundred of Corby, N. division of the county of Northampton, 8 miles (W. S. W.) from Wansford; containing, with Bulwick-Short-Leys, extra-parochial, 487 inhabitants. This parish is situated on the road from Stamford to Kettering, is watered by the Willow brook, and comprises by computation 2000 acres, of which about 200 are wood: the soil, near the village, is of sandy quality, and in other parts a fertile clay. Limestone and iron-ore are found, and the latter appears to have been wrought, as vestiges of ancient mines may still be traced. The living is a rectory, valued in the king's books at £18. 7. 1.; net income, £366; patron, Thomas Tryon, Esq. The greater portion of the tithes was commuted, some time since, for 300 acres of land: there is a good glebe-house. The church is partly in the decorated and partly in the later English style, with a finely-proportioned tower and spire; it contains three stone stalls and some screen-work, and has lately been re-pewed. Charles Tryon, Esq., in 1705 bequeathed £200, which, in 1805, were invested in the purchase of £400 three per-cent. consols., with a portion of the interest of, which, together with the rental of some lands, a school is supported. Near Bulwick Hall is a chalybeate spring.

BUMPSTEAD-HELION (St. Andrew), a parish, in the union of Risbridge, hundred of Freshwell, N. division of Essex, 3¼ miles (S. W. by S.) from Haverhill; containing 906 inhabitants. It comprises by measurement 3120 acres, of which 2390 are arable, and the remainder, with the exception of a small portion of pasture, chiefly woodland. The living is a vicarage, valued in the king's books at £13, and in the patronage of Trinity College, Cambridge; impropriators, the

who aided in the destruction of the Spanish Armada, in 1588. The church was fired by a detachment from the royal garrison at Cholmondeley House, on the 20th of June, 1643, and sustained considerable injury. The above Sir Hugh, about 1386, founded and endowed in the church a college for a master and six Secular chaplains ; and at the Dissolution, the establishment consisted of a dean, five vicars, and two choristers, whose clear revenue was valued at £48. 2. 8.: the buildings stood in a field about 200 yards north-west of the church. Thomas Aldersey, citizen of London, purchased the rectory and advowson from Queen Elizabeth, and afterwards leased the tithes for £130 per annum, of which he directed that £20 should be given to a schoolmaster, £10 to an usher, 100 marks to a minister (each to have a house and a certain portion of land in addition), £20 to a curate, and £10 to the poor. A chapel was built, in 1735, in the township of Burwardsley; and a church at Tilston-Fearnall, in 1836. There is a place of worship for Wesleyans. The school was rebuilt in 1812, at the expense of Samuel Aldersey, Esq.; and a second school, now conducted on the national plan, is supported by an endowment assigned by Mr. Thomas Gardener in 1750. Bunbury Heath, by some considered to be the place described in a poem entitled the "Ancient English Wake of Jerningham," is the scene of festivity on the Sunday preceding the festival of St. Boniface.

BUNCTON, a chapelry, in the parish of ASHINGTON, hundred of WEST GRINSTEAD, rape of BRAMBER, W. division of SUSSEX, 2½ miles (N. W.) from Steyning; containing 72 inhabitants.

BUNDLEY, or BONDLEIGH (ST. JAMES), a parish, in the union of OAKHAMPTON, hundred of NORTH TAWTON, South Molton and N. divisions of DEVON, 2 miles (N. N. W.) from North Tawton; containing 342 inhabitants. It is situated on the river Taw, and comprises 1479 acres, of which 167 are common or waste. A small number of persons are employed in weaving and glove-making. Stone is quarried for the roads. The living is a rectory, valued in the king's books at £10. 17. 8½., and in the patronage of the Wyndham family ; net income, £232. The church has some remains of Norman architecture, and an ancient font. There is a place of worship for Bible Christians.

BUNGAY, a market-town, in the union and hundred of WANGFORD, E. division of SUFFOLK, 40 miles (N. N. E.) from Ipswich, 40 (N. E. by E.) from Bury St. Edmund's, and 109 (N. E. by N.) from London, on the road to Yarmouth; containing 4109 inhabitants. This place is said to have derived its name from the term le-bon-eye, signifying "the good island," in consequence of its being nearly surrounded by the river Waveney, which was once a broad stream. Soon after the Norman Conquest, a castle was built, which, from its situation and the strength of its fortifications, was deemed impregnable by its possessor, Hugh Bigot, Earl of Norfolk, in the reign of Stephen ; but that monarch, in the 6th of his reign, in the year 1140, came with his army and took it. In 1154 also, the 1st year of Henry IL, the fortress was yielded by the same earl; but it was restored in 1163, and in the following year he again took up arms against the king, and fortified himself in the castle, which he was compelled to deliver up, and permit to be demolished : on its site a mansion was erected, which, in the 22nd

year of Edward I., 1293, Roger Bigot embattled, by
royal permission. The form of the castle, the remains
of which belong to the Duke of Norfolk, appears to have
been octangular. Portions of the west and south-west
angles are still standing, as are also three sides of the
main keep, situated nearly at the back of the two portal
towers; the walls are from 7 to 11 feet thick, and from
15 to 17 feet high : in the midst is a well of strongly impregnated mineral water, long since disused. Near Saint
Mary's church are the ruins of a Benedictine nunnery
founded about the year 1160, in the reign of Henry II.,
by Roger de Glanville and the Countess de Gundreda,
his lady : at the Dissolution the revenue was estimated
at £62. 2. 1¼.; there were then a prioress and 11 nuns.
In March 1688, a fire broke out, and the flames spread
with such rapidity that the whole town, with the exception of one small street, was reduced to ashes, and
property, to the amount of nearly £30,000, together with
most of the ancient records of the castle, as is supposed,
was destroyed. One house, which escaped the conflagration, is still standing near the nunnery, to which it is
supposed to have been attached, as the hospital for
travellers and strangers.

The TOWN is pleasantly situated on the river Waveney, which here forms the line of boundary between the
counties of Norfolk and Suffolk, and over which are two
neat bridges. The streets diverging from the market-
place in the centre of the town towards the principal
roads are spacious, well paved, and lighted with gas :
the houses are in general modern, having been built
since the fire; and the inhabitants are amply supplied
with water from springs. The theatre, a neat edifice
erected in 1827, is opened occasionally ; and there is an
assembly-room ; also a book-club, established in 1770.
On the northern side of the town is an extensive common, nearly surrounded by the Waveney, along the edge
of which, on the Norfolk side, is a pleasant promenade,
one mile and a half in length, leading to a cold bath,
where a bath-house has been built, and requisite accommodation provided. The trade is principally in
corn, malt, flour, and coal; and a new corn-hall has
lately been opened: there are several flour-mills, and
malting-houses, on a large scale; also a paper-mill, a
large silk-manufactory, and an extensive printing-office.
The Waveney is navigable from Yarmouth, whence the
town is supplied with coal, timber, and other articles of
consumption. The market is on Thursday; and fairs
are held on May 14th and September 25th. In the
market-place is an octagonal cross, surmounted by a
dome, on the top of which is a fine figure of Justice : so
late as the year 1810, the ancient cross, called the Corn
Cross, was standing. The town is within the jurisdiction
of the county magistrates, who hold petty-sessions
every Thursday; and a town-reeve is appointed annually,
who, and the feoffees, are trustees of the estates and
rent-charges devised for the benefit of the town : courts
leet and baron for the three manors of Bungay Soke,
Priory, and Burgh, are usually held twice a year.

Bungay comprises the parishes of *St. Mary* and the
Holy Trinity ; the former containing 2248, and the latter
1861, inhabitants. The living of St. Mary's is a perpetual curacy; net income, £115, with a house ; patron,
the Duke of Norfolk. The church is a handsome and
spacious structure, with a fine tower, having been chiefly
rebuilt between 1689 and 1701, of flint and freestone :

BURBAGE (*ALL SAINTS*), a parish, in the union of PEWSEY, hundred of KINWARDSTONE, Marlborough and Ramsbury, and S. divisions of WILTS, 4¾ miles (E. by N.) from Pewsey; containing 1455 inhabitants. The living is a vicarage, valued in the king's books at £7. 3. 1½.; net income, £257; patron, the Prebendary of Hurstborne and Burbage in the Cathedral of Salisbury.

BURCOMBE, SOUTH, a parish, in the union of WILTON, hundred of CAWDEN and CADWORTH, Salisbury and Amesbury, and S. divisions of WILTS, 2 miles (W. by S.) from Wilton; containing, with the tything of North Burcombe and part of the hamlet of Ditchampton, 402 inhabitants. The parish is on the road from Salisbury to Shaftesbury, and comprises by computation 1500 acres, the soil of which is partly chalk, and partly clay, alternated with sandy loam; the surface is hilly, and the lower grounds are watered by the river Nadder. The living is a perpetual curacy, with the chapel of St. John, in Wilton, and has a net income of £52; the Earl of Pembroke is impropriator, and the Master of St. John's hospital, Wilton, patron. The tithes have been commuted for £170, and the glebe consists of 15 poles of land. On the downs are several large barrows.

BURCOTT, a hamlet, in the parish of WING, union of LEIGHTON-BUZZARD, hundred of COTTESLOE, county of BUCKINGHAM; containing 170 inhabitants.

BURCOTT, a hamlet, in the parish and hundred of DORCHESTER, union of ABINGDON, county of OXFORD, 5 miles (E. by S.) from Abingdon; containing 183 inhabitants. The village is situated on the river Thames.

BURCOTT, a tything, in the parish of ST. CUTHBERT, city and union of WELLS, hundred of WELLSFORUM, E. division of SOMERSET; containing 103 inhabitants.

BURDON, a township, in the parish of BISHOP-WEARMOUTH, union and N. division of EASINGTON ward, N. division of the county of DURHAM, 3¾ miles (S. S. W.) from Sunderland; containing 114 inhabitants. The ancient family of Burdon, of knightly dignity, derived their name from this place; which also gave name to a local family, who, however, never passed the rank of yeomanry. The township lies on the south verge of the parish, near the road from Sunderland to Stockton, and comprises 1109a. 3r. 22p. The village is pleasantly situated on an eminence. The tithes have been commuted for £140. 17.

BURDON, GREAT, a township. in the parish of HAUGHTON-LE-SKERNE, union, and S. E. division of the ward, of DARLINGTON, S. division of the county of DURHAM, 2 miles (N. E. by E.) from Darlington; containing 117 inhabitants. It comprises 589 acres, of which 312 are arable, 264 grass-land, and 14 acres roads and waste. The whole of the township is leased under the Dean and Chapter of Durham: the tithes were commuted in 1838 for £131. 6. The Stockton and Darlington railway passes on the south.

BURE, a tything, in the parish, union, and hundred of CHRISTCHURCH, Ringwood and S. divisions of the county of SOUTHAMPTON, 2¼ miles (E.) from Christchurch; containing 786 inhabitants.

BURES (*ST. MARY*), a parish, in the union of SUDBURY, hundred of BABERGH, W. division of SUFFOLK, 5 miles (S. E. by S.) from Sudbury; containing 1596 inhabitants. This parish, including a hamlet of the

3 K

same name, containing 612 persons, and locally in the county of Essex, comprises by measurement 4127 acres, of which 2542 are in that part of the parish separated from Essex by the navigable river Stour. The living is a vicarage, valued in the king's books at £12. 16. 0½.; patron and impropriator, O. Hanbury, Esq. The great tithes have been commuted for £574, and the vicarial for £246: the impropriate tithes of the hamlet of Bures have been commuted for £387, and the vicarial for £81; the vicar's glebe comprises 13 acres.

BURES, MOUNT (St. John), a parish, in the union of Lexden and Winstree, Colchester division of the hundred of Lexden, N. division of Essex, 6 miles (S. S. E.) from Sudbury; containing 282 inhabitants. This place takes its distinguishing affix from an artificial mount near the church, one acre in extent at the base, and planted on its summit with stately oak-trees and other timber. The parish is pleasantly situated on the banks of the river Stour, and comprises by measurement 1420 acres, of which 1193 are arable, 130 pasture, and 13 woodland. The living is a rectory, valued in the king's books at £13. 6. 8., and in the patronage of the Rev. John Brett: the tithes have been commuted for £445, and the glebe comprises 22 acres. The church is an ancient edifice, consisting of a nave and chancel, with a tower between them, surmounted by a wooden spire. There was formerly a chantry, to which belonged a small chapel in the churchyard, now converted into two tenements.

BURFORD (St. John the Baptist), a market-town and parish, in the union of Witney, hundred of Bampton, county of Oxford, 18½ miles (W. N. W.) from Oxford, and 73 (W. N. W.) from London, on the road from Oxford to Cheltenham; containing, with the hamlet of Upton with Signett, 1862 inhabitants, of whom 1644 are in the town. This

Corporation Seal.

place is of considerable antiquity, and was by the Saxons called *Beorford*, of which its present name is a variation. In 685, an ecclesiastical synod was held here by the kings Ethelred and Berthwald, at which Aldhelm, Bishop of Sherborne, was ordered to write against the error of the British Church respecting Easter. In 752, a battle was fought at Battle-edge, a little westward from the town, between Ethelbald, King of Mercia, and Cuthred, King of the West Saxons, who had revolted against his authority: Ethelbald was defeated, and the royal standard, bearing the device of a golden dragon, captured; which event was commemorated for several ages by an annual festival, on Midsummer-eve, when the inhabitants paraded the streets, bearing the figures of a dragon and a giant. Soon after the Conquest, the town was bestowed on Robert, Earl of Gloucester, natural son of Henry I. In 1649, an encounter took place here between Fairfax and the royalists, the former of whom was victorious.

The town is pleasantly situated on the banks of the small river Windrush: the houses are indifferently built; the inhabitants are well supplied with water. Races were formerly held, but they have been discon-

ohn Fortesque, who sold it to Sir Lawrence Tanfield, by hom the Priory and manor were left to his grandson, ord Falkland, who was born here, and was killed in ie battle of Newbury. The property was afterwards urchased by Mr. Speaker Lenthall, who enlarged ie Priory, and built a beautiful chapel adjoining it: enthall died here, in 1661, and was interred in the .mily vault. The eminent cosmographer, Dr. Peter eylin, was born at Burford in 1600. The town gives ie inferior title of Earl to the Duke of St. Alban's.

BURFORD (ST. MARY), a parish, in the union of ɛNBURY, hundred of OVERS, S. division of SALOP, ; mile (W. by S.) from Tenbury; containing, with the wnships of Buraston, Greet, Nash, Stoke, Tilsop, eston, Whatmore, and Whitton, 1031 inhabitants, of hom 297 are in the township of Burford. Licence for weekly market and an annual fair was granted by enry III. The Leominster canal crosses the parish, on ie northern side of the village. The living is a rectory, ivided into three portions : the first is valued in the ing's books at £9. 13. 4., and has annexed to it the apels of Buraston and Nash; the second portion, to hich Whitton chapel is annexed, is valued at £8, and ie third, containing the mother church, at £8. 13. 4. hey are all in the patronage of Capt. George Rushout, st Life Guards. The tithes of Burford township have een commuted for £261, and the glebe consists of 65 cres. The church is interesting from its antiquity, and ts monuments to the Cornewall family. In the townhips of Nash and Burford are daily and Sunday schools; ınd at Whitton is a Sunday school.

BURGATE (ST. MARY), a parish, in the union and ıundred of HARTISMERE, W. division of SUFFOLK, 2½ niles (E.) from Botesdale; containing 369 inhabitants, ınd comprising 2076 acres, of which 61 are common or ʋaste. The living is a rectory, valued in the king's ɔooks at £13. 10. 10., and in the patronage of the Bishop ɔf Ely : the tithes have been commuted for £550, and he glebe, to which a good house is attached, comprises ₹4 acres. The church is a handsome structure in the ater English style, with a square embattled tower, and :ontains a finely sculptured font, and in the chancel a nonument to William de Burgate and his lady, whose ₁ffigies are engraven in brasses.

BURGATE, MIDDLE, NORTH, and SOUTH, :hree tythings, in the parish and union of FORDING-ȝRIDGE, Ringwood and S. divisions of the county of ȝOUTHAMPTON; containing, respectively, 657, 129, and ȝ09 inhabitants.

BURGH (ST. MARY), a parish, in the union of AYL-ıHAM, hundred of SOUTH ERPINGHAM, E. division of ᴺORFOLK, 2 miles (S. E. by E.) from Aylsham; con-:aining 314 inhabitants. The parish is situated on the ¹iver Bure, which is navigable from Aylsham to Yar-nouth, and on the banks of which is an extensive flour-mill : it comprises 788a. 1r. 37p., whereof 616 acres are ırable, 135 pasture and meadow, and 19 woodland and ɔlantations. The living is a discharged rectory, valued n the king's books at £7. 17. 1., and in the patronage ɔf Mr. Holley : the tithes have been commuted for £255. 19., and the glebe comprises 13 acres. The :hurch contains portions of the early and decorated styles, and has a square embattled tower; the font, ʍhich is very handsome, is elaborately sculptured with ¹epresentations of scriptural subjects. Numerous urns,

435

coins, and other antiquities, have been found in the neighbourhood.

BURGH, a district comprising the consolidated parishes of St. Margaret and St. Mary, in the EAST and WEST FLEGG incorporation, hundred of WEST FLEGG, E. division of NORFOLK, 4 miles (N. E. by E.) from Acle; containing 506 inhabitants. The village is situated on the old road from Norwich to Yarmouth, and the district is bounded on the south-west by the navigable river Bure. The whole consists of 1606a. 2r. 6p,. of which about 789 acres are arable, upwards of 100 water, 23 wood, and the rest pasture. Henry III. granted permission to hold a free market on Monday, and a fair on the eve and festival of St. Margaret, and six following days ; both of which have long been discontinued. The living of St. Mary's is a discharged rectory, with that of St. Mary's annexed, the former valued in the king's books at £8. 13. 4., and the latter at £4; patron, the Rev. W. Lucas : the tithes have been commuted for £458. 3., and the glebe comprises 22½ acres. The church of St. Mary has long been in ruins. There is a place of worship for Wesleyans. Thomas Wymer, in 1505, bequeathed land for the poor, of which the rental is £22 ; and other lands for the same purpose are let for about £60 per annum.

BURGH (ST. PETER), or WHEATACRE-BURGH, a parish, in the union of LODDON and CLAVERING, hundred of CLAVERING, E. division of NORFOLK, 6¾ miles (E. N. E.) from Beccles ; containing 312 inhabitants. This parish is bounded on the north, south, and east by the river Waveney, which separates it from the county of Suffolk; and comprises by measurement 860 acres, whereof 583 are low marshy grazing-land, about 15 wood, and the remainder arable. The living is a discharged rectory, valued in the king's books at £7. 6. 8.; patron and incumbent, the Rev. W. Boycatt: the tithes have been commuted for £370, and the glebe comprises 15½ acres. The church is an ancient structure in the early English style, with a tower of brick. There is a place of worship for Wesleyans. Thirteen acres of land were allotted to the poor at the inclosure of the parish, in 1811. In a field adjoining the churchyard are some remains of what is supposed to have been a religious house.

BURGH (ST. BOTOLPH), a parish, in the union of WOODBRIDGE, hundred of CARLFORD, E. division of SUFFOLK, 3¾ miles (N. W.) from Woodbridge ; containing 266 inhabitants. This place is by most antiquaries identified with the Combretonium of Antoninus, as the distances in the Itinerary correspond with it exactly, and not with Brettenham, as some have supposed. The parish comprises by measurement 1225 acres : the soil is partly of a mixed quality, and partly a heavy clay ; and the surface is level. The living is a discharged rectory, valued in the king's books at £8. 3. 4., and in the patronage of Frederick Barne, Esq. : the tithes have been commuted for £348. 15. 6., and the glebe comprises 11 acres. The church, a neat ancient structure in the decorated English style, with a square embattled tower, is built within a Roman encampment, of which part of the vallum still remains visible. There was anciently a commandery of the order of the Knights of St. John of Jerusalem.

BURGH-APTON, in the hundred of CLAVERING, county of NORFOLK.—See BERGH-APTON

3 K 2

BURGH, CASTLE (St. Peter), a parish, in the hundred of Mutford and Lothingland, E. division of Suffolk, 4½ miles (W. S. W.) from Yarmouth ; containing 327 inhabitants. This place, anciently *Cnobheresburg*, is supposed to be the Roman *Garianonum*, (which some writers have placed at Caistor, on the opposite side of the river,) a station founded by Publius Ostorius Scapula, and garrisoned, under the command of a *præpositus*, by a troop of cavalry called the Stablesian horse. The ramparts form three sides of an area of upwards of five acres and a half ; and various coins, urns, *fibulæ*, domestic utensils, and military weapons, have been found in the adjoining fields. The walls of the station are among the most perfect remains of Roman architecture in the kingdom ; two sides are very perfect, one end has partly fallen, and the side next the river appears not to have been fortified. Bede relates that in the reign of Sigebert, Furseus founded a monastery within the walls of the encampment ; but the incursions of the Saxons, and consequent danger to monasteries, caused him, and his brother, to whom he had intrusted the institution, and the monks, to abandon it almost as soon as formed ; and no trace of it remains. The parish comprises by measurement 1498 acres, of which 834 are arable, 649 pasture and marsh, and 15 acres roads ; much of the grass-land is level, ascending gradually towards the south, and being escarped towards the west. The soil is very various, affording specimens of almost every quality : the scenery, though naked, has been rather improved by recent planting ; there is a fine view over Norfolk, and more than sixty churches may be seen from one point. The navigable river Waveney flows on the western side, and, opposite the village, unites with the Yare, forming Breydon Water, which runs on the northern side, and is navigable. The living is a discharged rectory, valued in the king's books at £6. 13. 4., and in the patronage of the. Crown ; net income, £400. The church, an ancient structure in the Norman style, has, with the exception of the tower, which is circular, been rebuilt in the later English style.

BURGH-IN-THE-MARSH (St. Peter), a parish, in the union of Spilsby, Marsh division of the wapentake of Candleshoe, parts of Lindsey, county of Lincoln, 8 miles (E. by S.) from Spilsby ; containing 1095 inhabitants. The parish is situated on the road from Spilsby to Skegness, and comprises 4237a. 2r. 12p., about 3000 acres of which are meadow and pasture, 166 common or waste, and the rest arable. The village is large ; and fairs are held in it on the second Thursday in May, and the 26th September. The living is a discharged vicarage, to which that of Winthorpe was united in 1729, valued in the king's books at £13. 6. 8. ; patron and appropriator, the Bishop of Lincoln ; net income, £126. The appropriate tithes have been commuted for £304 ; the appropriate glebe consists of 76 acres, and the vicarial glebe comprises 14½ in this parish, and 17¾ in the adjoining parishes of Croft and Winthorpe. The church is a commodious edifice, with a lofty tower at the west end, and has a handsome nave with good clerestory windows. The united parishes, before the Reformation, belonged to the monastery of Bolington ; and there was a second church called St. Mary's, of which there is no vestige remaining. The Baptists and Wesleyans have each a place of worship. There is an endowed school, founded by Mrs. Jane Palmer in 1727, the funds of

lurgh-Wallis, and part of that of Sutton, 245 inhabitants. The latter part of the name of this place was added in consequence of the family of Wallis settling ere, probably about the time of Henry III. The parish is situated a mile to the east of the great north road, nd comprises about 1400 acres of land, chiefly arable, but including a considerable portion of wood and pasture; the scenery is very picturesque. The living is rectory, valued in the king's books at £14. 6. 10½.; et income, about £280; patron, M. A. Tasburgh, Esq. he tithes were commuted for land and a corn-rent, under an inclosure act, in 1813; the glebe comprises etween 80 and 90 acres. The church is a neat and ery ancient structure, of a mixed style, from that of he 12th to that of the 16th century.

BURGHAM, a tything, in the parish of WORPLESON, union of GUILDFORD, First division of the hunred of WOKING, W. division of SURREY; containing 14 inhabitants. This place is mentioned in Domesday ook under the name of Borham. It passed in the 13th entury to the family of Wintreshull, who continued to ossess it until the 16th century, when it was sold to Sir John Wolley, who filled the office of Latin secretary o Queen Elizabeth.

BURGHCLERE (ALL SAINTS), a parish, in the union, and partly in the hundred, of KINGSCLERE, but hiefly in the hundred of EVINGAR, Kingsclere and J. divisions of the county of SOUTHAMPTON, 9 miles S.) from Newbury; containing with Earlstone tything, 145 inhabitants. This parish abounds with limestone f superior quality, which is wrought to a considerable xtent: the surface is diversified with hills, on the ighest of which was formerly a beacon, and there are till some traces of a camp. A court of petty-session is eld at Whitway, in the parish, on the second Friday n every month. The living is a rectory, with the living f Newtown annexed, valued in the king's books at £30, nd in the patronage of the Earl of Carnarvon: the ithes have been commuted for £1073: and the glebe omprises 118⅞ acres. The old church is disused, and new one has been erected in the centre of the parish, it an expense of £2700; it is a handsome cruciform tructure in the later English style, with a square embattled tower, and was consecrated on the 24th October, 1838.

BURGHFIELD (ST. MARY), a parish, in the union of BRADFIELD, hundred of THEALE, county of BERKS, 5 miles (S. W.) from Reading; containing 1115 inhabitants. It is bounded on the north by the navigable iver Kennet, and comprises 3478a. 1r. 20p.: there are thout 300 acres of common or waste land. Coal was supposed to form part of the substratum, and in an unuccessful attempt some years since to explore it, a bed f cockle-shells, firmly concreted with sand, was discovered about 12 feet beneath the surface. The living s a rectory, valued in the king's books at £14. 19. 2.; net income, £810; patron, the Earl of Shrewsbury. The church, a very ancient structure, was rebuilt in 1843, at a cost of £2500, and is now a handsome edifice of cruciform design, in the Anglo-Norman style; the interior s embellished with a finely-painted window in the chancel representing the Virgin Mary, and contains a pulpit and reading-desk of stone, each of appropriate character. There are places of worship for Primitive and Wesleyan Methodists.

437

BURGHILL (ST. MARY), a parish, in the hundred of GRIMSWORTH, union and county of HEREFORD, 4 miles (N. W. by N.) from Hereford; containing, with the township of Tillington, 863 inhabitants. The parish comprises by admeasurement 3674 acres, of which 1800 are arable and garden-ground, 1400 meadow and pasture, and nearly 400 woodland; the surface is undulated, and the soil consists of clay, loam, and gravel. The road from Hereford to Weobley and Pembridge passes through. The living is a discharged vicarage, valued in the king's books at £6. 18. 2.; net income, £94; patron, B. Biddulph, Esq., to whom, with others, the impropriation belongs: the glebe consists of 27 acres, exclusive of augmentation lands. The church, which contains 350 sittings, was thoroughly restored about twenty years ago, at a cost of £2000: among the antiquities in the interior are a curious font of metal, a rood-loft, and the altar-tomb of Sir John Milbourne and his lady. There is a barrow adjoining the churchyard.

BURGHSTED, county of ESSEX.—See BURSTEAD.

BURHAM (ST. MARY), a parish, in the union of MALLING, hundred of LARKFIELD, Upper South division of the lathe of AYLESFORD, and W. division of KENT, 1¾ mile (N. N. W.) from Aylesford; containing 380 inhabitants. It is bounded on the west by the river Medway, and on the east by a range of chalk hills, near which are the Burham Downs, which intersect the parish. The area is 1718 acres, whereof 179 are common or waste, and 151 woodland; about 20 acres are planted with hops. The living is a discharged vicarage, valued in the king's books at £8; net income, £191; patrons and impropriators, Edward Kingsley, Esq., and others. The church is situated near the river. A spring, called Holy Garden, anciently attracted numerous pilgrims by the supposed miraculous efficacy of its waters.

BURIAN, ST., a parish, in the union of PENZANCE, W. division of the hundred of PENWITH and of the county of CORNWALL, 6 miles (S. W. by W.) from Penzance; containing 1911 inhabitants. This place, which is of very great antiquity, derives its name from a collegiate church founded by King Athelstan, in honour of St. Buriena or Bæriena, who had an oratory and was interred here. Athelstan bestowed on the church the privilege of sanctuary, and other immunities. The college was in existence at the Conquest, and the establishment consisted of a dean and three prebendaries till the Reformation, when the lands with which it was endowed were seized to the king, and there was no longer any support for the prebendaries; but the rectories of Burian, St. Levan, and Sennan, remained to the dean, forming his sole estate. In 1663, Seth Ward, Bishop of Exeter, possessed the deanery in commendam, and it was so held by his successors till the year 1709: but the king. Of the collegiate buildings the church only remains. The parish comprises 5468 acres, of which 1570 are common or waste: the soil is of light quality, resting on a substratum of granite; the surface is undulated, and the scenery in many parts picturesque. The village is neatly built, containing many good houses, and there are several small hamlets scattered over the parish. The living is a rectory, with the rectories of St. Levan and Sennan united, and a royal peculiar, valued in the king's books at £48. 12. 1., and in the patronage of the Crown : the consolidated tithes have been commuted for £1050. The church, which is situated on an eminence nearly 400 yards above the level of the sea, is a spacious structure, with a lofty tower 88 feet high, forming a conspicuous landmark to mariners; it was repaired in 1812, when a handsome carved screen and other relics of antiquity were removed. Near the south porch is an ancient cross, and there is another close to the churchyard. On the estate of Boslevan are some vestiges of a chapel, called the Sanctuary. At Boscawen, Rosemoddrep, Chyangwanga, and other places in the parish, are Druidical remains.

BURITON (St. Mary), a parish, in the union of Petersfield, hundred of Finch-Dean, Petersfield and N. divisions of the county of Southampton, 2¼ miles (S. by W.) from Petersfield; containing, with the tythings of Nursted and Weston, 993 inhabitants. It is situated on the road from London to Portsmouth, and comprises by measurement 6151 acres, of which 2305 are arable, 1594 meadow and pasture, 786 woodland, and 1405 uninclosed common. The manufacture of parchment is carried on to a small extent. The living is a rectory, with the living of Petersfield annexed, valued in the king's books at £32. 16. 10½.; net income, £1194 ; patron, the Bishop of Winchester. The tithes of Buriton have been commuted for £1084. 7., and there is a glebe of 62 acres. The church is an ancient structure in the Norman style, with a square tower, which was rebuilt, after having been destroyed by fire about the year 1721; the interior is neatly arranged, and contains a monument to the Rev. William Lowth, rector of the parish; and father of Bishop Lowth. Gibbon, the Roman historian, spent his early years on his patrimonial estate in the parish.

. . BURLAND, a township, in the parish of Acton, union and hundred of Nantwich, S. division of the county of Chester, 2½ miles (W.) from Nantwich; containing 639 inhabitants, and comprising 1520 acres, of which 400 are common or waste. The soil is clay and sand. The Whitchurch branch of the Chester canal crosses the township. The impropriate tithes have been commuted for £58. 10., and the vicarial for £35. 13.

BURLESCOMBE (St. Mary), a parish, in the union of Wellington, partly in the hundred of Bampton, but chiefly in that of Halberton, Cullompton and N. divisions of Devon, 5 miles (S. W. by W.) from Wellington; containing 958 inhabitants. This parish comprises 3768a. 16p. of land, of which about 200 acres are wood, and the rest arable and pasture in nearly equal portions; the soil is various, and in general of inferior quality. The Exeter and Bristol railway, and the small river Lyner, run through. The road from Wellington to Exeter, also, passes for four miles through the parish, which it enters near the Red Ball Inn, on Maiden Down : skirting Uffculm Down, it follows the track of the Roman portway from the city Uxella (Taunton) in its progress to Isca Danmoniorum (Exeter). Maiden Down was inclosed in 1803, and Lyner Moor in 1810. There are considerable mountains of primitive limestone, of which great quantities are burnt, and sent away by the Grand Western canal, whose summit level is in the parish. Small pieces of pure silver have been found ; manganese is supposed to abound, and there are indications of the existence of coal. The woollen manu-
438

facture was formerly carried on, but the only trade at present is the making of chairs.

The living is a discharged vicarage, valued in the king's books at £11. 15. 10.; patron and impropriator, E. Ayshford Sandford, Esq. The great tithes have been commuted for £235, and the small for £330 ; the vicar's glebe consists of 3¼ acres. The demesnes here of the ancient abbey of Canonsleigh, comprising more than 800 acres, are tithe-free. The church is a venerable structure in the later style of English architecture, with a tower of four stages, embattled, and crowned with a turret ; it consists of a nave, chancel, and north and south aisles. The stone steps to the ancient rood-loft, and the screen separating the chancel from the nave, are still remaining; the latter is richly ornamented with crockets, finials, and roses. Within the rails of the communion is an altar-tomb, with monks bearing shields under enriched canopies, erected by Nicholas Ayshford, in 1500; and in the north aisle are four more ancient monuments to the Ayshford family, who had a chantry chapel at the east end of the aisle. Attached to the villa of Ayshford is a chapel, for which an endowment has been charged upon the estate. There is a place of worship for Wesleyans.

A priory for Augustine canons was founded at Leigh, thence called Canonsleigh, in the parish, in the reign of Henry II., by William de Claville. It was originally dedicated to the Virgin Mary and St. John the Evangelist; and there is now at Exeter a deed dated prior to 1247, to which is appended the seal of the convent, representing the Virgin Mary and St. John. In 1284, the establishment was surrendered to Maud, Countess of Gloucester and Hereford, who converted it into a nunnery dedicated to St. Etheldreda; and in 1286 the abbess obtained the grant of a weekly market. It continued to flourish till the Dissolution, when its revenues were estimated at £202. 15. 3.: the remains consist principally of the porter's lodge, which is entire, and the gateway, in which is a fine Norman arch. Attached to the establishment were the chapels of St. Thomas and All Saints. At Westleigh was a chapel dedicated to the Holy Trinity, now converted into two cottages ; there was also a church in the parish in honour of St. Theobald, long since razed to the ground ; and the remains of an ancient chapel are discernible on the farm of Fenacre, near the site of the abbey. The water of a spring at Ayshford possesses properties similar to those of the sulphureous waters of Harrogate, in the county of York.

BURLESTON, a parish, in the union of Dorchester, hundred of Piddletown, Dorchester division of Dorset, 6 miles (E. N. E.) from Dorchester ; containing 65 inhabitants. It comprises by admeasurement 364 acres, and is situated on the river Piddle, which skirts the southern side of the village. The living is a rectory, united to that of Admiston, and valued in the king's books at £3. 17. 1.: the tithes of Burleston have been commuted for £115.

BURLEY (Holy Cross), a parish, in the union of Oakham, hundred of Alstoe, county of Rutland, 2 miles (N. E. by N.) from Oakham; containing 252 inhabitants. The manor came, by purchase, into the possession of Villiers, first duke of Buckingham, who greatly enlarged and embellished the mansion here, in which he successively entertained James I. and Charles I.,

BURL

BURM

ith their respective courts. This stately edifice, on
e breaking out of the civil war, was garrisoned by
small body of parliamentarian troops, who, unable to
astain an attack of the royalists, set fire to the house,
hich was burnt to the ground; the site is now occupied
y an elegant modern mansion. The living is a vicarage,
alued in the king's books at £10. 13. 1½.; net income,
350; patron and impropriator, G. Finch, Esq.

BURLEY, a tything, in the parish and union of
INGWOOD, N. division of the hundred of NEW FOREST,
ingwood and S. divisions of the county of SOUTHAMP-
ON, 5 miles (E.) from Ringwood; containing, with the
lle of Bistern-Closes, and the extra-parochial place of
urley-Lodge, &c., 571 inhabitants. A species of con-
rete stone, called Burley rock, is found in great abun-
ance, and is quarried for the foundations of houses.
. church, dedicated to St. John the Baptist, has been
uilt at an expense of £2400, including £1000 for en-
owment; patron, the Bishop of Winchester; net in-
ome, £100 per annum. There is a place of worship
r Independents.

BURLEY, with HEADINGLEY.—See HEADINGLEY.

BURLEY, a chapelry, in the parish of OTLEY,
pper division of the wapentake of SKYRACK, W. riding
f YORK, 2½ miles (W. by N.) from Otley; containing
736 inhabitants. This chapelry comprises 3190 acres,
f which about one-half is uninclosed and uncultivated;
he surface is boldly varied by hill and dale, and the
cenery in many parts is highly picturesque, and beau-
lfully diversified with wood and water. The village is
ituated in the vale of the Wharfe (the river flowing on
he east), under the lofty acclivity of Rombald's moor.
he inhabitants are chiefly employed in the cotton
nanufacture, for which there are two extensive mills;
he worsted manufacture is carried on upon a limited
cale, and there are a scribbling-mill and a corn-mill.
he chapel, a small structure erected about the year
630, being inadequate to the wants of the increasing
opulation, was rebuilt in 1842, at a cost of about
1700, raised by subscription, aided by grants from the
ncorporated and Diocesan Societies. It is in the early
inglish style, with a handsome spire, and is lighted on
he north and south sides by lancet windows of ground
lass, and on the east by a beautifully painted window.
he living is a perpetual curacy; net income, £80. The
mpropriate tithes of the chapelry have been commuted
or £126. There are places of worship for Independents
nd Wesleyans.

BURLEY-DAM, a chapelry, in the parish of ACTON,
mion and hundred of NANTWICH, S. division of the
ounty of CHESTER, 3½ miles (W. by S.) from Audlem.
n the civil war in the reign of Charles I., a skirmish
etween a party of Lord Capel's forces from Whit-
hurch, and about 1000 of the parliamentary garrison
t Nantwich, took place in this vicinity, on April 11th,
643. Burley-Dam chapel was built originally by the
Cotton family, not long after the dissolution of Com-
ermere Abbey, for the accommodation of their tenants.
The present chapel, built not far from the site of the old
ne, was consecrated in 1769. The living is a perpetual
uracy; income, £100; patron, Viscount Combermere.

BURLEY-LODGE, an extra-parochial liberty, in the
mion of RINGWOOD, N. division of the hundred of NEW
FOREST, Ringwood and S. divisions of the county of
SOUTHAMPTON; containing 21 inhabitants.

439

BURLINGHAM (ST. ANDREW), a parish, in the
union and hundred of BLOFIELD, E. division of NOR-
FOLK, 2 miles (W. by S.) from Acle; containing 214 inhabitants. It is situated on the road from Norwich to
Yarmouth, and comprises by measurement 743 acres, of
which 528 are arable, and 214 pasture and plantation.
The living is a discharged rectory, with that of Burlingham St. Edmund annexed, valued in the king's
books at £12, and in the patronage of Mrs. C. Burroughes : the tithes of the parish have been commuted
for £296. 15., and there is a good glebe-house, with
about 11 acres of land. The church has an embattled
tower, and in it are the remains of a carved screen with
representations of the Apostles.

BURLINGHAM (ST. EDMUND), a parish, in the
union and hundred of BLOFIELD, E. division of NOR-
FOLK, 3 miles (S. W.) from Acle; containing 98 inhabitants. It comprises about 645 acres, of which 623
are arable, and 22 wood and pasture. The living is a
discharged rectory, annexed to that of Burlingham St.
Andrew, and valued in the king's books at £12 : the
tithes have been commuted for £207. 11., and the glebe
consists of about 11 acres. The church, which is chiefly
in the early English style, has an embattled tower; the
nave is separated from the chancel by the remains of
a beautiful carved screen; the southern entrance is
through a decorated Norman doorway.

BURLINGHAM (ST. PETER), a parish, in the union
and hundred of BLOFIELD, E. division of NORFOLK,
2 miles (W. by S.) from Acle; containing 91 inhabitants.
It is situated on the road from Norwich to Yarmouth,
and comprises 399 acres, of which 275 are arable, and
124 pasture and plantation. The living is a discharged
rectory, valued in the king's books at £5, and in the
gift of H. N. Burroughes, Esq. : the tithes have been
commuted for £148. 13., with a glebe of 10 acres. The
church is chiefly in the decorated style, and has a circular
tower the upper part of which is octagonal : there are
neat monuments to members of the Burroughes family,
who reside at the Hall, a handsome building situated in
a tastefully laid out park.

BURLINGTON, YORK.—See BRIDLINGTON.

BURMARSH (ALL SAINTS), a parish, in the union
and liberty of ROMNEY-MARSH, though locally in the
hundred of WORTH, lathe of SHEPWAY, E. division of
KENT, 4½ miles (W. S. W.) from Hythe; containing 130
inhabitants. It comprises 1760 acres. The living is a
rectory, valued in the king's books at £20. 10. 10., and
in the patronage of the Crown; net income, £220. The
church is a neat edifice of stone, with a square embattled tower.

BURMINGTON (ST. NICHOLAS), a parish, in the
union of SHIPSTON-UPON-STOUR, Brails division of the
hundred of KINGTON, S. division of the county of
WARWICK, 1½ mile (S.) from Shipston; containing 188
inhabitants. The parish comprises 801 acres, of which
216 are common or waste. It is situated on the borders
of Gloucestershire and a detached portion of the county
of Worcester, and is intersected by the road from
Birmingham to Oxford; the river Stour flows along its
western boundary. The living is a rectory; net income,
£197; patrons, the Warden and Fellows of Merton
College, Oxford; incumbent, the Rev. E. Griffith. The
church, having fallen into ruins, was rebuilt on a
smaller scale, in 1693.

BURN, a township, in the parish of BRAYTON, union of SELBY, Lower division of the wapentake of BARKSTONE-ASH, W. riding of YORK, 2¾ miles (S. by W.) from Selby; containing 281 inhabitants. It comprises by computation 2370 acres : the new line of road from Doncaster to Selby passes through the village, near which is the Selby canal.

BURNAGE, a township, in the parish of MANCHESTER, union of CHORLTON, hundred of SALFORD, S. division of the county of LANCASTER, 5 miles (S. S. E.) from Manchester; containing 489 inhabitants. It lies equidistant between the roads from Manchester to Congleton and to Stockport; and comprises by measurement 610 acres.

BURNASTON, a hamlet, in the parish of ETWALL, union of BURTON-UPON-TRENT, hundred of APPLETREE, S. division of the county of DERBY, 5½ miles (S. W. by W.) from Derby; containing 143 inhabitants. In 1672 the Bonningtons sold the manor to Sir Samuel Sleigh; it was inherited by his grandson, Samuel Chetham, Esq., and afterwards devolved to the Cottons. The township comprises 888 acres, of a strong soil, and lies a little to the south of the Derby and Uttoxeter road. It pays a tithe-rent of £59. 18. 6. A small chapel or lecture-room was built in 1839. The old hall is an ancient half-timbered house, with pointed gables.

BURNBY (ST. GILES), a parish, in the union of POCKLINGTON, Wilton-Beacon division of the wapentake of HARTHILL, E. riding of YORK, 2¾ miles (S. E. by E.) from Pocklington; containing 110 inhabitants. The parish comprises 1700 acres, of which equal portions are arable and meadow, and about 300 acres wold land, with a small quantity of wood : the soil is generally a rich clay, the surface undulated, and the scenery in many situations very picturesque. The living is a discharged rectory, valued in the king's books at £7. 15. ; net income, £318; patron, the Duke of Devonshire. The church is a small ancient fabric, with a Norman bell-gable and door at the west end.

BURNESIDE, a chapelry, in the parish, union, and ward of KENDAL, county of WESTMORLAND, 2 miles (N. by W.) from Kendal; comprising the townships of Strickland-Ketel and Strickland-Roger, and containing 878 inhabitants. The manor, sometimes written Burns-head, belonged to an ancient family of that name, with whose heiress it passed to the Bellinghams, by whom it was long held; it afterwards came to the Braithwaites, Shepherds, and Lowthers. The chapelry is pleasantly situated on the river Kent, which flows through the village, separating it into two parts connected by a bridge. The area is 5427a. 2r. 19p., whereof 3133 acres are arable, 600 meadow and pasture, 65 woodland and plantations, and the remainder land newly inclosed ; the scenery is picturesque, and the soil a light sand. The Kendal and Windermere railway passes through the chapelry, at a distance of 200 yards from Burneside. In the village is a paper manufactory, commenced in 1832, and employing between thirty and forty hands. The living is a perpetual curacy, with a net income of £109; patrons, the Landowners; impropriators, the Warden and Fellows of Trinity College, Cambridge : the college tithes have been commuted for £216. 10., and those of the vicar of Kendal for £36. 1. The chapel was rebuilt between 1823 and 1826, and consecrated in the latter year; of the expense, £1300, about £900 were

ravel. The village is pleasantly situated on rising ground, about two miles east of the river. Near it is a brick-field, from which were obtained the bricks for the erection of the bridge carried over the Thames, near Maidenhead, as a viaduct for the Great Western railway. There are some extensive market-gardens, and a considerable part of the female population is employed in making lace by hand. A court leet for the manor is held every third year; and a statute-fair on October 2nd. The living is a vicarage, valued in the king's books at £16. 13. 4., and in the patronage of Eton College; impropriators, Sir C. H. Palmer, Bart., and others. The great tithes of the parish, exclusively of Lower Boveney, have been commuted for £750, and the small for £635; the vicar has a glebe of 24 acres. The church is a handsome structure. There is a place of worship for Independents. The remains of the abbey are, some ruinous walls, converted into a barn; part of the abbot's dwelling-house; and the fish-pond, now attached to the vicarage garden. There are also the remains of an ancient encampment, in the woodland called Burnham Beeches. Robert Aldrich, Bishop of Carlisle in the reign of Henry VIII., was a native of the place.

BURNHAM (St. Mary), a parish, in the union of Maldon, hundred of Dengie, S. division of Essex, 12 miles (S. E.) from Maldon; containing 1735 inhabitants. It takes its name from a small stream running near the church, and comprises 4277a. 3r. 16p. The village is situated on the northern bank of the river Crouch, near its estuary, and has a commodious quay, to which vessels of 250 tons' burthen can come up: there are vessels of 1000 tons' aggregate burthen belonging to Burnham, employing 100 seamen. The oyster-beds, both in the river and on the coast, are extremely productive; they are held under lease from Lady St. John Mildmay by a company, and in addition to the home consumption, a considerable quantity of oysters is exported to Holland and Belgium : about 300 persons are engaged in the fishery. The living is a vicarage, endowed with a portion of the rectorial tithes, and valued in the king's books at £22. 13. 4., with a net income of £558: it is in the patronage of Lady St. John Mildmay, to whom also the impropriation belongs. The church, built in 1525, stands about a mile from the village, on an elevated site; its altar-piece is embellished with a good painting of the Lord's Supper, and the pulpit and font are elaborately carved. Divine service is also performed in a national schoolroom, by license of the bishop; the school is endowed with about £80 per annum. There is a place of worship for Baptists. Several Roman coins, fragments of ancient masonry, and urns containing burnt ashes, have been found on a farm at the edge of the marsh. Burnham formerly conferred the inferior title of Baron on the Fitzwalter family.

BURNHAM, a hamlet, in the parish of Thornton-Curtis, union of Glandford-Brigg, N. division of the wapentake of Yarborough, parts of Lindsey, county of Lincoln; containing 75 inhabitants.

BURNHAM, a hamlet, in the parish of Haxey, union of Gainsborough, W. division of the wapentake of Manley, parts of Lindsey, county of Lincoln; containing 160 inhabitants. It is situated a mile and a half north of the village of Haxey.

BURNHAM (St. Andrew), a parish, in the union of Axbridge, hundred of Bempstone, E. division of Somerset, 9¾ miles (W. S. W.) from Axbridge; containing, with the hamlet of Edithmead, part of that of Highbridge, and part of the tything of Aston-Morris, 1469 inhabitants. It lies on the coast of the Bristol Channel; and its pleasant watering-place, and fine sandy beach seven miles in length, have induced many respectable families to make it their résidence during the summer months. The views are exceedingly good, including Bridgwater bay, and the Glamorgan, Quantock, Mendip, and Brent hills. The Bristol and Exeter railway passes through the parish. Two medicinal springs, one saline, with a chalybeate impregnation, and the other sulphureous, with a saline principle, are much esteemed, the former for its efficacy in relieving obstinate complaints of the stomach and bowels and obstructions of the liver, and the latter for its singular property of softening the skin and removing troublesome eruptions. There are spacious hot, shower, and vapour baths, elegantly fitted-up, and conducted by Mr. Johns. A good fishery is carried on, and cod and other white-fish are taken; the parish is also celebrated for its cider. On the shore are, a lighthouse 23 feet, and another 91½ feet, above the level of the sea at high-water mark, with revolving lights. On Trinity Monday and Tuesday is an annual fair. The living is a vicarage, valued in the king's books at £16. 11. 10½.; patrons and appropriators, the Dean and Chapter of Wells : the great tithes have been commuted for £190, and the vicarial for £635; the glebe comprises two acres, with an excellent parsonage-house. The church, dedicated in 1316, is a spacious edifice with a lofty tower, and has been lately enlarged by the addition of 471 sittings. It contains a fine altar-piece, of white marble, in the Grecian style, designed by Inigo Jones for the chapel of the intended palace of Charles II. at Whitehall, and afterwards placed in Westminster Abbey, by the Dean and Chapter of which it was presented to Dr. King, Bishop of Rochester, for many years incumbent of this parish, who erected it in the church at his own expense. A school is conducted on the national plan.

BURNHAM-DEEPDALE (St. Mary), a parish, in the union of Docking, hundred of Brothercross, W. division of Norfolk, 2½ miles (N. W.) from Burnham-Westgate; containing 109 inhabitants. The parish comprises by measurement 1038 acres, of which 630 are arable, 55 woodland and plantations, and the remainder marsh, for draining which last an act was obtained in 1821, whereby 250 acres have been inclosed by a wall, 70 feet broad at the base, and 10 feet high, to protect it from the sea. The village, which joins the marsh, is sheltered on the south by a range of hills clothed with plantations. The living is a discharged rectory, valued in the king's books at £11, and in the patronage of the Trustees of the late Mr. Blyth: the tithes have been commuted for £250, and the glebe contains 27 acres, with a handsome house, erected in 1840. The church is chiefly in the early English style, and consists of a nave and chancel, with a circular tower; its north aisle was taken down in 1796. On the shore are various artificial eminences, the supposed tombs of Saxons and Danes who fell in battle in the vicinity; and at a short distance are the vestiges of a fortification, probably raised by the Saxons, after the sanguinary battle between them and the Scots and Picts, at Stamford, in Lincolnshire.

BURNHAM, EAST, a liberty, in the parish and hundred of BURNHAM, union of ETON, county of BUCK-INGHAM, 4 miles (N. by W.) from Eton; containing 312 inhabitants. The manor of East Burnham, or Allards, was the seat of the Eyre family for more than 400 years: from them it devolved to the Sayers. This place lies south of Burnham common.

BURNHAM-MARKET, or BURNHAM-WESTGATE (ST. MARY), a parish, in the union of DOCKING, hundred of BROTHERCROSS, W. division of NORFOLK, 36½ miles (N. W.) from Norwich, and 120 (N. N. E.) from London; containing 1126 inhabitants. This parish derives its name from the small river Burn, on which it is situated, and takes the adjunct Westgate to distinguish it from adjoining parishes of the name of Burnham. It is pleasantly situated in a fertile valley, environed by a range of hills on the west and south, within 3 miles of the sea; and comprises 3047a. 2r. 1p., of which about 2533 acres are arable, 184 pasture and meadow, 169 woodland, and 68 waste. The town or village, the lower part of which is in the parishes of Burnham Sutton and Ulph, has experienced considerable improvement of late years, though its market has been discontinued, and the buildings appropriated to that purpose converted into dwellings; the houses are in general well built, and the inhabitants amply supplied with water. A small manufactory for iron and brass has been established, and hempen cloth is prepared to a limited extent. Fairs for toys are held on Easter Tuesday and Wednesday, and August 1st and 2nd. The county magistrates hold petty-sessions here on the last Saturday in the month; and courts baron are occasionally held. The LIVING is a rectory, with a mediety of the consolidated rectory or rectories of Burnham Norton and Ulph united, valued jointly in the king's books at £20. 16. 8., and in the patronage of Christ-Church College, Cambridge. The tithes of the parish have been commuted for £361 payable to the rector, and £361 to the college; the glebe comprises 84 acres, and there is a rent-charge of £38. 5. payable to the rector of Burnham-Sutton. The church is a neat structure of stone and flint, chiefly in the early style, consisting of a nave, chancel, and aisles, with a square embattled tower ornamented with sculptured figures: in the north aisle is a whole-length figure of a priest, rudely sculptured in stone. The site of another parochial church, dedicated to St. Edmund, is now occupied by a shop. All Saints' church, Burnham-Ulph, is used as a chapel to the church of Burnham-Westgate. There is a place of worship for Independents.

BURNHAM-NORTON (ST. MARGARET), a parish, in the union of DOCKING, hundred of BROTHERCROSS, W. division of NORFOLK, 1½ mile (N.) from Burnham-Westgate; containing 166 inhabitants. It comprises 3226a. 3r. 36p., of which about 607 acres are arable, 506 pasture and meadow, and 2062 woodland, salt-marshes, common, &c. The living, consolidated with that of Burnham-Ulph, is a rectory divided into medieties, partly annexed, with the living of Burnham-Overy, to that of Burnham-Sutton, and partly annexed to the living of Westgate. The tithes of Norton have been commuted for £253, and the glebe comprises 32¼ acres. The church, which is situated about half a mile to the south

nd the glebe comprises 30 acres, with a commodious nd handsome house, erected by the Rev. D. Everard. The church is chiefly in the decorated and later English tyles, with a square embattled tower; in the chancel is fine monument of brass to Sir William de Calthorp, lso a monument to the Rev. Edmund Nelson, father of Lord Nelson, the renowned naval commander, who was orn here, on the 29th of Sept., 1758, during the incumency of his father.

BURNISTON, a township, in the parish of SCALBY, nion of SCARBOROUGH, PICKERING lythe, N. riding of YORK, 3¼ miles (N. W.) from Scarborough; containing 49 inhabitants. It is situated on the eastern coast, nd comprises by computation 1900 acres: the village s on the road from Scarborough to Whitby. There is place of worship for Wesleyans.

BURNLEY, a market-town and parochial chapelry, nd the head of a union, in the parish of WHALLEY, higher division of the hundred of BLACKBURN, N. division of the county of LANCASTER, 25 miles (N.) from Manchester, 53 (E. N. E.) from Liverpool, and 210 N. N. W.) from London; comprising the townships of Burnley, Habergham-Eaves, Ightenhill Park, Reedley-Hollows, Briercliffe-cum-Extwistle, Worsthorn-with-Hurstwood, and Cliviger; and containing 23,505 inhabitants, of whom 10,699 are in the township of Burnley. This place, anciently *Brunley*, derives its name from the river Burn, on which it is situated, near the confluence of that stream with the river Calder; and, from the numerous coins, fragments of pottery, and urns containing ashes and burnt bones, that have been found in the neighbourhood, is supposed to have been a Roman station. Several Saxon remains have also been discovered; and at a short distance to the east of the town is a place called *Saxifield*, said to have been the scene of a battle n the year 597. About the same period, Paulinus is stated to have visited Burnley, on a mission for converting the natives to Christianity; and the remains of an ancient cross, erected to commemorate his preaching, still exist.

The TOWN is pleasantly situated on a tongue of land formed by the Burn and Calder; the greater part is of recent erection, and the houses are neatly built of free-stone found in the neighbourhood. The streets are paved, and lighted with gas, under an act obtained in 1819 for the improvement of the town; and the inhabitants are well supplied with water: another act for accomplishing these objects more effectually, was passed n 1846. The barracks, standing in the adjoining township of Habergham-Eaves, were erected in 1819, at an expense of £5500, of which sum £2500 were subscribed by the inhabitants. The trade was formerly confined to he manufacture of woollen-cloth and worsted goods; but that of cotton has been introduced, and large establishments for spinning, weaving, and printing cotton, have been erected. Coal, flagstone, and slate, are found n abundance within a short distance. The Leeds and Liverpool canal, which winds nearly round the town, as contributed greatly to the promotion of its trade. The East Lancashire railway now runs by the town; and there is a branch line from Burnley to the Manchester and Leeds railway at Todmorden: this branch is 4½ miles long, and belongs to the Manchester and Leeds company. The market, granted in the 22nd of Edward I. to Henry de Lacy, Earl of Lincoln, is on Monday and

443

Saturday, the former day being the principal; and on every alternate Monday is a market for cattle, established in January, 1819. Fairs are held on March 6th, Easter-eve, May 9th and 13th, July 10th, and Oct. 11th, for horses, cloth, and pedlery. Petty-sessions for the division are held here: the powers of the county debt-court of Burnley, established in 1847, extend over part of the registration-district of Burnley.

The township comprises 1128 acres of land. The LIVING is a perpetual curacy; net income, £770; patron, R. Townley Parker, Esq.; impropriator, Earl Howe. The chapel, dedicated to St. Peter, was erected soon after the Conquest, but, having been rebuilt, and enlarged at different times, combines various styles of architecture: it is a spacious structure, and contains several monuments of the Townley family, among which is one to the memory of Charles Townley, Esq., a celebrated patron of the fine arts, whose collection of marbles was purchased by the British Museum for £20,000. A church district named St. James', and another named St. Paul's Lane-Bridge, have been endowed by the Ecclesiastical Commissioners; patrons, the Crown and the Bishop of Chester, alternately. A church for St. James' district was commenced in August, 1846; and other churches are situated at Briercliffe, Habergham, Holme, and Worsthorn. There are places of worship for Baptists, Independents, Primitive Methodists, Wesleyans, and Roman Catholics, for which last the foundation stone of a new chapel was laid in April, 1846, by the Rt. Rev. Dr. Brown. The free grammar school was founded in the reign of Edward VI., and endowed, in 1578, by Sir Robert Ingham; the endowment has been considerably augmented by benefactions, and now produces about £130 per annum: the school has an interest in thirteen scholarships founded in Brasenose College, Oxford, by Dr. Nowell, Dean of St. Paul's, London, in 1572. The Rev. W. Whitaker, D.D., the learned master of St. John's College, Cambridge, received the rudiments of his education in the school. National schools have been established: an institution for the relief of poor married women in childbirth was commenced in 1819; and there is a Strangers' Friend Society. The interest of £1244. 15. three per cent. consols., given by Mrs. Elizabeth Peel in 1800, and of £450 by Mrs. Thompson, is expended in clothing. The union of Burnley comprises 26 townships and chapelries in the parish, and contains a population of 54,192.—See HABERGHAM-EAVES, &c.

BURNOP, with HAMSTEELS, a township, in the parish and union of LANCHESTER, W. division of CHESTER ward, N. division of the county of DURHAM; containing 154 inhabitants. Burnop, which probably derives its name from "Brunehop," the gill or hollow of the Brune or Browney, lies on that river; Hamsteels is situated across the water westward nearer Esh. The impropriate tithes have been commuted for £81. 7. 10. There is a place of worship for Wesleyans.

BURNSALL (ST. *WILFRID*), a parish, in the union of SKIPTON, E. division of the wapentake of STAINCLIFFE and EWCROSS, W. riding of YORK, 9½ miles (N. N. E.) from Skipton; containing 2726 inhabitants, of whom 284 are in the township of Burnsall with Thorpe-sub-Montem. The parish comprises the townships of Apple-tree-wick, Burnsall with Thorpe-sub-Montem, Cracoe, Hartlington, and Hetton with Boardley; and the chapelries of Rilston, and Coniston with Kilnsay; the whole

3 L 2

forming an area, by computation, of 25,950 acres, of which 2680 are in the manors of Burnsall and Thorpe. The soil, in the valley, is rich, but on the high grounds poor turbary earth, with heath ; the surface is varied, and the scenery mountainous and romantic. There are three factories, two for cotton and one for wool, employing about 120 hands. The village of Burnsall is situated on the river Wharfe, over which is a bridge of three arches, built in 1827 ; and the village of Thorpe in a deep glen beneath the mountains of Thorpe Fell and Burnsall Fell. The parish, it is probable, anciently formed part of that of Linton, to the rector of which it still pays a modus in lieu of corn-tithes. The living is a rectory in two medieties, valued together in the king's books at £36 ; net income of the first, £315 ; patron, the Rev. J. Graham ; and of the second, £276 ; patron, the Earl of Craven. The church is an ancient structure, partly Norman, and partly in the English style, with a square embattled tower : on each side of the entrance of the choir are a pulpit and reading-desk. The grammar school was founded on the 26th of May, 1602, by Sir William Craven, Knt., who endowed it with a rent-charge of £20, to which, on 16th of June, 1624, Elizabeth Craven added a bequest of £200. Sir William improved the church, in 1612 ; built four bridges, for the repair of which and the highways he left a rent-charge of £8 ; and was a great benefactor to the parish, of which he was a native and resident. Various beautiful pieces of quartz and other variegated fossils, and spar, are dug from Greenhow hill, which has been a rich lead-mining district.

BURNTWOOD, a chapelry district, in the parish of St. Michael, Lichfield, union of Lichfield, S. division of the hundred of Offlow and of the county of Stafford, 2 miles (W. by S.) from Lichfield ; containing, with the hamlets of Edgehill and Woodhouses, 744 inhabitants. It lies on the eastern side of Cannock Chase, and comprises 2456a. 1r. 20p. of inclosed land, and about 1000 acres of common on the chase ; 1716 acres are arable, 655 meadow and pasture, 12 woodland, 5 in pools and ponds, and 60 in homesteads. The land is in good cultivation. About 150 hands are employed in nail-making, but the population is mostly engaged in agricultural pursuits. There are several neat and pleasant mansions, one of which is Edgehill or Edial Hall, a square brick building with a cupola and balustrades, celebrated as the house in which the eminent lexicographer, Samuel Johnson, opened an academy in 1736 ; not meeting, however, with sufficient encouragement, he did not long continue here. At a short distance on the south of the chapelry passes the Wyrley and Essington canal. The living is a perpetual curacy; net income, £100 ; patron, the Vicar of St. Mary's, Lichfield ; appropriators, the Dean and Chapter of Lichfield : the glebe consists of about six acres, valued at £9 per annum, and a house. The chapel, dedicated to Christ, and erected in 1820, is a neat edifice of brick, with a square tower, and contains 250 sittings, whereof 140 are free. A school was endowed in 1765 by Mrs. Elizabeth Ball, with £600, of which £200 were expended in erecting the school-house, and the remainder was secured on land. Among other benefactions, the annual sum of £14 is paid out of a farm, as interest of two legacies left by the same lady, for the poor of the three hamlets comprising this township, and of the hamlet of Hammerwick.

elevations terminating in a high ridge in the centre of the parish, which commands very extensive views: the soil is in general clayey and wet, except in the vicinity of Newmarket Heath, where it is dry and chalky, and of .very inferior quality. The living is a rectory, valued in the king's books at £18. 10., and in the patronage of Charles Porcher, Esq.: the tithes have been commuted for £527. 14. 10., and the glebe comprises 62 acres, with a good glebe-house. Schools are supported by an endowment. Editha, consort of Edward the Confessor, had a palace here.

BURROW with BURROW, a township, in the parish of TUNSTALL, hundred of LONSDALE south of the Sands, N. division of the county of LANCASTER, 2½ miles (S. by E.) from Kirkby-Lonsdale; containing 177 inhabitants. These hamlets are also called Nether Burrow and Over Burrow; and when held by the Tunstalls, in the reign of Elizabeth, both places were styled manors. The estates passed to the Girlingtons, Tathams, and Fenwicks, successively; and more recently came to the Lamberts, who took the name of Fenwick. The township is situated on the east side of the river Lune, and on the road from Tunstall to Kirkby-Lonsdale; the villages are distant from each other about a mile. The long fertile bank on which is Burrow or Over Burrow Hall, is the site of the Roman station *Bremetonacæ*. A Roman military way connects Over Burrow and Ribchester; and various monuments of ancient date, such as stones with inscriptions, tessellated pavements, and Roman coins, have been discovered here, tending to remove the doubts that had existed as to this place being the *Bremetonacum* of the Itineraries.

BURROW-ASH.—See BORROWASH.

BURROWGATE, a division, in the parish and union of PENRITH, LEATH ward, E. division of CUMBERLAND; containing 712 inhabitants.

BURSCOUGH, an ecclesiastical district, including portions of Lathom and Scarisbrick, in the parish and union of ORMSKIRK, hundred of WEST DERBY, S. division of the county of LANCASTER, 3 miles (N. E. by N.) from Ormskirk, on the road to Preston; the township of Burscough containing 2228 inhabitants. The area of the township is 2309 acres, whereof 1353 are arable, 936 pasture, and 20 wood; the surface is generally level, and the soil good. The Liverpool canal and the Liverpool, Ormskirk, and Preston railway, pass through. The living is a perpetual curacy, in the patronage of the Vicar of Ormskirk; income, £100. The church (St. John's) was built in 1833, at a cost of £3500, and is in the early English style, with good schools attached. At Burscough Hall is a place of worship for Roman Catholics; it is dedicated to St. John, and is in the Grecian style, with a neat altar, above which are four paintings, one by Murillo, and the others by Italian artists: the farm adjacent forms an endowment for the priest, the Rev. John Anderton. There is also a small meeting-house. A priory of Black canons was founded here in the time of Richard I., by Robert Fitz Henry, lord of Lathom, and dedicated to St. Nicholas: at the Dissolution there were a prior, five brethren, and forty servants, and the revenue was estimated at £129. 1. 10. Previously to that period, it was the burial-place of the noble family of Stanley; and subsequently the cemetery, in which stands the mutilated central arch of the church, the only relic of the conventual buildings, became a place of interment for Roman Catholic families. The eight bells of the priory were removed to Ormskirk. A school is endowed with £18. 15. per annum.

BURSLEDON, a chapelry, in the parish of HOUND, union of SOUTH STONEHAM, hundred of BISHOP'S-WALTHAM, Southampton and S. divisions of the county of SOUTHAMPTON, 4¾ miles (E. S. E.) from Southampton; containing 548 inhabitants. It comprises 519 acres, whereof 98 are common or waste; and lies at the head of the estuary of the river Hamble, which is crossed by a bridge on the road from Southampton to Portsmouth. Several large vessels have been built for the navy, the creek being very commodious for that purpose, and the water deep enough for eighty-gun ships. The village is irregularly built, on the bank of the river. The chapel, dedicated to St. Leonard, has been enlarged.

BURSLEM (ST. JOHN THE BAPTIST), a market-town and parish, forming, with WOLSTANTON, a poor law union, in the hundred of NORTH PIREHILL, N. division of the county of STAFFORD, 2½ miles (N. E.) from Newcastle, 19 (N.) from Stafford, and 151 (N. E.) from London; containing, with the lordship of Hulton-Abbey, the hamlet of Sneyd, and the vill of Rushton-Grange or Cobridge, 16,091 inhabitants, of whom 12,631 are in the township of Burslem, which includes Longport. In Domesday book this place is named Barcardeslim, but in subsequent records Burewardeslyme, signifying, according to the best opinion, "a bower or dwelling near the Lyme," in allusion to the Lyme woodlands which formerly separated Staffordshire from Cheshire. It has long been celebrated as the seat of the earthenware manufacture. Dr. Plot, in his Natural History of Staffordshire, published in 1686, first noticed it as such; but it is supposed, with great probability, to have been entitled to this distinction from the Saxon era, if not from the time of the Roman dominion in Britain. The abundance of coal which the parish and neighbourhood yield, was, no doubt, a primary cause of the establishment of the business here, as it still continues to be the mainstay and support of it. The manufactures, however, did not acquire any celebrity, and were wrought altogether from the native clays, till after the commencement of the eighteenth century, when the finer clays of Dorsetshire and Devonshire were introduced. Josiah Wedgwood, who was born here in 1730, and commenced business about the year 1756, advanced the pottery wares to a higher degree of perfection and importance; and since his time the manufacture of porcelain has been established, which now occupies at least one-fourth of the industry and capital of the district. The Grand Trunk canal, which passes through the parish, and has a branch up to the town, has tended greatly to advance its prosperity: that work was commenced near Burslem in July, 1766, and completed in 1777.

The TOWN is for the most part situated on a gentle eminence, and contains several large manufactories of imposing appearance, and some handsome villas and residences within its immediate vicinity. An act of parliament was obtained in 1835 for regulating the market, establishing a police, and lighting the streets. The town-hall, which stands in the centre of the spacious market-place, was erected by subscription in 1761, and is a handsome building, lately improved. The trustees of the market erected near it, in 1836, at an expense of

northern part of the village is the ancient hamlet of Skeckling, and the manor of Burstwick, with its members, parks, and free warren, was anciently called the "Dominion of Holderness." The wife of Robert Bruce, King of Scotland, was confined here for some time, by order of Edward I. The living is a vicarage, valued in the king's books at £7; net income, £219; patron and impropriator, Sir T. A. Clifford Constable, Bart. The tithes were commuted in 1773, for land and a money payment. The church, principally in the later style, is a small ancient edifice, with an embattled tower at the west end. There is a place of worship for Primitive Methodists.

BURTHOLME, a township, in the parish of LANERCOST-ABBEY, union of BRAMPTON, ESKDALE ward, E. division of CUMBERLAND, 3¼ miles (N. E. by E.) from Brampton; containing 330 inhabitants. In this township are situated the ruins of Lanercost Abbey.

BURTHORPE.—See EAST-LEACH-MARTIN.

BURTON, a township, in the parish of TARVIN, union of GREAT BOUGHTON, Second division of the hundred of EDDISBURY, S. division of the county of CHESTER, 3¾ miles (W. N. W.) from Tarporley; containing 79 inhabitants. This township comprises 399 acres; the soil is sandy. The tithes have been commuted for £49. 11., payable to the Dean and Chapter of Lichfield, and £22. 13. to the vicar of the parish.

BURTON (ST. NICHOLAS), a parish, and formerly a market-town, in the union, and Higher division of the hundred, of WIRRALL, S. division of the county of CHESTER; containing, with the township of Puddington, 428 inhabitants, of whom 282 are in the township of Burton, 2½ miles (S. E. by S.) from Great Neston. The parish is situated on the river Dee. The manor for many generations belonged to the Bishops of Lichfield and Coventry, of whom Bishop Alexander de Savensby, in 1238, appropriated the tithes to the hospital of Denwall, in the parish, which, with all its revenues, Henry VII. about the year 1494 gave to the hospital of St. John the Baptist, Lichfield, to which establishment the property still belongs. The township of Burton comprises 1340 acres; the soil is a light sandy clay. At Denwall is a colliery, opened about the year 1750, and still in operation; the mine extends for nearly a mile and three-quarters under the river: the produce is sent chiefly to Ireland. There are also some quarries of excellent freestone; and facilities of communication with Chester and Liverpool are obtained by railway. The market, granted in 1298 to Bishop Langton, and a fair for three days on the festival of St. James, have both been discontinued. The living is a perpetual curacy; net income, £54; patron, Richard Congreve, Esq. The church, with the exception of the chancel, was rebuilt in 1721. There is a Roman Catholic chapel at Puddington. A free school was founded in 1724, by Dr. Wilson, the pious and benevolent Bishop of Sodor and Man, who was born here in 1663, and who gave £200, and his son, Dr. Thomas Wilson, rector of St. Stephen's, Walbrook, £200 more, towards the endowment.

BURTON, a township, in the parish of BAMBROUGH, union of BELFORD, N. division of BAMBROUGH ward and of NORTHUMBERLAND, 5½ miles (E. by S.) from Belford; containing 111 inhabitants. It lies about a mile and a half south-by-west from Bambrough, and consists of a farm and some cottages. The North Sea is on the east.

BURTON, a chapelry, in the parish and liberties of WENLOCK, union of MADELEY, Southern division of SALOP, 3 miles (S. W. by S.) from Wenlock; containing 181 inhabitants. The chapelry is situated on the road from Wenlock to Ludlow, and comprises by computation 1800 acres. The soil is various, but fertile; the surface is boldly undulated, and the lower grounds are watered by a small stream called the Corse. There are quarries of stone for building; and the rocks abound with fossil remains. The living is a perpetual curacy; net income, £50; patron, the Vicar of Wenlock. Here is a Roman camp in excellent preservation.

BURTON, a hamlet, in the parish of STOGURSEY, union of WILLITON, hundred of CANNINGTON, W. division of SOMERSET; containing 75 inhabitants.

BURTON, STAFFORD.—See RICKERSCOTE.

BURTON, or BODEKTON, in the union of SUTTON, hundred of ROTHERBRIDGE, rape of ARUNDEL, county of SUSSEX, 3½ miles (S. by W.) from Petworth; containing 7 inhabitants. It comprises by measurement 776 acres, and is bounded on the north-east by the river Rother, over which is a bridge at Stopham. The living is a rectory, with that of Coates consolidated, discharged from the payment of first-fruits, but paying tenths to the bishop, and valued in the king's books at £7. 3. 11½.; net income, £113; patron, Colonel Wyndham. The tithes of Burton have been commuted for £88. The church, which is beautifully situated in the Park, is a handsome structure in the later English style, and contains several ancient brasses, under enriched canopies, to the memory of the Gorings, and other families: divine service has not been performed for many years. Attached to the mansion is a Roman Catholic chapel.

BURTON, with WALDEN, a township, in the parish of AYSGARTH, wapentake of HANG-WEST, N. riding of YORK, 7¼ miles (W. by S.) from Middleham; containing 523 inhabitants, and comprising 6790 acres, whereof about 1800 are common or waste. The village is situated in a district abounding with fine scenery, on a small stream which falls into the river Ure, and contains a great quantity of salmon: the Bishop's-dale and Walden rivulets unite below the village. The hamlet of Walden has some scattered houses in its romantic dale, extending up the Walden stream to the distance of five miles south of Burton, between lofty moors and fells. Wool-combing is carried on. There is a place of worship for Wesleyans.

BURTON-AGNES (ST. MARTIN), a parish, in the union of BRIDLINGTON, wapentake of DICKERING, E. riding of YORK; comprising the townships of Burton-Agnes, Gransmoor, Haisthorpe, and Thornholm; and containing 603 inhabitants, of whom 322 are in the township of Burton-Agnes, 6½ miles (N. E. by E.) from Great Driffield. The parish comprises 7167 acres, of which 3323 are common or waste. The Hall, a noble brick mansion, and the seat of the ancient family of Boynton, was built about the year 1703. The living is a vicarage, with the living of Harpham annexed, valued in the king's books at £20. 6. 3.; patron, Thomas Raikes, Esq.; appropriator, the Archbishop of York. The tithes have been commuted for £865. 16. payable to the archbishop, and £735. 10. to the vicar, who has

is clayey, and in most situations suitable for the growth of wheat; and the surface generally level, but in some parts undulated: about a third comes under the denomination of wold land. The living is a rectory, valued in the king's books at £23. 6. 8.; patron, Robert Ramsden, Esq.: the tithes have been commuted for £1050, and the glebe comprises 25a. 3r. 27p. The church, a small ancient edifice with a square tower, has traces of Norman and early English architecture; it was repaired in 1842. There is a place of worship for Wesleyans.

BURTON-COGGLES (St. Thomas à Becket), a parish, in the union of Grantham, wapentake of Beltisloe, parts of Kesteven, county of Lincoln, 1¾ mile (W. N. W.) from Corby; containing 260 inhabitants. It comprises 2476 acres, and has a pleasant village seated on an eminence beneath which a small rivulet flows. Limestone of a soft quality is quarried. The living is a rectory, valued in the king's books at £16. 12. 3½.; and in the patronage of the Crown: the tithes have been commuted for £530, and there is a good glebe-house, with a glebe of 104 acres. The church is an ancient structure in the early English style, and contains the figures of two crusaders in good preservation. A school has an endowment of £21 per annum, arising from a bequest of land at Quadring by John Speight, in 1734, and by Catherine Chomeley, in 1773.

BURTON-CONSTABLE, a hamlet, in the parish of Swine, union of Skirlaugh, Middle division of the wapentake of Holderness, E. riding of York, 8 miles (N. E.) from Hull; containing 71 inhabitants. In the time of the Conqueror, this place was part of the possessions of the Archbishop of York; it shortly afterwards came to the family of Constable, who are the present owners. The hamlet comprises 1247a. 3r. 2p. of land, lying in West Newton township, in the parish of Aldbrough, but usually returned with Ellerby township, in Swine parish. Burton-Constable House, the seat of Sir Thomas Aston Clifford Constable, Bart., is a splendid mansion, said to have been partly erected so early as the reign of Stephen, but the two principal fronts of which, east and west, each about 130 feet long, have been built upon, and added to, an ancient edifice probably of the time of Henry VIII. The apartments are of exceedingly handsome design, and appropriately embellished, and the whole buildings are of a character suitable to a residence of distinction : the parks, also, and the gardens, are excellently kept.

BURTON-CONSTABLE, a township, in the parish of Fingall, union of Leyburn, wapentake of Hang-West, N. riding of York, 4¼ miles (N. E.) from Middleham; containing 252 inhabitants. It comprises 2572 acres of land, chiefly the property of Marmaduke Wyvill, Esq., lord of the manor, who has a handsome seat, standing in a picturesque valley, with fine park land attached.

BURTON-DASSETT, or Dassett Magna (All Saints), a parish, and formerly a market-town, in the union of Southam, Burton-Dassett division of the hundred of Kington, S. division of the county of Warwick, 4 miles (E.) from Kington; containing 614 inhabitants. This place, now reduced to a very small hamlet, is supposed to have been destroyed about the time of the battle of Edge-Hill, which place is distant 2 miles. The parish is situated on the Warwick and Banbury road, and comprises by measurement 4500

3 M

acres. Large stone-quarries are wrought, the material
of which is used for buildings. The living is a vicarage,
valued in the king's books at £14 ; net income, £167 ;
-patrons, Lord Willoughby de Broke, and W. R. Blencow, Esq., of whom the former is impropriator : the
glebe consists of 90 acres, with a good glebe-house. The
church is a very spacious and handsome structure.

BURTON-EXTRA, a township, in the parish and
union of BURTON-UPON-TRENT, N. division of the hundred of OFFLOW and of the county of STAFFORD ; contiguous to the southern part of the town of Burton, and
containing 1193 inhabitants. This place, called also
Bond-End, comprises the district of Shobnal, distant
one mile to the west, and forming in monastic times an
abbey grange. Here is a chalybeate spring.

BURTON-FLEMING, or NORTH BURTON (ST.
CUTHBERT), a parish, in the union of BRIDLINGTON,
wapentake of DICKERING, E. riding of YORK, 7 miles
(N. W. by W.) from Bridlington ; containing 460 inhabitants. It comprises by computation 3590 acres : the
soil, opening to the south-west, is chalky, producing all
kinds of grain of an excellent quality, and turnips in
great abundance. The living is a perpetual curacy,
valued in the king's books as a discharged vicarage at
£6. 4. 2.; net income, £95 ; patron, Capt. Robert Mitford, R.N. The tithes were commuted for land and a
money payment in 1768. The church is a neat edifice,
consisting of a nave and chancel, with a low tower ; it
contains a beam perfectly sound, marked "June, 1574."
There are places of worship for Wesleyans and Primitive
Methodists.

BURTON-GATE (ST. HELEN), a parish, in the union
of GAINSBOROUGH, wapentake of WELL, parts of LIND-
SEY, county of LINCOLN, 5 miles (S. S. E.) from Gainsborough ; containing 126 inhabitants. It is situated on
the banks of the Trent, and intersected by the Lincoln
and Gainsborough road. The living is a discharged
rectory, valued in the king's books at £8. 10. 10.; net
income, £88 ; patron, W. Hutton, Esq. The glebe consists of about 16 acres, with a good glebe-house. A
small petrifying spring has been discovered.

BURTON-HASTINGS (ST. BOTOLPH), a parish, in
the union of HINCKLEY, Kirby division of the hundred
of KNIGHTLOW, N. division of the county of WARWICK,
3 miles (S. S. W.) from Hinckley ; containing 276 inhabitants. The parish is situated on the line of the Roman
Watling-street, and intersected by the Ashby-de-la-
Zouch canal. It comprises by admeasurement 1335
acres, about one-third of which is arable, and the rest
pasture ; the surface is rather flat, the soil of medium
quality, and the scenery (the parish being well wooded),
is picturesque. The living is a perpetual curacy ; net
income, £105 ; patron and incumbent, the Rev. William
Samuel Bucknill. The church is ancient, with a square
tower. Connected with it is a Sunday school.

BURTON-HILL, a tything, in the parish, union, and
hundred of MALMESBURY, Malmesbury and Kingswood,
and N. divisions of the county of WILTS, ¾ of a mile
(S.) from Malmesbury ; containing 257 inhabitants.

BURTON-IN-KENDAL (ST. JAMES), a parish, partly
in LONSDALE ward, and partly in KENDAL ward, union
of KENDAL, county of WESTMORLAND ; and partly in
the hundred of LONSDALE south of the Sands, N. division of the county of LANCASTER ; comprising the township of Dalton, in Lancashire, and the townships of

THURGARTON and of the county of NOTTINGHAM, 5 miles (N. E. by E.) from Nottingham; containing, with the chapelry of Bulcote, 764 inhabitants. This place, in Domesday book called *Bertune*, belonged in the reign of Henry II. to the family of Jorz, from whom it derives the adjunct to its name, and from whom it descended to the ancestors of the Earl of Chesterfield. The village is pleasantly situated on the north bank of the river Trent, the vale of which is bounded by a range of lofty hills that shelter it on the north. The Nottingham and Lincoln railway has a station here, 5½ miles from the Nottingham station. The living is a discharged vicarage, valued in the king's books at £4. 19. 2.; net income, £145; patron and impropriator, the Earl of Chesterfield: the tithes were commuted for land in 1768. The church is an ancient spacious structure, with a spire: in a niche of the north aisle is an upright effigy of an armed knight, standing on a lion, and bearing a shield on the left arm, said to represent Robert de Jorz, who lived in the reign of Edward I.; and in the chancel are two altar-tombs of members of the family of Stapleton, with inscriptions in Saxon characters. There is a place of worship for Wesleyans.

BURTON, KIRK (ST. JOHN THE BAPTIST), a parish, in the union of HUDDERSFIELD, Upper division of the wapentake of AGBRIGG. W. riding of YORK; containing 8,452 inhabitants, of whom 3474 are in the township of Kirk-Burton, 5 miles (S. E.) from Huddersfield. This parish comprises the townships of Cartworth, Foulston, Hepworth, Kirk-Burton, Shelley, Shepley, Thurstonland, Wooldale, and part of Cumberworth-Half; the whole forming an area of 15,990 acres, whereof 1260 are in Kirk-Burton, which includes the hamlets of Dogby-ane, Green-Grove, Linfit-Lane, Spring-Grove, and Haddock; and the village of High Burton. The village of Kirk-Burton is of considerable size, and pleasantly seated on a declivity at the junction of two narrow ravines, or valleys. The woollen and fancy-waiscoating manufactures are carried on to a great extent, affording employment to about 2600 persons: edge-tools, and spades and shovels, are manufactured in High Burton; and there are coal-pits and good stone-quarries. Fairs for cattle are held on the last Mondays in April and October. The living is a vicarage, valued in the king's books at £13. 6. 8., and in the patronage of the Lord Chancellor; net income, £276; impropriators, the Governors of Sheffield Hospital. The tithes were commuted for land in 1799. A sum of £4 is annually paid by Kirk-Burton to the vicar of Dewsbury, as a mark of its dependence upon that ancient church. The parochial church, built in the reign of Edward III., is a large and commanding edifice, with a square tower; an organ was erected in 1836, at a cost of £300. At Holmfirth and New-Mill are district churches, the former an ancient structure; and at Thurstonland is an episcopal chapel. Here are places of worship for Independents, Wesleyans, and Primitive Methodists. A school, established in 1714, was endowed in 1721 by the Rev. Henry Robinson, with a bequest of £100; and in the following year with a bequest of £360, by J. Horsfall, Esq.; which sums, having been invested in land and houses, produce about 80 per annum: the school was rebuilt in 1840.

BURTON-LATIMER (ST. MARY), a parish, in the union of KETTERING, hundred of HUXLOE, N. division of the county of NORTHAMPTON, 6 miles (N. W.) from
451

Higham-Ferrers; containing 965 inhabitants. This place derives its distinguishing appellation from the barons Latimer, who had a residence here. The parish is intersected by the road from Higham-Ferrers to Kettering, and comprises by computation 2300 acres. The soil is a free loam, and very good except in the wold, where it is cold stiff land. The immediate locality is not picturesque, owing to the land having been but lately inclosed; but the surrounding country is very pretty, well wooded, and undulated. Limestone of the oolite formation, with fossils, is abundant. A mill for spinning worsted-yarn affords employment to about 100 persons; and there is a large manufactory for Brussels and Kidderminster carpets, in connexion with it. The living is a rectory, valued in the king's books at £29. 10.; patron, David Bevan, Esq.; incumbent, the Rev. D. Barclay Bevan. The tithes were commuted for land, under an inclosure act, in 1800: the glebe now comprises 700 acres; and the parsonage is a good house, much enlarged and improved by the present rector. The church is a handsome structure, partly in the Norman and partly in the early English style, and contains a richly carved oak screen: a new east window has been put up in the chancel by the Rev. Mr. Bevan, by whom, also, stalls have been erected. There are places of worship for Baptists and Wesleyans. The free school was founded in the reign of Elizabeth, by Margaret Burbank, and William Vaux, Lord Harrowden, the former of whom endowed it with 10 acres of land, and the latter with a house. The Rev. S. Barwick, in 1792, left an endowment of 7 acres, producing £20 per annum, for preparing children for the free school; and an infants' school has been lately established by the incumbent. The rent of 40 acres of land is distributed among the industrious poor, and 70 acres are set apart in lieu of the right of cutting furze.

BURTON-LAZARS, a chapelry, in the parish and union of MELTON-MOWBRAY, hundred of FRAMLAND, N. division of the county of LEICESTER, 1¾ mile (S. E. by S.) from Melton-Mowbray; containing 262 inhabitants. The chapel is dedicated to St. James. In the reign of Stephen, an hospital dedicated to the Blessed Virgin Mary and St. Lazarus, was founded here by a general collection throughout England, the principal contributor being Roger de Mowbray: it was dependent on the great house at Jerusalem, and was the chief of all the lazar houses in England; and the revenue, in the 26th of Henry VIII., was estimated at £265. 10. 2. The buildings stood near a spring, the water of which was in high repute for curing the leprosy; a bath and a drinking-room were built about 1760. The land in this lordship is peculiarly fine.

BURTON-LEONARD (ST. HELEN), a parish, in the Lower division of the wapentake of CLARO, W. riding of YORK, 5 miles (N. N. W.) from Knaresborough; containing 455 inhabitants. It comprises 1739a. 2r. 39p., of which 1100 acres are arable, and the remainder grassland; the soil is of an inferior kind, and the surface generally undulated: stone of excellent quality is burnt for lime. Many of the inhabitants were formerly employed in the flax and linen trade, but it has entirely ceased. The living is a discharged vicarage, valued in the king's books at £3. 1. 0½.; net income, £140; patrons and appropriators, the Dean and Chapter of York: a glebe-house was erected in 1839, and there are 45 acres of glebe. The church is a small plain structure, built in 1782. There are places of worship for Primitive and Wesleyan Methodists.

BURTON, LONG (St. James), a parish, in the union and hundred of Sherborne, Sherborne division of Dorset, 3 miles (S. by E.) from Sherborne; containing 386 inhabitants. It is situated on the great road between Bath and Weymouth, and comprises by measurement 1026 acres. The females are chiefly employed in making gloves for the Yeovil and other manufacturers. There are extensive stone-quarries, from which are obtained limestone, and excellent stone for building. The living is a discharged vicarage, with the perpetual curacy of Holnest annexed, valued in the king's books at £10. 15.; net income, £275; patron, C. Cosens, Esq.; impropriator, R. Gordon, Esq.: there is a good glebe-house, with 20 acres of land. The church was built more than 200 years ago. There are places of worship for Primitive and Wesleyan Methodists.

BURTON-ON-THE-WOLDS, a township, in the parish of Prestwold, union of Loughborough, hundred of East Goscote, N. division of the county of Leicester, 3½ miles (E. N. E.) from Loughborough: containing 448 inhabitants. The Wesleyans have a meeting-house.

BURTON-OVERY (St. Andrew), a parish, in the union of Billesdon, hundred of Gartree, S. division of the county of Leicester, 7½ miles (S. E. by E.) from Leicester; containing 449 inhabitants. It comprises by computation 1800 acres, and has an undulated surface, with a strong clay soil. The living is a rectory, valued in the king's books at £18. 5. 10.; net income, £497; patron and incumbent, the Rev. R. Thorp. The tithes were commuted in 1765 for land, and the glebe now consists of 272 acres, to which there is a good glebe-house.

BURTON-PEDWARDINE (St. Andrew), a parish, in the union of Sleaford, wapentake of Ashwardhurn, parts of Kesteven, county of Lincoln, 4½ miles (S. E. by E.) from Sleaford; containing 125 inhabitants, and comprising by computation 1800 acres. The living is a vicarage, valued in the king's books at £7. 12. 8½.; patron and impropriator, H. Handley, Esq.: the glebe comprises 263; acres, valued at £332 per annum. The church is a plain edifice, built in 1802, to replace the former structure, which had been erected in 1340, on the site of a still more ancient foundation; one of the chapels of the old church is still existing. There are some remains of the seat of Thomas Horseman, taster to Queen Elizabeth; and several tumuli.

BURTON-PIDSEA (St. Peter, or St. Mary), a parish, in the Middle division of the wapentake of Holderness, E. riding of York, 5 miles (E. by N.) from Hedon; containing 400 inhabitants. The name of this place is a corruption of *Burton per Sea*, or *by the Sea*: it is one of the manors that have remained, as part of the original fee of Drogo the Norman, in possession of the succeeding lords of the seigniory of Holderness to the present day. The parish contains about 1980 acres by measurement: the soil is rich and fertile; and the village is picturesque, situated on ground commanding an extensive prospect, and surrounded by some fine trees. Chatt House, in the parish, the residence of a family of that name in the 17th century, has been

Stretton; and containing 8136 inhabitants, of whom 4863 are in the market-town of Burton, 24 miles (E.) from Stafford, and 124 (N. W. by N.) from London. This place derived its name from having been a Saxon burgh of some importance, and its adjunct from being situated on the river Trent. In the ninth century, St. Modwena, who had been expelled from her monastery in Ireland, came hither, and, having obtained an asylum from King Ethelwulph, in reward for a miraculous cure that she is said to have performed on his son Alfred, erected a chapel, and dedicated it to St. Andrew: the site, still called St. Modwena's Garden, is the only part visible. In 1004, Wulfric, Earl of Mercia, founded an abbey for monks of the Benedictine order, which, from the vestiges still to be traced, appears to have been one of the most considerable in the kingdom: it was a mitred abbey, richly endowed, and invested with extensive privileges; and its revenue, at the Dissolution, was £356. 16. 3. The remains consist principally of some fine Norman arches that formed part of the cloisters, which included an area 100 feet square, and of part of the entrance gateway, now converted into a shop. In 1225, a large portion of the town was destroyed by an accidental fire. In the reign of Edward II., Thomas, Earl of Lancaster, posted himself at Burton, and endeavoured to defend the passage of the river against the king; but being unsuccessful in his attempt, he fled with his forces into Scotland. During the parliamentary war, the town and neighbourhood were frequently the scene of action between the contending parties.

BURTON is pleasantly situated in a fertile vale, on the western bank of the Trent, which is navigable from Gainsborough for vessels of considerable burthen, and over which is a noble bridge of freestone, 512 feet in length, having 37 arches, built prior to the Conquest, and substantially repaired in the reign of Henry II. The town consisting principally of one street, parallel with the river, is well paved, lighted with gas, and plentifully supplied with water; the houses are in general modern and well built. There is a subscription library and newsroom; and assemblies and concerts take place occasionally in the town-hall. The main branch of trade is that of brewing ale, for which the town has been highly celebrated for more than a century, large quantities being sent to London, China, and the East Indies. An ancient water-mill in the vicinity of the town, noticed in the Norman survey, is partly appropriated to the grinding of corn, and partly used as a manufactory for safes: a few articles in iron are also made, particularly screws. A company was established for regulating the navigation of the river; but a canal has been constructed, which joins the Grand Trunk canal, and affords a more direct medium for the transport of goods. Here is a principal station of the Birmingham and Derby railway, which passes on the west side of the town: in 1846 an act was passed for a railway from Burton to Nuneaton; and another act, for effecting railway communication with Uttoxeter and the Potteries. The market is on Thursday; and fairs are held on February 5th, April 5th, Holy-Thursday, July 16th, and October 29th, for cattle and cheese: the last continues six days, and is a great horse-fair.

The government is vested in a high steward, deputy-steward, and bailiff, appointed by the Marquess of

453

Anglesey, lord of the manor, who holds a court leet and view of frankpledge in October, at which the police are appointed. The bailiff is a justice of the peace, having concurrent jurisdiction with the county magistrates, and acts also as coroner; the corporation formerly had power to try and execute criminals, and to hold courts of pleas to any amount. The Genter's court is held every third Friday before the steward, or his deputy, for the recovery of debts not exceeding 40s. The powers of the county debt-court of Burton, established in 1847, extend over the greater part of the registration-district of Burton. The inhabitants, by virtue of letters-patent granted in the 11th of Henry VIII., are exempt from serving the office of sheriff, and from being summoned as jurors at the assizes and sessions for the county. The town-hall is a handsome building, erected at the expense of the Marquess of Anglesey, and containing, in addition to the offices for transacting the public business, a suite of assembly-rooms.

The parish comprises about 8000 acres, whereof two-thirds are arable, and the rest meadow, with about 250 acres of wood and plantations. The LIVING is a vicarage, in the patronage of the Marquess of Anglesey, the impropriator; net income, £192. The ancient church belonged to the abbey, and was made collegiate by Henry VIII.: having been greatly damaged in the parliamentary war, it was taken down, and the present edifice, a well-built structure with a tower, though less embellished than the former, was erected on its site, in 1720. Attached to the church is a lectureship, endowed with £31 per annum, and in the patronage of the Bailiff and principal inhabitants. A second church, dedicated to the Holy Trinity, and to which a district has been assigned, was erected in 1823, on land given by the noble marquess; it is a very handsome structure in the decorated English style, and highly ornamental to the town. The church was built and endowed by the executors of Isaac Hawkins, Esq., and contains 1100 sittings, of which 750 are free: the living is a perpetual curacy; net income, £261; patron, the Marquess. Christ Church, erected in 1844 on ground given by his lordship, and to which a district has been also assigned, is a beautiful structure in the early English style, with a square tower surmounted by a graceful spire, and contains 1000 sittings, whereof 750 are free; the cost, £3000, was raised by subscription, aided by public grants. The living is a perpetual curacy, in the patronage of the Vicar of Burton; and has a parsonage, of which likewise the marquess gave the site. A church was built at Stretton in 1829. There are places of worship for General and Particular Baptists, Independents, and Primitive and Wesleyan Methodists.

The free grammar school was founded in 1520 by William Beane, abbot (whose tombstone was found in the churchyard when making alterations in 1830), and endowed by him with land producing at present £375 per annum; the head master receives £250 a year, and the second master £125: the school-house was rebuilt in 1838. Richard Allsop in 1728 bequeathed property with which land was purchased, now producing £24 per annum, to found a school for the instruction of boys; and a national school, established in 1826, is supported by subscription. Besides these, are, a school for 550 children, built in 1844; and capacious national schools attached to Trinity church. Almshouses were founded and endowed in 1634, by Ellen Parker, for six widows or maidens; and there are some others, founded in 1591 for five unmarried women, and endowed by Dame Elizabeth Pawlett, the present income of which is about £80. Of various other charities, the principal, derived from land left by Mrs. Almund, yields about £72 per annum. A savings' bank was established in 1818; and a self-supporting dispensary in 1830. The poor law union comprises 53 parishes and places, of which 13 are in the county of Stafford, and 40 in that of Derby; and contains a population of 28,878: the workhouse stands at the north-western extremity of the town, in the township of Horninglow; it was built in 1839, at a cost of £8000, and is capable of accommodating upwards of 400 inmates. Isaac Hawkins Browne, a poet of minor celebrity, was born here about 1705.

BURTON-UPON-URE, a township, in the parish of MASHAM, union of LEYBURN, wapentake of HANG-EAST, N. riding of YORK, 1 mile (N.) from Masham; containing 200 inhabitants. It is chiefly on the eastern bank of the river Ure, and comprises by computation 2920 acres of land, extending southward to Northcote, to Nutwith, to Ilton Grange (allotted to Burton from Ilton Common), and to Aldbrough. In the last place is Aldbrough Hall, a mansion built near the site of a castle founded by William le Gros, Earl of Albemarle, who, having gained the battle of the Standard, was created Earl of York, in 1138. The tithes have been commuted for £55 payable to Trinity College, Cambridge, and £2 to the vicar.

BURTON, WEST (ST. HELEN), a parish, in the union of GAINSBOROUGH, North-Clay division of the wapentake of BASSETLAW, N. division of the county of NOTTINGHAM, 3¼ miles (S. S. W.) from Gainsborough; containing 35 inhabitants. The parish is situated on the river Trent, which forms its eastern boundary; and comprises 936a. 39p. The living is a perpetual curacy; net income, £65; patron, John Barrow, Esq. The church is a plain edifice.

BURTON, WEST, a tything, in the parish and hundred of BURY, union of SUTTON, rape of ARUNDEL, W. division of SUSSEX; containing 201 inhabitants.

BURTONWOOD, a chapelry, in the parish and union of WARRINGTON, hundred of WEST DERBY, S. division of the county of LANCASTER, 5 miles (N. W.) from Warrington; containing 836 inhabitants. Burton-wood manor was held by the barons of Warrington, by the annual service of one penny at Easter; and is named in the 12th of Henry III. in the perambulation by twelve knights of the county, who returned that (among other woods) "Burton Wode" ought not to be disforested. The families of Haydock, Legh, and Bold are also named in connexion with the place. The chapelry comprises 3814 acres, whereof about 700 are arable, and the remainder pasture and meadow, with 38 acres of common or waste; the surface is nearly a perfect level, and the soil for the most part a heavy marl, but in the south lighter and more valuable. The chief proprietors are Lord Lilford and H. Bold Hoghton, Esq., the latter of whom is lord of the manor. About a mile and a half of the Liverpool and Manchester railway, and more than half a mile of the Liverpool and Birmingham line, pass through the chapelry, the former in the northern, and the latter in the eastern, part; and the Sankey canal crosses it in the direction of St. Helen's.
454

The living is a perpetual curacy; net income, £90, derived partly from two farms in the neighbouring townships of Croft and Hindley, and partly from Queen Anne's Bounty; patron, the Rector of Warrington. The tithes have been commuted for £421. The chapel, built about 1736, is a plain brick edifice with a semicircular chancel, and has been lately enlarged. There is a small school, with a house for the master. At Bradley Hall, once the manor-house, is some ancient stone work, called the "Castle;" it must have been very strong, from the thickness of the walls remaining, and it is highly probable that it supported a drawbridge, as the house is surrounded by an ancient moat.

BURWARDSLEY, a chapelry, in the parish of BUNBURY, union of NANTWICH, Higher division of the hundred of BROXTON, S. division of the county of CHESTER, 2 miles (S. E. by S.) from Tattenhall; containing 458 inhabitants. The manor was given by the abbot of St. Werburgh's at Chester to Roger de Combre or Fitz-Alured, on condition that he should champion for the monastery; and his daughter and coheir brought the whole or part of the estate to the Touchet family. Robert, Lord Cholmondeley, is described as lord in 1662. Of late years the manor has been esteemed as subordinate to that of Tattenhall, which belonged also to the Touchets. Burwardsley was sold in 1804 by John Crewe, Esq., afterwards Lord Crewe, to Thomas Tarlton, Esq., of Bolesworth Castle. The chapelry comprises 998a. 3r. 14p.; the surface is finely undulated, the soil clay and a light loam, and the views very extensive. There are numerous quarries of white and red sandstone, the material of one of which is of excellent quality for buildings. Many of the inhabitants are employed in the manufacture of shoes. The Tattenhall station of the Chester and Crewe railway is distant about three miles only. The living is a perpetual curacy; net income, £46. 12.: patrons, sixteen Trustees; impropriator, Samuel Aldersey, Esq., but who will be eventually succeeded by the Haberdashers' Company. A rent-charge of £100 has been awarded as a commutation for the tithes. There is neither glebe nor glebe-house in the chapelry; but at Tattenhall is a plot of about fifteen acres. The chapel, dedicated to St. John, and beautifully situated, is a small stone building, erected by subscription in 1735. The Primitive Methodists have a place of worship.

BURWARTON (ST. LAWRENCE), a parish, in the union of BRIDGNORTH, hundred of STOTTESDEN, S. division of SALOP, 9 miles (S. W.) from Bridgnorth; containing 151 inhabitants. It is situated on the road from Bridgnorth to Ludlow, and comprises by computation 1240 acres, mostly pasture and woodland; about 300 acres are occupied in sheep-walks. The surface is undulated and mountainous: good ironstone is obtained. The Hon. Gustavus Hamilton is the proprietor; his mansion, built in 1840, is in the Italian style, and commands beautiful views of the Abberley, Malvern, Titterstone, and Clee hills. The living is a discharged rectory, valued in the king's books at £4. 6. 8.; patron and incumbent, the Rev. John Churton: the tithes have been commuted for £102, and the glebe comprises 20 acres, with a house. The church, an edifice in the pure Norman style of architecture, was restored by Mr. Hamilton, in 1843; the eastern window is of stained glass. There is a place of worship for Wesleyans.

BURW / BURY

BURWASH (*St. Bartholomew*), a parish, in the union of Ticehurst, partly in the hundred of Shoyswell and Henhurst, but chiefly in that of Hawkesborough, rape of Hastings, E. division of Sussex, 8 miles (S. by W.) from Lamberhurst; containing 2093 inhabitants. The parish is on the road from Lewes to Cranbrook, which intersects the village; and comprises 7000 acres, whereof 685 are common or waste: the neighbourhood abounds with ironstone, for the smelting of which a blast-furnace formerly existed. The village is pleasantly situated on an eminence, surrounded by hills of greater elevation, and consists of one long street, containing several respectable houses. A fair for cattle and sheep is held on the 12th of May. The living consists of a sinecure rectory and a vicarage, the former valued in the king's books at £8. 10., and the latter at £18; patron and incumbent, the Rev. J. Gould: the tithes have been commuted for £1125, and the glebe comprises 80 acres. The church is partly in the early and partly in the later English style, with a square embattled tower surmounted by a low spire. There are places of worship for Calvinists and Independents; and a national school supported by an endowment of about £35. 10. per annum. On Goodsial farm is a mineral spring.

BURWELL (*St. Mary*), a parish, in the union of Newmarket, hundred of Staploe, county of Cambridge, 4 miles (N. W. by W.) from Newmarket; containing 1820 inhabitants. The parish comprises 7232 acres, of which 3036 are common or waste. The village consists principally of one irregular street, nearly two miles long; the houses are built with stone obtained in the vicinity, in which pyrites and shark's teeth, in good preservation, have been found. An act for draining fen lands, and for improving the navigable cuts, was passed in 1841. A great fair for horses is held on Rogation-Monday, at Reach, once a market-town, now an insignificant hamlet, partly in the parish. The living is a discharged vicarage, with the rectory of Burwell St. Andrew consolidated, valued jointly in the king's books at £50. 14. 2.; net income, £335; patrons, the Chancellor, Masters, and Scholars of the University of Cambridge (the impropriators), for two turns, and the Heirs of the late Sir E. North, for one. The church is a beautiful edifice, in the decorated English style: the rent of 100 acres of land is appropriated for its repair. There are places of worship for Independents and Wesleyans. Here are the ruins of a castle surrounded by a moat, which was besieged in the war between Stephen and the Empress Matilda, by Geoffrey de Mandeville, Earl of Essex, who was shot by an arrow from the walls. The parish register contains the record of a fire on September 8th, 1727, when 78 persons lost their lives. The church of St. Andrew Burwell has long been demolished, and the cemetery converted into pasture-ground.

BURWELL (*St. Michael*), a parish, in the union of Louth, Wold division of the hundred of Louth-Eske, parts of Lindsey, county of Lincoln, 5¼ miles (S. by E.) from Louth; containing 174 inhabitants. This place, which is situated on the road from London to Louth, appears to have been formerly of more importance than it is at present: a grant of a weekly market and two annual fairs, was made in the reign of Edward III., and confirmed in that of Elizabeth; and the ancient market

455

cross is still remaining, in a very perfect state. The fairs are held on May-day and the festival of St. Michael (O. S.) The parish comprises 2009a. 3r. 29p. The living is a discharged vicarage, with the livings of Walmsgate and Muckton annexed, valued in the king's books at £8; net income, £159; patron and impropriator, Matthew Bancroft Lister, Esq. The church is partly of Norman architecture. There are the remains of a small alien priory of Benedictine monks, founded by John de Hay, and given by some of the lords of Kyme to the abbey of St. Mary Sylvæ Majoris, near Bordeaux. This is the birthplace of Sarah, Duchess of Marlborough, who was grand-daughter of the wife of Sir Martin Lister, ancestor of the present proprietor of the estate.

BURY (*Holy Cross*), a parish, in the union of St. Ives, hundred of Hurstingstone, county of Huntingdon, 1½ miles (N. N. E.) from Huntingdon; containing 359 inhabitants. This place formed part of the possessions of Ramsey Abbey; and there is a strong stone bridge of two arches over a small branch of the river Nene, which is supposed to have been built by one of the abbots. The living is a perpetual curacy, in the patronage of Lady O. B. Sparrow, with a net income of £167: the tithes have been commuted for £140. A portion of land in the parish of Riseley, Bedfordshire, purchased by Queen Anne's Bounty, belongs to the living. The church is composed of the eastern part of a large cruciform edifice, and exhibits a mixture of Norman and early English architecture; the entrance to the chancel from the nave is under a carved wooden screen.

BURY (*St. Mary*), a borough, parish, and the head of a union, chiefly in the hundred of Salford, S. division, and partly in the Higher division of the hundred of Blackburn, N. division, of the county of Lancaster; comprising the chapelries of Edenfield, Heywood, and Holcombe, the hamlet of Ramsbottom, and the townships of Bury, Coupe with Lenches, Elton, Heap, Musbury, Tottington Higher-End, Tottington Lower-End, and Walmersley with Shuttleworth; the whole containing 62,125 inhabitants, of whom 20,710 are in the town, 48½ miles (S. E. by S.) from Lancaster, 9 (N. N. W.) from Manchester, and 195½ (N. N. W.) from London. Some antiquaries suppose this to have been a Roman station: it was certainly a Saxon town, as its name implies. Leland notices the remains of a castle near the church, the site of which, still called Castle Croft, was not far from the ancient bed of the river Irwell. This castle, one of the twelve baronial castles in the county, was finally demolished about the year 1644, by the parliamentary troops, who laid siege to the town, and battered down the small remains that were then existing: fragments of it are still occasionally discovered.

The town occupies a gentle acclivity rising from the eastern bank of the Irwell, over which is a stone bridge, and is skirted on the east by the river Roche, which falls into the Irwell about two miles and a half to the south. It is seated in a salubrious and open country, beyond which are lofty and majestic mountains; and the district abounds with coal and water, rendering it extremely eligible for the numerous establishments in which the population is engaged. The town has been greatly improved of late years; and contains a public subscription library, three newsrooms, a mechanics' institution, and a medical society re-established in 1846. The woollen-trade was introduced in the reign of Edward III., and increased so as to constitute the staple trade of the town in the reign of Elizabeth, who stationed one of her alnagers here, to stamp the cloth; it is still carried on to a considerable extent. In 1845, there were in the borough, in active operation, twelve woollen manufac-tories, twenty-six cotton-mills for spinning and weaving, six iron-foundries, and four paper-mills; in which 6022 hands, and 1599-horse power, were employed. Besides these, were twelve calico bleachers and printers, a branch of business introduced here by the late Sir Robert Peel, Bart., using machinery of 431-horse power, and em-ploying 3131 hands; also five dyers and logwood-grinders. The manufactures indeed are so many and various, that if depression or stagnation occur in one branch, the working-classes find employment in another; and distress is consequently less felt in Bury than in other places where only one article is made. Among the works is the Wood Hill cotton-mill, belonging to Messrs. Thomas Calrow and Sons, established sixty years ago, and employing 800 hands; it is worked by two of the largest water-wheels on the Irwell, the wheels being 43 feet high and 16 wide, with 18-inch buckets, and equal to 284-horse power, besides which are two steam-engines of 80-horse power. The Hud-Car mill of Messrs. William Greg and Company employs 500 hands in spinning and weaving, using 25,000 lb. of cotton, and consuming 60 tons of coal, per week. The Butcher-lane mill of Messrs. Charles Openshaw and Son, which em-ploys 550 hands, spins per week 20,000 lb. of cotton, and consumes 80 tons of coal; it has two engines of 50 and 60 horse power. A branch of the Manchester and Bolton canal was constructed in 1791; and the follow-ing railways have a station at Bury: 1st., the Liverpool, Wigan, Bolton, and Bury; 2nd., the East Lancashire; and 3rd., the Bury and Heywood branch of the Man-chester and Leeds railway. The market is on Saturday; and fairs are held in March, May, and September. An act was passed in 1839 for regulating the markets and fairs, and also providing a market-place, which has since been erected by the Earl of Derby. One mile from the town, on the Bolton road, are commodious barracks, built in 1845, on a site given by the earl, and capable of accommodating 350 men and 48 horses; and near these barracks is the Wellington hotel, erected the same year.

By the act of the 2nd of William IV., cap. 45, the town was constituted a BOROUGH, with the privilege of sending a member to parliament, the right of election being vested in the £10 householders: the limits of the borough comprise by estimation 3660 acres; the re-turning officer is appointed by the sheriff. The town is within the jurisdiction of the county magistrates, who hold petty-sessions on every Monday and Friday: the powers of the county debt-court of Bury, established in 1847, extend over the registration-district of Bury. Courts leet are held in April and October, and at Whit-suntide; and a court baron every third week for the recovery of debts under 40s. The county police was introduced 12th August, 1841. The LIVING is a rectory, valued in the king's books at £29. 11. 5½.; net income, £1937; patron, the Earl of Derby. The tithes of Bury township have been commuted for £80, and the glebe

456

consists of 89 acres. The parochial church was taken down and rebuilt in 1776, and in 1844 a beautiful stone tower and a graceful spire were erected. St. John's church, a neat edifice, was erected in 1770: the living is a perpetual curacy, with a net income of £150, and in the patronage of the Rector. St. Paul's church was built at a cost of £7000, in 1841, and a district was assigned to it in 1842; it is a neat stone structure in the early English style, with a tower: the living is a perpetual curacy, in the patronage of Trustees, with a net income of £150, and a house. Other livings are maintained at Edenfield, Elton, Heap, Heywood, Hol-combe, Musbury, Ramsbottom, Shuttleworth, Totting-ton, and Walmersley. There are places of worship for Independents, Primitive Methodists, Wesleyans, New Connexion of Methodists, Presbyterians, Baptists, and Unitarians; and a Roman Catholic chapel, erected in the year 1840.

The free grammar school was founded in 1726, by the Rev. Roger Kay, who endowed it with estates now pro-ducing nearly £500 per annum. It is divided into a classical school, of which the head master must be a graduate of one of the universities, and an English school, with two masters; and is under the direction of trustees, thirteen in number, including the Dean of Manchester, the rectors of Bury and Prestwich, and four incumbents of parishes within ten miles of Bury. There are two exhibitions attached to the school, origi-nally of £25 each, but now augmented by a benefaction of the late Dean Wood's, and varying from £30 to £35, at the pleasure of the trustees; they are limited to the colleges of St. John's, Cambridge, and Brasenose, Ox-ford. A school was founded in 1748, by the Hon. and Rev. John Stanley, a former rector, who, on three occa-sions, gave £300, and whose lady gave £68, towards its support; in 1803 the late Sir Robert Peel contributed £100, and other persons have added various sums, making the investment at present £1108: the total in-come is £199. Several other large schools are in con-nexion with the Church. A savings' bank was esta-blished in 1822, and a dispensary in 1829; and there is also a lying-in charity. The union of Bury contains a population of 77,496. The Rt. Hon. Sir Robert Peel, lately first minister of the crown, was born, in 1788, at Chamber Hall, a mansion in the parish, at present the residence of the family of Hardman.

BURY, a parish, in the union of SUTTON, hundred of BURY, rape of ARUNDEL, W. division of SUSSEX, 7 miles (S. by E.) from Petworth; containing, with the tything of West Burton, 611 inhabitants. This parish, which comprises 3397a. 3r. 18p., is bounded on the east by the river Arun, and on the north by the Rother, and is intersected by the road from London to Bognor and Arundel: an act for inclosing lands was passed in 1841. The living is a discharged vicarage, valued in the king's books at £7. 5. 5.; net income, £100; patron, the Prebendary of Bury in the Cathedral of Chichester. The tithes have been commuted for £485, and there is a good glebe-house, with about 20 acres of land. The church is an ancient edifice in the later English style, consisting of a nave, north aisle, and chancel, with a square embattled tower surmounted by a low shingled spire : in the north window are the arms of Richard, Earl of Arundel, who purchased the manor from the abbey of Fescamp, in Normandy, in 1392.

Arms.

BURY ST. EDMUND'S, a borough and market-town, having exclusive jurisdiction, locally in the hundred of THINGOE, West division of SUFFOLK, 26½ miles (N. W. by W.) from Ipswich, and 72 (N. E. by E.) from London; containing 12,538 inhabitants. This was a place of importance before the introduction of Christianity into Britain, and is by some antiquaries supposed to have been the *Villa Faustini* of the Romans. That it was in the possession of that people is evident, from the discovery of many Roman antiquities. Soon after the settlement of the Saxons it was made a royal borough, and called *Beodrics worthe,* signifying "the dwelling of Beodric:" it subsequently belonged to Offa, King of East Anglia, who,. at his death, bequeathed it to EDMUND, afterwards canonized as a martyr, from whom it was named St. Edmund's Bury. Edmund, having succeeded to the kingdom of East Anglia on the death of Offa, was crowned here, in the fifteenth year of his age ; but, being taken prisoner by the Danes, who in 870 made an irruption into this part of the country, he was cruelly put to death. The circumstances attending his death and burial are thus superstitiously related : on his refusal to become a vassal to the conquerors, they bound him to a tree, pierced his body with arrows, and striking off his head, threw it into a neighbouring forest. After the enemy had retired, the East Anglians assembled to perform the funeral obsequies to the remains of their sovereign ; and having found the body, they went into the forest to search for the head, and discovered it between the fore-paws of a wolf, which immediately resigned it on their approach. The head, on being placed in contact with the trunk, is then said to have re-united so closely, that the juncture was scarcely visible. The subject of this story has been assumed for the device of the corporation seal.

Forty days after his death, the remains of Edmund, which had been interred at Hoxne, in a small chapel built of wood, were, from the report of miracles wrought at his tomb being promulgated and believed, removed to this place in 903 ; and a new church was built in honour of him, by some Secular priests, who were incorporated by King Athelstan, about the year 925, and the establishment made collegiate. The town and church having been nearly destroyed by Sweyn, King of Denmark, in 1010, were restored by Canute, who raised the town to more than its original splendour, rebuilt the church and monastery, which he endowed with great possessions, and, expelling the Secular canons, placed in their stead monks of the Benedictine order. The monastery of St. Edmund in process of time became one of the most splendid establishments in the kingdom ; and, in magnificent buildings, costly decorations, valuable immunities, and rich endowments, was inferior only to that of Glastonbury. In the year 1327, the townsmen and neighbouring villagers, assembling to the number of 20,000, headed by their aldermen and capital burgesses, made a violent attack upon it, and reduced a considerable part to ashes : they wounded the monks, and pillaged the coffers, from which they took the

charters, deeds, and other valuable property, including plate, £5000 sterling, and 3000 florins of gold. The king, on being informed of the outrage, sent a military force to quell the tumult ; the aldermen and twenty-four of the burgesses were imprisoned, and thirty carts loaded with rioters were sent to Norwich. Of these, nineteen were executed ; thirty-two of the parochial clergy were also convicted as abettors ; and the inhabitants were adjudged to pay a fine of £140,000, which was afterwards mitigated on the restoration of the stolen property. The monastery remained in the possession of the Benedictine monks for 519 years ; it contained within its precincts the churches of St. Margaret, St. Mary, and St. James, and its revenue, at the Dissolution, was £2336. 16. The remains consist chiefly of the abbey-gate, still entire, and displaying some elegant features in the decorated English style; the abbey bridge, in good preservation ; and detached portions of the walls, which still exhibit traces of former magnificence. About 1256, a fraternity of the Franciscan order came to Bury, but they were compelled by the abbot to remove beyond the precincts of the town, where their establishment continued till the Dissolution.

Henry I., on his return from Chartres, repaired to the shrine of St. Edmund, where he presented a rich offering, in gratitude for his safe return to his dominions. In 1173, Henry II., having assembled a large army at this place, to oppose his rebellious sons, caused the sacred standard of St. Edmund to be borne in front of his troops ; and to its influence was ascribed the victory that he obtained in the battle of the 27th of October. In 1214, King John was met here by the barons. Henry III. held a parliament at Bury in 1272, which may be regarded as the outline of a British house of commons ; and in 1296, Edward I. visited the town, where he also held a parliament. In 1381, Sir John Cavendish, lord chief justice, was brought hither and beheaded by the Suffolk and Norfolk insurgents, amounting to 50,000 men, who afterwards attacked the abbey, executed the prior, Sir John Cambridge, and continued their career of lawless outrage till they were finally dispersed by the exertions of Spencer, the martial Bishop of Norwich. In 1526, the Dukes of Suffolk and Norfolk assembled their forces here, to quell a dangerous insurrection of the inhabitants of Lavenham and the adjacent country ; and on the death of Edward VI., in 1553, John Dudley, Duke of Northumberland, made this place the rendezvous of his forces, when he caused Lady Jane Grey to be proclaimed successor to the throne. In 1555-6, twelve persons were burned at the stake, in the persecutions during the reign of Mary : in 1583, her successor, Elizabeth, visited Bury, where she was magnificently entertained.

The TOWN is delightfully situated upon a gentle eminence, on the western bank of the river Larke, also called the Bourne, in the centre of an open and richly cultivated tract of country ; the streets are spacious, well paved, and lighted with gas. The houses are in general uniform, and handsomely built, and the inhabitants are amply supplied with water ; the air is salubrious, the environs abound with interesting scenery, and the peculiar cleanliness of the town, and the number and variety of its public institutions, render it desirable as a place of residence. The subscription library, formed by the union of two separate establishments, one of which was founded in 1790, and the other in 1795, contains a valuable collection, and is liberally supported: there are also a newsroom, four circulating libraries, a mechanics' institute, and a billiard-room. The botanic garden, to which the abbey-gate forms the principal entrance, is an agreeable promenade, supported by an annual subscription of two guineas from each member. The theatre, a neat building erected in 1819, is opened during the great fair, by the Norwich company of comedians. Concerts take place occasionally in the old theatre, built in 1780, which has been converted to this use; and assemblies are held during the season at the subscription-rooms, erected in 1804, and handsomely fitted up. The spinning of yarn was formerly the principal source of employment for the poor, and the halls in which the wool was deposited are yet standing; but no particular branch of manufacture is at present carried on. About a mile from the town the river Larke becomes navigable to Lynn, whence coal and other commodities are brought hither in small barges. A railway to Ipswich, communicating with the line from Ipswich to London, was opened in Dec. 1846. The market-days are Wednesday and Saturday, the former for corn, &c. and the latter for meat and poultry. Fairs are held on the Tuesday in Easter-week, for toys, &c.; and on October 1st, and December 1st, for horses, cattle, butter, and cheese: the great fair commences on the 10th of October, and generally continues about three weeks.

Corporation Seal.

The GOVERNMENT, by charter of incorporation granted in the 4th of James I., and extended in the 6th and 12th of the same reign, and the 20th of Charles II., was vested in an alderman, six assistants, twelve capital burgesses, twenty-four common-councilmen, a recorder, coroner, town-clerk, four serjeants-at-mace, and subordinate officers; but by the act of the 5th and 6th of William IV., cap. 76., the corporation now consists of a mayor, six aldermen, and eighteen councillors, and the total number of magistrates is sixteen. The freedom is acquired by apprenticeship to a freeman, and by birth. The borough first received a precept to return representatives to parliament in the 30th of Edward I., but made no subsequent return till the 4th of James I., since which it has continued to send two members. The right of election was formerly vested exclusively in the aldermen, burgesses, and common-councilmen; but, by the act of the 2nd of William IV., cap. 45, was extended to the £10 householders of the parishes of St. Mary and St. James, which constitute the borough, and comprise 3000 acres. The mayor is returning officer. The corporation hold courts of session for the trial of capital offenders, under a grant from William IV.; and a court of record, which embraces all pleas where the cause of action has arisen within the precincts of the borough, and the damages do not exceed £200, is held once a month. Petty-sessions occur weekly; and a court for the recovery of debts under 40s. is holden under the chief steward of the liberty. The assizes for the county and liberty, the latter of which comprises seven hundreds within

458

the county, are held here and at Ipswich alternately, there being always a separate commission for the borough and liberty; also the general quarter-sessions are held here for a certain district of the county. The powers of the county debt-court of Bury, established in 1847, extend over the registration-districts of Bury and Thingoe, and part of the district of Stow. The shire-hall, on the site of the ancient church of St. Margaret, is a neat modern building, containing two courts for civil and criminal causes. The guildhall, where the borough courts are held, has a beautiful ancient porch of flint, brick, and stone, on which are sculptured the arms of the borough. The town bridewell, situated on the Hog Hill, was formerly a synagogue; the circular windows bespeak its antiquity, and it appears, from other parts, to be of Norman origin. The county gaol, erected in 1805, is a spacious building upon the radiating principle, surrounded by a stone wall, inclosing an octagonal area, the diameter of which is 292 feet : the house of correction near the gaol is arranged with a due regard to classification.

Bury comprises the parishes of St. Mary and St. James, each containing 6269 inhabitants. The living of each is a donative, the former in the patronage of J. Fitz-Gerald, Jun., Esq., and the latter in that of H. Wilson, Esq. : net income of St. Mary's, £110; and of St. James, which is commonly called a preachership, £106. The church dedicated to *St. Mary*, completed about the year 1433, is a spacious and elegant structure chiefly in the later English style, with a low massive tower; the north door is in the decorated style, and the porch, the roof of which is singularly beautiful, of later date. On the north side of the altar is a modern tablet of white marble to the memory of Mary Tudor, third daughter of Henry VII., wife of Louis XII. of France, and afterwards of Charles Brandon, Duke of Suffolk. The reredos, or carved screen behind the communion-table, presented by a lady whose name is not divulged, was finished in 1847, and is a beautiful piece of stone-work, harmonizing with the general character of the edifice. A painted window, a memorial of the families of the Bishop of London and the late John Smith and James Conran, Esqrs., of the town, has been fixed over the screen, and forms a fine termination of the vista of this noble building. The church of *St. James* is a large and handsome edifice, in the later style of English architecture, of which the western end is a rich specimen; the church gate, leading to the precinct of the abbey, is surmounted by a Norman tower. A district church dedicated to *St. John* has been erected in the parish of St. James; the patronage is vested in the Bishop of Ely. There are places of worship for Independents, Baptists, the Society of Friends, Methodists, Unitarians, and Roman Catholics.

The grammar school, founded by Edward VI., in the fourth year of his reign, and placed under the control of 16 governors, is open to the sons of inhabitants, upon the payment of two guineas entrance, and the same sum per annum, if taught Latin and Greek; the annual income is £411. 15. The school has four exhibitions, tenable for four years, of the annual value of £20 each, founded by Edward Hewer in the 11th of Elizabeth; two others, of the value of £25 each, founded under a bequest by Dean Sudbury in 1670, to either of the Universities; a scholarship at Corpus Christi; and another at Jesus College, Cambridge. The residue of the funds of Dean Sudbury's bequest, which amount in the aggregate to £154 per annum, is applied in apprenticing four children. A new school-house has been erected, over the entrance to which is a bust of the founder, with an appropriate inscription. The school produced Archbishop Sancroft; the three judges, Sir Edward Alderson, Sir John Patteson, and Sir R. M. Rolfe; Bishop Blomfield, and his brother, the Rev. Edward Valentine Blomfield; the distinguished Romilly, and Kemble. The feoffees of the Guildhall estate hold in trust, for charitable uses, certain buildings, lands, and rent-charges, producing an annual income of £2038 : a part of the estates was given by John Smyth, Esq., an inhabitant and a great benefactor to the town. The affairs were some years ago in chancery, and in 1842 a new distribution of the funds was ordered to be made. Clopton's asylum was founded for the support of six aged widowers, and the same number of widows, in 1730, by Poley Clopton, M.D., who endowed it with property producing £730 per annum ; it is a neat brick building with projecting wings, having the arms of the founder over the entrance in the centre. Some minor charities, amounting in the whole to a considerable sum, are distributed among the poor. The Suffolk general hospital, established in 1825, and supported by subscription, was originally built by government for an ordnance depôt, but was afterwards purchased and converted to its present use.

The abbey remains have been already noticed. Near the north gate of the town, on the road to Thetford, are the ruins of St. Saviour's hospital, founded in the reign of King John, with an income of 153 marks, and where the "good" Duke of Gloucester is believed to have been murdered. A little beyond it stood St. Thomas' hospital and chapel, now a private dwelling ; and about half a mile distant may be traced the site of the old Franciscan priory. Various other ruins, connected with the abbey and its early history, are visible. Many minor institutions were dependent on it, of which there are not at present any remains : among these may be noticed a college of priests, dedicated to the Holy Name of Jesus, founded in the reign of Edward IV., suppressed in that of Edward VI. ; an hospital dedicated to St. John, established by one of the abbots in the reign of Edward I. ; an hospital dedicated to St. Nicholas, founded also by an abbot of St. Edmund's, and the revenue of which, at the Dissolution, was £6. 19. 11. : and St. Peter's hospital, instituted in the latter part of the reign of Henry I., or the beginning of that of Stephen, and the revenue of which, at the Dissolution, was £10. 18. 11. Sir Nicholas Bacon, Bishops Gardiner and Pretyman, and Dr. Blomfield, the present Bishop of London, were born at this place. It contains the title of Viscount on the family of Keppel, earls of Albemarle.

BURYTHORP (*ALL SAINTS*), a parish, in the union of MALTON, wapentake of BUCKROSE, E. riding of YORK, 4 miles (S.) from Malton ; containing 226 inhabitants. The parish is situated on the road from Malton to Pocklington, at the base of the Yorkshire Wolds, and comprises about 1200 acres, of which two-thirds are arable, and the remainder meadow, pasture, and woodland; the surface is hilly, the soil various, and in general good, and the scenery in many situations very beautiful. Stone is quarried for burning into lime, and

for the roads. The living is a discharged rectory, valued in the king's books at £6. 16. 3., and in the patronage of the Crown : the tithes have been commuted for £264. 9. 9., and the glebe comprises 25 acres. The church is an ancient edifice with substantial buttresses. There is a place of worship for Wesleyans. In 1768, Francis Consith died here, at the extraordinary age of 150 years.

BUSBY, GREAT, a township, in the parish and union of STOKESLEY, W. division of the liberty of LANGBAURGH, N. riding of YORK, 2¼ miles (S.) from Stokesley; containing 114 inhabitants. The manor of this place, which was ancient demesne of the crown, was granted by the Conqueror to Robert de Brus, of Skelton Castle, and his descendants continued lords till the death of Peter de Brus, the fourth, without issue, when the lands came to the family of de Roos, who held of the king *in capite*. Among the other principal proprietors in former times, occur the family of de Mowbray, and the monks of Rivaulx and of Fountains. The township is situated a little to the south-west of the road from Stokesley to Thirsk ; and comprises, with Little Busby formerly united with it, 2090 acres of land. The tithes have been commuted for £201.

BUSBY, LITTLE, a township, in the parish and union of STOKESLEY, W. division of the liberty of LANGBAURGH, N. riding of YORK, 2½ miles (S.) from Stokesley; containing 34 inhabitants. It is a small hamlet, distant about a mile from the village of Great Busby, and contains Busby Hall, a handsome stone mansion occupying a commanding eminence. The tithes have been commuted for £73.

BUSCOT, or BURWASCOT (*ST. MARY*), a parish, in the union of FARRINGDON, hundred of SHRIVENHAM, county of BERKS, 1½ mile (S. by E.) from Lechlade ; containing 405 inhabitants, and comprising 2684a. 2r. 31p. About 100 acres are cottages and waste. Buscot-Park House, beautifully situated on the bank of the Thames, was built in 1781, by Pryse Loveden, Esq. ; prior to which, the family mansion of the Lovedens was near the church. Mr. Loveden took the name of Pryse, on coming into possession of property in Wales, as heir to his maternal grandfather. The living is a rectory, valued in the king's books at £21. 2. 8½., and in the patronage of Pryse Pryse, Esq. : the tithes have been commuted for £535, and the glebe consists of 64 acres.

BUSHBURY, or BYSHBURY (*ST. MARY*), a parish, in the union of PENKRIDGE, partly in the E. division of the hundred of CUTTLESTONE, and partly in the N. division of that of SEISDON, S. division of the county of STAFFORD, 3 miles (N. by E.) from Wolverhampton ; containing, with the township of Essington, and the hamlet of Moseley, 1509 inhabitants. This parish comprises 6400 acres, mostly arable land, well wooded. The surface is undulated, and partly elevated ; and from Bushbury hill, 650 feet above the level of the sea, are most extensive and beautiful views, embracing the Cley hills on the south-west, the Wrekin on the west, and Stafford, &c., on the north. The population is almost entirely agricultural. The Staffordshire and Worcestershire canal, and the Grand Junction railway, pass through the parish. The village is sheltered on the east by the hill, which is covered with a profusion of yew and other trees ; and in the vicinity are some handsome mansions. The living is a discharged vicarage, valued in the king's books at £7. 11. 5½., and in the patronage of the Landowners; net income, £159. The church, which has a square tower, belonged to the priory of St. Thomas, near Stafford; it was built about 1460, and was repaired and enlarged in 1834, when 250 sittings were gained. A school is supported by subscription. Near the village appears a considerable tumulus.

BUSHBY, a hamlet, in the parish of THURNBY, union of BILLESDON, hundred of GARTREE, S. division of the county of LEICESTER, 4¼ miles (E. by S.) from Leicester; containing 86 inhabitants. It lies on the road from Leicester to Uppingham; and comprises 665 acres, whereof 161 are arable, 483 meadow and pasture, 18 acres homesteads and gardens, and 3 woodland. The tithes have been commuted for £50. The poor share in a bequest of £100, the interest of which is distributed yearly.

BUSHEY (ST. JAMES), a parish, in the union of WATFORD, hundred of DACORUM, though locally in the hundred of CASHIO, or liberty of ST. ALBAN's, county of HERTFORD, 1¼ mile (S. E.) from Watford; containing 2675 inhabitants. This place appears to have attained some importance at an early period; and in the third of Edward I., David de Jarpanville, in answer to a writ of *quo warranto* issued by that monarch, claimed the privilege of holding a market here. The parish comprises 3188 acres, of which 970 are arable, and nearly all the rest meadow and pasture; 267 acres are common or waste: it is intersected by the London and Birmingham railway, which passes within a mile of the church. The living is a rectory, valued in the king's books at £18. 2. 1., and in the patronage of Exeter College, Oxford: the tithes have been commuted for £765, and the glebe contains 35 acres, with a house. At Bushey Heath is St. Peter's church, consecrated in June, 1837, a handsome edifice in the early English style, containing 400 sittings, of which 200 are free: the Rector is patron.

BUSHLEY (ST. PETER), a parish, in the union of UPTON-UPON-SEVERN, Lower division of the hundred of PERSHORE, Upton and W. divisions of the county of WORCESTER, 1½ mile (N. W.) from Tewkesbury; containing 334 inhabitants. The parish is situated on the river Severn, by which it is bounded on the east, and which, on the opposite bank, receives the waters of the Avon, a little above Tewkesbury, in the county of Gloucester. It comprises 1681 acres, more than two-thirds of which consist of pasture and orchards; the lands are well-wooded, and the soil fertile. The village lies a little to the north of the Tewkesbury and Ledbury road. The living is a perpetual curacy; net income, £53; patron and impropriator, J. E. Dowdeswell, Esq. The present church, consecrated in June, 1843, stands on rising ground, and is a handsome edifice of cruciform design, with a spire: the walls are built of blue stone procured in the parish; the ornamental parts are of freestone. A small school is supported by the Dowdeswell family.

BUSLINGTHORPE, a parish, in the union of CAISTOR, wapentake of LAWRESS, parts of LINDSEY, county of LINCOLN, 4 miles (S. W. by S.) from Market-Rasen; containing 50 inhabitants. The living is a discharged rectory, valued in the king's books at £2, and in the patronage of the Governors of the Charter-house, London: the tithes have been commuted for £235.

atives of the parish. There is a chalybeate spring, but in disuse.

BUTLEY, a township, in the parish of PRESTBURY, union and hundred of MACCLESFIELD, N. division of the county of CHESTER, 2¾ miles (N. by W.) from Macclesfield; containing 602 inhabitants. At the time of the Norman survey, this place, then the property of Ulluric, a Saxon free-man, was exempted, and is consequently unnoticed in Domesday book; a mark of clemency which the owner probably acquired by some signal service to the Conqueror. The township comprises 1470 acres of land, the soil of which is clay and sand. The manufacture of silk is carried on to some extent. There is a place of worship for Wesleyans, with a school attached. Some tumuli were discovered in the vicinity a few years since. This is the birthplace of Thomas Newton, a distinguished writer in the sixteenth century.

BUTLEY (ST. JOHN THE BAPTIST), a parish, in the union of PLOMESGATE, partly in the hundred of PLOMESGATE, but chiefly in that of LOES, E. division of SUFFOLK, 7¼ miles (E. by N.) from Woodbridge; containing 764 inhabitants. It is bounded on the east by a branch of the river Ore, called Butley Creek or Eye, over which are two ferries to Orford. The living is a perpetual curacy, with the living of Capel; net income, £135; patrons and impropriators, the Trustees of P. Thellusson, Esq. A priory of Black canons, dedicated to the Blessed Virgin, was founded in 1171, by Ranulph de Glanvill, a celebrated lawyer, and afterwards justiciary of England: the revenue, at the Dissolution, was £318. 17. 2. There are only some trifling remains of the buildings of the priory, but the gate-house is still in good preservation.

BUTSFIELD, a township, in the parish and union of LANCHESTER, W. division of CHESTER ward, N. division of the county of DURHAM, 11 miles (W. by N.) from Durham; containing 252 inhabitants. Two Roman aqueducts, for supplying the station at Lanchester, may be traced in the neighbourhood, particularly in the grounds belonging to Thomas White, Esq., who, on the inclosure of the common lands in 1773, purchased a part which was sold to defray the expense incurred in carrying the act of parliament into effect, and out of a barren waste succeeded in raising, in the course of a few years, the thriving and well-planted estate of Woodlands. Mr. White also built a good mansion-house, laid out pleasure-grounds and gardens, and made the neglected waters of the aqueducts supply his fishponds and reservoirs.

BUTTER-BUMP, a hamlet, in the parish of WILLOUGHBY, union of SPILSBY, Wold division of the hundred of CALCEWORTH, parts of LINDSEY, county of LINCOLN; containing 3 inhabitants.

BUTTER-CRAMBE, a chapelry, in the parish of BOSSALL, union of YORK, wapentake of BULMER, N. riding of the county of YORK, 9½ miles (N. E. by E.) from York. The chapelry comprises by computation 1500 acres, of which the soil is very productive, and the scenery pleasing and picturesque. The village is situated on the western bank of the navigable river Derwent, which is crossed by a stone bridge; and in the vicinity is Aldby Park, originally the site of a Roman station, and subsequently that of a royal Saxon ville, the summer retreat of Edwin the Great, where that prince was assaulted by an assassin whom Quichelm, King of the West

Saxons, one of Edwin's secret enemies, had suborned to murder him. The chapel is a small plain edifice. In the park, and on the banks of the Derwent, are still vestiges of the Saxon ville; and those of an old castle erected on an eminence, were visible in Camden's time.

BUTTERLAW, a township, in the parish of NEWBURN, union and W. division of CASTLE ward, S. division of NORTHUMBERLAND, 5¼ miles (N. W. by W.) from Newcastle; containing 16 inhabitants. It comprises about 240 acres, and is the property of the Duke of Northumberland.

BUTTERLEIGH, a parish, in the union of TIVERTON, forming a detached portion of the hundred of CLISTON, locally in the hundred of HAYRIDGE, Cullompton and S. divisions of DEVON, 3¼ miles (S. E. by S.) from Tiverton; containing 155 inhabitants. It is situated on the old road from Tiverton to Exeter, and comprises about 450 acres by computation. The living is a discharged rectory, valued in the king's books at £10. 8. 8., and in the gift of the Crown: the tithes have been commuted for £85 per annum, and the glebe comprises 69 acres of land. The church is a substantial edifice.

BUTTERLEY, a hamlet, in the township of RIPLEY, parish of PENTRICH, union of BELPER, hundred of MORLESTON and LITCHURCH, S. division of the county of DERBY, 3 miles (S.) from Alfreton. This hamlet lies at the north-east extremity of the township, and on the Alfreton and Derby road. Here are extensive ironworks, belonging to a company formed in 1792, and producing all the heavier articles in cast-iron, and machinery of various kinds : the ore and coal are conveyed to the spot by railways, and by the Cromford canal, which, by means of a tunnel, 2966 yards in length, passes under the works. In the neighbourhood is a reservoir covering 70 acres, for supplying the Nottingham canal. Butterley Hall is a handsome mansion, three-quarters of a mile from Ripley.

BUTTERMERE, a chapelry, in the parish of BRIGHAM, union of COCKERMOUTH, ALLERDALE ward above Derwent, W. division of CUMBERLAND, 8¼ miles (S. W. by W.) from Keswick; containing 84 inhabitants. The village lies in a deep winding valley environed by high rocky mountains, above the lake of Buttermere, noted for its char, and Crummock water, and in a district celebrated for picturesque and romantic beauty. Mines of lead and copper were formerly worked in the mountains; and many labourers are still occupied in the extensive quarries of fine blue slate in Honister Crag. The living is a perpetual curacy ; net income, £56; patron and impropriator, the Earl of Lonsdale. The chapel is a neat edifice, of modern construction.

BUTTERMERE (ST. JAMES), a parish, in the union of HUNGERFORD, hundred of KINWARDSTONE, Everley and Pewsey, and S. divisions of WILTS, 5¼ miles (S.) from Hungerford; containing 130 inhabitants. The living is a rectory, valued in the king's books at £10, and in the patronage of the Bishop of Winchester: the tithes have been commuted for £293. 10.

BUTTERSHAW.—See WIBSEY.

BUTTERTON, an ecclesiastical district, partly in the parishes of SWINNERTON and TRENTHAM, union of STONE, and partly in the parish and union of STOKE-UPON-TRENT, N. division of the hundred of PIREHILL and of the county of STAFFORD, 2½ miles (S. by W.)

461

from Newcastle-under-Lyme; containing about 300 inhabitants, of whom 56 are in Butterton township. This district lies on the road from Drayton to Newcastle; the surface is undulated, and the scenery picturesque, the land being well wooded. The living is a perpetual curacy, in the patronage of the Owners of the Butterton estate: the income is derived from 22 acres of land, and other sources. The church, a cruciform edifice in the Norman style, with a Flemish tower, was built in 1844, at an expense of £2200, entirely obtained from the Butterton estate. A national school is supported by the family.

BUTTERTON, a chapelry, in the parish of MAYFIELD, S. division of the hundred of TOTMONSLOW, N. division of the county of STAFFORD, 7 miles (E.) from Leek; containing 388 inhabitants. The river Manifold runs through the district, which comprises by computation 1300 acres: limestone is quarried, and a small quantity of gritstone; and a lead-mine is in operation. Portions of copper-ore, stalactites, fossil shells, and an ore called by the miners "brown end," convertible into zinc, are found; and there is a mineral spring strongly impregnated with sulphur. The living is a perpetual curacy; net income, £90; patron, the Vicar of Mayfield: impropriator, the Duke of Devonshire. The chapel, a neat stone edifice with a tower, was built in 1780. William Mellor, in 1754, bequeathed property now producing £16 a year, for which children are taught to read.

BUTTERWICK, a township, in the parish and union of SEDGEFIELD, N. E. division of STOCKTON ward, S. division of the county of DURHAM, 11 miles (S. E.) from Durham; containing 51 inhabitants. This place formerly belonged to the see of Durham, and in the 13th century was granted by Bishop Nicholson, under the designation of Buterwyk, to the family of Sadberge; from them the estate passed to the Hotons, and among subsequent owners occur the families of Belasyse, Yong, Baynbrigg, and Salvin. The chantry of St. Katherine in the church of Sedgefield, also had land here, which was attached to it at the period of the Dissolution. The township comprises 1495 acres. The tithes have been commuted for £113. 11. 8.

BUTTERWICK (ST. ANDREW), a parish, in the union of BOSTON, wapentake of SKIRBECK, parts of HOLLAND, county of LINCOLN, 1 mile (N. N. E.) from Bennington; containing 579 inhabitants. It is situated on the road between Boston and Wainfleet, and comprises 1766a. 26p. The living is a discharged vicarage, united in 1751 to that of Frieston, and valued in the king's books at £8. 4. 2.: the tithes have been commuted for land. There is a place of worship for Wesleyans. A grammar shool was endowed in 1665, by the Rev. Joshua Pinchbeck, with the rent of 130 acres of land, now valued at £280 per annum; besides which, there are various minor sums for the poor.

BUTTERWICK, a chapelry, in the parish of FOXHOLES, union of DRIFFIELD, wapentake of DICKERING, E. riding of YORK, 10¼ miles (N. by W.) from Great Driffield; containing 100 inhabitants. It comprises about 1645 acres, of which 1470 are arable, 95 grass, and 80 plantation: the village, which is neat, is situated on the banks of a small rivulet. The living is a perpetual curacy; net income, £47; patron, the Rector of Foxholes. The tithes were commuted for land in 1771.

In the church, which is a small ancient edifice, is a Knight Templar's monument at full length.

BUTTERWICK, a township, in the parish of BARTON-LE-STREET, union of MALTON, wapentake of RYEDALE, N. riding of YORK, 6 miles (N. W.) from Malton; containing 64 inhabitants. It is situated on the river Rye, and comprises about 500 acres of land. The tithes have been commuted for £150, and there is a glebe of 8 acres.

BUTTERWICK, EAST, a township, in the parishes of BOTTESFORD and MESSINGHAM, union of GLANDFORD-BRIGG, E. division of the wapentake of MANLEY, parts of LINDSEY, county of LINCOLN, 10¾ miles (W.) from Glandford-Brigg; containing 378 inhabitants. It comprises 604 acres; 263 acres are common or waste. The Bottesford beck and another large drain merge into the Trent at this place, and there is a ferry to West Butterwick. The village is seated on the east bank of the river. There is a place of worship for Wesleyans.

BUTTERWICK, WEST, a chapelry district, in the parish of OWSTON, union of GAINSBOROUGH, W. division of the wapentake of MANLEY, parts of LINDSEY, county of LINCOLN, 4½ miles (E. N. E.) from Epworth; containing, with the hamlet of Kelfield, 865 inhabitants. The living is a perpetual curacy; net income, £80; patron, the Vicar of Owston. The chapel is dedicated to St. Mary, and is a handsome edifice; the east windows contain ten coats of arms, executed in stained glass, of those persons by whose benevolence it was built, among whom were the Archbishop of York, the Bishop of Lincoln, the Archdeacon of Stow, and Sir Robert Sheffield. There is a place of worship for Wesleyans.

BUTTERWORTH, a township, in the parish and union of ROCHDALE, hundred of SALFORD, S. division of the county of LANCASTER, 2 miles (E. by S.) from Rochdale; containing 5088 inhabitants. The first lord of Butterworth upon record is Reginald de Bot'worth, who built the original mansion, called Butterworth Hall, in the reign of Stephen or Henry II. In Edward L's reign, Sir Baldwin Teutonicus or de Tyas, a knight of St. John of Jerusalem, and private secretary to John of Gaunt, granted all his lands in the township to Sir Robert de Holland in free marriage with his daughter Joan, who, surviving her husband, married, secondly, Sir John de Byron. The Ellands, however, as lords of Rochdale, claimed a superiority in the manor; but by an inquisition taken in the reign of Charles II., it was found that there was no manor at all. The Butterworth family resided here for several centuries. The township comprises 3752 acres, mostly pasture and moorland; 1752 are in the Freehold Side, and 2000 in the Lordship Side. Coal-mines and stone-quarries are in operation; the poor-rates are numerous, and, with bleach and calico works, afford extensive employment to the population. The Leeds and Liverpool canal, and the Manchester and Leeds railway, pass through the township.— See MILNROW.

BUTTOLPHS, a parish, in the union and hundred of STEYNING, rape of BRAMBER, W. division of SUSSEX, 1½ mile (S. E.) from Steyning; containing 48 inhabitants. The parish is bounded on the east by the navigable river Adur; and the Roman road from Bognor to Lewes probably passed near it. The living is a discharged vicarage, united to the rectory of Bramber : the church is an ancient edifice with a low embattled tower, and consisted formerly of a nave, chancel, and north aisle, which last was divided from the nave by arches, now filled up. About 1830 a considerable number of Roman bricks, tiles, and pottery, was discovered by the plough, on the downs.

BUTTSBURY (St. Mary), a parish, in the union and hundred of Chelmsford, S. division of Essex, 7 miles (S. W. by S.) from Chelmsford; containing 521 inhabitants. At the time of the Norman survey, the lands were the property of Henry de Ferrers; at present not less than seven manors are either wholly or partly within the limits of the parish. The living is a perpetual curacy, annexed to the rectory of Ingatestone : the impropriate tithes have been commuted for £323. 6. 8., and the glebe consists of 8 acres. The church is a small ancient building with a tower of stone surmounted by a shingled spire.

BUXHALL (St. Mary), a parish, in the union and hundred of Stow, W. division of Suffolk, 3¼ miles (W. by S.) from Stow-Market; containing 533 inhabitants. It is situated on the river Gipping, and comprises 2249 acres; the surface is moderately undulated, and the soil a stiff, rich, fertile clay. The living is a rectory, valued in the king's books at £20. 0. 5., and in the patronage of the family of Hill : the tithes have been commuted for £668, and the glebe comprises 39 acres. The church is a spacious and handsome structure, in the decorated English style, with a square embattled tower : there are some remains of ancient stained glass in the windows, and in the chancel are some memorials of the Hill family.

BUXTED (St. Margaret), a parish, in the union of Uckfield, hundred of Loxfield-Dorset, rape of Pevensey, E. division of Sussex, 1¾ mile (N. N. E.) from Uckfield; containing 1574 inhabitants. This parish is situated on the road from Lewes to Tonbridge-Wells, and comprises 8208 acres, of which 829 are common or waste; it abounds with sandstone and iron-stone, and it is said that the first pieces of ordnance cast in England were produced here. Buxted Park, the seat of the Earl of Liverpool, is an elegant mansion, in an ample and richly-wooded demesne. The living is a rectory, with the living of Uckfield annexed, valued in the king's books at £37. 5. 2½., and in the gift of the Archbishop of Canterbury : the tithes of Buxted have been commuted for £960, and there is a glebe of 50 acres. The church, beautifully situated within the grounds of the park, is a spacious and venerable structure in the decorated English style, with a square embattled tower surmounted by a lofty spire. A district church was erected at Hadlow Down, in 1836. There is a place of worship for Wesleyans. Dr. Saunders, rector of Buxted, in 1719 bequeathed land now producing £70 per annum, for the establishment of a free school at Uckfield, and six boys of this parish and six of Uckfield. His successors in the benefice have been eminently distinguished for their talents : of these may be noticed the Rev. William Clarke, author of a work on the connexion of the Roman, Saxon, and English coins, and his son Edward, who published Letters concerning the Russian Nation, and other productions, and who was interred here : a later rector was Dr. D'Oyly, whose successor was Dr. Wordsworth, master of Tri-

463

nity College, Cambridge, who died in 1846. That celebrated scholar Dr. W. Wotton, father-in-law of the Rev. William Clarke, lies interred in the churchyard; and the accomplished and intrepid traveller, Dr. E. D. Clarke, grandson of the Rev. William Clarke, was born, and passed his boyhood, in the parsonage-house. There are several chalybeate springs.

BUXTON, a market-town and chapelry, in the parish of Bakewell, union of Chapel-en-le-Frith, hundred of High Peak, N. division of the county of Derby, 33 miles (N. W.) from Derby, and 159 (N. W. by N.) from London, on the high road from Derby to Manchester; containing 1569 inhabitants. Antiquaries agree in considering this to have been a Roman station, although they have not been able to ascertain its name. The place was subsequently called Bawkestanes, supposed to be a corruption of Bathanstanes, signifying "the bath stones;" and one of the Roman roads noticed below still retains the appellation Batham-gate. The Romans, attracted by the temperature of the waters, constructed a bath, the wall of which, covered with red cement, and other parts, were remaining until some years ago, when they were removed to make way for improvements; and several Roman coins have been discovered. Near this spot two great military roads intersected, one connecting Little Chester and Manchester, and the other leading from Middlewich to Brough, and thence to York and Aldborough.

The town is situated near the source of the small river Wye, in a valley surrounded by bleak elevated tracts of moorland; but several plantations have been formed on the adjacent eminences, which, with other improvements, have materially altered the appearance of the immediate vicinity. The older part, occupying the high grounds, consists chiefly of houses built of limestone, without order, and of mean appearance; the more modern, situated in the vale, comprises lodging-houses and hotels, erected and fitted up with every regard to the comfort of the numerous visiters. The old Hall, built in the sixteenth century by the Earl of Shrewsbury, for several years afforded temporary accommodation to visiters of rank, and for some time was the abode of Mary, Queen of Scots, who, while in the custody of the earl, accompanied him and his countess in an excursion to this place. The house underwent considerable alteration and enlargement in 1670, and is still one of the principal hotels; it has stairs communicating directly with the natural baths. The Crescent, erected in 1781, by the Duke of Devonshire, is a fine range of building in the Grecian style, erected of gritstone obtained near the spot, fronted with freestone brought from a quarry about a mile distant. At the eastern extremity, and contiguous to the Great Hotel, hot baths have been constructed, which are supplied from Bingham's Well. The new square, nearly adjoining, has an arcade communicating with that of the Crescent, and forming a continued promenade; it contains many handsome lodging-houses, and there are others in various parts of the town. St. Anne's Well, near the Crescent, the resort of those who drink the waters, is inclosed within a building in the style of a Grecian temple : the water issues from the spring into a marble basin, and opposite to it is a double pump, by which both hot and cold water are simultaneously raised from springs lying within a few inches of each other; the hot spring has a temperature of 82° of Fahrenheit. The waters are saline, holding nitrogen gas in solution, and are efficacious in gout, rheumatism, and indigestion, and in nervous, scorbutic, and nephritic diseases : the season commences early in June, and continues generally till the end of October. There is also a chalybeate spring, the water of which is strongly impregnated with iron held in solution by acidulous gas. The environs abound with picturesque and romantic scenery, and with pleasant walks and rides : of the former is the Serpentine, beautifully wooded, following the course of the Wye ; and of the latter, the Duke's Ride, on the Bakewell road, extending over the summit of a rock called the Lover's Leap, is a favourite excursion.

The principal branch of trade consists in the manufacture and sale of many beautiful ornaments in marble, fluor-spar, alabaster, and other mineral productions of the Peak ; and a great quantity of lime, noted for its strength, is burnt to the west of the town, the workmen and their families living in huts excavated in the cinders, which cement firmly together, and become as hard as the rock itself. In the vicinity passes the Cromford and High-Peak railway ; and an act was obtained in 1846 for a railway from Stockport, by Buxton, to Ambergate, on the Midland line. The market is on Saturday ; fairs are held on Feb. 3rd, April 1st, May 2nd, and Sept. 8th, for cattle. The LIVING is a perpetual curacy ; net income, £105 ; patron, the Duke of Devonshire. A new church or chapel, an elegant structure near the town, was erected in 1812, at the expense of his Grace. There are places of worship for Independents, Wesleyans, and Unitarians. A school, now conducted on the national system, was founded towards the close of the seventeenth century, and re-opened in 1817, after a suspension of 25 years, during which period its affairs had been in chancery : the income, arising from land and property in the funds, is £80 per annum ; the school is held in an excellent room provided by the Duke of Devonshire. The Bath charity, for the benefit of poor invalids coming hither for the use of the waters, is liberally supported by subscription, and the benefit it confers is proved by the numbers who are annually claimants for its aid : in 1844 as many as 1491 persons were admitted, of whom 970 were cured or much relieved, 341 were relieved, 67 only derived no benefit, and 113 remained under cure. About three-quarters of a mile to the south-west of the town is *Pool's Hole*, a dark and dreary cavern, narrow and very low at the entrance, but lofty and presenting an exceedingly interesting appearance within, abounding with stalactites, representing various natural forms; near the extremity is a rude mass, called the Pillar of Mary, Queen of Scots, beyond which few persons advance. About one mile and a half beyond the cavern is *Diamond Hill*, so called from the detached crystals found there in profusion, denominated Buxton diamonds : their form is hexagonal, and their surface and angles well defined, but of bad colour; when first found they are hard, but they soon lose their property.

BUXTON (St. *Andrew*), a parish, in the union of AYLSHAM, hundred of SOUTH ERPINGHAM, E. division of NORFOLK, 3¼ miles (N. W.) from Coltishall ; containing 713 inhabitants. The village is pleasantly situated on the western bank of the navigable river Bure. The living is a discharged vicarage, united, with the living of Oxhead, to the rectory of Skeyton, and valued

464

in the king's books at £5. 13. 9. : the tithes of Buxton have been commuted for £256. 16., of which £145 belong to Sir E. Stracey, Bart., £12 to the Dean and Chapter of Norwich, and £99. 16. to the incumbent, who has also a glebe of 35½ acres. The church is in the later English style, and has a square embattled tower : the nave, which is lighted with clerestory windows, is separated from the chancel by the remains of a carved screen ; and on the north side of the chancel is a beautiful piscina, with stone stalls for three priests. There are places of worship for Particular Baptists and Wesleyans. Thomas Bulwer, in 1694, left £200 for the poor, which, with the bequests of Sir John Picto and others, produce about £60 per annum. This was a subordinate Roman station, and several remains have been discovered.

BWLCH, a township, in the parish of CWMYOY, union, division, and hundred of ABERGAVENNY, county of MONMOUTH ; containing 87 inhabitants. It comprises 724 acres, of which 200 are common or waste; and on the north-east is connected by a bridge over the river Munnow with the county of Hereford : the surface is undulated and well wooded, but the soil rather under the average fertility. The tithes have been commuted for £32. 2. payable to the perpetual curate of Cwmyoy, £24. 4. 9 to the incumbent of Oldcastle, and £12 14. to the incumbent of Llancillo. There are the remains of a square camp.

BYAL-FEN, an extra-parochial liberty, in the hundred of ELY, ISLE OF ELY, county of CAMBRIDGE ; containing 33 inhabitants. The tithes belonging to the crown for Byal, West, Hale, and Grunty Fens, have been commuted for £400.

BYERS-GREEN, a township, in the parish of St. ANDREW AUCKLAND, union of AUCKLAND, S. E. division of DARLINGTON ward, S. division of the county of DURHAM, 4 miles (N. N. E.) from Bishop-Auckland ; containing 489 inhabitants. It was anciently a part of the possessions of the family of Neville. The Byers-Green branch of the Clarence railway diverges from the Durham branch at Ferry Hill, about 6 miles distant, and terminates at this place. A district church dedicated to St. Peter has been built, and endowed by the Bishop of Durham, for the townships of Byers-Green and Newfield, and part of Binchester. The tithes have been commuted for £57 payable to the impropriators, £51 to the bishop, and £21 to the rector of Whitworth, and £6 to the rector of Brancepeth.

BYFIELD (Holy Cross), a parish, in the union of DAVENTRY, hundred of CHIPPING-WARDEN, S. division of the county of NORTHAMPTON, 7¼ miles (S. W. by S.) from Daventry ; containing 1079 inhabitants. The parish is situated on the borders of Warwickshire, which partly bounds it on the north ; and consists of 2962a. 16p., the surface being generally level, and the soil of full average fertility. It is crossed from south to north by the road from Banbury to Daventry. The living is a rectory, valued in the king's books at £28 ; net income, £917 ; patrons, the President and Fellows of Corpus Christi College, Oxford : the tithes were commuted for land and a. money payment in 1778.

BYFLEET (St. Mary), a parish, in the union of CHERTSEY, First division of the hundred of GODLEY, W. division of SURREY, 3 miles (W. N. W.) from Cobham ; containing 672 inhabitants. At the time of the

and ship and boat building, yards. Of these manufactures an extensive export trade is carried on, and the pottery-ware is much esteemed in the north of Europe; while the India vessels built at St. Peter's dock by Messrs. Smith, are among the finest specimens of our commercial marine. The living was formed under the 6 & 7 Victoria, c. 37, and is in the gift of the Crown and the Bishop of Durham alternately. A handsome church is about to be erected, for which a subscription has been opened, aided by grants from the Incorporated Society and the Church-Building Commissioners; and Sir M. W. Ridley, Bart., has given a site, nearly in the centre of the township. A tithe rent-charge of £80 is paid to the Bishop of Carlisle, one of £80 to the Dean and Chapter, and one of £35 to the vicar of Newcastle. There are six places of worship, nearly all belonging to the different Methodist connexions.

BYLAND-ABBEY, a township, in the parish of COXWOLD, union of HELMSLEY, wapentake of BIRDFORTH, N. riding of YORK, 7 miles (S. W. by W.) from Helmsley; containing 97 inhabitants. The township comprises 1527a. 3r. 30p., of which 444 acres are arable, 414 meadow and pasture, and 669 wood, water, and common. A monastery and church were founded here, in 1177, by the abbot and monks of Furness in Lancashire, who, having been disturbed by the Scots, fled to this part of the country, and were well received by Roger de Mowbray, at Thirsk Castle, who assigned lands at Byland for their support: at the Dissolution the revenue was estimated at £238. 9. 4. Of the abbey, which was a magnificent structure, the western front and other parts yet remain, in a high state of preservation, and afford a beautiful specimen of early English architecture: on the removal of a quantity of rubbish in the year 1818, was found a stone coffin, containing a perfect skeleton, conjectured to be that of Roger de Mowbray; and at the same time, fragments of a tessellated pavement were discovered.

BYLAND, OLD, a parish, in the union of HELMSLEY, wapentake of BIRDFORTH, N. riding of YORK, 5 miles (W. N. W.) from Helmsley; containing 185 inhabitants. The parish comprises by measurement 2200 acres of arable land, and by computation 800 acres in wood, and is chiefly of a red light soil; the aspect of the land is in many situations mountainous and wild. Freestone is quarried for building. The living is a donative; net income, £55; patron and impropriator, George Wombwell, Esq., of Newborough Park. The church is an ancient edifice with a square tower, and is supposed to have been attached to Rivaulx Abbey; the whole of the pavement is tessellated, and wrought with a variety of figures.

BYLAUGH (ST. MARY), a parish, in the union of MITFORD and LAUNDITCH, hundred of EYNSFORD, E. division of NORFOLK, 5¼ miles (N. E.) from East Dereham; containing 85 inhabitants. It comprises 1544a. 2r. 19p., of which 1100 acres are arable, 200 pasture, and 200 woodland and heath. The living is a perpetual curacy; net income, £82; patron and impropriator, E. Lombe, Esq., whose tithes have been commuted for £200. The church, which is in the later English style, with a tower circular in the lower and octangular in the upper part, was thoroughly repaired in 1809, when the chancel was rebuilt and transepts added by the late Sir John Lombe, who lies buried in the north transept.

BYLEY, with YATEHOUSE, a township, in the parish of MIDDLEWICH, union and hundred of NORTHWICH, S. division of the county of CHESTER, 1¼ mile (N. E. by N.) from Middlewich; containing 149 inhabitants. The manor of "Bively" was given by Richard de Aldford to the abbey of Pulton. After the dissolution of religious houses, it was purchased of the crown by Geffrey Shakerley, ancestor of the present family. The township comprises 1002 acres of land, the soil of which is clay. The impropriate tithes have been commuted for £128. 15. 9.

BYRNESS, a chapelry, in the parish of ELSDON, union of ROTHBURY, S. division of COQUETDALE ward, N. division of NORTHUMBERLAND, 13¾ miles (N. N. W.) from Bellingham. This place is situated on the road from Newcastle to Jedburgh, and is watered by the Rede river: coal-mines, freestone, and limestone are worked. The living is a perpetual curacy; net income, £75; patron, the Rector of Elsdon. The income is paid from Queen Anne's Bounty and the rent of 16 acres of land; there is a good glebe-house, with about 3 acres of land attached. The chapel was built by subscription, in 1793, in an ancient burial-ground; it is 34 feet long, by 22 wide, and has a very small chancel, and a porch at the west end. Here was a Druidical temple, but every vestige of it has disappeared.

BYROME, or BYRAM, with POOL, a township, in the parish of BROTHERTON, Lower division of the wapentake of BARKSTONE-ASH, W. riding of YORK, 1¾ mile (N. N. W.) from Ferry-Bridge; containing 79 inhabitants. It is situated on the east of the river Aire, and comprises by computation 850 acres, including the hamlet of Pool. Byram Hall is a handsome mansion, in a fine and well-wooded park of about 200 acres.

BYSHOTTLES, in the parish of BRANCEPETH, and county of DURHAM.—See BRANDON.

BYTHAM, CASTLE (ST. JAMES), a parish, in the union of BOURNE, wapentake of BELTISLOE, parts of KESTEVEN, county of LINCOLN, 5 miles (S. by W.) from Corby; containing, with the chapelry of Holywell with Aunby, and the hamlet of Counthorpe, 855 inhabitants. This place derives its name from an ancient castle, the origin of which is generally attributed to the Romans: it appears to have been strongly fortified; and within the foundations have been dug up, at various times, stone coffins, and other relics of antiquity. In 1080, Odo, Earl of Albemarle and Holderness, having married Adelina, sister of William the Conqueror, obtained a grant of the castle and adjoining territory for the purpose of enabling them to feed their infant son, Stephen, with wheaten bread; from which circumstance a close, constituting a part of the territory, still retains the name of "Wheaten Close."· In 1340, William de Fortibus, Earl of Albemarle, rebelling against Edward III., fortified his castle of Bytham, and plundered the surrounding country; but the castle being soon afterwards besieged by the royal forces, was taken and levelled with the ground. The living is a discharged vicarage, consolidated with the rectory of Little Bytham, and valued in the king's books at £7. 13. 6.: the tithes were commuted for land and a money payment in 1803. At Holywell is a chapel of ease. There is a place of worship for Wesleyans; and a school is partly supported by £25 per annum, from an estate belonging to the parish.

BYTHAM, LITTLE (ST. MADARDUS), a parish, i the union of BOURNE, wapentake of BELTISLOE, par of KESTEVEN, county of LINCOLN, 5 miles (S.) fro Corby; containing 311 inhabitants. The parish con prises about 1100 acres of land: Lord Willoughby Eresby is lord of the manor and chief owner of the so The village, which is ancient, is seated on an acclivit near the confluence of the river Glen with one of i tributary streams. The living is a rectory with t vicarage of Castle Bytham consolidated, valued in t king's books at £4. 8. 4., and in the alternate patrona of the Bishop and the Dean and Chapter of Lincoln; r At the inclosure in 1804, land w allotted in lieu of tithes, and 11½ acres were given for t repairs of the church.

BYTHORN (ST. LAWRENCE), a parish, in the uni of THRAPSTON, hundred of LEIGHTONSTONE, county HUNTINGDON, 6½ miles (N. W. by N.) from Kimbolto containing 322 inhabitants. It is situated on the ro from Huntingdon to Northampton, and comprises measurement 1500 acres. The living is united, wi that of Old Weston, to the rectory of Brington: t tithes have been commuted for £20. There is a pla of worship for Particular Baptists. John Mason Hus wait, in 1816, bequeathed £300, the interest of which appropriated to the teaching of children.

BYTON (ST. MARY), a parish, in the union KNIGHTON, hundred of WIGMORE, county of HER FORD, 4 miles (E. S. E.) from Presteign; containing l inhabitants. The parish comprises by measureme 847 acres, of which 359 are arable, 400 meadow, a 88 woodland: there are also about 70 acres of co mon. It is bounded on the north by the river L and intersected from north to south by the road betwe Leintwardine and Kington. The living is a discharg rectory, valued in the king's books at £5, and in t patronage of the Crown; net income, £115.

BYWELL (ST. ANDREW), a parish, in the union HEXHAM, E. division of TINDALE ward, S. division NORTHUMBERLAND; containing 452 inhabitants, whom 51 are in part of the township of Bywell, 4 mil (E. S. E.) from Corbridge, and 13½ (W. by S.) fro Newcastle-upon-Tyne. The parish is on the north a south sides of the river Tyne, and comprises the tow ships of Bearl, Broomhaugh, Riding, Stocksfield-Ha Styford, and part of Bywell; the whole forming an are by computation, of 3680 acres. It is intersected by tl road from Newcastle to Hexham; and the Newcast and Carlisle railway also passes through the paris The living is a discharged vicarage, valued in the king books at £3. 9. 2., and in the patronage of T. W. Bea mont, Esq.; impropriators, R. Trevelyan and H. Witha Esqrs. The great tithes have been commuted for £4 and the small for £100; the vicar has a glebe of acres. The church is a small edifice with a lof steeple.

BYWELL (ST. PETER), a parish, in the union HEXHAM, E. division of TINDALE ward, S. division NORTHUMBERLAND; containing 1512 inhabitants, whom 131 are in part of the township of Bywell, miles (E. S. E.) from Corbridge, and 14 (W. by S.) fro Newcastle-upon-Tyne. This parish, which is about miles in length, and from 2 to 3 in breadth, is on tl north and south sides of the Tyne, and comprises tl townships of East Acomb, Apperley, Broomley, Espe ields, High Fortherley, Healey, Newton, Newton-Hall, ewlands, and Stelling; the chapelry of Whittonstall; nd part of the township of Bywell; the whole form-ng an area, by measurement, of about 14,000 acres, of hich 7000 are arable, about 4850 pasture, and 2150 oodland. The north and north-west parts are inter-cted by the parish of Bywell St. Andrew: a portion f the land is very fertile and beautifully diversified by entle swells, and wood and water; but much consists f wild moors, of which nearly 3000 acres have been closed. The Mansion-House, the seat of Mr. Beau-ont, stands in a lawn adorned by forest-trees, having he river on its south side, with a beautiful islet, and on he opposite bank are extensive plantations. The village, hich is partly in the parish of Bywell St. Andrew, and artly in that of St. Peter, is pleasantly situated on the orth bank of the Tyne : it was formerly noted for the anufacture of saddlers' ironmongery, which was in a ourishing state in the 16th century, and is mentioned a their report by the commissioners of Queen Elizabeth; ut which has now wholly declined. The Newcastle and arlisle railway has a station here; and Mr. Beaumont as erected a handsome stone bridge of seven arches, t a cost of £10,000. The living is a vicarage, valued in he king's books at £9. 18. 1½.; net income, £119; atrons and appropriators, the Dean and Chapter of)urham, whose tithes have been commuted for £1358, nd who have a glebe of 21 acres. The church is an ncient edifice of large dimensions, with a tower, standing ear the church of St. Andrew. At Whittonstall is a eparate living. There are places of worship for Japtists, Roman Catholics, and Wesleyans. At a short istance from the Hall are the ruins of the old baronial astle of Bywell, once a very strong fortress; the fine quare tower is entire, and from its top is an extensive rospect.

C

CABOURN (St. Nicholas), a parish, in the union of Caistor, wapentake of Bradley-Haverstoe, parts of Lindsey, county of Lincoln, 1¾ mile (E. N. E.) from Caistor; containing 166 inhabitants. This parish, which s situated on the road from Caistor to Great Grimsby, and in a small vale in the heart of the Lincolnshire Wolds, omprises 2492a. 3r. 35p. of land, the subsoil of which s chalk, used for manure, and for the roads. The village is small, but from the numerous foundations of uildings in a field adjoining the vicarage, appears to ave been formerly of considerable extent. The living is a discharged vicarage, valued in the king's books at £5. 18. 4.; patron and impropriator, the Earl of Yar-orough : the income, arising from land allotted in 1811, is about £200. The church is a very ancient nassive structure with details of Norman architecture, and contains a large antique font.

CABUS, a township, in the parish and union of Garstang, hundred of Amounderness, N. division of the county of Lancaster, 2 miles (N.) from Gar-tang; containing 253 inhabitants. This place lies on the road from Garstang to Lancaster, and comprises 1323 acres of land. The Lancaster canal runs through. The court baron for Barnacre, Cabus, Cleveley, Holleth, Nateby, and Wyresdale is held here.

CADBURY (St. Michael), a parish, in the union of Tiverton, hundred of Hayridge, Cullompton and N. divisions of Devon, 8½ miles (W. by S.) from Cul-lompton; containing 251 inhabitants. It is situated on the road from Tiverton to Crediton, and comprises by computation 1697 acres, of which about 1000 are arable, 500 meadow and pasture, 72 orchard, and 136 wood-land and waste; the surface is hilly, and the soil in general light, resting upon a stony substratum. The living is a discharged vicarage, valued in the king's books at £9. 4. 3., and in the patronage of the Crown; net income, £163 ; impropriator, G. S. Farston, Esq. The benefice is endowed with half of the great tithes, and there is a good glebe-house, with five acres of land. On the summit of a high hill called Cadbury Castle, is an inclosure nearly circular, consisting of a single vallum and fosse, supposed to be either of British or of Roman origin; near it some Roman coins were found in 1827.

CADBURY, NORTH (St. Michael), a parish, in the union of Wincanton, hundred of Catsash, E. division of Somerset, 3¼ miles (S.) from Castle-Cary ; containing, with the hamlets of Galhampton and Wool-ston, 1075 inhabitants. The living is a rectory, valued in the king's books at £28. 17. 3½., and in the patronage of Emmanuel College, Cambridge : the tithes have been commuted for £489. 12. 2., and the glebe comprises 143½ acres. The church is a stately and beautiful pile, pleasantly situated on the ridge of a hill. Overlooking the village is an intrenchment of an oval form, surrounded by a large double rampart, composed of loose limestone, the produce of the spot.

CADBURY, SOUTH (St. Thomas à Becket), a parish, in the union of Wincanton, E. division of Somerset, 4½ miles (S.) from Cas-tle-Cary; containing 254 inhabitants. The living is a rectory, valued in the king's books at £10. 3. 1½., and in the patronage of James Bennett, Esq.: the tithes have been commuted for £250, and there is a glebe of 29½ acres. Near the village are the remains of one of the most famous ancient fortifications in England : it was situated on the northern extremity of a ridge of hills, and was encircled by four trenches; its figure in-clined to a square, but conforming to the slope of the hill; the area is upwards of thirty acres. A higher work within, surrounded by a trench, is called King Arthur's Palace : the rampart is composed of large stones covered with earth, with only one entrance, from the east, guarded by six or seven trenches. Numerous Roman coins have been discovered ; and the origin of the place may, with much probability, be ascribed to that people.

CADDINGTON (All Saints), a parish, in the union of Luton, partly in the hundred of Flitt, county of Bedford, but chiefly in the hundred of Dacorum, county of Hertford, 2 miles (W. S. W.) from Luton; containing 1747 inhabitants. It comprises 4515a. 2r. 27p., of which about 540 acres are meadow and pasture, 3700 arable, and 140 wood and coppice; the soil con-sists of clay, gravel, and chalk, and the timber is chiefly oak and ash. A pleasure-fair is held on Whit-Tuesday. The living is a vicarage, valued in the king's books at £10 ; net income, £319 ; patrons and appropriators, the Dean and Chapter of St. Paul's, London. The tithes were commuted for land and corn-rents in 1798, and the glebe consists of 30 acres, with a good house. In addition to the parochial church, there is a chapel of ease near Market-Street. Here is a school with an endowment.

CADEBY (*All Saints*), a parish, in the union of MARKET-BOSWORTH, hundred of SPARKENHOE, S. division of the county of LEICESTER, 1¼ mile (E. S. E.) from Market-Bosworth; containing, with the township of Osbaston, 387 inhabitants. It comprises 797a. 3p., of which about 240 acres are arable, 530 meadow and pasture, and 25 wood and plantations; part is a light soil well suited to turnips, and part good corn-land. The living is a rectory, valued in the king's books at £4. 10. 2½., and in the patronage of Sir W. W. Dixie, Bart.: the tithes have been commuted for £175, and there is a glebe-house, with 54 acres of land.

CADEBY, or CATEBY, a township, in the parish of SPROTBROUGH, union of DONCASTER, N. division of the wapentake of STRAFFORTH and TICKHILL, W. riding of YORK, 4½ miles (W. S. W.) from Doncaster; containing 153 inhabitants. The priory of Bretton and the establishment at Nostal held lands here; and among the families that have possessed property, occurs that of Metham, who settled at Cadeby about the reign of Edward II., and continued to hold it in the time of Elizabeth. The township is situated in the south part of the parish, and upon the river Don, opposite to Conisbrough, with which place it is connected by the King's ferry.

CADELEIGH (*St. Bartholomew*), a parish, in the union of TIVERTON, hundred of HAYRIDGE, Cullompton and N. divisions of DEVON, 4¼ miles (S. W.) from Tiverton; containing 403 inhabitants. The living is a rectory, valued in the king's books at £13, and in the patronage of Mrs. Moore: the tithes have been commuted for £193, and the glebe consists of 53 acres, with a house. In the church is a curious ancient monument to the memory of Sir Simon Leach, Knt.

CADLEY.—See SAVERNAKE-FOREST.

CADNAM, a hamlet, partly in the parish of ELING, hundred of REDBRIDGE, and partly in the parish of MINSTEAD, N. division of the hundred of NEW FOREST, Romsey and S. divisions of the county of SOUTHAMPTON, 4½ miles (N.) from Lyndhurst; containing 154 inhabitants. A chapel of ease to Eling was erected a few years since; and there is a place of worship for Wesleyans.

CADNEY (*All Saints*), a parish, in the union of GLANDFORD-BRIGG, S. division of the wapentake of YARBOROUGH, parts of LINDSEY, county of LINCOLN, 2¾ miles (S. S. E.) from Glandford-Brigg; containing, with the township of Housham, 438 inhabitants. The living is a discharged vicarage, valued in the king's books at £7. 18. 4.; net income, £230; patron and impropriator, the Earl of Yarborough. In the church are a beautiful screen of carved oak, and a font of great antiquity noticed by Camden. A farmhouse in the parish, called Newstead Abbey, was a priory of Cistercian monks.

CAENBY (*St. Nicholas*), a parish, in the E. division of the wapentake of ASLACOE, parts of LINDSEY, union and county of LINCOLN, 3 miles (E. by S.) from Spital; containing 185 inhabitants. The parish lies upon a slope, and comprises about 1600 acres, two-thirds of which are arable, 50 acres wood, and the rest

re conveyed to Newport by the river, in vessels of small urthen. The market is on Thursday; and fairs are eld on July 31st and October 2nd, the latter being a rge fair for horses. The market-house is a dilapidated difice, supported on four massive pillars of the Tuscan rder, which are supposed to have belonged to some loman structure, two bases of similar dimensions and haracter having been dug up near the walls. The ounty magistrates hold a petty-session once a fortight. There are places of worship for Baptists, Indeendents, and Wesleyans; and a free school for 25 oys and 25 girls, founded and endowed in 1724, by harles Williams, Esq. Several remains of the Roman tation are still visible, and numerous minor relics have een discovered, consisting of parts of columns, altars, ssellated pavements, coins, urns, a statue of Jupiter, ortions of the baths, &c. To the north of the town is n extensive quadrilateral encampment, with seven maller camps near it; and on the banks of the Usk are onsiderable remains of the amphitheatre, called by the nhabitants King Arthur's Round Table. St. Amphialus, tutor of the proto-martyr St. Albanus; and the nartyrs St. Julian and St. Aaron, were born at this lace. The renowned King Arthur is stated to have een interred here.

CAERTON-ULTRA-PONTEM, a hamlet, in the parish f CHRISTCHURCH, union of NEWPORT, Lower division f the hundred of CALDICOT, county of MONMOUTH; ontaining 267 inhabitants.

CAER-WENT (ST. STEPHEN), a parish, in the union nd division of CHEPSTOW, hundred of CALDICOT, ounty of MONMOUTH, 5½ miles (W. S. W.) from Cheptow, on the road to Newport; containing, with the amlet of Crick, 446 inhabitants. The parishes of Caervent and Llanvair-Discoed comprise by estimation 736a. 7p., of which 953a. 1r. are arable, 511a. 20p. asture and meadow, and 271a. 2r. 27p. woodland: for he most part, the surface is level, and the soil dry and ravelly. Caer-went, now an inconsiderable village, was nciently a Roman station, the *Venta Silurum* of Antoinus' Itinerary, and is supposed to have been the site f the capital city of the Britons in Siluria: it is still artially environed by the original Roman walls, inclosng an area about a mile in circumference. The turnike-road to Newport, the course of which here runs pon part of the Akeman-street, passes through the entre, where formerly stood the eastern and western ates; and coins, fragments of columns, statues, and ome beautiful tessellated pavements, belonging to the lomans, have been discovered. The village is pleasantly ituated upon ground somewhat elevated above the level ract around it; and at a small distance are the magnicent remains of Caldicot Castle, formerly possessed by he Bohuns, earls of Hereford. The living is a discharged vicarage, endowed with the rectorial tithes, and vith the perpetual curacy of Llanvair-Discoed annexed; t is valued in the king's books at £7. 11. 8., and is in he gift of the Dean and Chapter of Llandaff: the tithes lave been commuted for £249. 2., and the glebe comrises 6 acres, with a house attached. The church, conisting of a nave and chancel, with a square embattled ower, exhibits portions of the early and decorated English styles. There is a place of worship for Particular 3aptists. At Crick is a house, now a farm residence, in vhich King Charles was concealed for some time.

CAINHAM (ST. MARY), a parish, in the union of LUDLOW, hundred of STOTTESDEN, S. division of SALOP, 3 miles (E. S. E.) from Ludlow; containing 973 inhabitants. The parish is situated on the road from Leominster to Bridgnorth, and comprises by computation 2700 acres, in equal portions of arable and pasture, with numerous orchards : the river Letwytch, celebrated for fine trout, crosses its southern extremity. Stone is quarried for drains and buildings; and coal-mines, limeworks, and iron-foundries, are in operation. The living is a discharged vicarage, valued in the king's books at £4. 13. 4.; net income, £338; patron and incumbent, the Rev. J. Mainwaring; impropriators, the landowners. There is a glebe-house, with 120 acres of land. The church is ancient; in the churchyard is a cross. A church was consecrated in 1840, to which an ecclesiastical district called St. Paul's, Knowbury, has been assigned. There is a place of worship for Wesleyans; also a Sunday school. The remains of a Roman encampment are visible.—See KNOWBURY.

CAIN'S-CROSS, a hamlet, partly in the parish of STROUD, hundred of BISLEY, and partly in the parishes of STONEHOUSE and RANDWICK, hundred of WHITSTONE, E. division of the county of GLOUCESTER, 2 miles (W.) from Stroud. A district church, dedicated to St. Matthew, erected at an expense of £3600, raised chiefly by subscription, was consecrated on the 29th of January, 1837. The living is a perpetual curacy, in the patronage of Colonel Daubeny, who endowed it with £1000, vested in the funds; the district comprises the villages of Cain's Cross, Ebley, Westrip, Dudbridge, and Pakenhill.

CAISTOR, or CASTOR (ST. PETER AND ST. PAUL), a market-town and parish, and the head of a union, partly in the N. division of the wapentake of WALSHCROFT, but chiefly in the S. division of the wapentake of YARBOROUGH, parts of LINDSEY, county of LINCOLN, 23 miles (N. N. E.) from Lincoln, and 153 (N.) from London; comprising the chapelries of Holton-le-Moor and Clixby, and the hamlets of Audleby, Fonaby, and Hundon; and containing 1988 inhabitants. This was evidently a station of the Romans, of whom numerous coins and other relics have been discovered. According to tradition, Hengist, after having repulsed the Picts and Scots, obtained from Vortigern the grant of so much land as he could encompass with the hide of an ox : having divided the hide into small thongs, he was enabled to inclose a considerable area, forming the site of the town, which, from that circumstance, was called by the Saxons *Thuang Ceastre* or *Thong Ceastre*. Dr. Stukeley, however, derives the prefix from the Saxon *thegn*, a thane or nobleman. The marriage of Rowena, daughter of Hengist, to Vortigern, was solemnised here in 453. Egbert, who finally brought the several kingdoms of the heptarchy under his dominion, obtained a signal victory at this place over Wiglof, King of Mercia, in 827 ; in commemoration of which a cross was erected on the castle hill, where many bodies have been dug up, and a stone with a mutilated inscription, apparently recording the dedication of the spoils by the victor to some sacred purpose.

The TOWN, which commands extensive prospects over the vale of the Ancholme and the western ridges of the Wolds, is well supplied with water from four springs issuing out of a grey-stone rock, three of which unite their streams on the western side of it, and fall into the Ancholme ; the other flows into the same river near the junction of the Kelsey canal with that to Glandford-Brigg. Its market is on Saturday ; and fairs are held on the Saturdays before Palm-Sunday, Whit-Sunday, and Old Michaelmas-day. The town is within the jurisdiction of the county magistrates : the powers of the county debt-court of Caistor, established in 1847, extend over the sub-registration-district of Caistor. The parish comprises an area of 3220a. 3r. 28p. of land, including Caistor moor, which extends three miles west, and was inclosed in 1798 ; the soil is partly sandy, generally fertile, and well cultivated. The LIVING is a discharged vicarage, with the living of Clixby annexed, valued in the king's books at £7. 6. 8., and in the gift of the Prebendary of Caistor in the Cathedral of Lincoln, with a net income of £250. The tithes of Caistor were commuted at the inclosure for 91 acres of land to the impropriator, and 80 acres to the vicar ; but the hamlets of Audleby, Fonaby, and Hundon pay a yearly modus of £252. 7. to the former, and one of £180 to the latter. The church is a spacious structure in the early English style, with some remains of Norman architecture : it has a fine tower, with a chapel on the south side, now used as a vestry-room ; and stands within the area of the ancient castle, with the materials of which it is partly built. A singular ceremony has been long observed, on the performance of which is said to depend the tenure of an estate in the parish of Broughton. The holder sends an agent on Palm-Sunday, who cracks a whip three times in the north porch of the church, while the minister is reading the first lesson ; after which, attaching a small purse to the thong, he enters the church, and on the commencement of the second lesson, flourishes the whip thrice, and on the conclusion of it retires into the chancel : when the service is ended, the whip and purse are deposited in the manor-house at Hundon. The ceremony, however, was not observed in the year 1847. There are places of worship for Independents and Methodists. The free grammar school was founded in 1630, by the Rev. Francis Rawlinson, who endowed it with £400, afterwards laid out in the purchase of a portion of the great tithes of Beesby, now producing £130 per annum ; besides which there are £60 a year, arising from land bought with a donation by Wm. Hansard, Esq. The school has an exhibition of £10 per annum to Jesus College, Cambridge : the building was thoroughly repaired in 1838, at a cost of £200, raised by subscription. The poor law union of Caistor comprises 76 parishes or places, and contains a population of 27,068.

CAISTOR (ST. EDMUND's), a parish, in the union and hundred of HENSTEAD, E. division of NORFOLK, 3½ miles (S.) from Norwich ; containing 147 inhabitants. This place, though at present inconsiderable, was one of the most flourishing cities of the Britons, and the residence of the kings of the Iceni ; it was also the *Venta Icenorum* of the Romans, and the principal station of that people in the territory of the Iceni, from the ruins of which the present city of Norwich gradually rose. The walls of the ancient city, which was deserted after the departure of the Romans in 446, were in the form of a parallelogram, inclosing an area of about 32 acres, within which foundations of buildings may be traced. The remains consist of a single fosse and val-
470

lum, and were surrounded by a strong wall as an additional rampart, built upon the vallum, the inclosed space being capable of containing 6000 men. On the north, east, and south sides, are large mounds raised from the fosse, and the west side has one formed on the margin of the river Taas, as are also the remains of the Water-Gate. Within the area of the camp, at the south-east angle, stands the church, the materials for building which were evidently taken from the ruins of the rampart. The parish comprises about 1045 acres : the river Taas, which once filled the whole valley, is now an inconsiderable stream. The living is a rectory, with that of Merkshall or Mattishall-Heath united, valued in the king's books at £9, and in the patronage of Mrs. H. Dashwood : the tithes have been commuted for £445, and the glebe comprises 58½ acres, with a house. The church is partly in the early style, with a square embattled tower, and has a font exhibiting very curious sculpture.

CAISTOR NEAR YARMOUTH (ST. EDMUND), a parish, in the EAST and WEST FLEGG incorporation, hundred of EAST FLEGG, E. division of NORFOLK, 19½ miles (E.) from Norwich ; containing 909 inhabitants. The name is a corrupted Saxonism of *Castrum* ; it being clear, from the visible remains of fortifications, and the discovery of numerous coins, that the Romans had a camp here, opposite to, and connected with, *Garianonum.* The manor was anciently in the possession of the family of Fastolf ; and Sir John Fastolf, a celebrated warrior and an estimable man, whose character some consider Shakspeare to have pervertedly drawn in his Sir John Falstaff, was born here. He was the founder of the castle, the cost of which was defrayed with money obtained for the ransom of the Duke d'Alençon, whom he had taken prisoner at the battle of Agincourt ; it was supposed to be one of the oldest brick mansions in the kingdom, and was a castellated edifice in the form of a parallelogram, of which nothing now remains, except a circular tower about 90 feet high, with portions of the north and west walls. Eastward of the castle stood a college, forming three sides of a spacious square, with two circular towers ; it was established in the reign of Edward I. by one of the Fastolfs, and afterwards patronized by the founder of the castle, and his successors, till its dissolution : the remains have been converted into stables and a barn. Caistor was formerly in two parishes, Trinity and St. Edmund's, which were consolidated September 22nd, 1608 ; the church belonging to the former has been suffered to fall into ruins. The living is a rectory, valued in the king's books at £10 ; net income, £875 ; patron and incumbent, the Rev. G. W. Steward, who lately erected a handsome glebe-house. The church is chiefly in the decorated style, and consists of a nave, chancel, and south aisle, with a square embattled tower. The Wesleyans and Primitive Methodists have places of worship. The sum of £105, the rental of land devised by Elizabeth Blennerhaysett, Sir William Paston, and others, is annually applied in relief for the poor. A line of sand-hills called the *Meals* or *Marum Hills*, commences here, and extends, with occasional interruptions, to Hapsbury Point, and thence to Cromer bay.

CAISTRON, a township, in the parish and union of ROTHBURY, W. division of COQUETDALE ward, N. division of NORTHUMBERLAND, 4½ miles (W.) from Rothbury ; containing 54 inhabitants. This pleasant village, around which is a fertile alluvial soil, is situated on the brink of the Coquet, one mile south-by-west from Flotterton. It was formerly the property of three persons of the name of Hall, called respectively in the neighbourhood, duke, lord, and lawyer, and one of whom bequeathed, in 1779, the annual sum of £4. 15. to be paid out of his estate towards the support of a schoolmaster in the place. A school-house was erected in 1792, with money left by the Rev. John Tomlinson and others.

CAKEMORE, a township, in the parish of HALES-OWEN, union of STOURBRIDGE, Upper division of the hundred of HALFSHIRE, Hales-Owen and E. divisions of WORCESTERSHIRE ; containing 357 inhabitants. This place, which was until lately in the county of Salop, is situated on the borders of Staffordshire, and north-east of the town of Hales-Owen.

CALBOURN (ALL SAINTS), a parish, in the liberty of WEST MEDINA, Isle of Wight division of the county of SOUTHAMPTON, 5¼ miles (W. S. W.) from Newport; containing, with the chapelry of Newton, 750 inhabitants. The parish derives its name from the beautiful stream by which it is intersected : it comprises 5370 acres, whereof 200 are common or waste ; the surface is varied, and the scenery abounds with interest. Stone of very durable quality is extensively quarried for building purposes, for which it is in great repute. The living is a rectory, valued in the king's books at £19. 12. 8½., and in the patronage of the Bishop of Winchester : the tithes have been commuted for £660, and the glebe comprises 80½ acres. The church is a handsome structure in the early English style, and contains an ancient tomb, inlaid with brass, representing a knight in complete armour, with his feet resting on a dog ; considerable improvements were lately made. Dr. Fisher, Bishop of Salisbury, was a native of the parish, of which his father was rector.

CALCEBY (ST. ANDREW), a parish, in the union of SPILSBY, Marsh division of the hundred of CALCE-WORTH, parts of LINDSEY, county of LINCOLN, 4¾ miles (W.) from Alford; containing 52 inhabitants. This parish is situated on the road from Wainfleet to Great Grimsby, and comprises about 618 acres ; it lies towards the southern extremity of the chalk formation of the county, of which a bold line of bills in the neighbouring parish of Drily forms part of the eastern escarpment towards the sea. The living is a discharged vicarage, united, in 1774, to the rectory of South Ormsby, and valued in the king's books at £5. 10. 2¼. ; impropriator, C. B. Massingberd, Esq.

CALCETHORPE (ST. FAITH), a parish, in the union of LOUTH, Wold division of the hundred of LOUTH-ESKE, parts of LINDSEY, county of LINCOLN, 6 miles (W. by N.) from Louth ; containing 69 inhabitants. It comprises by computation 1100 acres, which are all arable, with the exception of 150 acres of grass land. The living is a sinecure rectory, valued in the king's books at £6. 2. 6. ; net income, £16 ; patron, W. Briscoe, Esq. The church is a ruin.

CALCUTT, a hamlet, in the parish of LOWER HEY-FORD, union of BICESTER, hundred of PLOUGHLEY, county of OXFORD ; containing 146 inhabitants.

CALDBECK (ST. KENTIGERN), a parish, in the union of WIGTON, ALLERDALE ward below Derwent W. division of CUMBERLAND; containing 1553 inha-

bitants, of whom 282 are in High, 646 in Low, and 567 in Haltcliffe, Caldbeck ; 8 miles (S. E.) from Wigton. This parish comprises a mountainous tract of 18,000 acres, not more than 6000 of which are inclosed, the remainder being appropriated to pasturing numerous flocks of sheep. The hills contain various mineral productions, principally lead and copper ores, limestone, and coal ; and there are several establishments for working the mines : a considerable proportion of silver is occasionally extracted from the lead-ore. The river Caldbeck flows through the village, about half a mile from which, in a romantic glen called the Howk, where is a natural bridge of limestone, the stream dashes impetuously over rocks, and forms two interesting cascades, by the sides of which are singular excavations named the Fairies' Kirk and Fairies' Kettle. A manufactory for blankets, flannels, &c., has been long established ; and there are a brewery, a small paper-mill, a fulling-mill, a gingham and check manufactory, and a dye-house. Hesket-Newmarket, in the division of Haltcliffe, is a smaller village, but more compact than Caldbeck, from which it is about a mile and a quarter distant to the east ; it is situated on the south side of the river Caldew, which divides this parish from that of Castle-Sowerby. The living is a rectory, valued in the king's books at £45. 13. 6¼.; net income, £436 ; patron, the Bishop of Carlisle. The church bears date 1112, and was founded soon after the establishment of an hospital for travellers, by the prior of Carlisle, with the permission of Ranulph D'Engain, chief forester of Inglewood : it stands in the township of Low Caldbeck, and was new roofed and greatly embellished in 1818. There are three meeting-houses for the Society of Friends, who settled here in the time of George Fox, their founder, who resided for some time at Woodhall; but their number, although formerly considerable, is now reduced to a few families. Robert Sewell, a natural philosopher of considerable repute, was a native of the parish.—See HESKET-NEW-MARKET.

CALDBRIDGE, a township, in the parish of Co-VERHAM, union of LEYBURN, wapentake of HANG-WEST, N. riding of YORK, 3¼ miles (S. W.) from Middleham ; containing 95 inhabitants. This place, also named Caldberg, comprises 2724 acres, of which 2300 are common or waste ; and includes the hamlet of East or Little Scrafton, which occupies the acclivities on the east of the river Cover. Lead-ore is obtained, in small quantity, on the moors that adjoin Witton Fell. Here is a well called St. Simon's, formerly in great estimation, but the properties of which are unknown ; and it is probable that the monks of Coverham, who had land here, valued at £7. 13. 4. per annum, possessed near this well an oratory, designated St. Simon's chapel. The tithes have been commuted for £15.

CALDECOT (VIRGIN MARY), a parish, in the union of SWAFFHAM, hundred of SOUTH GREENHOE, W. division of NORFOLK, 4 miles (N. E.) from Stoke-Ferry ; containing 48 inhabitants, and comprising about 640 acres. The living is a discharged sinecure rectory, valued in the king's books at £3. 1. 10¼.; net income, £6 ; patron and impropriator, Sir H. R. P. Bedingfield, Bart. The church has been in ruins upwards of a century and a half, and the village has disappeared.

CALDECOTE (ST. MICHAEL), a parish, in the union of CAXTON and ARRINGTON, hundred of LONGSTOW, county of CAMBRIDGE, 4 miles (E. by S.) from Caxton; containing 117 inhabitants. The living is a discharged vicarage, annexed to the rectory of Toft, and valued in the king's books at £3. 11. 0½.: the tithes have been commuted for £69. A school, built by subscription, is endowed with £18 per annum left by a late rector.

CALDECOTE (ST. DAVID AND ST. CHAD), a parish, in the union of NUNEATON, Atherstone division of the hundred of HEMLINGFORD, N. division of the county of WARWICK, 1½ mile (N. N. W.) from Nuneaton; containing 93 inhabitants. The parish comprises by measurement 668 acres of excellent land, in equal portions of arable and pasture : the surface is level, and is intersected by the river Anker and the Coventry canal. On the north-east the parish is bounded by the Watling-street, which separates it from Leicestershire; and on the south-west by the road between Nuneaton and Atherstone. The living is a discharged rectory, valued in the king's books at £6. 15., and in the gift of Kirkby Fenton, Esq. : the tithes have been commuted for £170. The church is an ancient edifice with a tower, and contains monuments to the Purefoy family. In 1647, George Abbot bequeathed land, directing the annual produce, about £4. 10., to be expended in teaching children.

CALDECOTT, a township, in the parish of SHOCK-LACH, union of GREAT BOUGHTON, Higher division of the hundred of BROXTON, S. division of the county of CHESTER, 5½ miles (N. W.) from Malpas; containing 69 inhabitants. The river Dee flows on the west of this township, which comprises 595 acres of land. The soil is clay.

CALDECOTT (ST. MARY MAGDALENE), a parish, in the union of HITCHIN, hundred of ODSEY, county of HERTFORD, 3½ miles (N. by W.) from Baldock; containing 41 inhabitants. It comprises by measurement 319 acres, chiefly arable. The living is a discharged rectory, valued in the king's books at £8, and in the patronage of W. Hale, Esq. : the tithes have been commuted for £70, and the glebe comprises 14 acres. In the year 1724, several Roman urns containing burnt bones and ashes, were discovered.

CALDECOTT, a hamlet, in the parish of CHELVES-TON, union of THRAPSTON, hundred of HIGHAM-FER-RERS, N. division of the county of NORTHAMPTON; containing 101 inhabitants.

CALDECOTT, a chapelry, in the parish of LID-DINGTON, union of UPPINGHAM, hundred of WRANDIKE, county of RUTLAND, 4¾ miles (S.) from Uppingham; containing 260 inhabitants. The Welland, which here separates the county from Northamptonshire, and the small river Eye, flow through the chapelry; which comprises 1089 acres of, in general, good land. The chapel is dedicated to St. John.

CALDER-BRIDGE, a hamlet, in the parish of BECKERMET, ST. BRIDGET, union of WHITEHAVEN, ALLERDALE ward above Derwent, W. division of CUM-BERLAND, 5 miles (S. E.) from Egremont. This place owes its origin and name to a bridge over the river Calder; and is celebrated for the remains of an abbey founded for Cistercian monks, by Ralph de Meschines, second earl of Chester and Cumberland, in ˙1134' in honour of the Virgin Mary, and the revenue of which, at the suppression, was £64. 3. 9. The beautiful ruins are situated in a sequestered and well-wooded vale, and

nother entrance, through a fine hexagonal tower with machicolated battlement. Within are the ruins of everal apartments, particularly the baronial hall. At he northern angle is a circular tower on a mound of arth, evidently the keep, encircled by a ditch; and nother dilapidated circular tower stands at the southern ngle : the whole is still surrounded by a moat.

CALDICOTE (*St. Mary Magdalene*), a parish, in he union of Peterborough, hundred of Norman-'ross, county of Huntingdon, 1¼ mile (W. S. W.) from tilton; containing 52 inhabitants. It is situated on he great road from London to York. The living is discharged rectory, valued in the king's books at :7. 3. 6.; present net income, £156; patron, William Vells, Esq.

CALDICOTT, a hamlet, in the parish of Northill, undred of Wixamtree, county of Bedford, 1½ mile N. W. by N.) from Biggleswade; containing 509 inha- itants, of whom 270 are in Upper, and 239 in Lower, aldicott.

CALDWELL, a township, in the parish of Stan- rick St. John, union of Richmond, wapentake of rilling-West, N. riding of York, 5¼ miles (E.) from rreta-Bridge; containing 209 inhabitants. This was rrmerly a place of much greater importance than it is t present. The township comprises by computation 000 acres, the soil of which is light and fertile: the 'ees flows on the north, at the distance of about three riles from the village. A chapel of ease has been built. . Roman military road passed through the township; nd a variety of coins have been found in the vicinity.

CALKE, Derby.—See Caulk.

CALKERTON, a tything, in the parish of Rod- iarton, union of Cirencester, hundred of Long- ree, E. division of the county of Gloucester; con- aining 145 inhabitants.

CALLALEY, with Yetlington, a township, in the arish of Whittingham, union of Rothbury, N. divi- ion of Coquetdale ward and division of Northumberland, 0½ miles (W. by S.) from Alnwick; containing 306 in- abitants, and comprising 3610 acres, of which 450 are ommon or waste. This place anciently gave name to s possessors; and was granted, by Gilbert de Callaley, 1 the reign of Henry III., to Robert Fitz-Roger, Baron f Warkworth and Clavering, an ancestor of the present amily of Clavering, one of the most ancient in the ounty. Callaley Castle, their residence, stands in a rge and beautiful park, and the scenery around is truly icturesque. Attached is a place of worship for Roman 'atholics. The village of Yetlington is three and a half riles west-south-west of Whittingham. On Castle Hill, conical eminence embosomed in woods, is a circular ntrenchment with vestiges of buildings, denoting a British or Saxon position.

CALLERTON, BLACK, a township, in the parish f Newburn, union and W. division of Castle ward, 3. division of Northumberland, 6¼ miles (N. W.) from Newcastle-upon-Tyne; containing 158 inhabitants. It is situated not far distant from the road between New- astle and Rothbury, and 3½ miles north-by-east from Newburn; and comprises 1377 acres, of which 1145 are rable, 197 meadow, 15 plantation, and 18 road. The ectorial tithes of the township have been commuted for yearly rent-charge of £220, and for the vicarial a mo- us of £6 is paid.

CALLERTON, HIGH, a township, partly in the parish of Ponteland, and partly in that of Newburn, union and W. division of Castle ward, S. division of Northumberland, 7½ miles (N. W.) from Newcastle- upon-Tyne; containing 131 inhabitants. It comprises by computation 989 acres: the village stands a consider- able distance south of the church of Ponteland. The tithes have been commuted for £116. 1. 8. payable to Merton College, Oxford, and £11 to the vicar of Ponte- land. Lady's Land, in the township, consisting of about eight acres, belongs to Morpeth free school.

CALLERTON, LITTLE, or LOW, a township, in the parish of Ponteland, union and W. division of Castle ward, S. division of Northumberland, 7¾ miles (N. W. by W.) from Newcastle-upon-Tyne; containing 34 inha- bitants. It is situated on the Pont, and comprises 573 acres, of which 380 are arable, 150 pasture, and 43 wood and water: the soil is a strong clay, suitable for the culture of wheat. The tithes have been commuted for £77 payable to Merton College, Oxford, and £10 to the vicar of the parish.

CALLINGTON (*St. Mary*), a market-town and parish, and formerly a borough, in the union of Lis- keard, Middle division of the hundred of East, E. division of Cornwall, 10½ miles (S. by E.) from Laun- ceston, 14 (N.) from Plymouth, and 213 (W. S. W.) from London; containing 1685 inhabitants. This town, an- ciently called *Calweton, Calvington*, and *Killington*, is situated on a gentle acclivity, and consists principally of two spacious streets; the houses are in general of mean appearance, and irregularly built, but the town is paved, and amply supplied with water. The inhabit- ants had a considerable trade in wool, which has of late declined: mining is carried on to some extent, there being several copper-mines in operation, the chief of which are those at Holm-bush and Redmoor, the former employing more than 100 persons; and in the vicinity are also some manganese mines. The market days are Wednesday and Saturday, of which the former is for corn and provisions, and the latter for meat only; and a cattle-market is held on the first Wednes- day in every month. An excellent market-place has been opened, together with a corn-market 90 feet long, by the present lord of the manor, Lord Ashburton; it is a very commodious building, ornamented with a colon- nade round it, supported on granite pillars. The fairs, chiefly for cattle and sheep, are on the first Thursday in May and September, and the first Wednesday and Thursday in November. The county magistrates hold a petty-session on the first Thursday in every month; and a portreeve and other officers for the town are appointed annually at the court leet of the lord of the manor. The court-house, a commodious edifice, was built by Lord Clinton. The borough received the elective franchise in the 27th of Elizabeth, from which time it continued to return two members of parliament, till it was disfranchised by the act of the 2nd of William IV., cap. 45. The parish comprises 2235 acres, of which 607 are common or waste. The living is a perpetual curacy, annexed to the rectory of South-Hill: the glebe comprises 50 acres. The church, a spacious structure containing three aisles, and constructed entirely of granite, was chiefly built at the expense of Nicholas de Asheton, one of the judges of the court of king's bench, who died in 1645, and to whose memory a marble tomb is·in the chancel : in the churchyard is the, shaft of an ancient cross, on the upper part of which is a representation of the Crucifixion. There are places of worship for Independents and Wesleyans ; and·a school erected by subscription, which is highly ornamental to the eastern and southern entrances to the town.

. CALLOW, a hamlet, in the parish and hundred of WIRKSWORTH, S. division of the county of DERBY, 2½ miles (S. W.) from Wirksworth ; containing 112 inhabitants. It comprises about 1000 acres of land, and has a small village. Callow Hall was an ancient moated mansion of considerable extent, of which a small portion remains, occupied as a farmhouse ; the moat and part of the bridge are still visible. ~The rectorial tithes have been commuted for £154.

CALLOW (St. MICHAEL), a parish, in the hundred of WEBTREE, union and county of HEREFORD, 4 miles (S. S. W.) from Hereford ; containing .171 inhabitants. It is situated on the road from· Hereford to Ross, and comprises by measurement 582 acres ; the surface is moderately undulated and well wooded, and the soil is nearly of average fertility. The living is a perpetual curacy, endowed with the rectorial tithes, and annexed to the vicarage of Dewsall ; 22 acres of land are tithe-free, having belonged to the fraternity of St. John of Jerusalem. The tithes havé been commuted for £86. 2. 10.; in addition to which, £12 a year are received from fourteen acres of land, purchased a few years ago, with an allowance from Queen Anne's Bounty. The church is pleasantly situated on the summit of a hill overlooking, at a short distance, the high road ; it was rebuilt about the year 1831. The rent of four acres of land bought with £100 bequeathed by Henry Pearle, Esq., a native, is given to the poor on St. Thomas's day, when a distribution is also made of the interest of £80 in the savings' bank at Hereford, the produce of timber cut down on the land a few years since. There are the remains of two Roman camps.

CALMSDEN, a tything, in the parish of NORTH CERNEY, hundred of RAPSGATE, E. division of the county of GLOUCESTER, 5¼ miles (N. N. E.) from Cirencester ; containing 65 inhabitants.

Corporation Seal.

CALNE (St. MARY), a borough, market-town, and parish, and the head of a union, in the hundred of CALNE, Chippenham and Calne, and N. divisions of WILTS, 30 miles (N. N. W.) from Salisbury, and 87 (W. by S.) from London, on the road to Bath and Bristol ; comprising the tythings of Blackland, Calstone, East-mead-Street, Quemerford, Stock, Stockley, Studley, Whetham, and Whitley ; and containing 5128 inhabitants, of whom 2483 are in the borough. This place is of very remote origin, and is supposed to have risen from the ruins of a Roman station on the opposite side of the river, near Studley, where numerous Roman antiquities have been 'discovered. It is said by tradition to have been the residence of the West Saxon monarchs ; but no vestiges exist of their palace or castle, the remembrance of which, is preserved only in the name· of a field· thought to have

been its site, and of· a street which probably led to it, A synod was assembled here in 977, for adjusting the differences then prevailing between the monks and the secular clergy, at which Dunstan, Archbishop of Canterbury, presided. During the controversy the floor of the chamber gave way, and several of the secular priests were killed ; but Dunstan, and the monks whose cause he advocated, escaped unhurt ; their preservation was regarded as a miraculous interposition of Heaven, and they were allowed to take immediate possession of the religious houses throughout the kingdom, to the exclusion of the secular clergy.

The TOWN consists principally of one long street, lighted with gas ; the houses are in general well built of stone, and the inhabitants are amply supplied with water from springs, and from the river Marden, which, after passing through the town, falls into the Avon. It has been much improved under the auspices of the Marquess of Lansdowne, whose extensive and stately mansion is in the adjoining liberty of Bowood ; and the environs abound with pleasing scenery. The woollen-manufacture, formerly carried on to a great extent, is now conducted on a very limited scale ; the articles are principally broad-cloth, kerseymere, and serge. A branch of the Wilts and Berks canal comes up to the town, and, uniting with the Kennet and Avon canal, and with the Thames at Abingdon, affords a facility of communication with London, Bristol, and the intermediate places. The market is on Wednesday ; and fairs are held on May 6th and September 29th, for cattle and sheep. The CORPORATION formerly consisted of two guild stewards, and an indefinite number of free burgesses, who annually appointed two constables ; but the government is now vested in a mayor, four aldermen, and twelve councillors, under the act of the 5th and 6th of William IV., cap. 76. The borough first sent members to parliament in the 23rd of Edward I. ; from that time it made irregular returns until the reign of Richard II., after which it uninterruptedly returned two members ; but, by the act of the 2nd of William IV., cap. 45, the number was reduced to one. The right of election, formerly in the members of the corporation, was, by the above act, extended to the £10 householders of the borough, the limits of which were increased from 800 to 8080 acres : the mayor is returning-officer. The powers of the county debt-court of Calne, established in 1847, extend over the registration-district of Calne. The town-hall is a neat and commodious building, erected by the lord of the manor, and has been repaired, and an upper story added, by the Marquess of Lansdowne ; the lower part is used as a market-place.

The LIVING is a vicarage, with the living of Berwick-Basset annexed, valued in the king's books at £8. 5.; net income, £769 ; patron, the Bishop of Salisbury. A portion of· the vicarial tithes was commuted for land in 1813. The church is a venerable structure in the early English style, with a square embattled tower. A district church, of which the first stone was laid in 1839, by the Marquess of Lansdowne, attended by a large concourse of the nobility and gentry, was completed ·at Derry Hill in 1840 ; it is an elegant edifice in the later English style, with a spire, and contains 500 sittings, of which 400 are free, for the benefit of the inhabitants of Derry Hill, Studley, and Pewsham, many of whom are, four miles distant from the mother church. · The living as augmented in 1842 to £120 per annum, by the Ecclesiastical Commissioners; patron, the Vicar. There are places of worship for Baptists, the Society of Friends, Methodists, and Unitarians. A free school was founded in 1660, by John Bentley, who endowed it with property, afterwards sold, and the produce vested in the purchase of annuities amounting to £50. Sir Francis Bridgman, Knt., in 1730 founded six scholarships, of the value of £50 per annum each, in Queen's College, Oxford; two of which are for natives of this town. The poor law union of Calne comprises 11 parishes or places, and contains a population of 9324. An hospital dedicated to St. John existed here in the reign of Henry III., the revenue of which, at the Dissolution, was £2. 2. 8. At the distance of three miles to the east of the town is the figure of a horse, cut in the chalk hill, 157 feet long.

CALOW, a township, in the parish and union of CHESTERFIELD, hundred of SCARSDALE, N. division of the county of DERBY, 2 miles (E. by S.) from Chesterfield; containing 536 inhabitants. The township comprises 1280 acres of land: the village is pleasantly situated on the Clown road, at its junction with the Sutton road. There are extensive collieries in the neighbourhood, and a furnace for smelting iron-ore. The Earl Manvers occasionally holds a manor court at Billmore House.

CALSTOCK (ST. ANDREW), a parish, in the union of LISKEARD, Middle division of the hundred of EAST, E. division of CORNWALL, 5¼ miles (E.) from Callington; containing 2553 inhabitants. This place anciently belonged to the Cotcheles, of whom the last heiress, more than three centuries since, conveyed it by marriage to the Edgcumbe family, whose descendant, the Earl of Mount-Edgcumbe, is the present proprietor. In the reign of Richard III., Sir Richard Edgcumbe, a zealous adherent to the Earl of Richmond, erected a chapel in the grounds of his baronial mansion of Cotehele, in commemoration of his escape from the partisans of Richard II., by whom he had been pursued. Charles II. passed several nights in this residence; and, in 1789, it was visited by the Princess Royal, and the Princesses Augusta and Elizabeth. The house is a spacious and highly interesting quadrangular structure, having on the north side a lofty square tower, containing the state apartments, with all their ancient furniture, which has been carefully preserved. The chapel erected by Sir Richard Edgcumbe has been much defaced by modern alterations, and externally retains but little of its original character.

The parish is separated from Tavistock and Beer-Alston, in Devon, by the navigable river Tamar, which forms its boundary on the east and south, and over which are a ferry and a bridge: the scenery is diversified, and near Cotehele House is singularly beautiful. The tide flows nearly to the centre of the parish, where a weir; and a very productive fishery is carried on, of salmon and trout of excellent quality, with which the Tamar abounds. A steamer runs three times a week to Plymouth, distant upwards of twenty miles. The parish comprises 6133 acres, of which 1397 are common or waste: the surface in the hilly parts is shelfy, and the soil light; the remainder is tolerably good corn-land. Mines of copper and tin are in operation; and a lead-mine, the ore of which is richly intermixed with silver, has been opened: the mineral Uranium is likewise procured, and there is a quarry of fine granite, of which considerable quantities were used in the erection of Waterloo Bridge. The living is a rectory, valued in the king's books at £26. 7. 8½., and in the patronage of the Crown, in right of the duchy of Cornwall; net income, £510. The church is an ancient structure, with a lofty embattled tower crowned with pinnacles; it stands upon a hill, and commands fine prospects. The parsonage-house was built in 1710, by Launcelot Blackburn, Archbishop of York, then rector. There are several places of worship for dissenters. On Hengist Down are several tumuli: here was fought a great battle between the Saxons and ancient Britons.

CALSTONE, a tything, in the parish, union, and hundred of CALNE, Chippenham and Calne, and N. divisions of WILTS; containing 219 inhabitants.

CALSTONE-WELLINGTON (ST. MARY), a parish, in the parliamentary borough, union, and hundred of CALNE, Chippenham and Calne, and N. divisions of WILTS, 3 miles (S. E. by E.) from Calne; containing 31 inhabitants. It comprises 183 acres; the surface is hilly, and the soil various, in some parts chalk, and in others a fertile loam. The living is a discharged rectory, valued in the king's books at £4. 13. 4.; net income, £192; patron, the Marquess of Lansdowne. A portion of the vicarial tithes was commuted for land in the year 1813.

CALTHORPE, LEICESTER.—See CATHORPE.

CALTHORPE (ST. MARGARET), a parish, in the union of AYLSHAM, hundred of SOUTH ERPINGHAM, E. division of NORFOLK, 4 miles (N. by W.) from Aylsham; containing 214 inhabitants. It comprises 1048 acres, of which 40 are common or waste; the soil is in general rich and loamy: a small tributary of the river Bure forms the boundary of the greater part. The living is a discharged vicarage, in the patronage of the Corporation of Norwich; impropriator, the Earl of Orford. The great tithes have been commuted for £195, and the vicarial for £138; the impropriate glebe consists of 34 acres, and the vicar's comprises 23 acres.

CALTHWAITE, a township, in the parish of HESKET-IN-THE-FOREST, union of PENRITH, LEATH ward, E. division of CUMBERLAND, 7 miles (N. N. W.) from Penrith; containing 206 inhabitants. The river Petterill, over which a bridge of one arch was built by subscription in 1793, flows on the eastern side of the village, and the Lancaster railway runs through the township.

CALTON, a chapelry, partly in the parish of BLORE, N. division, and partly in the parishes of CROXDEN, MAYFIELD, and WATERFALL, S. division, of the hundred of TOTMONSLOW, N. division of the county of STAFFORD, 5¼ miles (W. N. W.) from Ashbourn, on the road to Leek; containing 244 inhabitants. It comprises about 1400 acres, of which the surface is hilly, and the soil in general rich and productive; the substratum is limestone, which abounds with fossil shells. This is a dairy-farming country, and mostly laid out in grass-land and sheep-walks. The river Hamps, which separates the chapelry from Waterfall, is said to disappear at Waterhouses, and, after running underground for upwards of five miles, again to make its appearance near Ilam. The living is a donative, in the patronage of the Inhabitants; net income, £86, with a parsonage-house. The chapel, a small edifice, is dedicated to St. Mary.

CALTON, a township, in the parish of KIRKBY-IN-MALHAM-DALE, union of SKIPTON, E. division of the wapentake of STAINCLIFFE and EWCROSS, W. riding of YORK, 7 miles (N. W.) from Skipton; containing 79 inhabitants. It comprises by computation 1730 acres, of which the surface is varied, and chiefly in pasture. Calton Hall, now a farmhouse, was the residence of the Lambert family, of whom General Lambert was one of the principal leaders of the parliamentarians in the reign of Charles I.

CALVELEY, a township, in the parish of BUNBURY, union of NANTWICH, First division of the hundred of EDDISBURY, S. division of the county of CHESTER, 6 miles (N. W. by N.) from Nantwich; containing 190 inhabitants. The township lies on the road from Nantwich to Tarporley, and comprises 1416 acres, of a clayey soil. The Chester canal and the Chester and Crewe railway pass in the vicinity of the village; and the railway has a station here, 8 miles distant from the great station at Crewe. This was the birthplace and residence of the famous Sir Hugh Calveley, whose niece in 1360 married Arthur, sixth son of Sir John Davenport, of Merton, whose descendants have resided here up to the present time. A school is supported by Mrs. Davenport.

CALVER, a township, in the parish and union of BAKEWELL, hundred of HIGH PEAK, N. division of the county of DERBY, 1 mile (E. S. E.) from Stoney-Middleton; containing 573 inhabitants. There are extensive lime-works; also some cotton-mills, in which from 200 to 300 persons are employed. The village is situated on the river Derwent,

CALVERHALL, a chapelry, in the parish of PREES, union of WEM, Whitchurch division of the hundred of NORTH BRADFORD, N. division of SALOP; containing, with Willaston and Millenheath, 262 inhabitants. The living is a perpetual curacy; net income, £65; patron and impropriator, John W. Dodd, Esq. The chapel is dedicated to St. Bartholomew.

CALVERLEIGH (ST. MARY), a parish, in the union and hundred of TIVERTON, Cullompton and N. divisions of DEVON, 2 miles (N. W.) from Tiverton; containing 81 inhabitants. It comprises by measurement 500 acres, about 50 of which are woodland, and the rest arable and pasture in nearly equal portions. The living is a rectory, valued in the king's books at £12, and in the patronage of G. W. Owen, Esq.: the tithes have been commuted for £85. 13., and the glebe comprises 72 acres. In the church is a curious monument to a former proprietor named Southcot, dated 1638. There is a Roman Catholic chapel.

CALVERLEY (ST. WILFRID), a parish, in the union of BRADFORD, wapentake of MORLEY, W. riding of YORK, 5 miles (N. E.) from Bradford; containing, with the township of Bolton and the chapelries of Idle and Pudsey, 21,039 inhabitants, of whom 4142 are in the township of Calverley cum Farsley. This extensive parish, which is within the honour of Pontefract, belonged at the time of the Conquest to the Lacys, by whom the manor was given to Gospatrick, Earl of Northumberland, one of whose daughters and co-heiresses conveyed it by marriage, in the reign of Stephen, to the family of Scot, whose descendants assumed the name of Calverley. In 1754, Sir Walter Calverley, who took the surname of Blackett, sold it, with the whole of the estates, to the

great-uncle of Thomas Thornhill, Esq., the present lord. The parish comprises 8644a. 3r. 14p.; the soil is fertile, the surface is pleasingly varied, and the higher grounds command extensive and interesting views of the country adjacent. The village is beautifully situated, partly on the brow of an acclivity on the south side of Airedale, and partly on the bank of the river, and near the Leeds and Liverpool canal. The population is principally employed in the woollen-manufacture, for which there are extensive establishments; and within the parish are also some stone-quarries and coal-mines. The living is a vicarage, valued in the king's books at £9. 11. 10.; net income, £150, with a good glebe-house; patron, the Crown. The church is a venerable structure in the later English style, with a square embattled tower crowned by pinnacles, and contains several handsome monuments. Other churches have been erected at Farsley, Idle, and Pudsey; and there are some places of worship for dissenters.

CALVERTON (ALL SAINTS), a parish, in the union of POTTER's-PURY, hundred of NEWPORT, county of BUCKINGHAM, 1 mile (S.) from Stony-Stratford; containing 493 inhabitants. This parish once included the western portion of Stony-Stratford, which was separated from it by act of parliament: the manor belonged to Simon Bennet, Esq., who, during the commonwealth, built the manor-house on the site of a more ancient structure. The parish comprises about 2000 acres, whereof two-thirds are arable and the rest pasture; both the surface and the soil are considerably varied: the river Ouse skirts it on the north. The substrata are chiefly limestone and sandstone; the former, which abounds with numerous fossil shells, is quarried for burning into lime and for building purposes. The living is a rectory, valued in the king's books at £26. 2. 11.; net income, £346; patron, the Earl of Egmont: the tithes were commuted for land and a money payment in 1782. The church is a neat plain edifice, erected in 1818, by Lord Arden and the Rev. George Butler, D.D., then rector; it has been embellished with stained glass by the Rev. C. G. Perceval, the present incumbent, and the interior has a neat and pleasing appearance. The rectory-house, built by Lord Arden in 1820, occupies the site of a small Roman camp, and numerous fragments of Roman pottery, with arrow-heads, and a spear, have been discovered. Six small almshouses were built in 1830. A chalybeate spring, called the Bloody Hawk, was formerly much resorted to by persons who, on those occasions, formed groups for dancing to the violin.

CALVERTON (ST. WILFRID), a parish, in the union of BASFORD, S. division of the wapentake of THURGARTON and of the county of NOTTINGHAM, 7 miles (N. N. E.) from Nottingham; containing 1339 inhabitants. The parish is separated from that of Oxton by a small stream called Dover beck, which rises in the forest of Sherwood, and runs in a south-eastern direction into the Trent; it comprises by measurement 3300 acres, whereof two-thirds are arable, and the rest pasture and woodland. The chief manufactures are those of stockings and lace, which afford employment to about 600 persons. The village is of considerable extent, and situated in a picturesque valley. The living is a discharged vicarage, valued in the king's books at £4, and in the alternate patronage of the Archbishop of York and the Prebendary of Oxton in the Collegiate Church of Southwell; net ncome, £127 : the tithes were commuted for 203 acres of and, under an inclosure act passed in 1779. The church, erected in 1774, is a neat and substantial edifice with a tower. There are places of worship for Baptists and Wesleyans, and for a sect peculiar to the parish, founded in the latter part of the last century, by John Roe. A school is endowed with £6 per annum; and £40 per annum, a house and garden, and four tons of coal, are also allowed by the trustees of Mr. Jonathan Labray's hospital.

CALWICH, a township, in the parish of ELLASTONE, S. division of the hundred of TOTMONSLOW, N. division of the county of STAFFORD, 3½ miles (S. W. by W.) from Ashbourn; containing 131 inhabitants. A hermitage was established here, which was given to the priory of Kenilworth before the year 1148, by Nicholas de Greselei Fitz-Nigell, and a small number of Black canons placed therein. The house was assigned by Henry VIII. to the monastery of Merton, in Surrey, in exchange for the manor of East Moulsey, and as parcel of the monastery was again granted by that monarch to John Fleetwood. The township is on the western side of Dovedale, and comprises 655 acres, including the hamlet of Northwood. Calwich Abbey is the seat of the Hon. and Rev. Augustus Duncombe, by whom it was purchased of Court Gran-ville, Esq., in 1842. Attached to the mansion are a beautiful lawn and pleasure-grounds, and a fine sheet of water supplies excellent fishing. Handel, the composer, was a frequent guest here.

CAM (ST. GEORGE), a parish, in the union of DURS-LEY, Upper division of the hundred of BERKELEY, W. division of the county of GLOUCESTER, 1 mile (N.) from Dursley; containing 1951 inhabitants. This place is distinguished as the scene of a battle fought between the Saxons and the Danes, in the reign of Edward the Elder. The parish takes its name from a rivulet that divides it into Upper and Lower, and falls into the Severn at Frampton: it comprises 2531a. 1r. 26p., of which 2025 acres are pasture, £63 arable, and 242 common land; the soil is in general a strong clay. There are several quarries of white and of brown freestone, which, when kept dry, is of good quality for building; and facility of communication is afforded by the Glou-cester and Bristol railway, which crosses the lower part of the parish. A considerable portion of the land lies low, but the meadows afford excellent pasture, and the district is noted for the superiority of its cheese. The majority of the inhabitants are employed in the finer branches of the clothing-trade, and the weavers of the place are among the best workmen of this part of the kingdom. The living is a vicarage, valued in the king's books at £6. 13. 4.; net income, £150; patron and im-proprietor, the Bishop of Gloucester and Bristol. The great tithes have been commuted for £500, and the bishop's glebe consists of 23a. 2r. The church, which has been improved and newly pewed at a considerable expense, is an ancient structure in the later English style: in the porch was a figure of the patron saint carved in wood, which, in the reign of Edward VI., was taken down and removed to Colnbrook, from which circumstance the George inn in that town received its name. There are places of worship for Independents and Wesleyans. In 1730, Mrs. Frances Hopton be-queathed an estate for a school, now producing nearly £200 per annum.

CAMBERWELL (ST. GILES), a parish and union, in the E. division of the hundred of BRIXTON and of the county of SURREY, 3¼ miles (S.) from London; con-taining, with the hamlets of Dulwich and Peckham, 39,868 inhabitants. This place, in the Norman survey called Cambrewell, and in other ancient records Camerwell, appears to have been known to the Romans, whose legions are by some antiquaries supposed to have here forded the Thames, and to have constructed the cause-way leading from the river through the marshes in this parish, of which a considerable part, consisting of square chalk-stones, and secured with oak piles, was discovered fifteen feet below the surface of the ground, in digging the bed of the Grand Surrey canal in 1809. In Domes-day book mention is made of a church; and in the register of Bishop Edington at Winchester, a com-mission dated 1346, for "reconciling Camberwell church, which had been polluted by bloodshed," is still in existence. The village or town is pleasantly situated, and the beauty of its environs has made it the residence of many wealthy merchants of the metropolis: it is paved, and lighted with gas; and the inhabitants are amply supplied with water from springs, and from the works of the South London Company. The ancient part of the village contains several spacious mansions in detached situations; the more modern is built on rising ground to the south-east, and comprises the Grove, and Champion, Denmark, and Herne Hills, which are occupied by elegant villas in a pleasing style. A literary and scientific institution was founded in 1846. There are several coal and coke wharfs, and a limekiln on the banks of the Surrey canal, which terminates in the parish, through which the London and Croydon railway also passes. By the act to "amend the representation," the whole parish, except Dulwich, was included within the limits of the borough of Lambeth. The magistrates for the district hold a meeting every alternate week.

The parish comprises 4342 acres, of which 55 are common or waste. The LIVING is a vicarage, valued in the king's books at £20, and in the gift of the Rev. J. Williams: the great tithes have been commuted for £80, and the vicarial for £1100; the glebe comprises 21 acres, with a good glebe-house. The church, an ancient struc-ture in the later English style, with a low embattled tower surmounted by an open lantern-turret rising from the centre, was destroyed by an accidental fire on the morning of Monday, the 8th of February, 1841, and only the roofless walls left standing: a meeting of the parishioners was held on the 13th for the appointment of a committee, who, at a subsequent meeting, were em-powered to raise £12,000 for the erection of a new edifice. The new church, which is the most magnificent edifice of London, is of cruciform design, with a central tower and spire, and in the style of the latter half of the 13th century. The mass of the walls is built of rubble-work of Kentish ragstone, mixed with the materials of the old church; the exterior is faced with hammer-dressed stone from Yorkshire, with dressings of Caen stone. The general character of the building is bold and massive, rather than highly ornamented. The nave is supported on each side by five arches, resting on alternately round and octagonal pillars with carved capitals: the pulpit and some other portions of the in-terior are of oak, the communion-table is of stone; there is a fine organ, and the west window contains some stained glass, chiefly ancient.

The district church dedicated to St. George is situated on the bank of the Surrey canal, and is a handsome structure in the Grecian style, erected in 1824, at an expense of £17,000, of which £5000 was a grant from the Commissioners for Building New Churches; it is adapted for a congregation of 1700 persons. The living is a perpetual curacy; net value, £500. *Emmanuel* district church, situated in the High-street, near the old mansion-house, and of which the first stone was laid in 1841, was completed at an expense of £6000, of which £2000 were contributed by the Metropolitan Church-Building Society, £1000 by the Incorporated Society, and £1900 by Sir Edward Bowyer Smith, who also gave the site and a house for the minister, and presented the organ. It is a handsome structure of white brick, in the Norman style, with two towers surmounted by small spires at the east end, where is the principal entrance; the interior is well arranged, and contains 1000 sittings, of which 500 are free. The first stone of *St. Paul's* church, Herne-Hill, was laid in June, 1843. It is a brick building faced with Sneaton stone, in the English style, with a tower and spire 115 feet in height : the extent of the plan is 115 feet from east to west, and the internal length of the nave 80 feet, and its breadth, including the aisles, 50; the windows are of stained glass. The edifice affords accommodation to 700 persons; the cost was £4958, independently of numerous gifts of fittings-up. The living is in the gift of the Rev. J. G. Storie; income, £500. Two churches have been erected at Peckham, where are also two proprietary episcopal chapels. Camden chapel, built in 1795, and subsequently enlarged, is a handsome edifice of brick, with a campanile turret; it was under proprietary management previously to November, 1844, when it was consecrated. Besides these, is a chapel dedicated to St. Matthew, on Denmark Hill, and which, though locally in this parish, is dependent on that of Lambeth. There are places of worship for Baptists, Independents, and Wesleyans.

The free grammar school, originally intended for 12 boys, was founded in 1618, by the Rev. Edward Wilson, vicar of the parish, who built the premises, and gave seven acres of land for its endowment, which are let on lease for £60 per annum, paid to the master, who has also a house rent-free, and the privilege of taking boarders. The school is under the management of governors, who are a body corporate, and have a common seal. The Camberwell collegiate school, founded in 1834, is a proprietary establishment, on the principles of King's College, London, and under the patronage of the Bishop of Winchester; the buildings, to which are attached two acres of garden and play ground, are situated in the Grove, and are in the collegiate style, with a cloister in the centre of the front, forming the principal entrance. On the south of the village is Ladland's Hill, on which are the remains of a Roman camp, defended on the south side by a double intrenchment; and in a field in the neighbourhood, called Well Hill, three large wells, 36 feet in circumference, and lined with cement, have been discovered, from which the place probably derived its name. A head of Janus, 18 inches high, was found about a century since, at a place designated St. Thomas' Watering, where pilgrims used to stop on their way to

478

Becket's shrine; and near it is a hill, called Oak-of-Honour Hill, from an oak under which Queen Elizabeth is said to have dined. Dr. Lettsom, an eminent physician, lived for many years in a beautiful cottage in the Grove, where he had an extensive library and philosophical apparatus. The uncle of George Barnwell, the hero of Lillo's tragedy, resided in an ancient house of which there are still some vestiges remaining.

CAMBLESFORTH, a township, in the parish of DRAX, union of SELBY, Lower division of the wapentake of BARKSTONE-ASH, W. riding of YORK, 2¾ miles (N.) from Snaith; containing 321 inhabitants. There is a charity school, with an endowment of £6 per annum; likewise almshouses for six people, endowed with £100 per annum. The poor children also participate in the advantages of the grammar school at Drax.

CAMBO, a township, in the parish of HARTBURN, union of MORPETH, N. E. division of TINDALE ward, S. division of NORTHUMBERLAND, 11½ miles (W.) from Morpeth; containing 99 inhabitants. The township comprises 630 acres, of which the greater part is rich pasture-land. The village is on the road from Hexham to Alnwick : there is a small subscription library. The tithes have been commuted for £17. 10. payable to the impropriator, and £19 to the vicar of Hartburn. A district chapel has been built, the living of which is in the gift of the Vicar. Launcelot Brown, the landscape gardener, received his early education here. In the village are the ruins of a peel-house, or fortalice.

CAMBOIS, a township, in the parish and division of BEDLINGTON, union of MORPETH, N. division of NORTHUMBERLAND, 7½ miles (E. by S.) from Morpeth; containing 109 inhabitants. The lands extend along the sea-shore, between the rivers Blyth and Wansbeck; and the village is situated among rich pastures on a dry green knoll, formed by the banks of the sea and the Wansbeck, which has here a ferry over it. There is a small harbour, where corn, timber, and grindstones are shipped. Some spacious granaries were built during the war with France, at which period a great quantity of grain was exported. About half a mile south-east of the Wansbeck is a cluster of rocks, named Cambois ridge, the tops of which are dry at low water; but as this part of the coast is little frequented, except by small vessels, accidents seldom occur.

CAMBORNE (ST. MARTIN), a market-town and parish, in the union of REDRUTH, E. division of the hundred of PENWITH, W. division of CORNWALL, 4 miles (W. S. W.) from Redruth, and 267 (S. W.) from London, on the road from Truro to Penzance; containing 10,061 inhabitants. This town, which is situated in the centre of an extensive district abounding with copper, tin, and lead mines, consists of several streets, uniformly built, but indifferently supplied with water : two book-clubs have been established. The Dolcoath copper-mine has been sunk to the depth of 1000 feet, and extends laterally for more than a mile, in a direction from east to west; the number of persons employed exceeds 1500, and the annual expenditure of the proprietors is more than £50,000. There are several other mines, on a smaller scale : the neighbourhood abounds with granite; and an iron-foundry, and a manufactory for safety-fuzes used by miners in blasting, together employ about sixty persons. Here is a station on the Hayle and Redruth railway. The market is on Saturday : the market-ouse, a shed supported on pillars of granite, was erected at the expense of Lord de Dunstanville. The fairs are on March 7th, June 5th and 29th, and November 12th, and are principally for cattle. The county magistrates hold a petty-session for the district every alternate Tuesday; and a court leet is held in November, at which constables are appointed.

The parish comprises by computation 6000 acres, of which 1120 are common or waste. The LIVING is a rectory, valued in the king's books at £39. 16. 10½., and in the patronage of Lady Bassett: the tithes have been commuted for £900, and the glebe comprises 40 acres. The church is an ancient structure, principally in the later English style, and contains several monuments to the family of Pendarves; the altar-piece is of marble handsomely sculptured, and the pulpit of oak curiously carved. A church district, called All Saints, Tuckingmill, and including part of the parish of Illogan, was formed in 1844, and endowed by the Ecclesiastical Commissioners: another district, named Penponds, was formed in 1846. At Treslothan is a district church dedicated to St. John, the living of which is in the gift of E. W. Pendarves, Esq. There are places of worship for the Society of Friends, Wesleyans, and Bryanites. Mr. Arthur Woolf, an eminent civil engineer, who died in 1837, was born here about the year 1765; he made considerable improvements in the construction of steam-engines, and took out a patent for the application of two cylinders. Mr. Richard Trevithic, who was born at Camborne in 1775, and died in 1835, in conjunction with Captain Andrew Vivian, now residing here, constructed the first locomotive engine, for which they took out a patent, in 1802; they also constructed a high-pressure steam-engine, and invented the cylindrical boiler with a single tube, which is very economical in the use of fuel. Mr. Bickford, resident here, invented, with Mr. Thomas D'Arcy, the patent safety-fuze used by miners for blasting. John Stackhouse, Esq., of Pendarves, who was born in the parish in 1748, and died in 1819, was author of the *Nereis Britannica*, and editor of the *Theophrasti Plantarum Historia*.

Seal and Arms.

CAMBRIDGE, a university, borough, and market-town, having separate jurisdiction, and forming a union and hundred of itself, in the county of CAMBRIDGE, on the river Cam, 51 miles (N. by E.) from London; containing 24,453 inhabitants. This ancient town was the *Grantan-brycge, Granta-bricge,* or *Grante-brige,* of the Saxon Chronicle, signifying the Bridge over the Granta," the ancient name of the river Cam: by the substitution of cognate letters, the Saxon compound was altered after the Norman Conquest to *Cantebrige,* since contracted into *Cambridge.* The earliest authenticated fact in its history is its conflagration, in 871, by the Danes, who established on its isolated site one of their principal stations, which they occasionally occupied until the year 901. When the Danish army quartered here had submitted to Edward the Elder, that monarch restored the town; but, in 1010, the Danes again laid it waste. During the period that the Isle of Ely was held against William the Conqueror, by the Anglo-Saxon prelates and nobles, William built a castle at Cambridge, on the site, as it is supposed, of the Danish fortress, including also the sites of twenty-seven other houses, which, according to Domesday book, were then destroyed. In 1088, the town and country were ravaged by Roger de Montgomery, Earl of Shrewsbury, who had espoused the cause of Robert, Duke of Normandy. Upon the agreement made during the absence of Richard I. in Palestine, between Prince John and Chancellor Longchamp, the castle was among those which the chancellor was allowed to retain. The town was taken and despoiled by the barons, in 1215. King John was at Cambridge about a month before his death: soon after his departure, the castle was taken by the barons, and on his decease a council was held here between them and Louis, the Dauphin. In 1265, the inhabitants of the Isle of Ely being in rebellion against Henry III., the king took up his abode in the town, and began to fortify it; but being suddenly called away by the tidings of the Earl of Gloucester's success, he left Cambridge without a garrison, in consequence of which it was plundered by the rebels in the isle, the townsmen having fled at their approach. On the death of Edward VI., the Duke of Northumberland, at that time chancellor of the university, aiming to place Lady Jane Grey on the throne, came hither with an army to seize the Lady Mary, who, being at Sir John Huddleston's house at Sawston, and receiving intelligence of his design, escaped into Suffolk. The duke advanced towards Bury, but finding himself almost deserted by his forces, he returned with a small party to Cambridge, and proclaimed Queen Mary in the market-place: he was nevertheless arrested for high treason the same night in King's College. In 1643, Cromwell, who, before he acquired any celebrity as a public character, was for some time an inhabitant of the Isle of Ely, and twice returned for the borough of Cambridge, took possession of it for the parliament, and placed in it a garrison of 1000 men: in August, 1645, the king appeared with his army before Cambridge, but it continued in the possession of the parliamentarians until the close of the war. The town has suffered several times from accidental calamities: in 1174, the church of the Holy Trinity was destroyed by fire, and most of the other churches injured; in 1294, another conflagration destroyed St. Mary's church, and many of the adjoining houses. In 1630, the plague raged so violently that the summer assizes were held that year at Royston, the university commencement was postponed till October, and there was no Stour-bridge fair.

Situated in a fenny agricultural district, CAMBRIDGE owes its chief picturesque attractions to the number and variety, and in several instances the magnitude and beauty, of the buildings connected with the university; and to the walks and gardens attached to them. It is upwards of a mile in length, is one mile in its greatest breadth, and lies chiefly on the south-eastern side of the river: notwithstanding recent alterations, the streets in general are narrow and irregularly formed; but on the whole its aspect has been much improved by many elegant additions to the several colleges and university buildings. The town was paved under an act passed in 1787, and has lately been drained at a great expense: the streets, and many of the public buildings, are well

CAMB

lighted with gas; an act having been obtained, in 1834, to incorporate a company for affording a better supply. Water is procured from a conduit in the market-place, erected in the year 1614, by the eccentric and benevolent Thomas Hobson, carrier, and supplied by a small aqueduct communicating with a spring about three miles distant. Dramatic exhibitions are not permitted, within nine miles of the town, at any other period than that of Stourbridge fair, when, for three weeks, the Norwich company of comedians perform in a commodious theatre at Barnwell. Several public concerts are held in term-time, usually at the town-hall, when the best performers are engaged; and at the Public Commencements, which generally take place every fourth year, grand musical festivals are given. A choral society on an extensive scale has been formed; and there are several book societies, the largest of which has been established many years.

Cambridge has become a considerable thoroughfare, since the draining of the fens, and the formation of excellent roads towards the east and north-east coasts, over tracts previously impassable: the Eastern Counties railway, also, runs by the town, and has a principal station here; and in 1845 an act was passed for making a branch, 17½ miles long, from the town to Huntingdon. There is no manufacture; but a good trade in corn, coal, timber, iron, &c., is carried on with the port of Lynn, by means of the Cam, which is navigable up to Cambridge. A great quantity of oil, pressed at the numerous mills in the Isle of Ely, from flax, hemp, and cole seed, is brought up the river; and butter is conveyed hither weekly from Norfolk and the Isle of Ely, and sent to London. The markets, which are under the control of the university, though the tolls belong to the corporation, are held every day in the week, Saturday's being the largest, and are excellently supplied with provisions: the market-place consists of two spacious oblong squares. There are two fairs: one of them, for horses, cattle, timber, and pottery, beginning on the 22nd of June, and commonly called Midsummer or Pot fair, is proclaimed by the heads of the university, and the mayor and corporation, successively. The other, called Stourbridge fair, anciently one of the largest and most celebrated in the kingdom, is proclaimed on the 18th September by the vice-chancellor, doctors, and proctors of the university, and by the mayor and aldermen, and continues upwards of three weeks: the staple commodities exposed for sale are leather, timber, cheese, hops, wool, and cattle; the 25th is appropriated to the sale of horses. Both the fairs have been for some years declining.

The town is a BOROUGH by prescription: it was first incorporated by Henry I., in the early part of his reign; and 24 other charters, none of which, however, with the exception of that of the 5th of Richard II., caused any material change in the municipal government, were granted previously to the charter of the 7th of Charles I., under which the officers of the corporation consisted of a mayor, four bailiffs, twelve aldermen, twenty-four common-councilmen, and two treasurers. Other officers not named in the charter were, a high steward, recorder, deputy-recorder, four councillors, two coroners, a town-clerk, and deputy town-clerk. The government is now, under the act of the 5th and 6th of William IV., cap. 76, vested in a mayor, ten aldermen, and thirty councillors;

University Arms.

King of the East Angles, with the assistance of Bishop Felix, constituted within his dominions a school in imitation of some that he had seen in France. It is certain, that at a very early period the town was the resort of numerous students, who at first resided in private apartments, and afterwards in inns, where they lived in community under a principal, at their own charge. Several of these houses were at length deserted, and fell into decay; others were purchased in succession by patrons of literature, and, obtaining incorporation with right of mortmain, received permanent rich endowments. It is believed that a regular system of academical education was first introduced in 1109, when, the abbot of Crowland having sent some monks, well versed in philosophy and other sciences, to his manor of Cottenham, they proceeded to the neighbouring town of Cambridge, whither a great number of scholars repaired to their lectures, which were arranged after the manner of the university of Orleans. The first charter known to have been granted to the university is that in the 15th of Henry III., conferring the privilege of appointing certain officers, called *taxors*, to regulate the rent of lodgings for students, which had been raised exorbitantly by the townsmen: this was about 50 years before the foundation of Peterhouse, the first endowed college. In 1249, the discord between the scholars and the townsmen had arrived at such a pitch, as to require the interference of the civil power; and in 1261, dissensions arose in the university between the northern and the southern men, which were attended with consequences so serious that a great number of scholars, in order to pursue their studies without interruption, withdrew to Northampton, where a university was established, and continued four years. In 1270, Prince Edward came to Cambridge, and ordered an agreement to be drawn up, by virtue of which certain persons were appointed by the town and the university, to preserve the peace between the students and the inhabitants. In 1333, Edward III. granted some important privileges to the university, making its authority paramount to that of the borough, and ordaining that the mayor, bailiffs, and aldermen, should swear to maintain its rights and privileges. These eminent favours caused the townsmen to be more than ever jealous of its authority; and their discontents broke out into open violence in the succeeding reign, when, taking advantage of the temporary success of the rebels of Kent and Essex, in 1381, the principal townsmen, at the head of a tumultuous assemblage, seized and destroyed the university charters, plundered Benedict College, and compelled the chancellor and other members of the university to renounce their chartered privileges, and promise submission to the authority of the burgesses. These lawless proceedings were put an end to by the arrival of the Bishop of Norwich with an armed force; and the king soon after punished the burgesses, by depriving them of their charter, and bestowing all the privileges which they had enjoyed upon the university, together with a grant that no action should be brought

against any scholar, or scholar's servant, by a townsman, in any other than the chancellor's court. In 1430, Pope Martin V. decided, from the testimony of ancient evidence, that the members of the university were exclusively possessed of all ecclesiastical and spiritual jurisdiction over their own scholars. Richard II. restored to the burgesses their charter, with such an abridgment of their privileges as rendered them more subordinate to the university than they had previously been. On the first symptoms of an approaching war between King Charles and the parliament, the university stood forward to demonstrate its loyalty, by tendering the college plate to be melted for his majesty's use. In 1643, the Earl of Manchester, at that time chancellor of the university, came to Cambridge, and, after a general visitation of the colleges, expelled all the members that were known to be zealously attached to the king and to the Church discipline. In March, 1647, Sir Thomas Fairfax visited the university, and was received with all the honours of royalty at Trinity College; on the 11th of June he kept a public fast at the place.

Queen Elizabeth visited Cambridge, Aug. 5th, 1564, and stayed five days, during which she resided at the provost's lodge, King's College, and was entertained with plays, orations, and academical exercises. On the 7th of March, 1615, James I., with his son Henry, Prince of Wales, was here, and was lodged at Trinity College, which has ever since, on the occasion of royal visits, been the residence of the sovereign: King James honoured the university with another visit in 1625; and Charles I. and his queen were here in 1632, when they were entertained with dramatic exhibitions. It was also visited by Charles II., Oct. 14th, 1671, and Sept. 27th, 1681; by William III., Oct. 4th, 1689; by Queen Anne and the Prince of Denmark, April 16th, 1705; by George I., Oct. 6th, 1717; and by George II., in April, 1728; on all which occasions the royal guests were entertained by the university in the hall of Trinity College; and it was customary for the corporation to present them with 50 broad pieces of gold. Her present Majesty honoured the town with a visit, accompanied by his Royal Highness, Prince Albert, Oct. 25th, 1843; and in 1847 the Prince was elected chancellor.

The University is a society of students in all the liberal arts and sciences, incorporated, in the 13th of Elizabeth, by the name of the "Chancellor, Masters, and Scholars of the University of Cambridge." It is formed by the union of seventeen colleges, or societies, devoted to the pursuit of learning and knowledge, and for the better service of the Church and State; and each college is a body corporate, and bound by its own statutes, though controlled, as in Oxford, by the paramount laws of the university. The present statutes are given by Queen Elizabeth, and, with former privileges, were sanctioned by parliament. Each of the seventeen departments, or colleges, in this literary republic, furnishes members both for the executive and the LEGISLATIVE branch of its government; the place of assembly is the senate-house. All persons who are masters of arts, or doctors in one of the three faculties, *viz.*, divinity, civil law, and physic, having their names upon the college boards, holding any university office, or being resident in the town, have votes in the assembly. The senate is divided into two classes or houses; and according to this arrangement they are denominated *regents* or *non-regents*, with a view to some particular offices allotted by the statutes to the junior division. Masters of arts of less than five years' standing, and doctors of less than two, compose the regent or upper house, or, as it is sometimes styled, the " White-hood house," from its members wearing hoods lined with white silk ; and all the rest constitute the non-regent or lower house, otherwise called the " Black-hood house," its members wearing black silk hoods. But doctors of more than two years' standing, and the public orator of the university, may vote in either house according to their pleasure. Besides the two houses, there is a council named the *Caput*, chosen on October 12th, by which every university grace must be approved before it can be introduced to the senate; and this council consists of a vice-chancellor, a doctor in each of the three faculties, and two masters of arts, the last representing the regent and non-regent houses. No degree is ever obtained without a grace for that purpose: after the grace has passed, the vice-chancellor is at liberty to confer the degree. The university confers no degree whatever, unless the candidate has previously subscribed a declaration that he is *bona fide* a member of the Church of England, as by law established ; for all degrees, except those of B.A., M.B., and B.C.L., it is necessary that persons should subscribe to the 36th canon of the Church of England, inserted in the registrar's book.

The EXECUTIVE branch of the university government is committed to a chancellor, high steward, vice-chancellor, and other officers. The *Chancellor* is the head of the whole university, and presides over all cases relative to that body ; his office is biennial, or tenable for such a length of time beyond two years as the tacit consent of the university chooses to allow. The *High Steward* is elected by the senate, and has special power to try scholars impeached of felony within the limits of the university (the jurisdiction of which extends a mile each way, from any part of the suburbs), and to hold a court leet according to the established charter and custom ; he has power, by letters-patent, to appoint a deputy. The *Vice-chancellor* is elected on Nov. 4th, by the senate : his office, in the absence of the chancellor, embraces the government of the university, according to the statutes ; he acts as a magistrate both for the university and the county, and must, by an order made in 1587, be the head of some college. A *Commissary* is appointed by letters-patent under the signature and seal of the chancellor ; he holds a court of record for all privileged persons, and scholars under the degree of M.A. The *Public Orator* is elected by the senate, and is the oracle of that body on all public occasions ; he writes, reads, and records the letters to and from the senate, and presents to all honorary degrees with an appropriate speech : this is esteemed one of the most honourable offices in the gift of the university. An *Assessor* is specially appointed, by a grace of the senate, to assist the vice-chancellor in his court, *in causis forensibus et domesticis*. Two *Proctors*, who are peace-officers, are elected annually on Oct. 10th, by the regents only, from the different colleges in rotation, according to a fixed cycle. A *Librarian, Library-keeper*, and *Assistant Library-keepers*, are chosen by the senate, for the due management of the university library. The *Registrar*, elected also by the senate, is obliged, either by himself or deputy, to attend all congregations,

to give requisite directions for the form of such graces as are to be propounded, and to receive them when passed in both houses. Two *Taxors* are elected on Oct. 10th, by the regents only : they must be masters of arts, and are regents by virtue of their office; they are appointed to regulate the markets, and to lay the abuses thereof before the commissary. *Scrutators* are chosen at the same time by the non-regents only ; they are *ex-officio* non-regents, and attend all congregations, read the graces in the lower house, gather the votes, and pronounce the assent and dissent. Two *Moderators*, nominated by the proctors, and appointed by a grace of the senate, officiate in the absence of the proctors. Two *Pro-proctors* are appointed, to assist the proctors in that part of their duty which relates to the preservation of the public morals : this office was instituted by a grace of the senate, April 29th, 1818, and bachelors in divinity, as well as masters of arts, are eligible. *Classical Examiners* are nominated by the several colleges, according to the cycle of proctors, and the election takes place at the first congregation after Oct. 4th. There are three *Esquire Bedells*, whose duty it is to attend the vice-chancellor. The *University Printer*, and the *School-keeper*, are elected by the body at large : the *Yeoman Bedell* is appointed by letters-patent under the signature and seal of the chancellor ; and the *University Marshal*, by letters-patent of the vice-chancellor. The *Syndics* are members of the senate chosen to transact all special affairs relating to the university.

The PROFESSORS have stipends allowed from various sources ; some from the university chest, and others from her Majesty's government, or from estates left for the purpose. *Lady Margaret's Professorship of Divinity* was instituted in 1502, by Margaret, Countess of Richmond, mother of Henry VII., the election to be every two years. The *Regius Professorship of Divinity* was founded by Henry VIII., in 1540; the candidates may be either bachelors or doctors in divinity. The *Regius Professorship of Civil Law* was also established by Henry VIII. in 1540; the professor is appointed by the Queen, and continues in office during Her Majesty's pleasure. The *Regius Professorship of Physic*, instituted at the same time, may be held for life; the appointment is by the Queen. The *Regius Professorship of Hebrew* was likewise founded at the same time : a candidate must not be under the standing of M.A. or B.D. ; but doctors of all faculties are excluded. A Professorship of *Arabic* was established by Sir Thomas Adams, Bart., in 1632. The *Lord Almoner's Reader and Professorship of Arabic* is in the gift of the lord almoner, and the stipend is paid out of the almonry bounty. The *Lucasian Professorship of Mathematics* was instituted in 1663, by Henry Lucas, M.P. for the university ; a candidate must be M.A. at least, and well skilled in mathematical science. The Professorship of *Casuistry* was founded in 1683, by John Knightbridge, D.D., fellow of St. Peter's : a candidate must be a bachelor or doctor in divinity, and not less than 40 years of age. The Professorship of *Music* was established by the university, in 1684 ; that of *Chemistry* by the university, in 1702 ; of *Astronomy and Experimental Philosophy*, in 1704, by Dr. Plume, Archdeacon of Rochester ; and of *Anatomy*, by the university, in 1707. The Professorship of *Modern History* was established by George I., in 1724 : the professor is appointed by the Queen, and holds the office during Her Majesty's pleasure ; he must be either a master of arts, or bachelor in civil law, of a superior degree. The Professorship of *Botany* was founded by the university, in 1724, and has since been made a patent office. That of *Geology* was instituted by Dr. Woodward, in 1727 ; only unmarried men are eligible. The Professorship of *Astronomy and Geometry* was founded by Thomas Lowndes, Esq., in 1749. The *Norrisian Professorship of Divinity* was founded by John Norris, Esq., of Whitton, in the county of Norfolk, in 1768 : the professor cannot continue in office longer than five years, but may be re-elected ; he may be a member of either university, may be lay or clerical, but cannot be elected under his 30th, nor re-elected after his 60th year. The Professorship of *Natural and Experimental Philosophy* was established in 1783, by the Rev. Richard Jackson, M.A. ; a member of Trinity College is to be preferred, and next, a candidate from the counties of Stafford, Warwick, Derby, or Chester. The *Downing Professorship of the Laws of England,* and the *Downing Professorship of Medicine,* were founded in pursuance of the will of Sir George Downing, Bart., K.B., in 1800. The Professorship of *Mineralogy* was instituted by the university, in 1808, and afterwards endowed by Her Majesty's government. That of *Political Economy* was conferred by a grace of the senate in May, 1828, on George Pryme, Esq., M.A., late fellow of Trinity College, and is to be a permanent professorship.

Lady-Margaret's Preachership was founded in 1503 ; doctors, inceptors, and bachelors of divinity, are alone eligible, one of Christ's College being preferred. The *Barnaby Lectureships,* four in number, *viz.* in mathematics, philosophy, rhetoric, and logic, are so called from the election taking place on St. Barnabas' day, June 11th: the mathematical lecture was founded at a very early period, by the university ; and the other three were endowed in 1524, by Sir Robert Rede, lord chief justice of the court of common pleas in the reign of Henry VIII. The *Sadlerian Lectureships in Algebra,* seventeen in number, were founded by Lady Sadler, and the lectures commenced in 1710 : the lecturers were required to be bachelors of arts at least ; the lectureships are tenable only for ten years, and no one can be elected unless previously examined and approved by the mathematical professor. The Rev. John Hulse, who was educated at St. John's College, and died in 1789, bequeathed his estates in Cheshire to the university, for the advancement and reward of religious learning ; the purposes to which he appropriated the income being, first, the maintenance of two scholars at St. John's College ; secondly, to recompense the exertions of the Hulsean prizemen ; thirdly, to found and support the office of Christian advocate ; and fourthly, that of the Hulsean Lecturer, or Christian Preacher. The *Christian Advocate* must be a learned and ingenious person, of the degree of master of arts, or of bachelor or doctor of divinity, of thirty years of age, and resident in the university ; he has to compose yearly, while in office, some answer in English to objections brought against the Christian religion, or the religion of nature, by notorious infidels. The office of the *Hulsean Lecturer,* or *Christian Preacher,* is annual ; but the same individual may, under certain circumstances, be re-elected for any number of successive years not exceeding six : the preacher is afterwards ineligible to the office of Christian Advocate : his duty is, to preach and print twenty sermons in each year, the object of them being

483

to show the evidences of revealed religion, or to explain some of the most obscure parts of the Holy Scriptures. William Worts, M.A., of Caius College, formerly one of the esquire bedells of the university, gave two pensions, of £100 per annum each, to two junior bachelors of arts, who are required to visit foreign countries, to take different routes, and to write, during their travels, two Latin letters each, descriptive of customs, curiosities, &c. : the annuity is continued for three years, the period they are required to be absent.

The PRIZES for the encouragement of literature, the competition for which is open to the university at large, amount annually to nearly £1200 in value, three-fourths of which are given for the classics and English composition, and the remainder for mathematics. The amount of the annual prizes in the different colleges is upwards of £300, two-thirds of which are for the encouragement of classical literature. Two gold medals, value £15. 15. each, are presented annually by the chancellor to two commencing bachelors of arts, who, having obtained senior optimes at least, show the greatest proficiency in classical learning : these prizes were established in 1751, by the *Duke of Newcastle,* then chancellor. The members of parliament for the university give four annual prizes, of £15. 15. each, to two bachelors of arts and two under-graduates, who compose the best dissertations in Latin prose : these were founded by the *Hon. Edward Finch* and the *Hon. Thomas Townsend. Sir Edward Browne, Knt., M.D.,* directed three gold medals, value £5. 5. each, to be given yearly to three under-graduates on the commencement day ; the first to him who writes the best Greek ode in imitation of Sappho ; the second for the best Latin ode in imitation of Horace ; the third for the best Greek and Latin epigrams, the former after the manner of the Anthologia, the latter on the model of Martial. The Rev. Charles Burney, D.D., and the Rev. John Cleaver Bankes, M.A., only surviving trustees of a fund raised by the friends of the late *Professor Porson,* and appropriated to his use during his lifetime, transferred to the university by deed, bearing date Nov. 27th, 1816, the sum of £400 Navy five per cents. upon trust, that the interest should be annually employed in the purchase of one or more Greek books, to be given to such resident under-graduate as should make the best translation of a proposed passage selected from the works of Shakspeare, Ben Jonson, Massinger, or Beaumont and Fletcher, into Greek verse. The *Rev. Robert Smith, D.D.,* late master of Trinity College, left two annual prizes, of £25 each, to two commencing bachelors of arts, the best proficients in mathematics and natural philosophy. *John Norris, Esq.,* founder of the divinity professorship, bequeathed a premium of £12 per annum, of which £7. 4. are to be expended on a gold medal, and the remainder in books, to the author of the best prose essay on a sacred subject, to be proposed by the Norrisian professor. The *Rev. John Hulse,* mentioned above, directed that, out of the rents and profits of the estates which he bequeathed to the university, an annual premium of £40 should be given to any member under the degree of M.A., who should compose the best dissertation on any argument proving the excellence of the Christian religion. The *Rev. Thomas Seaton,* fellow of Clare Hall, bequeathed an estate, producing a clear income of £40, to be given yearly to a master of arts for the best English poem on a sacred subject.

3 Q 2

The university SCHOLARSHIPS are as follows. *John, Lord Craven*, founded two classical scholarships, tenable for fourteen years, of £25 per annum each : by a decree of the court of chancery, in 1819, the income of the scholars has been augmented to £50, and three additional scholarships founded, which are tenable for seven years only. *William Battie, M.D.*, left an estate producing £18 per annum, to endow a scholarship similar to the preceding. *Sir William Browne* left a rent charge of £21 for a scholarship tenable for seven years. The *Rev. Jonathan Davies, D.D.*, provost of Eton College, bequeathed, in July, 1804, the sum of £1000 three per cents., to found a scholarship similar to Lord Craven's for the greatest proficient in classical learning. The *Rev. William Bell, D.D.*, late fellow of Magdalen College, in 1810, transferred £15,200 three per cents. to establish eight new scholarships, for sons or orphans of clergymen. By a grace of the senate, Dec. 9th, 1813, it was directed that the sum of £1000, given by the subscribers to Mr. Pitt's statue, for the purpose of founding the *Pitt scholarship*, and afterwards augmented by a donation of £500 from the Pitt Club, should be placed in the public funds until the syndics were able to vest it in land, the clear annual income to be paid to the scholar. The *Rev. Robert Tyrwhitt, M.A.*, fellow of Jesus' College, who died in 1817, bequeathed £4000 Navy five per cents. for the encouragement of Hebrew learning ; and in the following year the senate decreed the foundation of three Hebrew scholarships, which number, in 1826, was increased to six, a scholar of the first class receiving an annual stipend of £30, and one of the second class a stipend of £20, for three years. The number of scholarships and exhibitions in the university is upwards of 700.

The annual *Income* of the university chest is about £16,000, including about £3000 of floating capital : it arises from stock in the funds, lands, houses, fees for degrees, government annuity (for the surrender of the privilege of printing almanacs), profits of the printing-office, &c. The expenditure is about £12,000, disbursed to the various officers, the professors, the library, and schools, the university press, and in taxes, donations, to charities, &c. The whole is managed by the vice-chancellor for the year, and the accounts are examined by three auditors appointed annually by the senate.

There are two *Courts of Law*, namely, the consistory court of the chancellor, and the consistory court of the commissary. In the former the chancellor, or vice-chancellor, assisted by some of the heads of colleges, and one doctor or more of the civil law, administers justice in all personal pleas and actions arising within the limits of the university, wherein a member of the university is a party, which, excepting only such as concern mayhem and felony, are to be here solely heard and decided. The proceedings are according to the course of the civil law, and from the judgment of the court an appeal lies to the senate. In the commissary's court, the commissary, by authority under the seal of the chancellor, sits both in the university, and at Midsummer and Stourbridge fairs, to proceed in all cases, except those of mayhem and felony, wherein one of the parties is a member of the university ; excepting that within the university all causes to which one of the proctors or taxors, or a master of arts, or any one of superior degree, is a party, are reserved to the sole jurisdiction

f B.A., M.B., or B.C.L., is granted unless a certificate e presented to the Caput that the candidate for such egree has passed, to the satisfaction of the examiners, ome one of these examinations. The student having assed this preparatory step, has next to perform the ercises required by the statutes for the degree which e has in view. The number of members of the university at the present time is 6487, of whom 3451 are of the nate.

Among the principal PUBLIC BUILDINGS are, the nate-house, the schools, and the library; the first rming the north, and the others the west, side of grand quadrangle, which has Great St. Mary's urch on the east, and King's College chapel on the uth. The *Senate House* is an elegant building of rtland stone, erected from a design by Sir James urrough, at the expense of the university, aided by an tensive subscription; its foundation was laid in 1722, it it was not entirely completed until 1766. The exrior is of the Corinthian order, and the interior of the oric. Near the centre of one side of the room is a arble statue of George I., by Rysbrach, executed at the pense of Viscount Townshend; and opposite to it is at of George II., by Wilton, executed in 1766, at the st of the Duke of Newcastle: at the east end, on one de of the entrance, is a statue of the Duke of Somerset, y Rysbrach; and on the other one of William Pitt, by ollekens, erected by a subscription at Cambridge, nounting to upwards of £7000. The *Public Schools*, which disputations are held and exercises performed, ere commenced on their present site in 1443, at the pense of the university, aided by liberal benefactions. hey form three sides of a small court, the philosophy hool being on the west, the divinity school on the rth, and the schools for civil law and physic on the uth; on the east is a lecture-room for the professors, ted up in 1795. Connected with the north end of e philosophy school, is an apartment containing the luable mineralogical collection presented by Dr. Woodard, in 1727. The magnificent *Library* occupies the hole quadrangle of apartments over the schools, and nsists of four large and commodious rooms, conining upwards of 100,000 volumes : at the commenceent, it occupied only the apartment on the east side, it it was afterwards extended to the north side. s most important acquisition was in the early part of e last century, when George I., having purchased of e executors of Dr. Moore, Bishop of Ely, that prelate's llection of books, amounting to upwards of 30,000 lomes, for £6000, gave them to the university, at the me time contributing the sum of £2000 towards fitting) rooms for their reception. The upper part of a muated colossal statue, from the temple of Ceres, at leusis, the gift of Messrs. Clarke and Cripps, of Jesus' ollege, by whom it was brought to England, is placed the vestibule. The rents of the university's estate at vington, in the county of Norfolk, are appropriated to e purchase of books, that estate having been bought ith money given in 1066, by Tobias Rustat, to be so nployed. William Worts, M.A., bequeathed the annual irplus of the produce of his estate at Landbeach, to ambridgeshire, to be applied to the use of the library; id a quarterly contribution of one shilling and sixpence om each member of the university, excepting sizars, also made towards its support. The superintendence

485

of the university press is committed by the senate to syndics, who meet to transact business in the parlour of the printing-office, and cannot act unless five are present, the vice-chancellor being one.

Richard, Viscount Fitzwilliam, of Trinity Hall, who died in 1816, bequeathed to the university his splendid collection of books, paintings, drawings, engravings, &c., together with £100,000 South Sea annuities, for the erection of a *Museum* to contain them ; and the collection has since been augmented by many valuable donations. The building was commenced in 1838, from the designs of Mr. G. Basevi, and forms nearly a square of 160 feet ; the principal or east front is a rich composition, with 14 columns of the Corinthian order, surmounted by a pediment. The ground floor contains three rooms for libraries, extending along the west front, and communicating with two others, one to the south for medals, and that to the north for terra-cottas, &c. ; the upper hall is 70 feet by 46, and will contain casts from the antique, &c. There are also three picture galleries, the floors of which, and also those of the libraries, are of Dutch oak. The *Botanic Garden* occupies between three and four acres on the south-east side of the town, conveniently disposed and well watered ; it was purchased, with a large old building that originally belonged to the Augustine friars, for £1600 by the late Richard Walker, vice-master of Trinity College. The building having been sold, a new one has been erected for the use of the lecturers in chemistry and botany. The garden is under the government of the vice-chancellor, the provost of King's College, the masters of Trinity and St. John's Colleges, and the professor of physic.

The *Anatomical School*, situated near Catherine Hall, contains a large collection of rare and valuable preparations, including the museum of the late professor, Sir B. Harwood, and a set of models beautifully wrought in wax, imported from Naples ; it is a small building conveniently fitted up, with a theatre for the lectures on anatomy and medicine, which are delivered in Lent term. Measures for the establishment of an *Observatory* were adopted in 1820, when a sum of £6000 was subscribed by the members of the university, to which £5000 were added out of the public chest by a grace of the senate. The building was commenced in the year 1822, and completed at an expense exceeding £18,115 : it stands on an eminence, about a mile from the College walks, on the road to Madingley, and is in the Grecian style ; the centre, surmounted by a dome, is appropriated to astronomical purposes, and the wings for the residence of the observers. The superintendence is vested in the Plumian professor, under whose direction are placed two assistants, who must be graduates of the university, and are chosen for three years, being capable of re-election at the expiration of that term. The *Philosophical Society* was instituted Nov. 15th, 1819, for the purpose of promoting scientific inquiries, and of facilitating the communication of facts connected with the advancement of philosophy and natural history ; it consists of fellows and honorary members, the former being elected from such persons only as are graduates of the university, and no graduate or member of the university can be admitted an honorary member. Attached to the society is a reading-room, supplied with the principal literary and scientific journals, and the daily newspapers.

St. Peter's College, commonly called Peter-house, was founded in 1257, by Hugh de Balsham, Bishop of Ely. There are sixteen fellowships on the foundation, to which no person can be elected who is not M.A., or of sufficient standing to take that degree; and not more than *Arms.* two fellows can be chosen from any one county, except those of Cambridge and Middlesex, each of which may have four: one-fourth of the foundation fellows are required to be in priest's orders. By Queen Elizabeth's licence the five senior clerical fellows may hold, with their fellowships, any living not rated higher than £20 in the king's books, and within twenty miles of the university. There are ten bye-fellows distinct from the former, and not entitled to any office or vote in the affairs of the college, but eligible to foundation fellowships. There are fifty-nine scholarships, of different value, which are paid according to residence; also an exhibition from the Company of Clothworkers, and one from the Ironmonger's Company. The Bishop of Ely is visiter, and appoints to the mastership one of two candidates nominated by the society. The number of members on the boards is 228. The college buildings, which stand on the west side of Trumpington-street, consist of three courts, two of which are separated by a cloister and gallery: the largest of these is 144 feet long, 84 broad, and cased with stone; the least, next the street, is divided by the chapel, and has on the north side a lofty modern building faced with stone, the upper part of which commands an extensive prospect of the country towards the south; the third was completed in 1826, by means of a donation from a late fellow, the Rev. Francis Gisborne, from whom it is called the Gisborne Court. The chapel, a handsome structure, erected by subscription in 1632, is chiefly remarkable for its fine east window of painted glass, representing the Crucifixion. Among the eminent persons who have been members of this society, or educated at the college, may be enumerated Cardinal Beaufort; Archbishop Whitgift; Andrew Perne, Dean of Ely; Bishops Wren, Cosin, Walton (editor of the Polyglot Bible), and Law; Moryson, the traveller; Crashawe, the poet; Dr. Sherlock, Dean of St. Paul's; Sir Samuel Garth; Jeremiah Markland; the poet Gray; and Lord Chief Justice Ellenborough.

Clare Hall was founded in 1326, by Dr. Richard Badew, afterwards chancellor of the university, by the name of University Hall; but having been burned to the ground about the year 1342, it was rebuilt and munificently endowed, through the interest of Badew, by Elizabeth de *Arms.* Burgh, one of the sisters and coheiresses of Gilbert, Earl of Clare, and from her received its present name. The society consists of a master, ten senior or foundation fellows, nine junior, and three bye-appropriation, fellows; the senior and junior fellowships are open to all counties. The master is elected by the senior and junior fellows, and must be either a bachelor or a doctor in divinity; and the seniors must all be divines, except two, who, with the consent of the master and a majority of the fellows, may practise law

mong the college plate is preserved a curious gilt silver
p, the gift of the foundress in the reign of Ed-
rd III. The chapel, built by Dr. Matthew Wren,
shop of Ely, from a design by his nephew Sir
ristopher, and consecrated by that bishop in 1655, is
e of the most elegant and best-proportioned in
e university. Of the more eminent members, &c.,
ay be reckoned, Archbishops Grindal and Whitgift;
shops Lindwood, Fox, Ridley and Andrews; the
artyrs, Rogers and Bradford; the poets, Spenser,
ray, and Mason; Dr. Long, the astronomer; Stanley,
itor of *Æschylus*; and the illustrious statesman, Wil-
m Pitt.

GONVILLE AND CAIUS COLLEGE,
originally styled Gonville Hall, was
founded in 1347, by Edmund, son of
Sir Nicholas Gonville, of Terrington,
in the county of Norfolk; in 1558,
the hall was consolidated with the
new foundation by Dr. John Caius,
and under the charter then obtained

Arms.   the united foundations received the
me they now bear. There are 29 fellowships, of
hich 21 are open to all counties, and 17 to laymen;
o of the fellows must be physicians. The college has
3 scholarships, open to all counties; three are of the
lue of £56 per annum each, six of £40, six of £36,
x of £30, one of £24, one of £22, and three of £20.
here are also, a scholarship in chemistry, of the value
£20 per annum; and four studentships in physic, of
e annual value of £113 each, founded by C. Tancred,
sq., who died in 1754, and who likewise founded four
udentships of nearly the same value, appropriated to
w, to be held by students of Lincoln's Inn, who are
t required to be members of the university. In addi-
on to these, are fourteen exhibitions of different value.
he visiters are, the masters of Corpus Christi College,
e senior doctor in physic, and the master of Trinity
all; the number of members on the boards is 317.
he college stands on the west side of Trinity-street,
aving Trinity College on the north, Trinity Hall on the
est, and the senate-house on the south; it consists of
ree courts. The south court, and three remarkable
ates of Grecian architecture, built by Dr. Caius, are
pposed to have been designed by John of Padua,
rchitect to Henry VIII., and to be the only works of
is now remaining in the kingdom: of the principal
urt, part has been rebuilt, and the rest cased with
one and elegantly ashed. The chapel, though small,
admired for its beauty: on the south wall is a monu-
ent of Dr. Caius, under a canopy; also a monument
f Stephen Perse, M.D., a great benefactor to the uni-
ersity, who died in 1615; and in the ante-chapel is
e gravestone of Sir James Burrough, Knt., formerly
aster, an ingenious architect, who designed the senate-
ouse and other public buildings in Cambridge, and
ied in 1774. The library is small, but contains some
cceedingly valuable books and manuscripts, particu-
rly in the departments of heraldry and genealogy.
The college has been a celebrated seminary for pro-
ssors of medicine and anatomy, ever since the time of
s second founder, the learned physician, Dr. Caius. Of
ose who have most eminently conferred honour on the
ciety in this faculty, may be enumerated, Dr. Francis
lisson; Sir Charles Scarborough; William Harvey,

the discoverer of the circulation of the blood; and Dr.
William Hyde Wollaston. Among other distinguished
members, or students, have been Dr. Branthwaite, one
of the translators of the Bible; Sir Thomas Gresham;
Sir Peter le Neve, the herald and antiquary; Richard
Parker, author of the Σκελετὸς *Cantabrigiensis*; Dr. Brady,
the historian; Henry Wharton, author of the *Anglia
Sacra*; Sir Henry Chauncy and Francis Blomefield, the
historians of Hertfordshire and Norfolk; the celebrated
Bishop Taylor; Bishop Skip, one of the compilers of
the Liturgy; Jeremy Collier; the learned Dr. Samuel
Clarke; Thomas Shadwell, the poet; and Lord Chancellor Thurlow.

TRINITY HALL was founded in 1350,
by William Bateman, Bishop of Norwich. There are twelve fellowships,
which are ordinarily held by graduates in civil law; ten of the fellows
are usually laymen, and two in holy
orders. The lord chancellor is visiter;
the number of members on the boards
is 149. The Hall stands behind the   *Arms.*
senate-house, near the river, and on the northern side
of Clare Hall: the principal court is very neat, being
faced with stone both within and without; the second
is a convenient and handsome pile of brick and stone.
The chapel is chiefly worthy of notice for its finely-
painted altar-piece. The library contains, among other
valuable books, a complete body of the canon, Roman,
and common law. Of remarkable persons who have
been members, or students, may be named Bilney, the
martyr; Gardiner, Bishop of Winchester; Bishops
Barlow, Halifax, and Horsley; Thomas Tusser, the
writer on husbandry; Sir Peter Wyche, the traveller;
Dr. Haddon, master of the requests to Queen Elizabeth; Sir Robert Naunton, secretary of state to James
I.; Philip, the celebrated Earl of Chesterfield; Sir William de Grey, chief justice of the common pleas; and
several other eminent lawyers, who have recently filled
distinguished offices.

CORPUS CHRISTI COLLEGE was
founded in 1351, by the brethren of
two guilds in Cambridge, bearing the
names of Gilda Corporis Christi, and
Gilda Beatæ Mariæ Virginis. There
are twelve fellowships, four of which
are appropriated, two for pupils from
the school at Norwich, and two for
natives of the county of Norfolk; the   *Arms.*
rest are open, with the restriction only that four of the
candidates shall, if possible, be natives of Norfolk: all
the fellows are required to take orders within three
years after their election. The visiters are, the vice-
chancellor, and the two senior doctors in divinity; in
extraordinary cases the sovereign is visiter. The present
number of members on the boards is 283.
This college, frequently called Bene't College, from its
proximity to the church of St. Benedict, is situated
opposite to Catherine Hall: the extent and magnificence
of its buildings give it a high rank among the recent improvements which have added so much to the splendour
of the university. It consists of two large courts, the
old and the new, the latter having been lately erected
out of the funds which had accumulated for that purpose, from the munificent bequests of Archbishop Her-

ring, and Bishops Mawson and Green, formerly masters of the college. The new buildings were commenced in July 1823 : the grand west front is 222 feet long, with a lofty massive tower at each extremity, and a superb entrance gateway, in the centre, flanked by towers corresponding with the former ; the court is 158 feet long, and 129 broad, having the chapel on the east side, the library on the south, and the hall on the north. The chapel, begun in 1579 by the Lord Keeper Bacon, is 66 feet long, and its exterior is richly adorned with sculpture. The library is a fine lofty room, 88 feet long, and contains the valuable manuscripts bequeathed to the college by Archbishop Parker, comprising a collection of papers upon ecclesiastical affairs, made on the dissolution of religious houses by Henry VIII., with other interesting documents relating to the Reformation, and the original record of the Thirty-nine Articles. The old court, situated behind the hall, is a very ancient pile of building, entirely appropriated to the students. Among the college plate is a curious drinking-horn, which belonged to the guild of Corpus Christi.

Of the distinguished members may be reckoned Archbishops Parker, Tenison, Herring, and Sterne ; Bishops Allen, Fletcher, Jegon, Greene (Thomas), Bradford, Mawson, Green (John), Ashburnham, and Yorke; Sir Nicholas Bacon; Roger Manners, fifth earl of Rutland ; Philip, second earl of Hardwicke ; his brother, the Right Hon. Charles Yorke; Sir John Cust, Bart., speaker of the house of commons; Fletcher, the dramatic poet ; Stephen Hales, the natural philosopher ; Nathaniel Salmon, the topographer ; and Dr. Stukeley, Robert Masters (the historian of the college), and Richard Gough, celebrated antiquaries.

KING'S COLLEGE was founded in 1441, by King Henry VI. The society consists of a provost and seventy fellows and scholars ; the latter are supplied by a regular succession from Eton College, and, at the expiration of three years from the day of their admission, are elected fellows. The college possesses some remarkable privileges and exemptions. By charter it appoints its own coroner, and no writ of arrest can be executed within its walls; the provost has absolute authority within the precincts. By special composition between the society and the university, the members are exempt from the power of the proctors and the university officers, within the limits of the college ; by usage they keep no public exercises in the schools, nor are they in any way examined for the degree of bachelor of arts. The Bishop of Lincoln is visiter; the present number of members on the boards is 121.

Arms.

The *Buildings* stand on the west side and near the centre of King's Parade, between it and the river, over which is a handsome stone bridge, communicating with the shady walks on the other side. They consist principally of the old court, now uninhabited, and purchased by the university to be taken down, in order to enlarge the public schools ; and the grand court, lately completed, having Gibbs' building on the west, the magnificent chapel on the north, the library and hall on the south, and a grand entrance from Trumpington-street on the east ; forming altogether the most superb group of buildings in Cambridge. The old court, built of

,xcepted, from which there may be three; there may lso be one fellow beyond the prescribed number from /liddlesex, Essex, Cambridge, and Kent, in which the ollege has property sufficient for the maintenance of a ellow : two fellows may remain laymen, and within welve years from M.A., one of the two must proceed to).C.L., the other to M.D. The vice-president and the ve senior fellows hold their fellowships with property ; he others quit the society when possessed of a stated nnual income. The five senior divines may hold livings ated in the king's books at not higher than £20 per nnum, and within twenty miles of .Cambridge. Every ther fellow must resign his fellowship at the expiration f a year after he has become possessed of preferment ated in the king's books at £10 per annum or upwards, r of real property producing an income of £100 per nnum, clear of all deductions. There is one bye-llowship, which is perfectly open, may be held by a yman, and is tenable with any property or prefer-ent ; but the holder has no vote in the society. The cholarships have been consolidated into twenty-six, and ugmented by college grants, many of them having pre-iously been inconsiderable : they are payable weekly ccording to residence. The president must be elected y a majority of the whole existing body, must have raduated B.D. at least, and must possess property to he amount of £20 per annum. The sovereign is visiter : he number of members on the boards is 339. The uildings are situated to the West of Catherine Hall, n the banks of the Cam, and consist of three courts of onsiderable magnitude. The entrance to the outer or rincipal. court, which is 96 feet by 84, is through an legant tower gateway ; the inner court is furnished with loisters about 300 yards in circumference, and extends) the bank of the river : Walnut-tree court has build-igs on one side only. The front of the college, next the 'am, was rebuilt a few years since, in an elegant style. he grove and gardens are particularly beautiful, and, ring on both sides of the stream, are connected by a 'ooden bridge of one arch, built in 1746, and much dmired for the ingenuity of its construction. Amongst minent members, or students, of the college, have been .rchbishop Grindall; Bishops Fisher, Davenant, Spar-)w, and Patrick ; Sir Thomas Smith, the statesman;)r. Thomas Smith, the ecclesiastical historian ; Thomas rightman, author of a treatise on the Revelation ; ohn Weever, author of the *Funeral Monuments*; Thomas uller, author of the *Worthies of England*, and other orks, historical and ecclesiastical ; and Dr. John Wallis, he mathematician. The celebrated Erasmus, also, was r some time a student.

CATHERINE HALL was established in 1475, by Robert Woodlark, D.D., chancellor of the university, and provost of King's College. There are six fellowships on the founda-tion, which may be increased or di-minished in number, in proportion to the revenue of the college : there cannot be more than two fellows om any one county at the same time ; and two of them t least must be in priest's and one in deacon's orders. herc arc eight other fellowships, in filling up six of hich, " a preference is to be given to persons born in the ty of York, if duly qualified." The scholarships are

Arms.

43 in number, varying in value from £2 to £35 per annum each ; thirteen are appropriated, and to several scholarships chambers rent-free are attached. The num-ber of members on the boards is 223. The Buildings form three sides of a quadrangle, 180 feet by 120, the fourth side being open towards Trinity-street, and having iron palisades, and a piece of ground planted with lofty elm-trees ; the front is towards the west, and has an elegant portico in the centre. The library, a very hand-some room, was fitted up at the expense of Dr. Thomas Sherlock, Bishop of London, who bequeathed to the college his large and valuable collection, and also left a stipend for the librarian. Amongst eminent members and students have been Archbishops Sandys and Dawes ; Bishops Overall, (who compiled a work called " The Convocation Book," wrote the sacramental part of the Church Catechism, and assisted in the translation of the Bible,) Brownrigg, Leng (author of the Cambridge *Terence*), Blackall, Hoadley, and Sherlock ; John Brad-ford, the martyr ; John Strype, the ecclesiastical his-torian and biographer ; Ray, the naturalist ; and Dr. John Lightfoot, the orientalist, and author of the *Horæ Hebraicæ*.

JESUS COLLEGE was founded by John Alcock, Bishop of Ely, in 1496, on the site of a Benedictine nunnery, established about the year 1130, and dedicated to the Virgin Mary, St. John the Baptist, and the Virgin St. Rhadegund, the endow-ment of which was augmented by Malcolm, fourth king of Scotland, and the possessions of which, on its dissolution in the reign of Henry VII., were granted to the bishop. There are sixteen foundation fellowships : eight of the fellows are to be natives of the northern, and eight of the southern counties, and six in priest's orders ; and by a late statute, granted by the Bishop of Ely, and with the king's licence, the society has been empowered to elect fellows from any part of England and Wales, without restriction. On each vacancy the master and fellows nominate two candidates, of whom the Bishop appoints one. There is one fellowship to which the bishop has an exclusive right both to nominate and appoint ; he is also visiter, and appoints the master. The college has 46 scholarships and exhibitions, varying in value from £9 to £70 per annum, and of which 27 are ap-propriated. The number of members on the boards of the college at the present time is 197.

Arms.

The *Buildings*, which are situated at the extremity of the town, consist of a principal court, 141 feet by 120, which is built on three sides ; and a small court sur-rounded by a cloister : an addition has lately been made to the eastern side of the college. The grand front looks towards the south, and is 180 feet long, being regularly built and sashed. Both the master and fellows have spacious gardens. The library contains many scarce and valuable editions of the classics. The chapel, anciently the conventual church of St. Rhadegund, ex-hibits, particularly in the chancel and the interior of the tower, considerable remains of the original structure ; the altar-piece, representing the Presentation in the Temple, was given in 1796, by Dr. Pearce, master of the college. In the south transept of what is now the ante-chapel are the tombs of one of the nuns, named

Berta Rosata, and of Prior John de Pykenham, the latter of which is supposed to have been removed hither from the neighbouring convent of Franciscans: in the north transept is the monument of Tobias Rustat, yeoman of the robes to King Charles II., a benefactor to the college, and who was equally remarkable for his great wealth and his extensive charities.

Amongst eminent members and students may be reckoned Archbishops Cranmer, Sterne, Herring, and Hutton; Bishop Bale, the biographer; Dr. John Nalson, the historian; Roger North, the biographer; John Flamsteed, the astronomer; Fenton, the poet; Dr. Jortin; the witty Lawrence Sterne; Tyrwhitt, the founder of the Hebrew scholarships; Gilbert Wakefield, the classical editor and critic; and the celebrated traveller, Dr. Edward Daniel Clarke.

 CHRIST'S COLLEGE was originally founded in 1456, by Henry VI., under the name of God's House; but in 1505, the Lady Margaret, Countess of Richmond and Derby, changed the name, incorporated the former society with the present college, and endowed it liberally for the maintenance of a master and *Arms.* twelve fellows. This foundation is for divinity, and the fellows are required to take priest's orders within twelve months after they have attained the requisite age. The only appropriation is to the counties of England and Wales; the restrictions are, that there shall not be two of the same county, and that there shall be six, and only six, from nine specified shires in the north of England collectively. Edward VI. added another fellowship, the holder of which participates in the emolument of the original foundation; he may be from any county, and is not obliged to take holy orders. Sir John Finch and Sir Thomas Baines founded two more fellowships unappropriated as to county, but with preference to the kindred of the founders: the revenues are independent of the college. These fifteen fellows have an equal claim to the college patronage, and are allowed by the statutes to hold preferment with their fellowships, provided it does not exceed the value of ten marks, after the deductions found in the king's books. Lady Margaret founded 47 scholarships, now augmented to 15s. per week during residence; there can only be three scholars of one county. Three were added by Edward VI.: various other scholarships and exhibitions have been founded by private benefactors; and four divinity studentships, the present value of which is £113 per annum each, were established by C. Tancred, Esq., who also founded a scholarship, value about £35 per annum, with preference to a native of Newmarket, secondly to the county of Cambridge. The visiters are the vice-chancellor and the two senior doctors of divinity; or, if the vice-chancellor be of this college, the provost of King's. The number of members on the boards is 301.

The *Buildings* stand north of Emmanuel College, and opposite to St. Andrew's church; and consist of the principal court, a handsome quadrangle, 130 feet by 120, and a second court, built on two sides, of which that next the garden and fields is an elegant and uniform pile of stone, about 150 feet long. The chapel is 84 feet long, with a floor of marble: in the east window are portraits of Henry VII., and some others of the family
490

of the foundress; and within the rails of the altar is the gravestone of Dr. Ralph Cudworth, author of the *Intellectual System*, and master of the college, who died in the year 1688. The garden has a bowling-green and a cold bath, and contains a large mulberry-tree, planted by Milton, when he was a student here.

Besides the great poet just mentioned, the following eminent persons have been members of the society, or students at the college: Leland, the antiquary; Archbishop John Sharp; Bishops Latimer, Law, and Porteus; Hugh Broughton, and Dr. Lightfoot, the orientalists; the poets, John Cleland, and Francis Quarles; Dr. Joseph Mede, an eminent divine; Dr. Thomas Burnet, author of the *Theory of the Earth*; Dr. Lawrence Echard, the historian; Dr. Saunderson, the mathematician; and Archdeacon Paley.

ST. JOHN'S COLLEGE was founded in 1511, by the executors of Margaret, Countess of Richmond and Derby: the original endowment was for 50 fellows, but part of the foundation estates having been seized by Henry VIII., the funds were found to be sufficient only for 32 fellowships. These, by letters-patent from *Arms.* George IV., are now open to natives of England and Wales, without any restriction or appropriation whatsoever; one of them is in the appointment of the Bishop of Ely. Candidates must have taken the degree of B.A. at least; and none are superannuated, provided they have proceeded regularly to their degrees. This being a divinity college, all the fellows are obliged to be in priest's orders within six years from the degree of M.A., except four, who are allowed by the master and seniors to practise law and physic; and the others must proceed to the degree of B.D. at the regular time: the electors are the master and eight senior resident fellows, in whom is vested the entire management of the college concerns. There are also 21 appropriated fellowships, which have all the privileges of the foundation fellowships, and an equal claim to the college patronage; and besides these, are three fellowships founded by Mr. Platt, and subsequently increased to nine by the society, which are open to all candidates; but the fellows are not allowed to hold any college preferment. Of the 114 scholarships, nine, founded by the Duchess of Somerset, have been augmented by the society to sixteen, which are appropriated to Manchester, Hertford, and Marlborough schools; and four, founded by Mr. Platt, have been increased by the college to nine, tenable, like the above-mentioned fellowships founded by him, by candidates born in any county. There are numerous exhibitions, varying from £70 each downwards. All livings under £30 in the king's books are tenable with the college preacherships, of which there are thirteen. The Bishop of Ely is visiter; the number of members on the boards at the present time is 1318.

The older *Buildings* are situated to the north of Trinity College, and occupy the whole space between Trinity-street and the river, consisting of three courts, built for the most part of brick. The first, which is the most ancient court, is about 228 feet by 216, and is entered from the street by a handsome gateway, with turrets coeval with the foundation; the second court, about 270 feet by 240, built by the benefaction of Mary,

Countess of Shrewsbury, is very handsome, and chiefly consists of fellows' apartments; the third, next the river, is of smaller dimensions than the others. The north side of the first court is occupied by the chapel, that of the second by the master's lodge, and that of the third by the library; extending altogether, from east to west, about 480 feet. The chapel is 120 feet long: in the ante-chapel is the tombstone of Thomas Baker, D.D., commonly called " Socius Ejectus," some time fellow of the college, and who wrote its history; and in the chapel is a tablet in memory of the learned Dr. Whitaker, master, who died in 1595. In the master's lodge is a spacious ancient gallery, nearly 155 feet long, with a richly ornamented ceiling, now divided into a suite of rooms, containing numerous portraits of benefactors and members of the college. The library, built by Archbishop Williams, contains one of the most valuable and extensive collections of books in the university, among which are those left by Dr. Baker, and those presented to the college by Matthew Prior, consisting chiefly of the works of the French historians. The spacious gardens and walks lie on the west side of the river, over which a stone bridge of three arches, leading from the inner court : the fellows' garden has a bowling-green. A large and splendid addition to the college has been lately completed, from a design by Rickman and Hutchinson, on the western side of the river, consisting of a spacious court, united to the three ancient courts by a covered stone bridge. The inner and the eastern and western fronts are all varied; the cloister extends from the east to the west wing, and has a lofty entrance in the centre : this building affords additional accommodation for one hundred and seven students, including ten suites of apartments for fellows of the college.

Amongst eminent members, &c., have been Roger Ascham ; Sir John Cheke; Sir Thomas Wyat ; Lord Treasurer Burleigh; Lord Keeper Williams; Dr. John Dee ; Thomas Wentworth, Earl of Strafford ; Lord Falkland ; Dr. William Whitaker ; Dr. William Cave ; Archbishop Williams ; Bishops Day, Gauden, Gunning, Jeremy Taylor, Stillingfleet, and Beveridge; Dr. Jenkins, who wrote on the reasonableness of Christianity ; Mr. Powell ; Dr. Balguy ; Dr. Ogden ; Thomas Stackhouse, author of the *History of the Bible ;* Dr. William Wotton, and Dr. Bentley, the critics ; Ben Jonson ; the poets, John Cleland, Ambrose Philips, Prior, Otway, Broome, Hammond, Mason, and Henry Kirke White; Martin Lister, the naturalist ; Francis Peck, and Thomas Baker, the antiquaries; the late Dr. Heberden ; and Herschel, the Queen's astronomer.

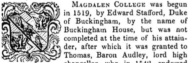

Arms.

MAGDALEN COLLEGE was begun in 1519, by Edward Stafford, Duke of Buckingham, by the name of Buckingham House, but was not completed at the time of his attainder, after which it was granted to Thomas, Baron Audley, lord high chancellor, who, in 1542, endowed it for a master and four fellows. here are thirteen bye-fellowships; two of them are appropriated, one of the two being a travelling fellowship, founded by the Rev. Drue Drury, and worth upwards of £200 per annum, but tenable for only nine years, and appropriated to the county of Norfolk : the master has the sole appointment to this fellowship, 491

and the person must either be in holy orders or designed for such. The other was founded by Dr. Millington, for the benefit of Shrewsbury grammar school. All the fellows, except those of the two last-mentioned fellowships, must take orders within three years after election, if the master think fit. The mastership is in the appointment of the possessor of the estate at Audley-End, now Lord Braybrooke. There are 42 scholarships, varying in value from £3 to £70 per annum each ; 12 of which are appropriated. The possessor of Audley-End is visiter ; the number of members on the boards is 207. This is the only college which stands on the north side of the river ; it consists of two courts, the larger being about 110 feet by 78. On the north side of the second court is a stone building, the body of which comprises the Pepysian library, given to the college by Samuel Pepys, secretary to the admiralty in the reigns of Charles II. and James II., and which contains many valuable curiosities ; in the wings are the apartments of the fellows. Among distinguished members, &c., may be named Archbishop Grindal ; Dr. Thomas Nevile, who erected the beautiful court in Trinity College which bears his name ; Pepys, the founder of the library ; Dr. Duport, the celebrated Greek professor ; the Lord Keeper Bridgeman ; Bishop Walton, editor of the *Polyglot Bible ;* Bishop Rainbow ; Dr. Howell, the historian ; Bishop Cumberland ; Dr. Waterland ; and Professor Waring.

TRINITY COLLEGE stands on ground formerly occupied by seven hostels and two colleges, Michael House and King's Hall. The former college was established in 1324, by Hervey de Stanton, chancellor of the exchequer to Edward II. ; the buildings of the latter, founded by Edward III., in 1337, for a master and 32 scholars, are said to have been of sufficient magnitude to accommodate Richard II. and his court, when he held a parliament at Cambridge, in 1381. Both these colleges were suppressed in 1546, and in the same year the present magnificent one was instituted by Henry VIII., for a master, 60 fellows, and 69 scholars, whose endowment was considerably augmented by his daughter, Queen Mary. The fellows are chosen from the scholars, ineligible if M.A., or of sufficient standing to take that degree; they are all required to go into priest's orders within seven years after they commence masters of arts, except two appointed by the master, one of whom is supposed to study law, the other physic. The scholarships, except four or five, are open to persons of any county. The government is vested in the master and eight seniors; and to so many of these as are absent the resident fellows next in seniority act as deputies : the mastership is in the gift of the sovereign, who is visiter. The number of members on the boards at the present time is 2044.

Arms.

The extensive Buildings of the college are situated between those of St. John's and Caius Colleges, occupying the space between Trinity-street and the river, and consisting of three quadrangular courts. The first court, which is the largest, forms a magnificent assemblage of buildings : on the north side is the chapel; on the west, the hall and the master's lodge ; while the other two sides comprise apartments for fellows and students. The south end of the west side has been rebuilt in a handsome style. The second court, called *Nevile's Court*, built in 1600, chiefly by the benefaction of Dr. Thomas Nevile, master of the college and Dean of Canterbury, is more elegant than the former, though less spacious. The library, forming the west side, is of later date, having been built chiefly through the exertions of Dr. Barrow; and the north and south sides, containing fellows' and students' apartments, have been almost wholly rebuilt: the library, and the cloisters which extend along the north, west, and south sides, were designed by Sir Christopher Wren. Beyond Nevile's Court is a newly erected quadrangle, called *King's Court* in honour of George IV.; the building of which was commenced in 1823, and completed in 1825, at an expense of upwards of £40,000, partly defrayed by a subscription, headed by a donation of £2000 from that monarch. It is from designs by William Wilkins, Esq., M.A.; and the principal front, with a tower gateway, faces the College walks, in a line with the library. The *Chapel*, upwards of 200 feet long, and in the later style of English architecture, was begun by Queen Mary, and finished by Queen Elizabeth: on each side of the choir are rows of very elegant stalls for the masters and scholars, with carved work by Gibbons; and the thrones for the master and the vice-master are remarkably grand. Among the monuments in the ante-chapel, the most interesting are, a statue of Bacon, by Weekes; a statue of Sir Isaac Newton, by Roubilliac, presented to the society by Dr. Robert Smith, master of the college; a tablet in memory of the eminent mathematician, Roger Cotes, Plumian professor, who died in 1716; another in memory of Isaac Hawkins Browne, celebrated for his poem on the Immortality of the Soul, and other works, who died in 1762; and a bust and tablet, by Chantrey, in memory of Professor Porson. The *Hall*, built in the later English style, is about 100 feet long, and 50 high. The *Master's Lodge*, which contains some magnificent apartments, has, since the reign of Elizabeth, been the residence of the sovereign, when the university has been honoured with a royal visit; and the judges always reside in it during the assizes. The *Library*, a splendid room, 200 feet long, and proportionately lofty, was built by subscription, amounting to nearly £20,000. The collection of books is large and valuable, and among the busts are those of Bacon, Newton, Ray, Willoughby, Roger Cotes, and Edward Wortley Montagu: there is a statue of Byron, by Thorwaldsen; also a statue of Charles Seymour, Duke of Somerset, for sixty years chancellor of the university, executed by Rysbrach in 1754; and at the upper end is a curious statue of Æsculapius, found at Samæ, about fourteen miles from Rome. Of the portraits, the most interesting is an original half-length of Shakspeare, by Mark Garrard, The room is paved with marble; and at the south end, opposite to the entrance, is a window of painted glass, from a design by Cipriani, representing the presentation of Sir Isaac Newton to George II.; for the execution of which, £500 were bequeathed by Dr. Robert Smith.

Amongst eminent members and students of the college have been, Archbishops Whitgift and Fowler; Bishops Powell, Wilkins, Hacket, Pearson, Pearce, Hinchcliffe, and Watson; Robert Devereux, Earl of Essex; Sir Francis Bacon; Sir Edward Coke; Fulke Greville; Lord Brooke; Charles, Earl of Halifax; Sir *m*; Joshua Barnes; Dr. Wallis, the mathematician; r Robert Twiston, the antiquary; John Morton, the storian of Northamptonshire; Sir Francis Pemberton; r William Temple; Anthony Blackwall, author of *The cred Classics Defended and Illustrated*; Dr. Farmer, to ıose memory there is a tablet in the cloister, near the apel; and Dr. Parr.

Arms.

SIDNEY-SUSSEX COLLEGE was instituted in 1598, pursuant to the will of Frances Sidney, Countess of Sussex, who died in 1589. It has nine foundation fellowships, open to natives of any part of her Majesty's dominions; besides which there are two established by Mr. Peter Blundell, and appropriated to his scholarships

the college, and one the nomination to which is sted in the Company of Fishmongers, London. No low derives any benefit from his fellowship unless he M.A. complete; and this being a divinity college, all e fellows must take orders within three years from e time of their election, and the degree of B.D. at the gular period. There are twenty foundation scholar-ıps, value 7*s.* per week during residence; and two unded by Mr. Blundell, appropriated to Twerton hool. Sir John Shelley Sidney, Bart., is visiter, as e representative of the foundress; but, by the statutes, e vice-chancellor and the two senior doctors in divinity e visiters in some cases, and the vice-chancellor, with e masters of Christ's and Emmanuel Colleges, in others. e number of members on the boards is 118. The build-gs are situated on the east side of Sidney-street, and ınsist of two courts built of brick, and completed in 598. The chapel and the library were rebuilt in 1780; ıd the hall and the master's lodge have lately been ised with stone, and greatly improved. The grounds ːe spacious, and the fellows' garden has a large bowl-ıg-green. Amongst eminent members or students may e recorded Oliver Cromwell; Archbishop Bramhall; ishops Seth Ward, Montagu, and Garnet; Thomas uller, the historian; Lord Chief Baron Atkins; Sir oger L'Estrange; Gataker, the critic; Dr. Comber, 'ean of Durham; Thomas Woolston, who wrote against iracles; and William Wollaston, author of *The Reli-on of Nature Delineated.* In the master's lodge is a ɔrtrait in crayons, of Cromwell, by Cooper; and in ıe library, a bust by Bernini, from a cast taken after ıe usurper's death.

DOWNING COLLEGE was founded by Sir George Downing, Bart., of Gamlingay Park, Cambridgeshire, who, by will dated in 1717, devised his estates in the counties of Cam-bridge, Bedford, and Suffolk, first to Sir Jacob Garrard Downing, and afterwards to other relatives, in suc-cession, and, in failure thereof, to

Arms.

ɔund a college in the university, upon a plan to be ɔproved by the two archbishops and the masters of St. ɔhn's College and Clare Hall. Sir Jacob died in 1764, ıe other devisees having died previously without issue; ut the estates being held by Lady Downing, and after-ards by her devisees, though without any real title, the niversity was obliged to sue in Chancery for the estab-shment of the college, in favour of which a decree was

493

obtained in 1769, and, after much litigation, a charter in Sept. 1800. A piece of land comprising nearly thirty acres, situated between Emmanuel and Pembroke Colleges, having been purchased for the site, the first stone was laid on May 18th, 1807, since which time the building has proceeded at intervals, at an expense of more than £60,000. The object of the foundation is stated in the charter to be the study of law, physic, and other useful arts and learning; and the society will consist of a master, professors of law and medicine, sixteen fellows (of whom two only are to be clerical), and six scholars. At present, however, only the master, the professors and three fellows are appointed, to take possession of the estates, administer the revenues, and superintend the erection of the college; the appointment of the remain-ing fellows is reserved until the completion of the build-ings. The scholars will also be elected after that period, but not more than two in each year. There are two chaplains nominated by the master, who is directed to be chosen, by the archbishops of Canterbury and York, and the masters of St. John's College and Clare Hall, from amongst those who are, or have been, professors or fellows. The visiter is the sovereign, by the Lord Chan-cellor; the number of members on the boards is 53. The whole buildings, when finished, will form a quad-rangle, larger than the principal court of Trinity College, in the Grecian style, and faced with Ketton stone; the master's lodge is of the Ionic, and the entrance to the college will be of the Doric, order : the designs are by Mr. Wilkins. Mr. John Bowtell, of Cambridge, be-queathed to the college a collection of books, manu-scripts, and antiquities.

The TOWN is divided into four distinct wards, named respectively Bridge ward, Market ward, High ward, and Preacher's ward; and contains the fourteen PARISHES of All Saints, in which are 1231 inhabitants; St. Andrew the Great, 1983; St. Andrew the Less, 9486; St. Bene-dict, 1022; St. Botolph, 723; St. Clement, 1039; St. Edward, 619; St. Giles, 2087; St. Mary the Great, 1013; St. Mary the Less, 704; St. Michael, 432; St. Peter, 627; St. Sepulchre, 638; and the Holy Trinity, 2189. The university, by custom and composition, is exempt from episcopal and archidiaconal jurisdiction. The living of *All Saints* is a discharged vicarage, valued in the king's books at £5. 6. 3.; net income, £120; patrons and impropriators, the Master and Fellows of Jesus College. The church contains a fine bas-relief, by Chantrey, to the memory of Kirke White. The living of *St. Andrew's the Great* is a discharged vicarage; net income £120; patrons and impropriators, the Dean and Chapter of Ely : the tithes were commuted for land in 1807. The church was repaired, and a great part of it rebuilt, in 1643, chiefly by aid of a benefaction by Christopher Rose, and has lately been rebuilt and enlarged; in the north transept is a cenotaph in memory of the celebrated navigator, Captain Cook, and his three sons. The living of *St. Andrew's the Less*, or *Barnwell*, is a donative; net income, £48; patron, the Rev. C. Perry : the tithes were commuted for land in 1807. The old church stands eastward from the town, and is supposed to have been built from the ruins of the priory at Barnwell. The village of Barnwell has suffered from repeated fires, the last and most destructive of which was on the 30th of Nov. 1731, when the greater part of the houses were consumed. A chapel of ease was erected a few years since ; and an additional church, dedicated to Christ, a handsome edifice in the later English style, and now used as the parish church, was consecrated on the 27th of July, 1839 : it contains 1400 sittings, of which 700 are free. At New Town, also in the parish, a church was erected in 1841, at an expense of £5180, in the same style of architecture as the former, and containing 900 sittings, half of which are free, the Incorporated Society having granted £450 in aid of the expense. The living of *St. Benedict's* is a perpetual curacy, valued at £4. 7. 11. ; net income, £151 ; patrons and impropriators, the Master and Fellows of Corpus Christi College. In the church was interred Thomas Hobson, the well-known Cambridge carrier. The living of *St. Botolph's* is a discharged rectory, valued at £2. 14. 4½. ; net income, £87 ; patrons, the President and Fellows of Queen's College. The living of *St. Clement's* is a perpetual curacy, valued at £4. 5. 7½. ; net income, £102 ; patrons, the Master and Fellows of Jesus College. The church stands a little south of the great bridge. The living of *St. Edward's* is a perpetual curacy, valued at 3s. 4d. ; net income, £66 ; patrons and impropriators, the Master and Fellows of Trinity Hall. The church is to the west of Trinity-street. The living of *St. Giles'* is a vicarage not in charge, to which the perpetual curacy of *St. Peter's* is united ; net income, £170 ; patron and appropriator, the Bishop of Ely : the tithes were commuted for land and a money payment in 1802. St. Giles' church stands at the north end of the town ; St. Peter's, opposite to it, has been disused for many years.

The living of *St. Mary's the Great* is a rectory not in charge ; net income, under £100 ; patrons, the Master and Fellows of Trinity College : the tithes were commuted for land in 1807. The church, commonly called the University church, is situated nearly in the centre of the town, on the east side of Trinity-street, and opposite to the public schools and library ; it is in the later English style, and consists of a nave, the dimensions of which are about 120 feet by 68, two aisles, and a chancel with a lofty tower surmounted by pinnacles, and containing twelve bells. The rebuilding of the church, by contribution, was begun in 1478, and finished in 1519, except the tower, which was not completed until 1608. In it was interred the celebrated reformer, Martin Bucer, whose body was taken up in the reign of Mary and burned, with that of Paul Phagius, in the market-place. Academical exercises were anciently performed, and public orations delivered, here ; and, in 1564, Queen Elizabeth was present at the disputations held in it : the university sermons are still preached here. William Worts, Esq., who died in 1709, left the sum of £1500, to accumulate for the purpose of building the galleries, and £20 per annum for keeping them in repair. The living of *St. Mary's the Less* is a perpetual curacy ; net income, £95 ; patrons and impropriators, the Master and Fellows of St. Peter's College, whose tithes were commuted for land in 1807. The church was built in 1327, on the site of a former edifice, dedicated to St. Peter, which gave name to the adjoining college. The living of *St. Michael's* is a perpetual curacy ; net income, £95 ; patrons and impropriators, the Master and Fellows of Trinity College. The church stands on the east side of Trinity-street, opposite to Caius College : in the spacious chancel are held the

disposed of in loans of £20 each, bearing no interest for twenty years, to ten young men, to set them up in trade. After the sum of £200 had been set apart, the donor ordered that the rents of the estates should be applied to the relief of persons confined for debt, and of old men and women of good character. Cambridge is also one of the twenty-five cities and towns to which Mr *Thomas White* gave, in rotation, the sum of £104, of which £100 were to be lent, in sums of £25 each, to four young freemen for ten years, without interest, preference being given to clothiers. *Thomas Hobson*, by a will dated in 1628, left houses, and £100, to purchase land for building and maintaining a house of correction, and a workhouse for setting the poor to work; which bequest has been increased by several others.

The RELIGIOUS HOUSES at Cambridge were numerous. The most ancient was that of *Augustine canons*, founded near the castle in 1092, by Picot, the sheriff, and augmented, and removed to Barnwell, by Payne Peverel, standard-bearer to Robert, Duke of Normandy; its revenue, at the Dissolution, was valued at £351. 15. 4. Some remains of the buildings have been converted into farm-offices. The *Benedictine* nunnery of St. Rhadegund appears to have been established about the year 1130, and was originally dedicated to Mary, but was re-dedicated to Rhadegund by Malcolm IV., King of Scotland, who augmented its revenue, and about the year 1160 built the conventual church, the remaining portion of which forms the chapel of Jesus College. For the purpose of founding that college, the nunnery was granted to Bishop Alcock by Henry VII., having escheated to the crown in consequence of its being deserted by the nuns. The monastery of the *Grey friars* or Franciscans, the site of which is occupied by Sidney-Sussex College, was instituted about 1224, and was very flourishing. The *Bethlemite* friars settled in Cambridge in 1257, in a house in Trumpington-street, of which they had procured a grant : the friars *De sacco*, or *De pænitentiâ Jesu Christi*, whose order was suppressed in 1307, settled in the same street in 1258 ; and the brethren of *St. Mary*, in the parish of All Saints, near the castle, about 1274. The priory of the *Black friars*, the site of which is occupied by Emmanuel College, was founded before 1275. The *Augustine friars* are supposed to have settled here about 1290 ; and their convent, which was in the parish of St. Edward, was established by Sir Geoffrey Pitchford, knt. The *White friars*, or Carmelites, the site of whose convent is occupied by the garden of the provost of King's College, settled first at Chesterton, and afterwards (about 1249) at the adjoining hamlet of Newenham, from which they removed, in 1316, to a spot of ground just within the walls, given them by Edward II. A small priory of *Gilbertines* was founded by Bishop Batzwalter, in 1291: the society occupied the old chapel of St. Edmund, opposite to Peter-House.

The *Castle*, built in the reign of William the Conqueror, on the site of a Roman station afterwards occupied by a Danish fortress, was, in early times, an occasional residence of the English sovereigns : after it had ceased to be so occupied, the buildings, which were extensive, went to decay ; though, during the civil war, it was made a garrison for the parliament. The county was in possession of it, subject to a fee-farm rent, so early as 1660 ; and the quarter-sessions were regularly held here from that time until after the build-
495

ing of the shire-hall. The remains of the ancient building, consisting of a gate-house, which was long used as a prison, until the erection, about forty years ago, of a county gaol within the limits of the castle, were levelled with the ground, to afford space and supply materials for the new county courts. Some of the earthworks that surrounded it are undoubtedly Roman. A somewhat curious piece of architectural antiquity exists in the mansion-house of *Merton Hall*, in the parish of St. Giles, which has long borne the name of Pythagoras' School, though for what reason is unknown : the most remarkable part of the building is a large hall, measuring 61 feet by 22, and which had formerly an undercroft, with circular arches and plain pillars, apparently constructed in the early part of the twelfth century.

Amongst *Eminent Natives* of Cambridge have been, Sir John Cheke, tutor, and afterwards secretary of state, to Edward VI. ; Dr. Thirlebye, first and only bishop of Westminster, and afterwards, successively, bishop of Norwich and of Ely; the eloquent Jeremy Taylor ; Dr. Goldisborowe, Bishop of Gloucester; Dr. Townson, Bishop of Salisbury ; Dr. Love, Dean of Ely ; Thomas Bennett, who suffered martyrdom at Exeter, in 1530 ; and Richard Cumberland, the dramatist. Prince Adolphus Frederick, fifth and youngest surviving son of King George III., was created Duke of Cambridge, November 27th, 1801.

CAMBRIDGE, a hamlet, in the parish of SLIMBRIDGE, union of DURSLEY, Upper division of the hundred of BERKELEY, W. division of the county of GLOUCESTER, 4 miles (N. by W.) from Dursley. This place, which derives its name from a bridge over the river Cam, is situated on the great road from Bristol to Gloucester. There is an endowed place of worship for Independents.

CAMBRIDGESHIRE, an inland county, bounded on the north-west by the county of Lincoln, on the north-east by Norfolk, on the east by Suffolk, on the south by the counties of Essex and Hertford, and on the west by those of Bedford, Huntingdon, and Northampton. It extends from 52° 2' to 52° 45' (N. Lat.) and from 28' (E. Lon.) to 18' (W. Lon.), and contains 858 square miles, or 549,120 statute acres. The county contains 33,095 inhabited houses, 1227 uninhabited, and 236 in the course of erection ; and the population within its limits amounts to 164,459, of which number, 81,611 are males, and 82,848 females.

At the time of the Roman invasion, Cambridgeshire formed part of the kingdom of the *Iceni*, being, according to Whitaker, inhabited by a tribe of that people, called the *Cenomanni*. In the first division of Britain by the Romans it was included in *Britannia Superior ;* in the second in *Britannia Prima;* and in the last, in *Flavia Cæsariensis*. During the heptarchy it was part of the kingdom of the East Angles ; and on the subsequent division of England into three great districts, it was comprised in that styled *Denelege*, or the Danish jurisdiction. The county consists of the archdeaconry of Ely and a small part of that of Sudbury, in the diocese of Ely, and province of Canterbury, comprising the deaneries of Barton, Bourne or Knapwell, Cambridge, Camps, Chesterton, Ely, Shengay, and Wisbech; the number of parishes is 162. For civil purposes it is divided into the hundreds of Armingford, Chesterton, Cheveley, Chilford, Ely, Flendish, Longstow, Northstow,

CAMB

Papworth, Radfield, Staine, Staploe, Thriplow, Wetherley, Whittlesford, Wisbech, North Witchford, and South Witchford. It contains the city of Ely; the university, borough, and market-town of Cambridge; the market-towns of Linton, March, Thorney, and Wisbech; and part of those of Newmarket and Royston. Three knights are returned to parliament for the shire, and two representatives each for the university and borough. It is within the Norfolk circuit; and the assizes are held at Cambridge, where stands the county gaol and house of correction.

The SURFACE exhibits little variety. The parts adjoining the counties of Suffolk, Essex, and Hertford, have gently rising hills, with downs, and open corn-fields, and a considerable portion of wood in the part contiguous to Suffolk, from Wood-Ditton to Castle-Camps; but in other parts there is a scarcity of timber. Gogmagog hills, commencing about four miles southeast of Cambridge, though of no great elevation, yet, being the highest in the county, command extensive prospects. The northern part of the county, including what is called the Isle of Ely, is for the most part fen land, and quite level, intersected by numerous canals and ditches, and containing many windmills, like those of Holland, and steam-engines, for conveying the water from the land into channels for carrying it off to the sea; the inclosures are chiefly formed by ditches, and there are few trees except pollard willows. The great expanse of fen land in the district comprises nearly half of that extensive agricultural tract called the BEDFORD LEVEL, the remainder of which is situated in the counties of Norfolk, Lincoln, Northampton, and Huntingdon. From the various remains that have been discovered in constructing the channels, it is conjectured, that at some remote period the county was all firm land, reduced to a marshy state by frequent inundations of the sea, and by the obstruction of the old natural outlet, at Wisbech, of the rivers Ouse, Nene, and Granta. To prevent subsequent inundations, commissions were issued, from time to time, to enforce the repair of banks and sewers. The most important work of this kind executed before the reign of James I., was the channel made by Bishop Morton, which carried off the overflowings of the Nene, and furnished water-carriage from Wisbech to Peterborough. From the reign of Henry VI. to that of James I. various commissions were granted for a general drainage; but no great progress was made. In 1630, Sir Cornelius Vermuyden, a Dutchman, agreed to undertake the work; but the landowners rejected his offer, and petitioned Francis, Earl of Bedford, who had a large property in the fens, to undertake it, to which that nobleman acceded; and a deed of agreement, the foundation of the laws by which the *Bedford-Level Corporation* is still governed, having been made and ratified at a session of sewers held at Lynn, in 1631, the earl associated with himself others, to whom he assigned shares. So rapid was the progress of the work that, in about three years, the Great Level was adjudged to be drained according to the Lynn law, and 95,000 acres were allotted to the parties as a compensation for the trouble and expense they had incurred. However, at a session of sewers held at Huntingdon, in 1639, the whole proceedings were annulled, the drainage was adjudged to be defective, and it was determined that the earl and his associates were not entitled to the
496

Cambridge; and the Nen or Nene, also navigable : the Lark falls into the Old Ouse at a place called Prick-willow, near the eastern border of the county, and is navigable to Bury St. Edmund's. The *Canals* intersecting the Isle of Ely were made for the purpose of drainage, but many of them are likewise navigable. Vermuyden's canal, commencing at Ramsey, enters the Isle near Ramsey mere, and extends to Welche's dam; it there joins the Old Bedford river, and, proceeding in the course of that river, leaves the county a little to the west of Welney. The New Bedford river is the main channel for barges passing from the upper to the lower parts of the Ouse. The Old Bedford river, which runs parallel with the last from Earith to Denver sluice, is now seldom navigated, excepting the lower part of it; having been almost choked up since the construction of the New Bedford line. A canal from Outwell to Wisbech was made about the end of the last century. There is also a canal from Peterborough to the Old Nene, a little below Benwich, and thence to March; besides short cuts from the Ouse to Soham, Reach, and Burwell. The county is well furnished with railway communication, which has been wholly effected by the Eastern Counties Company. Their main line enters the county, from Essex, at its southern boundary, and proceeds northward, by Cambridge, to Ely, a few miles from which it quits for Norfolk. Near Cambridge a line branches off in a north-west direction to Huntingdonshire; and from Ely there are branches, northward towards Lynn in Norfolk, north-westward to March and Peterborough, on the borders of Cambridge and Northampton, and south-westward to Huntingdonshire.

Few Roman antiquities have been discovered, except on the site of the station at Cambridge, the only one of importance within the limits of the county. The principal ancient roads that crossed the county were, the Ikeneld-street, the Ermin-street, and the great Roman way from Colchester to Chester; the first and last may be distinctly traced in different parts of their course. Before the Reformation the county comprised 32 religious houses, including two preceptories of the Knights Templars, two commanderies of the Knights Hospitallers, and three alien priories; of which there are various remains. Of ancient castles but little is left, except the earthworks. The most considerable encampment is that called Handlebury, on the highest part of Gog-magog hills, supposed to be of British origin. The most remarkable earthworks are the trenches that extended from the woods on the east side of the county to the fens: the most entire is the Devil's Ditch, which runs seven miles, from Wood-Ditton to Reach, in the parish of Burwell, nearly in a straight line; and parallel with it, extends another trench, called Fleam Dyke, at the distance of seven miles, stretching from the woodlands at Balsham to the fens at Fen-Ditton, but a large part of which has been levelled. The Isle of Ely gives the title of Marquess to the reigning sovereign.

CAMDEN-TOWN, a chapelry, in the parish of St. Ancras, Holborn division of the hundred of Ossulstone, county of Middlesex, 3¼ miles (N. W.) from St. Paul's; containing 14,987 inhabitants. This place takes its name from the Marquess Camden, lessee of the rebendal manor of Cantelows, in which it is situated. The principal part has been erected within the last few years; the houses are in general well built and regular,

and the crescent, terrace, and other ranges in the upper part of it, are of handsome appearance, and command a partial, but pleasing, view of the Hampstead and Highgate hills. Among the most recent improvements, those in the direction of the road to Holloway, along the sides of which many elegant residences are still in progress of erection, are particularly deserving of notice, and, together with the formation of buildings in other parts of the neighbourhood, have contributed greatly to increase the importance and enlarge the limits of this appendage to the western part of the metropolis. The streets, which are wide and regularly formed, are lighted and partially paved; and the inhabitants are supplied with water from a conduit, into which it is conveyed from Hampstead. The Camden-Town station of the Birmingham railway forms one of the most extraordinary assemblages of buildings in the country. Besides twelve acres at Euston-square, thirty acres are occupied here by the company, who have lately made most extensive alterations in their works, and just completed new buildings of remarkable size, at this station. The Regent's canal passes through the northern part of the district. A veterinary college, in which lectures are delivered on the anatomy and diseases of the horse, was established in 1791, and subsequently confirmed by royal charter; the premises, which are neatly built of brick, include a spacious area, and comprise a school for the instruction of pupils, a theatre for dissections and the delivery of lectures, a museum for anatomical preparations, and an infirmary, in which is stabling for 60 horses, with paddocks adjoining.

The chapel, erected in 1828, on ground given by the Marquess Camden, is a neat edifice of brick, with a handsome stone portico of the Ionic order at the west end, above which rises a circular turret with a cupola. The living is a perpetual curacy, in the gift of the Vicar; income, £200. A temporary church was opened in 1845; and a second, at Agar Town, in April 1847. Near the chapel are a chapel and cemetery belonging to the parish of St. Martin in the Fields, in connexion with which parish, also, are nine almshouses in Bayham-street. The Independents and Wesleyans have each a place of worship. On the eastern side of Haverstock-hill is a range of neat and commodious almshouses, in the Elizabethan style, erected for decayed journeymen tailors by the master tailors of the metropolis; the ground was given by Mr. Stultz, who also built a chapel, which was consecrated in June 1843, and to which there is a chaplain, who has apartments on the spot. At Haverstock-hill are also the buildings of the Orphan Working School, which was removed hither from the City-road in 1847.

CAMEL, QUEEN (St. Barnabas), a parish, in the union of Wincanton, hundred of Catsash, E. division of Somerset, 7 miles (N. N. W.) from Sherborne; containing 739 inhabitants. This was a place of some note previously to its being burnt, about the close of the sixteenth century; and a charter was anciently possessed for a market to be held twice a week, and four fairs annually: the former has long been discontinued, and only two of the latter are now held, one on Trinity-Tuesday, and the other on Oct. 25th. The parish comprises by admeasurement about 2500 acres. The living is a vicarage, valued in the king's books at £17. 16. 8., and in the gift of P. S. J. Mildmay, Esq.: the great tithes, payable to the family of Rogers, have been commuted for £337, with a glebe of 73 acres; and those of the incumbent for £177, with a glebe of 41½ acres. There is a place of worship for Wesleyans. Opposite the hamlet of Wales, near the bank of the river Camel, is a spring, the water of which has been successfully used in scrofulous cases.

CAMEL, WEST (*ALL SAINTS*), a parish, in the union of YEOVIL, hundred of SOMERTON, W. division of SO-MERSET, 4 miles (E. N. E.) from Ilchester; containing 344 inhabitants. This parish, which is within a quarter of a mile of the road from London to Exeter, comprises by admeasurement 2034 acres. Stone of good quality for building is extensively quarried. The living is a rectory, valued in the king's books at £13. 8. 9., and in the patronage of the Bishop of Bath and Wells: the tithes have been commuted for £250, and the glebe comprises about 65 acres, with a good house, mostly rebuilt in 1836. The church is a very ancient edifice, and has a pulpit of stone, and a handsome sculptured font. There is a place of worship for Wesleyans. Near the close of the last century, in a hill about half a mile to the north of the church, were discovered two cata-combs, in which were several human bodies, arranged in rows.

CAMELEY (*ST. JAMES*), a parish, in the union of CLUTTON, hundred of CHEWTON, E. division of SOMER-SET, 12 miles (S. by E.) from Bristol; containing 643 inhabitants. It is thought to have been the site of a Roman station, where, in the time of Ostorius, was a temple in honour of Claudius Cæsar, from which cir-cumstance, Temple-Cloud, a tything in the parish, de-rived its name, supposed to be a corruption of *Templum Claudii*; and this opinion is in some degree confirmed by the frequent discovery of relics of Roman antiquity. The parish is on the road from Bristol to Wells, and comprises by measurement 1633 acres, mostly fertile land in profitable cultivation: stone of a peculiarly good quality for flagging, and of which considerable quantities are sent to Bath, is extensively quarried. In Temple-Cloud are a respectable inn and a post-office: a considerable business is carried on by a firm as cheese-factors and wool-staplers; and many of the inhabitants of the parish, of whom the greater number reside in this part, are employed in collieries in the neighbourhood. The living is a rectory, valued in the king's books at £6. 18. 4., and in the patronage of the family of Hip-pesley: the tithes have been commuted for £218. 12., and the glebe comprises 96 acres. The church has been enlarged by the erection of a gallery.

CAMELFORD, an in-corporated market-town, having separate jurisdiction, and the head of a union, in the parish of LANTEGLOS *cum* CAMELFORD, locally in the hundred of LESNEWTH, E. division of CORNWALL, 16 miles (W. by S.) from Launceston, and 228 (W. S. W.) from London; contain-ing 705 inhabitants. This place, supposed to have been the *Guffelford* of the Saxon Chronicle, takes its name from a ford on the river Camel. It is generally thought to be the scene of a memorable battle between King

Seal and Arms.

Arthur and his nephew Mordred, about the year 542, when the former was mortally wounded, and the latter, killed on the spot; and about a mile to the north of the town, where the road crosses a small brook, is a place called "Slaughter Bridge" in allusion to the carnage which then ensued. In 823, a battle took place between the Britons and the Saxons under Egbert, the former of whom were defeated with great loss. The TOWN, though in a dreary part of the county, has a pure air, and is considered healthy: it is indifferently built, and consists principally of one street, part of which is spa-cious, and was macadamized a few years since; it is well lighted, and the inhabitants are amply supplied with water. The Camel is noted for its trout and salmon-peel, and is much resorted to by anglers. There is a manufactory on a small scale for the making of serge; and the spinning of yarn affords employment to a few persons. The market is on Friday: fairs are held on the Friday after March 10th, May 26th, July 17th and 18th (the former day being noted for the sale of sheep and lambs), and Sept. 6th, chiefly for cattle; another fair has been lately established, on the second Wednesday in November.

Camelford was made a free BOROUGH by Richard, Earl of Cornwall: its privileges were confirmed by charter of Henry III., in 1259; and in the 21st of Charles II. it received a charter of incorporation, by which the government is vested in a mayor, nine capital burgesses, and an indefinite number of free burgesses, assisted by a recorder, town-clerk, sergeant-at-mace, and subordinate officers. The mayor, who is elected on the Monday after Michaelmas, by the capital burgesses, from their own body, is a justice of the peace. The county debt-court of Camelford has jurisdiction over the registration-district of Camelford. The elective franchise was granted in the reign of Edward VI., from which time the borough returned two members to par-liament, until disfranchised by the act of the 2nd and 3rd of William IV., cap. 64: the right of election was vested in the free burgesses, being householders, re-siding in the borough, and paying scot and lot, in number about twenty; the mayor was returning officer. The town-hall, begun in June, 1806, was built at the expense of the Duke of Bedford, then proprietor of the borough; the lower part forms the market-place. The ancient chapel, dedicated to St. Thomas à Becket, has long been desecrated, and a new chapel has been built. There is a place of worship for Wesleyans. A school was founded in 1672, by Sir James Smyth, and endowed with the tenement of Great Tregarth, now producing £28 per annum; the schoolroom was rebuilt in 1823, at the expense of the Duke of Cleveland, on land be-longing to the corporation. There is an estate worth £60 per annum, which are distributed in clothing among the poor. The union of Camelford comprises 14 parishes or places, and contains a population of 8063. The renowned King Arthur is said to have been born at Tintagel Castle, about five miles north-west from the town.

CAMERTON (*ST. PETER*), a parish, in the union of CLUTTON, hundred of WELLOW, E. division of SOMER-SET, 7 miles (S. W. by S.) from Bath; containing 1647 inhabitants. The parish comprises by computation 1810 acres; the Somersetshire coal canal crosses it, and an old Roman fosse-way traces its south-eastern

498

oundary. Here is a coal-mine, where impressions of rn, rushes, and other plants, have been dicovered. he living is a rectory, valued in the king's books at 15. 9. 2.; patron, John Jarrett, Esq. : the tithes have en commuted for £408, and the glebe consists of 53 res. There are meeting-houses for Baptists and Wesyans. Various relics of the Britons, Romans, and txons, have been found in the vicinity.

CAMERTON, YORK.—See RYHILL.

CAMMERINGHAM (St. MICHAEL), a parish, in e W. division of the wapentake of ASLACOE, parts f LINDSEY, union and county of LINCOLN, 7¼ miles N. N. W.) from Lincoln ; containing 139 inhabitants. limestone is obtained. The living is a discharged icarage, valued in the king's books at £5. 4. 2.; net ncome, £140; patron and impropriator, Lord Monson. he glebe comprises about 60 acres, which, with an nnual money payment, were awarded in lieu of tithes. he church is a modern building, constructed with the materials of a former edifice.

CAMMERTON, a parish, in the union of COCK-RMOUTH, ALLERDALE ward below Derwent, W. division of CUMBERLAND; containing 941 inhabitants, of hom 154 are in the township of Cammerton, 2 miles E. N. E.) from Workington. The parish comprises 384a. 2r. 20p., and is bounded on the north by the olway Firth, and on the south by the river Derwent, hence passes a canal to the Seaton iron-works ; there re some mines of coal within its limits. The living is perpetual curacy ; net income, £100 ; patrons and ppropriators, the Dean and Chapter of Carlisle, whose thes have been commuted for £327. 1. 6., and who ave 18 acres of glebe. The church, rebuilt in 1794, ontains an effigy in full length, the feet resting on a mb, of a person called " Black Tom of the North," hose seat here, according to tradition, was Barrow astle, now in ruins.

CAMPDEN, BROAD, a hamlet, in the parish of HIPPING-CAMPDEN, union of SHIPSTON, Upper division of the hundred of KIFTSGATE, E. division of the ounty of GLOUCESTER, 1 mile (S. E.) from Chipping-ampden ; containing 230 inhabitants.

CAMPDEN, CHIPPING (St. JAMES), a parish, in ie union of SHIPSTON, Upper division of the hundred f KIFTSGATE, E. division of the county of GLOUCES-ER ; containing, with the hamlets of Berrington, road Campden, and Westington with Combe, 2087 ihabitants, of whom 1521 are in the market-town of hipping-Campden, 29 miles (N. E. by E.) from Glou-ester, and 90 (N. W. by W.) from London. This place, hich is of very great antiquity, is supposed to have de-ived its name from an encampment formed prior to a attle between the Mercians and the West Saxons. In 89, a congress of the Saxon chiefs, confederated for ie conquest of Britain, was held here. In the four-enth century it became noted as a staple town for 'ool, and was the residence of many opulent merchants, ho exported a great quantity of that article to Flanders ; ut on the emigration of the Flemings, who settled in ugland, and introduced the manufacture of woollen-loth, Campden lost its trade with Flanders, and its im-ortance from that time rapidly declined. Sir Baptist liekes erected a magnificent mansion here in the fif-enth century, which cost £29,000, and, with the offices, ccupied a site of eight acres ; and which, at the com-

499

mencement of the civil war in the reign of Charles I., its loyal owner demolished, to prevent its being garri-soned for the parliamentarians.

The TOWN is pleasantly situated in a fertile vale sur-rounded by hills richly wooded, and consists principally of one street, nearly a mile in length ; the houses are in general ancient, and some of them fine specimens of the style of domestic architecture prevailing about the time of Elizabeth : the inhabitants are amply supplied with water from numerous springs. On Dover Hill, about a mile from the town, athletic exercises, in imitation of the Olympic games, were instituted in the reign of James I., by Robert Dover, and were resorted to by the nobility and gentry resident in the adjacent country ; prizes were awarded to such as excelled in the games, which were continued until the time of the common-wealth. The manufacture of silk and rugs is carried on. In 1845 an act was passed for the construction of a railway from Oxford, by Chipping-Campden, to Wolverhampton. The market is on Wednesday; and fairs are held on Ash-Wednesday, April 23rd, August 5th, and December 11th. In the 3rd of James I., Campden received a charter of incorporation, by which the government was vested in two bailiffs, a steward, and fourteen capital and twelve inferior burgesses, who had power to hold a court of session, and a court of record for pleas and debts limited to £6. 13. 4. ; but the charter has fallen into disuse, and though the bailiffs are still appointed on the Wednesday before New Michaelmas-day, they exercise no authority. A court leet is held once a year, in a court-house situated nearly in the centre of the street.

The LIVING is a vicarage, endowed with two-thirds of the great tithes of the parish of Winfrith-Newburgh, in the county of Dorset, and valued in the king's books at £20. 6. 8.; net income, £640; patron and impropriator, the Earl of Gainsborough. The tithes of Campden were commuted for land and a money payment, in 1799. The church, situated to the north of the town, in the hamlet of Berrington, is a spacious and handsome struc-ture in the decorated style of English architecture, with a lofty tower : some portions of the finely-carved oak roof are still preserved in the north aisle, but in other instances the beauty and character of the interior have been defaced by modern alterations and repairs. It contains monuments to the memory of Sir Baptist Hickes, first Viscount Campden; Noel, Earl of Gains-borough ; and other distinguished persons. There are places of worship for Baptists and Wesleyans. The free grammar school was founded in 1487, and endowed by John Fereby or Verhey with a moiety of the manor of Lynham, in Oxfordshire ; but owing to mismanage-ment, the estate was sold, and another purchased, pro-ducing only £60 per annum, and which in 1627 was vested in trustees. It has an interest in eight scholar-ships established in Pembroke College, Oxford, by George Townsend, by will dated in 1682, for boys from the schools of Gloucester, Cheltenham, Campden, and Northleach. A Blue school for girls was endowed with £1000 by James Thynne, Esq. ; and there is a national school for boys, which has been incorporated with an ancient foundation by George Townsend. Almshouses for six aged men and the same number of women were endowed by the first Viscount Campden, who rebuilt the market-house, and during his life gave £10,000 for

3 S 2

charitable uses; he died in 1629. George Ballard, author of *Memoirs of Learned British Ladies,* was a native of Campden. There are some petrifying springs in the neighbourhood.

CAMPSALL (*St. Mary Magdalene*), a parish, in the union of Doncaster, Upper division of the wapentake of Osgoldcross, W. riding of York; containing 2149 inhabitants, of whom 385 are in the township of Campsall, 8 miles (N. N. W.) from Doncaster. The parish consists of the townships of Askerne, Campsall, Fenwick, Moss, Norton, and part of Sutton; and comprises by computation 9700 acres, of which 1470 are in the township of Campsall,, including the hamlet of Barnsdale. The village is pleasantly situated on a gentle acclivity, about seven miles distant from the river Don on the south, and on the north the same distance from the Aire. Stone of good quality is quarried. Camps Mount, the seat of George Cooke Yarborough, Esq., is an elegant mansion, standing at the head of a fine lawn, and embowered in luxuriant foliage; and Campsall Park is also a handsome residence. The living is a perpetual curacy, valued in the king's books at £16. 16. 8.; net income, £128; patron and impropriator, Mr. Yarborough. The tithes were commuted for land in 1814. The church is a large ancient edifice, and has some fine specimens of Norman architecture. The remains of a Roman road may be traced.

CAMPSEY-ASH, county of Suffolk.—See Ash.

CAMPTON (*All Saints*), a parish, in the union of Biggleswade, hundred of Clifton, county of Bedford, 6 miles (S. W.) from Biggleswade; containing 1390 inhabitants, of whom 889 are in the town of Shefford. The manor in which the small village of Campton, formerly called Camelton, is situated was anciently possessed by the noble family of Lisle : the manor-house is now occupied as a school. The parish is watered by the river Ivel, and comprises 1350 acres, about three-fourths of which are arable, and the rest pasture and wood; the surface is in general flat, and the soil runs through the several varieties of sand, gravel, and clay. Many females are engaged in making straw-plat, which is sold at Shefford market on Fridays, for the manufacturers of bonnets at Luton and Dunstable; a few hands are also engaged in making pillow-lace. · Fairs for cattle, pigs, sheep, &c., are held on Jan. 23rd, March 25th, and May 19th; and a pleasure-fair on October 11th. The living is a rectory, valued in the king's books at £11. 9. 7.; net income, £374; patron, Sir J. Osborne, Bart. The tithes were commuted for land and corn-rents in 1797; the glebe contains 65 acres, with a glebe-house. The church is in the later English style. The chapel of ease at Shefford, dedicated to St. Michael, was enlarged about twenty years ago; the late rector, the Rev. Edmond Williamson, contributing £600, the Incorporated Society £200, and the Duke of Bedford £50 : there are 600 sittings, all free. The Roman Catholics have a chapel, and there is a place of worship for Wesleyans. A national and infant school was erected in 1840, by the Misses Williamson, the Rev. Dr. Williamson, master of Westminster school, and the Rev. W. Williamson, tutor of Clare Hall, Cambridge; by whom also it is entirely supported. Robert Bloomfield, author of the *Farmer's Boy*, died at Shefford, in August 1823, and was buried at Campton, where a neat stone was erected to his memory by Archdeacon Bonney.

aste; the surface is finely varied, and the village is
leasantly situated on rising ground commanding an
\teresting view over the surrounding country. A fair
held on the 24th of June. Canewdon creek, which
navigable for small craft, is in the northern part of
\e parish. The living is a vicarage, valued in the king's
books at £34. 1. 8.; net income, £495; patron, the
\ishop of London; impropriator, Thomas Laver, Esq.
he church is a large structure, in the later style of
\nglish architecture, with a massive western tower. A
\ational school is partly supported by funds arising from
\nd.

CANFIELD, GREAT, a parish, in the union and
\undred of Dunmow, N. division of Essex, 5 miles
\. W.) from Dunmow; containing 496 inhabitants.
\he parish obtained the appellation of *Canfield ad
'astrum*, from a castle supposed to have been founded
ere by the De Veres, but of which there are no re-
\ains. It comprises 2471a. 3r. 6p.; the soil is fertile,
\nd the surrounding country is agreeable, and in some
\arts enriched with wood. The living is a discharged
\icarage, valued in the king's books at £13; net in-
\ome, £140; patron and impropriator, J. M. Wilson,
\sq. The church is a small ancient edifice, with a tower
\f stone.

CANFIELD, LITTLE, a parish, in the union and
\undred of Dunmow, N. division of Essex, 2¾ miles
\W. by S.) from Dunmow; containing 258 inhabitants.
\he living is a rectory, valued in the king's books at
\12. 0. 7½., and in the gift of Christ's College, Cam-
\ridge : the tithes have been commuted for £410, and
here is a glebe of 70 acres. The church, which for-
\erly belonged to the priory of Lewes, in the county of
\ussex, consists of a nave and chancel, with a small
\elfry surmounted by a spire of wood.

CANFORD, GREAT, a parish, in the union of
'OOLE, hundred of Cogdean, Wimborne division of
\ORSET, 2¼ miles (S. E. by E.) from Wimborne-Min-
ter; comprising the chapelries of Kingston and Park-
tone, and the tything of Longfleet; and containing
957 inhabitants. The parish is situated on the south
\ank of the river Stour, and on the road from Poole to
\outhampton; and comprises by measurement 12,395
\cres. The living is a vicarage, valued in the king's
\ooks at £11. 9. 9½.; patron, Sir Josiah John Guest.
'he parish, with respect to tithes, is separated into the
\astern, middle, and western divisions : the tithes of the
astern division have been commuted for £380, and are
\ayable every third year to the vicar, and in the two
ther years to the impropriator; the tithes of the
\estern division have been commuted for £286 payable
very third year to the vicar, and £133 two years in
\hree to the impropriators; and those of the middle
\ivision for £295 payable every third year to the vicar,
\nd £35 payable two years in three to impropriators.
'he glebe comprises 86 acres. The church consists of a
\ave and chancel, with a north aisle to each, and a
\ower between the two aisles; also a south aisle to the
\ave, and a south chapel to the chancel : the font, of
\urbeck marble, is of great antiquity. There are other
\hurches at Kingston, Parkstone, and Longfleet, form-
\ng separate incumbencies. The Independents have a
\lace of worship. A small portion of the ancient
\nanor-house, called John of Gaunt's Kitchen, is still
\emaining.

CANN (St. Rumbold), a parish, in the union of
Shaftesbury, hundred of Sixpenny-Handley, Shaston division of Dorset, 1½ mile (S. E.) from Shaftesbury; containing 524 inhabitants. The living is a
rectory, valued in the king's books at £9. 2. 1., and in
the gift of the Earl of Shaftesbury : the tithes have
been commuted for £250, and there is about an acre of
glebe.

CANNINGS, BISHOP'S (St. Mary), a parish, in
the union of Devizes, hundred of Potterne and Cannings, Devizes and N. divisions of Wilts, 3 miles
(N. E.) from Devizes; containing, with the tythings of
Bourton with Easton, Chittoe, Coate, and Horton, and
the chapelry of South Broom, 3843 inhabitants. The
manor belongs to the Bishop of Salisbury, whose predecessors had a residence here. The parish comprises by
measurement 11,026 acres. The living is a vicarage,
in the patronage of the Dean and Chapter of Salisbury,
valued in the king's books at £17. 19. 2.; net income,
£351; impropriator, under the bishop, T. G. B. Est-
court, Esq. The church is a handsome structure in the
early English style, supposed to have been either erected
or rebuilt about the same time as Salisbury Cathedral,
which it much resembles in its details. There are other
livings at Chittoe and South Broom.

CANNINGTON (St. Mary), a parish, in the union
of Bridgwater, hundred of Cannington, W. division
of Somerset, 3½ miles (N. W. by W.) from Bridgwater;
containing 1349 inhabitants. This place is of considerable antiquity, having given name to the hundred, and
was formerly of much greater importance than it is at
present. Camden derives its name from its having been
occupied by a tribe of Britons, called the *Cangi*. The
navigable river Parret flows on the north and east sides
of the parish. The living is a vicarage, valued in the
king's books at £7. 10. 10.; net income, £371; patron
and impropriator, Lord Clifford, whose tithes have been
commuted for £965. There is a Roman Catholic chapel
at Court House. A national school, erected at an expense of £290, has an endowment of £19. 12. per annum. Mr. Rogers bequeathed £300 per annum, directing that £6 each should be annually given to twenty
poor men, and the remainder to the poor generally.
A Benedictine nunnery was founded in the reign of
Stephen, by Robert de Courcy, and dedicated to the
Blessed Virgin; it consisted of a prioress and six or
seven nuns, whose revenue was estimated at £39. 15. 8.
The buildings are now occupied by a society of nuns,
who support a school.

CANNOCK (St. Luke), a parish, in the union of
Penkridge, E. division of the hundred of Cuttlestone, S. division of the county of Stafford, 8 miles
(N. by W.) from Walsall; containing, with the townships of Cannock-Wood, Hednesford cum Leacroft,
Huntington, and Great Wyrley, 2852 inhabitants, of
whom 1125 are in the township of Cannock. This place
was a forest or chace belonging to the Mercian kings,
and is supposed to have derived its name from Canute,
the first Danish king of England. The parish is situated
on the road between Walsall and Stafford, and comprises by computation 20,000 acres, about half of which
is still unenclosed on Cannock Chace, a heath about
12 miles long, and from 3 to 5 wide. Of the tithable
lands, 4497 acres are arable, 1830 meadow and pasture,
668 wood, and 2993 common : in Cannock township are

1510*a*. 3r. 26*p*. There are collieries at Wyrley, Church-Bridge, and other places, in some of which is found a peculiar description of ironstone, called Cannock stone, which oxygenates so rapidly as to be capable of much useful application; and a fine white gravel is found, excellently adapted to ornamental walks. The Liverpool and Birmingham railway passes through Penkridge, about four miles from the village of Cannock; and a canal has been cut at a great expense, by the Staffordshire and Worcestershire Canal Company, from Church-Bridge, to meet the canal at Galey, three miles off. The village is supplied with water by means of a conduit, and leaden pipes from Leacroft, about a mile distant, constructed by Bishop Hough.~ There is a manufactory for edge-tools at Wedges-Mill, which affords employment to about 100 persons; the coal used is from the immediate neighbourhood. A market was formerly held on Tuesday, but is discontinued; fairs, however, are held on May 8th, August 24th, and October 18th, principally for cattle and sheep.

The LIVING is a perpetual curacy, in the patronage of the Dean and Chapter of Lichfield, and has a net income of £144: the tithes have been commuted for £1217. 6.; a good glebe-house was built in 1842, and attached to it is half an acre of glebe land. The church is a very ancient edifice of stone, in the early English style, with a square tower. The parish is remarkable as having been the first curacy held by the famous Dr. Sacheverell. At Wyrley is a living in the gift of the Incumbent of Cannock. There are places of worship for Independents and Wesleyans. A school founded by John Wood was, in 1727, enfeoffed by Thos. Wood with land, the income of which is £8 per annum; and John Biddulph, Esq., gave a meadow for the use of the master. In 1725, Mrs. M. Chapman bequeathed a small sum for education; the endowment altogether produces about £20 per annum, with a house and two acres of land. A national school was endowed by Mrs. Walhouse (mother of Lord Hatherton), who died in 1843. Castle Ring, situated on the summit of Castle Hill, near Beaudesert Park, the seat of the Marquess of Anglesey, part of which is in the township of Cannock, is supposed to have been a British encampment: it is nearly a circular area of eight or ten acres, surrounded by a double trench occupying three or four acres more; and near it are the remains of a moat inclosing an oblong of about three acres, named the Old Nunnery, where a Cistercian abbey was founded in the reign of Stephen, which was shortly after removed to Stoneleigh, in Warwickshire. A similar inclosure at a small distance is called the Moat Bank. At Leacroft was formerly a mineral spring of great repute.

CANNOCK-WOOD, a township, in the parish of CANNOCK, union of PENKRIDGE, E. divison of the hundred of CUTTLESTONE, S. division of the county of STAFFORD; containing 275 inhabitants, and comprising 1214*a*. 20*p*. of land.

CANNONBY, CROSS (ST. JOHN), a parish, in the union of COCKERMOUTH, ALLERDALE ward below Derwent, W. division of CUMBERLAND; comprising the town of Maryport, and the townships of Birkby, Cross-Cannonby, and Crossby; the whole containing 5731 inhabitants, of whom 59 are in the township of Cross-Cannonby, 2½ miles (N. E. by E.) from Maryport. This parish, which is situated on the shore of the Solway Firth,

Canterbury was the metropolis of the Saxon kingdom Kent, and the residence of its kings, of whom Ethel- rt, having married Bertha of France, who had been ucated in the principles of Christianity, allowed her ʳ treaty the free exercise of her religion, and suffered ʳr to bring over a limited number of ecclesiastics. The ʳristian religion had been partially promulgated during e occupation of the city by the Romans, and two ʳurches had been built in the second century, one of ʳich, on Bertha's arrival, was consecrated for her use ʳ the Bishop of Soissons, and dedicated to St. Martin. uring the reign of this monarch, AUGUSTINE, who had en sent by Pope Gregory to convert the Britons to ʳristianity, took up his station at Canterbury, where, rough the influence of Bertha, he was courteously re- ived. His mission was attended with success: theᵢ ng, who soon became a convert, resigned his palace, ʳich Augustine converted into a priory for brethren of s own order; and, in conjunction with Ethelbert, he onded an abbey without the city walls, dedicated to . Peter and St. Paul. Being invested by the pope th the dignity of an archbishop, he made this city the at of the metropolitan see, which distinction it has tained for more than twelve centuries, under an unin- rrupted succession of ninety archbishops, many of ʳom have been eminent for their talents and their vir- es, and distinguished by the important offices they ᵢve held in the administration of the temporal affairs the kingdom. Among these may be noticed Dunstan, ʳo governed the kingdom with absolute authority ʳring the reigns of Edred and Edwy; Stigand, who, r his opposition to William the Conqueror, was dis- aced from his see; Lanfranc, his successor, who built the cathedral, and founded several religious tablishments; the celebrated Thomas à Becket; ephen Langton, who was raised to the see in defiance King John; Cranmer, who, for his zeal in promoting e Reformation, was burnt at the stake in the reign of ary; and Laud, who, for his strenuous support of e measures of his sovereign, Charles I., was beheaded ʳring the usurpation of Cromwell. The abbey was tended as a place of sepulture for the successors of e archbishop in the see of Canterbury, and for those the monarch in the kingdom of Kent: the cathedral, ʳich was not completed at the time of Augustine's cease, was dedicated to Our Saviour, and is still ually called Christ-Church.
The city suffered frequently from the ravages of the ANES, of whom, on their advancing against it in 1009, e inhabitants, by the advice of Archbishop Siricius, ʳrchased a peace for the sum of £3000, obtaining from em an oath not to renew their aggressions; but in ᵢ11, they again landed at Sandwich, and laid siege to e city, which, after a resolute defence for three weeks ᵢ the part of the inhabitants, they took by storm and duced to ashes. In this siege, 43,200 persons were ᵢin, more than 8000 of the inhabitants were massacred, ᵢd among the prisoners whom the Danes carried off to eir camp at Greenwich was Alphege, the archbishop, ʳom they afterwards put to death at Blackheath, for fusing to sanction their extortions. Canute, after his ʳurpation of the throne upon the death of Edmund onside, contributed greatly to the rebuilding of the ty, and the restoration of the cathedral; and, placing s crown upon the altar, gave the revenue of the port
503

of Sandwich for the support of the monks. From this time the city began to revive, and continued to flourish till the NORMAN Conquest, when, according to Stowe, it surpassed London in extent and magnificence. In Domesday book it is described, under the title *Civitas Cantuariæ*, as a populous city, having a castle, which, as there is no previous mention of it, was probably built by the Conqueror, to keep his Saxon subjects in awe: the remains now visible are evidently of Norman character. In 1080, the cathedral was destroyed by fire, but was restored with greater splendour, and dedicated to the Holy Trinity, by Archbishop Lanfranc, who rebuilt the monastic edifices, erected the archbishop's palace, founded and endowed a priory, which he dedicated to St. Gre- gory, and built the hospitals of St. John and St. Nicholas. In 1161, the city was nearly consumed by fire, and suffered materially from a similar calamity at several subsequent periods. In 1171, the memorable murder of *Thomas à Becket* was perpetrated in the cathedral, as he was ascending the steps leading from the nave into the choir: his subsequent canonization tended greatly to enrich the city and the church, by the costly offerings of numerous pilgrims of all ranks, who came not only from every part of England, but from every place in Christendom, to visit his shrine. From this source a rich fund was obtained for the enlargement and embel- lishment of the cathedral, which rapidly recovered from the repeated devastations to which it had been exposed, and from which it invariably arose with increased mag- nificence. Four years after the murder of Becket, Henry II. performed a pilgrimage to Canterbury, where, prostrating himself before the shrine of the martyr, he submitted to be scourged by the monks, whom he had assembled for that purpose. In 1299, the nuptials of Edward I. and Margaret of Anjou were celebrated with great pomp in this city; which, in the reign of Edward IV., was constituted a county of itself, under the desig- nation of the "City and County of the City of Canter- bury." Little variety henceforward occurs in the civil history of the city, whose interests were so closely inter- woven with the ecclesiastical establishments, that, upon their dissolution in the reign of Henry VIII., its pros- perity materially declined.
The *Jubilees*, which, by indulgence of the pope, were celebrated every fiftieth year, in honour of St. Thomas à Becket, caused a great influx of wealth into the city, which owed much of its trade to the immense number of pilgrims who came to visit his shrine: according to the civic records, more than 100,000 persons attended the fifth jubilee, in 1420, when the number and richness of their offerings were incredible: the last of these jubilees was celebrated in 1520. The dissolution of the priory of Christ Church was effected gradually: the festivals in honour of the martyr were successively abolished; his gorgeous shrine was stripped of its costly ornaments, and the bones of the saint were, according to Stowe, ultimately burnt to ashes, and scattered to the winds. The revenue, at the Dissolution, was estimated at £2489. 4. 9., a sum much inferior to the actual value of its numerous and extensive possessions. At this period, part of the monastery of St. Augustine was converted by Henry VIII. into a royal palace, in which Queen Elizabeth held her court for several days. During her reign, the *Walloons*, driven from the Netherlands by persecution on account of their religious tenets, found

an asylum at Canterbury, where they introduced the weaving of silk and stuffs; their descendants are still numerous in the city and its neighbourhood, and continue to use, as their place of worship, the crypt under the cathedral, which was granted to them by Elizabeth, and where the service is performed in the French language. *Charles I.*, in 1625, solemnized his marriage with Henrietta Maria of France at this palace. During the war in the reign of that monarch, the city was occenpied by a regiment of Cromwell's horse, that committed great havoc in the ecclesiastical buildings, and wantonly mutilated and defaced the cathedral, which they used as stabling for their horses. A political tumult occurred in 1647, in which originated the celebrated Kentish Association in favour of Charles I., that terminated in the siege of Colchester, and in the execution, after its capture, of Lord Capel, Sir Charles Lucas, and Sir George Lisle. *Charles II.*, on his return from France at the Restoration, held his court at the royal palace at Canterbury, for three days; and in 1676, that monarch granted a charter of incorporation to the emigrant silk-weavers settled in the city, who, on the revocation of the edict of Nantes, in 1685, were joined by a considerable number of other artisans from France.

The CITY is pleasantly seated in a fertile vale environed with gently rising hills, from which numerous streams of excellent water descend; and is intersected by the river Stour, which, dividing and re-uniting its channel, forms several islands, on one of which, anciently called Birmewith, the western part of the town is built. It still occupies the original site, and is of an elliptic form. The walls with which the Romans surrounded it, appear to have been built of flint and chalk, and to have included an area a mile and three-quarters in circumference, defended by a moat one hundred and fifty feet in width; of these walls nearly the whole is remaining, and on that part which forms the terrace of the promenade called Dane John Field, are four of the ancient towers in good preservation. The arches over the river have been taken down at various times; and of the six gates that formed the principal entrances, only the western, forming the entrance from the London road, is now standing. It is a handsome embattled structure, erected about the year 1380, by Archbishop Sudbury, who also rebuilt a considerable portion of the city wall; and consists of a centre flanked by two round towers, having their foundations in the bed of the western branch of the Stour, over which is a stone bridge of two arches, that has been widened for the accommodation of carriages and foot passengers, an approach having been cut through the city walls for each. The principal streets, which intersect at right angles, and also the smaller streets, were originally paved, under an act of parliament obtained in the reign of Edward IV.; they were subsequently made more convenient by an act passed in 1787, for the improvement of the city, and are now lighted with gas by a company established under an act obtained in 1822. The inhabitants are amply supplied with water conveyed into their houses from the river, by a company established in 1824 by act of parliament, and with excellent spring water brought from St. Martin's Hill into a spacious conduit in one of the ancient towers on the city wall, whence it is distributed to the most populous parts of the city, at the expense of the corporation. The houses in some parts retain their ancient

504

appearance, with the upper stories projecting. The greater part of the old Chequers Inn, mentioned by Chaucer as frequented by pilgrims visiting Becket's shrine, has been converted into a range of dwelling-houses, extending from St. Mary Bredman's church nearly half-way down Mercery-lane; and the remains of the palace of Sir Thomas More, in the dancing-school yard in Orange-street, are now used as a warehouse for wool. In other parts, the houses are in general handsome, and many of them modern and well built. An act was passed in 1844 for the general improvement of the city.

The ENVIRONS are pleasant, and the scenery is agreeably diversified with simple and picturesque beauty. On the road leading into the Isle of Thanet are extensive *Barracks* for cavalry, artillery, and infantry of the line. The cavalry barracks, erected in 1794, at an expense of £40,000, are a handsome range of brick building, occupying three sides of a quadrangle, and, with the several parades and grounds for exercise, comprise sixteen acres, inclosed with lofty iron palisades; the barracks for 2000 infantry, erected near the former, in 1798, have been since made a permanent station for detachments of the royal horse and foot artillery. The barracks erected on the site of St. Gregory's Priory, and in other parts of the city, have been taken down, and new streets of small houses occupy their places. To the south is *Dane John Field*, so called from a lofty conical mount said to have been thrown up by the Danes when they besieged the city; or, more probably, from its having 'been the site of a keep, or *donjon*. It is tastefully laid out in spiral walks and shrubberies, and planted with lime-trees: on the city wall, by which it is bounded to the south-east, is a fine broad terrace, with declivities covered with turf; and on the promenade is a sun-dial, supported on a marble pedestal sculptured with emblematical representations of the seasons, by Mr. Henry Weeks, a native artist. On the summit of the mount, from which a panoramic view of the city and its environs is obtained, a stone pillar has been erected, with tablets recording, among other benefactions, a vote of £60 per annum by the corporation for keeping the promenade in order.

The *Philosophical and Literary Institution* is a chaste and elegant edifice of the Ionic order, with a handsome portico of four columns, erected by subscription in 1825, after the model of a temple on the river Ilissus, in Greece. The members possess a spacious museum, in which is an extensive and valuable collection of minerals, fossils, and natural curiosities, scientifically arranged, and in an order peculiarly adapted to assist the student in natural history; it has recently been enriched by a collection of Greek and Egyptian antiquities, the gift of Viscount Strangford. The institution has also an extensive library, and a theatre in which lectures are delivered once a week throughout the year. The *Theatre*, a neat and commodious edifice, erected by Mrs. Sarah Baker, was opened in 1790: opposite to it is a concert-room belonging to the Catch Club, but now used by the members of the Apollonian Club for their concerts every Friday evening. The original Catch Club is at present held in the new concert-room in Guildhall-street. Assemblies are held in a suite of rooms built by subscription; and races take place in the month of August, upon Barham Downs, within three miles of the city.

he course, on which there is a commodious stand, has
een greatly enlarged.

The manufacture of silk, established by the Walloons,
nder the auspices of Queen Elizabeth, and which
ourished in such a degree as to obtain from Charles II.
charter of incorporation, gave place, in 1789, to the in-
oduction of the cotton manufacture by Mr. John Cal-
way, master of the company of weavers, who discovered
method of interweaving silk with cotton in a fabric
ill known by the name of Canterbury, or Chambeny,
uslin. A considerable trade in long wool is carried
, and there is an extensive manufactory for parch-
ent; but the principal source of employment for the
bouring class is the cultivation of hops, for the growth
? which the soil is peculiarly favourable, and with
tensive plantations of which the neighbourhood
ounds. A great quantity of corn is also raised in the
cinity. The city is geologically situated on the plastic
ay of the London basin, with which red bricks and
les are made; and at a short distance to the south-
st, flint imbedded in chalk is found in abundance,
om which lime of an excellent quality is produced.
here are numerous mills on the banks of the river,
veral of them extensive, particularly that called the
bbot's Mill from its having anciently belonged to the
bey of St. Augustine; it is now the property of the
rporation, by whom it was purchased in 1543. Can-
rbury has been long celebrated for its brawn. Frequent
tempts, attended with considerable expense, have been
ade to improve the navigation of the river Stour; and
a act was obtained in 1825, to make it navigable to
andwich, and to construct a canal from that port to a
arbour to be formed near Deal; but the undertaking
as not been commenced. The Canterbury and Whit-
able railway, which is chiefly for the conveyance of
oal from Whitstable, was opened in 1830; it is six
iles and a quarter in length, and runs nearly in a
raight line from North Lane to Whitstable, where it
rminates at the harbour. The railway from Ashford to
 amsgate, opened in 1846, passes through the city; it
as a station near the cathedral, and communicates
ith the Whitstable line. The market for cattle, corn,
ops, and seeds, is on Saturday, and the market for pro-
isions daily. The cattle-market is held on the site of
ie ancient city moat, in the parish of St. George with-
ut the walls; the corn, hop, and seed market is held
i a spacious room in the Corn and Hop Exchange, a
andsome building of the composite order, erected a few
ears since, and ornamented with the city arms and
ppropriate devices, behind which is a spacious area for
ie daily market for meat and vegetables. The market
or eggs, poultry, and butter, is held in the ancient
utter-market, near Christ-Church gate; and there is a
onvenient market-place for fish in St. Margaret street.
hese markets are under the regulation of the corpora-
on, by an act passed in 1824. The Michaelmas fair
ommences on the 10th of October, and continues
uring three market days.

The city, which at the time of the Conquest was
overned by a *præpositus*, or prefect, appointed by the
ing, received from Henry II. a charter, conferring
eculiar privileges, in addition to those it previously
njoyed. Henry III. granted the city to the inhabitants,
t a fee-farm rent of £60, and empowered the citizens
o elect two bailiffs; who were superseded by a mayor

Old Corporation Seal.

Obverse.   *Reverse.*

in the reign of Henry VI., who added the privilege of
choosing a coroner. Edward IV. confirmed the preceding charters, remitted £16. 13. 4. of the fee-farm
rent, and constituted Canterbury a county of itself:
Henry VII. limited the number of aldermen to twelve,
and the common-councilmen to twenty-four; and Henry
VIII., by an act of the 35th of his reign, empowered the
mayor and aldermen to levy a fine of six shillings and
eightpence per day upon all strangers who should keep
shops, or exercise any trade, in the city. James I., in
the sixth year of his reign, confirmed all the former
charters and privileges, and re-incorporated the citizens,
under the title of the "Mayor and Commonalty of the
city of Canterbury."

By the act of the 5th and
6th of William IV., cap. 76,
the corporation now con-
sists of a mayor, six aldermen, and eighteen councillors; and the council ap-
points a sheriff and a clerk
of the peace. By that act
also the city is divided into
three wards, called West-
gate, Dane-John, and Northgate, instead of six as before;
and there are nine justices

New Corporation Seal.

of the peace, including the mayor, who is a justice
during his mayoralty and the year following. The freedom of the city is inherited by birth, or acquired by
servitude, or marriage with a freeman's daughter. The
city has returned two members to parliament since the
23rd of Edward I.: the right of election was formerly
vested in the freemen and citizens at large, in number
about 2000; but by the act of the 2nd of William IV.,
cap. 45, the non-resident voters, except within seven
miles, were disfranchised, and the privilege extended to
the £10 householders; and by the act of the 2nd and
3rd of William IV., cap. 64, the limits of the parliamentary borough, which had comprised 2780 acres,
were enlarged to an extent of 4250 acres. Courts of
quarter-sessions are held for the trial of offenders, but
the capital jurisdiction is taken away; there is likewise
a court of petty-session on the first Thursday in every
month, for determining minor offences. The mayor's
court, which is also a court of record, is but rarely
held: the last instance of its exercising jurisdiction in
civil pleas was in February, 1793. The guildhall is an
ancient and lofty building, the interior of which is
decorated with portraits of the most distinguished bene-

factors to the city, and with various pieces of armour. In 1453, Henry VI. granted to the corporation the custody of his gaol at Westgate, which gate, from that time at least, if not previously, has been used as a city gaol; considerable additions have been made to it, and a house for the gaoler was erected in 1829, in a style corresponding with the character of the original building. The quarter-sessions for the eastern division of the county are regularly held here, and petty-sessions on the first Saturday in every month; and a king's commission of sewers, having jurisdiction over the several limits of East Kent, sits four times in the year at the sessions-house. The powers of the county debt-court of Canterbury, established in 1847, extend over the registration-districts of Canterbury, Blean, and Bridge. The sessions-house, and common gaol and house of correction, form an extensive pile of building within the precinct of the abbey of St. Augustine. Canterbury is the principal place of election for the eastern division of the county.

Arms of the Archbishopric.

The PRIMACY, though immediately delegated by the pope to the see of Canterbury, was not maintained without considerable difficulty; its establishment was violently opposed by the native British prelates, who refused to acknowledge the supremacy either of the archbishop or the pope. Offa, King of Mercia, attempted to divide the jurisdiction, and the archbishops of York persevered in asserting their claims; but the Archbishop of Canterbury was ultimately acknowledged Primate and Metropolitan of all England. In this dignity he ranks as first peer of the realm, and, with the exception of the royal family, takes precedence of all the nobility and chief officers of state; at coronations he places the crown upon the head of the sovereign. The Bishops of London, Winchester, Lincoln, and Rochester, are respectively his provincial dean, sub-dean, chancellor, and chaplain; he is a privy councillor in right of his primacy, and has the power of conferring degrees in the several faculties of divinity, law, and physic, except within the immediate jurisdiction of the Universities of Oxford and Cambridge. The province of Canterbury comprehends the sees of 21 bishops, including the four Welsh sees. The diocese, pursuant to the provisions of the act of the 6th and 7th of William IV., cap. 77, founded on the reports of the Ecclesiastical Commissioners, consists of the county of Kent, except the city and deanery of Rochester, and certain parishes in the diocese of London; and of the parishes of Croydon and Addington, and the district of Lambeth Palace, in the county of Surrey. The ecclesiastical establishment consists of an archbishop, dean, two archdeacons, nine (to be reduced to six) canons, six preachers, six minor canons, six substitutes, twelve lay clerks, ten choristers, two masters, fifty scholars, and twelve alms-men. The archbishop's patronage comprises the archdeaconries, two of the canonries, and the preacherships; the patronage of the Dean and Chapter consists of the minor canonries.

Under the whole building is a spacious and elegant ypt, the several parts of which correspond with those the cathedral; the western part is in the Norman ·le, and the eastern in the early English. The vaulted)f is about 14 feet in height, and supported on mas- e pillars, whose prevailing character is simplicity and ength, though occasionally sculptured with foliage d grotesque ornaments. Near the south end of the stern transept, Edward the Black Prince in 1363 unded a chantry, and endowed it for two chaplains th his manor of Vauxhall, near London: there are me remains of the chapel, consisting of the vaulting the roof, sustained by one central column. Near e centre of the crypt are the remains of the chapel the Virgin, in a niche at the east end of which s her statue, supported on a pedestal sculptured in sso-relievo with various subjects, among which the nunciation may be distinctly traced. The western rt of the crypt is called the French church, from its ving been given by Queen Elizabeth to the Walloons d the French refugees, and from the service being still rformed there in the French language.

The cathedral contains many interesting *Monuments*, d other memorials, of the archbishops, deans, and other gnitaries of the church, and of illustrious persons who ve been interred within its walls. In the arches sur- unding the chapel of the Holy Trinity are, the tomb Henry IV. and his queen, Joan of Navarre, whose cumbent figures, arrayed in royal robes, and crowned, e finely sculptured in alabaster; the mónument of e Black Prince, whose effigy in complete armour and a recumbent posture, with the arms raised in the .titude of prayer, is executed in gilt brass, and sur- ,ounted by a rich canopy, in which are his gauntlets id the scabbard of his sword; and the cenotaph of rchbishop Courteney, with a recumbent figure of ıat prelate in his pontificals. In the north aisle of ıe choir are the splendid monuments of the Arch- ishops Chicheley and Bourchier. The chapel of the irgin contains monuments to the memory of six of the ɛans; and in that of St. Michael are those of the Earl ¨ Somerset, and the Duke of Clarence, second son ¨ Henry IV., whose effigy, with that of the duchess ι her robes and coronet, is beautifully sculptured in ıarble; also the monuments of Archbishop Langton ıd Admiral Sir George Rooke. In the south aisle ¨ the choir are those of the Archbishops Reynolds, /alter Kemp, Stratford, Sudbury, and Meopham; and ithin an iron palisade, on the north side of Becket's rown, is the tomb of Cardinal Pole, the last of the :chbishops who were buried in the cathedral. There ɛe several monuments in the crypt, among which are ɔme to distinguished persons that have been connected 'ith the county.

The precincts of the cathedral comprehend an area ıree-quarters of a mile in circumference. The prin- pal entrance is on the south side, through *Christ-'hurch gate*, erected by Prior Goldstone in 1517, and chibiting, though greatly mutilated, an elegant spe- imen of the later style of English architecture; the 'ont is richly sculptured, and ornamented with cano- ied niches, and consists of two octangular embattled ɔwers, with a larger and a smaller arched entrance etween them, the wooden doors of which are carved 'ith the arms of the see, and those of Archbishop

Juxon. On the north side is the *Library*, containing a valuable collection of books, and a series of Grecian and Roman coins; in the centre is an octagonal table of black marble, on which is sculptured the history of Orpheus, surrounded with various hunting-pieces. A passage from the north transept of the cathedral to the library leads into a circular room, called *Bell Jesus*, the lower part of which is of Norman character; it is lighted by a dome in the centre, under which is placed the font, removed from the nave of the cathedral. On the east side of the cloisters is the *Chapter-house*, a spacious and elegant building, containing a hall 92 feet in length, 37 in width, and 54 in height: on the sides are the ancient stone seats of the monks, surmounted by a range of trefoil-headed arches supporting a cornice and battlement; the east and west windows are large, and enriched with tracery, and the roof of oak is panelled, and decorated with shields of arms and other ornaments. The *Cloisters* form a quadrangle, on each side of which are handsome windows of four lights; the vaulted stone roof is elaborately groined, and ornamented at the points of intersection with more than 700 shields. Against the north wall is a range of stone seats, separated from each other by pillars sup- porting canopied arches: on the east side are, a door- way leading into the cathedral, highly enriched, and an archway leading to the chapter-house; on the west side is an arched entrance to the archbishop's palace, the only remains of which are the porter's gallery and the surveyor's house. The *Treasury* is a fine building, in the Norman style of architecture, the staircase to which, in the same style, is of very curious design.

The city comprises the PARISHES of All Saints, con- taining 377 inhabitants; St. Alphage, 1073; St. An- drew, 509; St. George the Martyr, 1113; Holy Cross Westgate (part), 191; St. Margaret, 761; St. Martin 198; St. Mary Bredman, 402; St. Mary Bredin, 754; St. Mary Magdalene, 419; St. Mary Northgate, 4273; St. Mildred, 1900; St. Peter, 1094; and St. Paul, 1480; also the extra-parochial precincts of the archbishop's palace, containing 184; Christ-Church, 248; East- bridge Hospital, 46; St. John's Hospital, 46; Old Castle, 39; and the Almonry, 328. The living of *All Saints'* is a rectory, with which that of *St. Mary's in the Castle* is consolidated, valued together in the king's books at £80, and united with that of *St. Mildred's*, valued at £17. 17. 11.; it is in the gift of the Crown, and the net income is £150. The living of the parish of *St. Alphage* is a rectory, united to the vicarage of *St. Mary's Northgate*, the former valued at £8. 13. 4., and the latter at £11. 19. 4½.; net income, £150; patron, the Archbishop; impropriator of St. Mary's Northgate, G. Gipps, Esq. *St. Andrew's* is a rectory, with that of *St. Mary's Bredman* united, valued toge- ther in the king's books at £22. 6. 8., and in the patronage of the Archbishop for two turns, and the Dean and Chapter for one; net income, £224. The living of *St. George the Martyr's* is a rectory, with that of *St. Mary Magdalene's* united, the former valued at £7. 17. 11., and the latter at £4. 10.; net income, £150: patrons, the Dean and Chapter. *St. Margaret's* is a royal donative, in the gift of the Archdeacon; net income, £87. The living of *St. Martin's* is a rectory, united to the vicarage of *St. Paul's*, the former valued at £6. 5. 2½., and the latter at £9. 18. 9.; net income,

£300 : it is in the alternate patronage of the Archbishop and the Dean and Chapter, the appropriators;
and the tithes have been commuted for £210. *St. Mary's
Bredin* is a vicarage, valued at £4. 1. 5½.; net income,
£149; patrons and impropriators, the family of Warner.
The living of *St. Peter's* is a rectory, with the vicarage
of *Holy Cross* parish united, the former valued at
£3. 10. 10., and the latter at £13. 0. 2¼.; net income,
£161; patrons, alternately, the Archbishop and the
Dean and Chapter; impropriators, the Archbishop, and
the Corporation of Eastbridge Hospital, jointly : the
glebe consists of nearly 2 acres, with a glebe-house.

Of the several churches, few possess any distinguishing architectural features. *St. Martin's* is said to have
been founded during the occupation of Canterbury by the
Romans, and consecrated for the celebration of the
Christian service prior to the conversion of Ethelbert,
who is thought to have been baptized in it. The
materials of the building, particularly the chancel, are
chiefly Roman tiles : the chancel is supposed to be the
original church, and the other part of less antiquity. The
whole has been beautifully restored by the taste and
munificence of the Hon. Daniel Finch, and it is now a
perfect specimen of early architecture. It contains a
very handsome monument to the Lord-Keeper Finch,
who was compelled to leave the kingdom to escape the
malice of the republicans, before the death of Charles I.,
but returned at the Restoration, and lived to pass
sentence on the regicides; the inscription is a remarkably elegant specimen of monumental Latinity,
written with great power and spirit. There are places
of worship for Baptists, the Society of Friends, Independents, Wesleyans, and Roman Catholics; also a
synagogue.

The King's Free Grammar School, coeval with the present establishment of the cathedral, was founded by Henry
VIII. on the recommendation of Cranmer, for fifty scholars from all parts of the kingdom; the management is
vested in the Dean and Chapter. Belonging to it are
two scholarships of £3. 6. 8. per annum each, founded
in Corpus Christi College, Cambridge, and endowed
with a portion of the revenue of Eastbridge Hospital, by
Archbishop Whitgift, in 1569; one of three exhibitions
of about £15 per annum each, founded in that college
by Archbishop Parker, in 1575; a medical scholarship, founded by the same archbishop in Caius College,
Cambridge; and one of three scholarships founded in
the college by John Parker, in 1580. It has also four
scholarships at either university, founded in 1618, by
Robert Rose, who endowed them with twenty-six acres
of land in Romney Marsh; two exhibitions to any
college in Cambridge, founded in 1635, by William Hey-
man; four scholarships of £10 per annum each, established in St. John's College, Cambridge, by a decree of
the court of chancery, in 1652, in lieu of two fellowships
and two scholarships founded in that college by Henry
Robinson, in 1643; five exhibitions of £24 per annum
each, to Emmanuel College, Cambridge, founded in 1719,
by Dr. George Thorpe, prebendary of Canterbury; two
Greek scholarships of £8 per annum each, founded in
the same college by the Rev. John Brown, B.D.; and
one exhibition of £9 per annum, to any college in Cambridge, founded in 1728, by Dr. George Stanhope, Dean
of Canterbury. By the liberality of the members of a
society of gentlemen educated at the school, a fund has

owed with an estate, by John Cogan, for six clergy-men's widows; but the only property derived from his bequest was the site of the hospital, and the institution is indebted to subsequent benefactions for the whole of its income. *John Aucher, D.D.*, by deed in 1696, gave a rent-charge of £60 for six clergymen's widows, with reference to those in Cogan's Hospital; and a society raises annually by subscription £36, which is divided among three widows of clergymen. *Harris' Almshouses*, in Wincheap, were founded in 1726, by Thomas Harris, who endowed them with houses and land, producing £21 per annum, for five poor families. The Kent and Canterbury *Infirmary* was opened for the reception of patients on the 26th of April, 1793, under the auspices of Dr. William Carter; the building, which is spacious and well adapted to the purpose, stands on part of the cemetery of St. Augustine's Abbey, and contains apartments for a house-surgeon and 60 patients.

Of the numerous MONASTIC ESTABLISHMENTS that flourished here, the principal was the abbey which Austine, in conjunction with King Ethelbert, founded for monks of the Benedictine order, and dedicated to *St. Peter and St. Paul*; the revenue, at the Dissolution, was £1412. 4. 7. The remains consist principally of the gateway entrance, a beautiful specimen of the decorated style of English architecture, with two embattled octagonal turrets, relieved with canopied niches, and enriched with bands, mouldings, and cornices; between these turrets is the entrance, through a finely pointed arch, in which are the original wooden doors richly carved. One of the towers, called St. Ethelbert's Tower, was a fine structure in the Norman style, ornamented in its successive stages with a series of intersecting arches; part of it fell in 1822, and part was subsequently taken down from apprehension of danger. The cemetery gate is still standing; it was repaired, some years ago, in a creditable manner, by Mr. J. Mears, a native of the city. At the north-west of the cemetery are the remains of the chapel of St. Pancras, built in 1387, on the site of a chapel said to have been a pagan temple resorted to by Ethelbert before his conversion. The remains of this once splendid abbey have been restored, and now form part of the Church Missionary College. In Northgate-street was a religious house founded in 1084, by Lanfranc, for Secular priests, and dedicated to *St. Gregory;* the revenue, at the Dissolution, was £166. 4. 5.: the remains, consisting of parts of the walls, arches, and some windows in the Norman and early English styles of architecture, have been converted into a pottery, and tobacco-pipe manufactory. To the south-east of the city was a Benedictine nunnery, founded by Archbishop Anselm, and dedicated to *St. Sepulchre;* the revenue, at the Dissolution, was £38. 19.7. This convent obtained celebrity from the pretended inspiration of Elizabeth Barton, one of the nuns, called " the Holy Maid of Kent," who, for denouncing the wrath of the Almighty upon Henry VIII., for his intended divorce of Catherine of Arragon, was hanged at Tyburn, with her confederate, Richard Deering, cellarer of Christ-Church. To the right of the city, on the road to Dovor, was an hospital dedicated to *St. Lawrence*, for leprous monks, founded by Hugh, abbot of St. Augustine's, in 1137, and endowed for a warden, chaplain, clerk, and sixteen brothers and sisters, of whom the senior sister was prioress; the revenue, at the Dissolution, was £39. 8. 6. In the parish of

509

St. Peter was an Hospital founded by William Cockyn, citizen, and dedicated to *St. Nicholas and St. Catherine;* which, in 1203, was united to that of St. Thomas East-bridge. In the parish of St. Alphage was a priory of *Dominicans*, or Black friars, founded about the year 1221 by Henry III., the only remains of which are the hall, now a meeting-house for Baptists; and near the hospital for poor priests was a priory of *Franciscans*, or Grey friars, founded by the same monarch in 1224, which was the first house of that order established in the kingdom : the remains consist chiefly of some low walls and arches. There are also slight vestiges of a convent of *White friars* that once existed here.

Numerous relics of British and Roman antiquity have been discovered. Among the latter are aqueducts, tessellated pavements, vases, and coins; and a Roman arch, called Worthgate, considered to be one of the finest and most ancient structures of the kind in England, has been carefully removed from that part of the castle yard which was crossed by the new road from Ashford, and re-constructed in a private garden. There are some chalybeate springs, and one slightly sulphureous, in the extensive nursery-grounds of Mr. W. Masters, near the West gate; and without the North gate is a fine spring of water, where a bath, called St. Rhadigund's bath, has been constructed, with the requisite accommodation. The natives of Canterbury include, Dr. Thomas Linacre, founder of the Royal College of Physicians, in London; Dr. Thomas Nevile, master of Magdalen College, and afterwards master of Trinity College, Cambridge, who was sent by Archbishop Whitgift to tender the English crown to King James; William Somner, author of the *Antiquities of Canterbury*, and of a Saxon Glossary; and W. Frend, M.A., author of the *Ephemeris*. Of other literary characters that have flourished here, may be noticed, the Primate Langton, who first divided the Old and New Testaments into chapters; Osbern, a monk in the eleventh century, who wrote in Latin the life of St. Dunstan, and who, from his skill in music, was called the English Jubal; and John Bale, Prebendary of Canterbury and Bishop of Ossory, the Protestant historian and biographer. Isaac Casaubon, whom, on account of his learning, James I. invited over from France; and Meric, his son; were both installed prebendaries of the cathedral.

CANTERTON, a tything, in the parish of MINSTEAD, union, and N. division of the hundred, of NEW FOREST, Romsey and S. divisions of the county of SOUTHAMPTON; containing 38 inhabitants.

CANTLEY (*St. Margaret*), a parish, in the union and hundred of BLOFIELD, E. division of NORFOLK, 4½ miles (S. by W.) from Acle; containing 210 inhabitants. It is bounded on the south and south-west by the navigable river Yare, and comprises 1850a, of which 877 acres are arable, and 900 pasture, heath, marsh, and wood. The railway from Norwich to Yarmouth passes through the parish. The living is a rectory, valued in the king's books at £14, and in the gift of W. A. Gilbert, Esq.: the tithes have been commuted for a rent-charge of £300, and there is a good glebe-house, with 43 acres of land. The church is chiefly in the later English style, and has a tower; the entrance to the chancel is through a decorated Norman doorway. The poor have the benefit of 19 acres of land, allotted at the inclosure.

CANTLEY (*St. Wilfrid*), a parish, in the union of DONCASTER, S. division of the wapentake of STRAFFORTH and TICKHILL, W. riding of YORK, 3 miles (E. by S.) from Doncaster; containing 651 inhabitants. This parish, of which large portions were anciently possessed by different religious foundations, including those of Worksop, Kirkstall, and Hampole, comprises about 5160 acres, and contains the hamlets of Branton, Bessecar, High and Low Ellers, Gatewood, and Kilholme. The surface is level, and in some parts is well wooded. The parish is intersected by the road between Doncaster and Bawtry, which leaves it at Rossington bridge; and the Torn forms its southern boundary, dividing it from those portions of Finningsby parish which are in Yorkshire. The living is a discharged vicarage, valued in the king's books at £6. 6. 5½., and in the patronage of John Walbanke Childers, Esq., who is the impropriator: the vicarial tithes have been commuted for land producing £175 per annum, and there is a good glebehouse. The church was formerly in the hands of a religions community; it is a small cemented structure, with a low tower.

CANTSFIELD, a township, in the parish of TUNSTALL, union of LANCASTER, hundred of LONSDALE south of the Sands, N. division of the county of LANCASTER, 5 miles (S. by E.) from Kirkby-Lonsdale; containing 114 inhabitants. Cantsfield gave name to an ancient family, whose heiress married one of the Harringtons, of Aldingham; but in the time of Edward III. it was in the possession of the Tunstalls. In the 17th century a younger branch of the Cantsfields inhabited the Hall, and a daughter of Sir J. Cantsfield, marrying Sir William Gerard, Bart., brought the estate to that family. The township, which lies on the road from Lancaster to Richmond in Yorkshire, comprises 1221*a.* 2*r.* 18*p.* of land. Within its limits is Thurland Castle, built by Sir Thomas Tunstall, who obtained permission from Henry IV. to fortify and kernell it: the building stands on a slightly elevated site which rises from a level bounded on the south by the Greta and on the north by the Cant; and its wings, towers, and battlements, with a deep circular moat, give it quite a fortresslike aspect. This castle sustained a long and obstinate siege, which left it a ruin, during the civil wars. The great tithes of the township have been commuted for £42, and the small tithes for £46.

CANVEY ISLAND, a chapelry, partly in the parishes of NORTH and SOUTH BENFLEET, BOWERS-GIFFORD, LAINDON, PITSEA, and VANGE, union of BILLERICAY, hundred of BARSTABLE, and partly in the parishes of LEIGH, PRETTLEWELL, and SOUTHCHURCH, union and hundred of ROCHFORD, S. division of ESSEX; containing 277 inhabitants: the chapel is 6¼ miles (W. S. W.) from Leigh. This island is situated near the mouth of the Thames, and contains 3600 acres: it is encompassed by branches of that river, which, on the south side, is two miles broad; while on the other side there is a passage over the strand at low water, and at high water a ferry-boat is used. A fair is held on the 25th of June. The living is a perpetual curacy; net income, £58. 10.; patron, the Bishop of London. The tithes have been commuted for £190. The chapel is dedicated to St. Catherine. Service was formerly performed by the vicar, or curate, of South Benfleet; but, in 1837, a perpetual curate was inducted by the bishop.
510

CANWELL, an extra-parochial liberty, in the union of TAMWORTH, S. division of the hundred of OFFLOW and of the county of STAFFORD, 5¼ miles (S. W. by W.) from Tamworth; containing 27 inhabitants, and comprising 260 acres of land. In 1142, a priory of Benedictine monks was founded by Geva Riddell; it subsequently went to decay, became a poor cell for one monk, and was granted to Cardinal Wolsey by Henry VIII. towards the endowment of his two intended colleges. In Queen Mary's time, the manor was held by the Bishop of Exon; more recently it became the property of the Lawley family, by whom was built the spacious and beautiful mansion, Canwell Hall, at a cost of £60,000.

CANWICK (*All Saints*), a parish, in the wapentake of LANGOE, parts of KESTEVEN, union and county of LINCOLN, 1¾ mile (S. E. by S.) from Lincoln; containing 190 inhabitants. It comprises 2039*a.* 27*p.*, the chief part of which is arable; having on its western side a large common. The corporation of Lincoln are lords of the manor, but the greater part of the parish belongs to Col. Sibthorp, whose seat, Canwick Hall, is a large stone mansion with pleasant grounds, built by the late Col. Coningsby Waldo Sibthorp, who died in 1822. The house stands partly on the site of the old Hall, which had long been the seat of the Sibthorps, many of whom have represented Lincoln in parliament since the reign of George II. The village is neat, and situated on a bold eminence. The living is a discharged vicarage, valued in the king's books at £5. 6. 8.; net income, £231; patrons and impropriators, the Mercers' Company, London. The church was nearly all rebuilt many years ago, and appears from some remaining pillars and arches to have been a Norman structure; it has several neat monuments to the Sibthorp family: there are nearly 20 acres of church land. Some springs here are strongly impregnated with iron.

CAPEL (*St. Thomas à Becket*), a parish, in the union, and partly in the lowey, of TONBRIDGE, but chiefly in the hundred of WASHLINGSTONE, lathe of AYLESFORD, W. division of KENT, 3½ miles (E. S. E.) from Tonbridge; containing 516 inhabitants. It is crossed by the South-Eastern railway, and comprises 1584*a.* 2*r.* 14*p.*, about 70 acres of which are hop-grounds, and 90 acres in wood. The living is a vicarage, united with that of Tudeley: the rectorial tithes of Capel have been commuted for a rent-charge of £158, and the vicarial for £132. The church was formerly a chapel of ease to Hadlow.

CAPEL (*St. Andrew*), a hamlet, in the parish of BUTLEY, union of WOODBRIDGE, hundred of WILFORD, E. division of SUFFOLK, 2¾ miles (W. by S.) from Orford; containing 222 inhabitants. This was formerly a distinct parish, but the church is now in ruins, and the living, a perpetual curacy, has been consolidated with Butley.

CAPEL (*St. Mary*), a parish, in the incorporation and hundred of SAMFORD, E. division of SUFFOLK, 7 miles (S. W.) from Ipswich; containing 608 inhabitants. It comprises by measurement 1876 acres. The living is a rectory, with that of Little Wenham consolidated, valued in the king's books at £13. 18. 4.; patron and incumbent, the Rev. J. Tweed. The tithes have been commuted for £522, and the glebe comprises 22 acres, with a good glebe-house.

CAPEL (St. John the Baptist), a parish, in the
.ion of Dorking, Second division of the hundred of
'otton, W. division of Surrey, 6 miles (S. by E.) from
)rking; containing 989 inhabitants. It comprises
22 acres, of which 105 are common or waste; 813
res are exempt from tithes. The lands are principally
able, producing good crops of wheat and oats, and the
il is also well adapted to the growth of timber. Broom
all here, is an elegant edifice, on the south-eastern
nfines of Leith Hill. The living is a donative, in the
tronage of Charles Webb, Esq., with a net income of
$4 : the tithes have been commuted for £610. The
urch was enlarged in 1836, at the expense of J. S.
oadwood, Esq.

CAPEL-LE-FERNE (St. Mary), a parish, in the
ion of Dovor, hundred of Folkestone, lathe of
iepway, E. division of Kent, 3¼ miles (N. N. E.) from
)lkestone; containing 247 inhabitants. The parish is
the road from Folkestone to Dovor, and comprises
36a. 3r. 3p., of which 227 acres are common or waste :
e South-Eastern railroad runs at the foot of the cliff
the south side. The surface was originally little else
an a waste. The living is annexed to the vicarage of
kham : the tithes of Capel have been commuted for
175 payable to the Archbishop of Canterbury, £41.10.6.
the impropriators, and £100 to the incumbent, who
is also nearly an acre of glebe. The church is sur-
unded by handsome firs, which give it a very solemn
d retired character; it consists of only an aisle and
iancel, and is a good specimen of massy ancient archi-
cture. On a flat stone in the chancel is a brass to the
emory of a family named Gubbiss.

CAPERNWRAY, a manor, in the chapelry of Over
ellet, parish of Bolton-le-Sands, hundred of Lons-
ale south of the Sands, N. division of the county of
ancaster, 9½ miles (N. N. E.) from Lancaster. This
ace (anciently Coupmanwrara, as appears from deeds
the time of King John,) gave name to a family, of
hom Thomas de Coupmanwrara is mentioned in 1273.
is situated on the river Keer, is four miles north-east
om the Carnforth station of the Lancaster and Carlisle
ilway, and the Lancaster and Kendal canal passes
rough the property : the land is hilly and woody, with
nestone and freestone rocks. The manor is within the
anor of Over Kellet, of which George Marton, Esq.,
hose family has been long connected with Capernwray,
the lord; he is the principal proprietor of the soil, and
vner of the Hall. In the park is a chapel, dedicated
St. George, and supported by Mr. Marton; it is a
at structure in the early English style, from a design
r Sharpe, of Lancaster.

CAPESTHORNE, a chapelry, in the parish of
restbury, union and hundred of Macclesfield, N.
vision of the county of Chester, 6 miles (N. by W.)
om Congleton; containing 95 inhabitants. This place
the principal residence of the oldest, and now the
ily, branch of the Davenport family; it comprises by
mputation 800 acres, 600 of which are meadow and
isture, and 100 arable. The living is a perpetual
iracy; net income, £76; patron and impropriator,
. D. Davenport, Esq. The chapel, dedicated to the
oly Trinity, was erected by Mr. Ward, of Capesthorne,
)out the year 1726, in the Grecian style.

CAPHEATON, a township, in the parish of Kirk-
[?]melpington, union of Castle ward, N. E. division
511

of Tindale ward, S. division of Northumberland, 13
miles (W. S. W.) from Morpeth; containing 213 inhabitants. The township comprises 2213 acres, and forms
a very picturesque and highly cultivated district, a possession of the Swinburne family from the 13th century.
The castle is first mentioned in the 15th century, and is
styled by Leland "a faire castle," and "the oldist house
of the Swinburnes;" it was taken down in 1668, and
the present beautiful mansion, Capheaton Hall, now the
seat of Sir John Swinburne, Bart., F.R.S., and F.S.A.,
erected on its site. The village is exceedingly neat; and
directly in its front is an artificial lake, comprehending,
with its islands, between 40 and 50 acres. The impropriate tithes have been commuted for £87. 16., and the
vicarial for £23. 2. 9. Several Roman coins, silver
vessels, and ornaments, were discovered near the Hall,
by some labourers, in 1745.

CAPPENHURST, a township, in the parish of
Shotwick, union of Great Boughton, Higher division
of the hundred of Wirrall, S. division of the county
of Chester, 5¾ miles (N. N. W.) from Chester; containing 154 inhabitants. The manor belonged in the
reign of Edward I. to a family of the same name. In
the year 1701, Lord Cholmondeley held two-thirds of
it, which his ancestors had enjoyed from the time of
Henry VII.; and Sir James Poole the other third, with
the Hall, by inheritance from his ancestors : the manor
was purchased by the Richardson family in 1790. Cappenhurst comprises 1150 acres of land, of a clayey soil.
The Chester and Birkenhead railway passes close to it.
The tithes have been commuted for £100.

CARBROOKE (St. Peter and St. Paul), a parish,
in the union and hundred of Weyland, W. division of
Norfolk, 3 miles (E. N. E.) from Watton; containing
807 inhabitants. The parish comprises 3012a. 2r. 32p.,
of which 2162 acres are arable, 765 meadow and pasture, and 30 woodland. The living is a discharged
vicarage, valued in the king's books at £7. 12. 6.;
patron, R. Dewing, Esq. : the great tithes have been
commuted for £517. 4., and the vicarial for £22. 4.
Tithes upon 218 acres of land in Great Ellingham belong
to this parish. The church, rebuilt in the early part of
the reign of Henry VI., has a lofty square tower, a nave,
two aisles, and a chancel, which is separated from the
nave by an early English screen; the roof of the church
is splendidly carved and painted, and ornamented with
roses. There were formerly 16 stalls in the chancel.
The Knights Templars had a preceptory here, founded
by Roger, Earl of Clare, who died in 1173, and subsequently given by Maud, his widowed countess, who
amply endowed it, to the Knights Hospitallers of St.
John of Jerusalem, as a commandery : at the Dissolution
it was valued at £65. 2. 9., and the revenues, with the
house and church, were granted to Sir Richard Gresham
and Sir Richard Southwell. There are places of worship
for Independents, and Primitive and Wesleyan Methodists. An allotment to the poor, of 55 acres of land, was
made under an inclosure act, in 1801.

CARBURTON, a chapelry, in the parish of Edwin-
stowe, union of Worksop, Hatfield division of the
wapentake of Bassetlaw, N. division of the county of
Nottingham, 4¼ miles (S. S. E.) from Worksop; containing 193 inhabitants, and comprising 1516 acres.
The Duke of Portland is lord of the manor, and sole
owner, with the exception of about 40 acres which be-

CARD

long to the Duke of Newcastle, and are inclosed in Clumber Park. The village is on the west side of the park, on the small river Wollen, and near the Ollerton road. The chapel is a small edifice, with a burial-ground.

CAR-COLSTON (St. Mary), a parish, in the union and N. division of the wapentake of Bingham, S. division of the county of Nottingham, 9 miles (S. W. by S.) from Newark; containing 276 inhabitants. The living is a discharged vicarage, valued in the king's books at £6. 1. 10½.; net income, £203; patron and incumbent, the Rev. J. C. Girardot; impropriator, the Rev. R. Lowe: the glebe contains about 20 acres, with a house. The church has a handsome tower with four bells. There is a meeting-house for Wesleyans. This place was the residence of Dr. Thoroton, author of the *History and Antiquities of Nottinghamshire.*

CARDEN, a township, in the parish of Tilston, union of Great Boughton, Higher division of the hundred of Broxton, S. division of the county of Chester, 4½ miles (N. N. W.) from Malpas; containing 233 inhabitants. It comprises 617 acres, of a sandy soil. The village lies about a mile north of Tilston. A detachment of dragoons from the parliamentary garrison at Nantwich, on the 12th of June, 1643, plundered Carden Hall, and made its owner, John Leche, Esq., a prisoner.

CARDESTON (St. Michael), a parish, in the union of Atcham, hundred of Ford, S. division of Salop, 6 miles (W.) from Shrewsbury; containing, with part of the township of Wattlesborough, 372 inhabitants. It comprises about 2000 acres of land, some portions of which are occasionally flooded by the river Severn, that runs not far distant on the north. The soil is cold, resting chiefly on a stiff clay; coal and limestone exist, and the latter is worked. The living is a discharged rectory, valued in the king's books at £3; net income, £274; patron, Sir B. Leighton, Bart.

CARDINGTON (St. Mary), a parish, in the union of Bedford, hundred of Wixamtree, county of Bedford, 3 miles (E. S. E.) from Bedford; containing, with the township of Eastcotts, 1466 inhabitants. This parish is bounded on the north by the river Ouse, and comprises 5170 acres, of which 200 are common or waste. The manufacture of lace is carried on, affording employment to about 250 females, who work at their own houses. The river is navigable for barges to Bedford. The living is a discharged vicarage, valued in the king's books at £7. 17.; patrons and impropriators, the Master and Fellows of Trinity College, Cambridge. The great tithes have been commuted for £1350, and the vicarial for £250: the impropriate glebe consists of about 5 acres, and the vicarial of 2 acres; there is a good glebe-house. The church contains a tablet in memory of John Howard, the eminent philanthropist, who lived some years at this place, and served the office of sheriff for the county in 1773; and also a splendid monument by Bacon, the last of his works, erected in 1799, to the memory of Samuel Whitbread, Esq., whose family first settled here in 1650, at a house called the Barns. There are places of worship for Independents and Wesleyans, and at Cotton-End one for Particular Baptists. A parochial school is supported by subscription; and there are some almshouses, founded by John Howard and Mr. Whitbread, and endowed with about £30 per annum.

512

llished with a large painting of the *Salvator Mundi*, by e Rev. J. R. Deverell, late rector, who also presented a e toned organ ; in the chancel is a monument to Sir hn Hatcher, whose statue is beautifully executed in me. An excellent parsonage-house has been built.

CARGO, or CRAGHOW, a township, in the parish of ANWIX, union of CARLISLE, CUMBERLAND ward, . division of CUMBERLAND, 3¼ miles (N. W.) from arlisle ; containing 259 inhabitants.

CARHAISE.—See MICHAEL, ST., CARHAISE.

CARHAM (ST. CUTHBERT), a parish, in the union f GLENDALE, W. division of GLENDALE ward, N. division of NORTHUMBERLAND, 3½ miles (W. S. W.) from oldstream ; containing 1274 inhabitants. This place, ccording to Leland, was the scene of a sanguinary attle between the Saxons and the Danes, in which eleven ishops and two English counts were killed ; and in 018, a fierce conflict occurred here between the English and the Scots, the latter of whom were victorious : he loss of the English was severe, and this event, according to some writers, made so deep an impression on he mind of Aldun, Bishop of Durham, that he died of a roken heart. In 1296, the Scots, under William Wallace, ncamped on a hill in the neighbourhood, since called ampfield, and reduced to ashes an abbey of Black anons, which had been founded at a period unknown, s a cell to the priory of Kirkham, in the county of 'ork. In 1370, a battle took place between the Scots nder Sir John Gordon, and the English commanded by ir John Lelburne ; in which, after an obstinate conflict, he former were victorious, and the English general and is brother were made prisoners. The parish is pleasantly ituated at the north-western extremity of the county, nd is bounded on the north and west by Scotland ; it omprises, according to a recent survey, 10,262 acres. 'he surface, generally undulated, rises in some parts to considerable elevation ; and the scenery is enriched vith fine plantations, and enlivened by the river Tweed, n the south bank of which the village is situated. The iving is a perpetual curacy ; net income, £233 ; patrons nd impropriators, the heirs of A. Compton, Esq., of arham Hall. The great tithes of the township of arham have been commuted for £260, and the incumbent's for £22 ; the incumbent has 5½ acres of glebe. The church, erected in 1791, is a very neat edifice : in 832, a porch, and a vestry-room, which is now used or a Sunday school, were added ; and in 1839, the vhole of the interior was newly arranged and repewed.

CARHAMPTON (ST. JOHN THE BAPTIST), a parish, n the union of WILLITON, hundred of CARHAMPTON, W. division of SOMERSET, 1½ mile (S. E.) from Dunster ; ontaining 682 inhabitants. This place, which gives ame to the hundred, probably received its appellation rom the British saint Carantacus, or Carantac, who was the son of Keredic, Prince of Cardigan, and who etired hither, built an oratory, and spent the remainder of his life in acts of devotion. In the grounds of the vicarage have been found numerous skeletons, and also he foundation of an ancient building, supposed to be he remains of the oratory, which is stated to have been ised as the parochial church. The parish is situated on the road between Minehead and Bridgwater, and comprises 5199 acres, of which 599 are common or waste : stone is quarried for the roads. The petty-sessions for the division are held here. The living is a discharged

vicarage, valued in the king's books at £11. 8., and in the gift of the Luttrell family : the great tithes have been commuted for £505. 10,. and the vicarial for £280. 8. ; the glebe consists of about 2 acres. There is a handsome screen in the church, separating the nave from the chancel. In addition to the church, is a chapel of ease at Rod-Huish, a hamlet about 2 miles distant. The Wesleyans have a place of worship. Near Dunster Park is an old encampment, in excellent preservation ; it is octagonal, with double ramparts and a ditch, and has several outworks in connexion with it. In making a road through the parish, an ancient cairn was removed, when a perfect sepulchre, seven feet long, was discovered, containing a human skeleton.

CARISBROOKE (ST. MARY), a parish, in the liberty of WEST MEDINA, Isle of Wight division of the county of SOUTHAMPTON, 1 mile (W. S. W.) from Newport ; containing with the hamlet of Bowcombe, and part of that of Chillerton, 5613 inhabitants. This parish derives importance from its CASTLE, situated on a commanding conical eminence occupying about twenty acres. Its foundation is very remote : some writers even ascribe its origin to the Romans, as a few of their coins have been discovered in the neighbourhood ; but the style of its architecture, especially of the keep, clearly shows that it is principally a Norman erection. The whole was greatly improved in the time of Elizabeth, and surrounded by an extensive fortification, with five bastions and a deep moat, around which is a terrace-walk three-quarters of a mile in circuit : these works were raised by the inhabitants, and those who did not labour were obliged to contribute pecuniary aid. The castle was attacked and taken by Stephen, in 1136, when Baldwin, Earl of Devonshire, had taken refuge here, after declaring in favour of the Empress Maud ; and, in the reign of Richard II,. it successfully resisted an attack of the French, who plundered the island. Carisbrooke Castle is, however, most remarkable as the place in which Charles I. was confined for thirteen months, previously to his being delivered up to the parliamentary tribunal, after having made one or two unsuccessful attempts to escape : his children were also subsequently imprisoned in it. This ancient fortress, a rectangular parallelogram including the keep, an irregular polygon, occupies about an acre and a half of ground ; the keep is raised on an artificial mound, to which there is an ascent of 72 steps, and commands from its summit an extensive and beautiful prospect, embracing a great portion of the island, and parts of the New Forest and Portsdown hill opposite. Within the castle, which is considered as the residence of the governor, are the ruins of an ancient guard-house ; and also the chapel of St. Nicholas, built in 1738, on the site of a more ancient one, and in which the mayor and high constables of Newport are sworn into office annually : the appointment of a chaplain, whose stipend is £24, is in the Governor of the isle.

The parish is partly bounded on the east by the river Medina, is nearly 20 miles in circumference, and altogether irregular in its outline, encompassing the town of Newport on three sides, and containing about one-fourth part of it ; the surface is undulated, and the scenery very picturesque, and the soil consists of chalk, marl, and clay. The village is pleasantly situated at the foot of the Castle Hill, on the banks of a rivulet on which are five corn-mills, and which falls into the

CARL

Medina at Newport. It was of much more consequence formerly than it is at present, having been a market-town, and considered the capital of the island, until superseded by the town of Newport, on account of the more eligible situation of the latter, up to which the river Medina is navigable, and where the nearest wharf is situated. The LIVING is a vicarage, with the livings of Newport and Northwood annexed, valued in the king's books at £23. 8. 1½.; net income, about £1000; patrons, the Provost and Scholars of Queen's College, Oxford; impropriators, several landowners. Opposite to the castle, on a rising ground, stands the church, an ancient structure with an embattled tower, to which was formerly annexed a monastery of Cistercian monks, founded by William Fitz-Osborn, marshal to the Conqueror, who captured the island at the same time that William conquered the kingdom; the remains of the monastery have been converted into a farmhouse, called the Priory. There is a small glebe, comprising, with the site of the vicarage house and garden, nearly 2 acres. A district church, dedicated to St. John, was erected in that part of the parish which adjoins the town of Newport, at an expense of £4000, by the Rev. Dr. Worsley, of Finchley, and endowed with £1000 by Major-Gen. Sir H. Worsley; it was consecrated in 1837, since which period a district has been assigned to it, comprising a population of about 2500. The church is a handsome edifice of stone, in the early English style, containing 830 sittings, of which 230 are free; the tower included in the original design, has not yet been added, for want of funds. The living is in the gift of the Rev. Richard Hollings. There are places of worship for Independents, Baptists, Wesleyans, &c.

CARKIN, a township, in the parish of FORCETT, union of RICHMOND, wapentake of GILLING-WEST, N. riding of YORK, 7½ miles (E. by N.) from Greta-Bridge; containing 55 inhabitants. It is set out in farms, and comprises by computation 770 acres of land.

CARLATTON, an extra-parochial liberty, in ESK-DALE ward, E. division of CUMBERLAND, 9½ miles (E. S. E.) from Carlisle; containing 61 inhabitants, and comprising 1600 acres. Several coins, supposed to be Roman, have been discovered in ploughing a field forming part of the Low Hall estate; and at a farm called Saugh-tree-gate is a cairn.

CARLBY (ST. STEPHEN), a parish, in the union of BOURNE, wapentake of NESS, parts of KESTEVEN, county of LINCOLN, 5 miles (N. by E.) from Stamford; containing 216 inhabitants. It lies near the borders of Rutland, and comprises 1336a. 9p. of land. The village is scattered. The living is a discharged rectory, valued in the king's books at £9. 1. 10½.; net income, £195; patrons, the Marquess of Exeter and Sir John Wyldbore Smith, Bart. The tithes were commuted for land and a money payment in 1804: there is a good glebe-house. The church has a tower crowned by a spire.

CARLEBURY, a hamlet, in the parish of CONIS-CLIFFE, union of DARLINGTON, S. E. division of DAR-LINGTON ward, S. division of the county of DURHAM, 5½ miles (W. by N.) from Darlington; containing 44 inhabitants. Tradition informs us that this and several neighbouring villages were burnt in an incursion of the Scots. At Carlebury hills, in the time of Charles I., a severe battle was fought between the royalists and a party of the parliamentary forces; and some human

ARKSTONE-ASH, W. riding of YORK, 1½ mile (N. by E.) om Snaith ; containing 802 inhabitants. It comprises ?88a. 2r. 39p. of land, of a variety of soil, and produces 1 kinds of grain of excellent quality. An act was ussed in 1800 for inclosing 380 acres of waste in the wnship. There is a wooden bridge across the Aire, 1 the road to Snaith, built by Thomas Stapleton, Esq., ho also, in 1774, greatly improved Carleton Hall, the mily seat, in which is a Roman Catholic chapel, and hich is now occupied by Lady Throckmorton, lady of ιe manor, and sister to the late Miles Stapleton, Esq. ιe village, which is large and well built, is agreeably tuated on the north side of the river Aire, and on the ιad from Snaith to Selby. The living is a perpetual ιracy ; net income, £168 ; patrons, the Trustees of ;essrs. J. Day and Cave.

CARLETON, a township, in the parish of PONTE-ιACT, Upper division of the wapentake of OSGOLD-ιOSS, W. riding of YORK, 1¾ mile (S. by E.) from ɔntefract ; containing 179 inhabitants. It comprises ɼ computation 620 acres : the village is pleasantly situ-ed in a fertile vale, to the west of the road from Don-ιster to Ferry-Bridge. The tithes were commuted for ɔrn-rents, under an act of inclosure, in 1797.

CARLETON (ST. MARY), a parish, in the union of KIPTON, E. division of the wapentake of STAINCLIFFE ιd EWCROSS, W. riding of YORK, 2 miles (S. W.) from kipton ; containing 1242 inhabitants. The parish com-:ises 5090a. 3r. 24p., of which 173 acres are arable, ιout 85 wood, 3517 pasture, and 1250 common or ιoor ; the soil of the lands under cultivation near the ver is fertile, but on the high hills poorer. The popu-tion is chiefly employed in the worsted and cotton ιanufactures. The village is pleasantly situated in a ιcturesque vale, near the confluence of a stream with ιe river Aire. The living is a discharged vicarage, ιlued in the king's books at £5. 2. 1. ; patrons and ɔpropriators, the Dean and Canons of Christ-Church, ʹxford. The vicarial tithes have been commuted for 300, and there is a glebe of 65 acres, with an excellent ιebe-house ; the appropriate tithe rent-charge is £30. ιe church, rebuilt in the 16th century, is in the later ιnglish style, with a square embattled tower, and con-ιins 250 sittings, of which 70 are free ; it was repaired, ιd a new gallery added, in 1841, by the Rev. Walter ιevett, vicar, and the principal landowners ; and Mrs. ιusfield presented a complete set of communion service. . church dedicated to Christ was erected in Lothersdale, ι 1838. An hospital was founded for 12 widows of ιis parish and that of Market-Bosworth, by Ferrand pence, Esq., who endowed it with property, now pro-ucing an income of £280. The free school here was ιtablished by Francis Price and Elizabeth Wilkinson, in 709, and endowed with 99 acres of land, at present ɾorth £120 per annum, of which £55 are paid to a ιaster for teaching boys.

CARLETON-FOREHOE (ST. MARY), a parish, in he incorporation and hundred of FOREHOE, E. division f NORFOLK, 3 miles (N. N. W.) from Wymondham ; ɔntaining 151 inhabitants. The distinguishing appella-ion Forehoe is derived from four hills, supposed to have ʹen artificially constructed, and on one of which the ɔurt for the hundred was formerly held. The parish ɔmprises about 700 acres, of which 385 are arable, 180 ιasture and meadow, and 35 woodland : the road from

Norwich to Watton passes through it. The ancient manor-house, which was surrounded with a moat, has long been a ruin. The living is a discharged rectory, valued in the king's books at £5. 17. 1. ; net income, £120 ; patron, Lord Wodehouse. The tithes were commuted for land in 1766 ; the glebe now contains 131 acres, of which 37 were obtained, by purchase, with £200 given in 1724 by the Rev. James Champion, and £200 from Queen Anne's Bounty. The church is a handsome structure in the later English style, with a square embattled tower.

CARLETON-IN-CLEVELAND, a parish, in the union of STOKESLEY, W. division of the liberty of LANG-BAURGH, N. riding of YORK, 3¼ miles (S. S. W.) from Stokesley ; containing 259 inhabitants. The parish is about three miles in length from north to south, and two miles broad : the inclosed lands incline gently towards the north, and are in general fertile ; the fields are well fenced, and the appearance of the country is highly pleasing. Extensive alum-works were formerly carried on, but since the discovery of richer beds of that mineral on the coast near Whitby, they have been dis-continued. The village is situated at the foot of a con-siderable eminence, about a quarter of a mile south-west of the road leading to Stokesley, Thirsk, and Northal-lerton ; the houses are scattered irregularly on the banks of a small mountain rivulet that runs through the village, and afterwards joins the Leven. The living was, per-haps, once endowed with rectorial rights, but having been given to Whitby monastery, to which it was made appropriate, it was reduced at the Dissolution to a per-petual curacy ; it is in the patronage of C. Reeve, Esq., the impropriator, and has a net income of £56. The church is a small modern structure. There is a place of worship for Wesleyans. Various petrifactions of shells and fishes have been found.

CARLISLE, an ancient city and inland port, having separate jurisdiction, and the head of a union, situated in the ward, and E. division of the county, of CUMBERLAND (of which it is the chief town), 302 miles (N. N. W.) from London, on the great western road to Edinburgh and Glasgow ; containing 23,012 inhabitants. It was anciently called Caer-Luil, or Caer Leol, signifying "the city of Luil," a British potentate, who is reputed to have been its founder. The Romans, on selecting it for a station, changed the name to Lugovallum, which is probably derived from Lugus or Lucu, a "tower" or "fort," in the Celtic tongue, and Vallum, in allusion to Adrian's vallum, which passed near. From its earliest foundation till the union of the English and Scottish kingdoms, the town suffered those shocks of incursive warfare to which, as a border town, it was peculiarly exposed, and by which it was repeatedly overwhelmed. In the reign of Nero, it is stated, by the Scottish historians, to have been burned by the Caledonians, during the absence of the Romans ; who, in the time of Agricola, repaired it and constructed fortifications, as a barrier against the future attacks of the invaders. Soon after the final departure

Arms.

of the Romans, it was probably again destroyed ; for, in the seventh century, we find that Carlisle was rebuilt by *Egfrid*, King of Northumbria, in whose reign it rose into importance. About the year 875, it was demolished by the Danes, and lay in ruins till after the Norman Conquest, when it was restored by *William Rufus*, who, in 1092, built and garrisoned the castle, and sent a colony from the south of England to inhabit the city, and cultivate the circumjacent lands. The construction of the defensive works, however, advanced but slowly ; as, when *Henry I.* was here, thirty years afterwards, he ordered money to be disbursed for their completion. They were most probably finished by David, King of Scotland, who, in 1135, took possession of Carlisle for the Empress Matilda, and resided here for several years, the entire county having been subsequently ceded to him by *Stephen :* the Scottish historians attribute the building of the castle and the heightening of the walls to their monarch. After the disastrous battle of the Standard, in 1138, the city was the asylum of David, who occupied it with a strong garrison, and was here joined by his son ; and in September of the same year, Alberic, the pope's legate, arrived here, and found him attended by the barons, bishops, and priors of Scotland. This envoy obtained from the king a promise that all female captives should be brought to Carlisle and released before St. Martin's day ; and that in future the Scots should abstain from the violation of churches and the perpetration of unnecessary cruelties. In 1149, the city was the head-quarters of David, during the hostilities which he maintained against King Stephen ; and in the following year, a league was here entered into against the latter monarch, by David, Henry Plantagenet (afterwards *Henry II.* of England), and the Earl of Chester ; on which occasion Henry was knighted by the King of Scotland, and swore that when he should ascend the throne he would confirm to him and his heirs the territories held by the Scots in England. In 1152, David, and his son Henry, the latter of whom died this year, met John, the pope's legate, at Carlisle ; and in the following year, or the next after, the Scottish monarch expired in the city, and was succeeded by his son, Malcolm IV.

The counties of Cumberland and Northumberland having been ceded to Henry II. by Malcolm, in 1157, Carlisle was besieged in 1173, by William the Lion, brother and successor to Malcolm ; but on hearing that William de Lucy, the justiciary and regent during the king's absence in France, was advancing with a large army, he abandoned the enterprise. In the following year he again invested the place ; and after a siege of several months, the garrison, being reduced to extreme distress, agreed to surrender the castle at a fixed period, if not previously relieved ; from which engagement they were released during the interval by the capture of William, at Alnwick. In 1186, King Henry stationed himself at the city, with a strong body of forces, to aid the Scottish king in subduing Roland, a rebellious chieftain of Galloway. In 1216, Carlisle was besieged by Alexander, William's successor, and surrendered to him by order of the barons in rebellion against John ; but in the next year, after the accession of *Henry III.*, it was given up to the English. In 1292, a great part of it was destroyed by a conflagration, originating in the vindictive malice of an incendiary,

hich had been destroyed in the conflagration of 1292. n attempt was made on the city in 1380 by some Scotsh borderers, who fired one of the streets by discharg\g burning arrows, but were compelled to retreat by a port that a numerous army was approaching to its lief. It was attacked without success in 1385, by the hited Scottish and French forces; and, two years fterwards, it was again attacked, but with the like want success. In the year 1461, Carlisle was assailed by a cottish army in the interest of *Henry VI.*, which burned e suburbs; and this is the only event respecting it hat occurred in the war between the houses of York hd Lancaster. In 1537, during Aske's rebellion, it as besieged by an army of 8000 insurgents, under icholas Musgrave and others, who were repulsed by e inhabitants, and afterwards defeated by the Duke of orfolk, who commanded seventy-four of their officers be executed on the city walls: Musgrave, however, caped. In 1568, Mary, Queen of Scots, in the hope finding an asylum from the hostility of her subjects, ok fatal refuge in the castle. Next year, Lord Scrope, e lord warden, held Carlisle against the Earls of orthumberland and Westmoreland, then in open rebeln; and in 1596, Sir William Scott, afterwards Earl Buccleuch, attacking the castle before day-break, to scue a noted borderer celebrated in the ballads of ose times as "Kinmont Willie," surprised the garrison, id triumphantly bore him away. In the following ar, the city was visited by a pestilence, which deroyed more than one-third of the population, and casioned great distress among the survivors. On the aion of the two kingdoms, and the accession of James the English throne, the importance of Carlisle as a ontier town having ceased, the garrison was reduced.

At the commencement of the CIVIL WAR in the 17th ntury, the citizens embraced the royal cause. In 544, the city was threatened by a force which had asmbled from the circumjacent country, but which, being rsued by the *posse comitatûs* towards Abbey Holme, iickly dispersed and fled. At this period it afforded asylum to the Marquess of Montrose and his army, ho had retreated before the victorious arms of the arl of Callendar. After the capture of York in July the same year, Sir Thomas Glenham, with the garrin of that city, retired to Carlisle, where he assumed the mmand; and about the end of September, Sir Philip lusgrave and Sir Henry Fletcher, with the remnant of eir forces, which had been defeated by the Scots at alkeld, reached this place with some difficulty, being ird pressed by Gen. Lesley, who, however, did not en stay to invest the city, thus enabling the citizens make ample preparations for a siege. In October he turned with part of his forces, and besieged the place; it the garrison and inhabitants made a vigorous denee, suffering incredible hardship from the scarcity of ovisions: having held out until all hopes of relief cre destroyed by the fatal issue of the battle of Naseby, ey surrendered on honourable terms, on the 25th of ine, 1645. During the siege, one-shilling and threeilling pieces were issued from the castle, which, though ry scarce, are still to be met with in the cabinets of the rious. In October, Lord Digby and Sir Marmaduke angdale were defeated by Sir John Brown, governor of e city, at Carlisle Sands. On the general evacuation fortified towns by the Scottish garrisons, this city

517

was relinquished to the parliament, in 1647; but about the end of April, 1648, it was taken by surprise by a royalist force commanded by Sir Thomas Glenham and Sir Philip Musgrave; and soon afterwards, a considerable army was assembled for the king's service, under the command of Sir Marmaduke Langdale, on a heath, five miles from the city: this army retreating towards Carlisle, the citizens, dreading the recurrence of a famine, petitioned the governor, Sir Philip Musgrave, to refuse it admittance. The Duke of Hamilton, arriving with his Scottish army early in July, superseded Musgrave in the command, which he conferred on Sir William Levingston; and the duke's forces, which were quartered in the neighbourhood, having been joined at Rose Castle by those under Langdale, pursued their march southward. Musgrave, returning shortly after with his forces to Carlisle, was refused admittance by the new governor. Towards the close of the war, on the 1st of October, the city was surrendered by treaty to Cromwell, by whom it was garrisoned with 800 infantry and a regiment of cavalry. A garrison of 600 infantry and 1200 cavalry was afterwards established here, for the purpose of suppressing the insurrections of the moss-troopers. A dreadful famine, caused by the consumption of the garrison, in 1650, compelled the inhabitants to petition parliament for assistance. In 1653, the celebrated George Fox, founder of the Society of Friends, was imprisoned in the dungeons of the castle, on account of his religious tenets.

During the rebellion in 1745, the vanguard of the young Pretender's army encamped, on Nov. 9th, within four miles of Carlisle, which was garrisoned by the militia of Cumberland and Westmorland. Being joined on the following day by the main body, they summoned this place to surrender, and on the 13th commenced the siege, which was conducted by a body of forces under the Duke of Perth, who compelled the place to surrender on the 15th, when the mayor and corporation, on their knees, presented to the young Pretender the keys of the city, and proclaimed his father king, and himself regent, with all due solemnity. The rebel army remained here for several days, during which much dissension prevailed among its leaders; and then resumed its march southward, leaving in the castle a garrison of 150 men. But it was compelled to retreat on the approach of the Duke of Cumberland, part retiring into the castle here, and the remainder pursuing its flight across the border; and the duke, having laid siege to the city, forced the garrison to surrender at discretion. The officers of the rebel troops were sent to London, where having suffered death as traitors, their heads were sent down and exposed in the public places of the city. Cappock, whom the Pretender had created Bishop of Carlisle, was hanged, drawn, and quartered; and nine others concerned in the rebellion were executed in the city.

CARLISLE is pleasantly situated on a gradual eminence, at the confluence of the rivers Eden and Caldew, which, with the Petterel, almost environ it. The four principal streets diverge from the market-place, and have several minor ones branching from them; they are well paved, and lighted with gas by a company formed pursuant to an act obtained in 1819, who erected works at the cost of £10,000. The houses in general are regular and well built. A very handsome bridge of white freestone was erected over the Eden, in 1812, from a design by

R. Smirke, jun., at an expense to the county of about £70,000; it consists of five elliptical arches, and is connected with the town by an arched causeway. Two stone bridges, each of one arch, were built over the Caldew, on the west side of the city, in 1820; and a bridge of three arches over the Petterel, about a mile from the town, was erected a few years since. The CASTLE is situated at the north-west angle of the city, on the summit of a steep acclivity overlooking the Eden. It is of an irregular form, and consists of an outer and inner ward; the former, two sides of which are formed by part of the city wall, is quadrangular, and contains no buildings of importance, except an armoury, in which 10,000 stand of arms were formerly deposited, and which is now converted into barracks for the infantry of the garrison, the cavalry being quartered on the innkeepers. The inner ward is triangular, and contains the keep, or dungeon tower, into which the armoury has been removed; it is square, and of great strength, having a circular archway leading from the outer into the inner ward, and is, no doubt, that portion of the castle built by William Rufus. The other parts are evidently of later date, and correspond with the times of Richard III., Henry VIII., and Elizabeth, by all of whom the castle was repaired and partly rebuilt: a great part of the buildings erected by Elizabeth has been taken down. It is the head of the ancient royal manor of the soccage of Carlisle, now held by the Duke of Devonshire as grantee of the crown, and which includes part of the city, and 500 acres of land in its immediate vicinity. The environs abound with genteel residences: the view embraces the course of the river Eden, as it winds through a fertile and well cultivated tract of country. In 1818 and 1819, a subscription was begun for the relief of the poor, who by this means were employed in completing and forming various walks near the town, the most interesting of which are, the promenade on the slope and summit of the hill on which the castle stands, a terrace-walk on the opposite bank of the Eden, and a raised walk along the south margin of that river.

A subscription library was established in 1768, and a newsroom has been added to it: in Jan. 1830, some ground was purchased opposite the Bush Inn, for the erection of a new subscription library and newsrooms, which have been since built. A commercial newsroom was opened in 1825; and an academy of arts, for the encouragement of native and other artists in sculpture, painting, modelling, &c., was instituted in 1823; but the latter has been discontinued. A mechanics' institute was established in 1824; and a literary and philosophical society has more recently been formed, for which an appropriate edifice has been erected by a proprietary company. The theatre, which was built about 30 years since, is constantly open during the races, and at other stated periods. The races were commenced about the middle of the last century, and the first king's plate was given in 1763; they continue to be held in the autumn upon a fine course called the Swifts, situated on the south side of the Eden, and are generally well attended.

The TRADE principally consists in the manufacture of cotton, spinning and weaving being carried on to a considerable extent. There are about 300 power-looms in the town, and from 1600 to 2000 hand-looms in the town and its immediate vicinity, employed in the manu-

m, and thirty councillors, and the city was divided :o five wards. The mayor is a justice of the peace *ex icio* for two years, and the total number of magistrates ten; they meet for business on three days in each ek. The freedom of the city is inherited by birth, and quired by an apprenticeship of seven years to a resi- nt freeman. The citizens first exercised the elective

Corporation Seal.

Obverse.	*Reverse.*

anchise in the 23rd of Edward I., since which time ey have regularly returned two members to parlia- ent. The right of election was formerly in the free irgesses previously admitted members of one of the ;ht fraternities, whether resident or not, in number out 1000; but by the act of the 2nd of William IV., p. 45, the non-resident voters, except within seven iles, were disfranchised, and the privilege was extended the £10 householders: the limits of the city, also, ere enlarged for elective purposes, from 80 to 1800 acres. ie mayor presides at a court of record every Monday, the recovery of debts to any amount, and at a arterly court for the recovery of debts under forty illings; these courts are held in the town-hall, in the ntre of the town. The powers of the county debt- urt of Carlisle, established in 1847, extend over the gistration-districts of Carlisle, Brampton, and Long- wn. There are eight fraternities or companies, *viz.*, erchants, Tanners, Skinners, Butchers, Smiths, Wea- rs, Tailors, and Shoemakers; who hold a general eting on Ascension-day. The assizes for the county, d the Christmas and Midsummer quarter-sessions, are ld in the new court-houses, erected in 1810, by act of rliament, at an expense of £100,000, from a design by bert Smirke, jun., on the site of the ancient citadel it flanked the eastern gate; and consisting of two ge circular towers, one on each side of the entrance o the city, in the decorated style of English archi- ture. From one of the court-rooms is a subterra- ous passage, for conducting the prisoners to and from county gaol and house of correction, a noble pile of ilding, completed under the same act, in 1827, at a st of £42,000, and surrounded by a stone wall 25 feet rh; it occupies the site of the convent of the Black ars, and serves as a prison both for the city and unty. Carlisle is the principal place of election for ? eastern division of Cumberland.

The DIOCESE of Carlisle originally formed part of at of Lindisfarn; but the see being removed from the ter place to Durham, and considerable inconvenience ing felt on account of the distance of Carlisle from that y, Henry I., in 1133, constituted it a distinct bishop- :, and appointed to the episcopal chair Athelwald,

519

his confessor, who was prior of a monastery of Augus- tine canons founded here in the reign of William Ru- fus, by Walter, a Norman priest, and completed and endowed by this monarch. By the act of the 6th and 7th of William IV., cap. 77, the Ecclesiastical Commission- ers named therein were em- powered to carry into effect the report of two bodies of

Arms of the Bishopric.

commissioners previously appointed by the crown, by which it had been proposed that the diocese of Carlisle should consist of the old diocese, of those parts of Cum- berland and Westmorland which were in the diocese of Chester, of the deanery of Furness and Cartmel, in the county of Lancaster, and of the parish of Alston, then in the diocese of Durham. The bishop, or his chan- cellor, exercises sole ecclesiastical jurisdiction over the benefices, the powers of the archdeacon having been anciently resigned to him for an annual pension, in con- sequence of the smallness of the diocese rendering their concurrent jurisdiction inconvenient. The revenue of the priory above mentioned, in the 26th of Henry VIII., was estimated at £482. 8. 1. This monarch dissolved the monastic establishment in 1540, and instituted a dean and chapter, composed of a dean, four prebendaries or canons, and a number of minor canons, and endowed the body with the whole, or the greater part, of the pos- sessions of the dissolved priory, constituting the bishop, by the same charter, visiter of the chapter: he also appointed a subdeacon, four lay clerks, a grammar mas- ter, six choristers, a master of the choristers, and in- ferior officers. The advowson of the canonries has, since 1557, belonged to the bishop, who has also the patronage of the archdeaconry and chancellorship. The dean and four canons compose the chapter, which has the patronage of the minor canonries; the deanery is in the gift of the Crown.

The *Cathedral*, dedicated to St. Mary, is a venerable structure, exhibiting different styles. It was originally cruciform, but the western part was taken down, in 1641, to furnish materials for the erection of a guard- house; and during the interregnum, part of the nave and conventual buildings was also pulled down, for repairing the walls and the citadel: it has a square em- battled central tower, and the east end is decorated with pinnacles rising above the roof. The interior consists of a choir, north and south transepts, and two remaining arches of the nave, walled in at the west end, and used as a parish church. The choir is of decorated English architecture, with large clustered columns enriched by foliage, and pointed arches with a variety of mouldings; the clerestory windows, in the upper part, are filled with rich tracery, and the east end has a lofty window of nine lights, of exquisite workmanship, exhibiting great ele- gance of composition and harmony of arrangement, which render it superior to almost every other in the kingdom. The aisles are in the early English style, with sharply pointed windows and slender shafted pil- lars; the remaining portion of the nave, and the south transept, are of Norman architecture, having large mas- sive columns and circular arches, evidently built in the reign of William Rufus. There are monuments to the memory of some of the bishops, and one to Archdeacon Paley, who wrote some of his works while resident in this city, and who, with his two wives, was buried in the cathedral.

Carlisle is comprised within the two parishes of *St. Mary* and *St. Cuthbert*, which respectively contain, including parts without the city, 13,576 and 10,965 inhabitants. The living of St. Mary's is a perpetual curacy; net income, £90; patrons, the Dean and Chapter; appropriators, the Bishop, and the Dean and Chapter. The church is part of the nave of the cathedral. The living of St. Cuthbert's is a perpetual curacy; patrons and appropriators, the Dean and Chapter; net income, £157, with a glebe-house. The church, dedicated to St. Cuthbert, Bishop of Lindisfarn, is a plain edifice, built in the year 1778, at the cost of the inhabitants, upon the site of the ancient structure. Two district churches, namely, Trinity, in the parish of St. Mary, and Christ-Church, in that of St. Cuthbert, were completed in Sept. 1830, at an expense of £13,212, of which £4030 were subscribed by the inhabitants, and the remainder granted by the Parliamentary Commissioners; the first stone of each was laid on Sept. 25th, 1828: they are in the early style of English architecture, each having a tower surmounted by a spire. The patrons of both are the Dean and Chapter. Upperby and Wreay, also, form separate incumbencies. There are meeting-houses for Baptists, the Society of Friends, Independents, Wesleyans, and Presbyterians; and a Roman Catholic chapel. The *Grammar School* was founded by Henry VIII., on instituting the dean and chapter, and has an endowment of £120 per annum, of which the dean and chapter contribute £20; the remainder arising from an estate in the parish of Addingham, purchased in 1702, with a gift of £500 by Dr. Smyth, a former bishop: the management is vested in the Dean and Chapter. Dr. Thomas, Bishop of Rochester, left £1000 stock, directing the dividends to be applied to the benefit of two sons of clergymen, instructed here, and sent to Queen's College, Oxford; if not claimed by clergymen's sons from this school, they are given to others from St. Bees. Dr. Thomas, Dr. Tully, and the Rev. J. D. Carlyle, a learned orientalist, received the rudiments of their education here; the last is interred in the church of St. Cuthbert. A general infirmary for the county has been erected; and there are various benevolent societies, schools for the poor, and charitable donations. The union of Carlisle comprises 19 parishes or places, and contains a population of 36,084.

Near the city was an hospital dedicated to St. Nicholas, founded prior to the 21st of Edward I., for thirteen leprous persons, and which, at the Dissolution, was assigned towards the endowment of the dean and chapter. In the city walls, near the castle, an ancient vaulted chamber, having a recess at each end, and accessible only by an opening through the wall, has been discovered; it is supposed to have been a reservoir, or fountain, in the time of the Romans. In the reign of William III., a Roman *Triclinium*, with an arched roof, still existed, which, from an inscription on its front which Camden read " *Marti Victori*," is supposed to have been a temple in honour of Mars. A large altar was lately found, inscribed *Deo Marti Belatucardro*; and, a few years since, a *præferculum*, ten inches and a quarter high, having

nnexed to the curacy of Husthwaite. The impropriate thes have been commuted for £214. 15., payable to rinity College, Cambridge; and there is a glebe of bout 4 acres.

CARLTON, a township, in the parish of COVERHAM, nion of LEYBURN, wapentake of HANG-WEST, N. riding f YORK, 4 miles (S. W. by W.) from Middleham; con-ining 303 inhabitants. This village, which was for-ierly of much greater extent than it is at present, and ad a capital messuage called the Hall, is situated on ie north-west of the river Cover; and the township, sually styled Carlton Town to distinguish it from a eighbouring district of the same name, comprises about 380 acres, chiefly high moors and fells. A school-ousc was erected in 1835, where divine service is per-irmed, under a licence from the bishop; and there is place of worship for Wesleyans; also a close desig-ated Quaker Garth, where it is probable that sect had ace a meeting-house and burial-ground.

CARLTON, with LOFTHOUSE.—See LOFTHOUSE.

CARLTON, a township, in the parish of GUISELEY, pper division of the wapentake of SKYRACK, W. riding f YORK, 2 miles (S. E.) from Otley; containing 205 habitants, including the inmates of a workhouse erected ere in 1818 for an incorporation under Gilbert's act, imprising forty townships. It consists of about 1270 res of land, and has a small scattered village, lying at ie distance of 2 miles to the north of Guiseley. The thes were commuted for land and a money payment, nder an inclosure act, in 1772.

CARLTON, a township, in the parish of ROYSTON, apentake of STAINCROSS, W. riding of YORK, 3 miles V. N. E.) from Barnsley; containing 411 inhabitants. he monastery of Bretton had possessions here; and at t. Ellen's Well, in the township, was a house belonging) that establishment, which was used as a place of re-rement by the prior: there were also a chapel, where priest said the morning mass; and a well "to which," ys Dodsworth, "they used to come on pilgrimage." he township comprises by computation 2090 acres of rtile land, of which upwards of 200 are wood and plan-tions: Lord Wharncliffe is lord of the manor, and rincipal owner of the soil. The village is situated near ie Barnsley canal, and the road from Barnsley to Vakefield passes on the west of it, at the distance of bout two miles. In the neighbourhood are several andsome residences.

CARLTON, CASTLE (HOLY CROSS), a parish, in the nion of LOUTH, Marsh division of the hundred of .OUTH-ESKE, parts of LINDSEY, county of LINCOLN, miles (S. E. by S.) from Louth; containing 52 inhabit-nts. This place, which was once a populous market-iwn, enjoying many privileges granted by Henry I., erives its distinguishing appellation from an ancient astle, the baronial residence of Sir Hugh Bardolph, ccupying one of three artificial mounts, each sur-ounded by a moat still visible. The parish comprises y computation 443 acres, of which 336 are arable, bout 77 pasture, and 30 wood. The living is a rectory ot in charge; net income, £69; patron, John Forster, :sq. The church has been enlarged by the addition of chancel, and repewed.

CARLTON-COLVILLE (ST. PETER), a parish, in he incorporation and hundred of MUTFORD and LOTH-NGLAND, E. division of SUFFOLK, 3¼ miles (S. W. by W.)

from Lowestoft; containing 785 inhabitants. The parish has Mutford broad on the north, and the navigable river Waveney on the north-west; it comprises by measure-ment 2902 acres. The living is a discharged rectory, valued in the king's books at £12. 10. 7½., and in the gift of the family of Anguish: the tithes have been com-muted for £387, and the glebe comprises 17½ acres. The church is a handsome structure chiefly in the early English style, with a square embattled tower; it has a curiously sculptured font, and displays some details of a later period.

CARLTON-CURLIEU (ST. MARY), a parish, in the union of BILLESDON, hundred of GARTREE, S. division of the county of LEICESTER, 7½ miles (N. N. W.) from Market-Harborough; containing, with the chapelry of Ilston-on-the-Hill, 208 inhabitants, of whom 57 are in Carlton-Curlieu. The ancient manor-house affords a specimen of the Elizabethan style of architecture, though, from a date, it does not appear to have been finished until the time of Charles I.; it is chiefly built of fine stone from Ketton, in Rutlandshire, and was purchased at the termination of the civil war, by Sir Geoffrey Palmer, the first baronet. The living is a rectory, va-lued in the king's books at £18. 15. 10.; net income, £242; patron, Sir J. H. Palmer. There is a chapel of ease at Ilston.

CARLTON, EAST, comprising the united parishes of St. Mary and St. Peter the Apostle, in the union of HENSTEAD, hundred of HUMBLEYARD, E. division of NORFOLK, 5 miles (S. W. by S.) from Norwich; con-taining 310 inhabitants, and including 850 acres. The corporation of Norwich purchased the principal manor, and holds it upon condition of carrying yearly to the king's house, wherever he may be, provided he be in England, twenty-four pies or pasties, containing a hun-dred herrings, which latter the town of Yarmouth is bound to supply. The living of St. Mary's is a dis-charged rectory, valued in the king's books at £4, and till lately in the patronage of the Corporation; net in-come, £176. St. Peter's is a discharged sinecure rec-tory, valued at £6, and in the gift of the Crown; net income, £188. The two churches stood within fifty yards of each other; that of St. Peter has fallen into ruins. St. Mary's is chiefly in the early English style, and has a tower surmounted by a wooden spire.

CARLTON, EAST (ST. PETER), a parish, in the union of KETTERING, hundred of CORBY, N. division of the county of NORTHAMPTON, 7 miles (E. by N.) from Market-Harborough; containing 68 inhabitants. The parish is bounded on the north by the river Welland, and comprises 1600a. 5p., of which about 1000 acres are meadow and pasture, 188 wood, and the rest arable: it is crossed by the road from Harborough to Rockingham. The living is a rectory, valued in the king's books at £12. 16. 3.; net income, £108; patron, Sir J. H. Pal-mer, Bart. The church and the family mansion were rebuilt by the late proprietor: attached to the latter is a small park, which has been much improved by the addition of some beautiful grounds in the adjoining township of Middleton. An hospital, now occupied by five women, was founded in 1668, by Sir Geoffrey Pal-mer, who endowed it with forty-six acres of land in the forest of Leighfield; and Lady Mary Palmer, in 1711, bequeathed the principal part of a fund of £32 per an-num for apprenticing children.

CARL

CARLTON, GREAT (*St. John the Baptist*), a parish, in the union of LOUTH, Marsh division of the hundred of LOUTH-ESKE, parts of LINDSEY, county of LINCOLN, 7½ miles (E. S. E.) from Louth; containing 352 inhabitants. It comprises by computation 2196 acres, of which about 1327 are arable, and the rest pasture. The village, which is pleasant and well built, is situated near the source of a rivulet. The living is a vicarage, not· in charge, endowed with the rectorial tithes, and in the patronage of the Dean and Chapter of Lincoln; net income, £571, arising from 300 acres of land, and the tithes which have been commuted for £61. The church is an ancient edifice, lately repaired and beautified. There is a plâce of worship for Wesleyans. A school, erected by Sir Edward Smith, Bart., in 1716, is endowed with £20 per annum; four acres of land, yielding a rent of £6, were added on inclosing the lordship of Carlton Castle.

CARLTON-HIGHDALE, a township, in the parish of COVERHAM, union of LEYBURN, wapentake of HANG-WEST, N. riding of YORK; varying from 6½ to 16 miles (S. W. by W.) from Middleham, and containing 385 inhabitants. This district, which is co-extensive with the chapelry of Horsehouse, and comprises about 12,480 acres of land, consists chiefly of wild and romantic tracts, a large portion occupying the sides of Coverdale. It includes the hamlets of Arkleside, Blackrake, Coverhead, Bradley, Gammersgill, Horsehouse, Swineside, Woodale, and Pickle; all on the banks of the river Cover. Lead-ore is found in some of the lofty moors.

CARLTON-IN-LINDRICK (*St. John*), a parish, in the union of WORKSOP, Hatfield division of the wapentake of BASSETLAW, N. division of the county of NOTTINGHAM, 3¾ miles (N. by E.) from Worksop; containing, in the north and south divisions, 1047 inhabitants. This appears to have been a place of some importance before the Conquest, from the many vestiges of antiquity still visible. A considerable trade is carried on in malt, which is chiefly disposed of at Manchester and Stockport. The parish comprises 4073a. 25p.: the great road between Doncaster and Nottingham runs through the village, and the Chesterfield canal within three miles. The living is a rectory, valued in the king's books at £15. 13. 4.; net income, £576; patron, the Archbishop of York. The tithes were commuted for 541 acres of land in 1767, and there is an excellent glebe-house. The church, which is a spacious edifice chiefly in the Norman style, has a fine arch at the principal entrance; the tower and the nave are in a later style, and the north and south aisles have been erected within the last few years.

CARLTON ISLEBECK or MINIOTT, a chapelry, in the parish and union of THIRSK, wapentake of BIRD-FORTH, N. riding of YORK, 2½ miles (W. by S.) from Thirsk; containing 313 inhabitants. It comprises 1533 acres, of which 25a. 2r. 29p. are roads and waste: the village is pleasantly situated on the road from Thirsk to Ripon, and about one mile west of the York and Newcastle railway. The living is a perpetual curacy, with a net income of £103, and in the patronage of the Archbishop of York, who is appropriator, and whose tithes have been commuted for £247; those of the perpetual curate of the parish produce £73, and those of the rector of Kirby-Knowle £16. The chapel is small. There is a place of worship for Wesleyans.

KESTEVEN, county of LINCOLN, 7 miles (N. N. E.) om Grantham ; containing 219 inhabitants. It is the road from Grantham to Lincoln, and comprises 47a. 27p. of land. The village, which is straggling, seated on a declivity of the Wolds, in the vicinity of small rivulet. The living is a rectory, valued in the ng's books at £13. 1. 5½. ; patrons, Earl Brownlow, r Robert Bromley, Bart., and George White, Esq., 10 present in turn. The tithes have been commuted r £380, and the glebe comprises 39 acres, with a ebe-house. The church is an ancient structure ; the wer part of the tower is Anglo-Norman, and there is large arch, of the same style, opening into the nave.

CARLTON, SOUTH, a parish, in the wapentake of LWRESS, parts of LINDSEY, union and county of LIN-LN, 3½ miles (N. N. W.) from Lincoln ; containing 6 inhabitants. This was the principal seat, until eir removal to Burton, of the Monson family, of 10m Sir Thomas Monson was master falconer and aster of the armoury to James I., by whom he was eated one of the first baronets. The parish comprises out 2000 acres, and has a pleasant village seated ar the foot of an abrupt acclivity, about a mile south the village of North Carlton. The living is a per-tual curacy, with a net income of £200, in the patron-e of the Bishop of Lincoln. The church, an ancient ructure, underwent extensive repairs in 1812 : beneath a vault, still the burial-place of the Monson family ; d there are several mural monuments to the Monsons d others, in the church. A school was built and dowed in 1678, by John Monson. Two widows of is parish are inmates of the almshouses at Burton.

CARLTON-UPON-TRENT, a chapelry, in the parish NORWELL, union of SOUTHWELL, N. division of the pentake of THURGARTON, S. division of the county NOTTINGHAM, 6¾ miles (N.) from Newark ; contain-230 inhabitants. It is situated on the great north d, and comprises upwards of 1000 acres of land. the distance of a quarter of a mile east of the village, a ferry over the Trent, which bounds the chapelry. rlton House, built in the last century, was long the t of Sir William Earle Welby, Bart. The tithes re commuted for land in 1765. The chapel is a all ancient building, with a brick tower.

CARNABY (ST. JOHN THE BAPTIST), a parish, in union of BRIDLINGTON, wapentake of DICKERING, riding of YORK, 3½ miles (S. W. by W.) from Brid-gton ; containing 185 inhabitants. This place, which situated on the road between Bridlington and Drif-d, comprises about 2000 acres : good limestone is arried. Sir George Strickland, Bart., is lord of the nor, and chief owner of the soil. The living is a charged vicarage, valued in the king's books at . 8. 11½., and with the perpetual curacy of Frais-orpe annexed ; net income, £82 ; patron and impro-ator, Sir George Strickland. The church is a small ifice, with an embattled tower.

CARNFORTH, a township, in the parish of WAR-N, union of LANCASTER, hundred of LONSDALE south the Sands, N. division of the county of LANCASTER, niles (N. by E.) from Lancaster, on the road to Ken-l ; containing 306 inhabitants. This place, which longed at an early period to the family of Urswick, erwards passed to the crown, and was held by Mar-ret, Countess of Richmond and Derby ; the Coopers,

Warrens, and others, subsequently possessed the pro-perty. Carnforth is the south-western township of the parish, and is chiefly remarkable as the scene of a great aquatic depredation ; several hundred acres of the salt-marsh adjoining the south bank of the Keer, having been washed away within the last century. The area is 1446 acres. Here is a well-known quarry of sand-stone used as an ingredient in making mortar. The Lancaster and Carlisle railway passes through the town-ship, and has a station at the village : from Hest Bank, passing Bolton-le-Sands, to this place, the line proceeds over a peat-moss, twenty feet in depth, by an embank-ment which is twenty feet higher than the surface ; beyond Carnforth it enters a cutting half a mile long, and averaging fifty feet in depth.

CARN-MENELLIS, an ecclesiastical district, in the parish of WENDRON, union of HELSTON, W. division of the hundred of KERRIER and of the county of CORN-WALL ; containing about 3000 inhabitants. This district, the centre of which is about six miles north-east from Helston, comprises 5330 acres of land, standing high, for the most part poor and uncultivated, and chiefly of a mining character ; the turnpike-road from Truro and Penryn to Helston forms the south-eastern boundary. Numerous small tin-mines are wrought, and there are some considerable tin stream-works. The district was constituted in December, 1845, under the act 6th and 7th Victoria, cap. 37 : divine service is at present performed in a licensed schoolroom. There are several places of worship for dissenters. On the top of Carn-Menellis hill are some hollowed stones, usually termed Druidical altars ; also a huge barrow or mound of stones, which forms the apex of the eminence ; and in the north of the district are nine large upright stones in a circle, called the " Nine Maidens," popularly said to have been girls turned into stone for dancing upon a Sunday.

CARPERBY, a township, in the parish of AYS-GARTH, wapentake of HANG-WEST, N. riding of YORK, 9 miles (W. by N.) from Middleham ; containing, with Thoresby, 354 inhabitants. It comprises 4783 acres, of which 40 are common or waste ; and its village, which is long, and well built, is pleasantly seated on the north side of Wensley-dale, under lofty moorland hills. The impropriate tithes have been commuted for £120, pay-able to Trinity College, Cambridge. Here was a chapel of ease, of which some remains exist. There are places of worship for Primitive Methodists and Wesleyans.

CARRINGTON, a township and chapelry, in the parish of BOWDON, union of ALTRINCHAM. hundred of BUCKLOW, N. division of the county of CHESTER, 10 miles (S. W.) from Manchester ; the township contain-ing 559 inhabitants. The manor was held for more than three centuries by a family of the same name. In the reign of Elizabeth, a female heir brought it in marriage to Sir George Booth, of Dunham-Massey, from whom it descended to the earls of Stamford and War-rington. The township lies on the south side of the Mersey, which separates the county from Lancashire ; and comprises by admeasurement 1394 acres, of which 960 are arable, 424 meadow and pasture, and 10 wood-land : the soil is sand, clay, and moss. The two villages of Carrington and Partington form the chapelry. The living is a perpetual curacy ; net income, £375 : patron, the Bishop of Chester. The tithes have been commuted for £130 payable to the bishop, and £20 to the vicar of the parish. The chapel, dedicated to St. George, is a plain brick building, erected in 1759, chiefly at the cost of Mary, Countess of Stamford.

CARRINGTON, a parochial chapelry, in the union of BOSTON, E. division of the soke of BOLINGBROKE, parts of LINDSEY, county of LINCOLN, 1½ mile (S.) from New Bolingbroke; containing 229 inhabitants. It was formerly in the parish of Helpringham, but was constituted a parochial chapelry in 1812, by an act of parliament, on the occasion of a very extensive drainage of fen lands. The living is a perpetual curacy, with the township of West-Ville; net income, £86; patrons, certain Trustees. The tithes were commuted for land under the act of inclosure. The chapel was consecrated in 1818.

CARRINGTON, a village, in the parish and union of BASFORD, hundred of BROXTOW, county of NOTTINGHAM, 2¼ miles (N. W. by N.) from Nottingham; containing 853 inhabitants. This village, which is of recent origin, consists partly of handsome villas, occupied by merchants and lace manufacturers, who have warehouses in Nottingham. A church dedicated to St. John was consecrated in 1841: the income of the incumbent is £150, and the Bishop of Lincoln is patron.

CARSHALTON (*ALL SAINTS*), a parish, and formerly a market-town, in the union of EPSOM, Second division of the hundred of WALLINGTON, E. division of SURREY, 3 miles (W.) from Croydon; containing 2228 inhabitants. In Domesday book this place is styled *Aulton*, signifying Old Town; and it retained that appellation until the reign of John, when it was called Kersalton, of which the present name is a variation. The parish comprises 2015a. 1r. 19p. The village is pleasantly situated near Banstead Downs, on a dry and chalky soil; the river Wandle runs through the parish, and being joined in its course by other streams, forms in the centre of the village a broad sheet of water: a bridge was erected in 1828, which cost £500. The environs are diversified, and contain numerous mansions, inhabited principally by London merchants. Carshalton House, a handsome mansion, occupies the site of an ancient edifice in which Dr. Radcliffe, the munificent benefactor to the University of Oxford, resided during the time of the plague, in 1665. Near the churchyard is a fine spring, called Queen Ann Boleyn's Well; it is arched over with stone, and kept in good repair. A calico-printing establishment formerly carried on has been discontinued; but there are bleaching-grounds, and, on the banks of the river, several mills for the manufacture of snuff, paper, flocks, and leather, besides three large flour-mills: there are also some lime-kilns. The market, granted in the reign of Henry III., has long been discontinued; a pleasure-fair only is held, on the 1st and 2nd of July. The LIVING is a vicarage, endowed since 1726 with the rectorial tithes, and valued in the king's books at £11. 12. 6.; net income, £600; patron, John Cator, Esq. The church is an ancient structure of brick, containing portions in the early and decorated styles of English architecture; the chancel, which is built of flint, appears to be the oldest part. The interior is neat, and contains some interesting monuments to the families of Fellowes and Scawen; and two brasses, representing Sir Nicholas Gaynesford and his lady, with a group of children: it has been repaired, and the galleries enlarged, by subscription.

524

188, William Mareschall, Earl of Pembroke, founded a riory for Regular canons of the order of St. Augustine, edicated to the Blessed Virgin, and endowed it with ll his lands at "Kertmell," and with other possessions, esides many privileges, among which was the exclusive ght of appointing guides to conduct travellers over the xtensive sands that bound the parish on the south. he establishment, at the Dissolution, consisted of ten .ligious, and forty-eight servants, and the revenue was itimated at £212. 11. 10.: the conventual church, hich was also parochial, was purchased by the parish-ners.

The TOWN is situated in a vale surrounded by lofty lls of varied aspect, behind which the vast fells of oniston rise majestically to the north; the houses, with e exception of a row erected some years since on the orth side of the town, of modern and handsome ap-:arance, are in general built of stone, rough-cast and hite-washed. The environs abound with scenery rikingly diversified by richly-wooded eminences and irren. hills. The parish comprises the townships of pper and Lower Allithwaite, East Broughton, Cartmel-ell, Upper and Lower Holker, and Staveley. It is)unded on the south by the bay of Morecambe, into hich it extends for a considerable distance, and where, low water, is a passage over the sands to Bolton. ıe longer course across is nine miles; the shorter, ong that part called the Leven sands, is four: guides c usually waiting to conduct over both. The district ounds with rocks of limestone and marble, but very :tle trade is carried on; there are cotton-mills at pper Holker. The market is on Tuesday: fairs are eld on Whit-Monday and the Monday after October 3rd; and cattle-fairs on the Wednesday before Easter, nd November 5th.

The LIVING is a perpetual curacy, in the gift of the !arl of Burlington, with a net income of £113: the ithes were commuted for land in 1796. The church ı a spacious cruciform structure, in the early English tyle, with a curious tower. After having been suffered) remain in a state of neglect for nearly a century from he dissolution of the priory, during which time the onventual buildings had been removed, it was substan-ially repaired, in 1640, by George Preston, of Holker. 'he chancel contains some richly-carved stalls and fine abernacle work: on the north side of the altar is the ɔmb of William de Walton, one of the priors, and on he opposite side a magnificent altar-tomb with recum-ent figures of one of the Harringtons and his lady, upposed to be Sir John Harrington, who accompanied :dward I. into Scotland; besides many other monu-ıents. The Earl of Burlington also presents to the ıcumbencies of Broughton, Cartmel-Fell, Flookborough, .indale, and Staveley. The free grammar school, built ı 1790, in Upper Holker township, is supported by an ndowment of £125 per annum, arising from donations ıd legacies. Dr. Edmund Law, Bishop of Carlisle, /hose father was curate of one of the chapels in the arish for forty-nine years, received the rudiments of is education in the school. In a wood in the vicinity, bout forty years ago, 680 Roman coins were dug up, ated from 193 to 253; and at Broughton, a coin of he Emperor Adrian has been discovered. Three miles ɔ the south of the town is a spring, called Holy Well, he water of which is efficacious in gout, and in neph-

525

ritic and cutaneous diseases; and at Pit Farm, in the parish, is an intermitting spring.

CARTMEL-FELL, a chapelry, in the parish of CARTMEL, union of ULVERSTON, hundred of LONS-DALE north of the Sands, N. division of the county of LANCASTER, 8 miles (W. S. W.) from Kendal; containing 356 inhabitants. It is situated on the borders of West-morland, and on the Winster river. The road from Townhead in Staveley to Bowness, which traverses six miles, possesses many choice views of Windermere, and of the Coniston and Langdale mountains. The living is a perpetual curacy; net income, £67; patron, the Earl of Burlington, as lessee under the Bishop of Chester. The chapel is dedicated to St. Anthony. There is a small school, with an endowment of £8 per annum.

CARTWORTH, a township, in the parish of KIRK-BURTON, union of HUDDERSFIELD, Upper division of the wapentake of AGBRIGG, W. riding of YORK, 7¼ miles (S. by W.) from Huddersfield; containing 2247 inhabit-ants. This township, which comprises about 2820 acres, includes part of the villages of Hinchliffe-Mill and Holmfirth, and extends upwards of two miles north-ward from the latter place, along the romantic dale of the Holme stream: much of the land is high moor, in-closed under an act, in 1827. The manufacture of woollen-cloth is carried on to a considerable extent. The head of a brass Roman spear was dug up in the bog on the moor, in 1820.

CARWOOD.—See SIBDON-CARWOOD.

CARY-COATS, a township, in the parish of THOCK-RINGTON, union of BELLINGHAM, N. E. division of TINDALE ward, S. division of NORTHUMBERLAND, 12 miles (N.) from Hexham; containing 51 inhabitants. It adjoins the Bavington estate, on the north-west; and was probably at some period the appanage of a younger branch of the ancient house of Shafto: at the close of the last century it was the estate and residence of one of that family.

CASHIO, or CASHIOBURY, a hamlet, in the parish and union of WATFORD, hundred of CASHIO, or liberty of ST. ALBAN'S, county of HERTFORD, 1½ mile (N. W.) from Watford; containing, with the hamlet of Leavesden, 1548 inhabitants. In the time of the early Britons this was a place of importance, being the seat of Cassi-belaunus, King of the Cassii. The Saxon kings of Mer-cia also made it their residence; Offa included it in the possessions that he gave to the monastery of St. Alban's, and called the hamlet Albaneston, which was again changed by the Normans into Caisho, since converted into Cashio. Edward IV. constituted it a liberty, and it continued annexed to the crown from the period of the Dissolution until James I. granted the whole liberty of the monastery of St. Alban's to Robert Whitmore and John Eldred.

CASSINGTON (ST. PETER), a parish, in the union of WOODSTOCK, hundred of WOOTTON, county of OX-FORD, 6¾ miles (N. W.) from Oxford; containing, with the hamlet of Worton, 381 inhabitants. The manor formerly belonged to the Montacutes, one of whom, in the reign of Henry II., obtained leave to convert the mansion into a castle, of which some remains existed till within the last 50 years, when the materials were used in building the parsonage-house. The living is a discharged vicarage, valued in the king's books at £12;

patrons and appropriators, the Dean and Canons of
Christ-Church, Oxford. The tithes have been commuted for £210, and the glebe consists of 55 acres. The
church, which is in the Norman style, was originally
built in the reign of Henry II., by Geoffrey Clinton,
chamberlain to that monarch : the arch supporting the
tower, and the groined roof of the chancel, of Norman
character, are remains of the ancient building.

CASSOP, a township, in the parish of KELLOE,
S. division of EASINGTON ward, union and N. division
of the county of DURHAM, 4½ miles (S. E. by E.) from
Durham; containing 1076 inhabitants. This place,
anciently called Cazhope, and included within the limits
of Queringdonshire, was formerly the residence of the
family of Reed, and of that of Busby, and is at present
held under the see of Durham. The village stands, with
a northern aspect, on a high swell of limestone hills,
separated from Quarrington on the south by a broad
hollow vale, and commanding an extensive prospect of
a variegated tract in the north-western direction. The
produce of Cassop and Cassop-moor collieries is shipped
at Hartlepool. The impropriate tithes have been commuted for £104. 18. 8., payable to Christ's Hospital,
Sherburn, and the vicarial for £17. 4.

CASTERN, a hamlet, in the parish of ILAM, N. division of the hundred of TOTMONSLOW and of the county
of STAFFORD, 5¼ miles (N. W.) from Ashbourn; containing 45 inhabitants. This place lies on the borders of
Derbyshire, and on the east side of the Manifold river,
about a mile and a half north-west of the village of
Ilam. The Hall is now a farmhouse.

CASTERTON, a township and chapelry, in the
parish of KIRKBY-LONSDALE, union of KENDAL, LONS-
DALE ward, county of WESTMORLAND, 1½ mile (N. E.)
from Kirkby-Lonsdale; containing 623 inhabitants.
This place, which is supposed to have received its name
from an ancient castle, of which every vestige has been
removed, is situated on the river Lune, and on the road
from Lancaster to Sedbergh. The surface is diversified
with mountain, hill, and dale ; the soil is of light and
fertile quality, and in the valley is limestone rock, of
which, and of red conglomerate, there are quarries. The
line of the North-Western railway passes through. The
living is a perpetual curacy, in the patronage of Trustees :
there is a glebe-house. The chapel was erected in 1833,
and has a square tower, lancet windows, and a good
organ. The Clergy Daughters' school established here
in 1823, as a means of assisting clergy of limited incomes in the education of their daughters, is a prosperous and efficient institution, very liberally sustained by
donations of the nobility and gentry, and annual subscriptions. About 100 pupils are received from all
parts of the kingdom, and are lodged, clothed, boarded,
and educated, on the easy terms of £14 per annum; the
school is under the management of twelve trustees, the
instruction very comprehensive, and many accomplished
governesses, among others, have been educated here. A
preparatory school for extending the benefits of the
Clergy Daughters' school, and rendering the instruction
in the latter more effectual, by first training younger
pupils for it, was opened in 1837, and is wholly confined
to the children of clergymen with the smallest incomes;
about 35 children are at present in this school. There
are also here, a school for training girls as servants and
teachers, which was instituted in 1820, and receives 100

IREO, parts of KESTEVEN, county of LINCOLN, 3 miles .) from Grantham; containing 51 inhabitants. It nsists of three farms.

CASTLE-ACRE (ST. JAMES), a parish, in the union d hundred of FREEBRIDGE-LYNN, W. division of ɔRFOLK, 4 miles (N.) from Swaffham; containing 95 inhabitants. This place, called *Acre* at the time the Domesday survey, is noted chiefly for the remains its ancient castle and priory, from the former of ich it takes the prefix to its name. It appears, from ! vestiges of a Roman road leading from Thetford to ancaster, the discovery of a tessellated pavement, and, ely, of several coins (among which were some of spasian and Constantine), to have been a Roman tion, on whose site the castle was probably erected. is fortress was built by William Warren, first earl of rrey, to whom the manor, with 149 others, had been en by the Conqueror, and who made it the head of all ; lordships; it was perhaps enlarged by his descend- t, who, in 1297, entertained Edward I. here. The PARISH comprises 3249 acres, of which 2639 ! arable, 461 meadow and pasture, 13 wood, and 79 mmon; the land is in general rich, and boldly undu- ed. The village consists of two good streets, on the rth bank of the river Nar. Fairs for toys and pedlery ! held on St. James's day and August 5th; and petty- ssions once a fortnight. The living is a discharged :arage, valued in the king's books at £5. 6. 8.; patron d impropriator, the Earl of Leicester: the great hes have been commuted for £610, and the vicarial £168; the glebe comprises 3½ acres. The church, uated on the crown of the acclivity above the ·lory, is a spacious structure in the decorated and ter English styles, with a lofty embattled tower, ıd exhibits, in many of its details, fine specimens ' ancient architecture; the font, which is said to ıve been removed from the priory, is surmounted ; a beautiful piece of tabernacle work. There are aces of worship for congregations of Baptists, Primi- ve Methodists, and Wesleyan Methodists. Sufficient remains exist to indicate the extent of the ıstle, which, with its appendages, comprised an area of ore than eighteen acres, inclosed ·by ·an embattled all seven feet in thickness, strengthened by three fty buttresses built over the broad and deep moat by hich the castle was surrounded: the buildings were ' a circular form, and on the slope of a gentle eminence. ɔ the east of the castle are the ruins of the priory, ıtablished by Earl Warren, in 1085, for monks of the luniac order, dedicated to the Blessed Virgin, and sub- ·dinate to a similar establishment by the same founder, ; Lewes, in the county of Sussex. The revenues, which ıd become very considerable by successive augmenta- ɔns, were seized under pretence of its being an alien ·iory, but were subsequently restored; and in the reign ' Edward II., it was secured against further molestation y a royal order, as coming within the class of indigenous ıtablishments. Its income, at the Dissolution, was 324. 17. 5., and, with the site, was granted to Thomas, ·uke of Norfolk; it is now the property of the Earl of eicester. The priory church was a spacious cruciform ructure, with two towers at the west end, and a massive :ntral tower; the greater portion of the west front is ill remaining, and, with the exception of a large window f later insertion over the entrance, is an elegant specimen

527

of the most enriched style of Norman architecture. The conventual buildings are. at present a farmhouse and offices: a large room, called the prior's dining-room, and now a granary, has a fine oriel window. On making excavations within the walls of the chapter-house, in 1841, were found some beautifully embossed tiles, with heraldic devices, and some bulls of the Popes Honorius and Innocent.

CASTLE-ASHBY, county of NORTHAMPTON.—See ASHBY, CASTLE.—*And other places having a similar distinguishing prefix will be found under the proper name.*

CASTLE-CAMPS (ALL SAINTS), a parish, in the union of LINTON, hundred of CHILFORD, county of CAMBRIDGE, 5¾ miles (S. E. by E.) from Linton; con- taining 854 inhabitants. This place was the seat of the Veres, earls of Oxford, one of whom received it by grant from Henry I., as lord high chamberlain of England; the site of their magnificent castle is now occupied by a farmhouse, but the moat and some slight vestiges are still visible. The estate was subse- quently purchased by Thomas Sutton, founder of the Charter-house in London, who made it a portion of the endowment of that institution. The parish is situ- ated near the road from Cambridge to Colchester, and comprises by computation 2800 acres. The living is a rectory, valued in the king's books at £16. 4. 2., and in the gift of the Governors of the Charter-house, the tithes have been commuted for £630, and the glebe comprises 71 acres. The church is a handsome structure, in the later English style. There is a place of worship for Baptists.

CASTLE-CARROCK (ST. PETER), a parish, in the union of BRAMPTON, ESKDALE ward, E. division of CUMBERLAND, 4½ miles (S. by E.) from Brampton; containing 351 inhabitants. The parish comprises about 5500 acres, the soil of which on the west is dry, gravelly, and very stony; and on the east, which is rugged and mountainous, good for grazing, resting on extensive beds of limestone and freestone. It is bounded on the east and north by the small river Gelt, which rises in the royal forest of Geltsdale, a hilly tract of moorland. The living is a discharged rectory, valued in the king's books at £5. 12. 11.; net income, £159; patrons, the Dean and Chapter of Carlisle. The tithes were com- muted for land in 1801. The church is a neat struc- ture, built of freestone in 1828. The former edifice is supposed to have been built out of the ruins of an ancient castle that stood within an intrenchment near the village, the lines of which are distinctly visible: there is another intrenchment at a short dis- tance. Upon the summit of a long and lofty fell, forming the northern point of the range of mountains extending from Cross Fell, near Alston, are two cairns, one of which, called Hespeckraise, is of considerable magnitude: on the removal of another cairn near Gelt Bridge, about 1775, a human skeleton was discovered in a species of coffin made of rude stones. Near the church is a mineral spring, the water of which is of the same quality as that of Gilsland spa.

CASTLE-CARY (*ALL SAINTS*), a market-town and parish, in the union of WINCANTON, hundred of CATS- ASH, E. division of SOMERSET, 11 miles (E. N. E.) from Somerton, and 113 (W. S. W.) from London; containing, with the hamlets of Clanville, Cockbill, and Dimmer, 1942 inhabitants, of whom 50 are in Clanville, and 116 in Cockbill and Dimmer. Castle-Cary probably derived its name from an ancient castle originally belonging to a lord of the name of Carey, which was defended against King Stephen by its owner, Lord Lovell, one of whose descendants having embraced the cause of the deposed monarch, Richard II., it became forfeited to the crown. The site is still called the Camp, and weapons of iron have been found in it occasionally : the only remains are some slight traces of the intrenchments. Charles II., after the battle of Worcester, took refuge in the manor-house. The TOWN is pleasantly situated, and consists of two parts, extending together nearly a mile : the houses are neatly built, and amply supplied with water; the air is salubrious, and the environs abound with pleasing scenery. The market, which is on every alternate Tuesday, is well attended,· and supplied with sheep and cattle of all kinds, from October till the spring fairs, which are on the Tuesday before Palm-Sunday, May 1st, and Whit-Tuesday; a fair is also held on the first Tuesday after the 19th of September, for cattle, broad-cloth, and other merchandise. The parish comprises by admeasurement 2572 acres. The living is a discharged vicarage, valued in the king's books at £11. 16. 3.; patron, the Bishop of Bath and Wells; impropriator, Sir H. R. Hoare, Bart. The great tithes have been commuted for £301. 10., and the vicarial for £378; the impropriate glebe consists of 65 acres, and the vicarial of 10 acres. The church is a handsome structure, occupying an elevated situation; the arch-deacon holds his visitations in it. There are places of worship for Independents and Wesleyans.

CASTLE-CHURCH (ST. LAWRENCE), a parish, in the.E. division of the hundred of CUTTLESTONE, union, and S. division of the county, of STAFFORD, 1 mile (S. W.) from Stafford; containing, with the townships of Forebridge, and Rickerscote with Burton, 1484 inhabitants. The parish derives its name from the ancient baronial castle of Stafford, to which its church was originally an appendage; and comprehends a portion of the town of Stafford. It is a fertile district, on the south side of the river Sow, and comprises nearly 4000 acres of land. The Liverpool and Birmingham railway passes through. The living is a perpetual curacy, with a net income of £120; it is in the patronage òf the Crown, and Lord Stafford and others are impropriators. The church, of which the nave and chancel were rebuilt in 1845, at a cost of £2000, is in the Norman style. At Fore-bridge is a separate incumbency; and near the town is a Roman Catholic chapel, built in 1822, by the late Edward Jerningham, Esq.

CASTLE-COMBE (ST. ANDREW), a parish, in the union and hundred of CHIPPENHAM, Chippenham and Calne, and N. divisions of WILTS, 6½ miles (N. W. by W.) from Chippenham; containing 600 inhabitants. The village, which is very considerable, was anciently cele-brated for a castle, built in the early part of the thirteenth century, by Walter de Dunstanville, son-in-law of Reginald, Earl of Cornwall, and which was dis-mantled before the close of the fourteenth; it stood on a hill north of the village, where the remains of its in-trenchments are still discernible. A market was obtained by Bartholomew, Lord Badlesmere, which has been dis-continued; but the market-cross remains in the centre of the village. The living is a rectory, valued in the king's books at £9; patron, William Scroop, Esq.

ained in confinement, from the year 1330, until her ease, in 1358. It passed from the family of Albini he barons of Montalt, the last of whom died without e, when his widow surrendered the lordship for 10 per annum, to Queen Isabella, at that time regent,) was visited here, in 1340, by her son, Edward III., his queen. Edward III., on the death of his mother, led Castle-Rising on his son Edward ; it afterwards sed to the Howards, dukes of Norfolk, and subse- ntly to the Berkshire branch, who, in 1745, succeeded the title of Earl of Suffolk. The principal remains the shell of the keep, a square tower, the walls of ich are three yards in thickness, with some orna- nted doorways and windows in the Norman style of hitecture, though greatly dilapidated ; the site of the at hall, and some vestiges of the state apartments, may o be traced : the chief entrance is over a ruined bridge ne circular arch, defended by a tower gateway. his was once a considerable sea-port, inferior in this nty only to Lynn and Yarmouth ; but the harbour oming choked up with sand, its trade declined, and n the consequent decrease of its population, the mar- , which was held twice a week, has been discontinued many years. The vicinity was formerly subject to ndations of the sea, to prevent which an embankment been constructed. The government was originally ted in a mayor, twelve aldermen, and an indefinite nber of burgesses, aided by a recorder, high steward, ; but the corporation has gradually fallen into ay. Of the rank which the place held as an ancient ough, it still retains a memorial, in the precedence en to the name of the mayor in the commission of e peace for the county. The elective franchise was nferred in the last year of the reign of Philip and ary, from which time the borough returned two mem- rs to parliament till disfranchised by the 2nd of Wil- m IV., cap. 45 : the right of election was vested in the e burgesses, the number of whom had been reduced to o or three ; and the mayor was returning officer. The rish is situated on the road from Lynn to Wells, and mprises 2096a. 2r. 21p., of which 1008 acres are able, 865 meadow and pasture, and 223 woodland ; e soil is of a sandy and clayey nature. A trout stream ns through the parish, called the Rising river. The LIVING is a discharged rectory, with that of Roy- n consolidated, valued in the king's books at £8, and the gift of the family of Howard. The tithes have en commuted for £320, and the glebe comprises acres, with a glebe-house. The church is an ancient 'ucture, with a tower rising from between the nave d chancel ; it exhibits fine specimens of the Nor- m style, and has an east window in the decorated iglish style : the entrance is enriched with varied)uldings, and on each side of the large window above are series of intersecting arches ; the font is very cient, and highly ornamented. Near the church is an spital, containing thirteen apartments, a large hall, d a chapel, built in 1613, by Henry Howard, Earl of rthampton, who endowed it with a rent-charge of 00 for twelve aged women and a governess. To the st of the castle is a square mount, one acre in extent, d to the east of it a circular mount surrounded by a tch ; the former is by some supposed to have been a man camp, though others think both were thrown up ' the people of Lynn, when they besieged the castle, Vol. I.—529

and compelled the Earl of Arundel to relinquish his claim to one-third of the customs of their port. There are some chalybeate springs in the parish.

CASTLE-THORPE (St. *Simon and St. Jude*), a parish, in the union of Newport-Pagnell, hundred of Newport, county of Buckingham, 3 miles (N. N. E.) from Stony-Stratford ; containing 365 inhabitants. This place derives its name from the ancient castle of the barony of Hanslope, the site of which exhibits traces of very extensive buildings : it was taken and demolished in 1217, by Fulke de Brent, when it had been garrisoned by its owner, William Manduit, one of the barons who were in arms against Henry III. The London and Bir- mingham railway passes within a short distance. The living is annexed to the vicarage of Hanslope. Thomas Tyrell, one of the judges in the court of common pleas in the reign of Charles II., resided here, and was interred in the chancel of the church, where a handsome monu- ment was erected by his widow.

CASTLE-THORPE, a township, in the parish of Broughton, union of Glandford-Brigg, E. division of the wapentake of Manley, parts of Lindsey, county of Lincoln, 1½ mile (W.) from Glandford-Brigg ; containing 346 inhabitants. The Roman road from Lincoln to Win- teringham-on-the-Humber passes a short distance east of the village.

CASTLEFORD (*All Saints*), a parish, in the Upper division of the wapentake of Osgoldcross, W. riding of York ; containing 1850 inhabitants, of whom 1414 are in the township of Castleford, 3 miles (N. W.) from Pontefract. This place is by some writers supposed to have been the site of the Roman station *Legiolium*, or *Lagetium*, described in Antonine's *Itinerary* as being situated on the river Aire, where it was crossed by a ford, on the line of the Herman-street between Doncaster and York : Roman antiquities have been frequently disco- vered, including a scarce *denarius* of Caracalla, with a lion on the reverse. It is related, that the citizens of York, being pursued by Ethelred's army, in 750, turned at this place, and committed great slaughter on their pursuers. After the Norman Conquest, the parish was given to Ilbert de Laci, the heiress of whose family con- veyed it by marriage, with the whole honour of Ponte- fract, to John of Gaunt, Duke of Lancaster.

The village is situated on the south bank of the river Aire, at a short distance from its junction with the Calder, the latter of which, in 1698, was made navigable to Wakefield, and the Aire to Leeds. The united rivers are crossed by a handsome stone bridge of three arches, which was rebuilt in 1808, and connects Castleford with the village of Allerton-Bywater on the north side of the river. The parish comprises the townships of Castleford and Glass-Houghton, and contains 1534a. 2r. 18p., of which 517 acres are in Castleford ; 300 of these are arable, and 213 meadow and pasture. It has a station of the York and North-Midland railway. There is a dock-yard for building sloops, and a dry-dock for re- pairs : many owners of small craft reside here ; and among the manufactories and branches of trade are a timber-yard, some oil and corn-mills, several granaries, a pottery of black and stone ware, a whiting-mill, and glass-bottle works. A court leet, baron, and view of frankpledge, is held in May and October. The living is a rectory, valued in the king's books at £20. 13. 1½., and in the patronage of the Duchy of Lancaster ; net income, £555 : the tithes were commuted for corn-rents, under an inclosure act, in 1816. The church is thought to stand on part of the Roman camp above mentioned; it is a cruciform structure, with a tower rising at the intersection. There is a place of worship for Wesleyans in each of the townships.

CASTLETON (ST. EDMUND), a parish, in the union of CHAPEL-EN-LE-FRITH, hundred of HIGH PEAK, N. division of the county of DERBY, 4½ miles (N.) from Tideswell; containing 1500 inhabitants, of whom 941 are in the township of Castleton. This parish consists of the townships of Castleton and Edale. The former is said to have taken its name from a CASTLE built by William Peverell, natural son of the Conqueror, which, from its situation upon a steep and high peak, was called the *Castle of the Peak*, or Peak Castle; but from various records it appears that a castle existed pre-viously, supposed to have been erected by Edward the Elder, or his heroic sister Ethelfleda, and which, in the reign of Edward the Confessor, was the property of Earl Gundeburne. The castle remained with the Peverells until the attainder of the third William, when it was granted by Henry II. to John, Earl of Montaigne, after-wards King John; and during the absence of the earl's brother Richard I., Hugh Nonant, Bishop of Coventry, held it. In 1204, King John appointed Hugh Neville governor; but the disaffected barons seized it and kept possession until the reign of Henry III., from which period it had various occupiers, until settled by Edward III. upon his son, the Earl of Richmond, com-monly called John of Gaunt, who was created Duke of Lancaster, in 1362, when the castle became part of the duchy of Lancaster. The Duke of Devonshire now pos-sesses it, as lessee under the crown. The extent of the ruins evinces the former magnitude of the building; the castle-yard, the walls of which are in some places twenty feet high and nine feet thick, occupying nearly the whole summit of the hill. The keep, consisting of two stories almost entire, and standing at the south-western point of this high and precipitous limestone rock, towering above the mouth of the great cavern of the Peak, is fifty feet in height.

The PARISH, exclusively of Edale, comprises about 2900 acres, exhibiting a very hilly surface, and several varieties of soil : the township of Castleton occupies the western extremity of the large and deep valley which commences at Mam Tor, and runs eastward to join the valley of the Derwent. The great limestone district of Derbyshire has its northern termination at Castleton, the hills to the north being upon gritstone, and those to the south on limestone : the soil on the south side is very superior. The village, which is situated at the foot of the Castle hill, was fortified by a rampart, and the ditch is still visible, extending from the ravines at the base of the rock, to the outworks connected with the castle. The inhabitants principally derive their support from the mining district by which the village is sur-rounded. The living is a discharged vicarage, valued in the king's books at £6. 7. 6.; net income, £186; patron and appropriator, the Bishop of Chester. The great tithes have been commuted for £100, and the vicarial for £50; the appropriate glebe consists of 87½ acres, and the vicarial of 22 acres. The church is a small ancient edifice : the arch, with its mouldings entire, separating the nave from the chancel, is a fine specimen

ve formed an elevated mount in the valley, called tle Mam Tor. On its summit are the remains of a p, supposed to be Saxon, with the greater part of the part entire; and on the south-west side are two rows, in one of which, when opened some years ce, were found a brass celt and fragments of an un- ced urn. Near this mountain is the *Water Hull Mine*, ere is procured the beautiful and peculiar fluor-spar, most esteemed kinds of which are the violet-blue and e-coloured, which are worked into elegant vases, urns, . Here is also found, between the schistus and lime- ne, a species of elastic bitumen, that burns with a ght flame; another variety, less elastic, is formed of ments, and is called wood bitumen. About half a e midway in this mountainous ravine, which exhibits many places proofs of volcanic origin, is a place called Cove, where large masses of basaltic rocks are con- cuous, in which are imbedded quartz, crystals, &c. ch an assemblage of natural curiosities renders the ghbourhood of Castleton one of the most interesting tricts in the kingdom.

CASTLETON (St. Mary Magdalene), a parish, in union and hundred of Sherborne, Sherborne ision of the county of Dorset, 1 mile (E. N. E.) m Sherborne; containing 113 inhabitants. It com- ses 50 acres, chiefly pasture, and lies contiguous to park and residence of Earl Digby, lord lieutenant of county. The living is a perpetual curacy; net in- e, £81; patron, Earl Digby.

CASTLETON, a township, in the parish and union Rochdale, hundred of Salford, S. division of the nty of Lancaster; including part of the town of chdale, and containing 14,279 inhabitants. This ice derives its name from a castle which arose here in xon times, and which, it is highly probable, was one the numerous sacrifices in the conflicts between the xons and the Danes; the site is still to be traced by a ty mound called the Castle-hill, the fosse appearing und it in distinct lines. In Edward II.'s reign, nry de Lacy possessed the manor of Castleton. On ? dissolution of monasteries it was granted to the Rad- ffs, of Langley, and subsequently passed by purchase the Holts, of Stubley, who about 1640 took up their idence at Castleton Hall, and by whom the present fice was built soon after the Revolution. The Chet- ms, of Turton, succeeded by purchase to the estate in 13, since which time it has been successively held by ? Winstanleys, Smiths (an opulent mercantile family), l Burdetts. The river Roche, which divides the town Rochdale, bounds Castleton on the north; and the id to Manchester, the Rochdale canal, and the Man- :ster and Leeds railway, pass through. A large num- : of the inhabitants are employed in the woollen and ton manufactures of the vicinity. The parish church l glebe, on which latter the new part of Rochdale is ilt, are within the township.

CASTLETON, York.—See Danby.

CASTLE-VIEW, an extra-parochial liberty, in the ion, and adjoining the borough, of Leicester, hun- :d of Guthlaxton, S. division of the county of Lei- ster; containing 120 inhabitants.

CASTLEY, a township, in the parish of Leathley, per division of the wapentake of Claro, W. riding York, 4½ miles (E. by N.) from Otley; containing 0 inhabitants. It comprises by computation 480
531

acres; and is bounded on the south, and partly on the east and west, by the river Wharfe.

CASTON (*Holy Cross*), a parish, in the union and hundred of Wayland, W. division of Norfolk, 3½ miles (S. E.) from Watton; containing 513 inhabitants, and comprising about 1600 acres. The living is a rec- tory, united to the rectories of Rockland All Saints and St. Andrew, and valued in the king's books at £11. 19. 2.: the glebe comprises 59 acres. The church is a spacious edifice in the decorated and later English styles, with a tower; the interior contains a monument of the founder, supposed to be one of the Castons. There is a place of worship for Wesleyans.

CASTOR, county of Lincoln.—See Caistor.

CASTOR (St. Keneburgha), a parish, in the union and soke of Peterborough, N. division of the county of Northampton, 4½ miles (W.) from Peterborough; containing 1313 inhabitants. This village, and the op- posite one of Chesterton, occupy the site of the Roman station *Durobrivæ*, by the Saxons called *Dormancester*; and a great quantity of coins from Trajan to Valens, fragments of urns, tiles, &c., have been discovered. The Roman Ermin-street commenced here, and, pro- ceeding some distance, branched off into two divisions, the remains of which are still visible; one leading to Stamford, and the other, by Lolham-Bridges, through West Deeping, into Lincolnshire. *Lady Keneburgha's way* is supposed to have been a paved way from a fort- ress on the river Nene, which runs through the parish, to a castle on the hill, where the Roman governor re- sided. The place was destroyed by the Danes. The parish comprises about 3600 acres, and is considerably diversified in its surface, some parts being flat, and others very much elevated. The Northampton and Peterborough railway passes through. The living is a rectory, valued in the king's books at £52. 12. 8½., and held *in commendam* with the see of Peterborough: there are about 150 acres of glebe, and a glebe-house. The church, dedicated in 1124 to St. Keneburgha, who founded a nunnery here, is a spacious cruciform edifice, with a beautiful Norman tower of two stages, rising from the intersection, and surmounted by a spire. There are chapels of ease at Sutton and Upton, in the parish; a day school, having a master and mistress, is supported by the Earl Fitzwilliam, and a Sunday school, in the same building, by the bishop. John Landen, an eminent mathematician, was born here in 1719. Some tessellated pavement dug up in the parish is now laid down in the dairy at Milton Hall, the residence of Lord Fitzwilliam.

CASWELL, a tything, in the parish of Portbury, union of Bedminster, hundred of Portbury, E. divi- sion of Somerset; containing 74 inhabitants.

CATCHBURN, a township, in the parish and union of Morpeth, E. division of Castle ward, S. division of Northumberland, 1½ mile (S. by E.) from Mor- peth; containing, with Morpeth Castle, Park-House, and Stobhill, 145 inhabitants. At this place, which is situated on the east of the great road, Roger de Merlay, the second, built an hospital dedicated to St. Mary Magdalene, probably for the use of wayfaring people, and which is mentioned in a deed of the year 1282, An inquest taken after the death of Ralph, Lord Grey- stock, in the 17th of Edward II., enumerates its advow- son among his possessions; and John, Lord Greystock,
3 Y 2

in 1346, ordained by will that it should be given, with all its goods and ornaments, to a chaplain. There are no remains.

CATCHERSIDE, a township, in the parish of KIRK-WHELPINGTON, union of BELLINGHAM, N. E. division of TINDALE ward, S. division of NORTHUMBERLAND, 15 miles (W.) from Morpeth; containing 12 inhabitants. This place, anciently written Calcherside, has been the property of the Fenwicks, Blacketts, and Trevelyans; and, though now still and lonely, appears to have been once of some little importance. Tradition says there was a mill here: the "Scotch street" ran through the place; and in the last century it had an ale-house where carriers stopped, and villagers assembled for rural sports. On Camp Hill were traces of a British camp, which were removed a few years since.

CATCLIFFE, a township, in the parish and union of ROTHERHAM, S. division of the wapentake of STRAF-FORTH and TICKHILL, W. riding of YORK, 3 miles (S.) from Rotherham; containing 252 inhabitants. It comprises by computation 930 acres: the village is on a gentle eminence above the river Rother, on its western side. Here is a manufactory for glass, established about the year 1780.

CATCOMB, a tything, in the parish of HILLMARTON, union of CALNE, hundred of KINGSBRIDGE, Chippenham and Calne, and N. divisions of the county of WILTS; containing 68 inhabitants.

CATCOTT, a chapelry, in the parish of MOORLINCH, union of BRIDGWATER, hundred of WHITLEY, W. division of SOMERSET, 7 miles (E. N. E.) from Bridgwater; containing 750 inhabitants. This place is situated on the north side of the Polden hills, within two miles of the Glastonbury and Bridgwater canal: very fine blue lias for building is quarried. The living is a perpetual curacy, in the patronage of Aldborough Henniker, Esq., with a net income of £100: the chapel is a plain edifice, in the later English style, and has a very fine old font. There is a place of worship for dissenters. A bequest of £20 per annum is regularly distributed among poor widows.

CATEBY, county of YORK.—See CADEBY.

CATERHAM, or KATERHAM (ST. LAWRENCE), a parish, in the union of GODSTONE, Second division of the hundred of TANDRIDGE, E. division of SURREY, 3¼ miles (N. by W.) from Godstone; containing 477 inhabitants. The parish is situated on the road from Croydon to Godstone, and intersected by the London and Brighton railway; and comprises by admeasurement 2386 acres, of which 1462 are arable, 269 meadow and pasture, 175 woodland, and 468 uninclosed common. The surface is hilly, and the soil has several varieties, consisting of chalk, clay, and black mould: building-stone is quarried extensively. A fair for toys is held in July. The living is a rectory, valued in the king's books at £8. 0. 1½.; patron and incumbent, the Rev. James Legrew, whose tithes have been commuted for £400, and who has a glebe of 5 acres. The church was repaired in 1832, and a beautiful monument erected on the north side of the chancel to the memory of Mrs. Elizabeth Legrew. There is an encampment on the top of Whitehill, called the Cardinal's Cap, said to have been formed by the ancient Britons.

CATESBY (ST. MARY), a parish, in the union of DAVENTRY, hundred of FAWSLEY, S. division of the

esidence of the abbots of Bath till the dissolution of nasteries, when the manor was granted to the Hargtons. A paper-mill is in operation, giving employnt to a few hands. The living is a perpetual curacy, 1exed to the vicarage of Bath-Easton: the tithes have :n commuted for £50 payable to the incumbent, £31 the impropriator, and £15 to the Dean and Chapter Christ-Church, Oxford. In the chancel is a handsome mument to the memory of some of the Blanchard ily.

CATHERINGTON (St. *Catherine*), a parish, and : head of a union, in the hundred of Finch-Dean, tersfield and N. divisions of the county of South-pton, 6¾ miles (S. W. by S.) from Petersfield; con-ning 1003 inhabitants. It comprises by admeasure-nt 5035 acres, of which 2800 are arable, 1400 pas-re, 615 woodland, and 95 common or waste. The ing is a discharged vicarage, valued in the king's oks at £9. 5. 10., and in the gift of J. Hayward, Esq.: e great tithes, belonging to Sir L. Curtis, Bart., have en commuted for £614, and those of the incumbent : £280; there is a glebe of 2 acres. The church, uated on an eminence, has some rich Norman arches, d contains a monument to Nicholas Hyde, chief justice the court of queen's bench: a gallery was erected in 34. The poor law union comprises 5 parishes or ices, and contains a population of 2356.

CATHERSTON-LEWSTON (St. *Mary*), a parish, the union of Bridport, hundred of Whitchurch-nonicorum, Bridport division of Dorset, 2¾ miles . E.) from Lyme-Regis; containing 36 inhabitants. is place was the residence of a branch of the Wad-ms, by one of whom, Nicholas Wadham, and Dorothy s wife, Wadham College, Oxford, was founded. The irish is situated on the great road from London to lymouth, adjoining the post-town of Charmouth, and mprises by measurement 248 acres. The living is a scharged rectory, valued in the king's books at 2. 16. 10½.; net income, £67; patrons, the Executors Jones Ross, Esq. The church, rebuilt lately by sub-ription of the rector and his friends, is a neat small lifice.

CATHORPE (St. *Thomas*), a parish, in the union of utterworth, hundred of Guthlaxton, S. division of ie county of Leicester, 4½ miles (S. by E.) from Lut-rworth; containing 167 inhabitants. The parish is tuated on the river Avon, and on the road from Rugby Market-Harborough; and comprises 625a. 10r., of hich 462 acres are pasture, and the rest arable: the irface is varied, some parts being flat, and others rising a considerable elevation; and the soil is chiefly gravel, ith a little clay. The Roman Watling-street crosses ie south-western extremity. Three-fourths of the opulation are stocking-frame knitters. The living is a ctory, valued in the king's books at £5. 5. 2½.; net come, £226; patron and incumbent, the Rev. L. arper. The church is an ancient structure, in the ter English style. Dyer, the poet, was for some time cumbent.

CATMORE (St. *Margaret*), a parish, in the union Wantage, hundred of Compton, county of Berks, ½ miles (W. by S.) from East Ilsley; containing, with ie tything of Lilley, 96 inhabitants. It comprises out 720 acres; the surface is elevated, and the soil irions, in some parts chalk, and in others clay. Here
533

was formerly a market on Monday, granted in 1306 by Edward I., together with a fair on the festival of St. Margaret. The living is a rectory, valued in the king's books at £5. 5. 7½.; net income, £180; patron, C. Eyre, Esq.: the glebe consists of about 14 acres.

CATON, a parochial chapelry, and a township, in the parish of Lancaster, hundred of Lonsdale south of the Sands, N. division of the county of Lancaster, 5 miles (N. E. by E.) from Lancaster; containing 1195 inhabitants. The manor was a possession of the Gernets, the ancient foresters of Lancaster: there was also here a family named Caton, who held the manor by homage and service; and in connexion with the place, are mentioned, successively, the families of Curwen, Chorley, Stanley, Dalton, Riddell, Rawlinson, and Ed-mondson. The chapelry comprises four districts or quarters, viz.: Brookhouse, Caton Green, Littledale, and Town-End; and contains by measurement 8373a. 2r. 16p., whereof 600 acres are arable, 3300 meadow and pasture, 400 woodland, and about 4000 moorland. It lies on the road from Lancaster to Hornby, and on the eastern bank of the river Lune, which is here crossed by a bridge, with a road from it leading to Halton. The beauty of the diversified scenery elicited a warm eulogium from the poet Gray, in a letter to Dr. Warton; and Dr. Whitaker, in describing the beauties of the Vale of the Lune, says, "Immediately on approaching Caton, its cha-racter as the first of northern valleys is established by the beautiful windings here of the river, the fruitful alluvial lands upon its banks, the wooded and cultivated ridge that bounds it on the north-west, the striking appearance of Hornby Castle in front, and above all the noble form of Ingleborough, presenting an assemblage of features not united to compose any rival scenery in the kingdom." On the top of the moor are several freestone-quarries, and an inferior stone is found on the surface. There are two silk-mills, two cotton-mills, and a flax-mill, in operation, employing in all 400 persons; and at Grass-yard Hall is a corn-mill. Scarthwaite, on the bank of the Lune, is the seat of Adam Hodgson, Esq., command-ing the whole extent of the vale, and the winding course of the river; the precise spot selected by Mr. Hodgson for his house and terrace, under the auspices of Mr. Gilpin and Sir John Nasmyth, has long been distin-guished as "Gray's Station," and shares in all the ex-quisite scenery that gives celebrity to the vale. The Elms, and the land around it, are the property of John Walmsley, Esq., of Richmond House, near Lancaster, who is also owner of Caton mill. John Edmondson, Esq., is lord of the manor.

The living is a perpetual curacy; net income, £140, with a house erected in 1844; patron, the Vicar of Lan-caster. The ancient chapel was built about the year 1245; of this structure, the beautiful Saxon gateway and the font alone remain: the present edifice was erected about 300 years ago, and has a square tower. There are places of worship for Wesleyans and Inde-pendents; and a national school supported by subscrip-tion. The interest of £250 was left in 1838, by Richard Sparling Berry, Esq., for parents who educate their children without parochial relief: four cottages are free of rent for poor persons; and about £5 are annually distributed to the poor. In 1803, a Roman mill-stone, eight feet long, was found in Artle beck, bearing the name of the Emperor Adrian; and subsequently a stone with consonants on it, which, when supplied by the vowel *e*, form an ingenious monitory couplet.

CATSFIELD (*St. Lawrence*), a parish, in the union of Battle, hundred of Ninfield, rape of Hastings, E. division of Sussex, 3½ miles (S. W.) from Battle; containing 589 inhabitants. It is intersected by the road from Lewes to Hastings, and comprises 2938 acres, of which 875 are arable, 1447 meadow and pasture, 520 woodland, and 50 acres hops : the surface is alternated with hill and dale, and enriched with woods and plantations. The living is a rectory, valued in the king's books at £7. 9. 4½., and in the patronage of the Earl of Ashburnham : the tithes have been commuted for £370, and the glebe comprises 34 acres, with a glebe-house. The church is a handsome structure, partly in the early and partly in the decorated English style, with a square embattled tower surmounted by a low shingled spire : in the chancel is an elegant monument to the memory of J. Fuller, Esq., by Nollekens. At the gate of the churchyard is a remarkably fine oak, more than 40 feet in girth at a few feet from the ground.

CATSHILL, an ecclesiastical district, in the parish and union of Bromsgrove, Upper division of the hundred of Halfshire, Droitwich and E. divisions of the county of Worcester, 2¼ miles (N.) from Bromsgrove, on the road to Stourbridge; containing about 3000 inhabitants. This district is formed of the north part of the parish, and includes the celebrated Bromsgrove Lickey, from which is a most extensive and diversified prospect. The greater part of the population is employed in the manufacture of nails, and the rest in agriculture. The living is a perpetual curacy, in the patronage of the Vicar of Bromsgrove; net income, £150, including an augmentation from the Ecclesiastical Commissioners. The church, dedicated to Christ, was built in 1838, at a cost of nearly £2000; it is in the early English style, with a tower, and has 546 sittings, whereof 404 are free. There are places of worship for Baptists, Primitive Methodists, and Wesleyans; and a Sunday school in connexion with the church.

CATTAL, a township, in the parish of Hunsingore, Upper division of the wapentake of Claro, W. riding of York, 5¼ miles (N. E. by N.) from Wetherby; containing 193 inhabitants. It is situated on the north of the river Nidd, whose course here is very devious; and comprises by computation 950 acres : the road from York to Knaresborough passes on the north, about two miles distant from the village.

CATTERAL, a township, in the parish and union of Garstang, hundred of Amounderness, S. division of the county of Lancaster, 1¾ mile (S. S. W.) from Garstang, on the road to Preston; containing 1102 inhabitants. The family of Catteral were in possession of this place for a considerable period; from them it passed by marriage to the Sherburnes, and subsequently came to the Banisters, Winckleys, and others. The township is situated at the confluence of the West Calder with the river Wyre, and comprises 1341*a*. 3*r*. 4*p*. of good land; the surface is level, running up by a gradual ascent towards Bleasdale : at the higher end is a good stone quarry. A cotton-mill, belonging to S. L. Behrens, Esq., of Catteral House, employs 438 hands; and there is another cotton-mill, carried on by Messrs. Jackson; also a bobbin-turning manufactory. The Preston and Lancaster railway and canal both pass through the

g the finest writing and printing paper. Near the mlet is the old manor-house; but the adjacent stone alls, barns, and out-houses have far more the aspect of mote age than the dwelling, which is brick and tile, ough substantially constructed. The old walls are rongly built, and are apparently coeval with the reains of the *Lady Chapel* at the back; the general rangement having the character of an ancient grange. pleasure-fair is held on Holy-Thursday.

CATTISTOCKE (St. Peter and St. Paul), a pah, in the union of Cerne, hundred of Cerne, Totmbe, and Modbury, Cerne division of Dorset, 9 iles (N. W.) from Dorchester; containing 549 inhabitts. It is situated on the road from Dorchester to ;ovil, and comprises 2938a. 1r. 6p. The living is a ctory, valued in the king's books at £13. 13. 9., and the patronage of Mrs. Still: the tithes have been mmuted for £510, and there is a glebe-house, with out 28 acres of land. On a hill in the eastern part of e parish is an ancient circular fortification of about ur acres, called the Castle, surrounded by a double mpart, with entrances at the north-east and west: wards the middle of the area the ground rises into a ng barrow; and near the north entrance is a round mulus, the top of which consists of flint stones.

CATTO, with Landmoth.—See Landmoth.

CATTON, a township, in the parish of Croxall, ion of Burton-upon-Trent, hundred of Repton d Gresley, S. division of the county of Derby, 7½ iles (S. W. by S.) from Burton; containing 47 inhatants. It comprises 1064a. 2r. 14p., of strong good heat land. The village, which is scattered, is situated 1 the Trent, about a mile and a half north-west from le village of Croxall. The Hall is a noble brick mansion, leasantly seated in a fine park on the east bank of the rent. The vicarial tithes have been commuted for a :nt-charge of £91. 15.

CATTON (St. Margaret), a parish, in the union of r. Faith's, hundred of Taverham, E. division of 'orfolk, 2 miles (N.) from Norwich; containing 650 ihabitants. It comprises 904a. 2r. 35p., a consider-le part of which consists of woodlands, and garden 1d pleasure grounds, interspersed with numerous manons and villas, forming together a beautiful suburban llage. The living is a discharged vicarage, valued in le king's books at £4. 3. 9.; patrons, the Dean and hapter of Norwich. The landowners have purchased le impropriate tithes of the Dean and Chapter; the icarial tithes have been commuted for £170, and the .ebe contains 13 acres. The church, of which the most icient part is in the later English style, consists of a ave, chancel, and north aisle, with a circular tower, le .upper part octagonal; in the interior are several :at memorials. The Wesleyan Methodists have a place f worship.

CATTON, a grieveship, in the parish of Allendale, nion of Hexham, S. division of Tindale ward and of 'orthumberland; containing 535 inhabitants.

CATTON (All Saints), a parish, in the union of ocklington, partly in the wapentake of Ouse and 'erwent, and partly in the Wilton-Beacon division of le wapentake of Harthill, E. riding of York; conining, with the townships of East and West Stamrd-Bridge, and Kexby, 1078 inhabitants, of whom 185 re in the township of High Catton, and 186 in that of

Low Catton, 7½ miles (E. N. E.) from York. The parish comprises 7664 acres, whereof 1640 are in High, and 1264 in Low, Catton. The surface is generally level, and there is some fine land, the soil varying from a very good to a very inferior quality; the scenery, though not particularly striking, is yet pleasing, and some parts present a beautiful view of the Wolds, by which the parish is bounded on the east. The village of Low Catton is situated in the vale of the Derwent; and that of High Catton on a gentle acclivity, at the distance of a mile from the former. The living is a rectory, valued in the king's books at £21. 12. 8½.; net income, £410; patron, Col. Wyndham : the tithes were commuted for land in 1760. The church is an ancient edifice with a large tower. There are places of worship for Wesleyans at High Catton and East Stamford-Bridge.

CATTON, a township, in the parish of Topcliffe, union of Thirsk, wapentake of Birdforth, N. riding of York, 5 miles (S. W.) from Thirsk; containing 136 inhabitants. It is on the east bank of the river Swale, and comprises by computation 770 acres of land : the Leeming-Lane road passes at the distance of about a mile and a half to the west of the village. The tithes have been commuted for £160 payable to the Dean and Chapter of York, and £26. 15. to the vicar.

CATWICK (St. Michael), a parish, in the union of Skirlaugh, N. division of the wapentake of Holderness, E. riding of York, 8 miles (N. E. by E.) from Beverley; containing 191 inhabitants. The parish comprises 1493 acres : the soil is various, but chiefly clay and gravel; the surface is undulated, and the scenery diversified, and in some situations of pleasing character. Tiles, chimney-pots, and bricks are manufactured to some extent. The living is a rectory, valued in the king's books at £10. 5., and in the patronage of the Crown; net income, £149 : the tithes were commuted for a money payment on the inclosure of the parish. The church is an ancient edifice in the later style of English architecture, repaired in 1842. There is a place of worship for Wesleyans.

CATWORTH, GREAT (St. Leonard), a parish, in the union of St. Neot's, hundred of Leightonstone, county of Huntingdon, 4 miles (N. by W.) from Kimbolton; containing 637 inhabitants. It is situated on the London and Oundle road, and comprises about 2000 acres. The living is a rectory, valued in the king's books at £17. 16. 10½.; net income, £337; patrons, the Principal and Fellows of Brasenose College, Oxford. The tithes were commuted for corn rents, under an inclosure act, in 1795; the glebe contains 60 acres, with a glebe-house. The church is in the early English style, and ornamented with a spire. The Baptists and Wesleyans have places of worship. Sir Wolstan Dixie, lord mayor of London in 1585, was born here.

CATWORTH, LITTLE, a chapelry, in the parish of Longstow, union of St. Neot's, hundred of Leighton-stone, county of Huntingdon, 3¾ miles (N. by E.) from Kimbolton; containing 75 inhabitants.

CAUGHALL, a township, in the parish of Backford, union of Great Boughton, Lower division of the hundred of Broxton, S. division of the county of Chester, 3⅓ miles (N. by E.) from Chester; containing 16 inhabitants, and comprising 310 acres. The manor belonged for several generations to a family of the same name, of whom Roger de Caughall, who died in the early part of the 15th century, left two daughters, through whom it passed into the families of Massey and Osbaldeston. One moiety afterwards came to Sir Thomas Stanley Massey Stanley, and the other became vested in the feoffees of the grammar school at Whitchurch. The Ellesmere canal flows on the west of the township.

CAULDON (ST. MARY), a parish, in the union of CHEADLE, N. division of the hundred of TOTMONSLOW and of the county of STAFFORD, 7 miles (N.) from Cheadle; containing 326 inhabitants. The parish comprises about 1500 acres of land, in a barren and dreary part of the moorlands; and is separated from the parish of Waterfall by the river Hamp, which in its course enters the ground at Waterhouses, continuing a subterraneous progress for upwards of five miles. At Cauldon Lowe, a lofty hill, are lime-works from which the greater part of the surrounding country is supplied; the lime is conveyed by railway to Froghall, and thence by canal, and much of it is used in the iron districts for the smelting of ore, being peculiarly adapted for that purpose: about 150 hands are employed on the works at Cauldon Lowe. The village is formed of straggling houses on a declivity. The living is a perpetual curacy, with a net income of £85; patron, A. Henniker, Esq.: the church is a small building, with a tower. A school is supported by subscription. Curious fossils are found here in abundance.

CAULDWELL, a chapelry, in the parish of STAPENHILL, union of BURTON-UPON-TRENT, hundred of REPTON and GRESLEY, S. division of the county of DERBY, 5¼ miles (S. by E.) from Burton; containing 153 inhabitants. The manor was sold by William, Lord Paget, in 1565, to Peter Collingwood, Esq., from whose family it passed by successive marriages to the families of Sanders and Mortimer; it afterwards came by purchase to Henry Evans, Esq., of Burton. The township comprises 1040 acres of land, east of the Trent. The impropriate tithes have been commuted for £257, and the vicarial for £146. 10. The chapel is dedicated to St. Giles, and is a small structure with a tower. The Baptists have a place of worship.

CAULK, or CALKE (ST. GILES), a parish, in the union of ASHBY-DE-LA-ZOUCH, hundred of REPTON and GRESLEY, S. division of the county of DERBY, 4¼ miles (N. by E.) from Ashby; containing 55 inhabitants. A convent of Augustine friars, in honour of St. Mary and St. Giles, was founded here before 1161; of which the Countess of Chester was a principal benefactor, on the condition that it should be subject to the priory of Repindon, or Repton. The site was granted by Edward VI., in 1547, to John, Earl of Warwick; and the Caulk estate subsequently came to the Wensleys, Bainbrigges, and Harpurs. Of the last-named family, Henry Harpur was created a baronet in 1626; and Sir Henry Harpur, the seventh baronet, took in 1808 the name of Crewe, in right of his great-grandmother, Catharine, daughter and coheiress of Thomas, Lord Crewe.

The parish comprises by measurement 900 acres. Quarries of limestone, in which, occasionally, much lead is found, are extensively wrought; and large quantities of the stone are burnt into lime, for the conveyance of which facility is afforded by the Swannington railway, to Ashby and Leicester, and by canal to other places. A handsome and substantial stone mansion, of the Grecian order, called The Abbey, has been erected amidst the

CAUNDLE-WAKE, a tything, in the parish of ISHOP-CAUNDLE, union of SHERBORNE, hundred of ROWNSHALL, Sturminster division of DORSET; containing 36 inhabitants. It takes its adjunct Wake from noble family which anciently possessed the manor of e place.

CAUNTON (ST. ANDREW), a parish, in the union of UTHWELL, N. division of the wapentake of THURRTON, S. division of the county of NOTTINGHAM, miles (N. W. by N.) from Newark; containing 539 habitants. It is situated on the Worksop road, and mprises by measurement 2900 acres, of which 1600 e in the manor of Caunton, 800 in that of Beesthorpe, d 500 in the manor of Knapthorpe; the scenery is ≥asing, the soil chiefly clay, and the land well cultited. Coal is supposed to exist, and various attempts ve been made to discover it, but without success. The ing is a discharged vicarage, in the patronage of the ebendary of North Muskham in the Collegiate Church Southwell, valued in the king's books at £4. 2. 1.; t income, £142; impropriator, Lord Middleton. The hes were commuted for land under an inclosure act, 1795. The church is a neat structure of stone. ιere are places of worship for Primitive and Wesleyan ethodists; and a school built by subscription.

CAUSEY-PARK, a township, in the parochial chalry of HEBBURN, union of MORPETH, W. division of ORPETH ward, N. division of NORTHUMBERLAND, 6½ íles (N. by W.) from MORPETH; containing 116 inhabitts. This place, which has its name from an ancient ved way that led along its eastern boundary, and on the e of the present great north road, was formerly in the rish of Felton; and comprises 1030 acres of land, exnpt from tithes, paying only a modus of £3 per annum. he House here was built in 1589 by James Ogle, and is some gardens which are very productive, and well ocked with fruit-trees. A little to the west of the ɔuse is a fine broad dyke, of compact whinstone, which as been much quarried for the roads; it has the millone grit on its north cheek, and beds of slaty sandone, bituminous shale, &c., on the south. There was ιce a chapel dedicated to St. Cuthbert, with which the ace was probably honoured on account of the monks ˙ Durham having rested here in their flight from that ty, with the body of St. Cuthbert, to Holy Island, in ɔ69. Henry Ogle, in 1760, bequeathed a rent-charge ˙ £15 for a school.

CAUTLEY and DOWBIGGIN, an ecclesiastical disict, in the parish of SEDBERGH, W. division of the apentake of STAINCLIFFE and EWCROSS, W. riding of ORK, 3 miles (N. E.) from Sedbergh, on the road to irkby-Stephen; containing about 500 inhabitants. his district was formed out of Sedbergh township; it is ιostly grass land, the soil various, and the scenery ιountainous: the river Rawther, which passes through, ses about four miles eastward. Flagstone and building-ɔne are obtained, and at Hebblethwaite Hall is a ɔbbin-mill. The living is a perpetual curacy; net inɔme, £40; patron, the Vicar of Sedbergh: the church as built in 1846, at an expense of £750, and is in the ecorated style, with a campanile tower. There is a lace of worship for a congregation of Wesleyan Methoists. In the vale of the Rawther is a picturesque ιscade called Cantley Spout, the water of which falls ˙om a great height.

CAVE, NORTH (ALL SAINTS), a parish, partly in the union of HOWDEN, and partly in that of POCKLINGTON, Hunsley-Beacon division of the wapentake of HARTHILL, E. riding of YORK, 10 miles (E. N. E.) from Howden; containing 1217 inhabitants, and comprising the chapelry of South Cliffe, and townships of North Cave, and Drewton with Everthorpe. This parish is situated on the main road from Hull and Beverley to Wakefield and the West riding, about 4 miles from the Hull and Selby railway, and 2 from the Market-Weighton canal. It comprises 6913a. 1r. 8p., of which 2025 acres are in the chapelry of South Cliffe: about 4702 are arable, 1006 pasture and meadow, 230 wood, 935 warren, and 13 common; the soil is various, being chalky in the high, blue lias in the lower, and oolite in the intervening lands. The living is a discharged vicarage, valued in the king's books at £10. 7. 6.; net income, £247; patrons and impropriators, Henry Burton, Esq., and Mrs. Sarah Burton. The great tithes for part of the township of North Cave were commuted for land in 1764; a tithe rent-charge of £155 is paid to the impropriators, and one of £57 to the vicar, who has a glebe, of an acre and a half. The church is a commodious edifice with a handsome tower, and contains a full-length figure of a knight in armour, supposed to represent Sir Thomas Matham, whose family were formerly seated here, but of whose mansion there are no remains. At South Cliffe is a chapel of ease; and there are places of worship in the parish for the Society of Friends, Primitive Methodists, and Wesleyans.

CAVE, SOUTH (ALL SAINTS), a parish, in the unions of HOWDEN and BEVERLEY, Hunsley-Beacon division of the wapentake of HARTHILL, E. riding of YORK; containing 1852 inhabitants, of whom 1288 are in the market-town of South Cave, 27 miles (S. E.) from York, and 183 (N. by W.) from London. This parish comprises 7103a. 2r. 30p., and includes the townships of Broomfleet and Faxfleet; it is situated at the western extremity of the Wolds, and on the river Humber, which forms its boundary for three miles. The township of South Cave comprises 4323a. 1r. 20p. The surrounding country is very pleasing; the eminences affording many delightful views of Lincolnshire, and of the river, with the scenery on its banks. At the market, which is held on Monday, considerable quantities of corn are sold for the supply of the manufacturing towns in the West riding; it is shipped on the Humber, and the return cargoes consist of coal, freestone, lime, flags, and a variety of other necessary commodities. There is a fair on Trinity-Monday. The petty-sessions for the wapentake of Howdenshire take place here; and a manorial court is held in October, at which a constable is appointed. The town consists principally of three long streets, of which the longest is on the northern acclivity of a valley: from being anciently washed by the tides of the Humber, it obtained the name of Cove, afterwards corrupted to Cave. In the vicinity is Cave Castle, the seat of H. G. Barnard, Esq., a splendid embattled structure, with numerous turrets; the interior exhibits a corresponding style of magnificence, and is enriched with a noble collection of paintings by the first artists, including a fine portrait of Washington, whose ancestors possessed a portion of the estate, and resided here prior to their emigration to Virginia, in the middle of the seventeenth century. The living is a discharged vicarage, valued in the king's books at £8; net income, £168; patron and impropriator, Mr. Barnard: the great tithes have been commuted for £465, and the vicarial for £95. The church is a neat edifice, erected in 1601, and consists of a nave, north aisle, south transept, and chancel, with a fine tower. There are three places of worship belonging to Methodists, and a Roman Catholic chapel at Cave Castle.

CAVENDISH (St. Mary), a parish, in the union of Sudbury, hundred of Babergh, W. division of Suffolk, 2½ miles (E. N. E.) from Clare; containing 1353 inhabitants. This parish, at a very early period, was the property of the Cavendish family, of whom John Cavendish, being in attendance on Richard II., despatched the rebel Wat Tyler, whom William Walworth, lord mayor of London, had stunned with a blow of his mace. The populace of this neighbourhood, in retaliation, seized Sir John Cavendish, uncle of the former, and lord chief justice of the king's bench, whom, together with the prior of Bury, they beheaded at the market-cross in that town. The parish comprises 3351a. 1r. 24p.: the village is situated on the river Stour. The living is a rectory, valued in the king's books at £26; net income, £547; patrons, the Master and Fellows of Jesus College, Cambridge. Thomas Grey, in 1696, gave 78 acres of land for teaching poor children. The noble family of Cavendish, of which the Duke of Devonshire is the representative, derives its name from this place.

CAVENHAM (St. Andrew), a parish, in the union of Mildenhall, hundred of Lackford, W. division of Suffolk, 4½ miles (S. E.) from Mildenhall; containing 277 inhabitants. The river Lark is navigable on the north of this parish, where it is crossed by Temple bridge. The living is a discharged vicarage, valued in the king's books at £5. 5. 10., and in the patronage of the Crown; net income, £113; impropriator, H. S. Waddington, Esq. The vicarial tithes were commuted for land in 1801. The sum of about £22 per annum, the rental of 80 acres of land under an inclosure act, is applied to the purchase of coal for the poor.

CAVERSFIELD (St. Lawrence), a parish, in the union of Bicester, hundred of Ploughley, county of Oxford, 2 miles (N.) from Bicester; containing 178 inhabitants. It comprises 1438a. 2r. 3p., the soil of which is light and stony. The living is a discharged vicarage, valued in the king's books at £6; net income, £69; patrons and impropriators, the Trustees of the late Joseph Bullock, Esq. The glebe contains about 60 acres. Some suppose this to have been the place where Carausius, the Roman commander, assumed the purple in 287, and where he was afterwards slain by Caius Alectus: on Bayard's Green, about a mile from the church, are faint traces of a camp.

CAVERSHAM (St. Peter), a parish, in the union of Henley, hundred of Binfield, county of Oxford, 1 mile (N.) from Reading; containing 1642 inhabitants. This place, during the civil wars, was the scene of a sharp skirmish between the royalist and parliamentarian forces; and Charles I., who had fallen into the hands of his enemies, was, for a short time, kept in confinement here. The parish comprises 4490a. 1r. 5p., of which 3191 acres are arable, 702 meadow, 361 wood, and 200 common. The village is pleasantly situated on the northern bank of the Thames, the high grounds commanding a fine view of the town of Reading; and is

rge of high treason, by the Earl of Northumberland. : castle was dismantled, and in part demolished, at conclusion of the parliamentary war; since which e, being abandoned by the archbishops, it has reined in a state of gradual dilapidation : the remains :he great gateway, and some few fragments, are now only vestiges. The TOWN is pleasantly situated near western bank of the river Ouse, over which is a ry : the houses are neatly built, and the inhabitants ply supplied with water. The market, which was on :dnesday, has been discontinued for many years ; fairs cattle are held on May 12th and December 19th. e parish comprises 2000 acres : the surface is flat, l subject to inundation from the river; the soil is efly a fertile loam, and the lands are generally in a :d state of cultivation. The living is a perpetual acy; net income, £120; patron, the Prebendary of stow in the Cathedral of York. The tithes were muted for land and a money payment, in 1776. : church, situated near the Ouse, is a neat structure h a tower. There is a place of worship for Wesans. A school for girls was founded in 1731, by the v. Samuel Duffield, who endowed it with land now lding a considerable annual income; and £20 per 1um are paid for the instruction of children, out of an ate producing £213 per annum, vested in trustees for repair of the highways, and the preservation of the bankments. Dr. Harsnett, Archbishop of York, who d in 1631, gave land for teaching poor boys. An shouse was founded about 1723, by William James, q., who endowed it with land worth £76 per annum, aged persons; and an almshouse for six aged persons Wistow and Cawood not having received parochial lief, was founded in 1819, by James Waterhouse aith, Esq.

CAWSTON (ST. AGNES), a parish, in the union of ILSHAM, hundred of SOUTH ERPINGHAM, E. division NORFOLK, 3¼ miles (E. by N.) from Reepham, and . the road from Norwich to Holt; containing 1130 habitants. The manor is held in free socage of the >wn, in right of the duchy of Lancaster, in token of 1ich two maces are carried before the lord, or his :ward, one bearing a brazen hand surmounted by a >ugbshare, and the other a bearded arrow. Fairs are ld on Feb. 1st, and the last Wednesdays in April and 1gust, that in August being a large sheep-fair. The ing is a rectory, valued in the king's books at .5. 13. 11½.; net income, £808; patrons, the Master d Fellows of Pembroke Hall, Cambridge; the glebe ntains 14 acres, with a glebe-house. The church is handsome cruciform structure with a lofty tower, in e later English style, built by Michael de la Pole, Earl Suffolk : there is a chapel on its north side, the :erior of which is elaborately ornamented. The Inpendents, and Primitive and Wesleyan Methodists, ve places of worship. At the inclosure, in 1802, an otment of 100 acres was awarded to the poor for el.

CAWTHORNE, a chapelry, in the parish of SILKONE, wapentake of STAINCROSS, W. riding of YORK, miles (W.) from Barnsley; containing 1437 inhabitts. This chapelry, which is chiefly the property of hn Spencer Stanhope, Esq., and partly of Thos. Went>rth Beaumont, Esq., lord of the manor, comprises by mputation 3440 acres. Coal is abundant; sandstone

and gritstone are quarried, and great quantities of limestone, brought up the Barnsley canal, are burnt into lime : there are also some seams of ironstone of excellent quality. The surface is varied, and the lower grounds are watered by several brooks that flow into the river Dearne. Cannon Hall, the seat of Mr. Stanhope, is a spacious mansion, situated in a park which abounds with timber and with beautiful scenery. The village is pleasantly seated on a gentle acclivity forming the southern boundary of a picturesque valley. At Barnby bridge the Barnsley canal terminates in a spacious basin, on the banks of which are wharfs, warehouses, and a wet-dock, with conveniencies for boat-building and limeburning; and from the basin is a railway to the several collieries here and in other parts of the parish. The living is a perpetual curacy, in the gift of the proprietors of certain estates, and is worth £150 per annum. The chapel, dedicated to All Saints, is a neat edifice, in the later English style, with a square embattled tower; a south aisle was added in 1828, when 276 additional sittings were obtained, of which 216 are free. There is a place of worship for Wesleyans. The water of a mineral spring here is slightly impregnated with sulphuretted hydrogen.

CAWTHORPE, a hamlet, in the parish and union of BOURNE, wapentake of AVELAND, parts of KESTEVEN, county of LINCOLN, 1¼ mile (N. by W.) from Bourne; containing 94 inhabitants.

CAWTHORPE, near LOUTH, county of LINCOLN.— See COVENHAM (ST. BARTHOLOMEW).

CAWTHORPE, LITTLE (ST. HELEN), a parish, in the union of LOUTH, Marsh division of the hundred of CALCEWORTH, locally in the hundred of LOUTH-ESKE, parts of LINDSEY, county of LINCOLN, 2¾ miles (S. E. by S.) from Louth; containing 196 inhabitants. It comprises 468a. 20p., chiefly arable land. The living is a discharged vicarage, valued in the king's books at £3. 4. 4½.; the rectorial tithes have been commuted for £68. 3. 6., and the rectorial glebe comprises 13 acres.

CAWTON, a township, in the parish of GILLING, union of HELMSLEY, wapentake of RYEDALE, N. riding of YORK, 5½ miles (S. S. E.) from Helmsley; containing 101 inhabitants. It comprises by computation 1020 acres of land, and contains some beds of excellent limestone. The tithes have been commuted for £190.

CAXTON (ST. ANDREW), a market-town and parish, in the union of CAXTON and ARRINGTON, hundred of LONGSTOW, county of CAMBRIDGE, 10½ miles (W. by S.) from Cambridge, and 49 (N. N. W.) from London; containing 558 inhabitants. This place, which is one of the oldest post-towns in the county, is situated on the Roman Ermin-street : the buildings are in general irregular and of mean appearance, consisting principally of poor cottages and decayed inns, though there are a few good houses. The market, granted to Baldwin Freville in 1247, is on Tuesday; and fairs, principally for pedlery, are held on May 5th, and October 18th. The parish comprises about 2300 acres. The living is a discharged vicarage, valued in the king's books at £7. 12. 4.; net income, £80; patrons, the Dean and Canons of Windsor, to whom an allotment of land and a money payment were assigned, in lieu of tithes, by an inclosure act, in 1830 : the glebe contains about 9 acres. The living was a rectory previously to 1353, at which time it was appropriated to the chapel royal of Windsor. The church has a piscina in tolerable preservation. There is a place of worship for dissenters. Robert Langwith, in 1581, bequeathed £31. 10. per annum for the benefit of poor housekeepers, and for sermons to be preached quarterly in the church. The union comprises 26 parishes or places, and contains a population of 10,080. Matthew Paris, a Benedictine monk, who flourished in the reign of Henry III., and wrote a history of the world from the creation to the year of his death, which happened in 1259, was a native of the place. It has been stated, also, that Caxton, who introduced the art of printing into England, was born in the parish; but his own memoirs refer his birth and education to the county of Kent.

CAYTHORPE (ST. VINCENT), a parish, in the union of NEWARK, wapentake of LOVEDEN, parts of KESTEVEN, county of LINCOLN, 9 miles (N. by E.) from Grantham; containing, with the hamlet of Friston, 821 inhabitants. This parish, which is bounded on the east by the Roman Ermin-street, comprises 4207a. 1r. 35p. The land is in general well wooded; the scenery interesting; and fine views may be obtained of Belvoir Castle, Newark, and Lincoln Cathedral, from the Beacon, an eminence near the road from Grantham to Lincoln, on which the village is situated. There are several beds of limestone, and stones are quarried for the roads. The living is a rectory, valued in the king's books at £20. 11. 10½.; net income, £976; patron, C. J. Packe, Esq. The church is a curious cruciform structure, principally in the decorated English style, and has a very lofty spire rising from the centre, supported by four magnificent arches. It contains two handsome monuments to the Hussey family; and at the east end is a large painting on the plaster, in fresco, representing the Last Judgment, and which was discovered by scraping the wall a few years ago. There are a chapel of ease at Friston, and a place of worship for Wesleyans.

CAYTHORPE, a township, in the parish of LOWDHAM, union of SOUTHWELL, S. division of the wapentake of THURGARTON and of the county of NOTTINGHAM, 8¾ miles (N. E. by E.) from Nottingham; containing 315 inhabitants. It comprises about 350 acres of land. The Independents have a place of worship.

CAYTON (ST. LEONARD), a parish, in the union of SCARBOROUGH, PICKERING lythe, N. riding of YORK, 4 miles (S. by E.) from Scarborough; containing, with the township of Osgodby, 572 inhabitants, of whom 503 are in the township of Cayton. The parish is situated on the road from Scarborough to Bridlington, and is bounded on the north-east by the German Ocean: the soil is chiefly clay, suited to the growth of wheat; and the scenery, which is diversified by a range of lofty hills, is very picturesque. Stone is extensively quarried for building purposes, and for burning into lime. The living is annexed to the vicarage of Seamer: the church is an ancient edifice with a tower. There are places of worship for Primitive and Wesleyan Methodists.

CERNE, or CERNE-ABBAS (ST. MARY), a market-town and parish, and the head of a union, in the hundred of CERNE, TOTCOMBE, and MODBURY, Cerne division of DORSET, 8 miles (N. N. W.) from Dorchester, and 120 (S. W. by W.) from London; containing 1342 inhabitants. The name of this place is derived from its situation on the river Cerne, and the adjunct from its

ho ravaged this part of the country, and was killed by e peasants. The figure is occasionally repaired by the habitants of the town.

CERNE, NETHER, a parish, in the union of DOR-ESTER and CERNE, hundred of CERNE, TOTCOMBE, d MODBURY, Cerne division of DORSET, 5¾ miles . N. W.) from Dorchester; containing 71 inhabitants. e living is a perpetual curacy; net income, £60; trons, the Sheridan family.

CERNE, UPPER, a parish, in the union of DOR-ESTER and CERNE, hundred of SHERBORNE, Sher-rne division of DORSET, 9 miles (N. N. W.) from rchester; containing 107 inhabitants. This place s for some time the property of Sir Walter Raleigh: ire are still remains of the ancient manor-house. e parish is watered by a branch of the river Cerne, d comprises by computation 1200 acres. The living a discharged rectory, valued in the king's books at . 18. 4., and in the patronage of John White, Esq.: : tithes have been commuted for £160; the glebe nprises 15 acres, with a glebe-house. The church is ery old structure, and contains a font of large dimen-ns.

CERNEY, NORTH (ALL SAINTS), a parish, in the ion of CIRENCESTER, hundred of RAPSGATE, E. divi-in of the county of GLOUCESTER, 4 miles (N.) from rencester; containing, with the tythings of Calmsden d Woodmancote, 668 inhabitants. It comprises 3931a. . 24p., the principal part of which is arable. Races e annually held. The living is a rectory, valued in e king's books at £21. 10. 7½., and in the patronage University College, Oxford: the tithes have been mmuted for £730, and the glebe comprises 104 acres, ith a glebe-house. The Roman Fosse-way traces the istern boundary of the parish, in which may also be en vestiges of a Roman fortress, with circumvalla-ons.

CERNEY, SOUTH (ALL HALLOWS), a parish, in the nion of CIRENCESTER, hundred of CROWTHORNE and [INETY, E. division of the county of GLOUCESTER, 3¾ iles (S. E. by S.) from Cirencester; containing 1077 ihabitants. It comprises by measurement 2924 acres; mestone abounds, and is quarried for manure. The hames and Severn canal passes through the parish, id the Cheltenham branch of the Great Western rail-ay through a parish adjoining. The living is a dis-iarged vicarage, valued in the king's books at 6. 16. 8.; net income, £231; patron and appropria-ir, the Bishop of Gloucester and Bristol. The tithes ere commuted for land and corn-rents in 1808. The iurch is a fine specimen of Norman architecture, with ter additions, and consists of a nave, chancel, north isle, and north transept, with a low central tower and iire: at the south porch is a beautifully enriched arch rnamented with grotesque heads terminating the iouldings. Between the nave and the chancel is a ointed arch rising from slender columns, the capitals of hich are decorated with foliage; the chancel, with a ne east window of three lights, is of later date than the ther parts of the edifice. There is a place of worship ir Primitive Methodists; and a national school has een established, chiefly through the munificence of Irs. Ann Edwards, who gave £1500 for its foundation nd endowment, and £1000 more for building houses ir the master and mistress. Mrs. Edwards, in 1834,

541

bequeathed the residue of her property in trust to the charity for the support of widows and orphans of clergy-men of the diocese; in 1837, one-half of the bequest was appropriated to the erection of an asylum, and a very handsome edifice has been built, called Edward's College, on a site given for the purpose by a near rela-tive of the deceased, for the reception of distressed fami-lies of clergymen.

CHACEWATER, an ecclesiastical district, partly in the parish of KENWYN, and partly in that of ST. KEA, union of TRURO, W. division of the hundred of Pow-DER and of the county of CORNWALL, 5 miles (W. by S.) from Truro. This place is situated on the road from Truro to Penzance, and in the heart of a district abound-ing with mineral wealth. In the neighbourhood are several rich tin and copper mines, from the workings of the latter of which, near the surface, silver has been ex-tracted in quantities greater than was anticipated. A considerable customary market for provisions is held on Saturday. The living is a perpetual curacy; patron, the Vicar of Kenwyn; net income, £150. The church, a handsome edifice, dedicated to St. Paul, in the later English style, with a lofty tower, was erected in 1828, the Parliamentary Commissioners granting £2000. There are places of worship for Baptists, Bryanites, and Pri-mitive and Wesleyan Methodists.

CHACKMORE, a hamlet, in the parish of RADCLIVE, union, hundred, and county of BUCKINGHAM, 1½ mile (N. N. W.) from Buckingham; containing 238 inhabit-ants. The tithes were commuted for land in 1773. Here was formerly a chapel of ease.

CHACOMBE.—See CHALCOMBE.

CHAD, ST., a chapelry, in the parish of MALPAS, union of WREXHAM, Higher division of the hundred of BROXTON, S. division of the county of CHESTER, 2¼ miles (E. by S.) from Malpas, and on the road between Tushingham and Hampton. This place, called in Webb's Itinerary Chad-wick, had, probably, a chapel at a very ancient date, for the Chapel-field is mentioned in a deed of 1349: the present structure was built in 1689, principally by a benefaction of John Dod, mercer and citizen, of London. The living is a perpetual curacy; net income, £144; patron, the Rector of Malpas.

CHADBURY, a tything, in the parish of NORTON, union of EVESHAM, Lower division of the hundred of BLACKENHURST, Pershore and E. divisions of the county of WORCESTER, 3 miles (N. by W.) from Evesham; con-taining 28 inhabitants.

CHADDENWICKE, a tything, in the parish, union, and hundred of MERE, Hindon and S. divisions of the county of WILTS, 1¼ mile (E.) from Mere; contain-ing 16 inhabitants.

CHADDERTON, a township, in the parish of PRESTWICH cum OLDHAM, union of OLDHAM, hundred of SALFORD, S. division of the county of LANCASTER, 7 miles (N. E. by N.) from Manchester; containing 5397 inhabitants. This place is chiefly distinguished for its two ancient mansions, Fox-Denton Hall and Chadder-ton Hall, and for the families by whom they were occu-pied. Both mansions were possessed by the Traffords, in the reign of John; Geoffrey de Trafford assumed the name of Chadderton, and Margaret, his great-grand-daughter, being married to John de Radcliffe, of Rad-cliffe Tower and Fox-Denton, the manor passed as a dowry into that family. Chadderton Hall was the birthplace of Dr. Laurence Chadderton, an eminent divine at the period of the Reformation, of which he was a zealous promoter; he lived to the great age of 103 years, and died at Cambridge on the 16th November, 1640. The township is situated to the west of Oldham, and forms a right angle with the township of Royton. The spinning of cotton, weaving of silk, and manufacture of hats, are carried on; and coal abounds, which, by means of a branch of the Ashton canal, is conveyed to Manchester, Stockport, and other towns in the vicinity. The township is also intersected by the Rochdale canal, the Manchester and Leeds railway, and the Oldham and Middleton road. At Hollinwood, a large manufacturing village in the township, about two miles from Oldham, is a chapel dedicated to St. Margaret, the living of which is a perpetual curacy, with a net income of £150, and a house; patron, the Rector of Prestwich. In 1845 two districts or ecclesiastical parishes were formed under the 6th and 7th Victoria, cap. 37 : the church of St. John, to which one of these districts has been assigned, is in the early English style; the other church is dedicated to St. Matthew. The livings of both are in the patronage of the Bishop of Chester and the Crown alternately; net income of each, £150. To each church are attached schools; and at Hollinwood is a school, endowed by the Rev. John Darbey with £8 per annum in 1808, and £7 by another benefactor. The tithes have been commuted for £120. On the lawn in front of Chadderton Hall is a tumulus, on lowering which, at different periods, relics of antiquity have been discovered.

CHADDESDEN (St. Mary), a parish, in the union of Shardlow, hundred of Appletree, locally in that of Morleston and Litchurch, S. division of the county of Derby, 2½ miles (E.) from Derby; containing 472 inhabitants. Among the families who were anciently seised of this manor were the Grenes, Plumptons, Cliffords, and Newtons; and the Wilmot family have had their seat here for many generations. The parish is intersected by the road from Derby to Nottingham; and the Derby canal also passes through. The living is a perpetual curacy; net income, £89; patron, Sir H. S. Wilmot, Bart.; impropriator, the Duke of Devonshire. In the church are some memorials to the Wilmot family. In 1638 an almshouse for six persons was founded and endowed by Edward Wilmot; and in 1813 John Berrysford left property, now producing £16. 4. per annum, to be distributed amongst widows and orphans.

CHADDESLEY-CORBETT (St. Cassyon), a parish, in the union of Kidderminster, Lower division of the hundred of Halfshire, Kidderminster and W. divisions of the county of Worcester, 4½ miles (S. E. by E.) from Kidderminster; containing 1434 inhabitants. It comprises 5908a. 3r. 14p., of which 252 acres are woodland; and is intersected by the roads from Stourbridge to Stourport and from Kidderminster to Bromsgrove, which cross each other at the western extremity of the parish. Winterfold House, surrounded with 600 acres, is the property and residence of the Rev. Thomas Harward; in the grounds are some fine elms and oaks, and some deer. The living is a vicarage, valued in the king's books at £17. 3. 4.; patron, the Crown; impropriators, the Corporation of Warwick. The tithes were commuted for land and a money payment in 1797; and under the late act, the impropriate tithes have been

St. Chad, to which numerous pilgrimages and offerings were made.

CHADWELL (St. MARY), a parish, in the union of ASETT, hundred of BARSTABLE, S. division of ESSEX, miles (E. by N.) from Grays; containing 236 inhabitts. It comprises 1753 acres, chiefly arable, and is unded on the south by the river Thames : the soil is nerally deep and heavy, the surface considerably eleted above the marshes, and the surrounding lands ound with chalk. At the time of the Norman survey, e parish belonged principally to the Bishop of London, d some portions to Odo, Bishop of Bayeux, and others. e living is a rectory, valued in the king's books at 7.' 13. 4.; patron and incumbent, the Rev. J. P. Hergham, whose tithes have been commuted for £480 : e glebe contains 40 acres. The church is pleasantly uated on the brow of a hill. In a wood near the high-ly leading to Stifford, are several ancient excavations, :med Danes' Holes.

CHADWELL, a ward, in the parish of BARKING, ion of ROMFORD, hundred of BEACONTREE, S. divi-n of ESSEX, 9½ miles (N. E. by E.) from London ; con-ning 758 inhabitants.

CHADWELL, a chapelry, in the parish of ROTH-Y, union of MELTON-MOWBRAY, hundred of EAST ɔSCOTE, N. division of the county of LEICESTER, 5 iles (N. N. E.) from Melton-Mowbray ; containing, with e hamlet of Wycombe, 118 inhabitants, of whom 60 e comprised in Chadwell. The chapel is dedicated to . Mary.

CHADWICK, a hamlet and manor, in the parish d union of BROMSGROVE, Upper division of the hun-red of HALFSHIRE, Droitwich and E. divisions of the ɔunty of WORCESTER, 3½ miles (N. by E.) from Broms-rove, on the road to Birmingham. This place com-rises about 1500 acres, mostly arable, with a good deal f coppice wood ; the surface is undulated, the soil ravelly, and the scenery picturesque. The population estimated at about 1000, chiefly nailers and agricul-ural labourers. Woodrow, with about 400 acres of .nd, is freehold, and occupied by George Francis ldins, Esq.; the Manor Hall is the property of Francis . Rufford, Esq., who is the chief proprietor, under the 'ean and Chapter of Christ-Church, Oxford, who are 'rds of the manor. There are a Wesleyan and a Pri-itive Methodist place of worship. Here was formerly chapel, now in ruins.

CHAFFCOMBE (St. MICHAEL), a parish, in the nion of CHARD, hundred of SOUTH PETHERTON, W. ivision of SOMERSET, 3¼ miles (S. by W.) from Ilmin-:er ; containing 288 inhabitants. The living is a dis-arged rectory, valued in the king's books at £9. 10. 2½., id in the patronage of Earl Poulett : the tithes have een commuted for £155, and the glebe consists of 28 :res.

CHAGFORD (St. MICHAEL), a market-town and arish, in the union of OAKHAMPTON, hundred of WON-ORD, Crockernwell and S. divisions of DEVON, 15 miles ß. W. by W.) from Exeter, and 186 (S. W.) from Lon-on ; containing 1836 inhabitants. This place, origi-ally held by Dodo, a Saxon, was given by William the 'onqueror to the Bishop of Constance, and in 1328 was ɪade one of the stannary towns by Edward III., who ɪvested the lords of the manor with the power of in-icting capital punishment. In 1643, an action took

place between the royalists and the parliamentarians, in which Sidney Godolphin was killed ; and in the same century a fire occurred, when the charter for holding the market, and other records, were destroyed. The town is pleasantly situated near the river Teign, and sheltered by hills of romantic form ; the houses are irregularly built : the environs abound with picturesque scenery. On the banks of the Teign is a large woollen-manufactory. The market is on Thursday ; and there are fairs on the last Thursday in March, the first Thurs-day in May, and the last Thursday in September and October. The stannary court, in which the principal business of the mines is transacted, is held here. The parish comprises by measurement 8000 acres, of which 1200 are commons ; two-thirds of the remainder are arable, and the rest pasture and woodland. The living is a rectory, valued in the king's books at £39. 0. 10., and in the patronage of Mrs. Grace Hames ; net income, £442. The church is a handsome structure, and con-tains a richly-executed monument to the memory of Sir John Widdon, chief justice of the court of king's bench in the reign of Mary. At the hamlets of Great Weeke and Teigncombe, in the parish, are the remains of ancient chapels, and there was a chapel also at Rushford.

CHAIGELEY, or CHAIGLEY, with AIGHTON and BAILEY, a township, in the parish of MITTON, union of CLITHEROE, Lower division of the hundred of BLACK-BURN, N. division of the county of LANCASTER, 5 miles (W. by N.) from Clitheroe ; containing 1798 inhabitants, of whom 266 are in the hamlet of Chaigeley. Of this place, anciently St. Chad's Ley, little appears in early records in an authentic form. In the reign of James I., Thomas Osbaldeston, who was accounted a felon for having slain his brother-in-law, forfeited his possessions here. Among other proprietors, were the Holdens, whose family were long owners ; and the Sherburnes. Chaigeley stretches from the east-north-east brow of Longridge Fell, to the banks of the Hodder, and to Bowland, in Yorkshire ; the river here separating the counties of Lancaster and York. The surface of the land is undulating, the scenery woody and picturesque, and from the higher grounds are extensive views : there are good limestone and freestone quarries. Of the chief pro-prietors are, the Earl of Derby, and William Winstanley, Esq., M.D., the latter of whom is lord of the manor, and holds 1200 acres in the hamlet, his son residing at the Manor House. Chaigeley Hall, a plain stone edifice, was the seat of the Holdens. The Independents have a chapel ; with a school attached, endowed with £65 per annum, derived from a farm in the township, money in the funds, and houses in Ribchester. Two mineral springs here are resorted to by invalids. Within the last sixty years were standing the ruins of an ancient chapel ; and some fields near the place are still called St. Chad's meadows.—See AIGHTON and BAILEY.

CHAILEY (St. PETER), a parish, and the head of a union, in the hundred of STREET, rape of LEWES, E. division of SUSSEX, 6½ miles (N. by W.) from Lewes ; containing 1064 inhabitants. It is situated on the road from London to Lewes, and comprises 5889 acres, of which 828 are common or waste : sandstone of good quality is found, and quarried for building purposes ; the soil is generally fertile, and about 20 acres of land are under cultivation for hops. The living is a rectory, valued in the king's books at £9. 4. 2., and in the patronage of Mrs. Hepburn and Mrs. R. W. Blencowe: the tithes have been commuted for £682. 10.; the glebe comprises 5 acres. The church is a neat edifice, chiefly in the early English style, with a square embattled tower surmounted by a spire; the rectory-house is a very ancient building, surrounded by a moat. There are several chalybeate springs.

CHALBURY, a parish, in the union of WIMBORNE and CRANBORNE, hundred of BADBURY, Wimborne division of DORSET, 5 miles (N. by E.) from Wimborne-Minster; containing, with the tything of Didlington, 152 inhabitants. It comprises by measurement 1355 acres, of which about 584 are arable, 274 down, pasture, and meadow, 176 woodland, and 279 common. The village is situated on rising ground, commanding a fine view of the Needles and the British Channel. A particular sort of fine sand, used by founders, is obtained. The living is a rectory, valued in the king's books at £7. 10. 2½., and in the gift of the Earl of Pembroke: the tithes have been commuted for £180, and the glebe contains about 30 acres, with a glebe-house. At Didlington was a chapel, now a farmhouse, near which foundations of houses are often discovered in turning up the ground. There is a chalybeate spring.

CHALCOMBE, or CHACOMBE (ST. PETER AND ST. PAUL), a parish, in the union of BANBURY, hundred of KING'S SUTTON, S. division of the county of NORTHAMPTON, 3¾ miles (N. E. by E.) from Banbury; containing 488 inhabitants. This parish, which is bounded on the north and west by a portion of Oxfordshire, comprises 1641a. 1r. 8p.; the arable lands are rich, the dairy-farms well managed, and butter is sent in considerable quantities to the London market. The manufacture of lace and silk-stockings, and the weaving of shag, are carried on; but the trade is gradually declining. Freestone of tolerable quality is found, and the quarries have furnished materials for most of the houses in the parish. The living is a discharged vicarage, valued in the king's books at £7. 17.; patron, C. Wykeham Martin, Esq.: impropriators, the landowners. The great tithes have been commuted for £199. 16., and the vicarial for £240; the glebe comprises 7¼ acres, with a house, repaired in 1843. The church is a plain structure in the decorated English style, with a square tower. There is a place of worship for Wesleyans.

CHALDON (ST. PETER AND ST. PAUL), a parish, in the union of REIGATE, First division of the hundred of WALLINGTON, E. division of SURREY, 5 miles (N. E. by E.) from Reigate; containing 197 inhabitants. It comprises 1653a. 1r. 10p., of which upwards of 1000 acres are arable, 104 meadow, 347 wood, and 84 common; the surface is diversified throughout by depressions and elevations, and the leading soil is chalk, with occasional admixtures of gravel resting upon a substratum of chalk. Here are some quarries of a soft species of stone, not much used. The living is a rectory, valued in the king's books at £7. 10. 7½.; patron and incumbent, the Rev. James Legrew, whose tithes have been commuted for £335. 11. 3., and who has a glebe of 31 acres, with a glebe-house. The church, occupying a slightly-elevated site, with the command of agreeable scenery, is believed to have been founded at least eight centuries ago: a tower and spire were added in 1843.

CHALDON-HERRING (ST. NICHOLAS), a parish, in the union of WAREHAM and PURBECK, liberty of

ich he made a resting-place on some occasions. The ish comprises about 3600 acres ; the surface is undu- :d, and the soil, consisting of chalk, gravel, and clay, :onsidered poor. The living is a rectory, valued in king's books at £19. 9. 4½., and in the gift of the hop of Lincoln : the tithes have been commuted for)0, and the glebe comprises 54¼ acres, with a glebe- lse. The church is of very great antiquity. Here are :es of worship for the Society of Friends and Inde- dents, in the cemetery attached to the former of ch lie the remains of William Penn, founder of the)ny of Pennsylvania. A school, now conducted on national system, has been endowed by Sir Hugh liser with £30 per annum, and by Mrs. Molloy with) per annum ; and there are eight almshouses. ring the plague that raged in London in 1665, Milton ded at this place, where he completed his celebrated m of *Paradise Lost;* the house in which he lived is v occupied by a poor family. Here are the remains ι monastery, whose chapel is attached to the mansion Vach, which appears to have been so named from the nor, shortly after the Conquest ; and in the park ι monument erected by the late Sir Hugh Palliser the memory of Capt. Cook, the circumnavigator, ιn which is a long inscription composed by Admiral ·bes.

CHALFONT (ST. PETER'S), a parish, in the union λMERSHAM, hundred of BURNHAM, county of BUCK- :HAM, 1½ mile (N. N. E.) from Gerrard's-Cross ; con- ιing 1483 inhabitants. The rectory, the manor, and i7 acres of land, belonged to Missenden Abbey ; and :e sold, at the Dissolution, to Sir Robert Drury and ers, from whom they passed into the Bulstrode ily. The parish is intersected by a tributary stream he Colne, called Missbourne, upon which there is a -mill, affording employment to about fifty women. omprises about 4564 acres, of which 4100 are arable, wood, and 178 uninclosed common : the surface is gular ; the soil on the higher grounds is gravel, with ayey tenacious subsoil, and the lower grounds are ercd with a thin coat of alluvial bog earth. The petty- ions for the division are holden here. The living is carage, endowed with part of the rectorial tithes, and ιed in the king's books at £15. 17. 1.; net income, 0 ; patrons, the President and Fellows of St. John's lege, Oxford. The remainder of the great tithes ιngs to three proprietors of land. The church, rebuilt 7?6, is a plain brick edifice, with an embattled tower ?nty feet high, containing a peal of six well-toned s ; the quoins and window and door cases, of stone, e brought from the ruins of the Roman station of *ulam,* now St. Alban's.

CHALFORD, a hamlet, in the union of STROUD, tly in the parish and hundred of BISLEY, and partly he parish of MINCHINHAMPTON, hundred of LONG- :E, E. division of the county of GLOUCESTER, 4 miles E. by E.) from Stroud. This populous and thriving ·e is situated in a rich and fertile vale, abounding ι pleasing scenery, and is intersected by the river ome, which pursues a beautifully winding course ιugh luxuriant meadows, and here separates the parishes in which Chalford is situated. The manu- ure of woollen-cloth, still carried on to a great extent, introduced at an early period ; and in the reign of ιe there were three mills in the hamlet that retained

exclusively the use of some advantageous discovery in the process of the manufacture. The road from Stroud to Cirencester, and the Thames and Severn canal, pass through the village ; and the vicinity is thickly studded with the dwellings of persons employed in the factories. A district church, situated in the vale, and dedicated to Christ, was consecrated in September, 1841 : net income of the incumbent, £150; patron, the Archdeacon of Gloucester. There are places of worship for Baptists, Independents, and Wesleyans. At St. Mary's Mill, in the hamlet, was a chapel or .religious house, in which, according to Camden, Friar Bacon was educated ; it has given place to a modern building, but a room in the present house, called Bacon's room, is supposed to have been the study of that learned monk.

CHALFORD, a township, in the parish of ASTON- ROWANT, union of THAME, hundred of LEWKNOR, county of OXFORD, 2 miles (E. S. E.) from Tetsworth ; containing 58 inhabitants. This place formed part of the possessions of the monastery of St. Alban's, and on the Dissolution was granted by Henry VIII., for the sum of £413. 17. 6., to Bartholomew Piggot, from whom it passed to various families.

CHALGRAVE (ALL SAINTS), a parish, in the union of WOBURN, hundred of MANSHEAD, county of BED- FORD, 3¼ miles (N. by W.) from Dunstable ; containing, with the hamlets of Tebworth and Wingfield, 818 inha- bitants. The living is a discharged vicarage, united in 1772 to the rectory of Hockliffe, and valued in the king's books at £12 ; the impropriation belongs to Trinity Hall, Cambridge. The church is a venerable edifice in the ancient English style, and contains two antique tombs with statues of knights in armour. There is a place of worship for Wesleyans at Tebworth ; where was for- merly a chapel, endowed with 36 acres of land. The parish contains endowed almshouses for six maidens, and two for six widows.

CHALGROVE (ST. MARY), a parish, in the union of THAME, hundred of EWELME, county of OXFORD, 4 miles (N. N. E.) from Bensington ; containing, with Rufford liberty, 691 inhabitants. This place was distinguished in the civil war as the scene of an action that occurred at Chalgrove Field, in June, 1643, between the royalists under Prince Rupert, and a detachment of the parlia- mentarian army under the Earl of Essex ; in which the latter were defeated, several officers killed, and the cele- brated Hampden mortally wounded. In 1843, precisely two centuries afterwards, a monument was erected to the memory of Hampden, on the spot where he received his death-wound. The parish comprises 2364 acres, whereof 167 are common or waste inclosed under an act passed in 1843. The living is a vicarage, valued in the king's books at £10. 5. 5.; net income, £276; patrons, the Dean and Canons of Christ-Church, Oxford. Tithes were commuted for land and a money payment in 1797 ; and under the recent act, the tithes belonging to Christ- Church have been commuted for £435. 2., those belong- ing to the Dean and Canons of Windsor for £164. 6., and the vicarial tithes for £158. 1.: the appropriate glebe contains 65½ acres, and the vicarial 3½ acres, with a glebe-house. The church, whose steeple was struck down by lightning in 1727, contains some interesting monuments, and a curious ancient font. There are a chapel of ease at Berrick-Salome, in the parish, and a place of worship for Baptists.

CHALK (*St. Mary*), a parish, in the union of NORTH AYLESFORD, hundred of SHAMWELL, lathe of AYLESFORD, W. division of KENT, 1¾ mile (E. S. E.) from Gravesend; containing 385 inhabitants. This parish, which is bounded on the north by the Thames, and intersected by the Thames and Medway canal, comprises 1941 acres, whereof 45 are woodland ; the soil is chalk, with a little gravel. There was formerly a considerable manufactory for gun-flints, esteemed the best in Europe. A fair is held on Whit-Monday. The living is a discharged vicarage, valued in the king's books at £6. 3. 8., and in the patronage of the Crown ; impropriator, the Earl of Darnley. The great tithes have been commuted for £481. 10. 10., and the vicarial for £198. 10. ; the impropriate glebe contains upwards of 30 acres. The church is very ancient, and has various figures carved over the entrance, the origin and meaning of which have caused much controversy.

CHALLACOMBE (*Holy Trinity*), a parish, in the union of BARNSTAPLE, hundred of SHERWILL, Braunton and N. divisions of DEVON, 10 miles (N. E. by E.) from Barnstaple; containing 305 inhabitants. The parish comprises 5342a. 1r. 22p., nearly one-half of which is common : the South-Molton and Combmartin road passes through its western extremity. Slate and stone are quarried, the former of inferior quality. The living is a rectory, valued in the king's books at £11. 9. 2.; and in the patronage of Earl Fortescue : the tithes have been commuted for £189, and the glebe contains nearly 60 acres, with a glebe-house. The church is a small edifice in the later English style, and has a fine stone font, of curious workmanship. About a mile and a half south-east of the church, is an encampment called Showlsborough or Shrewsbury Castle, of an oblong form, containing about two acres, surrounded by a mound of earth.

CHALLOC (*St. Cosmus and St. Damien*), a parish, in the union of EAST ASHFORD, hundred of FELBOROUGH, lathe of SHEPWAY, E. division of KENT, 6 miles (S.) from Faversham; containing 429 inhabitants. It comprises by measurement 2739 acres, of which upwards of 1000 are arable, 694 wood, and 970 meadow and pasture, the larger part of the last being park land. A fair is held on the 8th of October, for horses, cattle, and pedlery ; a grant for which, and for a market now disused, was obtained in the 38th of Henry III., by Henry de Apulderfield, then lord of the manor, whose mansion is said to have stood upon a spot called Apulderfield's garden, in the Earl of Winchilsea's park. The living is annexed to the vicarage of Godmersham : the church is a spacious edifice in the early English style, with an embattled tower, a spire, and beacon-turret.

CHALLOW, EAST, a chapelry, in the parish of LETCOMB REGIS, union of WANTAGE, hundred of KINTBURY-EAGLE, county of BERKS, 1¼ mile (W.) from Wantage ; containing 336 inhabitants. The chapelry comprises 1293a. 14p. It is crossed by the Wilts and Berks canal, and the Great Western railway approaches within 1¼ mile of the chapel ; which is dedicated to St. Nicholas.

CHALLOW, WEST, a chapelry, in the parish of LETCOMB REGIS, union of WANTAGE, hundred of KINTBURY-EAGLE, county of BERKS, 2 miles (W. N. W.) from Wantage; containing 248 inhabitants. The chapelry comprises 666 acres; the Wilts and Berks canal
546

intersects it, and the Great Western railway passes within a mile. The chapel is dedicated to St. Lawrence; the living is a donative, in the gift of Miss Ferard.

CHALTON, a hamlet, in the parish of TODDINGTON, union of WOBURN, hundred of MANSHEAD, county of BEDFORD ; containing 224 inhabitants.

CHALTON, or CHALKTON (*St. Michael*), a parish, in the union of CATHERINGTON, hundred of FINCH-DEAN, Petersfield and N. divisions of the county of SOUTHAMPTON, 3 miles (N. E.) from Horndean ; containing, with the chapelry of Idsworth, 659 inhabitants. The parish is situated chiefly on the downs; the soil is unfavourable. There is a small iron-foundry at Idsworth. The living is a rectory, with that of Clanfield united, valued in the king's books at £20. 0. 10., and in the patronage of King's College, Cambridge : the tithes have been commuted for £218, and the glebe contains 77 acres, with a glebe-house. The Independents have a place of worship.

CHALVEY, a hamlet, in the parish of UPTON, union of ETON, hundred of STOKE, county of BUCKINGHAM, 1¼ mile (N.) from Eton; containing 674 inhabitants. The tithes were commuted for land and a money payment in the year 1808. Here is a place of worship for Independents.

CHALVINGTON (*St. Bartholomew*), a parish, in the union of WEST FIRLE, hundred of SHIPLAKE, rape of PEVENSEY, E. division of SUSSEX, 10½ miles (S. by E.) from Uckfield; containing 192 inhabitants. It comprises about 730 acres, of which 446 are arable, 259 meadow, and about 15 wood; the surface is altogether flat, and the soil has several varieties. The living is a discharged rectory, valued in the king's books at £8, and in the gift of Augustus Elliott Fuller, Esq. : the tithes have been commuted for £190, and the glebe comprises 29 acres. The church is principally in the decorated English style.

CHANDLINGS, an extra-parochial district, in the union of ABINGDON, hundred of HORMER, county of BERKS, 3 miles (N. by E.) from Abingdon ; containing 11 inhabitants. It lies on the road from Abingdon to Oxford, and comprises 75 acres of land.

CHAPEL, ESSEX.—See PONTISBRIGHT.

CHAPEL-ALLERTON, or CHAPELTOWN, a chapelry, in the parish of ST. PETER, liberty of LEEDS, W. riding of YORK, 2 miles (N. by E.) from Leeds, on the road to Harrogate ; comprehending the villages of Chapeltown, Meanwood, Gledhow, and Moor-Allerton; and containing 2580 inhabitants. It abounds with picturesque scenery, and is noted for the salubrity of its air. The lands, which comprise by admeasurement 2763 acres, are well cultivated ; and from the gentle undulation of the surface, embellished with villas and plantations, the district has a strikingly beautiful aspect. Stone of good quality abounds, and the quarries have afforded materials for the erection of the church, and several of the principal residences. The great tithes have been commuted for £260, and the small for £28. The living is a perpetual curacy ; net income, £361; patron, the Vicar of Leeds. The church, which is in the Grecian style, was enlarged and repaired in 1840, at a cost of £1200, raised by subscription. There is a place of worship for a congregation of Wesleyans ; and at Meanwood is a school where divine service is performed by license from the bishop.

CHAPEL-EN-LE-FRITH (ST. THOMAS à BECKET), market-town and parish, and the head of a union, in hundred of HIGH PEAK, N. division of the county DERBY, 41 miles (N. W. by N.) from Derby, and (N. W. by N.) from London, on the road from Sheffield to Manchester; containing 3199 inhabitants, and comprising the townships of Bowden-Edge, Bradshaw-Edge, and Coombs-Edge. The town is pleasantly situated the acclivity of a hill rising from a vale embosomed the mountains that bound this extremity of the county; it is partially paved, and amply supplied with water. A small subscription library was established a few years since. The principal branch of manufacture that of cotton, in which more than 300 people are employed: about 100 persons are engaged in the manufacture of paper, chiefly for the London newspapers; there are a rope-walk and an iron-forge near the town; also several coal-mines in the parish. The Peak forest canal passes three miles to the north-west, and, by means of a railway, communicates with the Peak forest limeworks, about three miles to the east of the town: there is a reservoir in the parish that occasionally supplies the canal with water. The market, which on Thursday, has greatly declined: the fairs, most of which are insignificant, are on the Thursday before February 13th, on March 24th and 29th, the Thursday before Easter, April 30th, Holy-Thursday, and the third Thursday after, for cattle; July 7th, for wool; the Thursday preceding August 24th, for sheep and cheese; the Thursday after September 29th, and the Thursday before November 11th, for cattle. The High Peak court, for the recovery of debts under £5, at which the steward of the Duke of Devonshire presides, is held every third week: the powers of the county debt-court of Chapel-en-le-Frith, established in 1847, extend over the registration-district of Chapel-en-le-Frith, and part that of Hayfield and Glossop. The parish comprises about 8370 acres, the surface of which is in general hilly. The LIVING is a perpetual curacy, in the patronage of the resident Freeholders, of whom a committee of chosen in equal numbers from the three "edges," or hamlets, into which the parish is divided, elect the minister by a majority; net income, £145. The glebe contains about 60 or 70 acres, with a glebe-house. The church is a neat edifice in the later English style, with a square embattled tower, which, with the south front, was rebuilt in the beginning of the last century, at the expense of the parishioners. There is a place of worship for Wesleyans. The union of which the town is the head, comprises 17 parishes or places, and contains a population of 11,349. At Barmoor-Clough, about two miles to east, is an ebbing and flowing well; and on a hill two miles to the south, are the vestiges of a Roman encampment, from which a Roman road leads to Brough, about eight miles distant.

CHAPEL-HILL, a chapelry, in the parish of SWINESHEAD, wapentake of KIRTON, parts of HOLLAND, county LINCOLN; containing 213 inhabitants. The living is a perpetual curacy; net income, £47; patron, the Vicar of Swineshead. The chapel was erected by subscription, one year 1826.

'HAPEL-HILL, a parish, in the union and division of CHEPSTOW, hundred of RAGLAN, county of MONMOUTH, 5 miles (N.) from Chepstow; containing 521 inhabitants, several of whom are employed in the manu-

547

facture of iron wire. This parish, consisting of 820 acres, is romantically situated on the right bank of the Wye, in a district abounding with richly varied and beautiful scenery. It contains the venerable and stately remains of Tintern Abbey, founded for Cistercian monks by Walter de Clare, in 1141, and dedicated to St. Mary: at the Dissolution, the revenue was estimated at £256. 11. 6., and the site was granted to the Earl of Worcester, from whom it has descended to the Duke of Beaufort. The remains consist principally of the walls of the abbey church, which are almost entire, and richly mantled with ivy; and the exterior of the building, though defaced by mean cottages built with the materials of the abbey, forms a striking object as seen from the opposite bank of the river. The clustered columns, of light and graceful proportion, which separated the south aisle from the nave, and the sharply pointed arches that supported the roof, are yet entire; and those of loftier elevation which sustained the central tower, though dilapidated, still retain their grandeur of effect. The ranges of pillars and arches in the transepts are also in good preservation. The east window, which occupies nearly the whole of the end of the choir, is beautifully enriched with tracery; and the interior generally, from the beauty of the style (the early English in its richest state, merging into the decorated), the symmetry of its parts, the harmony of its arrangement, and the richness and elegance of its details, is unsurpassed by any specimen in the kingdom. The living is a perpetual curacy; net income, £60; patron and impropriator, the Duke of Beaufort.

CHAPEL-LE-DALE.—See INGLETON.

CHAPEL-SUCKEN, a township, in the parish of MILLOM, union of BOOTLE, ALLERDALE ward above Derwent, W. division of CUMBERLAND, 12 miles (S. E. by S.) from Ravenglass; containing 214 inhabitants.

CHAPEL-THORPE, a district chapelry, in the parish of GREAT SANDALL, union of WAKEFIELD, Lower division of the wapentake of AGBRIGG, W. riding of YORK, 3 miles (S. by W.) from Wakefield; containing 1479 inhabitants. It comprises the township of Crigglestone, and is separated from Horbury by the river Calder; the number of acres is 3000, and the district is rich in coal and freestone. The living is a perpetual curacy: net income, £200; patron, the Vicar of Great Sandall; impropriator, R. Allatt, Esq. The chapel, dedicated to St. James, is a neat plain edifice, built 80 years since, by parochial rate.

CHAPELTOWN, a church district, in the parish of ECCLESFIELD, union of WORTLEY, wapentake of STRAFFORTH and TICKHILL (N. division), W. riding of YORK, 6 miles (N.) from Sheffield; containing about 3000 inhabitants. The district is three square miles in extent, and contains two villages. It lies on the new line of road called the Sheffield, Barnsley, Wakefield, Pontefract, and Goole road, which passes through the village of Chapeltown, as do the turnpike-road from Sheffield to Barnsley and Leeds, and the Rotherham, Worsley, and Penistone road. Coal and ironstone of good quality are obtained; and the Chapeltown Company's and Thorncliffe Company's iron-works respectively several hundred hands. Good stone, also, is quarried for building. The district was constituted in Sept. 1844, under the act 6th and 7th Victoria, cap. 37; and the erection of a church was commenced in the summer of 1847: it is in the

4 A 2

decorated style, the cost being estimated at £2500. There are three Wesleyan places of worship. At the Thorncliffe works is an excellent chalybeate spring; and in the garden of Howsley Hall is a fine old cork-tree in full growth, supposed to be the only one in England, with the exception of that at Windsor Castle.

CHARBOROUGH (St. Mary), a parish, in the union of BLANDFORD, hundred of LOOSEBARROW, Wimborne division of DORSET, 6¼ miles (S. S. E.) from Blandford. The living is a discharged rectory, annexed to the vicarage of Morden, and valued in the king's books at £7. 3. 6½. The church, a handsome and interesting edifice, is the burial-place of the Drax family. Over the door of a small arched building in the grounds of Charborough House is a tablet put up by Thomas Erle Drax, Esq., in 1780, with an inscription commemorating the meeting, in 1686, of some patriotic individuals who here concerted the plan of the Revolution.

CHARCOMBE, an extra-parochial liberty, in the hundred of KILMERSDON, county of SOMERSET; containing 30 inhabitants.

CHARD (St. Mary), a borough, market-town, and parish, and the head of a union, in the hundred of KINGSBURY-EAST, W. division of SOMERSET, 12 miles (S. E. by S.) from Taunton, and 139 (W. S. W.) from London; comprising the tythings of Forton and Tatworth; and containing 5788 inhabitants, of whom 2877 are in the borough, 1331 in the tything of Old Chard, 517 in Crim-Chard, and 471 in South Chard. This was a place of considerable importance during the heptarchy, and was by the Saxons called Cerdre (subsequently Cherde or Cerde), a name supposed to be derived from Cerdic, the founder of the kingdom of Wessex. In the 14th of Edward I. it was incorporated by Bishop Joslin, who set apart fifty-two acres out of his manor of Cherde, which he constituted the borough, giving leave for any person to settle here except Turk or Jew. It made eight returns of members to parliament, the franchise being exercised until the 2nd of Edward III., when the privilege was discontinued. In the civil war of the seventeenth century a battle took place, in which a party of royalists, under the command of Colonel Penruddock, was defeated.

The TOWN is situated at the southern extremity of the county, and upon the highest ground between the Bristol and English Channels, both of which are visible from Windwhistle Hill, about three miles to the east. It is in a flourishing state, and consists principally of two streets, intersecting each other, and lighted with gas; the houses are in general well built, and the inhabitants are supplied with water conveyed by leaden pipes into four conduits, from a spring at its western extremity, which furnishes a clear stream of water running through it. A handsome and commodious hotel, called the Chard Arms, has been erected in the Fore-street, at an expense of £5000. The clothing-trade was formerly the staple trade of the town, but it has been almost superseded by the manufacture of lace, for which several large works have been built within a few years, and which at one time employed 1500 of the inhabitants; this also is now on the decrease. Two attempts to find coal have been made in the vicinity, one in 1793, the other in 1827, when, after boring to the depth of 378 feet, without penetrating through the lias formation, the operations were discon-

CHARDSTOCK (St. *Andrew*), a parish, in the ion of Axminster, hundred of Beaminster, Brid-rt division of Dorset, 3 miles (S. S. W.) from Chard; ntaining 1405 inhabitants. The parish comprises 00 acres, of which 1018 are common or waste. It is ersected by the road from Bristol to Lyme Regis, and that from Chard to Honiton; and is bounded on the ıth-east by the river Axe. Limestone is quarried, and rnt chiefly for manure. Great quantities of cider are de. The living is a discharged vicarage, in the patron-: of the Bishop of Salisbury, and valued in the king's)ks at £14. 2. 6.; impropriator, and lord of the nor, Lord Henley. The great tithes have been com-ted for £490, and the vicarial for £490; the impro-ate glebe consists of 65 acres, and the vicarial contains)ut an acre, with a glebe-house. The church, rebuilt 1839, is a handsome structure in the later English le: the pulpit is of stone, and the altar-screen, also of ne, is richly carved, and embellished with canopied hes: the windows of the chancel are of painted ss. A district called All Saints was formed in 1841, l attached to a chapel at the southern extremity of the ·ish; it comprises a population of about 400 persons, f of whom reside in this parish, and half in that of Ax-nster. The chapel was consecrated April 23rd, 1840: bert Williams, Esq., presented an elegant service of mmunion-plate. The income of the living, which is a rpetual curacy, was augmented in 1842 to £80 per num by the Ecclesiastical Commissioners. There is place of worship for Wesleyans.

CHARFIELD (St. *James*), a parish, in the union of ıornbury, Upper division of the hundred of Grum-ıld's-Aśh, W. division of the county of Gloucester; ıntaining 471 inhabitants. The Gloucester and Bristol ılway has a station here, two miles from the Wickwar ation. The living is a rectory, valued in the king's)oks at £10. 1. 3.; patron, J. Neeld, Esq.: the tithes ave been commuted for £304, and the glebe contains 5 acres, with a glebe-house. The church is principally ı the later English style, with a low tower.

CHARFORD, NORTH (St. *Peter and St. Paul*,) parish, in the union and hundred of Fordingbridge, .ingwood and S. divisions of the county of Southamp-ɔn, 3½ miles (N. by E.) from Fordingbridge; contain-ıg 116 inhabitants, of whom 62 are in the tything of outh Charford. In the Saxon annals this place is ılled *Cerdickford*, from Cerdic, who defeated the Britons ear a ford on the Avon, and subsequently became the)under of the West Saxon kingdom. The living is a erpetual curacy, valued in the king's books at £5. 13. 4.: ıe church is in ruins.

CHARING (St. *Peter and St. Paul*), a parish, in ıe union of West Ashford, hundred of Calehill, ıthe of Shepway, E. division of Kent, 12½ miles (E. , E.) from Maidstone, on the road from London to olkestone; containing 1241 inhabitants. On the divi-ion of the possessions of the monastery of Christ-'hurch, Canterbury, in the time of Archbishop Lanfranc, 'haring was allotted to the archbishop, who had a palace ere, the ruins of which are still standing near the hurchyard. It is uncertain when and by whom the alace was built, but it was of great antiquity, and must ave been extensive: it is reported to have been the esidence of King John. Archbishop Morton rebuilt it ı the reign of Henry VII., and in March, 1507, lodged 549

and entertained that monarch here; Henry VIII., also, slept in it on the 23rd of May, 1520, when on his way to the continent to have his celebrated interview with Francis I. of France, in the Field of Gold Cloth. The parish is in the bailiwick of Chart and Longbridge, and comprises 4551a. 19p., of which about 2414 acres are arable, 1229 pasture, 60 acres hop-grounds, 684 wood, and 72 common. The Hill of Charing contains an in-exhaustible supply of chalk, immense quantities of which are yearly converted into lime, principally consumed in the Weald of Kent. It also abounds with fossil exuviæ of marine production; and some beautiful specimens of palatal and other teeth of Plychodus, Polygyrus, and other varieties of extinct species of fossil sharks, with spongia, oysters, echinites, vertebræ, ammonites, plagi-ostoma, spinosum, &c., have been procured from the chalk. In the galt below the hill, ammonites, belem-nites, hamites, and other chambered shells, enamelled scales, and various bivalve shells, are plentiful. Its summit affords a beautiful, varied, and extensive pros-peet of the surrounding country, with the British Chan-nel in perspective. Fairs are held at the village on April 29th and October 29th, for cattle (mostly Welsh) and pedlery.

The living is a vicarage, valued in the king's books at £13; patrons, the Dean and Chapter of St. Paul's, London. The rectory is valued in the king's books, with the annexed chapel of Egerton, at £47. 5. 4., and is held on lease under the Dean and Chapter by the executors of Mrs. Cassandra Marshall. The great tithes have been commuted for £735, and the vicarial for £480; the glebe contains 29 acres. The church consists of an aisle, transept, and lofty chancel, with a chapel on the south side of it (built by Amy Brent in the reign of Richard II.), and a square tower with a turret at the south-eastern angle; it is chiefly in the later style of English architecture, and has twice sus-tained injury by fire. The arms of Hugh Brent, and a rose, the badge of Edward IV., are still visible in the belfry. There is a place of worship for Wesleyans. A free school, founded by a bequest of Elizabeth Ludwell, who died in 1765, is endowed with £25 per annum, and has two exhibitions to Oriel College, Oxford. Urns, coins, and other evidences of a Roman station, have been found in the parish.

CHARLBURY (St. *Mary*), a parish, in the union of Chipping-Norton, partly in the hundred of Chad-lington, and partly in that of Banbury, county of Oxford, 6¾ miles (W. N. W.) from Woodstock; con-taining 2982 inhabitants, and comprising the ancient chapelries of East Chadlington and Shorthampton, the tything of West Chadlington, and the hamlets of Fawler, Finstock, and Walcott. This parish, in old records called *Ceorlcbury*, signifying in the Saxon language "the settlement of free labourers," belonged to the bishops of Lincoln, whose seat was at Dorchester, in this county; and was afterwards given in exchange for other lands, to the monastery of Eynsham; founded by King Ethelred. It continued to form part of the endowment of Eynsham till the Dissolution, when the manor, and subsequently the vicarage, were purchased by St. John's College, Oxford. Canbury Park, adjoin-ing Charlbury, was once part of the demesne forest of the king, and extended for nine miles, both in length and breadth; it afterwards became the property of

Jasper, Duke of Bedford, from whom it passed to the Duke of Northumberland, and subsequently to Henry, Lord Danvers, who built the present mansion, a spacious and handsome edifice, with a chapel in which are some elegant specimens of carved oak. The estate, after the Restoration, came to the Earl of Clarendon, who took his title of viscount from the place; it was subsequently sold to the trustees of John, Duke of Marlborough.

The village was formerly a market-town of note, but the market has been for some time discontinued; fairs are still held on the 1st of January, the second Friday in Lent, and the second Friday after the 12th of May, for live-stock, and on the 10th of October for cattle and cheese. The living is a vicarage, with the chapels of Chadlington, Finstock, and Shorthampton annexed, valued in the king's books at £25. 5. 10.; net income, £800; patrons, the President and Fellows of St. John's College, who are also impropriators of Chadlington. The tithes were commuted for land and a money payment in 1811. The church is an ancient and venerable structure, with a square embattled tower; it is partly in the Norman and partly in the early English style, and contains some memorials of the Jenkinsons, ancestors of the Earl of Liverpool, and a mural monument to Elizabeth, Viscountess Dowager of Hereford, and her grandson, Lord George Henry Somerset. There is a place of worship for Wesleyans. A free grammar school was endowed by Mrs. Ann Walker with £40 per annum, payable out of an estate that produces £200 per annum, from which also are paid two exhibitions of £5 each for scholars from this school, which is under the visitation of Brasenose College, Oxford; a school-house has been erected at an expense of £600.

CHARLCOMBE (St. Mary), a parish, in the union of Bath, hundred of Hampton and Claverton, locally in that of Bath-Forum, E. division of Somerset, 1 mile (N.) from Bath; containing 84 inhabitants, and comprising by measurement 523 acres. The living is a discharged rectory, valued in the king's books at £5. 15. 10., and annexed to the mastership of the free grammar school at Bath : the tithes have been commuted for £134, and the glebe consists of 14 acres, with a glebe-house. The church is a very small ancient edifice : according to tradition it was formerly the mother church of Bath, and received an annual acknowledgment of a pound of pepper from the abbey there.

CHARLCOTE (St. Leonard), a parish, in the union of Stratford-on-Avon, Warwick division of the hundred of Kington, S. division of the county of Warwick, 4½ miles (E. by N.) from Stratford; containing 267 inhabitants. The name is in Domesday book written Cerlecote, and is supposed to be derived from a possessor in the Saxon times. William, the son of Walter de Cerlecote, assumed the surname of Lucy about the close of the 12th century, and ever since that period the Lucy family have been the lords. The parish is bounded on the west by the river Avon, which on the south receives the waters of a stream called the Huile : it comprises 1949 acres, of which 1495 are arable, and 450 pasture; the surface is in general level, and the soil a sandy loam. The grounds of Charlcote Park, the seat of the family of Lucy, abounding with elms of stately growth, and well stocked with deer, add greatly to the beauty of the scenery. The mansion-house, a noble structure of brick and stone, was built by Sir

d a mile and three-quarters in breadth. The soil is iefly light; the land pleasingly wooded; and there much hill and dale, intersected with many rivulets, which seven mills of various kinds are worked. The er Etherow separates the district from the parish of ›ttram, in the county of Chester; and the Etherow duct on the Manchester and Sheffield railway, unites ⱳith that parish. Several cotton-mills are in opera- n, and an extensive coal-trade is carried on. The ᴀses of the upper town of Charlesworth are very old, ny of them having been built in the 16th and 17th ᵼturies; but the new town, or rather village, is quite dern. The district was constituted in June, 1845, ᴊer the act 6th and 7th Victoria, cap. 37; and a ᵼm has been licensed for divine service. The oldest ce of worship here, is one for Independents; it was ce a chapel of ease under Glossop church, but in ne way, now unknown, fell into the hands of the ᴊependents, who still retain it: the churchyard, how- ›r, is the burial-place of the inhabitants. There are, o, another place of worship for Independents, one for ptists, and three for Methodists.

CHARLETON (Sᴛ. Mᴀʀʏ), a parish, in the union ᴋɪɴɢsʙʀɪᴅɢᴇ, hundred of Cᴏʟᴇʀɪᴅɢᴇ, Stanborough d Coleridge, and S. divisions of Dᴇᴠᴏɴ, 2½ miles E.) from Kingsbridge; containing 703 inhabitants. e living is a rectory, valued in the king's books at 1. 8. 4., and in the patronage of Lord Ashburton: e tithes have been commuted for £550, and the glebe mprises 30 acres, with a glebe-house. The church ntains, over the altar, a good painting of Our Saviour d the Twelve Apostles, by Mr. Lethbridge, a native of ıe parish.

CHARLETON, QUEEN (Sᴛ.˙Mᴀʀɢᴀʀᴇᴛ), a parish, ı the union and hundred of Kᴇʏɴsʜᴀᴍ, E. division of ᴏᴍᴇʀsᴇᴛ, 2¾ miles (N. N. E.) from Pensford; contain- ᵼg 190 inhabitants. This parish obtained its distin- ᴊishing appellation from having been settled on Cathe- ne Parr, Queen of Henry VIII. The salubrity of the r made it a place of considerable resort, particularly in ᴧ74, when the plague swept away 2000 persons at ristol. The parish comprises 952 acres: the road to ath formerly intersected the village. A fair, granted y Elizabeth, on her progress through the place, in ᴧ73, is held on the 20th of July. The living is a ïcarage not in charge, in the patronage of Miss ᴊickenson, to whom also the impropriation belongs; ᵼt income, £48. In 1760, Mary Freeman left £500, roducing £25 per annum, for clothing and teaching ᴡenty boys.

CHARLEY, or Cʜᴏʀʟᴇʏ, an extra-parochial liberty, ı the union of Lᴏᴜɢʜʙᴏʀᴏᴜɢʜ, hundred of Wᴇsᴛ ᴊᴏsᴄᴏᴛᴇ, N. division of the county of Lᴇɪᴄᴇsᴛᴇʀ, 4¼ ᴊiles (S. W. by W.) from Loughborough; containing 53 ᴊhabitants. The ancient forest of Charley, or Charn- ᵼood, twenty miles in circuit, was disafforested soon fter the Conquest; its privileges were restored by ᴊenry II., but finally abolished by Henry III. The berty lies in the heart of the forest, and chiefly in the ᴊmantic vale of a rivulet: the area is about 500 acres; ᴊe soil on the south side is light, in the middle rather ᴛiff, but, all considered, good useful land. The Hall is plain brick building, with pleasant grounds. A society f eremites, of the order of St. Augustine, settled here in he reign of Henry II., by the favour of Robert Blanch-
551

mains, Earl of Leicester; but in the time of Edward II. it was united to one at Ulverscroft, where a priory of Regular canons, dedicated to the Blessed Virgin Mary, continued until the Dissolution, when its revenue was estimated at £101. 3. 10.

CHARLEY, a hamlet, in the parish of Fᴀʀᴇᴡᴇʟʟ, union of Lɪᴄʜꜰɪᴇʟᴅ, S. division of the hundred of Oꜰꜰ- ʟᴏᴡ and of the county of Sᴛᴀꜰꜰᴏʀᴅ, 4 miles (W. by N.) from Lichfield; containing 158 inhabitants. It lies on the eastern side of Cannock Chase, and west of the village of Farewell. Charley Hall is an ancient mansion.

CHARLINCH (Sᴛ. Mᴀʀʏ), a parish, in the union of Bʀɪᴅɢᴡᴀᴛᴇʀ, hundred of Cᴀɴɴɪɴɢᴛᴏɴ, W. division of Sᴏᴍᴇʀsᴇᴛ, 4 miles (W. by N.) from Bridgwater; containing 215 inhabitants. This parish stands partly on a high ridge of land, and partly in a valley, and com- prises 1432a. 2r. 7p., of which about 844 acres are arable, 491 meadow and pasture, 45 woodland, and 18 common; the soil in the lower part is chiefly clay, and in the upper the earth rests upon greywacke and sand- stone. The living is a rectory, valued in the king's books at £9. 15. 5., and in the patronage of the family of Starky: the tithes have been commuted for £268. 3. 8., and the glebe comprises 82 acres. Gothelney House, a building of the fifteenth or sixteenth century, is now occupied as a farmhouse.

CHARLTON, a hamlet, in the parish, union, and hundred of Wᴀɴᴛᴀɢᴇ, county of Bᴇʀᴋs, ¾ of a mile (N. E.) from Wantage; containing 329 inhabitants, and comprising 1368a. 8p.

CHARLTON, a tything, in the parish, and Upper division of the hundred, of Hᴇɴʙᴜʀʏ, union of Cʟɪꜰ- ᴛᴏɴ, W. division of the county of Gʟᴏᴜᴄᴇsᴛᴇʀ, 5¼ miles (N.) from Bristol; containing 319 inhabitants.

CHARLTON (Sᴛ. Pᴇᴛᴇʀ ᴀɴᴅ Sᴛ. Pᴀᴜʟ), a parish, in the union of Dᴏᴠᴏʀ, partly in the hundred of Bᴇᴡs- ʙᴏʀᴏᴜɢʜ, but chiefly within the liberty of the cinque- port of Dᴏᴠᴏʀ (of which it is a member), lathe of Sᴛ. Aᴜɢᴜsᴛɪɴᴇ, E. division of Kᴇɴᴛ, 1 mile (N. N. E.) from Dovor; containing 2513 inhabitants. This place, it is conjectured, was the Portus Dubris of the Romans, several anchors and fragments of wreck having been discovered at various times. The parish consists of 381 acres. The living is a discharged rectory, valued in the king's books at £32; net income, £99; patron, the Rev. John Monins. The church has been enlarged by the addition of 258 free sittings.

CHARLTON (Sᴛ. Lᴜᴋᴇ), a parish, in the union of Lᴇᴡɪsʜᴀᴍ, hundred of Bʟᴀᴄᴋʜᴇᴀᴛʜ, lathe of Sᴜᴛᴛᴏɴ- ᴀᴛ-Hᴏɴᴇ, W. division of Kᴇɴᴛ, 6½ miles (E.) from London; containing 2655 inhabitants. This place, in ancient records called Cerletone and Ceorletone, is sup- posed to have derived that name from Ceorle, the Saxon term for husbandman. The manor appears to have be- longed, from the close of the eleventh century till the Dissolution, to the monks of Bermondsey, to whom Henry III. granted a charter for a weekly market, and an annual fair on the eve of the Holy Trinity, to be held here. In 1665, the town, which at that time was of considerable importance, suffered severely from the ravages of the plague, and, together with the neigh- bourhood, sustained much injury from a violent tempest. The parish comprises by admeasurement 1400 acres, of which 528 are arable, 460 pasture, 165 marsh, and 30 woodland; and is delightfully situated in the heart of a fertile district, abounding with picturesque scenery, interspersed with elegant villas, and commanding from the higher parts extensive prospects. The village, which is on rising ground, retains much of its rural character; nearly opposite to the church is the manor-house, erected in 1612, a spacious and stately building, in front of which is a row of cypress-trees, said to have been the first planted in England. The market has long been discontinued; the fair, now held on St. Luke's day, is called Horn fair, from the numerous articles of that material brought for sale.

The LIVING is a rectory, valued in the king's books at £10. 7. 8½., and in the gift of Sir T. M. Wilson, Bart.: the tithes have been commuted for £600, and the glebe comprises 13 acres. The church, rebuilt of brick in 1640, and enlarged in 1839, is a neat edifice with an embattled tower: the windows are embellished with armorial bearings in stained glass, and the building contains various pieces of ancient armour, and numerous handsome monuments, among which are one to Lady Catherine Puckeringe; one to Brigadier-General Richards, surveyor of the ordnance in the reign of George II.; and one to the Right Hon. Spencer Perceval, who was interred in the church. The church of St. Peter in Blackheath Park, and Morden College, are both in the parish; and the district of St. Thomas', Woolwich, endowed in 1845 by the Ecclesiastical Commissioners, includes part of Charlton. A parochial school was built by Sir William Langhorne, who in 1714 endowed it with £300, now producing £8 per annum; it is conducted on the national plan. Sir William also bequeathed £1000 to augment the rector's income.—See BLACK-HEATH.

CHARLTON, a hamlet, partly in the parish of NEW-BOTTLE, and partly in that of KING's-SUTTON, union of BRACKLEY, hundred of KING's-SUTTON, S. division of the county of NORTHAMPTON, 4 miles (W. by S.) from Brackley; containing 446 inhabitants. On a neighbouring hill, called Rainsborough, is an oval camp with a double intrenchment, about half a mile in circumference, having two entrances on the north, and two on the south: urns, glass vessels, and other relics, have been discovered; and a little eastward, near a smaller intrenchment, a gold coin of Vespasian and several coins of Constantine have been found.

CHARLTON, a hamlet, in the parish, union, and hundred of ANDOVER, Andover and N. divisions of the county of SOUTHAMPTON; containing 323 inhabitants. It lies north-west of the town of Andover.

CHARLTON, a hamlet, in the parish of SINGLETON, union of WESTHAMPNETT, hundred of WESTBOURN and SINGLETON, rape of CHICHESTER, W. division of SUSSEX; containing 223 inhabitants.

CHARLTON, a tything, in the parish and hundred of DOWNTON, union of ALDERBURY, Salisbury and Amesbury, and S. divisions of WILTS; containing 300 inhabitants.

CHARLTON (ST. JOHN THE BAPTIST), a parish, in the union and hundred of MALMESBURY, Malmesbury and Kingswood, and N. divisions of WILTS, 2¼ miles (N. E. by E.) from Malmesbury; containing 683 inhabitants. It comprises about 5000 acres, of which the surface is in general flat, and the soil mostly clayey, and in some parts stony; there is a lake of 60 acres at Braden. Charlton Park, the seat of the Earl of Suffolk,

CHARLTON, EAST-QUARTER, a township, in the parish and union of BELLINGHAM, N. W. division of ·DALE ward, S. division of NORTHUMBERLAND, 1¾ ɛ (N. W. by W.) from Bellingham; containing 173 abitants. The village is pleasantly situated on the h side of the North Tyne. A small stream tributary hat river flows here.

CHARLTON-HORETHORNE, or CANFIELD (ST. 'ER AND ST. PAUL), a parish, and formerly a market- a, in the union of WINCANTON, hundred of HORE- RNE, E. division of SOMERSET, 5½ miles (S. W.) from ιcanton; containing 569 inhabitants. This parish, :h is situated on the road from Bath to Weymouth, prises about 2500 acres. Stone of good quality is ensively quarried for building, and repairing the ds; and a considerable number of the inhabitants employed in the manufacture of dowlas. The mar- was obtained in the 22nd of Edward I., by Henry de :y, who had by the same charter a grant for a fair on eve and morrow of St. Thomas the Martyr; the fair till held. The living is a discharged vicarage, valued he king's books at £8. 10. 5.; net income, £384; ron and impropriator, the Marquess of Anglesey: glebe comprises 40 acres. The church is a hand- e edifice in the early English style, but has been ɪtly disfigured by the insertion of windows of modern racter. There was anciently within the manor a ntry chapel, dependent on Kenilworth priory.

CHARLTON, KINGS (ST. MARY), a parish, in the on and hundred of CHELTENHAM, E. division of the ɴty of GLOUCESTER, 2 miles (S. S. E.) from Chelten- ; containing 3232 inhabitants. This place partici- ted in the hostilities of the parliamentary war during ɛ reign of Charles I.; and a hill since called Battle- wns, was the scene of a sanguinary conflict in which ɪny of the inhabitants, who adhered to the royal ɑse, were slain. The parish is situated on the road ɪm London to Gloucester, at the base of the Cotswold ls, and comprises 3214a. 2r. 4p.: the soil is chiefly a ɑdy loam, with a little yellowish clay; the lands are ɪtered by the Chelt, which flows hence into the parish Cheltenham. A small part of the population is em- ɔyed in the making of gloves. Stone of the oolite rmation is quarried for rough building, and for roads. ɪe living is a perpetual curacy; net income, £177, th an excellent glebe-house of recent erection; patrons, ɛ Principal and Fellows of Jesus College, Oxford; im- opriator, C. W. Lovesy, Esq. The church is a hand- me structure, in the later English style. There is a ɪce of worship for Wesleyans. The sum of £6 is paid ɾ instruction out of the rental of land producing £30 ɾ annum, given by Samuel Cooper about the year 43; the remainder is applied to the relief of the poor. mslhouses have been built; and there is a fund arising ɔm several benefactions, of £100 a year, which is dis- buted among the deserving poor. A mineral spring, ɴilar in its properties to the Cheltenham water, was ːely discovered.

CHARLTON-MACKREL (ST. MARTIN), a parish, in ɛ union of LANGPORT, hundred of SOMERTON, W. vision of SOMERSET, 3 miles (E.) from Somerton; ɴtaining 405 inhabitants. It is bounded on the south ɾ the river Cary, across which is a bridge of two ɔhes, on the line of a modern road that passes along ɔ course of the Roman fosse-way. The living is a

rectory, valued in the king's books at £16. 0. 2½.; net income, £499; patron and incumbent, the Rev. W. T. P. Brymer. The church is a handsome edifice, in the ancient style of English architecture, repaired and em- bellished at the expense of the present incumbent.

CHARLTON-MARSHALL, a parish, in the union of BLANDFORD, hundred of COGDEAN, Blandford divi- sion of DORSET, 1¾ mile (S. S. E.) from Blandford; con- taining 395 inhabitants. The living is annexed to the rectory of Spetisbury: the tithes were commuted for land in 1799. The church contains some monuments to the family of Bastard, and one to the memory of Dr. Sloper. Some fossils, and Roman and Grecian coins, were found in 1831.

CHARLTON-MUSGRAVE (ST. STEPHEN), a parish, in the union of WINCANTON, hundred of NORTON- FERRIS, E. division of SOMERSET, 1 mile (N. N. E.) from Wincanton; containing 409 inhabitants. The living is a rectory, valued in the king's books at £13. 10., and in the gift of the family of Lier: the tithes have been com- muted for £450, and the glebe comprises 52 acres, with a glebe-house. Dr. William Musgrave, physician and antiquary, was born here in 1657.

CHARLTON, NORTH, a township, in the parish of ELLINGHAM, union of ALNWICK, S. division of BAM- BROUGH ward, N. division of NORTHUMBERLAND, 6½ miles (N. by W.) from Alnwick; containing 238 inhabit- ants. The village is situated on the road from Alnwick to Belford. Charlton Hall stands near a stream which, after a short course, falls into the North Sea. There are some curious barrows.

CHARLTON, SOUTH, a township, in the parish of ELLINGHAM, union of ALNWICK, S. division of BAM- BROUGH ward, N. division of NORTHUMBERLAND, 5½ miles (N. by W.) from Alnwick; containing 188 inhabit- ants. This place is on the great north road, and com- prises 1823 acres, of which 941 are common or waste: the soil is light, and rests generally upon a limestone substratum; the surface is undulated and pleasing. Here was formerly a chapel, of which there are no re- mains. A great portion of North and South Charlton is covered with ancient roads and earthworks; and graves of rude workmanship are frequently discovered, containing bones, urns, and armour.

CHARLTON-UPON-OTMORE (ST. MARY), a parish, in the union of BICESTER, hundred of PLOUGHLEY, county of OXFORD, 6 miles (S. S. W.) from Bicester; containing, with the hamlets of Fencot and Murcot, 658 inhabitants. It comprises by measurement 1840 acres, of which 1291 are arable, and nearly all the rest pasture. The living is a rectory, valued in the king's books at £21. 9. 4½.; patrons, the Provost and Fellows of Queen's College, Oxford. The church is partly in the early and partly in the decorated English style: a portion of the ancient rood-loft, of exquisite beauty, is remaining; and in the chancel, which is lighted by elegant windows with flowing tracery, are some stone stalls highly en- riched.

CHARLTON, WEST-QUARTER, a township, in the parish and union of BELLINGHAM, N. W. division of TINDALE ward, S. division of NORTHUMBERLAND, 3 miles (W. N. W.) from Bellingham; containing 176 inhabitants. This place, which comprises about 400 acres, is situated at the confluence of the Tarset burn and the North Tyne river. Here anciently stood a castle, the walls of which were of ashlar stones four feet thick; its magnitude and strength are said to have impressed the popular mind with the notion of its having been the abode of some giant, and it is believed that there still exists a subterraneous passage beneath the bed of the Tyne, from this castle to another known as Dally Castle, distant from it southwards about a mile.

CHARLTON-WOODLANDS, a hamlet, in the parish and union of SHEPTON-MALLET, hundred of WHITSTONE, E. division of the county of SOMERSET; containing 86 inhabitants.

CHARLWOOD (ST. NICHOLAS), a parish, in the union, and First division of the hundred, of REIGATE, E. division of SURREY, 7 miles (S. S. W.) from Reigate, and on the borders of the county of Sussex; containing 1291 inhabitants. This place was the scene of a sanguinary battle between the Danes and the men of Surrey and Sussex, that occurred near a bridge since called Kilman Bridge, and in which the Danes were defeated with great slaughter. It comprises about 7000 acres. The London and Brighton railway intersects the southeastern part of the parish, as does also the road from London to Brighton by way of Crawley; and the river Mole winds through and bounds some parts of it. An act for inclosing lands was passed in 1843. The living is a rectory, valued in the king's books at £19. 16. 8.; patron and incumbent, the Rev. H. Wise: the tithes have been commuted for £900, and the glebe consists of 22 acres, with a glebe-house. The church contains several ancient monuments of the family of Sanders and others, and is in the Norman and early English styles; the south aisle is separated from the chancel by the remains of a very handsome and elaborately carved screen. There is a place of worship for Independents.

CHARMINSTER (ST. MARY), a parish, in the union of DORCHESTER, hundred of GEORGE, Dorchester division of DORSET, 2 miles (N. W. by N.) from Dorchester; containing 827 inhabitants. The living is a perpetual curacy, with the living of Stratton annexed; net income, £137; patrons and impropriators, the Pickard family. The great tithes have been commuted for £510, the perpetual curate's for £12, and the tithes of the landowners for £155. The church has been enlarged by the addition of 174 free sittings.

CHARMOUTH (ST. MATTHEW), a parish, and formerly a market-town, in the union of AXMINSTER, hundred of WHITCHURCH-CANONICORUM, Bridport division of DORSET, 2 miles (N. E. by E.) from Lyme Regis; containing 620 inhabitants. This place derives its name from its situation at the mouth of the river Char, which here falls into the English Channel. It was the scene of a sanguinary battle in 833, between the Saxons, under Egbert, and the Danes, who, though many of them were killed in the action, yet maintained their post, and made good their retreat to their ships. Another battle was fought in 840, when the Danes defeated the Saxons under Ethelwolf, but, without improving their victory, precipitately embarked, leaving their booty behind. In the 7th of Edward I. the abbot of the monastery of Ford, in the vicinity, obtained for the inhabitants the grant of a weekly market and an annual fair. After the battle of Worcester, Charles II. and his suite fled to the place, intending to escape into France; but, being frustrated in that expectation, quitted it without delay. On this occasion, a blacksmith having

; containing 784 inhabitants. ˙ This place was held moieties by the Charnocks and Banasters : afterwards manor came to the Lee family; and by marriage h the daughter of Sir Henry de Lee, a moiety de- ved to the Hoghtons, who subsequently became pos- sed of the whole. The township is separated from ath-Charnock by the township of Duxbury ; it lies the road from Preston to Wigan, and the river Yar- ʋ and North-Union railway pass through it. Coal stone are wrought. The tithes have been commuted £246..1. A school is partly supported by the land- ners.

CHARSFIELD (St. Peter), a parish, in the union Woodbridge, hundred of Loes, E. division of Suf- ₌ₖ, 5½ miles (N. by W.) from Woodbridge; contain- 551 inhabitants, and comprising by measurement)9 acres. The living is a perpetual curacy ; net in- e, £106; patron and impropriator, Earl Howe, ose tithes have been commuted for £160. There is a ce of worship for Particular Baptists.

CHART, or Churt, a tything, in the parish of ensham, hundred of Farnham, W. division of Sur- y, 5¼ miles (N. W.) from Haslemere ; containing 432 abitants. A manufactory for coarse earthenware is ·ried on to a limited extent. A chapel was erected 1838, by subscription, aided by a grant from the Pas- al Aid Society : the chaplain is appointed by the in- ꞏmbent of Frensham, and his stipend is paid by the ꞏiety.

CHART, GREAT (St. Mary), a parish, in the union West Ashford, hundred of Chart and Long- idge, lathe of Shepway, E. division of Kent, 2 miles . by S.) from Ashford; containing 714 inhabitants. ꞏis parish, called by the Saxons Sybertes Chert, and in omesday book Certh, lies chiefly on the Quarry hills, ꞏe southern part being within the Weald, the boundary ' which runs east and west, to the north of the church. he parish comprises 3281 acres, whereof 150 are in ꞏood, and 160 common. The town, which was burnt ꞏ the Danes, was anciently of some importance, having weekly market, and a great fair on the 5th of April r sheep and oxen; the market is disused, but the re- ains of the market-house were formerly visible in the ꞏld where the fair is still held. Chart is now a small llage; which, from its elevated situation, commands ꞏ extensive and picturesque view of the surrounding ꞏuntry. On the 1st of May, 1580, a violent earth- ꞏake was felt here. The living is a rectory, valued in ꞏe king's books at £25. 6. 0½., and in the patronage of ꞏ the Archbishop of Canterbury : the tithes have been ꞏmmuted for £700, and the glebe comprises 13 acres, ith a glebe-house. There is a place of worship for a ꞏngregation of Wesleyans.

CHART, LITTLE (St. Mary), a parish, in the union ꞏ West Ashford, hundred of Calehill, lathe of ꞏepway, E. division of Kent, 2 miles (S. W. by W.) om Charing ; containing 300 inhabitants. It com- ꞏises 1607a. 2r. 30p., of which 207 acres are in wood ; ꞏd the South-Eastern railway passes about three miles om the village. The living is a rectory, valued in ꞏing's books at £13. 10. 10., and in the patronage of ꞏe Archbishop of Canterbury : the tithes have been ꞏmmuted for £400, and the glebe contains about 30 ꞏres, with a glebe-house. The church, which is ancient, ꞏntains some handsome monuments to the Darell

family, and one to the memory of a descendant of Cam- den, the historian, which is remarkable for the elegance of the inscription.

CHART, SUTTON (St. Michael), a parish, in the union of Hollingbourn, hundred of Eyhorne, lathe of Aylesford, W. division of Kent, 5 miles (S. E. by S.) from Maidstone; containing 604 inhabitants. This parish, in Domesday book called Certh, is inter- sected from east to west by the Quarry, or northern range of bills, here forming the boundary of the Weald. It comprises by measurement 2165 acres, the soil of which on the hills is light and spongy, and on the lower grounds clay ; the whole land, excepting the pastures, is employed in the cultivation of fruit and hops. The southern declivity, both from its genial aspect and the richness of the soil, is well adapted to the culture of vines. The living is a vicarage, valued in the king's books at £8. 12. 8½., and in the gift of the Dean and Chapter of Rochester : the glebe contains 8½ acres. The church, which stands near Sutton-Valence, on the sum- mit of the acclivity upon which the village is built, was, with its beautiful spire, destroyed by lightning in 1779, but was rebuilt ; it belonged to Leeds Priory.

CHARTERHOUSE-HINTON, county of Somerset. —See Hinton, Charterhouse.

CHARTERHOUSE-on-Mendip, a district, in the union of Axbridge, liberty of Wytham Friary (though locally in the hundred of Winterstoke), E. division of Somerset, 5½ miles (E. N. E.) from Axbridge; con- taining 99 inhabitants. Here was a cell to the priory of Witham, which, as part of the possessions of that esta- blishment, was granted away in the 36th of the reign of Henry VIII.

CHARTERIDGE, a hamlet, in the parish of Ches- ham, union of Amersham, hundred of Burnham, county of Buckingham ; containing 404 inhabitants.

CHARTHAM (St. Mary), a parish, in the union of Bridge, hundred of Felborough, lathe of Shepway, E. division of Kent, 3 miles (S. W. by W.) from Can- terbury ; containing, with the chapelry of Horton, 974 inhabitants. It comprises 4530 acres ; and is situated on the river Stour, over which, near the village, is an ancient structure of five arches, called Shalmsford Bridge. About 700 acres are covered with wood. The manufacture of paper is carried on to a moderate extent, and there are also some seed-mills. The living is a rectory, valued in the king's books at £41. 5. 10., and in the gift of the Archbishop of Canterbury : the tithes have been commuted for £800, and there is a glebe of 34¾ acres. The church is of early decorated architecture, with very fine windows, and some remains of richly- stained glass ; the roof is of wood and the tower of flint, both being of later date than the stone-work. It con- tains a monumental arch and some old brasses, one in particular of Sir Robert Septvan, having the alæ of the knight's armour, and in other respects peculiar ; in the chancel lie the remains of Dr. John Reading, chaplain to Charles I., and author of some religious tracts. There is a place of worship for Wesleyans. Numerous tumuli, raised over the slain in the decisive conflict between Cæsar and Cassivelaunus, lie scattered at the distance of about three-quarters of a mile from the church, on the road to Canterbury.

CHARTINGTON, in the parish of Rothbury, county of Northumberland.—See Cartington.

CHARTLEY-HOLME, an extra-parochial liberty, locally in the parish of STOWE, S. division of the hundred of PIREHILL, union, and N. division of the county, of STAFFORD, 7½ miles (N. E. by E.) from Stafford; containing 71 inhabitants. In this liberty are about 2000 acres of the Chartley estate, of which nearly 1000 are in Chartley Park, a mile and a half north from Stowe. The park is in a state of nature, inclosed within an ancient oak paling, and studded with a few aged trees and several small plantations; it is celebrated for its breed of wild cattle, the superiority of its venison, and the abundance of its black game. On the summit of an artificial hill, stand the remains of Chartley Castle, built in 1220 by Ranulph Blundeville, Earl of Chester, whose sister (he dying without issue) carried his extensive estates in marriage to William de Ferrers, Earl of Derby. The castle seems to have soon fallen into decay, and its remains now consist chiefly of the fragments of two massive round towers, partly covered with ivy, and rising amid the foliage of numerous full-grown yew-trees that have weathered the storms of many centuries. The noble owners afterwards built, a little below the old castle, a more convenient mansion in the half-timbered style, curiously carved, and embattled at the top; but it was destroyed by fire in 1781, and little now remains to mark its site but the moat by which it was surrounded. Since then, another but a smaller house was raised near the same spot, which was, till lately, the occasional residence of the Earl Ferrers. Chartley Moss, comprising about 100 acres, is prolific in cranberries.

CHARWELTON (HOLY TRINITY), a parish, in the union of DAVENTRY, hundred of FAWSLEY, S. division of the county of NORTHAMPTON, 5 miles (S. W. by S.) from Daventry; containing 227 inhabitants. This place is partly bounded on the west by a portion of Warwickshire, and comprises by measurement 2258 acres, chiefly rich pasture land, with about 20 acres of wood; it contains excellent gravel, and stone is quarried for agricultural purposes, and for common buildings. The river Cherwell, from which the place took its name, rises in the cellar of a farmhouse in the parish, called Cherwell House. The village is intersected by the road from Daventry to Banbury. The living is a rectory, valued in the king's books at £20. 2. 11.; net income, £582; patron, Sir Charles Knightley, Bart. The church consists of a nave, north and south aisles, and a small side chapel; the arches are in the early English style, and the tower is remarkably well built and proportioned. The font is octagonal, and is a curious piece of workmanship; the church contains some good monuments of brass, and has a handsome one of marble to the memory of the Andrew family, the ancient possessors of the manor-house. The village, now situated at the distance of three-quarters of a mile from the church, is supposed to have been originally adjoining it, which opinion is confirmed by traces of foundations discovered near the church.

CHASELEY (ST. JOHN THE BAPTIST), a parish, in the union of TEWKESBURY, Lower division of the hundred of PERSHORE, Upton and W. divisions of the county of WORCESTER, 3 miles (S. W. by W.) from Tewkesbury; containing 364 inhabitants. The parish lies at the southern extremity of the county, and is bounded on the south-east by the river Severn, and on all other sides, except the north-west, by the shire of

CHATHAM (St. Mary), a borough, market-town, d parish, and the head of the Medway union, partly hin the jurisdiction, and adjoining the city, of Rochester, but chiefly in the hundred of Chatham and Llingham, N. division of the lathe of Aylesford, division of Kent, 8 miles (N. by E.) from Maidstone, 30 (E. by S.) from London; containing 21,939 inhabitants. This place, anciently called *Ceteham* and *tham*, derives its name from the Saxon *Cyte*, a cottage, *Ham*, a village; and, till it rose into importance as seat of one of the principal naval arsenals in the gdom, was only an inconsiderable village. At the iquest, the lord of the manor espoused the cause of ·old, and for his loyalty to that prince was deprived is possessions, which were conferred upon Crevecœur, o accompanied the Conqueror to England. The TOWN iituated on the south-east bank of the river Medway, l on the north side of Chatham Hill; and, though ensive, is irregularly built, partly from the nature of ground, which, in every direction, is very hilly, and ·tly from the large space occupied by its vast naval ablishments. The dockyard for the royal navy was menced in the reign of Elizabeth, when it occupied site of the present ordnance wharf, and was protected Upnor Castle, which that queen caused to be erected its defence. In 1622, it was removed to its present .ation, and greatly enlarged by Charles I., who cted capacious storehouses, and constructed new cks, to enable ships to float in with the tide. It was l further improved by Charles II., in whose reign the tch Admiral de Ruyter, having cast anchor at the re with fifty sail of the line, sent his vice-admiral, n Ghent, with seventeen of his lightest vessels and ght fire-ships, to destroy the shipping in the river edway : the vice-admiral attacked and took Sheerness, ough gallantly defended by Sir Edward Spragge, blew up e fortifications, burnt the storehouses, &c., and, sailing ⟩ the Medway with six men of war and five fire-ships, me in front of Upnor Castle, at that time defended by ajor Scot, whose warm reception of the assailant ıstrated his attempt on Chatham.

The dockyard occupies an extensive area, nearly a ile in length, inclosed on the land side by a high wall, d defended by strong fortifications, principally of ɔdern erection; the entrance is through a spacious teway, flanked by two embattled towers. The houses the superintendent and the principal officers are spa- ɔus and handsome buildings, and the various offices the several departments of the yard are neat and mmodiously arranged. The numerous storehouses, e of which is 660 feet in length, contain an immense antity of every article necessary for the building and uipment of ships of the largest dimensions, all dis- sed with such order and exactness, that upon any ıergency a 'first-rate man of war may be equipped for a in a few days. The mast-house is 240 feet in length, d 120 feet wide; and the new rope-house 1110 in ıgth, and 50 wide. At the north-eastern extremity of e dockyard are the saw-mills, erected on a very ex- nsive scale, under the superintendence of Mr. Brunel, an expense of nearly £57,000, and worked with werful machinery propelled by steam. To the north the mills is a canal, which, on entering the rising ound, passes under a tunnel 300 feet long, into an liptic basin, from which the timber, having been floated

from the river, is raised by machinery with extraordi- nary velocity. Connected with the steam-engine of the saw-mills are water-works, for the supply of the dock- yard, the infantry and marine barracks, and Melville hospital. There are four wet-docks sufficiently capacious for first-rate men of war, two of which, lately constructed, are of stone; besides two others for smaller vessels. There are also six slips or launches, for building ships of the largest dimensions; and among the many fine vessels launched from this dockyard are some of the first-rate men of war in the royal navy. In time of war the number of artificers and labourers employed exceeds 3000. Within the walls is a neat brick chapel, erected in 1811, at an expense of £9000. The ordnance wharf occupies a narrow site of land between the church and the river, to the west of the dockyard, and is still called the Old Dock. A large building has been erected in the dockyard for the grinding of paint, and the rolling and smelting of lead by steam.

Prior to the year 1760, the defence of the arsenal was entrusted principally to guard-ships in the river, to forts on its banks, especially at Sheerness, to Upnor Castle, built by Queen Elizabeth, and to a small fort below Gillingham, erected by Charles I.; but in 1758, an act of parliament was passed for the erection of such works as might be requisite for more perfect security, under the provisions of which act the extensive fortifications, called the Lines, were constructed. These works commence above the ordnance wharf, on the bank of the Medway, and are continued round an area one mile in extent from south to north, and half a mile from west to east (including the church of Chatham, the village of Bromp- ton, which is principally inhabited by the artificers in the yard and the barracks, magazines, &c.), to beyond the northern extremity of the dockyard, where they again meet the river. The fortifications were enlarged during the American war, and strengthened by the erec- tion of a strong redoubt on the summit of an eminence commanding the river; and in 1782, an act was pro- cured for their further improvement, under which con- siderable additions have been made to the Lines, which now constitute, next to those of Portsmouth, the most complete and regular fortification in the kingdom. Forts Pitt and Clarence, two redoubts flanking the southern extremity of the Lines, are situated on the heights overlooking the town, and command the upper part of the river; since the conclusion of the war, the former has been used as an hospital for invalids, and the latter as an asylum for lunatics. The lower or ma- rine barracks, adjoining the upper extremity of the dockyard, consist of a uniform range of brick building, inclosing a spacious quadrangle : the upper barracks are also neatly built of brick, and are extensive and commo- dions. The new artillery barracks, in Brompton, built in 1804, are a fine range, forming three sides of a qua- drangle, and containing apartments for the officers, lodg- ings for 1200 men, and requisite stabling; the open side of the quadrangle commands a good view of the Medway in the foreground, and of the Thames in the distance. The artillery hospital, a neat building, erected in 1809, contains wards for one hundred patients.

The TOWN was much improved under the provisions of an act passed in 1772, for paving and lighting it; but the streets are still narrow and inconvenient for carriages. A philosophical and literary institution was established in 1827, the members of which have spacious premises ; and a mechanics' institute was opened in 1837. There are two subscription libraries, one the United Service library, and the other the Marine library ; and a horticultural society has been formed for Rochester, Chatham, and the vicinity. Races are held in August, on the extensive plain without the Lines. There is ready communication with Gravesend by means of the Rochester and Gravesend railway, which commences at Strood, on the left bank of the Medway. The market is on Saturday : fairs, for three days each, were held on May 15th and Sept. 19th, but they have fallen into disuse. Chatham is partly within the jurisdiction of the county magistrates, and partly included in the limits of the city of Rochester. By the act of the 2nd of William IV., cap. 45, it was constituted a borough, with the privilege of sending a member to parliament : the right of election is vested in the £10 householders of a district comprising 1670 acres ; the returning officer is appointed by the sheriff for the county.

The parish, exclusively of the ground whereon the town is built, comprises 3960 acres, of which the surface is in general broken, and the soil a thin chalky earth ; there are tracts of woodland in different parts, covering 1051 acres. The LIVING is a perpetual curacy ; net income, £961 ; patrons and appropriators, the Dean and Chapter of Rochester. The parochial church is a neat plain structure of brick. The original edifice having been destroyed by fire, at the commencement of the fourteenth century, a new one was built under the sanction of a bull from the pope, who granted an indulgence of one year and forty days to all who should contribute to the work. In 1635 it was repaired and enlarged, and the steeple was rebuilt by the commissioners of the royal navy : in 1788, the body of the church was taken down, and rebuilt of brick upon a larger scale ; and the churchyard being found too small, the Board of Ordnance subsequently gave three acres of ground, at a short distance from the church, for a cemetery, which was consecrated in 1828. St. John's church, of the Doric order, with a tower, and containing 1624 sittings, of which 1090 are free, was completed in 1821, at an expense of nearly £15,000, by grant of the Parliamentary Commissioners : the living is a perpetual curacy, in the gift of the Incumbent of Chatham, who also presents to the perpetual curacy of Christ Church. The living of the dockyard chapel is a perpetual curacy, in the patronage of the Lords of the Admiralty. There are places of worship for Baptists, Independents, Primitive and Wesleyan Methodists, and Unitarians ; also a Jews' synagogue. " The Rochester and Chatham Commercial and Mathematical School" was instituted in 1827 ; the building, which was opened on Oct. 1st, 1828, is situated on the Chatham and Maidstone road, and cost £1600. Melville or Marine hospital is a handsome range adjacent to the dockyard, begun in 1827, and finished in the following year, at an expense of £70,000, for the use of the whole naval department ; it is built of brick and stuccoed. St. Bartholomew's Hospital was originally founded in 1078, by Gundulph, Bishop of Rochester, as a lazarhouse : the estate has been invested in the , Dean of Rochester, who is governor and patron ; the institution consists of five persons, namely, the patron or master, and four brethren, two in holy orders, the other two being the town-clerk of Rochester and another layman.

sters, and the whole is surmounted with open balus-
es, divided into sections adorned with urns and
aes. The south front is also very imposing, and has
ouble flight of steps in the centre. The taste and
nificenee of the present duke have been displayed
;he erection of the great northern wing, from the
gns of Wyatville. This splendid wing is 385 feet in
th, and forms a continuation of the east front,
ing the whole line 557 feet, and presenting one of
best specimens of masonry in the kingdom. The
rior is classically beautiful; the northern termina-
being distinguished by an elegant Italian tower, in
construction of which the Doric, the Ionic, and the
inthian orders have been tastefully employed.
he grand entrance to the mansion commands an ex-
sive and varied view of scenery of uncommon beauty :
magnificent hall is adorned with rich paintings, and
nd three sides of it is a gallery defended by open
ustrades. The buildings comprise, besides numerous
tes of apartments for visiters, a large number of
te rooms, including a gorgeous banqueting-hall, great
ing-room, and drawing-room; a sculpture-gallery, in
ich are the finest works of art; a gallery of paintings,
taining rare specimens of the ancient masters; a
:ndid library, 90 feet in length; a music-room, bil-
d-room; armoury; and chapel, which is seated and
d throughout with cedar-wood; and suites of pri-
e apartments for the duke and household. In the
dens, lawns, and shrubberies, are fine pieces of sculp-
:, with water-works and fountains; the orangery is
feet long, and a conservatory covers about an acre
land. Her Majesty, her royal consort, and the court,
ited the Duke of Devonshire on December 1st, 1843;
d remained at Chatsworth till the 4th.

CHATTERIS (St. Peter and St. Paul), a parish,
the union and hundred of North Witchford, Isle
Ely, county of Cambridge, 8¾ miles (E. by N.) from
imsey; containing 4813 inhabitants. This place, which
situated near the river Ouse, is of great antiquity.
980, a Benedictine nunnery was founded here, and
dowed by Alfwen, wife of Earl Ethelstan, and sister
Ednod, first abbot of Ramsey, who was raised to the
: of Dorchester, and was murdered by the Danes in
16 : the nunnery continued to flourish till the Disso-
:ion, when its revenue was estimated at £112. 3. 6.
,e parish comprises 13,454a. 26p., of which about
00 acres are upland and dry, and the remainder, with
: exception of the site of the village, flat, but well
ained; the soil is gravel, alternated with sand and
,y, of which last excellent bricks are made : consider-
le improvement, both in the agriculture and in the
il, has taken place since the inclosure in 1812. Chat-
·is is a franchise under the Bishop of Ely, who holds
:ourt leet for appointing officers, in a house called the
ildhall, given to the parish, with other premises and
ıds, producing together nearly £70 per annum, which
e distributed amongst infirm old men and widows.
ıe living is a vicarage, valued in the king's books at
l0 ; net income, £1370; patron and incumbent, the
:v. M. A. Gathercole : impropriator, Charles Chol-
ondelcy, Esq. The tithes were commuted for land and
rn-rents, under the inclosure act. There are places of
orship for Particular Baptists and Wesleyans. At
unny farm are the subterraneous remains of a chapel,
pposed to have contained the bones of St. Huna. In
559

1757, on opening a tumulus near Sòmersham Ferry,
several human skeletons, some military weapons, an urn,
and a glass vase, were found.

CHATTERLEY, a township, in the parish of Wolstanton, union of Wolstanton and Burslem, N. division of the hundred of Pirehill and of the county of
Stafford, 2 miles (N.) from Newcastle, on the road to
Sandbach; containing 374 inhabitants. It includes the
ancient vills of Dimsdale and Bradwell, and comprises
1563 acres. The houses are scattered.

CHATTISHAM (All Saints and St. Margaret),
a parish, in the incorporation and hundred of Samford,
E. division of Suffolk, 5½ miles (E. by N.) from Ipswich; containing 215 inhabitants, and comprising 713a.
3r. 7p. The living is a discharged vicarage, valued in
the king's books at £4. 13. 5.; patrons and appropriators, the Provost and Fellows of Eton College. The
vicarial tithes have been commuted for £142. 10., and
the glebe comprises 21 acres, with a glebe-house. There
is a place of worship for Wesleyans.

CHATTON (Holy Cross), a parish, in the union of
Glendale, E. division of Glendale ward, N. division
of Northumberland, 4 miles (E.) from Wooler, on
the road to Belford; containing 1725 inhabitants. This
parish, which is intersected by the river Till, comprises
by measurement 15,830 acres, whereof 7035 are arable,
8311 pasture, and 484 woodland. It abounds with limestone and coal, the working of which affords employment to a considerable number of the population; the
latter is chiefly for home consumption. Clay of good
quality is found for the making of bricks and tiles, which
is carried on to a moderate extent; and there are several
quarries of freestone of excellent quality for building.
A large fair is held at Weetwood Bank, on the third
Tuesday in May, for all kinds of stock, and also for
cloth, shoes, hardware, and various other articles. The
living is a vicarage, valued in the king's books at
£12. 16. 0½.; net income, £198; patron, the Duke of
Northumberland; impropriators, the Earl of Tankerville and others. The church was rebuilt about 1763.
A curious stone coffin was discovered in the churchyard
a few years since, while digging a grave, and has been
placed in the chancel of the church; it contained some
human bones, pieces of armour, and a coin of Robert
Bruce. There are vestiges of encampments in various
parts of the parish; and numerous fossils are found in
the limestone-quarries.

CHAWLEY, a tything, in the parish of Cumner,
union of Abingdon, hundred of Hormer, county of
Berks, 5½ miles (N. N. W.) from Abingdon; containing
94 inhabitants.

CHAWLEY (St. James), a parish, in the union of
Crediton, hundred of North Tawton, South Molton
and N. divisions of Devon, 2 miles (S. E. by E.) from
Chulmleigh; containing 850 inhabitants. The parish
comprises 4350 acres, of which 540 are common or
waste. Fairs for cattle are held on May 6th and Dec.
11th. The living is a rectory, valued in the king's,
books at £25. 14. 2.; net income, £455; patron, the
Hon. N. Fellowes. The church has a low steeple
covered with oak shingles, and contains some elegant
screen-work.

CHAWSON, a hamlet, in the parish of Roxton,
hundred of Barford, union and county of Bedford;
containing 195 inhabitants.

CHAWTON (St. Nicholas), a parish, in the union
and hundred of Alton, Alton and N. divisions of the
county of Southampton, 1¼ mile (S. S. W.) from Alton;
containing 460 inhabitants. This parish, which consists
by computation of 2600 acres, whereof several hundred
are rich woodland, and 60 common or waste, is situated
in a district abounding with picturesque scenery. It
comprises a beautiful and fertile valley, watered by
numerous springs that occasionally spread over the
adjacent lands ; and within its limits is one of the
sources of the river Wey. There is a quarry of stone
for building walls and cottages. The village, through
which the high road passes, contains several handsome
houses. The living is a rectqry, valued in the king's
books at £11. 5. 5., and in the gift of Edward Knight,
Esq.: the tithes have been commuted for £500, and
the glebe comprises 70 acres, with a glebe-house. The
church, which was enlarged in 1839 at an expense of £900,
contains a handsome monument to Sir Richard Knight.

CHEADLE (St. Mary), a parish, partly in the union
of Stockport, and partly in that of Altrincham,
hundred of Macclesfield, N. division of the county
of Chester, 7 miles (S.) from Manchester ; containing
10,145 inhabitants, of whom 5463 are in Cheadle-Bulkeley, 2288 in Cheadle-Moseley, and 2394 in Handforth
with Bosden. The parish comprises by measurement
5469 acres, chiefly arable and pasture land ; of these,
1666 acres are in Cheadle-Bulkeley, and 2745 in Cheadle-Moseley. The village, situated near the Mersey, is
remarkable for the beauty and salubrity of its situation,
and its neat appearance. The chief employment of the
inhabitants of the parish is the spinning, bleaching, and
printing of cotton. The Manchester and Birmingham
railway passes through Cheadle-Bulkeley, and the Macclesfield branch diverges from it there; another railway,
from Birkenhead, joining the Manchester and Birmingham railway at Stockport, also passes through a part of
the parish. The living is a rectory, valued in the king's
books at £13. 0. 7½.; net income, £635; patron, the
Rev. D. Broughton : there is a good rectory-house, with
a small glebe. The church is principally in the later
English style, with aisles and a tower, and contains
some monuments of the Brereton and Bulkeley families.
Parts of the screen-work in one of the chapels, and the
roof of the chancel, are supposed to belong to a church
much older ; the date of 1369 can be traced. A church
has been built at Handforth. There are places of worship for Methodists and Roman Catholics. A school at
Cheadle-Moseley, built by subscription, was endowed by
Mr. J. Robinson, in 1785, with three acres of land. A
neat Church of England school, near the church, is
supported by subscription ; and opposite the chapel is a
Roman Catholic school.

CHEADLE (St. Giles), a market-town and parish,
and the head of a union, in the S. division of the hundred of Totmonslow, N. division of the county of
Stafford, 14 miles (N. N. E.) from Stafford, and 147
miles (N. W. by N.) from London; containing 4399
inhabitants. This place is situated in a valley environed
by hills, which, though formerly barren, have been planted
with forest-trees, and have assumed the appearance of
verdure and cultivation. The town, which is intersected
by the roads from Newcastle to Ashbourn, and from
Leek to Uttoxeter, consists of one principal and four
smaller streets : the houses in the main street have, for

chimney and flower pots, affords employment to eral hands. The living is a rectory, valued in the g's books at £17. 5. 5., and in the patronage of St. in's College, Oxford : the tithes have been commuted £625, and the glebe comprises 26 acres, with a be-house. The church, an ancient and spacious fice, was, with the exception of the tower, rebuilt of ck in 1740; the chancel contains several monuments the Lumleys. Sir Edmund Yates, Knt., many years 2 of the justices of the king's bench and common as, noticed with eulogium by Junius in his letters, ided and was interred here ; Bishop Watson was also ried in the parish, of which he had been rector. Of successive rectors, from 1581 to 1662, five became hops, viz., Watson, Andrews, Mountain, Senhouse, l Hackett.

CHEAPSIDES, an extra-parochial liberty, in the ion of Howden, wapentake of Howdenshire, E. ing of York, 5½ miles (E.) from Howden; contain- 47 inhabitants. This place, which adjoins Scalby, prises about 10 acres, being cottages, and plots of d attached to them, on Walling Fen, built and inclosed viously to the general inclosure.

CHEARSLEY (St. Nicholas), a parish, in the union Aylesbury, hundred of Ashendon, county of Buck- ;ham, 3½ miles (N. N. E.) from Thame; containing 3 inhabitants. The parish is supposed to have been scene of a battle which Cerdic and Cynric fought h the Britons in 527, mentioned in the Saxon Chro- le as having occurred at Cerdicesleagh. It comprises measurement 914 acres, about two-thirds of which arable, and the rest pasture. The living is a perpetual racy, in the gift of Miss Grubbe ; net income, £46.

CHEBSEY (All Saints), a parish, in the union 'one, S. division of the hundred of Pirehill, N. vision of the county of Stafford, 2 miles (E. by S.) om Eccleshall; containing, with the township of Cold- orton, 442 inhabitants. The parish comprises about 112 acres of land, whereof 2812a. 3r. 18p. are in iebsey township, which includes the hamlet of Shal- wfield. The village, which is small and ancient, lies in narrow valley near the confluence of the Eccleshall iter with the river Sow. The Liverpool and Birming- m railway passes through the parish. The living is a carage, valued in the king's books at £5. 7. 6.; trons and appropriators, the Dean and Chapter of chfield : the great tithes have been commuted for £63, and the vicarial for £70; the vicar has a glebe 90 acres. The church is an ancient structure, stand- g above the village. In the churchyard was formerly tall pyramidal stone, supposed to be the memorial of bishop slain near this place.

CHECKENDON (St. Peter and St. Paul), a pa- ;h, in the union of Henley, hundred of Langtree, unty of Oxford, 7¼ miles (W.) from Henley-on- iames ; containing 398 inhabitants. The number of res is 3063, of which 2158a. 3r. 39p. are titheable ; iout 746 are beech-woods, and 73 common or waste. ie living is a rectory, valued in the king's books at 19. 9. 4½., and in the patronage of University College, xford : the tithes have been commuted for £560, and .e glebe comprises 117¾ acres. The church is a highly teresting edifice in the Norman style, with a circular ist end and a low embattled tower : there are two fine orman arches, with columns having highly enriched

capitals ; and on the floor are two ancient brasses, dated respectively 1404 and 1424, with engraved effigies. In the chancel is a curious monument to the memory of Christiana, wife of Richard Braybrook, who died in 1629 ; also a monument to the memory of T. Stanyan, Esq., author of a History of Greece, who died in 1751.

CHECKLEY, with Wrinehill, a township, in the parish of Wybunbury, union and hundred of Nant- wich, S. division of the county of Chester, 7 miles (S. E. by E.) from Nantwich ; containing 213 inhabitants. It comprises 1431a. 3r. 31p. The impropriate tithes have been commuted for £140, and the vicarial for £23. 6.

CHECKLEY (St. Mary and All Saints), a parish, in the union of Cheadle, S. division of the hundred of Totmonslow, N. division of the county of Staf- ford, 4 miles (S. S. E.) from Cheadle ; containing, with part of Foxt, 2322 inhabitants. It comprises by mea- surement 6034 acres, whereof 4700 are meadow and pasture, about 850 arable, and 390 woodland : the soil is of a fertile quality. The parish is in three divisions, namely, Tean, Madeley-Holme, and Foxt ; the village of Checkley, which is seated on the north side of the river Tean, is in the first-named division. Beamhurst, Dead- man's-Green, and Fole are hamlets in the parish. The living is a rectory, valued in the king's books at £20. 2. 6.; net income, £576 ; patron and incumbent, the Rev. William Hutchinson : there is a glebe of con- siderable value. The church is an ancient structure, with a tower : the porch and an early English arch leading to the interior are worthy [of notice; there is some painted glass, also a very handsome Saxon font, and a marble tomb with recumbent figures to Sir Jeffrey Fol- jambe. In the churchyard are three crosses, or pyra- midal stones, said to have been erected to the memory of three bishops who fell in a battle between the Saxons and Danes. At Tean is a separate incum- bency. Attached to the church is a Sunday school.—See Tean.

CHEDBURGH (All Saints), a parish, in the union of Thingoe, hundred of Risbridge, W. division of Suffolk, 5½ miles (S. W.) from Bury St. Edmund's ; containing 284 inhabitants, and comprising 566a. 1r. 16p. The living is a discharged rectory, in the gift of the Marquess of Bristol, valued in the king's books at £4. 2. 8½. : the tithes have been commuted for £143. 2., and the glebe consists of nearly 28 acres. The church is a small structure, with an east window in the deco- rated style ; a chancel was built by subscription in 1839, and in 1840 a beautiful tower and spire were added by the marquess, in the early English style. The Hon. William Hervey, in 1812, bequeathed property for the endowment of a school, for which a house has been built at the expense of the Marquess of Bristol.

CHEDDER (St. Andrew), a parish, in the union of Axbridge, hundred of Winterstoke, E. division of Somerset, 2½ miles (E. S. E.) from Axbridge ; contain- ing 2325 inhabitants. This place is of considerable antiquity, having been the occasional residence of the Saxon monarchs, and in the possession of Alfred the Great, who bequeathed his hunting-seat at Chedder, together with his brugge of Ax, and the wet moor, now Nedmore, to his son. The name is generally deduced from Ced, a brow or height, and Dwr, water ; a broad, clear, and rapid stream flows through the parish, and turns some paper-mills. The surface comprises 6697 a. 3r. 24p.; about 1140 acres are arable, 3136 meadow and pasture, 159 woodland, and 2261 in sheep-walks. Chedder Cliff, a vast chasm more than a mile in length, and appearing as if the mountain had been rent by an earthquake from the summit to the base, exhibits a combination of rocky precipices and gloomy caverns, some of the rocks towering 800 feet above the level of the valley. The principal cavern is about 100 feet high at the entrance, and afterwards sinks 300 feet beneath the rocks, branching out into several collateral apartments, and producing a perfect and pleasing echo; the sides and roof are covered with stalactites that have assumed a variety of fanciful forms. The village consists of three or four irregular streets, in one of which stands a dilapidated hexagonal market-cross: it was once a considerable market-town, the grant having been made to Joceline, Bishop of Wells, in the 19th of Henry III.; but it is now principally celebrated for its excellent cheese. Several of the inhabitants are employed in the tanning of leather, and the knitting of worsted stockings; and fairs for horned-cattle and sheep are held on May 4th and Oct. 29th. The living is a vicarage, valued in the king's books at £23. 16. 8.; patrons and appropriators, the Dean and Chapter of Wells: the appropriate and the vicarial tithes have been commuted for £400 each, and the glebe consists of 41 acres, with a glebe-house. The church is a large and handsome structure, with a tower 100 feet high, surmounted by pinnacles. There is a place of worship for Wesleyans. In 1751, Sarah Comer bequeathed £6052 three per cents., producing a dividend of £181. 11., which is applied to the instruction and the relief of the poor. A Sunday school was supported for 40 years, by the celebrated Hannah More.

CHEDDINGTON (St. Giles), a parish, in the union of Leighton-Buzzard, hundred of Cottesloe, county of Buckingham, 4½ miles (N. W.) from Tring; containing, with part of Seabrook hamlet, 439 inhabitants. It comprises by computation 1389 acres, of which 1023 are arable, 215 meadow and pasture, and 140 common. The London and Birmingham railway passes about a mile to the east of the village, and near this place the branch railway to Aylesbury commences. The living is a rectory, valued in the king's books at £15. 9. 7., and in the patronage of the Trustees of the Earl of Bridgewater: the tithes have been commuted for £300, and the glebe contains 81 acres, with a glebe-house.

CHEDDLETON (St. Edward), a parish, in the union of Cheadle, N. division of the hundred of Totmonslow and of the county of Stafford, 3½ miles (S. by W.) from Leek; comprising the townships of Basford, Cheddleton, and Consall or Cunsall; and containing 1824 inhabitants, of whom 1285 are in the township of Cheddleton. The parish consists of 8850 acres, whereof 1000, probably, are woodland, and the remainder chiefly pasture; in some parts sand prevails, in others clay, with peat or a dark soil on the surface, and the scenery is very beautiful. Coal is wrought, and grit-stone and burr-stone quarried; there are also a silk-throwing-mill, a paper-mill established a few years since, a dye-house, a brewery, and some coal and lime wharfs. The river Churnet intersects the parish; and the Churnet Valley railway, and Caldon and Uttoxeter branches of the Trent and Mersey canal, also pass through.

ircely a level field; the hills are composed of a hard
rable fossil rock, and afford rich and extensive views.
e river Parret rises in the parish, and, with the Axe,
ds greatly to the fertility and beauty of the district.
e living is a rectory, valued in the king's books at
. 8. 4., and in the gift of William Trevelyan Cox,
q.: the tithes have been commuted for £128. 10.,
d the glebe comprises 46¾ acres, with a glebe-house.
e church is a handsome edifice, erected on a new site,
1840, chiefly at the expense of Mr. Cox. On one of
: hills are the remains of a Roman encampment, and
the fields below it, is the site of a Roman villa. The
v. Thomas Hare, translator of *Horace*, was rector.

CHEDISTON (St. Mary), a parish, in the union
d hundred of BLYTHING, E. division of SUFFOLK,
miles (W.) from Halesworth; containing 433 inha-
ants, and comprising 2378a. 34p. The living is a
charged vicarage, united to the rectory of Halesworth,
d valued in the king's books at £6. 7. 6.: the impro-
ate tithes have been commuted for £230, and the
arial for £13. 14. 6.; the glebe comprises 61½ acres.
e church is chiefly in the perpendicular style, con-
ting of a nave and chancel, with a Lady chapel on the
rth; it has an embattled tower, and contains a font
Caen stone, curiously sculptured. An almshouse was
1575 vested in trustees, by Henry Claxton, for three
or families.

CHEDWORTH (St. Andrew), a parish, in the
ion of NORTHLEACH, hundred of RAPSGATE, E. divi-
n of the county of GLOUCESTER, 4½ miles (W. S. W.)
m Northleach; containing 983 inhabitants. It com-
ises by.computation 5000 acres, the soil of which is
iefly light, and good barley land. The living is a
carage, valued in the king's books at £7. 8. 4., and in
e patronage of Queen's College, Oxford. The vicarial
hes have been commuted for £278. 7., with a glebe of
0 acres; and the impropriate for £371. 2. payable to
e master, and £185. 11. to the usher, of Northleach
ammar school: the masters also have 118¼ acres of
be. The church contains a handsome stone pulpit,
d is supposed to have been built in the reign of
enry VI. In 1760, a Roman hypocaust was discovered
Lestercomb Bottom, in the parish, with a brick floor
d pillars, a spring, and a cistern, the bricks of which
re the inscription "*a'rviri.*" On a hill a little above
a large tumulus, in which, on the removal of a stone
: upright at its mouth, a great quantity of human
nes was exposed. Chedworth gave the title of Baron
the family of Howe, which became extinct on the
ath of John, Lord Chedworth, in 1804.

CHEDZOY (St. Mary), a parish, in the union of
IIDGWATER, hundred of NORTH PETHERTON, W. divi-
n of SOMERSET, 2¾ miles (E. by N.) from Bridg-
iter; containing 507 inhabitants. It is situated about
mile and a quarter from the Bath and Exeter road,
d comprises 1655a. 2r. 36p.: the soil is rather of a
ndy nature, but tolerably fertile. The river Parret,
ich runs through Bridgwater, affords facility for the
nveyance of coal; and the Bristol and Exeter railway
within three miles of the village. The living is a rec-
ry, valued in the king's books at £38. 7. 11., and in
e gift of the Rev. Richard James Luscombe: the tithes
ve been commuted for £380, and the glebe comprises
acres, with a glebe-house. The church is a spacious
uciform structure in the Norman style, with a lofty

embattled tower, and a north and south porch, over the
latter of which is the date 1579. Roman coins have
frequently been discovered; and in 1701, some earthen
urns and a fibula were dug up near the church.

CHEESEBURN-GRANGE, a township, in the parish
of STAMFORDHAM, union of CASTLE ward, N. E. division
of TINDALE ward, S. division of NORTHUMBERLAND,
12 miles (N. W. by W.) from Newcastle-upon-Tyne;
containing 56 inhabitants. This township, anciently
called Chyseburgh, is situated on the river Pont, and
comprises 795a. 2r. 39p. of high table land, upon a substratum of blue mountain limestone: it is the property
of Edward Riddell, Esq., high sheriff for the county in
1841, to whose ancestor the estate passed, in the female
line, from Sir Thomas Widdrington. Mr.·Riddell has a
beautiful seat here, which has been much improved, and
attached to the mansion is a Roman Catholic chapel.
The township having been annexed to the abbey at
Hexham, it is free from large tithes: the vicarial tithes
have been commuted for £8. 13., and 10s. are payable to
the Bishop of Durham.

CHEETHAM, a township, in the parish and union
of MANCHESTER, hundred of SALFORD, S. division of the
county of LANCASTER, 2 miles (N. by W.) from Manchester; containing 6082 inhabitants. The township
lies on the new and old roads to Bury; is beautifully
situated on rising ground; and comprises 954 acres, all
pasture land. It abounds with the private residences of
Manchester merchants and others, among which is
Green Hill, the seat of Edward Loyd, Esq., banker of
that town. The views of the surrounding country are
very extensive. The river Irwell separates the township
from Salford. St. Mark's church here was built in
1794, at the expense of the Rev. Charles Ethelston: the
living is a perpetual curacy, patron and incumbent, the
Rev. Hart Ethelston, M.A., grandson of the founder;
net income, £350. An ecclesiastical district is assigned
to the church, including portions of Crumpsall and
Broughton. St. Luke's church, built on land given by
the Earl of Derby, was consecrated in October, 1839; it
cost £15,000, and is an elegant structure in the decorated
English style, with a tower surmounted by a graceful
spire, forming a conspicuous object in the scenery: the
interior is particularly neat. The living is a perpetual
curacy, in the patronage of Mr. Loyd and four other
Trustees; net income, £300, with a good glebe-house.
St. Thomas's church, at the corner of Derby-street,
Redbank, was commenced in 1843, by the Manchester
and Eccles Church Building Society. The living is a
perpetual curacy, in the gift of the Bishop of Chester.
There are two meeting-houses for Wesleyans, with a
burial-ground and a school attached to one of them;
also a place of worship for Associated Methodists. St.
Chad's Roman Catholic chapel, in York-street, was commenced in the spring of 1846, and completed in August
1847, at a cost of £8500: it is an elegant edifice of the
14th century, 134 feet long, and has a fine tower. Connected with St. Mark's church are good schools, towards
the enlargement of which a government grant was made
in 1844; they contain a useful village library. Excellent
schools are also attached to St. Luke's.—See CRUMP-
SALL.

CHELBOROUGH, EAST, or LUCCOMBE, a parish,
in the union of BEAMINSTER, hundred of TOLLERFORD,
Sherborne division of DORSET, 16 miles (N. W.) from

Dorchester; containing 96 inhabitants. The parish was anciently called Luccombe, and East Chelborough was a hamlet within its limits. It comprises 948*a*. 1*r*., of which about 258 acres are arable, 594 pasture, 62 wood and plantation, and 23 orchard and garden-ground. The living is a rectory, valued in the king's books at £8, and in the gift of the Rev. Blakeley Cooper; the tithes have been commuted for £160, and the glebe comprises 110 acres, with a glebe-house.

CHELBOROUGH, WEST, a parish, in the union of BEAMINSTER, hundred of TOLLERFORD, Sherborne division of DORSET, 2½ miles (W. N. W.) from Evershot; containing 58 inhabitants, and consisting of 578*a*. 3*r*. 28*p*. The living is a discharged rectory, valued in the king's books at £4. 15. 7½., and in the gift of the family of Rolle, and John Bragge, Esq. : the tithes have been commuted for £82, and the glebe comprises 29¼ acres.

CHELDON (ST. MARY), a parish, in the union of SOUTH MOLTON, hundred of WITHERIDGE, South Molton and N. divisions of DEVON, 4 miles (E. by S.) from Chulmleigh; containing 90 inhabitants, and consisting by estimation of 1012 acres, of which 332 are common or waste. There are quarries of stone, which is chiefly used for the roads. The living is a discharged rectory, valued in the king's books at £4. 18. 6½., and in the patronage of the Hon. N. Fellowes : the tithes have been commuted for a yearly rent-charge of £77, and the glebe comprises 35 acres of land. The church is a small neat edifice.

CHELFORD, a chapelry, in the parish of PRESTBURY, union and hundred of MACCLESFIELD, N. division of the county of CHESTER, 5 miles (S. E. by E.) from Knutsford; containing, with the township of Old Withington, 392 inhabitants, of whom 201 are in Chelford township. This township comprises 1161*a*. 34*p*., of which about a fourth is arable land, of a level surface, and a sandy soil. It lies on the Knutsford and Macclesfield road, and five roads meet in the village. The Birtles and Henbury brooks unite immediately below the chapel, forming in Astle Park a fine sheet of water, which empties itself into a brook called Peover-leve. Here is a station on the Manchester and Birmingham railway. Astle Park is the seat of J. Dixon, Esq. The living is a perpetual curacy; net income, £128; patron and impropriator, Mr. Dixon : there is a glebe-house, with 11½ acres of glebe; and in Newton, near Middlewich, are also 30 acres. The chapel, rebuilt in 1776, is a plain edifice. In 1754, John Parker, Esq., erected a school, and endowed it with £50, to which Thomas Moss and Samuel Brook added each £100.

CHELL, a township, in the parish of WOLSTANTON, union of WOLSTANTON and BURSLEM, N. division of the hundred of PIREHILL and of the county of STAFFORD, 2 miles (N.) from Burslem; containing 737 inhabitants. It is divided into two townsteads, called Great and Little Chell, containing 740 acres: coal-mines are wrought on the confines. The village, which is seated on an eminence, and on the road from Newcastle to Congleton, is chiefly occupied by potters. There is a place of worship for Primitive Methodists. The workhouse for the parishes of Wolstanton and Burslem, lately erected here, is a fine capacious structure of gabled architecture. At Turnhurst, in the township, James Brindley, the eminent engineer, died in 1772.

iefly inhabited by persons engaged in dredging for
ne, which is found on a ledge of rocks six or seven
les out at sea, east of Harwich, and is made into
man cement; nearly thirty boats are employed in the
de. The living is a discharged rectory, valued in the
ig's books at £8. 10., and in the patronage of the
own : the tithes have been commuted for £346. 10.
ere are places of worship for Baptists and Wesleyans.
e noted John Henley, familiarly termed " Orator
enley," was for a short time rector.

CHELMSFORD (St. Mary), a market-town and
rish, and the head of a union, in the hundred of
IELMSFORD, S. division of Essex, of which it is the
ief town, 29 miles (N. E. by E.) from London, on the
ad to Yarmouth; containing, with the hamlet of
oulsham, 6789 inhabitants. This place, which is
thin a short distance of the *Cæsaromagus* of the Ro-
ans, derives its name from an ancient ford on the
ielmer, near the natural confluence of that river with
e Cann, into which its stream is previously diverted
an artificial channel near the bridge. In the reign of
lward the Confessor, and at the time of the Norman
rvey, it was in the possession of the bishops of Lon-
n; and two buildings, still called Bishop's Hall and
shop's Mill, seem to indicate its having been either
rmanently or occasionally their residence. In other
spects it was an inconsiderable place till the reign of
enry I., when Maurice, Bishop of London, built a stone
idge of three arches over the river Cann; and, divert-
g the road, which previously passed through Writtle,
ade Chelmsford the great thoroughfare to the eastern
arts of the county, and to Suffolk and Norfolk. From
iis period the town increased in importance; and its
rade so much improved, that, in the reign of Edward
II., it sent four representatives to a grand council at
Vestminster. A convent for Black, or Dominican, friars
xisted at an early date, the foundation of which has
een erroneously attributed to Malcolm, King of Scot-
ind : its revenue, at the Dissolution, was £9. 6. 5. In
his convent, of which only the site is visible, Thomas
.angford, a friar, compiled a Universal Chronicle, from
he creation to his own time. During the late war with
`rance, two extensive ranges of barracks, for 4000 men,
vere erected near the town, both of which have been
aken down; and at a short distance from it, a line of
mbankments, defended by star batteries, of which some
races are still remaining, was raised to protect the ap-
roaches to the metropolis from the eastern coast.

The TOWN is surrounded by interesting scenery. It
s well paved, and lighted with gas : the houses, several
f which, on both sides of the town, have gardens
xtending to the river, are in general modern and well
iuilt; and the inhabitants are amply supplied with
vater. Considerable improvements have been made of
ate years in the appearance of the neighbourhood : a
iandsome iron bridge has been erected over the Chelmer;
ind more recently a road has been formed, which, com-
nencing at the twenty-eighth milestone on the London
oad, and crossing the river Cann by an elegant iron
ridge (about one hundred yards from the stone bridge,
rected in 1787, and connecting Chelmsford with the
iamlet of Moulsham), enters the town about the centre
if the High-street. A building called the Institute has
een erected for the delivery of lectures, for concerts,
ind public meetings; and near the Eastern Counties
565

railway, which passes a little to the west, numerous
villas have been erected : this railway has a station here,
21 miles from the Colchester station, and 30 from the
London terminus. Races, which continue for two days,
are held in August, on Galleywood Common, about two
miles distant, where is an excellent two-mile course.

The trade consists principally in corn, which is sent
to London, and in the traffic arising from the situation
of the town as a great public thoroughfare : there are
several large corn-mills on the banks of the Chelmer.
A navigable canal to the river Blackwater, twelve miles
distant, was constructed in 1796. The market is on
Friday, for corn, cattle, and provisions; and fairs are
held on May 12th and November 12th. The town is
within the jurisdiction of the county magistrates, who
hold petty-sessions for the division every Tuesday and
Friday; and constables and other officers are appointed
at the court leet of the lord of the manor, who also holds
a court baron occasionally. The powers of the county
debt-court of Chelmsford, established in 1847, extend
over the registration-districts of Chelmsford and Witham.
The assizes and sessions for the county, and the election
of knights for the southern division of the shire, take
place here. The shire-hall is an elegant and commodious
structure, fronted with Portland stone, and having a
rustic basement, from which rise four handsome pillars
of the Ionic order, supporting a triangular pediment;
the front is ornamented with appropriate figures, in
basso-relievo, of Wisdom, Justice, and Mercy : in the
lower part is an area for the corn-market. The old
county gaol, a spacious stone building, in Moulsham,
was completed in 1777, at an expense of upwards of
£18,000; it is appropriated exclusively to the reception
of persons confined for debt, and for prisoners committed
for trial. Adjoining the gaol, and incorporated with it,
is the house of correction, for convicted female prisoners;
it was built in 1806, at a cost of about £7500. The new
convict gaol at Springfield Hill, on the road to Colchester, is a very extensive and well-arranged edifice of
brick ornamented with stone, completed in 1825, at an
expense of £55,739; and since enlarged. A building
has been erected within the last few years for the reception of vagrants.

The parish comprises 2348 acres, the soil of which is
generally a deep rich loam, occasionally intermixed with
gravel, and producing fair average crops. The LIVING
is a rectory, valued in the king's books at £31. 2. 6.,
and in the patronage of Lady St. John Mildmay : the
tithes have been commuted for £500, and the glebe
contains 15¾ acres, with a glebe-house. The body of
the church has been rebuilt, at an expense of £13,000,
the former having fallen down in 1800, from the un-
skilfulness of some workmen who, in digging a vault,
undermined two of the principal pillars: it is a stately
structure in the later English style, with a square embattled tower, crowned with pinnacles, and surmounted
by a lofty spire. A chapel in a modern style has been
erected at Moulsham, on a site given by Lady Mildmay.
There are places of worship for Independents, Baptists,
Irvingites, the Society of Friends, Wesleyans, and Roman Catholics. The free grammar school was founded
and endowed, in 1551, by Edward VI. : the income is
about £488; and, in common with the schools at
Maldon and Brentwood, it has an exhibition of £6 per
annum to Caius College, Cambridge. The school-house

was built by R. Benyon, Esq., in 1782, on the site of a more ancient one erected by Sir John Tyrrell, Bart. Philemon Holland, translator of Camden's *Britannia*, and a native of Chelmsford ; John Dee, the celebrated mathematician ; Sir Walter Mildmay, Bart., founder of Emmanuel College, Cambridge ; and Dr. Plume, Archdeacon of Rochester, received the rudiments of their education in the establishment. The union of Chelmsford comprises 31 parishes or places, and contains a population of 30,603. The inhabitants of an island in the river have from time immemorial practised the form of electing a representative, on a dissolution of parliament or the vacation of a member for the county : the ceremony concludes with the chairing of the successful candidate, who is dipped in the river, and the chair broken to pieces.

CHELSEA, a suburb of the metropolis, comprising the parishes of St. Luke and Upper Chelsea, in the Kensington division of the hundred of Ossulstone, county of Middlesex ; containing, with part of the chapelry of Knightsbridge, 40,179 inhabitants. This place was anciently called *Chelcheth* or *Chelchith*, probably from the Saxon *Ceosl*, or *Cesol*, sand, and *Hythe*, a harbour ; from which its present name is derived. In 785, a synod for the reformation of religion in England was assembled here by the legates of Pope Adrian. The beauty of its situation on the Thames, which is wider here than in any other part above London bridge, made it, at an early period, the residence of illustrious persons, whose superb MANSIONS procured for it the appellation of the " village of palaces." Among these was the residence of the chancellor, Sir Thomas More, at the north end of Beaufort-row ; which, after being successively in the occupation of several distinguished characters, was taken down by Sir Hans Sloane, in the year 1740. The bishops of Winchester had a palace at the upper end of Cheyne-walk, which, under an act of parliament passed in 1823, enabling the bishop to alienate it from the see, was taken down in 1824. Queen Elizabeth had also a palace here ; and Sir Robert Walpole resided for some time in a mansion previously belonging to the crown, on the site of which a fine edifice was erected in 1810, by Gen. Gordon. The mansion and gardens of the Earl of Ranelagh were converted into a place of public amusement, which after having been fashionably attended for a considerable time, was closed in 1805, and the buildings taken down ; the site is now occupied by dwelling-houses. Just above Battersea bridge, near the western extremity of Chelsea, are Cremorne Gardens, occupying the grounds of a villa that stood here belonging to Viscountess Cremorne, which was built by Theophilus, Earl of Huntingdon, in the reign of George II.

CHELSEA comprehends the old town on the bank of the Thames, over which is a bridge of wood leading to Battersea, in Surrey ; the new buildings, erected since 1777, and called Hans Town, in honour of Sir Hans Sloane, a former lord of the manor ; and several ranges of building of recent erection in various directions. In the old town is Cheyne-walk, which contains many handsome houses, commanding an interesting view of the river and the scenery on its opposite bank ; in the new town are, Sloane-street, a regular range of respectable houses, nearly a mile in length, Sloane-square, and Upper and Lower Cadogan places. The streets are partially paved,

566

and well lighted with gas, under the superintendence of 40 commissioners, including the rector and the churchwardens, appointed annually by act of parliament obtained about the year 1820 : an act for more effectually paving, lighting, and otherwise improving the parish of St. Luke, exclusively of the district of Hans Town, was passed in 1845. The inhabitants are supplied with water by the Chelsea Water-Works Company, incorporated in 1724. There are a soap-manufactory, two breweries, a manufactory for papier-maché, and an extensive floorcloth manufactory : a considerable trade is carried on in coal ; and in the neighbourhood are large tracts of ground cultivated by market-gardeners. The county magistrates hold a petty-session here for the hundred every Tuesday ; and four headboroughs, nine constables, and other officers are appointed at the court for the manor. The *Botanic Gardens* were established in 1673, by the Company of Apothecaries, to whom Sir Hans Sloane granted, at a quit-rent of £5 per annum, four acres on the bank of the river ; they contain a great variety of medicinal plants systematically arranged, a hot-house, green-houses, and a library, in which are many volumes of natural history: Lectures are delivered periodically to the students, by a demonstrator appointed for that purpose. In the centre of the gardens is a fine statue of Sir Hans Sloane, by Rysbrach ; and in the front opposite to the river are two remarkably fine cedars of Libanus. A second botanic garden, occupying more than six acres, and well stocked with plants arranged after the Linnæan system, in seventeen compartments, was established in 1807, near Sloane-street, where lectures are delivered in May and June.

The Royal Hospital for veteran soldiers, a handsome structure of brick ornamented with columns, quoins, and cornices of stone, erected after a design by Sir Christophen Wren, at an expense of £150,000, towards defraying which the projector, Sir Stephen Fox, grandfather of Charles James Fox, contributed £13,000, was begun in the reign of Charles II., and completed in that of William III. The buildings occupy a spacious quadrangle, in the centre of which is a statue in bronze of Charles II. ; the east and west sides, which are 360 feet in length, comprise wards for the pensioners, and the governor's house. In the centre of the north side is a large vestibule lighted by a handsome dome, with the great hall on one side, in which the pensioners dine, and on the other, the chapel, a neat and lofty edifice, containing a handsome altar-piece with a good painting of the Resurrection. The south side of the quadrangle is open to the river, affording a fine view of the extensive gardens, which reach to its margin. There are smaller quadrangles, in which are the infirmaries and various offices, formed by the addition of wings to the extremities of the north side of the large quadrangle. On the north side of the hospital is an inclosure of thirteen acres, planted with avenues of trees. The number of inpensioners is about 500, and of out-pensioners indefinite ; the annual expenditure is from £700,000 to £800,000. *York Hospital*, also in the parish, is a receptacle for wounded soldiers arriving from foreign stations, who are waiting for a vacancy in the royal hospital. The *Royal Military Asylum* was founded in 1801, by the Duke of York, for the support and education of the orphan children of soldiers, and of those whose fathers are serving on foreign stations : at present the number boys is 350.˙ There were formerly nearly 1000 boys the institution, and 300 girls ; but the latter, in 1823, re removed to Southampton, where a cavalry barrack, ich had been previously converted into an asylum 400 boys, was appropriated to their use. The pre- ses, which are of brick ornamented with stone, m three sides of a quadrangle : the west front con- ts of a centre, with a stone portico of the Doric order, mected with two wings by an arcade; and within the munds is a handsome chapel.

The ancient parish of Chelsea has lately been divided o two distinct and separate parishes. The living of . LUKE's is a rectory, valued in the king's books at 3. 6. 8.; net income, £1003 ; patron, Earl Cadogan. e church, erected in 1824, at an expense of £40,000, which the Parliamentary Commissioners granted 785, is a magnificent structure in the decorated and er styles of English architecture, with a tower crowned dome turrets at the angles ; the west front is strik- ly beautiful. The interior has an impressive grandeur effect, arising from the loftiness of the nave, which ι a triforium and a fine range of clerestory windows three lights, and is separated from the aisles by stered columns and pointed arches : the altar-piece ornamented with shrine-work of elegant design, and th a painting of the Descent from the Cross ; the east ndow is lofty and of graceful character, and the roof the building is groined. The living of UPPER CHEL- A is a rectory not in charge ; net income, £840 ; tron, Earl Cadogan. The church, situated in Sloane- reet, and dedicated to the Trinity, is a handsome edi- e in the later English style, with two minaret turrets , the west end, erected in 1830, at an expense of 5849, by grant from the Commissioners.

The old church, now used as a *Chapel*, is a small edi- ːe, partly in the early and partly in the decorated nglish style, with a low tower surmounted by a cam- anile turret : it is chiefly of brick, and was built in ιe early part of the sixteenth century ; it was enlarged, ιd the tower added, about 1670. At the end of the orth aisle is a chapel in the decorated style, and at the ttremity of the south aisle is one erected by Sir Thomas fore, in 1520. Among the many interesting monu- ents are those of Sir Thomas More; Dr. Edward hamberlayne, author of *The Present State of England*; homas Shadwell, poet-laureate in the reign of William ιd Mary ; Sir Hans Sloane; and others. The living a perpetual curacy ; net income, £300; patron, the .ector of St. Luke's. An episcopal chapel, called *Park* ιapel, was built by Sir Richard Manningham, in 1718, ιd is in the gift of J. D. Paul, Esq. *Christ Church*, tuated in Queen-streward, and consecrated in June, 1839, a neat edifice of brick, in the early English style, with campanile turret surmounted by a dwarf spire ; it was ·ected by the Trustees of Miss Hyndman, at a cost of early £4000, and will accommodate 1200 persons. The ving is in the gift of the Trustees. *St. Saviour's* dis- ·ict church, behind Hans-place, in Upper Chelsea, was lso built for a congregation of 1200 persons, at an esti- mated expense of £5000, of which one-half was ranted by the Metropolitan Church Building Society, nd the remainder raised by voluntary contributions; ː was consecrated in May, 1840. A district church edicated to *St. Jude* has been since erected in Turk's- ɔw, in the parish of Upper Chelsea. The two livings
567

are in the gift of the Rector. *St. Mark's College*, Stanley Grove, is a training institution for masters of national schools, with a chapel annexed, and nearly 60 young men have been prepared here since the foundation. At Whitelands is an institution for training schoolmis- tresses ; the building will accommodate ˙75 young women, and in connexion with it is a large school taught by the pupils in training. There are places of worship for Baptists, Independents, Wesleyans, and Roman Catholics. John King, A.M., editor of some of the tragedies of Euripides ; and Dr. Thomas Martyn, F.R.S., an eminent antiquary and natural philosopher, and regius professor of botany at Cambridge for sixty-four years, were natives of the parish.

CHELSFIELD (ST. MARY), a parish, in the union of BROMLEY, hundred of RUXLEY, lathe of SUTTON-AT- HONE, W. division of KENT, 6¼ miles (S. E.) from Bromley ; containing 1541 inhabitants. It comprises 4692 acres, of which 578 are woodland. The living is a rectory, valued in the king's books at £24. 14. 2., and in the patronage of All Souls' College, Oxford : the tithes have been commuted for £820, and the glebe comprises 53 acres, with a glebe-house. The church is in the early English style, with a tower and spire at the north-east angle of the nave. At Farnborough, in the parish, is a chapel of ease.

CHELSHAM (ST. LEONARD), a parish, in the union of GODSTONE, Second division of the hundred of TAN- DRIDGE, E. division of SURREY, 6 miles (S. E.) from Croydon ; containing 347 inhabitants. It is ecclesias- tically consolidated with Warlingham (*which see*), under the title of Warlingham with Chelsham. The church is in the early English style, and capable of accommodating about 200 persons ; the chancel is separated from the body of the building by an oak screen of great beauty and elaborate carving. At Ledgers, in the parish, at a short distance from the dwelling-house of the proprietor, is a moat, in which, on its being partially cleared out a few years ago, several mutilated remains of ancient vases were discovered.

CHELSWORTH.—See CHELLESWORTH.

CHELTENHAM (ST. MARY), a borough, market- town, and parish, and the head of a union, in the hun- dred of CHELTENHAM, E. division of the county of GLOUCESTER, 9 miles (E. N. E.) from Gloucester, and 95 (W. N. W.) from London ; containing, according to the census of 1841, 31,411 inhabitants ; and now consider- ably more. This place takes its name from the small river Chelt, which rises at Dowdeswell, in the vicinity, and runs through the town in its course to the Severn. The manor belonged to Edward the Confessor, and was afterwards held by the Conqueror; in 1199 it was granted to Henry de Bohun, Earl of Hereford, who ex- changed it with King John for other lands : it was next given to the abbey of Feschamp, in Normandy, and sub- sequently to the nunnery of Sion, in Middlesex, on the dissolution of which it reverted to the crown. Chelten- ham derives its importance from its mineral springs. The oldest of these was noticed in 1716, and since that time various others have been discovered, possessing different proportions of chalybeate, aperient salts, chiefly sulphate of soda, sulphate of magnesia, and oxyde of iron held in solution by carbonic acid ; the last˙ was dis- covered in 1803, by Dr. Thomas Jameson, according to whose analysis it contains a greater proportion of sulphureous gas than the others, and, in many instances, bears a strong affinity to the Harrogate water. They are efficacious in the cure of jaundice and other diseases of the liver, in dyspepsia, and in the complaints arising from the debilitating influence of hot climates. In 1721, the old well, or spa, to the south of the town, was inclosed; and in 1738 Captain Henry Skillicorn erected over it a brick pavilion supported on four arches, built a pump-room, and laid out walks for the accommodation of visiters. In 1780, the number of lodging-houses amounted only to thirty; but since the visit of George III., with the queen and princesses, in 1788, Cheltenham has been rapidly rising into celebrity as a place of fashionable resort; and at present it is eminent for the elegance of its buildings, the extent and variety of its accommodations, and the rank and number of its visiters, of whom, in the course of the season, there are generally not less than 15,000. It now assumes, also, more the character of a permanent residence of the gentry than formerly.

The TOWN is pleasantly situated on an extensive plain, sheltered on the north and east by the Cotswold Hills, and consists of numerous fine streets, the principal of which is more than a mile and a half in length, containing many excellent ranges of building, interspersed occasionally with houses of more ancient date and less pretending character. To the south of this street are a crescent and colonnade, and the upper and the lower promenade, lately built; and on each side are dwellings displaying much beauty and variety of architectural decoration. The masonic hall, in Portland-street, is a handsome edifice in the style of a Roman mausoleum, completed in 1823, and decorated in front and on one side with the insignia of the order of freemasonry. The streets are well paved, and lighted with gas, under an act procured in the 59th of George III. and amended in the 2nd of George IV.: the Gas-light and Coke Company was formed pursuant to an act passed in 1819; and in 1824 an act was obtained for the establishment of water-works, under the direction of a company. An act was also passed, in 1833, for the better sewerage, draining, and cleansing of the town. About half a mile towards the south is the Montpelier spa: the pump-room, a spacious rotunda, has a noble colonnade in front, above the centre of which is the figure of a lion couchant. Nearer the town stood the Imperial spa, an elegant building in the Grecian style of architecture, opened in 1818; this, however, has disappeared, and on its site has been erected the Queen's Hotel, one of the largest hotels in Europe. The Old well, or original spa, was enlarged by the erection of a new pump-room in 1803. There are also the chalybeate spa, opened in 1802; the Cambray chalybeate spa, discovered in 1807; and Alstone spa, opened in 1809. On the north side of Cheltenham is Pittville, where a new town has been planned on a magnificent scale, by Joseph Pitt, Esq.: the pump-room, of which the first stone was laid on the 4th of May, 1825, is a grand edifice, erected at an expense of more than £20,000. A fine assemblage of houses, also, has been formed to the south of the Montpelier pump-room, on the Lansdowne and Suffolk estates; it consists of a crescent of 48 handsome houses, and of elegant terraces, and parades, constituting by far the most splendid part of the town. Cheltenham contains warm, cold, medicated, and vapour

e structure in the later English style, was erected by scription, but finished by Lord Sherborne, and was secrated in 1823. This is a chapel of ease to the mother rch, and is served by stipendiary curates. *St. Paul's* rch, an edifice of the Grecian-Ionic order, with a tico and tower, was completed in 1831, at a cost of 00, half of which was defrayed by a grant from the liamentary Commissioners. This, also, is a chapel of e to the parent church. *St. James'* church, Suffolk-are, *St. John's*, Berkeley-street, and *Christ-Church*, sdowne, were erected under what is called the Forty rs' act, 5 George IV., cap. 5, by which the patronage n Trustees for forty years, after which period it will se to the incumbent of Cheltenham. The livings are petual curacies, but without districts assigned ; and income of each is derived from pew-rents, having no er endowment. Another church, *St. Peter's*, on the kesbury road, was commenced in 1847, in the Nor-n style ; a district has been assigned to it under the 6th and 7th Victoria, cap. 37, and on the consecration he church the district will be constituted an eccle-tical parish. A spacious burial-ground has been pur-sed by the parishioners. There are places of worship Baptists, the Society of Friends, the Connexion of Countess of Huntingdon, Independents, Wesleyan l other Methodists, and Roman Catholics. The ptist meeting-house has a burial-ground attached to and there is a fund of £25 per annum, for distri-ion among the poor of that congregation.

The *Free Grammar school* was established and endowed 1574, by Richard Pates ; the endowment, augmented Queen Elizabeth, produces a salary of £30 per um to the master, who is appointed by Corpus risti College, Oxford. There are eight scholarships Pembroke College, Oxford, founded in 1682, by George wnsend, for boys from Gloucester, Cheltenham, ipping-Campden, and Northleach, with preference in sentation to his donatives of Uxbridge and Coln-ok : the same benefactor instituted and endowed school here, for poor boys, and similar schools in the isbes of Winchcomb, Chipping-Campden, North-eh, and Nether Guyting, or Blockley, and for ap-nticing them he appropriated part of the income, ich amounts to £207. The Rev. William Stanley, in 04, gave land producing £25 per annum, subject to a t-charge of £8, the residue being applied to the same rpose. A portion of an endowment by Lady Capel, ounting to £37. 10. per annum, is paid for the in-uction of poor children. There are also national, ncasterian, and infants' schools, maintained by sub-iption. A proprietary college, the object of which is supply a good general education, founded on sound igious principles, was opened on the 22nd of June, 43 : the building is entirely of stone raised from dswell-hill, near the town, and has a façade 240 feet length ; the cost of its erection exceeded £8000. It ntains 300 boys, "the sons of noblemen and gentle-n," who are prepared for the universities in the clas-al department, and for the professions in the civil and litary departments. Almshouses for six persons were nded and endowed by Richard Pates, in 1574. A lispensary and casualty ward," established in 1813, d lately enlarged, is supported by subscription; and ere are many other charitable institutions, among ich may be noticed the female orphan asylum, the

Coburg Society for the relief of indigent married women in child-birth, and the Dorcas Society. The poor law union of Cheltenham comprises 13 parishes or places, and contains a population of 40,221.

CHELVESTON (*St. John the Baptist*), a parish, in the union of Thrapston, hundred of Higham-Ferrers, N. division of the county of Northampton, 2 miles (E. by N.) from Higham-Ferrers ; containing, with the hamlet of Caldecott, 372 inhabitants. This parish, which consists of 1754a. 3r. 36p., extends from the river Nene to the border of Bedfordshire, and the road from Higham-Ferrers to Kimbolton crosses it. The living is united to the vicarage of Higham-Ferrers : the tithes were commuted for land in 1801. A school was founded in 1760, by Abigail Bailey and Ann Levett, who endowed it with land, producing £12 per annum. James Sawyer, in 1708, endowed almshouses with £18 per annum.

CHELVEY (*St. Bridget*), a parish, in the union of Bedminster, hundred of Hartcliffe with Bedmin-ster, E. division of Somerset, 9 miles (W. S. W.) from Bristol; containing 54 inhabitants. It comprises 442a. 1r. 39p., and is intersected by the Bristol and Exeter railroad. The living is a discharged rectory, valued in the king's books at £4. 9. 7., and in the patronage of C. K. K. Tynte, Esq. : the tithes have been commuted for £95, and the glebe comprises 24 acres, and a house. The church is a neat edifice with a handsome tower.

CHELWOOD (*St. Leonard*), a parish, in the union of Clutton, hundred of Keynsham, E. division of Somerset, 2 miles (S. E.) from Pensford ; containing 260 inhabitants. It abounds with coal. The living is a discharged rectory, valued in the king's books at £5. 7. 6., and in the patronage of the Bishop of Bath and Wells : the tithes have been commuted for £175, and the glebe comprises 38 acres, with a glebe-house. The tower of the church was rebuilt in 1772. There is an endowed chapel belonging to the Independents.

CHELWORTH, a hamlet, in the parish of Crud-well, union and hundred of Malmesbury, Malmesbury and Kingswood, and N. divisions of Wilts ; containing 58 inhabitants.

CHENIES, anciently Isenhamsted, or Eastman-sted (*St. Michael*), a parish, in the union of Amer-sham, hundred of Burnham, county of Buckingham, 4 miles (E. by N.) from Amersham ; containing 625 inhabitants. This parish once belonged to the family of Cheynes, lords of the manor ; and the old manor-house, which was much improved in the reign of Henry VIII., by Lord Russell, into whose family it had come by mar-riage with the Cheynes', is still in tolerable preservation. The parish comprises about 1400 acres, nearly all belonging to the Duke of Bedford : the surface is hilly, and the soil a gravelly loam, resting on chalk. The manufacture of paper is carried on extensively. The living is a rectory, valued in the king's books at £12. 16. 0½., and in the gift of his Grace : the tithes have been commuted for £411. 6. 8., and the glebe com-prises 30 acres, with a glebe-house. Attached to the church is a chapel, built in 1556 by Anne, Countess of Bedford, pursuant to the will of her deceased lord, John, Earl of Bedford, and containing many very interesting and some superb monuments of the Russell family, espe-cially one to Lord William Russell, beheaded in 1683, and who lies interred in the vault beneath, with his heroic wife, Lady Rachel : in the vault are upwards of fifty coffins, with inscriptions bearing dates from 1591 to the present time. There is a place of worship for Baptists. An almshouse for ten poor persons was founded and endowed in 1603, by Anne, Countess of Warwick, daughter of the second earl of Bedford. John Russell, ancestor of the Duke of Bedford, was raised to the peerage in 1538-9, by the title of Baron Russell of Chenies, which his descendants continue to bear.

CHEPSTOW (ST. MARŸ), a port, market-town, and parish, and the head of a union, in the hundred of CALDICOT, county of MONMOUTH, 16 miles (S. by E.) from Monmouth, and 131 (W.) from London ; containing, with the hamlet of Hardwick, 3366 inhabitants. This place, called by the Britons *Cas Gwent*, and by most antiquaries supposed to have risen from the ruins of the ancient city *Venta*, about four miles to the west, derives its present name from the Saxon *Chepe*, a market, and *Stowe*, a town. It obtained also the name Striguil from the earls of Pembroke, to whom it belonged at the time of the Conquest, and who, from their residing in a neighbouring castle of that name, were called lords of Striguil, by which designation the manorial courts are still held. Soon after the Conquest, a strong castle was erected, probably by William Fitz-Osborn, Earl of Hereford, on the summit of a rocky precipice overhanging the river Wye : there are considerable remains, richly overspread with ivy, and forming a stately object from various points of view. About the same time the town was fortified with strong walls, portions of which, together with the bastions erected for their defence, are still remaining. In the reign of Stephen, a priory of Benedictine monks was founded here, and dedicated to St. Mary ; the revenue, at the Dissolution, was £32. 4. During the parliamentary war, the inhabitants adhered firmly to the royal cause, and the castle was taken, retaken, and again taken ; in which conflicts it sustained considerable damage. On the restoration of Charles II., Henry Marten, one of those who had sat in judgment on Charles I., was confined in the castle till his death.

The TOWN is situated on the river Wye, near its confluence with the Severn, and is built on the slope of a hill, among the lofty cliffs that rise abruptly from the western bank of the river, over which a handsome iron bridge of five arches was erected in 1816, at the joint expense of the counties of Gloucester and Monmouth, of which the river forms the line of separation. It is much resorted to by visiters on account of the beautiful scenery wherewith it abounds; and consists of several spacious and well-paved streets, in which are many handsome houses : it is lighted with gas, and supplied with water conveyed from Chepstow Park, four miles distant, by iron pipes. The trade is principally in navy timber, oak-bark, iron, and coal : formerly ship-building was carried on to a considerable extent, but at present vessels are only refitted and repaired. A steam-packet plies to and from Bristol during the summer months. The market-days are Wednesday and Saturday : great markets are held on the last Monday in every month, for horses, cattle, sheep, pigs, and wool; and fairs on the last Monday in February, Friday in Whitsun-week, the Saturday before June 20th, August 1st, and the Friday before October 29th. There is a convenient

: living is a perpetual curacy, in the gift of the Bishop of Salisbury, with a net income of £80. On the summit of a hill near the village is Oldborough, or Oldbury, up, to which it is supposed the Danes retreated after battle of Ethandune ; and on its slope is the figure of a white horse, 157 feet long, in the attitude of trotting, cut out of the turf on the chalk rock. It was executed about half a century since, under the direction, and at the expense, of Dr. Christopher Allsop, an eminent physician of Calne ; and, from its lofty situation, is being the highest land between London and Bath, is visible at the distance of twenty or thirty miles, in several directions.

CHERINGTON (St. Nicholas), a parish, in the division of Tetbury, hundred of Longtree, E. division of the county of Gloucester, 4 miles (N. N. E.) from Tetbury ; containing 220 inhabitants. The ancient manor-house was built by Sir John Turner ; the park contains a great number of deer. The living is a rectory, valued in the king's books at £13 ; net income, £176 ; patron, the Rev. W. George. The church is a small edifice, with a nave, chancel, south transept, and low tower at the west end, exhibiting in some parts traces of the early English style. The Rev. Joseph Trapp, professor of poetry at Oxford, and the translator of *Virgil*, was born here in 1672.

CHERITON (St. Martin), a parish, in the union of Elham, hundred of Folkestone, lathe of Shepway, division of Kent, 1 mile (W. N. W.) from Sandgate; containing 1178 inhabitants. This parish, which comprises 1788a. 2r. 28p., and includes the principal portion of the chapelry of Sandgate, is intersected by the South-Eastern railway, and the Grand Military canal. There are 102 acres of woodland. The living is a rectory, with the vicarage of Newington united, valued in the king's books at £16. 12. 6.; patron, the Rev. W. Brockman. The tithes have been commuted for £515, and the glebe contains 8 acres, with a glebe-house. The church is in the early English style, and contains several monuments, supposed to be the most ancient in the county.

CHERITON (St. Michael), a parish, in the union of Alresford, hundred of Fawley, Winchester and S. divisions of the county of Southampton, 3 miles (S. by W.) from Alresford ; containing, with the tything of Beauworth, 709 inhabitants. This parish participated in the conflicts of the civil war, and a battle took place here, called the battle of Alresford. It is situated on the road from Winchester to Petersfield, and comprises 2880 acres, the soil of which is in general chalky ; 135 acres are common or waste. The living is a rectory, with Kilmeston and Titchbourn livings annexed, valued in the king's books at £66. 2. 6., and in the patronage of the Bishop of Winchester : the tithes of Cheriton and Beauworth have been commuted for £625. 10., and the glebe comprises 160 acres, with a glebe-house. The church was erected in 1745.

CHERITON, BISHOP (St. Mary), a parish, in the union of Crediton, hundred of Wonford, Crockernwell and S. divisions of Devon, 11 miles (W. by N.) from Exeter ; containing 848 inhabitants. It comprises by admeasurement 4800 acres, of which about 4000 are arable, 610 woodland and copse, 100 pasture, and 90 orchard. The living is a rectory, valued in the king's books at £22. 13. 4., and in the patronage of the
571

Bishop of Exeter : the tithes have been commuted for £390, and the glebe comprises 50 acres, with a glebe-house.

CHERITON-FITZPAINE (St. Mary), a parish, in the union of Crediton, hundred of West Budleigh, Crediton and N. divisions of Devon, 4¾ miles (N. E. by N.) from Crediton ; containing 1156 inhabitants. It includes parts of the tythings of Bradley and Fulford, and comprises by measurement 5365 acres, of which 50 are common or waste. The living is a rectory, valued in the king's books at £37. 6. 8.; patron and incumbent, Rev. William Harris Arundell, whose tithes have been commuted for £992, and whose glebe comprises 31 acres. The church contains a stained-glass window; the gift of the incumbent, raised at the east end in 1846. There is an almshouse for six poor people, founded and endowed in 1594 by Andrew Scott ; the income is £45.

CHERITON, NORTH (St. John the Baptist), a parish, in the union of Wincanton, hundred of Horethorne, county of Somerset, 2½ miles (S. W. by S.) from Wincanton ; containing 290 inhabitants. This parish, which is situated on the great road from London to Exeter, comprises 1088a. 2r. 6p. : stone of good quality is quarried for building and for the roads. The living is a discharged rectory, valued in the king's books at £8. 12. 1.; patron and incumbent, the Rev. Thomas Gatehouse : the incumbent's tithes have been commuted for £195. 17., and a rent-charge of £46. 15. is paid to an impropriator ; the glebe comprises 29 acres, with a glebe-house.

CHERITON, SOUTH, a hamlet, in the parish of Horsington, union of Wincanton, hundred of Horethorne, E. division of Somerset, 3¼ miles (S. S. W.) from Wincanton ; containing 414 inhabitants. Here was formerly a chapel.

CHERRINGTON, a township, in the parish of Edgemond, union of Newport, Newport division of the hundred of South Bradford, N. division of Salop ; containing 189 inhabitants.

CHERRINGTON (St. John the Baptist), a parish, in the union of Shipston-upon-Stour, Brailes division of the hundred of Kington, S. division of the county of Warwick, 4 miles (S. E.) from Shipston ; containing 340 inhabitants. In the 52nd of Henry III., Ralph de Wylington held the manor by the service of a knight's fee, of the Earl of Warwick, as of the manor of Brailes. It was the property of Sir William Lucy early in the reign of Edward III. ; from which time it continued to his descendants. The area of the parish is 808a. 1r. 22p. A tributary of the Stour runs through from east to west. The living is a rectory, valued in the king's books at £11. 10. 7½.; net income, £259 ; patron, Daniel Turner, Esq. The tithes were commuted for land and money payments in 1805.

CHERRY-BURTON, county of York.—See Burton, Cherry.—*And other places having a similar distinguishing prefix will be found under the proper name.*

CHERTSEY (All Saints), a market-town and parish, and the head of a union, in the Second division of the hundred of Godley, W. division of Surrey, 13 miles (N. N. E.) from Guildford, and 20 (W. S. W.) from London ; containing 5347 inhabitants. During the heptarchy, the South Saxon kings had their residence in this town ; and it became noted for a Benedictine monastery, founded in 666 by Erkenwald, afterwards Bishop of London, and which, having been burnt to the ground in the war with the Danes, was refounded by King Edgar, and dedicated to St. Peter. In this abbey Henry VI. was privately interred; but his remains were subsequently removed, and deposited, with appropriate solemnities, in the royal chapel at Windsor. At the Dissolution, its revenue was £774. 13. 6.: some portions of the outer walls remain, and on the site, and with part of the materials, of the abbey, a private mansion, called the Abbey House, was erected, but this was pulled down some years ago.

The TOWN is pleasantly situated upon the Thames, over which is a handsome stone bridge of seven arches, built in 1785, at an expense of £13,000, defrayed jointly by the counties of Surrey and Middlesex : the houses are in general neatly built of brick ; the streets are partially paved, and lighted, and the inhabitants are plentifully supplied with water from springs. A neat building, of which the first stone was laid in November, 1838, by the high sheriff of the county, has been erected for a literary and scientific institution. The trade is principally in malt and flour; the manufacture of coarse thread, and the making of iron-hoops and brooms, are carried on to a considerable extent; and a great quantity of bricks is also made in the neighbourhood. The town is about three miles from the Weybridge station of the South-Western railway; and an act was passed in 1846 for a branch railway from that station to Chertsey and to Egham. The river Wey navigation and canal passes within two miles, and joins the Thames a little to the north of Weybridge, affording facility of conveyance for the several articles of manufacture, and for large quantities of vegetables, which are cultivated in the environs for the London market. The market, chartered by Queen Elizabeth in 1559, is on Wednesday : the fairs are on the first Monday and Tuesday in Lent, for cattle; May 14th, for sheep; and August 6th and September 25th, for toys and pedlery. A court of pie-poudre is attached to the fair in Lent. The county magistrates hold a meeting for the division on the first and third Wednesdays in every month; and headboroughs and other officers are appointed on Tuesday in Whitsun-week, at the court leet of the lord of the manor, who also holds a court baron on the following day at Hardwick Court, now a farmhouse, but once the manorial mansion, in which Henry VI. resided when a child. The powers of the county debt-court of Chertsey, established in 1847, extend over the registration-district of Chertsey, and part of the districts of Staines and Windsor.

The parish comprises about 10,020 acres. The LIVING is a vicarage, valued in the king's books at £13. 12. 4.; net income, £307; patrons, alternately, the Haberdashers' Company, and the Governors of Christ's Hospital; impropriators, the landowners. The church, a handsome structure in the later English style, with a square embattled tower, was built with money raised on annuities, in 1808; it contains a tablet to the memory of the celebrated orator and statesman, Charles James Fox, and several monuments to the Mawbey family. A church has been built at Addlestone (which see) ; and there are places of worship for Independents and Methodists. A school was founded in 1725, by Sir William Perkins, who endowed it with £3000 Bank

;he parish comprises by computation 12,650 acres, ich, excepting about 500 of wood and 143 common waste, are chiefly arable : the surface is in general 'y, and the soil on the high lands abounds with flint l chalk, which latter is obtained for manure. The |ING is a discharged vicarage, formerly consisting the medieties of Chesham-Leicester and Chesham-|burn, each valued in the king's books at £13. 1. 5½., consolidated in 1767 ; patron, the Duke of Bedford. ; great tithes have been commuted for £2326, and vicarial for £550 ; there are 2¼ acres of vicarial be. The church is an ancient cruciform structure, |h a square embattled tower surmounted by a low |re : in the chancel is a monument from an elegant |ign by Bacon, to the memory of Nicholas Skottowe, |. At Latimer is a chapel of considerable antiquity, |ich has lately been rebuilt ; it is supposed to have |n endowed by the Cavendish family. There are |r places of worship for dissenters, two of which are Baptists. A chalybeate spring was discovered in !0. At Asheridge, a college for a rector and twenty thren was founded in 1283, by Edmund, Earl of |nwall ; the revenue of which, at the Dissolution, was 17. 18.

CHESHAM-BOIS (St. Leonard), a parish, in the |on of Amersham, hundred of Burnham, county of ckingham, 1½ mile (N. E. by N.) from Amersham ; |taining 218 inhabitants. It comprises 905a. 3r. 32p., which about 620 acres are arable, 150 woodland, and common or waste ; the situation is hilly, and the soil, general a stiff clay resting on chalk, produces excel- t wheat. The parish is intersected in the northern rtion of it by a branch of the river Colne, on the |ks of which are a corn-mill and a mill for the manu- ture of paper. The living is a donative rectory, lued in the king's books at £5. 6. 8., and in the t of the Duke of Bedford : the tithes have been com- ited for £160, and the glebe comprises 2¼ acres, with ;lebe-house. The church was formerly a chapel of |e to the vicarage of Chesham, and is supposed to ve been originally a private chapel to the adjoining |nsion belonging at that time to Lord Cheney, whose nily monuments are in the church, the records of |ich extend back as far as to the year 1560 ; the pulpit d a painted window are great curiosities, and exhibit |ch skill and ingenuity.

CHESHIRE. a maritime county, bounded on the rth by the estuary of the Mersey, the county of |ncaster, and a small part of the county of York ; the east by the counties of Derby and Stafford ; on e south by the county of Salop, and a detached por- |n of Flintshire ; on the west by the counties of Den- ;h and Flint, and the estuary of the Dee ; and on the rth-west by the Irish Sea. It extends from 52° 56′ 53° 32′ (N. Lat.), and from 1° 48′ to 3° 10′ (W. Lon.) ; d includes 1052 square miles, or 673,280 statute res. Within the limits of the county are 73,444 in- bited houses, 5844 uninhabited, and 547 in progress erection ; and the population amounts to 395,660, of |om 193,646 are males, and 202,014 are females. The name is a contraction of Chestershire. At the ne of the Roman invasion, the county formed part of e territory occupied by the Cornavii ; in the first divi- |n of Britain by the Romans it was included in Bri- |nia Superior, and in their subsequent subdivision be-

573

came part of Flavia Cæsariensis. Under the Saxons it was a portion of the powerful kingdom of Mercia ; and upon the division of England into three great dis- tricts by Alfred, it was comprehended in that called Mercenlege, or the " Mercian jurisdiction." Cheshire is within the diocese of Chester, and province of York ; it comprises the deaneries of Chester, Frodsham, Maccles- field, Nantwich, Malpas, Middlewich, and Wirrall, con- taining 87 parishes. For purposes of civil jurisdiction it is divided into the hundreds of Broxton, Bucklow, Eddisbury, Macclesfield, Nantwich, Northwich, and Wirrall. It contains the city of Chester (which however forms a county of itself) ; the large manufacturing towns of Macclesfield and Stockport, recently created parliamentary boroughs ; and the other market-towns of Altrincham, Birkenhead, Congleton, Frodsham, Knutsford, Malpas, Middlewich, Nantwich, Northwich, Sandbach, and Tarporley. Under the act of the 2nd of William IV., cap. 45, the county was divided into two parts, the Northern and Southern, each sending to parliament two knights of the shire. Two citizens are returned for the city of Chester, and two burgesses each for Macclesfield and Stockport ; and the village of Farndon, bordering on Denbighshire, is included within the limits of the adjacent borough of Holt, and shares in the election of one member for the district of boroughs comprising Denbigh, Ruthin, and Holt. Under the act of the 1st of William IV., cap. 70, for the more effectual administration of justice in England and Wales, the assizes were directed to be held in Cheshire and each of the counties of Wales, in the same manner as such courts had been held in the counties of England having no palatine jurisdiction ; one of the two judges ap- pointed by Her Majesty's commission to hold the assizes within the county of Chester and principality of Wales proceeding to hold such assizes in North Wales, and the other in South Wales, and both holding the assizes in and for the county of Chester, as in other English counties. The assizes, and the Epiphany and Easter quarter-sessions, are held at Chester, where stands the county gaol; and the Midsummer and Michaelmas quarter-sessions, at Knutsford, where is the house of correction.

William the Conqueror, having granted the county to his nephew, Hugh Lupus, the latter was constituted the first hereditary earl in England, that dignity having previously been an office of the executive government of the realm. By the terms of the grant, Lupus acquired jura regalia within the county, in the exercise of which he created eight parliamentary barons (one of whom was hereditary constable, and another hereditary steward), assembled parliaments, and established courts of law. His descendants continued to enjoy this sovereignty until the death of John, Earl of Chester, in 1237, without male issue ; in consequence of which, Henry III. seized on the county of Chester, gave other lands in lieu to the sisters of the deceased earl, and bestowed the earldom on his son, Prince Edward. Richard II. having erected Cheshire into a principality, added to his other titles that of Princeps Cestriæ ; but this act was abrogated by his successor, and it again became a county palatine, and continued, under the king's eldest sons, as earls of Chester, to be governed, as in the time of its ancient earls, by a jurisdiction separate from, and independent of, the parliament of England. The ancient privileges of the palatinate were much abridged in the 27th of Henry VIII., prior to which time the lord high chancellor of England had not appointed justices of the peace, justices of the quorum, or of gaol delivery, in the county; the authority of the earl within the palatinate being as absolute as that of the king throughout the realm, and so extensive that he had power to pardon for treason and felony, to rescind outlawries, and to appoint justices of eyre, assize, gaol delivery, and of the peace; and all original and judicial writs, and indictments, for treason and felony, with the process thereon, being made in his name. In consequence of this curtailment of its privileges, the county petitioned that it might send knights and burgesses to the parliament of the realm; in accordance with which, a statute was passed in 1542, enacting that thenceforward two knights should be returned for the county palatine, and two burgesses for the city of Chester. The authority of the judges and officers of the great session of the county palatine, which, says Lord Coke, "is the most ancient and honourable remaining in England," extended over the counties of Chester and Flint, for both which one seal was used; and the king's writ did not run in the palatinate, all writs from the superior courts being directed to the chamberlain of Chester, who issued his mandate to the sheriff. The chamberlain had, within the county palatine and the county of the city of Chester, the jurisdiction of chancellor; and the court of exchequer, at Chester, was the chancery court, whereof the chamberlain, or his deputy, was the sole judge in equity: he was also judge at the common law within the said limits. The other officers of the court were the vice-chamberlain, baron, seal-keeper, filizer, examiner, six clerks or attorneys of the court, and some inferior officers. But by the recent statute above mentioned, the whole of these jurisdictions have been abolished, and the subjects of them transferred to the courts at Westminster.

The general appearance of the SURFACE is that of an extended plain, thickly covered with wood; so that, from some points of view, the entire county wears the aspect of a vast and continued forest. The most elevated lands are on the eastern border, and in the western part from Malpas to Frodsham. There are several small lakes, called meres or pools, of which Combermere is a fine sheet of water, nearly two miles in length and half a mile in breadth, close to the site of Combermere Abbey. The soils are intermingled; the prevailing species are clay and sand, a tolerably strong and retentive clay existing in the largest proportion. The subsoil is commonly clay or marl; but in some places it is found to consist of sand, rammel, foxbench, gravel, and red rock: the rammel is a hard argillaceous substance, very unfavourable to the vegetation on the surface; as also, in a still greater degree, is the foxbench. The proportion of land in tillage is much inferior to that of many counties possessing the same degree of fertility: wheat and oats, but principally the latter, are the chief objects of culture; and in a considerable tract bordering on Lancashire, into which county it also extends, potatoes are a more common agricultural crop than in any other part of the kingdom. The ordinary artificial grasses are red and white clover, rye-grass, trefoil, rib-grass, and vetches. As the making of cheese is a principal object of husbandry, the proportion of pasture land is

dstone peculiarly adapted to the formation of flags
l hones. *Limestone* is no where found but at New-
d-Astbury, where large quantities are burned with
l brought from Staffordshire. *Marl* exists almost in
ry part, and *Gypsum* is found in some places.
From its proximity to Manchester, the county has
ticipated in the great extension of the cotton manu-
ture, and there are now few situations within its
its favourable for the purpose where mills have not
n erected; which is more especially the case in the
thern part of the county, where the cotton trade has
dered Stockport one of the most important towns in
kingdom : the trade is also of considerable extent at
ecclesfield, Marple, and Congleton. A large quantity
muslin is made at Macclesfield, and in Stockport and
neighbourhood. There are numerous silk-mills at
ngleton, Macclesfield, Stockport, and Sandbach; the
aving of ribbon forms the staple trade of Congleton,
l that of silk-handkerchiefs of the more important
vn of Macclesfield, where also silk-ferret is made.
Knutsford is a manufacture of thread; and the
nufacture of hats for exportation at Stockport, Mac-
sfield, and Nantwich, and that of shoes at Sandbach,
each considerable. Some woollen-cloths are made
the north-eastern extremity of the county, in the
ish of Mottram; and tanning isvery extensively
ried on.
The principal RIVERS are the Dee, the Mersey, and
: Weaver; to which the minor streams of the Dane,
: Bollin, the Peover, the Wheelock, and the Tame,
: tributary. The *Dee*, a little below the city of Ches-
, enters an artificial channel, by which it is carried
ough the marshes in the north-eastern extremity of
ntshire, by Hawarden, to its expansive estuary, which
n some parts seven miles in breadth, but so full of
ıds that at low water the channel is almost entirely
ı: this opens to the Irish Sea near Hilbree Island,
ere it is about five miles in breadth. Prior to the
ır 1449, the navigation of the Dee had become so
ıch obstructed by sand, as to cause the stream fre-
ently to change its channel, and occasion the ruin of
: haven of Chester; to obviate which, a new quay or
ven was made nearly six miles from Chester, about
: middle of the following century : on its completion,
goods conveyed from and brought to the port of
ester were there shipped and landed. In 1700, an
: was obtained to enable the mayor and citizens to
over and preserve the navigation of the Dee; and
ıther act being passed in 1734, empowering some
ıtlemen, willing to undertake the work, to inclose a
ge tract of the banks of the river, called the White
ıds, on the condition of making a navigable line from
: sea to Chester, the present artificial channel was
npleted in 1740, in which year the undertakers were
orporated by the name of "The Company of Proctors of the Undertaking for recovering and preserving
: Navigation of the river Dee." In 1763, 1411 acres
land were recovered; in 1769, 664; and in 1795,
3; and this reclaimed tract has been greatly aug-
ıted by subsequent embankments.
The *Mersey* forms the boundary between this county
l Lancashire, and above Warrington, where it meets
: tide, begins to expand until it reaches Runcorn Gap,
.ere it is suddenly rendered narrow by a projection
m the Lancashire side. Beyond this point it imme-

diately opens into a grand estuary, three miles in width,
which gradually contracts until it arrives at Liverpool,
where it is only three-quarters of a mile in width, but
forms a fine channel, at least ten fathoms deep at low
water, and very commodious for shipping. At the distance of about five miles further, measuring by the Cheshire coast, it falls into the Irish Sea, through different
inlets, separated and much obstructed by sands; but
the passage is rendered secure by means of various
landmarks, buoys, and lighthouses, and the good system
of pilotage established by the Liverpool merchants. The
Weaver rises on Bulkeley Heath, in the south-western
part of the county, and pursues its entire course within
its limits. This river in its natural state, being navigable only at high tides, and but for six miles above Frodsham bridge, a company of Cheshire gentlemen, in 1720,
entered into a subscription to procure an act of parliament for extending the navigation from Frodsham
bridge to Winsford bridge; and all incumbrances
brought on by this undertaking were discharged in 1778.
Since that time a considerable surplus revenue, arising
from tonnage, &c., has been annually paid into the
county treasury in aid of the rate, as provided by the
act; and the returns are now estimated at about £20,000
per annum. The total length of the Weaver navigation
is nearly 24 miles; and the extensive trade upon it in
salt and coal, and in flint and clay for the Staffordshire
potteries, makes the tonnage greater than perhaps that
of any river of its size in the kingdom.
The CANALS that intersect Cheshire in various directions, are, the *Duke of Bridgewater's*, commenced under
an act passed in 1759, and completed, with its several
branches, under various others; the *Trent and Mersey*,
or Grand Trunk canal, begun under an act obtained in
1766, which has been amended by numerous subsequent
acts; the *Ellesmere and Chester* canal, commenced under
an act procured in 1772, and finished under many
others, with different branches; the *Peak Forest* canal,
the first act for which was passed in 1794; and the
Macclesfield canal, the act for constructing which was
obtained in 1825. The *Huddersfield* canal also pursues
its course for some distance within the northern confines
of the county, on the south side of the valley of the
Tame; and there is a branch canal from Stockport,
communicating with the Manchester, Ashton, and Oldham canal, which at Ashton approaches close to the borders of Cheshire, and in the vicinity of that town is
connected with the Peak-Forest and Huddersfield canals.
Several RAILWAYS, also, have been formed. The *Birmingham and Liverpool* railway enters the county at
Blackenhall, between Checkley and Wrinehill, and proceeds in a direction north-north-west to the west of
Crewe Hall, where it is joined by the Manchester and
Birmingham, and the Chester and Crewe, railways; it'
afterwards pursues its course to the river Mersey, at
Warrington. The *Manchester and Birmingham* railway
runs by Stockport and Sandbach, to Crewe, and has a
considerable branch to Macclesfield. The *Chester and
Crewe* railway runs from the station in Chester to Crewe,
a distance of 20½ miles; it is carried over the river
Weaver, and several bridges, by an extensive viaduct,
and at Christleton passes under the Ellesmere canal.
The *Chester and Birkenhead* railway commences at Chester, and proceeds to Birkenhead, on the Mersey, opposite
to Liverpool, a distance of 16 miles; it passes over

several extensive embankments, and by a viaduct of 11 arches over the Ellesmere canal. The *Sheffield, Ashton, and Manchester* railway crosses the north-eastern angle of the county, which interposes between Lancashire, Yorkshire, and Derbyshire; it is of recent construction, and is a line of great importance. Cheshire also includes part of the *Chester and Holyhead, Chester and Shrewsbury,* and *Altrincham and Manchester,* lines.

Few *Roman remains* have been discovered, except within the walls of Chester, which city, under the name of *Deva,* was for more than two centuries the station of the twentieth legion, vestiges of whose occupation are even yet numerous. The site of no other station within the county has been clearly ascertained, though it is conjectured by Whitaker, on interesting local evidence, that the station of *Condate* was at Kinderton, and that there were likewise fortified posts at Stockport, Stretford, and Warrington. Many Roman roads traversed the territory, of which the principal were, one from Manchester to Kinderton, one from Kinderton to Wroxeter, one from Kinderton southward by the vicinity of Sandbach, one from Kinderton to the station at Chesterton, near Newcastle-under-Line; one from Kinderton to Chester; the ancient Watling-street, originally of British construction, from the south-eastern coast of the island to Chester; and a great road called by Sir R. C. Hoare the *Via Devana,* from Chester southward : but the existing remains of these are few, scattered, and imperfect. Prior to the Dissolution, Cheshire contained 13 *Religious Houses,* including one commandery of the Knights Hospitallers; there were, besides, two colleges and nine hospitals. Of some of these houses considerable remains yet exist, especially of the abbey of St. Werburgh, Chester. The principal remains of *Castles* are those of Chester and Beeston, though the former were much diminished in 1790, for the purpose of erecting on their site the present noble county hall, gaol, and barracks; vestiges of those of Halton, Alford, Shotwick, and Shotlach are also traceable. There are several remarkable ancient mansions, namely, Doddington, Bramhall, Saighton, Little Moreton, Dutton, Poole, Brereton, and Crewe Halls; and many of the modern seats are elegant edifices. At Buglawton is a saline and sulphureous spring, efficacious in the cure of scorbutic diseases : at Shaw Heath, near Stockport, is a strong chalybeate spring; and some of the brine springs already noticed have also chalybeate properties.

CHESHUNT (ST. MARY), a parish, and formerly a market-town, in the union of EDMONTON, hundred and county of HERTFORD, 8 miles (S. by E.) from Hertford; containing, with Cheshunt-street, Waltham-Cross, and Woodside wards, 5402 inhabitants. In this parish was formerly a bank separating the kingdoms of Mercia and East Anglia during the heptarchy, the lands on one side of which the elder brother still inherits, and the younger those on the other side. Cardinal Wolsey possessed the united manors of Andrews and Le Mote, in the parish, and received from the crown the appointment of bailiff of the honour, and keeper of the park, of Cheshunt. Here stood the palace called Theobalds, the favourite residence of Lord Burleigh, and afterwards of James I., who died in it in 1625; it was also the occasional resort of Charles I., who here received the petition from both houses of parliament in 1642, a short time before he placed himself at the head of the army. The
576

FINGHAM, W. division of SURREY, 3 miles (S.) from ngston; containing 226 inhabitants. The parish nprises by admeasurement 1223 acres, of which 970 arable, and about 200 pasture; the soil is chiefly y. It is annexed to the vicarage of Malden, and the arden and Fellows of Merton College, Oxford, are im- priators: the tithes have been commuted for £305, d the glebe contains 25 acres. The church is in the ly English style. There is a strong chalybeate spring, led Jessop's Well.

Arms.

CHESTER, a city, port, and county of itself, locally in the hundred of BROXTON, S. division of the county of CHESTER, of which it is the capital, 17 miles (S.) from Liverpool, 36 (S. W.) from Manchester, and 197 (N. W.) from London; contain- ing 23,115 inhabitants, and, including those portions of the parishes of St. Mary on the Hill, St. Oswald, and

e Holy Trinity, which are without the limits of the y, 25,613. The origin of this ancient city has been cribed to the Cornavii, a British tribe who, at the time the Roman invasion, inhabited that part of the island hich now includes the counties of Chester, Salop, Staf- rd, Warwick, and Worcester; and its British name ier *Leon Vawr*, "city of Leon the Great," has been re- rred to Leon, son of Brût Darian Là, eighth king of ·itain. But there is no authentic account of Chester ior to the period when it was made the station of the rentieth Roman legion, after the defeat of Caractacus; d the more respectable historians deduce its names, ter *Leon Vawr*, "city" or "camp of the great legion," d *Caer Leon ar Dwfyr dwy*, "the city of the legion on e Dee," from its connexion with the Roman people. was also called *Deunana* and *Deva*, from the same ver. The Romans occupied it from the year 46 till eir departure from the island in 446, when it reverted the Britons, from whom it was taken by Ethelfrith, ng of Northumbria, who in 607 defeated them with e king of Powysland, with great slaughter. Having gained the place, the Britons continued to hold it till !8, when Egbert, as sole monarch of England, annexed to his other possessions. By the Saxons the city was lled *Legancester* and *Legecester*. It suffered greatly om the Danes in the ninth century: on their retreat, e walls were repaired by Ethelfreda, Countess of Mer- a: and after her death the Britons once more became i masters, but were again driven out by Edward the lder. In 971-3, Edgar assembled a naval force on the ee, on which occasion that king, as mentioned by some riters, was rowed from his palace on the southern bank the river to the conventual church of St. John, by ght tributary kings, he himself taking the helm, to note his supremacy.

On the division of England between Canute and Ed- und Ironside, in 1016, Canute retained possession of ercia and Northumbria; and Chester, which was in- uded in Mercia, continued to form part of it till the orman Conquest, when William bestowed it, with the rldom, on his kinsman, Hugh Lupus. At this time, cording to Domesday book, the city contained 431

rateable houses. For more than two centuries after the Conquest, it was the head-quarters of the troops em- ployed to defend the English border against the incur- sive attacks of the Welsh, and, on account of its im- portance as a military station, was more or less favoured by the reigning monarchs. In the war between Henry III. and the barons, Chester was captured by the Earl of Derby, in the year 1264, and held for the crown till the battle of Evesham, in which the barons were defeated with the loss of their leader, and an end put to the con- test. On the subjugation of Wales, in 1300, by Ed- ward I., several of the Welsh chieftains did homage to his son, Edward of Carnarvon, then an infant, in Chester Castle. Richard II., by an act of parliament which was rescinded by his successor, erected the earldom of Ches- ter into a principality, to be held only by the king's eldest son.

The city, in common with the whole county, suffered considerably from the sanguinary conflicts between the houses of York and Lancaster, during which it was visited by Margaret of Anjou. In 1554, the inhabitants experienced the severity of the persecution by which the reign of Mary was distinguished; and the martyrdom of George Marsh, a clergyman who was burnt for preach- ing the tenets of Protestantism, was rendered memor- able by an attempt of one of the sheriffs to rescue him, which was defeated by the other. In 1634, the city suffered dreadfully from the plague; during its conti- nuance the court of exchequer was removed to Tarvin, and the court of assize to Nantwich, and the fairs were suspended. In the memorable siege of the city by Sir William Brereton, in 1645, when the garrison was com- manded by Lord Byron, the inhabitants experienced great privations for their adherence to the cause of Charles I., who had the mortification to witness, from the Phœnix tower and the great tower of the cathedral, the entire defeat of his army under Sir Marmaduke Langdale, and its pursuit by the enemy even to the very walls. The noble commander, after a gallant resistance, surrendered on honourable terms, February 3rd, 1646. In 1659, Sir George Booth surprised and took possession of the city, but it was soon given up to the parliamentary forces under General Lambert. In 1688, the Roman Catholic lords, Molyneux and Aston, raised a force, and made themselves masters of Chester, for James II.; but his abdication rendered further efforts useless. Under William III. it was chosen one of the six cities for the residence of an assay-master, and allowed to issue silver coinage. In the rebellion of 1745, it was fortified against the Pretender, the last military event of importance re- corded of a place celebrated as the rendezvous of troops from the earliest times.

Situated on a rocky elevation, on the northern bank of the Dee, and half encircled by a fine sweep of the river, the appearance of CHESTER is remarkable and picturesque. The city is entirely surrounded by a wall, and comprises four principal streets, diverging at right angles from a common centre, and extending towards the cardinal points; at the extremities of the streets are gates, after three of which are respectively named East- gate-street, Northgate-street, and Watergate-street. This plan, strictly conformable to the Roman style of building, affords strong presumptive evidence of a Roman origin. Within the liberty of the city is an extensive southern suburb, called Hanbridge, which in feudal times generally fell a prey to the predatory incursions of the Welsh, and thence obtained, in their language, the appellation of *Treboeth*, "the burnt town." The streets of Chester, being cut out of the rock, are several feet below the general surface, a circumstance that has led to a singular construction of the houses. Level with the streets are low shops, or warehouses, over which is an open balustraded gallery, with steps at convenient distances into the streets; and along the galleries, or, as they are called by the inhabitants, "rows," are houses with shops: the upper stories are erected over the row, which, consequently, appears to be formed through the first floor of each house; and at the intersection of the streets are additional flights of steps. The rows in Bridge and Eastgate streets, running through the principal part of the city, are much frequented as promenades. Pennant considered these curious galleries to be remnants of the vestibules of Roman houses; but other writers are of opinion that they were originally constructed for defence, especially against the sudden inroads of the Welsh. The fronts of such of them as have not been modernised are bounded by a heavy wooden railing; and immense pillars of oak, supporting transverse beams, sustain the weight of the upper stories. Many of the houses in Bridge and Eastgate streets, having been rebuilt, are considerably improved and enlarged, and their appearance rendered light by iron-railing. The streets are well lighted with gas; they are indifferently paved, but the inconvenience to foot passengers, to whom the rows afford a sheltered walk, is little felt: the inhabitants are plentifully supplied with water, and the city, both within and without the walls, has been much improved of late by the addition of well-built houses. The new bridge, consisting of one arch of 200 feet in the span, is constructed of Peckforton stone, with quoins of granite, at an expense of £50,000, from a design by Mr. Thomas Harrison: the old bridge, consisting of seven arches, has, within the last few years, been considerably widened. In 1845 an act was passed for further improving the city, and for establishing new market-places. Fine views of the peninsula of Wirrall, the Welsh hills, and the estuary of the Dee, are obtained from the walls, which afford a delightful and favourite promenade. There are two public libraries: the theatre, a small neat edifice, is open during the races, and generally throughout the summer; and grand musical meetings are held at distant periods. The races, which attract much company from Wales and the neighbouring counties, commence on the first Monday in May, and terminate on the Friday following; they take place on the Rood-eye, a fine level beneath the city walls, well adapted to the purpose.

The PORT is not of much importance, owing to the shallowness of the water; but, by the exertions of the River Dee Company, the channel has been deepened, the navigation improved, and a tract of ground, formerly sands, but now arable land, has been gained by altering the course of the river, and making embankments, the last of which was completed in 1824. The commerce, both domestic and foreign, was once somewhat extensive, but is now chiefly confined to Ireland, though a few ships trade with the Baltic, Spain, Portugal, and the Mediterranean shores. The articles imported are, linen, butter, provisions, timber, hides, tallow, feathers, iron, hemp, flax, kid and lamb skins, fruit, oil, barilla, and wine; those shipped, chiefly coastwise, are cheese

,wed to trade in the city. Besides these fairs, are ers for the sale of live-stock, held on the last Thurs- in April, the first Thursday in September, and the last ırsday in November ; and for the sale of cheese and er agricultural produce, on the days preceding all the s. The Linen Hall, built about the year 1780, is a cious pile of building, forming an oblong, and com- ies more than one hundred shops.

The city is one of the most ancient corporate towns in England. At the Conquest, it ranked as a *Guilda Mer- catoris*, a constitution some- what similar to that of modern municipal corpora- tions ; it was chartered by its Norman earls, and ad- ditional immunities were conferred on the inhabitants by charter of King John. Edward III. granted to the ̣poration all the vacant lands within the liberty of ̣city ; and Richard II. authorized the mayor, sheriffs, ̱ commonalty, to hold courts of common law and ̱er courts, which privileges were confirmed and ex- ̣ded by Henry IV. and VI. Henry VII., besides ̤nting a more extensive charter, remitted four-fifths of ̣ fee-farm rent of £100 per annum, which Henry III. ̣ Edward I. had claimed from the citizens in con- ̣eration of continuing their privileges ; and constituted ̣city a county of itself, under the style of the " City ̣ County of the City of Chester." Charles II. dis- ̣nchised it in 1684-5 ; but its liberties were after- ̣rds restored, with a discretionary power in the crown ̣ displace the officers of the corporation. James II., ̣iling himself of this prerogative, displaced the mayor, ̣order, and other functionaries, but was induced, at ̣ approach of the Revolution, to restore them to ̣ce. By the act of the 5th and 6th of William IV., ̣. 76, the government is vested in a mayor, 10 alder- ̣n, and 30 councillors ; the council appoint a sheriff ; ̣ the city, formerly in 12 wards, is by that act divided ̣ 5 only : the number of magistrates is 15. No fewer ̣n 24 guilds or trade companies, headed by aldermen ̣ wardens, hold charters of incorporation under the ̣ seal. The freedom of the city is inherited by all ̣ sons of freemen, and acquired by servitude. On ̣ abridgment of the privileges of the county palatine, ̣ 1541, an act was passed, empowering the county to ̣urn two knights, and the city two burgesses, to par- ̣nent. The election for the city was vested in the ̣yor, aldermen, and common-councilmen, whether ̣ident or not, and freemen resident in the city a year ̣ eeding, in number about 1300 ; but by the act of ̣ 2nd of William IV., cap. 45, the right of voting ̣ extended to the £10 householders ; and the limits ̣he borough, which anciently comprised 3000 acres, ̣ ̣e enlarged, so as, for electoral purposes, to include ̣t of the township of Great Boughton, and compre- ̣d 3080 acres. The sheriff is the returning officer. By ̣ient usage, confirmed by the several charters, the ̣yor, assisted by the recorder, held crown-mote and ̣t-mote courts : the recorder has been sole judge ̣ce the passing of the act of the 5th and 6th Wil- ̣n IV. The earliest rolls in these courts are of the

Corporation Seal.

579

date 1277 : the jurisdiction of the crown-mote extends to all crimes except that of high treason, the mayor having had power to pass sentence of death, and order execution, independently of the crown ; and in the port- mote, pleas to any amount are cognizable. There are two other ancient courts ; one called the " Pentice court," which has cognizance of personal actions to any amount ; and the other the "Port-mote court," held before the mayor, to which records are removable from the Pentice court, by command of the mayor, without writ. The courts of quarter-sessions are held in the exchange, where the town officers and the members for the city are elected ; and the assizes for the county are held in the castle. The powers of the county debt- court of Chester, established in 1847, extend over the registration-district of Great Boughton. The exchange is a handsome brick building, finished in 1698 ; it is fronted with stone, supported by columns, and sur- mounted by a glazed cupola. On the ground-floor are the record-room and shops ; and on the first floor the council and assembly rooms, which are decorated with a picture of George III. by Reynolds, and portraits of members of the Grosvenor, Cholmondeley, Bunbury, and Egerton families, and of several charitable indivi- duals. The city gaol contains twelve wards, day-rooms, and airing-yards, and eight work-rooms.

Of the ancient CASTLE, built by the Conqueror, there remains only a large square tower, called "Julius Agri- cola's Tower," now used as a magazine for gunpowder. Though of modern appearance, having been newly fronted, it is undoubtedly of great antiquity, and interest- ing as the probable place of confinement of the Earl of Derby, and the place in which Richard II., and Mar- garet, Countess of Richmond, were imprisoned. In the second chamber James II. heard mass, on his tour through this part of the kingdom, a short time previously to the Revolution. This apartment, when opened after many years of disuse as a chapel, exhibited, from the richness of its decorations, a splendid appearance, the walls being completely covered with paintings in fresco, as vivid and beautiful as when executed ; and the roof, from the fine effect produced by the ribs of the groined arches, springing elegantly from slender pillars with capitals in a chaste and curious style, was equally striking. The remainder of the original structure, which was pulled down in 1790, contained a room termed Hugh Lupus' Hall, that was regarded as a superb speci- men of baronial grandeur. The new edifice, which has excited general admiration, was erected from a design by Mr. Harrison, and under his inspection : the principal entrance is of the Doric order, resembling the Propylæa at Athens. Opposite to the great gate is the shire-hall, a magnificent structure : on the right of the hall is the entrance to the gaol, which is appropriated to debtors and felons of the county. At the eastern side of the yard are barracks for 120 men, fronted with white free- stone, and ornamented with Ionic pillars ; on the western side is a corresponding building, used as an armoury, which will contain 30,000 stand of arms. The castle is a royal fortress : the establishment consists of a governor, lieutenant-governor, ordnance-keeper, and barrack-mas- ter. The constableship of the tower is held by patent, and is free from municipal control.

Chester, with part of the kingdom of Mercia, at an early period gave name to a DIOCESE, which afterwards

Arms of the Bishoprie.

was incorporated with that of Lichfield. In 1075, Peter, Bishop of Lichfield, restored the episcopal chair to Chester, whence it was a second time removed to Lichfield, by his successor, Robert de Lindsey. Chester again became a distinct diocese under Henry VIII., who named it one of the six new sees created in 1541, and endowed it with a portion of the possessions of the abbey of St. Werburgh, the revenue of which, at the Dissolution, was £1073. 17. 7. The first bishop was John Bird, previously a provincial of the Carmelites, and Bishop of Bangor, who, in 1547, granted the manors and demesnes of the bishopric to the king, accepting impropriations of little value in exchange, and thus rendered it one of the least valuable of the English sees. Its temporalities in Chester consist only of the palace, which was rebuilt in 1752, by Bishop Keene, and its appendages, and two houses near St. John's church. The act of the 10th and 11th Victoria, cap. 108, provides that the diocese of Chester shall consist of the county of Chester, and of the rural deanery of Warrington, in Lancashire. The bishop has the patronage of the canonries, of the honorary canonries, and the archdeaconries and chancellorship. The Dean and Chapter have the patronage of the minor canonries. The CATHEDRAL, originally the conventual church of St. Werburgh, was at first dedicated to St. Peter and St. Paul, but subsequently placed by Ethelfreda under the patronage of the Saxon saint Walmgha, daughter of Wulphere, King of Mercia: that princess, and Leofric, Earl of Mercia, were great benefactors to the church, as well as Hugh Lupus, who substituted Benedictine monks for Secular canons. On the suppression of the abbey, a dean, six canons or prebendaries, and six minor canons, were appointed in lieu of the abbot and monks, the last abbot being made dean: there are now a dean, four canons, four honorary canons, four minor canons, two archdeacons, a chancellor of the diocese, registrar, sacrist, and precentor. At the Dissolution the cathedral was dedicated to Christ and the Blessed Virgin. It stands on the eastern side of Northgate-street, and exclusively of some interesting remains of the abbey, the present building was erected in the reigns of Henry VII. and Henry VIII. With the exception of the western end, it is externally a heavy irregular pile: the tower in the centre, originally intended to sustain a spire, is supported by massive piers, and is in the later style of English architecture. The interior is elegant and impressive, and exhibits portions in the Norman and the early and decorated English styles. The piers of the nave are in the decorated style, with flowered capitals; and the clerestory, which is in the later style, has a fine range of windows. To the east of the north transept are traces of some chapels in the early English style; the south transept, which is larger than the north, and consists of a centre and two aisles, is in the decorated style, and, being separated from the cathedral by a screen, forms the parish church of St. Oswald. The choir has a chequered floor of black and white marble, and the stalls are adorned with light tabernacle-work

irch, dedicated to *Christ*, built in 1835 : the living is erpetual curacy in the gift of the Bishop, with a net ome of £150. There are places of worship for Bap- :s, the Society of Friends, the Connexion of the untess of Huntingdon, Independents, Welsh and :sleyan Methodists, New Connexion of Methodists, idemanians, Unitarians, and Roman Catholics. The *Free Grammar school* was founded by Henry VIII., o, in the 36th year of his reign, endowed it with a it-charge of £108. 16., for two masters and twenty- ir boys, from amongst whom the choristers of the hedral are chosen : it has an exhibition for a scholar one of the Universities. The schoolroom, originally : refectory of the monastery, is a fine specimen of the ly English style, but retaining little of the ancient fice, except a stone pulpit, and a staircase in good servation. The *Blue-coat school* was founded in 1700, the recommendation of Bishop Stratford, and en- wed for the maintenance of thirty boys : it is sup- rted by the interest of money arising from bene- tions, legacies, surpluses of musical festivals, rent of d, and annual subscriptions. In 1781, the revenue ng augmented, a plan was adopted for educating day scholars in addition ; hence the origin of the een-cap school. A similar school for girls was esta- shed in 1718, to which in 1793 Mary Tilley be- eathed £400, paid in 1815. In 1811, the late Mar- ess of Westminster founded a school for boys, and e marchioness a school for girls ; the rooms are unted near St. John's church. There are two dio- san schools, one of which, the Diocesan Central school, is instituted in 1812, under the patronage of Bishop w ; also a day school supported by endowment ; a ining college, with a commercial, agricultural, and echanical school under the same roof ; and various 'ants' and Sunday schools which are maintained by bscription.
St. John's Hospital, a very ancient institution, founded obably before the reign of Henry III., was demolished iring the siege of Chester, but was rebuilt in the reign Charles II., and its revenues conferred by charter the corporation, in trust for the poor in the hospital ; e charter also included the revenues of St. Giles's ospital in Spital Broughton. In consequence of ex- :me neglect and misapplication, the property belong- g to this charity has been greatly reduced. The ildings which now occupy the site of St. John's Hos- tal form, towards the front, three sides of a qua- angle, separated from North-street by iron-railings ; e south wing is used for the church of Little St. John's, e Blue-coat school occupies the centre, and the re- aining wing contains the master's house, at the back which is an inclosed yard, whereof one side contains : dwellings for poor women, who represent the sister- od of the hospital. Six almshouses founded by Sir iomas Smith in the reign of Henry VII., are inhabited widows of freemen ; four were founded by Robert etcher, in 1674, for widows ; and almshouses con- ming 16 rooms, in St. John's lane, are tenanted by as iny poor women. In 1658, William Jones, of the iddle Temple, granted buildings containing 10 rooms, d endowed them for six poor women and four men ove 55 years of age ; the houses are situated in Pepper- cet, and the income amounts to £67. 16. per annum. iere are various endowments and bequests belonging
591

to dissenters of the Presbyterian denomination, among which are almshouses for four women, in Trinity-lane, erected and endowed with property bequeathed by Mrs. Jane Dean, in 1729. The house of industry, built in 1751, is pleasantly situated near the Rood-eye. The general infirmary, a well-built commodious structure, on the western side of the city, originated in 1756, from a bequest of £300 by Dr. John Stratford, and its expendi- ture is now nearly £3000 per annum : the establishment of fever wards was proposed in 1774, and a few years afterwards carried into execution, chiefly through the exertions of Dr. Haygarth. There is also a lying-in institution, supported by subscription ; and a county asylum for lunatics, capable of accommodating 96 patients, has been erected on the Liverpool road, from a design by Mr. William Cole, jun., at a cost of £25,125.
The *Walls* of Chester rank amongst its principal ANTI- QUITIES, and are the only specimen of this species of ancient fortification in Britain remaining entire ; they comprise a circuit of nearly two miles, and, in the nar- rowest parts, are sufficiently wide for two persons to walk abreast. Of the small towers, or turrets, erected within bow-shot of each other, only the *Phœnix* and *Water* towers exist. To keep the walls in repair, a small murage duty was granted by Edward I. on all merchan- dise brought to the town by sea, but this revenue is not now very productive, in consequence of the principal articles of commerce being landed at Liverpool, and conveyed hither by canal ; the corporation, however, continue the repairs. Besides the city gates before enumerated, which, in comparison with the walls, are modern erections, is a fifth, or postern, between East gate and Bridge gate, called *New gate.* The military im- portance of the city rendered the custody of four of the gates, for centuries, an honourable and lucrative office ; it was held successively by the Earls of Shrewsbury, Oxford, and Derby, and Lord Crewe, and that of the fifth by one of the magistrates for the city. The custody of Water gate, connected with the office of issuing process for offences committed on the Dee, was sold in 1778, by the Earl of Derby, to the corporation. Among the ancient *Religious Establishments* may be no- ticed the monastery, or abbey, of St. John the Baptist, founded in 906 by Ethelred, Earl of Mercia, the revenue of which, at the Dissolution, was £88. 16. 8., and the remains of which now constitute the parish church of St. John ; the monastery of St. Mary, of uncertain founda- tion, for Benedictine nuns, mentioned in Domesday book, and the revenue of which was £99. 16. 2. ; the mo- nastery of St. Michael, of which mention occurs in the charter of Roger, constable of Chester, and also in the reign of Henry II. ; a house of Grey friars, in the parish of the Holy Trinity, probably founded by Henry III. ; a house of Carmelites, and another of Black friars, in the parish of St. Martin ; and, without the North gate, the hospital of St. John, which had a sanctuary and extensive privileges, and the revenue of which was £28. 10. In the neighbourhood of the castle were formerly numerous *Roman antiquities*, particularly at Nunsfield, where remains of a tessellated pavement have been discovered. The esplanade, when cleared of the ancient parts of the castle, was given by government to the county, for the erection of the splendid public buildings which now ornament the site ; but the right

of establishing a fortification, whenever necessary, was reserved for the crown. The eastern wall is built over part of a Roman wall ; but a segment of the wall is left outside the esplanade, for the purpose of clearing it. In a cellar belonging to the Feathers hotel is a Roman hypocanst, in a remarkably perfect state ; and in a close at the southern end of the bridge, termed Edgar's field, the supposed site of Edgar's palace, and adjoining a cavity in a rock, is a stone figure of the goddess Pallas, a relic alluded to by ancient writers. Remains of Roman altars, with figures and inscriptions, have also at different times been discovered. Randle Higden, Roger of Chester, and Bradshaw, mention subterraneous passages under the city; one of these was discovered about the commencement of the present century, extending in a southeastern direction from the ruins of the abbey, but it was soon closed up. On taking down an old house lately in Eastgate-street, a silver coin of Titus was found among the rubbish, and while digging for the foundation of the new building, a pavement was discovered about eight feet below the present road, giving authority to the prevalent opinion that the level of the city was formerly the same as that of the cathedral, the descent to which is now made by several steps.

This ancient city has been the birthplace of several eminent men, the most distinguished of whom were, four antiquaries of the same family, all named Randle Holme; Dr. William Cowper, who made collections for a History of Chester; and the celebrated mathematicians, Edward Brerewood and Samuel Molyneux, the latter a friend and correspondent of Locke. In the church of the Holy Trinity were interred, Matthew Henry, the commentator on the Bible, and a pastor in the city from 1687 to 1713, to whose memory a brass tablet has been placed over the communion-table ; and Parnell, the poet. Chester gives the title of Earl to the Prince of Wales, eldest son of the sovereign.

CHESTER-LE-STREET (St. Mary and St. Cuthbert), a parish, and the head of a union (though a portion of the parish is in the union of Lanchester), partly in the N. division of Easington ward, but chiefly in the Middle division of Chester ward, N. division of the county of Durham ; comprising the chapelries of Birtley, Lamesley, Pelton, and Tanfield, and the townships of Chester, Edmondsley, Harraton, Hedley, Kibblesworth, Lambton, Great and Little Lumley, Ouston, Plawsworth, Ravensworth, Urpeth, and Waldridge; the whole containing 16,359 inhabitants, of whom 2599 are in the township of Chester, 6 miles (N.) from Durham. This place occupies the site of the Roman station Condercum, and was called by the Saxons Conceaster, from which its present appellation is derived, as is its adjunct from its position on the line of the Roman military way to Newcastle : several Roman coins (especially a Gordian in gold, in the possession of the family of the late Mr. Surtees, of Mainsforth), and an altar much defaced, have been found; and specimens of antiquity are still frequently turned up. It was made the head of the ancient see of Lindisfarne by Eardulph, eighteenth prelate, who in 882 removed hither the relics of St. Cuthbert, and founded a church which continued under a succession of eight bishops to be the cathedral of the diocese, till the removal of the see, in 995, to the city of Durham. At this period the church became parochial, and in 1286, Bishop Anthony Beck founded in it a collegiate

CHESTERBLADE, a chapelry, in the parish of ᴇʀᴄʀᴇᴇᴄʜ, hundred of Wᴇʟʟꜱ-Fᴏʀᴜᴍ, E. division of ᴍᴇʀꜱᴇᴛ, 4¼ miles (E. S. E.) from Shepton-Mallet; ᵼtaining 57 inhabitants. The chapel is dedicated to Mary. There are vestiges of a Roman encampment a small hill in the vicinity.

Seal and Arms.

CHESTERFIELD (*ALL SAINTS*), a parish, and the head of a union, in the hundred of Sᴄᴀʀꜱᴅᴀʟᴇ, N. division of the county of Dᴇʀʙʏ; comprising the incorporated market-town of Chesterfield, which has a separate jurisdiction, and the townships of Calow, Hasland, Newbold with Dunston, Tapton, Temple-Normanton, and Walton; the ᵼole containing 10,451 inhabitants, of whom 6212 are the town, 24 miles (N. by E.) from Derby, and 151 . N. W.) from London, on the road to Leeds. This ᵼce, from its Saxon name *Ceaster*, appears to have been ᴿoman station; its Roman name is said to have been *ᵼtudarum;* and there is reason to suppose that in ᵼman times it was an emporium of the mining districts ᵼDerbyshire. At the period of the Norman survey it ᵼs called *Cestrefeld*, and was only a bailiwick to Newᵼld, the latter being now a small hamlet in the parish; ᵼt within a century from the Conquest, it seems to have ᵼen into such importance as to have obtained from ᴺg John, who conferred it upon William de Briwere, charter of incorporation, with the privilege of two ᵼrkets and a fair. In the reign of Henry III., a decisive ᵼtle was fought here between Henry, nephew of that ᵼnarch, and the barons: it terminated in the defeat of ᵼe latter, several of whom were slain; and Robert de ᵼrrers, Earl of Derby, who had espoused their cause, ᵼing taken prisoner, was sent in chains to Windsor, ᵼd afterwards, by act of parliament, degraded from his ᵼnours and deprived of his estates. During the parᵼmentary war, another conflict took place, between the ᵼyalists, under the command of the Earl of Newcastle, ᵼd the parliamentarians, in which the former obtained ᵼignal victory.

The ᴛᴏᴡɴ is situated on an eminence, and the borough ᵼbounded on the south and south-west by the Hipper, ᵼd on the east by the Rother, which are here inconᵼlerable streams: the houses are of brick, roofed with ᵼne; the streets are indifferently paved, but well lighted ᵼth gas, by an act of parliament obtained in 1825, and ᵼe inhabitants are plentifully supplied with water. ᵼere is a subscription library, a mechanics' institute, ᵼd a theatre; and races take place in autumn. An ᵼricultural society was established in 1819, the members ᵼwhich hold their meetings alternately at Chesterfield ᵼd Bakewell, generally in October. Some of ᵼhe inhaᵼtants are engaged in tambour-work, and the ᵼanufacᵼre of bobbin-net lace and hosiery; there is a silk-mill ᵼthe town, and in the neighbouring village of Little ᵼampton a cotton-wick mill, called the bump-mill, and ᵼmall-ware manufactory. In the vicinity are productive ᵼines of ironstone and coal, and some foundries; also ᵼveral potteries, chiefly for coarse brown and yellow ᵼne ware, which afford employment to upwards of 200

men. The Chesterfield canal, communicating with the Trent and the Humber, was completed in 1777, at an expense of £160,000: the Midland railway passes by the town, a little to the east of which is a station. The market is on Saturday: fairs, principally for cattle, are held on Jan. 27th, Feb. 28th, the first Saturday in April, May 4th, July 4th, Sept. 25th, and Nov. 25th, the last being toll-free; those in May and September, at the latter of which a great quantity of cheese is sold, are attended by clothiers from Yorkshire.

The ɢᴏᴠᴇʀɴᴍᴇɴᴛ, by charter of incorporation, granted by King John, ratified by succeeding monarchs, enlarged by Queen Elizabeth, and confirmed by Charles II., was vested in a mayor, six aldermen, six brothers, and twelve capital burgesses, assisted by a town-clerk, chamberlain, two meat inspectors, and a serjeant-at-mace. The corporation now consists of a mayor, four aldermen, and twelve councillors, under the act of the 5th and 6th of William IV., cap. 76: the limits of the borough are co-extensive with the township of Chesterfield. The mayor for the time being, and for the previous year, are justices of the peace *ex officio;* and there are two others. The petty-sessions for the division are held here; and a court of record, for the recovery of debts not exceeding £20, is held under the lord of the manor, by letters-patent granted by King John to William de Briwere, and confirmed by Charles I., in the seventh year of his reign, to William, Earl of Newcastle, and Sir Charles Cavendish, then lords of the manor: the jurisdiction extends over the hundred of Scarsdale, eight miles round Chesterfield. The powers of the county debt-court of Chesterfield, established in 1847, extend over the greater part of the registration-district of Chesterfield. The town-hall, standing in the market-place, was built in 1790; on the ground-floor is a prison for debtors. There is also a house of correction, under the superintendence of the county magistrates.

The ʟɪᴠɪɴɢ is a vicarage, valued in the king's books at £15. 0. 2¼.; net income, £204; patron, the Bishop of Lichfield. The church is a spacious cruciform structure, principally in the decorated, but partly in the early, and partly in the later, style of English architecture, with a tower rising from the intersection, and surmounted by a grooved or channelled spire of wood covered with lead. The clerestory windows of the nave, and the east window of the chancel, are fine compositions in the later style; and in the south transept are a beautiful screen and rood-loft: there are two very antique monuments in the nave, and three in the chancel, to members of the family of Foljambe. The interior of the edifice was renovated in 1842, at a cost of £4000; and it now gives accommodation to 1800 persons. Portions of the hamlets of Walton and Newbold, and the contiguous parts of the parish of Brampton, have been consolidated as a district to the church of St. Thomas, Brampton. In 1838, a church was built and dedicated to the Holy Trinity; it is in the early English style, with a tower, and cost £3700. To this church a district has been assigned, having a population of 3000: the living is a perpetual curacy, in the patronage of certain Trustees: net income, £90, with a glebe-house. There are places of worship for Baptists, the Society of Friends, Independents, Wesleyans, and Unitarians. The free grammar school, for the endowment of which Godfrey Foljambe, in 1594, appropriated £13. 6. 8. annually, was founded in the reign of Elizabeth, and placed under the management of the corporation; the endowment, augmented by benefactions, produces annually £109. 10. 9. : the master is chosen by the trustees of charities, subject to approval by the Archbishop of York. The schoolhouse was rebuilt by subscription in 1710, and was again rebuilt only a very few years since. The school, in common with the schools of Ashbourn and Wirksworth, has the preference, after the founder's relatives, to two fellowships and two scholarships, founded by the Rev. James Beresford, in St. John's College, Cambridge. A school intended originally as preparatory to the grammar school, was founded in 1690, and endowed by Cornelius Clarke; the endowment was subsequently augmented by John Bright, senior, and John Bright, junior, Esqrs., and the income is now £74. A national school was built in 1814, and a Lancasterian school in 1819. The Victoria school, just erected, is intended for the children of the district annexed to the parish church; of these children 50 boys and 50 girls are now clothed and educated at the expense of the vicar, the Rev. Thomas Hill. Judith Heathcote, and other members of the family, in the year 1619 appropriated estates, producing an income of about £114 per annum, to the apprenticing of children.

Thomas Large, in 1664, gave lands and tenements, now worth about £45 per annum, for the foundation and endowment of three almshouses, to which two more were added in 1751, by Mrs. Sarah Rose, who left £200 for their endowment. Almshouses for six aged persons were founded in 1668, by George Taylor, who endowed them with property at present yielding £22 per annum. The dispensary, erected in 1800, is liberally supported by subscription. Godfrey Foljambe, in 1594, bequeathed the rectory of Attenborough, and an estate at Ashover, producing together about £640 a year, which sum, after paying £40 per annum to the minister, £13. 6. 8. to the master of the grammar school, £20 to Jesus College, and £13. 6. 8. to Magdalen College, Cambridge, is appropriated to the relief of the poor. Godfrey Wolstenholme, in 1682, gave a house, let for £38. 5. per annum, which sum is distributed in coats and gowns; and Sir Godfrey Webster, in 1720, bequeathed £1100 South Sea stock. Mrs. Hannah Hooper, in 1755, gave £2000 three per cent. consols., and Mrs. Elizabeth Bagshaw, in 1802, £2000 three per cent. consols.; the dividends on which are distributed to the poor. The union of Chesterfield comprises 34 parishes or places, and contains a population of 39,379. An hospital for lepers, founded prior to the 10th of Richard I., and dedicated to St. Leonard, existed here till the reign of Henry VIII.; and there was a guild or fraternity, dedicated to St. Mary and the Holy Cross, founded in the reign of Richard II., the revenue of which, at the Dissolution, was £19. The chantry of St. Michael, founded by Roger de Chesterfield in 1357, and the chantry of the Holy Cross, founded in the reign of Edward III., were also among the ancient religious establishments of this place. There were besides, prior to the Reformation, three free chapels, dedicated respectively to St. James, St. Thomas, and St. Helen on the site of the last, the grammar school was built. Chesterfield gives the title of Earl to the family of Stanhope; a title conferred Aug. 4th, 1628, on Sir Philip, Baron Stanhope, a firm supporter of the royal cause during the civil war.

CHESTERHOPE, a hamlet, in the parish of COR-SIDE, N. E. division of TINDALE ward, S. division NORTHUMBERLAND, 5 miles (E. N. E.) from Belling-·. This place, which derives its name from the Ro-ι castra, Habitancum, or Risingham, being situated at foot of it, is of considerable antiquity. The church Hexham had some property here at an early period : 294 the prior of the hospital of St. John of Jerusa-claimed extensive privileges over lands he possessed Chesterhope; and the Halls, Forsters, and others have sequently been owners of estates in the district. Park Head are the remains of the celebrated figure ·d Robin of Risingham, cut in bas-relief in a rock, which may certainly be assigned to the Roman era Britain; and stones bearing Latin inscriptions have n found, which are supposed to be relics of the station he adjoining village of Risingham.

CHESTERTON (ST. ANDREW), a parish, and the d of a union, in the hundred of CHESTERTON, county CAMBRIDGE, 1¼ mile (N. E.) from Cambridge; con-ing 1617 inhabitants. The name of this place is de-·d from a castrum, or fortification, called Arbury np, at a small distance from the village, three parts the vallum of which are still remaining, inclosing a are area of nearly six acres, where many Roman coins ·e been found. It appears that every one who kept a here, in 1154, was bound to pay an Ely farthing, as was called, to St. Peter's altar, in the cathedral of r; and the fourth farthing arising from this town and ·t of Grantchester used to be paid to the castle of rwich, by the name of Ely ward penny, because that ·ce received it before. The parish is watered by the er Cam, and comprises 2729 acres, of which 169 are nmon or waste; the soil is in general a gravelly earth, ·h a subsoil of clay. In 1837, an act was passed for losing waste lands. The living is a vicarage, valued the king's books at £10. 12. 3½.; net income, £206; ·rons and impropriators, the Master and Fellows of nity College, Cambridge. The great tithes have been nmuted for £500, and the vicarial for £180; the im-·priate glebe consists of 90½ acres, and the vicarial con-ns 27⅞ acres, with a glebe-house. The church is ncipally in the decorated and later English styles. e poor law union of Chesterton comprises 38 parishes places, and contains a population of 21,608. The nains of Cambridge Castle are in the parish.

CHESTERTON (ST. MICHAEL), a parish, in the ion of PETERBOROUGH, hundred of NORMAN-CROSS, ınty of HUNTINGDON, 4½ miles (N. N. W.) from Stil-ı; containing 129 inhabitants. The parish is situated the great north road, which is here crossed by the ·d from Lynn to Northampton. It comprises by ad-asurement 1330 acres, consisting of arable and pas-e land in nearly equal portions; the soil is in some ·ts a rich clay, mixed with red sand, and in others ılk of fertile quality. The living is a rectory, valued the king's books at £17. 3. 4., and in the gift of the ırquess of Huntly: the tithes have been commuted £417. 11., and the glebe comprises 4¼ acres, with ;lebe-house. The church is principally in the early glish style. Midway between this and Castor is the ? of the ancient city of Durobrivæ, the fort of which s placed on the Huntingdonshire side of the river ne; and at Castle Field is a large tract inclosed by a ch and rampart, with the Roman Ermin-street run-

ning through it obliquely. On making a road across the site of Durobrivæ, several stone coffins, urns, and coins were dug up; and by the side of the high road near this place, in 1754, was found a coffin of yellowish stone, six feet two inches long, within which were a skeleton, three glass lachrymatories, some coins, and scraps of white wood inscribed with Greek and Roman letters.

CHESTERTON (ST. MARY), a parish, in the union of BICESTER, hundred of PLOUGHLEY, county of OX-FORD, 2 miles (W. by S.) from Bicester; containing 393 inhabitants. The living is a discharged vicarage, valued in the king's books at £7. 8. 9.; net income, £210; patrons and appropriators, the Warden and Fellows of New College, Oxford. The tithes were commuted for land in 1767. The church was consecrated in 1238. The Roman Akeman-street crosses the parish.

CHESTERTON, an ecclesiastical district, partly in the parish of AUDLEY, union of NEWCASTLE-UNDER-LYME, but chiefly in the parish of WOLSTANTON, union of WOLSTANTON and BURSLEM, N. division of the hun-dred of PIREHILL and of the county of STAFFORD; con-taining upwards of 2000 inhabitants, of whom 1207 are in the township of Chesterton, 2 miles (N. by W.) from Newcastle. The name of Chesterton evidently has refe-rence to the ancient Roman fortress situated here, the Mediolanum of Antonine; the site is still clearly marked out, and a large fosse exists along the north side of the station. Camden calls the place Chesterton-under-Lyme. The district comprises 2700 acres, whereof 843 are in Audley parish, and 1857 in the parish of Wolstanton; the township of Chesterton, which is wholly in Wolstan-ton, contains about 1100 acres, lying on the north side of that parish. The surface is hilly, and consists of such land as is usual above iron and coal mines; parts are wooded, and the views are extensive. The road from Newcastle to Liverpool passes on the east; and Sir Nigel Gresley's canal (now belonging to R. E. Heath-cote, Esq.) runs through. Considerable quantities of blue bricks, tiles, and pipes for drains and conduits, of superior hardness, are manufactured here; and potteries have been established at Red-street, in the northern part of Chesterton township, for a long period. There are iron and coal mines, several blast-furnaces for smelting the ironstone, and extensive iron-works belonging to Mr. Heathcote. The district was constituted in July, 1846, under the act 6th and 7th Victoria, cap. 37: the living is in the gift of the Crown and the Bishop of Lichfield, alternately. At Chesterton are places of wor-ship for Wesleyans and Independents; at Alsager's Bank, about two miles and a half west of that village, is another place of worship for dissenters, and at Red-street a small Unitarian meeting-house. The site of an ancient castle of John of Gaunt's, is to be seen behind an old mansion in Chesterton, called the Old Hall: the castle was removed to Newcastle, from which circumstance that place derived its name.

CHESTERTON (ST. GILES), a parish, in the union of SOUTHAM, Warwick division of the hundred of KING-TON, S. division of the county of WARWICK, 6 miles (N. N. E.) from Kington; containing 192 inhabitants. This place, which was once a populous town, is situated on the line of the Roman fosse-way, and derives its name from a Roman camp, within the limits of which coins have been discovered. The manor, long possessed by the Peto family, now belongs to Lord Willoughby de Broke. The parish comprises 3566 acres, chiefly pasture and woodland, and of which the surface is hilly, and the soil mostly clay: the road from Warwick to Banbury passes through. The living is a perpetual curacy; net income, £82; patron and impropriator, Lord Willoughby de Broke. The church is an ancient edifice, and contains some handsome monuments to the Petos.

CHESWARDINE (St. Swithin), a parish, in the union of Drayton, Drayton division of the hundred of North Bradford, N. division of Salop, 4½ miles (S. W.) from Drayton; containing 1015 inhabitants, and comprising 5724 acres, of which 96 are common or waste. The living is a discharged vicarage, valued in the king's books at £5. 6. 8., and in the gift of the family of Harding: the tithes have been commuted for £1015. 10., of which £197. 10. belong to the incumbent, with a glebe of 30 acres. The church was rebuilt a few years since. There is a school, which has a bequest of £4 per annum; and a sum of about £36 per annum, the interest of bequests, is appropriated to the purchase of wheat, distributed among the poor.

CHESWICK, a township, in the parochial chapelry of Ancroft, union of Berwick-upon-Tweed, Islandshire, N. division of Northumberland; containing 290 inhabitants. The tithes have been commuted for £347.—See the article on Ancroft.

CHETNOLE, a chapelry, in the parish and hundred of Yetminster, union of Sherborne, Sherborne division of Dorset, 7 miles (S. W. by S.) from Sherborne; containing 222 inhabitants. The chapel is dedicated to St. Peter. A school is supported by endowment.

CHETTISCOMBE, a chapelry, in the parish, union, and hundred of Tiverton, Cullompton and N. divisions of Devon, 2 miles (N. E. by N.) from the town of Tiverton. The chapel is dedicated to St. Mary.

CHETTISHAM, a chapelry, in the parish of St. Mary, city, union, and Isle of Ely, county of Cambridge, 2 miles (N. by W.) from Ely; containing 90 inhabitants. Here is a station of the Ely and Peterborough railway. The living is a perpetual curacy; net income, £79; patrons and appropriators, the Dean and Chapter of Ely. The chapel is dedicated to St. Michael.

CHETTLE (St. Mary), a parish, in the union of Wimborne and Cranborne, hundred of Monckton-up-Wimborne, Wimborne division of Dorset, 6 miles (N. E.) from Blandford; containing 122 inhabitants. It is situated within a mile of the road from Exeter to London, through Blandford and Salisbury, and comprises 1113a. 3r. 25p., with a level surface and chalky soil. A stately mansion, in the style of Sir John Vanbrugh, and probably the old manor-house, is in tolerable preservation. The manor and whole parish, with the mansion, and also the advowson of the church, were sold in 1846 to Edward Castleman, Esq., for £24,400. The living is a discharged rectory, valued in the king's books at £8. 2. 9.: the tithes have been commuted for £180, and the glebe contains about 21 acres: The church is partly in the early and partly in the later English style, and has a very ancient and handsomely carved pulpit. There is a large tumulus or barrow, which, from its extent, is called the "Giant's grave."

CHETTON (St. Giles), a parish, in the union of Bridgnorth, hundred of Stottesden, S. division of

ns; and a school, now conducted on the national
, is endowed with lands producing £38. 12. per
m. Sambrook is said to be the birthplace of Com-
ore Anson.

CHEVELEY (St. Mary), a parish, in the union of
vMARKET, hundred of CHEVELEY, county of CAM-
DGE, 3 miles (E. S. E.) from Newmarket; containing
inhabitants, and comprising by measurement 2526
s. An act for inclosing lands was passed in 1841 :
e is quarried for the roads. The living is a rectory,
ed in the king's books at £16. 8. 1½., and in the
of the Rev. James Thomas Bennet : the tithes have
commuted for £704, and the glebe contains 27
s of fertile land, with a glebe-house. The church is
iciform structure, with a central tower supported by
es and containing five bells; it has a very beautiful
screen, and some curious old monuments to the
ly of Folkes. A school was endowed with an estate
fohn Ray, by will dated 1558, and in 1709 Lord
or added other land; the former is let for £60 a
, and the latter produces £20. In Cheveley Park is
old castle, surrounded by a fosse. A very remark-
fossil tooth or tusk was found in a gravel-pit a few
s ago, six feet in length, with a curvature nearly
ilar ; it is now in the museum at York.

CHEVENING (St. Botolph), a parish, in the union
EVEN-OAKS, hundred of CODSHEATH, lathe of SUT-
-AT-HONE, W. division of KENT, 3½ miles (N. W.)
Seven-Oaks ; containing 1003 inhabitants. The
ish comprises by computation 3774a. 3r. 15p., of
ch 1065 acres are arable, 1244 meadow and pasture,
6 woodland, and 96 in hop-grounds. It is distin-
shed as the residence of the Stanhope family, who
'e a fine seat, at which the late earl, who was cele-
ted for his discoveries in mechanics and natural
losophy, established the improved printing-press
iring his name : his lordship died here, in 1816. A
· is held on May 16th. The living is a rectory, valued
the king's books at £21. 6. 8., and in the gift of the
:hbishop of Canterbury : the tithes have been com-
ted for £761, and the glebe contains 23 acres, with a
be-house. The church is adorned with several elegant
numents of the Lennard family, and one to Lady
:derica Stanhope. Various bequests by the Stanhope
iily are applied in apprenticing children. The Pil-
ms' path, which led towards Becket's shrine at Canbury, passes in the vicinity, and forms a boundary of
: Weald of Kent.

CHEVERELL, GREAT (St. Peter), a parish, in
: union of DEVIZES, hundred of SWANBOROUGH, Dees and N. divisions of WILTS, 6 miles (S. by W.)
m Devizes ; containing 557 inhabitants. The parish
nprises by computation nearly 2000 acres ; the manor
ms part of the endowment of the almshouse at Hey-
bury, founded by one of the Hungerford family. A
all part of the population is engaged in the manufac-
·c of edge-tools. A pleasure-fair is held in the first
ck after the festival of St. Peter. The living, once
: property of Queen's College, Cambridge, to which it
s given by Bishop Davenant, is valued in the king's
oks at £16 ; patron and incumbent, the Rev. R. M.
kinson : the tithes were commuted in 1797, for 307
rcs of land, now valued at £350 per annum. The
urch is a plain neat structure. There is a place of
irship for Independents ; and a school is endowed
587

with an acre of land and a cottage, for the instruction
of six boys. Many Roman coins have been found in
the parish. The late Dr. Lawrence, distinguished for
his Bampton lectures, and last archbishop of Cashel,
was for some time rector.

CHEVERELL, LITTLE (St. Peter), a parish, in
the union of DEVIZES, hundred of SWANBOROUGH, Devizes and N. divisions of WILTS, 5½ miles (S.) from
Devizes ; containing 295 inhabitants. The parish is
immediately under the northern edge of Salisbury Plain,
and comprises by measurement 1006 acres. The living
is a rectory, valued in the king's books at £11. 7. 3½. ;
net income, £405; patron, the Earl of Radnor. The
tithes were commuted for land and a money payment in 1797.

CHEVETT, a township, in the parish of ROYSTON,
wapentake of STAINCROSS, W. riding of YORK, 4¼ miles
(S. S. E.) from Wakefield ; containing 52 inhabitants.
This place is of considerable antiquity, and styled in
Domesday book Cevet; in the early part of the 14th
century there was a chapel. The township comprises
about 850 acres. The mansion here was built in the
reign of Henry VIII., and is an irregular edifice having
several interior courts ; the south front was added by
the Neviles, who put the whole into repair. The Midland railway is carried over a viaduct of thirteen arches,
each 21 feet in span, near Sandal, and afterwards under
a tunnel 700 yards in length, 22 feet wide, and 26 feet
high, in the formation of which, five shafts of 9 feet
diameter were sunk : the total expense of the work was
calculated at about £35,000.

CHEVINGTON, in the county of NORTHUMBER-
LAND.—See CHIVINGTON.

CHEVINGTON (All Saints), a parish, in the union
and hundred of THINGOE, W. division of SUFFOLK, 6
miles (S. W. by W.) from Bury St. Edmund's ; containing 624 inhabitants, and comprising 2429a. 15p. The
living is a rectory, valued in the king's books at
£16. 3. 9.; patron and incumbent, the Rev. J. White :
the tithes have been commuted for £580, and the glebe
consists of 32 acres, with a glebe-house. The church
has some Norman remains. The sum of £20, the rental
of land and cottages purchased with benefactions, is
annually distributed among poor families.

CHEW MAGNA (St. Andrew), a parish, and anciently a borough and market-town, in the union of
CLUTTON, E. division of CHEW, E. division of SOMERSET,
6½ miles (S.) from Bristol ; containing, with the tythings
of Bishop-Sutton, Knowle with Knighton-Sutton, North
Elm, and Stone, 2096 inhabitants, and comprising 4797
acres, of which 37 are common and waste. The village
is beautifully situated on an eminence to the north of
the river Chew, and commands extensive views of the
surrounding country. At the north-eastern extremity
of the parish is a ville, called Norton Hautville or Hawk-
field, supposed to have been the property of Sir John
de Hautville, who lived in the time of Henry III. : in
Knighton-Sutton, at the southern extremity, stands
Sutton Court, an ancient edifice pleasingly situated, by
some thought to have been the residence of Fielding's
Squire Western. The population is partly employed in
coal-mines in Bishop-Sutton, and in the manufacture of
stockings and of edge-tools to a limited extent ; formerly
there was a considerable manufactory for cloth. The
living is a vicarage, endowed with a portion of the rec-
· 4 F 2

torial tithes, with the living of Dundry annexed, valued in the king's books at £30. 13. 4., and in the patronage of the Bishop of Bath and Wells, and others, in turn; impropriator of the remainder of the great tithes, George Smyth, Esq. The tithes belonging to the vicar have been commuted for £416. 15., and those of Mr. Smyth for £98. 3. The church is a massive and spacious edifice with a nave and aisles, 106 feet in length by 60 in breadth, and having a tower at the west end 103 feet high. In the eastern corner of the south aisle is a handsome monument of the Baker family, who formerly had large possessions in the parish, and from whom the manor of Chew-Baker has its name; and inserted in a window of the aisle, is a wooden effigy, supposed to be of Hautville: in the eastern corner of the north aisle are monuments to the Strachy family. There are places of worship for Baptists, the Society of Friends, and Wesleyans. At the western extremity of the parish, adjoining North Whitcomb, on an eminence which commands a fine view towards the Bristol Channel, is Bow Ditch, or Burledge, a circular camp with triple intrenchments. To the north of the village is a well called Bully well, the water of which is said to be efficacious for diseases of the eye.

CHEW-STOKE (St. Andrew), a parish, in the union of Clutton, hundred of Chew, E. division of Somerset, 4¼ miles (W. S. W.) from Pensford; containing 825 inhabitants. This parish, which is situated on the road from Bristol to Wells, and on the river Chew, comprises 2092 acres, whereof 32 are common or waste. It abounds with limestone, and with stone of a reddish granulated texture, in which are found imbedded a few fossils and cornua ammonis; they are both extensively quarried, the former for agricultural, and the latter for building, purposes, and there are also some quarries of white lias, which is used for paving. The living is a discharged rectory, valued in the king's books at £7. 3. 4., and in the gift of the Rev. William Wait: the tithes have been commuted for £270. 12., and the glebe comprises 7 acres. The rectory-house, formerly used as a workhouse, has been restored at an expense of £400 by the incumbent, and is a very singular edifice, considered by antiquaries as one of the most interesting antiquities in the county. There is a place of worship for Wesleyans. A parochial school was founded in 1718, by a few inhabitants who raised funds for its erection and endowment; the income, augmented by subsequent benefactions, is £106. On the lands of Mr. Gray, in the parish, are some remains of a Roman military station, and coins have been found there.

CHEWTON, a tything, in the parish, union, and hundred of Keynsham, E. division of Somerset; containing 138 inhabitants. It is situated on the left bank of the river Chew, about midway between Compton-Dando and Keynsham.

CHEWTON, a tything, in the parish of Milton, union of Lymington, hundred of Christchurch, Lymington and S. divisions of the county of Southampton, 4¼ miles (E. by N.) from Christchurch; containing 633 inhabitants.

CHEWTON-MENDIP (St. Mary Magdalene), a parish, in the union of Wells, hundred of Chewton, E. division of Somerset, 5¾ miles (N. E. by N.) from Wells, containing, with the tything of Widcombe, 1216 inhabitants. The village is situated amidst the Mendip

n, who took possession of this portion of Britain, de the place his head-quarters, and threw up an in-nchment three miles in extent, some traces of which : still apparent. In the reign of Claudius Cæsar, the mans, as appears from an inscription upon a stone g up in 1723 (now in the possession of the Duke of chmond, at Goodwood), erected a temple here, and obably surrounded their station with walls. Other oman inscriptions have been discovered; and a curious ece of tessellated pavement, and several Roman coins, ere in 1727 found in the bishop's garden. Towards the ose of the fifth century the city was taken from the ritons by Ella, whose son Cissa rebuilt it, and called after his own name, *Cissa's ceaster*, fortifying it also ith a strong intrenchment. It subsequently became ie seat of the South Saxon kings, in whose possession e place remained till the middle of the seventh cen-ry, when Wulfhere, the Mercian, invaded it, and took thelwald, its king, prisoner; but on his embracing hristianity, he was reinstated in his dominions, which ² held until he was slain in battle by Ceadwalla, a prince ? Wessex, who subjugated the kingdom of the South axons. On the union of the Saxon kingdoms by gbert, in the year 827, Chichester was of considerable portance; but it suffered greatly from the Danes; and, : the time of the Conquest, had declined so much, that had scarcely a hundred houses within the walls. On he transfer of the South Saxon see from Selsey, where it ad remained for more than 300 years, to this place, the own regained its former importance, and after the Con-uest it was bestowed on Roger de Montgomery, who .rected a castle adjoining the ramparts, and four gates, ind gave the south-western quarter of the city for the iite of the cathedral and residence of the clergy. In the reign of Henry I. a cathedral was built by Bishop Ralph, which being destroyed by fire, that prelate erected a iecond edifice far exceeding the former in magnificence, ì considerable portion of which is incorporated with the present building. In 1189, the greater part of the city was destroyed by fire, and the cathedral, having sus-tained great injury, was repaired and enlarged by Siffred, the seventh bishop, whose effigy in marble was placed in a niche within the building. The castle was ordered to be demolished by King John, but the sentence was not carried into effect till the first of Henry III., 1216; after which a Franciscan convent was founded on its site.

During the civil war in the reign of Charles I., Sir Edward Ford, the sheriff, with the loyal gentry of the county, by assurances of raising a large force in Sussex for the royal cause, invited Lord Hopton from the west, and Chichester, being a walled town, was fixed upon for their head-quarters. While employed in col-leeting troops, improving their resources, repairing the fortifications, and strengthening their position, they were surprised by the sudden appearance of Sir William Waller, the parliamentary general, whose forces had been joined by several troops of horse, commanded by Col. Morley and Sir Matthew Livercy, and who imme-diately commenced a siege. The place was defended for some time with obstinate courage; but after an ineffectual resistance for ten days, the citizens were compelled to surrender on the 29th of December, 1642. The ca-thedral was partly demolished by the parliamentary forces, and the conventual buildings plundered and

589

nearly levelled with the ground; the churches of St. Bartholomew and St. Pancras were battered down, and the houses of the most eminent of the citizens destroyed. Waller made the convent of the Grey friars his head-quarters, and his soldiers were quar-tered in the cathedral. The city remained in the hands of the parliamentarians for six years after its surrender, and in 1648, the ordnance was removed to Arundel Castle, the garrison withdrawn, and the fortifications de-molished.

The CITY is pleasantly situated on a gentle eminence, nearly surrounded by the small stream Lavant, and consists chiefly of four streets, meeting nearly at right angles in the centre of the town, where is an octagonal cross in the decorated English style, which is consi-dered, in design and execution, equal to any structure of its class in England. The streets were formerly ter-minated by four gates in the ancient embattled walls with which the city was encircled: the last of these gates was taken down in 1773; and of the walls, some portions are remaining on the north and east sides, where spacious terraces were raised in 1725, covered with gravel, and shaded with rows of lofty elms, afford-ing a pleasant promenade for the inhabitants, and highly ornamental to the city. The houses are in general well built; and the streets are paved, and lighted with gas, under an act of parliament obtained in 1791 for the general improvement of the town, which is amply sup-plied with water. At the north entrance are the barracks, a spacious building adapted to the accommodation of 16 officers and 328 privates of cavalry, with stabling for 340 horses, and also of 48 officers and 888 privates of infantry; with grounds for exercise and parade. With-out the walls, a new suburb has arisen called Summers-town, which consists of several spacious streets of hand-some houses, and forms a pleasing appendage to the city. The theatre, a neat plain edifice, was built in the year 1791; the assembly-rooms, in which assemblies and concerts are held, were built by subscription in 1781. A public subscription library, situated in the churchyard, was established in 1794. A mechanics' institute was formed in 1824, for which a building has been erected at the extremity of South-street: it is 50 feet long, and 25 feet wide, built of brick, and faced with cement; the interior, which is lighted by two ranges of Grecian windows, contains on the ground-floor the library and apartments for the librarian, and on the upper floor a lecture-room. A literary and philosophical society was established in 1831, and holds its meetings in a house in South-street, built by Sir Christopher Wren, and con-taining a valuable museum, reading-room, and other re-quisite apartments. Races are held at Good-wood, about five miles north of the city; the Grand Stand, lately built, is a quadrilateral building, 120 feet long, and 70 feet wide, surrounded by a colonnade of the Doric order, and capable of accommodating nearly 3000 persons.

The TRADE consists principally in malt, corn (of which a considerable quantity is sent coastwise), flour, timber, and coal. The Lavant empties itself into the sea at Dell-quay, two miles distant from the town, where is a small harbour, into which vessels can enter at high water, and where a collector of customs is stationed to super-intend the transactions of the port; which carries on a small foreign trade, chiefly in timber. Lobsters and prawns, caught at Selsey, about seven miles south of the town, and esteemed the finest on the coast, are sent in great quantities to the London market ; and a large quantity of salt is made at Birdham, about three miles from Chichester. There is railway communication with Worthing and Brighton, on the east, and with Havant and Portsmouth, on the west; the station here is 79½ miles distant from London, by way of Brighton. A branch from the Portsmouth and Arundel canal, on the south side of the town, also contributes to facilitate and promote its trade. The market days are Wednesday and Saturday ; and on every alternate Wednesday is a large market for cattle, sheep, and hogs. The market-house, a convenient structure, was built in 1807 : the corn-market is held on Wednesday at the Corn Exchanges in North and East streets. The Exchange in East-street, erected in 1837, after a design by Mr. Elliot, is a handsome building, 250 feet in depth ; the principal entrance is by a Doric portico of six columns, projecting over the pavement, resting upon square plinths, and supporting a triangular pediment, with entablature and cornice : between the corresponding pilasters of the same order, and the antæ, three large folding-doors lead into the hall, which is 80 feet long, 50 feet wide, and lighted by a range of windows on each side ; and behind are ample stores for the corn which is deposited for sale. There are fairs held annually on St. George's day, Whit-Monday, St. James' day, Old Michaelmas-day, and the 20th of October, the last of them being called the Sloe fair.

The earliest charter of INCORPORATION extant is one by King Stephen : numerous others have been bestowed at various times, the principal of which were granted in the reigns of Henry II., Edward II. and III., Henry VI. and VII., and James I. and II. By the act of the 5th and 6th of William IV., cap. 76, the body corporate was made to consist of a mayor, six aldermen, and eighteen councillors; the borough is divided into two wards, and the municipal and parliamentary boundaries are co-extensive. The elective franchise was conferred in the 23rd of Edward I., since which time the city has returned two members to parliament. The right of election was formerly vested in the corporation, in the freemen at large, and in the inhabitants paying scot and lot within the city and liberties, about 600 in number, with the exception of those of the extra-parochial district of Newton, which, nevertheless, was within the walls, and subject to the jurisdiction of the city magistrates. By the act of the 2nd of William IV., cap. 45, the non-resident freemen, except within seven miles, were disfranchised; and the right of voting was extended to the £10 householders of a district which was incorporated with the borough. The old borough comprised 445 acres, but the limits of the new contain 604. The mayor is returning officer. The mayor for the time being and for the previous year are justices by virtue of their office, and there are six others. The recorder holds sessions for the city and liberties, and a court of record every Monday for the recovery of debts to any amount : there is also a court leet, on the last Monday in November ; and petty-sessions are held every Monday for the borough, and by the county magistrates every Saturday. The Michaelmas quarter-sessions for the western division of the county likewise take place here. The powers of the county debt-court

ith a profusion of gilding. The east end terminates in wainscoted altar-screen, with panels of crimson velvet; and beyond the altar-screen is the presbytery, the of of which is supported by arches of graceful form, ising from clustered columns of Petworth marble, with circular window at the end. The *North Transept* is parated from the cathedral, and appropriated as the arish church of St. Peter the Great. The *Lady Chapel*, hich is of later date, and ornamented with a Catherine-heel window, has been divided into two portions, of hich the upper forms the vestibule of the Chapter brary, and the lower the mausoleum of the Lennox mily; and on the east of the south transept is the cristy, now used as a chapter-house. The *South ransept*, which contains a remarkably fine monument the memory of Bishop Langton, and the shrine which anopies the tomb of St. Richard, has an elegant window ? seven lights, in the decorated style, and is adorned ith two large and interesting historical paintings, for hich it is indebted to the munificence and skill of ishop Sherborne, and which, though defaced by the words of Cromwell's soldiers, are considered very fine pecimens of early painting; also with a series of portraits of several bishops of Chichester, and of the kings f England from the Conquest, concluding with George II. One of the paintings represents the foundation of he see at Selsey by Ceadwalla; the other, Bishop Sherorne, attended by his ecclesiastics, petitioning Henry II. for a confirmation of the charter granted by Ceadalla. There are several monuments and ancient pieces ? sculpture in the cathedral: at the west end of the iddle south aisle is a fine whole-length statue of *Mr. Iuskisson*; and in the same aisle is an interesting monument to the memory of the poet *Collins*, executed in white marble by Flaxman, and erected by subscription. The *Cloisters*, occupying three sides of an irregular quadrangle, are in the later style. Within the last few years, considerable improvements have been made in the interior of the cathedral, which has been repaired and partly restored. Thick coats of whitewash and plaster, which had accumulated for ages, have been removed, monuments restored, and several of the finer portions of the embellishments of the edifice brought to light, among which are some arches over the entrance to the Lady Chapel; the choir has been enlarged and beautified, and many of the old seats and other obstructions have been removed from the nave.

The *Bishop's Palace*, situated in some pleasant grounds near the cathedral, bounded by part of the ancient ramparts of the city, after undergoing numerous changes in its external appearance, was repaired in 1725, and now presents a modern front, consisting of a centre and two wings connected by an open corridor; attached is a handsome chapel, in the early English style. The principal entrance to the palace court is through the Canon-gate, erected in the reign of Richard II., above which was the ecclesiastical prison. The *Deanery* was built by Dean Sherlock, afterwards Bishop of London, in 1725. Of the ancient houses for the canons, only two are now remaining, which have been assigned to the two senior residentiaries; in one of these is a fine Norman arch, with highly enriched mouldings. The house in which the precentor lives, is said to have been the residence of William D'Albini, the fourth earl of Arundel.

591

Chichester comprises the PARISHES of All Saints, or the Pallant or Palatinate, containing 327 inhabitants; St. Andrew, 625; St. Martin, 282; St. Olave, 238; St. Pancras, partly within and partly without the walls, 1065; St. Peter the Great, or the Subdeanery, 5021; St. Peter the Less, 349; and St. Bartholomew Without, 297; with the precinct of the Cathedral Close, 145. These parishes were, by act of parliament in 1753, united for the better maintenance of the poor, under the inspection of guardians. There are also an extra-parochial district called Newton, formerly the Black friars, containing 123 persons; and a small extra-parochial plot beyond the walls, called St. James', and containing 40 inhabitants. The living of *All Saints'* is a discharged rectory, valued in the king's books at £5. 17. 6.; net income, £55; patron, the Archbishop of Canterbury. *St. Andrew's* is a discharged rectory, valued at £4. 13. 4.; net income, £102; patrons, the Dean and Chapter of Chichester. The church is a neat edifice, in the later English style. *St. Martin's* is a discharged rectory, valued at £1. 6. 8.; net income, £67; patrons, the Dean and Chapter. The church, which was rebuilt by Mrs. Dear, of the city, is a handsome structure in the decorated English style: the interior is richly ornamented, and contains a fine monument lately erected to the memory of that lady. The living of *St. Olave's* is a discharged rectory, valued at £4. 18. 9.; net income, £85; patrons, the Dean and Chapter. The living of *St. Pancras* is a discharged rectory, valued at £8. 10. 8.; net income, £120; patrons, the Trustees of the Rev. C. Simeon. The church, which was destroyed during the parliamentary war, was rebuilt by subscription in 1750. *St. Peter's the Great* is a discharged vicarage, valued in the king's books at £16. 8. 4.; net income, £150; patrons and appropriators, the Dean and Chapter. The church is formed of the north transept of the cathedral. The district church dedicated to St. Paul is situated in the centre of a spacious cemetery, in the suburb of Summerstown, near the north gate: it is a handsome edifice in the later English style, with a lofty embattled tower; was built at an expense of £4500, raised by subscription, and was opened for divine service on the 13th of October, 1836. The living is in the patronage of the Vicar, after whose demise it will be in the Dean and Chapter; net income, £150. The living of *St. Peter's the Less* is a discharged rectory, valued in the king's books at £1. 6. 8.; net income, £56; patron, the Dean of Chichester. The church is an ancient edifice in the early English style. *St. Bartholomew's Without* is a perpetual curacy; net income, £65; patron, the Dean. The church, which was demolished during the parliamentary war, has been lately rebuilt. At Newton, a proprietary chapel, dedicated to *St. John the Evangelist*, was erected in 1813, on the lands of the monastery of the Black friars, at an expense of £7000, raised partly in shares and partly by subscription: it is of white brick, with a campanile turret, and two porches of Roman cement; the interior is well arranged, and contains 900 sittings, of which 250 are free. By act of parliament passed in 1812, the Dean and Chapter, the mayor, and all subscribers of £100, are perpetual trustees, and appoint the minister, whose fixed stipend of £80 is augmented by the rent of six pews producing £35 per annum, and an endowment of £200 by the Rev. S. Barbut, and £300 Queen Anne's Bounty. There are places

CHIC

of worship in the city for the Society of Friends, Huntingtonians, Independents, Wesleyans, and Unitarians.

The Free Grammar School was founded in 1497, by
Bishop Story, chiefly for the training of youth intended
for holy orders, and is endowed with tithes and land;
the management is vested in the bishop, who confirms
the appointment of a master nominated by the Dean and
Chapter. Archbishop Juxon; the learned Selden; Collins, the poet; and Dr. Hurdis, professor of poetry in
the University of Oxford, received the rudiments of
their education in the school. The *Diocesan Theological
College* was founded in 1839, under the sanction of
Bishop Otter, and in connexion with the cathedral, for
the preparation of candidates for holy orders; the
students must be graduates of the universities, or such
other persons as are recommended by the bishop, and
they are expected to remain one year. A free school
for affording nautical education to boys, was founded in
1702, by Oliver Whitby, who endowed it with lands now
producing £1230 per annum: charity schools are supported by subscription; and there are also national and
Lancasterian schools. *St. Mary's Hospital*, founded by
one of the deans in the reign of Henry II., for two men
and six women, was re-founded by Queen Elizabeth, in
1562, for a warden or custos in holy orders, two men,
and three women; the warden has a stipend of £160,
and each of the inmates an allowance of £30 per annum: the building consists of a refectory, on each side
of which are rooms for the inmates, and at the east end
a chapel, in which divine service is performed twice every
day. A dispensary, established in 1784; and a noble
infirmary, in 1827, about a mile north of the city; are
supported by voluntary contributions. The latter, which
is denominated the *West Sussex or East Hampshire
General Infirmary and Dispensary*, forms a handsome
range in the Grecian style, 120 feet in length; a wing
has been added, for the erection of which the sum of
£1000 was presented by Charles Dixon, Esq. Mr. John
Hardham, of London, bequeathed property producing
£700 per annum, to be applied to the diminution of
the poor rates.

An hospital for lepers was founded in the reign of
Richard I.: and to the south-east of the city was
a house of Black friars, established by Eleanor, queen of
Edward I., and dedicated to St. Mary and St. Vincent.
At St. Roche's hill, where was a chapel dedicated to that
saint, may be traced the remains of a circular Danish
encampment. At Gowshill, about half a mile further,
is an oblong camp; and on the same side, though nearer
to the town, is another of similar form, but larger, surrounded by a strong rampart and a single moat: they
are both supposed to be Roman, and were, perhaps,
occupied by Vespasian, when he landed on this coast.
Near the vicarage in South-street is an ancient crypt in
fine preservation, to which is a descent of six steps from
the level of the pavement; its history is very imperfectly
known, but it is supposed to have belonged to the
monastery of St. Peter. It is 36 feet in length, 24 in
breadth, and 11 feet high; the roof, which is groined, is
supported in the centre by a range of circular dwarf columns with capitals, and the arches terminate in corbels on
the walls. Bradwardine and Juxon, archbishops of Canterbury; Lawrence Somercote, a great canonist and
writer; and the poets Collins and Hayley, were natives
of the city. The learned Chillingworth was buried in

CHIDDINGLY, a parish, in the union of HAIL-AM, hundred of SHIPLAKE, rape of PEVENSEY, E. 'ision of SUSSEX, 7 miles (S. E.) from Uckfield; con-ning 930 inhabitants. The parish is situated on the d from London to Eastbourne, and comprises 4393a. 16p., of which about 2100 acres are arable, 975 mea-w and pasture, 1051 wood, and 80 in hop-grounds; surface is pleasingly undulated, and from Peake Hill richly diversified prospects. Dicker Common, which s inclosed by act of parliament in 1813, is now fine n land. The living is a discharged vicarage, valued the king's books at £8, and in the patronage of Earl herst; impropriator, A. E. Fuller, Esq. The great ies have been commuted for £550, and the vicarial for 52. 3.; the impropriate glebe comprises 34½ acres, d the vicarial 7 acres. The church is a handsome fice, chiefly in the later style, with a square embattled ver of the early English style, surmounted by a spire; the east end of the south aisle is a chapel in which is splendid, though mutilated, monument to Sir John fferay, Knt., lord chief baron of the exchequer in the ign of Elizabeth.

CHIDDINGSTONE (ST. MARY), a parish, in the ion of SEVEN-OAKS, hundred of SOMERDEN, lathe of TTON-AT-HONE, W. division of KENT, 8 miles (S. S. W.) m Seven-Oaks; containing 1405 inhabitants. The rish in the Textus Roffensis is called Cidingstæne, and other records Chiding-stone; according to tradition, om a large stone supposed to have been the spot where dicial affairs were transacted by the ancient Britons. comprises 5705a. 1r. 19p.; and is bounded on the uth by a branch of the Medway, and intersected by ie river Eden, about a mile south of which, on an ninence, is the village. The South-Eastern railway asses a little to the north. There are 210 acres of oodland. The living is a rectory, valued in the king's ooks at £28. 9. 4½., and in the patronage of the Arch-ishop of Canterbury: the tithes have been commuted r £868, and the glebe comprises 7 acres, with an ex-ellent glebe-house. The church is a very neat building, hiefly in the later English style, and contains some andsome monuments to the Streatfield family, and a eal of bells; the tower is considered the finest in the ounty.

CHIDEOCK (ST. GILES), a parish, in the union of RIDPORT, hundred of WHITCHURCH-CANONICORUM, ridport division of DORSET, 2¾ miles (W.) from Brid-ort; containing 826 inhabitants. It is bounded on the outh by the English Channel. The living is a perpetual uracy, annexed, with the livings of Marshwood and tanton St. Gabriel, to the vicarage of Whitchurch-anonicorum. There is a place of worship for Roman atholics.

CHIDHAM, a parish, in the union of WEST BOURNE, undred of BOSHAM, rape of CHICHESTER, W. division f SUSSEX, 6 miles (W. by S.) from Chichester; con-ining 325 inhabitants. This parish, which forms a eninsula on the coast, is bounded on the east by osham creek, on the west by Thorney channel, and n the south by the harbour of Chichester. It has been ttempted several times to open a more direct communi-ation between this place and Bosham, by means of an mbankment of the sea, but without success; the last mbankment, which was 550 yards in length, and 15 :et high, was swept away by the memorable storm of

1822. The soil is a marl of the richest kind, producing wheat and oats of superior quality; and the Chidham white, or Ledge-wheat seed, which is in so great estima-tion, takes its name from having been first raised in this parish. The living is a discharged vicarage, valued in the king's books at £10. 19. 2.; net income, £114; im-priators, the landowners. The church is in the early English style, with later additions.

CHIDLOW, a township, in the parish of MALPAS, union of WREXHAM, Higher division of the hundred of BROXTON, S. division of the county of CHESTER, 2 miles (S. E.) from Malpas; containing 12 inhabitants. The township comprises 135 acres; the soil is clay and sand. The tithes have been commuted for £18. 10.

CHIEVELEY, or CHEVELIE (ST. MARY), a parish, in the union of NEWBURY, hundred of FAIRCROSS, county of BERKS, 4½ miles (N. by E.) from Newbury; containing 1936 inhabitants, and consisting of the cha-pelries of Leckhampstead, Oare, and Winterbourne, and the tythings of Courage and Snelsmore. This place was the residence of the prior of Abingdon, whose ancient seat still retains the name of Prior's Court. The parish comprises 8925a. 3r. 5p.; the surface is in general flat, and is watered by the Winterbourne rivulet. The living is a vicarage, valued in the king's books at £26. 11. 3.; net income, £1174; patrons, alternately, John Thomas Wasey, Esq., and the Rev. Christopher Capel; impro-priators, various landowners. There are chapels at Leckhampstead, Oare, and Winterbourne; and a place of worship for Wesleyans. In 1759, Thomas Henshaw granted an annuity of £10, with a school-house at North Heath, and in 1805 Catherine Mather bequeathed £800, both sums for educating children; the school was rebuilt in 1839, and placed in union with the Na-tional Society.

CHIGNAL (ST. JAMES), a parish, in the union and hundred of CHELMSFORD, S. division of ESSEX, 3½ miles (N. W.) from Chelmsford; containing 252 inhabitants. The soil is generally inferior; a considerable quantity is a deep wet loam resting on a clayey marl, which, even under the best management, is far from being pro-ductive. The living is a rectory, with that of Mashbury united, valued in the king's books at £10. 14. 7.; net income, £430; patrons, the Executors of the late Rev. B. Hanbury. The church is a small edifice, partly of brick and partly of stone, with a spire of wood; near it is the parsonage-house, a handsome edifice. There was formerly a church dedicated to St. Mary, but it was taken down long since; and the churchyard is now a small field, called St. Mary's croft.

CHIGNAL-SMEALY (ST. NICHOLAS), a parish, in the union and hundred of CHELMSFORD, S. division of ESSEX, 4¾ miles (N. W. by N.) from Chelmsford; con-taining 94 inhabitants. This is one of the smallest parishes in the county, containing not more than 300 acres of land, the greater part of which is of very inferior quality. The living is a discharged rectory, valued in the king's books at £5. 6. 8.; net income, £120; patrons, alternately, F. Austen, Esq., and the family of Coke. The church is of brick, with an embattled tower, and con-tains some ancient monuments.

CHIGWELL (ST. MARY), a parish, in the union of EPPING, hundred of ONGAR, S. division of ESSEX, 6 miles (S.) from Epping, and 12 (N. E.) from London; containing 2059 inhabitants. This place was originally within the bounds of the great forest of Waltham, and in ancient records is styled *Cingwella*, supposed to imply the King's Well, a purgative spring here, from which its present name is derived. In the adjacent forest was a royal mansion, designated Potteles, or Langfords, the only memorial of which is preserved in the name of the site, King's Place Farm. The parish comprises 4522 acres, and, with the exception of 700 acres of common or waste, consists of land in a high state of cultivation, and of great fertility; the scenery is pleasingly rural, embellished with rich woods and thriving plantations; and in the immediate neighbourhood are several handsome seats and villas. The village consists principally of one long street, on the road from London to Ongar and Dunmow, and contains many substantial houses. At a distance of a mile to the south-east of the church is a range of detached villas and good houses, called Chigwell Row, forming one of the most populous and respectable parts of the parish. From these dwellings, and particularly from the top of Hog-Hill House, a hunting-seat, built by Sir James Tylney Long, Bart., is a splendid panoramic view, embracing St. Paul's Cathedral, the line of the Thames for many miles, Norwood, Shooter's Hill, Greenwich Hospital and Park, Woolwich Arsenal, and a large portion of the county of Kent down to Gravesend. The air is very salubrious, owing to the elevated position of the parish, and the inhabitants are noted for longevity. A road made across Hainault Forest from Chigwell Row to Romford, by subscription, in 1809, affords great facilities for traffic to the agriculturists and others of Essex, Herts, Middlesex, and Bucks, to the great market of Romford. Rolls Park, in the parish, was purchased by Eliab Harvey, in the beginning of the seventeenth century, and was the residence of his descendant, Admiral Sir Eliab Harvey, K.G.C., who distinguished himself in the battle of Trafalgar, when his own ship, the Téméraire, was boarded by two French ships, both of which, after a severe struggle, were captured and taken in tow as prizes.

The LIVING is a vicarage, valued in the king's books at £18; patron, the Prebendary of St. Pancras, in the Cathedral of St. Paul, London. The great tithes have been commuted for £900, and the vicarial for £500; the impropriator's glebe contains 56½ acres, and the vicar's nearly 11 acres, and there is a glebe-house. The church is an ancient structure, exhibiting in the south entrance and other parts some remains of early Norman architecture, with a wooden belfry and spire. On the north side of the chancel is an effigy in brass of Dr. Samuel Harsnet, many years vicar of the parish, and successively Bishop of Chichester and of Norwich, and Archbishop of York, who was buried here in 1631; on the south side is a monument in alabaster to the memory of Thomas Coleshill, an officer in the courts of Edward VI., Queen Mary, and Queen Elizabeth, and inspector of the customs at the port of London, who died in 1595. There are several other ancient monuments. St. John's chapel at Buckhurst Hill, consecrated in April, 1837, is an elegant building erected at a cost of about £2000, raised by subscription, including a grant of £200 from the Incorporated Society; the site was given by the lady of the manor, Mrs. Hatch Abdy, of Claybury Hall, who died in 1838, and to whom a monument has been erected in the chapel. The living is in the gift of the Bishop of London. At Chigwell

CHILCOMPTON (St. John the Baptist), a parish, the union of Clutton, hundred of Chewton, E. vision of Somerset, 6¾ miles (N. N. E.) from Shepn-Mallet; containing 618 inhabitants. The name of e parish is derived from its situation in a cold, though cturesque, vale. A clear stream flows through the llage, forming at intervals small cascades; and several easing villas add to the general neatness of the place. ɔal is obtained. Imbedded in the red rock in the vale, e found calcareous spar, iron-ore, branches of coral, d a few *cornua ammonis*: and there are quarries of mmon stone for rough building and the roads. The ing is a perpetual curacy, with a net income of £129: e patronage and impropriation belong to Miss Tooker. ɩe church has been rebuilt on a larger scale. There is place of worship for Wesleyans. On Blacker's Hill e vestiges of a quadrangular intrenchment, inclosing ɩout fifteen acres; and near it are several tumuli, tween which and Broadway are three subterranean vities, supposed to have been iron-pits, but called by e inhabitants "The Fairy Slats."

CHILCOTE, a chapelry, in the parish of Clifton-ampville, union of Tamworth, hundred of Repton d Gresley, S. division of the county of Derby, ¦ miles (S. W. by W.) from Ashby-de-la-Zouch; conining 162 inhabitants. The manor is described in the omesday survey as a hamlet of Repton; it belonged, ɩ early as the reign of Richard I., to the Berkeley family, ho held it under the earls of Chester. The heiress of ir Thomas Berkeley brought the property in the 15th entury to Sir Thomas Brydges, and it was subseuently possessed by the family of Milward, from whom ɩ passed in marriage to the Clarkes. The chapelry is ɩounded on the east by the river Mease, and comprises 325 acres, whereof 771 are arable, 533 meadow and ɩasture, and 20 plantation; the surface is undulated, nd the soil varies from stiff upland to sandstone. At he south entrance to the village is a small piece of ɩasture, on which a tithe-barn anciently stood. The hapel has been lately repaired by Francis Robertson, £sq. Chilcote Hall, formerly the seat of the Milwards, nd afterwards of the Clarkes, has been pulled down.

CHILCOTT, a tything in the parish of St. Cuth-ɩert, city and union of Wells, hundred of Wells-ʳorum, E. division of the county of Somerset; con-aining 70 inhabitants.

CHILDERDITCH (All Saints and St. Faith), a ɩarish, in the union of Billericay, hundred of Chaf-ʳord, S. division of Essex, 2½ miles (S. S. E.) from 3rentwood; containing 247 inhabitants. It is about ɩ½ miles in length and one in breadth, and comprises he manors of Childerditch and Tillingham. The living s a discharged vicarage, valued in the king's books at £8; patron and impropriator, Lord Petre. The tithes ɩave been commuted for £172; the glebe comprises ɩearly 18 acres, with a glebe-house. The church is a ɩeat plain edifice, with a tower of brick surmounted by ɩ shingled spire.

CHILDERLEY (St. Mary), a parish, in the union ɩnd hundred of Chesterton, county of Cambridge, ⁻4 miles (W. N. W.) from Cambridge; containing 54 nhabitants. After the capture of Charles I. by Cornet ʳoyce, in 1647, he was conveyed hither by order of 3romwell, who visited him, in company with Fairfax, ɔoth of them disavowing all participation in the seizure

of his person, and, at the king's request, caused him to be removed to Newmarket. The living is a rectory, valued in the king's books at £6. 9. 2.; income, £20; patron, N. Calvert, Esq. The church is in ruins.

CHILDREY (St. Mary), a parish, in the union and hundred of Wantage, county of Berks, 2½ miles (w.) from Wantage; containing 546 inhabitants. The parish is situated on the Ickleton-way, part of the Ikeneld-street; and comprises 2719a. 18p., of which about 2151 acres are arable, and the rest pasture. The soil, in the lower lands, is a rich black loam, with a substratum of clay; in the middle lands, a whitish loam, resting on soft freestone; and in the uplands, a very shallow light black mould on a white rubble. The surface is intersected by the Wilts and Berks canal, and, to the north of the church, by the Great Western railway. The village is pleasantly situated, and was for one night the abode of Charles I., who, escorted by his own troop, took up his quarters here. The living is a rectory, valued in the king's books at £33. 14. 7.; net income, £604; patrons, the President and Fellows of Corpus Christi College, Oxford. The tithes were commuted for land and a money payment in 1772. The church exhibits some remains of Norman architecture, and contains several ancient monuments, and a curious circular font of lead, divided into compartments, in each of which is the figure of an abbot; the windows have some old stained glass; and there are effigies in brass, inlaid with lead, of William Fyndern and his wife, with the date 1444. Here is a place of worship for Wesleyans; also a few almshouses.

CHILD'S-ERCALL, county of Salop.—See ERCALL, CHILD'S.—*And other places having a similar distinguishing prefix will be found under the proper name.*

CHILDWALL (All Saints), a parish, partly in the union of Prescot, and partly in that of West Derby, hundred of West Derby, S. division of the county of Lancaster; comprising the chapelries of Aigburth, Garston, Hale, Wavertree, and Much Woolton, and the townships of Allerton, Childwall, Halewood, Speke, and Little Woolton; the whole containing 10,714 inhabitants, of whom 186 are in the township of Childwall, 4½ miles (E. by S.) from Liverpool. *Childwall* is supposed to comprise the name of the Saxon chieftain by whom it was first occupied. The manor was held in the 13th century by the de Grelles and Delawarres; subsequently by the de Hollands, de Lathoms, and Sotheworths; and in the 15th century by the Stanleys, from whom it was sequestrated during the war of the Commonwealth. It afterwards became the property of the Le Greys, who sold the manor in the 18th century to Mr. Green, of Liverpool; and more lately it came to the Gascoynes. The heiress of the last-named family married the present Marquess of Salisbury, who assumed, in consequence, the name of Gascoyne.

The parish is bounded on the west and south by the river Mersey, to which the rivulets of Childwall are tributary, and comprises by computation 14,870 acres, of which 680 acres are in Childwall township. The soil is various; in the higher lands a light clay upon red rock, in some few parts sandy, and in the remainder a reddish marl alternated with blue clay. The Manchester railway passes about a mile to the north of the church. Childwall Hall (which, with nearly the whole of the township, is the property of the Marquess of

Salisbury, and entailed upon his second son,) is the splendid residence of John Shawe Leigh, Esq., and is in the castellated style, after a design by Nash; the park and grounds are in beautiful taste, and the scenery forms a panorama almost unrivalled in beauty and extent. The living is a vicarage, valued in the king's books at £5. 11. 8.; net income, £456; patron and appropriator, the Bishop of Chester. The church has some early English piers and decorated windows, but the greater portion is of modern date: the tower is handsome, surmounted by a spire, and of neater stonework than the rest of the edifice. Six other livings are maintained in the parish. There is an endowed school; and various bequests have been made for charitable uses. A cell of monks, here, from the monastery of Up-Holland, had the great tithes before the Reformation. Jeremiah Markland, son of a rector of the parish, a learned critic and classical scholar, was born at Childwall in 1693.

CHILFROOM (*Holy Trinity*), a parish, in the union of DORCHESTER, hundred of TOLLERFORD, Dorchester division of DORSET, 9 miles (N. W. by W.) from Dorchester; containing 128 inhabitants. The living is a rectory, valued in the king's books at £5; net income, £180; patrons, Sir G. Bamfylde, and, W. Fryer, Esq. A school was founded in 1774, by George Brown, who endowed it with a rent-charge of £21.

CHILGROVE, a tything, in the parish of WEST DEAN, union of WEST BOURNE, hundred of WEST-BOURN and SINGLETON, rape of CHICHESTER, W. division of SUSSEX; containing 130 inhabitants.

CHILHAM (*St. Mary*), a parish, and formerly a market-town, in the union of EAST ASHFORD, hundred of FELBOROUGH, lathe of SHEPWAY, E. division of KENT, 6 miles (W. S. W.) from Canterbury; containing 1165 inhabitants. The parish comprises 4332 acres, of which 560 are in wood. Chilham Castle is supposed to have been a post of the ancient Britons, and afterwards a military station of the Romans, there being evident proofs of the latter in the discovery of coins, foundations of houses, and other remains. It is of great antiquity, and was a strong fortress and palace of the kings of Kent, till destroyed by the Danes, in the middle of the ninth century; at the Conquest it was rebuilt by Fulbert de Dover, on whom it had been bestowed. The present stately edifice was erected by Sir Dudley Digges, in 1616, and the interior of the Norman keep made applicable to domestic purposes. On the north-west side are traces of a deep fosse, inclosing an area of eight acres. It is asserted that Cæsar, on his second invasion, here defeated the Britons, who retreated and intrenched themselves in an adjoining wood, where vestiges of their rude and extensive works are still visible; and on a hill at the south-east side of the river, and eastward from the castle, is a tumulus, termed *Julaber's Grave*, supposed to be the place of sepulture of Quintus Laberius Durus, a tribune, who was slain in the conflict. The house, which is in the Elizabethan style, is finely situated on the slope of a hill, commanding an extensive view of the valley of the Stour. On the same eminence, to the north-east of the house, stands the village, protected on one side by the castle and on the other by the church. The Chilham station of the Ashford and Canterbury part of the South-Eastern railway is nine miles distant from the Ashford

und before the time of the Romans; the animals are bite, with a tinge of red on the ears. The living is a carage as to the townships of Chillingham and New-wn, and a rectory as to Hebburn, and is valued in e king's books at £4; patron, the Bishop of Durham; propriator of the remainder of the great tithes, the arl of Tankerville. The tithes have been commuted r £384, and the glebe comprises nearly 2 acres, with a lcbe-house. The church is an ancient and small edifice, ith a Norman doorway; in the chancel is a richly-:ulptured monument, *temp.* Henry VII., to Sir Ralph rey, whose father was killed at the battle of Towton, ad whose grandfather was beheaded by Henry V., ith Lord Cobham, after the Lollard outburst. On an ninence eastward from Chillingham Park is a double trenchment, called Ros Castle, supposed to be a ritish fort; in the park is an ancient camp. At New-ıwn is a cross, termed the Hurle Stone, which is twelve et high.

CHILLINGTON (St. James), a parish, in the union f Chard, hundred of South Petherton, W. division f Somerset, 4 miles (W. by N.) from Crewkerne; ontaining 321 inhabitants. It is situated in a beautiful alley, to the north of the great London road, and com-rises 882a. 1r. 1p., of which 27 acres are common or aste. The living is a perpetual curacy; net income, 60; patron and impropriator, Earl Poulett, whose thes have been commuted for £237.

CHILLINGTON, a liberty, in the parish of Bre-·ood, union of Penkridge, E. division of the hundred f Cuttlestone, S. division of the county of Staf-ord, 2 miles (S. W.) from Brewood. A convent of enedictine nuns was founded by Isabel Lander, and :alled Black Ladies, from the colour of the nuns' dress, ıs a similar sisterhood of Cistercians, about two miles :o the east, in Shropshire, had the name of White Ladies, from the nuns' white habits. The Giffard family were seated here at a very early period. Chillington Hall, a beautiful mansion, long their seat, stands on an elevated site in a spacious park with fine pleasure-grounds and plantations. On the estate is an excellent quarry of brown and white freestone.

CHILMARK (St. Margaret), a parish, in the union of Tisbury, hundred of Dunworth, Hindon and S. divisions of Wilts, 12 miles (W. by N.) from Salisbury; containing, with the tything of Rudge, 593 inhabitants. This parish, which is situated on the ancient Ikeneld-street, belonged to the abbey of Wilton; it was granted by Henry VIII. to William Herbert and his wife, sister to Catharine Parr, and is still the property of their de-scendants, the earls of Pembroke. The parish comprises 3032a. 3r. 14p., and contains clay of excellent quality for bricks and for pottery. The celebrated quarries of freestone, from which was raised the stone for the erec-tion of Salisbury cathedral, have almost fallen into dis-use, being superseded by the Bath stone, which is more easily wrought. The river Nadder, and several of its tributaries, flow through the parish, which is also inter-sected by the Wilts and Berks canal. A fair, chiefly for cheese and horses, is held on the 31st of July. The living is a rectory, valued in the king's books at £19. 13. 4., and in the gift of the Earl of Pembroke: the tithes have been commuted for £411, and the glebe comprises 24 acres. The church is cruciform, with a tower rising from the intersection, surmounted by a

handsome spire; some parts of the building are in the early English style, others of later date. This is the birthplace of John de Chilmarke, a celebrated mathe-matician and philosophical writer who lived in the thir-teenth century.

CHILSON, a tything, in the parish of Charlbury, union of Chipping-Norton, hundred of Stone, W. division of county of Oxford, 5¼ miles (S. by W.) from Chipping-Norton; containing, with the adjacent tything of Pud-licott, 287 inhabitants.

CHILSWELL, a liberty, in the parish of Cumner, union of Abingdon, hundred of Hormer, county of Berks, 5 miles (N. by W.) from Abingdon; containing 12 inhabitants. Here was formerly a chapel.

CHILTERN, county of Wilts.—See Chittern.

CHILTHORNE-DOMER (St. Mary), a parish, in the union of Yeovil, hundred of Stone, W. division of Somerset, 3 miles (N. W.) from Yeovil; containing 291 inhabitants, and comprising by measurement 1395 acres. The living is a discharged vicarage, endowed with the rectorial tithes, and valued in the king's books at £5. 7. 1.; net income, £235; patron, the Rev. John Bayly. The glebe contains 16 acres of land, with a glebe-house.

CHILTINGTON, EAST, a village, in the parish of Westmeston, union of Chailey, hundred of Street, rape of Lewes, E. division of Sussex, 5 miles (N. W. by N.) from Lewes; containing 271 inhabitants. Here is a chapel of ease, a neat edifice in the later English style of architecture.

CHILTINGTON, WEST, a parish, in the union of Thakeham, partly in the hundred of East Easwrith, rape of Bramber, but chiefly in that of West Eas-writh, rape of Arundel, county of Sussex, 9 miles (E. S. E.) from Petworth; containing 747 inhabitants. It comprises by computation 3444 acres, of which 2817 are arable; a portion towards the South Downs is un-inclosed common. The surface is generally flat, but is intersected by a ridge of considerable elevation, ex-tending for nearly half a mile, and commanding good views. The soil near the downs is sandy, resting on a substratum of ironstone: on the steep banks which overhang the roads, are found circular nodules of blue limestone imbedded in clay; and in the lower parts are some pits of Sussex marble of fine quality. The living is a rectory, valued in the king's books at £12. 16. 10½., and in the patronage of the Earl of Abergavenny: the tithes have been commuted for £770, and the glebe comprises 12 acres, with a glebe-house. The church is a handsome structure, chiefly in the early English style, with later additions; it has a spire rising from between the nave and chancel, and a highly-enriched Norman arch at the north entrance. A school was founded in 1634, by William Smyth, who endowed it with land now producing £47 per annum.

CHILTON (All Saints), a parish, in the union of Wantage, hundred of Compton, county of Berks, 3¼ miles (N.) from East Ilsley; containing 309 inhabitants, and comprising 1374a. 2r. 36p. The living is a rectory, valued in the king's books at £13. 8. 4., and in the gift of the family of Heneage; net income, £400.

CHILTON (St. Mary), a parish, in the union of Thame, hundred of Ashendon, county of Bucking-ham, 3½ miles (N. by W.) from Thame; containing, with the hamlet of Easington, 364 inhabitants. The

living is a perpetual curacy, net income, £67; patron
and impropriator, Charles Spencer Ricketts, Esq. The
church contains some fine monuments to the Croke
family, of whom Sir George Croke, Knt., the celebrated
lawyer, famous for his determined opposition to the
tax of ship-money, in the reign of Charles I., was born
and lies buried here. Nicholas Almond, in 1628, gave
property now producing £26. 16. per annum, for distribution among the poor; and there is a small fund for
apprenticing children.

CHILTON, a township, in the ecclesiastical district
of FERRY-HILL, parish of MERRINGTON, union of
SEDGEFIELD, S. E. division of DARLINGTON ward, S.
division of the county of DURHAM, 9 miles (S. by E.)
from Durham; containing 189 inhabitants. The village
of Great Chilton is situated about a mile to the north-
east of Rushyford, and occupies a hilly region: it formed
part of the forfeitures of William de la Pole, Earl of
Suffolk, in 1388. There is a branch of the Clarence
railway from the Durham branch, about three furlongs
in length. The tithes have been commuted for £166. 19.
payable to the Ecclesiastical Commissioners, and £68 to
the vicar of the parish.

CHILTON, a parish, in the union of SUDBURY,
hundred of BABERGH, W. division of SUFFOLK, 1½ mile
(N. E. by E.) from Sudbury; containing 98 inhabitants.
It comprises 979a. 1r. 8p. The living is a discharged
rectory, valued in the king's books at £5. 6. 5½., and in
the gift of the family of Windham: the tithes have been
commuted for £280, of which £80 belong to the rector
of Great Waldingfield; and there are nearly 26 acres of
glebe.

CHILTON, or CHIPLEY, a hamlet, in the parish of
CLARE, union and hundred of RISBRIDGE, W. division
of SUFFOLK, 1 mile (W. by N.) from Clare; containing
150 inhabitants. A small priory of Augustine canons,
dedicated to the Blessed Virgin Mary, was founded
here; but the income not exceeding £10 per annum,
and the buildings becoming dilapidated, it was given, in
1468, to the Dean and Chapter of the College of Stoke:
the remains have been converted into a dwelling-house.
There was also a chapel.

CHILTON-CANDOVER, county of SOUTHAMPTON.
—See CANDOVER, CHILTON.

CHILTON-CANTILO (ST. JAMES), a parish, in the
union of YEOVIL, forming a detached portion of the
hundred of HOUNDSBOROUGH, BARWICK, and COKER,
but locally in that of HORETHORNE, E. division of
SOMERSET, 4 miles (N. by E.) from Yeovil; containing,
with the chapelry of Nether Adbeer, 134 inhabitants.
It comprises 616 acres, and is washed on its western
boundary by the river Yeo. The living is a discharged
rectory, valued in the king's books at £9. 11. 5½.; net
income, £260; patrons, the Goodford family.

CHILTON-FOLIATT (ST. MARY), a parish, in the
union of HUNGERFORD, partly in the hundred of KINT-
BURY-EAGLE, county of BERKS, but chiefly in the hundred of KINWARDSTONE, Marlborough and Ramsbury,
and N. divisions of WILTS, 2¼ miles (N. W. by W.) from
Hungerford; containing, with the hamlet of Leverton,
in Berks, 727 inhabitants. The parish derives its name
from the river Chilt, a small stream by which it is intersected. Here is the residence of Lieut.-Col. Popham,
which is remarkable for its antiquity and the elegance
of its style, and has attached a spacious chapel. The

rk is an ancient residence of the Knights Templars, anted to them by Ralph de Sudley.

CHILWELL, a hamlet, in the parish of ATTEN-)ROUGH, union of SHARDLOW, S. division of the apentake of BROXTOW, N. division of the county of OTTINGHAM, 4¾ miles (S. W. by W.) from Notting-ım; containing 772 inhabitants. The manor was ciently divided; in Domesday book it is called East d West Chilwell, and the parts do not appear to have ?een united until the reign of Elizabeth. In the hamlet ˀe 1475 acres, including the portion covered by the rent (which divides it into two unequal parts) and by s back-water, the Holme-Pit, which is partly in Chil-ell and partly in the parish of Clifton. The soil is ostly of a superior quality, consisting of darkish-red arl, clayey loam, and gravelly loam, with a small ıantity of black peat; the land is divided into arable, ısture, and nursery-grounds, but of late years the pas-re and meadow have considerably increased. The in-ıbitants are chiefly employed in the manufacture of ockings and lace, the latter being of recent introduc-)n. The Midland railway passes through the parish, ıd has absorbed a great portion of the former traffic rough the village, which stands on the old coach-ad between Nottingham and Birmingham. There are, place of worship for Methodists, a Sunday school sup-ırted by subscription, and two endowed almshouses.

CHILWORTH, a hamlet, in the parish of GREAT ILTON, union of THAME, hundred of BULLINGTON, ıunty of OXFORD, 3½ miles (W. N. W.) from Tetsworth; ontaining 93 inhabitants.

CHILWORTH, a parish, in the union of SOUTH TONEHAM, hundred of MAINSBRIDGE, Southampton ınd S. divisions of the county of SOUTHAMPTON, 5 miles ˈS. E. by E.) from Romsey; containing 177 inhabitants. ˈt is pleasantly situated, and comprises about 1200 ıcres, of which 200 are wood and meadow, and the rest :hiefly arable; the soil is peculiarly favourable to the ʒrowth of oak. The living is a perpetual curacy; net ncome, £53; patron and impropriator, John Fleming, Esq. The church is a neat and beautiful edifice, built a ˈew years since, by the late patron, P. Serle, Esq.

CHILWORTH, SURREY.—See MARTHA (ST.).

CHIMNELL, a township, in the parish of WHIT-:HURCH, Whitchurch division of the hundred of NORTH BRADFORD, N. division of SALOP, 1¾ mile (N. N. E.) ᵗrom Whitchurch; containing 16 inhabitants.

CHIMNEY, a hamlet, in the parish and hundred of BAMPTON, union of WITNEY, county of OXFORD, 6¼ miles (S. by W.) from Witney; containing 36 inhabit-ınts. The river Isis flows past the village. An ancient :hapel here was taken down in 1758.

CHINEHAM, a tything, in the parish of MONKS-ȘHERBORNE, union and hundred of BASINGSTOKE, Ba-ıingstoke and N. divisions of the county of SOUTH-ʌMPTON, 1½ mile (N. N. E.) from Basingstoke; contain-ing 34 inhabitants.

CHINGFORD (ALL SAINTS), a parish, in the union ɔf EPPING, hundred of WALTHAM, S. division of ESSEX, 9½ miles (N. N. E.) from London; containing 971 in-habitants. This parish lies on the borders of Epping Forest, in which is a house called Queen Elizabeth's Lodge, where the courts under the Forest laws are held. It is separated on the west from the parish of Edmonton, in the county of Middlesex, by the river Lea; and com-

599

prises 2459 acres of land, whereof 1505 are pasture and meadow, 462 arable, and 492 woodland, of which last 142 are inclosed. The surface is diversified, rising in some parts to a considerable elevation, and commanding richly varied views; and from the situation of Ching-ford on the borders of the Forest, and the number of handsome mansions in its vicinity, it abounds with pictu-resque scenery. The name appears to have been derived from a ford over the river Lea, called the King's Ford; and the principal manor, which belonged to Edward the Confessor, was given by that sovereign to the Cathedral of St. Paul, London, from which it was separated at the Reformation. In the manor-house, now the residence of the Rev. R. B. Heathcote, is the oak table on which James I. is said to have knighted the sirloin of beef on his re-turn from hunting; also an oak panel, supposed to have belonged to the coach in which Queen Elizabeth rode to return thanks after the defeat of the Spanish Armada. A pleasure-fair is held on Whit-Monday. The living is a rectory, valued in the king's books at £14. 5. 5.; patron and incumbent, the Rev. Mr. Heathcote, whose tithes have been commuted for £560, and whose glebe comprises 18 acres. The old church, beautifully situated, is a small ancient building of flint and stone, with a low tower, and in the later English style. In a corner are deposited the remains of Mr. and Mrs. Ramsden, who gave the pulpit, a very handsome one, and were buried about 1590: he was an officer in the household of Queen Elizabeth, and left bequests to this and several adjoining parishes. Sir John Sylvester, recorder of the city of London, and the late Col. Cooke, of the Bengal army, with his lady, are interred here; and there are several very old tablets. A new parish church was lately erected.

CHINLEY, a township, in the parish of GLOSSOP, union of CHAPEL-EN-LE-FRITH, hundred of HIGH PEAK, N. division of the county of DERBY, 2½ miles (N. by W.) from Chapel-en-le-Frith; containing, with the hamlets of Brownside and Bugsworth, 996 inhabitants. It com-prises 3707 acres, of which 98 acres are waste and roads. The impropriate tithes have been commuted for £63.ʹ9., and the vicarial for £11. 5. There is a place of worship for dissenters.

CHINNOCK, EAST (ST. MARY), a parish, in the union of YEOVIL, hundred of HOUNDSBOROUGH, BAR-WICK, and COKER, W. division of SOMERSET, 4½ miles (S. W. by W.) from Yeovil; containing 735 inhabitants. It is situated on the road from Yeovil to Crewkerne, and comprises by measurement 1350 acres. The manu-facture of sail-cloth is carried on to a considerable extent; and stone is quarried, chiefly for rough walls. The living is a vicarage, valued in the king's books at £6. 7. 8¼., and in the patronage of the Crown, with a net income of £140; the impropriation belongs to Corpus Christi College, Cambridge: the glebe comprises 45 acres. The church has been enlarged, and now con-tains 450 sittings, of which 350 are free. There is a place of worship for Wesleyans. Property producing about £60 a year is applied to charitable purposes. About a mile west of the church is a spring of brackish water, from which salt may be extracted.

CHINNOCK, MIDDLE (ST. MARGARET), a parish, in the union of YEOVIL, hundred of HOUNDSBOROUGH, BARWICK, and COKER, W. division of SOMERSET, 3½ miles (N. E. by N.) from Crewkerne; containing 222 inhabitants. It comprises 468a. 3r. 31p., of which about 214 acres are arable, and 254 pasture. The living is a rectory, valued in the king's books at £7. 9. 7., and in the gift of the Earl of Ilchester : the tithes have been commuted for £112. 12., and the glebe contains 39 acres. The church, which has a Norman arch over the southern entrance, has been considerably enlarged by subscription, aided by a grant from the Incorporated Society.

CHINNOCK, WEST (St. Mary), a parish, in the union of Yeovil, hundred of Houndsborough, Barwick, and Coker, W. division of Somerset, 3 miles (N. E. by N.) from Crewkerne; containing 561 inhabitants. The living is annexed to the rectory of Chiselborough : the tithes have been commuted for £160. 4. 8,, and the glebe contains 15½ acres. The church has been rebuilt. There is a place of worship for Wesleyans.

CHINNOR (St. Andrew), a parish, in the union of Wycombe, hundred of Lewknor, county of Oxford, 3½ miles (N. E. by E.) from Watlington; containing, with the liberty of Henton, 1308 inhabitants. The parish comprises 2485 acres, of which 150 are common or waste. The living is a rectory, valued in the king's books at £26. 0 5., and in the patronage of Sir James Musgrave, Bart. : the incumbent's tithes have been commuted for £701. 12., and the glebe contains upwards of 15 acres, with a glebe-house; a rent-charge of £50 is paid to the Dean and Canons of Windsor. The church is an elegant structure, partly in the early and partly in the decorated English style, with an embattled tower strengthened by buttresses; it contains some brasses and interesting monuments. The Roman Ikeneld-street enters the county at this place, and crossing the Thames, points towards Goring.

CHIPCHASE, with Gunnerton, a township, in the parish of Chollerton, union of Hexham, N. E. division of Tindale ward, S. division of Northumberland, 9 miles (N. N. W.) from Hexham; containing 372 inhabitants. Chipchase Castle, a large and beautiful structure, stands upon a lofty eminence, at the foot of which flows the North Tyne. Of the ancient building only a tower remains : it has a projecting battlement resting on corbels, and there are openings for missiles; some tattered fragments of paintings on the walls are exceedingly curious. A private chapel, in which the vicar performs divine service four times in the year, was rebuilt by John Reed, Esq., in 1732, on the lawn of the castle.—See Gunnerton.

CHIPPENHAM (St. Margaret), a parish, in the union of Newmarket, hundred of Staploe, county of Cambridge, 4½ miles (N. N. E.) from Newmarket; containing 666 inhabitants. William de Mandeville, Earl of Essex, gave this manor to the society of Knights Hospitallers, who fixed a subordinate establishment here. Charles I., during the civil war, enjoyed the diversion of bowling at Chippenham Park, the seat of Sir William Russel; and George I. was entertained here by Admiral Russel, Oct. 4th, 1717. About the middle of the seventeenth century the estate was possessed by Sir Francis Russel, Bart., whose daughter was married to the fourth son of the Protector Cromwell. The parish comprises 4205 acres, of which 43 are common or waste. The living is a discharged vicarage, valued in the king's books at £11. 12. 6.; patron and impropriator, John Tharp, Esq. : the vicarial tithes have been commuted for £325,

separated from that of Whalley, some years before the reign of Edward the Confessor. In Edward III.'s reign, John de Chepin granted the homage and service of thirteen vassals to Richard Knolle; and, with a short interval, in which the property was seized into the hands of the crown for felony, it continued in the Knolle family until the 7th of Henry VIII., when a female heir brought the estate to the knightly family of Sherburne, of Stonyhurst, from whom it passed to the Welds, and recently to the Earl of Derby. The parish is picturesquely situated in the ancient forest of Bowland, and is inclosed by Whitmoor hills and Longridge Fell. It comprises 8763a. 1r. 26p., whereof about 836 acres are arable, 5439 meadow and pasture, 90 wood and plantations, and a great part of the remainder common and waste: the township of Chipping contains 5582a. 2r. 24p. The soil is rather light, in some parts inclining to moor and peat, and the lands are watered by two rivulets called Lunde and Chipping brooks: limestone, in which fossils are found, is obtained in abundance. There are two cotton-mills, of which one, belonging to John Evans, Esq., has been established more than half a century, and is propelled by water and steam power; the other is the property of Simon Bond, Esq., and began working in 1806, water-power only being used.

The living is a discharged vicarage, valued in the king's books at £36. 13. 4.; patron, the Bishop of Chester, as appropriator of the rectory, which is valued at £24. 16. 5½. The income of the vicar is £120; it is derived, in part, from lands in Dutton and Whittingham, producing £38, and includes £33. 13. 4. assigned in lieu of tithes. The great tithes of Chipping township have been commuted for £399; and the bishop's glebe consists of 13 acres. The church was built in 1520; it is in the early English style, with a tower, and contains a polygonal font, of ancient date, with a carved inscription: in the churchyard is a stone cross, dated 1705, and surmounted by a dial. There are places of worship for Independents and Presbyterians; also one for Roman Catholics, built in 1827, on a site given by George Weld, Esq., of Leagram Hall. In 1684, John Brabbin left lands in Chipping, now producing £68 per annum, to clothe and educate 24 boys; and an estate now yielding £45 per year, to place them out as apprentices. He also founded an almshouse for six aged females, who each receive 12s. per month, and coal; and there are several minor charities.

CHIPPING-CAMPDEN. — See CAMPDEN, CHIPPING.—*And all places having a similar distinguishing prefix will be found under the proper name.*

CHIPPINGHURST, a hamlet, in the parish of CUDDESDEN, union of HEADINGTON, hundred of BULLINGTON, county of OXFORD, 7¼ miles (N. by W.) from Bensington; containing 18 inhabitants.

CHIPSTABLE (*ALL SAINTS*), a parish, in the union of WELLINGTON, hundred of WILLITON and FREEMANNERS, W. division of SOMERSET, 3 miles (W. by S.) from Wiveliscombe; containing 389 inhabitants. It is situated on the road from Taunton to Barnstaple, through Bampton, and comprises nearly 2200 acres: the meadows are irrigated by the waters flowing from Hedon and Byballs Hills, causing the growth of a luxuriant herbage; and the river Tone runs through the parish. Stone of the greywacke kind is quarried for the repair of the roads. The living is a rectory, valued in the king's books at £11. 1. 8., and in the gift of James Templer, Esq. : the tithes have been commuted for £275, and the glebe consists of 35 acres, with a glebe-house. The church, with the exception of the tower, which is handsome, is in a very dilapidated state, through age. The remains of a Roman encampment may be seen.

CHIPSTEAD (ST. MARGARET), a parish, in the union, and Second division of the hundred, of REIGATE, E. division of SURREY, 2¾ miles (N. by E.) from Gatton ; containing 666 inhabitants. It consists of arable and woodland, with some upland pastures : chalk in general forms the subsoil. The London and Brighton railway passes a little to the east of the church. The living is a rectory, valued in the king's books at £17. 13. 11½.; patron, Sir W. G. Hylton Jolliffe : the tithes have been commuted for £410, and there is a glebe of 43 acres. The church was restored in 1827; on the north side is a fine Norman arch. Here is a school endowed by Mary Stephens, in 1746, with land producing £70 per annum. Sir Edward Banks, Knt., the great contractor for public works, lies buried in the churchyard, the quiet and beauty of which fixed his attention in early life while he was employed as a labourer on the Merstham railway; he died in 1835.

CHIRBURY (ST. MICHAEL), a parish, in the hundred of CHIRBURY, S. division of SALOP, 3¼ miles (E. N. E.) from Montgomery ; containing 1593 inhabitants, of whom 278 are in the township of Chirbury. This is a place of considerable antiquity, and was distinguished during the heptarchy for its stately castle, erected by Ethelfreda, Countess of Mercia, to check the incursions of the Welsh. A priory of the order of St. Bennet was founded by Robert de Boulers, in the reign of John, or beginning of that of Henry III., at Snede; but it was shortly removed to this spot, where it continued to flourish until the 9th of Edward I., when the establishment was transferred to the place of its original institution, still retaining the name of Chirbury. The monks appear to have held considerable property in the neighbourhood ; and in the 7th of Edward II. that monarch confirmed their rights and privileges. But few other notices of the priory occur until the Dissolution, when its revenue was returned at £87. 7. 4., and the site was given to Edward Hopton.

The parish is situated on the road from Montgomery to Shrewsbury, and comprises by measurement 10,648 acres ; the largest stream is the Camblad. On the borders of the parish are some lead-mines : stone of a greyish green colour, and of very hard quality, is quarried for building and ornamental uses ; and white spar is found at Wotherton, of which great quantities are shipped to America. The living is a vicarage, valued in the king's books at £9. 6. 8.; stipend of the minister, £179; patrons, the Bishop of Lichfield (ex officio visiter of Shrewsbury grammar school), the Earl of Powis, J. A. Lloyd, Esq., Sir A. V. Corbet, Bart., and R. A. Slaney, Esq., as trustees. The impropriation is vested in the governors of Shrewsbury school, and furnishes its chief endowment ; the tithes have been commuted for £1000. The church is in the early English style, with a tower, surmounted by open battlements, and crowned with eight pinnacles. A chapel has been built, containing 280 sittings, of which 249 are free, the Incorporated Society having granted £150, and the Diocesan Society a like sum, in aid of the expense. There are places of

on of Essex, 5 miles (E.) from Royston; containing 6 inhabitants. It·comprises 2480a. 1r. 38p. The llage is situated on a hill of considerable elevation, mmanding a fine view of the surrounding district, iich is highly cultivated, and enriched with woodland enery. The living is a discharged vicarage, valued in e king's books at £10; net income, £173; patron d impropriator, J. Wilkes, Esq. The tithes of Great d Little Chishall were commuted for land and corn-nts, in 1811. The church is an ancient edifice, with tower surmounted by a small spire.

CHISHALL, LITTLE (St. Nicholas), a parish, in e union of Royston, hundred of Uttlesford, N. vision of Essex, 5½ miles (E. by S.) from Royston; ntaining 96 inhabitants. It consists chiefly of low nds, and comprises 1167a. 1r. 37p., of which about)58 acres are arable, 24 pasture, and 85 woodland; e soil is clay and chalk in some parts, and in others, ipecially the flat portions, a dry light gravel. The ving is a rectory, annexed to that of Haydon, and alued in the king's books at £14. 10. The church a small but lofty edifice of great antiquity, with a orch of freestone, and a tower partly of stone and artly of wood. John de Chishal or Chishull, Bishop ? London, who died in the year 1279, took his name om the place.

CHISLEBOROUGH (St. Peter and St. Paul), a arish, in the union of Yeovil, hundred of Hounds-dRough, Barwick, and Coker, W. division of Somer-et, 4 miles (N. N. E.) from Crewkerne; containing 540 habitants. It is intersected by the river Parret, and omprises about 730 acres, of which the surface is high nd the soil sandy. A fair for horses, cattle, and toys, s held on the last Tuesday in October. The living is a ectory, with that of West Chinnock annexed, valued in he king's books at £14. 5. 7½., and in the patronage f the family of Wyndham: the tithes have been com-nuted for £246. 17., and the glebe comprises 36 .eres.

CHISLEDON (Holy Cross), a parish, in the union f Highworth and Swindon, hundred of Kings-iRidge, Swindon and N. divisions of Wilts, 3½ miles S. E.) from Swindon; containing, with the tythings of 3adbury and Hodson, 1176 inhabitants. The living is i discharged vicarage, valued in the king's books at 18. 8. 9.; net income, £173; patron and impropriator, *. Calley, Esq.

CHISLEHAMPTON (St. Katherine), a parish, in he union of Abingdon, hundred of Dorchester, ounty of Oxford, 6 miles (N. by W.) from Bensing-on; containing 153 inhabitants. This parish, which is ituated on the Thame, comprises 901a. 39p.: the sur-ace is varied, rising into hills in some parts, and being n others level; the soil is clayey but fertile. Chisle-iampton Lodge is a handsome residence, in the grounds round which is one of the largest and finest elm-trees n the county. The living is. a perpetual curacy, with hat of Stadhampton; net income, £135; patron and mpropriator, Charles Peers, Esq.

CHISLET (St. Mary), a parish, in the union of 3lean, hundred of Bleangate, lathe of St. Augus-'ine, E. division of Kent, 7 miles (N. E.) from Canter-iury; containing 1097 inhabitants. It comprises 6675 .cres, of which 1054 are in wood. The living is a vicar-ige, valued in the king's books at £29. 19. 9½.; net in-

come, £231; patron and appropriator, the Archbishop of Canterbury. The church is in the early English style: the parsonage-house was rebuilt by the incum-bent, in· 1834. In 1811, the archbishop demised cer-tain land, which lets for £40 per annum, for the edu-cation of children; the income is applied to a national school.

CHISWICK (St. Nicholas), a parish, in the union of Brentford, Kensington division of the hundred of Ossulstone, county of Middlesex, 4½ miles (W. by S.) from London; containing 5811 inhabitants. This place is pleasantly situated on the margin of the Thames, to the left of the great western road from London, and contains many elegant seats belonging to the nobility and gentry, the principal of which, Devonshire House, is adorned on each side with fine rows of cedars : in this mansion died Charles James Fox, in 1806, and George Canning, in 1827. Here are the extensive gardens be-longing to the Horticultural Society of London, incor-porated by charter in 1808, for the improvement of hor-ticulture in all its branches. The living is a vicarage, in the patronage of the Dean and Chapter of St. Paul's, London (the appropriators), valued in the king's books at £9. 18. 4.; net income, £601. In the churchyard are some ancient tombs, and a monument to the memory of Hogarth. At Turnham-Green is a second church. The late Rev. H. F. Cary, the translator of Dante, was for some time curate, and afterwards lecturer, of Chis-wick, where he resided in the house once occupied by Hogarth, which he had purchased.

CHISWORTH, a township, in the parish and union of Glossop, hundred of High Peak, N. division of the county of Derby, 9 miles (N. N. W.) from Chapel-en-le-Frith; containing 532 inhabitants. It comprises 844 acres, and has an old romantic village, seated about four miles south-west of Glossop. There, are a colliery, a cotton-spinning factory, and an establishment for candle-wicks. A Methodist place of worship was built in 1831. The ruins of an old chapel and monastery still exist at this place.

CHITHURST, a parish, in the union of Midhurst, hundred of Dumpford, rape of Chichester, W. divi-sion of Sussex, 3¼ miles (W. N. W.) from Midhurst; containing 232 inhabitants. It is intersected by the river Rother, and comprises 1047 acres, of which 275 are common or waste. The living is a rectory, annexed to that of Iping: the church is in the early English style of architecture.

CHITTERN (All Saints), a parish, in the union of Warminster, hundred of Heytesbury, Warminster and S. divisions of Wilts, 4 miles (E. N. E.) from Hey-tesbury; containing 403 inhabitants. It is situated on the road from Amesbury to Bristol, and comprises by measurement 4288 acres; the lands are watered by several springs, which, during part of the year, rise in the parish and neighbourhood, and, uniting, form a con-siderable stream. The living is a discharged vicarage, with the vicarage of Chittern St. Mary, and is valued in the king's books at £7. 0. 10.; net income, £319; pa-trons, alternately, the Bishop and the Dean and Chapter of Salisbury; impropriators of All Saints', the family of Serle. The tithes of both parishes were commuted for land and corn-rents, in 1815, and the great tithes of All Saints' have been, under the recent act, commuted for £113. The church is an ancient structure. Westward from the place is a small Roman camp, named Knooke Castle, and near it an irregular ditch running in various directions, as if intended to form some ancient boundary line; there are also some remains of a convent in the parish. Commodore Michel, who circumnavigated the globe with Captain Cook, was born and buried here.

CHITTERN (ST. MARY), a parish, in the union of WARMINSTER, hundred of HEYTESBURY, Warminster and S. divisions of WILTS, 3¾ miles (E. by N.) from Heytesbury; containing 180 inhabitants. It comprises by measurement 1075 acres, and is in every respect similar to the parish of Chittern All Saints; they both form one village of a single street, each side of which is respectively in its own parish. The living is a discharged vicarage, united to that of All Saints, and valued in the king's books at £6: the appropriate tithes, belonging to the Dean and Chapter of Sarum, have been commuted for £125; the vicarial glebe consists of 164 acres. There is a place of worship for dissenters.

CHITTLEHAMPTON (ST. URITH), a parish, in the union and hundred of SOUTH MOLTON, South Molton and N. divisions of DEVON, 5¼ miles (W.) from South Molton; containing 1893 inhabitants. This parish, which is situated on the river Taw, and intersected by the new Exeter road, comprises 8673 acres, of which 150 are common or waste. It is enlivened with some beautiful scenery on the banks of the river, especially at Head Wood; and the grounds of Hudscott, one of the seats of the Rolle family, add materially to the interest of the view. Culm is obtained within its limits, and limestone is found, imbedded in thick slate or flagstone. A fair is held on the third Thursday in March. The living is a vicarage, valued in the king's books at £34. 18. 11¼.; net income, £413; patrons and impropriators, the family of Rolle. The church is in the later English style, and has a handsome embattled tower: the pulpit is richly ornamented with figures of saints and with foliage finely carved, and the window above the altar is embellished with painted glass; there are some beautiful monuments to the Giffards and the Rolle family. A chapel, dedicated to St. John, was built in 1838, by subscription, aided by a grant of £200 from the Incorporated Society, and was endowed by Lord Rolle, who also built a residence for the minister. At Brightley are to be seen some remains of an ancient mansion and a chapel.

CHITTOE, a tything, in the parish of BISHOP'S-CANNINGS, union of DEVIZES, hundred of POTTERNE and CANNINGS, Devizes and N. divisions of WILTS, 5 miles (N. W.) from Devizes; containing 207 inhabitants. Here is a church, dedicated to St. Mary, and having a consolidated chapelry attached; it is built on a site given by Mrs. Starkie, is in the old English style, was consecrated in October, 1845, and contains 170 sittings. The living is a perpetual curacy, in the gift of the Bishop of Salisbury.

CHIVELSTONE (ST. SYLVESTER), a parish, in the union of KINGSBRIDGE, hundred of COLERIDGE, Stanborough and Coleridge, and S. divisions of DEVON, 6 miles (S. E. by S.) from Kingsbridge; containing 591 inhabitants. It comprises 2547 acres, of which 555 are common or waste. The living is annexed to the vicarage of Stokenham. At Ford is a meeting-house for dissenters.

CHIVESFIELD, HERTFORD.—See GRAVELEY.

e village. The living is a rectory, valued in the king's oks at £11.0.7½., and in the patronage of Oriel College, ¢ford: the tithes have been commuted for £267, and e glebe contains 9 acres, with a glebe-house lately ilt. A new church has been erected near the site of e old one. Anthony Cratcherode, Esq., in 1753, queathed £12 per annum for charitable purposes.

CHOLLERTON (St. Giles), a parish, in the union HEXHAM, N. E. division of TINDALE ward, S. division NORTHUMBERLAND; containing, with the chapelry Birtley, and the townships of Barrasford, Colwell ith Swinburn, and Gunnerton with Chipchase, 1129 habitants, of whom 155 are in the township of Chol-rton, 6 miles (N.) from Hexham. The living is a carage, valued in the king's books at £6. 14. 4½.; net come, £361; patron and incumbent, the Rev. C. Bird; proprietors, the Mercers' Company and others. The eat tithes of the township of Chollerton have been mmuted for £233, and the small for £76; the vicar s a glebe of 7 acres. The church contains an east ndow of stained glass. At Birtley is a separate in-umbency. About a mile from the village of Chollerton ·as the line of the walls and fosse erected by the Romans nd South Britons, at various times, to protect them-elves from the incursions of the Picts.

CHOLMONDELEY, a township, in the parish of IALPAS, union of NANTWICH, Higher division of the undred of BROXTON, S. division of the county of HESTER, 7½ miles (W.) from Nantwich; containing 60 inhabitants. Cholmondeley House was garrisoned n 1643, by 400 royalists, who, in the month of April, vere attacked and defeated by the parliamentary troops rom Nantwich, losing 50 men and 600 horses; it was ifterwards recaptured by the royalists, who were driven rom it again on the 30th of June, 1644. The present ıplendid seat of the Marquess of Cholmondeley, about ıalf a mile from the former house, was begun in 1801, ınd completed in 1804; a chapel, to which the tenants ınay resort, is attached to it. The township comprises 1691 acres; the soil is clay, with a little sand. The :ithes of the township, with those of Bickley, Bulkeley, ınd Larkton, have been commuted for £342 payable to :he impropriators, and £32. 8. to the rector of Malpas.

CHOLMONDSTONE, a township, in the parish of ACTON, union and hundred of NANTWICH, S. division of :he county of CHESTER, 4½ miles (N. by W.) from Nant-wich; containing 206 inhabitants. It comprises 1740 ıcres, of which the soil is clay.

CHOLSALL, a hamlet, in the parish of ST. HELEN, ınion of ABINGDON, hundred of HORMER, county of BERKS; containing 16 inhabitants.

CHOLSEY (St. Mary), a parish, in the union and ɔarliamentary borough of WALLINGFORD, hundred of READING, though locally in the hundred of MORETON, :ounty of BERKS, 3 miles (S. W.) from Wallingford; :ontaining 1191 inhabitants. This place was distin-ɡuished for its monastery, founded in 986, by Ethelred, ıs an atonement for the murder of his brother, Edward :he Martyr, and which, together with the village, was destroyed by the Danes in 1006. The manor belonged :o the abbots of Reading, who had a splendid seat here, which was granted in 1555 to Sir Francis Englefield, ınd afterwards conveyed by the crown to William Knollys, Viscount Wallingford, subsequently created Earl of Banbury: the great barn, which measured 301

605

feet in length, 54 feet in breadth, and 51 in height, was taken down some years since, and four smaller ones were erected in its place. The parish comprises 4118a. 3r. 8p., of which 2971 acres are arable, 533 meadow, 340 common, 130 down, and 143 wood; it is intersected by the Great Western railway. The living is a vicarage, with that of Moulsford united, valued in the king's books at £18. 9. 9½., and in the patronage of the Crown; net income, £375; impropriators, the family of Minshull. The church contains some portions of Norman archi-tecture.

CHOLSTREY, a township, in the parish and union of LEOMINSTER, hundred of WOLPHY, county of HERE-FORD; containing 160 inhabitants.

CHOPPINGTON, a township, in the parish and divi-sion of BEDLINGTON, union of MORPETH, county of NORTHUMBERLAND, 4 miles (E. by S.) from Morpeth; containing 167 inhabitants. The township consists of East and West Choppington, both situated on the way side between Morpeth and the Stakeford, and of part of the hamlet of Sheepwash, where is a bridge of four arches over the Wansbeck, from which the prospect is very beautiful. The whole estate comprises about 625 acres, tithe-free.

CHOPWELL, a township, in the parish of RYTON, union of GATESHEAD, W. division of CHESTER ward, N. division of the county of DURHAM, 11½ miles (W. S. W.) from Gateshead; containing 320 inhabitants. It was given by Bishop Hugh to the abbey of Newminster, and at the Dissolution was held under that establishment by the Swinburns, who are supposed to have received from the crown a grant of the fee simple; it afterwards belonged to the families of Constable, Clavering, and Cowper, and now is the property of various owners. The township contains some coal; and at Black-hall, on the river Derwent, is a manufactory for German steel, which is stated to have been first carried on by some emigrants from Germany.

CHORLEY, a township, in the parish of WILMSLOW, union and hundred of MACCLESFIELD, N. division of the county of CHESTER, 5¾ miles (N. W. by W.) from Macclesfield; containing 561 inhabitants. This was a seat of the Davenports from about the year 1400 until 1612, when it was purchased by the Downes family; and in 1640 it came, also by purchase, to the Stanleys of Alderley. The Hall was an ancient timber mansion, within a moated site, but latterly became a farmhouse. The township comprises 1242 acres, whereof 194 are common land or waste; the soil is clay. The tithes have been commuted for £169. 10.

CHORLEY, a township, in the parish of WRENBURY, union and hundred of NANTWICH, S. division of the county of CHESTER, 5¼ miles (W. by S.) from Nantwich; containing 183 inhabitants. The manor was possessed by the Harcourt family in the reign of Edward II., when the two coheiresses of Robert Harcourt married into the Cholmondeley family. Isabel brought a moiety to Hugh Cholmondeley, whose daughter and heiress married Roger Bromley, of Basford; after continuing in the Bromley family for several descents, it was purchased, in 1561, by the Cholmondeleys of Cholmondeley, ances-tors of the present Marquess of Cholmondeley. The other moiety passed with Maud to the ancestor of the Cholmondeleys of Chorley, and came to the marquess's family by purchase, in the reign of Henry VI. The township comprises 1288 acres, of which the soil is clayey. The Primitive Methodists have a place of worship, and a Sunday school. The impropriate tithes have been commuted for £81, and the vicarial for £28. 17. 11., payable to the incumbent of Acton.

CHORLEY (ST. LAWRENCE), a market-town and parish, and the head of a union, in the hundred of LEYLAND, N. division of the county of LANCASTER, 32 miles (S. by E.) from Lancaster, and 208 (N. W. by N.) from London; containing 13,139 inhabitants. The name of this place is derived from its situation on the river Chòr, about a mile from its confluence with the Yarrow, and from the Saxon word Ley, a field; or from the family of Chorley, who were its ancient proprietors. The chief lordships of Chorley were subsequently held by the noble families of Ferrers and Lacy. A moiety of the manor was at a still later period possessed by the Sherburnes, and the other half by the Stanleys: the Sherburne portion afterwards passed to the Welds of Lulworth, who sold it about 1806 to Thomas Gillibrand, Esq. of Chorley Hall, whose ancestor, in the 17th century, had married into the Chorley family. On his death in 1829, the manor came in moieties to his widow and son. In 1644 Prince Rupert passed through the town at the head of a large army, on his march to York; and in 1648 Cromwell, after the battle of Ribblesdale, slept at Astley Hall, in the parish: by this route, also, General Carpenter, in 1715, advanced to Preston, nine miles distant, to meet the Scottish rebels, whom he defeated at that place.

The TOWN is pleasantly situated on the summit of a hill, on the road from Bolton to Preston; and though in Leland's time it is described as having "a wonderful poore, or rather no market," it is now a large and thriving place, being indebted to the excellent coal-mines and stone-quarries in the neighbourhood, and more recently to its extended cotton manufacture, and the enterprising spirit of its inhabitants, for a rapid rise into importance. It was at first lighted with gas by Mr. Timothy Lightoller, from his private works, but is now lighted by a public company; and is amply supplied with water, for which purpose works were erected in 1823, and a new company was incorporated in 1846, having a capital of £15,000. The appearance of the town has of late been very much improved; among other recent changes, the unsightly thatched buildings which stood in the most central part of one of the main thoroughfares, have been taken down, and are succeeded by handsome and commodious shops. The environs abound with diversified scenery, and the views, which are extensive, embrace Rivington Pike, &c. The principal branch of manufacture is that of cotton, of which the chief articles made are muslins and calicoes. There are at present eight mills, whereof two, belonging to Messrs. James Wallwork and Company, and one, the property of John Wilkinson, Esq., employ 800 persons; two, the property of Messrs. Richard Smethurst and Company, employ 560; two, belonging to Messrs. Lightoller, 480; and one, belonging to Richard Anyon, Esq., 150. There are also several printing and bleaching works, a logwood-mill, a corn-mill, and four iron-foundries; together with four collieries in operation. The Lancaster and the Leeds and Liverpool canals unite to the south-west of Whittle-le-Woods, and pass within a mile of the town; and there is a station on the North-Union railway, which was

opened in June, 1843. A grant of a market and fairs was obtained in the reign of Edward IV.: the market is on Tuesday; and fairs are held on March 26th, May 5th, and August 20th, principally for cattle; and on Sept. 4th, 5th, and 6th, for woollen-cloth, hardware, and pedlery. The county magistrates hold a petty-session every Tuesday; and the lord of the manor a court leet once a year: the powers of the county debt-court of Chorley, established in 1847, extend over the registration-district of Chorley. The town-hall, a stone building, under which the butter-market is held, was erected in 1802, at the expense of the late John Hollinshead, Esq.; and adjoining it is a small prison for the confinement of offenders prior to their committal to the county gaol.

The parish comprises 3571 acres, of which the soil is, for the most part, a stiff loam. The surface rises into hills in the eastern part, where the land is sterile; but westward it is simply undulated, and productive: about one-fourth is arable, and the remainder pasture and wood. Among the seats is Gillibrand Hall, a fortress-like edifice, built in 1807 by Thomas Gillibrand, Esq., and the seat of his son, Henry Hawarden Fazakerley, Esq., now lord of the manor, who assumed the latter name some years since. Astley Hall, a venerable mansion built in 1600, is seated in a park on the north-west margin of the Chor. Baganley Hall is a fine old house, built in 1633; and Burgh Hall, a brick edifice, built in 1740, partaking much of the modern style of architecture, with pleasure-grounds and gardens attached. About a mile from the town, and pleasantly situated on the banks of the Yarrow, is Yarrow House, the seat of Richard and George H. Lightoller, Esqrs.: South Cottage is occupied by Alexander Bannerman, Esq.; Willow House, by Thomas Cameron, Esq.; and Park Place is the residence of Richard Smethurst, Esq.

Chorley was originally a chapelry in the parish of Croston, from which it was separated in 1793, when that extensive district was divided into three distinct parishes. The LIVING is a rectory, not in charge, with a net income of £1022; patron, the Rev. Streynsham Master, A.M.: the tithes of the parish have been commuted for £264. The church is an ancient structure, retaining several features of Saxon character, of which the south entrance is a fine specimen; it is castellated, pinnacled at the east and west ends, and has a large tower supported by buttresses. The edifice formerly contained some relics, said to have been the bones of its tutelar saint, which were brought from Normandy by Sir Rowland Stanley, Knt., and presented to the parish by his brother. St. George's church, standing in an open area, on the east side of the town, was completed in October, 1825, at an expense of £13,707, defrayed by the Parliamentary Commissioners and by subscription; it is a handsome and spacious structure in the later English style, with a square embattled tower, and consists of a nave, with north and south aisles, and a choir: attached is a large burial-ground. The living is a perpetual curacy, in the patronage of the Rector. There are places of worship for Independents, Wesleyans, Primitive Methodists, Baptists, Unitarians, and Roman Catholics. The Roman Catholic chapel, dedicated to St. Gregory, was built in 1774, rebuilt in 1816, and aisles were added in 1831; it stands on an eminence called Weldbank, about a mile south-west of the town, and is in the omanesque style of architecture: adjoining is a house, ith 16 acres of ground, belonging to the priest, the Rev. enry Greenhalgh. The grammar school was originally established by the urchwardens, who, in 1634, built a school-house; it as an endowment of £11 per annum, arising from subsequent benefactions: a new school-house was built in 824. A large national school, and a school for Roman atholics, are supported by subscription; and there are so infants' and Sunday schools in connexion with the established Church. An almshouse was built and endowed in 1682, by Hugh Cooper, for six aged persons: enry Banister, of Hackney, Middlesex, left £600 in 625, for charitable purposes; and there are several inor charities, and a dispensary instituted in 1828. he poor law union of Chorley comprises 26 parishes nd townships, and contains a population of 38,836. At arrow Bridge is an alkaline spring, on the property of ohn Wilkinson, Esq.: its fame attracts numerous perons, and especially the poor, to drink the water, and any instances of the benefit derived from its use, have een authenticated; among others, a remarkable case of ropsy. The water has been recently analyzed by an minent chemist in Leamington, who has confirmed a revious analysis of the medicinal virtues peculiar to it. Baths are open to the public at a moderate charge.

CHORLEY, Stafford.—See Charley.

CHORLTON, a township, in the parish of Back-ford, union of Great Boughton, Higher division of he hundred of Wirrall, S. division of the county of Chester, 3 miles (N.) from Chester; containing 85 inhabitants. It comprises 506 acres of land, chiefly pasture, and of which the soil is sand, gravel, and clay; the surface is undulated, and the scenery embraces extensive views. The Ellesmere canal passes through the township. The tithes have been commuted for £100. Chorlton Hall, rebuilt in the year 1845, may be mentioned as the place where George Ormerod, Esq., wrote his History of Cheshire.

CHORLTON, a township, in the parish of Malpas, union of Wrexham, Higher division of the hundred of Broxton, S. division of the county of Chester, 2¼ miles (W. by N.) from Malpas; containing 150 inhabitants. The manor was held by the Birds, and afterwards by the Claytons, under the St. Pierres and their successors. The township comprises 447 acres, of a sandy and gravelly soil, with some clay. The tithes have been commuted for £60. Roman coins of the reigns of Valerian and Posthumus were dug up in a field here, in March, 1818.

CHORLTON, a township, in the parish of Wybunbury, union and hundred of Nantwich, S. division of the county of Chester, 5¾ miles (E. by S.) from Nantwich; containing 141 inhabitants. The manor was part of the ancient inheritance of the Delves family, and came by maternal descent to the Rev. Delves Broughton, Bart. The township comprises 811a. 32p. of land; it is intersected by the Liverpool and Birmingham railway, and the road from Nantwich to Newcastle passes close by. The impropriate tithes have been commuted for £74, and the vicarial for £14.

CHORLTON, a chapelry, in the parish of Manchester, union of Chorlton-upon-Medlock, hundred of Salford, S. division of the county of Lancaster, 3¼ miles (S. S. W.) from Manchester; containing, with 607

Hardy, 632 inhabitants. The township lies on the north side of the Mersey, and east of the road from Manchester to Chester, which passes through the village of Stretford, about a mile from Chorlton. The Duke of Bridgewater's canal, and the Manchester and Altrincham railway, also pass a short distance westward of the township. The living is a perpetual curacy; net income, £103; patrons and appropriators, the Dean and Canons of the Collegiate Church of Manchester. In 1741, Margaret Usherwood bequeathed £160 for teaching children.

CHORLTON, a chapelry, in the parish of Eccleshall, union of Newcastle-under-Lyme, N. division of the hundred of Pirehill and of the county of Stafford; comprising the townships of Chapel-Chorlton and Hill-Chorlton; and containing 365 inhabitants, of whom 243 are in Chapel-Chorlton, 6 miles (S. S. W.) from Newcastle. The chapelry consists of 1921a. 1r. 36p. of land, and lies west of the Sow, from which the village of Chapel-Chorlton is distant about half a mile. The Liverpool and Birmingham railway passes through. The living is a perpetual curacy; net income, £71; patron, the Bishop of Lichfield: the tithes have been commuted for £244. The chapel, dedicated to St. Lawrence, was rebuilt in 1827, at a cost of £800, raised by subscription and a grant from a Church Society. Near Hill-Chorlton is a place of worship for Primitive Methodists.

CHORLTON-UPON-MEDLOCK, a township, and the head of a union, in the parish of Manchester, hundred of Salford, S. division of the county of Lancaster; containing 28,336 inhabitants. The name of this place, formerly Chorlton-Row, was changed, on an act of parliament being obtained for the township, to Chorlton-upon-Medlock, as a better than its ancient designation, the river Medlock (which separates it from the township of Manchester) forming its entire boundary on the north. The old name, too, conveyed the idea of a very circumscribed population, which, in fact, it had about sixty years ago. The township was then chiefly occupied as an agricultural estate connected with the ancient Chorlton Hall, which is still standing near St. Luke's chapel, and which was the residence of the Minshull family, to whom nearly all the township originally belonged. The estates of Chorlton Hall, Garrat Hall, Ancoats Hall, and Ardwick Manor-House, once opposite sides of the river, once formed landscape scenery of the finest description.

In 1793 the Minshull estate was purchased, chiefly as a speculation for building, by Messrs. Cooper, Marsland, and Duckworth, by whom it was laid out in the main streets, Oxford-road, Grosvenor-street, Sidney-street, York-street, Ormond-street, &c.; and Grosvenor-square, now occupied by All Saints' church and churchyard, was at that time planted in the most ornamental style, and laid out as a pleasure-ground. But the anticipation of raising a new and beautiful town, with buildings corresponding with those erected by Peter Marsland, Esq., Roger Holland, Esq., Ottiwell Wood, Esq., and others, having failed, the proprietors sold the land for cotton-mills and cottages, which quite altered the character of the district, and became the main cause of the vast increase of population in all those parts which lie contiguous to the river. The place affords an instance of the extraordinary rise in the value of property throughout the county. The Chorlton Hall estate was sold by Edmond Trafford, in 1590, to Ralph Sorocold, for £320, and in 1644 was again sold to Thomas Minshull, apothecary, for £300; while in 1793, or twenty years after the introduction of the cotton manufacture, the estate, as before mentioned, was purchased by Messrs. Cooper, Marsland, and Duckworth, for £42,914. The annual value of the township at the period of the land-tax (about 1690) was £256. 4. 2.: in 1815 its value had increased to £19,484; in 1829, to £66,645; and in 1841, to £137,651, the last being an increase on the first of 53,000 per cent. Guided by the county assessment, and computing the property to be worth 25 years' purchase, its value in two centuries has increased from £300 to upwards of £3,000,000 sterling.

The town now consists of several good streets, well lighted with gas, paved, and amply supplied with water; and is inhabited by many of the merchants and manufacturers of Manchester, in the trade of which it largely participates. An act to regulate and improve the district was passed in 1822-3, and amended in 1832; under this, police commissioners and constables are appointed. The town-hall, a constable's dwelling-house, and a dispensary, are connected in one building, erected at a cost of £4500. A Lyceum for educational purposes was formed in 1838; and an Institute for popular instruction in 1840. The township comprises 632 acres, and is divided into two ecclesiastical districts, All Saints' (including St. Luke's as a licensed chapel) and St. Saviour's. The first church or chapel erected was St. Luke's, which was built in 1804 by the Rev. Edward Smyth, and is a plain building, with a cemetery of considerable extent adjoining. The elegant and commodious church of All Saints' was erected by the Rev. Dr. Burton, the present minister and patron, at an expense of £13,000; it is of the Doric order, and is built of stone, with an oak roof, and window frames of copper. The pulpit cost £450, and the organ £800: over the communion-table is a beautiful painting on glass of the Saviour's Passion in the Garden, executed by Eginton, of Birmingham. The steeple, terminating with a dome and copper-gilded cross, 145 feet in height, is much admired. This church was consecrated in April, 1820, and contains 1800 sittings, of which 400 are free. The square, purchased for £2000, and consecrated as a cemetery, has an area of 12,000 square yards, whereof a fourth part is appropriated by the patron to the burial of the poor. The catacombs beneath the church are convenient and elegant; the main aisle is a broad passage between two walls of marble monuments and inscriptions, and the side aisles are remarkably wide and lofty: many respectable families have places of sepulture here. St. Saviour's church was consecrated in November, 1836. There are meeting-houses for Evangelical Friends, Presbyterians, General Baptists, Independents, Primitive Methodists, Unitarians, and Wesleyans. A general cemetery for the interment of persons of all religious denominations, comprising four acres surrounded by a wall, was opened in 1821, at an expense of £6000; the buildings are of the Grecian-Ionic order, and the entrance is from Rusholme-road, through a handsome iron-gate, on the left of which is a chapel. There are numerous daily, Sunday, and infants' schools. The poor law union comprises 16 townships, and contains a population of 93,736.

Seal and Arms.

CHRISTCHURCH (*Holy Trinity*), a borough, sea-port, market-town, and parish, and the head of a union, in the hundred of CHRISTCHURCH, Ringwood and S. divisions of the county of SOUTHAMPTON, 21½ miles (S. W. by W.) from South-ampton, and 100 (S. W. by W.) from London; contain-ing 5994 inhabitants, and comprising the tythings of ure, Burton, Street, Winkton, Hurn, Iford, Parley, nd Tuckton, and the chapelry of Hinton-Admiral. his place is of great antiquity, and, from some relics iscovered in the church, is supposed to have been of oman origin; by the Saxons it was called *Twyneham-lourne*, and *Tweon-ea*, from its situation between two ivers. The earliest historical notice of it occurs in the axon Chronicles, which record its occupation by Ethel-old, during his revolt against his kinsman, Edward he Elder. In Domesday book it is mentioned, under he appellation of *Thuinam*, as a burgh and royal manor, ontaining 31 messuages. The present name is derived rom a priory, founded before the Conquest for a dean nd twenty-four Secular canons, and dedicated to the Holy Trinity, and which was rebuilt in the reign of William Rufus, and dedicated to Our Saviour Christ, by Ralph Flambard, Bishop of Durham, and originally dean f the priory. It was largely endowed by Richard de Redvers, Earl of Devon, to whom Henry I. gave the manor. Earl Baldwin, son and successor to Earl Richard, placed Canons regular of the order of St. Augustine in the priory, which flourished till the Disso-ution, when its revenue was £544. 6.: it was granted by Henry VIII. to the inhabitants for their parochial hurch. Some portions of the walls that inclosed the onventual buildings still remain; the ancient lodge is ccupied as a dwelling-house, and the site of the refectory nay be traced by the remnants of its wall. The town vas fortified by Richard de Redvers, who either erected r rebuilt the castle, of which there are some remains o the north of the priory. These consist chiefly of the uins of the keep on the summit of an artificial mount the walls of which are more than ten feet in thickness), nd part of the range that comprised the state apart-nents; the Norman style prevails, and the arches of ome remaining windows are divided by pillars of that haracter.

CHRISTCHURCH is situated on the borders of the New Forest, and between the rivers Avon and Stour, which, niting their streams at a short distance below, expand nto a broad sheet of water and fall into Christchurch ay, in connexion with which they form a harbour. The urrent of the Avon, to the east of the town, is inter-epted and divided into two parts by an island, from ach side of which a bridge to the opposite bank of the iver forms the continuation of the road to Lymington. The harbour is accessible only at high tides to vessels rawing not more than from five to six feet of water, he entrance being obstructed by a bar, or ledge of sand, xtending from Henigsbury Head, on the Hampshire ide (where Hengist, King of the Saxons, landed), to St. Catherine's Cliffe, in the Isle of Wight. The quay is

about two miles from the mouth of the harbour. In this harbour, as in the neighbouring port of Poole, there is high water twice at every tide, a peculiarity arising from the situation of the coast with respect to the Isle of Wight, and from the projection of the point of land on which Hurst Castle is situated. The river Avon was made navigable to Salisbury in 1680, but the accumula-tion of sand has rendered the navigation useless. Some of the labouring class have for years past been employed in drawing their nets for salmon at the mouth of the haven; the rivers are royalties, the property of the Rt. Hon. Sir G. H. Rose.

The town is partly lighted, and amply supplied with water; it is much frequented during the summer months as a place of pleasant resort, and the lofty cliffs in the vicinity afford delightful views. Several of the female inhabitants were formerly employed in the knitting of stockings, but this branch of industry has declined. There are two breweries; also two manufactories for watch fusee chains, at each of which about 50 persons are employed, chiefly women and girls; and almost every cottager is engaged in preparing the work con-nected with this branch of manufacture. The market is on Monday; fairs are held on Trinity-Thursday and October 17th, for cattle and horses, and for pleasure. The GOVERNMENT is vested in a mayor, recorder, and an indefinite number of free burgesses, assisted by a town-clerk and others; but the officers do not exercise magisterial authority, the town being wholly within the jurisdiction of the county justices. The borough was summoned in the 35th of Edward I. and the 2nd of Edward II., but made no subsequent return till the 13th of Elizabeth, from which time it regularly sent two members to parliament, until the 2nd of William IV., when, by the Reform act, it was destined thenceforward to send only one. The right of election was exercised by the mayor and free burgesses; but by the act above named, the non-resident electors, except within seven miles, were disfranchised, and the privilege was extended to the £10 householders of an enlarged district of 5332 acres, including the parish of Holdenhurst, which was for elective purposes incorporated with the former bo-rough of Christchurch, which comprised only 123 acres. The mayor is returning officer. A court leet for the manor is held twice a year by the steward. The powers of the county-debt court of Christchurch, established in 1847, extend over the registration-district of Christ-church.

The parish comprises by computation 30,000 acres, of which the surface is in general flat, and the soil in the vicinity of the rivers particularly fertile. The LIVING is a vicarage, with that of Holdenhurst annexed, valued in the king's books at £16; patrons, the Dean and Chap-ter of Winchester; impropriator, the Earl of Malmes-bury, whose mansion of Heron Court is within the parish. The great tithes of the two parishes have been commuted for £3200. The church is a magnificent cru-eiform structure, partly Norman, and partly in the early and later English styles, with a finely-proportioned and embattled tower at the west end, which was erected by the Montacutes, earls of Salisbury, in the fifteenth cen-tury. The piers and arches of the nave, which is of Norman character, are bold and simple; the clerestory is of later date; the northern entrance is a fine specimen of the early, and the chancel of the later, English style.

The altar is decorated with a rude, but interesting, representation of the genealogy of Christ, carved in the style of the age in which the church was founded : to the north of it is a beautiful sepulchral chapel, built in the reign of Henry VII., by the celebrated Countess of Salisbury, who, in the 70th year of her age, was beheaded by Henry VIII. ; and at the east is a spacious chapel dedicated to the Virgin Mary, erected in the fourteenth century by the ancestor of Lord Delawarr. There are some other chapels of fine execution, chiefly later English. The west front, principally in the early style, in which a large and handsome window has been lately inserted, is ornamented with a figure of Christ in a canopied niche. The length of the church is 311 feet, and its breadth at the western extremity 60 feet, and along the transepts 104 feet ; the height of the vaulted roof is 57 feet. It was repaired in 1841. There are, an endowed chapel at Hinton, built about half a century ago ; a chapel at Bransgore, a neat modern edifice ; one erected in 1834, at High Cliffe ; a fourth at Burton, erected in 1836 ; a chapel in the later English style, at Hightown, built at the expense of Lord Stuart de Rothesay and others ; and a chapel at Bournemouth. The Independents and Wesleyans have places of worship, and at Burton is a Roman Catholic chapel. The union of Christchurch comprises 3 parishes, and contains a population of 7828.

An intrenchment, 630 yards in length, extends across the isthmus that connects Hengistbury Head with the main land ; and near its northern extremity is a large barrow, in which human bones and an urn have been found. On Catherine Hill, about a mile and a half to the north of the town, and a mile to the west of the Avon, are traces of an exploratory camp, 55 yards square, round which are six small tumuli ; and near the base of the hill are ten large barrows, whereof one has been discovered to contain human bones. To the north of the camp is an elliptical earthwork, of which the greater diameter is 35, and the less 25, yards ; and the remains of other intrenchments may be traced in the vicinity. Somerford Grange, about two miles to the east of the town, belonged to the priory : part of the ancient buildings remained until about 25 years since, including the chapel, a stone edifice with a handsome arched roof of carved oak. Hordwell Cliff, between Christchurch and Milford, is famous for the fossil remains of tropical shells, sharks' teeth, &c. &c. Tutter's Well, at Stanpit, is celebrated for the purity of its water, and for its efficacy in weakness of sight.

CHRIST-CHURCH, a parish, in the union of St. Saviour's, partly in the E. division of the hundred of Brixton, but chiefly within the borough of Southwark, E. division of Surrey ; containing 14,606 inhabitants. This parish was anciently termed the liberty of Paris Garden, and formed a part of the parish of St. Saviour until 1706, when it was made distinct by act of parliament. It is situated on the south side of Blackfriars bridge, and has several ranges of good houses on both sides of Great Surrey-street, including Nelson-square on the east, and a portion of Stamford-street on the west. There are manufactories for hats, for glass, and for various articles of statuary in Roman cement ; extensive saw-mills ; a large cooperage ; and works for refining antimony, and making albata. At the end of the bridge is a building originally called the Leverian

610

Museum, and subsequently the Rotunda, which has been used for various purposes. Christ-Church constituted a portion of the borough of Southwark, under a charter of Edward VI., though the inhabitants did not for many years vote for its parliamentary members, having allowed the privilege to fall into disuse ; they have, however, been re-invested with the franchise, by the act of the 2nd of William IV., cap. 45.

The living is a rectory not in charge, in the patronage of the Trustees of Marshall's charity : the church is a neat edifice of brick, with a tower surmounted by a cupola. Surrey chapel, built by the late Rev. Rowland Hill, is within the parish ; and there are also places of worship for Baptists and Unitarians, the latter of which, in Stamford-street, has a fine portico of six fluted Doric columns supporting a triangular pediment. The parochial schools, on the national system, in Green Walk, were rebuilt in 1836, at an expense of nearly £2000. The British and Foreign school, situated in an alley opposite the workhouse, contains a spacious schoolroom for boys, and one of smaller dimensions for girls. The workhouse, since the incorporation of the parish with the union of St. Saviour's, has been enlarged at an expense of nearly £8000. Almshouses in Green Walk were founded and endowed by Mr. Charles Hopton, for 28 poor men, each of whom has a separate house of two rooms ; and in Church-street are almshouses for 45 women, endowed by Mr. Edward Edwards in 1753, the buildings consisting of four separate ranges of neat houses, erected successively in 1753, 1777, 1786, and 1791. There are various charities for general purposes, all of minor account except Marshall's charity, founded by John Marshall in 1627, and producing nearly £900 per annum ; Hammerton's, producing £230 per annum ; and Boyse's, producing £160 per annum.

CHRISTIAN-MALFORD (All Saints), a parish, in the union of Chippenham, partly in the hundred of Chippenham, but chiefly in the N. division of the hundred of Damerham, Chippenham and Calne, and N. divisions of Wilts, 5 miles (N. E. by N.) from Chippenham ; containing, with the tything of Avon, 1198 inhabitants. This place is situated on the river Avon, commencing at a bridge over an ancient ford across that stream, from the badness of which it is supposed to have derived its name ; its prefix most probably originated from the fact of Christianity having been promulgated here at a very early period. The parish comprises by computation 2762 acres ; between 300 and 400 are arable, 140 wood, and the rest pasture. The village, in the centre of which is an ancient cross, is situated on the river, which here turns two cloth-mills ; and the parish is intersected by the road from Oxford to Bath, and by the Great Western railway. The living is a rectory, valued in the king's books at £27, and in the patronage of the Bishop of Bath and Wells : the tithes have been commuted for £700, and the glebe comprises about 100 acres, with a glebe-house. Attached to the benefice are a copyhold of 60 acres held on lives, and a manor of which the rector is lord. The church has been repaired and repewed. There is a place of worship for Independents, said to be the oldest in the county.

CHRISTLETON (St. James), a parish, in the union of Great Boughton, Lower division of the hundred of Broxton, S. division of the county of Chester, comprising the townships of Christleton, Abbots-Cotton,

munds-Cotton, Littléton, and Rowton; and contain-
875 inhabitants, of whom 625 are in the township of
ristleton, 2 miles (E. by S.) from Chester. This place,
the time of the Norman survey, is said to have been
ry populous; it continued to be of some importance,
d was fortified for the parliament, and made the head-
arters of Sir William Brereton. At Rowton Moor a
ttle was fought between the royalist and parliamentary
rces, in which the former were defeated; and on the
ge of Chester being raised, in February, 1645, Christon was, in a sally of the citizens, very nearly deroyed by fire. The parish is situated on the road from
ndon to Shrewsbury, via Whitchurch, and comprises
admeasurement 3000 acres, whereof 1392 are in the
wnship; the soil is sand, loam, and clay. The Chester
d Ellesmere canal passes close to the village, and, at
tle more than a quarter of a mile from the bridge, is
ossed by a viaduct of the Chester and Crewe railway.
e living is a rectory, valued in the king's books at
39. 5.; net income,-£827; patron, the Hon. E. M. L.
ostyn : the glebe consists of about 40 acres, with a
ebe-house. The church, which is picturesquely covered
ith ivy, existed prior to the Conquest : the body was
built of brick in 1738, but the stone tower bears the
ate 1530; it has a peal of eight bells. There is a place
worship for Independents. In 1779, John Seller, of
ittleton, left about £10 per annum for teaching chil-
ren; and a school-house was built in 1800, by sub-
ription.

CHRISTON, a parish, in the union of AXBRIDGE,
undred of WINTERSTOKE, E. division of SOMERSET,
miles (N. W. by W.) from Cross; containing 92 inha-
itants, and comprising 572 acres, of which 84 are com-
ion or waste. The living is a discharged rectory, valued
ι the king's books at £6. 1. 8., and in the gift of Sir
ohn Smyth, Bart., and the family of Gore : the tithes
ave been commuted for £95, and the glebe consists of
4 acres. The church is principally in the early English
yle.

CHRISTOW (ST. JAMES), a parish, in the union of
T. THOMAS, hundred of WONFORD, Wonford and S.
ivisions of DEVON, 7½ miles (S. W.) from Exeter; con-
ining 624 inhabitants. The parish is situated on the
iver Teign, and comprises by measurement 3200 acres, of
hich 700 are common or waste : there are many excel-
nt cherry-orchards. Mines of manganese are worked,
nd a lead-mine has been discovered, which affords
ome beautiful specimens of mundic, &c. The living is
discharged vicarage, valued in the king's books at
.8. 6. 8.; patron and impropriator, Viscount Exmouth.
he great tithes have been commuted for £99. 10., and
he vicarial for £169. 19. : an excellent glebe-house has
een erected, at the expense of the incumbent; and at-
ached to the vicarage, is a glebe of 22 acres, in the
arish of Bovey-Tracey. The church, the arches of
hich are in the pointed style, has a Norman font, and
ome fine screen-work across the nave and aisles. It is
aid to have been mainly erected by Lord Russell, in the
eign of Henry VIII., of which monarch he purchased
he parish for £200 : the tower, 80 feet high, and much
dmired, is supposed to be of later erection. There is a
lace of worship for Baptists. The poor receive bread
very Sunday from the rents of an estate called Smith-
ayes, producing about £40 per annum, left by a cler-
yman named Stocke, in the latter part of the 17th

century; the residue, after affording small payments to
two adjoining parishes, belongs to the vicar. Lord
Exmouth takes the title of Baron Exmouth, of Canon-
teign, from his seat in the parish : the ancient mansion
was besieged by Cromwell's army, and the loop-holes are
still to be seen, through which the muskets were fired by
the besieged. Pope House is said to have been a cell to
the priory of Cowick, near Exeter.

CHUDLEIGH (ST. MARTIN), a market-town and
parish, in the union of NEWTON-ABBOTT, hundred of
EXMINSTER, Teignbridge and S. divisions of DEVON,
9 miles (S. S. W.) from Exeter, and 182 (W. S. W.) from
London; containing 2415 inhabitants. This place, anciently called Chidleighe, was the residence of the bishops
of Exeter, who had a sumptuous palace, of which there
are some small remains. In the year 1309, Bishop
Stapleton procured the grant of a weekly market and
an annual fair. During the parliamentary war, the
army under General Fairfax was quartered in the town.
In 1807, nearly half of it was destroyed by fire, the loss
of property being estimated at £60,000 value. It is
pleasantly situated on an eminence near the eastern
bank of the river Teign, and consists principally of one
long street; the houses are in general modern and
neatly built : the inhabitants are indifferently supplied
with water. The environs are pleasant, and abound
with woodland scenery; antimony and cobalt are among
the mineral productions, and there are quarries of argillaceous slate, in which many organic remains have
been discovered.

The trade, which consisted mainly in the manufacture of woollen-cloth, has lately declined : extensive
quarries of good marble and limestone, which abound in
the vicinity, afford employment to many of the inhabitants; and the neighbourhood is famed for cider of
superior quality. The market is on Saturday : the fairs,
chiefly for cattle and sheep, are on Easter-Tuesday, the
third Tuesday and Wednesday in June, and October
2nd, unless it falls on Saturday, Sunday, or Monday, in
which case the fair is postponed till the Tuesday following. The parish comprises 5188 acres, whereof 1660
are common or waste. The LIVING is a vicarage,
valued in the king's books at £21, and in the patronage
of Trustees for the inhabitants; the impropriate tithes,
belonging to Lord Clifford, have been commuted for
£250, and the vicarial for £550; the glebe comprises
one acre, with a glebe-house. There is a place of worship for Independents; also a Roman Catholic chapel
at Ugbrooke, in the parish. The free grammar school
was founded in 1668, by John Pynseut, of Combe, in
the county of Surrey, who endowed it with a rent-charge
of £30 per annum, founding also three exhibitions for
its benefit at Cambridge, of £5 each, tenable for four
years. Half a mile from the town is Chudleigh Rock,
a stupendous mass of limestone, in which is a cavern
of considerable extent; and near it are very perfect
remains of an elliptical encampment, supposed from its
form to be of Danish origin, but, from its proximity to
a Roman road, to have been previously occupied by that
people. Chudleigh confers the title of Baron on the
family of Clifford.

CHULMLEIGH (ST. MARY MAGDALENE), a market-
town and parish, in the union of SOUTH MOLTON, hundred of WITHERIDGE, South Molton and N. divisions of
DEVON, 21¼ miles (N. W.) from Exeter, and 194 (W. by

S.) from London; containing 1647 inhabitants. This place was anciently called *Chimleighe*; in the reign of Henry III., John de Courtenay, Earl of Devonshire, obtained for it the grant of a weekly market. During the parliamentary war, a skirmish took place here in 1645. The town, a considerable portion of which was destroyed by fire in 1803, is situated on an eminence rising gently from the eastern bank of the river Taw; the houses, with the exception of a few that are modern and well built, are low and covered with thatch. The market is on Friday; and fairs are held on the third Friday in March, the Wednesday in Easter-week, and the last Wednesday in July. A portreeve, whose office is merely nominal, and other officers, are appointed annually at the court leet and baron of the lord of the manor. The parish comprises 6835 acres, of which 1244 are common or waste. The living is a rectory, valued in the king's books at £20. 18. 1½.; net income, £415; patron and incumbent, the Rev. George Hole. In the church are five prebends, endowed with glebe and a portion of the tithes, *viz.*, Brookland, valued at £4. 8. 4.; Denes, at £4. 6. 8.; Higher Heyne, at £5. 13. 4.; Lower Heyne, at £5; and Penels, at £5. These prebends were permanently annexed to the rectory by the act 3rd and 4th Vict., cap. 113. The church, which was damaged by lightning in 1797, is an ancient and spacious structure in the decorated English style, with a square embattled tower; the interior is fine, and contains a screen of oak richly carved. There are places of worship for Independents and Wesleyans.

CHUNALL, a township, in the parish and union of GLOSSOP, hundred of HIGH PEAK, N. division of the county of DERBY, 7½ miles (N. by W.) from Chapel-en-le-Frith; containing 111 inhabitants.

CHURCH, a township, in the parish of WHALLEY, union, and Lower division of the hundred, of BLACK-BURN, N. division of the county of LANCASTER, 4¾ miles (E.) from Blackburn; containing 1545 persons. This township, and the townships of Huncoat and Oswaldtwistle, form the parochial chapelry of Church-Kirk, comprising 8667 inhabitants. The district is subject to the honor of Clitheroe, and yields suit and service to the court of Accrington. The printing of calicoes, and power-loom and hand-loom weaving, are the principal manufactures. The Leeds and Liverpool canal, which extends along the northern margin of Church and Oswaldtwistle, opens a communication to the eastern and western seas. The living is a perpetual curacy; net income, £218; patrons, the Trustees of William Hulme: the chapel is dedicated to St. James, and is a plain structure with an antique castellated tower; the body was rebuilt in 1804. Emmanuel church was built at Oswaldtwistle in 1837; the patronage is vested in five Trustees. There is a place of worship for Wesleyans. At Church, Oswaldtwistle, Cabin-End, and Daisy-Green, are national schools; and at Fox-Hill Bank is an infants' school.

CHURCH, a tything, in the parish of DOWNTON, union of ALDERBURY, hundred of DOWNTON, Salisbury and Amesbury, and S. divisions of WILTS; containing 319 inhabitants.

CHURCHAM (ST. ANDREW), a parish, in the union of WESTBURY, partly in the Lower division of the hundred of DUDSTONE and KING's-BARTON,. E. division, but chiefly in the hundred of WESTBURY, W. division,

vision of SOMERSET, 4¾ miles (N. by E.) from Ax-idge; containing 970 inhabitants. This is a very cient place, occurring in old deeds under the names of *richill, Cheuchill,* and *Cherchill.* Immediately after e Conquest it was held by Roger de Leon, who came er with the Conqueror, and who appears to have as-med the name of Courcill, or Curcelle, from his pro-rty : he is said to have been the remote ancestor of hn Churchill, the great Duke of Marlborough. The rish comprises 2541 acres, of which 166 are common waste. The living is a perpetual curacy; net income, 98; patrons and appropriators, the Dean and Chapter Bristol. The church is a handsome structure, with embattled tower, and contains a fine altar-piece re-esenting the Lord's Supper, and several interesting onuments. On a very high point of the Mendip hills, ove the village, is an encampment called Dolberry astle, which forms a parallelogram of 540 yards by 20, inclosed by a ditch on all sides but the south-east, here the steepness of the hill rendered it unnecessary; ithin it many Roman and Saxon coins and fragments weapons have been found.

CHURCHILL (ST. JAMES), a parish, in the union of IDDERMINSTER, Lower division of the hundred of ALFSHIRE, Stourbridge and E. divisions of the county f WORCESTER, 3½ miles (N. E. by E.) from Kidder-inster; containing 164 inhabitants. It is partly ounded by Staffordshire, and is crossed, from north to uth, by the road from Stourbridge to Kidderminster; contains 955 acres. The living is a discharged rec-ry, valued in the king's books at £5. 6. 8., and in the ift of the Rev. J. Turner : a portion of the tithes was ommuted in 1773 for land, of which there are 95 acres, alued at about £100 per annum; the remainder was ecently commuted for a rent-charge of £166, and there a glebe-house. The church formerly stood on an ele-ation still called Churchill; the present edifice was uilt in the valley, in 1470. Richard Penne and Roger ennet, in 1602, bequeathed property producing about 30 per annum, chiefly for teaching children.

CHURCHILL (ST. MICHAEL), a parish, in the union f PERSHORE, Lower division of the hundred of OSWALD-LOW, Worcester and W. divisions of the county of VORCESTER, 5½ miles (E. by S.) from Worcester; con-aining 115 inhabitants. The parish is intersected from est to east by the road from Worcester to Alcester, nd bounded on the west by a stream which falls into he Avon. It consists of 660 acres, whereof two-thirds re arable, and the remainder pasture, and is well ooded : much of the land was inclosed about 1776. he living is a discharged rectory, valued in the king's ooks at £13. 6. 8.; net income, £167; patron, Robert Berkeley, Esq. The church is situated on an eminence n the side of the road. There is a mineral spring.

CHURCH-KIRK, LANCASTER.—See CHURCH.

CHURCHOVER (HOLY TRINITY), a parish, in the nion of RUGBY, Rugby division of the hundred of KNIGHTLOW, N. division of the county of WARWICK, 4¼ niles (N. by E.) from Rugby; containing 339 inhabit-nts. At a very early period the monastery of Combe ad a great portion of the lands here, the gift of Robert le Wavre, confirmed by Henry II. After the Dissolu-ion the property is supposed to have been granted by he name of a manor, to Mary, Duchess of Richmond, nd it was afterwards held by the Dixons, of Coten, in

613

the neighbourhood. The parish is bounded on the west by the river Swift, and on the east by the Roman Wat-ling-street; and comprises by computation 1500 acres, in equal portions of arable and pasture. The surface is varied, rising in some parts into hills of considerable elevation, and in others being flat; the soil is clayey, with some gravel. The living is a rectory, valued in the king's books at £15; net income, £270; patron, Henry Grimes, Esq. There are 170 acres of glebe, and a glebe-house. The church is a small edifice, with a spire. The Independents have a place of worship.

CHURCH-STANTON (ST. PAUL), a parish, in the union of TAUNTON, hundred of HEMYOCK, Cullompton and N. divisions of DEVON, 11 miles (N. by E.) from Honiton; containing 1085 inhabitants. The village of Churchenford, which is noted for its cider, has cattle-fairs on Jan. 25th and March 6th. The living is a rectory, valued in the king's books at £26. 5. 5.; net income, £421; patron, the Rev. R. P. Clarke. The tithes were commuted for land and corn-rents in 1779. The church has been enlarged by the addition of 237 sittings. There is a small endowed school.

CHURCHSTOW (ST. MARY), a parish, in the union of KINGSBRIDGE, hundred of STANBOROUGH, Stanbo-rough and Coleridge, and S. divisions of DEVON, 2 miles (N. W. by W.) from Kingsbridge; containing 542 inha-bitants, including 211 in the union workhouse, situated in the parish. It is bounded on the north-west by the river Avon, and comprises 1650 acres, of which 20 are common or waste. The surface is irregular, rising in some parts into hills of considerable height; and the soil is extremely various, in some places exuberantly rich, and in others sterile and unproductive. The living is a discharged vicarage, with that of Kingsbridge an-nexed, valued in the king's books at £16. 16. 11., and in the patronage of the Crown, with a net income of £200 : the impropriation belongs to the Corporation of Exeter, as trustees for a charity. The tithes have been commuted for a rent-charge of £325, and the glebe consists of 14 acres.

CHURCH-TOWN, a hamlet, in the parish of BACK-WELL, union of BEDMINSTER, hundred of HARTCLIFFE with BEDMINSTER, E. division of the county of SOMER-SET; containing 82 inhabitants.

CHURSTON-FERRERS, a parish, in the union of TOTNES, hundred of HAYTOR, Paignton and S. divisions of DEVON, 1½ mile (N. W.) from Brixham; containing, with the hamlet of Galmpton, 772 inhabitants. The parish comprises 2434 acres, of which 197 are common or waste. It is situated on the coast of the English Channel, and is bounded on the north by Torbay, and on the west by the river Dart, which is here navigable. The living is a perpetual curacy, annexed to the vicarage of Brixham : the impropriate tithes have been commuted for £212, and the vicarial for £180. The church con-tains an ancient wooden screen.

CHURT, county of SURREY.—See CHART.

CHURTON, a township, in the parish of ALDFORD, union of GREAT BOUGHTON, Higher division of the hun-dred of BROXTON, S. division of the county of CHESTER, 4½ miles (S. E. by S.) from Chester; containing 254 in-habitants. It comprises 553 acres, the soil of which is sand and clay. The place is within the limits of the manor of Farndon, and has been long a possession of the Barnston family.

CHUT

CHURTON, a township, in the parish of FARNDON, union of GREAT BOUGHTON, Higher division of the hundred of BROXTON, S. division of the county of CHESTER, 7 miles (S. by E.) from Chester; containing 132 inhabitants. It belonged to the Barnstons as early as the reign of Richard II., and the Hankeys were seated here for many generations. There are 465 acres of land, of which the soil, like that of the preceding township, is clay and sand. Churton Hall, the former residence of the Barnston family, was built in 1569. The tithes have been commuted for £70, payable to an impropriator, and £1 to the minister of the parish.

CHURTON, or CHIRKTON (ST. JOHN THE BAPTIST), a parish, in the union of DEVIZES, hundred of SWANBOROUGH, Devizes and N. divisions of WILTS, 4¼ miles (N. E. by E.) from East Lavington; containing, with Conock tything, 428 inhabitants, of whom 268 are in the township of Churton. The living is a discharged vicarage, valued in the king's books at £11. 0. 5., and has a net income of £168; it is in the patronage of the Crown, and the impropriation belongs to the trustees of Heytesbury almshouse.

CHURTON-HEATH, or BRUERA, a chapelry, in the parish of ST. OSWALD, CHESTER, union of GREAT BOUGHTON, Lower division of the hundred of BROXTON, S. division of the county of CHESTER, 5¼ miles (S. E. by S.) from Chester; containing 3 inhabitants; and comprising 130 acres, of a clayey soil. The chapelry was the original seat of a rectory, to which St. Oswald, a vicarage, was subordinate. The living is now annexed to that of St. Oswald; the incumbent whereof receives a rent-charge of £17, for which the tithes of the chapelry have been commuted. The chapel, dedicated to St. Mary, is an ancient structure, with a Norman arch between the nave and chancel, and a rich Norman door at the south end; several carved stones are conspicuous in the walls.

CHURWELL, a township, in the ecclesiastical district of MORLEY, parish of BATLEY, wapentake of MORLEY, W. riding of YORK, 3 miles (S. W. by S.) from Leeds; containing 1198 inhabitants. This township, which is situated on the road from Leeds to Huddersfield, comprises by computation 540 acres of land, and abounds in excellent coal. It is chiefly inhabited by persons employed in collieries, in a woollen-cloth mill, and a tan-yard. There is a place of worship for Independents, also a school.

CHUTE (ST. NICHOLAS), a parish, in the union of ANDOVER, hundred of KINWARDSTONE, Everley and Pewsey, and S. divisions of WILTS, 3¾ miles (N. E.) from Ludgershall; containing 525 inhabitants. It comprises 3000 acres : the surface is hilly, and the scenery pleasingly varied; the soil is chiefly light and stony. The living is a vicarage, in the patronage of the Bishop of Salisbury, valued in the king's books at £11; net income, £244. The late Mr. George Soley, of Kimpton Lodge, near Andover, bequeathed £200 to be vested in the funds, and the proceeds divided among the poor. Jeremy Corderoy, a divine of some celebrity in the 17th century, was born here.

CHUTE-FOREST, an extra-parochial district, in the union of ANDOVER, hundred of KINWARDSTONE, Everley and Pewsey, and S. divisions of WILTS, 4¼ miles (N. E. by N.) from Ludgershall; containing 135 inhabitants. It comprises 1800 acres; the surface is boldly

th other persons of distinction, entered into a con-
iracy to assassinate the king, and restore the deposed
onarch, Richard II. Henry, being informed of this,
d an army against them, when some of the principal
nspirators, with the forces under them, retired to
rencester, where they encamped : here they were sur-
ised by the townsmen, and the Duke of Surrey and
e Earl of Salisbury were taken and immediately be-
aded, on which the troops dispersed. The explosion
hostilities against Charles I. is stated to have occurred
this town, upon a personal attack on Lord Chandos,
ho had been appointed to execute the commission of
ray on behalf of the king ; and it was soon afterwards
rrisoned by the parliament. It was assaulted by
ince Rupert, and captured, after a sharp conflict of two
urs, on the 2nd of February, 1642-3 ; but was reco-
red for the parliament by the Earl of Essex, on the
5th of September in the following year : it again fell
to the hands of the royalists, but was ultimately sur-
ndered to the parliament. On the landing of the
rince of Orange, in 1688, the inhabitants, influenced
y the Duke of Beaufort, declared for James II. ; and
ord Lovelace, on his march through the town with a
rty to join the prince, was attacked by Captain Lorange,
f the county militia, made prisoner, and sent to Glou-
ster gaol. In this encounter flowed the first blood
hat was shed in the Revolution.

The TOWN is pleasantly situated, and consists of four
rincipal, and several smaller, streets. It was anciently
f much greater extent, the walls having inclosed an
rea two miles in circuit. The houses, which are chiefly
f stone, are well built, and many of the more respect-
ble are detached ; the place is lighted, the foot-paths
re paved with small stones, and the inhabitants well
upplied with water. There is a society called the Ciren-
ester and Gloucestershire Agricultural Association ; and
commodious Hall for temperance and other meetings
ot involving theological or political controversy, has
een erected by Mr. Christopher Bowly, at a cost of
1500. Races were once held annually near the town.
But little trade is carried on, the cloth manufacture,
ormerly extensive, having declined : some knives of a
eculiar and superior quality are made for the use of
urriers ; and there are a small carpet-manufactory, and
hree breweries. The Thames and Severn canal passes
n the vicinity, and has a branch to the town : the
Cheltenham and Great Western Union railway, also,
as a branch to Cirencester, opened in May, 1841.
The market is on Monday, for corn and provisions,
nd on Friday for provisions only ; the latter was once
onsiderable for wool, but since the decline of the
voollen manufacture, it has been much neglected. Fairs
re held on Easter-Tuesday and Nov. 8th, and statute-
airs on the Monday before and the Monday after Oct.
11th. By charter granted by Henry IV., Cirencester was
onstituted a separate hundred, co-extensive with the
BOROUGH, the privileges of which still exist, and two
igh constables are annually chosen, though the town is
within the jurisdiction of the county magistrates, who
hold petty-sessions here. It sent representatives to a
great council in the 11th of Edward III., but did not
acquire the permanent privilege of returning two burgesses until the year 1571, by grant from Elizabeth.
The right of election was formerly vested in the resident
householders not receiving alms (except " inhabitants of
615

the abbey, the Embury, and Sperringate-lane "), about
500 in number ; but the limits of the borough, which
comprised only 84 acres, were for elective purposes increased by the act of the 2nd and 3rd of William IV.,
cap. 64, so as to embrace the whole of the parish, comprehending by estimation 5100 acres, and the franchise
was extended to the £10 householders. The steward
and bailiff of the manor are returning officers. There
is a court leet annually, at which the steward for the
manor appoints two high, and fourteen petty, constables,
two of the latter being for each of the seven wards into
which the borough is divided. The powers of the
county debt-court, established in 1847, extend over the
registration-district of Cirencester.

The LIVING is a vicarage not in charge, in the patronage of the Bishop of Gloucester and Bristol : the impropriate tithes have been commuted for £99, and the
vicarial for £240. The church is a magnificent structure in the decorated English style, erected in the
fifteenth century, with a lofty embattled tower, crowned
by pinnacles ; its interior and exterior are richly adorned,
and it contains several chapels of exquisite beauty, and
many monuments. A fund, producing £267 per annum,
was bequeathed for keeping it in repair. Two other
churches, one dedicated to St. Cecilia, and the other to
St. Lawrence, have long been in ruins. There are places
of worship for Baptists, the Society of Friends, Independents, Wesleyans, and Unitarians. The Royal Agricultural College of Cirencester was incorporated by
charter in March, 1845, and suitable buildings have since
been erected at Port Farm, on Earl Bathurst's estate,
and near the junction of the Stroud and Tetbury roads.
The edifice is in the Tudor style, having two bold fronts,
the principal or southern front being 190 feet long, and
its centre occupied by a fine tower 80 feet in height, with
a turreted newel of 100 feet, used as an observatory for
meteorological and other scientific purposes. The buildings are three stories high, and include a large dining-
hall, class-rooms, a laboratory, and a museum, with
ranges of sleeping apartments for the pupils. The
college is under the management of a head master and
of professors ; and besides instruction in agriculture,
conveyed by lectures, individual study, and practical
working, the pupils are taught botany, natural history,
physics, mathematics, drawing, mechanics, dynamics,
surveying, building, hydrostatics, and hydraulics, particularly as they refer to agriculture. There are professors, also, for the various branches of general education.
The Free Grammar school was founded by Bishop Ruthal,
and the original endowment was augmented by Queen
Mary with £20 per annum, payable out of the exchequer ;
the master is appointed by the Lord Chancellor. The
Blue-coat school, established in 1714, was afterwards
endowed by Thomas Powell, Esq., with £15 per annum,
part of an annuity issuing from the exchequer for 99
years, and a moiety of the revenue of Maskelyne's estate :
the Lord Chancellor, in 1737, added £20 per annum, out
of property left for charitable purposes by Mrs. Rebecca
Powell ; and in 1744 Mrs. Powell's executor assigned the
interest of £562 as a provisional supply after the expiration of the annuity. The Yellow-coat school was
founded and endowed in 1722, by Mrs. Powell ; the income is about £320.

St. John's hospital, for three men and three women,
was founded by Henry I., and endowed with land and

reserved rents amounting to between £30 and £40 per annum. *St. Lawrence's* hospital, for a master and two poor women, was founded in the time of Edward III., by Edith, proprietress of the manor of Wiggold ; it has a small endowment, and is under the control of Earl Bathurst. *St. Thomas's* was erected by Sir William Nottingham, attorney-general to Henry IV., and endowed with £6. 18. 8. per annum. The union of Cirencester comprises 39 parishes or places, of which 33 are in the county of Gloucester, and 6 in that of Wilts ; and contains a population of 20,726. There are a few antiquities. Henry I., in 1117, built an abbey for Black canons in honour of the Blessed Virgin Mary, which he and his successors richly endowed; it was a mitred abbey, and in the 26th of Henry VIII. its revenue was estimated at £1051. 7. 1. : the remains consist of two gateways and a large barn. In a field called the Querns, to the west of the town, near the Roman wall, are the remains of an amphitheatre. Grismond's Tower, a circular hill about a quarter of a mile westward, converted into an ice-house by Earl Bathurst, was discovered, on examination, to be a Roman tumulus, containing several large urns full of ashes and burnt bones. Richard of Cirencester, author of a History and Itinerary of Britain in the time of the Romans; Thomas Ruthal, Bishop of Durham, and counsellor to Henry VII. ; and, lately, Caleb Hillier Parry, M.D., eminent in his profession, and father of Capt. Sir Edward Parry, R.N., the celebrated navigator, were natives of the place.

CLACKHEATON.—See CLECKHEATON.

CLACTON, GREAT (*St. John the Baptist*), a parish, in the union and hundred of TENDRING, N. division of ESSEX, 14½ miles (S. E. by E.) from Colchester; containing 1296 inhabitants. This parish, which was formerly the residence of the bishops of London, is bounded on the south by the North Sea, and comprises an area about fifteen miles in circumference. The soil in some parts is light and of inferior quality, and in others, especially towards the coast, a fine strong loam, producing abundant crops. A fair is held on the 29th of June. The living is a discharged vicarage, with the donative of Little Holland annexed, valued in the king's books at £10, and in the patronage of F. Nassau, Esq. ; impropriators, Col. Harding and others. The great tithes have been commuted for £1146. 7., the vicarial for £250, and a rent-charge of £66 is paid to Travers' Knights of Windsor; the glebe contains 4½ acres, with a glebe-house. The church is a plain edifice, with a tower surmounted by a shingled spire. There is a place of worship for Wesleyans. Some horns and bones of enormous size were lately found in the clay which forms the cliffs on this part of the coast; among them were the grinding-tooth of an elephant, some colossal horns of the wild bull, and part of the skull of a rhinoceros.

CLACTON, LITTLE (*St. James*), a parish, in the union and hundred of TENDRING, N. division of ESSEX, 12½ miles (E. S. E.) from Colchester; containing 547 inhabitants. It forms part of a small district mentioned in the Norman survey under the name *Clackintuna* ; the lands are low, and of a great portion of them the soil is strong and heavy. The village is pleasantly situated round a small green, on which a fair is held on the 25th of July. The living is a discharged vicarage, valued in the king's books at £6. 13. 4. ; patron and impropri-

1830, at a cost of £3345, in the early English style, th a tower; and from the want of sufficient aecom-)dation for the increasing population, it is expected it another chapel will be shortly built at Fernall Heath. ,me schools are supported; and a fund of about £35 ', annum, arising from bequests, is applied to the pur- `ase of clothing, bread, &c., for the poor. On Elbury |ll is the site of a Roman camp, which completely over-)ked and would defend the city of Worcester: this np appears to have been first described by Mr. Allies his *Antiquities of Worcester*. A remarkable relic of)man-British antiquity, supposed to have been used a torque or ornament worn round the neck, was lately nd at Perdiswell, the seat of Sir O. P. Wakeman; d other relics have been discovered in the parish.

CLANABOROUGH (St. Petrock), a parish, in the ion of Crediton, hundred of North Tawton, South olton and N. divisions of Devon, 5½ miles (W. by N.))m Crediton; containing 69 inhabitants, and consist- ʒ of 740 acres, of which 104 are common or waste. ne living is a rectory, valued in the king's books at 5. 17. 3½., and in the patronage of the Crown: the hes have been commuted for £95, and the glebe com- 'ises about 45 acres, with a glebe-house.

CLANDON, EAST, a parish, in the union of Guild-)rd, Second division of the hundred of Woking, W. vision of Surrey, 4 miles (E. N. E.) from Guildford;)ntaining 293 inhabitants. It comprises by computa-)n 1430 acres, of which between 400 and 500 are ncultivated. On the north side the soil is chiefly clay, d there is a common where the oak grows freely; the)uthern. part consists of arable land and downs, and as a chalky soil. Within the parish is the elegant :sidence of Hatchlands; the park is extensive, and the ardens finely laid out. The living is a rectory, valued ι the king's books at £10. 6. 10½.; net income, £152; atron, the Earl of Lovelace. The church is a small lifice, with a low wooden tower and shingled spire.

ᐟCLANDON, WEST, a parish, in the union of Guild- ord, Second division of the hundred of Woking, V. division of Surrey, 3 miles (N. E. by E.) from ʋildford; containing 407 inhabitants. It comprises 37 acres, of which 384 are arable, 338 meadow and asture, 80 woodland, and 117 common. Clandon louse, the principal seat of the Earl of Onslow, was ʳected about 1730, and is one of the finest mansions in ιe county; it is of red brick with stone dressings, and ιe apartments are in general stately and commodious. lis lordship resides, however, at a smaller seat in the ljacent village of West Clandon. The living is a rectory, alued in the king's books at £13. 10., and in the atronage of the Earl of Onslow · the tithes have been ʋmmuted for £160, and the glebe contains 20 acres, ·ith a glebe-house. The church is in the early English tyle. with a low tower on the north side.

CLANFIELD (St. Stephen), a parish, in the union f Witney, hundred of Bampton, county of Oxford, miles (N.) from Farringdon; containing 584 inhabit- nts. The living is a discharged vicarage, valued in the ing's books at £7. 6. 5½.; patrons, H. Elliott and Villiam Aldworth, Esqrs.; impropriators, G. H. Elliott nd H. Collett, Esqrs. The great tithes have been com- ιuted for £300, the vicarial for £50, and tithes payable ɔ the vicar of Bampton for £100; the glebe comprises even acres. The church is in the early English style,

and has, in the chancel, a brass recording the death of Leonard Wilmot at Clanfield, in 1608.

CLANFIELD (St. James), a parish, in the union of Catherington, hundred of Finch-Dean, Petersfield and N. divisions of the county of Southampton, 5¾ miles (S. W.) from Petersfield; containing 239 inhabit- ants. This parish, which is about three miles to the south-west of Butser Hill, comprises 1363 acres, whereof 386 are common or waste. It consists of various quali- ties of soil; much of the surface is open, and in the lower grounds the land is rich and fertile. The village is pleasantly situated within a mile of the road to Peters- field. The living is a rectory, united to that of Chalton, and valued in the king's books at £11: the tithes have been commuted for £178, and the glebe contains nearly 63 acres.

CLANVILLE, Somerset.—See Castle-Cary.

CLAPCOT, a liberty, in the parish of Allhallows, Wallingford, union of Wallingford, hundred of Moreton, county Berks; containing 43 inhabitants.

CLAPHAM (St. Thomas à Becket), a parish, in the hundred of Stodden, union and county of Bedford, 2⅔ miles (N. W. by N.) from Bedford; and containing 370 inhabitants. The living is a discharged vicarage, valued in the king's books at £5. 13. 4.; net income, £270; patron, Lord Carteret. The church is a very ancient structure, with a tower remarkable for the simplicity of its architecture; it is mostly of rude Saxon, and has a Norman belfry. Clapham was formerly a chapelry in the parish of Oakley. J. Thomas Daw- son, Esq., of Woodlands, in the parish, has given a piece of ground for a school. Ursula Taylor, in 1722, be- queathed property for apprenticing poor boys, directing the ministers of St. Paul's and St. John's, Bedford, to be trustees; it consists of 41 acres of land, producing about £50 per annum.

CLAPHAM (Holy Trinity), a parish, in the union of Wandsworth and Clapham, E. division of the hundred of Brixton and of the county of Surrey, 4 miles (S.) from London; containing 12,106 inhabit- ants. This village has, for many years, been one of the most respectable in the environs of the metropolis. The road from London, particularly that part of it called Clapham Rise, has on each side large and elegant houses with gardens and lawns in front, forming a con- tinuous line leading to the common, which occupies a space of 190 acres, surrounded by noble mansions and villas, and which, from the improvements that have been made by the formation of carriage-drives, and the plantation of trees and shrubs, assumes the appearance of a park. On the east of the common a handsome cres- cent has been formed, opposite to which is a range of houses named the Grove; the area is tastefully laid out, and the approach from the common is formed by a well- constructed iron palisade, on each side of which is a stately mansion. In that part of the parish formerly called Bleakhall Farm, considerable alterations have also taken place: new roads have been made; a church and several villas have been erected, and the spot is now de- signated Clapham New Park. Great improvements have likewise been made towards the north-east, by the erection of numerous neat houses and cottages.

The parish is within the limits of the metropolitan police establishment; and is lighted with gas, main pipes having been laid down by the Phœnix Gas Com-

CLAP

pany, from which a sufficient quantity is distributed to every part of the village and its vicinity. The inhabitants are supplied with water from the South Lambeth water-works, and from an excellent spring on that side of the common leading to Wandsworth, opened in 1825, near another which had supplied the village for more than a century : this spring, the water of which is pecu-. liarly soft, provides upwards of 600 hogsheads per day, and nearly twenty families derive employment by conveying it to the houses of the inhabitants at a moderate expense. The subscription library, to which a commodious reading-room has been added, contains a well-assorted and extensive collection; it has been established for nearly half a century, and is liberally supported. Clapham is within the jurisdiction of the county magistrates, who hold a petty-session at the office of their clerk, every Saturday. The acting coroner for the district is appointed at the court of the duchy of Lancaster, within the jurisdiction of which a part of the parish is comprehended : the parochial affairs are under the direction of a select vestry.

The parish comprises 1233 acres. The LIVING is a rectory, valued in the king's books at £8. 0. 10., and in the patronage of the family of Atkins: the tithes have been commuted for £488. 14., and the glebe comprises 11 acres. The church, which belonged to the priory at. Merton, was, with the exception of the north aisle, which was left standing for the performance of the burial service, taken down under an act of parliament in 1774, and a new church erected in the following year, at an expense of £11,000, on the north side of the common. It is a neat structure of brick relieved with stone, with a dome turret, and having a handsome portico of stone, extending the whole width of the western front, which was added in 1812 : the interior is characterised by a chaste simplicity of style ; the east end is ornamented with a well-executed painting on glass, and there are some monumental tablets. The remaining aisle of the old church, which was situated in that part of the village leading to Wandsworth, near the old manor-house, was taken down in 1815, and a neat chapel, in some respects dependent on the mother church, was erected, under an act of parliament, at a cost of £5000, and dedicated to St. Paul. The living is a perpetual curacy; net income, £200; patron, the Rector. The burial-ground, which is spacious, contains many ancient tombs and monuments. St. James's church, in the Park, was built in 1829, and is an elegant structure in the decorated English style, with a graceful and richly-crocketed campanile turret ; the western front is ornamented with panelled buttresses relieved by tracery, dividing it into three doorways under richly moulded arches. The living is a perpetual curacy, in the patronage of Trustees; net income, £500. On the west side of the Clapham road is a fourth church, dedicated to St. John, and opened in May, 1842 ; it is of white brick with stone dressings, and has a stone portico formed by Ionic columns supporting a pediment. The living is in the gift of the Rector. There are places of worship for Independents, Wesleyans, and Baptists.

CLAPHAM, a parish, in the union of SUTTON, hundred of BRIGHTFORD, rape of BRAMBER, W. division of SUSSEX, 5 miles (N. W.) from Worthing; containing 262 inhabitants. The parish is situated on the road from Portsmouth, by way of Arundel, to Brighton; and

618

itants. The living is annexed to the rectory of urton-on-the-Water.

CLAPTON, a hamlet, in the parish of St. John, ckney, union of Hackney, Tower division of the ndred of Ossulstone, county of Middlesex, 3 miles by E.) from London; containing 5475 inhabitants. is place is divided into Upper and Lower Clapton. e latter consists of various ranges of handsome build-s, with several large detached mansions and villas on h sides of the road, extending from Hackney church about a mile, and occasionally interspersed with ges of smaller houses and shops. The former, from wer Clapton to Stamford Hill, consists of numerous ll-built and spacious houses of modern erection, with unds tastefully laid out, and comprises much rraces, the latter of which forms a lofty and extensive e. The houses are supplied with water from a reservoir Lower Clapton belonging to the East London Water-orks Company, into which it is conveyed from the er Lea by a steam-engine. There is no trade, except at is requisite for the supply of the immediate neigh-urhood; the nursery-grounds are extensive, and the jacent country is richly wooded, and comprises much asing scenery. A proprietary chapel was built at pper Clapton in 1777, which has lately been enlarged; d in 1841, a church was built upon a piece of ground ven by the Rev. T. B. Powell, at a cost of £6300, in dition to which, a considerable sum derived from pri-te sources was expended on embellishments: it is dicated to St. James, and the living is in the Rector's ft. There are places of worship for Independents and esleyans. The London Orphan Asylum at Lower apton, founded in 1813, for the maintenance and edu-tion of destitute orphans, of whom about 400 are now the institution, is a handsome edifice of light-loured brick, the centre of which, forming a chapel, s an elegant portico of four lofty fluted columns of the recian-Doric order, supporting a triangular pediment.

CLAPTON (St. Peter), a parish, in the union of Rapston, hundred of Navisford, N. division of the unty of Northampton, 5¼ miles (E. N. E.) from rapston; containing 119 inhabitants. This parish, hich is situated on the borders of the county of Hun-gdon, consists of 1850 acres, and is intersected by e road between Oundle and Huntingdon. The living a rectory, valued in the king's books at £17. 3. 9., d in the gift of the Shedden family: the tithes have en commuted for a yearly rent-charge of £295. 16., d there are 46 acres of glebe.

CLAPTON, a tything, in the parish and hundred of Rewkerne, union of Chard, W. division of Somer-t; containing 90 inhabitants.

CLAPTON, a hamlet, in the parish of Maperton, aion of Wincanton, hundred of Catsash, E. division Somerset; containing 38 inhabitants.

CLAPTON, a tything, in the parish of Midsomer-orton, union of Clutton, hundred of Chewton, E. ivision of Somerset, 6¾ miles (N. by E.) from Shepton-Iallet; containing 147 inhabitants.

CLAPTON-in-Gordano (St. Michael), a parish, i the union of Bedminster, hundred of Portbury, E. ivision of Somerset, 9¼ miles (W.) from Bristol; con-ining 138 inhabitants. In this parish are 1066 acres, hereof 169 are common or waste: within its limits is e tything of Clapton-Wick, which belongs to the parish
619

of Portbury, and has a population of 45. The living is a discharged rectory, valued in the king's books at £10. 9. 2., and in the patronage of James Adam Gordon, Esq.: the tithes have been commuted for £200, and the glebe comprises 43 acres.

CLARE (St. Peter and St. Paul), a market-town and parish, in the union and hundred of Risbridge, W. division of Suffolk, 15 miles (S. S. W.) from Bury St. Edmund's, and 55½ (N. E. by N.) from London; containing, with the hamlet of Chilton, 1700 inhabitants. This place, which is of great antiquity, derived consider-able importance during the Saxon heptarchy from being on the frontier of the kingdom of East Anglia; and after the Conquest it was distinguished as giving the title of Earl to the family of De Clare, and that of Duke to Lionel, third son of Edward III., who was created Duke of Clarence. George III. revived the title in the person of his third son, Prince William Henry, who, in 1789, was created a peer of the realm as Duke of Clarence. To the south of the town are the ruins of a castle, for-merly the baronial residence of the earls of Clare, and equal to any of such structures in feudal grandeur and magnificence: the site of the fortifications, which may be distinctly traced, comprehended an area of 30 acres. On the summit of a high mount evidently of artificial construction, are the remains of the keep, a circular building of flints strongly cemented with mortar, strength-ened with buttresses; it is supposed to have been erected either prior to or during the heptarchy. The honour of Clare is now annexed to the duchy of Lancaster.

The town is situated on the river Stour, which sepa-rates this county from Essex, on the south; the houses are in general old, but many new ones have been erected. The ancient market-place was lately considerably en-larged, by pulling down many unsightly buildings; and a handsome corn-exchange was erected in 1838. The streets are spacious; the inhabitants are amply supplied with water; and the approaches to the town are gradu-ally improving. The market is on Monday; fairs are held on Easter-Tuesday and July 26th, chiefly for toys and pedlery. The county magistrates hold monthly and petty sessions for the division here; and the courts baron of Erbury, and Stoke with Chilton, and a court for the duchy of Lancaster, are also held at this place. The parish comprises by computation 2178 acres. The living is a discharged vicarage, valued in the king's books at £4. 18. 9., and in the patronage of the Queen, in right of the duchy of Lancaster; net income, about £200. The church is a large, handsome, and ancient structure, chiefly in the decorated English style, with a tower strengthened by buttresses, and of an earlier date than the body. The interior, which has been improved by heightening the nave, and the addition of aisles, is richly ornamented, and contains an elegantly-designed font in the later English style, and a brass eagle on a pedestal, with wings displayed, forming the reading-desk. In the chancel are said to have been interred the remains of Lionel, Duke of Clarence, who died in 1368, at Piedmont, and who is supposed to have been born here. There are places of worship for Baptists and In-dependents. William Cadge, in 1669, bequeathed a farm now let for £74, appropriating £10 per annum to a master for teaching boys, and £15 per annum to the clothing of widows; and there are several other charitable bequests for distribution among the poor, who
4 K 2

have also the privilege of depasturing 40 milch-cows on a common, comprising 62 acres of land.

To the south-west of the town are the remains of *Clare Priory*, founded by Eluric or Alfric, Earl of Clare, for Secular canons, and which Gilbert de Clare, in 1090, gave to the Benedictine abbey of Bec, in Normandy, to which it was a cell till 1124, when his son Richard removed the monks to the village of Stoke. Joan d'Acre, daughter of Edward I., and wife of Gilbert de Clare, who was a great benefactress to this establishment, is traditionally said to have been interred in the chapel, which has been converted into a barn : the priory building, now a private residence, though it has undergone considerable repairs and alterations, still retains much of its original character. A monastery for *Augustine* monks is said to have been founded here in 1248, but by whom is not known ; and according to Robert Aske, who wrote in the reign of Henry VIII., the following persons were, among others of less distinction, buried in it, namely, Richard, Earl of Clare; Lionel, Duke of Clarence ; Joan d'Acre, and her son, Sir Edward Montheimer ; Dame Alice Spencer ; Sir John Beauchamp, Knt.; William Capel, and Eleanor, his wife; the Lady Margaret Scroope ; Sir Edmund, last of the Mortimers, earls of March ; Sir Thomas Grey, and his first wife ; and Sir Thomas Clopton, and his wife. To the north-west of the town are evident marks of a Roman camp.

CLAREBOROUGH (St. John the Baptist), a parish, in the union of East Retford, North-Clay division of the wapentake of Bassetlaw, N. division of the county of Nottingham, $2\frac{1}{2}$ miles (N. E. by E.) from East Retford ; containing, with the hamlets of Bollom, Gringley, Little Gringley, Moorgate, and Walham, 2207 inhabitants. This parish, which is situated on the great north road, intersected by the Chesterfield and Gainsborough canal, and skirted on the west by the river Idle, comprises 3407a. 2r. 21p., whereof the township of Clareborough contains 1230a. 3r. 20p. The soil is in general a good productive clay. The living is a discharged vicarage, valued in the king's books at £9. 15. 4. ; net income, £331 ; patrons, the Trustees of the late Rev. C. Simeon ; impropriators, the family of Hutchinson, and others. The tithes were commuted for land and a money payment in 1776 ; the glebe contains altogether 90 acres, with a glebe-house. The church is a small edifice, built by Archbishop Roger, and endowed by Sewell, Archbishop of York, in 1258 ; it consists of a nave, chancel, and aisles, with a square embattled tower. A handsome chapel of ease was opened in 1829, which is dedicated to St. Saviour, and contains 1065 sittings.

CLARENCE-PORT, a small port, in the parish of Billingham, union of Stockton, N. E. division of Stockton ward, county of Durham. This port was lately formed, at the base of Haverton Hill, on the north of the river Tees, near its mouth, for the greater facility of shipping the coal conveyed by the Clarence railway. The quantity of coal averages 400,000 tons annually ; and by means of four drops constructed for the purpose, 81 keels can be loaded in the short space of twelve hours.

CLARENDON-PARK, an extra-parochial liberty, in the union and hundred of Alderbury, Salisbury and Amesbury, and S. divisions of Wilts, $3\frac{1}{2}$ miles (E. by S.) from Salisbury ; containing 181 inhabitants. At this place were anciently two palaces, termed the King's and

nd Andover canal. The manufacture of paper is carried on to some extent, and there is an iron-foundry. The living is a rectory, valued in the king's books at £22, nd in the patronage of the Rev. Edward Frowd: the tithes have been commuted for £525, and the glebe comprises 38 acres. At Bury Hill, in the parish, are he remains of an encampment.

CLATTERCOTT, an extra-parochial liberty, in the nion and hundred of BANBURY, county of OXFORD, 6 iles (N.) from Banbury; containing 15 inhabitants. ere was a small religious house, dedicated to St. eonard, and endowed by Beauchamp, Earl of Warwick, r brethren of the Sempringham order; it was once an ospital for lepers, and the establishment, at the Dissolution, consisted of a prior and four canons, whose evenue was estimated at £34. 19. 11. per annum. here are some very slight remains.

CLATWORTHY (ST. MARY), a parish, in the union f WILLITON, hundred of WILLITON and FREEMANERS, W. division of SOMERSET, 3 miles (N. W.) from Wiveliscombe; containing 309 inhabitants. It is situated on the small river Tone, which falls into the Bristol Channel at Bridgwater, in confluence with the river 'arret; the number of acres is 2943, whereof 280 are r were common and waste. The soil is tolerably fertile, nd has a substratum of clay-slate, interspersed with white flint or quartz: slate for roofing was formerly quarried. An act for inclosing lands was passed in 842. The living is a rectory, valued in the king's books t £13. 10. 5., and in the gift of G. W. Carew, Esq.: he tithes have been commuted for £268, and the glebe omprises 93 acres. The church is a very ancient tructure. There is an encampment about 14 acres in xtent, but whether of Roman or British origin is not learly known.

CLAUGHTON, with GRANGE, a township, in the nion, and Lower division of the hundred, of WIRRALL, . division of CHESHIRE; containing, in 1841, 240 inhabitants. The manor was the property of the convent f Birkenhead, upon the dissolution of which it was ranted to the Worsleys, and thus descended to F. R. 'rice, Esq., by whom the manors of Birkenhead and Claughton were lately sold to William Jackson, Esq., .P. The township is situated to the north-west of Birkenhead, and comprises 575 acres, the soil of which s a loamy clay. The whole of it, with a small part of he township of Oxton, has by a recent act of parliament been annexed to the adjoining town, the three laces now forming one district or township under the ontrol of commissioners. The surface is dotted over vith villas and other handsome suburban residences, mongst which is the Manor-House, lately called Claughton Hall, the seat of Mr. Jackson. Stretching own from this mansion, in a south-eastern direction, es the fine public park of Birkenhead; and almost pposite the park entrance are the house and grounds f J. R. Pim, Esq., by whom a meeting-house for the ociety of Friends has been erected on his own property. everal churches, also, and other public buildings, have een raised; an account of which will be found under he head of BIRKENHEAD.

CLAUGHTON, a township, in the parish and union f GARSTANG, hundred of AMOUNDERNESS, N. division f the county of LANCASTER, 2 miles (S. S. E.) from Garstang; containing 772 inhabitants. This place gave

name to a local family, of whom Richard de Clacton appears in a deed without date as a benefactor of Cocker-sand Abbey. The Banastre family held a moiety of the manor in Edward II.'s reign; and Claughton is afterwards found in possession of the Brockholes, whose descendant, in the last century, devised his estates to William Fitzherbert, Esq., of Swynnerton Hall, Staffordshire, with injunction to take the name and arms of Brockholes. The township lies on the road from Lancaster to Preston, and comprises 3785a. 2r. 4p. of land: the Lancaster and Preston railway and canal also pass through it. Claughton Hall, the seat of the family of Fitzherbert Brockholes, is a noble stone mansion, surrounded by a well-wooded park of 500 acres, abounding with game, and commanding beautiful views. The vicarial tithes have been commuted for £350. At a short distance from the Hall is a Roman Catholic chapel, a neat building in the Grecian style; the interior is very handsome, especially the altar: adjoining is the house of the priest, the Rev. Henry Gradwell. There is a small cotton-mill.

CLAUGHTON (ST. CHAD), a parish, in the hundred of LONSDALE south of the Sands, N. division of the county of LANCASTER, 7 miles (N. E. by E.) from Lancaster, on the road to Hornby, containing 118 inhabitants. This place was early erected into an independent parochial township, with its own lords, probably the Kellets. It would appear from an inquisition, 18th of Edward II., that the manor had passed to Hugh de Carnetbye; and a John de Claughton, and subsequently the Flemings, are mentioned as proprietors here. The Crofts were lords of a third part of the manor in the 15th and 16th centuries, and in the reign of Henry VIII.: Simon Croft appears afterwards to have held the whole manor. In 1712 the Fenwicks became lords of Claughton. The parish comprises a large tract of land, which is beautifully diversified, rising on one side into hills, and on the other spreading into a rich and fertile vale, through which the river Lune pursues its serpentine course. The soil is favourable for grazing; and there are some good quarries of flagstone. Claughton Hall is an interesting specimen of the domestic architecture of the reign of Elizabeth; the north-west front is ornamented by two square towers rising some height above the building, evidently erected for the purpose of enjoying the fine prospects up and down the valley of the Lune. It was in possession of Sir W. Croft in the time of Charles I., of whose cause he was a firm supporter. The living is a discharged rectory, valued in the king's books at £9. 13. 10., and in the patronage of the Heir of the late Thomas Fenwick, Esq.; net income, £145. The original church was built in 1070; the present edifice in 1815. There is a day and Sunday school.

CLAVERDON (ST. MICHAEL), a parish, in the union of STRATFORD-ON-AVON, Henley division of the hundred of BARLICHWAY, S. division of the county of WARWICK, 3½ miles (E. by S.) from Henley; containing, with the hamlet of Langley, 711 inhabitants. The parish is situated on the road from Henley to Warwick, and comprises by measurement 3580 acres; its northeastern boundary is skirted by the canal from Stratford to Birmingham. The living is a discharged vicarage, with that of Norton-Lindsey annexed, valued in the king's books at £5. 12. 1.; net income, £265; patron, the Archdeacon of Worcester. The great tithes have been commuted for £672. 3., and the vicarial for £229. 10.; the impropriator's glebe comprises 33 acres, and the vicar's 5 acres, with a glebe-house. The church, with the exception of the chancel and tower, was rebuilt in the years 1827-8, and contains a handsome monument, in the chancel, belonging to the Spencer family, who formerly possessed a large mansion in the parish. John Matthews, about the year 1526, left property for the repair of the church, now worth about £96 per annum, out of which a village school is also supported.

CLAVERING (St. Mary and St. Clement), a parish, in the union of Saffron-Walden, hundred of Clavering, N. division of Essex, 7½ miles (N. by W.) from Bishop-Stortford; containing 1172 inhabitants. The parish borders on the county of Hertford, and comprises by computation 3691 acres, of which about 500 are in woods and plantations; the soil is various, consisting of chalk, clay, sand, and a light gravel. A small stream, rising in Arkesden, unites with a rivulet from Langley, and pursues its course through the parish to the river Stort. The village is irregularly built, but contains some respectable houses, and the surrounding scenery is agreeably diversified. The living is an endowed vicarage, with that of Langley annexed, valued in the king's books at £22. 13. 11½.; patrons and impropriators, the Governors of Christ's Hospital: the great tithes have been commuted for £504, and the vicarial for £465. 6., and the glebe contains 7¼ acres, with a glebe-house. The church is a spacious and handsome edifice of stone, with an embattled tower. There is a place of worship for Independents.

CLAVERLEY (All Saints), a parish, in the union of Bridgnorth, Hales-Owen division of the hundred of Brimstree, S. division of Salop, 6 miles (E.) from Bridgnorth; containing 1669 inhabitants. This parish comprises the townships (for highway purposes) of Beobridge, Broughton, Gatacre, Ludstone, Shipley, and Sutton, which, in the manor court of Claverley, are denominated "foreign towns," being distinct manors; and Ashton, Dallicott, Farmcott, Heathton, Hopstone, and Woundale, which are called "king's towns," and are part of the forest of Morfe. The lordships of Beobridge and Broughton were part of the possessions annexed to the abbey of Haughmond, but after the Dissolution they became the property of the Levesons, who also became possessed of Ludstone. Throughout the copyhold lands, the Borough-English custom prevails, of descent to the younger son. The parish lies on the eastern confines of the county, and consists of 8141a. 3r. 28p., about three-quarters of which are arable, and the rest pasture, with 43 acres of waste. The living is a perpetual curacy; net income, £300; patrons and impropriators, the family of Whitmore: the great tithes have been commuted for £2060, and the remainder for £12. The church is a handsome structure in the later English style, with a high tower surmounted by pinnacles; the pews have been lately re-arranged, and galleries built. A school was founded in 1659, by Richard Dovey, who endowed it with an estate; in 1702, John Sanders devised £5 a year for clothing the boys; and Richard Bennett, in 1794, left £100 in aid of the charity, which is now united with a national school. In Gatacre-Park House, here, the Earl of Derby took shelter immediately after the battle

ued in the king's books at £5. 3. 1½.: the church is small thatched building. Here are vestiges of a man camp, and several tumuli covered with trees.

CLAXBY (St. Mary), a parish, in the union of Istor, N. division of the wapentake of WALSHCROFT, rts of LINDSEY, county of LINCOLN, 4 miles (N. E.) m Market-Rasen; containing 220 inhabitants. It nprises by measurement 1679 acres. Coal is supsed to exist, but no attempt has been made to work there are quarries of stone of good quality for roadking, and great quantities are raised for the supply the neighbourhood. A pleasure-fair is held about end of August or beginning of September. The ing is a discharged rectory, to which the rectory Normanby-on-the-Wolds was united in 1740, valued the king's books at £8. 10. 10.; net income, £844; trons, the family of Atkinson. The church is in the rly English style, and contains some ancient monuents. There is a place of worship for Wesleyans. veral Roman coins, one of them of the reign of Contine, and some Roman pavements, have been discvered.

CLAXBY-PLUCKACRE (St. Andrew), a parish, the union of HORNCASTLE, hundred of HILL, parts of NDSEY, county of LINCOLN, 4 miles (S. E. by E.) from rncastle; containing 29 inhabitants. It is situated the road from Horncastle to Boston, and comprises computation 900 acres, with a light sandy soil apted to barley and oats, which form the chief proce. The living is a discharged rectory, valued in the ng's books at £6. 10. 10., and in the gift of the family Dymoke: the tithes have been commuted for £140. ie church fell down some years since, and has not en rebuilt: the inhabitants have sittings in Moorby urch by consent of the rector and parishioners, and annual payment of £5 is made to the minister of oorby as officiating minister.

CLAXTON, a township, in the parish of GREATHAM, lion of STOCKTON-UPON-TEES, N. E. division of STOCKIN ward, S. division of the county of DURHAM, 7 miles !. N. E.) from Stockton; containing 52 inhabitants. branch of the Norman family of Heriz, settling here, sumed the local name; and numerous notices of the axtons occur in the records during the 13th, 14th, d 15th centuries: from this family Thomas Claxton, celebrated antiquary, and the friend and correspondent Camden, was descended. Of the ancient manoruse, which was deserted for Horden, no traces exist. ie township comprises 866 acres: the great tithes have en commuted for £125, and the vicarial for £33.

CLAXTON, or LONG CLAWSON (St. Remigius), a rish, in the union of MELTON-MOWBRAY, hundred FRAMLAND, N. division of the county of LEICESTER, miles (N. N. W.) from Melton-Mowbray; containing ;8 inhabitants. It is situated in the vale of Belvoir, d comprises by admeasurement 2800 acres: the canal wigation from Nottingham to Grantham runs from :st to east, through the lower part of the manor. The 'ing is a discharged vicarage, valued in the king's oka at £9. 10. 2.; net income, £105; patron, Lord odolphin: 126 acres of land belong to the vicarage, id there is a glebe-house, with an acre of glebe. Here aptists and Wesleyans have places of worship. Here c two free schools, towards the endowment of which athony Wadd in 1758 gave land, the rent of which
6‌23

is now £62. 8.; in 1772, Mrs. Briggs bequeathed £100, for the same purpose.

CLAXTON (St. Andrew), a parish, in the union of LODDON and CLAVERING, hundred of LODDON, E. division of NORFOLK, 2¼ miles (N. W. by N.) from Loddon; containing 200 inhabitants, and comprising by computation 920 acres. A charter for a market on Monday, and for a fair on the eve of the festival of St. John the Baptist, to continue four days, was granted in the reign of Edward III., to the Kerdiston family; but both have long been discontinued. The living is a vicarage, endowed with a small portion of the rectorial tithes; net income, £60; patron, Sir Charles Rich, Bart.: the glebe contains about 24 acres. The church, which consists of a nave and chancel, with a tower, is partly in the early, and partly in the decorated style, and appears, by some arches now filled up, to have had a north aisle. There is a place of worship for Baptists. Extensive ruins still remain of the seat of the Kerdiston family, whose manor-house Edward III. permitted to be converted into a castle.

CLAXTON, a chapelry, in the parish of BOSSALL, union of YORK, wapentake of BULMER, N. riding of YORK, 8½ miles (N. E. by E.) from York; containing 168 inhabitants. It comprises by computation 813 acres of land: the village is situated about a mile to the east of the road between York and Malton. The pettysessions for the division are held at Lobster House. The chapel is a small edifice. There are places of wor ship for Wesleyans and Primitive Methodists.

CLAYBROOKE (St. Peter), a parish, in the union of LUTTERWORTH; comprising the townships of Great and Little Claybrooke, the chapelry of Wigston Parva, the hamlet of Ullesthorpe, and the liberty of Bittesby, in the hundred of GUTHLAXTON, S. division of the county of LEICESTER; and the chapelry of Wibtoft, in the Kirby division of the hundred of KNIGHTLOW, N. division of the county of WARWICK; the whole containing 1417 inhabitants, of whom 519 are in Great Claybrooke, 4 miles (N. W. by W.) from Lutterworth, and 104 in Little Claybrooke. The parish is situated on the road from London to Hinckley and Atherstone; the surface is pleasingly undulated, and the soil in some few places sandy, but in general a rich loam. A part of the population is employed in the stocking manufacture, which is carried on to a considerable extent. The Midland railway passes through the parish, and the Ullesthorpe station is within its limits. The living is a vicarage, valued in the king's books at £30. 10. 5., and in the patronage of the Crown; impropriators, the Earl of Denbigh, Trinity College, Cambridge, and others; net income, £451, with a glebe-house. The church is at Little Claybrooke, and is partly in the decorated and partly in the later English style. There are chapels of ease at Wibtoft and Little Wigston; and the Independents have a place of worship. A school was endowed by Mark Smith with £26 per annum, and is aided by an annual sum of £26 from Alderman Newton's charity: J. E. Dicey, Esq., of Claybrooke Hall, has erected a school for females, which he supports. This was the Roman station Benonæ, or Vennones; and at a place termed High Cross, two miles westward, two great Roman roads intersect, which traversed the kingdom obliquely.

CLAYCOATON.—See COATON, CLAY.

CLAYDON, a chapelry, in the parish of CROPREDY, union and hundred of BANBURY, county of OXFORD, 6½ miles (N.) from Banbury; containing 337 inhabitants. The chapel is dedicated to St. James, and is a small edifice, with a north aisle divided from the nave by four arches of Norman character; the tower is of the 15th century. The village is situated in the northern extremity of the county: a small spring which rises in it has the peculiarity of emitting the largest quantity of water in the driest weather. Here is found the *pyrites aureus*, or golden firestone; also the *asteria*, or star-stone, called by Gesner *sigillum stellæ*, from its use in sealing: in splitting some of these, the figure of a rose is plainly discernible.

CLAYDON (ST. PETER), a parish, in the union and hundred of BOSMERE and CLAYDON, E. division of SUFFOLK, 3½ miles (N. N. W.) from Ipswich; containing 418 inhabitants. The Stow-Market and Ipswich navigation crosses the parish. The living is a rectory, with that of Akenham united, valued in the king's books at £10, and in the patronage of Miss Drury: the tithes of the two parishes have been commuted for £510, and there are 31 acres of glebe in Claydon, and 20 in Akenham. The church stands on a very high site, commanding an extensive prospect: the parsonage-house and grounds, which adjoin the churchyard, are neatly arranged, and ornamented with fine timber.

CLAYDON, EAST (ST. MARY), a parish, in the union of WINSLOW, hundred of ASHENDON, county of BUCKINGHAM, 2¾ miles (S. W. by W.) from Winslow; containing 378 inhabitants. The living is a discharged vicarage, annexed to that of Steeple-Claydon, and valued in the king's books at £7. 17. The church was demolished during the civil war, by Cornelius Holland, one of the judges who sat upon the trial of Charles I.

CLAYDON, MIDDLE (ALL SAINTS), a parish, in the hundred of ASHENDON, union and county of BUCKINGHAM, 4 miles (W. S. W.) from Winslow; containing 127 inhabitants. The living is a rectory, valued in the king's books at £15; net income, £540; patron, Sir Harry Verney. The church contains a monument to the memory of Sir Edmund Verney, standard-bearer to Charles I., who was killed at the battle of Edge-Hill, in 1642; and a monument, by Chantrey, to Gen. Sir Harry Calvert, adjutant-general of the British army, and father of Sir Harry Verney, the present baronet. Almshouses for six widows were built in 1694, by Sir Ralph Verney, who endowed them with a rent-charge of £15. 12.

CLAYDON, STEEPLE (ST. MICHAEL), a parish, in the union, hundred, and county of BUCKINGHAM, 5½ miles (W.) from Winslow; containing 849 inhabitants. At the period of the Conquest, this was the most populous place in the hundred; in an adjoining wood, an earthen vessel filled with coins of Carausius and Alectus, has been discovered. The living is a vicarage, with that of East Claydon annexed, valued in the king's books at £13. 3. 9.; net income, £300; patron, Sir Harry Verney, Bart. The tithes were commuted for land and a corn-rent in 1795. Thomas Chaloner, in 1656, built a school, and endowed it with £12 per annum; but the gift has long been lost.

CLAYHANGER (ST. PETER), a parish, in the union of TIVERTON, hundred of BAMPTON, Cullompton and N. divisions of DEVON, 4¾ miles (E. by N.) from Bamp-

ne other plains in the neighbourhood, was once ered.

CLAYTON, LANCASTER.—See DROYLSDEN.

CLAYTON, a township, in the parish and union Stoke-upon-Trent, N. division of the hundred of REHILL and of the county of STAFFORD, 2 miles (S: E.) from Newcastle; containing 155 inhabitants. e township comprises 734 acres, whereof about 50 are odland, and the remainder arable and pasture in nearly ual portions : it is the property of J. Ayshford Wise, q., in right of his lady, the heiress of the Lovatt family, ated here since the reign of Henry VIII. The village composed of five farmhouses and a few scattered cotes, and is delightfully situated on a woody eminence rth of Trentham Park, over which is a fine view of afford Castle, Cannock Chase, &c.

CLAYTON (ST. JOHN THE BAPTIST), a parish, in the ion of CUCKFIELD, hundred of BUTTINGHILL, rape of EWES, E. division of SUSSEX, 2¼ miles (S. S. E.) from urst-Pierrepoint ; containing 747 inhabitants. It is uated on the road from London to Brighton, by way Cuckfield, and intersected by the London and Brigh n railway, which proceeds for about a mile and a arter under Clayton Hill, through a tunnel that comences near the church. The area consists of 2353 res, whereof 201 are common or waste. The southern rtion of the parish is fine down, and the northern mprises some rich arable, pasture, and woodland ; the enery is pleasing, and the views from Clayton Hill are xtensive. Fairs are held on St. John's Common, for attle and sheep, on the 6th of July, and the 26th of eptember. The living is a rectory, with that of Key er annexed, valued in the king's books at £21. 0. 10., nd in the patronage of Brasenose College, Oxford : the ncumbent's tithes have been commuted for £400, and he glebe comprises 25 acres ; certain impropriate tithes ave been commuted for £39. The church is of the arly English style, with some Norman details, among hich is a fine arch separating the chancel from the ave ; it was repaired in 1838. The Roman road from ortus Adriani passed over Clayton Hill to St. John's ommon ; and on opening a barrow near Clayton wind ill, in 1805, the remains of a camp-kitchen were found, which was a vessel of embaked clay, containing bones f various animals. In the rectory grounds, some years nce, a Roman bath was discovered by the plough, with beautiful tessellated pavement ; celts and various ruidical relics have been found near Layton Mill, and umerous fossils in the chalk-pits.

CLAYTON, a township, in the parish and union of RADFORD, wapentake of MORLEY, W. riding of YORK, ½ miles (W. by S.) from Bradford ; containing 4347 inabitants. This place, which is noticed in the Domesay survey, where it is written Claitons, as part of the anor of Bolton, comprises by computation 1600 acres, f which about 150 are arable, and the remainder high nd affording tolerable pasture, with four or five acres f wood. It contains the straggling villages of Clayton nd Clayton-Heights, situated on the acclivities, and art of Queen's-Head on the summit, of a bold emience ; and the population is chiefly employed in the anufacture of worsted goods, and in hand-loom weav g. There are seven quarries of slate and flagstone, of hich two are worked underground ; the stone is of ccellent quality, and is brought up through a shaft in

the same manner as coal. In the upper part of the township, called the Mountain, is a valuable coal-mine. The Leeds and Halifax old road passes through the township. A living has been instituted, which is in the gift of the Vicar of Bradford ; and there are places of worship for Baptists and Wesleyans.

CLAYTON, with FRICKLEY.—See FRICKLEY.

CLAYTON-GRIFFITH, a township, in the parish of TRENTHAM, union of STONE, N. division of the hundred of PIREHILL and of the county of STAFFORD ; containing 56 inhabitants. This township adjoins the south-western suburbs of Newcastle-under-Lyme, and has a few scattered houses in the vicinity of the canal.

CLAYTON-LE-DALE, a township, in the parish, union, and Lower division of the hundred, of BLACK-BURN, N. division of the county of LANCASTER, 4¼ miles (N. by W.) from Blackburn ; containing 511 inhabitants. In the reign of Henry VIII. John Talbot, of Salesbury, was the proprietor of this estate, which is now held by the noble family of Warren. Showley Hall, here, was once the seat of the Walmesley family. The township lies on the road from Preston to Clitheroe, and the river Ribble passes through it on the northwest, in which part there is much elevated land.

CLAYTON-LE-MOORS, a township, in the parish of WHALLEY, union, and Lower division of the hundred, of BLACKBURN, N. division of the county of LANCASTER, 5½ miles (N. E. by E.) from Blackburn ; containing 2602 inhabitants. Clayton-le-Moors, "the clayey district among the Moors," gave the name of Clayton to a family, who resided here as early as the reign of Henry II. From this family the manor came by female heirs to the Grimshaws and de Rishtons, and from them it descended in moieties to the Lomaxes and Walmesleys : by the marriage of Catherine Walmesley, who died in 1785, with the seventh lord Petre, a moiety passed to his lordship and devolved to his descendants. The township lies on the road from Blackburn to Burnley, and the village is distant about a mile and a half north-by-west from the town of Accrington. The river Henbury passes on the west side of the township. A district church, All Saints', was erected in 1839 : the living is in the gift of Trustees. The Wesleyans have a place of worship ; and at Enfield is a Roman Catholic chapel. The Baptist congregation originally at Oakenshaw, in Clayton-le-Moors, removed to Accrington in 1735. Three schools are supported by subscription.

CLAYTON-LE-WOODS, a township, in the parish and hundred of LEYLAND, union of CHORLEY, N. division of the county of LANCASTER, 4 miles (N. by W.) from Chorley, on the road to Preston ; containing 795 inhabitants. This place was possessed by the Clayton family as early as the 11th century : a moiety passed by marriage to the Lees, and from them to the Hoghtons ; and the second moiety has been held by various families, among whom have been the Orrells and Andertons. The township comprises 1450a. 1r. 21p., mostly pasture and meadow ; about 24 acres are wood : the land is elevated, the soil various, and the views pleasing. The river Lostock flows through. Clayton Villa, with 40 acres around it, is the seat of Francis Anderton, Esq. ; and at Clayton Green is the neat residence of Thomas Dewhurst, Esq. The tithes have been commuted for £100 payable to Lord Skelmersdale, and £82 to the vicar. The Wesleyans have a place of worship ; and there is a Roman Catholic chapel, built in the year 1824. A school has the aid of an endowment of £9. 6. per annum.

CLAYTON, WEST, a township, in the parish of HIGH HOYLAND, wapentake of STAINCROSS, W. riding of YORK, 9 miles (S. E. by E.) from Huddersfield; containing 1440 inhabitants. The township is situated on the Wakefield and Denby-Dale road, and comprises by computation 1080 acres, belonging to various proprietors. Several coal-mines are in operation. The manufacture of fancy silk and worsted goods, for waistcoats, trowsers, and ladies' dresses, is carried on to a considerable extent, and large mills have been erected for these branches of industry, in which the greater part of the population is employed: there is an extensive worsted spinning-mill; and clogs are also manufactured. The village is situated on a declivity, and the surrounding scenery is pleasingly diversified. There are places of worship for Independents, Baptists, Wesleyans, and Methodists of the New Connexion.

CLAYWORTH (ST. PETER), a parish, in the union of EAST RETFORD, North-Clay division of the wapentake of BASSETLAW, N. division of the county of NOTTINGHAM, 6 miles (N. N. E.) from East Retford; containing 627 inhabitants. This parish, which is bounded on the west by the river Idle, and intersected by the Chesterfield canal, comprises the townships of Clayworth and Wiseton, the former containing 2076, and the latter 930, acres of fertile land; the soil of Clayworth being a rich clay, and that of Wiseton a fine red sandy mould. The living is a rectory, valued in the king's books at £26. 10. 10.; net income, £604, with a house; patron, the Bishop of Lincoln. The tithes have been commuted for a rent-charge of £3. 5. only, the greater part of the parish being tithe-free under an inclosure act passed at the close of the last century, when 281 acres were allotted to the incumbent, now called Clayworth-highfield, or the Tithe-farm. The church contains many ancient monumental inscriptions. There is a place of worship for Wesleyans. The Rev. William Sampson, in 1700, bequeathed land now producing £57 per annum, as an endowment for a school.

CLEADON, a township, in the parish of WHIT-BURN, union of SOUTH SHIELDS, E. division of CHESTER ward, N. division of the county of DURHAM, 3½ miles (N. by W.) from Sunderland; containing 257 inhabitants. Cleadon, or, as anciently written, Clivedon, Tower, which was taken down at the close of the last century, is mentioned so early as 1587, and was a square building of two stages, leaded, and with a spiral stone staircase to the top; it was attached to the east end of the present old mansion, and commanded a very extensive prospect. Limestone is obtained; and near Marston rock is found a species of indurated marl, in thin laminæ, very pliant, and hence termed flexible limestone.

CLEARWELL, a chapelry, in the parish of NEW-LAND, union of MONMOUTH, hundred of ST. BRIAVELL'S, W. division of the county of GLOUCESTER, 7 miles (W. by N.) from Blakeney; containing 674 inhabitants. A considerable number of persons belonging to Clearwell are employed in the coal and iron mines in the parish and in the adjacent Forest of Dean. A church has been built and endowed, containing 460 sittings, 380 of which are free. There is a curious stone cross.

CLEASBY, a parish, in the union of DARLINGTON, wapentake of GILLING-EAST, N. riding of YORK, 3½ miles (W. by S.) from Darlington; containing 164 inhabitants. The parish is bounded on the north by the river Tees, and comprises by computation 839 acres, mostly arable land; the surface is generally flat, but with a singular and very high embankment, which runs through the parish on the south side. The living is a perpetual curacy; net income, £188; patrons, the Dean and Chapter of Ripon. The old church, a small and inferior structure, built with the parsonage-house, by Dr. John Robinson, a native of the parish, a distinguished plenipotentiary, and Bishop of London, was replaced in 1828 by an edifice in a superior style of architecture, containing a curious monument to the prelate. Dr. Robinson also founded a school in 1723, and endowed it with 16 acres of grass land, of the annual value of £22, free for six boys. Mrs. Cornwallis, a step-daughter of the bishop, left in 1785 funds now producing £10. 15. for the relief of poor housekeepers.

CLEATHAM, a township, in the parish of MANTON, union of GLANDFORD-BRIGG, wapentake of CORRING-HAM, parts of LINDSEY, county of LINCOLN, 6 miles (S. W.) from Glandford-Brigg; containing 99 inhabitants. It comprises about 1087 acres, of which the soil is light and sandy. The tithes have been commuted for £206.

CLEATLAM, a township, partly in the parish of STAINDROP, partly in that of GAINFORD, and partly in that of WINSTONE, union of TEESDALE, S. W. division of DARLINGTON ward, S. division of the county of DURHAM, 2 miles (S. S. W.) from Staindrop; containing 95 inhabitants. The township comprises 1098a. 1r. 28p., of which 612 acres are arable, 451 meadow and pasture, and 34 woodland. The soil is mostly a strong clay, and the surface chiefly elevated ground, commanding extensive views of the surrounding country, including the castles and parks of Raby and Streatlam, and in the distance the Cleveland hills: freestone is quarried for building purposes. In the centre of the village is an ancient cross. The tithes have been commuted for £131. 12. payable to the rector of Winstone, and £21 to the vicar of Gainford: the Duke of Cleveland is impropriator of the lands situate in the parish of Staindrop.

CLEATOR (ST. LEONARD), a parish, in the union of WHITEHAVEN, ALLERDALE ward above Derwent, W. division of CUMBERLAND, 5 miles (S. E. by S.) from Whitehaven; containing 763 inhabitants. The manor-house was that about 1315, by a party of Scots under James Douglas. The parish comprises 2693a. 1r. 38p. of which about 1162 acres are arable, 32 wood, and 1500 inclosed common. Coal, limestone, and iron-ore are wrought, and a great quantity of lime is burnt and sent to Scotland: here are also forges for the manufacture of spades and other edge-tools, and an extensive establishment for spinning hemp and tow, making sewing-thread, &c. The living is a perpetual curacy; net income, £77; patron and impropriator, T. R. G. Braddyll, Esq. The church was rebuilt in 1841, when 272 sittings were added. A Roman causeway passed through the parish, from Egremont to Papcastle, near Cockermouth; but few traces of it are apparent.

CLECKHEATON, a township, in the parish of BIRSTAL, union of BRADFORD, wapentake of MORLEY, riding of York, 9 miles (W.) from Leeds; contain-4299 inhabitants. This township, which is situated a rich and fertile vale, includes the hamlets of Oaken-w and Scholes, and comprises by admeasurement 36 acres; Miss Currer is lady of the manor. Several l-mines of excellent quality are in operation, and a rry of freestone of inferior kind is worked. From its ourable situation on the Leeds and Elland, Leeds and lifax, and Bradford and Dewsbury roads, the place well adapted for the woollen and worsted manufac-es, which, together with the making of cards and chinery used in the woollen-trade, are carried on to reat extent; there are also two iron-foundries. Vast antities of cloth for the army are made. The village situated on the slope of a hill commanding a fine w of the vale, whose acclivities are richly wooded, d of the surrounding country, which abounds with turesque scenery. It is neatly built and well lighted th gas from works established in 1837, at an expense £4000, by a proprietary of £10 shareholders; a news-m is supported by subscription, and there is a chanics' institution, established in 1838. Consider-le improvements have recently taken place in the lage, and numerous villas have been erected in the mediate vicinity. Fairs for cattle, which are well ended, are held on the first Thursday in April, and the last Thursday in August.

The chapel called the White chapel, about a mile m the village, was rebuilt about a century since, by r. Richardson, of Bierley, and again, on a larger scale, 1821; it is a neat edifice in the early English style, d contains 800 sittings, of which 186 are free. The ring is a perpetual curacy, in the patronage of Miss urrer; net income, £150. A district church dedicated St. John was erected on a site given by the late Mrs. eaumont, of Bretton Hall, by a grant from the Parlia-entary Commissioners, at an expense of £2700, and nsecrated in 1832; it is in the early English style, ith a square embattled tower crowned by pinnacles, and ntains 500 sittings, of which 60 are free. The living a perpetual curacy, in the patronage of the Vicar of irstal; net income, £150, with a glebe-house. The dependents and Wesleyans have places of worship. here were some remains of a Roman camp, which ve long been obliterated by the plough; and many ins, chiefly of the Lower Empire, have been found on e site. Several coins, also, were discovered in earthen rs near Scot Lane, in 1818 and 1830.

CLEE (Holy Trinity), a parish, in the parliamentary rough of Grimsby, union of Caistor, wapentake of Bradley-Haverstoe, parts of Lindsey, county of Lin-oln, 2 miles (S. E. by E.) from Grimsby; containing, ith the township of Cleethorpe, and the hamlets of hrunscoe and Weelsby, 1002 inhabitants. The parish bounded by the river Humber on the north and east, d comprises by computation 3400 acres, the surface which is rather flat, excepting towards the sea, where ere is a considerable elevation commanding a fine view the Yorkshire coast and German Ocean. An act for closing land was passed in 1840. In the parish are any of the fountains called Blow Wells, which are ep circular pits, supplying a continual flow of water. he living is a discharged vicarage, valued in the king's oks at £8; net income, £93; patron and appropriator, e Bishop of Lincoln: there is about an acre of glebe.

The church has some fine Norman piers and arches, and an ancient circular font: an inscription on one of the pillars in the south aisle contains a memorial of the dedi-cation of the church to the Holy Trinity in the reign of Richard the First, 1192. There is a place of worship for Wesleyans.

CLEE (St. Margaret's), a parish, in the union of Ludlow, hundred of Munslow, S. division of Salop, 8¼ miles (N. E. by N.) from Ludlow; containing 269 inhabitants. The living is a perpetual curacy, valued in the king's books at £2. 8. 4.; net income, £172; patron, Mrs. F. Thursby. There is a place of worship for Roman Catholics at Clee Hills.

CLEER, ST., a parish, in the union of Liskeard, hundred of West, E. division of Cornwall, 2½ miles (N. by W.) from Liskeard; containing 1412 inhabitants. It comprises 7370 acres, of which 2673 are uninclosed common and coppice, with some oak woods; the soil in general is light, with the exception of some boggy peat soil: there is a great quantity of granite, locally termed moor-stone, and of porphyry; and a copper-mine has been opened. The river Fowey runs through the parish, and several rivulets empty themselves near Looe. The living is a vicarage, valued in the king's books at £19. 6. 8., and in the patronage of the Crown; impro-priator, E. P. Bastard, Esq.: the great tithes have been commuted for £330, and the vicarial for £330; the impropriate glebe contains 2 acres. The church is a handsome and spacious structure, in the early English style. There are a few chalybeate springs; also an ancient Druidical monument, called the Hurlers, con-sisting of rude upright stones arranged in three circles, their centres in a right line, and the middle circle the largest.

CLEETHORPE, a township, in the parish of Clee, union of Caistor, wapentake of Bradley-Haverstoe, parts of Lindsey, county of Lincoln, 3 miles (E. S. E.) from Grimsby; containing 803 inhabitants. This town-ship, which comprises the hamlets of Far and Near Cleethorpe, contains about 700 acres of land, and is pleasantly situated on the south shore of the Humber, near the confluence of that river with the German Ocean. It is much resorted to as a bathing-place, for which it is highly eligible; the air is pure, the scenery good, and besides a few lodging-houses and smaller inns, there is a large hotel, built some years since, on an eminence embracing extensive views of the sea, the Humber, and the Yorkshire coast. Many of the population are em-ployed in the oyster-fisheries. There is a place of wor-ship for Wesleyans.

CLEEVE, BISHOP'S (St. Michael), a parish, form-ing the hundred of Cleeve or Bishop's-Cleeve, in the union of Winchcomb, E. division of the county of Gloucester; comprising the township of Bishop's-Cleeve, and the hamlets of Gotherington, Stoke-Orchard, Southam with Brockhampton, and Woodmancote; and containing 1944 inhabitants, of whom 682 are in the township, 3 miles (N. by E.) from Cheltenham. This parish derives its name Clive or Cleeve from the Saxon Clic, "a steep ascent;" and its adjunct, distinguishing it from Prior-Cleeve, from its having been the property of the bishops of Worcester, whose ancient palace is now the rectory-house. It comprises 8746a. 1r. 2p., of which more than 1000 acres are common. The village is seated on an eminence, on the road from Cheltenham to

CLEE

Evesham; and the Birmingham and Gloucester railway crosses the common. The living is a rectory, valued in the king's books at £84. 6. 8.: patron and incumbent, the Rev. W. L. Townsend, D.D.: the rectorial tithes have been commuted for £1278, and the impropriate for £107. 6., and there are 181 acres of rectorial glebe. The church is a curious and spacious structure, principally of Norman architecture, with a noble arch of exquisite workmanship in that style over the western entrance: the spire fell down in 1696, and caused considerable dilapidation, but in 1700 it was replaced by the tower that now rises from the centre of the building. There is a chapel of ease at Stoke-Orchard. On the ridge of Cleeve-Cloud Hill is a large double intrenchment called the Camps, in the form of a crescent, 350 yards in length, but accessible only in front. Within the parish are some springs, the water of which is strongly saline.

CLEEVE, OLD (St. Andrew), a parish, in the union of Williton, hundred of Williton and Free-manners, W. division of Somerset, 18 miles (N. W.) from Taunton; containing, with the chapelry of Leighland, 1351 inhabitants. The parish adjoins the Bristol Channel, and is remarkable for its craggy rocks, which abound with alabaster; it comprises by measurement 4700 acres, whereof about 2900 are arable, 1500 meadow, pasture, and orchard, 200 woodland, and 100 uninclosed. On the beach a great quantity of kelp is gathered and burnt for the market at Bristol. Lodging-houses have been erected for the accommodation of persons resorting hither for the benefit of sea-bathing. The living is a discharged vicarage, endowed with the rectorial tithes, and valued in the king's books at £7; patron and incumbent, the Rev. W. Newton, whose tithes have been commuted for £600, and whose glebe comprises 3¼ acres, with a glebe-house. At Leighland is a distinct incumbency. There is a place of worship for Wesleyans. A Cistercian abbey, in honour of the Virgin Mary, was founded here in 1188, by William de Romara, the revenue of which, in 1534, was valued at £155. 9. 4½.: there are still some remains, part having been converted into a private mansion, called Cleeve Abbey. At the hamlet of Chapel-Cleeve was a chapel, also dedicated to the Virgin; it stood on a rock, and was the resort of numerous pilgrims.

CLEEVE, PRIOR (St. Andrew), a parish, in the union of Evesham, Upper division of the hundred of Oswaldslow, locally in the Upper division of that of Blackenhurst, Pershore and E. divisions of the county of Worcester, 5½ miles (N. E.) from Evesham; containing 366 inhabitants. The parish is situated on the navigable river Avon, which here receives the waters of the Arrow, on its entering the county. It comprises 1454a. 3r. 17p., whereof 900 acres are arable, and 500 meadow and pasture; the soil is a clayey loam, resting upon blue limestone, and the scenery is rich and pleasing, and abounding with fine orchards. There are quarries of lias and blue limestone, which are wrought for building, slabs for hearthstones, and various other purposes; and also a species of marble susceptible of a high polish, and resembling that of Derbyshire. The village is beautifully situated on an eminence rising from the southern bank of the Avon; the grounds immediately around it are flat, and the meadows occasionally subject to floods. The living is a vicarage, valued in the king's

w building, in the Norman style, has been erected by)scription, on ground given by Sir Joseph Lock; it situated near the margin of the Cherwell, and, as seen m Magdalene bridge, forms an interesting feature in) vale. Stone's hospital, here, for poor persons, was inded pursuant to the will of William Stone, principal New Inn Hall, dated May 12th, 1685, for eight)men ; Boulter's almshouses were established agree-ly to the will of Cutler Boulter, dated March 21st, 36, for eight single men. Various lands and tene-ents, producing at present about £14 per annum, .t capable, on the expiration of the present leases, of crease to the amount of £300 per annum, have been 't, in moieties, for the benefit of the poor, and for pairing the church. Adjoining the parish, but on tra-parochial ground, is the hospital of St. Bartho-mew, founded by Henry I., in 1126, for infirm lepers, ld which, having suffered considerable impoverishment, as granted by Edward III. to Oriel College, on condi-)n that the society should maintain a chaplain and ght almsmen in perpetuity. About the time of the ege of Oxford, the house was demolished, and rebuilt / the society ; the remains are now appropriated to [abling and cow-houses. Here were preserved relics of irious saints, the supposed efficacy of which, in per-)rming miraculous cures, attracted numerous pilgrims. [n the demesne lands of Mr. Morrell, a skeleton of a igantic horse was discovered in 1821, completely capa-soned in the Roman costume.

CLENCHWARTON (St. Margaret), a parish, l the union of Wisbech, hundred of Freebridge-Marshland, W. division of Norfolk, 3 miles (W.) rom Lynn ; containing 597 inhabitants. At the time f the Norman survey this place was called *Ecleuuartuana*, ignifying a watery situation by a river. The parish com-rises by admeasurement about 2880 acres, two-thirds of /hich are arable ; 160 acres consist of the old bed of the iver Ouse, formed into pasture ground : salt-marshes xtend to the Wash between Terrington and North Lynn. .bout 1100 acres are titheable only to the livings of Vest and North Lynn. The living is a rectory, valued l the king's books at £14. 6. 8., and in the patronage f Mrs. Goldfrap ; net income, £337 : the glebe contains 2 acres. The church is in the later English style, with square embattled tower. There is a place of worship)r Wesleyans.

CLENNELL, a township, in the parish of Allenton, nion of Rothbury, W. division of Coquetdale ward, 7. division of Northumberland, 10¼ miles (W. N. W.) rom Rothbury ; containing 18 inhabitants. This place /as the seat and manor of the family of Clennell, and in he 18th of Edward I. was possessed by Thomas Clennell, /ho in that year obtained a grant of free warren. Luke 3lennell, Esq., who resided here, was high sheriff of the ounty in 1727 ; and William Wilkinson, Esq., who ame to the property by marriage, filled the same office l 1758. The township consists entirely of steep por-hyritic hills, covered with short grass, and occupied as heep-walks, and is situated on the east side of the dwine, one mile north from Allenton.

CLENT (St. Leonard), a parish, in the union of 3romsgrove, Lower division of the hundred of Half-shire, Stourbridge and E. divisions of the county of Vorcester, 4 miles (S. S. E.) from Stourbridge ; con-aining 918 inhabitants. It contains the two manors of

Upper or Church-Clent, and Nether Clent; is com-posed principally of a group of lofty hills ; and comprises 2365a. 2r. 33p., of which about 1414 acres are arable, 565 pasture, 57 woodland, and 255 common. The living is a vicarage, with that of Rowley Regis annexed, valued in the king's books at £8. 16. 5½., and in the patronage of the Crown ; impropriator, J. Amphlett, Esq. The great tithes have been commuted for £340, and the vicarial for £315. The church is an ancient structure, with a tower. There are places of worship for Baptists and Wesleyans. A free school was founded by John Amphlett, Esq., in 1704 ; and a Sunday school by Thomas Waldron, Esq., who, at his death in 1800, bequeathed £500 for its support. The infant king of Mercia, St. Kenelm, is supposed by some to have been murdered here, in 819, by order of his sister Quen-drida ; others think that he was slain accidentally.—See Rowley Regis.

CLEOBURY-MORTIMER (St. Mary), a market-town and parish, and the head of a union, in the hundred of Stottesden, S. division of Salop, 32 miles (S. S. E.) from Shrewsbury, and 137 (N. W.) from Lon-don, on the road to Ludlow; containing 1730 inhabitants. The name of this place is derived from its situation in a district abounding with clay, and from the Saxon word *byrig*, a town ; the adjunct, by which it is distinguished from North Cleobury, in the same county, is taken from its ancient possessor, Ralph de Mortimer, who held it at the time of the general survey. Hugh de Mortimer, his son, built a castle here, which, when he revolted in favour of the heir of Stephen, he fortified against Henry II., who, with a powerful army, besieged and entirely de-molished it. During the war between Henry III. and the barons, Cleobury suffered greatly from the incursions of the Welsh, who at that time made frequent irruptions into this part of the country. The town is situated on an eminence rising gradually from the western bank of the river Rea, over which is a neat stone bridge, and consists principally of one long street, containing many good houses, and the mutilated remains of an old cross ; the inhabitants are plentifully supplied with excellent water from a spring that has its source in the Brown Clee hills, and falls into a spacious basin in the lower part of the town. From its retired situation, in a dis-triet almost inaccessible in consequence of the badness of the roads, the trade is rapidly declining ; formerly there were some important iron-works, but there are now only two forges. A few of the inhabitants are em-ployed in the manufacture of paper, for which there are two mills. On the Clee hills, about three miles west of the town, are large collieries, producing excellent coal; and on the higher part of them is a remarkably fine, though not extensive, vein of cannel coal, of which many beautiful specimens have been worked into snuff-boxes and ornaments of various kinds. Common stone is also quarried. The market, granted to Sir Francis Lacon in 1614, is held on Wednesday ; the fairs are on April 21st, Trinity-Monday, and October 27th. The powers of the county-debt court of Cleobury, established in 1847, extend over the registration-district of Cleobury.

The parish comprises about 6000 or 7000 acres. The living is a vicarage, valued in the king's books at £13 ; net income, £448 ; patron, William Lacon Childe, Esq.; impropriators, the Earl of Craven, Mr. Childe, and others, with the exception of the corn-tithes of a small part of the parish, which belong to the lay deacon. The church is an ancient structure, with a plain tower, surmounted by an octagonal spire of wood, considerably curved from the perpendicular. There are two places of worship for Wesleyans; and a Roman Catholic chapel attached to Mawley Hall, the mansion of Sir Edward Blount, Bart., within a mile of the town. A free school was founded pursuant to the will of Sir Lacon William Childe, Knt., dated in 1714, whereby he bequeathed the residue of his personal estate, after the death of his lady, for its endowment : the income is about £500, including the interest of £1000 given by Mr. John Winwood, in 1810. An infants' school is endowed with £15 per annum. The poor law union of which the town is the head, comprises 17 parishes or places, namely, 13 in the county of Salop, 3 in that of Worcester, and one in that of Hereford ; and contains a population of 8708. To the east of the free school are the remains of a Danish encampment; and within the distance of a mile and a half were the three castles of Cleobury, Toot, and Walltown, of which there is not a single vestige. An old farmhouse here is said to have been the first settlement of the Augustine friars. Robert Langford, author of the *Visions of Pierce Plowman*, a satirical poem on the clergy of the fourteenth century, was a native of the town.

CLEOBURY, NORTH (St. Peter), a parish, in the union of Bridgnorth, hundred of Stottesden, S. division of Salop, 1 mile (N. by E.) from Burwarton ; containing 176 inhabitants. It comprises by admeasurement 1145 acres, exclusive of about 430 of uninclosed land forming part of the Brown Clee hill, once a forest, and which is the highest hill in the county, rising to an elevation of 1805 feet. Coal-mines are worked, but they are supposed to be nearly exhausted; and good stone is quarried for buildings. The living is a rectory, valued in the king's books at £5. 12. 3½., and in the gift of Henry George Mytton, Esq. : the glebe comprises 75 acres, with a glebe-house. The church was enlarged and thoroughly repaired in 1834. Upon the summit of the Brown Clee hill are the remains of an encampment, partly in the parish of North Cleobury, supposed to be a work of the Britons when besieged by the Roman army ; and on the Burfs, which is the highest peak of the hill, and between a mile and a mile and a half distant from the village, is a poetical inscription, celebrating the independence, valour, and love of liberty of the ancient Britons, written by the Rev. Thomas Warter, a man of great literary attainments, and many years rector of the parish.

CLERKENWELL, an extensive parish, in the Finsbury division of the hundred of Ossulstone, county of Middlesex; separated from the city of London on the south by the intervening parish of St. Sepulchre, and on the west by the liberties of Saffron-Hill and Ely-Rents ; and containing, with the chapelry of Pentonville, 56,756 inhabitants. This place derives its name from an ancient well, round which the clerks, or inferior clergy, of London, were in the habit of assembling at certain periods, for the performance of sacred dramas, as noticed in the reign of Henry II. by Fitz-Stephen, who calls the well *Fons Clericorum.* The site appears to have been well adapted for the purpose, being in the centre of gently rising grounds, that formed an extensive natural amphitheatre, for the accommodation of the numerous specta-

630

tors who attended. The most celebrated of these festivals occurred in 1391, in the reign of Richard II., and continued for three days, during which several sacred dramas were performed by the clerks, in presence of the king and queen, attended by the whole court. Soon after the year 1100, Jordan Briset and Muriel his wife founded a priory here for nuns of the Benedictine order, dedicated to St. Mary, and the site of which is now occupied by St. James's church : the revenue, at the Dissolution, was £282. 16. 5. The same Jordan and his wife founded an hospital for the Knights Hospitallers of the order of St. John of Jerusalem, which was munificently endowed with lands, and invested with many privileges by several successive monarchs; the lord prior had precedence of all lay barons in parliament, and power over all commanderies and smaller establishments of that order in the kingdom ; the revenue, at the Dissolution, was £2385. 12. 8. The institution was partly restored in the reign of Philip and Mary, but was again suppressed in that of Elizabeth. The remains are, the gate, in the later English style, restored in 1846, and the greater part of which is now occupied as a tavern ; and the vaults of the old church, which were cleared out some years since, when a beautiful crypt in the Norman style was discovered. St. John's church occupies part of the site. The establishment of these monasteries naturally drew around them some dependent dwellings, but the parish made little progress in the number of its inhabitants prior to the time of Elizabeth, in whose reign, besides several "banqueting and summer houses," it contained a few straggling cottages, and some good residences in the immediate neighbourhood of the religious houses : its increase was afterwards more rapid, and in 1619 noblemen and gentlemen were among its inhabitants. Since that time, the formation of numerous streets, and the recent laying out of Spafields and the New River Company's estate in a variety of streets and squares, have rendered this one of the most populous districts in the vicinity of the metropolis.

The parish is lighted with gas, and the pathways are well flagged and kept in repair, under the superintendence of two separate Boards of Commissioners, one for each division of the parish, appointed under special acts : it is within the limits of the metropolitan police establishment. The inhabitants are supplied with water by the *New River* Company, whose works are situated in the parish, where the river terminates. This stupendous undertaking was projected in the reign of Elizabeth, and in the following reign an act of parliament was obtained, enabling the mayor and commonalty of London to carry it into effect; but the commissioners, dreading the difficulty and expense, made no advances for some years. In 1609, Hugh Myddelton, a citizen and goldsmith of London, made proposals to the common-council of the city to undertake the work at his own risk, and to complete it in four years, for which purpose the commissioners transferred to him the powers with which they had been invested by the act. After having persevered in the enterprise till the water was brought to Enfield, the city refusing to grant him any pecuniary assistance, Myddelton applied to the king, who advanced sums of money, amounting in the whole to £6347, with which assistance the work was completed on the 29th of September, 1613. The river, from its source at Amwell in Hertfordshire to Spafields, is 38¾ miles and 16 poles

CLER

ength; there are nearly 300 bridges over it, and its rse is continued through the varying levels of the tricts through which it passes, by means of 40 ices. The Regent's canal passes on the north side the parish.

Of the numerous *Wells* with which the parish abounded, eral were in great repute for their medicinal proper-, and houses of public entertainment were erected ir their site. Of these houses, which generally had -gardens, and were rendered more attractive by sical performances, the chief were Bagnigge Wells, hite Conduit House, and New Tunbridge Wells, or ington Spa, all still remaining. Of those which have many years been discontinued were, the Pantheon, Spafields, now a chapel belonging to the Countess of intingdon's Connexion; the Cold Bath, in Coldbath- lds, of which the bath alone is still frequented; the lberry and Vineyard gardens, now covered with build- s, and the names of which probably denote the pur- se to which the ground was anciently appropriated; celebrated bear-garden at Hockley in the Hole; d Sadler's Wells, near the New River Head, which has many years been converted into a theatre for dra- tic representations. *Fons Clericorum*, or the *Clerks' ll*, is thought by some to have been situated in Ray- eet, where the spot is marked by a pump with an in- ription; but it is more probable that the original well, on which a pump was afterwards erected, was in the ntre of Clerkenwell-Green, between the two religious uses; a supposition partly confirmed by the tenor of deed of grant of the ground by the ancestor of the arquess of Northampton, wherein the right is reserved the inhabitants of drawing water from this pump, the e of which is distinctly laid down in Stowe's Survey London.

The manufacture of clocks and watches, of which the veral parts form distinct and separate departments of e trade, has for more than a century been carried on re to a considerable extent: when the duty on clocks d watches was imposed in 1791, not less than 7000 the inhabitants were deprived of employment, and liged to have recourse to parochial aid. There is a rge manufactory for tin goods, which during the late ir supplied the chief of the government contracts; so some extensive distilleries and soap manufactories. e parish, with the exception of a detached portion of out 100 acres locally situated in the parish of Horn- y, was, by the act of the 2nd of William IV., cap. 45, nstituted part of the newly-enfranchised borough of nshury, the elections for which take place on Clerken- ll-Green. The sessions for the county, and the eetings of the magistrates for the assessment of the unty rates, and for other affairs, are held at the Ses- ns-house on the Green, which was erected at an ex- nse of £13,000, and was repaired and beautified a few ars since: it is a spacious and handsome edifice, with stone front, having in the centre four pillars of the nic order, rising from a rustic basement and support- g a pediment. A new police-court for the district of erkenwell, the business of which was formerly carried at Hatton-Garden, was built in Bagnigge Wells road, der the 2nd and 3rd of Victoria, cap. 71, and opened ecember 16th, 1841: the building is a neat structure, ith a frontage of 260 feet, and consists of two distinct rts almost perfectly square, united by a bold archway.

631

The Clerkenwell prison was erected near the site of the old Bridewell, which was incorporated with the new building; it was enlarged and partly rebuilt in 1818, and considerably extended in 1830 by the removal of several adjoining houses. The buildings were, however, pulled down in 1845; and in the spring of 1847 a model prison was completed, for the detention of persons remanded from police courts, and committed for trial: there are 1000 cells. The house of correction for the county, in Coldbath-Fields, was erected in 1794, at a cost of £70,000, including the purchase of the site, and has lately been much enlarged; it is a spacious brick building inclosed with high walls, and the average num- ber of prisoners is about 1000.

The churches of St. James and St. John, formerly the only churches, have each a distinct parochial dis- trict attached, and the parish of St. James is subdivided into three parts, viz., the district of St. James', of St. Mark's, and of St. Philip's. The living of *St. James'* is a perpetual curacy, with Pentonville chapel; net income, £712; patrons, the Inhabitants of Clerkenwell generally, paying church and poor's rates. The church is a sub- stantial structure of brick with a handsome stone steeple, erected between the years 1788 and 1792, on the site of the ancient church of the priory of St. Mary, which had been previously modernised, and which, at the time of its being taken down for the erection of the present edifice, retained many vestiges of its Norman character, and contained the ashes of the last prioress of the nun- nery; the last prior of St. John's; Weever, the anti- quary; Bishop Burnet; and many other distinguished characters. This conventual church, on being made parochial, at the time of the dissolution of the priory, was dedicated anew to St. James the Less. The living of *St. John's* is a rectory not in charge, in the patronage of the Crown; net income, £260. The church, with large curtailments and alterations, is the choir of that belonging to the priory of the Knights Hospitallers. The ancient edifice was purchased of the Aylesbury family, in 1721, by Mr. Simon Michell, who, having repaired the choir, built the present west front, and covered the whole with a new roof, disposed of the church and ad- joining grounds, in 1723, for £2950, to the commis- sioners for building fifty new churches in Queen Anne's reign, who constituted it a parish church, and caused it to be consecrated on St. John's day, December 27th. The interior of the building was much improved in 1845. Notwithstanding that it enjoys the privilege of religious rites, the incumbent of St. James' is entitled to the sur- plice fees, which he has received since the year 1771, when a lawsuit was successfully prosecuted for their recovery: there are separate churchwardens for St. John's church, but the inhabitants of both districts con- tribute to the repairs of the two churches, and the same overseers of the poor act for the whole.

St. Mark's, in Myddelton-square, containing 1622 sittings, of which 847 are free, was erected in 1826, by a grant from the Parliamentary Commissioners, at an ex- pense of £16,000, and is a neat edifice in the later English style, with a handsome western front containing a square tower having pierced parapet and pinnacles: the cost of furnishing it, which amounted to £2000, was defrayed by a rate voted by the vestry. The living is a district incumbency; net income, £480; patron, the Bishop of London. *St. Philip's*, in the later English style, with a campanile turret, built in Granville-square, at an expense of £4418, and to which an ecclesiastical district has been assigned out of the district of St. Mark, was consecrated on January 1st, 1834, and was furnished by subscription : net income, £420 ; patron, the Bishop. The chapel at *Pentonville*, a neat edifice of brick, ornamented with stone, and having a small cupola, was opened in 1788, under the provisions of the Toleration act, and continued as a private chapel till 1791, when it was purchased by the parish for £5000, and consecrated as a chapel of ease to St. James'. Spafields chapel, formerly the Pantheon, as before noticed, was appropriated for a place of worship by the Countess of Huntingdon, who for many years occasionally resided at the chapel-house adjoining ; and at her decease here in 1791, it was, agreeably to her will, vested in trustees, with other chapels in various parts of the kingdom. There are likewise meeting-houses for Baptists, the Society of Friends, Independents, and Wesleyan and other Methodists, besides a chapel in which the service is performed in Welsh. The parochial school, founded about the year 1700, has been removed from the school-house in Aylesbury-street, to more convenient premises in Amwell-street, erected in 1829, at an expense exceeding £3000, and forming a spacious and handsome range in the Elizabethan style, capable of accommodating 1000 children. The London Female Penitentiary at Pentonville, established in 1807, is a large building, comprising an infirmary, and apartments for 100 females. In addition to the two religious establishments previously noticed, a convent of Benedictines was founded in St. John's-square, in the reign of James II., by one "Father Corker," which was destroyed in the Revolution of 1688. A portion of the Roman Watling-street, and the river of Wells (the *Fleta* of the Romans), form part of the boundaries of the parish. Among the distinguished natives and residents of Clerkenwell may be enumerated Sir Thomas Chaloner, Bishop Burnet, Sir John Oldcastle, and Baron Cobham ; and Edward Cave, who established the *Gentleman's Magazine*, had his printing-office in St. John's Gate, an engraving of which has, since the commencement of that publication, adorned the first page of its numbers.

CLETHER (ST.), a parish, in the union of CAMELFORD, hundred of LESNEWTH, E. division of CORNWALL, 7 miles (E.) from Camelford ; containing 221 inhabitants. The living is a discharged vicarage, valued in the king's books at £6. 11. 10½.; net income, £165 ; patrons, J. Carpenter and T. J. Phillips, Esqrs.; impropriator, the perpetual curate of St. Thomas', near Launceston.

CLEVEDON (ST. ANDREW), a parish, in the union of BEDMINSTER, hundred of PORTBURY, E. division of SOMERSET, 12 miles (W. by S.) from Bristol ; containing 1748 inhabitants. This parish is pleasingly situated on the shore of the Bristol Channel, at the influx of the river Yeo, and comprises 2986a. 1r. 20p., chiefly meadow and pasture land ; the soil is various, consisting in nearly equal portions of sand, loam, and clay. From its favourable situation on the coast, the village has lately become a bathing-place ; the climate is remarkably mild, and myrtles and other delicate shrubs flourish in the open air at all times of the year. Clevedon Court, the seat of Sir Abraham Elton, Bart., is a spacious mansion in the later English style, and one of the finest

ted to have been annexed to Madresfield, in 1595: e chapel has been demolished.

CLEVELY, a township, partly in the parish of)CKERHAM, hundred of LONSDALE south of the Sands, t chiefly in the parish of GARSTANG, hundred of SOUNDERNESS, union of GARSTANG, N. division of the unty of LANCASTER, 4¼ miles (N. by E.) from Gar- ing; containing 124 inhabitants. It comprises 617 res, the whole the property of the Duke of Hamilton. Shire's Head, or Shire Side, is a chapel built of stone 1800, on the site of a former edifice which had fallen to utter ruin: the living is a perpetual curacy, in the tronage of the Vicar of Cockerham; net income,)3. A school has been erected on ground given by e duke.

CLEVERTON, a hamlet, in the parish of LEA, ion and hundred of MALMESBURY, Malmesbury and ngswood, and N. divisions of WILTS, 3¼ miles (E. S.) from Malmesbury; containing 116 inhabitants.

CLEWER (ST. ANDREW), a parish, in the union of INDSOR, hundred of RIPPLESMERE, county of BERKS, mile (W.) from Windsor; containing 3975 inhabit- ts. This parish, situated on the south bank of the hames, contains part of the town of Windsor, and com- ises 1666a. 1r. 12p., of which about two-thirds are eadow-land, and nearly all the rest arable. On a tent roll of the 13th of Edward II. is a grant to John e Hermit, of the chapel of St. Leonard, of Loffield, in indsor Forest, to inclose some land, parcel of the rest, which probably gave name to St. Leonard's Hill, a elegant mansion built by the Duchess of Gloucester, hen Countess Waldegrave, on the site of a cottage. A urt leet is held annually; and a fair for toys and dlery takes place on the 29th of May. The living is a ctory, valued in the king's books at £14. 1. 0½., and the patronage of Eton College: the tithes have been mmuted for £468. 19. 9., and the glebe contains arly 24½ acres, with a glebe-house. The church con- ins several ancient memorials, among which are some rses on a brass plate, commemorating Master Expence, famous archer, who shot a match against one hundred en in Bray. There is a room in the village of Ded- rth (one-half of which is in this parish), licensed by e bishop for divine service, and also used as an infants' hool; it was erected by subscription, on land given ' W. B. Harcourt, Esq., and is a neat building, suitable r a small chapel of ease. A Roman Catholic chapel s erected and is supported at the sole expense of W. Riley, Esq. In 1809, Sir James Poultney, Bart., left ' will £666. 13. 4. in the three per cent. consols., for a hool; and in 1815, Earl Harcourt conveyed two cot- ges, a schoolroom, and £500 Navy five per cents., for struction. A mineral spring was lately discovered.

CLEY (ST. MARGARET), a small sea-port, a parish, d formerly a market-town, in the union of ERPING- AM, hundred of HOLT, W. division of NORFOLK, 26 les (N. N. W.) from Norwich, and 124 (N. N. E.) from ndon; containing 828 inhabitants. In 1406, Prince mes of Scotland, on his voyage to France, to receive education, was driven by stress of weather upon this ast; and, being detained here, was sent to London by der of Henry IV., who committed him to the Tower. e surface of the parish is boldly undulated, and some the elevations command very fine views by sea and d. The town is situated on the banks of a small

river that falls into the harbour, at the north-eastern extremity of the county, and consists principally of one street, in the centre of which is the custom-house, a neat and commodious edifice. It is plentifully supplied with water from springs. The trade of the port, which is called Blakeney and Cley, consists mainly in coal, tim- ber and deals, hemp, iron, tar, tallow, oil-cakes, &c., of which the importation is considerable; a small trade is also carried on in malt: the exports are chiefly corn and flour. The navigation of the Cley is both narrow and of small depth, but in its course to the sea it forms a junction with the Blakeney channel. Under an act of inclosure, obtained in 1822, a large quantity of land has been recovered from the sea by an embankment. The market, held on Saturday, has long fallen into disuse; but a fair for horses is held on the last Friday and Saturday in July. The living is a rectory, valued in the king's books at £22. 13. 4., and in the patronage of John Winn Thomlinson, Esq.: the tithes have been com- muted for £400, and the glebe comprises 18½ acres. The church is a fine spacious structure, in the early Eng- lish style, with portions of later date; the south porch is highly decorated, and has a fine groined roof: the nave is lighted chiefly by oriel windows of elegant de- sign; the font has sculptured representations of the seven sacraments of the Church of Rome. There are places of worship for Wesleyans and Primitive Metho- dists.

CLEYGATE, a manor, in the parish of THAMES- DITTON, Second division of the hundred of KINGSTON, union of KINGSTON, E. division of SURREY, 1¾ mile (E. S. E.) from Esher; containing 940 inhabitants. It was given to the convent of Westminster by Tosti, probably the son of Earl Godwin, and the grant was confirmed by Edward the Confessor. The Domesday survey records that "Claigate" was then still held by the monks, and the lands continued in their possession until the Disso- lution. A district church was consecrated in Decem- ber, 1840, and dedicated to the Trinity; it is a compo- sition of the later Norman and early English styles, and has a square tower crowned by an octagonal spire at the north-east angle: the cost was £1600.

CLIBURN (ST. CUTHBERT), a parish, in the WEST ward and union, county of WESTMORLAND, 6 miles (S. E.) from Penrith; containing 251 inhabitants. The parish is pleasantly situated between the rivers Eden and Lavennet, which bound it on two sides, and is inter- sected by the small river Lethe. It comprises 1769a. 2r. 11p., whereof about 120 acres are woodland, and the remainder arable and pasture; the soil is partly of a dry, light, and sandy quality, partly moor, and partly a strong loam. In the parish is the small hamlet of Gilshaughlin, where, during the prevalence of the plague at Appleby, in 1598, the market for that town was held. The living is a discharged rectory, valued in the king's books at £9. 1. 5½.; net income, £188; patron, the Bishop of Carlisle. The tithes were commuted for land in 1806. The church is a small neat edifice, with a low tower. A school is endowed with an allotment of land, producing £21 per annum.

CLIDDESDEN, a parish, in the union and hundred of BASINGSTOKE, Basingstoke and N. divisions of the county of SOUTHAMPTON, 1¼ mile (S. by W.) from Basing- stoke; containing 306 inhabitants. The living is a rec- tory, with that of Farleigh-Wallop united, valued in the king's books at £10. 16. 3., and in the gift of the Earl of Portsmouth, with a net income of £685 : the tithes of Cliddesden have been commuted for £550, and there is a glebe of 10½ acres. There is a school, endowed with £10 per annum by the Earl of Portsmouth.

CLIFF, with Lund, a chapelry, in the parish of Hemingbrough, union of Selby, wapentake of Ouse and Derwent, E. riding of York, 3½ miles (E.) from Selby; containing 540 inhabitants. The township comprises 2618 acres, of which 543 are open, but fertile, common. The village is of some length, and usually called Long Cliffe. One of the stations on the Hull and Selby railway, which passes close to the village, is situated here. An act for inclosing lands was passed in 1843. There is a place of worship for Wesleyans. In 1708, Mary Ward bequeathed £220 for a school, towards the further support of which Mr. Whittall gave £100.

CLIFFE (St. Helen), a parish, in the union of North Aylesford, hundred of Shamwell, lathe of Aylesford, W. division of Kent, 5 miles (N. by W.) from Rochester ; containing 842 inhabitants. The parish is bounded on the north by the Thames, and comprises 5660 acres, whereof 180 are woodland, about 2000 arable, and the remainder pasture, including a considerable portion of marshy land. The village, which is supposed to take its name from the cliff or rock on which it stands, was formerly of much greater extent, a great part of it having been destroyed by fire in 1520 : it was the scene of several provincial councils. A pleasure-fair is held on September 28th. The living is a rectory, valued in the king's books at £50 ; net income, £1297 ; patron, the Archbishop of Canterbury : the glebe contains 20 acres. The church is considered one of the finest in the county, being a large handsome cruciform structure in the early English style; with an embattled central tower, and containing several curious monuments and remains of antiquity, together with six stalls that belonged to a dean and five prebendaries, it having been formerly collegiate.

CLIFFE (St. Thomas).—See Lewes.

CLIFFE, a township, in the parish of Manfield, union of Darlington, wapentake of Gilling-West, N. riding of York, 5¾ miles (W. by N.) from Darlington ; containing 54 inhabitants. It is on the south bank of the Tees, near Peirse Bridge, and comprises about 970 acres. The estate was for centuries the property of the family of Witham, but was lately sold, since which a Roman Catholic chapel here has been disused.

CLIFFE, KING'S (All Saints), a parish, in the union of Oundle, hundred of Willybrook, N. division of the county of Northampton, 7 miles (W. S. W.) from Wansford ; containing 1278 inhabitants. This was anciently the head of a bailiwick in the forest of Rockingham, called the Clive, and had a royal mansion, in which the kings of England passed some days in their progresses or hunting excursions, prior to the year 1400. The parish is situated on a slope, and surrounded by woods ; it comprises by measurement 2200 acres. A small number of the population is employed in the manufacture of wooden-ware ; and there are quarries of freestone and limestone, for building and manure. A market, not much frequented, is held weekly, on Tuesday ; and a fair for cattle, horses, and cheese, on the

29th of October : the market cross was demolished in 1834. The living is a rectory, valued in the king's books at £13. 16. 3.; net income, £525; patron, the Earl of Westmoreland : the tithes were commuted for land and a money payment in 1809 ; the glebe contains 477 acres, with a glebe-house. The church is a spacious cruciform structure, in the early and later English styles, with a tower rising from the centre, and contains some beautiful details ; the pulpit, reading-desk, and open sittings, were formed out of carved oak originally in the collegiate church at Fotheringay, and placed here in 1818. There are places of worship for Independents and Wesleyans. Schools, and almshouses for six aged women, were respectively endowed by Mrs. Elizabeth Hutcheson and the Rev. William Law, with land comprising together 409 acres, producing an income of £407 ; in addition to which, an accumulation of £517. reduced annuities yields £15 per annum. There are other almshouses, founded by John Thorpe, in 1688, for three aged women. Dr. Michael Hudson, chaplain to Charles I., was rector for a short time ; and the Rev. William Law, author of the Serious Call, was born in 1686, at this place, where he resided during the last twenty years of his life, and was buried. A Roman cemetery has been discovered, on an ancient road called " John's Wood Riding," which runs through the parish.

CLIFFE, NORTH, a township, in the parish of Sancton, union of Pocklington, Hunsley-Beacon division of the wapentake of Harthill, E. riding of York, 3 miles (S.) from Market-Weighton; containing 74 inhabitants. It comprises by computation 1480 acres : the village is situated near the foot of an abrupt acclivity rising from a sandy plain, and is on the road from Market-Weighton to North Cave.

CLIFFE-PYPARD (St. Peter), a parish, in the union of Cricklade and Wootton-Bassett, chiefly in the hundred of Kingsbridge, but partly in that of Elstub and Everley, Swindon division, and partly in that of Potterne and Cannings, Chippenham and Calne division, of Wilts, 4 miles (S.) from Wootton-Bassett ; containing 933 inhabitants. The parish comprises by computation 4000 acres, of which the greater portion is meadow and pasture. The northern part is divided from the southern by a high and very steep ridge or cliff, from which the place takes its name, and which consists of a kind of chalkstone, whereof part is used for manure, and part of a harder land is quarried for building and paving. The living is a vicarage, valued in the king's books at £9 ; patron and impropriator. H. N. Goddard, Esq. : the great tithes have been commuted for £435. 18., and the vicarial for £590. The church is an ancient edifice, with a good tower of free-stone : the nave is separated from the aisles by a range of five pillars and arches, supporting a richly-carved open roof of oak, and in the chancel are an old monument to one of the Goddard family, and a handsome monument of marble to Thomas Spackman, a carpenter who, having realized an ample fortune, bequeathed an endowment for a free school in the parish ; the monument cost £1000. Sarah, Duchess Dowager of Somerset, in 1686 left the manor of Thornhill, in the parish, to Brasenose College, Oxford, for the foundation of certain scholarships ; and the manor of Broadtown to trustees for apprenticing poor boys of the county

Wilts. Various Roman and Saxon coins have been und.

CLIFFE, SOUTH, a chapelry, in the parish of ORTH CAVE, union of POCKLINGTON, Hunsley-Beacon vision of the wapentake of HARTHILL, E. riding of ORK, 3½ miles (S.) from Market-Weighton; containing 36 inhabitants. It comprises 2025a. 1r. 8p., mostly of light sandy soil, and situated under the western ridge the Wolds; a large portion is rabbit-warren. On the est is the Market-Weighton canal, and on the east the ad between Sancton and South Cave. The chapel, ilt in 1782, is endowed with land for its repair.

CLIFFE, WEST (ST. PETER), a parish, in the union Dovor, hundred of BEWSBOROUGH, lathe of ST. UGUSTINE, E. division of KENT, 2¾ miles (N. E.) from ovor; containing 116 inhabitants. It is situated on e road from Dovor to Deal, and comprises by measure-ent 1170 acres, of which 150 are meadow and pasture, d the remainder arable, with a few acres of wood-nd; the surface is gently undulated, and the soil in ost parts chalky. The living is a discharged vicarage; et income, £34; patrons and appropriators, the Dean d Chapter of Canterbury, whose tithes have been com-uted for £391, and whose glebe contains 13 acres. he church is small, and roofed with tiles.

CLIFFORD (ST. MARY), a parish, in the union of AY, hundred of HUNTINGTON, county of HEREFORD, miles (N. E.) from Hay; containing, with part of the ownship of Vowmine, 892 inhabitants. The parish is ituated on the borders of Wales, from which it is eparated, on the west, by the Wye, the river also ounding it on the north and north-east; it comprises y measurement 5500 acres, and the soil is in general lay and a sandy loam. The living is a discharged icarage, valued in the king's books at £4. 10.; net ncome, £300; patron and incumbent, the Rev. John rumper; impropriators, the landowners. There is a lace of worship for Independents. Some portions of lifford Castle are still remaining, in a ruinous con-lition: it stood on a bold eminence, projecting over the Vye, and was the baronial residence of the lords de lifford for two centuries, and also, it is supposed, the irthplace of Fair Rosamond. Here was likewise a onvent of Cluniac monks, founded by one of the lords, s a cell to the priory of Lewes, in Sussex: at the Dis-olution its revenue was estimated at £75. 7. 5. Lord le Clifford derives his title from the parish.

CLIFFORD, with BOSTON, a township, in the parish f BRAMHAM, Upper division of the wapentake of BARK-TONE-ASH, W. riding of YORK, 3½ miles (S. E. by S.) rom Wetherby; containing 1566 inhabitants. The pinning of yarn and the manufacture and bleaching of loth are carried on to some extent; the mill is pro-elled by the Bramham beck, which flows through the ownship. There are also quarries of good building-tone. A sheep-fair is held on the Wednesday after Michaelmas-day. A district church, very eligibly situ-ted, and forming a prominent object to the neighbour-100d, has been erected: it is a handsome, but small, ruciform structure of stone, built by subscription, at an xpense of £1200, on a site given by George Lane Fox, Esq., who contributed £100 of the amount; it is dedi-ated to St. Luke, was consecrated by the Archbishop f York on the 8th of June, 1842, and contains 300 sittings, of which about one-third are free. Mr. Lane

635

Fox also contributed £1000 towards its endowment, and £500 towards the erection of a parsonage-house. The living is in the gift of that gentleman.—See BOSTON.

CLIFFORD-CHAMBERS (ST. HELEN), a parish, in the union of STRATFORD-UPON-AVON, Upper division of the hundred of TEWKESBURY, though locally in that of the hundred of KIFTSGATE, E. division of the county of GLOUCESTER, 2½ miles (S. by W.) from Stratford; con-taining 309 inhabitants. This parish, which is situated on the river Stour, and on the Birmingham and Oxford road, comprises about 2500 acres, nearly equally divided between arable and pasture; about twenty acres are gorse. The living is a rectory, valued in the king's books at £18. 15. 7½.; net income, £172; patron, the Rev. T. G. Tyndall; incumbent, the Rev. F. Annesley: the tithes have been commuted for £44. 12., and the glebe consists of 64 acres, and a glebe-house. The church is a small structure, with a south door of Nor-man architecture. A Sunday school is supported by a bequest of £10 per annum.

CLIFTON (ALL-SAINTS), a parish, in the union of BIGGLESWADE, hundred of CLIFTON, county of BEDFORD, 1½ mile (E. by N.) from Shefford; containing 865 inha-bitants. It comprises by measurement 1450 acres, of which about 200 are pasture; the surface is generally level, and the soil in some parts clay, in others gravel. The river Ivel flows through the parish, and is naviga-ble to Shefford. The living is a rectory, valued in the king's books at £20. 2. 11.; net income, £439; patron and incumbent, the Rev. D. J. Olivier. The church contains some monumental brasses, and a fine altar-tomb in memory of Sir Michael Fisher, lord of the manor, who died in 1549. A school was founded and endowed in 1827, by the Rev. D. S. Olivier, late rector.

CLIFTON, or ROCK-SAVAGE, a township, in the parish and union of RUNCORN, hundred of BUCKLOW, N. division of the county of CHESTER, 2¼ miles (N. N. E.) from Frodsham; containing 34 inhabitants. This place has been called Rock-Savage, since the erection of a splendid house by Sir John Savage, in 1565. The township comprises 577 acres, whereof the prevailing soil is clay; and consists of only the manorial mansion and its demesne land, now in the possession of the Mar-quess of Cholmondeley, who enjoys the title of Earl of Rock-Savage. A tithe rent-charge of £91 is paid to the Dean and Chapter of Oxford.

CLIFTON, a chapelry district, in the parish of ASHBOURN, hundred of MORLESTON and LITCHURCH, though locally in the hundred of WIRKSWORTH, S. divi-sion of the county of DERBY, 1¼ mile (S. W.) from Ashbourn; containing, with the hamlet of Compton, 839 inhabitants. This place is mentioned in Domesday book under the name of Cliptune; and in the reign of Henry VII. belonged to the Cokaynes, and of Ashbourn. The ancient chapel here was taken down about 1750, and part of the materials were used to repair the chancel of the parish church: the present chapel is dedicated to the Trinity, and was consecrated in 1845. The living is in the gift of the Vicar.

CLIFTON (ST. ANDREW), a parish and favourite watering-place, and the head of a union, in the county of the city of BRISTOL, 1¼ mile (W.) from Bristol, 14 miles (N. W.) from Bath, and 121 (W. by S.) from Lon-don; containing 14,177 inhabitants. This place, by

4 M 2

some antiquaries supposed to have been a British town prior to the Roman invasion, and to have been called *Caeroder*, or the " city of the chasm," derives its present name from its romantic situation on the acclivities and summit of a precipitous cliff, apparently separated by some convulsion of nature from a chain of rocks on the Somersetshire coast. The river Avon, which at spring tides rises to the height of 46 feet, and is then navigable for ships of very large burthen, flows with a rapid current through this natural chasm, forming the southern and western boundaries of the parish, and dividing the counties of Gloucester and Somerset. The lower part of the town, called the HOT WELLS, and formerly the more populous, is situated at the base of the cliff, and has a mild and genial atmosphere, peculiarly adapted to delicate and consumptive constitutions. It first rose into importance from the efficacy of its hot springs, originally noticed in 1480 by William of Worcester, the topographer of Bristol, and brought into general celebrity in 1632, when the water was applied externally in cases of cancer and scrofula, and internally in cases of inflammation, dysentery, and hemorrhage. These waters issue from an aperture in the rock, about ten feet above low-water mark; their mean temperature is about 71° of Fahrenheit; they contain a portion of sulphuric-acid, but are peculiarly soft and pleasant to the taste, and free from any offensive smell. At the time of the earthquake at Lisbon, the water became so red and turbid for some days, as to be unfit for use. A new pump-room, with hot and cold baths, and containing also apartments for the residence of invalids, a neat building of the Tuscan order, has been erected at an expense of £8000, by the Society of Merchants of Bristol, who are lords of the manor of Clifton, near the site of the old house, which was built by subscription in 1770. Gloucester House, formerly the only hotel of any note, and whence the steam-packets to Ireland regularly sail, is still much frequented, from its proximity to the Hot Wells. Dowry square and parade, Hope-square, Albemarle-row, and St. Vincent's parade, all contain respectable lodging-houses, fitted up with a due regard to the accommodation of visiters of every rank, and of which some have not unfrequently been the temporary residence of royalty. At Mardyke, on the lower road to Bristol, is a saline mineral spa, said to have been found efficacious in visceral complaints.

On the south-western brow of the hill, and protected on the north and east by the summit of the cliff, is situated that part of the town properly called CLIFTON, about half a century since consisting only of a few scattered dwellings, but now of piles of stately edifices of Bath stone, forming, from the beauty of their architecture, a conspicuous and imposing feature in the landscape for many miles. This portion, like the Hot Wells, owes its origin and rapid increase to the efficacy of a similar spring issuing from the rock into a well 320 feet in depth, sunk at an immense expense, in 1772, and from which 30,000 gallons of water are daily raised by a powerful steam-engine, and afterwards propelled to an additional height of 120 feet, and distributed through pipes to most of the respectable houses on the hill. There are some splendid ranges of buildings, and handsome hotels, with every requisite accommodation, and commanding beautiful and extensive views. Near the summit of St. Vincent's Rock, so named from an
636

ancient chapel dedicated to that saint, was a snuff-mill, which, by a grant from the lords of the manor, Mr. West, an ingenious self-taught artist, has converted into an observatory, furnished with powerful telescopes and a camera; it embraces a most widely extended and diversified prospect, comprehending not only the romantic scenery in the immediate neighbourhood, but a distant view of the Bristol Channel and the Welsh mountains, and the pleasing villages with which the county of Gloucester is thickly studded. The nursery-grounds of Mr. Miller comprise more than 60 acres, beautifully laid out, and forming one of the most favourite resorts of this attractive place. There are some elegant private mansions, among which may be noticed that of Mr. Goldney, and that built by Sir William Draper, the opponent of Junius, in the front court of which are a plain monument to the distinguished Earl of Chatham, and a cenotaph to the memory of those officers and men of the 79th regt. who fell in India. The town is well lighted with gas, and improvements are constantly in progress. The Society of Merchants have formed a beautiful road, winding round the side of the rocks from the Hot Wells to Clifton Down; the extensive commons, also, have been partially planted. There is no regular market; but from its proximity to Bristol, the town is well supplied with provisions of every kind; and the prices of all articles, either of clothing or food, may be considered on an average full 15 per cent. lower than those of the metropolis. The £10 householders are entitled to vote for the representation of Bristol. The parish contains 910 acres, comprehending the site of the town and adjacent buildings. The LIVING is a perpetual curacy; net income, £782; patrons, the Trustees of the late Rev. C. Simeon; impropriator, James Taylor, Esq. The church, a spacious structure in the later English style, was erected in 1822. A church dedicated to the Holy Trinity, and accommodating 1600 persons, has been built at the Hot Wells, for the poor; and there are a private Episcopal chapel, and a district church dedicated to St. John the Evangelist, the latter in the later English style, and erected by the Bristol Diocesan Association. Christ church, at Clifton Park, was consecrated in Oct. 1844; it is of the style which prevailed about the middle of the 13th century, and affords accommodation to 1000 persons. The livings of Holy Trinity church, Christ church, and St. John's, are perpetual curacies, the two first in the patronage of Simeon's Trustees, and the last in the gift of the Bishop of Gloucester and Bristol. There are places of worship for the Countess of Huntingdon's Connexion and Wesleyans; also a floating chapel for seamen, called the Clifton Ark; and a Roman Catholic chapel in a superb style of Grecian architecture. The poor law union of Clifton comprises 12 parishes or places, and contains a population of 66,233.

On the summit of St. Vincent's Rock are the remains of an encampment of three or four acres, defended by three ramparts and two ditches; the inner rampart, which is in no part more than five feet in height, is supposed to have been surmounted by a wall. Its extent, from one side of the rock to the other, is 293 yards, and on the side next the river is a deep trench, thought to have been cut during the civil war of the seventeenth century. Its origin is ascribed to the Romans, who are said to have placed here the first of that chain of forts hich they erected to defend the passage of the Severn. ۱ the immediate neighbourhood, and in various parts ؛ the parish, numerous Roman and Saxon coins have ۱en found; and at a short distance, in the parish of ۱estbury, are the remains of a Roman way. In the ۱cks, lead and a very rich iron-ore have been dis-۱vered, but not in sufficient quantity to be worth ۱orking; and in the fissures of the rock, and more ۱pecially in digging the foundations of houses, are ۱und the beautiful quartz crystals called Bristol dia-۱onds, remarkable for their naturally formed and ۱ghly polished hexagonal surfaces, and equalling in ۱ansparency those of India, to which they are inferior ۱ly in hardness and durability: they are generally im-۱edded in nodulæ of ironstone, of the same colour as ۱e soil. Anne Yearsley, who in the humble situation ۱f a milk-woman, displayed great poetical talent, and ۱roduced several literary works, was a native of this ۱lace; she died in 1806, at Melksham, in the county of ۱Vilts. Sir Humphrey Davy commenced his career here, ۱s assistant to Dr. Beddoes, an eminent physician; and ۱mong the numerous distinguished persons who have ۱ade it their retreat was Mrs. Hannah More, who here ۱nded a life devoted to literature and good works.

CLIFTON, with SALWICK, a township, in the parish ۱f KIRKHAM, union of the FYLDE, hundred of AMOUN-۱ERNESS, N. division of the county of LANCASTER, 3 ۱iles (E. S. E.) from Kirkham, on the road to Preston; ۱ontaining 538 inhabitants. The manor of Clifton has ۱een held from remote antiquity by the knightly family ۱f the same name: the ancient Hall has long disap-۱eared,.but an elegant mansion has lately been erected ۱y Thomas Clifton, Esq. The township comprises 3403a. 1r. 37p.: it is bounded on the south by the river Ribble; the Lancaster canal passes through, and there is a station on the Fleetwood and Preston railway. The Hall is the residence of Edward Pedder, Esq. The village, which stands rather high, consists of a street of farmhouses, cottages, and out-buildings; it overlooks the Ribble, and the air is very salubrious and healthy. Salwick occupies the northern part of the township, and contains Salwick Hall. The township is included in the ecclesiastical district of Lund: the tithes have been commuted for £530 payable to the Dean and Chapter of Christ-Church, Oxford, and £75. 6. to the vicar. In 1682, John Dickson left a small bequest for teaching children, and a school has lately been built, by aid of a grant of £50 from the National Society, with which it is in union.

CLIFTON, a township, in the parish of ECCLES, hundred of SALFORD, S. division of the county of LAN-CASTER, 5 miles (N. W. by W.) from Manchester, on the road to Bolton; containing 1360 inhabitants. The Cliftons of Westby were in possession of this place in the 20th of Edward I.; the manor subsequently came to the Hollands, and afterwards, by purchase, to the Gaskell family. The township comprises 850 acres of land, in equal portions of arable and pasture, and of which the soil is of a clayey nature. It is situated in a luxuriant vale, and is bounded by the river Irwell, which flows on the north-east. The Manchester and Bolton railway passes through; and a line quits this railway here, and proceeds through Bury to Rossendale and other parts of the county; it was opened to Rawtenstall, a distance of 14 miles, in Sept. 1846, and has since been

extended. The inhabitants are mostly employed in nine collieries. A school has been built by the proprietor's trustees.

CLIFTON, with COLDWELL, a township, in the N. division of the parish of STANNINGTON, union and W. division of CASTLE ward, S. division of NORTHUMBER-LAND, 2½ miles (S.) from Morpeth. It is situated on the road between Morpeth and the township of Stan-nington, and is the property of the Earl of Carlisle. In the 12th century lands' were held at Clifton, under Roger de Merlay, by William of Clifton: in the year 1240 the Conyers family appear to have been proprie-tors; and of subsequent owners have been the Ogles, Howards, and Greys. At Coldwell, which is now ex-tinct, the monks of Newminster had possessions, and among others who had an interest in the same place may be named the families of Conyers and Heron.

CLIFTON (ST. MARY), a parish, in the union of BASFORD, N. division of the wapentake of RUSHCLIFFE, S. division of the county of NOTTINGHAM, 4¼ miles (S. W. by S.) from Nottingham; containing, with the hamlet of Glapton, 419 inhabitants. The village is situated on a level tract, near which is Clifton Hall, commanding extensive prospects over the river Trent, the town of Nottingham, and the adjacent counties of Derby and Leicester. The Hall is now much modern-ised; its principal front is ornamented with 10 hand-some Doric columns, and the interior comprises several magnificent apartments. The living is a rectory, valued in the king's books at £21. 6. 10¼.; net income, £500, arising chiefly from land, with some annual payments to the rector from Barton, Normanton, Keyworth, and Stanton; patron and impropriator, Sir Juckes Clifton, Bart. There is an excellent rectory-house, with exten-sive gardens. The church is a fine structure; having become dilapidated, it was restored, and re-opened for divine service in May 1846: it has a massive tower, and contains several monuments to the Clifton family. There are almshouses for six poor widows. Here was a small college for a warden and two priests, dedicated to the Holy Trinity, founded in the time of Edward IV. by Sir Gervase Clifton: at the Dissolution it was valued at £20 per annum.

CLIFTON, a township, in the parish of DEDDING-TON, union of WOODSTOCK, hundred of WOOTTON, county of OXFORD, 1¼ mile (E.) from Deddington; con-taining 277 inhabitants. There is a place of worship for a congregation of Wesleyans.

CLIFTON (ST. CUTHBERT), a parish, in WEST ward and union, county of WESTMORLAND, 2½ miles (S. E. by S.) from Penrith; containing 288 inhabitants. It derives its name from the situation of the village on a rocky eminence in the vale of the river Lowther, by which the parish is bounded on the north and west. At Clifton Moor, now inclosed, a slight skirmish oc-curred between the Duke of Cumberland's dragoons and the rear-guard of the Pretender's army on its retreat to Scotland. The parish comprises 1676a. 2r. 39p., of which about 35 acres are woodland; the soil is various, in some parts a dark brown mould on a substratum of gravel, in others a strong red soil resting on clay, and in some parts light and sandy. There is a station of the Lancaster and Carlisle railway, called the Clifton-Moor station. The living is a rectory, valued in the king's books at £8. 3. 4.; net income, £150; patron, the

Bishop of Carlisle. The tithes were commuted for land in 1811. The church is a small ancient structure, with a low tower. When excavating for the railway, a Roman altar, in a high state of preservation, was dug up. There is a medicinal spring, the water of which is efficacious in the cure of scorbutic complaints.

CLIFTON, a township, partly in the parish of St. Michael-le-Belfrey, and partly in that of St. Olave, Mary-Gate, union of York, wapentake of Bulmer, N. riding of the county of York, 1½ mile (N. W.) from York; containing 1242 inhabitants. The village, which is large and handsome, forms a suburb to the city. In 1820, two massive Roman stone coffins, each 7½ feet in length, and bearing a short inscription, were found in the grounds of David Russell, Esq., and deposited in the cathedral of York.

CLIFTON, with Norwood, a township, in the parish of Fewston, Lower division of the wapentake of Claro, W. riding of York, 6 miles (N. by E.) from Otley; containing 387 inhabitants. The township comprises 3510 acres of moor and pasture land, with a little arable. Church service is performed on every Tuesday in a schoolroom.

CLIFTON, with Newall—See Newall.

CLIFTON, a township, in the chapelry of Harts-head, parish of Dewsbury, union of Halifax, wapentake of Morley, W. riding of York, 5 miles (N. N. E.) from Huddersfield; containing 1779 inhabitants. The village extends to the western verge of the township, and from its elevated situation commands extensive views of the vale of the Calder, and of the surrounding country. The population is chiefly engaged in the manufacture of cards for machinery. A school is endowed with £10 per annum.

CLIFTON-CAMPVILLE (St. Andrew), a parish, in the union of Tamworth, partly in the hundred of Repton and Gresley, S. division of the county of Derby, but chiefly in the N. division of the hundred of Offlow and of the county of Stafford, 6 miles (N. E. by N.) from Tamworth; containing 921 inhabitants, of whom 341 are in the township of Clifton-Campville. This parish consists of the townships of Clifton-Campville and Haunton, and the chapelry of Harleston, in the county of Stafford; and of the chapelry of Chilcote, in that of Derby. It comprises by computation 6300 acres; the surface is undulated, and the soil in some places a rich fertile marl, and in others a strong clay. The village, which is large, is situated in the vale of the Mease, and on the road from Elford to Ashby-de-la-Zouch. The living is a rectory, valued in the king's books at £30, and in the gift of Henry John Pye, Esq., to whose ancestor, Sir Charles Pye, Bart., the manor was sold by the Coventry family in 1700. The tithes of Clifton-Campville and Haunton have been commuted for £717. 1. 1., those of Harleston for £370, and of Chilcote for £258; the glebe contains 150 acres, with a good glebe-house. The church is adorned with one of the finest spires in the kingdom; and has two chancels separated by a handsome screen: there are some paintings on glass, one of which represents St. Mark; and in the south chancel is an ancient monument with recumbent effigies to the memory of Sir John Vernon and his lady. At Harleston and Chilcote are chapels of ease; and a parochial school is supported by the patron and incumbent. In the eastern extremity of the parish is a

d South Clifton, on a small eminence on the banks the Trent, is an ancient structure in the later English style, with a handsome embattled tower. There is chapel of ease at Harby, where also, and in South Clifton, are places of worship for Wesleyans. A schoolmaster receives £10. 10. per annum from land bequeathed by Simon Nicholson, in 1669, for instructing children; a schoolroom and dwelling-house were built. by subscription, in 1779. There is also a school at Harby.

CLIFTON-REYNES (ST. MARY), a parish, in the union of NEWPORT-PAGNELL, hundred of NEWPORT, county of BUCKINGHAM, 1½ mile (E. by S.) from Olney; containing 213 inhabitants. The principal manor here was given by William the Conqueror to Robert de Odeni, one of the companions of his expedition, and afterwards passed into the family of Reynes, from whom the place takes the adjunct to its name. An heiress of the family of Reynes conveyed the property to the Lowes, who sold it to the celebrated Serjeant Maynard; it subsequently passed to the noble family of Hobart, and about 1750 was disposed of by the Earl of Buckinghamshire to the Small family. Another manor here was anciently possessed by the Mordaunts. The parish, which is situated on the eastern bank of the river Ouse, comprises 1395a. 23p.; the surface is irregular, and the lower lands are subject occasionally to inundations of the river. The living is a rectory, valued in the king's books at £13. 6. 10½.; patron and incumbent, the Rev. H. A. Small. By a recent inclosure act, land of the value of about £150 per annum, was given in lieu of a portion of the tithes. There is a small glebe also, part of which is in the adjoining parish of Newton-Blossomville; with a glebe-house. The church, a handsome edifice, is supposed to have been erected about the time of Edward I.; it has a square tower, and contains an ancient font, and some tombs to the family of Reynes. A school was built in 1844.

CLIFTON-UPON-DUNSMOOR (ST. MARY), a parish, in the union of RUGBY, Rugby division of the hundred of KNIGHTLOW, N. division of the county of WARWICK, 2 miles (E. N. E.) from Rugby: containing, with the chapelry of Brownsover and the hamlet of Newton and Biggin, 699 inhabitants. The parish is situated on the banks of the Avon, and comprises by admeasurement 3465 acres, of which 835 are in Brownsover; two-thirds are arable, and the remainder pasture. It is intersected by the road from Rugby to Harborough, and the London and Birmingham railway has a first-class station at Rugby; the Oxford canal traverses the parish, and the river Swift separates it from the parish of Newbold. The living is a discharged vicarage, valued in the king's books at £8. 1. 8.; net income, £119; patron, the Earl of Bradford: the impropriation belongs to two schools and 21 individuals; the glebe contains about 15 acres, with a house. The church is in the later English style, and had formerly a handsome spire. There is a chapel of ease at Brownsover. A parochial school is supported by subscription and a small legacy, and the inhabitants have the privilege of sending their children free to Rugby school. Christopher Harvey, author of a collection of poems called the *Synagogue,* and other works, was vicar, and was buried here in 1663; Thomas Carte, author of an elaborate History of England, was born here in 1686.

CLIFTON-UPON-TEME (ST. KILLOM), a parish, in the union of MARTLEY, Upper division of the hundred of DODDINGTREE, Hundred-House and W. divisions of the county of WORCESTER, 10¼ miles (N. W. by W.) from Worcester; containing 512 inhabitants. The parish is situated near the river Teme, and comprises by measurement 2853a. 1r. 16p.: stone of good quality for building and the roads, and flagstone, are quarried. The village, which is beautifully situated on a steep cliff, overlooking the serpentine course of the Teme, was made a free borough by Edward III., who also granted a weekly market, now disused. Ham Castle, formerly the residence of the family of Jefferies, and which was nearly destroyed in 1646 by the parliamentary troops, was completely restored, indeed nearly rebuilt, by the proprietor, in 1840. The living is a discharged vicarage, valued in the king's books at £6. 19. 2.; patron and impropriator, Sir T. E. Winnington, Bart.: the tithes have been commuted for £235, of which £207. 10. are payable to the vicar; and the glebe consists of two acres, with a house, built in 1845. The church has a square tower, surmounted by a spire which is a landmark to the country around; the interior was restored in 1844: among some ancient monuments is one to a Knight Templar, supposed to be Sir Roger de Wysham. A school is supported by subscription. There was anciently a chapel at Noverton, in the parish; but in 1532, Charles, Bishop of Hereford, with the consent of the vicar of Clifton and the inhabitants, united Noverton to the parish of Stanford, reserving to the vicar an annual pension of 13s. 4d., in lieu of tithes and offerings due from the inhabitants of the chapelry. At Woodmanton, still in the parish, was another chapel.

CLIFTON-UPON-URE, a township, in the parish of THORNTON-WATLASS, union of LEYBURN, wapentake of HANG-EAST, N. riding of YORK, 4 miles (S. W.) from Bedale; containing 39 inhabitants. The manor passed from the lords Scrope, of Masham, to Sir Ralph Fitz-Randolph, and subsequently to the Wyvilles, Daltons, and Prestons, of whom the last-named sold it to the family of Hutton, in 1735. The township, which is situated on the eastern acclivities of the vale of the Ure, comprises by computation 592 acres of land. Clifton Castle, a handsome mansion, stands in a fine park.

CLIMPING, a parish, in the union of EAST PRESTON (under Gilbert's act), hundred of AVISFORD, rape of ARUNDEL, W. division of SUSSEX, 7 miles (S. S. W.) from Arundel; containing 279 inhabitants. This parish includes all that remains of the ancient parish of Cudlow, of which not more than one hundred acres have escaped the encroachment of the sea. It is bounded on the south by the English Channel, and on the east by the river Arun, over which is a ferry; and is intersected by the road from Bognor to Littlehampton. The living is a vicarage, valued in the king's books at £9. 11. 0½., and in the gift of Eton College: the great tithes have been commuted for £422, and the vicarial for £224; there is an impropriate glebe of 7 acres. The church is a handsome cruciform structure, chiefly in the early English style, with a fine Norman tower at the end of the south transept.

CLINCH, a tything, in the parish of MILTON-LILBOURNE, union of PEWSEY, hundred of KINWARDSTONE, Everley and Pewsey, and S. divisions of WILTS; containing 106 inhabitants.

CLINCH, with FAWDON.—See FAWDON.

CLINT, a township, in the parish of RIPLEY, Lower division of the wapentake of CLARO, W. riding of YORK, 1¼ mile (W. by S.) from Ripley; containing 393 inhabitants. The township includes the hamlet of Burnt-Yates, and comprises 1835a. 1r. 25p.: the village is a short distance from the river Nidd, which passes on the south. Here are the remains of an ancient mansion, called Clint Hall. The Roman road from Ilkley, through the forest of Knaresborough, branched in two directions at this place, one leading to Catterick, the other to Aldborough. A free school was founded by Rear-Admiral Robert Long in 1760, which received at the same time, and subsequently, several endowments, the total now producing upwards of £200 a year.

CLIPPESBY (ST. PETER), a parish, in the EAST and WEST FLEGG incorporation, hundred of WEST FLEGG, E. division of NORFOLK, 3 miles (N. E.) from Acle; containing 123 inhabitants. The parish comprises 861a. 1r. 24p., of which about 447 acres are arable, and 372 marsh and pasture; the old road from Norwich to Yarmouth runs through it. The living is a discharged rectory, valued in the king's books at £6. 13. 4., and in the patronage of H. Muskett, Esq.: the tithes have been commuted for £245, and the glebe contains 3¾ acres. The church is partly in the early and partly in the later style, and the chancel contains an altar-tomb to the memory of John Clippesby and his lady, whose effigies are inlaid in brass. There is a place of worship for Wesleyans. The old Hall, an ancient relic, is still standing, with some slight remains of the moat.

CLIPSHAM (ST. MARY), a parish, in the union of STAMFORD, soke of OAKHAM, locally in the hundred of ALSTOE, county of RUTLAND, 9¾ miles (N. E. by E.) from Oakham; containing 206 inhabitants. The living is a rectory, valued in the king's books at £10. 0. 5., and in the patronage of the coheiresses of Mrs. Snow: the tithes have been commuted for £250, and the glebe comprises 51 acres, with a glebe-house.

CLIPSTON (ALL SAINTS), a parish, in the union of MARKET-HARBOROUGH, hundred of ROTHWELL, N. division of the county of NORTHAMPTON, 4 miles (S. S. W.) from Market-Harborough; containing 859 inhabitants. This parish comprises 2900 acres, whereof two-thirds are in pasture or meadow, the remainder being arable land. The country is hilly and undulated; the scenery is that of a rich agricultural district, and is greatly improved by the woodlands of the adjoining parishes of Kelmarsh and Haselbeech. The sub-soil of the hills is formed on the escarpment of the inferior oolite, and the surface soil is soft, sandy, ferruginous, of a brown colour, and good fertile quality, and easily worked. The valleys repose upon the lias formation, intersected with deep ravines of diluvial gravel, from which specimens of almost every rock in England may be collected; their surface soil is a tenacious, sandy, calcareous clay, expensive to work, and generally in old pasture. Grazing occupies the chief attention of the farmer, and tillage is here far behind the general state of that description of culture elsewhere. No good stone has yet been discovered in the parish; the roads are repaired with gravel of an inferior kind, and the expense of digging and carriage for a large extent of road becomes a serious burthen to the inhabitants.

The living is a rectory in three portions, two of which are valued in the king's books at £11. 12. 8½., and the third at £6; present net income, £600; patrons, the Master and Fellows of Christ's College, Cambridge. In 1776 an act was obtained for inclosing the parish, till then open field; by which, land exceeding 500 acres was awarded in lieu of tithes, which had been paid in kind. An excellent rectory-house was built in 1841, with funds borrowed from the governors of Queen Anne's Bounty. The Anabaptists have a place of worship. In 1647 Sir George Buswell, Knt., founded a school and hospital, which he endowed with 186 acres of land, producing £260 per annum, to which an annual dividend of £20 on £688 three per cent. consolidated annuities has been added by other benefactors. In the school, from 20 to 40 boys are instructed; and in the hospital are maintained twelve aged single men or women, who receive from 4s. to 5s. per week, and per year a suit of clothes and an allowance of coal. The head master must be a clergyman of the Church of England, and a graduate of one of the two universities: his salary is £100, with a garden, and apartments in the centre of the building, in the wings of which the almspeople reside; he may take a curacy in the neighbourhood, and is allowed an usher, whose salary is £50. The institution is open to the inhabitants of Clipston, Marston-Trussel, East Farndon, Oxendon, Kelmarsh, and Haselbeech; but the almspeople are usually chosen from this parish, and pupils from the other places seldom attend the school. The confirmation of the appointments to both school and hospital is vested in Lady W. Horton, of Rosliston, in the county of Derby, a descendant of the founder. Adjoining the parish, on the west, is an inship of several houses, called Newbold or Nobald, ecclesiastically united to the parish, but in other respects extra-parochial.

CLIPSTON, a township, in the parish of PLUMTREE, union, and S. division of the wapentake, of BINGHAM, S. division of the county of NOTTINGHAM, 6¾ miles (S. E.) from Nottingham; containing 86 inhabitants. Richard I., after returning from the captivity brought on by his crusade to the Holy Land, had an interview with the King of Scotland, in 1194, at this place, where they spent several days.

CLIPSTONE, a township, in the parish of EDWINSTOW, union of SOUTHWELL, Hatfield division of the wapentake of BASSETLAW, N. division of the county of NOTTINGHAM, 3¾ miles (W. S. W.) from Ollerton; containing 286 inhabitants, and comprising 1648 acres. On an eminence above the village are some remains of a palace that belonged to the Anglo-Saxon kings, and which is said to have been erected by one of the kings of Northumbria. It was frequently the residence of King John, both before and after his accession to the throne; and to it, also, all the sovereigns of England down to Henry V. appear to have repaired for the diversion of hunting in the royal forest of Sherwood. A parliament was held here by Edward I. in 1290, and an old oak at the edge of the park is still called the Parliament Oak.

CLIST (ST. GEORGE), a parish, in the union of ST. THOMAS, hundred of EAST BUDLEIGH, Woodbury and S. divisions of DEVON, 1½ mile (N. E. by E.) from Topsham; containing 370 inhabitants. This parish, formerly called Clistwick, from its situation on the river Clist, comprises by computation 1000 acres: the surface is undulated, except near the banks of the river; the il is in some parts a rich loam, in others clayey, and in me light and sandy, the whole being in a state of good ltivation. The living is a rectory, valued in the king's oks at £17. 16. 8.; net income, £348; patron and cumbent, the Rev. W. R. Ellicombe. In the windows the church are some remains of stained glass. A hool was founded in 1703, by Sir Edward and Dame ward, and has an exhibition of £4 per annum at either the universities.

CLIST (St. Lawrence), a parish, in the union of r. Thomas, hundred of Cliston, Woodbury and S. visions of Devon, 5½ miles (S. by E.) from Cullomp- n; containing 168 inhabitants. This parish, which is uated on the river Clist, and in the fertile vale of that me, comprises 968 acres, of which 65 are common or aste; the soil is luxuriantly rich, consisting chiefly of a rong deep loam, producing the heaviest crops of corn d the finest cider in this portion of the county. Veins iron-ore are discernible in some parts. The living is rectory, valued in the king's books at £9. 4. 4½.; net come, £244; patrons, the Trustees of St. John's ospital, Exeter. The glebe comprises about 46 acres; e glebe-house, originally a portion of some religious tablishment, has been partly rebuilt. The church is a ndsome structure in the later English style, with a fty embattled tower, and contains a richly-carved oak reen; in a niche in the north-east wall is a *Madonna*, d in the churchyard are the remains of a fine cross. he tower was struck by lightning in three places, in larch, 1846. The whole of the manorial rights and the nds were bequeathed by Eliza Hele, lady of the manor, r charitable purposes. There is a strong mineral pring at the base of a hill in the western part of the arish, said to be efficacious in diseases of the eye.

CLIST (St. Mary), a parish, in the union of St. homas, hundred of East Budleigh, Woodbury and . divisions of Devon, 2¼ miles (N. E. by N.) from Top- ham; containing 197 inhabitants. It is memorable as he scene of one of the principal contests between the dherents of the old religion and the reformers during he rebellion, in 1549. The inhabitants took part against he king's forces, and defended the long bridge here gainst them with great bravery for some time; but ere at length defeated, and pursued, with great aughter, through the village to the adjoining heath. he parish is intersected by the river Clist, and com- rises 534 acres by admeasurement. The living is a ctory, valued in the king's books at £5. 1. 3., and in ie gift of the family of Strong: the tithes produce 150, and the glebe comprises 26 acres.

CLIST, BROAD (St. John the Baptist), a parish, the union of St. Thomas, hundred of Cliston, 'onford and S. divisions of Devon, 5 miles (N. E.) om Exeter; containing 2407 inhabitants. This place as burnt down by the Danes in 1001. The old man- n of Columbjohn, in the parish, was garrisoned for harles I. by his loyal adherent, Sir John Acland. The imber of acres is about 9000; the surface is undulated, d the soil partly a strong clay, and partly a deep light ndy earth. The river Clist runs through the parish; e Culme flows on the north-west, and turns a paper- ill. Good cider is made. The living is a vicarage, dowed with part of the rectorial tithes, and valued in e king's books at £26; net income, £407; patron, r T. D. Acland; impropriator of the remainder of the

VOL. I.—641

rectorial tithes, the Rev. Dr. Troyte. The church is a handsome edifice in the later English style, containing three stone stalls having rich canopies, with an effigy in plate armour. Sir T. D. Acland has built a chapel in the Norman style, on his estate at Killerton, at a cost of about £3000; it was consecrated in September, 1841. On the manor of Clist-Gerald is a barn, once the chapel of St. Leonard; and there were also chapels in the parish dedicated to St. David and St. Catherine. A school, founded in 1691, is supported partly by an endowment of about £15 per annum. An almshouse for twelve persons was built by Mr. Burrough, who endowed it, in 1605, with £23. 11. per annum. John, Duke of Marlborough, is said to have been born at Churchill, in the parish.

CLIST-HONITON, a parish, in the union of St. Thomas, hundred of East Budleigh, Woodbury and S. divisions of Devon, 4½ miles (E. by N.) from Exeter; containing 467 inhabitants. The parish is situated on the river Clist, a small, but rapid stream that has given its name to almost every place through which it flows. It comprises 1721 acres, whereof 85 are common or waste; the soil is chiefly sandy, with some portions of rich vegetable mould on a stratum of pebbles. The village, which is on the bank of the river, suffered greatly from an accidental fire in 1825, that destroyed the greater part of it. The living is a perpetual curacy, in the patronage of the Dean and Chapter of Exeter, the appropriators; the tithes attached to the living have been commuted for £165, and the great tithes for £265. The church, erected since the Reformation, contains what is supposed by antiquaries to be the original Saxon font.

CLIST-HYDON (St. Andrew), a parish, in the union of St. Thomas, hundred of Cliston, Woodbury and S. divisions of Devon, 4 miles (S. S. E.) from Cul- lompton; containing 325 inhabitants. The living is a rectory, valued in the king's books at £20. 0. 7½., and in the patronage of Mrs. Huyshe: the tithes have been com- muted for £350, and the glebe contains 86 acres. A school is endowed with about £20 per annum, principally from a bequest by Robert Hall, D.D., in 1667.

CLIST-SACKVILLE (St. Gabriel), an ancient chapelry, in the parishes of Farringdon and Sowton, union of St. Thomas, hundred of East Budleigh, Woodbury and S. divisions of Devon, 2¼ miles (N. by E.) from Topsham; containing 286 inhabitants. This place was mortgaged by Sir Ralph Sackville to Walter Browns- comb, Bishop of Exeter, to enable him to proceed with Edward I. on a crusade to the Holy Land, promising to refund the money at a fixed period, and to defray all charges on the estate during his absence. The bishop erected a palace, still standing, and fenced the ground at great charge, so that the expense exceeded the value of the land, in consequence of which it remained with him and his successors, until Bishop Vesey alienated it to the Earl of Bedford. The chapel has been demolished; it had two chaplains endowed by Bishop Brownscomb, and Bishop Stapeldon annexed to it an hospital for twelve superannuated clergymen. Clist-Sackville, then called Bedford House, was made one of the garrisons for the blockade of Exeter, in 1645: Sir Thomas Fairfax sent an engineer to draw a line of fortifications round it.

4 N

Arms.

CLITHEROE (St. Mi-
chael), an unincorporated
borough, market-town, and
parochial chapelry, and the
head of a union, in the parish of WHALLEY, Higher
division of the hundred of
BLACKBURN, N. division of
the county of LANCASTER,
on the eastern bank of the
Ribble, 30 miles (N.) from
Manchester, 49 (N. E.) from
Liverpool, 26 (S. E.) from
Lancaster, and 216 (N. N. W.) from London ; the township containing 6765 inhabitants. The ancient name of
this town, *Cliderhow*, is of a mixed derivation from the
British *Cled-dwr*, which signifies *the hill* or *rock by the
waters*, and the final syllable *how*, a Saxon word for *hill ;*
being descriptive of its situation on an isolated eminence,
terminating in one direction in a lofty rock of limestone
whereon stands the keep of a castle, the original erection of which is involved in considerable obscurity.
The place was the scene of an engagement, in 1138, between a small party of the English army and the Scots,
in which the former was totally defeated by superior
numbers ; and traces of this sanguinary conflict have
been discovered near Edisforth Bridge, and along the
banks of the Ribble.

Some ascribe the foundation of the CASTLE to Robert
de Lacy the first ; but, on the authority of a manuscript
in the Bodleian Library, it is assigned to Robert de
Lacy the second, in 1179, which account is confirmed by
Dugdale, who states that the castle and the chapel of St.
Michael annexed thereto, were built by the latter. Dr.
Whitaker, however, in his *History of Whalley*, considers
it to be of earlier date. The castle originally consisted
of a keep, with a tower, and arched gateway, and was
surrounded by a strong lofty wall, built on the margin
of the rock ; it was used as a species of fortress for dis-
pensing justice and receiving tribute by the Lacys, who
were lords paramount of the honour. This honour,
which extends over the parishes of Whalley, Blackburn,
Chipping, and Ribchester, the forest of Bowland, and the
manors of Tottington and Rochdale, and includes 28
manors, formed part of the possessions of the house of
Lancaster, from the time of the marriage of Thomas
Plantagenet, Earl of Lancaster, with Alice, sister and
heiress of Henry de Lacy, until the Restoration, when
Charles II. bestowed it upon General Monk, Duke of
Albemarle, for his services : it has a court for the
recovery of small debts, extending over the hundred of
Blackburn ; and a similar court is held for the wapentake of Bowland. During the wars of the Roses,
Henry VI., on his deposition, sought a temporary refuge
here among the hereditary dependents of the house of
Lancaster, but was betrayed to his rival by the Talbots
of Bashall and Colebry, and sent bound to London. In
the civil war the fortress was among the last surrendered
to the parliament, by whose directions, in 1649, it was
dismantled ; the keep, a square tower, being all that
remains. The site, and a certain portion of ground
occupied by the demesne and forests of the baronial
edifice, are extra-parochial, and commonly designated
the Castle parish. A modern castellated edifice has
been erected within the precincts of the castle. An

The chapelry consists of the townships of Chathurn, itheroe, Heyhouses, Mearley, and Worston. The VING is a perpetual curacy, in the patronage of the v. J. H. Anderton; net income, £127, with a glebe-use. The church has been rebuilt, with the exception the tower and the east window, which form a good ecimen of the later English style: the Incorporated ciety granted £1500 towards defraying the expense. e former edifice was of great antiquity, being designated, in a deed of the 13th of Edward IV., the church St. Mary Magdalene; against the south wall of the ve was a brass plate, bearing a curious enigmatical igram, and an inscription in Latin to the memory of :. John Webster, the celebrated judicial astrologer, and rate of Clitheroe, who was interred here, June 21st, 82. In 1838, an additional church, dedicated to St. mes, was erected by subscription, aided by James iomson, Esq., of Primrose, who, and his family, were e principal contributors: the living is in the gift of ve Trustees. At Chatburn and Heyhouses are other urches. There are places of worship for Independents, Methodists, and Roman Catholics. The free ammar school was founded in 1554, by Philip and ary, and endowed with the rectorial tithes of the rish of Almondbury, and with certain lands in the strict of Craven, in Yorkshire; the head master receives a salary of £200, and has a handsome residence, d the second master is allowed £100. The poor law nion of Clitheroe comprises 33 parishes or places, of 'hich 19 are in the West riding of York, and 14 in the ounty of Lancaster; and contains a population of 3,018. Heyhouses is in Burnley union. The Rev. ames King, chaplain to the house of commons, and ather of Captain James King, who accompanied Captain look in his voyage of discovery round the globe, and of Valker King, Bishop of Rochester, was, during the early art of his ministry, incumbent of Clitheroe.

CLIVE, a township, in the parish of MIDDLEWICH, nion and hundred of NORTHWICH, S. division of the ounty of CHESTER, 2 miles (W. by S.) from Middle- rich; containing 117 inhabitants. The manor was the ncient inheritance and seat of the family of Clive, or lliffe, from whom it passed, or a part of it, by marriage, o the Wilbrahams. The Congletons, Weevers, Stan- eys, and Hulses, were also connected with the place. he township comprises 462 acres, of a chiefly clayey oil: the Liverpool and Birmingham railway passes brough. The impropriate tithes have been commuted or £45. 14. An old house here, standing near Wins- ord bridge, and called the Nuns' House, belonged, pro- ably, to the nuns of Chester.

CLIVE, a chapelry, in the parish of ST. MARY, liber- ies of the town of SHREWSBURY, union of WEM, N. livision of SALOP, 3½ miles (S.) from Wem; containing !73 inhabitants. The living is a perpetual curacy, with net income of £66, and in the gift of the Bishop of Lichfield (ex officio visiter of Shrewsbury grammar chool), the Earl of Powis, J. A. Lloyd, Esq., Sir A. V. Corbet, Bart., and R. A. Slaney, Esq. The chapel is ledicated to All Saints. William Wycherley, the poet, vas born here in 1640.

CLIVIGER, a chapelry, in the parochial chapelry of BURNLEY, parish of WHALLEY, union of BURNLEY, digher division of the hundred of BLACKBURN, N. livision of the county of LANCASTER, 3½ miles (S. E. by

S.) from Burnley; containing 1395 inhabitants. This place was granted by Henry de Lacy, who died in 1159, to the abbot of Kirkstall. Sir Ralph de Elland claimed it as part of his manor of Rochdale; and the then abbot, Lambert, who was elected in 1191, admitting the justice of his claims, the grange of Accrington was substituted for "Clivachir" by Roger de Lacy. The Clivachers also possessed lands here; of this family, Cecilia de Clivacher, about the reign of Edward I., appears to have been the last. Various other families subsequently held property in the manor, and among them were the de Holmes, who held the portion now known as Holme, in Cliviger. The chapelry comprises 6631 acres, whereof 1119 are common or waste. The river Irwell has its rise here, running to Bacup, and thence to Bury and Manchester, a circuitous course of twenty-five miles. The village lies on the road from Todmorden to Burnley. The living is now a district incumbency; net income, £101; patrons, the family of Whitaker. The chapel, situated at Holme, and of the time of Henry VII., was rebuilt in 1788. There is a place of worship for Wesleyans; and a school is conducted on the national plan. William Whitaker, a controversial divine, was born at Holme in the year 1547.

CLIXBY, a chapelry, in the parish and union of CAISTOR, S. division of the wapentake of YARBOROUGH, parts of LINDSEY, county of LINCOLN, 2½ miles (N. by W.) from Caistor; containing 45 inhabitants. The living is annexed to the vicarage of Caistor.

CLOATLY, a hamlet, in the parish of HANKERTON, union and hundred of MALMESBURY, Malmesbury and Kingswood, and N. divisions of WILTS, 3½ miles (N. E.) from Malmesbury; containing 77 inhabitants.

CLODOCK (ST. CLEODOCUS), a parish, in the hundred of EWYASLACY, county of HEREFORD, 10 miles (N. N. E.) from Abergavenny; containing, with the chapelries of Crasswall, Llanveynoe, and Longtown, and the township of Newton, 1762 inhabitants. The parish comprises 1800 acres, about three-fourths of which are pasture and meadow land, and 200 acres woodland. The surface is very irregular, rising into numerous hills of various elevation, and a considerable portion of it extends along the side of the Black Mountain, or Hatterel hills; the soil is generally light. The rivers Olchon and Munnow have their source within the parish, which is also traversed by the Eskley, a stream that abounds with trout of excellent quality, and is much frequented by anglers. Fairs are held on the 29th of April, 22nd of June, and 21st of September. The living is a vicar- age, not in charge; net income, £149; patron, Mr. Wilkins, Esq.; impropriator, Sir V. G. Cornewall, Bart. There are chapels of ease at Longtown, Llanveynoe, and Crasswall, in the patronage of the vicar; and a fourth chapel has been lately built.

CLOFFOCK, an extra-parochial liberty, in the union of COCKERMOUTH, in ALLERDALE ward above Derwent, county of CUMBERLAND; containing 4 inhabitants. It consists of a tract of common, about 80 acres, lying on the north side of the town of Workington, and com- pletely surrounded by the river Derwent and a small stream. Races are held annually; and at the western extremity of the place are a quay and a patent-slip. A portion of the ground is called Chapel Flat, and is thought to have been the site or property of a religious house.

CLOFORD (St. Mary), a parish, in the union and hundred of Frome, E. division of Somerset, 4½ miles (S. W.) from Frome; containing 253 inhabitants. The living is a discharged vicarage, valued in the king's books at £7. 17. 6.; patron and impropriator, T. Horner, Esq. The great tithes have been commuted for £40, and the vicarial for £135; the glebe comprises 6 acres. There is a place of worship for Wesleyans.

CLOPHILL (St. Mary), a parish, in the union of Amphill, hundred of Flitt, county of Bedford, 1 mile (N. by E.) from Silsoe; containing 1066 inhabitants. It comprises by computation 2340 acres, of which about 1400 are arable, and 700 pasture. The soil is light and sandy, with some portions of gravel, clay, and moorland; the surface is rather hilly, and the lower grounds are subject to inundation from the river Ivel, which flows through the parish. The living is a rectory, valued in the king's books at £12; net income, £522; patron, Earl de Grey. The tithes have been commuted for £239, and the glebe contains 70 acres, with a glebe-house. The church stands upon an eminence at some distance from the village. There is a place of worship for Wesleyans. At Cainhoe are vestiges of the moated castle of the barons d'Albini: the hill on which it stood is high and steep, and overgrown with coppice-wood. Here was also a religious house, probably a cell to St. Alban's Abbey.

CLOPTON, a hamlet, in the parish of Mickleton, union of Shipston-upon-Stour, Upper division of the hundred of Kiftsgate, E. division of the county of Gloucester; containing 27 inhabitants.

CLOPTON (St. Mary), a parish, in the union of Woodbridge, hundred of Carlford, E. division of Suffolk, 4 miles (N. W.) from Woodbridge; containing 389 inhabitants. It comprises by measurement 2107 acres; the soil is partly strong clay and partly of a mixed quality, the surface rather hilly, and the scenery varied: a small stream winds through the lower grounds. The living is a rectory, valued in the king's books at £16. 13. 4.; net income, £538; patron and incumbent, the Rev. George Taylor. The church is ornamented with four beautiful windows in the later English style, and has a handsome tower. There are about 14 acres of land and four tenements, the rent of which is applied to the expenses of the church, and the relief of the poor.

CLOPTON, a hamlet, in the parish of Old Stratford, union of Stratford, Stratford division of the hundred of Barlichway, S. division of the county of Warwick, 1 mile (N. W.) from Stratford.. This place includes the manors of Upper and Lower Clopton. Clopton House, with its grounds, comprising about 400 acres, was the ancient seat of the Clopton family, who were great benefactors to Stratford, and who built the bridge across the Avon in 1490, and the chapel. The mansion was fast falling to decay when Charles Thomas Warde, Esq., the present proprietor, purchased it; and for the last few years he has been enlarging it considerably, and repairing and restoring the older parts, in the ancient style, with carved-oak wainscot and oak floors. He has built a new suite of drawing-rooms of spacious dimensions, a complete range of offices of every description, stables, and a conservatory; and has enriched numerous apartments with panelling and ceilings in the c or Louis XIV. style. These improve-

CLOUGHTON, a chapelry, in the parish of SCALBY, ion of SCARBOROUGH, PICKERING lythe, N. riding of ᵣRK, 4¼ miles (N. W. by N.) from Scarborough; con- ning 454 inhabitants. This township is situated on ᵣ road from Scarborough to Whitby, and bounded on ᵣ east by the North Sea; it comprises about 3510 res, of which a portion is moorland hills. Quarries excellent freestone are wrought. The chapel has been ᵦuilt. There is a place of worship for Wesleyans; ᵢo a school rebuilt in 1835.

CLOVELLY (*ALL SAINTS*), a parish, in the union of ᵢDEFORD, hundred of HARTLAND, Great Torrington ᵢd N. divisions of DEVON, 11 miles (W. by S.) from ᵢdeford; containing 950 inhabitants. At this place ᵢs a Roman *trajectus* from Carmarthen; and till within ᵢe last few years, the remains of a fort, erected by the ᵦmans for the defence of the pass, were plainly discern- ᵢe. The village is romantically situated, in a district ᵦounding with geological attractions, on the acclivities ᵢa shelving and precipitous rock, rising abruptly from ᵢe Bristol Channel to the height of several hundred ᵢt above the harbour, and crowned with luxuriant ver- ᵢre. The harbour, which is an appendage to the port ᵢ Bideford, and, though small, remarkable for its secu- ᵢy, is partly formed by a substantial pier erected by a ᵢember of the family of Carew, by whose ancestor the ᵢanor was purchased in the reign of Richard II. A ᵦnsiderable trade is carried on in the herring-fishery, ᵣr which Clovelly is the most noted place on the coast; ᵢe herrings are esteemed the finest taken in the Chan- el, and the fishery furnishes employment to the principal art of the labouring class. The parish comprises 2578 ᵢres, of which 300 are common or waste. The living is rectory, valued in the king's books at £19. 11. 5¼., ᵢd in the patronage of Sir J. H. Williams, Bart.: the thes have been commuted for £200, and the glebe con- ᵢins 78 acres. The church, which was made collegiate ᵣr a warden and six chaplains, by the family of Carew, ᵢ the 11th of Richard II., contains some handsome ᵢonuments. There is a place of worship for Wesleyans. ᵢn the heights above the village is a large encampment, ᵢlled Dichen, or the Clovelly ditches, consisting of ᵢree trenches or dykes, inclosing a quadrilateral area 60 feet in height and 300 in breadth.

CLOWN (*ST. JOHN THE BAPTIST*), a parish, in the ᵢnion of WORKSOP, hundred of SCARSDALE, N. divi- ᵢon of the county of DERBY, 9 miles (E. N. E.) from ᵢhesterfield; containing 677 inhabitants. It comprises ᵦout 1855 acres, of which 1262 are arable, 521 pasture, ᵢd 58 wood. The greater portion is high ground, and ᵢe remainder undulated; the soil on the high lands is thin loam, with a substratum of limestone, and in the ᵢwer inclined to clay. There are numerous springs of ᵢccellent water, which, uniting their streams, fall into ᵢ brook flowing to Welbeck. The living is a rectory, ᵢlued in the king's books at £7. 0. 10., and in the ᵢtronage of the Crown. Tithes were commuted for ᵢnd and a money payment in 1778, and under the re- ᵢnt act a commutation has been made for a rent-charge ᵢf £330; the glebe contains 67 acres, with a glebe- ᵢouse. The church has Norman portions, amidst various ᵢter styles. Charles Basseldine, in 1730, founded a ᵢhool, with an endowment of thirteen acres of land, ᵢow producing £26 per annum. There is a chalybeate ᵢpring.

645

CLUN (*ST. GEORGE*), a market-town and parish, and the head of a union, in the hundred of PURSLOW, S. di- vision of SALOP, 26 miles (S. W.) from Shrewsbury, and 157 (N. W. by W.) from Lon- don; containing 2077 inha- bitants. This place takes its name from the river Colun or Clun, which, ris- ing in the forest of that name, 6 miles to the west,

Corporation Seal.

divides the town into two parts, and pursues an easterly course towards Ludlow. In the reign of Stephen, or, according to Camden, in that of Henry III., a castle was erected by Fitz-Alan, afterwards Earl of Arundel, on a lofty eminence overlooking the river, the proprietor of which possessed the power of life and death over his tenants; it was demolished by Owain Glyndwr in his rebellion against Henry IV. The remains present an interesting and picturesque object in the surrounding landscape, consisting of the lofty walls of the keep and the banquet-hall; and considerable masses of the ruins in various parts of the area indistinctly mark out both the ancient form and extent of this once stately pile. In the reign of Henry VIII. the parish was by statute made part of the newly formed county of Montgomery, from which it was afterwards severed, and included in that of Salop. An act was passed in 1837, for inclosing 8600 acres in the forest of Clun, and in 1839, one for inclosing 1700 in the township of Clun; several acres are set apart for the recreation of the inhabitants.

The TOWN is romantically situated, on a gentle emi- nence surrounded by hills of bolder elevation, and con- sists principally of one long irregular street on the north bank of the river, over which is an ancient stone bridge of five sharply-pointed arches, leading to that part of the town where the church stands. The market is on Tuesday: the fairs are on the 11th May, Whit-Tuesday, and Sept. 23rd, for cattle, sheep, and pigs; and Nov. 22nd, which is a statute and a large cattle fair. Clun was formerly a lordship in the marches, and was first incorporated by the lords marchers, whose charter was confirmed to Edmund, Earl of Arundel, in the reign of Edward II., at which time its prescriptive right was admitted; but the charter not having been enrolled in chancery, and all the records of the lords marchers having been destroyed, its being an incorporated borough was proved by parole evidence. The government is vested in two bailiffs, a recorder, two serjeants-at-mace, and subordinate officers; and the bailiffs hold a court of record for the recovery of debts. The hundred court, for the recovery of debts under 40s., is held every third Wednesday, and courts leet in May and October; at that in October constables are appointed. The town-hall is a neat modern stone building, supported on arches.

The LIVING is a vicarage, valued in the king's books at £13. 10. 5.; net income, £680; patron and impro- priator, the Earl of Powis. The church, which was dependent on the priory of Wenlock, is a very ancient structure, in the earliest period of the Norman style, and has evidently been of much greater extent than it is at present, having had several chapels. It has a low tower of very large dimensions and of great strength, with a pyramidal roof, from the centre of which rises another tower of similar form, but smaller; the arch under the tower, forming the western entrance, bears a strong resemblance to the Saxon, and it is not improbable that this part of the building existed before the Conquest. The northern entrance is under a highly ornamented Norman arch, on the east side of which is an arched recess, richly cinquefoiled, and probably intended for the tomb of the founder. St. Mary's chapel of ease, at Chapel Lawn, was built in 1844, at a cost of £1200; it is in the early English style, with a campanile tower. There is a place of worship for Wesleyans. *Clun Hospital,* dedicated to the Holy Trinity, was founded, in 1614, and endowed by Henry Howard, Earl of Northampton, with tithes now producing a revenue of £1600 per annum. The establishment consists of eighteen poor brethren and a warden, and the management is vested in the bailiff, vicar, and churchwardens, the steward of the lordship, the rector of Hopesay, and the warden of the hospital; the Bishop of Hereford is visiter. The buildings comprise a quadrangle 40 yards in length, and the same in breadth: in 1845 they were extended on the east side of the quadrangle, by the erection of a chapel, a house for the warden, and a dining-hall. The poor law union of Clun comprises 19 parishes or places, namely, 17 in the county of Salop, one in Salop and Montgomery, and one in Montgomery; and contains a population of 10,024.

Within a quarter of a mile to the north-west of the town, is a single intrenchment, said to have been raised by Owain Glyndwr, as a shelter for his troops during their attack on the castle; and within half a mile to the south, is Walls Castle, the station from which it was battered. About two miles and a half to the north-east, is the camp of Ostorius, the station occupied by that general in his last battle with Caractacus; and about five to the south-east, near the confluence of the rivers Clun and Teme, and within 4 miles of Walcott, the seat of the Earl of Powis, are the Caer or Bury Ditches, the station of the British hero, and the scene of his last effort against the Roman power. The camp, which is of elliptic form, comprehends an area of from three to four acres, on the summit of a very lofty eminence, commanding an extensive view of the surrounding country; the steep acclivities are defended by a triple intrenchment of amazing strength, which, though overgrown with turf, is still entire. This fortification, evidently a work of prodigious labour, is one of the most interesting in the country, and, under the care of the Earl of Powis, is preserved with a due regard to its historical importance. In making a road from Clun to Bishop's-Castle, in 1780, several cannon-balls were found.

CLUNBURY (ST. SWITHIN), a parish, in the union of CLUN, hundred of PURSLOW, S. division of SALOP; containing 994 inhabitants, of whom 258 are in the township of Clunbury, 6½ miles (S. S. E.) from Bishop's-Castle. This parish, which is situated in the heart of a sequestered district abounding with romantic scenery, comprises by computation 6000 acres, exclusively of woods and common. There are some quarries of stone for building and for mending the roads. The village is beautifully situated at the foot of a lofty hill, and surrounded with woods and plantations. The living is a perpetual curacy; net income, £120; patron and impropriator, the Earl of Powis. The church is a neat

CLYTHA, a hamlet, in the parish of LLANARTH, ion of ABERGAVENNY, division and hundred of RAGN, county of MONMOUTH, 3 miles (W. N. W.) from glan; containing 335 inhabitants. This place, which situated on the left bank of the river Usk, and interted by the high roads leading from Abergavenny to mmouth and Usk, contains by estimation 1503a. 17p., of which 683 acres are arable, 776 pasture and adow, and 44 woodland. The vicarial tithes have n commuted for £115, and there is a glebe of about acres. Clytha House is a handsome mansion in the ecian style, with a noble portico, standing in tastefully d-out grounds; near it are the remains of an ancient apel, and on the brow of a lofty eminence contiguous nds a castellated building, erected in 1790, by the e William Jones, Esq., to the memory of his lady, and ence is a beautiful and extensive view of the vale of Usk, with the Blorange, Sugar Loaf, and Skirrid untains in the distance. Upon the summit of another inence, at the extremity of the Clytha hills, is a all encampment called Coed-y-Bunnedd, which retains rks of having been strongly fortified.

COAL-ASTON, a township, in the parish of DRONELD, union of CHESTERFIELD, hundred of SCARSDALE, division of the county of DERBY, ¾ of a mile (N. by) from Dronfield; containing 352 inhabitants.

COAL-PIT-HEATH, an ecclesiastical parish, partly the parish of FRAMPTON-COTTERELL, hundred of ANGLEY and SWINEHEAD, and partly in the parish of ESTERLEIGH, hundred of PUCKLE-CHURCH, union of HIPPING-SODBURY, W. division of the county of GLOUESTER, 1½ mile (S. by E.) from Frampton-Cotterell; ntaining about 2300 inhabitants. It lies on the nks of the river Frome, and on the Bristol and Biringham railway; and the road from Bristol to Sodbury sses through its centre. There are seven coal-pits, in e possession of the lords of the manor, who derive a rge revenue from the estate. The parish was constited in 1845, under the act 6th and 7th of Victoria, p. 37; and on the 9th October, in that year, the urch, called St. Saviour's, was consecrated. It is in e early decorated style, with a nave, chancel, rth and south aisles, and tower; the chancel is paved ith encaustic tiles, many of the windows are of painted ass, and there is a fine organ: the cost of the edifice ceeded £3000. The living is a perpetual curacy, in the tronage of the Bishop of Gloucester and Bristol; net come, £150.

COALEY (ST. BARTHOLOMEW), a parish, in the union 'DURSLEY, Upper division of the hundred of BERKEEY, W. division of the county of GLOUCESTER, 3 miles t. N. E.) from Dursley; containing 979 inhabitants. comprises 2463 acres, of which 1900 are pasture, 300 able, 90 woodland, and 81 common or waste. The ing is a discharged vicarage, valued in the king's books £8. 2. 2., and in the patronage of the Crown; improiator, S. Jones, Esq. Tithes were commuted for land d a money payment in 1801; and under the recent t, impropriate tithes have been commuted for a rentarge of £56. 14., and vicarial for one of £300. There a place of worship for Wesleyans.

COANWOOD, EAST, a township, in the parish and ion of HALTWHISTLE, W. division of TINDALE ward, division of NORTHUMBERLAND, 5 miles (S.) from altwhistle; containing 139 inhabitants. The name was

647

anciently Collingwood, which, in its Welsh form of Collen-gwydd, means hazel-trees or hazel-wood, with which the district abounded, until, in consequence of the mining operations in the vicinity (converting the wood into charcoal), the article became scarce, existing now only in certain places. The township contains the hamlets of High and Low Ramshaw, and Gorbet-hill, and comprises 2040 acres, of which about 1000 are common or waste: it has a coal-mine, called the Rig-pit, in operation. There is a place of worship for the Society of Friends.

COAT, a hamlet, in the parish and hundred of MARTOCK, union of YEOVIL, W. division of the county of SOMERSET; containing 175 inhabitants.

COATE, a tything, in the parish of BISHOP's-CANNINGS, union of DEVIZES, hundred of POTTERNE and CANNINGS, Devizes and N. divisions of WILTS; containing 303 inhabitants.

COATE, a tything, in the parish of LIDDINGTON, union of HIGHWORTH and SWINDON, hundred of KINGSBRIDGE, Swindon and N. divisions of the county of WILTS; containing 43 inhabitants.

COATES (ST. MATTHEW), a parish, in the union of CIRENCESTER, hundred of CROWTHORNE and MINETY, E. division of the county of GLOUCESTER, 3½ miles (W. by S.) from Cirencester; containing 373 inhabitants. It is bounded on the north by the high road from Stroudwater to London, and on the east by that from Cirencester to Bath. Stone of excellent quality is quarried for buildings, and for general purposes. The Thames and Severn canal passes through the parish. The living is a rectory, valued in the king's books at £9. 6. 8.; net income, £369; patron, Earl Bathurst. The tithes were commuted for land and a money payment, in 1792: the glebe contains 509 acres, chiefly arable, with an excellent glebe-house. At Trewsbury, in the parish, near the place where a castle formerly stood, the remains of which, with the intrenchments, may yet be seen, is a well, supposed to be the source of the Thames, and called the Thames Head.

COATES (ST. EDITH), a parish, in the union of GAINSBOROUGH, W. division of the wapentake of AsLACOE, parts of LINDSEY, county of LINCOLN, 9½ miles (N. W. by N.) from Lincoln; containing 47 inhabitants. The living is a discharged vicarage, valued in the king's books at £3. 16. 8.; net income, £50; patron and impropriator, Sir J. Ramsden, Bart.

COATES, a parish, in the union of SUTTON (under Gilbert's act), hundred of BURY, rape of ARUNDEL, W. division of SUSSEX, 4 miles (S. E. by S.) from Petworth; containing 67 inhabitants. It is bounded on the north by the Rother navigation, and comprises by measurement 346 acres; the surface is diversified, and, from the higher grounds, especially from Coates Castle, the views are extensive. The living is consolidated with the rectory of Burton: the tithes have been commuted for £69. 12., and the glebe contains nearly 5 acres. The church is in the early English style.

COATES, a township, in the parish of BARNOLDSWICK, union of SKIPTON, E. division of the wapentake of STAINCLIFFE and EWCROSS, W. riding of YORK, 8 miles (W. S. W.) from Skipton; containing 101 inhabitants. The township is situated in a district abounding with limestone of good quality, and comprises by measurement 385 acres. The village, which is near the parochial church, is neatly built. Coates Hall, a large Elizabethan mansion, now neglected, was the residence of the Bagshaw family.

COATES, GREAT (*St. Nicholas*), a parish, in the union of Caistor, wapentake of Bradley-Haverstoe, parts of Lindsey, county of Lincoln, 4 miles (W.) from Great Grimsby; containing 245 inhabitants. The living is a rectory, valued in the king's books at £11. 10. 10., and in the gift of Sir R. Sutton, Bart.: the tithes have been commuted for £654. 5., and the glebe contains 76¼ acres, with a glebe-house.

COATES, LITTLE (*St. Michael*), a parish, in the union of Caistor, wapentake of Bradley-Haverstoe, parts of Lindsey, county of Lincoln, 3¼ miles (W. by S.) from Great Grimsby; containing 40 inhabitants. The living is a discharged vicarage, valued in the king's books at £4. 18. 4., and in the gift of Trinity College, Cambridge: the college receives a tithe rent-charge of £140, and the vicar one of £112.

COATES, NORTH (*St. Nicholas*), a parish, in the union of Louth, wapentake of Bradley-Haverstoe, parts of Lindsey, county of Lincoln, 11 miles (N.N.E.) from Louth; containing 225 inhabitants. The parish comprises 2061 acres, of which 507 are common or waste: the Louth and Humber canal runs through. The living is a rectory, valued in the king's books at £12. 10. 10., and in the patronage of the Crown, in right of the duchy of Lancaster: the tithes have been commuted for £470. 18.; and the glebe contains half an acre. The church, which has a tower, consists of a nave, chancel, and aisles, with a chapel. There are some of those wells, usually called " Blow wells."

COATHAM, EAST, a hamlet, in the parish of Kirk-Leatham, union of Guisborough, E. division of the liberty of Langbaurgh, N. riding of York, 6¼ miles (N. by W.) from Guisborough; containing, with West Coatham, 371 inhabitants. This is a small fishing village near the mouth of the Tees, formerly much resorted to for sea-bathing, but now eclipsed by the neighbouring town of Redcar: the sands in the neighbourhood are well adapted for the promenade or the carriage, and the prospect is often rendered pleasing from the number of trading-vessels sailing in the offing. A school is supported by an income of £47, arising principally from the revenues of Kirk-Leatham school.

COATHAM-MUNDEVILLE, a township, in the parish of Haughton-le-Skerne, union of Darlington, S. W. division of Stockton ward, S. division of the county of Durham, 4 miles (N.) from Darlington, on the road to Durham; containing 138 inhabitants. The place takes its distinguishing name from the family of Amundeville, to whom it belonged in the first or second century after the Conquest. A chapel dedicated to St. Mary Magdalene existed here at a very early period, and it is probable that it continued for several centuries, being mentioned so late as the year 1680, when, however, it seems to have been in ruins. The township comprises 1466 acres, of which 771 are arable, 668 grass land, 12 wood, and 15 road and waste. On the river Skerne is a manufactory for spinning flax and shoe-thread. The Stockton and Darlington railway passes through the township, on its way to the collieries and the Aucklands. The tithes have been commuted for a yearly rent-charge of £95. 17., and there is a glebe of 16 acres.

its and brasses to the noble families of Cobham and oke. In 1362, John, Lord Cobham, made it collate, and, contiguous to the churchyard, erected a ege, which he amply endowed for five chaplains, rwards increased to eleven : at the suppression the ege was valued at £128. 1. 2., and was confirmed by crown to George, Lord Cobham, whose executors, in)8, built upon the site the present college, and enved it with the former possessions, for the maintence of 20 persons. It is a neat quadrangular building stone, comprising part of the ancient structure. The irse of the Roman Watling-street is visible in the ish ; and on a hill in Cobham Park is a splendid usoleum, of the Doric order, erected by the late Earl Darnley, at an expense of £15,000. The place confers ; title of Baron on the Duke of Buckingham.

COBHAM (ST. ANDREW), a parish, in the union of SOM, Second division of the hundred of ELMBRIDGE, ! division of SURREY, 10 miles (N. E.) from Guildford, d 20 (S. W.) from London ; containing 1617 inhabitts. It comprises 5193a. 1r. 37p., of which about 60 acres are arable, 1217 meadow, and nearly 800)od ; and is bounded by the river Mole, which is ssed by a bridge on the road from Portsmouth to)ndon. This river was anciently called the Emley, and ve name to the hundred, properly Emley-Bridge : it ounds with pike, trout, perch, and other fish, and its nks are adorned with several elegant villas. The vilge near the church is called Church-Cobham, and about lf a mile from it, on the Portsmouth road, is Streetbbham, where is a post-office. A fair is held on the [th of December. The living is a discharged vicarage, lued in the king's books at £9. 17. 11.; net income, 162 ; patrons, the family of Simpkinson : there are iree acres of glebe. The church has a handsome Noran arch at the principal south entrance ; its walls are iilt with gravel cemented into a hard mass, at least a ird in thickness, and cased with plaster : on taking wn the north wall for the enlargement of the church, i 1826, its foundation was discovered to be scarcely, if ; all, lower than the level of the floor inside. There is saline chalybeate spring near the brook which separates ie parish on the north from Esher ; and a little to the est of Cobham is a barrow, near which a considerable umber of Roman coins of the Lower Empire was loughed up in 1772.

COBLE-DEAN, a hamlet, in the township of CHIRON, parish, borough, and union of TYNEMOUTH, E. division of CASTLE ward, S. division of NORTHUMBERAND, 1 mile (W.) from North Shields. It is situated n the north bank of the Tyne, and contains a steam our-mill, a manufactory for whiting, and a raft-yard ; eam tug-boats, also, are built here. An act was passed i 1846, for constructing docks and other works, to be illed the Northumberland Docks.

COBLEY, with TUTNAL.—See TUTNAL.

COBRIDGE, a village, partly in the parish of BURSEM, and partly in that of STOKE-UPON-TRENT, N. division of the hundred of PIREHILL and of the county of TAFFORD, 2¼ miles (N. N. E.) from Newcastle ; the ville urslem portion containing 1584 inhabitants. The ville f Rushton, which has been superseded by Cobridge, is escribed in Domesday book under the name of Rise-)ne; it was given by Henry de Audley to Hulton .bbey, to which it became the grange, and since the

Dissolution has been in the possession of the ancient family of Biddulph. Cobridge is in the Staffordshire Potteries, situated on an eminence, midway between Burslem and Hanley, and contains several manufactories and collieries. A neat district church, dedicated to Christ, has been erected by the rector of Burslem, aided by the Church Commissioners and the Diocesan Society ; it is in the English style, with a tower, and affords accommodation to about 560 persons. The living is in the gift of the Rector. There are a chapel belonging to Roman Catholics, and a meeting-house for the New Connexion of Methodists. Schoolrooms were erected by subscription in 1766.

COCKEN, a township, in the parish of HOUGHTON-LE-SPRING, union of CHESTER-LE-STREET, N. division of EASINGTON ward and of the county of DURHAM, 4 miles (N. N. E.) from Durham ; containing 65 inhabitants. Cocken was separated from the constablery of West Rainton, and made distinct in 1726. It is situated on the river Wear, and comprises by measurement 380 acres, of which 250 are arable, 120 meadow and pasture, and 10 waste : coal is obtained in the neighbourhood. The whole township is the property of William Standish Standish, Esq., of Duxbury Park, Lancashire. The manor-house, which is surrounded by beautiful scenery, became, at the commencement of the present century, the residence of a convent of nuns of the order of St. Theresa, who were driven by the revolutionists from their former settlement at Lier, in Flanders. After residing here for upwards of twenty years, they removed to Field House, near Darlington. Mrs. Standish has established a dame's school, at her own expense, within the grounds.

COCKERHAM (ST. MICHAEL), a parish, in the unions of GARSTANG and LANCASTER, partly in the hundred of AMOUNDERNESS, but chiefly in the hundred of LONSDALE south of the Sands, N. division of the county of LANCASTER ; comprising the chapelry of Ellel, and part of the townships of Cleveley, Forton, and Holleth ; the whole containing about 3500 inhabitants, of whom 847 are in the township of Cockerham, 7 miles (S.) from Lancaster. The name is compounded of coker, a quiver, and ham, a village. Soon after the Conquest the place was in the possession of the Lancasters, barons of Kendal ; the abbot of St. Mary de Pratis established a cell or priory here, which existed in the 20th of Edward I., but it merged in the superior house long before the Dissolution. The manor afterwards passed into the family of Charteris, and was sold by Lord Wemyss, about 1798, to Messrs. Green, Atkinson, Dent, and Addison. The parish is bounded on the west by Morecambe bay, and comprises above 10,000 acres, mostly arable land, with an undulated surface. The river Cocker, the principal water in the district, issues from the hills above Ellel Chapel ; runs by Galgate, Holleth, and Forton ; and after verging first to the west, and then to the north, washes the township of Cockerham on the south. To the west of the village, the river passes under a well-built bridge, and widens into a spacious estuary, terminating near the mouth of the Lune, from which it is separated by a long and narrow neck of land, the site of the ruins, and of the extraparochial precincts, of Cockersand Abbey. The Wyro flows near the eastern borders of the parish, where it receives a small rill from Cleveley ; and the Lancaster and Preston railway passes through. A market is mentioned among the customs of the manor in the reign of Edward III. : a fair is yet held; as are courts leet and baron. The living is a discharged vicarage, valued in the king's books at £10. 16. 8.; patrons, the Lords of the Manor : the tithes were commuted under a private act in 1827, for £600; the vicarage-house was rebuilt in 1843, in the Elizabethan style. The church was probably founded by the first William de Lancaster : the present edifice is a re-erection, in 1814, on the site of a building of the reign of James I. or Charles I.; it consists of a body, aisles, chancel, and tower, the last more ancient than the other parts, and castellated. There are chapels at Ellel, Dolphinholme, and Shirehead, forming separate incumbencies. A school is supported by subscription, aided by £12 per annum from lands.

COCKERINGTON (St. Leonard), a parish, in the union of Louth, Wold division of the hundred of Louth-Eske, parts of Lindsey, county of Lincoln, 4¼ miles (E. N. E.) from Louth; containing 246 inhabitants. It comprises by computation 2000 acres, and contains Cockerington Hall, the seat of William Scrope, Esq., a neat mansion in grounds tastefully laid out. The living is a discharged vicarage, valued in the king's books at £5. 1. 5½.; net income, £163; patron, the Bishop of Lincoln; appropriators, the Dean and Chapter of Lincoln. The greater portion of the tithes were commuted for land in 1765, and by the recent act a commutation has been made of the remainder for a rent-charge of £17; the glebe consists of 160 acres. The church is a plain edifice with a tower, and contains the mausoleum of Sir Adrian Scrope, ancestor of the present family of that name. There is a place of worship for Wesleyans. An almshouse for six widows was founded and endowed with £20 per annum, by Sir A. Scrope.

COCKERINGTON (St. Mary), a parish, in the union of Louth, Wold division of the hundred of Louth-Eske, parts of Lindsey, county of Lincoln, 4 miles (N. E.) from Louth; containing 227 inhabitants, and comprising by computation 1000 acres. The living is a perpetual curacy, annexed to that of Alvingham : the Bishop of Lincoln holds about 300 acres of land in the parish, allotted in lieu of tithes in 1765. The church, rebuilt in 1841, is situated in the same churchyard as that of Alvingham, and was formerly the chapel to the abbey of that place.

COCKERMOUTH (All Saints), an unincorporated borough, market-town, and parochial chapelry, and the head of a union, in the parish of Brigham, Allerdale ward above Derwent, W. division of Cumberland, 25 miles (S. W.) from Carlisle, and 305 (N. W. by N.) from London; containing 4940 inhabitants. The name is derived from the situation of the place at the *mouth* of the river *Cocker*, which here unites with the Derwent. The town was taken by surprise, in 1387, by an army of Scottish borderers, who remained here three days. Mary, Queen of Scots, after her escape from the castle of Dunbar, rested some time at Cockermouth, on her way from Workington to Carlisle, and was also hospitably entertained at Hutton Hall, then belonging to the Fletchers. During the civil war of the 17th century, the castle was besieged in August, 1648, by a body of 500 Cumberland royalists, but was relieved on September 29th by Lieut.-Col. Ashton, whom Cromwell had

market-place, and on Saturday is a market for visions, &c. Fairs for cattle are held on every rnate Wednesday from the beginning of May till end of September; and there is a great fair for horses d horned-cattle on the 10th of October; also two great rs, or statutes, for hiring servants, on the Mondays Whitsuntide and Martinmas. The town has no arate jurisdiction: the chief officer is a bailiff, who is sen at Michaelmas, at the court leet for the manor, m among the burghers, by a jury of burghers appointed for regulating the affairs of the town; he acts clerk of the market, but exercises no magisterial ctions, and has no local authority. In the 23rd of ward I. the borough returned members to parliament, t from that date till the 16th of Charles I. the elective nchise was suspended; it was then restored by a solution of the house of commons, and from that riod has been exercised without intermission. The ht of voting for the two members was formerly vested the burgage tenants, about 300 in number; but, by act of the 2nd of William IV., cap. 45, was extended the £10 householders of an enlarged district, which elective purposes was substituted for the ancient rough: the old borough comprised 3000 acres, and boundaries of the new contain 9500: the bailiff is turning officer. The county magistrates exercise jurisction within the borough, and hold a petty-session ery Monday. The steward of the manor holds a court ery three weeks, for the recovery of debts under 40s., d a court leet at Michaelmas and Easter; and aided r commissioners appointed for the government of the veral manors within the honour, he also holds, at hristmas, a court of dimissions in the castle. The wers of the county debt-court of Cockermouth, established in 1847, extend over the greater part of the gistration-district of Cockermouth. The Epiphany arter-session for the county is held here in January; d this is the principal place of election for the eastern vision of the county. The Moot-hall, an old dilapidated ructure inconveniently situated in the market-place, has en rebuilt in a commodious manner, and on a more gible site. There is a small house of correction in :. Helen's street.

The living is a perpetual curacy; net income, £132; tron, the Earl of Lonsdale. The tithes of the chapelry ere commuted for land in 1813, and under the recent t for a rent-charge of £150; the glebe contains acres. The old church or chapel, erected in the ign of Edward III., was taken down, with the excepon of the tower, and the present edifice of freestone ilt by means of a brief, in 1711, and dedicated to All ints; it was enlarged in 1825. There are places of orship for the Society of Friends, Independents, and 'esleyans. A free grammar school was founded in 76, by Lord Wharton, Sir Richard Graham, and hers, the income being £24 per annum. Other schools e supported by subscription, and the poor have the oduce of several benefactions. The union of Cockeouth comprises forty-seven parishes or places, and ntains a population of 35,676. The hills on each side the Derwent are interesting to the naturalist, consistg of calcareous stone, almost entirely composed of ells of the genus *ammoniæ*. On the north side of the wn is a tumulus, called Toot-hill; and one mile westard are the rampart and ditch of a fort or encamp-
651

ment, triangular in form, and nearly 750 feet in circumference. William Wordsworth, the eminent poet and laureate, was born here in 1770.

COCKERSAND-ABBEY, an extra-parochial liberty, in the union of LANCASTER, hundred of LONSDALE south of the Sands, N. division of the county of LANCASTER, 7 miles (S. W. by S.) from Lancaster. The earliest notice connected with the celebrated abbey of Cockersand, appears to be in the charter of William de Lancaster, who granted to Hugh, a hermit, certain lands and his fishery upon the Lune, to maintain an hospital. This was followed by other grants; and Theobald Walter, among other donors, gave to the hospital the moss of Pilling. A grant was subsequently obtained from the abbey at Leicester, and in 1190 Pope Clement III. elevated the house into a monastery, as the abbey of St. Mary, of the Præmonstratensian order, of Cockersand. The numerous grants which followed extended its possessions very widely, and in point of revenue it ranked the third among the religious houses of Lancashire; yet in a petition, 2nd Richard II., for a confirmation of their charters, the monks style themselves "the king's poor chaplains," and "pray for a consideration of their poverty, and that they are daily exposed to the perils of drowning and destruction by the sea." On the Dissolution the site was leased by the crown, and afterwards became possessed by various families, among whom, in the reign of Philip and Mary, were the Daltons, to which family it continues to belong. The ruins of the abbey stand on a neck of land which projects into the sea on the sands of Cocker. Originally the buildings covered nearly an acre of land, but the octagonal chapter-house, 30 feet in diameter, used for the burial-place of the Daltons, alone remains; and the windows of even this small portion no longer retain their glass: a finely clustered column in the centre of the interior supports moulded arches resting upon smaller columns of the angles. The area of the ruins is strewed with parts of walls, massive stones, and obliterated ornaments. The site is a rock of red friable freestone, which might once have fortified it against the encroachments of the sea, but which is now often beaten against by the fury of the tides, and the bones of the cemetery washed away.

COCKERTON, a township, in the parish and union of DARLINGTON, S. E. division of DARLINGTON ward, S. division of the county of DURHAM, 1¼ mile (N. W. by N.) from Darlington; containing 482 inhabitants. The soil, which is loamy, is in general good. The village is neatly built; its inhabitants were formerly employed in the linen manufacture, but the trade has been removed to Barnsley. Divine service is performed every Wednesday, by permission of the bishop, in the national schoolroom, built in 1825; and there is a place of worship for Wesleyans. A gold coin, and several copper coins, were found in a large stone jar, in the beck, in 1836.

COCKEY-MOOR.—See AINSWORTH.

COCKFIELD, a parish in the union of TEESDALE, S. W. division of DARLINGTON ward, S. division of the county of DURHAM, 12 miles (N. W. by W.) from Darlington; containing, with the township of Woodland, 944 inhabitants. This parish comprises 4416a. 20p., whereof 400 acres form a common of uninclosed land; the soil is clay, with a substratum of freestone of a most
4 O 2

excellent and durable quality, the ancient church of Darlington, which was built with it, being still in high preservation. The great basaltic dyke, bisecting a dyke of earlier formation, runs through the parish; and there is coal, the mines of which, though they have been wrought for nearly five centuries, are even now slightly productive. An extension of the Stockton and Darlington railway, from St. Helen's station to Cockfield, is of great convenience for the transport of produce. The living is a discharged rectory, with the vicarage of Staindrop, lately annexed, valued in the king's books at £9. 18., and in the gift of the Duke of Cleveland: the tithes of the parish have been commuted for £220, and the glebe consists of 16 acres, with a house. There is a place of worship for Wesleyans. On Cockfield Fell are traces of ancient intrenchments. This was the birthplace of the ingenious Jeremiah and George Dixon, of whom the former, more particularly, was employed in scientific investigations of importance.

COCKFIELD (St. Peter), a parish, in the union of Cosford, hundred of Babergh, W. division of Suffolk, 4¼ miles (N. by W.) from Lavenham; containing 951 inhabitants. The living is a rectory, valued in the king's books at £30, and in the patronage of St. John's College, Cambridge; net income, £635. The church has a large and handsome tower.

COCKHILL, Somerset.—See Castle-Cary.

COCKING, a parish, in the union of Midhurst, hundred of Easebourne, rape of Chichester, W. division of Sussex, 2½ miles (S.) from Midhurst; containing 464 inhabitants. It is situated on the road from London through Midhurst, to Chichester, and comprises 2267 acres, including a portion of the Downs. The living is a vicarage, valued in the king's books at £13. 6. 8., and in the patronage of the Bishop of Chichester. The church is in the early English style, with some later additions.

COCKINGTON, a parish, in the union of Newton-Abbot, hundred of Haytor, Paignton and S. divisions of Devon, 2½ miles (W.) from Torbay; containing 203 inhabitants. This place is of considerable antiquity, and appears to have obtained a degree of importance at an early period; in 1297, the inhabitants received the grant of a market and a fair, both which have long been discontinued. The living is a perpetual curacy, annexed to that of Tor-Mohun; impropriator, the Rev. Roger Mallock. The church contains an octagonal font and a wooden screen. Queen Elizabeth leased the rectory of Tor-Mohun, and the church of Cockington, to Sir George Cary, who in 1609 erected almshouses here for seven persons, with an endowment of £30 per annum.

COCKLAW, a township, in the parish of St. John Lee, union of Hexham, S. division of Tindale ward and of Northumberland, 4½ miles (N. by E.) from Hexham; containing 172 inhabitants. It is chiefly distinguished for its strong old fortress, called Cocklaw or Cockley Tower, in 1567 the principal seat of the family of Errington, who derived their name from a small hamlet on the Erring burn, where they were seated in 1372. The township extends from the North Tyne along the eastern side of the burn, and the Roman Watling-street passes on the east a small distance from the village. The impropriate tithes have been commuted for £224.

ndon, through Ipswich, to Norwich, and bounded the south-west by the Stow-Market and Ipswich navigation; it comprises 2585a. 3r., of which 1721a. 1r. ?. are in Crowfield, and contains some extensive chalk-s. Petty-sessions are held monthly. The living is a arage, endowed with the rectorial tithes, and valued the king's books at £12. 0. 5.; patron, the Rev. J. nge: the tithes have been commuted for £637. 7. 6., d the glebe contains nearly 29 acres, and a house. e church is a handsome structure in the decorated nglish style, with a square embattled tower at the st end of the north aisle; the window of the chancel embellished with stained glass, the gift of the family Longe. The Rev. Balthazar Gardemau, vicar, vested e impropriation in trustees for the use of the vicar r ever; and in 1758, his widow, Lady Catherine, ected a commodious school, with an endowment in d now producing a rental of £70 per annum.

CODDINGTON (St. Mary), a parish, in the union Great Boughton, Higher division of the hundred Broxton, S. division of the county of Chester; mprising the townships of Alderley, Chowley, and ddington; and containing 324 inhabitants, of whom 9 are in the township of Coddington, 2 miles (S. S. W.) om Handley. This place is supposed to have been a bitation of the Britons. In 1093, it appears to have en held by two brothers, Hugh and Ralph, the former whom was Baron of Hawarden, and the Earl of Ches-r's chamberlain, and the latter the earl's butler. In e 31st of Edward III., Hawiss, widow of Ralph Botiler, aimed to have a market here every Monday, and a ir on the eve and festival of the Exaltation of the Holy ross. The parish comprises 2957a. 1r. 5p., about one-ird of which is arable: in Coddington township are 337 acres, whereof the soil is clay. The living is discharged rectory, valued in the king's books at .5. 4. 2., and in the gift of the Dean and Chapter of hester: the incumbent's tithes have been commuted r £247, and the glebe consists of 3 acres; certain nppropriate tithes have been commuted for £128. The te church, an ancient structure with a wooden belfry, upposed to have been founded in the eleventh century, as granted, with the living, to Chester Abbey, by itz-Hugh, and was one of the few possessions remain-g to the abbey that were confirmed to the Dean and hapter by Queen Elizabeth. This church was taken own in 1833, and a new edifice erected at a cost of 1600. In the middle of a field called the Mudd-field, a tumulus of uncertain origin, which has never been pened: iron bits of a very large size have been found a a corner of the same field, and a causeway has been raced under ground. John Stone, rector of this parish, nd sacrist of the cathedral of Chester, brought hither he communion-plate of that cathedral, and buried it in he church, underneath a seat in the chancel, during the ebellion in 1745.

CODDINGTON (All Saints), a parish, in the union f Ledbury, hundred of Radlow, county of Here-ord, 3 miles (N.) from Ledbury; containing 158 in-abitants, and consisting of 1064 acres. The living is discharged rectory, valued in the king's books at 4. 18. 4., and in the patronage of the Bishop of Here-ord: the tithes have been commuted for a yearly rent-harge of £180, and the glebe comprises 34 acres, with a lebe-house.

653

CODDINGTON (All Saints), a parish, in the union of Newark, S. division of the wapentake [of Newark and of the county of Nottingham, 2¼ miles (E. by N.) from Newark; containing 436 inhabitants. It com-prises by measurement 1500 acres: limestone is quarried for building and for burning into lime. The living is annexed, with that of Syerston, to the vicarage of East Stoke: the tithes were commuted for land in 1760. The church is a small structure, principally in the early and decorated English styles. There is a place of wor-ship for Wesleyans. Joseph Birch, in 1738, bequeathed 98a. 2r. 8p. of land, part of the proceeds of which is paid to a master for teaching children, and the remain-der distributed among the poor.

CODFORD (St. Mary), a parish, in the union of Warminster, hundred of Heytesbury, Warminster and S. divisions of Wilts, 2 miles (N. W.) from Wily; containing 338 inhabitants. This parish, situated on the river Wily, and the road from Bristol to Portsmouth, comprises 2123 acres, of which 661 are common or waste; the soil is chalk, of which there are some pits, whence are taken materials for building cottages and for the roads. The living is a rectory, valued in the king's books at £18, and in the patronage of St. John's Col-lege, Oxford: the tithes have been commuted for £345, and the glebe, including a portion of downland, com-prises about 95 acres. The church was nearly rebuilt in 1844; it was a very ancient structure, supposed to have been built anterior to the Conquest, and had a Norman arch, surmounting one of plainer character, thought to be of Saxon architecture. There is a place of worship for Independents. The remains of a British camp are to be seen.

CODFORD (St. Peter), a parish, in the union of Warminster, hundred of Heytesbury, Warminster and S. divisions of Wilts, 3 miles (E. S. E.) from Hey-tesbury; containing, with the township of Ashton-Gifford, 394 inhabitants, and consisting of 1614 acres. The living is a rectory, valued in the king's books at £17. 15.; net income, £380; patrons, the Master and Fellows of Pembroke College, Oxford: the glebe com-prises about 8 acres.

CODICOTE (St. Giles), a parish, in the union of Hitchin, hundred of Cashio, or liberty of St. Alban's, though locally in the hundred of Broadwater, county of Hertford, 1½ mile (N. N. W.) from Welwyn; con-taining 906 inhabitants. The parish is intersected by the London and Bedford road, and comprises 2433 acres; the soil is gravel, alternated with clay. At Sissifernes, in the parish, the soil is particularly favour-able to the growth of walnuts. Many females are occupied in making straw-plat for hats and bonnets. There were formerly a chartered market on Friday, and a fair on St. James' day, both of which are discontinued; but a small market for the sale of straw-plat is held on Thursday, and a pleasure-fair on Whit-Monday. The living is a discharged vicarage, valued in the king's books at £7. 5. 10., and in the gift of the Bishop of Ely: the vicarial tithes have been commuted for £150, and tithes belonging to the bishop for £500; there is a glebe of 30 acres. The church is a small building, with a chapel attached, and has an embattled tower sur-mounted by a spire. Here is a place of worship for Baptists. On Codicote heath are the remains of a Roman fortification.

CODNOR, with Loscoe, an ecclesiastical parish or district, partly in the parishes of DENBY and PENTRICH, union of BELPER, but chiefly in the parish of HEANOR, union of BASFORD, hundred of MORLESTON and LITCHURCH, S. division of DERBYSHIRE, 2 miles (N. by W.) from Heanor. This district comprises the township of Codnor and Loscoe, in Heanor parish, containing 1738 inhabitants, of whom 1314 are in Codnor; the extra-parochial liberty of Codnor-Park, with 815 inhabitants; and portions of Denby and Pentrich. The township comprises 1894 acres, and the liberty 1320. The manor of Codnor was held at the Domesday survey, under William Peverel; and belonged to the family of Grey as early as 1211, when Codnor Castle became the seat of the elder branch of that noble house. Richard de Grey was one of the loyal barons in the reign of Henry III.; and John, Lord Grey, distinguished himself in the Scottish wars, in that of Edward III. The last lord Grey, of Codnor, died about 1526; he was a philosopher and alchymist, and had a licence to practise the transmutation of metals. The estate eventually devolved to Sir John Zouch, who sold it in 1634 to Archbishop Neile and his son Sir Paul; and their descendant disposed of the manor and castle, with the members, to Sir Streynsham Master, high sheriff in 1712, who occupied the castle. The park contained about 3200 acres; and it is said that six farmhouses, with their out-buildings, were raised with the materials taken from the ruins of Codnor Castle.

The district lies on the eastern confines of the county, and the land is nearly equally divided between arable and pasture; the higher parts command extensive views. Coal and ironstone are wrought, employing many of the population, and the Butterley Iron Company have three blast-furnaces here; there is also a manufactory of stone-ware bottles, and frame-work knitting is carried on. Facility of conveyance is afforded both by canal and railway. The parish was formed by the Ecclesiastical Commissioners, under the act 6 and 7 Victoria, cap. 37; the living is a perpetual curacy, endowed with £150 per annum, and in the gift of the Crown and the Bishop of Lichfield, alternately. The church, dedicated to St. James, was consecrated in 1844, and is a neat building with a tower. There are places of worship for Baptists and Wesleyans; and good schools on the national system. The sum of £11 per annum was left in 1731 by Jonathan Tantum, two-thirds to the poor, and one-third to the Society of Friends. Loscoe Park has been long disparked, and the house, for several generations the seat of the Draycotts, pulled down.

CODSALL (ST. NICHOLAS), a parish, in the union, and S. division of the hundred, of SEISDON, S. division of the county of STAFFORD, 5 miles (N. W.) from Wolverhampton; containing, with the township of Oaken, 1096 inhabitants. The parish comprises 2869 acres, whereof 1568 are in Codsall township; the soil is loamy; about one-third pasture, and the rest arable: stone is quarried for building. The road from Wolverhampton to Shrewsbury passes along the south-western boundary. The village is picturesquely seated on an eminence, and there are several neat villas. The living is a perpetual curacy; net income, £146; patron, Lord Wrottesley; impropriator, the Duke of Sutherland, whose tithes have been commuted for £172. 13. 6. The

l the chancel is a handsome altar-tomb. In 1695, illiam Blake bequeathed land producing about £50 annum, chiefly for instruction. To the south of the rch, on a spot called Castle Yard, foundations, supped to be those of a castle, are frequently dug up; l at Wilcot, in the parish, is an old chapel, in which the arms of the family of Pope, and a mural tablet the memory of John Price, keeper of the Bodleian rary at Oxford.

COGGESHALL, GREAT (St. Peter), a marketwn and parish, in the union of Witham, Witham ision of the hundred of Lexden, N. division of sex, 3 miles (N.) from Kelvedon, and 44 (N. E.) from ndon; containing 3408 inhabitants, of whom 443 are the hamlet of Little Coggeshall. This place is supsed by some to have been the Roman station *Ad Anm*, and by others the *Canonium* of Antoninus, with the stance of which latter from *Cæsaromagus* its situation cisely corresponds : numerous vestiges of Roman tiquity have been discovered. The present town pears to have risen from the establishment of an bey in 1142, by King Stephen and his Queen Matilda, r monks of the Cistercian order, and in honour of e Blessed Virgin; to the abbot and monks of which ng John granted several privileges, including, probly, the power of life and death, as is inferred from e ancient name of one of the streets, still by some lled Gallows-street. Henry III. granted them free arren, a weekly market, and an annual fair for eight ys. The revenue of the abbey at the Dissolution was ?98. 8. : the remains, which exhibit specimens of early nglish architecture, are now occupied as a farmhouse; e exterior has lancet-shaped windows in good prervation, and in the interior are some good windows id vaulted and groined roofs. Near the abbey is an cient bridge of three arches, built by Stephen, over canal cut for conveying water from the river to the onastery.

The town is situated near the river Blackwater, from hich it rises gradually to a considerable elevation, and nsists of several narrow streets; it was first lighted th gas in 1837, and the inhabitants are amply supied with water from springs in the neighbourhood. e manufacture of baize and serge, formerly extensive, now extinct; the principal branch of trade is silkeaving, which has been established within the last 30 ars. In 1838, Mr. John Hall erected a silk-throwing ill, capable of employing 500 persons, and Messrs. 'estmacott and Co. have 100 looms at work weaving oad silks and velvets; in 1826, Mr. Bankes commenced the tambour-work on lace-net, in which about)0 females are engaged, and in 1838 introduced a imber of machines for weaving lace-net. An extensive on-foundry and steam flour-mill have been erected by harles Newman, Esq. The place is noted for its getables and garden-seeds. The market is on Thursy: the market-place is spacious, and contained an d cross, which was taken down in 1787. A fair for ittle and pedlery is held on Whit-Tuesday.

Coggeshall anciently comprised the parishes of Great id Little Coggeshall, at present consolidated : in the tter were two churches, built by the monks; one for eir own use, which has been entirely demolished, and e other for a parochial church, the remains whereof ive been converted into a barn. The parish comprises

655

by computation 2300 acres, 300 of which are wood-land; the soil is various, in some parts a strong loam resting on a clay bottom, in others a stiff wet loam on a whitish marl, and in the neighbourhood of the town a rich deep loam of great fertility. The living is a vicarage, valued in the king's books at £11. 3. 4.; net income, £215; patron, Peter Du Cane, Esq., lord of the manor; impropriators, Charles Skingley, Esq., and Mrs. Caswell. The church is a spacious handsome structure in the later English style, with a large tower; the aisles are embattled, and strengthened with empanelled buttresses : the interior contains several ancient monuments. There are places of worship for Baptists, the Society of Friends, Independents, and Wesleyans. A school, under the direction of Pembroke Hall, Cambridge, was founded in 1636, by Sir Robert Hitcham, Knt., who bequeathed land producing £300 per annum. Silver and copper coins of Ethelwulph, and a massive gold ring, have been dug up on the Highfields estate.

COGSHALL, a township, in the parish of Great Budworth, union of Northwich, hundred of Bucklow, N. division of the county of Chester, 3½ miles (N. N. W.) from Northwich; containing 108 inhabitants. The manor was possessed by the Lacys, from whom it reverted to the crown as parcel of the duchy of Lancaster; the lands were purchased in fee-farm in 1612. Burges Hall, now Cogshall Hall, belonged to the ancient family of Burges, from whom the estate passed to the Starkeys, Booths, Ashtons, and others. The township comprises 560 acres, of a clayey and sandy soil. Tradition reports, that on a steep sandy eminence called Butter Hill, the market people from the hundred of Wirral deposited their butter and other produce when the plague excluded them from the market-place at Chester.

COKER, EAST (St. Michael), a parish, in the union of Yeovil, hundred of Houndsborough, Barwick, and Coker, W. division of Somerset, 3 miles (S. W. by W.) from Yeovil; containing, with the hamlet of North Coker, 1334 inhabitants, and comprising by measurement 2081 acres. Nearly one-half of the population is employed in the manufacture of sail-cloth, which is carried on to a great extent; and limestone, and stone for building and for the roads, are quarried. The living is a vicarage, valued in the king's books at £12. 6. 3.; patrons, the Dean and Chapter of Exeter; impropriator, W. Helyar, Esq., as lessee under the Dean and Chapter. The rectorial tithes have been commuted for £335, and the vicarial for £267. 10.; the glebe comprises 7 acres, with a glebe-house. The church is a neat cruciform edifice, with a central tower. There is a place of worship for Baptists. The foundations of a Roman building were discovered in a field in 1753; one of the rooms had a beautiful pavement representing persons lying on a couch, beneath which were found a hypocaust, several coffins, burnt bones, &c. There are remains of a religious house, called Nash Abbey, in the parish, supposed to have been an appendage to that of Montacute. Dampier, the celebrated circumnavigator, was born here in 1652.

COKER, WEST (St. Martin), a parish, in the union of Yeovil, hundred of Houndsborough, Barwick, and Coker, W. division of Somerset, 3½ miles (S. W. by W.) from Yeovil; containing 1046 inhabitants, and consisting of about 1300 acres. The living is a rectory, valued in the king's books at £12. 19. 7.; patron, R. Raven, Esq.: the tithes have been commuted for £425, and the glebe comprises 17 acres, with a glebe-house. The church has been enlarged, by the addition of 316 sittings. There is a school, endowed with the interest of a bequest of £100; also almshouses for five persons, founded about 1719, pursuant to the will of William Ruddock.

COLAN (St. Colan), a parish, in the union of St. Columb Major, hundred of Pyder, E. division of Cornwall, 3½ miles (S. W. by W.) from St. Columb Major; containing 217 inhabitants, and comprising 1481 acres, of which 150 are common or waste. The barton of Colan belonged to the ancient family of Colan or St. Colan, whose last heir-male, about the year 1500, left two daughters, the elder married to one of the Blewetts, of Holcombe-Rogus, in Devonshire, and the other to a member of the family of Trefusis. The Blewetts resided here for several generations, and one of the family, Major Colan Blewett, distinguished himself as an active officer under Charles I., and is said to have had four brothers engaged in the same service. The parish contains the villages of Bezoan, Melancoose, and Mountjoy. The living is a discharged vicarage, endowed with a portion of the rectorial tithes, and valued in the king's books at £6. 13. 4.; net income, £163; patron, the Bishop of Exeter; impropriator of the remainder of the rectorial tithes, Sir R. Vyvyan, Bart. The church contains a monument to the memory of Thomas and Elizabeth Blewett, with a brass plate, on which their effigies, and those of their thirteen sons and eleven daughters are engraved. There are two places of worship for Wesleyans. In the parish is a celebrated spring, called Our Lady of Nantz' Well.

COLBOURNE, a township, in the parish of Catterick, union of Richmond, wapentake of Hang-East, N. riding of York, 2½ miles (S. E. by E.) from Richmond; containing 142 inhabitants. This place, which derives its name from a stream, or burn, that falls into the river Swale a little below the village, comprises by computation 1240 acres of land. The ancient Hall, now a farmhouse, was a seat of the D'Arcy family; and near it are the remains of a Roman Catholic chapel, which was dedicated to St. Ann.

COLBY (St. Giles), a parish, in the union of Aylsham, hundred of South Erpingham, E. division of Norfolk, 3¼ miles (N. E. by N.) from Aylsham; containing 346 inhabitants. It comprises 1115a. 1r. 18p., of which about 868 acres are arable, 177 pasture and meadow, and nearly 28 wood and plantation. The living is a discharged rectory, valued in the king's books at £8. 15. 10., and in the gift of Lord Suffield: the tithes have been commuted for £360, and the glebe contains 7a. 27p., with a glebe-house. The church had a north aisle, which was taken down in 1748, when the church was thoroughly repaired; the font is elaborately sculptured, and to the south side of the chancel is attached a beautiful piscina. Thomas de Colby, D.D., Bishop of Lismore and Waterford, who died in 1460, was a native of the parish.

COLBY, a township, in the parish of St. Lawrence, Appleby, East ward and union, county of Westmorland, 1½ mile (W. by N.) from Appleby; containing 156 inhabitants. The village is situated on an eminence, at the base of which flows the river Eden.

COLCHESTER, a borough and market-town, having separate jurisdiction, and the head of a union, locally in the Colchester division of the hundred of Lexden, N. division of Essex, 22 miles (N. E. by E.) from Chelmsford, and 51 (N. E. by E.) from London; containing, with the parishes of Bere-Church, Greenstead, Lexden, and

Arms.

Mile-End, all within the liberties, 17,790 inhabitants. This place, which by some antiquaries is supposed to have been the *Camalodunum* of the Romans, derives its name either from its having been one of the *Coloniæ* established by that people in Britain, or from its situation on the river Colne. It was called by the Britons *Caer Colun*, and appears to have been a town of considerable importance prior to the invasion of the Romans, who, according to Tacitus and other historians, having, under the conduct of Claudius, subdued the Trinobantes and taken possession of this town, garrisoned it with the second, ninth, and fourteenth legions, styled by him the conquerors of Britain. The Roman name of the place is said to have been derived from an altar dedicated to Mars, under the name of Camulus, by which also that divinity is designated on some coins, still extant, of Cunobeline, King of the Trinobantes, who, prior to the conquest by the Romans, had his residence here. Claudius, having reduced the neighbouring country to a Roman province, appointed Platins his proprætor, and returned in triumph to Rome. After his departure, Boadicea, queen of the Iceni, taking advantage of the absence of part of the Roman legions, attacked *Camalodunum*, which, after a feeble resistance, she entirely demolished; but according to Pliny, and the evidence of Roman coins and other ancient inscriptions, it appears to have been soon rebuilt with increased splendour, and to have been adorned with public edifices, a temple to Claudius, a triumphal arch, and a statue to the goddess of Victory; and Constantine the Great is traditionally said to have been born in the city, which continued to flourish as a principal station of the Romans till their final departure from Britain. The Saxons, by whom it was afterwards occupied, gave it the name of *Colne-ceaster*, and it retained its consequence as a place of strength for a considerable time, but began to decline in proportion as London rose into importance. On the irruption of the Danes, it became a principal residence of that people, who, by treaty with Alfred, were established in the city and country adjacent; but re-commencing their barbarous system of plunder and devastation, Edward the Elder, in 921, took the town by assault, and putting them all to the sword, re-peopled it with West Saxons. According to the Saxon Chronicles, he repaired the walls in 922, at which time he is stated to have erected the castle, now falling to decay; but the remains of that edifice are evidently of Norman character.

Colchester was a considerable town at the time of the Norman survey, but suffered greatly in the wars of th succeeding reigns. During the turbulent reign of John Saher de Quincy, Earl of Winchester, having assemble n army of foreigners, laid siege to the place in 1215; ut on the approach of the barons, who were advancing om London to its relief, he drew off his forces and rered to Bury St. Edmund's : he afterwards got posseson of the town, and, having plundered it, left a garrison the castle, which, being invested by the king, was ompelled to surrender. The castle was subsequently esieged and taken by the troops of Prince Louis, whom he barons had invited into England to their assistance, nd who, thinking the opportunity favourable for conuest, kept possession of it for himself, and hoisted the anner of France upon its walls ; but the barons, having ubmitted to their new sovereign, Henry III., retook the astle from the prince, and expelled him from the kingom. In the reign of Edward III., the town contriuted 5 ships and 170 mariners towards the naval armanent for the blockade of Calais. The inhabitants, during he attempt to raise Lady Jane Grey to the throne, stedastly adhered to the interests of Mary, whose cause hey supported with so much zeal, that, very soon after er accession, the queen visited the town for the express urpose of testifying her gratitude : she was received with every public demonstration of joy, and, on her departure, was presented with a silver cup, and £20 in gold. During her reign many of the Protestant townspeople were put to death on account of their religious tenets. In 1648, the inhabitants, who during the contest between the king and the parliament had generally espoused the cause of the latter, for whose support they had raised considerable supplies of money, finding it necessary to restrain its inordinate power, formed an alliance with the royalists, who, being closely pressed by the parliamentarians, took up their station in the town, into which they were admitted by the inhabitants by treaty. The town was soon afterwards besieged by the army under Fairfax, who had been joined on his march by Col. Whalley and Sir Thomas Honeywood with 2000 horse and foot ; and after a close blockade for eleven weeks, during which period the place was gallantly defended by the Earl of Norwich, Lord Capel, Sir Charles Lucas, and Sir George Lisle, the garrison, reduced to the extremity of want and suffering, surrendered to Fairfax, when Sir Charles Lucas and Sir George Lisle were shot under the castle walls.

The TOWN is built on the summit and northern acclivity of an eminence rising gently from the river Colne, over which are three bridges ; and occupies a quadrilateral area inclosed by the ancient walls, within which the houses to the south and south-east are irregularly disposed. The streets are spacious, and the High-street contains many excellent houses ; the town is well paved, lighted with gas, and supplied with water by an engine worked by steam. A splendid hotel was erected in 1842-3, adjoining the railway terminus, in the Italian style. The theatre, a neat and commodious edifice, erected in 1812, is opened annually by the Norwich company. A botanical society was instituted in 1823 ; and there is a medical society, established in 1774. The barracks here, with a park of artillery, were capable of accommodating 10,000 troops ; but since the conclusion of the war they have been taken down. The woollenmanufacture appears to have been carried on so early as the reign of Edward III.; the weaving of baizes, for which the town was afterwards distinguished, was probably introduced by the Flemings in the reign of Eliza.

beth, and at that time employed a considerable number of the inhabitants. This manufacture was subject to certain regulations prescribed by the Baize-hall ; it has been transferred to other towns. A large silk-throwing mill, established in 1825, affords occupation to about 300 hands ; and there is a distillery, employing about 50 men ; also a rectifying-house. The oyster-fishery on the river Colne, granted to the free burgesses by Richard I., confirmed by subsequent charters, and for the preservation of which courts of admiralty were and are still occasionally held at Mersea Stone, about 8 miles from the borough, but now generally at the town-hall, affords employment to about 600 licensed dredgemen ; and numerous smacks are engaged in conveying to London the oysters, for which there is a very great demand, especially for those of Pyfleet, which are found in a small creek, and are remarkable for their flavour. The river is navigable to the suburb called the Hythe, where are a spacious quay and a custom-house. The Eastern Counties railway from London extends to this town ; and, in junction with that line, commences the railway between Colchester and Ipswich, which was opened in June 1846. The markets are on Wednesday and Saturday, the latter being the principal for corn and provisions, and also a large mart for cattle and sheep : the market-place is on the north side of the High-street, and is commodiously arranged. The corn-exchange, erected a few years since, is a handsome building ; the interior is 78 feet by 47, and is lighted by 19 skylights along the sides of the hall, and a clerestory lantern over the centre of it. The fairs are on July 5th and the following day ; July 23rd and two following days, for cattle ; and Oct. 20th for cattle, and the three following days for general merchandise. There was formerly another fair, called the Tailors' fair, from its having been granted by William III. in the same charter which incorporated the tailors of Colchester, December 15th, 1699.

[Corporation Seal.

Obverse.   *Reverse.*

This is supposed to be a BOROUGH by prescription : it was first incorporated in 1189, by charter of Richard I., who conferred on the inhabitants many valuable privileges, which were confirmed by succeeding sovereigns, and extended by Henry V. : the charter having been forfeited on several occasions, was renewed by George III. in 1818. By the act of the 5th and 6th of William IV., cap. 76, the corporation now consists of a mayor, six aldermen, and eighteen councillors ; and the borough is divided into three wards, the municipal and parliamentary boundaries being co-extensive. The mayor for the time being. and for the previous year, are justices by virtue of office ; and there are seven others. The borough first exercised the elective franchise in the 23rd of Edward I., since which time it has, with occasional intermissions, returned two members to parliament. The right of election was formerly vested in the free burgesses generally, whose number was about 1400; but by the act of the 2nd of William IV., cap. 45, non-resident burgesses, except within seven miles, were disfranchised, and the privilege was extended to the £10 householders of the borough, the limits of which comprise 11,055 acres. The mayor is returning officer. The recorder presides at quarterly courts of session for the borough and liberties, together extending over sixteen parishes; and the mayor and recorder hold two courts of pleas for the recovery of debts to any amount, the jurisdiction of which was extended by Edward IV. to the adjoining parishes of Bere-Church, Greenstead, Lexden, and Mile-End. These two courts are held at stated periods: one, styled the Law Hundred, for actions against free burgesses, is on Monday; and the other, called the Foreign Court, for actions against strangers or non-freemen, is on Thursday. The petty-sessions for the division are also held in the town, every Saturday. The powers of the county debt-court of Colchester, established in 1847, extend over the registration-districts of Colchester, and Lexden and Winstree, and part of Tendring district. The Town-hall, erected from the designs of Messrs. Blore and Brandon, was opened March 1st, 1845: it is of the Roman-Doric order; the front is divided by pilasters into five compartments, and is surmounted by a bold cornice and balustrade with a central compartment bearing the borough arms.

Colchester, upon very disputed authority, is supposed to have been the seat of a diocese in the early period of Christianity in Britain: Henry VIII. made it the seat of a suffragan bishop, and two bishops were successively consecrated. The town comprises within the walls the twelve PARISHES of All Saints, containing 492 inhabitants; St. James, 1603; St. Martin, 937; St. Mary-at-the-Walls, 1272; St. Nicholas, 1087; St. Peter, 1916; St. Runwald, 444; the Holy Trinity, 768; St. Botolph, 3003; St. Giles, 1987; St. Leonard, or the Hythe, 1119; and St. Mary Magdalen, 365. The four parishes without the walls, namely, Lexden, Bere-Church, Mile-End, and Greenstead, are considered as part of the town, but are described under their respective heads. The living of *All Saints'* is a rectory not in charge, with a net income of £291, and is in the gift of Balliol College, Oxford: the tithes have been commuted for £35. The church, erected in the year 1309, near the east gate of the monastery of Grey friars, which had been founded by Robert Fitzwalter in that year, consists of a nave, north aisle, and chancel, with a handsome tower of flint and stone; the south wall, now covered with cement, is of Roman bricks laid in the herring-bone style. The living of *St. James'* is a discharged rectory, valued in the king's books at £11. 10., and in the patronage of the Crown; net income, £98. The church is a spacious structure, built prior to the reign of Edward II.; it consists of a nave, north and south aisles, and a chancel, with a tower of Roman brick and stone, and has a fine altar-piece representing the Adoration of the Shepherds. *St. Martin's* is a discharged rectory, valued at £6. 13. 4.; net income, £102: the patronage is in dispute. The church, which was much damaged during the siege of the town in 1648, was repewed in 1841, when 50 free sittings were added; the steeple, 658

built with Roman bricks, is in a ruinous state. The living of *St. Mary's-at-the-Walls* is a rectory, valued at £10; net income, £212; patron, the Bishop of London. The tithes have been commuted for £105, and the glebe consists of 14 acres. The church was rebuilt in 1713, with the exception of the ancient steeple, which, becoming ruinous, was repaired in 1729; it contains some ancient monuments: the churchyard is surrounded with avenues of lime-trees, and is much frequented as a promenade. *St. Nicholas'* is a discharged rectory, valued at £10; net income, £92; patrons, the Master and Fellows of Balliol College, Oxford. The church is ancient; the tower some years since fell down upon the nave and chancel, the latter of which is still in a ruinous state. The chapel of St. Helen, in this parish, rebuilt by Eudo in 1076, was lately used as a place of worship by the Society of Friends, and is now a Sunday school. *St. Peter's* is a discharged vicarage, valued at £10; net income, £285; patrons, the Trustees of the late Rev. Charles Simeon. The church, an ancient structure, was erected before the Conquest, and in Domesday book is noticed as the only church in Colchester; it was extensively repaired and modernised in 1758, when the tower at the west end was erected, and was some time since greatly beautified at an expense of £3000: the altar-piece is embellished with a fine painting, by Halls, of the Raising of Jairus' Daughter. *St. Runwald's* is a discharged rectory, valued at £7. 13. 4.; net income, £160; patron, Charles Grey Round, Esq. The church, which is small, was erected about the close of the thirteenth century, and is partly of brick and partly of stone, with a wooden turret rising from the centre. The living of the parish of the *Holy Trinity* is a discharged rectory, valued at £6. 13. 4.; net income, £158; patrons, the Master and Fellows of Balliol College, Oxford. The tithes have been commuted for £24. The church was erected in the year 1349, and consists of a nave, south aisle, and chancel, with a tower. Only a part of the tower, the west door (now closed up), and a small portion about it, are of early date; but this small part is curious from its near approximation to Roman work, being plastered over bricks, and also from its having a straight-lined arch: the arch into the church is semicircular, and of flat tiling. The edifice contains several ancient and interesting monuments, among which is one to the memory of Dr. William Gilbert, chief physician to Queen Elizabeth and James I., and author of many learned works. *St. Botolph's* is a perpetual curacy, in the patronage of Balliol College, and has a net income of £21: the tithes have been commuted for £230. 7. A new parish church in the Norman style, built under the superintendence of Mr. Mason, of Ipswich, at a cost, including the purchase of the site, of above £7000, was consecrated on the 25th of October, 1837; the doorway and other portions of the western elevation are designed from the Norman tower at Bury St. Edmund's: there are 1079 sittings, of which 815 are free, the Incorporated Society having granted £1000 towards the expense. The old church, which has been in ruins since the siege in 1648, exhibits indications of its original magnificence, and of the antiquity of its style, which appears to have been the early Norman, and of the same date as the neighbouring priory; it was built with bricks of extraordinary hardness, supposed to have been taken from the Roman station. The ving of *St. Giles'* is a discharged rectory, valued at 30; patron and incumbent, the Rev. John Woodrooffe organ, whose tithes have been commuted for £200, d whose glebe comprises one acre and a half, with a ebe-house. The church, a very ancient structure hich has been repaired and enlarged, contains a monument to the memory of Sir Charles Lucas and Sir George isle, who were shot under the walls by order of Fairfax, ter the siege of the town. The living of *St. Leonard's* a discharged rectory, valued at £10; net income, 129; patrons, the Master and Fellows of Balliol Colge. The church is a spacious structure in good preervation, and was once remarkable for the exquisite urved-work of the roof, which, having fallen into decay, as removed. The living of *St. Mary Magdalen's* is a ectory, valued in the king's books at £11, and in the ift of the Crown: the church is small, and pleasantly ituated on Magdalen Green. On the site of the chapel f St. Anne, which stood in the parish of St. James, nd was originally a hermitage, a barn has been erected, art of the chapel being incorporated with the building. here are places of worship for Baptists, Independents, he Society of Friends, and Wesleyans.

The *Free Grammar School* was founded and endowed y the corporation, to whom Queen Elizabeth, in the 6th year of her reign, granted certain ecclesiastical evenues for that purpose: the income amounts to 181. 10. Dr. Harsnet, Archbishop of York, received ie rudiments of his education in the school. *John innock* in 1679 endowed almshouses for aged widows rith a rent-charge of £41, to which several other beneactions were added subsequently; the income now amounts to £235. *Arthur Winsley* in 1726 founded and endowed almshouses for widows whose husbands have since been added. In 1791, *John Kendall* erected and endowed eight almshouses for widows whose husbands have died in Winsley's almshouses, or in default of such, for other single women: the small original endowment having been considerably augmented, the annual income amounts to about £166, and eight additional houses have been erected. Four almshouses for aged women were endowed in 1552 by Ralph Fynch with £6. 6. 8. per annum, to which £5 per annum have been added by John Lyon, and the interest of £262. 10. new four per cent. annuities by W. Godwin, together with £1000 three per cent. consols. for four additional houses: the income amounts to £51. The Essex and Colchester general hospital, completed in 1820, and supported by subscription, is a neat building of white brick, on the south side of the London road. The poor law union of Colchester comprises the twelve parishes within, and the four without, the walls.

Of the monastic establishments anciently existing here, was the hospital founded (at the command of Henry I.) for a master and leprous brethren, and dedicated to *St. Mary Magdalen*, by Eudo, who had been a principal officer of the household to William the Conqueror and his two sons, William and Henry. The revenue at the Dissolution was £11. This hospital was refounded in 1610, by James I., for five poor brethren and a master, who is always the clergyman of the parish. The almshouses have been lately rebuilt, and are now tenanted by five widows, who receive one shilling per week each; the remainder of the income, which is very considerable, being appropriated to the master's use.
659

Of the other establishments, the principal was *St. John's Abbey*, founded in the reign of Henry I. by the same Eudo, for monks of the Benedictine order, and the revenue of which, at the Dissolution, was £523. 17.: of this only the gateway is remaining, a handsome structure in the later English style, either built since the foundation of the abbey, or a subsequent addition to it. To the south of the town was a monastery of Augustine canons, founded in the reign of Henry I., and dedicated to *St. Julian and St. Botolph*, by Ernulphus, who afterwards became prior; at the Dissolution its revenue was £113. 12. 8.: the only remains are its stately church, now in ruins. Without the walls was an hospital, or priory, of *Crutched Friars*, an order introduced into England about 1244; the revenue of which, at the Dissolution, was £7. 7. 8. The priory of *Franciscan* or *Grey Friars* was founded in 1309, by Robert Fitz-Walter; the only probable remains are the parish church of All Saints.

Of the *Walls* by which the borough was surrounded, and in consideration of repairing which Richard II. is recorded to have exempted the burgesses from sending members to three of his parliaments, considerable portions still remain. They were strengthened by bastions, and defended on the west by an ancient fort of Roman construction, the remaining arches of which are built with Roman bricks; the north and west sides, where the town was most exposed, were protected by deep intrenchments. The entrance to the town was by four principal gates and three posterns, which have been mostly demolished. The ruins of the *Castle* occupy an elevated site on the north side of High-street; the form is quadrilateral, and the walls of the keep, twelve feet in thickness, are almost entire. The building is of flint, stone, and Roman brick intermixed, and is supposed to have been originally erected by the Romans, and subsequently repaired by Edward the Elder; the solidity of the structure has frustrated repeated attempts to demolish it, for the sake of the materials. The town and environs abound with relics of antiquity, among which is a quantity of Roman bricks in several of the churches and other buildings; and tessellated pavements, sepulchral urns, statues, lamps, rings, coins, medals, and almost every other species of Roman antiquities, have been discovered. Wm. Gilbert, born in 1540, physician to Elizabeth and James I., and author of a work on the qualities of the loadstone, entitled *De Magnete*, and other publications; and Dr. Samuel Harsnet, Archbishop of York; were natives of the place. The Rt. Hon. Charles Abbot, speaker of the house of commons (whose father was rector of All Saints), was elevated to the peerage, June 3rd, 1817, by the title of Baron Colchester, which is now enjoyed by his son.

COLD-ASHBY, county of NORTHAMPTON.—See ASHBY, COLD.—*And other places having a similar distinguishing prefix will be found under the proper name.*

COLDCOATS, a township, in the parish of PONTE-LAND, union and W. division of CASTLE ward, S. division of NORTHUMBERLAND, 9¼ miles (N. W.) from Newcastle; containing 36 inhabitants. It is situated on the road from Newcastle to Rothbury, and consists of East, West, South, and Middle Coldcoats, comprising together about 1020 acres of farm land. The impropriate tithes have been commuted for £138. 9. 8., payable to Merton College, Oxford, and the vicarial for £24. 3.
4 P 2

COLD

COLDCOTES, a hamlet, in the township of SEA-CROFT, parish and borough of LEEDS, Lower division of the wapentake of SKYRACK, W. riding of YORK; containing 16 inhabitants. A tithe rent-charge of £27 is paid to the Dean and Chapter of Oxford.

COLD-DUNGHILLS, an extra-parochial district, adjoining the parish of ST. CLEMENT, in the borough and union of IPSWICH, E. division of SUFFOLK; containing 66 inhabitants.

COLDHURST, an ecclesiastical parish or district, in the parish of PRESTWICH-CUM-OLDHAM, union of OLD-HAM, hundred of SALFORD, S. division of the county of LANCASTER, 7 miles (N. E. by N.) from Manchester. It is nearly three miles in circumference, and is principally pasture and meadow land, of hilly surface. The turn-pike-road from Oldham to Rochdale passes through it. Coal-mines are wrought, and cotton and hat manufactories carried on. An old Hall here, belonging to Abram Crompton, Esq., is now converted into cottages. The district was constituted in October, 1844, under the act 6th and 7th Victoria, cap. 37, and the erection of a church was commenced in the summer of 1847; it is in the early English style, and built on a site presented by Mr. Crompton. The living is a perpetual curacy; net income, £150; patrons, the Crown and the Bishop of Chester, alternately. Within the district are some fine springs. Coldhurst is said to have been the scene of an action in the rebellion, in which the parliamentarians were defeated.

COLD-MARTIN, a township, in the parish of CHAT-TON, union of GLENDALE, E. division of GLENDALE ward, N. division of NORTHUMBERLAND, 1 mile (E. by S.) from Wooler. The vicarial tithes have been commuted for £16. 12. 7.

COLDMEECE, a township, in the parish of ECCLES-HALL, union of STONE, N. division of the hundred of PIREHILL and of the county of STAFFORD, 3 miles (N. N. E.) from Eccleshall; containing 56 inhabitants. This place, with Millmeece, lies in the Cotes quarter of the parish, and on the east side of the river Sow. Mill-meece is three miles north from Eccleshall, and on the road from that town to Swinnerton.

COLDRED (ST. PANCRAS), a parish, in the union of DOVOR, hundred of BEWSBOROUGH, lathe of ST. AUGUS-TINE, E. division of KENT, 5 miles (N. W. by N.) from Dovor; containing 157 inhabitants. It comprises 1532 acres, of which 60 are in wood. The living is a vicarage, annexed to that of Sibbertswold, and valued in the king's books at £6. 2. 6. The church is surrounded by a trench, inclosing about two acres, with an artificial mount on the northern side, which tradition ascribes to Ceoldred, King of Mercia, from whom the parish is named, and who fought a battle near this spot, in 694, with Ina, King of the West Saxons : it is, however, probably of Roman origin, various relics of that people having been discovered on the site.

COLDREY, an extra-parochial liberty, attached to the parish of FROYLE, in the union and hundred of ALTON, Alton and N. divisions of the county of SOUTH-AMPTON; containing 18 inhabitants, and comprising 194 acres of land.

COLDWELL, a township, in the parish of KIRK-WHELPINGTON, union of BELLINGHAM, N. E. division of TINDALE ward, S. division of NORTHUMBERLAND, 14 miles (W.) from Morpeth; containing 8 inhabitants.

COLEBY, a hamlet, partly in the parish of BURTON-PON-STATHER, and partly in that of WEST HALTON, nion of GLANDFORD-BRIGG, N. division of the wapen-ke of MANLEY, parts of LINDSEY, county of LINCOLN; ntaining 68 inhabitants.

COLEDALE, with PORTINGSCALE, a township, in e parish of CROSTHWAITE, union of COCKERMOUTH, LLERDALE ward above Derwent, W. division of CUM-ERLAND, 3 miles (W.) from Keswick; containing 262 habitants.

COLEFORD, a market-town and chapelry, in the arish of NEWLAND, union of MONMOUTH, hundred of T. BRIAVELL'S, W. division of the county of GLOU-ESTER, 20 miles (W. S. W.) from Gloucester, and 124 W. by N.) from London; containing 2208 inhabitants. his place, which is pleasantly situated on the verge of e county, next Monmouthshire, and bounded on the orth and east by the Forest of Dean, obtained the grant f a market from James I. During the parliamentary ar, a skirmish took place previously to the siege of loucester, between a party of royalists, commanded by ord Herbert, and the parliamentary forces under Col. arrow, when the market-house was destroyed, and Sir ichard Lawdy, major-general of South Wales, and veral officers, were killed: at a subsequent period, uring the same war, the ancient chapel was demolished. he town is situated on the old turnpike-road between loucester and Monmouth, and consists principally of ne spacious street, in which is the market-place; the ouses are in general neat and well built. The environs re pleasant, in some points beautifully picturesque; and n the vicinity are several elegant mansions. Many of the labouring class are employed in extensive iron-works in the neighbourhood. Here is a pottery for the manu-facture of various articles of common ware; and sand-stone is quarried to a considerable extent, the best of which is used for troughs, millstones, &c., and that of inferior quality for drains and walls. There is a tram-road to Monmouth, about five miles distant, for the conveyance of coal and lime: Coleford lies on the edge of the Forest of Dean coal-basin, and some pits have been sunk within its boundary. The market is on Friday; and fairs are held on June 20th for wool, and Dec. 5th for cattle and pedlery; the market-house was rebuilt in 1679, Charles II. contributing £50 towards defraying the expense. The county magistrates hold a petty-session here for a portion of the Forest division. The living is a perpetual curacy; net income, £150; patron, the Bishop of Gloucester and Bristol. The chapel, a very plain structure, built in the reign of Queen Anne, who contributed £300 towards its erection, and rebuilt of stone in 1821 at a cost of £3000, is dedi-cated to All Saints; it has accommodation for about 1000 persons: a new organ was lately erected. There are places of worship for Baptists, Independents, and Wesleyans; and a national school, built in 1837, is sup-ported by subscription. A sum of £200 was bequeathed by Colonel Ollney, the interest to be distributed among the poor at Christmas, in coal and blankets. Vestiges of Offa's Dyke may be distinctly traced in some parts of the town.

COLEFORD, a hamlet, in the parish and hundred of KILMERSDON, E. division of SOMERSET, 6¼ miles (W. by N.) from Frome; containing 825 inhabitants. A market was anciently held here, which has been long

discontinued, and the fair of Coleford, which was much frequented, is now almost entirely disused. A coal-mine near the church, the most southern in the coal-basin of the district, yields chiefly small coal. This place, with the neighbouring hamlets of Lypeat and Kilmersdon, was constituted a chapelry in 1831, when a chapel was erected: the living is a perpetual curacy, in the patron-age of the Vicar of Kilmersdon; net income, £120. There are places of worship for Wesleyans and Inde-pendents; and a school in connexion with the National Society, erected by subscription in 1835. Some remains exist of an ancient church, consisting of the chancel and part of the nave, near the present chapel; and in the village are the ruins of a turret with a stone staircase, and piscina.

COLEMORE, a parish, in the union of PETERS-FIELD, hundred of BARTON-STACEY, Andover and N. divisions of the county of SOUTHAMPTON, 5¾ miles (S. by W.) from Alton; containing 144 inhabitants. This parish, noticed in the Domesday survey and other re-cords under the name of Colmere, is supposed to have derived that appellation from the situation of the greater portion of it, formerly, near the western mere or boun-dary of the ancient forest of Wolmer, where great quan-tities of charcoal were made. It comprises about 1400 acres, of which the soil is fertile, the surface is elevated, and the scenery abounds in sylvan beauty. The living is a rectory, with the living of Prior's-Dean united, valued in the king's books at £22. 9. 4½.; patron and incumbent, the Rev. John Bury Bourne. The tithes have been commuted for £500, and the glebe consists of about 30 acres, with an excellent glebe-house. The church, a plain edifice, was completely restored in 1845. The living was held from 1608 for many years, by the Rev. John Greaves, the astronomer and mathematician, who was a native of the parish; and subsequently it was held by Dr. Richard Pococke, the celebrated eastern traveller, fellow of New College, Oxford.

COLE-ORTON (ST. MARY), a parish, in the union of ASHBY-DE-LA-ZOUCH, hundred of WEST GOSCOTE, N. division of the county of LEICESTER, 2 miles (E.) from Ashby; containing 601 inhabitants. This parish is beau-tifully situated on the Ashby and Loughborough road, between the romantic scenery of Charnwood Forest, on one side, and the less diversified country beyond Ashby, towards Staffordshire, on the other. It comprises by measurement 2600 acres, of which the surface is un-dulated. The village is at the extremity of the forest, and, with the church, and the handsome mansion of the Beaumont family, forms an interesting and prominent feature in the landscape. In the park grounds is an epitaph by Wordsworth to Francis Beaumont, the poet, who was born in an extra-parochial district adjoining: the neighbourhood was one of Wordsworth's favourite places of resort, and much of it has been the subject of his muse. The living is a rectory, valued in the king's books at £10. 6. 0½.; net income, £267; patron, Sir G. H. W. Beaumont, Bart.: the glebe contains about 7 acres, with a glebe-house. The church is a compact structure in the later English style, with a square em-battled tower, surmounted by a handsome spire, and was thoroughly repaired in 1812: the altar-piece is embellished with a fine painting of the Angel delivering St. Peter from Prison, presented by the late Sir George Beaumont, who also ornamented the south-east window

661

with rich stained glass, brought from Rouen. In an aisle railed off from the rest of the church is an elegant monument of alabaster, with two reclining figures, to the memory of Sir Henry and Lady Elizabeth Beaumont, the former of whom died in 1607, and the latter in 1608: there is also a tablet, by Chantrey, to Sir G. Beaumont and his lady. Thomas, Viscount Beaumont, in 1702 founded a school for children, and an hospital for six widows, which he endowed with the great tithes of Swannington, valued now at about £193 per annum: the school is in connexion with the National Society.

COLERIDGE (St. Mary), a parish, in the union of Crediton, hundred of North Tawton, South Molton and N. divisions of Devon, 10 miles (W. N. W.) from Crediton; containing 677 inhabitants. The parish is situated on the river Taw, abounding with excellent trout, and comprises 3181 acres, of which 604 are common or waste. About forty persons are employed in the weaving of serge by hand-loom. Facility of communication is afforded by a road through the centre of the parish, connecting Bideford with Exeter. A fair is held on the first Monday after the 19th of September, when a few cattle and sheep are exposed for sale. The living is a discharged vicarage, valued in the king's books at £7. 8. 9.; net income, £142; patron, the Bishop of Exeter; impropriator, the Hon. N. Fellowes: the rectorial tithes have been commuted for £200; the glebe comprises 16 acres. The church is a handsome early English structure, with the exception of the chancel and the east end of the north aisle, which are of the later English style, and were erected by John Evans, supposed to have been lord of the manor, and whose monument, with a recumbent figure, is placed in the latter; the east window is embellished with stained glass, in which is a full-length portrait of Edward VI., with the sceptre and a Bible. There is a place of worship for Baptists. On Trinity Green was an ancient chapel, now converted into a dwelling-house; and there are some remains of a Roman encampment, near the Taw.

COLERNE (St. John the Baptist), a parish, in the union and hundred of Chippenham, Chippenham and Calne, and N. divisions of Wilts, 7 miles (W. by S.) from Chippenham; containing 1209 inhabitants. This place, formerly called Coldhorn, derives its name from its bleak situation upon the summit of one of the highest hills in the vicinity of Bath. The neighbourhood was the scene of many sanguinary conflicts between the Saxons and the Danes. About eighty years ago the village was destroyed by fire, and rebuilt of stone, without much regard to uniformity. The parish comprises by computation 3652 acres: stone of good quality for ordinary purposes is abundant, but is not quarried. A small fair for sheep and pigs is held annually. The Great Western railway passes about a mile and a half to the south of the church. The living is a discharged vicarage, valued in the king's books at £9. 16.; net income, £92; patron, the Warden of New College, Oxford. There is also a sinecure rectory, valued at £16. 11. 10½., and annexed to the wardenship. The church is a handsome structure in the later English style, with a stately tower. Here is a place of worship for Independents; and a school is supported by subscription. The late Hon. Mrs. Forrester bequeathed property, which was expended in the purchase of thirty

mprises 1992a. 1r. 24p., chiefly pasture land. The ing is a vicarage, valued in the king's books at 7. 11. 8. : patron and impropriator, the Earl of Radr : the great tithes have been commuted for £400, d the vicarial for £350; the glebe contains 1a. 18p., th a glebe-house. The church has at the west end an battled tower with pinnacles, and contains some ndsome monuments; the window of the chancel exbits some fine stained glass representing the Nativity, esented by the Earl of Radnor in 1787. Lord Simon gby, in 1694, gave £500 for teaching children and her charitable purposes; in the same year, Offalia awlins made a donation of £100; and in 1705, the ev. John Pinsent, vicar, gave an estate, now producing out £28 per annum, for apprenticing children. The nds having increased considerably by a benefaction the Earl of Radnor's, the income now amounts to 73. Coleshill gives the title of Baron to the Earl adnor, who has a splendid mansion here, called Colesll House.

COLESHILL (ST. PETER AND ST. PAUL), a marketwn and parish, in the union of MERIDEN, Coleshill vision of the hundred of HEMLINGFORD, N. division f the county of WARWICK, 18 miles (N. by W.) from Varwick, and 103½ (N. W.) from London; containing 172 inhabitants. This place derives its name from its tuation on the acclivity and summit of an eminence, ising gradually from the south bank of the river Cole, ver which is a neat brick bridge of six arches leading nto the town : it consists principally of one long street, rom the centre of which a shorter one, of considerable idth, diverges towards the church, affording a convelient area for the market-place, in which is a portico of rick. The houses are in general well built, and several f them handsome and of modern date; the inhabitants re amply supplied with water from springs, and from he rivers Cole and Blyth, which run through the parish. he Midland railway has a station here. The market s on Wednesday; and there are fairs on the first Monlay in January for cattle and sheep, on Shrove-Monday or horses, which is the principal fair, and on May 6th, he first Monday in July, and first Monday after Sept. 5th, all for cattle. Petty-sessions are held every alterate Wednesday; and two headboroughs, two clerks of he market, and two pinners, are chosen at the court of he lord of the manor, the Earl Digby, held in October. he bishop holds his triennial visitation in August; nd a court of probate is held half-yearly in April and)ctober. Part of the workhouse is appropriated to the onfinement of malefactors previously to their committal. he town is the place of election for the northern divi-ion of the county.

The parish is intersected by the roads from Lichfield o Coventry, and from Birmingham to Atherstone and Juneaton; and comprises 5272 acres, of which two-hirds are arable land, and the remainder pasture : a oortion is attached to Coleshill Park, about a quarter of ι mile west of the town. The river Tame runs through, nd forms a boundary on the north, separating the arish from the parish of Curdworth. The LIVING is a icarage, valued in the king's books at £10. 1s. 6½., and n the patronage of the Earl Digby (the impropriator), vith a net income of £718 : the tithes were commuted or land and a money payment in 1779. The church is ι spacious structure, in the decorated English style, with
663

a north-east chancel, and a lofty tower surmounted by an octagonal spire, crocketed at the angles, part of which was taken down and rebuilt in the same style in 1812; it contains an ancient Norman font, with an effigy of St. Peter, and a representation of the Crucifixion rudely sculptured on it. There are places of worship for Independents, Wesleyans, and Roman Catholics. The free grammar school was founded in the reign of James I., by Lord Digby, who, with some of the parishioners, endowed it with 70 acres of land and several houses; the management is vested in thirteen trustees, of whom the earl nominates three. A school was endowed in 1694, by Simon, Lord Digby, with £500, which have been vested in the purchase of land, for instructing children; a new school-house has been erected, and under the same trust is an endowment for two almshouses, &c. A large building, the property of the earl, is appropriated as a boys' and an infants' school. Coleshill gives the title of Viscount to Earl Digby.

COLEY, a chapelry, in the township of HIPPER-HOLME, parish and union of HALIFAX, wapentake of MORLEY, W. riding of YORK, 3 miles (N. E. by E.) from Halifax. The living is a perpetual curacy; net income, £150; patron, the Vicar of Halifax : there is a good glebe-house. The chapel, originally founded in 1529, was rebuilt in 1711, and again in 1816, in the later English style; it stands on an eminence, has a square tower ornamented with pinnacles, and accommodates 950 persons.

COLKIRK (ST. MARY), a parish, in the union of MITFORD and LAUNDITCH, hundred of LAUNDITCH, W. division of NORFOLK, 2½ miles (S.) from Fakenham; containing about 460 inhabitants. The parish comprises 1487a. 21p., of which 955 acres are arable, 392 meadow and pasture, and 140 woodland; the surface is elevated, and the scenery interesting. The living is a discharged rectory, with that of Stibbard annexed, valued in the king's books at £10, and in the patronage of the Townshend family : the tithes have been commuted for £456. 16. 9., and the glebe comprises 46 acres, with a glebe-house. The church is in the later English style, with a square embattled tower. There is a place of worship for Primitive Methodists. The poor have £25 per annum from a house bequeathed by Samuel Collison and another, in 1767; also 7 acres of land, let for £7 per annum.

COLLIERLY, a township, in the parish and union of LANCHESTER, W. division of CHESTER ward, N. division of the county of DURHAM, 10¼ miles (S. W.) from Gateshead; containing, with the villages of Dip-ton and Pontop, 853 inhabitants. About sixty years ago this township was nearly all waste and uninclosed land, and very thinly inhabited; but by the recommencement of coal-mining (formerly carried on to a considerable extent, and employing numerous people), and the formation of a railway, it has acquired its present importance and increased population. The township comprises by computation 1700 acres, of which about 500, mostly arable, are the property of the Marquess of Bute; the soil is chiefly clay, and, though cold and inferior, produces good oats. The surface is generally elevated; Pontop Pyke is the highest ground in the district, being upwards of 1000 feet above the level of the sea. The Pontop Pyke colliery was first opened in the year 1743, and the working of it was renewed in 1834 by the Stanhope and Tyne Railway Company: the railway passes through the district, and conveys the coal to the shipping at Shields. The townships of Collierly, Kyo (containing the populous village of Annfield), Billingside, and part of Greencroft, were formed, in 1842, into a district parish for ecclesiastical purposes, with a population of 2000. A church dedicated to St. Thomas had been consecrated in 1841; it is a neat structure in the early English style, with a campanile tower and lancet windows, and contains 300 sittings, of which 250 are free. The living is a perpetual curacy; net income, £150; patron, the Bishop of Durham. There are places of worship for Primitive Methodists and Wesleyans.

COLLIERS-END, a hamlet, in the parish of STANDON, union of WARE, hundred of BRAUGHIN, county of HERTFORD; containing 233 inhabitants.

COLLINGBOURN-DUCIS (ST. ANDREW), a parish, in the union of PEWSEY, hundred of ELSTUB and EVERLEY, Everley and Pewsey, and S. divisions of WILTS, 9 miles (S. E.) from Pewsey; containing 518 inhabitants. This place was formerly part of the duchy of Lancaster, from which it acquired the adjunct to its name; Henry VIII. alienated it to the Earl of Hertford, afterwards Duke of Somerset, and Protector of England, upon whose attainder it reverted to the crown, and was granted by Queen Elizabeth to Edward, Earl of Hertford. The parish is on the road between Andover and Marlborough, and comprises by measurement 3241 acres, the soil of which is generally of a light clayey nature; the surface is varied, rising in several parts into hills of considerable elevation, and the village, situated on a plain, is watered by a small rivulet. The living is a rectory, valued in the king's books at £16. 6. 8., and in the gift of the Marquess of Ailesbury: the tithes have been commuted for £626, and the glebe contains about 58 acres, with a glebe-house.

COLLINGBOURN-KINGSTONE (ST. MARY), a parish in the union of PEWSEY, hundred of KINWARDSTONE, Everley and Pewsey, and S. divisions of WILTS, 4 miles (N. N. W.) from Ludgershall; containing 933 inhabitants. The living is a vicarage, valued in the king's books at £15. 7. 3½.; net income, £261; patrons and appropriators, the Dean and Chapter of Winchester. There is a place of worship for Wesleyans. John Norris, eminent as a divine and philosopher, was born at the vicarage-house, in 1567.

COLLINGHAM (ST. OSWALD), a parish, in the Lower division of the wapentake of SKYRACK, W. riding of YORK, 1½ mile (S. S. W.) from Wetherby; containing 324 inhabitants. The parish is bounded on the north by the river Wharfe, and contains some beautiful scenery; it comprises about 2500 acres, of which 150 acres are woodland, and about two-thirds of the remainder arable. Sandstone of excellent quality is found in abundance. Beilby-Grange, in Micklethwaite, the seat of Alexander Browne, Esq., was purchased from Lord Wenlock in 1841; the noble mansion is surrounded by an extensive park, and the present owner has added much to its beauty. The living is a discharged vicarage, endowed with the rectorial tithes, valued in the king's books at £3. 11. 5½., and in the gift of Mrs. Wheler, with a net income of £414: the vicarage-house is picturesquely situated. The tithes were commuted for land and a money payment in 1814.

A school was founded in 1738, and is endowed with £34 per annum, from funds arising from a bequest by Lady Elizabeth Hastings.

COLLINGHAM, NORTH (ALL SAINTS), a parish, in the union, and N. division of the wapentake, of NEWARK, S. division of the county of NOTTINGHAM, 5 miles (N. N. E.) from Newark; containing 911 inhabitants. This place is situated a mile from the river Trent, and on the Midland railway; the surface is level, and generally well wooded. The living is a discharged vicarage, valued in the king's books at £8. 14. 2.; net income, £92; patrons and appropriators, the Dean and Chapter of Peterborough. The church is partly of the early English style; the tower, aisles, porches, and clerestory were added in the 15th century. The Particular Baptists have a place of worship; and a school is £39 per annum. There are considerable remains of the village cross, a plain and solid structure, apparently an erection of the 14th century.

COLLINGHAM, SOUTH (ST. JOHN THE BAPTIST), a parish, in the union, and N. division of the wapentake, of NEWARK, S. division of the county of NOTTINGHAM, 5½ miles (N. N. E.) from Newark; containing 721 inhabitants. This parish, which is situated on the road from Newark to Gainsborough, and bounded on the west by the river Trent, consists of 2862a. 2r. 25p.; the surface, though generally flat, acquires a degree of elevation towards the east. The soil is extremely various, comprising almost every variety, from the richest loam to the most sterile heath; near the village it is sandy, but well adapted to the growth of early vegetables, of which large quantities are raised. In the centre of the village is a magnificent elm, planted in 1745 to commemorate the retreat of the Pretender from Derby. The Collingham station of the Nottingham and Lincoln railway is 10½ miles from the Lincoln station, and 5¼ from that of Newark. The living is a rectory, valued in the king's books at £14. 1. 10½.; gross income, £426; patron, the Bishop of Peterborough. The tithes were commuted for land and money payments in 1790. The church was built at various periods, the most ancient part being the piers and arches on the north side, which are of the 12th century, very massive and richly ornamented with zigzag and other mouldings; the piers of the south side are of the early English style, with plain pointed arches. The chancel is of the 14th century, with square-headed windows; the east window, which is large and of five lights, was added late in the 15th century: the tower, aisles, porch, and clerestory are of the same period. There are two places of worship for Wesleyans; and a national school supported by subscription. Here is a place called Potter's Hill, where many Roman relics have been found; and south of this, on the Fosse-road, on the Lincolnshire boundary, is the site of the Crocolana of Antoninus, now occupied by the village of Brough, where coins, termed Brugh pennies, have been ploughed up, and ancient foundations often discovered. Human bones, with remains of coffins, have also been turned up in a place called the Chapel Close, in the scattered hamlet of Danethorpe; where was formerly a chapel connected with the priory of Thurgarton.

COLLINGTON (ALL SAINTS), a parish, in the union of BROMYARD, hundred of BROXASH, county of HERE-

RD, 4½ miles (N.) from Bromyard; containing 160 inhabitants. It is intersected by the road from Bromyard to Tenbury, and comprises 936 acres. The living is a discharged rectory, valued in the king's books at £18. 10., and in the gift of W. Lacon Childe, Esq.: the tithes have been commuted for £140. 1. 9., and the glebe contains 42 acres.

COLLINGTREE (ST. COLUMBUS), a parish, in the union of HARDINGSTONE, hundred of WYMMERSLEY, S. division of the county of NORTHAMPTON, 3½ miles (S.) from Northampton; containing 232 inhabitants. The parish comprises by admeasurement 646 acres, of varied surface: the soil is various, part being a strong clay; near the village, rich grazing-land; and in other parts sandy. The village is within two miles of the Blisworth station on the London and Birmingham railway; and the road from Northampton to Stony-Stratford intersects the parish. The living is a rectory, valued in the king's books at £16. 10. 5.; net income, £331; patron and incumbent, the Rev. Benjamin Hill. The tithes were commuted for land and a money payment in 1779; the glebe contains about 238 acres, and a glebe-house. Besides the church, there is a place of worship for Wesleyans.

COLLOW, a hamlet, in the parish of LEGSBY, union of CAISTOR, W. division of the wapentake of WRAGGOE, parts of LINDSEY, county of LINCOLN; containing 23 inhabitants. It lies south of Legsby village.

COLLUMPTON.—See CULLOMPTON.

COLLY-WESTON (ST. ANDREW), a parish, in the union of STAMFORD, hundred of WILLYBROOK, N. division of the county of NORTHAMPTON, 3½ miles (S. W. by S.) from Stamford; containing 434 inhabitants. This place is situated on a very high hill, rising from the river Welland, and is intersected by the Stamford and Kettering road; it consists of 1321a. 2r. 16p. There are extensive quarries, the material of which becomes excellent slate when exposed to the frost, and supplies the neighbourhood for many miles around. An act for inclosing lands was passed in 1841. The living is a rectory, valued in the king's books at £12. 9. 7., and in the patronage of the Crown: the tithes have been commuted for £302. 10., and the glebe contains 50 acres, with a glebe-house.

COLMWORTH (ST. DENIS), a parish, in the hundred of BRADFORD, union and county of BEDFORD, 5½ miles (W. by S.) from St. Neot's; containing 575 inhabitants, and comprising by measurement 2300 acres. The living is a rectory, valued in the king's books at £18; patron and incumbent, the Rev. W. Gery. The tithes were commuted, at the recent inclosure of the parish, for about 450 acres of land, valued at 15s. per acre per annum. The church is a handsome structure with a lofty spire, in the early English style: the chancel has an elegant window of large dimensions, and contains a monument in alabaster to Sir William Dyer, descendant of Judge Dyer; in the wall is a brass with the date 1389. A school on the national plan is supported by a bequest of £300 three per cents. by the late Rev. R. S. Hill, rector.

COLN ST. DENIS, a parish, in the union of NORTHLEACH, Upper division of the hundred of DEERHURST, though locally in the hundred of BRADLEY, E. division of the county of GLOUCESTER, 3 miles (S. W. by S.) from Northleach; containing 200 inhabitants. It is bounded

on the south-west by the river Coln, and on the north-west by the old Roman Fosse-way; and comprises by computation 1800 acres, of which the soil is light and stony, and the surface hilly: stone is quarried for common buildings, and the repair of roads. The living is a rectory, valued in the king's books at £9. 19. 4½.; net income, £450; patrons, the Master and Fellows of Pembroke College, Oxford. The tithes were commuted for land and corn-rents, in 1797; the glebe contains 70 acres, with a glebe-house.

COLN ST. ALDWIN'S (ST. JOHN THE BAPTIST), a parish, in the union of NORTHLEACH, hundred of BRIGHTWELLS-BARROW, E. division of the county of GLOUCESTER, 3 miles (N.) from Fairford; containing 428 inhabitants. It is pleasantly situated on an eminence, rising gently from the river Coln, and comprises by computation 2000 acres. The living is a discharged vicarage, valued in the king's books at £8. 19. 4½.; net income, £90; patrons and appropriators, the Dean and Chapter of Gloucester. The tithes were commuted for land in 1769. The church is an ancient structure, partly in the Norman and partly in the early English style.

COLN-ROGERS (ST. ANDREW), a parish, in the union of NORTHLEACH, hundred of BRADLEY, E. division of the county of GLOUCESTER, 4 miles (S. W. by S.) from Northleach; containing 137 inhabitants. It is bounded on the north-east by the river Coln, and comprises about 1400 acres, of which the surface is irregular, and the soil is in some portions clayey and wet, and in others stony. The living is a rectory, valued in the king's books at £7. 0. 5., and in the gift of the Dean and Chapter of Gloucester; the tithes have been commuted for £250, and the glebe contains about 40 acres, with a house.

COLNBROOK, a chapelry, and formerly a market-town, partly in the parish of STANWELL, hundred of SPELTHORNE, county of MIDDLESEX, but chiefly in the parishes of HORTON, IVER, and LANGLEY-MARISH, hundred of STOKE, union of ETON, county of BUCKINGHAM, 46 miles (S. E. by S.) from Buckingham, and 17 (W. by S.) from London, on the road to Bath; containing 1050 inhabitants. This place, which is of great antiquity, is supposed to have been the station Ad Pontes of Antoninus: it derives its name from the river Colne, by which it is separated from Middlesex, and is intersected by different branches of that river, over each of which is a small bridge. The town consists principally of one long street, and the houses are in general neatly built, and of respectable appearance. The trade chiefly arises from its situation as a great thoroughfare, and till lately it was a considerable posting town; it is about a mile and three-quarters distant from the Great Western railway. The market has long been discontinued, and the market-house and the chapel, which were inconveniently situated in the narrower part of the town, have been removed by the commissioners of the turnpike-roads, who have built a new chapel, a neat edifice, dedicated to St. Mary. Fairs are held on April 5th and May 3rd, for cattle and horses. The government, by charter of Henry VIII., renewed in the reign of Charles I., is vested in a bailiff and burgesses. The living is a donative; net income, £103; patrons, Trustees of the late George Townsend, Esq., for fellows of Pembroke College, Oxford. There is a place of worship for Baptists;

and several charitable bequests have been made, the principal of which is one by Thomas Pitt, in the year 1657, of some land now producing £32 per annum, for distribution among the poor.

COLNE (St. Helen), a parish, in the union of St. Ives, hundred of Hurstingstone, county of Huntingdon, 5 miles (N. E.) from St. Ives; containing 544 inhabitants. It comprises about 2000 acres, of which the surface is very flat, and the soil among the finest in the kingdom, land letting for about £3 per acre. The living is annexed, with that of Pidley, to the rectory of Somersham: the tithes have been commuted for £540. The church is in the early English style, with a western tower, and contains some remains of figures and armorial bearings in stained glass.

COLNE, a market-town and parochial chapelry, in the parish of Whalley, union of Burnley, Higher division of the hundred of Blackburn, N. division of the county of Lancaster, 35 miles (S. E.) from Lancaster, and 217 (N. N. W.) from London; containing 20,761 inhabitants, of whom 8615 are in the township of Colne. This place is supposed by the geographer of Ravennas to have been a Roman station, the site of which is referred by Whitaker, the historian of Manchester, to Caster Cliff, a lofty eminence about a mile south of the town, where are still the vestiges of a quadrilateral camp, 120 yards in length, and 110 in breadth, surrounded by a double vallum and fosse. The camp is considered by Dr. Whitaker, the historian of the parish of Whalley, only as the castra æstiva of the primary station, which, perhaps on better authority, he places in the low grounds beneath the town and near the bank of the Colne water, but of which every vestige has been obliterated by cultivation. Numerous Roman coins have been found at various times, and among them several of Gordianus and other emperors, inclosed in a large silver cup turned up by the plough in 1696.

The town seems to have arisen with Lancaster, Manchester, and other places in the county, soon after its conquest by Agricola, in the year 79, and derives its name either from Colunio, the supposed name of the Roman station, or from the Saxon Culme, coal, with which the neighbourhood abounds. It is situated on an elevated point of land between the river Calder and the Leeds and Liverpool canal; the streets are paved, and the inhabitants are amply supplied with water. A subscription library was established in 1793. The woollen-manufacture was carried on here previously to the arrival of the Flemings in England in the time of Edward III., as appears from the rent-roll of the last Henry de Lacy, lord of the manor in 1311, in which a fulling-mill is returned as being valued at 6s. 8d. per annum; and the manufacture of shalloons, calimancoes, and tammies, was also extensively carried on. A Piece-hall was erected in 1775, a substantial stone building, for many years the principal mart in the district for woollen and worsted goods, but now appropriated to the sale of general merchandise at the fairs only. The cotton-manufacture is at present the principal branch of business; the chief articles are calico and mouselin de lain for the Manchester market, both of them being made to a considerable extent. The Leeds and Liverpool canal passes through a tunnel a mile in length, at a small distance from the town, affording a facility of conveyance for the coal, freestone, slate, and lime, with which the neighbouring hills abound,

666

and for the produce of the factories; and the East Lancashire railway and the Bradford Extension both terminate at this place, in a common station. The market days are Wednesday and Saturday; on the last Wednesday in every month is a market for cattle, and the fairs are March 7th, May 13th, for cattle, and 15th for pedlery, October 11th, and December 21st. The town is within the jurisdiction of the county magistrates: the powers of the county debt-court of Colne, established in 1847, extend over the sub-registration-districts of Colne and Pendle.

The chapelry includes the townships of Barrowford, Foulridge, Great and Little Marsden, and Trawden, and comprises by computation 23,040 acres, chiefly pasture and meadow land: of this area, 4526 acres are in the township of Colne. The living is a perpetual curacy; net income, £179, with a good glebe-house; patrons, Hulme's Trustees. The chapel, dedicated to St. Bartholomew, is a very ancient structure, erected probably soon after the Conquest, and in the reign of Henry I. given to the priory of Pontefract by Hugh de Val. It was repaired, or partly rebuilt, in the reign of Henry VIII., when the only remains preserved of the original edifice were the finely-carved screen at the entrance and the sides of the choir, and three massive circular columns in the north aisle, one of which, having been undermined by some interments, suddenly gave way in 1815, and endangered the whole building, which has since been rendered firm and secure. There is a church or chapel at Little Marsden; and since 1835 four additional churches have been erected in this chapelry, viz.: Christ Church, Colne, built in 1836; St. Thomas', Barrowford, in 1838; St. Mary's, Trawden, in 1844; and St. John's, Great Marsden, in 1847. A district has been assigned to each of the five churches, and the benefice of each augmented by the Ecclesiastical Commissioners to £150. The livings of Little Marsden, Christ Church, and Barrowford, are in the gift of Hulme's Trustees, and those of Trawden and Great Marsden in that of the Crown and the Bishop of Chester, alternately. In the same period five national schools have been built, capable of accommodating 1700 children. There are places of worship for Baptists, Independents, Wesleyans, and Primitive Methodists. The grammar school, of very uncertain foundation, is endowed with about £15 per annum, for which six boys are taught free, four of them by means of a bequest of £40 from Thomas Blakey in 1687; the old schoolroom was taken down, and on its site a new one erected by subscription, in 1812. There is a tradition that Dr. Tillotson, Archbishop of Canterbury, received the rudiments of his education at the school. A school was founded, and endowed with £16 per annum, in 1746, at Laneshaw Bridge, by John Emmot, Esq.

COLNE, EARL'S (St. Andrew), a parish, in the union of Halstead, Witham division of the hundred of Lexden, N. division of Essex, 3½ miles (E. S. E.) from Halstead; containing 1385 inhabitants. This parish takes the prefix to its name from the family of De Vere, earls of Oxford, to whom it belonged at the time of the Domesday survey; and its name, in common with others in the district, from the river Colne, over which is a bridge on the line of the Roman road from Colchester. It is about ten miles in circumference, and consists chiefly of elevated ground; the soil is a kind of loam, partially mixed with sand, and, though not of great tenacity, erably fertile. A fair is held on March 25th. The ing is a vicarage, endowed with a portion of the :torial tithes, and valued in the king's books at). 10. 10.; patron, and impropriator of the remainder the rectorial tithes, H. H. Carwardine, Esq. The eat tithes have been commuted for £242. 14. 9., and e vicarial for £670. The church is a handsome ancient ifice, with a massive tower partly of flint, and is orna- nted with several monuments of the De Veres, which re removed from the church of a Benedictine priory anded here in the eleventh century by Aubrey de Vere, ho became one of the monks : the priory was dedicated St. Mary and St. John the Evangelist, and was ade a cell to the abbey of Abingdon, in Berkshire; at e Dissolution it had a prior and ten monks, with a venue of £175. 14. 8. There are places of worship r Particular Baptists and the Society of Friends. Cer- in land was bequeathed by the Rev. Christopher vallow, who died in 1539, for the support of a grammar hool; the proceeds amount to £188 per annum. homas Audley, lord chancellor of England in the reign Henry VIII., was born in the parish.

COLNE, ENGAIN (St. Andrew), a parish, in the ion of Lexden and Winstree, Witham division of e hundred of Lexden, N. division of Essex, 2¾ miles .) from Halstead; containing 685 inhabitants. This rish, which derives the affix to its name from the mily of Engain, proprietors of the manor, comprises 444a. 2r. 5p., whereof about 1896 are arable, 297 pas- re, 15 in hops, and 148 wood and plantations. The nds are in general elevated, and the soil is of light uality, consisting of loam, mixed with sand. The river olne forms the southern boundary, near which passes e Roman road from Colchester. A fair for toys is eld on Whit Monday and Tuesday. The living is a ctory, valued in the king's books at £13. 17. 6., and the gift of the Governors of Christ's Hospital: the thes have been commuted for £750, and the glebe com- rises 56 acres, with a house. The church, a plain edifice ith a good tower of brick, is pleasantly situated; the arsonage-house is a handsome residence.

COLNE, WAKES (All Saints), a parish, in the ion of Lexden and Winstree, Witham division, e hundred of Lexden, N. division of Essex, 5½ miles . by S.) from Halstead; containing 444 inhabitants. his parish, which is situated on the road from Col- ester to Halstead, derives its distinguishing epithet om one of its former proprietors. It is about eight iles in circumference, and consists generally of low nd; the soil is loam of various kinds, intermixed with ay. The Roman road from Colchester passes through e parish, to the south of which flows the river Colne. he living is a rectory, valued in the king's books at 12. 0. 5., and in the patronage of the Earl of Verulam : e tithes have been commuted for £574, and the glebe ntains 18½ acres, with a glebe-house. The church is a plain edifice, with a steeple of wood.

COLNE, WHITE (All Saints), a parish, in the ion of Halstead, Witham division of the hundred of exden, N. division of Essex, 4 miles (E.) from Hal- ead; containing 419 inhabitants. It comprises 1467a. ·. 33p., chiefly arable, and is bounded on the south y the river Colne; the lands are generally elevated, id the soil of light quality. The living is a perpetual racy, or donative; patrons and impropriators, the

family of Hume : the impropriate tithes have been com- muted for £345, and the perpetual curate's for £135; the glebe comprises a quarter of an acre. The church, by the name of Colne mi Blanc, was assigned by Aubrey de Vere, founder of Colne Priory, and confirmed by Aubrey, his son, to the monks at Colne : after the Dis- solution it was given to John, Earl of Oxford, and became a donative or curacy. It is an ancient building, with a square embattled tower formerly surmounted by a spire. The Roman road from Colchester passes on the south of the parish.

COLNEY (St. Andrew), a parish, in the union of Henstead, hundred of Humbleyard, E. division of Norfolk, 2¾ miles (W. by S.) from Norwich; contain- ing 110 inhabitants. This parish, which is bounded on the north-east by the river Yare, and intersected by the road from Norwich to Hingham, comprises about 900 acres. The living is a discharged rectory, valued in the king's books at £6. 13. 4., and in the gift of J. Scott, Esq. : the tithes have been commuted for £219, and the glebe contains 38 acres. The church, a small edifice with a circular tower, has been repewed ; the font is richly sculptured.

COLNEY (St. Peter).—See London-Colney.

COLNEY-HATCH, a hamlet, in the parish of Fryern-Barnet, union of Barnet, Finsbury division of the hundred of Ossulstone, county of Middlesex; containing 216 inhabitants. This village lies a little to the east of the great north road; it contains some hand- some houses, and the environs abound with pleasing scenery.

COLSTERWORTH (St. John the Baptist), a pa- rish, partly in the wapentake of Beltisloe, and partly in that of Winnibriggs and Threo, union of Gran- tham, parts of Kesteven, county of Lincoln, 8 miles (S.) from Grantham ; containing, with the hamlets of Twyford and Woolsthorpe, 1017 inhabitants. The village is situated in a beautiful valley, through which winds the river Witham, and is remarkable for the salubrity of the air. The living is a rectory, valued in the king's books at £14. 10. ; net income, £585 ; patron, H. Mirehouse, Esq. The tithes were commuted for land and corn- rents in 1805. The church is a small structure of early English architecture, with a good tower in the later style, and contains a gallery erected at the expense of Sir Isaac Newton, who was born at Woolsthorpe on Christmas- day, 1642. There is a place of worship for Wesleyans. The Roman road called High Dyke, passes through the parish.

COLSTON-BASSET (St. Mary), a parish, in the union of Bingham, S. division of the wapentake of Bingham and of the county of Nottingham, 10 miles (S. E. by E.) from Nottingham; containing 403 inhabit- ants. It is situated on the road from Nottingham to Waltham, and comprises about 2500 acres, the soil of which is chiefly a strong clay ; the river Smite and the Grantham Canal pass within half a mile. Limestone is quarried, and sent, when burnt, in considerable quanti- ties to the surrounding districts. The ancient cross in the village was rebuilt in 1831, to commemorate the coronation of William IV. The living is a vicarage, valued in the king's books at £8. 7. 6., and in the pa- tronage of the Crown ; net income, £270 ; impropriator, H. Martin, Esq. The glebe contains about 44 acres, and a good house has been built by the incumbent. The

4 Q 2

church is an ancient and beautiful cruciform structure in the later English style, standing on a hill at a short distance from the village; it contains a remarkably handsome screen of oak. There are places of worship for Roman Catholics and Methodists.

COLTISHALL (St. John the Baptist), a parish, in the union of Aylsham, hundred of South Erpingham, E. division of Norfolk, 7 miles (N. N. E.) from Norwich; containing 897 inhabitants. The parish comprises 1129a. 29p., whereof about 1065 acres are arable, 30 pasture, and 34 woodland. It is situated on the river Bure, and the road from Norwich to North Walsham runs through the village, the west side of which is in the parish of Great Hautbois. Here is a brewery; and a considerable trade is carried on in malt, corn, coal, and timber, for which the river affords facility of conveyance. A fair for pedlery is held on Whit-Monday. The living is a rectory, valued in the king's books at £7. 2. 6., and in the patronage of King's College, Cambridge: the tithes of this parish, with those upon certain lands in South Ruston and Scottow, have been commuted for £340, and the glebe contains about 27 acres. The church, chiefly in the early style, has a lofty embattled tower: the nave is separated from the chancel by a carved screen; the font is Norman, and the building contains several neat memorials. There is a place of worship for Wesleyans. John Chapman, in 1718, bequeathed £10 per annum and a house, to which in 1815 the Rev. Dr. Grape added £360 three per cent. consols., making the income £20. 16., for teaching boys.

COLTON (St. Andrew), a parish, in the incorporation and hundred of Forehoe, E. division of Norfolk, 7½ miles (W. by N.) from Norwich; containing 282 inhabitants. This parish, which is bounded on the south by a stream tributary to the river Yare, forms part of the manor of Costessey, and comprises 900a. 2r. 29p.; about 726 acres are arable, and 169 pasture. The living is a discharged rectory, valued in the king's books at £6. 9. 9½., and in the patronage of the Crown, with a net income of £348; there are 25½ acres of glebe. The church is in the later English style, and has an embattled tower. The Rev. Henry Rix, in 1726, bequeathed land for the endowment of a school and other charitable purposes, the income of which, with a subsequent gift, amounts to £15. 10.; and the poor receive £17. 5. per annum from ten acres of land allotted for fuel, at the inclosure, in 1801.

COLTON (St. Mary), a parish, in the union of Lichfield, S. division of the hundred of Pirehill, N. division of the county of Stafford, 2 miles (N. by E.) from Rugeley; containing 672 inhabitants. This parish, which is bounded on the north by the river Blythe, and on the south by the Trent, comprises by measurement about 3000 acres, in equal portions of arable and meadow: the soil is of average quality. The Grand Trunk canal passes through the south-western part of the parish. The living is a rectory, valued in the king's books at £5; net income, £461; patron and incumbent, the Rev. Charles Landor. The glebe comprises 40 acres. The church is an ancient structure, with a tower; the north aisle was rebuilt in 1801. There is a place of worship for Wesleyans; also a school founded by contributions in 1763, and since endowed with £500 by John Spencer, Esq.; and a school for younger children, endowed by Mr. Webb with land producing £5 per annum.

COLUMB, ST., MINOR (St. Columb), a parish, in e union of St. Columb Major, hundred of Pyder, division of Cornwall, 5¼ miles (W. by S.) from St. lumb Major; containing 1681 inhabitants. The rish comprises 5535 acres, and is bounded on the west the bays of Towan and Watergate, in which are the all harbours of New Quay and Porth, on the Bristol ιannel. The cliffs on this part of the coast are very ¡ty, and over them proceeds a narrow path, which scends to a fine sandy beach, stretching to Mawgan ιrth: in the rocks are many curious caverns, formed the action of the sea. The pilchard-fishery is carried extensively at New Quay, the harbour there having ιen formed for the vessels employed in that concern, in hich the principal part of the population is either terested or engaged. Lead-ore is found in several ιrts, and three mines have been opened, of which vo, at New Quay and Narrow Cliff, are still worked ith moderate success; but the third, at Watergate, ¦ter a large outlay in the buildings and machinery, ιs been abandoned. There are also quarries of slate- one well adapted for common building purposes, and a uarry of stone partaking of the properties of granite, hich is much valued. A fair for cattle held here on ιe 9th of June, is one of the chief cattle-fairs in the ιunty. The living is a perpetual curacy; net income, 117; patron and impropriator, Sir J. B. Y. Buller, art. The church is a spacious and ancient structure, ith a very lofty tower; the roof is of oak. There are laces of worship for Wesleyans and Baptists. Consi- erable remains exist of Rialton Priory, a cell to the ιriory of Bodmin, built by Thomas Vivian, prior of 3odmin, about the close of the 15th century; they con- ¡ist of the archways leading into three courts, and are ιmbattled, and mantled with ivy. There are also some ιarthworks, the principal of them being at Porth Island; ιnd several barrows, in one of which, on a farm at Tre- haras, five urns containing bones were found a few ʹears since.

COLVESTON (St. Mary), a parish, in the union of Swaffham, hundred of Grimshoe, W. division of Nor- ʹolk, 6½ miles (N. by E.) from Brandon; containing ¡2 inhabitants. It lies near the road from Brandon to Swaffham; and comprises 800 acres, the property of Lord Berners, by whose family the manor has long been ιeld. The living is a discharged rectory, consolidated ʋith the vicarage of Didlington, and valued in the king's ɔooks at £9. 0. 2½.: the church, which was dependent ɔn that of St. Bartholomew at Ickburgh, was, with the ʹillage, long since demolished.

COLWALL (St. James), a parish, in the union of Ledbury, hundred of Radlow, county of Hereford, 1½ miles (N. E. by N.) from Ledbury; containing 940 ιnhabitants. This parish is supposed to have derived ts name from Collis Vallum, "a fortified hill," which is lescriptive of the situation of the place. The Hereford- ihire beacon, an ancient encampment on one of the ιighest of the Malvern hills, and the lines of the circum- ʹallation of which are still very distinct, is thought to ιave been formed by the Britons to repel the Romans; ιnd some antiquaries are of opinion that here Caractacus ʋas taken prisoner. Near the place a coronet of gold ʋas discovered in 1650, said by some to have belonged ɔ a British prince; it was sold for a very large sum. Γhe parish is traversed by the two roads from Malvern

to Ledbury, the one through Malvern-Wells, and the other through the Wyche; it comprises 3458a. 3r. 26p. Limestone is quarried, which, as well as other strata, contains fossil remains; and common stone is quarried for roads and buildings. From forty to fifty people are employed in glove-making. The living is a rectory, valued in the king's books at £20. 6. 8., and in the gift of the Bishop of Hereford: the tithes have been com- muted for £480; there is an excellent glebe-house, and the glebe contains 61 acres. The church is an ancient structure with a handsome tower, and contains portions in the early and decorated English styles. There is a place of worship for Plymouth Brethren; also a free grammar school, founded in 1612 by Humphry Walwyn, and under the patronage of the Grocers' Company.

COLWELL, with Great Swinburn, a township, in the parish of Chollerton, union of Hexham, N. E. division of Tindale ward, S. division of Northumber- land, 8¾ miles (N. by E.) from Hexham; containing 393 inhabitants. Colwell, Great and Little Swinburn, and Whiteside Law, form two contiguous townships in the parish, situated near the intersection of the Cambo road and the Watling-street. The tithes of Colwell with Great Swinburn have been commuted for £213 payable to the Mercers' Company, London, and £116 payable to the vicar.

COLWICH (St. Michael), a parish, in the S. divi- sion of the hundred of Pirehill, union, and N. division of the county, of Stafford, 3 miles (N. W. by N.) from Rugeley; containing, with Fradswell chapelry, the town- ships of Bishton, Moreton, Shugborough, and Wolseley, and part of those of Drointon, Great and Little Hay- wood, and Hixon, 2015 inhabitants, of whom 205 are in the township of Colwich. This parish, which is situated on the banks of the Trent, and intersected by the road from London to Liverpool, comprises by measurement 6492 acres. The scenery is very delightful, the river flowing through a vale of the richest verdure, adorned with a variety of elegant villas, among which are the charming seats of Shugborough and Wolseley. There are two quarries from which a durable stone is obtained for building. The Staffordshire and Worcestershire canal forms a junction with the Grand Trunk canal near Great Haywood: the Trent-Valley railway passes through the parish; and in 1846 an act was obtained for a rail- way from this place, through the Potteries, to Maccles- field. The living is a discharged vicarage, valued in the king's books at £6. 0. 5.; patron, the Bishop of Lich- field: the great tithes have been commuted for £700, and the vicarial for £500; the glebe consists of about 6 acres, 4½ of which are in the parish of Stowe. The church is of some antiquity, and contains a monument to the memory of the celebrated navigator, George, Lord Anson, who was interred in the family cemetery at this place, June 14th, 1762. At Great Haywood is a paro- chial chapel, and there is an endowed chapel at Frads- well. The Independents have a place of worship. In 1837 was established here the Mount Pavilion convent of Benedictine nuns; attached to it is a private chapel. The remains of Haywood Abbey, situated in the parish, have been converted into a gentleman's seat.

COLWICK (St. John the Baptist), a parish, in the union of Basford, S. division of the wapentake of Thurgarton and of the county of Nottingham, 2½ miles (E.) from Nottingham; containing 109 inhabitants. This parish, which is situated on the river Trent, comprises by computation 1235 acres; the surface is varied, the soil on the hills is a strong clay, and the remainder rich pasture and meadow land. The manor is the property of John Musters, Esq., who has a splendid house here; the village is pleasantly situated under a long range of bills on the north bank of the Trent. The living is a rectory, valued in the king's books at £6. 1. 0½.; net income, £220; patron, Mr. Musters. The church, which stands embosomed in foliage, contains some ancient monuments of the Byron and Musters families.

COLYFORD, a hamlet, in the parish and hundred of COLYTON, Honiton and S. divisions of DEVON, one mile (S. S. E.) from Colyton. This place was made a borough before the reign of Edward I., and is still governed by a mayor, who is annually chosen at the court of the lord of the manor. The corporation consists of the mayor and burgesses; and the mayor, who holds office for one year, and is constable the next, is possessed of a small field, and has the tolls of a well-attended cattle-fair, held on the first Wednesday after March 12th. The road from Exeter to Weymouth runs through the village. There are lands still called Chapel Lands, but the existence of the chapel is known only by tradition: the great tithes within the limits of the borough belong to the vicar of Colyton. A Roman road passed through the place, the remains of which are sometimes dug up. Sir T. Gates, who discovered the Bermuda Isles, was born here.

COLYTON, or CULLITON (ST. ANDREW), a market-town and parish, in the union of AXMINSTER, hundred of COLYTON, Honiton and S. divisions of DEVON, 5 miles (S. W.) from Axminster, and 151 (W. S. W.) from London; containing 2451 inhabitants. This place derives its name from the river Coly, on which it is situated, near the confluence of that stream with the Axe. In the reign of Edward III. it obtained the grant of a weekly market and an annual fair. During the civil war, the royal forces in possession of the town were attacked and defeated by a detachment of the parliamentarian army stationed at Lyme. The TOWN is pleasantly seated on the road between Axminster and Sidmouth, in a fertile vale, containing some fine pasture land and orchards, and abounding with excellent timber; the houses, many of which are very ancient, are in general irregularly built of flint, with thatched roofs. The inhabitants are supplied with water from two conduits connected with springs a little south of the town. The principal branch of manufacture was that of paper, which is at present on a reduced scale, there being but one establishment, in which only ten persons are employed: a tan-yard gives employment to about thirty hands. The market is on Thursday, and there are smaller markets on Tuesday and Saturday. Two small fairs are held under the control of feoffees, by charter of Henry VIII.; one on the first Thursday after the 1st of May, and the other on the first Thursday after the 14th of October; and there is likewise a fair at Colyford on the first Wednesday after the 12th of March. The petty-sessions for the division are held here; and two constables and a tythingman are annually appointed at the court leet of the lord of the manor.

The parish comprises 6430 acres, of which 140 are common or waste. The LIVING is a vicarage, with the

ne 18th and the Wednesday before December 11th. he living is a vicarage, valued in the king's books at 15. 4. 4½.; patron, the Bishop of Bath and Wells. he great tithes have been commuted for £315, and the carial for £440; the glebe contains 13 acres, with a ebe-house. The church has been repaired, and the llery enlarged.

COMBE (St. Swithin), a parish, in the union of UNGERFORD, hundred of Pastrow, Kingsclere and . divisions of the county of Southampton, 6 miles :. by S.) from Hungerford; containing, with the ham- t of East Wick, 203 inhabitants. The parish is situ- ed at the head of a valley, stretching towards Hurst- burne-Tarrant, and at the south base of Wallborough ill, belonging to the chain of the north downs; it bmprises by measurement 2074 acres. The living is a ischarged vicarage, endowed with a portion of the recto- al tithes, and valued in the king's books at £6. 13. 4.; atrons, the Dean and Canons of Windsor; impropria- brs, the Provost and Fellows of King's College, Cam- ridge. The church, which was formerly much larger, as attached to a monastic establishment in the vicinity, he remains whereof have lately been converted into a armhouse. Round the summit of Wallborough Hill re a fosse and mound, marking the site of a Roman or British encampment.

COMBE, a tything, in the parish of Enford, union f Pewsey, hundred of Elstub and Everley, Everley nd Pewsey, and S. divisions of Wilts, 8¼ miles (W.) rom Ludgershall; containing 79 inhabitants.

COMBE, ABBAS.—See Abbas-Combe.

COMBE, ENGLISH, a parish, in the union of Bath, hundred of Wellow, E. division of Somerset, 3 miles 'S. W.) from Bath; containing 486 inhabitants. This parish, which comprises by computation 1796 acres, is iituated near the Great Western railway, and about two miles from the London and Exeter road, from the river Avon, and the Kennet and Avon navigation. There are several quarries, from which stone is obtained for build- ng and the repair of roads. The living is a discharged vicarage, valued in the king's books at £9. 3. 11½., and n the gift of the family of Radford: the impropriate ithes, belonging to Mrs. Salisbury, have been commuted or £187, and the vicarial for £170; the glebe contains about 15 acres, with a glebe-house. The church is a very handsome structure, and has been repaired at a considerable expense. There are places of worship for Baptists and Lady Huntingdon's Connexion. The Gur- nays had a castle here, but little more than the fosse which encompassed it is visible. The ancient road Wansdyke crosses the parish, passing by an eminence called Roundbarrow or Barrow Hill, which has been er- roneously considered of artificial construction.

COMBE-FIELDS, or Combe-Abbey, an extra- parochial liberty, in the union of Rugby, Kirby division of the hundred of Knightlow, N. division of the county of Warwick, 5¼ miles (E.) from Coventry; containing 195 inhabitants, and comprising 3656 acres. It is well watered by two branches of the river Sow, which partly bound it on the east and west; the Oxford canal winds through the district, and it is also intersected by the road from Coventry to Lutterworth. Richard de Cam- villa, in 1150, founded here a Cistercian abbey, which was dedicated to St. Mary, and richly endowed; at the Dissolution it contained about fourteen monks, and was

671

valued at £343. 0. 5. per annum. The site, which was granted by Edward VI. to the Earl of Warwick, is oc- cupied by the manor-house: there are still some vestiges of the cloisters. The present noble mansion, the seat of the Earl of Craven, was chiefly erected by Lord Har- rington in the reign of James I., but has since received many additions, rendering it one of the finest seats in the country; the apartments are sumptuously fur- nished, and are adorned with paintings by the best masters. The park is beautifully diversified, enriched with wood and water, and embracing wide prospects.

COMBE-FLOREY (St. Peter), a parish, in the union of Taunton, hundred of Taunton and Taunton- Dean, W. division of Somerset, 6 miles (N. E. by E.) from Wiveliscombe; containing 304 inhabitants. It comprises by computation 1600 acres: there are quar- ries of sandstone and conglomerate of good quality, for building. The living is a rectory, valued in the king's books at £11. 13. 9., and in the patronage of the Crown: the incumbent's tithes have been commuted for £220, and a rent-charge of £44 is paid to an impropriator; the glebe comprises 70 acres, with a glebe-house. The church is a neat plain edifice. The able and eccentric writer, Sydney Smith, who died in 1845, was incum- bent of the parish.

COMBE-HAY, a parish, in the union of Bath, hun- dred of Wellow, E. division of Somerset, 3½ miles (S. by W.) from Bath; containing 239 inhabitants. The parish comprises by measurement 1080 acres. The sur- face in some parts is hilly, and the soil in these is a light stone brash, but in the valleys fertile; the district abounds with fine timber. Stone of inferior quality is quarried for building cottages, and for the roads; and fullers'-earth is found in abundance. A small brook flows through the parish into the Avon, and the Somer- setshire coal-canal also intersects it. The living is a rectory, valued in the king's books at £9. 12. 3½., and in the gift of the Hon. H. Hanbury Tracey: the tithes have been commuted for £240, and the glebe comprises 38 acres. The church is a neat edifice. There is a place of worship alternately used by Baptists and In- dependents. The Roman Fosse-way passes near; the ditch on each side is here very perfect.

COMBE-HILL, with Healy.—See Healy.

COMBE, LONG (St. Lawrence), a parish, in the union of Woodstock, hundred of Wootton, county of Oxford, 5 miles (W. by S.) from Woodstock; contain- ing 605 inhabitants. The living is a rectory, in the patronage of Lincoln College, Oxford, the impropriators; net income, £90. The church is in the early English style, with a square embattled tower having angular pinnacles surmounted by vanes; it contains some inte- resting details, and near the stone steps leading to the rood-loft is a stone pulpit, finely sculptured. It an- ciently occupied a very low situation, but was rebuilt on its present site in 1395.

COMBE-MARTIN (St. Peter), a market-town and parish, in the union of Barnstaple, hundred of Braun- ton, Braunton and N. divisions of Devon, 5 miles (E.) from Ilfracombe, and 176 (W. by S.) from London; containing 1399 inhabitants. This place derives its name from its situation in a valley, and its adjunct from its proprietor at the time of the Conquest. In the reign of Edward I., some mines of lead, containing a con- siderable portion of silver, were discovered, and 377 men from the Peak in Derbyshire were brought to work them ; in the reign of Edward III. they produced such a quantity of that metal as to assist the king materially in defraying the expense of carrying on the war with France. These mines, after remaining in a neglected state for many years, were re-opened in the reign of Elizabeth, and worked with considerable advantage under the direction of Sir Bevis Bulmer. They were unsuccessfully explored in 1790 : in 1813 a more profitable attempt was made, which, after four years, however, was discontinued : the works have been since renewed, and the mines are at present in operation. Some iron and copper are also found ; and limestone is quarried and burnt for agricultural use to a great extent. There is a variety of geological productions in one of the hills, as well as numerous fossils.

The TOWN is situated in a deep romantic glen, extending in a north-west direction, and opening into a small cove on the Bristol Channel, which is capable of being converted into a good harbour, and which formed a convenient port for shipping the mineral produce, and still affords the inhabitants the means of conveying coal and lime to other towns, whence they receive corn and bark in return. The houses, many of which are in ruins, and overgrown with ivy, extend for nearly a mile, in an irregular line, along the side of the vale : the surrounding scenery is strikingly magnificent. The market has been discontinued ; but the charter, granted to Nicholas Fitz-Martin by Henry III., in 1264, is still retained by the exposure of some trifling articles for sale on the market-days : the market-house is rapidly falling to decay. Fairs are held on Whit-Monday and Lammas feast ; and the county magistrates hold a petty-session for the division, on the first Monday in every month, at a small inn. The parish comprises 3600 acres, of which 1837 are common or waste. The living is a rectory, valued in the king's books at £39. 8. 9., and in the gift of the family of Toms : the tithes amount to about £400 per annum, and the glebe contains 60 acres, with a glebe-house. The church is a handsome structure with a tower, built about the time of Henry III. ; the nave is separated from the chancel by a screen. Here are places of worship for Wesleyans and Independents. A school was endowed in 1733, by George Ley, Esq., with land producing £25 per annum : the premises were rebuilt a few years since, by George Ley, Esq., grandson of the founder. There are three rings of stone on the summit of one of the hills in the parish, called Hangman Hill, the height of which is 1189 feet. Dr. Thomas Harding, a learned Roman Catholic divine and controversialist, was born here in 1512.

COMBE, MONCTON (St. Michael), a parish, in the union of Bath, hundred of Bath-Forum, E. division of Somerset, 3½ miles (S. E. by S.) from Bath ; containing 1107 inhabitants. The manufacture of paper is carried on ; and on Combe Down are extensive quarries, where stone was obtained for erecting many of the best houses in Bath : clusters of hexagonal brown crystals are found in the cavities of the stone, and in the fissures of the rocks are some fine and curiously frosted stalactites. The living is a perpetual curacy, in the gift of the Rector of South Stoke. On the brow of the hill which surmounts the village, and forming a conspicuous feature in the landscape, is an elegant chapel in the decorated English style, with a tower and spire 90 feet

rker. The tithes were commuted for land and a ney payment in 1803. The church stands on the rth side of the village; it is an ancient structure, ely repaired.

COMB-PYNE, a parish, in the union and hundred AXMINSTER, Honiton and S. divisions of DEVON, 3¾ les (E. S. E.) from Colyton; containing 143 inhabitts. This place was anciently called Comb-Coffin, m the Coffin family; its present adjunct is derived m the Pynes, its later possessors. The living is a ¡charged rectory, valued in the king's books at . 11. 8., and in the gift of Messrs. Knight, Cuff, and ¡wards : the tithes have been commuted for £115, and ere is a glebe of 28 acres.

COMB-RAWLEIGH (ST. NICHOLAS), a parish, in e union of HONITON, hundred of AXMINSTER, Honin and S. divisions of DEVON, 1½ mile (N. N. W.) from oniton; containing 276 inhabitants. This parish, hich is separated from that of Honiton by the river tter, comprises 1740a. 3r. 2p., and is intersected by e old road to Taunton. The living is a rectory, valued the king's books at £20. 0. 10., and in the gift of . Simeon Drewe, Esq. : the tithes have been commuted r £300, and the glebe comprises 40 acres, with a ebe-house. The church is a handsome structure in e later English style, and contains a monument to the emory of John Sheldon, Esq., F.R.S., and anatomical rofessor, who died in 1808.

COMBROOK, a chapelry, in the parish of KING-ON, union of STRATFORD-UPON-AVON, Kington diviion of the hundred of KINGTON, S. division of the ounty of WARWICK, 2¼ miles (W. by N.) from King-on; containing 282 inhabitants, and comprising 1137 cres. The tithes were commuted for land in 1772. ¡he chapel, dedicated to St. Margaret, has been rebuilt. ¡here is a place of worship for Wesleyans; and a chool, endowed by a late Lord Willoughby with £5 ¡er annum, is further supported by Lord Willoughby de ¡roke. In 1763, Lady Tryphena Verney, agreeably to bequest of £300 by her husband, George Verney, Esq., onveyed an estate for the maintenance of two scholars at 'rinity College, Cambridge, to be chosen from this school, r, in default, out of the grammar school at Warwick.

COMBS (ST. MARY), a parish, in the union and hun-¡red of Stow, W. division of SUFFOLK, 1¼ mile (S. by N.) rom Stow-Market; containing 1064 inhabitants. The ¡arish is situated on the road from Bury St. Edmund's ¡o Ipswich, and on the river Orwell, which forms its ¡orth-eastern boundary, and is navigable from Ipswich ¡o Stow-Market. It comprises by measurement 2770 cres. The soil is generally a strong clay, but near the iver light, and inclined to moor; the surface is very ¡neven, rising into hills of considerable elevation; the ¡wer grounds afford excellent pasture. A large tannery ¡as been established for more than 150 years. The ¡ving is a rectory, valued in the king's books at ¡25. 17. 8½., and in the gift of the Earl of Ashburnham, ¡ith a net income of £511 : the glebe comprises 30 cres, and a handsome rectory-house has been built by ¡he Rev. Richard Daniel. The church is in the decorated ¡nglish style, with a square embattled tower; the win-¡ows retain some fine portions of ancient stained glass. 'here is a place of worship for Independents.

COMMON-DALE, a township, in the parish and ¡nion of GUISBOROUGH, E. division of the liberty of

LANGBAURGH, N. riding of YORK, 6½ miles (S. E.) from Guisborough; containing 79 inhabitants. The name of this place is corrupted from Colman-dale, so called from Colman, Bishop of Lindisfarne, who had a hermitage here. It was given to the priory of Guisborough by the founder, and continued with that establishment until the Dissolution, when it passed to the Chaloner family, by whom the lands were afterwards divided and sold. The township is in the district called Cleveland, occupy-ing the south part of the parish, and comprising a narrow secluded vale, surrounded by high and heathy moors; it contains by computation 2630 acres of land, mostly the property of Viscount Downe. In the township is the hamlet of Skelderskew-Grange, which belonged to the priory of Basedale, and which probably derives its name from skell, a rivulet, and skew, wood-ground stand-ing on a hill; terms precisely descriptive of the posi-tion of the hamlet.

COMPSTALL, a village, in the parish and union of STOCKPORT, hundred of MACCLESFIELD, N. division of the county of CHESTER, 5 miles (E.) from Stockport. It lies on the west bank of the Etherow, which here sepa-rates the county from Derbyshire, and over which is a bridge from the village. The inhabitants are chiefly employed in spinning, power-loom weaving, bleaching, and printing, and the remainder principally at extensive coal-works in the neighbourhood. Forty years since, Compstall consisted of only a few straggling cottages, but since the establishment of the cotton-manufacture, it has been gradually rising to its present thriving con-dition. There is a place of worship for Wesleyans.

COMPTON (ST. NICHOLAS), a parish, in the union of WANTAGE, hundred of COMPTON, county of BERKS, 2¼ miles (E. S. E.) from East Ilsley; containing 544 in-habitants, and comprising by admeasurement 3600 acres. The living is a discharged vicarage, valued in the king's books at £11. 14. 4½.; net income, £330; patron, John Thomas Wasey, Esq.; impropriators, the Rev. James Best, and Messrs. Palmer.

COMPTON, a hamlet, in the parish of ASHBOURN, hundred of MORLESTON and LITCHURCH, though locally in the hundred of APPLETREE, S. division of the county of DERBY, ¼ a mile (S. E.) from Ashbourn. This place forms a suburb of the town of Ashbourn, from which it is separated by a small brook called the Schoo. Sion Chapel, with six almshouses attached to it, under the direction of the trustees of the Countess of Huntingdon's College, was built here by John Cooper, who, by deed in 1801, endowed them with £4500 three per cent. re-duced annuities, yielding a dividend of about £130 per annum. The premises were repaired in 1824.

COMPTON, a tything, in the parish and union of NEWENT, hundred of BOTLOE, W. division of the county of GLOUCESTER; containing 504 inhabitants.

COMPTON, a tything, in the parish of HENBURY, union of CLIFTON, Upper division of the hundred of HENBURY, W. division of the county of GLOUCESTER; containing 144 inhabitants.

COMPTON (ALL SAINTS), a parish, in the union of WINCHESTER, hundred of BUDDLESGATE, Winchester and N. divisions of the county of SOUTHAMPTON, 2 miles (S. W.) from Winchester; containing 304 inhabitants. The parish comprises by measurement 2099 acres; and the Itchen navigation, the London and Southampton road, and the London and South-Western railway, pass through it. The living is a rectory, valued in the king's books at £23. 6. 8.; net income, £329; patron, the Bishop of Winchester. The church, which is small, has portions in various styles, the Norman predominating; and contains a handsome monument, by Westmacott, to Dr. Huntingford, Bishop of Hereford, and Warden of Winchester College.

COMPTON, a liberty, in the parish of TETTENHALL REGIS, union of SEISDON, N. division of the hundred of SEISDON, S. division of the county of STAFFORD, 2 miles (W.) from Wolverhampton; containing 641 inhabitants. Here is a neat village, adjoining the Staffordshire and Worcestershire canal, and near Tettenhall-Wood, where a considerable quantity of sand is obtained for the use of the iron-founders, and for mixing with mortar. Several handsome houses and a great number of cottages have been built at Tettenhall-Wood since its inclosure in 1809; the cottages are mostly occupied by lock-makers. There is a small dissenting meeting-house.

COMPTON (ST. NICHOLAS), a parish, in the union of GUILDFORD, First division of the hundred of GODALMING, W. division of SURREY, 3½ miles (S. W. by W.) from Guildford; containing 522 inhabitants. It comprises 1971 acres, of which 77 are common or waste, and extends to the top of the chalk hill reaching from Guildford to Farnham; the soil is chalk, sand, and a little clay. The living is a rectory, valued in the king's books at £15. 4. 9½.; patron and impropriator, the Rev. George M. Molyneux: the tithes have been commuted for £421. 15., and the glebe contains nearly 72 acres, with a glebe-house. The church has a low tower and spire, and contains a curious chancel, with a groined roof, and a chapel over it; these portions are in the early English style, but there are others of decorated character. Dr. Edward Fulham, who attended Charles II. during his exile, and was the first canon of Windsor appointed after the Restoration, was born here in 1604.

COMPTON (ST. MARY), a parish, in the union of WESTBOURNE, hundred of WESTBOURNE and SINGLETON, rape of CHICHESTER, W. division of SUSSEX, 10 miles (N. W.) from Chichester; containing 274 inhabitants. The parish is bounded on the west by the county of Southampton, and the village is situated on one of the roads from Petersfield to Chichester. The living is a vicarage, endowed with a small portion of the rectorial tithes, with the living of Up-Marden annexed, and valued in the king's books at £13. 6. 8.; patron, and impropriator of the remainder of the rectorial tithes, M. R. Langdale, Esq. The great tithes have been commuted for £130, and the vicarial for £131; the glebe comprises 4 acres. The church is in the early and decorated English styles, and contains some neat monuments to the families of Peckham and Phipps. Edward Flower, in 1521, founded a free grammar school, with an endowment of £100 to be laid out in land; Thomas Pelham gave £80, with a rent-charge of £20, and in 1528, William Spicer conveyed lands in furtherance of the charity, the total income of which amounts to £28.

COMPTON, a tything, in the parish of ENFORD, union of PEWSEY, hundred of ELSTUB and EVERLEY, Everley and Pewsey, and S. divisions of WILTS; containing 73 inhabitants.

COMPTON-ABBAS, or WEST COMPTON (ST. MICHAEL), a parish, in the union of DORCHESTER, hundred of CERNE, TOTCOMBE, and MODBURY, Dorchester

674

Mendip range, presenting a very picturesque appearance : the village of Cross, in the parish, has a General st-Office. The living is a discharged vicarage, valued the king's books at £11 ; patron, the Prebendary of mpton-Bishop in the Cathedral of Wells : the great hes have been commuted for £71. 2., and the vicarial £203. 17.; the rectorial glebe contains 82½ acres, d the vicar's nearly 7 acres, with a glebe-house. The urch has a handsome stone pulpit, and the exterior ch of the porch is in the Norman style : in the church-rd is an ancient cross. A little to the south-west of mpton is a spacious natural cave, entered by a per-ndicular shaft ; and proceeding by a difficult winding ssage, a still more extensive cavern opens to the ght : from the roof, which expands into a kind of arch, ng formerly some beautiful stalactites ; and various crustations, assuming the most fantastic shapes, lay attered about; but all have been defaced or removed y visiters.

COMPTON-CHAMBERLAIN (St. Michael), a pa-sh, in the union of Wilton, S. division of the hun-ed of Damerham, S. division of Wilts, 8 miles (W.) om Salisbury ; containing 350 inhabitants. It abounds ith green sandstone, used for building. The living is discharged vicarage, valued in the king's books at 13 ; net income, £99 ; patron and impropriator, J. H. enruddock, Esq. : the rector is entitled to a rent-charge f £67. 12. out of the tithes of the parish of Tisbury. he church is an ancient cruciform structure, in the ecorated English style, with a square embattled tower n the south side, forming in the lower part a porch. olonel Penruddock, who was executed at Exeter, in 655, for an attempt to restore Charles II. to the throne, sided in the parish.

COMPTON-DANDO (St. Mary), a parish, in the nion and hundred of Keepesham, E. division of omerset, 2 miles (E. by N.) from Pensford ; contain-g, with part of Woolard hamlet, 359 inhabitants. It situated on the river Chew, and comprises 1845 acres, f which 25 are common or waste : there are some quar-es of stone, but of a quality fit only for the roughest uildings and for the roads. The living is a discharged icarage, valued in the king's books at £5. 10. 5. ; net come, £180 ; patron and appropriator, the Bishop of ath and Wells : the glebe comprises 50 acres, with a ouse. The church is a handsome structure in the de-rated and later English styles, with a square embattled wer ; at the north-east angle of the building is an en-ched buttress, the lowest portion of which is formed of e remains of a Roman altar, displaying in one of its ces a statue of Hercules Pacificator, and in the other, ne of Apollo. There is a place of worship for Wes-yans. A cold spring here is slightly impregnated with on. The Wansdyke traverses the parish in a north-est direction.

COMPTON-DUNDON (St. Andrew), a parish, in e union of Langport, hundred of Whitley, W. divi-on of Somerset, 2½ miles (N.) from Somerton ; con-ining, with the tythings of Compton and Dundon, and e hamlet of Littleton, 679 inhabitants, of whom 355 re in Compton tything. It comprises 2568 acres, of hich 1146 are arable, 1289 pasture, and 133 woodland. he living is a discharged vicarage, valued in the king's ooks at £9. 6. 10. ; net income, £201 ; patron, the ishop of Bath and Wells. The church stands in the

675

village of Dundon. The ruins of a mansion that for-merly belonged to the family of Beauchamp adjoin the churchyard. An adjacent hill is called Dundon Beacon, from a beacon having anciently stood on it.

COMPTON-DURVILLE, a tything, in the parish and hundred of South Petherton, union of Yeovil, W. division of Somerset, 1½ mile (W. N. W.) from South Petherton ; containing 136 inhabitants.

COMPTON, FENNY (St. Peter), a parish, in the union of Southam, Burton-Dassett division of the hun-dred of Kington, S. division of the county of War-wick, 8 miles (N. by W.) from Banbury ; containing 615 inhabitants. By measurement made in 1836, this parish comprises 2077 acres, which are chiefly pasture : the Oxford canal passes through it, and there is a wharf for coal. Within the limits of the parish are some quarries of good building-stone. The village lies at the northern base of the Dassett hills, part of which range is included in the parish : to the east of the village were formerly two windmills ; one was burnt down about eighteen years since, the other still remains. The living is a rectory, valued in the king's books at £15. 8. 4., and in the patronage of the President and Fellows of Corpus Christi College, Oxford, who purchased the ad-vowson in 1733. The tithes were commuted for land in 1778; the glebe comprises altogether 412 acres, and there is a glebe-house, built in 1842. The church is a very ancient structure, and is mentioned by Dugdale as having been given in the time of Henry I. to the canons of Kenilworth : in the chancel were formerly three in-scriptions in brass to the memory of the family of Willis ; one only of these now exists. The Wesleyans have a place of worship; and a national school is sup-ported by subscription. On the summit of Gredenton Hill, in the parish, are vestiges of a British camp in the form of a horse-shoe, 228 yards in length, and defended with six lines of ramparts, between which were fosses round the steep declivity of the hill. Sir Henry Bate Dudley, a comic writer of some note, was born here in 1745.

COMPTON-GIFFORD, a tything, in the parish of Charles the Martyr, Plymouth, union of Plympton St. Mary, hundred of Roborough, Roborough and S. divisions of Devon, 1½ mile (N. N. E.) from Plymouth ; containing 271 inhabitants. Here is a chapel connected with the Establishment. The vicarial tithes have been commuted for £225, of which £160 are payable to the vicar of St. Charles the Martyr's, and £65 to the vicar of St. Andrew's.

COMPTON-GREENFIELD, a parish, in the union of Clifton, Upper division of the hundred of Hen-bury, W. division of the county of Gloucester, 6¼ miles (N. by W.) from Bristol; containing 65 inhabit-ants. It comprises 650a. 2r. 2p. of which 39¼ acres are arable, and 610 pasture : the navigable river Severn flows on the western side. The living is a discharged rectory, valued in the king's books at £7, and in the gift of Caius Lippeucot, Esq. : the tithes have been com-muted for £140, and the glebe contains 50 acres, with a glebe-house.

COMPTON, LITTLE (St. Denis), a parish, in the union of Chipping-Norton, hundred of Kington, S. division of Warwickshire, 4½ miles (N. w. by W.) from Chipping-Norton; containing 301 inhabitants. The parish adjoins that of Long Compton, and within its

4 R 2

limits is a spot of land which marks the junction of the shires of Gloucester, Oxford, and Warwick. It comprises by computation 1600 acres; the soil is chiefly clay and rocky. The living is a perpetual curacy; net income, £66; patrons, the Dean and Canons of Christ-Church, Oxford. The tithes were commuted for land and a money payment, under an inclosure act, in 1794. Here is a mansion which was the residence of Bishop Juxon, chaplain to Charles I.

COMPTON, LONG (St. Peter and St. Paul), a parish, in the union of Chipping-Norton, Brailes division of the hundred of Kington, S. division of the county of Warwick, 4¼ miles (N. N. W.) from Chipping-Norton; containing, with the hamlet of Weston, 829 inhabitants. The parish is situated on the road from London to Birmingham through Oxford, and comprises 3750a. 2r. 11p. It had a weekly market and an annual fair, granted by Henry III. in the 15th of his reign, both of which are now disused: the village is a polling-place for the southern division of the county. The living is a discharged vicarage, valued in the king's books at £12. 15. 7½.; net income, £191; patrons and impropriators, the Provost and Fellows of Eton College. The tithes were commuted for land in 1811; the glebe contains 125 acres, with a glebe-house. There are places of worship for Wesleyans and Independents. About a mile southward is that remarkable monument of antiquity called Rollerich, or Rowlright, stones.

COMPTON-MARTIN (St. Michael), a parish, in the union of Clutton, hundred of Chewton, E. division of Somerset, 8 miles (N.) from Wells; containing 601 inhabitants. This parish, anciently Coomb-Martin, is situated on the north side of the Mendip hills, and comprises by computation 2200 acres. The scenery is remarkable for its richness, variety, and beauty; and at Highfield, near the entrance of the village, is a view commanding a romantic vale, extending to the Bristol Channel, with the mountains of Monmouthshire and Glamorganshire in the distance. The river Yeo has its source here, issuing from a pond in the centre of the village; and the road from Bristol to Wells passes through the parish. The living is a rectory, with that of Nempnett-Thrubwell annexed, valued in the king's books at £10. 6. 8.; patron and incumbent, the Rev. W. H. Cartwright: the tithes have been commuted for rent-charges of £265 each for Compton and Nempnett, and the glebe comprises 27 acres. The church is an ancient structure; the chancel is Norman, and the nave, aisles, and a private chapel, are of the later English style.

COMPTON, NETHER (St. Nicholas), a parish, in the union and hundred of Sherborne, Sherborne division of Dorset, 2¾ miles (W. N. W.) from Sherborne; containing 456 inhabitants. The living is a discharged rectory, with that of Over Compton annexed, valued in the king's books at £7. 18., and in the gift of John Goodden, Esq.: the tithes of the parish produce £243. 16. 3., and the glebe comprises 22 acres.

COMPTON, OVER (St. Michael), a parish, in the union and hundred of Sherborne, Sherborne division of Dorset, 3½ miles (W. by N.) from Sherborne; containing 151 inhabitants. The living is a rectory, annexed to that of Nether Compton, and valued in the king's books at £11. 9. 4½.: the tithes have been commuted for £87. 3., and the glebe comprises 52¼ acres.

58; patrons, the Rev. W. Bishop, and others: the hes were commuted for land and a money payment in 77. The church is a very ancient structure. CONDOVER (St. Andrew), a parish, in the union Atcham, hundred of Condover, S. division of Lop, 4½ miles (S.) from Shrewsbury; containing 1550 habitants. The parish comprises by measurement 7545 res, about two-thirds of which are arable, and 790 res are tithe-free; the soil is in some parts light and avelly, in others a stiff clay, and in others good mea-w-land. The surface is undulated, and rather hilly; e lands are watered by a copious stream called Cond-er brook, and there is a small lake named Bosmere, and near which have been found several botanical ants not known elsewhere in England. Coal exists ar the boundary of the parish, and a mine has been ened. The living is a discharged vicarage, valued in he king's books at £4. 14.; patron and impropriator, . W. Smythe Owen, Esq., of Condover Hall. The great thes have been commuted for £1092, and the vicarial r £210; the glebe contains nearly 7 acres.

CONEYSTHORPE, a township, in the parish of arton-in-the-Street, union of Malton, wapentake : Bulmer, N. riding of York, 4 miles (N. by W.) from hitwell; containing 170 inhabitants. The township omprises about 1150 acres, the soil of which is chiefly ght, and on a substratum of limestone; the surface is enerally undulated, and the scenery in many situations ery beautiful. A church built here in 1837, by the Earl f Carlisle, is a neat edifice with a campanile tower.

CONEYTHORPE, a township, in the parish of soldsborough, Upper division of the wapentake of Claro, W. riding of York, 4¼ miles (E. N. E.) from Knaresborough; containing 118 inhabitants. It com-rises by computation 800 acres of land, mostly the roperty of Lord Stourton. At this place is a large umulus called Claro Hill, which either gives its name o, or receives it from, the wapentake of Claro, and on vhich, it is said, the councils of the wapentake were of ld wont to be held.

CONEY-WESTON.—See Weston, Coney.

CONGERSTON (St. Mary), a parish, in the union f Market-Bosworth, hundred of Sparkenhoe, S. livision of the county of Leicester, 3¾ miles (N. W. y W.) from Market-Bosworth; containing 267 inha-litants. The parish comprises 587a. 2r. 17p., and is rather more than half of the lordship of Congerston. The surface is varied, and the soil, which is generally good, is well adapted in some parts for corn; a consi-lerable portion of land is meadow and pasture. The Ashby-de-la-Zouch canal flows through the parish. The iving is a rectory, valued in the king's books at £5. 3. 6½., and in the gift of Earl Howe, with a net in-come of £218: the tithes were commuted for land and a money payment in 1822. Charles Jennings, in 1773, eft £333 for teaching children; the school is in union with the National Society, and is assisted by Earl and Countess Howe.

CONGHAM (St. Andrew), a parish, in the union and hundred of Freebridge-Lynn, W. division of Norfolk, 7 miles (E. N. E.) from Lynn; containing 326 nhabitants. It comprises 2850a. 2r. 22p., of which thout 1887 acres are arable, 487 pasture, and 358 wood and plantations, the last chiefly in the vicinity of Cong-ham Lodge; there is a sheep-walk of 97 acres: the com-

mon was inclosed in 1812. The living is a rectory, with that of Congham St. Mary consolidated in 1684, valued together in the king's books at £12. 10.; patron and incumbent, the Rev. J. Wright. The tithes have been commuted for £565, out of which £25 are payable to the rector of Roydon; the glebe comprises 35 acres, with a glebe-house. The living was endowed in 1718, by Ellen Spelman, with lands then worth £53. 18. per annum. The church of St. Mary has been demolished; that of St. Andrew is chiefly in the early style, and has a chapel on the north side. The learned antiquary and historian, Sir Henry Spelman, was born at this place, in 1561, and served as high sheriff of the county in the year 1604; he died in London in 1641, and was buried in the south transept of Westminster Abbey.

CONGLETON, an in-corporated market-town, a chapelry, and the head of a union, in the parish of Astbury, having separate jurisdiction, locally in the hundred of Northwich, S. division of the county of Chester, 31 miles (N. E. by S.) from Chester, and 161 (N. W. by W.) from Lon-don; containing 9222 in-habitants. Some writers have considered this the site of Condate, an aboriginal settlement of the Cornavii; but Whitaker, in his History of Manchester, has convincingly refuted this opinion, and fixed that station at Kinderton. The place is noticed in the Domesday survey, under the designation of Cogle-tone; but its origin has not been satisfactorily ascer-tained. In the beginning of the fourteenth century, a free charter was bestowed upon it by Henry de Lacy, Earl of Lincoln, who in 1282 had procured the grant of a weekly market. In the reign of Henry VI., an inun-dation having done considerable damage to the town, the inhabitants obtained permission to divert the course of the river; and subsequently they had a grant of the king's mills, which stood on its banks. The town is situated in a valley embosomed in richly-wooded hills, on the south bank of the river Daven or Dane, over which a bridge was built in 1782, and, notwithstanding some recent improvements, consists of narrow and irre-gularly formed streets. The houses in the eastern part are old, and chiefly of timber and brick-work; those in the western part are in general modern and of handsome appearance. The inhabitants are supplied with water from springs, and from the rivulet Howtey or Howey, which intersects the town; in 1833, an act was obtained for lighting the streets with gas. The environs abound with scenery beautifully diversified by the windings of the river, on the banks of which are numerous elegant mansions and villas.

The manufacture of gloves, and of leather laces called Congleton Points, for which the town was celebrated, has given place to the throwing of silk, the spinning of waste silk and of cotton, and the manufacture of ribbons, handkerchiefs, and other silk goods. Forty mills for silk have been erected since 1753, when that branch of manufacture was introduced by Mr. Pattison, of London, who built the first mill here, an edifice now comprising five stories, 480 feet in length, and of proportionate

Corporation Seal.

width, and which is considered in point of extent the second in the kingdom. In this mill, ribbons and hand-kerchiefs are made to a great extent by the power-loom, a thousand hands being employed; it is the property of Samuel Pearson and Son, and is the second mill built in England, one having been built previously at Derby. A canal from Marple to join the Grand Trunk canal at Lawton, has been constructed, which, passing within a quarter of a mile of the town, materially facilitates its trade; and an act was passed in 1846 for a railway from Macclesfield, by Congleton, to the Potteries. The market is on Saturday; the fairs, chiefly for cattle, are on the Thursday before Shrovetide, May 12th, July 12th, and Nov. 22nd. The market-house, in High-street, a neat and commodious structure containing a handsome assembly-room, was built in 1822, at the expense of Sir Edmund Antrobus, Bart.; the market-place has recently been enlarged by the corporation, and is one of the best in the county.

The GOVERNMENT, by charter of incorporation granted by James I., in 1625, was vested in a mayor, 8 aldermen, 16 capital burgesses, a high steward, town-clerk, and subordinate officers. By the act of the 5th and 6th of William IV., cap. 76, the corporation now consists of a mayor, 6 aldermen, and 18 councillors; the borough is divided into three wards, being co-extensive with the township of Congleton; and the number of magistrates is nine. The corporation formerly held quarterly courts of sessions for trying prisoners charged with misdemeanors and felonies not capital; and courts of record are still held for the recovery of debts to any amount, by the high steward, an officer appointed by the corporation. A court leet, also, is held in August, at which the high steward, or his deputy, presides. The county debt-court of Congleton, established in 1847, has jurisdiction over the registration-district of Congleton. The guildhall, a neat brick building, was built in 1805.

The township comprises 2380 acres, the soil of which is loam and sand. The LIVING is a perpetual curacy; net income, £147; patrons and impropriators, the Mayor and Corporation. The chapel, dedicated to *St. Peter*, was rebuilt of brick, in 1740; a square tower of stone was added to it in 1786, and it was enlarged by the addition of two galleries in 1840, when the church-yard was also extended: the chapel stands on elevated ground, and commands a fine prospect. There was formerly another chapel at the end of the bridge, on the opposite side of the river Dane, which, having long since become desecrated, was appropriated to the reception of the poor; it was pulled down in 1810. At Congleton Moss, a church dedicated to the *Holy Trinity* was erected in 1845, at a cost of £1500, raised by public grants and by subscription, on a site given by the Rev. James Brierley, M.A.: the living is a perpetual curacy, in the patronage of the Rector of Astbury; income, £100. Two districts or ecclesiastical parishes have been formed under Sir Robert Peel's act: in the one, *St. Stephen's* district, a chapel has been purchased from the dissenters, and licensed by the bishop; in the other, *St. James'*, a church has been erected on a site given by Edward Lowndes Mallabar, Esq. The first stone of the church was laid on the 29th of May, 1847: the building is in the style which prevailed in the latter part of the 13th century, and cost about £3500, exclusively of the tower, which it is proposed to add hereafter at an expense of

CONHOPE, a township, in the parish of AYMES-EY, hundred of STRETFORD, union of LEOMINSTER, nty of HEREFORD, 4½ miles (N. by E.) from Pemdge; containing 72 inhabitants.

CONINGSBY (ST. MICHAEL), a parish, in the union d soke of HORNCASTLE, parts of LINDSEY, county of NCOLN, 8 miles (S.) from Horncastle; containing 59 inhabitants. This parish, which is situated on ‹ rivers Bain and Witham, and on the road from aford to Horncastle, comprises by computation)0 acres; the surface is flat, and the soil chiefly .d and gravel. An act for more effectually draining lands was obtained in 1840. The living is a rectory, ued in the king's books at £39. 10. 2½., and in the t of Sir Gilbert Heathcote, Bart.: the tithes were nmuted at the inclosure in 1802, for 600 acres of d, valued at £644 per annum. The church is a hand-ne structure, in the early English style. There are ces of worship for General Baptists, and Primitive d Wesleyan Methodists. The poet Dyer, who was for years resident in this parish, of which he was rector, s buried in the churchyard.

CONINGTON (ST. MARY), a parish, in the union ST. IVES, hundred of PAPWORTH, county of CAM-IDGE, 3¼ miles (S. by E.) from St. Ives; containing 6 inhabitants. The living is a rectory, valued in the ng's books at £9. 15. 10.; net income, £238; patron, e Bishop of Ely. The tithes were commuted for land 1799. There is an endowed school. Traces of the oat surrounding the site of an ancient fortress, called ruce Castle, may be discerned.

CONINGTON (ALL SAINTS), a parish, in the hun-red of NORMAN-CROSS, union and county of HUNT-‹GDON, 3 miles (S. E. by S.) from Stilton; containing 24 inhabitants. The lordship, together with the ancient 1stle, of which there are some vestiges in the village, as given by Canute to Turkill, a Danish lord, who, 1king advantage of his residence among the East ngles, invited over Sueno to plunder the country. fter Turkill's departure it fell to Waldeof, Earl of luntingdon, who married Judith, niece to the Con-ueror, from whom it descended to the royal line of cotland, and thence to the Cottons, ancestors of Sir .obert Cotton, celebrated for his valuable collection of ooks and MSS., known by the name of the Cottonian ibrary. The parish is situated near the north road, etween Alconbury Hill and Stilton, and comprises 089 acres, which consist partly of highland and partly f fen, the former a clayey soil, and the lower parts ex-remely fertile, with some excellent meadow and pas-1re. The living is a rectory, valued in the king's books t £19. 6. 8., and in the gift of J. Heathcote, Esq.: the thes have been commuted for £450, and the glebe ontains 27 acres, with a glebe-house, lately built. The hurch is a large handsome structure, erected in the ›ign of Henry VII., and has an embattled tower with ctagonal pinnacles; the interior has lately undergone xtensive repairs, and contains many monuments to the ‹ottons, and an inscribed tablet to the memory of Prince lenry of Scotland, Lord of Conington, &c. The Rev. ames Oram, in 1769, left £1000 for the endowment of wo schools, one being at this place. Sir Robert Cotton, n making an excavation for a pond, found the skeleton f a sea fish, twenty feet long, lying in perfect silt, about ix feet below the surface of the ground.

CONISBROUGH (ST. PETER), a parish, in the union of DONCASTER, S. division of the wapentake of STRAFFORTH and TICKHILL, W. riding of YORK, 6¼ miles (N. E. by E.) from Rotherham; containing 1445 inhabitants. This place, which is situated on the road from Sheffield to Doncaster, is of high antiquity, and has been connected with all the different dynasties by which Britain has been governed: it is stated to have been the seat of a civil jurisdiction, comprising twenty-eight towns, and is famed for the ruin of its Saxon castle, which stands upon a conical hill rising abruptly from the Don, and consists of the body of a circular tower encompassed by the ordinary concomitants of strong fortifications. Conisbrough is first mentioned as a fortress belonging to Hengist, the Saxon leader, who was defeated here in 487, by Aurelius Ambrosius, and again in 489, at which period, according to Geoffrey of Monmouth, he was made prisoner and beheaded at the northern gate of the citadel, where a tumulus is said to cover his relics: some, however, suppose that the pre-sent pile was érected by Earl Warren, to whom William the Conqueror gave the manor. In this castle, Richard, Earl of Cambridge, second son of the Duke of York, and grandson of Edward III., was born; he was be-headed for conspiring against Henry V. The round tower, or keep, is almost perfect, the remaining part forming a picturesque ruin: one of the principal scenes in Sir Walter Scott's romance of Ivanhoe is laid here. The parish comprises about 4000 acres of fertile land, in the vale of the Don, and abounds with beautiful scenery. Limestone of good quality is quarried to some extent, and the inhabitants are partly employed in the manu-facture of linen checks. The living is a discharged vicarage, valued in the king's books at £8. 12. 8½.; patron, the Archbishop of York; impropriators, Sack-ville Lane Fox, Esq., and others. The great tithes have been commuted for £366. 16., the vicarial for £223. 6., and a rent-charge of £1. 11. is paid to the archbishop; the glebe contains 66½ acres, with a glebe-house. The church is of Norman character, combined with the early, decorated, and later styles of English architecture; and had formerly a chantry, founded in the fifteenth of Ed-ward II.: there are several monuments, and the mu-tilated statue of a knight, together with a curious stone adorned with many hieroglyphics. Here is a place of worship for Wesleyans.

CONISCLIFFE (ST. EDWIN), a parish, in the union of DARLINGTON, S. E. division of DARLINGTON ward, S. division of the county of DURHAM; containing, with the townships of Carlebury and Low Coniscliffe, 422 inhabitants, of whom 244 are in the township of High Coniscliffe, 4 miles (W. by N.) from Darlington, on the road to Barnard-Castle. The village of High Coniscliffe, in which stands the church, is situated on the north bank of the Tees, occupying an eminence nearly sur-rounded by quarries. The living is a vicarage, endowed with a portion of the rectorial tithes, and valued in the king's books at £7. 18. 1½.; patron, the Bishop of Durham; impropriator of the remainder of the rectorial tithes, P. H. Howard, Esq. The great tithes have been commuted for £179, and the small for £182; the vicar has a glebe of 60 acres. The church is a very ancient structure, partly in the Norman and partly early Eng-lish, with a Norman tower surmounted by a handsome spire. There is a place of worship for Wesleyans.

CONISCLIFFE, LOW, a township, in the parish of CONISCLIFFE, union of DARLINGTON, S. E. division of DARLINGTON ward, S. division of the county of DURHAM, 3 miles (W.) from Darlington; containing 134 inhabitants. This place is on the north bank of the Tees, and on the road from Darlington to Carlebury. Thornton Hall, within the township, now a farmhouse, was the seat of the Tailbois, the Thornton, the Bowes, and Honeywood families.

CONISHOLM (ST. PETER), a parish, in the union of LOUTH, Marsh division of the hundred of LOUTH-ESKE, parts of LINDSEY, county of LINCOLN, 8¼ miles (N. E. by E.) from Louth; containing 146 inhabitants. The living is a discharged rectory, valued in the king's books at £9. 13. 6½., and in the gift of the Earl of Ripon: the tithes have been commuted for £180. 2. 6., and the glebe contains 64 acres. There is a place of worship for Wesleyans.

CONISTON, a township, in the parish of SWINE, union of SKIRLAUGH, Middle division of the wapentake of HOLDERNESS, E. riding of YORK, 5½ miles (N. E. by N.) from Hull; containing 110 inhabitants. The abbey of Thornton had possessions at this place (styled in Domesday book *Coiningsesbi*) in the 12th century; the monastery of Swine held land here at a later period; and among other proprietors in former times occurs the family of Cobbe. The township consists of about 600 acres; the village is pleasantly situated on the road from Hull to Hornsea. The tithes were commuted for land and a money payment in 1789.

CONISTON, with KILNSAY, a chapelry, in the parish of BURNSALL, union of SKIPTON, E. division of the wapentake of STAINCLIFFE and EWCROSS, W. riding of YORK, 12 miles (N. by E.) from Skipton; containing 172 inhabitants. The chapelry comprises by computation 5380 acres, a great portion of which is open moorland, affording tolerable pasture. Kilnsay Craggs, a lofty range of limestone rocks rising to the height of 170 feet, presenting a rugged front more than half a mile in length, and in places overhanging the line of their base nearly forty feet, form a strikingly grand and romantic feature in the scenery of Wharfdale. The chapel, dedicated to St. Mary, is a small neat edifice.

CONISTON, COLD, a township, in the parish of GARGRAVE, union of SKIPTON, E. division of the wapentake of STAINCLIFFE and EWCROSS, W. riding of YORK, 7 miles (W. N. W.) from Skipton; containing 242 inhabitants. This place was distinguished during the Border warfare for the intrepid conduct of its inhabitants, who in an attempt to resist the progress of an army of Scottish invaders at a spot called Sweep Gap, on the northern side of Coniston Moor, were nearly all killed. The township comprises by computation 1710 acres, chiefly moorland affording excellent pasture; the village is situated on the road to Settle, and the surrounding scenery is pleasingly diversified. Here is a church dedicated to St. Peter, the living of which is a perpetual curacy, in the gift of J. G. Garforth, Esq.: a consolidated chapelry is annexed, comprising part of the parishes of Gargrave and Kirkby-Malhamdale.

CONISTON, MONK, with SKELWITH, a township, in the parish of HAWKSHEAD, union of ULVERSTON, hundred of LONSDALE north of the Sands, N. division of the county of LANCASTER, 4 miles (W. by N.) from
680

Hawkshead; containing 470 inhabitants, of whom 259 are in Monk-Coniston. This place consists of various groups of houses and neat cottages, roofed with slate from the adjacent mountains, and beautifully scattered round the head of Coniston Lake, anciently called Thurston Water, which is about six miles in length from north to south, about half a mile in its greatest width, and about twenty-seven fathoms in depth. The lake abounds with char, said to be of finer flavour than the char of other lakes; and at the head, on the margin of the water, is an inn for the accommodation of visiters, where post-horses, carriages, and pleasure-boats are always in readiness. The scenery around abounds with every variety of picturesque and romantic grandeur. A church was erected and endowed by Mr. Redmayne, on the Brathey Hall estate, here, in 1835, and consecrated the year following; it is a neat edifice on the road from Hawkshead to Ambleside, near Brathey Bridge, where are two pleasing cascades.

CONISTONE, CHURCH, a chapelry, in the parish and union of ULVERSTON, hundred of LONSDALE north of the Sands, N. division of the county of LANCASTER, 6 miles (S. W.) from Ambleside; containing 1148 inhabitants. The manor, which was held by the Urswicks, passed by marriage in the reign of Henry III. to the le Flemings, and became the seat of seven descents of the family. About the 10th of Henry IV., Thomas le Fleming married one of the four daughters of Sir John de Lancaster, by whom he acquired the manor of Rydal, in Westmorland; and for seven generations more, Rydal and Conistone vied to fix the family in Westmorland or Lancashire. Sir Daniel Fleming, Bart., died in 1821, leaving his lady his estates. The township is the most northern part of the county, stretching to the shire-stone near the hills of Wrynose and Hard-Knot; within its limits are Yewdale and the reputed lordship of Tilberthwaite. The population of the village has increased from the flourishing state of the copper-mines and slate-quarries here. A fair for cattle is held on the third Saturday in September. The chapel was consecrated in 1586, and re-erected in 1819, when 230 additional sittings were provided: the living is a perpetual curacy, in the patronage of T. R. G. Braddyll, Esq.; net income, £100. To the north-west of the village is the Old Man, the most elevated mountain in the county, 2576 feet above the level of the sea; on its summit are three heaps of stones called the Old Man, his Wife, and Son, supposed relics of the Sabæan superstition.

CONOCK, a tything, in the parish of CHURTON, union of DEVIZES, hundred of SWANBOROUGH, Devizes and N. divisions of WILTS, 4½ miles (N. E. by E.) from East Lavington; containing 160 inhabitants.

CONONLEY, a township, in the parish of KILDWICK, union of SKIPTON, E. division of the wapentake of STAINCLIFFE and EWCROSS, W. riding of YORK, 3 miles (S.) from Skipton; containing 1159 inhabitants. The township formerly constituted a joint township with Farnhill, from which it was separated in 1838; it comprises by computation 1500 acres. The village is pleasantly situated on the western acclivity of Airedale, and the surrounding scenery is pleasingly diversified. A lead-mine was opened in 1840. Tithe rent-charges have been awarded amounting to £62. 3., of which £33. 14. 6. are payable to the Dean and Chapter

Christ-Church, Oxford, and £28. 8. 6. to the vicar the parish.

CONSALL, STAFFORDSHIRE.—See CUNSALL.

CONSIDE, or CONSETT, with KNITSLEY, a township, in the chapelry of MEDOMSLEY, parish and union LANCHESTER, W. division of CHESTER ward, N. division of the county of DURHAM, 14½ miles (N. W. by W.))m Durham; containing 195 inhabitants. This place, ciently Conkesheved, was successively in the possession various families, and once belonged to the Halls, of 1om several had a taste for literary pursuits, espe- 1lly John Hall, born in 1627, who was a man of very nsiderable talent, and is commemorated by Antony à ood. The township comprises 2353 acres, of which .61 are arable, 520 pasture, and 272 woodland. Ex- nsive iron-works are carried on at Consett, being a cent revival of the ancient manufacture of which this ighbourhod was the seat; the Romans, and, about '0 centuries ago, a colony of Germans who had set- :d at Shotley-Bridge, having worked the mines, the oduce of which, known as the Derwent iron, is very perior. Coal is also abundant, and, being the out- op of the Durham coal-field, is probably worked at 1s expense than that of any other part of the kingdom. re-bricks are manufactured; and besides the coal d iron, a considerable traffic exists in lead, lime, and nber. The Stanhope railway, in connexion with the)ntop and Shields railway, intersects the township.

CONSTANTINE (ST. CONSTANTINE), a parish, in e union of FALMOUTH, E. division of the hundred of ERRIER, W. division of CORNWALL, 5½ miles (N. E. y E.) from Helston; containing 2042 inhabitants. 'his parish, which is bounded on the south by the 1avigable river Hel, and includes a part of the port of iweek, comprises 8000 acres by computation : the soil 1ear the river is rich and fertile, but in the higher parts terile rock ; the hills are chiefly of granite. The village 1 pleasantly situated on an eminence nearly surrounded 1y tin-works, and commands some delightful views of he river, with its numerous creeks, the banks of which re finely clothed with wood. A copper and tin mine, alled Wheal-Vyvyan, is worked ; and large masses of ;ranite are scattered over the surface of the lands, of ize sufficient for building bridges. Great quantities of ysters are sent from Merthen, on the river, to Rochester. ;he petty-sessions for the division are held here. The iving is a discharged vicarage, valued in the king's)ooks at £19. 3. 10½., and in the gift of the Dean and Chapter of Exeter, who are also appropriators : the ithes have been commuted for £480 payable to the ap- ropriators, and £485. 12. to the incumbent, who has a ;lebe of 11 acres. The church contains an ancient monu- nent, with a brass, to the family of Gervis. There are 1laces of worship for Wesleyans and Bryanites. On he estate of Mayere, in the parish, is a vast rock of ;ranite computed to weigh 750 tons, called the Tolmen, n the shape of an egg, with several excavations on the op, curiously poised upon two others ; and at a short 1istance is another mass, of circular form, resembling a :ap. The sites of decayed chapels are discernible at 3onallock and Budockvean; and near the church, 1 bag, full of silver coins of Arthur and Canute, was 'ound about the close of the seventeenth century.

COOKBURY (ST. JOHN THE BAPTIST), a parish, in .he union of HOLSWORTHY, hundred of BLACK TOR-

RINGTON, Holsworthy and N. divisions of DEVON, 4¼ miles (E. N. E.) from Holsworthy ; containing 301 inha- bitants. The parish comprises 1833 acres, of which 1083 are common or waste. The living is a perpetual curacy, annexed to the rectory of Milton-Damerell.

COOKHAM (HOLY TRINITY), a parish, the head of a union, and formerly a market-town, in the hundred of COOKHAM, county of BERKS, 3½ miles (N. by E.) from Maidenhead; containing 3676 inhabitants. This parish, extending south-westward to Maidenhead Thicket, and comprehending the whole of that waste, is situated on the river Thames, by which it is bounded on the north and east; and comprises by measurement about 10,000 acres, of which nearly 4000 are arable, more than 1000 grass, 93 in orchards, 151 wood, and 884 common. There is a considerable hamlet called Cookham-Dean, about a mile and a half to the west of the village, border- ing upon Bisham, and consisting of scattered cottages; it is noted for its orchards, rural scenery, and woodland ; and the wildness of its character, in the midst of a highly cultivated neighbourhood, renders it the more attractive to the lover of nature in her simpler form. A bridge has been built across the Thames, which greatly facilitates traffic, and affords ready access out of Buckinghamshire to the Great Western railway. The manufacture of coarse paper is carried on; fairs are held on May 16th and October 11th. The living is a vicarage, valued in the king's books at £14. 14. 2.; patron, John Rogers, Esq.; impropriators, the land- owners. The great tithes have been commuted for £1252, and the vicarial for £480; there is a vicarial glebe of 7½ acres. Near the entrance into the chancel of the church is a brass plate to the memory of Sir Ed- ward Stockton, vicar of the parish, who died in 1534, and is styled " Pylgrym of Jerusalem, and canon pro- fessed of the House of our Lady at Guisbro' in York- shire :" this no longer appears, being probably concealed by a pew. Several descendants of General Washington, and Mr. Hooke, the historian of the Roman empire, are interred in the church. There is an episcopal chapel in that part of Maidenhead situated in the parish ; and at Cookham-Dean is a church dedicated to St. John, which has a chapelry district attached. The Independents and Wesleyans have places of worship. The poor law union of Cookham comprises 7 parishes or places, and contains a population of 11,060.

COOKLEY (ST. MICHAEL), a parish, in the union and hundred of BLYTHING, E. division of SUFFOLK, 2½ miles (W. S. W.) from Halesworth ; containing 324 inhabitants, and comprising by computation 1664 acres. The living is a discharged rectory, united to that of Huntingfield, and valued in the king's books at £6. 13. 4. The church is chiefly in the later English style, and consists of a nave and chancel, with an embattled tower ; the font is curiously sculptured, and there is a Norman doorway on the north side filled up. A school was founded by Thomas Neale, in 1701.

COOKLEY, a hamlet, in the parish of WOLVERLEY, union of KIDDERMINSTER, Lower division of the hun- dred of OSWALDSLOW, Kidderminster and W. divisions of the county of WORCESTER, 3 miles (N. by E.) from Kidderminster. The soil here is of light quality, and good for the cultivation of turnips and barley ; the surface is undulated, and the scenery very pleasing. The river Stour and the Staffordshire and Worcestershire canal pass through the hamlet. The village lies about a mile higher up the stream than Wolverley; it is a busy manufacturing place. The Cookley iron-works, established two centuries ago, and now the pro-perty of Messrs. John Knight and Company, employ 550 hands in making iron and tin plates, and all kinds of best iron; and the Wood-Screw Company employ 150 hands. The cottages of the workmen and villagers are very neat. The Wesleyans have a place of worship; and an infant school is supported by the Sebright charity.

COOKNOE, NORTHAMPTON.—See COGENHOE.

COOLING (ST. JAMES), a parish, in the union of Hoo, hundred of SHAMWELL, lathe of AYLESFORD, W. division of KENT, 6 miles (N. by E.) from Rochester; containing 144 inhabitants. This parish, originally called *Colniges* or *Colnegcs*, from its bleak situation, and at a later period *Cowling*, contains the remains of a castle built in 1331, formerly of great strength, but long since dismantled; they occupy eight acres. The parish is bounded on the north by that part of the Thames named Sea-reach, and comprises 1544 acres of land, the substratum of which is chalk: there are 30 acres of wood. The living is a rectory, valued in the king's books at £14, and in the gift of T. Best, Esq.: the tithes have been commuted for £570, and the glebe contains about 9 acres. In the church is a tomb of Lord Cobham.

COOLING (ST. MARGARET), a parish, in the union and hundred of RISBRIDGE, W. division of SUFFOLK, 8¼ miles (N. N. W.) from Clare; containing 882 inha-bitants. There are fairs on July 31st and October 17th. Branches Hall, in the parish, is a large and handsome mansion. The living is a perpetual curacy; net income, £100; patrons and impropriators, the Master and Fel-lows of Trinity Hall, Cambridge. Wm. Deynes, in the 35th of Elizabeth, bequeathed estates here, the proceeds to be equally divided among the parishes of Cooling, Hargrave, Barrow, and Moulton.

COOL-PILATE, a township, in the parish of ACTON, union and hundred of NANTWICH, S. division of the county of CHESTER, 4 miles (S.) from Nantwich; con-taining 59 inhabitants. In this township were two Halls, with considerable estates annexed to each; one belonging to the Whitneys, and more recently to the Darlingtons and Tomkinsons; the other, to the St. Pierres, and subsequently to the Davenports, whose representative sold it in 1786. The township com-prises 635 acres, of a clayey soil. The river Weaver passes on the east. The impropriate tithes have been commuted for £45, and the vicarial for £12. 18.

COOMBE, a township, in the parish of PRESTEIGN, union of KNIGHTON, hundred of WIGMORE, county of HEREFORD, 2½ miles (E. S. E.) from Presteign; con-taining 121 inhabitants. It consists of 608 acres, and is intersected by the river Lug, which partly separates it on the north-west from Wales, and is joined here by the brook Endwell. Many vestiges of British encamp-ments are to be seen in the vicinity.

COOMBE, a hamlet, in the parish of HUISH-EPIS-COPI, union of LANGPORT, E. division of the hundred of KINGSBURY, W. division of SOMERSET; containing 25 inhabitants.

COOMBE, a tything, in the parish and hundred of EAST MEON, union of PETERSFIELD, Petersfield and N.

egular area, about thirteen miles in circumference.
e lands are generally low, in some parts undulated,
d the soil is gravelly, producing fair average crops;
e scenery is in general pleasing, and enlivened with
veral fine sheets of water. The manor was the pro-
rty of the bishops of London from a remote period
l the time of the Conquest. The living is a rectory,
lued in the king's books at £15. 3. 4., and in the pa-
nage of the Crown: the tithes have been commuted
£660, and the glebe comprises 74 acres, with a glebe-
use. The church, an ancient structure, is principally
Norman architecture; the walls are of unusual thick-
ss, and the chancel is circular. Bonner, Bishop of
ndon, who was lord of the manor, resided for a con-
lerable time at Copford Hall.

COPGROVE (St. Michael), a parish, in the Lower
vision of the wapentake of Claro, W. riding of York,
miles (S. W. by W.) from Boroughbridge; containing
3 inhabitants. It comprises 1000 acres, the surface
which is hilly, and the soil gravelly: a small stream,
tributary to the Ure, passes on the west, and separates
e place from the parish of Burton-Leonard. The
ing is a discharged rectory, valued in the king's books
£5. 9. 7., and in the gift of T. Duncombe, Esq., of
opgrove Hall: the tithes have been commuted for
170, and the glebe contains 23 acres, with a glebe-
ouse. St. Mongah's Well, in the village, was formerly
lebrated for its medicinal properties.

COPLE (All Saints), a parish, in the union of
Edford, hundred of Wixamtree, county of Bedford,
miles (E. by S.) from Bedford; containing 551 inha-
itants. This parish, which is intersected by the road
·om Oxford to Cambridge, and bounded on the north
y the navigable river Ouse, comprises by computation
108 acres, whereof 1350 are arable, 580 pasture, and
0 wood. The living is a discharged vicarage, valued
1 the king's books at £7; net income, £215; patrons
nd appropriators, the Dean and Canons of Christ-
'hurch, Oxford: the glebe consists of 7 acres, with a
lebe-house. The church is in the later English style,
nd contains some brasses. There is an old house for-
nerly belonging to the family of Luke, one of whom,
ir S. Luke, employed Butler, the poet, as secretary, and
vas ridiculed under the character of Hudibras.

COPMANTHORPE, a chapelry, in the parish of
T. Mary-Bishopshill-Junior, E. division of Ainsty
vapentake, union and W. riding of York, 4 miles (S. W.
y S.) from York; containing 284 inhabitants. This
hapelry, called in old documents Temple-Copman-
horpe, comprises by measurement 1652 acres, of which
337 are arable, 236 meadow and pasture, 30 woodland,
nd 47 common. The York and North-Midland railway
asses through. The living is a perpetual curacy, with
he living of Upper Poppleton annexed; patron, the Vicar
f the parish; net income, £100. The tithes have
een commuted for £498. 15., of which £430 are payable
o the Dean and Chapter of York, and £68. 15. to the
ear, the former having also a glebe of 25 acres, and
he latter a glebe of one acre. The chapel is a small
lain building: a faculty was granted in 1750, for in-
losing a chapelyard for the interment of the dead.
'here is a place of worship for Wesleyans. Adjoining
he hamlet is a field called "Temple field," in which,
ccording to tradition, stood a temple; of what descrip-
ion, or to whom dedicated, there is no record; but

stones, evidently parts of pillars, and others curiously
carved, have been found in the field, and in the fields
adjoining, and similar ones appear also in the walls of
some of the oldest houses.

COPP.—See Eccleston, Great.

COPPENHALL (St. Michael), a parish, in the
union and hundred of Nantwich, S. division of the
county of Chester; comprising 2629 acres, and containing, in 1841, 747 inhabitants, of whom 544 were in
the township of Church-Coppenhall, 5 miles (N. E.)
from Nantwich, and 203 in that of Monks-Coppenhall.
The manor of Church-Coppenhall belonged soon after
the Conquest to the family of Waschett; about the end
of the thirteenth century it is supposed to have passed
to the De Orrebys, and among subsequent owners have
been the families of Corbet, Hulse, Shaw, and Broughton.
Monks-Coppenhall appears to derive its prefix from
having belonged at an early period to the monks of Combermere: of the families that have held the property
since, may be named those of Crue, Burnell, Vernon,
and Cholmondeley. The Liverpool and Birmingham
railway extends for nearly 2½ miles in the parish, the
Chester and Crewe railway for a mile and a half, and
the Crewe and Manchester for nearly two miles. (See
Crewe.) The living is a rectory, valued in the king's
books at £6. 10., and in the patronage of the Bishop
of Lichfield: the tithes have been commuted for £275,
and the glebe comprises 10 acres. The church, built of
wood and plaster, in the style which prevailed in the reign
of Elizabeth, was taken down, and rebuilt of brick, in
1821. There is a place of worship for Wesleyans.

COPPENHALL, a chapelry, in the parish and union
of Penkridge, E. division of the hundred of Cuttlestone, S. division of the county of Stafford, 3 miles
(S. by W.) from Stafford; containing 119 inhabitants.
It comprises 963a. 2r. 5p., about three-fourths of which
are arable, and the rest pasture and meadow. The living
is a perpetual curacy; net income, £85; patron and
impropriator, Lord Hatherton. The chapel, dedicated
to St. Lawrence, is built of timber and brickwork, of
the reign of Elizabeth.

COPPINGFORD (All Saints), a parish, in the
hundred of Leightonstone, union and county of
Huntingdon, 7 miles (N. W. by N.) from Huntingdon;
containing 45 inhabitants. It comprises by measurement 807 acres, of which 537 are arable, 200 pasture,
and 70 wood. The living is a rectory, consolidated
with that of Upton, and valued in the king's books at
£18. 13. 1½.: the church is in ruins.

COPPIN-SIKE, with Ferry-Corner, an extra-
parochial liberty, in the union of Boston, wapentake of
Kirton, parts of Holland, county of Lincoln; containing 42 inhabitants.

COPPULL, a township, and an ecclesiastical district,
in the parish of Standish, union of Chorley, hundred
of Leyland, N. division of the county of Lancaster,
4 miles (S. S. W.) from Chorley; the township containing 1031 inhabitants. Richard Fitz-Thomas, lord of
Coppull, before the general use of dates in charters,
gave to the priory of Burscough a part of his land, and
"pannage in the woods of Coppull, with common of
pasture, and all the easements and liberties appertaining
to the town of Coppull." In the 5th of Charles I.,
Edward Rigbye held the manor, which was subsequently
sold to the Hodgson family. The township was originally

skirted by a copse, and hence, probably, derived its name ; it is of level surface, and commands fine views of the Rivington hills. There is an extensive coal-mine, also some print-works ; see *Birkacre.* One of the stations of the North-Union railway is situated here. The ecclesiastical district includes the townships of Charnock-Richard and Welsh-Whittle : the living is a perpetual curacy ; net income, £120 ; patron, the Rector of Standish. The church was built in 1657, rebuilt and enlarged in 1758, and repaired in 1840. ' The tithes of Coppull have been commuted for £261. 12. 6. A national school was built in 1847.

COPSTON MAGNA, a chapelry, in the parish of MONKS-KIRBY, union of LUTTERWORTH, Kirby division of the hundred of KNIGHTLOW, N. division of the county of WARWICK, about 5 miles (S. S. E.) from Hinckley ; containing 113 inhabitants. This place, called Great Copston, to distinguish it from Copston Fields, or Copston Parva, a hamlet in the parish of Wolvey, owes its name to one Copst, who possessed it in the time of the Saxons. It comprises 1080 acres, whereof two-thirds are arable, and the remainder meadow and pasture. The chief proprietor is the Earl of Denbigh. The chapel is part of a larger edifice.

CORBETSTYE, a hamlet, in the parish of UPMINSTER, union of ROMFORD, hundred of CHAFFORD, S. division of ESSEX ; containing 177 inhabitants.

CORBRIDGE (ST. *ANDREW*), a parish, in the union of HEXHAM, E. division of TINDALE ward, S. division of NORTHUMBERLAND ; comprising the townships of Aydon, Aydon-Castle, Clarewood, Corbridge, Dilston, Halton, Halton-Shields, Thornborough, and Great and Little Whittington ; and containing 2103 inhabitants, of whom 1356 are in the township of Corbridge, 4½ miles (E.) from Hexham. This place, which is of great antiquity, appears to have been known to the Romans, who, at a short distance to the west, had a station on the line of the Watling-street, supposed by Camden to have been the *Curia Ottadinarum* of Ptolemy, and by Horsley the *Corstopitum* of Antoninus, and which is now called Corchester. In 1138, David, King of Scotland, who made frequent incursions into the English territories, encamped his forces at this place ; which was subsequently burnt by the Scots in 1296, and again in 1311. From its great importance, King John, expecting to find concealed treasure, directed a search to be made here, but without effect. This monarch, in the 6th year of his reign, bestowed the manor upon Robert de Clavering, Baron of Warkworth ; and the last baron having granted his Northumberland estates to the crown in reversion, they were given by Edward III. to Henry Percy, in whose line they continue to this day. During the parliamentary war, a battle was fought here between the royalists and the Scottish forces. The place was formerly a borough and market-town, had extensive privileges, and returned members to parliament. Some vestiges of its ancient consequence are still apparent : to the south of the church is a venerable tower, once used as the town gaol; and a little to the east is an eminence called Gallow Hill, the place of execution for criminals. It early carried on a considerable trade, and that it was originally of much greater extent, is evident, from the former existence of three additional churches, severally dedicated to St. Mary, St. Helen, and the Holy Trinity, the sites of which are well known.

great plenty; the stone is used also for the roads. e ancient family of the lords Latimer held property the parish in early times; the manor is now vested in ꞓ Earl of Cardigan. The living is a rectory, valued in ꞓ king's books at £13. 16. 3., and in the gift of the rl. The church is a uniform and beautiful specimen the decorated style, and consists of a chancel, nave, uth aisle, and south porch, with a western tower and ire; it was probably erected at the commencement of e 14th century. The porch is entirely of stone, the of being supported by two arched stone ribs. The ifice was internally in a very dilapidated state, but s been successfully restored; the piers, arches, and ndows have been scraped, and relieved from many ats of whitewash, and new open seats have been put , possessing the character of the old oak seats. In ꞓ church is a tomb, supposed to cover the remains of ord Latimer; and in the churchyard is a monument old date, remarkable for the beauty of its design, d its picturesque effect. The Independents have a all place of worship. There is a national school, pported by the Earl of Cardigan; also a British and ꞏreign school for boys and girls, endowed by Mr. ꞏwlatt, a former inhabitant of the village.

CORBY, GREAT, a township, in the parish of ETHERAL, union of CARLISLE, ESKDALE ward, E. ivision of CUMBERLAND, 6¼ miles (E. S. E.) from Carsle; containing 806 inhabitants. The village is pleaꞏntly situated on the east bank of the Eden; and conguous to it, on the summit of a precipitous cliff, stands orby Castle, anciently the seat of the Salkelds, who nherited it from Hubert de Vallibus, Baron of Gilsland, ꞏnd from whom it passed by purchase to its present ꞏossessors, the Howards, a branch of the Norfolk family. The mansion was much modernised and improved in ꞏ813, and the scenery and walks surrounding it abound n natural beauties. The Corby viaduct for conveying ꞏhe Newcastle and Carlisle railway over Corby, or Dryꞏeck, valley, consists of seven arches spanning 40 feet ꞏach; the height from the ground is 70 feet, the whole ength 480 feet, and as a specimen of architecture it is ittle inferior to Wetheral bridge. A school was enꞏlowed in 1720 with 25 acres of land, yielding about £20 ꞏer annum.

CORBY, LITTLE, a township, in the parish of WARWICK, union of BAMPTON, ESKDALE ward, E. diꞏision of CUMBERLAND, 5½ miles (E. by N.) from Carꞏisle; containing 283 inhabitants. The village is situꞏated at the junction of the Eden and Irthing rivers.

CORELY (ST. PETER), a parish, in the union of CLEOBURY-MORTIMER, hundred of STOTTESDEN, S. diꞏision of SALOP, 4½ miles (E.) from Tenbury; ꞏontaining 525 inhabitants. It is picturesquely situated ꞏt the base of the Clee hills, on the road from Ludlow ꞏo Cleobury, and comprises 2174 acres, whereof 877 are ꞏommon or waste; the soil is principally clay; the ꞏultivated land is mostly pasture. Several coal-mines are in operation. The living is a discharged rectory, valued in the king's books at £5. 5. 10., and in the patronage of W. Hall, Esq. : the tithes have been commuted. The church was rebuilt about 70 years ago, with the exception of the tower, which is ancient. There is a national school.

CORFE, a parish, in the union of TAUNTON, hundred of TAUNTON and TAUNTON-DEAN, W. division of

SOMERSET, 3 miles (S.) from Taunton; containing 279 inhabitants. It comprises 1127 acres of land, whereof 348 are common or waste. Stone is quarried, to be burnt into lime. The living is a perpetual curacy, with a net income of £66, and is in the gift of Lady Cooper, who owns the tithes, which have been commuted for £89. 13.

CORFE-CASTLE (ST. EDWARD THE MARTYR), an incorporated town and parish, in the union of WAREHAM and PURBECK, possessing separate jurisdiction, locally in the hundred of CORFE - CASTLE, Wareham division of DORSET, 23 miles (E. S. E.) from Dorchester, and 120 (S. W.) from London; containing 1946 inhabitants. This place, which in the Saxon Chronicle is termed Corve and Corvesgeate, appears to have derived its importance from a formidable CASTLE erected by Edgar prior to the year 980, at the gate of which Edward the Martyr, when calling to visit his step-mother Elfrida, was by her order treacherously murdered. In the reign of Stephen the castle was taken by Baldwin de Rivers, Earl of Devonshire, who held it against the king : it was frequently the residence of King John, who here kept the regalia, and by whose orders twenty-two prisoners, some of them among the principal nobility of Poitiers, were starved to death in its dungeons; and Edward II., after his deposition in 1327, was removed from Kenilworth to this fortress, where he was detained for a short time prior to his tragical death at Berkeley Castle. During the parliamentary war, Lord Chief Justice Bankes, who then resided in the castle, being with the king at York, Sir Walter Earl and Sir Thomas Trenchard assaulted the place, thinking to obtain easy possession of it for the parliament; but it was heroically defended by Lady Bankes and her daughters, with the assistance only of their domestics, until, on the approach of Charles to Blandford, Captain Lawrence was sent to her assistance, when, having raised a small guard of her tenantry, she sustained a siege for six weeks, and, with the loss of two men only, preserved the castle for the king. In 1645, the castle was again besieged by the parliamentary forces, under Fairfax, when, by the treachery of Lieutenant-Colonel Pitman, an officer of the garrison, who deserted from the king's service, it was taken and demolished. The remains of this stupendous edifice are extensive and interesting, and plainly indicate its former prodigious strength; they occupy the summit of a lofty and steep eminence to the north of the town, with which they are connected by a bridge of four narrow circular arches, crossing a deep ravine, and leading to the principal entrance between two massive circular towers. The walls, which inclose a spacious area divided into four wards, were defended by numerous circular towers at convenient distances, of which several have declined from the perpendicular line, owing to the attempts made to undermine them at the siege, and of which, as well as of the walls, vast fragments have fallen into the vale. At the western angle are the remains of the keep, a massive octagonal tower, and in the inner

Seal and Arms.

ward those of the king's and queen's towers, between which is part of the chapel, with two pointed windows; the east end of the king's tower, which is separated from the main building, is overgrown with ivy, and forms a picturesque feature in these extensive ruins, which, from their elevated situation, are conspicuously grand and majestic.

The TOWN stands on an eminence, nearly in the centre of the Isle of Purbeck, and consists principally of two streets diverging from the market-place, in the centre of which is an 'ancient stone cross; the houses are in general built of stone, obtained from the neighbouring quarries, and are approached by a flight of steps; the inhabitants are well supplied with water. The bridge connecting the castle with the town is called St. Edward's bridge, and is said to be the spot where Edward, fainting from the loss of blood, fell from his horse and expired. At the entrance from the London road is an ancient stone bridge over the small river Corfe, by which the town is bounded on the east. The population is chiefly employed in the quarries and clay-pits for which the isle is celebrated; and from the principal of these, called Norden, about a mile from the town, a railway has been constructed, to facilitate the communication with Poole harbour, where the clay is shipped for the Staffordshire and other potteries. A few of the female inhabitants are engaged in the knitting of stockings. The market, which was held on Thursday, has been for some time discontinued; the fairs are on May 12th and October 29th. The lord of the manor of Corfe was anciently hereditary lord-lieutenant of the Isle of Purbeck, and had the power of appointing all officers, and determining all actions or suits by his bailiff or deputy; he was also admiral of the isle, and exercised the authority of lord high admiral, in which capacity he was entitled to all wrecks, except in cases where there was a special grant to the contrary. These privileges ceased on the passing of the Militia act, in 1757, Mr. Bankes, then lord of the manor, having omitted to enforce his claims. Though a borough by prescription, the town was not incorporated till the 18th of Queen Elizabeth, who invested it with the same powers as were enjoyed by the cinque-ports. Under the existing charter of Charles II., the corporation consists of a mayor, who is elected at the court leet of the lord of the manor, held at Michaelmas, and eight barons, who have previously served the office of mayor; the mayor and the late mayor are justices of the peace. The elective franchise was granted in the 14th of Elizabeth, from which time the borough returned two members to parliament, till it was disfranchised in the 2nd of William IV.

The parish comprises 7193 acres, of which 1479 are common or waste. The LIVING is a rectory, valued in the king's books at £40. 14. 7.; net income, £685; patron, William Bankes, Esq. The church is a spacious and ancient structure, partly Norman, and partly in the early English style, with a lofty embattled tower, crowned by pinnacles, and ornamented with niches in which are some sculptured decorations of singular design; it contains a few old monuments and several altar-tombs of Purbeck marble. The parish is in the centre of a district of considerable extent, in which the earliest of the Sunday schools were established, under the auspices of William Morton Pitt, Esq., of Kingston House. Several schools are supported by subscription.;

CORNARD, LITTLE (*ALL SAINTS*), a parish, in the
on of SUDBURY, hundred of BABERGH, W. division
SUFFOLK, 3 miles (S. E.) from Sudbury; containing
3 inhabitants. It is bounded on the south-west by
navigable river Stour, and comprises about 1400
es. The living is a rectory, valued in the king's
ıks at £8. 2. 8½., and in the patronage of Mrs. Green:
tithes have been commuted for £492, and there is a
be of 50 acres.

CORNBROUGH, a township, in the parish of
ERIFF-HUTTON, union of MALTON, wapentake of
LMER, N. riding of YORK, 11 miles (N. by E.) from
rk; containing 63 inhabitants. The township com-
ises 920 acres by measurement, divided between arable
d pasture.

CORNELLY (*ST. CORNELIUS*), a parish, in the union
TRURO, W. division of the hundred of POWDER and
the county of CORNWALL, ¾ of a mile (W. by S.) from
egoney; containing 119 inhabitants, and comprising
out 1047 acres. The living is a perpetual curacy; net
come, £47; patron, the Vicar of Probus; impropria-
rs, the principal inhabitants: the glebe contains 12
res. It was anciently annexed to Probus, from which
was separated in 1532, the incumbent paying 6s. 8d.
nually to the vicar of that parish, as an acknowledg-
ınt. The Bishop of Exeter receives a tithe rent-charge
£134, and the incumbent one of £15.

CORNEY (*ST. JOHN THE BAPTIST*), a parish, in the
ion of BOOTLE, ALLERDALE ward above Derwent, W.
ivision of CUMBERLAND, 4 miles (S. E. by S.) from
avenglass; containing 273 inhabitants. This parish
situated on the coast of the Irish Sea, and comprises
bout 3000 acres, of which 1000 are common or waste;
: is bounded on the east by a lofty range of fells
tretching on the south to the mountain of Black Comb.
he surface is boldly varied, and the scenery in many
arts strikingly picturesque; the higher grounds com-
and diversified prospects, and from Corney Hall is an
xceedingly fine view of the sea and numerous interest-
ıg objects. On the lands of the Hall are several veins
f iron-ore of very rich quality, but of limited depth,
'hich were wrought to some extent about 80 years
ince. The living is a discharged rectory, valued in the
ing's books at £9. 17. 1.; net income, £140; patron,
ıe Earl of Lonsdale. To the north of the village are
ome extensive ruins, of which the history is unknown,
nd in the neighbourhood were numerous Druidical re-
ıains. Mr. Troughton, an eminent philosophical in-
trument maker, was a native of the parish.

CORNFORTH, a township, in the parish of
lISHOP'S-MIDDLEHAM, union of SEDGEFIELD, N. E.
ivision of STOCKTON ward, S. division of the county of
)URHAM, 6¼ miles (S. S. E.) from Durham; containing
00 inhabitants. It comprises about 1570 acres. Coal
ı obtained, which is shipped on the Tees; and a vast
uantity of limestone is quarried from a hill, at the bot-
ɔm of which the village lies, in a low and warm situa-
on: the houses are disposed in the form of a square,
'ith a green of several acres in the centre. The impro-
riate tithes have been commuted for £108. 6. 6., and
ıe vicarial for £28. 10. Dr. Hutchinson, a learned
'riter, was born here. An extensive burial-ground was
iscovered a few years since, in a field on the summit of
ıe high ground on the south of the village: the graves
re made in all directions, and at no great depth, in the

687

magnesian limestone; in one was found the umbo of a
shield, and in another the head of a spear.

CORNHILL, a parish, in the union of BERWICK-
UPON-TWEED, in NORHAMSHIRE, N. division of NORTH-
UMBERLAND, 1½ mile (E. by S.) from Coldstream; containing 823 inhabitants. It comprises about 4430 acres,
of which the soil is productive and chiefly arable, and the
scenery of a romantic character. The village, which is
pretty and salubrious, is separated from Scotland by the
Tweed only; Coldstream is the first town over the
border, and the river is crossed by a noble stone bridge.
There is a good hotel for the sporting gentlemen who
resort here to hunt in great numbers during the winter
months. A fair is held on December 6th. The living
is a perpetual curacy, in the patronage of the Dean and
Chapter of Durham, who are the appropriators. The
church, dedicated to St. Helen, was rebuilt in 1751,
when a stone coffin, containing fragments of a human
skeleton, and two urns of coarse earthenware, were
found; it was again partly rebuilt in 1840, at a cost of
about £500, and is principally in the early English style,
with a campanile bell-tower. The castle here was demolished by the Scots in 1385, and again in 1549, when
a considerable booty fell into their possession; the remains are built up in a modern mansion. To the south-
east is an encampment of unusual construction; and a
quarter of a mile westward is another large collection of
earth-works, the most remarkable north of the Wall for
variety and extent. In a wood is St. Helen's well, the
water of which is serviceable in scorbutic and gravel
complaints; but it is not much used.

CORNSAY, a township, in the parish and union of
LANCHESTER, N. W. division of DARLINGTON ward,
S. division of the county of DURHAM, 6¼ miles (N. E.)
from Wolsingham; containing 201 inhabitants, and
comprising 2141 acres, of which 200 are common or
waste. The impropriate tithes have been commuted for
£119. 10. In 1811, Wm. Russell, Esq., of Brancepeth
Castle, gave an endowment of £20 per annum for a
schoolmaster, and built and endowed almshouses for six
men and six widows.

CORNWALL, a maritime county, bounded on the
north by the Bristol Channel, on the west by the Atlantic
Ocean, on the south by the English Channel, and on the
east by Devonshire. It extends from 49° 57′ 30″ to
50° 55′ 30″ (N. Lat.) and from 4° 10′ to 5° 44′ (W. Lon.),
and contains 1327 square miles, or 849,280 statute
acres: within its limits are 65,574 inhabited houses,
4962 uninhabited, and 926 in the course of erection;
and the population amounts to 341,279, of whom 164,757
are males, and 176,522 females. The part of Britain
including this county and a portion of Devonshire, from
its shape was called by its ancient British inhabitants
Kernou, or, as it is written by the Welsh, *Kerniw*, signifying " the horn," which word was Latinized to *Carnu-
bia* or *Cornubia*; and when the Saxons gave the name of
Weales to the Britons, they distinguished those who had
retired into Kernou, or Cornubia, by that of *Cornwealas*,
and their country was thus called Cornwall, or Cornwall, that is, " Cornish Wales." At the time of the
Roman Conquest, the northern part was inhabited by
the *Cimbri*, the eastern by the *Danmonii*, and the remaining portion by the *Carnabii*, of whom the Danmonii
had subdued the two other tribes, and taken possession
of their territories; but on the completion of the Roman

Conquest, the whole became included in the great province of *Britannia Prima*. During the aggressions of the Saxons, various acts of hostility occurred between them and the Cornish Britons, and the latter were obliged to invoke the assistance of the Danes, who arrived on this coast in 806. King Egbert, nevertheless, overran the whole territory; and the Britons were at length finally reduced by Athelstan, prior to which time they had occupied a great part of Devonshire, and inhabited Exeter in common with the Saxons.

Cornwall is within the diocese of Exeter, and province of Canterbury; and forms, with three parishes in Devonshire, an archdeaconry, comprising the deaneries of East, Kerrier, Penwith, Powder, Pyder, Trigg-Major, Trigg-Minor, and West, and containing 203 parishes: the Scilly Islands are also in the archdeaconry of Cornwall. The office of rural dean, which in most parts of the kingdom has become nearly nominal, is here an efficient office; the rural deans are appointed annually, perform regular visitations to every church within their deaneries, and report the state of each at the archdeacon's visitations. For civil purposes the county is divided into the hundreds of East, Kerrier, Lesnewth, Penwith, Powder, Pyder, Stratton, Trigg, and West. It contains the borough and market towns of Bodmin, Falmouth, Helston, Launceston, Liskeard, Penryn, St. Ives, and Truro; the following market-towns, also ancient boroughs, but deprived of their privilege of sending representatives to parliament by the act of the 2nd of William IV., cap. 45, *viz.*, Bossiney, Callington, Camelford, East Looe, Fowey, Lostwithiel, St. Mawes, Saltash, and Tregoney; four decayed boroughs having no markets, deprived in like manner, *viz.*, Newport, St. Germans, St. Michael, and West Looe; and twelve market-towns which are not boroughs, *viz.*, Camborne, Grampound, Marazion, Padstow, Penzance, Polperro, Redruth, St. Agnes, St. Austell, St. Columb, Stratton, and Wadebridge. Of the above towns, twelve are sea-ports, *viz.*, Falmouth, Fowey, Looe, Marazion, Padstow, Penryn, Penzance, Polperro, St. Agnes, St. Ives, Truro, and Wadebridge; besides which, there are the smaller ports of Boscastle, Bude, Charlestown, Gweek, Hayle, Helford, Mevagissey, New Quay, Porth, Port-Isaac, Portleven, Portreath or Basset's Cove, and Trevannance. By the act above named the county was divided into two portions, called the Eastern and the Western divisions, each sending two representatives to parliament: the boroughs Bodmin and Truro continue to return two members each, as also does Penryn, in conjunction with Falmouth, which, prior to the passing of the act, enjoyed no share in the representation: Helston, Launceston, Liskeard, and St. Ives, each now return only one. Cornwall is included in the Western circuit: the spring and summer assizes, and the quarter-sessions, are held at Bodmin, where stand the county gaol and house of correction; and the Easter quarter-sessions at Truro.

Cornwall is a royal duchy, settled by act of parliament on the eldest son of the sovereign; and its immediate government is vested in the duke, who has his chancellor, attorney-general, solicitor-general, and other officers, and his court of exchequer, with the appointment of sheriffs, &c. The important concerns of the tin-mines are under a separate jurisdiction, the tin-miners being, by ancient privilege confirmed by Edward III., exempt from all other civil jurisdiction than that of the *Stannary*

ops usually cultivated are wheat, barley, and oats, including the naked oat, called in Cornwall *pillis* or *pilez*, word signifying "bald." The green and root crops nsists principally of turnips, *ruta baga*, potatoes, in me places the flat-pole or drum-head cabbage, and :llow clover, trefoil, and rye-grass, the last here called :ver. The dry, light, friable and porous soils of Cornall, and its moist and mild climate, are particularly vourable to the growth of potatoes, which have here een cultivated to a great extent longer than in any ther parts of the kingdom ; in the vicinity of Penzance ie land produces two crops in the year, and an acre has een known to yield 300 bushels of the early kidneyotatoes at the first crop, and 600 bushels of appleotatoes at the second : a large quantity is sent to ondon, Plymouth, and Portsmouth. The natural eadows are comparatively of small extent, and lie attered throughout the county ; the only pasture nds consist of the wastes, and of the fields of artificial rasses. Many of the valleys are well wooded, parcularly in the south-eastern part of the county, and in ie vicinity of Lostwithiel and Bodmin ; and there are ctensive plantations at Tregothnan, Clowance, Tehidy, ort Eliot, Carclew, Trelowarren, Boconnock, Heligan, c. : the principal landowners having of late years irected their attention to planting, chiefly in elevated ituations, the face of the country, in the course of wenty or thirty years, will present extensive woodland cenery. Nearly a fourth part of the surface, from 50,000 to 200,000 acres, consists of uninclosed moors, owns, and *crofts*, as the waste lands are here generally .alled.

Cornwall has been celebrated for the produce of its ꓵINES from a remote period of antiquity. Strabo, Ꮋerodotus, and other ancient writers relate that the ?hœnicians, and after them the Greeks and the Romans, raded for TIN to Cornwall and the Scilly Islands, under he name of the islands *Cassiterides*, from a very early ꞓeriod ; and Diodorus Siculus, who wrote in the reign ꞓf Augustus, gives a particular account of the manner n which the tin-ore was dug and prepared by the Bri ons. At what time the coinage of the tin procured here ꞷas established is uncertain, but it was practised as :arly as the reign of King John. In that of Edward I. t was first ordered, for better securing the payment of he duty to the earl, that all tin should be brought to :ertain places appointed for that purpose, to be weighed ꞷnd stamped, or, as it is usually termed, *coined*; and that ꞷo tin should be sold until the stamp had been affixed. Ꮯhe term *coinage*, by which this process has always been lesignated, appears to have been derived from cutting ꞷff a *coign*, or corner of each block, to ascertain its ꞷurity. The average annual quantity raised from these ꞷines in the years 1799, 1800, and 1801, was 16,820 ꞷlocks, each weighing about 3¼ cwt.; in 1811, the ꞷuantity produced was only 14,698 blocks, but in 1824, t had increased to 28,310, and in 1831 it was 25,155, he average of the eight years from 1824 to 1831 inclusive being 26,647 blocks. The mineral rights of tin in he duchy manors were sold, about 35 years ago, for a :rm of years. The tin-ore has always been smelted n the county, at first in blast-furnaces, the buildings for ꞷhich were called "blowing-houses ;" but reverberatory ꞷurnaces being introduced early in the last century, the ꞷre has since been smelted in them with pit-coal from

South Wales, the produce being called "common tin." The blowing-houses are now used for smelting the diluvial or stream tin, in which charcoal alone is employed ; and the produce is called "grain tin," being of purer quality, and bearing a higher price than the common kind. The *Copper* mines were not extensively worked until the close of the 17th century, since which the quantity of ore raised has been gradually increasing : in 1824, 110,000 tons of ore were obtained, producing 8417 tons of copper, of the value of £743,253 ; in 1826, 128,459 of ore, producing 10,450 of copper, of the value of £755,358 ; in the year ending June, 1831, 146,502 of ore, producing 12,218 of copper, of the value of £817,740 ; and in 1837, 140,753 of ore, producing 10,823 of copper, of the value of £908,613. The produce of the *Lead* mines is inconsiderable, and the only mine from which silver is extracted is in the parish of Calstock. The various mines employ a fourth of the entire population, and the wages paid from the copper-mines alone, exceed half a million annually ; the steam-engines employed at the mines annually consume 80,000 tons of coal.

Much use is made of the various kinds of stone found in the county ; and the Cornish slate is a considerable article of commerce. Of this, the principal quarries are those on the southern coast, those between Liskeard and the Tamar, those in the parishes of Padstow and Tintagel, and the celebrated quarry of Delabole, or Dennybal, in the parish of St. Teath, the produce of which is held in the highest esteem, and is shipped in large quantities from Port Isaac, about five miles distant, both coastwise and to the continent : the quartz crystals found in this quarry are of great brilliancy. There is a large quantity of stone suitable for building in various parts of the county ; it is principally taken from the porphyry dykes, or elvan courses, which traverse both the granite and slate strata ; the granite, or moor-stone, which abounds on the surface of the moors, has of late years been exported for the erection of bridges and other public buildings. Steatite, or soap rock, of a fine soft texture, is found imbedded in the serpentine, near the Lizard, and is the most curious of all the earthy substances found in Cornwall ; it is of various colours, but the pure white is most esteemed for the porcelain manufacture, for the use of which much of it is exported. An abundance of felspar-clay, resulting from the decomposition of granite, is obtained in the parishes of Roche, St. Stephen, and St. Denis ; and is likewise shipped, chiefly at the neighbouring ports of Charlestown and Pentuan, for the manufacture of china and fine earthenware. A yellow sandy clay, which, from its resisting intense heat, is called fire-clay, found near Lelant, is sent to Wales, for laying the bottoms of copper furnaces. In the parish of St. Keverne is a yellow clay used to make moulds for casting metals ; and near Liskeard is found a clay of a slaty nature, but of a soapy texture, which has fertilizing properties. Among the Cornish ornamental stones may be enumerated its serpentine or porphyry, its marbles, talc, stalactites, and the asbestos and small gems : its fossils are of great variety, many of them beautiful in colour, and some clear and transparent, from which they have obtained the name of Cornish diamonds.

The abundance of *Fish* on the coast constitutes an important source of trade. The most esteemed species for the table, such as the turbot, dory, piper, sole, red mullet, whiting, &c., are plentiful; but the most important of the fisheries are those of mackerel, herrings, and pilchards, particularly of the last, which are peculiar to this coast, the opposite coast of Britanny, and the south of Ireland. After supplying the inhabitants with their winter stock, the great mass of pilchards are salted, the oil is then pressed out of them, and they are packed in hogsheads for exportation, principally to the ports of Italy. The chief stations of the pilchard-fisheries are Fowey, Looe, Mevagissey, St. Mawes, the coves of the Lizard, and in Mount's bay, on the south coast; and St. Ives and New Quay, on the north coast. About 21,000 hogsheads are annually produced; 2000 tons of mackerel are also taken. Oysters are found in great abundance in the creeks of the Hel, and exported to the Medway, where they are laid down to fatten for the London market.

There are few branches of *Manufacture*, except such as relate to the smelting and preparation of the metals. The manufacture of carpets is carried on at Truro, and coarse woollen-cloths are made at Truro and Perran-Arworthal; there are iron-foundries at Perran-Wharf and Hale, and manufactories for gunpowder at Kennall Vale, in the parish of St. Stythians, and at Cosawes, in that of St. Gluvias. With regard to the state of the *Harbours*, the mouths of nearly all the tide rivers on the north coast have been almost choked with sand cast up by the surge, or drifted in by the north-westerly winds. The principal RIVERS are, the *Tamar*, which forms, from the sea up to its source (excepting only for the space of about three miles) the boundary between this county and Devonshire, and is navigable as high as New Quay, about 24 miles above Plymouth; the *Lynher* or *Lyner*, which becomes navigable at Noddetor or Notter Bridge, and spreads into the Lynher creek, four miles below which it falls into the Tamar; the *Tide*, or *Tidi*, which becomes navigable two miles above St. Germans creek, which forms a junction with the Lynber creek; the *East Looe* river, which is navigable up to Sand-place; the *Duloe*, a tributary of the East Looe, and navigable up to Trelawnwear; the *Fowy*, which becomes navigable, at high water, at Lostwithiel, three miles below which it joins the Leryn creek, and forms a wide and deep haven, falling into the sea below Fowey; the *Fal*, which about a mile below Tregoney spreads into a wide channel, and soon afterwards opens into the broad expanse of Falmouth harbour, through which it empties itself into the sea, being navigable in all its creeks; the *Hel*, which at high water becomes navigable at Gweek, and, being joined in the latter part of its course, by several small creeks, forms Helford haven, within a mile below which it falls into the sea, through an estuary about a mile broad; the *Heyl*, which at St. Erth spreads into the estuary of Hayle, the latter about two miles further opening into St. Ives' bay; the *Alan* or *Camel*, which is navigable up to Polbrock; and the *Seaton*.

A canal was constructed from *Bude* harbour to *Thornbury*, in the county of Devon, by a company formed in 1819. It has divers branches: from Red Post a branch, nineteen miles in length, extends down the western bank of the Tamar to Druxton Bridge, about three miles north of Launceston; and from Burmsdon there is a branch, nearly a mile and a half in length, up the west bank of the Tamar to Moreton Mill,

where it receives a feeder from a reservoir on Langford Moor. In 1825, an act was obtained for the construction of the *Liskeard and Looe canal*, which commences at Tarras Pill, and terminates at Moorswater, being five miles and seven furlongs in length, and having twenty-five locks: there is a branch, about a mile in length, to Sand-place. In 1824, an act was obtained for making a railway from *Redruth* to *Point Quay*, in the parish of St. Feock, with several branches; also for restoring, improving, and maintaining the navigation of Restrongett creek. The *Redruth and Chacewater railway*, commencing at the town of Redruth, proceeds in an eastern direction to Nangiles, where it is joined by a branch from the mines near Scorrier Hall. The *Hayle railway*, chiefly for the conveyance of minerals from that place to Redruth, with a branch to Portreath, joins the Redruth and Chacewater railway; it has been bought by the West Cornwall Railway Company, and will form part of their line from Truro to Penzance. The *Bodmin and Wadebridge railway*, for the conveyance of minerals and passengers, was opened in 1834: the line is 12 miles in length.

Cornwall abounds with rude monuments of its aboriginal inhabitants, much resembling those found in Ireland, Wales, and North Britain, consisting of large unwrought stones placed erect, either singly or in circles, or with others laid across, and of tumuli of stones or earth: the numerous circles of erect stones are generally termed *Dawns-mên*, " the stone dance." There are also two circular inclosures of stone, or earth, one at St. Just near the Land's End, and the other at Peranzabuloe, within which are rows of seats, having formed amphitheatres, originally designed for the exhibition of various sports, and where, in later times, the Cornish plays were acted: these are called " rounds," or *plan an quare*, " the place of sport." Tumuli are to be seen in all parts of the county. Another kind of rude stone monument, most probably sepulchral, occurs in many places, viz., the cromlech, which consists of a large flat stone laid horizontally upon several others fixed upright in the ground, and which is provincially called the " quoit," or the " giant's quoit." Celts have been found here more abundantly than in any other part of the kingdom. Several artificial caves, or subterranean passages have been discovered, consisting of long galleries extending in various directions, formed of upright stones with others laid across. In 1749, a great number of gold coins, believed to be British, was found in the middle of the ridge of Carnbrè Hill. In several parts of the county may be seen rude stones of granite, with inscriptions, supposed to be ancient British, and some of them coeval with the time of the Romans. The Roman antiquities consist mostly of coins, which of late years have been discovered in abundance in the western part of the county; and of spear-heads, swords, and other weapons of mixed metal, which have frequently been found in the ancient mines and stream-works. The situation of any of the Roman stations has not been ascertained. Ancient roads, or fragments of them, are visible in various parts of the county: one of these, believed to be British, traverses the hills, with barrows at intervals along its line, from the Land's End towards Stratton and the north of Cornwall, passing near the great British station of Carnbrè. Two Roman roads enter the county from Devonshire, one of which was a tinuation of the great road from Dorchester and :ter; the other appears to have led from Torrington the northern part of Devonshire towards Stratton. ps and earthworks are particularly numerous, the ater part of them being nearly round or oval. In ny places along the coast a single vallum runs across m the edge of one cliff to that of another, with a ditch the land side. There are considerable remains of a lum called the "Giant's Hedge," which appears to e been originally about seven miles and a half in gth, extending in an irregular line from the river Looe, ittle above the town of West Looe, to Leryn.

Before the Reformation, there were about twenty igious establishments, including two alien houses, and e commandery of the Knights Hospitallers ; there were o eleven colleges and seven hospitals: but the nastic remains are few, and, excepting those of St. rmans Priory, not remarkable. Small chapels, or itories, erected over wells or springs to which extraordinary properties have been attributed, abound in st parts of the county, the greater part of them however in ruins; and throughout the whole of it are ancient one crosses, not only in the churchyards, but on the oors, and in other solitary situations. There are also, rticularly in the narrowest parts of the county, from . Michael's Mount to the Land's End, remains of veral rude circular buildings on the summits of hills, very remote antiquity, and still denominated Castles; gether with several cliff castles, formed by stone walls nning across necks of land from one cliff to another the sea-coast. Of more regular fortresses the prinpal remains are those at Launceston, Carnbrè, Tintagel, 'rematon, and Restormel, all of high antiquity, and the rst believed to be of British origin. The most perfect pecimen of ancient domestic architecture is Cothele louse, built in the reign of Henry VII. Many others f the houses of the landed proprietors are also fine old imily mansions, of very antique structure, though some f them have been altered, enlarged, and modernised. Notwithstanding the abundance and variety of the mineal strata, there are few springs possessing mineral proerties. The Cornish men were formerly much addicted o sports and pastimes, especially to the miracle play, rrestling, and hurling; the practice of wrestling still revails. Cornwall, as before noticed, gives the title of)uke to the eldest son of the sovereign.

CORNWELL, a parish, in the union of CHIPPINGJORTON, hundred of CHADLINGTON, county of OXFORD, , miles (W.) from Chipping-Norton; containing 97 inabitants. The living is a discharged rectory, valued in he king's books at £7. 4. 2., and in the patronage of the 'rown; net income, £140.

CORNWOOD (St. MICHAEL), a parish, in the union f PLYMPTON St. MARY, hundred of ERMINGTON, Erington and Plympton, and S. divisions of DEVON; ontaining, with the village or post-town of Ivy-Bridge, 080 inhabitants. The parish comprises 10,680 acres, f which 7459 are moor, common, and waste; it is inersected by the river Yealm, and bounded on the northast by the Erm. About 5000 acres of moor are, for nine nonths in the year, appropriated to the pasture of large uantities of cattle and sheep. Granite is found in abunlance, and extensively quarried for building. Cattleairs are held on the first Monday in May, and the fourth Monday in September. The living is a vicarage, valued

691

in the king's books at £33. 4. 7.; net income, £405; patron, the Bishop of Exeter; impropriator, Sir J. L. Rogers. The glebe comprises about 80 acres. The church is in the ancient English style, and has three stone stalls and a piscina. There is a chapel for the district of Ivy-Bridge, at the extremity of the parish : the living is in the gift of Sir J. L. Rogers. A school on the national plan is aided by an endowment of £10 per annum by the Rev. Duke Yonge, the late vicar, who also bequeathed £20 per annum for affording medical assistance to the poorer inhabitants. The Rook charity, comprising upwards of 27 acres, produces a rent of £44, which is distributed among the poor. The aunt of Sir Walter Raleigh resided at Fardd, in the parish.

CORNWORTHY (St. PETER), a parish, in the union of TOTNES, hundred of COLERIDGE, Stanborough and S. divisions of DEVON, 4½ miles (S. E. by S.) from Totnes; containing 554 inhabitants. The parish is situated on the navigable river Dart, and separated from Ashprington by the river Harborne, which falls into the Dart. It comprises by estimation 1600 acres : the soil is fertile in some parts, in others poor ; there are some good pastures, and productive orchards. About fifty persons are employed in the paper manufacture. Here are quarries of limestone, which is raised for building purposes, but chiefly for burning into lime, and for the roads. The living is a discharged vicarage, valued in the king's books at £10; net income, £210; patron, the Rev. Charles Barter ; impropriators, Edward Holdelet, J. Peete, and H. Tucker, Esqrs. The church is a neat structure in the later English style, and contains a monument to Sir Thomas Harrison. A school, now conducted on the national plan, was founded in 1609, by Elizabeth Harris, and endowed by her with land producing about £25 per annum. Sir John Peters bequeathed a small sum from the great tithes, to be distributed to poor people ; and there are some cottages erected on land given for that purpose by Sir Peter Edgecumbe. A priory for seven nuns of the order of St. Augustine, said to have been founded by the family of Edgecumbe, and valued at the Dissolution at £63 per annum, formerly stood here : two of the arched gateways still remain.

CORPUSTY (St. PETER), a parish, in the union of AYLSHAM, hundred of SOUTH ERPINGHAM, E. division of NORFOLK, 6 miles (W. N. W.) from Aylsham ; containing 449 inhabitants. The parish is on the road from Norwich to Holt, and comprises 1018 acres, whereof 49 are common or waste : the village is situated on the south side of a branch of the river Bure, on which is a flour-mill. The living is a discharged vicarage, valued in the king's books at £4. 12. 8½.; net income, £62 ; patron, the Bishop of Norwich ; impropriator, J. R. Ives, Esq., whose tithes have been commuted for £256. The church, which stands on an eminence commanding very fine views, is chiefly in the decorated style, and consists of a nave and chancel, with a square embattled tower ; the nave is separated from the chancel by the remains of a carved screen, and there is a handsome sculptured font. The Wesleyans and Primitive Methodists have each a place of worship.

CORRIDGE, a township, in the parish of HARTBURN, union of MORPETH, W. division of MORPETH ward, N. division of NORTHUMBERLAND, 11 miles (W. by S.) from Morpeth ; containing 22 inhabitants. The

4 T 2

families of Aynsley, Robson, and Carr have held lands here. The township is divided into two farms, East and West, and comprises 329a. 1r. 19p., of which 67 acres are arable, 262 pasture, and the remainder woodland; the river Wansbeck passes on the north. A rent-charge of £24 is paid to the vicar of Hartburn.

CORRINGHAM (ST. MARY), a parish, in the union of ORSETT, hundred of BARSTABLE, S. division of ESSEX, 3 miles (E.) from Horndon-on-the-Hill; containing 255 inhabitants. The parish is situated between Tilbury Fort and Canvey Island, and bounded on the south by the river Thames: at the time of the Norman survey it belonged to the Bishop of London. The living is a rectory, valued in the king's books at £22. 13. 4.; patron and incumbent, the Rev. J. H. Stephenson, whose tithes have been commuted for £830, and whose glebe contains 29 acres. The church, situated on the Green, is an ancient building, with a low tower surmounted by a shingled spire.

CORRINGHAM (ST. LAWRENCE), a parish, in the union of GAINSBOROUGH, wapentake of CORRINGHAM, parts of LINDSEY, county of LINCOLN, 4 miles (E. by N.) from Gainsborough, on the road to Louth; comprising the hamlets of Aisby, Dunstall, and Yawthorpe, the township of Little Corringham, and the chapelry of Somerby; and containing 564 inhabitants, of whom 189 are in Little Corringham. This parish is in the Norman survey called *Coringeham*; it gives name to the wapentake, and is the head of a deanery, the original establishment of which, though not exactly known, must have been prior to the year 1100. The hamlet of Great Corringham comprises 1889 acres; that of Little Corringham 987: including respectively 595 and 275 acres of common or waste. The village is seated between two branches of the small river Eau. The living is a vicarage, valued in the king's books at £12, and in the patronage of the Bishop of Lincoln: the great tithes have been commuted for £532. 12. 11., and those of the vicar for £170. 18. The church, which belonged to the Knights Templars, is an ancient stone structure in the Norman style, with later additions, and has a tower; the south doorway has a richly ornamented Norman arch, and there are several similar arches within the church, which evidently consisted originally only of a nave and chancel. Here are two places of worship for Wesleyans.

CORSCOMBE (ST. MICHAEL), a parish, in the union and hundred of BEAMINSTER, Bridport division of DORSET, 3½ miles (N. E.) from Beaminster; containing 810 inhabitants. The parish comprises by computation 5000 acres; the soil is various, in some parts chalky, in some clayey, and in others a rich black mould. The village is situated on the north side of a hill, and commands extensive views over the county of Somerset to the Bristol Channel, and the mountains of Wales. The Court-house, belonging to the lord of the manor, and now occupied as a farmhouse, is nearly encompassed by a moat, over which was a drawbridge. The living is a rectory, valued in the king's books at £21. 3. 4., and in the gift of W. Maskell, Esq.: the tithes have been commuted for £573, and the glebe comprises 61 acres. The church is a neat edifice, erected about 1675.

CORSE (ST. MARGARET), a parish, in the union of NEWENT, Lower division of the hundred of WESTMINSTER, E. division of the county of GLOUCESTER, 6 miles (N. N. W.) from Gloucester; containing 482 inhabitants.

their paying the annual sum of 110 marks; and the iginal charter, which is deposited with the court rolls, in excellent preservation. The bailiffs of this manor e chosen by the tenants from among themselves; they e invested with the powers of sheriff and coroner thin the parish, and the tenants of the rectory manor e suit and service to their court leet.

The TOWN principally consists of one long street, the uses of which, built chiefly of freestone, have a very at appearance: its situation is dry and healthy, and ₂ free access which the inhabitants have to Corsham rk renders it desirable as a place of residence. Cor- am House, the seat of Lord Methuen, lord of the ꞁnor, who was raised to the peerage by the title of ꞁron Methuen, of Corsham, July 13th, 1838, was built the site of the ancient palace, in 1582, and was con- ꞁerably enlarged by the late Mr. Methuen, in order to ceive the extensive gallery of pictures which had been llected by Sir Paul Methuen. The manufacture of ꞁollen-cloths was formerly carried on, and in the last ntury had obtained some degree of celebrity, but it ꞁs since that period altogether disappeared. The mar- ꞁt has been discontinued; but fairs for cattle are held ꞁ March 7th and September 4th. A new market- ꞁuse, which is also a court-house, was built with a view ' reviving the market, in 1784, in the centre of the wn. The Great Western railway runs in the vicinity. he parish comprises 6498a. 3r. 14p., of which more ꞁan 2200 acres are arable, nearly 3800 pasture, and 228 oodland: the peasantry are partly occupied in raising tone from the numerous quarries in this parish and that f Box.

The LIVING is a discharged vicarage, valued in the ꞁing's books at £10. 16.; patron, Lord Methuen; im- ꞁropriators, the landowners. The vicarial tithes have ꞁeeꞁ commuted for £299. 10.; the vicar enjoys some ꞁeculiar privileges, and possesses an official seal. The ꞁhurch is an ancient structure, with a tower rising from our massive piers and arches in the centre, between the ꞁave and the chancel, and formerly surmounted by a ꞁfty spire, which, being deemed insecure, was taken ꞁown in 1812. The aisles are separated from the nave ꞁy low Norman pillars and small arches: in the north ꞁisle is a small chapel, divided from it by a stone screen ꞁf handsome design; and on the north-western side is he ecclesiastical or consistory court of the incumbent. ꞁhere are places of worship for Baptists and Independ- nts. At the south-east entrance to the town is a free ꞁhool, with an almshouse for six aged poor, built and ꞁdowed by Lady Margaret Hungerford, in 1668, and ꞁoth under the superintendence of a master, who ocen- ꞁies a lodge adjoining the schoolroom. The first master, ꞁppointed by Lady Hungerford, was the Rev. Edward ꞁells, vicar of the parish, and father of the learned ꞁuthor of Sacred Geography; and Mr. Hasted, the his- orian of the county of Kent, who died here in 1812, ꞁeld the same appointment. Some valuable lands are ꞁested in trustees for repairing the church, sustaining the ꞁoor in the parish-dwelling, and for the repair of the ꞁridges. Richard Kirby, of Islington, in 1672 be- ꞁueathed his interest in an estate near Dublin, to be ꞁistributed among eight poor persons; and Lady James' ꞁharity, producing £57. 8. per annum from the three ꞁer cents., of which the parish receives two-thirds, is ꞁppropriated to the distribution of blankets and coats. .

693

Bishop Tanner states that here was an alien priory, and that William the Conqueror gave the church of this place to the abbey of St. Stephen, at Caen, in Normandy, the monks of which held it until, as parcel of the late possessions of that foreign house, it was assigned by Henry VI. to King's College, Cambridge; but he is at a loss to reconcile this fact with the gift of the church and other possessions by Henry II. to the Benedictine monks of Marmonstier, in Tourrain, who had a cell here. During the wars with France, this priory was in the custody of the Bishop and Chapter of Exeter. It was given, in the 1st of Edward IV., towards the endowment of the monastery at Sion, and as parcel thereof was granted by James I. to Philip Moore; the revenue was £22. 13. 4. There was also a nunnery, which occupied the present site of the Methuen Arms inn.

CORSLEY (ST. MARGARET), a parish, in the union and hundred of WARMINSTER, Warminster and S. divi- sions of WILTS, 3¼ miles (W. N. W.) from Warminster; and containing 1621 inhabitants. The parish comprises by measurement 2580 acres. Stone for building and road-making is quarried; and the weaving of cloth employs about thirty persons. Fairs are held on Whit- Tuesday and the first Monday in August, for cheese, pigs, and toys. The ancient manor-house, in which it is said Sir Walter Raleigh passed much of his time in concealment, is now occupied as a farmhouse. The living is a discharged rectory, valued in the king's books at £11. 0. 10.; net income, £215; arising chiefly from 98 acres of land allotted under an act for inclosing the parish, in 1780; patron and impropriator, the Mar- quess of Bath. The present handsome church was erected on the site of a former structure, at an expense of £3500, and was opened for divine service on the 22nd of October, 1833. On the summit of Clea Hill are re- mains of a strong intrenchment, to which the Danes are said to have fled from Edindon, where they had been attacked by Alfred; numerous fossils are found im- bedded in the chalk of which the hill consists.

CORSTON (ALL SAINTS), a parish, in the union of KEYNSHAM, hundred of WELLOW, E. division of SOMER- SET, 3¼ miles (W.) from Bath; containing 604 inhabit- ants. The river Avon bounds the parish on the north- east, and the Great Western railway intersects it; the area is 1145 acres. Cornua ammonis and various petri- fied shells abound in the quarries. The living is a dis- charged vicarage, valued in the king's books at £6. 3. 9.; net income, £150; patron, the Bishop of Bath and Wells; impropriators, the family of Langton.

CORSTONE, a chapelry, in the parish, union, and hundred of MALMESBURY, Malmesbury and Kingswood, and N. divisions of WILTS, 2½ miles (S. by W.) from Malmesbury; containing 273 inhabitants. The chapel, dedicated to All Saints, exhibits some portions of early English architecture.

CORTON (ST. BARTHOLOMEW), a parish, in the in- corporation and hundred of MUTFORD and LOTHING- LAND, E. division of SUFFOLK, 2 miles (N.) from Lowes- toft; containing 442 inhabitants. This parish, which comprises 1149a. 1r. 39p., is situated on the coast of the North Sea, and has doubtless participated in the devastation occasioned by the encroachment of the waves upon the land, by which the adjoining parish of Newton has been almost destroyed. From the remains of a church still visible at a place called the Gate, and the ruins and old foundations of houses in other parts, the village of Corton is presumed to have been much more extensive than at present, and probably the resort of fishermen, when the mouth of Yarmouth harbour reached nearly to this place. The living is a discharged vicarage, in the patronage of the Crown; impropriators, the heirs of Thomas Fowler,' Esq.: the great tithes have been commuted for £242, and the vicarial for £120. The church is partly in ruins, the porch and the walls of the nave being nearly overspread with ivy; but divine service is still performed in the chancel: from its beautiful tower, which is yet perfect, and serves as a landmark for mariners, and from its extensive ruins, there is reason to presume that it was a structure of much magnificence. Coins, fossils, &c., have been found within the base of the cliff, which borders on the sea, on its being undermined by the tide; and a stratum of oak, several feet thick, and extending in length more than 200 yards, was exposed to the view, after a severe storm, in 1812. About the same time, a part of the *pelvis*, or haunch bones, of the mammoth, together with other antediluvian remains, was found half a mile northward of the place.

CORTON, a township, in the parish of BOYTON, union of WARMINSTER, hundred of HEYTESBURY, Warminster and S. divisions of WILTS, 2½ miles (S. E. by S.) from Heytesbury; containing 205 inhabitants.

CORTON-DENHAM (ST. ANDREW), a parish, in the union of WINCANTON, hundred of HORETHORNE, E. division of SOMERSET, 4 miles (N.) from Sherborne; containing 480 inhabitants. The parish is romantically situated in a valley at the foot of a range of hills, whose highest point is Beacon Hill, or Corton-Ash Beacon, which rises 655 feet above the level of the sea. Nearly the whole of the lands have been held by the ancestors of Lord Portman since about the year 1600. Large quantities of marl of rich quality are obtained, which are used as a good top-dressing on high lands; and at the sides of the hill is an immense mass of building-stone, but the great labour required to work it to a fine surface, on account of its veins of iron, renders it useless. There is a manufactory for dowlas. The living is a rectory, valued in the king's books at £13. 9. 4½., and in the gift of Lord Portman: the tithes have been commuted for £366, and the glebe comprises 32½ acres, with a glebe-house. The church is a neat structure; the body is supposed to have been built in 1541, and the tower, from a date over the entrance door, in 1685. Some workmen, in 1723, discovered a Roman urn in the vicinity, containing coins in good preservation, of the emperors from Valerian and Gallienus to Probus; and there are traces of extensive fortifications about half way under the hill, which are thought to have been connected with South Cadbury Castle, about two miles distant.

CORYTON (ST. ANDREW), a parish, in the union of TAVISTOCK, hundred of LIFTON, Lifton and S. divisions of DEVON, 6¼ miles (N. by W.) from Tavistock; containing 374 inhabitants. The living is a rectory, valued in the king's books at £8. 13. 9.; net income, £208; patron, Sir Robert Newman, Bart.

COSBY (ST. MICHAEL), a parish, in the union of BLABY, hundred of GUTHLAXTON, S. division of the county of LEICESTER, 7 miles (S. S. W.) from Leicester; containing, with part of the hamlet of Little Thorpe,

1013 inhabitants. It comprises 2000 acres, consisting of arable and pasture land in about equal portions: the manufacture of stockings is carried on. The living is a discharged vicarage, valued in the king's books at £4. 15.; net income, £138, arising from land allotted under an inclosure act, in 1767, in lieu of tithes; patron, J. Pares, Esq.; impropriators, W. Hubbard, Esq., and others.

COSCOMB, a hamlet, in the parish of DIDBROOK, union of WINCHCOMB, Lower division of the hundred of KIFTSGATE, E. division of the county of GLOUCESTER; containing 18 inhabitants.

COSELEY, an ecclesiastical district, in the parish of SEDGLEY, union of DUDLEY, N. division of the hundred of SEISDON, S. division of the county of STAFFORD; comprising the villages of Coseley and Brierley, with part of the village of Ettingshall, and containing 5683 inhabitants. This place is situated in the heart of a district abounding with mines of coal and ironstone; and the inhabitants are principally employed in the various branches of the iron-trade and other works in the neighbourhood, and in the manufacture of nails and screws, which is carried on to a great extent. A new branch of the Birmingham canal has been cut from Wolverhampton, passing through the district. The church, dedicated to Our Blessed Saviour, was erected in 1829, at an expense of £10,537, by grant of the Parliamentary Commissioners, and is a spacious building in the later English style, with a square embattled tower. The living is a district incumbency, in the patronage of Lord Ward; net income, £138, with a parsonage. There are places of worship for Particular and General Baptists, Wesleyans, and Unitarians. A Unitarian school, built in 1753, is endowed with £31 per annum; and there are some national schools, erected in 1833, at an expense of £580.

COSFORD, a hamlet, in the parish of NEWBOLD-UPON-AVON, union of RUGBY, Rugby division of the hundred of KNIGHTLOW, N. division of the county of WARWICK, 3 miles (N. by W.) from Rugby; containing 82 inhabitants. A part of the lands here belonged to the monks of Pipewell, and Edward VI. in 1553 granted them to John Green of Westminster, and Ralph Hall of London; they afterwards came to Elizabeth and Thomas Wightman, and from the last passed to Sir Thomas Leigh, Knt. The hamlet lies on the west side of the river Swift; and the Midland railway passes close by the place.

COSGROVE (ST. PETER), a parish, in the union of POTTERSPURY, hundred of CLELEY, S. division of the county of NORTHAMPTON, 2 miles (N. N. E.) from Stony-Stratford; containing 701 inhabitants. The parish is situated on the border of Buckinghamshire, the Buckingham canal passing on its southern side and there joining the Grand Junction canal, which enters the county here by crossing the Ouse near the confluence of the Tow with that river. It consists of 1559a. 1r. 33p., and the road from Northampton to Stony-Stratford intersects it from north to south. The living is a rectory, valued in the king's books at £14. 11. 3., and in the patronage of Mrs. Mansell; net income, £363. In digging for the Grand Junction canal, some skeletons were found here; also an earthen pot containing Roman coins, chiefly of the later emperors. There is a mineral spring.

COSMUS, ST., and DAMIAN-IN-THE-BLEAN (ST. SMUS AND ST. DAMIAN), a parish, and the head of the ion of BLEAN, in the hundred of WHITSTABLE, lathe ST. AUGUSTINE, E. division of KENT, 1½ mile (N. W. N.) from Canterbury; containing 606 inhabitants. is parish, which includes some lands belonging to the aster of Eastbridge Hospital, and others held under e Dean and Chapter of Canterbury, all tithe-free, is tersected by the Canterbury and Whitstable railroad, d comprises 2260a. 1r. 15p., of which 704 acres are able, 347 pasture, 657 wood, and 26 in hop-grounds. he living is a vicarage, endowed with the rectorial thes, valued in the king's books at £10, and in the atronage of the Master of the Hospital: the tithes ave been commuted for £537, and the glebe consists of acres. There is a place of worship for Wesleyans. he union of Blean comprises 16 parishes or places, and ontains a population of 13,745.

COSSAL (ST. CATHERINE), a parish, in the union of ASFORD, S. division of the wapentake of BROXTOW, N. ivision of the county of NOTTINGHAM, 6½ miles (W. N. .) from Nottingham; containing 334 inhabitants. The ottingham canal proceeds through the parish north-ard, in a serpentine direction; and the river Erewash ns on the west side, separating it from Derbyshire. he living is a perpetual curacy, annexed to the rectory f Wollaton. In the village is an hospital, founded by he ancient family of Willoughby, for four old men and our women.

COSSEY, or COSTESSEY (ST. EDMUND), a parish, in he incorporation and hundred of FOREHOE, E. division f NORFOLK, 4 miles (N. W. by W.) from Norwich; con-aining 1074 inhabitants. The parish is bounded on the north by the river Wensum, and comprises 3040 acres, of which 1500 are arable, 640 meadow and pasture, 550 woodland, and the remainder common and waste. Cos-ey Hall, the seat of Lord Stafford, lord of the manor, is a spacious quadrangular mansion, erected by Sir Henry ferningham, Bart., and contains many stately apart-nents; it is situated in a well-wooded park; and conti-ruous to the house is the family chapel, dedicated to St. Augustine, and richly embellished with stained glass. The living is a perpetual curacy, in the patronage of the frustees of the Great Hospital, Norwich: the tithes have been commuted for £337, and the glebe comprises 60 acres. The church is a handsome structure in the later English style, with a square embattled tower surmounted by a spire. There is a place of worship for Baptists; and a Roman Catholic chapel in the early English style, erected in 1841.

COSSINGTON (ALL SAINTS), a parish, in the union of BARROW-UPON-SOAR, hundred of EAST GOSCOTE, N. livision of the county of LEICESTER, 2 miles (S. E. by E.) rom Mountsorrel; containing 310 inhabitants. It is founded by the rivers Soar and Wreake, and comprises by computation 1500 acres, about two-thirds of which are arable, and the rest pasture, with the exception of 20 acres of woodland. The soil, though various, is fer-ile and productive; the surface is generally elevated, put in some parts flat, and subject to inundation from he rivers. The living is a rectory, valued in the king's books at £17. 7. 6.; net income, £448; patron and ncumbent, the Rev. J. Babington. Near the Wreake is large oblong tumulus, 350 feet long, 120 broad, and 0 high, called Shipley Hill.

695

COSSINGTON (ST. MARY), a parish, in the union of BRIDGWATER, hundred of WHITLEY, W. division of SOMERSET, 4¼ miles (N. E. by E.) from Bridgwater; containing 248 inhabitants. The village is one of the neatest in the county, the cottages being fitted up in a tasteful style, and the gardens ornamentally laid out. The living is a rectory, valued in the king's books at £13. 10.; net income, £254; patron and incumbent, the Rev. J. S. Broderip.

COSTOCK, or CORTLINGSTOCK (ST. GILES), a pa-rish, in the union of LOUGHBOROUGH, S. division of the wapentake of RUSHCLIFFE and of the county of NOTTINGHAM, 6 miles (N. N. E.) from Loughborough; containing 470 inhabitants. This parish is situated on the road between Nottingham and Leicester, and watered by a brook which divides it into two parts: it comprises by computation 1500 acres, of which one-third is wold, and the remainder in nearly equal portions arable and pasture land. Limestone is quarried for the uses of agriculture and building, and for the repair of roads. About thirty persons are employed in stocking-making, and a few women in spotting and running lace. The living is a rectory, valued in the king's books at £7. 18. 4.; net income, £395; patron, the Rev. Dr. Sutton. The tithes were partly commuted for land in 1760, about 450 acres still remaining subject to tithe; there is a good glebe-house, with about 200 acres of land. The church, which is supposed to have been built about the year 1300, appears to have lost much of its ancient beauty, having been probably desecrated during the troubles of the seventeenth century; it is now a plain edifice, the principal ornament of which is the window in the chan-cel. There is a place of worship for Wesleyans.

COSTON (ST. ANDREW), a parish, in the union of MELTON-MOWBRAY, hundred of FRAMLAND, N. division of the county of LEICESTER, 3½ miles (S. E.) from Waltham; containing 147 inhabitants, and comprising by computation 1800 acres. The living is a rectory, valued in the king's books at £16. 6. 3., and in the patronage of the Crown; net income, £360. The church is a handsome structure, in the early and decorated Eng-lish styles, with a tower surmounted by a spire, in the later English style.

COSTON (ST. MICHAEL), a parish, in the incorpora-tion and hundred of FOREHOE, E. division of NORFOLK, 4½ miles (N. W.) from Wymondham; containing 48 inhabitants. It comprises 345 acres, of which 243 are arable, 90 meadow and pasture, and 9 woodland. The living is a rectory, annexed to the archdeaconry of Nor-folk: the tithes have been commuted for £93, and the glebe comprises about 8 acres. The church is in the early English style, with a square embattled tower.

COSTON-HACKET, or COFTON (ST. MICHAEL), a parish, in the union of BROMSGROVE, Upper division of the hundred of HALFSHIRE, Northfield and E. divisions of the county of WORCESTER, 6 miles (N. E.) from Bromsgrove, and 7 (S. W.) from Birmingham; contain-ing 211 inhabitants. The parish comprises 1251a. 3r. 19p., of land, of which 600 acres are arable, 460 pasture, 170 woodland, and 21 water. Part of it extends over the range of hills called Bromsgrove Lickey, commanding extensive views of the surrounding counties, and in se-veral places it is ornamented with large quantities of oak and fir. The population is chiefly employed in agricul-ture. The Birmingham and Gloucester railway passes through. The living is annexed to the rectory of North-field ; the tithes have been commuted for £244, and the glebe consists of 56 acres. The church is a small edifice with a bell gable, having some decorated portions in the later English style. There is an excellent Sunday school in connexion with it. On three succeeding Sundays after Midsummer, a wake is kept, called Bil-berry wake, from a fruit which grows very luxuriantly on Cofton hill. Partly here, and partly in the parish of King's-Norton, is Groveley, the residence, beautifully situated, of John Merry, Esq. Charles I. slept at Cofton Hall, now a farmhouse, on the 14th of May, 1645, the day when Hawksley House was taken.

COTCLIFF, an extra-parochial district, locally in the parish of LEAKE, union of NORTHALLERTON, wapentake of ALLERTONSHIRE, N. riding of YORK, 4 miles (E. by S.) from Northallerton; containing 15 inhabitants. It is situated on the east bank of the small river Coldbeck, and consists of an extensive acclivity, terminating in a boldly rising cliff, which is well wooded : the Bishop of Ripon is lord of the manor and owner of the soil.

COTE, a tything, in the parish of OLVESTON, union of THORNBURY, Lower division of the hundred of LANGLEY and SWINEHEAD, W. division of the county of GLOUCESTER ; containing 17 inhabitants.

COTE, county OXFORD.—See ASTON.

COTES, a hamlet, in the parish of PRESTWOLD, union of LOUGHBOROUGH, hundred of EAST GOSCOTE, N. division of the county of LEICESTER, 1½ mile (N. E. by E.) from Loughborough; containing 75 inhabitants.

COTES, a township, in the parish of ECCLESHALL, union of STONE, N. division of the county of STAFFORD, 4½ miles (N. by E.) from Eccleshall; containing 328 inhabitants. This place is situated on the road from Newcastle to Eccles-hall, and on the railway from Liverpool to Birmingham. The living of the district church of St. James, Cotes-Heath, is a perpetual curacy ; net income, £100; patron, the Vicar of Eccleshall : there is a parsonage-house. A national school has a small endowment.

COTES-DE-VAL, a hamlet, in the parish of KIM-COTE, union of LUTTERWORTH, hundred of GUTHLAX-TON, S. division of the county of LEICESTER, 3½ miles (E. N. E.) from Lutterworth; containing 6 inhabitants.

COTGRAVE (ALL SAINTS), a parish, in the union, and S. division of the wapentake, of BINGHAM, S. division of the county of NOTTINGHAM, 6 miles (S. E. by E.) from Nottingham ; containing, with the hamlet of Strag-glethorpe, 850 inhabitants. The parish comprises 3500a. 2r. 35p., exclusively of 102 acres of roads ; a portion called the Wold, formerly an uncultivated tract, has been converted into rich arable land. The greater part of the surface is flat ; the soil is partly a tenacious clay and partly a rich loam, and the high grounds on each side of the village abound in blue marl, intermixed with layers of red clay. Limestone of the blue lias forma-tion is abundant, and is quarried for building and the roads, and for burning into lime; gypsum is also found. The Nottingham and Grantham canal intersects the parish. The "Court of St. John of Hierusalem," which was anciently held at Shelford, under the prior of St. John of Jerusalem, and then styled the "Master and Lieutenant's Court of Shelford," is held here, and has a common seal : its jurisdiction extends over various parishes, for which all wills are proved in this court,

and to the tenants of which charters of exemption from toll throughout the king's dominions are granted. The living is a rectory, consisting of two consolidated medieties, the first valued in the king's books at £10. 7. 3½., and the second at £9. 14. 9½.; net in-come, £628 ; patron, Earl Manvers. The tithes were commuted for land and a money payment in 1790 ; the glebe altogether consists of 555 acres, with a glebe-house. The church is a handsome structure in the later English style, with a square embattled tower crowned with pinnacles, and surmounted by a lofty octangular spire; the nave is parted from the aisles by slender clustered columns, and lighted by an ele-gant range of clerestory windows. There is a place of worship for Wesleyans.

COTHAM (ST. MICHAEL), a parish, in the union, and S. division of the wapentake, of NEWARK, S. division of the county of NOTTINGHAM, 4 miles (S.) from Newark ; containing 87 inhabitants. It comprises 1210 acres of land, and has a small village on the east bank of the Devon. The knightly families of Leek and Markham had long their seat here. The living is a donative, valued in the king's books at £7. 18.; net income, £35 ; patron, the Duke of Portland. The church was partly rebuilt in 1831, when a porch was added.

COTHELSTON, a parish, in the union of TAUNTON, hundred of TAUNTON and TAUNTON-DEAN, W. division of SOMERSET, 7 miles (N. W. by N.) from Taunton ; containing 104 inhabitants. The parish is situated on the road to Bridgwater. Limestone strata of blue lias are found ; and some indications of copper being ob-served, an attempt at mining was made, but soon dis-continued. Cothelston Hill is 1250 feet above the level of the sea, commanding an extensive view over eleven counties ; on the summit is a round tower of great antiquity. The living is a perpetual curacy ; net income, £58 ; patron, the Vicar of Kingston, to which church this was once a daughter church : the tithes are appro-priate to the Dean and Chapter of Bristol, and have been commuted for £68. The church contains some interesting monuments to the Stowells, formerly pos-sessors of the manor, which are placed in an aisle now belonging to the family of Esdaile.

COTHERIDGE (ST. LEONARD), a parish, in the union of MARTLEY, Upper division of the hundred of DODDINGTREE, Worcester and W. divisions of the county of WORCESTER, 3¾ miles (W.) from Worcester, on the road to Bromyard ; containing 228 inhabitants. This place, which was connected with the priory of Westwood, is bounded on the south by the river Team, and consists of 2129a. 2r. 11p.; wheat, beans, and some hops, are the principal produce. The small scattered village lies on the margin of the river. The Rev. John Rowland Berkeley is the owner of the whole parish, about ten acres excepted. The living is a perpetual curacy, valued in the king's books at £5. 16. 8. ; patron and incumbent, the Rev. J. R. Berkeley. Sir Rowland Berkeley, in 1694, gave a rent-charge of £6 for ap-prenticing children.

COTHERSTON, a township, in the parish of Ro-MALD-KIRK, union of TEESDALE, wapentake of GIL-LING-WEST, N. riding of YORK, 3½ miles (N. W. by W.) from Barnard-Castle ; containing 566 inhabitants. The township comprises 8228 acres, of which 5084 are com-mon or waste. The village is pleasantly situated on the uth bank of the Tees, and is celebrated for the making cheese, similar in quality to "Stilton." There is a anufactory for carpets. Here are the remains of a stle that belonged to the Fitz-Hughs, lords of the anor, but was destroyed in one of the devastating inads of the Scots. The tithes have been commuted for 108. There are places of worship for the Society of ·iends, Independents, and Wesleyans; and a national hool.

COTHILL, a hamlet, in the parish of MARCHAM, ιion of ABINGDON, hundred of OCK, county of BERKS; ntaining 45 inhabitants.

COTLEIGH, a parish, in the union of HONITON, andred of COLYTON, Honiton and S. divisions of the EVON, 3 miles (E. N. E.) from Honiton; containing 69 inhabitants. It comprises 1216a. 18p., of which 61 acres are arable, 625 pasture, and 30 woodland. he living is a rectory, valued in the king's books at 9; patron and incumbent, the Rev. W. Michell: the thes have been commuted for £200, and the glebe ɔnsists of 23 acres.

COTMANHAY, an ecclesiastical parish or district, the union of BASFORD, hundred of MORLESTON and ITCHURCH, S. division of the county of DERBY, 1½ ιile (N.) from Ilkeston; containing 2200 inhabitants. his district comprises the liberty of Shipley, in Heanor arish, and the hamlet of Cotmanhay, in the parish of keston; and is bounded on the east by the river Ereash, which is also the boundary here between the ɔunties of Derby and Nottingham. It lies along the alley of the Erewash; and parallel to the river are the rewash canal and the Erewash-Valley railway, which ɔonnect'the coal districts of Derbyshire and Nottingham ᴠith the Trent navigation and the Midland railway, reᵻpectively. The Nutbrook canal, which joins the Ereᴠash canal, terminates in the centre of this district; it ᴠas made for the transit of minerals from the extensive ɔoal-fields of Shipley, Ilkeston, and West Hallam. The ɟistrict abounds in coal and ironstone: the latter, in ɔonsequence of the increased trade in iron, is of more ⱱalue than formerly; furnaces have been lately erected n the neighbourhood, and the population has been much ncreased by the influx of labourers employed in raising ⱳhe stone. The manufacture of stockings is extensively ɔarried on. The district was formed in November 1845, ınder the act 6th and 7th of Victoria, cap. 37 : the living s in the gift 'of the Crown and the Bishop of Lichfield, ılternately; net income, £150. The church was erected n 1847, at a cost of about £2400.—See SHIPLEY.

COTNESS, a township, in the parish and union of ꞀowDEN, wapentake of HowDENSHIRE, E. riding of Ꞁork, 5 miles (S. E.) from Howden; containing 38 inꞀabitants. It comprises by computation 240 acres, ex-Ꞁlusive of about 250 acres on Walling Fen: the river Ꞁuse passes on the south.

COTON (Sᴛ. PETER), a parish, in the union of ɔHESTERTON, hundred of WETHERLEY, county of CAM-ᴣRIDGE, 3 miles (W. by N.) from Cambridge; containing ϧ07 inhabitants. The living is a discharged rectory, ⱱalued in the king's books at £6. 12. 11.; net income, £213; patrons, the Master and Fellows of Catherine Ꞁall, Cambridge. The tithes were commuted for land ind a money payment in 1799. Dr. Andrew Downes, ᴣreek professor at Cambridge, and translator of the Ꞁpocrypha, died here in 1627.

COTON, a township, in the parish of HANBURY, union of BURTON-UPON-TRENT, N. division of the hundred of OFFLOW and of the county of STAFFORD, 6¾ miles (S. E. by S.) from Uttoxeter; containing 72 inhabitants. This place is generally called Coton-under-Needwood, to distinguish from others of the same name. It lies about a mile south of the river Dove, and the like distance north-west of the village of Hanbury. Coton Hall is a neat mansion, erected in 1790. William Wollaston, author of The Religion of Nature Delineated, was born here in 1650.

COTON, with HOPTON, a township, in the parishes of Sᴛ. MARY and Sᴛ. CHAD, STAFFORD, S. division of the hundred of PIREHILL, union, and N. division of the county, of STAFFORD, 5¾ miles (E. by S.) from Stone ⅃, containing 464 inhabitants. Upon Hopton Heath, now inclosed, a most severe battle was fought in 1643, between the king's forces under the Earl of Northampton, and the parliamentary army commanded by Sir John Gell and Sir William Brereton. The earl, notwithstanding the superiority of his adversaries, attacked them with great impetuosity, and a long and obstinate contest followed, in which, after performing prodigies of valour, the earl's horse having been shot under him, he was surrounded and slain. The royalists, however, continned the battle, and, according to their own account, gained a decided victory; but the parliamentary army, on the other hand, asserted that, though worsted at first, they were in the end successful : be this as it may, it is certain that out of 600 dead found on the field next morning, 500 were royalists. The township is a fertile district, containing a number of scattered houses ex-ṭending from the hamlet of Littleworth, on the eastern side of Stafford, to the confines of Ingestre, the beautiful seat of the Earl Talbot, who is lord of the manor and owner of most of the soil. On the north bank of the river Sow, in the hamlet of St. Thomas, are some remains of a priory of Black canons, founded about 1180. The Staffordshire General Lunatic Asylum is situated in the township.

COTON-IN-THE-ELMS, a township, in the parish of LULLINGTON, union of BURTON-UPON-TRENT, hundred of REPTON and GRESLEY, S. division of the county of DERBY, 6¼ miles (S. by W.) from Burton; containing 351 inhabitants. The township comprises 1176a. 1r. 34p. The impropriate tithes have been commuted for a yearly rent-charge of £230.

COTTAM, with LEA, ASHTON, and INGOL, hundred of AMOUNDERNESS, LANCASTER.—See ASHTON.

COTTAM, a chapelry, in the parish of SOUTH LE-VERTON, union of EAST RETFORD, North-Clay division of the wapentake of BASSETLAW, N. division of the county of NOTTINGHAM, 8 miles (E. by S.) from East Retford; containing 89 inhabitants, and comprising 625 acres. The chapel is dedicated to the Holy Trinity.

COTTAM, a chapelry, in the parish of LANGTOFT, union of DRIFFIELD, wapentake of DICKERING, E. riding of the county of YORK, 5¼ miles (N. N. W.) from Driffield; containing 41 inhabitants. The chapelry comprises 2600 acres, of which 1800 are arable, meadow, pasture, and sheep-walks, and 800 rabbit-warren. The living is a perpetual curacy, annexed to the vicarage of Langtoft : the chapel is a small and very plain edifice.

COTTENHAM (ALL SAINTS), a parish, in the union and hundred of CHESTERTON, locally in NORTHSTOW hundred, county of CAMBRIDGE, 6¾ miles (N.) from Cambridge; containing 1833 inhabitants. This place was the residence of the monks sent here by Geoffrey, Abbot of Crowland, and who first established a regular course of academical education at Cambridge. The village was nearly destroyed in 1676 by an accidental fire, which consumed more than two-thirds of the buildings. The parish comprises by measurement 7037 acres. The Adventurers' land, chiefly inclosed from the river Ouse and the common adjoining, was sometimes subject to inundation, but in consequence of late improvements, this has been in a great measure prevented; acts for inclosing other lands, and for draining certain fen land and low ground in the parish, were passed in 1842. The dairies, which are numerous, are famed for producing excellent cheese. A branch of the Ouse passes near the village. The living is a rectory, valued in the king's books at £36. 15., and in the gift of the Bishop of Ely: the tithes have been commuted for £765, and the glebe comprises 133 acres. The church is a handsome structure, in the later English style. There is a place of worship for Particular Baptists. A school was founded in 1703, by Mrs. Catharine Pepys, who gave a house, and £100 to purchase land; and it has several other small endowments. This is the birthplace of Archbishop Tenison, who died in 1715. Charles Christopher Pepys, lord high chancellor, was raised to the peerage by the title of Baron Cottenham, Jan. 16th, 1836.

COTTERED (ST. MARY), a parish, in the union of BUNTINGFORD, hundred of ODSEY, county of HERTFORD, 3 miles (W.) from Buntingford; containing 465 inhabitants. It comprises by measurement 1755 acres, and is intersected by a cross-road between Baldock and Buntingford. The living is a rectory, with that of Broadfield annexed, valued in the king's books at £20. 8. 6½.; net income, £348; patron, W. Brown, Esq.: the tithes were commuted for 315 acres of land, under an inclosure act, in 1806, and there are 10 acres of ancient glebe, with a glebe-house. The church consists of a nave and chancel, in the later English style, but has, by various alterations, been deprived of its general unity of design; it contains a beautiful marble font. Schools were built by Mr. Henry Soames, in 1829, and endowed with a rent-charge of £40.

COTTERSTOCK (ST. ANDREW), a parish, in the union of OUNDLE, hundred of WILLYBROOK, N. division of the county of NORTHAMPTON, 2 miles (N. N. E.) from Oundle; containing 204 inhabitants. The parish is situated on the left bank of the river Nene, and consists of 675a. 2r. 6p. The living is a discharged vicarage, with that of Glapthorn united; net income, £91; patron and impropriator, the Earl of Westmoreland: the tithes were commuted for land and a money payment in 1813. The church, with its tower, is an interesting edifice, exhibiting portions in every style of English architecture, and some remains of stained glass in the fine tracery of the windows. It anciently had a college for a provost, twelve chaplains, and two clerks, founded in 1336, by John Gifford, a canon in the cathedral of York; three stone stalls still remain in the chancel. In 1658, Clement Bellamy bequeathed land, producing about £20 per annum, for two exhibitions to scholars at Cambridge, and for apprenticing children; this parish is entitled to a fourth share. In the vicinity are numerous vestiges of Roman works, and of a continued chain of

fortification extending from Gloucester to Northampton, erected by Ostorius Scapula, pro-prætor of Britain in the reign of the emperor Claudius: a Roman tessellated pavement of great beauty was discovered in the parish within the last fifty years.

COTTESBACH (ST. MARY), a parish, in the union of LUTTERWORTH, hundred of GUTHLAXTON, S. division of the county of LEICESTER, 1½ mile (S. by W.) from Lutterworth; containing 82 inhabitants. The parish is situated on the Banbury and Lutterworth road; it is bounded on the west by the Watling-street, and on the north-west by the little river Swift, and comprises by computation 1220 acres, which consist principally of rich pasture land, ornamented with oak, ash, and elm trees. The living is a rectory, valued in the king's books at £10. 6. 8.; net income, £106; patron and incumbent, the Rev. J. P. Marriott: the glebe consists of about 25 acres, with a glebe-house. The church is in the decorated style. Several Roman antiquities were discovered in the vicinity of the Watling-street a few years ago, comprising spear-heads, urns, beads, clasps, skulls, &c. In one part of the parish, the springs have the quality of petrifying whatever falls into them. Dr. Edward Wells, author of the well-known Geography of the Old and New Testaments, and several other works, was rector of the parish for many years.

COTTESBROOKE (ALL SAINTS), a parish, in the union of BRIXWORTH, hundred of GUILSBOROUGH, S. division of the county of NORTHAMPTON, 9¾ miles (N. N. W.) from Northampton; containing 252 inhabitants. It is situated between the roads leading from Northampton to Market-Harborough and to Welford, and on the north-west side adjoins Naseby Field, where the celebrated battle so disastrous to Charles I., and decisive of his fate, was fought in 1645. The parish comprises 2747a. 3r. 16p.; the surface is diversified with hill and dale, the soil is generally clayey, and chiefly in meadow and pasture: the lands are watered by two brooks which flow in a south-eastern direction. Cottesbrooke Park is the seat of Sir James Hay Langham, Bart.; the mansion, a handsome structure of stone and brick, and having two wings, was built about 1712. The living is a rectory, valued in the king's books at £26. 0. 10., and in the gift of Sir James H. Langham: the tithes have been commuted for £646. 12., and the glebe consists of about two acres, with a glebe-house. The church, which is admired for its architecture, is in the decorated style; it has a tower containing seven bells, and in the interior are several ancient monuments, some of which were defaced and mutilated by Cromwell's soldiers after the battle of Naseby. An hospital for two widowers and six widows was founded by Alderman Langham (afterwards Sir John Langham) in 1651, and endowed with 53 acres of land. A cell of Præmonstratensian canons existed here, foundations of which have been dug up, the site appearing to have been surrounded by a moat. In the autumn of 1836, as some labourers were digging a well close to the park walls, they threw up some fossil bones, highly mineralized, in the midst of the lias clay which forms the bed of the stratum in that place; they have proved to be the vertebræ and coracoid bones of a species of plesiosaurus, and have been deposited in the Clarendon, at Oxford.

COTTESFORD (ST. MARY), a parish, in the union of BICESTER, hundred of PLOUGHLEY, county of Ox-

ORD, 6 miles (N.) from Bicester; containing 187 inhabitants. The living is a discharged rectory, valued in e king's books at £6. 13. 4.; net income, £344; atrons, the Provost and Fellows of Eton College.

COTTESMORE (ST. *Nicholas*), a parish, in the nion of OAKHAM, hundred of ALSTOE, county of RUTAND, 4¼ miles (N. N. E.) from Oakham; containing, /ith the chapelry of Barrow, 670 inhabitants. The arish is situated on the road from the great north road o Oakham, and comprises 3379a. 2r. 20p. The surface s mostly flat, except on the west side, where it forms a ill of considerable elevation; the soil is in general a ight clay, and in some parts a reddish loam, resting on ed sandstone, or on limestone rock. The parish is inersected by the Oakham canal. The living is a rectory, alued in the king's books at £25. 16. 3.; net income, 893; patron, the Earl of Gainsborough. The tithes ere commuted for land and a money payment in 1799; ie glebe comprises 785a. 3r. 29p., with a glebe-house. t the hamlet of Barrow, a very neat chapel of ease has een built by the Rev. H. W. Nevile. Richard Westrook Baker, Esq., of agricultural celebrity, and who was presented with a valuable service of plate in 1841, as a testimonial of respect, by eleven hundred subscribers, has his residence in the parish.

COTTINGHAM (ST. *Mary Magdalene*), a parish, in the union of KETTERING, hundred of CORBY, N. division of the county of NORTHAMPTON, 2 miles (S. W. by W.) from Rockingham; containing, with the township of Middleton, 1033 inhabitants. The parish comprises by measurement 3286 acres of arable and pasture, and about 845 of woodland : this includes a portion of Rockingham Forest (1279 acres), by the addition of which the parish was enlarged in 1833. The road from Rockingham to Market-Harborough passes through. The village stands about half a mile to the south of the Welland, which bounds the parish. The living is a reetory, valued in the king's books at £23. 7. 3½.; net income, £426; patrons, the Principal and Fellows of Brasenose College, Oxford : there are 53 acres of glebe, and a house. The church, built in the 14th century, is a neat structure with a spire; the interior was restored, and two galleries added, in 1839. The Methodists have a place of worship; and a parochial school is endowed with £10 per annum. In an ancient record it is stated that a house for leprous persons existed here in the time of Henry III. A massive ring of pure gold was found in 1841, on the borders of Rockingham Forest, apparently of great antiquity, and in good preservation; it is inscribed in Saxon characters with legends supposed to be of talismanic character, and was probably worn as an amulet.

COTTINGHAM (ST. *Mary the Virgin*), a parish, and formerly a market-town, in the union of SCULCOATES, Hunsley-Beacon division of the wapentake of HARTHILL, E. riding of the county of YORK, 4½ miles (N. W.) from Hull; containing 2618 inhabitants. This place is of considerable antiquity, and was known as of some importance when Domesday book was compiled. Leland, in his *Collectanea*, states that William d'Estoteville or Stuteville, sheriff of Yorkshire, entertained King John here, and obtained from that monarch, in the year 1200, permission to hold a market and fair, and to embattle and fortify his residence. This noble mansion, called Baynard Castle, continued for ages a distinguished

monument of feudal grandeur ; it was in the possession, successively, of the Stutevilles, the Bigods, and de Wakes. It is stated on credible authority, that Henry VIII., when at Hull, learning that the lady of Lord de Wake, the then owner of the castle, was remarkable for her beauty, sent to apprise her lord of his intention to dine with him on the following day ; but Lord de Wake, apprehending that the object of the king was the dishonour of his wife, directed his steward, on the night on which the intimation was received, to set fire to the castle, which was accordingly burnt to the ground, and the royal visit thus prevented. In the 15th of Edward II., Thomas, Lord de Wake, began to establish here a monastery for Augustine canons, which, about the year 1324, was removed to the extra-parochial liberty of Newton, or Howdenprice ; its revenue at the Dissolution was estimated at £178. 0. 10. : there are no remains.

The parish comprises 9495a. 3r. 8p., of which 4562 acres are arable, 4536 meadow and pasture, 144 wood, and 251 garden land, a large portion of the last being appropriated to the cultivation of vegetables and other horticultural produce for the market at Hull, which place is also in a measure supplied with milk and butter from this neighbourhood. A great part of the parish is a plain, lying between the Wolds and the river Hull, which forms the eastern boundary, and separates Cottingham from the parishes of Sutton and Waghen; about 2000 acres are upon the declivity of the hills, lying immediately on limestone rock. There is much diversity of soil, from a light gravel to a strong tenacious clay. The village is large, very agreeably situated at the eastern foot of the Wolds, and contains several highly respectable houses : there are two breweries, and a carpet manufactory ; and the Tweeddale Patent-Tile Company have lately erected extensive works for the manufacture of bricks and tiles by steam. The Hull and Bridlington railway has a station here, about midway between the stations of Hull and Beverley ; and the river affords easy conveyance for agricultural produce, coal, lime, &c. The market and one of the fairs have been discontinued, but a fair is held on the festival of St. Martin.

The LIVING is a vicarage, with the perpetual curacy of Skidby annexed, valued in the king's books at £106. 13. 4., and in the patronage of the Crown ; net income, £124; appropriator, the Bishop of Chester. The great tithes of Cottingham have been commuted for £918, and the bishop's glebe consists of 442 acres. The church is a spacious and handsome edifice built in 1272, with a light and beautiful tower rising from the centre ; and contains several elegant monuments, particularly of the family of Burton, and in the chancel an ancient tombstone to the memory of the founder, Nicholas de Stuteville. A small additional church was built by subscription, at Newland, in 1833. There are places of worship for Independents, Primitive Methodists, and Wesleyans. A free school is principally supported from · a bequest of land, now producing about £45 per annum, by Mr. Mark Kirby, in 1712. Some remains exist of the ramparts and ditches of Baynard Castle. Adjoining the ancient road called Keldgate, are intermitting springs, which sometimes flow copiously after remaining quiescent for several years.

COTTINGWITH, EAST, a chapelry, in the parish of AUGHTON, union of POCKLINGTON, Holme-Beacon

division of the wapentake of HARTHILL, E. riding of
YORK, 8½ miles (S. W. by W.) from Pocklington; containing 308 inhabitants. It is situated on the left bank
of the river Derwent, and comprises by computation
1140 acres of land, inclosed in 1773, at which time the
tithes were commuted for allotments and a yearly
modus. The chapel, rebuilt about 60 years since, is a
neat edifice with a tower on which is a spherical cupola.
There are places of worship for Wesleyans and the
Society of Friends; and the poor have 18 acres of land,
let for £28 per annum.

COTTINGWITH, WEST, a township, in the parish
of THORGANBY, union of YORK, wapentake of OUSE and
DERWENT, E. riding of YORK, 9¾ miles (S. E.) from
York; containing 201 inhabitants. This place is situated on the Derwent, and forms the northern portion of
the long and straggling village of Thorganby. The tithes
were commuted for land and a money payment, under
an act of inclosure, in 1810.

COTTLES.—See CHALFIELD, LITTLE.

COTTON, a township, in the parish of SANDBACH,
union of CONGLETON, hundred of NORTHWICH, S. division of the county of CHESTER, 2¾ miles (E. by N.) from
Middlewich; containing 101 inhabitants. It lies about
a mile west of the road from Brereton to Knutsford,
and comprises 323 acres, of a sandy soil. The vicarial
tithes have been commuted for £25. 5.

COTTON, a township, in the parish and union of
WEM, Whitchurch division of the hundred of NORTH
BRADFORD, N. division of the county of SALOP; con-
taining 439 inhabitants.

COTTON, a township, in the parish of ALVETON,
union of CHEADLE, S. division of the hundred of TOT-
MONSLOW, N. division of the county of STAFFORD, 5½
miles (N. E.) from Cheadle; containing 519 inhabitants.
It includes the hamlets of Upper and Lower Cotton,
and comprises 2272 acres of land. Here is abundance
of excellent limestone, of which extensive quarries are
worked by the Trent and Mersey Canal Company. At
Lower Cotton is a chapel dedicated to St. John the
Baptist, built in 1795, at the expense of the late Thomas Gilbert, Esq., who partly endowed it, and left the
payment of the repairs a charge upon his property.
The living is a perpetual curacy; net income, £44;
patron, Thomas Gilbert, Esq.; impropriator, John
Bill, Esq.

COTTON (ST. ANDREW), a parish, in the union and
hundred of HARTISMERE, W. division of SUFFOLK,
6 miles (N. N. E.) from Stow-Market; containing 545
inhabitants. It comprises 1921 acres, of which 58 are
common or waste; the surface is in general flat, and
the soil heavy. The living is a rectory, valued in the
king's books at £15. 10. 2½.; patron and incumbent,
the Rev. Peter Eade: the tithes have been commuted
for £480, and the glebe consists of 18½ acres, with a
glebe-house, much improved by the present incumbent.
The church is a handsome structure in the decorated
style, with an embattled tower, and a fine south porch;
the nave is lighted by clerestory windows. There is a
place of worship for Wesleyans.

COTTON, county of YORK.—See COTTAM.

COTTON, or COULTON, a township, in the parish of
HOVINGHAM, union of HELMSLEY, wapentake of RYE-
DALE, N. riding of YORK, 8 miles (S. by E.) from
Helmsley; containing 158 inhabitants. It comprises

undary of Scotland, half a mile east of Yetholm, e impropriate tithes have been commuted for 6. 17. 6., and the vicarial for £17. 17.

COULSDON (St. John the Evangelist), a parish, the union of Croydon, First division of the hundred Wallington, E. division of Surrey, 5 miles (S. by .) from Croydon; containing 1041 inhabitants. This rish, which is situated on the road from London to ighton, occupies an elevated position, and commands tensive and varied prospects; it comprises 3648 res, exclusively of 550 of down land, and the Brighton ilway passes a little to the west. The living is a rectory, valued in the king's books at £21. 16. 5½., and· the gift of the Archbishop of Canterbury: the tithes ιve been commuted for £858, and the glebe comprises)¾ acres. The church, consisting of a nave, chancel, ιd aisles, with a tower and spire, has been thoroughly paired and stuccoed, and is a very pleasing object. he Roman road out of Sussex passed through the arish : on Farthing Downs are dykes which seem to ave been thrown up as a barricade, and on the high art of the downs are several small barrows.

COULSTON, EAST (St. Thomas à Becket), a parish, in the union of Westbury and Whorwelsdown, undred of Whorwelsdown, Whorwelsdown and N. ivisions of Wilts, 8 miles (S. W.) from Devizes; conaining 105 inhabitants. It comprises 864 acres, of ιhich 276 are arable, 362 pasture, 168 down, and woodland. The living is a rectory, valued in the king's books at £7. 14. 2., and in the patronage of the rown : the tithes have been commuted for £175. 5., and he glebe consists of 31 acres, with a glebe-house.

COULSTON, WEST, a tything, in the parish of Edington, union of Westbury and Whorwelsdown, aundred of Whorwelsdown, Whorwelsdown and N. divisions of Wilts; containing 144 inhabitants.

COULTON (Holy Trinity), a parish, in the union οf Ulverston, hundred of Lonsdale north of the Sands, N. division of the county of Lancaster; con:aining, with the chapelries of Haverthwaite and Rusland and the parochial chapelry of Finsthwaite, 1983 nhabitants. East Coulton is 5½ miles (N. N. E.), and West Coulton 5 (N. by E.), from Ulverston. This is οne of the most modern parishes in Lancashire. Dr. Whitaker, by whom its origin was investigated, does not carry the parochial claim higher than to the year 1676, when it was probably severed from the parish of Hawkshead, in which it was previously a parochial chapelry. The parish is bounded on the east and south by the lake Windermere, and the river Leven, which issues from it; and on the west by the lake Coniston, and the river Crake, which, with the Leven, falls into Morecambe bay. The scenery is diversified by cheerful valleys, and rocky but moderate acclivities with hanging woods every where clothing their sides almost to their summits. The road from Ulverston to Kendal runs through the southern part of the parish, within the limits of which, at Backbarrow, extensive cotton-works are carried on; there are also iron-works, and works for the preparation of acid, and of gunpowder. The living is a perpetual curacy; net income, £84; patrons and appropriators, the Landowners, who pay their quotas for the minister's stipend. The church is a small plain building on the summit of a bleak hill; it consists of an embattled tower, a body with aisles, and a chancel. The

chapels of Haverthwaite, Rusland, and Finsthwaite, form separate incumbencies. There is a meeting-house for the Society of Friends; and a parochial school is endowed with 50 acres of land given by Adam Sandys, Esq., besides a small bequest from Bartholomew Penington.

COUND (St. Peter), a parish, in the union of Atcham, hundred of Condover, S. division of Salop, 6½ miles (S. E. by S.) from Shrewsbury; containing, with the chapelry of Cressage, 808 inhabitants. The parish is situated on the road from Shrewsbury to Worcester, and washed on the north-east by the navigable river Severn. It abounds with richly diversified and wildly romantic scenery, and comprises by computation 5071 acres, of which 1543 belong to Cressage; the surface is slightly undulated. There are two quarries, from which is obtained a species of white freestone, lately used in rebuilding the chapel at Cressage. The living is a rectory, valued in the king's books at £33, and in the patronage of Mrs. Frances Thursby : the tithes have been commuted for £619, and the glebe consists of 93 acres, with a glebe-house. The church is in the later English style, and contains monuments to the memory of the Cresset, Fowler, Dod, Wilde, and Langley families; the pulpit is a handsome specimen of ancient carved oak. Dr. Edward Cresset, Bishop of Llandaff, who had been rector of this parish, and possessed the principal property in it, lies buried here.

COUNDON, a township, in the parish of St. Andrew Auckland, union of Auckland, N. W. division of Darlington ward, S. division of the county of Durham, 2 miles (E. by S.) from Bishop-Auckland; containing 475 inhabitants, when the census was taken in 1831, but now increased to 990, in consequence of the extended working of its coal-mines. A church and parsonage-house have been erected, and the living has been endowed by the Bishop of Durham, and a district assigned comprising the townships of Coundon, Windleston, and Westerton : the Bishop presents.

COUNDON, a hamlet, in the parish of the Holy Trinity, Coventry, union of Meriden, Kirby division of the hundred of Knightlow, N. division of the county of Warwick; containing 181 inhabitants, and comprising 1000 acres. An act for inclosing waste lands was passed in 1841. The impropriate tithes have been commuted for £245.

COUNDON-GRANGE, a township, in the parish of St. Andrew Auckland, union of Auckland, S. E. division of Darlington ward, S. division of the county of Durham, 1½ mile (E. S. E.) from Bishop-Auckland; containing 313 inhabitants. This place is situated on an eminence, and commands an extensive view of Weardale : the river Gaunless passes on the west. The impropriate tithes have been commuted for £93. 12.

COUNTESS-THORP, a chapelry, in the parish and union of Blaby, hundred of Guthlaxton, S. division of the county of Leicester; containing 815 inhabitants. It comprises 1200 acres of land, the soil of which is chiefly a strong clay. The manufacture of stockings is carried on. Here is a station of the railway between Rugby and Derby, situated 5½ miles south from the Leicester station. The chapel, dedicated to St. Andrew, was rebuilt in 1841, when 212 sittings were gained.

COUNTHORPE, a hamlet, in the parish of Bytham-Castle, union of Bourne, wapentake of Beltisloe, parts of KESTEVEN, county of LINCOLN, 3½ miles (S.) from Corby; containing 85 inhabitants.

COUNTISBURY (ST. JOHN THE BAPTIST), a parish, in the union of BARNSTAPLE, hundred of SHERWELL, Braunton and N. divisions of DEVON, 15½ miles (E. by N.) from Ilfracombe; containing 185 inhabitants, and comprising 3227 acres, whereof about 2000 are common or waste. This parish, which is situated on the shore of the Bristol Channel, and near the junction of the counties of Devon and Somerset, is bounded for some miles on the south and west by the small, rapid, river Lyn. The spring tides here rise to the height of 30 feet. The scenery is of bold and rugged character, softened occasionally by woodland and pastures. Stone of good quality is abundant, and is quarried for the use of the immediate neighbourhood. The living is a perpetual curacy, annexed to that of Linton : the tithes have been commuted for £105, and the glebe comprises 14 acres.

COUPE and LENCHES, with NEWHALL-HEY, and HALL-CARR, a township, in the parish of BURY, union of HASLINGDEN, Higher division of the hundred of BLACKBURN, N. division of the county of LANCASTER, 4¼ miles (S. S. E.) from Haslingden; containing 1716 inhabitants. These places comprise 1545 acres, of which 230 are common or waste; they lie on the banks of the Irwell, and on the confines of the hundred of Salford. The inhabitants are actively engaged in the cotton and woollen manufactures. Coupe Law is a bold eminence commanding an extensive view. Part of the township is in the ecclesiastical district of Rawtenstall. The tithes have been commuted for two rent-charges of £2. 12. 6. each, payable to the rectors of Bury and Prestwich-cum-Oldham.

COUPLAND, a township, in the parish of KIRK-NEWTON, union of GLENDALE, W. division of GLENDALE ward, county of NORTHUMBERLAND, 4½ miles (N. W.) from Wooler; containing 109 inhabitants. The township is bounded on the east by the river Till, and on the south-west by the Glen, and comprises about 800 acres, mostly arable land, with 70 acres of plantation; the surface is level, and the soil of a light gravelly quality. Coupland Castle was enlarged in 1820, from a peel-house, of which the walls have been preserved. The impropriate tithes have been commuted for £106. 10., and the vicarial for £40. 10.

COURAGE, a tything, in the parish of CHIEVELEY, union of NEWBURY, hundred of FAIRCROSS, county of BERKS, 4½ miles (N. N. E.) from Newbury; containing 277 inhabitants. The vicarial tithes have been commuted for £342.

COURT, a tything, in the parish of PORTBURY, union of BEDMINSTER, hundred of PORTBURY, E. division of SOMERSET; containing 59 inhabitants.

COURTEENHALL (ST. PETER AND ST. PAUL), a parish, in the union of HARDINGSTONE, hundred of WYMERSLEY, S. division of the county of NORTH-AMPTON, 5½ miles (S.) from Northampton; containing 143 inhabitants. This place is situated between the two roads from Northampton to London, one by Newport-Pagnell and the other by Stony-Stratford, and is within a mile of the Roade station of the London and Birmingham railway : the Grand Junction canal passes within two miles. The number of acres is 1314, mostly pasture. There is a quarry of limestone used for build-

d has a considerable village. The Staffordshire and orcestershire canal, and the Liverpool and Birmingm railway, pass through the liberty. A chapel of ease s built in 1839 by Edward Monckton, Esq., of Somerd Hall, and fitted up by the inhabitants. There is a ce of worship for Wesleyans; also a national school, ached to the chapel.

COVENEY (St. Peter), a parish, in the hundred South Witchford, union and Isle of Ely, county Cambridge, 6 miles (W. N. W.) from Ely; contain-, with the chapelry of Manea and the hamlet of ardy-Hill, 1505 inhabitants. It stands on an emince overlooking the Fens. The manor belonged to e monks of Ely, and having been for some time wrong-lly withheld from them, was recovered by Bishop igell before the year 1169 : among subsequent owners, cur the families of Lisle, Scrope, and Robinson. The ing is a rectory, valued in the king's books at £5, d in the gift of Lord Rokeby, with a net income of 09 : the tithes have been commuted for £227. 14.; d there is a glebe of 30 acres. The church is an ant edifice with a thatched roof. The chapel at Manea ms a separate cure. There is a national school suprted by subscription ; and about £50 per annum, the ount of various bequests, are distributed among the or on St. Thomas's day. Great numbers of oak, and a w other trees, have been discovered buried at various pths below the surface, and some almost petrified are und in various places.

COVENHAM (St. Bartholomew), commonly called awthorpe, a parish, in the union of Louth, wapen-ke of Ludborough, parts of Lindsey, county of incoln, 6 miles (N. N. E.) from Louth ; containing 77 inhabitants. It comprises 1434a. 1r. 28p., and is atered at its eastern extremity by the river Ludd, from hich a canal runs to Tetney Haven, at the mouth of he Humber. The living is a discharged rectory, valued 1 the king's books at £17. 12. 8.; net income, £287 ; atrons, the Heirs of Sapsford Harold, Esq., for one urn, and of the Rev. C. D. Holland, for two turns. The thes of this parish, and of Covenham St. Mary, were ommuted for corn-rents, under an inclosure act, in 793. The glebe consists of about 62 acres in this arish, and 2½ in that of Grainthorpe. The church ontains a curious octagonal font, much admired by ntiquaries ; and in the chancel is an effigy in metal f John Skypwyth, Knt., who was interred here in July, 415. The church-land comprises 26 acres, allotted at he inclosure. There are places of worship for Primitive fethodists and Wesleyans.

COVENHAM (St. Mary), a parish, in the union of outh, wapentake of Ludborough, parts of Lindsey, ounty of Lincoln, 5½ miles (N. N. E.) from Louth ; ontaining 169 inhabitants, and comprising 973a. 1r. 26p. he living is a discharged rectory, valued in the king's ooks at £10, and in the patronage of the Crown ; net ncome, £197. The church is an ancient edifice, with a ower : in the north wall of the chancel is an arched ompartment, ornamented with tracery, and supposed to ave formerly contained a tomb. The church-land omprises 17a. 1r. 5p., allotted at the inclosure of the arish, and the rent is applied as far as necessary to the epair of the church, the residue being given to the poor. Iere was a cell belonging to the monastery of St. Cari-phus, in the diocese of Mains.

COVENTRY, an ancient city, in the hundred of Knightlow, N. division of the county of Warwick, 10 miles (N. E.) from Warwick, 18 (S. E.) from Birmingham, and 91 (N. N. W.) from London, on the road to Holyhead ; containing, with the hamlets of Radford, Whitley, and Keresley, 31,430 inhabitants. In ancient records this place is called

Arms.

Coventre, and Conventrey, probably from the foundation of a convent, of which St. Osberg was abbess in the year 1016, when it was burnt by Canute, King of Denmark, and Edric the traitor, who, having invaded Mercia, destroyed many towns in Warwickshire. On the site of this convent, Leofric, Earl of Mercia, and his countess Godiva, about the beginning of the reign of Edward the Confessor, erected a monastery, which they munificently endowed, and decorated with such a profusion of costly ornaments, that, according to William of Malmesbury, the walls were covered with gold and silver. About this time, Leofric, at the intercession of his countess, granted the citizens a charter conferring various privileges and immunities, which grant was commemorated in the south window of Trinity church, by portraits of the earl and countess, with a poetical legend. Leofric died in 1057, and was interred in the monastery which he had founded. Shortly after the Norman Conquest, the lordship of Coventry became vested in the earls of Chester, of whom Ralph, the third earl of that name, married Lucia, grand-daughter of Leofric. Their son Ralph having espoused the cause of the Empress Matilda, his castle of Coventry was occupied by the forces of Stephen : the earl besieged it, but the king came in person to its relief, and repulsed him after an obstinate conflict. In 1141, Robert Marmion, the inveterate enemy of the Earl of Chester, took possession of the monastery, from which he expelled the monks ; fortified the church ; and cut deep trenches in the adjoining fields, concealing them only with a slight covering : on the earl's approach to dislodge him, Marmion drew out his forces, but forgetting the exact situation of the trenches, his horse fell with him to the ground, and in this situation his head was severed from his body by a private soldier. In the reign of Henry III., the twelve noblemen and prelates elected to decide upon the terms by which such as had forfeited their estates during the baronial war might be again admitted to enjoy them, met here ; and their decree is called the *Dictum de Kenilworth*, from its having been published in the king's camp at Kenilworth, during his siege of the castle, in 1266. In 1355 was commenced the erection of the city walls, which were of great height and thickness, and subsequently extended to three miles in circuit; they were strengthened with thirty-two towers, and contained twelve principal gates, each defended by a portcullis.

In 1397, Richard II. appointed this town for the decision, by single combat, of the quarrel between the Dukes of Hereford and Norfolk ; and magnificent preparations were made on Gosford Green for this encounter, which, however, was prevented by the banishment of the combatants, a measure that ultimately caused the deposition of the king. In 1404, the Duke of Hereford, who had become Duke of Lancaster by the death of his father, John of Gaunt, on his return from exile, having succeeded to the crown by the title of Henry IV., held a parliament here, which, from the exclusion of all lawyers, was called *Parliamentum Indoctorum*. In 1411, the Prince of Wales, afterwards Henry V., was arrested at the priory by John Horneby, mayor of the city, proba- bly for some tumultuous excess, the particulars of which are not recorded. In 1459, Henry VI. held a parliament in the chapter-house of the priory, which, from the num- ber of attainders passed against the Duke of York and others, was, by the Yorkists, called *Parliamentum Dia- bolicum;* the acts made in it were annulled by the suc- ceeding parliament. In 1467, Edward IV. and his queen kept the festival of Christmas at Coventry; two years after, Earl Rivers and his son, who had both been seized by a party of the northern rebels at Grafton, were beheaded on Gosford Green, to the east of the city. In the war between the houses of York and Lan- caster, Richard, Earl of Warwick, marched with all his ordnance and warlike stores into this city, where he remained for a short time, during which Edward IV., on his route from Leicester, attempted to force an en- trance. Being repulsed, the king passed on to War- wick, and thence to London; and having gained the battle of Barnet, in which the Earl of Warwick was slain, and that near Tewkesbury shortly after, he re- turned to Coventry, and deprived the citizens of their charter, for the restoration of which they were compelled to pay a fine of 500 marks. In 1474, Edward IV. and his queen kept the festival of St. George here; and subsequently, in 1485, Henry VII., on his route from Bosworth Field, was received here with every demon- stration of respect.

In the early part of the sixteenth century, Coventry became the theatre of religious persecution : the Bishop of Chester, coming to examine persons accused of heresy, condemned seven to the stake, which sentence was exe- cuted in the Little Park. In 1554, Mr. Hopkins, sheriff for the city, was confined in the Fleet prison, on a charge of heresy, but was liberated after great intercession, and fled the kingdom ; in the following year, Laurence Saunders, Robert Glover, A.M., and Cornelius Bongey, were burnt for their religious tenets. In 1565, Queen Elizabeth visited the city; and in 1569, Mary, Queen of Scots, on her removal from Tutbury Castle for greater security, was for some time at the Bull inn, in the cus- tody of the Earls of Shrewsbury and Huntingdon. In 1607, the city suffered considerable damage from an inundation, which entered 257 houses, washing away furniture and property of various kinds : the flood rose to the height of three yards, and after remaining for three or four hours, suddenly subsided; clusters of white snails were afterwards found in the houses and in the trees, supposed to have collected prior to the influx of the water, which, though observed at the distance of nearly a mile from the town, was so instantaneous in its approach, as to preclude all means of precaution. King James, attended by a large retinue of the nobility, visited the city in 1617, when a cup of pure gold, weighing 45 ounces, and containing the sum of £100, was presented to him by the corporation, which his majesty ordered to be preserved with the royal plate for the heirs of the crown.

about 200 members, and is well regulated by a com-ittee: the theatre, a neat and conveniently arranged ilding, is opened occasionally; and assemblies and ncerts take place periodically at St. Mary's and Dra-rs' Halls. The barracks, erected in 1792, on the site the old Bull inn (where Henry VII. slept on his route om the victory of Bosworth Field), are a handsome nge of building, fronted with stone, and ornamented th the royal arms over the principal gateway; the tablishment is for a field-officer and fifteen subalterns, d comprises a riding-house, an hospital, and stabling r 188 horses.

The making of caps was the principal TRADE of the wn prior to the year 1436, when the manufacture of oollen and broad cloth was introduced, which continued flourish till the end of the sixteenth century: at this me Coventry was celebrated for a superior blue dye, hich from the permanence of its colour, obtained the pellation of "Coventry true blue." About the begin-ng of the eighteenth century, striped and mixed tam-ies, camlets, shalloons, and calimancoes, were manu-ctured to a considerable extent; to which succeeded le throwing of silk, the weaving of gauze, broad silks, d ribbon, and the manufacture of watches. The eaving of ribbon at present forms the staple trade: a ast supply is furnished weekly to the wholesale houses London, and to every part of the United Kingdom, by eans of commercial agents; and large quantities are xported. In 1808 there were 2819 silk and ribbon ooms in the city alone, exclusively of those in the adja-ent villages: since that time the number has consider-bly increased, affording employment to nearly 16,000 persons in the city and suburbs; and from the intro-duction of the French looms and machinery, an infinite variety in the pattern and an elegance in the texture have been attained, which give a distinguished superior-ity to the ribbon manufactured here. The manufacture of watches, for which Coventry was so long celebrated, has of late undergone great improvement; and many gold watches of superior construction are supplied to the first houses in that branch of trade. The situation of the town is peculiarly advantageous for trade, being central to the ports of London, Liverpool, Bristol, and Hull, and having by means of the Oxford and Coventry canals, which form a junction at a short distance to the north, a direct communication with the manufacturing districts of Lancashire and Yorkshire. On the south side of the town is a station of the London and Birming-1am railway; there is a railway to Leamington, and an act was passed in 1846 for a railway to Nuneaton, 10½ miles in length.

The market, which is on Wednesday and Friday, is 1eld in various parts of the town; for corn, in the Cross-cheaping, a spacious area enlarged by the removal of a middle range of old houses, and in which was the ancient cross, one of the most beautiful in the kingdom, juilt by Sir William Holles, Knt., in 1544, and taken lown in 1771; for cattle, in Bishop-street; for pigs, in Cook-street; and for butter, eggs, and poultry, in an area behind the mayor's parlour, or police-office, where a market-house has been erected. Fairs for three days :ach commence April 21st, Aug. 16th, and Oct. 21st, or cattle and merchandise; to these fairs are attached :ourts of pie-poudre, and the corporation is entitled to he same tolls as are taken at Smithfield market, in

London: there are also monthly fairs for cattle. The great show-fair takes place on the Friday after Corpus Christi-day, and continues for eight days, on the first of which the commemoration of Lady Godiva's procession is occasionally revived, by a representative obtained for that purpose. This ceremony has its origin in a tradi-tion, that, the citizens having been greatly oppressed by the severe exactions imposed upon them by Leofric, his countess undertook to intercede for their relief, but was apparently frustrated in her suit by a promise of exemp-tion only upon the condition of her riding naked through the city on horseback. It is further recorded in the tra-ditionary legends of the city, that, having obtained her husband's permission, and trusting for concealment to the length of her hair, and to the discretion of the inha-bitants, who were ordered, upon pain of death, to shut themselves up in their houses, she performed the task, and obtained for the city a charter of "freedom from servitude, evil customs, and exactions." The tradition also records that a tailor, who disobeyed the injunction, was instantly struck blind; and a figure, called Peeping Tom, carved in wood, and placed in an opening at the corner of a house in High-street, is still preserved in memory of this event, which has become closely inter-woven with the history of the place, though not invented till the time of Charles II.

New Corporation Seal.   *Old Corporation Seal.*

Ranulph, Earl of Chester, in the reign of Henry II., granted a CHARTER to the inhabitants, confirming their possessions in free burgage as they held them in the time of his father and ancestors, with liberty to elect a bailiff, and to have a portmote, or town court of record, in which the bailiff should preside for the trial of all pleas amongst themselves; bestowing on them, also, all such freedoms as the burgesses of Lincoln enjoyed. This charter was confirmed by the reigning sovereign; and in a subsequent charter, granted by Edward III., Coventry, with a considerable district around it, was termed a city, and liberty was given to elect a mayor and two bailiffs, who presided in the portmote, which was from that time called the "Court of the Mayor and Bailiffs." Henry VI. made the bailiffs sheriffs also, and converted the city into a county, separating it from the county of Warwick, and conferring many other privi-leges. Under the last charter, that of James I., the corporation consisted of a mayor, 10 aldermen, a coun-cil of 31, a recorder, two sheriffs and bailiffs, a coroner, steward (always a barrister), two chamberlains, two wardens, a town-clerk, sword-bearer, mace-bearer, and subordinate officers. By the act of the 5th and 6th of William IV., cap. 76, the government is now vested in a mayor, 10 aldermen, and 30 councillors. The city is divided into 5 wards, instead of 10 as formerly; and comprises 13 fraternities, or trading companies, the numbers of which, with the exception of the Drapers' Company, who still retain their hall, have been greatly reduced. There are 19 justices of the peace; and a police force, consisting of a superintendent, inspector, sergeant, and 16 constables. The freedom is obtained by a servitude of seven years to any branch of trade within the city and liberties. Among the privileges enjoyed by the freemen is that of pasturing cattle upon the "Lammas Grounds," a tract of about 1100 acres, appropriated to that use from Lammas to Candlemas by especial grant. The city first exercised the elective franchise in the 26th of Edward I.: there were partial intermissions until the 31st of Henry VI., since which time it has regularly returned two members to parliament. The right of election was formerly vested in the freemen, in number about 3000; but by the act of the 2nd of William IV., cap. 45, the non-resident freemen, except within seven miles, were disfranchised, and the privilege was extended to £10 householders within the city: the mayor is returning officer. The boundaries of the city were defined by the act passed in the year 1842 for re-annexing Coventry to the county of Warwick, and abolishing the distinction of "county of the city," conferred by Henry VI. The corporation formerly held quarterly courts of session, at which the recorder presided, and they had power to try capital offenders; but the courts of quarter-sessions are now held here by the magistrates of the county, and the assizes by the judges of the Midland circuit, for the "Coventry division," which comprises the greater part of North Warwickshire. Petty-sessions are held by the Warwickshire magistrates every alternate Thursday; and the city magistrates attend at the police-office every day except Tuesday. The powers of the county debt-court of Coventry, established in 1847, under the provisions of a general act of parliament, extend over the registration-district of Coventry, and part of the districts of Foleshill and Meriden.

The County Hall is a neat modern building faced with stone, and ornamented with pillars of the Tuscan order, rising from a rustic basement, and supporting a handsome cornice in the centre of the front. Adjoining is the gaoler's house, a neat brick edifice; and behind it are the prison and bridewell, which were rebuilt a few years since, at an expense of £16,000. St. Mary's Hall, appropriated to the larger meetings and civic entertainments of the corporation, is a magnificent structure in the later English style, originally built by the master and wardens of the Trinity Guild, in the fourteenth century. The exterior of the edifice, with its richly decorated windows, and elaborately groined archway, has an imposing grandeur of effect. The interior, which is replete with the richest ornaments of the decorated style, comprises a splendid banquet-hall, adorned with well-painted portraits of several of the sovereigns who have been entertained within its walls; the windows, the tracery of which is gracefully elegant, are ornamented with painted glass: at the upper end is a fine piece of tapestry, worked in compartments; and on the north side is a small recess, with a beautiful oriel window, of which the original carved roof is still entire. The council-chamber is fitted up in the ancient style, and

706

eple, the whole forms an interesting architectural feae in the town. The church was completed in 1832, d dedicated to Our Blessed Saviour. The living is a rpetual curacy; net income, £179; patron, the Vicar St. Michael's.

The parish of the *Holy Trinity* comprises 1771*a*. 2*r*. *p*. of land. The living is a vicarage, valued in the ng's books at £10, with a net income of £396; it is the patronage of the Crown, and the impropriation longs to the corporation. The church, which is of rlier date than the more recent part of St. Michael's, a venerable cruciform structure, in the later English yle, with a well-proportioned tower rising from the intersection, and surmounted by a handsome octagonal ire. The proportions of the interior are more massive an those of St. Michael's; and though less elaborate its details, this church preserves throughout a consistant unity of design: the oak roof is panelled, and derated with gilded mouldings; the pulpit, which is of one, has been recently restored, and is a beautiful specimen of enriched sculpture, in the later style. The first one of another church, dedicated to St. Peter, and to hich a district has been assigned, was laid on the 7th :ptember, 1840: the edifice cost £3200, and was ened for divine service on the 28th October, 1841; e design is in the later English style, and the building ntains 1354 sittings, 695 of which are free. The living a perpetual curacy; net income of the incumbent, l50; patron, the Vicar of Holy Trinity. The living of '. *John's* is a rectory not in charge, annexed to the headastership of the free school, and including also a lecreship for the second master; net income, £83. The hureh, ·formerly a chapel, erected in honour of Our Saviour, upon ground given by Isabel, queen-mother of Edward III., is an interesting structure, quadrangular n the lower part and cruciform in the upper; from the entre rises a square embattled tower, with circular turets at the angles, and supported on four finely-clustered iers and arches of singular beauty: the interior is chaacterised by a simple grandeur of style. A church district named St. Thomas' was formed out of the parish of St. John, in 1844, by the Ecclesiastical Commissioners: he living is in the gift of the Crown and the Bishop of Vorcester, alternately. There are places of worship in he town for congregations of Baptists, the Society of Friends, Independents, Wesleyans, Unitarians, and Roman Catholics.

The *Free Grammar school* was founded in the reign of Henry VIII. by John Hales. His original muuificent ntentions were frustrated by the opposition of the then :orporation, and Coventry school was thereby deprived of university endowments which would have made it the ival of Eton and Winchester. At his death, however, his benefactor endowed it with lands and houses to the value of 200 marks per annum, which now produce an ncome of £870. It was placed by the Municipal act mder the management of Church-Charity Trustees, who ippoint the masters. There are several exhibitions, which have been much increased in value of late years, md will probably continue to increase; they are five in 1umber, and worth about £40 per annum during resilence at the university. There are also two fellowships it St. John's College, Oxford, and one at Catherine Hall, Cambridge, appropriated to this school. The school-:oom is the only remaining portion of the hospital of St.

John, founded in the reign of Henry II., and was the chapel of that religious house: its east window is a magnificent specimen of flowing decorated tracery, and the side windows of the ancient chancel are of the same date, probably 1320. The roof, which is now concealed by a coved plaster ceiling, is a fine specimen of joiners' work, and contains a vast amount of timber. The beautiful double row of oak stalls were removed by Hales from the choir of the church belonging to the monastery of Grey friars, for the use of the scholars. The western end of the school was taken down about fifty years ago to widen the street, and was rebuilt in the worst style of pseudo-Gothic then prevalent; one stone alone retains the characteristic Norman ornament, which proves the antiquity of the old west front. Sir William Dugdale the celebrated antiquary, and Archbishop Secker, received their education in this school; and the quaint old physician, Philemon Holland, who was called the Translator General of the age, was master here. The present masters are, the Rev. T. Sheepshanks, M.A., of Trinity College, Cambridge, and the Rev. W. Drake, M.A., late fellow of St. John's, in the same university. *Bablake school* occupies one side of the quadrangle of Bond's hospital. It was founded in 1566 by Thomas Wheatley, ironmonger, and mayor of the city, in consequence of an accidental acquisition of wealth, by the delivery of barrels of cochineal and ingots of silver in mistake for steel gads, which he sent his agent to purchase in Spain; the original endowment, increased by subsequent benefactions, produces £938 per annum.

Bond's hospital was founded in 1506, by Thomas Bond, draper, who endowed it with lands for the maintenance of ten poor men and one woman: the number of pensioners, in consequence of the improvement of the income, has been increased to forty-six, of whom are resident. The building, occupying one side of the Bablake quadrangle, is an ancient edifice of timber frame-work, in the Elizabethan style; it has undergone great improvement, under the superintendence of Mr. Rickman, and the entire building is now restored to its original character. The *Grey-friars' hospital*, so called from its proximity to the monastery of that order, was founded in 1529, by William Ford, who endowed it for five aged men and one woman; from the increased amount of the income, there are at present 34 poor persons in the establishment. The buildings, which form a long and narrow quadrangular area, almost darkened by the projection of the upper stories, are in the style of domestic architecture prevailing in the reign of Elizabeth; the timber frame-work, richly carved, and decorated with cornices and canopies over the central windows and doorways, is as perfect as when first erected, and these beautiful almshouses are deservedly admired as the most entire and elegant specimen of the kind in the kingdom. The *House of Industry* occupies the site, and includes the remains, of a monastery of Carmelites, founded in 1342, by Sir John Pulteney, lord mayor of London, and the clear revenue of which, at the Dissolution, was £7. 13. 8. Part of the arched cloisters, beautifully groined, also the refectory and dormitory, are still remaining, with the beautiful entrance gateway, richly groined and ornamented with three canopied niches in front; to these remains has been added a large and handsome brick building, well adapted to the purpose. The management of this establishment, which is also a comfortable asylum for the aged poor, is vested in a body of guardians, under a local act, which extends over the parishes of St. John the Baptist and St. Michael, and part of that of the Holy Trinity, the whole union containing a population of 27,070. The trustees of the church and general charities have altogether at their disposal funds to the amount of £3000 per annum, for distribution among the poor : the charity of Sir Thomas White has arisen chiefly from his donation of £1400 in the reign of Henry VIII., exclusively of considerable sums to be lent for nine years to apprentices of good character, on the expiration of their indentures ; in this loan, natives of Leicester, Northampton, Nottingham, and Warwick participate. At Allesley, about a mile distant, is a petrifying spring, not much used. Walter of Coventry, a Benedictine monk and eminent early historian ; William Macclesfield, created cardinal by Pope Benedict XI. ; John Bird, Bishop of Chester, who was deprived of his see in the reign of Mary ; Humphrey Wanley, the antiquary ; and Nehemiah Grew, the botanist, were natives of the city. It gives the title of Earl, created in 1697, to the family of Coventry.

COVERHAM (*Holy Trinity*), a parish, in the union of LEYBURN, wapentake of HANG-WEST, N. riding of YORK, 12 miles (W.) from Bedale, and 1½ (S. W.) from Middleham ; containing 1254 inhabitants. This place was distinguished for its abbey, which was founded at Swainby, in the parish of Pickhall, near the southern point of Richmondshire, prior to 1189, by Helewisia, daughter and heiress of Ranulph de Glanville, lord chief justice of England, and was removed hither in 1214 by the son of that lady, Ralph Fitz-Robert, lord of Middleham. The institution was of considerable celebrity, and received various endowments from families of rank, possessing, among other lands, nearly the whole of the valley of Coverham ; at the Dissolution its revenue was returned at £207. 14. 8. The situation of the priory was highly appropriate for the purposes of the foundation, and from the spot is obtained a view of the outline of Whernside and Penhill, which is very majestic, but it does not appear that the buildings were ever magnificent ; the remains, situated on the north side of the Cover, consist principally of some shattered arches of the nave, and the gateway, a very picturesque structure.

The parish extends over a space of forty superficial miles, and is divided into the High dale and Low dale. The former contains 12,480 acres, and includes the townships of Gammersgill, Swineside, Arkleside, Blackrake, Bradley, Coverhead, Pickle, and Woodale, with the village of Horsehouse, which gives name to a chapelry that consists of the preceding townships. The latter comprises 9640 acres, and includes, besides Caldbridge, East Scrafton, Carlton, Melmerby, and West Scrafton, the hamlet of Coverham Abbey, in the vicinity of which stand the ancient church and mill of the monks, and which, with Agglethorpe Hall and its dependencies, forms the township of Coverham, with 1090 acres of rich land. The river Cover, which confers its name upon the district, is a rapid stream abounding with trout ; the dale through which it runs is supposed to have been the birthplace of Myles Coverdale, Bishop of Exeter, born in Yorkshire in 1488, and who, in 1535, published the first edition of the Bible ever printed in English. Both coal and lead are found in the parish. The living is a perpetual curacy, endowed with the tithes of Arkleside,

708

General Dyson, owner of the estate of Peakill, in the parish, has lately erected two elegant tablets in the chancel, one in memory of his father, James Dyson, Esq., for many years solicitor to the Admiralty and Navy; and has also presented an excellent organ, and a beautiful altar window. There is a place of worship for Wesleyans.

COWDEN (ST. MARY MAGDALENE), a parish, in the union of SEVEN-OAKS, hundred of SOMERDEN, lathe of SUTTON-AT-HONE, W. division of KENT, 9 miles (W.) from Tonbridge-Wells; containing 695 inhabitants. It comprises 3232 acres, whereof 760 are woodland. One of the four principal heads of the Medway, which rises at Gravelly Hill, in Sussex, directs its course eastward along the southern side of the parish, and separates it from the county of Sussex. Iron-ore is found. The living is a rectory, valued in the king's books at £9. 18. 11½., and in the gift and incumbency of the Rev. T. Harvey : the tithes have been commuted for £544, and the glebe consists of 4 acres. The church is a small building, with a handsome spire; a north aisle has been added to it, and 134 additional sittings have been provided.

COWDON or COLDEN, GREAT and LITTLE, an ancient parish, in the union of SKIRLAUGH, partly in the Middle, but chiefly in the N., division of the wapentake of HOLDERNESS, E. riding of YORK, 3½ miles (S. by E.) from Hornsea; containing 151 inhabitants, of whom 19 are in Little Cowdon. Great Cowdon is described in Domesday book as a berewick, belonging, in the Confessor's time, to St. John of Beverley; and the manor was in the possession of the Archbishop of York at an early period subsequent to the Conquest. At Little Cowdon was a parochial chapel dedicated to St. John the Evangelist, anciently given to the monks of St. Martin, Albemarle, who conveyed it in the 18th of Richard II. to the convent of Kirkstall; the patronage before this time had been exercised by the knightly family of Despencer. The parish is commonly considered a township, sometimes called Cowdons-Ambo, partly in the parish of Aldbrough, but chiefly in that of Mappleton : it comprises by measurement 1503 acres, of which about 800 are in Great Cowdon; one-fourth is pasture, and the remainder arable. The village of the latter place is situated at the very edge of the cliffs, on the German Ocean, and is occupied by a few farmers and persons employed in obtaining gravel from the cliffs. The chapel, with a portion of the village, suffered from the devastations of the sea, and was swept away about half a century since : the living, however, exists, and is a discharged rectory, valued in the king's books at £2. 13. 4., and annexed to the living of Aldbrough. Some time since, the incumbent received £3000 in satisfaction of his claim to tithes.

COWES, EAST, a parochial district, in the parish of WHIPPINGHAM, liberty of EAST MEDINA, Isle of Wight division of the county of SOUTHAMPTON, 5 miles (N.) from Newport; containing 880 inhabitants. The village is situated on the eastern side of the mouth of the river Medina, by which it is separated from West Cowes, and owes its origin to a fort or blockhouse, erected in the reign of Henry VIII., for the defence of the harbour, but of which no vestiges are now discernible. Until of late here was an establishment of the Customs, which has been removed to West Cowes, and
709

the buildings are now occupied as a station for the men employed in the preventive service. Ship-building is carried on to a considerable extent; and good building-stone is obtained in several parts of the vicinity, particularly at Osborne Park, where it was raised in large quantities for the erection of the Southampton docks. The neighbourhood abounds with interesting features and finely-varied scenery; and on the brow of a hill near the village is East Cowes Castle, a handsome structure, consisting of one square and two circular embattled towers, erected by the late eminent architect, Mr. Nash, ' for his own residence, and commanding a fine sea-view. Osborne House was purchased in 1845 from Lady Isabella Blanchford by Her Majesty as a royal residence: the estate comprises 376 acres, and, with Barton farm, 817 acres; having an indented line of sea-shore about a mile and a half in extent. Important additions have been made to the house, and the grounds in various ways embellished. The church, dedicated to St. James, and of which the first stone was laid by Her present Majesty, when Princess Victoria, who was also present at its consecration in 1831, was erected at an expense of £3000, raised by subscription, towards which Her Majesty and the Duchess of Kent contributed liberally, and which was also aided by a grant of £375 from the funds of the Incorporated Society; it is a handsome edifice, in the Norman style, and contains 668 sittings, of which 370 are free. The living is a perpetual curacy, in the patronage of the Rector of Whippingham, with a net income of £135. There is a place of worship for Independents. At Barton was an oratory of Augustine monks, founded by John de Insula, in 1282, and the beautiful remains of which have been converted into a farmhouse.

COWES, WEST, a sea-port and chapelry, in the N. division of the parish of NORTHWOOD, liberty of WEST MEDINA, Isle of Wight division of the county of SOUTHAMPTON, 5 miles (N.) from Newport, and 86 (S. W.) from London; containing 4107 inhabitants. This place owes its origin to the erection of a small castle in 1539, by Henry VIII, on the western bank of the river Medina, commanding the entrance of the harbour; the fortress is a small edifice with a semicircular battery mounting eight pieces of heavy ordnance, and contains accommodation for a captain and a company of artillery. From the excellence of the harbour, in which ships may find shelter in stormy weather, and from which they may sail out either to the east or west, as the wind may serve, Cowes has become a populous and flourishing town; and from its advantageous situation for ship-building, several private yards have been established, in which men-of-war have been built for the royal navy. The town is romantically situated on the acclivity of an eminence: the streets are narrow, and the houses in general inelegant, but, rising above each other from the margin of the river to the summit of the eminence on which they are built, they have a pleasing and picturesque appearance from the opposite bank, and are seen with peculiar advantage from the sea, of which they command interesting and extensive views. The excellence of its beach, the pleasantness of its situation, and the salubrity of the air, have rendered it a fashionable place for sea-bathing, for which purpose several respectable lodging-houses have been erected, and numerous bathing-machines are ranged on the beach, to the west of the castle. The parade, terminated at one extremity by the castle, and at the other by the Marine hotel, forms a favourite promenade. The Royal Yacht Club, consisting of about 160 noblemen and gentlemen, established here for many years, celebrate their regatta annually in August, on which occasion more than 200 yachts and other vessels are assembled, forming a spectacle truly splendid. The club-house, situated on the parade, is a handsome building with a spacious veranda, commanding a fine view of the sea, and having in front an inclosure, within which are several pieces of cannon, and a semaphore, with apparatus for the display of signals to the vessels in the roadstead, belonging respectively to the several members of the squadron. An extensive trade is carried on in provisions and other articles for the supply of the shipping : the principal exports of the island are wheat, flour, malt, barley, wool, and salt, large quantities of which are shipped for France, Spain, Portugal, and the Mediterranean shores. Packets sail several times a day to Southampton, Ryde, and Portsmouth, and passage-boats to Newport. A market-house was erected in 1816, and the market is well supplied with meat, fish, and vegetables; a fair is held on the Thursday in Whitsun-week. The town is partly in the jurisdiction of the borough of Newport, and partly in that of the county; the upper part of the market-house is appropriated as the town-hall.

The living is a perpetual curacy; net income, £256; patron, the Vicar of Carisbrooke. The chapel, erected in the year 1657, and consecrated in the year 1662, is on the summit of the hill : in 1811 it was enlarged and improved at an expense of £3000, by the late George Ward, Esq., who added the tower at the west end, the lower part of which, opening into the church, forms the pew and the mausoleum of that family, and contains an elegant monument to the late Mrs. Ward ; the building was further enlarged in 1832. A district church, erected on the west cliff, at the expense of Mrs. Goodwin, at a cost of £5000, including endowment, and dedicated to the Holy Trinity, was consecrated in 1832 : it is a handsome building of white brick, ornamented with stone, in the later English style, and has an embattled tower crowned with pinnacles; the interior is lighted by a range of lofty windows, enriched with tracery, and is embellished with an east window of stained glass, and other appropriate details. The living is a perpetual curacy in the patronage of Mrs. Goodwin; net income, £85. There are places of worship for Independents and Wesleyans, and a Roman Catholic chapel.

COWFOLD, a parish, in the union of CUCKFIELD, hundred of WINDHAM and EWHURST, rape of BRAMBER, W. division of SUSSEX, 7 miles (S. S. E.) from Horsham; containing 943 inhabitants. It is on the road from London, by way of Horsham, to Brighton, and comprises by measurement nearly 3000 acres, the soil of which is chiefly a stiff clay, though in some parts of a lighter quality. The village is pleasantly situated, and a market for corn is held in it every alternate Wednesday. The living is a vicarage, endowed with the rectorial tithes, valued in the king's books at £10. 6. 8., and in the patronage of the Bishop of Chichester : the tithes have been commuted for £580, and the glebe comprises 33 acres. The church is a handsome structure, in the early and later English styles, with a low embattled tower; in the nave is a magnificent monument of brass

710

to the memory of Thomas Nelond, prior of Lewes, who died in 1433.

COWGILL, an ecclesiastical district, in the parochial chapelry of DENT, parish and union of SEDBERGH, W. division of the wapentake of STAINCLIFFE and EWCROSS, W. riding of YORK, 9 miles (S. E. by E.) from Sedbergh; containing about 500 inhabitants. It lies south of Rysell Fell, and partakes much of the scenery of the chapelry at large : the river Dee passes in the vicinity. Here are some small collieries, of which the veins of coal are from six to fifteen inches deep. The living is a perpetual curacy, in the patronage of five Trustees; income, £100. The church stands at the head of a picturesque vale, four miles east from Dent, and is a small neat structure with a campanile turret, built by subscription, in 1838, at a cost of £750 : to the building and endowment, Professor Sedgwick contributed £100. There is a place of worship for the Society of Friends, in which Fox has preached, and attached to which is a school. A Sunday school is connected with the church.

COWGROVE, or KINSON, a tything, in the parish of WIMBORNE-MINSTER, union of WIMBORNE and CRANBORNE, hundred of BADBURY, Wimborne division of DORSET, 2 miles (W.) from Wimborne; containing 752 inhabitants.

COW-HONEYBOURNE, county of GLOUCESTER.— See HONEYBOURNE, Cow.

COWICK, a chapelry, in the parish and union of ST. THOMAS THE APOSTLE, EXETER, hundred of WONFORD, Wonford and S. divisions of DEVON, 1 mile (S. W. by S.) from Exeter. The chapel is dedicated to St. Thomas à Becket. A Benedictine monastery, a cell to the abbey of Bec, in Normandy, was established here by William, son of Balwine, in the time of Henry II.; but there are not any remains of it.

COWICK, a township, in the parish of SNAITH, union of GOOLE, Lower division of the wapentake of OSGOLDCROSS, W. riding of YORK, half a mile (S. E. by E.) from Snaith ; containing 882 inhabitants. The township comprises by computation 8970 acres, and includes East and West Cowick, and the hamlets of Newbridge and Greenland. Cowick and Snaith have a peculiar jurisdiction, which extends over several neighbouring places. The Hall, a seat belonging to Viscount Downe, is a handsome mansion, in an extensive park. At West Cowick is an Independent meeting-house.

COWLAM, a parish, in the union of DRIFFIELD, wapentake of BUCKROSE, E. riding of YORK, 2 miles (N. E.) from Sledmere ; containing 44 inhabitants. This place, which appears to have been formerly a large village or town of some importance, is the property of the Rev. T. F. F. Bowes, to whose brother, General Bowes, killed at the head of his brigade in Spain, after being severely wounded at the storming of Badajos, a monument was voted by parliament, and erected in the Cathedral of St. Paul, London. The parish comprises by computation 2200 acres, of which about 300 are pasture, and 100 woodland. The surface is very irregular, and intersected with deep valleys of romantic character ; the soil is chalky, with some portions containing flints, but generally producing good crops. The living is a discharged rectory, valued in the king's books at £11. 11. 3.; net income, £30; patron and incumbent, the Rev. T. F. F. Bowes. The church contains a curious ancient font.

COWLEY, a hamlet, in the parish of PRESTON-BISSET, union, hundred, and county of BUCKINGHAM; containing 31 inhabitants.

COWLEY (ST. MARY), a parish, in the union of CHELTENHAM, hundred of RAPSGATE, E. division of the county of GLOUCESTER, 5 miles (S. by E.) from Cheltenham; containing 317 inhabitants. It comprises 1835 acres, of which about 200 are pasture, 100 woodland, 39 common or waste, and the rest arable. The living is a rectory, valued in the king's books at £9. 1. 10½., and in the patronage of the Crown: the tithes have been commuted for £300, and the glebe consists of 73 acres, with a glebe-house.

COWLEY (ST. LAWRENCE), a parish, in the union of UXBRIDGE, hundred of ELTHORNE, county of MIDDLESEX, 1½ mile (S. by E.) from Uxbridge, near the Great Western railway; containing 392 inhabitants. The living is a rectory, valued in the king's books at £11, and in the gift of J. Hilliard, Esq.: the tithes have been commuted for £197, and the glebe consists of 12 acres, with a glebe-house.

COWLEY (ST. JAMES), a parish, in the union of HEADINGTON, hundred of BULLINGTON, county of OXFORD, 2½ miles (S. E.) from Oxford; containing 606 inhabitants. The living is a perpetual curacy; net income, £64; patrons and appropriators, the Dean and Canons of Christ-Church, Oxford. Part of the parish is called Temple-Cowley, from some lands having been given by Matilda, in the reign of Stephen, to the Knights Templars, who had a preceptory here, which was afterwards removed to Sandford. To the north of Cowley Marsh are some remains of an hospital, dedicated to St. Bartholomew, and thought by Tanner to have been founded by Henry I., when he built his palace at Beaumont; it was granted by Edward III. to Oriel College, as a retreat for the students in time of pestilence.

COWLEY, a township, in the parish of GNOSALL, union of NEWPORT, W. division of the hundred of CUTTLESTONE, S. division of the county of STAFFORD, 5 miles (E.) from Newport. This is a quarter in the parish, and contains a number of scattered houses, and the hamlets of Coton, Befcott, and Plardiwick, extending from nearly one to two miles south-west of Gnosall. At Coton is an Independent meeting-house, built in 1823.

COWLING, county of SUFFOLK.—See COOLING.

COWLING, with BURRELL.—See BURRELL.

COWLING, an ecclesiastical parish, in the parish of KILDWICK, union of SKIPTON, E. division of the wapentake of STAINCLIFFE and EWCROSS, W. riding of YORK, 2½ miles (W. by S.) from Cross Hills; containing about 2500 inhabitants. This district borders westward on Lancashire. It includes a portion of the large tract of upland moor stretching across the western part of Craven, and partly slopes down towards the valley of the Aire, into which river it sends a stream of some magnitude. The area is about 5500 acres: the reclaimed land is almost entirely pasture-ground, the number of acres under tillage being very small; in parts the rocks rise abruptly to a considerable height, probably about 1000 feet, and there are several glens of great natural beauty. Good building-stone is quarried, some of which was used for the construction of the Liverpool docks. The road from Colne to Keighley passes through; and at Cross Hills is a station on the Leeds and Bradford Extension railway. The population is principally employed

711

in hand-loom weaving: there is also a small cotton-mill. Car Head, the seat of W. B. Wainman, Esq., with its woods and grounds, adds much to the attractions of the place. The parish was constituted in September 1845, under the act 6th and 7th Victoria, cap. 37: the living is in the gift of the Crown and the Bishop of Ripon, alternately; income, £150. The church is in the later English style, and consists of a nave, chancel, north and south aisles, and western tower; it is a handsome structure, on a good site, and forms a very pleasing object from several points of view: the total cost of the building, which was designed by Chantrell, was nearly £2000. There are two places of worship for Wesleyans, and two for Baptists. On the moor is a stone, called the Hitchin stone, supposed by some to have been used in Druidical rites; it is about ten feet high, in its general figure is rather cubical, and has a large hole passing through it in a sloping direction, as if drilled, and another joining the former in the centre, of sufficient size to admit a man.

COWPEN, or COOPEN, a township, in the chapelry of HORTON, union of TYNEMOUTH, E. division of CASTLE ward, S. division of NORTHUMBERLAND, 8 miles (E. S. E.) from Morpeth; containing 2464 inhabitants. This township, which is called in old records Cupum, Cupin, Copun, or Couperum, comprises about 1553 acres, and extends nearly two miles along the southern bank of the Blyth, which is navigable. The canons of Brinkburn and the monks of Tynemouth had salt-mines here, the latter being also owners of much of the land, and there were formerly several other salt-works near the river; but they have all long since disappeared. That portion of the Bedlington iron-works in which engines are constructed, is in this township, adjoining the river, and employs numerous hands: there are also four corn-mills, two of which are worked by steam; a large colliery; and at Cowpen quay a ship-building yard. The village lies about a mile west of the port of Blyth, on the highway between that place and Newcastle, and about a quarter of a mile from the Blyth river; it contains several good houses, all of modern date except the Hall, at present in the occupation of a farmer. The impropriate tithes have been commuted for £295, payable in moieties to the Duke of Northumberland and M. J. F. Sidney, Esq., and the vicarial for £36, payable to the vicar of Woodhorn. There are places of worship in the township for congregations of Burghers, Methodists of the New Connexion, Primitive Methodists, and Roman Catholics.

COWPEN-BEWLEY, a township, in the parish of BILLINGHAM, union of STOCKTON-UPON-TEES, N. E. division of STOCKTON ward, S. division of the county of DURHAM, 4½ miles (N. E. by N.) from Stockton; containing 196 inhabitants. It lies to the north-east of Billingham, towards the marshes, and comprises 2640 acres, including the large farm of Saltholme; 530 acres are common or waste. The lands are the property of the Dean and Chapter of Durham. In Cowpen-marsh, a pasture of from 400 to 500 acres, are several large earthen mounds, now covered with herbage, the remains of the old salt-works that were carried on in this angle of the county: the abbot of Guisborough had his salt-works on the opposite coast. The tithes have been commuted for £173. 3., of which £30 are payable to the vicar of the parish.

COWT

COWSBY, a parish, in the union of THIRSK, wapentake of BIRDFORTH, N. riding of YORK, 6¼ miles (N. N. E.) from Thirsk; containing 108 inhabitants. The parish comprises 1167a. 1r. 30p., of which about 510 acres are arable, 429 meadow and pasture, and 134 moor; the surface is beautifully diversified with hill and dale, and richly clothed in many parts with wood. Cowsby Hall, an excellent mansion, is the seat of the Lloyd family, who are lords of the manor, and proprietors of the lands. The living is a discharged rectory, valued in the king's books at £5. 11. 0½., and in the patronage of Mrs. Lloyd: the tithes have been commuted for £125, and the glebe comprises 19 acres. The church was taken down and rebuilt, and consecrated in April, 1846: it is in the Norman style, with a tower and spire, and of exceedingly chaste design: the cost was defrayed by the Lloyd family. Here is an hospital for four parishioners, endowed with £10 per annum, and supposed to have been founded by Lord Crewe.

COWTHORN, a township, in the parish of MIDDLETON, PICKERING lythe and union, N. riding of YORK, 5 miles (N. N. W.) from Pickering; containing 20 inhabitants. The soil is light and sandy, and the substratum in some parts limestone; the scenery is bold, with extensive views from the higher grounds. Good stone is quarried for building purposes. There are some Roman antiquities.

COWTHORP (ST. MICHAEL), a parish, in the Upper division of the wapentake of CLARO, W. riding of YORK, 3¾ miles (N. E. by N.) from Wetherby; containing 115 inhabitants. It is situated on the river Nidd, about a mile from the road between Boroughbridge and Wetherby. The living is a discharged rectory, valued in the king's books at £4. 15. 10.; net income, £130; patron, R. F. Wilson, Esq. The church is an ancient structure, consisting of a nave and chancel, in the latter of which is a monumental brass with the effigies of a man and woman, bearing between them a model of a church, and supposed to be Brian Rowcliff, a baron of the exchequer, and his lady, the founders of the building. Near the manor-house stands a gigantic oak-tree, one of the largest in England; it measures 60 feet in girth, and when entire, its branches are said to have overspread an acre of ground: twenty-four persons have sat down within its hollow trunk.

COWTON, EAST (ST. MARY), a parish, in the union of NORTHALLERTON, wapentake of GILLING-EAST, N. riding of YORK, 7 miles (N. E. by E.) from Catterick, and 8 (N. W. by N.) from Northallerton, the post-town; containing 454 inhabitants. It comprises 3144a. 3r., of which 1743 acres are arable, and the remainder meadow and pasture: the surface is low, but undulated, with many commanding prospects: the soil is clay, partially gravelly, with beds of sand. A station on the York and Newcastle railway has been established at the place. The living is a discharged vicarage, valued in the king's books at £4. 6. 10½.: the patronage is attached conditionally to the Mastership of Kirkby-Ravensworth Hospital; otherwise it belongs to the Wardens and Hospitallers. The impropriate tithes have been commuted for £270, and the vicarial for £213. 6. 8.; the glebe consists of half an acre. The church is a small edifice. There is a place of worship for Primitive Methodists. A free school, founded by the Dakyn family in 1556, has

rence railway. There are two limestone-quarries, and a good seam of clay used in the manufacture of brown earthenware ; a small foundry, also, employs some hands. A church has been erected ; and there are places of worship for Wesleyans and Primitive Methodists.

COXLEY, a tything, in the parish of St. CUTHBERT, city and union of WELLS, hundred of WELLS-FORUM, E. division of SOMERSET ; containing 272 inhabitants. Here is an incumbency, in the gift of the Vicar of Wells.

COXLODGE, a township, in the parish of GOSFORTH, union and W. division of CASTLE ward, S. division of NORTHUMBERLAND, 2 miles (N.) from Newcastle ; containing 924 inhabitants. The township comprises 800a. 1r. 14p., of which 691 acres are arable, 106 meadow and pasture, and 2½ wood. The surface is rather level, but rising gradually from the south towards the north ; the soil is a strong clay, and, though much of it requires good draining to render it more productive, grows fair crops of wheat. The views embrace in the distance the Simonside and Cheviot hills. From the openness of the country to the west and north, and the extent of town moor on the south, the air is very salubrious, and is considered the best in the neighbourhood of Newcastle. An excellent seam of coal has been in work here for fifty years past ; a railway conveys the coal to the river Tyne, and the great north road passes on the east of the township. The Newcastle races are run on the adjoining moor, which, with the Leazes, contains 1600 acres. There is a windmill-pump in the township, for raising water to supply a reservoir on the moor, near Newcastle. The tithes have been commuted for £85. 9. 9. payable to the Bishop of Carlisle, a similar sum to the Dean and Chapter, and £17. 3. 2. to the vicar of Newcastle.

COXWELL, GREAT (St. GILES) a parish, in the union and hundred of FARRINGDON, county of BERKS, 2 miles (S. W.) from Farringdon ; containing 351 inhabitants. This parish comprises by admeasurement 1426 acres. The surface is a gentle acclivity, and the soil varies greatly on the north and west sides of Bradbury Hill ; it is chiefly a strong clay, in some parts poor and boggy, and on the south and east a rich loam. Limestone of a soft nature, in which numerous fossils are imbedded, is plentiful ; and on the hill is a' yellowish sandstone, hard enough for sharpening scythes. The village is pleasantly situated on the southern acclivity of the hill. The living is a discharged vicarage, valued in the king's books at £7. 7. 11.; patron, the Bishop of Salisbury ; impropriator, the Earl of Radnor. The vicarial tithes have been commuted for £198, and the impropriate for £21 : there are 4 acres of vicarial glebe. The Rev. John Pynsent, in 1705, bequeathed land producing about £20 per annum, for apprenticing children ; and there is a curious bequest from the Earl of Radnor, in 1771, charging his land with an annuity of £45, to be applied to the apprenticing of children of Coleshill and this parish, so often as the vicar of Coleshill should be absent from the parish more than 60 days in any one year, and should accept any other preferment with the cure of souls. The remains of a religious house built here by the abbots of Beaulieu, to whom the manor was granted by King John in 1205, are now a farmhouse : the barn is 148 feet long, and 40 feet wide, the roof sup-

ported on two ranges of timber pillars resting upon stone pedestals ; the walls are 4 feet thick, and of excellent masonry. On Badbury Hill is a circular encampment, supposed to be Danish.

COXWELL, LITTLE, a chapelry, in the parish, union, and hundred of FARRINGDON, county of BERKS, 1½ mile (S.) from Farringdon ; containing 315 inhabitants, and comprising 842a. 3r. 13p. The chapel is dedicated to St. Mary. The tithes were commuted for land and a money payment in 1801. The remains of a camp, apparently in the form of a square, are visible here, the double ditch on the western side being nearly entire ; and in an inclosed field of about fourteen acres are 273 pits, called Cole's Pits, excavated in the sand, and varying in depth, supposed to have been habitations or hiding-places of the ancient Britons.

COXWOLD (St. MICHAEL), a parish, partly in the union of EASINGWOULD, and partly in that of HELMSLEY, wapentake of BIRDFORTH, N. riding of YORK ; containing 1076 inhabitants, of whom 325 are in the township of Coxwold, 6 miles (N.) from Easingwould. The parish comprises the townships of Angram-Grange, Birdforth, Byland cum Membris, Coxwold, Newbrough, Oulston, Thornton cum Baxby, Wildon-Grange, and Yearsley, and consists of 12,025a. 2p. of fertile land, whereof about 3005 acres are arable, 7919 grass land, and 1099 wood, water, common, &c.; the township of Coxwold contains 1369a. 1r. 21p. The village is pleasantly situated on an eminence, amidst beautiful scenery of hill and dale, and woodland, and about 6 miles to the east of the York and Newcastle railway : there is a large cattle and sheep fair on the 25th of August, and races are held on the Monday after Michaelmas-day. The living is a perpetual curacy ; net income, £351 ; patrons and impropriators, the Master and Fellows of Trinity College, Cambridge, whose tithes in Coxwold township have been commuted for £353. The church is a small ancient structure, with an octagonal tower, and is said to have been erected so early as 700 ; the chancel was rebuilt in 1777, by the Earl of Fauconberg : there is some stained glass in the windows, and the building contains many handsome monuments of the Belasyse family. A chapel of ease was built at Yearsley, in 1839 ; and there is a separate incumbency at Birdforth. A free grammar school was founded in 1603, by Sir John Harte, alderman of London, who endowed it with £36. 13. 4. per annum ; and an hospital for ten poor men was founded in 1696, by Thomas, Earl of Fauconberg, the endowment of which consists of a rent-charge of £59. There are several other charities. Sterne wrote his *Tristram Shandy* and some other works at Shandy Hall, in the village, where he resided about seven years.

CRAB-WALL, with BLACON.—See BLACON.

CRACKENTHORPE, a township, in the parish of BONGATE, or St. MICHAEL, APPLEBY, EAST ward and union, county of WESTMORLAND, 2½ miles (N. W.) from Appleby ; containing 104 inhabitants. At a place called Chapel-hill are the ruins of a chapel dedicated to St. Giles. On the road from this place to Kirkby-Thore, and southward of the ancient Roman road, are traces of a quadrilateral camp ; and further on is a small outwork, named Maiden-hold.

CRACOE, a township, in the parish of BURNSALL, union of SKIPTON, E. division of the wapentake of STAINCLIFFE and EWCROSS, W. riding of YORK, 6 miles

(N.) from Skipton; containing 153 inhabitants. It comprises 1876 acres of pasture and moorland, divided among various proprietors, of whom the Duke of Devonshire is lord of the manor; 523 acres are common or waste. Abundance of good limestone and freestone is obtained in the mountainous parts. The tithes have been commuted for £97. There is a place of worship for Wesleyans.

CRADLEY (St. James), a parish, in the union of BROMYARD, hundred of RADLOW, county of HEREFORD, 8¼ miles (W. by N.) from Malvern; containing 1504 inhabitants. The parish is situated on the borders of Worcestershire, which bounds it on the north, east, and south; it is intersected by the road from Worcester to Hereford, and comprises by measurement 5966 acres, of which 1008 are woodland, about 140 hop-grounds, and 90 common or waste. A small stream, running from south to north, divides the district into two nearly equal portions, called East Cradley and West Cradley. At Ridgway Cross are quarries of old red sandstone, excellent for building; and there are also quarries of limestone and of Ludlow rock. The living is a rectory, valued in the king's books at £18, and in the gift of the Bishop of Hereford : the tithes have been commuted for £1001, and the glebe comprises 110 acres, with an excellent glebe-house. The church is a plain edifice with a low tower. There is a place of worship for Lady Huntingdon's Connexion. A free school was founded in the reign of Charles II., and endowed with £20 per annum from the Vinesend estate, in the parish. Several interesting fossils are found among the strata, including asaphus caudatus, the orthoceratites, and the encrinites.

CRADLEY, a chapelry, in the parish of HALES-OWEN, union of STOURBRIDGE, Lower division of the hundred of HALFSHIRE, Stourbridge and E. divisions of the county of WORCESTER, 1 mile (N. W. by N.) from Hales-Owen; containing 2686 inhabitants. This place is situated on the river Stour, by which it is separated on the north and north-west from the county of Stafford; it consists of 781a. 1r. 20p. of well-cultivated land, and is intersected by the road between Stourbridge and Hales-Owen. The surface is hilly, and the vicinity abounds with diversified and highly picturesque scenery. The Cradley iron-works were established two centuries ago, and in 1839 works were erected for chain-cables, anchors, anvils, &c.: the manufacture of nails, traces, gun-barrels, and various other articles in iron, is carried on to a considerable extent. There are also mines of coal in the township, but of inferior quality. The Dudley canal passes at the distance of two miles. About a mile from the village is a remarkable salt-spring, and an attempt was made to introduce the manufacture of salt, but without success : the water was subsequently analyzed, and found to be strongly impregnated with sulphate of soda, magnesia, and other mineral substances; and warm and cold baths were erected on the spot, now called Cradley Spa, and, from the beauty of their situation, much frequented. The living is a perpetual curacy; net income £150; patrons and impropriators, certain Trustees. The chapel was erected about the year 1789, and is situated on the brow of a hill commanding an agreeable prospect; it is a neat brick building, and underwent a thorough repair in 1824-5. There are places of worship for Baptists,

714

Wesleyans, and Unitarians. In a large wood, called Cradley Park, are vestiges of a moat which surrounded some ancient building.

CRAFTON, a hamlet, in the parish of WING, union of LEIGHTON-BUZZARD, hundred of COTTESLOE, county of BUCKINGHAM; containing 83 inhabitants.

CRAIKE, or CRAYKE (St. CUTHBERT), a parish, in the union of EASINGWOULD, W. division of the wapentake of BULMER, N. riding of YORK, 3 miles (E. by N.) from Easingwould; containing 579 inhabitants. Egfrid, King of Northumbria, in 685 gave this place, with land extending three miles round it, to St. Cuthbert; and a monastery is mentioned by Simeon of Durham as existing here, at the time of the Danish invasion in 883, when the bones of St. Cuthbert were brought to Craike, villam vocabulo Crecam, for refuge. Etha, a hermit, who lived here at an earlier period, is noticed as a famous saint by the same authority. The parish comprises by measurement 2756 acres, about three-fifths of which are arable, and the remainder pasture, with the exception of 10 acres of plantation. Above the village, on an eminence, stand the ruins of Craike Castle, probably built by Bishop Pudsey in Stephen's reign, now converted into a farmhouse : the estate, which was in the hands of the bishops of Lindisfarne first, and of Durham after the removal of the see, from the time of St. Cuthbert to the prelacy of Bishop Van Mildert, was sold by the latter, by virtue of an act of parliament. The ruined castle is a picturesque object to the country around, and commands a view which is only bounded by the horizon of the plain of York, and extending to the Wolds of the East riding, and the hills of Craven'on either side. The living is a rectory, valued in the king's books at £10, and in the patronage of the Bishop of Ripon : the tithes have been commuted for £678, and the glebe comprises 52 acres, with a good residence. The church is a neat edifice of the fifteenth century, with a tower. There is a place of worship for Wesleyans.

CRAKEHALL, a township, in the parish and union of BEDALE, wapentake of HANG-EAST, N. riding of YORK, 1¾ mile (N. W. by W.) from Bedale; containing, with Rands-Grange, 576 inhabitants. The village forms a spacious quadrangle, inclosing an extensive and pleasant green ornamented with stately trees; on which stands a district church, built by subscription in 1839, at the cost of £1000, of which sum £300 were contributed by the Church Building and Ripon Diocesan Societies. The living is the gift of the Rector of Bedale : the district assigned includes Crakehall, Langthorne, and East Brompton. There are places of worship for Baptists and Wesleyans.

CRAKEHILL, with ELMER.—See ELMER.

CRAKEMARSH, a township, in the parish and union of UTTOXETER, S. division of the hundred of TOTMONSLOW, N. division of the county of STAFFORD, 2¼ miles (N. by E.) from Uttoxeter. This is a fertile township watered by the river Dove, and lying on the road from Uttoxeter to Rocester. Crakemarsh Hall, the seat of Sir Thomas Cotton Sheppard, Bart., is a delightfully situated mansion, near the Dove.

CRAMBE (St. MICHAEL), a parish, in the union of MALTON, wapentake of BULMER, N. riding of YORK; containing, with the townships of Barton-le-Willows and Whitwell-on-the-Hill, 610 inhabitants, of whom 191 are in the township of Crambe, 1 mile (S. E.) from

Whitwell. The parish is bounded by the river Derwent on the east, and situated one mile from the York and Scarborough turnpike-road. It comprises 4000 acres, of which the portions of arable, and of meadow and wood-land, are nearly equal; the soil is generally rich, the surface undulated, and the scenery very pleasing. Stone is quarried for building purposes and for burning into lime. The river is crossed by a stone bridge of three arches. The living is a discharged vicarage, valued in the king's books at £9. 1. 8.; patron and appropriator, the Archbishop of York. The great tithes of Crambe and Barton have been commuted for £343, and the small for £211; the vicar has a glebe of 39 acres. The church is an ancient structure with a tower, and con-taining a handsome font. There is a place of worship for Wesleyans.

CRAMLINGTON, a parochial chapelry, in the union of TYNEMOUTH, E. division of CASTLE ward, S. division of NORTHUMBERLAND, 5 miles (N. W.) from Earsdon; containing 2657 inhabitants. It comprises by measure-ment 3357 acres, of which 2640 are arable, 600 pasture, and 110 woodland. The surface presents the appear-ance of a ridge, having a descent both to the north and south; the soil is strong, and for the most part wet, unless when drained, owing to a bed of blue clay, from 30 to 110 feet in depth, lying immediately beneath. The views are very extensive: to the south and west are seen the churches and buildings of Newcastle, and the valley of the Tyne; on the east the ports of Seaton-Sluice and Blyth, and the sea; and to the north the Simonside hills. The chapelry is intersected by the Newcastle and Bedlington road, and the great north road passes to the west, within one mile of the village, which is situated on a pleasant slope, and has gradually risen to its present improved state from the opening of the adjacent coal-mines. Excellent freestone, also, is in abundance. The living is a perpetual curacy, with a net income of £66, and in the gift of Sir M. W. Ridley, Bart.; the tithes have been commuted for £266. 13. payable to the Bishop of Carlisle, a similar sum to the Dean and Chapter, and £102 to Sir M. W. Ridley. The chapel is dedicated to St. Nicholas. There are places of worship for Primitive Methodists and Wesleyans. In the black shale, which usually forms the roof of each seam of coal in the mines, shells of the class *unio* are frequently met with; while *palmæ, fernæ,* and *equisetæ* are not uncommon: the water from the mines holds in solution carbonate of iron.

CRANAGE, a township, in the parish of SANDBACH, union of CONGLETON, hundred of NORTHWICH, S. divi-sion of the county of CHESTER, 3¼ miles (E. N. E.) from Middlewich; containing 512 inhabitants. The town-ship comprises 1736 acres, of a light soil. In the reign of Henry VI. a bridge of stone was erected across the river Dane here, at the expense of Sir John Nedham, but a few years ago it gave place to the present struc-ture, from a design by Mr. Harrison, of Chester. A beautiful viaduct of 23 arches, carries the Manchester and Birmingham railway over the valley of the Dane. The great tithes have been commuted for £44, and the vicarial for £111. Thomas Hall, Esq., erected two schools, one of which he endowed with £10, and the other with £4, per annum.

CRANBORNE (ST. BARTHOLOMEW), a market-town and parish, in the union of WIMBORNE and CRAN-
715

BORNE, chiefly in the hundred of CRANBORNE, but partly in that of MONCKTON-UP-WIMBORNE, Wimborne division of DORSET, 30 miles (N. E. by E.) from Dor-chester, and 92 (W. S. W.) from London; containing 2551 inhabitants, and comprising the tythings of Alder-holt, Blagdon, Boveridge, Holwell, Monckton-up-Wim-borne with Oakley, and Verwood. This place, which is of great antiquity, derives its name from the Saxon *Gren,* a crane, and *Burn,* a river; either from the tortuous windings of a stream, which, rising in the parish, falls into the Stour, or from the number of cranes that fre-quented its banks. In 980, Ailward de Meaw founded here a Benedictine monastery, dedicated to St. Bar-tholomew; but in 1102, the abbot retired with his brethren to Tewkesbury, where Robert Fitz-Hamon had founded a magnificent abbey, to which the original establishment became a cell. The old manor-house, being embattled, was called the Castle, and was the oc-casional residence of the king, when he came to hunt in Cranborne Chace, an extensive tract reaching almost to Salisbury: the chace courts were regularly held in it, and it contained a room, called the dungeon, for the confinement of offenders against the chace laws.

The TOWN is pleasantly situated at the north-eastern extremity of the county, in the centre of a fine open expanse of champaign land; the houses are in general neat and well built, and the inhabitants are amply sup-plied with water. Ribbon-weaving formerly flourished here, but has declined, and the majority of the labouring class are now employed in agriculture. The market is on Thursday; and fairs are held on Aug. 24th and Dec. 6th, for cheese and sheep. The town is within the jurisdiction of the county magistrates, and is divided into the liberties of the tything, the priory, and the borough, for which a constable, tything-man, and bailiff, are appointed respectively. The parish is the largest in the county, and comprises 13,052a. 3p., whereof 5006 acres are arable, 2094 pasture, 1347 woodland, and 4604 common and heath; the soil is chiefly chalk, gravel, and clay, of which last a species found at Crendall is used for making earthenware.

The LIVING is a discharged vicarage, valued in the king's books at £6. 13. 4.; net income, £151; patron and impropriator, the Marquess of Salisbury. The church, formerly the church of the priory, is an ancient structure, partly Norman, and partly in the early Eng-lish style, with a large and handsome tower in the later style, and a highly enriched Norman arch at the north-ern entrance: the pulpit is of oak, richly carved, and supported on a pedestal of stone; there are some re-mains of stained glass in the large window of the south aisle, representing the Virgin Mary and the heads of some of the saints, and in the chancel are monuments to the Hooper and Stillingfleet families. The chapel of ease at Verwood was erected in 1829; that at Bove-ridge has been rebuilt. The first stone of a handsome chapel, connected with the Establishment, was laid in Sept. 1841, at Alderwood, in the parish: the building has been completed at the expense of the Marquess of Salisbury. An almshouse was founded and endowed in 1661, by Thomas Hooper, for three single persons, now increased to five. On Castle Hill, to the south of the town, is a circular fortification, consisting of two deep trenches and ramparts, and including an area of six acres, in which is a well; and in the environs are nu-
4 Y 2

merous barrows, some of which have been opened and found to contain urns with bones. The learned Bishop Stillingfleet was born here in 1635. Cranborne gives the title of Viscount to the Marquess of Salisbury.

CRANBROOKE (ST. DUNSTAN), a market-town and parish, and the head of a union, in the hundred of CRANBROOKE, Lower division of the lathe of SCRAY, W. division of KENT, 7 miles (E.) from Lamberhurst, and 48 (S. E. by E.) from London; containing 3996 inhabitants. This place, anciently *Cranebroke*, derives its name from its situation on a brook called the Crane. When the manufacture of woollen-cloth was introduced into England by Edward III., it was principally carried on in the Weald of Kent; and Cranbrooke, situated in the centre of that district, became, and continued to be for centuries, a very flourishing town, and the chief seat of the clothing trade, by the removal of which into the counties of Gloucester and Somerset, within the last seventy years, its trading importance has been almost annihilated. ¡The TOWN consists chiefly of one wide street, extending three-quarters of a mile in length, from which a smaller street branches off at right angles; it is indifferently paved, but contains some well-built houses, is lighted with gas, and amply supplied with water. The trade is now principally in hops and corn, which are sold to a considerable extent; and there is a small manufactory for making hop-bagging, sacking, &c. The Staplehurst station of the South-Eastern railway is a few miles to the north. The market is on Wednesday, and there is also a cattle market on alternate Wednesdays. The market-house, a neat octagonal building, supported on double columns at the angles, and surmounted by a cupola, was erected by the late William Coleman, Esq., a great benefactor to the town. The fairs are on May 30th and Sept. 29th, for horses and cattle; the latter being also the great hop-fair.

The parish comprises 9862 acres, of which 2100 are in wood. The LIVING is a vicarage, valued in the king's books at £19. 19. 4½.; patron, the Archbishop; appropriators, the Dean and Chapter of Canterbury. The great tithes have been commuted for £994, and the vicarial for £64. 16. 5.; the appropriate glebe consists of 52 acres, and there is one acre of vicarial glebe, with a house. The church is a spacious handsome structure, in the later English style, with a square embattled tower: in the year 1725, one of the columns giving way, a part of the church fell down; it was repaired at an expense of £2000. A church dedicated to the Trinity has been erected in the hamlet of Milkhouse-street, by subscription, aided by a grant from the commissioners, and endowed with more than £1000; it was consecrated in Sept. 1838, and the living is a perpetual curacy, in the patronage of Trustees. There are places of worship for Particular Baptists, Huntingtonians, Independents, Wesleyans, and Unitarians. The free grammar school was founded in 1574, by Simon Lynch, and endowed by Queen Elizabeth with land producing at present about £140 per annum, which has been augmented by benefactions to £300 per annum. The poor law union of Cranbrooke comprises 6 parishes, and contains a population of 13,163. In Milkhouse-street are the remains of an ancient chapel dedicated to the Holy Trinity. There are several mineral springs in the vicinity, similar to those of Tonbridge-Wells. Sir Richard Baker, author of the *English Chronicles*, was born in the parish,

about the year 1568, at Sissinghurst Castle, which was used as a receptacle for French prisoners during the late war; and William Huntington, founder of the sect called Huntingtonians, who died in 1813, was born at a place in the parish named "The Four Wents."

CRANFIELD (ST. PETER AND ST. PAUL), a parish, in the union of AMPTHILL, hundred of REDBORNE-STOKE, county of BEDFORD, 7 miles (W. N. W.) from Ampthill; containing 1371 inhabitants. It comprises by measurement 3933 acres, the soil of which is generally light, and in parts clayey: some persons are employed in the lace manufacture. The living is a rectory, valued in the king's books at £33. 2. 1.; net income, £376; patrons, the family of Harter. The tithes were commuted for 692 acres of land, under an inclosure act, in 1837. The church is a handsome structure, in the early and decorated English styles. There are places of worship for Baptists and Wesleyans; and a school, endowed with £20, arising from land. A chalybeate spring rises in the parish.

CRANFORD (ST. DUNSTAN), a parish, in the union of STAINES, hundred of ELTHORNE, county of MIDDLESEX, 2½ miles (N. W. by W.) from Hounslow; containing 370 inhabitants. The parish is situated on the river Colne, over which is a bridge at the village, which from that circumstance takes the name of Cranford-Bridge; it comprises by measurement 721 acres, whereof about 323 are arable. The Great Western railway passes about three-quarters of a mile to the north of the church. The living is a rectory, valued in the king's books at £16, and in the patronage of the Earl Fitzhardinge: the tithes have been commuted for £250, and the glebe comprises 13 acres. The church was built previously to the time of Henry VIII., and contains portions of different styles.

CRANFORD (ST. ANDREW), a parish, in the union of KETTERING, hundred of HUXLOE, N. division of the county of NORTHAMPTON, 4¼ miles (E. by S.) from Kettering; containing 257 inhabitants. It is bounded on the south by Cranford St. John, and consists of 1089 acres. Lace-making is carried on by the females. Good limestone abounds. The living is a rectory, valued in the king's books at £9. 9. 7.; net income, £150; patron and incumbent, Sir G. Robinson, Bart. This benefice was consolidated with that of Cranford St. John, by an order in council, of the 21st of Aug. 1841. The tithes have been commuted for land, under an inclosure act, and the glebe contains about 100 acres, with a 'glebe-house. The church has been repaired and beautified at the expense of the rector.

CRANFORD (ST. JOHN), a parish, in the union of KETTERING, hundred of HUXLOE, N. division of the county of NORTHAMPTON, 4 miles (E. S. E.) from Kettering; containing 341 inhabitants. This parish is intersected by the road from Kettering to Thrapston, and the navigable river Nene runs within two miles of its eastern boundary: it comprises 1149 acres. Good limestone is abundant. The living is a rectory, valued in the king's books at £12; net income, £198. The church has been thoroughly repaired and beautified at the expense of the rector.

CRANHAM (ALL SAINTS), a parish, in the union of ROMFORD, hundred of CHAFFORD, S. division of ESSEX, 4 miles (S. E. by E.) from Romford; containing 280 inhabitants. This parish, which was formerly known by the names of Bishop's-Ockingdon and Cravenham, comprises 1875a. 22p., whereof upwards of 1000 acres are arable, 647 meadow and pasture, and 91 woodland. The surface rises towards the north; the soil is stiff and clayey in some parts, and in others of lighter quality. The living is a rectory, valued in the king's books at £13. 13. 4., and in the patronage of St. John's College, Oxford: the tithes have been commuted for £560, and the glebe comprises 36 acres, with a glebe-house. The church is an ancient edifice, containing some monuments.

CRANHAM (St. James), a parish, in the union of Stroud, hundred of Rapsgate, E. division of the county of Gloucester, 2½ miles (N. E. by E.) from Painswick; containing 428 inhabitants. It comprises by measurement 1823 acres. A few persons are employed in the manufacture of earthenware; and there are quarries of stone of good quality for building, and also for paving. The road from Cheltenham to Bath passes on the north-west, and that from Cheltenham to Stroud on the south, of the parish. The living is a discharged rectory, consolidated with that of Brimpsfield, and valued in the king's books at £6. 6. 8. The church is a neat ancient structure. There is a place of worship for Baptists.

CRANLEY (St. Nicholas), a parish, in the union of Hambledon, Second division of the hundred of Blackheath, W. division of Surrey, 8 miles (S. W.) from Guildford, on the road to Brighton; containing 1357 inhabitants. The parish comprises 7494 acres, of which 4500 are arable, upwards of 500 meadow and pasture, and the remainder in about equal portions of woodland and waste: the village extends for more than a mile over the common. The living is a rectory, valued in the king's books at £20. 18. 1½.; patron, F. Sapte, Esq.: the tithes have been commuted for £1582, and the glebe consists of above 200 acres. The church is a large and handsome edifice in the ancient English style, having a richly ornamented chapel, inclosed with curious and elegant lattice-work, at the termination of each aisle. There is a small meeting-house. At Vatchery are foundations, encompassed by a moat, of the baronial residence of the lords of Shere; and near them is a large reservoir of water, comprising about 70 acres, for supplying the Wey and Arun Junction canal, which passes through the parish. Cranley gives the title of Viscount to the Earl of Onslow.

CRANMORE, EAST (St. James), a parish, in the union of Shepton-Mallet, hundred of Frome, E. division of Somerset, 4¼ miles (E.) from Shepton-Mallet; containing 66 inhabitants. The district which now comprises East and West Cranmore was exempted from all suit and service to the hundred courts, and raised into a liberty by Henry I. The living is annexed to the vicarage of Doulting; impropriator, J. M. Paget, Esq.; the vicarial tithes have been commuted for £71. 4. The church was taken down in April, 1845, and a new edifice consecrated in August, 1846; it is built of freestone, and is of graceful design. The inhabitants bury at West Cranmore.

CRANMORE, WEST (St. Bartholomew), a parish, in the union of Shepton-Mallet, hundred of Wells-forum, E. division of Somerset, 3½ miles (E.) from Shepton-Mallet; containing 319 inhabitants. It is situated on the road from Wells to Frome, and comprises

717

1867a. 11p.: there are quarries of good freestone. The living is annexed to the vicarage of Doulting; impropriator, R. C. Strode, Esq. The vicarial tithes have been commuted for £145, and the glebe comprises nearly 53 acres: a rent-charge of £1. 5. is paid to the impropriator. The church is a handsome structure in the later English style.

CRANOE (St. Michael), a parish, in the union of Market-Harborough, hundred of Gartree, S. division of the county of Leicester, 6 miles (N. N. E.) from Harborough; containing 137 inhabitants. The living is a rectory, valued in the king's books at £8. 16. 8.; net income, £181; patron, the Earl of Cardigan. The tithes were commuted for land and a money payment, in 1825. The church was rebuilt in 1847.

CRANSFORD (St. Peter), a parish, in the union and hundred of Plomesgate, E. division of Suffolk, 3 miles (E. N. E.) from Framlingham; containing 303 inhabitants, and comprising by computation 1000 acres. The living is a discharged vicarage, valued in the king's books at £6. 13. 4.; and in the patronage of the Pooley family: the tithes have been commuted for £330, and the glebe consists of 44 acres.

CRANSLEY (St. Andrew), a parish, in the union of Kettering, hundred of Orlingbury, N. division of the county of Northampton, 3 miles (W. S. W.) from Kettering; containing, with the hamlet of Little Cransley, 319 inhabitants, and consisting of 2046a. 1r. 24p. The living is a discharged vicarage, valued in the king's books at £8. 5.; net income, £98; patron and impropriator, William S. Rose, Esq. The glebe contains about 40 acres, with a glebe-house. The church is a handsome structure, beautifully situated in the midst of rich wooodland scenery; the tower has crocketed pinnacles, and is surmounted with a spire: there are monuments and tablets to the Rose family, and also to the family of Sir J. Robinson, lords of the manor. A school was founded in 1824, by the Rev. G. Anderson, vicar, who erected an appropriate building, and endowed it with a rent-charge of £25.

CRANTOCK (St. Cadock), a parish, in the union of St. Columb Major, hundred of Pyder, W. division of Cornwall, 1 mile (S. W.) from New Quay; containing 450 inhabitants. This parish comprises by measurement 2465 acres, of which 150 are common or waste, and is bounded on the north by the Bristol Channel. It has a small harbour at the mouth of the river Gannel, which runs through the parish, where a number of vessels discharge their cargoes of coal; and sand, coal, slates, and various articles of merchandize, are carried in barges about three miles up the river. The living is a perpetual curacy; net income, £78; patron and impropriator, Sir J. B. Y. Buller, Bart.: the tithes have been commuted for £380, and the glebe consists of 33 acres. The church is very ancient, and has a chancel unusually large in proportion to the nave; the arches, and the principal parts of the tower, are built of sandstone: the font bears the date of 1474. In the time of Edward the Confessor, the church was made collegiate for secular canons, who continued till the Dissolution, when the revenue of £89. 15. 8. was divided amongst the dean, nine prebendaries, and four vicars-choral. In the churchyard, which covers an area of three acres, is a stone coffin: whenever the ground in the vicinity is dug up for foundations, or any excavation made, human skeletons are found. There are two places of worship for Wesleyans.

CRANWELL (St. ANDREW), a parish, in the union of SLEAFORD, hundred of FLAXWELL, parts of KESTE-VEN, county of LINCOLN, 4 miles (N. W.) from Sleaford; containing 230 inhabitants. It is situated about half a mile west of the great north road, and comprises by computation 2506a. 3r. 30p., nearly all arable. The wide extent of flat ground to the west and north, formerly covered with heath, and the open level of rich land to the east, before sprinkled with fen, are now well cultivated. The surface in some parts towards the south is undulated, and the soil in general throughout the parish is a stiff clay. There are several quarries of stone of the oolite formation, with which most of the houses in the neighbourhood are built. The living is a discharged vicarage; net income, £199; patron, the Bishop of Lincoln; impropriator, Sir J. E. Thorold, Bart. The glebe, which is chiefly in the parish of North Ranceby, contains about 230 acres. The church is a small structure, with heavy Norman pillars and arches.

CRANWICH (St. MARY), a parish, in the union of THETFORD, hundred of GRIMSHOE, W. division of NOR-FOLK, 6 miles (N.) from Brandon; containing 108 inhabitants. It comprises 1800 acres, of which 1000 are arable, 400 meadow and pasture, 100 woodland, and 200 heath. The living is a discharged rectory, with the vicarage of Methwold annexed, valued in the king's books at £8. 9. 7.; net income, £450; patron, Lord Berners. The tithes have been commuted for £180, and there is a glebe-house, with 19½ acres of land. The original church was a very ancient structure, supposed to have been erected by Harold, one of whose freemen held a moiety of this place in the time of Edward the Confessor; the present structure is chiefly in the early English style, with a circular tower, and contains, in the chancel, a piscina, and some monuments to the Partridge family.

CRANWORTH (St. MARY), a parish, in the union of MITFORD and LAUNDITCH, hundred of MITFORD, W. division of NORFOLK, 2 miles (S. S. E.) from Shipdham; containing 340 inhabitants. The parish is bounded on the south by a tributary to the river Yare, and comprises 1127 acres, of which 809 are arable, 279 pasture, and 5 woodland. The living is a rectory, with that of Letton consolidated, valued in the king's books at £5. 18. 6½., and in the gift of T. T. Gurdon, Esq. : the tithes have been commuted for £214. 8., and the glebe comprises 28 acres, with a handsome rectory-house. The church is in the early and later English styles, with a tower surmounted by a neat spire; there are several monuments to the Gurdon family. About 11 acres of land are let to the poor by the rector, in small allotments.

· CRASSWALL, a chapelry, in the parish of CLODOCK, union of DORE, hundred of EWYASLACY, county of HEREFORD, 5 miles (S. E.) from Hay; containing 374 inhabitants. This chapelry comprises by measurement 5116 acres, of which 4007 are inclosed land, consisting of good arable and pasture, with a small portion of wood, and the remaining parts are mountain and common, affording pasturage for sheep and cattle. It is situated on the borders of Brecknockshire, among the Black mountains, and near the source of the Munnow river. There is a quarry of fine stone in the neighbourhood.

The living is a perpetual curacy; net income, £47; patron, the Vicar of Clodock. The chapel is dedicated to St. Mary. About the close of the reign of King John, a monastery was founded here, probably by Walton de Lacy, for a prior and ten religious of the order of Grand-mont, in Normandy : it was valued at 40s. per annum, and granted, in the 2nd of Edward IV., to God's House, now Christ's College, Cambridge.

CRASTER, a township, in the parish of EMBLETON, union of ALNWICK, S. division of BAMBROUGH ward, N. division of NORTHUMBERLAND, 6¼ miles (N. E.) from Alnwick; containing 247 inhabitants. In 1272 the manor was held by William de Craucestr', by the service of half a knight's fee, and it has continued in his family to the present time; his descendants in the 14th century altered their name to Craster. Craster Tower, the seat of Thomas Wood Craster, Esq., is surrounded with plantations, and commands fine land and sea views. The village, which is called Craster Sea-Houses, is situated on the coast.

⁓ CRATFIELD (St. MARY), a parish, in the union and hundred of BLYTHING, E. division of SUFFOLK, 7 miles (W. S. W.) from Halesworth; containing 720 inhabitants, and comprising 2085 acres, of which 103 are common or waste. The living is a discharged vicarage, with that of Laxfield annexed, valued in the king's books at £5. 7. 11., and in the gift of the Rev. E. Hollond : the impropriate tithes, belonging to the Hudson family, have been commuted for £403, and the vicarial for £115; there is a glebe-house, with about 6 acres of land. The church, which is chiefly in the later English style, consists of a nave, chancel, and aisles, with an embattled tower; the font has some curious sculptures, representing scriptural subjects. There is a place of worship for Independents. A national school was endowed with £9. 6. 8. per annum, under the will of Mrs. Mary Leman, dated 1805; and there are town lands, which let for about £200 per annum, applied to the repairs of the church, and to general purposes.

CRATHORNE (ALL SAINTS), a parish, in the union of STOKESLEY, W. division of the liberty of LANG-BAURGH, N. riding of the county of YORK, 4 miles (S. S. E.) from Yarm; containing 304 inhabitants. This place, which is in the district called Cleveland, and situated on the western side of the vale of the river Leven, anciently belonged to the Crathorne family, who were settled here for many generations, and of whom Sir William Crathorne, Knt., died in the early part of the 14th century. The parish comprises about 2450 acres, of which 1722 are arable and in good cultivation, 500 meadow and pasture, and 200 woodland and planta-tions. The surface is generally level, the scenery en-riched with wood, and in many situations very pleasing; the soil near the village, and on the banks of the Leven, which here abounds in trout, is a gravelly loam, but in most other parts a poor clay. Good white freestone, used for building purposes, is obtained from the bed of the river. The village is situated on the road to Thirsk : many of the inhabitants were formerly employed in the linen manufacture, which was carried on to a conside-rable extent, and there was also a spacious bleach-ground in the parish. The living is a rectory, valued in the king's books at £10. 11. 10½., and in the patronage of Mrs. Tasburgh, with a net income of £205. The church is a small ancient structure, in the chancel of which is the recumbent effigy of a knight, supposed to be Sir William Crathorne. There is a Roman Catholic chapel, originally founded by the Crathorne family, and rebuilt about 1825. Near the village is a chalybeate spring.

CRAWCROOK, a township, in the parish of RYTON, union of GATESHEAD, W. division of CHESTER ward, N. division of the county of DURHAM, 7 miles (W.) from Newcastle-on-Tyne; containing 290 inhabitants. The township is intersected by the railway from New-castle to Carlisle, and bounded on the north by the river Tyne, from which the land gradually rises, commanding pleasing views, and being for the most part undulated; the soil is of good quality, producing turnips and excellent barley, for which latter the district is celebrated. Craw-crook townfields, consisting of 700 acres, were divided by act of parliament in 1794. The tithes have been commuted for £236. The Wesleyans and Presbyterians have places of worship here; and there are schools for boys and girls, the master of which has £30, and the mistress £20 per annum, each with a house and garden, Mr. Simpson having left the interest of £1000 to the institution.

CRAWFORD, TARRANT (St. Mary), a parish, in the union of BLANDFORD, hundred of BADBURY, Wim-borne division of DORSET, 4 miles (S. E. by E.) from Blandford; containing, with the tything of Preston, 67 inhabitants, and comprising about 1000 acres. The living is a donative; net income, £50; patron and impropriator, J. S. W. S. E. Drax, Esq. Richard Poor, successively Bishop of Chichester, Salisbury, and Dur-ham, founded an abbey of Cistercian nuns, in honour of the blessed Virgin and All Saints, about 1230; at the Dissolution its revenue was estimated at £239. 11. 10.

CRAWLEY, a township, in the parish of EGLING-HAM, union of ALNWICK, N. division of COQUETDALE ward and of NORTHUMBERLAND, 9¼ miles (W. N. W.) from Alnwick; containing 20 inhabitants. It was anciently called Crawlawe, from Caer-law, a fortified hill. Crawley Tower, a Roman structure, stands on an emi-nence near an old and strong intrenchment, which is thought to be the Alauna Amnis of Richard of Ciren-cester, though some place this station at Alnwick, and others at Glanton: it commands a fine view of the vale of Whittingham, with the river Breamish from its source to Horton Castle; and there are the remains of not less than seven British and Saxon fortifications within four miles round the spot. The impropriate tithes have been commuted for £6. 10., and the vicarial for 6s. 6d.

CRAWLEY, a hamlet, in the parish and union of WITNEY, hundred of BAMPTON, county of OXFORD, 1¾ mile (N. W. by N.) from Witney; containing 252 inha-bitants, a few of whom are employed in the manufacture of blankets. It comprises 1116 acres, of which 504 are arable, 75 pasture, 410 woodland, and the remainder waste. The tithes have been commuted for £205.

CRAWLEY (St. Mary), a parish, in the union of WINCHESTER, hundred of BUDDLESGATE, Winchester and N. divisions of the county of SOUTHAMPTON, 4 miles (E.) from Stockbridge; containing 483 inhabit-ants, of whom 372 are in that portion of the parish ex-clusively of the chapelry of Hunton. It comprises about 3490 acres, of which 2803 are arable, 420 meadow and down, and 257 wood. The living is a rectory, valued in the king's books at £35. 13. 4., and in the gift of the Bishop of Winchester: the tithes have been commuted

719

for £657. 10., and the glebe comprises 10 acres. The church has been repaired at an expense of £270, towards which the Bishop contributed £50, the rector £200, and the parishioners £20.

CRAWLEY (St. John the Baptist), a parish, in the union of EAST GRINSTEAD, hundred of BUTTING-HILL, rape of LEWES, E. division of SUSSEX, 9½ miles (N. by W.) from Cuckfield; containing 449 inhabitants. The parish comprises 769a. 2r., of which 185 acres are arable, 119 pasture, 129 plantation, and 318 waste. Crawley is a post-town, consisting of one wide street, in which stands a remarkably fine old elm-tree of immense girth: the houses on the west side of the village are in the parish of Ifield. The London and Brighton road passes through; and not far distant is the Three-Bridges station of the London and Brighton railway, where the Horsham line branches off. Fairs for horned-cattle are held on May 8th and September 29th. The living is a discharged rectory, valued in the king's books at £6. 15., and in the gift of the family of Clitherow: the tithes have been commuted for £86. 14., and the glebe contains nearly 29 acres, and a glebe-house. The church is partly in the decorated and partly in the later English style; a gallery was erected in 1827.

CRAWLEY, HUSBORN, county of BEDFORD.— See HUSBORN-CRAWLEY.

CRAWLEY, NORTH (St. Firmin), a parish, in the union of NEWPORT-PAGNELL, hundred of NEWPORT, county of BUCKINGHAM, 3¼ miles (E. by N.) from New-port-Pagnell; containing 865 inhabitants. The manor is the property of the Lowndes family, to whom it was conveyed about the year 1710, and the advowson in 1723. The living is a rectory, valued in the king's books at £27. 10., and in the patronage of William Selby Lowndes, Esq.: the tithes were commuted for land in 1780. The church has been enlarged by the addition of 106 free sittings. A monastery dedicated to St. Firmin is mentioned in Domesday book as having been founded here before the time of Edward the Confessor, and was in existence after the Conquest.

CRAWSHAW-BOOTH.—See HIGHER BOOTHS.

CRAY (St. Mary), a parish, in the union of BROM-LEY, hundred of RUXLEY, lathe of SUTTON-AT-HONE, W. division of KENT, 2 miles (S. by W.) from Foot's-Cray; containing 997 inhabitants. The district of the Crays, so called from the river Cray, which runs through it, is reckoned one of the most beautiful tracts in Kent, and produces a vast quantity of birch: it comprehends four parishes, distinguished by their prefixes. St. Mary's had the privilege of a market in the reign of Edward I.; but the market-house having been destroyed by a tempest in 1703, the market has not since been held. The parish consists of 2010 acres, whereof 532 are in wood. The living is annexed to the vicarage of Orpington: the church contains several ancient brasses and some me-morials of the Mannings.

CRAY, FOOT'S (All Saints), a parish, in the union of BROMLEY, hundred of RUXLEY, lathe of SUTTON-AT-HONE, W. division of KENT, 12¼ miles (S. E.) from London; containing 358 inhabitants. This place pro-bably derived its prefix from Fot or Vot, its proprietor in the time of Edward the Confessor, and has its name from the river Cray, which runs by the eastern end of the village, turns an extensive paper-mill, and then directs its course towards North Cray. The parish comprises by measurement 798 acres, of which about 380 are arable, 300 meadow and pasture, and 66 woodland. The living is a discharged rectory, valued in the king's books at £8. 3. 4., and in the patronage of the Crown: the tithes have been commuted for £264, and the glebe comprises 2 acres, with a glebe-house. The church is a small plain building, supposed to be of high antiquity. At Sidcup is a separate incumbency.

CRAY, NORTH (ST. JAMES), a parish, in the union of BROMLEY, hundred of RUXLEY, lathe of SUTTON-AT-HONE, W. division of KENT, 1 mile (N. by E.) from Foot's-Cray; containing 517 inhabitants. The parish is situated on the road from London to Maidstone, and comprises 1444 acres, of which 339 are woodland; it is pleasingly diversified with villas and well cultivated domains, of which North Cray Place and Mount Mascall are the principal. In 1723, a subterraneous fire broke out, and the inhabitants for several days employed themselves with waggons in conveying water from Bexley, to quench the flames. A small fair is held on the 29th May. The living is a rectory, valued in the king's books at £13. 9. 9½., and in the gift of Lord Bexley; the tithes have been commuted for a rent-charge of £392, and the glebe comprises 48 acres, with a glebe house. The church, a small building, is said to have been the chapel of a monastery which stood on the site of the present North Cray Place.

CRAY, ST. PAUL'S (ST. PAULINUS), a parish, in the union of BROMLEY, hundred of RUXLEY, lathe of SUTTON-AT-HONE, W. division of KENT, 1 mile (S.) from Foot's-Cray; containing 564 inhabitants. It is situated on the small stream of the Cray, which here turns a paper-mill employing about 30 men and 40 women. The parish comprises 1651 acres, of which 191 are woodland. The living is a rectory, valued in the king's books at £12. 13. 4., and in the gift of Viscount Sidney: the tithes have been commuted for £486, and the glebe contains upwards of 12 acres, with a glebe-house. The church has some interesting specimens of architecture; it is supposed to have been built about the middle of the 13th century, and its vestry, part of the walls of which are of Roman brick, to have been originally a chapel. There is a place of worship for Wesleyans. In a wood near Paul's-Cray Common is a strong chalybeate spring, formerly of some repute in the neighbourhood, but now almost entirely disused; its waters resemble those of Tonbridge-Wells. Lord Wynford resides at the seat called Leesons, in the parish, which is delightfully situated on the border of the common, commanding extensive views over the country towards Essex.

CRAYFORD (ST. PAULINUS), a parish, and formerly a market-town, in the union of DARTFORD, hundred of LESSNESS, lathe of SUTTON-AT-HONE, W. division of KENT, 13 miles (E. by S.) from London; containing, with the hamlets of Northend and Slade-Green, 2408 inhabitants. This place is so called from Creccanford, an ancient ford on the river Creccan, now Cray. In the immediate vicinity some antiquaries have placed the Roman station Noviomagus, near which a great battle was fought in 457, between Hengist the Saxon and the British king Vortimer, which ended in the secure establishment of the kingdom of Kent under the rule of the former. The parish comprises by measurement 2458 acres, of which 136 are in woodland: the surface is varied with hill and dale: the soil in general is gravel, resting

720 ·

in some parts on strata of loam, beneath which is chalk. The river Cray flows through the parish in two separate branches, and the meadows in its vicinity are occasionally subject to inundation: upon its banks are several extensive establishments for printing calico, silk, and chalis; and a very large flour-mill. The village consists of an irregularly formed street, branching off from the London and Dartford road. One of the archbishops of Canterbury, who formerly had possessions here, procured a weekly market on Tuesday, and a fair on Our Lady's Nativity; the market has long been disused, but a fair is still held on the 8th of September. The living is a rectory, valued in the king's books at £35. 13. 4., and in the gift of Thomas Austin, Esq.: the tithes have been commuted for £850, and the glebe comprises nearly 57 acres, with a house. The church, which stands on an eminence at the upper end of the village, is a plain structure, adorned with an elegant altar-piece. There is a place of worship for Particular Baptists. In the parish are many ancient caves, some of which are from fifteen to twenty fathoms deep, increasing in circumference from the mouth downwards, and containing several large apartments, supported by pillars of chalk: it is conjectured that they were used as places of security for the families and moveable goods of the Saxons, during their wars with the Britons. The manor-house, which was built by Sir Cloudesley Shovel, is now tenanted by a farmer.

CREACOMBE (ST. MICHAEL), a parish, in the union of SOUTH MOLTON, hundred of WITHERIDGE, South Molton and N. divisions of DEVON, 8¼ miles (S. E. by E.) from South Molton; containing 58 inhabitants. The living is a discharged rectory, valued in the king's books at £4. 18. 9., and in the gift of the Rev. W. Karslake: the tithes have been commuted for £44. 11. 6., and the glebe consists of 100 acres.

CREAKE, NORTH (ST. MARY), a parish, in the union of DOCKING, hundred of BROTHERCROSS, W. division of NORFOLK, 3 miles (S. E. by S.) from Burnham-Westgate; containing 648 inhabitants. It comprises 3601a. 1r. 17p., of which 3179 acres are arable, 126 pasture and meadow, and 69 woodland: the road from Fakenham to Burnham runs through the village. The living is a rectory, valued in the king's books at £33. 6. 8., and in the gift of Earl Spencer and the Bishop of Norwich, alternately: the tithes have been commuted for £1025, and the glebe consists of 187 acres, with a glebe-house. The church, which is in the decorated and later English styles, consists of a nave, chancel, north aisle, and embattled tower: on the south side of the chancel are three stone stalls, with a piscina of elegant workmanship, and opposite is an altar-tomb, under a decorated canopy: the font is very ancient, and on the floor of the nave is a fine brass of a priest. There are places of worship for Wesleyans and Primitive Methodists; also a national school, endowed with £10 per annum by the late Mr. Herod. At Lingerscroft, between Creake and Burnham, Sir Robert de Narford in 1206 founded a church, and subsequently a chapel and hospital dedicated to St. Bartholomew, in which he placed a master, four-chaplains, and thirteen poor lay brethren. The foundation soon afterwards acquired the distinction of a priory of Augustine canons, and, in the 15th of Henry III., was elevated into an abbey: that monarch also confirmed the grant of a fair previously made, changing the period to the eve and festival of St. Thomas the Martyr; and in the 14th of Edward I., the abbot claimed the right of holding four fairs annually at Creake. In consequence of the death of the abbot, and there being no convent to elect another, the abbey was dissolved; and its possessions were granted, in the 22nd of Henry VII., to the Countess of Richmond, by whom they were given to Christ's College, Cambridge. Remains of the choir and other parts of the abbey still exist, and exhibit some very fine arches.

CREAKE, SOUTH (ST. MARY), a parish, in the union of DOCKING, hundred of BROTHERCROSS, W. division of NORFOLK, 4 miles (S. S. E.) from Burnham-Westgate; containing 940 inhabitants. It comprises 4090a. 30p., of which nearly 3078 acres are arable, 273 pasture and meadow, 39 woodland, and 700 common used as a sheep-walk : the Fakenham road runs through the village. The living is a discharged vicarage, valued in the king's books at £22, and in the gift of the family of Townshend, the impropriators : the great tithes have been commuted for £675, and the vicarial for £440; the vicarial glebe contains 3 roods, with a glebe-house. The church contains portions of the early, decorated, and later English styles, with a tower. There is a place of worship for Independents. The sum of £100 per annum, derived from land, is partly applied to the relief of the poor, and partly in support of a national school. In the neighbourhood is a Saxon fortification, the way leading from which is called Blood-gate, from the dreadful slaughter there in a battle between the Saxons and the Danes.

CREATON, GREAT (ST. MICHAEL), a parish, in the union of BRIXWORTH, hundred of GUILSBOROUGH, S. division of the county of NORTHAMPTON, 7¼ miles (N. N. W.) from Northampton; containing 505 inhabitants. The parish is intersected by the road from Northampton to Welford, and comprises 938 acres; the soil is partly red sand, and partly loam, alternated with clay. The population is entirely agricultural, with the exception of a few persons employed in the making of lace. The village is built on the north side of a hill, at a short distance from the public road; in the centre of it is a pleasant green, formerly covered with wormwood. The living is a rectory, valued in the king's books at £11. 1. 8., and in the gift of the Rev. E. T. Beynon : the tithes were commuted in 1782, for 148a. 3r. 37p. of land, now valued at £260 per annum. The church is situated on an eminence. There is a place of worship for Independents. Near the church is a national school for boys and girls, with a master's house, built in 1845, on a rood of the rectory ground; it is supported by subscription. In 1825, six cottages for the accommodation of aged people were built on the green by the Rev. Thomas Jones, fifty years minister of the parish.

CREATON, LITTLE, a hamlet, in the parish of SPRATTON, union of BRIXWORTH, hundred of SPELHOE, S. division of the county of NORTHAMPTON, 7¾ miles (N. N. W.) from Northampton; containing 77 inhabitants, and comprising 333 acres of rich land. It is situated in the northern part of the parish, and close to the village of Great Creaton.

CREDENHILL (ST. MARY), a parish, in the hundred of GRIMSWORTH, union and county of HEREFORD, 5 miles (N. W. by W.) from Hereford; containing 192 inhabitants. The road from Hereford to Kington runs

through the parish, which comprises by measurement 1215 acres; about 517 are arable, 500 meadow and pasture, and 170 woodland. The scenery is picturesque; the soil is a rich sandy loam, and the prevailing kinds of timber are elm and oak. There is a quarry of excellent stone on Creden Hill, not now in operation, but the material of which was formerly used for building castles and churches. The living is a discharged rectory, valued in the king's books at £17. 19. 4., and in the gift and incumbency of the Rev. John Eckley, whose tithes have been commuted for £354, and who has a glebe of 27 acres, with a house. The church is a strong ancient structure, in the later English style. On the summit of the hill, the declivity of which is well wooded, are the remains of an almost inaccessible camp, having an outer and an inner trench, inclosing an area of about 50 acres, and supposed to have been constructed by the Romans for the defence of their adjacent station at Kenchester, the *Magna Castra* of Antoninus : the view from it is one of the most extensive and beautiful in the county.

CREDITON (HOLY CROSS), a market-town and parish, and the head of a union, in the hundred of CREDITON, and extending also into that of WEST BUDLEIGH, Crediton and N. divisions of DEVON; comprising the tythings of Cannon-Fee, Crediton, Knowle, Rudge, Town, Uford, Uton, and Woodland; and containing 5947 inhabitants, of whom 2245 are in the borough and tything of Crediton, 8 miles (N. W.) from Exeter, and 180 (W. by S.) from London. This place, which takes its name from its situation near the river Creedy, was for many years the seat of a diocese, of which a collegiate church founded here in 905, and dedicated to the Holy Cross, became the cathedral. In the reign of Canute, Levinus, Bishop of Crediton, prevailed upon that monarch, with whom he had great influence, to annex the see of St. Germans to that of Crediton; and the united see was removed to Exeter by Edward the Confessor, in 1049. A chapter, consisting of a dean and twelve prebendaries, continued to be maintained in the old collegiate church under the jurisdiction of the Bishop of Exeter, the revenue of which, at the Dissolution, was £332. 17. 5.: the church, with some lands belonging to it, was granted to twelve of the inhabitants, who were incorporated as governors in the reign of Edward VI. In the reign of Edward I. this borough sent members to a parliament held at Carlisle; and in 1310, Bishop Stapleton obtained. for it a grant of a weekly market and three annual fairs. Towards the middle of the sixteenth century, the opponents of the Reformation assembled their troops at Crediton, but were compelled to withdraw by Sir Peter Carew, who was sent against them with a superior force. In 1644, Charles I. reviewed his soldiery at this town, which was subsequently held by the army under Sir Thomas Fairfax. In 1743, a fire destroyed a considerable part of it; a similar calamity occurred in 1769, and in 1840 a fire broke out in the eastern portion of the town, by which 22 houses were consumed.

CREDITON is pleasantly situated in a vale near the Creedy, which unites with the river Exe between this place and Exeter. It is divided into two parts, east and west, of which the former, containing the church, is the more ancient, and the latter the more extensive; these have been connected by a line of road lately constructed, and the town now consists chiefly of one main street, nearly a mile in length, containing low cottages at each extremity, with a few well-built houses in the centre. A new market-place has been erected in North-street, by J. W. Buller, Esq., lord of the manor, and many other improvements have been made within the last few years, under an act obtained in 1836. Assemblies and concerts take place occasionally, during the winter, in a good assembly-room, conveniently fitted up. The town has long been celebrated for the manufacture of serge, chiefly for exportation, but the business has much declined, and the principal trade is now in making coarse linen-cloth, called brin. An act was passed in 1845 for making a railway to Exeter, and another act in 1846 for a railway to Barnstaple. The market, which is well attended, is on Saturday; and on the Saturday preceding the last Wednesday in April is a large market for cattle, at which more than 1000 head are frequently sold. Fairs for cattle are held in the eastern division of the town, on May 11th and Sept. 21st; and on St. Lawrence's Green, in the western division, on the 21st of August, if it happen on Tuesday or Wednesday, if not, the fair is postponed till the following Tuesday: this fair continues for three days. The town is within the jurisdiction of the county magistrates, who hold a petty-session every month; and its local affairs are under the superintendence of a portreeve, bailiff, and constables, chosen annually by a jury at the court leet of the lord of the manor. The powers of the county debt-court of Crediton, established in 1847, extend over the registration-district of Crediton.

The parish is ten miles in length from east to west, and about four miles in extreme breadth, and comprises 10,469 acres, of which 569 are common or waste. The soil in the northern and central portions is a rich red loam, well adapted for grain, with some excellent pasture, and in the southern portion of a clayey nature, coarse, and alternated with copse and brake. The surface is hilly, and richly wooded; the elm grows profusely in the hedge-rows, and the scenery, enlivened with the streams of the Creedy and Exe, is finely varied. At Posberry is a quarry of trapstone, of excellent quality for building and road-making. The LIVING is a vicarage, valued in the king's books at £30, with a net income of £425, and in the patronage of the twelve Governors, by whom the church is kept in repair, to whom the impropriation belongs, and who elect a chaplain to assist the vicar: the great tithes have been commuted for £1770. The church, rebuilt in the reign of Henry VII., is a spacious and magnificent cruciform structure, in the later English style, with a square embattled tower rising from the centre. The nave is separated from the aisles by massive columns with ornamented capitals, supporting arches of the decorated English style, and is lighted by an elegant range of clerestory windows with flowing tracery; the original roof of oak, richly carved, and ornamented with transverse ribs and bosses at the intersection, is now concealed by a flat plain ceiling. On the south side of the choir are three stone sedilia; a piscina of a highly interesting character is still remaining, and the church has many ancient monuments, altar-tombs, and brasses. At Posberry is a church dedicated to St. Luke, forming a separate incumbency. There are places of worship for Baptists, Independents, Wesleyans, and Unitarians.

722

The grammar school was founded and endowed by Edward VI., and further endowed by Queen Elizabeth, who by her charter vested the patronage in the twelve governors of the church, directing them to elect four boys, under the name of Queen Elizabeth's Grammar Scholars, to each of whom 40s. are annually given: there are three exhibitions, of £6. 13. 4. each, to either of the universities, tenable for five years. The Blue-coat school, founded about the year 1730, by subscription, and since endowed with various benefactions, was united with an English school in 1814, and placed under one master, in a house erected in 1806 by the trustees of Sir John Hayward's charity: the annual income is £116. A mathematical school was established in 1794, by Mr. Samuel Dunn, who endowed it with £600 stock, now in the four per cents. The poor law union of Crediton comprises 29 parishes or places, and contains a population of 22,076. Near the church are some slight remains of the episcopal palace; and part of a chapel dedicated to St. Lawrence, connected with one of the prebends of the collegiate church, has been formed into cottages: in the Dean's street is an ancient building said to have formed part of the dean's house, in a portion which, supposed to have been the refectory, the old ceiling is still preserved. At Yeo is the gable of a barn, formerly a chapel, the east window of which is in good preservation; and on the hill above Posberry is a triple intrenchment of great antiquity. Winifred, Archbishop of Mentz, and legate under several of the popes, who was eminently successful in promulgating Christianity among the Mercians, and suffered martyrdom in the year 354, was a native of this place.

CREECH, or CREKE (ST. MICHAEL), a parish, in the union of TAUNTON, hundred of ANDERSFIELD, W. division of SOMERSET, 3½ miles (E. N. E.) from Taunton; containing 1296 inhabitants. This parish, which is situated on the river Tone, and intersected by the road from Plymouth to Bath, comprises by measurement 2218a. 2r. 13p.: there are quarries of stone of a reddish hue, of good quality for building and other purposes. The tide flows up to the Half-Locks, on the Coal-Harbour estate, where a very extensive traffic in salt, &c., was formerly carried on. The village has much improved since the formation of the Bridgwater and Taunton canal, which is here crossed by a well-built bridge of brick. A new cut from this canal has been formed under an act obtained in 1834, terminating at Chard, and communicating with the old canal wharfs near the bridge: it is carried over the river Tone by a handsome and extensive aqueduct, which crosses the lower road and moor, near the parish of Ruishton. The line of the Bristol and Exeter railway passes under the aqueduct. Here, also, commences the railway projected in 1846, to Ilminster, and which will run in the line of a portion of the Chard canal. The living is a vicarage, endowed with a portion of the rectorial tithes, and valued in the king's books at £16. 18. 9.: patron, the Rev. H. Cresswell; impropriators of the remainder of the rectorial tithes, Mrs. Dyer and the Rev. Miles Formby. The tithes have been commuted for £383, and the glebe comprises 72 acres. The church, a spacious and handsome edifice with a tower, is pleasantly situated on an eminence above the Tone. There is a place of worship for Baptists. Here was a monastery of the Cluniac order, part of which is still perfect.

CREECH, EAST, a tything, in the parish of CHURCH-KNOWLE, union of WAREHAM and PURBECK, hundred of HASILOR, Wareham division of DORSET, 3¾ miles (S.) from Wareham; containing 183 inhabitants. It is about a mile north-west of the parochial church.

CREED (ST. CREED), a parish, in the union of ST. AUSTELL, W. division of the hundred of POWDER and of the county of CORNWALL; including nearly the whole of the town of Grampound, and containing 758 inhabitants, of whom 265 are in that portion exclusive of Grampound. The parish is situated on the river Fal, by which it is bounded on the west, and comprises 2450 acres, of which 23 are common or waste. The living is a rectory, valued in the king's books at £13. 6. 8.; net income, £351; patron, C. H. T. Hawkins, Esq. Besides the parochial church, there is a small chapel of ease at Grampound, in a ruinous condition. On the estate of Nantellon are vestiges of two intrenchments, each inclosing about one acre.

CREED, a tything, in the parish of BOSHAM, union of WEST BOURNE, hundred of Bosham, rape of CHICHESTER, W. division of the county of SUSSEX; containing 64 inhabitants.

CREEKSEA, or CRIXETH (ALL SAINTS), a parish, in the union of MALDON, hundred of DENGIE, S. division of ESSEX, 2 miles (N. W. by W.) from Burnham; containing 199 inhabitants. This parish is bounded by the river Crouch, over which is a ferry to Wallasea Island, from the south side of the parish, where the marshes are protected from inundation by strong embankments nine feet in height. Near the mouth of the river is a creek flowing from the sea, from which the place is supposed to have derived its name. The living is a discharged rectory, with the vicarage of Althorne united in 1811, valued in the king's books at £9. 8. 10.; patron, J. Robinson, Esq. The tithes of Creeksea have been commuted for £241, and the glebe consists of 21 acres. The church is a neat plain edifice.

CREETING (ALL SAINTS), a parish, in the union and hundred of BOSMERE and CLAYDON, E. division of SUFFOLK, 1½ mile (N.) from Needham-Market; containing 286 inhabitants. The road from Ipswich to Norwich runs through the parish on the north-east, and the Stow-Market and Ipswich navigation passes along the south-western boundary. The living is a discharged rectory, annexed to the rectories of Creeting St. Mary and St. Olave, and valued in the king's books at £10. 0. 5. The church, which stood within thirty yards of that of St. Mary, and in the same churchyard, was pulled down by faculty upon condition of two full services being performed in the latter, the only church now standing in the three consolidated parishes.

CREETING (ST. MARY), a parish, in the union and hundred of BOSMERE and CLAYDON, E. division of SUFFOLK, 1½ mile (N. N. E.) from Needham-Market; containing 196 inhabitants. The road from Ipswich to Norwich, and the Stow-Market and Ipswich navigation, run through the parish. The living is a discharged rectory, with those of Creeting St. Olave and All Saints consolidated, valued in the king's books at £7. 14. 2., and in the patronage of Eton College: the tithes have been commuted for £750, and the glebe comprises 62 acres, with a glebe-house. The church was enlarged when that of All Saints was taken down; the entrance on the south is by a Norman doorway, and the font is

723

of Caen stone, curiously sculptured. About 42 acres of town-land are applied to the use of the poor, to whom Mrs. Uvedale, the lady of Rear-Admiral Uvedale, left in 1814 £300. Here was a cell to the abbey of Bernay, in Normandy, the revenue of which, at the suppression of alien establishments, was applied towards the endowment of Eton College.

CREETING (ST. OLAVE), a parish, in the union and hundred of BOSMERE and CLAYDON, E. division of SUFFOLK, 2½ miles (N. N. E.) from Needham-Market; containing 30 inhabitants. The living is a discharged rectory, annexed to those of Creeting St. Mary and All Saints, and valued in the king's books at £4. 17. 8½.: the church has been long demolished. Robert, Earl of Morton, gave the manor to the abbey of Grestein, in Normandy, and it was under the care of some monks of that abbey.

CREETING (ST. PETER), or WEST CREETING, a parish, in the union and hundred of STOW, W. division of SUFFOLK, 2 miles (N. by W.) from Needham-Market; containing 213 inhabitants. It is bounded on the south by the Stow-Market and Ipswich navigation, and comprises 1335a. 3r. 31p. The living is a discharged rectory, valued in the king's books at £10. 2. 6.; patron and incumbent, the Rev. Edward Paske, whose tithes have been commuted for £400, and whose glebe comprises 6 acres, with a glebe-house. The church is in the early English style, and has an embattled tower.

CREETON (ST. PETER), a parish, in the union of BOURNE, wapentake of BELTISLOE, parts of KESTEVEN, county of LINCOLN, 3¾ miles (S. by E.) from Corby; containing 164 inhabitants. The living is a discharged rectory, valued in the king's books at £4. 15. 10., and in the patronage of the Crown. The incumbent's tithes have been commuted for £138, and the glebe contains 31 acres, with a glebe-house; a rent-charge of £26 is paid to the Dean and Chapter of Lincoln.

CRENDON, LONG (ST. MARY), a parish, in the union of THAME, hundred of ASHENDEN, county of BUCKINGHAM, 2¼ miles (N. by W.) from Thame; containing 1656 inhabitants, a few of whom are employed in the manufacture of needles. The living is a perpetual curacy; net income, £134; patron, Lord Churchill. The tithes were commuted for land and a money payment in 1824. The church is a spacious edifice, with a tower rising from the centre. There is a place of worship for Particular Baptists. Sir John Dormer, Knt., who was buried in the church, bequeathed a rent-charge of £26, which is distributed among the poor. Walter Giffard, Earl of Buckingham, and his countess, in 1162 built and endowed the abbey of Nutley here for Regular canons of the order of St. Augustine; it was dedicated to the Virgin Mary and St. John the Baptist, and at the Dissolution possessed a revenue valued at £495. 18. 5.: the remains have been converted into a farmhouse.

CRESLOW (HOLY TRINITY), a parish, in the union of AYLESBURY, hundred of COTTESLOE, county of BUCKINGHAM, 5¾ miles (N.) from Aylesbury; containing 7 inhabitants. The living is a rectory, valued in the king's books at £3: the church is dilapidated, and the inhabitants attend divine service at Whitchurch. There are remains, chiefly consisting of an embattled tower, of the ancient mansion of Creslow House, in which is a crypt; it was long in the possession of the lords De Clifford. Silver and copper Roman coins have been found.

4 Z 2

CRESSAGE, a chapelry, in the parish of COUND, union of ATCHAM, hundred of CONDOVER, S. division of SALOP, 3½ miles (N. W. by N.) from Much Wenlock; containing 297 inhabitants, and comprising by computation 1543 acres. The tithes have been commuted for £208. 15. 10., and there are 23 acres of glebe. The chapel has been taken down, and another built, in a more convenient situation, of white freestone obtained in the neighbourhood. Near Cressage are the remains of an ancient oak, supposed to have sheltered Christian missionaries previously to the building of churches; it was then called *Chrest ach* (Christ's oak), from which the name of Cressage is said to be derived.

CRESSING (*ALL SAINTS*), a parish, in the union of BRAINTREE, hundred of WITHAM, N. division of ESSEX, 3 miles (S. E.) from Braintree; containing 560 inhabitants. This parish, which was anciently included within that of Witham, comprises by measurement 2365a. 31p.; the soil is generally heavy, but fertile, and in some parts are indications of iron-ore. The living is a discharged vicarage, valued in the king's books at £7. 15. 5.; patron, the Vicar of Witham; appropriator, the Bishop of London. The great tithes have been commuted for £343, the vicarial for £287; and the glebe comprises 2¼ acres. The church contains an alabaster monument to the memory of several members of the Neville family. Cressing Temple, a preceptory of the Knights Templars, was given by King Stephen, with the advowson of the church, in perpetual alms to that order: the possessions subsequently passed to the Knights Hospitallers of St. John of Jerusalem, and reverted to the crown at the general suppression.

CRESSINGHAM, GREAT (*ST. MICHAEL*), a parish, in the union of SWAFFHAM, hundred of SOUTH GREEN-HOE, W. division of NORFOLK, 12 miles (N. N. E.) from Brandon; containing 476 inhabitants. This parish derives its name from a small river or creek, called by the Saxons *Grecca*: it comprises 2426a. 2r. 27p. The living is a discharged rectory, with the rectory of Bodney united, valued in the king's books at £17. 18. 1., and in the patronage of the Crown. The tithes of Great Cressingham have been commuted for £502. 10., and the glebe consists of 52½ acres, with a glebe-house. The church is a handsome structure in the early and later English styles, with a well-proportioned tower at the west end: the chancel contains a piscina of elegant design, and some sepulchral brasses. At the inclosure in 1801, 35 acres were allotted to the poor, for fuel. About a mile from the village, in a field called Stone Close, is the site of an ancient parochial chapel dedicated to St. George, where the rector has a fair for horses and toys on the first Wednesday and Thursday in August. William Barlow, Bishop of Chichester, and George Mountaine, Archbishop of York, were rectors of the parish in 1525 and 1602, respectively.

CRESSINGHAM, LITTLE (*ST. ANDREW*), a parish, in the union of SWAFFHAM, hundred of SOUTH GREEN-HOE, W. division of NORFOLK, 3 miles (W.) from Watton; containing 244 inhabitants. It is situated on the declivities of a rich valley, and comprises by computation 1810 acres, of which 1350 are arable, 200 pasture, and about 230 woodland. Clermont Lodge, a neat mansion, stands on an eminence encompassed by a beautiful park. The living is a discharged rectory, valued in the king's books at £13. 12. 6.; net income, £284; patrons,

£1200, with a house for the priest, by the late Dowager Lady Stourton. Sir Edward Vavasour, Bart., the proprietor of the soil, supports a school. A Roman Catholic establishment has existed at this place ever since the period of the Reformation.

CRETINGHAM (St. ANDREW), a parish, in the union of PLOMESGATE, hundred of LOOES, E. division of SUFFOLK, 8 miles (N. N. W.) from Woodbridge; containing 411 inhabitants, and comprising by admeasurement 1600 acres. The living is a discharged vicarage, valued in the king's books at £9. 10. 10., and in the patronage of the Crown; net income, £142; impropriator, T. Chenery, Esq.: there is a glebe-house, with about 23 acres of land. The church contains portions in the early and later English styles, and has in the chancel some memorials of the Cornwallis family. Here was formerly a chapel, dedicated to St. Mary Magdalene.

CREWE, a township, in the parish of FARNDON, union of GREAT BOUGHTON, Higher division of the hundred of BROXTON, S. division of the county of CHESTER, 6¼ miles (N. W.) from Malpas; containing 67 inhabitants. It comprises 284 acres, whereof the soil is clay; and is bounded on the west by the river Dee, which separates the parish from Wales.

CREWE, a township, in the parish of BARTHOMLEY, union and hundred of NANTWICH, S. division of the county of CHESTER, 4½ miles (S. W. by S.) from Sandbach; containing, according to the census of 1841, 396 inhabitants. The town of Crewe, which but a few years since consisted of only one house, now assumes the appearance of a rapidly increasing place; and its population, swelling with its size, amounts to about 5000. It lies near the road from Nantwich to Sandbach; is built, for the most part, on ground belonging to Oak Farm, in the adjoining parish of Coppenhall; and consists of several hundred dwelling-houses, occupied, almost exclusively, by persons connected with the railway lines to which the place owes its present importance. The houses are arranged in four classes, viz.: lodges, in the villa style, for the superior officers; ornamented Gothic buildings, for the next in authority; detached mansions, which accommodate four families, with separate entrances to each; and cottages, with four apartments, for the work-people. The first, second, and third classes have all gardens and yards, and the fourth gardens, also; and the whole presents a remarkably neat specimen of a model town. Each house and cottage is supplied with gas, and water is abundant: there are baths, a playground, a newsroom, a library, and an assembly-room.

The Grand Junction or Liverpool and Birmingham Railway Company, desirous of having a central position for their works, selected Crewe; and from their station here, now serving as a general station, diverge the Chester and Crewe railway, taking a west-north-west direction to Chester; and the Crewe and Manchester railway. The whole lines now belong to the London and North-Western Company. The entire railway-works cover a space of thirty acres, and employ about 1100 persons, of whom 800 are engaged in the engineering department, and the remainder in the coach-building department. Among the various buildings is the forge, where the iron-work is executed, the *fan* being used instead of the bellows; and in another portion is the coach-building room, in continuation of which are the

725

repairing-shop and smithy. Another wing is appropriated to the locomotive branch, presenting the aspect of a vast polytechnic institution, and in which are all the implements of engineering. In the extreme wing is the brass and iron foundry; and an immense space is allotted to trains of carriages, and to steam-engines, some of which are kept always ready under steam pressure, in case of accident.

The township comprises 1913 acres, of which the prevailing soil is sand and clay. It has been the inheritance of the Crewe family from a very early period. The Hall, the seat of Lord Crewe, exhibits a good specimen of the more enriched style of architecture which prevailed in the early part of the 17th century: it was begun in 1615, and completed in 1636, and the ceilings and wainscots of many of the rooms, and the principal staircase, retain their original decorations. The gallery, a hundred feet in length, is fitted up as a library, and contains a number of family portraits, and fine pictures: the mansion has also a private chapel, where divine service is performed every Sunday morning, and where is a large painting of the Last Supper, with two beautiful specimens of ancient stained glass. The park is embellished with a charming sheet of water covering 90 acres, and the scenery of the domain is strikingly picturesque. A church was consecrated in the town in December, 1845; it is in the Anglo-Norman style, in the form of a cross, and has an elegant tower: the whole is of Newcastle blue brick, with freestone angles. There is an endowment of £200 per annum for the minister. The tithes of the township have been commuted for £110 payable to the impropriator, and £30 to the rector of the parish. A school was founded in 1729, pursuant to the will of Thomas Leadbeater, Esq., who bequeathed £30 for the erection of a house, and £120 for the maintenance of a master; and there have been erected schools for the children of the artisans who are engaged on the works.

CREWKERNE (St. BARTHOLOMEW), a market-town and parish, in the union of CHARD, hundred of CREWKERNE, W. division of SOMERSET, 10 miles (S. W. by S.) from Ilchester, and 132 (W. S. W.) from London; comprising the tythings of Clapton, Coombe, Easthams, Furland, Hewish, Laymore, and Woolminstone; and containing 4414 inhabitants. This place, being a royal manor, anciently enjoyed many privileges, and in the reign of Henry II. was exempt from taxation. The town is pleasantly situated in a fertile valley, watered by branches of the rivers Parret and Axe, and sheltered by hills richly planted. It has five principal streets, diverging from a spacious market-place, in the centre of which is a large and commodious market-house; the houses are in general well built and of handsome appearance, and the inhabitants are amply supplied with water. Sailcloth, stockings, and dowlas, are manufactured. An act was passed in 1846 for a railway to this town, 8½ miles in length, from the Yeovil branch of the Bristol and Exeter line. The market, which is well supplied with corn, is on Saturday; and a fair is held on the 4th of September, for horses, bullocks, linen-drapery, cheese, and toys. The powers of the county debt-court of Crewkerne, established in 1847, extend over part of the registration-districts of Chard, Beaminster, and Yeovil. The living is a perpetual curacy; net income, £158; patrons, the Dean and Chapter of Winchester; impropriator, J. Hussey, Esq. The church is a spacious cruciform structure in the decorated English style, with a highly enriched tower rising from the intersection, crowned with battlements and ornamented with angular turrets; the interior is finely arranged, the windows are large, and filled with tracery, and the piers and arches which support the tower are lofty and of graceful elevation. There are places of worship for Particular Baptists and Unitarians. The free grammar school was founded in 1449, by John de Combe, precentor of the cathedral of Exeter, who endowed it with land now producing £300 per annum : it has four exhibitions, of £5 per annum each, to any college at Oxford, founded by the Rev. William Owsley, who gave a rent-charge of £20. There are two other schools, endowed with £9. 12. per annum, and two almshouses, one of which, for twelve aged men and women, was in 1707 endowed with a rent-charge of £29 by Mrs. Mary Davis.

CRICH (St. Mary), a parish, in the union of Belper, partly in the hundred of Morleston and Litchurch, partly in that of Scarsdale, and partly in that of Wirksworth, N. and S. divisions of the county of Derby; containing, with the township of Wessington and the hamlet of Tansley, 3698 inhabitants, of whom 2619 are in the township of Crich, 5 miles (W. by S.) from Alfreton. This is a place of some antiquity, and coins of Adrian and Diocletian have been found in an adjacent lead-mine, from which circumstance it is conjectured that lead was obtained here by the Romans. It is situated on an eminence commanding extensive prospects, on the road from Alfreton to Wirksworth, and near the river Derwent. The parish comprises about 3400 acres, the substratum of which has long been a source of considerable wealth : the lead-mines, several of which are now in operation, produce a metal of the finest quality, and appear to have been wrought continuously since the time of the Norman survey, when "Leuric had a lead-mine at Cric." The manor of Wakebridge, in the parish, belonged to Darley Abbey, and still enjoys the privilege of exemption from king's duty on lead-ore, the mine of which, in the manor, is considered the richest in the county. The parish contains also limestone and gritstone quarries, the stone of the latter of which was in demand for the use of the Midland railway, and is applied to building and other purposes.

The village not long since was inconsiderable, but rose into importance from the establishment of a cotton-manufactory at Frichly in 1793, and in 1810 received the grant of a market, which however was discontinued on the decline of the factory. The chief employment at present is frame-work knitting; there are also manufactories for the spinning of candle-wicks, and one for bobbin-turning. Cattle-fairs are held on the 6th April and 11th October. The Cromford canal passes along the western side of the parish, and, by a tunnel on the south, joins the Nottingham canal; the Midland railroad runs through the eastern part, and a branch has been laid down to a limestone-quarry at the top of the village, for the purpose of conveying the stone to twelve kilns lately built. The living is a discharged vicarage, valued in the king's books at £6. 10. 10, ; net income, £98 ; patron and impropriator, Sir W. W. Dixie, Bart. : the tithes were commuted for land in 1776. The church is a fine structure, with a tower surmounted by a spire,

and contains several ancient monuments of the Dixie family; it is beautifully situated, commanding an extensive prospect. Among the old monuments is one supposed to be of Sir W. de Wakebridge, who fought in the Holy Land. A church has been built in the hamlet of Tansley; and there are places of worship for Wesleyans, Independents, and Baptists. About one mile north of the village is Crich Cliff, a lofty hill, upon which an observatory was erected in 1789.

CRICK, a hamlet, in the parish of Caerwent, union and division of Chepstow, hundred of Caldicot, county of Monmouth, 4 miles (S. W. by W.) from Chepstow; containing 148 inhabitants. The road leading from this village to Caerwent was a Roman way. The village contains a house, now a farmhouse, where Charles I. was concealed for some time.

CRICK (St. Margaret), a parish, in the union of Rugby, hundred of Guilsborough, S. division of the county of Northampton, 6½ miles (N. by E.) from Daventry; containing 1006 inhabitants. This place was visited by the army of Fairfax, which rested here on the night previous to the battle of Naseby, when the church and rectory-house were unroofed and otherwise damaged. The parish is situated on the borders of Warwickshire,' and intersected by the road from Northampton to Coventry : it comprises by measurement 3271 acres; the surface is rather hilly, and the soil various, in some parts clayey, in others gravelly and sandy. The manufacture of worsted stockings was formerly carried on to some extent, but has been discontinued. Coarse limestone is found, and used for flags, and occasionally for building. A nameless rivulet, which flows into the Avon near Dovebridge, has its source within the parish; and the Grand Union canal, connecting Leicester with the Grand Junction canal, passes through a tunnel 1524 yards in length. The Crick station on the London and Birmingham railway is within two or three miles. The living is a rectory, valued in the king's books at £32. 13. 1½.; net income, £890; patrons, the President and Fellows of St. John's College, Oxford : the tithes were commuted for 560 acres of land in 1776. The church is a spacious and handsome structure, in the decorated English style, with a square embattled tower; the window of the chancel has been lately restored, and is a very beautiful specimen of flowing tracery : the stained glass with which the windows generally were embellished was destroyed by the soldiers of Fairfax. There are places of worship for Independents and Wesleyans. The Roman Watling-street skirts the western boundary of the parish, where Roman antiquities have been found; and there are tumuli in various parts. Archbishop Laud was rector of the parish for seven years.

CRICKET (St. Thomas), a parish, in the union of Chard, hundred of South Petherton, W. division of Somerset, 3 miles (E.) from Chard; containing 78 inhabitants. This parish is situated on the Exeter and London road, in a district of much natural beauty; and the handsome seat and extensive domain of the Hood family form an interesting feature in the surrounding scenery. A fair is held on Whit Monday and Tuesday, for cattle. The living is a discharged rectory, valued in the king's books at £9. 17. 6., and in the gift of Lord Bridport : the tithes have been commuted for £92, and the glebe comprises 30 acres, with a glebe-house.

CRICKET-MALHERBIE (St. Mary Magdalene), a parish, in the union of CHARD, hundred of ABDICK and BULSTONE, W. division of SOMERSET, 2¾ miles (S.) from Ilminster; containing 36 inhabitants. The parish stands on elevated ground, and comprises by computation 520 acres: the Creech and Chard canal passes at the distance of a mile. The living is a discharged rectory, valued in the king's books at £6. 6. 3.; net income, £77; patron, Stephen Pitt, Esq. : the glebe consists of about 20 acres.

CRICKLADE, a borough and market-town, in the union of CRICKLADE and WOOTTON-BASSET, hundred of HIGHWORTH, CRICKLADE, and STAPLE, Cricklade and N. divisions of WILTS, 48 miles (N. by W.) from Salisbury, and 83 (W. by N.) from London; containing 2128 inhabitants. This place, which is of great antiquity, is by some supposed to have derived its name from the British *Cerigwâld*, signifying a country abounding with stones; and by others from the Saxon *Cræcca*, a brook, and *Lædian*, to empty, the small rivers Churn and Rey here discharging themselves into the river Isis. It is thought by Dr. Stukeley to have been a Roman station, from its position on the Roman road which connected *Corinium*, now Cirencester, with *Spinæ*, now Speen. About the year 905, Ethelwald, opposing the election of Edward the Elder to the throne, collected a large body of troops, consisting principally of East Angles, and advanced on a predatory excursion to this place, from which he retreated with his plunder before Edward, who was marching to attack him, reached the town. In 1016, Cricklade was plundered by Canute the Dane; since which it has not been distinguished by any event of historical importance.

The TOWN is situated in a level tract of country, on the south bank of the Isis, which has its source in the vicinity; it consists principally of one long street, and is paved from the fund called the Cricklade-Way lands, varying from £150 to £170 per annum, and arising from an early bequest. Water-works have been constructed, and pipes laid down in the main street, by a spirited individual. The market is on Saturday; there is also an extensive market for corn and cattle on the third Tuesday in every month, and a pleasure-fair is held on the 23rd of September. The Thames and Severn canal runs to the north of the town, and is connected with the Wilts and Berks line by the North Wilts canal, which passes the town to the south-west; the Swindon and Gloucester branch of the Great Western railway runs a few miles to the south. The county magistrates hold a meeting on the first Saturday in every month; and a bailiff and other officers are appointed by a jury at the court leet of the lord of the manor, who also holds a court every third week for the recovery of debts under 40s. Cricklade is a borough by prescription, and exercised the elective franchise from the reign of Edward I., with various intermissions, till that of Henry VI., since which time it has uninterruptedly continued to return two members to parliament. In consequence of notorious bribery, the franchise was in 1782 extended to the adjoining divisions of Highworth, Cricklade and Staple, Kingsbridge, and Malmesbury. The polling-places are Cricklade, Brinkworth, and Swindon.

Cricklade comprises the parishes of *St. Samson* and *St. Mary*, the former containing 1642, and the latter 486, inhabitants, and consisting together of nearly 8000
727

acres, about two-thirds of which are arable; the soil is generally a rich loam, producing fine crops, and the surface is mostly flat. The living of *St. Samson's* is a vicarage, valued in the king's books at £18. 11. 10½.; net income, £460; patrons, the Dean and Chapter of Salisbury, who are also appropriators of the rectory, of which the Rev. T. Heberden is lessee. The church is a spacious and ancient cruciform structure, with a handsome embattled tower, rising from the intersection, crowned by a pierced parapet and pinnacles, and highly ornamented with niches and pedestals: the south porch was formerly a chapel, built by the Hungerford family; and towards the east is another porch, with large battlements, having in the centre the figure of a lion couchant. The interior is of corresponding character; the piers and arches that support the tower are lofty and of graceful elevation. A stone cross, which once stood in the principal street, was removed into the churchyard when the old town-hall was taken down. The living of *St. Mary's* is a discharged rectory, valued at £4. 14. 0½.; net income, £83; patron, the Bishop of Gloucester and Bristol. The church is a very ancient structure; the chancel is separated from the nave by a circular Norman arch, and the interior contains many vestiges of its original character. In the churchyard is a handsome stone cross of one shaft on a flight of steps; the head is richly ornamented with small sculptured figures in canopied niches. There are places of worship for Independents and Wesleyans. Near St. Samson's churchyard is a building erected in 1652, by Robert Jenner, goldsmith, of London, for the purpose of a school, but which for many years was used as a poor-house, and has only lately been restored to its original purpose. Among the several charities is one of a hundred acres of land granted by Charles I., out of the forest of Braydon, and now producing about £125 per annum, of which one-half is given to decayed tradespeople, and the other, in equal portions, applied to the apprenticing of children, and distributed among the poor. A benefaction called Dunches' charity, consisting of lands worth £30 a year, is also, by the will of the donor, appropriated to eight decayed tradespeople not receiving parochial aid. The union comprises fourteen parishes or places, and contains a population of 13,165. In the parish of St. Mary are the remains of the priory of St. John the Baptist, founded in the reign of Henry III., now converted into a private residence. There was also an hospital dedicated to the same patron, the revenue of which, at the Dissolution, was £4. 10. 7. : some land, belonging to it, in the parish of St. Samson, is still called the Spital.

CRIDLING-STUBBS, a township, in the parish of WOMERSLEY, union of PRESTON (under Gilbert's act), Lower division of the wapentake of OSGOLDCROSS, W. riding of YORK, 4¾ miles (E.) from Pontefract; containing 159 inhabitants. It is chiefly of the same limestone bed as Womersley township, and comprises by computation about 900 acres.

CRIGGLESTONE, a township, in the chapelry of CHAPELTHORPE, parish of GREAT SANDALL, union of WAKEFIELD, Lower division of the wapentake of AGBRIGG, W. riding of YORK, 3¼ miles (S.) from Wakefield; containing 1479 inhabitants. This township lies on the Wakefield and Manchester road, in a picturesque and fertile district, and comprises 2950 acres of profitable land. It abounds in coal, which is shipped to supply the London market: Messrs. Pope and Co., of London, in 1843 opened an excellent coal-pit here, at an outlay of £30,000 to effect the "winning." There are several villages in the township, the principal being that of Chapelthorpe, so called from the chapel, a neat edifice, the living of which is a perpetual curacy, in the patronage of the Vicar of Sandall. The annual sum of £19. 13., arising from bequests, is appropriated to the support of a Sunday school, and the relief of the poor, who have also an interest in the liberal bequest made by Alderman Scholey to the parish.

CRIMPLESHAM (St. Mary), a parish, in the union of Downham, hundred of Clackclose, W. division of Norfolk, 2 miles (E.) from Downham; containing 358 inhabitants. It comprises 1658a. 1r. 7p., whereof 1058 acres are arable, 488 pasture, and 59 woodland. Crimplesham Hall is a handsome mansion, in the grounds of which was formerly a church. The living is a discharged perpetual curacy, valued in the king's books at £8; net income, £90; patron and appropriator, the Bishop of Ely: the tithes have been commuted for £525. 1. 8., and the glebe contains 58 acres. The church is an ancient structure in the early and decorated English styles, with a tower; the north and south entrances are in the Norman style. At the inclosure in 1806, twelve acres were allotted to the poor, the proceeds of which, amounting to £23 per annum, are distributed in coal.

CRINGLEFORD (St. Peter), a parish, in the union of Henstead, hundred of Humbleyard, E. division of Norfolk, 3 miles (S. W. by W.) from Norwich; containing 191 inhabitants. It comprises about 1200 acres, chiefly arable; and derives its name from an ancient gravelly ford, which has been superseded by a stone bridge, over the river Yare, separating the liberties of Norwich from the county. The living is a perpetual curacy; net income, £205; patrons and impropriators, the Trustees of St. Giles' Hospital, Norwich. The church is in the later English style, with a square embattled tower. Within the parish was once a free chapel, dedicated to St. Ethelred, to which pilgrims used to resort in great numbers.

CRIPTON, a hamlet, in the parish of Winterbourn-Came, union of Dorchester, hundred of Culliford-Tree, Dorchester division of Dorset, 3½ miles (S. by E.) from Dorchester; containing 17 inhabitants.

CRITCHILL, or CRICHEL, LONG (St. Mary), a parish, in the union of Wimborne and Cranborne, hundred of Knowlton, Wimborne division of Dorset, 6½ miles (W. S. W.) from Cranborne; containing 120 inhabitants. This parish, which received its distinguishing appellation from its greater length in comparison with the adjoining parish of More-Critchill, is divided into two tythings, Critchill-Gouis and Critchill-Lucy, so named from their ancient lords. It comprises 1867 acres, of which 730 are common or waste. The living is a rectory, united in 1774 to that of More-Critchill, and valued in the king's books at £12. 13. 8½.; the glebe consists of 110 acres. The church has a good tower at the west end, with a massive buttress on its north side. Some vestiges of a Roman road may be traced.

CRITCHILL, MORE (All Saints), a parish, in the union of Wimborne and Cranborne, hundred of Badbury, Wimborne division of Dorset, 6 miles (N. by W.) from Wimborne; containing, with the hamlet of Manswood, 316 inhabitants, and comprising by admeasure-
728

ment 1649 acres. The living is a rectory, with that of Long Critchill united, valued in the king's books at £10. 9. 7.; net income, £371; patron, Henry Sturt, Esq. The church is a small ancient structure, having an embattled tower, with a porch of modern erection, and has been lately beautified with a western window in the later English style, and otherwise much improved at the expense of the patron: it had a chantry, well endowed with land by John de Bridport, in the 2nd of Edward III., for a chaplain to pray daily for his soul. Traces of the Roman road from Badbury-Rings to Old Sarum may be seen in the parish.

CRIXETH, county Essex.—See Creeksea.

CROBOROUGH.—See Blackwood.

CROCK-STREET, a hamlet, in the parishes of Ilminster and Donyatt, hundred of Abdick and Bulstone, union of Chard, W. division of Somerset, 3 miles (W. S. W.) from Ilminster; containing 54 inhabitants. A quantity of coarse earthenware is made.

CROCKER-HILL, a hamlet, in the parish of Boxgrove, union of West Hampnett, hundred of Box and Stockbridge, rape of Chichester, W. division of Sussex; containing 52 inhabitants.

CROCKERN-WELL, a hamlet, partly in the parish of Bishop-Cheriton, and partly in that of Drewsteignton, hundred of Wonford, Crockern-Well and S. divisions of Devon, 7 miles (S. W.) from Crediton. It abounds with beautiful scenery. Here was formerly a chapel, of which there are no remains.

CROCKERNE-PILL, a hamlet, in the parish of Easton-in-Gordano, union of Bedminster, hundred of Portbury, E. division of Somerset, 5½ miles (N. W.) from Bristol; containing 1748 inhabitants, This hamlet, which had its rise in the seventeenth century, is situated on the banks of the Avon, near the junction of that river with the Severn, and is chiefly inhabited by mariners, engaged in piloting vessels to and from Bristol, and along the Channel, under the regulations of the Company of Merchant Adventurers of Bristol.

CROFORD, a tything, in the parish of Wivelis-combe, union of Wellington, W. division of the hundred of Kingsbury and of Somerset; containing, with the tything of Nunnington, 455 inhabitants.

CROFT (St. Michael), a parish, in the union of Leominster, hundred of Wolphy, county of Hereford, 5½ miles (N. N. W.) from Leominster; containing, with the detached township of Newton, 144 inhabitants. The parish comprises 1581 acres; it is of undulated surface, and the scenery is extensive and beautiful. The land is divided into equal portions of arable and pasture, with some excellent oak-timber, particularly at Croft Park, surrounding the mansion. There is a limestone-quarry. The living is a discharged rectory, with the vicarage of Yarpole annexed, valued in the king's books at £7. 11. 3., and in the patronage of W. T. K. Davies, Esq.; net income, £330. The tithes of Croft have been commuted for £120; and there is a glebe of 71½ acres, with a house. The church is ancient, and contains a beautiful monument to one of the Croft family. A national school is supported by subscription. At Castle Park, on an eminence to the north-west of the village, is Croft-Ambury, an ancient British camp, with a double ditch and rampart.

CROFT, with Southworth (Christ Church), a parish, in the union of Warrington, hundred of West

)ERBY, S. division of the county of LANCASTER, 5 miles N. N. E.) from Warrington; containing 1155 inhabitants. The Croft family held lands in Croft in the reign of Edward III.; Southworth gave name to the knightly amily of Southworth, and both manors were possessed by Sir John Southworth in the 39th of Elizabeth. They subsequently passed to other families, and also belonged o the Roman Catholic establishment at Stonyhurst. This is a new parish formed out of the parish of Winwick by act of parliament, in 1845. It comprises 1851 acres, whereof 1288 are meadow and pasture, and the remainder nearly all arable; the surface is level, and the soil clay and peat. The population consists partly of handloom weavers. The living is a rectory, in the patronage of the Earl of Derby: the tithes have been commuted for a rent-charge of £230; and there is a glebe-house, built at the expense of the rector of Winwick. The church, which is in the later English style, with a tower and spire, was erected in 1833, at the cost of £4000, defrayed by the rector of Winwick, aided by society grants. There are places of worship for Unitarians and Methodists; and a Roman Catholic chapel. A school is endowed with £6. 10. per annum, and a house and garden.

CROFT, a parish, in the union of BLABY, hundred of SPARKENHOE, S. division of the county of LEICESTER, 6¼ miles (E. by N.) from Hinckley; containing 321 inhabitants. The parish comprises by computation 1000 acres. The soil is various; to the north of the village, light; with some good pasture land near the borders of a brook which flows through the parish; and on the south of the village, a stiffish clay. There is a large quarry, supplying an excellent material for building and for the repair of roads; and about one-fourth of the population is employed in frame-work knitting. The village is situated on a granite rock rising from the edge of the brook, and continuing in a ridge northward, until it terminates in a remarkable conical hill, covered with verdure, and conspicuous for many miles round. The living is a rectory, valued in the king's books at £12. 3. 4.; net income, £582; patron and incumbent, the Rev. Robert Thomas Adnutt. A portion of the tithes have been commuted for land, and the remainder for a rent-charge of £70. 8.; the glebe comprises altogether 250 acres, with a glebe-house.

CROFT (ALL SAINTS), a parish, in the union of SPILSBY, Marsh division of the wapentake of CANDLESHOE, parts of LINDSEY, county of LINCOLN, 1¾ mile (N. N. E.) from Wainfleet; containing 649 inhabitants. The living is a vicarage, valued in the king's books at £23. 7. 3½.; net income, £388; patron and impropriator, Lord Monson.

CROFT (ST. PETER), a parish, in the union of DARLINGTON, wapentake of GILLING-EAST, N. riding of YORK; containing 744 inhabitants, of whom 422 are in the township of Croft, 3½ miles (S.) from Darlington. The parish comprises the townships of Croft, Dalton-upon-Tees, part of Great Smeaton, and part of Stapleton; and consists by measurement of 6384 acres, of which 5032 are in tillage, and 1352 meadow and pasture. It has been latterly much resorted to for the benefit of its sulphureous springs, which are similar to those of Harrogate. The spa is in the township of Croft, and on the property of Sir William Chaytor, Bart.: it was first brought into notice in 1668, and so

early as 1713 the water had acquired such fame that it was sold in London in sealed bottles at an exorbitant price. In 1808 the proprietor erected a capacious hotel, with suitable conveniences, and a number of lodging-houses for the accommodation of visiters; and over the spring is a splendid suite of baths, built in 1829. The air is remarkably pure; the surrounding country is pleasant, and the views on the banks of the Tees are delightful, commanding an extensive tract in the highest possible state of cultivation.. The village is neatly built, and situated on the river, over which is a handsome stone bridge of seven arches, about 200 yards distant from the spa; it is 414 feet in length, and from the bed of the river to the top of the iron-railing 59 feet high. At about a quarter of a mile below the village, the York and Newcastle railway crosses the Tees by a splendid oblique viaduct of four arches, at an angle of 45°, and 54 feet above the level of the river; the Croft station is only about one hundred yards from the village, although locally in the parish of Hurworth. The living is a rectory, valued in the king's books at £12. 8. 4., and in the patronage of the Crown; net income, £825. The church is an ancient edifice, and exhibits specimens of various styles of English architecture; it contains an altar-tomb to a member of the Milbank family, and another to the family of Clervaux, the ancestors of Sir William Chaytor. Burnet, the author of the Theory of the Earth, was born here in 1635.

CROFTON, a township, in the parish of THURSBY, union of WIGTON, CUMBERLAND ward, and E. division of CUMBERLAND, 3¼ miles (E. N. E.) from Wigton; containing 80 inhabitants. It is situated on the river Wampool, and near the road from Wigton to Carlisle, and the railway from Carlisle to Maryport.

CROFTON, a district incumbency, in the parish and hundred of TITCHFIELD, union of FAREHAM, Fareham, and S. divisions of the county of SOUTHAMPTON, 2½ miles (S. W. by W.) from Fareham; containing 809 inhabitants. The living is a perpetual curacy, in the patronage of the Vicar of Titchfield: the chapel, dedicated to the Holy Rood, is a very ancient edifice, lately thoroughly repaired. A school, in connexion with the National Society, was built in 1839, at the expense of the Rev. David Haynes. .

CROFTON, with WOLFHALL, a tything, in the parish of GREAT BEDWIN, union of HUNGERFORD, hundred of KINWARDSTONE, Marlborough and Ramsbury, and S. divisions of WILTS; containing 180 inhabitants.

CROFTON (ALL SAINTS), a parish, in the union of PRESTON (under Gilbert's act), Lower division of the wapentake of AGBRIGG, W. riding of YORK, 3¼ miles (E. S. E.) from Wakefield; containing 389 inhabitants. This parish is in the honour of Pontefract, and comprises about 970 acres of fertile land, including the hamlet of Birkwood: the roads from Doncaster and Pontefract to Wakefield form a junction here. Coal-mines were extensively wrought for several years, and have been discontinued for some time, though much coal yet remains. The village is pleasant and well built, and has an ever-flowing fountain in the centre. At Oakenshaw, in the parish, the Midland railway is carried over the Barnsley canal by a viaduct of five segmental arches of 60 feet span each, and at the height of 60 feet above the level of the water; the whole is constructed of brickwork with stone quoins. Here, also, one of the most extensive cuttings in the whole line was made through rock, shale, and bind, the greatest depth being 50 feet, and the quantity of earth removed amounting to 600,000 cubic yards, most of which was used to form the Oakenshaw embankment. The living is a rectory, valued in the king's books at £10. 0. 2½., and in the patronage of the Crown, in right of the duchy of Lancaster; net income, £334. The church is a small cruciform structure in the later English style, with a low central tower. The original church stood on low swampy ground, nearly a mile from the present site: the only remains of it are the names of "Church Field" given to a field of the glebe land, and "Church Hill" to the particular spot where it stood. Dr. Richard Fleming, founder of Lincoln College, Oxford, was a native of this place; the remains of his arms, carved in stone, still appear over the porch of the present church.

CROGLIN (St. John the Baptist), a parish, in the union of Penrith, Leath ward, E. division of Cumberland, 5 miles (N. N. E.) from Kirk-Oswald; containing 336 inhabitants. The parish derives its name from the river Croglin, by which it is bounded on the south; the surface is very uneven, and rises in some places into eminences of mountainous elevation, the highest being Croglin Fell. The substrata are chiefly limestone, and freestone of a reddish colour, which are both quarried, with some porphyry; and veins of coal are likewise found. The living is a discharged rectory, valued in the king's books at £8; net income, £223; patron, the Rev. John Jackson. A school, built by subscription in 1724, and conducted on the national plan, is endowed with the interest of £50 given in 1723 by the Rev. J. Hunter, rector, and an allotment of 24 acres appropriated on the inclosure, and yielding about £14 per annum.

CROMER (St. Peter and St. Paul), a parish, and formerly a market-town, in the union of Erpingham, hundred of North Erpingham, E. division of Norfolk, 21 miles (N.) from Norwich, and 130 (N. N. E.) from London: containing 1240 inhabitants. This place, originally of much greater extent, included the town of Shipden, which, with its church and a considerable number of houses, forming a parish, was destroyed by an inundation of the sea in the reign of Henry IV. Of the numerous ravages of the ocean the last occurred in 1837, when a large portion of the cliffs and houses of Cromer, with part of the jetty was washed away. In 1838, on the eastern side, a groin about 150 yards in length was laid down, running out from the cliff to the north, and which, aided by a sea-wall there erected, it is expected will prevent the recurrence of a similar catastrophe in that quarter; the security of the cliffs immediately below the town was provided for by a breast-work of stone and flint, with winding approaches to the beach and jetty. An act for the erection of other works, was passed in 1845.

The TOWN commands a fine view of Cromer bay, which, from its dangerous navigation, is by seamen called the "Devil's Throat." It was formerly inhabited only by a few fishermen, but, from the excellence of its beach, the salubrity of its air, and the beauty of its scenery, it has become a bathing-place of some celebrity; many of the houses are badly built and of mean appearance, but
730

those near the sea are commodious and pleasant, and there are several respectable lodging-houses and inns for visiters. The town has a circulating library and a subscription news-room; and a regatta is occasionally celebrated. Attempts have often been made to construct a pier, but the works have invariably been carried away by the sea: the jetty of wood, about 70 yards long, erected in 1822, forms an attractive promenade, as well as the fine beach at low water, which, on account of the firmness of the sand, and its smooth surface, affords also an excellent drive for several miles. Cromer is within the limits of the jurisdiction of the port of Cley: vessels of from 60 to 100 tons' burthen discharge their cargoes of coal and timber on the beach, and there are 18 large vessels and 20 herring-boats belonging to the place, besides about 40 boats employed in the taking of lobsters and crabs, which are abundant and of superior flavour. A fair, chiefly for toys, is held on Whit-Monday. The county magistrates hold a meeting every alternate Monday. The living is a discharged vicarage, valued in the king's books at £9. 4. 9.; patron and appropriator, the Bishop of Ely. The church was built in the reign of Henry IV., and was in ruins from the time of Cromwell till about 50 years ago, when it was newly roofed and repaired: it is a handsome structure of freestone and flint, in the later English style, with a lofty embattled tower; and the western entrance, the north porches, and the chancel, though much dilapidated, are fine specimens. There is a place of worship for Wesleyans. A free grammar school was endowed in 1505 by Sir Bartholomew Read, and further by the Goldsmiths' Company in 1821; but no application being made for classical instruction, it was remodelled by the company on the national plan. Roger Bacon, a mariner of Cromer, is said to have discovered Iceland in the reign of Henry IV.

CROMFORD, a chapelry, in the parish and hundred of Wirksworth, union of Bakewell, S. division of the county of Derby, 1 mile (N. by E.) from Matlock; containing 1407 inhabitants, and comprising 1308 acres, of which 125 are common or waste land. This place, which is pleasantly situated on the river Derwent, was an inconsiderable village prior to the year 1776, when Sir Richard Arkwright, having purchased the manor, erected mills, which were the first ever put in motion by water, and established a cotton-manufactory of large extent. Since this period it has greatly increased, and at present it is a flourishing place, consisting chiefly of neat and commodious dwellings for the persons engaged in the factories, many of them built round an open space where a small customary market is held on Saturday, and others chiefly in detached situations. The cotton manufacture affords employment to more than 1000 persons; there are a manufactory for hats, one for ginghams on a small scale, and a paper-manufactory. In the neighbourhood are extensive mines of lead and calamine, and quarries of marble and limestone: a great quantity of lapis calaminaris is exported annually. The Cromford canal communicates with the Erewash canal near Langley bridge, and commodious wharfs and warehouses have been constructed on its banks. The Cromford and High Peak railway, for the conveyance of minerals and merchandise, commences at this place, and pursues its course to the Peak-Forest canal, near Whaley bridge; the whole line is thirty-hree miles, in which it attains a rise of 990 feet above he level of the Cromford canal : it was opened in 1830. The chapel, a small neat building in the Grecian style, begun by Sir Richard Arkwright, in 1794, and completed by his son, Richard Arkwright, Esq., who endowed it with £50 per annum, was consecrated in 1797. The living is a perpetual curacy; net income, £96; patrons, the family of Arkwright : the great tithes have been commuted for £90, and the vicarial for £11. The Wesleyans have a place of worship.

CROMHALL (St. Andrew), a parish, in the union of Thornbury, Upper division of the hundred of Berkeley, W. division of the county of Gloucester, 1½ miles (N. W. by W.) from Wickwar; containing, with the tything of Cromhall-Lygon, 732 inhabitants. It is situated on the road from Wotton-under-Edge to Bristol; and derives the name Abbotts, affixed to one of its tythings, from its having belonged to the abbots of St. Augustine's in Bristol, to whom it was given by Lord Berkeley in 1148. The parish comprises 2579 acres, whereof 272 are common or waste. The high lands abound with excellent limestone, of which a great quantity is burnt into lime; and a coal-mine has been opened within the last few years, but being on the edge of the coal basin the veins are broken, and the produce is small and slaty. The living is a rectory, valued in the king's books at £16. 9. 2., and in the gift of Oriel College, Oxford : the tithes have been commuted for £452, and the glebe comprises 85 acres with a glebe-house. The church, with the exception of the tower, which is of earlier date, and placed on the north side, is a handsome structure in the later English style. There are some remains of a cell on Abbotside Hill.

· CROMPTON, a township, in the borough, parochial chapelry, and union of Oldham, parish óf Prestwich-cum-Oldham, hundred of Salford, S. division of the county of Lancaster, 3 miles (N. by E.) from Oldham; containing, with the villages of Shaw, High Compton, and Cowlishaw, 6729 inhabitants. This, the most northern part of the chapelry, has the largest population of any of the townships connected with Oldham, and its growth in trade has fully kept pace with the other parts of this flourishing district. A bleak situation, and somewhat sterile soil, have produced a race of hardy and laborious men, and the close connexion with Saddleworth has given to the people much of the manners and character which prevail in that hilly country. The population is employed in the spinning and manufacture of cotton, the making of hats, and in collieries and stone-quarries. The ancient mansion of Crompton Hall, having fallen into decay, has lately been rebuilt by the owner, Henry Travis Milne, Esq., a descendant of the feudal family of Crompton. Shaw, which lies on the east side of the village of Crompton, has a parochial chapel. The former edifice was of great antiquity, and was twice enlarged and re-edified during the last century; the present structure was built in the latter part of it, by subscription, aided by a grant. The living is a perpetual curacy in the patronage of the Rector of Prestwich; net income, £250. In 1845 a district parish was formed under the 6th and 7th of Victoria, cap. 37, called East Crompton; and a church, dedicated to St. James, was built in 1847 : the edifice is in the pointed style, with a tower, and contains 586 sittings. The living is a perpetual curacy; net income, £150;

patrons, the Crown and the Bishop of Chester, alternately. The tithes of the township have been commuted for £93. There are various places of worship for dissenters; and several schools.

CROMWELL (St. Giles), a parish, in the union of Southwell, N. division of the wapentake of Thurgarton, S. division of the county of Nottingham, 5¼ miles (N.) from Newark; containing 203 inhabitants, and comprising about 1400 acres. The living is a rectory, valued in the king's books at £13. 2. 3½.; net income, £430; patron, the Duke of Newcastle. The tithes were commuted for land in 1773; the glebe consists of 248 acres, with a good glebe-house. The tower and chancel of the church, which are ancient, are in the early English style, and a window in the chancel is a beautiful specimen of the decorated. A boys' and girls' school is held in a room belonging to the rector, and is chiefly supported by him.

CRONDALL (All Saints), anciently Crundelle-Halle, a parish, in the union of Hartley-Wintney, hundred of Crondall, Odiham and N. divisions of the county of Southampton, 3½ miles (W. N. W.) from Farnham; containing, with the tythings of Crookham, Dippenhall, Ewshott, and Swanthorpe, 2199 inhabitants, of whom 423 are in the township of Crondall. The parish comprises by computation nearly 10,000 acres, of which 4612 are arable, 740 pasture and meadow, 904 woodland, and 3650 common. Almost every variety of soil is to be found, from barren shingly gravel and sand, to rich alluvial mould, productive marls, and dry clays on a chalk substratum, yielding abundant crops of corn, clover, turnips, &c., and hops almost rivalling the produce of the celebrated " Hart-ground " at Farnham. In some spots chalk or marl stones are dug, adapted for rough buildings; and a stratum of fine chalk runs diagonally through the southern end of the parish. A rivulet has its source in the village, and flowing through the parish, forms a tributary to the river Loddon; the London and South-Western railway and the Basingstoke canal cross the parish. The living is a vicarage, valued in the king's books at £22. 5. 7½.; net income, £441; patrons and impropriators, the Master and Brethren of the Hospital of St. Cross, Winchester, who have leased the great tithes to the Marquess of Winchester. The church of great antiquity, the nave being of early and the chancel of later Norman, with zig-zag mouldings; it contains several monuments, some with Saxon inscriptions, and others with figures in brass, and is said to have suffered much during the wars of the Commonwealth. A district church in the early English style, built by subscription, has been consecrated; and there are places of worship for Independents, Ranters, and Bryanites. The late Henry Maxwell, Esq., of Ewshott House (the principal residence in the parish), presented a building for a school in connexion with the Establishment, and bequeathed £1250 for the maintenance of a master. At the north-eastern extremity of the parish is Cæsar's camp, a spot of singular and commanding position; the earthworks are of considerable extent, with deep ditches, and in the centre is a spring.

CRONTON, a township, in the parish and union of Prescot, hundred of West Derby, S. division of the county of Lancaster, 3¼ miles (S. S. E.) from Prescot; containing 402 inhabitants. In the 4th year of Elizabeth, this place appears as a manor in the possession of

Thomas Holte ; and in the reign of James I., it was the
property of James Lawton. The Hall belonged to the
Wrights for several generations, and was sold by their
heirs in 1821. The township comprises 1108 acres, of
which 21 are common land or waste: the surface is
principally flat; but on the east side is Pex Hill, the
residence of Thomas Brancker, Esq., from which a most
extensive view is obtained, embracing the Cheshire hills
and the Welsh mountains. There is an excellent redstone quarry. The road from Liverpool to Warrington
passes through ; and the place has the advantage of
railway communication by a branch from Huyton on the
Liverpool and Manchester line. The impropriate tithes
have been commuted for £105, payable to King's College, Cambridge, and the vicarial for £52. 10. The Wesleyans have a place of worship.

CROOK, with BILLY-ROW, a township, in the parish of BRANCEPETH, union of AUCKLAND, N. W. division of DARLINGTON ward, S. division of the county of
DURHAM, 5½ miles (N. W. by N.) from Bishop-Auckland ; containing 538 inhabitants. The township comprises by computation 4310 acres. Crook is a scattered
village, situated on the road between Willington and
Wolsingham, and partly extending into the adjoining
township of Helmington-Row. Coal is worked. A
branch of the Clarence railroad, from Ferry-Hill upwards, affords an easy communication with the coast ;
and the Bishop-Auckland and Weardale railway terminates here, after a course of eight miles, from the Stockton and Darlington line. The Incorporated Society, in
1841, granted £50 in aid of the expense of building a
district chapel, containing 306 free sittings : it is dedicated to St. Catherine, and the living is in the gift of
the Rector of Brancepeth. The tithes have been commuted for £68. 16. 8. An eminence in the township,
called Billy Hill, is seen by mariners in very clear weather, though so distant from the sea.

CROOK, a chapelry, in the parish, union, and ward
of KENDAL, county of WESTMORLAND, 4¾ miles
(W. N. W.) from Kendal ; containing 257 inhabitants.
It lies on the road from Kendal to Bowness, and comprises 2067 acres, of which the surface and scenery are
mountainous and rugged, and the soil mostly a light
gravel. The population is agricultural, with the exception of about 40 hands employed in the woollen manufacture, established about fifty years since in the hamlet
of Crook-Mill, where, also, the turning of bobbins is
carried on. In the mountainous part of the district is a
small vein of lead, containing barytes, similar to that
used in the manufacture of Wedgwood's jasper vases.
The living is a perpetual curacy ; net income, £77 ; patron, the Vicar of Kendal : there is a glebe-house. The
tithes belong to Trinity College, Cambridge, and amount
to £64. 14. The chapel, an ancient building with a
tower, stands in the centre of the chapelry. The Society
of Friends had formerly a meeting-house here, which
was taken down about seven years ago, and they have
still a burial-ground near How. The village school has
a small endowment.

CROOKDAKE, a hamlet, in the township and
parish of BROMFIELD, union of WIGTON, ALLERDALE
ward below Derwent, W. division of CUMBERLAND, 6½
miles (S. W.) from Wigton ; with 191 inhabitants.

CROOKDEAN, a township, in the parish of KIRK-
WHELPINGTON, union of BELLINGHAM, N. E. division of

nd drives with delightful prospects, and a serpentine ake a mile long. The living is a rectory, with that of Pirton united, valued in the king's books at £7; net income, £488; patron, the Earl. The church, rebuilt in 1763, is a neat edifice in the later English style, with a tower to the west and a chancel to the east, in which last are splendid monuments to the Coventry family, removed from the former church.

CROOME, EARL'S (St. Nicholas), a parish, in the union of Upton-on-Severn, Lower division of the hundred of Oswaldslow, Upton and W. divisions of the county of Worcester, 2 miles (N. E. by E.) from Upton; containing 194 inhabitants. This parish is partly bounded on the north-west by the river Severn, and is intersected from north to south by the road from Worcester to Gloucester. It comprises by measurement 1138 acres, in equal portions of arable and pasture; the surface is undulated, the soil a rather stiff clay, and the scenery picturesque and beautiful: excellent limestone is obtained for building and for manure. There are several respectable houses: Earl's-Croome Court, an ancient half-timbered mansion in the Elizabethan style, is the seat and property of the Hon. William Coventry. The living is a discharged rectory, valued in the king's books at £7. 8. 1½.; patron and incumbent, the Rev. Charles Dunne, M.A., whose tithes have been commuted for £235, and whose glebe comprises 5 acres, with a glebe-house. The church stands on the road from Upton to Pershore, and is an ancient building in the Norman style, with a noble arch. The tower was rebuilt in 1832, when the edifice was repaired and enlarged by subscription and a rate; the east window, of stained glass, representing the Crucifixion, was inserted at the expense of the rector, in 1844. Margaret, daughter and heir of Jeffries, of Earl's-Croome, in 1570 was married to Sir Thomas Coventry, father of Lord-Keeper Coventry; Dr. Butler, author of *Hudibras*, was clerk to a subsequent Mr. Jeffries, and is supposed to have written most of his works under the roof of Earl's-Croome Court.

CROOME, HILL (St. Mary), a parish, in the union of Upton-on-Severn, Lower division of the hundred of Oswaldslow, Upton and W. divisions of the county of Worcester, 3¼ miles (E.) from Upton; containing 201 inhabitants. The parish lies on the east of the river Severn, and consists of 977 acres; the surface is elevated, and the soil of full average productiveness. The living is a rectory, valued in the king's books at £7. 10. 5. and in the patronage of the Crown: the tithes have been commuted for £115; the glebe contains nearly 61 acres, with a glebe-house. The church is a mile south of the village of Boughton, and is a stone edifice with a tower.

CROPREDY (St. Mary), a parish, in the union, and chiefly in the hundred, of Banbury, but partly in the hundred of Bloxham, county of Oxford, and partly in the Burton-Dasset division of the hundred of Kington, S. division of the county of Warwick, 4 miles (N. by E.) from Banbury; comprising the chapelries of Claydon, Wardington, and Mollington, and the township of Bourton; and containing 2727 inhabitants. This place is memorable as the scene of an engagement that occurred in 1644, between the forces of the royal army and those of the parliament, near Cropredy bridge, of which structure some portions still remain, consisting of a projecting pier, a pointed arch, and a round arch, the

last built in 1697. The parish is situated on the river Cherwell, and comprises by computation 7000 acres; the soil is chiefly a rich loam, producing abundant crops, and there is a considerable portion of meadow and pasture land. The Oxford canal passes through the parish. The living is a discharged vicarage, valued in the king's books at £26. 10. 10.; net income, £592; patron and appropriator, the Bishop of Oxford. The tithes for the greater portion have been commuted for land, under various acts of inclosure; a rent-charge of £121 is paid to the bishop, and one of £123 to the vicar. The church is mostly in the decorated English style, and contains monuments to the families of Danvers, Loveday, Gostelow, and Taylor. There are chapels of ease at Claydon, Mollington, and Wardington; and places of worship for Independents and Wesleyans. Walter Calcott, in 1575, endowed a free school at Williamscott, *which see*.

CROPSTON, a township, in the parish of Thurcaston, union of Barrow-upon-Soar, hundred of West Goscote, N. division of the county of Leicester, 3¼ miles (S. W. by S.) from Mountsorrel; containing 111 inhabitants.

CROPTHORNE (St. Michael), a parish, in the union of Pershore, Middle division of the hundred of Oswaldslow, Pershore and E. divisions of the county of Worcester, 3 miles (W. N. W.) from Evesham; containing, with the hamlets of Charlton and Netherton, 732 inhabitants. This parish is situated on the river Avon, and intersected by the road from Evesham to Pershore; and comprises by measurement 3735 acres, of which 1479a. 1r. 7p. are in the portion exclusively of Netherton and Charlton. There are quarries of blue limestone, which is used for paving floors and for burning into lime. From Court House is a beautiful view of the river and the adjacent country. The living is a vicarage, valued in the king's books at £14. 17. 3½., and in the patronage of the Dean and Chapter of Worcester. The tithes of Cropthorne and Charlton were commuted for land and money payments, under inclosure acts, in 1776 and 1779; and those of Netherton were commuted in 1844, for a rent-charge of £84. 8. 2. The glebe comprises about 300 acres. The church, with the exception of the tower, was rebuilt in the reign of Henry VIII.; it contains several interesting monuments to the Dineley family. Mrs. Mary Holland, in 1735, bequeathed £50 for the erection, and £200 for the endowment of a school.

CROPTON, a chapelry, in the parish of Middleton, union and lythe of Pickering, N. riding of York, 4¼ miles (N. W. by N.) from Pickering; containing 335 inhabitants. The township comprises by computation 3824 acres, of which about 2000 are open moorland: the village adjoins Cawthorn, on the eastern acclivities of the dale of the small river Seven. Excellent limestone is obtained, and burnt into lime for building and agricultural purposes.' The tithes were commuted for land in 1765. Here is a chapel of ease; also a place of worship for Wesleyans; and an estate, producing about £23 per annum, is appropriated to the support of a school. There are various tumuli, thought to be British, and a high mount called Cropton Castle; and at Cawthorn, within two miles, are vestiges of a Roman camp.

CROPWELL, BISHOP (St. Giles), a parish, in the union, and S. division of the wapentake, of Bingham, S. division of the county of Nottingham, 4 miles

(S. W.) from Bingham; containing 533 inhabitants. The parish comprises by measurement 1550 acres. There are quarries of blue lias, which is used for building, and for burning into lime; and also several beds of gypsum, of which great quantities are sent into different parts of the country to be made into plaster for flooring. Facility of conveyance is afforded by the Nottingham and Grantham canal, which runs through the parish. The living is a discharged vicarage, valued in the king's books at £5. 3. 4.; net income, £172; patron, the Bishop of Lincoln. The church is a handsome edifice, with a lofty embattled tower. There is a place of worship for Wesleyans. The old Fosse-road intersects the parish.

CROPWELL-BUTLER, a chapelry, in the parish of TITHBY, union, and S. division of the wapentake, of BINGHAM, S. division of the county of NOTTINGHAM, 8¼ miles (E. S. E.) from Nottingham; containing 678 inhabitants. This place was anciently called Crophill-Botiller, from a circular hill situated between it and Bishop-Cropwell, and from its early possessors, the Botillers, or Butlers, of Warrington, in Lancashire. The chapelry comprises 1800 acres, of which 30 were allotted to the incumbent, at the inclosure in 1788, in commutation of tithes. There is a place of worship for Wesleyans.

CROSBY, a township, in the parish of CROSS-CANNONBY, union of COCKERMOUTH, ALLERDALE ward below Derwent, W. division of the county of CUMBERLAND, 3 miles (N. W. by W.) from Maryport; containing 272 inhabitants. There is a school, endowed by John Nicholson with £10 per annum.

CROSBY, a township, in the union of GLANDFORD-BRIGG, partly in the parish of FLIXBOROUGH, N. division, but chiefly in the parish of BOTTESFORD, E. division, of the wapentake of MANLEY, parts of LINDSEY, county of LINCOLN, 8¼ miles (N. W. by W.) from Glandford-Brigg; containing 199 inhabitants.

CROSBY, a township, in the parish of LEAKE, union of NORTHALLERTON, wapentake of ALLERTONSHIRE, N. riding of YORK, 5¾ miles (N. by W.) from Thirsk; containing 37 inhabitants. It comprises 1430 acres of land, of a generally fertile soil. The hamlet, consisting of only a few houses, is situated on the Cod beck, and on the road from Knayton to Northallerton.

CROSBY-GARRET (St. Andrew), a parish, in East ward and union, county of WESTMORLAND, 6½ miles (W. by S.) from Brough; containing 274 inhabitants, of whom 202 are in the township of Crosby-Garrett. This parish, which comprises the townships of Crosby-Garrett and Little Musgrave, separated by the intervening chapelry of Soulby, is bounded on the north-east by the river Eden, and on the south-west by a lofty verdant hill, called Crosby Fell. The village is situated at the foot of the Fell, in a deep and romantic valley. The living is a discharged rectory, valued in the king's books at £19. 4. 4½.; net income, £122; patron, William Crawford, Esq., lord of the manor. The church, which occupies an eminence overlooking the village, is a spacious and venerable structure, containing portions of the Norman style.

CROSBY, GREAT, a chapelry, in the parish of SEFTON, union and hundred of WEST DERBY, S. division of the county of LANCASTER, 6 miles (N. by W.) from Liverpool; containing, in the year 1846, 2194 inhabitants.

Among the families early connected with Great Crosby, were those of De Aynosdale, Molyneux, Ferrers, and De Walton, of whom Robert De Walton took the name of Blundell, and was ancestor of the Blundells of Little Crosby, and the Blundells of Ince-Blundell. William Blundell, Esq., is now lord of the manor and principal proprietor. The chapelry comprises 2066 acres, whereof 561 are common land or waste. The population has very considerably increased within the last thirty years. The living is a perpetual curacy, in the patronage of the Rector of Sefton; income, £200. The chapel, dedicated to St. Luke, is a brick building with a tower, re-erected in 1774, and enlarged in 1847, at a cost of £250. The tithes have been commuted for £280. A Roman Catholic chapel dedicated to St. Peter was built in 1826: the Rev. William Brown was the first appointed priest, and still officiates. The grammar school here was founded in 1620, by John Harrison, merchant of London, a native of the township, and has an endowment of £50 a year, and a house and garden; the mastership is in the gift of the Merchant Taylors' Company, London, and the present head master is the Rev. Joseph Clark, appointed in 1829: the school is a good building of freestone. A school for girls, founded under the will of Catherine Halsall, is endowed with lands of the value annually of £40. Here is a spring, called St. Michael's.

CROSBY, LITTLE, a township, in the parish of SEFTON, union and hundred of WEST DERBY, S. division of the county of LANCASTER, 7¾ miles (N. by W.) from Liverpool; containing 394 inhabitants. Paganus de Villers was the first lord of Little Crosby, which, in the reign of Stephen, came by marriage to the family of De Molines. The daughter of Sir John, or Sir William, Molyneux was married to David Blundell (living in the reign of Edward I.), and thus conveyed the manor into that family. Nicholas Blundell died in 1737, leaving two daughters; the surviving one married Henry Pepard, Esq., of Drogheda, and upon her death in 1772, Nicholas, the then eldest son, took the name of Blundell. William Blundell, Esq., is now lord of the manor, and owner of the township, which comprises 1740 acres, and of which the surface is level, with a light sandy soil. His seat, Crosby Hall, was built by his ancestors in 1500, and has since been altered and improved at various times, a portion bearing the date 1647; the park is gracefully laid out, and well wooded, and among the trees the laurel is unique. Mr. Blundell served the office of high sheriff of Lancashire in 1838. The tithes have been commuted for £196. 10. The Roman Catholic chapel here, dedicated to the Blessed Virgin, was rebuilt in 1847, at the sole cost of Mr. Blundell, amounting to £2500; it is a handsome structure of stone, in the early English style, with a tower surmounted by a spire. The interior is richly ornamented: the windows are of painted glass, with the arms of the benefactors; and the east window, of stained glass, by Barnett, of York, represents Our Lady and Child in the centre, with St. William and St. Catherine on the right and left. The roof contains the Litany of Loretto; and the chancel arch is a fresco painting, by Nicholas Blundell, Esq., of the Day of Judgment. The priest has a house, nine acres of land, and an annuity charged upon the estate. A school, built on land given by Mr. Blundell, is supported by subscription. At Harkirk, an ancient burial-ground, a number of Saxon and other ancient coins, of which à print is preserved in the British Museum, were found in April, 1611 ; and in 1847 were discovered the remains of an arched window.

CROSBY-RAVENSWORTH (St. Lawrence), a parish, in West ward and union, county of Westmorland, 4 miles (N. by E.) from Orton ; containing, with the townships of Mauld's-Meaburn, Reagill, and part of Birbeck-Fells, 909 inhabitants, of whom 323 are in the township of Crosby-Ravensworth. The parish comprises 8942a. 3r. 19p. of inclosed land, whereof 3399 acres are in Crosby-Ravensworth township. It is celebrated for its breed of hogs ; the hams are noted for their peculiarly fine flavour. Limestone is quarried extensively. The village is situated in a fertile valley, watered by the rivers Birbeck and Lyvennet, which latter has its source at a place called Black Dub, where Charles II. halted with his Scottish army. The living is a discharged vicarage, valued in the king's books at £7. 13. 14.; net income, £150; patrons, the family of Howard ; impropriator, the Earl of Lonsdale : the glebe consists of 28 acres, with a glebe-house. The church, a handsome structure with a tower, was built in 1814 : near it stands the ancient manorial mansion, a tower-building embosomed in trees, and formerly moated. A school was founded and endowed by the Rev. William Willan, in 1630 : the schoolroom was rebuilt in 1784, by William Dent, Esq., who, with others, raised the income to £30. Another school is partly supported by an endowment of £25 per annum, accruing from land ; and a third, for females, is endowed with £6 per annum. On the eastern side of Black Dub is a heap of stones, called Penhurrock, probably a tumulus of the Britons.

CROSBY-UPON-EDEN (St. John), a parish, in the union of Carlisle, Eskdale ward, E. division of Cumberland, 4 miles (N. E. by E.) from Carlisle ; containing 403 inhabitants, of whom 146 are in the township of High Crosby, and 133 in that of Low Crosby. This place is supposed to have derived its name from an ancient cross, to which, in the time of Henry I., the inhabitants resorted for prayer, previously to the erection of the present church on its site. The parish is finely situated on the river Eden, by which it is bounded for nearly three miles, and is intersected by the military road from Newcastle to Carlisle ; the southern portion forms part of the fertile vale of Eden, and towards the north the surface rises to a considerable elevation, commanding extensive and richly varied prospects. Freestone of a reddish colour, and of a fine compact texture, is obtained in the neighbourhood. The living is a discharged vicarage, valued in the king's books at £3. 11.5½.; net income, £100; patron and appropriator, the Bishop of Carlisle. The church, situated in the village of Low Crosby, is a small ancient edifice. An additional church has been erected ; and a national school, built in 1806, is supported by subscription. In the northern part of the parish, the sites of the Roman wall built by Severus, and of the ditch by Adrian, are plainly discernible.

CROSCOMBE (St. Mary), a parish, and formerly a market-town, in the union of Shepton-Mallet, hundred of Whitestone, E. division of Somerset, 3 miles (S. E.) from Wells ; containing 804 inhabitants. The parish comprises by admeasurement 1436 acres, and is watered by a small river, which in its course turns several mills, whereof two are for grinding corn, one for winding silk, and another used as a stocking manu-
735

factory. A market was granted by Edward I. ; it has been long discontinued, but there is a fair on Lady-day. The living is a discharged rectory, valued in the king's books at £12. 6. 10½., and in the patronage of five Trustees : the tithes have been commuted for £200, and the glebe comprises 15 acres, with a glebe-house. The church is beautifully situated, and is a handsome edifice in the later English style, having a tower surmounted by a good spire; the pews are of carved oak. There is a place of worship for Particular Baptists, near which stands an ancient cross, fourteen feet high. In the vicinity are to be seen vestiges of a Roman encampment, called Mashury Castle.

CROSS, a tything, in the parish of Portbury, union of Bedminster, hundred of Portbury, E. division of Somersetshire ; containing 98 inhabitants.

CROSS, St., Hampshire.—See Winchester.

CROSSCRAKE.—See Stainton.

CROSSENS, a hamlet, in the parish of North Meols, union of Ormskirk, hundred of West Derby, S. division of Lancashire, 3½ miles (N. E.) from Southport; containing 582 inhabitants. The surface here is generally level ; the soil is various, much of it of good quality, and chiefly arable. The village is prettily situated on slightly rising ground, at the mouth of the Ribble ; the population principally consists of farmers, labourers, and hand-loom weavers. A church (St. John's) was erected in 1837, for the accommodation of the inhabitants, and those of the adjoining hamlet of Banks, which has a population of 840 ; it is a neat structure with a tower. The living is a perpetual curacy, in the patronage of Trustees; there is a parsonage house. A good national school has been established ; and at Banks is another national school, in which divine service is performed by the minister of Crossens.

CROSSLAND, North and South, in the parish of Almondbury, union of Huddersfield, Upper division of the wapentake of Agbrigg, W. riding of York, 3 miles (S. W.) from Huddersfield ; containing 2826 inhabitants. The scenery in this neighbourhood is beautifully varied, consisting to a great extent of hill and dale, and the soil is rich and fertile. The chapelry of South Crossland comprises by measurement 1840 acres, of which about 250 are arable, 1100 meadow and pasture, 290 woodland, and 192 common : stone of excellent quality is extensively quarried. The manufacture of woollen-cloth is carried on to a considerable extent. The chapel, lately made a district church, was erected in 1828, with lancet windows and a tower, at the expense of £2321, by the Commissioners for Building Additional Churches ; it is dedicated to the Holy Trinity, and contains 650 sittings, of which 300 are free. The living is a perpetual curacy, in the gift of the Vicar of Almondbury, with a net income of £150.

CROSSTONE, a chapelry, in the parish and union of Halifax, wapentake of Morley, W. riding of York, 11½ miles (W.) from Halifax ; containing 11,685 inhabitants. This place, which derives its name from an old cross, now fallen to decay, comprises the townships of Stansfield and Langfield, and is intersected by the Manchester and Leeds railway ; the surface is mountainous, and the scenery romantic. The population is largely employed in the cotton and worsted manufactures. The living is a perpetual curacy, in the gift of the Vicar of Halifax, with a net income of £150 : the chapel, or district church, was rebuilt in the early English style in 1836, at a cost of £3000, defrayed by the Church Commissioners, and contains 1030 sittings, of which 430 are free, and 405 appropriated to different farms.

CROSS-WAY-HAND, an extra-parochial district, in the union of OUNDLE, hundred of WILLYBROOK, N. division of the county of NORTHAMPTON, 4 miles (N. W.) from Oundle; containing 8 inhabitants, and comprising 849 acres of land.

CROSTHWAITE (ST. KENTIGERN), a parish, in the union of COCKERMOUTH, ALLERDALE ward below Derwent, W. division of CUMBERLAND, ½ a mile (N. by W.) from Keswick; containing 4759 inhabitants, and comprising the townships of Borrowdale, Braithwaite, Coledale, Newlands, Thornthwaite, St. John's Castlerigg with Wythburn, Keswick, and Underskiddaw. This parish comprises 28,000 acres, of which 18,800 are common or waste; it produces copper and lead ores, with plumbago or black-lead, and abounds with interesting objects, noticed in the article on Keswick. The living is a vicarage, valued in the king's books at £50. 8. 11½.; net income, £312; patron, the Bishop of Carlisle; impropriators, Sir John B. Walsh, Bart., and others. The church, an ancient fabric, was roofed with slate in 1812, having been previously covered with lead: here lies buried the poet Southey, on whose monument is an inscription by the laureate Wordsworth. Adjoining the churchyard is a free school, founded and endowed prior to 1571' and having an income of about £100 per annum. There are separate incumbencies at Borrowdale, Newlands, Thornthwaite, St. John's Castlerigg, Wythburn, and Keswick. Two saline springs here were formerly in great repute among the inhabitants.

CROSTHWAITE, a parochial chapelry, in the parish of HEVERSHAM, union and ward of KENDAL, county of WESTMORLAND, 4 miles (W. S. W.) from Kendal; containing, with the constablewick of Lyth, 717 inhabitants. This extensive chapelry is bounded on the southwest by the mountainous ridge called Lyth Fell, or Whitbarrow Scar. The village of Churchton, near the chapel, is small, but neatly built, and is situated in a picturesque and fertile vale. The manufacture of paper is carried on to a moderate extent, and there are a malting establishment and a corn-mill: in the hamlet of Raw are several limekilns; and at Pool-bank is a manufactory of wooden-hoops. The living is a perpetual curacy; net income, £113. The chapel, dedicated to the Virgin Mary, and rebuilt in 1813, at the expense of the landholders, is beautifully situated. George Cocke, in 1665, bequeathed £60 for a school; and the endowment arising from the bequest, augmented by the interest of £300 bequeathed by Tobias Atkinson in 1817, and £13 out of a general fund, now amounts to £37 per annum. In Lyth Moss several large trees have been discovered beneath the surface.

CROSTON (ST. MICHAEL), a parish, and formerly a market-town, in the unions of CHORLEY and WIGAN, hundred of LEYLAND, N. division of the county of LANCASTER; containing, with the townships of Bispham, Bretherton, Mawdesley, and Ulnes-Walton, 3939 inhabitants, of whom 1456 are in the township of Croston, 6½ miles (W.) from Chorley. In the third year of King John, 1201, Nicholas Pincerna, or Butler, is recorded as rendering "an account of 100s. in the town of Croston, for three parts of the year," probably the chief rent

of his possessions; and at a very early date several other considerable families held lands here, among whom were the Fittons, Heskeths, and Ashtons. In a recent year the manor became the property, in moieties, of the Traffords, and of Thomas Norris, Esq., the latter by purchase of the Hesketh moiety about 1825. Croston anciently formed one of the most extensive and valuable benefices in the county; and for many ages the limits of the parish remained unaltered; but, at various periods since, it has been divided, by authority of parliament, into six independent parishes, viz.: Croston; Hoole,' separated in 1642; Chorley, and Rufford, detached in 1793; and Tarleton, and Hesketh with Becconsall, detached in 1821.

The length of the parish is about eight miles, and its breadth four; the township of Croston comprises 2273 acres. The river Douglas forms the western boundary of the parish, discharging its stream into the estuary of the Ribble at Hesketh Bank, on the north; the Yarrow bounds the village of Croston on the south and southwest, and is joined by the Lostock half a mile below it. From the point of confluence of the Douglas and the Yarrow to the estuary of the Ribble, these waters are sometimes known by the name of the Asland, and are navigable, though they are not navigated. The market has fallen into disuse; but there is a cattle-fair on the Monday before Shrove-Tuesday. The LIVING consists of a rectory and a vicarage, valued in the king's books at £31. 11. 10½.; patron, the Rev. Robert Mosley Master. The tithes have been commuted for £250; and the glebe contains 232 acres, with a glebe-house. The church stands upon the margin of the river Yarrow, and consists of a nave, aisles, chancel, and two chapels, with a strong tower, castellated, and adorned with pinnacles; the chancel, the roof of which is arched, is divided from the nave by a tall screen of ornamented oak: the font has the date 1663. This edifice was restored in 1743, at an expense of £1834, defrayed by a brief. At Bretherton and Mawdesley are separate incumbencies. The Rev. James Hiet, in 1660, built a school in the churchyard (rebuilt in 1827), and endowed it with £400; and a school of industry was established in 1802, to which Elizabeth Master in 1809 bequeathed £200.

CROSTWICK (ST. PETER), a parish, in the union of ST. FAITH'S, hundred of TAVERHAM, E. division of NORFOLK, 5 miles (N. N. E.) from Norwich; containing 147 inhabitants. It comprises 690a. 3r. 7p., of which 600 acres are arable, 52 pasture and home-stalls, 8 plantation, and 30 common. The living is a discharged rectory, valued in the king's books at £2. 17. 6., and in the gift of the Bishop of Norwich: the tithes have been commuted for £190, and the glebe comprises 4 acres.

CROSTWIGHT (ALL SAINTS), a parish, in the TUNSTEAD and HAPPING incorporation, hundred of TUNSTEAD, E. division of NORFOLK, 3½ miles (E. by S.) from North Walsham; containing 69 inhabitants. It comprises 777 acres, of which 481 are arable, and 66 common or waste. The living is a discharged rectory, valued in the king's books at £5. 6. 8., and in the gift of M. Shephard, Esq.: the tithes have been commuted for £150, and the glebe comprises 12 acres. Near the Hall, considerable remains are to be seen of the ancient manor-house, occupied by a branch of the Walpole family, the heiress of which married an ancestor of Lord Cholmondeley, by whom the estate was sold.

CROUCH-END, a hamlet, in the parish of HORNSEY, union of EDMONTON, Finsbury division of the hundred of OSSULSTONE, county of MIDDLESEX, 5 miles (N. by W.) from London. This agreeable hamlet is situated on the road from London to the village of Hornsey, in a neighbourhood embellished with beautiful scenery, and consisting of the rich pasture and meadow for which the northern environs of the metropolis are remarkable.

CROUGHTON, a township, in the parish of ST. OSWALD, CHESTER, union of GREAT BOUGHTON, Higher division of the hundred of WIRRALL, S. division of the county of CHESTER, 4½ miles (N. by E.) from Chester; containing 27 inhabitants. It comprises 271 acres, of a clayey soil. The Ellesmere canal passes through the township.

CROUGHTON (ALL SAINTS), a parish, in the union of BRACKLEY, hundred of KING'S-SUTTON, S. division of the county of NORTHAMPTON, 4 miles (S. W.) from Brackley; containing 472 inhabitants. This place, which forms the most southern parish in the county, and is bounded on the south by a part of Oxfordshire, comprises by admeasurement 2200 acres, whereof about 100 are pasture, and the rest arable, with 30 acres of plantation. It is crossed from east to west by the road between Buckingham and Deddington. The living is a rectory, valued in the king's books at £15. 3. 6½.; net income, £324; patron, Viscount Ashbrook. The tithes were commuted for land and a money payment in 1807. Dr. John Friend, the learned author of the History of Physic, was born here in 1675.

CROWAN (ST. CREWENNE), a parish, in the union of HELSTON, E. division of the hundred of PENWITH, W. division of CORNWALL, 6 miles (N. by W.) from Helston; containing 4638 inhabitants. The parish contains several copper-mines, of which the principal, called Binner-Downs, affords employment to 780 persons. Clowance, the seat of the family of St. Aubyn, is in the parish. A fair for cattle is held at the village of Penge. The living is a vicarage, valued in the king's books at £11. 9. 2.; patron and impropriator, the Rev. H. M. St. Aubyn: the great tithes have been commuted for £490, and the vicarial for £470; the glebe contains 40 acres, with a glebe-house. The church was beautified in 1832, when 190 additional sittings were provided; it has several handsome monuments of the St. Aubyn family. There are places of worship for Wesleyans and Bryanites; and a spacious schoolroom erected at an expense of £1000, by the late Sir John St. Aubyn. From Crowan Beacon, a heap of stones of a conical form, and probably a cairn, are fine views of the surrounding country. Near the farms of Tregear and Drym are slight remains of an encampment; at Burneston are vestiges of an ancient chapel; and on the Barton of Boletto is a singular spot called Hangman's Barrow.

CROWBOROUGH.—See BLACKWOOD.

CROWCOMBE (HOLY TRINITY), a parish, in the union of WILLITON, hundred of WILLITON and FREE-MANNERS, W. division of SOMERSET, 10 miles (N. W. by N.) from Taunton; containing, with the hamlet of Flaxpool, 673 inhabitants. This parish is situated on the road from Taunton to Minehead, and comprises 3177 acres, of which 683 are common or waste land: the surface is finely varied, and the hills command an extensive view of the greater part of Somersetshire, the Bristol Channel, and the Welsh coast. Some veins of copper

have been found in the sides of the Quantock hills, and in the churchyard; and coal is supposed to exist in the western portion of the parish. Stone is quarried for building, and for burning into lime. The place was formerly of greater importance than it is at present; it was a borough, and the inhabitants enjoyed various privileges: a portreeve is still annually chosen at the court leet of the lord of the manor. At the entrance of the village is an ancient cross, in good preservation. A weekly market was granted in the reign of Henry III., and three annual fairs were once held; but the market has been long discontinued, and of the fairs, only one is held, on the 31st of October. The living is a rectory, valued in the king's books at £32. 14. 4½.; patron, Robert Harvey, Esq. The church is an ancient edifice, built of hewn stone, and having a tower surmounted by an octagonal spire, which was struck down by lightning in 1723, and repaired at a cost of £231: the interior was neatly fitted up in 1534, with well carved oak; and the north aisle, a handsome addition to the original structure, was built by the Carews, to whom there are several fine monuments. Fragments of a cross are visible in the churchyard, and opposite to the church are the remains of another. Thomas Carew, in 1733, founded and endowed a school, of which the income amounts to £41; and there is another, supported by a bequest by the Rev. Dr. James, with which land was purchased, now yielding about £12 annually: they are on the national system. In the vicinity of the courthouse is a spring which ebbs and flows with the tide. Near the village is some land called the Field of Battle, where an engagement is said to have taken place during Monmouth's rebellion.

CROWELL (ST. MARY), a parish, in the union of THAME, hundred of LEWKNOR, county of OXFORD, 5 miles (E. S. E.) from Tetsworth; containing 169 inhabitants. It is situated at the foot of the Chiltern hills, and comprises 987 acres, of which three-fourths are arable, and the remainder woodland, with 62 acres of common or waste: the soil on the hill is chalky, and on the low lands light. The living is a rectory, valued in the king's books at £7. 9. 9¾., and in the patronage of Baroness Wenman: the tithes have been commuted for £240, and the glebe consists of 9½ acres, with a glebe-house. The Roman Ikeneld-street passes through the parish.

CROWFIELD, a chapelry, in the parish of COD-DENHAM, union and hundred of BOSMERE and CLAYDON, E. division of SUFFOLK, 6 miles (E. N. E.) from Needham-Market; containing 385 inhabitants. It is situated near the road from Ipswich to Debenham. The living is annexed to the vicarage of Coddenham; impropriator, Sir W. F. F. Middleton, Bart. The chapel is dedicated to All Saints.

CROWHURST (ST. GEORGE), a parish, in the union of GODSTONE, First division of the hundred of TAND-RIDGE, E. division of SURREY, 4 miles (S. E.) from Godstone; containing 350 inhabitants. It is crossed by the Dovor railway, and comprises by computation 2000 acres, of which 1150 are arable, and 780 meadow and pasture. The living is a perpetual curacy; net income, £65; patron and impropriator, George Rush, Esq., whose tithes have been commuted for £261. 7., and who has a glebe of nearly 2 acres. The church is in the early style, with a tower and spire; in the interior are

several brasses to the Gaynsfords and others, and the
windows contain remains of stained glass. According
to tradition, Henry VIII., on his way to Anna Boleyn at
Hever Castle, visited Crowhurst Place, formerly the seat
of the Gaynsfords, an old mansion surrounded by a
moat.

CROWHURST (St. George), a parish, in the union
of Battle, hundred of Baldslow, rape of Hastings,
E. division of Sussex, 2¾ miles (S.) from Battle; containing 326 inhabitants. This parish is beautifully diversified with hill and dale: about 70 acres are planted with
hops. The chief substrata are limestone, sandstone, and
ironstone, which last is abundant, and was formerly
wrought extensively, and smelted: there are some pow-
der-mills in the parish. The village is in a picturesque
valley, in which also the church forms a pleasing feature.
The living is a rectory, valued in the king's books at £10,
and in the gift of T. Papillon, Esq.: the tithes have been
commuted for £253, and the glebe comprises 24 acres,
with a glebe-house. The church, the nave of which was
rebuilt in 1794, is a handsome structure in the early and
decorated English styles, with a square embattled tower:
in the churchyard is a fine yew-tree, measuring 27 feet
in girth at a height of four feet from the ground. Near
the church are some interesting remains of a religious
house; the chapel is still in tolerable preservation.

CROWLAND, or Croyland (St. Bartholomew and
St. Guthlac), a parish, and formerly a market-town,
in the union of Peterborough, wapentake of Elloe,
parts of Holland, county of Lincoln, 8 miles (N. by
E.) from Peterborough, and 89 (N.) from London; containing 2973 inhabitants. During the heptarchy this
place was the retreat of St. Guthlac, who in the reign
of Cenred, eighth king of Mercia, retired from the persecution of the pagan Britons into a hermitage, near
which Ethelbald, in 716, founded a Benedictine monastery to the honour of St. Mary, St. Bartholomew, and
St. Guthlac. He endowed it with a considerable sum
of money; with "the whole island of Croyland, formed
by the four waters of *Shepishea* on the east, *Nena* on the
west, *Southea* on the south, and *Asendyk* on the north;
with a portion of the adjoining marshes; and with the
fishery of the Nene and Welland." This monastery,
which, from the marshy nature of the soil, was built
upon a foundation of piles, having been destroyed by
the Danes in 870, was rebuilt by King Edred in the
year 948. In 1091 it was by an accidental fire reduced
to a heap of ruins, from which, under the influence of
its abbot, who granted a plenary indulgence to such as
should contribute to its restoration, it was again rebuilt,
in 1112; but the whole was destroyed by a like cause
about forty years afterwards. It was a third time restored, with increased splendour; and continued to flourish till the Dissolution, when its revenue was £1217.
5. 11. The conventual buildings, which, from neglect,
were gradually falling to decay, were almost entirely
demolished during the parliamentary war, when the
monastery was occupied as a garrison.

The town, which is accessible only by artificial roads,
consists chiefly of four streets, separated by water-
courses, and communicating with each other by means
of an ancient triangular stone bridge of singular construction, erected in the reign of Edward II. The bridge
has one principal and finely groined arch, from which
diverge three pointed arches over the streams Welland,

738

here are places of worship for Independents and Wesleyans; and a school with an endowment in land producing £42 per annum. In 1747, the body of a woman was found in an erect position in the peat moor near the town; it appeared to have been there for several centuries.

CROWLE (St. John the Baptist), a parish, in the union of Droitwich, partly in the Upper division of the hundred of Halfshire, but chiefly in the Middle division of that of Oswaldslow, Worcester and W. divisions of the county of Worcester, 5 miles (E.) from Worcester; containing 526 inhabitants. This place is situated in a district abounding with picturesque scenery; the approach from Worcester is by a beautiful range of hills, forming an amphitheatre, and commanding extensive prospects. The parish comprises 1690a.2r.25p., of which two-thirds are arable, and the remainder pasture, with 100 acres of woodland; the soil is a strong rich clay: on the south side are extensive quarries of blue lias, which burns into excellent lime. About 100 persons are employed in the manufacture of gloves. The rivulet Bow skirts the parish on the east, and falls into the Avon near Pershore; the Worcester and Birmingham canal passes within a mile, and the Spetchley station of the Gloucester and Birmingham railroad is within two miles. Crowle Court, the interior of which shows it to have been a religious house, is a very ancient edifice, surrounded by a deep moat. The living is a vicarage, valued in the king's books at £16; net income, £306; patron and incumbent, the Rev. Edwin Crane, M.A.; impropriator, George Farley, Esq. The tithes were commuted for land in 1806; the glebe consists of about 180 acres, with a glebe-house. The church is an ancient structure with a square tower, and contains a lectern of carved stone, of the reign of Rufus. A parochial school is supported by subscription.

CROWLEY, a township, in the parish of Great Budworth, union of Runcorn, hundred of Bucklow, N. division of the county of Chester, 6¾ miles (N.) from Northwich; containing 175 inhabitants. It comprises 1375 acres, of which 22 are common or waste land. Crowley Lodge, a neat brick edifice, was formerly a seat of the Pickering family.

CROWMARSH-BATTLE, a hamlet, in the parish of Bensington, union of Wallingford, hundred of Ewelme, county of Oxford; with 93 inhabitants.

CROWMARSH-GIFFORD (St. Mary Magdalene), a parish, in the union and parliamentary borough of Wallingford, hundred of Langtree, county of Oxford, ½ a mile (E.) from Wallingford; containing 330 inhabitants. The living is a rectory, valued in the king's books at £12. 6. 0½., and in the gift of the Trustees of Dr. Barrington, late Bishop of Durham: the tithes have been commuted for £247, and the glebe consists of one acre. The church is a small Norman edifice, with two circular windows at the west end. In the parish are some remains of fortifications, supposed to have been raised by Stephen, either in 1139, when he besieged the Empress Matilda in Wallingford Castle, or in 1153, when he laid siege to that town.

CROWNTHORPE (St. James), a parish, in the incorporation and hundred of Forehoe, E. division of Norfolk, 2 miles (N. W. by W.) from Wymondham; containing 111 inhabitants. It comprises 685 acres, of which 462 are arable, 154 pasture, and 68 wood; the

common land was inclosed in 1777. The living is a discharged rectory, valued in the king's books at £4. 12. 6., and in the gift of Lord Wodehouse: the tithes have been commuted for £145, and the glebe contains 16 acres.

CROWTON, a township, in the parish of Weaverham, union of Northwich, Second division of the hundred of Eddisbury, S. division of the county of Chester, 5¼ miles (W. by N.) from Northwich; containing 454 inhabitants, and comprising 1250 acres. The soil is partly clay and partly sand. The river Weaver bounds the township on the north.

CROXALL (St. John the Baptist), a parish, in the union of Tamworth, partly in the N. division of the hundred of Offlow and of the county of Stafford, and partly in the hundred of Repton and Gresley, S. division of the county of Derby, 7½ miles (N.) from Tamworth; containing, with the township of Catton, in Derby, and that of Oakley, in Stafford, 258 inhabitants. It comprises 3219 acres, in about equal portions of arable and pasture, with hedge-row timber; the surface is undulated, the soil rich, and the scenery picturesque. The village lies on the east side of the Mease, a tributary to the Trent. The Birmingham and Derby railway crosses the Thame and Trent near their junction in the parish, by a viaduct a quarter of a mile in length, supported on piles driven fifteen feet below the bed of those rivers. The living is a vicarage, endowed with the rectorial tithes of Oakley, valued in the king's books at £5, and in the patronage of the Crown; net income, £499; impropriators of the remainder of the rectorial tithes, the family of Princeps. The tithes of the township of Croxall have been commuted for £180 payable to the vicar, and £159 payable to the impropriators: the vicar has a glebe of one acre. The church is a very ancient edifice, and contains many monuments to the Curzon and Horton families. There is a school in union with the National Society.

CROXBY (All Saints), a parish, in the union of Caistor, S. division of the wapentake of Walshcroft, parts of Lindsey, county of Lincoln, 5¼ miles (E. S. E.) from Caistor; containing 106 inhabitants. The parish is situated on the road between Caistor and Louth, and comprises about 1500 acres; the soil is heathy on the hills by which the surface is diversified, and there are some fine plantations. In the western portion of the parish is a large sheet of water, abounding with carp, tench, eels, and perch. The living is a discharged rectory, valued in the king's books at £6. 4. 2., and in the patronage of the Crown: the tithes have been commuted for a yearly rent-charge of £310, and the glebe comprises 12 acres.

CROXDALE, a chapelry, partly in the parish of Merrington, and partly in the parish of St. Oswald, Durham, union of Durham, S. division of Easington ward, N. division of the county of Durham, 3½ miles (S. by W.) from Durham; containing, with the township of Hett, 494 inhabitants. The manor came into the possession of the Salvin family prior to 1474, and has ever since continued in their hands. Here flows a small rivulet called Croxdale beck, the channel of which is a romantic dell of great depth and narrowness. A cross erected at this place gave name to the adjoining lands. The living is a perpetual curacy, endowed with the rectorial tithes; patrons, the Dean and Chapter of Durham.

5 B 2

The chapel, dedicated to the Holy Cross, is now a district church. There is a private Roman Catholic chapel at the Hall.

CROXDEN (ST. GILES), a parish, in the union of UTTOXETER, S. division of the hundred of TOTMONSLOW, N. division of the county of STAFFORD, 4 miles (E. S. E.) from Cheadle; containing, with part of Calton chapelry, 293 inhabitants. It comprises by admeasurement 2588 acres, of which 1638 are grass land, 480 arable, 270 wood and plantations, and 200 common; and has a number of scattered farmhouses and cottages. The village lies in a narrow but fertile vale, watered by the Peake rivulet. The living is a perpetual curacy; net income, £92; patron, the Earl of Macclesfield. The church is a small decayed building, with a wooden belfry. Bertram de Verdun, in 1176, gave the monks of Aulney, in Normandy, a piece of land at Chotes or Chotene (probably Cotton) to build a Cistercian abbey, which three years afterwards was removed to Croxden, where he and his family were buried. It was dedicated to the Blessed Virgin, and at the general dissolution had an abbot and twelve religious, whose revenue was valued at £103. 6. 7. The remains of this once stately and sumptuous edifice exhibit good specimens of the early English style.

CROXTETH-PARK, an extra-parochial liberty, in the union and hundred of WEST DERBY, S. division of LANCASHIRE, 4 miles (W. N. W.) from Prescot. This place anciently belonged to Robert Fitz-Henry, ancestor of the family of Lathom. It came subsequently into the possession of Edmund, Earl of Lancaster, son of Henry III., and remained in the crown until 1446, when Henry VI. by letters-patent granted Croxteth to Sir Richard Molyneux, whose descendants, now represented by the Earl of Sefton, have ever since held the property. There are few dwellings in the liberty; the area of which is 953 acres. A tributary of the little river Alt bounds it, and flows through the park attached to Croxteth Hall: the road from Liverpool to St. Helen's passes on the south. The Hall, erected in 1702, and situated in the adjoining district parish of West Derby, is of brick, with stone dressings, and has a terrace in front, ascended by a broad flight of steps: the back part, formerly of wood and plaster, was rebuilt in 1805 of brick. There is a stone-quarry. The tithes of the liberty have been commuted for £152.

CROXTON (ST. JAMES), a parish, in the union of CAXTON and ARRINGTON, hundred of LONGSTOW, county of CAMBRIDGE, 3½ miles (W. N. W.) from Caxton; containing 264 inhabitants. The parish is situated on the road from Cambridge to Oxford, and its general appearance is flat; it comprises by computation 2000 acres of land, the soil of which is clayey and cold, but produces good crops of wheat. Croxton Park contains 150 acres of land, with a handsome residence. The living is a rectory, valued in the king's books at £14. 8. 6½.; net income, £185; patron, Samuel Newton, Esq. The tithes were commuted for land in 1811; the glebe comprises 347 acres, including 310 given as the allotment, and there is a glebe-house. The church, which is elegantly fitted up, has been extensively repaired by the patron. Edward Leeds, founder of the celebrated Leeds family, was buried here; he was vice-chancellor of Cambridge university, and master of Clare Hall, about the year 1540.

CROXTON, a township, in the parish of MIDDLEWICH, union and hundred of NORTHWICH, S. division of the county of CHESTER, 1 mile (N. N. W.) from Middlewich; containing 48 inhabitants. It comprises 523 acres, of which the soil is sand and clay. The Grand Trunk canal passes in the vicinity.

CROXTON (ST. JOHN THE EVANGELIST), a parish, in the union of GLANDFORD-BRIGG, E. division of the wapentake of YARBOROUGH, parts of LINDSEY, county of LINCOLN, 7 miles (N. E. by E.) from Glandford-Brigg; containing 105 inhabitants. It comprises 1476a. 1r. 1p., of which about 1194 acres are arable, 179 meadow and pasture, and 103 woodland. The living is a discharged rectory, valued in the king's books at £5. 14. 2., and in the patronage of the Crown, with a net income of £358: the tithes were commuted for land in 1809. Upon a lofty eminence about half a mile westward of the village, are the remains of a large intrenchment called Yarborough Camp, supposed, from the discovery of coins, to be a Roman work.

CROXTON, a chapelry, in the parish of FULMODESTON, union of WALSINGHAM, hundred of GALLOW, W. division of NORFOLK, 4 miles (E. by N.) from Fakenham; containing 68 inhabitants. The chapel is dedicated to St. John the Baptist.

CROXTON (ALL SAINTS), a parish, in the union of THETFORD, hundred of GRIMSHOE, W. division of NORFOLK, 2 miles (N.) from Thetford; containing 330 inhabitants. There is an extensive rabbit-warren. The living is a discharged vicarage, valued in the king's books at £6. 13. 4.; net income, £98; patrons and impropriators, the Master and Fellows of Christ's College, Cambridge. The tithes were commuted for land in 1813; the glebe consists of 32 acres. The church is in the decorated style; the lower part of the tower is circular, and the upper part octagonal: the south aisle was removed more than half a century since. There is a place of worship for Wesleyans.

CROXTON, a township, in the parish of ECCLESHALL, union of STONE, N. division of the hundred of PIREHILL and of the county of STAFFORD, 3¾ miles (N. W. by W.) from Eccleshall; containing 887 inhabitants. The village, which is large, lies on the road from Eccleshall to Nantwich. Tithe rent-charges have been awarded amounting to £371. 16.

CROXTON-KEYRIAL (ST. JOHN), a parish, in the union of GRANTHAM, hundred of FRAMLAND, N. division of the county of LEICESTER, 7 miles (S. W.) from Grantham; containing 650 inhabitants. It is the property of the dukes of Rutland, of whose ancient mansion there are some remains, situated in a park in which races are celebrated at Easter. The living is a discharged vicarage, valued in the king's books at £7. 14. 7.; net income, £206; patron and impropriator, the Duke of Rutland: the tithes were commuted for land in 1766. The church is a very handsome structure in the later English style, with a tower rising from the centre. William Smith in 1711 bequeathed land, producing a rent of £11. 8., for which children are taught. W. Rymington left an estate, now worth £120 per annum, to the poor of this and three other parishes; G. Ashburne, a rent-charge of £15 to poor parishioners; and Anna Parnham, £300 for the poor, and £200 for the free school. Croxton Abbey was founded in 1162, by William Porcarius de Linus, for Præmonstratensian canons, whose evenue at the Dissolution was valued at £458. 19. 11. : one of the abbots was physician to King John, whose bowels were interred in the church.

CROXTON, SOUTH (*St. John the Baptist*), a parish, in the union of BARROW-UPON-SOAR, hundred of EAST GOSCOTE, N. division of the county of LEICESTER, 9¼ miles (N. E. by E.) from Leicester ; containing 297 inhabitants. It comprises 1400 acres, of which about 400 are arable, and 10 woodland. The living is a dis-charged rectory, valued in the king's books at £8. 3. 4. ; net income, £130 ; patron, the Duke of Rutland.

CROYDON (*All Saints*), a parish, in the union of CAXTON and ARRINGTON, hundred of ARMINGFORD, county of CAMBRIDGE, 6 miles (S. by E.) from Caxton ; including the ancient parish of Clapton, and containing 441 inhabitants. It is situated on the road from Royston to Huntingdon, and comprises by measurement 2711 acres. The living is a discharged vicarage, endowed with part of the rectorial tithes, with the rectory of Clap-ton consolidated, and valued in the king's books at £7. 9. 7. ; patron and impropriator of the remainder of the rectorial tithes, J. F. Gape, Esq. The rectory of Clapton is valued in the king's books at £4. 9. 7. The incumbent's tithes have been commuted for £531, and there is a glebe-house, with 10 acres of land. Some re-mains are visible of a mansion of the Downing family, many members of which were buried in a vault under the church. Sir George Downing, Bart., of Gamlingay, was the founder of Downing College, Cambridge, for which he left nearly 1800 acres of land in this parish.

CROYDON (*St. John the Baptist*), a market-town and parish, and the head of a union, in the First division of the hundred of WALLINGTON, E. division of SURREY, 9½ miles (S.) from London; containing, with part of Norwood, 16,712 inhabitants. This place, called by Camden *Cradeden*, and in ancient records *Croindene* and *Croiden*, derives its present name from *Croie*, chalk, and *Dune*, a hill, denoting its situation on the summit of an extensive basin of chalk. By some antiquaries it has been identified with the *Noviomagus* of Antonine ; and the Roman road, from Arundel to London, which passed through that station, may still be traced on Broad Green, near the town. At the time of the Conquest it was given to Lanfranc, Archbishop of Canterbury, whose successors had for several centuries a residence here, which is said to have been originally a royal palace. During the war between Henry III. and the barons, in 1264, the citizens of London, who had taken up arms against their sovereign, after being driven from the field at Lewes, retreated to this town, where they endeavoured to make a stand ; but part of the royal army, then stationed at Tonbridge, marched hither, and attacked and defeated them with great slaughter. The archiepis-copal palace,which in 1278 was in its original state,built chiefly of timber, was enlarged by Archbishop Stafford, and improved by his successors in the see, of whom Archbishop Parker, in 1573, had the honour of enter-taining Queen Elizabeth and her court for several days here. The palace having afterwards fallen into a state of dilapidation, was alienated from the see by act of par-liament, and sold in 1780 : the gardens have been con-verted into bleaching-grounds, the proprietor of which occupies the remains of the palace. With the produce of the sale, and other funds, was purchased in 1807 Ad-dington Park, three miles and a half from Croydon.

741 ·

The parish is pleasantly situated on the border of Banstead Downs, and within its limits are two of the three sources of the river Wandle, a stream abounding with excellent trout. The TOWN consists principally of one long street, and is paved, lighted with gas, and watched, under the direction of commissioners appointed by an act passed in the 10th of George IV. for its general improvement : the inhabitants are plentifully supplied with water. The houses are mostly substantial and well built, and many of them are handsome and of modern erection. In the vicinity are several mansions, with parks and pleasure-grounds, numerous detached residences, and ranges of neat dwellings inhabited by highly respectable families ; the salubrity of the air, and the convenient distance from the metropolis, rendering this place a chosen retreat for merchants and retired tradesmen. A literary and scientific institution was established in 1838. The barracks, erected in 1794, contain accommodation for three troops of cavalry, with an hospital, infirmary, and all the requisite stables, shops, &c. Within a mile east of the town is Addis-combe House, formerly the residence of the first lord Liverpool, which, in 1809, was purchased by the East India Company, for the establishment of their military college, previously formed at Woolwich Common, for the education of cadets for the engineers and artillery, but since 1825 open to the reception of cadets for the whole military service of the company, with the excep-tion of the cavalry. There are generally from 120 to 150 students, and under the auspices of the court of directors, the establishment has obtained a rank equal to that of any military institution in the kingdom. The buildings which have been at various times added to the original mansion, for the completion of the college, have cost more than £40,000.

The trade is principally in corn : the calico-printing and bleaching businesses, which were formerly carried on extensively, have materially declined. A large brewery has been established more than a century ; and there are others of more recent date. The London and Croy-don railway, which was opened on June 5th, 1839, has its first station contiguous to that of the Greenwich railway, near London Bridge, and pursues the line of that railway for nearly a mile and a half : it then diverges from it by a viaduct, and pursues its course to New Cross, Sydenham, Penge, and Norwood, and thence to this town. The Croydon station and depôt, formerly the premises of the canal company, whose property was purchased for the formation of the railway along the bed of the canal, is a spacious establishment, covering nearly five acres of ground. The whole course of the line amounted, in 1840, to £615,160, averaging for the expense of its construction, about £70,000 per mile. The Brighton line turns off from the terminus at Croy-don, and passes on the east side of the town, in a southerly direction towards Sussex. The Croydon Company and the Brighton Company were amalgamated in 1846. A railway was opened from near Croydon to Epsom in May, 1847 ; it is eight miles in length. An act was passed in 1846 for a railway to Wandsworth. The market is on Saturday : fairs are held on July 6th for cattle, and Oct. 2nd for horses, cattle, sheep, and pigs ; at the latter, which is also a large pleasure-fair, a great quantity of walnuts is sold. The town is within the jurisdiction of the county magistrates, of whom those acting for the division hold a petty-session every Saturday; and a head constable, two petty constables, and two headboroughs, are appointed at the court leet of the Archbishop of Canterbury, who is lord of the manor. `The powers of the county debt-court of Croydon, established in 1847, extend over the registration-district of Croydon. The summer assizes for the county are held here and at Guildford, alternately; and Croydon is the principal place of election for the eastern division of the county. The town-hall, a neat stone edifice surmounted by a cupola, was erected in 1807, at an expense of £10,000, defrayed by the sale of waste lands belonging to the parish. The prison was erected by subscription among the inhabitants, on the site of the old town-hall, and is a large and substantial building, of which the lower part, containing several rooms, is used as the town gaol, and for the confinement of prisoners during the assizes, and the upper part let for warehouses. Near the town-hall is a convenient market-house for butter and poultry.

The parish comprises about 2000 acres, the larger portion of which is arable land. The LIVING is a discharged vicarage, valued in the king's books at £21. 18. 9., and in the patronage of the Archbishop; net income, £587; impropriator, A. Caldcleugh, Esq. The church, begun by Archbishop Courteney, and completed by Archbishop Chichely, is a spacious and elegant structure of freestone and flint, in the later English style, having a lofty embattled tower with crocketed pinnacles. In it are deposited the remains of Archbishops Grindall, Sheldon, Potter, and Herring, and there are some very fine monuments, of which that of Archbishop Sheldon, bearing his effigy in episcopal robes, exceeds all in beauty of workmanship; there are likewise some ancient brasses. Its finely-painted windows were wantonly destroyed during the Commonwealth. Two new churches were, in 1827-9, erected partly by a grant of £300 from Queen Anne's Bounty, and partly by aid from the Parliamentary Commissioners: `one, on Croydon common, dedicated to St. James, is a handsome edifice in the later English style, with a small campanile tower, and contains 1200 sittings, of which 400 are free; the other is at Beulah Hill, Norwood. The livings are perpetual curacies, in the patronage of the Vicar; net income of St. James', £300. A district chapel, dedicated to St. John, was erected at Shirley, in 1836, at a cost of £1300: the living is in the gift of the Archbishop. There are places of worship for Baptists, the Society of Friends, Independents, and Wesleyans. The free school was founded and endowed in 1714, by Archbishop Tenison, and has an income of £130 per annum; schoolrooms were erected in 1792, at an expense of nearly £1000, on a piece of land adjoining the old school-house, which, having become unfit for the purpose, was let. The Society of Friends have a large establishment, removed to this place, in 1825, from Clerkenwell, where it had existed for more than a century, for the maintenance and education of 150 boys and girls. A free school originally founded and endowed by Archbishop Whitgift, in conjunction with the hospital of the Holy Trinity, is now a national school; and a school of industry for girls is kept in the chapel belonging to the old archiepiscopal palace.

The hospital of the *Holy Trinity* was founded and endowed by Archbishop Whitgift, in 1596, for a warden,
742

schoolmaster, chaplain, and any number above 30; and not exceeding 40, of poor brothers and sisters, not less than 60 years of age, of the parishes of Croydon and Lambeth, who were to be a body corporate and have a common seal. It is under the inspection of the Archbishop of Canterbury; the income, originally not more than £200, has increased to £2000 per annum, and there are 34 brothers and sisters now in the hospital. The building, occupying three sides of a quadrangle, in which is a small chapel, is a handsome specimen of the domestic style prevailing at the time of its erection. *Davy's* almshouses, for seven aged men and women, were founded in 1447, by Elias Davy, citizen of London, who endowed them with land, now producing about £180 per annum: the premises were rebuilt about 80 years since. *The Little Almshouses*, containing originally nine rooms, were erected principally with money given by the Earl of Bristol, in consideration of land inclosed on Norwood common; they have been enlarged by the addition of fifteen apartments, at the `expense of the parish, for the poor. In 1656, *Archbishop Laud* gave £300, which sum, having been invested in the purchase of a farm and in the funds, produces £62 per annum,/ applied to the apprenticing of children. *Henry Smith*, of London, in 1627 left lands and houses yielding an income of £213, of which about £150 are distributed among the inmates of the Little Almshouses; and there are various other charitable bequests for the relief of the poor. The union of Croydon contains 11 parishes or places, and contains a population of 27,721.

On a hill towards Addington is a cluster of 25 tumuli, one of which is 40 feet in diameter; they.appear to have been opened, and, according to Salmon, to have contained urns. On Thunderfield common is a circular encampment, including an area of two acres, surrounded by a double moat. At Duppas Hill, it is said, a tournament took place in 1186, when William, only son of John, the 7th earl Warren, lost his life. In 1719, a gold coin of the Emperor Domitian was found at Whitehorse farm, in the parish, where also, some years ago, a gold coin of Lælius Cæsar, in good preservation, and several others, were discovered; and in digging for a foundation in the town, in 1791, two gold coins of Valentinian, and a brass coin of Trajan, were found.·

CROYLAND.—See CROWLAND.

CRUCKTON, `a township, in the parish of PONTESBURY, union of ATCHAM, hundred of FORD, county of SALOP, 4 miles (S. W. by S.) from Shrewsbury; containing 155 inhabitants. A church dedicated to St. Thomas, being a chapel of ease to the second portion of the rectory of Pontesbury, was built by subscription in 1840, at an expense of £900; it is in the early English style, and contains 280 sittings, of which 160 are free. .

CRUDWELL (*ALL SAINTS*), a parish, in the union and hundred of MALMESBURY, Malmesbury and Kingswood, and N. divisions of WILTS, 6 miles (E.) from Tetbury; containing, with the hamlets of Chedglow, Chelworth, Eastcourt, and Murcott, 681 inhabitants. It comprises 4782a. 2r. 3p., of which about 2266 acres are arable, 2314 pasture, and 128 wood. The living is a rectory, valued in the king's books at £17. 5. 2½.; net income, £487; patron, the Rev. W. Maskelyne. The church is a large and handsome edifice, in the Norman style; on one side of the nave the columns are short and massive, and on the other lofty .and light. A hool is endowed with land worth £18 per annum. ear this place runs the old Fosse-way to Cirencester.

CRUMPSALL, a township, in the parish and union of MANCHESTER, hundred of SALFORD, S. division of LANCASHIRE, 2½ miles (N. by W.) from Manchester, on the road to Bury; containing 2745 inhabitants. It comprises 826 acres, nearly the whole of which is pasture land, occupied chiefly by farmers who supply the town of Manchester with milk and other dairy produce. The surface is undulated; and being highly favourable for the erection of villas, cottages ornées, &c., many have been built by the merchants and shop-keepers of Manchester, in pleasant situations. The river Irk, a tributary to the Irwell, bounds the township; and several considerable works have been established on its banks. There are, a spinning and weaving mill, built in 1832, and enlarged in 1845, the property of John Brooks, Esq., and occupied by Messrs. Simpson, Thompson, and Company, having 170-horse steam-power, and employing 900 hands; a calico-printing establishment, carried on by Thomas Fielden, Esq.; and some Turkey-red dye-works, the property of, and conducted by, Messrs. Louis and Michael Delaunay, whose father, a native of France, commenced the first dye-works for that colour in the neighbourhood. Crumpsall Hall was the residence of the ancestors of the ducal family of Howard.

The "village" comprehends portions of the townships of Crumpsall, Cheetham, and Broughton, and is commonly known by the name of Cheetham-Hill; it contains two inns, and as many as twelve beer-houses. The tithes of the township belong to the Dean and Canons of Manchester, and amount to £90 per annum. The Wesleyans have a large and handsome meeting-house, with a commodious day and Sunday school; and the Methodists two places of worship. In 1785 three cottages were built, out of the rent of which the sum of £13 is paid in support of St. Mark's school, in Cheetham. Humphrey Cheetham or Chetham, the founder of the Blue-coat hospital in Manchester, was born here in 1580: five of the boys are eligible from this place. The township can boast of another benefactor in George Clarke, who bequeathed to the poor the rents of three farms within it, to be distributed yearly in clothing, bedding, &c. The trustees of this charity some years ago obtained an act to enable them to sell the land for building on, which greatly increased the income of the estate, now about £2000 per annum; the cost of the farms having been £300 only, at the time of Mr. Clarke's purchase of them. The distribution of the proceeds is made every winter by the boroughreeve of Manchester, under the title of the Boroughreeve's Charity.—See CHEETHAM.

CRUNDALE (ST. MARY), a parish, in the union of EAST ASHFORD, hundred of WYE, lathe of SHEPWAY, E. division of KENT, 9 miles (S. W. by S.) from Canterbury; containing 278 inhabitants. It is partly bounded by the river Stour on the west, and comprises 1572a, 36p., of which about 980 acres are arable, 180 pasture, 250 wood, and 150 rough down. The living is a rectory, valued in the king's books at £11. 10. 10., and in the gift of Sir Edmund Filmer, Bart.: the incumbent's tithes have been commuted for £371. 9. 6., and a rent-charge of £23. 10. is paid to an impropriator; the glebe consists of about 18 acres, with a glebe-house. At Crundale Green, considerable remains of a Roman

sepulchre were discovered in 1703, with several skeletons, urns, and other vessels, both of earthenware and glass.

CRUTCH, an extra-parochial district, in the Upper division of the hundred of HALFSHIRE, Droitwich and E. divisions of the county of WORCESTER, 2 miles (N.) from Droitwich; containing 9 inhabitants, and comprising 240 acres. It lies to the east of the road from Droitwich to Kidderminster.

CRUWYS-MORCHARD (HOLY CROSS), a parish, in the union of TIVERTON, hundred of WITHERIDGE, Cullompton and N. divisions of DEVON, 5¼ miles (W.) from Tiverton; containing 670 inhabitants. This place takes its name from the ancient family of Cruwys, whose seat, Morchard House, near the church, was originally built in 1199, and is now inhabited by their descendant, the Rev. G. S. Cruwys. The parish is situated on the new road from Tiverton to Barnstaple, and comprises by computation nearly 6000 acres. The living is a rectory, valued in the king's books at £21. 11. 8.; patron and incumbent, the Rev. G. S. Cruwys, whose tithes have been commuted for £524, and whose glebe comprises 150 acres, with a glebe-house. The church was in 1689 struck by lightning, which rent the steeple and melted the bells; it contains a finely-carved oak screen, and some ancient monuments to the Anerays, and one to the memory of the Rev. Edmund Granger. In the churchyard is the burial-ground of the Cruwys family, the area of which is bounded by fir-trees, marking out the site of the old family chapel, destroyed by Cromwell's soldiers: large pieces of alabaster, being fragments of broken monuments, have been dug up on the spot.

CRUX-EASTON (ST. MICHAEL), a parish, in the union of KINGSCLERE, hundred of PASTROW, Kingsclere and N. divisions of the county of SOUTHAMPTON, 7 miles (S. S. W.) from Newbury; containing 102 inhabitants. The parish comprises by measurement 994 acres, of which 696 are arable, and about 200 woodland: the road from Andover to Newbury passes through the village. The living is a rectory, valued in the king's books at £12. 12. 6.; net income, £180; patron, the Rev. James Bagge: there is a glebe-house, with about 23 acres of land. The church was repaired about a century since by casing the old walls. There is a chapel of ease, called New Chapel; and a school is supported by the Earl of Carnarvon. In the neighbourhood are remains of several encampments. Here was the celebrated grotto constructed by the nine daughters of Edward Lisle, Esq., and commemorated by Pope; it has been suffered to go to ruin, the shell only remaining.

CUBBERLEY (ST. GILES), a parish, in the union of CHELTENHAM, partly in the hundred of BRADLEY, but chiefly in that of RAPSGATE, E. division of the county of GLOUCESTER, 4½ miles (S. by E.) from Cheltenham; containing 231 inhabitants. This place during the parliamentary war afforded an asylum for one night to Charles II., who, travelling in disguise after the battle of Worcester, slept at the parsonage-house the evening before he effected his escape. The parish is situated within a quarter of a mile of the new road from Cheltenham to Cirencester, and comprises by measurement 3421 acres: stone of inferior quality is quarried. The principal source of the river Thames, called the Seven Springs, is in the parish: the stream turns a mill within half a mile from the spot whence it issues. The living is a rectory, valued in the king's books at £10, and in

CUBL . CUCK

the gift of Henry Elwes, Esq.: the tithes have been commuted for £470, and the glebe comprises 17½ acres, with a glebe-house. The church, said to have been rebuilt in 1330, by Sir Thomas de Berkeley, is a handsome structure in the decorated English style, and contains several ancient and interesting monuments : the statue of Sir Thomas is still remaining in a niche in the south aisle; against the north wall, under a recess, is the figure of a knight in bold relief; and there are also the effigies of a crusader, and of a lady in the dress of the fourteenth century. There is a place of worship for Baptists.

CUBBINGTON (St. Mary), a parish, in the union of Warwick, Kenilworth division of the hundred of Knightlow, S. division of the county of Warwick, 5 miles (N. E. by E.) from Warwick ; containing 830 inhabitants. It is bounded on the south, and partly on the east, by the river Leame, is intersected by the road from Warwick to Rugby, and comprises 1858 acres of rich and productive land. The living is a discharged vicarage, valued in the king's books at £6. 6. 8.; net income, £207 ; patron and impropriator, Lord Leigh. The church has been enlarged. A national school was established in 1821 ; and a bequest by John Glover, in 1762, of £250 for educating children, and one by Hannah Murcott, in 1775, of £100 for the establishment of a school, are applied towards its support.

CUBERT (St. Cuthbert), a parish, in the union of St. Columb Major, W. division of the hundred of Pyder and of the county of Cornwall, 10 miles (N. E.) from Truro ; containing 368 inhabitants. It is situated on the shore of the Bristol Channel, and comprises by admeasurement 2440 acres, of which a portion is common or waste: along the coast are several curious caverns, and a very large sand-bank between 200 and 300 feet high ; and there is a well, called Holy Well, on the beach, much resorted to for children diseased or weak in their limbs. A small cattle-fair is held on the 3rd of June. The living is a discharged vicarage, valued in the king's books at £8. 6. 8., and in the gift of the Rev. T. Stabback : the tithes have been commuted for £178, and the glebe consists of 20 acres, with a glebe-house. There is a place of worship for Wesleyans. The remains of two encampments, supposed to be Danish, may be traced.

CUBLEY (St. Andrew), a parish, in the union of Uttoxeter, hundred of Appletree, S. division of the county of Derby, 6 miles (S. by W.) from Ashbourn ; containing 425 inhabitants. It comprises 2227 acres of land, mostly of a strong soil, with some gravelly loam ; and has two pleasant villages, one north of the church, called Big Cubley, the other on an eminence west of the church, named Little Cubley. This was the chief seat of the Montgomery family, and for a time the seat of the Stanhopes ; but the mansion was long since pulled down. A fair, held on November 30th, was long noted for fat hogs. The living is a rectory, with that of Marston-Montgomery annexed, valued in the king's books at £13. 16. 3., and in the gift of the Earl of Chesterfield : the tithes have been commuted for £380, and the glebe comprises 5¼ acres, and a glebe-house. The church is an ancient structure with a fine tower ; in the chancel, which was repaired in 1845, is the figure of a Knight Templar : the edifice is seen to good effect on the road from Sudbury to Ashbourn.

744

CUBLINGTON (St. Nicholas), a parish, in the union of Aylesbury, hundred of Cottlesloe, county of Buckingham, 6¾ miles (N. by E.) from Aylesbury; containing 290 inhabitants. It comprises 1200 acres, chiefly pasture land. The living is a rectory, valued in the king's books at £9. 16. 3. ; net income, £289; patrons, the Rector and Fellows of Lincoln College, Oxford. The tithes were commuted for land and a money payment, in 1769.

CUBY (St. Keby), a parish, in the union of Truro, W. division of the hundred of Powder and of the county of Cornwall ; adjoining the town of Tregoney, and containing 161 inhabitants. The parish is situated on the road from St. Austell to St. Mawes, and is bounded by the river Fal ; it comprises 2000 acres, all arable, except about 8 acres of coppice. The living is a vicarage, annexed to the rectory of Tregony cum St. James, valued together in the king's books at £10. 4. 2. The church, with the exception of the porch and tower, was rebuilt in 1828 ; the interior is exceedingly neat, and contains a font curiously sculptured.

CUCKFIELD (Holy Trinity), a market-town and parish, and the head of a union, in the hundred of Buttinghill, rape of Lewes, E. division of Sussex, 25 miles (N. E. by E.) from Chichester, and 38 (S.) from London, on the road to Brighton ; containing 3444 inhabitants. This place is situated on a pleasant eminence, nearly in the centre of the county. The pathways in the town are laid with bricks of a very firm and durable quality, formed of red clay, which is found within the distance of four miles, as are strata of pipe-clay of peculiar whiteness : sandstone also is found in the parish. The London and Brighton railway, after being carried across the valley of the Ouse by a stately viaduct of 37 arches, passes within a mile and a half of the town, and for its further progress a bridge and embankments have been constructed at Vale Pool. The market is on Friday ; and fairs are held on Whit-Thursday and Sept. 16th, for horses and cattle. The county magistrates hold petty-sessions for the division on alternate Mondays ; and the town is a polling-place for the eastern division of the county : the powers of the county debt-court of Cuckfield, established in 1847, extend over the registration-district of Cuckfield, and the parish of Wivelsfield. Cuckfield Place is an ancient mansion, erected in the latter part of the sixteenth century. The living is a vicarage, valued in the king's books at £20. 14. 2.; net income, £414 ; patron, the Bishop of Chichester ; impropriators, the landowners. The church is a large and handsome structure in the decorated English style, with a tower surmounted by a spire covered with shingles, which, from its elevated situation, has been frequently injured by lightning. There are places of worship for Independents and Unitarians. The free grammar school was founded in 1528, and endowed by Edward Fuller, of London, and the Rev. William Spencer, of Balcomb, with the manor of Redstone, in the parish of Reigate, and other property ; the income is £28 per annum. Lady Dorothy Shirley erected the school-house, which adjoins the churchyard ; also a gallery in the church for the scholars. The poor law union of Cuckfield comprises 15 parishes or places, and contains a population of 17,132.

CUCKLINGTON (St. Lawrence), a parish, and formerly a market-town, in the union of Wincanton, hundred of NORTON-FERRIS, E. division of SOMERSET, 2¾ miles (E. by S.) from Wincanton; containing 339 inhabitants. The manor belonged to Henry de Ortiaco or L'Orti, to whom Edward I., in the 32nd of his reign, granted a market on Tuesday, and a fair on the eve, day, and morrow, of the festival of All Saints, and for seven successive days; both of which have been long discontinued. The living is a rectory, with that of Stoke-Trister united, valued in the king's books at £12. 19. 4½., and in the gift of William Phelips, Esq., lord of the manor: the tithes of the two parishes have been commuted for £594. 6., and the glebe comprises 99¼ acres.

CUCKNEY, or NORTON-CUCKNEY (ST. MARY), a parish, in the union of WORKSOP, Hatfield division of the wapentake of BASSETLAW, N. division of the county of NOTTINGHAM, 5½ miles (S. S. W.) from Worksop; containing 1697 inhabitants, of whom 625 are in the township of Norton-Cuckney. The parish is watered by the river Poulter, and comprises 5284a. 3r. 21p., of good land, all inclosed, and consisting of extensive pastures and some plantations: the township contains 1095 acres. The village is of considerable extent; and some worsted and cotton mills give employment to a large number of children from the Foundling Hospital, London. There is also a mill for polishing marble. A market and a fair were formerly held, but both have been long discontinued. The living is a discharged vicarage, valued in the king's books at £9. 8. 6½.; patron, Earl Manvers; impropriators, the Duke of Portland, and others. The great tithes have been commuted for £726. 18., and the vicarial for £212. 5.; the glebe contains 19 acres, with a glebe-house. The church, a large ancient structure, with a handsome tower, was thoroughly repaired and repewed in 1831.

CUCKNOE.—See COGENHOE.

CUDDESDEN (ALL SAINTS), a parish, in the union of HEADINGTON, hundred of BULLINGTON, county of OXFORD, 6½ miles (E. S. E.) from Oxford; containing, with the chapelries of Denton and Wheatley, and the hamlet of Chippinghurst, 1483 inhabitants, of whom 305 are in the township of Cuddesden. This place has been for many years distinguished as one of the residences of the bishops of Oxford. According to Wood's Athenæ, a palace was built in 1635, by Bishop Bancroft, at an expense of £3500, exclusively of a large grant of timber from Shotover Forest, by Charles I.; this edifice was burnt down by Colonel Legge, in 1644, from an apprehension that it might be converted into a garrison by the parliamentarians, and was rebuilt in 1679, by Bishop Fell. Extensive repairs and improvements were made in 1846-7, a neat chapel added, and the gardens enlarged. The living consists of a vicarage and rectory, annexed to the bishopric, and valued in the king's books at £17. 0. 5.; the tithes have been commuted for £315, and the glebe contains nearly 30 acres. The church is a spacious and handsome cruciform structure, chiefly Norman, with some later portions; the west entrance is a fine specimen of the Norman style, and the arch under the tower is highly enriched with zig-zag mouldings and other details: there are some interesting monuments to Bishop Bancroft (who was interred near the south wall of the chancel) and Bishops Moss and Jackson. At Wheatley is a separate incumbency, in the gift of the Bishop.

VOL. I.—745

CUDDINGTON (ST. NICHOLAS), a parish, in the union and hundred of AYLESBURY, county of BUCKINGHAM, 5½ miles (W. S. W.) from Aylesbury; containing 626 inhabitants. The parish is situated on the river Teme, by which it is bounded on the north-west; and according to computation comprises 1240 acres, whereof the greater portion is arable, and the remainder excellent pasture-land. Stone of good quality for building is extensively quarried. The living is annexed to the vicarage of Haddenham: the impropriate tithes have been commuted for £275, and the vicarial for £180; the impropriate glebe consists of nearly 18 acres, and the vicarial of 14 acres. There is a place of worship for Particular Baptists.

CUDDINGTON, a township, in the parish of MALPAS, union of WREXHAM, Higher division of the hundred of BROXTON, S. division of the county of CHESTER, 2¼ miles (W. by S.) from Malpas; containing 240 inhabitants. It lies on the south-western border of the county, and comprises 1258 acres, of which the soil is sand and clay. The tithes have been commuted for £163.

CUDDINGTON, a township, in the parish of WEAVERHAM, union of NORTHWICH, Second division of the hundred of EDDISBURY, S. division of the county of CHESTER, 4¼ miles (W. by S.) from Northwich; containing 253 inhabitants. It comprises 1031 acres, of a sandy soil. The road from Tarporley to Weaverham passes through.

CUDDINGTON (ST. MARY), a parish, in the union of EPSOM, Second division of the hundred of COPTHORNE and EFFINGHAM, W. division of SURREY, ¾ of a mile (N. N. E.) from Ewell; containing 158 inhabitants. This place is noticed in Domesday book under the appellation of Codintone, and anciently gave name to a family supposed to have been a branch of the Wateviles: Sir Simon de Codington was knight of the shire in the reign of Edward III., and the family held the manor till the 16th century. The living, now extinct, was a vicarage, valued in the king's books at £7. 12. 3½.: the tithes are impropriate, and have been commuted for £381. 15. The church has been demolished. The celebrated palace of Nonsuch, built by Henry VIII., was situated in the parish.—See EWELL.

CUDHAM (ST. PETER AND ST. PAUL), a parish, in the union of BROMLEY, hundred of RUXLEY, lathe of SUTTON-AT-HONE, W. division of KENT, 7 miles (S. E. by S.) from Bromley; containing 776 inhabitants. The parish comprises 5113 acres, whereof the soil is in general poor, and abounds with large flints; it contains many extensive woods, covering 1089 acres, and the most considerable of which is that called Cudham-Lodge Wood. The living is a discharged vicarage, valued in the king's books at £13. 2. 2., and has a net income of £190; the patronage and impropriation belong to the Crown. A grant for a weekly market to be held here, was made by Henry III.

CUDWORTH (ST. MICHAEL), a parish, in the union of CHARD, hundred of SOUTH PETHERTON, W. division of SOMERSET, 3 miles (S. S. E.) from Ilminster; containing 155 inhabitants. It comprises 436 acres of arable land, 520 pasture, and 98 wood. The prevailing timber is elm and Scottish fir; the surface is rather hilly, and the soil rests upon chalk: limestone is quarried. The Creech and Chard canal passes within two miles. The living is a perpetual curacy, in the patron-

5 C

age of the Bishop of Bath and Wells; net income, £63: the tithes have been commuted for £200, and the glebe contains 32 acres. The church is in the later English style of architecture.

CUDWORTH, a township, in the parish of ROYSTON, wapentake of STAINCROSS, W. riding of YORK, 4 miles (N. E. by E.) from Barnsley; containing 552 inhabitants. Mention of this place first occurs in the chartularies of Nostal and Bretton, both which monastic establishments possessed lands here; and among the families that have been connected with the spot as landed proprietors, occur those of Stapleton and Jobson, which were of considerable note. Lands, too, here and in some neighbouring manors, were included in the endowment of the Savoy Hospital, founded by Henry VII. The township comprises by computation 1680 acres of land, and contains the villages of Upper and Lower Cudworth. There is a place of worship for Wesleyans.

CUERDALE, a township, in the parish, and Lower division of the hundred, of BLACKBURN, union of PRESTON, N. division of the county of LANCASTER, 3¾ miles (E.) from Preston; containing 106 inhabitants. This place belonged to a family of the same name from the earliest times. About the reign of Richard II. it passed by marriage to the Molyneuxs, and since 1582 it has been the property of the Asshetons, of Downham, who formerly resided at Cuerdale Hall, a fine building of red brick with stone dressings, erected in a beautiful situation by William Assheton, in 1700. The township lies on the river Ribble, and comprises 660 acres of richly cultivated land, the property of William Assheton, Esq. The road from Preston to Samlesbury passes through. A few years ago, in digging earth here, a large mass of silver, consisting of ingots or bars of various sizes, was found by the workmen, together with silver armlets, tolerably entire, and several antique ornaments of different kinds, cut into pieces, the whole amounting to upwards of 1000 ounces; also about 6000 coins of various descriptions, but chiefly Anglo-Saxon pennies. This treasure had been deposited, it is supposed, about the year 910, in a leaden chest, which was so decomposed that only small portions of it could be secured.

CUERDEN, a township, in the parish and hundred of LEYLAND, union of CHORLEY, N. division of the county of LANCASTER, 4½ miles (S. S. E.) from Preston; containing 573 inhabitants. The manor was given by Roger de Poictou to Vivian Molinaux or Molyneux, who had followed him from Normandy; and afterwards devolved to various families, among whom were the Banastres, Charnocks, Langtons, and more recently, the Fleetwoods. The township comprises 800a. 1r. 19p. of land, of various soil; and is situated on the Lostock river, on the banks of which are two cotton-mills, one belonging to William Clayton, Esq., and the other to William Eccles, Esq., together employing more than 700 persons. The Preston and Parkside railway, and the Preston and Wigan road, pass through. Cuerden Hall is the seat of Robert Townley Parker, Esq., whose family and tenantry attend Bamber-Bridge church, on the opposite side of the Lostock. The vicarial tithes have been commuted for £55; and the impropriate, payable to Mr. Parker, for £39. 12. 4. A school is endowed with land of the annual value of £6, and is further supported by £7 per annum from the Lostock Hall estate, and £5 from Crooke's bequest.

746

CUERDLEY, a township, in the parish of PRESCOT, union of WARRINGTON, hundred of WEST DERBY, S. division of the county of LANCASTER, 4½ miles (W. by S.) from Warrington; containing 221 inhabitants. This place was early in the possession of the barons of Manchester, from whom it appears to have reverted to the crown. The lordship was sold by Edward VI. to Richard Brooke, of Norton, in the county of Chester; ancestor of Sir Richard Brooke, Bart., the present chief owner of the soil. The township lies on the north side of the river Mersey, and south of the road from Warrington to Liverpool; and comprises 1425 acres of land. Marks of an encampment were formerly visible on Cuerdley marsh, near the edge of the Mersey. The impropriate tithes have been commuted for £128, payable to King's College, Cambridge, and the vicarial for £81. 11.

CUGLEY, a tything, in the parish and union of NEWENT, hundred of BOTLOE, W. division of the county of GLOUCESTER, 8 miles (W. N. W.) from Gloucester; containing 490 inhabitants.

CULBONE, or KILNER (ST. CULBONE), a parish, in the union of WILLITON, hundred of CARHAMPTON, W. division of SOMERSET, 4 miles (W. by N.) from Porlock; containing 34 inhabitants. This parish, which is bounded on the north by the Bristol Channel, and exhibits the most romantic scenery, comprises 1502 acres, whereof 760 are common or waste. The village, from the steepness of the surrounding hills, was until within the last few years scarcely approachable, except on foot. The living is a discharged rectory, valued in the king's books at £3. 18. 11½., and in the gift of the Earl of Lovelace: the tithes have been commuted for £35, and the glebe comprises 32 acres, with a glebe-house.

CULCHETH, a township, in the parish of NEWCHURCH, union of LEIGH, hundred of WEST DERBY, S. division of the county of LANCASTER, 6 miles (N. E. by N.) from Warrington; containing 2139 inhabitants. It comprises 5362 acres of land, whereof 3384 are meadow and pasture, 924 arable, 100 wood, and 954 road and waste; the surface is undulated, and the soil partly moss and partly clay. At Bury Lane, in the township, is a cotton-mill; also a station on the Liverpool and Manchester railway. Holcroft Hall, here, was formerly the abode of the Holcrofts, the traffickers in monastic property in the reign of Henry VIII.; and Hurst Hall, now a farmhouse, was the residence of Thomas Holcroft, a member of this family, in 1692. There are places of worship for Dissenters. A school at Twiss Green, founded by John Guest, was endowed by Henry Johnson in 1727 with about £25 per annum, to which other bequests have been added; and sixteen boys belonging to the township, who are occasionally clothed, receive instruction on this charity. Ambrose Yates, in 1772, bequeathed a house and about three acres of land, the rent now producing about £14, to be given to the poor annually on the 2nd of February; and several small benefactions are distributed on St. Thomas's day.—See NEWCHURCH.

CULFORD (ST. MARY), a parish, in the union of THINGOE, hundred of BLACKBOURN, W. division of SUFFOLK, 4¾ miles (N. N. W.) from Bury St. Edmunds; containing 352 inhabitants. The parish is bounded on the south by the river Lark, which is navigable for small craft from Lynn to Bury; and comprises 2209 acres, whereof 106 are common or waste. The surface is undulated, and the scenery diversified; the soil is generally light and sandy, but clay is found in some parts, and also a strong earth well adapted for making white bricks. Culford Hall, the seat of R. B. De Beauvoir, Esq., lord of the manor, is an elegant mansion, situated in a spacious park. The living is a discharged rectory, consolidated with the livings of Timworth and Ingham, valued in the king's books at £8. Lord Cornwallis, who for his brilliant achievements as commander-in-chief in India, was created a marquess in 1792, and to whom parliament voted a monument in St. Paul's Cathedral, was born here.

CULGAITH, a chapelry, in the parish of KIRKLAND, union of PENRITH, LEATH ward, E. division of CUMBERLAND, 7 miles (E.) of Penrith; containing 361 inhabitants. It comprises 2697a. 2r. 26p., the whole arable, except 150 acres of woodland. From the Crowdundle quarries, here, is raised red freestone of excellent quality for building, of which blocks of immense size are obtained for pillars and other uses. The living is a perpetual curacy; net income, £80; patron, the Vicar of Kirkland; impropriator, the Rev. R. Rice. The chapel is dedicated to All Saints.

CULHAM (ST. PAUL), a parish, in the union of ABINGDON, hundred of DORCHESTER, county of OXFORD, 1 mile (S. S. E.) from Abingdon; containing 404 inhabitants. This place, which is nearly surrounded by the river Isis, was the occasional retreat of the abbots of Abingdon; and in the ancient manor-house, now occupied as a farmhouse, is a room still called the Abbot's chamber. The living is a vicarage not in charge; net income, £100; patron and appropriator, the Bishop of Oxford.

CULLERCOATS, a township, in the parish and union of TYNEMOUTH, E. division of CASTLE ward, S. division of the county of NORTHUMBERLAND, 2 miles (N. by W.) from Tynemouth; containing 738 inhabitants. This is a small sea-port, artificially constructed, inhabited chiefly by fishermen, and remarkable for being, perhaps, the smallest township and manor in England, not extending further than the village and a plot of adjoining ground, and the whole of the land, exclusive of that covered by houses, not exceeding seven acres. It is a mesne manor, and is included in the parliamentary borough of Tynemouth. In the bathing season the village is much frequented; the beach is a firm sand, and suitable accommodation is afforded by lodging houses for visiters. A school is used on Sundays as a place of worship by dissenters: there is a small burial-ground belonging to the Society of Friends.

CULLINGWORTH, a hamlet and church district, in the township of BINGLEY cum MICKLETHWAITE, parish of BINGLEY, union of KEIGHLEY, Upper division of the wapentake of SKYRACK, W. riding of YORK, 7 miles (N. W.) from Bradford. The lands have been inclosed, and afford good crops of corn, and excellent pasturage: stone is quarried for building. The village is pleasantly situated on an eminence commanding fine views of the vale below, and is chiefly inhabited by persons employed in worsted-spinning and the Heald-yarn manufacture, for which there are large mills established in 1810. The living is a perpetual curacy, endowed by the ecclesiastical commission, and in the gift of the Crown and the Bishop of Ripon, alternately. There

are places of worship for Baptists, Wesleyans, and Primitive Methodists; and a school endowed with £10 per annum, under the inclosure act. At Spring-head is a Roman encampment.

CULLOMPTON (ST. ANDREW), a market-town and parish, in the union of TIVERTON, hundred of HAYRIDGE, Cullompton and N. divisions of DEVON, 12 miles (N. E. by N.) from Exeter, and 166 (W. by S.) from London; containing 3909 inhabitants. This place, which derives its name from its situation on the river Culme, or Columb, was held in royal demesne during the heptarchy; and a collegiate church was founded here by one of the Saxon monarchs, which was annexed by William the Conqueror to the abbey of Battle, in Sussex. In 1278 the inhabitants obtained from Edward I. the grant of a market, which was confirmed by his successor in 1317, with the addition of an annual fair. The TOWN is pleasantly situated in an extensive vale, surrounded by a large tract of level country, and consists of one principal street, roughly paved, from which some smaller streets diverge; the inhabitants are amply supplied with water, and the environs abound with pleasant walks. It suffered severely by an alarming fire that broke out July 8th, 1839, from the roof of a thatched tenement on the western side of the main street; 132 houses and cottages were reduced to ashes, including the whole of New-street. The chief articles of manufacture are broad and narrow woollen-cloth, kerseymere, and serge, the production of which affords employment to several hundred persons: on a stream between the river and the town are two flour-mills, a paper-mill, and a mill for spinning yarn; and there are other manufacturing establishments, and four tanneries. The Bristol and Exeter railway passes through. The market is on Saturday; the fairs are on the first Wednesdays in May and November, and are large marts for bullocks and sheep. The county magistrates hold a petty-session here monthly for the division. Three high constables are chosen for the hundred, of whom one acts for this and the adjoining parish of Kentisbeare; and six petty constables are annually appointed by the parishioners, three for the town, and three for the rest of the parish.

The parish comprises about 9000 acres: the surface is greatly diversified with hill and dale, and the lower lands are subject to occasional inundation from the river Columb; the soil comprehends almost every variety. The LIVING is a vicarage, valued in the king's books at £47. 4. 2.; net income, £351; patron, R. B. De Beauvoir, Esq.; impropriators, the proprietors of estates. The church is an elegant and spacious structure, in the later English style, with a lofty tower, strengthened by highly enriched buttresses, and crowned with pierced battlements and crocketed pinnacles: opening into the south aisle is a beautiful chapel, erected in 1528, in the richest style of that period, by John Lane, whose remains are deposited in it: the roofs of the nave and aisle of the church are of oak, finely carved, and decorated with gilding. There are places of worship for Baptists, Bryanites, the Society of Friends, Independents, Wesleyans, and Unitarians. A fund of nearly £70 per annum arising from land bought with a donation from George Spicer, in 1624, is appropriated to the apprenticing of children; and £54. 10. per annum, arising from land purchased with a donation from John and Henry Hill, Esqrs., are given in clothing to aged men. There are several other benefactions, by means of which £100 are annually distributed among the poor. At Langford-Barton are to be seen the remains of an ancient chapel.

CULM-DAVEY, a hamlet, in the parish and hundred of HEMYOCK, union of WELLINGTON, Cullompton and N. divisions of DEVON. Here is a chapel of ease to the rectory of Hemyock.

CULMINGTON (*ALL SAINTS*), a parish, in the union of LUDLOW, hundred of MUNSLOW, S. division of SALOP, 5½ miles (N. by W.) from Ludlow; containing 541 inhabitants. It lies on the road from Ludlow to Wenlock, and comprises 3500 acres, whereof two-thirds are arable land, and the remainder pasture: stone is obtained for building, and for the roads. The river Corve flows through the parish. The living is a rectory, valued in the king's books at £18. 9. 2.; patron and incumbent, the Rev. W. Johnstone: the tithes have been commuted; and there are 40 acres of glebe and a glebe-house. The church, built about two centuries ago, is in the early English style, with a tower surmounted by a spire, which has a pleasing effect in the scenery. Near the church are vestiges of a moat and a keep.

CULMSTOCK (*ALL SAINTS*), a parish, in the union of WELLINGTON, hundred of HEMYOCK, Cullompton and N. divisions of DEVON, 7 miles (N. E.) from Cullompton; containing 1446 inhabitants, several of whom are employed in the woollen manufacture. The parish comprises 3365 acres, of which 417 are common or waste. Fairs for cattle are held on the 21st of May, and the Wednesday after the 29th of September. The living is a discharged vicarage, in the patronage of the Dean and Chapter of Exeter, the appropriators, and valued in the king's books at £16: the great tithes have been commuted for £320, and the vicarial for £355; the glebe contains 4¼ acres, with a glebe-house. The church contains a handsome stone screen, with a doorway enriched and canopied with foliage; it was enlarged in 1824. There are meeting-houses for Baptists, the Society of Friends, and Wesleyans.

CULPHO (*ST. BOTOLPH*), a parish, in the union of WOODBRIDGE, hundred of CARLFORD, E. division of SUFFOLK, 3½ miles (W. by N.) from Woodbridge; containing 70 inhabitants. The living is a discharged perpetual curacy, valued in the king's books at £5. 7. 11.; income, £55; patron and impropriator, T. T. Gurdon, Esq., whose tithes have been commuted for £15.

CULVERLANDS.—See TILFORD.

CULVERLEY, an extra-parochial district, adjacent to the parish and liberty of DIBDEN, union of NEW-FOREST, Southampton and S. divisions of the county of SOUTHAMPTON; containing 46 inhabitants.

CULVERTHORPE, a chapelry, in the parish of HAYDOR, union of SLEAFORD, wapentake of ASWARD-HURN, parts of KESTEVEN, county of LINCOLN, 5½ miles (S. W. by W.) from Sleaford; containing 139 inhabitants. The chapel is dedicated to St. Bartholomew.

CULWORTH (*ST. MARY*), a parish, in the union of BRACKLEY, hundred of KING'S SUTTON, S. division of the county of NORTHAMPTON, 7¼ miles (N. E.) from Banbury; containing 713 inhabitants. It is situated near the borders of Oxfordshire, and comprises 2214 acres of a rich and productive soil. The living consists

of a rectory and vicarage, valued in the king's books at £10, and in the gift of the Rev. John Spence: the rectorial tithes have been commuted for £509, and the vicarial for £191; the rectorial glebe contains nearly 24 acres, and there is a glebe-house. The church has a new chancel, built in 1845, by the rector. A school built by Mrs. Danvers was endowed in 1795, with an annuity of £65, by Martha and Frances Rich; it is in union with the National Society.

CUMBERLAND, the extreme north-western county of England, occupying a maritime situation, bounded on the east by Northumberland and Durham; on the south-east by Westmorland and Lancashire, from the former of which it is partly separated by Ulswater and the river Eamont, and from the latter by the river Duddon; on the west by the Irish Sea; and on the north by Scotland, from which it is divided by the Solway Firth and the rivers Sark, Liddell, and Kershope. It extends from 54° 12′ to 55° 10′ (N. Lat.), and from 2° 19′ to 3° 37′ (W. Lon.), and contains 1478 square miles, or 945,920 statute acres: within its limits are 34,574 inhabited houses, 2386 uninhabited, and 200 in the course of erection; and the population amounts to 178,038, of whom 86,292 are males.

This county, in Saxon orthography *Cumbra-land*, signifying "the land of the Cumbrians," derives its name from having been occupied, after the settlement of the Saxons in Britain, by a remnant of the ancient Britons, styled *Cumbri* or *Cymry*. It was also designated *Caerleyl-schire*, or *Caerlielleshire*, from its chief town *Caerleyl*, now Carlisle. At the time of the Roman invasion, it was, according to Whitaker, inhabited by the *Volantii* or *Voluntii*, a "people of the forests," and the *Sistuntii*, both tribes of the *Brigantes*, whose territory was not subjugated by the Romans until the reign of the Emperor Vespasian. In the division of the island by the victorious Romans, Cumberland was chiefly included in the great province of *Maxima Cæsariensis*, which was separated from that of *Valentia* by the fortified wall crossing the northern part of the county. During the heptarchy it formed part of the kingdom of *Northumbria*, composed of the two smaller states of *Bernicia* and *Deira*. About the middle of the tenth century, it was ceded to the Scots, together with the greater part of Bernicia; and from that period it was sometimes under the dominion of their monarchs, and sometimes under that of the English sovereigns, till the year 1237, when it was finally annexed to the crown of England by Henry III.

Its border situation has caused it to be the subject of many remarkable transactions, and the scene of numerous interesting historical events. Even after the Scottish dominion over the northern counties of England had finally ceased, the feuds between the two kingdoms raged with unabated violence for more than three centuries, during which this county was seldom long exempted from the horrors of invasion, or the cruelties and depredations of border warfare. Life and property could only be preserved by a most vigilant system of watch and ward, and the construction of numerous fortresses: almost every gentleman's residence, partienlarly on the sea-side or near the border, had its fortified tower, sufficiently capacious to afford refuge to the inhabitants of the domain; and in some parishes the church towers were so constructed as to serve for

748

his object. The border service and laws were instituted in the reign of Edward I.; the former for the purpose of keeping a strict watch, establishing beacons, and regulating the musters in time of war; and the latter for the punishment of private rapine and murders committed by individuals of either nation on those of the other in time of peace. A lord warden of the marches, whose authority was partly civil and partly military, was appointed on each side of the borders; the first English lord warden being nominated in 1296. The English borders were divided into three districts, called Marches, namely, the Eastern, Middle, and Western; and Cumberland was included in the last. The wardens held courts, but offenders were frequently executed without trial. The union of the two kingdoms, under James VI. of Scotland and I. of England, having put an end to the devastating inroads and sanguinary retaliations which defile the border annals, that monarch took active measures for ensuring the peace of the harassed district; and to abolish as much as possible the distinction between the kingdoms, he ordered that the counties of England and Scotland which had been called the Borders should be styled the Middle Shires, and thus described them in his proclamation. He soon after banished the Græmes or Grahams, a numerous clan occupying what was called "the debateable ground," near the river Esk, who had long been an annoyance both to their own countrymen and the inhabitants of Cumberland. Notwithstanding these precautionary measures, outrages and robberies continued to be perpetrated for some time after James' accession to the English throne, which caused him to issue several special commissions, under which various beneficial regulations were adopted. All persons, "saving noblemen and gentlemen unsuspected of felony or theft, and not being broken clans," in the counties lately called the Borders, were forbidden to wear any armour, or weapons offensive or defensive, or to keep any horse above the value of 50s., on pain of imprisonment. Slough-dogs, or blood-hounds, for pursuing the offenders through the mosses, sloughs, or bogs, were ordered to be kept at the charge of certain districts; and the laws were enforced against the moss-troopers, as they were called, with the utmost severity: nevertheless, they were not finally extirpated until the reign of Queen Anne.

Cumberland is in the diocese of Carlisle, and province of York, and contains 104 parishes. For purposes of civil jurisdiction it is divided into five wards (a term peculiar to the border counties), respectively denominated Allerdale above Derwent, Allerdale below Derwent, Cumberland, Eskdale, and Leath. It comprises the city and inland port of Carlisle; the ancient borough and market-town of Cockermouth; the sea-port, market-town, and newly-enfranchised borough of Whitehaven; the market and sea-port towns of Maryport, Ravenglass, and Workington; the small but thriving sea-port of Harrington; and the market-towns of Alston-Moor, Aspatria, Bootle, Brampton, Egremont, Hesket-Newmarket, Keswick, Kirk-Oswald, Longtown, Penrith, and Wigton. By the act of the 2nd of William IV., cap. 45, the county sends four representatives to parliament, and for that purpose is divided into two portions, called the Eastern and Western divisions; the former composed of the wards of Cumberland, Eskdale, and Leath; and the latter of those of Allerdale above and below Derwent.

749

Carlisle and Cockermouth each return two members; and Whitehaven, by the act, is invested with the privilege of sending one. Cumberland is included in the Northern circuit: the assizes and the Easter and Midsummer quarter-sessions are held at Carlisle, where stands the common gaol and house of correction; the Epiphany sessions, at Cockermouth; and the Michaelmas sessions, at Penrith.

The SURFACE of the county is beautifully diversified with level plains and swelling eminences, deep sequestered vales and lofty mountains, open heathy commons and irregular inclosures, in some parts richly decorated with tufted groves and thriving plantations, and the whole enlivened with almost innumerable streams and extensive lakes. The mountainous and the level districts form its marked natural divisions. The latter occupy chiefly the northern and western parts, and though well cultivated and fertile, do not afford any interesting scenery, except along the courses of the several rivers. The mountainous lands, between which and the plains there are generally lower ranges of smooth hills, may be divided into two extensive districts, equally incapable of agricultural improvement, but differing considerably in character. The entire eastern and north-eastern sides of the county, bordering on Durham and Northumberland, form the highest part of the mountainous chain that runs through the centre of the island from Staffordshire to Linlithgow, and are chiefly comprised under the designations of Cross Fell, Hartside Fell, Geltsdale Forest, and Spade-adam Waste, amongst which, Cross Fell rises preeminently to the height of 2902 feet, and though steep on its western side, has a very gentle declivity eastward. These mountains, to the south-east, are separated by the level tracts bordering on the rivers Eden, Eamont, Petterill, and Caldew, from those occupying the southern part of the county, which are among the most elevated in Britain, and present a great variety of grand and picturesque forms, their sides being steep and rugged, and in some places ornamented with woods; while the deep vales, mostly rich and in a high state of cultivation, and in many parts well wooded, contain, in numerous instances, lakes of considerable extent; the whole forming some of the most romantic scenery in the kingdom, deservedly eulogized in the descriptive tours of several ingenious writers, and comprehending a pleasing variety of subjects for the pencil.

The most valuable of the MINERALS are coal and lead; in addition to which, the county produces the singular mineral substance called wad or black-lead, slate, copper, iron, and lapis calaminaris. The coal district is supposed to occupy an extent of about 100 square miles: the principal collieries on the coast are those at Whitehaven and Workington, which supply by far the chief portion of the coal imported into Ireland. The singular species called "cannel coal" is procured in different parts, particularly in the parishes of Caldbeck and Bolton. The most important lead-mines are those at Alston-Moor, which were discovered and worked by Francis, first earl of Derwentwater; and, on the attainder of the third earl, were, together with the manor and his other estates, forfeited to the crown, and appropriated to the endowment of Greenwich Hospital. The ore contains a proportion of silver, averaging from eight to ten oz. per ton: copper-ore has sometimes been found in the same vein with the lead, and this metal was formerly exported from the county in large quantities, being likewise found at Caldbeck, Melmerby, and Hesket. It is also in the lead-mines that the *lapis calaminaris* is found. Iron-ore of a rich quality is procured in the mines of Whitehaven, and exported to South Wales: there are iron-mines at Crowgarth, in the parish of Cleator, and at Bigrigg, in that of Egremont; and on the sea-shore, near Harrington, ironstone is collected, and a few hundred tons annually sent to Ulverston. The celebrated mine of "wad" at the head of Borrowdale, is described in the account of that place.

The limestone near the sea-coast is burned in great quantities for exportation, particularly at Over-end, near Hensingham, and at Distington, from each of which places about 350,000 bushels are sent every year to Scotland. At Allhallows, Brigham, Cleator, Hodbarrow-in-Millom, Ireby, Plumbland, Sebergham, Uldale, &c., are lime-works for inland consumption; and the barony of Gilsland is supplied from the parishes of Castle-Carrock, Denton, and Farlam. Gypsum, or alabaster, is more especially abundant in the parishes of Wetheral, St. Cuthbert (Carlisle), and St. Bees, on the sea-coast, about a mile from Whitehaven, whence 500 or 600 tons are annually exported to Dublin, Glasgow, and Liverpool, where it is principally used in the composition of stucco. Of the freestones, which abound and are worked in most parts of the county, there are two quarries producing some of an excellent quality, both red and white, in the neighbourhood of Whitehaven, from which place much of their produce is shipped for Ireland, Scotland, and the Isle of Man. At Negill and Barngill, near the same port, are export quarries of grindstones; and in the townships of Bassenthwaite, Borrowdale, Buttermere, Cockermouth, and Ulpha, are quarries of excellent blue slate: that obtained in Borrowdale is of the best quality. Numerous mineral substances of minor importance, and a great variety of spars and metallic fossils, are found; and divers extraneous fossils, also, are discovered imbedded in the limestone strata in several places.

The *Manufactures* are various. That of cotton, at present the principal, was first established at Dalston, and soon extended to Carlisle and Penrith, at all which places are large works: the spinning of cotton, which is nearly of equal magnitude, is carried on at Carlisle, and has been the means of greatly increasing the population. At Cleator, Egremont, and Whitehaven, sailcloth is manufactured; and at Keswick, coarse woollen cloths and blankets. Coarse earthenware is made at Dearham and Whitehaven, and bottles at the Ginns, near that town; and there are iron-foundries at Carlisle, Dalston, and Seaton near Workington; paper-mills at Cockermouth, Egremont, and Kirk-Oswald; and several yards for ship-building at Maryport, Whitehaven, and Workington, besides every kind of manufacture necessary for the shipping. The *Fisheries*, too, are of some importance: there are herring-fisheries at Allonby, Maryport, and Whitehaven, the last on a very extensive scale; and a great quantity of cod is taken on this coast. In the Esk, Eden, and Derwent are valuable salmon-fisheries, the produce of which is sent from Carlisle and Bowness to London, to which place the char caught in the lakes is also forwarded after being potted at Keswick. The pearls, still occasionally found in the muscles of the Irt, were once highly esteemed.
750

The two principal *Rivers* are the Eden and the Derwent, the former of which, after being augmented in different parts of its course by the Eamont, Irthing, Caldew, and Petterill, empties itself into the Solway Firth. In its lower reaches it was made navigable up to Carlisle bridge, to which the tide ascends, a distance of somewhat more than ten miles, under the authority of an act of the 8th of George I.; but the passage was so much impeded by shoals as to form a very imperfect line of navigation, and its use is now almost wholly superseded by the *Carlisle Canal*, which was constructed under an act obtained in 1819, and, commencing at Carlisle, communicates with the Solway Firth at Fisher's Cross, near Bowness. There are also the Esk, the Liddell, the Levon or Line, and a vast number of smaller streams. The county is furnished with excellent *Railway* communication. Four lines have their termini at Carlisle; namely, the Newcastle, which runs eastward, by Brampton, and quits the county for Northumberland near the great Roman wall; the Caledonian, which runs northward into Scotland; the Maryport, which runs south-westward, by Wigton, to the coast; and the Lancaster, which proceeds southward, by Penrith, into Westmorland. Other railways connect the coast towns of Maryport, Workington, Whitehaven, and Ravenglass; and there is a line from Workington, inland, to Cockermouth.

The REMAINS of distant ages are numerous and interesting. There is a considerable number even of the rude memorials of the aboriginal inhabitants, the largest and most complete of which is the circle of stones vulgarly called "Long Meg and her Daughters," in the parish of Addingham. About a mile and a half south-east of Keswick is a smaller circle, having an oblong inclosure on the east side; another, named the "Grey Yawd," is in the parish of Cumwhitton, and a third at a place designated Swinside, near Millom, with part of another near it. Kistvaens, and rude weapons and tools of the ancient British inhabitants, have been found in various places, especially in the south-western part of the county, near the sea-coast. Cumberland is thought to have contained several British cities, of which Carlisle is enumerated by Richard of Cirencester as one; and it was formerly crossed by a great trackway, probably of British construction, that extended from the banks of the Eamont through Carlisle, nearly in the line of the present turnpike-road. The "Maiden-way," from Kirby-Thore to Bewcastle, which seems to have been another British road, may still be traced across the moors in the eastern and north-eastern extremities of the county, in its course into Scotland.

The celebrated ROMAN WALL, constructed by the Emperor Severus, nearly in the line of a vallum of earth previously raised by Adrian, to check the incursions of the northern barbarians, crossed the northern portion of the county, and may yet be traced in different parts of its course, particularly near Burdoswald, Lanercost Priory, and within about a mile of its termination on the shore of the Solway Firth. Of the stations along the line of this barrier, the first that occurs in following its course westward from the border of Northumberland is that at Burdoswald, which, from the numerous inscriptions and other relics, appears to have been the one called in the Notitia *Amboglana*, occupied by the *Cohors Prima Œlia Dacorum*, and the remains of which evince its former extent and importance. The next is at Castle-

:eads, or Cambeck Fort, six miles and a quarter fur-
ter, which is supposed to have been the *Petriana* of
te Notitia; three miles beyond is Watchcross, con-
:ctured to have been *Aballaba*. The next was that of
ongaveta, at Stanwix, just opposite Carlisle. At Burgh-
n-the-Sands, about four miles and a half further, was
te station *Axelodunum*, on the site of which urns,
ltars, and inscriptions have frequently been found: at
)rumburgh are evident remains of another station, pro-
ably *Gabrocentum*; and the last remains of the wall
oint to a spot supposed to be the site of the station
'unnocelum, the last on this line of defence. Of the
tationes per lineam valli, placed so as to afford support
o the garrisons of the stations on the wall, Cumberland
ontained six, whereof that at Ellenborough, the name
f which is doubtful, was one of the most important:
n its site the greatest number of Roman antiquities has
een found. At Papcastle, near Cockermouth, was
tnother, supposed to have been called *Derventio*. At
)ld Carlisle was one more considerable, of which there
tre extensive remains; as also of that at Old Penrith,
r Plumpton-wall, the *Voreda* of Antonine and Richard
f Cirencester: at Moresby was one, thought to have
)een *Arbeia*; and the sixth was the station *Bremetenracum*,
he site of which has not been ascertained. There are
tikewise remains of two advanced stations on the north
tide of the wall; one at Bewcastle, and the other at
Netherby, on the Esk. Carlisle was the *Luguballium* of
the Romans; and, from the great number of military
stations, no county in England, except Northumberland,
has produced so many Roman altars and inscribed
stones as Cumberland, besides a profusion of miscellaneous Roman antiquities.

The principal Roman road across the county, which
has been designated "the larger road of Severus," ran
nearly parallel with the wall, a little to the south of it;
and is yet visible from Willowford across the Irthing to
Walburs, a little beyond which place, after being for
some distance very conspicuous, all trace of it is lost
for some miles until near Watchcross, where it re-
appears for a short distance. Both the British track-
ways above-mentioned were subsequently important
Roman roads, especially the first, which passed by the
stations at Plumpton-wall and Carlisle, and crossed the
Roman wall at Stanwix, through which it proceeded by Longtown and Solway Moss into Dumfries-shire: from Longtown a branch diverges north-eastward, towards the
station at Netherby, thence to a Roman post at the
junction of the Esk and Liddell, and onward to that of
Castle-Over, in Dumfries-shire. No fewer than three
Roman roads diverged from the station at Ellenborough,
one along the coast towards Bowness, another to Papcastle, and the third north-eastward to the station at
Old Carlisle, which it passed to the left, proceeding in a
direct line towards Carlisle cathedral. A Roman road
that connected the stations at Ambleside (in Westmorland) and Plumpton-wall, is still visible in various
places, especially near the Whitbarrow camp, which was
a post of some consequence between the two Roman
towns: at this point terminates a road from the station
at Brougham, situated near the town of Penrith, but in
the county of Westmorland. Another Roman road,
formed of pebbles and freestone, extends from the parish
of Egremont through Cleator, Arlochden, and Lamplugh,
towards Cockermouth.

751

Prior to the Reformation, there were eleven *Religious
Houses*, besides two collegiate establishments and two
hospitals, within the limits of the county. Of these,
there yet remain the churches of the monasteries of St.
Bees, Carlisle (now the cathedral), and Lanercost; part
of the church of Holme-Cultram; and various ruined
buildings of Calder Abbey, the priories of St. Bees,
Carlisle, and Wetheral, and the nunnery of Seaton.
The remains of Holme-Cultram, and of Lanercost, exhibit specimens of the earliest English architecture,
having the pointed arch united with the massive Norman pillar; those of Seaton have lancet-shaped windows
and slender pillars. The ancient *Castles*, owing to the
border situation, are remarkably numerous; but most
of them are now either in ruins or in a state of considerable dilapidation. Independently of these, few of
the ancient mansions present any remarkable feature,
except the large square tower of three or four stories
attached to most of them, intended to afford refuge for
the family on any sudden predatory inroad of the Scots.
The most remarkable *Mineral water* is the sulphureous
spring at Gilsland, celebrated for the cure of cutaneous
disorders, and long resorted to on account of its valuable properties: besides a considerable portion of sulphur, its waters contain a small quantity of sea-salt, and
a slight admixture of earthy particles. There is also a
strong sulphureous spring in the township of Biglands,
in the parish of Aikton; and a saline spring at Stanger,
two miles north of Lorton, nearly resembles the Cheltenham water, turning white on the infusion of spirit of
hartshorn, and precipitating particles, chiefly saline, on
the application of oil of tartar. There are many other
mineral springs, but their properties have not been
accurately ascertained. Cumberland gives the title of
Duke to the King of Hanover, fifth son of George III.,
who was created Earl of Armagh, and Duke of Cumberland and Tiviotdale, in the year 1799.

CUMBERWORTH (*St. Helen*), a parish, in the
union of Spilsby, Marsh division of the hundred of
Calceworth, parts of Lindsey, county of Lincoln,
4¼ miles (S. E. by E.) from Alford; containing 183 inhabitants, and comprising 1228*a*. 31*p*. The living is a
discharged rectory, united in 1733 to the rectory of Anderby, and valued in the king's books at £10. 10. 2½.
The tithes were commuted for land and a money payment, in 1819; the glebe comprises 215 acres. The
church was rebuilt at the expense of the incumbent, the
Rev. John Lodge, and opened for divine service in 1839;
it is a handsome structure in the decorated English
style. Here is a place of worship for Wesleyans.

CUMBERWORTH, a chapelry, partly in the parish
of High Hoyland, and partly in that of Silkstone,
wapentake of Staincross, W. riding of York, 8 miles
(W.) from Barnsley; containing 1867 inhabitants. This
chapelry, which is divided into Upper and Lower, comprises 2360 acres, principally the property of T. Wentworth Beaumont, Esq.: the population is chiefly agricultural, but partly employed in the woollen and fancy
manufactures. The villages of Upper and Lower Cumberworth are both of considerable antiquity, and in the
former is the chapel of St. Nicholas, an ancient building
situated on a high hill. The living is a donative, in the
patronage of Mr. Beaumont. The tithes, which were
commuted for 40 acres of land in 1800, at the inclosure
of the commons, originally belonged to the ancestors of

the patron, the Wentworths of Bretton Park, who were lords of the manor, and obtained a grant of the donative in consideration of their endowing the living with the tithes of the township. They afterwards augmented the benefice by inclosing 34 acres of land from the waste.

CUMBERWORTH-HALF, a township, partly in the parish of EMLEY, Lower division of AGBRIGG wapentake, and partly in the parish of KIRK-BURTON, union of HUDDERSFIELD, Upper division of AGBRIGG wapentake, W. riding of YORK ; containing 1480 inhabitants. The township includes part of the hamlets of Skelmanthorpe and Scissett, and comprises 800 acres.

CUMDEVOCK, a township, in the parish of DALSTON, union of CARLISLE, CUMBERLAND ward, and E. division of the county of CUMBERLAND, 6 miles (S. S. W.) from Carlisle ; containing 361 inhabitants.

CUMMERSDALE, a township, in the parish of ST. MARY, liberty and union of CARLISLE, E. division of CUMBERLAND, 2¼ miles (S. by W.) from Carlisle ; containing 620 inhabitants.

CUMNER (ST. MICHAEL), a parish, in the union of ABINGDON, hundred of HORMER, county of BERKS ; comprising the tythings of Bradley, Chawley, Henwood, Hillend, Stroud, Swinford, and Whitley, the liberty of Chilswell, and the township of Cumner ; and containing 1058 inhabitants, of whom 608 are in the township, 5¼ miles (N. N. W.) from Abingdon. This was one of the appendages to the abbey of Abingdon, whose abbots had a residence here called Cumner Hall, now in ruins, which is noted as the place of the murder of the Countess of Leicester by the direction of her husband, the favourite of Queen Elizabeth : many of the scenes of Sir Walter Scott's *Kenilworth* are connected with the locality. The parish comprises 6637a. 2r. 38p. ; the surface is very elevated, and the greater portion consists of the hills of Cumner and Wytham, rising nearly 300 feet above the level of the river Thames, which bounds the parish for nearly three miles. The soil is various ; in some parts clayey, in others sandy, alternated with stone brash. The living is a discharged vicarage, valued in the king's books at £24. 17., and in the gift of the Earl of Abingdon : the tithes were commuted for land and money payments, in 1795 and 1814. The church is an ancient structure, containing some interesting monuments, among which are those of two abbots of Abingdon, and a monument to Anthony Foster, a retainer of the Earl of Leicester's, by whom the countess was murdered. A mineral spring here was formerly much frequented for its reputed virtues, but is now disused.

CUMREW, a parish, in the union of BRAMPTON, ESKDALE ward, E. division of CUMBERLAND, 7 miles (S. by E.) from Brampton ; comprising the townships of Cumrew Inside and Outside, the former containing 112, and the latter 71, inhabitants. The parish is bounded on the east by the river Gelt, and comprises 2694a. 2r. 10p., of which about 950 acres are arable, and the rest, with the exception of 30 acres of wood, high moorland pasture inclosed about 35 years ago. The soil on the level grounds is a good loamy earth ; and in the western district, which is mountainous, there is good limestone. The living is a perpetual curacy ; net income, £81 ; patrons and appropriators, the Dean and Chapter of Carlisle. The tithes have been commuted for £89. 13. 4., and the glebe comprises 17½ acres. There are several cairns, one of which, Car-

duneth, on the summit of a hill, is of immense size ; and near the river are the ruins of a large castle formerly belonging to the Dacres.

CUMWHINTON, a township, in the parish of WETHERAL, union of CARLISLE, CUMBERLAND ward, E. division of the county of CUMBERLAND, 4 miles (S. E. by E.) from Carlisle ; containing 339 inhabitants. There is a place of worship for Wesleyans.

CUMWHITTON (ST. MARY), a parish, in the union of BRAMPTON, ESKDALE ward, E. division of CUMBERLAND ; comprising the townships of Cumwhitton, Moorthwaite, and Northsceugh ; and containing 533 inhabitants, of whom 242 are in the township of Cumwhitton, 9 miles (E. S. E.) from Carlisle. The parish comprises 5400a. 2r. 29p., the whole of which is arable, with the exception of about 140 acres of meadow, the ground occupied by a few Scottish firs and larches, and the plantations on the banks of the Eden. The living is a perpetual curacy ; net income, £102 ; patrons, the Dean and Chapter of Carlisle. The church is in the Norman style, and consists of a nave, chancel, and north aisle ; a tower was built in 1810, and the ancient lancet windows have been displaced for others of larger dimensions. On an eminence called "King Harry" is a Druidical temple, the stones of which, 90 in number, are placed in a circular position ; and the lines of intrenchments may be traced on the common.

CUNDALL (ST. MARY AND ALL SAINTS), a parish, comprising the townships of Cundall with Leckby, and Norton-le-Clay, in the wapentake of HALLIKELD, and the township of Fawdington in that of BIRDFORTH, N. riding of YORK ; and containing 387 inhabitants, of whom 188 are in Cundall with Leckby, 5 miles (N. N. E.) from Boroughbridge. The parish is on the banks of the river Swale, and comprises by computation 3480 acres, of which about 2120 are in Cundall with Leckby : the soil is gravelly ; the scenery is pleasingly diversified with wood and water. The hamlet of Cundall is on the western side of the river, and about 5 miles distant from the Sessay station of the York and Newcastle railway. The hamlet of Leckby is about a mile north from Cundall. The living is a vicarage, valued in the king's books at £3. 6. 8., and in the patronage of the Bishop of Ripon, with a net income recently augmented to £96 : the church is an old and dilapidated building, fast falling into ruins. A small chapel of ease was erected in 1839, at Norton-le-Clay.

CUNSALL, a township, in the parish of CHEDDLETON, union of CHEADLE, N. division of the hundred of TOTMONSLOW and of the county of STAFFORD, 3¾ miles (N. N. W.) from Cheadle ; containing 190 inhabitants. It contains 2122 acres, and has a small village. At Cunsall Wood the Caldon canal passes through a deep glen, in which are extensive limekilns.

CUNSCOUGH.—See MELLING.

CURBAR, a township, in the parish and union of BAKEWELL, hundred of HIGH PEAK, N. division of the county of DERBY, 1½ mile (E. by S.) from Stoney-Middleton ; containing 412 inhabitants. It is situated on the eastern bank of the river Derwent.

CURBOROUGH, with ELMHURST, a township, in the parish of St. CHAD, LICHFIELD, union of LICHFIELD, N. division of the hundred of OFFLOW and of the county of STAFFORD ; containing 227 inhabitants. The two hamlets extend from one to two miles from Lichfield, and form a township of scattered houses, comprising about 2000 acres, of which 860 are in Elmhurst. Near Stitchbrook, in the township, is Christian Field, where tradition says 1000 British Christians were massacred.

CURBRIDGE, a hamlet, in the parish and union of WITNEY, hundred of BAMPTON, county of OXFORD, 2¼ miles (W. S. W.) from Witney; containing 387 inhabitants. It comprises 2907 acres, of which 1941 are arable and 955 pasture. The tithes have been commuted for £685, and there is a glebe of 124½ acres. Six almshouses situated here are endowed with £110 per annum.

CURDRIDGE, a tything, in the parish and hundred of BISHOP's-WALTHAM, union of DROXFORD, Droxford and N. divisions of the county of SOUTHAMPTON; containing 397 inhabitants. A separate incumbency has been founded here, in the gift of the Rector.

CURDWORTH (ST. NICHOLAS), a parish, in the union of ASTON, Birmingham division of the hundred of HEMLINGFORD, N. division of the county of WARWICK, 8 miles (N. E. by E.) from Birmingham; containing 693 inhabitants. This parish, which includes the hamlet of Minworth, is bounded on the south by the river Tame, and intersected by the road from Birmingham to Tamworth, and the old road from Coventry to Lichfield. It comprises by computation 3170 acres, of which 1620 are in the township of Curdworth, and 1550 in Minworth, into which districts the parish is divided by a portion of Sutton-Coldfield intervening between them. The surface is generally level, and the soil chiefly suited to the growth of turnips and barley; around the village and towards the river are rich meadow and pasture grounds. The Birmingham and Fazeley canal passes through the parish, and the Birmingham and Derby railway proceeds for about half a mile through Minworth. The living is a vicarage, valued in the king's books at £5, and in the patronage of the Rev. W. Wakefield, the present incumbent, and others; net income, £289; impropriators, the Rev. W. Wakefield, and C. B. Adderley, Esq. The tithes (with the exception of those for the manor of Dunton, about 500 acres, which still pays great and small tithes to the vicar of Curdworth) were commuted for land under an inclosure act passed in the year 1791. The church is an ancient structure, in the later English style, with a tower; a noble Saxon arch separates the chancel from the body of the edifice: Dr. Sacheverel was married in this church. There is a place of worship for Wesleyans, and at Minworth is one for Independents. A battle was fought here between the parliamentarians and Charles I.

CURLAND (ALL SAINTS), a parish, in the union of TAUNTON, hundred of ABDICK and BULSTONE, W. division of SOMERSET, 5¾ miles (S. E. by E.) from Taunton; containing 228 inhabitants. The living is annexed to the rectory of Curry-Mallet: the tithes have been commuted for £84, and the glebe contains 12 acres. There is a place of worship for Wesleyans.

CURRY, EAST, and CURRY-LOAD, tythings, in the parish of STOKE ST. GREGORY, union of TAUNTON, hundred of NORTH CURRY, W. division of SOMERSET; containing respectively 686 and 184 inhabitants.

CURRY-MALLET (ALL SAINTS), a parish, and formerly a market-town, in the union of LANGPORT, hundred of ABDICK and BULSTONE, W. division of SOMERSET, 6 miles (N. N. W.) from Ilminster; containing 630

inhabitants. The manor, in the time of Edward II., belonged to Hugh Poyntz, to whom that monarch granted a weekly market, and a fair on the eve, day, and morrow of the festival of All Saints; and who, in the 18th of that reign, was summoned to parliament by the title of Lord Poyntz, of Curry-Mallet. In the second year of Edward III. this place was annexed to the duchy of Cornwall, by the same act of parliament which vested the duchy in the eldest son of the king, and it has ever since continued to form a part of it. The parish abounds with lias stone, which is extensively quarried for lime, and for building; and the Chard canal passes through. The living is a rectory, with that of Curland annexed, valued in the king's books at £24. 1. 3., and in the patronage of the Crown, in right of the duchy of Cornwall; net income, £392. The church is a handsome structure in the later English style.

CURRY, NORTH (ST. PETER AND ST. PAUL), a parish, in the union of TAUNTON, hundred of NORTH CURRY, W. division of SOMERSET, 7 miles (E. by N.) from Taunton; comprising the tythings of North Curry, Knapp, Lillesdon, and Wrantage; and containing 2028 inhabitants, of whom 950 are in the tything of North Curry. This place appears to have been known to the Romans, an urn containing a quantity of silver coins of that people having been discovered in 1748 : it was subsequently held by the Saxon kings, and retained in demesne by the Conqueror. King John granted it a market, which was held on Wednesday, but has been long discontinued. The parish comprises by admeasurement 5500 acres, of which about 1600 are arable, 90 woodland, and the rest pasture; the navigable river Tone passes in the vicinity. Newport, in the parish, anciently possessed the privileges and officers of a corporate town, and is still called a borough; it had also a chapel. The living is a discharged vicarage, with that of West Hatch annexed, in the patronage of the Dean and Chapter of Wells, valued in the king's books at £21; impropriator, C. Holcombe Dare, Esq. The great tithes have been commuted for £650, and the vicarial for £220; the glebe consists of 2½ acres, with a glebe-house. There are places of worship for Particular Baptists and Wesleyans.

CURRY-RIVELL (ST. ANDREW), a parish, in the union of LANGPORT, hundred of ABDICK and BULSTONE, W. division of SOMERSET, 2 miles (W. S. W.) from Langport; comprising the tythings of Hambridge and Portfield, part of those of Burton-Pynsent and Weck, the entire hamlet of Langport-Westover, and Westmoor, an extra-parochial place; the whole containing 1660 inhabitants. The parish is situated on the river Parret, and intersected by the road from Barnstaple to London; it comprises 4001 acres by measurement, and contains several quarries of blue limestone and white lias, in which bivalve shells of different sorts are frequently found. Fairs for cattle and sheep are held on the last Wednesday in February, the Monday next after Lammas, and the 5th of August. The living is a vicarage, with the chapelry of Weston, endowed with the rectorial tithes of the latter, and valued in the king's books at £13. 16. 0½.; patron and impropriator, W. Speke, Esq. The vicarial tithes have been commuted for £310, and the impropriate for £200; the glebe comprises only the site and gardens of the ancient vicarage-house. The church is an old edifice in the early English style. At

Westport is a separate incumbency, in the gift of R. T. Combe, Esq.

CURY (ST. NINIAN), a parish, in the union of HEL-STON, W. division of KERRIER hundred and of CORN-WALL, 4¾ miles (S. S. E.) from Helston; containing 541 inhabitants. It is situated on the shore of Mount's bay. The old living is a vicarage, annexed, with the livings of Germoe and Gunwalloe, to the vicarage of Breage: the great tithes have been commuted for £279, and the vicarial for £190. A perpetual curacy has been lately instituted, which is in the gift of the Rev. Canon Rogers, and includes the parishes of Cury and Gunwalloe. The church has a fine Norman arch over the south door. There is a place of worship for Wesleyans. In a field on the estate of Trevessec was discovered, a few years since, an earthen vessel containing several hundred copper coins of various Roman emperors. .

CUSOP (ST. MARY), a parish, in the union of HAY, hundred of EWYASLACY, county of HEREFORD, 2 miles (E. S. E.) from Hay; containing 223 inhabitants. On the west and south the parish is bounded by a portion of Wales, the river Wye separating it in the former, and the river Dulas in thé latter, direction. It comprises 2294 acres, of which 900 are common or waste; and is intersected by the road from Hereford to Hay. The living is a discharged rectory, valued in the king's books at £5. 19. 7., and in the gift of the Earl of Oxford: the tithes have been commuted for £210.

CUSTHORPE, a hamlet, in the parish of WEST-ACRE, union and hundred of FREEBRIDGE-LYNN, S. division of the hundred of GRENHOE, W. division of NORFOLK, 4¼ miles (N. W.) from Swaffham. Here are the ruins of a chapel, dedicated to St. Thomas à Becket, and supposed to have been founded by the monks of West-Acre priory, who received permission to hold a fair on the 7th of July: connected with it was a house, the residence of a custos and one or two monks.

CUTCOMBE (ST. JOHN), a parish, in the union of WILLITON, hundred of CARHAMPTON, W. division of SOMERSET, 5¼ miles (S. W. by S.) from Dunster, and on the road from Minehead to Exeter; containing 843 inhabitants. The parish comprises 7231 acres, of which 1852 are common or waste. The surface is strikingly diversified, rising in some parts into hills of mountainous elevation, and on the summit of Dunkery, one of the highest mountains in the western counties, and 1696 feet above the level of the sea, are the remains of several large hearths belonging to the beacons formerly erected to alarm the country in times of civil discord or foreign invasion. Limestone is extensively quarried for building and for burning into lime; and iron-ore, which is wrought in the adjoining parish, is supposed also to exist here. Fairs are held at Wheddon Cross on the 22nd, and at Luckwall Bridge on the 29th, of September. The living is a vicarage, endowed with part of the rectorial tithes, with the living of Luxborough annexed, and valued in the king's books at £14. 0. 7½.; it is in the patronage of the Crown. The impropriate tithes have been commuted for £114. 14. 6., and the vicarial for £295; the glebe comprises about 1¼ acre. There is a place of worship for Wesleyans. A parochial school has an endowment of £35 per annum, arising from a bequest by Richard Elsworth, in 1729; and commodious schoolrooms, with a residence for the master and mistress, have been erected.

754

CUTSDEAN, a chapelry, in the parish of BREDON, union of WINCHCOMB, Upper division of the hundred of OSWALDSLOW, Blockley and E. divisions of the county of WORCESTER, 7 miles (W. by S.) from Moreton-in-the-Marsh; containing 172 inhabitants. It comprises 1505a. 2r. 20p., and forms a detached portion of the parish, entirely surrounded by the county of Gloucester. The chapel is a small edifice containing 72 sittings, and stands about 14 miles east-south-east of the parish church. There is a place of worship for Baptists. A schoolmistress receives £7. 16. per annum, left by a member of the Tracey family.

CUTTHORPE, a hamlet, in the parish of BRAMPTON, union of CHESTERFIELD, hundred of SCARSDALE, N. division of the county of DERBY, 1½ mile (N. by E.) from Brampton village; containing 333 inhabitants. The hamlet is pleasantly situated on an eminence commanding fine views, and forms the north side of the parish. The road from Chesterfield to Chapel-en-le-Frith passes through. The Hall, now a farmhouse, is a very ancient building.

CUXHAM (HOLY ROOD), a parish, in the union of HENLEY, hundred of EWELME, county of OXFORD, 5 miles (S. S. W.) from Tetsworth; containing 222 inhabitants. It comprises 497 acres, of which 29 are common or waste. The living is a rectory, valued in the king's books at £9. 10. 5.; net income, £275; patrons, the Warden and Fellows of Merton College, Oxford. The tithes have been commuted for a rent-charge of £182; there is a good glebe-house, and the glebe contains nearly 24½ acres.

CUXTON (ST. MICHAEL), a parish, in the union of NORTH AYLESFORD, hundred of SHAMWELL, lathe of AYLESFORD, W. division of KENT, 3 miles (W. S. W.) from Rochester; containing 376 inhabitants. This parish comprises 1685 acres, of which 24 are common or waste, and 382 in wood: the river Medway, which has a wharf, passes within a quarter of a mile. The chalk-pits in the neighbourhood supply material for lime, and bricks are made to a limited extent. The living is a rectory, valued in the king's books at £14. 15. 5., and in the gift of the Bishop of Rochester: the tithes payable to the incumbent have been commuted for £380. 16., with a glebe of 28½ acres; a rent-charge of £32. 1. is paid to an impropriator, and one of £43. 5. to the Dean and Chapter of the Cathedral of Rochester.

CUXWOLD (ST. NICHOLAS), a parish, in the union of CAISTOR, wapentake of BRADLEY-HAVERSTOE, parts of LINDSEY, county of LINCOLN, 4 miles (E.) from Caistor; containing 62 inhabitants. It lies in the eastern part of the Wolds, and comprises 1670 acres of land. The road from Caistor to Great Grimsby passes on the north of the parish. The living is a discharged rectory, valued in the king's books at £5. 7. 6., and in the gift of H. Thorold, Esq.: the tithes have been commuted for £314. 17. 8., and the glebe comprises one acre and a quarter.

CWMCARVAN, a parish, in the division of TREL-LICK, hundred of RAGLAN, union and county of MON-MOUTH, 5 miles (S. S. W.) from Monmouth; containing 315 inhabitants. The parish is in the eastern part of the county, and contains 2908 acres, of which 939 are arable, 1498 pasture and meadow, and 394 woodland, the remainder consisting of roads and waste. The surface exhibits considerable varieties of elevation, some parts being boldly undulated, and others tolerably level; and from Cwmcarvan Hill the views are extensive and pleasing. A battle was fought here between Henry V. and Owen Glyndwr, the latter of whom was defeated. The living is annexed to the rectory of Mitchel-Troy : a rent-charge of £193 has been awarded as a commutation for the tithes, of which sum £20 are payable to the Bishop of Llandaff; and there is a glebe of 10 acres of land belonging to the rector. The church is an ancient structure, containing a pulpit which is elaborately carved.

CWMYOY (St. Michael), a parish, in the union, division, and hundred of Abergavenny, county of Monmouth, 8 miles (N. by W.) from Abergavenny; containing, with the hamlets of Bwlch-Trewyn and Toothog, 718 inhabitants. Soon after the year 1108, a priory, dedicated to St. John the Baptist, and afterwards known by the name of Llanthony Abbey, was founded here by Hugh Lacy, for canons regular of the order of St. Augustine, many of whom, on account of

755

the privations and hardships which they sustained in this place, removed, first to the episcopal palace at Hereford, and afterwards, in 1136, to Hyde, near Gloucester; leaving a few of their brethren at the original settlement at Llanthony, whose revenue, in the 26th of Henry VIII., was estimated at £100. The parish is about eight miles in length, and one mile in breadth, forming a rich and fertile valley, inclosed on both sides by lofty hills, which extend from one extremity of the parish to the other, and watered by a rivulet called the Honddu, along the bank of which is the road to Abergavenny. Nearly in the centre of this picturesque vale are the ruins of the abbey, consisting of the gateway, and part of the conventual building. The chapel of Llanthony, a plain edifice, is situated close to the ruins. The living is a perpetual curacy; net income, £68; patron, R. Powell, Esq. There are places of worship for Welsh Methodists and Baptists; and a school supported by subscription. At the extreme part of the Black mountain is a fine specimen of a Roman encampment.

END OF VOLUME I.

GILBERT & RIVINGTON, PRINTERS, ST. JOHN'S SQUARE, LONDON.

Lightning Source UK Ltd.
Milton Keynes UK
UKHW021338041218
333417UK00008B/149/P